BASS & STOGDILL'S

Handbook of Leadership

BERNARD M. BASS IS DISTINGUISHED PROFESSOR OF MANAGEMENT and director of the Center for Leadership Studies at the State University of New York, Binghamton. He was former director of the Management Research Center at the University of Pittsburgh (1965–68) and the University of Rochester (1969–72). He is listed in *Who's Who in America, Who's Who in the World,* and *American Men and Women of Science.* He served as president of the Division of Organizational Psychology of the International Association of Applied Psychology (1978–82).

Books by Bernard M. Bass

1960 *Leadership, Psychology, and Organizational Behavior*
1965 *Organizational Psychology*
1966 *Training in Industry: The Management of Learning* (with J. A. Vaughan)
1972 *Man, Work and Organizations* (with G. V. Barrett)
1979 *Organizational Psychology* (with E. Ryterband)
1981 *Stogdill's Handbook of Leadership* (second edition)
1982 *Interpersonal Communications in Industry* (with R. Klauss)
1983 *Organizational Decision-Making*
1985 *Leadership and Performance Beyond Expectations*

Edited Works

1959 *Objective Approaches to Personality Assessment* (with I. A. Berg)
1959 *Leadership and Interpersonal Behavior* (with L. Petrullo)
1961 *Conformity and Deviation* (with I. A. Berg)
1970 *Current Perspectives for Managing Organizations* (with S. D. Deep)
1970 *Managing for Accomplishment* (with R. C. Cooper and J. A. Haas)
1972 *Studies in Organizational Psychology* (with S. D. Deep)
1987 *Advances in Organizational Psychology: An International Review* (with P. J. D. Drenth and P. Weissenberg)

THE LATE RALPH M. STOGDILL (1904–78) was professor emeritus of management science and psychology at Ohio State University, where he had served earlier for many years as associate director of the Ohio State Leadership Studies. Included among his numerous publications were *Individual Behavior and Group Achievement* (1959) and *Managers, Employees, Organizations* (1965). He was recognized by *American Men and Women of Science, Leaders in American Science, Who's Who in Science,* and *Who's Who in American Education* and was a former management history director of the Academy of Management. A biannual prize for the best contribution to the study of leadership was named in his honor.

BASS & STOGDILL'S
Handbook of Leadership

THEORY, RESEARCH, AND MANAGERIAL APPLICATIONS

Third Edition

by
Bernard M. Bass

THE FREE PRESS
A Division of Macmillan, Inc.
NEW YORK

Collier Macmillan Publishers
LONDON

The Free Press
A Division of Macmillan, Inc.
866 Third Avenue, New York, N. Y. 10022

Collier Macmillan Canada, Inc.

Printed in the United States of America

printing number
 2 3 4 5 6 7 8 9 10

Library of Congress Cataloging-in-Publication Data

Bass, Bernard M.
   Bass & Stogdill's handbook of leadership: theory, research, and
managerial applications / Bernard M. Bass.—3rd ed.
      p.   cm.
   Rev. ed. of: Stogdill's handbook of leadership. ©1981.
   Includes bibliographical references.
   ISBN 0-02-901500-6
   1. Leadership—Abstracts.   2. Leadership—Bibliography.
I. Stogdill, Ralph Melvin, 1904–1978.   II. Stogdill, Ralph Melvin,
1904–1978. Stogdill's handbook of leadership.   III. Title.   IV. Title:
Bass and Stogdill's handbook of leadership.
HM141.S83   1990
016.3033′4—dc20   89-17240
                                                          CIP

TO
John W. Gardner,
who has shown that what can be done
from a research-based scholarly understanding of leadership
and a dedication to public service

Contents

PART VIII
Improving Leadership and
Leadership Research

Preface to the Third Edition

What's New in This Edition

This third edition reflects the growth and changes in the study of leadership and its broadening as a subject of inquiry since the 1981 edition. There have been shifts in both content and method. Substantively, during this period we have seen many more field reports on leaders at higher levels. Executives and senior officials have become an increasing subject of inquiry, while the proportionate number of studies on college students and younger participants has continued to decrease. Distinctly separate fields of inquiry, such as political science and psychology, have come to make greater use of each other, to build a broader appreciation of the phenomenon of leadership (see, for example, House, 1988a).

The treatment of leadership as a phenomenon in organizational and social psychology has broken out of its normal confinement to the study of the behaviors seen previously mainly in leader-group interactions in the field and laboratory. Cognitive science has provided the freedom to explore leader-follower thoughts and feelings. Organizational science has increased the sophistication of examinations of leadership that are contingent on the context in which leadership occurs. Political science has provided new objective insights into the contrasts of leadership, politics, and administration. Throughout this third edition, the contributions from cognitive social psychology and the social, political, communications, and administrative sciences have been expanded.

Methodology has become more sophisticated. More field and longitudinal studies have appeared, along with many helpful meta-analyses. Culture and environment, both inside and outside the organization, have taken on a renewed prominence (Ungson, James, & Spicer, 1985).

Societal changes have been reflected in the growth of a research literature on leading health professionals, hospital and nursing administrators, data processing supervisors, and police officials. Studies of the supervision of services, the maintenance of information systems, and project teams have become more common.

New journals that are partially or fully devoted to the subject of leadership, such as *Group and Organizational Studies*, the *Leaders Magazine*, and the *Leadership Quarterly* have emerged. "Pop" leadership books, including *In Search of Excellence* and *The One-Minute Manager* have led the best-seller lists. Biographies and autobiographies of business, political, and military leaders have also become prominent features of best-seller lists, as have popularized versions of leadership theories and the results of research. Autobiographies (Bass, 1981) and biographies (Ruiz de Gauna, 1988) have appeared as contributions to the history of leadership theory and research in the past half-century.

The Center for Creative Leadership has become a mature major force in the training and application of research to management. The internationalization of the research on leadership has expanded. Along with the continuing base in the Anglo-American world are substantially more research studies from Europe, Japan, Israel, and India.

Some popular books on leadership, such as that by Clemens and Mayer (1987), who connected lore from the classics with the modern boardroom, although interesting and informative about the art of leadership, failed to appreciate it as a science. They misinterpreted a conclusion from the first edition of the handbook to suggest that, as of 1974, little was known about the subject despite the 3,000 pre-1974 publications reviewed and that so much more was still to be learned. A lot was known by 1974, but, as in any science, the information that was available generated more questions than it answered.

Worse still are the "know-nothings" who simply know little about the subject and do not take the time to find out. Yet, they declare that we know nothing about leadership. Or, what we know does not matter. Or, leadership does not exist. Or, if it does, it is antidemocratic and interferes with good team efforts. This book should demonstrate the absurdity of such know-nothingism.

Certain phenomena, first recognized in the 1970s, have emerged in the 1980s as salient for study. They include transformational leadership, envisioning, implicit theory, prototypicality, empowerment, delegation, substitutes for leadership, upward influence, and within- and between-group analyses of leader-follower relations. In the marketplace for leadership training programs, Hersey and Blanchard's situational leadership and Sorcher's behavioral modeling have joined Blake and Mouton's, Fiedler's, Vroom and Yetton's, and Reddin's as being most popular, although the dearth of controlled research on the Hersey-Blanchard, Blake and Mouton, and Reddin models remains bothersome.

There has been a rise in college courses and curricula devoted to leadership. Currently, over 600 universities and colleges provide such courses (Clark, Freeman, & Britt, 1987). It has been recognized that an important purpose of higher education is to help prepare its graduates for positions of leadership and active participation in a democratic nation and its institutions. Additionally, community leadership training for adults and for high school students has been widely promoted by national associations that focus on this need.

Plan of This Book

A multiplicity of themes is likely to appear in any study of leadership. Leadership itself may be the independent, dependent, or intervening variable. In organizing the studies and seeking to extract generalizations from the organization, I hoped to avoid the structure of a Wagnerian opera in which different themes continually appear, disappear, and reappear. As much as possible, I have attempted to compile findings into tight thematic bundles.

A handbook should promote both understanding and application. One cannot understand leadership in a

vacuum. Thus, an appreciation of effective leadership in modern West Germany requires an understanding of what kinds of participatory practices have been legislated since World War II, as well as what firmly entrenched traditions, accepted by both leaders and subordinates, about the "leadership principle" have been carried forward from the Second Reich of a century ago. For example, on matters of routine, the subordinates' jobs are spelled out in detail in West Germany. When delegated by superiors to carry out such routines, subordinates are obligated to give unquestioning obedience but are left alone to complete the task. For unprogrammed activities, however, superiors are supposed to consult with their subordinates. When the superior finally decides, it is the subordinate's duty to accept the decision. A similar mix of tradition and modern improvements has emerged in the Japanese Ringi method of circularizing ideas among subordinates and gaining their inputs before a seemingly "unanimous" decision is announced by their leader. And, it should be noted that although the German and Japanese post-1945 economic miracles were due to much more than effective leadership, such leadership did play an important part.

In restructuring the handbook for the third edition, I tried to integrate the available literature. This edition, as does the second edition, begins with a consideration of the definitions and concepts used, the gross typologies, and a brief review of some of the better-known theories, mainly of the past. Then attention is focused on the personal traits, tendencies, attributes, values, and ascriptions of leaders, moving from the broad treatment of the research findings up to 1970 in the first edition to a consideration of the activity and energetic behavior commonly observed in emerging leaders and then to the knowledge, intellectual competence, and technical skills required for leaders. Next come the leaders' socioemotional talents, interpersonal competencies, and attention to relationships and the differences in these characteristics in leaders who are imbued with ideologies, especially authoritarianism, Machiavellianism, and self-aggrandizement. A fuller examination of the values, needs, and satisfactions of leaders follows. Singled out for special attention are competitiveness and the preferences for taking risks.

The chapters on personal characteristics that transcend situational considerations examines the esteem that others generally accord to leaders as a consequence of the leaders' personalities, regardless of circumstances. In this section, Stogdill's original 1948 piece on the traits of leadership has been slightly revised as Chapter 4. It introduces a more general review in subsequent chapters that brings the issues about traits up to date. The more general examination of the personal factors associated with leadership has been extensively reorganized and expanded in the chapters that follow. Both here and later on, increased attention has been paid to knowledge, information, and intellectual ability, as well as to power orientation and political tactics.

In the preface to the first edition, Stogdill (1974) noted that not a word would be found about charisma because it had not been subjected to experimental verification or to quantitative measurement. But the many developments in theory and research about charisma since 1974 have now made possible an entire chapter devoted to charismatic and inspirational leadership. Also in this chapter (Chapter 12) and elsewhere, it is argued that a new paradigm of leadership—transformational leadership—has arisen that makes possible the inclusion of a much wider range of phenomena than when theory and modeling are limited to reinforcement strategies.

Next, leadership is examined as a more dynamic interactional phenomenon. That is, one's position provides power and knowledge. Such power and knowledge are distributed equally or unequally among people who work or play together. The distribution is either legitimated or is a source of conflict. Questions emerge about the responsibility and authority of leaders and how much should be and can be delegated. However, delegation is discussed more fully in Chapter 22 as a style of management.

The interaction, itself, becomes the next focus of attention. The leader is dependent on the reactions of followers, as well as on the leaders' and followers' implicit theories of leadership. When leadership is a matter of an exchange, contingent reinforcement is seen as the main explanation of what makes the leadership effective. Chapters 17–19 examine leadership as a mutually reinforcing exchange relationship and provide a detailed review of contingent reinforcement and its limitations. In this regard, cognitive theory is found to be helpful in understanding the reactions of leaders to their subordinates.

Chapter 20 concentrates on the extent to which leaders must manage and managers must lead. The review of management styles in Chapter 21 begins with its most general dichotomization as autocratic or democratic. Within this conceptualization, leaders and managers are directive or participative and task or relations oriented and behave by initiating structure or by showing consideration.

Chapter 22 attends to the locus of decision making by leaders: directive or participative. Chapter 23 is concerned with the focus of leadership: tasks or relationships. Added to the discussion on the controversy over Fiedler's contingent model is the Blake-Mouton versus Hersey-Blanchard dispute about whether there is one best way to lead or whether the situation is paramount in determining the most appropriate style to employ. Chapters 24 and 25 conclude this discussion with reviews of what is known about leaders' tendencies to initiate structure or to show consideration, to want to manage or to abdicate such responsibilities.

If one falls back to description rather than prescription, it is clear that the extent to which a style is effective compared to alternative styles depends on the environment and organization in which the leadership is enacted, on the immediate group of followers, on the characteristics of the task, on spatial arrangements and networks, on how much stress is being generated and on whether substitutes for leadership exist in the situation.

The 1980s saw an explosion of interest in the culture of organizations. The interaction of leaders and their organizational culture take on prominence when situational considerations that affect leadership are reviewed in Chapter 26. The importance of the immediate group and the nature of the task are the subjects of Chapters 27 and 28, respectively. The role of leadership and organization in dealing with stress, crisis, and disaster are discussed in Chapter 29. In Chapter 30, the newer technological advances in communications and accessibility to information contribute to the need for looking more extensively at spatial considerations, networking, and substitutions for leadership. In the same way, the availability of CRISP tapes and other financial data banks has increased the flow of sophisticated analyses of the leadership-succession phenomenon. The discussion about succession has been extensively expanded in Chapter 31.

Studies of women increased dramatically during the 1980s. Therefore, Chapter 32 on women and leadership has been considerably expanded over the chapter in the second edition. I had hoped that by the late 1980s there would be a similar increment in post-1980 studies of leadership among disadvantaged groups, such as black Americans, Hispanics, and the handicapped. However, the increase has only been modest. In Chapter 33, I have been able to add to the chapter in the second edition only modest reviews of leadership and management among Hispanics, Native Americans, Asian Americans, Jewish Americans, and the handicapped.

The accelerating internationalization of management has been reflected in the growth of research on leadership that crosses national boundaries. This research, a considerable amount of which has been generated by European and Japanese investigators, is presented in Chapter 34.

The expansion of Chapter 35 was necessary because of the increased attention to theory and research on the development and education of leaders and managers and its application to coaching and mentoring. New Chapter 36, on assessment, reflects the maturing of the area and the completion of a number of large-scale long-term studies, such as the A T & T and Stanford 20-year follow-ups. Finally, newer substantive developments and more promising newer methods have been added in Chapter 37 to provide a picture of the broad array of tools, methods, measurements, and techniques that are now available for the study of leadership and the most salient substantive problems that await solutions.

Inclusion of Unpublished Research

This handbook differs considerably from the reviews one finds in the *Annual Review of Psychology* because of a constraint usually imposed on what is covered in the latter. In addition to covering one to a few years of work, the annual reviews concentrate on archival publications. Leadership is one of the fields for which it is difficult to accept for publication unorthodox views, qualitative research, or new paradigms. New ideas alone are insufficient. Factors with which the field is comfortable, such as initiation and consideration or variants in labeling, dominate the published literature. Descriptions of more subtle, less well documented, less evident phenomena are not considered acceptable for the scientifically more rigorous journals. These phenomena are more likely to be found in unpublished manuscripts, dissertations, and books in a variety of fields that have not had the benefit of the surgery of expert referees.

In this handbook, I have included many unpublished reports that offer fresh points of view, sometimes grander and sometimes heretical, that are likely to be less acceptable to experimental scientists but more in line with the traditions of social science scholarship, as well as with what is in the heads of practicing leaders. Although the field has come far as a science since Terman (1904), experimental scientists still have plenty of catching up to do with the intuitive understanding of leadership present among many of the most successful and effective leaders.

Glossary

A glossary has been included in this third edition because of the wider array of disciplines represented to help readers from one field who may be unfamiliar with some of the terms used in another.

Acknowledgments

In 1966, the Smith Richardson Foundation suggested that Ralph Stogdill undertake a systematic analysis and review of the literature on leadership. The result was the first edition of the *Handbook of Leadership* (1974), a sourcebook of experimental products up to 1973. It was an attempt to assemble all the published evidence on a given topic and to summarize the findings.

The task of reviewing and abstracting the literature on leadership was begun in 1946, under a grant from the Office of Naval Research. One result of the navy-sponsored survey was "Personal Factors Associated with Leadership: A Survey of Literature" (1948), which, as revised, is the basis of Chapter 4. Systematic abstracting continued with support from the College of Administrative Science, Ohio State University. In 1966, a two-year grant from the Smith Richardson Foundation permitted a full-time attack on the task.

More than five thousand abstracts were prepared. Only those with a direct bearing on leadership were included in the survey. Stogdill was assisted in the demanding task of abstracting by Kathleen Koehler Haas, William G. Nickels, and Adele Zimmer. Unlike the second and third editions, the inspirational and advisory literature was ignored, as were small-group studies that were only indirectly related to leadership. A chapter on the charismatic leader was deliberately omitted in this first edition because, prior to 1980, this important variant of the leadership role was not a willing or frequent subject of research that involved measurement or experimentation.

Shortly before he died in 1978, Ralph Stogdill asked me to collaborate with him on a new edition of the handbook. I accepted the assignment willingly, but I have had to carry on alone and take full responsibility for the assignment.

I have attempted to maintain some of the essence of the first edition. Nevertheless, in addition to a considerable amount of new material from the industrial management and political science literatures, the second and third editions have been updated by the incorporation of an extensive amount of relevant publications that appeared between 1974 and 1990. I have relaxed the criteria that Stogdill employed for including or excluding material in the first edition, for I believe that much of the understanding about leadership occurs from testable ideas that have not been, as yet, fully tested. On occasion, I have put more weight on generalizations that are emerging from the body of softer literature dealing with organizational and management development than on some of the seemingly harder, antiseptic, laboratory studies of dragooned college students in brief encounters with an experimenter. Also, issues that were given little or no attention in the first edition, such as power politics, upward influence, substitutes for leadership, transformational leadership, and leadership among women, blacks, and people of other cultures now are discussed in separate chapters.

Among the most helpful general reviews for the third

edition were those of Faucheux (1985), Hollander (1985), House (1984), and House and Singh (1987). Gardner's (1986, 1988) masterful series of essays on the nature of leadership was equally stimulating. Earlier works that are of particular importance include those of Paige (1977) and J. G. Hunt's series of symposium works on leadership.

A search of the computerized files of the abstracts of The Educational Resources Information Center (ERIC), Management Abstracts, the Psychological Abstracts, the Sociological Abstracts, Dissertation Abstracts, and Dissertation Abstracts International uncovered an important list of abstracts of consequence that were published since 1967. Journals such as the *Journal of Applied Psychology, Administrative Science Quarterly, Academy of Management Journal, Academy of Management Review, Group and Organizational Studies, Personal Psychology,* and many others were searched for the 1960–89 period. A comparable number of reprints, preprints, and papers presented at meetings that crossed my desk also figured in the final literature that was surveyed, along with many earlier items not included in the original handbook. The original 3,000 references cited in the first edition have increased to 7,500 in this third edition.

I wish to thank Jerry Hunt, Peter Weissenberg, Tom Harrell, Fred Fiedler, Marvin E. Shaw, and David O. Van Fleet and his students for their many useful suggestions on ways to improve chapters in the *Handbook.* Others who have been helpful include the late Rensis Likert, Jack Miner, Richard Franke, Frank Heller, Ed Fleishman, Robert Blake, Chet Schriesheim, Jerri Frantzve, Michael Manning, and William Fox.

It is impossible to acknowledge all those who assisted in preparing this third edition. Particularly useful were Susan Harrington and Janet Page's comments on selected chapters; Lena Massy, Lisa Schumann, and Don Bernardo's assistance in checking references; Jane Hendrickson's and Marion Aldrich's help in preparing the reference list; and the following personnel in the University Manuscript Center—Phyllis Antos, Patricia Foreman, Lois Orzel, Betty Regan, and Carrie Roy—who prepared the many drafts of the manuscript.

Bernard Bass
Binghamton, New York

Introduction to Concepts and Theories of Leadership

1

Concepts of Leadership

Leadership is one of the world's oldest preoccupations. The understanding of leadership has figured strongly in the quest for knowledge. Purposeful stories have been told through the generations about leaders' competencies, ambitions, and shortcomings; leaders' rights and privileges; and the leaders' duties and obligations.

The Beginnings

Leaders as prophets, priests, chiefs, and kings served as symbols, representatives, and models for their people in the Old and New Testaments, in the Upanishads, in the Greek and Latin classics, and in the Icelandic sagas. In the *Iliad*, higher, transcendental goals are emphasized: "He serves me most, who serves his country best" (Book X, line 201). The *Odyssey* advises leaders to maintain their social distance: "The leader, mingling with the vulgar host, is in the common mass of matter lost" (Book III, line 297). The subject of leadership was not limited to the classics of Western literature. It was of as much interest to Asoka and Confucius as to Plato and Aristotle.

Myths and legends about great leaders were important in the development of civilized societies. Stories about the exploits of individual heroes (and occasionally heroines) are central to the Babylonian *Gilgamesh, Beowolf,* the *Chanson de Roland,* the Icelandic sagas, and the Ramayana (now they would be called cases). All societies have created myths to provide plausible and acceptable explanations for the dominance of their leaders and the submission of their subordinates (Paige, 1977). The greater the socioeconomic injustice in the society, the more distorted the realities of leadership—its powers, morality and effectiveness—in the mythology.

The study of leadership rivals in age the emergence of civilization, which shaped its leaders as much as it was shaped by them. From its infancy, the study of history has been the study of leaders—what they did and why they did it. Over the centuries, the effort to formulate principles of leadership spread from the study of history and the philosophy associated with it to all the developing social sciences. In modern psychohistory, there is still a search for generalizations about leadership, built on the in-depth analysis of the development, motivation, and competencies of world leaders, living and dead.

Written philosophical principles emerged early. As can be seen in Figure 1.1, the Egyptian hieroglyphics for leadership (*seshemet*), leader (*seshemu*) and the follower (*shemsu*) were being written 5,000 years ago.

In 2300 B.C. in the Instruction of Ptahhotep, three qualities were attributed to the Pharoah. "Authoritative utterness is in thy mouth, perception is in thy heart, and thy tongue is the shrine of justice" (Lichtheim, 1973). The Chinese classics, written as early as the sixth century B.C., are filled with hortatory advice to the country's leaders about their responsibilities to the people. Confucius urged leaders to set a moral example and to manipulate rewards and punishments for teaching what was right and good. Taoism emphasized the need for the leader to work himself out of his job by making the people believe that successes were due to their efforts.

Greek concepts of leadership were exemplified by the hereos in Homer's *Iliad.* Ajax symbolized inspirational leadership and law and order. Other qualities that the Greeks admired and thought were needed (and sometimes wanting) in heroic leaders were (1) justice and judgment (Agamemnon), (2) wisdom and counsel (Nestor), (3) shrewdness and cunning (Odysseus), and (4) valor and activism (Achilles) (see Sarachek, 1968). (Shrewdness and cunning are not regarded as highly in contemporary society as they once were.)

Figure 1.1. Egyptian Hieroglyphics for Leadership, Leader, and Follower

Seshemet-Leadership

Seshemu-Leader

Shemsu-Follower

Later, Greek philosophers, such as Plato in the *Republic*, looked at the requirements for the ideal leader of the ideal state (the philosopher king). The leader was to be the most important element of good government, educated to rule with order and reason. In *Politics*, Aristotle was disturbed by the lack of virtue among those who wanted to be leaders. He pointed to the need to educate youths for such leadership. Plutarch, although he was involved with prosocial ideals about leadership, compared the traits and behavior of actual Greek and Roman leaders to support his point of view in *The Parallel Lives* (Kellerman, 1987).

A scholarly highlight of the Renaissance was Machiavelli's (1513/1962) *The Prince*. Machiavelli's thesis that "there is nothing more difficult to take in hand, more perilous to conduct, or more uncertain in its success, than to take the lead in the introduction of a new order of things" is still a germane description of the risks of leadership and the resistance to it. Machiavelli was the ultimate pragmatist. He believed that leaders needed steadiness, firmness, and concern for the maintenance of authority, power, and order in government. It was best if these objectives could be accomplished by gaining the esteem of the populace, but if they could not, then craft, deceit, threat, treachery, and violence were required (Kellerman, 1987). Machiavelli is still widely quoted as a guide to an effective leadership of sorts,

which was the basis for a modern line of investigation with the Mach scale (Christie & Geis, 1970). A 1987 survey of 117 college presidents reported that they still found *The Prince* highly relevant.

In the same way, a fundamental principle at West Point today can be traced back to Hegel's (1830/1971) *Philosophy of Mind* which argued that by first serving as a follower, a leader subsequently can best understand his followers. Hegel thought that this understanding is a paramount requirement for effective leadership.

Universality

Leadership is a universal phenomenon in humans and in many species of animals.

Animal Origins. Leadership predates the emergence of humankind. Allee (1945, 1949, 1951) maintained that all vertebrates that live in groups exhibit social organization and leadership. High-ranking males feed more freely than do other members of the group and tend to have more ready access to females. In some cases, high status involves guard duty and protection of the herd.

Pecking Order. Individual animals dominate or submit their local spaces to others in the well-known pecking order. In one of the early experiments on animal social relations, Murchison (1935) placed roosters at opposite ends of a narrow runway and measured the distance that each advanced toward the other. As a result of successive pairings, he was able to determine a strict hierarchy of dominance. Rooster A invariably dominated all the remaining subjects. At the bottom of the hierarchy was the rooster who yielded to all the others.

Douglis (1948) removed hens from their home flocks and placed them in other flocks for short periods. The hens' pecking order in each flock was observed. It was found that a hen can become an assimilated member in at least five different flocks and have a different status in each. The hen can recognize and react to the status or esteem of as many as 27 individuals. Highly dominant hens become assimilated within three days, but hens that were not dominant required three to six weeks to become assimilated. Once established, a hierarchy tended to maintain itself.

Dominance Effects in Primates. Miller and Murphy (1956) and Warren and Maroney (1969) tested pairs of monkeys who were competing for food in an area and observed strict dominance hierarchies. Subordinate animals were more successful in obtaining low-preference, rather than middle- or high-preference, foods. Bernstein (1964) noted that when the dominant male was removed from a group of monkeys, the activities of other males increased. After the dominant male returned, he resumed his dominant status and the activities of other males decreased.

Carpenter (1963) studied societies of monkeys and apes. His general findings suggested that the leader tended to control the group's movement in its search for food and shelter, regulate intragroup status, defend the group, and maintain its integrity in its contacts with other organized groupings. When the dominant male was removed from the group, the territory covered by the group was markedly reduced. Thus, the leader enlarged the freedom of the group's movement. But the dominant male tended to be avoided by low-ranking males. In some bands, the one or two males that were next in rank stood by the leader to ward off intruders and were permitted to groom him on occasion.

Again, Mason (1964) reported that leaders among groups of monkeys and apes appeared to have the primary function of initiating progressions and determining the line of march. The dominant males quelled intragroup fights, protected the females and young, were attractive to all members, were sought out by females, and influenced the size of the group's territorial range.

Zajonc (1969) interpreted the fact that fighting disappears almost entirely in primate groups after a hierarchy of dominance has been established as evidence that such groups develop norms. The norms are learned by group members, are stable but can be changed, and are complied with by the majority of members. Koford (1963) observed that the relative dominance of two bands of monkeys that meet at an eating place is usually determined by the relative dominance of the leaders of the bands. Once the dominance of a band has been established, it is observed by the other group, even in the absence of the other leader. Experimentation and observation in natural settings suggest that groups of animals develop strongly differentiated status hierarchies that their members recognize and observe. In primate groups, leaders obtain privileges that tend to bolster their dominance. Their presence is an advantage to the group in gaining possession of a desired territory and in expanding the area of free movement for the group. However, whether these findings and similar results reported for packs of wolves and hyenas, elephant matriarchies, bands of gorillas, and pods of whales are relevant to understanding the human condition remains controversial.

Humans. Parenthood, a condition that unarguably cuts across cultural lines, makes for ready-made patterns of leadership. Nevertheless, the patterns of behavior that are regarded as acceptable in leaders differ from time to time and from one culture to another. Citing various anthropological reports on primitive groups in Australia, Fiji, New Guinea, the Congo, and elsewhere, H. L. Smith and Krueger (1933) concluded that leadership occurs among all people, regardless of culture, be they isolated Indian villagers, nomads of the Eurasian steppes, or Polynesian fisherfolk. Lewis (1974) concluded, from a more recent anthropological review, that even when a society does not have institutionalized chiefs, rulers, or elected officials, there are always leaders who initiate action and play central roles in the group's decision making. No societies are known that do not have leadership in some aspects of their social life, although many may lack a single overall leader to make and enforce decisions.

Leaders, such as Abraham, Moses, David, Solomon, and the Macabees, were singled out in the Old Testament for a detailed exposition of their behavior and relations with God and their people. God was the supreme leader of his Chosen People who clarified, instructed, and directed what was to be done through the words of his Prophets and arranged for rewards for compliance and punishment for disobedience to the laws and rules He had handed down to Moses. In Islam, the ideal caliphate leadership was based on religious law (Rabi, 1967).

In *The Parallel Lives,* Plutarch (1932), in about A.D. 100, tried to show the similarities between 50 Greek and Roman leaders. Latin authors, such as Caesar, Cicero, and Seneca to name just a few, wrote extensively on the subject of leadership and administration. Their influence was considerable on the medieval and Renaissance periods, which looked back to the classics for guidance. Their influence on Thomas Jefferson and James Madison has an impact on the design of the U.S. government as we know it, as did such Renaissance scholars as Montesquieu in his *The Spirit of Laws* (1748).

Military writings about leadership stretch from the Chinese classics to the present. Napoleon listed 115 qualities that are essentials for a military leader. Meyer (1980) called for a renaissance in the concern for military leadership, in contrast to the focus on the "overmanagement" of logistics. Resources must be managed by the military leader but are no substitute for effective leadership.

Theory versus Problem Orientation

The earliest social science literature on leadership was concerned predominately with theoretical issues. Theorists sought to identify different types of leadership and to relate them to the functional demands of society. In addition, they sought to account for the emergence of leadership either by examining the qualities of the leader or the elements of the situation.

Earlier theorists can be differentiated from more recent ones in that they did not consider the interaction between individual and situational variables. Also, they tended to develop more comprehensive theories than do their more recent counterparts. Between 1945 and 1960, students of leadership devoted more of their efforts to empirical research and, as a consequence, ignored various issues that the theorists regarded as important. But research on leadership became theory driven again from the 1970s onward, although these theories tended to focus on a few phenomena and were less ambitious than those of the past.

Research on leadership in some segments of the population (students, military personnel, and business managers) was heavy but sparse on other segments (such as leaders of volunteer agencies, police officers, and health administrators). Because of the growing employment in the health, social service, and protection fields, there has been an upsurge in studies of leadership among nurses, social workers, and the police. In

the same way, the increase and upgrading of minorities in the U.S. labor force has resulted in an examination of leadership among women and minorities. Cross-cultural studies of leadership have burgeoned as well.

The emerging propositions about leadership maintain their validity over time in strong cultures. Nonetheless, they also are subject to change because of cultural changes. Thus, over 50 percent of over 1,000 students from 8 U.S. universities who were surveyed about their attraction to the television series, "MASH," indicated that watching the program had modified their attitudes or behavior about organizational life. All but 5 percent considered "MASH" to be a realistic portrayal of organizational values and processes. The respondents felt an increased desire to work with superiors who treat subordinates with understanding and respect (Dyer & Dyer, 1984).

The Importance of Leaders and Leadership

Napoleon expressed his feelings about the importance of leadership in his quip that he would rather have an army of rabbits led by a lion than an army of lions led by a rabbit. Surveys of job satisfaction from the 1920s onward illustrated the importance of leadership.[1] They uniformly reported that employees' favorable attitudes toward their supervisors contributed to the employees' satisfaction. In turn, employees' favorable attitudes toward their supervisors were usually found to be related to the productivity of the work group (see, for example, Lawshe & Nagle, 1953). Since then, countless surveys can be cited to support the contention that leaders make a difference in their subordinates' satisfaction and performance. Leaders also can make the difference in whether their organizations succeed or fail.

The usual efforts to estimate the number of leaders in the United States use census data on proprietors and officials. But Gardner (1986c) noted that although owners, managers, and officials are in the position to do so, they do not necessarily act as leaders. Cleveland (1985) estimated the number of opinion leaders in the United States and how they grew in number between 1955

---

[1]Bergen (1939), Houser (1927), Kornhauser and Sharp (1932), and Viteles (1953).

and 1985. In 1955, he estimated that there were 555,000 opinion leaders, whereas in 1971, he guessed that at least 1 million Americans could be classified as opinion leaders. He considered seven out of ten public executives to be opinion leaders—policymakers in public, philanthropic, voluntary, and large-scale "private" enterprises—in 1971. By 1985 he estimated the number to have multiplied to 1 out of every 200 Americans.

As Cleveland (1985, p. 4) stated: There are some 83,000 government units in the United States, and about 175,000 corporations each doing more than $1 million worth of business a year. The galloping rate of growth of complexity means that a growth curve of the requirement for leaders (if anyone were clever enough to construct such an index) would show a steeper climb than any other growth rate in our political economy.

Is Leadership a Figment of the Imagination? Some critics argue that all the effects of leadership are in the eyes of their beholders. Followers attribute effects that are due to historical, economic, or social forces to leadership, as in romantic fiction (Meindl & Ehrlich, 1987; Meindl, Ehrlich, & Dukerich, 1985). Other critics, such as Pandey (1976), regard leadership as a useless concept for understanding social influence. For Calder (1977), the objective contributions of the "leader" to outcomes may be more interesting than true. The extreme position taken by some attribution theorists is that organizational outcomes are determined primarily by other factors, but leaders are credited with what happened after the fact.

Organizational leaders who are perceived to be exerting leadership on organizational performance are merely the subjects of misperceptions, some critics contend. That is, organizational outcomes are objectively determined by environmental and organizational factors in which leadership, at best, can play only a minor role. For instance, M. C. Brown (1982, p. 1) concluded that "once other factors influencing effectiveness are accounted for, it is likely that leadership will have little bearing on organizational performance."

Pfeffer (1977) took a similar but not as extreme position: Leadership is a sense-making heuristic to account for organizational performance and is important primarily for its symbolic role in organizations. Leaders are selected or self-selected to fulfil the fate of the organization and are highly constrained by organizational and external factors. Therefore, they can have only a limited impact on organizational outcomes compared to external factors. Leaders are able only to react to contingencies, to facilitate the adjustment of the organization in its context, and to alter that environment to some limited extent. Also they have no control over many factors that affect organizational performance and they typically have unilateral control over few resources.

Despite these constraints, management and leadership seem to have a substantial effect on some organizational outcomes. Thus, when Lieberson and O'Connor (1972) examined the effects of top management on the success of 167 firms over a 20-year period, they found that the effects depended on which outcomes were considered. Managers had the greatest effect on profit margins but the least effect on sales; they also were of less consequence in capital-intensive industries. In the same way, Salancik and Pfeffer (1977) showed that the mayors of 30 U.S. cities had considerable influence only on those budgetary issues, such as libraries and parks, that were not in the domain of important special-interest groups, such as the police, fire fighters, and highway maintenance personnel. In all, Pfeffer concluded that since people want to achieve the feeling that they are in control of their environment, they find it useful to attribute outcomes of their group and organizational performance to leaders, rather than to the complex internal and external environmental forces that actually are most important. Meindl and Ehrlich (1987) showed that if performance outcomes of firms were attributed to the leadership of the top management, rather than to the employees, market conditions, or the government, the judges gave better evaluations of the outcomes. Meindl and Ehrlich attributed this finding to the judges' assumption that leaders have a reliable and potent impact on outcomes.

Even when the true causes of outcomes were logically not determinable, Meindl, Ehrlich, and Dukerich (1985) showed that there was a tendency to view leadership as the likely cause of the outcomes. This study and the one by Meindl and Ehrich (1987) were thought to demonstrate that leadership is more of a romantic notion than a phenomenon that truly affects group and organizational outcomes.

Then there is evidence that would-be followers, subordinates, and groups of employees are so constrained by technology, rules, job requirements, and organizational policies that there is little discretionary room for a superior or leader to make much of a difference in how things get done (Katz & Kahn, 1966). Furthermore, subordinates may have much more effect on the behavior of their superiors than vice versa (Goodstadt & Kipnis, 1970).

Miner (1975, p. 200) was ready to abandon the concept of leadership, stating that "the concept of leadership itself has outlived its usefulness. Hence, I suggest that we abandon leadership in favor of some other, more fruitful way of cutting up the theoretical pie." In 1982a, Miner recanted this statement but still maintained that the concept has limited usefulness because so much of the empirical research has been on emergent leadership in small groups, rather than within more complex organizations. For Miner, the fragile, distressed, leadership that arises in the small, temporary group to develop, maintain, and enforce the norms of the group may have little relevance for leadership in the impersonal "task system" of the traditional organization.

Leaders Do Make a Difference. Despite the skepticism about the reality and importance of leadership, all social and political movements require leaders to begin them. As Tucker (1981, p. 87) put it, "in the beginning is the leadership act. A 'leaderless movement' is naturally out of the question." This does not mean that formal, institutionalized leadership is required. In fact, no leader in an institutional form appeared in the numerous peasant revolts from the sixteenth to nineteenth centuries in Southern Germany. The same was true for journeymen's strikes during the eighteenth century. Leadership remained informal and egalitarian. Only in the middle of the nineteenth century did definite leaders, such as Ferdinand Lasalle, emerge. Lasalle placed himself at the head of the German workers' movement and worked out its explicit ideology, along with the myth that he founded the movement (Groh, 1986). This behavior is consistent with most cases of institutional development: Leaders determine the direction they will take. The historical records of the early British Royal Society of the seventeenth century illustrate that its secretaries were responsible for who joined the society and what kinds of science were sponsored (Mulligan & Mulligan, 1981).

Indeed, leadership is often regarded as the single most critical factor in the success or failure of institutions. For instance, T. H. Allen (1981) argued that the school principal's leadership is the most important factor in determining a school's climate and the students' success. Sylvia and Hutchison (1985) concluded that the motivation of 167 Oklahoma teachers depended considerably on their perceptions of the quality of their relationships with their superiors. And Smith, Carson, and Alexander (1984) found that among the 50 Methodist ministers they studied, some were more effective leaders than were others. The effectiveness of these ministers was evidenced by the differential impact that their ministries had on church attendance, membership, property values, and contributions to the church.

In the business and industrial sector, Maccoby (1979, p. 313) concluded, from his observations of the manager as a game-playing politician, that the need of firms to survive and prosper in a world of increasing competition, of technological advances, of changing governmental regulations, of changing worker attitudes, requires "a higher level of leadership than ever before." When an organization must be changed to reflect changes in technology, the environment, and the completion of programs, its leadership is critical in orchestrating the process (Burke, Richley, & DeAngelis, 1985). Mintzberg and Waters (1982) examined the evolution of a retail firm over a 60-year-period and found that a senior executive could successfully reorient the firm by intervening to change previous strategies and organizational structures. In the same way, Day and Lord (1986) noted that when confounding errors are controlled in studies of the effects of executive succession, differences in executive leaders can explain as much as 45 percent of their organizations' performance. Agreeing with Chandler (1962), they stated that historical analyses of changes of leadership over significant periods have shown that leadership has a profound influence on an organization. Concurrent correlational analyses of a sample of executives and their organizations at the same point in time reach similar conclusions, although the effects are not as strong.

In a review of experiments in the United States on the productivity of workers between 1971 and 1981, Katzell and Guzzo (1983) concluded that supervisory methods seemed particularly effective in increasing output. In Sweden, Westerlund (1952a) observed that the high-quality performance of supervisors improved that attitudes and performance of telephone operators. Also in Sweden, Ekvall and Arvonen (1984) found that leadership styles accounted for 65 percent of the variance in organizational climate in the 25 units they studied. Virany and Tushman (1986) stated that the senior managers of better-performing minicomputer firms were systematically different from those of firms that performed poorly. The senior management in the better firms had had previous experience in the electronic industry and was more likely to include the founder of the firm who still served as chief executive officer. Although most attention has been paid to industrial leaders as developers and builders, Hansen (1974) pointed out that the success with which a firm, such as the Ford Motor Company, closed a plant without much human dislocation depended on effective leadership.

Leadership has been considered a critical factor in military successes since records have been kept; that is, better-led forces repeatedly have been victorious over poorly led forces. Thus, not unexpectedly, morale and cohesion among Israeli and U.S. enlisted soldiers correlated with measures of the soldiers' confidence in their company, division, and battalion commanders (Gal & Manning, 1984).

Personnel of the Mississippi Cooperative Extension reported that they felt less job stress if they saw their supervisors displaying more leadership in structuring the work to be done and showing concern for the subordinates' needs (Graham, 1982). In a study of 204 innovations in state programs, Cheek (1987) found that the governors came up with 55 percent of the innovations and the agencies with only 36 percent.

Studies by Tucker (1981), Hargrove and Nelson (1984), and Hargrove (1987) concluded that the style and performance of a U.S. president makes a big difference in what happens to legislation, policy, and programs. Successful presidents are more sensitive to the inherent politics of policy-making. They define and publicize the policy dilemmas facing the country and earn widespread public and Congressional support for their positions. They construct their policy agendas with the felt needs of the country in mind and create political support for their agendas; they also realize that timing is important (Tucker, 1981). But like Jimmy Carter, they can fail if they push for what they deem to be right but what is not politically feasible and if they favor comprehensive integrated solutions, rather than incremental steps (Hargrove, 1987). Presidents can make decisions that are not implemented because they or their assistants do not follow them up. For example, as part of the agreement to resolve the Cuban missile crisis, President Kennedy ordered the removal of U.S. missiles from Turkey on the border of the Soviet Union. Six months later, he was astonished to learn that the missiles were still in place (Manchester, 1988). Although presidents spend relatively little time trying to make major reorientations in policy, they have an important impact on the smaller substantive decisions that affect the larger overall strategies (Neustadt, 1980). History may be drastically altered by a sudden change in presidents. Before leaving Washington, D.C., for his fateful trip to Texas in November 1963, Kennedy signed the first order for a phased withdrawal from Vietnam. On assuming office after Kennedy's assassination, Lyndon Johnson rescinded the order. The war continued for another decade.

According to Richard Nixon's "Silent Majority" speech in 1969, presidents may have to take an unpopular stand, but when they do, they can strengthen acceptance by explaining their reasons, soliciting support, and winning approval (Safire, 1975). Presidents also provide symbolic support for the development of norms, values, and beliefs that contribute to subsequent national and organizational development (Sayles, 1979). As Gardner (1988a) noted, for a society to function, its people must share beliefs and values regarding the standards of acceptable behavior. Leaders can revitalize those shared beliefs and help keep the values fresh. "They have a role in creating the state of mind that is the society" (Gardner, 1988a, p. 18). They conceive and articulate goals that move people from their own interests to unite for higher ends.

Often, the effects of leadership are indirect. For example, Katzell (1987) showed through a path analysis that although supervisors' direct influence on their subordinates was modest, they exerted indirect influence and increased the employees' morale by providing rewards, relating rewards to performance, and treating employees equitably; the increased morale, in turn, improved the employees' performance.

Jongbloed and Frost (1985) modified Pfeffer's (1977) reasoning to argue that leaders still have an important general role to play. What leaders really manage in organizations are the employees' interpretations or understanding of what goes on in the organizations. The leaders manage meanings and, therefore, exert a strong impact on organizational outcomes. Jongbloed and Frost showed how the laboratory director in one Canadian hospital, compared to another in a second hospital with the same formal assignments and the same absence of control of issues, successfully lobbied for the importance of pathology and convinced the hospital administrators to allocate more funds for operations and budget than were allocated in the second hospital.

The importance of leadership is attested by academic and lay interest in leadership as a subject for development, training, and education (Campbell, 1977).[2] Although U.S. college presidents believe that our educational institutions are reluctant to incorporate leadership education into their curricula (Cronin, 1984), the college landscape is not bleak. Gregory's (1986) survey of all known U.S. degree-granting institutions of higher learning uncovered 53 that offered an academic course on leadership, 70 that made it possible to major or concentrate in the subject, 181 that incorporated the study of leadership in an academic course or a student-affairs

program, and 81 that offered the subject in continuing education or professional programs.[3]

Leadership as a Subject of Inquiry

The importance of leadership is also demonstrated by its place in social science research. According to Mitchell (1979) and DeMeuse (1986), leadership has been one of the frequent subjects of empirical research, concentrating on the antecedents of leaders' behavior and the factors that contribute to its effectiveness. Leadership is a featured topic in almost every textbook on organizational behavior (McFillen, 1984–87). The scholarly books on leadership number in the hundreds, and articles, reports, and essays number in the thousands.

Several different schools of thought have prevailed simultaneously since leadership first was studied. The early sociological theorists tended to explain leadership in terms of either the person or the environment. Later researchers tended to view leadership as an aspect of role differentiation or as an outgrowth of social interaction processes. Recently, the naïve theories of leadership we hold have been considered most important in explaining what is going on. But this is as it should be. Theory and empirical research should move forward together, each stimulating, supporting, and modifying the other. Neither can stand alone. An elegant theory without prospects of elegant data gathering makes for a sketchy theory. Early in a line of investigation, crude data and theory may be useful. Later, as understanding develops and practice improves, more stringent standards are required (Bass, 1974).

Assumptions

The research discussed in the following chapters is based on a wide variety of theoretical assumptions. Despite differences in the philosophies that guide them and the research methods used, there is remarkable convergence of findings on many problems. This convergence, when it occurs, can be regarded as strong evidence of the validity of the findings.

An almost insurmountable problem is the question of the extent to which we pour old wine into new bot-

---

[2]Recognition of the importance to the nation of leadership and its development for all types of organizations is witnessed by the Alliance for Leadership Development, which includes the following members: American Leadership Forum of Houston; Association of American Colleges of Washington, D.C.; Association of Governing Boards of Universities and Colleges; Center for Creative Leadership of Greensboro, N.C.; Coro Foundation of St. Louis; International Leadership Center of Dallas; National Association of Secondary School Principals of Reston, Va.; and the National Executive Service Corps of New York. The Alliance's programs include the promotion of research on and teaching of leadership, related conferences and publications, a clearinghouse of information on leadership programs at universities and secondary schools, leadership development programs in the community, and development programs for corporate executives.

[3]Details about these can be found in Clark, Freeman, and Britt (1987).

tles when proposing "new" theories. For instance, Julius Caesar's descriptions of his leadership style in the Gallic Wars in the first century B.C. are clear, succinct endorsements of the need for what Blake and Mouton (1964) conceived as "9-9" style—a style that Fleishman (1953a) described in terms of high initiation and consideration and that in the year 2500 some new theorist will give a new name. When does a field advance? Are we beyond Caesar's understanding of how to lead infantry shock troops?

My hope in this book is to catalog what is known about leadership and to suggest some of the things that we do not know and should try to find out. Although I agree with Burns (1978, p. 2) that "leadership is one of the most observed . . . phenomena on earth," I disagree with Burns that "it is one of the least understood."

The Meaning of Leadership

The word leadership is a sophisticated, modern concept. In earlier times, words meaning "head of state," "military commander," "princeps," "proconsul," "chief," or "king" were common in most societies; these words differentiated the ruler from other members of society. A preoccupation with leadership, as opposed to headship based on inheritance, usurpation, or appointment, occurred predominantly in countries with an Anglo-Saxon heritage. Although the *Oxford English Dictionary* (1933) noted the appearance of the word "leader" in the English language as early as the year 1300, the word "leadership" did not appear until the first half of the nineteenth century in writings about the political influence and control of British Parliament. And the word did not appear in the most other modern languages until recent times.

Defining Leadership

There are almost as many different definitions of leadership as there are persons who have attempted to define the concept.[4] Moreover, as Pfeffer (1977) noted,

[4]Different definitions and conceptions of leadership have been reviewed briefly by Morris and Seeman (1950), Shartle (1951a, 1951b, 1956), L. F. Carter (1953), C. A. Gibb (1954, 1969a), Bass (1960), Stogdill (1975), and Schriesheim and Kerr (1977b).

many of the definitions are ambiguous. Furthermore, the distinction between leadership and other social-influence processes is often blurred (Bavelas, 1960; Hollander & Julian, 1969). The many dimensions into which leadership has been cast and their overlapping meanings have added to the confusion. Therefore, the meaning of leadership may depend on the kind of institution in which it is found (Spitzberg, 1986). Nevertheless, there is sufficient similarity among definitions to permit a rough scheme of classification. Leadership has been conceived as the focus of group processes, as a matter of personality, as a matter of inducing compliance, as the exercise of influence, as particular behaviors, as a form of persuasion, as a power relation, as an instrument to achieve goals, as an effect of interaction, as a differentiated role, as initiation of structure, and as many combinations of these definitions.

Leadership as a Focus of Group Processes

Early on, definitions of the leader tended to view the leader as a focus of group change, activity, and process. Cooley (1902) maintained that the leader is always the nucleus of a tendency, and (that) all social movements, closely examined, will be found to consist of tendencies having such nuclei. Mumford (1906–07) observed that "leadership is the preeminence of one or a few individuals in a group in the process of control of societal phenomena." Blackmar (1911) saw leadership as the "centralization of effort in one person as an expression of the power of all." Chapin (1924b) viewed leadership as "a point of polarization for group cooperation." According to L. L. Bernard (1927), leaders are influenced by the needs and wishes of the group members; in turn, they focus the attention and release the energies of group members in a desired direction. Regarding the dominance of the leader's personality M. Smith (1934) commented that "the social group that express its unity in connected activity is always composed of but two essential portions: the center of focal activity, and the individuals who act with regard to the center." For Redl (1942), the leader is a central or focal person who integrates the group.

As a nation develops, it needs a centralized locus for its operation which can only be achieved by a single leader (Babikan, 1981). All important decisions and their implementation center on the cult of the leader even when, as in parliamentary democracies, actual decision making is diffuse. The leader embodies the collective will. This single leader sorts out the essential problems, offers possible solutions, establishes priorities, and launches developmental operations.

J. F. Brown (1936) maintained that "the leader may not be separated from the group, buy may be treated as a position of high potential in the field." Following in the same tradition, Krech and Crutchfield (1948) observed that "by virtue of his special position in the group he serves as a primary agent for the determination of group structure, group atmosphere, group goals, group ideology, and group activities." For Knickerbocker (1948), "when conceived in terms of the dynamics of human social behavior, leadership is a function of needs existing within a given situation, and consists of a relationship between an individual and a group."

This emphasis on the leader as the center, or focus, of group activity directed attention to group structure and group processes in studying leadership. On the one hand, some of the earliest theorists, such as Cooley and Mumford, were sophisticated in their concept of leadership. On the other hand, several of the definitions placed the leader in a particularly fortuitous, if not helpless, position, given the inexorable progress of the group. Leaders were thought to have to stay one pace ahead of the group to avoid being run over. Centrality of location in the group can permit a person to control communications, and hence is likely to place him or her in a position of leadership, but centrality, in itself, is not leadership.

Leadership as Personality and Its Effects

The concept of personality appealed to several early theorists, who sought to explain why some persons are better able than are others to exercise leadership. A. O. Bowden (1926) equated leadership with strength of personality: "Indeed, the amount of personality attributed to an individual may not be unfairly estimated by the degree of influence he can exert upon others." Bingham (1927) defined a leader as a person who possesses the greatest number of desirable traits of personality and character. According to L. L. Bernard (1926), "Any person who is more than ordinarily efficient in carrying psychosocial stimuli to others and is thus effective in conditioning collective responses may be called a leader"; the leader must possess prestige and "must know what stimuli will condition adequate responses for his purposes and develop a technique for presenting these stimuli." Tead (1929) regarded leadership as a combination of traits that enables an individual to induce others to accomplish a given task.

The personality theorists tended to regard leadership as a one-way effect: Leaders possess qualities that differentiate them from followers. But these theorists did not acknowledge the extent to which leaders and followers have interactive effects by determining which qualities of followers are of consequence in a situation. What theorists now see is that the personal qualities of a would-be leader determine his or her *esteem* in the eyes of potential followers. Some personality traits, such as ascendancy or social boldness, more often than not go hand in hand with being esteemed and attaining leadership, but social boldness is not leadership. At the extreme, in times of crisis, followers *endow* a highly dominant figure who is empathic to their critical needs with charisma. The hero's personality then makes it possible for him or her to perform enormous feats of leadership (Stark, 1970).

Leadership as the Art of Inducing Compliance

Munson (1921) defined leadership as "the ability to handle men so as to achieve the most with the least friction and the greatest cooperation. . . . Leadership is the creative and directive force of morale." According to F. H. Allport (1924), "leadership . . . is personal social control." B. V. Moore (1927) reported the results of a conference at which leadership was defined as "the ability to impress the will of the leader on those led and induce obedience, respect, loyalty, and cooperation." Similarly, Bundel (1930) regarded leadership as "the art of inducing others to do what one wants them to do." According to T. R. Phillips (1939), "leadership is the imposition, maintenance, and direction of moral unity to our ends." Warriner (1955) suggested that "leadership as a form of relationship between persons requires that one or several persons act in conformance with the request of another." For Bennis (1959), "leadership can be defined as the process by which an agent induces a subordinate to behave in a desired manner."

The compliance-induction theorists, perhaps even more than the personality theorists, tended to regard leadership as a unidirectional exertion of influence and as an instrument for molding the group to the leader's will. They expressed little recognition of the rights, desires, and necessities of the group members or of the group's traditions and norms. This disregard for the followers and the group was rejected by various other theorists, who sought to remove, by definition, any possibility of legitimating an authoritarian concept of leadership. Yet, regardless of the sentiments of some behavioral scientists, one cannot ignore that much leadership is authoritarian, directive, and even coercive. Its effects are seen in public compliance but not necessarily in private acceptance.

Leadership as the Exercise of Influence

Use of the concept of influence marked a step in the direction of generality and abstraction in defining leadership. J. B. Nash (1929) suggested that "leadership implies influencing change in the conduct of people." Tead (1935) defined it as "the activity of influencing people to cooperate toward some goal which they come to find desirable." Stogdill (1950) termed it "the process of influencing the activities of an organized group in its efforts toward goal setting and goal achievement."

Shartle (1951a, 1951b) proposed that the leader be considered an individual "who exercises positive influence acts upon others" or "who exercises more important influence acts than any other members of the group or organization." Similarly, Tannenbaum, Weschler, and Massarik (1961) defined leadership as "interpersonal influence, exercised in a situation and directed, through the communication process, toward the attainment of a specified goal or goals." This definition was expanded by Ferris and Rowland (1981), who conceived of the leadership-influence process as a contextual influence that has an impact on subordinates' attitudes and performance through effects on

the subordinates' perceptions of their job characteristics.

The interactive aspect became apparent as leadership was linked by definition to influence processes. Haiman (1951) suggested that "direct leadership is an interaction process in which an individual, usually through the medium of speech, influences the behavior of others toward a particular end." According to Gerth and Mills (1953), "leadership . . . is a relation between leader and led in which the leader influences more than he is influenced: because of the leader, those who are led act or feel differently than they otherwise would." For Cartwright (1965), leadership was equated with the "domain of influence." Katz and Kahn (1966) considered "the essence of organizational leadership to be the influential increment over and above mechanical compliance with routine directions of the organization." They observed that although all supervisors at the same level of organization have equal power, they do not use it with equal effectiveness to influence individuals and the organization. In the same way, Hollander and Julian (1969) suggested that "leadership in the broadest sense implies the presence of a particular influence relationship between two or more persons."

According to Hemphill (1949a) and Bass (1960), an individual's effort to change the behavior of others is attempted leadership. When the other members actually change, this creation of change in others is successful leadership. If the others are reinforced or rewarded for changing their behavior, this evoked achievement is effective leadership. The distinctions between attempted, successful, and effective leadership are important because the dynamics of each are quite different.

The concept of influence recognizes the fact that individuals differ in the extent to which their behaviors affect the activities of a group. It implies a reciprocal relationship between the leader and the followers, but one that is not necessarily characterized by domination, control, or induction of compliance by the leader. It merely states that leadership exercises a determining effect on the behaviors of group members and on activities of the group. The definition of influence also recognizes that leaders can influence group members by their own example. The Israeli lieutenant leads with the call, "Follow me." Leaders serve as models for the followers. As Gandhi suggested: "clean examples have a curious method of multiplying themselves" (quoted in Paige, 1977, p. 65).

Defining effective leadership as successful influence by the leader that results in the attainment of goals by the influenced followers, that is, defining leadership in terms of goal attainment (to be discussed later in the chapter) is particularly useful, for it permits the use of reinforcement theory to understand leader-follower behavior.

Limited to Discretionary Influence. Numerous theorists wanted to limit leadership to only that influence which is not mandated by the leader's role. As noted before, Katz and Kahn (1966) defined leadership as an influential increment over and above compliance with the routine directives of the organization. J. A. Miller (1973a) saw leaders exerting influence "at the margin" to compensate for what was missing in the specified process and structure. Jacobs and Jaques (1987) conceived and viewed leadership in complex organizations as "discretionary action directed toward dealing with unanticipated events that otherwise would influence outcomes of critical tasks at the actor's level" (as did Osborn, Hunt, & Jauch, 1980). It is influence over and above what is typically invested in the role—influence beyond what is due to formal procedures, rules, and regulations. Thus, managers are leaders only when they take the opportunity to exert influence over activities beyond what has been prescribed as their role requirements.

Leadership as an Act or Behavior

One school of theorists preferred to define leadership in terms of acts or behaviors. For L. F. Carter (1953), "leadership behaviors are any behaviors the experimenter wishes to so designate or, more generally, any behaviors which experts in this area wish to consider as leadership behaviors." Shartle (1956) defined a leadership act as "one which results in others acting or responding in a shared direction."

Hemphill (1949a) suggested that "leadership may be defined as the behavior of an individual while he is in-

volved in directing group activities." Fiedler (1967a) proposed a somewhat similar definition:

> By leadership behavior we generally mean the particular acts in which a leader engages in the course of directing and coordinating the work of his group members. This may involve such acts as structuring the work relations, praising or criticizing group members, and showing consideration for their welfare and feelings.

Leadership as a Form of Persuasion

Both Presidents Eisenhower and Truman emphasized the persuasive aspect of leadership. According to Eisenhower, "leadership is the ability to decide what is to be done, and then to get others to want to do it" (quoted in Larson, 1968, p. 21). According to Truman (1958, p. 139), "a leader is a man who has the ability to get other people to do what they don't want to do, and like it." And for Lippmann (1922), such persuasiveness is long lasting: "The final test of a leader is that he leaves behind him in other men the conviction and the will to carry on." Several theorists defined leadership as successful persuasion without coercion; followers are convinced by the merits of the argument, not by the coercive power of the arguer. Neustadt (1960) concluded, from his study of U.S. presidents, that presidential leadership stems from the power to persuade. Schenk (1928) suggested that "leadership is the management of men by persuasion and inspiration rather than by the direct or implied threat of coercion." Merton (1969) regarded leadership as "an interpersonal relation in which others comply because they want to, not because they have to." According to Cleeton and Mason (1934), "leadership indicates the ability to influence men and secure results through emotional appeals rather than through the exercise of authority." Copeland (1942) maintained that

> leadership is the art of dealing with human nature. . . . It is the art of influencing a body of people by persuasion or example to follow a line of action. It must never be confused with drivership . . . which is the art of compelling a body of people by intimidation or force to follow a line of action.

Odier (1948) differentiated between the value and the valence of a leader. Valence is the power of a person to act on the feeling or value of another person or group of persons, of modifying (strengthening or weakening) it in one fashion or another. Thus, valence is defined not by the value of the leader's personality but by the quality of the influences he or she exerts on the members of a group. Koontz and O'Donnell (1955) regarded leadership as "the activity of persuading people to cooperate in the achievement of a common objective."

Persuasion is a powerful instrument for shaping expectations and beliefs—particularly in political, social, and religious affairs. The definition of leadership as a form of persuasion tended to be favored by students of politics and social movements and by military and industrial theorists who were opposed to authoritarian concepts. It was also the province of rhetoricians and communications theorists. Research on persuasion, persuasibility, and communications has paralleled research on leadership (W. Weiss, 1958). Persuasion can be seen as one form of leadership. Much of what has been learned from studies of persuasion can be incorporated into an understanding of leadership.

Leadership as a Power Relation

Most political theorists, from Machiavelli through Marx to the academic political scientists of the twentieth century, have seen power as the basis of political leadership. Social psychologists J. R. P. French (1956) and Raven and French (1958a, 1958b) defined leadership in terms of differential power relationships among members of a group. For the latter, interpersonal power—referent, expert, reward based, coercive, or legitimate—is conceived "as a resultant of the maximum force which A can induce on B minus the maximum resisting force which B can mobilize in the opposite direction." Similarly, Janda (1960) defined "leadership as a particular type of power relationship characterized by a group member's perception that another group member has the right to prescribe behavior patterns for the former regarding his activity as a member of a particular group."

M. Smith (1948) equated leadership with control of the interaction process. Thus, "the initiator of an interaction, A, gives a stimulus to the second participant, B. A asserts his control by interfering with B's original course of action."

Power is regarded as a form of influence relationship. It can be observed that some leaders tend to transform any leadership opportunity into an overt power relationship. In fact, the very frequency of this observation, combined with the often undesirable consequences for individuals and societies, has induced many theorists to reject the notion of authoritarian leadership. Nevertheless, many of those who were most committed at one time to trust building, openness, and participatory approaches, like Bennis (1970), have faced the world as it is, not as they would like it to be, and have come to acknowledge the importance of power relations in understanding leadership.

The power relationship may be subtle or obscure. "As a power relation, leadership may be known to both leader and led, or unknown to either or both" (Gerth & Mills, 1953). For instance, myths and symbols about the master-slave relationship may unconsciously influence superior-subordinate relationships in modern organizations (Denhardt, 1987).

Leadership as an Instrument of Goal Achievement

Numerous theorists have included the idea of goal achievement in their definitions. Several have defined leadership in terms of its instrumental value for accomplishing a group's goals and satisfying its needs. According to Cowley (1928), "a leader is a person who has a program and is moving toward an objective with his group in a definite manner." Bellows (1959) defined leadership as "the process of arranging a situation so that various members of a group, including the leader, can achieve common goals with maximum economy and a minimum of time and work." For Knickerbocker (1948), "the functional relation which is leadership exists when a leader is perceived by a group as controlling means for the satisfaction of their needs."

The classical organizational theorists defined leadership in terms of achieving a group's objectives. R. C. Davis (1942) referred to leadership as "the principal dynamic force that motivates and coordinates the organization in the accomplishment of its objectives." Similarly, Urwick (1953) stated that the leader is "the personal representation of the personification of common purpose not only to all who work on the undertaking, but to everyone outside it." K. Davis (1962) defined leadership as "the human factor which binds a group together and motivates it toward goals."

For Jacobs and Jaques (1987), leaders give purpose to others to expend and mobilize energy to try to compete. Cattell (1951) took the extreme position that leadership is whatever or whoever contributes to the group's performance; it is the group's *syntality*, resulting from its members and the relations among them. To measure each member's leadership, Cattell noted, remove him or her from the group, one at a time, and observe what happens to the group's performance. In a similar vein, as noted earlier, both Calder (1977) and Pfeffer (1977) stated that leadership is mainly influence and is even attributed to participants after the fact. The attributions may be based on implicit theories of leadership (Rush, Thomas, & Lord, 1977). Outcomes are attributed more readily to the leader, thus, when things to wrong, the leader is likely to be blamed and even removed (Hollander, 1986).

For Burns (1978), Bennis (1983), Bass (1985a), and Tichy and Devanna (1986), leadership transforms followers, creates visions of the goals that may be attained, and articulates for the followers the ways to attain those goals. As Luiz Muñoz Marín, former governor of Puerto Rico, said: "A political leader is a person with the ability to imagine non-existing states of affairs combined with the ability to influence other people to bring them about" (quoted in Paige, 1977, p. 65).

Envisioning the goals involves intuition, fantasy, and dreaming, not just analytical, systematic, conscious thought processes. For Jack Sparks, the chief executive officer who transformed the Whirlpool Corporation,

> ... the vision came after years of mulling over the kind of organization that Whirlpool could be, and after his constant interaction with people in other organizations and academics. The vision was his; and the strategic planning process became the vehicle for implementing that vision, not its source. (Tichy & Devanna, 1985, p. 138)

Tucker (1981) observed that most current politicians must focus the attention of their constituents on short-term goals and programs. More statesmanlike opinion leaders are necessary to arouse and direct a democracy toward achieving longer-term goals, such as stabilization of the population, improvement of the environment, and arms control.

Leadership as an Emerging Effect of Interaction

Several theorists have viewed leadership not as a cause or control of group action but as an effect of it. Bogardus (1929) stated that "as a social process, leadership is that social interstimulation which causes a number of people to set out toward an old goal with new zest or a new goal with hopeful courage—with different persons keeping different places." For Pigors (1935), "leadership is a process of mutual stimulation which, by the successful interplay of individual differences, controls human energy in the pursuit of a common cause." For H. H. Anderson (1940), "a true leader in the psychological sense is one who can make the most of individual differences, who can bring out the most differences in the group and therefore reveal to the group a sounder base for defining common purposes."

This group of theorists was important because they called attention to the fact that emergent leadership grows out of the interaction process itself. It can be observed that leadership truly exists only when it is acknowledged and conferred by other members of the group. Although the authors probably did not mean to imply it, their definitions suggest that this quality amounts to little more than passive acceptance of the importance of one's status. An individual often emerges as leader as a consequence of interactions within the group that arouse expectations that he or she, rather than someone else, can serve the group most usefully by helping it to attain its objectives.

Leadership as a Differentiated Role

According to role theory, each member of a society occupies a position in the community, as well as in various groups, organizations, and institutions. In each position, the individual is expected to play a more or less well-defined role. Different members occupying different positions play different roles. Birth and class may force the differentiation of roles. According to the leader of Ponape, Heinrich Iriarte, some Micronesians are born to rule while others are born to serve (Paige, 1977, p. 65).

Leadership may be regarded as an aspect of role differentiation. H. H. Jennings (1944) observed that "leadership . . . appears as a manner of interaction involving behavior by and toward the individual 'lifted' to a leadership role by other individuals." Similarly, C. A. Gibb (1954) regarded group leadership as a *position* emerging from the interaction process itself. For T. Gordon (1955), leadership was an interaction between a person and a group or, more accurately, between a person and the group members. Each participant in this interaction played a role. These roles differed from each other; the basis for their difference was a matter of influence—that is, one person, the leader, influenced, and the other persons responded.

Sherif and Sherif (1956) suggested that leadership is a role within the scheme of relations and is defined by reciprocal expectations between the leader and other members. The leadership role is defined, as are other roles, by stabilized expectations (norms) that, in most matters and situations of consequence to the group, are more exacting and require greater obligations from the leader than do those for other members of the group.

Newcomb, Turner, and Converse (1965) observed that members of a group make different contributions to the achievement of goals. Insofar as any member's contributions are particularly indispensable, they may be regarded as leaderlike; and insofar as any member is recognized by others as a dependable source of such contributions, he or she is leaderlike. To be so recognized is equivalent to having a role relationship to other members.

Much of the research on the emergence and differentiation of roles pertains equally well to leadership. As Sherif and Sherif (1956) indicated, roles are defined in terms of the expectations that group members develop in regard to themselves and other members. Thus, the theory and research pertaining to the reinforcement, confirmation, and structuring of expectations applies also to the leadership problem. Of all the available definitions, the role conception of leadership is most firmly buttressed by research findings.

The recognition of leadership as an instrument of goal attainment, as a product of interaction processes, and as a differentiated role adds to the development of a coherent theory that fits much of the facts available to date. Leadership as a differentiated role is required to integrate the various other roles of the group and to maintain unity of action in the group's effort to achieve its goals.

Leadership as the Initiation of Structure

Several commentators viewed leadership not as the passive occupancy of a position or as acquisition of a role but as a process of originating and maintaining the role *structure*—the pattern of role relationships. M. Smith (1935a) equated leadership with the management of social differentials through the process of giving stimuli that other people respond to integratively. Lapiere and Farnsworth (1936) observed that situations may be distinguished from one another by the extent to which they are organized by one member of the group. Such organization is usually spoken of as leadership, with its nature and degree varying in different social situations.

Gouldner (1950) suggested that there is a difference in effect between a stimulus from a follower and one from a leader. The difference is in the probability that the stimulus will structure the group's behavior. The stimulus from a leader has a higher probability of structuring a group's behavior because of the group-endowed belief that the leader is a legitimate source of such stimuli. Gouldner disagreed with C. A. Gibb (1947) regarding the notion that once the group's activity is dominated by an established and accepted organization, leadership tends to disappear. Thus, Bavelas (1960) defined organizational leadership as the function of "maintaining the operational effectiveness of decision-making systems which comprise the management of the organization."

Homans (1950) identified the leader of a group as a member who "originates interaction." For Hemphill (1954), "to lead is to engage in an act that initiates a structure in the interaction as part of the process of solving a mutual problem." And Stogdill (1959) defined leadership as "the initiation and maintenance of structure in expectation and interaction."

This group of theorists attempted to define leadership in terms of the variables that give rise to the differentiation and maintenance of role structures in groups. Such a definition has greater theoretical utility than do those that are more concrete and descriptive to a lay person: It leads to a consideration of the basic processes involved in the emergence of the leadership role.

Again, what must be kept in mind is that leadership is more than just the initiation of structure. As Gouldner (1950) noted, we need room for acts of leadership in the completely structured group. Stogdill's (1959) inclusion of maintenance of structure is important. Furthermore, if structure is the consistent pattern of differentiated role relationships within a group, we must be sure also to consider the persons, resources, and tasks within the differentiated roles.

Leadership as a Combination of Elements

Naturally, some scholars combine several definitions of leadership to cover a larger set of meanings. Bogardus (1934) defined leadership as "personality in action under group conditions . . . not only is leadership both a personality and a group phenomenon, it is also a social process involving a number of persons in mental contact in which one person assumes dominance over the others." Previously, Bogardus (1928) described leadership as the creation and setting forth of exceptional behavioral patterns in such a way that other persons respond to them. For Jago (1982), leadership is the exercise of noncoercive influence to coordinate the members of an organized group to accomplishing the group's objectives. Leadership is also a set of properties attributed to those who are perceived to use such influences successfully. Other definitions, such as Barrow's (1977), combine interpersonal influence and collective efforts to achieve goals into the definition of leadership. Dupuy and Dupuy (1959) add to this combination of definitions that leadership also involves obedience, confidence, respect, and loyal cooperation from followers. Still others prefer to discuss leadership as a collection of roles that emerge from an interactional process. For Tichy and Devanna (1986), the combination of power with personality defines the transformational leader as a skilled, knowledgeable change agent with power, legitimacy, and energy. Such a leader is courageous, considerate, value driven, and able to deal with ambiguity and complexity.

The search for the one and only proper and true definition of leadership seems to be fruitless, since the appropriate choice of definition should depend on the methodological and substantive aspects of leadership in which one is interested. For instance, if one is to make extensive use of observation, then it would seem important to define leadership in terms of acts, behavior, or roles played; its centrality to group process; and compliance with the observed performance, rather than in terms of personality traits, perceived power relations, or perceived influence. Contrarily, if extensive examination of the impact of the leadership was the focus of attention, then it would seem more important to define leadership in terms of perceived influence and power relations.

Leadership and Headship

The concepts of leadership and headship can be completely differentiated. Holloman (1968, 1986) conceived headship as being imposed on the group but leadership as being accorded by the group. In similar fashion, C. A. Gibb (1969a, p. 213) distinguished leadership from headship as follows:

1. Headship is maintained through an organized system and not by fellow group members' spontaneous recognition of the individual's contribution to group progress.
2. The group goal is chosen by head persons in line with their interests and is not internally determined by the group itself.
3. In headship, there is little or no sense of shared feeling or joint action in pursuit of the given goal.
4. In headship, there is a wide social gap between the group members and the head, who strives to maintain this social distance as an aid in the coercion of the group.
5. The leader's authority is spontaneously accorded by fellow group members and particularly by followers. The authority of the head derives from some extra-group power which he or she has over the members of the group, who cannot meaningfully be called followers. They accept domination

for fear of punishment, rather than follow in anticipation of rewards.

Kochan, Schmidt, and de Cotiis (1975) agreed with Gibb because they saw that managers, executives, an agency officers must be both leaders and heads.

In its conception, leadership can include headship. Defined more broadly, leadership includes the many ways it is exerted by leaders and heads and the various sources of power that make it work (Bass, 1960). With the broader definition, *heads* lead as a consequence of their status—the power of the position they occupy. Without such status, *leaders* can still gain a commitment to goals and can pursue arbitrary coercive paths with their power if their esteem—their accorded value to the group—is high. Both status and esteem are not all-or-none quantities. In any group, members will vary in both. Therefore, leadership will be distributed among them in similar fashion.[5] Although there is usually one head of a group, one cannot ordinarily attribute all leadership that occurs in a group to just one of its members. Until an "academy of leadership" establishes a standard definition, we must continue to live with both broad and narrow definitions, making sure to understand which kind is being used in any particular analysis.

An Evolving, Expanding Conceptualization

Definitions can be used to serve a variety of purposes. Bass (1960) noted that the definition used in a particular study of leadership depends on the purposes of the study. Consistent with this, Yukl (1981, p. 5) concluded that "leadership research should be designed to provide information relevant to the entire range of definitions, so that over time it will be possible to compare the utility of different conceptualizations and arrive at some consensus on the matter."

Either by explicit statement or by implication, various investigators have developed definitions to serve the following different purposes: (1) to identify the object to be observed, (2) to identify a form of practice, (3) to satisfy a particular value orientation, (4) to avoid

a particular orientation or implication for a practice, and (5) to provide a basis for the development of theory. (The hope is that the definitions will provide critical new insights into the nature of leadership.)

The definitions indicate a progression of thought, although historically, many trends overlapped. The earlier definitions identified leadership as a focus of group process and movement, personality in action. The next type considered it as the art of inducing compliance. The more recent definitions conceive of leadership in terms of influence relationships, power differentials, persuasion, influence on goal achievement, role differentiation, reinforcement, initiation of structure, and perceived attributions of behavior that are consistent with what the perceivers believe leadership to be. Leadership may involve all these things.

Applicability

Leadership research faces a dilemma. A definition that identifies something for the factory manager or agency head is not necessarily the most useful one for the development of a broad theory. Thus, a definition that enables the research to identify a group leader—the person whose behavior exercises a determining effect on the behavior of other group members—may not provide much insight into the processes and structures involved in the emergence and maintenance of leadership. But if the research results are to be applied by the factory manager or agency head, then the definitions must be couched as closely as possible to their ways of "wording the world" (Van de Vall & Bolas, 1980).

A definition should do more than identify leaders and indicate the means by which they acquire their positions. It should also account for the maintenance and continuation of leadership. Thus, few groups engage in interaction merely for the purpose of creating leaders and dropping them as soon as they emerge. For the purposes of this handbook, leadership must be defined broadly.

The Handbook Definition. Leadership is an interaction between two or more members of a group that often involves a structuring or restructuring of the situation and the perceptions and expectations of the members. Leaders are agents of change—persons whose acts affect other people more than other people's acts affect them. Leadership occurs when one group member modifies the motivation or competencies of others in the group. Research in the 1970s and 1980s often expressed this idea as the directing of attention of other members to goals and the paths to achieve them. It should be clear that with this broad definition, any member of the group can exhibit some amount of leadership, and the members will vary in the extent to which they do so.

The introduction of the concepts of goal attainment and the solution of problems in certain definitions recognizes the fact that leadership serves a continuing function in a group. But these concepts do not account for the continuation of leadership. The concepts of role, position, reinforcement of behavior, and structuring expectation serve better to account for the persistence of leadership. For the purposes of theory development, it would seem reasonable to include variables in the definition of leadership that account for the differentiation and maintenance of group roles. Finally, room is needed for a conception of leadership as an attribution that is consistent with the implicit theories about it that are held by the individuals and groups who are led.

Summary and Conclusions

The study of leaders and leadership is coterminous with the rise of civilization. It is a universal phenomenon. It is not a figment of the imagination, although there are conditions in which the success or failure of groups and organizations will be incorrectly attributed to the leaders, rather than to environmental and organizational forces over which the leaders have no control. In industrial, educational, and in military settings and in social movements, leadership plays a critical, if not the most critical role, and as such, is an important subject for study and research.

How to define leadership can be a long-drawn-out discussion that dominates the early portion of deliberations of a scholarly meeting on the subject of leadership. In this chapter, we have seen the rich variety of possibilities, which leads to our conclusion that the definition of leadership should depend on the purposes to be served by the definition. Leadership has been seen as the focus of group processes, as a personality attribute, as the art of inducing compliance, as an exercise of influence, as a particular kind of act, as a form of persuasion, as a power relation, as an instrument in the attainment of goals, as an effect of interaction, as a differentiated role, and as the initiation of structure. Definitions can be broad and include many of these aspects or they can be narrow. A distinction may be made between headship and leadership. One complex definition that has evolved, particularly to help understand a wide variety of research findings, delineates effective leadership as the interaction among members of a group that initiates and maintains improved expectations and the competence of the group to solve problems or to attain goals. Types of leaders can be differentiated according to some of these definitions, more often on the basis of role, functional, or institutional differences.

Typologies and Taxonomies
of Leadership

After defining leadership to suit their purposes, earlier scholars and more recent popularizers usually developed a handy classification. This was either a simple typing of leaders or a multilayered taxonomy with formal rules for classifying the leaders by their characteristics or behavior. In *The Republic,* Plato offered three types of leaders of the polity: (1) the philosopher-statesman, to rule the republic with reason and justice, (2) the military commander, to defend the state and enforce its will, and (3) the businessman, to provide for citizens' material needs and to satisfy their lower appetites. This early typology has been followed by a long line of typologies of leadership, some of which are probably being formulated right at this moment for presentation in the popular press. A respite from new leadership typologies is unlikely in the forseeable future, for although typologies lack rigor, they are appealing, convenient, and easy to discuss, comprehend, and remember.

Different types of leaders have been studied according to the groups they lead. Often attempts have been made to extrapolate conclusions from the one special type of leader and group studied to leadership in general. The types of leaders studied have included college presidents, chief executive officers, military officers, school principals, student leaders, task leaders, technical leaders, hospital and nursing administrators, religious leaders, revolutionaries, leaders of crowds, criminal leaders, managers at all levels in business and industry, consumer-opinion leaders, experimental small-group leaders, women leaders, black leaders, public officials, athletic leaders, child and adolescent leaders, leaders of social movements, political leaders (heads of state or government), and administrators at all levels of various public agencies and private institu-tions. Typologies have been created within and among these specializations.

Examples of Classifications

Leaders of Crowds

Leaders of mobs and crowds were the first to be given social psychological classification. LeBon (1897) described the crowd leader as a persuasive person of action whose intense faith and earnestness resists all reasoning and impels the mob to follow. Influenced by LeBon, Conway (1915) observed three types of crowd leaders: (1) the "crowd-compeller" inflames followers with his or her point of view, (2) the "crowd-exponent" senses what the crowd desires and gives expression to it, and (3) the "crowd-representative" merely voices the already formed opinions of the crowd.

Since these early views about leadership of a crowd, spontaneous crowds have frequently been replaced by organized demonstrations complete with television reporters. In such demonstrations, the leader must add considerable administrative effort to this overall performance; usually, the leader here is Conway's third type—the crowd-representative—speaking to the already converted.

Educational and Student Leaders

Harding (1949) distinguished 21 types of educational leaders: the autocrat, cooperator, elder statesman, eager beaver, pontifical type, muddled person, loyal staff person, prophet, scientist, mystic, dogmatist, open-minded person, philosopher, business expert, benevolent despot, child protector, laissez-faire type, community-minded person, cynic, optimist, and democrat. As a result of observations and interviews, Spaulding (1934) classified elected student leaders into the following five types: the social climber, the intellectual success, the good fellow, the big athlete, and the leader in student activities. From then on, the typing of students as social, political, athletic, or intellectual leaders became a common practice.

Benezet, Katz, and Magnusson (1981) classified college presidents as founding presidents, explorers, take-charge presidents, standard-bearers, organization presidents, and moderators. A founding president is a rarity today. The explorer brings on new programs and risky new plans, the take-charge president holds together an institution that is facing great difficulties, the standard-bearer leads the institution that has "arrived," the organization president is a pragmatic administrator, and the moderator is an egalitarian administrator who consults with and delegates a great deal to faculty members and student leaders.[1]

Public Leaders: Statesmen, Politicians, and Influentials

Credit is also due Plato for the first typology of political leaders. Plato classified such leaders as timocratic (ruling by pride and honor), plutocratic (ruling by wealth), democratic (ruling by popular consent on the basis of equality), and tyrannical (ruling by coercion) (Shorey, 1933). This classification fits well with much of what will be analyzed in later chapters about the bases of influence and power. Plutocratic, democratic, and tyrannical leaders remain in the popular lexicon of political leadership.

With respect to public leadership, Bell, Hill, and Wright (1961) identified formal leaders (who hold official positions, either appointed or elected), reputational leaders (who are believed to be influential in community or national affairs), social leaders (who are active participants in voluntary organizations), and influential leaders (who influence others in their daily contacts). Haiman (1951) suggested that five types of leaders are needed in a democracy: the executive, the judge, the advocate, the expert, and the discussion leader.

[1]See also Astin and Scherrei (1980) for an empirical classification of college presidents based on factor analysis.

Kincheloe (1928) distinguished prophets from non-prophets. Prophets are leaders without offices. Although they may arise in times of crisis, they create their own situation. Their real ability is to arouse their followers' interest so that the followers will accept prophetic goals and support them enthusiastically. Prophets become a symbol of the movement they have initiated, and their authoritative words tend to release inhibited impulses within their supporters. Kiernan (1975) clustered leadership patterns in African independent churches into two types: (1) preachers and prophets and (2) chiefs, prophets, and messiahs.

City mayors were placed in five categories by Kotter and Lawrence (1974) on the basis of the agendas the mayors set, the networks they built, and the tasks they accomplished. Ceremonial mayors set short-run agendas of small scope; they were individualistic and had a personal appeal but no staffs. Personality/individualistic mayors also had no staff, but the scope of their agendas was greater and the time involved in them was longer. Caretakers had short-run agendas of large scope with loyal staffs and were moderately bureaucratic. Executive mayors set agendas of large scope and of longer range, had staffs, were bureaucratic, and had a mixed appeal. Program entrepreneurs set the agendas of the largest scope, had staff resources, and built extensive networks with mixed appeals.

Pursuing a purely empirical approach, Bass and Farrow (1977a) generated six types of political leaders. Pairs of judges independently completed a 135-item questionnaire to describe the leaders on 31 factors after they had read considerable amounts of biographical literature written mainly by the immediate subordinates of the leaders. The 15 leaders were intercorrelated according to their scores on the 31 factors through use of the Bass and Valenzi systems model (Bass, 1976). An inverse factor analysis generated six clusters in relation to the behavior of leaders and subordinates, with the highest loadings for clustered figures as follows:

Autocratic-submissive: Adolf Hitler, Joseph Stalin, Nicholas II, and Louis XIV.

Trustworthy subordinates: Hirohito, Alexander the Great, Franklin Delano Roosevelt.

Clear, orderly, relationships: Winston Churchill.

Structured, sensitivity to outside pressures: Fiorello LaGuardia, John F. Kennedy, and Franklin Delano Roosevelt.

Satisfying differential power: Nikolai Lenin.

Egalitarian, analytic: Thomas Jefferson.

Legislative Leaders. J. M. Burns (1978) classified legislative leaders as ideologues, tribunes, careerists, parliamentarians, or brokers. *Ideologues* speak for doctrines (economic, religious, or political) that may be supported widely throughout their constituency but more typically are held by a small but highly articulate minority. *Tribunes* are the discoverers or connoisseurs of popular needs, the defenders of popular interests or the advocates of popular demands, aspirations, and governmental actions. *Careerists* see their legislative careers as a steppingstone to higher offices, provided they do a job that impresses their constituents and observers. *Parliamentarians*, as political technicians, either expedite or obstruct legislation. They bolster the parliament as an institution of tradition, courtesy, and mutual forbearance and protection of fellow members. *Brokers* mediate among antagonistic legislators, balancing interests to create legislative unity and action.

Transactional versus Transformational Public Leaders. As Buckley (1979) noted, the successful political leader is one who "crystallizes" what the people desire, "illuminates" the rightness of that desire, and coordinates its achievement. But such leadership can be transactional or transformational. This distinction has become of considerable importance to the study of leadership in general. The transformational-transactional differentiation has formed the basis of sundry other books since Burns's seminal work (Bass, 1985a; Bennis & Nanus, 1985; Tichy & Devanna, 1986). In exchanging promises for votes, the transactional leader works within the framework of the self-interests of his or her constituency, whereas the transformational leader moves to change the framework. Forerunners of this distinction are to be found in Hook's (1943) differentiation of the *eventful* man and the *event-making* man. The eventful political leader was swept along by the tides of history; the event-making political leader initiated the actions that made history. President Lincoln's predecessor, Buchanan, was

content to stand by and allow the Union to disintegrate slowly; Lincoln was determined to hold the Union together and to reverse what seemed at the time to be the inexorable course of Southern secession.

Downton (1973) discussed the leadership of rebels in terms of the transactional-transformational distinction. And Paige (1977) concluded that it would be useful to classify political leaders according to the changes they sought and achieved. *Conservative* leaders tend to maintain the existing political institutions and policies, *reformist* leaders promote moderate changes in institutions and policies, and *revolutionary* leaders strive for fundamental changes in existing institutions and policies.

For Burns (1978, p. 3), who first provided a comprehensive theory to explain the differences between transactional and transformational political leaders, transactional leaders

approach followers with an eye to exchanging one thing for another: jobs for votes, or subsidies for campaign contributions. Such transactions comprise the bulk of the relationships among leaders and followers, especially in groups, legislatures, and parties.

Burns noted that the transformational leader also recognizes the need for a potential follower, but he or she goes further, seeking to satisfy higher needs, in terms of Maslow's (1954) need hierarchy, to engage the full person of the follower. Transforming leadership results in mutual stimulation and elevation "that converts followers into leaders and may convert leaders into moral agents." If the follower's higher-level needs are authentic, more leadership occurs.

Burns went on to classify transactional political leaders as opinion leaders, bargainers or bureaucrats, party leaders, legislative leaders, and executive leaders. Transformational leaders were categorized as intellectual leaders, leaders of reform or revolution, and heroes or ideologues.

Most experimental research, unfortunately, has focused on transactional leadership (see, for example, Hollander, 1978), whereas the real movers and shakers of the world are transformational leaders. Although both types of leaders sense the felt needs of their followers, it is the transformational leader who raises consciousness (about higher considerations) through articulation and role modeling. Through transformational leaders, levels of aspiration are raised, legitimated, and turned into political demands.[2]

Women Leaders

Influential women have been classified in a number of ways, some unflattering, many fitting stereotypes about women in the workplace.[3]

In the community, women have been classified as fashion leaders and trend setters, in contrast to those who are content to accept, ignore, or resist change. For example, in determining opinion leadership among women in a community, Saunders, Davis, and Monsees (1974) found it useful to classify 587 women who attended a family planning clinic in Lima, Peru, as early or late adopters and as pre- or postacceptors of family planning.

Hammer (1978) singled out four negative stereotypes of women leaders in the workplace. The earth mother brings home-baked cookies to meetings and keeps the communal bottle of aspirin in her desk. The manipulator relies on feminine wiles to get her way. The workaholic cannot delegate responsibilities. The egalitarian leader denies the power of her leadership and claims to relate to subordinates as a colleague. Similarly, Kanter (1976, 1977a, 1977b) discerned four stereotypes of women leaders who work primarily in a man's world. The mother provides solace, comfort, and aspirin. The pet is the little sister or mascot of the group. The sex object fails to establish herself as a professional. The iron maiden tries too hard to establish herself as a professional and is seen as more tyrannical than she actually is.

Sociopsychological Classifications

The classification of leaders according to some model of the social or psychological dynamics of leaders and subordinates was pioneered by Nafe (1930). Nafe presented a perceptive analysis of the dynamic-infusive leader who directs and redirects followers' attention to the perceptual and ideational aspects of an issue until thought has been transferred into emotion and emotion into action. According to Nafe "the attitude of the leader toward the led and toward the project is found to be a problem in name only. The leader needs only to have the appearance of possessing the attitude desired by the followers." The real problem is the attitude of the led toward the leader. The attributes of leadership exist only in the minds of the led: "The leader may be this to one and that to another, but it is only by virtue of having a following that he or she is a leader." The adhesive leader (who seems to share the followers' attitudes) is opposite in every respect to the infusive (inspiring and influential) type, according to Nafe, who added the following additional categories to his taxonomy: static versus dynamic, impressors versus expressors, volunteer versus drafted, general versus specialized, temporary versus permanent, conscious versus unconscious, professional versus amateur, and personal versus impersonal.

Using analogies with genetics, Krout (1942) identified the social variant leader, who arises out of the group's need to agree about its goals and what to do about its lagging forms of behavior. Krout also described hybrid leaders, who seek to change the social structure through discontinuous methods to achieve the group's goals, and mutants—innovators who redefine the cultural patterns of their group and may set new goals to achieve their objectives for the group.

Jones (1983) described four types of leadership in terms of the kinds of control that the leaders exert that affect a follower's reactions. The leader can control the process or the output, and can be obtrusive or unobtrusive, situational or personal, and paternalistic or professional. The taxonomy can be used to explain how groups can be both satisfied with their situation and yet low in productivity.

Psychoanalytic Taxonomies

Pursuing a psychoanalytical orientation, Redl (1942) suggested that instinctual and emotional group processes take place around a member whose role may be that of patriarch, leader, tyrant, love object, object of aggression, organizer, seducer, hero, bad example, or good example. Continuing in the same vein, Zaleznik (1974) contrasted charismatic leaders with consensus

---

[2]Transformational leadership is discussed in detail in Chapter 12; transactional leadership in Chapters 17, 18, and 19.
[3]See Chapter 32.

leaders. Charismatic leaders are inner directed and identify with objects, symbols, and ideals that are connected with introjection. They are father figures. Consensus leaders "appear" to be brothers or peers, rather than father figures.

Kets de Vries and Miller (1984b, 1986) presented a fivefold psychopathological classification of executives to account for their dysfunctional performance: persecutory preoccupation, helplessness, narcissism, compulsiveness, and schizoid detachment.[4] Narcissists were included with resentfuls and highly likeable low achievers among the three types of flawed managers described by Hogan, Raskin, and Fazzini (undated).

The Myers-Briggs Types. Jung's (1971) psychoanalytic conceptualization was the basis of the popular Myers-Briggs fourfold classification of the thought processes of leaders and managers when faced with decisions and problems. The Myers-Briggs Type Indicator (Myers & McCaulley, 1985) sorts leaders into 4 types and 16 subtypes based on their responses to the indicator. Leaders are either extroverted or introverted, sensing or intuitive, thinking or feeling, and judging or perceiving. The extrovert prefers the outer world of people, things, and activities, whereas the introvert prefers the inner world of ideas and concepts. The extrovert is gregarious and people oriented; the introvert seeks accomplishment working with few key colleagues. The sensing type of leader is oriented toward facts, details, and reality; the intuitive leader is focused more on inferences, concepts, and possibilities. The thinking types prefer analysis, logical order, and rationality and are seen as "cold" by feeling types, whereas the feeling types, who value feelings and harmony, are described as too "soft" by the thinking types of leaders. The judging types prefer to make decisions rapidly and move on to the next issue, but the perceiving types seek to delay decisions.

A sample of 875 U.S. managers who were tested by the Center for Creative Leadership (Osborn & Osborn, 1986) between 1979 and 1983 found them distributed as follows: extroverts (50 percent), introverts (50 percent), sensors (52 percent), intuitives (48 percent), thinkers (82 percent), feelers (18 percent), judgers (70 percent), and perceivers (30 percent).

[4]These will be discussed more fully in Chapter 10.

The four Myers-Briggs types generate 16 subtypes of managers. The 875 managers were concentrated in four of the subtypes: ISTJ (introverted-sensing-thinking-judgers), ESTJ (extroverted-sensing-thinking-judgers), ENTJ (extroverted-intuitive-thinking-judgers), and INTJ (introverted-intuitive-thinking-judgers). Delunas (1983) showed that for 76 federal executives and managers from private industry, the Myers-Briggs types (sensors-perceivers, sensors-judgers, intuitives-thinkers, and intuitives-feelers) were significantly linked with their most or least preferred administrative styles.

Data from almost 7,500 managers and administrators showed that the majority were types who were more likely to reach closure (judges) than to miss nothing (perceivers). They were more likely to be impersonal, logical, and analytical (thinkers) than more concerned with personal and human priorities (feelers). The subtypes that were most likely to be concerned with enhancing human performance (the intuitive-feelers) were underrepresented except in human development departments. Those who were involved in the production of tangible products or in following established procedures tended to be practical sensing types. Those who provided long-range vision tended to be the imaginative, theoretical intuitive types (M. H. McCaulley & Staff, 1989).

Personality Types

Other typologies of personalities have developed around the scores that examinees obtain on various assessments of their personalities. For instance, using scales developed for the California Personality Inventory (CPI), Gough (1969, 1987, 1988) described four types of individuals who are found in diverse samples of students and adults. Leaders and innovators are extroverts, but leaders are also ambitious, enterprising, and resolute, while innovators are adventurous, progressive, and versatile. Saints and artists are introverted, but although the saints are steadfast, trustworthy, and unselfish, the artists are complex, imaginative, and sensitive. Leaders and saints accept the norms; innovators and artists question them. Although 25 to 30 percent of the general population of students and adults were classified by the CPI as leaders, 66 percent of West Point cadets were so typed.

Leaders and innovators at West Point had a higher aptitude for service than did the saints or artists.

Organizational and Institutional Leaders

Presentations of types of leaders in organizations coincided with the appearance of essays on effective management and are likely to continue. Bogardus (1918) distinguished four types of organizational and institutional leaders: (1) the autocratic type, who rises to office in a powerful organization, (2) the democratic type, who represents the interests of a group, (3) the executive type, who is granted leadership because he or she is able to get things done, and (4) the reflective-intellectual type, who may find it difficult to recruit a large following. J. H. Burns (1934) proposed the following types: the intellectual, the business type, the adroit diplomat, the leader of small groups, the mass leader, and the administrator.

Cowley (1931) differentiated between leadership and headship. This particularly important and useful distinction was articulated by Gibb (1969a), as was noted in Chapter 1. Leadership emerges as a characteristic of the individual; headship, as a characteristic of office and position.

Influenced by Leopold's (1913) analysis of prestige, Chapin (1924a) differentiated political-military leaders, who imbue the masses with their personality, from socialized leaders, who influence their followers to identify themselves with the common program or movement. In Bartlett's (1926) threefold classification, institutional leaders are established by virtue of the prestige of their position, dominative types gain and maintain their position through the use of power and influence, and persuasive types exercise influence through their ability to sway the sentiments of followers and to induce them to action.

Sanderson and Nafe (1929) proposed four types of leaders. The static leader is a professional or scientific person of distinction whose work influences the thoughts of others. The executive leader exercises control through the authority and power of position. The professional leader stimulates followers to develop and use their own abilities. The group leader represents the interests of group members.

In seminal German publications in 1921 and 22,

Weber (1947) delineated three types of legitimate authority in organizations and institutions, each associated with a specific type of leadership. Bureaucratic leaders operate with a staff of deputized officials and are supported by legal authority based on rational grounds. Their authority rests on beliefs in the legality of normative rules and in the right of those who are elevated to authority under such rules to issue commands. Patrimonial leaders operate with a staff of relatives rather than officials. They are supported by traditional authority that rests on the sanctity of immemorial traditions and the legitimacy of status of those who exercise authority under them. Charismatic leaders operate with a staff of disciples, enthusiasts, and perhaps bodyguards. Such leaders tend to sponsor causes and revolutions and are supported by charismatic authority that rests on devotion to the sanctity, heroism, or inspirational character of the leaders and on the normative patterns revealed or ordained by them.

Jennings (1960) subdivided these charismatic and patrimonial leaders differently. The great men who are rule breakers and value creators are supermen, those who are dedicated to great and noble causes are heroes, and those who are motivated principally to dominate others are princes. The princes may maximize the use of their raw power, or they may be great manipulators. Heroes come in many varieties also: heroes of labor, consumption, and production; risk-taking heroes; and so on. Supermen may or may not seek the power to dominate others.

Several commentators have noted that types of leadership are classifiable according to the model of organization in which the leadership occurs. Golembiewski (1967) proposed that the *collegial* model of organization permits leadership to pass from individual to individual at the same level in the organization. The traditional model implies that leadership is retained within the positions established by a hierarchy of authority relationships.

Possibly influenced by Burns and Stalker (1961), Sedring (1969) suggested that political leaders in the organismic model of organization[5] are characterized by interdependence, evolutionary change, and domina-

---

[5]See glossary for definition of organismic.

tion by factors that involve the whole organization of which their unit is a part. In the mechanistic model of organization, leaders are classified by the lack of integration, conflict in relationships, and dominance by factors in their own units. Morrow and Stern (1988) typed managers according to their performance in assessment programs.[6] The stars were smart, sensitive, social, self-assured, sustained, self-starters. The next best in assessments were the adversaries, who were able, analytic, argumentative, adamant, abrupt, and abrasive. The least adequate, according to their assessments, were the persevering, painstaking producers and the phantoms (polite, passive, and perturbed).

Bass (1960) noted that, in U.S. industry, task-oriented leaders dominated production up to 1950, when everything that was produced could be easily sold. In the 1950s, these leaders gave way to interaction-oriented leaders, who had to find markets for what was produced in an "outer-oriented" nation of conformists. For a nation turned inward, self-oriented leaders were expected to follow, but not as quickly as actually happened in the late 1960s and 1970s in the "me-too" generation of drugs and flower children. Despite the insecurities posed by the threats of the corporate raiders, which promote the need for protective self-orientation, the most effective of industrial leaders can be found who integrate a concern about production, particularly the quality of goods, with caring about the people involved.[7]

Maccoby (1979) posited three ideal types of leaders of business and industry in a longer view of production in the United States in the past 200 years. The types matched the ideals of the prevailing social character of the time, which was linked to the mode of production then dominant and the leaders' functions in production and service. The independent craftsman was the prototypical social character in Jefferson's idealized democracy of farmers, craftsmen, and small businessmen. Leaders were independent lawyers, physicians, small businessmen, and farmers. They espoused egalitarian, autonomous, disciplined, and self-reliant virtues.

After the Civil War, the paternalistic empire builder came to the fore, reflecting the "rags-to-riches" entre-preneurial spirit of the Horatio Alger stories. In this post-1865 social and economic environment,

> . . . ambitious boys had to find new fathers who had mastered the new challenges, leaving behind their own less adapted [craftsman] fathers. . . .
>
> The paternalistic leader . . . appealed to the immigrant . . . in need of a patron. . . . The still-independent craftsmen . . . were forced into increasingly routinized factory jobs [and] struggled [by unionizing] against the paternalistic jungle fighter. . . . (Maccoby, 1979, p. 308)

This second ideal of the empire builder as a lionlike jungle fighter with patriarchal power gave way to the third ideal of the *gamesman.* The gamesman emerged in the twentieth century when social character became more self-affirmative and the spirit more meritocratic. Adventurous and ambitious but fair and flexible leadership became the dominant ideal.

> With a boyish, informal style, he controls subordinates by persuasion, enthusiasm and seduction rather than heavy and humiliating commands. Fair but detached, the gamesman has welcomed the era of rights and equal opportunity as both a fair and an efficient climate for moving the "best" to the "top." (Maccoby, 1979, p. 309)

The gamesman type of leader enjoys challenges. The gamesman is daring, willing to innovate and to take risks (Maccoby, 1976). But the gamesman can become a liability to a firm when one person's gain can be another person's loss. Leadership is needed that values caring and the assurance that no one will be penalized for cooperation. Both sacrifice and reward need to be shared equitably (Maccoby, 1981).

Managers Typed by Their Leadership Style. The most popular classification of management styles—the alternative ways that leaders pattern their interactive behavior to fulfill their roles as leaders—was that of Blake and Mouton (1964). Extremes of task- and relations-oriented leadership[8] were seen to generate the five styles as follows:

---

[6]See Chapter 36.
[7]See Chapter 23.

[8]To be discussed in detail in Chapter 23. The numbers refer to the coordinate points on a grid whose axes are scaled from 1 to 9.

Type of Leadership Style	Relationship Orientation	Task Orientation
9, 1—Tough-minded, no-nonsense production-prodder	Extremely low	Extremely high
1, 9—Country-club leader	Extremely high	Extremely low
1, 1—Laissez-faire, abdicator of responsibility	Extremely low	Extremely low
5, 5—Compromiser	Moderate	Moderate
9, 9—Integrator of task accomplishment with trust and commitment from followers	Extremely high	Extremely high

Managers were seen to have basic and "backup" styles.

Reddin (1977) further advanced this popular taxonomy of management in relation to eight types, each of which is a consequence of being low or high in Blake and Mouton's two dimensions of relationships and task orientation and a third dimension—effectiveness. Managers come in the various combinations of this three-dimensional typology as follows:

Type of Leadership	Relationship Orientation	Task Orientation	Effectiveness
Deserter	Low	Low	Low
Autocrat	Low	High	Low
Missionary	High	Low	Low
Compromiser	High	High	Low
Bureaucrat	Low	Low	High
Benevolent autocrat	Low	High	High
Developer	High	Low	High
Executive	High	High	High

An equally compelling typology of managerial styles has developed, starting with Tannenbaum and Schmidt (1958), around the issue of who shall decide—the leader or the follower. The types could be seen along an authoritarian–democratic continuum: the leader who announces the decision, the leader who sells the decision, the leader who consults before deciding, the leader whose decisions are shared, and the leader who delegates the decision making.[9]

Bradford and Cohen (1984) typed styles of managers into the manager as technician, manager as conductor, and manager as developer. The manager as technician relates information to subordinates who are committed to the leader because of the leader's technical competence and depend on the leader for the answers to problems. The manager as conductor is a heroic figure "who orchestrates all the individual parts of the organization into one harmonious whole" (p. 45) with administrative systems for staffing and work flow. The manager as developer "works to develop management responsibility in subordinates and . . . the subordinates' abilities to share management of the unit's performance" (pp. 60–61).

Sorting managers into those who emphasize rationality and quantitative analysis, Leavitt (1986) identified three types of managers according to their stylistic emphasis. *Pathfinders* are creative and visionary; they use instinct, wisdom, and imagination to meet their goals and know how to ask questions and search out problems. *Problem solvers* are analytic, quantitative, and oriented toward management controls. *Implementers* are political and stress consensus, teamwork, and good interpersonal relationships.

Quinn, Dixit, and Faerman (1987) developed a taxonomy of management roles to indicate conditions under which playing them would be most conducive to effectiveness. The patterns observed gave rise to seven types of managers. The same managers could play roles conceived to be opposite in value, and the roles could be placed at two ends of a continuum. The four bipolarities were

Mentor versus Director

Facilitator versus Producer

Coordinator versus Innovator

Monitor versus Broker

Effective leaders were typed as masters, conceptual producers, aggressive achievers, peaceful team builders, long-term intensives, and open adaptives. *Masters*

---

[9]See Chapter 22.

are high in all eight roles. *Conceptual producers* are almost like masters, except that they are lower in monitoring and coordinating. *Aggressive achievers* are high in monitoring, coordinating, directing, and producing but are lower in the other roles, particularly facilitating. *Peaceful team builders* are high in six of the roles but lower in the broker and producer roles. *Long-term intensives* are high in the innovator, producer, monitor, and facilitator roles and fall nearer the mean on the mentor and director roles. *Open adaptives* are much less likely to monitor and coordinate. Ineffective managers were typed with the same kind of analysis of management roles into chaotic adaptives, abrasive coordinators, drowning workaholics, extreme unproductives, obsessive monitors, permissive externals, and soft-hearted indecisives.

Cribbin (1981) classified effective managers into the following types: entrepreneur ("We do it my way and take risks"), corporateur ("I call the shots, but we all work together on my team"), developer ("People are our most important asset"), craftsman ("We do important work as perfectly as possible"), integrator ("We build consensus and commitment"), gamesman ("We run together, but I must win more than you").

Lewis, Kuhnert, and Maginnis (1987) sorted military officers into three styles of character. *Operators* have a personal agenda that they pursue without concern for others, lack empathy, and cannot be trusted. *Team players* are highly sensitive to how others feel about them and value decisions according to what others will think or say, rather than to the merits of the case. In contrast, *self-defining leaders* are personally committed to ideals and values and pursue what they regard as the right and most worthy solutions.

Typologies of Leaders by their Functions, Roles, and Behaviors

The functions, roles, and behaviors of leaders in interpersonal interaction in small groups and as managers in larger organizations resulted in the creation of many taxonomies of leadership functions, roles, and behaviors in these two kinds of settings.

Leadership in Small and Experimental Groups. The study of group and organizational processes began to require taxonomies of leadership and management based on functions, roles, and behaviors. Thus, Pigors (1936) observed that leaders in group work tend to act either as masters or as educators. Cattell and Stice (1954) identified four types of leaders in experimental groups: (1) persistent, momentary problem solvers, who have a high rate of interaction, (2) salient leaders, whom observers think exert the most powerful influence on the group, (3) sociometric leaders, who are nominated by their peers, and (4) elected leaders. Bales and Slater (1955) observed that the leader performs two essential functions; the first is associated with productivity and the second is concerned with the socioemotional support of the group members. Benne and Sheats (1948) suggested that group members who exert leadership play three types of functional roles: (1) group-task roles, such as initiator, gatekeeper, and summarizer, (2) group-building and group-maintenance roles, such as harmonizer, supporter, and tension reducer, and (3) individual roles, such as blocker, pleader, and monopolizer. Bales (1958a) noted that the first two roles are the major functions of leadership in experimental groups. For Hemphill (1949a), the leader's behavior could be typed according to how much he or she set group goals with the members, helped then to reach the goals, coordinated the members' efforts, helped members fit into the group, expressed interest in the group, and showed humanness. Analyses of the behavior of leaders also produced a variety of other categorizations of the behavior of leaders in small groups, which will be detailed in many of the later chapters (see, for example, Reaser, Vaughan, & Kriner, 1974; Schutz, 1961b).

From another point of view, Roby (1961) developed a mathematical model of the functions of leadership that was based on response units and information load and developed the following classification of leadership functions: (1) to bring about congruence of goals among the members, (2) to balance the group's resources and capabilities with environmental demands, (3) to provide group structure that will focus information effectively on solving the problem, and (4) to make certain that all needed information is available at a decision center when required. Again, according to Schutz (1961b), the functions of leadership could be classified as follows: (1) to establish and recognize a hierarchy of group goals and values, (2) to recognize and integrate the various cognitive styles that exist in the group, (3) to maximize the utilization of group members' abilities, and (4) to help members resolve problems that involve adapting to external realities as well as the fulfillment of interpersonal needs.

S. Levine (1949), who directed most of his attention to small groups, named four types of leaders: (1) the charismatic leader, who helps the group rally around a common aim but tends to be dogmatically rigid, (2) the organizational leader, who emphasizes effective action and tends to drive people, (3) the intellectual leader, who usually lacks skill in attracting people, and (4) the informal leader, who tends to adapt his or her style of performance to the group's needs.

Clarke (1951) proposed three types of leaders: (1) popular leaders, who wield influence because of their unique combination of personality traits or ability, (2) group leaders, who through their understanding of personality, enable group members to achieve satisfying experiences, and (3) indigenous leaders, who arise in a specific situation when group members seek support and guidance.

Getzels and Guba (1957) offered three types of leadership, two of which are associated with separate dimensions of group activity: (1) nomothetic leadership, which is involved with the roles and expectations that define the normative dimensions of activity in social systems, (2) ideographic leadership, which is associated with the individual needs and dispositions of members that define the personal dimensions of group activity, and (3) synthetic leadership, which reconciles the conflicting demands that arise from the two contrasting systems within a group. Bowers and Seashore (1967) maintained that the functions of leadership are support of members, the facilitation of interaction and of work, and the emphasis on goals. Cattell (1957) observed that the leader performs the following functions: services in maintaining the group, upholding role and status satisfactions, maintaining task satisfactions, keeping ethical (norm) satisfactions, selecting and clarifying goals, and finding and clarifying means of attaining goals.

Using a factor analysis of behavioral ratings, Oliverson (1976) identified four types of leaders in 24 encounter groups: technical, charismatic, caring-interpersonal, and peer oriented. The technical leader emphasizes a cognitive approach, the charismatic leader stresses his or her own impressive attributes, and the last two types of leaders accentuate the facilitation of interpersonal relations with caring and friendship. After observing 16 group-therapy leaders of various theoretical persuasions, Lieberman, Yalom, and Miles (1973) formulated three types of group leaders: (1) charismatic energizers, who emphasize stimulation, (2) providers, who exhibit high levels of cognitive behavior and caring, and (3) social engineers, who stress management of the group as a social system for finding intellectual meaning. Three other styles—impersonal, manager, and laissez-faire types—were variants of the initial three. Therapeutic change in participants was highest with providers and lowest with managers. Casualties were highest with energizers and impersonals and lowest with providers. Again from observations of therapy groups, Redl (1948) suggested that the leader may play the role of patriarch, tyrant, ideal, scapegoat, organizer, seducer, hero, and bad or good influence.

Komaki, Zlotnick, and Jensen (1986) provided a sophisticated and rigorous approach to classifying the behavior of supervisors on the basis of a minute-by-minute time sampling of coded observations in a small-group setting. Their taxonomy, which was constructed to provide observers with a way to categorize specific supervisory behaviors, includes seven categories of supervisory behavior. The first three categories are derived from operant conditioning theory; they are related to effective supervision: (1) performance consequences, indicating knowledge of performance, (2) performance monitors, collecting information and performance, (3) performance antecedents, providing instructions for performance, (4) own performance, referring to the manager's own performance, (5) work related, referring to work but not performance, (6) nonwork related, not pertaining to work, and (7) solitary, not interacting with others. The categories are linked as shown in Figure 2.1.

Organizational Leadership

Many attempts have been made to categorize organizational leaders and managers specifically according to the kinds of functions they perform, roles they play, or behaviors they display. Numerous classification

Figure 2.1. Operant Taxonomy of Supervisory Behavior

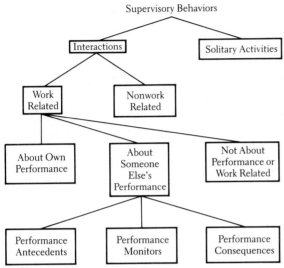

SOURCE: *J. L. Komaki, S. Zlotnick, and M. Jensen, "Development of an Operant Based Taxonomy and Observational Index of Supervisory Behavior,"* Journal of Applied Psychology *(1986). Copyright 1986 by the American Psychological Association. Reprinted by permission of the publisher and author.*

schemes have appeared. Many of them prescribe the functions for the ideal organizational leader. Others are derived from empirical job analyses or factored behavioral descriptions of the actual work performed by actual managers and administrators. For example, both approaches have concluded that the organizational leader may play the role of final arbitrator, the superordinate whose judgment settles disputes among followers. This function was often considered to be critical for the avoidance of anarchy in many political states. The maintenance and security of the state, it was believed, depended on the existence of a legitimate position at the top to which all followers would acquiesce to avoid the continuation of conflict against them.

Idealized versus Empirically Determined Classifications. On the one hand, the classical theories of ideal management indicated that the primary functions of executives could be typed as planning, organizing, and controlling. Although coordinating, supervising, motivating, and the like were added to the list, they were seen merely as variations of the organizational-control function.

On the other hand, leadership functions based on behavioral descriptions of actual managers included defining objectives and maintaining goal direction, providing means for attaining goals, providing and maintaining the group structure, facilitating action and interaction in the group, maintaining the cohesiveness of the group and the satisfaction of members, and facilitating the group's performance of tasks.

The functions identified by the behavioral descriptions grew out of research on basic group processes and on the emergence of the leadership role and its contribution to the performance, interaction, and satisfaction of members who are engaged in a group task. The classical functions of planning, organizing, and controlling were concerned with the rationalized processes of formal organizations. Although these functions are generalized and abstract, they are by no means unreal; however, they tend to ignore the human nature of members of the organization and the limited rationality with which the manager must operate. Yet, organizations strive for rationality. Understanding the purposes of a leader in an organization requires a consideration of his or her planning, directing, and controlling. However, many more behaviors emerge in large-scale descriptive surveys of and interviews with leaders.

Mooney and Reiley (1931) identified the three functional processes in any organization as being the same as in any governmental entity: legislative, executive, and judicial. Coffin (1944) suggested that the three functions of organizational leadership were formulation (planning), execution (organizing), and supervision (persuading). Barnard (1946b) identified the functions of organizational leadership as (1) the determination of objectives, (2) the manipulation of means, (3) the instrumentation of action, and (4) the stimulation of coordinated effort. Davis (1951) was in agreement with many others in declaring that the functions of the business leader are to plan, organize, and control an organization's activities. In a study of leadership in Samoa, Kessing and Kessing (1956) identified the following leadership functions: consultation, deliberation, negotiation, the formation of public opinion, and decision making. Gross (1961) proposed these functions: to define goals, clarify and administer them, choose appropriate means, assign and coordinate tasks, motivate, create loyalty, represent the group, and spark the membership to action.

Selznick (1957) suggested that the functions of organizational leadership include the (1) definition of the institution's mission and goals, (2) creation of a structure to achieve the institution's purpose, (3) defense of institutional integrity, and (4) reevaluation of internal conflict. Katz and Kahn (1966) advocated three functions for organizational leadership: (1) policy formation (the introduction of structural change), (2) the interpretation of structure (piecing out the incompleteness of the existing formal structure), and (3) administration (the use of a formal structure to keep the organization in motion and operating effectively). Wofford (1967) proposed that the following functions of management be selected: setting objectives, organizing, leading, and controlling. For Krech and Crutchfield (1948), a leader could be an executive, planner, policymaker, expert, representative of the external group, controller of internal relationships, purveyor of rewards and punishments, arbitrator and mediator, exemplar, symbol of the group, surrogate for individual responsibility, ideologist, father figure, and scapegoat.

T. A. Mahoney (1955, 1961) and colleagues (Mahoney, Jerdee, and Carroll, 1965) typed managers according to their main functions. According to a survey of 452 managers in 13 firms, supervising was the main function of 51 percent of lower-level supervisors, 36 percent of middle managers, and 22 percent of top managers. Top managers were more likely to be generalists and planners than were lower-level managers. Figure 2.2 shows how managers could be typed according to their main function. As can be seen, the type of manager depended on the organizational level.

Williams (1956) focused on dealing with knowledge, decision making, interaction with others, character, organization over person, and policies and records. Koontz, O'Donnell, and Weihrich (1958) wrote about planning, organizing, motivating, and controlling. McGrath's (1964) fourfold classification concerned monitoring, forecasting, taking direct action, and creating conditions. For Bennett (1971), the taxonomy included deciding, planning, analyzing, interacting with people, and using equipment. For Hemphill (1950a), who used factor analytical approaches to type the behavior of leaders, the functions of supervisors, managers, and ex-

Figure 2.2. Distribution of Assignments Among Job Types at Each Organizational Level

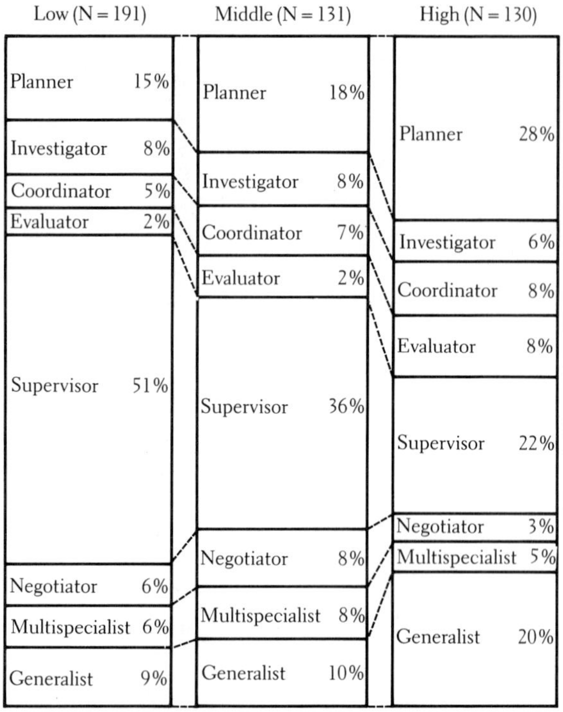

(NOTE: *Totals do not add up to 100 percent because of rounding.*)

SOURCE: *Mahoney, Jerdee, and Carroll (1965).*

ecutives were initiation, representation, fraternization, organization, domination, recognition, production, integration, communication down,[10] and communication up.[11] For Hemphill (1960), supervisors, managers, and executives dealt with providing staff services for nonoperations areas; supervising work; controlling business, technical markets, and production; human, community, and social affairs; long-range planning; exercising broad power and authority; business reputation, personal demands, and preservation of assets. For Fine (1977), who employed job analyses, the functions were analyzing, negotiating, consulting, instructing, and exchanging information. For Dowell and Wexley (1978), they included working with subordinates, organizing their work, planning and scheduling work, main-

[10]Downward in the organization.
[11]Upward in the organization.

taining efficient and good-quality production, maintaining equipment, and compiling records and reports.

An outstanding example of a large scale long-term analysis of management functions was Tornow and Pinto's (1976). The taxonomy involved long-range thinking and planning; the coordination of other organizational units and personnel; internal control; responsibility for products and services, finances, and board personnel; dealing with public and customer relations, complexity, and stress; advanced consulting, maintaing the autonomy of financial commitments; service to the staff; and supervision.[12]

The categorizations became more fine tuned and numerous. Winter (1978) generated 19 leadership competencies, ranging from conceptualizing to disciplining.[13] Metcalfe (1984) came up with 20 classes of leaders' behavior, ranging from proposing procedures to shutting out other persons' efforts to participate. Finally, Van Fleet and Yukl (1986a) emerged with a detailed breakdown of 23 functions, ranging from showing consideration to monitoring reward contingencies. Subsequently these were combined by Yukl (1989) into 11 functions: networking, supporting, managing conflict and team building, motivating, recognizing and rewarding, planning and organizing, problem solving, consulting and delegating, monitoring, informing, and clarifying.

Mintzberg (1973) created the best-known taxonomy of managerial roles in which managers were seen to engage in three sets of roles: interpersonal, informational, and decisional. Within each of these sets, specific roles were conceived. The interpersonal set included the figurehead, leader, and liaison. Within the informational set were the monitor, disseminator, and spokesman. Within the discussional set were the entrepreneur, disturbance handler, resource allocator, and negotiator.

Commonalties in Taxonomies

Despite the plethora of taxonomies of leadership some common themes appear. The leader may help set and clarify the missions and goals of the individual member, the group, or organization. The leader may energize and direct others to pursue the missions and goals. The leader may help provide the structure, methods, tactics, and instruments for achieving the goals. The leader may help resolve conflicting views about the means and ends. The leader may evaluate the individuals, group's, or organization's, as well as his or her own, contributions to the effort.

Some types that are common among many of the taxonomies include the authoritative, dominating, directive, autocratic, and persuasive. Other types are the democratic, participative, group developing, supportive, and considerate. Still other types include the intellectual, expert, executive, bureaucrat, administrator, representative, spokesperson, and advocate. These taxonomies are the subject of leadership styles in Chapters 21 to 24. It is possible to encapsulate many of these typologies into the autocratic versus democratic dichotomy. The autocratic type correlates with the directive type, and the democratic type correlates with the participative or considerate type. The executive is not regarded as a separate type but is classified as either task oriented (autocratic) or relations oriented (democratic). The persuasive pattern of behavior is a subclass of task-oriented or initiating behavior. However, in many situations, the representative (spokesperson's) pattern of behavior is independent of task orientation and relations orientation. The intellectual type, the expert, often ignored early on, was soon seen[14] to be required for any comprehensive theory of leadership.

Yukl (1987a) showed the strong similarities across these taxonomies of the behavior of leaders, dealing with leadership in both the small group and in the large organization. Figure 2.3 shows the approximate correspondences.

Yukl (1987b) demonstrated that the descriptive scales of his taxonomy shown in Figure 2.3 that were used by subordinates to describe their leaders were highly reliable and accurately discriminated among supervisors being described.

An Integrated Model. Mumford, Fleishman, Levin, et al. (1988) summarized and integrated these efforts into a taxonomic model. Their summary classification

---

[12]More about this taxonomy will be discussed in Chapter 20.
[13]This taxonomy will be discussed in detail in Chapter 20.

[14]As detailed in Chapter 7.

Figure 2.3. Approximate Correspondence Among Major Taxonomies

YUKL (1989)	MINTZBERG (1973)	MORSE & WAGNER (1978)	STOGDILL (1963)	BOWERS & SEASHORE (1966)	HOUSE & MITCHELL (1974)	LUTHANS & LOCKWOOD (1984)	PAGE (1985)
Supporting			Consideration	Leader Support	Supportive Leadership		
Consulting					Participative Leadership		
Delegating			Tolerance of Freedom				
Recognizing						Motivating & Reinforcing	
Rewarding							
Motivating	Leader Role	Motivating & Conflict Handling	Production Emphasis	Goal Emphasis	Achievement-oriented Leadership		Supervising
Managing Conflict & Team Building			Integration	Interaction Facilitation		Managing Conflict	
Developing		Providing Development				Training & Developing	
Clarifying			Initiating Structure		Directive Leadership		
Planning & Organizing	Resource Allocator; Entrepreneur	Organizing & Coordinating		Work Facilitation		Planning & Coordinating	Planning & Organizing; Strategic Planning
Problem Solving	Disturbance Handler	Strategic Problem Solving	Role Assumption; Demand Reconciliation			Problem Solving & Deciding	Decision Making
Informing	Disseminator	Information Handling				Exchanging Information	Consulting
Monitoring	Monitor					Monitoring/ Controlling	Monitoring Indicators, Controlling
Representing	Spokesman; Negotiator; Figurehead		Representing; Influencing Superiors			Interacting with Outsiders; Socializing & Politicking	Representing
Networking & Interfacing	Liaison	Managing Environment & Resources					Coordinating

Indicates behavior not included in the earlier taxonomy.

SOURCE: *Adapted from Gary Yukl,* Leadership in Organizations *(Engle-wood Cliffs, N.J.: Prentice-Hall, 1989), p. 95.*

included (1) the search for and structuring of information (acquisition, organization, evaluation, feedback, and control), (2) the use of information in problem solving (identifying requirements, planning, coordinating, and communicating), (3) managing personnel resources (acquisition, allocation, development, motivation, utilization, and monitoring), and (4) managing material resources (acquisition, maintenance, utilization, and monitoring). Figure 2.4 shows how their taxonomy was integrated into a working model, just as it was possible

for Winter (1978, 1979b) to do with tests and competency measures of leaders, as will be discussed in the next chapter.

Summary and Conclusions

Early in the scientific process, efforts were made to classify phenomena. Investigators have focused attention on classifications of leaders of crowds, institutions,

Figure 2.4. Interrelationships Among the Leader-Behavior Dimensions

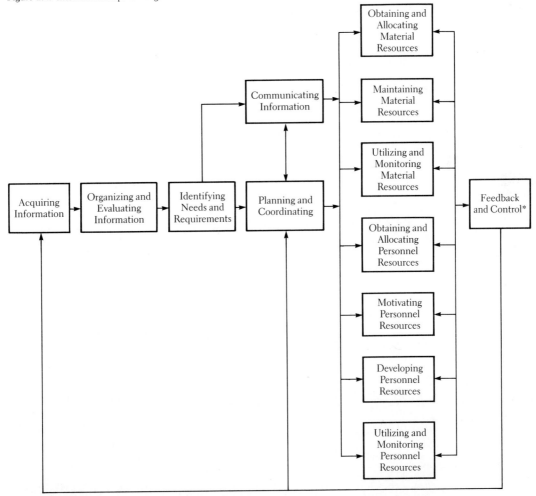

NOTE:* *The category feedback and control is presented to reflect its role in actual leadership activities.*

SOURCE: *Mumford, Fleishman, Levin, Korotkin, and Hein (1988).*

industry, education, politics, legislative opinion, and communities. They have made an important distinction between transactional leaders, who concentrate on an exchange relation of what they and their followers want, and transformational leaders, who strive to arouse and satisfy the higher-level needs of their followers. Various sociopsychological classifications of small-group leaders are also available, many of which can be seen in terms of either a task or relations orientation.

Many functional typologies have also been developed. Those for organizational leaders expand on the functions of leaders of small groups.

Taxonomies of leadership remain popular because they simplify and provide labels for easy communication, comprehension, and recall. But they may also result in overgeneralization and faulty inferences. With continued research, they give way to more sophisticated conceptualizations.

An Introduction to Theories and Models of Leadership

Theories of leadership attempt to explain the factors involved either in the emergence of leadership or in the nature of leadership and its consequences. Models show the interplay among the variables that are conceived to be involved; they are replicas or reconstructions of the realities. Both theories and models can be useful in defining research problems for the social and political scientist and in improving prediction and control in the development and application of leadership.

Despite complaints to the contrary, there has been no shortage of modeling and theorizing about leadership. However, relatively few models and theories have dominated the research community, and many have been restatements of the obvious. On the other hand, progress has been made when the models and theories have been built on astute observation and assumptions that are consistent with a more general body of propositions from the social sciences. Thus, theories about reinforcement leadership have been built from what is generally known about reinforcement; theories about transformational leadership have similarly benefitted from motivational theory.

Nothing is supposed to be as practical as a good theory, but nothing seems more impractical than a bad one (Bass, 1974); a theory may be good for one purpose and bad for another, for theory is supposed to be a way of trying to understand the facts. Unfortunately, leadership theories sometimes obscure the facts. Much effort then has to be expended in coping with the obscurity.

A dilemma arises. If a theory of leadership is to be used for diagnosis, training, and development, it must be grounded theory—grounded in the concepts and assumptions that are acceptable to and used by managers, officials, and emergent leaders (Glaser & Strauss, 1967). But such a theory is likely to lack rigor. There

will be a loss of generality and the opportunity to employ standardized measurements.

I begin here with an introductory survey of some of the better-known theories and models of leadership, reserving details about them for later chapters.

Personal and Situational Theories

Great-Man Theories

For many commentators, history is shaped by the leadership of great men. Without Moses, the Jews would have remained in Egypt. Without Winston Churchill, the British would have given up in 1940. The eighteenth-century rationalists felt that luck had to be added to the personal attributes of great men to determine the course of history. The Russian Revolution would have taken a different course if Nikolai Lenin had been hanged by the Old Regime instead of exiled. For the romantic philosophers, such as Friedrich Nietzsche, a sudden decision by a great man could alter the course of history (Thomas Jefferson's decision to purchase Louisiana, for example). To William James (1880), the mutations of society were due to great men, who initiated movement and prevented others from leading society in another direction. The history of the world, according to James, is the history of Great Men; they created what the masses could accomplish. Carlyle's (1841) essay on heroes tended to reinforce the concept of the leader as a person who is endowed with unique qualities that capture the imagination of the masses. The hero would contribute somehow, no matter where he was found. (Despite the examples of Joan of Arc, Elizabeth I, and Catherine the Great, great women were ignored.) Dowd (1936) maintained that "there is no such thing as leadership by the masses.

The individuals in every society possess different degrees of intelligence, energy, and moral force, and in whatever direction the masses may be influenced to go, they are always led by the superior few."

The great-man theory of leadership is currently espoused by those who show how faltering business corporations are turned around by transformational leaders, such as Lee Iacocca. Military leaders, such as Douglas MacArthur, and political figures, such as John F. Kennedy, are treated similarly. Martin Luther King is considered to be the "great man" whose leadership inspired the black civil rights movement.

Influenced by Galton's (1869) study of the hereditary background of great men, several early theorists attempted to explain leadership on the basis of inheritance. Woods (1913) studied 14 nations over periods of five to ten centuries and found that the conditions of each reign approximated the ruler's capabilities. The brothers of kings (as a result of natural endowment, of course) also tended to become men of power and influence! Woods concluded that the man makes the nation and shapes it in accordance with his abilities. Wiggam (1931) advanced the proposition that the survival of the fittest and intermarriage among them produces an aristocratic class that differs biologically from the lower classes. Thus, an adequate supply of superior leaders depends on a proportionately high birthrate among the abler classes. Jennings (1960) completed a survey and analysis of the great-man theory of leadership.

Trait Theories

If the leader is endowed with superior qualities that differentiate him from his followers, it should be possible to identify these qualities. This assumption gave rise to the trait theories of leadership (Kohs & Irle, 1920). L. L. Bernard (1926), Bingham (1927), Tead (1929), Page (1935), and Kilbourne (1935) all explained leadership in terms of traits of personality and character. Bird (1940) compiled a list of 79 such traits from 20 psychologically oriented studies. A similar review was completed by Smith and Krueger (1933) for educators and by W. O. Jenkins (1947) for military leaders.

Until the 1940s, most research about leaders and leadership focused on the individual traits of consequence. Leaders were seen to be different in various attributes and tested personality traits than were non-leaders. Two questions were posed: What traits distinguish leaders from other people? What is the extent of those differences?

The pure trait theory fell into disfavor. Stogdill's (1948) critique (see Chapter 4) concluded that both person and situation had to be included to explain the emergence of leadership. But as will be seen in Chapters 5 through 12, traits of leadership, as such, still are of paramount importance to the subject.

Situational Theories

In direct opposition to trait theorists, situational theorists suggested that leadership is all a matter of situational demands, that is, situational factors determine who will emerge as leader. Particularly in the United States, situationalism was favored over the theory that leaders are born, not made. According to situationalism, the leader is the product of the situation, not the blood relative or son of the previous leader (Stogdill, 1975).

The controversy over which is more important, personality or situation, is an ancient one. Plutarch's *The Parallel Lives* (c. A.D. 100) suggested that for each type of leader who emerged in Greece, one emerged in parallel conditions in Rome; thus, Alexander the Great had his counterpart in Caesar. The great-man theorists believed that it was all a matter of personality and personality development—that Alexanders and Caesars would surface no matter what conditions surrounded them. The situationalists thought otherwise. For instance, they sought to identify those states of affairs that gave rise to the emergence of the "man on the white horse," the dictator who appears following revolutionary upheaval, chaotic politics, social and economic distress, and the weakening of traditional institutions.

The situationalists advanced the view that the emergence of a great leader is a result of time, place, and circumstance. For Hegel, the great man was an expression of the needs of his times. What the great man did was automatically right to do because he fulfilled what was needed. The great man actually could not help what he did, since he was directed and controlled by his historical environment. For example, the need for civil peace made it mandatory for Octavian to form the Roman Principate and destroy republicanism.

For Herbert Spencer, societies evolved in a uniform, gradual, progressive manner. No great man could change the course of this development. The American Civil War was an inevitable clash caused by the conflicting economic interests of North and South. For Engels, Marx, and their successors, economic necessity made history. For these economic determinists, the obstacles to expanding production had to be overcome. The greater the obstacles, the greater the need and the more capable the required leader. But who he turned out to be was irrelevant (Hook, 1943). Mumford (1909) agreed that the leaders who emerged depended on the abilities and skills required at the time to solve the prevailing social problems. Although the abilities and skills were innate as well as acquired, the leadership, as such, stemmed from the organized phases of the social process or the habitual ways in which people adapt to each other.

Thus, according to the situationalists, the national condition determined the development and emergence of great military figures. For A. J. Murphy (1941), leadership did not reside in a person but was a function of the occasion. The situation called for certain types of action; the leader did not inject leadership but was the instrumental factor through which a solution to a problem was achieved. J. Schneider (1937) noted that the number of great military leaders in England was proportional to the number of conflicts in which the nation engaged. Spiller (1929) concluded that a sweeping survey of the field of human progress would show that 95 percent of the advance was unconnected with great men. Rather, great men like Mahatma Gandhi appeared at a critically important advancement of a socially valued cause, devoted himself to it, and profited greatly from the work of many others.

Bogardus (1918) presented the view that the type of leadership that develops in a group is determined by the nature of the group and the problems it must solve. Hocking (1924) went even further in suggesting that leadership resides in the group and is given to leaders only when they put forth a program that the group is willing to follow. Person (1928) advanced two hypotheses to account for leadership: (1) any particular situation plays a large part in determining leadership quali-

ties and the leader for that situation and (2) the qualities in an individual that a particular situation may determine to be leadership qualities are themselves the product of a succession of previous leadership situations that have developed and molded that individual. Bennis (1961) concluded that theories to explain who emerges and succeeds as a leader in an organization have to take into account the following circumstances: (1) the impersonal bureaucracy, (2) the informal organization and interpersonal relations, (3) the benevolent autocracy that structures the relationship between superiors and subordinates, (4) the job design that permits individual self-actualization, and (5) the integration of individual and organizational goals.

Personal-Situational Theories

Although wars and other crises present opportunities for the acquisition of leadership by persons who would otherwise remain submerged in the daily round of routine activities, various theorists have maintained that the situation is not in itself sufficient to account for leadership. How many crises arise that do not produce a person who is equal to the occasion? A combination of personal and situational elements needs to be considered.

James (1880) pointed out that the great man needs help—that his talents needed to fit with the situation. Ulysses S. Grant, for instance, was a continuing failure in private life before his emergence as the Union's great military commander, and he failed again as president. His rise to commanding general of the Army of the Potomac was delayed by the many political appointees who came before him and took turns displaying their ineptitude before exasperated President Lincoln turned to Grant. Grant's leadership in the Vicksburg campaign brought victory, despite the orders of his superior, General Halleck, to fall back toward New Orleans. But it was Grant's persistence, helped by congressmen, that overcame the inertia of the political appointment system, and this trait of persistence and confidence in his success marked the style with which he hammered out his military victories (Williams, 1952).

Both the great-man theorists and the situational theorists attempted to explain leadership as an effect of a single set of forces and overlooked the combining effects of individual and situational factors. In reaction, Westburgh (1931) suggested that the study of leadership must include the affective, intellectual, and action traits of the individual, as well as the specific conditions under which the individual operates. Case (1933) maintained that leadership is produced by the conjunction of three factors: (1) the personality traits of the leader, (2) the nature of the group and of its members, and (3) the event confronting the group. J. F. Brown (1936) proposed five field-dynamic laws of leadership. Leaders must (1) be identified as members of the group they are attempting to lead, (2) be of high potential interpersonally, (3) adapt themselves to the existing structure of relationships, (4) realize the long-term trends in the structure, and (5) recognize that leadership increases in potency at the cost of reduced freedom of leadership.

Hook (1943) noted that there is some restriction in the range of traits that a given situation permits the emergent leader to have. Thus, heroic action is decisive only when alternative courses of action are possible. On Elba, Napoleon had alternatives; on St. Helena, he had none.

Bass (1960) argued that the great-man-versus-the-environment controversy was a pseudo-problem. For any given case, some of the variance in what happens is due to the situation, some is due to the individual, and some is due to the combining effects of the individual and the situation. Thus, Mao Zedung played a critical role in the Chinese Revolution, but without the chaotic state of Chinese affairs under Kuomintang leadership, his rise to power would not have been possible. As will be discussed in Chapter 37, Dansereau, Alutto, and Yammarino (1984), provided a complete statistical formulation of models to examine the interplay of leader, follower, and situation. Their WABA methodology makes it possible to break into components and to index the variation and covariation in leadership and outcomes at the level of the leader and the individual member, the leader and the group, the leader and the group at different times, and the leader in a larger assemblage of groups, as well as all the statistical combinations of effects at the different levels of analysis.

Personal-situational theorists argue that theories of leadership cannot be constructed for behavior in a vacuum. They must contain elements about the person as well as elements about the situation. Any theory of leadership must take account of the interplay between the situation and the individual. Barnard (1938) and many others (C. A. Gibb, 1947; Jenkins, 1947; Lapiere, 1938; Murphy, 1941) attempted to resolve the situation-personality controversy by suggesting that leadership behavior is a less consistent attribute of individuals than such traits as nonsuggestibility, energy, and maturity, which are empirically associated and theoretically linked with overt leadership behavior. Such a trait as consistency results in some consistency in the behavior of individual leaders that transcends situations.

As will be detailed in the next chapter, Stogdill (1948) concluded that the leaders' traits must bear some relevant relationship to the characteristics of the followers. An adequate analysis of leadership involves a study not only of leaders, but of the situation. Stogdill's position strongly influenced the theorization that followed. According to Gerth and Mills (1952, p. 405–6),

> to understand leadership, attention must be paid to (1) the traits and motives of the leader as a man, (2) images that selected publics hold of him and their motives for following him, (3) the features of the role that he plays as a leader, and (4) the institutional context in which he and his followers may be involved.

C. A. Gibb (1954, p. 914) suggested that

> leadership is an interactional phenomenon arising when group formation takes place. The emergence of a group structure, whereby each of its members is assigned a relative position within the group depending upon the nature of his interrelations with the other members, is a general phenomenon and a function of the interrelation of individuals engaged in the pursuit of a common goal.

Stogdill and Shartle (1955) proposed that leadership needs to be studied in terms of the status, interactions, perceptions, and behavior of individuals in relation to other members of an organized group. Leadership should be regarded as a relationship between persons, rather than as a characteristic of the isolated individual. Data for all the members of a group should be combined and interrelated to study leadership in terms of the structural and functional dimensions of the organized interrelationships.

Wofford (1981) presented an elaborate integration of concepts and research results from the behavioral studies of ability, motivation, role perception, environmental constraints, determinants of the behavior of leaders, and environmental influences. This leader-environment-follower interaction theory conceived of the leader as a person who analyzes current deficiencies in the conditions that determine the performance of followers and takes corrective action. This theory appears to concentrate heavily on the practice of management by exception.

As will be seen in Chapter 36, the personal-situational approach has come to dominate the practice of forecasting the leadership potential of prospective supervisors and managers. The effort builds on the attempt to match the individuals' personal history, competencies, and traits with the requirements of the job.

Psychoanalytic Theories

Freud (1922), as well as many other psychoanalytically oriented writers such as Erikson (1964), Frank (1939), Fromm (1941), and H. Levinson (1970), addressed the leadership issue at length. Favorite interpretations conceived the leader as father figure, as a source of love or fear, as the embodiment of the superego, and as the emotional outlet for followers' frustrations and destructive aggression (Wolman, 1971). Freud (1913) proposed that the beginnings of civilization required a struggle with the leader of the primitive clan. In his study of Moses, Freud (1922/1939) tried to account for the rise of monotheism.

Much of this psychoanalytic theorizing about leadership attempted to explain the leader's political behavior from early childhood and family developments. Thus, for Freud and Bullitt (1932), Woodrow Wilson was obsessed with his father. Wilson buried his resentments of his articulate and impressive father under his intense idealization of him and publicly played out his private fantasies of Christlike greatness by attempting to become a grandiose new savior of the world.

For Freud, the father of the family defined the leader's psychological world. He is everyone's own private leader, who mediates the "transition . . . from inner to outer, from psychology to politics" (Strozier & Offer, 1985, p. 43). For Fenichel (1945), obedience to the "father" provided protection. The father could become the savior in times of crisis (Bychowski, 1948).

Mother figures can be as important as father figures. Strong mothers or absent fathers figured strongly in the career developments of Franklin Delano Roosevelt, Douglas MacArthur, and many other world-class leaders. These parental effects will be discussed further in Chapter 35.

Psychohistory. Psychoanalysis had a marked influence on psychohistorians' attempts to understand adult political leaders in terms of their childhood deprivations, cultural milieu, and relationships with parental authority and the psychodynamic needs of their followers that they fulfill. Illustrative of this approach is the variety of psychoanalytic treatises that have been written on Adolf Hitler alone, such as those of Langer (1972), Gatzke (1973), and Waite (1977). Other favorite biographical subjects of psychoanalysts have been Abraham Lincoln, Martin Luther, and Mahatma Gandhi.

Kernberg (1979) focused attention on the schizoid, obsessive, paranoid, and narcissistic character structures of leaders. Kohut (1976, 1977) saw charismatic leaders as narcissists, who use their followers to maintain their self-esteem. The followers' shame, jealousy, and hate are buried by their idealization of the leader. The pathology of leadership was also explored by Kets de Vries (1980, 1984) among others. Indeed, although the psychoanalytic study of leadership has accentuated psychopathological issues, "it is . . . patently absurd to label all leaders as pathological" (Strozier & Offer, 1985, p. 6). There is an imbalance in the psychoanalytical attention given to the neurotic and psychotic aspects of leaders' behavior and the ignoring of the healthy and creative in world-class leaders. Therefore, the psychoanalytic view needs to be refocused to explain "that elusive fit between the *leader* and the *led* in the full richness of the unique moment of the past" (Strozier & Offer, 1985, p. 7). For example, in contrast to immature leaders, Alexander (1942) and Erikson (1964) considered mature leaders to have innate abilities to command attention, to be free from irrational conflicts, and to be sensitive to the needs of others and be able and willing to relate emotionally to them.

Using the methods of psychohistory to delve deeper into questions concerning social insight, G. Davis (1975) showed how the psychodynamics of Theodore Roosevelt's childhood found expression in his "affective" insights as an adult leader. Personal recollections, published accounts, journalism, and biographies about Roosevelt as a child were meshed with an analysis of the relevant cultural developments that occured in the United States at the same time. Davis concluded that Roosevelt's psyche resolved the childhood experiences of his generation.

Crises and Charisma. Psychoanalytical theory was also used by Kets de Vries (1980) and by Hummel (1975) to show how the interaction of the personalities of leaders and the situations is dramatized in times of crisis. For Kets de Vries (1980), charismatic leaders arise in crises out of a sense of their own grandiosity and the group's sense of helpless dependency. Whether they serve well as leaders depends on whether they can transform their "paranoid potential" and sense of omnipotence into reality testing. In fragmented societies, such charisma may give rise to an integration of institutions and loyalties or it may spawn opposition movements (G. T. Stewart, 1974).

For Hummel, projection by the followers is at the root of their intense love for the charismatic leader. Followers see the leader as a superhuman hero because they cannot become consciously aware of their unconscious projections. Zaleznik (1977) proposed that the true leader, in contrast to the manager, has resolved the conflicts of his id and superego and has developed the strong ego ideals embodied in his confidence and self-determination.[1]

Group Dynamics. Psychoanalysis has much to say about the leader-follower development in the small group. According to Freud (1922), group members act like family siblings, in developing their ego-identifications. They form a common libidinal connection with

their leader (father) by incorporating his image into their superegos. For Redl (1942), the central person in the group (not necessarily the group leader) becomes an object of the members' identification on the basis of love or fear, an object of aggression, and a support for their own egos. The central person can become a model to be admired, the members' ego-ideal. The followers may internalize his standards of conduct or come to fear him as an aggressor. What had the most influence on the course of subsequent research on, education in, and the practice of group dynamics was Bion's (1948, 1961) sorting of leader-member relations into four "cultures": task oriented, dependent, fight-flight, and pairing.

Psychoanalysis also has much to say about leadership in therapeutic groups, although opinions differ on whether the group therapist is the group leader. For instance, Scheidlinger (1980) argued that the therapist's leadership is important to the way the group will function, as well as how much the group can contribute to successful treatment by providing a climate of safety and support for the reenactment of family-child and parent-child encounters.

Political Theories of Leadership

Political theorists, from Plato onward, had explanations, either explicit or implicit, and prescriptions for leadership. Marxism-Leninism, with its focus on economic determination of the course of history coupled with the dictatorship of the proletariat, laid out strong messages about who shall lead and what is expected of the leadership. Mao Zedung's mass-line leadership was much more explicit. It incorporated operant conditioning, consciousness raising in small groups, confession and self-criticism, and critical feedback. For Mao, the scattered and unsystematic ideas of the masses were to be studied to turn them into concentrated and systematic ideas that the leadership was to take back and explain to the masses until they became committed to the ideas and then implemented and tested them (Barlow, 1981).

Nazi ideology was centered on the *Führerprincip.* According to the Nazis, unquestioning obedience and loyalty to superiors produces the order and prosperity that would be shared by those who were worthy by race to

[1]More on theories about the charismatic leader will be found in Chapter 12 and later. Psychoanalytic concepts of leadership and group dynamics have figured strongly in the work of Maslow (1965) and other humanistic theorists. Some of these will be considered further in Chapters 7 and 27.

participate in the New Order. The other races were to be enslaved or exterminated. Emperor worship in Japan and fascism in Spain, Italy, and elsewhere had a similar blend of feudalistic, authoritarian, and ethnocentric ideologies. Like kings with divine rights, like the Emperor of China who pursued the Will of Heaven, the national dictator could do no wrong, so each successive level of leadership below him was equally infallible. Superiors' decisions were to be obeyed, not questioned. In contrast, the leadership espoused in the democratic world of constitutionally elected representatives who are responsible to their constituencies makes decisions based on the vote of the majority but the rights of the minority are respected and protected.[2]

Humanistic Theories

Grounded in American ideals of democracy and individual freedoms, the theories of McGregor, Argyris, Likert, Blake and Mouton, Maslow, and Hersey and Blanchard were concerned with development of the individual within an effective and cohesive organization. The human being is by nature a motivated organism. The organization is by nature structured and controlled. It is the function of leadership to modify the organization to provide freedom for individuals to realize their motivational potential for the fulfillment of their needs and to contribute to the accomplishment of organizational goals.

McGregor (1960, 1966) postulated two types of organizational leadership—Theory X and Theory Y. The former, based on the assumption that people are passive and resistant to organizational needs, attempts to direct and motivate people to fit these needs. Theory Y, based on the assumption that people already possess motivation and a desire for responsibility, attempts to arrange organizational conditions in such a manner as to make it possible for them to fulfill their needs while directing their efforts toward achieving organizational objectives.

In his maturity-immaturity theory, Argyris (1957, 1962, 1964a) perceived a fundamental conflict between the organization and the individual. It is the nature of organizations to structure members' roles and to control their performance in the interest of achieving specified objectives. It is the individual's nature to be self-directive and to seek fulfillment through exercising initiative and responsibility. An organization will be most effective when its leadership provides the means whereby followers may make a creative contribution to it as a natural outgrowth of their needs for growth, self-expression, and maturity. Most organizations pursue a one-way model in the way people are supposed to relate to others. The model contains a single loop or one-way link from the more powerful to the less powerful. In this model, there is preference for (1) unilateral control, (2) a win-or-lose orientation toward others, (3) a concealment of feeling, and (4) a rational censoring of information, freedom, and risk. In contrast, the model espoused by Argyris (1983) is double looped in that it comprises a (1) learning orientation, (2) a low-defensive, high-information environment, and (3) joint control by the more powerful and the less powerful with free and informed choice. This second double-looped model will be more effective in the long run for both the individual and the organization.

Likert (1961a, 1961b, 1967) suggested that leadership is a relative process in that leaders must take into account the expectations, values, and interpersonal skills of those with whom they are interacting. Leaders must present behaviors and organizational processes that the followers perceive to be supportive of their efforts and of their sense of personal worth. Leaders will involve followers in making decisions that affect their welfare and work. They will use their influence to further the task performance and personal welfare of followers and will enhance the cohesiveness of the group and the members' motivation to be productive by providing subordinates with freedom for responsible decision making and the exercise of initiative.

Blake and Mouton (1964, 1965) conceptualized leadership in terms of a managerial grid in which concern for people represents one axis and concern for production represents the other axis. Leaders may be high or low on both axes, or they may be high on one and low on the other. The leader who rates high on both axes develops followers who are committed to the accomplishment of work and have a sense of interdependence through a common stake in the organization's

---

[2]More will be said about these divergent political theories of leadership in Chapter 9.

purposes. Relationships of trust and respect for the leader emerge as well.

Maslow's theory of eupsychian management (1965) was derived from his observations of people at work in industry. Maslow stressed that it is important for managers to develop their subordinates' self-esteem and psychological health and emphasized the need for self-actualization so that everyone would have the opportunity to become what he or she had the capacity to become. Eupsychian management distinguishes between the person who is trying to be a democratic superior and one who is spontaneously democratic. According to this theory, the unconscious and the depths of personality have to be probed in the search for enlightened management. On the basis of these probes, different leaders will be chosen for different situations, as was the case with the Blackfoot Indians. Thus, power should be given to a leader only on an ad hoc basis for the situation in which it is warranted. Such leadership must not be left to self-seekers with neurotic needs for power, but should be given to those who are best suited to be leaders for the designated situation—those who can set things straight, who can do what needs to be done.[3]

Hersey and Blanchard's (1969a, 1972) life cycle theory of leadership synthesizes Blake and Mouton's (1964) managerial grid, Reddin's (1977) 3-D effectiveness typology, and Argyris's (1964a) maturity-immaturity theory. According to this theory, the leader's behavior is related to the maturity of the subordinates. As the subordinates mature, the leader's behavior should be characterized by a decreasing emphasis on task structuring and an increasing emphasis on consideration. As the subordinates continue to mature, there should be an eventual decrease in consideration. Maturity is defined in terms of subordinates' experience, motivation to achieve, and willingness and ability to accept responsibility.[4]

Interaction and Social Learning Theories

Interaction and social learning theories explain the leader-follower relationship as a consequence of the leader's interaction with the followers, as well with the circumstances involved. Interaction theories of leadership such as Gibb's (1958) are characterized by a complex and gross combination of the leader's personality; the followers' needs, values, attitudes, and personality; and the group's structure of interpersonal relations, character, as such, task, and environmental setting. What happens may be explained in terms of the leader's role and its attainment, reinforcement of change, paths to goals, and the effects of contingencies.[5]

Leader-Role Theory

According to leader-role theory, the characteristics of the individual and the demands of the situation interact in such a manner as to permit one or perhaps a few persons to emerge as leaders. Groups become structured in terms of positions and roles during the course of the members' interactions. A group is organized to the extent that it acquires differentiated positions and roles. Leadership represents one or more of the differentiated positions in a group. The occupant of a leadership position is expected to play a role that differs from the roles of other group members.

Leaders behave according to what is expected of them, and how they perceive their roles are defined. The leader's (and follower's) perceptions and expectations of his or her role are affected by the organization's formal policies and procedures, informal communications with colleagues, past experience, and his or her own needs and values (Kahn & Quinn, 1970). As will be detailed in Chapter 15, managers ordinarily must cope with conflicts among the different sources of information about their roles. Another line of reasoning states that what is routinely prescribed for the leader is not leadership; rather, leadership involves only the discretionary activities that the leader performs when the prescriptions fail to tell him or her what to do (Osborn & Hunt, 1975a). So it is the discretionary aspects of the leader's role that need to be emphasized.

Hunt, Osborn, and Martin (1981, p. 3) presented a well-supported theory to explain why some leaders act

---

[3]More will be said about this theory in Chapter 10 and later chapters.
[4]A full discussion of experimental and field studies based on these humanistic theories is presented in Chapters 21 and 23.

[5]Chapters 17, 18, and 19, in particular, detail much of the relevant research on the subject.

efficiently in response "to specific opportunities and problems which the unit is not designed to handle." The rules and procedures created by the organization can make the leader redundant. Kerr and Jermier (1978) pioneered the analysis of the substitutes for leadership; a discussion of this is saved for Chapter 30. Nevertheless, the wrong inference can be drawn here, namely, that more available regulations necessarily reduce the discretionary behavior of leaders. On the contrary, Hunt, Osborn, and Martin (1981) predicted and found that leaders in units in which more rules, policies, and procedures are used were expected to respond with more discretionary use of those rules and procedures and actually did so. Jones (1983) analyzed the leader's role in terms of the controls provided by it. Jones argued that such control of the work flow, of the way the task is structured, and of the way jobs are formalized may provide the leader with as much influence over what goes on as does his or her ability to promise or deny rewards and punishments.

Homans (1950) developed a theory of the leadership role using three basic variables: action, interaction, and sentiments. He assumed that an increase in the frequency of interaction by group members and their participation in common activities was associated with an increase in their sentiments of mutual liking and in the clarity of the group's norms. The higher the status of persons within the group, the more nearly their activities would conform to the group's norms, the wider would be their range of interactions, and the larger the number of group members for whom they would originate interactions.

Theories of the Attainment of the Leadership Role

These theories attempt to explain who emerges as a leader of a group and why. For Hemphill (1954), leaders emerge in situations in which components of group tasks are interdependent and are related to the solution of a common problem among group members. Fundamental to his theory is the concept of the structure in interaction or predictable interaction activity. The role structure of the group and the office of the leader are defined by institutionalized expectations with respect to this initiation of structure in interaction. The probability of the success of an attempted act of leadership is a function of the members' perceptions of their freedom to accept or reject the suggested structure in interaction. When such a structure leads to the solution of mutual problems, it acquires value and strengthens the expectation that all group members will conform to it. Thus, acts of leadership initiate structure in interaction and successful leadership is the act of successfully initiating such structure.

Consistent with Hemphill, Stogdill (1959) developed an expectancy-reinforcement theory of such role attainment. This theory attempted to explain the emergence and persistence of leadership in initially unstructured groups, as well as what leadership is and how it comes into existence. As group members interact and engage in the performance of mutual tasks, they reinforce the expectation that their actions and interactions will continue in accord with their previous performance. Thus, the members' roles are defined by mutually confirmed expectations of the performances and interactions they will be permitted to contribute to the group. The leadership potential of any given member is defined by the extent to which he or she initiates and maintains structure in interaction and expectation.

Another attempt to explain the emergence of leadership was proposed by Stein, Hoffman, Cooley, and Pearse (1979), who presented a valence model. According to this model, emergent leaders are the group members who are most willing and able to perform those roles and functions that enable the group to accomplish its tasks and that guide and encourage others to contribute to the process. Such leadership will appear in phases that parallel Tuckman's (1965) stages of group development: orientation, conflict, and emergence. Some emergent leaders take charge early, others move ahead with collaborators, and still others fail to maintain their initial success as leaders.

Reinforced-Change Theory

In a theory proposed by Bass (1960), leadership is the observed effort of one member in a group to change the motivation, understanding, or behavior of other members. A change will be observed in other members if the initiating member is successful. Motivation is increased by changing the members' expectations of being rewarded or punished. People become a group if the group's existence is rewarding to them or enables them to avoid punishment. The behavior of group members changes to increase the rewards the members receive for performance. Leaders acquire their position by virtue of their perceived ability to reinforce the behavior of group members by granting or denying rewards or punishments. Since the group's effectiveness is evaluated in terms of its ability to reward its members, leaders are valued when they enable a group to provide expected rewards. The congruence of a leader's perceived status—value of the position held and esteem—value as a person regardless of the position, and ability can account for the leader's success. Incongruence generates conflict and failure. This emphasis on congruence is found also in Halal's (1974) general theory. A particular style of leadership is congruent with specific technologies of tasks and specific motivation of subordinates. Adaptation occurs to achieve greater congruence.

Bass argued that the emergence of leadership and what would promote effectiveness (the members' actual achievement of their goals of reward or the avoidance of punishment) depended on the interaction potential in the situation—the physical, psychological, and social distance among individuals. The likelihood that individuals will interact depends on the size of the group and the geographic and social proximity of the individuals, their opportunity for contact, intimacy and familiarity, mutuality of esteem and attraction, and homogeneity of abilities and attitudes. Monge and Kirste (1975) extended the examination of proximity as a time-and-space opportunity, again showing the positive association of proximity with the potential to interact as well as its contribution to satisfaction with the interaction.

The conditions affecting the potential to interact will be examined again more fully, particularly in Chapter 30. The importance of reinforcement in the leader-follower relationship will be examined in various contexts in many of the later chapters that deal with power relationships and exchange relationships. It is central to path-goal theory.

Path-Goal Theory

The reinforcement of change in the subordinate by the leader is a prominent aspect of path-goal theory. Georgopoulos, Mahoney, and Jones (1957) and M. G. Evans (1970a) suggested that the successful leader shows a follower the rewards that are available to him or her. The leader also shows the follower the paths (behaviors) through which the rewards may be obtained (House, 1971). The leader clarifies the goals of the followers, as well as the paths to those goals. This clarification enhances the psychological state of the followers and arouses them to increase their efforts to perform well. Thus, the followers achieve satisfaction from the job to be done. The leaders may enhance satisfaction with the work itself as well as provide valued extrinsic rewards, such as recommendations for pay increases that are contingent on the subordinates' performance. (The leader needs to be able to control the rewards that subordinates value.)

The situation determines which type behavior by the leader will accomplish these path-goal purposes. Two situational aspects of consequences are the competence of the subordinates and environmental forces, such as how highly structured is the task to be done (House & Dessler, 1974). To reconcile the theory with experimental results, House (1972) proposed that the effects of a leader's behavior are contingent on three kinds of moderator variables: (1) task variables, such as role clarity, routine, and externally imposed controls, (2) environmental variables, (3) and individual differences, such as preferences, expectations, and personality.[6]

Contingency Theory

Along with the path-goal theory, Fiedler's contingency theory (1967a) dominated much of the research on leadership during the 1970s. For Fiedler, the effectiveness of task-oriented and relations-oriented leaders is contingent on the demands imposed by the situation. Leaders are assessed as task oriented or relations oriented according to the way they judge their least-pre-

[6]Empirical studies dealing with path-goal propositions will be discussed in detail in Chapters 24 and 28.

ferred co-worker. The task-oriented leader is most likely to be effective in situations that are most favorable or most unfavorable to him or her. The relations-oriented leader is most likely to be effective in situations between the two extremes. A situation is favorable to the leader if the leader is esteemed by the group to be led; if the task to be done is structured, clear, simple, and easy to solve; and if the leader has legitimacy and power owing to his or her position.

Most person-situation theorists focus on how the person needs to be developed to adapt best to the needs of the stuation. But Fiedler's research and theory tended to emphasize the need to place the person in the situation for which he or she is best suited. Task-oriented people should be selected to lead very favorable or unfavorable situations, and relations-oriented people should be selected to lead situations that are neither high nor low in favorability. And so, Fiedler, Chemers, and Mahar (1976) developed a method to help a leader "match" his or her situation. The leader of a designated orientation is helped to change the situation or to adjust better to the favorability or unfavorability of the situation. The Fiedler, Chemers, and Mahar (1976) leadership-training program consists of first identifying the trainee's particular style—task- or relations orientation and then teaching the trainee how to analyze and classify leadership situations for their favorableness, or situational control. The next elements that are considered are the best fit of the situation and style and how to change one's style to suit the occasion or how to change the situation to fit one's style better. Fiedler's four decades of work involved a progression from empirical discoveries to the formation of the theory to the practical application of the theory and to validation of the application.[7]

Theories and Models of Interactive Processes

Numerous additional elaborations have appeared to account for leadership and for leader-follower relations as an interactive process. For instance, Fulk and Wendler (1982) and Greene (1975) agreed that if subordinates (followers) perform well, the leader displays more consideration, which then leads to increased satisfaction for the followers. If the followers do not perform well, the leader displays more structuring behavior and the followers' satisfaction does not increase.

Multiple-Linkage Model

Yukl (1971) proposed that the leader's initiation of structure enhances the subordinate's ability to cope with the situation; the leader's consideration for the welfare of the subordinate enhances the subordinate's satisfaction with the situation. Yukl (1970, 1981) greatly expanded the interaction framework. Yukl's multiple-linkage model proposed that the subordinate's effort and skill in performing the task, the leader's role, the resources available, and the group's cohesiveness all moderate the effects of the leader's behavior on group outcomes. The Yukl model also differentiated between leadership required for short-term and for long-term effectiveness. Yukl and Kanuk (1979) provided evidence that, in contrast to performance outcomes, the subordinates' satisfaction came about from different patterns of behavior by the leader and mediating conditions.

Multiple-Screen Model

Another interaction approach to understanding the relations of the leader and the led is the multiple screen model, which attempts to explain the relationship between the leader's intelligence and his or her group's performance. Thus, Fiedler and Leister (1977) suggested and provided empirical support for the proposal that intelligent leaders can generate effective groups if the leaders have good relations with their bosses. If relations are poor, then it is experienced rather than intelligent leaders who bring about more productive groups. Experience is more important to effective leadership if leader-boss relations are poor.[8]

---

[7]A section of Chapter 23 is devoted to a review of research based on Fiedler's theory, and a section of Chapter 35 discusses its applications.

[8]Chapter 29 will discuss this model further.

Vertical-Dyad Linkage

The vertical dyad of boss and subordinate is an interaction linkage of mutual influence. It emphasizes the relationship between the leader and each individual follower, rather than between the leader and the group as a whole. Graen (1976) assumed that the leader behaves differently toward each follower and that these differences must be analyzed separately. This theory is in opposition to most earlier theories, which assumed that the leader behaves in much the same way toward all group members and that behavioral descriptions from group members can be averaged to obtain an accurate description of the general behavior of the leader. According to Graen, leaders categorize followers as belonging to an in-group or an out-group, and the leader behaves differently toward members of these two groups. In-group members can be more independent of the leader and receive more attention from the leader, as well as more of the other rewards. As a consequence, in-group members perform better and are more satisfied than are out-group members (Vecchio & Gobdel, 1984). Extensive investigations by Graen and associates of the effects of vertical dyads effects have been published and will be discussed more fully, particularly in Chapter 17.

Exchange Theories

Graen's (1976) vertical-dyad linkage (subsequently called leader-member exchanges) was one of many interaction theories that were based on the assumption that social interaction represents a form of exchange.[9] Exchange theories propose that group members make contributions at a cost to themselves and receive benefits at a cost to the group or other members. Interaction continues because members find the social exchange mutually rewarding. Blau (1964) began with the fact that most people consider being elevated to a position of high status to be rewarding and that it is also rewarding for members to associate with their high-status leaders. But leaders tend to deplete their power when members have discharged their obligations to the leaders. The leaders than replenish their power by rendering valuable services to the group. They benefit as much as anyone else does from following their good suggestions, rather than somebody else's poorer ones. The compliance that the leaders' contributions earn them constitutes a surplus profit of leadership.

T. O. Jacobs (1970) formulated a social-exchange theory and buttressed it with a wide range of research findings. According to Jacobs, the group provides the leader with status and esteem in exchange for the leader's unique contributions to the attainment of the group's goals. Authority relationships in formal organizations define role expectations that enable group members to perform their tasks and to interact without the use of power. Leadership implies an equitable exchange relationship between the leader and the followers. When role obligations are mutually acknowledged, each party can satisfy the expectations of the other on an equitable basis.

Exchange can be built on differences in power between the leader and the led (Lasswell & Kaplan, 1950)—the subject of Chapter 13—or it can be a consequence of a successful chain of interaction experiences (Hollander & Julian, 1969)—discussed in detail in Chapter 18.

Behavioral Theories

As early as 1929, Aaronovich and Khotin (1929) reported using differential cued reinforcement to alter the leadership behavior of monkeys in uncovering boxes of food. Mawhinney and Ford (1977) reinterpreted path-goal theory in terms of operant conditioning. W. E. Scott (1977) saw the need to replace the conception that leadership is due to influence or persuasion with an analysis of the observable behaviors of leaders that change the behavior of subordinates. All these behavioral theories emphasized reinforcement and making the receipt of rewards or the avoidance of punishment contingent on the subordinate behaving as required. According to Davis and Luthans (1979, p. 239):

> The leader's behavior is a cue to evoke the subordinate's task behavior. The subordinate's task behavior, in turn, can act as a consequence for the leader which, in turn, reinforces, punishes, or extinguishes the leader's subsequent behavior. Similarly, the sub-

[9]See, for example, Gergen (1969), Homans (1958), March and Simon (1958), and Thibaut and Kelley (1959).

ordinate's behavior has its own consequences ... which serve to reinforce, punish, or extinguish this behavior. The consequences for the subordinate's behavior may be related to the leader's subsequent behavior, [to] the work itself, and its outcomes, or [to] other organization members.

Supervisors do not directly cause subordinates' behavior; they merely set the occasion or provide a discriminative stimulus for the evocation of it. The behavior of subordinates depends on its consequences. Environmental cues, discriminative stimuli, behaviors, and consequences form a behavioral contingency for analysis.

But Davis and Luthans left room for cognitive processes to enter the scenario "to assign concepts to behavior and to infer relationships between events." Their functional analysis of the leader-subordinate dynamic uses Luthans's (1977) S-O-B-C model, in which S is the antecedant stimulus, O is the organism's covert processes, B is the behavior, and C is the consequence.

Sims (1977) conducted one of the many investigations to be reviewed in Chapter 17 which demonstrated that a leader's positive rewarding behavior will improve a subordinate's performance, particularly if the reward is contingent on the quality or quantity of the performance.

Other behavioral models and theories concentrated on the followers' reactions. For example, Sheridan, Kerr, and Abelson (1981) developed a model to represent extreme, rather than ordinary, leader-subordinate interactions. The day-to-day behavior of the leader may be relatively unimportant to the supervisor-subordinate relationship compared to the leader's behavior when a subordinate experiences an intense demand or when the leader experiences a highly unexpected response. This model shows that subordinates can become so accustomed to frequent leadership activity that the effects of this activity are minimal and even dampening.

Communication Theories

Communications and rhetoric provide another point of departure for theories about leader-follower interactions. For example, Sharf (1978) created a rhetorical framework based on a theory by Burke (1969) to ana-

lyze the relative success of emerging leaders in small groups in obtaining cooperation from the other members of the groups and in resolving the struggle for leadership status. When applied to recorded discussions of small, leaderless task groups, the analyses reveal the importance of going beyond the symbolic divisions in the emergence of leadership.

Perceptual and Cognitive Theories

An early theoretical emphasis on the perceptual and cognitive aspects of leadership was provided by Goffman (1959), who analyzed social behavior as theater. That is, Goffman evaluated the roles, membership, and phenomena of groups in terms of actors, audience, frontstage, and backstage. For Goffman, social learning creates a disparity between the leader's intentions and the followers' understanding of what the leader is trying to do.

Quinn and Hall (1983) constructed an integrated theory of leadership on the basis of such perceptual and cognitive dimensions as the flexibility versus the control of leaders and the internal versus the external focus of leaders. Carrier (1984) constructed cognitive maps to locate traits of leadership in reference to these dimensions. For example, the trait of dominance was placed in a location that is high in both control and in internal focus.

Perceptual and cognitive theories offer several advantages. They make use of the major strides in cognitive psychology and are immediately applicable in diagnosis and leadership education.[10] They include theories about attribution, information processing, systems analysis, and rational-deductive decision trees and will be presented briefly in this chapter.

Attribution Theories

Each leader and follower is seen to have his or her own implicit theory of leadership. If we want to understand the behavior of individual leaders, we must begin by attempting to find out what they are thinking about the situation in which they would be leaders (Pfeffer, 1977). And whether they are seen to act like leaders

[10]For details, see Chapter 35.

depends on their and their followers' implicit theories about leadership (Eden & Leviatan, 1975). We observe the behavior of leaders and infer the causes of these behaviors to be various personal traits or external constraints. If these causes match our naive assumptions about what leaders should do, then we use the term "leadership" to describe the persons who we observed. Thus, for Calder (1977), leadership changes from a scientific concept to a study of the social reality of group members and observers—a study in how the term is used, when it is used, and assumptions about the development and nature of leadership. Attributions of leadership by observers and group members are biased by their individual social realities (Mitchell, Larson, & Green, 1977; H. M. Weiss, 1977), which accounts for the low correlations that are often found between supervisors', peers', and subordinates' ratings of the same leaders,[11] as well as for the confounding of evaluations of the performance of subordinates and the behavior of leaders (Rush, Thomas, & Lord, 1977).

Green and Mitchell (1979) formulated a model to study such attributional processes in leaders. They explained that the leader's behavior is a consequence of the leader's interpretation of the subordinate's performance. Thus if presented with an incident of a subordinate's poor performance, such as low productivity, lateness, a missed deadline, or disruptive behavior, the leader forms an implicit theory about the subordinate and the situation, judging that the cause of the incident was the subordinate's personality, ability, or effort or an externality, such as the lack of support, a difficult task, or insufficient information. Causality is attributed more to the subordinate than to the situation if the subordinate has had a history of poor performance and if the effects of the poor performance have severe outcomes (Mitchell & Wood, 1979). In such circumstances, the leader will focus remedial action on the subordinate, rather than on the situation, even if the situation was the cause of the problem. Meindl, Ehrlich, and Dukerich (1985), along with Pfeffer (1977) and Calder (1977), agreed that there is a tendency to attribute more of the cause than is actually warranted to the subordinate rather than to the situational circumstances.[12]

Information Processing

Following Newell and Simon's (1972) theory that focused attention on the problem solver's subjective "problem space," which contains the encodings of goals, initial situations, intermediate states, rules, constraints, and other relevant aspects of the task environment, Lord (1976) saw the utility of studying the shared problem spaces of leaders and followers when they tackle a common task. For example, a leader was expected to devote more effort to developing an orientation and definition of the problem or the group when the actual task lacked structure.

Social cues and symbols take on more importance for an understanding of leadership if this information-processing approach is employed. In addition to encoding, information processing involves selective attention, comprehension, storage, retention, information retrieval, and judgment. Both theory and evidence show that the perceptions of leaders are based largely on spontaneous recognition. Moreover, the cognitive category, leadership, is hierarchically organized. Perceptions and expectations of the attributes and behavior of leaders are widely shared (Lord, 1976, 1985; Lord, Binning, Rush, & Thomas, 1978).

Open-Systems Analysis

An open-systems point of view implies sensitivity to the larger environment and organization in which leaders and their subordinates are embedded. To convert inputs into outputs, flows of energy and of information must occur in the system. In open systems, the effect of the outputs on the environment are feedback and new inputs. The relations within the system grow and become more intricate with repeated input-output cycles. The cyclical conversion process can be increased in rate and intensity. Leaders or followers can import and introduce more information. Directive leaders do it alone; if followers are included, the proc-

---

[11]See, for example, Bernardin and Alvares (1975), Ilgen and Fujii (1976), and T. R. Mitchell (1970a).

[12]More will be discussed about attributional processes in Chapters 18, 19, and elsewhere.

ess is participative. Energy levels can be increased by selecting as leaders and followers more highly motivated individuals or by increasing the reinforcements that accrue from outputs (Katz & Kahn, 1966).

Bryson and Kelley (1978) created a systems model for understanding the emergence, stability, and change in organizations in which the formal leaders are elected, such as cooperatives, professional associations, and legislatures. They constructed a list of clusters of individual, processual, structural, and environment variables that were likely to be of consequence to each other on the basis of earlier formulations by Peabody (1976) and Van de Ven (1976).

Therapeutic Groups. Lieberman (1976a) explained change-induction groups, such as psychotherapy groups, encounter groups, self-help groups, and consciousness-raising groups, in terms of systems analysis. Five structural characteristics of the system were seen to affect the change-induction process: (1) the level of psychological distance between the participant and the leader, (2) felt causes, sources, and cures of psychological misery, (3) the extent to which the group is seen as a social microcosm, (4) the degree to which members stress differentiation rather than similarity, and (5) the relationship between the cognitive and expressive behavior of the leader.

Incorporating Macro- and Micro-levels. Many models and theories of leadership have been embedded in larger organizational models and theories. For example, Bowers and Seashore's (1966) four-factor theory of leadership (described earlier) is part of a larger systems theory of organizations. Osborn and Hunt (1975a, 1975b) formulated an adaptive-reactive model of leadership to incorporate such macrovariables as environmental constraints or organizational demands as antecedents of the behavior of leaders. Likewise, Bass and Valenzi (1974) used systems theory to construct an open-systems model of leader-follower relationships. According to their model, the systems are open to the outside environment and are sensitive to the contraints imposed on them by the outside. The system imports energy (power) and information from the outside, converts it, and exports goods and services to the outside. The Bass-Valenzi model (Bass, 1976) proposes that

whether leaders are directive, negotiative, consultative, participative, or delegative depends on their perceptions of the system's inputs and within-systems relations. The leader and his or her immediate work group form an open system of inputs (organizational, task, and work-group variables), within-system relations (power and information differentials), and outputs (productivity and satisfaction). For instance, the Bass-Valenzi model posits that leaders will be more directive if they perceive that they have more power and information than do their subordinates. They will consult if they perceive that they have the power but that their subordinates have the necessary information to solve the group's problems. They will delegate when they perceive that their subordinates have both power and information, and they will negotiate when they perceive they have the information but not the power. A small-space analysis of empirical data by Shapira (1976) supported these propositions.

Starting with open-systems theory and Jaques's (1978) general theory of bureaucratic organizations, Jacobs and Jaques (1987) formulated a theory to explain the requirements of leadership at successively higher echelons of large bureaucratic organizations. To compete successfully, the organizations must have an appropriate structure, which Jacobs and Jaques specified as no more than five operating levels and two additional higher headquarters levels. At each level, the complexity of the environment must be understood and clearly transmitted to the next level below to reduce uncertainties at that level. Such a reduction of uncertainty will add value to productivity at that level and define how it must adapt to remain competitive. At each level, the role of the leadership is to ensure the accuracy of the uncertainty-reduction process and the availability of resources for the required adaptive changes. To accomplish this goal, leaders at the successively higher echelons increasingly must have "the capacity to deal with more uncertain and more abstract concepts" and with longer time spans for accomplishment and evaluation. At the lowest three echelons, leaders must focus on how they can contribute to the organization's productivity above and beyond the rules and policies that have been laid down for them by higher authority. At the next two echelons, leaders must concern themselves with how to maintain and improve their organizational arrangements. At the highest echelons, leadership involves strategic decision making in a "nearly unbounded environment."[13]

Rational-Deductive Approach

Vroom and Yetton (1974) rationally linked some of the accepted facts about leadership into a prescription of the kind of leadership style that is most likely to succeed. They posed ten questions that leaders should ask themselves in deciding whether to be directive or participative in decision making with their subordinates and whether to do so primarily with individual subordinates or with the whole group at once. Essentially, they argued that supervisors ought to be directive when they are confident that they know what needs to be done and when their subordinates do not have this knowledge. Furthermore, they suggested that in this situation, the subordinates will accept a decision made by the supervisor. However, if the subordinates have more information than does the supervisor, if their acceptance and commitment are of paramount importance, and if the subordinates can be trusted to concern themselves with the organization's interests, the supervisor should be participative.[14]

Hybrid Explanations

Cognitive, behavioral, and interactional explanations are likely to be needed to account fully for leader-follower relations and outcomes from them. Gilmore, Beehr, and Richter (1979) instructed leaders in an experimental laboratory to display either a lot or a little initiative and a lot or a little consideration. Although the participants who were subjected to the leadership failed to perceive that their leaders actually differed in their behavior, a lot of actual (but not perceived) initiative, coupled with a lot of actual (but not perceived)

consideration by the leaders, resulted in a better quality of work by the participants. The quality of the participants' work was lower when the leaders displayed a great deal of initiative but little consideration. It would seem that under certain conditions, it is more profitable to make use of behavioral theories to understand the behavior of leaders. Under other circumstances, such as when leaders and subordinates must act on the basis of their interpretations of a situation, perceptual and cognitive theories are more useful. Some theories or aspects of them may account better for the leadership that handles short-term disturbances; other theories may deal better with the leadership that corrects chronic deficiencies in the long term.

Winter (1978, 1979a) developed a complex model that combines aspects of the trait, reinforcement, behavioral, and cognitive approaches and the feedback loops of systems analysis. Winter's model was based on a battery of tests of skills and behavioral competency measures for over 1,000 naval personnel and their leaders. Figure 3.1 shows the emergent model that links different skills with particular performances. The model is based on empirical cluster analyses and subsequent regression analyses. Greater optimization (assigning tasks to those subordinates who are most likely to do them well and making tradeoffs between the requirements of the tasks and individual needs) and goal setting both contributed to more delegation by the leader. Increased monitoring by the leader resulted in more positive expectations, disciplining, and the giving of advice and counsel. It also contributed to more feedback, which, in turn, led to more disciplining and giving more advice and counsel.

Johnston (1981) used many of the preceding theories to construct a model of the "holistic leader/follower grid." To represent the leader-follower interchange adequately, Johnston borrowed from Jung's (1968) psychoanalytic theory of life cycles, Berne's (1964) transactional analysis, McGregor's (1960) theory X and theory Y, Rogers's (1951) nondirective counseling, and Tannenbaum and Schmidt's (1958) model of decision making. Tomassini, Solomon, Romney, and Krogstad (1982) also constructed a cognitive/behavioral model in which the leader's influence was seen to interact with the subordinate's work behavior and identified the situations that circumscribe what the leader can do.

---

[13]More will be said about these propositions in Chapters 20 and 26.
[14]Empirical research in support of the validity of the Vroom and Yetton model is presented in Chapter 22.

Figure 3.1. Flow Chart of the Navy Leadership and Management Processes in Terms of the Cross-Validated Competencies

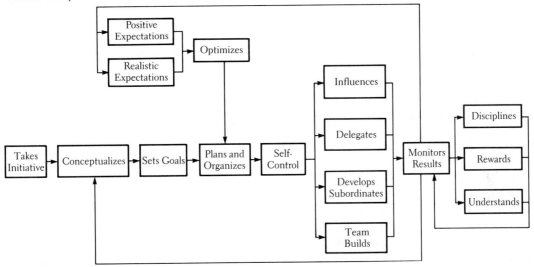

SOURCE: *Adapted from Winter (1978).*

Transformational Leadership

By 1960, the dominant paradigm for the study of leadership had evolved from research on the traits and situations that affect leadership to something more dynamic. Leadership was now seen to be contingent on a condition of traits and situations involving a transaction or exchange between the leader and the led (Hollander, 1986). In this view, leaders exchange promises of rewards and benefits to subordinates for the subordinates' fulfillment of agreements with the leader. Even the psychoanalysts conceived of followers as complying with the leader to obtain the leader's love.

Freud (1922) suggested that there was more to the concept of leadership than a mere exchange. For the leader embodied ideals for the follower with which the follower identified. Barnard (1938) noted that personal loyalty was more powerful than "tangible inducements." But along with Downton (1973), Burns (1978) presented the new paradigm of the transformational as opposed to the transactional leader. The transformational leader asks followers to transcend their own self-interests for the good of the group, organization, or society; to consider their longer-term needs to develop themselves, rather than their needs of the moment; and to become more aware of what is really important.

Hence, followers are converted into leaders. Among 90 transformational leaders, Bennis (1984) found evidence of competence to manage attention and meaning, to articulate visions of what was possible, and to empower the collective effect of their leadership.

Burns conceived leaders to be either transformational or transactional, but the paradigm was modified by Bass (1985a, 1985b), who proposed that transformational leadership augments the effects of transactional leadership on the efforts, satisfaction, and effectiveness of subordinates. Many of the great transformational leaders, including Abraham Lincoln, Franklin Delano Roosevelt, and John F. Kennedy, did not shy away from being transactional as well as transformational. They were able to move the nation as well as play petty politics. Waldman and Bass's (1985) analysis of surveys of senior military officers and business managers confirmed the fidelity of the model. Tichy and Devanna (1986) described the hybrid nature of transformational leadership. According to them, transformational leadership is not due just to charisma. It is

a behavioral process capable of being learned and managed. It's a leadership process that is systematic, consisting of purposeful and organized search for changes, systematic analysis, and the capacity to move resources from areas of lesser to greater productivity ... [to bring about] a strategic transformation. ... (p. viii)

Kuhnert and Russell (1989) designed a four-stage model of how the transformational leader develops, based on Kegan's (1982) theory of the evolving self.[15]

Factor analytic studies by Bass (1985a), Hater and Bass (1988), and Seltzer, Numerof, and Bass (1989) have suggested that transformational leadership can be conceptually organized along four correlated dimensions: charismatic leadership, inspirational leadership, intellectual stimulation, and individualized consideration. Chapter 12 details the antecedents and consequences of charismatic leadership, inspirational leadership, and intellectual stimulation, and Chapter 8 discusses individualized consideration. Factorially, transactional leadership is contingent reinforcement, expressed usually as contingent reinforcement and management by exception, which will be examined at length in Chapters 17 through 19.

Hater and Bass (1988) and Yammarino and Bass (1988) have shown that according to a leader's subordinates, colleagues, and superiors, the transformational factors correlate more highly with the leader's effectiveness, than does practicing contingent reward. Contingent reward, in turn, correlates more highly with the leader's effectiveness than do reactive management by exception and contingent punishment. Satisfaction with the leader follows a similar pattern (Bass & Avolio, 1989). Similar results can be obtained when different sources are used to describe the leader and to evaluate the outcomes of the leadership in effectiveness and satisfaction.

Transformational leadership is closer to the prototype of leadership that people have in mind when they describe their ideal leader and is more likely to provide a role model with which subordinates want to identify (Bass & Avolio, 1988). In practice, this means that leaders develop in their subordinates an expectation of high performance rather than merely spend time praising or reprimanding them (Gilbert, 1985). For Bradford and Cohen (1984), the manager must be more than a hero of technical competence and organizing skills. He or she must become a developer of people and a builder of teams.

Methods and Measurements

Theories of leadership have depended on different methods of verification, and models of leadership have depended on different methods of measurement. Research on the traits of leaders tended to rely heavily on the use of tests and questionnaires for the collection of data. With the development of interaction theories, it became important to know what was happening in the group. Expert or trained observers were used to keep a running record of the behavior of group members, and the members also might be asked to report their feelings and observations. In some cases, observers merely reported what they saw, in other cases, they were provided with checklists of behaviors or processes to be reported. The most widely used checklist is the set of behavioral categories developed by Bales (1950). Carter and associates (1951), Mann (1961), Bales, Cohen, and Williamson (1979), Bales and Cohen (1980), and Komaki, Zlotnick, and Jensen (1986), among others, also developed observational categories and procedures. Bass, Gaier, Farese, and Flint (1957) relied on the changes in correlations among members' judgments from before to after group discussion to measure how much each member had been influential.

Observational studies have identified a number of behaviors that the trait theorists did not anticipate. Whereas the trait theorists were interested in the subjective aspects of the dynamics of personality, the interaction experimenters were concerned with observable behaviors. The two approaches often produced results that were independent of each other. Nevertheless, Jacoby (1974) was able to demonstrate substantial construct validity based on agreement among three methods of assessing opinion leadership: self-designating, sociometric, and key informant.

Clinical interviews and individual case histories have dominated psychoanalytic explanations; laboratory experiments and field surveys have often been the method of choice in cognitive and behavioral investigations. By now, it is fair to say that every procedure

---

[15]More will be said about this development in Chapter 35.

known to social science in general has been applied specifically to the study of leadership. These procedures have included autobiographical analysis; biographical analysis; case studies; the evaluation of news records, memoranda, and minutes of meetings; the analysis of speeches; biodata analysis; studies of communication patterns; autologs and observers' logs of leaders' activities; ratings by observers, superiors, peers, subordinates, and clients; judgments of verbal protocols; and individual interviews. Increasingly, investigators are using two or more approaches to increase the confidence in their efforts. For example, Heller (1969a) first collected survey-questionnaire data from managers. After analyzing the results, he gathered them together in panels to interpret and confirm or refute the results. Again, focused interviews of panels of voters can provide the basic ideas for political media campaigns that are then followed up by public opinion polls of representative samples of voters (Kennan & Hadley, 1986).

Summary and Conclusions

The long history of reliance on great-man theories naturally led to the search for traits of leadership and theories of traits. In reaction, there arose an equally strong emphasis on environmental theories. Finally, syntheses were achieved in theories of interacting persons and situations, built around psychoanalysis, role attainment, reinforced change, paths to goals, or contingencies of leader and situation.

Theories have been built on the assumption that humankind is inherently good or inherently evil, on exchange relationships, and on behavioral, perceptual, or cognitive bases. Empirical and rational problem solving and systems analysis have also been used. Newer departures have occurred with theories that focus on social-information processing and on transformational leadership. However, empirical research on leadership began with studies of the personal factors that contribute to the emergence and success of a leader.

Personal Attributes of Leaders

Traits of Leadership: 1904–47

Smith and Krueger (1933) surveyed the literature on leadership to 1933. Developments in leadership methodology, as related especially to military situations, were reviewed in 1947 by Jenkins (1947). The present survey was concerned only with those studies[1] through 1947 in which some attempt was made to determine the traits and characteristics of leaders.

Methods

The primary methods that these studies employed to identify the personal characteristics of leaders were the following: (1) observation of behavior in group situations, (2) choice of associates (voting), (3) nomination or rating by qualified observers, (4) selection (and rating or testing) of persons occupying positions of leader-

[1]In many of the studies surveyed, leadership was not defined. In others, the methods used in the investigation appeared to have little relationship to the problem stated. An attempt was made here to include all studies bearing on the problem of traits and personal factors associated with leadership. The original book or article was read and abstracted in detail in all except four cases (one American and three German publications) in which the data were derived directly from abstracts.

Since evidence reported by fewer investigators was not regarded as providing a satisfactory basis for evaluation, the present survey dealt with only those factors that were studied by three or more investigators. Although it was realized that the number of investigations in which a factor was studied is not necessarily indicative of the importance of the factor, nevertheless, the frequency with which a factor was found to be significant appeared to be the most satisfactory single criterion for evaluating the data accumulated in this survey. Other criteria, such as the competence of the experimental methods employed and the adequacy of the statistical treatment of data, were regarded in evaluating the results of a particular study.

During the analysis of data obtained from various groups and by various methods, a question arose about the extent to which results may be influenced by differences in the social composition of the groups, differences in methodology, and differences in criteria for leadership. There was no assurance, for example, that the investigator who analyzed the biographies of great men was studying the same kind of leadership behavior that is revealed through observation of children's leadership activities in group situations. It is of interest, however, that some of the studies that used the two different methods yielded remarkably similar results. On the other hand, there were some factors that appeared only in certain age and social groups or only when certain methods were employed.

ship, and (5) analysis of biographical and case history data.

Observations and Time Sampling of Behavior in Group Situations

In these studies, the behavior of two or more individuals was observed in situations that permit the emergence of leadership activities. The situation was either highly structured in advance, as in the studies of children by Henning (1929), Luithlen (1931), Miller and Dollard (1941), and Terman (1925), or the situation was natural and uncontrolled, as in some of the boys' gangs studied by Thrasher (1927). The periods of observation ranged from five-second periods at definitely spaced intervals to an hour or more of continuous observation. Chapple and Donald (1946) devised a method for recording on a polygraph the frequency and duration of observed social contacts by executives. The relative merits of the various time-sampling methods were evaluated by Arrington (1943).

The observational studies that yielded the most relevant data on leadership were those of Chevaleva-Ianovskaia and Sylla (1929) and the pioneering investigation of Terman (1904). Henning (1929) devised a number of ingenious experimental situations for the study of leadership in pairs of children, but the investigations of

This chapter is a revision of "Personal factors associated with leadership: A survey of the literature," by Ralph M. Stogdill, which appeared in the *Journal of Psychology*, 1948, 25, 35–71. It is excerpted by permission of The Journal Press, Provincetown, Massachusetts. Research for the original article by Stogdill (1948) was supported by a grant from the Office of Naval Research (N6ori-17 T.0 III NR171123). The revision aimed to increase the consistency in style of the chapter with the rest of the book.

This classic is included here, as revised, for its publication marked a turning point in the study of leadership. Prior to this work, emphasis had been placed on the search for universal traits of leadership. After it, situation-specific analyses took over, in fact, dominating the field, much more than was argued for in this chapter, as can be seen clearly in its discussion and conclusions. Both individual traits and situational assessments are important, as well as the interaction between them. That was Stogdill's main thesis.—BMB children in which these methods were employed proved disappointingly unproductive.

Choice of Associates (Voting, Naming, Ranking, Sociometrics)

The usual procedure in these studies, most of which used children or students as subjects, was to ask the members of a group to name the persons who they would prefer as leaders, and, in some cases, to describe the characteristics of each nominee that made him or her desirable as a leader. Sociometrics was an extension of this method; it involved the construction of a "sociogram" or chart showing graphically the preferential relationship of each member to every other member of the group.

The outstanding investigation of this collection of studies was that of Jennings (1943), who combined observational with sociometric methods to produce an investigation of unusual human insight. Another study, characterized by insight into human behavior, was that of Buttgereit (1932). Other studies whose methodology and statistical treatment of data were superior were those of Dunkerley (1940), Partridge (1934), and Tryon (1939).

Nomination by Qualified Observer

In these studies, leaders were named by teachers, club leaders, or other adult observers who were regarded as being in a position to identify the leaders in the groups selected for study. The leaders were compared with the members of control groups.

Selection of Persons Occupying Positions of Leadership

Leadership in these studies was regarded as synonymous with holding office or some position of responsibility. The majority of the studies used high school or college subjects and defined leadership as holding some office, such as the presidency of the student body or of a fraternity or sorority, the captaincy of an athletic or debating team, the chairmanship of a club, and the like. In addition, a number of these studies dealt with adults in rural communities and small cities. The study

by Carlson and Harrell (1942) was concerned with congressmen, while that of Thurstone (1944) involved governmental administrators.

The most competent of these studies, from the point of view of methodology and the treatment of data, were those of Bellingrath (1930), Caldwell and Wellman (1926), Flemming (1935), Sward (1933), and Thurstone (1944).

Analysis of Biographical and Case-History Data

Ackerson (1942) and Brown (1931) based their studies on the analysis of case histories of delinquent children. The remaining studies were based on the analysis of biographical data; examples are the works of Merriam and Gosnell (1926, 1929) and of Michels (1915). Prominent contributions based on these methods were those of Ackerson (1942) and Cox (1926).

The Listing of Traits Considered Essential to Leadership

In all these studies, except that of Jones (1938), the authors asked different groups of persons, usually business executives and members of the professions, to list the traits they believed to be essential to leadership. Little uniformity was found among the items contained in such lists. Only intelligence, initiative, and responsibility were mentioned twice each among the top five items in the lists reported by Gowin (1915), Heath and Gregory (1946), Jones (1938), and Starch (1943).

Supplementary Aspects of Methodology and Sampling

Various supplementary measures were employed in an effort to determine the traits associated with leadership. The most frequently used were tests of intelligence and personality, but questionnaires, rating scales, and interviews were also utilized in some cases. The various studies employing these methods included intelligence tests (e.g., Reynolds, 1944), personality tests (e.g., Roslow, 1940), questionnaires (e.g., Brown, 1933), rating scales (e.g., Page, 1935), interviews (e.g., Chapin, 1945), and factor analysis (e.g., Brogden & Thomas, 1943). The age groups studied included preschoolers (e.g., Goodenough, 1930), elementary school children (e.g., Bonney, 1943), high school students (e.g., Bellingrath, 1930), college students (e.g., Zeleny, 1939), and adults (e.g., Winston, 1937).

Results

The results of the survey are presented in the form of discussions of the evidence accumulated on those factors that were studied by three or more investigators. When contradictory evidence occurred, those studies with positive, negative, and neutral results are presented separately.

Chronological Age

Leaders were found to be younger in six studies and older in ten investigations. No differences were found in two studies, and the results differed with the situation in one inquiry.

The evidence of the relation of age to leadership was quite contradictory. Pigors (1933) observed that leadership does not appear in children before age 2 or 3 and even then usually takes the form of overt domination. Active leadership of a group seldom appears before age 9 or 10, at which age the formation of groups and gangs may become a noticeable feature in the social development of children. According to Pigors, the following four states are necessary for the appearance of leadership in children: (1) development of determination and self-control, (2) grasp of abstractions and social ideals, (3) awareness of personalities, and (4) a sufficient memory span to pursue remote goals rather than immediate objectives. Arrington (1943), however, found no evidence from a survey of time-sampling experiments to support the proposition that leadership increases with age in preschool children.

Baldwin (1932), Finch and Carroll (1932), Garrison (1933), Hunter and Jordan (1939), and Remmelin (1938) found leaders to be younger than their followers. But only in the latter two studies were those differences statistically reliable. Bellingrath found girl leaders to be younger than nonleaders but boy leaders to be older. Leaders were found to be older than followers by Buttgereit (1932), Goodenough (1930), Gowin (1915), Moore (1935), Newstetter, Feldstein, and Newcomb

(1938), Nutting (1923), Parten (1933), Partridge (1934), and Zeleny (1939). Gowin (1918) found outstanding executives to be 12.2 years older on the average than the average of lesser executives. But Ackerson (1942) and Brown (1933) did not find leaders and followers to be differentiated on the basis of age. The correlation coefficients reported by a number of these authors are shown in Table 4.1. These correlation coefficients range from −.32 to .72, with an average coefficient of .21.

According to Caldwell and Wellman (1926), the relationship of age to leadership differs in various situations. Leaders in athletics were found to be close to the class average in age, while boy editors and student council members were younger than average, as were girl club leaders and student council and citizenship representatives. The correlation of chronological age with leadership appears to depend on other variables. For instance, it will automatically be highly positive in an organization if there is an age-rank lockstep but lower or even negative in many other circumstances.

Height and Weight

Leaders were found to be taller in height in nine studies and shorter in two and heavier in weight in seven studies and lighter in two. No differences in height or weight were reported in four studies, and the results depended on the situation in two studies.

Height. An inspection of Table 4.1 reveals correlations between height and leadership ranging from −.13 to .71. The general trend of these studies is to indicate a low positive relationship between height and leadership. The average correlation was about .30. Nevertheless, Hunter and Jordan (1939) and Garrison (1933) found student leaders to be somewhat shorter than were nonleaders, but Baldwin (1932) and Reynolds (1944) could find no relation to all between height and leadership in students.

Weight. The correlation coefficients shown in Table 4.1 suggest a low positive relationship between weight and leadership. The average correlation coefficient was about .23. But again, Hunter and Jordan (1939) found the reverse—that leaders were significantly lighter than were nonleaders. Garrison (1933)

Table 4.1 Correlation of Variables with Leadership

Author	IQ	Grades	Age	Height	Weight
Ackerson (1942) (boys)	.18		−.01		
(girls)	.32		−.11		
Bellingrath (1930) (boys)	−.14*	.05*	.27	.17	.25
(girls)			−.32	.44	.42
Drake (1944)	.47				
Eichler (1934)	.06	.12	.21		
Flemming (1935)	.44				
Garrison (1933) (School 1)		.30	−.12	−.02	−.02
(School 2)		.36	−.25	−.13	−.04
Goodenough (1930)	.10		.71	.71	.52
Howell (1942)	.08	.39			
Levi (1930) (Elementary school)	.26	−.27			
(Junior and senior high school)	.25	.00			
Newstetter, Feldstein, and Newcomb (1938)	.17		.45		
Nutting (1923)	.90	.11	.20		
Parten (1933)	.34		.67	.67	
Partridge (1934)	.54		.55	.43	.46
Reynolds (1944)	.22	.27			
Sheldon (1927)	.06	.19		.05	.02
Zeleny (1939)	.44		.49	.35	.20

*Total scores of boys and girls combined.

and Moore (1935) also reported leaders to be somewhat lighter than followers. Since height and weight tend to correlate positively, it was not surprising to find the same pattern of results for weight as for height.

Physique, Energy, Health

Physique was positively associated with leadership in five studies; athletic ability and physical prowess, in seven; energy, in five; and health in four. Moreover, health and physical condition were found to be a factor in four of the reviewed investigations.

Physique. Bernard (1928), Kohs and Irle (1920), Nutting (1923), Sheldon (1927), and Webb (1915) reported that superior physique was a characteristic of leaders. However, the correlation coefficients of .28, .18, .11, and .23 reported by Kohs and Irle (1920), Nutting (1923), Sheldon (1927), and Webb (1915), respectively, suggested that this relationship was slight but reliable. Nonetheless, Bowden (1926) concluded from the re-

sults of his study of college students that leadership was not the result of a dominating physique, and Baldwin (1937) found that high school leaders did not differ from followers in freedom from physical defects.

Health. Leaders, according to Baldwin (1932), Bellingrath (1930), Reals (1938), and Stray (1934), appeared to have some advantage over nonleaders in possessing better health, although Ackerson (1942) and Hunter and Jordan (1939) failed to find that health was a differentiating factor.

Athletic Prowess. Athletic ability and physical prowess did appear to be associated with leadership status in boys' gangs and groups. Evidence to this effect was presented by Buttgereit (1932), Flemming (1935), Partridge (1934), Puffer (1905), Spaulding (1934), Thrasher (1927), and Webb (1915). Correlations of .38, .62, and .40 between athletic ability and leadership were reported by Flemming (1935), Partridge (1934), and Webb (1915), respectively.

Energy. According to Bellingrath (1930), Brown (1934), Cox (1926), Stray (1934), and Wetzel (1932), leaders were also characterized by a high rate of energy output. But Cox (1926) found various groups of great leaders to differ markedly from each other in physique, energy output, and athletic prowess; only military leaders were outstanding in these traits.

Appearance

Leaders presented a better appearance in 11 studies. They were better dressed in two others but no relationship was found in 1 study, and appearance was negatively correlated with leadership in two studies. The results clearly depended on circumstances. Thus, Dunkerley (1940) found that students who were chosen as leaders in social activities differed significantly from nonleaders in appearance and dress, but students chosen as leaders in intellectual and religious activities did not differ markedly from nonleaders in these respects. A correlation of .21 between attractive appearance and leadership in high school students was reported by Flemming (1935), but the correlation between leadership and being seen as beautiful was only .05. Yet, Partridge (1934) found a correlation of .81 between ratings of appearance and leadership among adolescent boys, while in Goodenough's (1930) study, a negative correlation of −.20 was found between beauty and leadership in preschool children.

Tryon's (1939) analysis suggested that appearance is more closely associated with leadership in boys than in girls. Tryon reported correlations of .49 and .06, respectively, for 15-year-old boys and girls while the correlation coefficients for 12-year-old boys and girls were .31 and .08, respectively. Ackerson (1942) reported correlation coefficients of .12 and −.06 between leadership and being seen as slovenly for boys and girls, respectively, while a slovenly appearance and leading others into misconduct were correlated .32 and .31 for delinquent boys and girls.

Fluency of Speech

This trait was positively associated with leadership in all 12 studies that examined the relationship, although a few of the results were marginal.

Tone of Voice. Baldwin (1932) reported a definite trend for teachers to rate the tone of voice of leaders as confident and the tone of voice of nonleaders as lacking in confidence. Flemming's (1935) factor analysis of teachers' ratings of high school leaders revealed "pleasant voice" as one of the four factors found to be associated with leadership. The correlation was .28 between "pleasing voice" and leadership in high school students. Partridge (1934) reported that boy leaders could be reliably distinguished from nonleaders when in the presence of strange boys but hidden from view, so that judgments had to be made on speech alone. However, Fay and Middleton (1943), in repeating this experiment under somewhat similar conditions, found a correlation of only .08 between leadership ratings and degree of leadership, as estimated by voice alone. Likewise, Eichler (1934) reported a correlation of only .11 between voice and leadership.

Talkativeness. Talkativeness and leadership were reported by Tryon (1939) to be correlated .41 and .31 for 12-year-old boys and girls, respectively, while the coefficients for 15-year-old boys and girls were .15 and .44, respectively. In Goodenough's (1930) study, a correlation of .61 between talkativeness and leadership was found. Thurstone (1944) did not find highly paid administrators to surpass their lesser-paid associates in scores on tests of word fluency, but he did find a significant difference in their scores on tests of linguistic ability. Simpson (1938) also reported verbal ability to be correlated with the capacity to influence others; the correlation was .45.

Fluency. Chevaleva-Ianovskaia and Sylla (1929) noted that child leaders were characterized by longer durations of verbal excitation. Terman (1904) reported that leaders were more fluent of speech, and Leib (1928) observed that leaders excel in speaking ability. The same skills were reported in adult leaders by Bernard (1928) and Merriam (1929). Again, Zeleny (1939) reported a correlation of .59 between leadership ratings and total remarks made in class. Interesting conversation and leadership were correlated .28 in Flemming's (1935) study. Finally, Burks (1938) and Malloy (1936) found that vividness and originality of expression and facility of conversation were associated with successful social relationships.

Considering the size of the experimental groups, the competence of the experimental methods employed, and the positive nature of the evidence presented, it was apparent that fluency of speech, if not tone of voice, was a factor to be considered in the study of leadership. It has long been recognized that effective leadership cannot be maintained in an organization without an adequate system of intercommunication. Thus, it does not seem surprising that some of the most searching studies of leadership should reveal the capacity for ready communication to be one of the skills associated with leadership.

Intelligence

All except 5 of 23 studies presented evidence which indicated that the average leader surpassed the average member of his or her group in intelligence. However, five of the studies suggested that too great a difference in the IQ of the leader and the average member will militate against the leadership. Statistically reliable differences were reported, for example, by Hunter and Jordan (1939), Remmelin (1938), and Sward (1933). In most of these studies, there was a considerable overlapping of the scores of leaders and nonleaders on intelligence tests, which indicates that superior intelligence was not an absolute requirement for leadership. Nevertheless, the general trend of the findings suggested that leadership status was more often than not associated with superiority in intelligence. The correlations shown in Table 4.1 reveal a consistently positive relationship. The average of these coefficients was approximately .28.

Factorial studies demonstrated a number of points that may be of considerable significance for the study of leadership. Cattell (1946), for example, reported that the intelligence factor is heavily weighted with such character elements as being wise, emotionally mature, persevering, mentally alert, vigorous, and conscientious. These items correspond fairly closely to the factors discussed later, which were found in the present survey to be supported by an excess of positive over negative evidence. For example, Thorndike (1936) reported a correlation of .60 for 305 male members of European royal families between their intellectual abil-

ity and their estimability of character (which, in turn, is related to leadership). Thus, it appears that high intelligence may be associated with other characteristics that contribute to a person's value as a leader.

Limits. One of the most significant findings concerning the relation of intelligence to leadership is that extreme discrepancies between the intelligence of potential leaders and their followers militated against the exercise of leadership. Hollingworth (1926) found that, "among children with a mean IQ of 100, the IQ of the leader was likely to fall between 115 and 130 IQ. That is, the leader was likely to be more intelligent, but *not too much more* intelligent than the average of the group led." Observation further showed that a child with an IQ of 160 had little chance of being a popular leader in a group of children of average intelligence but might become a leader in a group of children with a mean IQ of 130. One of the difficulties in this connection seemed to be communication. The average child cannot comprehend a large part of the vocabulary employed by a child of unusually superior intelligence to express exact meanings in relation to his or her more mature and complicated interests. Differences in interests, goals, and activity patterns also act as barriers to joint participation, which is a necessary condition of group leadership.

Hollingworth's findings were confirmed by a number of investigations. Finch and Carroll (1932), studying groups of 66 gifted, 66 superior, and 66 average children, arrived at the conclusion that "given a superior group of children to lead, the leading will tend to be done by the gifted children," even though the leaders as a group tend to be younger than the group led. However, in an early study of the formation of boys' gangs, Warner (1923) found that leaders and followers differ much more in chronological age than in mental age. She observed that older boys with mentalities below normal tended to group with younger boys who had a mental age near their own and slightly higher, and that when groups of retarded delinquent boys contacted groups of brighter delinquents, the contacts were "so short and non-social that no noticeable event took place." Again, Maller (1925), studying cooperation and competition among children, found that homogeneity of intelligence, rather than level of intelligence, was important in cooperative behavior. McCuen (1929) studied leadership in 58 organizations of college students. He concluded that "the crowd seems to desire to be led by the average person. Evidently in a democratic society, the leader must not be too far detached from the group."

Two studies by Lehman (1937, 1942) are of interest in this connection. In the first study, Lehman determined the age intervals at which outstanding men in various professions made their best contributions. In the second study, he determined the optimal age intervals for eminent leadership. Chemists, for example, were found to make their best contributions during the age intervals 28–32 years, while the optimal ages for eminent leadership in chemistry were 45–49 years. Thus, it appears that even in science, individuals' contributions and communications must be understood by, and in accord with the thinking of, their contemporaries for them to rise to a position of leadership in their profession.

Scholarship

Leaders were found to have better scholastic records in 22 studies and poorer records only once. No differences were obtained in four investigations. It is not surprising that leaders were found, with a high degree of uniformity, to have better average scholastic grades than did nonleaders, for, as was just noted, leaders were found to be more intelligent, on the average, than were their followers. But the findings by Buttgereit (1932), Caldwell and Wellman (1926), and many others suggested that superior scholarship may not be a mere by-product of superior intelligence, but may have direct importance for leadership when it is one aspect of a general ability to get things done. It was also suggested that superior accomplishment in areas that were valued by the group had prestige value, which may also contribute some to leadership. At the same time, there was an abundance of evidence to indicate that a position of leadership was ordinarily not based on superior intelligence and accomplishment alone, since these two factors were present, to a high degree, in many persons who did not occupy positions of leadership.

Thus, overall, the magnitude of the correlations shown in Table 4.1 suggests that intelligence and scholarship account for only a fraction of the total complex of factors associated with leadership.

Knowledge

The results of all 11 studies dealing with leadership and knowledge implied that persons who are chosen as leaders tended to be those who knew how to get things done. Of particular interest was Caldwell's (1920) experiment in which he asked 282 high school pupils to nominate boy and girl leaders for three different situations: (1) a trip to the wharf, (2) the production and presentation of a program before a neighboring school, and (3) the reorganization of a program for administering athletics in the school. The nominations revealed "a clear judgment on the part of these pupils as to the members of the group best fitted to lead them." The most important abilities ascribed to these leaders were intelligence and practical knowledge about the situations for which they were chosen as leaders.

In this connection, it seems worthwhile to consider the findings of Baldwin (1932) and Burks (1938) in relation to the association between leadership and the ability to make constructive and creative suggestions. Burks, for example, found that the ability to present constructive ideas for difficult situations was closely associated with successful social relationships.

The studies of Cox (1926), Drake (1944), Flemming (1935), Stray (1934), and Thrasher (1927) found that constructive imagination was a characteristic of leaders. Additional evidence related to the ability to get things done was presented by Bellingrath (1930) and Dunkerley (1940). Cox (1926) and Peck (1931) reported that great leaders were characterized and differentiated from the average by a greater intensity of application and industry. In summary, the results of these various studies seemed to indicate that specialized knowledge and the ability to get things done were factors that contributed to leadership.

Judgment and Decision

Soundness and finality of judgment related to leadership in five studies, and speed and accuracy of thought and decision, in four analyses. In view of the positive correlations found between intelligence and leadership, it was not surprising to find a similar relationship between judgment and leadership. Bellingrath (1932), Drake (1944), and Webb (1915) reported correlations ranging from .34 to .69 between common sense and leadership, while Bellingrath (1930), Drake (1944), Flemming (1935), and Webb (1915) found correlations of .60, .34, .28, and .69, respectively, between judgment and leadership. Farsightedness and leadership were seen to be correlated .55, .25, .33 in the studies of Bellingrath, Drake, and Webb, respectively. Two of the factor-analytic studies, those of Cowley (1931) and Dunkerley (1940), revealed that soundness and finality of judgment was a factor that was common to leaders. In addition to the judgment factor, Cowley (1931) also uncovered three factors that appeared to represent speed of decision. Hanawalt, Richardson, and Hamilton (1943) found that leaders used the "?", or "undecided," response on the Bernreuter test significantly less frequently than did nonleaders, and this tendency was especially noticeable on the most discriminating items. In spite of the small number of studies bearing on judgment and decision, the general competence of the methods employed lent confidence to the results obtained.

Insight

Leadership was found to be related to aspects of insight as follows: keenly alive to environment, alert (six studies), ability to evaluate situations (five studies), social insight (five studies), self-insight (two studies), and sympathetic understanding (seven studies). Traditionally, insight has been regarded as one aspect of general intelligence. However, the discussion by Jennings (1943) and others suggested that insight may be socially conditioned to a high degree. Some of the most competent investigators of the leadership problem have contributed evidence leading to the inference that insight and awareness are factors associated with leadership ability. Brown (1931), Buttgereit (1932), Caldwell and Wellman (1926), Cox (1926), Dunkerley (1940), and Fauquier and Gilchrist (1942) found that leaders were characterized by alertness and keen awareness of their environment. The ability to evaluate situations was found to be a

factor in the studies of Bowden (1926), Buttgereit (1932), Chevaleva-Ianovskaia and Sylla (1929), Merriam and Gosnell (1929), and Thurstone (1944). Less clearly defined was social insight, reported to be a factor associated with leadership in the studies of Bowden (1926), Hanfmann (1935), Jennings (1943), Pigors (1933), and Zeleny (1939). Brogden and Thomas (1943) and Guilford and Guilford (1939) found that "studies the motives of others," was measured by Guilford's T factor of being thoughtful, which was described as a kind of intellectual leadership.

The results of these various studies suggested that alertness to the one's surroundings and an understanding of situations were intimately associated with leadership ability, yet little was understood about the nature of these processes. No worker who is responsible for improving the social effectiveness of individuals can fail to be impressed by the persistent blindness of maladapted individuals to the social situations in which they are attempting to adjust. From the point of view of understanding personal qualifications for leadership, it would appear that one issue that continues to be in need of thorough investigation is the fundamental nature of awareness and social insight.

Originality

Although only seven studies contained data on this trait, the magnitude of the positive correlations found suggested that the relationship between originality and leadership was worthy of further investigation. The correlations reported by Bellingrath (1930), Drake (1944), Flemming (1935), and Webb (1915) ranged from .38 to .70 and were higher, on the average, than were those for any other trait except popularity. At the same time, Cox (1926) found that great leaders rated unusually high in originality.

Adaptability

The ten studies involving adaptability and leadership suggested that ready adaptability to changing situations was a factor that might be associated with leadership, although the correlations of .13 and .21 reported by Eichler (1934) and Flemming (1935) were not impressive. The ability to adjust to situations has also been regarded traditionally as an aspect of general intelligence but, as described in the investigations considered here, this factor appeared to contain a large social component. This fact has long been recognized by clinical observers, who have repeatedly pointed out that persons of high intelligence may be rendered ineffectual in their vocational, social, and other adjustments through extreme self-preoccupation and inhibition to action. Such inhibition is negatively correlated with leadership.

Introversion-Extroversion

Leaders were found to be more extroverted in five studies and more introverted in three. No differences emerged in four studies.

The only studies that reported a marked relationship between extroversion and leadership were those of Goodenough (1930) and Sward (1933). Goodenough reported a correlation of .46 between extroversion and leadership in children. Sward found that leaders scored reliably higher than did nonleaders in extroversion on the Heidbreder scale. Richardson and Hanawalt (1943) observed that college leaders scored reliably lower in introversion than the Bernreuter norms and lower than nonleaders, although the difference between leaders and nonleaders was not significant. Hunter and Jordan (1939) and Remmelin (1938) also reported that introversion scores on the Bernreuter scale did not differentiate leaders from nonleaders. Middleton (1941) found that leaders scored low in extroversion, while Bellingrath (1930) and Drake (1944) found no significant correlations between introversion-extroversion scores and leadership.

All the groups of great leaders except soldier-statesmen in Cox's (1926) study were rated as introverted, with soldier-fighters rating very high in introversion. Thurstone's (1944) study of administrators in Washington, D.C., revealed that successful administrators rated higher than less successful administrators in Guilford and Guilford's (1939) T factor, which is measured by such items as, "introspective, analyzes himself"; "often in a meditative state"; "analyzes the motives of others"; and "not more interested in athletics than in intellectual pursuits." Brogden and Thomas (1943) added to this list such items as, "he does not want anyone to be with him when he receives bad news," "he does not try to find someone to cheer him up when in low spirits," "prefers to make hurried decisions alone." These items are of interest when considered in relation to the findings on mood control. In view of the diversity of findings, it appears doubtful that leaders can be described with any degree of uniformity in terms of introversion-extroversion.

Self-sufficiency. Much the same situation exists with regard to self-sufficiency. Hunter and Jordan (1939) and Richardson and Hanawalt (1944) found that leaders had high self-sufficiency scores on the Bernreuter test, but Dunkerley (1940), Remmelin (1938), and Richardson and Hanawalt (1943) obtained no significant differences.

Dominance

The evidence concerning the relationship of dominance to leadership is somewhat contradictory. Leaders were found to be more dominant and ascendant in 11 studies; were rejected as leaders if they were bossy, domineering persons in 4 studies, and no differences appeared in 2 studies.

Cox (1926) and Drake (1944) found "desire to impose will" to be associated with leadership, but Webb (1915) reported a zero-order correlation between those two factors. Ackerson (1942) reported a correlation of approximately .20 between bossiness and leadership in problem children. Leadership and bossiness were related, to some extent, in the children studied by Tryon (1939), who reported correlations of .28 and .29 between these two factors for 15-year-old boys and girls, respectively. Chapple and Donald (1946), Richardson and Hanawalt (1943, 1944), and Hunter and Jordan (1939) found leaders to be significantly more dominant than nonleaders. Small but positive differences in ascendance were reported by Bowden (1926) and Moore (1935). Eichler (1934), however, found that leaders and nonleaders did not differ in dominance. Still stronger contradictory evidence was presented by Broich (1929), Jennings (1943), and Hanfmann (1935), who concluded that bossy, domineering persons were rejected as leaders. Caldwell (1920) reported that high school pupils expressed preference for leaders who could keep order without being bossy. In all, these findings suggest that leadership cannot be defined in terms of personal dominance.

Initiative, Persistence, and Ambition

Initiative and a willingness to assume responsibility were related to leadership in 12 studies and persistence in the face of obstacles, in 12 other inquiries. Ambition and desire to excel were of consequence to leadership in 7 analyses, as were application and industry in 6 additional analyses.

Initiative. All except one of the studies in which initiative was found to be a trait ascribed to leaders were investigations in which student leaders were nominated by their associates and the traits that were thought to make them desirable as leaders were described. The study by Carlson and Harrell (1942) represented some departure from this method, in that 53 Washington correspondents were asked to name the 10 ablest senators and the 10 ablest representatives in rank order and to rate them from 1 to 10 on integrity, intelligence, industry, and influence. A factor analysis of these ratings revealed Factor I to be heavily loaded with industry and influence and might also have been called push or aggressiveness. Industriousness and leadership were correlated .55 and .16 in the studies of Bellingrath (1930) and Flemming (1935), respectively. Dunkerley's (1940) factor analysis also revealed a trait cluster, identified as initiative, which was descriptive of intellectual and social leaders but not of religious leaders. Finally, Drake (1944) and Sheldon (1927) reported correlations of .56 and .52 between aggressiveness and leadership.

Persistence. Cox (1926) found that great face-to-face leaders were characterized, to an outstanding degree, by "persistence in the face of obstacles," "capacity to work with distant objects in view," "degree of strength of will or perseverance," and "tendency not to abandon tasks from mere changeability." Pigors (1933) observed that the development of determination and a sufficient memory span to pursue remote goals, rather than immediate objectives, were necessary conditions for the appearance of leadership in children. The remainder of the studies that presented evidence on this point represented a variety of points of view.

Pinard (1932), in an experimental study of perseveration in 194 "difficult" children, ages 8–15, found that of 24 leaders, 17 belonging to the moderate nonperseverator group were rated as more reliable, self-controlled, and persistent and as the most constructive leaders. Drake (1944) and Webb (1915) obtained correlations of .23 and .59 between leadership and strength of will. Webb (1915) reported a correlation of .70 between leadership and "persistence in overcoming obstacles" and of .53 between leadership and persistence. In Bellingrath's (1930) study of high school students, persistance was correlated .68 with leadership, while Eichler (1934) and Sheldon (1927) found correlations of .23 and .34 between leadership and persistence. An interesting sidelight was presented in Ackerson's (1942) study of problem children, among whom stubbornness correlated .15 for boys and .12 for girls with leadership.

Ambition. Cox (1926) also presented evidence to indicate that great face-to-face leaders, such as soldiers, religious leaders, and statesmen, were characterized to an outstanding degree by a "desire to excel at performances." Hanawalt, Hamilton, and Morris (1934), in a study of 20 college leaders and 20 nonleaders, found that the level of aspiration of leaders was significantly higher than that of nonleaders. Correlations of .47, .29, and .64 between leadership and desire to excel were reported by Webb (1915), Drake (1944), and Bellingrath (1930), respectively.

That leadership is related to work, rather than to passive status or position, is suggested by the fact that a number of investigators have found leaders to rate high in application and industry. Cox (1926) observed great leaders to rank unusually high in this respect. The correlations reported by Bellingrath (1930), Flemming (1935), and Webb (1915) ranged from .16 to .55.

Responsibility

All 17 studies on the subject found responsibility to be related to leadership. Thus, student leaders were seen to rate somewhat higher than followers on dependability, trustworthiness, and reliability in carrying out responsibilities in the studies of Baldwin (1932), Bellingrath (1930), Burks (1938), Caldwell (1920), Dunkerley (1940), Moore (1932), Nutting (1923), Pinard (1932), and Wetzel (1932). Trustworthiness and leadership were correlated .64 in Webb's (1915) study, .37 in Drake's (1944) study, and .10 in Flemming's (1935) study. Correlations of .42, .21, and .53 between conscientiousness and leadership were reported by Webb (1915), Drake (1944), and Bellingrath (1930), respectively. Partridge (1934) observed a correlation of .87 between dependability and leadership. Jennings (1943) observed that the girls who were chosen as leaders tended to be those who inspire confidence. Cox (1926) found that all types of great face-to-face leaders rated high in trustworthiness and conscientiousness, with religious leaders rating outstandingly high in these traits.

Integrity and Conviction

Integrity and fortitude related to leadership in six studies and strength of convictions did so in another seven analyses.

Integrity. Intellectual fortitude and integrity of character represent traits that are apparently associated with eminent leadership in maturity. All the studies that contributed evidence on this point were concerned with outstanding adult leaders, except that of Middleton (1941), who found that "character" is one of the traits associated with leadership in college students. Michels (1915) reported that strength of convictions was also a characteristic of successful political leaders. Cox (1926) found that the great face-to-face leader was characterized, to an outstanding degree, by "absence of readiness to accept the sentiments of his associates." This trait was especially conspicuous in revolutionary statesmen. Webb (1915) obtained a correlation of $-.32$ between leadership and acceptance of the sentiments of others. Caldwell and Wellman (1926) noted that one of the characteristics of high school leaders was insistence on the acceptance of their ideas and plans.

Conviction. Adult leaders, in a community studied by Chapin (1945), appeared to hold opinions that were generally similar to those of the group, but they "expressed the trends of opinion of the rank and file more sharply, more decisively, and more consistently." Simpson (1938), in a study of those who influence and those who are influenced in discussion, found that influence scores correlated $-.41$ with influenceability scores. It appears that persons in various types of groups may be valued as leaders because they know what they want to accomplish and are not likely to be swayed from their convictions.

Liberalism or Conservativism. The evidence on liberalism-conservatism suggested that the attitudes that will be regarded as acceptable in leaders are largely determined by the nature of the situation. Hunter and Jordan (1939) found college student leaders to be somewhat more liberal than nonleaders in attitudes toward social questions. Newcomb (1943) reported that in a college where liberalism is a tradition and ideal, those women students who had the most prestige were regarded as most liberal. Middleton (1941), on the other hand, ascertained that campus leaders were low in radicalism. In Thurstone's (1944) study of Washington administrators, the Allport-Vernon Study of Values was found to be the most effective of a battery of 75 tests in differentiating higher-salaried from lower-salaried administrators. Successful administrators scored significantly higher in social and theoretical values and significantly lower in economic and religious values. Drake (1944) and Webb (1915) obtained low positive correlations between leadership and interest in religion.

Self-confidence

Almost all authors reporting data on the relationship of self-confidence to leadership were uniform in the positive direction of their findings. Self-assurance was associated with leadership in 11 studies, as was absence of modesty in 6 studies. The following correlation coefficients were reported: .58 by Bellingrath (1930), .59 by Drake (1944), and .12 by Webb (1915). Cowley (1931) found self-confidence to be one of six factors possessed in common by three widely different types of leaders. Cox (1926) noted that great leaders were characterized, to an unusual degree, by such traits as self-confidence, esteem of their special talents, and a tendency to rate their talents correctly. Buttgereit (1932), Moore (1932), and Zeleny (1939) also reported leaders to rate high in self-confidence. Tryon (1939) described student leaders as assured in class and as assured with adults. Richardson and Hanawalt (1943, 1944) found college and adult leaders to earn higher self-confidence scores on the Bernreuter test than did nonleaders, but Hunter and

Jordan (1939) and Remmelin (1938) failed to find that the self-confidence scores on the Bernreuter test differentiated between leaders and nonleaders.

Inferiority. Sward (1933) found that inferiority scores on the Heidbreder rating scale did not differentiate leaders from nonleaders, although women leaders rated themselves higher in inferiority atttitudes than did their associates. But Ackerson (1942) reported correlations of only − .02 and .08 between feelings of inferiority and leadership in boys and girls.

Modesty. The findings here suggested that leaders tend to be persons who are not handicapped by an excessive degree of modesty. Cox (1926) reported that great military leaders and statesmen were characterized, to a greater than average degree, by eagerness for the admiration of the crowd and desire for the limelight, although they exhibited offensive manifestations of self-esteem to a lesser degree than the average. Middleton (1941) also found leaders to rate low in modesty. But a correlation of − .09 between leadership and modesty was reported by Flemming (1935). Eagerness for admiration was correlated − .16 with leadership in Webb's (1915) study, while Drake (1944) obtained a correrlation of − .11 between conceit and leadership. Both Ackerson (1942) and Tryon (1939) found positive correlations between leadership and attention-getting or show-off tendencies. These correlations coefficients ranged from .15 to .30. The general trend of these findings suggested that leaders rate higher than their followers in self-confidence and self-esteem and slightly lower in modesty.

Control of Moods and Optimism

Associations with leadership were reported as follows: controlled in mood, seldom gloomy (four studies); moods uncontrolled (two studies); happy, cheerful disposition (four studies); and happiness not a factor (two studies). Nevertheless, in all six studies on the subject, leadership and a sense of humor were positively related.

Mood. Jennings (1943) stated that one of the characteristics of girl leaders in an institution was the ability to control their own moods so as not to impose their negative feelings, depressions, and anxieties on others.

Caldwell and Wellman (1926) and Malloy (1936) also found leaders to be constant in mood. Webb (1915) reported a correlation of − .45 between depression and leadership. Ackerson (1942) and Cox (1926), however, reported some association between leadership and moods of depression, although not to a significant degree, and the extent differed with different groups.

Drake (1944), Tryon (1939), and Webb (1915) found that a cheerful, happy disposition is associated with leadership. These authors reported correlations ranging from .29 to .60 between leadership and cheerfulness. However, Ackerson (1942) and Baldwin (1932) did not find cheerfulness to be a distinguishing factor in leadership. Ackerson (1942) noted that "unhappiness" and "leadership" were correlated − .03 for boys and .06 for girls.

Humor. Drake (1944), Flemming (1935), Tryon (1939), and Webb (1915) reported correlations ranging from .34 to .64 between leadership and sense of humor. Stray (1934) also found leaders to be characterized by a sense of humor. Goodenough's (1930) finding of a correlation of .53 between leadership and laughter was also relevant to this subject.

The scarcity of evidence concerning the relation of mood control to leadership cannot be regarded as confirmation of its unimportance. The evidence suggests that mood control may be significantly related to effective leadership and a sense of humor is certainly relevant. The topic appears to warrant thorough investigation.

Emotional Control

Leaders were found to be more stable and emotionally controlled in 11 studies and less well controlled in 5 studies. No differences were found in 3 other studies.

Self-Control. A number of manuals that outline the practical techniques for gaining friends and becoming a leader regard self-control as a very important prerequisite for attaining these goals. The evidence relating to this contention is divided. Eichler (1934) reported a correlation of .18 between leadership and self-control. Baldwin (1932), Pigors (1933), and Wetzel (1932) also found self-control to be a factor related to leadership. Bellingrath (1930) and Drake (1944) reported correlations of .70 to .38, respectively, between leadership and stability. Leaders were found by Middleton (1941) and Terman (1904) to rate low in emotionality, while Bowden (1926) and Caldwell and Wellman (1926) found leaders to be well balanced and self-composed in comparison with their followers. Webb (1915) reported correlations of −.25 between irritability and leadership, and −.36 between readiness for anger and leadership.

Excitability. Cox (1926), however, found great face-to-face leaders to rate high in excitability. This trait was present, to an unusual degree, in revolutionary statesmen. In problem children, Ackerson (1942) reported correlations of .12 for boys and .36 for girls between irritability and leadership. A correlation of .16 between leadership and excitability was found by Sheldon (1927). Fauquier and Gilchrist (1942) also noted that leaders were more excitable than nonleaders. But Zeleny (1939) could find no difference between leaders and nonleaders in the degree of emotional control, and Drake (1944) and Flemming (1935) reported correlations close to zero between leadership and excitability.

Anger. The data on the relationship between leadership and anger and fighting cast further light on this subject. Cox (1926) found great face-to-face leaders, except statesmen, to be characterized by a liability to anger and "a tendency to flare up on slight provocation." Ackerson (1942) reported that "temper tantrums" and "leader" were positively correlated, while "temper tantrums" and "follower" were negatively correlated. Webb (1915), however, found a correlation of −.12 between leadership and occasional extreme anger. Tryon (1939) reported correlations of .59, .48, .25, and .40 between fighting and leadership for 12-year-old boys, 15-year-old boys, 12-year-old girls, and 15-year-old girls, respectively. Ackerson (1942) found fighting and leadership to be correlated .13 for boys and −.17 for girls, but fighting and leading others into bad conduct were correlated .20 for boys and .36 for girls. Incorrigibility and defiance were also positively correlated with leadership and, to a still higher degree, with leadership in misconduct, while these traits were correlated negatively with "followers." These studies did not lead convincing support to the view that leaders are necessarily persons who are characterized by a high

degree of self-control or an incapacity for emotional expression.

Social and Economic Status

In 15 studies, the leaders came from higher socioeconomic backgrounds, and in 2 studies, no differences were found. Only two investigators, Baldwin (1932) and Goodenough (1930), reported negligible differences. However, the differences in the social and economic status of leaders and nonleaders were usually not extreme. Only Remmelin (1938) found differences that were large enough to be statistically reliable. Nonetheless, taken as a whole, the evidence presented in studies from a wide variety of leadership situations indicated that leaders tend to come from a socioeconomic background that is superior to that of the average of their followers.

Social Activity and Mobility

Leaders participated in more group activities in all 20 studies on the subject. They also exhibited a higher rate of social mobility in 5 additional studies.

Participation. Baldwin (1932), Brown (1933), Chapin (1945), Courtenay (1938), Richardson and Hanawalt (1943), Roslow (1940), Link (1944), Merriam and Gosnell (1929), Reals (1938), Smith and Nystrom (1937), Sorokin (1927), and Zeleny (1939) all found that leaders surpassed followers in the number, extent, and variety of group activities in which they participated. Zeleny (1939) reported correlations ranging from .17 to .68 between leadership and participation in extracurricular activities. Leadership was defined by a number of authors as "occupying one or more positions of responsibility in group activities."

Mobility. Physical and social mobility were observed by Sorokin (1927), Sorokin and Zimmerman (1928), and Winston (1932) to be associated with adult leadership. Sorokin and Zimmerman reported that farmer-leaders were characterized, to a high degree, by a tendency to shift from place to place and from one occupational or economic position to another and Winston (1937) observed the same tendency in inventors. On the other hand, social detachment appeared to be a factor in the formation of the boys' gangs studied by Thrasher (1927) and Warner (1923).

Biosocial Activity

Biosocial activities were related to leadership as follows: active in games (six studies); active, restless (nine studies); and daring, adventurous (three studies).[2]

Broich (1929), Brown (1931), Buttgereit (1932), and Reininger (1929) found that child leaders were more active in games than were nonleaders. In Tryon's (1939) study, leadership and "active in games" were correlated .52 to .74 for groups of 12- and 15-year-old boys and girls. Terman (1904), Thrasher (1927), and Tryon (1939) found leaders to be more daring and adventurous than followers. Correlations of .57 to .78 between daringness and leadership were reported by Tryon (1939). Cowley (1931) ascertained that motor impulsion was a factor common to different types of leaders. According to Chevaleva-Ianovskaia and Sylla (1929), leaders were characterized by a predominance of excitation over inhibition. Liveliness was reported by Leib (1928) and Brown (1931) to characterize leaders. Flemming (1935) found a correlation of .47 between leadership and liveliness, while Goodenough (1930) reported a correlation of .29 between physical activity and leadership. Ackerson (1942) and Tryon (1939) obtained correlations close to .20 between "restlessness" and leadership. These findings suggested that physical activity and mobility were associated with leadership.

Social Skills

Sociability was associated with leadership in 14 studies and diplomacy or tact in 8 others. Fairly high positive correlations between sociability and leadership were reported by Bonney (1943), Drake (1944), Flemming (1935), Eichler (1934), Goodenough (1930), Sheldon (1927), Tryon (1939), and Webb (1915). These correlation coefficients are shown in Table 4.2.

[2]This list of traits of biosocial activities is difficult to classify, since in few cases is the behavior clearly defined. The majority of investigators appeared to emphasize the social aspects of these behaviors, although some emphasized an underlying physical component of energy or vitality. This is merely one example of the difficulty mentioned by a number of investigators, of attempting to analyze human behavior by dividing it into distinct and separate traits.

Table 4.2 Correlation between Social Traits and Leadership

Investigator	Variable	Correlation with Leadership
Bonney (1943)	Social skills	.53
Drake (1944)	Sociability	.52
Flemming (1935)	Sociability	.33
Eichler (1934)	Social intelligence	.10
Goodenough (1930)	Sociability	.98
Sheldon (1927)	Sociability	.47
Tryon (1939)	Friendliness	.44 to .74
Webb (1915)	Sociability	.39

Burks (1938), Malloy (1936), Middleton (1941), and Prosh (1928) also found student leaders to rate higher than nonleaders in sociability. Ackerson (1942) observed that belonging to a gang was correlated .26 with being a leader and .21 with being a follower. Being a leader and within an intimate circle were correlated .39 in Webb's (1915) study. Moore (1932) and Newcomb (1945) reported friendliness and social skills, respectively, as factors that distinguished leaders from followers. Despite their higher introversion, Cox (1926) also noted that great leaders were rated above average, but not to an outstanding degree, in fondness for companionship and social gatherings.

Tact. Courtesy, tact, and diplomacy were found by Bernard (1928), Wetzel (1932), Drake (1944), Flemming (1935), Hanfmann (1935), Parten (1933), Stray (1934), and Webb (1915) to be traits that distinguished leaders from nonleaders. Drake, Flemming, and Webb reported correlations of .08, .27, and .73, respectively, between tact and leadership. However, Flemming (1935) obtained a correlation of only −.03 between rudeness and leadership for boys and girls, respectively. The correlations between rudeness and leading others into bad conduct were .24 and .40 for boys and girls, respectively. Ackerson determined that both bashfulness and seclusiveness were negatively correlated with leadership.

Ackerson (1942), Goodenough (1930), and Webb (1915) obtained correlations ranging from −.29 to .21 between offensive manifestations and leadership. Ackerson's (1942) findings suggested that misconduct is not necessarily a bar to leadership. Stealing, for example, was correlated .12 and .21 with leadership, while stealing and leading others into misconduct were correlated .46 and .16 for boys and girls, respectively.

Popularity and Prestige

Evidence from ten diverse studies indicated that leaders were persons who tend to rate higher than average in popularity. Evidence presented by Ackerson (1942), Bellingrath (1930), Carlson and Harrell (1942), Cox (1926), Garrison (1933), Michels (1915), Miller and Dollard (1941), Nutting (1923), Tryon (1939), and Zeleny (1939) all indicated that popularity and prestige were rather closely associated with leadership status. The correlations shown in Table 4.3 suggest that the relationship between popularity and leadership was fairly high. However, Nutting (1923) pointed out that popularity cannot be regarded as synonymous with leadership.

Cooperation

Cooperativeness was related to leadership in 11 studies and work for the group and corporate responsibility was so related in 8 others. The ability to enlist cooperation was related to leadership in 7 additional analyses.

Leaders were found by Baldwin (1932), Dunkerley (1940), Fauquier and Gilchrist (1942), Newcomb (1943), and Wetzel (1932) to rate higher in cooperativeness than were followers. Drake (1944) and Webb (1915) re-

ported correlations of .44 and .69 between cooperativeness and leadership. The ability to enlist cooperation and to control others in a group enterprise were found by Baldwin (1932), Caldwell (1920), Hanfmann (1935), Merriam and Gosnell (1926), and Nutting (1923) to be characteristics associated with leadership ability.

Broich (1929), Jennings (1943), Leib (1928), Nutting (1923), and Pigors (1933) observed that leaders tend to be persons who are able to work for the group's welfare, and Buttgereit (1932) noted that a sense of social responsibility is characteristic of leaders. Webb (1915) reported a correlation of .69 between leadership and corporate spirit. Cox (1926) also reported that great leaders rate outstandingly high in a sense of corporate spirit.

Patterns of Leadership Traits Differ with the Situation

There was a preponderance of evidence from a wide variety of studies (19 in all) that indicated that patterns of leadership traits differed with the situation. Ackerson's (1942) study revealed marked differences in the conduct and personality patterns of children who were regarded as leaders in general and children who were regarded as leaders in misconduct. Boys and girls in these two groups also differed somewhat. Bellingrath (1930) found marked differences in the extent to which leaders in athletics, student government, publications, and clubs participated in extracurricular activities and were chosen as leaders under various circumstances. The investigation of Caldwell and Wellman (1926) revealed athletic leaders to be tallest among the leaders and to excel in physical achievements, while editors were younger and shorter than average but ranked higher in scholarship than did the other groups of leaders who were studied. Cowley's (1928) study demonstrated large differences in the traits of criminal leaders, army leaders, and student leaders. The profiles of the average ratings of the traits of groups of great leaders studied by Cox (1926) differed markedly from one group to another, especially in physical and emotional traits, but much less so in traits that may be classified as intelligence, self-regard, and persistence. Dunkerley's (1940) factor analysis of the intercorrelations of 15 variables representing trait ratings of 167 women col-

Table 4.3 Correlation between Popularity and Leadership

Investigator	Variable	Correlation with Leadership
Ackerson (1942) (boys)	Popularity	.32
(girls)		.40
Bellingrath (1930)	Popularity	.80
Garrison (1933) (School 1)	Admiration	.82
(School 2)		.58
Nutting (1923)	Popularity	.60
Tryon (1939) (boys, age 12)	Popularity	.47
(boys, age 15)		.64
(girls, age 12)		.23
(girls, age 15)		.68

lege students, revealed a factor identified as social leadership and two factors identified as religious leadership.

Hanfmann (1935) observed three types of leaders among preschool children: (1) objective leaders who engage in constructive play and get what they want by saying why they need it, (2) social leaders, whose goal is to play with others rather than play in itself, and (3) gangsters, who get their way by force and a complete disregard for others. Schuler (1935) concluded that although teachers may ascertain with increasing reliability the dominant-submissive behavior of older adolescent boys in one situation, such as the school, it becomes less possible to predict those tendencies in another environment, such as the home.

Sward (1933) found that superior socioeconomic status, as well as higher intelligence and scholastic attainment, differentiated 125 campus leaders from 125 followers. However a classification of the leaders into subgroups demonstrated the following distinguishing differences: (1) bright, relatively unmotivated, unsocial, self-confident campus editors, (2) rather insecure, intellectual and very intelligent debaters, (3) strongly socialized and intellectually mediocre campus politicians, and (4) extroverted women leaders.

Terman (1904) found that children who were leaders in one experimental situation may not have been leaders when matched against different children in other situations. Children who were "automatons," or nonleaders, in most situations might achieve leadership in some situations. Those children who were leaders in most situations were said by their teachers to be characterized by intelligence, congeniality, liveliness, and goodness.

In Tryon's (1939) study, the clusters of traits that characterized boys and girls at age 12 differed from those found at age 15. This difference was especially noticeable for girls, who matured somewhat more rapidly in social interests than did boys. The leadership cluster for 12-year-old boys was composed of the items: daring, leader, active in games, and friendly, while that for 15-year-old boys contained the items: daring, leader, and active in games and fights. The leadership cluster for 12-year-old girls contained the items: daring, leader, and humor about jokes, while for 15-year-old girls the

following items appeared: popular, friendly, enthusiastic, happy, humor about jokes, daring, leader. The total weight of the evidence presented in this group of studies suggests that if there were general traits that characterized leaders, the patterns of such traits were likely to vary with the leadership requirements of different situations.

Transferability and Persistence of Leadership

Six follow-up studies, although yielding somewhat variable results, intimated a certain degree of persistence or transferability of leadership. Levi (1930) studied 230 leaders in elementary and junior high school, 206 of whom were studied again in senior high school. The correlation between leadership in elementary school and in senior high school was .19, while the correlation between leadership in junior high school and in senior high school was .52. There was a low negative correlation between athletic leadership in elementary school and in high school, but a correlation of .44 between athletic leadership in junior high school and senior high school.

Kohs and Irle (1920) completed a follow-up study of the military careers of 116 college students. Three faculty members rated these students on various traits. Correlations between the U.S. Army rank attained and various ratings in college ranged from .11 to .39. The best assessments for predicting military success were found to be the raters' estimates of the assessees' potential value to the service and raters' estimates of the assessees' intelligence. Assessments of leadership in college were correlated .11 with army rank attained, but scholarship was not predictive of army rank. Page (1935), studying cadets at West Point, found the first-year leadership rank to be correlated .67 with fourth-year leadership rank. Rank in bearing and appearance was most highly correlated with rank in leadership, while the ranks in athletic activities, tactics, and academic standing were correlated with leadership rank in progressively lesser degrees.

Clem and Dodge (1933) conducted a comparative study of the postschool success of 27 student leaders, 36 high-ranking student scholars, and 38 random pupils from six successive high school graduating classes. The student leaders ranked highest in subsequent outstanding achievements, number of honors received, and quantity of publications. The random group ranked highest in community leadership and the amount of money accumulated after graduation. In general, the student leaders tended to become more successful than the student scholars and the random group, although the differences were not impressive. Courtenay (1938) studied 100 women leaders and 100 nonleaders from 13 successive high school graduating classes. The 2 groups were matched as to socioeconomic background, ethnic heritage, scholarship, and age at graduation. Courtenay found that 72 student leaders but only 29 nonleaders went to college and that twice as many high school leaders as nonleaders were engaged as adults in professional work. The average salary of the adults who had been high school leaders exceeded that of those who had been nonleaders. The high school leaders were more active as adults in community work. Shannon (1929) compared student leaders, scholars (honor-roll members), and a random group from 5 high school graduating classes. Although, the graduates who were on the honor roll were little more successful than were the random group, Shannon concluded that "whatever is required to excel in the extracurricular life of the high school, seems to be the same thing that contributes most to success later."

These findings strongly suggested that leadership in school activities was somewhat predictive of later success. However, the extent to which leadership persisted and transferred was not clearly determined.

Summary and Conclusions

1. The following conclusions were supported by uniformly positive evidence from 15 or more of the studies surveyed:
   a. The average person who occupies a position of leadership exceeds the average member of his or her group in the following respects: (1) intelligence, (2) scholarship, (3) dependability in exercising responsibilities, (4) activity and social participation, and (5) socioeconomic status.
   b. The qualities, characteristics, and skills required in a leader are determined, to a large extent, by the demands of the situation in which he or she is to function as a leader.
2. The following conclusions were supported by uniformly positive evidence from ten or more of the studies surveyed:
   a. The average person who occupied a position of leadership exceeded the average member of his or her group, to some degree, in the following respects: (1) sociability, (2) initiative, (3) persistence, (4) knowing how to get things done, (5) self-confidence, (6) alertness to and insight into situations, (7) cooperativeness, (8) popularity, (9) adaptability, and (10) verbal facility.
3. In addition, a number of factors were found to be specific to well-defined groups. For example, athletic ability and physical prowess were found to be characteristics of leaders of boys' gangs and play groups. Intellectual fortitude and integrity were found to be associated with eminent leadership in maturity.
4. The items with the highest overall correlation with leadership were originality, popularity, sociability, judgment, aggressiveness, desire to excel, humor, cooperativeness, liveliness, and athletic ability, in approximate order of magnitude of the average correlation.
5. In spite of considerable negative evidence, the general trend of the results suggested a low positive correlation between leadership and such variables as chronological age, height, weight, physique, energy, appearance, dominance, and mood control. The evidence was about evenly divided concerning the relation to leadership of such traits as introversion-extroversion, self-sufficiency, and emotional control.
6. The evidence suggested that leadership exhibited in various school situations may persist into college and into later vocational and community life. However, knowledge of the facts related to the transferability of leadership remains meager and obscure.
7. The most fruitful studies, from the point of view

of understanding leadership, were those in which the behavior of leaders was described and analyzed on the basis of direct observation or the analysis of biographical and case-history data.

The factors associated with leadership could probably all be classified under the general headings capacity, achievement, responsibility, participation, and status:

1. *Capacity* (intelligence, alertness, verbal facility, originality, and judgment).
2. *Achievement* (scholarship, knowledge, and athletic accomplishments).
3. *Responsibility* (dependability, initiative, persistence, aggressiveness, self-confidence, and the desire to excel).
4. *Participation* (activity, sociability, cooperation, adaptability, and humor).
5. *Status* (socioeconomic position and popularity).
6. *Situation* (mental level, status, skills, needs and interests of followers, objectives to be achieved, and so on).

These findings are not surprising. It is primarily by virtue of participating in group activities and demonstrating his or her capacity for expediting the work of the group that a person consequently becomes endowed as a leader. A number of investigators were careful to distinguish between the leader and the figurehead and to point out that leadership is always associated with the attainment of group objectives. Leadership implies activity, movement, and getting work done. The leader is a person who occupies a position of responsibility in coordinatinig the activities of the members of the group in their task of attaining a common goal. This definition leads to a consideration of another significant factor.

A person does not become a leader by virtue of the possession of some combination of traits, but the pattern of personal characteristics of the leader must bear some relevant relationship to the characteristics, activities, and goals of the followers. Thus, leadership must be conceived in terms of the interaction of variables that are in constant flux. The factor of change is especially characteristic of the situation, which may be radi-

cally altered by the addition or loss of members, changes in interpersonal relationships and in goals, the competition of extra-group influences, and the like. The personal characteristics of the leader and of the followers are, in comparison, highly stable. The persistence of individual patterns of human behavior in the face of constant situational change appears to be a primary obstacle not only to the practice of leadership, but to the selection and placement of leaders. It is not especially difficult to find persons who are leaders. It is quite another matter to place these persons in different situations where they will be able to function as leaders. It becomes clear that an adequate analysis of leadership involves a study of leaders not only but of situations.

The evidence suggests that leadership is a relationship that exists between persons in a social situation and that persons who are leaders in one situation may not necessarily be leaders in other situations. Must it then be assumed that leadership is entirely incidental, haphazard, and unpredictable? Not at all. The very studies that provided the strongest arguments for the situational nature of leadership also supplied the strongest evidence to indicate that leadership patterns as well as nonleadership patterns of behavior were persistent and relatively stable. Jennings (1943, p. 210) observed that

the individual's choice behavior, in contrast to his social expansiveness, appears as an expression of needs which are, so to speak, so "central" to his personality that he must strive to fulfull them whether or not the possibility of fulfilling them is at hand or not.

A somewhat similar observation was made by Newstetter, Feldstein, and Newcomb (1938, p. 92):

Being accepted or rejected is not determined by the cordiality or antagonism of the individual's treatment of his fellows, nor evidently, is the individual's treatment of his fellows much affected by the degree to which he is already being accepted or rejected by them. Their treatment of him is related to their acceptance or rejection of him. Their treatment of him is, of course, a reaction to some or all of his behaviors, but we have been completely unsuccessful in attempting to measure what these behaviors are.

The authors concluded that these findings provided "devastating evidence" against the concept of the operation of measurable traits in determining social interactions. Although these findings do not appear to provide direct evidence either for or against a theory of traits, they do indicate that the complex of factors that determines an individual's status in a group is most difficult to isolate and evaluate.

The findings of Jennings and Newstetter, Feldstein, and Newcomb suggested that the problem of selecting leaders should be much less difficult than that of training nonleaders to become leaders. The clinician or group worker who has observed the fruitless efforts of socially isolated individuals to gain acceptance in a group or leadership status is aware of the real nature of the phenomena just described. Some individuals are isolated in almost any group in which they find themselves, while others are readily accepted in most of their social contacts.

A most pertinent observation on this point was made by Ackerson (1942, p. 45), who noted that "the correlations for 'leader' and 'follower'" are not of opposite sign and similar magnitude as would be expected of traits supposed to be antithetical." These may not be the opposite poles of a single underlying trait. Ackerson went on to say:

It may be that the true antithesis of "leader" is not "follower," but "indifference," i.e., the incapacity or unwillingness either to lead or to follow. Thus it may be that some individuals who under one situation are leaders may under other conditions take the role of follower, while the true "opposite" is represented by the child who neither leads nor follows.

The findings suggest that leadership is not a matter of passive status or of the mere possession of some combination of traits. Rather, leadership appears to be a working relationship among members of a group, in which the leader acquires status through active participation and demonstration of his or her capacity to carry cooperative tasks to completion. Significant aspects of this capacity for organizing and expediting cooperative efforts appear to be intelligence, alertness to the needs and motives of others, and insight into situations, further reinforced by such habits as responsibility, initiative, persistence, and self-confidence.

But the studies surveyed offered little information as to the basic nature of these personal qualifications. Cattell's (1946) analysis suggested that these qualifications could be based, to some degree, on basic intelligence, but Cattell and others also implied that these personal qualifications were socially conditioned to a high degree. The problems requiring thorough investigation are those that relate to factors that condition social participation, insight into situations, mood control, responsibility, and the transferability of leadership from one situation to another. Solutions to these problems seem basic not only to any adequate understanding of the personal qualifications of leaders, but to any effective training for leadership. The next 25 years set the stage for dealing with these issues.

Traits of Leadership: A Follow-up

This chapter reports the results obtained when Ralph Stogdill examined another 163 studies of the traits of leadership published between 1948 and 1970 and the ways in which such results could be meaningfully factor analyzed and clustered. The chapter provides a framework for many of the chapters that follow.

At the beginning of the twentieth century, leaders were generally regarded as superior individuals who, as a result of fortunate inheritance or social adventure, possessed qualities and abilities that differentiated them from people in general. The search for the specific qualities then occupied the next two generations of commentators and researchers. But in the 1940s, three reviews—by Bird (1940), and W. O. Jenkins (1947), and particularly by Stogdill (1948) just presented in the preceding chapter—sounded the seeming death-knell of a pure traits approach to the study of leadership. Bird (1940) analyzed 20 studies that considered 79 traits. Of these, 65 percent were mentioned in only a single study. Only four of the traits (extroverted, humor, intelligence, and initiative) appeared in five or more studies. W. O. Jenkins (1947) reviewed 74 studies of military leaders and found that although these leaders tended to have some superiority over followers in at least one of a wide variety of abilities, there was little agreement about the abilities that characterized the leaders. Jenkins concluded that military leadership was specific to the military situation under investigation. Stogdill (1948) also noted that some of the traits required of leaders tended to differ with the situation.

These reviews by Bird, Jenkins, and Stogdill were cited frequently after 1948 to support the view that leadership was entirely situational in origin and that particular personal characteristics could not accurately predict leadership. This view overemphasized the situational and underemphasized the personal nature of leadership. For instance, Carter (1953), Gibb (1954), and Shartle (1956) inferred that stable trait-leadership

relationships were for specific situations only. The view that leaders are born was rejected. Nevertheless, it was held that certain characteristics improve a leader's chances of success (Van Fleet & Yukl, 1986a). Thus, the question was: To what extent does the same trait-leadership connection remain true for a wide variety of situations? Evidence was amassed to indicate that different leadership skills and traits were required in different situations. The behaviors and traits that enable a mobster to gain and maintain control over a criminal gang are not the same as those that enable a religious leader to gain and maintain a large following. Yet certain general qualities—such as initiative and fortitude—appeared repeatedly to characterize both because particular personality traits contribute to a person's emergence as a leader in a wide variety of situations. This finding was supported in Mann's (1959) survey of research on the relation of personality to performance in small groups. Mann found positive relationships between personal traits (intelligence, adjustment, extroversion, dominance, masculinity, and sensitivity) and leadership in 71 to 80 percent of the studies. Kenny and Zaccaro (1983) concluded, from an analysis of studies on the subject, that 49 to 82 percent of the variance in the emergence of a person as a leader was due to some stable characteristic of the person.

Improvements in Methods and Measurements

Many new methods and measurements were introduced into the study of leadership in the decades after 1948. The one-variable-at-a-time experiment gave way to the factorial and multivariate experiment in which the effects of various contributions of treatments could be analyzed in the same experiments. Theory began to guide much of the data collection.

Questionnaire methodologists introduced a variety of techniques to reduce errors of halo, leniency, and social desirability and to increase the relevance and reliability of results, although their efforts often met with limited success. The critical-incidents technique, forced-choice checklists, behaviorally anchored rating scales, and semantic differentials were just a few of the specific new methods used. Factor analysis became the basic tool in the search and verification of the existence of traits of consequence. Other multivariate regression procedures also became commonplace in efforts to establish the relative importance of different traits to successful leadership.

The internationalization of efforts also became widespread. Whether the same traits of leadership were relevant to rural agricultural leaders in Chile and Mali or led to promotion to higher management in Norway, Italy, and Japan were subjects examined in the third quarter of the century. And in the United States, a topic of considerable interest was whether different leadership traits would emerge as being important for women and for racial and ethnic-minority leaders. (See Chapters 32, 33, and 34.)

The human-potential movement sparked awareness of the need to deal with leadership at a level of socioemotional feeling that was deeper than surface intellectual perception. Studies of such traits as self-exposure, empathy, psychic energy, intuition, and interpersonal competence blossomed.

The whole field of small-group research exploded with investigations beginning in the 1950s. At the same time, much more rigor was introduced into the measurements of individual role taking and behavior in small-group interactions. In addition, experimenters became much more aware of the many threats to the validity of their findings.

Just as situational leadership was becoming the primary theory used for management training, research was beginning to go in the opposite direction. There was a resurgence of interest in consistent individual differences across situations, braced with meta-analytic demonstrations of the validity and generalizability of a very limited battery of cognitive abilities tests for predicting successful performance in a wide variety of situations (Schmidt & Hunter, 1977). Meta-analytic the-

ory itself suggested that the situational variations frequently could and should be attributed not to substantive effects but to sampling error. Situational effects would have to be shown above and beyond what would be generated by the normal probability distribution of the means generated in the diverse situations. Strong inferences were drawn about personality and early developmental influences that have permanent effects on individuals and their behavior as leaders and followers.

Comparison of the Reviews of 1948 and 1970

The follow-up survey completed by Stogdill in 1970 was based on 163 studies of the characteristics of leaders reported 1948 through 70. Table 5.1 presents a comparison of findings from the 1948 survey (Chapter 4) with those of the 1970 survey.

The 1970 survey failed to record all negative findings since it is probable that many of the negative results were not published. For this reason, only positive findings are reported in column 3. Caution is urged in interpreting conclusions on the basis of the *published* findings.[1]

In the surveys, a positive, or significant, relationship means that (1) a given trait was significantly correlated with some measure of the effectiveness of leaders, (2) a sample of leaders was found to differ significantly from a sample of followers on the trait, (3) a sample of

---

[1]David Bakin pointed to the existence of a farcical but not necessarily fanciful prospect about positive and negative findings in social science. Suppose, he argued, that the true difference between A and B is really zero. Thus, in 95 percent of all studies of A and B, we would expect to reach a negative conclusion—a finding of no statistically significant difference between A and B at the 5 percent level of confidence. But 5 percent of all studies will reach a positive but erroneous conclusion that there is a difference between A and B. Who publishes? Only those with positive findings! So, if we depend on a count of publications of positive and negative findings, we will draw the wrong inference about the true difference between A and B.

Unfortunately, there is some truth to Bakin's burlesque: Researchers and journal editors are reluctant to publish negative findings and hence, there is little question that positive findings are more likely to be published than are negative ones. Let the reader beware. See, for example, Borg and Tupes (1958), Coates and Pellegrin (1957), Ghiselli and Barthol (1956), and J. S. Guilford (1952).

Personal Attributes of Leaders

Table 5.1 Characteristics of Leaders According to the 1948 and 1970 Surveys of Research Findings

Characteristics	Number of Positive Findings		Number of Zero or Negative Findings
	1948 Survey	1970 Survey	1948 Survey Only
Physical Characteristics			
Activity, energy	5	24	
Age	10	6	8
Appearance, grooming	13	4	3
Height	9		4
Weight	7		4
Social Background			
Education	22	14	5
Social status	15	19	2
Mobility	5	6	
Intelligence and Ability			
Intelligence	23	25	10
Judgment, decisiveness	9	6	
Knowledge	11	12	
Fluency of speech	13	15	
Personality			
Adaptability	10		
Adjustment, normality		11	
Aggressiveness, assertiveness		12	
Alertness	6	4	
Ascendance, dominance	11	31	6
Emotional balance, control	11	14	8
Enthusiasm		3	
Extroversion	5	1	6
Independence, nonconformity		13	
Objectivity, tough-mindedness		7	
Originality, creativity	7	13	
Personal integrity, ethical conduct	6	9	
Resourcefulness		7	
Self-confidence	17	28	
Strength of conviction	7		
Tolerance of stress		9	
Task-related Characteristics			
Drive to achieve, desire to excel	7	21	
Drive for responsibility	12	17	
Enterprise, initiative		10	
Persistence against obstacles	12		
Responsibility in the pursuit of objectives	17	6	
Task orientation	6	13	
Social Characteristics			
Ability to enlist cooperation	7	3	
Administrative ability		16	

Table 5.1 *(Continued)*

Characteristics	Number of Positive Findings		Number of Zero or Negative Findings
	1948 Survey	1970 Survey	1948 Survey Only
Attractiveness		4	
Cooperativeness	11	5	
Nurturance		4	
Popularity, prestige	10	1	
Sociability, interpersonal skills	14	35	
Social participation	20	9	
Tact, diplomacy	8	4	

effective leaders was found to differ significantly from a sample of ineffective leaders on the trait, or (4) a sample of high-status leaders (such as top managers) was found to differ significantly from a sample of low-status leaders (such as first-line supervisors) on the trait.

The discussion of Table 5.1 will be by clusters of individual traits: physical characteristics, social background, intelligence and ability, personality, task-related characteristics, and social characteristics.

Physical Characteristics

Measures of physical characteristics, such as age, height, weight, and appearance, showed both positive and negative findings in the 1948 survey. However, between 1948 and 1970, there was little concern with leaders' physical characteristics. Yet height and weight above the average of the peer group is certainly not a disadvantage in achieving leadership status. Many organizations like to be represented by impressive physical specimens. When faced with taller opponents in television debates, shorter presidential candidates, such as Jimmy Carter and Michael Dukakis, stand on raised platforms to equalize their height with those of their taller opponents. Frederick the Great required that all his soldiers be tall; on the other hand, Napoleon is often cited as an example of the fact that a man of small stature can rise to a position of great power. Thus, physical stature may complement a leader, or a leader may compensate for the lack of physical stature. Yet, there is a rational element involved. Robert Peel, who introduced the "bobbies" to London, made a

highly effective police force without firearms by choosing only large men who could dominate the scene of social conflicts. Conversely, it has been noted that smaller-sized policemen are more likely to suffer attack and injury.

Activity, Energy, Stamina. Results of the 1970 survey unearthed 25 studies[2]—many more than the 1948 survey—which suggested that the leader tends to be endowed with an abundant reserve of energy, stamina, and ability to maintain a high rate of physical activity. Even when handicapped by physical disability or poor health, highly successful leaders tended to exhibit a high rate of energy output.

Age. Age appeared in six studies reported between 1948 and 1970.[3] Age continued to be related to leadership in a complicated fashion, as was noted in Chapter 4. A survey by Lehman (1953) on the relation of age to achievement in science, art, politics, and other fields found that great men tended to exhibit signs of outstanding accomplishment at a relatively early age. Many, but not all, had the advantage of special education or training because of the early recognition of their talents. However, it usually takes time to rise to the top in a corporate or governmental structure. Standard and Poor's (1967) reported that 74 percent of

[2]The reader who is interested in the complete list of citations of these studies should consult Chapter 5 in the earlier editions of this handbook.
[3]See, for example, A. R. Bass (1964), Johnson, Peterson, and Kahler (1968), and Newcomer (1955).

66,336 American executives in its 1967 *Register of Corporations, Directors, and Executives* were over age 50. Only 168 executives were under age 30, while 8,085 were in the 71 to 80 age group. The two sets of findings indicate that the creative individual is likely to exhibit evidences of his or her ability at an early age; however, large organizations are not designed to use such creative gifts in administrative capacities. Rather, organizations tend to rely on administrative knowledge and demonstrations of success that come with experience and age.

Of course, there are many exceptional cases of young chief executive officers who reached the top early. Some examples include Jack Welch of General Electric Corporation, who was promoted rapidly from within; Michael Eisner of Disney Studios, who transferred from a high-level position elsewhere; and Steven Jobs of Apple and NeXt, who founded and built the corporations that he led. Nevertheless, the need for organizations to be more creative and flexible in competing in a world of rapid change and new technologies results in many organizations dipping down in their corporate structures for relatively younger executives to assume corporate leadership. In many firms and agencies with age-rank locksteps, it would appear that young persons who desire quick recognition of their talents might be advised to consider a profession in which prestige is based on individual accomplishment rather than an administrative career involving a long climb up the status structure of the organization. Legislation barring mandatory retirement will slow up the hierarchial promotion process even more as top executives who are older than age 65 remain with the firm or agency, thus preventing movement upwards of all who are below them. As will be noted in Chapter 34, which deals with cross-cultural issues, the age-rank lockstep seems to vary considerably from one country to another.

Social Background

Social Status. Studies of the socioeconomic background of leaders continued to proliferate between 1948 and 1970; 19 studies were found for this period.[4]

D. R. Mathews (1954) observed that from 1789 to 1934, 58 percent of the presidents, vice presidents, and cabinet members had fathers in the professional, proprietor, or official occupations, 38 percent had fathers who were farmers, but only 4 percent had fathers who were wage earners. It is apparent that high social status has provided an advantage in rising to high levels of political leadership. But Newcomer (1955) and *Scientific American* (1965) reported that, compared with 1900, more top executives in 1965 were beginning to come from the poorer and middle-income groups, rather than the wealthy strata of society. A. Porter (1965) found that the background of the father of an executive was significantly related to the executive's level in the organization and his authority for making policy. However, the father's background was not related to the size of the organization or to the executive's status in the business world or satisfaction with the progress of his career.

Miller and Dirksen (1965) reported that highly visible community leaders were differentiated from their less visible peers by being business oriented, Republican, member of the Chamber of Commerce, and named in the mass media. However, the hidden leaders were characterized as holding administrative or professional jobs; they were not owners of large businesses, natives of the city, or from families in the city that were not prominent. Again, R. M. Powell's (1969) large-scale survey of the executive-promotion process indicated that religious and ethnic background—usually linked with social status—were also important factors.

Studies of the social background of student leaders by Martin, Gross, and Darley (1952); Weinberg (1965); Krumboltz, Christal, and Ward (1959); and Kumar (1966) revealed few consistent relationships across samples, although Williamson (1948) found that fraternity members occupied a disproportionately large share of leadership positions on the college campus.

Mobility. Six studies dealt with the upward mobility of leaders.[5] Jennings's (1967a) study is illustrative of the work in this area; it presented an insightful analysis of the problems, stresses, and adaptations involved in rapid upward mobility in the large corporation. More

---

[4]See, for example, Ghiselli (1959), Hulin (1962), Lewis (1960), and Mathews (1954).

[5]See, for example, Hicks and Stone (1962), Powell (1969), and Roe (1956).

specifically, Cussler (1958) found that once women executives reached middle management, they found it difficult to rise higher in the industrial organization. Much more will be said in Chapter 32 about women's social status in organizations in relation to that of men and their difficulties in achieving a high rank.

Education. Fourteen studies showed the importance of education to leadership.[6] Reflecting the national rise in educational levels, senior managers with college degrees increased from 28.3 percent in 1900 to 74.3 percent in 1964 (*Scientific American*, 1965). In contrast, G. F. Lewis's (1960) review of several studies indicated that small businessmen have less education and more often start their careers as unskilled or semiskilled workers than do top executives in large firms. In regard to first-line foremen, Johnson, Peterson, and Kahler (1968) studied 496 foremen in a company from 1940 to 1961. They found that the average age of these foremen increased from 31.2 years in 1940–44 to 41.2 years in 1955–59 and that the years of schooling increased from 10.8 to 11.2 during the same period.

The conclusions drawn from these studies of social background were that (1) high socioeconomic status was an advantage in attaining leadership status, (2) leaders who rose to high-level positions in industry tended to come from the lower socioeconomic strata of society than they did a half century earlier, and (3) the leaders tended to be better educated now than formerly. The rise in the general level of education of the population is common knowledge. Requirements for managerial and administrative positions increasingly demand a graduate degree, such as the MBA. The trend toward reduced emphasis on social status and more emphasis on education is expected to accelerate as the effects of affirmative action manifest themselves. As firms and agencies aggressively promote women, blacks, and other minorities, one should expect to see a considerable increase in the upward mobility of these groups. For example, in 1960, women and blacks were hardly observed in MBA programs, but in 1980, women constituted 30–40 percent of MBA classes, and business schools were actively engaged in trying to achieve substantial increases in the number

of black and minority students in their programs. (More on this in Chapters 32 and 33. Chapter 11 attempts to explain the general impact on leadership of status.)

Intelligence and Ability

Intelligence. In 1970, 25 reports of a positive relationship between leadership, intelligence, and ability were found to have been published between 1948 and 1970,[7] compared to 17 studies correlating scores on intelligence tests with leadership status in the 1948 survey. The average correlation of .28 in the 1948 survey was corroborated in the 1970 survey. Five of the competent studies of 1948 had suggested, however, that large discrepancies between the intelligence of potential leaders and that of their followers militated against the exercise of leadership. Ghiselli (1963b, p. 898) reported supporting evidence. In a study of three groups of managers, he found that "the relationship between intelligence and managerial success is curvilinear with those individuals earning both low and very high scores being less likely to achieve success in management positions than those with scores at intermediate levels."

Thus, leaders can be too able for those they lead. Persons with higher abilities may suffer from extreme self-preoccupation, their abilities may make it difficult for them to communicate with those they are attempting to lead, and their ideas may be too advanced to be accepted by their potential followers (pioneers are seldom outstanding leaders). The discrepancy in abilities is likely to be paralleled by discrepancies in interests and goals. Also, Korman's (1968) extensive review on the prediction of managerial performance must be kept in mind. Korman reported that "intelligence, as measured by verbal ability tests, is a fair predictor of first-line supervisory performance, but not of higher-level managerial performance."[8] But one must also reckon that only those who already possess above-average intelligence are likely to have achieved top management positions in the organization. So there is a restriction in range, which makes it impossible for intel-

---

[6]See, for example, Feil (1950), Kumar (1966), Mandell (1949), and O'Donovan (1962).

[7]See, for example, Ghiselli (1964), Rowland and Scott (1968), Rychlak (1963), and Thornton (1968).

[8]Chapters 7, 12, and later show that higher levels of management call for a different kind of intelligence—fluid intelligence—which may be contrasted to the crystallized intelligence of import to lower levels of management.

ligence tests to discriminate the good from the bad performers at the top of the organization. Nevertheless, it
should be clear that a high-level intelligence test that
discriminates verbal intelligence among those at the
upper end of the population's intelligence, such as the
Miller Analogies (used for predicting success in graduate and professional schools), is also likely to be a valid
predictor of the potential to rise in firms, agencies, and
institutions.

Other Intellectual Abilities. Table 5.1 presents uniformly positive findings for studies completed between
1948 and 1970 which indicated that leaders are characterized by superior judgment and/or decisiveness (e.g.,
Roadman, 1964), knowledge (e.g., Colyer, 1951), and
fluency of speech (e.g., Burnett, 1951b).

Personality

Up to 31 studies in the 1970 survey dealt with personality and leadership. Several differences may be noted
in the 1948 and 1970 lists of personality characteristics.
These differences may well be attributed to changes in
theories regarding the structure of personality. The
only characteristics with uniformly positive findings in
the 1948 list were adaptability and strength of conviction. Those that appeared in the 1970 list were adjustment (e.g., Terrell & Shreffler, 1958), aggressiveness
or assertiveness (e.g., Hobert & Dunnette, 1967), independence (e.g., Hornaday & Bunker, 1970), objectivity
(e.g., Argyris, 1953), enthusiasm (e.g., Gibb, 1949), and
tolerance of stress (e.g., Lange & Jacobs, 1960). Characteristics that appeared with positive findings in both
the 1948 and 1970 lists were alertness (e.g., Porter,
1959), originality (e.g., Randle, 1956), personal integrity
(e.g., Stephenson, 1959), and self-confidence (e.g., Moment & Zaleznik, 1963).

Ascendance (e.g., Sanders, 1968), emotional balance
(e.g., Harville, 1969), and extroversion (e.g., Harrell,
1966) showed almost as many negative as positive findings in the 1948 survey. These results implied that
dominance, self-control, and outgoing personality may
characterize some leaders but not others.

Task-related Personality Characteristics. Both the
1948 and the 1970 reviews produced uniformly positive
results indicating that leaders are personally character-

ized by a need for achievement (e.g., Cummings &
Scott, 1965) and a sense of responsibility (e.g., Gordon,
1952). Leaders tend to be task oriented (e.g., Medow &
Zander, 1965) and dependable in the pursuit of objectives (e.g., Powell & Nelson, 1969). They display enterprise and initiative (e.g., Helfrich & Schwirian, 1968)
and are persistent in overcoming obstacles.

Social Personality Characteristics. The positive
findings on social characteristics in both 1948 and 1970
suggest that leaders are active participants in various
activities. They interact easily with a wide range of personalities (e.g., Krumboltz, Christal & Ward, 1959), and
this interaction is valued by others. They are not only
cooperative with others (e.g., J. S. Guilford, 1952) but
are able to enlist cooperation (e.g., Bentz, 1964) and to
execute (administer) projects (e.g., Kay, 1959). Interpersonal skills (e.g., D. S. Brown, 1964), including tactfulness (e.g., Tarnapol, 1958), make them attractive to followers (e.g., Price, 1948). Leaders are valued by group
members because they have such characteristics as
nurturance (e.g., Roff, 1950) and popularity (e.g., Harrell & Lee, 1964) that foster loyalty and cohesiveness
in the group.

Factor Analysis of the Traits of Leadership

As another follow-up to the 1948 survey, a review of
factorial studies of leadership published between 1945
and 1970 was completed to determine whether the
studies had identified many factors in common. The
analysis was based on 52 factorial studies, including
surveys of a large number of military and industrial personnel, studies of leadership in military and industrial
groups, and reports on experimental groups.[9]

Factors identified in three or more studies are listed
in Table 5.2. Factors found in only one or two investigations are not listed.

It should be emphasized that the factors that
emerged depended on the variables originally included
in the battery of traits measured or ignored by the investigators. For instance, if an investigator included
many measures of social distance, a common factor of

---

[9]The complete list of citations for the 52 factor analytic studies appears in Chapter 5 of the preceding editions of this handbook.

Table 5.2 Factors Appearing in Three or More Studies of the 52 Surveyed

Factor	Number of Studies Found	Example of Study
Technical skills	18	Borgatta & Eschenbach, 1955
Social nearness, friendliness	18	Hausman & Strupp, 1955
Task motivation and application	17	Creager & Harding, 1958
Supportive of the group task	17	Ghiselli, 1960
Social and interpersonal skills	16	Bartlett, 1959
Emotional balance and control	15	Carter, Haythorn, & Howell, 1950
Leadership effectiveness and achievement	15	Borgatta, 1955a
Administrative skills	12	Borg, 1960
General impression (halo)	12	Mandell, 1956
Intellectual skills	11	Grant, 1955
Ascendence, dominance, decisiveness	11	Klein & Ritti, 1970
Willingness to assume responsibility	10	Flanagan, 1961
Ethical conduct, personal integrity	10	Flanagan, 1951
Maintaining a cohesive work group	9	Cassens, 1966a
Maintaining coordination and teamwork	7	Wilson, High, Beem, & Comrey, 1954
Ability to communicate; articulativeness	6	High, Goldberg, & Comrey, 1956
Physical energy	6	Peres, 1962
Maintaining standards of performance	5	Bass, Wurster, Doll, & Clair, 1953
Creative, independent	5	Wofford, 1970
Conforming	5	Triandis, 1960
Courageous, daring	4	Palmer & McCormick, 1961
Experience and activity	4	Hussein, 1969
Nurturant behavior	4	Crannell & Mollenkopf, 1946
Maintaining informal control of the group	4	Sakoda, 1952
Mature, cultured	3	Stagner, 1962
Aloof, distant	3	Roach, 1956

social distance could emerge. If no measures of social distance were included, no common factor of social distance could be extracted. Likewise, if only a single reliable measure of social distance was included, it would not appear in a separate common factor of social distance, as such.

It may be observed in Table 5.2 that the most frequently occurring factors were descriptive of various skills of the leader. They included the following: social and interpersonal skills, technical skills, administrative skills, intellectual skills, leadership effectiveness and achievement, social nearness, friendliness, supportive of the group task, and task motivation and application.

These factors indicated that leaders differ from each other consistently in the effective use they make of interpersonal, administrative, technical, and intellectual skills. Some leaders could be described as highly task

motivated; others were most capable of maintaining close, friendly, personal relationships. The best leaders were able to do both. Chapter 7 will concentrate on the former and Chapter 8, on the latter.

The next most frequent set of factors was concerned with how leaders relate to their groups. The behaviors included maintaining the cohesiveness of the group, coordination, task motivation, task performance, and high quality of output. A concern for the group's performance was softened by nurturant behavior and the use of informal controls. These factors were as follows: maintaining a cohesive work group, maintaining coordination and teamwork, maintaining standards of performance, maintaining informal control of the group (group freedom), and nurturant behavior.

Next in frequency were factors concerned strictly with the personal characteristics of leaders. Leaders could be described in terms of how much they were emotionally well balanced, willing to assume responsibility, ethical in conduct, able to communicate readily, dominant, energetic, experienced, courageous, and mature.

If the order of frequency of factors is significant, it would appear that successful leadership involves certain skills and capabilities—interpersonal, technical, administrative, and intellectual—that enable leaders to be of value to their group or organization. These skills allow leaders to maintain satisfactory levels of group cohesiveness, drive, and productivity. Leaders are further assisted in the execution of these functions if they possess a high degree of motivation to complete tasks, personal integrity, communicative ability, and the like. In sum, the factorial studies seem to provide a well-balanced picture of the skills, functions, and personal characteristics of leaders in a wide variety of situations.[10]

[10]It should be kept in mind that the factors that emerged from the analysis of intercorrelations of items describing leaders depended, to a large degree, on (1) the kinds of items and variables for which descriptions were obtained, (2) the numbers of items and variables in different descriptive categories, and (3) the nature of the population of leaders who were described. Few factorial studies of leadership were comparable when matched against these three criteria. As a result, few studies produced identical factors; however, certain factors with the same or similar names appeared with considerable frequency

If factors with the same name appeared in two different studies, they did not necessarily contain loadings on identical items or variables. In other words, it could not be assumed that the factors described identical behaviors. A factor was identified or named on the basis of the nature of items or variables with the highest loadings on the factor. If several similar items or variables have high loadings, the element of the similarity of the item or variable is usually given heavy consideration in naming the factor.

The frequency with which a given factor appeared in the reports did not necessarily represent the frequency of its occurrence among leaders in general. An item or variable could not appear in a study unless measures were obtained on characteristics represented by the factor. Researchers, of course, differ in their ideas about what is important in the study of leadership. As a result, they tended to use different sets of items or variables in their efforts to measure leadership. Furthermore, it cannot be assumed that the listed factors constituted a complete catalog of the leader's qualities and abilities. One of the values of factor analysis is that it brings together in the same factor all items that act alike in describing the individuals in the samples. Thus, the resulting factor describes a generalized form of behavior, rather than the minute details of behavior.

It should also be kept in mind that factors can emerge only if leaders behave differently on different orthogonal dimensions. Thus, for initiation and consideration factors to emerge, there must be a low correlation between them. The same leaders who are high in initiation should

Summary and Conclusions

The differences between 1948 and 1970 may be due primarily to the larger percentage of studies in the 1970 survey than in the 1948 survey from the world of work rather than from children's and social groups.[11] The similarities of results make it reasonable to conclude that personality traits differentiate leaders from followers, successful from unsuccessful leaders, and high-level from low-level leaders. One practical application of this conclusion is the assessment center for determining leadership potential among candidates for managerial positions (Bray, Campbell, & Grant, 1974; Bray & Grant, 1966). By the mid-1970s, over 1,000 such assessment centers were in operation. In these centers candidates are observed for two to three days in interviews, leaderless group discussions, and other situational tests. They are also tested individually with personality and aptitude tests. The in-basket, a sampling of managerial action requirements, is also often used. Observers meet to try to pool their results on the basis of inferences from the test results and their observations to yield a picture of the total personality of the

vary in consideration from high to low. Those who are low in initiation should likewise vary from high to low in consideration. Conceptually, most leaders could be high in both and the factor could fail to appear, although the different behaviors could still be seen.

If the correlation is high between them, only a single factor generally will appear that contains items of both kinds. Nevertheless, the same leaders who are high in consultative behavior are also likely to participate in decision making. Only one factor, consideration, will appear. Consultation, in which the leader decides, and participation, in which decisions are consensual, are conceptually distinct, despite the fact that the same leaders who tend to use one of the approaches will also use the other approach. The distinctions are important both to theory and to practice. It may be particularly important for a leader to consult rather than participate in one circumstance but to share the decision making with fully participating subordinates in another situation. Nevertheless, the generalized behaviors described by the 26 factors produce a more meaningful, logical picture of the leader than would be provided by a list of 100 haphazardly selected items or variables that were all correlated with leadership status and effectiveness. The results of the factorial studies indicate that an infinitely large number of variables are not needed to obtain a well-balanced description of a leader. A relatively few of the 26 factors can be the basis for organizing a fairly complete examination of leadership traits and behavior.

[11]Stogdill suspected that the absence of some particular positive findings in the 1970 survey were due, in part, to the decisions of his abstracters. We also must be cautious about the volume of results obtained for some traits and not for others. Researchers tend to pursue fads. Also, changes occur over the decades in the names that are used to label the same traits of behavior.

candidate and his or her leadership potential in positions familiar to the observers. Much more will be presented about such assessment centers in Chapter 36.

The leader is characterized by a strong drive for responsibility and completion of tasks, vigor and persistence in the pursuit of goals, venturesomeness and originality in problem solving, drive to exercise initiative in social situations, self-confidence and a sense of personal identity, willingness to accept the consequences of his or her decisions and actions, readiness to absorb interpersonal stress, willingness to tolerate frustration and delay, ability to influence other people's behavior, and the capacity to structure social interaction systems to the purpose at hand.

The clusters of characteristics discussed in this chapter differentiate leaders from followers, effective from ineffective leaders, and higher-echelon from lower-echelon leaders. In other words, different strata of leaders and followers can be described in terms of the extent to which they exhibit some of the characteristics. Furthermore, research by Bass (1953), Moore and Smith (1953), and Tarnapol (1958) suggested that isolates—and, to less extent, followers—can be described by the antonyms of trait names attributed to leaders. The characteristics generate personality dynamics that are advantageous to the person seeking the responsibilities of leadership.

The conclusion that personality is a factor in differentiating leadership does not represent a return to the pure trait approach. It does represent a sensible modification of the extreme situationalist point of view. The trait approach tended to treat personality variables in an atomistic fashion, suggesting that each trait acts singly to determine the effects of leadership. The situationalist approach, on the other hand, denied the influences of individual differences, attributing all variance among persons to the fortuitous demands of the environment.

Again, it should be emphasized that some of the variance in who emerges as a leader and who is successful and effective is due to traits of consequence in the situation, some is due to situational effects, and some is due to the interaction of traits and situation. For example, suppose candidates for management positions are tested in three situations: social service agencies, industrial firms, and military organizations. We are likely to find in the aggregate that individual interpersonal competence is predictive of successful performance. But it is also most predictive in social service agencies and least predictive in military organizations. Considering the importance of competence to perform tasks and interpersonal competence at two stages in the careers of public accountants, engineers, and other kinds of technical specialists, one finds that both are important to performance. During the early years with a firm, a person's technical competence is most strongly indicative of successful performance, but after two to five years, interpersonal competence becomes more important.

The element of chance would appear to play a part in the rise of individual leaders. A given leader may be able to rise to the top of the hierarchy in competition with one group of peers, whereas he or she may be unable to do so in another group of peers. An individual's upward mobility would seem to depend, to a considerable degree, on being at the right place at the right time. Finally, it should be noted that, to a very large extent, our conceptions of characteristics of leadership are culturally determined, as will be elucidated in Chapter 34. Situational contingencies will be examined more fully in Chapters 26 through 31.

Yet, individuals differ and they differ consistently from each other. This statement implies that there are regularities in their abilities, interests, orientations, values, and personality that endure across time. Other differences of consequence may include age, sex, family background, physique, and so on. Since the beginning of the study of leadership, the question has remained: How much do these individual differences account for the emergence of leadership and its effectiveness, and do the effects transcend situational circumstances? Thus, some individuals will attempt to lead in most situations in which they find themselves, but others will avoid doing so whenever possible. And some individuals will attempt to be leaders only in certain situations, and their personal predispositions can be described. The same may be said about succeeding as a leader.

There is no overall comprehensive theory of the personality of leaders. Nonetheless, evidence abounds about particular patterns of traits that are of consequence to leadership, such as determination, persistence, self-confidence, and ego strength.

Chapters 4 and 5 canvassed the many traits and characteristics that have been found to be associated with leadership, as revealed in studies and reviews starting early in this century. This review forms a base for subsequent chapters on those particular personality complexes that affect the emergence of leadership, which have been singled out for continued attention. What shall be seen is that individuals with higher activity and energy levels, with relevant task and intellectual competencies, with relevant interactional skills, and with particular values and orientations tend to emerge as leaders more often than not. As a consequence of these attributes, they tend to be valued as individuals and placed in valued positions.

The mass of research findings about the traits of leaders compared to nonleaders and of successful and effective leaders compared to unsuccessful and ineffective ones include the following: activity level, rate of talk, initiative, assertiveness, aggressiveness, dominance, ascendance, emotional balance, tolerance for stress, self-control, self-efficacy, enthusiasm, and extroversion. Chapter 6 and several that follow will continue the examination of these traits.

Task competencies are associated with leading. They include intelligence, judgment, decisiveness, knowledge, fluency of speech, resourcefulness, technical abilities, intellectually stimulating qualities, vision, imagination, articulativeness, cognitive abilities, diagnostic skills, originality, and creativity. Chapter 7 presents a more detailed consideration of the task competence of leadership.

Interpersonal competencies are another cluster of consequences. They include the ability to enlist cooperation, administrative ability, attractiveness, cooperativeness, affiliativeness, nurturance, sociability, interpersonal skills, social participation, tact, diplomacy, empathy, social insight, and attributional accuracy. These are the focus of Chapter 8.

Authoritarianism and its opposite must be taken into account. Traits involve egalitarianism, Machiavellianism, power orientation, adaptability, adjustment, normality, and self-orientation. Chapter 9 deals further with these attributes of leaders and nonleaders.

Personal values also need to be considered, such as personal integrity, ethical conduct, task orientation, achievement orientation, desire to excel, competitiveness, independence, objectivity, tough mindedness, acceptance of responsibility, initiative, persistence against obstacles, determination, ego strength, inner direction, confidence, preference for risk, responsibility in the pursuit of objectives, and satisfaction with leadership. Discourse about these characteristics continues in Chapter 10.

Chapter 11 further examines personal factors in the context of the sociodynamic processes that contribute to one's status and esteem and, therefore, one's leadership by describing some individuals who are accorded more esteem, status, and power by their peers. Numerous personal characteristics are associated with this tendency to be accorded more esteem, status, and power. They may include chronological age, appearance, physical stature, education, social position, mobility, popularity, and prestige.

The personal factors that contribute to charismatic leadership are detailed in Chapter 12. Subsequent chapters elaborate further on the importance of such personal factors in understanding both leaders and their followers.

All the chapters beginning with the next examine more than just consistent individual differences in predispositions. They also consider the dynamics that move one individual to lead, another to follow, and still another to remain independent or isolated owing to different experiences and expectations.

Leadership and Activity Level

The importance of energy and activity to leadership was recognized in comments from Demosthenes to Galsworthy. By A.D. 100, Plutarch (1909) had summed up the classical wisdom that persuasive oratory is a matter of action, action, and then more action. According to Galsworthy (1931), political candidates are marvels of energy. This chapter explores the extent to which such energy and activity, manifested in rates of participation and the tendency to be assertive and dominant, accounts for attempts to lead. But the discussion is expanded to consider various antecedent conditions other than personal factors that make one individual lead and another avoid leadership. These factors may include, for example, previous success or greater rewards of the former individual as a leader. Or, the individual who leads may have been given specialized information relevant to the group's objectives.

Energy and Assertiveness

Energy Level and Indefatigability

Activism, forcefulness, and militant behavior characterized the great American presidents (Wendt & Light, 1976). More generally, Cleveland (1985, p. 160) noted that "leaders need the physical energy to concentrate harder and work harder than most of [their] associates." In an analysis of the development and careers of 15 world-class leaders, the first common characteristic that Willner (1968, p. 62) observed was "a high energy level and an extraordinary degree of vitality." This vitality took several forms. Some of these leaders were capable of dramatic bursts of energetic activity, followed by periods of lassitude. Others sustained a continuously high rate of activity; they could work long hours, maintain late hours, get along on little sleep, and do so without signs of fatigue. Their assistants were worn out and came close to collapse trying to keep up

with their indefatigable activity. For instance, Kemal Atatürk, the founder of modern Turkey, once went four nights without sleep. It was common for him to stay up late at night in animated conversation, drinking, and gambling. He sometimes dictated for over 24 hours at a time, exhausting one after another of his secretaries. Sukarno of Indonesia also needed little sleep and was known to complete a day of heavy activity with an equally active night of recreation. Ghana's Kwame Nkrumah also needed little sleep or food and could refresh himself with catnaps on two chairs. Fidel Castro was reportedly awake and at work for up to 20 hours daily during the first months of his regime. Nikolai Lenin seemed to work unceasingly. Gamal Abdel Nasser of Egypt frequently maintained a working schedule from early in the morning until early the following morning.

As was seen in Chapters 4 and 5, a high level of activity is common to leaders in a variety of different situations. Levy-Leboyer and Pineau (1981) reaffirmed this by finding that leaders of more successful French laboratories held more frequent meetings and more frequent evaluations. Okochi (1989a) noted in interviews with chief executive officers that they had to have a high energy level to keep up with the unlimited demands on their time for day-to-day business decisions, as well as the required ceremonial duties.

The majority of the rank-and-file members in most voluntary groups are both inactive and less interested in the means and ends of their groups than are the fewer highly active members. These inactive members are unlikely to emerge as leaders of the group. Rather, the leadership of a voluntary organization is drawn from those few members who are highly active in the organization and who strongly subscribe to the organization's purposes and activities. Thus, Seidman, London, and Karsh (1951) observed that it was the most active union members who were most convinced of the value of the union's aims and operations and were most ready to try to gain and maintain support for them. Adjectives used to describe both men and women who displayed leadership in initially leaderless group discussions included active, assertive, energetic, and not silent or withdrawn (Gough, 1988).

Dominance and Extroversion

Dominance. Activity and participation are usually associated with the traits of dominance and assertiveness, as well as with attempts to lead. Furthermore, group members who score high on psychological tests of assertiveness and dominance tend to emerge as successful leaders. Thus, Rohde (1951) reported that discussion groups that were composed of different combinations of dominant and submissive members tended to prefer members who tested high in dominance as leaders. Although tested dominants exhibited more controlling behaviors, they were better able to adapt themselves to the situational demands imposed by other members. They could be more agreeable and cooperative than tested submissives.

Megargee, Bogart, and Anderson (1966) studied pairs of participants, one scoring high and the other scoring low on a test of dominance. When instructions emphasized the task, tested dominants did not assume the leadership role significantly more often than did tested submissives. However, when leadership was emphasized, dominant participants emerged as leaders in 90 percent of the pairs. In the same way, Scioli, Dyson, and Fleitas (1974) found that a high degree of tested dominance correlated with leadership in 22 discussion groups of male and female college students, but these results had to be qualified since Dyson, Fleitas, and Scioli (1972) observed that dominant personalities emerged as leaders only if the environment required conformity and did not permit dissent.

Berkowitz and Haythorn's (1955) study of groups composed of dominant and submissive members found that submissive members tended to choose dominant members and reject submissive members as leaders. However, dominant members chose dominant and submissive members about equally.

In a study that used checklists of adjectives, Gough (1988), found that the ratings of emergent leadership that observers gave to 95 males and 98 females in initially leaderless group discussions correlated .62 and .67, respectively, with the participants' being aggressive and .85 and .84, respectively, with their being assertive.

Kremer and Mack (1983) showed that preemptive behavior by male and female students in mixed-motive experimental games was related to the students' subsequent nomination for leadership in five-person task groups. But earlier high levels of preemptive behavior were more predictive only of the emergence of females as leaders.

Extroversion. As was discussed in Chapters 4 and 5, extroversion is another generalized trait that is likely to increase one's tendencies to attempt to lead and to participate in group activities. Extroversion, in turn, is linked to self-monitoring behavior and a sense of self-efficacy, the sensitivity to cues about what it is appropriate to do.

Individuals differ in their willingness and ability to initiate and sustain interactions with other persons. Introverted individuals find almost all interactions stressful and unpleasant. Other individuals are more comfortable in face-to-face situations, in small informal groups, or in large formal organizations. Many skilled public speakers seem to exude joy in their encounters with large audiences.

In Gough's (1988) just-mentioned investigation, emerging as a leader correlated .65 for males and .59 for females with being outgoing, .76 and .80 with being outspoken, .62 and .39 with being sociable, and −.81 and −.65 with being shy. Lord, DeVader, and Alliger (1986) thought that Stogdill (1948) and Mann (1959) had both underestimated the correlation of the personal trait of extroversion and leadership. They completed a meta-analysis of reports of different types of subjects and situations that related extroversion and leadership. The meta-analysis adjusted the grand mean of results for the sample sizes and various errors attenuating each of the obtained correlations. These researchers estimated that the true mean correlation between extroversion and leadership was .26 across the different samples of subjects and situations. The results for dominance and leadership were less supportive of the importance of the trait of dominance across situations, however; the estimate of the true mean correlation was .13.

The Dynamics of Attempts to Lead

Activity, participation, and leadership are more than a matter of personal predilection. The dynamics involve one's personal experience and expectations, as well as the experience and expectations of those with whom one is interacting.

Leadership must be attempted if a person is to have the chance to be influential (Bugental, 1964). Gray, Richardson, and Mayhew (1968) found that the amount of influence exercised by group members tended to increase with increases in their attempts to be influential. Although extroverts are more likely to try to lead, whether they make the attempt will depend on whether they expect to be successful and to make a contribution to the group's effort to cope with its problems and whether their previous attempts have been successful. Also important is whether colleagues and fellow group members feel the same way about the person's efforts; if they do, empowerment occurs (Barton, 1984). There is a mutually satisfying integration of performance between persons and their groups.

Favorable reactions to one's attempts to lead will sustain the effort. Attempts to lead that result in effective coping with the group's problems and meeting its needs will be accepted and result in a continuation of such attempts (Jones, 1938). Furthermore, one who expects to be successful in influencing others will be more likely to attempt leadership. And members will be inclined to follow a particular leader whom they expect will achieve desired results (Bass, 1960). Hemphill, Pepinsky, Kaufman, and Lipetz (1956) showed that individuals are more likely to attempt interaction when the rewards and satisfaction they will receive for achieving success in working with others are greater. Consistent with this finding is Gerard's (1954) finding that if individuals are rewarded or avoid punishment through group activity and membership, they will increase their attempts to influence each other through interaction. In further support, Grossack (1954) contrasted the written communications of participants in

an experiment who were rewarded as a group with participants in groups who were rewarded as individuals. The participants who were rewarded as a group were more likely to send messages that attempted to influence others.

According to Good and Good's (1974) study of 48 undergraduates, one will be more inclined to want to lead in a group that one perceives is closer in attitudes to oneself and in which it should be easier to function as an effective leader. Hemphill, Pepinsky, Kaufman, and Lipetz (1957) studied groups whose members varied in their motivation to achieve their group goals and the members' expectations of success in achieving the goals. They found that group members attempt to lead more frequently when the rewards for mutual problem solving are relatively high and when there is a reasonable expectation that attempts to lead will result in contributions to task accomplishment.

At the same time, Banta and Nelson (1964) obtained results indicating that members' disagreements about who should lead decreased the attempts to lead. Unfavorable reactions to members' inactivity or attempts to lead also resulted in a reduction of subsequent attempts to lead and rejection of the members as leaders. Geier (1963) also studied the emergence and acceptance of leaders in successive stages of problem solving. Those members who were perceived to be uninformed, unparticipative, and rigid tended to be eliminated as potential leaders in the first stage. In the second stage, an intensive struggle for leadership was observed; contenders who were perceived to be authoritarian or offensive tended to be rejected.

Hemphill, Pepinsky, Shevitz, et al. (1954) demonstrated that attempts to lead depend on actual earlier success as a leader. In 16 groups, participants whose relevant knowledge helped to solve the group's problems were the members who exhibited initiative and attempted leadership of the group in subsequent trials. Conversely, participants whose knowledge hindered the group reduced their attempts to lead in subsequent trials.

Many additional different elements contributed to efforts to participate and attempt to lead. Hemphill (1961) summarized the results of four different experiments that were concerned with conditions under which group members will attempt to initiate acts of leadership and concluded that the following conditions facilitate attempts to lead: (1) the promise of large rewards for success in a task, (2) reasonable expectations of the successful completion of a task, (3) acceptance by others of one's attempts to lead, (4) tasks that require a high rate of group decision making, (5) possession of superior task-relevant information, and (6) previously acquired status as a group leader. This last condition was consistent with findings by Rock and Hay (1953) and Jackson (1953b), who observed in industrial field studies that members of a work group increased their participation when placed in the role of leader. It is not surprising to find strong associations between leadership and overall participation in the group's activities; members participate, to a considerable degree, if they have had previous successful experiences in influencing others to cope effectively with the group's problems (Hemphill & Pepinsky, 1955). And past contributors to a group's effective performance are more likely to become the acknowledged leaders of the group (Bunyi, 1982). The silent member usually has little influence on others in a group except as a possible threat to force the group to reconsider its deliberations if the silent member finally speaks out.

Talking and Leading

Schultz (1980) observed that in permanent groups, leaders emerged as a consequence of how well they fulfill various communication functions. Hollander (1978) noted that effective leadership depends on receiving, processing, retaining, and transmitting information, much of it through talking with others. Talking calls attention to the speaker. The sheer quantity of verbiage one emits increases the likelihood of emerging as a leader. But the quality of the talk also makes a difference.

Talking is a critical aspect of the performance of the appointed leader, as well as that of the emergent leader. As Stech (1983, p. 11) pointed out:

If a record is kept of activities on the job, the largest percentage of communication actions involve talking to other people—either face-to-face or over the telephone. . . . Written messages can be composed,

that is, mulled over, edited, revised, and thus carefully constructed. In responding to another person's messages orally, there is very little time to censor, modify, or edit. Reactions must be made in a matter of seconds (perhaps as little as one-tenth of a second). This implies that conversations are under less direct and immediate control. A subordinate's responses to a leader's messages are not always predictable, and the general tone and direction of the discussion depend upon both people. For this reason, inherent leadership style tendencies are likely to be seen more clearly by observing oral verbal behavior than reading memos or notes.

Even in so-called leaderless groups—self-managed production teams—Manz and Sims (1984) found that the informal team leader (whom they called the "unleader") relied heavily on frequent active communication with others.

Quantity of Talking

There seems to be a generalized rate of communicating in groups, rather than different rates for different aspects of the communication. For example, Bales, Strodtbeck, Mills, and Roseborough (1951) reported that if participants of a group are ranked in order of the total number of acts they initiate, they will also be ranked in the same order according to (1) the number of acts they receive, (2) the acts they address to specific individuals, and (3) the acts they address to the group as a whole. That is, the four types of talk will be positively correlated.

A convincing body of research indicates that the member who participates most actively in group activities that no one has been appointed or elected to lead is most likely to emerge as a leader. Research by Bass (1949, 1954a, 1955b, 1955c) on the leaderless group discussion indicated that the group member who talked most tended to emerge as a leader. The time spent talking in discussions correlated .65 to .96 with observers' ratings of a person's success as a leader.

When the measures of successful leadership were completely objective, success in leading a conference likewise was found to be strongly related to participation (Conference Research, 1950). Furthermore, Tryon (1939) reported correlations of .41, .31, .15, and .44 between talkativeness and leadership among adolescents. Goodenough (1930) and Chevaleva-Ianovskaia and Sylla (1929) found similar results in children. Confirming results were reported by Bales (1953), J. R. P. French (1950), and by many others.[1]

Consistent with these results, Chapple and Donald (1946) found executives to differ significantly from individuals in nonsupervisory positions in their rate of activity, quickness of response, speed of response when interrupted, and ability to speed up their rate of interaction in periods of interruption.

Finally, using Hemphill's (1954) definition of leadership as the initiation of structure in interaction, Bates (1952), Bass (1954a), Borgatta (1954), Berkowitz (1956b), and Riecken (1958) each reported results that indicated that the group member who emerges as a leader tends to exhibit a high rate of activity in initiating structure and in directing the activities of others. Likewise, Gronn's analysis (1983) showed that Australian school administrators accomplish their administrative purposes and adjust their controls mainly through talking with relevant others, which takes up much of their work day.

The 'Babble' Hypothesis

Bothered by these results, critics referred to the strong association between quantity of talk and leadership as evidence of a "babble" hypothesis of leadership. To emerge as a leader, they contended all that matters is how much one talks, not what one talks about. However, it should be kept in mind that in an initially leaderless discussion and in conferences, in general, members compete with each other for the group's attention. A "babbler" will be squelched by fellow members. The talking needs to be relevant to dealing with the group's task; the quality of the talk affects its quantity. Each group member's rate of talk is regulated by the other members of the group.

Regulation by Others of a Member's Rate of Talk.
Other members may increase a member's rate of talk merely because he or she may need to respond to nu-

merous questions from the others. Furthermore, as Olmsted (1954) and Talland (1957) found, groups tend to develop norms that regulate the length of time that is appropriate for members to talk. Talland suggested that the norm tends to reduce irrelevant loquacity. Olmstead observed that task-oriented groups differ from process-oriented groups in developing norms that permit longer speeches by members.

In a group where everyone tries to participate a great deal, each individual member's participation will be more limited than in a group where most other members talk infrequently. Borgatta and Bales (1953a) studied groups of nine men divided into subgroups, each with three members. The members of the subgroups rotated in different sessions until each of the nine men had worked with each of the others. In groups composed of all high participators, the members inhibited each others' interactions. Regardless of the members' characteristic performance in each of the groups, their rates of interaction were lower when the average rate of interaction of other members was higher. At the same time, each member revealed personal limitations, regardless of the group in which he happened to be. There seemed to be an upper bound on each individual's characteristic rate of interaction, no matter how much opportunity he had to participate in a particular subgroup.

Illustrating how one's attempts to lead are affected by the efforts of others, Bonjean (1966) observed that when a group of young, highly educated managers entered a predominantly rural community to staff a new firm, the established businessmen of the community tended to withdraw from community activities as the younger managers became increasingly active and influential.

Quantity versus Quality. The comparative importance to leadership of the quantity and quality of one's participation was examined by Sorrentino and Boutillier (1975), who planted trained confederates in problem-solving groups. The confederates varied their quantity and quality of verbal interaction. The confederates' quantity of verbal participation predicted their ability to lead and created a favorable impression about their motivation, perhaps because quantity is a clearer indication of a group member's intentions than is qual-

---

[1]Hurwitz, Zander, and Hymovitch (1953); Riecken (1958); Kirscht, Lodahl, and Haire (1959); Regula (1967); Burroughs and Jaffee (1969); Jaffee and Lucas (1969); Regula and Julian (1973); and Gintner and Linkskold (1975).

ity. But the quality of the confederates' verbal interaction predicted perceived differences among the other members on such variables as competence, influence, and contribution to the group's goals. Furthermore, according to McClintock (1963), a high rate of activity did not result in emergence as a group leader if the individual exhibited a large amount of negative affect and behavior that was detrimental to the group's movement. Ginter and Lindskold (1975) placed 72 female undergraduates in 4-person problem-solving groups to judge the quality of paintings. A confederate in each group was identified to the group as being either expert or inexpert. The confederates made expert or inexpert contributions, and talked either a lot or relatively little. Talking a lot increased the choice of the confederate as leader in the inexpert condition, but sheer talkativeness was not as important in emerging as a leader in the expert condition. Similar results were reported by Fiechtner and Krayer (1986) who experimentally varied leader-supplied information and found that its quality was more important than its quantity in relation to members' satisfaction with decisions. In an Australian study of 157 managers and graduate students, Bottger (1984) found that quantity of talk had more of an effect on the influence on others that was attributed to the participants, but the quality of the talk had more effect on the participants' actual influence.

Relevance. The relevance of the talk makes a difference. Salancik, Pfeffer, and Kelley (1978) showed that while communicating correlated with influence on purchasing decisions, the influential effect of the communication depended on its relevance. Communicating new information resulted in being most influential in decisions to purchase new equipment, communicating about needs resulted in being most influential in decisions to purchase additional equipment, and communicating about evaluating old equipment resulted in being most influential in decisions to replace old equipment.

Different Effects on Different Types of Leadership. Rates of talk correlate much more highly with task-oriented than with relations-oriented leadership. Stein and Heller (1979) analyzed 72 correlations re-

ported in the literature and found that the amount of verbal participation and leadership were much more likely to be highly correlated if task leadership rather than the maintenance of relationships was involved. The mean correlation of verbal participation with measures of task leadership was .69, whereas the mean correlation of verbal participation with maintenance leadership was .16.

The quality of talk becomes more important than the quantity for leadership that maintains relations.[2]

Time and Effort

Expenditures of Time

The sheer quantity or percentage of time spent in interaction and working with others seems to contribute to one's success as a leader. Thus, P. Miller (1953) found that of 250 high school principals, those spending more time in supervision and less in research and pupil affairs were rated as more adequate leaders. Studies of naval leadership revealed a correlation of .53 between nominations for success as leader and the number of times a naval officer was mentioned as one with whom others spent the most time getting work done (Shartle, Stogdill, & Campbell, 1949). Smith and Nystrom (1937) found that high school leaders devoted more time to extracurricular and leadership activities than did nonleaders. City political bosses were observed by Salter (1935) to be joiners, highly active in community groups. Similarly, Olmsted (1954) concluded that the more people participated in community activities, the more likely they were to be regarded as community leaders. Katz and Lazarsfeld (1955) noted that the opinion leaders—women most likely to influence personally the buying practices of others—were gregarious "joiners" with many friends. Again, in laboratory analyses of communication networks[3] Shaw and Gilchrist (1956) found a positive relation between the tendency to write letters to others and one's subsequent rank as a leader.

Thus, the data support the contention that participation and leadership are coincidental, both arising out

[2]More will be said about the quality of talk and interpersonal competence in Chapter 8.
[3]See Chapter 30.

of interpersonal interchanges that are directed toward achieving coordination and consensus. Yet, above and beyond the amount of participation, Burke (1974) suggested that leaders must maintain interpersonal control over participation.

Observed Behavioral Patterns of Attempted Leadership

Participation that contributes to leadership in both experimental and established groups includes such observed behavioral patterns as the initiation of spontaneity in groups, stimulation of a wide range of group actions, and the tendency to make others feel included in the group. As H. H. Jennings (1943) found in a study of leadership in a training school for girls, a leader, compared with average girls and isolates, actively protected and encouraged the weak, showed tactful consideration of others, inspired confidence, widened the field of participation for others, and established rapport quickly with a wide range of personalities.

Paraphrasing Yukl (1981), attempts to lead that contribute to one's emergence as a leader can include efforts to inspire others; to emphasize the importance of performing well; to display friendly, supportive behavior; to give praise and recognition to others for their accomplishments for the group; to point the way for members to achieve rewards; to encourage the sharing of ideas before decisions are reached; to clarify what needs to be done and who should do it; to set goals; to help train or coach others; to inform others about developments; to take the initiative in proposing solutions to problems; to prepare plans, schedules, and priorities; to coordinate and facilitate the work of others in the group and their interactions; to serve as the group's representative to other groups; to encourage the resolution of conflicts among members; and to criticize the poor performance of others.

Other researchers have identified similar behaviors. Some of the patterns for which the most evidence is available are initiation of spontaneity, widening boundaries, and acceptance of others.

Initiation of Spontaneity. H. H. Jennings (1943) observed that girl leaders, by virtue of their spontaneity, were valued because they stimulated spontaneity in

others. However, Newstetter, Feldstein, and Newcomb (1938) found that individual leadership attributed to a member in the group was determined more by the cordiality received from others than by cordial behavior toward others. Subsequently, Grosser, Polansky, and Lippitt (1951) and Bandura and Huston (1961) observed that group members act more spontaneously under a friendly than under an unfriendly or detached leader.

In a study of boys in a summer camp, Polansky, Lippitt, and Redl (1950a) found that members in high-prestige positions were more likely than others to act spontaneously in their groups and made more direct attempts to influence others. Their readiness to act spontaneously also resulted in their being more susceptible to behavioral contagion (being influenced without intention or awareness) than those of low prestige. Individuals who felt themselves lacking in prestige were more subject to contagion from others. Similar results were obtained by Lippitt, Polansky, Redl, and Rosen (1952) and by Lefkowitz, Blake, and Mouton (1955).

Widening Boundaries. Some but not all leaders have the competence to widen the range of actions by other members in the group. As was noted before, H. H. Jennings (1943) observed that the emergent leader tended to widen the field of participation for others. But Lippitt (1940) found that only democratic leaders tended to provide group members with freedom to make decisions and to act. J. R. P. French (1941) observed that group freedom was greater in organized than in unorganized groups. In addition, Cattell and Stice (1953) found that emergent leadership was associated with group unity, freedom to participate, influence, and interdependence. Results obtained by Gebel (1954) indicated that leaders differ from followers in their greater tolerance for "exposing the phenomenal field" and thus in providing for greater scope of action. Heslin and Dunphy (1964) and Reid (1970) suggested that members are more satisfied with a leader who provides freedom for participation, action, and expression of feeling.

Acceptance of Other Group Members. Again, some but not all leaders tend to make others feel included. Leaders identified by sociometric choice are characterized by a ready acceptance of other group members and, as was noted earlier, by protection of the weak and underchosen (H. H. Jennings, 1943). Ziller (1963, 1965a) found that leaders of effective groups differed from those of ineffective groups in being less severe in evaluating members who lacked the potential to achieve and in encouraging the development of those whose performance was marginal.

Bass (1967b) concluded, from a series of experiments and surveys, that task-oriented leaders, in comparison with self-oriented and interaction-oriented leaders, exhibited a relatively high tolerance for deviant opinions and conflicting ideas. Furthermore, several studies of conformity to norms suggested that leaders tend to be more tolerant of the deviate than are other group members. Similarly, A. R. Cohen (1958) found that high-status members who have consolidated their positions communicate more with low-status members than do leaders in unstable positions.

Other Observed Behavior. B. Schultz (1974) found that peer ratings of performance in five problem-solving sessions resulted in the following characteristics of leaders compared to nonleaders: giving directions, formulating goals, and being self-assured. Leaders were also rated lower than nonleaders on being more quarrelsome and less sensible. These characteristics of emergent leaders were assigned to them early and remained relatively consistent.

Summary and Conclusions

This chapter began by looking at how some personality traits, such as energy level and assertiveness, contribute to one's attempts to lead, participate, and interact. In turn, these attempts to lead are sustained by their positive consequences.

Group members who possess information that enables them to contribute more than other members to the solution of the group's task tend to emerge as leaders. However, a would-be leader who is overloaded with information may become handicapped.

Observational studies have identified several patterns of leader behavior that were not anticipated by the trait theorists. Emergent leaders in experimental and in natural groups tend to be valued because their spontaneity is contagious and they stimulate spontaneity in others. They widen the field of participation for others and expand the area of the group's freedom to make decisions and to act. They protect the weak and underchosen, encourage participation of less capable members, are tolerant of those who deviate, and accept a wide range of personalities of members.

As Block (1986) argued, leaders and managers need to empower themselves to shape their work environment. The simple fact that active, energetic, assertive people are more likely to influence the course of events around them and the "silent majority" are less likely to do so makes it difficult to accept the notion that leadership is a phantom of our imaginations. The data are compelling.

Leaders and managers need to be active, not passive. But merely being active is only a small part of the total explanation of who emerges and succeeds as a leader.

The immediately preceding chapters contained the seeds of two propositions: (1) to emerge as a leader, one must participate and (2) to remain acceptable to others as a leader, one must exhibit competence. This chapter reviewed theory and research about the first proposition and indicated how it needs to be qualified. The next two chapters deal with the second proposition and focus on how one's task and interpersonal competence affects one's success and effectiveness as a leader. Personal traits are important in explaining what happens, but antecendent conditions and the consequences of the attempts to lead are also important.

Task Competence and Leadership

Task competence and intelligence are important to leadership. But how and why?

The Meaning and Effects of Competence

Competence is the capability that a person brings to a situation. It may be a specific aptitude, ability, or knowledge that is relevant to meeting the requirements of the successful performance in a particular setting (Boyatzis, 1982). It may invoke a person's more generalized intelligence, which is of consequence to a broad spectrum of situations. Or it may concern a person's understanding of how to realign an entire organizational culture (Tichy & Ulrich, 1983).

Those who believe they have the competence to deal with the tasks (hereafter called task competence) facing the group will be likely to attempt leadership. If the others agree with them about who has the task competence, their attempts to lead will be successful. If the emergent leaders are actually task competent, as they and others believe, their leadership will be effective—that is, the group will attain its task objectives (Bass, 1960). If the would-be leader's opinion of his or her competence is not shared by the prospective followers, the unwise attempt to lead will fail. Michael Dukakis attempted to win the presidency. Although he believed he had the competence to be president, the majority of the electorate disagreed with him and failed to support his candidacy.

This contribution of the leader's task competence to the group's effectiveness has been given as one reason for the effectiveness of the technological innovations of Japanese organizations, in contrast to U.S. organizations. Although most tenth-grade Japanese students can solve simultaneous equations and graph the equations, far fewer U.S. university students are capable of

doing so. Japanese executives are more likely to have engineering degrees, whereas U.S. executives are more likely to have degrees in law or accounting (Tsurumi, 1983b).

The differences in the task competencies of such leaders as Robert F. Scott and Roald Amundsen go a long way to explain why Amundsen's team reached the South Pole first and returned in good order while Scott's team, although it managed with great struggle and fortitude to reach the pole, failed to survive the return trip. Amundsen knew, from his own experience in polar exploration and the experiences of others, that a small crew of men on skis, using sleds hauled by Greenland dog teams, offered the best chance of success. Scott, who had not profited from his own and Ernest Shackleton's past failures, tried to rely on Siberian ponies, motor sledges, and hauling by hand. Amundsen prepared for as many contingencies as he could; Scott, as on an earlier expedition, assumed the best and left little in reserve for emergencies (Huntford, 1984).

In distinguishing the transactional leader from the transformational leader, Downton (1973) noted that followers of the transactional leader are most willing to engage in "transacting goods" with the leader on the basis of their assessment that the leader can "grant them their most preferred choices." The leader's ability to do so requires task competence. As Downton (1973, p. 95) explained:

The greater a leader's competence as perceived by the follower, the greater the probability that the follower will transact goods with him. . . . We should expect the leader's information, skills, and personal temperament to be important factors influencing the formation and maintenance of follower commitments. . . . Competence to cope with the instrumental tasks of the group is an important criterion in selecting leaders, for it is through the leader's successful performance of his instrumental functions that rewards are accumulated by individual followers.

Hambrick and Mason (1984) observed that when the senior managers of organizations have entrepreneurial experience, the firms will engage in more innovation of products and expansion of markets. Also, when senior managers are more educated, innovation is more likely (Becker, 1970; Kimberly & Evanisko, 1981). Analyses by Child (1974) and by Hart and Mellons (1970) revealed that the younger a corporation's managers, the greater were the corporation's growth and volatility of sales and revenues. Profitability, however, was not affected.

In a study of over 1,500 senior managers in 129 large firms in eight countries, Heller and Wilpert (1981) reported that the managers' competence, as seen in their experience, qualifications, and skills, influenced the extent to which participative and democratic behavior occurred at other levels in their organizations. Nevertheless, such managerial competence tended to be underutilized, according the Heller and Wilpert.

Competence and Leadership

The quantity of participation forecasts a person's emergence as a leader because it is correlated with quality. Continued ignorant talk will not be reinforced or rejected by others. As was discussed in Chapter 6, Sorrentino and Boutillier (1975) and Gintner and Linkskold (1975) found that the "windbag" or compulsive talker who lacks interpersonal or task competence ultimately will fail in attempting to lead. Again, Hollander (1960) found that when a group is given tasks, its leader is usually evaluated with respect to his or her competence. This acknowledged competence builds up the leader's credit so the leader can subsequently depart from the group norms and move the group in novel ways, yet still be accepted by the group.

Task and Socioemotional Competence

As was noted in Chapter 5, the most frequently obtained leadership-skill factors tended to involve task or socioemotional performance. Thus, Hollander (1978)

observed that leadership competence included being a good facilitator, enabling others to make an effective contribution, having skill in handling the inner workings of the group, maintaining activities on a relatively smooth course, giving direction to activity, and acquainting followers with their roles in the main effort. The leader gives competent guidance to other group members concerning their jobs. He or she must be able to discriminate between good and bad work and to evaluate such work.

Limerick (1976) offered a rigorous way to sort leadership in small groups into performance influencing content and performance influencing process. Similarly, Dunphy (1963), in a study of adolescent peer groups in suburban areas, identified two mutually supportive roles—leader and sociocenter. The leader was influential in group activities, while the sociocenter relieved group tensions. Again, using Bales's method of observational ratings of the behaviors of actual leaders, Bales and Slater (1955) and Slater (1955) proposed that there are two types of leadership behaviors: socioemotional and task oriented.

As one rises in an organization, the task competence that is required changes from technical prowess to conceptual and abstract capabilities, as I will discuss shortly in more detail. But as will be covered in Chapter 8, the need for socioemotional competence remains much the same at all levels (Boyatzis, 1982).

Task Competence and Successful and Effective Leadership

The evidence continues to mount that generalized intelligence or mental ability is associated with a person's performance as a leader or manager. But the evidence also points to variations in the strength of the association for different situations. For example, Mandell (1950a) reported the following correlations between tested mental ability and performance as a civil service administrator: housing agency executives, .30 and .64; Veteran's Administration executives, .52; and Navy executives, .13. Again, traits that were checked on adjective checklists correlated respectively for 95 males and 98 females with their emergence as leaders in initially leaderless group discussions as follows: clear thinking, .38 and .43; clever, .49 and .54; and wise, .42 and .30 (Gough, 1988).

Intelligence and Leadership

Although intelligence generally is a positive indicator of competence, its creative component becomes more important for leadership at higher levels of management.

General Intelligence. Schmidt and Hunter (1977) introduced theory and method to support the validity of the same particular ability or trait for predicting performance across a wide variety of situations. They argued that much of the variations observed from one situation to another require correction for restriction in range and unreliability of the measurements. With this in mind, Cornwell (1983) and Lord, DeVader, and Alliger (1986) found from meta-analyses of the relationship that an even stronger conclusion could be reached than Stogdill's (1948) or Mann's (1959) about the importance of the personal trait of general intelligence to leadership. For instance, Lord, DeVader, and Alliger used the data from 18 studies, those reviewed by Mann in 1959, and others that were published subsequently through 1977. Both Cornwell (1983) and Lord, DeVader, and Alliger concluded from their meta-analysis, after adjusting the studies for different sample sizes and errors of measurement, that the true mean correlation of general intelligence and being perceived as a leader was .50 across the different situations. These samples included male and female students in high school, college, and graduate school; management trainees and military cadets; and managers and salesmen.

In addition to cross-sectional studies, there is support from longitudinal predictions. Ball (1938) found that intelligence measures yielding an initial .50 correlation with leadership increased to .75 over a ten-year period.

A follow-up of Terman's (1925) assessment of 1,000 gifted children reported that during their careers, the highly intelligent were far more likely than most to obtain leadership positions and to perform effectively in them, as indexed by such diverse criteria as admission to honorary societies and the acquisition of military medals. Howard and Bray (1988) noted the importance of initially tested intelligence to the success of managers in the careers at AT&T in 8- and 20-year follow-ups of the assessments of their accomplishments.

Creative Intelligence. General intelligence deals with how well one works with words, numbers, spatial orientation, and abstraction. According to Guilford (1967), there is also an independent factor of creative intelligence, which can be measured by such tests as those requiring the judgment of obvious consequences of actions and conditions and of remote consequences and asking for the generation of unusual uses of objects. As will be detailed more fully later, Rusmore (1984) showed that general intelligence is more important for success in lower-level management and creative intelligence is more important for success in higher-level management.

Technical Competence. Table 7.1 shows the level of management achieved after 20 years by college graduates and noncollege men in the AT&T Management

Table 7.1 Management Level Achieved After 20 Years of Employment at AT&T by 137 College Graduates and 129 Noncollege Graduates Hired into the First Level of Management

Management Level	Number		Percent	
	College	Noncollege	College	Noncollege
Sixth	3	0	2%	0%
Fifth	12	0	9%	0%
Fourth	27	4	20%	3%
Third	64	37	46%	29%
Second	27	61	20%	47%
First	4	27	3%	21%
TOTAL	137	129	100%	100%

Source: Adapted from Howard (1986).

Progress Study. College graduates clearly had the edge on promotion (Howard & Bray, 1989). Technical competence is expected in those appointed to positions of leadership. A sample of 12 nursing directors, 86 head nurses, and 267 staff nurses in 12 Egyptian hospitals agreed in their expectation that head nurses should have advanced education beyond the baccalaureate degree in clinical nursing and administration (Essa, 1983).

Many surveys document the importance of technical competence to a person's success and effectiveness as a leader. For instance, Penner, Malone, Coughlin, and Herz (1973) found that U.S. Army personnel were more satisfied with their officers and noncoms if they believed them to be technically competent. Farris (1971a) showed that among 117 professionals at the National Aeronautics and Space Administration, including 20 supervisors, those who were identified as the informal leaders in the informal organization were technically more competent and in more active contact with their colleagues. They were also more motivated by the technical aspects of their work, better rewarded, and more influential in their work.

Bass (1960) proposed that groups will be more effective if the hierarchy of influence in the group matches the members' abilities. Rohde (1954a, 1954b, 1954c) demonstrated this relationship in experimental groups in which members differed in their ability to perform a task. Rohde found that the group performed more effectively if the leader was qualified than if the leader was unqualified, regardless of the members' abilities and ideas. It was more difficult for an unqualified than for a qualified leader to retain control of the group, especially when the members were similar in ability.

The link between the technical competence of the leader and the effectiveness of the group was also seen by T. G. Walker (1976), who examined the leadership in state supreme courts. Walker found that when leaders were selected on the basis of their merit instead of their seniority, the courts generated less dissent with their rulings. Additional results reported by Jackson (1953b) and by Rock and Hay (1953) suggested that the emergence of leaders was not a matter of mere chance, unjust discrimination, or keeping the good person down. Both leaders and members appeared to recognize their comparative potential for advancing the purpose of their groups, and the groups were more effec-

tive if the leaders and members played the roles for which they were perceived to be best fitted.

Bugental (1964) found that participants who were trained in task-related skills emerged as leaders more often than did untrained participants. G. J. Palmer (1962a, 1962b) studied groups in which the members differed in their ability to perform tasks. Task ability was related to successful leadership (the successful influencing of the performance of others) and still more strongly to effective leadership (achieving the goals of the tasks). Hollander (1966) varied the characteristics of group leaders, including whether they were task competent or task incompetent, and found that leaders who were perceived by members to be task competent exerted significantly more influence than did those who were perceived to be task incompetent. Julian and Hollander (1966) reported that the willingness of group members to accept a leader's attempts to influence them depended on the leader's competence. However, Hollander and Julian (1970) found that a less-competent leader would continue to be tolerated if such a leader was seen to be highly motivated to perform the tasks of the group.

Hollander (1964) assigned an ambiguous task to groups. After a first trial, the groups were required to predict what would occur in the next trial. A planted confederate of the experimenter played a role of deviate from the group norms but was provided with the correct answers. The confederate's influence as a leader was measured by the number of trials in which the confederate's suggestion was accepted as the group's choice. Such influence increased as the trials progressed despite the confederate's violation of the group's norms. Thus, the members' perceptions of the confederate's ability influenced the confederate's emergence as a leader. Similarly, Goldman and Fraas (1965) assembled 32 student groups of four members each to solve discussion problems. The groups worked under four types of leadership: (1) leader appointed because of ability, (2) leader arbitrarily appointed, (3) leader elected by group members, and (4) no leader present. The groups worked best in situations in which they perceived the leader to have been correct in previous situations.

In surveys of 176 senior U.S. Army officers, 256 supervisors and managers, 23 educational administrators, and 45 professionals, Bass (1985a) found uniformly that subordinates who described their supervisor as intellectually stimulating also said they exerted extra effort, were more satisfied with their leader, and regarded him or her as more effective. The same findings appeared in data-feedback surveys in a variety of firms, such as IBM, Digital Equipment, General Electric, and Federal Express (Bass & Avolio, 1989). Superiors also thought that such intellectually stimulating supervisors and managers had greater leadership potential (Hater & Bass, 1988).

In a study of 95 employees of a nonprofit organization, Podsakoff, Todor, and Schuler (1983) showed that the expertise attributed to the leader was critical to whether the leader's instrumental and supportive behavior reduced the employee's role ambiguities. That is, ordinarily such considerations and structuring of the paths of employees to their goals would have been expected to clarify what employees needed to do to carry out their role arrangements. But when the employees did not perceive the leader as having expertise, their sense of role ambiguity could not be reduced.

Kemp (1983) analyzed 94 questionnaires and 20 interviews of senior industrial and military executives who were concerned with the development of high technology. It was found that successful projects were led by project managers who, among other things, fully understood the technology and the operational needs and could attract the support of professionally competent and experienced subordinates.

The Importance of Memory

Task competence takes many forms. Willner (1968) found that most of the world-class leaders she studied projected "the image of unusual mental attainments." Gandhi and Lenin were "genuine intellectuals," but most of the others were primarily action oriented. The majority displayed the ability to seize on information and ideas from many sources and to use their excellent memories to store and retrieve the information when they needed it.

Franklin Delano Roosevelt could soak up facts and ideas and impress coal miners with the details of their situation or business people with the complexities of their firms. He was constantly searching and storing information for use when he needed it. Likewise, Mussolini had a prodigious memory with which he could startle and impress others.

Repeatedly, general managers, senior officials, and chief executive officers are singled out for praise for practicing walk-around-management in which they can recognize individually a large number of their employees, call them by their first names, and remember small details about them.

Knowledge, Skills, and Abilities

Knowledge, such as how to evaluate a subordinate's performance; skill, such as how to prepare clear instructions; and ability, such as how to speak fluently, all may be involved in what a leader needs to help a group. In field studies with army combat squads who were performing a variety of field problems, Goodacre (1951); Greer, Galanter, and Nordlie (1954); and Havron and McGrath (1961) found that the characteristics of the squad leaders that were most highly associated with their unit's effectiveness included overall ability, knowledge of their jobs, and knowledge of their men.

Knowledge, skills, and abilities that are of consequence to leadership can be more fully detailed, given the multiple functions that may be involved in specific situations, such as serving as a prime minister, a general manager, a school principal, or a naval officer. Specific situations call for specific task competencies in the leader. Leaders with the specific competencies result in more effective groups. For instance, leaders of guidance groups that are made up of members with different kinds of problems must include among their competencies a great deal of flexibility (Hollander, 1978). At the same time, certain specialties provide an impetus to move individuals into positions of leadership. Almost half the members of the U.S. Congress are lawyers. Medical-school leadership tends to be in the hands of physicians who specialize in internal medicine; 42 percent of deans of medical schools in 1977 were so specialized (Wilson & McLaughlin, 1984).

To determine what distinguished the competencies of superior and average naval officers, Spencer (undated) and Winter (1978) identified officers' activities according to the motivation, skills, and activities that were required to carry them out. The information gathered could be applied to selection and training. An analysis of approximately 800 incidents of leadership and management performance among a cross-section of commissioned and noncommissioned naval officers identified 27 leadership and management competencies. The 27 competencies subsequently were grouped by factor analyses into five factors. Four of the five factors significantly predicted superior leadership and management performance in a new sample. These factors, which differentiated between superior and average leadership and management performance, were competence in achieving tasks, the skillful use of influence, management control, and advising and counseling.

Kaplan (1986) reported results of the content analysis of interviews with 25 general managers and executives who were asked to provide examples of effective and ineffective general managers. The respondents thought that effective general managers did better in strategic long-term thinking than in short-time crisis management and in communicating well. They judged the general managers to have more vision, a greater knowledge of business, and the ability to establish priorities. Similarly, Bryson and Kelley (1978) found that congressional leadership depends on a variety of competencies; personability, style, and skill, along with political "savvy," were deemed crucial in determining who becomes a congressional leader and who stays a leader. Clearly effective leaders need to be alert and sensitive to circumstances that suggest that a problem exists. Political leaders must be able to read the signals of discontent, of the seriousness of natural disasters, and of dangerous international currents. With the aid of their staffs, they must be able to diagnose properly the conditions of a problem so they can formulate appropriate policy responses (Tucker, 1981). This ability to diagnose the social and technical aspects of problems, to attribute causes accurately, and to identify the elements of consequence in a situation may depend, to a considerable degree, on intuition.

Intuition

Intuition is the ability to know directly without reasoning. It is an insight or a hunch. It is the experience of seeming to learn in one trial without much awareness of how we have learned what we know. Since it depends more on induction, intuition allows leaders to deal with complexity and limited rationality in the face of uncertainties and contributes to their innovative and creative abilities (Goldberg, 1983).

Barnard (1938) first called attention to the rational and the intuitive components of effective executive decisions. This work was carried forward and qualified by Simon (1947). Simon (1987) explained unconscious intuitive decision making, in contrast to conscious rational decision making, as being a consequence of the decision maker's myriad of earlier encounters with similar relevant circumstances. The acquisition of these many earlier experiences built up the relevent information that the decision maker could bring into play without awareness—the instantaneous flash of insight, intuitive feeling, or assured judgment. In support, Simon called attention to Bhaskar's (1978) demonstration that although experienced businessmen and novice business students reached the same conclusions about a business policy case, the businessmen did so much more quickly and intuitively. The novices were slower, more conscious, and more deliberate in their analyses.

In addition to explaining intuition in terms of relevant experiences, Simon (1987) noted that some of the limitations on the rationality of managerial decision making can be explained as the favoring of intuition over reason. Instead of rationally choosing between the lesser of two evils, managers will intuitively choose neither and delay making a decision. Unlike MBA students, experienced managers are likely to redefine problems on an in-basket test[1] rather than accept them as presented (Merron, Fisher, & Torbert, 1987). But the intuitive ability to recognize and diagnose quickly situations calling for remedial action is seen as being important to the effective decision making of managers. According to Litzinger and Schaefer (1986), effective managers achieve a balance between their analytical reasoning and their insight and spontaneity.

Agor (1986a, 1986b) surveyed several thousand managers in the public and private sectors. In comparison to lower-level managers, top managers indicated they were more likely to depend on intuition in making key decisions. But a follow-up of 200 of the most highly

[1]See glossary.

intuitive top managers reported that these managers mixed intuition with analytical reasoning in reaching key decisions. Intuition was most often brought into play in making decisions regarding uncertain situations, when little precedence existed, when facts and time were limited, when relevant variables were less predictable, and when several plausible possibilities could be entertained.

Bruce's (1986) in-depth interviews with chief executive officers (CEOs) of 11 large corporations established that the CEOs intuitively set the tone and direction for their firms. Although they had staff, senior management, and consultants to provide advice, the CEOs had to have the ability to make the important final strategic decisions by themselves. These intuitive decisions are difficult to articulate; as Simon (1987) suggested, they are likely to have been the consequence of the possession of a great deal of relevant information. The CEOs had a "tremendous reserve of knowledge about their companies" (p. 21). General George Patton replied to the accusation that he made snap decisions by saying:

I've been studying the art of war for forty-odd years . . . a surgeon who decides in the course of an operation to change its objective is not making a snap decision but one based on knowledge, experience and training.
. . . So am I.
—As quoted in Puryear (1971, p. 382)

CEOs use strategic planning to lay the foundation for convincing their boards of directors and senior management that their intuitively sensed direction for their firms is the right way to go. Justification for the plans are provided by logic and reason.

Closely allied to intuition are imagination, vision, and foresight. Imaginative ability was seen as being more important to Abraham Lincoln than intellectual brilliance (Hyman, 1954). Furthermore, this imagination is shown, according to Woodrow Wilson, in a president's capacity to predict the course of events, in the problems to which he calls national attention, in his sense of timing, in his appreciation of the gravity of the problem, and in the urgency he creates when he proposes a solution to it. Imagination is also shown in the way safety nets are built against misfortune and old forms are stretched to cover new functions without arousing excitement about a change.

Organizational Level and Required Task Competencies. McCall and Lombardo (1983) attributed the failure of executives when they were promoted to a higher level of management to limited task competencies; that is, the managers had competence that was suitable for one level but not for the next higher one. As McCall and Lombardo noted: "The charming-but-not-brilliant find that the job gets too big and problems too complex to get by on interpersonal skills" (p. 11). Cleveland (1985, p. 4) argued that managers need a broader range of competencies at higher levels: "Every person who seeks or assumes the role of executive leadership in an information-rich society must develop the aptitudes and attitudes of the generalist." Levinson's (1980) criteria for choosing chief executives include such task competencies as intelligence, good judgment, vigorous problem solving, articulate speech, and adaptability. According to the ratings of a questionnaire survey of 413 subjects just before the November 1984 presidential election, the presidential candidates fell far short of the level of competence that the respondents saw was required for the position (Butterfield & Powell, 1985). The public, aided and abetted by the media, seemed to be even more dissatisfied with the candidates in 1988. Both the public and the media appeared to be seeking the Great Man who was also completely technically competent and experienced.

For Jaques (1976), cognitive competence is the exercise of judgment within prescribed rules and regulations to achieve an objective. The time span of discretion in which a person works is measured by his or her assignment with the longest completion time. It increases systematically as one goes up the organizational ladder. The competence required to deal with cognitive complexity likewise increases systematically. Those who are unable to do so tend to view things as being black or white rather than as being in shades of gray. Moreover, they find it difficult to integrate conceptual data to develop original insightful or creative solutions to complex problems. The competence needed at higher levels of management to deal effectively with complex problems involves the ability to differentiate issues into their many shades, as well as to integrate the concepts involved (Harvey, Hunt, & Schroder, 1961).

At the first level of supervision, with a time frame of three months to one year, managers need to be able to reflect about the work done and articulate what is happening with an aggregate of tasks. They must be able to discriminate how situations make a difference in requirements.

At the next level, the departmental manager, with a time frame of one to two years, must be able to make trade-offs between carrying out current, known tasks and preparing for probable new ones. The departmental manager has to extrapolate from given rules (Stamp, 1981) and to fine-tune linear trends. Above this level, intuition begins to play an increasingly important role, as was already noted (Agor, 1986a, 1986b).

The general manager, with a time frame of two to five years, is the next level. He or she requires the cognitive competence to compare known systems to determine which may get the work done better. At the next higher level, the head of a smaller firm, with a time frame of five to ten years, deals with more cognitive complexity. He or she must make predictions about what the future may hold for the firm and how it should be planned for.

Still higher in level is the senior officer of a strategic division of a large corporation, with a time frame beyond 10 years. The senior officer must be able to impose on his or her world a cognitive ordering of what is deemed most relevant. Priorities must be kept effectively, and a friendly environment sustained. The senior officer also needs to have competence in networking with key individuals in many diverse fields. Finally, at the chief-executive level of a corporation, with a time frame of 20 years or more, the cognitive competence required includes managing a system to envision and carry out the development of a complex institution or to transform or divest such an institution (Jaques, 1976).

Klauss, Flanders, Fisher, and Carlson (1981a, 1981b) interviewed 31 senior federal executives whose colleagues had identified their "superior or exemplary" performance. These executives revealed a variety of higher-level task competencies. They were able to take a holistic systems view of and a strategic focus toward issues and situations. In critical incidents, they re-

vealed a proactive ability to anticipate events. In addition, they maintained a network of formal and informal contacts inside and outside their own agencies, which kept them informed about developments. Vansina (1988) observed some of these competencies in senior corporate executives. These executives were expected to deal with the interfaces of the company—its headquarters, business environment, and sociopolitical environment—in an integrated way and to "manage" all levels of their organization. They were also expected to be identified with the mission, purpose, or vision of the company; to see themselves as part of a system; and to use simple means to deal with the organization's complexities.

As noted earlier, Rusmore (1984) confirmed the extent to which organizational level made a difference in the requirements of task competence. When 208 executives in one firm were administered 7 mental abilities tests, two factors emerged: (1) general intelligence (based on tests of verbal, quantitative, and abstract reasoning) and (2) cognitive creativity (based on tests of obvious consequences, remote consequences, and unusual uses). Managers were classified as first-line supervisors, mid-level executives, and high-level executives. Mean factor scores ($\times$ 100) on general intelligence increased from -34 to 11 to 29 and on cognitive creativity from -34 to 17 to 24 with the increasing levels of managers in the organization. There was also a corresponding change in the correlations of each of the factors with the performance of the supervisors, middle managers, and higher-level executives. General intelligence contributed relatively more to the performance ratings of first-line supervisors than to those of high-level executives, and middle managers were in between in this regard. Conversely, cognitive creativity was relatively more important to the performance ratings of the high-level executives than to the first-line supervisors; again, results for the middle managers were in between. Further analyses reported by Rusmore and Baker (1987) showed that general intelligence declined in its correlation with managerial performance from .39 at the lowest level of management to .33 at the middle level. It was .19 for managers who were near the top and only .13 for the top-level executives. At the same time, creative intelligence increased in correlation with managerial performance for these four successive levels of management, as follows: −12, .19, .27, and .33. These findings occurred despite the fact that both general intelligence and cognitive creativity were higher among managers at the higher levels and lower among those at the lower levels. Similarly, Most (1988) reported that the scores of general line managers and administrators, as well as finance, insurance, and real estate managers on Guilford-Zimmerman (GZAS) tests of verbal comprehension and general reasoning were higher at successively higher levels of compensation.

Exclusive Possession of Task-Relevant Information

As was noted in Chapter 6, the possession of exclusive task-relevant information increases one's attempts to lead. It also provides one with an advantage in gaining leadership in a group. (However, an excess of information may operate as a disadvantage if it places a strain on the credulity of group members or makes the potential leader too superior to the other members.) Rudraswamy (1964) reported that participants who possessed task-relevant information exhibited a significantly higher rate of attempts to assume leadership than did uninformed subjects. Alford and Scoble (1968) found that less-educated, active leaders were better informed about community affairs than were higher educated nonleaders.

Bettin and Kennedy (1985) corroborated the importance of relevant information to successful leadership in a field study of 84 U.S. Army captains. Superiors' ratings of the captains' current performance as military officers correlated .26 with their total time in the military service but .41 with the relevance of their previous assignments to their current position.

In Chapter 6, I introduced evidence that showed that a group member's participation and attempts to lead a group were enhanced if the member had exclusive knowledge that was relevant to the group's reaching its goals. In a study by Hemphill, Pepinsky, Shevitz, et al. (1956), one member in each group was given information that would provide him or her with an advantage in the solution of the group's problem. Those who were given such special information scored significantly higher in their attempts to lead in assembly and construction tasks but not in discussion tasks. Shevitz

(1955), using construction and mathematical tasks, also found that the exclusive possession of information by a group member resulted in the member's making a greater number of attempts to lead, in the member's differentiating his or her position from that of the other members, and in the member's consolidation as the leader.

There are decided limitations on how important the possession of exclusive information will be to a member's emergence as a group's leader. Keller (1983) provided one member of three-person groups with exclusive information. The task involved using decision rules to admit applicants to graduate programs. The exclusive information had some influence on the group's decision. It had even more influence on the member's being seen as an expert, according to feedback that was given in one experimental condition.

Information Overload. When a member is overloaded with information, he or she can fail to lead effectively. Shaw and Penrod (1962) varied the amount of information provided to members of different groups. They found that the group's performance improved when moderate amounts of diverse information were given to individual members but it did not improve when these individuals received large amounts of such information. With large amounts of such information, the highly informed member's suggestions became implausible and unacceptable to the less-informed members. M. E. Shaw (1963a) obtained similar results in a comparison of groups in which one member was provided with either two units or six units of information. The specially informed member with two units of information entered the discussion earlier and initiated more task-oriented communication than did the rest of the members of that group, but the situation was reversed for the member who received six units. The informed member was named more often as a leader in the two-unit group than in the six-unit group. Evidently, six units of information became an overload that impeded the informed member's ability to lead.

Optimality of Intelligence and Competence

"A president or would-be president must be bright but not too bright, warm and accessible but not too folksy, down to earth but not pedestrian" (Cronin, 1980, p.

14). There is an optimal level for intelligence and competence. As was noted in Chapters 4 and 5, the leader cannot be too superior in intelligence to those to be led. The leader must be more able to solve the problems of the group, but not too much more able. In the same way, the previously cited work of Shaw and Penrod (1962) and M. E. Shaw (1963a) showed that prospective leaders could be given too much information as well as too little information for optimal performance.

A number of factors may militate against the "too superior" member becoming a leader. Communications and understanding may be made difficult by the intellectual disparity of the leader and followers. If he or she is vastly superior in competence, the would-be leader may no longer appreciate the group's problems or be concerned with helping to solve them. Rather than lead the group, he or she may withdraw from it. The ideas of the overly capable individual may call for too great a change in behavior by the group (Bass, 1960). Although the people who filled cabinet and other high governmental positions in the administration of John F. Kennedy were described as the "best and the brightest," Halberstam's (1983) study had to question why so many of their decisions and policies were later proved wrong. A lack of pragmatism in the very bright may be one reason.

Pragmatism. In a study of management students' abilities to set priorities properly, Gill (1983) concluded that the very bright spent too much time and put too heavy an emphasis on the exclusive use of logic and rationality in making their decisions. Those who were a bit lower in intelligence were more pragmatic. They could accept the fact that there were costs and limits to the search for alternatives and to their efforts to achieve completely logical solutions. If the brightest students had been more experienced, they might have been more willing to use less reasoning and more intuition in setting priorities.

Pondy (1983) and Weick (1983) considered such pragmatic thinking and action to be basic to the effectiveness of an executive. The ability to think and act incrementally characterizes successful executives, who must unite the intuitive and the rational and respond to behaviors, not intentions or preconceptions. These executives need to be ready to take actions, rather than depend on moving ahead solely by thinking about matters. In taking action, they need to pay close attention to what is happening and to take corrective steps as needed. They must be able to impose order and logic on situations when such order and logic do not exist to be able to interpret what happens consistently.

Moderators of the Effects of Task Competence

Task competence has its limitations in other ways. For example, Justis (1975) found that the competence of a leader had less of an impact on the performance of members when they were less dependent on the leader. The technical competence of a supervisor may be less important to the group's productivity if the supervisor consults with the members about decisions or allows them to share in the decision making. Thus, Reeder (1981) showed that for 78 clerks doing routine work and computer programmers doing nonroutine work for the U.S. Army in Germany, their supervisors' knowledge of their jobs was less causally related (according to path analyses) to the clerks' and the programmers' productivity than whether the supervisor was participative.

Election or Appointment. Election increases the demand for competence in a leader (Hollander, 1978). Hollander and Julian (1970) conducted a set of experiments that were concerned with competence and the election or appointment of a leader. Six hundred college students served as participants in various group discussion tasks. In the first experiment, the members' perceptions of the leaders' competence were more important than the manner in which the leaders gained office. In the second experiment, although only the leaders' competence was highly related to influence, the members tended to admit having been more influenced by elected than by appointed leaders. In the third experiment, the leaders were either elected or appointed to act as spokesmen for their groups. The elected incompetent leaders were rejected, regardless of the group's success or failure in the group's task, whereas the group's success increased the endorsement of the elected competent leaders. The acceptance or rejection of appointed competent leaders was unrelated to the effects of their group's success or failure, but incompetence resulted in rejection of the appointed leaders. Carter, Haythorn, Shriver, and Lanzetta (1951) also compared the performance of appointed and emergent leaders. Emergent leaders were more active then appointed leaders and tended to dominate the situation. Presumably, unlike the appointed leaders, they had to struggle for status.[2]

Relevence. Fundamental to situational analyses of leadership is the realization that the ability to solve the group's problems is a relative matter. An ability that is relevant to solving the problems of a group of farmers in Iowa may be irrelevant to solving the problems of a submarine crew, except to the extent that general intelligence may be important in both situations. As Bass (1960, pp. 174–175) noted:

A mathematician may be vastly superior to stevedores in the arithmetic of space, yet communication difficulties alone are likely to make it impossible for the math expert to supervise effectively the stevedores' loading of the hold of a ship. Similarly, the mathematician may successfully serve as a head of a mathematics department but remain inadequate to solve the problems of a department of agricultural statistics. Ability of a member to help a group must be considered in light of the group's problems. As J. F. Brown (1936) noted, the leader must be superior to other members in one or more characteristics relevant to the problems facing the group. And as Murphy (1941) concluded the choice of leader is dictated by the needs of the group.

Dubno (1963) observed that groups that required high-quality decisions did better with leaders who were slow to make decisions, while groups that were under pressure for speedy decisions were more effective with leaders who were fast decision makers. Similarly, Carter, Haythorn, Shriver, and Lanzetta (1951) found that the behavior of leaders differed according to the task of their groups. In groups that had a reasoning task, leaders asked for information or facts, but in groups with a mechanical-assembly task, they asked that things be done. In a discussion task, they asked for the expression of feelings or opinions.

Following his review of military leadership, W. O. Jenkins (1947) concluded that military leaders in a given field were superior to other members in skills that were pertinent to that field. To lead and earn esteem from skilled followers, it helps to be a master of the craft. Thus, in one of the early experiments on the relation of task ability to leadership, Carter and Nixon (1949a, 1949b) found that scores on mechanical tests were related to the emergence of a leader in groups performing mechanical tasks. On the other hand, scores on word-fluency and clerical-aptitude tests were correlated with the emergence of leaders in groups performing clerical tasks. However, no test of ability was uniquely related to the emergence of a leader in groups performing intellectual tasks.

Stein and Heller (1978) and Heller and Stein (1978) reviewed studies in which the group members' verbal interactions were categorized, through content analysis, according to the relevance of each of their statements to the ongoing group process. Emergent leaders were found to carry out a greater amount and variety of task-related behaviors than were nonleaders. Leaders were found to be significantly more active than were nonleaders in identifying problems; in proposing solutions to problems; in seeking information, opinions, or structure; in giving information or opinions; and in initiating procedures for the group's interaction or accomplishment of tasks.

Motivation, Stress, and Cognitive Resources. Fiedler and Leister (1977) developed a model to explain the limits of the contribution of a leader's intelligence to the task performance of a group. The model posits a series of screens of variable permeability that the leader's intellectual output must traverse before task performance can be affected. The screens are displayed in Figure 7.1. Leaders with greater intelligence will produce more task-effective groups if they are motivated and experienced, if there is little stress between them and their superiors, and if relations are good between them and their subordinates. A field study of 158 army-infantry squad leaders provided empirical support, as shown in Table 7.2. Thus, the intelligence and task performance of experienced squad leaders correlated .36, but they correlated only .15 for inexperienced leaders. Other correlations were .30 for motivated leaders, but only .14 for unmotivated ones; .40 for leaders who were not stressed by their superiors,

[2]See Chapter 15.

Figure 7.1. Schematic Representation of Multiple Screen Model

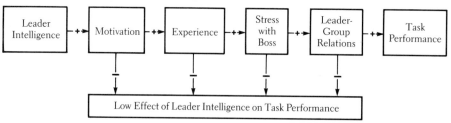

SOURCE: *Fiedler and Leister (1977a).*

but only .07 for stressed leaders; and .30 for the leaders who perceived that they had good relations with their subordinates, but only .15 for those who perceived they had poor relations. However, when leader-subordinate relations were evaluated by the subordinates, a reversal occurred. Good relations generated a correlation of .07 between the leader's intelligence and the group's performance, but .34 when the subordinates considered that the relations were poor. The model was supported subsequently in studies in the Coast Guard and elsewhere (Potter & Fiedler, 1981).

The effects of a leader's intelligence on group outcomes depends on what the leader does with his or her intelligence. For example, the correlation for 41 leaders in small volunteer public health teams in Honduras and Guatemala was close to zero between their tested intelligence and their team's performance, as rated by the project directors and their staffs. When the leaders were nondirective, shared leadership, or allowed a usurper to take charge, the correlations between the leaders' intelligence and their teams' performance were all negative; when the leaders were directive, their tested intelligence tended to correlate positively with their teams' performances (Fiedler, O'Brien, & Ilgen, 1969). Similarly, Blades (1976) found that in U.S. military samples, a leader's intelligence and technical

competence correlated with a group's performance only when the leader was directive. On the basis of these results, Fiedler's (1986) cognitive-resources-utilization theory of leadership specified the conditions under which the leader's intelligence and relevant task competencies would be effectively employed by the leader. The theory predicted that when leaders are directive, are not involved in conflict with their superiors, and enjoy the support of their followers, they will make most effective use of whatever cognitive resources they possess, and their groups will profit most from their direction. This theory is consistent with Plato's ideal of the philosopher king and with a demonstration by Bass, Flint, and Pryer (1957a) that a group will be more effective if there is a positive correlation between the leader's ability and the leader's influence on the group.

Other Contingencies. It would seem obvious that the more the group's task requires intellectual abilities for its effective completion, the more the leader's intelligence would be of importance to the group's success. However, such positive results were found to occur only if the leader was free of conflict with his superior. Where the leader was in stress because of the boss's meddling, the leader's intelligence was contraindicated

Table 7.2 Correlation of the Leader's Intelligence with Successful Performance of the Squad

Correlation	Condition	Correlation	Condition
.36	Experienced leader	.15	Inexperienced leader
.30	Motivated leader	.14	Unmotivated leader
.40	Unstressed leader	.07	Stressed leader
.30	Good relations with subordinates	.15	Poor relations with subordinates

SOURCE: Adapted from Potter and Fiedler (1981).

for bringing about the group's successful performance, the more the task had intellectual requirements (Blades, 1976). Thus, there is evidence that intelligence and competence must be combined with other contingent variables to produce successful and effective leadership.

Moment and Zaleznik (1963) used sociometric nominations to identify four sets of group members. The stars, who received many nominations, scored high in ideas and congeniality. Those who were selected as technical specialists were high in ideas and low in congeniality. Those who were chosen as social specialists were high in congeniality but low in ideas, and the generally underchosen were low in both ideas and congeniality. Stars were able to fuse the different leadership, task, and social demands made upon them and were the most participative, involved, and interdependent in their behavior. The technical specialists were the most independent and achievement oriented, participated least, and were unlikely to emerge as leaders. The social specialists were highest in interaction and were most dependent. The underchosen were most competitive and counterdependent but least interested. These results suggest that the perceived competence of a leader is highly related to the kind of role that he or she plays in a group. Similarly, according to Borgatta, Couch, and Bales (1954), who studied the same groups in repeated sessions, those participants with higher scores on intelligence tests tended to retain their leadership throughout the sessions if they also were sociometrically chosen as members with whom others enjoyed working. Groups that lacked such sustained leadership had a more inhibited response to the task situation, were tenser, withdrew more from active participation, and had less solidarity than groups that were continuously led by highly intelligent and highly acceptable leaders.

Summary and Conclusions

Task competence results in attempts to lead that are more likely to result in success for the leader, effectiveness for the group, and reinforcement of the tendencies. But, competence is relative, which suggests that a complete understanding of leader-group relations requires an examination not only of individual differences in competencies, such as in intelligence and experience, but of the relevance of the competencies for given situations. Intuition, which plays an important role in effective management and leadership, particularly at higher organizational levels, appears to be a consequence of the possession of relevant information based on experience.

On the one hand, the true correlation of intelligence with leadership is about .50 across a wide range of situations. Generally, more intelligent people are likely to be more task competent and emerge as leaders, regardless of the situation. Other personal characteristics also contribute to task competence and leadership in different situations. On the other hand, since the task requirements may vary from one situation to another, situational differences will also affect who emerges as a leader. Finally, other contingencies that moderate the competence-leadership relationship need to be considered. Task competence is not enough. Many bright, able, and technically proficient individuals fail as leaders because they lack interpersonal competence.

8

Interpersonal Competence
and Leadership

The traditional view of interpersonal competence emphasized the ability to socialize, to fit with group norms, to comply with authority, to avoid conflict, and to be polite and mannerly. A second meaning propounded by the human relations movement conceived of interpersonal competence as involving empathy, insight, heightened awareness, and the ability to give and receive feedback. Such competence implied an openness to discussions about one's feelings, consensual solutions to conflict, and the development of commitment to actions (Argyris, 1962). Managers with interpersonal competence were considered more willing to depend on trust and shared decision making than on power (Zaleznik, 1965b). It is the second meaning of interpersonal competence that will be accented here. A third meaning implying the competence to manipulate others will be considered here but looked at more fully in the next chapter.

Evidence of interpersonal competence has included a wide variety of behaviors, such as showing understanding, caring, and consideration for others; displaying authenticity, rather than transparency; communicating easily and clearly; fostering and maintaining good relations with others; and serving to increase harmony, reduce tensions, and resolve conflicts. Compared with incompetent managers, competent managers are influential but not dictatorial, good in dealing with people and in delegating, and trustworthy and credible rather than overly political (Kaplan, 1986). They promote group decisions, not to keep their subordinates happy but to take full advantage of their subordinates' knowledge and to increase their subordinates' commitment to the decisions (Lombardo, Ruderman, & McCauley, 1987).

Although an international sample of faster-climbing managers did not see as much value in being interper-

sonally competent as did managers whose advancement in their careers was slower, the faster climbers rated themselves higher in "understanding why I do what I do" than did the slower climbers (Bass, Burger, et al., 1979). According to Hall and Donnell (1979), who compared 1,884 managers who were either fast, medium, or slow in their career advancement, more rapid promotion was directly related to the self-rated ability to relate effectively with others. Similarly, Wolberg (1977) noted that the potential to be a group leader was directly linked to the ability to relate as a peer in role playing and to avoid immature "acting out" behavior during training.

Basic Interpersonal Skills

Everyday experience suggests that people differ in interpersonal competence. Yet beginning in 1920 with E. L. Thorndike (Thorndike & Stein, 1937), the effort to measure and thus be able to investigate interpersonal competence empirically has been difficult. Earlier researchers found it hard to discriminate social intelligence from general intelligence. But in 1980, Erez was able to assess the social intelligence of 45 Israeli managers and to show how it related to their tendency to be employee-centered rather than job-oriented leaders.

Empathic abilities have long been recognized as part of interpersonal competence, but as will be shown later in this chapter, the efforts to measure empathy have been fraught with difficulties (Dymond, 1949; Hogan, 1969). Virmani & Mathur (1984), conceived of "vivek," the cognitive ability to evaluate the implications of the attitudes, needs, desires, and intentions of others and oneself. Vivek, which is associated with effective leadership and management, is a fluid ability in that it can perceive complex relationships in human interactions in new environments.

The quality of one's verbal and nonverbal communication has been seen to contribute to one's overall interpersonal competence (Rosenthal, 1979b), along with the fear of negative evaluation (Watson & Friend, 1969) and apprehension about communication (McCroskey, 1977). Self-monitoring (Snyder, 1974) also may involve basic social skills (Lennox & Wolfe, 1984).

With support from a factor analysis of a lengthy self-report by 339 male and female undergraduates, Riggio (1986) found seven basic social skills to be of consequence: emotional expressivity ("I have been told that I have 'expressive' eyes), emotional sensitivity ("It is nearly impossible for people to hide their true feelings from me"), emotional control ("I am very good at maintaining a calm exterior, even when upset"), social expressivity ("I usually take the initiative and introduce myself to strangers"), social sensitivity ("While I was growing up, my parents were always stressing the importance of good manners"), social control ("I find it very easy to play different roles at different times"), and social manipulation ("If I really have to, I can 'use' other people to get what I want").

This chapter will discuss many of the interpersonal skills just mentioned in detail. However, social manipulation is covered in Chapter 9.

Competence in Communicating

In Chapter 6, I introduced the subject of one's quality of communication to point out that attempts and success in leading cannot be explained only by attention to one's quantity of communications. Being active as a communicator is not enough. This chapter extends the discussion by looking at the quality of communicating with others as an interpersonal competence. Although the quality of communication may also be a matter of task competence to some degree, it is one thing to know something but another thing to transfer the information to another individual and do so to the satisfaction of the other individual. A listener's acceptance of a message from a TV news anchorperson is likely to depend more on how the person looks and how the message is delivered than on the contents of the message. President Reagan was known as the "Great Communicator" more for the perceived sincerity in his delivery than for its accuracy.

Considerable evidence has accumulated to demonstrate the connections between competence in communicating and satisfactory performance as a leader and manager. For instance, from 200 interviews with successful corporate leaders, Kanter (1983) found that the leaders had a number of communication skills in common. They were constantly able to expand their thinking by their active soliciting of new ideas and feedback from others and were continuously reaching out for new information. Also, they knew how to persuade others about the quality of their ideas and had the ability to communicate persuasively to others and to enlist their support by persistently working for it.

Quality of Communications. The quality of one's talk does make a difference in one's success in emerging as a leader. Alpander's (1974) survey of 217 corporations to determine which training needs were the highest priorities for currently employed managers found that oral communication abilities rated the highest. Furthermore, Mold (1952) reported that 490 industrial supervisors stated that they needed the most development in "how to sell ideas to my superior." Consistent with this finding, Comrey, High, and Wilson (1955b) found that "high-producing" supervisors in the aircraft industry communicated effectively. And satisfaction with the effectiveness of officers and noncoms among over 30,000 U.S. Army personnel was strongly associated with their ability to communicate effectively with their subordinates, according to ratings by superiors and subordinates (Penner, Malone, Coughlin, & Herz, 1973).

In a field setting, Klimoski and Hayes (1980) clearly demonstrated the importance of the quality of communications over mere quantity. They surveyed 231 editorial subordinates and their 15 assistant managers who abstracted current technical publications. Among the supervisory behaviors noted were explicitness in giving instructions and frequency of communication about job-related matters. The managers' explicitness correlated significantly with the subordinates' expectations of success and reward in their jobs but frequency of communication did not. Explicitness correlated .57 with the subordinates' satisfaction with supervision, but frequency correlated only .19 with such satisfaction. The managers' explicitness correlated −.44 and −.30 with the subordinates' role ambiguity and role conflict, while frequency correlated .04 with each of these measures of problems in doing their jobs. The managers' explicitness contributed to their subordinates' self-rated effort; frequency did not.

Snyder and Morris (1984) were able to connect the quality of supervisors' communications in 12 offices of a social service agency with the quality of services rendered by the agencies and the lower costs of the operations. Colleagues used a reliable 4-item questionnaire that was based on previous work by Olmstead and Christensen to rate their supervisors on the quality of their communications. The overall quality of the supervisor as a communicator significantly contributed to the lower costs of operation, even after adjusting for the different numbers of clients served and the size of the different offices. Ward (1981) collected data from first-line supervisors in two manufacturing plants, three libraries, and two hospital nursing departments. The main concern was the supervisors' *rhetorical sensitivity*—their creative invention of effective discourse in writing and speaking. Ward found that the supervisors' rhetorical sensitivity correlated positively with the satisfaction of their subordinates.

Ability to Convey Meaning and to Enhance Retention. Getting across the meaning of a message is crucial and may require the development of innovative approaches. Not only do the feelings as well as the ideas in the message need to be communicated effectively (Bennis & Nanus, 1985), but messages have to be remembered. According to survey studies the messages sent by leaders that become memorable (become influential and remembered for a long time) are brief oral injunctions such as, "Work smarter, not harder" or "No matter what the other girls are doing, act like a lady" (Knapp, Stohl, & Reardon, 1981).

All 65 employees and managers of one firm interviewed by Stohl (1986) could recall such a memorable message. The messages were almost all single sentences and tended to be rules. The employees usually first heard the messages soon after they joined the firm and in a private one-to-one conversation. If an appropriate situation arose, the recipients said they would pass the message on in the same way. A majority of messages (in this organizational setting) dealt with one's role behavior and were applicable to various situations. One such message was, "If you're not helping, you're hindering."

These pithy memorable messages, usually from a sender of higher status to a recipient of lower status, provide sense-making structures and a guide to what behavior is appropriate in an organization. Memorable messages, content analyzed, provide information about the norms, values, expectations, rules, requirements, and rationality of an organization's culture. Clearly, the manager who includes such memorable messages in his or her communications is likely to have a much greater impact on subsequent events in the organization.

Consistency. Inconsistency of contributions may not be as deleterious as one might expect. Contrary to their hypothesis, Goldberg and Iverson (1965) found that the influence wielded by high-status members depended on their status, rather than on the consistency of their statements. They did not lose influence if they changed their opinions several times during a discussion.

Timing. The timing of participation makes a difference in the influence of the participation on other members (Leana, 1985). M. Smith (1935a) noted the importance of opportunity. He or she who succeeds as a leader may be but one of several who might have been just as successful had he or she been present to attempt leadership first. Hollander (1978) concluded that to emerge as a leader, one needs to participate early. But M. E. Shaw (1961) found that the group members who stated their opinions either early or late were better able to have their opinions accepted than those who stated their opinion in the middle of a discussion. Bass (1967a) experimented with groups of male managers in which the heads of the groups revealed their opinions at the beginning or end of a session, or not at all. The other group members were able to influence each other the most when the heads remained silent, but they exhibited greater coalescence around the heads when the heads revealed their opinions. Silent heads were most influenced by the other members and were most dissatisfied with their own final judgments.

Early presentation by the leader of his or her favorite

alternatives to group decisions foreclose other members' generation of additional alternatives (Maier & Sashkin, 1971). The search for alternatives is narrowed and the quality of the decision may suffer (Brillhart & Jochem, 1964). When leaders were trained by Maier and McRay (1972) to delay presenting their preferences, their groups were more productive in proposing high-quality alternatives.

Style. A number of studies focused attention on the consistent differences in managers' styles of communicating and the effects of these styles. Thus, replicating earlier work, McCroskey et al. (1981) showed that the communication style of upper managers and the immediate superiors of employees affected different aspects of their employees' satisfaction.

Klauss and Bass (1982) completed path analyses for the relationships among managers' communication styles, according to their supervisors, peers, and subordinates, in an information technology firm, a navy civilian agency, and a social service agency. Managers who were described as highly informative and trustworthy contributed considerably to their colleagues' role clarity, satisfaction with the managers, and evaluations of the effectiveness of the managers. Being seen as dynamic was of no consequence. In turn, trustworthiness or credibility tended to depend on being a careful listener, on being informal and open in two-way conversations. Informativeness tended to depend on being seen as a careful transmitter of information and using frank, open, and two-way communications. Similarly, St. John (1983) observed that the credibility of supervisors was enhanced by frankness, consistency, accessibility, keeping promises, accepting responsibility, personal style, and showing interest in others.

Luthans and Larsen (1986) directly observed the communication behavior of 120 managers from five organizational settings. They also gathered self-reports on how the managers communicated. Two dimensions emerged in analyses of the data. Consistent with the activity-leadership relationship discussed in Chapter 6, the first dimension was the extent to which the manager actively communicated and engaged in staffing and training activities, rather than remaining a passive isolate who was drawn into communication activities only when it was necessary to manage conflicts. The second dimension involved the extent to which a manager was informal, spontaneous, and oriented toward development, rather than formal and communicative mainly when controlling others with regularly scheduled monitoring activities.

Competence with Linguistic Forms. Drake and Moberg (1986) suggested that linguistic form may be more important than linguistic substance in affecting whether attempts to assume transactional leadership are accepted or rejected, that is, whether an exchange proposed by a superior to gain compliance from a subordinate will be accepted as such by the subordinate. Some forms can suppress the subordinate's tendency to calculate the costs and benefits of the exchange. For example, the subordinate may be "sedated." He or she may comply without thinking about the cost when told, "We've just got a last-minute rush order that needs to be filled before we leave tonight." (The semantically direct, "I want you to fill this rush order" might result in the employee's thinking about the cost of compliance and desiring an inducement for doing so.) Numerous other hints, prompts, teases, and semantic indirectness can serve to sedate the supervisee.

The leader can avoid responsibility for providing the inducements for compliance ("You may find it worthwhile to fix the oil gauge"). The leader's language can also be "palliative." For example, a staff manager, with no way of rewarding line employees for information she requires, may get the information by hedging. "This won't take long, but can you locate some good estimates of the prices for . . . ?"

Quality of Writing. The advent of electronic mail, when every employee is in instant contact with every other's personal computer terminal, suggests that the quality of writing will regain the status for distance communication that it had before the invention of the telephone. The storage and retrieval of transmitted information will also be greatly improved. Nonetheless, oral communication is likely to remain highly important.

Competence in Nonverbal Communication. Nonverbal communication is also important to leadership (Stein, 1975). For example, Remland (1984) demonstrated that superiors in videotaped interactions with subordinates would be seen as more considerate (and therefore more satisfying as leaders) if they used non-verbal means to reduce the status differences between themselves and their subordinates. Elsewhere, Remland (1981) pointed out that when nonverbal messages contradict verbal ones, the listener tends to trust the nonverbal message more than the verbal one. Thus, a manager who talks as if he or she wants to share in decision making with a subordinate but looks bored whenever the subordinate speaks, will be regarded as manipulative and insincere. And in investigating the effects of nonverbal and verbal communications among 151 college students on their perceptions of leadership, Gitter, Black, and Fishman (1975) concluded that nonverbal communications could be even more important than verbal ones.

Baird (1977) examined eight categories of nonverbal behavior in ten discussion groups of five students each. These categories included head agreement, head disagreement, eye contact, facial agreement, facial disagreement, postural shift, gesticulation of the shoulders or arms, and gesticulation of the hands or fingers. A significant relation was found, in particular, between perceived emergence as a leader and the tendency to gesticulate with one's shoulders or arms.

Friedman and Riggio (1981) examined the extent to which individuals differed in their nonverbal expressiveness and indicated that those who were more nonverbally expressive were more likely to influence the mood of those who were less nonverbally expressive. Such nonverbal expressiveness was also found to contribute to patients' satisfaction with the interpersonal manners of their physicians (Freedman, DiMatteo, & Taranta, 1980).

Promoting Individual Relationships in the Large Organization

Although interpersonal skills are important at every level of management in an organization, Jacobs and Jaques (1987) deduced different components of such skills that are required at different levels. At the lower production levels of the organization, managers must provide interpersonal feedback, try to create a supportive work atmosphere, "map" the interpersonal relations within the small work group and among work groups, and maintain equity within the work force.

They must also counsel and evaluate individuals and orient new personnel.

At the upper middle-management levels, interpersonal skills are required to build and maintain a consensus on objectives within the organization, to develop the capabilities of subordinates, and to begin the development of information networks that are essential for effectiveness. Organizational communication must be facilitated, along with a supportive environment. Personal problems of colleagues may need to be handled.

At the top, managers of systems need to be competent in their relations with outside agents, agencies, and the community. Again, they need to foster a climate that is supportive and motivating. Many executives at the top of the organization are able and willing to open and maintain interpersonal contacts all through their system. They practice management by "walking around" to meet employees—whatever their level in the organization—as they perform their tasks. Such one-on-one communications contribute substantially to the effectiveness of the organization and the satisfaction of employees (Peters & Austin, 1985).

Another tactic of top executives is to communicate directly with every employee in brief attention-grabbing notes. Admiral Elmo Zumwalt did so with his famous Z-grams to the various units under his command. Electronic mail, which instantly links every member of the organization with every other member, provides a ready opportunity for such contact between the top and the bottom levels of an organization. However, whether such one-on-one contact will enhance relationships will depend on whether overloading is avoided and the quality and interest of the messages remain high.

Klauss's (1981) study of 31 senior executives in government service found that a cluster of competencies, which involved sensitivity to individual and interpersonal dynamics, contributed to their effectiveness. When the effective executives spoke of critical incidents, they added to the technical or political aspects by clarifying information about the personalities involved and the human dynamics that influenced the situation. What was important to them was an understanding of the key actors involved—their general predispositions, biases, and orientations to given issues. The executives conveyed a sensitivity to the personal reactions and feelings of key officials who could be affected by or who could influence a course of action. Not only were they acutely aware of the personal and interpersonal factors that are important to each situation, they maintained informal networks to obtain insights into the predispositions and views of key higher-level officials.

Contact Time. How much time a manager believes should be spent interacting with subordinates may make a considerable difference in the effectiveness of the relationship. Whereas Speroff (1955) reported a correlation of $-.76$ between workers' satisfaction scores and the frequency of interviews between workers and plant managers, Klauss and Bass (1981) showed that greater communication between managerial and professional supervisors and their superiors, peers, and subordinates in various large organizations directly increased the judged trustworthiness of the focal person and, in turn, resulted in the greater satisfaction of colleagues with that person. Probably the most valid picture was provided by A. N. Turner (1955), who found that some personnel valued interaction because it signified a friendly relationship but that others preferred to be left alone and interpreted frequent interaction as interference and an indication of criticism.

Caring and Consideration

A sample of 97 first-line supervisors reported spending an average of 2.5 hours a week discussing personal problems—such as difficulties with co-workers; opportunities for advancement; dissatisfaction with their jobs; and financial, physical, family and emotional problems—with their subordinates. Some also mentioned problems with sex, alcohol, and drugs. The most common strategies of the supervisors were to offer support, to listen, and to ask questions. In these discussions, the subordinates and supervisors generated solutions and shared personal experiences (Kaplan & Cowen, 1981). From structural and factor analyses of the descriptions of helping behavior by 58 first-line supervisors and their 355 subordinates, Konovsky (1986) found one factor in the helping behavior of supervisors that involved offering support and sympathy and a second factor that involved assistance in problem solving.

Although better educated superiors were directly helpful, the supervisors' task competence and experience did not make any difference.

Consideration. Overall, the satisfaction of group members is enhanced when their leaders show that they care by demonstrating their consideration for their individual subordinates. Such consideration emerged early in factorial studies of the behavior of leaders (Fleishman, 1951) and has repeatedly appeared in subsequent analyses.[1]

Consideration can be seen in prosocial behavior, such as helping, sharing, donating, cooperating, and volunteering. Such behavior aims to produce and maintain the well-being and integrity of others. Leaders will manifest it by showing leniency in personnel decisions, practicing a considerate style, sacrificing their own interests, and spending time and energy for the good of the group or organization or the individuals within it (Brief & Motowidlo, 1986). The leader who displays prosocial behavior serves as a role model for a good organizational citizen who complies with the organization's requirements despite personal inconvenience, suggests improvements without personal benefit, and ignores hardships to carry on voluntarily (Smith, Organ, & Near, 1983). Thus, probation officers will have little effect on recidivism if they show empathic, warm regard for their cases but fail to demonstrate prosocial values and socially acceptable ways of achieving goals and do not model, encourage, and reinforce noncriminal alternatives (Ross & Gendreau, 1980).

Individuation. Within the immediate group, the interpersonally competent leader can individualize his or her relationships, avoid treating all subordinates alike (Meyer 1980), and discriminate between the more competent and less competent members in the group (Fiedler, 1964). Diffusion of responsibility in group decisions is avoided unless the group decisions serve useful purposes, such as gaining commitment from peripherally involved members. Equity is favored rather than equality; each member may be given equal opportunities, but rewards will be contingent on each individual's contribution to the group's success. Group pro-

[1]This will be discussed fully in Chapter 24.

ductivity is enhanced by such individuation (Ziller, 1964).

The interpersonally competent leader is oriented toward the individual development of his or her various subordinates, as well as the development of his or her team. Morse and Wagner (1978) showed that effective managerial behavior provided for the growth and development of both. Assignments are delegated to subordinates to provide such opportunities for development. Competent leaders take on responsibilities as mentors and coaches according to the differential needs of members for guidance and counseling.

For Bradford and Cohen (1984) the quintessence of "postheroic" transformational[2] managers is their orientation toward developing their subordinates. These managers build teams that share responsibility and visions of the future, as well as support the continuous development of individual skills. In so doing, they enhance the motivation, commitment, and performance of their subordinates. Individualized consideration was one of the transformational leadership factors which emerged from descriptions of leaders by their colleagues and subordinates using the Multifactor Leadership Questionnaire (Bass & Avolio, 1989). Individualized consideration involved showing concern for each subordinate as an individual and attending to the subordinate's development. The factor consistently correlated highly with subjective and objective measures of the leader's effectiveness (Bass, 1985; Hater & Bass, 1988; Yammarino & Bass, 1989).

Authenticity and Trust

Authenticity and trustworthiness are attributes that have been stressed frequently in theory and research on leadership. I have already noted the repeated appearance of "trust" as an important aspect of interpersonal communications. Again, in one of many such studies, Sgro, Worchel, Pence, and Orban (1980) obtained significant positive correlations between Rotter's Interpersonal Trust Orientation Scale for 41 cadet leaders and how satisfied their subordinates were with the leaders. The trust scores of their subordinates were related to positive evaluations of them on various

[2] The distinction between transformational and transactional leadership was introduced in Chapters 2 and 3 and its other factors discussed more fully in Chapter 12.

dimensions of behavior, such as consideration, tolerance for freedom, persuasion, and initiation of structure.

Smircich and Chesser (1981) constructed and evaluated a highly reliable standardized questionnaire for subordinates to use in describing their superiors. Convergent validity was demonstrated. The measure of authenticity dealt with existential aspects of the superior-subordinate relationship, for example, "My relationship with my superior is open and direct." It had sociological elements ("My superior shows flexibility in carrying out the role of supervisor"), empathic aspects ("My superior could step into my shoes and know how I feel"), and social-psychological issues ("When we talk, I know my superior really listens to me"). However, authenticity did not necessarily mean mutual understanding between superiors and subordinates, for the authenticity that was attributed to the superiors was of no consequence for 141 subordinates and 58 superiors in altering their lack of agreement about their ratings of the subordinates' performance.

Ability to Handle Conflict

Among the six factors that identified the effective manager, Morse and Wagner (1978) found one that involved the ability to deal with conflict among colleagues and associates and to avoid continuing conflicts that got in the way of completing assignments. Walton (1972) noted that effectiveness as a leader was associated with the ability to convert conflicts of interests among subordinates and colleagues into accommodations, conciliations, compromises, and, better yet, consensual agreements. Effective leaders did not run away from conflict nor try to deal with it arbitrarily (Walton, 1972).

Transformational leaders, in contrast with transactional leaders, seem to have more ability to deal with conflict. They are less readily disturbed by it, possibly because they are "more at peace with themselves." Gibbons (1986) reached this conclusion on the basis of in-depth interviews with 16 senior executives in a high-technology firm identified as transformational or transactional by peer nominations and by subordinates' descriptions of them on the Multifactor Leadership Questionnaire (Bass & Avolio, 1989).

Social Insight, Empathy, and Leadership

Leadership of a group depends, to some extent, on the leader's ability and motivation to estimate accurately the group's attitudes, motives, and current level of effectiveness. As Bass (1960, pp. 167–168) indicated:

It is not enough for a leader to know how to get what followers want, or to tell them how to get what they want. The leader must be able to know what followers want, when they want it, and what prevents them from getting what they want. . . .

Empathic success should increase with increased motivation to attend to clues. It should also increase with information available about others' behavior. Two persons may display the same success in guessing the motives of some other members. One estimator may be more apt; the other estimator may be more interested in the question because of momentary situational demands or acquired motives. . . . An alert teacher "senses" from facial expressions, questions or lack of them, restlessness, and lack of response whether he [or she] is continuing to meet the needs of the student audience. An effective orator or actor requires similar skills.

Many others have offered similar propositions. Wittenberg (1951) emphasized the need-estimating aspect of leadership. That is, the leader must know what the individual members need and then employ the group process so the members will satisfy these needs. Coyle (1948) suggested that to work with youths, group leaders must understand the various motives that draw the group together to "find the appropriate form to clothe their collective needs." For political and organizational leadership, Titus (1950) and J. M. Burns (1978) noted that the leader must be able to choose the group's objectives wisely and forecast the cost of obtaining the objectives, the likelihood of doing so, and the degree to which goal attainment will be satisfying to the members.

Lane (1985) moved matters further by suggesting that managers should examine their ability to be followers so that they can better understand the feelings and problems of their subordinates. Managers can do so by examining their own role as followers with different bosses. Leaders should appreciate whether their subordinates learn from them and whether their subordinates are comfortable sharing problems and confidences with them. They also need to know their subordinates' strengths and weaknesses. In the same vein, Haislip (1986) saw that a leader needs to be sensitive to those aspects of the work experience that illustrate how the organization values its employees' personal goals. Such sensitivity will keep the leader focused on helping to maintain the congruence of the goals of the employees and the organization and, thereby, the employees' commitment.

It is expected that leaders will be more insightful. Thus, Shartle, Stogdill, and Campbell (1949) found that nominations for "Popular Leader" were correlated .47 with predictions of "who will be most accurate in estimating group opinion." In a study of 153 supervisors in seven organizations, E. J. Frank (1973) observed that leaders who perceived their roles to require sensitivity to others also perceived themselves as being sensitive. Along with this felt sensitivity, the leaders appeared to feel that they were openly accepted by the group and that the working environment was pleasant. Alertness to changing circumstances and shifts in needs is also considered to be important to leadership (Hollander, 1978).

In all, from the early studies on, it has been thought that insight and empathy give the individual the competence to gain, hold, and maintain the position of leader. In traditional Japan, the head of a group ostensibly made the group's decisions, and once the leader made the decision, it was regarded as the "will of the group" and accepted without challenge. But if one looked more carefully, one saw that the leader had the responsibility to sense the will of the group in order to understand what was wanted, both intellectually and emotionally. He had to *hara de wakaru* or "understand with his belly" (Kerlinger, 1951). It appears that this is still required of the Japanese manager.[3]

Insight, Empathy, and Transactional and Transformational Leadership

Insight and empathic competence should be important if the leader is transactional[4] and engages in an ex-

---

[3]See Chapter 34.
[4]See note 2 and Chapters 17 and 19.

change relationship with followers. The leader needs to learn what the followers want so he or she can make the right offers to them for their compliance. But the transformational leader also can build from a stronger base if he or she understands the current interactions of prospective followers. The individually considerate transformational leader must have a sense of his or her followers' developmental needs and how the followers' current wishes differ from each other. The inspirational leader has a sense of which appeals will be heard most readily by followers. Since followers identify with charismatic leaders, the leaders should be able to be insightful about their followers' interests to the extent to which the leaders understand themselves.

Problems with Insight and Empathy

Despite the importance with which insight and empathy have been regarded, the empirical evidence of the association of these personal traits with leadership is often hard to establish. In comparison to others, the data suggest that leaders do not appear to exhibit a higher degree of generalized insight into the feelings or motivation of followers. Furthermore, a variety of measurement problems complicate the conclusions and many contingencies force the qualification of results. However, considerable positive evidence has been amassed about the insight of leaders into the feelings of their *immediate* followers and an understanding of the localized situation. Often, many contingencies force qualification of the results and a variety of measurement problems further complicates the outcomes.

In the most general sense, *empathy* refers to the awareness or appreciation and *insight* refers to understanding of what others are thinking and feeling about a matter. Empathy is "the ability to walk around in someone else's world" (Kilcourse, 1985, p. 23). Insight and empathy may be a matter of seeing others in relation to ourselves. But the linkages of empathic ability and social insight to leadership are complicated by the various definitions and ways of measuring empathy and insight.

Generalized Social Insight and Empathy

Empathy and insight can refer either to awareness and understanding of social phenomena at a general level (knowledge of cultural norms and social intelligence) or

to understanding of the most probable tendencies of prototypical others. History is replete with examples of political leaders whose success depended on their accurate sensing of the moods and desires of their constituencies.

Various researchers have developed measures of social insight and empathy at this general level. These measures require participants to estimate the percentage of people in a designated population who will endorse the items on a test of personality, attitudes, or job satisfaction. The participants' accuracy is measured by how well their estimates match the actual endorsement by a sample of the population.

Mixed Findings. Chowdhry and Newcomb (1952), Bell and Hall (1954), Nagle (1954), Trapp (1955), and Fleishman and Salter (1963) found that leaders were more accurate than nonleaders in estimating such responses in a general population. Kerr and Speroff (1951) and Van Zelst (1952) were able to forecast success as a salesman, union leader, and foreman with a brief test that purported to measure individual differences in empathic ability at the general level by the method just described. However, Sprunger (1949), Hites and Campbell (1950); Gage and Exline (1953); Talland (1954); Bugental and Lehner (1958); and Cohn, Fisher, and Brown (1961) did not find leaders to be significantly more accurate than nonleaders in such tested estimations. Along the same lines, Marchetti (1953) obtained no relation between grocery managers' ability to predict employees' responses on a test of attitudes in general and the managers' rated efficiency by their superiors. Finally, Shartle, Stogdill, and Campbell (1949) reported a slight negative relation between naval officers' popularity as leaders and their tested ability to estimate group opinion in general. Thus, decidedly mixed results have been found for the relations between generalized social insight, generalized empathy, and leadership.

It is even questionable whether generalized empathy exists. Although Cline and Richards (1960, 1961) found low but significant correlations between a variety of different measures of ability to judge the behavior of other persons, Ausubel and Schiff (1955), Bender and Hastorf (1950), and Crow and Hammond (1957) found no support for the hypothesis that there is an ability to predict interpersonal responses in general. For one thing, education, experience, and general intelligence are likely to affect respondents' performance on measures of generalized empathy and insight.

Localized Social Insight and Empathy

Different from generalized insight and empathy are specific perceptual sensitivities at a local level—in a designated group working with specific other members. A considerable array of positive findings supports Stogdill's (1948) conclusion in Chapter 4 that "alertness to the surrounding environment and understanding of 'social' situations are intimately associated with leadership ability." The ability to size up situations differentiated leaders from followers in six pre-1948 studies. Carter, Haythorn, Shriver, and Lanzetta (1951) also found that leaders were able to evaluate situations. Insight into motives, thoughts, feelings, and actions of others was found to characterize leaders in seven pre-1948 studies.

Empirical Support. Reviews of the literature on localized social insight and empathy generally affirmed the empathy-leadership connection, although they found that the effects were small and may have been nonexistent or negative in many cases.[5] Thus, for example, after surveying 15 studies that reported 101 results concerning leadership and empathy, R. D. Mann (1959) noted that 74 percent of the results were positive but researchers usually were unable to obtain statistically significant positive results in any single investigation.[6] To illustrate, Williams and Leavitt (1947a, 1947b); G. H. Green (1948); Greer, Galanter, and Nordlie (1954); and Lansing (1957) used sociometric nominations as a basis for studying insight. Group members were asked to nominate other members for leadership and to estimate the ranking that others would ascribe to them. Leaders were found to be more accurate than nonleaders in estimating their own sociometric rank (their esteem or value to the group in the eyes of the other members) or, in some studies, the rank of others.

Gallo and McClintock (1962) also found that leaders were more accurate than nonleaders in perceiving their esteem in the group. Furthermore, Fiedler's (1967a) theory of leadership[7] was first formulated around the linkage of empathy to leadership, and assumed similarity to others was the main measure of consequence. In studies of basketball teams and surveying teams, Fiedler (1953a, 1953b, 1954a) found that the teams were more effective if their esteemed members, who were likely to be the team leaders, perceived preferred members to differ from rejected members. Fiedler (1954b, 1955, 1959) obtained similar findings for B-29 bomber crews, tank crews, and groups in open-hearth steel shops. The groups were more effective if the crew leader or foreman discriminated more distinctly between members with whom he preferred to work and members whom he rejected.

Nagle (1954) reported high correlations between departmental productivity and the ability of departmental supervisors to estimate employees' attitudes. Anderhalter, Wilkins, and Rigby (1952) noted that candidates for the U.S. Marines Officers Candidate School who showed the highest ability to predict other candidates' future effectiveness were likely to make effective company officers themselves. Greer, Galanter, and Nordlie (1954) found leaders of infantry squads to be more accurate than other squad members in their perceptions of the esteem of other members. Schrage (1965) reported that accurate perception and interpretation of the environment were more important than the motivation for power or the need for achievement in differentiating successful from unsuccessful entrepreneurs. Finally, Jennings (1952a) showed that supervisors who did not understand the behavior of their subordinates felt inadequate and insecure; as their frustration increased, they became less able to obtain cooperation and satisfactory performance from their subordinates.

Negative Results. On the basis of a survey of managers and their subordinates, Hatch (1962) concluded that the empathic accuracy of the managers had limited practical significance. He found no significant differences between the empathic accuracy of the managers and the superiors' description of the managers as good or poor in maintaining satisfactory relations with their subordinates. Similarly, Jerdee (1964) reported

---

[5]Reviews were presented by D. T. Campbell (1955), Crow (1957a, 1957b), Hatch (1962), Kerr and Speroff (1951), R. D. Mann (1959), H. C. Smith (1966), Strunk (1957), Bronfenbrenner, Harding, and Gallwey (1958), Cline and Richards (1963), W. F. O'Connor (1963), and Shrauger and Altrocchi (1964).

[6]Meta-analysis would confirm the strength of the actual relationship.

[7]See Chapter 23.

that supervisors' predictions of subordinates' morale were negatively related to the employees' actual scores on morale. Andrews and Farris (1967) noted that subordinates' innovation was correlated negatively with their supervisors' effectiveness in planning if the supervisors were sensitive to individual differences, but the correlation was positive if the supervisors were insensitive to differences among people. Williams and Leavitt (1947a) observed that the more successful leaders they studied most underestimated the sociometric status accorded them by other group members. Finally, Shartle, Stogdill, and Campbell (1949) found that nominations for popular leaders were not correlated with error in estimating group opinion. Likewise, such errors scores failed to correlate with predictions of who would be most accurate. Popular leaders were not more accurate than unpopular leaders in estimating group opinion, although other group members expected them to be so.

Situational Contingencies

More often than not, positive or negative results have to be qualified by conditions. Only under particular situational circumstances is one likely to find that the leader was more insightful or empathic than the nonleader. Some of these variations in outcomes, of course, may be found to be due to random error when subjected to a meta-analysis.

Substance of Judgments. Foa (1960) found that workers' predictions of their foremen's responses to a projective (picture) test were more accurate when the foremen described the action in the ambiguous picture as positive and focused on the job rather than on interpersonal relations. Holmes (1969) compared leaders' estimates of the frequency of interaction and duration of speech of group members with recordings of the groups' performance. Leaders evaluated the duration of behavior by followers more accurately than the frequency of the behavior.

Relevance. Chowdhry and Newcomb (1952) found that leaders tended to judge group opinion better than do nonleaders or isolates, but the superiority of leaders over nonleaders was restricted mainly to issues that were relevant to the specific groups of which they were leaders. When matters concerned groups in which they

were not leaders, their superiority tended to disappear. Similarly, Northwood (1953) collected facts and opinions from a sample of residents in a housing project. Office holders were found to be significantly more accurate than informal (sociometrically nominated) leaders and followers as judges of fact and opinion (group norms); they were not superior judges of nonrelevant scores, however. Greer, Galanter, and Nordlie (1954) emphasized this type of contingent outcome, suggesting that they obtained positive results, whereas others, such as Hites and Campbell (1950), did not because the leaders in the inquiry by Greer, Galanter, and Nordlie were asked to estimate matters that were more relevant to the members' goals.

Cohesiveness. Since cohesive groups usually involve considerable mutuality of choice among their high-status members, the leadership clique was expected to exhibit higher accuracy about others in the group than the members of lower status. Exline (1960) assigned members to high- or low-congeniality groups to discuss a task and measured the members' accuracy of knowledge of each other's task-relevant and person-relevant opinions. Exline found that the leaders were more accurate judges of person-relevant opinions, such as popularity, only in cohesive groups. Lemann and Solomon (1952) also found that the accuracy of interpersonal perception was higher in cohesive groups than in uncohesive groups.

Familiarity. Studies of newly formed groups obtained negative results when they correlated a member's first impressions of others with the member's initial success as a leader (G. B. Bell, 1951; H. E. Hall, 1953). Hatch (1962) found that only if managers felt that they were well acquainted with a subordinate were they able to predict accurately the subordinate's attitudes beyond what would be predicted by chance.

The familiarity of members in a specific group was found to be directly related to the members' accuracy in judging each other's life goals. Filella (1971) divided 32 Indian college students who were together in summer school for 3 weeks into 4 groups of 8 members each. Members of each group were first asked to rank their own 11 life goals (to provide a criterion) and then to rank the life goals of each of the other group members, beginning with the person they felt they knew best, then the person they felt they knew second best, and so on, down to the person they felt they knew least. The mean correlations between estimators and the actual self-ranking systematically declined with decreasing familiarity, as follows:

	Most Familiar						Least Familiar
Order of familiarity of raters with the ratee	1	2	3	4	5	6	7
Mean accuracy of raters about the ratee	.54	.48	.43	.27	.21	.19	.12

Lupfer (1965) recorded group members' interactions in a business game. At the end of each session, each subject indicated, on a questionnaire, a prediction of and prescription for the behavior of every other member. As the sessions progressed, the members' role behavior tended to conform to prescriptive norms, and the prediction of behavior increased in accuracy.

In a reversal of these findings, Browne and Shore (1956) noted that although second-level departmental managers were less close to operating employees than were the foremen, the managers were somewhat more accurate than were the foremen in predicting the employees' attitudes.

Focused Attention. Lundy (1956) administered a scale of values to 52 students who later met in pairs to discuss a problem. Then each partner predicted the responses of the other, using the value scale, both with attention focused on the self and with attention focused on the partner. Lundy found that focusing attention on the partner increased the accuracy in predicting the partner's responses.

Assumed and Actual Similarity. Localized social insight and empathy often present a multiple measurement problem. Bass, Burger, et al. (1979) employed a model that was first formulated by Cronbach and Glaser (1953) to study managers' ability to judge the life goals of specific other managers with whom they had been working in small exercise groups for several days. The procedure was as follows: Participants ranked each of 11 life goals in order of importance to them. Then they ranked the goals in order of importance to each of the other members of their exercise group.

Three correlational indexes were calculated as being important to the discussion here:

1. Empathy or accuracy in judging others—the correlation between a participant's judgments about other members' life goals and the other members' self-judgments. (This assumed that participants generally had an accurate appreciation of their own goals.)
2. Projection or assumed similarity to others—the correlation between the ranking participants assigned to themselves and those they assigned to everyone else in the group.
3. Actual similarity to others—the correlation of a participant's self-ratings with the self-ratings of each of the other members. For the group as a whole, this is an index of the group's homogeneity.

In addition to the scoring biases pointed out by D. T. Campbell (1955), studies of empathy at the local level are also likely to suffer from the generalized tendency of judges to assume that they are similar to others. Thus, for 1,026 managers in 12 countries, Bass, Burger, et al. found that assumed similarity (the correlation of one's ratings with judgments of others' ratings) averaged .50. But true similarity or homogeneity, evidenced by the average correlation of self-rating among all participants, was only .21. Likewise, Lazar (1953), after a review of eight studies, concluded that in judging the attitudes of groups, people err in the direction of their own beliefs or opinions.

The amount of actual similarity or homogeneity also affected what kinds of outcomes were obtained by Bass, Burger, et al. This finding was consistent with Notcutt and Silva's (1951) study, which found that the smaller the difference between *actual* self-descriptions and others' self-descriptions, the smaller the error when pairs of persons predicted each other's responses.

Thus, it follows, both rationally and empirically, that we can be more accurate about others who happen to be like us because of the general tendency to assume that others are indeed like us. A leader's accuracy may be accounted for by the bias toward assumed similarity and the homogeneity of the leader and the group. In fact, to be a leader of a group, one must usually share many attitudes, values, and goals with the other members (Cartwright, 1951). By definition, the opinions of group members are more strongly influenced by the leaders of the group than by nonleaders. It follows that the forecasts of group opinion made by leaders will be more accurate than will estimates made by nonleaders, since the opinions are close to those held by the leaders. Thus, when leadership was defined in terms of influence on the group decision, Talland (1954) demonstrated that leaders are better estimators of final group opinion because it was closer to their own initial opinion. But leaders are not more accurate in estimating opinion before interaction. These confoundings of measurements need to be kept in mind when one considers the correlations obtained between leadership and localized measures of empathy and insight.

Organizational Considerations. E. L. Scott (1956) analyzed the organizational charts drawn by 696 officers and men aboard 10 submarines in which the status structure was thought to be well defined. He found marked differences in the accuracy of status perceptions of the men on the various ships and among the men in the various departments within the same ship. The most frequent type of error was to perceive superiors as peers, peers as subordinates, and persons outside one's department as subordinates in one's department. High-ranking personnel made fewer errors in their perception of superiors and peers, but not in total. The more widely superiors interacted with other persons, the greater was the perceptual error of their subordinates. The greater the disparity between an officer's rank and the level of his position aboard ship, the greater were the perceptual errors of his subordinates. At the same time, the subordinates were able to perceive status relationships more accurately when their superiors retained authority and delegated less. Scott's study pointed to some potent organizational factors that operate to determine the accuracy with which status is perceived in highly structured situations.

Summary and Conclusions

Interpersonal competence is fundamental to successful and effective leadership. What may by involved are the ability to communicate, the willingness and ability to promote individual relationships with others, authenticity, caring, the ability to handle conflict, and insight and empathy. Particular attention has been paid to the extent to which leadership requires insight and empathy.

The conclusion that leaders excel in the ability to diagnose situations and to understand the motives and actions of other individuals appears to be based on the observation that leaders are able to respond adequately to changing situations. It is perhaps natural to assume that such adequate coping responses are the outgrowth of prior, conscious diagnosis and evaluation of situations. But there are other possible explanations. Adequate coping behavior may be based on cognitions and information-processing behaviors that are not subject to high degrees of conscious or rational control.

Trying to assess individual differences in generalized empathy by asking a leader to guess how an entire population will respond to a personality test calls for a highly rationalized procedure, because all the cues that would enable a leader to respond adequately to face-to-face interaction are absent. The task of guessing would appear to measure calculation rather than a response to interpersonal situations. In trying to resolve some of the differences in conclusions reached by different investigators, one should keep in mind that successful leaders are not required to solve all problems or to be sensitive to all people; rather, they ought to be sensitive to those problems and people in the groups they lead. The findings on group cohesiveness and the influence of prescriptive behavior suggest that predictions become more accurate when groups develop norms to which the members comply. In this case, it would appear that predictive accuracy is a function of conformity to norms, rather than insight into situations. Leaders also tend to exceed followers in factual knowledge about persons and events. But factual knowledge is not synonymous with insight and empathy. The hypothesis that leaders are better able than are followers to diagnose social situations is neither well supported by research results nor easily rejected.

Therefore, new research designs are needed to provide definitive tests of the hypothesis that leadership and empathy are linked because any theory of leadership that is of consequence includes the notion that the leader fulfills some of the needs of the group by helping its members cope with the internal and external environment. Some theorists, like J. M. Burns (1978), think the needs include ways of dealing with any aspect of the group's performance. Structuralists like Hemphill (1954) and J. A. Miller (1974) limit leadership to the fulfillment of those needs that involve the structuring of the relationships among the members and their objectives. In either case, it seems obvious that leaders are likely to be more able to meet such needs of they can sense better than other members what is needed. Sensitivity, awareness, and empathy, one would think, would be likely to appear to a greater degree among leaders than among nonleaders and among more successful and effective leaders. Unfortunately, the evidence is decidedly mixed. Theories must be able to deal with the extent to which successful leaders may often be obtuse, to the detriment of their followers. Great men in the tragedies of history illustrate this phenomenon.

Fiedler, Warrington, and Blaisdell (1952) noted the importance of unconscious attitudes in sociometric choice. Thus, researchers may need to probe more deeply to test whether leaders are better able than are nonleaders to diagnose social situations. For instance, if as researchers suspect that empathy is often emotional, intuitive, and unconscious, then they must use fantasy and projective techniques more frequently to study it, rather than objective assessments, even though objective techniques tend to have greater validity and reliability and are more suitable for measurement and experiment.

Stimulated recall represents another untapped possibility, using audio- or videotape recordings to re-create for participants an event they have just experienced. During the re-creation, participants can freely associate and record their associations of what they were thinking during the original event.

Statistical controls should be employed more fre-

quently to eliminate contamination of the leadership-empathy relation by the correlation of both variables with a third, such as assumed similarity. More sophisticated analyses are also likely to help. As noted before, Barnlund (1962) had rotated 25 participants in groups of five in different combinations through six different task situations. With five members per group, he believed that a correlation of .88 was needed to establish statistically significant consistency in the extent to which the same members emerged as leaders despite the changing tasks. He concluded that the task and group composition determined the emergence of leadership, not anything that could be attributed with confidence to individuals. In reexamining Barnlund's (1962) data and conclusion, Kenny and Zaccaro (1983) noted that the average correlation in the leadership rank that individuals attained as members of the six groups was .64. This correlation was substantial evidence of personal consistency in the emergence of leadership across the six situations. Kenny and Zaccaro concluded more properly that the Barnlund results support the contention that between 49 and 82 percent of the variance in leadership could be accounted for by a stable personality trait that they inferred was "the ability to perceive the needs and goals of a constituency and to adust one's personal approach to group action accordingly" (p. 678).

Such differences in the ability to diagnose and understand the motives of others and to predict their subsequent actions accurately separates great statesmen from mediocre politicians. Because of the sentiment against war in Britain and France in 1938, British Prime Minister Neville Chamberlain and French Premier Édouard Daladier wanted to believe that Adolf Hitler could be conciliated over the Sudetenland, a local conflict, with goodwill and flexibility. In Winston Churchill's diagnosis, Hitler was using the local situation to destroy Czechoslovakia as a key bastion that was standing in the way of Hitler's plans to conquer Europe. At Munich, Chamberlain and Daladier completely misread Hitler's goals, values, and, most likely, subsequent actions; Churchill understood them accurately (Tucker, 1981). But the leadership and compliance displayed by all parties at Munich were strongly associated with the orientations of all the key figures to personal predilections, power, and politics.

Authoritarianism, Power Orientation, Machiavellianism, and Leadership

Many seek power and authority and depend on their use of power and authority, rather than on their competence, to lead (Jongbloed & Frost, 1985). It would seem reasonable to expect that those persons who strongly endorse the exercise of power and authority in dealing with subordinates would be motivated to lead. But as Christie and Cook (1958) pointed out, the authoritarian personality syndrome should not be confused with the overt exercise of authority. In the same way, the personal orientation to gain and hold power is not the same as having it to exercise. Nevertheless, Pinnell (1984) found that compared with leaders in positions that lack power and authority, leaders in positions of power and authority were more likely to perceive power to be good. Thus, when Pearson and Sanders (1981) conducted a survey of appointed career and political state executives in seven states using a questionnaire that contained six questions about authoritarianism, submissiveness, conventionality, power, and toughness, they found that the state executives, particularly the less educated executives with more state service, supported authoritarianism to a greater degree than they opposed it. They also found that public-safety executives were more authoritarian in attitude than were social-service executives.

The Authoritarian Personality

According to Samelson (1986), Wilhelm Reich was the first to use authoritarianism to explain Hitler's rise to power in Germany in 1933 in Marxist and Freudian terms. Erich Fromm (1941) expanded on the idea from an analysis of a survey of German workers. The concept moved from politics and psychoanalysis into social psychology (Sanford, 1986). Adorno, Frenkel-Brunswik,

Levinson, and Sanford (1950) postulated an authoritarian type of personality, which was characterized as politically and religiously conservative, emotionally cold, power seeking, hostile toward minority groups, resistant to change, opposed to humanitarian values, and the like.

F Scale

Adorno, Frenkel-Brunswik, Levinson, and Sanford (1950) devised the *F* Scale to measure authoritarianism. The statements in the scale included such ideological right-wing clichés as these: "People can be divided into two distinct classes, the weak and the strong"; "No weakness or difficulty can hold us back if we have enough will power"; "What a youth needs most is strict discipline, rugged determination, and the will to work and fight for family and country"; and "Most of our social problems would be solved if we could somehow get rid of the immoral, crooked, and feebleminded people." A political conservative, therefore, was likely to earn a higher authoritarian score than was a political liberal (Christie, 1954; Shils, 1954).

Authoritarianism or Acquiescence? All statements on the *F* Scale were couched in the same power-oriented terms. Endorsement of any statement implied support of an authoritarian ideological point of view. Bass (1955a) and Chapman and Campbell (1957b) completed research analyses suggesting that scores on the *F* Scale could be explained mainly by the response set of social acquiescence—the general tendency to agree with statements of attitudes. However, after an error in calculation was corrected, a flurry of subsequent studies indicated that the percentage of variance due to social acquiescence only accounted for about one-quarter of the variance in the scores on the *F* Scale. Although some of the responses to the *F* Scale could be attributed to social acquiescence, for the most part, the scores still provided a substantive measure of the authoritarian syndrome (Bass, 1970).

Factorial Validity. According to Bass and Valenzi (1974), authoritarianism, as measured by the *F* Scale, was one of the four personality factors that emerged empirically in a search to understand the system of variables describing the relations among leaders and followers and their organizational performance. It appeared independently of assertiveness, sense of fairness, and introversion-extroversion.

Construct Validity. Evidence of the construct validity of the *F* Scale was obtained by Campbell and McCormack (1957), who found that the scores of U.S. Air Force cadets were more authoritarian than those of college students. But, contrary to expectations, the cadets' scores on authoritarianism decreased with the time they were in the U.S. Air Force. Thus, according to Masling, Greer, and Gilmore (1955), authoritarians among 1,900 military personnel tended to rate other group members less favorably than did egalitarians. In turn, as was consistent with earlier studies by Jones (1954) and Thibault and Riecken (1955a), Wilkins and DeCharms (1962) reported that, as expected, authoritarians were influenced by external power cues in evaluating others and used fewer behavioral cues in describing others. Authoritarians were also more highly influenced by considerations of status in making evaluations.

Relation to Competence

On the basis of their reviews of the research literature, both Titus and Hollander (1957) and Christie and Cook (1958) concluded that authoritarianism, as measured by high scores on the *F* Scale, was negatively correlated with intelligence. Authoritarians tended to be not as bright as egalitarians and were also less educated. Courtney, Greer, and Masling (1952) administered the *F* Scale to a representative sample of residents of Philadelphia. Those who scored highest on authoritarianism were laborers and those with the least education. The lowest scores were make by managers, officials, and clerical and sales people. Professionals, semiprofessionals, and university students scored between these two groups.

Newcomb (1961) observed that authoritarians were less able than were egalitarians to determine which group members agreed with them, and their sociometric choices were determined accordingly. Authoritarians were also likely to be less popular with their peers. In studying 2,139 naval recruits, Masling (1953) found that authoritarianism was negatively related to their popularity.

Authoritarianism appears to decline with experience. Thus, Campbell and McCormack (1957) found that authoritarianism decreased with increasing military experience in various samples of military personnel, and Rohde (1952) discovered that authoritarianism was not highly valued by officers who attained the rank of air-crew commanders.

Authoritarianism and Leadership

Preferences in Leadership

Milton's (1952) data indicated that in 1952, authoritarian college students, as measured by their scores on the *F* Scale, supported the nomination for president of Douglas MacArthur, who symbolized and emphasized power and authority in leadership, whereas students with low *F* scores supported the nomination of Adlai Stevenson, who was portrayed as a more consultative problem solver. Sanford (1950) administered an authoritarian-egalitarian scale to 963 randomly selected adults in Philadelphia. Those who scored high on authoritarianism wanted a stern leader, but one who was competent, understanding, and helpful. Those who scored low preferred a leader who was kind, friendly, and guided by the people. The strong leader who tells people what to do was accepted by the authoritarians but rejected by the egalitarians; the egalitarians wanted either to be told nothing or to be told what to do but not how to do it. The authoritarians tended to choose a leader for his or her personal magnetism and high status, whereas the egalitarians preferred a humanitarian leader who did things for people. Thus, authoritarians favored being led by an autocratic, directive, structuring, task-oriented leader; egalitarians favored being led by a democratic, participative, considerate, relations-oriented leader.[1]

Medalia (1955), who studied enlisted men in the U.S. Air Force, found that authoritarians expressed greater acceptance of formal leaders than did egalitarians. Haythorn, Couch, Haefner, et al. (1956b) also found that authoritarians were more satisfied with appointed leaders and were less critical of their own group's performance.

Reactions to Leadership

Thibaut and Riecken (1955a) studied the effects on authoritarians and egalitarians of attempts to influence them by persons who were of different ranks in an organization. They found that the authoritarians were more sensitive to the rank of a leader then were the egalitarians. The results of E. E. Jones (1954) were similar. However, Jones found that egalitarians viewed the forceful-stimulus person as more powerful and the passive leader as less powerful than did those who scored high on the F Scale. The egalitarians were more highly sensitized to differences in personal power and to behavioral cues, while the authoritarians tended to differentiate in terms of institutional status.

Thibaut and Riecken (1955b) also studied group reactions to a leader's attempts to instigate aggressive behavior. They found that neither the authoritarianism of the group members nor the status of the leader influenced the members' initial acceptance of the leader. However, authoritarian participants became more submissive when they faced a high-status instigator, but tended to reject the efforts of a low-status instigator. In overt communication, the authoritarian members were less intense in their rejection of the higher-than the lower-status instigators. In a similar type of analysis, Lipetz and Ossorio (1967) found authoritarians to be less hostile toward high-status than to low-status target persons whether or not these persons attempted to instigate aggression. To investigate a similar effect, Roberts and Jessor (1958) used projective tests to study the attitudes of authoritarians toward persons who were frustrating to them. Compared with egalitarians, authoritarians tended to exhibit personal hostility toward low-status frustrators and to express indirect hostility toward high-status frustrators.

Authoritarianism and the Behavior of Leaders

Use of Reward and Punishment. Dustin and Davis (1967) asked participants to indicate whether they would use monetary rewards and penalties or evaluative communications to stimulate maximum performance in hypothetical followers. Compared with egalitarians, authoritarians used negative sanctions (monetary penalties and negative evaluations) significantly more often. W. P. Smith (1967a) also found that authoritarians tended more than did egalitarians to use punishment rather than reward as a method of inducing performance in others. Among chief petty officers, authoritarianism and the number of demerits given recruits were positively related (Masling, 1953). However, using a different scale to uncover authoritarianism, Baker, DiMarco, and Scott (1975) failed to find significant differences between the use of either monetary bonuses or penalties by those who were high and low in authoritarianism. More definitive work might be done in this area, although one would intuitively expect authoritarians to be more prone to make use of negative reinforcers.

Behavior of Emergent Leaders. Bass, McGehee, Hawkins, et al. (1953) demonstrated that authoritarian personalities, as measured by the F Scale, are least likely to attempt or exhibit successful leadership behavior in an initially leaderless discussion—a socially ambiguous situation that calls for considerable flexibility if one wishes to attempt to emerge as a leader in the situation. This finding was consistent with results reported by Bass and Coates (1952), who found significant correlations of .32 and .33 between the tendency of ROTC cadets to display successful leadership in initially leaderless group discussions and their scores on two measures of perceptual flexibility. Similarly, Geier (1963) observed that overly rigid members tended to be eliminated as leaders in the early stages of group discussion. Consistent with these findings, Hollander (1954) obtained nominations for a student commander from 268 naval aviation cadets that correlated −.23 with the cadets' scores on authoritarianism.

---

[1]These leadership styles will be discussed in Chapters 21 through 24.

Since egalitarians are more likely to become leaders in their communities, Courtney, Greer, and Masling (1952) reported that the community leaders they studied were significantly more egalitarian than the followers. Greer's (1953) interviews with 29 leaders in Philadelphia discovered that the leaders' scores on the authoritarian-egalitarian scale were significantly more egalitarian than were those of nonleaders. Tarnapol (1958) obtained similar results. It should be noted that the reverse may be expected in highly conservative communities.

Leadership Styles. Haythorn, Couch, Haefner, et al. (1956a) formed two groups, one with high ratings on the F Scale (authoritarian) and the other with low ratings on the F Scale (egalitarian). The 32 participants viewed a film and met in their groups to compose dialogue for the film. According to pairs of reliable observers, in their respective groups, the egalitarian leaders were significantly more sensitive to others, contributed more toward moving the group closer to goals set by the group, showed greater effective intelligence, and were more submissive in their attitudes toward other group members than were the authoritarian leaders. Using the same design, the same investigators (Haythorn, Couch, Haefner, et al., 1956b) again found that authoritarian leaders were less sensitive to others.[2]

Egalitarian leaders tended to promote more participation. Thus, when they emerged or were appointed in the Haythorn, Couch, Haefner, et al.'s (1956a, 1956b) experiments, followers tended to be able to exert more influence and to express more differences of opinion. Authoritarian leaders were described as being more autocratic, less democratic, and less concerned with the group's approval than were the egalitarian leaders.

Effects. Rohde (1952) administered the F Scale to 176 members of an air crew who were also rated by their crew commanders on three criteria. Authoritarianism was correlated $-.33$ with the commander's willingness to take the men into combat, $-.46$ with the commanders' perception of the desirability of the men

as friends, and $-.11$ with the commanders' confidence in the men as members of the crew.

Ley (1966) found a strong correlation of .76 between the turnover rate of employees in industry and the authoritarian scores of their supervisors. But contrary to Ley's hypothesis, a leader's authoritarianism was not significantly related to several measures of the effectiveness and performance of the group. Likewise, Hamblin, Miller, and Wiggins (1961) failed to find a significant correlation between a leader's authoritarianism and measures of his group's morale and success. To obtain such effects from authoritarian leaders, situational circumstances need to be taken into account.

Contingencies that Modify the Effects of a Leader's Authoritarianism

The effects of the authoritarianism of leaders tend to be moderated by their followers' authoritarianism or egalitarianism, as well as by various other situational factors. Researchers have often focused on the impact of the followers' authoritarianism on the leadership process, for submissiveness and obedience to a higher authority are firmly entrenched in the authoritarian personality. Thus, in a study of Israeli naval officers and crews, Foa (1957) concluded that authoritarian commanders should be in charge of subordinates with authoritarian expectations.

Match and Mismatch of Leaders and Followers: Effects on the Follower. Numerous attempts have been made to examine what happens when authoritarian and egalitarian leaders have to work with authoritarian and egalitarian subordinates. Systematic effects have been observed on both the followers and the leaders. Some effects depend on whether followers and leaders are matched or mismatched in personality. Thus, Vroom (1959, 1960a) found that authoritarian subordinates (according to their scores on the F Scale) tended to be less satisfied and less motivated to working under participative leaders than were egalitarian subordinates. In this study of a package-delivery firm, Vroom found that the extent to which employees were satisfied and effective under participative supervision depended on their being egalitarian and highly in need of independence. Campion (1969) confirmed Vroom's findings in an experimental study. But another replica-

---

[2]Sensitivity to others is a potential contributor to effective leadership as noted in Chapter 8.

tion of Vroom's study by Tosi (1970), using the same survey method as Vroom with a different organization and different jobs, failed to corroborate Vroom's results. However, Tosi noted that his respondents were different from Vroom's in terms of values, interests, and other personality characteristics, was well as sex.

Tosi (1973) tested a supervisory-subordinate congruency hypothesis. The hypothesis was that a personality match between the supervisor and subordinate could result in greater satisfaction and morale and in less conflict than a mismatch. Data were collected from 488 managers of consumer loan offices. Four samples were formed, high F and low F samples, of authoritarian and egalitarian employees that worked for bosses who rated either high or low in a tolerance for freedom on the Leadership Behavior Description Questionnaire, Form XII.[3] The congruency hypothesis was partially supported: Job satisfaction and degree of participation were highest for the authoritarian subordinates who worked for the bosses who lacked a tolerance for freedom. But egalitarian subordinates who worked for bosses who had a high tolerance for freedom unexpectedly were reported to have lowest levels of participation and satisfaction. These results suggest that some degree of structure or direction has to be present, whether in the boss or in the subordinate, to define the situation in which work is done.

Haythorn, Couch, Haefner, et al. (1956a) formed combinations of leaders and followers on the basis of high or low scores on the F Scale. They found that compared to egalitarian followers, authoritarian followers generally were rated by observers as less democratic and less sensitive to others, were more satisfied with their appointed leaders, and rated their groups higher in productivity and goal motivation. Unexpectedly, the authoritarian followers were not more submissive to the leaders than were the egalitarian followers, and they exercised more influence in their groups than did egalitarians. Observers rated the egalitarian followers lower than the authoritarian followers in productivity and goal orientation and higher in withdrawing from the field of activity.

Frey (1963) studied the disruptive behavior of differently composed groups under authoritarian and egali-

tarian leaders. The most disruption occurred in groups that were composed of both authoritarian leaders and followers; the least disruption occurred in groups that were composed of both egalitarian leaders and followers; the lowest performance occurred in groups that were composed of egalitarian leaders and authoritarian followers; and the highest performance occurred in groups that were composed of both authoritarian leaders and followers.

Match and Mismatch of Leaders and Followers: Effects on the Leaders. Bass and Farrow (1977b), using path analysis, showed how the authoritarianism of leaders and followers determined whether a leader would be *directive*, negotiative, consultative, *participative*, or delegative.[4] They administered a short form of the F Scale to 77 managers and their 409 subordinates from industry and public agencies and asked subordinates to describe their managers' styles of leadership as well. Bass and Farrow found that the authoritarianism of the managers or their subordinates did not affect the extent to which the managers were *directive*. However, authoritarian or egalitarian personality did determine the degree to which the managers were perceived to be negotiative (manipulative and opportunistic), as well as how often they tended to consult with their subordinates. Authoritarian subordinates viewed their managers as more negotiative, particularly if the managers had short-term, rather than long-term, perspectives. In turn, the managers' short- or long-term perspectives were an intervening variable influenced by authoritarianism. Specifically, managers with authoritarian personalities were short-term maximizers, and managers who were short-term maximizers more frequently used a negotiative style of leadership. On the other hand, managers were more likely to be seen as consultative when their subordinates were egalitarian and fair minded. As with directiveness, the other styles of leadership studied, *participation* and delegation, were unaffected by the authoritarianism of the managers or their subordinates.

---

[3]See Chapter 24.

[4]As defined in Chapter 22 *direction* (in italics) refers only to giving orders. Direction (roman) includes ordering, persuading, negotiating, and manipulating. *Participation* refers only to sharing in the decision process. Participation includes consulting, sharing, and delegating.

Other Situational Contingencies. Illustrative of situational moderations of the effects of authoritarian leadership was Harrell, Burnham, and Lee's (1963) demonstration that authoritarians tended to emerge as leaders in task-oriented groups and egalitarians tended to emerge as leaders in socioemotional groups. The size and structure of the group also makes a difference in the effects of the authoritarianism or egalitarianism of the leader. Authoritarian personalities appear to do better as leaders when interaction among members is constrained by the size of the group and the centralization of the organization's communications. In comparing large and small work groups Vroom and Mann (1960) found that supervisors who scored high on the *F* Scale were more readily accepted in large groups than in small groups and that egalitarian supervisors were better accepted in small groups. The employees described authoritarian supervisors as being more participative, exerting less pressure on employees, and creating less tension between themselves and higher management than egalitarian supervisors in large groups, but they viewed authoritarian supervisors in small groups as less participative and creating more tension between supervisors and subordinates than egalitarian supervisors. Vroom and Mann also examined the relationship between the authoritarianism of the supervisors and the satisfaction of their subordinates. Subordinates whose jobs were characterized by a low degree of interaction with their supervisors and by a low degree of interdependence had more positive attitudes about authoritarian supervisors.

M. E. Shaw (1955) studied the effects of authoritarian and egalitarian leadership in different communication nets. He found that groups under authoritarian leaders were highly productive but had low morale. M. E. Shaw (1959a) further reported that, as expected, groups with leaders who scored high in authoritarianism performed better in centralized networks, whereas groups with egalitarian leaders performed better in less highly centralized networks.

Overall, the evidence suggests that the presence of the authoritarian personality syndrome in the leader or the follower systematically affects the performance of both and their satisfaction with each other. Yet, by the 1980s, interest in the leadership performance of the authoritarian personality had dissipated. In its place was the more sharply focused interest in those who most often seek and acquire power, how they use it, and with what effects.

Power, Interpersonal Competence, and Leadership

Individuals differ in their attitudes toward power; they also differ in their abilities to seek and use it (Frost, 1986). Those with the motivation and willingness to use power in their dealings with others will use their interactions more consciously with others to get what they want and to gain control over situations. Those with skill in the use of power will embed that power in their communications with others and will use tactics to influence what happens. Such tactical maneuvering or organizational politics embodies " . . . the exercise of power [seen] . . . in the . . . tactics [members] use to get their way in the day-to-day, ongoing, present time functioning of [the] organization—it is *power in action*" (Frost, 1986, p. 22). According to a review by Dill and Pearson (1984), a model of such organizational politics better accounts for the effectiveness of managers of research and development projects than does a rational model. Kotter (1979) adds that such dynamics of power contribute to an organization's functioning.

Uses and Abuses of Power. Power can be wielded for personal aggrandizement. But it also can be used for purposes that are beneficial to others. For instance, *intrepreneurs* (individuals who behave innovatively in large, complex organizations) are task-oriented personnel who use power whenever they can to ensure that their ideas, inventions, and innovations are accepted in their organizations (Pinchot, 1985). Such intrepreneurs regard power as being instrumental for the accomplishment of tasks and as something they share with others, rather than as a basis for personal aggrandizement. Kanter (1983) described such individuals as "quiet entrepreneurs," who communicate in a collaborative/participative fashion. Although they could use their power to coerce others with threats and cajolery, they tend to be persuasive in their leadership style and to use much of the socially acceptable techniques of interpersonal competence discussed in Chapter 8, such as frequent staff meetings, frequent sharing of information, consulting with others, showing sensitivity to the interests of others, and a willingness to share rewards and recognition.

Motivation for Power

According to McClelland (1975), people gain emotional satisfaction from experiencing the effects of their use of power. Along with the feelings of pleasure, aggressive feelings may also appear, as may physiological reactions, particularly the release of catecholamines which is associated with emotional experiences.

Acquisition of Power. Some individuals strive to acquire power and to use it. Others obtain it, sometimes reluctantly, by being in a position of authority to deal with uncertainty, to negotiate the allocation of resources, and to maintain collaborative efforts.

Power can be exercised and emotional satisfaction gained from its use. Some individuals will seek such opportunities to exercise power; others will not. Power seekers will be more likely to make use of the power they gain if they believe their attempts to lead through power will be successful (Kipnis, 1976). Mowday (1978) provided support for these contentions, finding that managers who had revealed a high need for power employed it more frequently if they perceived it to be useful to do so. In general, such managers preferred assignments in which they could exert leadership and actively influence others.

Measurement of Power Orientation

Although, the need for power had been measured directly by questionnaires and personality inventories that assess manifest needs, power orientation and power needs have often been assessed by using respondents' answers to the Thematic Apperception Test. Scores on this test are based on how much power the examiners find in stories the respondents invent when shown ambiguous sketches such as one of a man seated at a desk. A power response to such an ambiguous sketch in the test would be: "He disapproved because he was determined to get his way." This response may be contrasted with the following, which projects the need for achievement: "He was busy working and didn't hear the bell." It also may be contrasted with a

response that projects the need for affiliation, such as: "He kept looking at the photos of his family on his desk and wishing he was with them." The Miner Sentence Completion Test is another projective technique in which examinees complete sentences beginning with such words as "I feel . . . ", "My job . . . ", and the like. Power orientation can be estimated from the themes of the completed sentences.[5] Power orientation has also been measured indirectly but objectively by Harrell and Stahl (1981) by asking for preferences to alternative job assignments. Respondents indicated their relative preference for jobs having characteristics that appealed to different needs including the need for power.

Power Orientation and Careers

The need for power was an important element in the "Leadership Motive Pattern" formulated by McClelland (1975) and found particularly important for success as a manager in a follow-up of 237 AT&T general managers in nontechnical areas (McClelland & Boyatzis, 1982). Power orientation, measured using the Miner Sentence Completion Test, also contributed to predictions of the respondents' plans to work as managers, according to Miner and Crane (1981). Although scientists and engineers were found to prefer jobs that provide opportunities to satisfy their need for achievement, successful executives had the highest need for power (Harrell & Stahl, 1981).

Cummin (1967) and Wainer and Rubin (1969) found that high power motivation, coupled with high achievement motivation, was associated with the success of managers. Stahl (1983) corroborated these findings in a large nationwide sample of managers in which the rating of the managers' performance and the managers' rate of promotion were connected with a great need for power and for achievement, as measured by an objective test. In a study of elected politicians in two local settings, Browning and Jacob (1964) observed that strongly power-oriented and achievement-oriented men were more likely to occupy political offices with greater potential to achieve and to exercise power. Those with little need for power and for achievement did not hold such offices.

[5]See Chapter 25.

Power-motivated individuals also pursue careers other than politics that allow them to exert significant influence over others, such as teaching, psychology, business, or journalism. Those with little power motivation choose careers with fewer opportunities to influence others.

Power Orientation and Leadership Behavior

Power motivation makes specific differences in the behavior of different leaders. For example, Fodor and Farrow's (1979) experiment found that participants who had a great need for power are partial toward followers who are ingratiating. Fodor (1984) reported that individuals who were strongly motivated for power became more active when supervising others than did those low in motivation for power. Active attempts to lead were highest when productivity was stressed and rewarded, but such attempts by participants with a high motivation for power to gain control of the situation and increase productivity were thwarted. McClelland (1985) noted that men with a high power motive displayed more instability in their interpersonal relations, had more arguments, were more impulsive, and engaged in more competitive sports. Furthermore, both men and women with a high motivation for power reported holding more offices than did those with a low motivation for power (Winter, 1973). Similarly, Kureshi and Fatima (1984) found that highly power-motivated Indian Muslim students were activists and showed concern for power in their everyday activities and in student elections.

Consistent with the effects of the personality traits of activity, dominance, and social boldness, those who are more oriented toward power would be expected to attempt to influence others in doing so. Thus, Veroff (1957) found that individuals who scored high on projective measures of power motivation also scored high on satisfaction with their status as leaders and were rated high in argumentation and attempts to convince others. However, Frantzve (1979) failed to find that power, measured by Stewart's social-maturity scale, predicted emergence as a leader in initially leaderless discussions among male and female students.[6]

[6]More detailed and compelling evidence about the relationship of power to attempted and successful leadership is presented in Chapter 13.

Power, Leadership, and Cognitive Complexity.

Along with such obvious personality traits as self-confidence, self-determination, and dominance, the acquisition and use of power to influence others is associated with the individual's cognitive complexity—the ability to differentiate and integrate abstract information. In a four-year study of insurance-company employees, Sypher and Zorn (1986) found that the cognitive complexity of individuals strongly contributed to their persuasive ability. Such personnel were promoted more often within the organization than were others. House (1984) observed that cognitively complex individuals are better able to identify power relationships. As is true of leadership in general, communication skills are important in the wielding of power.

Power, Leadership, and Communication Ability.

Communicative competence is required to articulate arguments, advocate positions, and persuade others, all useful for acquiring and using power (Parks, 1985). With such competence, many other strategies and tactics are available to exert influence using one's power (Marwell & Schmitt, 1967; Wiseman & Schenek-Hamlin, 1981). These strategies are detailed in a later section.

Power and Effectiveness of Leadership.

Although individuals who base their leadership on power may create conditions that are unsatisfying to some or all of their subordinates, they may successfully influence the course of events, which results in the fulfillment of tasks and the attainment of goals by their group or organization. Thus, Shaw and Harkey (1976) found that groups in which the leaders displayed ascendant tendencies did better than did groups in which nonascendant people were the leaders. O'Brien and Harary (1977) reported that those leaders whose power matched their desire for it were more effective as leaders. Batkins (1982) stated that among human service agency directors, those with a great need for power led more efficient agency operations than those with little need for power; the results for the need for affiliation was the opposite.

Fodor (1987) found that small, experimental groups of men in the ROTC that attempted to solve a subarctic survival situation did best if their leader had a strong need for power. However, Fodor and Smith (1982) obtained outcomes indicating that individuals with a high power motivation tended to inhibit group discussions more than did those with a low power motivation. The individuals with a high motivation for power brought fewer facts and proposals into the discussion that were available to them exclusively. As a consequence, fewer alternatives were considered and the quality of decisions was lower for groups led by such individuals. Consistent with these findings, House and Singh (1987) concluded that power motivation is predictive of effective leadership only when the assertion of one's social influence is critical and technical expertise is not.

The Imperial Motive

Leaders need to have some degree of self-control and the ability to inhibit their own need for power. For instance, Jennings (1943) observed that leaders in girls' schools controlled their own moods and did not inflict their anxieties and depressed feelings on others.

McClelland (1985) concluded that if power motivation is low, leadership potential generally will be absent. If power motivation is high and activity is uninhibited, the individual behaves like a conquistador and has thoughts of personal dominance and winning at someone else's expense. The tendency to inhibit activity is measured by obtaining the frequency with which the word "not" appears in stories written by an individual for the Thematic Apperception Test. *Activity inhibition* is thought to reflect the restraint the individual feels about using power impulsively or using power to manipulate or coerce others.

McClelland proposed that some successful leaders are high in power motivation, low in need for affiliation, and high in the inhibition of activity. This is the imperial motive pattern and signifies ruthless, efficient organizing that may sometimes be channeled into "selfless leadership" that is oriented toward doing good for others. Those who score low in inhibition of activity have thoughts of power that center much more on personal dominance, being a conquistador, and winning at someone else's expense. Those who score high in inhibition of activity reveal altruistic images of power.

McClelland found that male "imperials" were more likely to join more organizations than were male con-

quistadors and to argue more frequently. The women imperials were likely to be elected to more offices than were the women conquistadors and were likely to accept more reponsibility.

Since activity inhibition, based as it is on the number of "nots" in TAT protocols, has little theoretical support or empirical validation, Winter and Barenbaum (1985) decided to extract a measure of responsibility from the protocols based on whether the following were expressed in the protocols: moral-legal standards, obligations, self-judgments, concern for others, and concern about consequences.

Responsibility moderated the effects of power as predicted. For the same 422 managers in the original 1956 AT&T assessment study (Bray, Campbell, & Grant, 1974) analyzed for the imperial power motive by McClelland and Boyatzis (1982), 77 percent of the men with "responsible power" were at level 3 or higher 16 years later. Only 56 percent with other combinations lacking in both power motivation and responsibility reached this level (Winter, undated).

Self-monitoring and Leadership

Inhibition of activity is likely to be revealed in self-monitoring. Snyder (1974, 1979) suggested that individuals differ in the extent to which they monitor and control presentations of themselves in social situations. Self-monitors are sensitive to cues about the appropriateness of various types of behavior (Snyder & Mason, 1975) and use these cues to guide their interpersonal behavior.

Abilities associated with self-monitoring cut across the factors of sensitivity and control and have been found to contribute to a leader's effectiveness. Self-monitoring involves concern with social appropriateness, attention to social-comparison information, the ability to control and modify self-presentation, and the flexible use of this ability in particular situations (Snyder, 1974, p. 529). The elements of self-monitoring have been found to correlate with the ability to be a good actor and to be able to give impromptu speeches (Briggs, Cheek, & Buss, 1980). Those who score low in self-monitoring are controlled by their own consistent attitudes and are not molded to the demands of the situation. As measured by a revised self-report inventory, self-monitoring involves at least two independent components: sensitivity to others' behavior and the ability to modify one's behavior accordingly (Lennox & Wolfe, 1984).

Snyder suggested that high self-monitoring individuals may be more likely to emerge as the leaders of groups because of their ability to regulate the interpersonal relationships in group interactions. Kenny and Zaccaro (1983) further proposed that experienced leaders became sensitive to differences in group situations and pattern their approaches accordingly. They develop acuity in foreseeing the needs of their followers and alter their own behaviors to respond more effectively to those needs. Contributing to the self-monitoring-leadership linkage is the fact that high self-monitors present themselves in a socially desirable manner (Snyder, 1979) and construct an image of the ideal type of person for the situation they face. Using this ideal, the high self-monitors act according to the demands of this role (Snyder & Cantor, 1980).[7]

Considerable indirect evidence has emerged that generally supports the existence of a linkage between self-monitoring and the tendency to emerge and succeed as a leader in various situations. Ickes and Barnes (1977) found that high self-monitors tended to speak first in an interaction and to initiate more conversational sequences than did low self-monitors. They also were perceived to be more friendly, outgoing, and extroverted than were low self-monitors (Lippa, 1978) and were found to be more successful in performing as boundary spanners, which requires a greater adaptability to situational requirements (Caldwell & O'Reilly, 1982).

Garland and Beard (1979) tested whether the effects of self-monitoring on emergent leadership would depend on the nature of the task confronting a group: A high self-monitor was expected to emerge as a leader when the task emphasized discussion and when task competence was difficult to assess. Such effects occurred in all-female groups but not in all-male groups. In an unpublished field study of natural groups, Ellis, Adamson, Deszca, and Cawsey (undated) also found

that those who were high in self-monitoring were more likely to emerge as leaders. Mendenhall (1983) likewise reported that high self-monitors were more likely to emerge as leaders of initially leaderless groups if they perceived themselves to be leaders rather than being perceived as leaders by their peers. Nevertheless, peer-rated leadership of male students in semester-long mixed-sex study groups correlated .41 with the Lennox and Wolfe (1984) Revised Self-Monitoring scales (.26 with sensitivity to others' behavior and .40 with ability to modify one's behavior accordingly). But the correlations were lower for female participants, which was the reverse of Garland and Beard's (1979) results for all-male and all-female groups. The explanation put forth by Ellis, Adamson, Deszca, and Cawsey was that they were studying leadership in mixed groups in which females are more reluctant to assert leadership in the presence of males; Garland and Beard had studied all-male and all-female groups.

Foti and Cohen (undated) involved three-person same-sex groups of students containing one high, one moderate, and one low self-monitor in a manufacturing exercise. The emergent leader was highly self-monitoring in 41 of the 58 groups, moderate in 11 of the groups, and low in self-monitoring in only 6 of the groups. High self-monitors, as expected, adapted their leadership style to the situation. They exhibited more initiation of structure when instructions emphasized the importance of the task rather than relationships and more consideration when instructions emphasized developing good interpersonal relationships. Groups led by high self-monitors were somewhat more productive if the task was emphasized.

Power Orientation and Transformational Leadership

The good managers among McClelland and Burnham's (1976) imperials were oriented toward serving their organizations. They generated among their subordinates team spirit, clarity of purpose, and a sense of responsibility for their work. House, Woycke, and Fodor (1986) found that six charismatic U.S. presidents—Jefferson, Jackson, Lincoln, the two Roosevelts, and Kennedy—revealed significantly more power and achievement motivation in their inaugural addresses

---

[7]These propositions fit particularly well with the concept of the leader as transactional, providing followers with need fulfillment in exchange for their compliance.

than did six noncharismatic presidents—Tyler, Pierce, Buchanan, Arthur, Harding, and Coolidge.[8]

Among women, McClelland (1985) reported a correlation of .37 between maintaining the imperial motive pattern and accepting institutional responsibility. The comparable correlation for women conquistadors was close to zero.

Machiavellianism

The pursuit of power and its skillful use have been seen as fundamental to successful leadership by observers from Nicolo Machiavelli to Lasswell (1948) and Lane (1961). Although this power orientation is interpersonal, it is unlike the interpersonal competence discussed in the last chapter. As can be seen in the writings of Thomas Jefferson, Henry Thoreau, and Ralph Waldo Emerson, such interpersonal competence is based on a philosophy of the inherent goodness and perfectability of humankind. This orientation was espoused by well-known socially oriented management theorists, such as Lewin (1939), Gibb (1964), Argyris (1962), and Bennis (1964), who argued that influence can and should be exerted on others when there is a need for it, at which time, for the good of self and others, one should be open, frank, and candid in communications, share in decision making with them, openly commit oneself to positions so others will know where one stands, jointly select and identify mutually satisfying goals to work toward, develop and maintain mutual trust, and encourage group discussions including others above and below oneself in the organizational hierarchy. But there was an earlier scholarly view about interpersonal competence that is epitomized by the work of Machiavelli in *The Prince* (1513/1962) and in *The Discourses* (1531/1950). Caesare Borgia, a local dictator, was Machiavelli's model prince; he used all means at his disposal, including murder, to achieve and hold his political position. Machiavelli had served on diplomatic missions to such crafty rulers as Louis XII of France, the Holy Roman Emperor Maximilian, and Pope Julius II. The political tricks he observed first hand were included in his advice to the prince.

[8]Chapter 12 will look at length into the power-charisma-leadership relationship.

Machiavelli's Advice

Strong, ruthless, and cynical leadership is required of the prince because people are completely and inherently self-interested and self-serving. As a consequence, they will regularly subvert the state and reduce it to chaos. It is in their best interests for the prince to do whatever he can in whatever way he can to prevent chaos from occurring. Religious and ethical criteria for justifying the leader's actions are irrelevant.

Political calculation is required to control events rather than be victimized by them. For "reasons of state," the ends always justify the means. The ends are the welfare of the state. Whatever the leader does to help strengthen and preserve the state is good; whatever tends to work against the state is bad. The leader must be pragmatic, not idealistic, in facing problems. He must always keep in mind the particular interests of his own state.

In a sense, Machiavelli was an early amoral behaviorist who argued for studying what we do, rather than what we ought to do. He argued that "he who studies what might be done rather than what is done will learn the way to his downfall rather than to his preservation." He was also an early situationalist, for instance, giving different advice to the prince about how to deal with acquired political states, depending on whether the states were culturally and politically similar or different from his own.

According to Machiavelli, the prince must be ready to imitate the behavior of the fox, who can "recognize traps," and the lion, who can "frighten wolves." To obtain and maintain power, he needs a calculating attitude without any sense of guilt or shame. The prince should rely more on being feared than on being loved. If cruelty is required, it should be done all at once, not over an extended period. Although the prince does not need to have a moral character, he must seem to have one; he should appear to be merciful, faithful, humane, sincere, and religious, and avoid being despised. He has to uphold his dignity "which must never be allowed to fail in anything whatever." He should not pay attention to advice unless he has asked for it.

Machiavelli even had advice for those around the prince. Anyone with cleverness and some power who helped the prince to gain his position must be careful because the prince cannot tolerate any competent, powerful people close to him.

The Mach Scale

Statements from *The Prince*, as well as from *The Discourses*, were used by Christie and Geis (1970) to form the Mach scale, which measures the extent to which respondents subscribe to Machiavelli's dictums about how the leader should act toward others to be most successful in obtaining and maintaining compliance with his interests. An original list of 71 statements dealt with tactics ("A white lie is a good thing"), views ("It is hard to get ahead without cutting corners"), and morality ("No one has the right to take his own life"). The Mach IV scale, consisting of 20 such items, had a split-half reliability of close to .80.

Other versions of the Mach scale were formed to reduce the bias of social desirability that is inherent in the content. Obviously, to admit to being devious is not a socially desirable response.

Influence Behavior of 'High Machs'

Individuals who score high on the Mach scale ("high Machs") resist social influences and are concerned with getting the job done, rather than with emotional and moral considerations. They tend to initiate and control interactions with others. In contrast, people who score low on the Mach scale ("low Machs") are more susceptible to social influence and are distracted by interpersonal concerns (Epstein, 1969). High Machs frequently practice deception, bluff, and other manipulative tactics in competitive situations and in contexts of uncertainty. They also exhibit a "cool" task-directed syndrome during face-to-face competition that allows for improvisation in both substance and in the timing of responses to the task or to other people. High Machs are impervious to considerations that can interfere with manipulative behavior and effective bargaining (Christie & Geis, 1970).

In their study, Drory and Gluskinos (1980), varied the leaders' power as perceived experts with authority and the task so it was more structured or less structured to create situations that were more favorable or less favorable to the leaders. They found that as leaders, the high Machs generally gave more orders and reduced

tension more than did the low Machs. However, they became less directive and requested more assistance when they had less power and the task had less structure than when they had more power and the task was highly structured. In respect to their flexibility of response as conditions changed, high Machs were like egalitarians (low *F* Scale scores) who had been found to do the same by Bass and Farrow (1977b). Low Machs were similar to high authoritarians in their inflexibility of response to changing situations.

The impact of a Machiavellian outlook seems to depend on how much a manager interacts with others in the organization. Coates (1984) obtained reports of the frequency of the contacts of 79 managers with their superiors and peers. It was found that the rated influence of managers who were high Machs was likely to be higher than that of low Machs if the managers had frequent contact with their superiors and peers.

Other Political Tactics

The number of politically astute, devious, deceptive, artful, and crafty tactics leaders can employ is much more extensive than Machiavelli described. Many other tactics were mentioned in the Greek, Roman, and Chinese classics. However, Machiavellianism is a generic label for all such amoral political manipulativeness.

Martin and Sims (1956), Jameson (1945), and Pfiffner (1951) described these tactics according to their use in modern corporations. They suggested that managers need to withhold the release of information or time its release for when it will do the most good. These writers also noted that managers need to bluff, to act confidently even when they are unsure or lack the relevant information. Furthermore, managers need to make political alliances with those who have the power to protect their interests and can and should hide their real feelings about plans that are popular with others by starting to act on them but then retarding and delaying their implementation so that the plans are in process but are never completed. They should keep socially distant from subordinates and never become personally involved with them, always remaining the boss when interacting with them. Managers should openly compromise, yet secretly divert or delay plans that involve compromise so their aims will continue to be pursued despite public statements to the contrary. McCall (1978, p. 227) felt the same way about the need for creative leaders to be "crafty, grouchy, dangerous, feisty, contrary, inconsistent, evangelistic, prejudiced, and spineless."

Behavioral scientists have not paid much attention to this Machiavellian way of establishing and maintaining leadership. The very deviousness of Machiavellianism may make its widespread practice less visible, for, overall, the social approach to interpersonal competence is more popular and socially acceptable. Bass (1968c, 1970b) found that only a minority of MBA students and middle managers espoused the Machiavellian approach as the way "to get ahead in most large organizations" on a 12-item questionnaire, the Organizational Success Questionnaire (OSQ). While favoring political tactics, this minority of students and managers tended to reject to Gibb-Bennis-Argyris social humanistic approach to effective interpersonal relations. For the majority of the MBA students and managers, least popular were the tactics of retarding and delaying and of using compromises to divert plans. But published OSQ results for students in six countries and unpublished OSQ data, gathered from samples of managers in over a dozen countries, suggested that the different nationalities differ widely in their endorsement of these political and social approaches (Bass & Franke, 1972).

Influence Tactics. Kipnis, Schmidt, and Wilkinson (1980), who gathered data on what people at work say they do to influence others who work with them, found a mixture of both social and political approaches. In their first investigation, 165 lower-level managers wrote essays describing an incident in which they influenced their bosses, their co-workers, or their subordinates. A content analysis disclosed the use of 370 different influence tactics. The Machiavellian tactics that were uncovered included the following: lied to the target, acted in a pseudo-democratic manner, puffed up the importance of the job, manipulated information, made the target feel important, cajoled the target, pretended to understand the target's problem, became a nuisance, slowed down on the job, threatened to withdraw help, threatened to leave the job, blocked the target's ac-

tions, ignored the target, invoked past favors, waited until the target was in the right mood, was humble, showed dependence, invoked rules, obtained support informally from superiors, threatened to notify an outside agency, and made formal appeals to higher levels.

Ingratiation and Blocking. Kipnis and Schmidt extracted 58 tactics from the content analyses and then gave them to 754 part-time graduate students who worked fulltime during the day. The students were asked how frequently they had used any of these tactics during the past six months to influence others with whom they had worked. When the responses were factor analyzed, two manipulative factors emerged: ingratiation and blocking. Ingratiating tactics were used more frequently to influence co-workers and subordinates than superiors. The primary reason the students gave for using them was to get help on their jobs, to obtain benefits from these other persons, or to try to effect changes. The ingratiating tactics included:

Made him or her feel important ("only you have the brains, talent to do this").

Acted very humbly to him or her while making my request.

Made him or her feel good about me before making my request.

Inflated the importance of what I wanted him or her to do.

Waited until he or she appeared in a receptive mood before asking.

Pretended I was letting him or her decide to do what I wanted (act in a pseudo-democratic fashion).

Blocking tactics were generally less frequently used than most of the other approaches. They were used to get benefits and changes in decisions from one's boss. They included:

Threatened to notify an outside agency if he or she did not give in to my request.

Threatened to stop working with him or her until he or she gave in.

Engaged in work a slowdown until he or she did what I wanted.

Ignored him or her and/or stopped being friendly.

Distorted or lied about reasons he or she should do what I wanted.

Still other Machiavellian tactics that were used with some frequency included:

Pretended not to understand what needed to be done so that he or she would volunteer to do it for me.

Concealed some of my reasons for trying to influence him/her.

A favorite tactic was to form coalitions with others to exert the combined power reflected in the group, rather than in the lone voice of the individual. Another common tactic, found by Nuttin (1984), is to plan one's behavior in advance, imagining or playing through situations to time what one will do and to fit one's appeals to the imagined outcomes. Preserving and enhancing one's self-esteem seems to underlie much of these behaviors (Kelley & Michela, 1980).[9]

Game Playing. Frost (1986, p. 527) conceived tactical maneuvering to gain power and influence in terms of the sociopolitical games employees play in organizations:

An organizational game involves social actors, payoffs, and a set of interpretive strategies ... [that] specify the rules, data and successful outcomes in the game. Given the social construction around power that is involved in such games there is a degree of elasticity in the way the game is constructed and played. Invention and adaptation enter into the development and enactment of game rules and meanings, because they come alive in the service of actors' strategic actions in the game.

Table 9.1 presents a lengthy list of the possible games that organizational members can play to get their way, sometimes consciously for their own sake and sometimes consciously for the sake of others or for their organization. Organizational members may use such games to disguise their political intentions, to mobilize support, and to quiet opposition. Power-seeking members play at empire building by following the rules to

facilitate their upward mobility in their organizations. (Pfeffer, 1981b).

Specific individual games include "making it" (moving up the ladder of success), mentoring, sponsorship, empire building, and upward influence (see Table 9.1). Through such games, players seek justification for and meaning in their actions to allow them to increase their power and hence to participate in other organizational games.

Games such as "lording" (Mintzberg, 1983) are played by actors with little power, who "lord it over" those who are subject to their influence. Those who play these games hold onto the little power they have by establishing a context in which they interpret the rules and routines of organizations literally and see that the rules are strictly enforced and the routines are rigidly implemented. They get their way and resist change by invoking the rule book—the bureaucracy—and by threatening to go to a higher authority for decisions (Frost, 1986). On occasion, they invent rules, expecting no challenge about their existence because of the large complex book of rules that would have to be consulted to refute their argument. In these individual games, players manage impressions (Zerbe & Paulhus, 1985) and join and build networks and coalitions (Porter, Allen, & Angle, 1981).

Heresthetics. For Riker (1986), leadership, as practiced by successful politicians, is primarily political manipulation. According to this view, leadership is evident when a politician is able to change an issue in the minds of constituents and legislators, so the minority support for the older framing of the issue swells to a majority because of the politician's new interpretation of the issue. The politician-leader achieves this goal by imparting to his or her description the exact twist to reality that will gain majority approval of the issue. It is a matter not of persuasive rhetoric but of a "heresthetic" argument that shows how the proposal will serve the best interests of the majority. In Riker's case studies, heresthetic leaders manipulated support by setting and controlling agendas, calculating likely voting patterns, and then manipulating the values of importance. They made appeals to share organizational or societal purposes, but their private motives were paramount.

---

[9]These and still other tactics that those with lower status use to influence others with higher status will be examined in detail in Chapter 18. Self-serving impression management, which uses some of these tactics—including ingratiation, intimidation, and supplication (Jones & Pittman, 1982)—and which may create an illusion of control (Alloy & Abramson, 1982), will be considered more fully in Chapter 12.

Table 9.1 Some Games Employees Play in Organizations

Games Played	Political and Communicative Strategies and Tactics Used
Individual Games	
Sponsoring Protégés	Ingratiating
Mentoring Protégés	Impression management
Making It	Networking
Empire Building	Gatekeeping
Lording It over Others	Reasoning
	Rule citing
	Labeling
	Managing sanctions
	Appealing to a higher authority
	Covering up
	Manipulative persuading
	Asserting
Intraorganizational Games	
Rival Camps—"We versus They"	Co-opting
Making Out	Coalition building
Whistle Blowing	Agenda controlling
Young Turks	Leaking information
Insurgency-Counterinsurgency	Withholding support
	Scapegoating/defaming
	Isolating/terminating
	Developing champions
	Building consensus
	Supporting
	Framing perspectives

SOURCE: Adapted from Frost (1986).

As Riker (1986, p. 64) noted, "the heresthetic neither creates preferences nor hypnotizes. . . . He probes until some new alternative, some new dimension [is found] that strikes a spark in the preferences of others." He manipulates private incentives even while remaining idealistic.

Because of the isolationist sentiment in the United States in 1940, Franklin Delano Roosevelt could not gain approval from Congress to give 50 old American destroyers to Britain, which was being strangled by German submarines. But he did gain approval for lend-lease, in which the destroyers were exchanged for bases in Bermuda, the Bahamas, and elsewhere that could be viewed as a first-line offshore defense for the United States. He was able to convince Congress to pass the Lend-Least Act of 1941 by emphasizing the age and

outmoded condition of the destroyers and the advantages of obtaining the bases.

Summary and Conclusions

Leaders may be oriented toward the uses of power and political manipulation, rather than to the social approaches to influencing others. When they are, authoritarianism, power motivation, and Machiavellianism are aspects of their personalities that are of consequence. Measuring the authoritarianism of both leaders and followers has been helpful in understanding the preferences, performance, and satisfaction of these leaders, particularly as a function of the circumstances involved.

Authoritarian personalities tend to be rejected in sociometric choice. But this tendency does not necessarily prevent authoritarians from performing as leaders in task-oriented, emergent groups, as well as in formal organizations.

The personalities of leaders and followers interact. Authoritarian followers tend to evaluate leaders in terms of status, power, and position, whereas egalitarians evaluate leaders as persons in terms of behavioral and personality cues. With directive leaders, egalitarian followers tend to feel more comfortable in large, structured groups. With directive leaders, egalitarians tend to react more favorably in small, less highly structured groups. Egalitarian followers are somewhat more hostile toward leaders in high-status positions. Thus, the degree to which a leader is accepted and the degree of satisfaction that group members feel under authoritarian and egalitarian leaders generally is dependent on a matching of the leader's personality with the follower's personality, along with a congruent group structure.

Power-motivated leaders can be effective if they are task oriented, rather then concerned about interpersonal relationships, and if they can inhibit their need for power. These imperialists can use their power for their advancement or for the good of their organizations.

Machiavellians are cool in their performance as leaders and are not distracted by interpersonal considerations or social influences in competitive situations. The use of Machiavellian tactics is probably more widespread than acknowledged. However, many other personal values and orientations are also associated with the emergence and success of leaders.

Values, Needs, and Well-being of Leaders

Leaders, like most people, are multidimensional, complex personalities. Douglas MacArthur was, for his biographer William Manchester (1978), "a great thundering paradox of a man, noble and ignoble, inspiring and outrageous, arrogant and shy, the best of men and the worst of men, the most protean, most ridiculous and most sublime." So far I have detailed how the intricacies of the personal factor of leadership involve activism; task and interpersonal competence; and orientation toward authority, power, and manipulativeness. But much more needs to be said. This chapter examines how leaders see themselves; the next chapter discusses how others see them. Here, I explore the leader's self-ascribed personal values (what is regarded as right, important, and good) and valued activities, as well as his or her need for achievement and affiliation, locus of control, concepts of the self, preference for taking risks, cooperativeness-competitiveness, trust, health and well-being. Composite models of the motivation to manage and to lead emerge from these traits.

The attitudes of leaders in management positions toward their organization and their individual differences in satisfaction with their roles as managers are also examined here. Leaders see themselves differently from nonleaders in many ways. Thus, as Peppers and Ryan (1986) found, when 79 individuals who occupied positions of leadership were contrasted with 110 who did not, the leaders differed from the nonleaders in three general ways. First, they saw themselves as more talkative, aggressive, intelligent, committed, and ambitious. Second, they aspired to be more sensitive, democratic, fair, committed, imaginative, confident, and self-assured. And third, there was more congruence between the leaders' aspirations and self-perceptions than between the nonleaders'. Piotrowski and Armstrong (1987) concluded that all 30 chief executive offi-

cers they interviewed had clear values. Trow and Smith (1983) showed that those who volunteered to serve on the boards of directors of agencies that planned and advocated social change systematically differed in their values from those from the same community who did not volunteer to serve. Those who volunteered were much more likely to value good will and the need to eradicate sin and were much less likely to endorse a hard line in dealing with social problems. Generally, leaders more strongly endorse the values of their movements than do ordinary followers.

Values

Importance to Leaders

Baltzell (1980) illustrated how the directions leaders took were influenced by the values they assimilated. He contrasted the values of upper-class Protestant Boston and upper-class Protestant Philadelphia. Puritan Boston saw human beings as inherently sinful, in need of authoritative institutions headed by righteous leaders of superior education. Quaker Philadelphia saw human beings as inherently good, individually perfectable, without need of mediation by state or church, erudition, or professionalism. For Boston's Brahmins, but not for Philadelphia's, public service became obligatory; Boston's Adamses, Cabots, and Lowells produced a good many eminent political leaders; Philadelphia's Biddles, Cadwaladers, and Whartons did not. Baltzell attributed the difference to the original Puritan and Quaker values inculcated in succeeding generations of family members. The Bostonians, who pursued political leadership, and the Philadelphians, who pursued leadership in business and finance, clearly differed in their attitudes and opinions about what was important to them and what interested them.

In a review of available research, Ghiselli (1968a) noted that managers' personal values correlated from .25 to .30 with criteria of their effectiveness. England and Lee (1974) suggested six reasons for the influence of the personal values of rightness, goodness, and importance on a leader's performance. That is, these values affect (1) a leader's perception of the situations and problems to be faced, (2) a leader's decisions and solutions to problems, (3) the way in which a leader looks at other individuals and groups of individuals and thus interpersonal relationships, (4) the leader's perception of individual and organizational success, as well as of how to achieve them, (5) the leader's determination of what is and what is not ethical behavior, and (6) the extent to which a leader accepts or resists organizational pressures and goals.

Determinants of Leaders' Values

Education. Systematic differences in the values of managers are associated with differences in their education. Esser and Strother (1962) found that managers with average amounts of education tended to be rule oriented. Those with the least education were least rule oriented, followed closely by those with the most education. And England (1967a) observed that managers with less education placed more value on organizational stability. Those with college majors in the humanities, the fine arts, and the social sciences stressed the importance of the organizational goals of productivity and efficiency.

Cognitive Style. Organizational values seem to be linked to differences in the way managers sense, think, judge, and feel, according to the Myers-Briggs Type Indicator (Myers, 1962). Mitroff and Kilmann (1976) showed, in a content analysis of managers' stories about their ideal organization, that sensory-thinkers emphasized factual details, the physical features of work, impersonal organizational control, certainty, and specificity; intuitive-thinkers focused on broad, global issues built around theories of organization; and intuitive-feelers stressed personal and humanistic values in their ideal organization, which existed to serve man-

kind. Intuitive-feelers were also found to be bigger risk takers (Behling, Gifford, & Tolliver, 1980; Henderson & Nutt, 1980). The sensory-feelers described their ideal organization as one that focuses on facts and processes, with attention to human relationships and qualities.

Personal Considerations. A kind of discounting seems to occur on the basis of perceptions of abundance or scarcity. In a study of a hospital, Jensen and Morris (1960) found that supervisors valued leadership and executive ability more highly when these traits were less prevalent among them. And when the supervisors were socially adjusted and personable, they attached less value to these qualities.

What leaders value as an activity for its own sake obviously depends on their vocation. Distinct patterns of interests demarcate the different professions (E. K. Strong, 1943). Among governmental leaders, one is likely to see leaders with strong political values; in the military, leaders with strong interests in adventure; in business, strong interests in computational matters; and in science, strong preference for theoretical activities—understanding the "whys" of things. Managers and executives tend to score highest among the professions in economic and political values in contrast to scientific personnel, who value theory and understanding; to artists, who are more concerned with creativity; and to those in the helping professions, who have stronger social or religious values.[1]

Student leaders, mostly from the middle-class themselves, are more likely than are followers or isolates to identify with middle-class values (Martin, Gross, & Darley, 1952). Some strongly value academic and vocational activities and goals; others strongly value socializing (Brainard & Dollar, 1971).

Societal Developments. The values of business managers reflect societal and cultural trends. In developing industrial societies, the belief in social Darwinism (the survival of the fittest) fit with the doctrine that the "invisible hand" made the unrestricted free market the best economic system. This belief also meshed with the Calvinist doctrine of predestination (of being

---

[1]Allport, Vernon, and Lindzey (1960); Bedrosian (1964); Nash (1965); and Tagiuri (1965).

chosen by God for success) and with the value of frontier individualism. All these beliefs and values combined to justify so-called profit maximization—the "bottom line"—as the single objective of enterprise. Poverty, drudgery, and exploitative employment of the "unfit" (not chosen) for the longest possible hours at the lowest possible wages were justified as the best means to achieve the highest profits to enrich the employer, who was blessed by God to prosper and rightfully entitled to them. The constraints of governmental regulation and union movements were unnatural, uneconomic, unreligious, and immoral.

In reaction to the excesses to unconstrained profit maximization came the voting public's and legislatures' more sophisticated views of the government's regulatory role, the acceptance of unionism, and more socially conscious religion. Equally, if not even more important, came management's awareness that profit maximization was a chimera. Instead of that single objective function, came the realization that what managers should maintain and improve was the value of the systems for which they were responsible as stewards. Thus, managers needed to integrate the needs and interests of the constituencies of the system—the owners and shareholders; the employees, including the managers themselves; the suppliers; the clients and customers; and the community. Instead of valuing the longest working hours at the lowest possible wages, managers came to value the highest hourly productivity per employee at equitable and satisfying wages. Integration meant alignment of the employee's and the organization's interests in their mutual growth and development. More often than not, managers have come to view themselves as stewards. For example, in the technologically driven high-technology electronics industry, keeping abreast or ahead of competition in new products means maintaining a committed, loyal, and involved management, research and development, engineering, and manufacturing work force; satisfied investors; cooperative suppliers; and confident consumers. Mergers, acquisitions, leveraged buyouts, and corporate raiding force managements to keep their eyes on short-term results, current earnings, and the price of their shares in relation to their assets. Nevertheless, attention on longer term investment and outcomes must still be maintained for the firm to remain healthy and viable.

Balancing Values

Some of the balanced, salient values are likely to remain the same in profit-making enterprises as in government, education, health, and social service organizations, although specific objectives that are consistent with the purposes of the organization obviously need to be substituted. For instance, in health organizations, concern for the care of patients is substituted for a concern with the quality of products, but the organizational steward must keep alert to the employees's as well as the patients' interests. Maslow (1965, p. 131) captured an ideal set of balanced objectives for the management of any system:

> [The leader in the work situation] is the one who can get the job done best or who at least can help to organize things in such a fashion that the job gets done best . . . (p. 128).
>
> [At the same time, the need for balance is apparent. The good leader must also have the] ability to take pleasure in the growth and self-actualization of other people. . . . He must be strong, he must enjoy responsibility . . . ; he must be able to mete out discipline as necessary, to be stern as well as loving [like] a good father and a husband; he ought to be able to get great gratification out of watching his children grow up well and out of watching his wife develop her personality well and grow on toward greater maturity and self-actualization.

Quinn (1984) proposed that managers are faced with competing values that need to be kept under consideration. For example, they must make choices for expansion and adaptation, rather than for consolidation and continuity.They must choose between risk-taking inventiveness and conservative cautiousness and sometimes between the acquisition and allocation of resources and information gathering and distribution.

Darwinistic profit-maximizing values and objective-balancing, trustee-oriented values may have to compete with a third set of values (Hay & Gray, 1974). For a minority of managers, quality of life, environmental protection, and other social and political values (for instance, disinvestment in South Africa) override the other constituent interests of the firm. For socially directed managers, there can be no balanced compromise about the quality of a product, environmental pollution or the safety of workers. Likewise peace-minded investors avoid investing highly in the profitable military weapons industries and public health advocates refuse to work for tobacco firms.

But it is not enough to say that some executives are profit maximizers, others are systems balancers, and still others have social concerns that are paramount. There may be trade-offs between the three objectives that are not mutually exclusive. For instance, Osborn and Jackson (1988) presented data on the safety of 41 nuclear plants that suggested that the past experience of high profitability was associated with fewer major safety violations if the utility's total energy output was not committed to nuclear energy. However, if there was a relatively larger commitment to nuclear than to nonnuclear power, more major safety violations were likely with high profitability. Like riverboat gamblers, executives in the latter utilities appeared to be more willing to increase the risks of losing it all as profits increased. Nonetheless, a survey of 6,000 business managers by Posner and Schmidt (1984) found that the 2 most important of 11 values were organizational effectiveness and high productivity and the lowest in importance were organizational value to the community and service to the public. In another study of 803 public officials at the federal GS-15 level, Schmidt and Posner (1986) reported that effectiveness and productivity were first and third while service to the public and value to the community were seventh and eighth among the 11 values. The general public was tenth in ratings of the importance of constituents' interests; clients, bosses, self, technical personnel, managers, and co-workers were all more important. The evidence suggests that public and private administrators are relatively less concerned about their obligations to society than about their obligations to their organizations.

Evidence. There are data to support the contention that a multiplicity of values involving personal and organizational considerations lie beyond the objectives of management. For managers to restrict themselves to a single objective function—profit maximization—is a fictional convenience for classical economists and some operational research specialists. For example, when Dent (1959) asked a representative sample of 145 U.S. chief executive officers or their deputies in confidential "off-the-record" interviews, "What are the aims of top management in your company," only 36 percent mentioned as their first aim "to make money, profits, or a living." Three-fourths talked about multiple goals, including growth, public service, the welfare of employees and the quality of products. High-quality products and public service were mentioned more often by the executives in larger firms and the welfare of employees was cited more often in smaller nonunion and larger unionized companies. In firms with higher percentages of white collar, professional, or supervisory employees, fewer executives spoke of profitability and more spoke of growth. In addition, the willingness of managers to pursue noneconomic objectives may be a matter of how much their own income depends on the profitability of the firm. If they have alternative sources of income, they may express a broader range of valued objectives for the company (Hambrick & Mason, 1984).

Shartle (1956) conducted studies of the elements that executives in several kinds of organizations said they valued to various degrees. A factor analysis of item intercorrelations produced nine factors that described the value dimensions for business firms: (1) organizational magnitude, expansion, and structure, (2) internal consideration for welfare, health, and comfort, (3) the degree of competition, strategy, and shrewdness, (4) the degree of ethical and social responsibility, (5) the quality of the product or service, (6) the degree of change, (7) the degree of organization control over the identifications of members, (8) the degree of external political participation, and (9) the degree of equality and recognition of members.

In a survey of 1,576 first-time supervisors at Japanese National Railways, Furukawa (1981) isolated five valued objectives. Three were task related (to establish order, to increase motivation, and to accomplish goals) and two were interpersonally oriented (to establish and maintain dependable relationships and peaceful work units). To achieve the human relations objectives, the supervisors saw the need to be more considerate and less initiating; to achieve the task-oriented objectives, they considered more initiation of structure and less consideration to be instrumental.

Valuing nonprofitable activities, such as social programs, community programs, and employee welfare programs seem rooted more in individual differences than in socialization processes within the organization. This idea was inferred by Sukel (1983), who found that status as a top, middle, or first-level manager in manufacturing, banking, or retailing make no difference to the valuing of such socially relevant activities. At the same time, senior management could be seen as self-serving rather than more broadly interested in their organization. Such was seen in the rejection of the bid of its own senior management by the Board of Directors to buy control of the RJR-Nabisco conglomerate, although the bid matched an outsider's leveraged buy-out offer. The Board of Directors openly said they did not trust the management to protect the rights of the employees and to maintain the integrity of the firms' operations (Sterngold, 1988).

Priority of Profitablity and Performance

While maintaining some sense of balance, most managers and business leaders, if given the choice, do tend to place a higher priority on profitability and performance. England (1967a, 1967b) who studied managers in nine hierarchical levels, found that there was general agreement on the greater importance of the goals of organization effectiveness and productivity than of social welfare goals. Community leaders of middle-sized cities in the Midwest, most of whom were in business or banking, believed that economic development was the paramount goal of university extension services (Moss, 1974). A similar sample did not regard environmental concerns to be of much importance to their communities (Sofranko & Bridgeland, 1975). But community leaders in rural Georgia saw less of a need for economic exchange than for coordination than did rural heads of households with whom they were compared (Nix, Singh, & Cheatham, 1974).

Using England's (1967a) Personal Values Questionnaire, England and Weber (1972) contrasted the extent to which U.S. managers regarded various issues as "successful," as "right," and as "pleasant." From these judgments, managers were seen to emphasize either what is pragmatic, what is moral, or what is pleasurable. England and Lee (1974) then administered the Personal Values Questionnaire to almost 2,000 U.S., Australian, Indian, and Japanese managers. The success of these managers was measured by their income adjusted for their age. In all four countries, successful managers were more likely to hold pragmatic values emphasizing productivity, profitability, and achievement.

Bass (1975a) developed Exercise Objectives in which the performance of participants can be a gauge of their pragmatism or idealism. In Exercise Objectives, five budgeting decisions are required in dealing with questions about whether to budget money to deal with problems of safety, labor relations, the morale of managers, the quality of products, and environmental pollution. Bass's (1968c) study of 113 MBA students showed that the unwillingness to spend money to remedy any of the five problems was related to strong economic values and was significantly related to an attitude supporting an implicit economic theory of management and leadership, rather than a humanistic one. Conversely, the willingness to spend money for organizational needs was positively associated with a social orientation to trust others. It was negatively correlated with a political orientation to bluff and to maintain psychosocial distance (Bass, 1968c).

Fast-track Managers. From 46 to 77 percent of an international sample of 5,122 managers was willing to spend money for all five budgeting problems, but faster-climbing managers tended to exhibit more pragmatism than idealism in that they were less willing to spend money to handle the requests for safety, to settle a strike, to deal with morale, to improve the quality of products, or to eradicate pollution in a stream. Although they did not want to risk wasting money, faster-climbing managers did value generosity and fair-mindedness. Thus, the faster-climbing managers emerged as persons who wanted productive value for their expenditures (Bass, Burger, et al., 1979).

What managers judge to be important and valuable for success as a manager is related to their own success.

Managers who stress the importance of inner-directed behavior (imagination, self-confidence, and so on) are rated more effective in their jobs than are those who see their roles as demanding high degrees of other-directed behavior (cooperativeness, tactfulness, and so forth), according to Lawler and Porter (1967a, 1967b), Mitchell and Porter (1967), and Porter and Lawler (1968). Consistent with these results, Bass, Burger, et al. (1979) found that generosity, fair-mindedness, sharp-wittedness, and steadiness were judged to be more important for top management by those whose rate of advancement as managers was faster, and tolerance and adaptability were judged to be more important for top managers among those whose rate of advancement was slower.

The attributes that were considered most important for middle managers by those whose rate of advancement was higher were generosity, sharp-wittedness, and reliability. However, those whose rate of advancement was lower deemed tolerance, adaptability, and self-control to be most important for middle managers.

Managers whose rate of advancement was faster thought that the most important attributes of first-line supervisors were generosity and reliability. In contrast, those whose rate of advancement was slower judged fair-mindedness, tolerance, and adaptability to be most important for first-line supervisors.

Other attributes valued by faster-climbing managers —more than by those who were advancing more slowly—included objectivity and productivity. Compared with the slower-advancing managers, the faster-climbing managers valued a task orientation and a results orientation, being less dependent on a higher authority and decision making by higher-ups, a longer-range view of affairs, and a greater reliance on persuasiveness than on authority. However, the faster-climbing managers valued interpersonal competence less than did the slower climbers and did not prefer risk-taking activities under uncertainty any more than did the slower climbers.

The Valuing of Pay. In response to the traditionalists' overemphasis on pay as a motivator, humanist scholars overreacted in attempting to minimize the importance of pay to managers and their subordinates. According to reviews of research on pay and manage-rial motivation by Opsahl and Dunnette (1966), Dunnette (1967), and Porter and Lawler (1968), pay remains a strong motivator for managerial personnel. Lawler and Porter (1966) found that presidents and vice presidents stressed the importance of pay slightly less than did managers at lower levels, but pay was highly significant for all. Pay may satisfy not only lower-order needs, such as the need for safety and security, but higher-order needs, such as the need for autonomy and self-actualization. Porter and Lawler (1986) found that those managers who perceived that their pay depended on their job performance to a great degree tended to perform better on their jobs when both they and their superiors rated their performance. The relation between the probability of higher pay and their likely effort was stronger for those who attached a high reward value to pay. Effective performance was related to the extent to which it was seen as instrumental to higher pay.[2]

The Valuing of Technical Competence. Studies before 1965 indicated that first-line supervisors valued the technical aspects of their assignments more than their human relations responsibilities.[3] Their higher-level managers tended to agree with them (Rubenowitz, 1962). Increasingly, however, recognition of the importance of other attributes, such as interpersonal competence, has accompanied the valuing of technical competence in supervision. Such a shift in values (an increased subscription to pragmatism) occurred for managers in Western Australia in a period of 23 years. The change was attributed to changing Australian business conditions during the same period (Spillane, 1980).

Personal Priorities. Managers and leaders have their own personal priorities about what is important to them. In the aggregate, some personal goals, such as self-actualization, independence, and expertise, are more important than are others, such as duty, prestige, and wealth. There are wide individual differences among managers and leaders, depending on their organizational level, their nationality, whether they have

---

[2]More will be said about this in Chapter 17.
[3]Kelly (1964); Mandell and Duckworth (1955); Moore, Kennedy, and Castore (1946); and Sequeira (1962).

job security, and so on. Hofstede (1978) found that for the responses of 65,000 supervisors, salesmen, and service personnel to a worldwide survey of IBM employees, these individual differences could be accounted for by two factors. These factors were the valuing of personal assertiveness (leadership, independence, and self-realization) and the valuing of personal comfort (pleasure, security, and affection).

According to Bass, Burger, et al. (1979), for 3,082 managers in an international sample, the importance of 11 life goals was as follows (with 1.00 = most important, and 11.00 = least important): self-realization, 4.09; independence, 4.89; expertness, 5.17; affection, 5.21; leadership, 5.32; security, 5.50; service, 6.01; pleasure, 6.78; duty, 7.08; prestige, 7.65; and wealth to build a large estate, 8.27. But the standard deviations (from 2.6 to 3.3 for each goal) suggested that in the total group, some managers rated the same goal first in importance while others ranked it eleventh. Wide individual differences, particularly across the 12 countries studied were the rule.

Attitudes toward Corruption

Investigative journalism has, since its inception, put the spotlight on managerial and entrepreneurial corruption. Nonetheless, there has been a marked paucity of empirical research on managers' attitudes toward corruption and the ethics of their behavior. Pitt (1985) gave middle and senior managers in South Africa 15 scenarios involving ethical considerations and asked them to indicate whether they regarded the manager's behavior as wrong, how frequently such behavior had been observed, and what the company should do about it. Over 90 percent thought it was definitely wrong to accept a large bribe or to tell competitive bidders their rivals' offers for the managers' own material benefit. But 4 out of 10 thought it "understandable" for a firm that had just been awarded a contract by a project engineer to give the engineer an all-expense-paid trip. Similar proportions thought it was all right for a geologist to use inside information about new developments to purchase company shares and for a purchasing manager to accept an invitation from a supplier for a "night on the town" hosted by the supplier's secretary.

Over 90 percent said they had observed colleagues and friends accepting a potential supplier's invitation to lunch and a bottle of whiskey as a Christmas gift from a supplier. Half or more said they had seen colleagues or friends accepting free trips and entertainment from suppliers, as well as conducting insider trading.

Only 34 percent thought the company should take legal action in the case of large bribes, although 62 percent would fire the bribe taker. Similar reactions were registered for releasing information prematurely to rival bidders, but a plurality would only give such employees a warning for insider trading, accepting free trips, and filing false expense claims.

Although there is much divergence in ethical opinion among managers, a high set of standards can be described and appreciated. On the basis of six interviews with six leaders who were identified by well-informed observers as models of ethical leadership, Shapiro (1985) concluded that ethical leaders express a strong commitment to the mission of their organization, derive great satisfaction from progressing toward the mission, and empower others to contribute to the mission. Furthermore, they care for the various stakeholders in the organization, not only the owners and stockholders, and have a broad sense of community. They also remain informed about what is going on in their complex organizations. In all, they believe that bad means cannot be justified to gain good ends.

Values and Political Leadership

Again one has to look to journalists, historians, and essayists for the best understanding of the values that underlie the performance of political leaders. However, Rokeach (1972) completed a content analysis of four political leaders—Norman Thomas, socialist candidate for U.S. president; Barry Goldwater, a Republican conservative candidate for U.S. president; Nikolai Lenin; and Adolf Hitler. Each leader revealed distinctively different patterns of reference to the values of "freedom" and "equality" in his writings. For Thomas (a socialist), the values of freedom and equality were both highly salient. For Hitler (a fascist), they were seldom referred to. For Lenin (a communist), equality was much more important than freedom, and for conservative Republican Goldwater, freedom was prized over equality.

Paige (1977) offered a number of hypotheses about the importance of values to the behavior of political leaders.

1. Terminal values (the worthwhileness of the end-state) can be used by political leaders to justify contrary instrumental values (the worthwhileness of activities). Lenin argued that violence is justifiable to destroy the State to achieve the peaceful Communist society. Woodrow Wilson justified the U.S. entry into World War I because that war was to be the war to end all wars.

2. Values influence the scope of what is relevant. Those political leaders who sincerely value "One World" look at the same conflicts between nations differently from the way ardent nationalists look at them and try to act accordingly, say, on the subject of nuclear proliferation.

3. Political leaders and followers vary in the intensity of their value commitments. Both loyalty and treachery determine what happens to political movements in crises.

4. To achieve desired ends, political leaders may sacrifice the values of truth and honesty. "A good precinct captain [in Chicago] will always find a way to steal votes" (p. 124).

5. Values become salient to a political leader's behavior in reaction to circumstances and objectives. What a political leader says to get elected may be the opposite of what he does after he is elected. In his campaign for the presidency in 1932, Franklin Delano Roosevelt argued for the popular economic value of a balanced federal budget. When elected, he moved rapidly into federal deficit spending to stimulate the economy to deal with the Great Depression.

To be politically successful in the United States a leader must place a heavy emphasis on the value of individualism. Since two U.S. political parties cross social boundaries to a considerable degree, personalized entrepreneurship, rather than social and economic policy issues, dominate elections. The U.S. Constitution was designed to check runaway leadership; nevertheless, individual leadership is seen as the universal panacea. Individual initiative and responsibility are prized

in the U.S. culture; the role of leader is similarly valued. In the long-drawn-out electoral process and then after gaining office, the president has to "showcase and sell his own qualities" as a person to obtain and remain powerful and influential (Rockman, 1984).

Values of the Political Revolutionary. Certain values, including asceticism, appear to stand out among revolutionary leaders, such as Oliver Cromwell, Maximilien Robespierre, Nikolai Lenin, and Mao Zedung (Mazlish, 1976). All 32 revolutionary leaders studied by Rejai and Phillips (1979) were driven by a sense of justice and injustice and a corresponding attempt to right wrongs. Nationalism and patriotism were also important. When Rejai and Phillips (1988) contrasted 50 revolutionary leaders who aimed to overthrow their governments and 50 loyalist leaders who aimed to preserve them, the values, according to 96 scholars, that were more apparent in the revolutionaries than in the loyalists included an optimistic view of human nature but a fluctuating optimistic view of their countries. Revolutionaries tended to abandon religion and to become atheists.

Achievement Motivation and Task Orientation

The need for achievement, as measured by projective techniques, reflects a deep-seated fantasy about success and accomplishment. Task orientation is a self-report about conscious preferences measured by questionnaire inventories. Although the projected need and the conscious orientation are low in correlation with each other (Bass, 1967c), they both appear to contribute positively to the emergence and success of a leader. Successful accomplishment is rated highly as a personal goal by managers in diverse organizations and countries (Bass, Burger et al., 1979; England, 1967a, 1967b). The desire to achieve, to complete tasks successfully, is a personal trait associated with those who emerge and succeed as leaders.

Achievement Motivation

Relying on a projective measure, the Thematic Apperception Test, McClelland (1961) and McClelland and

Winter (1969) provided strong initial evidence to support the proposition that the need for achievement is an important value for effective leaders, particularly successful entrepreneurs.[4] Their data were corroborated by numerous studies, both in the United States and abroad which demonstrated that managerial and entrepreneurial success was predicted by the need for achievement.[5] Likewise, Cummin (1967) found that more successful executives had higher need for achievement. Similarly, Wainer and Rubin (1969) observed that the need for achievement of 51 technical entrepreneurs who founded and operated their own firms was related to the growth rate of their companies. The highest performing companies were those whose owners had a strong need for achievement and a moderate need for power. Furthermore, data from over 1,000 managers gathered by Hall and Donnell (1979) found that the managers' speed of career advancement was associated with their motivation to achieve. Mussen and Porter (1959) concluded that leaders who were effective in group discussions scored significantly higher than did those who were ineffective in the need for achievement and affiliation and in feelings of adequacy.

However, unlike most other investigations, Harrell and Harrell (1978) failed to find such a measured need for achievement in a Stanford University forecast of the subsequent success of MBA students in small business. And Litwin and Stringer (1968) found that although participants in a small-group experiments were more satisfied if their leaders had a high need for achievement, their groups experienced the same satisfaction if their leaders had a high need for affiliation.

Task Orientation

Bass (1960a, p. 149) conceived of task orientation as a characteristic of persons who in social settings "will [try] hardest to help obtain the group's goals, solve its problems, overcome barriers preventing the successful completion of the group's tasks, and who persist at . . . assignments." Task orientation is distinguished from interaction orientation (to have fun, work cooperatively, and be helpful) and from self-orientation (to be praised, recognized, respected, and have loyal associates). The Orientation Inventory (Bass, 1962b) was developed to measure the three valued approaches to working with others.

According to a review of research by Bass (1967b), those who were in higher-status positions in organizations uniformly were more task oriented. Thus, top managers scored higher than did middle managers, middle managers scored higher than did supervisors, supervisors scored higher than did nonsupervisory workers. In addition, the higher the task orientations revealed by college student leaders in sensitivity training groups, the more they were rated positively by their peers on behaviors that are relevant to leadership. The student leaders were seen to help other group members express their ideas, help the groups stay on target, help get to the meat of issues, give good suggestions on proceeding, provide good summaries, encourage high productivity, take the lead, work hard, and offer original ideas (Bass & Dunteman, 1963). Again, observers at an assessment center rated temporary supervisors who were under consideration for promotion as being more promotable if the supervisors were high in task orientation.

Task orientation was higher among second-line supervisors whose superiors rated them "best," rather than "less than best." Likewise, it was higher among top- and middle-performing first-line supervisors than among those whose performance was low (Dunteman & Bass, 1963).

A variety of other overlapping indicators of task orientation generally have been positively linked to attitudes and performance in work settings and their effects. For example, Rubenowitz (1962) found that superiors in an industrial situation tended to rate their subordinates higher in effectiveness when the latter were production oriented rather than person oriented.

Alternative Measurement of Conscious Task Orientation. Tziner and Elizur (1985) set out to design and evaluate an assessment instrument that was particularly relevant to managers' motivation to achieve, unlike previous measures that were derived from thematic apperception projective approaches or general self-reporting personality inventories like the Edwards

[4]See also McClelland (1965a, 1965b, 1969).
[5]Andrews (1967); Hornaday and Aboud (1971); Meyer and Walker (1961); and Meyer, Walker, and Litwin (1961).

Personal Profile or the Orientation Inventory. Their instrument consisted of 18 questions that asked 90 managers from a large Israeli corporation about how much they preferred to undertake difficult, problem-solving, high responsibility tasks involving calculated risks and how gratifying it was to do so if they were successful. The motivation to take calculated risks and solve problems correlated modestly with the rated performance of the managers, but no correlation was found between the motivation for responsible or difficult tasks and gratification for success with them.

Achievement and Power. Measured alone, achievement motivation and task orientation have been reasonably accurate in predicting the success of entrepreneurs and increases in their performance (McClelland & Winter, 1969). But each makes only a partial contribution to a full assessment of the motivation to manage. For a full assessment, as was noted in Chapter 9, one needs to return again to the issue of how individuals' orientation to power and its uses combines with their achievement motivation to account for their behavior as leaders. As Browning and Jacob (1964) observed, whether the need for achievement and for power directs individuals toward leadership in the economic or political arena depends on which arena in the community is open and available to them. In the political arena, as was noted in Chapter 9, dynamic, activist, and effective presidents gave inaugural addresses that scored high in both the need for achievement and the need for power. Inactive presidents, less highly regarded by posterity, gave inaugural addresses that were low in both needs (Winter & Stewart, 1975). In the American scene, power is for the individual to achieve. (However, as will be shown in Chapter 33, it is easier for those in the mainstream to gain power than it is for women or those of minority backgrounds.) Entrepreneurship is prized for the manager as well as the political leader at the top (Rockman, 1984).

Achievement and Willingness to Take Risks

Tasks with moderate risks are satisfying to those who have a great need to achieve. A risk-free task will lack challenge and a highly risky task harbors the likelihood of failure (Atkinson, 1964). However, a higher level of risk of failure will be entertained if the task is inherently interesting (Shapira, 1975). Leaders must take calculated risks using the limited information available to them. Thus, Cleveland (1985) emphasized that the generalist executive needs to be prepared to take risks if he or she is to take the lead in the "perilous, problematic and participatory climate for policy making of today's information-rich world."

Risk Taking

Some people enjoy taking risks, but others do not. Such preferences and behavior affect the leadership that emerges. Older leaders were found to be generally more conservative and more likely to avoid taking risks (Alluto & Hrebiniak, 1975). They want more information and higher probabilities of success and may be content with lower payoffs as a consequence. The contrast between older and younger leaders was illustrated by the two Roman consuls in 210 B.C.; Fabius who was older, was the delayer, whereas Maximus, who was younger, was eager to fight immediately to try to trap Hannibal's forces.

Along with higher-than-ordinary needs to achieve (McClelland, 1965c) and an internal locus of control (Borland, 1974), entrepreneurs and the founder-leaders of organizations also, have, as would be expected, higher risk-taking propensities than do managers, in general (Brockhaus, 1980). They also have a higher tolerance for ambiguity than do managers in general (Schere, 1981).

Wallach, Kogan, and Bem (1962) found that high risk takers were more influential in discussions than were low risk takers. Marquis (1962) and Collins and Guetzkow (1964) observed that high risk takers were more persuasive than more cautious members of a group.

For a random sample of 26 express-mail managers, Hater and Bass (1988) reported an average correlation of .47 between the extent to which each manager was described by three subordinates as a transformational leader (charismatic, individualizing, and intellectually stimulating) and the extent to which the same managers were judged to be high in risk taking by their bosses. But the correlation was .02 with risk-taking judged by the boss if the manager was described by subordinates as transactional in leadership (practicing contingent reward and management by exception).

Frost, Fiedler, and Anderson (1983) found that taking physical risks was also related to performance as a leader. In a questionnaire survey of 40 army leaders, they found that effective combat leaders engaged in more personally endangering acts than did ineffective combat leaders. Interviews with 19 fire-battalion chiefs and evaluations of 124 fire-service leaders again suggested that effective leaders exhibit more personal bravery than do ineffective leaders. Such personal bravery is expected of combat leaders, when, as in the Israeli Army, policy dictates that they are expected to go first into danger to be followed by their men.

Willingness to Trust

Closely associated with the willingness to take risks is the willingness to trust. In a study first mentioned in Chapter 8, Sgro et al. (1980) showed that the leadership behavior of 41 cadet officers, as described by their 149 cadet subordinates, was associated with the officers' scores on a self-inventory of interpersonal trust. Interpersonal trust correlated significantly with their consideration and tolerance of freedom and their subordinates' satisfaction with them. According to Devine (1977), who completed a survey of opinion leadership in three towns in Minnesota, both opinion leaders and opinion followers showed a willingness to trust others, but opinion isolates were less likely to do so. Rosenberg (1956) suggested that persons with low interpersonal trust would have difficulty establishing close friendships. As leaders, they would be less likely to permit freedom of action in their subordinates.

It may be that risk-taking, trusting leaders are able to maintain longer time spans in contrast to those who press for quick solutions and immediate feedback (Fram & DuBrin, 1981). Clearly, a willingness to risk and to trust others are required for meaningful delegation. More delegation should be seen in those leaders who are greater risk-takers and more willing to trust others. Conversely, the Machiavellian authoritarian, who expects others to share the same tendencies toward deception and surprise, is less likely to take chances on others.

Particularly salient in determining the proclivity to take risks is one's self-confidence. Both Clausen (1965) and Burnstein (1969) inferred that high risk takers tended to score high in self-confidence, which, in turn, led them to attempt and to succeed in influencing groups to follow their leadership. But many other aspects of one's self-concept enter into the emergence and success of a leader.

Concepts of the Self

Apart from what has been said so far, how people think, feel, and act about themselves affects their tendencies to lead. Thus, in contrast to others, transformational leaders value their capacity to learn from others and from their environment and believe they can learn more about themselves in doing so (Bennis & Nanus, 1985). Top business leaders, according to Levinson and Rosenthal (1984), have strong self-images and ego ideals.

Self-actualization

Maslow (1954) conceived of self-actualization as a higher level of maturity than the need for achievement. Compared to nonleaders, leaders tend to self-actualize more. They are more likely to perform up to their capacities and to develop themselves accordingly. This motivation was at the top of Maslow's (1954) need hierarchy. Maslow believed that the attainment of self-actualization is revealed in characteristics of psychological health and well-being, such as perceiving reality efficiently, accepting oneself, tolerating uncertainty, being problem centered rather than self-centered, and trying to identify one's defenses with the courage to give them up (Maslow 1965). For Burns (1978), self-actualizers were potential transformational leaders because of their flexibility and their capacity for growth. Through their drive toward self-actualization, they could continually be one step ahead of their followers and help their followers rise behind them, as measured by their upward movement on Maslow's hierarchy of needs, from a concern for safety and security toward a concern for achievement and self-actualization.

The Personal Orientation Inventory (POI) measures 12 interrelated aspects of self-actualization (Shostrom,

1974). POI assesses such self-concepts and values as self versus other directed, self-regard, self-acceptance, self-actualizing, responsiveness to one's own feelings and needs, capacity for intimate contact, and the extent to which one has a constructive view of humanity. In a survey of 58 executives in a high-technology firm, Gibbons (1986) found many strong correlations between subordinates' descriptions of the transformational-leadership behavior (charismatic, individually considerate, intellectually stimulating, and inspirational) of their superiors and the superiors' self-descriptions on the POI. Among these attributes, self-reported self-acceptance correlated .41 with being described as a charismatic and inspirational leader. The superiors' self-rated inner direction, self-regard, self-acceptance, and the capacity for intimate contact all correlated above .40 with the subordinates' ratings of their superiors' being seen as individually considerate as a leader. Inner direction and self-acceptance also correlated above .40 with being seen to display the transactional leadership factor of practicing contingent reward. Gaston (1983), too, found evidence to support the contention that those managers who were identified in POI interviews and by their colleagues as self-actualized tended to perform well as leaders even in less-than-optimum organizational systems.

Some of Maslow's elements of self-actualization have to be reconsidered as contributions to the performance of leaders. For example, Gibbons (1986) found that spontaneity generally was closer to zero in correlation with various leadership factors. This finding seems to be consistent with McClelland's argument that the motivation to lead includes a need for inhibiting power and, as shall be discussed later, the emergence and success of a leader calls for a high degree of self-monitoring.

Although rated before the 1980s as being most important in themselves, self-actualization and autonomy were the least well-satisfied managerial needs (L. W. Porter, 1961b).[6] Job security was less important and more readily satisfied (Centers, 1948).[7] This pattern changed in the 1980s with the increased concern for

security. With the "downsizing" of management in the 1980s, job security has become a more potent issue for lower and middle managers (McCormick & Powell, 1988).

Among 3,082 mostly middle managers from 12 countries, as noted before, Bass, Burger, et al. (1979) found that the managers had a clear set of preferences when they were asked to rank their life goals. The most important goals were self-realization (self-actualization) and independence (autonomy). Security was ranked much lower. The managers were sorted into those whose rate of advancement was higher and those whose rate of advancement was lower. Goals dealing with assertiveness and accomplishment were emphasized more often by faster-climbing managers, whereas those associated with comfort tended to be favored by slower-climbing managers. Similarly, Hall and Donnell (1979) found that in comparing 190 slow, 442 average, and 32 fast career-advancing managers, the fast advancers stressed the need for self-actualization, belonging, and esteem in motivating their subordinates. They paid only average attention to the need for safety and security. The slow managers emphasized mainly the need for safety and security, and the average managers were in between. This finding is consistent with Porter and Lawler's (1968) finding that differences in managerial performance were more highly related to the need for self-actualization and autonomy than to the need for security, belonging, and esteem.

Different Ways of Achieving Self-actualization. People differ in what they consider self-actualization to be. Executives may see it as the attainment of leadership; technologists, as the attainment of expertise; and entrepreneurs, as the attainment of wealth. Similarly, Maslow's social needs can be satisfied within the family and among friends through affection, on the job through service, and in the organization or community through duty. Wainer and Rubin's (1969) study of entrepreneurs who had started their own companies found that their strong need for achievement and their moderate need for power were associated with their companies' success. Ghiselli's (1986b) analysis of middle managers and hourly workers found that successful managers had less desire for security and financial rewards than did the unsuccessful ones.

---

[6]See also Haire, Ghiselli, and Porter (1963); Johnson and Marcrum (1968); and L. W. Porter (1962).
[7]See also Centers and Bugental (1966), Edel (1966), N. George (1958), and Raudsepp (1962).

Harrell and Alpert (1979) concluded that to maximize success and satisfaction, the need for autonomy should be strong among business entrepreneurs, moderate among tenured professors, and weak among bureaucrats. Appelbaum (1977) obtained data from 75 suburban supervisors in governments that strongly supported Harrell and Alpert's suggestion about bureaucrats. However, Henderson (1977) failed to find support for expectations about the effects of self-actualization on the choice of a leadership style.

Self-understanding

"Know thyself," a favorite piece of revealed wisdom to many classical Greek philosophers, continues to be important advice for leaders today. In most surveys, leaders tend to give themselves an inflated evaluation in contrast to their colleagues' descriptions of their performance (Bass & Yammarino, 1989). They believe they have more important jobs than their superiors think they have. Modesty is not usually a trait of managers. But self-understanding is essential even for the most successful leaders. As was already noted, the interpersonally competent manager is open to receiving feedback, the approach most likely to promote and maintain a manager's accurate self-understanding.

Concepts of the self can be perceived or actually be at variance with the outside world and affect a leader's performance. For instance, Ziegenhagen (1964) subjected 15 world-class political leaders' autobiographies to content analysis and showed that the leaders' ethnocentric behavior, conformity to in-group norms, and hostility to outgroups correlated highly with the inconsistencies in the leaders' self-conceptions. These inconsistencies were assessed by the lack of agreement between the leaders' self-conception and the conception that the individual leaders thought others had of them. As McCall and Lombardo (1983, p. 11) noted:

> Executives need to be able to handle their own success. They can be derailed when . . . success goes to their heads. After being told how good they are for so long, some simply lose their humility and become cold and arrogant. Once someone acts as if there is nothing more to learn, their information sources begin to dry up and people no longer wish to work with them.

There are often discrepancies of consequence between what leaders think about themselves and what others think of them. Wexley, Alexander, Greenawalt, and Couch (1980) studied manager-subordinate dyads and obtained a significant correlation between a subordinate's satisfaction with supervision and the congruence between the manager's self-description and the subordinate's description of the manager.[8]

Other self-concepts related to leadership that have been of particular interest include locus of control, field independence, self-efficacy, self-confidence, self-esteem, and self-understanding.

Locus of Control

Locus of control (LOC), internal or external, has been widely studied since the mid-1960s as a personal antecedent of consequence to a leader's and to a manager's behavior. To measure LOC, Rotter (1966) developed and evaluated a self-report assessment instrument, the I-E Scale, which discriminates between persons who are controlled by internal forces (persons for whom outcomes are contingent on themselves), and those who are controlled by outside influences (persons for whom outcomes are due to such forces as luck, fate, and powerful others whom they do not and cannot control). Unexpectedly, DeBolt, Liska, and Weng (1976) concluded, from a review of the literature, that internal control, as measured by the I-E Scale, failed to relate consistently to leadership in small groups of students. In the same way, Nystrom (1986) failed to detect much association between LOC and the performance of managers.

Anderson and Schneier (1978) disagreed, pointing particularly to results from many other studies of managers. Thus, Durand and Nord (1976) showed that the LOC of supervisors was linked to the extent to which their subordinates thought them to be considerate and initiating, In a simulated industrial setting, Goodstadt and Hjelle (1973) found that supervisors with an external LOC were more likely to rely on persuasion and those with an internal LOC were more likely to rely on personal power. Mitchell, Smyser, and Weed (1975) obtained similar results. They noted that supervisors with an external LOC were more likely to use coercion

---

[8]The importance of this congruence will be discussed again in the next and later chapters.

and legitimate authority, whereas those with an internal LOC used rewards, respect, and expert power. Pryer and Distefano (1971) confirmed that nursing supervisors with an internal LOC were more considerate than were those with an external LOC. In a study of 89 supervisors and their 345 subordinates, Johnson, Luthans, and Hennessey (1984) showed that the leaders' LOC affected their influence on their subordinates' productivity and satisfaction with them as leaders. Supervisors who rated themselves as internally controlled were also rated by their subordinates as significantly higher in persuasiveness and in their influence on higher authority.

Abdel-Halim (1980) also found that LOC affected how managers viewed their roles. Role ambiguity did not seem to bother managers with an internal LOC as much as it disturbed managers with an external LOC.

Confounds. Some of the relationship between LOC and the performance of managers may be accounted for by the finding that internally controlled managers are more task oriented (Anderson, Hellriegel, & Slocum, 1977). This finding is consistent with those of several other studies which showed that managers with an internal LOC individually put forth more task-centered effort and perform better than do those with an external LOC (Anderson, 1977).[9]

There are other confounding elements. Managers with an internal LOC have higher activity levels than do those with an external LOC (Brockhaus, 1975; Durand & Shea, 1974), appear more realistic about their aspirations (Phares, 1973), and perceive less stress under the same conditions (Anderson, 1977). They are also less dogmatic, more trustful, and less suspicious of others (Joe, 1971). Not unexpectedly, Coates (1984) found a complex statistical interaction between the LOC and Mach scores of 79 managers, the number of contacts they reported with superiors and peers, and superiors' rating of their influence.

Field Independence

A cognitive trait that is linked to inner directiveness and inner control is field independence. This trait is

[9]See also Andrisani and Nestel (1976); Heisler (1974); and Majumder, MacDonald, and Greever (1977).

measured by Witkin's Rod and Frame Test, in which field-independent people judge that it is the field, not them, that is being reoriented. Paper-and-pencil correlates of field independence have also been found, for example, in people who can readily see the whole figures on the Group Embedded Figures Test.

Field-independent Israeli managers with engineering backgrounds were more likely to be employee centered than job centered in their leadership styles (Erez, 1980). Results elsewhere indicated that field-independent hospital managers preferred to use participative and delegative, rather than directive, leadership styles, although more managers as a whole were field dependent than were field independent on the Group Embedded Figures Test.

Self-efficacy

As has already been noted, individuals who see themselves as masters of their own fate, rather than at the mercy of luck, fate, or powerful other people, tend to cope better with stress and generally make more effective and satisfying leaders. Such leaders are also likely to see themselves as more self-efficacious. Bandura (1982, p. 122) defined self-efficacy as a judgment of "how well one can execute courses of action required to deal with prospective situations." Self-efficacy is a broad set of expectations that are associated with beliefs about one's adaptability, ingenuity, and ability to work under stress, regardless of the ease or difficulty of the goals (Locke, Motowidlo, & Bobko, 1986). Bennis and Nanus (1985) saw the transforming leaders as one who has a strong, positive self-regard and who employs the Wallenda factor (Wallenda is the name of the family of high tightrope walkers), that is, who focuses on the risky task rather than being preoccupied with the possibilities of failure. Cleveland (1985) observed that the generalist executive in an information-rich world of work needs to be optimistic about what can be accomplished. Community leaders have more positive expectations about outcomes than do nonleaders.

Self-confidence

Self-efficacy is closely allied with self-confidence and self-esteem. Self-confidence was seen to be positively associated with leadership in the reviews reported in

Chapters 4 and 5. Bass (1985a) and Zaleznik (1977) showed that it is particularly strong in transformational leaders. Mowday (1979) found that the leadership of 65 elementary school principals in dealing with four decisions was related to their self-confidence and that the principals were more likely to be persuasive if they were self-confident. Conversely, Kipnis and Lane's (1962) results indicated that supervisors who lacked confidence in their leadership ability were significantly less willing than were self-confident supervisors to hold face-to-face discussions with subordinates and more often attempted to solve supervisory and development problems by the use of administrative rules or by referring the subordinates to a superior for a decision. According to Kaplan (1986), self-confidence weighed heavily in discriminating among those general managers who performed effectively from those who did not. The "effectives" were seen as personally secure, communicating their confidence to others and being decisive, while the "ineffectives" were characterized by incidents displaying their personal insecurity, their lack of "guts" and their unwillingness to make tough decisions or risk making enemies.

The self-confidence of supervisors affects what they do to influence others. Those who feel confident in their ability to influence others are likely to use rewards and promises of rewards; those who lack self-confidence are more likely to use coercion (Goodstadt & Kipnis, 1970; Kipnis & Lane, 1962).

Self-confidence can give rise to the stubbornness and obstinacy of Willner's (1968, p. 65) sample of charismatic world-class leaders whose

> . . . determination . . . would not permit them to lose sight of their goals or swerve from a particular tactic they had decided upon, no matter how remote from achievement the goals may have appeared to others or how unwise the tactic. Moved by some intuition or "inner voice," and undiscouraged by the obstacles that seemed insuperable to those around them, they pursued the courses they had set themselves.

Self-confidence can also result in an unrealistic, inflated evaluation of oneself. When coupled with extremely low self-esteem, the performance of such leaders is likely to be socially counterproductive (Reykowski, 1982).

Self-esteem

As was noted in Chapter 4, 17 pre-1948 studies had found self-esteem to be higher in leaders than in their followers. Additional support came from subsequent investigations that showed the positive relationship between self-esteem and leadership. Thus, market research studies concluded that a majority of fashion-opinion leaders and personal-grooming-opinion leaders are high in self-esteem. Hemphill and Pepinsky (1955) found attempted leadership to be higher among participants who felt personally accepted or esteemed. Andrews (1984) showed that among 64 undergraduates, those with high self-esteem were more likely to emerge as the leaders of their groups and were more likely to be rated as displaying such leadership behaviors as offering problem-relevant information, giving sound opinions, and making procedural suggestions.

Burns (1978) noted that the most potent sources of political leadership are the unfulfilled needs for esteem and self-esteem. For Erikson (1964), great leaders become leaders because they have personally experienced, in a way that is representative of their people, the identity struggle for a particular niche in society that is compatible with their self-respect and expectations. But Barber (1965) thought that deciding to become a candidate for political office is indicative of either very high or very low self-esteem.

Bass (1960) postulated that those with high self-esteem would be more likely to attempt leadership. Bennis and Nanus (1985) concluded, from 90 interviews with top-level leaders, that such self-esteem was likely to be transferred to their subordinates. The leaders then could operate without having to resort to criticism or negative reinforcement. Higher performance expectations and confidence were generated in subordinates as a consequence. Defensiveness was lower if self-esteem was high. Self-esteem, in leaders appears to be related to the ability to accept people as they are, rather than as one would like them to be; to focus on the present, rather than on the past; to be as courteous to close colleagues as to strangers; to trust others; and to do without the need for constant approval and recognition.

Other Related Self-concepts of Consequence

Successful leaders have revealed a more optimistic view of themselves and the world around them than have those who have failed and nonleaders. Content analyses of archival records by Zullow, Oettingen, Peterson, and Seligman (1988) found that nine of the ten losers of presidential elections between 1948 and 1984 tended to see the pessimistic side of issues in their nomination speeches. Other analyses have found that bold leadership was predicted by optimistic styles. Similarly, those individuals who have learned a sense of helplessness are much less likely to take the initiative in social situations (Abramson, Seligman, & Teasdale, 1978).

Health, Well-being, and Leadership

The amount of commentary and clinical and anecdotal literature is legion on how the health of individuals affects their performance as leaders. However, few controlled studies have been conducted (the subject was hardly mentioned in the previous editions of the handbook). Nevertheless, the acute and chronic ailments of political and organizational leaders are common sources of concern, as are issues related to the maintenance of their health, such as their diets, exercise regimens, medications, and lifestyles.

Physical Health

"A grain of sand in a man's flesh, and empires totter and fall." So wrote Emile Zola (1902) referring to Napoleon III's incapacitation by stones in his bladder. A chronic disorder can have a continuing impact on a leader's performance, and acute disorders can alter specific situations. Interpersonal relations, concentration on necessary details, energy level, and availability all depend on a leader's physical health and stamina. Countless examples of these effects on world-class leaders were described by L'Etang (1970).

The capacity of many of the major persons who were involved in escalating decisions to go to war in the 1914 summer was diminished by the state of their physical health. The Austrian archduke and archduchess were assassinated at Sarajevo on June 28, after which Austria issued its unacceptable ultimatum to Serbia. Count Szogyeni, Austria-Hungary's emissary to Berlin, was incapacitated by advanced age and was unable to transmit conversations accurately; it is said that in early July, he gave Austria a false picture of the support that Germany would provide if Austria went to war. The ambassador from Serbia's most important ally, Russia, Nicholas Hartwig, died of a heart attack on July 10. On July 25, Sergei Sazonov, an invalid since 1906, made the fateful recommendation to the czar that Russia should mobilize (even before Austria did). Lord Edward Grey, British foreign minister, was suffering from seriously impaired vision but had to read numerous documents involved in the justification of Britain's entry into the war in early August.

Additionally, of the other key decision-makers, Kaiser Wilhelm was not in the best of mental health, Czar Nicholas was distracted by the hemophilia and expectation of a shortened life of his one son and heir, and Emperor Franz Josef was 84 years old, having reigned since 1848.

Illness was an important factor governing the behavior of Presidents Wilson, Franklin Roosevelt, Eisenhower, and Kennedy. Wilson's arteriosclerosis was diagnosed as early as six years before he was elected to his first term of office in 1912. Wilson took toxic analgesics for his "blinding headaches" that affected his kidneys. What seems to have been a stroke in April 1919 brought about a sharp change in his personality and materially reduced his effectiveness in trying to win support for his League of Nations. A stroke on September 3, 1919, resulted in his complete incapacitation; thereafter, his wife, his physician, and Joseph Tumulty ran his office. None of his objectives could be met.

Franklin Delano Roosevelt's high blood pressure and other debilitating ailments made questionable his suitability for the presidency when he ran for his fourth term in 1944. His physician noted signs of hardening cerebral arteries before he went to meet Churchill and Stalin at the fateful Yalta Conference in February 1945.

Illness dogged President Eisenhower, limiting his activities at important international conferences. His weak heart caused acute problems at meetings at higher altitudes.

John F. Kennedy's chronic back pain was well known to the public, but he was also a victim of Addison's disease, which was treated with cortisone. Both the disease and treatment cause extreme mood swings and emotional instability at a time when Kennedy was dealing with the Bay of Pigs and the Cuban missile crisis.

Benito Mussolini's judgment was impaired by syphilis. By 1938–39, there was a noticeable deterioration in his intellectual capacity. In the four years before his downfall, he assisted Hitler at Munich, invaded Albania and Greece, and took Italy into a disasterous war with Britain.

Other examples of health problems that impaired the judgments of world-class leaders are those of Kemal Atatürk, Nikita Khrushchev, and George III of England. Kemal Atatürk suffered from Korsakoff's psychosis in which victims fill in gaps in their memory with imaginary events. Like many other world-class leaders, Nikita Khrushchev had to deal with high blood pressure.

King George III's porphyria first appeared during the first year of his 60-year reign. This genetic disorder periodically made him mentally deranged at a period when the British monarch not only reigned but ruled if he could manage Parliament. Intermittently, George III could do neither, and Britain lost its American colonies.

Park (1988) noted that the advanced age of leaders may be accompanied by a deterioration in judgment and temperament. That Paul von Hindenberg, Germany's president, became decrepit in the last years of the Weimar Republic made Hitler's rise to power that much easier. During these same years, Ramsey MacDonald, British prime minister, was a victim of Alzheimer's disease, which made his continued leadership of the Labor Party an embarrassment of ludicrous speeches and impaired judgment. Likewise, the premature aging of Poland's leader Marshal Josef Pilsudski contributed to his delusions about Poland's military strength and status in its foreign relations with Germany and Russia. Park suggested that governments with fixed terms of office require independent disability commissions to make judgments and recommendations about removing seriously mentally disabled leaders from office.

Many historical questions remain about how physical health influenced the leadership of generals, politicians, statesmen, and emperors. Was it lead poisoning that resulted in a sudden change for the worse in Caligula (lead was used by the Romans to seal wine bottles and for piping water)? How was John Foster Dulles's last year in office as Secretary of State affected by his carcinoma of the bowel? What was the impact on the course of events of Anthony Eden's acute obstructive colitis, which caused him to have a high fever during the Suez Crisis of 1956? Can effective leaders successfully mask or compensate for their debilitating illnesses? How are they affected by the medications they take to treat their conditions? How much of the success or failure of businesses can be traced to the ill-health of top executives? The impact of the sudden death of the chief executive officer will be discussed in Chapter 31 as a significant issue of succession.

Mental Health

Forms of mental maladjustment and ill-health, including neuroses, psychoses, and personality disorders, are the opposite of self-efficacy. Eysenck (1985) found neuroticism to be one of the two dimensions of central importance in accounting for large amounts of variance in social and leadership behavior. The other was introversion-extroversion. In contrast to the general population, Eysenck noted, managers and administrators were likely to be low in such neurotic tendencies and high in extroversion. Nevertheless, although such leaders are a minority, numerous linkages between pathological tendencies and leadership styles have been observed by clinical analysts. For example, Fernberg (1979) described frequently observed pathological character structures in administrators: schizoid, obsessive, narcissistic, and paranoid.

Managers with Type-A Personalities. The incidence of psychosomatic illnesses, such as hypertension and heart disease, tends to be higher in workaholic managers. Type-A managers are hostile, driven, competitive, time conscious, and frustrated in their sense of being blocked from full accomplishment. They hurry the speech of others; become unduly irritated when forced to wait; exhibit explosive speech patterns or frequent use of obscenities; make a fetish of always being on time; have difficulty sitting and doing nothing; play nearly every game to win, even when playing with children; become impatient while watching others do things they think they can do better or faster; and are prone to heart disease (Friedman & Rosenman, 1974).

In addition to hard-driving competitiveness, these Type-A managers' sense of urgency is accompanied by restlessness, multiple activities against deadlines, and impatience with delays and with others. These managers are self-centered and poor in interpersonal relationships.

In general, Type-A managers seem to have an overwhelming need to assert control over whatever happens. Nonetheless, when they lose control, they overreact with signs of helplessness. They react either with "all or nothing." In the process, they waste energy and strain themselves needlessly.

In a survey of 163 South African managers, Type-A behavior was found to be correlated with a strong feeling of exhaustion, role conflict, absence of friendliness, and anxiety/depression (reflecting joylessness). The behavior of these people as managers and leaders was affected accordingly, concomitant with effects on their hearts (Strumpfer, 1983).

The relationship between Type-A behavior and heart disease was demonstrated in a large number of studies (Jenkins, 1976, 1978). Men who were in the highest third in Type A scores on the Jenkins Activity Survey had 1.79 times the incidence of new coronary heart disease as did men who were in the bottom third of the distribution. When men who had had a single heart attack were compared with men who had had second heart attacks, Jenkins, Zyzanski, and Rosenman (1976) demonstrated that the Type-A score was the strongest single predictor of recurrent coronary heart disease.

Nevertheless, there are three important qualifications. First, as Strumpfer (1983) noted, the majority of people with Type-A behavior never develop heart disease. Second, it is difficult to control the confounding of Type-A behavior with other risk factors, such as smoking and obesity. Third, and most important, if it is a psychosomatic illness, the heart condition is a response to anger and frustration. The happy Type-A workaholic who enjoys his work and the challenges from it is not as likely to be at risk of heart disease. Also more likely to be free of heart disease may be Type-As who are emotionally expressive and genuinely confident in themselves and who laugh a lot and can be highly active (Hall, 1986).

The entire Type-A syndrome of anger, impatience, aggravation, and irritation may not be the culprit, but, rather, only one or more elements related to it. For instance a cynical, mistrusting attitude or intense self-involvement may be the particular risk factor of consequence (Fischman, 1987).

The Psychopathology of Leadership

According to Kets de Vries and Miller (1984a, p. 8), leader's wishes are articulated into fantasies. They are "scenes in the private theatre of [the leader's] subjective world." Those that dominate are the bases for specific styles of leadership. They may, in turn, become shared fantasies that can permeate all levels in a centralized organization, creating a specific organizational culture and determining decision making, strategy, and structure. On the basis of clinical observations of executives in four firms, five pathological leadership constellations were observed to emerge. Kets de Vries and Miller (1984a, 1986) identified them and provided generalizations about their different effects on their organization and their colleagues. These five constellations were feelings of persecution, feelings of helplessness, narcissism, compulsiveness, and schizoid detachment.

The Persecutory Preoccupation and Its Effects.
The dominant fantasy of such leaders is that they cannot really trust anyone and that menacing superior force exists that is out to "get" them. Thus, these leaders are quick to take offense and are always on guard. Along with their mistrust of others, they are suspicious, hypersensitive, and overconcerned with hidden motives and special meanings. They distort reality in an effort to confirm their suspicions. As Kets de Vries and Miller (1986, p. 269) stated:

The boss may feel hostile to those who report to him [or her and] may want to harm or attack others as a defensive reaction to his/her own feelings of persecution and mistrust. . . .

The leader sees . . . subordinates either as malingerers and incompetents, or as people who are deliberately out to raise his/her ire. As a consequence, he/she is likely to gravitate towards two extremes. He/she might try to exert a tremendous amount of control through intensive personal supervision, formal controls and rules, and harsh punishments. . . .

The second, less common, reactions of the hostile leader toward . . . subordinates may be one of overt aggression. He/she may be reluctant to provide emotional or material rewards, striving always to come out on the winning side of any "trades." . . . subordinates hold back their contributions and concentrate mostly on protecting themselves from exploitation.

In organizations that are dominated by paranoid leaders, emphasis is on management controls and continuous vigilance. Power is centralized and decision making is top-down, although information is sought from below. The organization is conservative and reactive to threats, rather than proactive to opportunities. Risk taking is low and is reduced by diversification, with an increased need for control, rather than constant goals, strategic plans, or unifying themes and traditions (Kets de Vries & Miller, 1984a).

Helplessness and Hopelessness and Their Effects. According to Kets de Vries and Miller (1986), the dominant fantasy is that it is hopeless to change the course of events in life; one is just not good enough. This depressive neurosis gives rise to a lack of self-confidence and initiative, feelings of dependence, and low self-esteem (Jacobson, 1971). Feelings of guilt, worthlessness, and inadequacy are exhibited in self-depreciation and feelings of inferiority. Feelings of learned hopelessness develop; the person believes that the malaise will last forever and that it will affect everything he or she does (Trotter, 1987). Kernberg (1979) noted that such depressive managers avoid responsibility, procrastinate about major decisions, and become passive and laissez-faire in their leadership style. Only routines get done; their groups stagnate, and goals are not clarified.

Narcissism and Its Effects. Of 32 revolutionary leaders, 23 were described as egotistical, narcissistic,

and searching for personal fame and glory (Rejai, 1980). Narcissists are dominated by the fantasy of getting attention and impressing others dramatically. Some are histrionic, with an excessive expression of emotions and an incessant drawing of attention to themselves. They are likely to be superficial and exaggerate their evaluations of others (Kets de Vries & Miller, 1984a). Narcissists who reject the object-relations in their fantasy exhibit severe and frequent defensive reactions, are demanding taskmasters, and gather sycophant subordinates around themselves. Narcissists who deceive themselves are overly sensitive to criticism and privately harbor grudges against dissenters. As Kets de Vries and Miller (1985, pp. 16–17) stated:

> Such leaders are hyperactive, impulsive, dramatically venturesome, and dangerously uninhibited. They live in a world of hunches and impressions rather than facts as they address a broad array of widely disparate projects, products, and markets in desultory fashion. The leaders' flair for the dramatic leads them to centralize power, allowing them to initiate bold ventures independently. . . . Instead of reacting to the environment (when at the top of the organization) the leader, often an entrepreneur, attempts to enact his own environment . . . [placing a] sizable proportion of the firm's capital . . . at risk. . . . Most of these . . . moves are made in the service of grandiosity. Unbridled growth is the goal. The organization's strategy is a function of its leader's considerable narcissistic needs—his desire for attention and visibility . . . the top man wants to be at center stage, putting on a show. . . . He wants to finally show "the others over there" how great an executive he really is.

Some degree of self-concentration appears to be important for effective leadership. Charismatic leaders carry around with them many self-assuring internal images with which they have a dialogue and form a basis for connections with their followers (Zaleznik, 1984). But concentration on the self may be a mixed blessing. Leaders may have highly inflated evaluations of themselves or severely negative self-images. As was noted earlier, in both instances of such self-concentration, prosocial leadership is unlikely to be attempted (Reykowski, 1982).

Compulsiveness and Its Effects. This neurosis is fueled by the fantasy "I don't want to be at the mercy of events. I have to master and control all the things affecting me." The fantasy is articulated by behaving as a perfectionist. The compulsive person is preoccupied with trivial details and insists that others submit to his or her way of doing things. He or she sees relationships in terms of dominance and submission and is characterized by a lack of spontaneity, inability to relax, meticulousness, dogmatism, obstinacy, and a constant preoccupation with losing control. "Every last detail of operation is planned out in advance and carried on in a routinized and preprogrammed fashion. Thoroughness, completeness, and conformity with standard and established procedures are emphasized. . . . Surprises must be avoided" (Kets de Vries & Miller, 1984a, p. 14).

Schizoid Detachment and Its Effects. The fantasy here is that "the world of reality does not offer any satisfaction to me. All of my interactions with others will eventually fail and cause harm so it is safer to remain distant" (Kets de Vries & Miller, 1984a, p. 11).

The manager with this problem is insecure, withdrawn, and noncommital. He or she discourages interaction because of a fear of involvement. The world is an unhappy place, filled with frustrating colleagues. Most contacts will end painfully, this manager believes. To compensate for this lack of fulfillment, he or she daydreams.

Again, the fantasy is articulated in ineffective, laissez-faire leadership.[10] The manager is detached and feels estranged from others. The cold, unemotional appearance is matched by an indifference to praise or reproof.

The Mentally Healthy Leader

A healthy self-concept contributes to one's effectiveness as a leader. Neurotic and disordered beliefs about oneself are most likely to result in leadership that is fraught with problems for colleagues and for the organization. But what is it for leaders to be in good mental health?

Effective, healthy leaders retain a balanced view of

themselves and how to deal with their work. They are at peace with themselves (Cleveland, 1985). They avoid maladaptive responses to the conflicts arising from their moving up the organization ladder. They help themselves by understanding their motivations, by establishing a firm sense of their identity, by maintaining continuity and predictability in their relations with their colleagues, by being selective in their activities and relationships, and by living appropriately with their own daily rhythms. They can face disappointments realistically and do not hide or deny their occurrence. They remain the masters of their fate and can tolerate their feelings of loss. They know when to withdraw and to reexamine their emotional investments in people and activities (Zaleznik, 1963).

Leaders' Organizational Values, and Orientation

Belonging, Identification, and Loyalty

One value of importance that many leaders and managers gain from their membership in an organization is a feeling of belonging to it and identification with it (Wald & Doty, 1954). For example, Mullen's (1954) survey of 140 clubs of foreman in 32 states found that 88 percent of the foremen wanted to feel identified with the company, and 71 percent reported that they were treated as if they were a part of management. D. D. Braun (1976) noted that identification with the community of Mankato, Minnesota, was strongly associated with community leadership, rather than mere participation, in community activities.

Orientation toward Superiors or Subordinates

Some leaders tend to feel closer to the attitudes, beliefs, and values of the higher authorities in their organization; others tend to identify with those below themselves. The best leaders are able to do both. Furthermore, the leaders' performance will be affected by how much the leaders identify with the organization's values.

D. T. Campbell and associates (1955, 1957, 1958, 1961) developed various methods of measuring orientation toward or identification with one's superiors and

[10]The experimental and survey evidence on the conterproductive effects of laissez-faire leadership is detailed in Chapter 25.

subordinates. With these methods, Campbell and Mc-Cormack (1957) compared attitudes of Air Force and civilian personnel. They found that colonels were significantly less oriented toward their superiors than were majors or college men, and majors were less so than Air Force cadets or their instructors. Air Force majors and lieutenant-colonels were significantly more subordinate oriented than were the other groups tested. Orientation toward superiors or toward subordinates appeared to be independent of tested information about leadership (Campbell & Damarin, 1961), nor were self-reported orientation measures consistent with the observed orientation to superiors or subordinates in a role-playing exercise (Burwen & Campbell, 1957a). However, orientation toward superiors did correlate with authoritarianism and with valuing discipline (Chapman & Campbell, 1957a). The leader's location in the organization affects his or her orientation toward those above or those below.[11]

Identification with the Values of Higher-ups. The alignment of the individual manager's goals and those of the organization is central to the manager's sense of belonging and identification with the organization (Culbertson & McDonough, 1980). Vroom (1960b) observed that the goals of a large firm are likely to be more accurately perceived by those executives who have more favorable attitudes toward the firm. Subordinates who resemble their superiors in the personality traits "sociable" and "stable" are better satisfied than are those who do not closely resemble their superiors in this respect. Furthermore, subordinates who identify themselves with their superiors and express interests similar to them are more satisfied than those who do not (Eran, 1966).[12] Such identification also helps their careers. Top managers generally prefer and rate as more effective those subordinates whose attitudes and values were similar to their own (R. E. Miles, 1964a; V. F. Mitchell, 1968). Identification with management also contributes to the likelihood that an employee will be promoted to a management position (J. C. White, 1964).

Lawler, Porter, and Tannenbaum (1968) found that interactions with superiors were more favorably valued than were those with subordinates. Balma, Maloney, and Lawshe (1958a, 1958b) concluded that foremen who identified with management were rated as having significantly more productive groups than were those who did not. But the employees' satisfaction with a foreman was not related to the foreman's orientation. R. S. Barrett (1963) also discovered that foremen who perceived that their approach to problems was similar to that of their immediate superiors tended to feel free to do things in their own way. Fleishman and Peters (1962) observed that the effectiveness of lower-level managers was identified with that of their immediate middle-level superiors. Read (1962) found that the successful upward mobility of managers was related to the degree of their problem-oriented communication with superiors. This tendency to communicate with superiors was associated with feelings of trust in their superiors and perceptions of their superiors' influence.

Henry (1949) and others found that rapidly promoted executives tended to identify themselves with their superiors as a primary organization reference group. Campbell, Dunnette, Lawler, and Weick (1970) suggested that "fast-trackers" tend to identify with fast-trackers higher-up in the organization and are less interested in their current group of subordinates and may even work against the best interests of their immediate subordinates to get promoted. But the extent to which superiors enhance their subordinates' sense of belonging to the organization tends to pay off in their subordinates' better performance. Habbe (1947) demonstrated that insurance agents who thought they were fulfilling their managers' expectations sold more policies and experienced fewer lapses than did those who thought they were not meeting these expectations.

Identification with the Values of Subordinates. Some evidence also suggests that for many leaders, satisfaction and success is connected with identification with those who are below them in the organization. According to R. E. Miles (1964a), managers did not regard lower-level supervisors as being highly promotable when they identified only with the company. Similarly, Mann and Dent (1954b) found that supervisors and employees agreed that the promotable supervisor is

[11]Cummings and ElSalmi (1968); Herzberg, Mausner, Peterson, and Capwell (1957); Porter and Lawler (1965); and Vroom (1965).
[12]See also Gruenfeld and Foltman (1967), Mordechai (1966), and M. S. Meyers (1966).

one who will stand up for employees and their rights, train them for better jobs, and let them know where they stand on matters that concern them. Pelz's (1952) study of industrial work groups indicated that first-line supervisors who are oriented to subordinates tended to be evaluated positively by workers, but only of they were perceived to have sufficient influence with superiors so they could satisfy the workers' expectations.

Supervisors who value belonging and identification do much to increase their subordinates' sense of "ownership" of activites (Habbe, 1947). Consistent with this finding is Anikeeff's (1957) that the greater the satisfaction of managers, the greater the similarity between the attitudes of managers and workers. Satisfied managers prevent a cleavage in attitudes between workers and management.

The favorable attitudes of leaders toward their subordinates are reciprocated. Obrochta (1960) reported that workers' attitudes toward foremen were favorable only when the foremen held favorable attitudes toward the workers. Murphy and Corenblum (1966) observed that loyalty to a superior was higher at all levels in an organization if the superior perceived his or her group of subordinates as a primary source of social support.

Hierarchical Differences in Attitudes, Needs, and Values

As one rises on the organizational ladder, one usually finds shifts in values that cannot be attributed to age, education, or seniority. Status differences emerge, and commitment to the organization is generally greater the higher one's level in the organization. Pfiffner and Wilson (1953) surveyed two levels of supervisors. Their results indicated that high-level supervisors felt at ease with superiors and were interested in duties involving management functions. Low-level supervisors identified with their work groups and were less critical of workers than were the high-level supervisors. Rosen and Weaver (1960) found four levels of management in agreement regarding the importance of factors that affect the effectiveness of jobs (authority, knowledge of plans, consultation) as opposed to the importance of a role in policy-making and communication with higher-ups. But first-line supervisors differed from higher levels of management in emphasizing the importance

of consideration and fairness. Compared with workers, managers at all levels regarded themselves as upholders of group norms (Fruchter & Skinner, 1966). W. K. Graham (1969) factor analyzed the intercorrelations among the job-attitude scores of personnel at three levels of organization in life insurance agencies. Higher-level managers differentiated managerial actions from the organizational climate, while supervisors and agents did not.

Needs. Many studies have found that the importance of self-actualization and autonomy (discussed earlier) increases with one's status in one's organization, whereas those remaining in lower-status positions attach more value to security and working conditions. For example, Porter (1963b) found that higher-level managers placed greater emphasis on the need for autonomy and self-actualization than did lower-level managers. Furthermore, there is considerable agreement with the finding that the higher the level of a manager's position, the greater the manager's need for achievement (Beer, Buckhout, Horowitz, & Levy, 1959).[13] Similarly, higher-level managers exceed those at lower levels in the desire to be inner directed (Eran, 1966).[14] Managers who attain higher organizational levels when young are more likely to value self-actualization and achievement (Bass, Burger, et al., 1979). But a relatively temporary rank may not make much difference in a population of students. Thus, F. J. Michaelson (1951), in a study of military cadets, found that those of high rank did not differ from those of low rank in a desire for advancement, human relations orientation, or identification with high socioeconomic status.

Meaning of the Job. Triandis (1960) factor analyzed the meanings attached to job descriptions by managers and workers. Six factors were isolated, five of which were similar for managers and workers. However, in a study of meanings attached to words describing jobs and people, Triandis (1959a) found that upper-level managers stressed the importance of status, polish, and education; lower-level managers stressed power and po-

---

[13]See also Henry (1949); McClelland (1961); Meyer and Walker (1961); Pellegrin and Coates (1957); Veroff, Atkinson, Feld, and Gurin et al. (1960); and Vroom (1965).
[14]See also Mordechai (1966), Porter and Henry (1964a), and Uris (1958).

sition; and workers stressed money and dependability. Lennerlöf (1965b), in comparing the attitudes of Swedish managers, superiors, and workers, discovered that workers value good personal relations to a greater extent than do supervisors and supervisors value it more than do their superiors. Also, the supervisors and their workers felt more strongly than did their superiors that the supervisor should strive to attain an independent and influential position.

Nonetheless, when Schwartz, Jenusaitis, and Stark (1966) compared the values of U.S. foremen and workers, they found that the two groups agreed in placing greater value on job security, wages, and working conditions than on interpersonal relations. Similarly, Friedlander (1966a) found few differences between the values of U.S. civil service employees at different levels of status.

Lifestyles. Bray, Campbell, and Grant (1974) reported on a comprehensive comparison of the assessed values of those who had advanced further in the Bell System with those who had not. Over the eight years of the survey, systematic changes occurred in the lives of 400 Bell System managers who were followed up after evaluations at an assessment center. Two contrasting lifestyles were identified: the "enlarger" and the "enfolder." The enlarger's lifestyle stressed innovation, change, self-development, and movement away from traditional ways of thinking and doing things. The enfolder's lifestyle was oriented more toward tradition and maintaining the close family and friendship ties that the individual had gained through adolescence and college. Enfolders were less likely to leave their hometown area and were much less likely to engage in any self-improvement activities. More successful managers were enlargers; less successful managers were enfolders. Enlargers gained occupational interests and lost concern for parents and family; enfolders either suffered small losses in such concerns or remained the same. Enlargers sharply reduced their interest in recreational and social activities; enfolders showed only a small loss in such interests.

Which is cause, and which is effect? As managers rise faster and higher, they may have less time for family ties and recreation. At the same time, as shall be emphasized later, they obtain increasingly greater satisfaction from their job as they rise in rank. Less successful managers are likely to derive less satisfaction from their jobs and have more time for family and recreation. However, one cannot ignore the evidence that successful people are more likely to be career oriented before they actually began to work, which suggests that they bring to their job at least some semblance of a lifestyle that will contribute to their success in the organization.

Satisfaction with the Leadership Role

Rank, Level, and Satisfaction

One of the most consistent findings in behavioral science is the positive correlation between the importance of one's position in an organization and one's satisfaction with it. Relying on early survey evidence, G. B. Watson (1942) was convinced that managers and supervisors tended to be more satisfied with their work than were rank-and-file employees. Furthermore, it became clear that top managers were generally more satisfied than were managers at lower levels (Bass, 1960). The results of many studies supported the contention that the higher the level of individuals' positions in the organization, the greater the degree of their job satisfaction.[15] And the reasons are not hard to find. Compensation is greater and, as was just noted, the need for self-actualization and autonomy is better satisfied at higher echelons of the organization (L. W. Porter, 1963a). Nevertheless, there are alternative or additional plausible explanations in some organizations in which status is unrelated to power and influence, for instance, organizations in which the top leaders are puppets or figureheads. Thus, Ritchie and Miles (1970) studied 330 managers in five levels of organization. They found that satisfaction did not differ as a consequence of the level of the position, but according to the amount of participation in decision making.

T. R. Mitchell (1970a, 1970b) studied line and staff officers of different ranks and in different commands abroad. Not only did satisfaction rise with rank, but line

[15]J. W. Campbell (1948), DeLora and Barber (1963), Edel (1966), Eran (1966), Johnson and Marcrum (1968), Kolstad (1944), E. L. Miller (1966a, 1966b), L. W. Porter (1961a, 1961b, 1962), Porter and Mitchell (1967), Renck (1955), Troxell (1954), and Vroom (1965).

officers of all ranks were found to be better satisfied than were those in staff positions (staff positions are usually accorded less importance than line positions); however, this feeling varied greatly from one situation to another. Porter and Lawler (1965) confirmed these findings in a review of the empirical literature. They concluded that line managers tended to be somewhat more satisfied than did staff members and perceived more fulfillment of their needs for self-actualization (Porter, 1963b). But satisfaction was not related to a manager's span of control.

In the laboratory, Guetzkow (1954) found that key persons in a communication network saw themselves as most important and were more satisfied than did members with less important positions. Bass, Pryer, Gaier, and Flint (1958) found that satisfaction was greater in a member assigned more power compared with four others with much less power. The attractiveness of a group was significantly lower for the average member when members were assigned control differentially, in contrast to groups in which all members were equal.

Clarity about Status and Role. It would seem obvious that a leader's satisfaction is strongly associated with the clarity of the position held and agreement about its importance, power, and what is required for satisfactory performance. This idea was corroborated by Gross, Mason, and McEachern (1958), who conducted an extensive study of the perceptions of role interactions between school board members and superintendents. The results indicated that the greater the degree of consensus among board members, the higher the board members rated the superintendent, the higher he rated the board, and the greater the superintendent's job satisfaction. The board's rating of the superintendent was not related to his measured personality or to his agreement with the board. Within both samples, the degree of consensus in expectations of a position was related to the extent to which the role demands of the position had been formally or legally codified.

Satisfaction with Compensation

One obvious reason why those of higher status in the organization tend to be more satisfied than do subordinates is that they ordinarily earn more pay. (But this is not always true. Deans may earn less than professors, and supervisors may earn less than skilled subordinates.) However, satisfaction with earnings is relative. One feels relatively deprived, depending on whom one compares oneself with. In a highly inflationary economy, dissatisfaction with pay is seen as being due primarily to inflation, governmental policy, and OPEC, not necessarily to one's employer. In a depression, relatively modest compensation may be highly satisfying. Furthermore, the greater the congruence between the managers' feeling about how pay should be determined and their perception of how it is determined, the greater their satisfaction with their pay (Lawler, 1966c, 1967b).

Penzer (1969) found that expectations regarding external opportunities were major determinants of managers' satisfaction with their pay. Those who attended college brought different expectations with them than did those who did not attend college, and those expectations, when compared with external reference groups, partially determined their satisfaction with their pay. Among the internal factors, commendations, rapid advancement, salary increases, and the like tended to inflate expectations. Thus, the managers' satisfaction with their pay is obviously related to how much they earn in an absolute sense, as well as to the correspondence between expected pay and actual pay. Managers prefer pay that is based on performance and merit, but they tend to define merit in terms of traits that they perceive themselves to possess.

More effective managers tend to feel more satisfied with their pay (Lawler & Porter, 1966; Porter & Lawler, 1968). Managers who score high in a preference for taking risks but not in achievement motivation prefer pay that is based on performance (Meyer & Walker, 1961). However, the higher managers rate themselves in comparison with their peers on variables such as education, experience, productivity, effort, and skill, the more importance they attach to these variables as determinants of pay.

Further support for the relationship between the satisfaction of managers and the extent to which their level of pay corresponds with their expectations for pay was obtained by Klein and Maher (1966). Middle managers overestimated the pay of subordinates and underestimated the pay of superiors. They believed that the difference between their pay and that of the persons above and below them was too small. The smaller the perceived difference between their pay and that of their subordinates, the less satisfied the managers were with their pay (Lawler, 1965, 1967b).

In a study of 919 low- to middle-level managers, Gorn and Kanungo (1980) isolated a job involvement factor (For me, mornings at work really fly by; I'll stay over-time to finish a job even if I'm not paid for it). Ninety-three managers were identified as being motivated most by their extrinsic need for adequate salary and security and 124, by their intrinsic need for interesting work, responsibility, and independence. Involvement was as high among the extrinsically motivated as among the intrinsically motivated, if their respective needs were being met.

Personal Factors Affecting Satisfaction

Although J. G. Mauer (1969) found that the job satis-faction of industrial supervisors was not related to their age, education, degree of involvement in work, income, or the size of their plant, more often than not, these factors have been found by others to affect the satisfac-tion of managers.

Education and Managerial Satisfaction. Many studies have found that the managers' satisfaction with their leadership role depends on their level of educa-tion. Higher pay may be expected but not necessarily forthcoming for those with more education. For exam-ple, Andrews and Henry (1963) and Klein and Maher (1966, 1968) reported that with more education, man-agers felt less satisfied with their pay. However, Stogdill (1965b) and Lawler and Porter (1966) reported studies in which no relation was found between the education of managers and their satisfaction with their pay. Bet-ter-educated managers may be dissatisfied for other reasons. Stogdill (1965a) studied 442 managers and su-pervisors in six departments of an aircraft plant. He found that the better-educated managers were less sat-isfied with the company and with their freedom on the job; however, their level of education was not consist-ently related to their attitudes about their pay. Accord-ing to Friedlander (1963), less well-educated supervisors

tended to derive satisfaction from the social and tech-nical, rather than the self-actualizing, aspects of their work.

Age and Managerial Satisfaction. Saleh and Otis (1964) asked 80 managers, aged 60–65, to think back over their careers and indicate the age at which they had derived the most satisfaction from their work. These managers said that their satisfaction increased to age 59, then showed a sharp decrease. Another sam-ple, aged 50 to 59, also reported an increase in satisfac-tion until age 59, but then anticipated a decrease in satisfaction after age 60. The authors interpreted the reduced enjoyment after age 60 to a blockage of chan-nels for further development and advancement.

Friedlander (1963) found that the older supervisors tended to derive more satisfaction from the social and technical aspects of their work and less satisfaction from self-actualization than did the younger supervi-sors. Results reported by England (1967a) indicated that older managers placed a higher value on social wel-fare and a lower value on organizational growth and leadership in the industry as goals of their organization. Gruenfeld (1962) found younger industrial supervisors to be more interested than were older ones in high wages and fringe benefits. Older supervisors were more concerned about regular hours and freedom from stress.

Stogdill (1965a), in his study in an aircraft plant, found that with increasing age, managers tended to be more satisfied with the company but less satisfied with the recognition they received. But J. G. Mauer (1969) failed to find any relation between the age and the sat-isfaction of industrial supervisors. Some studies failed to find that managerial satisfaction was affected by the manager's age or other factors.

Tenure and Managerial Satisfaction. In Stogdill's (1965a) survey, the number of years a manager re-mained in the same position tended to contribute to all the aspects of dissatisfaction that were measured but particularly to dissatisfaction with the failure to be pro-moted. However, Hall, Schneider, and Nygren (1970) reported that tenure, but not position, was related to identification with the organization and the satisfac-tion of needs in the U.S. Forest Service.

Performance and Satisfaction

Consistently, the evidence points to the fact that better-satisfied managers perform better. Lawler and Porter (1967b) found that the degree to which an individual's needs are satisfied is related to his or her job performance, as evaluated by peers and superiors, and that this relationship is stronger for managers than for nonmanagers. Porter and Lawler (1968) reported that managers who were rated high in performance by themselves and their superiors expressed a higher degree of need satisfaction than did those who were rated low in performance. Managers who were rated higher in effort also reported that they required a greater fulfillment of all their needs. Finally, Slocum, Miller, and Misshauk (1970) reported that high-producing foremen were better satisfied than were low-producing ones.

Summary and Conclusions

What leaders and managers regard as right, important, and good, shapes their performance. These values depend on occupational and societal influences. But a majority are likely to see themselves as pragmatically balanced in outlook.

Leaders differ in their values for many reasons. They may be selected by an organization because of their values or they may assimilate the organization's values after joining. Their profession and locale also make for obvious differences. Furthermore, their performance depends on their concepts about themselves, their pragmatism, their preferences for taking risks, and their valuing of short-term maximization or long-term gain.

Compensation is a strong motivator, but its effects are relative. Identification with the organization is also a strong motivator, as are commitment to the organization's goals and the managers' location in the organization.

Systematic differences in values separate radical from conservative political leaders and revolutionaries from loyalist leaders. Both the projected needs for achievement and task orientation contribute positively to the emergence of leaders. In turn, there is a linkage of such leadership to risk-taking propensities. Among the self-concepts that particularly affect the emergence and performance of leaders are the internal or external locus of control, the sense of self-efficacy, and self-confidence, self-esteem, and the valuing of self-actualization.

Researchers have generally ignored the physical health of leaders. Yet, physical health can be essential to a leader's performance. Physical and mental health meet in their effects on leadership when the Type-A personality is considered. Additional mental health problems are seen in leaders who feel persecuted, helpless, narcissistic, compulsive, or schizoid.

Satisfaction with the role of leader is associated with earnings and status and their accompanying power and control. Role clarity is particularly important. Although exceptions can be found, the higher one's status in an organization, the greater one's job satisfaction. Managers' satisfaction with their role in the organization and with their compensation often depend on their education, age, and tenure and correlate with their effective performance.

However, the leaders' successful performance also depends on how much others value them. Their self-concepts, needs, and values move them to lead; how much others value them and accord them esteem and status affect how likely these others will accept the leaders' efforts.

Accorded Status, Esteem, and Leadership

People are valued by others because of the position they occupy. Or, they may be valued as persons regardless of their position.

Meaning of Status and Esteem

Blaise Pascal (1660/1950) described a great nobleman as being valued for the status he had in society that made it possible for him to be "the master of objects that men covet" and for which objects deference was paid to him. But he was not esteemed by Pascal as a person, as was "M. N. [who] is a greater geometrician than I . . . [and who] I esteem for the enlightenment of mind, virtue, health and strength. . . ."

Pascal's nobleman was of worth to others because of his noble status, the hierarchical position he held in society. The nobleman's position gave him control, power, and influence. Pascal failed to recognize that a poor nobleman could still be accorded some status and influence. Even without control of wealth to distribute, a nobleman's position was still of more importance than a commoner's.

Pascal's mathematician was esteemed for his technical competence and personal qualities. Many noblemen of high status lacked such personal qualities and were held in low esteem by those who knew them personally or by reputation. Many ordinary folk who lacked status could be esteemed by others for their personal value.

The value that others accord members for their position in a group, organization, or society is the members' *status*. Status contributes to the members' success as leaders. The same is true for the members' *esteem*—the value accorded them by others for their personal qualities (Bass, 1960). Conflicts abound and ineffective-

ness increases in the group, organization, or society when the esteem and status of the members fail to be correlated.[1]

Shared Perceptions of Status and Esteem

It should be clear that the value of a perception or a person is in the eye of the beholder. "Pocketbook" voters will esteem a president for their perceptions of his effects on their personal economic life; "sociotropic" voters will evaluate a president on what he does for the national economy (Kinder, 1981). Nevertheless, extensive evidence points to the ease with which members share perceptions of each others' differences in status and esteem. Animals are quick to recognize the differences in their group and usually do not challenge the leader's dominance. If they do challenge it, a fight settles the issue; thereafter, the status structure exhibits considerable stability.

Among humans, even in the absence of symbols and signs of office, formal authority, and other common attributes of status in formal organizations, potential differences in esteem and status are quickly recognized by group members (Gronlund, 1955a) as well as by trained observers (Stein, 1971). Vielhaber and Gottheil (1965) studied 117 cadets who were rated by 4 judges after only 20–35 seconds of observation. The judges' ratings correlated .45 with the upper classmen's evaluations after 4 weeks of observation and correlated .31 with composite evaluations of aptitude for service made 14 weeks later!

Importance of First Impressions. Gronlund (1955a) observed that group members are about as well agreed on their relative esteem at the beginning of their inter-

---

[1]As will be detailed in Chapter 15.

action as they are after an extended acquaintance. In experiments with the self-esteem of members of dyads, Levinger (1959) also found that although later behavior influenced a partner's behavior more than did first impressions, first impressions tended to determine behavior throughout the experiment. Likewise, Barker (1942) demonstrated that after a few moments of getting acquainted, a group of strangers exhibited a high degree of agreement in choosing members for seatmates.

Self versus Others. Agreement is not high between self-esteem and the esteem that others accord one. Gronlund (1955b) correlated each individual's rank according to the others in a group with the individual's ranking of the other group members. The median rank-order correlations were only .40 for 104 graduate students. Blake, Mouton, and Fruchter (1954) studied 10 groups, each with 3 members, in a discussion task. Changes between Sessions 1 and 2 included varying the task, group membership, and identity of observers. Evaluations were made on a 12-item questionnaire. In both sessions, there was limited agreement between the individuals' ratings of themselves and the observers' ratings of them, as well as between the individuals' ratings of themselves and of other members for esteem and accorded status, as evidenced by leadership, contributions to the groups' decision, and the amount of clerical work performed.

Agreement among Others. Bass and White (1951), Bass and Coates (1952), and Bass and Wurster (1953a, 1953b) reported that pairs of observers tended to reach agreement on which member of an initially leaderless group emerged with the highest accorded status as a leader of the group. Correlations between observers ranged from .51 to .83. Similar results were obtained for ratings of cadet leaders. A reliability of .68 was obtained as an index of agreement among ratings by 2–17 ROTC cadets rating a total of 307 fellow cadets (Bass & Coates, 1953). Prien and Culler (1964) found, however, that observers agreed better on those who participated a little rather than on those who participated a lot.

The sociometric ratings among very young children were inconsistent from one period to the next (Lazar, 1953). But according to Newstetter, Feldstein, and Newcomb (1938), as the age of campers increased, the stability of their sociometric ratings increased as well.

Northway (1946) reported rate-rerate correlations of .8 to .9 when summer campers rerated each other a week after a first rating. Bjerstedt (1956) reported correlations of .82 between ratings and reratings 4 months apart among 867 Swedish schoolchildren aged 9 and older; even after 13 months, the rate-rerate correlation was .73. McGuire, Lammon, and White (1953) found a similar consistency among adolescents from one year to the next. Even when half the children, aged 6–12, in a group are replaced with new members, the remaining children's ratings of esteem were consistent, to some extent, with earlier ratings (E. Campbell, undated).

Status

Warner, Meeker, and Eells (1949) observed that all societies and social groups of any size or complexity have status systems. Status structure and the differentiation of function are necessary for the coordination of efforts. Even collectives that are designed to minimize functional specialization and the differential distribution of rewards develop well-defined status structures (E. Rosenfeld, 1951).

In traditional societies, younger people accorded the old man, regardless of who he was personally, particular status as the occupant of a position. Age was an important determinant of status. However, the details concerning what was expected of members of different ages—infants, boys, girls, young men, young women, old men, and old women—differed from one social organization to another (Linton, 1945).

Occupants of various positions are provided with cues, which makes it easy to identify their status. Status differences in military organizations are clearly visible. In many societies, the adolescent often is easily discriminated by dress from the preadolescent, as is the married woman from the unmarried woman. Until modern times, each profession had its own identifiable costume. And the signs and symbols of differential status in the modern industrial organization are familiar. The top managers have extra-large corner offices on the top floor, custom-made desks, large leather desk chairs, carpeting, coffee tables, couches, and special parking spaces for their cars; the first-line supervisors have small offices in the basement with wooden desks and chairs and park in the lot wherever they can (Barn-ard, 1952).

Status differences affect how members group. In a mixed social gathering, high-level officials will cluster, as will those who are lower in status. At a cocktail party, men often stay together in one corner of the room and the women, in another corner. In organizations, members tend to maintain some degree of physical distance between themselves and other members who differ from them in status.[2] Status also determines how people communicate with others who are working at a distance. Thus, members of organizations send memos to those above or below them in status but telephone those who are at their same level in status (Klauss & Bass, 1981).

Concomitants of Status

Some positions provide occupants with direct control over what is rewarding to others; occupants of such positions have greater status in the organization (Barnard, 1951). In turn, such status-derived power makes it possible for its possessors to exert leadership and influence over others. Some roles make it possible for the role players to have access to information and the ability to solve the group's problems.[3]

Sherif, White, and Harvey (1955) found that the higher the importance of a member's position, the greater his or her competence, as judged by other members. This finding fits with the facts of everyday life. Studies of the occupational-status hierarchy in social organizations show that positions accord their occupants more status if all occupants of those positions either acquire more knowledge once they occupy the position or are selected for the position only if they have the knowledge. Those occupations with the highest societal status (that is, value or importance to society), according to college students, include those of physician, lawyer, banker, engineer, and school administrator, all of which require a great deal of education and specialized knowledge. Low-status occupations include those of truck driver, coal miner, janitor, and ditch digger, all of which necessitate little or no educa-tion. The status of occupations is remarkably stable. For 25 occupations, the correlations in status in 1925, 1946, and 1967 were all above .9 (Hakel, Hollman, & Dunnette, 1968) and were as likely to be as high in 1990. Furthermore, miners' and laborers' perceptions of the differentiations of occupational status were similar to those of the college students (Cattell, 1942).

In primitive societies, the high status of the medicine man and the tribal elders was partly due to the knowledge held by anyone occupying such positions. In a world that had to depend on the memory of events and procedures without the availability of books and in which life expectancy was short, age was highly prized. Since wisdom required age and experience, age, status, and leadership were strongly linked. Conversely, the lower status of women and children was often due to their ignorance of magic, ritual, and tribal history.

Value of Positions. A price tag can be set on one's status in firms and agencies. Job evaluation establishes the worth of each position to the organization. One's pay, then, depends on the position's established value, regardless of who occupies the position. One's status and value to one's family, clan, or social organization were clearly fixed in Anglo-Saxon law. The "man-price," or wergild, varied with a man's status in society; it was to be paid to a man's relatives as retribution if he was murdered or killed by accident. The various social strata were valued by their respective prices. The church placed its own members on the wergild scale. It equated a priest with a thane. The price of a king was from 6 to 15 times that of a thane (Whitelock, 1950). Today, the executive who is incapacitated owing to the fault of another still sues for a far greater estimated loss of income than does the manual laborer. The estimates are based on the expected future earnings of executives and laborers in the same general circumstances.

Striving for Increased Status. The desire for upward mobility is associated with attaining a more important and valued position to increase one's influence. Those with lower status in a group are more likely to be concerned about raising their status than are those who already have attained leadership roles of importance. In three industrial plants, M. Dalton (1950) observed that the lower-status executives tried to get

[2]As will be noted in Chapter 30.
[3]As was already discussed in Chapter 7.

more personnel to supervise and tried to transfer from staff (less influential) to line (more influential) positions. The line executives, on the other hand, did not seek staff jobs and were more concerned about entering the management "eating circle" and about personal distinctions. Similarly, Bentz (undated) observed that members of college faculties who accorded themselves lower status tended to report more concern within their department about rank, status, and influence.

Upward striving for status may be reflected in a desire to identify with those of higher status or to accumulate the signs and symbols of higher status. Beshers (1962) called this striving "one-way status mirrors" when he observed the behavior of poor people of lower-class status aspiring to join the middle class.

Expectations of higher status are conducive to greater satisfaction. Kipnis (1964) reported that those who expect to move up are generally more satisfied with their work. Vroom (1966) studied master's degree students in a business school before and after they accepted positions and found that they rated organizations as attractive when they perceived that these organizations were instrumental to the attainment of their personal goals. H. H. Kelley (1951) found that high-status members with no possibility of promotion were least attracted to a group. Conversely, in yet another laboratory study, Spector (1953) reported that participants who were placed in a pseudo-military hierarchy and were promoted were the most satisfied. In the U.S. Air Force, Borgatta (1955b) noted that personnel who saw adequate opportunities for advancement to officer positions also were less critical of the rewards and punishments possible in the U.S. Air Force. However, those who were actually striving for advancement in status were more critical than were those who did not seek promotion.

Individuals not only like to occupy comfortably high-status positions within groups but enjoy, within limits, associating with high-status groups, since these groups are likely to have more power and influence in the organizations. J. W. Mann (1961) found that members of a group, especially low-status members, preferred to associate with groups of similar or higher status than theirs. Their expectations tended to focus on the group that was next highest in status.

This striving for status—usually positions of leadership—often involves the motivation to achieve congruence in status among the various positions one holds. Dissatisfaction with one's status in one organization may be due to one's status in another. Benoit-Smullyan (1944) hypothesized that individuals with different status in different groups would attempt to equalize their stature in the various groups. Thus, a business leader may endow an art institute to gain status in cultural circles. Fenchel, Monderer, and Hartley (1951) found that subjects' strivings for status in five groups to which they belonged were higher in those groups in which their current status was low.

Although the desire for upward movement in an organization may be the norm, nevertheless, it may require changes in residence, associates, and patterns of living. Upward mobility also may require a change in relationships with friends, associates, and former coworkers in the organization. In addition, a higher-status position involves changes in responsibility and accountability for results. It may even mean lower pay for some workers, who, if promoted to supervisor, will no longer be paid for overtime. Not all members of an organization welcome such upward mobility. For example, Springer (1956) found that 13 percent of 10,533 workers who were recommended for promotion to leadman, assistant foreman, or foreman refused the promotion.

A major factor in the emotional breakdown of medical officers in World War II was their promotion to a higher-level position of responsibility and status, according to Reider (1944). The young officer who depended on a superior for support not only lost it when he became a status peer of senior officers, but he was also expected to provide support for his subordinates.

Concern about Losing Status. Although D. W. Olmsted (1957) showed that members can drop from a position of leadership to the status of participant without reducing their activities or losing their liking for their group, most persons in important positions will be concerned about losing status. E. L. Thorndike (1940) noted that for many, perhaps most persons, political power is a habit-forming psychological drug. Abdications are rare. It is one's general status that is involved, not the specific position. A president of the

Teamsters' Union is tenacious about maintaining his union office because it is inconceivable for him to return to driving a truck after a term in such a high-status position. Yet, a cabinet secretary or the president of the American Association of University Professors can return to a high-status position in business or in academia after serving a term in office and so usually is not as reluctant to relinquish office (Selznick, 1943).

Lowered Status, Dissatisfaction, and Performance. Lowered status is likely to result in dissatisfaction and a decline in performance. H. H. Kelley (1951) studied the written communications of group members in high-status and low-status positions, with and without the possibility of status mobility, and found that low status was associated with relative dislike for the group task. The low-status members communicated their dissatisfaction to other low-status members. Furthermore, the high-status members who could lose their status made fewer positive comments than did those whose status was secure, and the low-status members with the possibility of upward mobility made fewer negative comments than did those who had no such opportunity.

Burnstein and Zajonc (1965a) observed that group members' performance tended to suffer when their status was decreased and tended to improve when their status was increased. Loss of status is likely to generate hostility. Lindzey and Kalnins (1958) asked students to compare themselves and other persons with figures in a picture test of projective attitudes. The students tended to identify themselves with hero figures, but identified other persons more often with nonhero figures. In the students' projections, changes in status after frustration revealed increased aggression by the hero against others and by others against the hero. Consistent with these findings, Worchel (1961) showed that expressions of hostility against others were reduced by restoring their lost status.

Status and Leadership

Substantial evidence and everyday experience support the strong connection between status and leadership so much that many confuse and merge the two concepts. The worth or value of a manager's position in the organizational hierarchy increases as he or she moves to higher echelons. Greater responsibility and authority accrue along with higher status. Thus, according to D. T. Campbell (1956), the descriptions of the behavior of leaders and the nominations for leadership of submarine officers were highly correlated with the officers' rank and the level of their positions.

A rise in status and status differentiation may be reflected in the use of effective leadership. In one Mexican village, economic development resulted in the emergence of a cohesive wealthier class. These wealthier members led the initiation of projects, mobilization of community support, and the successful completion of the projects. In a second village without such economic and class developments, little change was possible. Only the first village could deal effectively with outside influences that sought to control local decision making (Krejci, 1976).

Systematic differences are observed in the requirements for leadership with increases in status. The concern for routine production at the lowest levels becomes the concern for systems and the external environment at the highest levels. In the previous chapter, it was noted that satisfaction also increases with increases in status. Later chapters show that systematic changes also occur in the concern for interpersonal relations with immediate subordinates, and with the amount of delegation, as status increases.

Styles. Bass (1960) deduced that the power accruing from members' high status makes it possible for them to become coercive leaders. This power, coupled with information and the ability to help the group that stem from their high-status positions, allows them to persuade or to permit participation by others in decision making.

The higher-status member of an organization, Schell (1951) suggested, offers security, protection, and opportunity to the subordinate in turn for obedience and zeal. On the coercive influence associated with higher status in the industrial organization, Roethlisberger (1945, p. 287) remarked: "Personal dependence upon the judgments and decisions of his superiors, so characteristic of the subordinate-superior relation . . . makes the foreman . . . feel a constant need to adjust himself to demands of his superior and to seek approval of his superior."

Gerard (1957) found that participants with high status tended to be controlling in their behavior, whether their role relationships were clear or unclear. But low-status participants required a clearly defined set of role expectations to be effective. Without group goals, high-status participants assumed broader prerogatives, whereas low-status participants seemed bewildered. High-status participants also perceived themselves to have more freedom of action than did low-status participants.

Influence. The power of the higher-status boss to influence his lower-status subordinate foremen has been observed in numerous empirical studies. For instance, Jacobson, Charters, and Lieberman (1951) found that supervisors conformed to what they thought their bosses expected of them. Foremen who said their bosses expected them to be considerate tended to describe themselves as more considerate leaders and were so described by their subordinates (Fleishman, 1953b). Similarly, Mann (1951) found that foremen who changed more as a consequence of training in leadership received more encouragement from their superiors and felt more secure in their relations with their superiors. Bass (1960) reported finding that the higher a salesman's rank in a sales organization, the more likely was he to be nominated by the others as influential.

Attempts to lead were more likely to be successful when the members differed in accorded status and when they were highly motivated than under the opposite conditions (Bass, 1963). A correlation of .88 was obtained between the organizational level of 131 supervisors in an oil refinery and their success in initially leaderless group discussions for which no one was appointed chairman (Bass & Wurster, 1953b). If the problem concerned company matters, the correlation was even higher (Bass & Wurster, 1953a). A correlation of .51 was found between the rank of 264 ROTC cadets and their tendency to lead discussions among associates. When 180 cadets were retested in a new discussion among their associates a year after an initial discussion, those who had risen in rank from cadet noncommissioned officer to first lieutenant or higher during that year gained significantly more in observed success as leaders on the retest than did those who re-

ceived promotions to cadet second lieutenant only (Bass, 1964).

J. C. Moore (1968) found that when dyads worked on an ambiguous task, partners of lower status in the same experimental condition tended to defer to the choices made by their partners of higher status. Subsequently, J. C. Moore (1969) showed that agreement among partners tended to erode their expectations of differential performance that were activated by the differences in their status.

The influence of the leader's status may contribute to better performance among the leader's subordinates. Thus, Doyle (1971) showed how the process and productivity of schoolteachers was linked systematically to their principals' achieved status. And Tang, Tollison, and Whiteside (1988) reported that among 47 quality circles (QCs) the attendance rate by others was higher over a three-year period when these meetings were attended frequently by senior managers than when upper-management attendance was low. QCs with a high level of middle-management attendance attempted more QC projects and had a greater amount of cost savings. But the effect of lower-management attendance on QC effectiveness was not significant.

Influence accrues from high status because more attention is paid to high-status persons. Pedestrians at a traffic signal committed significantly more violations when they witnessed violations committed by an experimenter who was dressed to represent a person of high social status (Lefkowitz, Blake, & Mouton, 1955).

Vrugt (undated) showed that when a confederate who was introduced as a higher-status graduate student of psychology violated nonverbal rules in an experiment, it was more acceptable, since this behavior was considered to be intentional. But when a lower-status undergraduate did the same thing, the student's action was attributed to an inability to behave suitably. In the same way, it has been found that group members address more remarks to high-status than to low-status members (Katz, Goldston, & Benjamin, 1958; H. H. Kelley, 1951).

Influence accrues from high status because the behavior of persons with high status is more acceptable. Sabath (1964) presented a confederate as a new member of either high or low status to groups who were performing discussion and construction tasks. During the construction task, the new member exhibited disruptive behavior, followed by actions that enhanced or impeded the group's performance of the task. The high-status member was seen in a generally favorable manner, regardless of that person's behavior, while the low-status member was favorably viewed only when that person's performance enhanced the group's functioning. Consistent with these results, A. Pepitone (1958) concluded, from a research review, that the higher the status position of group members, the greater was the tendency to attribute good intentions to their positive and negative acts and to perceive their positive and negative actions as justified. Persons who were perceived to have high status were more acceptable as authority figures, and their idiosyncratic behavior received greater acceptance (Hollander, 1961a). Group members expected more of their high-status members and tended to overestimate the performance of these members (O. J. Harvey, 1953).

Effects of Self-accorded Status. To the extent to which self-accorded status mirrors actual status, it correlates with attempts to lead and to be successful as a leader. If there is a mismatch of self-accorded and accorded status, the attempts are likely to misfire. A common but not well-recognized phenomenon and source of potential conflict is the belief by all job occupants in a hierarchy that they have bigger and more important jobs than their bosses think they have (Haas, Porat, & Vaughan, 1969; Volkerding & Grasha, 1988). Guetzkow (1954) showed that key persons' ratings of their own importance to communication networks correlated with their influence behavior in the networks. Gold (1951–52) described how tenant-janitor interactions in a multiple dwelling changed when the janitor's concept of his status changed as he adopted "professional standards" and began earning a higher salary than some of his tenants. The stage was set for conflict with those tenants who did not appreciate the janitor's changed concept of the importance of his job.

Effects of Socioeconomic Status. Chapter 4 noted 15 studies through 1947 indicating that leaders come from a socioeconomic background according them higher status. For instance, C. A. Smith (1937) found the leaders of a Connecticut industrial town to be from wealthy families with "connections." Many additional

works followed in support. Hollingshead (1949) observed that Elmstown's youths displayed leadership behavior as a function of the social class of their family in Elmstown. Baltzell (1958) noted that the descendants of colonial merchants and statesmen, pioneering businessmen, and mining and railroad tycoons of Philadelphia all went to school with one another, lived in fashionable neighborhoods, were Episcopalian, joined the same clubs, intermarried, and eventually entered the elite class. They became the community leaders.

J. A. Davis (1929) found that only 19 percent of 163 Russian communist leaders had peasant fathers, while only 29 percent had working-class fathers.[4] Taussig and Joslyn (1932) observed that 70 percent of the fathers of 7,371 American business executives were businessmen, although businessmen constituted only 10 percent of the work force. Even labor leaders tended to be the sons of professionals and businessmen (Sorokin, 1927b).

An array of studies of opinion leaders attest to the strong linkage of socioeconomic status and leadership. Switzer (1975) showed that peasant leaders in a progressive, industrial-agrarian department of Colombia were more educated and more economically secure and had a clearer land title than were peasant leaders in a rural, conservative department. Farmers in Orissa, India, were more effective in motivating other farmers to improve their agricultural techniques if they were higher in socioeconomic status (Rath & Sahoo, 1974). In addition, Roy, Jaiswal, and Shankar (1974) reported that sociometrically identified leaders in four villages in Bihar, India, tended to be higher in caste and had greater land holdings than did followers. But Chesterfield and Ruddle (1976) warned that extension agents do not pay enough attention to the less-visible opinion leaders in rural Venezuela, such as relatives, symbolic kin, and older community members.

Changes in Socioeconomic Status. Systematic changes have occurred, both in the United States and abroad. After a decade of socialism, 96 percent of managers in Poland reported they came from the working or lower middle class (McClelland, 1961). In the United

---

[4]After three generations of socialism, leaders are now likely to emerge from the new privileged classes of party members, intellectuals, military officers, and managers.

States, the Air Force Command passed in the 1980s to officers whose background was quite different from those who engaged in World War II. According to Margiotta (1976), because of broader social recruitment in the 1950s and 1960s, U.S. Air Force leaders in the 1980s became more representative of the U.S. population in terms of socioeconomic origin, regional affiliation, size of their hometown, and religion. Just as with the military, American political, business, and educational leaders in the 1980s increasingly were drawn less often from those of mainstream British or north European backgrounds, and more often from those who are lower in status as a class than were the previous generation's leaders. But to some extent, leadership in many industries still remains somewhat closed to those not of British and northern European ancestry and to ethnic minorities outside the mainstream (Korman, 1988).

Confounds. Ability and status are likely to be confounded. For example, early studies (Davis, 1929; Sward, 1933; Taussig & Joslyn, 1932) found that intelligence, skill, and educational level tended to be higher among those who were higher in socioeconomic status.

Middle-class adolescents may become school leaders more often because they are somewhat higher in verbal aptitude than are working-class students. Regardless of the cause, most psychological studies indicate the existence of class differences in verbal aptitude. For example, among 140 college women, a significant correlation of .21 was obtained between verbal aptitude, as measured by the American Council on Education linguistic score, and socioeconomic status as measured by the father's occupation, parents' education, and religious affiliation (Bass, Wurster, Doll, & Clair, 1953).

The relation between leadership and socioeconomic status is also confounded with the tendency of higher socioeconomic status to be correlated with greater education and opportunity. The collateral interrelations were apparent to Jencks, Bartlett, Corcoran, et al. (1979), who looked at 13 demographic variables about fathers and sons and concluded that a father's occupation, family background, education, and intelligence are the best predictors of a son's occupational success. Although credentials, demonstrated by degrees in engineering, law, or business administration, provide ave-

nues to success in business leadership, it also helps to marry the boss's daughter. Middle-class students can pursue more extracurricular leadership opportunities; working-class students frequently have to put their time into part-time jobs.

The status-leadership concordance is also confounded by the relationship of both status and leadership to how much time people spend with each other. Stogdill and Koehler (1952) found that the extent to which persons in lower echelons mentioned an individual as one with whom they spent the most time correlated .82 with the mentioned person's level in the organization. However, these mentions of frequency of contact also correlated .31, .33, and .23 with being preferred as a leader. Time spent with persons in other units also correlated highly with the other person's level in the organization ($r = .69$). Similarly, Browne (1949) found that an executive who was mentioned frequently as one with whom others spent time was also an officeholder who described himself as being higher in authority and who was in a higher echelon in the organization.

Other confounds with status were noted by Jackson and Fuller (1966), who discovered that lower-class pupils liked middle-class teachers better. They also rated the middle-class teachers as less authoritarian.

Symbolic Value of Status. Did Pascal overstate the case when he suggested that his nobleman would lose all his influence if he lost the power to control what lesser men wanted. The symbols, signs, and privileges would still make the poor nobleman's position valuable in the eyes of others—a continued source of envy, deference, and respect. The rich commoner might still be willing to exchange places with the poor nobleman or to pay handsomely to have him as a son-in-law. Others' perception of the legitimacy and value of the nobleman's privileged position in society's hierarchy would still give him some influence, apart from his personal qualities. Thus, the poor nobleman's position would still provide referent power,[5] and the rich commoner might still want to identify with the nobleman, regardless of the nobleman's impoverishment, because of his ennobled rank in society.

---

[5]See Chapter 13.

Nevertheless, Pascal was right to some degree, for the absence of any real power attached to one's position generally results in the reduced ability to lead. Viteles (1953) talked about the first-level foreman as the "forgotten man," since the foreman was left only some of the symbols of status but little control of his subordinates. In a study of an electric utility company, Pelz (1951) found that supervisors who attempted leadership behavior failed to obtain changes in their subordinates if they, the supervisors, lacked influence with higher-ups; if they had no voice in decisions made by their superiors; if they lacked freedom from superiors' orders; and if their salary was low. Supervisors who were in positions that had more value and importance and had influence with higher authority were more successful when they made the same leadership attempts. Influential supervisors were seen by their subordinates as being more able to obtain rewards and provide punishments for their subordinates. Supervisors who were unable to grant or deny rewards, despite their title and position, had the signs of status but were unsuccessful in leading their subordinates.

Celebrities (not to be confused with the charismatic leaders, who are discussed in the next chapter) are an interesting case in point. As long as they remain highly visible, celebrities are extremely high in status and highly paid in relation to the general population. Their positions as superstars, playboys, aristocrats, or heroes of media hype are of much greater importance and value than are their personal qualities because of the public image of their positions that publicity agents create for them. That is, their image, rather than their talent, makes them influential. As long as they remain visible in their celebrated positions, the public will react toward them as if they were truly charismatic and want to identify with them (that is, want to be in their position as media stars) and ready to accept their opinions on both products and politics. But celebrity status tends to be ephemeral, declining with a decline in publicity.

Esteem

Esteem is the value of members as persons, regardless of their positions, to their group, to their organization,

or to society. It is the members' perceived potential to help the group, the organization, or society to attain their respective goals, independent of the position the members occupy.

The recognition of differences in esteem among members is established during the history of a natural group (Sherif, 1967) and increases in discrimination with the age of the group (Lippitt, Thelen, & Leff, undated). Such evaluations of the adequacy of group members are found among children aged 8 or even younger (Campbell & Radke-Yarrow, 1956).

Members with more personal ability, regardless of their position, will be more esteemed, since, through their personal ability to solve the group's problems, they can help the group attain its goals. In the same way, members with more personal power[6], regardless of their position, will be more esteemed, since they can directly give or deny love, friendship, security, and other interpersonal rewards. It is possible for them to coerce others by manipulating such rewards, but they are likely to lose esteem if they do. Members with esteem that is due primarily to their personal ability will be more successful in persuading others when they attempt to do so (Mowday, 1979). If their esteem depends on both personal ability and personal power, they may be more successful as participative leaders if they so choose (Bass, 1960).

Concomitants of Esteem

Popularity and Respect. People like, respect, and admire those who they esteem. The acceptance of a stranger is related to his or her esteem and prestige (Byrne, Griffitt, & Golightly, 1966). Santee and Vanderpol (1976) found a correlation of .83 between being liked and being respected and a correlation of .78 between being liked and being seen to be of value to the organization. In Bass's analysis (1960) of five sociometric ratings of 203 salesmen by their associates, being liked correlated .60 with being seen as of value to the firm and .49 with being seen as capable. Graves and Powell (1988) found that 398 college recruiters rated the applicants' subjective qualifications for being hired substantially higher if they personally liked the applicants.

[6]See Chapter 13.

Perceived Similarity. We esteem those in a group whom we regard as most similar to us in attitudes, interests, and abilities. We tend to reject those whom we regard as different or unlike us. Graves and Powell (1988) also found a significant correlation between the extent to which the recruiters felt themselves to be similar to the applicants and the extent to which they favorably rated the applicants' subjective qualifications.

Individuals tend to choose friends who are close to them or only slightly higher in socioeconomic status (Bonney, 1946a, 1946b; R. A. Ellis, 1956). Bechtel and Rosenfeld (1966) gave students incorrect information about their esteem and status in their dormitory and then asked the students to select new roommates from among ten levels of esteem and status. They also estimated their chances of being accepted as roommates. The students' estimates of being accepted decreased as the distance increased between their own esteem and that of their choice of roommates.

Many investigators have demonstrated that similarity in attitudes is a significant factor in sociometric choice.[7] For example, Byrne (1965) showed that the acceptance of a stranger was related to the similarity of attitudes. A stranger who was perceived to have similar attitudes to those of the raters was adjudged more intelligent, more moral, and better informed (Byrne, 1961). Furthermore, we particularly like others who are similar to us on socially desirable dimensions (Hendrick & Brown, 1971; Palmer & Byrne, 1970). We prefer those who share our group's norms and values (Stein, 1982b).

Perceived similarity in personality characteristics was also significantly related to interpersonal choices in numerous studies.[8] A review by Berscheid and Walster (1969) suggested that similarity of attitude and personality was associated with interpersonal attraction—mutuality of esteem.

Mutual Attractiveness. People tend to like those who like them (Newcomb, 1956). Furthermore, the extent to which people are attracted to each other and the extent to which they actually interact are enhanced by their perceived similarity in attitudes and personality and even more by the degree to which they like each other (Aronson & Worchel, 1966; Byrne & Griffitt, 1966a, 1966b). For instance, the expectation of being liked by a participant in an experimental task was significantly related to interpersonal attraction (Backman & Secord, 1959; Darley & Berscheid, 1967).

Similarity in competence also makes a difference in personal attractiveness. Thus, Zander and Havelin (1960) found that members of experimental groups tended to be most attracted to others whose competence was closest to their own.

Competence. M. A. Price (1948) studied esteem among 223 girls in a junior college. Girls who were esteemed by their schoolmates were mentioned on a "guess who" test as being like the person who has good ideas, expresses joy and satisfaction, keeps the central idea in mind, appeals for group loyalty, and makes others feel they will benefit by following her suggestions. Girls who were rejected were more frequently mentioned as being like the person who expresses fear and worry and embarrasses others. Bass and Coates (1953) found positive correlations between scores on intelligence tests and peers' ratings of esteem in the ROTC. The "ability" items that were listed on a peer-evaluation scale for assessing esteem among Marine OCS cadets included "well trained," "experienced," "performs well before the group," "has sound judgment," "thinks quickly," "exhibits imagination," "is well educated," and "is a fine athlete" (Hoffman & Rohrer, 1954). Likewise, H. H. Jennings (1943) noted that institutionalized girls who were "overchosen" (those who were more desired as associates) exhibited more ingenuity, planning, and organization. The more esteemed members of Whyte's (1943) street-corner society were known for their resourcefulness and the past success of their ideas. In the same way, Zeleny (1946–47) found that cadets with exceptional ability in flying were more likely to be chosen as flying partners. Similarly, Feinberg (1953) noted that regardless of economic background, esteemed adolescent boys were higher in athletic and scholastic proficiency than were those who were rejected by their peers. But in choosing friends,

---

[7]See for example Byrne and Clore (1966); Davitz (1955); Fensterheim and Tresselt (1953); Fiedler, Warrington, and Blaisdell (1952); and A. J. Smith (1957).
[8]Hoffman (1958), Izard (1960), Lindzey and Urdan (1954), Lundy, Katkovsky, Cromwell, and Shoemaker (1955), Secord and Backman (1964), and Steiner and Dodge (1957).

Riley and Flowerman (1951) suggested, we tend to select those who are "smart, but not too smart; pretty, but not too pretty."

Demonstrated competence increases one's esteem. Gilchrist (1952) found that persons became more attractive to others if they consistently succeeded on assigned tasks. Lippitt, Polansky, Redl, and Rosen (1952) reported that in a summer camp, boys with a history of success were most liked. Zander and Havelin (1960) showed that those who were highly competent in experimental groups were preferred over those who lacked competence. And Jackson (1953a) noted that when members of a formal organization judged other members of the work group, they tended to value most those they perceived contributed to the achievement of the group's goals and conformed to the group's standards.

An individual's ability to help the group can be increased, of course. R. E. Andrews (1955) suggested that supervisors should be given as much information about policies and decisions as possible to enhance their standing with their subordinates. Whyte (1943) noted that leaders can increase or maintain their perceived value to their group by making sure the group engages in activities at which they, the leaders, are most proficient.

Status. It is often difficult to sort out whether members' value and contribution to the group or organization is due to the information, control, and importance of their position or to their personal qualities. In fact, since more highly qualified people are ordinarily promoted and occupy higher-status positions in an organization, a positive correlation is expected between members' status and their esteem. Such a tendency was found in experimental groups (Flint, Bass, & Pryer, 1957b).

Status is often gained through personal ability, competition, and effort. Persons who are likely to be esteemed because of their personal characteristics are also likely to obtain positions that are of greater worth in formal hierarchical organizations. Thus, esteem often leads to the achievement of a higher status (Pellegrin, 1952). Promotion to a higher status in industrial and military organizations often depends on superiors' ratings of one's worth to the organization, although, of course, upward mobility in status can also be due to

chance, tradition, or favoritism, which are unrelated to one's esteem.

According to Sherif and Sherif (1953), those in positions of control (high status) are perceived by others to be endowed with superior personal traits. Perlmutter (1954) confirmed that the greater the perceived capacity of individuals to influence the perceiver, the greater the total number of traits will be assigned to them and the more desirable will be the traits assigned to them. In the same way, Courtney, Greer, Masling, and Orlans (1953) noted that military recruits who were given positions with the most responsibility and authority were most esteemed. Barnard (1951) agreed that abilities will be imputed to persons of higher status even when the abilities cannot be recognized. This, he suggested, is a way that low-status followers maintain their own self-esteem. The followers rationalize that they are being persuaded by the suggestions of the most capable members of the organization, rather than being coerced through mere differences in status.

Esteem was found to be higher for individuals with the status of owners and professionals in agricultural communities (Hooker, 1928). Likewise, among three canteen work groups, those living at higher socioeconomic levels were more esteemed (Mumford, 1959). Similarly, prestige and popularity were observed to be higher for persons who were heads of organizations in their communities (J. E. White, 1950). D. T. Campbell (1953) noted that among the crews of seven out of ten submarines, the commanding officer was most esteemed, receiving the most nominations as the person others wanted to see in command. Merit ratings (esteem) of military officers tended to be higher, the higher their military rank (Robins, Willemin, & Brueckel, 1954). A review of officer-efficiency ratings from 1922 to 1945 revealed a positive correlation between the rank of officers and their merit ratings; those at higher grades in the service received more favorable ratings of their performance in combat in Korea (U.S. Army, 1952). In the same way, in a study of 1,900 military personnel, Masling, Greer, and Gilmore (1955) found that the higher individuals ranked in the military organization, the greater the number of favorable sociometric mentions they tended to receive in regard to both military and personal matters.

The fact that status and esteem are correlated may be a valid assessment of the value of both the positions and personal qualities of the personnel involved. When the status and esteem of personnel are truly mismatched, the lack of correlation may reflect the overevaluation of esteem associated with an accurate appraisal of the status of the personnel. Thus, almost all high-ranking military officers are usually appraised as excellent or superior in performance. Less frequently, such an appraisal may reflect the overevaluation of the position because of the high esteem earned by the occupant. For example, although a paraprofessional has a lower status than a registered nurse, the importance of the position of paraprofessional may be raised substantially in the eyes of a patient if the patient thinks his or her comfort depends more heavily on the performance of the paraprofessional than of the nurse.

"Unearned" Esteem. Yet, it must be clear that one can be esteemed for a variety of reasons that have little or nothing to do with one's ability to help the group. Persons may gain esteem merely because of their similarity to stereotypes or popular conceptions of esteemed or popular figures. For instance, the youthful-looking, gray-haired, handsome man is a strong political asset in television campaigning, but immature facial characteristics (associated with infantile helplessness) will reduce a would-be leader's expected value (Berry & McArthur, 1986). Also, one's family name may carry great weight.

Duncan (1984) observed that managers who were first seen as friends by employees could then be admitted to the employee's "humor network." They could become initiators and foci of work-related jokes.

Experimentally, it was possible to raise or lower the esteem of a neutral stranger merely by attaching some false cues to the stranger; the results depended on others' attitudes toward those cues (Asch, 1946). H. H. Kelley (1950) introduced two persons to an audience, one as "warm," the other as "cold." The audience's perceptions of the personality of the two was altered by the adjective used in introducing them. The "warm" person became more esteemed.

Esteem and Conformity

Before new individuals can be accepted by the other members of an established group and rise in esteem, they usually must demonstrate that they will abide by the rules of the group and share its ways of behaving

and its goals (N. Anderson, 1923).[9] Thus, Bonney and Powell (1953) found that the highly esteemed children in sociometric analyses were more cooperative. Likewise, Marwell (1966) showed that experimental subjects chose those who had been cooperative on a first task assignment as partners for a second task assignment. And Christie (1952) found that if a new army recruit increased his acceptance of the prevailing authoritarian attitudes, he was more likely to be esteemed by his peers after six weeks in service. Similarly, Havighurst and Taba (1949) noted that adolescents who conformed best to the middle-class standards of a school were most likely to be esteemed by their middle-class peers. Following a survey of the literature, Northway, Frankel, and Potashin (1947) concluded that esteem was highest in children who were not extremely shy or so aggressive as to interfere with the group's activities. However Stein (1982b) theorized that highly esteemed members of a group only appear to conform to the group's norms, since they actually exemplify them. They do not have to move from their own points of view to be seen as conforming to the group's normative values and attitudes.

Meeting Expectations

We like and value those who behave according to our expectations. Thus, Sharpe (1956) reported that the evaluation of principals' effectiveness by teachers and staff was highly related to the principals' conformity to the expectations of the teachers and staff. In the same way, Jackson (1953) found that foremen were evaluated by subordinates according to the match between the foremen's behavior and the subordinates' expectations. Baumgartel (1956) reported the same kinds of results for the staff's evaluations of the directors of a medical research center. Foa (1956) asked Israeli factory workers what they thought was the best way for a foreman to handle difficult situations involving workers and the way their foremen usually dealt with such incidents. Favorable evaluations of their foremen increased as the discrepancies decreased in how the workers thought the foremen should behave and how the foremen usually behaved. Likewise, Tsui (1982) showed that for a sample of 217 middle managers, the managers' reputa-

[9]See also Merei (1949), Pellegrin (1953), Thrasher (1927), and Whyte (1943).

tion for effectiveness correlated with their bosses', subordinates', and peers' expectations about the managers' role.

Santee and Vanderpol (1976) correlated the degree to which professors conformed to students' expectations. One group of students rated their satisfaction with different professorial behaviors; another group of students indicated which behaviors were typical of their professors and rated the professors' esteem. The professors' conformity to the students' expectations correlated .56 with the students' ratings of respect and .61 with the students' ratings of the professors' value to the university.

Numerous exceptions have been reported. Mumford (1959) found more deviation among more highly esteemed canteen workers. Blau (1960) reported that when cases were unimportant, caseworkers deviated more from the norms about gossiping. Conformity to one's reference group's ideals may be more important than is conformity to opinions of a temporary or a particular local group (Sherif & Sherif, 1964). What is most important, as Hollander's (1978) theory and research demonstrated, is that the member with esteem who first conforms to the group builds up idiosyncrasy credit that permits him or her to deviate and to emerge as a group leader.[10]

Need for Esteem

Maslow (1954) called attention to the importance of the need for esteem. Just as we would like to occupy valued positions, most of us also desire to be valued as persons, particularly by those we value (Wurster, Bass, & Alcock, 1961). Lippitt, Thelen, and Leff (undated), hypothesized that we are more concerned about being criticized personally than about being criticized for the social role we play. This concern with one's value was implicit in Festinger's (1954) theory of social-comparison processes. It results in the practical advice to supervisors to criticize a subordinate's poor performance, not the subordinate's personal motives, attitudes, or value as a person.[11]

We are more satisfied with situations and groups that provide us with esteem. For instance, Van Zelst

(1951) indicated that highly esteemed workers were more satisfied with their jobs and with their firm, and Heyns (1950) noted that participants who felt they were accepted were more satisfied with the decisions of a conference. But Flint, Bass, and Pryer (1957a) failed to find any relation between esteem and attraction to problem-solving groups.

Esteem and Leadership

Interviews with 11 chief executive officers (CEOs) led Bruce (1986) to conclude that the CEOs' status and the power accruing from their top position in the firm was not enough to ensure their success in office. Their first task was to gain acceptance, to get a lot of people in the organization to know and trust them personally. They had to see the company and to be seen. The CEOs, as individuals, took control in such a way that their firms began to take on their personal character. Consistent with this finding, Bird (1940) concluded that leadership reflects the esteem in which the member is held. Similarly, Homans (1950) proposed that those of "higher social rank" in a group initiate the interaction. Lazarsfeld, Berelson, and Gaudet (1948) suggested that the influence of personal contact on opinion depended on trust in esteemed persons. Sims and Manz (1981) noted that esteemed leaders attract more attention to themselves and, therefore, can serve as models in organizational life. Rosenthal and Frank (1956) reasoned that the efficacy of psychotherapy depended on the patient's confidence in the therapist.

Brim (1954) discovered that mothers were more willing to adopt recommended child-rearing practices if they esteemed the physician who suggested the new methods. But esteem of the physician was not enough to sustain the new behavior; that required their husbands' approval and support as well. Lanzetta and Haythorn (1954) observed that the more students esteemed their instructors, the more their opinions would coalesce with those of their instructors.

Garrison (1933) obtained a correlation of .82 between the tendency of high school seniors to be admired and their tendency to be chosen as leaders. Page (1984) showed that U.S. presidents from the 1930s to the 1970s could move public opinion on such issues as inflation, energy, foreign policy, and civil rights only if

[10]See Chapter 17.
[11]See Chapter 19.

their performance in office was approved by the public. If their performance was disapproved, they either had no effect or actually pushed people farther from their positions.

Sociometric Evidence. In sociometric studies, members of a group nominate the person or persons in the group with whom they spend the most time or with whom they prefer to work, to play, and so on. "Stars" receive many nominations; isolates receive few or none. As more attractive persons, stars are higher in esteem.

In his seminal sociometric studies, Moreno (1934/1953) observed that the higher the esteem of group members, the more nominations they received and the greater was the volume of words expected and accepted from them by other members. The esteemed member was permitted more frequently to assume the initiative and to terminate activities. In the same way, H. H. Jennings (1947) found that the sociometrically "overchosen" in a girls' institution exhibited four times as much behavior "making new events happen" or "enlarging the extent of activities" than did the "average chosen." When the girls were free to choose a leader, H. H. Jennings (1943) observed, they tended to select someone who displayed spontaneity and enlarged the field of action for others. C. A. Gibb (1950) and Borgatta (1954) indicated that ratings of the effectiveness of leaders were highly related to the leaders' ratings as desired work partners but were unrelated to their ratings as persons who were desired as friends. The member who showed a great deal of initiative and participation attracted a large portion of the positive emotional responses of the other group members. Similarly, Newstetter, Feldstein, and Newcomb (1938) found that an individual's leadership in a group was determined largely by the cordiality received from others rather than by the leader's cordiality toward others.

The highly chosen tend to be successful leaders in future settings. This tendency has resulted in the use of ratings by buddies or nominations by peers to forecast the subsequent success of leaders in the military. From World War II onward, peer ratings of esteem by cadets in Officer Candidate School or at West Point have been found to be one of the best single predictors of subsequent success as a regular U.S. Army officer

(Haggerty, Johnson, & King, 1954). Thus, a correlation of .51 was obtained between esteem among peers at West Point and rated success as an infantry officer 18 months later. Likewise, a correlation of .42 was obtained between esteem among fellow trainees in Officer Candidate School and combat performance as a U.S. Army officer (Baier, 1947). Similar results were reported by the U.S. Air Force (1952) and the U.S. Marine Corps (Wilkins, 1953; Williams & Leavitt, 1947b). (More will be said about these results in Chapter 36).

Evidence from Leaderless Group Discussions (LGDs). A strong case can be made for the personal factor from studies using an initially LGD to assess esteem and leadership during the discussion and again in real life as much as two years later. In these small-group discussions, in which no member is appointed leader, high correlations were found between ratings by observers or peers of the value and contribution of members to the group and their influence and emergence as leaders of the group (Bass, 1954a). Moreover, those members who were esteemed most highly by their peers exhibited the most influence on the other members and on the group's decision, according to objective measurements of changes in opinion (Bass, 1955a). Elsewhere, Bass (1961c) reported that attempts to lead were more successful among able and esteemed leaders, especially when the congruence between the leaders' esteem and self-esteem was great.

Wurster, Bass, and Alcock (1961) obtained results with 95 LGD participants indicating that they felt more responsive toward the suggestions and opinions of persons whom they esteemed than toward those of people in general. Thus, the highly esteemed person had an advantage in opportunities to influence others because the others tended to feel responsive toward his or her behavior.

Bass (1954a) reported a median adjusted correlation of .51 for 17 studies of this emergence as leader in the LGD and subsequent appraisals of meritorious leadership performance from one week to two years later. The criteria included rated merit as a U.S. Army cadet and officer (Weislogel, 1953), nominations for positions of leadership in a sorority or fraternity (Bass & White, 1951), rated potential and general merit as a civil service administrator (Arbous & Maree, 1951), rated adequacy as a foreman (Mandell, 1950a; Wurster & Bass, 1953), and rated suitability for foreign service (Vernon, 1950). Similar findings were reported for British supervisors (Handyside & Duncan, 1954), Finnish foremen (Rainio, 1955), and military trainees (Gleason, 1957).[12]

Evidence of Perceived Helpfulness. Leaders will be successful to the degree that they are seen as having the potential to be helpful. In 72 business and governmental conferences, Crockett (1955) noted that emergent leaders were rated as members who were most needed by the group. In another study of industry N. A. Rosen (1969) obtained ratings of workers' preference for eight foremen. Foremen who were high and low in preference then changed places. The findings suggested that the new foremen were evaluated in terms of their ability to help the group. The greater the consensus among the workers in weeks 1 to 10 that the new foreman "is our leader," the greater was the increase in productivity and cohesiveness in weeks 11 to 16. Again, Rosen, Levinger, and Lippitt (1961) found that schoolchildren and college students rated helpfulness and fairness as the most important traits that enable individuals to influence others but that adults rated fairness first and helpfulness second in importance. Kelman (1970), Olsen (1968), and Sells (1968) placed particular importance on the confidence and trust that followers had in their leaders. In turn, such confidence and trust in the leader are linked to the competence of the leader. In a report on 72 men in the Antarctic for a year, P. D. Nelson (1964b) concluded that what differentiated leaders from the men in maintaining their esteem as leaders was their stronger motivational commitment to the group.

Feelings about the helpfulness of leaders are multidimensional. R. D. Mann, Gibbard, and Hartman (1967) obtained college students' expressions of feeling toward different leaders as well as descriptions of the followers' responses. The data were intercorrelated and factor analyzed. Among the factors that emerged were feelings about the leader as an analyst, as an authority figure, and as being committed to the leader-member relationship. The investigators found that the leaders were valued for supporting the members' independ-

dence, identification, and social closeness. But M. G. Evans (1973) and Lawler and Hall (1970) noted that such perceived esteem in leaders can be induced in subordinates by their own needs and desires for particular behaviors by leaders. The distortion becomes great in the charismatic leader who may be perceived by followers as a savior, as will be detailed in the next chapter. Leaders of therapy groups were seen as more helpful if they were evaluated as higher in self-disclosure and as better in their own mental health (May & Thompson, 1973). Bolman (1973) reported on the extent to which therapeutic improvement occurred according to individuals' and peers' ratings of the membres of therapy groups. The favorable characterization of the therapist helped, but Bolman failed to replicate previous findings in which liking the therapist as a person contributed to improvement in the members. Although how well one is liked or disliked may affect one's leadership to some extent (Schubert et al., 1974), being liked is not necessarily a substitute for esteem in contributing to the leader's performance.

Visibility, Popularity, Esteem, and Leadership. Numerous commentators have pointed out that it is important for aspiring managers to make themselves visible to those with higher authority to increase their prospects for promotion. Tagiuri and Kogan (1957) found that self-confidence enhanced an individual's visibility in a group. Although visibility made some contribution to a person's emergence and success as a leader, it did not make as much of a contribution as did the person's perceived value to the group.

Being liked, popular, and chosen as a friend tend to make some contribution to leadership, but not as much as does esteem. Thus, numerous investigators have found nominations received for leader and for friend to be positively correlated.[13] However, friendship tended to correlate less with leadership than did other variables, such as nominations for followership and amount of participation (Lana, Vaughan, & McGinnies, 1960).

Bass (1960) demonstrated that influence is more strongly associated with one's sociometrically rated value and ability than are one's sociometrically deter-

---

[12]As will be noted in Chapter 36, the LGD is now a routine part of management assessment centers.

[13]See, for example, Borgatta (1954), Burnett (1951a, 1951b), Hollander and Webb (1955), and M. A. Price (1948).

mined popularity and visibility. Table 11.1 shows the results of such a sociometric study of 203 salesmen. In each of their sales units, the salesmen nominated 7 others as being "liked as a co-worker" and rejected 7 people. They repeated these nominations in relation to "value to the company," "ability to solve the company's problems," and "influence." Each salesman's "score" was the number of his nominations less the number of rejections by others on each criterion. His "visibility" was based on the percentage of all salesmen in his division who knew him. Being of value and ability correlated .68 and .74 with influence, being visible correlated only .29 with influence, while being liked or popular correlated .50 with influence. Visibility and popularity were unrelated, but, as Riedesel (1974), stressed, popularity systematically confounds sociometric studies of the esteem-leadership relationship.

To examine conditions in which esteem, popularity, and leadership are or are not correlated, P. B. Smith (1963) classified group members in terms of their sociometric nominations of other members for competent ideas, leadership, and liking. The differentiation between the ratings for leadership and liking were related to the raters' attraction to the group. The raters were divided into four types:

Type 1. This type of rater was an active member attracted to the group. This type was most active in discussing the usefulness of meetings and in making rules for procedure. For this type, leadership was highly correlated with liking and ideas.

Type 2. This type of rater was low in activity and unattracted to the group. Seen as most active in attempting to draw people in, withdrawing from the group, and submitting to others' wishes, rating of leadership was highly correlated with ideas but not with liking.

Type 3. This type sought individual recognition and was unattracted to the group. For this type, leadership was highly correlated with liking but not with ideas.

Type 4. This type of rater was low in both activity and attraction to the group, and leadership ratings were not highly correlated with ideas or liking.

In all, it would appear that being liked and being visible may still be of some importance to one's influence, but, in general, perceived competence and values are of much more importance to leadership.

Maintaining Esteem and Status

Subordinates value and esteem leaders who are considerate of their needs and who avoid being domineering (D. T. Campbell, 1953). Esteemed leaders will lose their esteem if they fail their groups or if, as was mentioned earlier, they use their esteem to coerce members into accepting their influence to avoid being denied the leaders' support and affection. Conversely, the esteem of leaders will be enhanced if the leaders effectively contribute to their groups' success (Bass, 1960). In the same way, more important positions and higher status will be assigned to those who are seen to contribute or who have the potential to contribute to the well-being of others or the success of the organization. Demotion will be favored for those who fail to be of help or who use their status to coerce others.

Table 11.1 Median Intercorrelations among Five Sociometric Ratings of 203 Salesmen by Their Associates

Visibility	Popularity	Value	Ability	Influence
Visibility	−.05	.39	.38	.29
Popularity		.60	.49	.50
Value			.73	.68
Ability				.74

SOURCE: Adapted from Bass (1960), p. 282.

Esteem and Self-esteem

The last chapter detailed the importance to leadership of self-confidence and self-esteem. As was noted, Bass (1955b) found a correlation of .38 between self-esteem and emergence as a leader in initially leaderless groups, but the correlations between self-esteem and objective success as a leader were only .17 and .18 for a total of 95 participants. Moreover, self-esteem may be quite different from the esteem accorded by another person. For instance, one would expect that those with extremely low or extremely high self-esteem would be too preoccupied with their own concerns to be highly esteemed by others (Reykowski, 1982). Nonetheless, one would ordinarily expect some correlation between self-esteem and esteem. Shapiro and Klein (1975) found such a correlation in encounter groups, but only after two days of meetings and only for a composite profile of the leaders as seen by themselves and by the nonleaders. Similarly, Willerman and Swanson (1953) demonstrated that members' evaluations of themselves are related, to some extent, to other members' evaluations of them.

Leaders tend to be more accurate about their own esteem than are other members. But this tendency is not surprising, since everyone in the group can make more accurate judgments about the leader than about other members. The leader's behavior is more visible, more frequent, and more observable than is the behavior of most other members (Bass, 1949).

According to H. H. Jennings's (1943) sociometric analyses in a girls' school, a comparison of self-estimates with estimates by others showed that the "overchosen" (the stars) appraised themselves most accurately on having good ideas and making others feel benefited, while the "underchosen" (the rejectees and isolates) estimated themselves most accurately in expressing discouragement and being easily hurt.

Summary and Conclusions

The value of one's position in the eyes of others is one's status; the value of one as a person in the eyes of others is one's esteem. Consensus about the status and esteem of others is commonplace and is likely to be established quickly. More knowledge is usually associated with those in higher-status occupations and positions. Throughout history, the value of positions and the value of occupations have been scaled. Upward mobility is sought and downward mobility is dissatisfying. Individual members of a group or organization can be more coercive if their accorded status depends on their personal control of what is desired by others in the group. Such members will attempt more leadership. However, continued direction, particularly if it is coercive, may lead to resentment and the loss of esteem.

High-status people can also be more influential because others pay more attention to them and tend to judge their behavior as more acceptable. High-status people can break the rules more easily ("The king can do no wrong"). Conflict arises if accorded status is mismatched with self-accorded status, but the status accorded to figureheads without real power will still give them some influence.

Individuals tend to choose friends whose social status is similar to their own. Group members, however, tend to prefer highly esteemed and high-status persons for positions of leadership. Members interact with these highly esteemed high-status persons more frequently than they do with low-status members without esteem; they also accept them more readily as authority figures, more readily justify their actions on behalf of the group, and exhibit more tolerance of their deviant behavior. The highly esteemed members with high status are permitted to suggest innovations in the group, but they are not expected to interrupt or otherwise to behave inconsiderately toward low-status members with less esteem.

Members of a group quickly size up the leadership potential of a new member. Status evaluations that are made on first acquaintance are rather highly correlated with evaluations made several weeks later. Group members tend to choose other members, as well as leaders, whose values, interests, and personalities are similar to their own. They tend to regard leaders as more attractive than members of lower status and to consider both the positive and negative actions of high-status members as legitimate.

Group members tend to evaluate themselves in terms of the reactions of their fellow members. The more attractive the group, the greater its impact on the members' evaluations of themselves. For this reason, a loss of status is damaging to the members' self-respect, particularly if the downward mobility is interpreted as evidence of decreased liking by other group members. A loss of status may be accompanied by a decline in performance, reduced liking for the task and the group, and feelings of hostility. However, ordinary members may reject the opportunity to rise in status if doing so involves radical changes in responsibility and style of living that are in conflict with their self-concept and system of values. Thus, those who become leaders appear more willing to accept the responsibilities for the rewards of high status.

The concomitants of esteem include respect, admiration, being liked as a person, and being judged as competent. But esteem may also be earned or unearned for irrelevant reasons. Furthermore, esteem may be misjudged for status, and vice versa. Members can be more persuasive if their esteem depends on their being perceived as able to solve the group's problems, but to gain esteem, they first need to conform to the rules, after which they can begin to innovate and deviate without losing their esteem. Assumptions of similarity of sociometric status, attitudes, and values contribute to being esteemed and attractive to others. We lose esteem by violating others' expectations of us.

Considerable evidence from sociometric research; use of the initially LGD; and the success of students, salesmen, managers, school principals, military officers, and therapists all demonstrate the contributions of esteem and perceived helpfulness to success as a leader above and beyond considerations of visibility and likeability. The esteemed leader may achieve charismatic standing in the eyes of others.

Charismatic, Charismalike, and Inspirational Leadership

We are indebted to the German sociologist, Max Weber (1924/1947) for introducing the concept of charisma to the study of leadership in the early decades of this century. Charisma quickly became of interest in the sociological study of social and political movements, as well as in the psychoanalytical interpretations of history. But into the 1970s, charismatic leadership still had not become a subject for survey or experimental research in social or organizational psychology (Stark, 1977).

The Concept of Charismatic Leadership

Weber saw charismatic leaders as being extremely highly esteemed persons, who are gifted with exemplary qualities. Such individuals tend to exude confidence, dominance, a sense of purpose, and the ability to articulate the goals and ideas for which followers are already prepared psychologically (Fromm, 1941). The response of followers is likewise extreme. It is both cognitive and emotional, as well as devoted and unquestioning. Charismatic leaders have extraordinary influence over their followers, who become imbued with moral inspiration and purpose. The followers experience a magnetic attraction that transcends their usual experience. They become zealots and leaders in their own right (Trice & Beyer, 1986). For some writers, charismatic leadership implied radical innovation (Stark, 1969); for others, it implied pathology (Davies, 1954).

Although most attention has been paid to charismatic leaders in the religious and political arenas, such leaders also appear in organizational and military settings (Handy, 1976). On the basis of his observations of such successful leaders, Lawler (1982) concluded that their leadership occurs "through a combination of factors" that can be captured by words like "vision," "communication," "symbols," and "charisma." Such leaders are more concerned with doing the right things than with doing things right.

Charismatic leaders often emerge in times of crises as prospective saviors who, by their magical endowments, will fulfill the unmet emotional needs of their completely trusting, overly dependent, and submissive followers. If successful, charismatic leaders bring about radical transformations in their groups, organizations, or societies.

Burns (1978) preferred to speak about heroic leadership, believing that charisma had been overworked in usage. The highly esteemed individual is a hero. There is a

> belief in [heroic] leaders because of their personage alone, aside from their tested capacities, experience, or stand on issues; faith in the leaders' capacity to overcome obstacles and crises; readiness to grant to leaders the powers to handle crises; mass support for such leaders expressed directly—through votes, applause, letters, shaking hands—rather than through intermediaries or institutions. Heroic leadership is not simply a quality or entity possessed by someone; it is a type of relationship between leader and led. A crucial aspect of this relationship is the absence of conflict. (p. 244)

The heroic, transcending leader excites and transforms previously dormant followers into active ones. For example, leaders of an exodus heighten the followers' motivation, purposes, and missionary zeal. Followers become proselytizers, who, in turn, act as leaders as a consequence of their exalted awareness.

Types of Charismatics

The 'Office Charismatic' and the Personal Charismatic.

Etzioni (1961) and Hollander (1978) noted that charismalike leadership could be a property of one's position (celebrity status) as well as one's person. An American president has a lot of luster, some of which he loses after he leaves office. The "office charismatic" and the public celebrity attain extremely high status by virtue of the strong public image they have as holders of a valued role. Personal charismatics gain extremely high esteem by virtue of the extent to which others have faith in them as persons. (Holders of charismatic offices and celebrities may or may not be esteemed in the same way.) Furthermore, personal charismatics may be in high- or low-status positions. Thus, a personal charismatic can occupy the highly valued office of president, but a charismatic avatar can attract people to his person because of his sacrificial renunciation of all worldly power and possessions.

Etzioni (1961) suggested that although charismatic office frequently has to be achieved, "office charisma" is ascribed. Regardless of their ability or performance, incumbents obtain it with the office. Charisma can attach to any high social status, achieved or inherited, as is seen in aristocratic offices (witness the public reactions to a visit or the marriage of the Prince of Wales. The charisma as well as celebrity status goes with the role.)

Celebrities.

One cannot ignore the vicarious effects on a mass audience of the superstar who can be only an image and a name to identify with. For example, enlistment rates can go up substantially after a popular star appears in a war movie. As Schiffer (1983, p. 9) noted:

> To most people . . . political figures . . . are just like box-office attractions in the field of entertainment—this despite the fact that many politicians are often bearers of ideals and ideologies. . . . We embrace the images . . . popular actors, actresses, and musicians who, above and beyond their talents, have been given charismatic status despite—or perhaps because of—certain flaws in their character or theatrical skills.

Psychological projection and identification play important roles in the processes of this charismatic influence at a distance.

Weber believed that the personal charismatic creates the charismatic office to be filled by an uncharismatic successor. However, Etzioni (1961) pointed out that personal charisma may be revealed more forcefully when the holder of the office is an incumbent who follows uncharismatic predecessors in the same office, as was the case with Franklin Delano Roosevelt, who followed Warren Harding, Calvin Coolidge, and Herbert Hoover. Also nothing seems to preclude one charismatic succeeding another.

In their private lives, publically celebrated charismatics may have little charisma. As Etzioni (1961, p. 316) put it, "Top executives, heads of state, and kings, who have charisma in the eyes of the public . . . may have little or [none] in the eyes of [their] private secretaries, valets, and cabinet ministers." Visibility and name recognition provided by television and media events have been essential for political election.

Weber's Concept of Charisma

Weber's (1922/1963) concept of charisma was an adaptation of the theological concept of charisma, which involves endowment with the gift of divine grace. Weber's model for a charismatic leader was a mystical, narcissistic, and personally magnetic savior with a doctrine to promote who arises in times of crisis.

Weber (1924/1947) applied the concept of charisma to understand the development and maintenance of complex organizations in which the gift of extraordinariness as a person was now bestowed by colleagues and subordinates instead of by God. Trice and Beyer (1986) summed up Weber's conceptualization, as seen in his writings and in an exegesis of them, as having five components: (1) a person with extraordinary gifts, (2) a crisis, (3) a radical solution to the crisis, (4) followers who are attracted to the exceptional person because they believe that they are linked through him to transcendent powers, and (5) validation of the person's gifts and transcendence in repeated experiences of success.

For Weber, charismatic leaders inspired the creation

of organizations, which subsequently became traditionally or bureaucratically managed. After such routinization of the organization, charismatic offices, such as that of pope or hereditary chief, could arise. In most complex organizations, managerial bureaucrats would take charge. The charismatics formulated the basic purposes and principles for bureaucratic administrators to live by.

Weber's Legacy

Although many contradictions were seen in Weber's conceptualization (Downton, 1973), charisma has figured strongly since Weber as an explanatory concept in sociology, political science, and psychoanalysis. Weber's original concept has been modified, expounded on, and extended in numerous sociological, political science, and psychoanalytic treatises.[1] Charisma plays a major role conceptually in the psychoanalytical offshoot of psychohistorical analysis (see, for example, Demause, 1982). Weber's lead was also followed by a number of organizational theorists, who found charisma among some holders of offices in complex oganizations, particularly at higher levels.[2] Such charismatics were likely to be at the center of institutional structures and have the power to radicalize them (Berger, 1963).

The revisers of Weber's concept have seen the need to acount for both Weber's conception of the charismatic leader's break with continuity, as well as his or her dealing with the aftermath. They have also questioned the relative importance and meaning of charisma to democratic politics (Schiffer, 1973). For Weber (1924/1947) the charismatic leader is obeyed because of the moral authority with which he is endowed, not because of democratic consent.

Some commentators favor a highly restricted view of charisma. Thus, Friedrich (1961) would have charisma limited to inspirational leadership that entails the charismatic having a call from God for his or her mission. Trice and Beyer (1986) wanted to see all five Weberian components present before a condition was accepted as charismatic. They rejected labeling any leadership

as charismatic merely because it was inspiring or dynamic. They thought that Berlew's (1979) three characteristics of charismatic leadership (confidence building, shared vision, and creating valued opportunities) were "rather incomplete and pale in comparison to Weber's conception of charisma" (p. 122). They dismissed Solomon's (1977) discussion, which they stated, was of personalized, autocratic leadership, not charisma. And although George Washington was worshipped like a charismatic because he embodied the values of his society (Schwartz, 1983), they concluded that he was not charismatic because he and his situation lacked some of the other Weberian features.

Other extremists, like Bradley (1984), argued that the intense cohesiveness of the group was what would result in endowing leaders with charismatic qualities. At the end of another continuum, Dow (1969a) placed almost exclusive emphasis on the exceptional individual and his ideas, rather than on the social or political scene.

Toward a Pragmatic Concept of Charisma

As is the case with those who have defined leadership, we are confronted with absolutists who insist that their definition of charisma is the only proper one when, in fact, definitions should be created for their operational and explanatory utility (Bass, 1960). Nor does the meaning have to remain fixed with Weber and his interpreters. Some of the variance in the charismatic phenomenon is due to the exceptional individual, some to the exceptional situation, and some to the interaction of the exceptional individual and the exceptional situation.

There have been and continue to be considerable numbers of exceptional people. For example, it is likely that there were many other charismatic reformist preachers who were contemporaneous with the more famous ones, from Martin Luther to Martin Luther King. Although they were less publicized, each had dedicated followers, radical solutions, a mission, and self-confidence. In all walks of life and at all organizational levels, we are likely to encounter charismatic and charismalike interactions between confident, gifted leaders with seemingly radical solutions to critical problems and followers who are unquestioningly and mag-

---

[1]See, for example, Schiffer (1973), Schweitzer (1984), and Willner (1968).
[2]Blau and Scott (1962), Etzioni (1961), and Friedland (1964).

netically attracted to these leaders (Bass, 1985a; Smith, 1982). Such leadership is not merely inspiring or dynamic; it involves unusual follower reactions to the leadership. For purists, we may need to talk about the charismalike behavior of leaders or the charismalike devotion of followers. For the purposes in this chapter, the Weberian requirements and those of some revisionists will be regarded as sufficient but not all are necessarily essential in each instance. For example, continued unquestioning acceptance of the leader is not an absolute essential consequence of charismatic leadership. As Tucker (1970, p. 4) noted:

> Followers can be under the spell of a leader and can accept him as supremely authoritative without necessarily agreeing with him on all occasions or refraining from argument with him. In the highly argumentative atmosphere of a modern radical party, for example, a leader can be both charismatic and contested on specific points, as Lenin often was by his close followers. Indeed, he can even manifest some of his charisma in the inspired way in which he conquers dissent by the sheer power of his political discourse. Immense persuasiveness in argument may, in other words, be one of the extraordinary qualities by virtue of which a leader acquires charisma in his followers' eyes. . . .

In hi-tech industry, strong substantive arguments may be characteristic of charismatic leaders and their immediate technical subordinates, who never accept the leaders unquestioningly.

The charismatic relationship can appear in the absence of a crisis. For instance, dynamic leaders of financial investing have devoted, unquestioning followers. The leaders provide these followers with an exhilarating mission—to grasp an opportunity for improving the often already-wealthy followers' portfolios. The followers show every indication of wanting to identify with the leaders and their ideas. Just because there is no crisis, are these leaders other than charismatic? Boal and Bryson (1987, 1988) agree that visionary charismatics need no crisis.

What do we call charismatic leaders who have all the Weberian attributes except success? Early in their careers, Mao Zedung and Yassar Arafat suffered one defeat after another. Perhaps it was their successful escapes that were emphasized. What about the charismatic leader who is incompetent? Schiffer (1973) suggests it is easier for many followers to identify with a charismatic who displays a lack of talent, just as they do.

As the concept has spread from sociology and political science to psychoanalysis and psychology, increasing attention has been paid to the followers' need to identify with the leader and to the endurance of the charismatic, rather than to the routinization of the organization that was to follow according to Weber. It also has been observed that the charismatic leader inspires opposition and hatred in those who strongly favor the old order of things (Tucker, 1970). This view argues strongly for dyadic, rather than group, analyses of charismatic leader-follower relationships. One can see the subordinates of a single charismatic supervisor divided in the extent to which they love, fear, or hate him or her. The very behaviors and qualities that transport supporters into extremes of love, veneration, and admiration of the charismatic, may send opponents into extremes of hatred, animosity, and detestation (Bass, 1985a).

Charismatic leaders vary greatly in their pragmatism, flexibility, and opportunism and display different styles to achieve their impact. On the one hand, Charles de-Gaulle was always more concerned about being right than achieving immediate results and spoke of his "contempt for contingencies." Generally, his attitude was unbending (Hoffman & Hoffman, 1970). He became pragmatic only when forced to do so in order to resolve the Algerian crisis. Other inflexible charismatics of our time included Muammar Qaddafi of Libya and Ayatollah Khomeini of Iran. On the other hand, John F. Kennedy and Franklin Delano Roosevelt avoided speaking out to risk political battles which they thought they might lose. Nikolai Lenin also was a practical activist and a pragmatic organizer ready to reverse course when necessary (Tucker, 1970).

Personalized versus Socialized Charismatics. Charismatics can foster antisocial or prosocial behavior. One cannot exclude one or the other for valid scientific reasons; the dynamics may be similar (Bass, 1989). Freud (1922) distinguished between the true charismatics who directed followers toward transcendental purposes to totemic leaders whose worship as idols could satisfy the fantasies of their followers. Howell (1988) distinguished between personalized and socialized charismatic leaders. Personalized charismatic leaders use their powers of persuasion to obtain their followers' obedience and submission (McClelland, 1975). Such leaders are self-aggrandizing and maintain psychological distance from their followers, which increases their magical, supernatural, charismatic image. In contrast, socialized charismatic leaders are oriented to serving others. They develop shared goals with their followers and inspire the attainment of such goals. Psychological distance between leaders and followers is reduced, which enhances the followers' expectations of the equalization of power and mutual stimulation.

Followers accept the influence of personalized charismatic leaders to identify with them. Followers accept the influence of socialized leaders' ideas because these ideas are intrinsically rewarding (Kelman, 1958).

Howell deduced that personalized charismatic leaders must maintain a physical or psychological presence and satisfying relationship with their followers to continue to remain influential. Socialized charismatic leaders perpetuate their influence by the continued relevance of their ideas and mission to the subordinates' intrinsic satisfaction. To some degree, Howell's socialized charismatic leadership, with its emphasis on the mutuality of goals and its absence of the followers' identification with the leader, fits with what will be discussed later in this chapter as inspirational leadership.

Again, illustrating the need to look at the charismatic leader as exemplifying some but not all the Weberian characteristics, it is clear that the move toward routinization of leader-follower relations may be begun by the charismatic rather than by the followers. Marshall Tito of Yugoslavia was a good case in point, as were Augustus, Joseph Stalin, and Jawaharlal Nehru, who continued the routinization begun by the charismatic Julius Caesar, Nikolai Lenin, and Mahatma Gandhi and who had many, if not all, the charismatic qualities of their predecessors. Were not the successors as charismatic as the founders, even though cumbersome bureaucracies emerged under them?

Finally, it is interesting to note that Zablock (1980) was able to order four kinds of charismatic leadership in communes according to the completeness of the is-

sues covered by the leadership.[3] *Absolute* charismatic leadership was commonly found in selected religious communes. These communes concentrated authority about meanings, goals, strategies, norms, and alternatives. *Normative* charismatic leadership occurred in other religious communes that were similar except that authority about alternatives was missing. *Executive* charismatic leadership was found in some psychological, counterculture, and political communes in which concentrated authority about meanings, goals, and strategies but not about norms or alternatives was present in one or a few leaders. *Policy* charismatic leadership was particularly salient in counterculture and political communes in which authority was concentrated only about meanings or only about meanings and goals.

The Charismatic Relationship

Conger and Kanungo (1988) listed as behaviors of the charismatic leader being radical, unconventional, risk taking, visionary, entreprenurial, and exemplary. Nevertheless, of the elements associated with the charismatic relationship, two seem essential. The first is the pattern of abilities, interests, and personal traits that is common to most charismatic leaders. The second is the strong desire by followers to identify with the leader. Charismatic leaders have strong referent power. Often but not always, leaders present concise and radical solutions to crises. The followers' belief in the solutions comes as a consequence of their faith in the charismatic leader. Finally, if the effect of the emotion-driven charismatic relationship is to endure, it must therefore give way to a more rationally-driven routinization.

Characteristics of Charismatic Leaders

Requisite Abilities. Although followers endow a leader with charisma to fulfill their situational needs, they do not endow just anybody. The person who is so

---

[3]Descriptions of the communes could be Guttman scaled with a reproducibility of the hierarchy of 93. (A Guttman scale is a set of statements which can be ordered so that endorsement of a particular statment will predict endorsement of all those higher in the ordering and rejection of all those lower in the ordering of the statements. A perfect ordering has a reproducibility of 1.00.)

Table 12.1 Correlations between Ratings of Transformational and Transactional Leadership Factors and of Specific Performance as a Manager (According to Superiors) for 54 Managers Rated on the Multifactor Leadership Questionnaire by 306 Subordinates.

Subordinates' Description	Superior's Appraisal				
	Judgment and Decision Making	Financial Management	Communication	Persuasion	Risk Taking
Charismatic Leadership	.33*[a]	.36**	.32*	.33*	.45**
Intellectual Stimulation	.23	.35**	.29*	.24	.18
Contingent Reward	−.08	−.07	.18	.08	.01

*$p < .05$.
**$p < .01$.
[a]These data are from a sample of high performers and from a random sample drawn from a larger population. Differences between the samples have been removed by a partial correlation analysis.

SOURCE: Adapted from Hater and Bass (1988).

endowed must have abilities that are relevant to the situation. Thus, charismatic compared to noncharismatic presidents were judged by historians to be more highly esteemed by their contemporaries and able to accomplish more in their administrations (Maranell, 1970). As Table 12.1 shows, in an express mail business, the superiors of 54 managers rated the managers significantly higher in judgment, quality of decision making, financial management, communication, persuasion, and risk taking if the managers were described by their 306 subordinates as more charismatic on the Multifactor Leadership Questionnaire (MLQ).[4] No such significant correlations were found when the managers were described by their subordinates as practicing transactional contingent reward (Hater & Bass, 1988). Similar results were reported by Yammarino and Bass (1988) for naval officers, as shown in Table 12.2.

Personality Characteristics. Several empirical studies of charismatic and noncharismatic leaders revealed patterns of systematic differences that are consistent with the profile of the charismatic that has emerged from historical and sociological analyses. Thus, Hall (1983) completed a study of 10 leaders in the Atlanta area who were nominated for their charisma; in particular, these leaders described themselves as less accepting of authority than did 99 percent of a normative population. Labak (1973) asked 9,609 students to rate the charisma of their faculty at the University of Northern Colorado on a standardized questionnaire; 26 teachers, identified as charismatic, were matched with noncharismatic teachers. On standardized self-report inventories, the charismatic teachers described themselves as more enthusiastic, self-actualized, and tolerant of ambiguity and less defensive. Wilson (1975) reported that the following traits emerged in an analysis of charismatic heroes: self-esteem and self-possession, generosity, openness, honesty, and concern for others. A model and questionnaire test by Conger and Kanungo (1988, 1989) of the behavior of "a familiar person in the organization with leadership abilities" suggested that above and beyond their task orientation and relations orientation, leaders who were described as charismatic were also rated highly sensitive to the needs of followers, strongly articulate, willing to take personal risks, agents of radical change, and idealistic in their vision of the future.

Regardless of the situation, charismatic leaders are likely to display high levels of emotional expressiveness, self-confidence, self-determination, and freedom from internal conflict and are likely to have a strong conviction of the moral righteousness of their beliefs

[4]This questionnaire was developed to measure the factors in transformational and transactional leadership, one of which was charismatic leadership. The scale of charismatic leadership is described later in this chapter.

Table 12.2 Correlations of Subordinates' Ratings of Leadership Behavior and Superiors' Ratings of Successful Performance for 186 U.S. Navy Lieutenants and Lieutenants, Junior Grade.[a]

Subordinates' Ratings of Officers' Leadership Behavior	Superiors' Ratings of Performance	
	Cumulative Fitness-Report Evaluations	Cumulative Recommendation for Early Promotion
Transformational		
Charisma	.38**	.37**
Intellectual stimulation	.31**	.34**
Inspirational leadership	.25**	.28**
Individualized consideration	.21**	.24**
Transactional		
Contingent rewards (promises)	.17*	.17*
Contingent rewards (rewards)	.20**	.24**
Management-by-exception (active)	.22**	.28**
Management-by-exception (passive)	−.05	−.04
Nonleadership		
Laissez-faire	−.31**	−.31**

[a]$N = 186; r \geq .14$
*$p \leq .05; r \geq .19$
**$p \leq .01$.

SOURCE: Adapted from Yammarino and Bass (1988).

(House, 1977). Biographies, case studies, anecdotal material, and some quantitative research provide evidence of these characteristics.

Expressive Behavior. Friedman, Prince, Riggio, and DiMatteo (1980) suggested that charismatic leadership manifests itself in nonverbal emotional expressiveness. Expressive persons can use nonverbal cues "to move, inspire, or captivate others" (p. 133). Such expressiveness can be assessed with the self-reporting Affective Communication Test. Examples of items on the validated test include these: "I often touch friends during conversations," "I can easily express emotion over the telephone," "I [don't] usually have a neutral facial expression," and "I am [good] at pantomime in games like charades." Expressiveness is related to dramatic flair and experience in acting and in politics. Females score higher in emotional expressiveness, just as they tend to be seen as more charismatic than comparable males (Avolio & Bass, 1989). Emotional expressiveness corre-

lates .60 with the need for exhibition and .45 with the need for dominance. As will be seen, the latter are personality attributes of the charismatic leader.

For Bensman and Givant (1975) and Willner (1968), charismatic leaders project a powerful, confident, dynamic presence. The leaders' tone of voice is engaging and captivating, and their facial expressions are animated, yet they remain relaxed (Friedman & Riggio, 1981). Not only do they maintain direct eye contact, but their eyes have a magnetic attraction (Wilner, 1968). Riggio (in press) showed that extroverted and charismatic females were facially expressive, which led to their being evaluated more favorably than their nonexpressive counterparts. Spontaneously expressive females received more positive evaluations from judges but similarly expressive males did not; the judges viewed the emotional control of males in a more favorable light. Expressive cues included fluid, outward-directed cues, such as rate and fluency of speech; outward-directed gestural fluency and smiles; and cues of body emphasis, contact with the body, and inward-directed gestures.

Self-confidence. Charismatic leaders display complete confidence in the correctness of their positions and in their capabilities (Hoffman & Hoffman, 1970) and make this confidence a clear aspect of their public image. Even when personally discouraged and facing failure, they are unlikely to make such feelings public (Tucker, 1968). Such elevated self-esteem helps charismatics to avoid defensiveness in conflicting interpersonal situations and to maintain the confidence that their subordinates have in them (Hill, 1976). Charismatics tend to project onto likeminded loyal followers their continuing confident opinions of themselves (Bass, 1985a). They are great actors—always "on stage" —always projecting to their followers their extreme self-confidence and convictions so they become larger than life. They must be able to present themselves as miracle workers who are likely to succeed when others would fail (House, 1977).

Self-determination. For Weber (1924/1947), charisma was first a personal attribute of some leaders whose purposes, powers, and extraordinary determination set them apart from ordinary people. Friedrich Nietzsche's (1883/1974) superman had some of the same characteristics: inner-direction, originality, self-determination, sense of duty, and responsibility for the unique self. For Nietzsche, ordinary men conformed to the expectations of others. The superman could free himself from the expected. He was a point of contact with the future who created new values and goals. He was also a highly self-oriented narcissist. Weber's charismatic could also be a mystical ascetic, concerned with himself, rather than involved with others, and interested in promoting ideas for their own sake, rather than for material gain. According to Weber, the determined charismatic leader would set aside normal political life.

But self-determination can also imply obstinacy. Instead of being open to new ideas, some charismatic leaders may become closed-minded, dogmatic, and rigid. They may announce that they have provided the only true way to enlightenment. They think that their continued development is unnecessary and regard differences of opinion as heretical (Stark, 1969).

Insight. The charismatic leader can arouse, as well as articulate, feelings of need among followers and find radical solutions to their problems. Charismatics have insight into the needs, values, and hopes of followers (McClelland, 1975) and the ability to build on them through dramatic and persuasive words and actions. According to Gardner (1961), they are able to "conceive and articulate goals that lift people out of their petty preoccupations." Such leaders can unite people to seek objectives that are "worthy of their best efforts." For Yukl (1981), charismatics can say things publicly that followers feel privately but cannot express.

Freedom from Internal Conflict. Charismatic leaders maintain their confidence and determination, despite serious setbacks and defeats through a self-assurance that is "at one with their inner images" (Kets de Vries, 1984, p. 117). The confidence and determination of charismatic leaders stems from their greater freedom from the internal conflict that ordinary mortals are more likely to experience between their emotions, impressions, and feelings (Freud's id) and their controlling conscience (superego). Freedom from the id-superego conflict makes for strong ego ideals and assuredness about what the leaders value as good, right, and important. Convinced of the goodness, rightness, and importance of their own points of view, charismatic leaders are likely to be more forthright and candid in reprimanding subordinates and can maintain a clear conscience if they feel they must replace them (Keichel, 1983). (Ronald Reagan was an exception in this respect. As did Richard Nixon, he avoided such confrontations.) On the other hand, the ordinary manager is continuously victimized by self-doubts and personal traumas in such circumstances, regardless of the extensiveness or success of their careers (Levinson, Darrow, Klein, et al., 1978).

Eloquence. Because we are now in the era of speech writers, we no longer can readily attribute the emotional flair for expressive language to the leaders who use it. But it is known that highly charismatic Mario Cuomo writes his own colorful, incisive, inspiring speeches, such as the famous one he gave at the 1984 Democratic Convention. On television, Cuomo can respond extemporaneously to telephone questions in the same dynamic way. This facile use of language helped him win the record landslide vote in his 1986 gubernatorial reelection in New York. According to Bord (1975), charismatic leaders use high action verbs, short pauses between phrases and sentences, and reiteration in their speeches. Their messages are simple, focus on the collective identity of the speaker and the audience, and evoke a response from the audience.

Activity and Energy Levels. According to a three-year survey by the Group for the Advancement of Psychiatry (1974), the charismatic qualities needed by candidates for 100 vacant medical school chairs in psychiatry were a high energy level, optimism, fatherliness, and a capacity to inspire loyalty. Again, previously collected opinions of political historians demonstrated that charismatic presidents were more active and took significantly stronger actions than did noncharismatic presidents (Maranell, 1970).

Characteristics of Followers

Desire and Need to Identify with Charismatics. Weber (1924/1947, p. 328) wrote about the followers' "devotion to the specific and exceptional sanctity, heroism or exemplary character of an individual charismatic person, and of the normative patterns or order revealed or ordained by him." Willner (1968) saw followers as having an intense emotional and cognitive attraction to charismatic leaders above and beyond ordinary esteem, affection, admiration, and trust; this attraction involves "devotion, awe, reverence, and blind faith" (p. 6). Followers have an unqualified belief in the "man and his mission about what is, what should be, and what should be done" (p. 9).

More important than what charismatics do or say is what their different prospective followers feel about them. The same words or actions by a would-be leader can seem charismatic and extremely influential to ardent disciples but humbug to others.

For Madsen and Snow (1983), charismatic leadership depends as much on the "magnetizability" of the followers as on the magnetism of the leader. Those who are in psychological distress are prone to join a charismatic leader's coterie, according to Galanter's (1982) review of clinical evidence. For example, although he had been in prison for two decades, the magnetic murderer Charles Manson still could maintain a devoted following of misfit personalities on California's Russian River. The "Moonies," ardently devoted to their charismatic leader, the Reverend Sun Myung Moon, showed more feelings of helplessness, cynicism, and distrust of political action and less confidence in their own sexual identity, their own values, and the future than did a sample of college students (Lodahl, 1982). Charismatic gurus and leaders of sects attract insecure and lonely people, who join their coterie of followers and relinquish their rights to make decisions in exchange for strict, protective boundaries and security; the magnetism of the gurus often has a strong sexual component (Newman, 1983). Freemesser and Kaplan (1976) observed in interviews that those who joined a charismatic religious cult had lower self-esteem than a comparable set of others.

Corsino (1982) argued that the charismatic leadership of Malcolm X was due to his personality traits and the intellectual, moral, and emotional predispositions of his followers, who could identify with his experiences and who projected their own frustrations with white society onto him. After a content analysis of statements that followers made about Adlai Stevenson and Dwight D. Eisenhower during the 1952 presidential election campaign, Davies (1954) concluded that those who attributed special endorsements to their leader had a higher intolerance for indecision and crisis than did those who did not, used rigid categories of good and evil, and felt that other people were more in agreement with them than was actually the case.

The Identification Process. Freud (1922) accounted for the follower's identification with the charismatic leader and the follower's total commitment by suggesting that these were ways for the follower to resolve conflict between his or her ego and superego. Downton (1973) agreed, seeing that we resolve the conflict between our self-image and what we want and think it should be by making the leader the embodiment of our ego ideal. By accepting a leader with transcendental objectives, followers can fulfill their desires to go beyond their own self-interests and to become more noble and worthy. The leader is idealized and becomes the model of behavior to be emulated—the embodiment of the follower's aspirations. Commitment is directed to the person of the charismatic leader (whether the leader's goals are self-aggrandizing or prosocial). Through the leader, the follower can achieve the strongly desired ideal self (Marcus, 1961). Obedience to new attitudes and goals develops from the effort to emulate the leader's example and mission; at the same time, the follower's capacity to criticize the leader is impaired (Weber, 1924/1947).

Erikson (1968) conceived *identity confusion* as growing out of a failure to mature in adolescence and young adulthood and a failure to develop a strong ego ideal because of oppressive, weak, or absent parents. The lack of an ego ideal to guide one's behavior and interpersonal relationships arouses uneasiness and a sense of drift. Downton (1973) thought that identifying with the charismatic leader was a way of coping with such identity confusion, as well as with the conflict between the ego and the ego ideal. As a consequence, the charismatic leader benefits the follower by providing him or her with new goals and a positive identity and by enhancing the follower's self-esteem. The charismatic leader gives the follower a second chance to attain maturity. Young women's identification with Mother Theresa's aid of the poorest of the poor can give them an enhanced self-image and make them agents of contribution to a worthy cause. Identification with a maniacal murderer, Charles Manson, can likewise enhance a follower's self-image, but with a most unworthy cause.

Charisma, an endowment of spiritual grace from God, was converted by social science into an endowment of leaders by their followers of a high degree of esteem and referent power. The value, popularity, and celebrity status that others attribute to a leader engenders in followers strong emotional responses of affection and the leader's generalized influence beyond the immediate situation and beyond the ordinary exchange of compliance for promises of reward or threats of punishment. The vicarious satisfaction obtained from basking in the glory of the charismatic may be as sufficient a reward for the starstruck as doing God's work is for the pious. Admiration of the charismatic leader and the desire to identify and to emulate him or her are powerful influences on followers. Charisma is in the eye of the beholder and, therefore, is relative

to the beholder. Nevertheless, the charismatic leader actively shapes and enlarges his or her audience through energy, self-confidence, assertiveness, ambition, and opportunities seized (Bass, 1985a).

House (1977) described the dynamic process involved as follows: Self-confident in their own competence, convinced of their own beliefs and ideals, and strong in the need for power, charismatic leaders are highly motivated to influence their followers. Their self-confidence and strong convictions increase their followers' trust in their leaders' judgments. Charismatics engage in impression management to bolster their image of competence, increasing their subordinates' compliance and faith in them. They relate the work and mission of their group to the strongly held values, ideals, and aspirations that are part of their organization's culture. In organizational settings, they vividly portray for their subordinates an attractive vision of what the outcomes of their efforts could be. This portrayal provides subordinates with more meaning for their work and arouses their enthusiasm, excitement, emotional involvement, and commitment to the group's objectives. Roles are defined in ideological terms that appeal to the subordinates. What makes this process more than just inspirational is that charismatic leaders use themselves as examples for subordinates to follow. Thus, cadets at the U.S. Air Force Academy said they most wanted to emulate those squadron commanders whom they had described as highly charismatic on the MLQ (Clover, 1989).

In some instances, their very lack of talent may make some popular but untalented charismatic figures easier for their uncritical followers to identify with and to gain vicarious satisfaction from their own frustrated ambitions (Schiffer, 1973). Unlike Freud's (1922) Moses-like charismatic leader, who orients followers toward personal and moral growth and toward transcendental purpose and mission, the pseudocharismatic totemic leader operates as an idol who is easy to identify with at a superficial level because he or she caters to the whims and fantasies of the followers. Token identity and perfunctory rituals satisfy the followers' need to belong (Faucheux, 1984); logic-tight compartments in the followers separate what is not wanted in the leader from what is wanted, repress the former, and enhance the latter. Charisma depends on a regression to imagery. The childlike image of the faultless leader replaces a realistic appraisal (Schiffer, 1973); even when the leader's faults are recognized, as was the case with Ronald Reagan, supporters see them as illustrations of the leader's greater humanity and find it easier to forgive him or her for having their own shortcomings. This leniency connects with the fact that when they evaluate their superiors, subordinates often do not rate them as they have been asked to do; rather, they rate prototypes of a generalized leader that they carry around in their heads.

Reactions to charismatic leaders are likely to obey similar psychometric principles. Bass and Avolio (1987) obtained a correlation of .83 between subordinates' behavioral descriptions of the charismatic leadership of their superiors on the MLQ and the subordinates' ratings of the prototypical leader using the Lord, Foti, and Phillips (1982) prototypicality scale. Correlations of prototypicality with other leadership styles were much lower. Prototypicality correlations fell to .61 with practicing contingent reward and .38 with practicing management by exception.

At the crux of the phenomenon of charisma is the emotional response of the follower to the charismatic leader. As Schiffer (1973, p. 3) stated:

> Commonly, . . . some specific . . . unique personality is supposedly the true source of the process . . . [or] a standard-bearer for a new and exciting ideology . . . TV cameras and commentators . . . lend lustre and dimension to the whole happening; a strange hypnoid state begins to infiltrate the most vulnerable minds.
> . . . the social scientist looks for economic and cultural factors . . . to explain the new "miracle"; the intelligentsia dissect the personal mystique of the hero. . . .

The charismatic leader reduces the followers' resistance to changing their attitudes and frees their responses by arousing emotional responses toward him or her and a sense of excitement and adventure. But, as was noted before, the cost of such emotional responding may be impaired judgment if the followers uncritically accept the leader. The dependence generated by charismatic leadership is evident when the loss

of an inspiring, charismatic leader is accompanied by demoralization and disruption among the followers (Hays & Thomas, 1967).

The Mystique

The magical and the fantasy aspects of charisma and their costs need to be considered more fully. Charismatics are not merely self-confident, determined, and convinced of their own beliefs. They may believe they have supernatural missions and purposes. Martin Luther King really had a waking dream of what he was to accomplish. Downton (1973, p. 230) noted that "the charismatic relationship can be a two-way exchange in which the leader comes to see himself as charismatic and lives from day to day on the deferential treatment he sees as rightfully his."

Followers do not merely have favorable perceptions of the leader; for them, the charismatic leader may be larger than life. Furthermore, they can act like they have been mesmerized, suspending their ability to make critical judgments. If we cannot have the loved object, we try to imitate and emulate the object, to gain its approval and to meet its standards and expectations (Kets de Vries, 1984).

The sense of reality of both the charismatic leader and the followers can be distorted by psychodynamic mechanisms, such as projection, regression, and disassociation. The followers can project their processes and needs onto the charismatic leader, who may become the catalyst for the followers' rationalizations. John F. Kennedy is a case in point:

> John F. Kennedy ushered in a new Camelot complete with his Queen Guinevere and knights ready to do battle in Cuba, Berlin and Vietnam with the villainous foes of freedom, the Cuban devils and Soviet dragons. The depth of the public depression resulting from Kennedy's assassination can only be explained by the strong, emotional, idolization of the image of Kennedy as dragonslayer, savior, and creator of a new life on earth for the disadvantaged. In reality, he was an astute politician who changed a fictitious Soviet superiority in missiles—the so-called missile gap—into the beginning of a new arms race led by the United States. . . . His statesmen-like qualities grew with his experience in office. But for the

mass of the U.S. public, his image was that of the youthful world leader who was lifting the U.S. out of the stodgy Eisenhower years with the focus of a future of U.S. leadership among the nations of the world and in space (Bass, 1985a, pp. 56–57).

The Transformation of Followers

Although, as was mentioned earlier, Freemesser and Kaplan (1976) found that youths who joined a charismatic cult were lower in self-esteem than a comparison sample, the youths' self-esteem was raised in 6 to 12 months by membership in the cult. Avolio and Bass (1988) attempted to fine-tune this interactive process in terms of the follower's cognitive processes, using Smith and Ellsworth's (1985) cognitive dimensions that account for how emotions differ from each other. The novelty to the follower of the leader's message will increase the follower's attention to it. The follower's uncertainty in the current situation will also increase his or her attention to the leader's message.

The charismatic (as well as inspirational) leader concretizes a vision that the follower views as worthy of his or her effort, thereby raising the follower's excitement and effort. But Downton (1973) observed that people who seek to identify with the leader but who are at a distance from him or her may become only passingly committed and aroused and may not take action to conform to the leader's initiatives. If they are free to act and are not constrained by other commitments or the lack of opportunity, they will actually become committed to leaders even at a distance. Downton (p. 230) described this process as transformational, rather than transactional, noting its greater likelihood of taking effect:

> In the formation of a charismatic commitment, the opportunity for action is apt to be greater than strictly transactional relationships because the follower who identifies with a leader can transform his behavioral pattern without necessarily exchanging tangible goods with the leader. For example, the follower . . . can act when the leader initiates a new moral code that can be put immediately into practice, no matter how distant the leader and the opportunities for organizational activity.

Tension is reduced in the follower who strongly identifies with the charismatic leader. Since the leader has come to substitute for the follower's ego ideal, continuing, uncritical, acceptance of the leader's initiatives is a way of bringing the ego in line with the ego ideal. In the case of identity confusion, when the follower has been unable to "find himself" and to decide who he is and what he wants to be, the follower's intolerance of criticism of the leader counteracts the problems of identity. The follower protects the idealized identity of the leader as a defense. Such criticism is a challenge to the person who is defending the image, since it is by identifying with that image that the person develops a sense of who he is and what he wants to become.

Crises and Their Solutions

Some explanations of the charismatic relationship have emphasized that social crisis is the root cause of its emergence. According to this viewpoint, the charismatic appears in times of great societal distress to save society. This salvation from distress engenders "special emotional intensity of the charismatic response . . . followers respond to the charismatic leader with passionate loyalty because the [promise of] salvation . . . that he appears to embody represents the fulfillment of urgently felt needs" (Tucker, 1970, p. 81).

Among the five sociopolitical factors that accounted for half the variance in the degree to which charismatic leadership was attributed to twentieth-century heads of state, Cell (1974) isolated such factors as a national social crisis and disruptive youths. It is not only acute crisis that brings out the charismatic leader. Charismatic leadership also arises when the crisis is chronic, such as when the ultimate values of a culture are being devalued and radical social change is occurring (Hummel, 1973). Charisma carries with it a challenge to the old order; a break with continuity; a risky adventure; and continual movement, ferment, and change (Bass, 1985b). The empowered leaders can continue to influence these feelings to maintain their positions, but they need to provide new, usually radical, solutions to the crisis or to relate it "to a higher purpose that has intrinsic validity" for the followers (Boal & Bryson, 1987). The charismatic leader can also promote unlearning and the search for new actions. In highly ambiguous situations, such new solutions may be chosen precipitously (Hedberg, 1981).

Individuals who feel that they have lost control over their environment are more ready to accept the authority of a charismatic leader (Devereux, 1955). People become "charisma hungry" owing to the decline of old values and rituals; shocks to the culture; and growing fears, anxieties, and identity crises. For example, Mahatma Gandhi satisfied such "hunger" in Indians by giving them a new collective identity and new rituals (Erikson, 1969). Adolf Hitler arose as the savior of Germany in response to the disappointments of military defeat and social, political, and economic distress. Despite Italy's final victory in World War I, the rise of Benito Mussolini to power in 1922 illustrated the same theme of distress in Italy (Fermi, 1966). Martin Luther King and Jesse Jackson stirred disadvantaged blacks to believe that their personal efforts, combined with collective action, could reshape American society to advance their place in it, ultimately for the benefit of all Americans.

When organizational cultures are in transition, charismatic leaders appear in industry. They arise when traditional authority and legal, rational, and bureaucratic means cannot meet the organization's need for leadership. Old, highly structured, successful organizations are unlikely to need such leadership. Charismatic leaders are more likely to appear in failing organizations or newly emerging ones that are struggling to survive. In such organizations, charismatic leaders can radicalize from within, rather than in response to a challenge from outside (Berger, 1963). They create new cultures for their supporters by creating new meanings and beliefs for them.

In the absence of threats and the need for new strategies and reorientation toward them, the maintenance of the existing order and organizational culture can be accomplished by institutional processes and by symbolic acts of the leaders' reaffirmation of the organization's values and standards. But when the organization must change to survive, its reorientation requires substantive changes in the distribution of power, interruption of previously established commitments and beliefs, and the management of the development of a new set of values, norms, beliefs, and rationalizations

(Romanelli & Tushman, 1983). Many colleges in the 1980s were faced with declining enrollments and declining resources, coupled with increasing competition for available public and private funds. Charismatic presidents were needed. Delson's (1986) analysis of interviews in and news clippings of five schools suggested, among other things, that such presidents had to have a sense of purpose and recognize the need to build for the future. They had to choose strong deputies, be able to gain the active involvement of public officials, and seize opportunities that arose.

The rapid change in the nature of work and organizations in the 1980s and 1990s may give rise to new types of charismatic labor leaders, although such leaders may have particular difficulty institutionalizing changes in their unions (Spector, 1987). The change from smokestack industry to service and high technology industries may also presage the appearance of new charismatic labor leaders (Bass, 1985a).

But industrial change is driven by opportunity as well as threat. The opportunities present in changing market demands and technological developments can bring forth charismatic leadership of consequence and result in necessary organizational changes. As will be noted later, since different sorts of threats and opportunities exist at every organizational level, it is not surprising that charismatic leadership can be revealed at any organizational level.

Cultural Expectations. Charismatics appear in societies with traditions of support for them and expectations about their emergence. Thus, charismatic prophets and messiahs could arise in ancient Israel because they fit with a long prophetic tradition. They were being awaited. The intense spiritual relationship of the charismatic leader and his followers is distinctive in modern Islam, which flowed out of the Judeo-Christian tradition. The prophet is an extraordinary personality who emerges in a situation of social crisis, carrying a messianic message that becomes legitimated and routinized (Dekmejian & Wyszomirski, 1972). In the absence of such tradition, as in ancient China, the emergence of such charismatics is much less possible. The same appears to be generally the case in modern China; Mao Zedung was an exception. Hierarchy continues to be more important in determining leader-follower relations in China than the possibilities that charismatic leaders will arise. For the charismatic leader to resort to particular psychological mechanisms in his appeals, the followers must have shared norms. Since sinfulness is a shared norm in the Judeo-Christian world, the Western charismatic leader can stimulate guilt among followers. The importance of "face" is a shared norm in the Orient; if it were possible to do so, the Oriental charismatic leader would have to focus on shame. The use of rationalization and denial also requires that followers share norms and myths (Hummel, 1972).

According to Tsurumi (1982), an important aspect that accompanied the introduction of quality control circles in Japan was the American consultant Charles Protzman's emphasis on the need for a charismalike manager to "secure the faith and respect of those under him by his being an example of high purpose, courage, honor and independence." This focus conformed with the Japanese tradition of leaders as men of exemplary moral courage and selfsacrifice. In India, to attain charismatic status, one must use a wide range of sacraments to achieve supernatural stature. Such attainment can come from practicing asceticism, passive meditation, and physical austerity, which may or may not translate into leadership. But whatever develops as a consequence does not depend on a crisis (Singer, 1969).

Organizational Expectations. Executives at the top of the organization are expected to be transformational, that is, concerned with the ultimate purposes of their organization. Such leaders must be reflective about long-term issues and sensitive about how their organization must remain in tune with the external environment (Watson, 1988). Using the MLQ, a correlation of .23 was found for 45 New Zealand professionals between subordinates' descriptions of the charisma of their leader and the leader's level in the organizational hierarchy (Bass, 1985a). Bass, Waldman, Avolio, and Bebb (1987) reported similar results for the mean charismatic behavior described and required by subordinates of their leaders at two successive levels of the organization. However, such MLQ differences failed to

be found when junior and senior officers were compared in the U.S. Navy (Yammarino & Bass, 1988) and when majors were compared with colonels in the U.S., Canadian, and German armies (Boyd, 1989a).

Charisma without Crisis. Boal and Bryson (1987) suggested that charismatic effects can emerge not only in crises, but as a consequence of the charismatic's vision and its articulation, which create a sense of need for action by the followers. The visionary charismatic begins with ideological fervor and moves to action, unlike the crisis charismatic, who begins with solutions to a crisis and then develops ideological justifications for them.

Whether spurred by a crisis or an ideology, the charismatic leaders' solutions can take opposite directions. The dedicated follower of one charismatic can be uplifted and moved to a new and better life; the dedicated follower of another can be moved to murder or suicide. Thus, charismatic leadership can be beneficial or deleterious to society and to organizational life, depending on whether the followers' needs are authentic or contrived and whether the leader has prosocial or antisocial goals.

Routinization

History is replete with charismatic leaders whose revolutionary changes endured. As Bass (1985a, p. 41) noted:

> The known world was remade socially, culturally and politically by Alexander the Great in his own brief career. Simon Bolivar's efforts had lasting political effects on much of Latin America. Mohammed's effects transformed societies stretching from North Africa to Indonesia and left lasting works on cultures from Spain to Central Asia.

What makes for the lasting effects of charismatic leaders? Weber (1924/1947) attributed them to routinization. Focused on the expressive and the emotional, the relationship between the charismatic leader and the led is basically unstable; it must be routinized by the development of organizational rules and arrangements to achieve stability, Weber thought. The charismatic leader's mission can be routinized in several ways. For example, unless the leader is replaced by an equally charismatic successor, an administrative apparatus is created, along with rites and ceremonies, to provide continuity of the message and mission. Or oral and written traditions emerge to provide the endurance of the charismatic's effects. The charismatic, revolutionary hero, Napoleon Bonaparte became the Emperor Napoleon, with a new court, new legal codes, a new educational system, and a new administration. Mao Zedung, the permanent revolutionary, was succeeded by Deng Xiaoping, the administrator, who sought to maintain most of the bureaucratic political system created by Mao but not as much of Mao's economic system.

The charismatic leader is a hard act to follow. Institutional practices and the cultural imperatives built by the charismatic leader must replace him after he is gone. Marshall Tito of Yugoslavia planned carefully for the succession after his death but was not optimistic that any associate could accumulate the personal authority that his charisma had given him (Drachkovitch, 1964). Actually, the structures remain in place in Yugoslavia, but the excitement and commitment to them appear to be gone.

Continuity is also provided by key groups of believers and by distinctive practices and imagery in the form of visual art, ceremonies, and stories. In the survival and growth of Alcoholics Anonymous and the National Council on Alcoholism, both founded by charismatic leaders in 1935 and 1946, respectively, Trice and Beyer (1986) found (1) the development of an administrative apparatus that puts the charismatic's program into practice, (2) the transfer of charisma to others in the organization by rites and ceremonies, (3) the incorporation of the charismatic's message and mission into the organization's traditions, and (4) the selection of a successor who resembles the charismatic founder and has the esteem to achieve the charismatic's personal influence.

Charisma May Emerge from Routinization. The office may make the leader. Apart from "office charisma," the demands of the office may greatly elevate the esteem of the officeholder. For instance, profligate Prince Hal developed into charismatic Henry V in response to the demands of kingship.

Charisma grows from administrative routine. Such an interesting reverse effect was demonstrated by Scott (1978). Rather than supporting Weber's thesis that charismatic authority eventually contributes routinization, Scott found that routinization, as evidenced by years of tenure in a bureaucratic office, contributed to one's charismatic authority. In a random sample of Kentucky school superintendents, Scott found a correlation of .52 between their years in office and their charismatic authority. It was not until the thirteenth year of their tenure that the superintendents' charismatic authority was rated consistently high. A peak of charismatic authority was reached after 13 years of tenure and continued through the twenty-first year of tenure before declining slightly, just before the superintendents' retirement.

Using Mao Zedung as an example, Chang (1982) argued that the emergence of a charismatic leader is a long-term process of interaction between the leader and followers and their collective ability to accumulate political power. Mao's charismatic leadership was legitimated, reinforced, and maintained through institutional efforts, but institutionalization did not bring routinization, as Weber maintained. Thus, we need to allow for various possible relations between charismatic leaders, their immediate colleagues, and the public that may result in a more personalized leadership, rather than routinization of the leadership over time.

The Charismatic Leader in Complex Organizations: A Conceptual Examination

Charismatic leadership is no longer attributed solely to the founders of religious, social, or political movements. The concept is now used to understand lesser leaders and leadership in a wide variety of situations. Numerous theorists have used the concept of charisma to account for organizational members' emotional responses to work-related stimuli and to their trust and confidence in their leader and their leader's values, which result in their motivation to perform beyond expectations based on cost-benefit exchanges.[5]

[5]See, for example, Bass (1985a), Berlew (1974), Boal and Bryson (1987), House (1977), and Sashkin and Fulmer (1985).

Widespread Distribution

Charismatic leader-follower relations are widely found in political life, as well as in complex organizations. They appear not only "in extravagant forms and fleeting moments, but in an abiding, if combustible, aspect of social life that occasionally bursts into open flame" (Geertz, 1977, p. 151). Charismatic relationships have been reported in such diverse organizations as suburban school systems; communes; utopian communities; colleges; Alcoholics Anonymous; the National Council on Alcoholism; the Chippewa Indian tribe; a maternity home; a British manufacturing firm; Tanganyikan labor unions; and the royal courts of England, Java, and Morocco (Trice & Beyer, 1984). In the 1980s, these relations were of considerable interest to studies of educational institutions, the military, and business and industry.

As Shils (1965), Dow (1969a), and Oberg (1972) observed earlier, Bass (1985a, pp. 56–57) found in empirical surveys that charisma is widely distributed as an interpersonal relationship and is not limited only to world-class leaders or to those who found movements or head organizations:

> [Charisma] shows up with . . . Lee Iacocca at Chrysler convincing workers, suppliers, Congressmen, and customers that Chrysler could be turned around and doing it; the young Robert Hutchins recasting the prestigious University of Chicago in his own image; Hyman Rickover, taking on the whole Navy Department with an idea, the nuclear submarine, whose time had come. . . . [M]uch of what the Iacocca's, Hutchins' and Rickover's can do from the top of the organization, can occur in varying amounts and degrees all through complex organizations. Such charismatic effects can be studied and found or developed in supervisors at all levels of the complex organization.

Charisma, in turn, is a component—the most general and important component—of the larger concept of transformational leadership. In this regard, it is to be found, to a considerable degree, in industrial, educational, governmental, and military leaders at all organizational levels. In questionnaire surveys, many followers described their military or industrial superiors as persons who made everyone enthusiastic about assignments, who inspired loyalty to the organization, who commanded respect from everyone, who had a special gift of seeing what was really important, and who had a sense of mission and excited subordinates. Some of these subordinates had complete faith in the leaders with charisma and felt good to be near them. They were proud to be associated with the charismatic leaders and trusted the leaders' capacity to overcome any obstacle. The charismatic leaders served as a symbol of success and accomplishment for their followers (Bass, 1985a).

Charismatics may be more likely to appear in political and religious movements than in business or industry (Katz & Kahn, 1978), but they also appear at various levels in the complex organizations of business executives, educational administrators, military officers, and industrial managers. For Zaleznik (1983), charisma distinguishes the ordinary manager from the true leader in organizational settings. The true leader attracts intense feelings of love (and sometimes hate) from his or her subordinates, who want to identify with him or her. Feelings about ordinary managers are bland, but relations are smoother and more steady. However, like most intimate relationships, the relations between the charismatic leader and his or her followers tend to be more turbulent. Such "commando leaders" emerge to accomplish challenging and exhilarating tasks that need to be undertaken in an organization. Although they are highly effective, they may be "glamorous nuisances" (Handy, 1976).

Katz and Kahn (1978) argued that the charismatic relationship is strengthened to the degree that leaders distance themselves from their followers. This idea fits with Hollander's (1978) inference that charismatic leadership is less likely to emerge in complex organizations because of the close contact of superiors and subordinates, which prevents the maintenance of the magical properties of charisma. But many charismatic leaders, like Nikolai Lenin and Lyndon Johnson, for example, had close, immediate, lifelong, subordinates, who worshiped them with intense devotion. Social distance between leaders and followers is not essential for the maintenance of the charismatic relationship. In fact, Howell (1988) argued that socialized charismatics do not maintain such a distance.

Yukl (1981) attributed the presumed scarcity of charismatic leaders in business and industry to the lack of managers with the necessary skills. Berlew (1974) thought that many managers have the skills but do not recognize the opportunities available. Bass (1985a) suggested that such managers may be less willing to risk standing out so visibly among their peers in organizations when they believe that conformity may be more important for success. Nevertheless, House (1977) suggested that charismatics may be found throughout complex organizations; evidence of their effects on their followers includes the followers' trust in the correctness of the leader's beliefs, beliefs that are similar to the leader's, unquestioning acceptance of the leader, affection for the leader, willingness to obey the leader, emotional involvement in the mission of the organization, heightened goals for performance, and belief by the followers that they are able to contribute to the success of the group's mission.

Utility of Charismatic Leadership in Complex Organizations

Weber (1946) noted that charismatic leadership is a way to provide order and direction in complex organizations that were not bureaucratized or operated according to traditions. To meet the challenges of a rapidly changing work force, markets, and technologies in the past few decades, productive organizations increased their efforts to avoid bureaucratic and traditional rigidities by using ad hoc groups, temporary systems, and organicity (Robbins, 1983). Elaborate formal coordination and planning were replaced by teamwork and devoted, intense efforts by members. Increasingly, leader-subordinate relationships displayed more charismatic characteristics (Quinn & Cameron, 1983).

Shamir, House, and Arthur (1988) suggested that charismatic leaders generate more effort in their subordinates in a number of ways. These leaders enhance, for their subordinates, the intrinsic worth of the goals and activities required to reach the goals; instill in them faith in the future and the belief that the goals are beyond ordinary, rational purposes, and, in the process, raise their self-esteem.

The charismatic prophet's antiestablishment preaching can be destructive, but it also may contribute to

organizational renewal. Etzioni (1961) suggested that more charismalike leadership is needed in organizations to induce subordinates to accept guidance in expressive matters, in value judgments, and in decisions about purpose. Less charisma is needed to achieve agreement about instrumental means that usually are based on facts and rationales. More charisma is also needed if compliance depends on moral involvement; less is needed if it depends on material rewards or the avoidance of penalties. For Etzioni, personnel in the lower ranks are instrumental performers, decisions about means are relegated to personnel in the middle levels, and charismatic concerns for the ends should be restricted to the top levels. For him, lower-level charismatic leadership would be dysfunctional in service and production bureaucracies: "Development of charisma on levels other than the top is not only unnecessary but is likely to undermine the rational processes required to maximize organizational effectiveness" (p. 317).

But Etzioni saw that when decisions about ends remain important, such as for priests, shop stewards, and military combat officers who are lower in the hierarchy of their organizations, charismatic leadership still has utility. Empirical support can be found in Bass's (1985a) report that significantly greater amounts of charismatic leadership were seen by the surveyed subordinates of U.S. Army combat officers than among combat-support officers. Nevertheless, Etzioni's argument about business and industrial organizations requires that decisions about values, objectives, goals, and missions be limited to the top levels, when, in fact, participation in aspects of such decisions can be encouraged at all levels. Therefore, it is not surprising to find that subordinates in lower organizational ranks who describe their immediate supervisors as charismatic also think their units and their organization are more productive. And opinions about the effectiveness of lower- and middle-level charismatic leaders are shared by their superiors (Hater & Bass, 1988; Yammarino & Bass, 1988).

Differences in the Behavior and Accomplishments of Charismatics

Weber did not pay much attention to the individual differences in the personalities of charismatic leaders but saw only that routinization would follow from the development of the charismatic's religious or political authority. However, some charismatic leaders' sense of omnipotent personal power may prevent the institutionalization of charismatic authority into procedures and routines to be managed by subordinates and successors (Mitscherlich, 1967). This situation seems to have occurred with Kwame Nkrumah of Ghana but not with Jomo Kenyatta of Kenya. Both leaders were charismatic, but only Kenyatta could accept political opposition (Dow, 1969b). Thus, charismatic leaders may differ considerably from each other in what they do and what they can accomplish.

> Charismatic mentors will guide and support the personal growth of their disciples. Equally charismatic patrons will exchange support, protection and security for loyalty and service, keeping their clients in the same continued state of dependency. Charismatic, inspirational teachers will provide intellectual stimulation; charismatic celebrities who lack the intellect will not. Charismatic junior army officers with their cry of "follow me," will provide inspiration to take action; charismatic ascetics or mystics may foster escapism and lethargy. (Bass, 1985a, p. 52)

When Charismatic Leaders Fail. The situation may cause the charismatic leader to fail. For example, charismatic conductors of symphony orchestras will be seriously constrained by the unionization of the musicians they direct, as well as by the evaluation and control of employers, critics, business managers, and audiences (Kamerman, 1981). But more often, their personal weaknesses may lie behind their failure, as Bass (1985a, pp. 50–51) pointed out:

> Despite their self-confidence, self-determination, and freedom from inner conflicts, some charismatics will fail . . . as a consequence of particular deficiencies or exaggerated tendencies. Sometimes they may fail due to the overwhelming constraints they face and how they try to cope with them. Thus, how leaders with a sense of mission, self-confidence, ambition and other attributes of charisma handle the organizational constraints that frustrate their aims also makes a difference in whether they succeed in transforming organization managements, or fail in a dissatisfy-

ing standoff between what they want to see done and what can be done.

What McCall and Lombardo (1983) discovered in "derailed" promising young executives is illustrative. Unpredictability, insensitivity to others, the betrayal of trust, and the failure to delegate to staff effectively and to build a team abort the executives' move up the organizational ladder as expected. A political leader who operates at a distance from colleagues and constituents may get away with cronyism and extreme ambitiousness, but for the industrial executive, too many such flaws create among his more powerful colleagues strong antipathies to his subsequent promotion.

If the strong identification with a charismatic leader produces dependent, immature followers, rather than provides a model and inspiring support for self-actualizing followers (Musser, 1987), the early successes nourish unrealistic expectations, both within the leader and within the followers. If the problems become too great, the group's expectations may eventually surpass the leader's magical powers, causing the leader's downfall (Heifetz & Sinder, 1987).

Empirical Studies of Charismatic Effects

The earlier case studies, retrospective analyses, and commentaries about the impact of charismatic leaders on their followers have been augmented by a few questionnaire and interview surveys of the military, industry and education; of teams competing in a complex business game; and in a laboratory experiment.

Paucity of Empirical Research. Trice and Beyer (1986) were able to list nine sociological and anthropological field studies of charisma, as of 1977, that they regarded as relevant, but House (1977) was unable to unearth any controlled empirical efforts to investigate the phenomenon, as of 1976. The paucity of studies may explain why charisma was not indexed in *Psychological Abstracts*, as of 1969 (Stark, 1970). The lack of empirical research on charisma may justify Lawler's (1982) complaint that the thousands of available empirical studies of leadership offered little guidance to serious practitioners of the art.

At least two reasons may underlie the paucity of

such laboratory and field experiments and surveys until recently. First, many, if not most scholars, assumed charisma to be a rare attribute, limited to a few extraordinary leaders. Second, they thought it was impossible to bring charisma into the laboratory or to measure it with adequate validity. Both these assumptions have proved to be mistaken.

A Laboratory Experiment on Charisma

Howell (1985) succeeded in bringing the phenomenon of charisma into the laboratory. In the first such laboratory experiment, she compared the effects on subordinates of three types of leaders: charismatic, structuring, and considerate. The leaders' roles were played by one of two actresses, each of whom was trained for 30 hours. The actresses' training consisted of in-depth descriptions of their roles and a demonstration of the behaviors, emotional states, body language, facial expressions, and paralinguistic cues that they were to use in the experiment. The actresses also viewed videotapes of actual managers who portrayed the different styles of leadership and rehearsed extensively. Videotapes of the actresses enacting the three styles after training were rated by 203 judges; this manipulation check attested to the validity of the actresses' performance.

When playing the charismatic,

the leader articulated an overarching goal, communicated high performance expectations and exhibited confidence in participants' ability to meet these expectations, and empathized with the needs of participants. . . . The highly charismatic leader also projected a powerful, confident, and dynamic presence and had a captivating, engaging voice tone. . . . Nonverbally, the charismatic leader alternated between pacing and sitting on the edge of her desk, leaned toward the participant, maintained direct eye contact, and had a relaxed posture and animated facial expressions. . . .

The structuring leader . . . explained the nature of the task, provided detailed directions, emphasized the quantity of work to be accomplished within the specified time period, maintained definite standards of work performance, and answered any task related questions. . . . Nonverbally, the structuring leader sat on the edge of her desk, maintained intermittent eye

contact, and had neutral facial expressions and a moderate level of speech intonation. . . .

The considerate . . . leader engaged in participative two-way conversations, emphasized the comfort, well-being, and satisfaction of participants, and reassured and relaxed participants. The highly considerate leader was also friendly and approachable and had a warm voice tone. Nonverbally, the considerate leader sat on the edge of her desk, leaned toward participants, maintained direct eye contact and had a relaxed posture and friendly facial expressions. . . . (Howell, 1985, p. 8)

The laboratory task was an in-basket exercise requiring the completion of 15 memos in 45 minutes, followed by an optional task of 5 memos to be completed in an additional 15 minutes; most participants actually completed the optional task. Two co-workers who were confederates of the experimenter, plus the participant, made up the task group. The confederate co-workers (also trained) either encouraged the participant (high-productivity norming) or discouraged the participant (low-productivity norming).

A total of 144 undergraduates were allocated to the six experimental treatments, 24 participants per treatment, so that each type of leadership was combined with high- or low-productivity norms.

The most important finding was that only the charismatic leader was able to generate high productivity when confederate co-workers tried to discourage the participant. The leader who initiated structure did almost as well, but only if the co-workers encouraged high productivity. The structuring leader generated even less productivity than did the considerate leader when co-workers were discouraging and set low-productivity norms. In addition, in contrast to participants who worked under the leaders who initiated structure or were considerate, participants who worked under a charismatic leader had higher task performance; they suggested more courses of action, had greater satisfaction with the task, felt less role conflict, and were more satisfied with the leader. Also, the qualitative task performance of individuals with a charismatic leader was better than that of individuals with a considerate leader.

One component that was not specified in Howell's

operationalization of charisma was the extent to which the participants identified with the leader. Hence, if such identification distinguishes the true charismatic from the inspirational leader, as will be suggested later, Howell's results may better describe the impact of the inspirational leader if such identification did not occur.

Surveys and Interviews

To test House's (1977) theory of charismatic leadership, Smith (1982) identified, by nominations, a sample of 30 "charismatic" and 30 "noncharismatic" leaders, who represented a broad sample of formal work organizations in the business, industrial, and governmental sectors. Smith administered 38 scales to subordinates to describe their superiors' attitudes and behavior. A discriminant analysis and cross-validation revealed that 7 of 18 emergent dimensions, formed from the 38 scales, significantly differentiated the charismatic from the noncharismatic leaders. The charismatic leaders were seen to be dynamic (emphatic, active, fast, aggressive, bold, extroverted, energetic, and frank). Subordinates who worked for charismatic leaders developed more self-assurance than did those who worked for noncharismatic leaders. They said they experienced more meaningfulness at work if their leader had been nominated earlier as a charismatic. In addition, they worked longer hours per week, which suggests that their motivation was heightened, and revealed a higher level of trust and acceptance of the charismatic leader in their ratings of "self-disclosure" to the charismatic leader than did the subordinates of the noncharismatic leaders.

Along similar lines, O'Reilly (1984) found, in a survey of employees of Silicon Valley electronic firms, that the credibility of top managers, as judged by their dynamism, trustworthiness, and expertise, was significantly enhanced if the chief executive officers (CEOs) were regarded as charismatic. The employees' commitment was similarly elevated.

Development of the MLQ Scale of Charismatic Leadership.
Bass (1985c) developed a charismatic leadership scale of ten items of the MLQ (Bass & Avolio, 1988) dealing with both the leader's behavior and the follower's reactions. He began with Burns's (1978) definition of a transformational leader who raises the followers' level of consciousness about the importance and value of designated outcomes and ways of reaching them; gets the followers to transcend their own self-interests for the sake of the team, organization, or larger polity; and raises their level of need on Maslow's (1954) hierarchy from lower-level concerns for safety and security to higher-level needs for achievement and self-actualization.

Seventy senior executives (all male) were able to describe at least one such transformational leader they had known in their careers. Their descriptive statements, along with others about transactional leadership that featured an exchange of rewards for the follower's compliance with the leader, were sorted by 11 graduate students into transformational and transactional. The 73 statements on which the judges could agree were administered to 177 senior U.S. Army officers who were asked to describe their most recent superior, using a 5-point scale of frequency, from 0 = the behavior is displayed not at all to 4 = the behavior is displayed frequently, if not always.

The first factor that emerged was labeled charismatic leadership because it seemed to contain most of the components of such leadership. Highest item factor loadings (correlations with the factor) were the effects of the leader:

.87: I have complete faith in him.

.86: Is a model for me to follow.

.85: Makes me proud to be associated with him.

The behavior of such a leader was seen in such items that correlated with the charismatic factor as

.71 Has a special gift of seeing what it is that is really important for me to consider.

.71 Has a sense of mission that he transmits to me.

Sixty-six percent of the covariance of all the 143 items could be accounted for by this first factor of charismatic leadership (Bass, 1985a). An even larger amount was accounted for in a comparable sample of U.S. Air Force officers (Colby & Zak, 1988). Hater and Bass (1988) achieved similar results when they refactored the 70-item questionnaire that subordinates completed to describe their immediate management superiors. Onnen (1987) obtained similar findings from 454 parishioners who described their Methodist ministers. A ten-item scale of such items was included with Form 5 of the revised instrument (MLQ-R). High reliabilities (.85 and above) were routinely reported for descriptions of superiors by large samples of subordinates in military and industrial settings (Bass & Avolio, 1989). Hater and Bass showed that 28 managers who were identified by their superiors as "top performers" in an express-package shipping firm earned a significantly higher charismatic leadership score from their subordinates than did a random sample of 26 ordinary performers.

Relationship to Effective Leadership. For the samples of officers in the U.S. Army and Air Force, the MLQ charisma scale correlated .85 and .90 with the rated effectiveness of the officers and .91 and .95 with satisfaction with their performance as leaders. For a sample of Indian managers in an engineering firm and an American sample from high-tech companies, Waldman, Bass, and Einstein (1985) reported correlations of .72 and .81 between subordinates' ratings of the charisma of their leaders and the effectiveness of their leadership. This finding was in contrast to the correlations between rated effectiveness and how much contingent rewarding and management by exception the managers practiced. The average correlation between contingent reward and effectiveness was only .48 and .06 between ratings of the leaders' activity in practicing management-by-exception and the leaders' effectiveness.

Gibbons (1986) obtained similar results in a computer firm, Bass (1985a) for New Zealand educational administrators and professional personnel, Yokochi-Bryce (1989) for managers from 14 Japanese firms, and Boyd (1989b) for U.S., Canadian, and German NATO field grade officers. Similarly, Hoover (1987) reported correlations of .69 and .66 between the charisma on the MLQ of headmasters of private schools and their effectiveness and satisfied subordinates.

Seltzer and Bass (1987) obtained a correlation of .81 between charismatic leadership and effectiveness, according to 875 part-time MBA students who described their current boss, and according to the subordinates of 98 currently enrolled part-time MBA students. The correlation was .86 with satisfaction with the leader. This correlation was considerably higher than were the correlations of effectiveness and satisfaction with other measures of leadership behavior, such as consideration and the initiation of structure. A similar pattern emerged in determining how much stress and burnout was avoided in the subordinates of charismatic leaders (Seltzer, Numerof, & Bass, 1989). Among 264 retail chain-store employees, Peterson, Phillips, and Duran (1989) found that the MLQ charismatic leadership scores they gave their supervisors contributed more to the predictions of organizational commitment of the employees and their perceptions of store effectiveness than did any of the other leadership measures employed in the study which included P(erformance) and (M)aintainance leadership (see Chapter 23) and initiation and consideration (see Chapter 24).

Leaders with high scores on the MLQ-R, Form 5 were also seen to encourage self-actualization among subordinates. Correlations between charisma and measures of self-actualization ranged from .43 to .65 (Seltzer & Bass, 1987). Charismatic leadership also correlated highly with the transformational leadership measures of individualized consideration, with its strong component of orientation toward the development of subordinates. Charismatic leadership and intellectual stimulation were also highly correlated (Bass, 1985a). Intellectual stimulation will be discussed later in this chapter as a component of inspirational leadership, which overlaps charismatic leadership to a considerable degree.

Much of the foregoing correlational evidence was from the same source, the leader's subordinate. Avolio, Bass, and Yammarino (1988) showed that although the charisma-effectiveness connection was inflated, coming as it did from the same source, when one subordinate of the same leader provided the assessment of leadership and another the assessment of effectiveness, the connection remained, but to a lesser extent. Nor was the connection affected by a generalized feeling of satisfaction. Furthermore, only about 10 percent of the measure of charisma could be accounted for by the bias of leniency (Bass & Avolio, 1988). In addition, superiors agreed that charismatics, as described by subordinates, were more effective (Hater & Bass, 1988). As was seen in Table 12.1, superiors gave higher ratings of performance to managers who subordinates had described as charismatic on MLQ-R, Form 5. As is shown in Table 12.2, Yammarino and Bass (1989) found that better fitness reports and recommendations for early promotion from their superiors were earned by 186 naval officers whose subordinates had described the officers on MLQ, Form 11 as charismatic leaders. The subordinates' descriptions of the charismatic leadership of these officers, all graduates of the U.S. Naval Academy, were also predicted by the grades for overall military performance that the officers had earned at the academy.

In addition, subordinates' identification of charismatic leaders on the MLQ has been found to predict independent objective criteria of the leaders' effectiveness. Onnen (1987) reported a substantial correlation between the parishioners' descriptions of charismatic Methodist ministers on the MLQ and the parishioners' church attendance on Sunday. The charismatic leadership scores also correlated with the growth in church membership. And Avolio, Waldman, and Einstein (1988), as will be detailed later, showed that in a game played by MBA students, simulated business firms with charismatic presidents earned higher profits and stock prices and had a larger share of the market.

Biographical and Historical Analyses

Analyses by House (1977, 1985) based the definition of charismatic leadership on its effects on followers. A charismatic leader induces a high degree of loyalty, commitment, and devotion in the followers; identification with the leader and the leader's mission; emulation of the leader's values, goals, and behavior; a sense of self-esteem from relationships with the leader and the leader's mission; and an exceptionally high degree of trust in the leader and the correctness of the leader's beliefs. With the research strategy for studying U.S. presidents employed earlier by others,[6] House asked eight historians to use House's definition to classify ten charismatic and nine noncharismatic U.S. presidents and Canadian prime ministers. (Seven of the eight historians were in complete agreement.) The historians identified Thomas Jefferson, Andrew Jackson, Abraham Lincoln, Theodore Roosevelt, Franklin Delano Roosevelt, and John F. Kennedy as charismatic

presidents and Calvin Coolidge, Warren Harding, Chester A. Arthur, James Buchanan, Franklin Pierce, and John Tyler as noncharismatic presidents. They also listed the following charismatic Canadian prime ministers: Ramsey MacDonald, Sir Wilfred Laurier, John George Diefenbaker and Pierre Elliott Trudeau. Biographies of these presidents, prime ministers, and their cabinet members were content analyzed to compare the effects of the charismatics and the noncharismatics on the cabinet members. To measure the behavior of the presidents, House coded passages that indicated the leaders' display of self-confidence and their expression of expected high performance by their followers, confidence in their followers' ability and performance, strong ideological goals, and individualized consideration for their followers.

The inaugural addresses of the presidents were similarly content analyzed to assess the presidents' achievement, power, and affiliation motives. The cabinet members of charismatic presidents and prime ministers expressed more positive affect toward them than did the cabinet members of noncharismatic presidents. The need for achievement and the need for power were higher among the charismatics than among the noncharismatics. The charismatic leaders were more likely to be seen as great and as effective than were the noncharismatic leaders (House, Woycke, & Fodor, 1988). In another analysis, charisma, combined with power and other needs, accounted for 37 percent of the variance in the overall performance of 39 presidents, 41 percent of the economic performance of their administrations, and 45 percent of their domestic social performance (House, Spangler, & Woycke, 1989).

The same pattern of correlations emerged when the MLQ, Form 5 was used by sets of undergraduates to describe the leadership of 69 world-class political, military, and industrial leaders after the undergraduates had read biographies of them. The students completed the 70-item forms as if they were the immediate assistants of the world-class leader they were describing. The leaders that the students thought were higher in charisma were also described as much more satisfying and effective than were the leaders who were lower in charisma but higher in transactional factors, such as contingent reward and management-by-exception. Among the leaders who received the highest scores for cha-

---

[6]See, for example, Barber (1985), Simonton (1986), and Woodward (1974).

risma were Martin Luther King, Mahatma Gandhi, and John F. Kennedy; those who were rated lowest in charisma included President Gerald Ford, Henry Ford II, and J. Edgar Hoover (Bass, Avolio, & Goodheim, 1987).

A Simulated Business

The pattern of correlations was the same when the MLQ, Form 5 questionnaire was used by MBA students to rate the "presidents" of 27 "companies." Each firm was composed of 9 MBA students who were competing in a semester-long complex business game with students representing 2 other such "firms." Although the business game ran for 12 weeks, it simulated 8 quarters of performance. Leadership ratings of each team's president were collected at the end of the eighth quarter. The success of the presidents and their firms was announced at the end of each of the first 8 "quarters." Although each company began with equivalent assets, those companies that were led by presidents who rated high in charismatic leadership also performed significantly better on objective indexes of success, such as returns on investment, stock prices, and share of the market. The results were the same when independent raters used videotapes of the company meetings to complete the MLQ describing the presidents. The judgments of the raters of the videotapes were in agreement with those of the students who portrayed the colleagues of the company presidents (Avolio, Waldman, & Einstein, 1988).

Inspirational Leadership

Charismatic leadership? Inspirational leadership? What's the difference? According to Downton (1973), the difference is in the way followers accept and comply with the leader's initiatives. If the dynamics of the identification of the followers with the leader are absent and if the followers are drawn to the goals and purposes of the leader but not to the leader, as such, then the leader is inspirational but not charismatic. Followers believe they share a social philosophy with the inspirational leader (Downton, 1973). If the followers feel they are more powerful as a consequence of the leader's exhortations because the leader has pointed out desirable goals and how to achieve them—not because the powerful leader is their model—then the leader is inspirational, not necessarily charismatic (McClelland, 1975). Followers impute God-given powers to charismatic leaders and are incapable of criticizing them. But although followers may regard inspirational leaders as symbols of beliefs and shared problems, they can also roundly criticize them (Downton, 1973).

As was already noted, followers resolve their intrapsychic tensions by identifying with the charismatic leader, form a strong commitment to his or her person with uncritical and unquestioning obedience, and sometimes attribute supernatural powers to the leader. None of this is necessary for the followers of inspirational leaders. A serious problem in meaning for the followers creates the possibility that an inspirational leader will emerge. Followers perceive such an inspiring leader to be knowledgeable, enlightened, and sensitive to the problems at hand, and from these perceptions, their confidence in the leader grows. Their trust in the inspiring leader arises from the meaning the leader gives to their needs and actions. Followers share with the leader common beliefs about what is wrong, beliefs the leader articulates publicly for them. Unlike the charismatic leader, who substitutes for the followers' ego ideal, the inspirational leader provides symbols for it. Inspirational leaders help followers feel more powerful by setting forth desirable goals and providing the means to achieve them (McClelland, 1975).

Winter (1967) showed business students a film of President John F. Kennedy presenting his inaugural address. The stories that the students were asked to write after seeing the film were contrasted with those written by other students who saw a film about modern architecture. Kennedy inspired an uplifting of spirit and an elevation in the students' sense of power, not the responses to charisma of obedience, loyalty, and submission.

Although conceptual distinctions between charismatic and inspirational leadership can be made, they may be difficult to establish empirically. In reality, charismatic leaders tend to be highly inspirational, although inspirational leaders may not be charismatic. For instance, for Fromm (1941, p. 65), the charismatic leader not only embodies a more extreme and clearly defined personality for those who identify with him, but is able to "arrive at a clearer . . . outspoken formulation of . . . ideas for which his followers are already prepared psychologically." In military and industrial surveys of subordinates' descriptions of their superiors on questionnaires, Bass (1985a) was unable to obtain a consistent inspirational factor that was separate from a factor of charismatic leadership.

Behavior of Inspirational Leaders

As with charismatic leaders, the behavior of an inspirational leader may be perceived as inspirational by one person and as hokum by another. What is challenging for one follower is easy and dull for another. The inspirational leader has to have insight into what will be challenging to a follower and for what reasons. Inspirational leaders are perceived by others to display such behaviors as setting challenging objectives as standards; using symbols and images cleverly to get ideas across; providing meaning for proposed actions; pointing out reasons why followers will succeed; remaining calm in crises; appealing to feelings; calling for meaningful actions; stressing beating the competition; envisioning an attractive, attainable future; and articulating how to achieve that future.

The inspirational leader expresses goals that his followers want to attain (McClelland, 1975). But the leader has to express vivid goals that strengthen and uplift the followers (DeCharms, 1968). Such leaders "conceive and articulate goals that lift people out of their petty preoccupations, carry them above the conflicts that tear a society apart, and unite them in the pursuit of objectives worthy of their best efforts" (Gardner, 1965b, p. 98). According to Yukl and Van Fleet (1982, p. 90) inspirational behavior "stimulates enthusiasm among subordinates for the work of the group and says things to build their confidence in their ability to successfully perform assignments and attain group objectives."

Such leadership was mentioned frequently in 1,511 critical incidents collected by Yukl and Van Fleet about the behavior of effective leaders in the ROTC and 129 such incidents about U.S. Air Force officers in the Korean War. The inspirational behavior of leaders included instilling pride in individuals and units, using pep talks, setting examples with their own behavior of what is expected, and building confidence and enthusiasm. In these critical incidents, inspirational leadership

correlated with objective measures of effectiveness as a leader.

High levels of activity, coupled with strong self-confidence, determination, ego-ideals and a sense of mission, were seen to lie behind the inspiring success of CEOs in turning around their organizations. Peters (1980) reported on 20 companies that had "executed major shifts in directions with notable skill and efficiency. Their CEOs chose a single theme and almost unfailingly ... never miss[ed] an opportunity to hammer it home." They consistently supported the theme, usually over a period of years. In this way, they orchestrated a shift of attention throughout management. According to 413 management students, the good president of the United States exhibits the same kinds of inspirational qualities as does the good CEO. Such good leaders share high levels of energy, active involvement, and articulateness (Butterfield & Powell, 1985). Similarly, Fahey and Harris (1987) reported on the inspirational aspects of effective leadership in the U.S. Navy. Nearly 30 naval commands were nominated for their excellence by 300 naval officers. A total of 600 interviews were then held with the officers and enlisted personnel. Among other things, the leaders of these excellent commands were described as "passionate about their mission," and the messages they gave to their commands were that everyone could be a winner. High standards were to be maintained. Like the CEOs, they had points of focus, such as safety and cleanliness, when they made face-to-face contact throughout their commands.

Vaill (1978, p. 110) found that members in high-performing systems could relate "peak experiences in connection with their participation. They were enthused and communicated joy and exultation." When elated by inspiring leaders, euphoric subordinates would accept increased risks. Familiar are

the stirring preachers of evangelism, the lectern-pounding political orators, and the rousing after-dinner speakers.... Nowadays, of course, much of this arousal has been institutionalized in anonymous media messages. Social and political movements ... depend heavily in transforming a passive, inactive constituency into an aroused, alarmed, active one. (Bass, 1985a, p. 66)

Listening to audiotaped inspirational speeches, such as Winston Churchill's speech on Dunkirk, Thomas Jefferson's first inaugural address, and Henry V's speech in Shakespeare's play, generated more activation among subjects (according to their responses to an adjective checklist and their urinary epinephrine level—a physiological indicator of activation) than did listening to audiotaped travel lectures. However, the inspirational speeches also increased the subjects' need for power, which was reflected subsequently in their stories on the Thematic Apperception Test (Steele, 1973, 1977; Stewart & Winter, 1976).

Inspiring leaders have the ability to influence subordinates to exert themselves beyond their own expectations and self-interests. That extra effort is inspired by the persuasive appeal of the leaders' language, symbols, images, and vision of a better state of affairs. It is stimulated by the subordinates' perceptions that they and the leader have common purposes. It is reinforced by various ritualistic institutional practices and peer pressures. The main overlapping components of inspirational leadership behavior can be seen to include managing meaning and managing impressions, molding followers' expectations, envisioning, and intellectually stimulating followers.

The Management of Meaning

Heifetz and Sinder (1987) found a high degree of agreement among several hundred elected, appointed, and career officials at the local, state, and federal levels of the U.S. government, foreign government officials, military officers, and managers in the private sector when these respondents were asked what their constituents expected of them. Many answered that their constituents expected inspiration, hope, consistency, direction, and order. What the leaders felt was most often expected of them was that they would provide their constituents with meaning, security, and solutions to their problems. This ability to manage meaning was seen by Smircich and Morgan (1982, p. 261) to be particularly important to a leader:

Leadership works by influencing the relationship between figure and ground, and hence the meaning and definition of the context as a whole. The actions and utterances of leaders guide the attention of those involved in a situation in ways that are conciously or unconsciously designed to shape the meaning of the situation. They ... draw attention to particular aspects of the overall flow of experience, transforming what may be complex and ambiguous into something more discrete and vested with a specific pattern of meaning.... They ... frame and shape [and "punctuate"] the context of action in such a way that the members of that context are able to use the meaning thus created as a point of reference for their own action and understanding of the situation.

The leader must be able to deal with the equivocalities of many interactive situations and the intepretive schemes of those involved. They must then "embody through use of appropriate language, rituals, and other forms of symbolic discourse, the meanings and values conducive to desired modes of organized action" (Smircich & Morgan, 1982, p. 269). Levinson and Rosenthal (1984, p. 284) agreed: "The fundamental communication [by leaders] is that of the meaning of the organization." The meaning is found in the image of the organization, its place in the environment, and its collective purpose.

Inspirational leaders compare their groups with various referents such as (1) competitors—"we can do better than all of our competitors"; (2) ideals—"we can achieve our best performance"; (3) goals—"we can attain whatever we set our minds to do"; (4) the past—"we can do better than we've done before"; (5) traits—"this is what we should look like"; and (6) stakeholders—"we can make our employees our strongest advocates." New meaning can be provided by unfreezing old interpretations and creating new ones. New languages, new jargons, new lexicons, new arrangements can be introduced to provide the new meanings (Cameron & Ulrich, 1986).

Inspirational leadership has also been equated with demagoguery, manipulation, exploitation, and mob psychology, for it also tends to involve the emphasis on persuasive appeals and emotional acceptance. Riker's (1986) switching tactics, described in Chapter 9, may come into play. Meaning may become convoluted in the leader's efforts to resolve the rhetorical problems facing his or her followers. Simons (1970) listed the ways in which leaders of social movements may resolve rhetorically the problems a social movement has in attracting and maintaining followers, securing the adoption of its program by the larger society, and dealing with resistance from the larger entity. The radical goal images the leaders' depict may be crossed with the conservative ways they propose to attain them. Or the leaders may disavow the radical program they seek to achieve to gain a more widespread, diverse following. Insistence on maintaining the movement's values may require abandoning the tactics that would implement its program. Ethics give way to rationalized expediency.

Ideology built on logic gains intellectual respectability, but mass followings may find more meaning in oversimplified, magical beliefs about solutions to problems. Folk arguments, myths, and deceptions replace logical exposition.

Use of Symbols

Inspirational leaders make extensive use of symbols—representations of chunks of information. Symbols are signs that represent sets of cognitions; the cognitions are linked by overlapping functional associations (Eoyang, 1983). But as Tierney (1987) noted, symbols are more than objectifications of meaning. They are strategies for understanding, for making sense, consciously or unconsciously, of the organization or the environment. Leaders justify their existence and actions by their insignia, formalities, stories, ceremonies, conferences, and appurtenances. The symbols mark them as the center of attention and influence (Geertz, 1983).

Tierney (1987) collected interview data from 32 college presidents to focus attention on their symbolic purposes and performance. The presidents talked about themselves as metaphors. For example, they said that they provided "the glue so that their organization stuck together." They would give a personal computer to every faculty member as a physical symbol that teaching was going to be changed at the institution. The personal computer could become as much of a physical symbol as the school tie. Presidential concern was symbolized by the practice of walking-around management, knowing every faculty member by his or her first name, or meeting students "on their own turf."

Structural innovations, such as the creation of task forces, symbolized the prospects of a new brush for sweeping the organization. The president was a personal symbol of the campus when speaking to the community. He or she converted ideas about the institution's values into images that could be symbolized; thus, the diploma *mill* was changed to the *seat* of learning.

Symbols provide a greatly simplified message that can have inspirational meaning. For instance, the cross symbolizes Christianity, as well as its emphasis on suffering, sacrifice, and redemption. Gandhi's spinning wheel symbolized Indian self-reliance, the value of cottage industries, the rejection of the British Raj, and the demand for Indian independence.

Confusing, contradictory, or ill-understood ideas can be made into a coherent whole through symbols. The metaphor of a stack of falling dominoes substitutes for the complexities of appeasement versus conciliation or of trying to justify support for the rebels in Nicaragua and the loyalists in El Salvador. Inspirational leaders substitute symbols, as well as slogans and simple images, for complex ideas. Thus, the slogan "Never again!" conveys 2,000 years of Jewish history and the Holocaust. *Glasnost* and *perestroika* convey the opening of communications and the restructuring of Soviet society.

The conservative dress code for IBM employees, instituted by Thomas J. Watson, Sr., was intended to impress customers and employees alike. The code symbolized dedication to service, uniform high quality, and seriousness of purpose. Social and organizational realities are created from such codes and symbols (Stech, 1983).

The replacement of old symbols by new ones helps people recall new ideas and beliefs with new emotional values. For example, the Iranian revolutionaries who marched with flowers sticking out of their rifle barrels to signify a new era of peace and brotherhood marched again against Iraq with headbands to signify their readiness for martyrdom and war to the death.

Symbols can stand for inspirational solutions to problems. In the Soviet Union, the hammer and sickle signify the worker and peasant whose proletarian dictatorship would bring forth a communist utopia. The 13 stars and stripes in the American flag signal the federation of the original 13 sovereign states—the United States.

Inspirational leaders use symbols to draw attention to their leadership. The "crowns and coronations, limousines and conferences" circumscribe the arena on which their followers can focus, the arena in which leading ideas come together with leading institutions. The important events within the arena are seen by followers as what "translates intentions into reality" (Bennis, 1982, p. 56).

Impression Management

Impression management involves what we do to create and maintain desired impressions in others about ourselves (Schlenker, 1980). Such impressions will affect how much we are esteemed by others and, therefore, how much we can be successful in influencing them.

To illustrate, Wayne and Ferris (1988) arranged for 96 undergraduates to serve, in turn, as a supervisor of a confederate of the experimenters. The confederate acted as a subordinate in a simulated work setting in which mail orders were processed for a catalog marketing firm. Compared to a control, the "subordinate" impressed each of the 96 student subjects with self-enhancing communications, flattery, conformity, and doing favors for the supervisor. The "subordinate's" use of impression management increased substantially the supervisor's liking and "appraised" performance of the "subordinate," as well as satisfaction with the exchange relationship. The same kind of impression management by bank employees of their supervisors was reported in a survey of how much the subordinates reported they praised their supervisor and did personal favors for him or her. According to the 23 supervisors of the 84 bank employees, those employees who practiced impression management were better liked by the supervisors. Being better liked, in turn, resulted in higher performance appraisals for the subordinates and more satisfying exchange relations.[7] Impression management may also involve creating and maintaining desired impressions about organizations to promote the loyalty and commitment of others to the organizations.

Although some of the political leaders Willner (1968)

studied were primarily men of action and not of a scholarly bent, Wilner wrote of "their capacity to project the image of unusual mental attainments." These leaders could seize on information and ideas from many sources and, with their excellent memory, they would convey the impression of possessing a powerful mind and a wide range of knowledge. Illustrative, as noted in Chapter 7, were Franklin Delano Roosevelt and Benito Mussolini, who used their prodigious memories to impress listeners.

Confidence-building. It is a leader's *perceived* competence that determines whether his or her attempts to influence will be accepted by followers. Impression management, the enhancement of how one is viewed by others, is an important requirement for building followers' confidence in leaders (Adams & Yoder, 1985). To some degree, one's success as an inspiring (as well as a charismatic) leader may be due to how one presents oneself to the other members of the group (Goffman, 1959). For example, if would-be leaders give the impression that they have had previous experience (even if they have not) with the group's task, their views are more likely to be accepted. Of course, they have to be credible. In the same way, by paying attention to their own dress and speech, by an appropriate amount of name-dropping, by being seen with the "right" persons, among other similar means, people can raise their esteem in the eyes of their fellow members, which will contribute to followers' confidence in them. Political leaders, in contrast to statesmen, stand or fall at election time on how well they and their staffs manage the public's impressions of them. For example, President Gerald Ford actually was successful in bringing inflation down and reducing unemployment. However, he failed to win a second term in office, after his appointment to a first term following Nixon's resignation, partly because he lacked communication skills and the voting majority in 1976 perceived him to be the cause of a recession he actually had inherited (Sloan, 1984).

The president's wife is another illustration of the management of impressions. Her loyalty, discipline, and circumspection are all dramatically presented to the public on a continuing basis (Caesar's wife must be above reproach). The wife's visible presence alongside the president in rituals of public leadership assures the

---

[7] More will be said about influence-tactics in Chapter 18.

viewer symbolically of the morality and trustworthiness of the president (J. B. Gillespie, 1980).

Manipulation of Information. Impression management is aided by the fact that people are willing to draw inferences about the personal characteristics of others with only limited information (Schneider, Hastorf, & Ellsworth, 1979) about their physical appearance, expectations from the role or status, or expressive behavior, such as facial expressions (Goffman, 1959), and intensity of the voice (Allport & Vernon, 1933).

Television has both helped and complicated the building and maintenance of images. Thus, a short presidential candidate may have to avoid being seen with a tall opponent in a television debate, and may arrange to stand on a higher platform to make his height equal to that of taller candidates. The brevity and selective editing capabilities of television can be used to protect the leader's image, but the live camera is also a force for bringing reality into the living room. Events that are favorable to the person's image can be staged, but events that are unfavorable to the image can also dramatically show up, as if the leader was face to face with supporters. Impression management is effective up to a point; it then can backfire and have a "boomerang" effect (Jones & Wortman, 1973). Thus, according to a field survey of direct observations by Gardner and Martinko (1988), high school principals who flattered people more often were less adequate in their performance than were those who talked more about the organization.

Gardner and Martinko agreed with Schneider (1981) that the management of impressions is achieved through "the manipulation of information about the self by the actor," but it also can be achieved by manipulating information about the organization that the impression manager leads. The presentation can be verbal, nonverbal, or in the form of artifactual displays, such as dress and office decor. The preferred targets of the principals' verbal presentations about themselves were their superiors. The principals were more apologetic to familiar than to unfamiliar listeners and used descriptions of their organizations and of themselves more frequently in dyadic than in group settings and in interactions with those outside than inside their organization.

The annual reports of CEOs to stockholders are often efforts to impress the stockholders about the qualities of the firms' performance and future. Salancik and Meindl (1984) examined the annual reports of 18 U.S. corporations over an 18-year period and concluded that those CEOs whose firms operated in unstable environments and who therefore lacked real control over the organization's annual focus emphasized how much they were in control over organizational outcomes. For instance, they announced executive changes to imply that management was dealing with the organization's unstable environment. But these impressional explanations had a positive impact on the future performance of the firms that used these tactics. A similar effect was achieved by a bogus professor who delivered a nonsensical lecture on the application of mathematical game theory to the education of physicians. The bogus professor, a trained actor, was introduced to his audience as having degrees and publications (both of which were phony). The lecture consisted of doubletalk, contradictory statements, seductive gestures, humor, and meaningless references to unrelated topics. The "professor" earned high ratings from the 55 students, none of whom detected the hoax. However, when videotapes of a similarly seductive lecture included valid content, students actually learned more of the content from such a seductive lecturer (Scully, 1973).

Image-building. Impression management reaches its peak in image building. When contact with political leaders is mainly through interviews on television and the leader's image is systematically modified to suit the feedback obtained from public opinion polls, the voting public responds to the image created for that purpose. The 1988 Bush-Dukakis presidential election campaign clearly showed the manufacturing of images of leadership that were unrelated to reality. George Bush, the conservative "wimp," was converted overnight into the strong, decisive, patriotic, religious, forceful law-and-order candidate, who stood for mainstream American values of family, patriotism, and support of education and the environment. Michael Dukakis, the low-key pragmatist, was converted into a liberal ideologue by the same myth makers. Dukakis was pictured as a "card-carrying" member of the American Civil Liberties Union who furloughed murderers to repeat their crimes, would take away citizens' rights to own guns, and opposed the recital of the Pledge of Allegiance in public schools. Continued polling and the election itself reflected the extent to which voters chose one image over the other, rather than one person over the other.

Kennan and Hadley (1986) described in detail how the images of political candidates are created by media consultants. The consultants begin with analyses of the current image. For example, Jay Rockefeller, a West Virginia gubernatorial candidate in 1980, began as an individual whom the public saw as unforceful, ineffective, and a stranger—neither a leader nor a friend. As a member of the Rockefeller family, he was judged to be cold, elitist, uncaring, and manipulative. The media consultants carefully planned what Rockefeller would say, how he would say it, and when. They determined the exact language and terminology he would use in his speeches, press releases, and television commercials; the specific issues and subject matter that he would communicate to the voters; and his physical appearance, including his haircut and style of clothing. At the end of the campaign, the image of Jay Rockefeller was that of a casual, down-to-earth, warm, open, and friendly person. As a member of the Rockefeller family, he was not seen as powerful, forceful, effective, and influential. A Democrat, he won the election decisively, despite the Republican landslide everywhere else, in the wake of President Reagan's election in 1980.

Molding Follower's Expectations

According to Edwards (1973), the most effective supervisors are those who can create high expectations for performance for subordinates to fulfill. Less-effective supervisors fail to develop such expectations. And the more ambiguous the criteria for evaluating the group's performance, the greater is the leader's influence in defining expectations about the situation. Arvey and Neel (1974) showed that the performance level of 130 engineers was a function of their expectations that their effective performance of their jobs would be rewarded and that their supervisor was concerned about

their performance. Likert (1961a) also emphasized the importance for superiors to communicate their high expectations to their subordinates.

As molders of expectations, inspirational leaders can redirect their organizations with clear agendas of what needs to be done. They know enough not to be satisfied with easy panaceas. They also are able to avoid letting their enthusiasm trap them into creating unreasonable expectations in their subordinates and uninvited acceptance of their ideas (Tichy & Devanna, 1986). Harold Geneen, the former CEO who built IT&T, saw himself setting high expectations in a number of ways. He considered himself a leader who established hard, challenging goals for the organization and who served as a model of hard work and long working hours for his subordinates (Geneen & Moscow, 1984). Kanter's (1983) 200 change-masters (leaders who successfully changed their groups) reported that they led their teams to expect to share in the credit for the results of the changes. After the changes, they continued to inspire, encourage, and stimulate the teams who worked with them.

Closely allied to the preceding expectation setting is Vaill's (1982) concept of *purposing*, a continuous stream of actions by inspiring leaders in complex organizations that induces clarity, consensus, and commitment regarding the organization's basic purposes. Leaders of a high-performing system define and maintain a sense of purpose among all members of the system. Purposing is seen when the members can develop and express deep feelings about the system, its aims, the people in it, its history, and its future and, therefore, can focus on the issues and variables in the system that make a difference in its performance.

Using the Pygmalion and Galatea Effects. The Cyprian king and sculptor Pygmalion fell in love with the beautiful statue he carved. Aphrodite turned the statue into a real women, Galatea. Pygmalion's fantasy about Galatea became a reality.

The Pygmalion and Galatean effects have been seen in modern research. What managers expect of their subordinates strongly influences the subordinates' performance and progress. In turn, subordinates tend to do what they believe is expected of them (Livingstone,

1969). These effects were first demonstrated by Rosenthal and Jacobson (1968) in relation to schoolteachers' expectations about their pupils.

Groups can increase their effectiveness by harnessing the Pygmalion effect (Eden, 1984). Leaders who have confidence in their subordinates set difficult goals for the subordinates and arouse the subordinates' expectations about achieving them (Eden, 1988). Doing so encourages the self-fulfilling prophecy among the subordinates that they will succeed and, as a consequence, actually increases the likelihood that they will attain the goals (Livingstone, 1969). Schrank (1968); Rosenthal (1974); and Crawford, Thomas, and Fink (1980) reported results that generally but not conclusively supported the utility of enhancing leaders' expectations about their subordinates. Effects were seen more for men than for women.

The strongest evidence was obtained by Eden and Shani (1982), who found that the performance of leadership trainees in a field experiment in the Israel Defense Forces was improved by building up their instructors' positive expectations about them. The 105 trainees were assigned at random to one of three conditions: high, regular, or unknown "command potential." The instructors and assistants were led to believe that their trainees had one of the three levels of "command potential." The "expectancy induction" accounted for 73 percent of the variance in the trainees' objective achievement scores. Similar effects occurred for the trainees' attitudes. Those in the "high-potential" condition reported greater satisfaction with the course and more motivation to go on to the next course.

The instructors' expectations about the performance of the trainees appeared to transfer to the trainees' self-expectations—the Galatea effect. Sutton and Woodman (1989) established that when the 20 sales supervisors of 259 salaried sales employees, 84 percent of whom were female, were told which of their employees were supposedly "exceptional" and which were not, and suitable adjustment was made for separating full-time sales personnel from part timers, the Pygmalion effect emerged in the employees' sales performance over the next three months as well as in higher evaluations of their performance and in higher self-expectations. Again, Pfeffer and Salancik (1975) and At-water (1988) showed that supervisors' social and supportive leadership behaviors were correlated .48 and .38, respectively, with what the supervisors felt their bosses expected of them. Eden and Ravid (1982) had a psychologist inform trainees in advance that they had "high, regular, or unknown" command potential. Then the psychologist withdrew. Instructors were not preconditioned. Trainees who were given the most positive messages about their "command potential" did better than those who received less-favorable messages. But a clerical training program for women did not attain such results. Ignoring the sex differences, Eden (1984) concluded, as had Locke, Latham, Saari, and Shaw (1981), that managers need to be shown the utility of encouraging their subordinates with hard goals and high expectations.

Enabling and Empowering. Followers' expectations about what they may accomplish can be increased if their leader obtains or shows them how to obtain the resources that will enable them to reach their higher goals. Or the leader may reduce or remove constraints or show the followers how to do so. For instance, the leader can focus attention on the technical, political, and cultural resistances to change and can work with followers to overcome such resistances. Threats can be turned into opportunities. Followers can be empowered more by increasing their autonomy and discretionary opportunities and getting support from the higher authority for their efforts. Leaders can arrange for key employees and higher authorities to signal their public commitment to new goals. Encouragement and involvement can be stressed at all levels. Structure and systems can be modified to enable and empower subordinates to stretch to achieve greater accomplishments (Cameron & Ulrich, 1986).

Leaders can promote enabling by stressing that everyone can be a winner through constant learning and improvement. Risks can be taken, and mistakes can be tolerated. Performance can be steadily improved by incremental demands on subordinates. For starters, a half-mile run can be achieved by everyone. Then a mile run can be accomplished. Ultimately, everyone can run seven or eight miles (Harris, 1987). Enabling and encouraging others to act and showing the way requires inspiring a shared vision (Kouzes & Posner, 1987).

Envisioning

Envisioning a desired future state and showing followers how to get to it are basic components of the inspirational process. They require not only technical competence but artistry and creativity. Despite the thoroughness of the data and the complexities of the problem, the capable inspiring leader can reduce matters to a few key issues before asking others to consider what is to be done. Doing so does not necessarily mean the advocacy of simple solutions; rather, it means that complex problems are organized into a few central themes for discussion (Tichy & Devanna, 1986).

Envisioning is the creating of an image of a desired future organizational state that can serve as a guide for interim strategies, decisions, and behavior. It is fundamental to effective executive leadership. Without the ability to define a desired future state, the executive would be "rudderless in a sea of conflicting demands, contradictory data, and environmental uncertainty" (Sashkin, 1986, p. 2). Envisioning integrates what is possible and what can be realized. It provides goals for others to pursue and drives and guides an organization's development (Srivastva, 1983). Mikhail Gorbachev is illustrative in his efforts to politically democratize the Soviet Union and to envision a unified Europe stretching to the Urals.

Bennis and Nanus (1985) concluded, from in-depth interviews with 90 top directors and executives, that envisioning requires translating intentions into realities by communicating that vision to others to gain their support. Envisioning is the basis for empowering others, for providing them with the "social architecture" that will move them toward the envisioned state. It involves paying close attention to those with whom one is communicating, zooming in on the key issues with clarity and a sense of priorities. Risks are accepted, but only after a careful analysis of success or failure. However, it should be noted that envisioning focuses more on success than failure and more on action than on procrastination.

Rational and Emotional Elements. Cameron and Ulrich (1986) pointed to the rational and emotional ele-

ments of envisioning. The rational element articulates a vision in which questions about purpose, problems, missing information, and available resources are answered. The emotional element articulates a vision of a wholistic picture that is intuitive, imaginative, and insightful, using symbols and language that evoke meaning and commitment.

Strategic Planning. Other aspects of envisioning that are relevant in different ways at different levels of management in the complex organization include the formulation of strategies based on the contingencies of the threats and opportunities of the organization, its resources, and the interests of its constituencies. Leaders must be able to formulate and evaluate appropriate organizational responses and arrange for their implementation in operations and policies (Wortman, 1982). They will be more effective in doing so if they are proficient in gathering ideas, storing information, valuing, logical thinking, and learning from their mistakes (Srivastva, 1983). As they rise in their organizations, the abilities that are required of them will shift from dealing with concrete matters that have short-term consequences and for which all the parameters are known to more abstract issues with greater amounts of uncertainty and longer-term consequences (Jacobs & Jaques, 1987).

Consciousness Raising. Long-range visions need detailing. The leader must understand the key elements in the vision and consider the "spillover" effects of their future development. Furthermore, the leader must be able to communicate his or her vision in ways that are compelling, make people committed to it, and help make it happen. As Bennis (1982, 1983) concluded after his interviews with 90 innovative organizational leaders, the leaders could communicate their vision to clarify it and to induce the commitment of their multiple constituencies to maintaining the organization's course. These leaders also revealed the self-determination and persistence of charismatic leaders, especially when the going got "rough." Yet they emphasized their and their organizations' adaptability to new conditions and to new problems. They concentrated on the purposes of their organizations and on "paradigms of action." They made extensive use of metaphor, symbolism, ceremonials, and insignias as ways of concretizing and transmitting their visions of what could be. They pictured what is right, good, and important for their organization and thus contributed considerably to their organization's culture of shared norms and values.

This arousal of consciousness and awareness in followers of what is right, good, and important; which new directions must be taken; and why, is the most important aspect of intellectual stimulation. "The mass line" leadership of Mao Zedung illustrated its application to social and political movements. The scattered and unsystematic ideas of the Chinese masses about marriage, land, and the written language were to be converted by the Communist party leadership into a set of coherent, concentrated, and systematic ideas for reform that would be fed back to the masses until they embraced them as their own. Mao even seemed to practice this strategy in his one-on-one discussions with others (Barlow, 1981).

Intuitive Aspects. For Pondy (1983) envisioning begins with intuitive interpretations of events and data that give meaning to new images of the world that ultimately can be clarified into strategies for the firm. Symbols and phrases are invented to focus attention on the strategic questions that are needed to get others involved in the process. As Jim Renier of Honeywell suggested, although the vision that emerges may be that of the single-minded chief, it often evolves, in larger organizations, in particular, out of the chief's give-and-take with many others during repeated reviews of the possibilities of the desired future state. Renier (as quoted in Tichy & Devanna, 1986, p. 128) put it this way: "What you've got to do is constantly engage in iterating what you say [about the vision] and what they say is possible. And over a couple of years the different visions come together."

With their ability to provide images of the future state, inspiring leaders provide direction. A commonly used metaphor, a cliché favored by political leaders, is the path, road, or journey that must be taken that gives direction to the followers (Tucker, 1981). But metaphoric visions can boomerang into apocryphal anecdotes and reverse in meaning. For example, King Canute wanted to convey his limitations to his courtiers and used his lack of control over the tides to illustrate his point. History converted the metaphor into an illus-

tration of the king's foolish pomposity in trying to command the sea not to roll up the beach.

Envisioning is particularly important when the group or organization is facing ill-structured problems (Mitroff, 1978). Planful opportunism in leaders "can turn unpredictable events into building blocks of change" (Tichy & Devanna, 1986, p. 94). Inspiring leaders look ahead optimistically despite the current uncertainties of internal and external threats and opportunities to the organizations. Yet Bruce (1986, p. 20) noted,

> In the minds of CEOs . . . the vision is never clear, only a foggy haze and a multitude of conflicting signals. We see the future darkly, while ignorant armies of experts shout across a smoky field at one another.

Reformers and Revolutionists. Inspiring reformists of political movements are able to convey to others a vision of what the society would be like, how it would look, if its ideals were supported. They espouse the myths that sustain the political community and its professed ideal cultural patterns. Practices that depart from the ideals must be changed or eliminated in the desired future state. Inspiring revolutionary leaders, on the other hand, envisage a future in which the sustaining myths and current cultural patterns have been rejected and society has been fundamentally reconstituted (Paige, 1977). The future the revolutionaries envisage in their rhetoric of the new regime is surprisingly devoid of details or mention of justice, despite their focus on the injustices of the old regime they intend to overthrow by force (Martin, Scully, & Levitt, 1988).

Can Envisioning Be Developed? Mendell and Gerjuoy (1984) accepted the conventional wisdom that visionary leadership cannot be effectively taught. Unless the talent is there already, managers can only be prepared to anticipate possibilities. If this were true, then only recruiting and selection would ensure an adequate number of capable inspiring leaders with vision. But it is possible for managers to develop their ability to envision and to be more inspirational leaders, in general. Exercises that engage executives in envisioning their organization's future may help. In such exercises, executives are asked to talk about how they expect to spend their day at some future date, say five years hence, or what they expect their organization to look like at some future date. Or they may be asked to write a business article about their organization's future. From these visions, they can draw up mission statements and the specifications that must be met by such an organization (Tichy & Devanna, 1986).[8]

Intellectual Stimulation

Intellectually stimulating leaders see themselves as part of an interactive creative process (Brown, 1987). Not bound by current solutions, they create images of other possibilities. Orientations are shifted, awareness is increased of the tensions between visions and realities, and experiments are encouraged (Fritz, 1986). Although intellectual stimulation is inspiring and is often associated with charismatic leadership, it involves important differences. Intellectual stimulation contributes to the independence and autonomy of subordinates and prevents "habituated followership,"characterized by the blind unquestioning trust and obedience that are seen in charismatic leader-follower relations (Graham, 1987). Intellectual stimulation is much more than a matter of broadcasting good ideas. For instance, in the public sector, Roberts (1988) demonstrated that the intellectual generation of ideas and framing of problems were not enough. Makers of innovative policies had to serve as catalysts by mobilizing and building support for their ideas, by circulating their ideas through various media available to them, by collaborating with other highly visible and reputable groups and organizations, by creating demonstration projects, by sponsoring reforms in the legislature, by positioning and developing supporters in the government, by enlisting champions to introduce their proposed legislation, by influencing and creating public-interest groups and associations, and by monitoring and evaluating the extent to which the legislation that is passed conforms to the policies that were promoted.

Reformulations. Leaders move subordinates to focus on some things and ignore others. A pattern is imposed on a flow of events to simplify their complexity

and diversity. The real world is made easier to understand (Bailey, 1983). Intellectual stimulation can move subordinates out of their conceptual ruts by reformulating the problem that needs to be solved. Wicker (1985) provided numerous examples of what can be done. Ideas can be played with by applying metaphors and similes (for example, "interpersonal attractiveness is a magnetic field"). The scale can be changed; a city can be likened to a big village. The absurd can be considered, as can fantasy ("Suppose the stars did influence your success" or "suppose water floated on oil"). Alternative states could be imagined, such as particles becoming a wave. Nouns can be changed into verbs. The figure and ground can be transposed ("Concentrate on the space around the object, instead of the object"). Contexts can be enlarged or subdivided. Hidden assumptions can be uncovered (failures may be due to poor planning, not to lack of ability). Infante and Gordon (1985) noted that it was more satisfying to their subordinates if their supervisors argued for their own formulations and refuted other points of view, but it was more dissatisfying if the supervisors attacked others' self-concepts. Unfortunately, some people mistake argumentation with aggression and hostility. The former is favored in leaders; the latter is not.

Personal Creativity versus the Intellectual Stimulation of Others. There is a difference between possessing task competence, knowledge, skill, ability, aptitude, and intelligence and being able to translate these qualities into action as intellectual inspiration and the stimulation of others. Jimmy Carter and Herbert Hoover exemplified technically competent leaders who failed to inspire; John F. Kennedy and Franklin Delano Roosevelt are illustrations of presidents who were not as intellectually astute as Carter and Hoover, but were far superior in their ability to stimulate others intellectually, to imagine, to articulate, and to gain acceptance of and commitment to their ideas.

Styles. Quinn and Hall (1983) conceived that leaders provide intellectual stimulation in one of four ways: rational, existential, empirical, and ideological. Rationally oriented leaders emphasize ability, independence, and hard work; they try to convince colleagues to use logic and reason to deal with the group's or organization's

_____
[8]Such educational activities will be discussed further in Chapter 35.

problems. Existentially oriented leaders try to move others toward a creative synthesis by first generating various possible solutions in informal interactions with others and their common problems. Empirically oriented leaders promote attention to externally generated data and the search for one best answer from a great deal of information. Idealists encourage speedy decisions; they foster the use of internally generated intuition and need only to gather a minimum amount of data to reach a conclusion (Quinn & Hall, 1983). Chaffee (1985) proposed that three strategies are pursued in finding solutions to the organization's problems—linear, adaptive, and interpretive. If linear data are gathered and analyzed, alternative actions are formulated with expected outcomes if a particular action is taken. If an adaptive strategy is pursued, the effort will be to adjust the organization to environmental threats and opportunities by being particularly cognizant of the revenues and resources needed from the environment. If an interpretive strategy is pursued, reality is less important than are perceptions and feelings about it. Values, symbols, emotions, and meanings need to be addressed. Neumann's (1987) interview study of 32 college presidents found that with experience, the presidents tended to move toward more interpretive strategies if they had not initially emphasized them. The shift of experienced presidents away from purely adaptive strategies was most evident.

Central versus Peripheral Routing. Intellectual stimulation takes people on what Petty and Cacioppo (1980) conceived of as the central route to being persuaded, which occurs when people are ready and able to think about an issue. It may be contrasted with persuasion via the peripheral route, which occurs when people lack either motivation or ability. Persuasion through the central route produces enduring effects; persuasion via the peripheral route lasts only if it is bolstered by supportive cognitive arguments. If persuasion is by the peripheral route, it is only necessary for the source of the persuasion to be liked. The distinction between central and peripheral processing has much in common with the distinctions between deep versus shallow processing, controlled versus automatic processing, systematic versus heuristic processing, and

thoughtful versus mindless or scripted processing (Cialdini, Petty, & Cacioppo, 1981).

Factorial Independence. Although Bass (1985a) was unable to separate consistently an inspirational from a charismatic leadership factor in factorial analyses of U.S. Army officers' MLQ descriptions of their superiors, he did obtain a separate factor of intellectual stimulation. Hater and Bass (1988) replicated this finding with a sample of industrial managers. Items of this factor included such statements as "provides reasons to change my way of thinking about problems," "stresses the use of intelligence to overcome obstacles," and "makes me think through what is involved before taking actions." Subordinates in military, industrial, and educational organizations who described their superiors as frequently engaging in such actions tended to view the superiors as highly effective and satisfying. When covariance within units was ignored, Avolio, Bass, and Yammarino (1988) found correlations of .54 and .73 between intellectual stimulation and effectiveness for two samples of managers. Comparable correlations of the relation of the leadership to subordinate satisfaction were .48 and .67. Bass (1985a) and Seltzer and Bass (1987) reported correlations in the same range. As may be seen in Table 12.1, Hater and Bass (1988) found positive correlations between superior's evaluations of managers and the extent to which the managers were described as intellectually stimulating. In the same way, Avolio, Waldman, and Einstein (1988) obtained correlations between the extent to which the "presidents" of 27 complex business-gaming teams were intellectually stimulating and the teams' market share (.56), debt-to-equity ratio (−.56), returns on assets (.46), stock prices (.47), and earnings per share (.37).

Keller (1989) correlated the MLQ intellectual stimulation of 66 R&D project team leaders according to the team members with superiors' evaluations of the teams' effectiveness and the number of patents produced by the teams. Intellectual stimulation of the team leaders correlated .36 with the supervisors' evaluations of the team performance and .25 with patents produced by the teams. The effect was more specifically pinpointed in the case of patents produced when the results were subdivided for the 30 teams engaged in research projects and the 36 teams engaged in developmental projects. Intellectual stimulation of the leaders correlated .57 with patents produced by the research teams but only .01 for those engaged in more routine developmental activities. However, along with the benefits to teams and organizations of intellectually stimulating leadership, elsewhere a cost may have been revealed as well.

Intellectual Stimulation and Burnout. For a sample of 277 part-time MBAs who described their full-time supervisors in their work situation, the effects of other transformational factors (charismatic leadership and individualized consideration) contributed to reducing the feelings of stress and burnout. However, when these effects were controlled by partial correlation, intellectual stimulation appeared to *add* to feelings of stress and burnout among the MBAs (Seltzer, Numerof, & Bass, 1987).

Transformational Leadership: Charisma, Inspiration, and Intellectual Stimulation

According to Bass (1985a), the items describing leaders that judges generally found to be transformational, in terms of Burns's (1978) definition of transformational leadership, emerged as four factors in surveys of subordinates' ratings of their military or industrial superiors: (1) charismatic leadership ("Share complete faith in him or her"), (2) inspirational leadership ("Communicates high performance expectations"), (3) intellectual stimulation ("Enables me to think about old problems in new ways"), and (4) individualized consideration ("Gives personal attention to members who seem neglected"). The latter most factor was discussed in Chapter 8.

The pattern of factors provided a portrait of the transformational leader that Zaleznik (1977) independently drew from clinical evidence. Zaleznik's leaders attracted strong feelings of identity and intense feelings about the leader (charisma), sent clear messages of purpose and mission (inspirational leadership), generated excitement at work and heightened expectations through images and meanings (inspirational leadership), cultivated intensive one-on-one relationships and empathy for individuals (individualized consideration),

and were more interested in ideas than in processes (intellectual stimulation). Likewise, Posner and Kouzes (1988a) extracted a parallel profile of transformational leadership from interviews. They noted that transformational leaders challenged the process, inspired vision, enabled others to act, modeled the way and "encouraged the heart." Again, the visionary leader (Sashkin, 1988) and the empowering leader (Sashkin & Burke, 1988) reflect similar patterns of transformational leadership. Consistent with the view, Atwater and Yammarino (1989) found that a sample of 107 Annapolis midshipmen squad leaders evaluated by their 1,235 plebe subordinates as transformational described themselves as more likely to react emotionally and with feeling.

Although they are conceptually different and form independent clusters of items, the factors uncovered by Bass (1985a) are intercorrelated, and a single score on transformational leadership can be meaningfully calculated for selected studies and analyses (viz., Seltzer, Numerof, & Bass, 1987). The antecedents and effects of this transformational score have been compared with the effects of transactional leadership that is composed of the factors of contingent reward and management by exception, factors to be discussed in Chapters 17 to 19.

Effects of Transformational Leadership

The results of the extensive surveys of over 1,500 general managers, leaders of technical teams, governmental and educational administrators, upper middle managers, and senior U.S. Army officers that were discussed earlier for charismatic leadership are also relevant for transformational leadership. Subordinates of these leaders, who described their managers on the MLQ, Form 5, as being more transformational, were also more likely to say that the organizations they lead were highly effective. Such transformational leaders were judged to have better relations with higher-ups and to make more of a contribution to the organization than were those who were described only as transactional. Subordinates said they also exerted a lot of extra effort for such transformational leaders. If leaders were only transactional, the organizations were seen as less effective, particularly if most of the leaders practiced passive, reactive management-by-exception (intervening only when standards were not being met). Subordinates said they exerted much less effort for such leaders (Bass & Avolio, 1989).[9]

Similar conclusions were reached in more intensive studies of "presidents" of 27 MBA business-gaming companies (Avolio, Waldman, & Einstein, 1988), Methodist ministers (Onnen, 1987), and the principals of private schools (Hoover, 1987) and with biographical analyses of world-class industrial, military, and political leaders (Bass, Avolio, & Goodheim, 1987).

These findings were based mainly on subordinates' judgments of both the leadership and the outcomes. However, for the same leaders, sets of subordinates' ratings of their leaders were compared with other sets from different subordinates' ratings of the outcomes on the group and organization. The results obtained show that the leader-outcome correlations could not be attributed only to both sets of ratings coming from the same source (Avolio, Bass, & Yammarino, 1988).

Beyond this, Waldman, Bass, and Einstein (1987) showed that the performance appraisals of subordinates were higher if their leaders had been described as transformational. And, Hater and Bass (1988) and Yammarino and Bass (1989), as was noted before, demonstrated that those leaders who were described as transformational (more charismatic and intellectually stimulating, for example) rather than transactional by their subordinates were judged to have a much higher leadership potential by the leaders' superiors, as was shown earlier in Tables 12.1 and 12.2.

Similar conclusions were reached when data on the outcomes of leaders were examined. For instance, Litwin and Stringer (1966) demonstrated that transformation-like leadership resulted in more productivity at lower costs than did authoritarian or democratic styles imposed on simulated business firms. Onnen (1986) showed that Methodist ministers who were transformational tended to generate more growth in their church membership and greater attendance at Sunday services by their parishioners. The transformational "presidents" of simulated business firms generated more profitability, a greater share of the market, and

better debt-to-equity ratios (Avolio, Waldman, & Einstein, 1988) than did the transactional "presidents."

Specific additional relationships were found using the MLQ. Zorn (1988) reported that the transformational leaders among 73 pairs of small-business owners and their employees were more person centered and more complex in their interpersonal constructs. Singer (1985) showed that subordinates in New Zealand preferred working with leaders who were more transformational than transactional. Clover (1989) used an abbreviated version of the MLQ to correlate the descriptions of 3,500 subordinates at the U.S. Air Force Academy of their commissioned-officer squadron commanders and various measures of their squadrons' performance. A transformational leadership score was attained by combining the assessments of the commanders' charisma, inspirational leadership, intellectual stimulation, and individualized consideration. It was found that commanders who received higher ratings in transformational leadership led better-performing squadrons and were more likely to be seen as preferred role models by the cadets. Rosenbach and Mueller (1988) also used an abbreviated version of the MLQ to survey the descriptions of 110 fire chiefs by their 732 subordinates and again showed that the transformational-leader factors were more highly correlated with the subordinates' perceptions of effectiveness and satisfaction than were the transactional factors.

The Leader Behavior Questionnaire (LBQ), developed by Sashkin and Fulmer (1985) as a self-report of visionary leadership, includes scales of focused attention, long-term goals, clarity of expression, caring, propensity to take risks, and empowerment. Stoner-Zemel (1988) found that visionary leadership, as measured by the LBQ, correlated with employees' perceptions of the quality of their work lives. Ray (1989) showed that LBQ-assessed visionary leadership was related to a factory culture of organizational excellence. And Major (1988) obtained LBQ assessments in 60 high schools that linked the visionary leadership behavior of school principals with whether the schools performed high or low on various objective criteria.

Champions of Innovation. Radical military innovations require champions committed, persistent, and courageous in advocating the innovation (Schon, 1963).

---

[9]See additionally, Gibbons (1986), Hoover (1987), Medley (1966), and Murray (1988). See Bass and Avolio (1989) for a complete review.

The same entrepreneurial champions are required for the success of new business ventures according to Collins, Moore, and Unwalla's (1970) psychological profile of 150 entrepreneurs and by Rothwell, Freeman, Horsley, et al. (1974), Madique (1980), Miller (1983), and MacMillan and George (1985). In comparison to matched leaders of established businesses, such organizational champions were found by Ippoliti (1989) to score significantly higher on the four transformational MLQ scale scores combined provided by their subordinates, as well as higher on each of the scales: charisma (3.15 versus 2.48), individualized consideration (2.83 versus 2.35), intellectual stimulation (2.75 versus 2.44), and inspirational leadership (2.49 versus 1.87).

Transformational Leadership Augments Transactional Leadership

Burns (1978) believed that transformational leadership and transactional leadership are at opposite ends of a continuum. However, Bass (1985a) suggested that transformational leadership augments the effects of transactional leadership. To specify the effects more clearly, Waldman, Bass, and Einstein (1985) computed a hierarchical regression analysis of transactional and transformational leadership on self-reported measures of effort and performance for two samples of U.S. Army officers and one sample of industrial managers. By first entering the two transactional leadership scores for contingent reward and management by exception into the regression equation and then following with the entry of the interrelated transformational leadership scales of charismatic leadership (containing inspirational elements), intellectual stimulation, and individualized consideration, they demonstrated that transformational leadership had an incremental effect over and above transactional leadership. The incremental increases ranged from 9 to 48 percent for the different samples and outcomes predicted. For both outcomes and in all three samples, transformational leadership had a highly significant incremental effect, over and above transactional leadership. Seltzer and Bass (1987) obtained similar results for part-time MBA students' descriptions of their full-time superiors on

the scales of initiation and consideration[10] and the augmenting transformational scales. Finally, Waldman and Bass (1989) found the augmentation effect of transformational charismatic leadership on transactional contingent reward when predicting the fitness reports obtained by U.S. Navy officers.

Howell and Avolio (1989) obtained results of an even more complex model of the role of transformational leadership among 76 Canadian insurance managers in their contributing to their organizational effectiveness. A combination of their inner-directiveness measured by Rotter's measure of internal/external locus of control, their transactional and transformational leadership measured by their subordinates using MLQ-10, and their managers' perceptions of the organizational culture accounted for 36 percent of the variance in sales targets their units met a year later according to a hierarchical regression analysis. Transformational leadership alone accounted for one-third of the accuracy of the multiple prediction and augmented transactional leadership in predicting sales performance.

Summary and Conclusions

Since its conception, charismatic leadership has undergone considerable development, although until the 1980s, there was much commentary but little empirical research about it. Two attributes are seen to be essential for the charismatic relationship: The leader must be a person of strong convictions, determined, self-confident, and emotionally expressive and his or her followers must want to identify with the leader as a person, whether they are or are not in a crisis. Whether the charismatic leader is self-aggrandizing or prosocial, he or she generates extraordinary performance in the followers.

Inspirational leadership does not depend on personal-identification processes. Rather, mutual goals of leaders and followers are identified and encouraged by the leader. Inspirational leadership stems from the management of meaning and impression management. The in-

---

[10]See Chapter 24.

spirational leader builds the followers' expectations by envisioning a mutually describable future and articulating how to attain it. Leaders can use many intellectually stimulating ways to move followers out of their conceptual ruts. Intellectual stimulation, charismatic leadership, and inspirational leadership are major components of transformational leadership, which adds to transactional leadership in generating positive outcomes of the groups and organizations led. But above and beyond this, to understand the effects of such leadership requires a detailed examination of the leader's power.

Power and Legitimacy

13

Power and Leadership

Power has been of concern to priests, philosophers, and kings since the beginnings of civilization and to chiefs and medicine men before that. Who can influence whom clearly depends on who is more powerful and who is less so. Only with God on his side could Moses convince Pharoah to let his people go. Shakespeare's plays were filled with concern about power and innocence, failing power, and power and personality (Hill, 1985). "To say a leader is preoccupied with power is like saying that a tennis player is preoccupied with making shots his opponent cannot return" (Gardner, 1986a, p. 5). This chapter explores the meaning of social power, the bases of such power, and how such power contributes to leadership in societies, communities, formal organizations, and small groups.[1]

Definitions of Social Power

Power is the force that can be applied to work. It is the rate at which energy can be absorbed. Social power is the ability to take actions and to initiate interactions. It is a force underlying social exchanges in which the dependent person in the exchange relationship has less power and the person with more power is able to obtain compliance with his or her wishes. The compliant person depends on the more powerful other person for desired outcomes that cannot be obtained from other sources (Emerson, 1964).

Power as Force

Power was defined as "the production of intended effects" (Russell, 1938); "the ability to employ force" (Bierstedt, 1950); the right to prescribe behavioral pat-

terns for others (Janda, 1960); and the intended, successful control of others (Wrong, 1968). But as Gardner (1986a, p. 5) observed: "power does not need to be exercised to have its effect—as any hold-up man can tell you." Most behavioral theorists maintain that power can be exerted without intention. Cartwright (1965) conceived power in terms of the control of information and personal affection, while Bierstedt (1950) focused on prestige.

Simon (1957) saw power as a manifestation of an asymmetry in the relationship between A and B. For J. R. P. French (1956), as well as Cartwright (1959a, 1959b), the power of A over B equals the maximum force which A can induce on B minus the maximum resisting force which B can mobilize in the opposing direction. For Dahl (1957), "A has power over B to the extent that A can get B to do something that B would not otherwise do." For Pfeffer (1981), power is B's ability to change the course of action of A from what A would otherwise have done; B can overcome A's resistance or reluctance to act.

For Presthus (1960), power was a matter of A's and B's rapport with each other. Emerson (1964) emphasized the dependency relationship between A and B. If A is more dependent on B rather than vice versa, A has less power than B. A's dependence on B can be due to B's control of resources that A cannot obtain elsewhere. It can be due to B's ability to reduce uncertainties for A or to B's ability to cope with critical contingencies in the attainment of organizational goals based on the organization's strategy, environment, or technology (Daft, 1983). B can obtain A's compliance with B's wishes. Thus, Bagozzi and Phillips (1982) showed that 64 percent of the power that suppliers have over wholesale distributors can be accounted for by the inability of the distributors to find other suppliers, the critical value of the resources controlled by the suppliers, the countervailing power of the distributors, and

---

[1]Power and its effects on leadership were the subject of comprehensive reviews by Cartwright (1959a, 1959b, 1965), House (1984, 1988), Podsakoff and Schriesheim (1985a), and Yukl (1981), among others.

how much business was involved. According to Bennis and Nanus (1985, p. 17), power is "the basic energy needed to initiate and sustain action. [It is] the *capacity to translate intention into reality and sustain it.*" For Burns (1978), power can be wielded nakedly, as when people are treated as things, or it can be relational, collective, and purposeful, as revealed in social exchange.

Power and Social Exchange

Thibaut and Kelley (1959) regarded power as an exchange relation in which one member has control over another's behavior or fate. As Gardner (1986a, p. 5) put it,

> It is possible to think of the exercise of power as a kind of exchange. You want something from me and you have the power to produce in return certain outcomes that I want—or want to avoid. You can give me an A or flunk me. You can promote me to supervisor or reduce me to clerk. You can raise my salary or lower it. You can give or withhold love.

Individuals tend to maintain a balance in the exchange of social values (Homans, 1958). The differentiation of social roles that results in organizations is based initially on such exchange relations (Gouldner, 1960). Blau (1964) and Adams and Romney (1959) saw power as negative, in A's use of deprivation, aversive stimulation, and sanctions to control B's behavior. Harsanyi (1962a, 1962b) took a broader view and weighed social benefits against social costs in defining power relations. Bass (1960) defined the power of A and B as A's control of what B needs and values. If B is satiated or uninterested in what A controls, A loses power over B. Burns (1978) agreed. In this view, Cartwright (1965) emphasized the importance of ecological control: Power can be exercised by controlling resources or necessities, by occupying space, or by avoiding or boycotting a location. Thus, a leader's power is reflected in the ability to impose standards, limits, and boundaries on a group; to indicate what is expected of members for reward or the avoidance of harm; and to enforce such rules. The boundaries are likely to be areas of increasing threat and impenetrability, requiring judgment by those who are being controlled about how far

they can deviate without punishment (Timasheff, 1938).

The social exchange is seen in the exchange relationship between the Roman patron and his freedmen clients and between the ward boss and his neighborhood constituents. The clients' and constituents' votes and obedience provided the bases of power for the patron and the ward boss in return for which the followers received protection, security, and material support. The ethnic political leader in the United States disperses tangible divisible rewards, favors, and services to his or her constituents. For example, Borowiec's (1975) study of 83 Polish-American leaders in Buffalo indicated that they provided constituents with special information and personal assistance in dealing with public agencies.

The exchange calculus may be complex; leaders of more powerful followers are likely to be more powerful than leaders of less powerful followers. The leaders can mobilize the power of their followers and can be granted or deprived power by their followers. In combination with their followers, they can collectively acquire more power (Burns, 1978). This mutuality in the power relation is seen when followers must complete their assignments if the leader is to be rewarded, along with them. The slowdown or inattention of subordinates can result in the loss of benefits for the leader.

Power Is Not Synonymous with Influence

House (1984) proposed to operationalize the measurement of power by its effects. Power was equated with "the capacity to produce effects on others. These effects are achieved by the exercise of authority, expertise, political influence and charisma . . . each having a different base or source and each having different effects" (p. 26). But it is useful to maintain the distinction between power and influence although the boundaries between power and influence remain unclear (Faucheux, 1984). Unfortunately, power often is used synonymously with influence. Tautologies have been endemic. We observe that A leads B; therefore, we conclude that A has more power than B. Inferences about power and its effects must begin with measures of power that are completely independent of observed relations between A and B. The observed relations are a product of the power differences between A and B, not the behavior observed. Leadership can be conceived as the exercise of power (Berlew & Heller, 1983). Thus, Milewicz (1983) concluded, after interviews with purchasing agents about their relations with their many suppliers, that the tendency of the agents to exert leadership in dealing with suppliers was a consequence of the agents' self-perceived power. The agents had such power because they could, for example, control the length of the order cycle. Whether they fully used this power to exert leadership depended on their personal desire to be influential.

Leadership and influence obviously are a function of power. Power is the potential to influence. It is the probable rate and amount of influence of a person or the occupant of a position. Thus, for instance, Barber (1966) inferred that the power relations among members of a legislative committee could be accounted for by such factors as the rate of success in getting suggestions accepted and the rate of agreement received. Although Lord (1977) found that for 144 undergraduates, perceived leadership and social power were related, the unexplained variance required maintaining separate conceptual distinctions between them. Follert (1983) constructed a 20-item scale to measure the power of a manager. The scale scores obtained were related to the structuring leadership of the manager and the compliance of subordinates with requests, but were clearly distinguishable from the scale of power.

We need to separate the holding of power because of one's person, one's office, the willingness to exercise it, and the tendency actually to do so. Studies tend to confuse all four and sometimes even fail to distinguish between power and influence.

Power of Subordinates

Power is not an absolute amount. As was already noted, it depends on the power of those to be influenced, both positively and negatively. The power of those who are influenced adds to the total power available in the situation and can be increased by the synergistic action of the leader and the followers. The leader's power may be diminished to the extent that it can be offset by the power of individual followers. Bass and Valenzi (1973) developed one set of five-point scales to assess a boss's power and another set of five-point scales to assess a subordinate's power. The subordinate and boss each

described how frequently the boss could override or veto any decisions made by the subordinate, grant or deny promotion or salary increases to the subordinate, reverse the subordinate's priorities, control the size of the subordinate's budget, and get support from a higher authority for what he or she wanted to do. In turn, the superior and subordinate each described how frequently the subordinate could bring outside pressure to support what he or she wanted; do the opposite of what the boss wanted him or her to do, maintain final control over his or her plans, assignments, and targets, regardless of what the boss thought about them; ignore the boss and submit requests to a higher authority; and nominate or vote for who would be the boss. The differences in the power of superiors and subordinates then became the metric of importance in predicting the superiors' styles of leading the subordinates through, direction, consultation, negotiation, or the delegation of decision making (Chitayat & Venezia, 1984; Shapira, 1976).

Gardner (1986a, p. 16) pointed to the reversals that can occur between hierarchical rank in an organization and the power to accompany it: "Every experienced observer knows of cases in which such second and third level leadership is formidable—capable, for example, of paralyzing a newly appointed top executive." Gorbachev's difficulties in restructuring the Soviet Union's economy and politics arc illustrative. Gardner (1986a) concluded that the efforts to reform high school curricula in the 1960s failed because of the power of rank-and-file teachers whose support was not enlisted in the attempted improvements. The power of subordinates over their superiors is widespread when the skills and knowledge of the subordinates are hard to replace. On the one hand, superiors need to guard against becoming overly dependent on subordinates with power; on the other hand, they need to maintain good interpersonal relations, trust, and openness of communications with them (Kotter, 1985a).

Sources of Power

In examining the sources of power, one cannot avoid overlapping the discussion of empirical findings with that of the antecedents and consequences of power. Further overlapping is inevitable because power begets power. Power from one base can generate power in another. For example, the individuals whose power is based on the legitimacy of their positions can acquire additional power by controlling the rewards that accompany the legitimacy of the positions occupied. In the same way, group members tend to defer to those they perceive to be experts. Perceived expertness, in turn, tends to legitimate the leadership role (Goodstadt & Kipnis, 1970). Although we may be able to sort out conceptually the different bases of power, in nature they are likely to be intertwined.

Personal Power

Power can derive from one's person or one's position. Although it may seem otherwise, the evidence to date suggests that prospective followers tend to consider the personal power of the highly esteemed expert more important than the legitimacy and power to reward and punish that may derive from appointment to a position of leadership.

Those with personal power can grant affection, consideration, sympathy, recognition, and secure relationships and attachments to others (Bass, 1960). For example, Rosen, Levinger, and Lippitt (1961) asked teachers and emotionally disturbed boys to rank six items of power in order of importance. The two groups basically agreed on the relative importance of physical strength, sociability, expertness, fairness, fearlessness, and helpfulness as sources of power. But those with personal power also can punish others by becoming more distant, formal, cold, and businesslike.

Bass, Wurster, and Alcock (1961) demonstrated that we want to be valued and esteemed mainly by those we value and esteem. We endow such persons with personal power. In the same way, Hurwitz, Zander, and Hymovitch (1953) showed that we seek the affection and support of those we hold to be personally powerful. Professional personnel were continually reshuffled to form 32 sextets. The power to influence and the extent to which each member was liked after the first half-hour of interaction were assessed. Those with low esteem wanted most to be liked by those with high esteem.

Identification and Power. As was noted in the preceding chapter, the charismatic leader can serve as the focus of positive emotional feelings, as the ideal object for psychoanalytic transference and identification (Kelman, 1958). The transference of coping with problems to father figures provides followers with an escape from responsibility and making decisions—let the leader do it (Fromm, 1941). Followers identify with their successful superiors. Business executives see successful superiors as symbols of achievement (Henry 1949). Leaders of gangs of delinquents become the superego of the members. By submitting to the leader, members are relieved of all personal responsibility for their antisocial activities (Deutschberger, 1947).

The charismatic leader is the ultimate in personal power. The charismatic leader is personally endowed by followers with infallibility and wisdom. Personal power is manifested in the emotional bonding between the leader and followers and in the followers' dependence on the father figure; their endowment of the leader with omniscience, virtue, and supernatural powers; and in their deep-seated love and affection for the leader. Charismatics such as the Reverend Jim Jones and the Ayatollah Khomeini had the power to induce the most extremes of behavior—mass suicide and martyrdom—in their followers. Understanding such personal power requires an examination of strong emotional fixations that go beyond the ordinary considerations of social exchange, cognitions, rewards, and punishments.

Positional Power

The status associated with one's position gives one power to influence those who are lower in status. Custom, tradition, rules, and regulations assign power to incumbents of positions. Some superiors can be the "purveyors of rewards and punishments" to their subordinates (Krech & Crutchfield, 1948). Leaders with positional power can recommend punishments and rewards, instruct group members on what to do, and correct each member's job performance (Fiedler & Chemers, 1974). Such power can be wielded crudely or with sublety. It may be obtrusive or unobtrusive and overt or covert (Ford, 1980). Overtly, a superior may have the power to recommend or deny pay increases to subordinates; less obviously, a first-line supervisor, for example, may have power because of his or her influence with even more powerful leaders who are higher up in the organization (Pelz, 1951). This power, in turn, may be due to the higher-ups' attitudes about the role of supervisors who are lower in the organization, as well as to personal attributes and merit of specific supervisors. Pelz found that only those supervisors who had influence with higher-ups exhibited behavior that made a difference in their subordinates' satisfaction. Supervisors without influence "upstairs"—although they tried—were much less likely to have effects on their subordinates. Supervisors who had influence with higher-ups were much more likely to be able to obtain rewards for their employees. Their power was greater and, therefore, what they did in their own group made more of a difference to their subordinates.

Hollander (1978) pointed out how the supervisors' position in a hierarchy provides them with various sources of power. Supervisors command resources that are not ordinarily available to subordinates. They have discretion in assigning dirty and boring or interesting and challenging tasks. They can open or close doors to opportunities for the subordinates' growth and advancement. They have power to reduce uncertainty or to prolong anxiety in subordinates by providing or withholding hard information. They can act as a buffer to keep their subordinates from becoming too vulnerable to an unstable external environment and thus sustain their subordinates' optimism and hope. For Fiedler and Chemers (1974), the leader's positional power combines with the leader's esteem and orientation—task or relationship—to determine whether he or she will be effective in designated situations.

Function. As may be expected, Hambrick (1981) found that the executives' power over decisions depended on their functionally specialized roles. Accounting executives had more power over budgeting decisions; marketing executives had more power over decisions about advertising and distributing products. Extra power also accrued to those executives who were involved in activities that were critical to the firms' strategic success, that is, who scanned critical information and the environment for threats and opportunites, for example. Similarly, although meetings of clinical interdisciplinary teams of health professionals are supposed to be among equals, physicians dominate all de-

cisions about treatment, according to a survey of 137 team members' descriptions of 19 such meetings (Fiorelli, 1988).

One's position in an organization can provide power because occupancy of the position gives control or organizational resources and infornation of consequence to the organization. Control over resources, such as the size of the staff, budgetary expenditures, and evaluation procedures, may be involved (Gomez-Mejia, Page, & Tornow, 1982). With such control of resources, a manager may be able to maintain a good working relationship with subordinates, despite the subordinates' low level of trust in the manager (Novak & Graen, 1985). Power also accrues to positions that control critical contingencies that originate in the environment or technology of the organization. It hinges on the extent to which the position makes it possible to cope with the critical demands that the organization is facing (House, 1988b). The importance of positional power was illustrated when Geissler (1984) compared 131 women heads of university nursing programs with 108 women heads of other university departments. The heads of nursing felt significantly more powerful in their preferred roles than did the women who led other university departments.

Socialization Processes. Organizational members need to know how to use increases in their positional power (Taylor, 1986). Gouldner (1960) maintained that power is based on socializing norms, role differentiation, and organization that binds people together in the same social system. Gilman (1962) agreed that a power relationship is authoritative anywhere within the boundaries of a social system that gives it consensual support.

In many cultures, business transactions are conducted without written contracts because norms of obligation are regarded as binding (Macaulay, 1963). Similarly, politicians wield considerable power based on IOUs through which they can expect that favors they granted to other politicians in the past will be reciprocated when they call in their unwritten "chits" for past "services rendered."

Power Begets Power. House (1984) pointed out that individuals who are in positions of power not only can assert it successfully, but also can maintain and increase their level of power. Thus, power-oriented individuals who gain positions of power will strive to retain their power, since they are in a favored position to ensure that their power continues. (Over 99 percent of the U.S. House of Representatives are reelected every two years.) On the basis of interview data from a study of the California gubernatorial administrations of Ronald Reagan and Jerry Brown, Biggart and Hamilton (1987) added the corollary that for persons to sustain their power in an organizational setting, they must self-consciously exercise their power to signal those working for them to be aware of their obligations to carry out their assignments as expected.

Other Aspects of Power

Leaders may exercise both competitive and collective power. In a survey of 350 business and university managers, Roberts (1986) observed the widespread use of power to compete with bosses, peers, and subordinates, as well as the utilization of collective power to collaborate with others. McClelland (1975) saw the competitive exercise of power in the exertion of personal dominance or the search for victory over adversaries. This use of power was contrasted with joining with others to form shared goals to instill in the collective a sense of power to pursue such goals.

The power of supervisors could be scaled in four ways according to Jones (1983). Power could be obtrusive or unobtrusive, it could be situation based or personal, it could be professional or paternalistic, and it could be exercised over process or output. Ford (1980) agreed on the utility of looking at covert power and showed experimentally that dependent subjects in peripheral positions in a network will suppress decisions, particularly if they are uncertain about the preferences of the person in the central location in the network[2] who has covert positional power.

Power and Emergence as a Leader

Control and Power

Bass, Gaier, and Flint (1956) studied male ROTC groups in which members varied in the amount of con-

trol they could exercise over each others' avoidance of punishment—extra marching because of demerits. Each member drew a card which determined that he could exercise one, two, three, or four units of control to reduce the required marching for demerits. Members with four units of control attempted twice as much leadership as those with one unit of control under high motivation, but there was no difference when the groups were under low motivation. (These groups had no demerits requiring the extra marching.) Attempted leadership increased with the amount of control a member obtained in the lottery. But the amount of control a member had ceased to have import when what was being controlled was unimportant to him. Thus, members attempt more leadership acts when they have a lot of control and when they strongly desire what they can control. Hence, members have *power* to influence when they have *control* over what they desire (Bass, Pryer, Gaier, & Flint, 1958). Group members' attempts to lead increase with increases in their control and power, even if the control and power accrue from a lottery.

In the same way, whether undergraduates acting as managers in a simulated organization used their control of useful information to attempt to have constructive influence over subordinates depended on whether they saw themselves in a cooperative situation with their "subordinates" or in a competitive or individualistic one (Tjosvold, 1985a).

Power and Influence

Members of a group tend to be more influential than other members if they perceive themselves to have more power. Moreover, they tend to be more satisfied than are members who have little power. They are also better liked, and their attempts to influence are better accepted. Lippitt, Polansky, Redl, and Rosen (1952), who studied children in a summer camp, found that those children who had more power attributed to them by other children were better liked, made more attempts to influence others, and scored higher in the initiation of behavioral contagion (imitation without intent or awareness). The campers' perceptions of their own power were highly correlated with the power that others attributed to them. Consistent with these re-

---

[2]More will be said in Chapter 30 about the power and importance of central and peripheral positions in a network.

sults, Levinger (1959) demonstrated that members of experimental groups, informed that they had more power than other members, tended to perceive themselves as actually having more power. Also, they became more assertive and made more attempts to influence others.

Furthermore, Wolman (1956) found a strong relationship between a leader's power and the leader's acceptability to members, as seen by observers and in peer ratings. Ziller (1955) showed that group opinion was influenced more strongly by a high-power than by a low-power figure. Similarly, Levinger (1959) found that the perceived relative power of a member in a group correlated .55 with the number of attempts to influence others, .51 with the range of assertiveness, and .48 with the degree of assertiveness of the member. A change in attempts to influence tended to change along with a change in perceived power as the group continued with the problem. Dahl, March, and Nastair (1957) observed the power of some U.S. senators with their announced votes to influence other senators in roll-call votes as the other senators came to make their final decisions. Michener and Burt (1975a) examined components that determined the success of leaders in inducing compliance. They found that compliance was greater when leaders justified their demands as being good for the group, had power to punish persons who did not do as they had asked, and had a legitimate right to make demands on subordinates. However, neither the success nor failure of the groups nor the approval of the leaders by their subordinates affected the leaders' ability to be influential. Consistent with this, Gamson (1968) suggested that leaders would shift toward coercion of subordinates if they felt they lacked the subordinates' approval but had the legitimate authority to ask for compliance, although such coercive power is often counterproductive.

Power can be counterproductive in supporting one's efforts to be a leader because it can be threatening, particularly in unstructured situations. A. R. Cohen (1953, 1959) found that in the face of powerful leaders, followers felt more threatened in unstructured than in structured groups. Followers whose self-esteem was low also tended to feel more threat in the presence of power, and such felt threat was intensified in unstructured situations.

The Bases of Power

Etzioni (1961) conceived of power as being physical, material, or symbolic. He defined these three forms of power as follows, giving the bases of each:

> *Coercive* power rests on the application or . . . threat of . . . physical sanctions . . . ; generation of frustration . . . ; or controlling through force the satisfaction of needs. . . .
>
> *Remunerative* power is based on control over material resources and rewards. . . .
>
> *Normative* power rests on the allocation and manipulation of symbolic rewards and deprivations. . . . (p. 5)

For Parsons (1951), such normative power could be based on esteem, prestige, and ritualistic symbols or on acceptance.

Etzioni also pointed out that for a leader to emphasize remunerative power to followers who were already committed to the leader's choice of action would be a waste, since only normative symbolic rewards would be appropriate for such followers. Highly alienated followers would be inclined to disobey, despite material sanctions. Followers would be more likely to consider normative power to be legitimate and least likely to accept coercive power as legitimate.

The French-and-Raven Model

French and Raven (1959) identified five kinds of power that quickly became popular among investigators as the way to type the variations among the bases of power. Their five bases were as follows:

1. Expert power is based on B's perception of A's competence.

2. Referent power is based on B's identification with or liking for member A.

3. Reward power depends on A's ability to provide rewards for B.

4. Coercive power is based on B's perception that A can provide penalties for not complying with A.

5. Legitimate power is based on the internalization of common norms or values.

Rahim (1988) developed a leader power questionnaire from the answers of 1,256 respondents. The final inventory contained five factorially independent scales to measure each of the bases of power. Subsequent validations were completed with a national random sample of 476 executives and a sample of 297 employed college students.

Problems with the Five-Base Model. The French-and-Raven model had a number of problems. The five bases are not conceptually distinct. For example, expertise is valued highly so that sources of such as personal power, expert power and referent power, are likely to be correlated empirically, that is, lodged in the same people. In the same way, the position holder with the power to reward is also likely to have the power to punish. The position will give some degree of legitimacy as well. By definition, formal hierarchies are a structure of legitimate, reward, and coercive power relationships.

Further conceptual difficulties were noted by Patchen (1974), who suggested that the French-and-Raven classification was inadequate because the various bases of power were not defined in a conceptually parallel way. Thus, reward power and coercive power were defined in terms of resources that the influencer could apply. Referent and legitimate power were defined in terms of the characteristics and motives of the target person. Expert power depended on the characteristics of the influencer and on the information resources he or she personally possessed.

It was not surprising, therefore, to find that the five bases of power are empirically correlated. Thus Rahim (1986) obtained, in a national random sample of 477 executives, a correlation of .58 between the expert and referent power the executives attributed to their superiors. The superiors' control of rewards and coercive punishments correlated similarly with their legitimate power according to their subordinates. To complicate matters, Filley and Grimes (1967) emerged with an even finer set of distinctions. They studied 44 full-time professional employees in a nonprofit organization who reported to a single director and to an associate director. The employees were interviewed about hypothetical incidents that might require them to seek a decision from the director or the associate director. The respondents were asked to whom they should go for a

decision, to whom they would like to go, and to whom they would in fact go, and why. Answers to the "why" questions were classified according to the bases of power to which the organizational members appear to have responded. Twelve different bases were detected. For example, instead of one category for legitimate power, several emerged. Legitimate power could be based on formal authority, on responsibility, on control of resources, on bureaucratic rules, or on traditional rules.

Student (1968) also had problems with the French-and-Raven classification. He regarded referent power and expert power as sources of "incremental influence" that characterize the individual, whereas he thought that reward power, legitimate power, and coercive power were organizationally derived. He found that supervisors' scores on incremental influence, referent power, and expert power were positively and significantly related to the quality of the group's performance and to a reduction in costs. But average earnings declined with the reward power of the supervisor, and the maintenance costs of the group rose with coercion.

Hinken and Schriesheim (1989) attempted to address some of the methodological problems of the five-base French-and-Raven model by making sharper distinctions among the five bases of power as follows:

Expert power is the ability to administer to another person information, knowledge, or expertise.

Referent power is the ability to administer to another person feelings of personal acceptance or approval.

Reward power is the ability to administer to another person things he/she desires or to remove or decrease things he/she does not desire.

Coercive power is the ability to administer to another person things he/she does not desire or to remove or decrease things he/she does desire.

Legitimate power is the ability to administer to another person feelings of obligation or responsibility.

Table 13.1 presents the list of statements that emerged in factor analyses of the extent to which respondents agreed that the statements described their supervisors. The three samples of over 500 respondents were part-time employees who were enrolled in

Table 13.1 Final Scale Items Responding to the Statement, "My Supervisor Can..."

1. *Expert Power*
   Give me good technical suggestions.
   Share with me his/her considerable experience and/or training.
   Provide me with sound job-related advice.
   Provide me with needed technical knowledge.
2. *Referent Power*
   Make me feel valued.
   Make me feel like he/she approves of me.
   Make me feel personally accepted.
   Make me feel important.
3. *Reward Power*
   Increase my pay level.
   Influence my getting a pay raise.
   Provide me with special benefits.
   Influence my getting a promotion.
4. *Coercive Power*
   Give me undesirable job assignments.
   Make my work difficult for me.
   Make things unpleasant here.
   Make being at work distasteful.
5. *Legitimate Power*
   Make me feel that I have commitments to meet.
   Make me feel like I should satisfy my job requirements.
   Give me the feeling I have responsibilities to fulfill.
   Make me recognize that I have tasks to accomplish.

SOURCE: Adapted from Hinken and Schriesheim (1989), Table 1.

undergraduate business courses, full-time psychiatric hospital employees, and full-time employees taking MBA courses.

Despite the problems with it, the French-and-Raven classification has frequently been used in controlled experiments and field studies; therefore, I will use the classification to review research that focused on the antecedents and consequences of the use of each of the five bases of power.

Expert Power

In 1597, Sir Francis Bacon provided us with the adage that knowledge is power. And such expert power can lie behind, even unseen, effective leadership. Gardner (1986a, p. 12) quoted Lyndon Johnson as saying, "When the press talks about my successes as Senate Majority Leader they always emphasize my capacity to persuade, to wheel and deal. Hardly anyone ever mentions that I usually had more and better information than my colleagues."

Expert power may be manifest in information, knowledge, and wisdom; in good decisions; in sound judgment; and in accurate perceptions of reality (Watts, 1986). An item that is highly loaded (.78) on a factor of expert power is "has considerable professional experience to draw from in helping me do my work" (Rahim, 1986). In comparison with other bases of power, the use of expert power by leaders appears to be most acceptable to and most effective with followers. It most readily gains their compliance and is least likely to provoke their resistance (Podsakoff & Schriesheim, 1985a).

The power of revolutionary or reform leaders often begins with their perceived power as experts, which they use to define prevailing problems and to develop innovative solutions. Followers are persuaded that the leaders have the right answers to their problems and are organized to provide support (Gjestland, 1982).

In the physician-patient relationship, the physician wields expert power and the patient plays a distinctly subordinate role, particularly if the patient is also lower in socioeconomic status (Fisher, 1982). But whether the patient complies with the physician's expert advice will depend on what that advice entails, as well as the physician's referent power. It has already been noted (Hemphill, Pepinsky, Shevitz, et al., 1954) that those members of a group who have the relevant information about a task will attempt to lead the group. Such attempts are likely to be successful if the members are perceived to be expert and to be effective and if they really have the expertise. Groups tend to defer to the actual and the perceived expert. They are likely to be persuaded by the perceived expert, to accept both publicly and privately the expert's opinion (Bass, 1960).

H. T. Moore (1921) obtained experimental support for the idea that we accept readily the influence of those who we accept as experts. Moore observed that students shifted their judgments (about linguistic, ethical, and musical matters) toward what the experimenter led them to believe was the opinion of experts. When Mausner (1953) introduced one student as an art student and another as an art expert, the group's opinion was more strongly influenced by the art expert than by the art student. Knight and Weiss (1980) arranged for leaders of task groups to be seen as "expert" or "nonexpert" on the basis of how they were chosen. Those who were chosen as experts were better able to influence the group than were those who were chosen as nonexperts. The selection of leaders from inside or from outside the group made no difference.

In another experiment, Mausner (1954b) demonstrated that subjects tended to agree more often with a partner whom they observed to succeed than with one whom they observed to fail. In the same way, Luchins and Luchins (1961) demonstrated that an expert's opinion was more influential than the majority opinion of the group in determining the group's response to a judgmental task. Torrance (1952) and M. A. Levi (1954) both obtained greater improvement on survival problems when groups were fed back expert information after an initial training period.

Evan and Zelditch (1961) studied experimental groups with supervisors who differed in their knowledge of the task. Differences in the supervisors' knowledge did not affect the group's productivity; however, group members exhibited more covert disobedience and resistance to the least-informed than to the moder-

ately or well-informed supervisor. This effect was attributed to changes in the followers' attitudes toward the right of the poorly informed supervisor to occupy a position of leadership. Similar results were reported by G. M. Mahoney (1953), who found that workers were much more satisfied with a wage-incentive system when they thought the supervisor did a good job of explaining the reasons for changes in the system.

Caveats. The impact of expert power has its limits, as was expressed in the earlier admonition that would-be leaders must be able but not too much more able than their followers. Also many examples can be cited of experiments in which experts failed to be influential. C. B. Smith (1984) observed that the apparent technical and administrative expertise in a contrived short-term employment situation did not increase the experimental subjects' output as coders or their compliance with directives. Collaros and Anderson (1969) studied groups with one expert, all experts, and no experts. Groups in which all members were told that they were experts were more inhibited in their performance.

Although individuals can become more influential by acquiring more knowledge and expertise, the technological revolution in the spread of knowledge and the ease with which information can be transmitted can quickly alter who is expert about the available information and the resulting stability in patterns of influence. Thus, under some circumstances, a clerk with access to a computer program may become more expert and influential than a Ph.D. without the same program. Cleveland (1985) noted that information is expandable, compressible, substitutable, transportable, diffusable, and shareable. It is not necessarily a scarce resource. Expert power is becoming more fluid than fixed in a position or a person. It can be found in a computerized data bank or in a computer software program.

Some further qualifications are in order. The stronger status-leadership relation can override expert power. Torrance (1955a) found that the high status of a team member contributed more to influencing other members to accept the correct answer to a problem than did knowing the correct answer. Paradoxically, two supposed experts may generate less confidence than one alone. Torrance and Aliotti (1965) studied groups who were involved in information seeking who had one or two randomly selected students in the role of expert. They found that groups with two experts obtained more accurate information than did those with one expert, but the groups with two experts were less certain of their judgment.

Referent Power

Referent power is based on the desire of followers to identify with their leaders and to be accepted by them. The evidence is primarily indirect about the extent to which referent power contributes to influence and leadership. Many of the studies of consequence (as reported in Chapter 11) have focused on the extent to which the followers esteem and value their leaders, for such esteem and valuing are highly related to the leaders' referent power.

We also need to consider other indirect evidence of referent power that concerns ingratiation and the desire for acceptance by followers. For much of this indirect evidence, referent power is assumed from friendship or popularity. Thus, Rahim (1986) found factor loadings for referent power of .85 and .81 for such items as, "I like the personal qualities of my superior" and "My superior is the type of person I enjoy working with." As Podsakoff and Schriesheim (1985a) noted, none of the field studies of referent power has captured its essence in the desire of the less powerful to identify with those with referent power. For example, such referent power is clearly seen when a charismatic relationship exists between the leader and the follower, since what binds the follower to the leader is the desire to identify with the leader, as was discussed previously.

Chapter 11 reviewed the extent to which surveyed individuals who are generally esteemed as persons are more likely to be leaders. For instance, in 17 studies of executives in various types of organizations, esteem, as estimated by merit ratings received from superiors, was highly related to the criteria for "real-life" success as a leader (Bass, 1960). The same has been found true in controlled experimental settings, but with qualifications based on selected experimental manipulations of referent power—the degree to which followers like and respect the leader. Thus, for instance, French and Snyder (1959) found that more highly accepted leaders

in experimental groups attempted to exercise more influence and had more effective groups than did those who were less well accepted. Followers also attempted to use more influence when they were accepted by their leader. In a review of such studies (generally, studies of the effects of esteem), Podsakoff and Schriesheim (1985a) found that the use of referent power by leaders usually contributed to their subordinates' better performance, greater satisfaction, greater role clarity, and fewer excused absences.

Acceptance, Popularity, and Power. Zander (1953) and Zander and Cohen (1955) introduced two strangers to groups of persons. The one introduced as a high-prestige person felt better accepted and more at ease than the one assigned to a low-prestige role, as expressed by the group's responses. Hurwitz, Zander, and Hymovitch (1953) combined and recombined members of discussion groups of six members each. Each individual rated the others on the degree of liking and perceived power and participation. Members with a high degree of power were better liked and participated more often than did those with a low degree of power.

Ingratiation. As was mentioned earlier, Bass, Wurster, and Alcock (1961) demonstrated that we want to be esteemed by those we esteem. We are more concerned with being liked and accepted by those we respect and accept—those who have referent power. This concern, in turn, may lead to ingratiation—the striving by followers to be valued and rewarded by those they esteem or see as more powerful. A line of investigation by Jones and Jones (1964) suggested that followers who want to be liked by high-power figures employ subtle ingratiation tactics in an effort to gain acceptance. The use of flattery did not vary with experimental conditions. Jones, Gergen, Gumpert, and Thibaut (1965) showed that participants who faced the prospect of poor task performance attempted to ingratiate themselves with their experimental supervisor by presenting themselves as strong and competent, but only if the supervisor was open to influence. L. Wheeler (1964) demonstrated that low-power subjects remembered more autobiographical statements made by the high-power figure. However, Wheeler failed to find that participants who were highly dependent on their task leader used information seeking as a means of ingratiation or to increase their own power. Along similar lines, A. R. Cohen (1958) demonstrated that low-status members who could increase their status in the group tended to communicate in friendly, ingratiating ways. These tactics were designed to protect and enhance their relations with those who controlled the upward-mobility process. But those members with little perceived opportunity to increase their status made relatively few such attempts. There may be a rational payoff in ingratiating behavior; Kipnis and Vanderveer (1971) observed that leaders tend to reward their ingratiating followers.

Referent power can become coercive. Moreno (1934/1953) suggested that if A highly valued B, B could injure A. Bass (1960, p. 289) noted that

> [if] you can give me affection, self-esteem through association with you and vicarious satisfaction by identification ... although I may not privately accept what you say, I will publicly agree with you so that you will grant me what I want from you." (p. 289)

And such referent power may be lost as a consequence because "if I must continue to inhibit my own opinions ... I will begin to value you less, to dislike you and eventually reject you" (pp. 289–290). Such can also occur with the power to reward.

Reward Power

Reward power implies one's ability to facilitate the attainment of desired outcomes by others. An item highly loaded on a factor of reward power is "Can recommend a promotion for me if my performance is consistently above average" (Rahim, 1986). Marak (1964) studied some groups who were rewarded for a correct decision and others that were not. The results indicated that the ability to provide rewards was related to leadership, as measured by sociometric, interaction, and influence scores. The more valuable rewards a member could provide, the more closely this ability was related to leadership. Evidence for the emergence of a leadership structure was suggested by the finding that attempted leadership, actual influence, and rewards for initiating leadership increased as the sessions progressed. Similarly, Herold (1977) showed that the be-

havior of subordinates in 32 3-member groups depended on the manipulation of monetary rewards by group leaders. Dustin and Davis (1967) observed that when given a choice, leaders used monetary rewards twice as much as they used praise in a leader-subordinate experimental simulation. Kipnis (1972) also found that economic incentives were favored over other ways of improving subordinates' performance. As before, Hinton and Barrow (1975) found that when subordinates performed at high levels, supervisors tended to make more use of economic reinforcements than of praise. However, when subordinates performed poorly, leaders tended to make more use of reproof. (The denial of rewards or fining subordinates for poor performance is seen as the use of coercive power, which will be discussed later.)

Many of the critical behaviors that separate successful from unsuccessful noncommissioned officers in situational tests were found by Flanagan, Levy, et al. (1952) to be due to the differential reinforcements provided by these officers. Successful officers more often encouraged their men to follow rules and regulations, gave pep talks when the men were tired, and constantly checked the behavior of their men. However, S. Kerr (1975) noted that in their desire to achieve one kind of behavior, leaders, as well as organizations, unintentionally reward another kind.

Greene (1976a, 1976b) completed the first longitudinal study of the effects of rewarding behavior by leaders and concluded that such behavior could result in the improved performance of subordinates. Sims (1977), Sims and Szilagyi (1978), and Szilagyi (1980b) also found a causal relationship between reward behavior and performance in a series of longitudinal studies.

Justis (1975) examined effective leadership as a function of the extent to which followers' rewards depended on the leader's competence and performance. The leader's effectiveness and influence were greater the more the leader was seen to be competent and the more the followers' rewards depended on the leader's performance.[3]

Interdependence Effects. Berkowitz (1957b) studied pairs in which one or both members could earn a re-

---

[3]Chapter 17 will review the use of rewards and punishment by leaders in much more detail.

ward. The perception of interdependence increased the members' motivation when both were eligible for valued rewards. Participants were motivated to work toward their partner's reward even though they were not eligible. In the same way, Berkowitz and Daniels (1963) demonstrated that participants work harder for a "supervisor" whose success is dependent on their performance than when no such interdependence exists. Berkowitz and Connor (1966) varied both success and dependence for pairs who could win rewards. Participants who experienced failure expressed a stronger dislike for their partner the greater their feeling of responsibility toward the partner. Successful participants, however, worked harder for their dependent partner than did the control participants.

The leader may also have to share the power to reward with other authorities, especially in matrix or organizations where a subordinate reports to a functional leader and a project leader. In such a case, Hinton and Barrow (1975) found that leaders were more likely to use their reward power if they had to share its use than when they operated alone.

Distributing Rewards. A norm that is common to students and workers in the same small-group settings often is "to share and share alike." Thus, Morgan and Sawyer (1967) found that pairs of boys, when permitted to earn equal or unequal rewards, preferred equal rewards, whether their partners were friends or strangers. But their perception of the other's expectation played an important part in determining their preference. Even ingratiating subordinates who disparaged the competence of their student supervisors failed to modify the allocation of rewards by the supervisor (Fodor, 1974). And when Shriver (1952) gave leaders of discussion groups checks of various amounts with which they were required to reward the contributions of other members, some leaders solved the problem by drawing lots; others, after delay and emotional upset, passed out the checks quickly and departed. Shriver interpreted these results as indicating that there are limits to the reward power that an emergent leader can exercise with comfort. Nevertheless, W. P. Smith (1967b) found that participants with a highly valued outcome liked their partners less than those with less highly valued outcomes. Those with little power valued their outcome more highly and used their power more positively than did those with much power.

Yet, equity and loyalty considerations do have an impact on the situation. Thibaut and Faucheux (1965) varied equity and loyalty to one's group in bargaining for individual gain. Partners who were told that they had greater power tended to use it; other partners tended to acquiesce. Lower-power members appealed for "a fair share" when the high-power members could manipulate rewards, but they appealed to "loyalty" when rewards were manipulated by an outsider. Again, Thibaut and Gruder (1969) found that participants tended to form contractual agreements when they discovered that an agreement restricted the power of each to prevent their joint attainment of maximum outcomes. P. Murdoch (1967) observed that members tended to develop contractual norms when the divider of rewards was presented as being likely to withdraw from the relationship.

Butler and Miller (1965) and McMartin (1970) suggested that participants tend to distribute rewards in proportion to the difference in the average rewards received from others. Swingle (1970a) demonstrated that cooperative participants were exploited more when they were powerful than when they were weak, even when such exploitation resulted in reduced rewards for the exploiter.

Power affects promises to cooperate for mutual benefit. Tedeschi, Lindskold, Horai, and Gahagan (1969) studied reactions to participants who repeatedly promised to cooperate but who varied in credibility (their degree of cooperation following their promises). Powerful teammates ignored the promises and failed to cooperate. Equal-power participants were most cooperative with the willing member. Weak-power subjects became more exploitative as the credibility of promises increased. L. Solomon (1960) demonstrated that unconditional offers of cooperation by one member of an experimental pair are responded to by exploitative behavior and less liking of the partner when the two members are of equal power, but conditional offers of cooperation elicit greater cooperation and more liking of the partner. These differences are reversed in the unequal power situation.

Antecedents to Usage and Effects. Hinton and Barrow (1976) showed that leader-reward behavior was most frequently used by leaders who were responsible, confident, and enthusiastic. Studies by Barrow (1976) and Herold (1977) found that leaders were rewarding toward good performers and more punitive toward poor performers. Hunt and Schuler (1976), Oldham (1976), and Sims (1980) found similar responses. But, Greenberg and Leventhal (1976) reported that leaders will offer financial bonuses to poor performers to motivate them when that is the only sanction they have available.

Bennis, Berkowitz, Affinito, and Malone (1958) studied reward power in hospitals. They found that supervisors in hospitals in which the rewards that were given were congruent with those hoped for by the subordinates exercised more influence than did supervisors in hospitals in which the rewards were not congruent with the subordinates' hopes. Furthermore, the hospitals that gave rewards that were congruent with the subordinates' hopes were more effective. But supervisors exhibited little awareness of the subordinates' preferences for rewards.

To appreciate fully the effects of reward power, one must consider how it is used. On the one hand, as will be reported in later chapters, many studies have demonstrated the utility of rewards by supervisors in exchange for compliance by subordinates. Supervisors' recommendations for rewards that are contingent on the subordinates' performance have been widely found to contribute to productivity and effectiveness of operations. On the other hand, such rewards may be resented by subordinates and actually be coercive. In such cases, compliance will be public only, not private, especially when subordinates see the supervisors' use of rewards as capricious, arbitrary, and unfair, rather than reasonable, predictable, and fair.

Coercive Power

Epictetus declared:

> . . . no one is afraid of Caesar himself, but he is afraid of death, loss of property, prison, disenfranchisement. Nor does anyone love Caesar himself unless in some way Caesar is a person of great merit; but we love wealth, a tribuneship, a praetorship, a consulship. When we love and hate and fear these things, it needs must be that those who control them

are masters over us. . . . That is how at a meeting of the Senate a man does not say what he thinks, while within his breast his judgment shouts loudly. (Starr, 1954, p. 144)

The leader who uses coercive power controls the granting or denying of valued rewards or feared penalties; subordinates' private opinions and feelings remain hidden, but there is pressure on them to express publicly what they really feel. In hierarchical settings, coercion is manifest when the subordinate "holds in abeyance his own critical faculties for choosing between alternatives and uses the formal criterion of the receipt of a command or signal as his basis for choice" (Simon, 1947, p. 126). The extremes in coercive power were seen in Shaka, the Zulu King, who was known to have summarily executed his courtiers for a breach of etiquette, a smile at the wrong time, disagreeing with him over a minor point, or for one of many other slight causes of his displeasure (Morris, 1966).

Tannenbaum (1950) listed the ways in which an industrial executive may use his or her power over subordinates to restrict or inhibit their behavior. The executive may arbitrarily identify the organization's goals, set up criteria for evaluating alternative paths to the goals, rule out alternatives, limit the general activities in which subordinates are permitted to engage, identify the positions with control and power, give or withhold information, and set deadlines to be met to avoid punishment or to earn rewards.

Coercive power implies the ability to impose penalties for noncompliance. Rahim (1986) found that the endorsement of the statement "My superior can fire me if I neglect my duties" correlated .82 with a factor of coercive power. French and Raven (1959) demonstrated that conformity by followers (public acceptance but private rejection) is a direct function of earlier threats of punishment for noncompliance. Although coercion most commonly involves punishment and its threat, more subtle uses of power to coerce may involve promises of rewards for compliance. One will comply publicly but perhaps not privately as a consequence of such promises and one's concern about failing to obtain promised rewards in the absence of compliance. Thus, A has power over B if A can control whether B is rewarded or punished and B seeks rewards and wants to avoid punishment. A is coercive if B behaves publicly according to A's demands, although B privately rejects A (Bass, 1960).

Militant leaders of social and political movements apply coercive pressure on officials who are vulnerable to their attacks, such as executives whose business may suffer, "high-minded" university presidents, or elected politicians. In so doing, the leaders gain visibility and mobilize their supporters to support their coercive efforts, which are directed at changing the actions of their targets before changing their attitudes. Such leaders harass, threaten, cajole, disrupt, provoke, and intimidate in speeches, dress, manners, gestures, slogans, rituals, and violent confrontations (Simons, 1970).

A clear demonstration of the coercion that results from power was reported by French, Morrison, and Levinger (1960). In laboratory assignments in which supervisors could assess monetary fines, subjects serving as subordinates exhibited a much greater discrepancy between their public and private reactions than if no fines were established.

Usage. The use of coercive power is less popular with leaders and subordinates alike. Leaders tend to employ this form of power to deal with the unacceptable performance of subordinates, primarily when they do not have the power to reward subordinates for acceptable performance (Kipnis, 1976). McFillen and New (1979) demonstrated that leaders were less willing to exercise monetary sanctions for poor performance when they had the power only to punish than they were to use monetary rewards for good performance when they had the power only to reward their subordinates. But leaders were more inclined to use their coercive power when they were under pressure to maintain high-productivity schedules and had lost their power to reward for good performance (Greene & Podsakoff, 1981). Simon (1947) argued that the use of coercive power is hard to avoid in any formal hierarchy for five reasons: (1) subordinates develop expectations for obedience to symbols of higher status, (2) the superior can satisfy the subordinates' personal need for security from a substitute father or mother, (3) the subordinates may share the same goals as the superior and perceive that blind obedience provides a means to obtain the goals, (4) the subordinates are freed from the responsi-

bility for making difficult decisions and the superior bears the burden of these decisions for them, and (5) most simply, the superior may be able materially to reward or punish the subordinates.

Subordinates in an industrial organization are coerced by sources other than their immediate superiors. They may have to accept publicly, yet reject privately, the dictates of buyers of the organization's products, contractual agreements with labor unions or industrial cartels, and the demands of government, custom, and tradition (Bass, 1960). More often than not, coerciveness in the hierarchical setting is subtle. Subordinates may not even be aware that they are being coerced (Timasheff, 1938) and may repress their private feelings that are at odds with their public statements. For example, the executive may be reminded by the CEO of the costs in lost stock options if the executive quits, or a young executive with new ideas may be coerced by a superior who keeps emphasizing the possibilities of failure (Kets de Vries, 1980).

Although it may not be too subtle, pure political influence can be coercive when it displaces the rational and legitimate use of power with Machiavellian deception, divisiveness, defensiveness, or emotional appeals. Even the offer of rewards for political favors can be seen as coercive and require a strong countervailing conscience to resist. Power can be wielded by political manipulations, such as covertly denying, delaying, or distorting information that is sent to another member of the organization so that latter's choices are restricted (House, 1984).

Indirect Coercion. Observing vicariously how penalties are tied to the performance of one's colleagues may be more effective in maintaining performance in the short term than may direct threats. Schnake (1986) studied the effects of punishment on the attitudes and behavior of co-workers who observed a peer receiving the punishment. Students who were hired for temporary clerical employment observed a co-worker receiving a reduction in pay, a co-worker receiving a threat of a reduction in pay, or a co-worker who was not penalized. Those who observed a co-worker receiving a reduction in pay produced significantly more output than did those who observed a co-worker being threatened with a reduction in pay or not being penalized. Job satisfaction was not affected, and the effects held for at least a week.

'It's not what You Say, but the Way You Say it.'
Compliance that is actually due to coercion can occur without the feelings that one is being coerced as a consequence of the language employed in the attempted influence. A comprehensive review by Drake and Moberg (1986) detailed how both public and private compliance can accrue as a result of the language used by A to obtain B's compliance when ordinarily B would see A's request as exploitative and coercive. For instance, A can use sedating language, which suppresses B's tendency to analyze whether B will gain or lose by complying. Thus, A can be indirect (something needs to be done about the trash), rather than direct (take out the trash); in this case, A becomes the observer, not the leader. Or A's observations of the existence of a problem and related hints, prompts, and teases can substitute for a direct order. Or, A can first determine B's availability and willingness to comply before assigning new responsibilities to B. (But if A behaves this way routinely, B may interpret A's effort to be a characteristically annoying ploy and hence may lose trust in A.)

Giving orders or making requests without explanation is likely to produce less compliance and more sense of being coerced than is giving logical reasons. However, more compliance will occur and less coerciveness will be felt even if the reasons do not really make any sense. Such reasons can be substituted because cognitive processing is limited when decisions are made to follow orders in many seemingly legitimate situations. For example, Langer, Blank, and Chanowitz (1978) showed that personnel who were using a copying machine would allow a usurper to take over the copying machine from them for the irrelevant reason that "I have to make copies" when they would comply less often if no reason was given for the takeover.

Power is legitimated in the language employed. Hence, A increases his power over B by using rich, rather than redundant, vocabulary and by expressing less uncertainty in his appeals (Berger & Braduc, 1982).

Another approach to offset the potential coerciveness of a direct order is to use disclaimers preceding the order. As quoted by Drake and Moberg (1986, p.

578), Hewitt and Stokes (1975) outlined five forms of disclaimers:

Hedging (I'm not really committed): "I haven't given this much thought but...."
Credentialing (I'm not prejudiced): "Some of my best friends are...."
Sin licensing (I'm not a rule breaker): "I know this is against the rules but...."
Cognitive disclaimers (I'm not confused): "This may seem strange but...."
Appeal to suspend judgment (Don't get offended): "Don't get me wrong but...."

Excuses and justifications may also be employed to palliate the feelings of exploitation and to increase compliance. Compliance is also increased by avoiding messages of powerlessness. O'Barr (1982) reported that more convincing witnesses in court trials were *less* likely to use powerless language, such as intensifiers (e.g., "very") and hedges (e.g., "sort of ").

Conditions That Increase the Use of Coercive Power. Coercive power dominated supervisory-subordinate relations, according to Goode and Fowler (1949), in a factory where workers had a strong need to remain in the work group. These workers were marginal, handicapped, without skills, and unable to get jobs elsewhere. Although coercive power figured strongly in their performance, formal leaders also used other bases of power to maintain compliance. Kipnis and Cosentino (1969) studied the types of corrective actions used by military and industrial executives. Industrial supervisors tended to reprimand and to transfer offending employees, whereas military supervisors more often used instruction, reassignment, extra work, and reduced privileges as corrective measures.

Boise (1965) studied supervisors' attitudes in a city's police, street, and water departments. Police supervisors tended to disagree with the concept of a uniform penalty for unacceptable performances, while supervisors in the other departments agreed with the concept. Scores on the F Scale of authoritarianism were positively related to agreement with the uniform penalty concept. According to T. R. Mitchell (1979), supervisors' recourse to coercive power will depend on the reasons they give for their employees' noncompliance and poor performance (internal factors, such as the employees' ability and motivation, or external factors, such as policy or chance).

Coercive power is most likely to be used to deal with noncompliance. Katz, Maccoby, Gurin, and Floor (1951) found that the foremen of low-producing railroad section gangs were more punitive foremen. A longitudinal study by Greene (1976b) concluded that supervisors are punitive in reaction to their subordinates' poor performance. T. R. Mitchell (1979) further showed that more coercion was practiced if the supervisor attributed the poor performance to a lack of motivation, rather than to a lack of ability, or to policy changes or bad luck.

Goodstadt and Kipnis (1970) studied student work groups under different types of supervisory power. Student supervisors tended to use coercive power to solve disciplinary problems, but they used expert power to solve problems arising from ineptness. Sims (1980) concluded, from a review of both longitudinal field and laboratory studies, that punishment tends to be more a result than a cause of employees' behavior. More specifically, managers tend to increase punitive behavior in response to the poor performance of employees.

Punitive leadership was found by Sims and Szilagyi (1975) and Sims (1977) to be uncorrelated with the subordinate performance of professionals and technical personnel, but it had a significant inverse correlation with the performance of administrative and service subordinates. Szilagyi (1980b) found that higher levels of punishment tended to follow higher levels of absenteeism by employees. Studies by Bankart and Lanzetta (1970), Barrow (1976), and Hinton and Barrow (1975) also demonstrated the tendency of supervisors to become coercive as a consequence of the subordinates' inadequate performance.

Illustrating the use of punishment in reaction to other events, including the loss of other bases of power, Greene and Podsakoff (1979) found that after a contingent (positive reinforcement) pay plan at two paper plants had been abandoned, supervisors began to use rewards less and punishment more. Fodor (1976) likewise found that leaders were more authoritarian and coercive with disparaging and disruptive subordinates.

The leaders rated such subordinates lower and gave them less pay than they gave to other subordinates. In the same study, Fodor noted that supervisors who were subjected to group stress also tended to become more coercive and less rewarding.[4]

Support for Coercive Power. Legitimacy, coupled with coercion, will increase the public and private acceptance of coercive demands. In a study of experimental groups, Levinger, Morrison, and French (1957) found that the threat of punishment induced conforming behavior in group members before punishment but not after punishment. Most to the point was the fact that the group members' perceptions of the legitimacy of the punishment reduced their resistance to conform. Particularly important is the support of the status structure. When Iverson (1964) presented taped speeches by persons who were identified as high or low in status, those who listened to speakers who made punitive remarks formed more favorable impressions of the personalities of the high-status speakers than they did of the low-status speakers. The coercive demands of an attractive esteemed leader are more likely to be accepted, although continued use of coercive power will reduce such attractiveness and esteem. Another support for ready obedience to coercive power are immature participants. Kipnis and Wagner (1967) found that immature participants performed better than did mature participants under a leader whose decisions to administer punishment were backed up by superior authority. Brass and Oldham (1976) examined the reactions of first-line supervisors to an in-basket simulation.[5] Overall, the supervisors punished more often than they rewarded their subordinates. The more active supervisors, those who used both more reward and more coercive powers, were rated as more effective.

Situational variables, such as difficulty of the task and prospects for failure, increase a leader's tendencies to employ coercion (Michener, Fleishman, Elliot, &

---

[4]Chapter 19 will detail further conditions under which leadership will be punitive; Chapter 29, the effects of stress on leadership.
[5]A standard sample of memos, notes, letters, and bulletins requiring actions and decisions are likely to be found in a supervisor's inbasket. The adaquacy with which the problems in the correspondence are handled can be scored. See Chapter 36 for further detail.

Skolnick, 1976). That is, leaders who face failure will tend to become more coercive (Kipnis, 1976).

Leaders use coercion more easily when they rationalize that they are only following orders from higher authority without questioning the legitimacy of these orders. They are more coercive if they attribute the coercive action to their position, rather than to themselves as persons, and if they can maintain sociopsychological distance from those they are coercing as enemies, inferiors, and troublemakers. Adolf Hitler made coercion acceptable to the Germans by consolidating the attention of the German people as the Master Race against a single adversary and then lumping different opponents together in the same single category of all those who were antithetical to the Master Race (Paige, 1977).

Resistance to Coercive Power. When Milgram (1965b) instructed students to activate a device that supposedly administered electric shock to subjects who made errors in a learning experiment, the students were willing to administer "dangerous" degrees of shock on command. The students had a strong tendency to obey authority and to accept being coerced by it. But when students who were administering the electric shock were permitted to observe two other individuals who refused to do so, the number of refusals was significantly increased. Stotland (1959) found that when participants were required to work with a domineering supervisor, they tended to identify with the supervisor. However, when they were able to interact with a peer from another group, they would exert more independence from the power figure, show more hostility toward him, and exhibit greater motivation to reach the goal despite the supervisor's hindrance. French, Morrison, Levinger (1960) observed that the greater the threat of punishment, the less the resistance to comply, but the resistance increased after the threat disappeared.

A form of "group compensation" may arise, according to Stotland (1959), in resistance to attempts to be coerced if the opportunity is made available to do so. In Stotland's study individuals used models to design a city and were subject to the veto power of a "supervisor," who interrupted their work twice. Some of the participants were given the opportunity to meet pri-

vately in the absence of the "supervisor"; others were not. Those who met privately became much more aggressive and hostile toward the supervisor, whereas those who did not continued to accept the supervisor publicly. Private assembly permitted the formation of an informal organization to present a unified front against the "supervisor's" continued attempts to coerce the participants. In sum, group members were better able to resist coercive power when they had an opportunity to interact with peers in the absence of the supervisor or to observe other members who disobeyed orders. Resistance would be higher if the orders were judged to be illegitimate and the leader was personally unattractive.

Resisting attempts by superiors to exercise their coercive power may be productive. In an experiment by Horwitz, Goldman, and Lee (1955), students were frustrated by the arbitrary refusal of their teacher to repeat instructions. However, they shifted to more favorable attitudes toward the teacher, were less annoyed, and regarded the teacher as less coercive when the teacher read their opinions and agreed to repeat the instructions. These more favorable attitudes occurred less often when the teacher was informed by a "higher authority" that the instructions should be repeated. The students solved problems and learned best when they could take direct action to "reform" the coercive teacher; problem solving and learning were somewhat less efficient when the students could only state their grievances and were poorest when the students were led to believe that all the other students accepted the coercive teacher's refusals to repeat the instructions.

Unintended Consequences of Coercion. Those with coercive power will readily fall back on it when necessary. They are tempted to exploit their positions of power in demanding a greater share of available resources and rewards. The process is reinforced by colleagues' development of mistrust of the coercive power holder and by the power holder's counterreaction of suspiciousness about the colleagues' intentions, which results in his or her greater reliance on coerciveness (Kipnis, 1976). Coercive power can turn a mutually benevolent relationship into one of mutual hostility (Deutsch & Krauss, 1960).

The costs of depending on coercive power in formal

organizations are well known. For instance, satisfaction with supervision is almost uniformly lower. Thus, whereas the satisfaction of life insurance agents was related positively to their manager's use of referent and expert power, it was related negatively to their perceptions of the degree of reward, coercive, and legitimate power that the manager exercised (Bachman, Smith, & Slesinger, 1966). Weschler, Kahane, and Tannenbaum (1952) observed that a research laboratory headed by a coercive leader was more productive but less satisfying to its members than was a laboratory that was under less coercive leadership. Zander and Curtis (1962) indicated that participants in a coercive situation found each other less attractive, less well accepted, and less motivated than they were in a referent situation. Weiss and Fine (undated) found that participants who had experienced insult and failure were receptive to arguments to be hostile and punitive, whereas comparable participants who had satisfying experiences were more ready to accept communications to be lenient. Hostility toward power figures who can coerce other members was also found by Stotland (1959). Bachman, Bowers, and Marcus (1968) and Gemmill and Thamhain (1974) observed that coercion is linked to lower performance, and Ivancevich and Donnelly (1970b) reported that it is connected to a higher rate of absenteeism.

Participants may withdraw from the problems at hand to avoid being coerced. Riecken (1952) attributed such withdrawal to the frustrations of coercion. Oldham (1976) related punishment by leaders to evaluations of their subordinates' effectiveness. Generally, punishment was correlated not with the subordinates' performance, but with their lack of "motivational effectiveness."

A line of investigation beginning with Janis and Feshbach (1953) generally supported the contention that strong threats are less productive than are moderate or mild threats. In the prototype experiment by Janis and Feshbach, conditions of strong, mild, and minimal fear were included in propaganda about dental hygiene and resistance to counterpropaganda was measured. It was found that the arousal of minimal fear seemed to provide the most persistent influence, whereas the arousal of strong fear resulted in the ignoring or avoiding of attempts to influence (a form of withdrawal) or the development of conflicting tendencies to minimize the importance of the threatening propaganda. On the basis of similar findings, Kelman (1953) argued that when coercion is too great, interfering responses and hostility toward the coercer made participants less prone to accept the coercer's attempts to influence them. Yet the crushing of the prodemocracy movement in 1989 in China illustrates that credible strong threats followed by application of overpowering force and punishments can make for powerful deterrents. Nevertheless, subjugation to continued coercion is likely to contribute to dysfunctional outcomes, such as learned helplessness, feelings of powerlessness, alienation, and depression, or when possible, to generate verbal and interpersonal aggression and sabotage in those who are being coerced (Spector, 1975). Thus, in a study of 216 nurses and nurses' aides, Sheridan and Vredenburgh (1978a) found that the use of coercive power contributed to heightened tension among the hospital personnel.

Legitimate Power

Legitimate power is based on norms and expectations that group members hold regarding behaviors that are appropriate in a given role or position. The legitimation of a role is derived from such norms and expectations. Members are more likely to accept the position of the leader and his or her influence as legitimate when the leader holds attitudes that conform to the norms of the group or organization. For Read (1974), the legitimacy of leaders involves a complex set of attitudes toward the leaders and their source of authority; the leaders' actual behavior contributes to their continuing legitimacy. Thus, Bleda, Gitter, and d'Agostino (1977) observed that the satisfaction of enlisted personnel with army life was related more to the leadership of those they saw as the originators, rather than as the relayers, of daily orders to them.

French and Raven (1959) suggested three sources of legitimate power: (1) cultural values that endow some members with the right to exercise power, (2) the occupancy of a position organized to confer authority, and (3) appointment or designation by a legitimizing agent. An item that Rahim (1986) found to be highly correlated (.74) with a factor of legitimate power was, "My superior has the right to expect me to carry out her (his) instructions."

In goal-setting experiments, students and workers usually try to do what they are asked (Latham & Lee, 1986); they generally regard the requests from experimenters in laboratories and supervisors in work settings to be legitimate. The experiment is a "demand situation," and in the workplace, employees think it is legitimate for their supervisor to tell them what to do—that it is inherent in the employment contract (Locke, Latham, & Erez, 1987). The legitimacy of supervisors' orders was significantly related to the subordinates' intentions to work hard for an assigned goal in Oldham's experiment (1975).

A survey of 1,155 soldiers who had completed basic training to prepare them for action in the Korean War showed that the soldiers had a stronger "fighter spirit" to the degree that they perceived their leader had legitimacy (R. B. Smith, 1983). According to Michener and Burt (1975a, 1975b), studies of college students indicated that recognition of the authority of the leader's office was more important to their compliance than was endorsement of the leader's personal rights to exercise power.

House (1984) provided a rationale for the fact that although people accept leadership based on legitimate power, they do not do so with any special enthusiasm or as readily as they do when leadership is based on expert power. When influenced by legitimate direction, followers are being responsive to the source, not to the content, of the attempted leadership (Wrong, 1980). They tend to attribute the consequences of their compliance to external factors, not to themselves (Litman-Adizes, Raven, & Fontaine, 1978). They are less personally involved and can take less credit and satisfaction for success from their compliance. They do what is expected of them but not more than may occur in response to leadership based on referent or expert power.

Legitimacy through Appointment, Election, or Emergence. How the legitimacy of the office is established makes a difference. Appointment or election to a position tends to legitimate the leadership role to a greater extent than does emergence in the role through interaction or capture of the role by force. Thus, in an experiment with 82 groups of three to five male undergraduates, Burke (1971) found that the basis on which leadership was legitimated—election, emergence, or counterelection—was more important to the role differentiation that occurred within the groups then whether the goal was or was not established by consensus and whether pay was distributed equally or differentially. Again, Huertas and Powell (1986) found an increase of ingratiation and conforming statements among members if a leader was not appointed but was allowed to emerge.

Legitimacy was manipulated in an experiment by Goldman and Fraas (1965). Leaders of groups playing "Twenty Questions" were either elected, appointed by reason of their competence, or randomly appointed. Control groups had no formal leader. The groups' performance, as measured by the time required and the number of questions needed to reach the solution, was poorer if the leaders were randomly appointed or not put in place at all than if they were legitimated by election or appointment because of their competence.

Hollander and Julian (1969) and Firestone, Lichtman, and Colamosca (1975) demonstrated that leaders are in the best possible position to get things done if they first emerged informally as leaders in the group and then were elected by the members. Ben-Yoav, Hollander, and Carnevale (1983) similarly observed that elected leaders are more likely than are appointed leaders to contribute to the group's discussion and to receive greater responsiveness and support subsequently from other members. Group members regard elected leaders as more competent, more responsive to the members' needs, and more interested in the group's task. Election gives followers a greater sense of responsibility for leadership and heightens their expectations for the leader's performance (Hollander, 1978).

Legitimacy will give a leader who represents a group to higher authority or to other groups more latitude in negotiating. In turn, the legitimate leader will expect to receive more support from the group he or she is representing (Boyd, 1972). If elected leaders are also confident in themselves, they are likely to use their legitimate power and persuasion instead of punishment to correct their subordinates' poor performance (Goodstadt & Kipnis, 1970). Hollander, Fallon, and Edwards (1977) found that elected leaders had greater influence than did appointed leaders on small experimental groups that were perceived by their members to be failing, although the greater influence of a newly elected leader in a group that continued to fail was soon lost.

Winning an election establishes a much higher degree of legitimate acceptance of the elected president as the embodiment of the nation and as the head of state, government, and political party and commander-in-chief of the military than would be expected from the president's initial support from the voters. About half the U.S. electorate votes. Often, the difference between the votes given to the winner and loser is so close that the U.S. president, with his enormous powers, is legitimated by only about 25 percent of the eligible voters. Moreover, the president's nomination by his party for a second term of office is almost automatic (Hollander, 1985).

Other experiments have shown that legitimacy is enhanced through permanency rather than temporariness of office and appointment by higher authority rather than by election. Although the negotiation of leaders with a higher authority will have more legitimacy in the eyes of the members if the leaders are elected by the groups than are fortuitously appointed (Julian, Hollander, & Regula, 1969), arbitrarily appointed leaders can increase their legitimacy by consulting with the members (Lamm, 1973).

Appointed leaders in a hierarchical setting also are likely to have legitimate power from their appointment. The amount of their power is a direct reflection of the power, authority, and status of the legitimating authority. For example the commission of U.S. Army officers confers powerful legitimacy. The appointment of a university chancellor by a board of trustees does likewise, although when the legitimator is seen as incompetent and lacking in authority, the appointee's power and ability will be questioned (Knight & Weiss, 1980). Torrance's (1954) study of decision making in established and newly formed groups found that the members' influence on decision making depended on their position in the power structure of the group and was stronger in permanent than in transitory groups. Furthermore, although Raven and French's (1958a) examination of groups with elected and emergent leaders concluded that "the very occupation of a key position in a structure lends legitimacy to the occupant"

the authors noted that elected leaders were better liked than were emergent leaders and their influence was better accepted. Anderson, Karuza, and Blanchard (1977) observed that individuals who were elected to an undesirable leadership position had greater social power than were those elected to a desirable position but that appointment made no difference.

Julian, Hollander, and Regula (1969) found that the appointed leaders in experimental groups had a source of authority that was perceived to give them stability in their positions. But election made the leaders more vulnerable to censure if they later proved inadequate. Members were most willing for the leaders to continue in their positions when the leaders were competent in the task, interested in the group members, and involved in the group's activities.

Inner Circle versus Outer Circle. Vecchio (1979) showed that the leader's legitimate power was particularly important to the performance of those subordinates who were not part of the leader's "inner circle" of confidants and trusted assistants. At the same time, the subordinates in the inner circle did best when their superior did not possess power that was due to the superior's formal positions. The inner circle was most optimistic about its leader when the outer circle treated their leader in a friendly manner (Koulack, 1977).

Sources of the Enhancement of Legitimate Power. In a formal organization, legitimate power becomes equivalent to the authority vested in a position.[6] Illustrating the importance of such legitimate power, Klimoski, Friedman, and Weldon (1980) set up a laboratory simulation of an assessment center[7] that required the assessors in a group meeting to integrate their assessments. The chair holders of these integrative panel discussions either were or were not granted formal voting rights. If they were granted such rights, they were able to exert more influence on the panel, as evidenced by the assessment ratings assigned by the different panel members and in the final evaluations of the candidates that emerged.

Subordinates' trust of the legitimate authority makes

---

[6] A subject of Chapter 16.
[7] See Chapter 36.

a difference in the authority's power. Thus, Earley (1986b) showed that British tire workers who were assigned goals accepted them more when the reasoning for the goals was explained by their union steward, in whom they presumably felt more trust, than when the explanation was offered by their supervisors, whom they viewed as members of management—the untrustworthy opposition. The loss of such trust and confidence is particularly damaging to legitimate power.

Sources of Reduction in Legitimate Power. Mitchell and Scott (1987) examined the dramatic decline that occurred in the American public's confidence in the legitimate leaders of various institutions. In the late 1970s, President Jimmy Carter saw it as a "crisis of confidence." According to public opinion polls, the public's trust in government declined from about 80 percent in the 1950s to 33 percent in 1976 (just after the Watergate scandal). From the late 1960s to the late 1970s, the public's confidence in business leaders fell equally dramatically. It was the leaders of government and business who were seen as particularly untrustworthy, not the institutions as such. For example, in the 1980s, over a hundred political appointees of the Reagan administration were forced to resign in a cloud of scandals and indictments. The "sleaze" factor in the Reagan administration did not help to restore confidence in governmental leaders, nor did the Wall Street scandals, the Iran-contra affair, the many plant closings, and the stock market crash of 1987. Confidence in Ronald Reagan appeared to be maintained during his administration by his successful management of the impression of a personable, likeable, strong, and decisive leader.

Lipset (1985) found that the "great deal of confidence in the people running the various institutions" expressed in 1966 and in 1984 had declined as follows: physicians, 72 percent to 43 percent; educators, 61 percent to 40 percent; military leaders, 62 percent to 45 percent; religious leaders, 41 percent to 24 percent; members of the Supreme Court, 50 percent to 35 percent; CEOs of major companies, 55 percent to 19 percent; leaders of labor unions, 22 percent to 12 percent; members of Congress, 42 percent to 28 percent; and journalists, 29 percent to 18 percent.

The legitimacy of these institutional leaders is founded on the public's beliefs in their special expertise, in their serving as stewards with legal and moral responsibility for the management of their institutions in the best interests of their constituencies, and in their ability to innovate and to inspire progress. Mitchell and Scott (1987) suggested that the decline in confidence was due to the loss of belief that the institutional leaders had the expertise and motives that were once attributed to them. Rather than serving as stewards, the leaders had become self-serving.

With the decline in confidence has come the loss of legitimacy. The competence of the leaders is increasingly questioned. The leaders appear to be more self-aggrandizing. Their prospective innovations are increasingly constrained by the felt need to protect others from them. The decline in their legitimacy results in a public that feels much less "obligation or responsibility to believe in what their leaders tell them or to do what their leaders ask of them" (Mitchell & Scott, 1987, p. 449).

Countervailing power can reduce legitimacy; failures can offset it. Caplow (1968) observed that a majority coalition that is formed in opposition to the leader may not only undermine the legitimacy of his or her position but may assume the leadership function.

Worthy, Wright, and Shaw (1964) created groups in which a confederate of the investigators accused a naïve teammate of losing the game. When the accusation was legitimate, other members of the team were less willing to interact with the accused than with others; however, they were less willing to interact with either the accused or the accuser when the accusation was not legitimate.

Those with legitimate power may also be ready to give it up or to avoid exercising it. The tendency is more common in young low-level managers. In a survey of 569 managers, Veiga (1986) identified a variety of causes for giving up control: (1) the manager, especially the young low-level manager, may think the group lacks direction or the commitment or belief that it can do well, (2) the manager personally feels no commitment or responsibility for the outcome and nothing to gain from it, (3) the manager feels unwilling or unable to make a meaningful contribution to the decision, (4) the group's task may seem too ill-defined or too difficult, (5) the manager may believe that someone else in the group has more conviction, experience, ability, and willingness to take responsibility, (6) someone else's idea may be seen as similar to the manager's, (7) the manager may feel intimidated by an attack or by higher authority, (8) or the manager may wish to avoid damaging a relationship.

Kaplan, Drath, and Kofodimos (1985) noted that legitimate power may be counterproductive if the demeanor, isolation, and autonomy of the superior impedes the flow of criticism from the subordinate to the superior. The subordinate's performance may suffer if the leader's legitimacy results in an aura of power, in a tendency to monopolize discussions, or in an abrasive style. The use of such power in this way may increase social distance between the superior and the subordinate, which further restricts communication. If the subordinate perceives that the superior's power is an embodiment of the organization, he or she may interpret criticism of the superior as disloyalty to the organization.

Legitimacy will be counterproductive if powerful superiors appoint only subordinates who agree with them or if they exempt themselves from the formal appraisals that others who are less powerful must undergo. But knowingly or unknowingly, supervisors may give up some of the power to which they are legitimately entitled to their subordinates as a way of increasing overall satisfaction and responsibility. Blake and Mouton (1961a) asked a supervisor and a subordinate to rank lists of items in order of importance. The level of satisfaction and responsibility of both supervisors and subordinates combined was higher when they alternated in exercising power.[8]

Comparisons of the Bases of Power

Relative Importance

In 13 studies reviewed by Podsakoff and Schriesheim (1985a), large samples of respondents ranked the 5 bases of power according to their importance in the superior-subordinate relationship. Agreement was high among the respondents, regardless of whether they were sales people, members of a liberal arts faculty, in-

surance agents, or factory workers. For each sample as a whole, expert and legitimate power always ranked first or second in importance as the basis of superiors' power, with mean rankings tied at 1.6. The other bases were seen as far less important, with means rankings as follows: referent, 3.3; reward, 4.1; and coercive, 4.6. However, as will be noted later, Podsakoff and Schriesheim urged caution in interpreting these findings on their face value.

Relative Willingness to Use Powers

Leaders differ not only in the importance of the bases of their power but in their willingness to use power that is based on one source rather than another. Lord (1977) identified 12 functions that are typically performed by a leader, such as developing plans, proposing solutions, and providing resources. He watched to see how often each leader in a sample displayed the 12 functions; he also determined which of French and Raven's (1959) five bases of power the leaders employed in attempts to exert their power. Lord then correlated the occurrence of each leadership function with the basis of power the leader used. He found that task behavior to complete the work of the group correlated with the type of power used, but the leader's efforts to establish socioemotional relations did not. For example, the extent to which leaders relied on themselves as experts correlated with the extent to which they proposed solutions, but the extent to which the leaders tried to employ referent power with their socioemotional efforts did not increase their being liked.

Coerciveness is more likely to be used by those who have the power to do so and by insecure leaders who lack self-confidence. Thus, in a laboratory experiment, Instone, Major, and Bunker (1983) found that, compared to those whose self-confidence was high, those who lacked self-confidence tended to use coercion rather than expert power. House (1984) listed other personal attributes that contribute to a leader's tendency to use coercive power, including the leader's power orientation, Machiavellianism, and dogmatism. In another laboratory study, Goodstadt and Hjelle (1973) reported that individuals who perceived themselves to be externally controlled by their environment used punishment to maintain their influence much more

[8]Voluntary power sharing will be discussed in subsequent chapters.

frequently than did those who saw themselves as internally self-controlling. Such "internals" attempted to lead through their expertise rather than coercively.

Raven and Kruglanski (1970) suggested that those with power anticipate the consequences of using the various kinds of power they may have and avoid using those that are believed to be least effective. More specifically, for example, power holders who expect targets to resist will be tempted to employ more coercive power if they are capable of doing so (Kipnis, 1976). Support for this contention was found for managers in state agencies, industry, and the military (Kipnis & Cosentino, 1969; Kipnis & Lane, 1962), as well as in laboratory experiments (Goodstadt & Kipnis, 1970; Rothbart, 1968). In the Kipnis studies, supervisors were asked to describe an incident in which they had to correct the behavior of a subordinate. Which type of power was brought to bear on the situation depended on the supervisors' diagnosis of the subordinate's problem, the subsequent and most likely reactions of the subordinate, and what was likely to be best for the continuing relationship with the subordinate.

Culture, tradition, and organizational norms will also determine the type of power that may be employed to a given situation. For example, tradition may provide power to those with seniority and age that can be used and accepted by those who are younger and have less seniority. More authoritarian, coercive uses of power will come into greater use and acceptability during times of stress.

Legitimacy will be stressed by those who believe in "rules of law rather than rules of men." House (1984) suggested that the use of legitimate power will be favored over the use of arbitrariness and political influence because legitimate power provides more orderliness and predictability. Legitimacy has more clear-cut limitations; unbounded arbitrary power generates excess costs and inefficiencies. Legitimate power can be exerted impersonally without the buildup of the allegations of political exchanges. Legitimate power is ordinarily more acceptable to the subordinate and supported by the larger group than is power that is based on the personal arbitrary predilictions of the superior. House (1984) cited considerable support for the greater acceptability of legitimacy in studies in which employ-

ees were asked why they comply with managers' requests, suggestions, or directions.

Willingness to use one type of power rather than another was observed by Rosenberg and Pearlin (1962) in a study of the attitudes of 1,138 hospital nurses toward power. The percentage of nurses who stated they would make use of each of form of power was as follows: persuasion, 54 percent; benevolent manipulation, 38 percent; legitimate authority, 5 percent; contractual power, 1 percent; and coercive power, 2 percent. Kappelman (1981) reported that male school principals were more likely than were their female counterparts to use their reward and coercive power, although the women principals were likely to be described as more active leaders.

Since the bases of power are interrelated, changes in one will have effects on the others. For example, Greene and Podsakoff (1981) found that when the reward power of 37 supervisors in a paper mill was lowered by abandoning an incentive pay plan in which the supervisors' evaluation of the performance of 392 subordinates figured strongly, not only did the supervisors' reward power decline, but their referent, legitimate, and "organizationally-sanctioned" power declined as well, while the subordinates' perceptions of the supervisors' coercion increased significantly. No such changes in the bases of supervisory power were found in a second comparable paper mill that did not change its pay policy. Consistent with this, Gamson (1968) concluded that when leaders' efforts to succeed through their legitimacy failed, they resorted to their coercive power.

Effects of Different Bases of Power

Cooperativeness, benevolence, friendliness, and generosity are attributed to those in power who use rewards rather than penalties. The reverse attributions are made about those who use authority or political persuasion (Rubin, Lewicki, & Dunn, 1973).

Table 13.2 shows the correlations between the perceived power base of the first-line supervisors and their behavior as leaders that Martin and Hunt (1980) found for 289 professional personnel in a construction bureau and 118 in a design bureau of a midwestern state high-

Table 13.2 Correlations between the Perceived Basis of Power and Ratings of the Initiation of Structure and Consideration by First-line Supervisors

Basis of Power	Initiation of Structure[a]		Consideration[a]	
	Construction Bureau	Design Bureau	Construction Bureau	Design Bureau
Expert	.44	.41	.50	.48
Referent	.23	.16	.15	.10
Reward	.24	.06	.11	.02
Coercive	.10	.01	−.10	.01
Legitimate	.04	.11	−.03	.00

[a]See Chapter 24 for detailed definitions of initiation and consideration.

SOURCE: Adapted from Martin and Hunt (1980).

way department who responded to a mailed survey. As can be seen, of all the bases of power, expert power made the most important contribution to leadership. The effect was not always beneficial; design professionals who complied with their supervisor because of the latter's expert power signaled a greater intention to quit.

Ivancevich (1970) reported that the satisfaction of life insurance agents correlated .35 with the agency manager's use of referent power, expert power, and reward power, but satisfaction correlated −.28 with the use of coercive power and .14 with the use of legitimate power. Again, Bachman (1968) found that faculty members of colleges were better satisfied under deans with high power (control over college affairs) whose influence was based on expert and referent power than under deans who relied on reward, legitimate, or coercive power. However, in a study of salesmen's perceptions of branch managers' power, Ivancevich and Donnelly (1970a) found that coercive and legitimate powers were not related to productivity. Only the expert and referent powers of the branch managers were positively related to the salesmen's performance.

Podsakoff and Schriesheim's (1985a) review of these and other field studies of the relationship of the five sources of power of supervisors and the outcomes for subordinates concluded that unlike studies of the *actual* reward behavior of supervisors that usually generate positive outcomes, the supervisors' *power to reward*

was unrelated or even negatively related to such outcomes. But Podsakoff and Schriesheim attributed the difference in findings to the way these field studies measured power. Often the measure consisted only of respondent's rank ordering of the bases of power as defined. The power to reward was confounded with a sense of illegitimacy, used in exchange for compliance rather than for performance. Again coerciveness was seen to be confounded with the potentially illegitimate use of punishment. The actual narrow content of the scales of legitimate power failed to match French and Raven's broader conceptualization, and the desired identification of the subordinate with the superior was not included in measures of referent power, which often seemed no more than assessments of friendship.

Hinken and Schriesheim's (1989) surveys of three samples of students who described their part-time or full-time supervisors found that although coercive power was likely to correlate with legitimate power to some extent, it was likely to be independent of the other bases of power. The other bases—expert, referent, and reward—were likely to correlate with legitimate power as a base as well as with each other as bases.

Despite these shortcomings, seven of the field studies[9] emerged consistently with positive associations be-

[9]Bachman (1968); Bachman, Bowers, and Marcus (1968); Bachman, Smith, and Slesinger (1966); Burke and Wilcox (1971); Busch (1980); Hinken and Schriesheim (1989); and Slocum (1970).

tween supervisors' expert and referent power and subordinates' satisfaction and performance. The results
were uniformly negative or reversed for coercive power
and mixed for legitimate and reward power. Negative
correlations were found between the supervisors' expert and referent power and the excused absences of
production workers (Student, 1968), but none of the
power measures was related to unexcused absences or
turnover. However, Busch (1980) found that the expert
power of supervisors contributed to the subordinates'
lesser intentions to quit in the three companies studied. Less consistent findings emerged for referent and
legitimate power.

A similar pattern was noted by Gemmill and Thamhain (1974) in the outcomes of support by supervisors
and the commitment of subordinates to the work associated with supervisory powers. Only expert power
consistently was positively correlated with such outcomes and with the clarity of the subordinates' role.
Also, such role clarity appeared to be enhanced if the
superiors had referent power (Busch, 1980).

Most people are aware that the use of coercion is
met with dissatisfaction on the part of those coerced.
They may be somewhat less aware that, in general, subordinates are more satisfied when their superiors exercise expert and referent power (power that is due to
their person) than when they exercise coercive power
(power that is usually due to their position).

Yukl and Taber (1983) agreed with Podsakoff and
Schriesheim (1985) that the use of expert and referent
power is most efficacious. Nevertheless, the skill of application and appropriateness must be considered.
Leaders need to exercise authority with courtesy and
clarity and to verify compliance. Reward power should
be used to reinforce desirable behaviors after they occur. Coercive power should be used only when absolutely necessary, such as for deterring behavior that is
detrimental to the individual, group, or organization.
Leaders accumulate and foster expert and referent
power over time by showing that they are confident,
decisive, considerate, and protective of subordinates'
interests. In the same vein, Watts (1986, p. 286) suggested that "using too much power can express the
need to control, the flip side of which is the fear of
being out of control. Using too little power can express
a tremendous need to be liked, to avoid conflict." Fur-

thermore, leaders need to avoid promising more (based
on their reward power) than they can deliver, and they
need to avoid being corrupted by their power.

Power and Corruption

In the 1840s, Count Cavour, a future cofounding
statesman of modern Italy, wrote that "absolute power
inevitably corrupts," which Lord Acton later made famous as "power tends to corrupt; absolute power corrupts absolutely" (D. M. Smith, 1985, p. 26). The process was elucidated by Kipnis (1976). First, the desire for
power becomes an end in itself. Next, access to such
power tempts the officeholder to use institutional resources for illegitimate self-aggrandizement. Self-aggrandizement is followed by false feedback from others, which generates an elevated sense of self-esteem
in the leader, coupled with a devaluation of the worth
of others and a distancing from them.

Gardner (1986a) listed four ways that help to mitigate
the corruption of power in government. First, acceptance of the rule of law and the accountability of leaders
to abide within explicit and universally applicable constraints is required. Second, power needs to be dispersed, as in the U.S. system of checks and balances
of executive, legislative, and judicial powers. Third, a
strong private sector must be maintained. Finally, an
alert citizenry is essential.

So far, analyses of power and corruption have been
left to investigative journalists and the legal profession.
What is needed are controlled surveys and experiments
to increase our understanding of the interrelation of
the power-corruption relationship, its antecedents and
consequences for business, governmental, and other
institutions. How do the fear of being caught; public
humiliation; regulatory control; a sense of duty, obligation, patriotism, and loyalty; and internalized ethical
and professional standards inhibit the corruptive influences of holding power over others?

Summary and Conclusions

Studies of power are concerned with the means by
which one individual has the potential to influence
others. The most thoroughly researched sources of
power are personal—expert and referent—and posi-

tional—reward, coercive, and legitimate. Power represents but one aspect of role differentiation; it is not synonymous with leadership. The concept of power leaves unexplained much of what is involved in the leadership role.

The more-powerful members of a group ordinarily are better liked than are the less-powerful members. They attempt more influence and exercise more of it, and their influence is more accepted. Groups tend to be better satisfied when more-powerful members occupy the positions of leadership.

Followers react differently to leaders with different sources of power. They seek to be liked by those with referent and reward power. Although the threat of punishment tends to induce compliance, followers usually find leaders who use coercive power less attractive than they do those who use other forms of power. Furthermore, followers tend to respond to reward power either by developing contractual agreements or by forming coalitions that tend to equalize the bargaining positions of participants in the power structure. Appointment or election to a position tends to legitimate it to a greater degree than does the acquisition of a position by force or by the emergence of a leader in interaction.

All sources of power yield influence. In real-life situations, leaders draw consciously or unconsciously on multiple sources of power. Reward and coercive power are probably the sources that they manipulate most easily; leaders have less control over referent power—the extent to which group members like them and are attracted to them.

Self-confidence, self-esteem, and knowledge of the task enable subordinates to resist the effects of power. Interacting with peers and gaining support from reference groups strengthen the followers' resistance. The influence of a leader can be weakened by the followers' formation of coalitions with countervailing power. Followers can reduce the extent to which they are subject to influence by asking and receiving a clear definition of the situation. The power of a leader is weakened by the presence of members whose values and goals are in opposition to those of the leader and the organization and thus that challenge the legitimacy of the leadership role. Ingratiation may also be a means of private resistance.

The advantage in a power situation, however, resides with the holder of power. But leaders may be ready to give up or to share their power with subordinates for personal or organizational reasons. Although power can corrupt, a better understanding of the causes and consequences of this process await controlled examination. An important consideration is how power is distributed within a group, organization, or society.

Leadership and the Distribution of Power

The distribution of power and the leadership associated with it have been a main theme in both political history and the history of management-worker relations. Autocracies and oligarchies have represented concentrations of power; democracies, the wide distribution of power. At one extreme is the individual autocrat with a patronizing staff of subordinates dictating to a relatively powerless membership. The other extreme is the voluntary or legally mandated dispersion of power within organizations outward and downward from their original centers of power.

Importance of Differences in Power

Mulder (1976) focused attention on such differences in power in organizations and the tendency of those who are striving for more power to reduce them. Hofstede (1980) unearthed a power distance factor in a large-scale survey of employees' attitudes in 50 countries.[1] A large power distance was indicated, for example, in countries in which employees expressed fear of disagreeing with their supervisors. Hofstede suggested that under such circumstances, employees became either dependent or counterdependent. On the other hand, the maintenance by supervisors of a small power distance between themselves and their employees encouraged consultation and participation.

Power and Leadership Style. Differences in power in a group, organization, or society are reflected in the kind of leadership that can be attempted and whether the leadership is successful and effective. When differences in power are great, more directive leadership and more coercion are likely. Large differences within a group, organization, or society—particularly in coer-

cive power and, to a lesser extent, in personal, reward, and legitimate power—may guarantee public success and acceptance of the leadership efforts. But resistance, private at least, will bring about unintended consequences, such as resentment and apathy.

When differences in power are small, more participative leadership is likely. Many behavioral science theorists have observed that the sharing, leveling, and equalization of power among members of a group increases the members' participation and results in their full commitment and acceptance, both public and private, of the leader.[2]

Elitism versus Populism. Even within a society's democratic order there are wide differences in power. Populism competes with elitism. For populists, all citizens share equally in the opportunity to exert influence through political activity. For elitists, power is delegated to those who are committed to the rules of decision making and are highly knowledgeable and skillful in analysis, negotiation, persuasion, and manipulation. Populism calls for a high degree of citizen participation; elitism calls for a relatively passive, uninvolved citizenry, who, from time to time, "in a single elemental choice," elect the active officials who will be responsible for the stability, efficiency, and authority of the state (Summers, 1987).

Populism within the organization translates into shop-floor democracy, in which all employees share consultation and decision making with their immediate superiors. Elitism within the organization translates into the election of experienced and knowledgeable union officials and council representatives or heavy dependence on informal leaders from within the work force.

---

[1]See Chapter 34.

[2]See, for instance, Argyris (1957), Lawler (1986), R. Likert (1961a), Lippitt (1942), and McGregor (1960).

Distribution of Power in the Small Group

Populism within the small group translates into shared decision making by the group members; elitism translates into elected heads whose powers to decide are unchallenged by the members, who remain passive following the election. In elitist groups, most of the power resides in the leader; in populist groups, it is widely shared and equalized among the members and the leader. With such equalization of power, the members become as influential as the leader, and their effects on each other become important to the process of interpersonal influence. Thelen (1954) noted the power and control of the group over its members. Group agreements "have teeth in them." The determination of what is possible and at what cost or with what reward is under the control of the group. Leadership occurs in changing the agreements and working out new ones to fit the continual diagnosis of realities in the group-problem situation.

According to Tannenbaum and Massarik (1950), shared decision making increases the likelihood that workers will accept the goals desired by the management, which results in their greater satisfaction and increased efforts to move toward the selected goals. Likewise, McGregor (1944) argued that the effectiveness of workers will be increased when workers are given opportunities to participate in finding solutions to problems—to discuss actions that affect them and to assume responsibilities when they are ready to do so. If members of a group participate, to some extent, in setting goals, they will be more motivated to achieve the goals. If they have the capabilities, they can be delegated more responsibility or freedom to act without a review by a higher authority (Learned, Ulrich, & Booz, 1951).

When all members are equal in status and power, more communication of feelings will occur (Bovard, 1952). Status and power differentiation in a group results in the inhibition of the ventilation of feelings by members who are lower in the status and power hierarchy. Such inhibition can be detrimental to the group's functioning. Thus, Thibaut and Coules (1952) demonstrated that the communication of hostility toward instigators will reduce the residual hostility toward them. Again, power differences can offset the influencing effects of participation. Thus, although Bass, Flint, and Pryer (1957b) and Bass (1963) found that for an individual to influence a group's decisions, he or she had to participate and to attempt to lead, such active participation did not necessarily influence the group's decision when the members of a small group varied widely in power.

Caveats. This does not mean that all communications are easier and all outcomes are better when members are equal in status and power. Although some believe that power sharing and participation are a universal panacea for promoting change, productivity, and satisfaction, experimental researchers, such as Locke, Latham, and Erez (1987) suggested that considerable qualification is needed. For instance, the members' acceptance of hard group goals can be effected without the power sharing implied in group discussions and decision making if the leader is clear and supportive. More competition and persistence in the face of rejection are likely to be required of the would-be leader of a group in which all members are equal in status and power. Thus, Bovard (1951a) observed that in groups in which there is little status differentiation among members and all have similar power to influence each other, verbal interaction is higher and more influencing is attempted than when a single person of higher status directs the activities.

It may be that although communication seems easier when members are equal in power, it really is more difficult. Shepherd and Weschler (1955) studied work groups that differed in status stratification within the groups. The members of these groups felt they had fewer communication difficulties, but they actually experienced more such difficulties.

Formation of Coalitions. The distribution of power in a group is dynamic. Two or more members can combine their power to increase their joint power to influence the course of events. Thus, how reward power is distributed in the triad has been the focus of experiments regarding the bargaining process. Mills (1953) assembled triads in which one member was given high reward power; one, medium power; and one, low power. A strong tendency was found for two of the members to form a coalition that acted in opposition to the third member. Lawler (1975) found that expectations of support from others was an important cognitive determinant of the formation of a coalition against inequitable and threatening leaders.

Vinacke and Arkoff (1957) confirmed hypotheses advanced by Caplow (1956) that (1) when all members of a triad are equal in power, all possible combinations will be formed, (2) when two equal members who are stronger than the third member combine, they will form a coalition in opposition to the third member, (3) when one member is weaker than the two equal members, he or she will form a coalition with one of them, and (4) when one member is stronger than the other two combined, no coalition will ensue. Turk and Turk (1962) confirmed the fourth of these hypotheses. But Kelley and Arrowood (1960) found that the results reported by Vinacke and Arkoff depend on the clarity of the game and on whether a player is assured of a certain return whether or not the player joins a coalition.[3]

Coalitions are also organized as a tactic to increase one's upward influence. Kipnis and Schmidt reported that respondents exerted more upward influence on their boss by obtaining the support of their co-workers and subordinates to back up their request, or they arranged to organize a formal meeting at which they made their request. Such coalitions were used at about the same frequency to influence co-workers, subordinates, and the boss.

Stability of the Distribution of Power

House (1984) deduced that the distribution of power in organizations would tend to become stable over time and that it would change only if there were major shifts in environmental or technological demands on the organization. But even here, changes in the power distribution would come slowly because those in power are reticent to part with any of it. In fact, given the tendency of the powerful to gain more power, demands for change in the organization may bring about a greater concentration of power, rather than equalization of power.

The stability of the distribution of power begins early. In an observational study of kindergarten children, Hanfmann (1935) noted a stable power structure

[3]See Caplow (1968) for a detailed analysis of power relations in the triad.

that was similar to a pecking order. In the same fashion, Gellert's (1961) observations of pairs of preschool children during three play periods found that in a significant proportion of the dyads, the same child maintained the same position of dominance or submission during the three play periods, which again suggests that a pecking order was at work.

Structuralist versus Behavioralist Views

There are two opposing arguments about how power should be distributed in organizations. In the structuralist view, it is inherent in the nature of organizations that power is distributed unevenly, and as organizations develop, for power to accrue in varying amounts among the units and supervisors of the organization. Some units (and, therefore, their supervisors) obtain more power than do others in influencing the allocation of the organization's scarce resources (Pfeffer & Salancik, 1978). The units and supervisors with more power have control over strategic contingencies and the activities of other departments that are critical to their functioning, which makes it less likely that there will be any way of substituting for the more powerful unit's activities; they also provide information to the less powerful units to decrease the latter's uncertainties. Thus, more powerful units and supervisors are in the center rather than the periphery of information and work flow (Hickson, Hinings, et al., 1971). Hinings, Hickson, Pennings, and Schneck (1974) found support for these propositions in 20 subunits of 5 breweries. Saunders and Scamell (1982) obtain similar results with 62 vice presidents, deans, and directors of six universities.

The opposing behavioralist view suggests that the equalization of power in organizations is essential to the organization's health. The equalization of power is a basic tenet of modern organizational development (Bennis, 1965) and the human potential movement (Maslow, 1965). It has its roots in those aspects of democratic and egalitarian values that stress the importance of informal trusting relationships rather than a formal structure in which relationships depend on the authority of the position and the requirements of the role. Practical applications have included unstructured leadership, job enlargement, leadership sharing, participative management, consultative supervision, joint consultation, workers' councils, and other forms of industrial democracy. Thus, Patchen (1970), who administered questionnaires to 90 employees in plants operated by the Tennessee Valley Authority found that the degree of control that workers had over their jobs was significantly correlated with their general interest in their jobs, concern with innovations in their work, and pride in their work.

Whyte (1953) and Simon (1957) argued for structure, power differences, and status differentiation. They contended that hierarchical organization is the natural, biological, and sociological solution for ensuring a group's survival. R. B. Cattell (1953) hypothesized that status differentiation promotes speed in decision making and the faster attainment of goals. Communication-net studies,[4] such as the one by McCurdy and Eber (1953), have supported this contention. On the other hand, Argyris (1957) and McGregor (1960) were equally convinced that individuals, motivated by the basic desire for autonomy and self-actualization, are frustrated by organizational structure, specialization of work, and philosophies of management that assume that workers will remain complacent and unproductive unless they are subjected to controls that hamper unwanted initiatives from workers.

Implications for Organizational Design. The two opposing views have been the basis of opposing prescriptions for how organizations should be designed. Structuralism emphasizes designing organizations with power differences; behaviorism emphasizes designing organizations with power equalization. Legitimate differences in power are manifested in an organization in how much the positions of occupants in the organization are structured, that is, prescribed and bound by rules and regulations or the dictates and policies of a higher authority. An infantry squad is highly structured; an initially leaderless discussion group is not. In the infantry squad, there is a clear legitimate hierarchy of power from the squad leader down to the new private; there is no such legitimate hierarchy in the leaderless discussion group. Equalization of power is fostered by behaviorism in its support for informality, trust, learning, and the sharing of information.

Structuralism—as enunciated by such classical management theorists as Taylor (1911), Fayol (1916), Follett (1918), and Davis (1942)—depends on external constraints to gain the compliance and commitment of followers. Behaviorism, through the equalization of power, is expected to gain even more commitment as well as compliance through the individual's awareness of and insight into effective interpersonal relations and trust.

Structuralism calls for someone to be responsible for supervising all essential activities. The hierarchical pyramid of supervisor-subordinate relationships is mandated. Power sharing proposes that any group member can take on leadership responsibilities when he or she sees the need to do so. The autonomous team with no formally appointed leader is the extreme example.

Structuralism avoids the duplication or overlapping of responsibilities. However, overlapping, cross-training, rotation, and other forms of sharing responsibilities to increase the reliability of the system are encouraged by behavioralists when informal relationships are developed among workers who are committed to see that their group prospers.

The simplification of jobs is fundamental to a structuralist approach. According to this approach, no individual should be responsible for a wide assortment of unrelated acts. In contrast, behavioralists call for the enlargement and enrichment of jobs; they believe that subordinates become closer in power to superiors when they receive bigger jobs with greater responsibilities.

The extreme structural position calls for subordinates to receive clear, written job specifications and role assignments. The extreme behavioralist position calls for making goals clear and allowing subordinates, commensurate with their training and experience, to decide how to reach the goals.

Both structuralists and behaviorists agree that authority should be delegated so that decisions take place as close as possible to the action. For structuralists, the decision maker is the superior in the situation; for behavioralists, the decision is shared or delegated to the subordinates as much as possible.

Structuralists emphasize the chain of command. Behavioralists argue that organizations require much communicating, reporting, proposing, influencing, complying, and deciding in complex vertical, diagonal,

[4]See Chapter 30.

and horizontal paths that are not shown on the formal organizational charts. Again, participants need some sense of the equalization of power for this flow to occur effectively.

Neither the structuralists nor the behavioralists have a monopoly on the truth (Bass & Ryterband, 1979). Situational elements and individual preferences, as shall be shown later, strongly affect which approach pays off. Young professional workers, compared to older, unskilled employees, are likely to demand less structure and more equalization of power. Some pupils thrive in schools with a great deal of freedom to choose what and how to learn, but others do best in a highly structured environment. Juvenile delinquents who adjust most readily to institutionalization may have more difficulty avoiding antisocial, criminal behavior once they are back on the streets. The optimum differentiation of power is likely to lie between the extreme structuralist and extreme behavioralist positions, depending on the situation. In this pluralistic society, the only thing one can safely say is that wide differences in performance, attitudes, and response to hierarchy are likely to depend on task, time, place, immediate needs, and the like.

Distribution of Power in Communities and Organizations

The distribution of power provides the potential for leadership and influence over events and people. It shows itself and its effects in how it is distributed in communities, in formal organizations, and in smaller groups.

Community Power Structures

The earliest research on power was concerned with the identification of individuals with the potential to influence in their local communities. Lynd and Lynd (1929) pointed the way in their study of Middletown. F. Hunter (1953) used interviews in a large city to obtain a list of 175 persons who were mentioned as wielding influence in the community and for whom reasons were given for the belief that they had such potential to influence. A panel of experts reduced the list to 40

persons who were regarded as constituting a "monolithic" power structure in the city. However, Dahl (1961) maintained that the nominating technique hid important details that could be uncovered by a study of community issues. He concentrated on identifying those individuals who had played key roles in promoting or blocking the issues. His analysis of the data suggested that there was a pluralist power structure in the city. Using both the Hunter and Dahl methods, Freeman, Fararo, Bloomberg, and Sunshine (1963) and Presthus (1964) found that the two methods identified a common core of power figures and that the Dahl method revealed additional subgroups of individuals who could influence different issues.

The status and power structures of many communities were studied.[5] Consistently, those persons who were identified as having power also tended to rate high in social and economic status. Educational level, as such, was less important (Alford & Scoble, 1968). However, the acceleration of the importance of new technology in everyday life has given increased power to professionals in their communities. That is, as problems of health, economics, safety, and so on come to the fore, the expert power of professionals takes on increasing importance in the community.

When Hunter and Fritz (1985) studied the power structures in four Chicago suburbs, they found that the smaller communities contained less complex structures. This finding fit with V. Williams's (1965) conclusion that smaller communities may be able to function effectively without the differentiation of roles and individuals in specialization, power, and authority. Similarly, when the dispersion of power in small rural communities was described from 189 interviews and from the reconstructed history of a county in the southeastern United States since 1900 by Nix, Dressel, and Bates (1977), they noted that the initial bossism was replaced by informal cliques, organized pluralism, bifactionalism, multifactionalism, and amorphous leadership. As for the Chicago suburbs, the informal status structures were less complex in the richer suburbs than in the poorer ones (Hunter & Fritz, 1985).

[5]By Blumberg (1955), Bonjean (1963, 1964), Clelland and Form (1964), Fanelli (1956), Form and Sauer (1963), Lowry (1968), Olmsted (1954), Schulze (1958), and Wildavsky (1964), among others.

Interlocking Office Holding. Perrucci and Pilisak (1970) compiled a list of 434 organizations in a community with a population of 50,000. Of 1,677 executives in these organizations, 1,368 held a position in 1 organization. Twenty-six executives who occupied positions in 4 or more organizations were compared with 26 executives who occupied only 1 position. The multiorganizational leaders were regarded by both groups as being more powerful and as having more influence on actual and theoretical issues. These leaders were named more often as social and business friends and were found to constitute a powerful network of influence relationships. The concentration of power was seen in the city boss, studied in detail by Banfield and Wilson (1963), Moos and Koslin (1951), and Zink (1930). Mayor Richard Daley of Chicago epitomized the use of social exchange relationships with other bloc leaders and centers of community power to build the powerful political machine that claimed to "make Chicago work."

Power Systems

Power reveals itself in formal organizations in the extent to which it is associated with status and authority—the formal authority system—and the beliefs shared by the members in the organization's system of ideology. An organization's system of authority involves the way legitimate power is distributed and enacted in goals, rewards, sanctions, and the division of labor. Its system of expertise is more informally applied to solving the complex problems of the organization (Mintzberg, 1983). The interlocking among systems was illustrated by Majchrzak (1985), who found that the rates of unauthorized absences in units in 20 Marine Corps companies were significantly reduced, in contrast to 20 control companies, if policies were clarified and communicated effectively to all levels involved and there was a hierarchical consistency—agreement and understanding of the policies and requirements at the different levels.

The systems can offset each other. Although the authority system would dictate otherwise, the system of expertise may result in general managers being less influential than their subordinate staff experts. Thus,

B. Walter (1966) traced the transmission of influence in two municipal organizations. Superiors generally were found no more influential than their staff subordinates in making decisions; in fact, the subordinates were more influential when making novel decisions.

The political system operates outside the system of formal authority to benefit some constituents at the expense of others or at the expense of the organization (Mintzberg, 1983). Although the political system is likely to conflict with the other systems, it can also serve to mobilize power, when needed, for the acceptance and implementation of new strategies. The four systems of power can be observed in community settings as well. The system of authority is based on the legitimate power of the different roles and positions—the status and authority of the position holders.

Status and Power. One of the most consistent findings in social science research is the general tendency for those higher in status in an organization to wield more power to influence those who are lower in status. Naturally, there are exceptions, as was just noted in B. Walter's study of municipal organizations. Nevertheless, among many studies of the relationship, Blankenship and Miles (1968) found hierarchical position to be a more important determinant of managers' decision-making behavior than was the size of a company or the number of subordinates who were supervised. Bass (1960) argued that by creating greater differences in power and status between the leader and followers, one can increase the proportion of success in the leadership acts of leaders. This outcome was observed by Hemphill, Seigel, and Westie (1951) in a study of 100 groups that varied in status differentiation. Such leadership was also likely to be more dominating, directive, and coercive and more likely to define and structure the work for the membership. Again, as was expected, a related study of 212 aircrews by Rush (undated) found that aircrew commanders were much less considerate of their subordinates when the crews were highly stratified in status.

House (1988a) concluded that when social stratification (status differentiation) exists and the holders of authority feel strongly about their status, they will have fewer inhibitions against being coercive. The greater the social stratification, the more likely for them to be coercive to obtain compliance from those at lower levels in status.

Equal status and equal power are more commonly found when familiarity, homogeneity, and the potential to interact among members are high. Caplow and Forman (1950) observed that when neighborhoods contained families who were homogeneous in the duration of their residence, interests, and type of dwelling, no status differentiation occurred. Form (1945) reported similar findings for Greenbelt, Maryland, when it was a newly established community for federal white-collar employees of similar occupations, age, nativity, and housing. Similarly, Munch (1945) found that the homogeneous inhabitants of isolated Tristan da Cunha in the South Atlantic maintained their community without status differentiation and institutionalized government.[6]

Effects of the Total Amount of an Organization's Power and Control.

A. S. Tannenbaum (1956a, 1956b, 1968) suggested that the total power and control of an organization vary, rather than remain fixed in amount. They can be expanded by increasing authority—legitimate power—in one or two levels or in all levels of the organization. An organization tends to gain most in the total amount of its control of its members when authority is expanded all the way down the line, particularly to the lowest levels. In studies of two industrial plants (1956a) and four labor unions (1956b), Tannenbaum found that organizations of the same type can differ in the amount of authority exercised by executives at different levels and in the total amount of organizational control.

Smith and Tannenbaum (1963) studied 200 units of large firms. They found that the total amount of organizational control was positively and significantly related to the members' loyalty, morale, and judged effectiveness but not to objective measures of effectiveness. Nevertheless, member-officer agreement on the ideal amount of control and actual total amount of control over members was related to rates of effectiveness. On

the other hand, when Smith and Tannenbaum (1965) examined the effects of the total amount of control by the members of women's organizations, the total amount of control failed to increase the coordination of leadership, although such leadership contributed to the group's effectiveness.

In a study of insurance agencies, Bowers (1964b) found that total organizational control was related to the members' satisfaction and performance but not to the volume of business, the growth of business, or the turnover of personnel. Furthermore, the amount of power at different levels of an organization was not associated with effectiveness. Smith and Ari (1964) observed that a consensus among members of work groups and among superiors and subordinates was related to the total amount of organizational control but not to the amount of control of individuals at the work level.

Ivancevich (1970) also studied the effects of the total amount of organizational control and members' satisfaction in insurance agencies. The agents' satisfaction with status, autonomy, and growth was correlated about .30 with the manager's control over the agency, the agents' control over the agency, and the total amount of organizational control. Ivancevich found that agents were equally satisfied whether they or the manager exercised control. Likewise, in another study of insurance agencies, Bachman, Smith, and Slesinger (1966) found that the agents' satisfaction was highly related to the total amount of control, control by the manager, and control by the agents.

In addition to the effect of differences in the total amount of control exercised by members, the total amount of control is higher when exercised by members in all echelons than in one or two levels of the hierarchy. The total amount of control, but not control in the various echelons, is related to productivity and the satisfaction of members. Furthermore, given the effect of charisma, members tend to feel more satisfied in some organizations when the top-level leader exercises strong control over organizational activities (House, 1988).

Although not examined, it may be that the reason why high total control produces greater satisfaction and productivity is that goals and expectations are

---

[6]The antecedents and consequences of high interaction potential will be discussed more fully in Chapter 30.

much clearer for members and conflict is much lower than when organizational anarchy exists.

Measurement of the Distribution of Power

The distribution of power is ordinarily inferred from observing the variance among members of a group or organization in their success in efforts to influence each other. This inference leads to a tautology. Observed differences in influence indicate the distribution of power; differential power begets differential influence. The equalization of power is seen in shared leadership.

Power differences are also inferred from differences in status and esteem. The general has more power than the colonel. The admired parent will have more power in the family than an estranged one.

Measuring the responsibility, authority, and delegation associated with a position is a more direct way to tap an incumbent's power.[7] Another direct measure of power differentiation that is independent of observed influence and status was originated by Bass and Valenzi (1974), who asked subordinates and managers to describe the power—mainly legitimate—that the managers had over the system, which included the managers and their subordinates, and the power the subordinates had over the same system. Questionnaire items dealing with the managers' power over the system included the extent to which the managers had the power to override or veto any decisions the subordinates made, grant or deny promotion or salary increases to subordinates, reverse the priorities of subordinates, control the size of subordinates' budgets, and get the higher authority's support for what the managers wanted to do.

Although not ordinarily and formally recognized, the subordinate may have various amounts of power over the system, including the power to bring outside pressure to support what the subordinate wants; do the opposite of what the manager wants done; maintain final control over his or her own plans, assignments, and targets, regardless of what the manager thinks about them; ignore the manager and submit his or her own

requests to a higher authority; and nominate or vote for a manager.

Bass and Valenzi obtained alpha coefficients of .60 for the reliability of both management's and subordinates' power on the basis of a simple summation of responses to scales of extent. They found that on scores ranging from 1 to 9, superiors' power was typically above 6 while the subordinates' score was below 4. Shapira (1976), using small-space analysis, showed that the differences between the power of managers and subordinates, when combined with the information that each had, could predict, according to theoretical expectations, which style of leadership would be most often displayed by the managers. Managers with more power and information than their subordinates were most directive, managers with more power but less information were most consultative, managers with more information but less power were most negotiative, and managers with less power and information were most delegative.[8]

Kotter (1978) plied a different route to study power differences in organizations. His interviews focused on whom the incumbent in a particular management position felt dependent. Kotter also assessed the incumbent's efforts to obtain cooperation, compliance, and deference from others in the system. Integrating these concerns about power and dependence with a concern for the organization's goals was seen as the key to effective performance and was consistent, as was noted in Chapter 9, with McClelland and Burnham's (1976) demonstration that effective managers have a strong need for power but are oriented toward organizational goals rather than self-aggrandizement.

For their study of the distribution of power among departments at universities, Saunders and Scamell (1982) modeled their assessments after Hinings, Hickson, Pennings, and Schneck (1974). They were able to obtain valid measures of three determinants of how departments differed from each other in power. From data obtained in interviews and questionnaires, they indexed the department's centrality in the flow of work and information, the difficulty of substituting an alternative department for the department's activities, and

---

[7]See Chapter 16.

[8]See Chapter 22 for further details.

the extent to which the department had the ability to cope with uncertainties.

The Power of the Group

Power sharing with all members of a group does not necessarily mean increased initiative by and freedom for members. On the contrary, powerful groups can constrain and influence their individual members more strongly than can any individual leader with power. Mere membership in a group makes a difference. Deutsch and Gerard (1954) found that individuals in a group were more influenced by observed standards than were those who were not in a group. Katz and Lazarsfeld (1955) concluded that people are more likely to change their opinions if their family members or friends are undergoing a similar change. The changes are also more likely to persist if supported by such group affiliations. In the same way, individuals are more influenced by the mass media when they are listening in groups than when they are alone.

Socialization processes in organizations are a familiar observation. For example, after liberal students enter the world of work, they tend to adopt more conservative attitudes involving the norms of the firms they join. S. Lieberman (1954) found that workers who were promoted to foremen tended to shift their attitudes in favor of the management as they became members of management. Workers with the same attitudes of those who became foremen but who subsequently were elected as union shop stewards, shifted attitudes in the union's direction after 12 months as stewards.

The Tendency to Conform

Many early investigators demonstrated the tendency of members of a group to shift toward the attitudes and behavior of the group.[9] Subsequently, Bass (1957b), Hare (1953), and McKeachie (1954) found, in various experiments, that group discussions were more effective than was reading or listening to arguments in in-

creasing group members' agreement with each other, both publicly and privately. Generally, such group discussion leads to improvement in the members' understanding, commitment, and decision making. But the reverse is also true. Janis (1972) saw "groupthink" as the reason why highly competent members made extremely poor collective decisions, such as occurred in the Bay of Pigs fiasco. Highly cohesive, these members assumed a unanimous view when it did not exist; conformity occurred out of a sense of mutual loyalties to the group.

The signs of conformity of workers' performance as a consequence of the work group's power over its members are well known. The fear of "rate busting" and of the management's lowering of the price per piece paid to workers result in the distributions of outputs of workers that peak at an arbitrary limit set by the group. The variance in output is not a normal probability distribution; the distribution is truncated at the upper end.[10]

Subtle Influences. In a series of well-known experiments, Asch (1952) showed that conformity to the opinion of a simulated group can be induced even when the group decision defies the senses. A fair proportion of participants will agree that the clearly shorter of two lines is longer if they see all the other persons (all confederates) in the same situation stating that the shorter line is the longer one.

Subtler influences of group power were measured by M. L. Hoffman (1956) and Horwitz (1954). Hoffman confronted participants with group norms that alternately agreed and disagreed with the participants' responses. The psychogalvanic skin responses of participants suggested that tension was reduced when they believed they had conformed to the group instead of being in disagreement with others. Horwitz (1954) found that individual members were under the greatest tension, according to their greater recall of interrupted tasks (Zeigarnik effect), when they voted not to continue a task that the group had voted to continue.

The effects of conformity persist even after the group disbands. When partners are separated after ex-

[9]Bechterew and Lange (1924/1931); Conradi (1905); Hilgard, Sait, and Magaret (1940); Marple (1933); H. T. Moore (1921); Thorndike (1938); and Wheeler and Jordan (1929).

[10]Rothe (1946, 1947, 1949, 1960, 1961) and Rothe and Nye (1958, 1959).

periencing a judging situation together, they continue to exert a mutual influence on each other's judgments when asked to judge alone (E. Cohen, 1956). The tendency to be affected in this way was found by Bovard (1948) to persist for at least 28 days.

Power Sharing to Promote Change

The use of discussion in groups is an approach to increase power sharing in the decision-making process and to increase the influence of the group decision on its individual members. K. Lewin (1943) conducted a seminal experiment to demonstrate how group discussion influenced housewives' choice of meats for their families' meals. Group discussion will produce more change in members than will the arguments of individuals. It has been found superior to lecture techniques in reducing biases in the merit-rating tendencies of supervisors, prejudice, hostile attitudes, alcoholism, and emotional disturbances in children. Group discussion has also proved superior to lectures in reaching solutions to community problems and modifying food habits (Lichtenberg & Deutsch, 1954). In addition, Radke and Klisurich (1947) observed that mothers of newborn infants who engaged in discussions under the leadership of a dietitian adopted much more readily the desired behavioral patterns that coincided with the usual recommended procedures than did a control group who received individual instruction. Similarly, Levine and Butler (1952) significantly reduced the halo effect in merit ratings by foremen by permitting them to discuss and make decisions regarding more realistic evaluations. Torrance and staff (1955) found that B-29 crews were more likely to reach a state of efficiency that enabled them to go into combat if they had been observed to participate in decision making earlier in survival school.

Coch and French (1948), J. R. P. French (1950), and French and Zander (1949) reported the results of an experiment in a clothing manufacturing plant. The factory had experienced a considerable turnover of labor after each change in operating methods. The experimenters studied four groups of employees. For the control group, a change was merely announced. For the three experimental groups, the workers were given an opportunity to discuss the change, to offer suggestions, and to agree on the necessity for the change. Productivity increased and the turnover of personnel decreased in the experimental groups but not in the control group.

The same plant studied by Coch and French and a second plant acquired by merger were studied in 1962, 1964, and 1969 by Seashore and Bowers (1963, 1970) and by Marrow, Bowers, and Seashore (1968). Both managers and workers were given group training in joint problem solving. Although the employees' satisfaction did not change to a marked degree, their commitment to the task improved and the productivity norms were raised. Productivity also increased.

Ronken and Lawrence (1952) studied a firm that was experiencing difficulties in communication. When small groups and committees were formed to discuss and analyze the problem and to suggest solutions, communications became freer and operations were conducted more smoothly. Lawrence and Smith (1955) compared groups of workers who set their own production goals with other groups that merely discussed production problems. Groups who set their own goals showed significantly greater increases in productivity.

Lawler and Hackman (1969) reported experimental results using group power to develop a pay-incentive plan for maintenance crews. Three groups developed their own pay-incentive plans to reward good attendance on the job. The plans were then imposed on two other groups. One type of control group was given a lecture about job attendance and the other received no experimental treatment. Only those in the groups who developed their own plans increased their attendance.

Sharma (1955) surveyed 568 teachers in 20 school systems and found that their satisfaction was related to the extent to which they reported that they were involved in decision making as individuals or as groups. Zander and Gyr (1955) examined employees' attitudes toward a merit rating system. They found that a significant change in attitudes required monthly feedback and that consultation and discussion were somewhat more effective than were mere explanations of the system. In addition, under both conditions, changes in attitudes occurred only when subordinates described the supervisor as sincere, when the supervisor knew the plan and the issues, when the supervisor's and the subordinates' opinions were in agreement, and when the supervisor was skilled as a chairperson.[11]

Effects of Increased Group Power

The more power the work group has over its members, the fewer differences will be seen in the output of its members. Thus, Seashore (1954) found less variance in productivity among different members of the more cohesive of 228 factory groups.

The more members expect to be rewarded and to avoid punishment through membership in the group, the more they value the group and in the Asch line-judging experiment, the more the group will have the power to produce conformity (Deutsch & Gerard, 1954). Gerard (1954) noted that the greater the attraction of the members to a group, the more their opinions coalesced. Gorden (1952) observed more conformity by members who were identified most with the group. Similarly, Newcomb (1943) observed that the extent to which Bennington College students wanted to "belong" on campus determined the extent to which they shifted their social attitudes in the direction of the prevailing modal liberal attitudes on campus. Again, Rasmussen and Zander (1954) found that teachers' levels of aspiration conformed more to the ideal of their group the more they were attracted to the group, that is, saw the group as potentially rewarding.

Visibility and Salience of the Group. Groups will exert more power over their members when their members' behavior is visible than when it is unobservable (Deutsch & Gerard, 1954). The effects of conformity can be increased by giving the group more power and by making it more important to its mem-

bers. For example, Dickinson (1937) observed that the effectiveness of a group's wage incentives depends on mutual policing. Members who work for group rewards are more likely to keep up with each other in groups that are sufficiently small to permit effective mutual observation. Again, members of such groups, rewarded as groups, were found by Grossack (1954b) to demand more uniformity from each other than did individuals who were competing with others for rewards.

Significant to a group's power over its members is whether the members are clear about the modal or majority opinion of the other members. The clearer the members are as to what they must conform, the more they are likely to conform. In judging intelligence from photographs, participants tended to shift their judgments toward the group decision if they obtained knowledge of the decision (S. C. Goldberg, 1954). Gorden (1952) observed that when expressing their public opinion, members of a cooperative living project tended to be influenced by what they perceived to be the group's opinion. Bennett (1955) found more compliance with a request for volunteers among those who perceived most others doing the same thing. Pennington, Haravey, and Bass (1958) obtained the greatest objective increase in agreement among members in groups in which members made their initial opinions public in discussions or when a group decision was announced; agreement was less when either decision or discussion was absent, and it was least when both were absent. Similarly, in studies of autokinetic judgment, N. Walter (undated) found that agreement among participants decreased when they were no longer given information that was ostensibly based on the judgments of typical students of a prestigious school.

Power, Leadership, and Structure

As was noted earlier, differences in power are established in formal organizational structures. Some positions and roles are assigned more power than are others, and power increases as people move from the bottom to the top of the organization. Management-worker hierarchies and political bureaucracies replace traditional power structures that are based on family,

---

[11]For more on the sharing and redistribution of power to effect planned change, the reader may wish to examine Bennis, Benne, and Chin (1962); French, Bell, and Zawacki (1978); and Zollschan and Hirsch (1964)—all edited collections of readings on the theory and techniques of planned change—and such theoretical and technical reviews as those by Bavelas (1948); Bennis (1963, 1965, 1966a); Burns and Stalker (1961); Cartwright (1951); Ginzberg and Reilley (1957); Kanter (1983); Lippitt, Watson, and Westley (1958); Low (1948); McMurry (1947); Patchen (1964); Schein and Bennis (1965); Sofer (1955); Spicer (1952); Tannenbaum and Massarik (1950); Tichy and Devanna (1986); Winn (1966); and Zander (1949, 1950).

class, tribe, wealth, strength, and age. Even in a country with 370 years of democratic tradition, preferences for formal power structures vary. Some prefer highly structured settings, and others prefer highly unstructured ones.

Preferences for More Structure or Less Structure

In some situations, everyone wants total structuring. Automobile drivers on through streets want assurance that drivers coming from side streets halt at stop signs and red lights and that oncoming drivers stay on their side of the white dividing lines. Conversely, at a social gathering, the hostess may be faulted for trying to structure interactions. But in working and educational settings, much divergence of opinion occurs. Thus, Heron (1942) observed that if employees must learn by trial and error when they do not have access to information about rules and procedures, they are dissatisfied and afraid to take the initiative because of possible infractions and penalties. Seeman (1950) found that a majority of schoolteachers preferred a group-oriented style of leadership; however, they exhibited a substantial demand for a type of leadership that calls for the differentiation of power.

Bradshaw (1970) obtained ratings of the ideal, as well as the actual behavior of leaders in a professional organization. The rank order of the means for both observed and desired behavior was as follows: (1) structuring of expectations, (2) tolerance of freedom, (3) consideration, and (4) emphasis on production. The observed tolerance of freedom was close to ideal, but more structure was desired than was provided by supervisors. More autonomy and self-actualization were desired than realized. Bradshaw concluded that deficiencies in structure were associated with deficiencies in the satisfaction of higher-order needs; in other words, structure is needed for the satisfaction of these needs.

Wispe and Lloyd (1955) found that low producers preferred a more structured group, whereas high producers favored a less structured group and perceived their superiors to be less threatening than did low producers. Lowin and Craig (1968) studied supervisors in experimental groups and found that supervisors advocated more structure and closer supervision of subordinates who were incompetent, which is consistent with what has been noted about the impact of subordinates' incompetence on their supervisor's punitiveness.[12]

Structure and Effectiveness

If any sizable group is to reach a common objective, some degree of structure in the role relations within the group is required. Individuals need to be able to predict each other's behavior. Unless informal means are possible, the reliability of individual performance will be obtained only by distributing authority, power, and responsibility to holders of the various positions in the group through a structure, without which the group is likely to remain highly ineffective. Thus, Lucas (1965), who studied the effects of feedback on problem solving in groups, found that a group's effectiveness was related to the degree of the group's structure. Gerard (1957) observed that leaders tend to perform more effectively when they have a wider scope of freedom but that followers are more effective in a somewhat more highly structured situation. Gross, Martin, and Darley (1953) found that groups with strong formal leaders were more productive and more cohesive than were those with weak informal leaders. Again, Sexton (1967) studied 170 line workers in jobs whose structure varied widely, according to both the supervisors and the workers, and found that the degree of job structure was positively and significantly related to the employees' satisfaction of needs. Hickson, Pugh, and Pheysey (1969) studied a variety of organizations in England and found that the structuring of activities, role specialization, and functional specialization were positively and significantly related to the size and productivity of the groups. Similarly, in a study of manufacturing firms, Pheysey, Payne, and Pugh (1971) noted that formality and an orientation to rules were related to the employees' satisfaction with their promotion and with fellow workers and to the generation of greater involvement by the managers with the group. Bass and Valenzi (1974) also obtained a positive association between the perceived effectiveness of work groups and the extent

---

[12]In Chapters 13 and 18.

to which relations between managers and subordinates in such groups were structured.

Hobhouse, Wheeler, and Ginsberg (1930) rated the level and complexity of development of some 200 cultures. They found that efficient government, which resulted from a strong and stable leadership position or council of leaders, was positively correlated with high cultural achievement. Two opposing factors were found to reduce the power of the chief. In the less well-developed societies, the frequent absence of a permanent government deprived the chiefs of any effective structure for exercising power except for sporadic undertakings. In the more highly developed societies, the presence of a stable governing council limited the powers of the primary chief.

Fox, Lorge, et al. (1953) compared the effectiveness of six- to eight-man discussions of U.S. Air Force officers with groups of 12 to 13. Although smaller groups ordinarily would be more effective, here the larger groups yielded higher-quality decisions; the large groups overcame their disadvantage by organizing themselves to solve the problem to make maximum use of the larger number of participants. In the same way, F. L. Bates (1953) observed that the performance of four medium-size bomber wings was better when there was a greater use of authority and a greater frequency of production plans, orders, and instructions sanctioned by authority. Again, if additional members are not redundant in contributing to a group's decision and if efficient computerization can be arranged to process, establish priorities, distribute, and pool their individual contributions, groups of 35 may be able to become as effective in utilizing the informational resources of their individual members as can groups of six without the computerized and information-processing advantages.

Bureaucracy and the Distribution of Power. The theory of bureaucracy is concerned with problems involved in the structure of power relations in formal organizations. Weber (1924/1947) observed that bureaucracy is characterized by the continuous organization of official functions bound by rules, specified spheres of competence, the hierarchical ordering of authority relations, and impersonality. Responsibility and authority reside in the office, rather than in the person. Bureau-

cratic structure does not necessarily limit all autonomy for the organization's managers, although as expected, Engel (1970) found that the managers' autonomy was greater in organizations with moderate bureaucratic structures than in those with extreme ones. Numerous case studies[13] have suggested that when organizations become overly concerned with rules and formalities, they tend to lose touch with the external demands made on them and to become insensitive to the internal problems that they generate. (These defects are not confined only to bureaucracies.) Dissatisfaction and ineffectiveness are unintended effects. Although it is the rational purpose of a bureaucracy to use specialized talent effectively, bureaucratic organizations and institutions often emphasize formalisms and legalisms to such a degree that the perpetuation of the system takes precedence over the function the system was intended to perform. In agreement, Burns (1978, pp. 295–296) declared:

> Bureaucracy is the world of explicitly formulated goals, rules, procedures . . . specialization and expertise, with the roles of individuals minutely specified and differentiated . . . organized by purpose, process, clientele, or place. [It] prizes consistency, predictability, stability, and efficiency . . . more than creativity and principle. Roles and duties are prescribed less by superiors. . . . than by tradition, formal examinations, and technical qualifications. Careers and job security are protected by tenure, pensions, union rules, professional standards, and appeal procedures. The structure . . . approaches the . . . elimination of personalized relationships and . . . reciprocity, response to wants, needs, and values—that is, transactional leadership. . . .
>
> Through its methodical allotment of tasks, its mediating and harmonizing and "adjustment" procedures, its stress on organizational ethos, goals, and authority, bureaucracy assumes consensus and discounts and discredits clash and controversy, which are seen as threats to organizational stability. Bureaucracy discourages the kind of power that is generated by the tapping of motivational bases among

---

[13]See, for example, Bennis (1970); Merton, Gray, Hockey, and Selvin (1952); and Peabody and Rourke (1964).

employees and the marshaling of personal—as opposed to organizational—resources. Bureaucracy pursues goals that may as easily become separated from a hierarchy of original purposes and values as from human needs. And bureaucracy, far from directing social change or serving as a factor in historical causation, consciously or not helps buttress the status quo.

Thus, the status and power differentiation of a bureaucracy, initially organized to meet objectives expeditiously and efficiently, often experiences "hardening of the arteries" when it fails to adapt to changes in outside conditions and its own personnel. But a complete lack of power differentiation generates problems that are equally damaging to the group's and organization's performance.

Kingsley (1967) described a group of therapists that fell apart and disbanded after the demise of its structured power relations when the discussion leader left. Members were unable to maintain interactive relationships in the absence of the power structure provided by the leader. Similarly, over a period of one year, L. M. Smith (1967) observed an experimental elementary school whose administration, scheduling, curriculum, teaching, and discipline were highly unstructured and in which authority resided in the pupils. The teachers engaged in a ceaseless struggle for power, and there was continuous confusion, delay, noise, and frustration. All but two of the teachers decided to leave at the end of the year.

Industrial Democracy

Power may formally be redistributed by assigning worker representatives to management boards and committees. The redistribution may be voluntary on the part of management, as in the United States, or mandated by legislation, as in West Germany. Although some attempts had been made earlier in the United States and elsewhere, representative industrial democracy appears to have been initiated in Sweden in about 1938 from the deliberations of national representations of employees and workers in response to labor unrest that was more common to Sweden in the 1920s and 1930s than in most other countries. In West Germany, the occupying military authorities after World War II, interested in ensuring that resurgent German industry could not again be exploited for military purposes and the subversion of the democratic government, passed a law prescribing the *Mitbestimmung* (the representation of workers on a firm's supervisory board). The *Betriebsverfassungsgesetz* was also formally prescribed by law somewhat later to provide for the participation of employees in a wide range of matters. To signal Yugoslavia's break with Soviet state centralism in 1950, Marshall Tito introduced self-management, another early attempt to use legislation to guarantee employees representative participation in the management of production and administration (Stymne, 1986). In the United States, along with a century of trade unionism, came management-inspired efforts to establish representative democracy in industry. However, it has been within the past 15 years that legislated tax advantages have contributed to the growth of Employee Stock Option Plans (ESOPs) in which employees begin to share in the company's ownership. By 1986, 7,000 U.S. firms had ESOP plans (Meek, 1987). Also, representatives of the employees and consumers have been elected to serve on the boards of directors of corporations. Finally, groups of employees began to purchase control of their own firms, and the employees began to elect the directors who are responsible for the firm's management and policies. Hence, quite a few businesses became partly or fully employee owned.

This representative democracy is in contradistinction to power sharing at the workplace. In the workplace sharing of power, workers participate directly with their immediate supervisor in decisions that are of consequence to their own work and working situation. As Heller and Clark (1976) wisely noted, it is important to distinguish between real power sharing, in which employees actually participate in decision-making processes of consequence, and the semblance of participation that may not yield the same degree of commitment, motivation, and productivity. Workers may sit on the boards of directors in Yugoslavia, but, in fact, party members, financial experts, and technocrats exhibit most of the power, initiative, and influence (Obradovic, 1975). Moreover, as has already been discussed and as Heller and Clark observed, both individual preferences and situational considerations affect the optimum balance of self-direction and present structure.

Industrial cooperatives, such as Mondragon in Spain, became community-and-employee owned holding companies for subsidiary plants. ESOPs in the United States gave employees voting privileges and sometimes, control over management. In reaction to threatened plant closings, employees purchased the ownership of their own plants. Trade unions, such as Israel's Histadrut, became holding companies for large conglomerates of business and industrial establishments. But none of these formal developments necessarily means that a participative climate in superior-subordinate relations will develop as a consequence, nor do they necessarily produce a real equalization of power. For example, who owns the company may not be as important to a new employee who enters the firm at a low level as to an older employee with an important position in the company.

Although one purpose of the equalization of power is to increase the commitment of those who are initially lower in power, despite their desire for more power, Styskal (1980) failed to find the expected increased commitment when subunits were given more decision-making authority over the curriculum, program, employees, budgets, and work assignments in three federally sponsored temporary educational organizations in New York City.

Many other problems can be cited. Discussing efforts by U.S. corporations to introduce voluntary and obligatory participation, Kanter (1982b) noted such problems as the paternalistic imposition of democracy; the need for results of the participation to be visible; the concern by both management and the union about losing power; the time required; the lack of relevant knowledge by many employees; the limiting of participation to more abstract decisions that are remote from the employees' concerns at the workplace; tensions between innovation and democracy; the constraints of previous decisions; the need for leadership; the resistance to change of various interest groups; the tension between social, emotional, and business needs; and excessive expectations about the gains that may accrue from participation. Management may resist power sharing not only from the fear of losing its prerogatives, but because of a disinclination to learn new leadership styles involved in consensus building. Unions may not only fear a loss of power, but may remain suspicious of the management's motives. And employees may be satisfied with their current inefficiencies in getting the work done (Alexander, 1984).

Dixon (1984) proposed that some interrelated elements are necessary for any participatory program to succeed. First, an information system is required to provide feedback on the organization's performance. Ownership of the information must reside with the group, feedback must be timely, and results must be visible to all employees. Second, employees at all levels need to be represented. Representation calls for groups of competent employees to identify and solve problems, to have the power to act on their decisions, and to agree on a common vision. Finally, the organization's leadership needs to believe in the creativity and responsibility of the employees.

Voluntary Programs

Selekman (1924) reported the results of a management-sharing plan in a chemical firm. For management to gain a better understanding of the workers' point of view, two boards were created. The Board of Operatives was composed of elected workers and was responsible for working conditions, grievances, recreation, training, company housing, and the like. The Board of Management, which was composed of executives and stockholders, was responsible for production, wages, farm equipment, hours, and financial policies. Although the Board of Operatives was slow to accept responsibilities, it gradually participated in planning and decision making. Effects attributed to the experiment were a reduction in the turnover of personnel and greater cooperation to improve production.

Given (1949), a company president, experimented with a "bottom-up management" plan, in which he delegated authority down the line to employees and encouraged the employees to use their initiative and to assume responsibility. Results were good. Another company president worked directly with employees to stimulate their responsibility and initiative at the workplace. His activities placed foremen under great conflict and stress, but he worked with them until they accepted his philosophy of participation. He concluded that his organization became more informal and his workers more responsible and involved (Richard, 1959).

Joint Consultation. Wyndham and White (1952) found that workers in an Australian refinery tended to regard the elected representative to worker-management committees as an alternative to their foremen. The latter regarded their positions as threatened, even though they were members of the joint consultation committees. H. Campbell (1953) concluded that for joint consultation to be effective, the foreman must be involved in the process as an active participant.

A study by W. H. Scott (1952) of joint consultation in three British industrial firms also indicated that the procedure is subject to strains in different segments and levels of the organization. Although workers' representatives were generally well accepted in their discussions with management, both the workers and their representatives reported that little was accomplished because only trivial issues were discussed. The workers felt they were neither consulted nor kept informed by the representatives. The foremen reported they were bypassed in communications between management and workers' representatives. The workers and their representatives complained that the foremen failed to take action on many matters that could have been handled more effectively on the spot rather than being referred to joint consultation. Although the majority of workers' representatives were also union stewards, the union members complained that they were not adequately represented. Scott concluded that joint consultation resulted in few advantages that could not be produced as well as by responsible leadership.

Jaques (1952) completed an intensive case study of a single British factory that formed works councils and work committees to participate in management. The workers tended to feel dissatisfied with the performance of their elected representatives. The representatives were under heavy stress because of their different, conflicting demands; little authority for making decisions; and increasing separation from the workers. Similar problems were revealed, but the study threw greater light on details of the consultative procedure. Jaques's findings suggested that the difficulties encountered may result not so much from the unwilling-

ness of either management or employees to make the system work as from their confusion about their respective responsibilities. Management tended to feel that it should not trespass upon the responsibilities of workers' representatives on the Works Council, particularly in matters involving social relationships; hence, the managers tended to take passive roles. The workers' representatives tended to regard operative problems and policies as the responsibilities of management and adopted passive attitudes toward those matters. When the general manager of the factory accepted the idea that he was responsible for all aspects of organizational life and activity and that giving orders is not necessarily autocratic or unethical, he was able to "assume more fully his leadership mantle." In turn, his subordinates accepted theirs. With their responsibilities more clearly focused, they were able to initiate building a Works Council more broadly representative of the factory. Jaques's study suggested that members cannot act effectively in their own interests or in behalf of the group unless the leader exercises the functions of his or her role and takes the initiative in clarifying the definitions of roles throughout the system.

Power Sharing Cost-Reduction Plans. The Scanlon Plan is a means for sharing reductions in unit costs that are under the control of labor. Such reductions are determined first by establishing a normal labor cost for the factory. The labor cost may be arrived at by a joint worker-management agreement. Whenever labor costs fall below the norm, the workers receive anywhere from 50 to 100 percent of the amount. A second element of the Scanlon Plan is a suggestion system in which benefits that accrue from the reduction in the labor costs are shared with all workers in the plant. Reports indicate that as many as 80 percent of the suggestions submitted in a Scanlon Plan plant are accepted, while plants with individual suggestion plans commonly accept 25 percent. Furthermore, with the Scanlon Plan, there is no reason for the workers to withhold suggestions that will increase productivity; the only result is lower labor costs and consequently a bonus for everyone (Lesieur, 1958).

To determine the effects of the Scanlon Plan, Puckett (1958) surveyed 9 firms with 11 plants that produced many different products and whose workers' skills ranged from manual labor to highly technical. In the 11 plants that were followed over a 2-year period, the gain in productivity varied from 11 percent to 49 percent with a mean gain of 23 percent. Bonuses averaged 17 percent of the gross pay and were based on splitting the savings in labor costs, with 75 percent going to the workers and 25 percent to the company. Besides the direct benefits from increased production and higher profits, there were also better service to the customer, higher-quality products, an improved competitive position, and no decline in employment.

Many other power sharing cost-reduction practices now in evidence can be mentioned, some of which, such as suggestion systems, were first introduced by the Yale Manufacturing Company in 1892. The upward communication provided by quality circles and survey feedback systems are other examples.

Employee Stock Ownership Plans (ESOPs)

Rosen, Klein, and Young (1986) completed a survey of 2,804 employee owners of 37 firms with ESOPs. A majority of the respondents reported that stock ownership increased their interest in their company's financial performance, their personal identification with the company, and their desire to stay with the firm. However, the ESOP arrangement was seen to have less of an effect on their job satisfaction and their influence at the workplace or over company policy. Nor did it result in the managers treating them more like equals.

French and Rosenstein (1984) conducted a survey in a prosperous plumbing installation and services firm that began an employee stock ownership plan in 1958 and whose managerial employees held 76 percent of the shares, which have substantially increased in value. For 461 respondents, the amount of their equity in the firm correlated with their desire to be of influence in it. However, the extent to which they identified with the firm depended more on their status and perceived influence in the firm than on the amount of stock they held. Also, their amount of equity was unrelated to their job satisfaction, which correlated only with their perceived influence. But their interest in financial information about the firm did depend on their equity position and their white-collar status.

Mandated Programs

Legislative action in the United States has been directed toward establishing fairness in collective bargaining of employees and management and in employment practices. Elsewhere, power sharing through the representation of employees on supervisory and director's boards was legislatively mandated. Countries have tended to concentrate on one or two types of power-sharing legislation (Walker, 1975).

To illustrate, W. M. Blumenthal (1956) described the management of steel plants in Germany. Each plant was managed by a board of three men, one a union representative. The general trend was for the two management representatives to assume responsibility for production, while the union representative assumed responsibility for personnel, wages, and grievances.

Figures 14.1 and 14.2 describe the degree of legal support for individual workers and representative bodies in 12 European countries. For each country, the figures show the average right to participate in 16 specified decisions, ranging from such daily routine decisions as the assignment of tasks to workers to such long-range decisions as major capital investments. Each of the decisions was rated from "no right" to "final say," based on assessments of laws and collective bargaining agreements and on interviews with labor and legal experts and employers about company polic-

Figure 14.1. Workers' Legal Rights in 1976

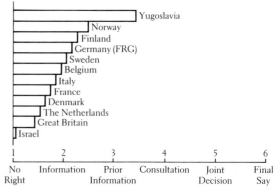

Average Right to Participate

SOURCE: *From "Industrial Democracy in Europe (IDE)." International Research Group,* Industrial Democracy in Europe. *Oxford: Clarendon Press, 1981.*

Figure 14.2. Legal Rights of Representative Bodies of Workers in 1976

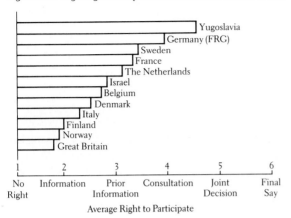

SOURCE: *From "Industrial Democracy in Europe (IDE)." International Research Group,* Industrial Democracy in Europe. *Oxford: Clarendon Press, 1981.*

ies. Then they were averaged (Industrial Democracy in Europe, International Research Group, 1981).

Effectiveness and Acceptance. Evaluations of the operations and effectiveness of workers' councils have been reported for West Germany (Hartmann, 1970; Wilpert, 1975), Norway (Thorsrud & Emery, 1970), Great Britain (K. Walker, 1974), Yugoslavia (Obradovic, 1970, 1975; Rus, 1970), Sweden (Link, 1971), and socialist countries (Sturmthal, 1961, 1964). Derber (1970) suggested that although effective power sharing implied in industrial democracy was considerable, it tends to be moderated by a number of factors. First, as managers become more professional, their professionalism imposes a barrier to involving employees in decision making. Second, the majority of employees are not strongly motivated to assume managerial responsibilities as long as their financial and other personal needs are satisfied. Third, when union officials and employee representatives become involved in management decision making, they stir up political and factional conflicts that weaken their influence with workers. Last, joint decision making involves too much of management's time for operations to run efficiently.

A number of other studies pointed to the differences among managers in their acceptance of industrial democracy and power sharing. In agreement with Derber,

Norrgren (1981a) found that Swedish managers who were young, had little seniority but much formal education, and were high in the hierarchy had positive beliefs and intentions about participation. Managers who were involved in white-collar union activities had positive beliefs and intentions and evaluated participative activities highly. Managers from several Canadian companies expressed more willingness to share power with employees if the managers felt they had more job security and influence and if they regarded their employees as competent (Long, 1982). Bass and Shackleton (1979) called attention to the exclusion of the lower- and middle-management levels from the participatory process when representatives of workers meet with top management. These lower-level managers, often ignored and eliminated from the mechanisms of industrial democracy, disassociate themselves from the participatory process and undermine its potential effectiveness.

After a carefully planned observational study of worker-management council meetings in Yugoslavia, Obradovic (1975) concluded that initiatives came mainly from the engineers, financial experts, and members of the Communist party, not from the rank-and-file employees serving as council representatives. The fewer attempts of ordinary workers to lead were unlikely to be successful. Consistent with this finding, Rubenowitz and Norrgren (1980) used survey questionnaires and interviews to study the effects of different forms of participation in 10 Swedish plants that varied in size from 40 to 830 employees. The actual participation of employees was much more of perceived consequence when formal agreements for power sharing included acceptance of a policy to promote decision making by employees in their daily work. Much less participation was perceived if it only involved formal participation by representatives of the employees. Rosenstein (1977) observed that just because a powerful trade union with a strong social mission is the entrepreneur and owner of industries, as is the case of the Israeli Histadrut, it does not necessarily mean that the participation of employees will be encouraged. Actually, the various power centers of the Histadrut—the managers, the trade union officials, the ideologists, and the politicians—have had to be persuaded and educated about the nature of the joint management program that is in effect. As of 1977, Histadrut had established such joint managements in 30 of its plants. Success depends on the continuing support of both top management and employees. Nevertheless, a 12-country longitudinal survey revealed extensive behavioral changes in organizational relationships that were derived from mandatory programs of industrial democracy (Industrial Democracy in Europe, International Research Group, 1979).

Selective Power Sharing. Bass and Rosenstein (1977) and Bass and Shackleton (1979) proposed that industrial democracy is most likely to work well for some issues, such as dealing with pay and benefits, career development, working conditions, and job security, but not for others, such as financial planning or marketing strategies. The 12-country consortium study (Industrial Democracy in Europe, International Research Group, 1981) revealed in detail the extent to which these arguments were valid. In the same way, a total of 103 top Scottish managers and shop stewards who were interviewed by Dickson (1980) tended to favor the direct participation of employees on safety committees and briefing groups and in dealing with the job enrichment of groups. The managers were less enthusiastic about the employees' participation through their representatives on company boards, works councils, and plantwide committees. However, shop stewards felt a bit more positive than the managers about the value of such representative participation. The managers saw the direct involvement of employees as a way to enhance communication and the acceptance of decisions. The shop stewards thought that both direct and representative participation were a moral right that contributed to the employee's morale if they were acknowledged by management.

A random sample of 7,832 employees from a total of 134 European firms in metal engineering, banks, and insurance were asked how much they were involved in the 16 decisions for which they had legal rights (see Figures 14.1 and 14.2). Their legally mandated involvement was more important in determining power sharing about long-term decisions. For workers in the 134 firms, the laws and regulations accounted for 24 percent of the variance in their involvement in short-term

decisions; 50 percent, in medium-range decisions; and 58 percent, in long-term decisions. With respect to the short-term decisions, the legal right of unions and other representative bodies to participate collectively in such decisions had a negative effect on the actual involvement of individual workers. As for the involvement of workers in medium- and long-term decisions, the right of both workers and their representatives to participate had a positive effect. The degree of power sharing that could be explained by legal norms was much higher than what could be explained by the firm's technology, organizational structure, or market conditions. It was concluded that the actual participation of employees depends on "an intricate interrelation of internal management practices and externally promoted support systems based on formal laws or collective bargaining agreements" (Industrial Democracy in Europe, International Research Group, 1981, p. 292).

Strauss and Rosenstein (1970) found the experience of introducing industrial democracy in different countries to be mixed:

> Most Indian plans have died, almost still-born. Israel had roughly the same experience in regards to the plant council program—and so did Norway with its work councils. In England, . . . "as shop stewards grow in importance, joint consultative committees either become negotiating committees indistinguishable from shop floor bargaining, or they fall into disuse." In France their effectiveness has been hampered by union-management and interunion rivalries, though in some instances they perform important welfare or shop-level bargaining functions.
>
> But most observers agree that participation has been a success, at least by very limited standards, in Yugoslavia, Sweden, the German iron and steel industry, and some American Scanlon Plan companies.

By success, Strauss and Rosenstein meant that in different locations, industrial democracy gave labor a sense of having won something. It broadened the scope of bargaining, strengthened management to the extent that the leaders of unions and workers were co-opted to advocate common goals, and to provide channels of communication and opportunities for training prospective new managers.

Power Sharing
at the Immediate Work-Group Level

Roethlisberger (1941) observed that any technological change by management may affect not only the physical but the social location of an individual in the organization. The possibility of social dislocation within the organization constitutes a severe threat to many members.

Individuals in leadership positions tend to feel more tolerant of change and stress than do those in follower positions. In addition to being more receptive, members in leadership positions usually have access to information that enables them to predict some consequences of change. The member in a follower position has less access to such information unless it is provided by the management. Rumor, imagination, and speculation often lead to grossly inaccurate evaluations of the effects of an announced change. Participation in planning change provides at least a minimum base of information on which a member may evaluate some possible effects of a given change on his or her work, status, and relationship to the organization. Considerations such as those discussed earlier have suggested the hypothesis that workers will feel more receptive to change if they are involved in planning it.

Reducing the power differences between superior and subordinate at the shop-floor level in the work group is a main theme of behavioral theorists and practitioners' interventions. "Every employee a manager" sums up M. S. Myers's (1968) changeover of supervisor-subordinate power relations. Formerly, the powerful supervisor fully planned for and controlled the performance of the powerless operator, whose only responsibilities were to carry out orders. Now, as much as possible, the operator becomes self-planning, self-directing, and self-controlling.

Legally mandated democracy is not a substitute for shop-floor democracy. The correlation between legally mandated democracy and participation in decisions that affect daily work was only .10 in the 12-country survey (Industrial Democracy in Europe, International Research Group, 1981). The workers' satisfaction with the firm was also unrelated to legally mandated democracy, which suggests that mandated democracy is not a substitute for participative management and democratic leadership. The newer Swedish Codetermination Act gave legal rights for employees to be consulted by their supervisors at the workplace. White- and blue-collar workers reported an increase in their own influence five years after the Swedish Codetermination Act was passed, but managers did not report increased power sharing with their bosses as a consequence of the act (Stymne, 1986).

Sharing the Power to Plan Change. Shifting the distribution of power results in a sharing of planning and control that have positive effects on the commitment, understanding, satisfaction, and productivity of workers. Structure still remains, but it is based not on differences in power but on structural design to which the workers have contributed. The utility of such self-planning was reaffirmed in a series of experiments by Bass (1970a), Bass (1977), and Bass and Leavitt (1963).

In a first simulation, Bass and Leavitt (1963) demonstrated the importance of self-planning, both to productivity and to satisfaction. Several simple exercises were devised. In each, trios of managers in training developed a plan for themselves and then exchanged plans with another trio. A counterbalanced order was used so that half the teams executed their own plan first and half executed the other team's plan first. Then they executed both plans. The result was that managers were more productive and satisfied with operating their own plan.

In a similar simulation, 1,416 managers in a training setting completed Exercise Organization (Bass, 1975h). As expected, the objective output and efficiency were significantly greater when they executed their own plans. Moreover, self-planning resulted in greater felt responsibility, job satisfaction, and satisfaction with the plan. However, the payoff was much greater when participants with practice (that is, more experience and knowledge) made their own plans than when those without practice did so.

The importance of maintaining some special elements that the supervisor can bring to the planning process, such as support, experience, and knowledge, was illustrated by Schlacter (1969), who studied 6 highway maintenance crews over 25 weeks. In two crews, the foremen assisted their supervisor in planning and reported results back to their crews. Two other crews assisted their superiors in planning. The third pair of crews assumed full responsibility for planning. The first two crews maintained stable job satisfaction scores and production records throughout the 25 weeks. The third pair of crews gained significantly in job satisfaction, but lost significantly in productivity. Similarly, Latham and Saari (1979) showed experimentally that supportive leadership resulted in higher goals being set by student participants than did nonsupportive leadership.[14]

Rationale. Reasons given by participants for the utility of reducing differences in power for the purposes of planning included these: (1) it reduces the sense of accomplishment when carrying out the plan, (2) it generates more efforts to confirm the validity of the plan by executing it successfully and more confidence to see that it can be done, (3) it may increase the commitment to see that the plan works well, (4) it may increase flexibility, room for modification, and initiative to make improvements, (5) it is likely to generate a greater understanding of the plan, (6) it may allow for the better use of human resources, (7) it may reduce communication problems and the consequent errors and distortions in following instructions, and (8) it may avoid competitive feelings among planners and those who must execute the plans (Bass, 1970a).

Utility of Self-managed Teams. Increasingly, project teams are being formed with informal leadership in which no one member is appointed as leader. Rather, power is fully shared in planning, operations, and control. Manz and Sims's (1980, 1984, 1986) research investigated the utility of such self-managed groups. More will be said about these groups elsewhere.[15]

The Redistribution of Power

House (1988) suggested that increased power sharing may come about through major shifts in environmental or technological demands that require the lodging of greater power with lower-status but expert employees.

Power sharing may come about through the replacement of managers and employees, by a deliberate redesign of the organization's structures and systems so critical information is broadly disseminated throughout the organization, by creating multiple centers of control, and by decoupling parts of the organization with different interests and unconnected requirements. However, the voluntary redistribution of power is likely to come about slowly and only after prolonged debate and conflict. Thus, Dalton, Barnes, and Zaleznik (1968) intervened to shift power downward from managers to scientists in departments of a research and development organization. The scientists at the different levels gained in functional power and favored an acceleration in the downward shift. But, at the same time, the managers at various levels experienced a reduction of their hierarchical power and consequently favored slowing the downward distribution of power.

The privileged, dominant coalitions in an organization will be reluctant to surrender power; they may shift technologies or move the organization into different environments to maintain their own competence-enhancing power.

Summary and Conclusions

The distribution of power in groups, organizations, and societies is a strong determinant of the leader-follower relationships that can and do occur. How power is distributed in the group or organization is associated with its structure of role relationships. Although the distribution of power is likely to be stable, behavioralists, in particular, argue for its equalization while structuralists favor its strengthening. However, personal and situational moderators need to be taken into account in determining whether differences in power need to be reduced or increased to promote effective operations and relationships. Different distributions of power are likely to exist side by side and to deal with the legitimacy, politics, expertise, and identification processes. The total power of a group, which can be increased or decreased, strongly affects the conformity of members, their persistence, and their changes in attitudes and behavior.

Group members exhibit a desire for structure, espe-

[14]Detailed discussions about supportive leadership will be found in Chapters 21, 23, and 24.
[15]See the index.

cially under conditions of stress, threat, and the pressure of tasks, but they also want to share power. The extent to which power sharing and structure are desired tends to vary with the personality of the individual and the demands of the situation. In general group and organizational members tend to feel more satisfied under moderate degrees of structure than under overly structured or totally unstructured conditions.

Power sharing, in the form of opportunities to discuss proposed changes, facilitates the acceptance of change by members who will be affected by it. Participation in planning and decision making regarding the change induces a still higher degree of acceptance. As a consequence, power-sharing programs and restructuring, both voluntary and legally mandated, have become common. Nevertheless, a variety of individual and situational factors moderate the impact of these power-sharing efforts. Individual managers and workers differ in their acceptance of power sharing. Their acceptance depends on the nature of the problems and decisions to be reached, as well as on whether the power sharing is voluntary or legally mandated, direct or through representatives. Much conflict may accompany the legitimation of such power sharing.

Conflict and Legitimacy in the Leadership Role

Although one president, Lyndon Johnson, wanted every American to love him, another president, Harry Truman, concluded that "if you can't stand the heat, stay out of the kitchen!" National leaders must settle for less than universal affection. They must be willing to be unloved and they must deal with conflict (J. M. Burns, 1978). And so must most other leaders, for conflict often attends the leadership role. No leader can be successful if he or she is not prepared to be rejected (T. O. Jacobs, 1970). Nonetheless, Levinson (1984, p. 133) pointed out that executives go to great lengths to avoid conflict because of their discomfort with feelings of anger:

> ... much of the irrational in management practices arises because of people's efforts to cope with their own anger and to avoid the anger of others. ... But the very fact that they have angry feelings, when they often feel it is wrong to be angry, leaves them feeling guilty.

To contend with these feelings of anger and guilt, they make irrational organizing and planning decisions to deny their anger and to appease their conscience.

Sources of Conflict

Appointed leaders with appropriate competencies and styles may still find their attempts to lead stymied because of numerous possible conflicts with their subordinates. The appointed leader may be resented as a representative of higher authority (Seaman, 1981), or subordinates may favor the appointment of someone else. The leader and the subordinates may have different opinions about the means and ends of their efforts, as well as other ideas. For example, college presidents and vice presidents may disagree about their institutions' goals, although they generally are more likely to agree about means (Birnbaum, 1987a).

Role Conflict

Sources of role conflict for leaders include the ambiguity of the role, personal inadequacy to meet the demands of the role, various incongruities, incompatibility among several roles, conflicting demands, mixed costs and benefits associated with playing the role, and discrepancies between actual and self-accorded status. Role ambiguity occurs when the leaders' roles are not clearly defined and the leaders cannot determine what they are expected to do (R. L. Kahn, Wolfe, Quinn, et al., 1964). Or leaders may not be able to meet the demands of the task or the interpersonal demands of their role (D. J. Levinson, 1959). An incongruence occurs when, for instance, old, experienced workers are assigned to young, inexperienced supervisors. The workers are likely to perceive a discrepancy between their seniority and their rank in the status hierarchy (S. Adams, 1953).

When an individual plays two or more roles in a group, the demands of the several roles may be incompatible (interrole incompatibility); for example, the role of group representative may be incompatible with the role of enforcer of discipline (Stouffer, 1949). Or there may be within-role conflict. That is, when different followers or subgroups make conflicting demands on a given leadership role, the occupant of the role will find it difficult to exhibit any course of action that will satisfy the various sets of expectations (Merton, 1940).

Conflict can occur if one would lose power, esteem, autonomy, or self-determination by joining or forming another group. For example, members may reject the opportunity to join suggested coalitions with others in three-way bargaining situations, even if it would be otherwise rewarding, because joining would cause them to lose esteem in relation to the other members (Hoffman, Festinger, & Lawrence, 1954). Similarly, analyses of French cabinets and college interfraternity councils led Holt (1952a, 1952b) to infer that otherwise mutually rewarding coalitions were rejected because the loss of autonomy or self-determination was involved.

Conflicts and disagreements may arise in the legitimation process—in the right to function as a leader. Thus, when kingdoms were reconstituted in the nineteenth century in such countries as Belgium, Bulgaria, Greece, and Sweden, outsiders from Germany, France, and Great Britain were legitimated as kings to avoid internal dissent. This selection of a presumably impartial outsider as constitutional monarch is consistent with the tendency for a leader to be acknowledged as the one organizational member with the legitimate power to play the role of final arbitrator, the superordinate whose judgment settles disputes among followers. This function was often believed to be critical for the avoidance of anarchy in political states. The maintenance and security of the state depended on the existence of a legitimate position at the top whose occupant could arbitrate conflicts among all followers. Daum (1975) looked at the impact of internal promotion versus bringing in an outsider to lead the group. The results were as expected. The selection of a leader from within the group tended to cause the remaining members to express lower overall satisfaction and to reduce their voluntary participation following the change.

If members can agree on the leadership structure, they are more likely to be satisfied with the group, according to results obtained by Shelley (1960b). Similarly, Bass and Flint (1958a) found that early agreement about who shall lead increases a group's effectiveness.

In the same way, Heslin and Dunphy (1964) noted that the satisfaction of members was high when the degree of status consensus among them was also high.

Organizational Locus

One's location in an organizational hierarchy will make a difference in how much role ambiguity one experiences. Culbert and McDonough (1985) suggested that much of the conflict observed in organizations starts at the top with excessive competition among the senior executives with special interests who are vying for power. Without their awareness, a "falling-domino effect" is created; the competitive conflicts at the top set off conflicts at each echelon below. Culbert and Mc-Donough (1985) attributed much of the conflict in industry to the failure of those who are in conflict to recognize that they actually had compatible interests. Sometimes they did not highlight one individual's contributions to another or to the organization and sometimes, they did not achieve a common frame of reference so that each could see that the other's efforts "made organizational sense."

In addition, more role ambiguity occurs for lower-level managers. The responsibilities and authority of first-line supervisors and middle managers are less clearly defined than those of top management. Uncertain about what they are allowed and expected to do, they experience more tension than do the top managers and feel less satisfied with their jobs. Thus, D. C. Miller and Schull (1962) reported that middle managers register more role stress than do top managers and more frequently state that they are unclear about the scope of their responsibilities and what their colleagues expect of them. Likewise, Brinker (1955) reported that first-line supervisors in industry work under more or less constant frustration because they are not given enough authority to believe they are part of management or to solve the problems presented by their subordinates. Supervisors of 140 management clubs wanted to be more closely identified with higher management because most of them felt that they did not know the company policy on many important matters and, as a result, they had to work in the dark (Mullen, 1954).

Moore and Smith (1953) found that it was noncommissioned officers in the military, rather than higher-ups, who felt constant pressure because of their inadequate authority, the lack of distinction between supervisors and technicians, and conflicts among the leadership philosophies of different levels of organization. Consistent with all these findings, Wispé and Thayer's (1957) study found less consensus about the functions of the assistant manager than those of the manager. The assistant manager's role was ambiguous in that both the manager and the assistant manager did not know whether certain functions were obligatory or optional. Strain and tension were higher for the assistant manager in the more ambiguous role.

Those at the bottom and top of their union hierarchy have unflattering opinions about each other. S. M. Peck (1966) found that union stewards saw corruption in their top union officials but justified the unethical activities of the top officials on the grounds that strong methods are required to cope with existing conditions and that corruption abounds everywhere. At the same time, Miles and Ritchie (1968) reported that although high-ranking union officials "agreed" that shop stewards and rank-and-file members should be encouraged to participate more in decision making and that such participation would result in improved morale, better decisions, and willingness to accept the goals of bargaining, they were "uncertain" whether stewards and rank-and-file members would be likely to set reasonable goals for themselves if given the opportunity.

Conflict arises between managers and professionals and between those in boundary-spanning activities that link activities outside and inside the organization, such as marketing, and those in internal operations, such as manufacturing. Interviews established that boundary spanners had interpersonal and cooperative orientations, while the line managers emphasized authority, power, and rationality (Anonymous, undated). Conflict arises between staff and line workers and between individuals, in general, who work in different parts of the same organization. For example, there is a continual tension between university administrators and faculty members and between hospital administrators and community physicians; much of this tension is due to

their differences in perception (Browne & Golembiewski, 1974), attributions (Sonnenfeld, 1981), and cognitive orientations (Kochan, Cummings, & Huber, 1976). Nystrom (1986) found systematic differences in the work-related beliefs of those middle managers who were responsible for the supervision of line personnel and those who were responsible for the "technostructure" of designing the work processes, specifying outputs, and controlling employees' skills in the same manufacturing organization. Middle line managers believed significantly more strongly in the desirability of structuring people's work activities than did the technostructure managers, who had significantly stronger beliefs in internal than external loci of control. The middle managers also were significantly more motivated to manage than were the technostructure managers.

Control of Resources

Another source of continuing conflict is over the limited control that managers have of the resources they need to get their work done (Pfeffer, 1981). In a study of laboratory directors of hospitals, Jongbloed and Frost (1985) found that the laboratory directors were constrained by numerous external individuals and groups, including the physicians who were responsible for ordering the laboratory's tests, the hospital's higher administration, and the head of the Department of Pathology, as well as accreditation councils, labor unions, and professional societies. One laboratory director coped satisfactorily with this conflict; another did not. The successful laboratory director devoted a lot of energy to lobby for increased resources and gained more needed funding. The unsuccessful director concentrated on the technical aspects of the laboratory operations and was forced to continue with a less-adequate budget.

Pfeffer and Salancik (1978) examined the amount of discretion mayors had in determining items for their cities' budgets. They found that mayors who dealt with powerful organized interest groups, such as businesses, professional societies, and labor unions, had less discretion over the budgets than did mayors whose cities had a higher proportion of nonwhites, governmental employees, and construction workers, and a lower median income.

Relation to Leaders' Performance and Satisfaction

It is not surprising that both role ambiguity and role conflict tend to be deleterious to the performance and satisfaction of leaders. Uncertainty about whether one's performance is adequate is a symptom of role ambiguity and is a source of ineffectiveness, according to Pepinsky, Pepinsky, Minor, and Robin (1959), who studied experimental groups working on a construction problem. The leaders of half the groups were required to work with a superior officer whose approval or disapproval of transactions could be predicted. The leaders of the other groups were required to deal with a superior whose behavior could not be predicted. The researchers found that the productivity of the team was higher under conditions of high predictability than under conditions of low predictability.

Rizzo, House, and Lirtzman (1970) found that with more perceived role ambiguity and conflict, less overall leadership behavior and less job satisfaction were reported in two industrial firms. Tosi (1971) also found that role conflict was negatively related to job satisfaction but not necessarily to the effectiveness of the group. Nevertheless, supervisors seem to be able to tolerate role conflict better if they do not have to interact much with their own immediate bosses. In a study of seven companies, supplemented by a national survey, R. L. Kahn, Wolfe, Quinn, et al. (1964) found that role conflict increased as the ambiguity of the situation increased and the rate of communication with one's superiors was high. Job satisfaction decreased under these same conditions. They inferred that the source of most role conflicts are in interactions with one's immediate superiors. Subsequent studies corroborated that as much as 88 percent of all role conflict was with one's boss.

In all, anyone in a hierarchy needs to act both cooperatively and competitively. Roberts (1986) surveyed 350 managers from three levels of management in two business firms and two universities. In all four organizations, managers reported using both cooperative and competitive styles in their relations with their bosses, peers, and subordinates. This is likely to be one of the reasons why, as will be detailed in Chapter 36, successful performance in a leaderless group discussion is a valid predictor of success in management positions (Bass, 1954a), since both situations call for cooperating and competing with the others.

Incongruities in Status, Esteem, and Ability

Status-Status Incongruence

Ordinarily, people have multiple roles and positions and are accorded status for each. Each status may be matched in value with the others or it may be incongruent. In organizations that are a mix of bureaucracies and collegial entities, conflict arises because the same individuals must play roles with various degrees of status and importance, depending on the decisions involved. For example, in a university hospital, the university president, the vice president for health sciences, and the medical school faculty will have more influence than will the hospital's governing board over the selection of the dean of medicine, the hospital director, and the chief of the medical staff, but the reverse will occur on issues about the financial integrity of the hospital. Among 26 such decision-making issues, Wilson and McLaughlin (1984) found that there was little correlation of the medical school department head's influence, the dean's influence, and the hospital director's influence. The influence of the incumbants of a particular position in the hospital depended mainly on the issue.

Conflict results if there is an incongruity between one's status in one situation and in another. For example, military enlisted personnel who had high-status civilian positions were more dissatisfied with their officers than were enlisted personnel who came from civilian jobs whose status was lower (Stouffer, Suchman, DeVinney, et al., 1949).

Search for Congruence. People tend to try to increase status congruence. In class-conscious Britain, 156 first-line supervisors varied in the social class to which they felt they belonged. Those who perceived themselves to be higher in social class more readily identified with their senior managers. And the more they thought that their role as supervisor was lower in status than the status of their social class, the more they identified with senior managers (Child, Pearce, & King, 1980). Jaques (1952) observed much anxiety and confusion when a British worker (low status) was assigned to chair (high status) a conference with management; relief and satisfaction came only after the managing director assumed the chair. In the same way, Trow and Herschdorfer (1965) demonstrated that groups with incongruent status structures that were free to change did so, whereas those with equally free but with congruent structures did not change. Furthermore, groups with high degrees of status incongruency were rated low in the performance of tasks and in the satisfaction of their members. Similarly, in a study of 50 workers in one department of a firm, Zaleznik, Christensen, and Roethlisberger (1958) found that members with high status congruence were most likely to meet the productivity standards of management. Likewise, S. Adams (1953) demonstrated that group members were better satisfied when leadership and other high-level positions were occupied by persons who ranked high in age, education, experience, and prestige. The group's productivity tended to suffer when the high-status positions were occupied by persons who ranked low in other aspects of status (age, education, experience, and social position). Yet Singer (1966) found that although status incongruence in groups was associated with tension, disorganization, and hostile communications, it did not result in lower productivity by the group or in the dissatisfaction of the group members.

Two Leaders. Groups with two appointed, elected, or emergent leaders are inherently likely to generate conflict. Osborn, Hunt, and Skaret (1977) looked at the potential conflicts between the two leaders—the chapter adviser and the elected president—in each of 33 local chapters of a national business fraternity whose duties overlapped. The authors concluded that organizational effectiveness would be enhanced if only one leader played an active role in influencing subordinates and exchanges with other units. Similar conclusions about the inherent conflict in the overlapping roles of

two leaders were reached by Whyte (1943), who examined these two-leader configurations in mental institutions.[1]

When coleaders are appointed as joint heads of social work training groups, conflicts between the leaders will block the group's development. But if the two leaders can work together and resolve their potential disagreements, advantages will accrue in the greater opportunities to vary their roles, the wider perspectives for solving problems, and better management of and support and reinforcement for the group (Galinsky & Schopler, 1980). Such duality is built into German firms, which are led by a technical director and a commercial director and have no single president, as in U.S. firms. Again, although conflicting loyalties may be created, the benefits of the organizational design include equal attention to the quality of the products and to commercial success.

Formal-Informal Incongruence

The mismatching of the formal and informal structures in any organization may be a threat to an organization (Selznick, 1948). Moreno (1934/1953) noted that formal groupings that a higher authority superimposes on informal, spontaneous groupings are a chronic source of conflict. In the same way, Roethlisberger and Dickson (1947) associated the relationship of workers' dissatisfaction with the discrepancies between the formal and informal organizations of workers in an industrial plant.

Cause and effect may be reversed. Inadequacy and dissatisfaction with the formal organization may give rise to an unrelated informal organization that is at variance with the formal one and that emerges as a means to resist the coercive demands of high-status members (Shartle, 1949b). Such an informal organization may arise if the formal organization cannot provide the members with rewards, such as recognition or opportunity (Pfiffner, 1951), and to bypass incompetent, high-status members to achieve the goals of the formal organization (Lichtenberg & Deutsch, 1954).

When the formal and informal structures are

---

[1]See also reviews by Hunt, Hill, and Reaser (1973); Kerr, Schriesheim, Murphy, and Stogdill (1974); and Nealy and Fiedler (1968).

merged, however, conflict is lower and the group's performance is better. Stouffer, Suchman, DeVinney, et al. (1949) observed that discussions were more satisfying to the participants when the informal leaders were given higher status by being placed in the position of discussion leaders. In the same way, Haythorn (1954a) reported that the performance and cohesiveness of bomber crews were highly related to the extent to which the aircraft commander (the formal leader) performed the informal leadership roles usually expected of the formal group leader.

Role-Role Incongruence

Playing a variety of roles is not necessarily stressful. The average individual learns to play the role of child, sibling, parent, subordinate, peer, and superior without apparent effort. However, some individuals play only dependent roles well, and others are content only when they play the role of superior. Professionals tend to assume the role of authoritative, independent agents. Professional actors seem to enjoy enacting a great variety of roles but can experience personal conflict in separating their real selves from the parts they play; that is, in separating their private lives from their public images. Although we may not be accomplished actors, we can play a variety of roles without apparent stress if the different roles are compatible. Nevertheless, we may find different roles to be incompatible with each other and, therefore, a source of conflict for us. Thus, Getzels (1963) found that schoolteachers were expected to maintain a socioeconomic role that was higher than their salaries would sustain. On the one hand, in their role as citizens, they were often expected to be more active in church affairs and less active in political affairs than the average citizen; on the other hand, in their professional roles, they were expected to be certified as experts in various fields of knowledge, but they could be challenged by any parent or taxpayer. Thus, teachers were subject to several sources of strain in each of several incompatible roles. Getzels and Guba (1954) also studied individuals with two or more roles that contained contradictory or mutually exclusive expectations. They found that such role conflict tended to increase when one of the individual's roles was perceived as illegitimate.

Status-Esteem Incongruence

Conflict ensues and the group's performance is adversely affected when the group members who are in positions of importance (high status) are not esteemed (Bass, 1960). J. G. Jenkins's (1948) study of two naval air squadrons—one with high morale and one with low morale—found that in the high-morale group, the squadron commander and executive officer were most often nominated as individuals with whom others would want to fly (that is, they were high in status and esteemed), but in the low-morale squadron, nominations were unrelated to the occupation of the positions of commander or executive officer. Conversely, Palmer and Myers (1955) found a correlation of .38 between the effectiveness with which 40 antiaircraft radar crews maintained their equipment and the extent to which they esteemed their key noncommissioned officers. Similarly, Bass, Flint, and Pryer (1957b) obtained a correlation of .25 between the extent to which status was correlated with esteem in an experimental group and the subsequent effectiveness of the group. Gottheil and Vielhaber (1966) also observed that groups performed more effectively when their leaders were esteemed. According to interview studies, Shils and Janowitz (1948) concluded that the German enlisted soldiers' high morale and motivation to resist surrender during World War II seemed to be due primarily to their esteem for their officers. In the same way, among the Israeli soldiers in Lebanon in 1982 who believed the incursion to be immoral, morale remained high only if they highly esteemed their officers (Gal, 1987).

Firestone, Lichtman, and Colamosca (1975) had college students elect their own group leader after participating in an initially leaderless group discussion. The groups that were subsequently most effective in an emergency were those that were led by the elected member with the highest ratings for performance in the leaderless group discussion. Those that were worst in the emergency were led by the person they believed had the lowest ratings for performance in the preceding leaderless group discussion.

Status-Influence Incongruence

Ordinarily, emergence and success of leaders are higher among those who are higher in status and become a source of conflict if a person of low status attempts to lead. Watson (1982) coded the taped interactions of 16 leader-subordinate dyads in a goal-setting discussion to discern their specific effects on each other. The dyads were made up of an elected leader of a student team and one randomly chosen subordinate team member. When the elected leaders attempted to dominate by an abrupt change of topic, by challenging a previous comment, or by an ideational or personal challenge, the subordinates were most likely to respond with deference and a willingness to relinquish some but not all behavioral options. When the subordinates tried to dominate, however, the leaders resisted and competed for control of the situation. Thus, when persons of higher status, the elected leaders, acted in congruence with their status, the subordinates complemented and completed the interaction with deference and simple agreement, but when the subordinates with lower status tried to dominate, the leaders resisted.

Inversions can occur in which those who are lower in status are able to be more influential than those who are higher in status. Such inversions can be a source of continuing resentment and hidden conflict when the high status figures grudgingly acquiesce to those who are lower in status. Obviously, subordinates can be more influential over leaders who abdicate their role. Pettigrew (1973) gave examples of situations in which subordinates or those who are otherwise lower in status have influence over those who are higher in status. Generally, in these situations, higher-status superiors became dependent on their subordinates (Mechanic, 1962). Physicians can become so dependent on attendants in hospital wards that the attendants can block reforms. Prison guards can become dependent on the inmates for the inmates' good behavior. Although guards can report prisoners for disobedience, too many such reports from the same guards create the impression among their superiors that they are ineffective. As a consequence, guards agree to let certain violations by prisoners go unreported in exchange for the prisoners' cooperation in other matters. Experts can keep their superiors dependent on them for information, particularly about risky innovations, and thereby maintain power over their superiors (Crozier, 1964). Soviet subordinates can hold their superiors hostage with the knowledge of the illegal acts their superiors committed

for their group to meet its production quotas (Granick, 1962).

Status-Competence Incongruence

It seems obvious that if those with high status are incompetent for their role assignments, the group will be less productive, successful, and satisfied. Conversely, competence at high-status levels should produce less conflict, more satisfaction, and group success. Yet, as was noted in Chapters 4, 5, and 7, some curvilinearity in outcomes may be expected, for leaders sometimes may be too able for the groups they lead. Nevertheless, strong positive associations between such congruence and effectiveness have been found in surveys and experiments. Woods (1913) related the judged ability (strong, mediocre, or weak) of 386 European sovereigns from the eleventh century to 1789 to their states' performance. A correlation of .60 was found between judged ability of a sovereign and ratings of the political, material, and economic progress of the state the sovereign headed. Similarly, Rohde (1954c) reported correlations up to .63 between the success of groups in learning to go through a maze and the adequacy of the pretest performance of the persons in charge of each of the groups. Furthermore, in a comparison of nine orientation discussion groups, Stouffer, Suchman, DeVinney, et al. (1949) observed that members were much more likely to say they "got a lot out of the discussion" when the member of the group who was chosen to lead the discussion was better educated. Bass (1961c) found that successful leadership was more highly related to ability in effective groups than in ineffective groups.

The choice of a competent leader is a major determinant of the effectiveness of a team and stimulates effective mutual influence among other group members (Borg, 1956). Thus, after analyzing a large number of small-group studies, Heslin and Dunphy (1964) concluded that group members are most likely to achieve consensus on the status structure of the group when (1) the leader is perceived to be highly competent, (2) a leader who is high in both group-task and group-maintenance functions emerges, or (3) two mutually supportive leaders emerge, one specializing in task functions and the other in group-maintenance functions. (But two leaders often present problems, as was noted earlier.)

The mismatching of status and competence in a group is likely to result in the downgrading of the group leader. Thus, Ghiselli and Lodahl (1958a) found that a supervisor was likely to be poorly regarded by higher managers if he was assigned to a group containing a line worker whose supervisory ability was superior to his. Goldman and Fraas (1965) noted the importance of matching competence and status in their comparison of groups whose leaders were elected, appointed for competence, or appointed randomly. They found that groups with leaders who were appointed for competence did best, groups with elected leaders did the next best, and groups without leaders or whose leaders had been appointed randomly did the worst.

Other Incongruities with Ability. Exline and Ziller (1959) assembled groups in which members held positions that were incongruent in competence and power and other groups, in which competence and power were congruent. The participants rated the congruent groups as significantly more congenial, as exhibiting stronger intermember agreement, and as involving less overlap of activities.

Evan and Simmons (1969) studied students who were hired to work as proofreaders. In the first experiment, their pay (supposedly an indicator of the worth and importance of their position) was inconsistent with their acknowledged level of competence. In the second experiment, their pay was inconsistent with their level of authority. Incongruity, particularly the underpayment of students in relation to their authority, resulted in a reduction in the quality of work and in conformity to the organization's rules.

A superior's and subordinate's differences of opinion about the difficulty of achieving competence in the superior's job may be another source of conflict. In an eight-country sample of 1,600 managers, the average time that senior executives thought it would take their subordinates to learn the senior executive's job was 18 months; their subordinates estimated it would take them fewer than 6 months (Heller & Wilpert, 1981).

Incongruence of Personality and Expectations

As may be expected, incongruities between the organization or group members' personality and the roles required of them result in reduced effectiveness. Smelser (1961) selected students who scored either high or low on a personality test of dominance. The least productive two-person groups were composed of pairs in which the personality-assessed submissive partner was assigned a role that required dominance and the personality-assessed dominant partner was given a role that required submissiveness. The most productive groups were those in which role assignments were consistent with the personality assessments of the members.

Requisite personality may be a matter of expectations. Violated expectations generate conflict. Lipham (1960) tested the hypothesis that personality traits that are compatible with the expectations about a leadership role will be related to the leader's effectiveness. In a study of school principals, Lipham found that those who scored high on expected characteristics, such as drive, emotional control, and sociability, were rated more effective than were those who scored high on unexpected characteristics, such as submissiveness and abasement.

In a study of insurance agencies, Wispé (1955, 1957) found that successful agents were characterized by a strong drive for success. But the same attitude toward success, when exhibited by the agency manager, was at variance with the agents' expectations of a more humane, considerate orientation toward their problems. Thus, the characteristic that was perceived to contribute to successful selling was not necessarily expected to contribute to effective management.

Overt conflict can be avoided (at a price) if those of lower status hide their abilities from those of higher status. College coeds used to "play dumb" on dates, just as black subordinates used to display "feeble-mindedness" in dealing with white superiors. Ordinarily, a better way for an organization to avoid conflict and to enhance satisfaction and performance is to develop suitable promotional policies that match the competence of employees with their status (Bass, 1960).

Within-Role Conflict

Culbert and McDonough (1980) stated that the failure of individuals to align their own needs for personal meaning, identity, and success with what they believe the organization needs to receive from those in their roles is at the heart of individual members' conflicts within an organization. Organizational and personal needs must be fused to allow both to reach high levels of achievement and satisfaction (Lester, 1981).

Brandon (1965) observed that the negative affect associated with status incongruence in groups is largely attributable to discrepancies between the role performance of the role players and their expectations. An individual experiences such stress when different individuals or groups make contradictory demands on his or her role that cannot be satisfied by any compatible course of action.

Discordant Expectations

Discrepancies between a role player's role expectations and the expectations of his or her subordinates, peers, superiors, and clients about the role have been studied extensively as fundamental sources of conflict. Similar attention has been paid to the discrepancies between what is done and what ought to be done. Thus, Colmen, Fiedler, and Boulger (1954) reported little agreement among 45 leaders in the U.S. Air Force in evaluating their own duties. Further confusion resulted from the discrepancy between what potential leaders thought they ought to do and what they actually did do. Halpin (1957b) found little relationship between how aircraft commanders and school superintendents said they might behave and how their subordinates said they actually behaved.

Stogdill, Scott, and Jaynes (1956) asked members of a large naval organization to describe what they did and what they ought to do. In addition, subordinates were asked to describe what their immediate superiors did and ought to do. Self-descriptions and self-expectations were rather highly related; the average correlation for 45 items of behavior was above .70. Not only did the superiors perceive themselves as behaving very much as they thought they should behave, but the subordinates also described their superiors as behaving very much as the subordinates expected them to behave. The average correlation between the subordinates' descriptions and expectations of superiors was above .50. However, the subordinates' *self-expectations* were much more highly related to their *expectations* for their superiors than their *self-descriptions* were related to their *descriptions* of their superiors; that is, subordi-

nates appeared to entertain similar expectations for themselves and for their superiors, although their descriptions of their own and their superiors' behavior were not as similar. Except for handling paperwork and other forms of individual effort, however, they did not perceive that their own behavior resembled that of their superiors. Only in the leader-behavior variables were the subordinates' self-descriptions somewhat close to their descriptions of their superiors' behavior.

Discrepancy scores were computed by subtracting the score that was based on the description of what they did from what they said they ought to do. The discrepancy score for each item for both superiors and subordinates was correlated with the superiors' degree of responsibility[2] according to their subordinates. Discrepancies between superiors' self-descriptions and their self-expectations were highly related to their level of responsibility. Superiors who obtained high scores for their level of responsibility from their subordinates perceived themselves as having too much responsibility and as acting as representatives of their followers more extensively than they should. They also reported spending too little time inspecting the organization and too much time in paperwork and engaging in all forms of leadership behavior more extensively than they should. Discrepancies between subordinates' self-descriptions and self-expectations were greater at higher organizational levels where their superiors were recipients of frequent interactions. Under these conditions, the subordinates perceived themselves to be doing more than they should in attending conferences, interviewing personnel, handling paperwork, and representing their own subordinates. When superiors delegated a great deal, their subordinates thought that they, the subordinates, had too much responsibility and spent less time than they should in coordination and professional activities.

Along similar lines, Triandis (1959a) found that the smaller the discrepancy between workers' ideal and actual descriptions of their supervisor's behavior, the better liked was the supervisor by the workers. Results obtained by Holden (1954) indicated that the greater the extent to which the leader's behavior conformed to the members' expectations, the greater was the productiv-

[2]See Chapter 16.

ity of the group. Havron and McGrath (1961) suggested that the leaders of highly effective groups either behave as expected or are successful in inducing group members to form ideals that are similar to the actual behavior of the leaders. Thus, Foa (1956), who studied supervisors and workers in Israeli factories, found that supervisors and workers agreed on the ideal behavior for a supervisor, but that they did not agree on what the supervisor actually did. The more there was agreement between the ideal and perceived behavior of the supervisor, the better satisfied were the workers with their supervisor. Workers who identified with their supervisor tended to attribute to the supervisor the ideals that they held. Ambivalent workers attempted to conform to the ideal attributed to their supervisor but were aware of the supervisor's deviation from the ideal. Indifferent workers felt less inclined to accept the ideal of the supervisor in their own behavior and were also less likely to notice discrepancies between the supervisor's ideal and real behavior. However, F. J. Davis (1954) failed to corroborate these effects among U.S. Air Force officers in that the successful adjustment of the followers did not depend on their agreement with the leader about the leader's role.

The Man or Woman in the Middle

Neuberger (1983) saw the supervisor as the focus of multilateral expectations that could be ambiguous, conflicting, and contradictory. Rules, regulations, and structure do not necessarily provide solutions to such conflicts, which can result in political behavior and unstable leadership behavior.

Conflict may arise because there are decided differences in what members who are at different levels of the organization expect is appropriate behavior for them. L. W. Porter (1959) reported that first-level supervisors saw themselves as careful and controlled in their approach to the job and to other people. Their second-level managers, in contrast, described themselves as enterprising, original, and bold. First-level supervisors differed from line workers as much as they differed from higher-level managers; they perceived themselves to be significantly more careful and controlled than the workers saw themselves. The first-level supervisory role imposed demands for behavioral patterns that differed from those of superiors and subordinates.

This is a common dilemma. Like everyone else at each successive level in an organizational hierarchy, the supervisor is a man or woman in the middle. Such persons face conflicting role demands from at least two sources—their superiors and their subordinates. Although the person in the middle is likely to be subjected to competing demands from numerous other sources—peers, higher authority, rules, suppliers, and customers—most attention has been paid to the conflicting demands from superiors and subordinates (Gardner & Whyte, 1945; Smith, 1948). Superiors expect results, initiative, planning, firmness, and structure. Subordinates expect recognition, opportunity, consideration, approachability, encouragement, and representation (Brooks, 1955). Thus, Pfeffer and Salancik (1975) demonstrated that their superiors expected more task behavior from first-line supervisors while their subordinates expected more socializing from them. Likewise, Snoek (1966) found that supervisors "in the middle" experienced more conflict than did operatives "at the bottom." Supervisors had a wider diversity of interactions than did the operating personnel, and the conflicting demands placed on them led them to experience more role strain.

In military organizations, officers above and enlisted personnel below disagree on what characterizes the good noncommissioned officer in between them (U.S. Air Force, 1952). Factor-analytic studies by J. V. Moore (1953) showed, for example, that subordinates of officers favored their being less strict, whereas superiors of the officers emphasized military bearing and ability. Halpin (1957b) found that commanders of aircrews who emphasized consideration were most highly rated by their subordinates, whereas those who initiated structure were more likely to be rated effective leaders by their superiors. Similarly, Zenter (1951) noted that 87 percent of the officers studied thought that a good noncommissioned officer follows orders, but only 44 percent of the enlisted men accepted this idea. At the same time, 49 percent of enlisted men believed that a good noncommissioned officer has to gain popularity, whereas only 7 percent of officers agreed with them. One discordant note to all these findings was the failure of Graen, Dansereau, and Minami (1972b) to find the expected discrepancy between subordinates' and superiors' role expectations of executives in the middle.

The conflicts of middle management were reflected in a 1982 opinion research poll which found that over half the respondents had "lost confidence in their superiors"; 69 percent saw too many decisions being made (and made poorly) at the top by persons who were unfamiliar with the particular problems (Fowler, 1982). Adding to the middle managers' malaise was the job insecurity brought on by the drastic reductions in middle-management positions in the 1980s (Clutterbuck, 1982a)—a happening predicted 30 years earlier by Leavitt and Whisler (1958), who forsaw that dramatic improvements in information processing would substitute for this level of management.

Other Sources of Within-Role Conflict

Differences in perceived needs, values, interests, and goals are a structural source of conflict among managers at different hierarchical levels as well as between leaders and followers in the community. For example, Fiedler, Fiedler, and Camp (1971) showed that whereas community leaders thought that poor government, neighborhood disunity, and the failure of public services were the concerns of consequence, householders believed that crime, immorality, traffic, and unemployment were the issues that needed attention. Managers and union leaders both generally overemphasize the importance of pay as a source of dissatisfaction of employees and underemphasize the importance of such concerns as security and opportunity (Bass & Ryterband, 1979).

Contradictory demands may stem from discrepancies between one's immediate work group and one's reference group. At some colleges, professors may be caught between the demands of their cosmopolitan, professional research-oriented reference groups and the role demands of their local campus for high-quality teaching and good relations with students. Industrial scientists may be caught between their professional reference groups' demands that they get their work published and their business firms' demands for secrecy. That these conflicts are a source of dissatisfaction are illustrated in an industrial study by Browne

and Neitzel (1952), who found that workers' satisfaction declined as the disagreement between what their leaders demanded of them and what was wanted by their reference groups increased. Similarly, Jacobson (1951) and Jacobson, Charters, and Lieberman (1951) studied foremen, union stewards, and workers. Foremen expected the stewards to play a passive role in the organization, whereas the stewards and the workers expected the stewards to play an active role on behalf of employees and the union. Foremen and stewards whose expectations deviated from the norm of their reference group got along more easily with each other.

Supervisors in training are often caught in a conflict when their superiors are opposed to what the supervisors are being taught by their trainers. The success or failure of the trainers depends on the trainees' supervisors. Trainers are more likely to succeed in modifying the supervisors' behavior if the supervisors' superiors show interest in the program, participate in its development, and take the course first (W. Mahler, 1952).

Politicians must continually cope with conflict between what they must do and what they would prefer to do. They must choose between what they find expedient and what they know is right. Personal integrity has to be sacrificed to unholy alliances. For Henry IV of France, the Protestant Huguenot, "Paris was worth a mass." For Adolf Hitler and Joseph Stalin, making a deal with each other bought time. For President Dwight D. Eisenhower, keeping silent in the face of Senator Joseph McCarthy's virulent attacks on George Marshall, Eisenhower's close friend, was justified as a means of maintaining the Republican coalition. Presidents Ronald Reagan and George Bush both embraced the agenda of the Far Right while campaigning for election but tended to give a lower priority to many of the right wing's demands once they were elected.

To some extent, role conflict and its effects are in the eye of the beholder. Maier and Hoffman's (1965) study of role-playing groups found that when the discussion leader perceived interpersonal conflict in terms of difficult subordinates, the group reached a lower-quality decision than it did when the leader saw disagreement as a source of innovation and new ideas.

Identification. Identification with superiors or subordinates appears to be a key to understanding the man or woman in the middle. Potential conflicts with supervisors and subordinates depend on with whom identification and similarity are sought. Thus, Pfeffer and Salancik (1978) observed that when leaders were more responsive to their subordinates' demands, the leaders' characteristics and activities were more like those of their subordinates. The leaders were more responsive to their boss's pressures to produce when the leaders' activities were more like those of their own superiors. A second study found that supervisors who were required to engage in a lot of peer-oriented interdepartmental coordination were less likely to be responsive to their subordinates.

D. T. Campbell and his associates developed various methods of measuring identification with superiors and subordinates. Of the variety of independent subscales that emerged (Campbell, Burwen, & Chapman, 1955), the most promising were identification with discipline, superior-subordinate orientation, and eagerness for responsibility and advancement. Identification with superiors rather than subordinates correlated .21 with authoritarianism, .25 with identification with discipline, and −.20 with cooperation (Chapman & Campbell, 1957a). Paradoxically, those of higher rank appear to be less concerned about their superiors and more concerned about their subordinates. Campbell and McCormack (1957) found that colonels in the U.S. Air Force were significantly less oriented toward superiors than were air force majors or college men and majors were less so than air force cadets or their instructors. Furthermore, air force majors and lieutenant-colonels were significantly more subordinate oriented than were the other groups tested.

Lawler, Porter, and Tannenbaum (1968) found that interactions with superiors were more valued than were those with subordinates. In addition, the managers reacted more favorably to interactions that their superiors initiated than to those initiated by others. Porter and Kaufman (1959) devised a scale for determining the extent to which supervisors described themselves as similar to top managers. Self-perceptions that were similar to those of top managers were associated with patterns of interaction that peers perceived to be similar to those of managers in high-level positions.

Subordinates whose attitudes and role perceptions were similar to those of superiors were preferred by their superiors (Miles, 1964a) and rated by them as more effective (V. F. Mitchell, 1968). In turn, subordinates who resembled their superiors in the personality traits "sociable" and "stable" were better satisfied than were those who resembled their superiors less closely. Henry (1949) and others found that it was the rapidly promoted executives who particularly tended to identify themselves with their superiors. On the other hand, Pelz (1952) showed that first-line supervisors who are subordinate oriented tended to be evaluated positively by their workers but only if they were perceived to have sufficient influence with superiors so they could satisfy the workers' expectations.

Balma, Maloney, and Lawshe (1958a, 1958b) studied more than 1,000 foremen in 19 plants. They found that foremen who identified themselves with management were rated as having significantly more productive groups than were those who did not identify with their superiors. However the employees' satisfaction with a foreman was not related to the foreman's orientation. R. S. Barrett (1963) discovered that foremen who perceived that their approach to problems was similar to that of their immediate superiors tended to feel free to do things their own way. Finally, Fleishman and Peters (1962) observed that top-level managers tended to connect the effectiveness of lower-level managers with that of these managers' immediate middle-level superiors.

Resolving Conflict

An ideal resolution of conflict is offered by the transformational leader when he or she moves adversaries to transcend their conflicting self-interests for the good of the larger entity. Both George Kennon and Mikail Gorbachev point to the need for the Soviets and the Americans to resolve the arms race by focusing more of their resources on the world's common problems of overpopulation, environmental pollution, and economic development. Loyalty to one's national interests can be advanced by loyalty to Planet Earth. But as Gorbachev (1988) argued, in his address to the United Nations, trust and predictability among the parties in conflict are mandatory if they are to join forces to work for common transcendental goals. Seven months later, the leaders of the seven largest First World nations followed up by resolving to try to deal cooperatively with the major threats to the global environment (Kilborn, 1989).

Dual Loyalties

Conflicting interests may be overridden by multiple identifications and allegiances. The potential conflicts may be reduced, avoided, and even resolved because people who are members of two groups or organizations with conflicting interests may consider themselves loyal to both. For example, Stagner (1954) obtained a correlation of .33 between the favorableness of workers' attitudes toward their company and toward the union. Purcell (1954) found that although more workers identified with the company than with the union, 73 percent of the men and women surveyed expressed loyalty to both. Foremen and stewards each tended to identify with the organization that they represented officially, but both foremen (57 percent) and stewards (88 percent) generally felt favorable toward the others' organization. In a case study of 18 supervisors of a British shoe factory, Amstrong (1983) was chagrined to find (because of his Marxist orientation) that despite the supervisors' resentment about their deteriorating income and status relative to the work force, they remained loyal to the senior management. For Armstrong, this continuing loyalty to senior management meant that the supervisors failed to recognize their interests as members of the working class who were exploited by the capitalist senior management.

Obrochta (1960) obtained results indicating that foremen and workers were most similar regarding their attitudes toward the company and least similar regarding their attitudes toward union leaders. The foremen's attitudes were more favorable toward both the union leaders and the company than were those of the hourly workers, and the attitudes of the hourly workers were more favorable toward the union than were the foremen's.

Reciprocities. Obrochta also found that the workers' attitudes were somewhat more favorable toward their foreman than were the foreman's toward them. Further evidence on reciprocity or the lack of it was gathered by Derber, Chalmers, Edelman, and Triandis

(1965) in a study of 37 industrial plants. The results of this study indicated that managers' attitudes toward the union and union leaders' attitudes toward the management were positively and significantly correlated; each group was moderately favorable in its attitude toward the other. Obviously, there are variations and exceptions. For instance Stagner, Chalmers, and Derber (1958), using separate scales for measuring attitudes toward the company and the union, found no relation between the management's attitudes toward the union and the union's attitudes toward the management. Yet, in many firms, managers and union officials regard each other in generally favorable terms, despite the conflict between them about substantive issues, particularly those involving their respective powers. Investigating managerial attitudes in a southern city, Alsikafi, Jokinen, Spray, and Tracy (1968) suggested that unfavorable managerial attitudes toward the union tended to be associated with the inclusion in labor contracts of union security clauses that the managers perceived challenged their authority to manage. At the same time, Spillane (1980) noted that in contrast to a 1959 survey, a 1978 survey of attitudes of Australian union leaders and Australian business executives had found that the gap in attitudes had narrowed substantially and that both groups in the later survey strongly supported arbitration as a way of resolving industrial disputes. On the other hand, Edwards and Heery (1985) noted that when the interests of shop-floor democracy in 35 British collieries came into conflict with the interests of the union officials or national interests, the local leaders upheld the concerns for shop-floor democracy.

Mutual Perceptions and Differing Interests. Conflict has a tendency to escalate and to be exacerbated by "mirror imaging"—attributing opposite qualities to the opposition. Thus, "we" are honest, just, rational and benevolent; "they" are dishonest, unjust, emotional, and malevolent. Leaders of groups, organizations, and nations tend to exploit and exaggerate these opposing attributions, as was seen among Americans who exhibited this mirror imaging of Iranians soon after the American hostages were seized in Tehran in 1979 (Conover, Mingst, & Sigelman, 1980). Despite this mirror imaging, K. F. Walker (1962) found that managers and union leaders were accurate in predicting each other's attitudes, but both perceived more conflict than actually existed. Foremen and shop stewards who wanted the company and union to coexist amicably experienced more stress than normal and tended to hold favorable attitudes toward each other (Purcell, 1954). However, the underlying bases for evaluating the management and the union differed. Stagner, Derber, and Chalmers (1959) surveyed the attitudes of two labor leaders and two managers in each of 41 establishments. When they computed a composite score for each establishment for each of 35 attitude and satisfaction variables, they found that the management's evaluation of the union emerged as a single general factor but the union's evaluations were denoted by two factors, one involving union-management relations and the other concerned with the union's achievements.

Remmers and Remmers (1949) and Miller and Remmers (1950) examined the attitudes of managers and labor leaders toward human relations-oriented supervision. Managers tended to overestimate labor leaders' scores, whereas labor leaders underestimated managers' scores. In a comparative study of managers and union officials, Weaver (1958) found, as expected, that union officials exhibited strong prolabor attitudes. But not as obviously, managers were neutral about grievances, arbitration, the labor movement, and working during a strike.

Schwartz and Levine (1965) compared the interests of managers and union officials in the same companies. The managers scored higher in an interest in supervisory initiative and production interests and the union officials scored higher on an interest in power seeking, propaganda, bargaining, arbitration, and disputation. Similarly, Bogard (1960) compared the values of management trainees and labor leader trainees and found that management trainees scored higher in aggressiveness and lower in altruistic values than did the union trainees.

Managing Conflict

The management of conflict is an important component of most management roles. Often it may involve transactional leadership to move the conflicting em-ployees, groups, or organizations to accept that the bargain that can be struck with the opposition can bring more benefits and less costs than can continuing the conflict.

Transformational leaders (socialized charismatics) will add to the transactional effort with more supportive, friendly, obliging, compromising, and integrative efforts to move the parties in conflict from a competitive to a cooperative stance with each other (Musser & Martin, 1988). The conflict between the felt security of employees in the old ways of doing things and changes required by new demands can be managed by the transformational leader who instills pride in the past, coupled with the need to meet the challenges of the future (Tichy & Devanna, 1986). Thomas and Schmidt (1976) reported that middle managers spent more than 25 percent of their time dealing with conflict between them and their organizational colleagues. The figures were even higher for first-line supervisors.

Diagnosis and Remediation

The diagnosis of the causes of a conflict is a rational way to begin to manage conflict. For example, if conflict is due to the failure to match status and esteem, it can be reduced by incorporating the results of subordinates' evaluations into promotional policies or building up the esteem of those of high status. If conflict is anticipated because of the rise in status of one member at the expense of the others, it can be avoided by bringing in an outsider to lead the group (Bass, 1960).

Kabanoff (1985a) proposed a typology of conflict situations. Each type suggested a relevant rationale for its management. For instance, if a diagnosis showed that the team members' esteem was lower than their actual ability and expertise, public praise could be used to increase their esteem. In addition, counseling could help peers increase their acceptance of the expert but unesteemed members.

Table 15.1 lists a number of these conflict situations and the implied strategy for handling them.

Multiple Orientation. Simultaneous upward and downward orientation and sensitivity are required of the effective supervisor. Sarbin and Jones (1955) reported that a successful foreman is not only competent in the eyes of his superiors but fulfills the expectations

Table 15.1 Conflict Situations and Implied Strategies for Reducing or Resolving Them

Type of Conflict	Example	Implied Strategy
Low esteem–high ability	A person's actual ability is greater than others' perceptions of his or her expertise.	Change a person's informal status to match his or her ability by using public praise to increase his or her status, counseling to increase his or her acceptance by peers, and so on.
Low commitment–high centrality	A person with little commitment to the group is placed in a central communication position.	Increase the person's commitment by tying his or her rewards to the group outcomes, reassign the group members so a committed person takes over the central position, or reduce the centralization of communication pattern.
Low popularity–high status	A disliked person exercises authority over others.	Increase the interpersonal skills of the disliked superior or reduce his or her authority.
Incompatibility–required collaboration	Persons with incompatible needs are required to collaborate in the performance of a task.	Reassign the task to compatible persons, redesign the task so it requires less collaboration, or have the supervisor collaborate with the incompatible persons to limit conflict.
Esteem-status	A person's esteem is mismatched with the importance (status) of his or her task in the flow of work.	Redesign the flow of work to decrease the dependence of the esteemed person on unesteemed persons.
Low ability–high required ability	A person's ability or knowledge is incongruent with the requirements of the job.	Retrain and provide more information to the incumbent or reassign the incumbent.
Low ability–high status	A person with little ability is in a position to exercise authority over others.	Retrain and provide more information to the person in authority or decrease the person's authority.
Low ability–highly critical task	A person of little ability is assigned to a highly critical task.	Train the person, change the assignment or the assignee, or redesign the task system to reduce the importance of the task.
Low status–highly critical task	A person in a low-status position is assigned a critical task.	Increase the authority of the position, reallocate the task to another position, or reduce the importance of the task.

SOURCE: Adapted from Kabanoff (1985b), pp. 133–134.

of his subordinates. According to Wray (1949), this is not an easy task, since superiors and subordinates present conflicting expectations that are difficult to reconcile. Nonetheless, in his study of an industrial plant, H. Rosen (1961a, 1961b) found that managers could exhibit an upward orientation toward the demands of their superiors while remaining sensitive to the demands of their subordinates.

The experience of supervisors in their subordinates' jobs has been seen to be of consequence. Maier, Hoffman, and Read (1963) compared managers who had previously held the jobs of their subordinates with peers who had not held these jobs. The subordinate's trust in mutual agreements about the current subordinate's problems appeared only with those managers

who had previously been in the subordinate's job, although the managers' previous assignment to the subordinate's job did not facilitate effective communication.

Three of every four first-line supervisors who were rated as promotable by their superiors were described by their subordinates as pulling for both the employees and the company. Only 40 percent of those seen as less worthy of promotion were so described (Mann & Dent, 1954b).

Conflict-Management Tactics

Filella (1971) queried 27 Spanish managers who formed the top three levels of their banking organization about how they dealt with disagreements with each other. In terms of the influence tactics described by Kipnis, Schmidt, and Wilkinson (1980), they used reasoning most often, followed, in order, by the formation of coalitions, friendliness, assertiveness, bargaining, and appeals to a higher authority. Subordinates used all these tactics except reasoning more often than did their superiors in trying to resolve disagreements with them. Rational justification appears to be particularly useful to superiors in heading off potential conflict and dissatisfaction when managers are faced with maintaining the status quo or with trying to promote change. Bies and Shapiro (1986) asked 137 evening MBA students who had full-time jobs during the day to recount an incident in which their current manager had rejected their proposal or request. The managers could reject the proposal or request without losing their subordinates' respect, trust, and esteem if the subordinates judged that the managers provided good and sufficient justifications for their decision. Such justifications were either that the issue was not in the manager's control or that the request did not fit with goals and priorities.

Managers who are facing the need to make changes likewise must be prepared to give their subordinates good and sufficient justification. Although resistance to change is a problem in all social settings, it is both endemic and fraught with increasing penalties in productive and service enterprises that must deal with rapidly changing markets and technologies. Tichy and Devanna (1986) suggested that senior managers can assuage middle managers' tensions about the need for stability and change by creating organizations that "embrace paradox." Such organizations can provide a balance between the need for adaptation and the need for stability and between the denial and acceptance of reality (for example, "We're not number 1 as yet, but we will be"). The old forms can be abandoned, but the new can be better.

Tichy and Devanna noted that senior managers must deal with technical reasons for resistance to change, such as habit, inertia, fear of the unknown, loss of organizational predictability, and sunk costs (the organization's investment of resources in the old ways). Senior managers must also deal with political reasons for resistance to change, including the threat to currently powerful coalitions of vested interests, win-lose decision making about scarce resources, and the need

for leaders to find fault with their own previous decisions. They must likewise deal with cultural reasons for resistance to change, as seen in the extent to which the organizational culture has highlighted old values and methods that now must be abandoned, the felt security in regressing to the "good old days," the absence of a climate for change, the demands for conformity to the old ways, and the lack of receptivity to new ideas.

In managing the rational and socioemotional conflicts associated with resistance to change in industrial firms, the senior managers must summarize the past and eulogize its value, as well as emphasize the continuities of the past with the future and justify the changes. To counter the political and socioemotional reasons, they must mobilize coalitions of support for the changes (Tichy & Devanna, 1986). Thus, Kanter's (1983) 200 "change-masters"—executives who could successfully bring about new developments in their organizations—knew how to build coalitions to get the funds, staff, and authorization to move ahead to carry out their innovations.[3]

Palliation. Experimental student subjects, whose anger and aggression had been aroused, could be induced to collaborate by introducing ways for them to control their anger and aggression. Baron (1984) arranged for undergraduate subjects to play the role of executives who discussed important issues with an accomplice of the experimenter. The accomplice disagreed strongly with the students in an arrogant and condescending manner, which angered the students. But subsequently, the accomplice palliated the situation by offering a token gift of a Life Saver candy, by generating sympathy with justification for his earlier aggressive behavior, or by asking for help with a humorous task (three experimental conditions); these palliative efforts increased the likeability of the accomplice. In contrast to the control condition in which such palliative efforts were not made, in the three experimental conditions, the subjects indicated that they would be more likely to try to collaborate with the accomplice and be less likely to avoid him if conflict arose in the future.

[3]Bass (1983b), Janis and Mann (1977), and Levi and Benjamin (1977), among others, also reviewed behavioral approaches that leaders can use to manage conflict.

Force and Avoidance. The use of force by superiors and avoidance by subordinates to manage the conflicts between them appears to be a matter of individual differences, for conflict is in the eye of the beholder. In some circumstances, some people see conflict with others but others do not. In a study of one supervisor and one subordinate each from 113 agencies for parks and recreation, Howat and London (1980) found that the supervisors and subordinates who perceived more frequent conflicts tended to see each other as being more likely to use force as a way of dealing with conflict. Supervisors who perceived more conflicts were also viewed by their subordinates as being likely to withdraw from conflict; subordinates who perceived more conflicts were viewed by their supervisors as likely to avoid confrontation and compromise. Those who saw a lot of conflict around them were rated unfavorably by others in their interpersonal relations.

Tactics Related to Identification. Halpin and Winer (1957) listed four ways for an airplane commander to manage the conflicts with his superiors and subordinates: (1) he could identify completely with the higher authority and disparage the need to be considerate of the welfare of his subordinates, (2) he could reduce intimacy with his subordinates to minimize any guilt feelings he might have about being inconsiderate of them, (3) he could be inconsiderate on the job but "pal around with them" off the job, or (4) he could focus completely on satisfying the needs of his subordinates. Evidence in support of these findings accrued from a factor analysis by Hites (1953) of the results of a survey of aircrews. Hites noted that leaders varied in their loyalty and deference to superiors and also varied in their loyalty to their subordinates. That is, some commanders were loyal to their superiors, some were loyal to their subordinates, some were loyal to both, and some were loyal to neither. Halpin's (1953) followup study of 89 commanders of B-29 aircraft found that the commanders were likely to be highly rated by their superiors and their subordinates if they exhibited consideration, friendliness, and warmth toward their subordinates and initiated clear patterns of organization and ways of accomplishing missions.

Pelz (1952) and Likert (1961a, 1961b) observed that the managers in the middle can perceive themselves as members of overlapping subgroups. Effective leaders can see themselves as members of two groups, one composed of their superior and their peers and the other, composed of their subordinates and themselves. They have sufficient influence with their superior to represent their subordinates' interests effectively; they are well enough identified with their subordinates to be supported by them. Thus, they are both good leaders and good followers, able to satisfy the expectations of both their subordinates and their superior.

Summarizing the results of organizational surveys, Kahn and Katz (1953/1960) inferred that effective leaders differ from ineffective ones in that they make it clear that their role differs from that of their subordinates. They do so by not performing the subordinates' function; by spending time on supervision but not closely supervising subordinates; and by concerning themselves with their subordinates' needs, rather than with rules.

A chain effect was illustrated by Bowers (1963, 1964a), who studied management-foremen-worker relations in an industrial firm. The more supportively the foreman's superior behaved toward him, the higher was the foreman's self-esteem. The higher the foreman's self-esteem, the less often he discussed his problems with subordinates and the better he perceived their attitudes toward him. The better the attitudes that the foreman perceived his superior and subordinates shared about him, the more he felt friendly toward his subordinates. The more friendly he felt, the more supportively he behaved toward his subordinates. Bowers concluded that the foreman's self-esteem converts the behavior of his superior into a mandate for the foreman's action. A study of nursing supervisors by Kamano, Powell, and Martin (1966) provided corroborative evidence. It reported that those who were evaluated more favorably by higher-level administrators likewise tended to rate their own subordinates more favorably.

Organizational Politics. The competing self-interests of different organizational members give rise to organizational politics. In this situation, the members vie for control in a struggle to obtain cooperation. Their different beliefs about desired actions and outcomes are complicated by their uncertainties over the means-to-ends linkages. The win-lose possibilities of political activity are threatening to the members' self-interests and are likely to arouse resistance if the politicking is open rather than concealed (Frost & Hayes, 1979).

Organizational politics may be seen in the performance of "intrapreneurs," who break the organization's rules to pursue new products and ideas in which they are personally interested (Pinchot, 1985). According to Frost (1986) politicking can be seen in the intentional building of frameworks, the rules and meanings of communication for systems of influence. Although the exertion of influence on the surface activities of the organization is primarily a matter of the appropriate open use of ability, power, and control of resources, organizational politics may be required, particularly if the deeper organizational structure requires reshaping. Reshaping is necessary when the organization can no longer function with the old arrangements for balancing members' self-interests and new alignments are needed to accomplish objectives in the face of likely resistance. Such legitimate politics can be seen in whistle-blowing (dissent based on principles) and bargaining.

Politicking is overtly rational but covertly caters to the self-interests of the political actor. It aims to confront others to gain their compliance by manipulative actions. At deeper organizational levels, it becomes an effort to shape conscious and unconscious organizational values, beliefs, and practices. Resistance from others is reduced by the concealment of the true self-interests of the political actor. Machiavellian tactics, such as those introduced in Chapter 9, are employed.

Machiavellian Tactics. Although it would seem that persons in the middle manage the contradictory demands placed on them by open compromise, actually they may employ more subtle or sometimes devious ways of momentarily reducing but not resolving conflict. First, the person in the middle may tell each conflicting party what he or she wants to hear. For example, when he addressed liberal audiences, President Lyndon B. Johnson would emphasize how much he admired Franklin Delano Roosevelt's liberal policies. When he met with his conservative financial backers, however, he would discourse on how much he was against the liberal policies (Caro, 1982).

Second, persons in the middle may withhold information from superiors or subordinates and mask their feelings. Thus, W. H. Read (1962) found that managers who communicated to their superiors with less-than-complete accuracy were more upwardly mobile. The relationship was conditioned by the extent to which managers trusted their superiors and perceived them to have influence with higher management. Walker, Guest, and Turner (1956) studied the problems of supervisors on an assembly line, where the workers were under constant pressure because of their inability to control the speed of their work. The most effective supervisors were found to absorb the pressures and criticisms from higher management without communicating their frustrations and tensions to the workers.

In her survey of 350 managers, Roberts (1986) noted that the managers said they were more inclined to try to impress their boss, somewhat less likely to do so with their peers, and least likely to do so with their subordinates. A negotiated solution was more often sought with their boss or peers than with their subordinates.

Jambor (1954) suggested that persons in the middle of conflicts between those above and those below them in the hierarchy often acquiesce to their more powerful superiors and rationalize their position with their less powerful subordinates. Jablin (1981) observed the same pattern but thought that such political behavior may result in the loss of support from the subordinates. Subordinates who perceived their supervisors to be highly political were both less open in their communications with their supervisors and less satisfied with them than they were with those supervisors whom they saw as less political. This same effect was also noted by Roff (1950). Such political behavior by combat officers resulted in their immediate subordinates rating them as less sincere, less impartial, and more concerned with personal advantage. Wickert (1947) also found that an officer had to appear sincere and consistent to be rated as a successful leader of a combat crew.

Elected officials are caught in a cauldron of conflicting demands from their various constituencies. Followers have difficulty checking on the authenticity of their leaders, who often can maintain office indefinitely without much need for sincerity and consistency. According to Titus (1950), hypocrisy may be necessary when dealing with followers but minimal use should be made of it. (One person's hypocrisy is another's tactfulness.) For Jameson (1945), leaders need to "wear masks" to disguise their own feelings and to live up to expectations, despite conflicting demands made on them. Political leaders contrive both conflicts and their resolutions. For instance, the Nazis set fire to the Reichstag in 1933 and pinned the guilt on the Communists, setting them up as criminal plotters against the government. In 1934, Joseph Stalin secretly arranged for the assassination of a Leningrad party leader, then dramatized it as a plot against the state, providing a rationale for the terroristic purge that followed. In 1964, the Johnson Administration contrived and magnified the Gulf of Tonkin incident into a major assault on the U.S. Navy to gain Congressional support for escalation of the U.S. response in Vietnam.

"Divide and conquer" is a classic tactic that Machiavellians use to gain and maintain their power over the opposition of subordinates who are weakened by the dissension within the opposition that keeps it from mobilizing effectively against those in control. Lawler (1983) examined how this tactic, by a contrived, imaginary leader, affected two female subordinates in a three-person group who were working under inequitable rates of pay. Conflicts of interest were increased between the subordinates, but co-optation tactics (promise of advancement) were more effective than threats in preventing their rebellion. The subordinate who was promised advancement was less susceptible to pressure from the other two subordinates to rebel against the imaginary leader.

Ignoring Dissonance. Political leaders may also avoid immediate conflict by ignoring the facts about the conflicting circumstances in favor of their strongly held beliefs, needs, and wishes. When Hitler broke the Treaty of Versailles, he promised to keep the Treaty of Locarno. When he broke the Treaty of Locarno, he promised no further territorial aggression in Europe. When he entered Austria by force, his government promised no interference in Czechoslovakia. At the time of the Munich crisis in 1938, when British Prime Minister Neville Chamberlain and French Premier Édouard Daladier were confronted with such interference and more territorial demands, they ignored all of Hitler's previous broken promises. For peace at any price and with an image of Hitler as the "bulwark

against Bolshevism," Chamberlain and Daladier engaged in wishful thinking. They appeased Hitler and relied again on his good faith.

Reserving Judgment. Barnard's (1938) "fine art of executive decision" noted that superiors' demands for conflict-laden decisions by the executive must be met, but responsibility for them can be delegated. Subordinates' demands for such decisions need be met only when the decisions are important, and they cannot be delegated. The tactful executive can avoid conflict-laden decisions on questions that are not pertinent, as well as premature decisions, impossible solutions, and decisions that others should make.

Political tactics often are employed in trying to resolve disagreements between individuals and groups at the same organization level. The formation of coalitions and the use of appeals to higher authority are two such frequently used strategies (P. J. Frost, 1986).

Dealing with the Boss. Kahn, Wolfe, Quinn, et al. (1964) found that 88 percent of all role conflict involves pressure from above. In the same way, D. E. Frost (1983) discovered that it was their boss's behavior that created most of the role conflict and ambiguity for first- and second-level leaders in an urban fire department. Again, their managers were the overriding reason for the role ambiguity and conflict experienced by 123 salaried employees of a metal fabricating firm who were surveyed by Deluga (1986a). At the same time, Jambor (1954) found that when supervisors' perceptions of their role differed from their superior's perception of it, the supervisors experienced more anxiety than when their role perception differed from their subordinates' perceptions of their role. Nonetheless, according to Deluga, the ambiguity of the employees' role was unrelated to the influence tactics they used in dealing with their boss. However, those who experienced more role conflict were more likely to use reason and assertiveness with their boss than try to bargain with them. If their manager continued to resist their efforts to influence, the subordinates who felt more role conflict tended to try ingratiation, impression management, flattery, and the creation of goodwill and attempted to gain the support of the higher authority and their coworkers. Fiedler (1984), as was noted in Chapter 7, amassed considerable evidence to show that when experienced leaders are in conflict with their boss, they tend to be able to maintain productive groups. But intelligent leaders without such experience are handicapped by their conflicts with their boss. Experience, not intelligence, helps leaders deal with the stress engendered by the conflicts they have with their own superiors.

Dealing with the Problem Subordinate. Using clinical observation and psychoanalytical theory, Zaleznik (1965a) conceived of four types of subordinates, each representing a type of personality that is in conflict and is attempting to cope with the demands of a higher authority. The *impulsive* subordinate rebels and strives to overthrow authority and its symbols; his or her unconscious effort may be to displace his or her father or to deal with painful loneliness. The *compulsive* subordinate likewise wants to dominate the struggle with authority but does so passively. This subordinate's behavior is rigid, and he or she avoids making decisions. Underneath, there are doubt, rapid shifts in feelings about interpersonal encounters, hidden aggression, and denial of responsibility, coupled with a powerful conscience and strong guilt feelings. Immature early development results in the *masochist*, illustrated by the accident-prone employee who evokes sympathy when hurt. The masochist's performance is inadequate and invites criticism and shame. His or her identity is with the oppressed, helpless, and weak. The *withdrawn* subordinate turns his or her interests inward and passively submits to a perceived malevolent world and untrustworthy superiors. Although this type of person may handle routine tasks well, he or she makes little effort to be innovative.

Zaleznik's advice for supervising these four types of malfunctioning subordinates is to avoid being trapped into their dynamics, for example, by reinforcing the doubting of the compulsive subordinate or losing control to the impulsive, rebellious subordinate. Conflict with such subordinates needs to be objectified and conflicting issues broken into their components. Realities need to be recognized.

Managing Conflict with Openness, Trust, and Confrontation

Shartle (1956) pointed to the efficacy of substitution. Leaders should have a balanced, flexible set of identifications with various organizational projects and plans.

If they find themselves blocked in one line of activity, they can shift to another, thus avoiding a sense of frustration and failure. J. M. Burns (1978, p. 39) saw conflict as an opportunity to display leadership. The leader (in contrast to the status quo administrator) converts the demands, values, and goals of conflicting constituencies into workable programs:

> Leaders, whatever their professions of harmony, do not shun conflict; they confront it, exploit it, ultimately embody it. Standing at the points of contact among latent conflict groups, they can take various roles, sometimes acting directly for their followers, sometimes bargaining with others, sometimes overriding certain motives of followers and summoning others into play.

What is required here is the belief that the discussion of conflict can be constructive and that conflicting parties can be trusted to work toward effective outcomes if communications between them are open. Culbert and McDonough (1980) stated that the awareness of every organizational member's self-interests and the need to deal with them is essential to organizational and individual effectiveness. They argued that subordinates need to confront their superiors about their needs. Out of this confrontation can come an alignment of the subordinates' needs and the organization's needs. The conflict between downward and upward demands can be best resolved through such open confrontation and discussion.

Evidence is mixed in support of this contention. On the one hand, according to a survey of 350 managers by Roberts (1986), the search for consensus was the most popular way for the managers to deal with their superiors, peers, and subordinates. Likewise, Friedlander and Margulies (1969) found that the task motivation and involvement of research personnel were maximized by their trust in management. Wilcox and Burke (1969) concluded that openness between workers and supervisors resulted in greater job satisfaction for both. Similarly, Klauss and Bass (1982) reported that colleagues were more satisfied with focal persons who they perceived were more open in their communications. In 147 established managerial work groups, Crouch (1986) found that managers were more willing to encourage the open expression of conflicting views and that they, as well as their subordinates, had little need to dominate. Strong dominant personalities evidently have a greater tendency to suppress such conflict. Crouch also found that the groups' performance was enhanced to the extent the managers legitimated such open expression of conflicts in points of view.

However, Rubin and Goldman (1968) found no difference in the openness of communication of effective and ineffective managers. And Willits (1967), who studied 20 small manufacturing firms, showed that although measures of the success of the firms were positively related to the president's openness in communicating ideas, as was expected, they were negatively related to his open communication of feelings. Furthermore, open communication by the other executives did not coincide with company success. Crouch and Yetton (1987) suggested that the benefits of open group discussions depend on the leader's skills in managing conflict.

Even if they have strong political or professional credentials, the new political appointees to senior-management positions in public bureaucracies move into a situation that is inherently full of conflict. They must confront long-established rules and regulations, entrenched cliques, and deception from career civil servants who become defensive, passively obstruct new policies, and withhold or delay providing information to and from the appointees (House & Covello, 1984). In turn, the career governmental executives often must keep the agency operating while they await a new political appointee as the new head of the agency. Potential conflicts between incoming newly appointed agency heads and their permanant civil servants are likely to be minimized by a mutual understanding that is established before the appointee takes office or is developed later.

> Civil servants have some ideas of the thinking and requirements of their [newly appointed heads], and [the agency heads] acquire knowledge of the dispositions of their civil servants. A civil servant who gives advice is likely to frame it on the basis of his understanding of the needs of [the agency head], and [the head] is likely to modify his policy preferences on the basis of his knowledge of what is . . . feasible. (Page, 1987, p. 133)

To reduce potential conflicts with the incoming new political head of the agency, Schmidt (1985) suggested

that while awaiting the new head, the federal career executive continue to make normal decisions about filling vacancies and about policies to be implemented or postponed, stress greater cooperation and a truce among antagonistic organizations, hold informational meetings, avoid the usurpation of power by bureaucratic processes, and try to keep rivalries about "turf" to a minimum.

Managing Conflict by Converting It to Problem Solving

Walton and McKersie (1965, 1966) and Likert and Likert (1978) thought that conflict could be managed best when it is converted from win-lose negotiations to a problem-solving situation from which both parties can emerge as winners. Furthermore, Likert and Likert saw that it was particularly important for conflicting parties to avoid becoming adversaries who debate solutions to the conflict before they have reached agreement on what outcomes they deem to be essential and desirable. This position is consistent with Bass's (1966b) finding that negotiators who began with committed solutions were much more likely to reach a deadlock than were those who entered negotiations without firm solutions in mind. It also fitted with Maier's (1967, 1970b) results, which indicated that an early focus on ready-to-apply solutions causes groups to avoid trying to find more creative ways of meeting their problems. Adversarial groups cling to their favorite solutions as they proceed with negotiations.

Maturing of Relationships

The potential for conflict is reduced when union and management relationships mature from competition over costs and benefits to cooperation toward increasing the returns both to management and to employees. Thus, the management invites joint decision making and profit sharing and supports the importance of seniority, security, pension benefits, and so on. The unions support the redesign of jobs and the introduction of cost-reduction techniques, coupled with the retraining of employees. Both the management and the unions collaborate on safety programs. Win-lose bargaining is converted into win-win problem solving.

At the level of the individual union and management representative, Rosen, Greenhalgh, and Anderson (undated) pointed out that studies have shown that union stewards may spend an average of 11 hours per week on socioemotional leadership functions, as do their counterparts in management in dealing with the absenteeism, insecurities, an grievances of employees.

A mature, collaborative approach substitutes a mutually acceptable culture and a common philosophy for minutely detailed agreements that cover all possible contingencies. Fixed periodic negotiations are replaced by joint study groups and more open discussions. A reward system is determined, not the levels of reward (Lawler & Mohrman, 1987). According to Long's (1988) survey of two Canadian firms, managers are most likely to favor such a collaborative approach if they are dissatisfied with the behavioral and attitudinal conditions in the firm and if they think that increasing the workers' influence on policy decisions would improve these conditions. In 1987, General Motors and the United Auto Workers agreed to establish continuous joint methods for addressing specific issues at each plant. The objective would be to design solutions that improve the efficiency of each plant and the quality of its particular products. Johnson (1988) thought that such continuous joint processes work well if the local manager is adept at mobilizing the skills and energies of the workers and providing them with sound direction. Continuous joint process emphasizes mutual listening and the sharing of information and ideas. But managers need to have more than just labor's interests in mind, for they are the custodian of the interests of the shareholders and various other constituencies of the corporation and its need to remain competitive in the international marketplace.

Promoting Congruence of the Formal and Informal Organization. The leader can avoid or reduce conflict by fostering the congruence of status, esteem, and competence within the group and its activities and the congruence between the informal and the formal organization. For example, formal-informal incongruencies were seen within technical units of the U.S. Air Force. On the one hand, the formal and informal organizations agreed that cooperation and pride in the formal organization were desirable and that the most competent personnel were most valuable. On the other hand, the formal and informal organizations had conflicting attitudes about punishment for laxity and the need for high standards of performance (Anonymous, 1945–46). Leadership increased the congruence in attitudes. According to Whyte and Gardner (1945), leaders of the formal organization foster such congruence by becoming aware of the informal organization, discovering the informal leader, and obtaining his or her cooperation and agreement to work toward common goals. Formal leaders use the informal organization constructively to convey attitudes, to locate grievances, and to maintain social stability (K. Davis, 1951). They identify the differences and values that buttress the informal compared to the formal organization.

Legitimation and Conflict

Legitimation of a role refers to others' perception of an individual's right to function in a given position. An individual's appointment to a given position legitimates his or her performance of the role, at least for those who do the appointing. Likewise, election to an office legitimates the role of the elected individual, in the eyes of those who voted for the candidate as well as for most others. In traditional societies, legitimacy can be provided by inherited status and rank as well as election or appointment. For instance, Vengroff (1974) noted that it did not make any difference in community participation in the development of 31 villages in Botswana whether the leaders were the elected councillors or were the traditional tribal chiefs. But conflict will arise when what is regarded as legitimate for one member in one situation is viewed as illegitimate for others in the same or different situations.

Although legitimation may be lost if the individual fails to perform as expected, legitimacy of one's appointment has to be sharply separated from competence or perceived competence to perform the role. C. B. Smith's (1984) experiment showed that the presence or absence of competence in appointed supervisors did not affect the legitimacy of their authority or the conformity of subordinates to organizational directives.

The Meaning Attached to Legitimacy. Legitimacy is affected by the culture in which the appointment is embedded. It is not just a matter of agreeing on a list of uniformly interpretable regulations about appropriate behavior in the organization. Indeed, it is a fundamental source of conflict in that what is legitimate depends on both written and unwritten rules whose creation and interpretation are a developing process of shared meanings. In analyzing the relationship between the CEO and vice presidents of a Bell Telephone operating company, Feldman (1986) noted that the meaning attached to the positions held by the executives is often overlooked. The meaning is provided by the cultural system of the bureaucracy. In turn, it restricts the courses of action that are open to position holders. Neilsen and Rao (1987) agreed that the meaning of legitimacy that emerges about a position is a dynamic process that develops as new ideas and understandings about it are accepted within the organization. The meaning is enhanced when it is given more credence from demonstrations of trustworthiness as hidden agendas surface. The language that reinforces the legitimacy of a leader's actions is multilayered. At the institutional level, shared meanings evolve from history and habit. For instance, many leaders may be legitimately consumer oriented rather than technology oriented because the business has been driven by customer loyalty and interests. At another level, such meanings may be supported by stories and myths (for example, a customer-oriented engineer convinces a new client about the product with a humorous demonstration). At a third level, theories are articulated that legitimately guide action (for instance, changing market conditions require even more response to clients' needs). Finally, "symbolic universes of meaning" buttress legitimacy (for example, modern professional management is market oriented; traditional management is not so focused).

Legitimation and Conflict in Different Settings

As was already observed, the discrepancies between what others expect and one's expectations will be a source of role conflict. A group's failure to achieve consensus in its expectations about its or others' requirements likewise causes conflict. Conversely, agreement about role requirements and conformity to normative expectations about what it is legitimate for the role player to do generally contribute to the effectiveness in organizational life.

Many research analysts point to the similarities and differences in opinions about what constitutes departures from legitimacy and the effects of doing so in po-litical, educational, military, and industrial settings. For example, Schein and Ott (1962) studied the attitudes of managers, union leaders, and college students toward the legitimacy of influencing various kinds of behavior. The three groups and a sample of U.S. Air Force personnel (F. J. Davis, 1954) agreed about the legitimacy of influencing job-related behaviors. All the groups considered it legitimate for a supervisor to try to influence the job performance and work environment of employees. However, they differed about the legitimacy of a supervisor trying to influence non-job-related behavior.

Substantive conflicts in the legitimation of the leader's rights can best be catalogued in the context of their social settings, in which numerous examples have been reported of the loss or lack of legitimacy owing to incongruities, discordant expectations, and within-role and between-role conflict. These incongruities resulted in dissatisfaction and ineffectiveness.

Public and Community Settings. Homemakers are faced with the same pressures to deal with new technologies and the ambiguities of standards of quality as are professionals and managers. However, because they are not accorded the social legitimacy that professionals and managers receive, they experience an unusual conflict (Chafetz & Dworkin, 1984). For instance, homemakers are likely to see themselves as lacking in any of the power and resources to confront a manufacturer of a shoddy product.

Conflict may be sharper in public bureaucracies because of their legal obligations to respond to clients who can exert pressure on them. Conflict within public bureaucracies is exacerbated when the external political climate restricts objective goal setting and even-handed decision making (J. M. Burns, 1978). Those who are at the outer boundaries of the bureaucracy are much more likely to face such politically based conflict than are those who are far inside the organization (Katz & Kahn, 1966).

Each of several resettlement communities in Israel that Eisenstadt (1954) studied had developed specific norms, although all the communities had also incorporated the norms of the surrounding culture. Norms were perceived as prescribing proper types of behavior for given roles and role situations. To some extent, reference group norms served as general standards by which various patterns of behavior were evaluated. Because of their wider range of reference groups, the leaders served as a medium for consolidating the subgroups and integrating them into an effective larger group. Leadership was found to be ineffective when followers were apathetic toward an issue that required integrative action, when the leaders' broader orientation did not correspond with the practical issues faced by the followers, when the leaders had no authority to deal with broader issues, and when the leaders were in conflict with other leaders.

Business and Industry. In a study of managers' attitudes, Schein and Lippitt (1966) found that those whose roles involved close supervision and centralization of responsibility regarded it as legitimate to influence subordinates in more areas than did other managers. Contrary to the hypothesis, managers whose subordinates had more visible roles and interacted more frequently with outsiders did not exercise more influence than did those whose subordinates had less visible roles.

Both superiors and subordinates expected communication, development, delegation, understanding, knowhow, and teamwork from supervisors, according to Brooks (1955). But for the superiors, their autonomy was more critical to them than was their legitimacy. In a study of first-line supervisors, Klein and Maher (1970) found that the supervisors' lack of autonomy was related to role conflict, but neither the perceived legitimacy of autonomy nor the discrepancy between legitimate and actual autonomy was so related. However, Ulrich, Booz, and Lawrence (1950) observed that superiors may make legitimate but conflicting demands on the manager's role.

Conflict was latent in Freeman and Taylor's (1950) survey in which 100 top executives said they looked for aggressive, energetic applicants for management positions in the company, even though they personally wanted "tactful subordinates." The top executives attributed their own success to "brains and character," but they preferred "emotionally controlled and balanced" subordinates, rather than overly bright or highly ethical ones. The conflict was illustrated most clearly when the top executives' self-perceptions were compared with those of middle managers. Whereas the top managers emphasized their self-determination, enterprise, and dignity, the 170 middle managers emphasized their discreetness, modesty, practicality, patience, deliberateness, and planfulness. Whereas the top executives disavowed stinginess, shyness, and a lack of ambition, the middle managers avoided describing themselves as reckless, disorderly, aggressive, and outspoken (Porter & Ghiselli, 1957). However, Bass, Waldman, Avolio, and Bebb (1987) generally found positive correlations between what subordinates in New Zealand said they required in the leadership of their supervisors and what the supervisors required of their bosses. This "falling-dominoes" effect suggests that, in reality, there tend to be more positive than negative associations in what is legitimated for supervisory roles at each successive level in the organization, although some strong bosses may prefer to keep their subordinates weak in power and autonomy.

Wernimont (1971) found that workers also tended to make contradictory demands on their supervisors. On the one hand, they expressed a desire for clear instructions and goals. On the other hand, they wanted considerable freedom to do work their own way. Similarly, Foa (1956) compared ideal and actual descriptions of the behavior of foremen and workers in Israeli factories. He found that the workers complained most frequently about their foreman's ineffective social relations but were more critical of their own conduct than of their foremen's conduct. But the foremen complained little about work behavior. The smaller the discrepancy between the workers' ideal for the foremen and their descriptions of the foremen's actual behavior, the better satisfied the workers were with the foremen. When the workers identified with their foremen, they attributed the same ideals to the foremen that they held for themselves.

There seems to be a fundamental difference in the ideals of managers' roles and how managers are actually required to enact the roles. Hortatory admonitions, managerial ideals, the popular literature, and normative expectations all counsel the need for system and deliberation at all levels. As McCall (1977) noted, they assume that managers are likely to be engaged in a small number of events with enough time to ponder about how they should behave in response to the events. In reality, however, the demands on a typical manager make such deliberation impossible. For example, Guest (1956) found that foremen ranged from 200 to 583 activities in a single day. S. Carlson (1951) reported that Swedish top executives were undisturbed for only an average of 23 minutes during a day. Mintzberg (1973) found that half the activities of 5 top executives lasted 9 or fewer minutes and concluded that the executives' activities were fragmented, brief and varied and that the executives had little control over them. Ninety-three percent of the executives' contacts were arranged on an ad hoc basis; they initiated only 32 percent of them.[4]

Educational Settings. Generally, students are prepared to accept direction from instructors if the instructors are behaving legitimately. Torrance (1959) studied groups that were under different degrees of pressure from instructors to accept a new food. He found that group members expected instructors to exercise influence and that they did not perceive that such influence was great pressure. In Lee, Horwitz, and Goldman's (1954) experiment, each of three instructors of classes of ROTC cadets was given more authority or less authority to decide whether certain instructions should be repeated. Most students voted to repeat the instructions, but in each class, the "planted" instructor arbitrarily decided not to repeat the assignment. The instructor met the greatest resentment and hostility when the students believed he had little authority to make a decision. Thus, the instructor who acted as if he had a great deal of authority but did not have it, according to the students, met with the greatest rejection. If the students believed the instructor had the authority, he could act in this manner and be less resented for doing so.

M. V. Campbell (1958) reported that when teachers' needs and role behavior were close to the principal's expectations for them, teachers tended to feel better satisfied, were more confident in the principal's leadership, and were rated as more effective by the principal. Seeman's (1953, 1960) study of principals and teachers in 26 communities found that although the teachers expected their principal to attend to matters within the school, the principal's success in improving the school

situation depended on his or her devoting time to public relations matters outside the school. When principal and teachers disagreed about the principal's role, the principal reported less indecision than did the teachers, for the principal was required to take action more often than were the teachers.

Gross, Mason, and McEachern (1958) and Gross, McEachern, and Mason (1966) studied role conflict in school superintendents. They found that the school superintendents differed in their perceptions of the legitimacy of the various expectations that others held of them. In particular, they differed about the severity of sanctions that might be applied if they did not comply with what they thought was expected of them. Those superintendents with a moralistic orientation tended to conform to what they regarded as legitimate expectations but rejected expectations they regarded as illegitimate, regardless of the sanctions that might be involved. Those with an expedient orientation tended to conform to those expectations that were attended by the strongest sanctions for noncompliance or compromised between what they actually would do and what they expected to do to minimize possible sanctions. A third type of superintendents gave equal weight to legitimacy and possible sanctions.

Gross, Mason, and McEachern (1958) also studied reference group identifications and consensus among superintendents and members of school boards. The superintendents were more strongly identified with external professional reference groups than were the school board members. In the division of responsibilities, both the superintendents and the members of the school boards assigned more tasks to themselves and expressed great approval for bypassing each other. Superintendents rated the school boards more highly and were better satisfied with them when there was consensus among the board members. In turn, the greater the consensus on the board, the higher was its rating of the superintendent.

Military Settings. Numerous military studies were done on the effects of role sanctions, legitimation, and conflict. For instance, Greer (1954) reported finding that only among the more effective of 26 infantry rifle squads in six hours of simulated combat did appointed leaders act more closely to what was desired and ex-

[4]More about this in Chapter 20.

pected of them by the rest of the squad. Failure to live up to subordinates' expectations resulted in conflict and the squad's ineffectiveness.

Stouffer, Suchman, DeVinney, et al. (1949) found that U.S. officers and enlisted personnel disagreed markedly during World War II on whether officers should maintain social distance from enlisted personnel. Although 82 percent of the enlisted personnel agreed that "an officer will have the respect of his men if he pals around with them off duty," only 27 percent of the captains, 39 percent of the first lieutenants, and 54 percent of the second lieutenants agreed. Similarly, E. L. Scott (1956) found that enlisted personnel on small ships perceived the organization's status structure more accurately when superiors interacted less extensively throughout the organization, retained authority, and delegated less freely.

Merton and Kitt (1950) found that enlisted personnel who expressed attitudes in conformity with the norms of the U.S. Army were promoted more rapidly. If the enlisted personnel accepted the status structure of the army as legitimate, they were more readily identified with others at their own or next-highest status level.

The effects of the presence of more legitimacy or less legitimacy were seen by Levy (1954), who contrasted aircrews who were led in periodic discussion by their own commanders with aircrews whose discussions were led by clinical psychologists. Members of the groups that were led by their commanders had more favorable attitudes toward their groups and a greater sense of well-being than did those of groups that were led by the clinical psychologists.

In the military, the most extreme conflicts between subordinates and higher authority are likely to arise when acts of collective insubordination occur, despite fears of reprisal. These acts seem to be due to unresolved grievances about impersonal conditions, such as slow demobilization, poor food, unacceptable discipline, or unfair discrimination, rather than from individual resentment (Gal, 1985). Personal conflict about goals and commitments (Rose, 1982), such as occurred for American servicemen in Vietnam and Israeli soldiers in Lebanon in 1982, will produce withdrawal or protest, rather than group revolt. Gal (1985) saw the need for legitimacy in military decision making to deal with such personal conflicts. Decisions must serve

proper goals, must be made through appropriate processes, and must be in accord with a common value system with which the individual soldier identifies.

Conditions Affecting Legitimacy and Conflict

Various conditions can be enumerated that enhance or reduce legitimacy and, therefore, affect the amount of conflict and inefficiency that occurs. For instance, legitimation depends on clear, accepted group norms. B. R. Clark (1956) found that high-status members of a group could not be fully legitimated as such if the group norms were not clearly defined and not well accepted by the members.

The differentiation of legitimate power can enhance the positive impact of a leader's legitimacy. The importance of legitimate power was illustrated in a Dutch experiment by Mulder, Van Dijk, Stirwagen, et al. (1966), who varied the power distance between leaders and followers by permitting leaders to distribute rewards of different amounts. The legitimate leader was elected by the group. The illegitimate leader (a confederate of the experimenter) forced himself into the experimental control booth and took over the leadership function. Under conditions of great power distance, the followers resisted the illegitimate leader more than they did the legitimate leader. In a similar fashion, P. B. Read (1974) demonstrated the importance of perceived differences in legitimacy in a study of mock trial juries. Paradoxically, organizations with excessive levels of hierarchy and dependence on the differentiation of power are "hotbeds" of politics and conflict (Culbert & McDonough, 1985). For communications to move through the excessive layers requires the illegitimate bypassing of channels. For timely decisions to be made, illegitimate actions may need to occur. For work to get done, the pursuit of creative ad hoc alternatives, rather than conformity to the rules, may be required.

Knapp and Knapp (1966) studied elected officers and nonofficers who served as group leaders in a verbal conditioning experiment. Officer-led groups exhibited a higher rate of response and conditioned more readily than did groups led by nonofficers. Thus, official status facilitated the groups' learning.

Election versus Appointment. Experimentation offers the opportunity to compare the legitimation of the leadership role by election and by appointment. When Rosen (1969), in an industrial field experiment used the preference of work group employees to reassign those who became their supervisors, all seven groups showed initial increases in productivity. Similarly Ben-Yoav, Hollander, and Carnevale (1983) gave a decision-making task to 21 groups of 4 college students each and compared leaders who were appointed or elected. Elected leaders were considered to be more responsive to the followers' needs, more interested in the group task, and more competent than those who were appointed and were favored as future leaders. Dellva, McElroy, and Schrader (1987) compared 64 formally appointed leaders with those who emerged in student groups at the U.S. Army Command and General Staff College. Over time, the formally appointed leaders tended to lose influence, while the emergent leaders gained influence. Raven and French (1957) instructed experimental groups to elect one of their members as supervisor and subsequently, replaced the supervisors of half the groups with appointed leaders. They found that in contrast to these appointed leaders, the elected leaders' personal attractiveness to the other members increased and their suggestions were more likely to be accepted by the groups. In the same vein, Hollander and Julian (1970) found that members of problem-solving groups were more willing to accept a selfish action by an elected leader than by an appointed one. In another experiment by Hollander and Julian (1970), team members ranked the relative importance of several items, and the leaders could accept the ranking or reverse it. Elected leaders deviated from their groups more than appointed leaders. Both types of leaders deviated more if they enjoyed strong rather than weak support from group members. The authors concluded that more is expected of the elected than of the appointed leader. The elected leader is given greater latitude to deviate and act on behalf of the group's goals, but he or she must be aware of this advantage to profit from it.

When spokespersons for a group were elected rather than appointed, their legitimacy was greater, but they were more likely to be rejected than were the appointed spokespersons if they were seen to be incompetent or unable to produce results. Nonetheless, the appointed spokespersons also had to be competent or

successful to satisfy the group members (Julian, Hollander, & Regula, 1969). According to Hollander (1978), election created greater demands by group members for their spokesperson's performance. The elected spokespersons showed greater firmness than did the appointed persons, who were as firm only if they could consult their members (Hollander, Fallon, & Edwards, 1977). Elected spokespersons also felt freer to yield (Boyd, 1972) and to accept or reject the decisions of the group they were representing (Hollander & Julian, 1970). This is consistent with finding that elected leaders evaluated their followers more highly than did appointed leaders (Elgie, Hollander, & Rice, 1988). But appointed leaders, when representing their own groups, could achieve agreement with each other about the solutions to problems more easily and with less conflict than could elected leaders in the same circumstances (Manheim, 1960).

The Struggle for Status and Legitimacy. When all members of a community, work unit, or experimental setting are initially equal in status (the value of their initial positions in their groups), a struggle for status will result. In an informal discussion, one does not initially have the "right to lead." Gaining the right to lead and obtaining the status of leader depend on individual initiative, assertiveness, competence, and esteem. To the degree that individuals strive for status, a struggle for such status is likely to occur unless a leader has been elected or appointed in advance. Many factors will affect this struggle, including each combatant's self-estimate and credibility. Furthermore, leaders seem more concerned than do followers about maintaining their status. Gallo and McClintock (1962) studied leaders and nonleaders in the presence of three accomplices who supported the participants in the first session but withdrew their support in the second session. They found that leaders initiated more task-oriented behaviors than did followers, especially when their positions were threatened in the second session; the leaders also exhibited more hostility and antagonism when their status was threatened. Gartner and Iverson (1967) informed experimental groups that one member would be selected for a superior position in another group. The chance for upward mobility in status interfered with the task performance in well-established groups but reduced the members' morale rather than productivity in newly formed groups.

The struggle for status is most likely among a group of strangers. But if the abilities and past performance records of members are made clear to all, if their esteem is made more visible, the conflict about who shall lead is reduced. Bradford and French (1948) emphasized that the productivity of group thinking depended on the ability of group members to perceive clearly each other's roles. Drucker (1946) observed that despite the informality of relations among executives in the different divisions of General Motors, the executives worked together with relatively little conflict. The absence of conflict was attributed to objective measures of the performance of the divisions, which made the effectiveness of the executives visible to each other.

Overestimated Status. The struggle for status is augmented by the general tendency of members of organizations and groups to overestimate their own status and power (Bass, 1960; Bass & Flint, 1958a)—that is, to believe that their positions are more important than others think the positions are. In this situation, role conflict is inevitable. Those at a designated organizational level think that all who are below them have "smaller" jobs than the job holders think they have, and all those who are above the person at the designated level perceive that person's job as being "smaller" than he or she perceives it to be (Haas, Porat, & Vaughan, 1969). This bias is more general. Thus, J. D. Campbell (1952) found that 250 Boston residents tended to rate the value of their own jobs higher than they did jobs that were similar to their own.

Conflict results when people who interact or work together overestimate the importance of their own positions and underestimate the importance of others with whom they interact. For example, a janitor of an apartment house may adopt "professional standards" and accord himself more status than his tenants grant that he has (Gold, 1951–52). When a foreman accords himself more status and authority than his unionized subordinates grant him, his attempts to lead his subordinates will meet with rebuff (Wray, 1949).

Bass and Flint (1958a) showed, with 51 groups of ROTC cadets, that although members of greater power attempted more leadership and were seen by others to have exhibited more success, as was expected, they actually were no more successful. Moreover, high-control[5] members significantly overestimated their esteem compared to low-control members. The control and power differences that were arbitrarily assigned to some of these participants were likely to have aroused hostility and resentment among those without control. Although low-control members perceived of themselves as submitting to the powerful members, a greater proportion of them actually rejected the attempts to lead by the arbitrarily more powerful members.

Credibility. Legitimation involves gaining credibility as being trustworthy and informative. Klauss and Bass (1982) found strong positive correlations in social service agencies, military organizations, and industrial firms between such subordinates' ratings of managers' credibility and the managers' success as leaders. One establishes one's trustworthiness by gaining "membership character," by being seen as loyal to the group, conforming to the prevailing norms, and establishing that one is motivated to belong and identify with the group (Hollander, 1958).

Stability of Legitimacy and Leadership. The stability of the distribution of legitimate power and the tendency of leaders to hold onto their offices are fostered by, at least, five factors: (1) the validators, (2) continuing redefinitions, (3) acquisition of relevant information, (4) control of the resources that are needed for change and thwarting the restructuring of the situation, and (5) higher authority. In regard to the first factor, Hollander (1978) pointed out that leaders have validators of their positions who can support the leader's legitimacy or withdraw it. The validators uphold the leader's right to office even when a leader's performance may be inadequate. Unable to admit their errors because they have an investment in and a sense of responsibility for the leader, they continue to support the failing leader (Hollander, Fallon, & Edwards, 1977). The second factor was demonstrated by A. R. Cohen (1958), who found that leaders who are threatened with losing their status

---

[5]Control refers to the extent one member can provide possible incentives for another member. If the other member values the incentives, the control becomes power.

can redefine their groups' boundaries to isolate themselves from the very members whose support they need. Cohen found that high-status members who faced the loss of status communicated less with low-status members than did high-status members who were not facing a loss of status. In relation to the third factor, which was suggested by Caro (1974), the incumbent leader amasses knowledge of rules and regulations, develops the required organizational contacts and contracts, acquires the trappings of power, and is more visible than those who are seeking the incumbent's office. The fourth factor involves high-status members' blocking the restructuring of the situation if a new structure would cause them to lose their status (Burnstein & Zajonc, 1965b). Those with the high status control the machinery for change. In authoritarian states, dictators coerce the opposition; in democratic states, elected officials use their legitimate power to reject electoral reforms in financing, redistricting, limited terms of office, and so on that would threaten their reelection. As reluctant as the Soviet party officials are to relinquish their power, privileges, and perquisites are the over 99 percent in the U.S. House of Representatives who were reelected to office in 1988 (Rosenbaum, 1988).

Higher authority is the fifth factor. Katz, Blau, Brown, and Strodtbeck (1957) studied groups of four members who first engaged in a discussion about the possible tasks. The members then chose a task for the next session, in which half the groups performed the chosen task and the other groups were required to complete tasks imposed on them. The chances of a member remaining a leader from the first discussion to the completion of the chosen or imposed task depended on whether the task of the leader's choice was chosen by the group or imposed by the experimenter. If the group's choice of task was guided by the leader, the imposition of a different task threatened his leadership. However, his position was strengthened if he did not enforce the imposed task that the group rejected. In addition, the more the leader stirred up controversy about the choice of tasks in the first discussion, the less he was likely to remain a leader during the task-completion phase. If the leader experienced little initial opposition to his choice of task and his choice was supported by the group, he was more likely to retain his leadership than if a different task was arbitrarily imposed on the group by the experimenter.

Changes in the Behavior of Leaders. Only after the struggle for status has ended and a stable hierarchy has been organized, can those who achieved the high status reduce their level of activity (Heinicke & Bales, 1953; Whyte, 1953). Once a person is fully recognized by the other members as the leader and has won the struggle for status, he or she needs to attempt less leadership to exhibit the same amount of successful leadership. Thus, Bass, Gaier, and Flint (1956) found that when all the members of a group of ROTC cadets had equal control over each other, any member had to attempt more than the average amount of leadership to exhibit more than the average amount of observable leadership. But when the members of a group differed initially in their control over each other, the successful leader did not require as many attempts to lead.

Usurpation. As was noted earlier in the chapter, when the legitimate leader continues to be inadequate in meeting the needs of the group, the role may be usurped. However, the usurper may not do as well in the leadership role as did the legitimate leader. According to Crockett (1955), who studied conference leadership, emergent leaders tended to take control when the designated chairperson failed to do enough goal setting, information seeking, solution proposing, and problem proposing. Usurpation also occurred when cliques with divergent goals were present. Similarly, Lowin and Craig (1968) found that members initiated more structure in work groups when their superiors were incompetent. Katz, Maccoby, Gurin, and Floor (1951) found the same usurpation of leadership in groups of men who were engaged in railroad maintenance work. Heyns (1948) observed that when the appointed leader of a group fails to perform his or her duties satisfactorily, the attempts by other group members to assume leadership are more readily accepted than when the leader is adequate. In the same way, P. J. Burke (1966a, 1966b) noted that disruptive behavior in experimental groups was significantly related to the leader's failure to establish an authority structure for the group. Stogdill (1965a) found that in metal shops in which the work was precise and a piece could be ruined by interference and horseplay, the workers applied pressure on deviant group members when the supervisor failed to provide structure. In textile mills, women operators of high-speed sewing machines who were paid on an output basis, applied pressure on deviant members if their supervisors were inexperienced or failed to keep order. Many other investigators concluded that members initiate needed actions in the group if the leader fails to do so.[6]

Replacement of Leaders. In addition to the democratically required replacement of heads of state, governmental, ministerial, and agency leaders are deposed as a consequence of their failure to serve their group or organization adequately. Leaders are deposed and replaced when their validators or a higher authority lose confidence in the leaders' competence to serve the needs of the organization or group, especially when the group's or organization's performance has deteriorated (Hollander, 1978). But empirical studies and cause-effect inferences to support this contention have been mixed.[7]

Personality Differences in Reactions to Conflict. People vary in their willingness to subject themselves to conflict and to legitimate various roles and differences in status. Those who are higher in task orientation and lower in interpersonal orientation, as measured by the Orientation Inventory, showed that they are more ready to engage in conflict in small group discussions (Bass, 1967c) and are more likely to accept being marginal in role. Marginal roles exist between groups with conflicting norms, values, and goals (Stonequist, 1937). Individuals who prefer such marginal roles have lower social needs (Ziller, 1973), are also less extroverted (Wonder & Cotton, 1980), and reveal a higher task orientation and a lower interpersonal orientation (Cotton & Cotton, 1982).

Other personality differences make some leaders more prone than others to generate conflict with their subordinates, with consequential losses in effectiveness. Tjosvold, Andrews, and Jones (1983) asked 310 medical technicians to describe the cooperative, competitive, and individualistic orientations of their imme-

diate superiors. The technicians' satisfaction, desire to perform well, and willingness to remain in their jobs were reduced substantially if they reported that their leaders were competitive and individualistic, rather than cooperative. Kohn (1986) came to similar conclusions after a review of other survey and experimental investigations. Even among business leaders, there seems to be more payoff from a cooperative than from a competitive outlook.

These personality differences in competitiveness and cooperativeness manifest themselves in feelings about conflict and reactions to it. They can be understood in a model created by Blake and Mouton (1964) and Thomas (1976). As Figure 15.1 shows, individuals differ in their concern for themselves and for others as well as in their assertiveness. Self-concern and assertiveness gives rise to competitiveness; self-concern and a lack of assertiveness, to avoidance and withdrawal; assertiveness and a concern for others, to collaboration; and a lack of assertiveness and a concern for others, to accommodation. Compromise is literally an in-between result. For Blake and Mouton (1964), ideal leaders are both assertive and concerned about others. They deal with conflict by integrating conflicting ideas through collaborative problem solving.

Kabanoff (1985a) validated the conflict model by asking 104 MBA students to describe their feelings, reactions, and preferred ways of dealing with the various overt or covert conflicts described in four scenarios. Four of the five ways of coping emerged as expected. The exception was the finding that accommodation was equally acceptable to the unassertive respondent

Figure 15.1. Reactions to Conflict

Assertive	Competition or Countervailing Power		Collaboration
		Compromise	
Unassertive	Avoidance or Withdrawal		Accommodation
	Self		Others

Concerned for Self or Others

SOURCE: *Adapted from Blake and Mouton (1964) and Thomas (1976).*

[6]See, for example, Carlson (1960), Hamblin (1958b), Helmreich and Collins (1967), Mulder and Stemerding (1963), and Polis (1964).
[7]This will be discussed in detail in Chapter 31.

whether he or she was self-concerned or concerned about others. However, a factor analysis by Rahim (1983) of the self-descriptions of a national sample of 1,219 executives on how they deal with conflict substantiated the *a priori* conceptualization of the five independent styles of coping with conflict.

A factor analysis by Kipnis, Castell, Gergen, and Mauch (1976) resulted in a modified version of the model for how husbands and wives resolve their disagreements. Using the model, Rim (1981) found that the spouses' values affected how they resolved conflicts with each other. For example, they were more likely to be accommodating if both the spouses valued broadmindedness, independence, loving, and true friendship but not self-control. An empirical personality assessment by Kilmann and Thomas (1975) provided further indirect support for the Blake and Mouton model. For example, introverts avoided conflict, and extroverts collaborated. Again, Terhune (1970) and Jones and Melcher (1982) found that those who had a high need for affiliation were more likely to accommodate than to compete. Chanin and Schneer (1984) reported more of a tendency to compromise or accommodate than to compete or collaborate by undergraduate seniors who were higher in feeling than in sensing, according to their scores on the Myers-Briggs Type Indicator.

Summary and Conclusions

Leaders face many conflicts. Role ambiguity and the lack of a clear definition of the task are associated with less job satisfaction and a reluctance to initiate action.

Their location in an organization predisposes leaders to engage in some conflicts more than others. Incongruities, discrepancies, and imbalances between roles and status and esteem and competencies give rise to many of these conflicts. Middle managers and first-line supervisors experience more role ambiguity than do top managers. Workers are better satisfied and more productive when their supervisors are able to predict the reactions of their superiors. The failure of a superior to support supervisors results in the decreased self-esteem of the supervisors and in reduced esteem for them by their subordinates. The supervisor's and superior's disagreement about the supervisor's role results in greater anxiety and disagreement between the supervisor and his or her subordinates.

Within their role, leaders are faced with contradictory demands from superiors, peers, subordinates, and others. Multiple identifications are a way of coping with the resulting conflicts. Conflicts are also reduced or resolved by rational cause-effect analyses, by open discussion of the conflicts to convert negotiations into problem solving, or by more devious means.

Conflict has been observed in business, industry, education, the military, and in the public sector when a leader's legitimacy is questioned. This legitimacy may be an outcome of a struggle for status or a matter of election or appointment. Its basis will affect its acceptance by followers. The leadership role is subject to a variety of conflicting expectations. The extent to which the leader is able to fulfill these expectations tends to determine the degree to which the groups concerned will legitimate the leadership role. Central to the legitimacy of formal leadership are the leader's authority and responsibility.

16

Authority, Responsibility, and Leadership

Authority appeared early in explanations of social and political behavior. In ancient Egypt, the *Instruction of Ptahhotep* (ca. 2300 B.C.) declared, "To resist him that is put in authority is evil" (Lichtheim, 1973). For Pericles in the Athens of fifth century B.C., a spirit of reverence and a respect for authority and the laws were what constrained public acts and inhibited wrong doing (Thucydides, 404 B.C./1910). Many intellectuals philosophized about the connection of authority to responsibility. For Edmund Burke (1790/1967), those appointed to the exercise of authority were assigned a holy function.

Recognized authority gives rise to power, and power brings responsibility with it. Thus Friedrich Nietzsche (1888/1935) declared that toward the summit, responsibility increases. In his second annual message to Congress, President Abraham Lincoln observed that those who have the power to save the Union, also bear the responsibility to do so.

The legitimate power of individuals in groups, organizations, and societies derives from their authority and responsibility. Whether viziers, company presidents, military officers, school principals, or first-line supervisors, their responsibility should be commensurate with their authority to minimize their role conflict. Often, it is not. Much variation and mismatching of authority and responsibility have been reported for people who hold the same kinds of positions. Surveys by Bass and Valenzi (1974) discovered many managers who thought that they were delegated responsibility without the necessary authority to go along with it. Interviews with 32 college presidents by Birnbaum (1988a) disclosed that responsibilities without authority made the presidents' leadership role most difficult. The presidents coped by accepting the ambiguities of their situation, by incrementally pursuing limited objectives, and by practicing management-by-exception.

A study by Munson (1981) of social work supervisors and their subordinates revealed differences between preferred and actual authority and in the structure of relations that were relevant to supervisory practices and control. In the same way, Aiken and Bacharach (1985) found considerable discrepancy between subordinates' self-reported authority to make decisions and the authority their superiors' said the subordinates had in 44 local governmental administrative agencies in Belgium. The discrepancy was increased if the local government was controlled by a coalition, the organization was open to outside influences, and the structure of control was fragmented.

The allocation of responsibility and authority to managers should reflect what is required to meet organizational objectives. However, in fact, responsibility and authority may be allocated as rewards or punishments, as political symbols, or as political gestures to imply that improvements are occurring in the organization (Benze, 1985).

Authority

Meaning of Authority

Traditionalists defined authority as the right to command and to induce compliance. They saw authority as a central feature of the structure of formal organizations that prescribed "expectations that certain individuals should exert control and direction over others within defined areas of competence." Authority is derived from implicit or explicit contracts about the individual's position or knowledge. The potential conflicts from incongruities between authority and positional responsibilities and between authority and knowledge are the same as for status-competence imbalances. The loss of positional authority because of the restructuring of the organization will be reflected in feelings of deprivation (C. S. George, 1972).

Behaviorists, influenced by Barnard (1938), maintained that leaders have authority only to the extent that followers are willing to accept their commands. Authority was defined operationally in terms of the areas in which members of an organization are free to carry out their responsibilities (Petersen, Plowman, & Trickett, 1962; Stogdill, 1957b, 1959).

Both traditional and behavioral definitions are phrased in terms of value judgments in support of two conflicting moralities or ideologies (Wells, 1963). Peabody (1962) found that executives in a city welfare agency emphasized legitimacy and position as the bases of authority, whereas the policemen in the same city stressed knowledge and competence. In a later study, Peabody (1964) found that supervisors in a police department, a welfare agency, and a public school tended to think of authority in terms of internal (superior-subordinate) relations, whereas the people supervised tended to think of it in terms of external (worker-client) relations. Supervisors in the police department accepted conflict-producing instructions without question more frequently than did those in the welfare agency or the school. The unacceptable use of authority was more common in the welfare agency than in the police department or the school.

Authority specifies an organizational member's perceived area of freedom of action and interaction, along with the formally delegated or informally recognized right to initiate action. Members act in accordance with their perception of (1) the degree of freedom allowed them and (2) the initiative that they feel they can safely exercise. Their perception may or may not coincide with the expectations of their supervisors, peers, or subordinates. Authority is also connected with the affirmation of certain values as illustrated by the inaugural oath of the U.S. President to preserve, protect, and defend the Constitution (Paige, 1977).

In general, group leaders perceive themselves to have a higher degree of authority than do the leaders of subgroups, and leaders of subgroups, in turn, perceive their authority to be higher than the perceived authority of individual members of the subgroups who are responsible for performing individual tasks. Authority gives legitimate power, which depends on the norms and expectations held by a group that are appropriate to a given role—the accorded rights, duties, and privileges that go along with appointment or election to a position.

Authority Dependent on Superiors and Subordinates

Authority depends on an interactional relationship between leaders and followers. Leaders can restrict the authority of subordinates by withholding their rights to act and decide or increase their subordinates' authority by delegating to them the rights to act. Followers can reduce the leader's authority by failing or refusing to accept the leader's decisions and can increase their leader's authority by referring matters to the leader for decision. The area of freedom of members of an organization depends not only on the behavior of their superiors and subordinates but on the members' perceptions of the behavior and expectations of their superiors and subordinates. The authority of professionals, for instance, stems from a wide variety of sources, such as their control of resources and their assigned responsibilities (Filley & Grimes, 1967).

Conflict results if colleagues think that a leader has misperceived or exceeded the limits of his or her authority (Pondy, 1967). For example, U.S. workers would find it unacceptable if their supervisors gave them orders about where they should live. According to Haas, Porat, and Vaughan (1969), an almost universal source of conflict is the tendency of individuals at any designated level to see themselves as having more authority and responsibility than their superiors believe they have. Lennerlöf (1965a) also reported a tendency for supervisors to rate themselves as having more authority than their superiors reported delegating to them.

Legitimacy may be awarded by higher officials, but it still depends on the acceptance of subordinates. Followers give a form of consent to legitimacy, which they can grant or withhold, sometimes at considerable cost (Hollander, 1978). For Barnard (1938), this meant that authority is delegated upward and is granted by one's subordinates. Furthermore, the perception that a superior has the right to give orders must be widely held and shared by other subordinates. Nor does one gain such support of one's authority from subordinates passively. Bendix (1974) thought that the compliance of subordinates with authority depends on the leader's active cultivation of the legitimacy of authority. Whitson (1980) suggested that there is a tense equilibrium between authority and the confidence followers have in the authority structure. Paradoxically, as confidence wanes, more formal authority and more coercion are applied, escalating the loss of confidence. Presumably, renewed confidence, accompanied by less coerciveness, is required before authority can be restored.

Zones of Indifference and Acceptance. Barnard expanded his argument about the extent to which authority derives from subordinates' acceptance of orders by noting the conditions that increase or decrease such compliance. Orders will be complied with to the extent they are understood, are consistent with the purpose of the organization, and are compatible with the personal interests of the subordinate and to the extent the subordinate is physically and mentally able to comply with them. But each subordinate has a "zone of indifference" within which orders are acceptable without the conscious questioning of authority. These zones of indifference are maintained by the interests of the group. In bureaucracies, they give the higher authority some latitude and autonomy in its dealings with organizational members (Downs, 1967).

A leader's authority, legitimated by his or her position, can bring about a wide or narrow zone of acceptance in subordinates by instilling in them the belief that the benefits of compliance will exceed the costs involved in remaining members in good standing in the organization. Using the Professional Zone of Acceptance Inventory (Hoy, Tarter, & Forsyth, 1978), Johnston (undated, b) surveyed 490 teachers in 55 elementary and secondary schools. In the 26 secondary schools, the teachers' zones of acceptance correlated .71 with their loyalty to the principals. However, the more authoritarian the principal, the lower was the teacher's zone of acceptance. The more the principal enforced the rules rationally and legitimately in the eyes of the teacher,

the larger was the teacher's zone of acceptance. This finding was consistent with Gouldner's (1954) observation that rational discipline was necessary for the efficient functioning of the work process, according to the factory workers he interviewed. Rational discipline maintained their loyalty to their supervisor. Workers thought it required being lenient and "not too strict" (p. 46). "(W)hen there's work to be done they expect you to do it, . . . otherwise they leave you alone" (p. 47). However, with professionals, Johnston found that the zone of acceptance was increased more by the extent to which the principals granted the teachers professional autonomy than by rational discipline and rule enforcement.

Authority versus Power

Authority is not power. "No amount of legal authority over the grizzly bears of British Columbia would enable you to get yourself obeyed by them out in the woods" (National Research Council, 1943). In supervisor-subordinate relationships, coercive and reward power, as well as legitimate power, are expected in the supervisor's position in addition to authority, but subordinates have learned to associate reward and punishment with the supervisory position and its symbols of status and authority. An analysis of authority and power requires an examination of attitudes and expectations about authority figures and symbols, as well as of the rules and regulations that describe what should be expected of holders of positions of authority (Bass, 1960).

Authority is power that is legitimated by tradition, religion, and the rights of succession; it is distinguished from force and coercion (J. M. Burns, 1978). In traditional societies, authority is the legitimate support for the father, the priest, and the noble. It comes from God, the Will of Heaven, or Nature. In modern societies, formal authority derives from man-made constitutions, compacts, charters, judges' rulings, and due process. The state has the authority to charter the board. The board has the authority to appoint the organization's president. The president has the authority to hire a staff, and so on. Decisions can be reversed in the same way. Those who appoint the leaders to a given position usually have the authority to revoke functions previously assigned, to remove units of the organization from the leaders' jurisdiction, and to dismiss them from office. Even when supported by their superiors, appointed leaders may find themselves frustrated and powerless when subordinates (like grizzly bears) refuse to obey their commands. Once-powerful elected or appointed leaders are likely to find that they no longer have influence after their followers and subordinates withdraw their support (as was the case with U.S. Attorney General Edwin Meese in 1988) or give it to opponents. Thus, the concept of role legitimation[1] calls attention to the fact that the power and influence of leaders are dependent on the acknowledgment of their authority by followers and, in some circumstances, by superiors or peers. Needless to say, the acceptance and exercise of authority will also depend on the interpretation by the individuals in authority of their rights, duties, obligations, privileges, and powers. Thus, for instance "President Eisenhower simply did not believe that he should be leading crusades of a moral, humanitarian, or civil rights nature. He believed that his job was to operate exclusively within the governmental powers of his office" (Larson, 1968, p. 21).

School principals can be seen to administer rules in three ways. In a study in 31 secondary and 39 elementary schools, Johnston (undated, a) observed that when principals enforced the rules with explanations and understanding, the compliance of the staff was high. When other principals enforced rules with discipline and punishment the staff complied grudgingly. When still other principals did not enforce the rules, the teachers did not obey the rules. The principal's influence and the felt loyalty of the teachers to their principal correlated .39 and .51, respectively, with the extent to which the principal used explanation and understanding to enforce the rules. The same correlations with the extent to which punishment was employed to maintain the rules were .01 and −.03, respectively, and the correlations with influence and loyalty were negative (−.31 and −.20, respectively) when the rules were neither enforced by the principal nor obeyed by the teachers. Venable (1983) corroborated the finding that the principals' exercise of nonpunitive legitimate authority (use of rule-administration behavior) correlated with the teachers' loyalty to the principals.

Some argue that authority and the concomitant differentiation of power are essential for cooperative efforts in organizations; others advocate equalization, leveling, and power sharing. At one extreme, Carney (1982) saw authority as the organization's universal panacea—the basis for keeping power in the hands of the few, rather than in the many, in an organization. The absence of such authority and the equality of the distribution of power in an organization makes improbable the spontaneous and comprehensive cooperation of the organization's members to work together toward common goals. Authority provides managers with the rights to control rewards and punishments; to maintain discipline, order, and security; and to avoid confusion and frustration. However, at the other extreme, Baker (1982) noted that when organizational members are committed to equality in the distribution of power, such as was seen in a radical feminist community, the maintenance of an encrusted bureaucracy was prevented, and a shifting cadre of leaders could emerge, both informally and formally, to generate policy and cooperation. Authority could be shared.

Strength and Ubiquity of Authority

Authority is pervasive in its effects, often accounting for unquestioning influence. Thus, in Milgram's (1965b) experiment, previously cited in Chapter 13, participants accepted without much consideration an experimenter's authority and delivered supposedly dangerous shocks to other student participants. Scheffler and Winslow (1950) found that persons in low-status positions did not reject authority any more than did those in high-status positions. W. E. Scott's (1965) study of the attitudes of workers in a professional organization that allowed little autonomy on the job found that workers tended to accept the system of restrictive supervision. However, those who were professionally (externally) oriented were more critical of the authority structure than were those who identified themselves as internally oriented. Self-confidence about one's interpersonal relationships also appeared to make a difference in one's responsiveness to authority. Thus, Berko-

---

[1]Discussed previously in Chapters 14 and 15.

witz and Lundy (1957) observed that individuals whose interpersonal confidence was high tended to be influenced more readily by authority figures than by peers, whereas the reverse was true for persons whose interpersonal confidence was low.

Authority is not confined to the leadership structure. All members of an organization possess or believe they possess some degree of authority to perform their respective jobs. In a study of more than 1,700 individuals in formal organization, Stogdill (1957a) found that only about 1 in 500 checked the statement "I have no authority whatsoever." Even unskilled mechanical workers rated themselves as having more than zero responsibility and authority. Furthermore, Zander, Cohen, and Stotland (1957) observed that the felt possession of authority and the exercise of authority tend to be highly correlated.

Motivational Effects on Acceptance of Authority. Control over what others want is what establishes power over them (Bass, 1960). For leaders, such power, rather than empty formal authority, depends on the extent to which they can activate the needs and motives of their subordinates (J. M. Burns, 1978). The stronger the motivational base the leader can tap, the more authority, power, and control he or she can exercise. Thus, Hollander and Bair (1954) reported that highly motivated members of a group tended to identify more strongly with authority figures than did members whose motivation was low. According to German Field Marshal Erwin Rommel, "The commander must try, above all, to establish personal and comradely contact with his men, but without giving away an inch of his authority" (as quoted in Mack & Konetzni, 1982, p. 3). Taylor (1983) suggested that leader-subordinate relationships in the U.S. Army were systematically undermined during the 1960s and the 1970s by the decrease in personal contact between leaders and subordinates because of the introduction of information technology; more detached, self-centered subordinates; and institutional policies that gave lower-level commanders more responsibility but less authority. An effort to restore personal contact and authority at each level was initiated in 1979. In the same vein, H. J. Bowman (1964) revealed that school principals who described their su-

periors high in consideration on the Leader Behavior Description Questionnaire tended to rate themselves high in responsibility and authority.

Scope of Authority and Its Effects

Bachand (1981) contrasted Canadian Crown corporations headed by government-appointed boards of directors (some of whom were governmental ministers) with Canadian private-sector corporations headed by boards of directors who were elected by stockholders. The boards differed in their scope of authority, which affected their actions and those of the executives who reported to them. The members of the Crown boards of directors, compared with those of the boards of directors of private corporations, believed they had the authority to do more than just give advice and counsel. The members of the Crown boards faced more potential for direct conflict between political and economic objectives and had to be more active than did members of the private-sector boards. As appointees of the government, the members of the Crown boards of directors believed themselves to be more independent than did the members of the private-sector boards. In turn, the chief executives of the Crown corporations sought their support for specific policies and decisions more often than the chief executives of private-sector corporations sought the support of their boards.

Boards of directors in five agencies were observed by D. E. Tannenbaum (1959) to enlarge or restrict the chief executive's role by their willingness or refusal to delegate authority to the executives to act and decide. S. Epstein (1956) studied the effects of this enlargement or restriction on supervisors in experimental groups who were given different degrees of freedom of action. Severe restriction induced the supervisors to restrict the behavior of their subordinates, to supervise them more closely, and to supervise in a management-oriented manner. But the absence of such restrictions induced the supervisors to give their subordinates more freedom and to supervise them less closely.

Dalton, Barnes, and Zaleznik (1968), as mentioned in Chapter 14, studied the effects of changes in the authority structure of some departments of a research organization when other departments were left unchanged. In those departments where authority was transferred from department heads to scientists and engineers, the scientists and engineers favored the change, but the department heads did not. Heightened expectations in the unchanged departments, triggered by the shifts in authority in the changed departments, resulted in the subordinates' dissatisfaction with superiors in the unchanged departments and in a greater tendency of those whose authority remained unchanged to seek positions elsewhere.

Throughout the Soviet system, the scope of authority of the formal organizational leadership has been limited by a parallel Communist Party structure. The dualism is seen in the parallel State and Party organizational structures, factory management and Party representatives, military commanders and political commissars. The recognition of the costliness of this dualism is beginning to result in its elimination in the military (Mack & Konetzni, 1982) and industry (Gorbachev, 1988).

Discretionary and Nondiscretionary Leadership. Birnbaum's (1988b) interviews with 32 college presidents revealed that the presidents' discretionary opportunities to lead are increasingly being constrained by governmental intervention, demographic trends, fiscal constraints, unrealistic public expectations, divergent interest groups on campus, and confusing patterns of authority. Beyond the presidents' nondiscretionary responsibility to balance their budgets, they still have discretion in how much they try to locate new sources of support.

Hunt, Osborn, and Schuler (1978) conceptualized leadership to consist of a discretionary and a nondiscretionary component. According to this concept, discretionary leadership is under the control of the leader, and nondiscretionary leadership is invoked by the organizational setting in which the leader operates. With civilian control and with concern about avoiding war-provoking incidents, U.S. military officers, in particular, are limited in their discretionary activities. Although they are fully accountable and responsible for the actions of their subordinates, they are held on a tight leash by the higher command (Mack & Konetzni, 1982).

Hunt, Osborn, and Schuler (1978) analyzed discretionary and nondiscretionary leadership in a large engineering division of a public utility. A leader's nondiscretionary score, derived from the results of a leadership survey, was that portion of the original score predicted by organizational practices. The discretionary score was equal to the difference between predicted and original scores. Table 16.1 shows the relative extent to which each of four original leader behaviors toward subordinates (approval, consideration, disapproval, and ego deflation) were accounted for as discretionary and nondiscretionary. It can be seen that in the public utility, the rewarding leadership behavior of managers had more of a nondiscretionary component than did disapproval or ego deflation.

Other efforts to measure a supervisor's discretionary leadership included a modification of items from the Leader Behavior Description Questionnaire, in which subordinates indicated the extent to which their supervisor "can and does," "could but doesn't," "can't and doesn't," and "can't but tries anyway" (Martin & Hunt,

Table 16.1 Percentage of Variance That Accounts for the Discretionary and Nondiscretionary Leadership Components of a Manager's Behavior

	Manager's Leader Behavior			
	Approval	*Consideration*	*Disapproval*	*Ego Deflation*
Discretionary	77	77	90	81
Nondiscretionary	20	22	9	1
Error	3	1	1	18

SOURCE: Hunt, Osborn, and Schuler (1978).

1981). Van de Ven and Ferry (1980) asked supervisors and employees to judge the amount of authority they have in making decisions in four areas of their jobs: (1) determining what tasks the employee will do, (2) setting quotas, (3) establishing rules and procedures, and (4) determining how exceptions to the usual work are to be handled.

Effective leaders increase the clarity of what is required of their subordinates through their discretionary leadership (Gast, 1984), but the subordinates may also display discretionary leadership behavior. Goodacre (1953) studied the performance of good and poor combat units on simulated performance problems. There was a greater tendency in good units for the men without authority to take the initiative for giving orders during the problem and to be better satisfied with their leaders' management of the problem than was the case in poorly performing units.

Changing Authority Patterns

Heller (1985, p. 488) summed up the decline in authority in Britain and elsewhere, both at the macro- and the microlevels in the past several decades, as the basis of relationships between the subordinate and the superior:

> The loss of authority is . . . evidenced by a decline in public confidence in institutions and institutional leaders, a loss of loyalty and commitment of organizational members, and a trend toward identification with multiple organizations. . . . the loss is [also] evidenced in a decline in willingness to be bossed as well as a loss of desire to be the boss, and in a trend toward rating oneself as "better than" the boss on desirable traits.

However, Heller noted that the loss of authority brings on a challenge for new bases for inducing compliance. One possibility is a return to strong personal, charismatic leaders. Industrial democracy, power sharing, and participative management, which focus on compliance that occurs as a consequence of the development of a commitment to goals, offer another alternative. The social network may be another substitute for authority.

In addition to cultural changes that have diminished authority as the basis of compliance, Zaleznik (1980) presented a number of cases of executives whose neuroses got in the way of their gaining compliance from subordinates. Sometimes, for example, the superior isolated himself, became tyrannical, and caused a palace revolution against his authority. In other cases, the executives could not exert their authority because of their obsessive fear of hurting their subordinates.

Responsibility

Meaning of Responsibility

Authority in organizations is meant to be used to fulfill assigned responsibilities (Hollander, 1978). The responsibilities are the members' perceptions of the organization's expectations that they will perform on behalf of the organization. Generally, leaders perceive their responsibilities to be broader and more far reaching than other group members perceive their own responsibilities. Leaders consider it their responsibility to make policies and to initiate action for themselves and for those members for whom they are responsible. The other members perceive themselves to be responsible for initiating action in specific subgroups or for executing individual assignments. Supervisors in naval organizations who are more conscious of their active leadership are perceived to be more responsible naval officers by their subordinates (Stogdill, Scott, & Jaynes, 1956).

Interdependence

Like authority, responsibility also depends on leader-follower relations. The leader can reduce the responsibility of other group members by failing or refusing to relinquish duties that others could perform, by overly close supervision, and by requiring consultation before others can perform. Other group members can reduce the leader's responsibility by performing tasks that the leader would be expected to perform. They can increase the leader's responsibility by failing to carry out assigned and expected duties. Even when responsibilities are closely defined, the actions of their leaders tend to condition the perceived responsibilities of the subordinates, while the performance of the subordinates tends to condition the responsibilities of the leader.

Relation to Effective Leadership

H. H. Meyer (1959) found that foremen and general foremen did not differ significantly on 77 items in their evaluations of the amount of the foremen's responsibilities. However, more effective foremen rated themselves significantly higher in responsibility than did ineffective foremen. In a later study in 21 plants, Meyer (1970b) found that the most effective foremen assumed that they had full responsibility when there was any ambiguity about who was in charge. Ziller (1959) studied group leaders' decision making regarding a difficult problem that risked the safety of their group. The leaders could base their actions on a throw of the die or by making a rational decision. Leaders who accepted responsibility for their group's action tended to be nonconformists and to possess personal resources that enabled them to take risks without undue stress and strain.

Accountability

Hollander (1978) pointed out that leaders are more likely than are others to be held accountable, despite the circumstances. A leader cannot evade the consequences of having more influence over others, more control over events, greater visibility and recognition, and greater responsibility for failures, misplaced efforts, or inaction in the face of an evident threat to the group's well-being. As Mack and Konetzni (1982, p. 5) noted:

> In navies in general, and in the United States Navy in particular, strict accountability is an integral part of command. Not even the profession of medicine embraces the absolute relationship found at sea. A doctor may lose a patient under trying circumstances and continue to practice; but a naval officer seldom has the opportunity to hazard a second ship.

The accountability of leaders to their group when they represent their group in negotiations has important effects on their status in negotiations (Lamm, 1973). However, leaders may try to avoid accountability or displace blame by resorting to collective responsibility vested in a committee, board, or shared authority.

Time Span. Jaques (1956) introduced time span—the length of time during which a manager or employee can be held accountable for decisions—to measure the manager's or employee's responsibility. Time span was found to correlate between .86 and .92 with the compensation that the job occupant judged to be fair (Richardson, 1971). It also is a good index of the location of a position in an organizational hierarchy. Thus, a supervisor may have a time span of 1 month; a department head, 1 year; a general manager, 3 years; and a chief executive officer of a corporation, 20 years. Similarly, in an army, the company commander may have a time span of 3 months; the battalion commander, 1 year; and the brigade commander, 2 years.

Delegation of Responsibilities

Delegation implies that one has been empowered by one's superior to take responsibility for certain activities. The degree of delegation is associated with the trust the superior has for the subordinate to whom responsibilities have been delegated.[2] When a group is the repository of authority and power, it likewise may delegate responsibilities to its individual members.

The delegation of responsibilities should not be confused with laissez-faire leadership[3] or abdication. A leader who delegates is still responsible for following up whether the delegation has been accepted and the requisite activities have been carried out.

The delegation of decision making implies that the decision making is lowered to a hierarchical level that is closer to where the decisions will be implemented. Such delegation is consistent with the encouragement of self-planning, self-direction, and self-control.[4]

Studies of Organizational Authority, Responsibility, and Delegation

The RAD Scales

Stogdill and Shartle (1948) developed the RAD scales to measure organizational responsibility (R), authority (A), and delegation (D). The self-rated responses by in-

---

[2]The relation of a leader's trust in subordinates and the tendency to delegate will be discussed more fully in Chapter 22.
[3]See Chapter 25.
[4]See Chapter 10.

dividual job occupants formed scales that exhibited high reliabilities (Stogdill, 1957a; Stogdill & Shartle, 1955). Correlational results were obtained in ten organizations that engaged in the production of chemicals, the manufacturing of metal products, and governmental work.

Relationship of Responsibility, Authority, and Delegation. As expected, the responsibility and authority of job occupants were uniformly positive in correlation in all 10 organizations. The correlations ranged from .13 to .63 with a mean of .45. But the relationships of responsibility and authority to delegation were not as consistently high. Responsibility averaged .17 in correlation with delegation in the 10 organizations (the range was from −.27 to .38). Authority averaged only .23 with delegation, in correlation within the organizations and ranged widely in correlation from organization to organization, from −.42 to .49.

A critical complaint of managers is that they are often delegated a great deal of responsibility by their superiors without the associated authority. Satisfaction and productivity, it would seem, are likely to be greater when responsibility, authority, and delegation are highly correlated. In the 1 organization of the 10 that Stogdill and Shartle studied, in which the correlation was −.42 between the managers' self-rated delegation and actual authority, dissatisfaction and ineffectiveness were rampant. In the 8 organizations in which delegation matched authority, satisfaction and effectiveness were much higher than in the 2 organizations in which they were mismatched. Similar inferences could be suggested about the wide range of correlations (from .13 to .63) obtained between responsibility and authority. In the organization in which responsibility and authority correlated .63, operations went much more smoothly than in the organization in which the correlation was only .13.

Some other patterns of interest emerged in the Stogdill and Shartle data and are a useful way to describe likely leadership and management differences among organizations. For instance, age and seniority varied from one organization to another in their relation to responsibility, authority, and delegation. For example, in one organization, authority was invested in older members, but in another organization, it was invested in younger ones. The correlation between age and authority within the organizations ranged from −.26 to .45. It does not take much imagination to contrast the organization in which self-estimated authority correlated .45 with age to the one in which the correlation was − .26. The organization with the negative correlation was a rapidly expanding technology firm; the organization with the high positive correlation was a stable agency with a strong age-promotion lockstep. More often than not, the educational level of an organization's managers correlated positively with their responsibilities and authority. The managers' own perceived responsibility and authority were unrelated to their subordinates' job satisfaction, but a mean correlation of .19 for the 10 organizations was found between the managers' perceived authority and the extent to which their superiors were seen as considerate in leadership behavior. Evidently, the higher members rise in authority in an organization, the more they are treated with consideration by their superiors. H. J. Bowman (1964) found similarly that school principals who rated themselves higher in responsibility, authority, and delegation described their superiors as being more considerate of them.

Status, Salary, and the RAD Scales

Kenan (1948) used the RAD scales to study large governmental organizations and found, as expected, that executives in higher-level positions described themselves as being higher in responsibility and authority than did those in lower-level positions. Correspondingly, Browne (1949) noted that executives' salaries related positively to self-estimates of responsibility and authority. D. T. Campbell (1956) reported that authority and delegation but not responsibility were positively and significantly related to one's level in various organizations, military rank, time in the position, and recognition for being in a position of leadership. Strong positive correlations should be expected between Jaques's (1956) time span of accountability and authority and responsibility as measured by the RAD scales.

RAD and Leader-Subordinate Relations

In four large naval organizations, Stogdill and Scott (1957) found that the responsibility and authority of subordinates were related to the responsibility of their superiors but not to the authority of their superiors. When superiors rated themselves as having a high level of responsibility, their subordinates rated themselves as having high levels of responsibility and authority, but these subordinates' self-ratings were unrelated to the authority of their superiors. However, the higher the responsibility and authority of their superiors, the less their subordinates tended to delegate. Yet, as might be expected, those superiors who delegated the most had subordinates who rated themselves highest in responsibility, authority, and delegation.

Stogdill and Scott (1957) analyzed the responsibility, authority, and delegation scores of commanding officers and executive officers (akin to chief administrators) and the average RAD scores of their junior officers on submarines and on landing ships. The executive officers tended to delegate more freely to those below them on both types of ships when the commanding officers exercised a wider scope of responsibility and authority and delegated more freely. But the relationship between commanding officers and executive officers on the submarines and landing ships differed substantially. Executive officers reported more responsibility and authority when their commanding officers were high in responsibility, authority, and delegation on the submarines, but the reverse was true on the landing ships.

At the same time, RAD scores of the junior officers were systematically related to the RAD scores of their executive officers and to those of their commanding officers. As the authority of their executive officer increased, the RAD scores of the junior officers tended to decrease. When their commanding officer delegated more freely, the junior officers reported an increase in responsibility on landing ships but a decrease in responsibility on submarines. Stogdill and Scott concluded that the commanding officers could increase or decrease the workloads and freedom of action of their executive officers. In the same way, junior officers tended to tighten their controls as superiors increased their own sense of responsibility and freedom of action. However, responsibility and authority did not flow without interruption down the chain of command. The responsibility, authority, and delegation of subordinates were more highly influenced by the sub-

ordinates' immediate supervisors then by their higher-level commanding and executive officers.

Expectations and Performance. Stogdill, Scott, and Jaynes (1956) also found that the performance and expectations of subordinates in the U.S. Navy were related to the responsibility and authority of their superiors. When the subordinates said their leaders had a great deal of responsibility, the subordinates said they also had a similar large amount of responsibility that required them to spend considerable time planning and attending meetings, but relatively little time teaching. With such enlarged responsibility, they thought they spent too much time in interpretation and in consulting with their subordinates and too little time in consulting with outsiders.

The subordinates' perceptions of the authority of superiors was more highly related to subordinates' expectations than to the subordinates' performance. When the superiors were perceived to have a high degree of authority, their subordinates rated themselves higher in responsibility and in spending comparatively large amounts of time planning and interpreting. They spent less-than-average amounts of time in supervision. When their superiors were seen to have a great deal of authority, these subordinates thought that they, themselves, ought to have more authority and that they ought to spend more time planning, attending meetings, and consulting with outsiders. These subordinates who believed that their superiors had a great deal of authority also thought that they, the subordinates, should spend less time in supervision and personal contacts. These subordinates also believed that they, the subordinates had too much responsibility and spent too much time in research, preparing procedures, negotiations, and training and too little time in coordination and professional consultation.

According to Stogdill, Scott, and Jaynes (1956) when U.S. Navy supervisors were perceived to delegate freely, their subordinates not only rated themselves higher in responsibility and authority but thought that they should have a high degree of responsibility and authority. However, the subordinates believed that they, the subordinates, spent too much time in inspections, preparing procedures, training, and consulting peers and not enough time in coordination and interpretation.

The responsibility of subordinates appeared to be more highly related than their authority to the responsibility and authority of their superiors. An increase in the responsibility of superiors had the effect of increasing the responsibility of their subordinates, but it did not necessarily increase the subordinates' authority. As was said before, this was a latent cause of dissatisfaction. An increase in the superiors' responsibility, authority, and delegation also appeared to require that the subordinates increase their coordination activities.

Discrepancies and Conflict. Browne and Neitzel (1952) found that the greater the difference between superiors and subordinates in estimating the superiors' responsibility, the lower was the subordinates' job satisfaction. However, disparities in these perceptions of the superiors' authority and delegation were not related to the subordinates' satisfaction.

Summary and Conclusions

Responsibility needs to be commensurate with authority. Authority is both allocated from above and acknowledged from below before it converts into power and leadership and becomes strong in its effects on leadership and wide in scope. Discretionary leadership is needed beyond that required by authority and responsibility, particularly as a consequence of changing patterns of authority.

Leaders' responsibilities are broader than those of their subordinates but are dependent on their subordinates. Responsibilities but not accountability can be delegated.[5]

Supervisors with more responsibility generate more responsibility among their subordinates, but the same is not true for the downward flow of authority. The responsibilities of superiors tend to influence the performance of subordinates, but their authority produces a stronger impact on the subordinates' expectations. When superiors have a great deal of responsibility and authority, their subordinates believe that the demands made upon them for coordination increase. However, when superiors delegate a great deal to their subordinates, the subordinates report that they are overburdened with responsibilities and need more authority than they possess. Subordinates do not view delegation as an unmixed blessing when they have critical or burdensome duties to perform. Delegation by superiors results in delegation by subordinates down to the lowest levels of supervision, more so in larger than in smaller organizations.

Organizational effectiveness can be determined by measurements of the responsibility, authority, and delegation and their interrelationships at different levels of the organization.

The linkage of the authority and responsibility of superiors and subordinates is embedded in the larger framework of superior-subordinate interdependence, the subject to which we now turn.

---

[5]Delegation will be a particular subject of managerial style in Chapter 22.

The Transactional Exchange

Leadership
as Contingent Reinforcement

As much as they claimed divine intervention in their leadership, the heroes of the *Iliad* most often engaged in transactions and offers to both men and the Gods to gain compliance with their leadership. Achilles, the greatest of the Achaean battle leaders, went off to sulk over the arbitrary confiscation of Briseis, a girl captured from Achilles by the king, Agamemnon. Briseis was taken from Achilles to compensate Agamemnon for the loss of his own prize, Chryseis, after public pressure was brought on Agamemnon to return Chryseis to her father, a priest of Apollo, to assuage the wrath of Apollo. Without Achilles, the Achaeans faced defeat. Agamemnon sent Odysseus and Ajax to lure Achilles back to take charge of the Achaean forces with promises by Agamemnon that Achilles would receive booty, land, and women if he achieved victory over the Trojans (*Iliad*, 1720/1943, Book IX).

Leadership as a Social Exchange

Although transformational leadership may transcend the satisfaction of self-interests, nevertheless, the dynamics of leadership-followership have most often been explained as a social exchange. The exchange is established and maintained if the benefits to both the leader and the followers outweigh the costs (Homans, 1958, 1961). This exchange is fair if "the leader gives things of value to followers such as a sense of direction, values, and recognition, and receives other things in return such as esteem and responsiveness" (Hollander, 1987, p. 16). Followers expect that the leader will enable them to achieve a favorable outcome and believe the exchange to be fair if the rewards are distributed equitably. However, they perceive the leader's failure to do so to be unjust, particularly if the leader has not

made an effort or is self-serving. "Fundamentally, there is a psychological contract between the leader and followers, which depends upon a variety of expectations and actions on both sides" (Hollander, 1987, p. 16).

The exchange or transaction cycle contains the following phases in crude and simple terms. The leader and the followers perceive each other as being potentially instrumental to the fulfillment of each other's needs, say, for the completion of a task. If necessary, the leader clarifies what the followers must do to complete the transaction (successfully complete the task) to obtain the material or psychic reward or to satisfy their needs.[1] The followers' failure to comply may move the leader to take corrective action. The followers' receipt of a reward or avoidance of punishment is contingent on their successful compliance and completion of the task. Satisfaction of the leader's need accrues from the followers' success. Wilson, O'Hare, and Shipper (1989) expanded the description of the task cycle for the tasks performed by personnel, their mainly transactional managers and more transformational leaders and executives in a service organization, as shown in Table 17.1.

Blanchard and Johnson (1982) set out the following rules for contingent reinforcement in the "one-minute manager's game plan." First, obtain the subordinate's agreement with the goal, including the appropriate behavior for achieving it. Check the subordinate's behavior to see whether it matches the agreed-on goal. Second, if the goal is achieved, provide praise (contingent reward) as soon as possible that is specific to what the subordinate did right. Indicate how the subordinate's action helps others and the organization. Third, if the subordinate's performance fails to match expectations, deliver a reprimand (contingent punishment) as soon

[1]As will be seen in Chapter 28, if the task is highly structured already, then little or no leader clarification will be needed.

Table 17.1 The Task Cycle Model

A Generic Task	Executives	Leaders	Managers	Personnel	
				Service	Sales
The Goal What do I do?	*The Goal* Clarify and direct mission achievement	*The Goal* Envision and initiate change for future	*The Goal* Clarify and communicate today's goals	*The Goal* Give service, keep one's own goals clearly in mind	*The Goal* Meet the client's needs, earn revenues
The Plan How do I do it?	*The Plan* Develop and communicate strategies	*The Plan* Solve novel problems resourcefully	*The Plan* Plan and solve problems that are encountered	*The Plan* Solve the client's problems as an adviser	*The Plan* Give service, be professional, analyze needs
Resources How do I carry out the plan?	*Resources* Develop a supportive culture	*Resources* Modeling, mentoring, and challenging	*Resources* Facilitate by coaching and training	*Resources* Professional/ technical skills	*Resources* Knowledge of the product, empathy, probing skills
Feedback How do I know I am performing?	*Feedback* Track and share information	*Feedback* Develop an awareness of the impact of the task	*Feedback* Obtain and give feedback on the subordinate's performance	*Feedback* Inquire about and follow up on the impact	*Feedback* Ask and identify questions and resistances
Adjustments How do I fix my mistakes?	*Adjustments* Direct/oversee other managers	*Adjustments* Use persuasion to gain and maintain commitment	*Adjustments* Correct the time and details to meet the goal	*Adjustments* Self-control to meet commitments to service	*Adjustments* Answer objections, ask for order
Reinforcement Satisfaction from achievement of the task	*Reinforcement* Share rewards for the organization's success	*Reinforcement* Share rewards for supporting the change	*Reinforcement* Recognize and reinforce the subordinate's performance	*Reinforcement* Recognize and reinforce cooperation	*Reinforcement* Express appreciation to clients
Result Task achieved	*Result* Mission accomplished	*Result* Change for the better	*Result* Today's goals achieved	*Result* Service rendered	*Result* A sale

SOURCE: Adapted from Wilson, O'Hare, and Shipper (1989), p. 2.

as possible after the failure. Despite the reprimand, it must be added, you should continue to think well of the subordinate but not of this specific performance. Fourth, the subordinate's success may call for setting a new goal; the subordinate's failure may require a review and clarification of the old goal.

Reinforcement Leadership and Followership

It takes at least two for leadership to occur. Someone has to act, and someone else has to react. Whether the actions and reactions will take place will depend on who the "someones" are, their needs, competencies, and goals. If one is perceived to be instrumental to the other's attainment of the goal as a consequence of greater competence or power, the stage is set for an interaction and leadership to occur.

In this transactional process, leaders are the agents of reinforcement for the followers. At the same time, the followers' compliance or noncompliance makes them the agents of reinforcement of the leaders. As Bass (1985a, pp. 121–122) explained:

Leader and subordinate accept interconnected roles and responsibilities to reach designated goals. Directly or indirectly, leaders can provide rewards for progress toward such goals or for reaching them. Or, they can impose penalties for failure ranging from negative feedback to dismissal. . . . Contingent positive reinforcement, reward if agreed-upon performance is achieved, reinforces the effort to maintain the desired . . . employee performance. Contingent aversive reinforcement . . . signals the need to halt the decline in speed or accuracy of the employee's performance, to modify or change the employee's behavior. It signals the need for a reclarification of what needs to be done and how.

Adams, Instone, Prince, and Rice (1981) collected West Point cadets' narratives about good or bad leadership incidents that occurred during summer training. High on the list of good incidents was contingent rewarding behavior. High on the list of bad incidents was punishing subordinates with or without provocation.

Utility of Contingent Reinforcement

According to Peters and Waterman (1982, p. 123), the managers of the excellent companies they examined exerted a good deal of effort to provide positive reinforcement for the successful completion of tasks. They made a conscious effort to reinforce any action that was valuable to the organization. The subordinates' satisfaction was increased the most, according to a field study by Reitz (1971), when their supervisors praised and rewarded them for acceptable performance (but reproved them for unacceptable work). For the 231 subordinates surveyed by Klimoski and Hayes (1980), particularly strong associations were found between their satisfaction with their supervisors and the supervisors' explicitness in giving instructions on what was required, support for efforts to perform effectively, and consistency toward the subordinates. The supervisors' explicitness and consistency also had moderate effects on reducing role ambiguity and role conflict. The supervisors' consistency contributed to some extent to the subordinates' performance and knowledge of the job, although these appeared to be enhanced by the subordinates' involvement in determining standards. Thus, the leaders' behaviors in the contingent-reward path-goal process contribute to the subordinates' efforts and performance by clarifying the subordinates' expectations that payoff will accrue to them as a conse-

quence of their efforts. To a lesser extent, some of the contingent-reward behaviors also contribute directly to the subordinates' improved performance and satisfaction with supervision by reducing role ambiguities and role conflicts.

Effects on Satisfaction. Podsakoff and Schriesheim (1985) completed a comprehensive review of field studies of the effects on subordinates of supervisors' contingent and noncontingent reinforcement.[2] Among the general conclusions they reached were that subordinates were more satisfied with their situation if their leaders provided them with rewards (positive feedback) that were contingent on their performance. Such satisfaction was not present if rewards were not contingent on their performance. (I feel well treated by my supervisor no matter what I do. In other words, it makes no difference how I perform; my supervisor will always arrange for me to be rewarded.) This noncontingent reward by the supervisor was not as satisfying as earning rewards because of the subordinates' good performance. Particularly dissatisfying to subordinates was noncontingent negative feedback, that is, not really being able to link reprimands with the behaviors that elicited them. This condition is likely to promote learned helplessness.

The field studies involved 17 large samples, with a median size of 275 cases, of financial managers, paramedics, engineers, white-collar employees of public utilities, registered nurses and nurses' aides, administrators of nonprofit organizations, city and state government employees, hospital pharmacists, and mental health employees. For the 17 samples, a mean positive concurrent correlation close to .50 was found between the subordinates' satisfaction with supervision and the extent to which the superiors practiced contingent reward. The corresponding mean correlation was near zero between satisfaction with supervision and the practice of contingent punishment. Again, noncontingent reward had little relation to satisfaction with supervision. At the same time, noncontingent punishment was negatively correlated with satisfaction with

---

[2]The studies included those of Bateman, Strasser, and Dailey (1982); Bigoness, Ryan, and Hamner (1981); Hunt and Schuler (1976); Keller and Szilagyi (1976); Podsakoff and Todor (1983a, 1983b); Podsakoff, Todor, Grover, and Huber (1984); Podsakoff, Todor, and Skov (1982); Reitz (1971); and Sims and Szilagyi (1975).

supervision in these samples. The mean correlation here was −.32 for 11 of the samples in which the measures were available.

Effects on Performance. Considerable evidence from laboratory experiments and field studies is also available concerning the contribution of contingent rewards to the effectiveness of subordinates and collegial groups. Spector and Suttell (1957) contrasted reinforcement leadership with authoritarian and democratic leadership of teams in a controlled, laboratory setting. The teams subjected to the reinforcement leader maximized positive reinforcement for correct plans produced by the teams of subjects. He was encouraging and expressed approval of good solutions to problems every time the teams reached them. When incorrect planning occurred, the reinforcement leader suggested how it could be improved. The authoritarian leader made the groups' decisions and did their planning. Under the democratic leader, the leader and the teams shared the responsibility for planning and decision making. The teams that received reinforcement leadership were the most productive, and members with little ability appeared to profit most from it.

Hunt and Schuler (1976) and Oldham (1976) observed that praise and recognition, as well as material rewards, that were contingent on acceptable performance promoted better performance and effectiveness. Giving rewards, such as praise, recognition, and recommendations for a pay increase, for subordinates' acceptable performance not only helps improve subordinates' performance (Keller & Szilagyi, 1976) but it enhances subordinates' expectations. The influence of the leader in the situation is also strengthened when contingent reward is practiced (Sims, 1977).

For 11 of the samples in the Podsakoff-Schriesheim (1985) review, the mean concurrent correlation was .32 between contingent rewarding supervision and the effectiveness of the subordinates', or work groups', performance. For 10 samples, the mean correlation was close to zero between contingent punishment by the leader and the subordinates' performance. (Luthans and Kreitner [1975] did find that contingent penalization for unacceptable actions improved performance but only when it was coupled with contingent reward for acceptable performance.) The mean correlation

was also close to zero between performance and noncontingent reward for 8 samples and −.12 between noncontingent punishment and performance.

Even after the same single source of variance was removed by removing the general factor of each individual's responses to all questions (the subordinate raters described the leaders' as well as their own satisfaction and performance), Podsakoff and Todor (1985) found there was still a positive association between contingent reinforcement leadership and a group's cohesiveness, drive, and productivity.

Causality. In cross-lagged causal analyses of 206 employees, Greene (1976a) was first to demonstrate that contingent rewarding by supervisors resulted in the improved subsequent performance and satisfaction of subordinates. The correlation was .48. The effect had some permanency and was not observable only in concurrent correlations of the supervisors' behavior and the subordinates' performance and satisfaction.

Using 61 working MBA students, Sims (1977) corroborated Greene's conclusion in a six-month longitudinal field study about how much contingent rewarding by supervisors contributed to the respondents' subsequent performance. The correlation was .50. Likewise, Szilagyi (1980b), in a three-month longitudinal study of 128 employees in a controller's department, obtained a comparable coefficient of .48.

The results were reversed or nil (−.23, −.12, −.07) for the effects of earlier contingent punishment by supervisors on the future performance of subordinates in Greene's, Sims's, and Szilagyi's studies. But future punitive supervision appeared to be more a consequence of past poor performance of subordinates; the correlations for the three studies were −.40, −.04, and −.59. Future contingent reward was not consistently a consequence of subordinates' earlier good performance; the correlation for the three studies were .26, .09, −.17.

Utility of Disciplinary Action

Although the overall implication of the field studies is that contingent reward leads to improved subordinate performance but contingent punishment has less consistent effects, the performance of subordinates obviously can improve as a consequence of the supervisor's correction and may improve from other forms of negative feedback (Arvey & Ivancevich, 1980).

Sims and Szilagyi (1975) suggested that negative sanctions may improve performance by reducing role ambiguity. According to Podsakoff (1982), high performing leaders use both contingent positive and contingent aversive reinforcement. O'Reilly and Weitz (1980) found that managers of high-performing units used negative reinforcers more quickly. Franke and Kaul (1978) reinterpeted the statistical inferences that could be drawn from the Hawthorne experiments (Roethlisberger, 1941) and concluded that managers' tightening of discipline was an important reason for the increased productivity of workers—a relationship that was ignored by the original investigators. O'Reilly and Puffer (1983) asked 142 sales representatives to describe critical incidents of a good and poor performance with and without supervisory reinforcement. They found that effort, satisfaction, and a sense of equity were enhanced as well by formal or informal reprimands for poor performance as by favorable recognition for good performance.

Following initial interviews with a random sample of 100 hourly refinery employees, Arvey, Davis, and Nelson (1984) surveyed 526 hourly employees. The employees were asked to describe their perceptions of their immediate supervisors' disciplinary behavior, as well as the kinds of factors that supervisors take into account when applying discipline. Twenty percent of the employees reported that they had experienced disciplinary actions. Both the punishment orientation and reward orientation of the supervisors contributed to employees' satisfaction with their supervisors. But the employees' evaluation of the supervisors differed strongly, depending on how much and in what ways the supervisors used punishment. The more the supervisors used formal punishment ("write you up for an infraction") or informal punishment ("yell at you"), the less satisfied their subordinates were with them. The employees' satisfaction with their supervisors correlated $-.46$ with too-harsh discipline and $-.50$ with discipline without giving a clear explanation. On the other hand, satisfaction with the supervisors correlated .31 with the supervisors' tendency to discipline people immediately after an infraction of the rules occurred; .60 with the tendency to maintain close and friendly

relations with employees they had disciplined, and .32 with consistency in disciplining employees from person to person and situation to situation.

Contingent punishment may take several forms when an employee fails to live up to expectations, such as when the employee deviates from the norms, his or her production falls below agreed-on standards or the quality of what is produced becomes unacceptable. The leader may call attention to the deviation. Being told of one's failure to meet standards may be sufficient to provide aversive reinforcement for what one did wrong. Being told why can be particularly helpful to the inexperienced subordinate, especially if the message includes further clarification of the desired performance. The leader may administer penalties, such as fines or suspensions without pay. Loss of support from the leader may occur or the employee may be discharged.

Management by Exception. When leaders take corrective actions and intervene only when failures and deviations occur, they are practicing management by exception. In practicing management by exception, some managers actively search for deviations and shortfalls. They set up standards and regularly monitor subordinate performance to see if the standards are being met. Others are more passive, asking no more than what is essential to get the work done (Hater & Bass, 1988). Management by exception is contingent aversive reinforcement, since leaders who practice it intervene only when something goes wrong. If a subordinate's performance falls below some threshold, at the emotionally mildest level, the leader feeds back information to the subordinate that the threshold has been crossed. The negative feedback may be accompanied by a contingent reward from the leader, in the form of reclarification and encouragement. At the other extreme, it may be accompanied by disapproval, a reprimand, a formal citation, suspension, or discharge. Management by exception is consistent with the cybernetics of negative feedback—feedback that signals the system to move back toward its steady-state base. The manager is alert for deviations and provides the negative feedback when needed.

In most surveys of descriptions of industrial leaders by their colleagues and subordinates, managing by exception does not contribute to appraisals of the leaders' effectiveness or satisfaction with the leaders (Bass, 1985a). However, it correlates .23 and .25 with the rated effectiveness of officers in the U.S. Army and Air Force and .29 and .31 with subordinates' satisfaction with the officers' leadership (Colby & Zak, 1988).

Particularly important is whether the management by exception is active or passive. The leader who arranges to monitor errors and deviances that need to be corrected is seen to be actively engaged in management by exception. The leader who waits to be informed about errors and deviances before taking action is seen as practicing passive management by exception. The correlations for 186 junior naval officers described by their subordinates as actively managing by exception were .50 and .54 with the subordinates' evaluation of the effectiveness of the officers and satisfaction with them, and .28 and .22 with fitness reports and recommendations for early promotions from their superiors. The same correlations with passively managing by exception were respectively .11, .19, $-.04$, and $-.05$. (Yammarino & Bass, 1988).

In interviews with 474 managers about their use of discipline, Beyer (1981) found that both personal and situational factors could account for the extent to which supervisors took disciplinary actions with problem employees. For example, managers who personally endorsed humane pragmatism—concern for both the employees' welfare and the company's productivity—were more likely to be constructive and confrontational with problem drinkers and less likely to take disciplinary action against these employees. At the same time, the judged seriousness of the drinking problem was the strongest determinant of whether disciplinary action, including issuing warnings in writing or ordering a suspension or discharge, would be taken. Union and management policies had systematic effects, as did the managers' expectations that their constructive or disciplinary efforts would or would not please higher authority. Unfortunately, the results were often different when the managers dealt with problem employees other than those who had drinking problems.

Observing co-workers who are being threatened or punished by supervisors can also provide vicarious reinforcement that promotes productivity of the onlook-

ers. Schnake (1986) hired students at $5.00 an hour ostensibly to perform clerical work, along with a confederate of the experimenter who made sure to perform more poorly than the student subjects. Threats to reduce the confederate's wage to $3.50 per hour for poor performance and actually cutting the confederate's pay resulted in significant increases in the output of the subjects.

Applying Contingent Reinforcement

According to Zaleznik (1967), contingent reinforcement with an emphasis on the exchange should be practiced by managers who are interested in efficient processes rather than substantive ideas. It will be facilitated by the managers' flexibility in using their powers to reward or punish to maintain or improve processes and organizational arrangements. Blanchard and Johnson (1982) suggested that inexperienced subordinates may need to be told by their superior what they did right and how their superior feels about their work, and encouraged to continue. Experienced subordinates may need to be told what they did wrong without diminishing their self-esteem. Furthermore, reprimand will work if it is timely and specific to the behavior involved, not to the person. It should focus on what was done wrong, how the supervisor feels about it, and the expectation that the subordinate's performance is going to improve. The subordinate's failure to appreciate what is expected calls for the clarification of requirements, rather than punitive actions. Failure that is due to a lack of knowledge calls for information giving, training, or transfer. Failure that is the result of insufficient challenge calls for enlarging the task, transfer, increased extrinsic incentives, or acceptance of reality by the subordinate. A lack of commitment requires that the employee's involvement in the planning or control process be increased. An overload of goals necessitates the establishment of priorities.

According to Scott and Podsakoff (1982), if leadership and followership can be conceived as behaviors, then the principles of operant reinforcement can be used to modify leader-follower behaviors. To begin with, leaders need to learn what reinforcers work with what kinds of followers. They also must be able to identify and specify the types of behavior by subordinates that will maximize the group's performance, or, if this is not possible, to identify and specify the desired results and to keep up with changes that are required. The shifting of control by the leader to self-control by the followers over time is salutory.

If extrinsic reinforcers are used, leaders must be able to link the reinforcement to the subordinates' performance. Leaders need to be consistent in their administration of reinforcements. Punishment must be delivered quickly and with reasons for it to stamp out undesirable responses. Environmental events that sustain the dysfunctional behavior need to be eliminated. McElroy (1985) also argued that reinforcement is not mindless. Rather, when reinforced, a subordinate will develop a reason for it that may be the same or different from the one given by the leader. It is likely that the subordinate will attribute the reward for the successful performance to his or her personal efforts but attribute penalties for failure to external causes, which, it is presumed, will result in the penalties having less of an effect on the subordinate's subsequent behavior.

Schedules of reinforcement will systematically affect causal attributes. For example, if one is rewarded only some of the time for good performance, one will tend to attribute the cause to effort or luck, rather than to ability.

Caveats. Caution is required in applying reinforcement theory that is based on animal research to human leader-subordinate relations. If faced with choices X and Y and reinforced 90 percent of the time for choosing X and 10 percent of the time for choosing Y, animals will choose X, 90 percent of the time. However, humans will take a cognitive leap, deducing that they will maximize their reward by choosing X, 100 percent of the time. Animals will earn rewards only 81 percent of the time; humans, 90 percent (Mawhinney, 1982).

Using contingent reward or punishment is a tricky business. A 100 percent schedule of praise for every success will probably lead to the subordinate's satiation and discounting of the supervisor, as well as to the subordinate's perception that the superior's behavior is ingratiating. Continued praise in front of associates may create considerable feelings of discomfort and defensive feelings. Too infrequent a schedule of contingent praise may raise questions about the superior's motivation. The subordinate's expectation of an extrinsic reward that is contingent on his or her performance may reduce the subordinate's intrinsic motivation to continue that performance (Deci, 1972). Thus, in a field study of 48 health care technicians for handicapped and mentally retarded children, Jordan (1986) showed that the intrinsic motivation of those whose rewards were contingent on performance decreased $2\frac{1}{2}$ months after the extrinsic incentive program started. The technicians' intrinsic motivation increased if the rewards of the incentive program were not contingent on performance. Their satisfaction with the extrinsic reward of pay was not affected, however.

Mild punishment in private, in the form of suggested corrections by the superior of the subordinate's behavior, may be salutory. Severe punishment, in the form of a suspension, may provoke hostility, resentment, and anxiety. Frequent contingent punishment may increase anxiety to the point where it interferes with the subordinate's performance. Too-infrequent contingent punishment may allow incorrect habits to become entrenched that will be difficult to eliminate.

In a nationwide survey of 5,000 employees, almost half the respondents said that the managers at their firm were too lenient with poor performers (Anonymous, 1988a). Nonetheless, according to Veiga (1988), a majority of executives are in favor of candor in dealing with problem subordinates. Unwanted behaviors and outcomes need to be clarified. Both the leader and the subordinate need to acknowledge their responsibilities for the situation. Clear-cut expectations about what will be changed need to be established, and positive support for making a small new change needs to be given.

On the basis of theory and research, Arvey and Ivancevich (1980) offered a set of propositions that outline the conditions under which punishment is likely to be effective in organizational settings. They stated that punishment should be delivered as close as possible to the time of the undesired subordinate behavior by an otherwise close and friendly supervisor and should be moderate in intensity. Furthermore, punishment should be accompanied by explanation. Alternatives to the undesired behavior should be available.

A Model for Contingent Reinforcement

Bass (1985a) presented a model of the most important linkages between contingent positive and aversive reinforcement by leaders and the resultant effort of their followers to comply and carry out the transaction. The model is displayed in Figure 17.1. As Bass (1985a, pp. 147, 149) noted:

Leaders ... reward followers to encourage the followers' acceptance of their work roles. Followers comply with the leaders' directions ... to gain the rewards promised by the leaders for such compliance. If the followers succeed, they earn material rewards, ... satisfaction and enhanced self-esteem. ... [In maintaining their] role behavior and ... [in] renewing their efforts ... [to] comply with what is expected of them ... the leaders also clarify such expectations. Such clarification promotes followers' understanding of their roles and builds followers' confidence, further contributing to their compliance.

If the followers fail to comply and the failure is attributed by the leaders [to a lack of] follower clarity

Figure 17.1. Contingent Reinforcement and Follower Effort

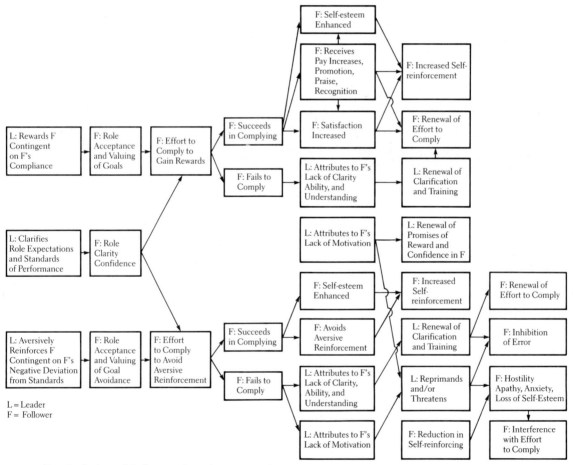

L = Leader
F = Follower

and understanding, then the leaders will renew their clarification of what they expect. If the leaders attribute the failure of their followers to lack of motivation [and they wish to be positively reinforcing] the leaders will renew their promises of reward and confidence in the followers . . . [or if the leaders wish to use] aversive reinforcement such as reprimand, they [run the risk] of followers' anxiety withdrawal.

Leaders practicing contingent aversive reinforcement . . . will foster followers' efforts to comply with the clarified standards to avoid negative consequences for failure. If followers succeed in complying, they avoid being aversively reinforced and may increase in self-esteem and self-reinforcement. If they fail and leaders attribute the failure to lack of clarity, ability, and understanding, the leaders will renew clarification and attempt to improve followers' ability through training, thus increasing the likelihood of ultimate successful performance by followers. On the other hand, if aversively reinforcing leaders attribute followers' failure to comply to lack of follower motivation, they are likely to reprimand or threaten, possible generating the unintended effects on followers of hostility, apathy, anxiety, and loss of self-esteem. In turn, there will be a reduction in self-reinforced effort and interference with the efforts of followers to comply.

The specific behaviors involved and the measurements needed to test the model are available from numerous sources.

Specific Behaviors and Measures of Contingent Reward and Punishment

Klimoski and Hayes (1980) found four of six behaviors of supervisors that 231 surveyed subordinates thought were ways in which their supervisors provided contingent reward: (1) being explicit when giving instructions, (2) allowing the subordinates to be involved in determining standards of performance, (3) giving support for efforts to perform effectively, and (4) being consistent toward subordinates. Only when the subordinates saw the supervisors as behaving in these four ways did they expect that their effort would lead to successful performance and that their successful performance would generate the commensurate rewards. The other seem-

ingly relevant behaviors of supervisors—frequency of communications and frequency of review—were actually irrelevant to these subordinates' expectations.

Yukl (1981) used content analysis to derive a category of "structuring reward contingencies"—the extent to which a leader rewards a subordinate's effective performance with tangible benefits, such as a pay increase, promotion, more desirable assignments, a better work schedule, or more time off. Examples of contingent reward structuring were as follows: "My supervisor established a new policy that any subordinate who brought in a new client would earn 10 percent of the contracted fee" and "My supervisor recommended a promotion for a subordinate with the best performance record in the group" (p. 122).

Another way in which the leader can establish the "contract" with the subordinate is to set goals. The leader emphasizes the importance of setting specific performance goals for each important aspect of a subordinate's job, measures the subordinate's progress toward reaching the goals, and provides concrete feedback. Yukl gave these examples: "The supervisor held a meeting to discuss the sales quota for next month" and "My supervisor met with me for two hours to establish performance goals for the coming year and to develop action plans" (p. 123).

According to factor analyses of survey results, Sims (1977) found that contingent reward takes two main forms: praise for work well done and recommendations for pay increases, bonuses, and promotions. Also, there may be commendations for meritorious effort and honors for outstanding service. The first positive-reward-behavior factor explained 37 percent of the variance among the supervisors. Items that most highly correlated with this first factor included:

Your supervisor would show a great deal of interest if you suggested a new and better way of doing things.
  Your supervisor would give you special recognition if your work performance was especially good.
  Your supervisor would personally pay you a compliment if you did outstanding work (p. 126).

The second factor, which accounted for 18 percent of the variance, dealt with recommendations for promotion and advancement. Items that were highly correlated with the second factor included:

Your supervisor would see that you will eventually go as far as you would like to go in this organization, if your work is consistently above average.

Your supervisor would recommend that you be promoted if your work was better than others who were otherwise equally qualified.

Your supervisor would help you get a transfer if you asked for one (p. 126).

Yukl and Van Fleet (1982) uncovered numerous critical incidents of management by exception and contingent punitiveness among ROTC officers, such as these:

Checks to see that tasks are accomplished satisfactorily.

Shows concern about the appearance of cadets.

Expresses disappointment that the unit did not perform better.

Explains to a person why he is being disciplined.

Sims (1977) uncovered a factor of supervisory behavior that dealt with contingent punishment. The items included, "Your supervisor would get on you if your work was not as good as the work of others in your department" and "Your supervisor would give you a reprimand (written or verbally) if your work was consistently below acceptable standards" (p. 126).

Scales of Contingent Reinforcement. The Contingency Questionnaire (Johnson, 1970; Reitz, 1971) assessed the extent to which subordinates perceive contingencies between their performance and how the organization responds to them. Three factors emerged: (1) supportive instrumentality—the contingency between the subordinate's behaviors and a supportive or rewarding organizational response, (2) punitive instrumentality—the contingency between the subordinate's undesirable behaviors and the administration of punitive events by the organization or the withdrawal of rewards, and (3) advancement instrumentality—the contingency between the subordinate's behavior and the subordinate's advancement in the organization. The three factors accounted for approximately 50 percent of the common variance in the scale of 20 items.

House and Dessler (1974) developed four-item scales to measure leader-contingent approval and leader-contingent disapproval behavior. Scales to assess

noncontingent reward and noncontingent sanctioning behavior were also added. Hunt and Schuler (1976); Fulk and Wendler (1982); and Podsakoff, Todor, and Skov (1982) likewise developed and evaluated the Leader Reward and Punishment Questionnaire, which had a total of 23 items to measure both contingent and noncontingent reinforcement by the leader. In typical items from the most recent report, supervisors were described in paraphase as follows:

Contingent Reward—personally compliments me when I do outstanding work.

Noncontingent Reward—praises me when I do poorly as when I do well.

Contingent Punishment—would reprimand me if my work was below standard.

Noncontingent Punishment—holds me accountable for things over which I have no control.

Schriesheim, Hinken, and Tetrault (1988) corroborated the factorial validity of the four dimensions of contingent reward, noncontingent reward, contingent punishment, and noncontingent punishment with the responses of 176 aircraft controllers and 375 employees of a psychiatric hospital to a questionnaire in which they were asked to describe their supervisors.

Bass (1985a) created and Bass and Avolio (1989) evaluated a scale of ten items within the Multifactor Leadership Questionnaire (MLQ) to measure contingent reward in an exchange context that contained items such as: "tells me what to do if I want to be rewarded for my efforts" and "there is close agreement between what I am expected to put into the group effort and what I can get out of it."

As was noted earlier, a contingent aversive or punitive factor is involved in the practice of management by exception. Hater and Bass (1988) and Yammarino and Bass (1988) created factored scales of active and passive management by exception within the MLQ. The active practice of management by exception dealt with monitoring and searching for subordinates' deviations from standards and making suitable corrections ("Checks to see if things are going along all right"). The passive practice by the manager involved only reacting when deviations are brought to his or her attention ("endorses the adage, 'If it ain't broken, don't fix it'").

Compared to other ways of measuring leadership

performance, these behavioral scales of contingent reinforcement behavior by leaders tend to be relatively free of the usual biases of respondents to rate according to the social desirability of the behaviors (Podsakoff, Todor, Grover, & Huber, 1984) or the implicit theories of leadership that the raters hold (Bass & Avolio, 1988).

Reinforcement and the Emergence of Leaders

In addition to the use by leaders of contingent reinforcement to develop and maintain effective follower compliance, contingent reinforcement processes also can explain who emerges as a leader. A variety of experiments have been conducted to show how reinforcement can increase individual members' attempts to lead and their process in such leadership.

Who attempts and continues to lead and who attempts and continues to follow in newly formed groups without appointed leaders can be explained by the differential reinforcement experiences of the various members of the groups. To be successful in influencing others, one must attempt to lead. Such attempts to lead are increased by the positive reinforcement of success as a leader and are decreased by failure and aversive reinforcement. The inhibition of the leadership attempts of one member by failure can increase the leadership attempts of others. The positive reinforcement of one member can result in "crowding out" the other members. Contrived reward has been applied in experiments to test its efficacy in reinforcing attempts to lead the interaction process as well as its efficacy in reinforcing the probabilities of successfully leading others.

Reinforcing Attempts to Lead

Bavelas, Hastorf, Gross, and Kite (1965) assessed the amount of activity of each participant in initial discussions. In a second session, only one particular member of each discussion group was reinforced for participation by the flashing of a green light. Additionally, in some of these groups, the participation of the remaining members was inhibited by the flashing of a red light. Without inhibiting other members with the

red flashing light, those who were positively reinforced with the green flashing light significantly increased their talking (highly correlated with attempts to lead). But it was necessary to both use positive reinforcement (the green flashing light) with the initially least-active talker and to inhibit (with the red flashing light) the initially most-active talker to increase the amount of talking by the originally least-active talker. The least active talker's gain was mostly at the expense of the originally most active talker.

Jaffee (1968) and Jaffee and Skaja (1968) reinforced the leadership acts of one member of pairs of experimental partners. The number of leadership attempts by the members who were reinforced by the appearance of a light significantly exceeded those by the nonreinforced and control participants. The effects lasted over a test period of one week and were found to generalize to a different experimental situation. Zdep and Oakes (1967) likewise demonstrated that reinforcement of a group member's leadership acts resulted in an increase in talking and leadership. In the same way, Binder, Wolin, and Terebinski (1965, 1966) and Wolin and Terebinski (1965) controlled the proportion of decisions as a leader for which each member of a group was reinforced. The resulting emergence as a leader fit a Markov model. Increases in leadership behavior were found to be responsive to changes in such rates of reinforcement.

Aiken (1965a) rewarded a group member in a second session who had talked the least in a previous session. The other three members were punished for speaking in the second session. The rewarded member's verbal output significantly increased in comparison with the output of unrewarded control group members, but punishment did not significantly decrease it. After the second session, the three unrewarded experimental group members rated the rewarded member higher than members of the control group rated each other in leadership, participation, and self-confidence.

Reinforcing Successful Leadership

In these experiments, mainly with school pupils and college students, group members whose leadership was reinforced with success rather than failure were more likely to increase their influence over the other members. Thus Mausner (1954a) gave participants either positive, negative, or no reinforcement when they were working alone on a judgmental task. When combined in pairs, the nonreinforced partners had a significant tendency to shift their judgments to comply with those of their reinforced partners, while the reinforced participants did not change. The participants who had received positive reinforcement were significantly less influenced by their partners than were those who had received negative reinforcement. Thus, Mausner demonstrated that the participants' perception of the success of their partners gave them prestige and reinforced their expectation of future success. The participants who worked with previously successful partners were significantly more influenced by them than were those who worked with previously unsuccessful partners in a judgmental task. Banta and Nelson (1964) showed that the probability of positively reinforced participants having their suggestions adopted increased over 60 trials, while the probability for negatively reinforced participants decreased. Kanareff and Lanzetta (1960) also demonstrated that the tendency to be imitated by others is related to the rate at which the imitated one is positively reinforced.

McClintock (1966) used paid accomplices who either supported, shifted support, or did not support the leaders of discussion groups. It was found that leaders evidenced more release of tension, more positive affect, and more task-oriented responses when they were supported than when they were not supported.

Cohen and Lindsley (1964) gave pairs of subjects a monetary reward for social responses or punished them by blackouts of the room for individual (nonsocial) responses. They rewarded acts of leadership by opening a panel that permitted subjects to see each other briefly. Differential leadership responses were established by the differential reinforcement procedures.

James and Lott (1964) rewarded some members of an experimental task group with six nickels, others with three, and did not reward still others. Those who were rewarded with six nickels chose each other significantly more often than did those who were rewarded with three nickels or those who were not rewarded. G. Gardner (1956) studied groups of boys who were assigned fictitious scores for success in operating switches that activated various combinations of lights. The scores

correlated .93 with their nomination as team captains. Observations of success appeared to reinforce the group's perception of a member's suitability for the leadership role. Katz, Blau, Brown, and Strodtbeck (1957) found that the greater the extent to which the leader's suggestions were reinforced by the follower's acceptance and support in the first session of a discussion task, the greater the extent to which the leadership was retained in later sessions. Likewise, York (1969) and Hastorf (1965) demonstrated that reinforcement of members' behavior in the group significantly increased their leadership. Gilchrist (1962) studied groups of four members in which two succeeded and two failed. These facts were communicated to group members, who then chose partners for the next problem. In the third session, the successes were made to fail and the failures were made to succeed. Both success (S) and failure (F) participants tended to choose other successes for further activities. Participants who succeeded twice (SS) chose other SS participants, while those who failed twice (FF) distributed their choices between SS and FF participants. In the third session, the mutually chosen successes (SS) were again combined and made to fail; the failures (FF) were made to succeed. These participants, now FFS, tended to choose other FFS participants. The experience of success after failure enabled the previously failing participants to choose each other. The eventual experience of success reinforced the expectation of success among those who had initially failed.

Hamblin, Miller, and Wiggins (1961) studied the effects of the leader's competence, reinforcement of the leader, and conflicting suggestions by group members on a group's morale. Reinforcement rate, perceptions of the leader's competence, manipulation of the leader's success, and the group's morale were all highly and significantly intercorrelated. The members' opposition to the leaders' suggestions was reduced by reinforcement of the leader, the leader's success and competence, and the group's morale.

Mausner and Bloch (1957) found that reinforcement of a partner and the partner's prestige interacted in a judgmental task. That is, both the partner's prestige and earlier reinforcement contributed to the partner's influence in a condition of success but not when failure was contrived. Reinforcement did not overcome the effect of a partner's failure to make correct judgments in a previous situation.

Caveats. Some qualifying considerations are in order. Reinforcements may have unintended and unwanted effects on attempted and successful leadership. Zdep (1969) assembled groups of four members in which one member scored either high or low in self-reported leadership (the Leadership Scale of the California Psychological Inventory). The participation rate of high scorers increased under the experimenter's reinforcement but it did not increase for the low scorers. As the high scorers' rate of participation rose, the subsequent leadership ratings by the other members increased. But the experimenter's reinforcement of one member built up expectations about that member among the others. Low scorers who failed to respond when given the reinforcement were rated as poorer leaders than were low scorers who were not so reinforced. Aiken (1965b) also demonstrated that the use of reinforcement for operant conditioning of specific behaviors, such as giving suggestions and asking for contributions, resulted in marked changes in leadership style but produced a tense, anxious leader. This finding suggested that simple reinforcement technology, by itself, may be inadequate for leadership training. The shaping of one member's responses must take into consideration the larger context of the interaction with other active participants.[3]

The Dynamics of the Exchange Relationship

The leader-follower transactional exchange was the essence of the dynamics of leadership for Hollander (1958, 1978), who concluded that the leader and the follower enter into an exchange that begins with negotiation to establish what is being exchanged and whether it is satisfactory. The exchange results in the follower's compliance for the leader's assistance in pointing the way toward the attainment of mutual goals.

[3]More about this will follow in Chapter 19 which is devoted to examining the limitations and constraints on the use of contingent reinforcement to shape subordinate and leader behavior.

Idiosyncracy Credit

In real life, there is no experimenter to reinforce the attempts of one member rather than another to lead. On a playing field, with similar personalities and a common situation, what, then, makes one member a leader and another a follower? For Hollander, it is a matter of how much idiosyncracy credit each member previously earned. The interplay that fashions who will lead and who will follow builds up idiosyncracy credit for the emerging leader relative to the follower. Both competence in the group's task and conformity to the group's norms earn idiosyncracy credit for a member and, as a consequence, emergence as leader or success as an appointed leader. A buildup of such credit makes subsequent initiatives even more likely to be accepted and strengthens the member's status as a leader. With idiosyncracy credit, the emerging leader can deviate from the group's norms in a way that those without such credit are not permitted to do. Newcomers, for instance, are unlikely to have the necessary credit, although some may bring derivative credit with them from another group as a consequence of their reputation in that group. There is a complex interplay between the requisite competence and the requisite conformity in maintaining idiosyncracy credit. Alvarez (1968) demonstrated that a leader's greater deviance from the norms was tolerated when it was accompanied by the group's success. In a study of a simulated organization, Alvarez found that the leader lost credit at a slower rate than did the followers, but only in successful organizations. The leader lost credit at a faster rate than followers in unsuccessful organizations.

Consistent with the concept of idiosyncracy credit, Zierden (1980) suggested that leading through the follower's point of view is the way to achieve success and effectiveness as a leader. The fundamental conformity of leaders to their followers' norms and values was seen by Litzinger and Schaefer (1982, p. 139) to be manifested in the way the Pope calls himself "The Servant of the Servants of God" and in Hegel's conception of leadership:

Leadership is possible . . . not only on the condition that followership has been learned, but on the more radical condition that the leader has known . . . the travail of the follower; he must here and now incorporate within himself all that the follower is. The school for leadership is indeed followership, a followership that is fully preserved within leadership, but transformed for having moved beyond itself. . . .

Litzinger and Schaefer also saw that good followership precedes good leadership in the West Point faculty doctrine that leadership is developed by first teaching cadets how to be good followers. Prior to their gaining powerful office, world-class leaders, from Otto von Bismarck to George Bush, were seen as "faithful takers of orders." To be elected, President Bush strongly espoused the norms of the majority of the electorate about law enforcement, the flag, taxes, education, the environment, and so on. Once elected, his actions could deviate to some extent from these espousals without losing too much of his majority constituency.

Limitations. With idiosyncracy credit, the leader can step out from the rest of the pack and suggest innovations that will bring about changes in the group. Nevertheless, although the leader is able to deviate from the group's norm, he or she must continue to pay attention to the group's norms, values, and standards to remain successful in influencing others. A leader will lose much of his or her idiosyncracy credit by an outrageous violation of the members' expectations. Some evidence is available about the possible limits of deviation from norms. Hollander (1961a) conducted an experiment in which his participants were given brief descriptions of persons who were to be ranked from high to low in accorded status. The participants were then given lists of behaviors that might be exhibited by the persons whom they had ranked. As the perceived status of those who were ranked increased, progressively less disapproval was shown for "suggesting changes from group plans" and "discussing group concerns with outsiders." However, "interrupting others to make comments" was increasingly disapproved for persons with increasing status. High-status members were permitted to innovate group changes but were not expected to interrupt low-status members.

Looking at the same issue, Michener and Lawler (1975) found that members were more likely to endorse the continuance of leaders in their positions when the groups were positively reinforced by being successful in their efforts, when the members got more rewards than did the leaders, or when the leaders were not permanently fixed in the office. But they were less enthusiastic about endorsing the continuance of leaders in office if the leaders were inconsistent in their competence or fairness. Polansky, Lippitt, and Redl (1950a) and Grosser, Polansky, and Lippitt (1951) showed that those group members who attempted to be more influential and those who were more successful in doing so were more susceptible to contagious influence from other members. Compared to those members who tried but failed to exert influence on the group, they were more likely to act in reference to the demands of the group situation than in terms of their own needs. Although they were able to react spontaneously to others and to initiate spontaneity in others, they also felt secure enough to resist direct attempts by others to influence them. They could maintain conformity to the steady state as well as enlarge the other members' freedom to act.

The holders of idiosyncracy credit have other limitations on the deviance that they are permitted. For example, they have less latitude to deviate from particular role obligations (Hollander, 1961a, 1961b), although they may deviate from norms with less cost than can other members. In effect, the leader's freedom to deviate from general norms is exchanged for conforming more closely to the expectation others have about the requirements of the leader's role.

Negotiation of Equity

In the social exchange, the followers may exert influence and make demands on the leader. Negotiation may be required about what will be done and by whom. The negotiation may consider the distribution of effort and rewards between the leader and the followers, including need, justice, merit, equity, and fairness. Dyer, Lambert, and Tracy (1953) observed that in the more effective of two bomber wings (in which the most successful leadership was likely), more favorable attitudes existed toward the method of allocating rewards and punishments. A satisfactory interchange between the leader and followers is enhanced by mutual trust

(Deutsch, 1973), a sense of fairness and equity, mutual support, involvement, and wider latitudes of acceptance (Dansereau & Dumas, 1977; Graen, 1976). But the interdependence of the followers affects how important equity is to the satisfactory exchange. According to Miller and Hamblin (1963), differential rewarding for relative achievement decreased a group's productivity when the members were highly interdependent but not when they were less interdependent.

True equity would require that rewards be commensurate with contributions. But equity is relative. Members judge the equity of their costs and benefits in comparison to the costs and benefits of others who they regard as similar to them (J. S. Adams, 1963).

Negotiations may be between the leader and the group or between the leader and each individual member. Graen and Cashman (1975) suggested that such individualized exchanges will be closer to the parties involved than would be an exchange between the leader and the group. Such closeness will increase acceptance of more responsible tasks by the individual members and the leader's greater assistance of the members. There will also be more support, sensitivity, and trust in the closer relationship.

Leader-Member Exchange

The superior-subordinate relationship was conceived as a social exchange or negotiated transaction. The conception led to a fully developed theory to explain the effects of leadership on the compliance of subordinates. Leader-member exchange implies an informally developed role—one that is negotiated between each individual group member and the leader (Graen, 1976).[4] Co-workers may get involved in the role definition, but the leader, in particular, has a vested interest in the member's role. The definition of a member's role defines what the member and the leader will ex-

pect the member to do. Such was demonstrated with 62 new nonacademic employees on a college campus by Graen, Dansereau, Minami, and Cashman (1973). Given the leader's control of reinforcements, the interpersonal exchange relationship of the member and leader is particularly important in shaping the member's performance.

Quality of the Exchange. The "quality" of the leader-member exchange, the satisfaction of either or both parties with it, should be a determinant of subsequent outcomes of joint efforts. For example, for 41 such leader-member dyads studied by Liden and Graen (1980), members with higher-quality relationships with the leader assumed more responsiblity for their jobs, contributed more to their units, and were rated higher in performance than were their colleagues who reported lower-quality relationships with their leader. According to Dienesch and Liden (1986), the quality of the exchange may be affected by the mutual trust of the leader and the member, mutual loyalty, their mutual influence on each other, the competence of one or the other, the perceived equity of the exchange, and the interpersonal attraction of the leader and member. Dienesch and Liden suggested three theoretically and methodologically appropriate dimensions that should be considered:

(a) Perceived contribution to the exchange—perception of the amount, direction, and quality of work-oriented activity each member puts forth toward the mutual goals (explicit or implicit) of the dyad; (b) Loyalty—the expression of public support for the goals and the personal character of the other member of the [leader-member exchange] dyad; . . . (c) Affect—the mutual affection members of the dyad have for each other based primarily on interpersonal attraction rather than work or professional values (pp. 624–625).

The three dimensions appear to be conceptually distinct, according to judges, but are empirically correlated (Dienesch, 1985). Each of the three dimensions would be expected to have a different impact. Mutually percieved contributions should result in the undertaking of more challenging assignments and joint efforts, mutual loyalty should be reflected in more shared

---

[4]First known as vertical-dyad linkage theory (Dansereau, Cashman, & Graen, 1973), the theory of leader-member exchange implies that there is a different exchange relationship between each individual member and the leader. An analysis of the leader's relation with the average member or the group cannot account for the differences in these exchanges. Leader-member exchange is likely to be coded as LMX in the literature to contrast it with theory and analysis based on the average group member's relation with the leader (ALS).

"confidences," and interpersonal attraction should generate greater warmth in the workplace and emotional support for nonwork problems.

Inner versus Outer Circle Members. According to the theory of leader-member exchange, the development of the members' roles will be differentially reinforced because the leader does not have the time to give all members equal attention. Furthermore, the leader differentially values subordinates and fosters the success of those he or she values most (Chassie, 1984). The leader also initiates more exchanges with highly competent subordinates (Kim & Organ, 1982) and establishes a close relationship with only a few key members—the inner group. For dealing with the outer group, the leader relies on formal authority (Graen, 1976). In agreement, Hollander (1978) among others, observed that it is commonplace in groups and organizations for an inner clique to form with whom the leader has closer relations than with the rest of the group. The inner clique gets more attention and more approval and possibly more status but is expected to be more loyal and committed to the leader and the group. The envy of members of the outer circle is likely to be aroused, and the inner clique must share more blame for the leader's failures.

Dansereau, Graen, and Haga (1975) interviewed 60 leaders and their individual subordinates four times over nine months. For members of the inner group, the leader-subordinate dyadic exchange was seen to be a partnership that was characterized by reciprocal influence, an extracontractual behavioral exchange, mutual trust, respect and liking, and a sense of a common fate. For the members of the outer group, the leader-member exchange was characterized by downward influence, role-defined relations, and a sense of loosely coupled fates. The leader was seen to be an overseer. The higher quality of the vertical-dyad linkage for inner-group members than for outer-group members was correlated with the leader's greater attention to the inner-group members. The energy and effort of the inner-group members was greater; they had fewer job problems.

Duchon, Green, and Tabor (1986) found that members of the inner group were more compatible with the leader and had a higher quality of relations with the leader than did members of the outer group, although outer-group members were not necessarily less satisfied with their leader or with their influence. Graen and Schiemann (1977) obtained results indicating that leader-member dyads in the inner group agreed more on the meaning of mutually experienced events than did leader-member dyads of the outer circle. In a study of first-level supervisors and their immediate superiors by Liden and Graen (1980), the outer-group members reported spending less time in decision making and were less likely to volunteer for special assignments and extra work.

Where outcomes have been based on criteria other than self-reports of the leaders and the members, the findings about inner-outer circle membership have been mixed. For instance, when the performance of the inner and outer circles was measured objectively, the expected differences for bank tellers or for enlisted airmen completing small-group tasks were not found. Nor was there a significant correlation between the quality of the leader-subordinate relationship and the turnover of the bank tellers (Vecchio, 1982, 1985). Rosse and Kraut (1983) studied 433 managerial dyads and found that the exchange that gave subordinates considerable latitude in negotiations was positively correlated with the subordinates' job satisfaction and was negatively related to their having job problems. But these researchers failed to confirm other predictions about job performance.

The quality of leader-member exchanges and productivity did improve as expected with special training among 106 governmental form-processing employees (Graen, Novak, & Sommerkamp, 1982). Also, for 45 supervisor-subordinate dyads in a business organization, Vecchio and Gobdel (1984) found that leader-member dyadic exchanges in the inner group were of a higher quality and were associated with the members' higher performance ratings, better actual job performance, less tendency to quit, and greater satisfaction with supervision. Inner-group members become trusted lieutenants. For a sample of 83 administrators in a large Midwestern hospital, Mael (1986) showed that such lieutenants have more latitude in negotiations in their dyadic exchange relationship with their leader and are more satisfied than are others with their job and their leader's performance.

Dyadic or Group Analysis?

Along with demonstrating the reality discussed earlier, that the inner and outer circles of subordinates are likely to be working for the same superior, a case was built for focusing on the leader-member exchange, in contrast to the average exchange relationship between the leader and the group (Graen, 1978; Graen & Cashman, 1975). Graen, Liden, and Hoel (1982), among others, provided evidence to support the importance of studying the dyadic exchange relationship. Graen, Liden, and Hoel (1982) showed that a group analysis alone might fail to detect important outcomes. For example, although the average way a leader related to the group did not predict the turnover of group members, the quality of the dyadic leader-member exchange did predict the tendency of 20 out of 48 individual members of an information systems department to quit. Ferris (1985) replicated this finding and showed again that the differences of the dyadic-exchange quality scores of the individual members *within* the groups predicted turnover. But the quality of the average exchange relationships of the groups and the leaders did not.

Graen, Orris, and Johnson (1973) found that supervisors established effective dyadic exchange relationships with some newly hired employees and established ineffective ones with others. Early on, the supervisors thought they could predict which newcomers would stay and which would leave within a few months, and they fulfilled their prophecy by acting on it. They invested most of their time and energy in the development of those who they thought would stay. Those newcomers who were expected to leave early remained unclear about what their supervisors expected of them, whereas those who worked for the same supervisors but were expected to remain were quite clear after the first week of employment. These results could not have been captured by analyzing only the supervisor's relation to the group of newly hired employees. In the same way, Crouch and Yetton (1988) looked at 323 manager-subordinate dyads in Australia in which 78 managers were involved. The same manager maintained a different relationship with subordinates, depending on the subordinates' performance. High-performing subordinates whose experience with the managers was friendly had more task contact with the managers; low performers had less contact and experienced less friendliness.

In the previously mentioned nine-month study of a management hierarchy by Dansereau, Graen, and Haga (1975), most of the dyadic relations were new at the beginning of the study. Again, the same manager developed different dyadic relations with different subordinates. The same manager's relations with different subordinates ranged from mentor-protégé to overseer-peon. The quality of each dyadic exchange relationship remained stable from the first month onward and could forecast career outcomes. Graen and Cashman (1975) showed again over a nine-month period of study that the different quality of the dyadic relationship of different subordinates with the same superior determined the role assignments of the subordinates. Subordinates who had a high-quality relationship with the manager carried out less-routine activities. They had more responsible administrative discretionary opportunities. They also had more resources at their disposal. The dyadic exchange was not just in the perceptions of the superior and subordinate who were directly involved. Peer observers tended to agree with the particular superior and subordinate about the quality of that relationship.

Graen, Cashman, Ginsburgh, and Schiemann (1978) showed that those managers who developed higher-quality dyadic linkages with their bosses produced greater resources for their subordinates than did those managers who developed lower-quality linkages. Liden and Graen (1980) obtained the same results with foremen. Some foremen appeared to collaborate with their bosses on unstructured tasks and to receive appropriate resources in return; others who were led by the same boss did not collaborate or obtain the resources.

Caveats. Despite this evidence, some investigators remain unconvinced that much is added by substituting dyadic relationships for average group-member relationships with the leader. For example, Fujii (1977) found that analyses of leader-subordinate relations in an experimental setting based on dyads did not differ greatly from analyses based on mean group results. Proponents of leader-group exchange further argue that most measures of leadership remain reliable and valid even though they are couched in terms of leader-group not leader-member relationships (for example, "He [she] recognizes *our* efforts," not "He [she] recognizes *my* efforts"; "He [she] shows the *group* what to do," not "He [she] shows *me* what to do" (Schriesheim, 1979a). Variations among members within a group are merely individual differences in describing the same leadership behavior (Nachman, Dansereau, & Naughton, 1985). In a study of public utility employees, Schriesheim (1979a) found little difference in the correlations of descriptions of leader-member relations with outcomes compared to correlations of leader-group descriptions with these same variables and concluded that distinguishing between leader-member and leader-group measurements, although theoretically meaningful, may have little practical utility; however, he favored continuing to use available leader-member descriptions rather than leader-group descriptions for theoretical purposes.

Both Dyadic and Group Analyses Needed

But it is not an either-or question. For example, most supervisors have learned to praise subordinates in public and to reprove them in private. Thus, one should expect that the extent to which the leader praises subordinates will be seen in the same way by the subordinates (whichever description is used), since praise is likely to be a public affair. In this case, the average member of the group of employees will provide a description of the leader that is equal in accuracy to the description provided member by member. But to describe the leader's contingent punishment, dyadic analysis should prove more fruitful, since such contingent punishment is more likely to be a private one-on-one exchange. In some circumstances, the effects on the group are likely to be more important; in others, individual exchanges will be more important. Much more "multiplex" examinations are required to take into account both possibilities as well as their statistical interaction (Dansereau, Alutto, Markham, & Dumas, 1982).

In an effort to examine both the group and individual effects, Katerberg and Hom (1981) correlated the satisfaction and role perceptions of 672 National Guardsmen and their leadership descriptions of their first sergeants and unit commanders. Between-units leadership effects were based on the usual correlations between scores averaged for each unit. Within-unit effects were obtained by means of a hierarchical regression analysis in which unit means were entered as the first step and the remainder were then regarded as being due to within-group effects. Considerable increases in explanatory covariance emerged when the within-group component was added to the leadership-satisfaction outcomes, despite the fact that the instrument used to assess leadership (The Leadership Behavior Description Questionnaire) was couched in terms of group, not individual members. This preliminary effort was followed shortly by the development by Dansereau, Alutto, and Yammarino (1984) of a theory and methodology for analyzing the variance in leadership, along with the covariance in leadership outcomes of leader-member relations and their effects for the dyad, the group, and higher organizational levels of analysis. Dansereau, Alutto, and Yammarino's DETECT computer program facilitated an examination of what had heretofore not been fully analyzed—the variances and covariances within the same group and in a set of groups, as opposed to the variance and covariances among these groups. Dansereau, Alutto, and Yammarino's strategy and program determined whether relationships are a function of (1) different styles of leaders described by their average subordinate, (2) leadership processes that occur within groups only, or (3) individualized differences in perceptions of the same leader's behavior.

Varient Theory. Members' reports may be similar about their leader or outcomes within a group but differ from the reports of the average members about their own leaders and outcomes. These *whole-group* differences lie between and not within groups. There are intergroup differences in responses, coupled with the homogeneity of responses within the groups. This condition fits with the average-member-exchange approach to studying leadership based on the average member of each group. For instance, the reinforcing style used by a leader with all the group members correlates with the leader's sense of security and personality (Hinton & Barrow, 1976).

In a *group-parts* condition, individuals' responses differ from one another within a group, but their average does not differ from the average responses provided by the members of other groups. Differences lie within groups, not between groups. There are intragroup differences and heterogeneity among the members within the groups. The leader-member-exchange approach is necessary to study the leadership and outcomes.

A third alternative is that the reports of the individuals may differ reliably and consistently both within or between the groups. This condition is *equivocal*, for the reports are codeterminable from both sources. Individual implicit theories, such as discussed in Chapter 19, may be dominant in an equivocal condition.

A fourth possibility is that members may not respond as a group but only independently; thus, their identity as a member of a particular group or the set of groups under analysis may be irrelevant. Here the results of interest are *inexplicable*, accounted for neither by systematic differences among individual member differences nor by the groups. There are no reliable differences among individuals within or between groups, and thus a null case is demonstrated.

Some WABA Results. Yammarino and Naughton (1987) completed within-and-between analyses (WABA I) of the variances in initiation and consideration of 70 members of a law enforcement organization on a university campus. Each member of the different hierarchically arranged units described his or her own immediate superiors. The investigators also completed corresponding analyses of within-and-between analyses (WABA II) of the covariances in the leadership-outcomes descriptions. Outcomes included satisfaction with supervision, satisfaction with rewards, supervisory control, adequacy of communications, efforts of subordinates, and stress on subordinates. The results for the WABA I analyses of variance indicated the existence of an equivocal or codeterminable condition. There was significant variance both within and between groups, as well as consistent individual differences in perceptions at work here, rather than just differences between leaders. On the other hand, the WABA II analyses of covariance generally supported the conclusion

for 10 of the 28 relationships that leader-outcome differences between whole groups dominated. This supported the acceptance of the average-leadership-style or whole-group approach. For example, members' satisfaction with rewards and the leader's initiation of structure correlated .67 among groups led by the different leaders and only .09 for members within groups led by the same leader. It did not matter if the descriptions were correlated in group terms ("The leader rewards the group if. . . . ") or in individual terms ("The leader rewards me if. . . . "). In the case of six variables, an equivocal condition was seen. For example, satisfaction with supervision emerged as codeterminable; there were covarying differences between leaders and outcomes as well as among members' descriptions within the groups of their leader. The correlations between initiation and consideration were particularly likely to emerge as equivocal in interpretation. Finally, in the case of 12 variables (such as leadership and communications), the results were inexplicable. There was no statisticaly significant between-or-within covariance.

Table 17.2 illustrates the importance of both a dyadic and group account of leader-outcome relationships based on members' descriptions. We need to ask the same questions about such relationships in two ways, dyadic and group. We need to examine both within-and-between covariances. As is seen in Table 17.2, satisfaction with rewards and with considerate leadership are correlated modestly (.26 to .42), regardless of the analytic component (between or within leaders) or type of description (leader-group or leader-member). Again, differences between leaders in initiation correlates with the average members' satisfaction with rewards. The same results apply for all the members, regardless of their group. However, the leaders perceived use of initiation correlates with satisfaction only between leaders' groups, not within leaders' groups.

In a similar fashion, it was concluded, in the replication of the Graen, Liden, and Hoel (1982) study, that the group effect was also of consequence when 81 registered nurses who quit or remained described their supervisors, although the dyadic effect on turnover was still the stronger (Ferris, 1985). To repeat, then, although the group or dyadic approach may be appropriate in some instances, only analyses that take both pos-

Table 17.2 Correlations between Leadership and Members' Satisfaction with Rewards

Members' Satisfaction with Rewards	Initiation		Consideration	
	Leader-Group Relation Described	Leader-Member Relation Described	Leader-Group Relation Described	Leader-Member Relation Described
Between Leaders	.67	.57	.42	.30
Within the Same Leaders	.09	.03	.27	.26

SOURCE: Yammarino and Naughton (1987).

sibilities into account are likely to explain fully what is happening.

Summary and Conclusions

Leadership can be understood as a transactional exchange of material, social, and psychological benefits. In a fair and profitable exchange, the benefits to both the leader and follower exceed their costs. In the transactional process, leaders and followers reinforce each other's behavior with either reward or punishment, preferably reward, and preferably reward that is contingent on fulfilling the transacted role arrangements. But the exchange may be less rewarding; it can involve management by exception or punitive discipline.

Differential reinforcement can by used to manipulate experimentally who, in a group, emerges as leader. It can be used to increase different members' attempts to lead and to affect whether their attempts will be successful in influencing the other members. In the dynamics of the exchange relationship, competence and early acceptance of the group's norms as a follower builds the idiosyncracy credit of a member, making it more likely that his or her attempts to lead will be successful. With enough idiosyncracy credit, one can begin to stand out in the group and be successful in introducing new ideas.

To understand many individual and organizational outcomes of leadership, it is necessary to focus attention on the dyadic leader-member exchange, for the same leader is likely to have different expectations and reactions about his or her different subordinates. These different perceptions and behaviors of leaders result in different levels of performance by subordinates who are working for the same leader that cannot be captured by looking only at leader-group relationships. However, it is not an either-or matter. What happens appears to depend on a combination of dyadic and group effects that need to be teased out if a full account is wanted. I now turn to a more detailed consideration of the interactive effects of leaders and their followers.

CHAPTER

18

Leader-Follower Interactive Effects

The last chapter emphasized that successful leaders influence their followers and bring about changes in their followers' attitudes and behavior by managing positive and negative reinforcements. These reinforcements are contingent on the followers' performance. The exchanges that occur vary considerably in nature and amount. Different leaders have different role relations with their followers; likewise, followers have different relations with their leaders.

As a consequence, leaders range from "all to none" in their effects on their followers. At the one extreme can be found the rule-governed, fully programmed administrators, the paper-pushing absentee supervisors, and the token officeholders without power. These leaders are glorified doormen, whose behavior is almost fully determined by others. At the other extreme are the disciplinarians; the rule makers; the monitors; the role changers; and the purveyors of praise, reward, or penalties. The followers can become better and more fully informed. Their interests may be enlarged. Their expectations may be developed, their preference for taking risks may be altered, and their satisfaction with their roles may be strongly influenced by the leadership. But followers and their performance may or may not benefit from the leadership exerted. The leader's successful influence on the followers may or may not be effective in achieving goals of consequence to the followers. This chapter examines in more detail the roles of both the transactional leader and the led in the exchange that takes place between them. Specifically, it looks at the leader in relation to the subordinate as a source of feedback, as a communicator, as a model, and as a source of influence. It also explores the upward influence of the subordinate as a source of feedback and the impact of compliance on the leader. Finally, it reviews the mutual effects of the interaction of the leader and the subordinate.

Contributions of Leadership to the Transactional Relationship

In the formal organization, the performance of individual employees or their work group depends on their energy and direction and their competence and motivation to perform what is required to reach the objectives of their positions in the system. The transactional leader may contribute to the adequacy of their performance by (1) clarifying what is expected of the employees, particularly the purposes and objectives of their performance, (2) explaining how to meet such expectations, (3) spelling out the criteria for the evaluation of effective performance, (4) providing feedback on whether the individual employee or work group is meeting the objectives, and (5) allocating rewards that are contingent on their meeting the objectives. Effective leadership develops understanding and agreement about the leader's and employee's roles in this process. For instance, if the leader engages in management by objectives, leadership may take the form of periodic discussions between the leader and the employee in which a review of past performance and obstacles to effectiveness are the basis for setting mutually acceptable objectives for the next period. Legitimacy for the roles of both the leader and the led is provided by those organizational policies that declare and support the roles.

Leaders as a Source of Feedback

Feedback about a subordinate's performance is the most common contingent reinforcement provided by a leader. Supervisory feedback is required to improve the subordinate's performance of the job and can affect either the subordinate's ability or motivation to do the job (Locke, Latham, Saari, & Shaw, 1981; Payne & Hauty, 1955). Cook (1968) found that the improvement in the attitudes and performance of managers who participated in a business simulation game was directly related to the frequency with which reports of their performance were fed back to them.

Rewarding when positive, feedback can be highly punitive when negative. However, negative feedback may quickly come to be interpreted as rewarding if it is seen as intended to be helpful and if it actually results in improved performance. Subordinates will find as fair and accurate negative feedback about their failures if the causes are attributed to bad luck or external circumstances rather than to their lack of ability or motivation and the feedback is about the task, not about them (Liden, Ferris, & Dienesch, 1988). Nevertheless, when subordinates suspect they are doing poorly they will seek feedback to short-circuit the buildup of negative feedback, to uphold their self-esteem by structuring how and when the feedback is given, and to mitigate blame (Larson, 1989). Feedback can also be neutral and nonreinforcing, as when the superior merely acknowledges that he or she has seen a subordinate's behavior or has heard a subordinate's statement without evaluating it.

According to a survey of 360 supervisor-subordinate dyads by Larson, Glynn, Fleenor, and Scontrino (1985), supervisors differ from each other in the timeliness, specificity, frequency, and sensitivity of their feedback. But these four dimensions are highly intercorrelated. Furthermore, negative feedback that is prefaced by the Drake-Moberg (1986) sedative or palliative statements will be accepted by subordinates with less sense that they are being negatively reinforced ("It's probably not necessary to say this, but ... ; I know it's hard, but ... ").

Types. Supervisory feedback can range from a grunt of acknowledgment of a message received or a pat on the back for a job well done to a formal annual appraisal interview. The grunt or pat has the advantage of occurring soon after the behavior about which the feedback is being given. The appraisal interview has the advantage of being systematic and of couching the feedback in the context of goals, needs, and plans for future action.

Impact. It is important that subordinates accept and agree with the performance feedback their supervisors believe they are giving them (Ilgen, Fisher, & Taylor, 1979). Naturally, agreement and acceptance are more likely if the feedback is positive (Jacobs, Jacobs, Feldman, & Cavior, 1973). Agreement and acceptance are also more likely if the feedback is clear and convincing and if the superior is highly credible and gives feedback frequently (Halperin, Snyder, Shenkel, & Houston, 1976; Shaw & Fisher, 1986; Tuckman & Oliver, 1968). The credibility of the superior's feedback is likely to be enhanced if the subordinate believes the superior is highly knowledgeable about the subordinate's job and has sufficient opportunities to observe the subordinate's performance (Landy, Barnes, & Murphy, 1978; Stone, Gueutal, & MacIntosh, 1984). The context in which feedback is delivered will affect whether subordinates interpret it as positive or negative. For example, if feedback is solicited, it may be received more positively than when it is volunteered unexpectedly.

Pavett (1983), among others, illustrated the positive effects of feedback on the performance of 203 staff nurses. Komaki, Collins, and Penn (1982) also found feedback to have a positive impact. To determine the effects of feedback, above and beyond just giving instructions alone, they monitored the safety performance of 200 employees over 46 weeks. After a baseline was established, safety rules were clarified in meetings in which considerable supervisory-subordinate interaction occurred. In contrast to the baseline record of performance, modest improvements occurred in only two of four departments as a consequence of the clarification efforts alone. Then safety performance feedback graphs were introduced. It was this feedback that produced significant improvements in safety over the baseline. Whether the feedback was delivered once a week or twice a week did not seem to matter. Both frequencies of feedback were equally effective in comparison to baseline or initial training meetings, according to a similarly designed investigation by Chhokar and

Wallin (1984) of the effects of feedback on improvements in safety among 58 employees over a ten-month period.

Leaders as Communicators

In addition to giving feedback, much of the remainder of supervisory behavior involves a variety of additional types of communication with others. Their communications distinguish leaders who are successful and effective from those who are not. As was noted in earlier chapters, emergent leaders are heavy contributors to the interactions that take place in their groups. They display more initiation of ideas, express more opinions, and ask more questions than do those members who do not emerge as leaders (Bass, 1954a; Morris & Hackman, 1969). Elected and appointed leaders would be expected to do likewise in discussions with their groups, as well as in separate dyadic interactions with each of their team members (Watson, 1982).

In a survey, chief executive officers of large businesses ranked face-to-face-communication as the most important source of their effectiveness (Anonymous, 1978). An intensive study of nine senior executives by S. Carlson (1951) over a four-week period noted that they spent approximately 80 percent of their time talking with others. Another detailed study of four departmental-level managers found that more than 80 percent of their time was spent in conversation. Zelko and Dance (1965) stated that when managers were asked how much of their work day was spent in communicating, their replies ranged from about 88 percent to 99 percent, with most saying that it was above 90 percent. Similar results were reported by Lawler, Porter, and Tannenbaum (1968); Mintzberg (1973); and P. A. Stewart (1967).

For Baird (1980), the credibility of a manager's communications depends on his or her competence, esteem, personality, dynamism, character, and perceived intentions. Empirically, Klauss and Bass (1982) established strong positive linkages between the trustworthiness and informativeness of supervisors and their careful communications to subordinates; their two-way, rather than one-way, communications; and their attentive listening. In turn, this trustworthiness, informativeness, and care contributed to their subordinates' role clarity, satisfaction with their supervision, and the effectiveness of their work groups.

Hain (1972) reported that among four General Motors plants, productivity and profitability showed the greatest increase in the plant that also showed the greatest improvement in communications. Similar parallel improvements in other General Motors plants were reported by Widgery and Tubbs (1975) and Tubbs and Widgery (1978). Hain and Tubbs (1974) found greater efficiency, fewer grievances, and lower absenteeism to be associated with employees' ratings of the effectiveness of their supervisors' communication. The effectiveness of supervisors' communication was the best predictor of low grievance activity in still another General Motors automotive assembly plant (Tubbs & Porter, 1978). Such effective communication included agreement that supervisors were friendly, easy to talk to, interested and paid attention to what one was saying, willing to listen to one's problem, and receptive to ideas and suggestions. They showed one how to improve one's performance.

These various communication behaviors are usually included in measures of leadership. It is not surprising that Klauss and Bass (1981) found correlations as high as .65 between the various communication styles of supervisors and the supervisors' leadership styles as described by their subordinates.

Leaders as Models for Their Subordinates

Although charismatic leaders are more likely to serve as models for subordinates who identify with them, transactional leaders may also serve as models. Porter and Kaufman (1959) devised a scale for determining the extent to which supervisors describe themselves as similar to top managers. Self-perceptions similar to those of top managers were associated with patterns of interaction that peers of the supervisor perceived to be similar to the interaction patterns of the managers in the top-level positions. Katz, Maccoby, and Morse (1950) noted that supervisors in an insurance firm tended to model their tendency to be coercive or participative on whether their bosses were coercive or permissive. Likewise, R. Cooper (1966) showed that workers tended to pattern their own behavior after that of their supervisors. Task-oriented leaders supervised groups in which workers made fewer errors in their work and exhibited lower rates of absenteeism and tardiness than was true for groups with leaders who did not have such a task orientation. In the same way, according to a study by Kern and Bahr (1974) of approximately 100 staff personnel in the Washington State Division of Parole, those parole officers who interacted a lot with their supervisors used their superiors as models for the way they, the parole officers, supervised their parolees. But such modeling did not occur when the parole officers interacted less frequently with their supervisors. H. M. Weiss (1977) studied 141 superior-subordinate dyads, obtaining from each member of the dyad a self-description of his or her supervisory behavior, along with the subordinate's evaluation of the superior's competence and success. These items were then correlated with the degree of similarity found in the self-descriptions of the superior-subordinate dyads. Weiss found that subordinates tended to choose for role models those superiors they saw as more competent and successful.

The characteristics of their superiors that subordinates modeled were found by Adler (1982) to depend on the self-esteem of the subordinates. Among the subordinates of 66 Israeli heads of bank departments, those with high self-esteem were more likely to model the heads whom they perceived to have reward and coercive power; those subordinates with low self-esteem were more inclined to model heads whom they perceived to have referent power. Modeling was also more apparent, regardless of the subordinates' self-esteem, of heads who displayed more initiation and consideration in their leadership behavior.

Behavioral contagion is less-obvious modeling. A crude boss can spawn a batch of crude subordinates. Sometimes, the subordinates unconsciously adopt the boss's expressions of speech, intonations, and peculiar nonverbal mannerisms.

Leaders as Cues. Followers may come to depend on their leader's view of reality as their prime source of

information and expectations. Beyond followers' modeling of their leader's behavior, Graen and Cashman (1975) noted that followers also enlarged their interests to match more closely with those of their leader. In other words, the followers attempted to increase their esteem in the eyes of their leader and to ingratiate themselves with the leader (E. E. Jones, 1964). Friedlander (1966b) asked members of a research and development organization to describe various aspects of members' interaction and the group's performance. The effectiveness of the group was associated with open discussion and with the leader's suggestion of new approaches to problems. At the same time, a member's influence on other members was associated with his or her influence with the leader. Members accepted the leader's influence when policies were clearcut and group tensions were low. The members tended to play their expected roles and discuss divergent ideas when the leader was oriented toward productivity and efficiency.

Daniels and Berkowitz (1963) experimentally varied supervisor-worker dependence for the attainment of goals, the degree of liking, and the time required for a supervisor to learn of a worker's performance. They found that participants worked hardest under independent conditions when they believed that the superior would learn about their performance quickly. They also worked hardest when they had to depend on a supervisor whom they liked. Similarly, Katzell (1987) showed from the results of a survey how complex is the impact on the morale, involvement, and performance of employees of the extent to which supervisors help employees achieve intrinsic and extrinsic rewards. The extent to which they do so is linked to the extent to which they cue the employees by setting goals for them, maintaining normative standards, and preserving equity.

Falling Dominoes; Modeling or Alternating? Do "strong" leaders at one hierarchical level alternate with "weak" leaders at the level below them? Or does the style of leadership cascade from one management level to another through modeling and other processes?

Do subordinates at each descending level below the

boss imitate their boss or do they complement their boss's leadership with compliance to fit it? If A kicks B, will B kick C or will B become solicitous of C after being kicked by A? Does modeling and matching one's superior make a difference, or is alteration from one level of supervision to the next more likely to be productive? The modeling of transactional leadership behavior is supported in a number of ways. When a manager's boss rewards the manager for performance or allocates requested resources to him or her, some of these rewards and resources make it easier for the manager to reward his or her subordinates for their performance in turn. Discipline applied by the boss usually will require similar disciplinary action by the manager. The manager's subordinates will be safer targets of the manager's displaced hostility, which is sparked by the hostility of the boss toward the manager. The boss's clarification of goals for the manager provides the means by which the manager clarifies goals for his or her subordinates. On the other hand, the threatening boss may create a manager who is attentive to rewarding subordinates in exchange for their support against the threatening boss. The inefficiencies of the boss who practices noncontingent reinforcement with the manager may result in the manager rejecting the boss's style in favor of contingently reinforcing his or her subordinates. In the case of transformational leaders, J. M. Burns (1978) argued for the former point of view, but Tichy and Ulrich (1984) argued for the latter position. For Burns, dedication, caring, and participation are multiplied outward from the leaders through their disciples; the leaders become the models to be imitated by successive expanding layers of followers. Tichy and Ulrich (1984) suggested otherwise. The organizational changes envisioned by top management executives require that lower-level managers adopt leadership behavior to support the practical implementation of their superiors' visions, rather than modeling their superiors.

Most evidence supports modeling rather than alternating. Bowers and Seashore (1966) found that leadership behavior patterns exhibited by executives in insurance agencies were reflected in similar behavioral patterns by the supervisors below them. The supervisors' emphasis on the facilitation of goals and interaction with their subordinates was related to the extent to which the executives did the same. Similarly, Stogdill (1955) obtained data to indicate that participatory leadership at lower levels in an organization was dependent on it being practiced at higher levels. Again, Ouchi and Maguire (1975) found that subordinates tended to use the same methods of control as their superiors for dealing with their respective subordinates. Summarizing his studies of Japanese managers from the 1960s onward, Misumi (1985) reported that the supervisory styles that emphasized performance or maintenance and were used by different levels of managers in a departmental unit tended to be similar.

Bass, Waldman, Avolio, and Bebb (1987) collected self-rated and subordinate-rated leadership descriptions of second-line managers, their first-line supervisors, and their subordinates in New Zealand. A cascading effect of leadership behavior emerged. The amount of transformational and transactional leadership behavior observed at one level of management tended to be seen at the next lower level as well. The leadership patterns of subordinate-superior dyads tended to match each other. The correlation of the actual leadership observed among levels was highest (.51) for the transactional exchange involved in providing contingent rewards.

To examine whether modeling of one's superior made a difference in the performance of one's group, Misumi (1985) calculated the capital growth rate in two Japanese banks with 25 and 54 branches, respectively. Pairs of high-producing and low-producing branches with similar socioeconomic characteristics were compared. First-line and second-line superiors were identified as being low or high in performance and in maintenance orientation. In one bank, 38 percent of the first- and second-line superiors matched each other in orientation in both the more-productive and less-productive branches, but in the second bank, 77 percent of the first- and second-line superiors in the less-productive branches matched each other's orientation and 33 percent did so in the productive branches. The probabilities of matching on a chance basis were 25 percent. If the matching was in high performance and maintenance orientation at both levels, effects were salutary, but if the matching was in low performance and maintenance orientations, effects were counterproductive.

The alternating approach was observed indirectly when the same performance by commanding officers of ships and their executive officers appeared to produce opposite effects. In a study of shipboard organizations, D. T. Campbell (1956) found that although the leadership scores and sociometric interaction scores of the commanding officers were positively correlated with measures of shipboard efficiency and morale, the leadership and sociometric interaction scores of the executive officers, the commanders' closest aides, were negatively correlated with shipboard efficiency and morale.

Complementary Linkages and Mixed Effects

The Importance of Supervisors Having Influence Higher Up. Pelz (1949, 1951, 1952) noted that when supervisors who had influence with their superiors took the side of their subordinates, the subordinates tended to feel more satisfied. But when a supervisor without such influence identified with the subordinates' interests, the subordinates tended to be more dissatisfied. Closeness to subordinates and taking their side increased the subordinates' job satisfaction only when the supervisors had enough influence with their superiors to provide conditions that could result in the fulfillment of the subordinates' expectations. Jablin's (1980) results concurred with Pelz's findings, particularly for supportive supervisors with upward influence rather than non-supportive supervisors with such influence. Again, Nahabetian (1969) found that group members were better satisfied in general under leaders who had influence with their superiors than under those without such influence. Influential leaders were seen to facilitate the group's task, whereas those without influence higher up were seen to hinder the accomplishment of the task. Ronken and Lawrence (1952) reported similar findings.

Combined Effects of Multiple Hierarchical Levels. As noted elsewhere, Misumi (1985) showed the combined effects of two layers of supervision on the performance of banking subordinates. Hill and Hunt (1970) observed that although the leadership behavior of supervisors one level removed from the employees

was not related to the employees' satisfaction, the combined behavior of first- and second-level supervisors did affect their satisfaction. Much initiative by both first- and second-level supervisors was significantly related to the employees' satisfaction with their own esteem and autonomy.

As evidence of the systematic connections between subordinates, supervisors, and their superiors, Stogdill and Goode (1957) found that when supervisors interacted frequently with their superiors, their subordinates thought that the leaders should spend more time than they did in interviewing personnel and in coordination. According to Stogdill and Haase (1957), more impersonal performance, such as inspection, by superiors, kept subordinates away from superiors. When superiors spent little time in preparing procedures and much time in technical performance, their subordinates tended to interact with peers, but when superiors spent more than average amounts of time in supervision, subordinates tended to interact with them. A high rate of communicating and integrating behavior by superiors enlarged the total number of interactions initiated by their subordinates, as well as received by them; increased reciprocated interactions within the subgroups; and decreased interactions with members outside the subgroups.

Stogdill (1955) studied the effects of interactions among three hierarchical levels of organizational members—subordinates, supervisors, and the superiors of the supervisors. The supervisors tended to interact more with their own subordinates when their superiors interacted more with them. The interactions of these supervisors with members outside their own subgroups were affected by whether their superiors were the initiators or the recipients of interactions within their own subgroups of supervisors. If their superiors were initiators rather than recipients of interaction with the subgroup of supervisors, the supervisors tended in interact less frequently with members outside their own subgroups. When their superiors interacted frequently with members outside the subgroups of supervisors, the supervisors also interacted with members outside this unit, but the supervisors interacted less often with their superiors.

When superiors interacted with the supervisors' peers, the supervisors tended to initiate more interactions with their superiors but tended to receive fewer interactions in return. In general, the superiors' interactions with the supervisors induced similar patterns of interaction between the supervisors and their subordinates. The supervisors' interactions with their superiors exerted the strongest effects in restricting the area of interaction of their subordinates.

In the previously mentioned study of three hierarchical levels of organizational members (Bass, Waldman, Avolio, & Bebb, 1987), those lower-level leaders who were seen as being more charismatic by their subordinates, in turn, required less, not more charisma, in their superiors. It appears that charismatic leaders would rather not have a charismatic superior with whom they may have to compete.

Other Combinatory Effects. Stogdill and Goode (1957) observed also that leaders who interacted frequently with peers had subordinates who believed that their leaders had too little responsibility, were less active than they ought to be in representing their subordinates, and spent too much time in planning. When leaders interacted extensively with persons outside their own units, their subordinates reported having to delegate and represent their groups too much. These followers also thought they ought to spend more time than they did in inspection, planning, and preparation.

In a study of a large naval organization, Stogdill and Haase (1957) found that the more time superiors actually spent in highly personal interactions with others, such as interviewing personnel, the less their subordinates actually interacted with their peers and initiated interactions with members of other subgroups with whom their interactions were reciprocated.

Explanations. The multilevel and falling-dominoes effects may be due to differential selection as well as modeling. Lower-level supervisors can be either self-selected, selected by their second-level manager, or selected by the organization for positions so they will be stylistically matched or be compatible with their superior. It is also possible that certain leadership behaviors are reinforced by the norms of organizational subunits; therefore, the cascading effects may be due to the subculture of norms, beliefs, and values within which the leaders operate. In the same way, the environmental and technical demands in one subunit may generate common job requirements and therefore dictate the differential leadership observed and required at the different levels of the subunit. Thus, Smith, Moscow, Berger, and Cooper (1969) found weak support for the hypothesis that under conditions of slow organizational change, good interpersonal relations between managers and superiors were associated with good relations between managers and subordinates. But strong support was found for the hypothesis that under rapid organizational change, good relations between managers and their superiors polarized into poor relations between the managers and their subordinates. No doubt, the greater need for rapid change put pressure on the managers to push their subordinates for greater performance and rapid responses. Superiors encouraged the managers in this regard; subordinates were disturbed by it.

Followers' Impact on Leaders

Heller and Van Til (1982, p. 405) proposed that "leadership and followership are linked concepts; neither can be comprehended without understanding the other." The compliance of followers is the mirror image of successful leadership. Just as successful leadership may be seen to influence the completion of tasks and socioemotional relations, so the compliance of followers can be seen as instrumental to the completion of tasks and both public and private socioemotional acceptance of the leadership effort. It also seems obvious that by their performance, subordinates control the nature of the feedback from their superior (Jablin, 1980). In the same way, just as the leader can influence subordinates by initiatives and information, so the subordinates can complete the process and influence their leaders by giving feedback to them. Thus, Hegarty (undated) demonstrated that feedback of subordinates' ratings to supervisors resulted in positive changes in the supervisors' behavior. The employees of the 58 supervisors in the experimental and control groups completed an information-opinion survey. The survey results were used to prepare feedback reports to the experimental but not to the control supervisors. A second survey was conducted ten weeks later to measure change. After adjusting for the initial scores, Hegarty found that all

17 measures of change shifted more in the expected direction in the experimental than the control supervisors, six significantly so. Such feedback has become common in many organizations as a means for improving the effectiveness of leaders and their operations.[1]

Followership and Leadership

Followers' expectations affect the performance of their leaders; followers' perception of their leaders' motives and actions constrain what their leaders can succeed in doing (Stewart, 1982b). Thus, from an analysis of a representative sample of 100 Swedish managers and their subordinates, Norrgren (1981a) found that the subordinates' levels of education and aspirations affected the managers' beliefs, intentions, and evaluations, particularly those of the younger managers. Furthermore, although older subordinates and subordinates with high aspirations and substantial seniority were most specifically favorable toward their managers who had beliefs and intentions to allow the subordinates to participate in decisions, it was the younger subordinates who were found by Norrgren (1981b) to react most negatively to managers with beliefs and intentions that were opposed to such participation by subordinates.

The compliance of subordinates is not automatic; it depends on the active cultivation of the leader's legitimacy. A leader's management style is affected by how the subordinates respond to it. The subordinates can actively work to undermine it, or they can work hard to support it because it makes it possible for them to serve their own interests. Self-interest, according to Biggart (1981), may account for the strong loyalties of most of Ronald Reagan's subordinates, despite his "hands off" management style when he served as governor of California or president of the United States.

The follower's influence on the leader also means that, contrary to popular notions, followership and leadership are highly similar, as are followers and leaders. Hollander and Webb (1955) showed that the same peers who are nominated as most desired leaders are also nominated as most desired followers. Again, Nelson (1964a) found that among 72 men on a U.S. Antarctic expedition, the characteristics that made the men

liked were about the same for the leaders as for the followers. There are no sharp boundaries between the roles of leader and follower (J. M. Burns, 1978). Both roles always must be played in any group. Leaders cannot exist without followers, nor can followers exist without leaders. Moreover, leaders and followers exchange roles over time and in different settings. Many persons are leaders and followers at the same time.

The interaction between the leader and the follower is not symmetrical. K. M. Watson (1982) coded the antecedent acts of the dyadic interactions of the subordinates and leaders. When the leaders attempted to initiate structure, the subordinates were most likely to comply with deference. However, whenever the subordinates attempted to initiate structure, the most common reaction of the leaders was to resist by responding with efforts to try to structure the situation differently, rather than to comply with the subordinates' initiative.

The Good Follower. Kelley (1988) enumerated the many elements that go into being a good follower. These elements are similar in many respects to what makes a good leader. Followers are active, independent, critical thinkers who can manage themselves. They are committed to the organization and to persons, principles, or purposes beyond themselves. Their personal and organizational goals are aligned. They are competent and avoid obsolescence with continuing education and development. They disagree agreeably. They build credibility. They can move easily into the leadership role and return again to the role of follower.

Antitheses of Leaders. If not the followers, then who are the opposites to the leader? They are those who are barred from the process (for instance, the underaged who are denied the vote). They are the isolates and the rejectees. They are those who exclude themselves from participation—the apathetic, the alienated, and the anomic. The apathetic may be too busy with other affairs or too busy just surviving. The alienated may reject and resist participation; they believe that the power to lead is in the hands of others for the benefit of others. The anomic feel powerless, normless, aimless and see the leaders as being indifferent to their needs (J. M. Burns, 1978). These nonleaders-nonfollowers, by their lack of involvement, can have a negative impact on their groups, organizations, and societies.

---

[1] See, for instance, Bass (1976), Bowers and Franklin (1975), Cammann and Nadler (1976), and Likert (1967).

Quoting deJouvenal ("A society of sheep must in time beget a government of wolves"), Gardner (1987b) noted that those who fail to follow but remain the antithesis of leadership invite the leader's abuse of power.

Upward Influence

However, despite the asymmetry of the relationship, followers exert a considerable amount of upward influence on their leaders (Gabarro & Kotter, 1980). Acts of moral courage by elected political leaders can be strongly pressured by constituencies, economic blocs, and organized letter writers (Paige,1977). On tour, Woodrow Wilson was first shocked, then braced, by hearing a voice from the crowd shout, "Atta boy, Woody" (Davies, 1963).

After they have been elected, U.S. presidents tend to ignore public opinion, to which their own campaign rhetoric may have been responsive, or to reinterpret it to fit their preferred policies. But, when public opinion is sufficiently aroused, the presidents become responsive and usually adopt the opinion of the strong public majority as their own.

In 1983, U.S. public opinion polls indicated that the public did not find much reason for placing U.S. Marines at risk in Lebanon, as a consequence of a presidential policy that had been in effect for at least a year. Despite the continuing lack of public approval, days before the terrorist bombing of the Marine barracks, President Reagan was publicly expressing his opinion that we would never "cut and run." Days after the bombing and loss of life that greatly aroused public opinion against the policy, the Marines were "redeployed offshore" (Gwertzman, 1983).

Upward influence is seen as an important contribution to organizational effectiveness (Gabarro, 1979) and a key to understanding organizational politics (Porter, Allen, & Angle, 1981). Subordinates have the responsibility to exert upward influence on their bosses for their mutual benefit and the benefit of the organization as a whole. Subordinates should challenge their superiors' proposals and help them avoid mistakes, but subordinates can do so only if they have contributed to building trust between their superiors and themselves. The subordinates must provide adequate information and account for their performance in carrying out dele-gated assignments. Effective subordinates will actively invite review, support, and feedback from their superiors (Crockett, 1981).

The Tactics of Upward Influence. The upward influence tactics used by subordinates were identified and scaled by Kipnis, Schmidt, and Wilkinson (1980) as subordinate assertiveness; reasoning; bargaining about the exchange of benefits; appealing to a higher authority; forming coalitions; or trying friendliness, ingratiation, and flattery.[2] For Schilit and Locke (1982), upward influence tactics included the logical or rational presentation of ideas; informal exchange not related to performance, such as ingratiating or praising the superior; promising rewards or threatening sanctions; adhering to rules; manipulating matters so the superior is unaware of being influenced; mobilizing coalitions of support among co-workers and higher-ups; and being persistent or assertive.

Usage. All 123 salaried employees in a metal fabricating firm surveyed by Deluga (1986a) used ingratiation, flattery, reason, and assertiveness much more frequently when trying to influence their superiors than they did bargaining and appeals to co-workers or to a higher authority. Elsewhere Deluga (1988) reported that when their first efforts to influence their transactional but not their transformational superiors did not work, the 117 managers and employees of a Northeastern manufacturing firm subsequently displayed significantly less friendliness and assertiveness toward their superiors and appealed less to a higher authority. According to Schmidt and Kipnis (1984), staff managers were more likely than were line managers to attempt more upward influence to achieve individual goals.

Subordinates' goals will determine which tactics they use. To affect policy, subordinates will be more likely to use reasoning and the rational presentation of ideas (Kipnis, Schmidt, & Wilkinson, 1980; Schmidt & Kipnis, 1984). Mowday (1978) found that elementary school principals who were power motivated were more likely to attempt upward influence. The need for power determined the particular power strategies that

[2]Hinken and Schriesheim (1986) and Schriesheim and Hinken (1986) reworked the original upward influence measures of Kipnis, Schmidt, and Wilkinson, which resulted in improving their factorial structure and content validity with a shorter set of 27 questionnaire items.

96 managers from the Indian public sector said they employed to influence their superiors; most of the strategies they tended to use were "soft and subtle" (Singh, Kumari, & Singh, 1988). To promote self-interests and to gain personal goals and benefits, the Indian managers were more likely to try ingratiation and promises for a satisfactory exchange with the superior based on their evaluation of the superior's preferences. In looking at the specific reasons why subordinates attempt to ingratiate themselves with their bosses, Ralston (1985) argued that ingratiation is more likely to be used by Machiavellian subordinates with autocratic superiors in an ambiguous setting. In an Indian experiment, Pandey and Bohra (1984) confirmed that subjects who acted as subordinates were much likely to endorse ingratiating tactics with executives who liked to have admirers around them, preferred employees who supported their views, praised their ideas and conformed to their policies uncritically, used subjective criteria in making decisions about employees' requests for benefits, and rewarded those who flattered and pleased them by their behavior. In contrast, less ingratiation was suggested as a viable tactic if one was supposedly working for an executive who was opposite in such respects.

Schilit and Locke (1982) asked employees and supervisors which were more and which were less successful ways for subordinates to influence their superiors. They noted that both subordinates and superiors agreed that subordinates use logical presentations more than any other tactic in upward influence attempts and agreed that the substance of the effort determined its success. But they disagreed on what caused upward influence attempts to fail. Although the supervisors attributed failure to the substance of the attempt, subordinates attributed failure to the closed-mindedness of the supervisors.

In an analysis of the diaries of 60 middle-level managers over a two-month period, Schilit (1987) also found that the middle-level managers who were high in tested need for power thought they had more upward influence on strategic decisions. Such felt upward influence coincided with a high need for achievement, self-control, and experience with their superiors. As a whole, the managers tended to believe themselves to be successful in their upward influence attempts, particularly those involving less-risky strategic decisions.

Rice (1986) offered suggestions on how to cope with a difficult boss. Subordinates should observe how others succeed in getting along with the boss. They should offer to be helpful. They need to keep track of their boss's mood swings, discussing his mistreatment of them in private when the boss is calm. Subordinates should avoid seeking the boss's approval when it is not required, but they should not dispute the boss's legitimate authority even if they disagree with his judgments. Considerable upward influence may occur in the course of the subordinate's feedback to the superior.

The Subordinate as a Source of Feedback

For effective superior-subordinate relations, feedback must flow both ways; a loop must be maintained. In their attitudes and behavior, leaders can hinder or help close the loop from the subordinates back to them (Kaplan, Drath, & Kofodimos, 1985). Superiors prevent their subordinates' criticisms from reaching them by monopolizing conversations, by an abrasive style, by emphasizing their own power and status, and by "adopting the mantle of their office when interacting with lower level managers" (Bruce, 1986). While leaders do not seem to evaluate subordinates differently if they, the leaders, receive positive feedback, they do evaluate less active subordinates less favorably if the feedback is negative (Elgie, Hollander, & Rice, 1988). They avoid discussing issues until they are ready to make a decision. They distance themselves from subordinates and become isolated and insulated from feedback from below by selecting subordinates to bolster their own thoughts and feelings.

Channels of communication dry up as one moves upward in an organization. Information gets increasingly filtered as it must flow through more levels. To promote the upward flow of information, superiors need to reduce perceived differences in power, make themselves more accessible, and open informal channels (Bruce, 1986). They need to reward, not punish, messengers with bad news or disturbing opinions. They need to be aware that despite the greater pressure to communicate upward than downward, their subordinates are considerably reluctant to risk the displeasure of being seen as the visible critics of the current state of affairs or the bearers of unpleasant messages. They can encourage systematic surveys of subordinates' attitudes that are a formal medium for upward feedback. They can institute a policy, as did the British Army in World War II, that each commander must pay frequent visits to all the unit commanders at the level immediately below them. They can practice "walk-around" management in which managers visit employees at their work stations. This type of policy can promote upward feedback informally if the employees recognize that their superiors, particularly those at high levels in the organization, may feel out of touch with those at the lower levels and would appreciate receiving positive, supportive feedback as well as constructive criticism. The higher-level receivers must make it clear that they are open to accept feedback; the lower-level senders must be ready to provide feedback that is free of the distortion commonly observed in upward messages in which subordinates tell the superiors what they believe the superiors want to hear (Jablin, 1980).

In addition to such motivated distortion, there is cognitive distortion because of the different meanings that superiors and subordinates attach to the same words and their different perceptions and broader views about the same issues (Smircich & Chesser, 1981).

Maturity of Followers

The dictum that more guidance of the learner is needed early in training and less guidance is needed later in training is axiomatic in learning theory and counseling. In the same way, more direction is required by the novice subordinate and less direction is required by the mature subordinate. Less can be delegated to the novice; more can be delegated to the mature subordinate. The subordinates' readiness and competence determine how much and what kind of leadership can be efficacious.[3]

Readiness and Maturity. Followers strongly affect the likelihood of a leader's success in influencing them as a consequence of whether they are ready for the leader. J. M. Burns (1978) suggested that followers could be ripe for mobilization by a leader or contrarily imprisoned by fixed beliefs that would make it impossi-

ble to lead them. In the same vein, Heller (1969a) pointed out that some level of agreement about procedures, interests, and norms among followers is necessary before effective participatory leadership can occur. Nie, Powell, and Prewitt (1969) found five sets of attitudes that were of consequence to such readiness among political followers in Germany, Italy, Mexico, the United States, and Britain: (1) a sense of duty, (2) information about politics, (3) a stake in political outcomes, (4) a sense of political efficiency, and (5) attentiveness to politics.

One's readiness to accept the suggestions of leaders will depend on one's immediately preceding experiences. For instance, negative arguments that were introduced before an attempt to persuade students to volunteer for civil defense work were found more likely to reduce the success of the positive arguments than if the negative arguments came later (Feierabend & Janis, 1954).

Another antecedent to determining the readiness of subordinates for a subsequent attempt to lead them is the extent to which the attempted leadership fits with previous experiences. Weiss and Fine (undated) found that groups who were first subjected to failure and insult were more influenced by suggestions to be punitive; groups first subjected to rewarding experiences were more likely to respond to suggestions to be lenient.

According to L. I. Moore (1976), fully effective leadership tends to depend on mature followership. Moore developed a maturity index based on observations of verbal and nonverbal behavior of followers in task groups. Dimensions of maturity were motivation to achieve, ability and willingness to take responsibility, task-relevant education or experience, activity level, dependence, the variety of behavior interests, perspective, position, and awareness. The leader's knowledge of the followers' maturity can facilitate and modify the followers' and the leader's behavior.

Effects of the Follower's Interest and Competence on the Leader. What subordinates seek in their jobs affects what their supervisor can and will do, according to Maier (1965). Jones, James, and Bruni (1975) showed that the degree to which trust and confidence of 112 engineering employees correlated with the behavior of their supervisors was affected by whether the employ-

[3]Hersey and Blanchard's Life Cycle Theory of Leadership is built on this premise and will be discussed in detail in Chapter 23.

ees were involved in their work. If the subordinates preferred to avoid risk, if they did not wish to become involved in the task, if they were uninterested in the task, and if such interest was of no relevance to getting the job done, leaders became directive. But if subordinates wanted to be involved and were more interested in what happened, more supervisory leadership occurred to engage them. Thus, when the British managers who were surveyed by Heller (1969a) saw a decision as being important to subordinates but not to the company, they used a high degree of power sharing. Conversely, when a decision was a matter of concern to the company but not to subordinates, they preferred the centralization of power.

If the time required for subordinates to participate in decision making is more expensive than the value of their contribution, effective supervisors will be more directive than participative with the subordinates (Tannenbaum & Massarik, 1950; Lowin, 1968). On the other hand, if the supervisors value the competence of their subordinates, they will be more participative (Likert, 1959). Thus, Hsu and Newton (1974) found that supervisors of unskilled employees in a manufacturing plant were more directive than were supervisors of skilled employees in the same plant. Similar results were obtained experimentally by Lowin and Craig (1968) with students who thought themselves to be in part-time jobs. When the students thought they lacked competence for the tasks to be done, they were more appreciative of close, directive supervision than when they considered themselves to be competent. Likewise, Heller (1969a) reported that whenever managers saw that their technical ability, decisiveness, and intelligence were much greater than those of their subordinates, they were more likely to use autocratic decision methods. On the other hand, when the subordinates were valued for their expertise, they were more likely to be invited to share in the decision process with their supervisors.

Ashour and England (1971) found, in experimental teams of supervisors and secretaries, that the perceived competence of followers was the major determinant in assigning of discretionary tasks. Supervisors allowed competent secretaries more discretion than they permitted incompetent secretaries. Another effect of the competence of subordinates on superiors was seen by Kim and Organ (1982) using an in-basket simulation.[4] "Supervisors" were more likely to initiate noncontractual social exchanges with competent "subordinates." Scandura, Graen, and Novak (1986) showed, in this regard, that supervisors were more willing to involve competent subordinates, particularly those with whom they also had good relations, in nontrivial decisions.

The competence of followers may produce resistance. Thus, Mausner (1954a) showed that participants with a past history of positive reinforcement in a given type of judgment were less influenced by their partners in a group-judgment situation than were participants with a history of negative reinforcement. Nevertheless, effective followers are those who, despite their own competence, can avoid being overly resistant to influence from others because of the followers' capacity and willingness to learn from others, to listen, to discriminate, and to be guided by others without feeling threatened or afraid of losing status (J. M. Burns, 1978).

The competence of followers affects the way they view their leaders' initiation and consideration. Cashman and Snyder (1980) reported systematic differences in the factor structure of 475 descriptions of supervisors by more competent and less competent subordinates. In the same way, Snyder and Bruning (1985) found that the competence of 815 employees of federally funded social service organizations correlated .24 with their evaluations of the quality of the dyadic linkage with their superiors. The same correlation was obtained by Bass (undated) for 220 manufacturing employees who were sorted by their supervisors into "best" and "less than best" and the employees' satisfaction with their supervision.

The subordinate's competence may affect the subordinates' ability to comply. Numerous studies have shown, as seems obvious, that the compliance of subordinates affects their superiors' attitudes and behavior toward them. In a laboratory experiment, Price and Garland (1981) demonstrated that when the group members were low in competence, they were much more willing to comply with their leader's suggestions. Nevertheless, in some situations, compliance can suffer because the member is unable, rather than unwilling, to comply. Kessler (1968) hypothesized that highly rated subordinates in a governmental agency would be

[4]See the glossary and Chapter 36.

highly motivated to act in accord with their superiors' expectations; instead, Kessler found that these subordinates were most independent. Consistent with this, Simmons (1968) observed that in a business game, students who were rated as very low, low, or average in performance complied more closely with the managers' expectations than did those who were rated high in performance. Evidently, the competent, highly valued subordinates felt greater freedom than did the less highly valued subordinates to deviate from managers' expectations.

Effects of Followers' Good or Poor Performance.

The quality of the subordinates' performance, whether good or poor, has obvious effects on whether their leaders will be supportive or punitive toward them (Podsakoff & Schriesheim, 1985). The evidence in this regard is overwhelming. Barrow (1976) and Herold (1977) found that leaders rewarded good performers and behaved more punitively toward poor performers. So did Farris and Lim (1969), who divided 200 graduate students into 20 groups of 4 members each to play a business-discussion game. Some leaders, appointed at random, were told that they had high-producing groups, and other leaders were told they had low-producing groups. Leaders who were told that their groups were high producers were significantly more likely than were leaders of low-producing groups to be seen by their groups as sensitive, nonpunitive, maintaining high standards, exerting less pressure to produce, allowing freedom, and emphasizing teamwork. The subordinates in the "high-performance" condition were better satisfied, felt they had more influence, and described their groups as more cohesive.

In a laboratory study, Lowin and Craig (1968) artificially established the level of subordinates' performance as either high or low. "Poor" performing subordinates tended to elicit from their appointed leader close supervision with frequent directions and checking. The ideas of the "poor" subordinates were ignored. These subordinates were held closely to prescribed procedures, were viewed by their leader as irresponsible, and treated with less consideration. The laboratory "supervisors" of the "poorly" performing subordinates criticized them more for their work and for taking unauthorized work breaks, ordered them to end their unauthorized breaks and return to work, and showed them less support than did supervisors of high-producing subordinates.

Similarly, in studying the behavior of 82 coaches of boys' baseball teams, Curtis, Smith, and Smoll (1979) observed that when compared to the behavior of winning coaches, proportionately more of the observed behaviors of coaches on losing teams were reactions to players' mistakes and misbehaviors. (Of course, players on losing teams usually make more mistakes.) But more important, players perceived the coaches of losing teams to be more punitive and less supportive than they did the winning coaches. With older-age teams, such perceptions by team members became more significant to their continuing performance as winners or losers.

Some obvious effects were confirmed. Lanzetta and Hannah (1969) found that when trainees responded correctly, the trainers administered reward, but when the trainees responded incorrectly, the trainers administered punishment. In the same way, Bankart and Lanzetta (1970) found that reward and punishment were systematically related to observed performance; rewards were given for high performance and punishments for low performance. Kipnis and Vanderveer (1971) concluded that "managers" in a simulated work setting rewarded superior performers more than average performers and average performers more than poor performers. Fodor (1973a) also reported that superior performers were given more rewards than were average workers, while Chow and Grusky (1980) observed, in a laboratory study, that supervision was less close for productive workers than for unproductive ones. Finally, Sims and Manz (1984) found that laboratory subjects who acted as the appointed superiors of "subordinates" who were confederates of the experimenters tended to provide positive verbal rewards for the "subordinates'" good performance and punitive and goal-setting verbal comments when "subordinates'" performance was poor. However, much more of the supervisory activity dealt with clarifying how the task could be accomplished than with evaluations of the subordinates' efforts.

Escalation of Effects.

Not as obviously, continued punishment may lead to a downward spiral in performance. Moreover, "learned helplessness" can occur. A particular area of poor performance will be dealt with even more punitively than usual if a subordinate is generally viewed as a poor performer (James & White, 1983). Overall performance will deteriorate further (Peterson, 1985a).

However, there is some buffering against the downward spiral. Rothbart (1968) found that when the use of rewards in a prior trial in an experiment produced improved performance, the administrator had a strong tendency to use reward again. But if punishment on a previous trial led to increased performance, it was unlikely to be used in the next trial.

Effects of the Causes Supervisors Attribute to Subordinates' Performance

Calder (1977) and Green and Mitchell (1979) proposed that to understand how a subordinate's performance affects a supervisor's reactions requires a determination of the cause identified by the superior of the subordinate's good or poor performance.[5] Four causes were seen as possibilities: competence, effort, luck, or external causes within or outside the subordinate's control. Competence and effort were causes that were internal to the subordinate; luck and noncontrollable causes were external.

Knowlton and Mitchell (1980) demonstrated, with 40 undergraduates who were "supervising" confederates of the experimenter, that if supervisors attributed the good performance of their subordinates to the subordinates' efforts, they evaluated the subordinates more highly than ordinary. But if the good performance was attributed to the subordinates' competence, the supervisors did not do so. Ilgen and Knowlton (1980) reached similar conclusions. Mitchell (1981) and Brown and Mitchell (1986) found that supervisors were more likely to blame subordinates for a poor performance and its consequences than for external causes. In doing so, the supervisors again gave more weight to information about the subordinates' lack of effort than the subordinates' lack of ability.

For "supervisors" in a role-playing simulation con-

ducted by Green and Liden (1980), the poor performance of subordinates in missing a deadline was described as being due either to their taking an overextended lunchbreak—an internal cause—or to a delay in receiving materials—an external cause. The "supervisors" attributed taking too much time for lunch to the subordinates' personal character and failure to take responsibility for their action. "Supervisors" were more intense in their punitive reactions to the subordinates who missed the deadline because they took a long lunch. The "supervisors" thought they should be more punitive than just talking to the subordinate about the matter, but the subordinates thought that such a discussion was sufficient. The "supervisors" were less likely to carry out stated corrective policies when the failure was due to the delay in receiving materials.

In similar studies, supervisors generally were found to be more punitive when they attributed poor performance to internal causes—subordinate ability or effort—rather than external causes. If the lack of effort was the diagnosed cause, punitive action was more likely than if the lack of ability was seen to be the cause. If the lack of ability was regarded as the cause of the subordinate's poor performance, then the training or replacement of the subordinate was indicated (Mitchell & Wood, 1980; Wood & Mitchell, 1981). At the same time, employees who were described as succeeding because of their ability were seen to have more potential for top management positions than were those who were thought to be successful because of their efforts, external conditions, or good luck (Heilman & Guzzo, 1978).

Brown and Mitchell (1986) showed that attributions of internal causes increased if poor performance was detected in just one of several employees. The employees did not have to be working on interdependent tasks for this to happen. However, in a laboratory experiment with undergraduates, Offerman, Schroyer, and Green (1986) showed that leaders advocated reward or punishment for actual success or failure, rather than for the reasons they attributed for the subordinates' performance. The leaders also increased their talking to subordinates whose success they attributed to luck, as well as to subordinates whose poor performance was attributed to a lack of effort.

[5]This comprehensive line of investigation grew from earlier theorization by Kelley (1973) and by Weiner, Frieze, Kukla, et al. (1971).

Effect of Supervisory Experience. In a laboratory experiment and in a field study with military officers, Mitchell and Kalb (1982) found that the superiors' experience made a difference. Experienced supervisors were more likely to emphasize external causes than causes that were internal to the subordinate as the reason for the subordinate's poor performance. Liden (1981) obtained similar findings for bank managers' explanations of the poor performance of subordinates; again, more experience resulted in more external attributions. On the other hand, Mitchell and Kalb argued that if the subordinate performed poorly on the same task before, if the subordinate also performed poorly on other tasks, and if co-workers are performing well on the task, supervisors would be expected to attribute the subordinate's poor performance to the subordinate, rather than to external causes, and to act accordingly. Finally, Gioia and Sims (1986) demonstrated with 24 experienced managers, each interacting with 4 different subordinates in simulated performance appraisal interviews, that the interview resulted in a more-lenient appraisal of the subordinate afterward. The managers attached less blame to their subordinates for failure and more credit for success after the meeting than before it.

Subordinates' Accounts. If subordinates apologize or provide an explanation of the external causes for their poor performance, they can affect their supervisor's interpretation and reaction to the poor performance. In an experiment with 109 nursing supervisors, Wood and Mitchell (1981) showed that although both tactics may work to reduce the supervisor's blaming of the subordinate, the subordinate's explanations were much more effective than were apologies. In another study, Mitchell and Liden (1982) established that a supervisor's punitive action for a subordinate's poor performance might be moderated by the subordinate's social skills and popularity.

Lenient reactions of supervisors, according to an Israeli study by Bizman and Fox (1984), may result because supervisors see good acts by subordinates, such as avoiding waste and the squandering of resources, performing duties with precision and thoroughness, and making efficient and practical use of information, as being more stable in occurrence than bad acts by subordinates such as setting up difficulties in planning and organizing work, creating unpleasantness, and not following supervisors' instructions.

Martinko and Gardner (1987) traced different likely outcomes from the combined attributions of leaders and subordinates about the subordinates' failure to perform adequately. As can be seen in Figure 18.1, for instance, if both the leader and the subordinate consider that the subordinate's failure was due to bad luck, the leader will take no action and the subordinate will not change. If the leader attributes the subordinate's failure to a lack of effort, if the subordinate does likewise, and the leader reprimands the subordinate, the subordinate will increase his or her effort. However if the subordinate continues to perform poorly or if the leader continues to punish the subordinate, he or she will attribute the continued failure to external conditions, including the leader's punitiveness.

Effects of Followers' Compliance on Leadership

It is evident that leaders tend to react in response to their subordinates' compliance or noncompliance. As expected, Hinton and Barrow (1975) found supervisors rewarded subordinates for compliance with the supervisors' requests and were punitive when subordinates did not comply. Fodor (1974) demonstrated, also as expected, that leaders became more authoritarian when faced with a disparaging and disruptive subordinate. Naturally, they rated that subordinate lower and gave the subordinate less pay than they did subordinates who did not engage in such behavior. In an experiment by Crowe, Bochner, and Clark (1972), male management students were asked to play the role of a leader. Each was confronted with accomplices of the experimenters who served as subordinates and acted either democratically or submissively. Democratic subordinates showed initiative by putting forth ideas and trying to set their own goals. Submissive subordinates avoided taking any initiative and asked for detailed instructions, which they followed without question. The leaders' behavior was affected accordingly. For example, the leaders were more autocratic with the submissive subordinates and more democratic with the democratic ones. In the same way, Chow and Grusky (1980) found that in laboratory-simulated organizational set-

Figure 18.1. Some Combined Subordinate's and Leader's Attributions for Poor Performance by the Subordinates and Expected Responses

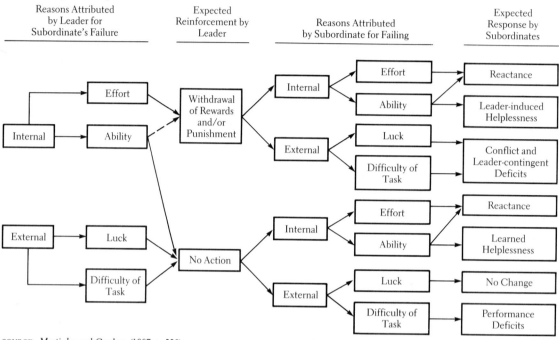

SOURCE: *Martinko and Gardner (1987, p. 238).*

tings, the subordinates' compliance generated employee-oriented supervision, while the subordinate's aggressiveness resulted in punitive supervision.

In a longitudinal field survey, Greene (1979a) reported similarly that the subordinate's compliance exerted considerable subsequent influence on the supervisor. If the subordinate was more compliant and performed better early on, the supervisor in the following three months was seen to display more considerate, supportive, and participative leadership. On the other hand, if the subordinate's performance was poor early on, the supervisor initiated more structure and role clarification later on. Poor subordinate performance by the subordinate, particularly the lack of compliance, generated the leader's greater use of punishment three or six months later.

At the same time, better supervisors tend to look for and to reward independent action in subordinates, whereas less effective supervisors tend to reward conformity and group action. The better supervisors are also less lenient (Kirchner, 1961; Kirchner & Reisberg, 1962).

Effects of Contrasting Subordinates. A supervisor's reactions to a subordinate's compliance appears to depend on the failure of other subordinates to comply. In a field study of the performance of clerical workers, Grey and Kipnis (1976) found that the supervisors' evaluations of compliant workers were higher in work groups with more noncompliant workers. Evaluations of noncompliant workers tended to be lower in work groups with more compliant workers. Goodstadt and Kipnis (1970) and Kipnis and Vanderveer (1971) found that in the presence of a poorly performing subordinate with a bad attitude, subjects allocated nearly twice as many pay raises to compliant workers as they did when the poorly performing subordinate was seen as simply inept, rather than disparaging.

Mutual Influence of Leaders and Followers

The preceding research examined the processes through which leaders affect their followers or the processes through which followers affect their leaders.

In fact, of course, both processes are occurring simultaneously and may be discussed as two-way dynamics. For example, as was described in Chapter 17, Graen (1976) examined the dyadic relation between the leader and each member of the group. He noted that the dyads form a behavioral interdependence between the respective roles. This interdependence includes the dyadic "partnership" engaged in reciprocal influence, its extracontractual behavioral exchanges, its role-defined relations, and its loosely coupled fates (Dansereau, Graen, & Haga, 1975). Graen and Schiemann (1978) observed that the manager's and subordinate's agreement about the relationship was higher if the quality of their behavioral interdependencies were high. Such interdependence of the manager and the subordinate is necessary for the leader to give and the subordinate to receive opportunities for growth on the job (Graen & Scandura, 1986). Subordinates with high needs for growth are more likely to collaborate in a closer and better-quality relationship with superiors on tasks that provide opportunities for growth.

But behavioral interdependence has its dark side. A superior and subordinate can share a delusion—a *folie à deux*—when both have a strong need to be dependent and are in an isolated position, say on a space-exploration mission. The delusion is likely to occur in more everyday settings if mutual trust and closeness are lacking. The subordinate may have the need to depend on the superior, but this need is frustrated if he or she cannot depend on the superior. In turn, the superior may want to depend on the subordinate but feels it unwise to do so. The world becomes dangerous, and the danger is compounded by the superior's and subordinate's lack of trust in each other. Each can trust only a few people but not each other. The superior and subordinate can elaborate their mistrust of each other into a common fantasy about an organizational betrayal of both of them. Thus, they become trapped by their shared delusion (Kets de Vries, 1984).

Models of Mutual Influence

Crouch (1987) and Zahn and Wolfe (1981) started with different assumptions and used different methods to construct different models to describe how mutual influence develops between superiors and subordinates. Crouch (1987) assumed that manager-subordinate rela-

tionships stem from the influence that the subordinates can exert in solving unstructured problems that they and the manager face. Over time, the model predicts the emergence of stable relationships. Either high- or low-performing groups will be developed to deal with outside demands on the groups. Zahn and Wolf (1981) provided Markov mathematical states-events models to describe the continuing interplay of the superior and the subordinate, showing how their emerging task and interactional relationships can predict future outcomes. Unexpected results appeared. Contrary to Crouch, the model predicted long-term behavior to be highly variable and versatile, rather than stable. The mutual biases of the superior and the subordinate were most salient in effect; both were likely to contribute to the cyclical maintenance of their relationships. Deterimining which model is closer to reality awaits the necessary long-term empirical research.

Two-way Impact

However, considerable empirical evidence is available to provide a cross-sectional picture of the two-way impact—the combined effects of the leader's and the follower's competence and compatibility, the interplay of the leader's style and the follower's personality and motivation, and the combined effects of the leader's and follower's concerns for the task and for their relationship with each other. Pratt and Jiambalvo (1982) showed that an understanding of the leadership of accounting auditors in working with their auditing assistants required consideration of aspects of the auditor, the assistants, and their interplay. Outcomes depended on the personal dominance of the auditors, the intolerance of ambiguity by the assistants, and the match between the perceived complexity of the task for the auditor and the assistants and the assistants' job experience.

Rao (1982) completed an experiment in which the leader could reward the subordinate. In addition, in one setting, the leader was to receive a bonus based on the subordinate's performance. The results were the leader's increased rewarding of the subordinate, large improvements in the subordinate's performance, and greater stability and cooperativeness between the leader and the subordinate. These results were different from those in the situation in which the leader was not offered any bonus for the subordinate's good performance.

The two-way nature of leadership and followership was investigated by Herold (1974), who carried out a double-substitution laboratory experiment in which both leaders' and subordinates' actual behaviors were intercepted and substituted with fully programmed supervisory and subordinate behaviors. Thirty-two groups of three persons each, consisting of one leader and two subordinates, were balanced in treatment so that the subordinates were powerful in half the groups and the leaders were powerful in the other half. The experimental task consisted of proofreading manuscripts and finding errors. The leader of each group received a "good product" from one of the subordinates and a "bad product" from the other. Within each group, one subordinate received a punitive communication following the performance, while the other received a supportive communication. Herold found strong mutual effects on the attitudes of the leaders and followers toward each other and toward the situation. Whether the leader received a good or bad product from a subordinate strongly affected what the leader did, but whether the subordinate received a punitive communication from the leader had somewhat less of an impact on the subordinate. The leader's power was important in its effects on subordinates, but the subordinates' power was not significant in affecting the leader's behavior.

This lack of symmetry was also seen by G. J. Palmer (1962a, 1962b), who studied leaders and followers in a difficult task situation. Palmer concluded that followership in such a situation is explained largely by the lack of ability. Leadership, on the other hand, requires a more complex explanation involving both individual and situational variables. For instance, the joint competence of the leader and the subordinate has to be considered. This conclusion was confirmed by Rohde (1958), who observed different combinations of qualified and unqualified leaders and followers under four conditions of reward and punishment. The leader's ability to perform the task was found to be more highly related to the group's performance than to the group's motivation. Not unexpectedly, the poorest performance was exhibited by groups with both unqualified leaders and unqualified followers. Almost equally poor

were groups with qualified leaders and two unqualified followers.

Blades (1976) also studied the joint effects of the leader's and subordinates' competence on their group's performance in servicing U.S. Army mess halls. Ratings of the group's performance by inspectors were correlated with ratings by 102 mess hall personnel of the intelligence, ability, and behavior of the leader. Blades found that the subordinates' intelligence, ability to perform the task, and motivation correlated positively with their performance only under participative management and when the subordinates were highly motivated. But the leader's intelligence correlated positively with the group's performance only under directive management with highly motivated leaders and subordinates. The leader's ability to perform the task and the leader's motivation correlated positively with the group's performance only with directive supervision of highly motivated subordinates. Blades concluded that competent, motivated subordinates can be led best if they are allowed to participate in the decision-making process, while competent, motivated leaders do best with a directive style if their subordinates' competence is limited.[6]

The Reciprocal Relationship

The leader and the follower depend on each other, for whoever leads and whoever follows stimulates and reinforces the other's behavior. The leader initiates, questions, or proposes; the follower complies, resists, or ignores.

Leadership and followership are mutual activities of influence and counterinfluence. Leaders and followers both give and both receive benefits. The relationship is maintained by this social exchange and this mutual influence (Hollander, 1978). As Hollander and Julian (1969) noted, when leaders are effective, they give something and get something in return. This transactional approach to leadership involves the trading of benefits. The leader provides a benefit by directing the group toward desirable results. In return, the followers provide the leader with status, the privileges of authority, influence, and prestige. However, the leader may demand from the followers what they regard as an ex-

[6] See Chapter 22 for an extended discussion of the different effects of participation and direction under different conditions.

cessive expenditure of energy by them. The followers' compliance may be tempered if desired outcomes do not match the perceived effort required. As members become less involved in the group's success, they complain less about obstacles to such success but more about demands for expending their time and energy (Willerman, 1954). Bass, Gaier, and Flint (1956) observed that ROTC cadets who were strongly motivated to enter advanced training complained about the difficulty of the test employed to screen applicants, whereas those whose motivation was low complained about having to take the test, rather than complaining about its difficulty.

Much of the differentiation of members' roles and the emergence of leadership in a group comes about as a result of the mutual reinforcement of intermember expectations. Because of their initiative, interaction, and contributions to the group's task, some members reinforce the expectations that they will be more likely than will other members to establish conditions that will promote the movement of the task, members' freedom and acceptance, and the group's cohesiveness. Other members, by compliance, reinforce the expectation that whoever has started and succeeded with it should continue in the leadership role, that is, "Don't change horses in midstream." Similarly, members build up expectations regarding the contributions that they are to make. The reactions of other members confirm the expectation that they are (or are not) to continue in the same role. The role system and the status structure of a group are determined by a set of such mutually reinforced intermember expectations. Thus, in a verbal learning experiment, Bachrach, Candland, and Gibson (1961) observed that the members of the group differentially reinforce the behavior of other members. Such differential reinforcement accounts, in large part, for individual differences in role specialization and conformity to norms.

Leader-follower interaction and mutual support are seen in the case of political leaders and their followers. The leaders activate and mobilize support for their objectives, control the communications media, and make use of intermediary opinion leaders. The followers may be actively interested in, to various degrees, or ready to be motivated to engage in political activity. Multilayered networks are formed of leaders and followers.

Those below yield an aggregate of public opinion to support the aims of those at the top. The importance of such followers' support for leaders was seen by Pepinsky, Hemphill, and Shevitz (1958), who studied experimental groups who were working on construction problems. When the leaders were made to believe that they were accepted by the members, the groups were more productive and exhibited high degrees of satisfaction and participation. When the leaders were made to feel that they were rejected, the groups made fewer and poorer decisions and exhibited less participation and satisfaction.

Effects of Language. More than direct cost-benefit calculations may lie behind an interaction between the leader and the followers. Drake and Moberg (1986) suggested that two adjustments in language can be made to change the cost-benefit calculations by a follower who is considering an attempt by a leader to influence him or her into compliance. First, sedating language, such as semantic indirectness, can be used in the leader's attempt to keep the follower from considering the costs of compliance. For example, instead of giving a direct order, the leader can hint at the need for action or prompt the follower by saying, for example, "It is getting warm in here" instead of "Please turn down the heat."

Second, the linguistic form of an influence attempt may palliate the follower to protect him or her from loss of respect that may occur if a more straightforward directive is used to correct a follower or to reverse a decision. Numerous positive polite strategies may be employed as palliatives, such as expressing admiration, claiming common viewpoints, displaying concern for the follower, and desiring cooperation. For palliatives, the influence attempt may be accompanied by efforts to reduce the differences in power between the leader and the follower. Instead of a direct order, "Check the switch again," the leader suggests "You *may want to try* to check the switch again."

Mutual Effects of the Task and Clarity of the Goal

Under some circumstances, clarification of what needs to be done may depend on the subordinates' participation with the leader in agreeing on the tasks and setting of the group's goals. Critical experiments described by Locke, Latham, and Erez (1987) suggested that such participation by subordinates in setting goals is important to their understanding, commitment and productivity if the leader is curt and unsupportive. The subordinates' participation in goal setting is not necessary if the leader assigns goals in a friendly and supportive manner. This may explain why Dossett, Cella, Greenberg, and Adrian (1983) found, in a laboratory study with 40 undergraduates, that although, as was expected, productivity on a clerical task was highest when a supervisor set high, clear, standards for them and gave them friendly support, the subordinates' participation in setting the goals did not contribute to their productivity by itself.

The failure of participation in setting goals to make a difference also may be explained by the character of the participation. Neider (1980) demonstrated, in a study of performance in retail stores, that only when the participation process clarified the linkage of effort and performance and only when the rewards given for high performance were valued were positive outcomes obtained from such participation.

The effects of clarification also depend on the competence of the leader. Podsakoff, Todor, and Schuler (1983) found that expert leaders who work at setting and clarifying goals did decrease their subordinates' sense of role ambiguity. But the reverse was true for the leaders who were inept; their efforts resulted in increasing their subordinates' sense of role ambiguity!

In a previously mentioned longitudinal survey by Greene (1979b) of the mutual effects of leaders and subordinates, 60 subordinates from five manufacturing organizations, were queried. These subordinates, had joined the management of their firms within the past three months and had never worked before for their immediate superiors. Greene assumed that because of the newness of their appointments, the subordinates' expectations were unclear and their full compliance was undeveloped. The subordinates described their leaders' behavior and indicated their own expectations, compliance, performance, and satisfaction. The data were gathered three times in three-month intervals to permit path analyses. Consistent with path-goal theory (see Chapter 28), early role clarification by a leader di-

rectly resulted in the greater satisfaction of and compliance by the subordinates three and six months later. Role clarification by the leader also was seen to enhance the subordinates' expectations that their greater effort would produce better performance.

Compatibility

It seems obvious that if leaders and their subordinates, individually or in groups, share the same approaches, values, and attitudes, they will be more satisfied with their relationship and experience less conflict and more mutual support. Such positive associations between the compatibility of the values of superiors and subordinates and satisfaction with their relationships were obtained by Duchon, Green, and Tabor (1986) in a field study of 49 Junior Achievement companies.

Fujii (1977) conducted an experiment in which the independent variables were manipulated by simulating a division of a greeting card company. Eighty paid male volunteers participated as work-group leaders or workers in the greeting card unit. The followers' performance, based on merit ratings by the leaders, but not on objective performance, was positively related to greater interpersonal compatibility between the leaders and the followers. Extrinsic satisfaction increased with leader-member compatibility. The relationship between leader-member compatibility and intrinsic and overall satisfaction was moderated by the amount of cooperation required by the task and the amount of experience with the task. Leader-member compatibility was positively related to relations-oriented leadership behavior but less so to task-oriented leadership behavior.

McLachlan (1974) reported a study of group therapy with 94 alcoholic inpatients in which patients and therapists were matched for conceptual compatibility on the basis of Hunt's Paragraph Completion Test. Matched pairs of patients-therapists were positively associated with outcomes, as evaluated by staff ratings 12 to 16 months later. Beutler, Jobe, and Elkins (1974) also investigated the effects of patient-therapist matching on attitudes. Matched attitude was associated with self-rated improvement (although some dissimilarity of attitudes resulted in more attitudinal changes in patients).

Similarly, Steiner and Dobbins (undated) completed a laboratory study of 111 management students and their "subordinates" in which high and low intrinsic and extrinsic work-related values were the manipulated bases of matched and mismatched "superiors" and "subordinates." When superiors and subordinates matched each other in high extrinsic or high intrinsic work values, the superiors were more likely to attribute the subordinates' past good performance to internal than to external causes.

Pulakos and Wexley (1983) examined 171 manager-subordinate dyads composed of the same and opposite sexes. Sex, as such, was not as important as perceived compatibility. The managers' leadership, particularly their facilitation and support of the work, was appraised higher by their subordinates when both the managers and the subordinates felt they were "similar kinds of people." Subordinates also were rated more favorably by their managers if they were perceived as similar. Conversely, lower performance appraisals occurred when the managers and subordinates were mutually perceived as dissimilar. When the subordinates saw themselves as similar to their managers, the managers gave higher dependability ratings to their female than to their male subordinates. But when subordinates said they were dissimilar to their managers, managers rated both males and females uniformly lower.

Similarity. The actual similarity between managers and their subordinates tends to correlate with the manager's appraisals of their subordinates' performance (Miles, 1964a; Senger, 1971); the subordinates' evaluations of their managers; as well as the subordinates' satisfaction with their managers (Weiss, 1977). Subordinates who more accurately perceive their superiors' attitudes toward work are rated more highly by their superiors and are more satisfied with their superiors (Greene, 1972; Howard, 1968; Labovitz, 1972).

Subordinates are more satisfied in general if their descriptions of their manager's attitudes more accurately match their manager's self-description. In turn, the subordinates receive higher evaluations from their manager if the manager's description of the subordinate's attitude matches the subordinates' self-descriptions (Wexley, Alexander, Greenawalt, & Couch, 1980).

Interplay of Leaders' Style and Subordinates' Motivation and Personality

Using Exercise Supervise (Bass, 1975c), approximately 3,500 managers in training workshops in 12 countries played one of three supervisory roles—authoritarian, persuasive, or participative—or one of three subordinate roles—highly involved, moderately involved, or uninvolved. Meetings took place between dyads that were composed of one supervisor and one subordinate. The three tasks were to decide which of 25 traits are most and least characteristic of lower, middle, and top managers. A Latin-Square design was completed so that data about all 9 supervisory-subordinate combinations of role play emerged. As might be expected, the uninvolved, apathetic subordinate was least preferred by supervisors as a whole and the participative supervisor was most preferred by the subordinates as a whole. At the same time, the fastest and easiest-to-complete interactions took place between the authoritarian supervisors and the uninvolved, apathetic subordinates. The dissatisfaction of subordinates and supervisors tended to be greatest for highly involved subordinates meeting with authoritarian supervisors; satisfaction tended to be greatest for highly involved subordinates meeting with participative supervisors. The interaction effects of persuasive supervision and subordinates at the three different levels of involvement fell in between in satisfaction and speed of decision (Bass, Burger, et al., 1979; Thiagarajan & Deep, 1970).

Sales, Levanoni, and Saleh (1984) contrasted the reactions of 226 intrinsically and extrinsically motivated clerical, technical, and professional employees to two types of supervision. General supervision provided broad specifications of goals and left the means of achieving them up to the subordinates. Close supervision involved giving detailed instructions at each stage in the process of completing a task and checking to see that instructions were carried out. The investigators found that intrinsically oriented employees expressed more satisfaction with their supervisors under general supervision than under close supervision; extrinsically oriented employees indicated the opposite. Similarly, Steiner and Dobbins (undated) experimented with the extrinsic and intrinsic work values of the subordinates of management students who were acting as their supervisors. Subordinates with high intrinsic work values were given more autonomy and more challenging assignments by their "supervisors" than were the other "subordinates."

W. W. Burke (1965) studied student leaders in 24 groups who were participating in an interfraternity contest. Each group performed a clerical and organizational task, as well as a decision-making task. Followers whose need-achievement scores were high and who were working with relations-oriented leaders reported more tension, regardless of the task, than did followers with high need-achievement scores who were working with task-oriented leaders. Those with low need-achievement scores who were working with task-oriented leaders reported more tension than did those who were working with relations-oriented leaders. The more relaxed situation occurred when the leader's personality was such as to meet the needs of the group of followers.

Misumi and Seki (1971), showed that Japanese subjects whose need for achievement was low demonstrated relatively high performance but low satisfaction with a task-oriented leader in experimental tasks. Subjects whose need for achievement was high were most productive and satisfied under high task- and relations-oriented leaders and performed worst under leaders whose task- and relations orientation were low. Misumi (1985) also noted that high-anxiety subjects did better under a relations-oriented than under a task-oriented leader.

Superiors were viewed as less active and directive by those hospital employees who were more concerned with power, achievement, and independence (Niebuhr, Bedeian, & Armenakis, 1980). Engineering personnel with high self-esteem who were in dyads with superiors of long duration saw more initiation and consideration in their superiors' leadership behavior (Neibuhr & Davis, 1984).

Greer (1961) reported that authoritarian infantrymen and airmen worked better under authoritarian leaders, while egalitarian men did better when led by egalitarians. A group's performance was positively related to followers' perceptions of the leader as a problem solver and the extent to which the leader met the followers' expectations. Again, Weed, Mitchell, and

Moffitt (1976) concluded, from a laboratory study, that supervision that was structuring generated higher performance by subordinates if the subordinates were higher in dogmatism. Considerate supervision generated higher performance in subordinates who were lower in dogmatism.

Concerns for Task or Relationships. Back (1948) analyzed the interactions of leaders and followers in two discussion groups—work centered and "emotionally toned." When the leaders emphasized work performance more than did the followers in period 1, the followers increased their work responses in period 2. When the leaders emphasized friendliness more than did the followers in period 1, the followers exhibited more friendly responses in period 2. The emotionally toned group devoted more time in period 1 to establishing stable intermember relations and a group structure. The work-oriented group spent more time in strengthening goal-directed activities. In period 2, the emotionally toned group spent more time maintaining participation among members and with leaders. In the work-oriented group, the leader tended to lose importance, whereas interactions between members were strengthened. Thus, it appeared that the leaders' behavior influenced the groups' response and, at the same time, the groups' response influenced the status of the leaders.

Bass and Dunteman (1963) studied sensitivity training groups that were composed of participants who were homogeneous in interaction orientation, task orientation, and self-orientation. Interaction-oriented groups tended to be most satisfied with their highly interaction-oriented leaders. The leaders who emerged in task-oriented groups tended to be even more highly task oriented than did the average member. However, the emergent leaders of the self-oriented groups were relatively low in self-orientation. Stimpson and Bass (1964) found that interaction-oriented participants in problem-solving groups, when compared with task-oriented and self-oriented participants, made it more difficult for their work partners to attempt and succeed as leaders, to reach agreement, and to feel responsible.

Bass (1967c) observed task-oriented and interaction-oriented followers under coercive and persuasive styles of leadership. He found that task-oriented followers produced greater quantities of work under persuasive leadership and that interaction-oriented followers produced high quantities of work of a high quality under coercive leadership. The followers' satisfaction with the task was significantly higher under a directive interaction-oriented leader than under a participative interaction-oriented leader. Conversely, their satisfaction was lower under a directive than under a persuasive task-oriented leader.

Summary and Conclusions

Leaders contribute to the transactional exchange with followers in numerous ways. They cue what needs to be done, provide feedback to subordinates on how well it is done, communicate needed information, and act as models for their subordinates.

Leaders play a mediating and connecting role between their followers and their own superiors. Their attempts to ally themselves with their subordinates and to work in behalf of their subordinates result in their subordinates' satisfaction if the leaders have enough influence with superiors to obtain the benefits sought for subordinates. To be successful, leaders must have influence "upstairs."

Leadership and followership are reciprocal. Different patterns of interaction among superiors vary in their effects on the performance and expectations of subordinates. When superiors interact with subordinates and with members within their own subgroup,

their subordinates report a loss of responsibility but feel overburdened with planning. When superiors interact with members other than their own subordinates and subgroup members, however, their subordinates feel under pressure to increase efforts in planning, coordination, inspection, and preparing procedures. These counterbalancing reactions appear to be logically consistent.

Groups operate more successfully when the task, the leader's personality, and the follower's personality are compatible. For example, groups with task-oriented leaders perform better than do those with person-oriented leaders when followers are also task oriented. Followers whose task orientation is low experience less tension under person-oriented leaders.

Followers affect, to a considerable extent, what their leaders may do and can do. The exertion of this upward influence takes many forms, ranging from ingratiation to establishing coalitions of influence. Important feedback can flow upward. Followers' effects on leaders depend on the followers' competence, maturity, readiness, and compliance, as well as the leaders' and followers' explanations for the followers' dispositions and performance. Still to be determined is whether the exchange relationship between the leader and subordinates becomes stable or remains variable in the long-term. How the exchange and its effects are moderated by circumstances is the subject which follows next.

Moderators of the Use and Effects of Contingent-Reinforcement Leadership

How much can a leader depend on using contingent reinforcement? What limits it? What moderates its use and its impact on subordinates?

Limits to Contingent Reinforcement

Like most other concepts and practices in social science, contingent reinforcement is neither a universal panacea nor of trivial importance. Rather, the limitations to its use and effectiveness need to be detailed. For instance, subordinates may take shortcuts to complete the exchange of reward for compliance. Quality may be sacrificed to obtain rewards for quantity of output. Complicated piece-rate, reward, and bonus systems generate ambiguities and are likely to induce "game playing" and the fear of "rate busting." Subordinates may react defensively. Reaction formation, withdrawal, or hostility may ensue. Also, the schedule of reinforcements, their timeliness, variability, and consistency will have considerable effect on the inducements (Bass, 1985a).

Perceptions of injustice may outweigh cost-benefit considerations. Tyler, Rasinski, and McGraw (1985) found that the changes in the governmental benefits that 584 undergraduates and 300 Chicago residents personally received were less important to them than were more abstract judgments of injustice when they endorsed their leaders. In the same way, federal managers regarded merit-based pay as inequitable and as undermining their agencies' effectiveness. However, they believed that performance appraisal and performance standards contribute to supervisor-subordinate communications and work planning, particularly if they focused on the subordinates' development (Gaertner & Gaertner, 1985). Silver-

man (1983) argued that the merit-pay contingent-reward system in the federal government failed for numerous political, economic, and psychological reasons, including open-ended regulations, drifting implementation policies, overcomplication, inconsistent treatment of employees, the compression of managers' pay, and simultaneous budget reductions. To this list could be added administrative blunders and unintended statutory provisions. Pearce, Stevenson, and Perry (1985) collected data two years before and two years after the introduction of a merit-pay program in the Social Security Administration and found no improvement in organizational performance.

Pay and Performance

As was already noted, contingent rewards for compliance may entail recommended increases in pay or advancement. If it is possible to make pay fully contingent on performance, such as by placing employees on a straight piece-rate or straight commission basis, productivity may rise as much as 30 percent, according to some studies. But in practice, for most work, there is likely to be little linkage between pay and performance, despite the revealed wisdom to the contrary. Often when workers are placed on a piece-rate or straight commission basis, the work group exerts strong pressure to restrict all its members to conform to the same standard output so that all earn the same pay (Rothe, 1960, 1961).

In Japan, a familiar practice is to link pay and promotion primarily to age and seniority, not meritorious performance. And in the United States, according to an interview study of a representative sample of 845 U.S. workers by Yankelovich and Immerwahr (1983), only 22 percent said there is a direct relationship between how hard they work and how much they get paid. A similar representative national survey of 5,000 employees found that only 28 percent saw a correlation between the salaries and performance of workers (Anonymous, 1988b). In the first survey, 61 percent said they preferred a closer link between performance and pay.[1] In the second survey, almost half the respondents found that managers at their firms were too lenient with underperformers and continued to reward them despite their continuing poor performance. Even when rewards have been found to be distributed according to merit, the linkages are modest. Lawler (1966c) surveyed 600 middle- and lower-level managers in several organizations and discovered only a small correlation between their pay and their performance ratings. In examining a single corporation's salary ranges, Patten (1968b) failed to find any statistically significant evidence that employees whose performance was rated more highly were also paid better. Nevertheless, Heneman (1973) reported one instance of a high performance–reward correlation of .65 for a sample of 51 managers. In line with these contradictory findings, Kopelman and Reinharth (1982) found much variation in the performance–reward correlation among ten branches of a large financial organization.

Contingent Recommendations

The compensation of chief executive officers (CEOs) is often related not to the CEOs' performance but, rather, to the size and scope of the organization for which they are responsible (Deckop, 1987). However, Gomez-Mejia, Tosi, and Hinkin (1987) showed that the compensation of CEOs was linked to their performance if the firms were owner controlled.

In simulations, recommended pay increases by 4,255 managers in an international survey correlated with meritorious performance, although they were modified extensively outside North America for other reasons, such as family considerations and personal circumstances (Bass, Burger, et al., 1979). Nonetheless, awarding more pay or less pay to subordinates seems to be a matter of the recommenders' values. Bass (1968a) re-

ported that students' value orientations were related to their generosity in recommending pay increases for fictitious engineers. Those who were lower in intelligence and ability and those who scored high in social and service values, as opposed to theoretical and economic values, were more generous in recommending salary increases. In the international survey, Bass, Burger, et al. (1979) found that more successful managers recommended significantly greater salary increases for an average meritorious fictitious engineer, but they were no different than their slower-climbing counterparts in their salary recommendations for engineers on other grounds. In another simulation, Martin (1987) showed that recommendations increased for both meritorious performance and for specialized expertise needed in a particular circumstance.

Moderating Conditions

According to managerial in-basket experiments by Martin and Harder (1988), students' financial-related rewards, such as profit sharing, office space, and company cars, are contingent on satisfactory performance, but interpersonal rewards, such as help or friendliness, are distributed equally according to subordinates' needs.

Managers may lack the necessary reward power required to deliver the necessary recommendations for pay increases. Those who can fulfill the self-interested expectations of their subordinates gain and maintain the reputation of being able to deliver pay, promotions, and recognition. Those who fail to deliver lose that reputation in the eyes of their subordinates and, therefore, no longer can be seriously seen as effective contingent-reward leaders (Tsui, 1982). Worse yet, they may be seen as having become more punitive, and their legitimacy and influence will be reduced (Greene & Podsakoff, 1979/1981).

Yukl (1981) enumerated the conditions that made it possible for managers to engage profitably in the contingent rewarding of their employees. As was already indicated, the managers needed substantial authority and discretion to administer tangible rewards to their subordinates. Their subordinates had to be dependent on them for access to the rewards that they, the subordinates, valued. It was necessary for performance out-

---

[1]Many other empirical studies support this conclusion. See, for instance, Hills (1979), Kearny (1979), and H. H. Meyer (1975).

comes to be determined primarily by the subordinates' efforts and skills, rather than by events beyond the subordinates' control. It was also necessary to be able to measure the subordinates' performance accurately. Finally, contingent reward was likely to have more of an impact if the work was "repetitive, boring, and tedious, rather than varied, interesting, and meaningful" (p. 141).

Positive versus Negative Reinforcement

Workers were fined in the Soviet Union for failing to meet production quotas. Workers everywhere face suspensions for infractions of rules. A sufficient cause for dismissal may be displeasing a domineering boss. Feedback can be negative as well as positive. Consistent with what was presented in earlier chapters, such contingent penalization, in general, is less effective than is contingent reward. After observing 126 incidents of feedback, Balcazar, Hopkins, and Suarez (1985–86) noted that feedback does not uniformly improve performance. Thus, according to a survey by Ilgen, Fisher, and Taylor (1979), the role ambiguity of 527 Australian employees was reduced much more by their receipt of positive rather than negative feedback about their performance. Although the effect of positive feedback is to reinforce behavior already displayed and hence to generate more of the same, for negative feedback to be effective, changes are required in performance as a consequence of changes in perception, motivation, or learning. Negative feedback also fails to work because of its unfavorable motivational impact on the subordinate's self-image.[2]

Disciplinary actions may cause emotional reactions and the deterioration of supervisory-subordinate relations instead of their intended correctional effects, according to a survey of 177 fire fighters in eight cities (Greer & Labig, 1987). The unintended results will occur if the administration of the actions is unpleasant, if poor relations already existed, and if the supervisor is judged to be inaccurate in his diagnosis and fails to represent adequate reasons for the disciplinary action.

Negative Reinforcement Used. Despite its potential to contribute to conflict and its relative lower contribution to the improvement of subordinates, negative re-

[2]This last point will be elucidated later as the Jackass Theory of Leadership.

inforcement is often employed. There are many reasons for "accenting the negative," despite the greater utility of emphasizing the positive and despite the decreased contribution of such leadership to the performance of subordinates. For instance, the supervisor may have a large span of control; as a consequence, the supervisor's time may be fully occupied with just monitoring deviations from the standard. Failure to pay attention to the deviations may invite disaster. A preoccupation with prospective failures will inhibit attention to the positive, particularly in the absence of clear goals, clear policies, and long-term objectives.

Managers may lack the power to provide or recommend rewards. Faced with continuing demands for productivity, they will increase their tendencies to use punishment especially since managers report less difficulty identifying poor performance than good performance (Podsakoff, 1982).

The performance of subordinates that is below standard is more salient for a supervisor than is the performance that exceeds the standard (Larson, 1980). Thus, subjects who were acting as supervisors were found, in a laboratory experiment by Fisher (1979), to require a smaller sample of work to evaluate a subordinate who was performing below average than to evaluate one who was performing above average. Larson (1980, p. 199) offered the following reasons for the greater sensitivity of supervisors to the failure rather than to the success of subordinates: "The criteria for minimally acceptable ... performance are frequently more clearly defined than are the criteria for superior performance, ... poor performance often has a more significant impact upon the work group's functioning than does superior performance."

Supervisors are likely to be more sensitive to their subordinates' failure if how well the supervisors do their job depends on how well the subordinates have completed assignments and if, as was noted earlier, the supervisors' pay, recognition, or promotion depend on the subordinates' performance (Larson, 1980).

Other Problems

Contingent reinforcement may fail because there is no clear differentiation of reinforcements for functionally adequate and functionally inadequate performance. Praise alone may not work without other accompanying rewards. The feedback may lack impact because goals have not been clearly set.

In addition, to understand the effects of reinforcement leadership, according to Fedor, Buckley, and Eder (undated), the impact on the subordinate's behavior of a supervisor's attempts at differential reinforcement of the subordinate will depend on the subordinate's perception of the supervisor's intentions: Does the supervisor want to dominate me, to focus my attention on unit standards, to support me, or to urge me to increase my productivity? A sample of 220 subordinates believed it was most likely that their supervisor wanted to dominate them, rather than to support or assist them in achieving higher performance levels. This belief may be due, in part, to the tendency of the subordinates, as the performers in the arrangement, to attribute situational causes, such as difficulties with the problem, equipment, or supplies, or bad luck to their poor performance. As the observers of the subordinates' behavior the supervisors, especially if they are unfamiliar with the specific tasks involved, are more likely to attribute the subordinates' poor performance to the subordinates' lack of ability or effort. Thus, Mitchell and Kalb (1982) showed that if the supervisor had no experience with the subordinate's job, he or she was less likely to act as an ex-performer and to accept situational reasons in making attributions about the subordinate's performance.

Whether the supervisor likes or dislikes the subordinate also makes a difference. According to an experiment and field study by Dobbins and Russell (1986), although leaders may attribute the same reason for the poor performance of subordinates they like and subordinates they dislike, they will tend to act more punitively toward the subordinates they dislike and will be less inclined to punish the subordinates they like.

A Jackass Theory? Many scholars, consultants, and practitioners find contingent reinforcement to be the full and sufficient driving force for predicting, controlling, and understanding leader-follower relations. Many others are considerably less confident. And still others find that the faults and failures override the successful applications enumerated in the preceding chapters. Thus, Levinson (1980) termed contingent reinforcement the "jackass theory" of leadership. When you as a subordinate are between a carrot and a stick, tempted by the carrot or threatened with the stick, it makes you feel like a jackass. Your self-esteem as a mature, conscientious, worthy individual is diminished. Furthermore, when you are between a carrot and a stick, you may see yourself as being in a contest that requires agility to reach the carrot or to avoid the stick. Or you may be immobilized by the uncertainties of whether the benefits of the carrot are outweighed by the costs of being beaten by the stick. Feelings of being manipulated may outweigh responsiveness to the contingent rewards. Drawing from the Russian writer Dostoyevsky, Vice-Admiral J. B. Stockdale (1981, p. 15) argued that people do not like to feel they are being programmed:

> You cannot persuade [people] to act in their own self interest all of the time. A good leader appreciates contrariness . . . some men all of the time and all men some of the time knowingly will do what is clearly to their disadvantage if only because they do not like to be suffocated by carrot-and-stick coercion. I will not be a piano key; I will not bow to the tyranny of reason.

As Maccoby (1988) noted, with increasing technology and its servicing, employees are expected to work and think as mature persons. They are expected to make judgments; to solve problems; to develop good working relationships with colleagues, clients, and customers; and to be committed to and understand what they are doing. These expectations require a broader view of what motivates people to work. About half the sample studied by Maccoby regarded themselves as experts who get much of their reward from doing the work itself. Being helpful to others and maintaining good relationships are important to many employees. Although about a fifth of the sample were interested in material rewards, their self-development of a full career and personal life was more important to them.

Simple carrot-and-stick supervisory reinforcement clearly has considerable limitations. It will not work well in the absence of a trusting relationship between superiors and subordinates. Subordinates need to trust that their leaders can fulfill their promises. Leaders must be able to trust that their subordinates will comply as expected rather than take short-cuts or superficial actions to achieve the promised rewards (Dwivedi, 1983). But many other forces constrain the superiors' intentions when they use reinforcement to deal with their subordinates' performance. These forces include information requirements, conflicting interests, biased perceptions, differential use of reward and punishment, and individual differences in reaction to contingent rewards.

Conflicts. Contingent reinforcement may fail to achieve the compliance of subordinates because intrapersonal or interpersonal conflicts may be involved. For instance, the leader may establish dyadic contingent reinforcement with each member of a group, although the members need to reach decisions in a highly coordinated fashion; the members may suffer from pluralistic ignorance, each subordinate not knowing every other member's views (Schanck, 1932). Or, the members may find the costs greater than the benefits promised and wishing to avoid confrontation with the leader, they may withdraw into anomie, apathy, or alienation. Followers may also rationalize the leader's excessive demands on them or the leader's incompetence. Ansbacher's (1948) interviews with German prisoners of war in World War II provided extensive evidence that although many continued to esteem Adolf Hitler and maintain confidence in him, they personally disagreed with him on many significant issues and interpreted his directions to suit their own needs. For example, Hitler demanded that Germany should never capitulate. But a majority of those who had confidence in him decided that he did not really want unnecessary bloodshed; therefore, they thought he would consider it his duty to end a lost war. And so, despite the fact that Hitler issued explicit orders that soldiers were to fight to the end, his supporters rationalized that it was all right to surrender.

Ephemeral or Negative Effects. Contingent reinforcement may succeed in only the short run or sometimes, not at all. In some circumstances, feedback about one's job performance actually may be counterproductive and yield negative results, as Kiggundu (1983) reported for 138 head-office employees.

Greene's (1979a) longitudinal study of new employees in their first nine months of work found that the subordinates' performance, compliance, and satisfaction improved because of contingent rewards by the leader. Satisfaction accompanied the leader's reward-

ing of subordinates for their good performance, and dissatisfaction emerged from the leader's punishment of the subordinates for their poor performance. But the effects mainly occurred earlier in the subordinates' employment. Contingent reinforcement may generate conflicting deleterious side effects that contribute to long-term failure. For example, subordinates may continue to accept the top managers' direction but displace their aggression onto less powerful targets. Purcell (1953) found that packinghouse employees were more ready to blame their lower-status supervisors than their top managers for the difficulties entailed in trying to comply with directions.

Biased Perceptions. Again, despite Peterson's (1985b) conclusion that, in general, rewards for good performance tend to be effective, many errors are likely to be made in the application of contingent reward. Leaders' performance evaluations are likely to be biased, and subordinates are likely to overestimate their own performance and that of their peers. Also biased judgments may work both ways. Subordinates may inflate the attractiveness of an order to justify their compliance with it (Campbell, Dunnette, Lawler, & Weick, 1970). Furthermore, subordinates' attributions of the reasons for the leader's behavior will affect the subordinates' satisfaction with it. And the leader whom subordinates judge to be willing but incompetent may be more forgivable than the leader who is judged to be competent but unwilling (Bass, 1982). The same leadership behavior, say initiation of structure, will be seen more favorably by managers than by graduate students, although a more punitive emphasis on production will be seen more unfavorably by both managers and students (Butterfield & Bartol, 1977).

Contingent Reinforcement May Be Avoided or Ignored. The use of contingent reinforcement is not essential for effective leadership and a productive organization. Jacoby, Mazursky, Troutman, and Kuss (1984) found considerable avoidance of opportunities for obtaining feedback or ignoring it if it was given. In their simulation, they had 17 security analysts decide which common stocks represent a good purchase. During a sequence of four periods, the analysts were able to request feedback about their performance. The feedback provided outcome results that could have predictive or explanatory value for the analysts. Some analysts did not request or consider any feedback, and other analysts were not consistent about doing so. The researchers found that the better performing analysts were more likely than were the poorer performing analysts to ignore outcome feedback that had no predictive or explanatory value.

Communes. When selected individuals and groups have a strong feeling of community, they have been able to maintain the high productivity that is associated with a strong work ethic without using reinforcement as the basis of their motivation to work. Communes depend even more strongly on trust relationships than do organizations whose motivation to work is based on contingent reinforcement. The Israeli kibbutz is an illustration:

> The underlying philosophy of the kibbutz insists that there must be no linkage between what a particular individual is able to contribute through his efforts and . . . and what rewards he is entitled to . . . In the kibbutz, everyone is entitled—as a human being and as a member of the community—to the comprehensive satisfaction of his needs . . . subject to limitations due to the economic capacity of the particular kibbutz. . . . This right is no way infringed if, because of health or for any other reason, he is unable to contribute to the kibbutz anything at all. In this respect the kibbutz constitutes a full-scale insurance system for every member. (Tsur, 1983, p. 24)

> [Although there may be some slackers] the large majority of kibbutz members generally perform at their best, and the prevailing differences in efficiency are the result of individual differences in ability, rhythm, [and] energy, . . . rather than of deficient motivation. . . . (Tsur, 1983, p. 26)

Moreover, the young people who leave the kibbutz to work elsewhere tend to be highly appraised by their employers because of the strong self-reinforcing work ethic they continue to maintain.

Group, Not Individual Rewarded. Curiously, there may be much more of this group effect in the U.S. industrial sector than one ordinarily supposes, which again points to the irrelevance of contingent reinforcement to the individual employee. For example, for the 71 managers and professionals of a manufacturing facility, Markham (1988) reported the the correlation was −.03 between their rated performance and their merit raises within their own units, but .45 between the performance ratings of all the members of a unit and the merit raises they received. In this facility, group, not individual, performance was being rewarded.

The Augmentation Effect. As was noted in Chapter 12, the simple social exchange—the short-term transaction between the leader and follower—is catalyzed by transformational leadership. Transformational leadership augments the effects of contingent reward (Bass, 1985a; Waldman, Bass, & Einstein, 1987; Waldman, Bass, & Yammarino, 1988). The leadership of Ernest Shackleton, whose men overcame superhuman obstacles in the Antarctic, or the leadership of Joan of Arc, Martin Luther King, Mahatma Gandhi, or Winston Churchill can only be conceived of as leadership that added to any cost-benefit exchange a transformation of the followers' needs from those at lower levels to higher-levels concerns for achievement, glory, humanity, fortune, country, faith, or family, which demanded excessive costs relative to tangible benefits. Self-interests were transcended; cost-benefit calculations were abandoned. It is difficult to conceive of the emotional response to the Ayatollah Khomeini and the rush to martyrdom by the Iranian masses merely as a social cost-benefit exchange between a leader and followers. On the positive side of reinforcement, appeals to self-interests alone will not result ultimately in leadership that is able to reward followers as much as they want. Continued attention to followers' self-interests alone will not permit a group, organization, or society to operate optimally. A culture of cooperation is needed, as is trust in the benefit of optimal organizational outcomes. A prosocial charismatic leader who appeals to interests that transcend the individual member will be more likely to create such a culture than will a leader who is limited to contingent reinforcement and the use of individual incentives (Miller, 1987). In the public sector, political leadership must appeal to both self-interests and shared values (Meier, 1988). In the 1990s and beyond, the shared environment is likely to become as powerful a political issue as self-interested economic gains.

Individual Differences. Contingent reinforcement may also be irrelevant if the subordinate attaches no importance or value to the reinforcement—if the subordinate is not interested in the rewards, promises of reward, or avoidance of punishment (Ilgen, Fisher, & Taylor, 1979). Subordinates' indifference may be due to low expectations that satisfactory levels can be attained to merit the rewards or that the promises of reward will be kept (Larson, 1984).

Above and beyond the specialized circumstance of communal living or group reinforcement, one finds that individuals differ in their preference for external or self-reinforcement. In a survey of 339 utility company managers, Parsons, Herold, and Turlington (1981) found that the managers varied in their preference for external feedback, that is, in their agreement with the statement, "Even though I may think I have done a good job, I feel a lot more confident of it after someone else tells me so." They also differed in their ability and tendency to reinforce themselves, that is, in agreeing that, "If I have done something well, I know it without other people telling me so" and, "As long as I think that I have done something well, I am not too concerned about how other people think I have done." In the same way, Bass (1967c) concluded that task-oriented subordinates and experienced subordinates are more likely to be self-reinforcing, whereas interaction-oriented and self-oriented subordinates are more likely to be sensitive to both positive and negative reinforcement from others.

One is likely to see personally counterdependent followers working in opposition to what the leader intended by contingent reward. But much of this reverse twist may also be seen in personally independent and even dependent followers. Among five styles of leadership—directive, manipulative, consultative, participative, and delegative—displayed by large samples of managers, Bass, Valenzi, Farrow, and Solomon (1975) found manipulative leadership least satisfying to subordinates and effective with them. But the managers' superiors may not find fault with the manipulative potentialities of the managers in practicing contingent reinforcement. In fact, manipulative managers are more successful with higher-ups in that they earn salaries,

after adjustment for their seniority, function, education, sex, and organization, that are higher than average (Farrow, Valenzi, & Bass, 1981).

Constraints on the Use and Impact of Feedback

Numerous factors constrain the use and impact of feedback, the most common way in which contingent reward is delivered by supervisors. These factors include problems with the performance-appraisal interview, the reluctance to give feedback, and coping with unintentional consequences.

Reluctance to Give Positive Feedback

Contingent reinforcement may be constrained by the reluctance of some supervisors to give positive feedback. Komaki (1981) offered numerous reasons for the reluctance to do so: time pressures, poor appraisal methods, doubts about the efficacy of positive reinforcement, the lack of skill, and discomfort to the leader and the subordinate. Feldman (1986, p. 39) offered a number of reasons why some supervisors may avoid giving positive feedback:

> Who among us has not found, much to our chagrin, that our praise, rewards, and favors often go unnoticed and unthanked? ... Consider the colleague who responds to subordinates' efforts above and beyond the call of duty with no comment, as if those efforts were simply his due. Consider the supervisor who compliments a subordinate for a job well done, and receives in return a comment like "No thanks to you."

Subordinates may interpret the feedback as a signal that the superior expects them to continue to perform at a high level. In such a case, the subordinates will regard the positive reinforcement as pressure to keep performing at the top of their capacity. Particularly when positive reinforcement is rare, subordinates may be ambivalent about receiving it for fear of becoming emotionally dependent on the good opinion of the supervisor, a good opinion that may easily be lost. Subordinates with low self-esteem will be jarred by the contrasting praise given them and will evaluate it as only a momentary departure from their generally poor performance. Furthermore, the positive feedback that is given often is actually trivial and meaningless, or it may be interpreted as such. The supervisor who gives it frequently may be seen as politically motivated, manipulative, ingratiating, and insincere. Feldman (1986) agreed that positive feedback will be less favorably received when it is given frequently and for trivialities than when it is given only for unusually good performance.

Subordinates who are in conflict with their supervisors may react defensively to positive feedback and even interpret it as negative feedback or a precursor of negative feedback. "When receiving praise, some people may be waiting, like Pavlov's dog, for the anticipated punishment to follow" (Feldman, 1986, p. 40).

Positive Feedback May Fail. Even if positive feedback is given, it may not provide the expected reinforcement. The subordinate may not believe that the positive feedback from the supervisor is a consequence of the subordinate's performance. Rather, the subordinate may perceive that the supervisor praises when he or she feels like doing so, not when the subordinate's performance is good, or that the positive reinforcement is too small or inequitable, which makes the subordinate angry because the subordinate believes that more reward should have been given for the performance. Finally, subordinates may feel the need to reciprocate and give unjustified, unwarranted positive feedback to the supervisor, and they will resent feeling pressured to do so.

Reluctance to Give Negative Feedback

Attitudes about Discipline, Reprimand, and Punishment. While some supervisors and subordinates may find even positive feedback discomforting, many more are reluctant to give and receive negative feedback (Larson, 1986; Sims & Manz, 1984). Although an experiment by C. D. Fisher (1979) with 168 college students indicated that "supervisors" gave feedback sooner when the "subordinates'" performance was poor than when it was good, Fisher believed that the results would be reversed in any long-term field study, since supervisors in real life are more likely to be reluctant to give negative feedback. It is one thing to say something negative to a stranger in one transient experience than to say it to someone with whom one will remain in close contact. Managers often are reluctant

to discipline employees because it is an unpleasant task for most of them. Discipline and friendship are difficult to maintain side by side (Harrison, 1982). Nevertheless, other studies have reported that numerous factors contribute to supervisors' willingness to use punishment. These factors include positive attitudes about punishment, in general (O'Reilly & Weitz, 1980), the supervisors' lack of dependence on their subordinates' performance (Ilgen, Mitchell, & Fredrickson, 1981), the subordinates' poor performance compared to co-workers (Ivancevich, 1983), and the supervisors' lack of reward power (Greene & Podsakoff, 1979/1981).

Salience of Poor Performance. It may take a considerable worsening in a subordinate's performance for a supervisor to overcome his or her reluctance to give negative feedback (Larson, 1986) although, as was mentioned earlier, their subordinates' poor performance is more salient to supervisors than is their subordinates' good performance.

The salience of the poor performance must outweigh how much the supervisor personally admires a subordinate. A supervisor may avoid giving negative feedback for poor performance to avoid risking a deterioration in his or her personal relationship with the subordinate. The supervisor may also be less likely to attribute the poor performance to the subordinate if relations with the subordinate are good (Bass, 1985a).

Use of Distortion. When supervisors are faced with a subordinate's poor performance that they attribute to the subordinate's lack of ability, they tend to "pull their punches." They distort their feedback and make it more positive than it should be (Fisher, 1979; Ilgen & Knowlton, 1980). Programmatic efforts to change the supervisor's feedback behavior have not been successful (Frank & Hackman, 1975; French, Kay, & Meyer, 1966). Some of this distortion may be due to the effort of the supervisor to act prosocially, to be more concerned with the subordinate's feelings than with the supervisor's or the organization's best interests. To avoid causing distress to the subordinate, the supervisor may remain lenient and avoid giving needed negative feedback.

The reluctance to give negative feedback is abetted by supervisors' tendencies to search for excuses and justifications for the poor performance of subordinates. Gioia and Sims (1986) arranged for 24 experienced managers to handle a simulated performance-appraisal interview. During the interviews, the managers tended to probe for excuses to justify the subordinates' performance; after the interviews, the managers reduced their blame of the poorly performing subordinates.

Other Factors. Still other factors make the supervisor reluctant to use negative feedback. The supervisor may be highly dependent on the subordinate to attain their mutual objectives (Tjosvold, 1985) or have limited authority to bring about a punishment (Beyer & Trice, 1984). Since negative reinforcement may cause the employee to quit (Parsons, Herold, & Leatherwood, 1985), the supervisors' reluctance may be based on that concern. Political considerations may deter a supervisor from giving negative feedback for fear of the employee's retaliation; an admonished employee may file a grievance for unfair discrimination or may complain to powerful friends in the organization. The supervisor's ability and motivation to correct a problem employee is also decreased if the performance of most of the work force is poor (Crawford, Thomas, & Fink, 1980).

Nevertheless, despite their reluctance, managers will become punitive with continuing poor performers and problem employees after asking questions and trying to solve the problems they believe are causing the poor performance (Fairhurst, Green, & Snavely, 1984). In the case of problem drinkers, for example, discipline by supervisors is widespread when the work context supports its use (Beyer & Trice, 1984). O'Reilly and Weitz (1980) found that supervisors who used informal warnings, formal warnings, and discharges led groups that performed better but Kipnis (1976) concluded, from research evidence, that supervisors are most likely to use such sanctions when they do not expect to be successful in using their influence to improve their subordinates' performance.

Subordinates as Moderators of Supervisors' Feedback

Subordinates, the intended receivers of the feedback, may also add to the reluctance of supervisors to give it (Greller, 1978) by expressing dissatisfaction with the process. They may discourage the supervisor from efforts to provide it by frequent rejections of the supervisor, displays of hostility, and displacement of the blame onto others. Many subordinates are likely to take personal responsibility for their successes but to attribute failures to external or situational causes, such as the difficulty of the task, bad luck, or the lack of cooperation and assistance from others (Greenwald, 1980; Sims & Gioia, 1984).

Interpretation and Acceptance. The contingency between performance and outcome may be more apparent to the subordinates when they are successful. Subordinates may expect success and tend to validate their expectations by reinterpreting as an actual success the failure that their supervisor sees. They may base their judgments of their performance on the desirability of the outcome to them personally, rather than on the explicit performance-outcome linkage (Miller & Ross, 1975).

Negative feedback may be interpreted as helpful and, therefore, may be regarded as a contingent reward, rather than as a contingent punishment. It all depends on how the feedback is presented, how much it is embedded in sedative and palliative language, and how open the subordinate is to feedback. The subordinate may fail to "hear" negative feedback because he or she will convert it into what he or she wants to hear.

Subordinates accept positive feedback more readily and recall negative feedback less accurately (Ilgen, Peterson, Martin, & Boeschen, 1981). Considerable discrepancy is found between the extent to which supervisors say they give feedback to their subordinates and the extent to which the subordinates say they receive such feedback. For example, in a survey of 178 managers and their subordinates by Mann and Dent (1954b), 82 percent of the managers said they gave "pats on the back" to their subordinates very often, but only 13 percent of their subordinates agreed with them. Eighty percent of the managers said they gave subordinates sincere and thorough praise very often, but only 14 percent of their subordinates agreed with them.

Context. Subordinates may ignore supervisors' feedback because it is not backed up with evidence, it is not consistent with feedback they received from co-workers, they judged it to be unimportant, or they regard self-reinforcement to be most relevant. Different working situations and levels of experience of the recipients of the feedback will determine which source of feedback the subordinates think is most useful and important to them (DeNisi, Randolph, & Blencoe, 1983). Although Greller and Herold (1975) found that a heterogeneous sample of working people attached more importance to feedback from a higher authority than from their peers, Pavett (1983) noted that in a hospital, feedback from patients and co-workers had a greater impact on nurses' perceptions of the connection between delivering high-quality care and valued outcomes than did feedback from supervisors. In a different work setting, Ivancevich and McMahon (1982) found that self-generated feedback about the attainment of goals did more than feedback from supervisors to improve the subordinates' performance, intrinsic job satisfaction, and commitment to the organization. And, according to Greller (1980), who surveyed 26 supervisors and 63 of their subordinates in the maintenance department of a metropolitan transit agency, the subordinates attached more importance than did the supervisors to feedback from the task itself (self-reinforcement), their own comparisons to the work of others, and to co-workers' comments about their work.

Insurance sales people have fewer contacts with each other than do metropolitan transit employees, for whom, as was just noted, feedback from co-workers is important. And so, Brief and Hollenbeck (1985) found that among the 62 insurance sales people they interviewed, the greatest amount of feedback on performance came from the supervisor and themselves, not from co-workers. Despite the general observation that we attribute our successes to ourselves and our failures to others and external conditions, most of the contingent self-reinforcement of the insurance employees was negative in the form of self-criticism, and it had detrimental effects on their performance.

Views about the Leader. The subordinates may rationalize the feedback as being due to the leader's need to complain, the leader's failure to understand the situation, or the leader's malevolence. According to Coye (1982), who conducted a laboratory experiment with undergraduates, subordinates are readier to accept feedback from a leader they perceive to be competent, rather than incompetent, particularly if the leader

has a strong need for achievement. If they perceive the leader to be incompetent, they will seek alternative sources of task-relevant information.

Self-esteem. The subordinates' self-esteem will moderate their request for feedback and their acceptance of it. Those with high self-esteem set higher goals, perform at a higher level, and experience more positive affect when performing well than do subordinates with low self-esteem (Taylor & Slania, 1981). Those with high self-esteem seek less information from others in making decisions and forming judgments; they are more self-reinforcing. Those with low self-esteem tend to be more dependent on social and environmental feedback (Weiss, 1977) and are more responsive to it. In the same way, inexperienced personnel prefer to receive feedback from their superiors, but experienced personnel prefer to be more self-reinforcing (Hillery & Wexley, 1974). However, in contrast to reinforcement only from the supervisor, a combination of both self and supervisory feedback, in which the subordinate first prepares a self-appraisal and then meets to compare it with the superior's feedback, appears to reduce the subordinate's defensiveness and to bring about greater subsequent improvement in the subordinate's performance (Bassett & Meyer, 1968). Whether the subordinate seeks feedback will also be affected by his or her role ambiguity and tolerance of ambiguity (Ashford & Cummings, 1981).

Feedback Characteristics as Moderators

Problems inherent with the feedback itself may cause it to fail to work as intended. In place of the summary ratings many supervisors use, Deets and Tyler (1986) introduced detailed feedback about the specific initiation and consideration behaviors[3] of supervisors at Xerox, along with interim evaluations of the supervisors' progress toward specific personal and professional goals that were given closer to the events involved. They found a marked improvement in attitudes toward the appraisal system and toward teamwork.

The accuracy, amount, distinctiveness, consistency, and method of giving feedback (oral, written, or face-to-face) may also matter (Duncan & Bruwelheide, 1985–

[3]Described in Chapter 24.

86). But, in a study of 360 pairs of managers and subordinates from over 50 organizations in three countries, Larson, Glynn, Fleenor, and Scontrino (1986) found it impossible to single out the specificity of feedback from other positive features of good-quality feedback, such as its timeliness, frequency, and sensitivity. However, Quaglieri and Carnazza (1985) showed that most subordinates paid attention to multiple aspects of feedback, including its accuracy, timeliness, attractiveness, and specificity, as well as to the trustworthiness, expertise, and power of the source. Furthermore, these and other features of feedback can be experimentally manipulated. Earley (1986a) completed a field experiment in which 60 subjects believed they were in a working situation processing subscriptions. Positive feedback increased their expectations of successful performance more than did negative feedback, as expected. The subjects' performance was better than anticipated if the feedback was specific, rather than general. In turn, specific feedback resulted in more planning by the subordinates, which contributed to the subordinates' better performance. However, the supervisors had less of an impact on the subordinates' performance than did self-generated feedback retrieved from computer storage, particularly if the positive or negative feedback was general. Only when the supervisors' feedback was specific and negative did its effect match that of self-generated feedback. Mediating these effects were the extent to which the subordinates trusted the computer feedback more than they did the supervisors' feedback.

Another important consideration is whether feedback from one source is discordant with feedback from other sources (Liden & Mitchell, 1985). If one colleague finds fault with a member's behavior, the impact is much less if other colleagues do not agree.

Coping with Unintended Consequences

Contingent negative feedback may have unintended consequences. Reprimands may serve not only to increase clarity about what is undesirable behavior and to correct it (Reitz, 1971), but they can generate unproductive anxiety. In turn, the anxiety can result in a variety of dysfunctional behaviors, such as reaction formation, guilt, and hostility, particularly in highly motivated subordinates who are already overloaded or under stress and who may interpret well-intentioned negative feedback as a personal attack (Bass, 1985a).

Komaki (1982) and Sims and Gioia (1984) suggested ways to cope with the unintended consequences and potential shortcomings of feedback processes and make better use of them. According to 60 professionals interviewed by Komaki, to increase the effective utilization of feedback, the long-term benefits of reinforcement need to be emphasized. More positive feedback should be used, but it should not be limited just to delivering praise; it should include connections to the performance involved. Reinforcement schedules have to be adapted to fit busy schedules. Standards of performance and of performance appraisals need to be clarified.

To reduce self-serving bias among subordinates and to increase the subordinates' acceptance of negative feedback, Sims and Gioia proposed that the supervisor needs to recognize and expect the biased reaction to negative feedback for poor performance. The subordinate's acceptance of negative feedback should be positively reinforced, and efforts to cover up mistakes should be rejected. Emphasis should be placed on determining the causes of and remedies for the poor performance.

Constraints on the Performance-Appraisal Interview

Problems and Possibilities

Contingent reinforcement may occur at the time the supervisor observes the subordinate's good or poor performance or in a performance-appraisal interview. An annual appraisal review seems to be the norm in the United States. However, more frequent appraisal interviews are suggested for poor performers (Kay, Meyer, & French, 1965) and for subordinates in nonroutine jobs in which goal setting is involved, progress is evaluated, and then goals are reset (Cummings & Schwab, 1973, 1978; McConkie, 1979). Numerous problems beset the efficacy of the feedback in this interview. Reinforcement theory would suggest that the feedback would be most reinforcing if it was given as soon as possible after the occurrence of the subordinate's good or poor performance, Yet, the delay caused by waiting to provide the feedback in a formal interview increases the reliability of the evidence to be discussed by the supervisor and the subordinate. Such a discussion can also take into account broader systematic issues and long-range goals and plans than could feedback given immediately after an incident. Since the supervisor and subordinate can both be better organized to give and receive the feedback, a more orderly, calm, and thoughtful exchange is possible than in the heat of the immediate operations. Of course, nothing precludes both timely feedback and feedback for an extensive period given during an appraisal interview in which the subordinates' performance during the six months or year preceding the interview is reviewed.

In this formal meeting of the superior and the subordinate, in which the subordinate's performance during a preceding period is reviewed, evaluations are made and suggestions for improvement are advanced. The meeting can involve the superior's and subordinate's sharing of information or it can be directed by the superior. The interview can be structured in a variety of ways around goals and their attainment or around traits and behavior.

Although it is an organized effort to provide positive reinforcement for good performance and negative feedback for poor performance, the performance-appraisal interview may fail to improve the subordinate's subsequent performance for numerous reasons. First, the formal feedback process tends to be constrained in use and impact by, for example, the superior's lack of familiarity with the subordinate's job. Second, the superior may not encourage the subordinate's participation and two-way communication in the interview (Cederblom, 1982). Other reasons for ineffective feedback during a performance appraisal include the lack of supervisory support, goal setting, focused discussion, and separation of administrative and developmental feedback (Ivancevich, 1982). The performance-appraisal interview may also fail to have an impact if no reward is linked to it (Burke, Weitzel, & Weir, 1978).

The lack of connection between performance appraisals and performance may be due to a variety of other goals that managers have in mind when they evaluate their subordinates (Longnecker, Sims, & Gioia, 1987). Supervisors may avoid discouraging poor-performing subordinates or confronting them with their inadequacies, seek favors from the subordinates, or discourage the top-performing employee from demanding a commensurate increase in salary. Thus, appraisals may be unrelated to performance even in the face of available objective evidence about the performance. For example, Leana (1984) discovered that the periodic evaluations of 98 claims adjustors by their 44 supervisors were not correlated with such objective measures of performance as the settlement ratio and the average cost of the claims that were settled.

Supervisors' and Subordinates' Evaluations of the Process

Lawler, Mohrman, and Resnick (1984) conducted a survey of over 300 supervisor-subordinate dyads regarding the extent to which the performance-appraisal interviews fulfilled their purposes. They found that although 82 percent of the supervisors said that all important matters had been discussed, most subordinates thought there had been less than a full discussion of their development, work, planning, or pay. Furthermore, they thought that not enough attention was being paid to documenting their performance. On the other hand, supervisors, in general, were unenthusiastic about discussing decisions about pay or documenting subordinates' performance in these interviews. Presumably, both these matters would be extremely important for leaders to cover as means of contingent reinforcement (Mohrman & Lawler, 1983). Consistent with these findings was the survey by Greller (1980), previously mentioned, which showed that supervisors actually overestimate the importance of the feedback they provide to subordinates and underestimate the value their subordinates place on feedback from sources under their own control, such as the task and the comparisons they make to the work of colleagues.

Avoidance

Many supervisors avoid conducting appraisal interviews. When forced by organizational policy, they often hold perfunctory, general discussions with subordinates, which the latter do not consider to be the formal feedback of a performance-appraisal interview (Meyer, Kay, & French, 1965). The failure to conduct high-quality performance-appraisal interviews with optimal frequency may militate against these interviews serving to provide effective contingent reinforcement. Most employees seek more such feedback opportunities than they receive (Ashford & Cummings, 1983).

Other Aspects of the Process

Frequent appraisals, however, particularly negative appraisals, may generate more resistance and defensiveness in subordinates (Burke, Weitzel, & Weir, 1978). If the feedback is not what the subordinate expected, it may arouse resistance (Bernstein & Lecomte, 1979) or be thought of as less accurate by the subordinate (Taylor, 1981). If the feedback is not as positive as expected, it may reduce the subordinate's commitment to the organization (Pearce & Porter, 1986). Decreased commitment is likely to be common, since subordinates ordinarily give themselves higher evaluations than do their superiors (Bradley, 1978).

Furthermore, subordinates' reactions to the performance-appraisal interview will depend on their opinions about the supervisor's credibility, knowledge, and trustworthiness, which parallel their reactions to informal feedback from their supervisor, as was mentioned earlier. Ilgen, Fisher, and Taylor (1979) noted that subordinates' judgments of their supervisors' credibility as an appraiser will influence how the subordinates react in performance-appraisal interview. If the subordinates think their supervisor is knowledgeable about their job and performance, they will regard the interview as fair and accurate, but those who judge their supervisor to be less knowledgeable will think the interview is unfair and inaccurate (Landy, Barnes, & Murphy, 1978). And, as Ilgen, Peterson, Martin, and Boeschen (1981) observed, subordinates who trust their supervisor will be more satisfied with the appraisal-interview process than will subordinates who do not trust their supervisor.

Herold and Greller (1977) added a number of other characteristics of feedback that recipients can discern in the performance-appraisal interview, including whether the feedback is helpful or unhelpful, clear or ambiguous, important or unimportant, and formal or informal. The utility of the feedback appeared to be most strongly related to its frequency, helpfulness, and importance.

In the interviews, ratings and discussions that focus on the past performance of the subordinates appear to be the most satisfactory to both superiors and subordinates (Fletcher & Williams, 1976; Mount, 1984). The subordinates' participation in the development of the rating forms also seems to help (Landy & Farr, 1980). Agreement on the meaning of scores and terms, such as "good" and "satisfactory," will help as well (Taylor, Fisher, & Ilgen, 1984). Supervisors who begin the interviews with positive feedback before giving negative feedback are seen as being more accurate by the subordinates than are supervisors who begin with the negatives before presenting the positive aspects of the subordinates' performance (Stone, Gueutal, & MacIntosh, 1984).

An Ideal System. Fox (1987–88) enumerated guidelines for an improved performance-appraisal system. First, credit should be given for good form. Second, emphasis should be on work-relevant behaviors that are known to be desirable and productive, rather than on outcomes that are often beyond the employee's total control. These behaviors should be determined from critical-incidents surveys of the occurrence of highly effective and highly ineffective job events. Third, the appraisals should be from multiple sources, not just from the boss. Fourth, ratings should be accompanied by evidence. For Fox, improvement in an employee's performance would stem from the ongoing defining of behaviors that need to be changed, setting goals for change, and administering feedback and other reinforcements on appropriate schedules.

Following a comprehensive review of the literature, Biddle and Fisher (1987) described an ideal procedure for promoting such contingent reinforcement from performance-appraisal interviews. First, there would be a pre-performance meeting in which the supervisor and subordinate reached an understanding of exactly how the subordinate's future performance was to be assessed. If rating scales were to be used, the meaning of each dimension and anchor point would be clarified. A performance monitoring system would be set up to assure that good data were available for the appraisal. The sources of feedback would be considered and the supervisor would arrange to collect data, as needed, from these sources, such as peers and clients, as well as to gather his or her own data. The subordinate would also keep track of his or her performance and accomplishments through self-monitoring.

Between interviews, the supervisor should give more timely frequent informal feedback and coaching so the formal performance-appraisal interview does not bring up much that is unexpected for the subordinate. The timeliness of the frequent informal feedback allows the subordinate to learn from and correct his or her errors immediately. It also affords opportunity to clear up differences in attributions for the same specific incidents of performance.

The actual performance-appraisal interview should begin with a self-appraisal, followed by the supervisor's sharing of his or her feedback with the subordinate and feedback collected from the other sources. Discussion should then center on how the subordinate might be able to do things differently and what additional support the superior might provide. Finally, new goals for the upcoming period should be discussed and established.

Implicit Theories of Leadership as Moderators

In this concluding section, I review the extent to which perceived and actual descriptions of the quality of the exchange, the causes of the exchange, and the consequences of the exchange may be obscured or magnified by the implicit theories of leadership that are held by the superiors and subordinates who are involved in the relationship.

Meaning of Implicit Theories of Leadership

Both the leader and the led are affected in their exchange relationship by the implicit theories of leadership they carry around in their heads.[4] If they both believe that leadership is mainly a matter of striking a deal for the payment for services rendered and monitoring the arrangements, then they are likely to judge that contingent reinforcement explains the motivation and performance of the leader and the subordinate. But if they believe leadership is mainly an inspirational proc-

ess, than they will judge contingent reinforcement as being of little or no consequence. Thus, Eden and Leviatan (1975) noted that people have preconceptions about what constitutes the appropriate behavior of leaders. Subordinates have expectations regarding the kind and amount of leadership behavior that is proper for given situations (L. R. Anderson, 1966b), as do the leaders themselves (Yukl, 1971). These preconceptions are important, according to Pfeffer and Salancik (1975), who obtained results showing that the leadership behavior of focal supervisors was affected by the expectations of both their superiors and their subordinates. In addition, subordinates attach their own individual specific value-laden meanings to the actions of their superiors (McConkie, 1984), while the leaders may regard their performance as leaders to be a matter of their traits, their power, or the way they act.

Birnbaum (1987c) collected the definitions of leadership provided in interviews with 32 college and university presidents. Almost all the presidents thought that leadership involves power, influence, and ways of behaving. About a quarter talked as well about traits of consequence, situational determinants, or the symbolism of leadership. Content analyses of the interviews suggested that about a third of the presidents believed that the goals of leadership stem from the mission of the institution; a few, from followers; and the rest, from the leaders themselves. Presidents saw themselves as either the heads of a bureaucracy; collegial in their relations with staff, faculty, and students; political manipulators; or occupants of a highly symbolic office. Some of the presidents had a single frame of reference about leadership, and about a quarter had multiple frames of reference (Bensimon, 1987). According to Bolman and Deal (1984), those with multiple frames of reference were better equipped to deal with the complexities of the modern college or community.

Implicit Theories of Leadership as Cognitive Frameworks. As was just mentioned, the implicit theories we hold about leadership and its antecedents and consequences join with our explicitly expressed attitudes, beliefs, values, and ideologies about leadership[5] to color strongly our judgments of specific leaders we describe or evaluate. Implicit theories are cognitive

---

[4]Enumerated by Bass and Barrett (1981).

[5]Enumerated by Bass and Barrett (1981).

frameworks or categorization systems[6] that are in use during information processing to encode, process, and recall specific events and behavior. An implicit theory can also be conceived as the personalized factor structure we use for information processing.

Effects on Raters of Leadership. Implicit theories of leadership facilitate the assimilation of specific events and behaviors into a collective interpretation. They help raters to categorize their stimulus environment into less complex classifications. Implicit theories make it possible to simplify complex information by enabling raters to process that information automatically, as well as to add missing details not observed in the actual behavior of the leader (Lord, Foti, & DeVader, 1984). The raters' application of their own implicit theory to observed events affects the truth of their observations. The result is that their responses to the survey questions are closer to their own implicit theories than to the actual events they observed. The impact of these implicit theories is greatest when raters are asked to recall the behavior and events they observed some time in the past.

Lord, Binning, Rush, and Thomas (1978) estimated that up to 40 percent of the variance in ratings of leadership can be accounted for by implicit theories. Thus, instead of describing the actual leadership behavior of the individual leader whose behavior is being judged, we respond in a way that is highly biased by our preconceptions about how leaders in general are supposed to behave. Support for this proposition first emerged when Eden and Leviatan (1975) applied D. J. Schneider's (1973) implicit personality theory to the study of leadership. Staw and Ross (1980) and McElroy (1982) provided additional support for the idea that the implicit conceptions we use in attributing what we observe to leadership seriously alter our attributions. Thus, an exchange may take place between a supervisor and a subordinate. The subordinate is actually complying with the supervisor's request to gain a recom-

mendation for promotion from the supervisor. But the subordinate has an implicit theory that says leaders are inspiring. The subordinate reports she is complying as a consequence of the way the supervisor inspired her to work with him. Thus, an actual transactional exchange is reported as a transformational event. Or, the reverse may occur. A subordinate is actually inspired to transcend her own interests. However, she holds an implicit theory that you get what you give, so she interprets her appraisal by the supervisor as compliance because she wants to be recommended by him for a promotion.

Effects on Leaders' Behavior. The supervisors are also clearly affected by the implicit theories of leadership they hold. Neubauer (1982) found, in a sample of 90 German supervisors, that implicit leadership theories are characterized by beliefs in participative management and acceptance of informal leader-member relations for workers who live up to the supervisors' expectations. But for workers who fail to live up to expectations, implicit theories emphasize control, the prevention of the development of informal leader-member relations, and the limiting of such workers to simple activities.

Managing the Effects of Implicit Theories

Implicit theories of leadership can be manipulated in advance to get raters to rate the same observed leadership behavior differently. If we are told and believe a leader to be effective in carrying out his or her assignment, it will influence how much and what type of leadership we judge to exist in the subsequent performance observed in that leader. In a laboratory study by Gioia and Sims (1985), subjects viewed the videotapes of contingently reinforcing leadership behavior by managers in action. When managers were presented to the subjects as effective leaders before the subjects saw the tapes, the subjects described the managers subsequently as being significantly higher in initiating structure than the managers who were presented to the subjects as ineffective before the same tapes were viewed. Similar results were reported by Rush, Thomas, and Lord (1977).

Other conditions can be arranged to increase the effect of implicit theories of leadership. Thus, the more

---

[6]Coghill (1981) examined the repertory grids of 90 South African managers that detailed the concepts they used to construct their cognitive worlds. (The repertory grid asks respondents to delineate the dimensions they use to describe the similarities and differences among colleagues.) As expected, the managers were found to reduce these complex worlds into a simple evaluative structure of models, implicit theories, and maps that systematically affected their perceptions and behavior.

ambiguous the leader's actual behavior, the more implicit theories will affect how we describe or evaluate it (DeNisi & Pritchard, 1978). In the same way, implicit theories of leadership will have more of an impact in less structured situations (Gioia & Sims, 1985). Halo effects can also be connected with implicit theories (Nathan & Alexander, 1985). In addition, subordinates are likely to fall back on their implicit theories of leadership when they lack information about the situation (Schriesheim & DeNisi, 1978).

Implicit theories of leadership need to take into account the causal expectations that leaders have about themselves and their followers, as well as the complementary theories held by the followers. The extent to which leaders will modify their reactions to the good and poor performance of subordinates, depending on whether they attribute the performance to the subordinates' competence or motivation, to external causes, or to luck, has already been addressed. The leaders are also likely to respond according to their own beliefs about the value of promises of reward for compliance or threats of punishment for noncompliance. As a consequence, one supervisor may praise a subordinate for the effort to reach desired standards that failed because of uncontrollable obstacles, and another supervisor may reprove the same subordinate for the failure despite the obstacles.

Larson (1980) suggested that supervisors vary in the implicit theories they have about feedback in general, as well as about the consequences of feedback to specific subordinates. Some supervisors may think that reprimands invite retaliation and that praise lacks credibility. Disapproval is more likely if rationality, objectivity, and certainty are regarded as more important than adaptability, if security is valued as more important than affiliation, and if the leaders see themselves aiming for homogeneity, regularity, standardization, safety, or consolidation (Quinn & Hall, 1983).

In the same way, subordinates will use various tactics to try to influence their leaders, according to the subordinates' beliefs about the likely effects on the leader of reason, ingratiation, excuses, and coalitions, as well as the implications for the subordinate's self-image involving their integrity and self-esteem. The organizational role they believe they are expected to play is also important.

The Prototypical Leader

Phillips and Lord (1981) concluded that implicit theories of leadership could best be understood in terms of cognitive categorization processes. ("In my head, Joe comes across as a dynamic leader. Dynamic leaders are a category containing such and such attributes. Therefore, Joe has these attributes.") They demonstrated this experimentally by using 128 undergraduates to view one or another of two videotapes of a 4-person problem-solving group in which the leader's salience and the group's performance were manipulated. Furthermore, Lord, Foti, and Phillips (1982) argued that implicit theories reflect the cognitive categories used to distinguish leaders from nonleaders. Such categories can be applied to explaining which information is connected to designated labels of leadership (Cronshaw & Lord, 1987; Lord, Foti, & Phillips, 1982).

For most people from the same culture, a common set of categories fits the image of what the typical leader is like. These categories describe the "prototypical" leader. A prototypical leader is *actively participating*; an antiprototypical leader *remains withdrawn*. Perceiving someone as a leader involves a relatively simple categorization of the stimulus person into a leader or nonleader. Such a categorical judgment, according to Rosch (1975), is made on the basis of the similarity between the stimulus person and the prototype of the category. The prototype is an abstract representation of the most representative features of members of the category.

Foti, Fraser, and Lord (1982) asked students to rate the extent to which phrases such as *"bright"* or *"sides with the average citizen"* (taken from a Gallup poll) fit their image of a leader, a political leader, an effective leader, or an effective political leader. The students' different prototypical categorizations helped considerably to account for changes in Gallup poll results of public support for Jimmy Carter at different times during his administration. If Jimmy Carter acted more like the students' prototype of an effective political leader, he received more support from the public. The mere social desirability of the categorizations was not as predictive.

People simplify, rather than describe or evaluate, their leaders in terms of many specifications. People form mental images of categories of leaders. As was noted before, they rapidly judge whether their leader falls into these categories according to their beliefs about the leader and how they see the leader acting (Phillips & Lord, 1981, 1982). Lord, Foti, and DeVader (1984) reported three studies that used 263 undergraduates to specify the internal structure of these leadership categories and how they relate to prototypicality. These studies showed how properties of the categories can be used to facilitate information processing, such as recalling information about a leader, and explain simplified perceptions about leadership.

In the first study, different students were each given five minutes to generate attributes of a particular type of leader or nonleader in 11 different situations: business, education, finance, labor, politics, the mass media, the military, minorities, the religions, in sports, and at the world level. Master lists of attributes of the frequency of mentions of specific clusters of traits were then assembled. Intelligence was seen as highest in "family resemblance," that is, attributed generally to leaders in almost all the 11 situations. Other categories with relatively high family resemblance for leaders included *honesty, outgoing, understanding, verbal skills, aggressiveness, determined,* and *industrious.* Most of the other 59 attributes, such as *caring, authoritarian,* and *decisive,* were limited to just one or two types of leaders.

In the second study, a different set of students judged how much these attributes were "prototypical" for leadership. The students rated the categories according to how well they "fit my image of a leader or a nonleader." Attributes "fitting the image of leader" included *intelligence, honesty, verbal skills, determined, informed, strong character, believable, concerned, goal oriented,* and *disciplined.* The family resemblance of these attributes correlated .40 with the attributes of the prototypical leader. A correlation of .42 was found between the speed of reaction in judging these attributes and their fitting the image of the prototypical leader. Such attributions of prototypicality were thus linked to implicit theories as "off-the-top-of-the-head reactions."

In the third study, Lord, Foti, and DeVader presented vignettes about a district store manager. One vignette ascribed to the manager four or five attributes of the prototypical leader, such as "provides information" and

talks frequently." Another vignette ascribed to the manager neutral attributes, such as "seeks information" or "explains actions." Still another vignette ascribed to the manager "antiprototypical" attributes, such as "admits mistakes" and "withholds rewards." Those who read the vignette containing the prototypical, rather than the neutral or antiprototypical, attributes perceived that the manager displayed more leadership and made much more of a contribution to the store's effectiveness and to the successful merchandising of a new product. The investigators inferred that attributes of causes and responsibility were a retrospective rationalization of events in which "leadership" was the central construct stimulated by the few prototypical attributes embedded in the vignette. However, Lord and Alliger (1985) failed to find that prototypicality weightings of the 12 functional leadership behaviors of members of small task groups had much impact on the often-found correlation between the sheer frequency of activity of group members and the leadership ratings they received.

Prototypicality and Contingent Reinforcement.

Bass and Avolio (1988) asked 87 part-time MBA students to describe their full-time supervisors' transactional and transformational leadership behavior with the Multifactor Leadership Questionnaire. They also had the students complete the prototypicality ratings developed by Lord and his associates about the attributes that "fit my image of a leader" and found that contingent reinforcement was less highly correlated with the prototypicality of the leader than was charismatic leadership, individual consideration, or intellectual stimulation. When the prototypicality ratings were statistically controlled by partial correlation, only charismatic leadership remained correlated significantly with effectiveness of operations (.34) and continued satisfaction with the leadership (.68). The partial correlation with contingent reinforcement was reduced to close to zero. Bass and Avolio concluded that the positive contribution that contingent rewarding by a leader is often seen to make with perceived effectiveness may be accounted for by the image of leadership held by the raters. The same may be true for the transformational effects of intellectual stimulation and individualized consideration. However, the charismatic effect cannot be accounted for in this way. Complicating these results may be the extent to which the followers' motivation affects their image of the ideal leader.

Imagined Ideal Leader and the Followers' Needs

Singer and Singer (1986) reported that among male undergraduates in New Zealand, the extent to which contingent reinforcement leadership was desired in an imagined ideal leader did not depend on the men's motivation. But those who had a higher need for affiliation were more likely to prefer transforming charismatic and considerate leaders. Nonconformists were more likely to prefer transforming intellectually stimulating leaders.

Summary and Conclusions

As an approach to effective leadership, contingent reinforcement has considerable limitations, although it may work well in many situations. Rewards for performance and disciplinary actions for failures may not work as expected for numerous reasons, ranging from the leader's lack of control over what the followers are seeking to the overriding impact of group norms. In the last analysis, the carrot-and-stick approach may make the subordinate feel denigrated and less than an adult person.

There are serious constraints on what can be accomplished with feedback. The timeliness, accuracy, attractiveness, and judged importance of feedback, as well as the trustworthiness, expertise, and authority of the source will affect its impact. Negative feedback is often distorted by both the leader who sends it and the subordinate who receives it. Many other factors related to superiors and subordinates will moderate its effects and generate unintended consequences.

Systematically affecting the meaning, interpretation, and understanding of the leader's efforts to provide contingent reinforcement will be the leader's and followers' implicit theories about leadership, particularly the prototypical leaders that fit their images of what leaders are like.

I conclude Chapters 17–19 about the transactional exchange and contingent reinforcement by noting that although the analyses of the exchange can explain much of what happens in many situations, the exchange still has considerable limitations. As was pointed out in Chapters 11–16, there is more to leadership than management of the simple exchange relationship. With this in mind, I now move on to examine the roles of leaders and managers and the styles they use.

Leadership and Management

CHAPTER 20

The Work of Leaders and Managers

What work do leaders do? What are the functions they serve? How does the organization and hierarchical level in the organization of the leaders affect these activities? Are their roles changing? What makes their activities more effective or less effective? Are managers leaders?

What Leaders and Managers Do

Leaders manage and managers lead, but the two activities are not synonymous. Leaders facilitate interpersonal interaction and positive working relations; they promote structuring of the task and the work to be accomplished. They plan, organize, and evaluate the work that is done (F. C. Mann, 1965). Managers plan, investigate, coordinate, evaluate, supervise, staff, negotiate, and represent (Mahoney, Jerdee, & Carroll, 1965). All these management functions can potentially provide leadership; all the leadership activities can contribute to managing. Nevertheless, some managers do not lead, and some leaders do not manage (Zaleznik, 1977).

Leadership in the Small Group or Team

As a way of sorting things out, it will be useful first to examine the functions of leadership in the group, ordinarily small. If the group is a project team, it is often autonomous and temporary. Contact is usually face to face. Regardless of whether they arise spontaneously or are elected or appointed, the members who emerge as leaders perform two essential functions: (1) they deal with the group's and the member's productivity and (2) they provide socioemotional support to the group members (Bales, 1958a; Bales & Slater, 1955).

Roles of the Leader. Any or all members can emerge as leaders, depending on how much of the functional roles they enact—the particular patterns of behavior they display in relation to the task of socioemotional development and operation of the group. Leaders enact these task-relevant and socioemotional group-building and maintenance roles. Nonleaders are more likely to enact individual roles, which are less functional for the group's development and maintenance. As formulated by Benne and Sheats (1948), task roles include those of initiator of the activity, information seeker, information giver, opinion giver, elaborator, coordinator, summarizer, feasibility tester, evaluator, and diagnostician. Group-building and maintenance roles include patterns of behavior, such as encouraging gatekeeping (limiting monopolistic talkers, returning the group to the agenda, and keeping the group on course), standard setting, expressing group feelings, consensus taking (sending up "trial balloons"), harmonizing, reducing tension (joking, "pouring oil on troubled waters"), and following. (This last role is consistent with what was said in earlier chapters about the positive correlation of leadership and followership.) Nonfunctional individual, self-concerned roles involve patterns of behavior such as aggression, blocking, self-confessing, competing, seeking sympathy, special pleading, disrupting, seeking recognition, and withdrawing.

Functions of the Leader. For the same context of the small interactive group but from another point of view, Roby (1961) developed a mathematical model of leadership functions based on response units and information load. According to Roby, the functions of leadership are to (1) bring about a congruence of goals among the members, (2) balance the group's resources and capabilities with environmental demands, (3) provide a group structure that is necessary to focus information effectively on solving the problem, and (4) make certain that all needed information is available at a decision center when required.

Consistent with this view, Stogdill (1959) suggested that it is the function of the leader to maintain the group's structure and goal direction and to reconcile conflicting demands that arise within and outside the group. For Stogdill, the functions of leadership also included defining objectives, providing means for attaining goals, facilitating action and interaction in the group, maintaining the group's cohesiveness and the member's satisfaction, and facilitating the group's performance of the task.

According to Schutz (1961b), the leader has the functions of (1) establishing and recognizing a hierarchy of group goals and values, (2) recognizing and integrating the various cognitive styles that exist in the group, (3) maximizing the use of group members' abilities, and (4) helping members resolve problems involved in adapting to external realities, as well as those involving interpersonal needs.

Bowers and Seashore (1967) maintained that the functions of leadership are the support of members, the facilitation of interaction, the emphasis on goals, and the facilitation of work. For Cattell (1957), the leader maintains the group, unholds role and status satisfactions, maintains task satisfactions, keeps ethical (norm) satisfactions, selects and clarifies goals, and finds and clarifies the means of attaining goals.

For Hollander (1978), goal setting was a particularly important function for the leader. And P. J. Burke (1966a, 1966b) showed that antagonism, tension, and absenteeism occurred when the leader failed in this function. According to Hollander, the leader also provides direction and defines reality, two more functions that are necessary for the group's effectiveness. If successful, such direction by the leader is a valued resource. As a definer of reality, the leader communicates relevant information about progress and provides needed redirection to followers.

Leadership in the Complex Organization

Somewhat the same, somewhat different, are the functions of the appointed leader—the managers, supervisor, head—of a group embedded in a larger organization of hierarchically arranged groups and individuals.

Insufficiency of the Classical Functions. As was noted in Chapter 2, for classical management theorists like R. C. Davis (1942), Urwick (1952), and Fayol (1916), the functions of the manager-leader in a formal organization were orderly planning, organizing, and controlling. These were completely rational processes. For

some, such as K. Davis (1951), the prescription for business leaders was the same as for managers—to plan, organize, and control an organization's activities. Little attention was paid to the human nature of the members constituting the organization. Although organizations strive for rationality, observation suggests that such rationality is limited (March & Simon, 1958). Nevertheless, understanding the purpose of the manager requires consideration of these planning, directing, and controlling functions of the manager for whom supervision and leadership may often be the most important but not the only aspect of his or her responsibilities. And so an empirical factored survey, such as was completed by Wofford (1967), could emerge with factors to describe managers' functions as setting objectives, planning, organizing, leading, and controlling. Managers in organizations do perform the functions of planning, organizing, and controlling. But limiting the analysis to such general functions inhibits a more searching type of inquiry into the nature of managerial performance—about what administrators, managers, and executives actually do as a whole. Not all of what they do is leadership, of course. But leadership remains an important component to the degree that management means getting work done with and through others. The overlapping needs of the organization, task, team, and the individual must be addressed. Thus, Coffin (1944) modified the classical functions as follows: formulation (planning), execution (organizing), and supervision (persuading). And Adair (1973) emerged with planning, initiating, controlling, supporting, informing, and evaluating.

Behavorial and Social Components. Barnard (1938) was most influential in introducing the need to include more behavioral, intuitive, and emotional components in the functional analyses of organizational leadership. Numerous other scholars incorporated behavioral, social, and political elements in their analyses of the functions of organizational leadership. Barnard (1946b) identified the functions of organizational leadership as (1) the determination of objectives, (2) the manipulation of means, (3) the instrumentation of action, and (4) the stimulation of coordinated effort. In this light, E. Gross (1961) elaborated on the functions of organizational leadership as follows: to define goals, clarify and administer them, choose appropriate means, assign and coordinate tasks, motivate, create loyalty, represent the group, and spark the membership to action. Similarly, Selznick (1957) suggested these as functions of organizational leadership: (1) definition of the institutional mission and goals, (2) creation of a structure for accomplishing the purpose, (3) defense of institutional integrity, and, (4) reevaluation of internal conflict. Again, in a study of leadership in Samoa, Kessing and Kessing (1956) identified as leadership functions: consultation, deliberation, negotiation, formation of public opinion, and decision making.

Katz and Kahn (1966) proposed three functions of leadership in terms of the organization's actual formal structure: (1) the introduction of structural change (policy formation), (2) the interpretation of structure (piecing out the incompleteness of the existing formal structure), and (3) the use of structure that is formally provided to keep the organization in motion and effective operation (administration).

Functional Overlap between Managing and Leading. This overlap is seen most clearly when one considers the human factor and the interpersonal activities involved in managing and leading. Skill as a leader and in relating to others is a most important requirement at all levels of management. It is clearly recognized at the first level of supervision; it is not as well known at the top of the organization. Nonetheless, interviews with 71 corporate executives by Glickman, Hahn, Fleishman, and Baxter (1969) revealed that at the top of the corporation, the group of consequence is relatively small. The group's members have highly personal relationships. They interact with each other, as in a small group; a high proportion of group involvement is usual and informal procedures supplant formal ones. Consistent with this finding, when Richards and Inskeep (1974) questioned 87 business school deans, 58 business executives, and 40 executives in trade associations about what kind of continuing education middle managers need most, these executives gave top priority to improving human relations skills and considered improving quantitative and technical skills to be of secondary importance. Similarly, Mahoney, Jerdee, and Carroll (1965) found that the single most important function of first-level managers is to supervise others.

Although they recognized eight important functions—planning, investigating, coordinating, evaluating, supervising, staffing, negotiating, and representing—their questionnaire survey of 452 managers from 13 companies in a variety of industries that varied in size from 100 to over 400 employees revealed that more time was spent on supervision than on any other function (28.4 percent). Supervising, along with the four other functions of planning, investigating, coordinating, and evaluating, accounted for almost 90 percent of all time the 452 managers spent at work.

Solem, Onachilla, and Heller (1961) lent further weight to the importance of the human factor by asking 211 supervisors to post and select problems for discussion in 26 discussion groups. In all, 58.8 percent of the first-line supervisors and 35.3 percent of the middle managers wanted to talk about the motivation of subordinates to follow instructions, to meet deadlines, or to maintain the quality of production. Over 40 percent of the staff supervisors were concerned about dealing with resistance to change, as were 36.4 percent of the middle managers and 22.7 percent of the first-line supervisors. The first-line supervisors were most concerned about disciplinary problems and problems of promoting, rating, and classifying employees, while the middle managers were most interested in talking about problems of selecting, orienting, and training employees.

Leaders as Boundary Managers. Gilmore (1982) saw leadership as being centrally concerned with the management of boundaries. Managing at the organizational level, the leader protects the organization from the risks of subversion by outsiders' values and practices. At the same time, the leader manages the importation into the organization of opportunities for learning. At the interpersonal level, the leader manages the boundary between maintaining the role requirements of self and others and making decisions based on personal considerations.

Managers as Linchpins. As will be detailed in the next chapters, the linchpin function of managers was stressed by R. Likert (1961a, 1967). As linchpin, the manager connects a group that is composed of the manager's superior, his or her peers, and with a group that is composed of the manager and his or her subordinates.

For Dagirmanjian (1981), leaders serve as managers by linking the whole organization with their subordinates. The leadership function in nursing was seen by Bernhard and Walsh (1981) to involve coordinating similar activities in two groups, those who seek care and those who give it.

Leaders or Managers? There is also a line of reasoning that draws a sharp distinction between leadership and management. It considers leadership to be the discretionary activities and processes that are beyond the manager's role requirements as mandated by rules, regulations, and procedures. Leadership is whatever discretionary actions are needed to solve the problems the group faces that are embedded in the large system (Osborn, Hunt, & Jauch, 1980). However, Grove (1986) soundly rejected the distinction, stating that the effective manager must have the clarity of purpose and motivation of the effective leader. Gardner (1986b, p. 7) agreed:

> Everytime I encounter an utterly first-class manager he turns out to have quite a lot of leader in him ... even the most visionary leader will be faced on occasion with decisions that every manager faces: when to take a short-term loss to achieve a long-term gain, how to allocate scarce resources among important goals, whom to trust with a delicate assignment.

For Gardner, the required distinction is between the leader-manager and the routine manager. Gardner's leader-manager, in contrast to the routine manager, thinks long term, can look beyond the unit he or she heads to see its relation to the larger system, and can reach and influence others outside their units. The leader-manager emphasizes vision, values motivation and renewal, and can cope with conflict. Gardner summed up the leader-manager's tasks as envisioning the group's goals, affirming values for the group, motivating the members, managing, achieving a workable unity among the members, explaining what needs to be done, serving as a symbol, representing the group, and renewing the group.

For the military, the leader-manager controversy about the importance of leading soldiers, rather than managing bureaucratic technological systems, continues. Advancement to senior levels may be due to tech-nological proficiency instead of leadership potential when the reverse may be needed. As Sarkesian (1985) noted, the low-intensity warfare of the 1980s and beyond calls for more leadership. Meyer (1983) saw the solution to be the development and maintenance of unit-based organizations that make strong, continuing leader-follower relationships possible.

Ideal Leaders versus Ideal Managers. From the psychoanalytic point of view, Zaleznik (1977) stated that leaders and managers differ in how they relate to their roles and their subordinates. Leaders, but not managers, are charismalike, they attract strong feelings of wanting to be identified with them and intense interpersonal relations. Leaders send out clear signals of their purpose and mission; managers tend to be more ambiguous or silent about their purpose. Leaders, but not managers, generate excitement at work. Managers are more likely to see themselves playing a role; leaders behave as themselves. Leaders are more concerned about ideas to be articulated and projected into images; managers are more concerned about process. Leaders for Zaleznik, are more likely to be transformational than are managers. On the other hand, managers will more readily practice contingent rewarding and management by exception, they will want to maintain a controlled, rational, equitable system. While managers tolerate the mundane, leaders react to it "as to an affliction."

A Leader-Management Model. MacKenzie (1969) illustrated the great variety of activities that a typical manager may perform, some of which, such as forecasting and budgeting, have little to do with leadership, as such, unless the latter is defined most broadly. Figure 20.1 shows the different elements, tasks, functions, and activities that may be part of the manager's job. At the center are people, ideas, and things, for these are the basic components of every organization with which the manager must work. According to MacKenzie, ideas create the need for conceptual thinking; things, for administration; people, for leadership.

Three functions—the analysis of problems, decision making, and communication—are important at all times and in all aspects of the jobs held by managers; therefore, these three functions are shown to permeate the entire work process. Also, at all times, managers

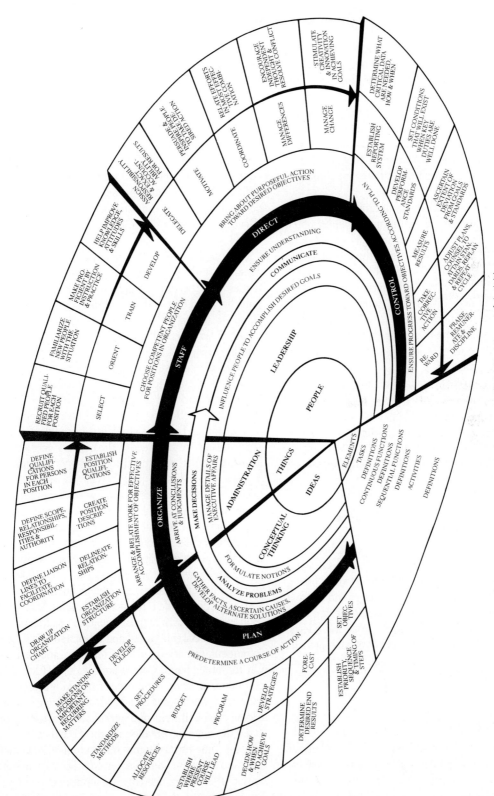

Figure 20.1. Leadership and Management Elements, Tasks, Functions, and Activities

SOURCE: *Reprinted by permission of the Harvard Business Review. "The Management Process in 3-D," by R. Alec MacKenzie (November–December 1969). Copyright © 1969 by the President and Fellows of Harvard College; all rights reserved.*

must sense the pulse of their organization. However, other functions occur ideally (but not necessarily in actual practice) in a predictable sequence; thus, planning, organizing, staffing, directing, and controlling are shown in that order on one of the bands. How much managers are involved in these sequential functions depends on their position and the stage of completion of the projects with which they are most concerned. The relevant activities and their definitions are shown on the outermost bands of the diagram.

We may quarrel with the idea of limiting leadership to the people element. More often, as will be noted later, the administrative and conceptual thinking required are so interlocked with the influence processes that the distinction is of academic rather than of practical consequence. However, the important aspect of the diagram is the sheer diversity of activities and their linkages to the functions and tasks of management. This diversity shows the inadequacy of any simple approach to capture what is involved in the managerial and leadership processes.

The diversity in how managers and organizational leaders spend their time, with whom they spend it, and what they do was corroborated by numerous investigators. For example, Stewart (1967) confirmed the diversity when she asked 160 managers to record all job-behavior incidents that occurred for them that were over five minutes in duration.

Methods of Studying What Managers Do

Chapters 4 and 5 described many of the methods that are available for studying leaders, mainly leaders as persons. Most of these methods are paralleled by procedures for studying the position of manager and the role of organizational leader. They include checklists, logs, diaries, and retrospective accounts from interviews, panel discussions, observations, and questionnaire surveys of focal leaders and their colleagues. Positions are analyzed, as well as functions, activities, and the work done.

Observation and Diaries

S. Carlson (1951) used self and assistants' recordings of the activities of 10 mainly Swedish executives for four weeks. For each action, the recordings noted the site, the person who was contacted, how the communications were conducted (face to face or otherwise), the issues involved, and the actions taken. Employing similar records, T. Burns (1957) collected 3 to 5 weeks of the diary entries of 76 British top managers. Dubin and Spray (1964) depended on the self-descriptions by eight executives of all "job behavior episodes" over a 2-week period, For each episode, they indicated its behavioral content, when it began and ended, who initiated it, with whom the interaction occurred, and how it was conducted. Horne and Lupton (1965) made use of checklist records of the activities of 66 managers for a 1-week period.

Carlson and James (1971) asked 88 insurance agency managers and 252 supervisors to record their work activities over 5 weeks and again 6 months later. Correlations between first and second measures ranged from .78 to .96, indicating a rather high degree of stability in reported work performance over time.

Kelly (1964) used activity sampling in a study of manufacturing executives. His results showed that managers who performed identical functions exhibited similar activity profiles. Likewise, Stogdill and Shartle (1955) asked U.S. Navy officers to keep a minute-by-minute log of their activities for a period of 3 days. After the logs were collected, the officers were asked to estimate the percentage of time they spent in different activities during the period. Correlations between logged time and estimated time were computed. The results indicated a fairly high correspondence between logged time and estimated time for objectively observable performances, such as talking with other persons, reading and answering mail, reading and writing reports, and operating machines. Less objective, less readily observable forms of behavior, such as planning and reflection, failed to yield estimates that corresponded highly with logged time. Nor was there a high correlation between logged and estimated behavior for infrequent activities, such as teaching and research. On the other hand, Carroll and Taylor's (1968, 1969) collection of brief self-reports from 21 managers on what they were doing at a randomly selected minute during each half hour of a period of investigation provided the same information for the 21 managers as did previous time estimates and other observational methods used by an outside observer. Komaki, Zlotnick, and Jensen (1986) introduced further sophistication into observational procedures by using microanalytical coding procedures that were again based on careful time sampling.

Best known are Mintzberg's (1973) structured observational studies of five executives whose activities were sampled over a period of a month. Mintzberg's studies led to numerous structured observational studies[1] centered on the frequency and importance of different roles taken by managers, such as those of figurehead, leader, liaison, and disseminator.

Limitations. Despite the face validity of observational approaches, Martinko and Gardner (1985) found a number of shortcomings in them. First, because sizes must of necessity remain small, the result is the questionable generalizability of conclusions. Second, these approaches often lack adequate reliability checks. Observers need to take account of the multiple purposes of a single action, whose coding often is unreliable. Third, observational reporting is usually simplistic, mechanistic, and narrow in perspective and tends to ignore variations among positions and their situational circumstances. Fourth, these approaches fail to remain consistent in using either an ideographic, a longitudinal, a case-by-case orientation, or a nomothetic approach that aggregates and averages observations across individual positions and situations.

In addition self-reporters and observers are likely to miss many fleeting, transient, actions. Usually observers can only infer the manager's purposes and the intentions of a manager's observable action. Moreover, much of a manager's behavior is cognitive and unobservable (Stewart, 1965). Observational studies need to pay attention to correcting the foregoing shortcomings of the observational approach and to be buttressed by interviews and questionnaires using larger samples.

Questionnaires, Interviews, and Panel Discussions

Managers or their associates may be asked to complete structured questionnaires organized by clusters, factors, or dimensions of activities in which ratings are made of how much time the managers spend on the different functions, tasks, and activities; with whom

they spend their time; and in what ways. The issues covered will be detailed later. Illustrative are investigations by Allen (1981), Korotkin and Yarkin-Levin (1985), and Sperry (1985). Allen collected self-rated questionnaire descriptions from 1,476 New York City government managers about their tasks. Korotkin and Yarkin-Levin used both interviews and questionnaires to generate lists of tasks describing the required activities of U.S. Army commissioned and noncommissioned officers. Sperry held a series of discussions with senior federal career managers to obtain information about their role orientation and job problems. As introduced in Chapter 2, Yukl (1989), among others, developed and evaluated a refined questionnaire, the Management Practices Survey, whose behavorial items make it possible for colleagues and the job incumbent to describe the relevance and importance of the manager's activities on behavioral dimensions, such as informing, monitoring, and supporting.

Critical Incidents. Flanagan (1951) originated the critical incidents technique in which respondents describe incidents of effective and ineffective job performance they had observed or in which they had been involved. The technique was applied to a study of the jobs of U.S. Air Force officers and research executives. It was possible to classify the incidents under the following major headings: supervision, planning and direction, handling administrative details, exercise of responsibility, exercise of personal responsibility, and proficiency in a given specialty. In the same way, Wallace and Gallagher (1952) analyzed the job activities and behaviors of 171 production supervisors in 5 plants. They collected 3,765 behavioral incidents, which they analyzed in terms of the topic involved, location of the incident, person contacted, and nature of the foreman's behavior during the incident. Along similar lines, Williams (1956) and Kay (1959), among others, were able to describe managerial jobs in terms of critical requirements. Williams collected over 3,500 incidents from a representative sample of 742 executives who were distributed proportionally by industry, company size, and geographic location. Kay collected 691 critical incidents of foremen's behavior from managers and rank-and-file employees.

In sum, in the study of the work of managers, attention may be directed toward the frequency, importance, and criticality to the organization of the manager's various activities, functions, and roles, as well as to the knowledge, skills, and ability required for the position. The informants may be observers, colleagues, or the managers themselves who report in structured interviews or surveys. These descriptions can be augmented by prescriptions about what managers ought to do. Finally, what managers ought to do may be sought empirically by comparing the work done by effective and ineffective managers.

Biases in Time and Work Methods of Study

According to a review by Carlson and James (1971) of the various methods employed to study what managers do, how they spend their time, and what functions they perform, adequate reliabilities and validities have been obtained.[2] Nonetheless, systematic biases can be noted.

Substantive Problems. An obvious error occurs if the description is more about a particular job incumbent than about the position as it is and should be performed by the average or typical incumbent. Another bias is due to the fact that managers in a hierarchy think they have a bigger job than their immediate superiors think they have, whereas managers think their subordinates have smaller jobs than the subordinates think they have (Haas, Porat, & Vaughan, 1969), so the importance of the position and its duties depends on who is describing them. Several investigations corroborated this fact.

Brooks (1955) asked 96 executives, their superiors, and their subordinates to rate the work performed by the executives as indicated by 150 functional items. The executives rated themselves higher than they were rated by their subordinates in such activities as defining authority, delegating, planning, and showing how jobs related to the whole picture. Again, supervisors and subordinates were found to differ in the requirements they saw for other aspects of the superior's job. According to Sequeira (1964), foremen perceived themselves as being required to perform duties that did

not legitimately belong to their jobs; among these duties were training new workers on the job, arranging wage agreements, and checking supplies. Workers expected their foremen to do more than the foremen required of themselves in the way of settling personnel problems and grievances, clarifying work difficulties, and improving work methods and conditions. A study by Yoga (1964) of 11 Indian plants in 3 industries (textiles, processing, and engineering) yielded similar results.

Methodological Problems. According to McCall, Morrison, and Hanman (1978), managerial behavior usually is described in global dimensions, such as planning and controlling, instead of actual observable behaviors because so many studies depend on interviews or questionnaires of the managers themselves. The results are then summarized with factor analyses. The responses of the managers provide only indirect information about what the managers do, in contrast to observations of what they actually do. The self-reports deviate considerably from observations and recordings of their behavior (Horne & Lupton, 1965; Kelly, 1964). Diaries, as self-reports, are also likely to deviate from summary estimates as well as from independent observers' descriptions (T. Burns, 1954). "Managers are poor estimators of their own activities" (Mintzberg, 1973, p. 222). Thus, although 12 university administrators estimated in a summary judgment that they had spent 47 percent of their time in meetings, their diaries for 5 weeks indicated that they had spent 69 percent of their time in such meetings (Lewis & Dahl, 1976).

The discrepancy between what managers say they do in response to questionnaires and what they actually do is to be expected. Managers do not consciously plan ahead to summarize all their activities in a retrospective survey and since the "managers' work activities are fragmented, brief, diverse, fast-paced and primarily oral, the sheer volume and nature of activities seriously hinders a manager's efforts to conscientiously observe and purposively memorize activities for accurate reporting on a future survey." (McCall, Morrison, & Hanman, 1978, p. 27). Furthermore, social desirability is likely to inflate results, regardless of the self-reporting method used (Weiss, Davis, England, & Lofquist, 1961).

[2] See also Anderson and Nilsson (1964); Carroll and Taylor (1968); Flanagan (1951, 1954); Hemphill (1959); Kay and Meyer (1962); Lau, Newman, and Broedling (1980); Lau and Pavett (1980); O'Neill and Kubany (1957); McCall, Morrison, and Hanman (1978); Pavett and Lau (1983); Shartle (1956); and P. A. Stewart (1967).

As with many other methodological problems, for confidence in the conclusions reached, the solution usually lies in using multiple methods that combine self-, colleagues, and observers' reports with a mix of logs or diaries and interviews or questionnaires.

Personal Preferences

It should be clear that not all the variations observed in describing the same positions are due to biases and error. Managers can occupy a position with the same requirements, yet still display considerable true differences in how they carry out their responsibilities. Stewart (1976b) observed that the activities of incumbents in management positions with the same function and at the same level can vary considerably because managerial jobs have a certain amount of choice beyond the basic demands of the job. To a considerable degree, managers can work on tasks of their choosing and when they want to. Stogdill and Shartle (1955) pointed out that naval officers spent the same amount of time on some activities, regardless of the different requirements of the new position to which they were transferred. In the same way, Castaldi (1982) found that ten chief executive officers (CEOs) who headed same-sized companies in the same industry (small furniture manufacturing firms) split seven to three on the importance they attached to Hemphill's (1959) operational activities. Seven attached more importance to strategic activities only. The majority's emphasis on strategic activities was seen to be a consequence of the static technology of the furniture industry, the heavy competitiveness between firms, and the long tenure of the CEOs. Nevertheless, three of the CEOs attached less importance to strategic activities.

Time Spent and Work Done by Managers

Use of Time

Most studies have focused on how managers spend their time, what work they do, and what roles they play. The frequency, importance, and criticality of these factors have been the usual gauges of consequence. Clearly, according to diaries and observational studies, managers work long hours, ranging from 50 to 90 hours per week, some of which may be carried on outside the office. Senior managers work longer than do lower-level managers but on fewer activities. Those with well-defined functions, such as accounting managers, can work fewer hours (McCall, Morrison, & Hanman, 1978). Shipping supervisors differ systematically from production supervisors in the time they spend in planning and scheduling work and in maintaining equipment and machinery (Dowell & Wexley, 1978).

With his background as a director of research on job and occupational information, Shartle (1934, 1949b) suggested that executive work could most meaningfully be quantified in terms of the amount of time that is devoted to various activities. Stogdill and Shartle (1955) compared the time-use profiles of 470 U.S. Navy officers and 66 business executives. They found that both groups spent more time (about 34 percent) with subordinates than with superiors or peers. Furthermore, both groups devoted about 15 to 20 percent of their time to inspections, examining reports, and writing reports and spent somewhat more time in planning than in other major administrative functions. The profiles suggested a high degree of similarity in administrative work between military and business organizations. Similarly, Jaynes (1956) analyzed variations in the performance of 24 officers in 4 submarines and 24 officers who occupied identical positions in 4 landing ships. He reported that variance in performance was more closely related to the type of position than to the type of organization in which the position was located.

In the previously cited study of executives in Sweden, S. Carlson (1951) found that they spent about 20 percent of their time in internal and external inspections and almost 40 percent of their time acquiring information. The remainder of their time was divided about equally between advising and explaining, making decisions, and giving orders. Most of the executives felt overworked, complaining that they had little time for family or friends.

According to Horne and Lupton's (1965) study of 66 managers, a large percentage of a manager's time is spent in discussions with others (informally with others, 44 percent; in formal meetings, 10 percent; and on the telephone, 9 percent). In contrast, only 2 percent is spent in reflecting, 10 percent in reading, and 14 percent in paperwork. At least half these activities occur in the manager's own office. The most frequent purposes are to transmit information (42 percent), discuss explanations (15 percent), review plans (11 percent), discuss instructions (9 percent), review decisions (8 percent), or give and receive advice (6 percent).

Time on Activity by Position. Stogdill, Shartle, Wherry, and Jaynes (1955) studied 470 U.S. Navy officers in 45 different positions or job categories. The officers were located in 47 different organizations. Data were obtained from all officers on the percentage of their working time that was devoted to the performance of 35 tasks, including personal contacts, individual efforts, and handling other major responsibilities. The results were related to the officers' level in the organization, military rank, scope or responsibility, scope of authority, and leadership behavior. Stogdill, Wherry, and Jaynes (1953) factor analyzed these naval officers' profiles to cluster the positions of officers doing similar work, such as public relations directors, coordinators, and consultants. Then, they correlated the scores for the specialties with how occupants spent their time. Eight factors emerged from the analysis. The officers spent their time in (1) high-level policymaking, (2) administrative coordination, (3) methods planning, (4) representation of members' interest, (5) personnel service, (6) professional consultation, (7) maintenance services, and (8) inspection. The officers' assignments and activities clustered as follows in these eight factors of the use of time: (1) technical supervisors (teaching, supervising, using machines and computing), (2) planners, such as operations officers (scheduling, preparing, procedures, reading technical publications, interviewing personnel, and consulting peers), (3) maintenance administrators (interpreting, consulting, attending meetings, and engaging in technical performances), (4) commanders and directors (representing, inspecting, and preparing reports), (5) coordinators, such as executive or staff officers (consulting juniors, supervising, scheduling, examining reports, and interviewing personnel), (6) public relations officers (writing for publication, consulting outsiders, reflecting, and representing), (7) legal or accounting officers (consulting juniors, professional consulting, interpreting), and (8) personnel administration officers (attending meetings, planning, and interviewing personnel).

T. A. Mahoney (1955) plotted the time-usage profiles of 50 company presidents against those of 66 business executives reported by Stogdill and Shartle (1956). The two profiles were almost identical. T. A. Mahoney (1961) next analyzed the performance of 348 business executives in terms of 8 functions. The performances with the percentage of time devoted to them were as follows: supervision (39 percent), planning (18 percent), generalist (14 percent), investigation (8 percent), coordination (6 percent), negotiation (5 percent), evaluation (4 percent), and miscellaneous (7 percent). Similar patterns of the usage of time were reported by Mahoney, Jerdee, and Carroll (1965) for a sample of 452 managers drawn from all organizational levels. A minimum amount of time was spent on each of these functions, although the percentage varied as a function of hierarchical level. For example, more time was spent in supervision at lower levels, and more time was spent in planning at higher levels. Replicated by Penfield (1975), these results were consistent with Stogdill, Shartle, Wherry, and Jaynes's (1955) findings for naval officers, and Haas, Porat, and Vaughan's (1969) findings for bank officials. Fleishman (1956) used the same kinds of data to analyze the differences between administrators in military and industrial organizations. He observed that differences *between* the patterns of administrative performance in industrial and naval organizations were generally no greater than differences *within* the two types of organizations. Taken together, all these studies indicated that time profiles of managerial positions tend to covary systematically with the hierarchical level of positions and the functional role of the positions in the organization. The patterns of time spent tend to be similar for positions that are comparable in level and function in different types of organizations.

Work Done

McCall, Morrison, and Hanman (1978) concluded, from diaries and observational studies such as by Brewer and Tomlinson (1964) and Horne and Lupton (1965), that contrary to both popular and classical images of management, much more managerial work involves handling information than making decisions. As Carroll and Gillen (1987) noted, the simple classical view of the manager as one who gets work done through prescribed and orderly planning, organizing, and controlling has given way to a more complex romantic view, stimulated by the seminal work of Mintzberg (1973), which is detailed later. Instead of the prescribed best ways to fulfill the managerial role, what we now have is a picture of harried executives putting out fires on demand, rather than systematically carrying out their prescribed functions in an orderly fashion. Both Guest (1956) and Ponder (1958) reached similar conclusions earlier from observational studies of production foremen who were seen to have to handle a variety of problems quickly. One problem followed the other with less than a minute for each on the average, according to Guest. More than 50 percent of the foremen's time was spent in face-to-face interactions, more often with subordinates than with outsiders, although the foremen had more total contacts with the latter. Landsberger (1961) also noted the same pattern of brief, varied, and fragmented activities with much lateral interpersonal interaction at the middle-management level. Numerous other empirical investigations continue to find the greater variety in the manager's functions and ways of conceptualizing them that describe what managers actually do, in contrast to the classical expectations that tend to limit the manager's work to rational planning, organizing, and controlling.

Managers do not behave according to textbook requirements for orderliness, planning, optimum decisions, and maximum efficiency. Rather, managerial processes, according to Mintzberg's (1973) in-depth study of five executives, are characterized by brevity, variety, and discontinuity. Managers rely on judgment and intuition, rather than on formal analysis, which makes it difficult to observe clearly their decision-making processes. Kurke and Aldrich (1983) supported Mintzberg's conclusions in a complete replication with four CEO's for one week. Yet Snyder and Glueck (1977), in a replication of Mintzberg's (1973) study, found managers to be more careful planners. But brevity in any one activity, interruptions of that activity, and discontinuity from one activity to the next are characteristic of what is gleaned from managers' diaries, recordings, and observations (Mintzberg, 1973). Although planning is regarded as a key element in the classical view of management, managers at all levels, according to diaries and observation, actually spend

less time at it because of interruptions and demands on their time for other activities (McCall, Morrison, & Hanman, 1978). Mintzberg concluded that managers are oriented toward action, not reflection.

There is a certain amount of ritualistic and regular duties in managerial work. Since personal communication is favored over written documents, managers spend a good deal of time on the telephone or in meetings. Klauss and Bass (1981) found that this tendency is increased when managers deal with peers. If the peers are at a distance, contact is by telephone; if they are close, the contact is face to face. But if the communication is with persons who are higher or lower in the organizational hierarchy, it is usually done through memos. Electronic mail is likely to substitute considerably for all three of these media of communication.

Effects of Hierarchical Level. Barnard (1938) focused attention on how the functions of the executive varied, depending on the location of the executive's position in the organizational hierarchy. Social and political considerations also affect what could be done.

Job-analytic studies were completed by Stogdill, Scott, and Jaynes (1956), who asked U.S. Navy officers to use Work Analysis Forms (Stogdill & Shartle, 1958) to indicate "What I Do" and "What I Ought to Do." Junior officers also indicted their perception of what their senior officer did and ought to do. Senior officers expected and were expected by the junior officers to engage more often than junior officers in such activities as attending conferences, consulting superiors, examining reports, planning, and coordination. Seniors expected and were expected by juniors to do less than junior officers in writing reports, reading technical publications, scheduling and routing, research, and engaging in technical and professional operations.

Both junior and senior officers tended to report that, compared with what they actually did, they should do more inspecting, research, planning, public relations, reflection, reading technical periodicals, and writing for publication. Both senior and junior officers reported that they should do less consulting with assistants and superiors, interviewing personnel, reading and answering mail, preparing charts, supervising, interpreting, and scheduling.

Sherif (1969) used the Work Analysis Forms in a

comparative study of three levels of managers in six diverse organizations. As would be expected, top managers consulted more with subordinates, while managers at the bottom consulted more with superiors and peers. Middle managers fell between the other two groups in contacts with superiors, peers, and subordinates. In regard to individual effort, examining reports and thinking increased with the level of the position, while writing reports, computation, and use of machines decreased with the level. With respect to major functions, preparing procedures, coordinating, and evaluating increased with the level of the position, and supervision and personnel activities progressively decreased. Haas, Porat, and Vaughan (1969) also used an adaptation of the Work Analysis Forms in a comparative study of three levels of organization. Planning and coordination were done most in top-level positions; negotiating, in middle-level positions; and supervising, at lower-levels. All levels combined did more investigating but less planning than they thought ideal.

Position Description Questionnaires. Hemphill (1960) studied the position of 93 business executives located in 5 companies with the Executive Position Description Questionnaire (EPDQ). The positions represented 3 levels of organization and 5 specialties (research and development, sales, manufacturing, general administration, and industrial relations). Data were obtained on 575 items that were classified as (1) position activities, (2) position responsibilities, (3) position demands and restrictions, and (4) position characteristics. Correlations were computed between positions (1) within each organization, (2) within each level of the organization, and (3) within each specialty. Again, systematic differences were associated with differences in the hierarchical levels in which the positions were located. The results indicated a greater degree of similarity between positions in the same specialty but in different organizations than between positions in different specialties within the same level of organization. Hemphill also factor analyzed the correlations between the 575 items. Ten factors emerged: (1) providing a staff service for a nonoperations area, (2) supervising work, (3) business control, (4) technical (markets and product), (5) human, community, and social affairs, (6) long-range planning, (7) exercise of broad

power and authority, (8) business reputation, (9) personal demands, and (10) preservation of assets.

With a heavier emphasis on the functional responsibilities of different managerial positions, Tornow and Pinto (1976) developed the Management Position Description Questionnaire (MPDQ) to provide a similar analysis for higher-level managers. Thirteen functions and associated work done for executives could be differentiated and evaluated as follows: (1) product, marketing, and financial-strategy planning—long-range thinking and planning, (2) coordination of other organization units and personnel—coordinating and efforts of others over whom one exercises no direct control, (3) internal business control—reviewing and controlling the allocation of personnel and other resources, cost reduction, performance goals, budgets, and employee relations practices, (4) products and services responsibility—planning, scheduling, and monitoring products and the delivery of services, (5) public and customer relations—promoting the company's products and services, the goodwill of the company, and general public relations, (6) advanced consulting—application of technical expertise to special problems, issues, questions, or policies, (7) autonomy of action—discretion in the handling of the job, making decisions that are most often not subject to review, (8) approval of financial commitments—authority to obligate the company, (9) staff service—fact gathering, the acquisition and compilation of data, and record keeping for a higher authority, (10) supervision—getting work done efficiently through the effective use of people, (11) complexity and stress—handling information under time pressure to meet deadlines, frequently taking risks, interfering with personal or family life, (12) advanced financial responsibility—preservation of assets, making investment decisions and large-scale financial decisions that affect the company's performance, and (13) broad personnel responsibility—management of human resources and the policies affecting it.

Tornow and his colleagues continued this line of investigation for 11 years in different industries, for different organizational levels, and in upwards of 20 countries involving more than 10,000 managers. The instrument they validated, the MPDQ, contains about 250 items of required activities, contacts, skills, knowledge, and abilities. In rating each item to describe the management position, the job analyst weighs the importance, the criticality, and the frequency of occurrence of the item. Managers indicated that 85 percent of their jobs were adequately described by the items of the MPDQ according to managers in both the United States and foreign countries (Page, 1985, 1987).

Seven large-scale studies that searched for factor-analytic solutions were carried out in a variety of industries, including banking, manufacturing, and retailing. Seven factors consistently emerged across these studies: planning, controlling, monitoring business indicators, supervising, coordinating, sales/marketing, public relations, and consulting.

Figure 20.2 shows the profiles of 10 factor scores obtained in Page and Tornow's (1987) study for the position of 108 executives, 125 managers, and 196 supervisors. Consistent with expectations, executive positions stood out in their planning, controlling, and monitoring business indicators and in their public relations activities. Supervisors' positions differed the most from those of the managers and executives in supervisory activities and their relatively low scores in comparison to the others on most of the other factors. The

managers' position tended to come closer to those of the executives in planning, controlling, coordinating, and consulting and closer to the supervisors in public relations.

Consistent with these findings, a factor analysis reported by Dunnette (1986) of 65 managerial tasks yielded seven factors: monitoring the business environment, planning and allocating resources, managing individuals' performance, instructing subordinates, managing the performance of groups, representing the group, and coordinating groups. Comparisons among 574 first-level, 466 middle-level, and 165 executive-level managers indicated that as the hierarchical level increased, so did the managers' functions of monitoring the business environment and coordinating groups. At the same time, the instruction of subordinates and the management of individuals' performance decreased. Managerial positions can be usefully profiled on these dimensions factored by Hemphill, Dunnette, Tornow and Pinto, and others and compared with norms for the different levels of management.

Yukl, Wall, and Lepsinger (1988) reported on the development and validation of the Managerial Practices

Figure 20.2. Factor Profiles for Different Levels of Management

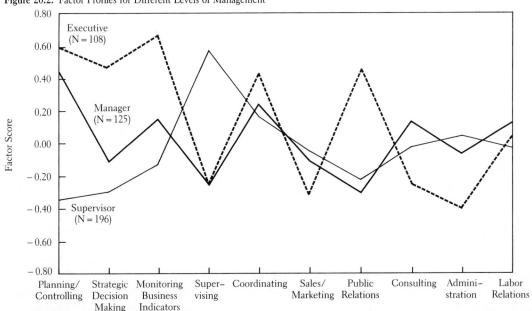

SOURCE: *Page and Tornow (1987, pp. 13–14).*

Survey (MPS). The survey focused on behavior, such as answers requests, invites participation, determines how to reach objectives, assigns tasks, praises, facilitates the resolution of conflicts, and develops contacts. Colleagues and job incumbents rate the importance and relevance of each behavior for carrying out the manager's responsibilities effectively. The 1988 version (Yukl, 1988) was grouped into 11 scales. The scales were developed using factor analysis and judges' categorizations of the items. The 11 scales assessed the following behavioral dimensions: informing, clarifying, monitoring, problem solving, planning and organizing, consulting/delegating, motivating, recognizing/rewarding, supporting, networking/interfacing, and conflict management/team building.

First-Level Supervisor Position. Specialized questionnaires were developed for the study of the position of first-level supervisor. Following Hemphill's (1960) work on the dimensions of managerial jobs, Prien (1963) constructed the Supervisor Position Description Questionnaire with items written by job analysts who were guided by an outline of general supervisory functions. Thirty supervisors indicated the extent to which each of the items was descriptive of their work. Prien extracted seven factors: (1) employee supervision, (2) employee contact and communication, (3) union-management relations, (4) manpower coordination and administration, (5) work organization, planning, and preparation, (6) manufacturing process supervision, and (7) manufacturing process administration.

Using a similar methodology, Dowell and Wexley (1978) factor analyzed the responses of 251 supervisors regarding the importance of 89 work activities of first-line supervisors. The factor structure obtained from the intercorrelations among ratings of importance was highly congruent with the factor structure obtained from the intercorrelations among the ratings of the amount of time spent in an activity. The 7 dimensions along which the positions of first-level supervisors could be ordered were as follows:

1. *Working with subordinates:* direct contact with subordinates, informing employees of the levels of performance that are expected, instructing workers in safe working habits, seeing that safety equipment is used, instructing workers in the proper use of materials and equipment, observing subordinates' work activities, listening to employees' ideas and problems, and settling disciplinary problems or potential grievances.

2. *Organizing the work of subordinates:* talking with supervisors in other departments about the levels of production, scheduling overtime, shifting people to other jobs to maintain production levels, establishing priorities on "down" equipment, and assigning employees to specific jobs.

3. *Work planning and scheduling:* consulting with the off-going supervisor about conditions on the shift, reading records of previous shifts' activities and planning production levels for the shift, and completing reports on the conditions at the end of the shift.

4. *Maintaining efficient and high-quality production:* checking the quality of production; finding the causes of low production or poor quality; determining production levels, the quality of the production, and the kinds and causes of waste; and soliciting suggestions from subordinates regarding improvements in work methods.

5. *Maintaining safe/clean work areas:* communicating Occupational Safety and Health Act regulations to workers, checking to see that walkways and fire exits are clear, completing maintenance records, and inspecting work areas for cleanliness.

6. *Maintaining equipment and machinery:* diagnosing problems with machines, adjusting machines, checking maintenance work when completed, inspecting machines for proper working order, and setting up machines.

7. *Compiling records and reports:* compiling miscellaneous reports, distributing tools or equipment, keeping personal records of job incidents, performing routine checks of safety devices, and notifying people of changes in schedules.

Dynamic Models. Wofford (1967, 1970, 1971) reached a somewhat simpler set of more psychologically defined dynamic factors to describe a manager's behavior: (1) order and group achievement—neatness and accuracy in planning, organizing, and controlling, (2) personal enhancement—use of power and pressure to achieve the employees' compliance, (3) maintenance

Figure 20.3. Interrelationships among the Leader Behavior Dimensions

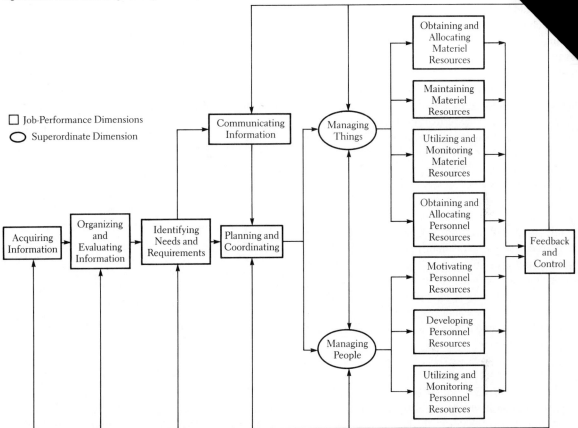

SOURCE: *Mumford, Fleishman, Levin, Korotkin, Hein (1988).*

of interpersonal relationships—personal interaction as a leader, (4) security and maintenance—reactions to or the avoidance of feelings of insecurity, and (5) dynamic and achievement orientation—aggression and setting specific goals.

Mumford, Fleishman, et al. (1988) started with a list of 156 tasks and 69 possible job-performance dimensions to describe the positions of U.S. Army officers. A total of 96 officers judged the importance, time spent, and freedom to decide on how, when, and where each of 13 job-performance dimensions was relevant. The most important dimension was setting an example for others to follow. Figure 20.3 displays the dynamic model the authors were able to organize to link the job-performance dimensions into a coherent design.

Networking and Boundary Management. Mumford, Fleishman, et al. (1988) modeled the leader-subordinate relation without much reference to persons outside the group except as imported information. However, McCall, Morrison, and Hanman (1978) concluded, from diary and observational studies,[3] that although lower-level managers spend most of their time within their own departments and organizations, senior managers have much more contact with those outside the organization. Luthans (1986), among others, paid special attention to the relations of the managers to others outside their immediate subordinates or immediate superior. He concluded from observing over

[3] The studies were by T. Burns (1954), Horne and Lupton (1965), Mintzberg (1970), and Stewart (1967).

ee clusters[4] of inside ac-
nost important was the
socializing, and "poli-
one's immediate col-
ared to be most impor-
of activities. Luthans,
985) inferred, from par-
ticipant observers records of 52 managers in a state
department of revenue, a manufacturing plant, and a
campus police department, that success in the organization was enhanced by networking with such outsiders, socializing, and playing politics. Consistent with
other studies, the investigators found that the successful managers also engaged more than did the less successful managers in conflict management, planning,
coordinating, and decision making. An in-depth study
of 15 successful general managers by Kotter (1982a)
again emphasized the importance of time spent with
outsiders as well as with others in their own organization. Kotter considered many of these contacts to be
network building. A manager's agenda could be more
readily implemented if he had developed a high-quality
network.

Sayles (1964) also focused particular attention on the
manager's lateral networking, which included relationships dealing with the work flow, with trading, with service, with giving or receiving advice, with evaluating
other groups or responding to the requests of those
evaluating one's group, with limiting or controlling decisions made by other managers, and with engaging in
innovations. McHenry (1986) generated two factors involving the importance ratings attached to a manager's
lateral activities for a sample of 400 managers—coordinating interdependent groups and representing one's
work group. In the same way, after agenda setting to
establish loosely connected goals and plans for short-,
medium-, and long-term responsibilities, Kotter (1982a)
saw general managers developing a cooperative relationship among those individuals they thought they
needed to satisfy their emerging agendas and to get the
networks to implement the agendas.

Mintzberg's Managerial Roles

Mintzberg (1973) presented a model of ten management roles that was dynamic and included both inside
and outside activities. It generated a great deal of interest and subsequent use.

Source of the Data

Mintzberg (1973) intensively studied five CEOs and
their organizations, along with a calendar of their
scheduled appointments for a month. Additional data
collected during a week of structured observations included anecdotal data about specific activities, chronological records of activity patterns, a record of incoming and outgoing mail, and a record of the executive's
verbal contacts with others.

The CEOs were found to work at an unrelenting
pace on a wide variety of tasks. They were subject to
frequent interruptions. They preferred specific, well-
defined activities of current importance over work on
general functions of less certainty and less immediate
relevance. In addition, they preferred verbal contact
with others to written contact.[5]

Ten Integrated Roles

On the basis of these data, Mintzberg divided managerial activities into interpersonal, informational, and decisional roles. The interpersonal category contained
three specific roles: (1) the figurehead role, (2) the
leader role, and (3) the liason role. In the figurehead
role, managers perform symbolic duties as heads of the
organization; in the leader role, managers establish the
work atmosphere and motivate subordinates to achieve
organizational goals; and in the liaison role, managers
develop and maintain webs of contacts outside the organization to obtain favors and information. The informational category also included three roles: (1) the
monitor role, (2) the disseminator role, and (3) the
spokesman role. In the monitor role, managers act as
collectors of all information that is relevant to the organization; in the disseminator role, managers transmit

---

[4] The three clusters were (1) routine communication associated with
processing paperwork and exchanging routine information, (2) planning, decision making, and controlling, and (3) human resource management activities, such as motivating, positively reinforcing, disciplining,
punishing, managing conflict, staffing, and training and developing.

[5] Many previously cited large-scale management surveys of communication patterns, time spent, and work done corroborated the tendency for
interpersonal interaction among managers in large organizations to be
primarily verbal rather than written.

information from the outside to members in the organization; and in the spokesman role, managers transmit information from inside the organization to outsiders.

Last, there were four specific decisional roles: (1) entrepreneur, (2) disturbance handler, (3) resource allocator, and (4) negotiator. Managers adopt the enterpreneurial role when they initiate controlled change in their organization to adapt to the changing conditions in the environment; the disturbance-handler role, when they are forced to deal with unexpected changes; the resource-allocator role, when they make decisions concerning the use of organizational resources; and the negotiator role, when they deal with other organizations or individuals.

The ten roles are an integrated set. Formal authority supports the three interpersonal roles, which in turn result in three informational roles. The authority and

informational roles enable the manager to play the four decisional roles. Table 20.1 is a summary of Mintzberg's ten executives roles.

To measure the extent to which managers had to be engaged in Mintzberg's roles, Pavett and Lau (1983) asked 48 manufacturing managers to indicate the importance of 69 activities in carrying out their duties and the approximate amount of time they spent on each activity. The roles of leader and entrepreneur were deemed most important and on which most time was spent. Time spent on a role and its importance correlated between .63 and .85.

Problems of Overlap. Although McCall and Segrist (1980) found that managers' performance in six of the roles correlated with the managers' rate of promotion, they obtained too much overlap in the activities among

Table 20.1 Summary of Mintzberg's Executive Roles

Role	Definition
Interpersonal	
Figurehead	Symbolic head; obligated to perform a number of routine duties of a legal or social nature.
Leader	Responsible for the motivation and activation of subordinates and for staffing, training, and associated duties.
Liaison	Maintains self-developed network of outside contacts and informers who provide favors and information.
Informational	
Monitor	Seeks and receives a wide variety of special information (much of it current) to develop thorough understanding of the organization and the environment; emerges as the nerve center of internal and external information of the organization.
Disseminator	Transmits information received from outsiders or from other subordinates to members of the organization. Some information is factual, some involves the interpretation and integration of diverse value positions of organizational influences.
Spokesperson	Transmits information to outsiders on the organization's plans, policies, actions, results, and so on; serves as an expert on the organization's industry.
Decisional	
Entrepreneur	Searches the organization and its environment for opportunities and initiates "improvement projects" to bring about changes; supervises the design of certain projects as well.
Disturbance handler	Responsible for corrective action when the organization faces important, unexpected disturbances.
Resource allocator	Responsible for the allocation of organizational resources of all kinds—in effect, the making or approval of all significant organizational decisions.
Negotiator	Responsible for representing the organization during major negotiations with others.

SOURCE: Adapted from Pavett and Lau (1982, p. 96).

Mintzberg's roles, which were supposed to be distinct. Snyder and Wheelen (1981) reported difficulty in assigning specific activities to specific roles. One activity appeared relevant to several roles, and the roles were not mutually exclusive. For instance, when one of the subordinates of a school superintendent attended a United Way campaign fund-raising meeting, she did so as the formal representative of the school system. The superintendent, if present at the meeting, attended as a figurehead. The superintendent took the opportunity to chat with an influential outsider about a problem to obtain advice. In this case, he was acting as liaison, monitor, and spokesperson.

Role Clusters. Shapira and Dunbar (1978) simulated the CEOs job as head of a firm of 6,000 employees with an in-basket test completed by 54 MBA students at Hebrew University. The "CEOs" could exercise each of the 10 managerial roles in dealing with the 16 memos in the in-basket and with the agenda he or she had prepared. A small space analysis indicated that the ten roles could be described meaningfully with 2 clusters. The first cluster was made up of the liaison, disseminator, spokesman, and figurehead roles. These roles were concerned primarily with the generation and transmission of information. The cluster corresponded with Mintzberg's (1975) notion of the executive as the general nerve center of the organizational unit. The second cluster of roles—entrepreneur, negotiator, leader, disturbance handler, monitor, and resource allocator—was concerned primarily with the active formulation and execution of decisions.

Role Factors. A number of investigators, such as Morse and Wagner (1978); Lau, Newman, and Broedling (1980); and Tsui (1984), used Mintzberg's role set to generate and factor specific leadership and management behaviors that could then be used for checklists of observed behaviors and questionnaire surveys. These then could be self-rated or completed by superiors, peers, or subordinates. When Lau, Newman, and Broedling (1980) factor analyzed a survey of the behavior of 210 governmental managers based on Mintzberg's 10-role model, 4 factors emerged: (1) leadership and supervision, (2) information gathering and dissemination, (3) technical problem solving and executive decision making, and (4) allocating resources. A factor analysis was completed by Tsui (1984) on the basis of

ratings by 1,080 personnel in the division of a large corporation of self, superiors, peers, or subordinates using survey questionnaires. The respondents rated how much the focal manager was observed to perform or carry out the role activity described. Table 20.2 presents examples of activities that loaded highly on the 6 factors that emerged.

It can be seen that care must be taken in interpreting the factor labels. For example, entrepreneurial activity appears to encompass planning, controlling, and implementing change, rather than its usual meaning of profit-oriented investment. And, although the role of liaison involves attending social functions, attendance at formal meetings in other units fits the role of spokesperson, rather than that of liaison.

Characteristics of the Managerial Processes

The characteristics of the process in which the manager engages are another way of analyzing what the manager does. Stewart (1967, 1982b) analyzed the duration of specific activities, the mode of communications used, and the particular persons contacted to detail the characteristics that distinguish among managers' positions.

Same Roles but Different Processes

The same role requirements may be met by managers in different ways with different characteristics of the process. For instance, Strauss (1962) found considerable difference in interpersonal patterns of contact and in oral versus written communications among purchasing agents with similar job descriptions. Similarly, Whitely (1985) demonstrated, with 70 managers studied for 7 consecutive days during 2 weeks, that managerial positions with similar behavioral content still allow incumbents considerable latitude in how they choose to play their roles. For instance, managers in accounting, management analysis, and reimbursements, who were all engaged in the function of internal business control, differed significantly in the frequency of their scheduled activities, activities lasting 60 minutes or more, and contacts with their boss and peers. As Stewart (1982a) emphasized, there is a need to distinguish between the demands placed on an incumbent to a job, the constraints within functions that must be carried

Table 20.2 Factor Structure of Observed Behavioral Items on Six Managerial Roles

Role and Abbreviated Descriptions of Items	Factors					
	1	2	3	4	5	6
1. Leader						
Evaluates the quality of the subordinate's job performance	69	−14	−04	−14	−03	−06
Resolves conflicts between subordinates	67	−03	−02	04	04	−04
Facilitates the subordinates' growth and development	73	−05	07	−07	09	−06
Alert subordinates to problems	72	08	−00	−04	−01	06
2. Spokesperson						
Serves as an expert to people outside the unit	−03	54	−01	−09	02	−02
Serves on committees, representing the unit	−06	62	−06	−08	01	−18
Provides information to others about the unit's activities	09	64	01	−09	06	02
3. Resource Allocator						
Distributes budgeted resources	07	−11	69	−19	03	−12
Allocates money within the unit	−05	−02	77	−12	03	−07
Decides which programs to provide resources	−02	21	60	−04	15	10
Allocates equipment or materials	15	02	65	19	08	01
4. Entrepreneur (Reversed scoring)						
Plans and implements changes	17	08	−20	−64	03	−05
Initiates controlled changes	25	23	−22	−50	−05	−18
Solves problems by instituting needed changes	37	14	−10	−41	09	04
5. Environmental monitor						
Keeps up with market trends	02	−08	08	−09	73	−18
Scans the environment for opportunities	−02	−05	−15	−07	77	04
Gathers information about customers and competitors	03	−02	−02	13	75	−07
6. Liaison (Reversed scoring)						
Attends social functions to keep up contacts	08	−01	00	−04	03	−82
Attends meetings in other units	−12	64	−07	−03	−09	−24
Attends social functions as a representative	03	13	−03	04	04	−73

SOURCE: Adapted from Tsui (1984, pp. 72–73).

out, and the choices that can be made in carrying them out. This information can be obtained from diaries, interviews, and time-sampling observations.

Thirteen reliably discriminable categories of characteristics of the process were obtained by Whitely in his study of 70 managers: scheduled activities, activities of fewer than 5 minutes' duration, activities of more than 60 minutes' duration, face-to-face contacts, self-initiated activities, activities carried out alone, contacts with 2 or more persons, the percentage of contacts

with the boss, contacts with peers, contacts with subordinates, contacts with external persons, information-seeking activities, and decision-making activities.

Operant Processeses

Characteristics of the process have also been categorized according to an operant taxonomy provided by Komaki, Zlotnick, and Jensen (1986), which was presented in Figure 2.1. The use of this taxonomy to differentiate effective from ineffective supervisors will be presented later.

Moderators of the Manager's Work, Function, and Roles

Considerable evidence has been amassed to show how management positions will differ, depending on their area of responsibility in the organization, their hierarchical level in the organization, changes within organizations, and differences among organizations.

Function of the Manager's Position

The managers' areas of responsibility make a considerable difference in how they spend their time, on what activities they work, and which are most critical and important to their success. For instance, as may be seen in Table 20.3, supervising is more significant to merchandizing managers than to data processing or finance managers. Thus, Alexander (1979b) found that the informational roles, as expected, were much more salient in staff positions, while the interpersonal roles

were more important in sales positions. Among the 225 managers studied in production, marketing, and accounting, Alexander noted that marketing and accounting managers reported themselves to be higher in requirements to enact the informational roles of monitor, disseminator, and spokesperson than did the production managers. Fewer differences were seen in the requirements of other roles.

Pavett and Lau (1983) reported on the self-ratings of 180 top, middle, and lower managers in southern California, on 54 items about the importance to their success of enacting Mintzberg's 10 roles plus an eleventh role of technical expert. The roles of leader and monitor were perceived to be highest in importance to sales and marketing; spokesperson and resource allocator, to accounting and finance; and technical expert, to research and development. For general managers, human and conceptual skills were seen as most important. In accounting and finance, the greatest importance was attached to technical skills, and in sales and marketing, it was apportioned to political skills.

In an in-depth report on 20 project managers, Spitz (1982) pointed out that the pattern of demands on a

Table 20.3 Correlations with Hierarchical Level (as Measured by Pay Grade) within Each Function of a Manager's Work in a Large Retail Organization

Activity	Job Function (N = 343)		
	Data Processing	Finance	Merchandising
Decision making	.25	.38	.46
Impact on the company	.15	.40	.34
Communication	.22	.35	.32
Supervision	.14	.02	.42
Knowledge	.32	.32	.51
Contacts	.35	.31	.36
Long-range planning	.19	.46	.44
Monitoring business indicators	.42	.49	.58
Customer relations/marketing	.16	.24	.21
Consulting	.22	.28	.48
Coordinating	.46	.62	.33
Controlling	.36	.36	.47
Products and services	.06	.26	.26
External contacts	.29	.33	.38
Supervising	.19	.05	.43

SOURCE: Adapted from McHenry (1986, pp. 12 and 14).

project manager may change over time as the project develops. That is, particular skills required for the project manager's integrative efforts will shift with the changing project. Vaughan (1981) concurred. Using structured interviews, she found that for expatriate matrix project managers in a large multinational firm, there were important shifts in roles owing to the matrix in which they worked and as a consequence of changes in the phases of the project. The project managers could best be described as boundary-spanning experts and focal managers of a developmental process.

More on the Importance of Hierarchical Level

In the preceding discussions about analyses of time spent and work done, organizational level has already been seen to be a major determinant. Much more can be said about the role requirements at different organizational levels.

Barnard (1938) noted that top management is concerned with broad policies, objectives, and plans. These purposes and objectives become more specific as they filter down to lower levels where the work is actually done. In addition, according to W. A. Scott (1967), unlike middle and lower managers, top managers are both the ultimate teachers and the judges of subordinates. They must be sensitive to the interactions among people below them and to their material resources. But at lower levels in the organizational hierarchy, Whyte (1956) observed that the primary function is to perceive one's task accurately and to conform to it. Technology and controls are most important. Nevertheless, if the broad objectives and policies set at the top are to be operationalized and successfully carries out, managers at lower levels must exhibit considerable initiative (Fiedler & Nealey, 1966).

On the one hand, Argyris (1964a) observed that the objectives of the job and interpersonal factors play more important roles in influencing the managers' effectiveness higher in the hierarchy. On the other hand, Pfiffner and Sherwood (1960) noted that, in particular, first-level supervisors work under considerable time pressure and have frequent and direct personal contact with the work. Nealey and Fiedler (1968) added more specifically that the typical functions of first-line supervisors are production, on-the-job training, contol of materials and supplies, and maintenance. Second-level supervisors are concerned with cost control, setting standards, selection and placement, coordination of work units, and formal training. The second-level manager needs less technical expertise about specific production processes than does the first-level supervisor, for the second-level manager may supervise several departments involving different technical processes.

A survey of 1,476 New York City managers revealed that those at higher levels reported having a considerably greater variety of activities to perform than did those at lower levels (Allen, 1981). Dubin and Spray (1964) analyzed the logs kept by executives over a two-week period. Lower-level executives were more likely than those at higher levels to concentrate their time on a single activity. At the same time, the sheer number of incidents per day in which a manager is involved is highest for first-line supervisors and declines with increasing levels of management. Thomason (1967) for example, reported the average number of activities for different levels of management as follows: foreman, 413; superintendent, 309; area superintendent, 274; general managers, 91.

Pfiffner and Sherwood (1960) noted other differences in activity and function between first-line and middle managers. First-line supervisors are more often in direct personal contact with subordinates, whereas middle managers see their subordinates less often. Middle managers spend more time with their superiors than do first-line supervisors. Middle managers use formal communications in their work to a greater extent than do first-line supervisors.

Roles Enacted. Paolillo (1981b) found that among 352 managers, the importance and time spent on 7 of the 10 roles identified by Mintzberg depended on the managers' level in the organizational hierarchy. Similarly, Klauss, Flanders, Fisher, and Carlson (1981b) asked 753 senior and 847 mid-level federal managers to indicate how important were Mintzberg's roles and how much time was spent on each of them. Seniors attached more importance than did mid-level managers to all the roles except leader, disseminator, and negotiator. They were particularly likely to spend more time acting as figureheads and spokespersons than were the mid-level managers.

In agreement with L. D. Alexander (1979a) and Paolillo (1981b), Pavett and Lau (1983) reported that hierarchical levels made a difference in the importance attached to the different roles. All three studies found that the roles of disseminator, figurehead, negotiator, liaison, and spokesperson were deemed more important at the higher managerial levels than at the lower levels. Consistent with these results, Hall, Bowen, Lewicki, and Hall (1975) reported that among the 10 roles carried out by 103 middle managers in manufacturing, the role of leader was most important and consumed the most time. Being a figurehead was least important and least time consuming.

P. Allen (1981) noted that among the task dimensions of 1,476 managers who were working for New York City, the analytical-evaluative task dimension (in which managers were required to analyze and evaluate laws, problems, programs, work procedures, processes, and reports) was more important for the highest-level managers than for managers at either the entry or the middle level. However, monitoring (in which managers develop and use mechanisms for ensuring adequate progress toward goals, maintaining appropriate records, and inspecting ongoing activities) was less important for the highest level than for the middle or lower levels. In L. D. Alexander's (1979a) previously cited study, hierarchical level made a considerable difference in 7 of Mintzberg's 10 role requirements. With increasing hierarchical level, there were increasing requirements for the roles of figurehead, liaison, monitor, disseminator, spokesperson, and entrepreneur. The negotiator role was seen as being required most by middle managers.

Level and Activity. T. A. Mahoney (1961) concluded, from several studies (for example, L. Strong, 1956; *Fortune*, 1946), that the higher the level of managers' positions, the more hours per week they devoted to their job and the more time they spent in planning and organizing, rather than in the technical work of the organization. This finding was confirmed in the previously cited survey of 452 managers in 13 firms by Mahoney, Jerdee, and Carroll (1965). Whereas supervising was the main activity of 51 percent of the lower-level supervisors, it was the main function of only 36 percent of the middle managers and 22 percent of the top managers. On the other hand, top managers were more likely to be generalists and planners than were lower-level managers.

Second-level managers appear to be more oriented toward their superiors and first-level managers, toward their subordinates (Pfiffner & Sherwood, 1960). T. Burns (1954) found that second-level managers spent more time with their superiors than with their subordinates, and Berkowitz and Bennis (1961), Guest (1956), and Piersol (1958) found that first-level supervisors spent more time interacting with their subordinates than with their superiors. Although face-to-face communication was the most frequent form of interaction for managers at all levels, high-level executives more often initiate than receive contacts, according to the logs they kept for two weeks (Dubin & Spray, 1964).

Time Lag between Decision and Consequences. Jaques (1956) advanced the hypothesis that high-level administrative work is characterized by longtime lags between the time a decision is made and the impact of the decision on the organization. If so, high-level managers would personally exhibit comparatively high degrees of future orientation and tolerance for delayed outcomes in their time perspectives. Jaques's proposition was supported in an investigation of 4 levels of supervisors and managers, from the shift foreman at the bottom to works managers at the top in the same British factory. Almost all decisions of a shift foreman were about matters that occurred within a 2-week period. On the other hand, only 3.3 percent of the decisions of the works manager involved questions of short duration; 50 percent of the decisions of the works manager involved policies with time perspectives of 1 year or longer. No one at lower levels was involved in decisions involving such periods of time (Martin, 1959). However, in a study of 141 managers at 6 levels of a plant, Goodman (1967) failed to find that future orientation and preference for delayed gratification were highly related to the level of an executive's position.

Despite Goodman's (1967) negative results, most other observers agreed with Jaques that the time perspective of managers at higher levels requires them to live with more uncertainty and lack of feedback, to consider longer-range goals, and to be able to remain for long periods without evaluating the effects of their decisions. Decisions at the highest levels involve especially high uncertainty and risk. Thus, W. A. Scott (1967) observed that "top management must have the ability to detach itself from the internal imperatives of coordination and to reflect on the general purposes and objectives of the company in its industry and society." Because of the nature of their role, top managers are often detached from outside judgment or objective criteria against which they can appraise their approach to problems, their decisions, and their philosophy. The production worker can be appraised against the tangible output and the lower-level manager against the department's performance. The long time span of the decision and the subjectivity of the job of the top manager make appraisals more difficult.

According to detailed interviews with 31 senior federal executives in 6 different agencies, Klauss (1981) concluded that the senior federal executive needs the following orientations: a systems view, a strategic focus, and a proactive stance. He or she needs the ability and willingness to maintain a network of formal and informal contacts, to support and encourage staff personnel, to manage diverse interests, to market and persuade, to take risks, and to maintain integrity and credibility. He or she most be concerned for broad-based sources of information. Persistence, persuasiveness, flexibility, open-mindedness, and self-confidence are also important.

Jacobs and Jaques (1987) argued that different critical tasks with different time lags between decisions and their consequences are required of leaders at different organizational levels. As leaders rise in the hierarchical level, the nature of their tasks changes systematically in the direction of requiring greater conceptual effort and the capacity to deal with more uncertain and more abstract constructs. Effectiveness at any given level thus depends on the capacity to learn the role behaviors demanded by the tasks at that level. As Rusmore (1984) demonstrated, fluid intelligence or creativity becomes more predictive of success at higher organizational levels; crystallized intelligence is more predictive of success at lower levels. Jacobs and Jaques (1987) spelled out the different types of activities performed by leaders at the lower, middle, and top echelons of a large corporation, as is shown in Table 20.4.

Leadership at each level has discrete tasks to perform that add value to each other level. The tasks have time spans, as is shown in Table 20.4.

Special Difficulties of Senior Managers. Along with the oft-cited "loneliness at the top" syndrome, as Bruce (1986, p. 19) noted, the tension between attention to the present and attention to the future is specific to CEOs: "if you do not satisfy the present, there will be no future." History judges the CEO on the strategic conceptualizations that contribute to future success, not on maintenance of the present situation. But the present imposes strong demands on the CEO's time, with its numerous review committees, preparations for board meetings and annual meetings, critical regulatory responses to governmental requests, and exorbitantly time-consuming internal and external ceremonial duties. Top corporate managers have to free themselves from these day-to-day operations and short-term goal orientations to focus more attention on long-term threats and opportunities, to provide long-term leadership on strategic issues and their analysis, on the formulation of implementation, on interpretation, and on evaluation (Wortman, 1982). Larger organizations establish a Chief of Organizational Operations to relieve the CEO of these day-to-day burdens.

Peters (1979) noted the peculiar difficulties involved in carrying out the role of CEO or senior executive and the remedies for each of these difficulties. For example, according to Peters, senior managers are given only one option, usually in accord with their preferences. However, over time, they can shape each option presented by subordinates in their review and contextual evaluation. Time is fragmented, but the senior manager can use the fragments as a succession of opportunities "to tackle bits of the issue stream." The fragments also provide a rich variety of information. Although major choices take months or years to emerge, the time provides opportunities to build a strong consensus and requirements for implementation. Peters concluded that top management's most important role is that of shaping the organization's values to provide coherence "in an untidy world, where goal setting, option selection, and policy implementation hopelessly fuzz together." This conclusion was illustrated in Kotter and Lawrence's (1974) study of the activities of city mayors. Effective mayors built consensus from among the key stake holders in favor of a few new directions. The ineffective mayors tended to make major commitments before they had developed the support for them.

Table 20.4 Functional Levels According to Discretionary Time Spans

Time Span	Stratum	Unit Led	Function
20 years	7	Corporation	Strategic: Operates in a nearly unbounded environment, identifies feasible futures, develops consensus on specific futures to create, and builds the required resource base to create open systems that can function in the environment. Conditions the environment to be "friendly" to the systems thus created. Creates a corporate culture and a value system that are compatible with societal values and culture, to serve as a basis for the organizational policies and climate.
10 years	6	Group of companies	
5 years	5	Company	Organizational: Stratum 5 individuals operate bounded open systems thus created. They are assisted by Stratum 4 individuals in managing the adaptation of those systems within the environment by the modification, maintenance, and fine tuning of internal processes and climate and by oversight of subsystems.
2 years	4	Division	
1 year	3	Department	Production: runs face-to-face (mutual-recognition or mutual-knowledge) subsystems—units or groups engaged in specific differentiated functions but interdependent with other units or groups, limited by context and boundaries set within the larger system.
More than 3 months	2	Section	
Less than 3 months	1	Shop floor	

SOURCE: Adapted from Jacobs and Jaques (1987, pp., 10, 11).

Effects of Level by Function. Using Hemphill's (1959) EPDQ, other investigators' have generally corroborated the influence of hierarchical level on a manager's activities.[6] But for positions within the functional areas of data processing, finance, and merchandising, McHenry (1986) reported mainly positive correlations between the pay grade of 343 first-level and middle-level managers in a large retail organization and their activities, depending on their functions. Table 20.3 shows how level makes a difference in what activities a manager performs, but it is also affected by the manager's functional area. For instance, the activity of supervising appears much more strongly linked with the hierarchical level of a position in merchandising than with positions in data processing and finance. On the other hand, long-range planning is related much more to the hierarchical level of a position in finance and merchandising; generally, the hierarchical level effect is less strong in data processing. At each level, the manager's constituents and interests are different. At the top, the manager is concerned with sponsors, clients, and the community, as well as with his or her own subordinates. At the bottom, the first-level supervisors are concerned with the interests of their superiors, their peers, and their subordinates, as well as with the interests of others, such as union stewards or outside inspectors. In all, managers spend relatively little of their time with their superiors, according to Brewer and Tomlinson (1963–64) and, as was just noted, much time may be spent with a wide variety of other parties, not just subordinates (M. W. McCall, 1974, 1977).

Importance of Difference among Organizations

Earlier, it was noted that, generally speaking, the manager with the same type of job in one organization will exhibit the same time profile and pattern of work as his or her counterparts in other organizations. Nevertheless, special characteristics of an organization can make an obvious difference in the manager's activities.

[6] See Liem and Slivinski (1975), Meyer (1961), and Rusmore (1961).

For instance, executives in public utilities will spend more time dealing with community relations than their counterparts in manufacturing. Katzell, Barrett, Vann, and Hogan (1968) studied the relationship between 9 executive role patterns and various organizational characteristics. The data were provided by 194 middle-management personnel working for the U.S. Army. The organizational dimensions that were most highly related to the roles performed depended on the level and mission of the organization within the army; the roles most affected were controlling, staffing, and time spent with other persons. Schneider and Mitchel (1980) used a mailed questionnaire to survey 1,282 field-agency managers working in 1 of 40 different life insurance companies. The investigators were able to identify 6 factors that could be used to describe the activities of the agency managers (general management, training and evaluation, supervising, goal setting, serving clients' needs, and enhancing the visibility and perceived capabilities of their agency and themselves as representatives of the insurance industry). Schneider and Mitchel obtained modest correlations between the frequency in which the agency managers engaged in the 6 factored activities and the characteristics of the agencies studied. General management activity and the enhancement of visibility were more frequent in agencies with a larger number of agents and supervisors. The managers' client-service activities depended on whether the agency was a branch or was independent. Differences in company policies and practices also made a difference in the managers' activities.

Interviews with senior executives of 24 Canadian companies and the executives' responses to questionnaires showed that general managers engaged in different activities, depending on their companies' particular strategies. If the companies were strategically trying to develop themselves by expanding their markets, personnel, and investments, the functions and activities that were most important to their general managers were marketing, finance, and research and development (R & D). If the companies were strategically trying to stabilize themselves by lowering costs and improving products, productivity, and investments, the particular functions of consequence to their general managers were production engineering, finance, and R & D. If the companies were trying strategically to "turn around" to reverse their declining markets, cash flows, and so forth, along with paying attention to finance and production, general managers needed to be flexible and able to deal with uncertainties and crises. Yet, regardless of the company's strategy, the general manager had to be an effective leader. This human resources function played an important integrative role in whatever other roles were assigned to the manager (Herbert & Deresky, 1987).

Changes in Organization, Technology, and Society

Changes in the managers' organization will result in considerable changes in their activities. In a study of production foremen in four plants, Wikstrom (1967) initially found that the foremen tended to make decisions like individual workers without reference to larger organizational considerations. Then, numerous specialists were introduced into the organization who influenced production in various ways. After the specialists were introduced, the foremen were required to coordinate and sequence the manufacturing processes. Since the foremen had to coordinate the impact of the various specialists, they had to assume managerial functions and decision-making responsibilities. K. W. Harris (1968) surveyed 23 school superintendents, each with more than 25 years of tenure in the same position. The superintendents reported spending much less time currently on curriculum and pupil personnel problems than they had done a quarter-century earlier and much more time on problems involving buildings, finance, and school-community relations. Clearly, the activities of the superintendents had changed within the same school districts with changes in societal requirements.

Baliga and Hunt (1988) detailed the finer tuning of requirements for leadership as the organization goes through its life cycle of gestation, birth, growth, maturity and revitalization or death. For gestation and birth, effective leadership at the top calls for developing a viable strategy and acquiring the resources to translate the strategy into an organizational reality. The representation of ideas and transformational leadership among external stakeholders are most salient here. Likewise recruitment and commitment from key personnel are critical. For lower-level managers, the socialization of subordinates is of primary importance, along with the selection of appropriate technologies and the design of information, control, and evaluation systems.

During the growth stage, Baliga and Hunt noted that although senior managers need to maintain transformational leadership with external stockholders, their transactional activities are of more consequence with subordinates. For lower-level managers, initiation, consideration, and task and relations-oriented leadership become most important.

At maturity, senior managers are required to pay more attention to subordinates, compared to their earlier emphasis on relations with external stakeholders. Ideally lower managers should be able to handle all problems that occur at levels below them. With decline and revitalization, more transformational attention by senior management is again needed with external stakeholders as well as with subordinates. Lower-level managers have to assist the seniors in this regard.

Computerization. Much of the research that is discussed in this chapter predated the computer and electronic revolutions. Today, most of the management decision making in many firms is computer assisted or even fully programmed. The personal data processor at the manager's desk may provide instant electronic contact with every other manager or professional in the firm, as well as instant contact with voluminous banks of information. Clearly, new descriptions of the way managers spend their time and the activities in which they engage are essential. Leavitt and Whisler (1958) and Uris (1958) anticipated that in the 1980s changes in the content and scope of the manager's role would occur because of the computer. They noted that the ranks of middle managers would be reduced and that top managers would communicate directly with lower-level managers through their computers. The "downsizing" of management in many U.S. firms in the 1980s through layoffs, "outplacements," and early retirement (McCormick & Powell, 1988) are a validation of these earlier prophesies about the decline of middle management. And the activities as well as the number of first-level supervisors may change. Kerr, Hill, and Broedling (1986) suggested that there will be an increased use of self-managed, autonomous work groups in which leadership is shared or at least informally provided by a team leader. Managers of such groups will be external to the groups. Their most important leadership behaviors will be to facilitate self-observation, self-evaluation, and self-reinforcement (Manz & Sims, 1987). Vanderslice (1988) goes further to propose flat, "leaderless organizational structures."

Computer-driven automation and information management will continue to increase at the workplace of first-level supervisors and their work groups. Specialized staff units will continue to grow in size and importance, adding to the prospects of increasing the traditional conflicts between the supervisors and the staff experts. The particular activities and characteristics of the management process of first-level supervisors are expected to be altered as a consequence. For example, first-level supervisors will be expected to spend more time with outside staff consultants who are involved with management information systems, new technologies, retraining workers, equal employment opportunities, and legal issues. They will also spend more time serving as participative leaders of their work groups.

Pedigo (1986) completed a survey of the impact of the computer on the manager's role. First-level managers were the heaviest computer users. However, over time, it is expected that as these first-level managers are promoted, usage will increase at higher levels. Pedigo may be underestimating upper-management's usage in that even though such managers may not use computers directly, they may be dependent on computer-generated information obtained from staff assistants. Again, as the college graduates of the 1980s and 1990s, who have "hands-on" experience with personal computers, move into middle- and senior-management ranks, one will, no doubt, ultimately see a personal computer being used at these levels by managers as much or more than the pencil, the memo, or the telephone.

Effective Managerial Activities and Role Taking

Managers in the same positions may be required to engage in somewhat different activities, or they may do so as a matter of personal competence or preference. They may be more effective or less effective, depending on the extent to which they emphasize certain activities and processes at the expense of other work they might do. Campbell, Dunnette, Lawler, and Weick (1970) proposed a person-process-product model of managerial effectiveness. The "person" in the model refers to the managers' competencies, such as those discussed in Chapters 7 and 8. The "product" is an organizational result, such as productivity. The "process" is the manager's on-the-job activities. All three components—person, process, and product—need to be understood in evaluating the manager's effectiveness, which depends on identifying and judging the observable actions and roles, which lead to the accomplishment of the organization's objectives (Porter, Lawler, & Hackman, 1975).

All college presidents have to engage in a lot of the same activities. Nonetheless, few are like Father Theodore Hesburgh of Notre Dame. Over a 35-year-period in office, Father Hesburgh's actions raised Notre Dame's endowment from under $10 million to over $300 million. At the same time, he greatly increased Notre Dame's scholarly mission at the expence of moving football (ordinarily a prime reason for alumni giving) from its preeminent niche to a more appropriate place in the university (Anonymous, 1987).

Weiner and Mahoney (1981) sampled the statistical performance of 193 manufacturing corporations. They concluded that what the top leadership did had a strong influence on the corporations' profitability.[7]

Effective school principals must contend with multiple demands placed on them daily. They must not only be instructional leaders, but administrators, head teachers, moral leaders, role models, community workers, social service providers, and even fund-raisers. Time for reflection on the need for systematic changes in the school is hard to find (Tewel, 1986). Allen (1981) formulated a model for the school principal's performance that showed how successful outcomes for the school depend on the principal's selection of appropriate roles to enact for a given situation. Support for the model was obtained from panels of experts.

Differences in Activity Rates. Recent quality evidence is consistent with the general conclusion that effective leaders are more active than are ineffective leaders,[8] although the contrary was found for first-level supervisors in dealing with production in less well-conducted investigations in the 1950s.[9] These supervisors of well-run work groups may have had more free time to plan and think ahead. They may have been more efficient in getting done what needed to be done, or they were better at delegating. Or, they may have had more competent subordinates. Martinko and Gardner (1985) suggested that the earlier findings about supervisors' activity rates were too frought with statistical problems to be accepted with any confidence. A much more strict study by Komaki, Zlotnick, and Jensen (1986) supported the more general conclusions that effective leaders are more active than are ineffective ones. They observed 24 managers in a medical insurance firm up to 20 times over the interval of the study, using a rigorous set of observational procedures, according to the operant-analysis categorizations and activity classifications shown in Table 20.5. Sets of observers were trained to achieve high interobserver agreement of 90 percent or better. Of the 24 managers, 12 were identified by their superiors as effective and 12 were identified as marginal.

Significantly more time was spent by the effective than the marginal managers in collecting information on employees' performance (monitoring). The effective managers were more likely to observe employees in action than to depend on self-reports or secondary sources. They more often sampled the employees' work, but they did not provide any more positive, neutral, or negative consequences. Komaki inferred that given their greater monitoring behavior, the effective managers were more likely to provide contingent reinforcement of the subordinates. Similar observational analyses were completed on the behavior of 19 sailboat racing captains by Komaki, Desselles, and Bowman (1989). The correlation of the order in which the boats finished the race (from first to last) was −.53 with amount of monitoring by their captains and −.59 with the amount they fed back consequences. Their coaches' ratings of the captains' effective handling of

---

Lieberson and O'Connor (1972) and Salancik and Pfeffer (1977) provided evidence that leadership influenced corporate performance less than did environmental or organizational factors. R. H. Hall (1977) maintained that such leadership activities are only important in times of organizational growth and crisis. The issue remains controversial and will be discussed more fully in Chapter 31.

[8] See Chapter 25.
[9] See, for example, Guest (1956), and Ponder (1958).

Table 20.5 Definitions and Examples of Categories on the Operant Supervisory Taxonomy and Index

Category	Definition	Example
Performance consequences	Indicates knowledge of someone else's performance.	"I noticed you showed the 1008 in your report." "You saved us from making a very big mistake."
Performance monitoring	Collects information about an individual's performance.	Listening to report given by subordinate. Watching women work on CRTs. "Did you set up the rehab audit?" "Mary, did Cathy find them?"
Performance antecedents	Instructs, reminds, or conveys an expectation of performance.	"You can just write 'no comment' in there if you want to." "Let's try to coordinate these two if we can."
Own performance	Refers to his or her own performance.	"I'm just amazed that I didn't notice it was there." "I'll tell Marilyn myself."
Work related	Refers to the work but not to the performance.	"We will never pay for the replacement of a prosthesis, is that correct?" "If they hear anything about HMOs, we will be interested in that."
Nonwork related	Does not refer to work issues or concerns.	"My sister found the blouse and she never finds me anything unless it's on sale."
Solitary	Occasions in which a manager is not interacting.	Working at one's desk on paperwork. Reading a booklet. Looking through a computer printout. Walking upstairs.

SOURCE: Komaki, Zlotnick, and Jensen (1986, p. 272).

their crews were related in the same way to their observed monitoring and "consequences" behavior.

Effective and Ineffective Supervisors' Activities. Observational studies of the work done by effective and ineffective production supervisors showed that the better performers compared to the poorer performers (as gauged by performance appraisals, group productivity, and the like) spent less time on purely production matters, gave more general work orders, initiated interpersonal contacts more frequently, and spent more time with staff and service personnel outside their work group (Ponder, 1958).

Differences in the Amount and Quality of Planning. Despite the general conclusions of Mintzberg (1973) and others that managers do not have much time for reflection and planning, how much time is spent on planning seems to differentiate effective from ineffective managers at the top as well as the bottom of the hierarchy. Stagner (1969) found that the time that 109 CEOs spent in organizational planning was

related to the firm's profitability. Similarly, General Electric (1957) foremen with better production records were seen to spend more time in long-range planning and organizing than were foremen with poorer production records. E. Williams (1968) compared the activity patterns and preferences of 30 effective and 30 ineffective executives. The effective executives scored significantly higher in planning, as well as in responsibility, human relations, decision making, and problem solving. Although the two samples differed in the time devoted to organizing and controlling, the ineffective executives spent less time in planning and rated organizing and controlling significantly higher in importance than did the effective executives. Apparently, the comparative deficiency in planning among the ineffective executives was accompanied by a perceived need for higher degrees of control.

The quality of planning has been assessed from the demonstrated skills of the planners. Bray, Campbell, and Grant (1974) showed that skill in planning, as measured in A T & T assessment-center exercises, was one of the best predictors of subsequent managerial success. Boyatzis (1982) also found competence in planning to be related to managerial effectiveness. Gillen and Carroll (1985) reported a correlation between planning skill and unit production of .34 in manufacturing firms and .43 in aerospace firms for a total sample of 103 unit managers in 10 firms.

Other Functional Differences. Gillen and Carroll (1985) also found that the production of the unit led by the manager correlated with the manager's supervisory skill (.46, .25), coordinating skill (.19, .30), and staffing skill (.23, .12). In addition to differences in planning, other functional differences were found by Heizer (1969) in managers assigned to the same line and staff positions, which correlated with their differential effectiveness. Heizer asked 200 managers to write incidents of effective and ineffective managerial behavior. Effective managers differed significantly from ineffective managers in planning, coordination, delegation, and staffing. In the same way, Kavanagh, MacKinney, and Wolins (1970) reported that the extent to which the department head fulfilled the functions of planning, investigating, coordinating, evaluating, supervising, and representing was related to the job satisfaction of the supervisors below the department head.

Alignment with the Surrounding Organization. Effective managers differ from ineffective ones in what they do to contribute to the surrounding organization. In a study of 345 R & D employees in a large chemical laboratory, Allen, Lee, and Tushman (1980) discovered that the overall performance of technical-service projects was better if the project manager took responsibility for linking the project with other parts of the organization. Ghiselli and Barthol (1956) found that successful supervisors differ from unsuccessful ones in perceiving themselves as planful, loyal to the company and to subordinates, and having the responsibility of working with people to achieve organizational goals. Unsuccessful supervisors saw themselves as good fellows, well liked, responsible for production, and able to rely on their ingenuity and resourcefulness, rather than on their planning or their loyalty to the company or to their employees, to get the job done. Successful supervisors identified with their work group and its members, whereas unsuccessful supervisors were interested in making a living.

Contact Patterns. According to Lake and Martinko (1982) and Martinko and Gardner (1984a, 1984b), who observed and coded the activities of highly effective and moderately effective school principals, the moderately effective principals spent more time with students and parents but less time with other outsiders than did the highly effective principals. The highly effective principals initiated 64 percent of the contacts; the moderates, 54 percent. While 47 percent of the moderates' contacts were judged to be human relations oriented, only 30 percent of the highly effective principals' contacts were so judged. Conversely, 66 percent of the highly effective principals' contacts were task oriented; 51 percent of the moderately effective principals' contacts were so designated.

Differences in Managerial Role Taking

Mintzberg's roles have been the basis of a number of studies of effective and ineffective managers. With a sample of managers drawn from different hierarchical levels, McCall and Segrist (1980) correlated an index of the managers' rate of advancement with the extent to which the managers carried out Mintzberg's roles. Significant correlations were found between the rate of promotion and carrying out the roles. The highest correlation was between the managers' rate of promotion and enacting the entrepreneur role ($r = .25$). Unexpectedly, the importance of the leader role was inversely related to the promotion rate ($r = -.15$). In all, it was possible to establish a multiple correlation of .39 between enacting six roles and the index of promotion rate.

Harrison (1978) compared the amount of time successful and unsuccessful CEOs spent in each of Mintzberg's 10 roles with a financial index of success based on six balance-sheet ratios. Data were collected for each executive using a work-diary method. The results indicated that the successful executives spent more time in leader and monitoring activities. They also spent more time in entrepreneurial and liaison activities than did they unsuccessful executives. However, the

successful executives spent less time in allocating resources and handling disturbances than did their unsuccessful counterparts. Similarly, Pavett and Lau
(1982) surveyed 48 middle- and lower-managers with 60
questionnaire items to assess their engagement in
these roles. Scores were correlated with reliable evaluations of the managers' performance independently obtained from three raters. The managers' judgment of
the importance and the time they spent in the liaison
role correlated with their rated performance. The leadership role and the role of technical expert were seen
as less important and as requiring less expenditure of
time by managers who were rated as better performers.

Although the managers collectively had indicated
that the leadership and entrepreneurial roles were most
important among all the roles on which they rated
themselves, the findings about the downgrading of the
role of leader by the better performing managers are
disquieting. Despite their consistency with those of
McCall and Segrist (1980), the findings are in considerable conflict with the results obtained by Harrison
(1978), Tsui (1984), and Morse and Wagner (1978) that
are presented in the following sections. The explanation may lie in the fact that, as Farrow, Valenzi, and
Bass (1981) reported, manipulative managers are most
likely to advance in salaries at a faster rate than is justified by their seniority, functional area, education, and
the like, although such manipulation is seen as unsatisfactory and ineffective by the managers' subordinates.
Manipulative behavior may be judged to fit the role of
entrepreneur but not that of leader. Another explanation is that the role of leader (motivating and activating
subordinates) may be counterproductive in a highly
mechanistic organization in which the behavior of subordinates is dictated by rules and regulations. As an
academic vice president told a dean's search committee in a highly bureaucratized university, "The dean
cannot be a leader!"

A Descriptive Questionnaire Analysis. Morse and
Wagner (1978) used the following modified list of 9 of
Mintzberg's (1973) managerial roles to classify managerial activities: (1) strategic problem solving, (2) resource
managing, (3) conflict handling, (4) organizing, (5) information handling, (6) motivating, (7) providing for

growth and development, (8) coordinating, and (9) managing the organization's environment. After several refinements by means of factor analysis, they constructed a list of 51 activities that could be used by
managers to evaluate another manager with whom
they worked closely. By rating managers on each activity, a colleague could evaluate the manager's behavior.
Six extracted factors covered the original 9 activities as
follows:

1. *Managing the organization's environment and its
resources.* Effective managers are proactive and stay
ahead of changes in their environment. They base
plans and actions pertaining to the organization's resources on clear, up-to-date, accurate knowledge of the
objectives of the company.

2. *Organizing and coordinating.* Effective managers
suit the amount of formal rules anf regulations in their
organization to the tasks to be done and to the abilities
and personalities of the people doing them. These
managers are not difficult to get along with or to coordinate with.

3. *Information handling.* Effective managers make
sure that information entering the organization is processed by formal reports, memos, and word of mouth on
a timely basis so it is usable, current, and provides rapid
feedback. They make sure that the person who has to
use the information clearly understands it.

4. *Providing for growth and development.* Effective
managers ensure, through career counseling and careful observation and recording, that their subordinates
are growing and developing in their skill for performing
their work. They guide subordinates by commending
the subordinates' good performance.

5. *Motivating and conflict handling.* Effective managers transmit their own enthusiasm for attaining organizational goals to others. They are not plagued by recurring conflicts of a similar nature that get in the way of
associates' efforts to perform their jobs.

6. *Strategic problem solving.* Effective manager periodically schedule strategy and review sessions involving the design of projects to improve organizational
performance and to solve organizational problems.
They spend considerable amounts of time looking at
their organization for problem situations and for opportunities to improve their subordinates' performance.

Evaluations of 231 managers by colleagues were higher among better performing managers on all six dimensions in three of six offices, according to objective criteria, such as net profit, budgeting data, and the volume of customer billing. The evaluations were correlated between .41 and .65 with superiors' rankings of how well the managers were performing. Multiple regression analyses suggested that the managerial activities that were of most consequence to the end results were, first, managing the organization's environment and resources and, second, motivation and conflict handling. But the consequences depended on the organization's objectives. Thus, according to multiple regressions, in contrast to other kinds of firms, in a data processing firm, accounting and handling financial records for clients, information handling, and strategic problem solving by the managers contributed the most to the appraised performance of the managers by their superiors.

A similar line of investigation was completed using the Management Practices Survey (MPS). Yukl and Kanuk (1979) showed that for 151 employees of beauty salons who described their salon managers, the average monthly profit margins of the salons correlated .47 and .49, respectively, with the extent to which managers were seen to engage in clarifying and motivating activities.

Numerous other examples can be provided. Thus, cadet sergeants' clarifying and motivating correlated .26 and .30, respectively, with the performance of the ROTC units for which they were responsible (Yukl & Van Fleet, 1982). Problem solving and recognizing/rewarding correlated .39 and .42, respectively, with the behavior of managers when the managers were responsible for the performance of insurance salespersons in retail department store outlets (Yukl & Carrier, 1986). For 24 school principals studied by Martinko and Gardner (1984b), whose managerial behavior was described by their schoolteachers, again problem solving, clarifying, monitoring, and motivating correlated with effectiveness (between .36 and .49), as did networking/interfacing (.47). Miles (1985) found that these and all the other 13 scales of activities of the MPS by 48 leaders of home economics programs correlated between .21 and .42 with the quality of the county programs they

administered. Similar results were found for department heads.

A Behavioral Checklist Analysis. Tsui (1984) pointed out that a manager's reputation for effectiveness depends on satisfying at least three constituencies: superiors, peers, and subordinates. The performance appraisals earned by a manager, merit pay increases, rate of promotion, and career advancement were highest when the manager's reputation for effectiveness was high among all three constituencies. Such threefold reputational effectiveness correlated with behavioral checklists of roles taken by a sample of managers. Mean correlatons for the threefold reputational effectiveness of managers and the extent to which the managers engaged in each of six roles were as follows: leader (.45), liaison (.23), entrepreneur (.37), environmental monitor (.34), resource allocator (.37), and spokesperson (.35). Multiple regression analyses indicated that almost 30 percent of the reputational effectiveness could be accounted for alone by the extent to which managers engaged in the roles of leader and entrepreneur. Expected differences emerged, however, among the constituencies in what role activities were important for reputational effectiveness. In a subsequent study, Tsui and Ohlott (1986) obtained results suggesting that the various constituencies have similar models of the elements of managerial effectiveness but they differ on the relative importance to attach to each. The roles of leader and entrepreneur (planner, controller, implementer of change) are most salient for managerial effectiveness in their models of what is important in the role repertoire of the focal manager they described.

A Three-Stage Model of Effective Leadership. Neider and Schriesheim (1988) developed a three-stage model that is presented in Figure 20.4. The three stages deal with precursor conditions, maintenance functions, and reassessment and monitoring. Precursor conditions are the organizational functions and tasks that take place to set the stage for effective leadership. They include a thorough job analysis, detailed compensation analysis, good selection strategies, and sound orientation training of the subordinates. In the first stage, effective leaders pay attention to the data that

Figure 20.4. A Diagnostic Model of Effective Leadership

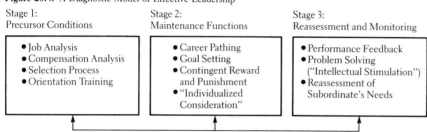

Stage 1:
Precursor Conditions

- Job Analysis
- Compensation Analysis
- Selection Process
- Orientation Training

Stage 2:
Maintenance Functions

- Career Pathing
- Goal Setting
- Contingent Reward and Punishment
- "Individualized Consideration"

Stage 3:
Reassessment and Monitoring

- Performance Feedback
- Problem Solving ("Intellectual Stimulation")
- Reassessment of Subordinate's Needs

SOURCE: *Neider and Schriesheim (1988).*

are necessary to clarify fully for subordinates how their efforts will result in the attainment of the objectives of the job. Equity and desired rewards that are contingent on performance are key considerations. Effective leaders see that the subordinate's knowledge, skills, and abilities match the requirements of the job. The second stage involves career pathing for the subordinate, goal setting, and performance-contingent and individualized consideration focused on the development of the subordinate through suitable delegation. The subordinate's self-esteem and the organization's attractiveness to the subordinate are enhanced.

In the third stage, the effective leader provides feedback and meetings at which the alignment of the subordinate's needs and performance with the organization are reassessed and misperceptions are corrected. Intellectually stimulating leadership here helps solve the subordinate's problems.

Summary and Conclusion

Executives must both manage and lead (Hosmer, 1982). Leaders manage and managers lead, but there are considerable variations in both and only some degree of covariation in what both do. Much depends on the level and function of the manager.

Diaries and observational studies compete with in-

terviews and questionnaire surveys in helping us to understand how leaders and managers spend their time and the work they do. There is much more to management than planning, directing, controlling, and supervising subordinates. However, the manager's effectiveness depends, to a considerable degree, on getting work done through others and networks of others. Activities are brief, fragmented, and discontinuous, rather than deliberate and reflective. Key activities include monitoring the environment, coordinating and representing others, and handling information and its sources. Interpersonal skills are needed at all hierarchical levels.

A manager's hierarchical level affects the time during which decisions are to be made and the lag in feedback about the effects. Work overload is a common experience at all levels as are systematic differences in the effective and ineffective performance of managers.

Earlier chapters delineated how leaders and managers differ in competencies, attitudes, and values. This chapter showed how their activities and roles have been described and prescribed and how organizational leaders and managers who are in the same position may differ in their models of what is required and how they will actually perform in the position. These differences in preferred and actual styles, their antecedents and consequences, are the subjects to which we turn next.

Autocratic and Authoritarian versus Democratic and Egalitarian Leadership

The duality has been seen throughout history. How should people be led? How should people be governed? How should people be guided? Two views prevailed (based on opposing doctrines about human nature). Either human nature was cursed by original sin or human nature was blessed with the inherent ability to find salvation. If people were essentially bad, they had to be controlled, directed, and uplifted by authority. If people were essentially good, they must be given the freedom in which to learn, to grow, and to overcome.

Two hundred years ago, the framers of the U.S. Constitution recognized the benefits and the costs of an independent executive and a democratic legislative body. They handled the dilemma posed by balancing the powers of the executive against the 2 elected senators from each of the sovereign 13 states and population-based representatives of the male, white, property-qualified electorate. This arrangement recognized the contribution of the democratic majority vote of state-wide and electoral district representatives to the commitment, interests, and satisfaction of the various constituencies. At the same time, the indirectly elected president could provide the need for order and for the execution and maintenance of federal laws, foreign affairs, and national defense. Much authority and power for direction and control were given to the president, but with safeguards. The president was commander-in-chief of the armed forces, but he had to face reelection and could be removed from office by the legislature. He could veto the legislative decisions of the representatives, but the veto could be overridden by the legislature.

This same dilemma confronts the individual leader today. How can the leader balance the advantages of a more democratic approach, which ordinarily contributes better to the commitment, loyalty, involvement, and satisfaction of followers, with a more authoritative approach, which contributes to order, consistency, and the resolution of conflict?

The Two Opposing Approaches

Leaders and managers vary in how they deal with the dilemma. A great many different concepts have been used to describe such variations. The concepts draw a distinction between work-related and person-related behavior; many seem to have the notion of autocracy at one extreme and democracy at the other. A list of different, but correlated, ways of describing the extremes is presented in Table 21.1.

These dichotomies are simplifications. Sweeney, Fiechtner, and Samores (1975) completed a factor analysis of the leadership focus of 103 male employed part-time college students that corroborated the high degree of complexity to be found in examining authoritative and democratic leadership. The factors included authoritarian role preference, authoritarian role pressure, egalitarian role preference, egalitarian role pressure, balanced manager, people-oriented manager, assumed similarity between opposites, contemptuous indulgence, supportive values, tolerance of people and organizational tolerance.

Nevertheless, the same persons who display one type of authoritarian behavior, say, initiation of structure, are also likely to be seen as displaying work facilitation and persuasion. The same persons who display one type of democratic behavior are likely to be seen as sup-

Table 21.1 Conceptions of Autocratic and Democratic Leadership

Source (by year)	Autocratic and/or Work-related Concepts	Democratic and/or Person-related Concepts
1938: Lewin and Lippitt	Authoritarian, autocratic	Democratic
1949: Nelson	Directive, regulative, manipulative	Democratic
1950: Katz, Maccoby, and Morse	Production centered	Employee centered
1951: Hemphill, Seigel, and Westie	Initiating structure	Considerate
1957a, 1957b: Fleishman	Production emphasis	Employee emphasis
1958: Kahn	Path-goal structuring, modifying goals, enabling achievement	Direct-need satisfaction
1960: Cartwright and Zander	Goal achievement oriented	Group maintenance oriented
1960: McGregor	Theory X	Theory Y
1960: Bass	Coercive, persuasive	Permissive
1964: Blake and Mouton	"9,1" (production, not employee concerned)	"1,9" (employee, not production concerned)
1964: Day and Hamblin	Punitive	Nonpunitive
1961a: R. Likert	High performance, technical, close supervision	Supportive, group methods, general supervision
1962: Blau and Scott	Distant, formal, aloof, cold	Close, informal, warm
1965: F. C. Mann	Administrative, technical	Human relations oriented
1966: Bowers and Seashore	Work facilitative, goal emphasizing	Interaction facilitative, supportive
1966a, 1966b: P. J. Burke	Directive	Nondirective
1967b: Bass	Task, self-oriented	Interaction oriented
1967a: Fiedler	Task oriented	Relations oriented
1967: R. Likert	Systems I and II	Systems III and IV
1969a: Heller	Coercive, directive	Joint decision making
1970: Wofford	Order, achievement, personal enhancement	Personal attraction, security and maintenance
1971: Yukl	Decision centralization, initiation	Considerate
1974: D. R. Anderson	Traditional, prescriptive	People centered, supportive
1974: Bass and Valenzi	Directive, negotiative (manipulative), persuasive	Consultative, participative, delegative
1974: Zaleznik	Charismatic	Consensual
1974: Vroom and Yetton	A (decisions)	C, G (decisions)
1976: Flowers	Closed	Open
1976: Keller and Szilagyi	Nonrewarding	Rewarding
1985: Misumi	(P)erformance leadership	(M)aintenance leadership

portive, considerate, and people oriented as well, but the correlation is far from perfect. As will be detailed later, empirical support for this contention was demonstrated by Edwards and Rode (1986), among others.

The Authoritarian Leadership Cluster

Although investigations use many terms that are not fully overlapping in meaning, generally, correlations will be high among those described in one or another of the authoritarian ways that involve organizing to get things done. That is, the same leaders who are described as autocratic or authoritarian (Lewin & Lippitt, 1938) will also be described as directive (Bass & Barrett, 1981; Heller, 1969a), "Theory X" (McGregor, 1960), coercive and persuasive (Bass, 1960), concerned with production (Blake & Mouton, 1964), lone decision makers (Vroom & Yetton, 1974), initiators of structure (Fleishman, 1953c), production centered (R. Likert, 1961a), goal emphasizers and work facilitators (Bowers & Seashore, 1966), task oriented (Fiedler, 1967a), and concerned about performance (Misumi, 1985).

The punitive task-directed leaders, say, the "bulls of the woods," the early twentieth-century shop foremen, the exploitative authoritarians (R. Likert, 1961a), make the decisions for their group and are concerned with what is needed to get the job done. Likewise, such leaders discourage subordinates' contributions to the decision process and pay little or no attention to the subordinates' needs. The more modern and less punitive task-focused leaders reserve decisions for themselves and remain more concerned about getting the job done than about the needs of their subordinates.

Task-directed leaders initiate structure, provide the information, determine what is to be done, issue the rules, promise rewards for compliance, and threaten punishments for disobedience. Leader-focused or task-focused leaders use their power to obtain compliance with what they have decided. Such directive and "regulative" leaders depend on their knowledge of policies and regulations and their official rank to regulate the behavior of their subordinates and their technical knowledge to solve problems to gain their subordinates' respect and willing compliance with their directives (Nelson, 1950). They are more often charismatic than consensual (Zaleznik, 1974).

The Democratic Cluster

The democratic or egalitarian cluster involves the leader's concern about the followers in many different ways. This democratic cluster will emerge for leaders who are considerate (Fleishman, 1953c), democratic (Lewin & Lippitt, 1938), consultative and participative (Bass, 1976), consensual (Zaleznik, 1974), employee centered (R. Likert, 1961a), concerned with people (Blake & Mouton, 1964) and the maintenance of good working relations (Misumi, 1985), supportive and oriented toward facilitating interaction (Bowers & Seashore, 1966), relations oriented (Fiedler, 1967a), and oriented toward joint decision making (Heller, 1969a) and group decision making (Vroom & Yetton, 1974). Democratic leaders are "Theory Y" ideologists (McGregor, 1960). They solicit advice, opinions, and information from their followers and share decision making with their followers. Democratic leaders use their power to set the constraints within which followers are encouraged to join in deciding what is to be done. Democratic leaders depend on their followers' skills, as well as on their own interpersonal ability and knowledge of their followers' individual needs, interests, and capabilities (Nelson, 1950).

Figure 21.1 displays the most salient of the distinctions in terms of three clusters. The authoritative cluster involves active leadership and more emphasis on the task than on relationships. The democratic cluster likewise involves active leadership but focuses more on relationships. The third cluster, to be fully examined in Chapter 25, involves laissez-faire, inactive leadership and no particular emphasis on task or relationships. Here, the leader abstains, withdraws, or abdicates responsibilities and shows none of the concerns seen in the authoritarian or democratic clusters.

Illustrating the meaningfulness of the clusters, Stanton (1960) reported higher scores for consideration and for a human relations orientation among managers of clerical employees of one firm that was known for more democratic supervision, compared to another firm that was known for more autocratic supervision. Conversely, the amount of initiation of structure was much higher in the autocratic than in the democratic firm.

Latent or Underlying Structure

Edwards and Rode (1986) asked 100 students, mainly in ROTC, to complete four different ways of measuring authoritative and democratic leadership preferences. The Leader Behavior Opinion Questionnaire[1] assessed how frequently they should initiate structure as leaders and how considerate they should be. Blake and Mouton's (1978) Managerial Grid was used to describe a concern for people and a concern for production. Hersey and Blanchard's (1973) LEAD-self questionnaire generated authoritative telling and selling scores and democratic, participating and delegating scores. Fiedler's (1967a) Least Preferred Co-worker (LPC) score was used to assess task and relations orientation.[2] The intercorrelations among the authoritative task measures were positive but rather low. The same was true

[1]See Chapter 24 and Fleishman (1960) for an extended discussion of the concepts and measurement of consideration and initiation of structure.
[2]For a discussion of Managerial Grid, the LEAD-self questionnaire, and the LPC score, see Chapter 23.

Figure 21.1. Conceptual Relations among Selected Styles of Leadership

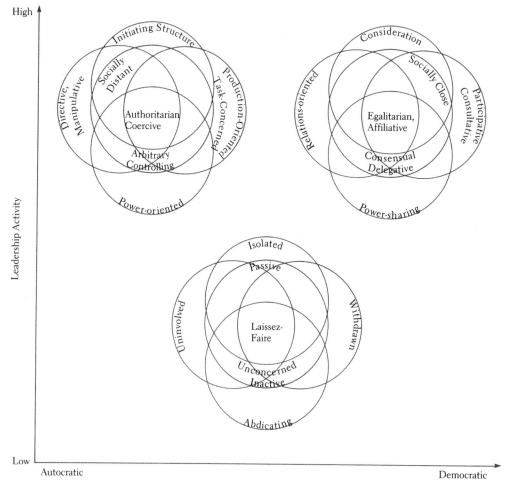

for the democratic measures. However, a path model of the intercorrelations, adjusted for measurement errors by Jöreskog and Sorbos (1978), suggested that the latent structure underlying the observed correlations was a continuum stretching from authoritative behavior at one end to democratic behavior at the other. This structure is consistent with the display hypothesized in Figure 21.1.

Distinctions among Styles of Leadership

This and the next four chapters will look at the following conceptions of the differences in leadership styles or patterns of leadership behavior and their effects: the overarching conception and evidence about authoritarian versus democratic leadership (this chapter), participative versus directive decision making (Chapter 22), relations versus task orientation (Chapter 23), consideration versus inition (Chapter 24), and laissez-faire leadership versus motivation to manage (Chapter 25).

What are the distinctions among these dichotomous conceptions? Authoritarian versus democratic leadership is the most multifaceted. It refers to the way power is distributed, whose needs are met, and how decisions are made. Participative versus directive leadership refers primarily to how decisions are made. Relations- versus task-oriented leadership focuses on whose needs are met. Consideration versus initiation of structure is a behaviorally factor-derived dichotomy. Consideration and initiation refer to how decisions are made and to the structuring of tasks, goals, and role relationships. Laissez-faire leadership and motivation to manage refer to the extent to which leadership is either avoided or attempted.

Karmel (1978) drew attention to the ubiquity of initiation and consideration in the study of leadership and efforts to theorize about it. What she primarily added was the importance of the total amount of both kinds of activity by leaders in contrast to inactivity. Thus, she brought us back full circle to Lewin and Lippitt (1938), who conceptualized leadership as authoritarian (initiating), democratic (considerate), or laissez-faire (inactive).

Authoritarian and Democratic Leadership

Why do we emerge with just two overarching clusters of leadership styles? Possibly because there are only two ways of changing a follower's behavior (apart from using drugs or physical force). The leader alters either the follower's information, understanding, and ability to cope with the task at hand or the follower's motivation to deal with the task. When the leader has more relevant knowledge than the follower, task-focused direction provides for the necessary transfer of information. Powerful leaders can arouse motivation. But in many situations in which followers have as much or more information than the leader or in which power is more widely shared, the motivation of followers is more likely to depend on involving them in decisions about handling the task and their concerns about it and themselves.

Misumi (1985) argued that the two fundamental dimensions, which he labeled P for the performance leadership function and M for the maintenance leadership function, underlie all the others in the clusters. Thus, for instance, participative and democratic leadership are situationally specific manifestations of the underlying maintenance function whose aim is to promote social integration and group stability. The manifestation of the maintenance function may appear as consideration if it is directed primarily toward satisfying subordinates' needs.

The Authoritarian Leader's Use of Power and Ability

MacIver (1947) and Bass (1960) noted that authoritarian leaders may depend on their power to coerce and their ability to persuade. An able leader successfully persuades others to follow him or her because they expect that following the leader's suggestions will result in solving the problems the group faces. A powerful person successfully coerces others to follow him or her because the power of the leader's position or the power of the leader as a person makes others expect that the leader will reward them for compliance or punish them for rejection. An able leader can indirectly reinforce the behavior of others. Such a leader can provide the cues that help them attain their goals. A powerful leader can directly reinforce the behavior of others by granting or denying them rewards or punishments for their behavior (Bass, 1960).

These types of authoritarian leadership were described by F. C. Bartlett (1926), who observed that leaders in any complex social group maintain their success, either because of the social prestige of their position and their personal capacity to impress and dominate or by virtue of their personal capacity to persuade their followers. Blau and Scott (1962) described the authoritarian supervisor as one who, among other things, uses his power to be strict rather than lenient, to supervise closely, and to ensure adherence to procedures. Parten (1932), observing the spontaneous play of nursery school children and, using one-minute sampling, found two types of leadership possible in the situation: persuasive leadership, which employs diplomatic, "artful" suggestion, and leadership through personal power, which uses brute force to dominate others. Zillig (1933) observed the same two types of leader in the German classroom: leaders who dominate and leaders who direct and guide.

Developmental Requirements for Democratic Leadership

Democratic leadership usually requires more maturity and some education in its processes. Some leaders may be identified as democratic on the basis of their use of parliamentary procedures and majority decision making. Others may consult; strive for consensus; and pursue an open, trusting, follower-oriented relationship. Such consensus leadership has deep roots in the American national character (Cooley, 1956). According to Zaleznik (1974), the idealized image of the leader in America is that of brother (or sister) rather than father (or mother). The leader is first among equals whose sense of timing may be more important than his or her expertise. The leader may be more dependent on the followers than the followers are on him or her. Compromise, caring, and a sense of responsibility and attachment to followers characterize the consensus leader.

Ideal Types

In the first studies to contrast the authoritarian and the democratic leader, the authoritarian leader dictated what was to be done and was unconcerned about the group members' needs for autonomy and development. The democratic leader shared the decision making with subordinates and was concerned about their need to contribute to deciding what was to be done. The authoritarian leader was personal in praise or reproof of each member; the democratic leader was factual and rational. The authoritarian leader emphasized his social distance from the members; the democratic leader deemphasized social distance.

Following the earlier experiments with authoritarian and democratic leadership, subsequent studies tended to concentrate on one of four aspects of the distinction between authoritarian and democratic leadership: (1) whether decision making was shared by the leader, (2) whether the followers were of primary concern to the leader, (3) whether social distance was maintained, and (4) whether punishment and coercion were employed.

It must be stressed that these are ideal types of authoritarian and democratic leadership. In practice, one is likely to find much variation and overlap. For instance, a benevolent autocrat, although he or she is likely to be dictatorial, may also be considerably concerned about the needs of his or her subordinates. The democratic manager may encourage group decision making but may also place a lot of emphasis on getting the job done, as well as on the needs of the group. The charismatic may rely on personal power and the followers' desire for identification, but also may choose to support democratic efforts and the attainment of pro-

social goals. Some researchers have taken greater care than others to define and "purify" the patterns of leadership behavior to be studied. But often it is difficult to determine whether a given pattern of leadership behavior examined was democratic, participative, considerate, relations oriented, or some combination of these characteristics.

Effects of Authoritative and Democratic Leadership

The Prototype Experiments

Consistent with Lewin's (1939) ideas about the dynamics in groups, two seminal experiments were completed (Lewin & Lippitt, 1938; Lippitt, 1940a) to explore the effects of democratic and authoritarian group atmospheres upon the behavior of group members. They were preceded by a report by Mowrer (1938) on how infractions of rules were reduced at the New Haven Children's Center in 1937 when a democratic approach was offered the children (aged 4 to 12) to deal with problems, in contrast to the authoritarian staff control that had been in place before.[3] Reporting on the studies, Lippitt (1940) defined what was meant by democratic and authoritarian leader behavior. By means of careful coaching and practice, the authoritarian leader was trained to determine all policy for group members, to dictate the methods and stages of goal attainment one step at a time, to direct the actions and interactions of group members, and to praise the members in a personal manner. The democratic leader was trained to encourage group members to determine their own policies, to give them perspective by explaining in advance the steps toward attaining the goals, to award them freedom to initiate their own tasks and interactions, and to praise them in an objective manner. The leaders were adults. The group members were 10-year-old boys and girls, who were closely matched on several control variables. Two groups of five members each worked on hobby projects. The behavior of leaders and members was recorded by trained observers.

Both the leaders and the group members initiated more actions in the authoritarian-led group. Members of the authoritarian-led group had more submissive re-

[3]Mentioned in Fox (1954).

actions to the leader, however, and treated him less as an equal than was the case in the democratic group. In the authoritarian-led group, members became progressively more submissive to the leader. Although they tended to respond to the leader, rather than to initiate interaction with each other, they hesitated to approach him because to do so might further reduce their personal power and freedom of movement. The democratic form of leadership, on the other hand, tended to increase the freedom of action of group members. The members of the democratically-led group exhibited less tension and hostility, and their subgroups were more cohesive and enduring than was the case for the authoritarian-led group.[4] Curfman (1939) replicated Lippitt's (1940a) first experiment with two clubs of fifth and sixth graders with similar results.[5]

Implications and Contrary Points of View

The research and development activities of R. Likert (1961a, 1967, 1977b) flowed from the direct inference from this prototype experiment that the democratic approach was to be advocated in organizations for the fostering of effectiveness and satisfaction. In this, Likert was joined by the entire human relations movement (see, for example, Argyris, 1957; McGregor, 1960). In counteraction, joining with the classical "scientific managers," Miner (1968) among others, argued for an emphasis on the manager-leader as a task-oriented, authority figure. Blake and Mouton (1964) pioneered the point of view that the best leaders and managers were both highly concerned for production and highly concerned for people and could integrate the two approaches. A fourth group of advocates, such as Fiedler (1967a), Vroom and Yetton (1974), and Hersey and Blanchard (1977), argued that which style was best depended on the situation.

As we shall see, in this and succeeding chapters, there is some truth in all these positions. The evidence has accumulated that in specified circumstances, authoritarian direction may, in fact, result in heightened productivity, particularly in the short term, but, overall, the democratic approach is likely to be more effective, particularly in the long run. And, in general, under

most conditions, working for a democratic supervisor will be more satisfying. This last conclusion is simplest to document.

Table 21.2 lists the empirical laboratory and field studies on the subject that were completed between 1953 and 1975. It can be seen that the satisfaction of members was the rule, rather than the exception, under democratic leadership. On the other hand, the more positive correlations were found between the authoritative leadership style and productivity. Fortunately, a more rigorous meta-analysis, including some of these findings as well as more recent reports, provided a greater opportunity to be more specific about these effects on productivity. In field studies, it could be concluded that a democratic style worked better. In the laboratory, however, the autocratic style resulted in more productivity.

As displayed in Table 21.3, Miller and Monge (1986) first completed such a meta-analysis of short-term laboratory experiments of the effects on productivity and satisfaction of "employees" of autocratic versus participative "supervisors" by Ivancevich (1974); Katzell, Miller, Rotter, and Venet (1970); McCurdy and Lambert (1952); and Shaw (1955). In these experiments productivity was greater, the more authoritarian than democratic was the leader in the laboratory manipulation. For the four short-term laboratory experiments in which the "supervisor" was trained to act autocratically or democratically, productivity was greater with authoritative, directive supervision. The mean correlation between productivity and authoritativeness was .33.

However, Miller and Monge (1986) also completed a meta-analysis (see Table 21.3) for 10 longer-term field studies. Consistent with what will be reviewed next, they found strong support in reports from 41 analyses, which generally dealt with longer-term results, that in such real-life settings, the mean correlation was .27 between democratic supervision and the productivity of the persons or groups supervised. They also concluded that more democratic supervisory styles correlated with the felt satisfaction of subordinates. The mean correlation was .34.

Consistent with this conclusion, as a consequence of the massive survey evidence accumulated by R. Likert (1977b) and his colleagues, we shall see that despite the fact that in the short run, in such selected circum-

[4]Laissez-faire leadership was introduced as a third leadership cycle by Lippitt (1940a) in his expansion of the experimental investigation. Its effects will be discussed in Chapter 25.
[5]Mentioned in Fox (1954).

Table 21.2 Positive, Zero, or Negative Correlations Obtained (1940–75) of Democratic and Autocratic Leadership with Members' Satisfaction and Productivity

Author	Democratic Leadership Correlated with		Autocratic Leadership Correlated with	
	Satisfaction	Productivity	Satisfaction	Productivity
Adams (1952)		0		0
Anderson (1959)	+	0		0
Argyle, Gardner, and Ciofi (1958)		+		
Beam (1975)	+			
Bergum and Lehr (1965)				+
Calvin, Hoffman, and Harden (1957)				+, 0
Day and Hamblin (1964)			−	−
Foa (1957)	+			
Hamblin, Miller, and Wiggins			0	
Harnquist (1956)	+			
Johnson and Smith (1953)		0		0
Ley (1966)				
Lippitt (1940a, 1940b)				
Lyle (1961)		+		+
McCurdy and Eber (1953)		0		0
Mahoney (1967)		0		+
Mullen (1965)	+	0	−	0
Mullen (1966b)	+	0	−	0
Patchen (1962)				+
Sales (1964)		0		0
Shaw (1955)	+			+
Snadowsky (1969)	+			−
Spector and Suttell (1956)		0		0
Torrance (1953)		0		+
White and Lippitt (1960)		0		0
Ziller (1957)	0	−		
Zweig (1966)		+		
Summary				
Positive relations (+)	8	3	0	7
Zero relations (0)	1	11	1	10
Negative relations (−)	0	1	3	2

stances as brief laboratory experiments, authoritarian supervision pays off in more productivity than does democratic supervision, in the long run, democratic approaches tend to generate larger improvements in an organization's productivity as well as in the satisfaction of its employees.

Effects of Leadership Style on Performance

As was already mentioned, results have been mixed in the short-term and concurrent studies of the effects of autocratic and democratic leadership on a group's per-

formance when the performance objectives are immediate productivity and the solution of a problem, rather than developing and motivating the capabilities of the team.

When Autocratic Leadership Is Better. Not unexpectedly, the military tends to value the use of authority more favorably. In a survey of 30,735 U.S. Army superiors, peers, and subordinates of commissioned and noncommissioned officers, Penner, Malone, Coughlin, and Herz (1973) found that leaders who established a high level of discipline were likely to be

Table 21.3 Correlations between Productivity and the Amount of More Democratic and Less Authoritarian Leadership in Field and Laboratory Settings

Setting	N	Correlation
Field Settings	1,193	.27
Abdel-Halim (1983a)	229	.29
Abdel-Halim and Rowland (1976)	106	.28
Fiman (1973)	170	.12
Jenkins and Lawler (1981)	58	.28
Neider (1980)	67	.30
Roberts, Miles, and Blankenship (1968)	6	.47
Schuler and Kim (1978)	383	.31
Veen (1972)	40	.33
Vroom (1960a)	108	.26
Yukl and Kanuk (1979)	26	.37
Laboratory Settings	209	−.33
Ivancevich (1974)	64	−.54
Katzell, Miller, Rotter, and Venet (1970)	76	−.21
McCurdy and Lambert (1952)	21	−.02
Shaw (1955)	48	−.39

SOURCE: Adapted from Miller and Monge (1986, p. 739).

rated much higher in their overall performance by their superiors. Consistent with this, Torrance (1953) reported that U.S. Air Force aircrews who were given feedback by highly authoritarian methods exhibited greater improvement in performance than did those who were given feedback by less highly structured methods.

Some supportive evidence was also found elsewhere. Hise (1968), studying simulated business groups, found that productivity was positively related to close rather than general supervision. M. E. Shaw (1955) obtained results that indicated that the speed and accuracy of a group's performance in a highly structured communications network were significantly higher under autocratic than under democratic leadership. In a study of groups in a formal organization, Shepherd and Weschler (1955) found that psychosocial distance between the leader and the followers was associated with fewer communication difficulties. Working closely together was related to greater difficulty in communication. Bergum and Lehr (1963) studied subordinates' monitoring performance under different conditions of supervision. They found that the vigilance of subordinates could be maintained at fairly high levels under authoritarian conditions.

Even in the short run, whether authoritarian leadership pays off will depend on the extent to which the leader has more knowledge about what needs to be done and control of the necessary resources. This payoff can be routinely demonstrated in leadership training exercises. Authoritarian leadership can be productive if the trainee who is assigned the role of autocratic leader happens, by chance, to know more about the problem to be solved than does the person who is playing the role of subordinate (Shackleton, Bass, & Allison, 1975). When authoritarian leaders know the correct answer to such exercises, they can better ensure highly accurate group outcomes than can democratic leaders. But authoritative leaders with misinformation can also lead their groups farther astray than can democratic leaders with the same degree of misinformation (Cammalleri, Hendrick, Pittman, et al., 1973).

When Autocratic Leadership Is Worse. More deleterious effects are likely when punitive and disciplinary actions are included in the autocratic leadership. In earlier chapters, we observed that supervisors tend to avoid disciplinary, punitive action even when confronted with poor performance by subordinates. Thus, for instance, Maier and Danielson (1956) reported that even when disciplinary rules call for punishment, supervisors tend to avoid it. They perceive that punishment will reduce productivity, even when it is used to control the violation of rules. In fact, Keller and Szilagyi (1976) found that punitive leadership, rather than improving performance, primarily increased role ambiguity. Day and Hamblin (1964) found punitive and close supervision to be connected with reductions in productivity and group harmony. They studied 24 groups of 4 members each, who had to follow elaborate blueprints to assemble models of molecules of pegs, springs, and various colored balls. In this complex task, the members were subjected to either punitive or nonpunitive supervision, as well as to close or general supervision. Punitive and close supervision, in contrast to nonpunitive and general supervision, tended to increase the subjects' feelings of aggression toward their co-workers, as well as toward their supervisor, which significantly lowered their productivity.

Numerous other experiments point to the deleterious main and side effects of punitive supervision. French (1957) examined the effects of the "supervisor" who obtained compliance by using the power to fine paid participants who were working at a simple task of sorting IBM punched cards according to the total number of holes the cards contained. The assignment was supposedly part of a research project. Participants were fined for their failure to maintain the standard of speed and accuracy. In comparison to participants who were rewarded with extra pay when they reached and maintained the standard, participants who were punished by fines for failure were more likely to show signs of resistance to maintaining production. After four working periods had occurred, punishment for failure become detrimental to speed and accuracy. The participants had a greater desire to leave the work and were more likely to want to do something else and to make suggestions for changing the work situation. Furthermore, they showed greater feelings of aggression, liked their supervisor less, and were less likely to accept the supervisor as competent to evaluate their work. In a similar experiment, Raven and French (1958b) levied fines when participants failed to conform to the demands of "supervisors." These fines led the participants to resist by overconforming to the suggestions of their supervisors. That is, metaphorically, if partici-

pants were ordered against their will to "polish the silverware," they rubbed so hard that they rubbed off all the silver.

Experiments by deCharms and Hamblin (1960) yielded similar results, finding that punitive supervision resulted in increased tension in and lower productivity by workers. These studies of the effects of punitive supervision are consistent with the general psychological findings that severe punishment tends to be disruptive and anxiety producing. Mild punishment, however, may provide, under certain circumstances, more appropriate attention to the failure to comply with authority and serve as a way to eliminate undesired acts. Thus, Georgopoulos (1965) observed higher productivity to be associated with a pattern of supervisors' disciplinary behavior that employees regarded as "just right" and "not too strict." Mild aversive reinforcements and negative feedback have their uses.

When Democratic Leadership Is Better. Comrey, Pfiffner, and Beem (1952) studied employees at six levels of organization in the U.S. Forest Survey. Supervisors of more effective departments were described as sympathetic, democratic, social, and willing to share information. Similarly, Comrey, High, and Wilson (1955a, 1955b) studied supervisors and workers in an aircraft factory. Supervisors of effective groups were characterized by adequate authority, communication downward, sympathy, lack of arbitrariness, and lack of hypercritical attitudes toward employees. Argyle, Gardner, and Ciofi (1958) also reported higher rates of productivity, reduced personnel turnover, and reduced absenteeism under democratic, nonpunitive supervision in work groups in seven British factories. Zweig (1966) found that democratic supervisors were rated by higher management as being more effective than supervisors exhibiting less democratic styles of behavior. Similarly, Hall and Donnell (1979) reported that the managers whose career advancement was the fastest were least likely to subscribe to "Theory X" beliefs[6] that workers are lazy, immature, and need to be carefully monitored and controlled; those who were advancing the slowest were more likely to do so.

---

[6]McGregor (1960) formulated Theory X (autocratic beliefs about how workers needed to be led) and Theory Y (democratic beliefs about how workers needed to be led).

Levy-Leboyer and Pineau (1981) obtained interview data from 151 French laboratory supervisors. The success of their laboratories was appraised subjectively and from research publication records. Leaders of more successful laboratories supervised less strictly, allowed for participation by technicians in decision making, and held more frequent meetings and evaluations.

In a federal agency, J. C. White (1972) observed that both the effective county office managers and the effective managers at headquarters used a more democratic style. The effectiveness of business supervisors and purchasing managers was also seen by H. C. White (1971a, 1972) to be associated with the extent to which they were more democratic and less autocratic. In the same way, Hollman (1973) and Tanimoto (1977) found that the effectiveness of management by objectives, as seen by subordinates, was greater when practiced by a more democratic than a more autocratic manager. Other studies have shown that democratic approaches in organizations have a favorable effect on the physical and mental health of the persons in those organizations (Caplan, Cobb, French, et al., 1975).

When Alternative Styles of Leadership Are Better. Contingent reinforcement and transformational leadership, as was noted in earlier chapters, may be more effective than is the emphasis on either authority or democracy. Ziller (1957) observed greater problems among members who were led democratically. Neither autocratic nor democratic leadership was as effective as a type of leadership that consistently reinforced the correct performance of members by approval and by suggestions for improvements. Spector and Suttell (1956) demonstrated that this type of leader resulted in better achievement by the group than did an authoritarian type who made decisions for the group or a democratic type who permitted maximum participation by members.

D'Angelo (1973) reported that a "human resources" style, which involves "striving to continually expand the areas over which the manager's subordinates have self-direction and self-control," was associated with more effective work groups before and after an organizational development program for 103 sales managers and their 360 salesmen subordinates than were the less effective autocratic or human relations styles. Again,

Howell (1985) showed that in contrast to task-structuring and considerate leaders, actors who were trained as charismatic leaders were most effective in enhancing productivity in the face of normative resistance among subordinates.

Prescient of the future interest in transformational leadership, as mentioned in Chapter 12, Litwin and Stringer (1966) organized 45 business students into three "firms." The firms competed in the construction and marketing of "radar equipment" manufactured from Erector Set materials. Three different climates were created: (1) *an authoritarian-structured* business, with a strong emphasis on the careful definition of duties, the exercise of formal authority, and so forth, (2) *a democratic-friendly* business, in which cooperative behavior, group loyalty, teamwork, freedom from punishment, and a loose informal structure were emphasized, and (3) an *achieving* (transformational) business, in which innovation was encouraged, competitive feedback was given, pride in the organization was fostered, a certain amount of risk taking was deemed desirable, and high personal goals were encouraged.

The "president" of each company was a member of the research staff and adopted an authoritarian, democratic, or achieving leadership style. The achieving (transforming) style resulted in the greatest dollar volume, number of new products, and cost-saving innovations. The authoritarian style did succeed in producing the finished goods with the highest quality, primarily by never deviating from the specifications. At the same time, consistent with most other findings, students who were working with a democratic president were more satisfied with their jobs than were the students in the other two firms.

No Differences. Still other investigators obtained no significant differences in productivity between democratically and autocratically led groups. Thus, both Lyle (1961) and Spector and Suttell (1956) found no differences in the performance of groups under democratic and autocratic leadership. However, Lyle (1961) observed a tendency for democratic groups to work faster under restricted communication, while authoritarian groups worked faster under open communication. Results obtained by S. Adams (1952) indicated that bomber crews performed more effectively under medium than under high or low degrees of democratic leadership. Sales (1964) obtained no significant difference in the performance scores of groups with democratic and autocratic leaders. Johnson and Smith (1953) studied classes taught traditionally and under democratic leadership. They found no significant differences in achievement gains or in the students' evaluations.

Mullen (1965, 1966b) also failed to find that group productivity was related to supervisory style. Likewise, T. A. Mahoney (1967) found no relationship between democratic supervision and measures of organizational effectiveness in a study of industrial organizations. Similarly, Swartz (1973) found that whether football coaches were autocratic, democratic, or laissez-faire was unrelated to their success in winning games. G. H. Graham (1969) conducted one class democratically according to Theory Y and another autocratically according to Theory X.[7] The two groups did not differ in examination scores. The top quartile of students did better when led by the democratic instructor but the lower 75 percent of students got better grades under the autocratic instructor.

Effects on Satisfaction

Ordinarily, satisfaction and morale are likely to be lower with autocratic supervision and higher with democratic supervision. Under autocratic leadership greater resentment, less loyalty, less commitment, less involvement, and less satisfaction are commonly found (Gouldner, 1954). Such subjective reactions to the supervisors and poorer relations with them affect the willing compliance of subordinates with their supervisors' initiatives (Barnard, 1938). In both the short term and the long term, subordinates generally will be more satisfied with democratic leaders.

When Democratic Leadership Is Better. Beam (1975) showed that enlisted personnel in the U.S. Navy had a strong desire to be treated democratically, regardless of the level of technology or physical activity in which they were involved. Mohr (1971) obtained similar results in 144 works groups from 13 local health de-

partments, as did Pennings (1975) in 40 branch offices of a large U.S. brokerage firm. The subordinates' satisfaction was strongly associated with democratic supervision in these as well as in many other large-scale field studies.

Baumgartel (1957) studied attitudes and motivations of scientists in governmental research-and-development labs under three leadership conditions (democratic, authoritarian, and laissez-faire). He found that scientists who worked under the democratic leadership held the most favorable attitudes and had a greater job motivation, whereas the least favorable attitudes were found among those who worked under the authoritarian leadership. In the same way, Harnquist (1956) observed that group members tended to feel more satisfied under democratic than under autocratic leadership, and Ziller (1957) found members to be least satisfied under autocratic leadership. Mullen (1965, 1966b) reported that the satisfaction of employees was associated with democratic supervision but saw no relationship between supervisory style and employees' requests for transfers. But in a study of personnel turnover, Ley (1966) found that the supervisor's authoritarian behavior was the factor that was most frequently associated with subordinates' quitting their jobs.

Mandell and Duckworth (1955) reported that the overall morale of 64 trade employees in civil service was high if the employees said that their "supervisor lets them know how they are doing." In a series of surveys to be discussed in more detail later, R. Likert (1961a) found that employees of public utilities revealed higher job satisfaction when their supervisors were more "personal" than "institutional" in their dealings and more "downward" or employee oriented and when the supervisors trained the subordinates for better jobs. Supervisors of high-morale groups differed from supervisors of low-morale groups in that they reviewed their subordinates' work more frequently, welcomed the discussion of mutual problems with subordinates, carried on group discussions, and kept subordinates posted on new information.

D'Angelo (1973), cited earlier, found that sales managers who believed themselves to be practicing a democratic, human relations style brought about more

[7]See McGregor (1960).

change in their subordinates in an organizational development program than did those who believed they were practicing either authoritarian or "human resources" leadership. H. H. Meyer (1968) studied two plants, one managed according to Theory Y and the other managed according to Theory X.[8] Workers under the more democratic (Theory Y) type of management reported higher felt responsibility, risk, reward, warmth, and identity. In the same way, Beehr and Gupta (1987) compared two manufacturing firms—one, formally democratic; the other, more traditional—that were similar in size and technology. They found that employees' perceptions, attitudes, and behavior were more favorable in the democratic firm.

Hendrix and McNichols's (1982) survey of 4,786 military and civilian personnel in the U.S. Air Force showed that managers who were described as self-enhancing, outspoken, and demanding and who used their authority as their primary means of influencing their subordinates were seen to contribute to a much less attractive organizational climate, to much less job satisfaction, and to much less perceived productivity than were other more democratic managers who tended to show concern for their subordinates and for group processes. Results were the same for three different work settings involving customer service, routine jobs, and unique jobs with a lot of autonomy.

Similarly, Brollier (1984) surveyed 93 directors of departments of occupational therapy and 348 staff therapists. The directors' democratic leadership had much more of a positive effect on the staff's satisfaction than on the staff's performance. A survey by Field (1984) of 295 human services professionals indicated that democratic leadership tended to promote greater job satisfaction among the staff, particularly satisfaction with salaries and career advancement.

Although the American public was led to believe that the 11,500 unionized air controllers went on strike in August 1981 for unreasonable economic demands and because of peer pressure, a U.S. Department of Transportation task force discovered that they struck because they wanted improvements in working conditions to alleviate job stress and because their managers practiced autocratic values and beliefs (Bowers, 1983).

[8]See McGregor (1960).

In 1989, the newly formed union of air controllers made the same claims that morale was low because of autocratic management (Cushman, 1989).

No Differences. Some studies have failed to find that democratic or autocratic supervision had any significant effect on satisfaction. Thus, with experimental groups of students, Hamblin, Miller, and Wiggins (1961) reported no relationship between authoritarian leadership and group morale. Again, J. D. White (1963) examined whether the morale of boards of directors was affected by how they were led. Although the power of members was found to be higher on boards with democratic than with autocratic leaders, morale was not related to the different styles of leadership.

In the case of sports' coaches, Browne and Mahoney (1984) concluded that it sometimes appears best for the coach to act in an authoritarian manner, but at other times, it is best for the coach to be more democratic by talking to players with individualized consideration and by allowing them to participate in goal setting.

Antecedent Conditions That Moderate the Effects

Taylor (1980) pointed out that immature, dependent, inexperienced subordinates are more likely to expect and accept authoritarian direction and that democratic leadership is likely to result in their more rapid development. Likewise, Nisbett (1986) suggested that a more democratic leadership is desirable as the work force becomes more educated and seeks greater participation, as business becomes more complex and requires a team of experts to deal with its problems, and as high technology increases in usage. Chapter 9 noted that authoritarian leadership works better with authoritarian followers and in authoritarian cultures. Other potential personal and interpersonal modifiers have also been discussed. Chapters 26 through 30 look at how situational conditions may affect the leader's style, and Chapters 32, 33, and 34 will examine how race, sex, and culture make a difference. In this chapter, I introduce some of the findings that have demonstrated that the effects of authoritarian and democratic leadership depend on these antecedent conditions.

Effects of Followers' Expectations, Orientation, and Competence

Evidence of the effect was provided by McCurdy and Eber (1953) who arranged for leaders to be coached in democratic and autocratic patterns of behavior. Authoritarian participants solved problems somewhat less speedily under democratic than under autocratic leadership.

According to French, Morrison, and Levinger (1960), autocratic leadership is likely to generate dissatisfaction and hostility in subordinates unless they see it as a legitimate part of the supervisor's role. Thus, Foa's (1957) study of groups of Israeli workers under democratic and autocratic leadership found that groups with authoritarian and democratic expectations were about equally well satisfied with democratic leaders. But when leaders were autocratic, crews with authoritarian expectations were better satisfied than were those with democratic expectations. Hemphill (1949b) noted that arbitrary inconsistency and reversal of opinion by the leader are more readily tolerated in groups that lack well-established rules and regulations, well-defined goal direction, and strong intermember cohesiveness.

Vroom and Mann (1960) studied industrial work groups that varied in size and in style of supervision. In the small groups, high rates of interaction occurred between workers and supervisors and egalitarian leaders were preferred. In the large groups, members interacted less frequently with each other and with their leaders and exhibited more positive attitudes toward authoritarian leaders. Calvin, Hoffmann, and Harden (1957) constructed experimental groups that differed according to their members' scores on tests of intelligence and the authoritarianism or egalitarianism of the leaders. The performance of groups composed of bright members did not differ under the authoritarian and egalitarian leadership. But dull members in authoritarian-led groups were more effective than were dull members in the egalitarian-led groups.

Circularity. Kruglanski (1969) reported that managers tended to supervise less closely those subordinates whom they trusted. However, a circularity occurs. Strickland (1967) found that laboratory "supervisors" came to mistrust "subordinates" whom they were directed to monitor closely and increased their trust of "subordinates" whom they were not instructed to watch closely. In the same way, McFillen (1978) and McFillen and New (1978) failed to find any significant relationship between supervisory rewards or punishment and subordinates' performance, but subordinates' performance caused a difference in closeness of supervision. Low-performing subordinates were more closely supervised. Finally, McFillen and New (1979) demonstrated experimentally that not only is mistrust increased under close supervision, but the supervisor attributes more success to the closely than to the generally supervised subordinate who succeeds and more failure to the closely supervised subordinate who fails.

Immediate Task Demands

Which leadership style works best depends on the task of the leader and the led. Thus, according to Rudin (1964), a punitive style of supervision leads to good performance on simple tasks and to poor performance on complex tasks. Becker and Baloff (1969) suggested that the optimum style of leadership is likely to depend on whether the task involves information processing or the generation of ideas.

In a laboratory experiment involving complex mechanical tasks under close or general supervision and punitive or nonpunitive styles, Day and Hamblin (1964) found that close supervision produced a large increase in aggressive feelings toward the supervisor. Close supervision did not affect satisfaction with the task, but production was significantly lower. The punitive style also resulted in increased aggressive feelings toward the supervisor, again without any effect on satisfaction with the task. As with close supervision, punitive supervision led to a decrease in production. On the other hand, Patchen (1962) obtained a positive relationship between close supervision and better performance in manual-type work when there was strong group cohesiveness and when the supervisor was seen as rewarding rather than punitive. Thus, although close supervision is usually considereed a part of a more autocratic style, its effects may depend more on whether it also includes a punitive component. (A benevolent autocrat would be more rewarding and less punitive.)

The phase in the group's work also makes a difference. R. C. Anderson's (1959) survey of leadership in experimental groups disclosed that groups under authoritarian leaders required less time in the planning phases, but were less efficient in the task-solution phases. Consistent with what was said earlier, democratic leadership resulted in greater satisfaction by members in both phases of problem solving. Subsequently, Doyle (1971) found that in group problem-solving tasks, egalitarian leadership was most effective in the analysis phase of problem solving, while in the final, synthesizing phase, in which coordination becomes more important, groups with powerful leaders were particularly effective.

Falling Dominoes Again

As was seen in Chapter 18, managers' behavior toward subordinates depends on how the managers' superiors act toward the managers. Thus, D. Katz (1951) found that highly productive groups had less close supervision from their foremen who, in turn, were less closely supervised by their superiors. Hunt, Osborn, and Larson (1975) observed that whether upper-level management is autocratic or not has an impact on what sort of leadership style is most effective at the lower levels. In the same way, Morse (1953) studied employees and supervisors in an office situation and found that although general supervision and delegation of authority facilitated the workers' satisfaction with the work group, they did not foster job satisfaction or satisfaction with the companay unless the supervisors' orientation toward employees was reinforced by higher management.

Large-scale, Long-term Comparisons of Autocratic and Democratic Systems

The outstanding application of democratic as opposed to autocratic influence processes in organizations has been the massive effort at the University of Michigan. Strong evidence was accumulated from over 500 studies completed between 1950 and 1977 that in the long run, democratic leadership pays off both in higher productivity and greater satisfaction by employees. The first study was completed by Katz, Maccoby, and

Morse (1950) in the home office of a large insurance company. Twenty-four work groups were studied, half of whom were high and half of whom were low in productivity. Each highly productive unit was matched with another unit that was low in productivity. Differences in supervisory behavior between the high- and low-productivity units were assessed by means of interviews with both supervisors and their subordinates. Highly productive supervisors more frequently were employee centered than production centered. They were more likely to exercise general rather than close supervision and they were more likely to differentiate their roles from those of their subordinates in terms of the duties they performed.

Next, Katz, Maccoby, Gurin, and Floor (1951) studied railroad maintenance-of-way workers. Again, the more productive supervisors were found to be more employee centered and to exercise more general supervision than those who were less productive. However, no difference in role differentiation was found. The line of investigation was continued by Morse and Reimer (1956), who showed that although authoritarian methods contributed more to increased productivity in an insurance firm during the first year of an experimental effort to change, a sizable drop in performance followed in subsequent years because of the adverse impact of the authoritarian approach on human factors.

These studies led to the formulation of a rationale for organizational improvement. This rationale relied partly on democratizing the leadership patterns in the organization, predicated on the efficacy of democratic over autocratic processes.

Rationale

Borrowing heavily from the original experimental concepts and results of Lewin and Lippitt (1938), R. Likert (1961a) conceived of four systems of interpersonal relationships in large organizations: (1) exploitative autocratic, (2) benevolent autocratic, (3) consultative, and (4) democratic.

These systems varied as System 1 to System 4 on a variety of criteria. Likert proposed and demonstrated that moving organizations away from System 1 and 2 and toward System 3 and 4 would result, given sufficient time for effects to take place, in increases in both the productivity and satisfaction of employees.

Method. The Profile of Organizational Characteristics (POC)—based on survey questionnaire results—generates an asssessment of where the organization is perceived to lie on the dimensions between System 1 and System 4. The leadership and influence processes in the consultative and democratic systems 3 and 4 are such that supervisors and subordinates trust each other a great deal, supervisors are very supportive, very easy to talk to, and virtually always get subordinates' ideas to try to make constructive use of them. There is an emphasis on economic and achievement motivation, as well as on personal worth. The subordinates' participation in goal setting is encouraged, along with bottom-up communication. Subordinates are influential in determining goals, tasks, and methods. Decisions and controls are decentralized.

As for leadership in the autocratic systems 1 and 2, the exploitative autocrat of System 1 emphasizes threats, fear, and punishment with some promise of reward. The benevolent autocrat of System 2 emphasizes more positive and less negative reinforcement. Top-down communication is stressed. Subordinates have little influence on goals and methods. Decisions and controls are centralized and are made person to person.

R. Likert (1967) applied Bowers and Seashore's (1966) four dimensions of leadership behavior to distinguish among autocratic and democratic leaders. He found that System 4 (democratic) leaders were highest and System 1 (autocratic) leaders were lowest on the four dimensions, as follows: (1) support—friendly, pays attention to what one is saying, listens to subordinates' problems, (2) team building—encourages subordinates to work as a team and encourages the exchange of opinions and ideas, (3) goal emphasis—encourages best efforts and maintains high standards, and (4) help with work—shows ways to do a better job; helps subordinates plan, organize, and schedule; and offers new ideas and solutions to problems. Figure 21.2 shows the major elements that differentiate the systems. The mean responses describing a System 1 organization would be found to the far left side of the profile. The mean responses in a System 4 organization would be

to the far right. For instance, there would be virtually no confidence in subordinates in a System 1 organization and a great deal of such confidence in a System 4 organization.

Overall Results. Correlations of the respondents' mean scores on the POC with the quality and quantity of organizational performance range from .3 to .6 (R. Likert, 1977a). In other words, in the more than 500 studies completed, positive associations generally have been found between measures of the organizations' performance and whether they are closer to democratic systems 3 and 4 than to autocratic systems 1 and 2. It is impossible to attribute particular effects exclusively to changes in leadership style. However, given the pattern of large-scale, long-term changes reported by R. Likert (1977b), which were associated with changes in both leadership and other aspects of organizational development, it seems most plausible to attribute some of these effects, at least, to the changes in leadership.

The correlations among the scales of leader, peer, subordinate, and organizational behaviors shown in Figure 21.1 range between .4 and .8. These correlations indicate that there is considerable consistency among these various assessments of the autocratic or democratic systems.

Industrial Studies

The more than 500 studies completed by 1977 were carried out in petroleum, automotive, pharmaceuticals, investment banking, insurance, delivery service, publishing, utilities, textiles, office equipment, packaging, paper making, and railroad companies. Research also was done in governmental organizations, hospitals, schools, colleges, correctional institutions, military organizations, and voluntary organizations. Data were obtained from more than 20,000 managers at all hierarchical levels and more than 200,000 nonsupervisory employees.

R. Likert (1975) reported that the shift from System 4 to System 1 between 1969 and 1970 at a General Motors plant resulted in substantial increases in direct labor efficiency in 1971 and 1972, and although indirect labor efficiency declined between 1970 and 1971, it sharply increased between 1971 and 1972.

Figure 21.2 Profile of Organizational Characteristics

Organizational Variables	System 1	System 2	System 3	System 4	Item No.
How much confidence and trust is shown in subordinates?	Virtually None	Some	Substantial Amount	A Great Deal	1
How free do they feel to talk to superiors about job?	Not Very Free	Somewhat Free	Quite Free	Very Free	2
How often are subordinates' ideas sought and used constructively?	Seldom	Sometimes	Often	Very Frequently	3
Is predominant use made of 1 fear, 2 threats, 3 punishment, 4 rewards, 5 involvement?	1, 2, 3, Occasionally 4	4, Some 3	4, Some 3 and 5	5, 4, Based on Group	4
Where is responsibility felt for achieving organization's goals?	Mostly At Top	Top and Middle	Fairly General	At All Levels	5
How much cooperative teamwork exists?	Very Little	Relatively Little	Moderate Amount	Great Deal	6
What is the usual direction of information flow?	Downward	Mostly Downward	Down and Up	Down, Up, and Sideways	7
How is downward communication accepted?	With Suspicion	Possibly with Suspicion	With Caution	With a Receptive Mind	8
How accurate is upward communication?	Usually Inaccurate	Often Inaccurate	Often Accurate	Almost Always Accurate	9
How well do superiors know problems faced by subordinates?	Not Very Well	Rather Well	Quite Well	Very Well	10
At what level are decisions made?	Mostly at Top	Policy at Top, Some Delegation	Broad Policy at Top, More Delegation	Throughout but Well Integrated	11
Are subordinates involved in decisions related to their work?	Almost Never	Occasionally Consulted	Generally Consulted	Fully Involved	12
What does decision-making process contribute to motivation?	Not Very Much	Relatively Little	Some Contribution	Substantial Contribution	13
How are organizational goals established?	Orders Issued	Orders, Some Comments Invited	After Discussion, by Orders	By Group Action (Except in Crisis)	14
How much covert resistance to goals is present?	Strong Resistance	Moderate Resistance	Some Resistance at Times	Little or None	15
How concentrated are review and control functions?	Very Highly at Top	Quite Highly at Top	Moderate Delegation to Lower Levels	Widely Shared	16
Is there an informal organization resisting the formal one?	Yes	Usually	Sometimes	No—Same Goals as Formal	17
What are cost, productivity, and other control data used for?	Policing, Punishment	Reward and Punishment	Reward, Some Self-guidance	Self-guidance, Problem Solving	18

SOURCE: *Adapted from Appendix 11 in* The Human Organization: Its Management and Value *by Rensis Likert. Copyright © 1967 by McGraw-Hill, Inc. Used with the permission of McGraw-Hill Book Company.*

These results need to be understood in terms of the differential impact of authoritarian and democratic systems on immediate, compared to long-term, labor costs. In three continuous-processing plants, autocratically imposed belt-tightening produced the immediate reduction in costs in one organization of 600. However, this reduction occurred at the expense of the employees' deteriorating motivation, dissatisfaction with company policy, and dissatisfaction with the leadership and was reflected in increased grievances, turnover, work stoppages, failure to meet delivery dates, and lower quality. In one study, it took three or more years for these effects to show up clearly.[9] The immediate savings of $250,000 actually produced losses of $450,000 in the longer term owing to the generation of more hostile, less motivated, and less individually productive employees as a result of the autocratic imposition (R. Likert, 1977b). Consistent with this finding, Dunnington, Sirota, and Klein (1963) noted that when engineered work standards were imposed on managers and supervisors at an IBM manufacturing plant, the employees in this plant resented the pressure, and the same kinds of adverse trends occurred in the measurements of the human consequences, as was reported for the three continuous-processing plants mentioned above. Yet, Dunnington, Sitrota, and Klein did find that employees whose particular supervisors were more democratic showed much less resentment of the work standards than did employees whose supervisors were more autocratic. The employees who worked for democratic supervisors felt less resentful because the democratic supervisors were more likely to try to do something if an employee complained that the work standard was unreasonable.

Contingency research, to be discussed in Chapter 26, supports the need for different organizational structures for different kinds of industry (see, for example, Lawrence & Lorsch, 1967a, 1967b; Woodward, 1965). Assembly plants (mass and batch production) have different organizational structures from oil refineries (continuous-processing). Nevertheless, Likert (1977b)

noted that regardless of industry, the better performing plant or department was likely to be closer to System 4 in its leadership processes, and the poorer performing plant or department closer to System 1 in its management system.[10]

Effects on Business Organizations. Results from 30 studies in 35 business firms involving some 260 sections, departments, or similar organizational units containing more than 50,000 employees were reported by R. Likert (1961a), Likert (1967), Likert and Likert (1976), and Likert and Fisher (1977). They demonstrated the efficacy of democratic as opposed to autocratic systems of management.

Nineteen of the studies, as summarized by Likert (1977b), were comparisons of democratic organizations that were closer to System 4 in their leadership and management with those that were closer to the autocratic System 1. The differences in productivity and earnings favoring System 4 over System 1 ranged from 14 to 75 percent. In 11 "before-after" studies, in which managment was helped to shift in the democratic direction toward System 3, productivity and earnings improved from 15 to 40 percent 1 or 2 years after the shift. In 2 comparisons in which control groups were available, no such improvements were obtained for the control groups.

These improvements continued if the democratic shift was maintained. In departments of fewer than 200 employees, the improvement resulted usually in annual savings of $50,000 to $100,000. In a large plant of 6,000 employees, the annual savings were more than $5,000,000. Guest (1962a) observed similar results for productivity, quality, and safety when a new manager of the poorest performing of 6 plants shifted the organization toward a democratic, Theory Y, leadership.

For 15 business firms, Taylor and Bowers (1972) reported the relations between their measures of organizational climate, derived from their survey of organizations, and various organizational outcomes, obtained from 6 months prior to the survey to 18 months afterward. Correlations between having democratic climates and efficiency reached as high as .8 and were

---

[9]Examples are replete of the extent to which the harmful attitudinal and performance effects of an autocratic leader linger long after the leader has left the organization. These coercive effects often do not surface until the autocratic leader has departed, since one of his or her techniques may include repressing dissent by means of threats to such dissidence (R. H. Solomon, 1976).

[10]Such results have been reported by R. Likert (1967); R. Likert and J. Likert (1976); Marrow, Bowers, and Seashore (1968); McCullough (1975); Mohr (1971); Roberts, Miles, and Blankenship (1968); and Toronto (1972).

somewhat lower between having democratic climates and reduced rates of absenteeism, minor injuries, ill health, and grievances.

Effects on Governmental Agencies. Heslin (1966) found that the high-producing units in a federal government agency, engaged in automatic data processing, were closer to Likert's System 4 in their management, as seen by the employees, than were the low-producing units. Operating bureaus of the Department of State were seen to provide better budgeting, space, travel, and personnel services if their managements (according to their own subordinates) were closer to System 4 than to System 1 (Warwick, 1975). Similarly, Likert (1977b) reported that city managers, when asked to compare the highest producing unit with a matched lowest producing unit they knew well, described the highest unit as between systems 3 and 4 and the lowest unit as pursuing a benevolent autocratic (System 2) management.

Effects on Military Organizations. In data from 20 ships and 18 shore stations of the U.S. Navy, Bowers (1975) found a strong relationship between an individual's intention to reenlist (which is a good predictor of actual reenlistment) and the extent to which the ship or station was closer to System 4 and farther from System 1. Again, Likert (1977b) reported that among 14 U.S. Navy crews, the absence of mishaps (accidents and disasters that are due to the operational failure of serviced aircraft) was associated with the extent to which supervisors facilitated the work and the team's development. In the same way, D. E. Johnson (1969) found that those among 93 U.S. Air Force ROTC units that were judged to be operating closer to System 4 than to System 1 units were also seen by a higher authority to be better performing units.

Effects on Educational Institutions. Summarizing 40 studies in school systems, Likert (1977b) concluded that school surveys of members of boards of education, superintendents, central staff, principals, department heads, teachers, students, and parents demonstrated that school systems that were closer to System 4, when compared to those closer to System 1, exhibited better communications, cooperation, and coordination (Lepkowski, 1970). They were more flexible and innovative

(Broman, 1974)[11] and more effective overall (Ferris, 1965; Riedel, 1974). Their personnel felt a greater sense of self-actualization and satisfaction from their work (Wagstaff, 1970).[12] Furthermore, they were judged as achieving superior educational results. They had better board-employee relations (R. C. Key, 1974) and union-management relations (Bernhardt, 1972; Haynes, 1972). Their students were more highly motivated and attained higher educational achievement for given IQ and socioeconomic levels (Belasco, 1973; A. K. Gibson, 1974). Their students had more favorable attitudes and were less likely to engage in disruptive behavior or acts of aggression against the schools (Cullers, Hughes, & McGreal, 1973; Morall, 1974).

Again, for 12 studies in institutions of higher education, Likert (1977b) concluded that institutions whose administrations were closer to System 4 than to System 1 experienced more favorable outcomes. The faculty members were more satisfied with administrative decision making (A. B. Smith, 1971).[13] There was less need for collective bargaining (Cline, 1974), more innovativeness (Bowers, 1976; Hanna, 1973) and commitment to college objectives (T. G. Fox, 1973; Laughlin, 1973), and more favorable student outcomes (Bowers, 1976; Gilbert, 1972).

Effects on Other Not-for-Profit Organizations. Munson (reported by Likert, 1977b) studied the relationship between the systems used by head nurses in 8 hospitals, according to the nurses reporting to them, and the nurses' satisfaction. On the basis of data from 351 nurses in 55 patient teams, Munson found that the closer the head nurse was to System 4 the more generally satisfied were the nurses. H. C. White (1971b, 1971c, 1971d) obtained similar results for peers who described effective and ineffective supervisors they had known. Again, System 4 was seen to be more effective than was System 1 in 3 outpatient clinics, according to an unpublished report by the National Tuberculosis and Respiratory Disease Association and by Ketchel

[11]See also, Gehrman (1970), Ladouceur (1973), and Naumann-Etienne (1975).
[12]See also Brindisi (1976), Byrnes (1973), Carr (1971), Chung (1970), Feitler and Blumberg (1971), Morall (1974), Prieto (1975), C. E. Shaw (1976), Smallridge (1972), M. C. Smith (1975), and D. E. Thompson (1971).
[13]See also, Gardner (1971), Javier (1972), and Lasher (1975).

(1972), who studied the effectiveness of volunteer health planning in 17 Ohio counties.

Studying the systems of 3 community-based reintegration centers for ex-convicts in Ohio, McGruder (1976) concluded that in comparison to the most autocratic center on Likert's POC, the most democratic center was most effective, as measured by graduation rates and low rates of recidivism and reincarceration. Similarly, Marchant (1976) obtained data on Likert's POC from staffs of 22 research-oriented university libraries. Staffs were more satisfied and faculty evaluations of service were higher the closer the libraries were to System 4 and the farther they were from System 1. Finally, Haggard (as reported by Likert, 1977b) found that as management of a YMCA shifted away from System 2 toward System 4, the growth in the number of persons served by the YMCA increased from 11,064 to 23,794, and the budget increased (from $173,000 to $303,000).

Interpretive Problems and Issues

Despite the amount of support attesting to the efficacy of democratic leadership in the long term, disquieting ambiguities remain. Thus, among the reasons why Miller and Monge (1986) excluded the results of 15 journal articles from their meta-analysis was their determination that the democratic approach had not been clearly measured or experimentally manipulated. They found additional methodological problems in 7 other studies.

Different Outcome Measures. Other difficulties arise reducing confidence in the reported conclusions owing to the extent to which differences occur from one study to the next in the definition and measurement of the satisfaction of followers and the productivity of groups. Some studies measure global satisfaction, whereas others measure satisfaction with leadership, the job, the group, or the organization. Some researchers count units of output or rates of performance as measures of productivity. Others use ratings of quantity or quality of output as productivity measures.

Circumstance. Leadership style may be a product of circumstances, rather than of personal preferences. For instance, Southern Baptist preachers may become authoritarian in response to the ambiguity of their role definition. Ingraham (1981) suggested that the ambiguity of the pastor's role in Southern Baptist churches results in the development of an authoritarian self-image among pastors. When the pastors are unsuccessful in influencing their congregations, they either withdraw from their attempts to lead or try to become manipulative authority figures.

Leader Affected. The leadership style that is adopted may affect the leader as well as the follower. Kipnis, Schmidt, Price, and Stitt (1981) randomly assigned 113 business students to act as authoritarian or democratic leaders of 5-person work groups that manufactured model airplanes. They found that those who acted as democratic leaders perceived their group members to be more internally motivated to work effectively than did those who acted as authoritarian leaders. As a consequence, the democratic leaders gave the members more favorable evaluations, although their productivity was not necessarily higher.

Confounding of Cause and Effect. Chapter 18 noted that followers condition a leader's behavior; that is, the leader of a productive group can afford to be more considerate of his or her subordinates than can the leader of a poorly performing group. In addition, Mitchell, Larson, and Green (1977) showed that subordinates' descriptions of a leader's initiation and consideration[14] are erroneously confounded with the perceived quality of his or her group's success and morale. The error is compounded because the same source of information about the leader's behavior provides the indicators of perceived group success and morale. Under these conditions, the correlations between democratic leadership, on the one hand, and group success and morale, on the other, are inflated above the true correlations.

In interpreting the findings, one faces the "chicken-or-the-egg" issue. A one-time concurrent study of leadership and its consequences may in reality by a one-time study of leadership and its antecedent conditions. Leaders may be authoritarian because their groups are unproductive or can afford to be democratic because

---

[14]For a detailed discussion of consideration and the initiation of structure, see Chapter 24.

their groups are productive. The needed longitudinal studies are few; the one-time studies are many. R. Likert's (1967) research with efforts to move organizations in a democratic direction suggests that the results may not be immediately apparent. One or two years may elapse before a change in leadership style exerts measurable effects on organizational performance.

Results Reflect Implicit Theories. The issue of what is cause and what is effect is complicated by the extent to which the correlations reflect the implicit leadership theories of the raters. That is, one may assume that subordinates will be more productive under a particular pattern of supervision. They may make their report about the supervisor as a consequence of how they see the group performing (Rush, Thomas, & Lord, 1977). Thus, in Mitchell, Larson, and Green's (1977) study, knowledge that a group performed well caused increases in the rated consideration and initiating of structure[15] of that group's supervisor, whereas knowledge that a group performed poorly caused large decreases in the supervisor's rated consideration and initiating of structure. These distortions in leadership ratings because of the knowledge of performance also occurred when raters of high- and low-performing leaders were exposed to identical and highly salient leadership behaviors (Lord, Binning, Rush, & Thomas, 1978).

Summary and Conclusions

A large cluster of styles can be included in democratic leadership and member-related behaviors: employee oriented, considerate, concerned with the satisfaction of needs, maintenance oriented, "1–9," rewarding and

[15]See Chapter 24.

nonpunitive, supportive, relations oriented, open, close, informal, warm, System 3 or System 4, and people centered. Included in autocratic leadership or work-related behaviors are opposites of those just mentioned: job centered, structuring, task oriented, "9–1," punitive, closed, distant, formal, cold, System 1 or System 2, and work centered.

The positive effects of democratic approaches are most apparent if one depends on the results of large-scale field surveys and lagged productivity measurements, rather than on small-group laboratory experiments with immediate, concurrent effects. Generally, the patterns of leadership behavior included in democratic leadership are more satisfying than those associated with autocratic leadership. But productivity in the short term may be enhanced more by autocratic leadership than by democratic leadership, particularly democratic leadership that ignores the task and concern for production goals. However, in the long term, the positive effects of democratic leadership are evident, especially if the employees' development, commitment, loyalty, and involvement are important to productivity. But numerous conditions, such as the authoritarianism of subordinates or the nature of the task, increase the utility of autocratic methods, particularly in the short run.

A sharper picture of leadership effects can be seen by looking at more distinctive components of democratic leadership, such as participation, relations orientation, and consideration for subordinates, as well as the counterpart components of autocratic leadership. A further understanding of what accounts for these differences in the effects of democratic and autocratic leadership may be gained from examining the decision processes involved, which are covered next.

Directive
versus Participative Leadership

Who decides? The leader? The led? Both? On what does the answer depend? What are the consequences? Should managers give directions and tell subordinates how to do the work, or should they share with subordinates the needs for solving problems or handling situations and involve them in working out what needs to be done and how?

The Continuum

Most managers do both, depending on the circumstances, but in different amounts. Tannenbaum and Schmidt (1958) suggested that direction and participation are two halves of a continuum, with many gradations possible in between. At one extreme of the continuum, the supervisor may give directions and orders to subordinates without even explaining why. The supervisor expects unquestioning compliance, and participation by subordinates is minimal. At the next gradation, the supervisor accompanies his or her directions with detailed explanations and expects to persuade and manipulate the subordinates or to bargain with them. At the third level (in between direction and participation), the supervisor consults with subordinates before deciding what is to be done. At the fourth gradation, full participation by both the supervisor and the subordinates occurs when both join in deciding what is to be done. At the fifth level, the supervisor delegates the task and how it is to be handled to the subordinates, and the supervisor's own participation is minimal. At this level, within the constraints set, whatever the subordinates decide is acceptable to the supervisor. At this

extreme of the continuum, some supervisors may completely abdicate their responsibilities.[1]

A score is sometimes generated to describe a point on the continuum. For instance, Drenth and Koopman (1984) did so for their influence-power continuum. The continuum ranged from pure leader direction—no reason or prior information is given to subordinates for a decision—to complete control of the decision by the subordinates. Scandura, Graen, and Novak (1986) did likewise.

Directive leadership implies that the leader plays the active role in problem solving and decision making and expects group members to be guided by his or her decisions. It can take many forms. Berlew and Heller (1983) suggested that to gain acceptance of their proposals, executives can try to use persuasion, reason, and logic. They can assert an expectation or need and offer rewards or exert pressure to gain acceptance. They can generate charismatic identification to motivate and build commitment. They can try partial disengagement by backing away from time-consuming issues with a lower priority and by concentrating colleagues' attention on more important issues.

Participative leadership, likewise, can take many forms. Berlew and Heller (1983) mentioned the possibilities of drawing others out, listening actively and carefully, and gaining acceptance through engaging colleagues in the planning or decision-making process.

Specific differences can be seen in the way directive and participative leaders communicate with their subordinates (Sargent & Miller, 1971). Different uses

[1]This will be discussed in Chapter 25 as laissez-faire leadership.

would be made of palliatives and sedatives. The brisk directive leader is likely to say, "I want you to . . ." The more sophisticated directive leader is likely to ask, "Would you be kind enough to . . . ?" The participative leader would ask, "Would it be a good idea if we . . . ?"

Meanings of Direction and Participation

Direction or directiveness has two meanings. First it is a distinct style in which the leader decides and announces his decision without consulting subordinates beforehand. Such direction can be with or without explanation. In this and subsequent chapters, "direction" is italicized when it is used in this way. Directiveness can also refer generally to that portion of the decision-making continuum in which the leader may manipulate, sell, persuade, negotiate, or bargain in lieu of giving orders. When used in this sense, the word will not be italicized.

Participation also has two distinct meanings, one encompassing the other. First, it may refer to a simple distinct way of leader-subordinate decision making in which the leader equalizes power and shares the final decision making with the subordinates. Consensus is sought. This specific style is italicized throughout this and later chapters. Participation is also commonly used as a general expression to refer to the half of the continuum of decision making in which subordinates are involved in some way in the decision process, either because they are consulted individually or in a group by their leader (who makes the final decision), they share with the leader in making the final decision, or they are delegated responsibility by the leader for making the decision. This general meaning of "participation" is not italicized.

Participative leadership suggests that the leader makes group members feel free to participate actively in discussions, problem solving, and decision making. It intimates the increased autonomy of workers, power sharing, information sharing, and due process (Lawler, 1986). But freedom does not mean license. In *participative* decision making, the leader remains an active member among equals.

Delegation. If participation takes the form of delegation, it does not mean that the leader abdicates his or her responsibilities. For instance, delegation may be followed up with, reclarification of what needs to be done, with support and encouragement, and with periodic requests for progress reports, as well as with praise and reward for subordinates' successful efforts (Bass, 1985a). Delegation should not be confused with laissez-faire leadership.[2] A leader who delegates still remains responsible for follow-up to see whether the delegation has been accepted and whether the requisite activities have been carried out.

Schriesheim and Neider (1988) distinguished among three types of delegation: advisory, informational, and extreme delegation. In advisory delegation, subordinates share problems with their supervisor, asking their supervisor for his or her opinions regarding solutions; however, the subordinates make the final decisions by themselves. With informational delegation, the subordinates ask the supervisor for information, then make the decisions by themselves. Extreme delegation occurs when subordinates make decisions by themselves without any input from their supervisor. A factor analysis of the surveyed responses of 196 nurses and 281 executive MBA students disclosed the independence of these three kinds of delegation. That is, leaders who used one kind of delegation did not necessarily use the others.

Delegation implies that one has been empowered by one's superior to take responsibility for certain activities. The degree of delegation is associated with the trust the superior has for the subordinate to whom the responsibilities have been delegated. When a group is the repository of authority and power, it likewise may delegate responsibilities to individual members.

Delegation of decision making implies that the decision making is lowered to a hierarchical level that is closer to where the decisions will be implemented. Such delegation is consistent with what was presented in Chapter 14 on the use of self-planning. Although delegation is a simple way to reduce time-consuming chores for a leader who is faced with a heavy work load,

[2]See Chapter 25.

it provides subordinates with learning opportunities and multiplies the executive's accomplishments (Anonymous, 1978), along with the desired latitude and freedom for subordinates (Strasser, 1983). The act of delegation is often directive, but it can be based on a prior participative decision as well. Nevertheless, Leana (1984) called attention to the need to avoid confusing the power relinquishment of delegation with the power sharing of *participation*. In agreement with Strauss (1963), Heller (1976), and Locke and Schweiger (1979), Leana (1987) also noted that delegation is more concerned with the autonomy and individual development of subordinates than is *participation*. According to the responses of 118 managers on how to handle 8 situations involving the assignment of a task to a subordinate engineer, there are some managers who are willing to delegate regardless of the circumstances. But other managers cluster in their lack of willingness to delegate around 1 of 3 considerations. Some do not delegate because they do not feel confident in the capabilities of the subordinates. Some avoid delegating because they think the task is too important to be left to the subordinates. Some are unwilling to delegate because of the technical difficulty of the task (Dewhirst, Metts, & Ladd, 1987).

Token Participation and Misuse of Participation.

When executives call meetings ostensibly to reach shared decisions but in actuality to inform and announce to subordinates their decision (Guetzkow, 1951), they are practicing token participation. They are also practicing it when they invite the wrong people to participate, knowing in advance that these people lack a genuine interest or have conforming tendencies.

Holding frequent group meetings does not necessarily imply participative leadership. Guetzkow and Kriesberg (1950) found that leaders may use meetings to "sell" and gain acceptance of their own solutions, as well as to explain their own preferences. These executives see meetings as a way to transmit information and to make announcements, rather than as an opportunity to share information and opinions or to reach decisions. According to Rosenfeld and Smith (1967), subordinates recognize this phoney participation and respond negatively to it.

If one can assume that followers in formal organizations appreciate autonomy, one should expect leaders who say they delegated freely to be described as considerate. The satisfaction of employees should also have been highly related to delegation. But the effects obtained by Stogdill and Shartle (1955) were marginal. Subordinates often feel that their superiors do not really delegate to them the authority to accompany the responsibilities they are given. Also, superiors may believe they are delegating, but their subordinates may see the same behavior as abdication—a most unsatisfying state of affairs for subordinates.

Some leaders risk participative decision making (consultation, *participation*, or delegation) only when a high-quality solution is not needed. Other leaders push for participation, regardless of the need for it and despite the extra time it takes (Wright, 1984–85). Participation has become an ethical imperative for some advocates, but Locke, Schweiger, and Latham (1986) argued that it should be seen as a managerial procedure that is appropriate in only some situations, for the effects, although generally satisfying to subordinates, may not necessarily contribute to the subordinates' productivity. In some circumstances, directive leadership may result in both higher productivity and greater satisfaction. Participation is usually thought to enhance the subordinates' compliance with decisions to change (Carson, 1985; Kanter, 1983); however, direction may be better for envisioning what needs to be changed.

Contextual Aspects of Participation

For Lawler (1986), participation is a way for U.S. business to offset foreign competition and to deal with increasingly specialized work and the higher labor costs associated with some of it. But clearer goals and directions could also help. The pressure for more participation in the workplace and involvement in decisions about work have been fostered in the United States by workers' greater expectations for upward mobility and the desire for more interesting work, but Lawler (1985) pointed out that education has not equipped many graduates to participate effectively at work. Participative management requires an appropriate organization design, as well as a design that is relevant to the employees' backgrounds, motivation, and abilities. Employees with more education are more concerned about participating in decisions that affect their work (Wright & Hamilton, 1979). In the shifting of the management of libraries from direction to participation, Sager (1982) noted that the roles of management and staff at all levels needed to be shifted, along with essential changes in regulations and policies.

Conceptual Distinctions and Empirical Overlaps

Tannenbaum and Schmidt (1958) thought of participation and direction as being based on how much authority was used by the superior in relation to how much freedom was permitted the subordinates. Bass (1960) noted that participative leadership requires leaders with power who were willing to share it. With their power, such leaders set the boundaries within with the subordinates' participation or consultation is welcomed. In contrast, with the powerless leader, as in the leaderless group situation, a struggle for status occurs among group members.

Numerous investigators have conceptualized the same directive-participative dimension in slightly different ways. Table 22.1 shows the comparable terms they have employed for Tannenbaum and Schmidt's (1958) original gradations.

Graves (1983) showed that two of the three categories of concepts used by students to cluster 23 supervisory behaviors as an indication of their implicit theories of leadership dealt first with task direction (such as "Sets goals for employee performance") and second, with participation (for instance, "Asks employees for opinions and suggestions"). The third category of concepts dealt with reward (for example, "Praises those who perform well"). Although conceptually independent, the dimensions of task direction and of participation correlated .53 for the students' implicit theories of leadership.

Similarly, Bass, Valenzi, Farrow, and Solomon (1975) found that according to subordinates' descriptions of their superiors, *direction* and persuasive negotiation were positively correlated. Even more highly intercorrelated were democratic consultation, *participation*, and delegation. However, 46 judges, using response-

Table 22.1 Conceptions of the Dimension of Participative versus Directive Leadership

Tannenbaum and Schmidt (1958)	Hersey and Blanchard (1969a, 1969b)	Sadler and Hofstede (1972)	Heller and Yukl (1969)	Bass and Valenzi (1974)	Vroom and Yetton (1974)
The leader decides and announces the decision.	*The leader* tells	*The leader* tells	*The leader uses* own decision with no explanation	*The leader is* directive	*The leader uses* AI, AII
"sells" the decision.	sells	sells	own decision with an explanation	persuasive—manipulative	
presents ideas and invites questions.		consults	consultation	consultative	
presents tentative decisions that are subject to modification.		consults	consultation	consultative	
presents problems, gets suggestions, makes decisions.		consults	consultation	consultative	CI, CII
defines limits and asks for a consensual decision.	participates	joins	joint decision	participative	GI, GII
permits followers to function within limits.	delegates		delegation	delegative	DI

allocation procedures, could readily and reliably discriminate among the specific behaviors involved in *direction* and negotiation, as well as among the behaviors involved in consultation, *participation,* and delegation. The five styles were found to be conceptually independent, although they are correlated empirically. For instance, the judges clearly saw consultation as a different pattern of behavior from, say, delegation; nevertheless, the same managers who were most likely to consult were also more likely to delegate, according to their subordinates' descriptions of the managers (Bass, Valenzi, Farrow, & Solomon, 1975). Similar results were reported by Filella (1971) for 77 Spanish managers, as well in Saville and Holdsworth's OPQ manual (Anonymous, 1985) for 527 British professionals and managers. Nevertheless, the three styles—consultation, *participation,* and delegation are distinctive and may, to some degree, have different antecedents and consequences. Factorial independence of each of the styles would make research with them easier; however, maintaining conceptually distinct but correlated styles remains viable and useful in the same way that analyses of body height and body weight continue to be separated, although height and weight are also empirically correlated. In general, tall people are heavier than short people, but it remains useful to talk about how people differ in height and how they differ in weight, rather than how they differ in the combination, stature.

More on Empirical Interrelations among Styles.
Additional evidence that the same managers empirically exhibit many of the conceptually different styles of decision making is obtained from examining the intercorrelations in style usage found in survey studies. Consultation, *participation,* and delegation are highly intercorrelated. That is, consultative managers also tend to be highly *participative* and delegative. The intercorrelations were above .6 for a sample of 343 to 396 respondents who described their organizational superiors. Even the extent to which managers are *directive* tends to correlate positively with the extent to which they are manipulative or negotiative, .25; consultative, .31; *participative,* .28; and delegative, .13. Consultation, the most popular style observed among 142 assistant school superintendents in Missouri, correlated highly

with *participation* (.64) and delegation (.47). Actually, all 5 styles have active leadership in common, and all are the opposites of inactivity and laissez-faire leadership.

Despite the intercorrelations among the leadership decision styles of the assistant school superintendents in Missouri, Wilcox (1982), using the Bass-Valenzi Management Styles Survey, reported systematic differences for the independent contributions of direction, consultation, and delegation to satisfaction with and the effectiveness of the leadership, even after the effects of many other organizational and personal variables of the leader and the led were removed.

Chitayat and Venezia (1984) completed a smallest-space analysis for 224 Israeli managers and executives from business and nonbusiness organizations and attained patterns for the Bass-Valenzi survey measures showing that *direction* and negotiation (persuasion and manipulation) were closer together but distant from delegation, *participation,* and consultation, which, in turn, were closer to each other in usage by the respondents.

Consistent with Bass, Valenzi, Farrow, and Solomon's (1975) and Wilcox's (1982) subordinates' descriptions of their superiors' styles, intercorrelations of .41, .33, and .51 were found among delegation, *participation,* and consultation and .23 between *direction* and negotiation for the Israeli managers. The correlations between decision styles within the two clusters were close to zero.

Managers may also tend to lean toward a style of inactivity. Whereas any of the preceding styles require activity, laissez-faire leadership or abdication do not. They call for doing little or nothing with subordinates, remaining passive or withdrawing, as will be discussed in Chapter 25.

Related Styles

I have already noted that participative decision making is a characteristic of democratic leadership. Direction is more often found in autocratic leaders. Clearly, participation is also likely to be seen with general, rather than close, supervision; with the equalization of power; and with nondirective leadership. Directive leadership is more likely to be exhibited by the same leaders who are also close supervisors, who do a lot of structuring, and who are manipulative and persuasive. This persuasive, manipulative emphasis was seen in political factors involving withholding information, bluffing, making alliances, publicly supporting but privately opposing particular views, compromising, and using delaying and diversionary tactics.[3]

Many elements of consideration[4] are part of participative decision-making leadership: asking subordinates for their suggestions before going ahead, getting the approval of subordinates on important matters, treating one's subordinates as equals, making subordinates feel at ease when talking with them, putting subordinates' suggestions into operation, and remaining easily approachable. For Graves (undated), implicit task direction correlated .61 with initiating structure and implicit participation correlated .81 with consideration, the two important dimensions of the Leader Behavior Description Questionnaire (LBDQ) that are examined in detail in Chapter 24. Many elements of direction are to be found on the LBDQ scale of the initiation of structure: making attitudes clear, assigning subordinates to particular tasks, and deciding in detail what shall be done and how.

Bass (1968c) contrasted MBA students' and managers' beliefs in how to succeed in business. Two social factors emerged: sharing decision making and emphasizing candor, openness, and trust. The factors involved making open and complete commitments, establishing mutual goals, and organizing group discussions. The factors coincided with ideal participative decision making, as proposed by Argyris (1962) and Bennis (1964).

Frequency

The popular stereotype of the ideal leader is the decisive, directive, heroic order giver. Burns (1978) saw such heroic leaders as transformational. Included in transformational leadership, as noted in Chapter 12, are the directive factors of charisma, inspirational leadership, and intellectual stimulation. The prototypical supervisor in the workplace of MBA students with full-time jobs had these directive transformational characteristics (Bass & Avolio, 1989). Yet in the behavioral sci-

ence literature, participative decision making is most commonly advocated. Actually, both Heller and Yukl (1969) and Bass and Valenzi (1974) have shown that neither extreme direction or extreme participation is reported most frequently by subordinates in describing their supervisor. Rather, subordinates see their supervisor as consulting with them most often. Thus, on a scale of frequency ranging from 1 (never) to 5 (always), according to over 400 subordinates from a variety of organizations, the average frequency with which superiors were observed to exhibit each of the styles on many items of supervisory decision-making behavior was as follows: consultation, 3.10; *participation*, 2.65; delegation, 2.46; *direction* with reasons, 1.97; *direction* without reasons, 1.90; and manipulation, 1.88 (Bass & Valenzi, 1974).

In agreement, H. R. Gillespie (1980) concluded, from self-reports of 48 manufacturing executives, that participation, particularly consultation, was more frequent, especially among executives at the top level. Kraitem (1981) likewise found that consultative leadership was favored in the self-reports of top executives in financial institutions and that there had been a shift away from more directive approaches.

Manipulation and negotiation were reported to occur least frequently, perhaps because of the greater subtlety of manipulative behavior, which is more difficult to discern when it happens. Obviously, the most artful manipulative behavior is that which is misperceived as participative. There is less reliability in judgments about manipulation than other decision-making style. Subordinates feel they are being manipulated when they think managers know in advance what they will decide and what they want the subordinates to do. The managers strike bargains and play favorites. Such manipulative behavior tends to be exhibited by *directive* managers but not by managers who generally tend to be participative (Bass, Valenzi, Farrow, & Solomon, 1975).

Multiplicity of Styles

For subordinates, the consistently autocrat or consistently laissez-faire leader for all situations is likely to be least satisfactory and effective. Generally, participative leadership will be favored by subordinates over direc-

---

[3]See Bass (1968c), Jameson (1945), and Martin and Sims (1956), as well as Chapter 9.
[4]See Chapter 24.

tive leadership. Nonetheless, subordinates may agree with their superior that supervisory *direction* is called for in a crisis and that consultation is indicated when subordinates are experts. The subordinates are likely to applaud their superior's flexibility in being directive in the first situation and consultative in the second. In fact, few managers use only a single style; most use a variety of styles, ranging from extreme direction to extreme participation. For 124 middle- and first-level supervisors, W. A. Hill (1973) found that only 14 percent of the supervisors were seen as likely to use the same one of 4 styles in 4 hypothetical situations.

Bass and Valenzi (1974) obtained sharper results with 124 subordinates, who described how frequently their superiors actually used 6 styles, ranging from deciding without explanation to delegating decisions to subordinates. A manager was classified as exhibiting a *single* managerial style if the subordinate indicated that only 1 of these styles was displayed by the manager "very often" or "always" and the remaining styles, "never" or "seldom." A manager was classified as exhibiting a *dual* approach if the managers were described by their subordinates as displaying 2 styles "very often" and/or "always" and the others, "never" or "seldom." A manager was classified as exhibiting a *multistyle* approach if he or she was described as displaying 3 or more of the 6 styles "sometimes," "fairly often," "very often," and/or "always." Of 124 subordinates, less than 4 percent indicated that their superior exhibited a *single* style or a dual approach; 117, or almost 95 percent, indicated that their boss exhibited a multistyle approach.[5]

Consistent with Bass and Valenzi's findings, Hollander (1978) noted that although political leaders, in particular, often try to project a consistent image to a wide audience based on a particular style that is uniform across situations, most change their style from the one they used before they were elected to the one they use after they were elected; they also change their style from one constituency to another.[6] History is replete with examples illustrating that the most powerful dictators may also be strong advocates of consultation. Lenin was seen by his biographers as a frequent consultant of his immediate subordinates (Bass & Farrow,

1977a). Mao Zedung urged party leaders to be consultative and instructed them carefully on how to carry out a doctrine stressing consultation:

> We should never pretend to know what we don't know, we should not feel ashamed to ask and learn from people below, and we should listen carefully to the views of the cadres at the lower levels. Be a pupil before you become a teacher; learn from the cadres at the lower levels before you issue orders. (Burns, 1978, p. 238)

Differences in Problems. The overwhelming tendency for managers to employ multiple decision-making styles is seen most clearly in studies of how the same managers use different styles, depending on the nature of the problem. Thus, McDonnell (1974) found that when 226 respondents were asked to choose whether they would be autocratic, consultative, *participative*, or laissez-faire, each respondent used a different style of reacting, depending on which of 12 problem situations was presented for consideration. Again, Heller and Yukl (1969) and Heller (1972a) demonstrated that a senior manager varies his or her style according to the nature of the required decisions. For example, prior consultation was the modal style for decisions that were critical to individual staff members but not to the organization. Participation in all 3 forms was most frequent for decisions of importance to subordinates and least frequent about decisions of importance to the company. Supervisory delegation and supervisory decision making without explanation were most frequent for decisions that were unimportant to both the leader and the subordinates. Figure 22.1 shows the obtained frequency distribution of decision-making styles.

Using a different method, to be detailed later, Vroom and Yetton (1973), emerged with similar results. Several thousand managers indicated the decision-making style they would employ if confronted with different kinds of cases requiring or not requiring high-quality solutions and subordinates' acceptance. Only about 10 percent of the variance in response could be attributed to the general tendencies of the managers to be more directive or more participative; 30 percent of their responses depended on whether high-quality solutions and subordinate acceptance were required. Hill and Schmitt (1977) tested a shortened version of Vroom

[5]3, or 2.4 percent, were unclassifiable.
[6]President Bush was extreme in this regard.

Figure 22.1. Percentage Frequencies of Participative and Directive Styles as a Function of the Importance of the Decision

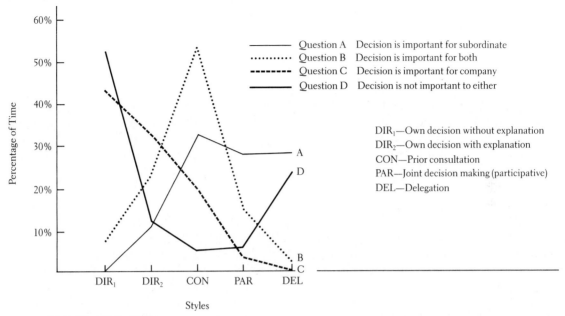

SOURCE: *Adapted from Heller (1972a).*

and Yetton's method and found that 37 percent of the variance in the leaders' decision-making style was due to case-requirement effects and only 8 percent was due to the effects of the respondents' individual dispositional differences. These results tended to be relatively insensitive to the hierarchical levels dealt with in the cases presented to the managers (Jago, 1978a). This was so despite the fact that, as was noted in Chapter 16, both the authority to be directive and the authority to be delegative increase as one rises in the organizational hierarchy (Stogdill & Shartle, 1955). Such increased authority makes it possible for superiors to delegate more responsibilities to subordinates. Paradoxically, it makes it possible for the superiors to be more participative as well.

Discrepancies between Self and Others' Descriptions

In Wilcox's (1982) dissertation, agreement was quite close between the superintendent's self-descriptions of their directiveness, participation, and delegation and descriptions provided by their subordinates. But the superintendents believed they were more consultative and less negotiative than their subordinates thought they were.

Generally, when managers' self-rated styles are contrasted with descriptions provided by their subordinates, one is likely to find many managers who see themselves favoring their subordinates' participation a lot more than their subordinates see such participation occurring. At the same time, many authoritarian leaders would be surprised to learn that they are judged to be far more directive by their subordinates than they believe themselves to be. Harrison (1985) studied 30 supervisors and their 234 college-educated subordinates in a large social service organization. There was little correspondence between the subordinates' feelings of participation in decision making and the supervisors' tendency to see themselves as participative in style. For the superiors, participation meant interacting with subordinates, but for the subordinates, it also meant that the subordinates could both send and receive information related to their own desires. Moreover, the subordinates' judgments of the extent to which their superior was participative correlated .61 with the interpersonal support they received from the superior, the team-building activities led by the superior (.59), and the accuracy of the information they felt they received from the superior (.30). The superior generally failed to recognize that any of these actions were connected to being participative.

A Harris (1987) poll revealed still another aspect of the discrepancy between managers and white-collar workers. Although 77 percent of the workers considered it very important for them to be allowed to participate in decisions that controlled their working conditions, only 41 percent of their superiors agreed with them.

Antecedents of Direction and Participation

As was already noted, different studies using a variety of methods showed that leaders in organized settings said they preferred to be consultative and were seen by their subordinates to be consultative most often. Such consultation involved their subordinates to some extent in the decision process, but the supervisors reserved the final decision for themselves. At the same time, a given leader was seen to use the whole range, from *direction* to delegation, in varying amounts. However, different patterns of usage were revealed; some leaders were more directive as a whole, while others were more participative. Both deductive and inductive research points to a variety of factors that predispose leaders to pursue one style rather than another. These antecedent conditions include the attributes of the leader and of the subordinates; their preferences, goals, tasks, and assignments; and the organizational and external environment.

Personality or Situation? Some argue that direction or participation will depend on the nature of the situation; others state that it depends on the leader's judgment of the situation (Hersey & Blanchard, 1977; Vroom & Yetton, 1973). Still others find that the predispositions of the leader are most significant (Fiedler, 1967a).

Situations have an obvious impact. On the one hand, crisis conditions may make any leader directive. On the other hand, a leader of a project team that is composed of experts from different fields will most likely benefit the project by being participative. Nevertheless, it may be that personality has more of an effect on a leader being directive but the situation has more of an effect on a leader being participative (Farrow & Bass, 1977). Both the contingency and the noncontingency theorists may be right. Frequency of direction may be mainly a matter of personality; frequency of participation may hinge mainly on contingent factors. Farrow and Bass (1977) found, for 77 managers who were described by their 407 subordinates, that situational factors, as seen by the managers or by the subordinates, were irrelevant in determining whether a manager would be *directive*. According to path analyses, managers who were most frequently *directive*, according to their subordinates, were highly assertive and regarded people as fundamentally unfair. Such managers were highly satisfied with their own jobs. If the managers had short-term rather than long-term objectives, their subordinates saw them to be manipulative and negotiative. These results transcended various organizational, intrapersonal, and personal attributes of the subordinates. On the other hand, the amount of participation seen by subordinates depended on the extent to which the manager perceived that the subordinates had discretionary opportunities and highly interdependent tasks.

Effects of the Leaders Themselves

Self-confidence and a personal sense of security are likely to have a strong effect on a leader's tendencies to be directive or participative (Bass & Barrett, 1981). Vroom (1960a) found that managers with authoritarian personalities, as measured by the F Scale of Adorno, Frenkel-Brunswik, Levinson, and Sanford (1950), were more directive. The lower their need for independence and the higher their degree of authoritarianism, the higher was their directiveness. Beliefs in the legitimacy of the manager's prerogatives to plan, direct, and control had similar effects. Managers who characterized themselves on personality inventories as unwilling to believe that people are fair minded were more likely to be *directive*, according to their subordinates. This finding was consistent with the proposition that managers will be directive because they believe in Theory X—employees cannot be trusted (McGregor, 1960).

Conversely, those who felt people were fair minded tended to be participative (Farrow & Bass, 1977).

Educational background also made a difference. Bass, Valenzi, and Farrow (1977) found a correlation of .37 between the educational level of 76 managers and their tendency to be participative.

Myers-Briggs Types. There is a consistent linkage between one's thought processes and the tendency to be directive or participative. For example, according to a study of 55 managers and executives by O'Roark (1986), who correlated scores on the Myers-Briggs Type Indicator with the Bass-Valenzi preferred management styles, individuals who emphasized "thinking" preferred to be directive more often, "feeling-oriented" individuals least preferred to be directive, "sensing" types least preferred negotiating, and "intuitives" preferred consulting but rejected participating. Schweiger and Jago (1982) also reported that of 62 graduate business students, "intuitive" Myers-Briggs types tended to choose fewer participative solutions to the problem set of Vroom and Yetton (1974), while "sensing" types tended to choose more such participative solutions. However, overall here, personality seemed less important than situational determinants in the choices that were made.

Risk Preferences and Propensities. Whether managers delegate certain duties to subordinates may depend on whether the managers enjoy doing the tasks themselves, as well as on their willingness to risk and wait for others to succeed (Matthews, 1980). Managers also need to feel secure and confident in themselves and in their subordinates (Hollingsworth & Al-Jafary, 1983).

The riskiness of a decision to a supervisor is decreased if it is to be implemented on a trial basis. In a simulation with 143 bank employees under such conditions, Rosen and Jerdee (1978) found the leaders to be more willing to engage in participation when decisions were to be implemented on a trial basis than when decisions implied permanent solutions.

The risk of decisions is increased for top managers who face intense competition from the marketplace. In such situations, the top manager tends to be more directive and highly controlling in some decisions, say about production, purchasing, and cost control, and more participative in others, such as those dealing with raising capital, research and development (R & D), policy changes, and marketing strategies (Khandwalla, 1973).

Power. Leaders with power can be more directive. Leaders who are esteemed and valued by subordinates, who are acknowledged as experts, and who are seen by subordinates to control rewards that the leaders can allocate among the subordinates have the power to be directive (Mulder, 1971; Raven, 1965b). In addition to the effects of expert, reward, and referent power, on being directive, coercive and legitimate power also do the same.

If the power of leaders is suddenly increased in an experiment, the amount the leaders can be directive is also increased, and, in fact, the leaders do tend to increase their directiveness (Shiflett, 1973). But, paradoxically, power is required to create participative circumstances. Whether power results in direction or participation depends on other factors. The results are decidedly mixed. Thus, Chitayat and Venezia (1984) noted that in Israeli business organizations, self-reported power contributed to being *directive*, but the reverse occurred in nonbusiness organizations (the armed forces and governmental agencies). In such highly bureaucratic organizations, powerful leaders were more participative because the rules and procedures required directiveness, and only executives with more power could be participative if they chose to be. But Hord, Hall, and Stiegelbauer (1984) found that more powerful school principals were more directive than were their less powerful assistant principals, teachers, or curriculum coordinators.

Experience. Heller and Yukl (1969) reported, in a study of 203 British managers at all hierarchical levels in 16 organizations, that senior managers, particularly those who were in their positions for a considerable time, and despite their greater power and status, were more likely than were junior managers to share in decision making with their subordinates. Seversky (1982) reported that more delegation was practiced by school superintendents who had more experience in their jobs. Likewise, Pinder, Pinto, and England (1973) found that older managers tended to be more participative, while younger managers tended to be more directive. Age, however, was unrelated to the participativeness of 48 manufacturing executives, according to H. R. Gillespie (1980).

Effects of the Superiors of the Leaders

There is a clear linkage between what a U.S. Navy executive officer of a ship can and does do and the responsibility, authority, and delegation of his immediate superior—the commanding officer. Stogdill and Scott (1957) correlated the responsibility (R), authority (A), and delegation (D) scores of commanding officers and executive officers with the average RAD scores of their junior officers on submarines and landing ships. The executive officers tended to delegate more freely to their subordinates on both types of ships when their commanding officers exercised wider scopes of responsibility and authority and delegated more freely. Commanding officers could increase or decrease the work load and freedom of action of their executive officers. Subordinates tended to tighten their controls as superiors increased their own responsibility and freedom of action. However, responsibility and authority did not flow without interruption down the chain of command. The responsibility, authority, and delegation of subordinates were more highly influenced by the subordinates' immediate supervisors than by the subordinates' higher-level officers.

Effects of the Subordinates

Some degree of agreement between the leader and the led about procedures, interests, and norms is necessary before effective participation can take place (Heller, 1969). In addition, they must concur that participation is relevant.

Relevance of Participation. Subordinates or followers vary in how much they would like to participate in decisions. As was noted earlier, Heller (1972a, 1976) found, in a number of samples in several countries, that managers used participation more frequently when decisions were more important to their subordinates than to the firm. Again, in an overall review of the literature, Hespe and Wall (1976) demonstrated that, although workers wanted to participate more than they actually were given the opportunity to do, they expressed the greatest interest in participating in

decisions that were related directly to the performance of their jobs, followed by matters concerning their immediate work units. They expressed little interest in participating in general policy decisions. This finding was corroborated by Long (1979), who found that workers in a Canadian trucking company that had become wholly owned by its employees increased their participation in company affairs after the employee takeover. According to Maier (1965), subordinates will prefer participation rather than direction if they are seeking personal growth, if they are striving to be more creative, and if they are highly interested in the objectives of the task. On the other hand, subordinates may prefer a great deal of direction, guidance, and attention from their supervisor until they have mastered the job, particularly if the job does not involve much creativity from them but only attention to routine details that must be learned (Bennis, 1966c).

Subordinates' Personality. Abdel-Halim (1983a), Abdel-Halim and Rowland (1976), and Vroom (1960a), among others, found that the personality traits of subordinates are of consequence to the participatory process. Just as authoritarian leaders want to be directive with their subordinates, so their authoritarian subordinates want to be directed by authoritarian leaders. Followers with authoritarian attitudes are likely to reject participative leadership. Highly authoritarian personalities wanted powerful, prestigious leaders who would strongly direct them.[7]

Subordinates' Competence. Raudsepp (1981) suggested that managers need a comprehensive inventory of subordinates' capabilities before deciding what duties they can delegate to subordinates and in which areas subordinates need further experience. Managers will consider participative approaches too risky when they have reservations about the competence and commitment of their lower-level employees (Rosen & Jerdee, 1977). Lowin (1968) showed that subordinates who perceived that they were not competent in the tasks to be completed were more appreciative of directive supervision than were those who thought of themselves as competent. Similarly, Heller (1969a) found that whenever managers reported a big difference in

[7]See Chapter 9.

skills between themselves and their subordinates, they were more likely to use *direction*. The differentials in skills that were of particular importance were technical ability, decisiveness, and intelligence. Managers were more likely to engage in participation when they esteemed the subordinates for their expertise and personal qualities. Heller (1976) also found that participative leadership was favored at senior organizational levels when the competence of subordinates was high. Similarly, on the basis of a study of members of 144 work groups in 13 local health agencies, Mohr (1977) concluded that supervisors favored participation when their subordinates had more training and were at higher technical and professional levels. Again, Sinha and Chowdhry (1981) found, in a survey of 135 Indian executives, that the executives tended to be participative if they believed their subordinates were better prepared but were more directive with subordinates whom they felt were less well prepared. Locke and Schweiger (1979) also concluded that leaders are more likely to be participative when they believe their subordinates have the necessary information to contribute to the quality of the decisions to be reached.

In a mass role-playing experiment, Maier and Hoffman (1965) observed that the "foreman" who regarded his "subordinates" as men with ideas was more likely to lead his crew toward an integrated solution to their problem on the basis of their participation in making the decision. However, if the "foreman" thought he was dealing with problem employees, he was more likely to direct them toward a solution he favored than to involve them extensively in the decision-making process.

Leana (1987) reported a correlation of .42 between the willingness of insurance supervisors to delegate responsibilities to their 122 subordinate claims adjusters and their judgment of the job capabilities of their subordinates. Tendencies to delegate correlated .27 with the subordinates' appraised trustworthiness. As was mentioned before, Dewhirst, Metts, and Ladd (1987–88) found strong indications that managers were less willing to delegate if the subordinates were incompetent or the tasks were difficult and highly technical.

In their prescriptive model (detailed later in this chapter), Vroom and Yetton (1973) deduced that leaders need to consider being more participative if they think they lack information that their subordinates are likely to have. In the same way, the Hersey and Blanchard (1977) model, which is detailed in Chapter 23, assumed that the subordinates' competence is the most important determinant of whether and when a manager should be directive or participative.

Superior-Subordinate Relations

The interplay of the superior and the subordinate contribute to the superior's tendencies to be directive or participative.

Differences in Power and Information. Bass and Valenzi (1974) proposed that the frequency with which a particular leadership style is used could be accounted for by the differences in power between the manager and the subordinates and by the differences in their competence or the information available to them. Shapira (1976) confirmed, through smallest-space analysis, the validity of Bass and Valenzi's deductions, namely, that given managers' power (P_m), subordinates' power (P_s), managers' information (I_m), and subordinates' information (I_s), then *direction* is more likely if $P_m > P_s$ and $I_m > I_s$, manipulation or negotiation is more likely if $P_m < P_s$ and $I_m > I_s$, consultation is more likely if $P_m > P_s$ and $I_m < I_s$, and delegation is more likely if $P_m < P_s$ and $I_m < I_s$.

Effects of the Quality of the Exchange Relationship. According to an analysis of 58 superior-subordinate paired questionnaires by Scandura, Graen, and Novak (1986), the quality of the superior-subordinate exchange may further complicate matters. Regardless of their competence, as rated by their superiors, subordinates who perceive they are in a more satisfying exchange relationship with their superiors also believe that their superiors allow them to participate much more in decision making. But subordinates who think they are in a dissatisfying relationship, will perceive such participation only if their performance has been rated highly by their superiors. If the relationship with superiors is poor and the subordinates' performance has been rated low, the superiors will be seen as much more directive. Superiors agree with this description of the exchange and its effects.

Effects of Constraints and Objectives

Policies, goals, task requirements, and functions constrain how directive or participative a leader can be. They also furnish objectives that the leader will see as being met more satisfactorily by either direction or participation. Both the leader and the subordinates may be constrained by rules, regulations, demands on their time, schedules, or fixed requirements for methods and solutions over which they have no control. The requirements of a decision may be highly programmed. Greater acceptance and change by the group may be desired or required. The manager may consider the objectives to be long range rather than a quick payoff; that is, the development of subordinates or the creation of a capable and effective operation for the long run may be more important than immediate profitability. According to Vroom (1976b), it "seems unlikely" that the same leadership style would be appropriate when one's objective was to save time than when one's objective was the long-term development of subordinates. If the cost of the time required of subordinates is more expensive than the value of the outcomes of their participation, directive approaches are more likely to be observed (Tannenbaum & Massarik, 1950).

Organizational Function. Chitayat and Venezia (1984) found, in their previously cited investigation of 224 Israeli executives, that the differences in the frequency of use of leadership styles were associated with differences in organizational norms, climate, and structure.

Since marketing is usually under shorter time constraints than is research, a directive style may be appropriate more often in work units in marketing than in research (Lawrence & Lorsch, 1967a, 1967b). Heller and Yukl (1969) found that production and finance managers tended to use directive decision making, whereas general and personnel managers were more participative.

In a study of 155 managers of police, Kuykendall and Unsinger (1982) found that the police managers stated that they would avoid delegating, regardless of the problem faced. Similar to managers in accounting, finance, and production, managers of police supervise more standardized, programmed types of jobs that permit less freedom and flexibility and allow for less meaningful participation by subordinates. Nevertheless, when accounting managers were faced with unprogrammed decisions, they tended to be more participative. A study of 212 chief accountants (McKenna, undated) found that although the chief accountants were generally more likely to be directive than participative, they were more likely to use consultation and *participation* than *direction* or delegation when they had to make unprogrammed decisions, rather than programmed decisions, and had to make decisions dealing with personnel, rather than with tasks. Similarly, the police managers were more likely to be participative than directive when faced with such decisions.

Service managers think that they generally face more unprogrammed decisions. Child and Ellis (1973) found, in a study of 787 managers in service organizations, that these managers saw their roles as less formal, less well defined, and less routine than did managers in manufacturing organizations. Similarly, Miner (1973) concluded that participative management was most likely to be found in organizations of professionals. Miller (1986) advocated such participativeness with R & D professionals.

Woodward (1965) studied the impact of technology on decision-making processes in 100 British firms. She concluded that in companies that were involved in mass or batch production, decision making was more likely to be directive but usually not precedent setting. On the other hand, in continuous-processing industries, such as petroleum refining, decisions were more likely to be made by committees with considerable participation by subordinates and that the decisions had long-term implications.

Organizational Level. Stogdill and Shartle (1955) reported correlations between the tendencies to delegate and the self-rated authority and responsibility of managers on the RAD scales in 10 organizations (Stogdill & Shartle, 1948). On the average, delegation correlated .17 with responsibility and .23 with authority. Since greater authority and responsibility naturally went with higher-level positions, it was not surprising to find that delegation was also higher among managers in higher-level positions. Moreover, delegation must be practiced at higher levels because organizations cannot afford to pay high-level executives to spend their time carrying out activities that could be performed by lower-paid staff (Major, 1984).

Using the RAD scales to study large governmental organizations, Kenan (1948) also found, as expected, that executives in higher-level positions described themselves as having a greater tendency to delegate than did those in lower-level positions. Correspondingly, Browne (1949) noted that the executives' salaries related positively to the executives' estimates of how much they delegated. D. T. Campbell (1956) reported that delegation was positively and significantly related to one's level in various types of organizations, as well as to one's military rank, time in position, and regard for being in a position of leadership.

Blankenship and Miles (1968) observed that the level of one's position is more important than is the span of control or size of the organization in determining the delegative behavior of managers. Upper-level managers not only reported greater freedom from their superiors in decisions but tended to involve their subordinates more in decisions than did managers at lower levels. H. R. Gillespie (1980) agreed, finding that among 48 manufacturing executives, those at the top level were more participative than were those at the next 2 levels below them.

A higher organizational level brings with it many of the conditions (mentioned earlier) that promote greater participation, and lower organizational levels do the reverse. Senior managers are concerned with longer-range problems and policies, norms, and values. They are dealing with more creative, more educated, higher-status subordinates, who expect more opportunities to participate and have a greater interest in long-term commitments and in their own development. Directive practices are more prevalent at lower levels, since managers are dealing with more routine types of work, more clearly defined objectives, and with less well-educated subordinates of lower status and fewer expectations about participating in the decision-making process (Selznick, 1957). Thus, in their intensive study of workers on the assembly line, Walker and Guest (1952) emphasized that supervision was likely to be more directive, particularly if the tasks to be performed were routine.

Other Characteristics of Tasks. Although Ford (1983) argued that there must be some way to measure the outcomes of tasks if tasks are to be delegated, Mohr (1971) found that the degree of "task manageability"

did not increase a manager's participatory style, but the task interdependence of the manager's subordinates did. Understandably, Leana (1986) reported that supervisors with heavier work loads were more likely to delegate work to their insurance claims adjusters than were supervisors with lighter loads.

Perceived Importance of Outside Environmental Influences. Managers differ in what aspects of the outside environment they regard as most important to their work and, as a consequence, they behave differently inside the organization. Bass, Valenzi, and Farrow (1977) asked 76 managers to describe the importance of economic, political, social, and legal influences on the work of their 277 immediate subordinates. These subordinates, in turn, described the frequency with which their own manager displayed *direction*, negotiation, consultation, *participation*, and delegation. Managers who tended to see economic events, such as inflation and taxes, as having strong effects on their work situation were more likely to be *directive* or negotiative. Managers who tended to see political, social, or legal issues as more important were more likely to be consultative or *participative*.

Higher Authority. If rules and regulations that are set by a higher authority or the central administration restrict subordinates' decisions, then supervisors dominate the group and make the decisions (Hemphill, Seigel, & Westie, 1951). A higher authority can indirectly prevent subordinates' participation in decisions by demanding immediate answers from supervisors and allowing the supervisors no time or opportunity to consult the workers. In addition, whether supervisors can be participative with their subordinates depends on the extent to which the higher authority requires the employees to be secretive about products, techniques, and business strategies. If people in the organization are supposed to know only "what they need to know," employees cannot be consulted about some decisions because much of the information required to discuss and consider such decisions cannot be revealed to them (Tannenbaum & Massarik, 1950).

The number of hierarchical levels at which participation is encouraged by policy will increase the tendency of supervisors to be participative throughout the system. Particularly important is the acceptance and promotion of the participative ideology by the sponsors of the organization and its top management (Marrow, Bowers, & Seashore, 1968).[8] The efforts of chief executive officers (CEOs) at General Motors, National Intergroup, and W. L. Gore & Associates demonstrated that participative leadership could be increased throughout their systems through the transformational leadership of their CEOs. The CEOs articulated a corporate mission and philosophy to encourage participation; they worked to gain acceptance of the approach by other key top executives and then those at lower levels. Participation at all levels was encouraged by changing the corporate culture, developing trust at all levels, and building the necessary skills for effective participation. The actions of top management resulted in increased employee commitment, job satisfaction, and role clarity (Niehoff, Enz, & Grover, 1989).

Corporate pressure to promote from within may also increase the need and importance of delegation at all levels in the organization to develop personnel for higher-level positions. The effectiveness of such delegation depends on setting early expectations about the results that are desired.

L. B. Ward's (1965) large-scale survey of top managements in the United States suggested strongly that the religious affiliation of the top managers in a firm affected the firm's personnel policies. Leadership at lower levels was more likely to be participative when the top management was not restricted to members of one religious group. When the top management was restricted to one religion, participation was most likely in all-Jewish-led firms and least likely in all-Catholic-led firms.

Organizational Size. Blankenship and Miles (1968), McKenna (undated), and Wofford (1971) reported systematic trends between the size of the organization and the leadership style observed in it. On the whole, the managers in larger firms exhibited more participation and less directiveness. However, a third variable may have been responsible, such as a greater amount of education among managers of larger firms, differences in policies, and so forth.

The results for small naval vessels differed markedly from those obtained for larger ships (Stogdill & Scott,

1957), particularly for delegation. The effects of delegation continued unbroken down the chain of command in the large organizations of the bigger vessels. On the small ships, the delegation process was broken or reversed in the third echelon down from the top. Characterized by a high rate of face-to-face interaction, the small ships were subject to greater interpersonal stresses and strains than were the large organizations. The formalized interactions in highly stratified larger organizations appeared to reduce some of the tensions found in the smaller organizations, where personal interaction is conducted on a less formal basis. A formalized interaction structure had the effect of enlarging members' area of freedom of action, whereas the contest inherent in face-to-face interaction tended to restrict freedom of action for some group members.[9]

General Effects of Directive and Participative Leaders

So far, this chapter has shown that the attributes of the leader and the led, as well as the constraints and objectives of the task and surrounding conditions, influence whether a leader will be directive or participative. This section examines the effects of direction or participation on (1) acceptance of the decision, (2) the subordinates' satisfaction, (3) the subordinates' involvement and commitment, and (4) the quality of the decision and productivity.

The evidence does not automatically favor one leadership style over the other. For instance, even the leadership that emerges in self-managed work groups, according to observations and group interviews by Manz and Sims (1984), needs to balance a "hands-off with a directive style if it is to be effective. Again, when asked about what managers do to appear fair, group members saw both direction with explanations and participative decision making as important. A survey of 815 managers by Greenberg (1988) found that to be seen as fair, 81 percent of the managers thought they needed to announce all pay raises and promotions; 76 percent, to explain how raises are determined; and 43 percent,

---

[8]See also, Maccoby (1981), O'Toole (1985), and Tichy and Devanna (1986).

[9]These findings are in accord with those reported by Cattell, Saunders, and Stice (1953); Shepherd and Weschler (1955); and others.

to explain why work assignments are made. At the same time, 55 percent declared that workers should be allowed to participate in decisions.

Benefits and Costs

Although considerable evidence can be marshaled in support of participation in general, Miner (1973, p. 348) suggested that the costs of participation may outweigh the benefits in many circumstances:

> The change in value structure required to implement participation on a large scale can be costly.... Many managers must be retrained to the participative leadership style; many others will find change difficult and end by seeking other employment. Among these latter may be individuals with considerable talent in aspects of the management process ... such as planning, coordinating, and controlling.... Individuals whose opinions are rejected by the group can become alienated both from the group and the organization; ... participation may yield a sense of closeness and belonging in a group that is mobilized behind objectives not in the best interest of the organization ... participative decision making is a slow process which may not be adequately responsive to rapid changes in an organization's environment.

Lawler (1986) strongly advocated participation as a means of decreasing workers' resistance to changes in procedures and increasing the flexibility of assignments. Nonetheless, he expected that salary and training costs would increase, as would resistance by some staff personnel and line managers to participative decision making.

A sampling of evidence now follows on the general effects of directive and participative leadership. Then evidence about contingencies that moderate the effects will be presented.

Effects of Participation on Acceptance

In general, the available evidence supports the contention that participative leadership promotes the acceptance of decisions and agreement to a greater extent than does directive leadership. When participative leadership is practiced in a group, R. Likert (1961a, 1961b) found that each member has the opportunity to gain recognition and a sense of self-worth. This type of leadership also creates conditions that allow each subordinate to observe how everyone else in the group feels about a matter under consideration. Such conditions reduce the individual's resistance to suggestions and changes of opinion. Thus, Bennett (1955) obtained results to indicate that students were much more likely to volunteer to serve as experimental subjects if they perceived that almost all other members of their class volunteered. Observing near-consensus and the opportunity to make public decisions increased volunteering more than did the opportunity for discussion. In a more tightly controlled experiment, Pennington, Haravey, and Bass (1958) showed that the followers' acceptance and change were greatest when both discussion and group decision were permitted, less when only discussion or announcements of group opinion were allowed, and least when only secret balloting was used.

Participatory leaders, who were instructed primarily to inhibit hasty decisions and domination of the group by any one member, were contrasted by Preston and Heintz (1949) with "supervisory leaders," who were directed to keep the group on the task. With more shared participation under participatory leaders, members as a whole showed more agreement with each other than did members without the opportunity to interact as much. The latter were more likely to be coerced—to show less acceptance of decisions privately than publicly. Again, Pennington, Haravey, and Bass (1958) found that groups under participative leadership achieved greater coalescence and changes in opinion than did those who where denied the opportunity to discuss and decide. Bovard (1951a, 1951b) observed that group-centered teams shifted their perceptions toward a common group norm more readily than did leader-centered groups. Hare (1953) found that although both participative and supervisory (directive) styles of leadership produced significant changes in the amount of agreement among group members, participative leaders were more in agreement with the group's rankings than were directive leaders. Likewise, Levine and Butler (1952) found participative leadership and group decision to be more successful in producing behavioral change than was a lecture or control condition.

In application, T. P. Wilson (1968) reported that prisoners make a better cooperative adaptation to prison life under participative than under bureaucratic management. Similarly, French, Kay, and Meyer (1966) observed that lower level managers' participation in an appraisal system facilitated their acceptance of the goal, the group's cohesiveness, and favorable attitudes toward the appraisal procedures. Jacobson, Charters, and Lieberman (1951) showed that workers who were involved in decision making by their foremen but not by their shop stewards tended to share the values and goals of management, whereas workers who were involved in decisions by their stewards but not by their foremen tended to share the goals and standards of the union.

In a demonstration of how to change housewives' meat-buying behavior (from steaks and chops to kidneys and liver) during World War II, Lewin (1947b) pointed the way toward the use of participative leadership to overcome resistance to change. Coch and French (1948) illustrated how a combination of participation in goal setting and the redesign of jobs resulted in the increased productivity of three groups of garment workers, with no such change obtained for a control group. Participation remains a key tool for those who cope with resistance to change (Lawler, 1986).

Effects of Participation on Satisfaction

Participation in all its forms has generally been found to generate greater satisfaction among subordinates. However, evidence has been gathered that *direction* can also be satisfying to subordinates, although to a lesser extent. Finally, examples can be cited for situations in which participation fails to be satisfying to subordinates.

Positive Effects. Preston and Heintz's (1949) previously mentioned study revealed the greater satisfaction of subordinates under participatory than under supervisory (directive) leaders. Similarly, Bass, Burger, et al. (1979) found that for an international sample of 1,641 managers who were engaged as subordinates in a training simulation, 51.7 percent preferred working again with a *participative* than with either of two kinds of directive supervisors (the choice by chance was 33.3 percent). Zimet and Fine (1955) contrasted the results of lectures given to 15 chief school administrators with

those of group-centered participative discussions. Although the administrators were initially more defensive in the discussions, subsequent sessions reduced their hostility and yielded increased warm, friendly behavior and more favorable attitudes toward themselves and others outside the meeting. Likewise, Ziller (1954) found that aircrews were more satisfied with decisions to simulated problems if they discussed the problem and their participative leader stated his opinion after the discussion. They were less satisfied when the decision was made authoritatively by a more directive leader. Again, according to Aspegren (1963), participatory leadership produced higher levels of satisfaction and task motivation among group members than did either directive or laissez-faire leadership. Storey's (1954) study of groups with participative leaders and groups with directive leaders found that members of participative groups were better satisfied with the group procedures, decisions reached, and intermember acceptance, although no significant differences were found in satisfaction with the leadership.

A. S. Tannenbaum (1963) reported the greater satisfaction among 200 clerks as a consequence of their increased opportunity to participate. Morse, Reimer, and Tannenbaum (1951) noted increased satisfaction with a new organizational arrangement that promoted more self-determination and group decision making by lowering by one echelon the authority to make and executive various decisions. What the supervisor had decided previously was now delegated to subordinates. In the same way, Mann and Baumgartel (1952) found that employees who felt free to discuss job-related and personal problems with their supervisors were better satisfied with the company, exhibited less absenteeism, and enjoyed membership in more cohesive work groups. Baumgartel (1956, 1957) found that scientists in research laboratories exhibited higher degrees of task motivation and job satisfaction under participatory than under directive supervisors. In a large metropolitan social service agency, Harrison (1985) obtained correlations of .42 and .47, respectively, between the extent to which the 30 superiors employed participative decision making and the 233 subordinates' desire to continue interacting with their leaders. Likewise, Mann, Indik, and Vroom (1963) reported that workers' satisfaction was highly related to their participation in decision making; their satisfaction and task motivation were especially low under directive supervision. In the same way, absences of white-collar workers related to how free they said they felt to discuss their job with their supervisor. Of the employees who were absent 4 or more times during a 6-month period, only 29 percent said they felt very free to talk with their boss, while 57 to 69 percent of those who were absent less often said they felt very free to hold such discussions (R. Likert, 1961a).

In a Dutch study, Drenth and Koopman (1984) obtained correlations for 175 municipal transport employees, 154 railway employees, and 153 steel workers of .44, .57, and .35, respectively, between the employees' participation in decision processes and the employees' satisfaction with the processes. Early participation in the decision process was particularly important to satisfaction.

Consistent with what was just presented, Weschler, Kahane, and Tannenbaum (1952) found that a research group that was led by a directive leader was less satisfied with its job. Dissatisfaction and high levels of job tension were also reported by Alutto and Belasco (1972) to be associated with "decision making deprivation."

Some Positive Effects of Direction

P. J. Burke (1966a, 1966b), as well as Katzell, Miller, Rotter, and Venet (1970), found that leadership direction could enhance group cohesiveness. Thiagarajan and Deep (1970) studied groups in which supervisors played three roles—*directive*, persuasive, and *participative*. The *directive* leader was more influential on coalescing agreement of follower and leader than the persuasive leader, and the persuasive leader was more influential than the *participative* one.

In an experiment with 47 executives, Bass (1967a) reported that the simulated advisory staff of a department head shifted and coalesced more if the department head announced his opinion, particularly if he did so at the beginning of the problem-solving meeting. In the same way, Anderson and Balzer (1988) showed for 19 teams in a university residence hall that were dealing with various problems, if the leaders immediately stated their opinions instead of withholding them until later in the discussion, fewer alternatives were

proposed, presumably indicative of a greater acceptance of the leader's point of view. However, T. A. Hill (1973) found that a consensus in student groups was more likely to be achieved when the leader was least opinionated. More will be said about the effects of directiveness on acceptance in the discussion of how contingencies modify the effects of participation and direction.

When Both Direction and Participation May Be Satisfying. Farrow, Valenzi, and Bass's (1980) analyses of approximately 1,400 subordinates' descriptions of their 350 managers in the Bass-Valenzi Management Styles Survey found that the managers' consultation correlated .34 with the subordinates' satisfaction with their jobs and .53 with the subordinates' satisfaction with their supervisors. The managers' *participation*, as seen by the subordinates, correlated .25 with their job satisfaction and .41 with their satisfaction with the leader. Comparable correlations of delegation with satisfaction were .32 and .46. However, *direction* also was positively correlated with satisfaction (.17 and .38). Only negotiation or manipulation was negatively related to job satisfaction (−.16) and satisfaction with the leader (−.16). Using the same Bass-Valenzi instrument with 147 assistant school superintendents' descriptions of their superintendents, Wilcox (1982) obtained similar results. The superintendents' frequency of *participation*, according to their assistant superintendents, correlated .37 with the assistants' job satisfaction and .41 with their satisfaction with the superintendents' leadership. The superintendents' *direction* correlated .20 with the assistant superintendents' job satisfaction, but .50 with their satisfaction with the superintendents' leadership.

In both the Farrow, Bass, and Valenzi and the Wilcox studies, consultation (when the leader seeks advice from subordinates but makes the final decision) and delegation (when the decision is left to the subordinates) were seen as more satisfying leadership styles than was *participation* (when the decision is shared between the leader and the subordinates). Thus, Wilcox obtained a correlation of .58 between consultation and satisfaction with the superintendents' leadership and .43 between delegation and such satisfaction. *Participation* and satisfaction correlated somewhat lower. A similar pattern of correlations with the same instrument translated into Turkish was obtained by Ergun and Onaran (1981) for 107 subordinates' descriptions of their supervisors in the Turkish Electrical Authority.

When Participation Is Not Satisfying. Pheysey and Payne (1970) found no relation between members' satisfaction and their amount of participation. Page and McGinnies (1959) showed a motion picture to groups of subjects who discussed the film under two styles of leadership—directive and nondirective. The directive leader was rated by the members as significantly more interesting, satisfying, purposeful, frank, industrious, and persuasive than was the nondirective leader. Levy (1954a, 1954b) also found that the satisfaction of members was higher under directive than under nondirective leadership. Likewise, Berkowitz (1953b) observed decision-making groups in business and governmental organizations and found that group cohesiveness and the members' satisfaction decreased with participative leadership and increased with directive leadership. Although one would expect to find that leaders who say they delegate a great deal generate greater satisfaction among their subordinates, often the subordinates fail to appreciate the delegation (Stogdill & Shartle, 1948). The subordinates may not appreciate it because they believe that they lack the authority to go along with the responsibilities that have been delegated to them. Also, superiors may believe they are delegating, but their subordinates may see the same behavior as dumping undesirable assignments on them. Or, they may think the delegation is marred by too close monitoring; the resources necessary to carry out the delegated task may not be provided; or the leader's instructions may be ambiguous. Some of the surrounding conditions that contribute to the failure of participation to be satisfying to subordinates can be a consequence of contingencies to be discussed later.

Effects of Participation on Involvement, Commitment, and Loyalty

According to D. Katz (1951), workers tend to enter or withdraw psychologically from groups as a function of their ability to make decisions in the respective groups. Many commentators (see, for example, Tichy & Devanna, 1986) have noted that the participation of em-

ployees is critical for the reorganization of a firm or agency and its successful implementation.

Kahn and Tannenbaum (1957) and Tannenbaum and Smith (1964) surveyed organized workers and members of women's clubs. The members' participation was facilitated by leaders who encouraged consultation and participation in activities. The members' loyalty to the organization was also strengthened by participation in activities. Likewise, in a study of technicians and laboratory testers at the Tennessee Valley Authority, Patchen (1970) found that participative management led to increased individual integration into the organization. Individuals became more involved in the work project when they were engaged in participative decision making. Siegel and Ruh (1973) reported similar results in a study of manufacturing employees; participative leadership was positively related to the employees' involvement in their jobs.

The opportunity to participate can be a mixed blessing. According to a nationwide survey by Gurin, Veroff, and Feld (1960), participation in the decision-making process increases both one's involvement in one's job and one's frustration with it. A. S. Tannenbaum (1963) studied 200 clerks who were given greater responsibility to make decisions. Despite their general increase in satisfaction, the clerks felt less of a sense of accomplishment at the end of the workday and less satisfied with their present level in the organization. In acquiring an increased feeling of responsibility for the work, the clerks developed standards of achievement that were harder to satisfy.

Locke (1968) began a long line of investigation by questioning whether the mere directive assignment of hard goals to people was sufficient to generate their heightened commitment and productivity; the people did not have to participate in the decision to set the hard goals. Considerable experimental support was obtained in U.S. studies (Latham & Baldes, 1975). Likewise, feedback appeared more important than participation in a study of the safety practices of 150 U.S. workers by Fellner and Sulzer-Azaroff (1985). But in Israeli experiments, Erez and Arad (1986) noted that involvement and commitment were required for the heightened productivity to occur, and such involvement and commitment could be obtained only if the experimental subjects participated in setting the goals. The U.S.-Israeli differences appear to have been resolved (Locke, Latham, & Erez, 1987) when it was discovered that participation was unnecessary in the United States for the required commitment to be achieved because the commitment seemed to have been gained by the friendly, supportive behavior of the experimenter is assigning the goals. In Israel, the experimenter who assigned the goals was curt and abrupt. Here, only with participation in the goal setting, was it possible to obtain the expected commitment and subsequent heightened performance. Thus, relations-oriented leadership, the subject of the next chapter, may substitute (as in the U.S. experiments) for actual participation in gaining the commitment of subordinates.

Effects on Task Performance

Generally, both participation and direction can affect subordinates' task performance and task outcomes. For example, Nutt (1986) examined 84 cases from service organizations, such as hospitals, governmental agencies, charities, and professional societies, in which managers had sponsored efforts to implement planned changes in their organizations. In 16 cases, the directive managers first acquired the necessary authority and then demonstrated or justified the changes with appropriate information; they were successful in their implementation efforts in 100 percent of these 16 cases. In another 14 cases, the participative managers first stipulated the needs, opportunities, and objectives and then set up task forces to develop recommendations; overall success occurred in 84 percent of the 14 cases. In 35 cases, managers used persuasion to sell the planned changes after the changes had been formulated by the staff or consultants; the success rate was 73 percent. In the remaining 19 cases, implementation was by management edict; least success was found. Here, the sponsor of the change used positional and personal power to issue directives ordering the changes; this approach achieved a success rate of 71 percent.

Effects on the Quality of Decisions

Experiments generally show that group decisions are superior to decisions reached by the average member of a group, although it is also true that the group decision may not be as good as that of the best member of

the group. But how often is the supervisor the best? If it could be guaranteed that the supervisor was always the best, then the quality of the decision might be better when decisions were made by the supervisor alone (Bass, 1960).

When 66 U.S. Air Force officers wrote decisions before a discussion and then met as an ad hoc staff to write the decisions, the decisions written by the staff were superior to the average quality of the decisions written by individuals without a discussion. At the same time, the quality was the same after the discussion, whether the decision was written by the staff or by the commander who had listened to the staff's discussion. Group discussions contributed to better decision making, whether the final decision was written by the group or by the person leading the group (Lorge, Fox, Davitz, & Brenner, 1958). Many others also studied the improved quality of decisions made by discussion groups.[10]

The quality of the decision was higher under participation than under a directive style of leadership that discouraged discussion. Lanzetta and Roby (1960) found that both time and error scores were better under participative than under directive leadership.

Leana (1983) engaged 208 undergraduate students in a role play of a business problem. In the 4-person groups, if the "vice president of operations," the formal leader of the group, was participative, rather than directive, the groups generated and discussed significantly more alternative solutions. The directive leaders tended to produce premature closure of the search for solutions, which presumably reduced the quality of the final decision that was reached. These effects were independent of the groups' cohesiveness. In the same way, Watson and Michaelsen (1984) demonstrated that participative leadership in a role-playing setting with 35 4-person student groups generated more effective problem solving than did directive leadership.

Effects on Productivity

If one searches for universal answers about the immediate effects of participation and direction on productivity, almost every possible alternative emerges. From

---

[10]These investigators included Blake and Mouton (1962b); Hoffman, Burke, and Maier (1965); Hoffman, Harburg, and Maier (1962); Hoffman and Maier (1967); Maier (1950); Maier and Solem (1952); and Solem (1953).

a review of the results of laboratory, correlational, and univariate field studies of the effects of leadership style on productivity, Locke and Schweiger (1979) concluded that they could find no overall trend favoring participative or directive leadership. As for field studies with multiple antecedent conditions and outcomes, they thought that other factors, such as training and reward systems, often could account for effects on productivity that were attributed to participation. Likewise, Erez and Arad (1986) demonstrated that appropriate information and involvement in goal setting were needed for a participative group discussion to generate higher-quality performance. Miller and Monge's (1986) meta-analysis confirmed several additional conclusions to be discussed later.

When Directive Leadership Is Better

Numerous specific studies can be cited in support of directive leadership, and a comparable number of studies can be cited in support of participative leadership. Katzell, Miller, Rotter, and Venet (1970) studied small problem-solving groups. More directiveness by leaders was positively associated with the greater effectiveness of groups. Kidd and Christy (1961) found that the avoidance of errors was greatest under directive leadership. Schumer (1962) obtained results which indicated that both the quality and quantity of productivity were enhanced by a directive form of leadership. Similarly, Torrance (1952) contrasted 5 types of critiques following 16 minutes of problem-solving activity by aircrews in survival school to see which resulted in the greatest improvement in the ability to solve subsequent problems. The largest gains were made when an expert directed the critique; the next largest, with guided discussion (participative leadership); and the least gain, with free discussion (laissez-faire leadership) in which no control was exerted.

Schlesinger, Jackson, and Butman (1960) found that committees are more effective in solving problems under directive than under nondirective leadership. Stagner (1969), who studied a large sample of corporation executives by questionnaire, observed that corporate profits were associated with more formality, more centralization of decision making, and less personalized management.

When Participative Leadership Is Better. In the well-known seminal experiment by Coch and French (1948), detailed in Chapter 14, the participation of pajama-manufacturing workers in decision making generated higher productivity and a lower turnover of personnel than did nonparticipation by a control group. A subsequent replication yielded comparable results (Marrow, Bowers, & Seashore, 1968). With groups of employees of a large supplier of aerospace electronics, Hinrichs (1978) obtained production increases of 20 to 30 percent and reductions in errors of 30 to 50 percent in 27 of 40 employee groups who were encouraged to participate over a 4-year period.

R. Likert (1977b), aiming toward long-range effects, involved various business and industrial groups in management by group objectives (MBGO). MBGO generates the participative sharing of data and the setting of a group's goals. A 27 percent increase in profits over the previous year from a retail sales division was reported. Such participation by teams of foremen resulted in a rise in productivity of 15 percent and a decrease in scrap from 7 to 14 percent in an auto assembly plant. In an early study reported by the Survey Research Center (1948), work groups were more productive among those first-level supervisors in an insurance company who encouraged their workers to participate in decisions. Indik, Georgopoulos, and Seashore (1961) showed that among 975 delivery men at 27 parcel delivery stations, the ease and freedom they felt in communicating with their superiors at a station correlated between .39 and .48 with the average deliveries the men completed daily in relation to the standard time allotted for completion.

R. J. Solomon (1976) demonstrated the greater effectiveness of participative library directors. The immediate subordinates of the directors evaluated the effectiveness of the services supplied by other departments. For instance, personnel in the acquisition departments evaluated the effectiveness of the circulation departments. Directors who were consultative and *participative* were the most conducive to high ratings of effective departments under them and directors who were manipulative were the least conducive. Similarly, Reeder (1981) employed path analysis to show that participative leadership by supervisors of U.S. Army clerks and programmers was more causally related to the subordinates' productivity than to the supervisors' knowledge of their subordinates' work.

When No Differences in Effects Were Found. In still other studies, both participation and direction were seen to have similar effects on task performance. According to Weschler, Kahane, and Tannenbaum (1952), a research group perceived itself to be less productive than one led by a participative leader. However, the leader's boss thought the group led by the directive leader was more productive. Lange and Jacobs (1960) and Lange, Campbell, Katter, and Shanley (1958) found that both directive patterns of leadership behavior and encouraging participation were positively and significantly related to the performance ratings of groups. Similarly, Farrow, Valenzi, and Bass (1980) found that effectiveness correlated positively with the amount of *direction* (.23) by about 250 managers, as seen by 1,400 subordinates. Effectiveness also correlated positively with various participatory approaches: consultation (.33), *participation* (.23), and delegation (.22). Only negotiation or manipulation by managers was negatively related to effectiveness (−.25).

McCurdy and Eber (1953) observed that groups in which free communication and decision making were practiced did not perform more effectively than did those in which the leader made all the decisions. Similarly, neither Spector and Suttell (1956) nor Tomekovic (1962) found differences in productivity between participative and nonparticipative groups.

In a study of 20 small shoe-manufacturing firms, Willits (1967) found that neither the degree of delegation by the president nor the extent of participation by executives in decision making was related to measures of the companies' success. Heyns (1948) and W. M. Fox (1957) also found no differences of consequence.

Effects on the Manager's Rate of Advancement

Hall and Donnell (1979) calculated the rate at which managers had been promoted by comparing their organizational level with their age. Over 2,000 subordinates indicated the extent to which the 731 managers allowed and encouraged them to participate in making and influencing work-related decisions. Although slowly and moderately advancing managers were seen to permit or encourage very little participation, faster advancing managers did a lot of it. On the other hand, Farrow, Valenzi, and Bass (1981) determined, for upwards of 1,200 managers and their subordinates, that the managers whose salaries were higher than would have been predicted from their function, their organization, their sex, and their seniority were seen by their subordinates to be persuasive, manipulative, and negotiative. Such managers were downgraded in effectiveness by their subordinates but evidently were pleasing to their bosses, who awarded them higher-than-expected salaries. Managers who were favored by their subordinates for their frequent consultation, *participation*, delegation, and *direction* were not similarly awarded salaries above the norms by their bosses.

Three Models in Support of Participation

Support for participative leadership is built into 3 models: cognitive, affective, and contingent (Miller & Monge, 1986). Cognitive models propose that participation contributes to subordinates' satisfaction and productivity because it improves the interchange of important information in the organization. For example, Anthony (1978) argued that workers have more knowledge than do their managers and their participation increases the information needed for high-quality decision making. Furthermore, as Melcher (1976) noted, workers will better under the requirements for implementing decisions if they have participated in the decision-making process. In a study of 12 R & D high-technology projects, McDonough and Kinnunen (1984) found that in the more successful projects, there was more discussion among the different levels of management about the projects' goals and more constant distribution of information about progress.

The satisfaction of employees is a side effect of such participation (Ritchie & Miles, 1970). Since the distribution of information is the crucial aspect of participation, Miller and Monge (1986) deduced that stronger effects should occur more for the participation of employees in decisions about the design of a job than in company-wide policy decisions. Satisfaction should occur only after the feedback of information about the consequences of the participation. Participation should not necessarily pay off in greater satisfaction merely for working in a participative climate or for a participative leader. It should pay off only when the exchange of knowledge is relevant to the decisions in questions.

The affective model, strongly endorsed by the human relations school of thought (see, for example, Maslow, 1965; McGregor, 1960), suggests that participation generates the satisfaction of higher-order needs in subordinates, which, in turn, increase the subordinates' motivation, satisfaction, and quality and quantity of performance.

The third model stresses various contingencies. One such contingency is the importance of the perception of participation. Another is the felt opportunity to participate. Still another is the number of issues involved. From all 41 weighted and adjusted estimates of the relation between the amount of participative leadership and the satisfaction of subordinates, Miller and Monge (1986) obtained a mean correlation of .34 in their meta-analysis cited earlier. The results were similar for students and organizational respondents. The correlation rose to .48 when the respondents *perceived* themselves to be participating on a multiplicity of issues (see, for example, Obradovic, 1970), while it dropped to .21 if only a single specific issue was involved (see, for instance, Alutto & Acito, 1974). The correlation was only .16 between *actual* participation and satisfaction. What makes participative leadership satisfying for subordinates is not so much their actual participation in the decision-making process as their feeling that they genuinely have the opportunity to do so if they want to contribute to making the decision. Only 50 percent of the American electorate actually votes in presidential elections; they are satisfied to remain on the sidelines. Yet, if they were denied the ballot, strong protests, cries of dictatorship, and a great increase in dissatisfaction with the system would ensue.

From 25 studies, the Miller-Monge meta-analysis yielded a mean of .15 between participative leadership and the productivity of subordinates. The mean rose to .27 for field studies (in contrast to laboratory settings). As was reported earlier, in those laboratory studies in which participants were subject to participative or directive leadership, the mean correlation was −.33 (productivity was higher with direction). When a friendly supervisor subjected the participants to arbitrarily assigned goals or to participation in setting the

goals, the mean correlation with productivity was −.01. It made no difference in these temporary conditions with a friendly experimenter whether arbitrary direction or participation was employed.

Miller and Monge did not find a change in these mean results for managers compared to lower-level employees or in different kinds of organizations, nor could they test the effects of personality. They concluded that with reference to such contingencies, they had found more support for the affective model than for the cognitive or contingent models. They reasoned in favor of the affective model because (1) they had found stronger effects between participation and satisfaction than between participation and productivity and (2) they had found stronger effects of a participative climate on the satisfaction of subordinates who were involved in multiple issues, rather than in a single one.

With reference to another contingency, they obtained mean correlations of −.33 versus .27 between participation and productivity in the laboratory versus the field studies. They inferred that directive leadership contributed to productivity in the laboratory because laboratory tasks tend to be simpler and have clear objectives and outcomes. They thought that participation yielded more productivity in the field because tasks in the real-life work setting are likely to be more complex and have unclear objectives and outcomes.

Wagner and Gooding (1987) uncovered another contingency. If single-source bias is present, in that the same respondent provides the data on participation and outcomes, mean correlations range from .34 to .42. But if one source provides the measure of participation and another source provides the data on outcomes, the range of correlations lowers to between .09 and .25.

Overall, the impact of participation, per se, on performance and satisfaction is evident.

Additional support for the contingent model stems from the fact that, as was noted earlier, a majority of managers actually are directive or participative, depending on the nature of the decision to be made. With this fact in mind, Hambleton and Gumpert (1982) found that, for 65 managers, their 189 subordinates, and their 56 supervisors, the adaptable, flexible manager who made a greater use of the variety of styles appropriate to different situations, according to the

Hersey-Blanchard model (1977),[11] emerged with significant and practical gains in the subordinates' performance.

Effects on Productivity. With reference to performance, Lawler (1986) integrated the models, suggesting that the effective participative process requires a multiplicative combination of the adequate flow of information, the requisite knowledge by employees of what needs to be done, shared power to decide, and satisfactory rewards for implementation. If any one of these elements is missing, the process will fail.

Contingent Effects of Directive and Participative Leadership

Is there one best way? Or do the different leadership decision-making styles differ in achieving mutual objectives, group goals, and the compliance of subordinates, depending on the circumstances? R. Likert (1977a) argued that if long-term measures of effectiveness are the criteria of consequence, then a democratic approach, including shared participative decision making, is universally more effective as long as the leader is task oriented. Blake and Mouton (1964) presented similar arguments for an integrated task- and relations-oriented approach. There are no contingencies for Likert or Blake. On the other hand, summarizing the previous literature, which was based mainly on short-term laboratory studies and surveys, Bass and Barrett (1981) noted that participative leadership is contraindicated for situations with short-term perspectives when interaction is restricted by the task, when the higher authority disapproves, when maximum output is demanded, when subordinates do not expect to participate, when leaders are unready for participation, and when emergencies occur.

Many comparable theories have been advanced on the basis of the postulate that effective leaders use participation or directive leadership styles to fit the situation. (See, as an example, Austin's [1981] style-flex model.) And countless commentaries and the inspirational management literature of the 1980s repeated the

virtues of the life-cycle theory (Hersey & Blanchard, 1969a) that the key situational factor for leaders to consider is the maturity of their subordinates (Carbone, 1981).

The evidence seen so far is that generally participative leadership enhances the quality of decisions and is more satisfying, but in the short run, at least, it may be less conducive to productivity than is directive leadership. Various contingencies must be taken into account to predict and understand more fully the impact of direction and participation. These contingencies include the differences between the leaders and their followers, the task objectives, and the environmental constraints under which they must operate.

Three bases for understanding exist. First, one can draw empirical inferences from surveys in which correlations have been run between the style of the leader and productivity or satisfaction under different contingencies. Second, one can draw further inferences from experiments in which each leadership style has been introduced under each contingency. Third, beginning with several acceptable assumptions that are consistent with what was said earlier about the impact of participation on the acceptance of followers and the quality of decisions, one can present models that prescribe which style of leadership is likely to be more effective. Empirical data supporting or refuting the propositions derived from the models can also be presented.

Superior-Subordinate Competence, Motivation, and Personality

Whether direction or participation is more effective as a leadership style has been found in a number of investigations to depend on the competence, motivation, and personality of the leaders and their subordinates. Probably the single most emphasized modifier in determining whether participative or directive leadership will be more effective is the ability of the subordinate relative to the leader and the information they each possess (Hersey & Blanchard, 1977). Mulder (1971) and Miner (1973) pointed out that it may be impossible and counterproductive for leaders to be participative in style if they are much more expert than their subordinates on the matters to be decided. What is important

---

[11]To be detailed in the next chapter.

to whether direction or participation work better is how much training and information the leader and the subordinate have (Filley, House, & Kerr, 1979; Locke & Schweiger, 1979). Blyth (1987) randomly assigned leaders to four conditions: The leaders were either trained or untrained in the use of survival gear and were instructed either to be directive or participative with their groups. Only the directive leaders who had been trained to use the survival gear had groups that performed well; participative leaders with the training performed no better than did those without training. When Blyth trained the group members but not the leaders to use the gear and then instructed the leaders to be directive or participative, the groups with participative leaders performed better than did those with directive leaders.

Communication network experiments, reported in Chapter 30, demonstrated that if leaders are in the center of a network, they are likely to be most informed, since they are in two-way contact with all the people at the periphery. Their network will be more effective if they are directive. On the other hand, if the leaders occupy peripheral positions, their network will be most effective if they are more participative (Shaw, 1954a).

Bass and Ryterband (1979) reported a study in which 18 wives of managers were asked to meet individually with a male manager (not their own spouse) to reach decisions about either company affairs or household affairs. The managers were instructed to be either directive or participative as the leaders in a counterbalanced design. The housewives felt responsibility for the household discussion regardless of the leader's style, but felt responsibility for the discussion about the company with the participative leader but not with the directive leader. The wives reported considerable hostility toward the directive leader in discussion of household affairs, and such meetings were the least satisfying experience for them. In contrast, the wives did not react negatively when leaders directed the decision-making process if the problem concerned company issues.

Latham and Baldes (1975) provided the strongest evidence to support the contention that both the ability and motivation of the leader, combined with the ability and motivation of the subordinates, determine what style of leadership will prove more effective. Latham and Baldes studied 49 groups of U.S. Army enlisted cooks. The cooks operated mess halls, each of which was led by a mess steward who was either directive or nondirective, according to behavioral descriptions of the steward by the group on such items as, "The mess steward decides what shall be done and how it shall be done." The tendency of the steward to enforce standards was measured by such items as, "The mess steward maintains definite standards of performance." Motivation was measured by responses to such questions as, "How hard do you work and do as good a job as possible?" The amount of ability of the stewards and cooks were obtained from a 50-item test. Measures of the quality of mess hall services were obtained from weekly inspections made by food service officers.

Nondirective participative leadership worked better when the cooks were both higher in ability and motivation. On the other hand, directive leadership resulted in a much more effective food service when the stewards were higher in ability and the cooks were highly motivated. Such directive leadership resulted in lower inspection ratings if the steward was lower in ability and the cooks were lower in motivation. Enforcement of standards by the steward generated the best food-inspection ratings either when the cooks were high in both ability and motivation or low in both ability and motivation. Particularly deleterious was the enforcement of standards when the cooks were high in ability but low in motivation.

The steward's tested intelligence contributed to the effectiveness of the mess halls but only when the steward was directive and the cooks were highly motivated. Furthermore, with highly motivated cooks, nondirective leadership resulted in a correlation of .56 between the cooks' level of ability as cooks and the effectiveness of operations. But here, directive leadership generated an opposite correlation of −.48 between the cooks' ability and effectiveness. With nondirective leadership, if the cooks' motivation was low, the cooks' ability correlated −.45 with the effectiveness of the mess halls; with directive leadership, the correlation was −.20. Parallel results were obtained when the tested intelligence of the cooks was used as an indicator of their ability.

Cognitive Resources Model. Blades's research was generated from the Fiedler cognitive resources model.[12] Fiedler and Garcia (1986) proposed that whether leaders are directive or participative depends on their personality and control of the situation. The leaders affect the groups' actions through such direction but only if the groups are supportive and accepting. If the leaders are participative, the members' intellectual abilities, motivation, and support will help determine the groups' actions. Outcomes of tasks are affected but not interpersonal relations.

Earlier support for the cognitive resources model came from Bons and Fiedler (1976), who found that among 138 U.S. Army squad leaders, the leaders' intelligence correlated .44 with their squads' performance of tasks. Yet the correlation fell to .04 when the squad leaders failed to be directive. Similar results were obtained by Fiedler, O'Brien, and Ilgen (1969) in a study of 41 small public health teams in Honduras. When the leader's direction was high, the leader's intelligence correlated .48 with community developments. When the leader's direction was low, the correlation fell to −.20. Intelligent, informed, able leaders can contribute more to the effectiveness of groups by being directive rather than participative, but only if their subordinates are already highly motivated and supportive of their efforts.

Personality. In Vroom's (1959) study of 108 supervisors in a retail parcel-delivery service, productivity was found to correlate with felt influence on decisions among egalitarians much more than among authoritarians. Satisfaction on the job was increased by participation, but only for subordinates with egalitarian attitudes. A. S. Tannenbaum (1958) noted that followers who were predisposed to participation tended to be satisfied under conditions of increased involvement. Those who were predisposed to dependence, however, reacted adversely to increased participation. Runyon (1973) and Mitchell, Smyser, and Weed (1975) found that, as might be expected, internally controlled subordinates were more satisfied with participative supervisors but externally controlled subordinates were more satisfied with directive supervisors.

[12]See Chapter 7.

Passive followers favored a more directive leader in Page and McGinnies's (1959) comparison of discussion groups led by directive and participative leaders. Likewise, in simulations (Bass, Burger, et al., 1979), apathetic subordinates were found to be relatively more comfortable with *directive* supervisors.

Saville (1984) proposed that supervisors who favored some form of direction or participation could be matched with subordinates who complemented them to maximize supervisory-subordinate compatibility and to minimize the development of serious problems between them. Receptive, dependent subordinates should be matched with *directive* supervisors; more reciprocating types of subordinates complement negotiative supervisors; more innovative, critical subordinates should be assigned to consultative supervisors; more affiliative, democratic subordinates should be matched with *participative* supervisors; and more self-reliant subordinates will fit best with delegative supervisors.

Bass, Valenzi, and Farrow (1977) found that for 244 managers and their 992 subordinates, judged effectiveness by both managers and subordinates correlated positively with delegative supervision (as seen by the subordinates) if the managers tended to regard the world as fair minded and if the subordinates were introspective but not assertive. The same was true for the effectiveness of *participative* leadership. In addition, it helped if the manager had an assertive personality. Consultation was more effective with introspective, unassertive subordinates and assertive managers. Manipulation and negotiation were particularly more effective with introspective managers and subordinates. The personalities of the managers or the subordinates were of no consequence to the effectiveness of *direction.* Likewise, in a consumer finance firm, Tosi (1970) failed to find that the subordinates' personalities made any difference.

Organizational and Interpersonal Relations

Bass, Valenzi, and Farrow (1977) developed discriminant functions for 244 managers and the 992 subordinates of work groups who were above and below the median in effectiveness who had responded to a questionnaire about the system of inputs, relations, and outputs under which they perceived themselves to operate. They found that the effectiveness of operations was higher if harmony and trust were higher. Nevertheless, a greater amount of harmony made consultative leadership even more conducive to effective operations, while a greater amount of trust in the organization contributed more to the impact on effectiveness of the leader's *participation*.

Power. Kipnis (1958) studied groups of children under different conditions of leadership, reward, and threat. Both reward and threat produced more public compliance than did the control condition. Participative leadership induced more children to change their beliefs when leadership was associated with the power to reward. Under threat of punishment for noncompliance, significantly fewer children changed their beliefs under participative leadership than under lecture conditions. The participative leader was better liked than the lecturer if he did not threaten. Similarly, Patchen (1962) found that directive supervision resulted in a group's high output only if the group was also cohesive and directed by a supervisor who was seen to be a rewarding figure.

Ergun and Onaran (1981) found that Turkish supervisors who were more active in either *direction* or *participation* were judged more effective when both the managers and the subordinates lacked power. Activity appeared to be a substitute for power.

Pelz (1951) observed that participative leadership by Detroit Edison managers generated satisfaction among employees only when the managers had influence "upstairs." But House, Filley, and Gujarati (1971) failed to replicate this finding for R & D managers in another firm.

Falling Dominoes Effects. The effectiveness of participatory leadership at lower levels in an organization will depend on the practice of such leadership also at higher levels, as well as in adjacent departments. Otherwise, conflict emerges (Lowin, 1968). Such conflict may be avoided if R. Likert's (1967) organization of overlapping groups is used. Here, every manager is a linchpin that connects the participatory group of the manager and his or her subordinates with the participa-

tory group of the manager's boss, the manager's peers, and the manager.

Constraints and Goals. Hemphill (1949b) found that directive behavior by leaders is most readily accepted in groups with a closely restricted membership, a stratified status structure, and members who are dependent on the groups. On the other hand, Murnighan and Leung (1976) obtained results indicating that participation helped performance only when subordinates thought the task was important. According to Ergun and Onaran (1981), the effectiveness of the unit, organization, and supervisor increased, particularly when the leader used *direction* when constraints were low, goals were clear, and the interdependence of tasks was high. *Participation* correlated more highly with the effectiveness for interdependent work teams with clear objectives and considerable discretionary opportunities.

Task Requirements. Shaw and Blum (1966) found that directive leadership was more effective in structured task situations, while nondirective leadership was more effective in less structured conditions. Roby, Nicol, and Farrell (1963) obtained indications that problems that required a reaction to environmental changes were more quickly solved under participative conditions, but that problems that necessitated coordinated action were solved more efficiently under directive leadership.

The leadership decision-making style in an organization is influenced by whether the organization must deal with a stable or turbulent market. Firms that operate in turbulent markets are more effective if they encourage participation and decision making at the lowest possible levels (Emery & Trist, 1965). Burns and Stalker (1961) contrasted the relatively stable environment of a rayon mill with the more unstable conditions faced by firms in the electronics industry. For the mill, in its stable environment, a "mechanistic" system with directive supervision was most effective. In the electronics field, with its rapidly changing environment, a more participative, "organic" system seemed most effective.

Similar conclusions were reached by Lawrence and

Lorsch (1967a, 1967b). For a container firm with a stable environment, effective decision-making processes within the firm were likely to be directive; in a plastics firm facing a more turbulent environment, effective decision-making processes were more likely to be participative. Nonetheless, Wagner and Gooding's (1987) meta-analysis of 118 correlational analyses on the extent to which the interdependence and complexity of tasks and performance standards moderate the effects of participation on employees' performance, motivation, satisfaction with, and acceptance of decisions revealed few differences in the effects of participation on outcomes if the task was complex rather than simple, if the task involved independence or interdependence, and if performance standards were present or absent.

Objectives. If the task has a practical rather than a theoretical outcome, directive supervision may be more effective. Korten (1968) observed that if the final product of a task was practical, more directive supervision was in order. On the other hand, if the outcome was theoretical, participation was of more utility. However, participative leadership needs to have a focus to affect productivity. Lawrence and Smith (1955) studied employees who were checkers and mail openers over a five-week period. Groups of each type of employee held participative discussions either about their work or to set the groups' goals. Only the goal-setting groups showed increased productivity, although both types of meetings were equally satisfying to the participants.

The increased productivity of the goal-setting groups was probably connected to the importance attached to the meeting in which the participative leadership occurred. Thus, Cosier and Aplin (1980) concluded, from an experiment with 84 undergraduate business students, that having the freedom to choose objectives about a task of prediction was important to them but having the freedom to schedule the procedure to be used was not. Delegation to them of the choice of objectives yielded a much better performance than assignment of the objectives, but delegation or assignment of the schedule to be followed made no difference to them. Similarly, Drenth and Koopman (1984) reported that among 56 Dutch employees, satisfaction with decisions was enhanced most by opportunities to participate for those employees who were unclear about their goals. For these same employees, however, satisfaction with the outcomes and implementation of the decisions correlated between .26 and .40 if the decisions were about tactical matters that were of consequence to them. But the parallel correlations ranged from −.11 to .13 if the decisions were about organizational strategies that the employees did not think were of such direct consequence to them. This finding lent confidence to arguments by Bass and Shackleton (1979) that participative management should be restricted to the kinds of decisions that are of direct concern to employees. Consultation with production employees about financial and marketing decisions may make little sense, in contrast to consultations about overtime policies.

When leaders overstep their authority by forcing an arbitrary decision on their groups, the expected resistance and hostility may fail to materialize if the leaders' behavior actually facilitates the achievement of the groups' goals. Whether leaders reach their objectives depends on whether the style of leadership they choose meets the needs of their subordinates to attain their goals and whether it clarifies for the subordinates the paths to achieve the goals (House & Mitchell, 1974). Participation may meet subordinates' needs but may fail to clarify goals without some direction from the leaders.

Time Perspective. If the supervisors' time perspective is short, that is, if they have some immediate objectives to attain, they are likely to find it most effective to be directive. Alternatively, if an important objective is the long-term efficiency of their groups, participation is more likely to pay off (Hahn & Trittipoe, 1961).

The Passage of Time. The passage of time itself may make a difference in the efficacy of early participation. Ivancevich (1976) demonstrated that, over time, the positive effects of involvement in goal setting may dissipate. Employees may become immersed in the job itself and forget their earlier involvement in decisions. The amount of participation by subordinates seems to reach an optimum. If actual participation is greater than expected, R. Likert (1959) noted that dissatisfaction will result. Ivancevich (1979) found that performance suffered when participation was above or below optimum.

A Deduced Model for Achieving Decision Quality or Subordinate Acceptance

Among the prescriptive models that indicate when leaders should be directive and when they should be participative, two have been particularly popular—that by Hersey and Blanchard (1977) and that by Vroom and Yetton (1974). Each model details the situations in which practicing managers should be directive and those in which they should be participative to maximize satisfaction and effectiveness. The former model is derived from empirical studies; the latter, from more rigorous deduction. The former is supported mainly by observation and commentaries of users and is seen to be fuzzy in its prescription and application; the latter is supported (and sometimes refuted) by controlled empirical surveys and experiments. Nevertheless, early on, criticisms were leveled at the Vroom-Yetton model for its lack of parsimony and applicability to management (Filley, House, & Kerr, 1976). Yet, unlike the Hersey-Blanchard model, the Vroom-Yetton model was more intellectually rigorous and lent itself more readily to empirical testing of its validity, although, as shall be seen, it is not without its serious flaws. The Vroom-Yetton model is examined in detail here; the Hersey-Blanchard model is discussed extensively in the next chapter.

Description of the Vroom-Yetton Model

The leadership decision style that is most conducive to effectiveness in the Vroom-Yetton model depends on the demand characteristics of the situation. Particularly important is whether the leader is aiming for a high-quality decision or for the subordinates' acceptance of the decision. Efforts have been made to show an adequate correspondence between deductions derived from the model and what can be induced empirically from managers' preferred and actual styles in dealing with problems containing various combinations of the demand characteristics.

The Direction-Participation Continuum. Vroom and Yetton (1973, p. 13) laid out the direction-participation continuum as follows:

AI: You solve problem or make decision yourself using information available to you.

AII: You obtain necessary information from subordinates, then decide on the solution to the problem yourself. Subordinates are not asked to generate or evaluate alternative solutions.

CI: You share the problem with relevant subordinates *individually*, getting their ideas and suggestions. Then you make the decision, which may or may not reflect your subordinates' influence.

CII: You share the problem with your subordinates *as a group*, collectively obtaining their ideas and suggestions. Then you make the decision, which may or may not reflect your subordinates' influence.

GI: You share the problem with relevant subordinates *individually*. Together you generate and evaluate alternatives and attempt to reach a solution. You do not try to influence the subordinate to adopt "your" solution and you are willing to implement any solution reached.

GII: You share the problem with your subordinates *as a group*. Together you generate and evaluate alternatives and attempt to reach a solution. You do not try to influence the group to adopt "your" solution and you are willing to accept and implement any solution which has the support of the entire group. Thus, CI and CII are consultative leadership either with each subordinate alone or all together. Similarly, GI and GII are *participative* either with each subordinate alone or all together.

Subsequently, Vroom and Jago (1974, p 745) added another choice:

DI: You delegate the problem to one of your subordinates, providing him with any relevant information that you possess, but giving him responsibility for solving the problem by himself. Any solution which the person reaches will receive your support.

The choice of AI is *directive*. AII is also directive and CI and CII are consultative. GI and GII are *participative* and DI is delegative.

The Situational Demands. The situational-demand characteristics and the requirements of the problem for the leader depend on whether the answers to the following seven questions are "yes" or "no":

1. Is there a quality requirement such that one solution is better than another?
2. Does the leader have sufficient information to make a high-quality decision?
3. Is the problem structured?
4. Is the subordinates' acceptance of the decision critical to effective implementation?
5. If the leader were to make the decision by himself or herself, is it reasonably certain that the decision would be accepted by the subordinates?
6. Do subordinates share the organizational goals to be obtained in solving this problem?
7. Is conflict among subordinates likely in preferred solutions?

The Feasible Sets. Seven rules are imposed to limit various styles of leadership to those feasible sets that can be deduced to protect the quality of the solution and acceptance of the decision: (1) AI is eliminated as a possible choice for the leader when the quality of the solution is important and the leader lacks information, (2) GII is eliminated from the feasible set of leadership styles if quality is important and subordinates do not share organizational goals, (3) AI, AII, and CI are eliminated when quality is important, the leader lacks information, and the problem is unstructured, (4) AI and AII are eliminated from the feasible set if the subordinates' acceptance of the solution is critical, (5) AI, AII, and CI are eliminated (a group approach is necessary to resolve conflicts) if the subordinates' acceptance is critical and subordinates are likely to disagree about the solution, (6) AI, AII, CI, and CII are eliminated if acceptance

but not quality is critical, and (7) AI, AII, CI, and CII are eliminated if acceptance is critical and subordinates share the organization's goals. Shared *participation*, GII, is deduced to be the only suitable leadership style.

Figure 22.2 shows the decision tree that must be followed, given the situational characteristics and the rules for eliminating choices of leadership styles. For example, in the flow chart in Figure 22.2, if the leader's answer to question 1 is that the problem does not require a high-quality decision, the leader's next decision is about whether the subordinates' acceptance is important (question 4). If a directive decision is seen to be unacceptable (question 5), the appropriate style for the leader to choose is GII, *participation* of the leader and all subordinates together in making the decision.

Development of Diagnostic Procedure

An initial roster of managers were asked to describe, in written form, a recent problem that they had to solve in carrying out their leadership role. The managers then specified the style (AI, AII, CI, CII, or GII) that came closest to the one they had actually used in dealing with that problem. They described the problem in terms of its quality and situational-demand characteristics. The diagnosis of the situation determined what styles the leaders used. There was considerable correspondence between what the managers said they had done and what was prescribed by the decision tree (Vroom, 1976) based on Vroom and Yetton's (1973) model.

The problems disclosed by these managers were used to prepare 30 to 54 standardized cases that were then given to several thousand managers to diagnose in terms of the seven questions and to decide which style they would use. As was noted earlier, most of the differences in the styles used depended on case differences rather than individual differences among the managers. Vroom and Yetton (1973) concluded that, on the average, managers said they would (or did) use exactly the same decision style as the decision-tree model in about 40 percent of the situations. In the two-thirds of the situations, the managers' behavior was consistent with the feasible set of styles proposed in the model. In other words, in only about one-third of the

Figure 22.2. Decision Process Flowchart (Feasible Set)

A. Does the problem possess a quality requirement?
B. Do I have sufficient information to make a high-quality decision?
C. Is the problem structured?
D. Is acceptance of the decision by subordinates important for effective implementation?
E. If I were to make the decision by myself, am I reasonably certain that it would be accepted by my subordinates?
F. Do subordinates share the organizational goals to be attained in solving this problem?
G. Is conflict among subordinates likely in preferred solutions?

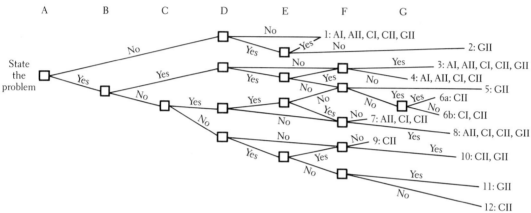

situations did their behavior violate at least one of the seven rules underlying the model.

Nevertheless, Vroom and Yetton also noted that the model called for more variance in style than the average manager recalled or proposed. Thus, if managers used the model as the basis for choosing their leadership styles, all would become both more directive and more participative. They would employ direction more frequently in situations in which their subordinates were unaffected by the decision and would use participative approaches more frequently when their subordinates' cooperation and support were critical or their subordinates' information and expertise were required.

Individual versus Group Problems. The frequency of the choice of process reflects strongly whether the problem concerned the group or its individual members. Table 22.2 shows how 98 managers, military officers, and heads of research departments dealt differently with the individual and group problems they faced. With group problems, managers more fre-

quently chose CII and GII; with individual problems, they more frequently chose AI, CI, GI, and DI (Vroom & Jago, 1974).

Consistent with the survey research summarized earlier in the chapter (Bass & Valenzi, 1974), the consult-

Table 22.2 Mean Frequency of the Choice of Process for Dealing with Group and Individual Problems (N = 98)

Choice	Group Problems	Individual Problems
AI	3.24	4.62[a]
AII	2.48	2.11
CI	4.05	5.99
CII	7.50	0.47
GI	0.09	6.30
GII	6.48	0.31
DI	0.16	4.20

[a]All individual versus group mean differences were significant at the .001 level except for AII means.

SOURCE: Vroom and Jago (1974).

ing styles CI and CII were the most popular solutions to the various problems presented. But a clear need was evident to distinguish between consulting with one's group or with individual members, depending on whether the problems concerned the group as a whole or particular members.

Evidence of Validity

Evidence to support or refute the validity of the model have been gathered in the field from numerous studies based on self-reports[13] and in the laboratory by Field (1982).

In Vroom and Jago's (1978) study of 96 managers who were unaware of the decision-tree model, the managers, who were from a variety of organizations, described 181 situations and their leadership behavior in these situations. The model was then employed to predict the ratings of the technical quality, the subordinates' acceptance, and the overall effectiveness of the final leadership styles chosen by the managers. The managers noted the extent to which their chosen leadership styles in the situation they described had resulted in a high-quality solution and the subordinates' acceptance. The logical Vroom-Yetton (1973) model and decision tree (Vroom, 1976) came up with prescribed leadership styles that matched what the managers reported they actually did in 117 (65 percent) of the 181 situations. Among the 117 situations, 80 (68 percent) were judged to be effective in the situation and 37 (32 percent) were judged to be ineffective. In 64 instances, the chosen leadership style was outside Vroom and Yetton's feasible sets for the situation described. In those cases, only 14 (22 percent) were seen by the managers to be effective leadership behavior and 50 (78 percent) were seen as ineffective. The more often Vroom and Yetton's 7 rules were violated, the solution was regarded as less effective, particularly when the subordinates' acceptance was involved.

Elsewhere Pate and Heiman (1981) reported the results of a survey of 530 supervisors, middle managers, and top administrators from 7 hospitals, most of whom were female. Three specially developed problem cases that were generated by the nurses and personnel directors were likely to call for autocratic (A), consultative (C), and delegative styles (D) to deal with them. When the respondents employed the Vroom-Yetton model and decision-tree, 71 percent of their choices were "within the model" and 29 percent were outside the model. These results were close to those of Vroom and Jago (1978) and Vroom and Yetton (1973).

Experimental Support. Field (1979) thought there was a need to examine the validity of the Vroom-Yetton model in circumstances that did not depend on the self-reports of managers. He conducted an experimental test in which 276 business students in 4-person groups solved 5 decision-making problems. However, the students also were instructed to use different decision processes of the model for each problem. This forced more solutions that diverged from the Vroom-Yetton feasible set. Field found that decisions fitting with the Vroom-Yetton feasible set were significantly more effective than were decisions made outside the feasible set. Of the 105 decisions in which the leader's behavior agreed with the feasible set, 51 (49 percent) were effective, whereas only 31 of 87 decisions (36 percent) outside the feasible set were effective. One of 3 quality rules and 3 of 4 acceptance rules had effects as predicted.

Scaling of Participation. According to Vroom and Yetton's (1973) model, the leadership decision styles could be judgmentally scaled according to the greater opportunities for subordinates to participate and to influence outcomes. The scale that emerged was roughly as follows: AI = 0; AII = 1; CI = 5; CII = 8; and GII = 10. Jago (1978a) scored the amount of participativeness by leaders, from 0 to 10 in choices of leaders' responses to 72 problems. He found that, as expected, subjects who employed a variant of the model displayed less participativeness (4.1) when the leader in a stated problem had all the information required to make a high-quality decision than when he did not (5.9). More participativeness occurred (7.6) when the subordinates' acceptance was required and was not likely to result from an autocratic decision. Less participativeness occurred it such acceptance was likely to result from an autocratic decision (5.0) or when such acceptance was irrelevant (3.3). Also, more participativeness occurred when subordinates expected to

---

[13]See, for example, Margerison and Glube (1979), Pate and Heiman (1981), Vroom and Jago (1978), and Vroom and Yetton (1973).

share organizational goals (5.8) than when such goal congruence was not expected (4.9).

Cautions. Mixed support for the model came from Clement (1983), who found that only the sixth rule (the subordinates' acceptance is more critical than the quality of the decision) significantly contributed to the model's validity. Clement also found that the seventh rule (subordinates share organizational goals) undermined the validity of the model in matching its prescribed leadership behavior with responses chosen by financial executives and managers of nonprofit organizations.

Although Field acknowledged the possibilities that subordinates may accept autocratic leadership in dealing with some of the Vroom-Yetton problems, experimental evidence gathered by Heilman, Cage, Hornstein, and Herschlag (1984) suggested that this may not occur. The latter researchers completed two experiments in which a leader's reported actions were either correct or incorrect according to the Vroom-Yetton model. Nevertheless, no matter what the circumstances, subjects who took the subordinate's point of view favored a participative solution even when the model prescribed an autocratic one. This finding is consistent with Sinha and Chowdhry's (1981) study, which found that although the Vroom-Yetton and Hersey-Blanchard models prescribe that leaders be more directive with less well-prepared subordinates, such autocratic leadership was detrimental to the group's efficiency and the subordinates' satisfaction.

Alternative Models

Model of Randomness. Pate and Heiman (1981, pp. 8–9) suggested that the level of matching of the model prescriptives with outcomes could have been due to random responding!

> By selecting a style at random it is possible to trace the style backwards through the model and compute the probability that a style will be "within" the model. . . . When this is done, the following probabilities result: .563 (A1 & A2), .680 (C1), .813 (C2), .750 (D), and .711 (any style). Thus, if a group of people chose any style and answered the decision

rule questions blindfolded, 71.1% of their responses would be "within the model."

Wedley and Field (1982) found similar results with the feasible-set choices of 102 undergraduates and 51 managers. However, they argued and showed that the different branchings that occurred to reach the various options were by no means random. In fact, the students and managers tended to prefer, to a high degree, the same particular branching of the decision tree leading to GII (*participation* with all subordinates together). This was only one branching among the 23 they could have followed.

Constructive Controversy. Tjosvold, Wedley, and Field (1986) proposed that a single concept, "constructive controversy," could account for the greater effectiveness of the decision making. Constructive controversy includes cooperation ("We seek a solution that is good and acceptable to all"), controversy ("Persons express their own views fully"), confirmation ("Persons feel understood and accepted by each other"), collaboration ("We all influence each other"), and differentiation ("All ideas are expressed before we began to evaluate them"). The investigators completed a study of 58 managers who retrospectively examined two previous problems. One decision was decidedly successful; the other was a failure. The managers applied the Vroom-Yetton model and described, on a 15-item questionnaire, how much constructive controversy had occurred in dealing with each of the two problems. Constructive-controversy scores accounted for 45 percent of the tendency to achieve a successful rather than a failing decision. Only 5 percent was attributable to the Vroom-Yetton model.

Model B. The original model, referred to here as model A, is predicated on the short-term objective of minimizing the time of the leader and the subordinates. A somewhat different model, Model B, is required if long-term objectives for the subordinates' development are involved. How a sample situation in which Model A or B is employed is illustrated below with a problem case in paraphase:

> You manage a region for a international consulting firm with a staff of six consultants. One of them is the subject of complaints from several clients that he

is not doing an effective job, although the clients are not explicit about what is wrong. For his first four or five years, the consultant's performance was superb. Now he has a "chip on his shoulder" and has lost identification with the firm and its objectives. You need to deal with the problem quickly to retain the client who most recently complained. What should you do?

The decision tree analysis is as follows:

A. (Quality?) = Yes
B. (Leader's information?) = No
C. (Structured?) = No
D. (Acceptance?) = Yes
E. (Prior Probability of Acceptance?) = No
F. (Goal Congruence?) = No

Given the fact that the problem is about an individual, not the group, the synthesized Model A and Model B solutions are these:

Feasible Set	CI, GI
Model A Behavior	CI (Individual Consultation)
Model B Behavior	GI (Individual *Participation*)

Maier's and Field's Models. Field (1979) suggested returning to an earlier, simpler fourfold model, developed by Maier (1970b) on the basis of earlier creativity and problem-solving experiments.[14] According to the model, a Type I problem has a quality requirement, acceptance is likely to be obtained easily, and the decision should be made by the leader. Type II problems do not have a quality requirement but acceptance is critical; therefore, these problems should be resolved by group decision. Type III problems do not have quality or acceptance requirements and should be decided by tossing a coin; participative approaches with this type of problem generate unnecessary conflicts. Type IV problems require both quality and acceptance and are solved by using persuasion or, better yet, by group discussion. Field also noted that in Figure 22.2, the deci-

[14]Maier (1960), Maier (1963), Maier and Danielson (1956), Maier and Hoffman (1960a, 1964), Maier and Maier (1957), and Maier and Solem (1962).

sion CII is in the feasible set for 19 of the 23 situations included in the 4 types of problems. But in the 4 situations in which CII is not in the feasible set, GII is in the feasible set. A more parsimonious rule that Field (p. 256) proposed to protect the quality of the decision and the acceptance of subordinates is this: "If acceptance of the decision by subordinates is critical to effective implementation and it is not reasonably certain that subordinates would accept an autocratic decision, but they share organizational goals (or decision quality is not important), use GII; otherwise, use CII." This simple model uses only 4 situation-demand characteristics instead of 7 and only 2 leadership styles, CII or GII, instead of the 5 of the Vroom-Yetton model. Also, this simple model offers a balance between the short-term time-efficient Model A and the long-term group-development Model B. Field concluded that what needs to be prescribed is either consultation with the group of subordinates or shared *participatory* leadership with the group unless it is certain that a directive decision would be acceptable to subordinates.

Jago and Vroom (1980) ran a comparative test of the Vroom-Yetton prescriptions with those of Field (1979) as well as those of Maier (1970b). For each prescription, the actual reported behavior of 96 managers dealing with 181 cases were collected. Sixty-five percent conformed to the Vroom-Yetton model, 79 percent conformed to Maier's prescriptions, but only 33 percent conformed to Field's. Of the 117 decisions that conformed to the Vroom-Yetton model, 80 percent fit Maier's model and 50 percent fit Field's. Furthermore, the Vroom-Yetton model provided more predictive power of effectiveness, quality, and acceptance of the decision by subordinates beyond what Maier's and Field's prescriptions did. Jago and Vroom (p. 354) concluded that although Field's

formulation guarantees conformity to the Vroom/Yetton prescriptions, yet his rules presumably are easier to learn and apply because they involve fewer situational variables and fewer normative contingencies. However, the apparent attractiveness may be misleading. The behavior of untrained managers violates Field's prescriptions substantially more often than such behavior violates the prescriptions of either Maier's model or the Vroom/Yetton model.

Because its highly participative prescriptions represent a large departure from the decision making style of most managers, implementing Field's model would require some rather dramatic behavioral changes that may meet with some resistance. Although its prescriptions are indeed easy to learn, Field's model may be quite difficult for some managers to internalize and practice. On the other hand, the Vroom/Yetton model may be more difficult to learn initially but more easily internalized and implemented.

Individual versus Situational Differences

Another issue that has been looked at extensively is how much the Vroom-Yetton situational requirements determine which choices of leadership style will be made and how much individual differences arise. For instance, will authoritarians be autocratic in choosing a response to any Vroom-Yetton problem, regardless of the Vroom-Yetton prescriptive rules and the nature of the problem? Vroom and Yetton (1973), Hill and Schmitt (1977), and Clement (1983) all demonstrated that situational main effects account for almost half the variance in choices, while individual differences are likely to account for less than 15 percent of the results. In dealing with problems about groups, 35 percent of the decisions were determined by the situation and 12 percent were due to individual differences in the preferences of the managers. In dealing with problems about individuals, 44 percent were due to situational elements and 9 percent to consistent individual differences among the managers (Vroom & Jago, 1974). Vroom and Yetton thought that these results suggested the need to talk more about autocratic and participative situations, rather than autocratic and participative persons. However, Jago (1978b) concluded, from an analysis of the differences among managers in the rules they used, that there was a need to focus on autocratic versus participative decision-making rules. Furthermore, Jago's results indicated that the decision maker cannot be fully represented as a linear processor who handles the rules in a simple additive fashion. Rather, the decision maker's choices interact, to some degree, so that a more complex configuration may provide a better portrait.

Vroom-Jago Model. Vroom (1984) summed up some of the strengths and weaknesses of the model's fit with actualities. Generally, the model was supported by consistencies between decision-making styles and superiors' and subordinates' perceptions of decision-making requirements based on characteristics of the decision process. Nevertheless, he pointed to several deficiencies for practical application owing to the simplicity in defining the variables that influence the decision-making process. Along with developing a differentiation for the group and individual problems faced by a manager (Vroom & Jago, 1974) and to take account of the failure of the original model to consider the importance of subordinates' knowledge, external influences outside the immediate work group, and the matter of time constraints, Vroom and Jago (1984) added the following questions to a determination of the feasible sets.

H. Do subordinates have sufficient information to make a high quality decision?

I. Does a severe time constraint limit your ability to involve subordinates?

J. Are the costs involved in bringing together geographically dispersed subordinates prohibitive?

According to a simulational analysis by Vroom and Jago (1984), the subordinates' knowledge, lack of time constraints, or lack of geographic dispersion greatly increased the expanded model's prescription for participative rather than directive leadership.

Vroom and Jago (1988) created a new model with considerably greater validity than the original Vroom-Yetton model by adding a number of objectives, such as cost reduction, that could be sought by the leader. Further, 5-point ratings were substituted for the yes-no responses. Multiple regression replaced deductions of the feasible sets. Effectiveness and commitment were introduced as alternative outcomes which might be sought by the leader. Also, they created conditions to encourage the reflection on past decisions.

Summary and Conclusions

This chapter has focused on the extent to which decisions are made by the superior, the subordinate, or both. Although conceptual distinctions are clearly maintained between *direction*, negotiation, *participation*, and delegation, most leaders exhibit all these modes with different patterns of frequency. Many antecedent conditions add to the variance found in these patterns. Participation is indicated when the subordinates' acceptance, satisfaction, and commitment are important and when subordinates have the required information. But direction can also be effective when structure is needed or when the leader has the necessary information and the quality of the decision is more important than is the commitment of the subordinates. In the same way, the delegative tendencies of the leader must be understood within the context of the larger organizational setting in which the leader must operate and the confidence that the leader has in the subordinates' competence. Both empirical and rational models are available for specifying the conditions under which either more direction or more participation is appropriate. The direction often may work as well or better than participation in short-term laboratory studies, but greater payoff from participative leadership appears in the field for longer-term relations and outcomes, although the effects remain modest when subjected to meta-analyses. As important as who decides (the leader, the led, or both) is for whose sake the decision is made. This issue is covered in the next chapter.

Task- versus Relations-Oriented Leadership

As was noted earlier, leaders differ from each other in their focus of attention. Some concentrate on the task to be accomplished, and some concentrate on the quality of their relationships with others. For instance, the behavior of project and team leaders can be described in terms of structuring patterns of communication and working methods for their groups. Their behavior can also be described in terms of their friendship and mutual trust building (Bergen, 1986). Most effective are leaders who do both; least effective are those who do neither. Thus, when Berkowitz (1953a) asked members of aircrews to describe their aircrew commander with a behavioral description inventory, a factor analysis of the results revealed factors concerned with both task and relationships, including maintaining standards of performance, acting on an awareness of situational needs, maintaining coordination and teamwork, and behaving in a nurturant manner.

Meanings

Task Orientation

Leaders differ in their concern for the groups' goals and the means to achieve the goals. Those with a strong concern are considered to be task oriented (Bass, 1967b; Fiedler, 1967a), concerned with production (Blake & Mouton, 1964), in need of achievement (McClelland, 1961; Wofford, 1970), achievement oriented (Indvik, 1986b), production oriented (Katz, Maccoby, & Morse, 1950), production emphasizing (Fleishman, 1957a), goal achieving (Cartwright & Zander, 1960), and work facilitative and goal emphasizing (Bowers & Seashore, 1966). The leaders' assumptions about their roles, purposes, and behavior reflect their interest in completing assignments and getting the work done. A high task orientation underlies selected types of leaders, such as Birnbrauer and Tyson's (1984) hard driver and persuader or Reddin's (1977) autocrat. Purely task-oriented leaders are likely to keep their distance psychologically from their followers and to be more cold and aloof (Blau & Scott, 1962). When coupled with an inability to trust subordinates, such concern for production is likely to manifest itself in close, controlling supervision (McGregor, 1960). Successful task-oriented leaders are instrumental in contributing to their groups' effectiveness by setting goals, allocating labor, and enforcing sanctions (Bales, 1958a). They initiate structure for their followers (Hemphill, 1950a), define the roles of others, explain what to do and why, establish well-defined patterns of organization and channels of communication, and determine the ways to accomplish assignments (Hersey & Blanchard, 1981).

Misumi (1985) conceived task-oriented leadership behavior as performance leadership—leadership behavior that prompts and motivates the group's achievement of goals (for example, when deadlines are necessary, the leader clearly specifies them and has a good grasp of how work is progressing). For Cleveland (1980), such a focus on the task is seen in strategic thinking, in projecting patterns of collective behavior, and in considering the whole situation. It is also seen in the leader's manifest curiosity about issues and methods and the system that can connect people and things to achieve objectives. Immediate supervision, combined with management as a whole, can foster a "culture of productivity"—a shared image of a highly productive work setting—in which supervisors, managers, and workers alike focus on the work being done and how to maintain successful operations. Akin and Hopelain (1986) described such a "culture of productivity" in three highly productive organizations.

Caveat. Although the various conceptualizations of task orientation have similar-sounding labels, their intercorrelations are not necessarily high. In fact, they may point to different attributes of an individual. Thus, the direct assessment of the task orientation of 81 Polish industrial personnel—using the Orientation Inventory (ORI), which asks examinees for their preferred activities—correlated only .32 with the need for achievement as measured by the Thematic Apperception Test, an assessment of the projected fantasies of the same examinees (Dobruszek, 1967). Similarly, Fiedler's (1967a) determination of task orientation, based on the leaders' rejection of the co-worker with whom they have found it more difficult to work, does not correlate as highly with other approaches to measuring task orientation. (In fact, the least preferred co-worker measure seems so unique that it will be treated separately in this chapter.) Thus, it is necessary to review results in the light of variations because of how task orientation and relations orientation are measured.

Relations Orientation

Leaders also differ in the extent to which they pursue a human relations approach and try to maintain friendly, supportive relations with their followers. Those with a strong concern are identified as relations oriented (Katz, Maccoby, & Morse, 1950), concerned for maintenance (Misumi, 1985) or group maintenance (Cartwright & Zander, 1960; Wofford, 1970), concerned for people (Blake & Mouton, 1964), people centered (D. R. Anderson, 1974), interaction facilitative and supportive (Bowers & Seashore, 1966), interaction oriented (Bass, 1967b), employee emphasizing (Fleishman, 1957a), and in need of affiliation (McClelland, 1961). Such leaders are expressive and tend to establish social and emotional ties (Bales, 1958a). Usually associated with a relations orientation are the leader's sense of trust in subordinates, less felt need to control them, and more general rather than close supervision of the subordinates (McGregor, 1960).

A strong relations orientation is the basis of Reddin's (1977) "missionary" and "developer" types of leader and with consideration for the welfare of subordinates (Hemphill, 1950a). For Hersey and Blanchard (1918), it

is linked to relationship behavior: maintaining personal relationships, opening channels of communication, and delegating to give subordinates opportunities to use their potential. It is characterized by involved support, friendship, and mutual trust. It is leadership that is democratic and employee oriented, rather than autocratic and production oriented. Misumi (1985, p.11) saw it as maintenance-oriented leadership behavior

> directed toward dispelling excessive tensions that arise in interpersonal relations within a group or organization, promoting the resolution of conflict and strife, giving encouragement and support, providing an opportunity for minority opinions to be expressed, inspiring personal need fulfillment and promoting an acceptance of interdependence among group members.

Relations-oriented supervision is seen in the communication patterns of supervisors and subordinates. Kirmeyer and Lin (1987) arranged for observers to record an average of 107 face-to-face interactions with the supervisors of 60 randomly chosen police radio dispatchers. Communications with the dispatchers' supervisors were facilitated if the dispatchers felt they were receiving social support from their superiors. Felt support correlated .33 with the dispatchers' communications about work to their superior and .48 with communications to their superiors about other matters. It correlated .55 and .26 with observed face-to-face communications from the superiors to the dispatchers about work and nonwork matters.

The concern for relations is manifest in different ways with different systems. Such concern that is involved in shifting organizations from autocratic systems 1 and 2 to democratic systems 3 and 4 (Likert, 1977) and in contributing to industrial democracy and participative management.[1] The concern for relations is central to humanistic management (Daley, 1986), which is dedicated to promoting the personal significance of work, the autonomy of employees, and fairness in appraisals. It is seen in Britain with Theory P, a deemphasis of traditional management-employee relationships in favor of management's increased awareness of employees' needs, increased involvement in the

[1]See Chapters 14 and 21.

community, and increased use of consultation (Jaap, 1982). It is seen in Japanese management and Theory Z, with its emphasis on long-term employment, unhurried evaluation and promotion processes, wide-ranging career opportunities, and consensual decision making (Ouchi, 1981).

Complications

Although measurements for research use, such as those of Fiedler (1967a) or Bass (1967b), often artificially force separation into the categories of task- or relations orientation, conceptually, leaders may have strong concerns for both task and relationships or for neither. At the same time, observers can accurately discriminate among the ratings for emerging task and socioemotional leadership earned by interacting members of experimental task groups (Stein, Geis & Damarin, 1973).

A strong concern for relationships and for task accomplishment may both be linked to some of the same kinds of leadership behavior. For instance, Hennigar and Taylor (1980) found that the assessed receptivity to change of 80 middle-management administrators of public schools was high if the administrators were either highly concerned for people or highly concerned for productivity. But a lack of concern for either was connected with a lack of openness to change.

Further complicating matters are the "switch-hitters." Although the autocratic leader is likely to be directive and caught up with getting the work done and the democratic leader is likely to be participative and concerned about maintaining relationships, nevertheless, some benevolent autocrats, who pursue a patronizing leadership style, are still likely to be concerned about their relationships and the needs of their followers. Likewise, highly task-oriented democratic leaders may encourage participation in decision making in the interests of reaching high-quality decisions. Presumably, they would be characterized as R. Likert's (1977) System 4 leaders.

Relations-oriented leadership is likely to contribute to the development of followers and to more mature relationships. However, task-oriented leadership can be the source of expert advice and challenging motivation for subordinates.

Although for the purposes of discussion and analysis, task- and relations orientation are treated separately here, Blake and Mouton (1964), Cleveland (1980), and many others, strongly advocated leadership that integrates both the task- and the relations orientations. Leaders have to be strong and decisive, yet sensitive to people (Calloway, 1985). Blake and Mouton (1964) argued that maximum leadership effectiveness occurs only when the leader, both highly concerned for production and highly concerned for people, integrates the human and task requirements of the job. The exclusively task-oriented manager is seen to treat employees as machines, to the detriment of the employees' commitment, growth, and morale. The exclusively people-oriented manager is viewed as running a "country club," to the detriment of productivity.[2]

Antecedents Contributing to Task Orientation and Relations Orientation

As with the tendencies and preferences for direction or participation, task or relations orientation tend to depend on the leader's personal characteristics as well as situational contingencies. These contingencies include the characteristics of the follower and of the organization and the task, goals, and constraints in the situation in which the leadership occurs.

Personal Antecedents

Following Bales (1958a) and Etzioni (1965), Downton (1973) surmised that instrumental (task-oriented) and expressive (relations-oriented) modes of leadership are assumed by individuals with different temperaments. Instrumental leaders are seen to be more aggressive, more able to tolerate hostility, and more anxious to be respected; expressive leaders are more accommodating, less able to tolerate hostility, and more anxious to be loved.

A variety of surveys and experiments demonstrated this linkage of personality to leadership orientation. For instance, Klebanoff (1976) made use of observers' and peers' rankings of the task- or relations-oriented behav-

[2]Kahn and Katz (1953), R. Likert (1977a), and Oaklander and Fleishman (1964), among many others, came to similar conclusions.

ior displayed by 160 participants in 40 small groups that were working on various tasks. Task-oriented leaders were more likely to have been first-born children; they felt more personal autonomy and tended to be more actively involved. Helmich and Erzen (1975) surveyed 108 corporation presidents and found that task-oriented leaders lacked fulfillment as presidents. The needs of relations-oriented presidents were better met by their assignment.

Results with the ORI. Preferences of the highly task-oriented examinee on the ORI (Bass, 1962c) included to be wise; to have the feeling of a job well done; to have bright, interesting friends; and to be a leader who gets things done. Interaction-oriented (relations-oriented) preferences included to have fun with friends, to have helpful friends, to work cooperatively, to make more friends, and to be an easy-to-talk-to leader. According to the scores on various personality inventories, personal factors significantly correlated with task orientation, as assessed by the ORI, included being more highly self-sufficient, resourceful, controlled in will power, aloof, not sociable, sober-serious, tough-realistic, and aggressive-competitive (Bass & Dunteman, 1963). Task-oriented leaders were more likely to show more restraint, ascendance, masculinity, objectivity, thoughtfulness, endurance, need for achievement, and heterosexuality (Bass, 1967b).

Task orientation was higher among men than among women and among those with greater maturity, education, status, and technical training. Task-oriented students were more likely to volunteer and to persist at tasks voluntarily until the tasks were completed (Frye & Spruill, 1965). They were self-reinforcers (Marston, 1964) and more likely to be seen as helpful to others in sensitivity training groups (Bass & Dunteman, 1963).

Relations or interaction orientation, as measured by the ORI, was higher among examinees who, according to various personality inventories, were socially dependent on the group, warm, sociable, and in need for affiliation (Bass & Dunteman, 1963). Such orientation also correlated with wanting to be controlled by others, to be close to others, to receive affection from others, to include others, and to be included with others (Bass, 1967b). Konovsky (1986) completed analyses of the extent to which supervisors of 484 hospital subordinates

were seen by their subordinates to provide emotional support and to help in solving the subordinates' problems. Supervisors offering such support and assistance also scored higher in personal competence, sociability, emotionality, and altruism.

In a Polish study, task orientation on the ORI was found to correlate positively as high as .41 with intelligence, as measured by a Polish version of the Army General Classification Test. Interaction (relations) orientation correlated negatively as low as − .32 (Dobruszek, 1967).

Immutable Conditions? These personal factors, seldom mentioned in the prescriptive literature of the past two decades, call attention to Fiedler's (1967a) argument that often one needs to find or change the situations to fit the leader's personality. These personal factors make managers and administrators skeptical about the possibilities of training and developing leaders to be both relations- and task oriented and about those who say they are already. Nevertheless, the correlations of task- and relations orientation with personality and intelligence are modest. Much can be changed in leadership orientation and behavior through learning, role modeling, and experience, reinforced by socialization processes and organizational culture.[3]

Situational Antecedents

Relations-oriented leaders are likely to emerge when they are more attentive to pleasing their subordinates than their superiors and, by definition, when they are more concerned about the needs of their subordinates. Managers who are "under the gun" to produce immediate results are more likely to be task oriented and less likely to devote time and energy to their relationships. But no specific experiments have been directed toward systematically trying to raise or lower such leaders' concerns. Brady and Helmich (1982) found, in a survey of chief executive officers (CEOs) and their boards of directors that CEOs were more task oriented than relations oriented if their boards were made up of outsiders. The reverse was true if the boards were composed of insiders.

Relations orientation is to be expected in organiza-

[3]See Chapter 35.

tions, such as the Israeli kibbutzim, communes, or religious orders, whose espoused beliefs emphasize providing for members according to their needs. Socioeconomic differencies between communities of workers are also likely to be of consequence. Thus, Blood and Hulin (1967) reported that workers in communities in which one would expect adherence to middle-class norms (for example, small suburban communities) tended to favor a human relations style of supervision. In the same way, strong organizational policies supporting either a relations or a task orientation (or both) particularly coincide with a top management that provides role models for lower management and engenders task, relations, or both orientations among the individual managers and supervisors. At the same time, the leaders' orientation is also likely to be affected by those below them.

Subordinates and Their Performance. Earlier chapters noted that the poor performance of subordinates appears to cause much of the observed punitiveness of leaders. In the same way, the good performance of subordinates appears to increase leaders' tendencies to be relations oriented. In a study of routine clerical workers and their supervisors in a life insurance company, Katz, Maccoby, and Morse (1950) found that supervisors of high-producing sections were significantly more likely to be employee oriented than production oriented. Barrow (1975) showed that increasing the performance of subordinates in a laboratory setting resulted in the leader becoming significantly more supportive. Decreasing the subordinates' performance caused the leader to become more task oriented. This finding is consistent with Bass, Binder, and Breed's (1967) findings for the performance of a simulated organization discussed below.

Farris and Lim (1969) showed that if the performance of groups was good in the past, the groups' leaders subsequently tended to be more relations oriented. The leaders were more sensitive to the needs and feelings of the members and more trusting and confident in the members. They allowed members more freedom and autonomy in their work. Members were encouraged to speak out and were listened to with respect. The leaders gave recognition for good work, communicated clearly, stressed pride in the group, and empha-

sized teamwork. The leaders of high-performing groups were also more task oriented than were the leaders of low-performing groups in that they maintained high performance standards without being punitive. They were less likely than were the leaders of low-performing groups to be critical of their groups' performance and less likely to exert unreasonable pressure for better performance.

Cause and effect could not be separated in a study of 112 engineering employees by Jones, James, and Bruni (1975). But the results are suggestive of the followers' influence on their leader's orientation and behavior, although the reverse possibility is also tenable.[4] Jones, James, and Bruni obtained correlations of from .41 to .55 between employees' confidence and trust in their supervisors and the extent to which their supervisors were seen to be high in support, emphasis on goals, facilitation of work, and facilitation of interaction. Again, as was noted in Chapter 9, Sanford (1951) found, in a survey of Philadelphia residents, that egalitarians wanted leaders who were warm and generally supportive, but authoritarians preferred leaders who would serve their special interests. Indirectly, one may infer that more relations-oriented leadership would be demanded by highly self-oriented followers, by followers with personal problems, by followers in need of nurturance, and by followers seeking affection. As shall be detailed later, the "psychological and job maturity" of one's subordinates dominate the Hersey-Blanchard (1977, 1981) prescriptions for determining whether leaders should be relations- or task oriented or both in their behavior toward subordinates.

Prior Effectiveness of the Organization. Commonly observed as well as deplored (see, for instance, R. Likert, 1977b) is the extent to which human relations concerns are abandoned when an enterprise's profits are seriously eroded. In such situations, akin to a stress response, task orientation is increased at the expense of relations orientation. Bass, Binder, and Breed (1967) demonstrated this phenomenon in a simulated budgeting exercise. The concern of decision makers for the satisfaction and well-being of employees and the willingness to accept more employee-centered

[4]See Katz, Maccoby, and Morse (1950), whose results are mentioned later.

solutions to problems in the areas of safety, labor relations, and management development were strongly influenced by whether the company had just finished a profitable year. MBA students were given one of three firms' year-end profit-and-loss statements. One firm showed a net loss of $86,000; another firm's statement showed that moderate profits had been earned. The third firm reported large profits. Three-quarters of the students in the profitable circumstances recommended buying safety equipment. Only half the students in the moderately profitable enterprise and only 25 percent of those in the firm that lost money in the previous year were willing to spend the required funds to settle a strike quickly. The goals emphasized in the most profitable situation were the welfare, goodwill, and satisfactory operations of employees. The goals stressed in the firm that had experienced a loss were meeting competition and raising profits.

General Consequences of Relations-Oriented and Task-Oriented Leadership

Three kinds of evidence are available. First, the extent to which relations- and task-oriented leaders are seen to be more meritorious or less meritorious by others can be examined. Second, the differential impact of these orientations on the satisfaction of subordinates can be reviewed. Third, the differential effects of these orientations on the performance of groups can be detailed. Care must be maintained about the validity of the evidence. Consistently, one sees managers who describe themselves as more both task- and relations oriented in leadership style than their subordinates perceive them to be (see, for example, Rees & O'Karma, 1980).

Evaluations as a Leader

Reports published on correlations of evaluations as a leader and relations or task orientation generally found both orientations to be of positive importance.

Relations Orientation. Shartle (1934) used interviews and questionnaires in a comparative study of supervisors who were rated as either effective or ineffective. Effective supervisors did not differ from their

ineffective peers in technical skills, but they were found to excel in their ability to interact effectively and in their interest in people. Similarly, Katzell, Barrett, Vann, and Hogan (1968) found that executives whose roles emphasized administrative, rather than technical, performance received higher performance ratings from their superiors.

Mann and Dent (1954b) studied supervisors who were rated for promotability by higher-level managers. Highly promotable supervisors were described by their employees as being good at handling people; approachable; willing to go to bat for employees; letting the employees know where they stand; pulling for both the company and the workers, rather than either alone; or using general, rather than close, supervision. In turn, the highly promotable supervisors saw their own superiors as being good at handling people, letting the supervisors know where they stand, and permitting the supervisors the freedom to make decisions.

H. H. Meyer (1951) observed that effective supervisors regarded others as individuals with motives, feelings, and goals of their own and did not avoid interactional stress. Similarly, Kay and Meyer (1962), using both questionnaire and observational methods, found that higher rated foremen were less production oriented and gave general, rather than close, supervision. Likewise, Walker, Guest, and Turner (1956) observed that effective supervisors established personal relationships with employees, stuck up for them, and absorbed the pressures from higher levels of authority. In the same way, A. N. Turner (1954) reported that workers regarded as good supervisors those who did not pressure their subordinates unnecessarily; were fair, friendly, and understanding; and did not tell their subordinates to quit if they did not like the conditions.

Among the 17 Americans on the 1963 Mount Everest expedition, all of whom were highly task oriented, those who were most interaction oriented and highest on FIRO-B Expressed Inclusion were rated highest in leadership. As Lester (1965, p. 45) noted:

> ... the results pointed to the importance ... of being emotionally responsive, affectionate and warm, inviting in manner, or placing primary value on the emotional give-and-take in face-to-face relations. The men reacted negatively to emotional constric-

tion, to too much emphasis on method, efficiency, productivity, and the imposition of high impersonal standards.

However, when interaction-orientation scores are high at the expense of task-orientation scores, such as when ipsative scoring[5] is used, task, rather than interaction or relations, orientation is likely to correlate with merit as a leader.

Task Orientation. Rubenowitz (1962) reported that job-oriented supervisors were regarded by higher management as more effective than person-oriented supervisors. Shortly afterward, Kelly (1964) found that the technical features of executives' behavior outweighed the effects of personal style.

According to Dunteman (1966), task orientation, as measured by the ORI, correlated with promotability ratings based on 3 days of assessment of 96 supervisors (but correlations were negative among the younger, temporary supervisors and the journeymen who were so assessed). For both 66 first-level and 27 second-level supervisors, task orientation significantly contributed to their high on-the-job performance ratings by their supervisors (Dunteman & Bass, 1963).

Many other studies, enumerated in Chapter 28, have shown that leaders who are concerned about the task in situations in which such a concern is relevant are likely to be evaluated highly by others. Furthermore, the plethora of studies of the need for achievement[6] provide additional evidence of the positive association of task orientation and success as a leader.

Impact on Subordinates' Satisfaction

Several investigations focused on the impact on subordinates' satisfaction of psychological and social closeness or distance, a component of relations orientation. The results were mixed. Julian (1964) found that job satisfaction was higher when there was psychological closeness between the leader and the led. However, Blau and Scott (1962) and E. P. Shaw (1965) reported that the cohesiveness of the group was strengthened

by the social distance between the leader and the followers, whereas Sample and Wilson (1965) found cohesiveness to be unrelated to such social distance. But the majority of reports from both field studies and laboratory experiments indicated that subordinates' satisfaction with their leaders was linked to their leaders' relations-oriented attitudes and behavior.

Field Studies. Hoppock's (1935) analysis of the early literature on job satisfaction indicated that workers tended to feel more satisfied when supervisors understood their problems and helped them, when needed. In a survey of more than 10,000 managerial, supervisory, and hourly personnel, Ronan (1970) obtained similar results, as did Roberts, Miles, and Blankenship (1968).

Stagner, Flebbe, and Wood (1952) found that railroad workers were better satisfied when their supervisors were good at handling grievances and communicating with employees. Likewise, Bose (1955) observed that workers under employee-centered supervisors had more pride in their groups than those under work-centered supervisors. Mann and Hoffman (1960) found that in two plants, one automated, the other not, employees were more satisfied with supervisors who were considerate of their feelings, recognized good work, were reasonable in their expectations, and stood up for their subordinates.

Stampolis (1958) showed that the more employees rated their supervisor as fair, able to handle people, giving of credit, ready to discuss problems, and keeping employees informed, the less the employees expressed a desire for their company to be unionized. Bass and Mitchell (1976) reported similar results for professional and scientific workers. Illustrative also is the inability, to date, of the United Auto Workers, to organize the highly relations-oriented, Japanese-owned, automobile plants in the United States (Gladstone, 1989).

Wager (1965) found that a supportive style of leadership assisted the supervisor in fulfilling and satisfying the employees' role expectations. In an aircraft factory, where team leaders devoted much of their time to facilitating the work of their team members and attending to the team members' personal problems, indicators of dissatisfaction, such as absenteeism and turnover, were lower (Mayo & Lombard, 1944).

---

[5]In ipsative scoring, the task score and relations score sum to a fixed total, say 100. If the task score is 65, then the relations score must be 35.

[6]See Chapter 10.

Numerous field studies continue to confirm the positive impact of a leader's relations orientation on the satisfaction of subordinates. For example, York and Hastings (1985–86) asked 172 employees working in North Carolina social services to complete the Survey of Organizations (D. G. Bowers, 1976). At all levels of the assessed maturity of workers, the facilitative and supportive performance of supervisors was associated with the subordinates' satisfaction and motivation to work. A review of nursing studies by Maloney (1979) concluded that people-oriented leaders generally were more satisfying to their employees. In addition, employees' grievances and turnover were lower when the leaders were seen as relations oriented.

When the socioemotional and task-oriented leadership of residence hall leaders were measured separately, both were linked by MacDonald (1969) to the satisfaction of students. However, the effects of task orientation on subordinates' satisfaction have usually been found to be somewhat less consistent. Task-relevant behavioral measures, which contain elements of the leaders' punitiveness, will generate dissatisfaction, grievances, and turnover (Schriesheim & Kerr, 1974). In a survey of several thousand employees, R. Likert (1955) found that job satisfaction decreased as the supervisors' pressure for production increased. On the other hand, it is not uncommon to find positive correlations for both the task- and relations-oriented behavior of supervisors and the satisfaction of their subordinates with supervisors. Generally, for nurse supervisors, for example, a strong task orientation that is not coupled with a high relations orientation results in less satisfied subordinates (Maloney, 1979). Gruenfeld and Kassum (1973) showed that nurses were satisfied with highly task-oriented supervisors, but only if the supervisors' people orientation was high as well. The strong task orientation of supervisors was dissatisfying when coupled with a medium or low orientation to people.

In a massive undertaking of over two decades, Misumi (1985) completed studies of over 150,000 Japanese employees working in banks, post offices, coal mines, shipyards, transportation, utilities and manufacturing, under supervisors with different performance (P) and maintenance (M) orientations. The supervisors were classified as P-type (above the median in P alone), M-type (above the median in M alone), neither type (pm)

or both types (PM). The subordinates of a PM supervisor had a more favorable attitude toward their supervisor than did the subordinates of an M-type or P-type supervisor. Least satisfying supervisors were those who were pm types. In a bank that had branches in Okinawa, Misumi and Mannari (1982) surveyed an average of 1,325 subordinates who described their 303 superiors' leadership. The P and M leadership orientations of the supervisors, as well as the subordinates' morale (interest in work and satisfaction with supervision) were collected 5 times in 15-month intervals. The supervisors were changed in 287 groups but not in 159 groups. It was found that there was less change in morale from interval to interval if the supervisor did not change. However, the morale of the subordinates rose if the P and M leadership orientation of the supervisor's successor was higher than that of the former supervisor. The previous morale of the subordinates had less of an effect on the incoming supervisor's leadership than vice versa.

Laboratory Experiments. Experiments may provide additional convincing evidence of the relationship between a leader's relations orientation and subordinates' satisfaction. As with the field studies, most experimental studies concluded that the satisfaction of subordinates was positively associated with the leader's relations-oriented behavior. Wischmeier (1955) found that group-centered, rather than task-centered, discussions resulted in a warm, friendly group atmosphere. T. Gordon (1955) also found that group-centered discussion was associated with members' sense of belonging, respect for others, ability to listen to and understand others, and loss of self-defensiveness. Similarly, Thelen and Whitehall (1949) and Schwartz and Gekoski (1960) reported that follower-oriented leadership enhanced satisfaction. Likewise, Maier and Danielson (1956) reported that an employee-oriented solution to a disciplinary problem produced greater satisfaction in groups of problem solvers than did one that was bound by legalistic restrictions.

Heyns (1948) coached one set of leaders to play a positive, supportive role that emphasized agreement, mutual liking, and cooperation. Another set of leaders was coached to play a negative role in which the leaders overtly displayed a misunderstanding of the members and made no effort to develop their groups' cohesiveness. Although the two styles produced no significant difference in the quality of the groups' decision or the members' satisfaction, the groups with positive leaders exhibited evidence of greater cohesiveness. W. M. Fox (1954) used scenarios to coach leaders in a similarly positive relations approach or a "biased, diplomatic persuasive" role. Groups with positively supportive leaders exhibited higher degrees of cohesiveness and members' satisfaction but were slower in solving problems. With a different group of participants, W. M. Fox (1957) also found that supportive leadership was associated with the members' satisfaction and the groups' cohesiveness.

Impact on the Group's and Members' Performance

It may be difficult to separate the impact of the leader's orientation on the members' satisfaction from its impact on the members' and the group's effectiveness. To illustrate, Medalia and Miller (1955) observed that human relations leadership and employees' satisfaction interact to influence the group's effectiveness. And although both a relations orientation and a task orientation are generally found to be positively associated with the group's productivity, attainment of goals, and followers' performance, there·are exceptions, as are noted later, which points to the possible need for a contingent approach. Some situations may call for more relations-oriented leadership and others for more task-oriented leadership; however it may be that in a vast majority of circumstances, strong doses of both types of leadership orientation are optimal.

When positive associations are found, it is usually inferred that the relations orientation or task orientation of the leader resulted in the improved performance of subordinates. But the reverse may be equally true. Few of the findings have been causal. The previous performance of subordinates is as likely to affect the orientation of the leader as the leader's orientation is likely to influence the subsequent performance of the subordinates (Bass, 1965c). Farris and Lim (1969), as was previously mentioned, showed that the past good or poor

performance of their groups determined, to a considerable degree, the task- and relations orientation of the group leaders.

Impact of Relations-Oriented Leadership on Performance. Pandey (1976) reported that groups led by relations-oriented leaders generated more ideas than did those led by task-oriented leaders. Katz, Maccoby, and Morse (1950) and Roberts, Miles, and Blankenship (1968) found that the performance of groups was higher under an employee-oriented style than under a more disinterested style of supervision. Philipsen (1965a, 1965b) also found that human relations leadership correlated positively with group effectiveness. But in a study of skilled tradesmen, Wison, Beem, and Comrey (1953) established that supervisors of both high- and low-performing shops were described as more helpful, sympathetic, consistent, and self-reliant than were those in medium-performing shops.

Abdel-Halim (1982) showed how much of the members' role conflict and role ambiguity that affected their intrinsic satisfaction with, involvement in, and anxiety about their jobs was moderated by the support they received from their supervisor. In the previously cited report by Konovsky (1986), supervisors who were judged by their 484 subordinates as helpful and emotionally supportive contributed to the subordinates' commitment to their hospital organization and to the supervisors' judged interpersonal effectiveness. In the same way, Riegel (1955) found that employees' interest in their company's success increased when their supervisor was seen to help them with their difficulties, to give necessary training and explanations, and to "take an interest in us and our ideas."

Indik, Georgopoulos, and Seashore (1961) studied the employees of a transportation company. Their results indicated that high levels of group performance were associated with satisfaction with the supervisors' supportiveness, open communication, mutual understanding, and autonomy of the workers on the job. As observed in Chapter 21, R. Likert (1961a, 1967, 1977b) concluded, from many surveys, that supportive attitudes toward employees, combined with the group's loyalty toward management, were associated with increased productivity and a desire for responsibility by the employees. With the introduction of a human relations approach to management, as well as high performance goals, long-term gains in productivity were achieved. Similarly, Daley (1986) surveyed 340 employees of Iowa public agencies and obtained uniformly positive associations between their perceptions of relations-oriented, humanistic management practices and the employees' evaluations of the effectiveness and responsiveness of their organizations to the public.

Supportive leadership increases the likelihood that organizations can police and correct themselves. Near and Miceli (1986) found that the felt support from their leaders was the most important factor in protecting employees from retaliation for calling attention to observed wrongdoing. Conversely, the perceived likelihood of suffering retaliation for whistle-blowing about observed wrongdoings was perceived by a random sample of 8600 federal employees to correlate with the lack of support from their supervisors and the higher management. These perceptions were realistic. Honest whistle-blowers were actually more likely to get punished than were their corrupt senior managers in Samuel Pierce's Housing and Urban Development Administration of 1981 to 1988 (as of late 1989).

Impact of Task-Oriented Leadership on Performance. R. Likert (1955) reported that a survey of several thousand workers indicated a tendency for productivity to be higher in the presence of higher pressure by supervisors for production. Similarly, Litwin (1968) noted that experimental groups whose leaders had a strong need for achievement were much more productive than were those whose leaders had a great need for affiliation or power. Dunteman and Bass (1963) studied foremen who had an interaction orientation or a task orientation. Groups who worked under task-oriented leaders were more productive than were those under interaction-oriented leaders. Likewise, Mann, Indik, and Vroom (1963) showed that the productivity of workers was associated with the supervisor's task orientation. R. Cooper (1966) also demonstrated that first-level supervisors, whose bosses judged them to be higher in "task relevance" tended to have more productive and more task-motivated subordinates.

For 14 U.S. Navy airplane-maintenance groups, R.

Likert (1977a) reported strong associations with the extent to which supervisors facilitated the work by helping with advanced scheduling and offering new ideas to solve problems in the job and the extent to which airplanes that were serviced by the groups were not involved in accidents and disasters because of operational failures.

Effects of a Combined Task- and Relations Orientation. Considerable theoretical and empirical support has been amassed for the idea that regardless of circumstances, the effectiveness of leadership is greatest when the leaders are both task oriented and relations oriented in attitudes and behavior. Thus, Patchen (1962) reported that the leader who maintained high-performance norms, encouraged efficiency, and attempted to obtain rewards for followers was likely to have a high-performing group. However, the maintenance of high performance standards alone and attempting to obtain rewards for followers alone each had a negative effect on productivity. Both patterns of behavior had to be combined to have a positive impact on productivity.

Numerous other studies and lines of investigation have supported the utility of a combined high task- and relations-oriented approach to leadership. Thus, Tjosvold (1984b) demonstrated, in an experiment with 56 college students, that the students were most productive in completing a subsequent task if they had experienced beforehand a leader who nonverbally conveyed warmth and who was directive about what was to be done. The experience of the warm leader, along with the absence of direction, was satisfying but the least conducive to subsequent productivity. Similarly, Klimoski and Hayes (1980) found that the effort, performance, and satisfaction of 241 assistants in the production department of a large information-processing firm was enhanced if the supervising editors were task centered in being explicit in their expectations and consistent in their demands, as well as supportive of their employees. In the same way, Daniel (1985) found that subordinates perceived that they were working in a more productive organization if their managers were concerned both about tasks and about people.

Hall and Donnell (1979) completed a survey study

of 2,024 subordinates who described their managers' attention to the demands of the task and concern for the quality of manager-subordinate relationships. The managers who were high in both earned high career-achievement quotients. (The quotient reflected the speed with which they had climbed their organizational ladder.) They were also the most collaborative in their leadership style. These results were consistent with Blake and Mouton's (1964) and J. Hall's (1976) findings for large samples. The moderately successful managers had a low relations orientation but a high task orientation, while those whose career success was lowest were low in both a task- and a relations orientation.

Erez and Kanfer (1983) argued that the relations orientation implied in allowing subjects to participate in goal setting enhanced the task-oriented impetus for more goal setting than did assigning goals to subjects without permitting them to participate in setting the goals. Erez, Earley, and Hulin (1985) obtained experimental evidence to show that such participation increased acceptance of the goals and hence increased productivity, although Erez (1986) found that the organizational culture from which the participants were drawn affected the need for such participation. Subjects from the Israeli private sector did better with assigned goals; subjects from the kibbutz sector did better with group participation in setting goals.

As described earlier in discussing the utility of participation, Locke, Latham, and Erez's (1987) critical experiment tried to understand why, in their respective investigative efforts and using the same standardized, experimental conditions, assigning goals to subjects, generated more productivity in the United States (Latham & Steele, 1983), while allowing the subjects to participate in goal setting generated more productivity in Israel (Erez & Arad, 1986). The one difference between the U.S. and Israeli situations that turned out to account for the highly significant difference in productivity was that the Israeli experimenter was curt and unsupportive in giving instructions, but the U.S. experimenter was friendly and supportive. The friendly, supportive experimenters' instructions facilitated the subjects' acceptance of the assigned goal without their participating in setting the goals.

Misumi (1985) and Misumi and Peterson (1985) consistently found, in the previously mentioned surveys and experiments of 150,000 Japanese employees in business and industry, greater productivity by employees under PM than under pm supervision, that is, under managers who were above rather than below the median in both performance orientation and maintenance orientation.

In one of these studies, P and M were systematically manipulated for coordinated first-level and second-level supervision in an experiment with 15 postal trainees working in trios. The PM-type first-level supervision generated more productivity than did either P or M alone. Second-level supervision, present only in the form of written instructions to the subjects from the second level, had the same effects, although with less statistical significance. For 215 of 500 groups of coal miners, when the second-level supervisor was actually present, the PM pattern in both the first and second levels of supervision was most typical for the high-producing groups. For 186 working groups of about 10 employees each, involving a total of 2,257 workers in a Mitsubishi shipyard, evaluations of group meetings were most positive under PM-type leaders (evaluation mean = 17.5), followed by M-type (mean = 16.4), P-type (mean = 15.3), and pm-type (mean = 14.5) leaders.

The rated performance of 92 squads in a bearing manufacturing firm was most often high if the squads were under PM leadership and least often if under pm leadership. The results for ratings above the median for P alone or above the median for M alone were in between. The same pattern emerged in a tire manufacturing firm, where, again, the success or failure rate of 889 project managers was strongly associated with their PM, P, M, or pm style of leadership, as shown in Table 23.1. The success rate was clearly highest (52 percent) and the failure rate was clearly lowest (5 percent) with the combined PM style.

Negative Evidence. A number of exceptions to the positive effects of task or relations orientation on productivity have been reported, particularly in short-range analyses. With reference to innovation, Andrews

Table 23.1 Relation of Types of Leadership to the Success or Failure of 889 Japanese Managers of Engineering Projects

Type	Number of Cases	Percentage	
		Success	Failure
Above the median on both performance (P) and maintenance (M) orientations	271	52	5
Above the median on P alone	192	26	17
Above the median on M alone	200	16	30
Below the median on both P and M	220	6	47

SOURCE: Adapted from Misumi (1985, p. 89).

and Farris (1967) found no evidence that innovation was higher when supervisors of scientific personnel were high in both task and human relations functions. Human relations skills had little moderating effect on the generally positive relationships between the leader's carrying out task functions and innovation. The most innovation occurred under supervisors who were neither high nor low in their attention to human relations, regardless of the task functions that were completed.

Lundquist's (1957) results indicated that regardless of whether supervisors were worker oriented, the sheer frequency of their interaction with workers increased their effectiveness. Weitz and Nuckols (1953) found that supervisors' scores on a test measuring human relations orientation were not related to the productivity of the group or the turnover of personnel. MacKinney, Kavanagh, Wolins, and Rapparlie (1970) found that both production-oriented and employee-oriented management were unrelated to the satisfaction of employees. Carp, Vitola, and McLanathan (1963) showed that supervisors of effective postal teams maintained their social distance from subordinates, an attitude that reduced the surfacing of emotional problems.

In a study of simulated management groups, Kaczka and Kirk (1967) established that the profitability of teams was associated with relations-oriented leadership. But this type of leadership also resulted in less pressure to accomplish tasks and less cohesiveness in the groups. Finally, C. A. Dawson (1969), studying the achievement of schoolchildren, observed that the chil-dren performed equally well under "cold" or "warm" leadership.

Blake and Mouton's Grid Theory®

Blake and Mouton (1964) are the best-known model builders who prescribe the integration of both task- and relations orientations as the one best way to achieve effective leadership. Their managerial grid (see Figure 23.1) is based on the concept that managers and leaders vary from 1 to 9 in their concern for people (the vertical axis of the grid) and from 1 to 9 in their concern for production (the horizontal axis). The measurement of these concerns is based on a manager's endorsement of statements about management assumptions and beliefs. But these concerns are interactive rather than independent. They are manifested in the five styles shown on the grid:

9,1: *Authority-Obedience Management.* The leader's maximum concern for production (9) is combined with a minimum concern for people (1). "Dictating to subordinates what they should do and how they should do it, the leader concentrates on maximizing production."

1,9: *"Country Club" Management.* The leader shows a minimum concern for production (1) but a maximum concern for people (9). "Even at the expense of achieving results, fostering good feelings gets primary attention."

Figure 23.1. The Managerial Grid®

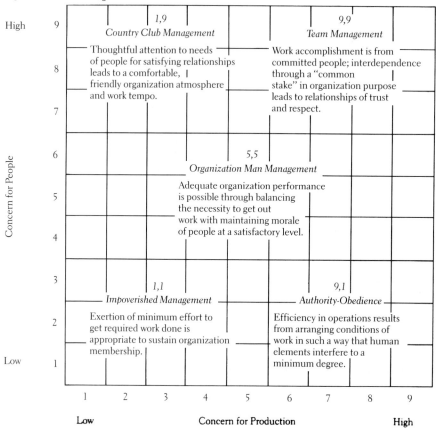

SOURCE: *The Managerial Grid figure from* The Managerial Grid III: The Key to Leadership Excellence, *by Robert R. Blake and Jane Srygley Mouton (Houston: Gulf Publishing Company), Copyright © 1985, p. 12. Reproduced by permission.*

1,1: *Impoverished Management.* The leader has a minimum concern for both production and people and puts forth only the least effort required to remain in the organization.

5,5: *"Organization Man" Management.* The leader goes along to get along, which results in conformity to the status quo.

9,9: *Team Management.* The leader integrates the concern for production and the concern for people at a high level; is goal centered; and seeks results through the participation, involvement, and commitment of all those who can contribute. This style can take the form of paternalism if the leader fails to integrate the concerns of production and people and the two are kept in logic-tight compartments. Paternalism occurs, for example, when the leader expresses a strong concern for the well-being of followers but does not consider their contributions to productivity, although he or she has an equally strong concern for production (Blake and Mouton, 1964, p. 10, in paraphase). They care as fathers (or mothers) for dependent subordinates from whom they expect unconditional loyalty.

Opportunistic leaders use several styles interchangeably, depending on the persons with whom they are dealing. Sometimes leaders masquerade as 9,9s when they really are paternalists or opportunists hiding behind facades.

The leader's dominant style is likely to be backed up by other styles. Thus, for instance, the 1,9 leader may begin a meeting in a casual, friendly way but quickly become the tough, no-nonsense, 9,1, which is his or her dominant style (Blake & Mouton, 1985c).

Team leadership (9,9) is what is prescribed. It is attained by behavioral science principles that involve participation, openness, trust and respect, involvement and commitment, open confrontation to resolve conflicts, consensus, the synergistic utilization of the human resources represented by the leader and followers, mutually determined management by objectives, mutual support, and change and development through feedback (Blake & Mouton, 1981a).

According to a study reported by Blake and Mouton (1985c), prior to a seminar, 68 percent of the managers saw themselves as 9,9; 10 percent, as 9,1; 19 percent, as 5,5; and 2-3 percent, as 1,9 or 1,1. After a seminar on the subject, a modal 41 percent admitted to being 5,5 and another 36 percent saw themselves as 9,1. Only 16 percent now believed they were 9,9. Blake and Mouton thought that these changes in results were indicative of the self-deception that occurs if understanding is impaired and feedback is not provided.

According to Blake and Mouton (1978), a 9,9 orientation has consistently proved to contribute positively to a variety of performance criteria in organizational development studies. In one of these studies, two matched subsidiaries of the same company were involved in a pre–post comparison over a ten-year-period. One subsidiary engaged in an extensive organizational development program that stressed 9,9 management; the other was not involved in any comparable program. The experimental subsidiary increased its profitability by 400 percent over the matched control.

In a study of 716 managers from a single firm, Blake and Mouton (1964) found that 9,9-oriented managers (after correcting for age differences) were more likely than were those with other dominant styles to advance further in their careers. J. Hall (1976) replicated these findings with an independent sample for 731 managers from a variety of companies.

Blake and Mouton (1985b) determined that the 9,9 style of team-management orientation characterized the leadership of the twentieth century U.S. presidents who had performed with greatness, in contrast to those who had not. This style was inferred from contemporary writings about the presidents' different ways of decision making, exercising initiatives, analyzing problems, taking advocacy roles, dealing with conflicts between themselves and their subordinates, and using critiques to increase their effectiveness in achieving results with and through subordinates.

Situational Contingencies Affecting Outcomes

Blake and Mouton did not leave much room for exceptions. Nevertheless, a substantial number of investigations of the impact of task- and relations orientation have been mixed or negative. Explanations for such findings have been sought in situational contingencies. These situational contingencies need to be examined for their moderating effects on the impact of relations- and task-oriented leadership on the satisfaction and productivity of followers. For instance, Miner (1982a, 1982b) suggested that the high-task–high-relations leadership orientation is most likely to be effective when organizations are a mix of systems of hierarchies and groups. The task orientation fits the hierarchies; the relations orientation fits the groups.

An illustration of a moderated result was the upward-influence tactics used by subordinates who were subjected to task- or people-centered leadership, according to Deluga's (1987b) study of 48 faculty members in a school of higher education. Deluga found that in the faculty members' first attempt to influence their superiors, only the superiors' relations orientation was of consequence. The faculty members said they were less likely to bargain or appeal to a higher authority if their superiors were more people centered. But if they failed to influence their superiors in their first attempt, in their second attempt, it was the task orientation of the leaders that was important. Here, the faculty members said they would be more likely to try friendliness, bargaining, assertiveness, appeals to a higher authority, and forming coalitions, the more they thought their superior was task centered.

The Subordinate as a Moderator

Although relations-oriented leadership was expected to generate more satisfaction among subordinates, moderating effects were seen in a number of investigations. In a study of community hospitals, F. C. Mann (1965) observed that the satisfaction of the nurses was related to the human relations skills of their supervisors, but the satisfaction of the nursing supervisors was related to the administrative skills of their superiors. At the same time, the satisfaction of the hospital technicians was related to their supervisors' technical and human relations skills. Tannenbaum and Allport (1956) studied two departments of women workers. One department was given more responsibility and authority for work and for decisions about the work and one department emphasized top-down line authority. A personality test was administered initially and scored as to the suitability of the workers' personality to the situation in which they worked. One year later, an attitude test was administered. The results of the test revealed that significantly more suited than unsuited workers in the situation with more authority and responsibility wanted the situation to continue, but suited and unsuited workers did not differ in their attitudes toward the program if they had not been given authority and responsibility. In another large-scale field study, Seashore (1954) found that supportive leadership with cohesive work groups paid off in higher productivity. However, the same group cohesiveness also resulted in lower productivity when the groups' supervisors were unsupportive.

The followers' need for achievement was seen by a number of investigators to make a difference in the way the followers reacted to particular styles of leadership. W. W. Burke (1965) discovered that followers with a high need to achieve who were led by socially close leaders rated their situation as more tense than did those with a high need to achieve who were under socially distant leaders. At the same time, followers with a low need to achieve who were led by socially close leaders rated their situation as more tense than did followers with a high need to achieve who were led by socially distant leaders. Followers with a high need to achieve rated socially close leaders high in authoritarianism, while those with a low need to achieve did the same for socially distant leaders. Misumi and Seki (1971) also studied the effects of leadership style on the performance of students who had a high or low need to achieve. Achievement-oriented students performed best under a leader who was high in both a P orientation and an M orientation. In groups whose members had a low need to achieve, the performance was best under a P-type leader.

Constraints and Goals as Moderators

Several studies obtained results suggesting that the style of supervision interacted with situational variables to influence productivity and satisfaction with the job. For example, Lundquist (1957) reported that foremen who are worker oriented produce better results in small than in large groups. In an Indian study of officers in central government departments, Srivastava and Kumar (1984) demonstrated that high task and high relationship styles of leadership both contributed to the effectiveness and adaptability of the middle-level officers; however, they did not do so for the junior-level officers. Nealey and Blood (1968) showed that among nurses in a Veterans Administration hospital, task-oriented first-level supervisors received higher performance appraisals, but it was the people-oriented second-level supervisors who received such higher performance appraisals. Although the subordinates' job satisfaction was correlated significantly at both levels with the supervisors' people orientation, task orientation contributed to the nurses' job satisfaction at the first but not at the second level of supervision.

The Task as a Moderator

W. W. Burke (1965) found that a group's performance of a coding task was completed more effectively under a production-oriented leader, but the completion of a decision task was carried out more effectively under a relations-oriented leader. Weed, Mitchell, and Moffitt (1976), among others, found that it was necessary to take the tasks into account to uncover the moderating of the linkage between a leader's relations orientation and the subordinates' satisfaction as a consequence of the subordinates' personality and orientation. Overall, they studied the effects of task- versus relations orientation on a group's performance and satisfaction with supervision as a function of the subordinates' personality and orientation. They compared leaders who scored high in human relations orientation and high in task orientation, low in human relations orientation and low in task orientation, low in human relations orientation and high in task orientation, and high in human relations orientation and low in task orientation. Each leader worked with subordinates who were high or low in dogmatism. Subordinates varied in their task- and relations orientations, as well. Regardless of their personality and orientations, the subordinates were significantly more satisfied with leadership behavior that was high in human relations orientation. But Weed, Mitchell, and Moffitt had also varied the ambiguity and difficulty of the tasks. The interacting effects of the leadership style—relations- or task oriented—and the subordinates' relations- or task orientation were strongest on difficult and ambiguous rather than clear and easy tasks. That is, the compatibility of the leader's and follower's personality made a difference only if the task was difficult and ambiguous.

Wofford (1971) obtained results indicating that a relations-oriented manager is likely to be more effective in terms of the productivity and morale of the group led in simple, centralized, structured operations. Schachter, Festinger, Willerman, and Hyman (1961) generated somewhat different and more convincing evidence in an experiment with work groups who were matched in age, productivity, seniority, and disciplinary records. For three weeks, managers were friendly and helpful to the favored group which they praised; they were threatening, reproving, and deliberately annoying in their demands on the unfavored group. The favor-

able and unfavorable relations ceased at the end of three weeks, when minor changes in work were instituted. Table 23.2 shows the percentage of assembled units requiring repair during each phase of the experiment. When the employees continued to work on old and familiar tasks, the unfavorable supervision had only slight effects on their performance. But when a changeover occurred that required work on new, unfamiliar tasks, the repair rates of the unfavored group jumped much higher than did those of the favored group. Equally important, although the favored group rapidly returned to its normal repair record by the end of the third week after the changeover, the unfavored group continued to exhibit a repair rate that was three times worse than what had been its normal record before the onset of the unfavorable supervisory relations. Unlike the results of surveys, this experiment demonstrated that unfavorable supervisory human relations cause decrements in performance primarily when new learning is required, not when accustomed tasks are performed.

Management Functions as Moderators

Woodward (1958) reported that friendly supervisors were rated as relatively more effective in service departments but relatively less effective in production departments. Consistent with this finding, B. Schneider (1973) noted that in social service agencies, supervisors set examples of how they expected their subordinates to relate to clients of the agencies. Satisfied clients coincided with the occurrence of friendly, concerned, su-

Table 23.2 Quality of Work before and after the Changeover of Work Groups that Were Subjected to Favored and Unfavored Supervisory Treatment

| | Percentage of Assembled Units Requiring Repair | |
Phase of the Experiment	Favored Group	Unfavored Group
During the first week of contrived disturbance	10.6	11.8
During the second two weeks of contrived disturbance	11.7	14.7
The first week after the changeover	21.1	31.4
The second week after the changeover	13.8	28.0
The third and fourth weeks after the changeover	11.6	29.0

SOURCE: Schachter, Willerman, Festinger, and Hyman (1961, p. 206).

pervisory relations with subordinates. Schneider also found that good customer relations with a bank reflected the good relations of the bank tellers with their superiors. Relations-oriented supervision thus would seem to be particularly indicated in service operations.

The manager and the coach of English football teams differ greatly in function. The manager has little continuous contact with the players, while the coach maintains a high degree of contact. Cooper and Payne (1967) found a correlation of .72 between the task orientation of the team coach and the success of the teams in winning games, but the same correlation was close to zero for managers.

Interrelations with Other Leadership Behaviors as Moderators

The effects of other types of behavior by the leader moderate the impact of the leader's task- or relations orientation. Thus, Larkin (1975) showed that elementary school teachers who were task oriented in their behavior created high morale among pupils, regardless of how much they also resorted to power. But teachers whose task-oriented behavior was low and who used power did generate rebellious pupils. Among supervisors of technical personnel, participative approaches (the provision of freedom) resulted in the most innovation if the supervisors were low in a task- or a human relations orientation (Andrews & Farris, 1967). In an experiment with small groups of ROTC students, Anderson and Fiedler (1964) found that those under task-oriented leaders were most productive and satisfied when the leaders were participative, but the satisfaction of students was greater when relations-oriented leaders were directive. Similarly, Pandey (1976) showed that the behavior and effectiveness of relations- and task-oriented leaders of discussion groups depended on whether the leaders were appointed, elected, or rotated, since the elected and rotated leaders tended to be more participative than did the appointed leaders.

A number of models of situational or contingent leadership have been constructed to provide advice to leaders on when they should be task oriented and hence directive and when they should be relations oriented and hence participative. The Hersey-Blanchard situational leadership model has been widely applied but has received little research support; the Fiedler contingency model has been more widely researched than applied. Both models remain highly controversial.

The Hersey-Blanchard Situational Leadership Model

Basis

The Hersey and Blanchard (1969a) situational leadership model was built on propositions that were based on Hersey and Blanchard's understanding of prior empirical research. These propositions were as follows:

1. Leadership styles vary considerably from leader to leader (Stogdill & Coons, 1957).
2. Some leaders' behavior primarily involves initiating structure to accomplish tasks, other leaders behave to build and maintain good personal relationships, and still others do both or do neither (Halpin, 1956a).
3. The most effective behavioral style of leaders is one that varies with the situation (Fiedler, 1967a; Korman, 1966).
4. The best attitudinal style is a high task- and a high relations orientation (Blake & Mouton, 1964).
5. The job and psychological maturity of the followers is most crucial in determining which behavioral style of leaders will result in the most effectiveness (Argyris, 1962).
6. Maturity relates to the stage in a group's life cycle or to the previous education and training of the followers.

Prescriptions

According to Hersey and Blanchard (1969a, 1969b, 1982a) a manager should be task oriented and tell or sell subordinates on what to do or a manager should be relations oriented and *participate*[7] with subordinates in joint decision making or delegate the deci-

---

As defined in the last chapter, *participation* (italicized) refers only to sharing in the decision process. Participation (romanized) includes consulting, sharing, and delegating. *Direction* (italicized) refers only to giving orders with or without explanation. Direction (romanized) includes ordering, persuading (selling), and manipulating.

sion to them depending on the subordinates' task-relevant maturity—their job maturity (capacity, ability, education, and experience) and their psychological maturity (motivation, self-esteem, confidence, and willingness to do a good job). The maturity levels manifest themselves in the subordinates' performance of their jobs. Newly appointed inexperienced employees on a job seek task-oriented direction from their superiors; they should be told what to do. As their "life cycle" on the job continues and their experience increases, they have to be sold to continue their performance. Later, relations orientation and *participation* become most efficacious with the subordinates' further development, to engage both their knowledge and their maturation. Finally, fully mature subordinates work best when the leaders delegate what needs to be done. The most effective leadership is conceived to depend on whether the leader's task-oriented or relations-oriented behavior matches the subordinate's maturity.

LASI or LEAD. The Leader Adaptability and Style Inventory (LASI)—later renamed the Leadership Effectiveness and Adaptability Description (LEAD)—provides brief vignettes (Hersey & Blanchard, 1974) of 12 situations, each with 4 alternatives, as shown in Figure 23.2.

For example, in situation 4, you supervise a group with a fine record of accomplishment whose members respect the need for change. You indicate from among four choices what supervisory action you would take to deal with the problem. One alternative, under answer C, is to delegate by allowing the group to work out the solution itself. This delegation is leadership behavior that is low in task orientation and low in relations orientation. The response adds 2 points to your self-rated delegation score. It also adds to your flexibility score,

for it best matches the requirements of the particular situation according to the model. The next best answer is A, to be *participative*, and is scored $+1$ for flexibility. It is a moderately adaptive leadership response, low in task orientation and high in relations orientation. The next best answer, D, to be persuasive, is scored -1 for flexibility; it is a response that is high in task- and high in relations orientation. Finally, the worst and least flexible answer is B, a highly *directive*, high task–low relations response; it is scored -2 for flexibility.

Subordinates and colleagues can also complete the form, indicating what they believe the focal manager would do; their responses can provide useful feedback to the focal leader (Hersey & Blanchard, 1981).

A curvilinear relationship between a leader's task- and relations orientation and the subordinates' maturity was postulated by Hersey and Blanchard (1977) as displayed in Figure 23.3. Unwilling and unable subordinates should be told what to do; willing but unable subordinates should be sold; unwilling but able subordinates should *participate*; and willing and able subordinates should be delegated assignments.

Subordinates' Maturity

Maturity is seen at four levels. Each level involves a different combination of attention to relations and task as in table below.

Positive Evidence

Despite problems with the model, some supportive empirical evidence has emerged for it along with contrary findings. Hersey, Angelini, and Carakushansky (1982) obtained support for the model as an approach to improve learning. The participants in their study were 60 managers who attended a management training semi-

Subordinates Level of Maturity	Leader's Behavior Should Be Oriented Toward		Prescribed Leadership Behavior
	Relations	Task	
1. Unable-unwilling	Low	High	Telling
2. Unable-willing	High	High	Selling
3. Able-unwilling	High	Low	Participating
4. Able-willing	Low	Low	Delegating

Situation	Alternative Actions
1 Your subordinates are not responding lately to your friendly conversation and obvious concern for their welfare. Their performance is in a tailspin.	A. Emphasize the use of uniform procedures and the necessity for task accomplishment. B. Make yourself available for discussion but don't push. C. Talk with subordinates and then set goals. D. Intentionally do not intervene.
2 The observable performance of your group is increasing. You have been making sure that all members were aware of their roles and standards.	A. Engage in friendly interaction, but continue to make sure that all members are aware of their roles and standards. B. Take no definite action. C. Do what you can to make the group feel important and involved. D. Emphasize the importance of deadlines and tasks.
3 Members of your group are unable to solve a problem themselves. You have normally left them alone. Group performance and interpersonal relations have been good.	A. Involve the group and together engage in problem solving. B. Let the group work it out. C. Act quickly and firmly to correct and redirect. D. Encourage group to work on problem and be available for discussion.
4 You are considering a major change. Your subordinates have a fine record of accomplishment. They respect the need for change.	A. Allow group involvement in developing the change, but don't push. B. Announce changes and then implement with close supervision. C. Allow group to formulate its own direction. D. Incorporate group recommendations, but you direct the change.
5 The performance of your group has been dropping during the last few months. Members have been unconcerned with meeting objectives. Redefining roles has helped in the past. They have continually needed reminding to have their tasks done on time.	A. Allow group to formulate its own direction. B. Incorporate group recommendations, but see that objectives are met. C. Redefine goals and supervise carefully. D. Allow group involvement in setting goals, but don't push.
6 You stepped into an efficiently run situation. The previous administrator ran a tight ship. You want to maintain a productive situation, but would like to begin humanizing the environment.	A. Do what you can to make group feel important and involved. B. Emphasize the importance of deadlines and tasks. C. Intentionally do not intervene. D. Get group involved in decision-making, but see that objectives are met.
7 You are considering major changes in your organizational structure. Members of the group have made suggestions about needed change. The group has demonstrated flexibility in its day-to-day operations.	A. Define the change and supervise carefully. B. Acquire group's approval on the change and allow members to organize the implementation. C. Be willing to make changes as recommended, but maintain control of implementation. D. Avoid confrontation, leave things alone.
8 Group performance and interpersonal relations are good. You feel somewhat unsure about your lack of direction of the group.	A. Leave the group alone. B. Discuss the situation with the group and then initiate necessary changes. C. Take steps to direct subordinates toward working in a well-defined manner. D. Be careful of hurting boss-subordinate relations by being too directive.
9 Your superior has appointed you to head a task force that is far overdue in making requested recommendations for change. The group is not clear on its goals. Attendance at sessions has been poor. Their meetings have turned into social gathering. Potentially they have the talent necessary to help.	A. Let the group work it out. B. Incorporate group recommendations, but see that objectives are met. C. Redefine goals and supervise carefully. D. Allow group involvement in setting goals, but don't push.
10 Your subordinates, usually able to take responsibility, are not responding to your recent redefining of standards.	A. Allow group involvement in redefining standards, but don't push. B. Redefine standards and supervise carefully. C. Avoid confrontation by not applying pressure. D. Incorporate group recommendations, but see that new standards are met.
11 You have been promoted to a new position. The previous supervisor was uninvolved in the affairs of the group. The group has adequately handled its tasks and direction. Group inter-relations are good.	A. Take steps to direct subordinates toward working in a well-defined manner. B. Involve subordinates in decision-making and reinforce good contributions. C. Discuss past performance with group and then you examine the need for new practices. D. Continue to leave group alone.
12 Recent information indicates some internal difficulties among subordinates. The group has a remarkable record of accomplishment. Members have effectively maintained long range goals. They have worked in harmony for the past year. All are well qualified for the task.	A. Try out your solution with subordinates and examine the need for new prices. B. Allow group members to work it out themselves. C. Act quickly and firmly to correct and redirect. D. Make yourself available for discussion, but be careful of hurting boss-subordinate relations.

Figure 23.2. The LASI Questionnaire

SOURCE: *From "So You Want to Know Your Leadership Style," by Paul Hersey and Kenneth H. Blanchard in* Training and Development Journal *(June 1981), p. 35. Copyright 1981, American Society for Training and Development. Reprinted with permission. All rights reserved.*

Figure 23.3. Hersey-Blanchard Model of the Relationship between Leader Style and Maturity of Followers

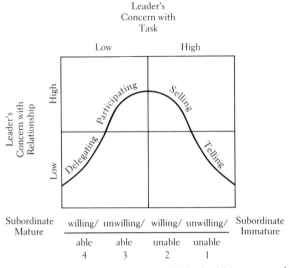

SOURCE: *From Paul Hersey and Kenneth H. Blanchard,* Management of Organizational Behavior: Utilizing Human Resources, *3e, © 1977, p. 170. Adapted by permission of Prentice-Hall, Inc., Englewood Cliffs, New Jersey.*

nar. The experimental groups were trained in four stages; a control group was not. Early on, the instructor engaged in a great deal of *direction*. The instructor next did some selling and then *participated* with the trainees in the learning process. Finally the instructor delegated the responsibility for learning to the trainees but remained available to support them. Thus, as the maturity of the trainees increased, the instructor decreased the task-oriented direction. The final examination at the end of training showed that the experimental group learned significantly more than did the control group.

Jacobsen (1984) found that LASI ratings by colleagues of the appropriate flexibility of the style of 338 managers correlated significantly with the progress of the managers' careers, as well as with selected performance criteria. Although the maturity level of their subordinates was found to moderate between the managers' behavior and effectiveness, it was less important than other situational variables. For 209 supervisors and managers from 5 organizations, Haley (1983) obtained positive correlations between the subordinates' LASI assessments of the adaptability of their superiors'

styles and the subordinates' ratings of the effectiveness of their own work groups. Hambleton and Gumpert (1982) found a statistically significant and practical gain in the job performance of 189 subordinates when their 56 supervisors applied the Hersey-Blanchard model correctly. High-performing managers rated higher than low performers on the effectiveness of their leadership and the flexibility of their style, both in their self-reports and in the appraisals by their subordinates and superiors. They also showed greater knowledge and use of the model of situational leadership.

Kohut (1983) found that the flexibility of 281 women managers, as measured by the LEAD, was related to their effectiveness and sex-role identity. Again, Vecchio (1987) surveyed 303 teachers from 14 high schools with the less controversial Leader Behavior Description Questionnaire (LBDQ), to be discussed in Chapter 24. Consistent with the Hersey-Blanchard model, Vecchio concluded that recently hired teachers, compared to those with more experience, may need and appreciate more initiation of structure from their supervisors.

Negative Evidence

Consistent with other studies with other instruments, such as with leaders' self-ratings on the LBDQ (Weissenberg & Kavanagh, 1972), Haley (1983) found response bias, low reliabilities, and lack of correlation between self- and others' LASI ratings of the focal managers. Narayanan, Venkatachalam, and Bharathiar (1982) could find no relation between the LEAD self-reports of 30 owners of small Indian hosiery knitting units and their employees' descriptions of the owners' styles. Nor could they find any connection with the productivity of the units.

York and Hastings (1985–86) surveyed 172 employees in three North Carolina social service departments to ascertain the effects of the supervisors' behavior on their subordinates' performance in the context of the subordinates' level of maturity. They found that regardless of the level of the subordinates' maturity, supervisors' supportive and work-facilitation behavior, as measured in the Survey of Organization contributed in the same way to the subordinates' performance.

Blank, Weitzel, and Green (1987) examined the situational leadership performance of 27 directors of residence halls (full-time professionals) who were responsible for 353 resident advisers (part-time paraprofessional students) in two large midwestern universities. A psychological maturity index was developed for the advisers, starting with 40 items about independence, the ability to take responsibility, and the motivation to achieve. Several factor analyses resulted in a refined single-factor scale of 11 items, such as, "acts conscientiously on the job," "follows through on job tasks," "takes care to do the job right," and "works hard on the job." Peer ratings on the items were obtained from other advisers to measure the psychological maturity of the advisers (the subordinates of the directors). Satisfaction with their work and supervision were obtained from the advisers, along with ratings of their performance by their directors. The psychological maturity of the advisers correlated .40 with their directors' ratings of their job performance. As predicted by the model, for those low in such psychological maturity work satisfaction increased linearly with the task-oriented, directive, and persuasive behavior of their directors. However, work satisfaction was much higher in advisers whose psychological maturity was high, regardless of the leadership behavior of their directors. The investigators concluded that their analyses as a whole lent little particular support for the Hersey-Blanchard model, although they agreed that further exploration of the relationships between the maturity of subordinates and the behavior of leaders would be useful.

Critique

The curvilinear model (Figure 23.3) has been roundly criticized because of the lack of internal consistency of its measures (Aldag & Brief, 1981), because of its conceptual contradictions, and because of its conceptual ambiguities (Graeff, 1983). The model appears to have no theoretical or logical justification (Graeff, 1983); nevertheless, the model has intuitive appeal. As was already noted, Blake and Mouton (1981a) argued that although situational leadership, as such, may be interesting, a preponderance of empirical evidence can be marshaled in support of their one best way, namely, leadership that integrates both a task- and a relations orientation. For example, in the just-mentioned research by Blank, Weitzel, and Green, the advisers' satisfaction with their supervision correlated .41 and .54, respectively, with the task- and relations behavior of their directors, regardless of the advisers' maturity. To this, Hersey and Blanchard (1982b) replied that Blake and Mouton deal with attitudinal models, while they deal with a behavioral model. Conflict only occurs when behavioral assumptions are drawn from the analysis of attitudinal models. Blake and Mouton (1981a, 1981b) countered with other difficulties with the Hersey-Blanchard model. They noted the extent to which task- and relations orientation and behavior tend to be interdependent, rather than uncorrelated with each other. Merely adding high task concerns to high relations concerns makes for benevolent paternalism, not teamwork. Qualitative differences at different ends of the continua in orientation and behavior need to be taken into account. For example, a high relations orientation of the kind that achieves high productivity (9,9) is characterized by openness, trust, respect, understanding, and mutual commitment. A high relations orientation that results in low productivity (1,9) is warm, friendly, and harmonious. To demonstrate this issue, Blake and Mouton (1981a, 1981b, 1982a) revised each of the 12 LEAD situations by adding fifth choices that reflected their 9,9 style. In paraphrase, the first Hersey-Blanchard situation was as follows:

> A group is not responding favorably to our friendly conversation and concern for their welfare. Their performance is going down quite quickly.

The prescribed Hersey-Blanchard answer is a high task–low relations orientation with the leader behaving according to response A. The least desirable choice is response D.

(A) Stress and apply uniform procedures and the need for accomplishing the task.

(B) Keep yourself on hand for discussion, but don't pressure subordinates to involve you.

(C) Set goals for subordinates after talking with them.

(D) Demonstrate your intentions by not interfering.

For this situation, Blake and Mouton thought the 9,9 style was the most efficacious: Initiate a critique session with the entire group to diagnose the underlying problems responsible for this rapidly declining production to decide what to do about it. From Blake and Mouton's point of view, the prescribed Hersey-Blanchard answer, A, is 9,1 behavior: telling subordinates what to do and pushing for production (Blake & Mouton, 1982a, 1982b).

One hundred experienced managers from 41 organizations completed the revised form without prior knowledge of the controversy. They ranked the choices for each of the 12 problems from most effective to least effective. The managers chose the fifth alternative, which reflects Blake-Mouton's 9,9 behavior (integration of the task- and relations orientation) between 72 to 90 percent of the time to handle each of the 12 situations. The managers chose the 9,9 alternative for situations, according to the four levels of the maturity of followers, from lowest to highest, 79 percent, 86 percent, 76 percent, and 78 percent of the time, respectively. They chose the appropriate alternative presented by Hersey-Blanchard, to reflect the followers' maturity, only 9 percent, 7 percent, 11 percent, and 5 percent of the time, respectively. Similar results were obtained with 36 mental health professionals.

In line with these results, Slocum (1984) suggested that the emphasis on the maturity of subordinates to determine when direction or participation is appropriate is of minor importance, in contrast to a number of other variables that deal with the subordinates' tasks, the technology employed, the information required, the managerial control and coordination systems in place, and the amount of self-control that is possible, as well as the extent to which the decision is operational and complex.

Efforts to Improve the Model and Its Measures

Nicholls (1985) suggested it may be possible to correct the model's logical flaws by required a smooth progression of the leader from the *parent* style of high task orientation–high relations orientation to the *developer* style of low task–high relations. In this developmental progression, the leader will maintain a balanced emphasis on both the task and relationships as long as the ability and willingness of the group are developing symmetrically. If ability and willingness develop asymmetrically, the leader may find it more appropriate to act highly task-oriented like a *coach* or a *driver*.

Boone (1981) improved the LEAD by modifying its scoring. The reliability of the LEAD self-report was increased by changing it from forced-choice scoring to scoring that captures the intensity of the endorsement of each alternative. In this way, for 249 managers from South Africa and the United States, more satisfactory test-retest reliabilities, ranging from .66 to .79, were obtained.

Should Leaders Be Consistent or Flexible?

A central question remains with the Hershey-Blanchard model: Should leaders vary their orientation and behavior to try to fit the demands of the situation or should they try to be consistent in their styles? If leaders recognize that different circumstances call for different actions on their part, do they risk being downgraded for being inconsistent and unpredictable? Do they cause subordinates to feel unsure about what is expected? The evidence is mixed. Bruce (1986) reported that CEOs placed a premium on being consistent and predictable in word and action. Staw and Ross (1980) asked 95 practicing managers and 127 undergraduates to read one of several case descriptions of administrators who were consistent or flexible and ultimately successful or unsuccessful in their actions. Although both sets of respondents assigned the highest ratings to administrators who were consistent, particularly those who also were successful, the practicing managers valued consistency more than did the undergraduates. Block and Kennedy (1986) asked 133 employees to rate leaders who were described as consistently autocratic, consistently participative, or flexible in their style, depending on the circumstances. The employees opted most often for the consistently participative manager than for the more flexible one. Graves (1985) obtained similar results for 141 undergraduate leaders. Those who persisted in one particular way were evaluated more favorably than were those who varied in their responses, despite the different levels of complexity with which they had to cope. Again supporting the utility of consistency, Aldag and Brief (1977) obtained strong negative correlations between an index of the variability of leaders' behavior and measures of subordinates' satisfaction, involvement with their jobs, organizational commitment, and experienced meaningfulness of the work. Blake and Mouton's (1982a) arguments for a consistent 9,9 leadership style have more empirical support than do Hersey and Blanchard's notions about how leaders must vary their style according to the situation.

Some exceptions need to be noted. James and White (1983) showed that 377 U.S. Navy managers were in favor of flexibility and varied their leadership behavior toward their subordinates, depending on their perceptions of what specifically caused their subordinates to perform inadequately. When 159 undergraduates judged systematically differing leadership descriptions, Knight (1984) found that the perceived competence among managers was more important in evaluating them than whether they were consistent or flexible.

One factor that seemed to account for the differences in support for consistency or flexibility was whether the evaluators of the leaders were the superiors or subordinates of the leaders. Appropriate flexible responses were more likely to be favored if one was a superior of the leader, but consistent participativeness was more likely to be favored if one was a subordinate of the leader, according to a simulation employed by Heilman, Hornstein, Cage, and Herschlag (1984). In addition, it seems that flexible leadership will be judged favorably if the shifts in a leader's style or behavior are meaningful and explainable to those who are evaluating the leader as shifts to accommodate the requirements of the circumstances. If no such change in requirements is perceived, consistency will be prized in a leader for the ease of its predictability and its fitting with colleagues' expectations.

Fiedler's contingency model, to be discussed next, avoids the problem of a leader's consistency in the face of situations with different requirements. Leaders are seen to have a personally consistent style. Either different types of leaders need to be chosen for various situations or the leaders need to change the situations to suit their particular personal style.

Why So Popular?

Given the competition for space in journals, many more studies of the Hersey-Blanchard model may have been conducted than were accepted for publication because of their theoretical problems or negative results. Nevertheless, the Hersey-Blanchard model has had remarkably widespread intuitive appeal to practicing managers and to leaders of management training programs, despite its theoretical inadequacies and the paucity of supportive empirical evidence. An understanding of its popularity with management may require an analysis of the sociology of knowledge, not of the model's theoretical or empirical validity.

Situationalism may be popular because it provides freedom from principles ("You can do your own thing as you see fit"). Principles are more complex to learn and practice. Situationalism allows a leader to keep all options open (Blake & Mouton, 1982b). Although LEAD lacks the desired level of reliability and its validity remains in doubt, its situations and choices seem to provide interesting discussion material for training. Its simplicity makes it possible to retain its prescriptions on a single small card. The simplicity may give managers a sense of quick mastery of a complex problem. For the personally authoritarian manager, it calls attention to the need for a flexible response. To the personally democratic manager, it gives legitimacy to be directive at times.

Fiedler's Contingency Model of Leadership

Fiedler's (1967a) contingency model of leadership has been the most widely researched model on leadership. It states that leaders with high Least Preferred Coworker (LPC) scores do best in situations moderately favorable to them; low scoring leaders do best in situations extremely favorable or extremely unfavorable to them. It is presented here as part of the discussion of relations- and task-oriented leadership. Nevertheless, controversy continues about whether Fiedler's LPC questionnaire measures task orientation or something else. This controversy, in turn, affects the ability to understand its contribution to effectiveness in different situations. On the surface, LPC measures how much each of 16 to 18 attributes reflect respondents' feelings about a person with whom they can work least effectively.

Development of the LPC Measurement

Starting in the early 1950s, Fiedler (1953a, 1953b, 1953c) began studying the success of therapists as a function of their accuracy and assumed similarity to their patients. This research was then extended to leaders and the effectiveness of the groups they led (Fiedler, 1954a, 1954b, 1955, 1956). A measure of Assumed Similarity between Opposites (ASo) was developed. ASo scores were obtained by computing the difference between two sets of semantic differential ratings. One set was the leader's description of his or her least preferred co-worker (LPC). The other set were ratings of the leader's most preferred co-worker. ASo scores were viewed as indicators of leadership style and were correlated with the performance of groups. The success in accurately predicting the performance of outcomes from ASo scores was mixed.

Eventually, the most preferred co-worker was abandoned as an assessment and attention focused on the LPC. In its standard version, the examinee is asked to think of everyone with whom he or she has ever worked and then to describe the one person with whom he or she could work least well. This description of one's LPC is made by marking 16 items, as shown in Table 23.3. The favorable pole of each scale is scored as 8 and the unfavorable pole is scored as 1 (Fiedler, Chemers, & Mahar, 1976). The sum of the scales of items constitutes the individual's LPC score. A relatively high LPC score (favoring the LPC) was most generally conceived by Fiedler (1967a, 1970b) to indicate a relationship-motivated person, whereas a low LPC score (rejecting the LPC) was conceived to indicate a task-motivated person.

Measurement Properties of LPC

A good deal of evidence is available concerning the internal consistency and stability of the LPC, but its validity remains a complex question.

Internal Consistency. Do the same people respond in the same way to the different items of the LPC scale? For earlier versions of LPC, Rice (1978a) obtained a mean split-half reliability of .88 for a variety of investigations. Fox, Hill, and Guertin (1973); Shiflett (1974); and Yukl (1970) discovered separate interpersonal and task factors in these earlier LPC scales, but the secondarily scored task factor was seen to be relatively unimportant. Therefore, a newer 18-item scale was designed to minimize task-factor items and, as a consequence, was somewhat higher in internal consistency (Fiedler, 1978). In 5 studies with the newer 18-item version, Rice (1979) reported coefficient alphas of .90, .91, .79, .84, and .89.

Table 23.3 The Least Preferred Co-worker Scale

Think of the person with whom you can work *least* well. This person may be someone you work with now or someone you knew in the past. This person does not have to be the person you like least well, but should be the person with whom you had the most difficulty in getting a job done.

Please describe this person as he or she appears to you by putting an "X" in the appropriate space on the following scales.

Pleasant	:___:___:___:___:___:___:___:	Unpleasant
Friendly	:___:___:___:___:___:___:___:	Unfriendly
Rejecting	:___:___:___:___:___:___:___:	Accepting
Helpful	:___:___:___:___:___:___:___:	Frustrating
Unenthusiastic	:___:___:___:___:___:___:___:	Enthusiastic
Tense	:___:___:___:___:___:___:___:	Relaxed
Distant	:___:___:___:___:___:___:___:	Close
Cold	:___:___:___:___:___:___:___:	Warm
Cooperative	:___:___:___:___:___:___:___:	Uncooperative
Supportive	:___:___:___:___:___:___:___:	Hostile
Boring	:___:___:___:___:___:___:___:	Interesting
Quarrelsome	:___:___:___:___:___:___:___:	Harmonious
Self-Assured	:___:___:___:___:___:___:___:	Hesitant
Efficient	:___:___:___:___:___:___:___:	Inefficient
Gloomy	:___:___:___:___:___:___:___:	Cheerful
Open	:___:___:___:___:___:___:___:	Guarded

SOURCE: Fiedler (1967, p. 41).

Stability. Do people's LPC scores remain the same over time? Rice (1978a) found 23 reports of test-retest reliability ranging from .01 to .91 with a median of .67. Stability indexed by high test-retest correlations was obtained by Chemers and Skrzypek (1972)[8] when the test and retest were separated by several weeks, at least. However, the time between the test and retest did not affect stability (as might have been expected), according to an analysis of studies in which the intervals between the test and the retest ranged from several days to over two years (Rice, 1978a). Hence, stability can be maintained over extended intervals of time. Bons (1974) obtained a test-retest reliability of .72 for 45 higher-level army leaders over a five-month period, and Prothero and Fiedler (1974) obtained a test-retest correlation of .67 for 18 faculty members of a school of nursing over a 16–24-month period. However, Fox (1976) found a decline in reliability when the retest was obtained 9 weeks instead of 4 weeks after the test. With intervals of 3–5 weeks, test-retest reliabilities ranged from .73 to .85. With intervals of 8–9 weeks, they ranged from .23 to .68; when the interval was 130 weeks, the test-retest reliability was only .45. In addition, Fox (1976) found that stability was reduced if the same least preferred co-worker was not described in the test and in the retest.

Thus, LPC is not necessarily as invariant an attribute of an individual as is a personality trait, such as sociability. Offerman (1984) and other investigators[9] obtained results suggesting that the LPC is more like a transitory attitude. For example, in a comparative experiment with male and female undergraduates who led opposite, mixed, or same-sex groups, Offerman (1984) found significant differences among the leaders as a consequence of the sex composition of the groups they had just led. The LPC scores of females who had just led male groups were most task oriented; the LPC scores of males who had just led female groups were most relations oriented.

Temporary shifts also can be induced by unsatisfactory work experiences in laboratory experiments. When instability has been found in such experiments,

it has been attributed to "implicit instructions" of training interventions as to how one should adapt toward poor co-workers (Rice, 1978a). LPC also appears sensitive to major life changes, such as being subjected to stressful contact assignments (Bons, Bass, & Komorita, 1970). In spite of the satisfactory median test-retest results, Schriesheim, Bannister, and Money (1979) remained unconvinced of the stability of LPC because of the wide variation in test-retest results within the various reported analyses. For instance, Schriesheim and Kerr (1977a) noted that a significant proportion of persons also changed category from high to low LPCs, or vice versa.

Parallel-Form Reliability. Do LPC scores remain the same if different attributes are included in the items? For instance, in one form, the choice may be between dull and bright. In the parallel form, the choice may be between stupid and smart. Rice (1978a) reported one study in which scales whose items had different content and that had different formats were fairly well correlated with each other. Different versions of the LPC have contained various amounts of task-oriented items, which may reduce their parallel-form reliability. This difference may account for some of the variations in correlations of the LPC version used with other tests and measures of the effectiveness of groups in attempts to determine the meaning of LPC (Schriesheim, Bannister, & Money, 1979). But Rice (1979) argued that since correlations of .79, .78, and .66 were obtained when items and formats to assess LPC had been changed, correlated parallel forms could be constructed successfully.

Content Validity. Are the items of the LPC scale biased? If LPC is a measure of the degree to which task-oriented individuals are negative about those with whom they cannot work, an attitude reflected by ascribing negative values to the LPCs on such attributes as pleasant-unpleasant that are not necessarily directed to their work, then task-oriented items, such as bright-dull, reduce the content validity of the LPC, since brightness and dullness are directly related to getting the work done (Schriesheim, Bannister, & Money, 1979). An 18-item version that omits such clearly task-relevant items is now operative. As was noted earlier, Shiflett (1974) and Yukl (1970), among others, demon-

---

[8]It was also obtained by Fiedler, O'Brien, and Ilgen (1969); Hardy (1971, 1975); Hardy and Bohren (1975); and Hardy, Sack, and Harpine (1973).
[9]Fishbein, Landy, and Hatch (1969a); E. J. Frank (1973); and Stinson and Tracy (1974).

strated that the earlier versions of the LPC contained two factors, one associated with interpersonal relations items; the other, with task-oriented items. Studies by Fiedler (1967a) and Schriesheim (1979b) have found LPC scores to be relatively free of social desirability, unlike so many other personality measures.

Construct Validity. What is really being measured by the LPC? How does the LPC logically and empirically link with other known entities? Fiedler and Chemers (1974, p. 74) observed that "for nearly 20 years, we have been attempting to correlate [LPC] with every conceivable personality trait and every conceivable behavior observation score. By and large these analyses have been uniformly fruitless."

But Rice (1978b), who sampled 66 out of 114 studies involving over 2,000 empirical relationships between the LPC and other variables, thought he could lay out the nomological network of empirical relationships of the LPC and other measures. He concluded more optimistically that although it remains unclear whether the LPC is a measure of social distance, personal need, cognitive complexity, or motivational hierarchy (as will be discussed later), LPC scores as measures of interpersonal relations versus task orientation is not in doubt.

The inconsistent results can be seen if one examines LPC's correlations with biographical data and then compares what Bass (1967b) reported about the correlations of direct measures of relations orientation and task orientation. In agreement with Bass's review, a low LPC score (task orientation) was higher with increasing age (Fiedler & Hoffman, 1962) and with experience (Bons, Bass, & Komorita, 1970). But opposed to Bass's conclusions, a high LPC score (relations orientation) was positively correlated with managerial level (Alpander, 1974) and with Protestant, rather than Catholic, affiliation (Fiedler & Hoffman, 1962). Above and beyond these results, no significant relations of biodata and LPC were found by Eagly (1970) and numerous other investigators.[10]

Schriesheim and Kerr (1974) have critically noted, as new evidence has emerged, that the LPC has been redefined as an orientation toward work, as an attitude,

as a cognitive complexity measure (E. J. Frank, 1973), as the ability to differentiate conceptually (Foa, Mitchell, & Fiedler, 1971), or as an index of a hierarchy of goals (Fiedler, 1972a). However, this redefinition could be a virtue rather than a fault. (Theoretical constructs like ether should wither away leaving behind empirical facts like the electrical discharge in lightning.) But critics fail to see that the new data justify the new interpretations (Hosking, 1978). For example, Evans and Dermer (1974) correlated the LPC scores for 112 business students, managers, and systems analysts with two measures of cognitive differentiation and cognitive complexity and found that low LPC scores were associated with cognitive simplicity. Nevertheless, high LPC scores were not unequivocally related to cognitive complexity.

LPC as a Measure of Relations and Task Orientation. A number of studies have supported the contention that a high LPC score is connected with relations orientation and a low LPC score is connected with task orientation.

Fiedler (1964, 1967a) proposed that high-LPC persons have a strong need to attain and maintain successful interpersonal relationships, whereas low-LPC persons have a strong need for successful task performance. Four sets of data generally gave some support for this interpretation (although many reversals were noted). The behavior of low-LPC leaders tended to be task oriented, and the behavior of high-LPC leaders was generally relations oriented. Members of groups with high- and low-LPC leaders tended to exhibit task-oriented and relations-oriented leadership. Higher levels of satisfaction and lower levels of anxiety were found among followers in groups with high-LPC leaders. Finally, data suggested that low-LPC persons gained self-esteem and satisfaction from the successful performance of tasks and high-LPC persons gained self-esteem and satisfaction from successful interpersonal relations. Fiedler (1978) inferred that for the individual who describes his or her least preferred coworker in negative, rejecting terms, the completion of the task is of such overriding importance that it completely colors the perception of all other personality traits attributed to the LPC score. His interpretation was as follows:

[10]See, for example, A. R. Bass, Fiedler, and Krueger (1964); Lawrence and Lorsch (1967a); Nealey and Blood (1968); Posthuma (1970); and Shiflett (1974).

"If I cannot work with you, if you frustrate my need to get the job done, then you can't be any good in other respects. You are unfriendly, unpleasant, tense, and distant, etc."

The relationship-motivated individual who sees his or her LPC in relatively more positive terms says, "Getting a job done is not everything. Therefore, even though I can't work with you, you may still be friendly, relaxed, interesting, etc.; in other words, someone with whom I could get along quite well on a personal basis." Thus, the high LPC person looks at [his or her least preferred co-worker] in a more differentiated manner—more interested in the personality of the individual than merely in whether this is or is not someone with whom one can get a job done. (p. 61)

LPC and Other Relevant Measures of Orientation. Vroom and Yetton (1973) and Sashkin, Taylor, and Tripathi (1974) reported that high LPC scores relate to the preference for participation in resolving conflict. Nebeker and Hansson (1972) found that high LPC scores correlate with support of the freedom that children should be given to use facilities. Alpander (1974) obtained results indicating positive relations between high LPC scores and the judged importance of people-oriented management functions. Similarly, Ayman and Chemers (1986) found that high-LPC Mexican managers described the ideal leader as a "people person" and low-LPC managers described the ideal leader as a task master; low-LPC managers were also more self-monitoring. However, Singh (1983) failed to find support in experiments with 53 Indian engineering students that high-LPC students would place greater importance on the equity of the distribution of rewards while low-LPC students would emphasize performance. In reverse of any expectations, Steiner and McDiarmid (1957) found that a high LPC score coincided with authoritarian beliefs, but Evans and Dermer (1974) and others[11] found LPC to be unrelated significantly to authoritarianism or dogmatism.

LPC and Observed Leader Behavior. Observers and other group members found a low LPC score to coincide, as expected, with initiating structure and

[11]See A. R. Bass, Fiedler, and Krueger (1964); Fishbein, Landy, and Hatch (1969a); and Sashkin, Taylor, and Tripathi (1974).

task-oriented leadership behavior and a high LPC score to coincide with relations-oriented behavior in a number of studies.[12] But complete reversals (Nealey & Blood, 1968) and negative results were also reported.[13] Interactions with situations had to be considered.[14]

LPC scores do not relate much to decision-making styles. McKenna (undated) obtained correlations between the LPC and style of decision making of 22 chief accountants, as follows: directive without explanation, −.12; *directive* with explanation, −.01; consultative, .06; *participative*, .03; and delegative, .13.

Mitchell (1970a) found that, as expected, high-LPC leaders gave more weight to interpersonal relations. Gottheil and Lauterbach (1969) studied military cadets and squads who were competing in field exercises and found that a leader's low LPC score was associated with a group's performance, while the leader's high LPC score was associated with a group's morale. But contrary to expectations, LPC scores were higher for leaders working under short-term than under long-term spans (Miller, 1970). Such complete reversals of results and the weakness of LPC scores as indicators of leadership behavior led Vroom (1976b) to suggest caution in characterizing leadership style on the basis of LPC score alone. For Fiedler (1967a), leadership style depends on combining LPC scores with measures of the situation in which the high- or low-LPC persons find themselves. A high LPC score, Fiedler (1978) noted, does not always predict that a leader will behave according to a relations orientation. Nor will a leader's low LPC score always predict that the leader will push for production, for completion of the task, or for more structuring. At any rate, while LPC may prove to discriminate among leaders in ways that are of consequence to their effectiveness in different contingencies, LPC is not directly symptomatic of the other styles of leadership behavior discussed earlier or yet to

[12]See Blades and Fiedler (1973); Chemers and Skrzypek (1972); Green, Nebeker, and Boni (1974); Gruenfeld, Rance, and Weissenberg (1969); Meuwese and Fiedler (1965); Sample and Wilson (1965); Sashkin (1972); and Yukl (1970).
[13]See L. R. Anderson (1964); Evans (1973); Fiedler (1967a); Fiedler, O'Brien, and Ilgen (1969); Fox (1974); Graen, Orris, and Alvares (1971); and Stinson (1972).
[14]W. W. Burke (1965), Chemers (1969), Fiedler (1967a, 1971b, 1971c, 1971d, 1972a), W. K. Graham (1970/1973), Green and Nebeker (1974), Nealy and Blood (1968), Rice and Chemers (1975), Shiflett and Nealy (1972), Shima (1968); and Yukl (1970).

be discussed. Hence, the results with LPC must stand alone. In fact, some question remains about whether LPC is measuring task- and relations orientation or something else.

Support for Alternative Meanings of LPC

LPC has gone through a series of reinterpretations on the basis of empirical studies of its characteristics. It has been conceived as a measure of social distance, of cognitive complexity, of motivational priorities and of a value-attitude.

LPC as a Measure of Social Distance. At first, Fiedler (1957, 1958) interpreted LPC—then called ASo, an index almost perfectly correlated with LPC— as a generalized index of psychological closeness. Low-LPC persons were conceived to be more socially or psychologically distant from other group members than were high-LPC persons. The assumed similarity data were drawn from person-perception research conducted in therapeutic settings. Fiedler (1953a, 1953b) inferred that respondents showed greater assumed similarity between themselves and group members they liked than between themselves and members they disliked. Analyses suggested that LPC was a measure of emotional and psychological distance, since high-LPC persons conformed more in the face of social pressure and were more closely involved with other group members. But following a review of studies of the reactions of others to high- and low-LPC persons, Rice (1978b) concluded that the data were contradictory.

LPC as a Measure of Cognitive Complexity. Foa, Mitchell, and Fiedler (1971) and Hill (1969a) argued that high-LPC persons are more cognitively complex (favoring the abstract over the concrete and using less broad categorizations) than are low-LPC persons. They based their proposal on the positive correlations they found between LPC and several measures of cognitive complexity. In addition, the intercorrelations among the factor scores of the LPC scale were lower for high-LPC persons, and greater responsiveness to interpersonal factors in the judgments and behavior of high-LPC persons was observed.

Although LPC was found to be correlated significantly with intelligence in only 1 to 14 analyses, in sev-

eral of 11 other analyses, LPC was related to specific cognitive tendencies. Thus, Mitchell (1970a, 1970b) found that high-LPC leaders gave more weight to power and structure in making discriminations, whereas low-LPC leaders gave more weight to interpersonal relations. Foa, Mitchell, and Fiedler (1970) observed that the high-LPC leader performed better in situations that present difficulties in either interpersonal or task relations and thus that require a high degree of cognitive differentiation between them. Jacoby (1968) found positive correlations between LPC and scores on the Remote Associates Test, a test of creativity. Similarly, Triandis, Mikesell, and Ewen (1962) reported a possibly positive correlation between LPC and the judged creativity of two written passages. Singh (1983) also obtained data to support LPC as a measure of cognitive complexity by demonstrating that high-LPC engineering students did better than did low-LPC students in obeying the precise prescriptions of a model for the equitable distribution of rewards.

The findings for cognitive complexity dealing with field independence-dependence, as measured by the Embedded Figures Test, were less consistent (Gruenfeld & Arbuthnot, 1968; Weissenberg & Gruenfeld, 1966). Furthermore, a number of other studies[15] found no evidence to support LPC as a measure of cognitive complexity.

LPC as a Measure of a Motivational Hierarchy. To account for so much variation in results, Fiedler (1972a) saw the need for a "hierarchical" conceptualization of LPC. Since, according to Fiedler, the high-LPC person needs to be related and socially connected to others, he or she will show concern for good interpersonal relations when the situation is tense and anxiety arousing and when his or her relations with co-workers seem tenuous. But when the goals of being related are secure, the relationship-motivated high-LPC person will then seek the self-oriented admiration of others and the attainment of prominence. In work groups, such goals can be attained by showing concern for the task-relevant aspects of the groups' interaction. In the same way, the major objectives of the low-LPC person are to

[15]See Fiedler (1954a, 1954b); Fishbein, Landy, and Hatch (1969b); Nealey and Blood (1968); Shiflett (1974); Shima (1968); and Larson and Rowland (1974).

accomplish a task and to earn self-esteem by doing a good job (D. W. Bishop, 1964). But when the completion of a task presents no problem, the low-LPC person will seek friendly, good interpersonal relations with co-workers, partly because he or she believes that good interpersonal relations are conducive to accomplishing the task (Fiedler, 1971b).

Nevertheless, this, like previous interpretations, remains controversial. Green and Nebeker (1977) presented data to support it. But evidence by Rice and Chemers (1975) failed to confirm predictions based on a motivational hierarchy. LPC as a measure of cognitive complexity better fit their results. Similarly, Kunczik (1976a, 1976b) found no support for the motivational hierarchy in studies of the relation of ASo with various personality measures among 1,590 German army recruits and 148 group leaders. Schriesheim and Kerr (1977b) concluded that neither sufficient theoretical nor empirical support emerged for this interpretation of LPC.

LPC as a Measure of a Value-Attitude. On the basis of a review of available evidence, Rice (1978b) agreed that the data did not support the shift in orientation required by the motivational hierarchy concept of LPC. Rather, according to Rice, the data better fit a simpler conceptualization of LPC as a value and an attitude, for LPC was more consistently and strongly related to attitudes and judgments than to behavioral manifestations. Therefore, LPC was seen as an attitude that reflects differences toward interpersonal relations and the accomplishment of tasks. One can make some general statements about the behavior of high- and low-LPC leaders, but situational variables have a strong influence.

How can Fiedler and Chemers's (1974) beliefs in the uniqueness of LPC be reconciled with Rice's conclusion that LPC is a value-attitude assessment? One problem was Rice's strategy of building his summary around published relationships that were statistically significant at the 5 percent level. As David Bakan has quipped in private communication, significant relationships are more likely to be published than are nonsignificant ones. The total universe of studies is probably far greater than what Rice compiled. And with so many studies in the significant pool at the margin of

significance, with no attention paid to the strength of the relationships that were found, it is difficult to accept Rice's evidence as compelling. However, Rice (1978b) concluded, as a consequence of his analysis of 313 reported relationships, that LPC was more strongly linked (that is, significant results at the 5 percent level were obtained) with values and attitudes. But even here, only 27 percent of the 313 relationships were significant. Yet even among these, some expected and reasonable inferences could be made with some conviction. Thus, as would be expected from relations-oriented individuals, high-LPC persons were found to make more favorable judgments of other group members—the leader, co-workers, and followers in general—[16] than were low-LPC persons in 18 of 20 analyses. Low-LPC persons tended to be more favorable than high-LPC persons in judgments of their best friends, more preferred co-workers, and loyal subordinates.[17] But negative results were also reported.[18]

Rice (1978b) concluded from these studies that low-LPC persons discriminated more sharply among other group members on task competence than did high-LPC persons. LPC was also related to judgments about oneself; low-LPC persons judged themselves significantly more favorably than did high-LPC persons in 34 of 102 analyses, particularly in direct evaluations (88 percent of the relationships were statistically significant).[19] A complete reversal (not necessarily unexpected) occurred in a Japanese study (Shima, 1968), and negative results were reported by others.[20]

Evidence that low-LPC persons value the successful completion of tasks was seen in the defensiveness of

[16]See, for example, Alpander (1974); Cronbach, Hartmann, and Ehart (1953); Godfrey, Fiedler, and Hall (1959); Hunt (1971); Wearing and Bishop (1976); and Wood and Sobel (1970).

[17]See A. R. Bass, Fiedler, and Krueger (1964); Bons, A. R. Bass, and Komorita (1970); Fiedler (1958, 1962, 1964, 1967a); Godfrey, Fiedler, and Hall (1959); Gottheil and Vielhaber (1966); Jones and Johnson (1972); and Shiflett (1974).

[18]See Bishop (1967), Chemers (1969), Gottheil and Lauterbach (1969), Hutchins and Fiedler (1960), and Steiner and Peters (1958).

[19]See, for example, D. R. Anderson (1964); Ayer (1968); A. R. Bass, Fiedler, and Krueger (1964); Bons, A. R. Bass, and Komorita (1970); W. W. Burke (1965); Fiedler (1972a); W. M. Fox (1974); and Shiflett (1974).

[20]Bishop (1967); Fiedler (1967a); Golb and Fiedler (1955); Gottheil and Lauterbach (1969); Gottheil and Vielhaber (1966); Gruenfeld and Arbuthnot (1968); Sashkin, Taylor, and Tripathi (1974); Steiner and McDiarmid (1957); and Strickland (1967).

their attributions about the cause of the failure of a task and their evaluation of the task-relevant ability of the group. In addition, low-LPC persons were found to be more optimistic about being successful in a task and about earning important rewards as a consequence. At the same time, high-LPC persons were more optimistic about the success of interpersonal relationships and the expectation that such success will lead to important outcomes (Fiedler, 1967a, 1972a).

Taking everything into account, Rice (1978b), on the basis of these mixed results, agreed with Fiedler that low-LPC persons value being successful in tasks and high-LPC persons value interpersonal success. But Fiedler concluded that any interpretation of the meaning of LPC must take into account situational considerations in determining how LPC will manifest itself in effective leadership. That is, Fiedler (1978) believed that the main effects of LPC on a leader's behavior are weak in comparison to the effects of the interaction of LPC with the favorableness of the situation to the leader.

Situational Favorability for the Leader

In Fiedler's (1967a, 1978) exposition of his model, low-LPC (task-oriented) leaders perform better and lead more effective groups when the quality of leader-member relationships, the degree of task structure, and the positional power of the leader are either altogether highly favorable or altogether highly unfavorable to the leader. High-LPC (relations-oriented) leaders are most effective when favorability is neither high nor low; that is, high-LPC leaders are expected to be most effective in moderately favorable circumstances. Fiedler envisaged eight situations (octants I through VIII), one for each combination of poor or good relations with group members, low or high structure of the group, and weak or strong power of the leader. The extremes of octants I and VIII are clearly determined in their location at the ends of the dimension of situational favorability. In octant I, leader-member relations are good, the task is highly structured, and the leader's positional power is strong. In octant VIII, leader-member relations are poor, the task is unstructured, and the leader's positional power is weak. But octants II and III, for instance, would change places on the dimension of favorability if one gave more weight to the task's structure than to the leader's positional power. The eight octants of the situational favorability dimension are shown along the horizontal axis of Figure 23.4.

Weighting. The relative importance of the three situational factors to the leader's situational favorability was reflected in a continuous scale constructed by Nebeker (1975). Nebeker's scale weighted standardized scores for each of the three situational variables such that the leader's situational favorability = 4 (leader-member relations) + 2 (task structure) + (positional power).

The theoretical combinations required by Fiedler for octant analysis fit the empirical multiple regression analyses completed by Nebeker (1975). Beach and Beach (1978) also reported findings that supported an independent, additive view of the three variables of leader-member relations, task structure, and leader's positional power. Beach and Beach (1978) asked students to estimate the probability of success and the situational favorability of a series of hypothetical leadership situations. Situations were presented as involving either good or poor leader-member relations, high or low task structure, and the leader's high or low positional power. A correlation of .89 was obtained between the estimated probability of the leader's success and the degree of situational favorability. A multiple correlation was then compared with situational favorableness as the criterion and the three situational favorability subscales as predictors. The beta weights obtained were .45 for leader-member relations, .33 for task structure, and .11 for positional power, comparable to the Nebeker formula of 4:2:1.

Earlier, situational favorability had been defined in terms of how much control the leader had in the situation. Support for the linkage of situational favorability and situational control came from a study by Mai-Dalton (1975) in which participants were asked to complete a leader's in-basket test. The study found that high-LPC leaders tend to be most effective and are most likely to ask for additional information in moderate-control situations, while low-LPC persons manifest the most information-searching behavior in high-control situations.

Figure 23.4. The Contingency Model of Leadership Effectiveness Based on Original Studies

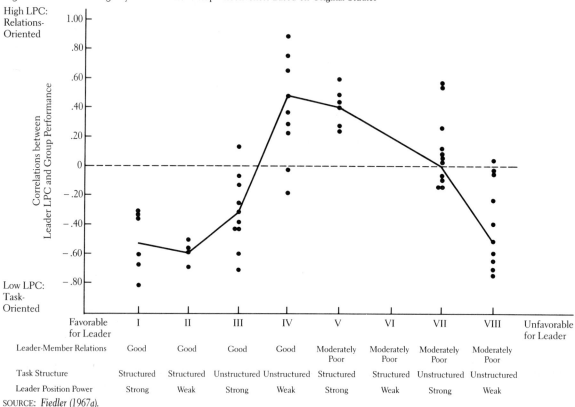

SOURCE: *Fiedler (1967a)*.

Determination of Situational Characteristics. In Fiedler's original studies, the quality of interpersonal relations was measured by sociometric choices and related measures of liking. Open-hearth steel crews were judged to be highly structured and boards of directors or transient student groups were judged to be highly unstructured. The leader's power was judged to be high for managers of gasoline stations and to be low for the informal leaders of basketball teams. Subsequently, Fiedler developed specific scales to provide measurements of the three situational variables for any leader-group situation. Other situational variables that have been assumed to determine the leader's situational control include stress, cultural and linguistic heterogeneity, and the amount of experience.[21]

To measure leader-member relations, a group-atmosphere scale was developed that correlated .88 with ear-

lier methods of estimating leader-member relations. It is presented in Table 23.4. To measure task-structure, a scale was created to obtain judgments about whether the goal was clearly stated, whether there was only one way to accomplish the task, whether there was one correct answer, and whether results are easy to check for correctness. To measure a leader's positional-power a scale questioned whether the leader could evaluate subordinates and recommend rewards, punishments, promotions, and demotions. (Fiedler, Chemers, & Mahar, 1976). Schriesheim (1979a) found the group-atmosphere scale to be free of social desirability, but the positional-power scale correlated .42 with social desirability.

Meaning of Situational Favorability. Situational favorability, with its high degree of control and influence, implies that the leaders are certain that their decisions and actions will have predictable results, will achieve the desired goals, and will satisfy the leaders (Fiedler,

[21]Ayer (1968); Fiedler (1966); Fiedler, Meuwese, and Oonk (1961); Fiedler, O'Brien, and Ilgen (1969); and Meuwese and Fiedler (1965).

Table 23.4 Group-Atmosphere Scale

Describe the atmosphere of your group by checking the following items.

Friendly	:___:___:___:___:___:___:___:___:	Unfriendly
Accepting	:___:___:___:___:___:___:___:___:	Rejecting
Satisfying	:___:___:___:___:___:___:___:___:	Frustrating
Enthusiastic	:___:___:___:___:___:___:___:___:	Unenthusiastic
Productive	:___:___:___:___:___:___:___:___:	Nonproductive
Warm	:___:___:___:___:___:___:___:___:	Cold
Supportive	:___:___:___:___:___:___:___:___:	Hostile
Interesting	:___:___:___:___:___:___:___:___:	Boring
Successful	:___:___:___:___:___:___:___:___:	Unsuccessful

SOURCE: Fiedler (1967, p. 267).

1978). At the favorable, high-control extreme and the unfavorable low-control extreme, the leaders know where they stand in relation to their groups. In-between relations are more cloudy for the leaders.

Schriesheim and Hosking (1978) found a number of problems with the measurement of situational favorability. The three variables are assumed to interact in a relatively simple way to determine the amount of influence the leader has over the group, an assumption subsequently supported by Beach and Beach's (1978) results. However, although Fiedler (1978) acknowledged the importance of other variables to situational control, he relied on just the aforementioned three among the many possible variables of consequence (Filley, House, & Kerr, 1976).

Situational Favorability and LPC

Between 1953 and 1964, Fiedler and his associates studied the effectiveness of leadership in a variety of groups and tested a contingency hypothesis from the results of those studies. Fiedler (1964) plotted the correlations and their medians between LPC scores (actually ASo) and group performance for the different octants—the different levels of situational favorability. He obtained a correlation between all the leaders in a particular study in a designated octant of situational favorability for the leaders and the effectiveness of their groups. A positive correlation indicated that high-LPC (relations-oriented) leaders coincided with more effective groups. A negative correlation showed that low-LPC (task-oriented) leaders ran more effective groups. A positive median correlation for all analyses

completed in a designated octant denoted the extent to which high-LPC leaders performed more effectively than did low-LPC leaders. A negative median correlation disclosed that the low-LPC leaders were superior for a designated octant. Fiedler theorized that the curvilinear relation (as seen in Figure 23.1) was an indication that low-LPC leaders were more effective than high-LPC leaders in very favorable and very unfavorable situations (e.g., octants I and VIII), whereas high-LPC leaders were more effective in situations of intermediate favorability (e.g., octants IV and V).

Validity of the Model

Fiedler (1971b, 1978) reviewed efforts to validate the contingency model.[22] The empirical investigations included field studies, field experiments, laboratory experiments, and octant analyses.

Field Studies. Field tests validating the model were completed with basketball teams, student surveying teams, bomber crews, tank crews, open-hearth shops, farm-supply cooperatives, training groups, departments of a large physical science research laboratory, a chain of supermarkets, and a plant that manufactured heavy machinery. W. A. Hill (1969a) reported analyses in a large electronics firm with assembly-line instructors. Fiedler, O'Brien, and Ilgen (1969) worked with public health volunteer groups in Honduras. Shima (1968) studied Japanese student groups; Mitchell (1970b), participants in a church-leadership workshop;

[22]Other such reviews were completed by Fiedler and Chemers (1974); and Mitchell, Biglan, Oncken, and Fiedler (1970).

and Fiedler (1971c), trainees of an executive development program.

Illustrative of the operational support of applied findings was Loyer and O'Reilly's (1985) study of Ontario community health supervisors. In favorable situations on the group-atmosphere scale, units led by low-LPC (task-oriented) supervisors were more effective (according to nursing directors' evaluations of the units) than were groups led by high-LPC supervisors. As predicted by the model, groups led by high-LPC (relations-oriented) supervisors, rather than those led by low-LPC (task-oriented) leaders, were more effective in situations that were moderately favorable to the supervisors. A similar confirmatory pattern was reported by Wearing and Bishop (1974) for the LPC scores of leaders and their U.S. Army combat-engineer training squads.

Kennedy (1982) reanalyzed data from 697 fire and military personnel in 13 studies. As the contingency theory postulated, low-LPC leaders did best, according to supervisors' and observers' evaluations, in very favorable and very unfavorable situations, and high-LPC leaders did best in the moderately favorable situations. However, Kennedy also observed that LPC leaders whose LPC scores were intermediate were generally more effective than were those whose LPC leaders scores were high or low, and their effectiveness was relatively unaffected by the favorability of the situation.

Conclusions supporting the validity of the contingency model were most likely to be reached if the criterion measure of effectiveness was limited to superiors' evaluations of the performance of high- and low-LPC persons in carrying out their tasks as leaders. Rice (1978b) reviewed the relevant correlations by octants

and found that almost all predictions fit the model. Table 23.5 presents Rice's results. However, Giffort and Ayman (1988) found that the contingency model was also supported when they used subordinates' satisfaction with co-workers as a criterion of effective leadership. The outcomes were dependent on situational favorability as expected, but two other measures of subordinates' satisfaction (with the job and with supervision) failed to be sensitive in the same way.

Field Experiments. A number of experiments and controlled field studies also tested the model. Fiedler (1966) studied 96 experimentally assembled groups of Belgian sailors, half of which were led by petty officers and half by recruits. Half the groups began with structured tasks (routing a ship convoy through 10 and then 12 ports), while the other half began with unstructured tasks (writing a recruitment letter). The results were consistent with the contingency model.

In a controlled experiment completed by Chemers and Skrzypek (1972) at West Point, leaders were chosen on the basis of sociometric choices by the members to determine in advance who the members would choose as a leader. Then half the groups were assembled with preferred leaders and half with nonpreferred leaders. This study, with carefully preselected leaders, replicated the predicted median correlations. The generally supportive results are displayed in Figure 23.5. Fiedler (1978) concluded that the results of field research on work groups almost uniformly supported the model but that the results of experimental group research were somewhat less supportive.

Laboratory Experiments. Gruenfeld, Rance, and Weissenberg (1969) studied leaders under high, me-

Table 23.5 Extent to Which the Contingency Model Fits Obtained Correlations of LPC and Superiors' Appraisals as a Function of Situational Favorability in Eight Octants

	I *Negative*	II *Negative*	III *Negative*	IV *Positive*	V *Positive*	VI *Positive*	VII *Positive*	VIII *Negative*
Predicted Direction:	*Negative*	*Negative*	*Negative*	*Positive*	*Positive*	*Positive*	*Positive*	*Negative*
Empirical Analyses:								
Correlation of superior's appraisal and LPC in the direction predicted by the model	14	1	18	—	12	0	2	16
Total number of analyses	17	1	18	—	12	1	2	16

SOURCE: Rice (1978b).

Figure 23.5. Median Correlations between Leader's Performance and Group Performance for the Original Studies, Validation Studies, and the Chemers and Skrzypek (1972) Study

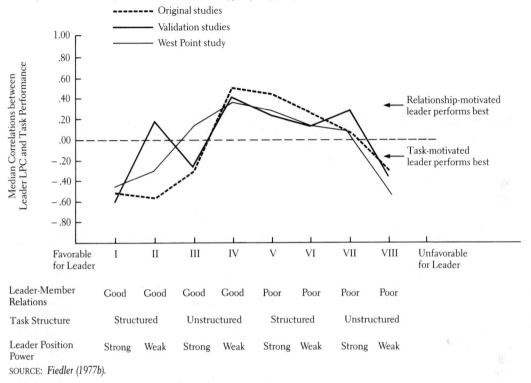

SOURCE: *Fiedler (1977b).*

dium, or low support in experimental groups. They found that low-LPC leaders behaved in a more dominant manner than did high-LPC leaders, regardless of the level of group support, but especially under medium support.

Exceptions to the predicted relations were found in octant II (good leader-member relations and structured, weak power of the leader), where the correlations between LPC and group effectiveness in the laboratory studies were positive rather than negative as predicted. The same results occurred in laboratory experiments by Hardy (1971, 1975) and Hardy, Sack, and Harpine (1973), who obtained LPC scores one or two weeks before their experiment. In two of these studies, leader-member relations were experimentally manipulated by assigning subjects to groups on the basis of preassessed sociometric scores. Rice, Bender, and Vitters (1980) completed a laboratory study of 72 4-person temporary groups of West Point cadets using female and male leaders. The LPC scores related significantly to the

groups' performance of tasks, according to the contingency model, in several cases, although the investigators qualified their findings because of the lack of direct measures of situational favorableness.

Singh, Bohra, and Dalal (1979) completed four experiments with male Indian engineering students and demonstrated that a much better fit with the contingency model could be obtained if the situational favorability of the octants was placed on the horizontal axis according to how much the ratings of the quality of leader-member relations, task structure, and position actually contributed to situational favorability. They discovered that ratings of the power relations declined in importance to situational favorability and ratings of leader-member relations increased in importance to situational favorability. They attributed the changes in the importance of the components of situational favorability to India's return to democracy after the emergency rule by Indira Gandhi, which coincided with the repeated data collection. These shifts called into question Nebeker's (1975) 4:2:1 fixed scheme for weighting the three variables that contribute to situational favorability.

Comparisons of the Octants. As shown in Table 23.5, a large number of studies have assessed the hypothesized relationships for designated octants. In these studies, usually efforts were made to select or create and compare two of the eight octant situations and to note the LPC of the leader in relation to the group's effectiveness. Thirty-eight of these studies have been generally supportive of the contingency model.[23]

Illustrative of additional supportive analyses of selected octants are dissertation studies of 122 child-study teams and their chairpersons in public schools (Jacobs, 1976), of 64 groups of secondary-school juniors (Smith, 1974), and of 40 task-oriented three-person experimental groups (Maher, 1976). Beebe (1975) manipulated the leader's positional power by instruction, structure, and task assignments. Only good leader-member relations were involved to determine the effectiveness of 37 three-person groups for octants II and IV. The correlation of LPC and group productivity was .01 in octant II and .40 in octant IV, both nonsignificant. Nevertheless, the result for octant IV was near the usual obtained in many other studies.

Unsupportive Results. Along with the field, laboratory, and octant studies that provide support for the validity of the contingency model have come a number of studies that have failed to find support for the model. Lanaghan's (1972) analyses of the effectiveness of 59 Illinois elementary schools and their principals and of the satisfaction of the teachers as a function of the behavior of the principals provided support for Fiedler's contingency-model predictions in only 6 of the 80 situations analyzed (at the 5 percent level of confidence). In 7 other situations, results for relations and task orientation were opposite to what would have been predicted by the model. Shiflett and Nealey (1972)

[23]W. W. Burke (1965); Chemers and Skrzypek (1972); Cleven and Fiedler (1956); Csoka (1974, 1975); Cummins (1970); Eagly (1970); Fiedler (1954a, 1955, 1966, 1967a, 1972a); Fiedler and Meuwese (1963); Fiedler, Meuwese, and Oonk (1961); Fiedler, O'Brien, and Ilgen (1969); Green and Nebeker (1977); Hardy (1971); Hawkins (1962); W. Hill (1969); Hovey (1974); Hunt (1967, 1971); Hutchins and Fiedler (1960); Ilgen and O'-Brien (1974); Julian (1964); Kunczik (1976a, 1976b); L. K. Michaelson (1973); Miller (1970); Nealey and Blood (1968); Reavis and Derlega (1976); Rice and Chemers (1973, 1975); Sample and Wilson (1965); Sashkin (1972); Schneier (1978); and Ziller (1963).

compared the performance of three-man college groups with very high intellectual ability and with moderate ability in creative tasks in octants III and IV (weak and strong positional power). The results of the moderate-ability groups supported the prediction of the model, but those of the very-high-ability groups were contradictory and nonsignificant.

Two laboratory experiments by Graen, Orris, and Alvares (1971) and a field study of tax examiners in the Internal Revenue Service by Fox (1982) also failed to find the expected outcomes. But Fiedler (1971a) and Chemers and Skrzypek (1972) attributed these failures to methodological manipulations that were inadequate to test the model. The results obtained by Utecht and Heier (1976) and Vecchio (1977) also failed to support the model, but Fiedler (1978) found that Vecchio's assignment of leaders to mixes of classmates whom the leaders ranked favorably and unfavorably was an invalid manipulation of good and poor relations. But again, Isenberg (1981) found no support for the model in a study of communications. When the LPC scores of 62 Indian woolen-mill supervisors were combined with task-structure and positional-power ratings of situational favorableness by Upmanyu and Singh (1981), they suggested that there was a need to reclassify the octants. A review by Rice (1981) concluded that followers were more satisfied when there were low-LPC (task-oriented) leaders in favorable situations and high-LPC (relations-oriented) leaders in unfavorable situations. Furthermore, contrary to the usual expectation that the homogeneity of the leader and followers would be more satisfying to the followers, Rice noted that the followers' satisfaction was highest when the leader and followers had dissimilar LPC scores.

Some unsupportive studies only indirectly tested the contingency model. Fiedler (1977b) pointed out that much research that was designed to test the model failed to use favorable and unfavorable situations that were different enough from each other to provide a valid test.

Criticisms and Rejoinders

In studies that employed only an approximate classification of situations—favorable, intermediate, or unfavorable to the leader—26 of 35 correlations of LPC and group effectiveness were as predicted by the model

(Fiedler, 1971b). But critics fault these conclusions. Some correlation coefficients were based on subsamples in the same study in which one subsample may have had good and the other may have had poor leader-member relations (Ashour, 1973a, 1973b; Graen, Alvares, Orris, & Martella, 1970).

A more general criticism is that most of the validations are based on concurrent measurements of LPC, leader-member relations, and group performance scores. Measures of leader-member relations and even LPC scores may be affected by the group's performance (Vroom, 1976b). This cause-effect criticism can be leveled at a good percentage of research on leadership, not just at those studies that have tested Fiedler's model (Kerr & Schriesheim, 1974), but Katz and Farris (1976) actually found specific evidence that group performance can cause variations in leaders' LPC scores.

Rice (1976) could find only one clear significant pattern relating the leader's LPC score to the group's effectiveness among 140 significant relations reported in the literature. When the leader described leader-member relations favorably, low-LPC leaders were clearly more effective; 23 of 26 significant effects (88 percent) under such conditions showed low-LPC leaders to be more effective than high-LPC leaders. When leaders described leader-member relations as poor, there was no clear pattern. This finding could be considered evidence that the group's performance affected the leader's judgment of the quality of relations with members. But a longitudinal study of 8 intramural basketball teams over a nine-week season by Konar-Goldband, Rice, and Monkarsh (1979) concluded that previously assessed LPC scores of the leaders and the groups' initial atmosphere did predict the groups' subsequent performance according to the contingency model. Increments in effective performance beyond the initial levels were most likely for groups with low-LPC leaders and a good group atmosphere. An additional 7 percent of the variance in effective performance was accounted for by the interaction of the groups' previous atmosphere and leaders' LPC scores. At the same time, the investigators also found that 10 percent of the increment in the groups' atmosphere beyond the initial levels was accounted for by LPC interacting with the groups' initial performance. They concluded that a systems approach that allows cause and effects to flow in both directions is required.

Differences in Octants. As was noted earlier, octant II, in toto, yielded mixed and widely diverging results. However, Fiedler (1978) argued that octant II, which requires a structured task with a powerless leader, may be created experimentally but is unlikely to exist in the field. Fiedler (1978) suggested that leaders who are placed under such circumstances will find the situation unmanageable. This suggestion, of course, fails to explain what is causing the varying results of octant II. A more important question is this: Why is octant II, for example, less favorable to a leader than is octant III, since in both octants, two of three variables favor the leader? What is required is differential weighting of the variables. The difference in task structure between octant II and octant III must be given more weight toward favorability than the leader's positional power as weak or strong. This weighting was provided by Nebeker (1975) and Beach and Beach (1978). However, except for permitting the graphics to remain the same, a rationale and evidence is needed to support the logic that task structure is twice as important to a leader's situational favorability than is the power of the leader's position. The same problem exists between octants IV and V, for which leader-member relations must be given more weight than task structure (as has been done).

Variations in Results. Empirically troublesome to some critics is the wide divergence of individual correlation coefficients in each octant, as can be seen in Figures 23.4 and 23.5. The median correlation for octant IV, for instance, may be .40, but the results that contribute to the median may range from .00 to .71. Another problem for which explanations are offered, but not necessarily accepted, is how to interpret some of the sudden shifts, say, from octant III to octant IV of the median of −.29 to the median of .40. Hosking (1978) believed that the most supportable inference about all octants except octant I is that medians are random departures from a true correlation of zero. Schriesheim and Kerr (1977b) agreed in a review of additional studies. Schriesheim and Hosking (1978, p. 500) concluded:

When the relevant studies are critically examined, and a distinction drawn between those that constitute adequate tests of the model and those that do not, the results are far from encouraging. Examining both the size and direction of the correlations in each of the eight octants of the situational favorableness dimension, reveals that Fiedler's model really has little empirical support.

However, Strube and Garcia (1981), using R. Rosenthal's (1978, 1979a) meta-analyses of the contingency model, thought that all but octants III and VII in Fiedler's original validation were supportable, but they ignored octant VI. Strube and Garcia identified 33 analyses from which the model was built and 145 subsequent tests of the validity of the model. A meta-analysis of these data strongly supported the model's validity. Vecchio (1983) believed that Strube and Garcia had used a biased sample of studies and suggested the need to qualify the conclusions they had reached, but Strube and Garcia (1983) rejected Vecchio's criticisms. Then, a less extensive meta-analysis by Peters, Hartke, and Pohlmann (1985) provided additional but somewhat less strong support for the validity of the model than Strube and Garcia obtained. Finally, after including almost twice the number of validation correlations than had been listed by Strube and Garcia (1981) and Peters, Hartke, and Pohlmann (1985), Nathan, Hass, and Nathan (1986) rejected the earlier supportive conclusions of both previous meta-analyses. Nathan, Haas, and Nathan based their rejection on the fact that the set of validity coeficients within each octant varied much too much. They stated:

> The confidence intervals are too broad to allow any one to expect, as the theory predicts, that low LPC leaders would be effective when situational favorability was good and high LPC leaders would be effective when situational favorability was moderately poor. Worse, the fairly stable finding in Octant II, that when situational favorability is very good, high rather than low LPC leaders will be effective is directly opposite to what the theory predicts. At best, one can conclude that over half the time, correlations are above and below zero as predicted. (p. 10)

Fiedler (1971a, 1971b, 1973, 1978) systematically dealt with many of the earlier criticisms of his methodology, of the statistical strength of evidence, of the conceptual meaning of the three variables defining situational favorability, and of the construct assessed by the LPC scales. He even anticipated many of the criticisms (Mitchell, Biglan, Oncken, & Fiedler, 1970). As T. R. Mitchell (1972) noted, if the validity of the hypothesized curvilinear relationship is to be tested, all eight octants must be assessed in a given study. Despite the difficulty of obtaining sufficient participants when the group, rather than the individual, is the unit of analysis, research designs must have adequate sample sizes and resulting statistical power (T. R. Mitchell, 1972).

Although the contingency model may still appear to be supported by a wide array of studies, the meaning of LPC remains unclear and controversial, and no adequate theoretical explanation of its effects has been presented. Moreover, the variability of the findings and the reverse results with octant II continue to trouble confidence in it. Yet, the model compares favorably with alternative models with which it has been compared analytically.

Comparison with Alternative Contingency Models. Schriesheim, Tepper, and Tetrault (1988) compared two alternative contingency models with Fiedler's contingency model. In the declining-octant model (Shiflett, 1973), the performance of both high- and low-LPC leaders should decline systematically from octant 1 to octant 8 as the situation becomes less favorable to the leader. In the declining-zone model, octants 1, 2, and 3 are most situationally favorable; octants 4, 5, 6, and 7 are the next most favorable; and octant 8 is the least favorable to the leader.

Fiedler's contingency model predicts that high-LPC leaders will be more effective in octant 4 than in octant 1, octant 2, octant 3, or octant 8. Four tests of the significance of the difference can be made to compare octant 1 with each of these other octants (2, 3, and 8). Four such tests can also be made for octants 5 against octants 1, 2, 3, and 8. Again, four such tests can be made for octant 6 and four more for octant 7. A comparable number of tests across pairs of octants can be made for low-LPC leaders who are predicted by the contingency model to be more effective in octants 1, 2, 3, and 8 and less effective in octants 4, 5, 6, and 7. Similar tests can be made for the rival models. In the declining-octant model, effectiveness is expected to decline from octant 1 to octant 8. Since octant 1 is the most favorable, it should coincide with the leader being more effective than in each of the other octants; octant 2 should yield better performance than each of the remaining octants, and so on.

Each octant was compared one at a time by Schriesheim, Tepper, and Tetrault (1988) with each relevant other octant using meta-analytic procedures. The data came from a variety of published investigations. Sixtytwo percent of 245 tests of the differences between pairs of octants fit the contingency model, 54 percent of 281 tests fit the declining-octant model, and 51 percent of 274 tests fit the declining-zone model. The investigators concluded that, overall, these results supported the greater validity of Fiedler's contingency model than of the proposed alternatives.

Other Situational Variables of Consequence

In a cross-cultural situation, Chemers (1969) trained leaders in the culture of their followers or in the geography of the country. Low-LPC leaders were more supportive and developed a more enjoyable group atmosphere in the culture-trained situation than the high-LPC leaders did in the geography-trained situation. These findings agreed with Fiedler's model in that in favorable situations, high-LPC leaders should tend to be concerned with the task, while low-LPC leaders should tend to behave in a relationship-oriented manner. In unfavorable situations, the high-LPC leaders should be concerned with relations and the low-LPC leaders, with task (Cummins, 1970).

Arrangements. Whether members of groups were coacting (performing side by side) or interacting did not seem to influence Hunt's (1967) or W. Hill's (1969a) generally supportive but nonsignificant findings.

Verbal Behavior. The behavior, as well as the effectiveness of followers, depends on the favorability of the situation and the leader's LPC. Fiedler (1967a) found that group members made more task-related comments in favorable situations and fewer such comments in unfavorable situations under a high-LPC leader. The reverse was true for group members under the low-LPC leader. Furthermore the group made more person-related comments in the unfavorable situation and fewer such comments in the favorable situation under the high-LPC leader.

Followers' LPCs. The followers' LPCs also may make a difference. Schuster and Clark (1970) studied first- and second-level supervisors in post offices. Under high-LPC second-level supervision, high-LPC firstlevel supervisors were better satisfied than were their low-LPC peers. With low-LPC second-level supervisors, the satisfaction of high- and low-LPC first-level supervisors did not differ.

Hunt (1971) assembled groups, each with a manager, two supervisors, and two workers, to play a business game. Although the effects of manager-supervisor interaction did not account for variance in the teams' performance, the effects of the manager and supervisor alone were each significantly related to the performance of the workers. Low-LPC managers and high-LPC supervisors had the best performing groups, while high-LPC managers and low-LPC supervisors had the poorest performing groups. The two-level interaction effect also predicted the satisfaction of workers better than did either LPC effect alone.

Leadership Experience. The leaders' experience with leadership changes the situational favorability to them (Bons & Fiedler, 1976). With continued experience, tasks become more routine and leaders get to know their subordinates and usually can work better with them. In addition, the leaders learn the expectations of the higher authority.

Although the effectiveness of leaders, as a whole, does not necessarily improve with experience (Fiedler, 1970a; Fiedler, 1972a), the contingency model predicts that leadership experience will have different effects on the performance of high- and low-LPC leaders. In a study of infantry squads by Fiedler, Bons, and Hastings (1975), 28 sergeants who served as squad leaders were evaluated at the time the units were formed and after they had had 5 months of experience. The sergeants' judgments about their situational favorability increased over the 5 months, as expected. The high-LPC leaders performed better at first when they had little experience and situational favorability than they did 5 months later. As predicted by the model, the low-LPC leaders performed relatively better after they had 5 months' experience and gained situational favorability. Similar results were found by Godfrey, Fiedler, and Hall (1959), for the general managers of 32 consumer cooperatives; by McNamara (1968), for Canadian elementary and secondary school principals; and by Hardy and Bohren (1975), for college teachers. Furthermore, the training of leaders, based on the contingency model, generates similar dynamics and results (Chemers, Rice, Sundstrom, & Butler, 1975; Fiedler, 1972a).[24]

Organizational Shifting. Changes in organization can have similar effects on situational favorability as can increased experience. Bons and Fiedler (1976) tested the contingency model using experienced leaders of army squads who were given new subordinates, new bosses, or new jobs.

In the stable condition of continuing with the same bosses, subordinates, and jobs, the experienced leaders who were low in LPC were unaffected, but the performance of experienced high-LPC leaders declined. When a change of boss, subordinates, or job moved leaders from moderate situational favorability to low situational favorability, the low-LPC leaders did again relatively better.

Implications

Fiedler's Contingency Model offers a remedial plan for increasing the effectiveness of leaders that is different from all other theories of leadership. Blake and Mouton (1964), Hersey and Blanchard (1969b), R. Likert (1977a), and Vroom and Yetton (1974), would see the need to educate leaders to improve their styles. In the case of Blake and Mouton, it would be toward the one best style—9,9. For Hersey and Blanchard, it would depend on the stage in the group's life cycle and the followers' maturity. For Likert, it would be toward a democratic style. For Vroom and Yetton, the decision process to use would depend on the problem situation. But Fiedler (1978) suggested an entirely different course of action. Because a leader's LPC is what matters, and LPC is not very changeable, then either one must identify and select leaders of high or low LPC to fit given situations or leaders need to know their LPC scores and in what situations they are most effective. Then, they can try to change the situation, rather than

---

[24]This issue will be discussed in Chapter 35.

themselves. Fiedler argued that changing leader-member relations, the structure of the task or a leader's positional power is easier than changing a leader's personality. Leader Match (Fiedler, Chemers, & Mahar, 1976), a training program that tries to do so is discussed in Chapter 35. The contingency model also has implications for leadership under stressful conditions, which is examined in Chapter 29.

Summary and Conclusions

In general, the leader who is more highly rated by superiors and peers, who is most satisfying to subordinates, and whose approach results in the good performance of the group is likely to be both relations oriented and task oriented in an integrated fashion. Blake and Mouton's theory is the strongest endorsement of this conclusion.

However, many situational contingencies have been found to moderate the effects. These contingencies include the makeup of the subordinates and the organizational constraints, tasks, goals, and functions in the situation. The popular but underresearched and controversial Hersey-Blanchard model has singled out the follower's psychological maturity and job experience as the most important contingencies affecting the leader's need to be task oriented or relations oriented.

Fiedler's widely researched contingency model states that (1) task orientation (as measured by LPC) works best in situations that are either extremely favorable or extremely unfavorable to the leader or in which the leader has very high or very low control and (2) relations orientation works best in situations that are moderately favorable to the leader or in which the leader has moderate control. Despite a vast array of publications on the reliability, validity, and meaning of LPC and situational favorableness and despite supportive tests of the model, the validity of the model continues to be disputed. Less controversial are the equally widely researched concepts and behavioral measures of the leaders' consideration of their subordinates and the leaders' initiation of structure for their subordinates, the subject of the next chapter.

Consideration, Initiating Structure, and Related Factors for Describing the Behavior of Leaders

In 1945, Shartle (1950b) organized the Ohio State Leadership Studies. Shartle's background had been the study of job requirements and job performance. He and his colleagues now applied this background to the study of leaders. At the time, no satisfactory theories of leadership existed. Before World War II, research had sought to identify the different traits of leaders. However, analyses of this research by Bird (1940), W. O. Jenkins (1947), and Stogdill (1948) had concluded that (1) attempts to select leaders in terms of traits had had little success, (2) numerous traits differentiated leaders from followers, (3) the traits demanded of a leader varied from one situation to another, and (4) the trait approach ignored the interaction between the leader and his or her group.

A Behavioral Approach

Since many investigators deemed the personality-trait approach to have reached a dead-end, an attempt was made to study the behaviors rather than the traits of leaders— in other words, to describe individuals' behavior while they acted as leaders of groups or organizations. Hemphill (1949a) had already initiated such work at the University of Maryland. After joining the Ohio State Leadership Studies, Hemphill and his associates, developed a list of approximately 1,800 statements, such as, "He insists on meeting deadlines," that described different aspects of the behavior of leaders. Most statements were assigned to several subscales. However, staff members agreed on 150 statements that could each be assigned to only one subscale. These statements were

used to develop the first form of the Leader Behavior Description Questionnaire—the LBDQ (Hemphill, 1950a; Hemphill & Coons, 1957). On the LBDQ, respondents rated a leader by using one of five alternatives to indicate the frequency or amount of the particular behavior that was descriptive of the leader being rated. Responses to items were simply scored and added in combinations to form subscales on the basis of the similarity of their content. These subscale totals were then intercorrelated and factor analyzed (Fleishman, 1951, 1953c; Halpin & Winer, 1957). Two factors were produced: consideration and the initiation of structure. These primary factors were identified by Halpin and Winer (1957) with Air Force officers and by Fleishman (1951, 1953c, 1957) with industrial supervisors.

The Two Factors That Describe Leadership Behavior

Consideration and the initiation of structure emerged in successive factor studies (Fleishman, 1973).

Consideration. This factor describes the extent to which a leader exhibits concern for the welfare of the other members of the group. The considerate leader expresses appreciation for good work, stresses the importance of job satisfaction, maintains and strengthens the self-esteem of subordinates by treating them as equals, makes special efforts to help subordinates feel at ease, is easy to approach, puts subordinates' suggestions into operation, and obtains subordinates' approval on important matters before going ahead. The support provided by considerate leaders finds them oriented towards relationships, friendship, mutual trust, and interpersonal warmth. Participation and the maintenance of the group accompany such support (Atwater, 1988). In contrast, the inconsiderate leader criticises subordinates in public, treats them without considering their feelings, threatens their security, and refuses to accept their suggestions or to explain his or her actions.

Initiation of Structure. This second factor shows the extent to which a leader initiates activity in the group, organizes it, and defines the way work is to be done. The initiation of structure includes such leadership behavior as insisting on maintaining standards and meeting deadlines and deciding in detail what will be done and how it should be done. Clear channels of communication and clear patterns of work organization are established. Orientation is toward the task. The leader acts directively without consulting the group. Particularly relevant are defining and structuring the leader's own role and those of the subordinates toward attaining goals.

The leader whose scale score in initiating structure is low is described as hesitant about taking initiatives in the group. He or she fails to take necessary actions, makes suggestions only when members ask for it, and lets members do the work the way they think best.

Psychometric Properties

Three Behavior-Description Questionnaires

The LBDQ, consisting of 40 statements, was made operational to measure the two factors of consideration and initiation (Hemphill & Coons, 1957). An industrial version, the Supervisory Behavior Description Questionnaire (SBDQ) followed (Fleishman, 1972), as did a shorter version, LBDQ-Form XII (hereafter referred to as LBDQ-XII), (Stogdill, 1963a). Each of the LBDQs had instructions such as these:

> . . . The following . . . are items that may be used to describe the behavior of your leader or supervisor. Each item describes a specific kind of behavior, but does not ask you to judge whether the behavior is desirable or undesirable. This is not a test of ability.

It simply asks you to describe, as accurately as you can, the behavior of your supervisor or leader. *Group* refers to an organization or to a department, division, or other unit of organization that is supervised by the person being described. . . . *Members* refer to all the people in the unit of organization that is supervised by the person being described.

THINK about how frequently the leader engages in the behavior described by the item.

DECIDE whether he (A) *always,* (B) *often,* (C) *occasionally,* (D) *seldom* or (E) *never* acts as described by the item.

Typical items are as follows:

1. He lets group members know what is expected of them.
2. He is friendly and approachable.

The intentions of the developers of the LBDQs and the SBDQ, particularly with regard to the initiation of structure, differed somewhat in the construction of the different versions. The LBDQ contained a subset of 15 items that asked subordinates to describe the actual structuring behavior of their leader. This structuring behavior was the leader's behavior in delineating relationships with subordinates, in establishing well-defined patterns of communication, and detailing ways to get the job done (Halpin, 1957b). The SBDQ consisted of 20 items that also asked subordinates about their leader's actual structuring behavior. The initiation of structure, as measured by the SBDQ, was intended to reflect the extent to which the leader organizes and defines interactions among group members, establishes ways to get the job done, schedules, criticizes, and so on (Fleishman, 1972). The SBDQ items for the initiation of structure included a wider variety of structuring behaviors drawn from the loadings on this factor, while such items on the LBDQ came mostly from original conceptualizations about communication and organization (Schriesheim, House, & Kerr, 1976). The revised LBDQ-XII had 10 items that measured the initiation of structure in terms of the actions of leaders that clearly define their own role and let followers know what is expected of them (Stogdill, 1963a).

Reliability and Validity

As Taylor, Crook, and Dropkin (1961) and Philipsen (1965a) noted, descriptions of the consideration and initiation of structure by leaders are highly stable and consistent from one situation to another. According to Schriesheim and Kerr's (1974) review of the psychometric properties of the LBDQ and SBDQ, the descriptions maintain the high internal consistency that was the basis for their construction. That is, items on the consideration-behavior scale of each instrument correlate highly with all the other consideration items and do not correlate with items on the initiation scale. Conversely, items on the initiation-of-structure scale, independent of the consideration items, are highly intercorrelated with all the other structuring items. Schriesheim (1979a) found, with a sample of 308 public utilities employees, that the consideration and initiation scales were so psychometrically robust that it did not make much difference in a supervisor's scores whether one asked a subordinate to describe how the supervisor behaved toward him or her personally (the dyadic approach) or how the supervisor behaved toward the whole work group (the standard approach).

Nonetheless, the scales left a lot to be desired. They suffered from halo effects and were plagued by a variety of other response errors, such as leniency and social desirability, as well as a response set to agree rather than to disagree (Schriesheim, Kinicki, & Schriesheim, 1979). It was not known whether they were valid measures of true consideration and initiation of structure. Most important, as research with the original LBDQ and SBDQ instruments continued, it became apparent that some of what leaders do had been missed. A great deal of the behavior of leaders was being lost in the emphasis on just two factors to account for all the common variance among items describing this behavior. Therefore, for LBDQ-XII, a variety of additional factored scales were constructed, possibly lacking complete independence from structuring and consideration, yet likely to include much of the missing information of consequence.

Comparison of the Three Forms. Although all three versions have been used extensively and each has been subjected to additional factor analyses (Bish & Schries-heim, 1974; Szilagyi & Sims, 1974a; Tscheulin, 1973), a direct comparison of all three became possible after a survey and factor-analytic study of 242 hourly employees by Schriesheim and Stogdill (1975). This comparison study was necessary since, as Korman (1966) and other had noted, the content of the scales varied, which caused differences in outcomes. The original LBDQ and particularly the SBDQ contained several items, such as "needles subordinates for greater effort," that measured punitive, arbitrary, coercive, and dominating behaviors and that affected the scores for the initiation of structure. The LBDQ-XII was considered to be freest of such autocratic items (Schriesheim & Kerr, 1974). As has usually been found, internal consistency reliabilities were high for scores on both factors that were derived from the items drawn according to their use in the LBDQ, SBDQ, or LBDQ-XII. For consideration and initiation, reliabilities were .93 and .81 for the LBDQ, .81 and .68 for the SBDQ, and .90 and .78 for the LBDQ-XII. (The reliability of .68 for the initiation of structure on the SBDQ was raised to .78 by removing three SBDQ punitive items from the scoring of the scale.) The primary factors that were extracted indicated that all three versions contained some degree of arbitrary punitive performance ("the leader demands more than we can do"). But as expected, the pattern was most marked in the SBDQ. A hierarchical factor analysis disclosed the existence of a higher-order factor of rater bias, which appeared in all three questionnaires.

According to Schriesheim and Kerr, the items loading highest on the SBDQ in initiating structure were these: "He insists that he be informed on decisions made by people under him" (.60), "He insists that people under him follow standard ways of doing things in every detail" (.65), and "He stresses being ahead of competing work groups" (.64). In fact, Atwater (1988) found that the items "demands a great deal from his workers" and "pushes his workers to work harder" correlated highest with the SBDQ factor she obtained and labeled *demanding behavior*. But on the LBDQ, the two items loading highest on initiating structure were as follows: "He maintains definite standards of performance" (.59), and "He lets members know what is expected of them" (.54).

What complicated matters further was that many researchers deleted items or modified the wording of items for use in a particular study, as Podsakoff and Schriesheim (1985) found in their review of studies that used the LBDQ. Also, many researchers failed to specify which version of the LBDQ they had used or how they had modified the scales (Hunt, Osborn, & Schriesheim, 1978).

Other Psychometric Issues

The items ask how the leader acts toward the work group, rather than toward specific individuals. Critics, such as Graen and Schiemann (1978), assume that there are large variations in the leader's behavior toward different individual members of work group and therefore the wording of items should allow for this. (But the previously cited findings of Schriesheim [1979a] suggested that the matter may be overblown.)

Individual differences also underly the ratings. D. M. Lee (1976) asked 80 students to judge the initiation and consideration of their English professors over an eight-week period. The results indicated that the individual students differed widely in the cues they used as the basis of their ratings of the same professors.

Other criticisms are that the questionnaires fail to weight the timing, appropriateness, importance, and specificity or generality of responses. They may assess the circumstantial requirements of the job, rather than the leader as a person with discretionary opportunities to behave in the manner indicated.

Leniency Effects. Seeman (1957) reported that the LBDQ scales suffered from halo effects. Even making items more detailed was of no help in reducing the halo. Schriesheim, Kinicki, and Schriesheim (1979) completed five studies of the extent to which consideration and initiation of structure were biased by leniency effects. They inferred from the results that leniency response bias, the tendency to describe others in favorable but probably untrue terms, did not particularly affect descriptions of initiation of structure. But even though consideration and leniency are conceptually distinct, they concluded that (1) consideration items were not socially neutral and were susceptible to leniency, (2) consideration reflected an underlying leniency factor when applied in a field setting, and (3)

leniency explained much or most of the variance in consideration. Leniency may explain why consideration tends to correlate higher with other evaluative variables than does the initiation of structure (Fleishman, 1973).

Implicit Theories. D. J. Schneider (1973) suggested, among others, that respondents report their implicit theories and sterotypes about leaders and leaders' behavior rather than the behavior of the specific leader they are supposed to be describing with the LBDQ. That is, respondents describe their idealized prototype of a leader, rather than the real one they should be describing (Rush, Thomas, & Lord, 1977). Thus, Eden and Leviatan (1975) noted that leader-behavior descriptions of a fictitious manager using the Survey of Organizations resulted in a factor structure that was highly similar to that obtained from descriptions of real managers reported by Taylor and Bowers (1972).[1] In the same way, Rush, Thomas, and Lord (1977) found a high degree of congruence between factor structures obtained from descriptions of a fictitious supervisor using LBDQ-XII and descriptions of real leaders from a field study by Schriesheim and Stogdill (1975). In both studies, the authors concluded that since practically identical factor structures emerged for fictitious and specific real leaders, the actual behavior of a leader is relatively unimportant for behavioral descriptions because descriptions are based mainly on implicit theories or stereotypes.

One might suggest that the tendency to project such results tells more about the subordinate than about the leader the subordinate is rating. But this tendency to project or to use implicit theories occurs as a consequence of ambiguity and the absence of specific information about the leader to be rated. Schriesheim and DeNisi (1978) studied 110 bank employees and 205 workers in a manufacturing plant who used the LBDQ-XII to describe supervisors in general after first describing their own supervisors. The investigators, as expected, found comparable factors emerging from the general and specific descriptions when each was analyzed separately. However, separate real and imaginary factors emerged when an analysis that provided the opportunity for statistical differentiation was made of the

[1]See Chapter 21 for a discussion of the Survey of Organizations.

combined data. As before, in both real and imaginary descriptions, the initiation of structure and consideration were correlated above .50, with reliabilities ranging from .84 to .87.

In a particularly important finding, Schriesheim and DeNisi discovered that although satisfaction with one's real supervisor correlated between .51 and .75 with descriptions of the actual consideration and initiation of the real supervisors, such satisfaction with one's real supervisor correlated only .23 and −.03 with scores for initiating structure and consideration for the stereotypes of supervisors.

Subsequent experimentation by Schriesheim and DeNisi (1978) with 360 undergraduates strongly supported the contention that as more specific information became available to respondents, the respondents' LBDQ responses became more accurate and were less likely to depend on implicit theories. These results are consistent with Bass, Valenzi, Farrow, and Solomon (1975), who showed that subordinates who described the same real leader were in much more significant agreement with each other than with subordinates who described other leaders.

Self-Ratings Unrelated to Subordinates' Ratings.
As many researchers, such as R. J. Solomon (1976), reported for self-rated directive versus participative leadership, for autocratic versus democratic leadership, or for task- versus relations-oriented leadership, D. T. Campbell (1956) and others[2] reported little relation between leaders' self-descriptions of their initiation and consideration and their subordinates' LBDQ descriptions of the leaders. Similarly, there is a low relation between what leaders say they should do, according to scores on the Leadership Opinion Questionnaire, and what they do, according to their subordinates' descriptions of them on the LBDQ (Schriesheim & Kerr, 1974).

Relation between Consideration and Initiation of Structure

Theoretically, given the original orthogonal factor structure, initiation and consideration should be independent, but such is not the case. Schriesheim, House,

[2]Bass (1957a), Besco and Lawshe (1959), Graham and Gleno (1970), and T. R. Mitchell (1970a).

and Kerr (1976) reexamined Weissenberg and Kavanagh's (1972) review of the data, along with work published subsequently. In 11 of 13 studies using the LBDQ, a positive correlation was reported. The median correlation for the 13 analyses was .45. Likewise, for the LBDQ-XII for 10 studies, the median correlation was .52 between the initiation of structure and consideration. The correlation was even higher when job pressure was strong in the situation. In addition, the correlations are positive between initiation and consideration both when group-by-group values are correlated and when the scores for individuals within the groups are correlated (Katerberg & Hom, 1981). But 11 of the 16 studies that used the SBDQ, which includes some "autocratic" items, yielded some significant negative correlations between consideration and initiation. However, the median correlation was −.05. Without the punitive items, consideration and initiation on the LBDQ tend to correlate more positively. A recent comprehensive review (Fleishman, 1989a), which included 32 studies with the SBDQ, showed a median correlation of −.02 between the consideration and structure scores.

Alternative and Additional Scales

Industrial Examples

Oldham (1976), among others, developed alternative and additional scales to provide a more detailed profile of leadership behavior. These scales included behaviors such as personally rewarding, personally punishing, setting goals, designing feedback systems, placing personnel, and designing job systems. These scales were higher in relation to effectiveness than were measures of consideration and the initiation of structure. In the same way, Seltzer and Bass (1987) showed that the transformational leadership factors of charisma, individualized consideration, and intellectual stimulation added substantially to the effects of initiation and consideration on subordinates' satisfaction and effectiveness. Initiation and consideration were conceived by Seltzer and Bass to be primarily transactional in nature.

Halpin and Croft (1962) also were not satisfied that the behavior of leaders could be adequately described with just two factors. Using items containing additional content about school principles, as well as LBDQ items, they extracted four factors to account for the common variance in the obtained descriptions of school principals' behavior: (1) aloofness, formality, and social distance, (2) production emphasis—pushing for results, (3) thrust—personal hard work and task structure, and (4) consideration—concern for the comfort and welfare of followers. These scales for describing the behavior of school principals were supplemented by the following four scales used to describe the behavior of teachers: (1) disengagement—clique formation, withdrawal, (2) hindrance—frustration from routine and overwork, (3) esprit—high morale, enthusiasm, and (4) intimacy, mutual liking, and teamwork.

When Halpin and Croft classified 71 schools into six categories according to school climate, they found that an open school climate was associated with the esprit of teachers under a principal who was high in thrust. An autonomous climate produced intimacy in teachers under an aloof principal. A controlled climate resulted in hindrance in teachers under a principal who pushed for production. A familiar climate was associated with the disengagement of teachers under a considerate principal. A climate with potential but with the disengagement of teachers resulted in a principal who exhibited consideration, along with an emphasis on production. A closed climate, also with the disengagement of teachers, was associated with an aloof principal. These results yielded considerably more insight into the dynamic interplay among the climate of schools, the behavior of leaders, and the response of teachers than could be produced by the use of just two factors to describe the behavior of leaders. The most direct expansion from initiation and consideration to a broader array of leader-behavior dimensions was the development of LBDQ-XII.

Leadership Behavior Description Questionnaire—Form XII

On the basis of a theoretical analysis of the differentiation of roles in groups, Stogdill (1959) proposed ten additional patterns of behavior involved in leadership, conceptually independent of consideration and initiation of structure, which should be included in the LBDQ-XII, along with consideration and the initiation of structure. These patterns are (1) representation—

speaks and acts as the representative of the group, (2) reconciliation—reconciles conflicting organizational demands and reduces disorder in the system, (3) tolerance of uncertainty—is able to tolerate uncertainty and postponement without anxiety or upset, (4) persuasiveness—uses persuasion and argument effectively, exhibits strong convictions, (5) tolerance of freedom—allows followers scope for initiative, decision, and action, (6) role retention—actively exercises the leadership role, rather than surrendering leadership to others, (7) production emphasis—applies pressure for productive output, (8) predictive accuracy—exhibits foresight and the ability to predict outcomes accurately, (9) integration—maintains a closely knit organization and resolves intermember conflicts, and (10) influence with supervisors—maintains cordial relations with superiors, has influence with them, is striving for higher status. The conception of the persuasiveness pattern anticipated the more recent focus on the measurement of charismatic and inspirational leadership.

Interdescriber Agreement. In a study of a governmental organization by Day (1968), high-ranking administrators were each described by two male and two female subordinates. Correlations were computed to determine the extent to which pairs of subordinates agreed with each other in their descriptions of their immediate superiors. The greatest agreement was shown by pairs of female subordinates describing their female superiors; their agreement was represented by correlations ranging from .39 (integration) to .73 (retention of the leadership role). The least agreement was shown by pairs of male subordinates describing their female superiors; their correlations ranged from −.02 (tolerance of freedom) to .53 (retention of the leadership role). Pairs of female subordinates tended to exhibit higher degrees of agreement than did male subordinates in descriptions of male superiors on 8 of the 12 scales. The exceptions occurred for representation, production emphasis, integration, and influence with superiors.

In general, the scales with the highest degrees of interdescriber agreement across groups of reporters, male or female, were demand reconciliation, tolerance of uncertainty, persuasiveness, role retention, predictive accuracy, and influence with superiors. The scales with the lowest degrees of agreement across samples were representation, tolerance of freedom, and integration.

Divergent Validities. To test the divergent validities of several scales of the LBDQ-XII, Stogdill (1969), with the assistance of a playwright, wrote a scenario for each of six scales (consideration, structure, representation, tolerance of freedom, production emphasis, and superior orientation). The items in each scale were used as a basis for writing the scenario for that pattern of behavior. Experienced actors played the roles of supervisor and workers. Each role was played by two different actors, and each actor played two different roles. Motion pictures were made of the role performances. Observers used LBDQ-XII to describe the supervisor's behavior. No significant differences were found between two different actors playing the same role. Still, the actors playing a given role were described as behaving significantly more like that role than the other roles. Stogdill concluded that the scales measured what they purported to measure.

Factor Validation.[3] Data collected by Stogdill, Goode, and Day (1963a, 1963b, 1964, 1965) used nine of the LBDQ-XII scales to obtain descriptions of the leadership behavior of United States senators, corporation presidents, presidents of international labor unions, and presidents of colleges and universities. For leaders in each setting, the scores for the scales were intercorrelated and factor analyzed. In general, the results suggested that each factor was strongly dominated by a single appropriate scale. For example, in all four analyses, the representation factor emerged with only the representation scale correlated highly with it. The representation scale correlated, respectively, with the representation factor, .80, .94, .92, and .92, in the four locales. Similarly, the role retention subscale correlated only with its own retention factor, .89, .93, .81, and .92. However, production emphasis tended to load highly on structuring as well as on production emphasis.

Reconciliation of conflicting demands failed to emerge as a factor differentiating college presidents, presumably, because they all were described similarly highly in this behavior. Orientation to superiors, of course, did not fit with the role of senators, nor did

[3]The glossary provides definitions of the factor analytical terms used in this and subsequent sections.

union presidents differ from each other in orientation to a higher authority. Finally, the differences in predictive accuracy generated the factor of predictive accuracy for only the corporate and union leaders, not for the senators and college presidents.

Slightly different results emerged when all the items of the LBDQ—Form XII were intercorrelated and factor analyzed for three additional locales. Eight factors emerged as follows: (1) general persuasive leadership, (2) tolerance of uncertainty, (3) tolerance of followers' freedom of action, (4) representation of the group, (5) influence with superiors, (6) production emphasis, (7) structuring expectations, and (8) retention of the leadership role. In addition, two distinct factors of consideration were extracted.

The most numerous and most highly loaded items on the first, a general factor, were measures of persuasiveness. Other scales with items on the factor were about the reconciliation of conflicting demands, structuring expectations, retention of the leadership role, influence with superiors, consideration, and production emphasis. These items represented the followers' general impression of the leaders. The items dealt with being persuasive, as well as being able to reconcile demands, structure expectations regarding the task to be performed, hold the leadership role, and influence superiors. In fulfilling these functions, leaders were seen as considerate of their followers' welfare. Each of the remaining factors tended to be composed of items from a single scale, but some contained stray items from other scales. Consideration broke down into two separate factors, to be discussed later in connection with J. A. Miller's (1973b) hierarchical factor analysis.

The first nine factors showed similar loadings across the three organizations. Retention of the leadership role appeared as a separate factor only in the state government organization. All scales except those dealing with tolerance of uncertainty, tolerance of freedom, and representation contributed some items to the general factor. However, all scales except persuasiveness and the reconciliation of conflicting demands emerged as separate factors differentiated from each other. These findings indicate that the behavior of leaders is indeed complex in structure and that followers are able to differentiate among different aspects of behavior. Although persuasiveness and the reconciliation of conflicting demands did not emerge as separate factors, their high loadings on the general factor provided valuable additional insight into the nature of leadership, strongly suggesting that this general factor may be particularly useful, given what will be said in the next chapter about laissez-faire leadership, its opposite.

Initiation and Consideration as Higher-Order Dimensions. A. F. Brown (1967) used the LBDQ-XII to obtain scores on each of the 12 factors for 170 principals described by 1,551 teachers in Canadian schools. He found that two higher-order factors accounted for 76 percent of the total factor variance for the 12 primary factors. The loadings for the two factors, when plotted against each other, assumed a form in which production emphasis, structure, and representation clustered about an axis of initiation and tolerance of uncertainty, tolerance of freedom, and consideration clustered about an axis of consideration. The loadings for the remaining factors fell between the clusters at the extremes of these two orthogonal axes.

A plot of factor loadings obtained for LBDQ-XII descriptions of university presidents (Stogdill, Goode, & Day, 1965) produced similar results. Representation, structure, production emphasis, and persuasiveness clustered around the first axis and freedom, uncertainty, and consideration clustered around the second axis.

Marder (1960) obtained a somewhat different pattern of loadings when military rather than educational leaders were studied. The data consisted of 235 descriptions of U.S. Army officers by enlisted men. Productivity and initiation of structure centered on one axis and freedom and uncertainty clustered around the other. Consideration was displaced toward the central cluster of items.

Psychometric Outcomes Depend on Factor Theory

There are different schools of thought regarding the use of factor analysis. One school maintains that as much of the total factor variance as possible should be explained in terms of a general factor. Another school holds that rotational procedures, such as the varimax, which reduces the magnitude of the general factor, are legitimate. The former school, while admitting that systems of events in the real world may involve a variety of factors, maintains that human perception contains a large element of bias and halo that should be removed in the general factor before attempting to determine the structure of measurements representing the real world. The second school argues that the apparent halo in the general factor has its equivalent in the opacity of the real world and that the purpose of research is to reduce this opacity by making full use of all the structure differentiated by human perception. The structure that is perceived should not be permitted to remain hidden in the general factor.

If one prefers a two-factor theory of leadership behavior, initiation of structure, production emphasis, and persuasiveness can define one of the factors; consideration, tolerance of freedom, and tolerance of uncertainty can define the other. A two-factor solution, which leaves a considerable amount of the total variance unexplained, can always be obtained in the analyses of leader-behavior descriptions. However, a multifactor solution should not be rejected until its consequences have been thoroughly explored and it has been proved untenable. Furthermore, the dilemma can be reconciled, as J. A. Miller (1973b) and Schriesheim and Stogdill (1975) did, by recourse to hierarchical factor analysis. The former exploited rotation and differentiation; the latter, the general evaluative bias factor. Finally, the positive association routinely found (as noted earlier) between consideration and the initiation of structure, as measured by LBDQ-XII, suggests that a single, general factor solution may be warranted. Nevertheless, with reference to the contents of the LBDQs, the two-factor framework for describing leadership behavior—consideration and the initiation of structure—emerges consistently from factor analyses when no additional contraints are placed on the analyses, such as first requiring the isolation of a general factor that, no doubt, has strong connections with the prototypes of leaders that the respondents hold.

Refining Initiation and Consideration

Consideration and the initiation of structure can be finely factored in a number of ways by adding detailed behaviors, other than those found on the LBDQ-XII, and pursuing reconceptualizations about initiation and consideration. As was just noted, Stogdill (1963a) added new content dealing with different domains of leadership behavior to obtain the ten additional LBDQ scales for LBDQ-XII. More detail about initiation and consideration can also result in the greater intensification of the analysis of the basic content of initiation and consideration and related measures. Yukl (1971) demonstrated the feasibility of a three-factor approach (consideration, initiation of structure, and centralization of decisions). Saris (1969) offered "responsibility reference" and Karmel (1978) offered an active engagement factor as the third dimension. Another three-factor approach—initiating structure, participation, and decision making—was pursued by R. H. Johnson (1973). Wofford (1971) expanded the framework of leadership behavior to five factor-analytically derived behavioral dimensions (group achievement and order, personal enhancement, personal interaction, dynamic achievement, security, and maintenance).

Using several thousand members of a nationwide business fraternity, who described their leaders on both a new instrument (FFTQ), and the comparable scales of the LBDQ-XII, Yukl and Hunt (1976) demonstrated some degree of communality between scales that purport to deal with similar dimensions; yet overall, the scales revealed an unfortunate lack of equivalence.

Hierarchical Factor Analysis. Because of earlier reported findings of such lack of equivalence between the LBDQ and supposedly similar instruments,[4] J. A. Miller (1973b) assembled 160 items from 9 frequently referenced standard instruments used in published research concerning leadership behavior (described in this and preceding chapters). The objective was to gain a better understanding of the similarities and differences in the measures of consideration and the initiation of structure. The original pool included items from the following: the LBDQ (Halpin & Winer, 1957), Survey of Organizations (Taylor & Bowers, 1972), interaction process analysis (Bales, 1950), the Job Descriptive Index (Smith, Kendall, & Hulin, 1969), the Orientation Inventory (Bass, 1963), scale anchors used to describe a "continuum of leadership behavior" (Tannenbaum & Schmidt, 1958), six categorical statements describing a continuum of decision-making styles (Vroom & Yetton, 1974), the five bases of social power (French & Raven, 1959), and adjectives used by Fiedler (1967a) for measuring the least preferred co-worker (LPC). Miller drew 73 nonduplicative items from the

pool of 160 that were most specific and that were descriptive, rather than evaluative, and then collected data from 200 respondents from 10 organizations, including social agencies, industrial firms, and military organizations.

The hierarchical solution was achieved by first completing a factor analysis stipulating a two-factor solution. Then, the process was repeated stipulating a three-factor solution, then a four-factor solution, and so on (Zavala, 1971). Miller then successively rotated all 12 principal components, using the varimax (orthogonal) rotation algorithm. At each level, interpretable solutions reflecting familiar leader-behavior factors emerged. The two-factor solution clearly paralleled consideration and the initiation of structure.

Other clearly identifiable factors that were discovered in previous research emerged when an additional factor in each successive level of analysis was called for. Production and goal emphasis and close supervision split apart as subfactors of the initiation of structure in the four-factor solution. Participation emerged at level 6, information sharing, at level 7 and supporting (the narrowly interpersonal interpretation of consideration), at level 8. Enforcing rules and procedures emerged as a subfactor of close supervision at level nine, and so forth. The emergence of the factors and the hierarchical linkages are shown in Figure 24.1. The two factor solution appears at level 2; the three factor solution, at level 3; and so on. A subsequent higher-order factor analysis, based on an oblique solution, obtained a higher-order factor of consideration and another of initiation of structure.

It can be seen from Figure 24.1 that consideration includes behavior that is ordinarily regarded as concern for the welfare of subordinates, such as supportive behavior and sharing information, but it also appears linked to participative group decision making, to abdication, and to delegation.

Behavioral Descriptions of the Ideal Leader

Ideal Form—What a Leader Should Do

Hemphill, Seigel, and Westie (1951) developed and Halpin (1957c) revised an ideal form of the LBDQ that asks respondents to describe how their leader *should* behave, not, as on the LBDQ, how they see their

[4]See Korman (1966), Lowin (1968), House (1972), and Yukl (1971).

Figure 24.1. The Hierarchical Structure of Leadership Behaviors

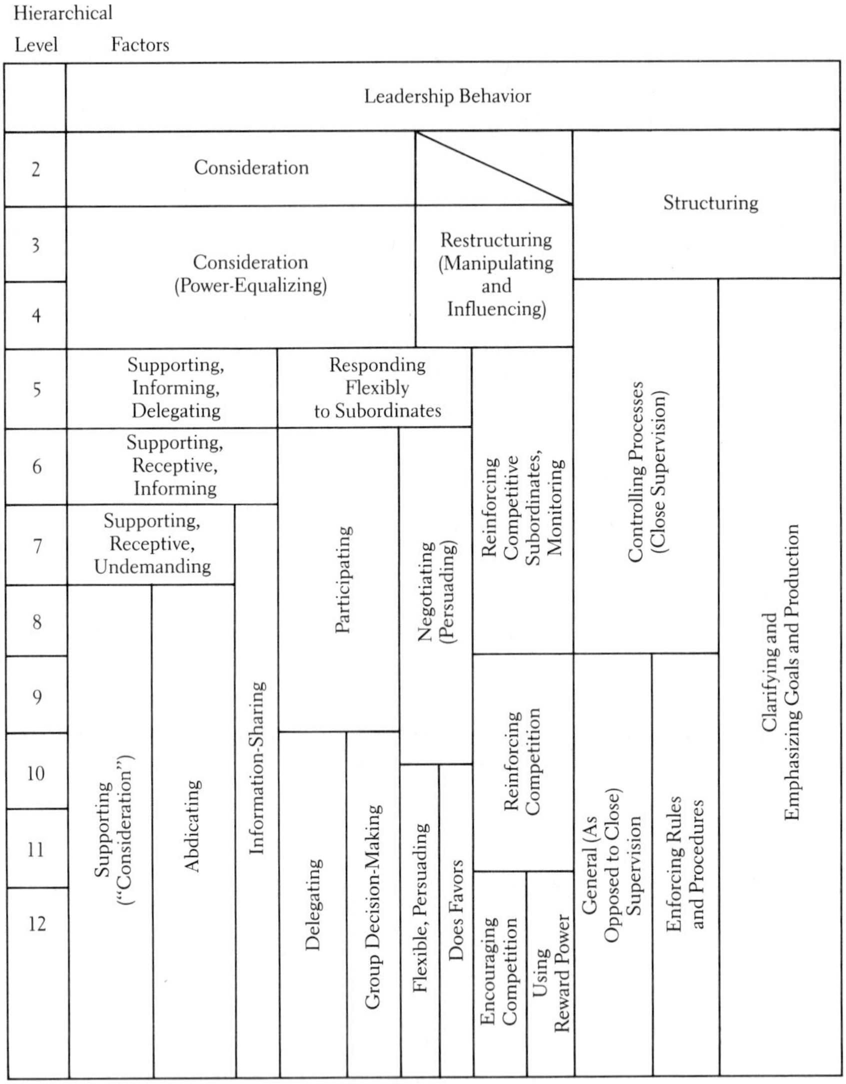

Hierarchical

Level   Factors

	Leadership Behavior
2	Consideration / Structuring
3	Consideration (Power-Equalizing) / Restructuring (Manipulating and Influencing)
4	
5	Supporting, Informing, Delegating / Responding Flexibly to Subordinates
6	Supporting, Receptive, Informing
7	Supporting, Receptive, Undemanding / Participating / Negotiating (Persuading) / Reinforcing Competitive Subordinates, Monitoring / Controlling Processes (Close Supervision)
8	
9	
10	Supporting ("Consideration") / Abdicating / Information-Sharing / Delegating / Group Decision-Making / Flexible, Persuading / Does Favors / Reinforcing Competition / Encouraging Competition / Using Reward Power / General (As Opposed to Close) Supervision / Enforcing Rules and Procedures / Clarifying and Emphasizing Goals and Production
11	
12	

SOURCE: *J. A. Miller (1973b).*

leader actually behaving. Thus, for example, in a study of 50 principals, J. E. Hunt (1968) found that teachers described principals as lower in actual consideration and structure than the teachers believed to be ideal. Such discrepancies between subordinates' descriptions of what their leaders should do and what the leaders actually do are more highly related to various measures of group performance than are desired or observed behavior alone. Such discrepancies are measures of dissatisfaction with the leaders' performance and, as a consequence, are more strongly related to various group outcomes.

Stogdill, Scott, and Jaynes (1956) studied a large military research organization in which executives and their subordinates each described themselves on the real and ideal forms of the LBDQ. In addition, subordinates described their superiors on the real and ideal forms. When superiors were really high in initiation of structure, according to their subordinates, the subordinates described their superiors on the ideal forms as having less responsibility than they should, as delegating more than they should, and as devoting more time than they should to teaching. When superiors were really high in consideration on the LBDQ, according to their subordinates, the subordinates on the ideal form expected the superiors to assume more responsibility than they perceived the superiors to assume, to devote more time than necessary to scheduling, and to devote less time to teaching and mathematical computation. When superiors were really high in initiating structure, as seen by their subordinates, the superiors perceived themselves to be devoting more time than they should to evaluation, consulting peers, and teaching and not enough time to professional consultation. When superiors were described as actually high in consideration, subordinates perceived themselves as having more responsibility than they should. The subordinates also reported that the superiors ought to devote more time than they do to coordination, professional consultation, and writing reports but less time to preparing charts. The leaders' initiation of structure was more highly related to subordinates' actual work performance. The leaders' consideration, on the other hand, was more highly related to subordinates' idealization of their own work performance.

In a similar type of study, Bledsoe, Brown, and Dalton (1980) showed that the actual behavior of school business managers, as described by 132 school superintendents, principals, and school board members, tended to differ considerably from the ideal initiation and consideration expected of the managers. Board members tended to describe the business managers as actually more considerate than did the school principals.

Ogbuehi (1981) surveyed 270 Nigerian managers' and administrators' self-descriptions of their ideal behavior using the LBDQ-XII. The results were consistent with their superiors' judgments of their effectiveness.

Leadership Opinion Questionnaire (LOQ). Fleishman's (1989a) LOQ differs from the ideal forms of Hemphill, Seigel, and Westie (1951) in that it asks the leaders themselves to choose the alternative that most nearly expresses their opinion on how frequently they should do what is described by each item on the questionnaire, and what they, as a supervisor or manager,

sincerely believe to be the desirable way to act. The LOQ also differs from the ideal form in that the LOQ scale for initiation of structure contains several items that Stogdill, Goode, and Day (1962) later found to measure production emphasis. Production emphasis correlates with initiating structure but is not identical with it.

Following a review, Schriesheim and Kerr (1974) concluded that the test-retest reliability of the LOQ had been adequately demonstrated over a one- to three-month period. Internal consistency reliabilities are also high (Fleishman, 1960, 1989b). In 60 studies, the median correlation between consideration and structure on the LOQ was $-.06$, with 57 of these correlations below .19 and only nine above .20 found significant (Fleishman, 1989). In a review of 20 LOQ validation studies (Fleishman, 1989b), a number of studies showed that supervisors higher in both consideration and structure were more likely to be higher on criteria of effectiveness, such as performance ratings, staff satisfaction, low stress, and burnout of subordinates.

Antecedents and Correlates of Consideration and Initiation of Structure

The internal consistency and test-retest reliability of the various scales of leader-behavior descriptions may be satisfactory, but to understand their effects, differences in content make it mandatory to distinguish whether the measures were based on the LBDQ, SBDQ, LOQ, or LBDQ-XII when reviewing the antecedent conditions that influence the extent to which a particular behavior is exhibited and concurrent conditions are associated with such behavior.

Interpreting Concurrent Analyses. Most of the available research consists of surveys in which leadership behavior and other variables about the leader or the situation were measured concurrently. However, it seems reasonable to infer that a relatively invariant attribute, such as the intelligence of the leader, is an antecedent to the leader's display of consideration or initiation, as seen by colleagues. The national origin of the leader's organization is antecedent to the leader's behavior. But the average leader's behavior in the organization cannot affect the origin of the organization. The leader's educational level is likewise obviously antecedent to the leader's behavior, since the leader's behavior cannot cause a change in his or her educational level. Similar inferences can be made about situational influences on the leader's behavior with less confidence, because the leader often can influence the situation, just as the situation is influencing the leader. If a concurrent association is found between company policy and the behavior of first-line supervisors, it seems reasonable to infer that the policy has influenced the supervisors, although it is also possible that the policy reflects the continuing behavior of the supervisors and is a reaction to their behavior. If an association is found between the leader's behavior and conflict in the work group, it is more likely that the leader is a source of the conflict; nevertheless, the continuing conflict is likely to be influencing the leader's behavior as well.

Suppose a positive association is obtained between a leader's consideration and the absence of conflict within a group. The most plausible hypothesis is likely to be that the leader's behavior contributes to the absence of conflict; nevertheless, the harmony within the group makes it possible for the leader to be more considerate. Therefore, in examining these concurrent results, the reader will have to decide on what meaning to draw from the reported associations. Such criteria of effectiveness as the subordinates' productivity, satisfaction, cohesion, and role clarity can be seen to be a consequence of the leader's behavior; yet, they may influence the leader's behavior as well.

Personal Attributes Related to Initiation and Consideration

In a study of ROTC cadets, Fleishman (1957a) found that the attitudes of cadets toward consideration and initiation on the LOQ were not related to the cadets' intelligence or level of aspiration. But among school principals described by 726 teachers, Rooker (1968) found that principals with a strong need for achievement were described as high in tolerance of freedom and reconciliation of conflicting demands on the LBDQ-XII. However, Tronc and Enns (1969) found that promotion-oriented executives tended to emphasize the initiation of structure over consideration to a

greater degree than did executives who were less highly oriented toward promotion. And Lindemuth (1969) reported that the level of consideration of college deans was related to the deans' scholarship, propriety, and practicality.

Experience and sex have been correlated with LBDQ scores. For 124 managers of state rehabilitation agencies who were described by their 118 subordinates, Latta and Emener (1983) found that the initiation of structure on the LBDQ increased directly with experience. At the same time, Serafini and Pearson (1984) reported finding that such initiation of structure was higher only among the 208 male nonadministrative supervisors and managers at a university. For the female leaders, consideration was higher, which is consistent with expectations that females are likely to be more relations oriented.

Personality, Values, and Interests. Although one might expect authoritarianism to coincide with the initiation of structure, such does not appear to occur. For example, Fleishman (1957a) observed that the leader's endorsement of authoritarian attitudes was negatively related to initiation of structure on the LOQ, but it was unrelated to consideration. Similarly, Stanton (1960) found no relation between consideration and authoritarianism. In the same way, Flocco (1969), who studied 1,200 school administrators, showed that consideration and the initiation structure, according to subordinates' responses to the LBDQ, were unrelated to the administrators' scores for dogmatism on a personality test.

Fleishman (1957b) also found that supervisors who favored consideration tended to have high scores on a personality scale of benevolence, whereas those favoring initiation were more meticulous and sociable. Also, Fleishman and Peters (1962) obtained results for supervisors indicating that the trait of independence was correlated negatively with both the initiation of structure and consideration and the trait of benevolence was positively correlated with the initiation of structure and consideration. Consideration was more highly related than initiation to ratings of social adjustment and charm, according to Marks and Jenkins (1965). Again, Litzinger (1965) reported that those managers who favored consideration tended to value support (being treated with understanding and encouragement), whereas those who favored initiation of structure tended to place a low value on independence. Atwater and White (1985) reported that the following personal characteristics were significantly correlated with demanding (SBDQ structuring) behavior by first-line supervisors: inflexible, aggressive, uncooperative, harsh, strict, tense, ambitious, and unforgiving.

Newport (1962) studied 48 cadet flight leaders, each described on the LBDQ by 7 flight members. Leaders who were perceived to be high in both consideration and initiation differed from those who were perceived to be low on both in their strong desire for individual freedom of expression, lack of resistance to social pressure, strong desire for power, strong cooperativeness, and strong aggressive attitudes.

In line with expectations, R. M. Anderson (1964) found, in a study of nursing supervisors, that those who preferred nursing-care activities were described as high in consideration but those who preferred coordinating activities were described as high in initiation. According to analyses by Stromberg (1967), school principals with emergent value systems were perceived by teachers as being high in initiating structure, whereas those with traditional value orientations were perceived as being high in consideration. Durand and Nord (1976) noted that 45 managers in a midwestern textile and plastics firm were seen by their subordinates as being higher in both the initiation of structure and consideration if the managers were externally, rather than internally, controlled—that is, if the managers believed that personal outcomes were due to forces outside their own control rather than to their own actions.

Fleishman and Salter (1963) measured empathy in terms of supervisors' ability to guess how their subordinates would fill out a self-description questionnaire. They found that empathy was significantly related to employees' descriptions of their supervisors' consideration but not their structuring. L. V. Gordon (1963a) showed that personal ascendancy was positively related to initiating structure but negatively related to consideration. Neither leader-behavior score was related to responsibility, emotional stability, or sociability, although sociability was correlated with initiating structure but not with consideration. However, Rowland and Scott (1968) failed to find any relation between consideration

on the LOQ and the social sensitivity of supervisors. Pierson (1984) failed to find any significant relations between the Myers-Briggs Indicator of perceptual and judgmental tendencies and consideration or initiation. Numerous other investigators[5] also failed to find LBDQ and LOQ scores related to any of the personality measures they employed. The situational factors, to be discussed later, may override or eliminate the effects of personality on initiation and consideration.

Cognitive Complexity. A number of studies of the influence of cognitive complexity and leadership behavior have obtained positive findings, particularly when the additional LBDQ scales have been used. W. R. Kelley (1968) reported that school superintendents who were high in cognitive complexity were also described as high in predictive accuracy and the reconciliation of conflicting demands. Likewise, Streufert, Streufert, and Castore (1968) found significant differences between emergent leaders whose scores on perceptual complexity varied in a negotiations game. Leaders who were lower in cognitive complexity scored higher on initiating structure, production emphasis, and reconciliation. Leaders who were higher in cognitive complexity scored higher on tolerance of uncertainty, retaining the leadership role, consideration, and predictive accuracy. Results obtained by Weissenberg and Gruenfeld (1966) indicated that supervisors who scored high in field independence endorsed less consideration than did those who scored high in field dependence. But Erez (1979) found that the self-described consideration of 45 Israeli managers with engineering backgrounds was positively related to field independence and to social intelligence, whereas initiating structure was negatively related to these two factors.

Preferences for Taking Risks. Risky decision making by supervisors was studied by Rim (1965), who reported that male supervisors who scored high on both consideration and initiating structure and head nurses who scored high in initiation of structure tended to make riskier decisions. Men and women who scored high in both attitudes tended to be more influential in their groups and to lead the groups toward riskier decisions. However, Trimble (1968) found that for a sample of

[5] See, for example, T. O. Bell (1969), Greenwood and McNamara (1969), and J. P. Siegel (1969).

teachers who described their principals as being higher in consideration than in initiating structure, neither of the principals' scores was related to the principals' perceptions of their own decision-making behavior.

Relations to Personal Satisfaction. Initiation and consideration are greater among more satisfied leaders, whose tendencies to make decisions and attempts to lead are also related. To some degree, these tendencies may be consequences rather than antecedents of initiation and consideration.

Managers who are more satisfied with their circumstances tend to earn higher LBDQ scores in their leadership behavior, according to Siegel (1969). Similarly, A. F. Brown (1966) reported that better satisfied school principals were described as being higher than were dissatisfied principals on all subscales except tolerance of uncertainty.

Relations to Other Leadership Styles

Chapters 21, 22, and 23 were devoted to democratic versus autocratic, participative versus directive, and relations-oriented versus task-oriented leadership styles. It should come as no surprise that consideration and initiation are related to these other leadership styles as well. Miner (1973) noted that concepts used in other studies, such as providing support, an orientation toward employees, human relations skills, providing for the direct satisfaction of needs, and group-maintenance skills are akin to consideration. Concepts that are similar to initiating structure are the facilitation of work, a production orientation, enabling the achievement of goals, differentiation of the supervisory role, and the utilization of technical skills. Miner further pointed out that with its emphasis on organizing, planning, coordinating, and controlling, initiating structure has much in common with the ideas of classical management.

Democratic and Autocratic Styles. Although factorially independent, the various scales of consideration and initiation contain the conceptually mixed bag of authoritarian and democratic leadership behaviors. Each scale contains a variety of authoritarian or democratic elements. Although they empirically cluster on one side or the other of authoritarian or democratic

leadership, they are conceptually distinct elements. The industrial version, SBDQ, particularly added strongly directive behaviors ("He rules with an iron hand") to its scale of initiating structure (House & Filley, 1971).

Yukl and Hunt (1976) correlated Bowers and Seashore's (1966) four leadership styles of support, the facilitation of interaction, emphasis on goals, and the facilitation of work with the LBDQ for 74 presidents of business fraternities. Support correlated .66 with consideration and .61 with the initiation of structure. On the other hand, the emphasis on goals correlated .64 with consideration and .76 with initiation, while the facilitation of work correlated .56 with consideration and .64 with the initiation of structure. Clearly, a large general factor of leadership permeates all these scales, which adds credence to what will be presented in the next chapter, namely, that the most important dimension empirically may be whether leadership generally is or is not displayed. This general factor becomes most apparent when the LBDQ rather than the LOQ is employed. Weissenberg and Kavanagh (1972) concluded from a review that although managers think they should behave as if consideration and initiating structure are independent, in 13 of 22 industrial studies and in 8 of 9 military studies, a significant positive correlation was found between these 2 originally independent factors of leadership behavior on the LBDQ, as completed by subordinates, particularly if LBDQ-XII was the version employed in the survey (Schriesheim & Kerr, 1974). Seeman (1957) noted that a school principal's overall leadership performance was seen to be a matter of how much consideration and initiation of structure was exhibited. When Capelle (1967) asked 50 student leaders and 50 nonleaders to fill out the LOQ, he found that leaders scored significantly higher than did nonleaders on both consideration and the initiation of structure. However, G. W. Bryant (1968) did not find that appointed and sociometrically chosen leaders (college students in the ROTC) differed significantly in their conceptions of the ideal leader on the LOQ. These results fit with the general contention that conceptually, initiation of structure is readily distinguishable from consideration, just as autocratic and democratic or relations-oriented and task-oriented leadership can be conceptually discriminated. But empirically, the same leaders who are high on one factor are often high on the other as well.

Task and Relations Orientation. The initiation-of-structure scale emphasized the concern with tasks ("insists on maintaining standards," "sees that subordinates work to their full capacity," "emphasizes the meeting of deadlines"), as well as directiveness ("makes attitudes clear," "decides in detail what should be done and how it should be done"). The scale of consideration emphasized the leader's orientation to followers ("stresses the importance of people and their satisfaction at work," "sees that subordinates are rewarded for a job well done," "makes subordinates feel at ease when talking with them"), as well as participative decision making ("puts subordinates' suggestions into operation," "gets approval of subordinates on important matters before going ahead"). Social distance was also minimized for considerate leaders ("treats subordinates as equals," "is easy to approach"). Conceptually in opposition to the initiation of structure is destructuring behavior (J. A. Miller, 1973a) that is, reducing the request for consistent patterns of relations within the group. The lack of initiation of structure implies allowing conditions to continue without structure and avoiding giving directions or being task oriented. Conceptually opposite to exhibiting consideration is leadership behavior that is exploitative, unsupportive, and uncaring (Bernardin, 1976).

Among 55 corporation presidents, a correlation of .55 was found between task-oriented production emphasis and the tendency to initiate structure, according to a member of their staffs. Similarly, the presidents' consideration correlated .49 with the relations-oriented representation of their subordinates' interests and .41 with the toleration of freedom of action for their subordinates (Stogdill, Goode, & Day, 1963a).

W. K. Graham (1968) found, as predicted, that high-LPC leaders (relations oriented) were described as being higher in consideration and structure than were low-LPC leaders (task oriented). Yukl (1968) also noted that low-LPC leaders tended to be described as high in initiation and low in consideration. However, Meuwese and Fiedler (1965) reported that leaders who were high and low on LPC only tended to differ significantly on specific items of the LBDQ, but not in the total scores

for consideration and initiating structure. Yukl (1971) and Kavanagh (1975) concluded that task-oriented behavior is implicit in initiating structure, but subordinates can still influence their superior's decisions.

Transactional and Transformational Leadership. Seltzer and Bass (1987) found that for 294 MBAs with full-time jobs who described their immediate supervisors, the scales of initiation of structure on the LBDQ-XII, according to subordinates, correlated .53, .55, .59, respectively, with charisma, individualized consideration, and intellectual stimulation on the Multifactor Leadership Questionnaire (MLQ), and .48 and .06, respectively, with the transactional measures of contingent rewarding and management by exception on the MLQ. However, consideration on the LBDQ-XII correlated .78, .78, and .65, respectively, with the same MLQ transformational leadership measures and .64 and −.23, respectively, with the same MLQ transactional leadership measures. Evidently, active leadership is common to initiation, consideration, transformational, and transactional leadership behavior, and there are particularly strong associations between transformational leadership and consideration. Nonetheless, adding the transformational scales to initiation and consideration increased substantially the prediction of outcomes of the rated effectiveness of leaders and satisfaction with the leadership.

Peterson, Phillips, and Duran (1989) found that the MLQ scale of charismatic leadership correlated higher with measures of consideration than measures of initiation of structure in a study of 264 retail chain-store employees describing their supervisors. Thus, charismatic leadership correlated .48 with maintenance orientation and .74 with support but only .16 with pressure for production and .22 with assigning work.

Power, Authority, and Responsibility of the Leader

Martin and Hunt (1980) obtained LBDQ evaluations by 407 professionals and quasi-professionals of their first-line supervisors in the construction and design units of 10 state highway department districts. Related data on morale were also collected. The expert power of the supervisors correlated .44 and .41 with their initiating structure and .48 and .51 with their consideration, but the other sources of power—referent, reward, coercive, and legitimate—correlated close to zero with the leadership measures. Foote (1970), who found that those members of the managerial staffs of television stations who tended to describe themselves on the RAD scales[6] as being high in responsibility and authority also tended to be described on the LBDQ-XII as being high in the tolerance of freedom. Those who delegated most freely were described as being high in production emphasis and low in representation orientation toward superiors.

Attempts to lead, manifest in one's emergence as a leader in a leaderless group discussion, were negatively related to consideration and positively related to the initiation of structure, according to Fleishman (1957a).

Situational Factors

The organization and the immediate group that is led affect the extent to which a leader initiates structure, is considerate, or both.

Organizational Policies. A clear-cut example of the impact of the organizational context on the behavior of the individual leaders within it was provided by Stanton (1960) in the case of two medium-sized firms. In one company, which was interested only in profits, authoritarian policies were dominant, and subordinates had to understand what was expected of them. The personal qualities of leadership were emphasized, and all information in the company was restricted to the managers except when the information clearly applied to an employee's job. The second firm, which had democratic policies, stressed participation as a matter of policy and was concerned about the employees' well-being, as well as about profits. This firm made a maximum effort to inform the employees about company matters. Supervisors in the firm with democratic policies favored more consideration, while supervisors in the firm with authoritarian policies favored more initiation.

The importance of the higher authority represented by the organization and its policies also can be inferred indirectly from results obtained in a progressive petro-

chemical refinery and in a national food-processing firm, where the extent to which supervisors felt they should be considerate was positively correlated with how highly they were rated by their superiors (Bass, 1956, 1958). Yet, in other companies no such correlation was found (Rambo, 1958).

Supervisors' perceptions of their superiors' and subordinates' expectations affect their leadership behavior. That is, supervisors will be more supportive or more demanding, depending on what they perceive their superiors and subordinates expect of them (Atwater, 1988).

Organizational Size. Vienneau (1982) examined the LBDQ scores of 33 presidents of amateur sports organizations, obtained from the responses of 85 members of their executive committees. Although the presidents' sex or language was of no consequence, both consideration and initiation were higher in the larger of the amateur organizations. This finding occurred despite the tendency of the presidents to agree on what was required of their ideal leader on the Ideal Leader Behavior Questionnaire, regardless of other organizational factors.

Functional Differences. D. R. Day (1961) found that upper-level marketing executives were described on the LBDQ-XII as being high in tolerance of freedom and low in structuring, but upper-level engineering executives were described as being low in their tolerance of freedom and high in initiation. In the same firm, the manufacturing executives were rated as being high and the personnel executives as being low in their tolerance of uncertainty.

Military-Civilian Differences. Holloman (1967) studied military and civilian personnel in a large U.S. Air Force organization and found that superiors did not perceive military and civilian supervisors to be different in observed consideration and initiation of structure, although they expected military supervisors to rank higher in initiation of structure and lower in showing consideration than they did civilian supervisors. Unexpectedly, Holloman found that subordinates—both military and civilian—perceived the military supervisors to be higher in consideration, as well as in initiating structure, than they did the civilian supervisors. Thus, in comparison to civilian supervisors, military supervisors were seen to display more leadership by both their civilian and military subordinates.

Halpin (1955b) administered the ideal LBDQ to educational administrators and aircraft commanders. Subordinates described their leaders on the real form of the LBDQ. The educators exhibited more consideration and less initiation of structure than did the aircraft commanders, both in observed behavior and ideal behavior. But, in both samples, the leaders' ideals of how they should behave were not highly related to their actual behavior, as described by their subordinates.

Attributes of Subordinates

Atwater and White (1985) and Atwater (1988) found that supportive (considerate) behavior by supervisors correlated highly with both the subordinates' loyalty and trust. Kerr, Schriesheim, Murphy, and Stogdill (1974) concluded, from a review of LBDQ studies, that if the subordinates' interest in the task and need for information are high, less consideration by the leader is necessary and more initiation of structure is acceptable to them. Consistent with this conclusion, Hsu and Newton (1974) showed that supervisors of unskilled employees were able to initiate more structure than were supervisors of skilled employees in the same manufacturing plant.

Gemmill and Heisler (1972) and Lester and Genz (1978) analyzed the impact of the locus of control of subordinates—internal or external—on subordinates' perceptions of their supervisors' leadership and their satisfaction with it. Internally controlled subordinates tended to see significantly more consideration and initiation in their supervisors' behavior (Evans, 1974). Again, although internally controlled subordinates in a textile and plastics firm tended to see their supervisors as initiating more structure, they also felt that their supervisors were less considerate (Durand & Nord, 1976). But Blank, Weitzel, and Green (1987) found zero correlations between the psychological and job maturity of 353 advisers of residence halls and the initiation and consideration, respectively, of their 27 residence-

hall directors (contrary to the Hersey-Blanchard model).

General Effects on Productivity, Satisfaction, and Other Criteria

As was noted earlier, except for a few cross-lagged analyses and experiments, most of the results reported here come from concurrent surveys of leadership behavior and criteria, such as the subordinates' productivity and satisfaction. Thus, for instance, Brooks (1955) found that all the items measuring consideration and initiation of structure differentiated excellently rated managers from those rated average or below average in effectiveness. Although one tends to infer that productivity and satisfaction are a consequence of leadership behavior, the effective outcomes modify the leader's behavior to some extent as well. Greene and Schriesheim's (1977) longitudinal study suggested that more consideration, early on, by a leader can contribute to good group relations, which, in turn, may result, later on, in higher productivity by the group.

Using an early version of the scales, Hemphill, Seigel, and Westie (1951) found that leader's organizing behavior (initiating structure) and membership behavior (consideration) were both significantly related to the cohesiveness of the group. Likewise, Christner and Hemphill (1955) noted that ratings of both the leaders' consideration and initiation, when made by subordinates, were positively related to ratings of the effectiveness of their units, but leaders' self-descriptions of consideration and initiation were not.

A sample of 256 MBA students who were working full time in many different kinds of organizations described the initiation and consideration of their immediate supervisors at work. They also completed a "burnout" questionnaire. Although their leaders' initiation correlated only $-.15$ with the MBA's feeling of being burned out; the leaders' consideration correlated $-.55$ with such feelings. Thus, considerate supervision appears to reduce substantially the sense of burnout among subordinates (Seltzer & Numerof, 1988).

In an extensive analysis of 27 organizations of 7 types involving more than 1,300 supervisors and 3,700 employees, Stogdill (1965a) found that the consideration of supervisors was related to the employees' satisfaction with the companies and to measures of the cohesiveness of the groups and the organizations. But, as with authoritarian and democratic leadership, neither the supervisors' consideration nor initiation of structure was consistently related to group productivity. Organizational differences had to be considered. The contribution to effectiveness of initiation and consideration appears quite variable and hence requires further examination of the context in which the data are collected.

Industrial Studies

Leader Behavior. Fleishman (1989a) reviewed more than 20 validity studies of the SBDQ. Fleishman, Harris, and Burt (1955) found that production foremen rated higher in performance by their managers were higher in initiation of structure and lower in consideration. But, absenteeism and turnover were greater in work groups that had foremen with this pattern. Many other studies with the SBDQ have confirmed this strong relation between leader consideration and worker job satisfaction in industry (Badin, 1974; Fleishman & Simmons, 1970; Skinner, 1969), hospitals (Szabo, 1981; Oaklander & Fleishman, 1964), educational settings (Petty & Lee, 1975), and government organizations (Miles & Petty, 1977).

The relationships between initiation of structure, as measured by the SBDQ, and performance criteria tend to vary with situations. Thus, both initiation of structure and consideration were positively related to proficiency ratings in non-production departments (Fleishman & Harris, 1955). Using the SBDQ, Hammer and Dachler (1973) showed that the leader's consideration was positively related to the subordinates' perceptions that their job performance was instrumental in their obtaining the desired outcomes but the leader's initiation of structure was negatively related to such perceptions. Likewise, Gekoski (1952) found that supervisors' initiation of structure, but not consideration, was related positively to group-productivity measures in a clerical situation.

Lawshe and Nagle (1953) obtained a high positive correlation for a small sample of work groups between group productivity and employees' perceptions of how considerate their supervisor was. In a study of the leadership of foremen, Besco and Lawshe (1959) found that *superiors'* descriptions of foreman's consideration and initiation of structure were both related positively to ratings of the effectiveness of the foremen's units. However, *subordinates'* descriptions of foremen's consideration, but not initiation of structure, were positively related to such effectiveness.

In later studies, the LBDQ or LBDQ-XII was more likely to be used. Trieb and Marion (1969) studied two chains of retail grocery stores. They found that the supervisors' consideration, as described by the workers, was positively related to productivity, cohesiveness, and satisfaction in both chains. The supervisors' initiation of structure was related positively to the productivity of subordinates and to cohesiveness in one chain, but not in the other. In a study of two companies, House and Filley (1971) found that the supervisors' consideration in both companies related significantly to the subordinates' satisfaction with the company and their jobs as well as to their freedom of action. In both companies, initiating structure was also related significantly to the subordinates' satisfaction with company and their jobs along with favorable family attitudes toward the company and their jobs. Again, Fleishman and Simmons (1970) showed that the effectiveness of Israeli supervisors was positively related to their initiation of structure and consideration.

M. G. Evans (1968) reported that both supervisors' consideration and initiation of structure were positively related to the importance of the goal to workers and to their job satisfaction. Under high supervisory consideration, a strong positive relationship existed between the supervisor's initiation of structure and the group's performance. In a later study, M. G. Evans (1970a) found that the supervisors' consideration and initiation were related to the workers' perceptions of opportunities to satisfy their need for security but not to their actual satisfaction with their job security. Weiss (1977) demonstrated that subordinates tended to be more likely to share values with their supervisors if the supervisors displayed considerate behavior toward them. But, Marks and Jenkins (1965) reported that the initiation of structure was more highly related than was consideration to global ratings of effectiveness. However, supervisors' initiation of structure and consideration were unrelated to the satisfaction of subordinates' needs for social esteem, autonomy, and self-actualization.

In a study of insurance sales supervisors, W. K. Graham (1970/1973) found that supervisory consideration was positively associated with group performance. Despite the somewhat similar setting—7 retail discount department stores—Hodge (1976), who studied the behavior of 21 second-level managers as reported on the LBDQ by 188 first-line managers, found that the satisfaction of subordinates' needs was positively associated with the higher-level managers' initiation of structure. Surprisingly, the relation was negative with consideration. These results were similar to what Patchen (1962) found for the supervision of manual workers but contrary to that reported by Fleishman and Harris (1962) for similar types of workers.

The source of the criteria makes some difference. Korman (1966) reviewed research in which the scores for consideration and initiating structure scores of industrial supervisors were related to various criteria of the supervisors' effectiveness and the work groups' performance. Generally, he found that the peer ratings of the groups' performance were unrelated to the peer ratings of the supervisors' consideration and initiation of structure. However, evaluations of the supervisors' effectiveness by superiors and subordinates, as well as evaluations based on objective criteria, tended to relate significantly to the supervisors' initiation and consideration, as described by subordinates.

A number of industrial studies were completed using the additional scales of LBDQ-XII. D. R. Day (1961) obtained 165 descriptions of executives in an aircraft manufacturing firm. The effectiveness of leaders correlated with a general factor, as well as with the predictive accuracy of LBDQ-XII, persuasiveness, role enactment, and the reconciliation of conflicting demands. According to R. E. Hastings (1964), leaders who were rated high in initiating structure and production emphasis supervised research teams that were rated high in the volume of work they completed. If the leaders were rated high in orientation to superiors, their groups were rated low in harmony. Leaders who were rated high in representation and role retention tended to supervise teams that were rated high in enthusiastic

effort, while leaders who were high in persuasiveness supervised teams whose quality of work was rated as high. Even after the effects of many other morale variables were removed, freedom and consideration by supervisors on LBDQ-XII were important contributors to the amount of innovative behavior displayed by 309 federal R & D aerospace scientists and engineers (Dalessio & Davis, 1986).

M. Beer (1964) used the LBDQ-XII to test McGregor's (1960) hypothesis that employees become motivated and are enabled to satisfy their higher-order needs (for autonomy, esteem, and self-actualization) only when supervisors allow them freedom from organizational structure and pressure. He found support in that the employees' satisfaction of the need for autonomy, esteem, and self-actualization was positively related to the supervisors' consideration and tolerance of freedom. However, contrary to his hypothesis, the leaders' considerate behaviors that resulted in the satisfaction of higher-order needs were not the ones that led to employees strong striving for the needs. Rather, the leaders' initiation of structure was the leaders' behavior that was associated with such striving.

Leaders' Attitudes. As with the effects of leaders' behavior, findings about the effects of leaders' attitudes were also mixed. Bass (1956) found that the effectiveness ratings by superiors of 53 supervisors were significantly related to their attitudes toward consideration but not toward the initiation of structure expressed two years previously on the LOQ. In a replication, a significant correlation of .32 was found between sales supervisors' attitudes toward consideration and effectiveness ratings by superiors three years later (Bass, 1958). But Bass (1957a) also reported that neither attitudes toward consideration nor toward initiation of structure were related to peer ratings of sales supervisors on criteria such as popularity, problem-solving ability, and value to the company. At the same time, Fleishman and Peters (1962) found no relation between LOQ measures of supervisors' attitudes toward leadership and their rated effectiveness as supervisors. Rowland and Scott (1968) also noted that LOQ measures of supervisory consideration were unrelated to employees' satisfaction.

According to T. C. Parker (1963), 1,760 employees of

a wholesale pharmaceutical company in 80 decentralized warehouses were more satisfied with their supervision, their recognition, and their job security when their supervisors felt that consideration and initiation were important, as measured by the LOQ. The correlations of subordinates' satisfaction and supervisors' attitudes were .51 with supervisory consideration and .22 with supervisory initiation. Although there was no relation of the supervisors' attitudes to such objective measures of group performance as productivity and errors in filling orders, the supervisor's favoring of the initiation of structure correlated .23 with pricing errors of the unit being supervised. Spitzer and McNamara (1964) also reported that managers' attitudes toward consideration and initiation were not related to a salary criterion of the managers' success, nor were such attitudes related to superiors' ratings of the managers' success. On the other hand, Gruenfeld and Weissenberg (1966) found that supervisors who scored high in favorable attitudes toward consideration and initiation were also more favorably inclined toward the personal development of their subordinates than were those with low scores. Generally, favored supervisors reveal this "hi-hi" pattern (Fleishman, 1989b) and it has been found related to low stress and "burnout" among subordinates (Duxbury, Armstrong, Drew, & Henly, 1984).

Military Studies

In the first extensive use of the LBDQ with U.S. Air Force personnel, Christner and Hemphill (1955) found that changes in the attitudes of crew members toward each other over time were related to the leadership behavior of the crew commander. When crew members described their commander as high in consideration, the crew members increased their ratings of each other's friendliness, mutual confidence, conversation on duty, and willingness to engage in combat. Crews that described their commander as being high in the initiation of structure increased their ratings of each other's friendship and confidence. But Halpin (1954) found that superiors tended to evaluate positively those aircrew commanders they described as being high in initiating structure and to evaluate negatively those described as being high in consideration. In training, the satisfaction of crew members was positively related to consideration ($r = .48$) and negatively related to initiat-

ing structure ($r = -.17$). In combat, however, both consideration ($r = .64$) and initiating structure ($r = .35$) were positively related to the same crew members' satisfaction. In a later study, Halpin (1957a) found that superiors' ratings of the commanders' effectiveness in combat were unrelated to crew members' descriptions of their commander's consideration. However, superiors' ratings, as before, were positively and significantly related to the commander's initiation of structure. Significantly, crew members' ratings of their commander on confidence and proficiency, friendship and cooperation, and morale and satisfaction were positively related to both consideration and the initiation of structure by their commander.

Fleishman (1957a) found that the consideration and initiation scores of ROTC leaders were positively and significantly related to peers' ratings of the leaders' value to their groups, but superiors' ratings were not related to either pattern of behavior. In a study of trainee leaders in the military, Hood (1963) found that the trainees reported more affiliation and less communication when their superiors were higher in initiating structure and consideration. Enlisted personnel attained higher scores on a pencil-paper test of military leadership when their leaders structured the situation and pushed for production. However, such higher attainment by the enlisted personnel was not related to their leaders' consideration.

Hooper (1968/1969) obtained results indicating that the attitudes of U.S. Air Force cadets toward consideration and initiation were not significantly related to their effectiveness ratings; the two scales, however, differentiated significantly between those scoring high and those scoring low on a composite leadership criterion.

Group Effects. C. H. Rush (1957) reported the effects of leadership behavior on other dimensions of the performance of 212 aircrews. Crew members described the leadership behavior of the crew leaders and conditions in the crews on Hemphill and Westie's (1950) Group Dimension Descriptions. The leaders' consideration was associated with more intimacy and harmony and less control and stratification in the crews. The leaders' high rating on the initiation of structure were related to greater harmony and procedural clarity and to less stratification in the crews.

In examining the satisfaction and the perceived initiation and consideration of their leaders, according to 672 U.S. Army National Guardsmen, Katerberg and Homs (1981) showed that it was necessary to account statistically for both the group effects and the individual dyadic effects of LBDQ descriptions of the first sergeants and the company commanders on the guardsmen's satisfaction with the sergeants and commanders. First sergeants and commanders who earned high mean LBDQ scores on initiation and consideration from their collective unit of subordinates also had units who displayed higher mean satisfaction. But beyond this, within the groups led by each leader, individual subordinates were more satisfied if they saw their leader exhibiting more initiation and consideration. The adjusted correlations between satisfaction and the initiation and consideration scores on the LBDQ were .37 and .47 for the group-by-group analyses for the first sergeant and commanders, respectively. The individual-within-group analyses added substantially to the leadership-satisfaction correlations. Although there were problems with Katerberg and Hom's failure to separate the group and dyadic effects completely (Dansereau, Alutto, & Yammarino, 1984), the strong associations with satisfaction found for both initiation and consideration in the military were supported by similar LBDQ evidence obtained for 30,000 U.S. Army personnel in 63 national and overseas installations (Marsh & Atherton, 1981–82).

Educational Studies

A variety of investigations have been completed for the leadership behavior of college administrators, school administrators, and school principals.

Administrators in Higher Education. Hemphill (1955) used the LBDQ to study the leadership of heads of academic departments in a university. The department head's reputation for administrative competence correlated .36 with consideration and .48 with initiation of structure. But Lindemuth (1969) failed to establish any relations between a college dean's initiation of structure and various measures of organizational climate.

School Administrators. Superintendents who were rated as effective leaders by both their staff and school board members were described as high in both consideration and initiation of structure (Halpin, 1956a). H. J. Bowman (1964) asked school principals to describe the leadership behavior of higher-level school executives and themselves. Principals perceived themselves as exercising high degrees of responsibility and authority and as delegating extensively when they described their own superiors as being high in consideration but not in the initiation of structure. Again, for school administrators studied by Flocco (1969), those described as higher in consideration and the initiation of structure by staff subordinates were rated more effective. Rated ineffective were those administrators who described themselves as being higher in consideration and the initiation of structure than their staff subordinates so rated them.

School Principals. A. F. Brown (1967) and Greenfield (1968) concluded, from reviews of Canadian studies, that the performance of pupils was associated with the principals' LBDQ scores. Keeler and Andrews (1963) studied the relation of principals' leadership to the performance of pupils and the cohesiveness of staffs in Canadian public schools. Both consideration and the initiation of structure by the principals, as described by the teachers, were significantly and positively related to the pupils' examination scores on a province-wide examination. The initiation of structure by the principals was positively related to the cohesiveness of their staffs, but consideration was not. Nevertheless, A. F. Brown (1966) reported that effective principals generally scored higher on the LBDQ-XII scales. Seeman (1957) found performance evaluations of the school principals' leadership positively related to consideration, initiation of structure, communication, and willingness to change and negatively related to domination and social distance. According to Fast (1964), consideration and the initiation of structure by principals, as described by teachers, were positively related to the teachers' satisfaction, although expected behavior was not. Again, Stromberg (1967) obtained a significant relation between teachers' morale and the attitudes of their principals toward consideration and the initiation of structure.

C. C. Wall (1970) studied four effective and four ineffective principals in terms of their dialogue, decision making, and action. Effective principals were described by their teachers as higher than ineffective principals in consideration and tolerance of freedom on the LBDQ-XII. Ineffective principals were described as high in production emphasis. Teachers in seven of the eight schools studied believed that the principals ought to initiate more structure than they were perceived to do. Teachers in the ineffective schools believed that the principals should exhibit more persuasion and demand more reconciliation and more integration of the group than they were perceived to do. Mansour (1969) found that these discrepancies between the expected and actual behavior of principals were negatively relatively to teachers' job satisfaction and participation. Fast (1964) also obtained results indicating that the greater the discrepancy between the teachers' expectations and observations of principals' behavior, the lower was the teachers' satisfaction.

Among different schools, Punch (1967) found that the principals' initiation of structure was positively related and the principals' consideration was negatively related to a measure bureaucracy in the school. At the same time, Mathews (1963) reported that the principals' initiation of structure and consideration was significantly related to Hemphill and Westie's (1950) measures of their staffs' stratification, control, homogeneity, cohesiveness, hedonic tone, and participation.

Hills (1963) obtained descriptions by 872 teachers, of 53 principals. Both consideration and initiating structure were highly correlated with two representative functions of the principals: (1) representing the teachers' interests to higher levels of the organization and (2) representing the teachers' interests to the schools' pupils and their parents. Hills concluded that consideration and the initiation of structure were not solely concerned with internal leadership but were reflected in the manner in which the principals, as leaders, dealt with outsiders and higher levels of authority.

On the other hand, Rasmussen (1976) failed to establish any significant relationship between the success of 25 elementary schools, the satisfaction of teachers, and the behavior of principals on the LBDQ. Bailey (1966) studied four principals who were described by their superintendents and four teachers as being higher in consideration than in initiating structure and four other principals who were described as being higher in initiating structure than in consideration. Each principal

and four teachers played a decision-making game. Although the principals' consideration was found to be significantly related to the teachers' satisfaction with the decision and support of it, neither the principals' consideration nor initiating structure scores were significantly related to the ability of a group to arrive at a decision or to perceptions that teachers had helped make the decisions.

Schoolteachers. In a large-scale Canadian study, Greenfield and Andrews (1961) obtained results indicating that consideration and the initiation of structure by classroom teachers were positively and significantly related to the scores of their pupils on achievement tests.

Hospital Studies

In a study of nurses and their supervisors, Nealey and Blood (1968) found that the satisfaction of subordinates was related to the consideration scores of both first- and second-level supervisors. The supervisors' initiation of structure contributed to the subordinates' job satisfaction at the first, but not at the second, level of supervision. Oaklander and Fleishman (1964) observed that when hospital administrators endorsed both high consideration and high initiation of structure on the LOQ, stress was lower in the units they supervised.

A path analysis by Sheridan and Vredenburgh (1979) for the descriptions by 372 nurses, practical nurses, and nursing aides of the behavior of their head nurses, disclosed a positive effect of the head nurses' initiation of structure on the subordinates' group relations. But these group relations did not affect the subordinates' performance or turnover rates. Good group relations also reduced the subordinates' felt job tension. However, such job tension had but a slight positive association with job performance or turnover rates. Yet, the head nurses' consideration had a direct positive effect, as well as an indirect effect, on the subordinates' performance. It also reduced the subordinates' felt job tension. However, such job tension had but a slight positive association with job performance. (This result fits with Weed, Mitchell, and Moffitt's [1976] laboratory finding that the leader's consideration makes for a pleasant working situation, although it may not necessarily contribute to the group's productivity.)

The critical importance of the leader's initiation and consideration to the performance of subordinates in health organizations was confirmed by Dagirmanjian (1981), Blaihed (1982), and Denton (1976). On the basis of a data analysis, Dagirmanjian (1981) concluded that the supervisors' initiation of structure and consideration was the central link between the organizational structure in mental health services and the staffs. Blaihed (1982) obtained the LBDQ-XII scores of chief executive officers (CEOs) and staffs of hospitals in Los Angeles and related the results to criteria of hospital performance furnished by the California Health Facilities Commission. The initiation of structure by the CEOs and staffs contributed to the efficiency of the hospitals and the quality of care they provided, as did a number of the other scale scores of the LBDQ. Similarly, for 80 professional mental health workers and their directors, Denton (1976) found significant and direct relationships between both supervisors' consideration and initiation of structure, on the one hand, and the workers' job satisfaction and satisfactory relations with clients, on the other hand. Duxbury, Armstrong, Drew, and Henly (1984) found that head nurses with low consideration–high structure LOQ scores had the lowest staff satisfaction and highest staff burnout.

Studies in Other Not-for-Profit Organizations

Cunningham (1964) observed that the most effective agricultural agents and 4-H club agents were above the median in both consideration and initiation of structure on the LBDQ. Similarly, Klepinger (1980) collected LBDQ and outcome data from a stratified sample of 35 executive directors of social service departments who were rated by their 227 employees. Directors who were rated high in initiation and consideration were also seen as highly effective managers, but their leadership behavior did not influence their employees' job satisfaction.

Bernardin (1976) found that for 501 police officers in a metropolitan department, consideration by supervisors was positively and linearly related to the police officers' satisfaction but not to their performance or absenteeism. To account for the results more adequately, additional descriptive data about the supervisors were required, such as the supervisors' specific reward orientation and punitiveness.

Stogdill (1965a) studied ten regional organizations in a department of a state government. He noted that throughout the ten organizations, executives who described their superiors as high in representation on the LBDQ-XII tended to manage groups that were rated high in support of the organization, and their subordinates tended to be satisfied with their pay. The tolerance of uncertainty by their superiors was related to harmony in the groups. Superiors were rated high in initiating structure supervised subordinates who were satisfied with the organization. When the state employees described their first-line supervisors, Stogdill found that the first-line supervisors who were described as high in the initiation of structure, consideration, and "influence upstairs" tended to supervise employees who were satisfied with the organization and groups that were rated strong in drive. Employees who described their supervisors as being tolerant of freedom expressed satisfaction with their own freedom on the job.

Hood (1963) found that trainees reported more affiliation and less communication when their leaders were rated as high both in initiating structure and in consideration. Furthermore, the trainees attained higher scores on a paper-and pencil test of performance when their leaders structured the situation and pushed for production. But such increased attainment was not related to the leaders' consideration.

Osborn and Hunt (1975a, 1975b) obtained data indicating that most aspects of the satisfaction of members in 60 chapters of a business fraternity were positively associated with their presidents' initiation and consideration. But Yukl and Hunt (1976) reported that in 74 chapters the correlations between LBDQ assessments of the chapter presidents' initiation and consideration and the chapters' efficiency in fulfilling specified requirements were only .12 and .10, respectively.

Summary Meta-Analysis

Fisher and Edwards (1988) completed a meta-analysis of studies in the computer abstracts of *Psychological Abstracts*. These studies presumably were published mainly after 1968. As can be seen in Table 24.1, after the mean findings were corrected for sample size, restriction in range, and unreliability, the adjusted mean correlation of LBDQ leader consideration with job per-

Table 24.1 Mean Correlations of Leader Consideration and the Initiation of Structure with Job Performance

Leadership Measure	Number of Respondents	Number of Correlations	Mean Correlation	
			Unadjusted	Adjusted
Consideration				
LBDQ	1,486	19	.19	.45
SBDQ	1,953	21	.19	.46
LBDQ-XII	1,424	11	.13	.27
Initiation of Structure				
LBDQ	1,486	19	.20	.47
SBDQ	1,953	21	−.02	−.06
LBDQ-XII	1,424	11	.09	.22

SOURCE: Adapted from Fisher and Edwards (1988, p. 202).

formance ranged from .27 to .45. The adjusted correlations of job performance with LBDQ initiation of structure were similar, but not with the SBDQ measure of initiation with its punitive elements.

Again, except for the SBDQ measure of initiation, considerably higher adjusted correlations were obtained, as expected, between initiation, consideration, job satisfaction, and satisfaction with supervision, as shown in Tables 24.2 and 24.3.

The patterns of results lent support to Larson, Hunt, and Osborn's conclusion, after examining 14 samples of first-line supervisors involving 2,474 respondents, that the multiple regression additive or interactive

combining of initiation and consideration was unwarranted, since it did not add sufficiently to the prediction of outcomes beyond what each measure could do alone. Part of this lack of augmentation of one measure by the other was due to the mean intercorrelation of .52 between them found for 10 samples on the LBDQ-XII by Schriesheim, House, and Kerr (1976). For four samples, Schriesheim (1982) obtained results indicating that consideration alone accounted for most of the effects on the satisfaction of subordinates. For samples of 230 hourly employees, 178 college seniors and graduate students with employment experience, 96 middle managers, and 258 clerks and middle managers who de-

Table 24.2 Mean Correlations of Leader Consideration and Initiation of Structure with Overall Job Satisfaction

Leadership Measure	Number of Respondents	Number of Correlations	Mean Correlation	
			Unadjusted	Adjusted
Consideration				
LBDQ	2,517	21	.34	.65
SBDQ	1,134	8	.47	.83
LBDQ-XII	4,347	25	.38	.70
Initiation of Structure				
LBDQ	2,517	21	.26	.51
SBDQ	1,134	8	−.02	−.04
LBDQ-XII	4,347	25	.23	.46

SOURCE: Adapted from Fisher and Edwards (1988, p. 202).

Table 24.3 Mean Correlations of Leader Consideration and Initiation of Structure with Satisfaction with Supervision

Leadership Measure	Number of Respondents	Number of Correlations	Mean Correlation	
			Unadjusted	Adjusted
Consideration				
LBDQ	632	7	.63	.99
SBDQ	1,048	10	.79	.99
LBDQ-XII	3,455	19	.57	.95
Initiation of Structure				
LBDQ	632	7	.29	.57
SBDQ	1,048	10	−.15	−.30
LBDQ-XII	3,455	19	.39	.73

SOURCE: Adapted from Fisher and Edwards (1988, p. 203).

scribed their supervisors' leadership behavior by means of the LBDQ and the SBDQ, Schreisheim found that the supervisors' consideration alone correlated between .62 and .77 with satisfaction with their jobs and with their supervisors. The results for the supervisors' initiation of structure, in multiple regression analysis, added only from 2 to 4 percent to the consideration effects in accounting for satisfaction. However, while Nystrom (1978) reached the same conclusion about consideration and the satisfaction of subordinates' needs, with a sample of 100 junior and senior managers, he noted that managers who were high in initiating structure and in consideration had relatively lower salary levels and progressed more slowly in their careers. Low initiation of structure, rather than high consideration, contributed the most to higher salaries and career advancement. Nystrom's results may say much about the culture and policies in the firm from which the 100 managers were drawn. Contingent factors need to be considered.

Contingencies in the Effects of Consideration and Initiation

Generally, the consideration of supervisors seems to be associated with subordinates' satisfaction with the supervisors, fewer absences and less likelihood of quit-

ting. But, as we have just seen, the correlations between a leaders' initiation of structure and the satisfaction and productivity of subordinates vary in outcome, depending on the instruments used to measure them. The constraints and goals in the situation also make a difference. The personnel involved may be particularly important. Followers in a wide variety of groups consider it legitimate for the leader to exercise influence on matters related to the performance of tasks and the work environment (Fleishman & Peters, 1962). At higher executive levels, initiation of structure is seen in planning, innovation, and coordination; at lower levels, it is seen in the push for production (Brooks, 1955).

Although too much initiation often increases the likelihood of grievances, absenteeism, and turnover (Fleishman & Harris, 1962), a certain amount of pointing out the "paths to successful effort" (Bass, 1965c) is characteristic of the effective supervisor. It yields the greatest effectiveness and satisfaction in the work group—especially when workers are untrained or unmotivated or both, for example, when the group lacks cohesiveness. Untrained personnel need more help; trained ones prefer less help.

The variety of mixed results noted in reviews[7] of the effects of consideration and initiation suggests that to

[7]See L. R. Anderson (1966a); Campbell, Dunnette, Lawler, and Weick (1970); and Korman (1966).

gain a better understanding of these effects, researchers need to specify the measures employed and the conditions involved (House, 1971; Kerr, Schriesheim, Murphy, & Stogdill, 1974). For example, the initiation of structure usually has been found to be associated with subordinates' role clarity, but somewhat less frequently with the subordinates' performance. The correlation varies considerably from study to study with the subordinates' satisfaction (Fleishman, 1973). Thus, the "leadership climate" under which the supervisors' work has been found related to the supervisors' own consideration and structure behavior and attitudes (Fleishman, 1953b).

Instrumentation

As was noted earlier, the differences in results obtained can be accounted for, to a considerable degree, by whether the investigator used the LBDQ, the SBDQ, the LBDQ-XII, or the LOQ.

Schriesheim, House, and Kerr (1976) did a masterful detective job in reconciling the mixed results obtained with the various versions of the LBDQ and SBDQ in measuring the initiation of structure. First, they pointed out that the LBDQ of Halpin (1957b) contained 15 items that asked subordinates to describe the actual initiating-structure behavior of their leader to establish well-defined patterns of communications and to set up ways to get the job done. But the revised LBDQ-XII (Stogdill, 1963a) contained 10 items for measuring the initiation of structure that dealt with the actions of the leaders in clearly defining their own roles and informing followers about what was expected of them. Even more substantial differences were found in the leadership behavior tapped by the SBDQ and the LBDQ in a comprehensive item-by-item analysis of 242 employees' descriptions of their supervisors. In addition to role clarification by the leader, as was noted earlier, the SBDQ included a cluster of items measuring punitive, autocratic, and production-oriented behaviors, such as, "He rules with an iron hand" or "He needles those under him for greater effort." Thus, the three scales—SBDQ and the earlier and later versions of the LBDQ—differed markedly in content. The initiation content of the LBDQ versions largely reflected communication and organization elements; the

SBDQ, on the other hand, consisted mainly of domination and production items.

An essential component of the initiation of structure in all the instruments involved role-clarification behaviors. A specific aspect of role clarification—establishing methods to get the work done—is mentionied in the LBDQs, but other aspects, such as scheduling and criticizing, are found only in the SBDQ. Schriesheim, House, and Kerr (1976, p. 301) concluded:

> When measured by the SBDQ, leader Initiation of Structure is generally positively related to performance ratings by superiors of manufacturing first-level supervisors' subordinates.... [8] This generalization also holds with regard to noncommissioned ... infantry officers[9] ... with Initiating Structure being measured in these studies by a form containing items similar to the autocratic behavior items of the SBDQ. A similar although much weaker pattern of relationships has been found concerning non-manufacturing supervisors of clerical workers doing routine tasks ... using selected items from the SBDQ in a laboratory experiment.[10]

> When the revised LBDQ Initiating Structure scale is used to measure leader behavior of first-line supervisors of non-manufacturing employees performing routine tasks, correlations with subordinate satisfaction are positive, although generally [lower] ... using a very modified version of the revised LBDQ.[11]

Meheut and Siegel (1973) demonstrated the differences by dividing the initiation-of-structure items of the SBDQ into those concerned with role clarification and those concerned with the autocratic behavior of leaders. They obtained a correlation of .26 between the leaders' role clarification and the subordinates' satisfaction, but a correlation of −.21 between the leaders' autocratic behavior and the subordinates' satisfaction.

Another source of error that accounts for variations in results with the SBDQ, according to Schriesheim, House, and Kerr, is the SBDQ's failure to provide op-

[8]Fleishman and Harris (1962); Fleishman, Harris, and Burtt (1955); Harris and Fleishman (1955); and Skinner (1969).
[9]Moore (1953), Moore and Smith (1956), and Stouffer (1949).
[10]Fleishman, Harris, and Burtt (1955); and Lowin, Hrapchak, and Kavanagh (1969).
[11]Beer (1966); Dessler (1973); Hunt and Hill (1971); Hunt, Hill, and Reaser (1971); and Hunt and Liebscher (1973).

portunity for respondents to describe the timing or appropriateness of the structuring of the particular task or of the context in which respondents work, even though empirical evidence indicates that timing may be more important than the frequency of specific leadership behaviors (see, for example, W. K. Graham, 1968; Sample & Wilson, 1965). In addition, leaders who have adequate knowledge of the demands of their subordinates' tasks may vary the amount of initiation of structure and the kind and timing of the structure they provide. Some tasks require more structure during the goal-setting (goal-clarification) stage, whereas others require more path clarification and feedback on performance. Furthermore, some subordinates need more administrative structure to relate their work to other employees, whereas other subordinates could benefit more from technical guidance. Leaders may have no control over standards. Their initiation of structure may depend on circumstances outside their purview. "He decides what shall be done and how it shall be done" may be physically impossible for leaders in some situations. Other initiation-of-structure items, such as, "He tries out his ideas in the group" are less likely to be affected by circumstances.

Some items deal with specific behavior and others deal with general tendencies. Such initiation-of-structure items as, "He schedules the work to be done" refer to specific actions; items such as, "He encourages overtime work" relate to general practices. Even further removed from specific behaviors and more concerned with the skills, traits, and personality attributed to the leader are such items as, "He makes accurate decisions" or "He is a very persuasive talker."

Organizational Contingencies

The impact of a leader's initiation and consideration will depend on the organization in which it occurs. House, Filley, and Gujarati (1971) found that both the leader's consideration and the leader's initiation of structure moderated the employees' satisfaction with freedom on the job, job security, and family attitudes in one firm, but not in another. Similarly, Larson, Hunt, and Osborn (1974) found that in one state mental health institution, the leaders' consideration was related to the performance of groups of personnel, but

that in another institution, initiating structure was more highly related to the groups' performance. The previously cited report by Marsh and Atherton (1981-82) of the results of a study of 30,000 U.S. Army personnel concluded that whether a military unit was mechanistic or organic moderated the extent to which the leader's initiation or consideration was related to the subordinates' satisfaction.

Differences in Function and Task. Fleishman, Harris, and Burtt (1955) noted that the leader's greater initiation of structure contributed to absences and grievances of subordinates in manufacturing departments and to heightened rates of turnover in nonmanufacturing departments. At the same time, Fleishman, Harris, and Burtt found that supervisors in manufacturing departments or in other departments that were working under time constraints were likely to receive higher merit ratings from their own supervisors if they tended to exhibit more initiation of structure, whereas the reverse was true for supervisors in service departments. In addition, in the nonmanufacturing service departments, the more considerate supervisors were seen as more proficient. "Pressure for production" was the moderator.

In Cunningham's (1964) study of county agricultural agents and 4-H club agents cited earlier, the agricultural agents' consideration was significantly related to effectiveness, but initiation of structure was not. In contrast, initiating structure was significantly related to the effectiveness of 4-H club agents, but consideration was not. However, as was noted earlier, the most effective agents in both organizations were those who were described as being above the median in both consideration and structure. Mannheim, Rim, and Grinberg (1967) reported that manual workers tolerated more initiation of structure by their supervisors than did clerical workers. Only clerical workers tended to reject the high-structuring supervisor when they expected the initiation of structure to be low. When high consideration was expected, both groups chose the leader who conformed to their expectations.

Hunt and Liebscher (1973) showed that the consideration of leaders was more strongly associated with subordinates' satisfaction in a construction bureau than in a bureau of design of a state highway department; the leaders' initiation of structure did not vary as much in its effects on satisfaction. Dagirmanjian's (1981) previously cited study of 126 mental health service personnel showed that when organizational differentiation was in force, the leaders' consideration generated employee satisfaction with supervision, but when organizational integration was involved, the leaders' initiation of structure generated such satisfaction.

Within-organizational Conditions

The relationships among the subordinates' satisfaction, the groups' performance, and the leaders' initiation and consideration depend strongly on who does the rating.

Leaders in the Middle. Although Rambo (1958) failed to find any significant differences in the initiation and consideration of executives at different echelons of the hierarchical structure, Halpin (1956a) saw such hierarchical differences when he examined the reactions of organizational members at different levels to the leader in between them in level. Halpin studied the leadership of school superintendents described by staff members, school board members, and themselves on both the real and ideal forms of the LBDQ. He found that the board members agreed among themselves and the staff members agreed among themselves in their descriptions of the superintendents' behavior, but the two groups differed significantly in their perceptions. Staff members saw the superintendents as less considerate than the superintendents saw themselves or the board members saw the superintendents. The board members described the superintendents as being higher in initiating structure than did the staff members or the superintendents. The staff members and the board members differed significantly regarding how considerate the superintendents should be, but they did not differ significantly about the extent to which superintendents should initiate structure. The board members expected the superintendents to act in a more considerate manner than the staff members considered ideal. There was a nonsignificant tendency for board members to expect more initiation of structure than either the staff members or the superintendents considered ideal.

Other studies in educational institutions by raters of

a leader in the middle were completed by Sharpe (1956), Carson and Schultz (1964), and Luckie (1963). Sharpe studied the leadership of principals as described by teachers, staff members, and the principals themselves. The three groups held similar ideals of leadership behavior, but the teachers and staff members perceived the principals as deviating less from the ideal norms than did the principals themselves. Occupants of high-status positions perceived the principals as deviating more from the ideal norms than did those in lower-status positions. Carson and Schultz (1964) obtained descriptions of junior college deans by college presidents, department heads, student leaders, and the deans themselves. The greatest discrepancies were found between the presidents' and student leaders' perceptions and expectations of the dean's behavior. The evidence suggested that the greatest source of role conflict for the deans was the discrepant expectations of their behavior. Luckie (1963) obtained 434 descriptions of 53 directors of instruction by superintendents, staff members, and the directors themselves. The results indicated that the instructional directors actually behaved at a lower level of consideration than superintendents, the directors themselves, and the staff members rated as ideal. The superintendents and the staff members expected the directors to exhibit higher degrees of structure than the directors considered ideal.

The conflict of the leader in the middle seems to reside in the question of how considerate to be, not how much structure to provide. Graen, Dansereau, and Minami (1972b) obtained data indicating that at lower organizational levels, both superiors and subordinates evaluated the leader in between them more highly if the leader initiated more structure. But the leader's consideration had more of an impact on subordinates than on superiors.

Lawrie (1966) used the scales of real and ideal consideration and initiation in a study of superiors' and subordinates' expectations of foremen in two departments. The convergence between real and expected behavior, as described by subordinates, was not related to ratings of the foremen's effectiveness. However, in one of the two departments, the foremen's ability to predict the superiors' expectations and the congruence between the foremen's and the superiors' expectations were related to ratings of the foremen's effectiveness.

Influence 'Upstairs.' Leaders' influence with higher authority has been found to affect the impact of their initiation of structure and consideration on their subordinates' satisfaction and performance. Consideration often involves promises of tangible rewards, and leaders may need influence "upstairs" to "deliver" on their promises. The initiation of structure involves setting forth goals and plans; influence "upstairs" adds to the leaders' ability to do so with authority and credibility. In one of two companies studied, House, Filley, and Gujarati (1971) found the expected strong positive relation between a supervisor's influence with a higher authority and an increase in the correlation of the supervisor's consideration with the subordinates' satisfaction. As Wager (1965) found earlier, in both the companies studied, the greater a supervisor's influence with higher authority, the greater was the supervisor's tendency to be considerate. Presumably, the influential leader could offer support and rewards with more certainty of providing them. Again, the more influential supervisor exhibited more initiation of structure in only one of the firms studied, but, generally, employees were more satisfied with most aspects of their jobs if their supervisors were more influential with higher authority.

Falling Dominoes Again. The falling-dominoes effect, discussed at length in earlier chapters, was observed by Hunt, Hill, and Reaser (1973) for results with the LBDQ-XII. In a school for the mentally retarded, an increase was found in the association of considerate supervision and the performance of aides when the LBDQ scores of the second-level and first-level supervisors were combined. In the same vein, Hunt, Osborn, and Larson (1975), with data from three mental institutions, showed that leaders' consideration had more of a positive impact on their groups' performance if the leaders' superiors were high in authoritarianism. However, group performance was higher if the leaders' initiation of structure was low, whether the leaders' superiors were authoritarian or egalitarian.

In his first study with the LOQ, Fleishman (1953a) found that the higher the supervisors' positions in the hierarchy of a plant, the less considerate the supervisors thought they should be and the more structure they thought should be initiated. These attitudes had an impact on those below them. Foremen whose superiors expected them to lead with less consideration and with more structuring revealed high grievance rates among their subordinates.

Size of Group Led. Ordinarily, one would expect that when the size of the group is enlarged, a leader would have to display more initiation of structure to be as effective as before the unit was enlarged (Bass, 1960). It would be expected that the leader would find it increasingly difficult to maintain the same level of consideration of the concerns of all subordinates as the group enlarged. Corollary results that are consistent with this expectation were found by Badin (1974), who showed that in the smaller of 42 work groups, the initiation of structure by the leader correlated negatively with the productivity of 489 manufacturing employees, but that the amount of a supervisor's initiation of structure was unrelated to productivity in the larger groups.

Osborn and Hunt (1975b), in their previously cited study of presidents of chapters of a business fraternity, found that the size of a chapter moderated the positive effects of initiation and consideration on the members' satisfaction. However, Sheridan and Vredenburgh (1979) failed to find any relation between the size of units led and the head nurses' leadership behavior, although size correlated with perceived job tension, which, in turn, was related to the subordinates' performance.

Structure of the Work Group. J. A. Miller (1973a) deduced that more initiation of structure would be contraindicated in a highly structured setting. Thus, for a supervisor to tell skilled crafts personnel how to do their job was expected to be detrimental to their performance. Consistent with this expectation, Badin (1974) found that when first-line supervisors initiated structure a great deal in the previously mentioned 42 work groups of the manufacturing firm, effectiveness was reduced in the already most structured of the 42 groups. The correlation of group effectiveness in these highly structured groups and the supervisors' initiation of structure was $-.56$. But in the less structured of the 42 work groups, the effectiveness of the groups was correlated .20 with the extent to which their first-line supervisor initiated structure.

Also consistent with Miller's argument, Jurma (1978)

demonstrated, in an experimental comparison, that workers in 20 discussion groups were more satisfied when leaders provided discussants with task-related information, gave guiding suggestions, helped groups to budget their time, and established group goals, particularly when the workers were faced with a debatable, ambiguous discussion task, rather than one with clear choices for making a decision.

Dyadic versus Group Relationships. By the late 1970s, considerable research had concentrated on the dyadic leader-subordinate relationship (Graen & Schiemann, 1978), instead of on the leader and the primary work group (Hunt, Osborn, & Schriesheim, 1978). Nevertheless, as was noted earlier, substantive differences in results from standard leader-group investigations often have failed to emerge. Thus, for example, in the case of the LBDQ, for 308 managerial and clerical employees in 43 work groups in a public utility, C. A. Schriesheim (1979a) found correlations of .77 and .89 between dyadic and group LBDQ descriptions of supervisors for initiation and consideration, respectively.

Cohesion. Among these 308 low- and middle-level managerial and clerical employees J. F. Schriesheim (1980), using a modification of the LBDQ-XII, asked subordinates to indicate how their superiors acted toward them as individuals rather than toward the group as a whole. In line with her expectations, she showed that when the cohesion of the work group was low, the leader's initiation of structure was positively related to the subordinates' satisfaction with supervision, role clarity, and self-rated performance. But when cohesiveness was high in the work group, the leader's consideration was positively related to the measures of satisfaction, clarity, and performance.

Alignment with Objectives. The contribution of initiation and consideration to productivity will depend on the extent to which the group of subordinates is supportive of the objectives of the productivity. In Howell's (1985) experiment, detailed in Chapter 12, the leader who initiated structure generated more than average actual productivity in the experimental subject if the confederate fellow worker established high norms for productivity. The experimental subject produced

much less if the confederate induced low norms for productivity. The leader's consideration had the same effect, but to a lesser extent. Similar results occurred for the effect of initiating structure on satisfaction and freedom from role conflict, but, here, the effects of consideration were not moderated by the productivity norms set by the confederates of the experimenter.

Hernandez and Kaluzny (1982) studied the leadership and performance of 20 work groups of public health nurses. They found that the supervisors' initiation of structure had a strong positive relationship to productivity but that consideration did not. Likewise, satisfaction was enhanced by the supervisors' and peers' initiation of structure. Instead of the amount of communication flow and group processing correlating positively with the groups' productivity and satisfaction, the reverse occurred. The explanation of these results lay in the lack of support by the nurses for the appropriateness of the services they offered.

Group Conflicts. Various kinds of conflict between the group and external agents, as well as within the groups, moderate the extent to which consideration and initiation will be effective. R. Katz (1977) found that considerate leadership was most effective when the group faced external conflicts but that initiation of structure by the leader was most effective in dealing with internal interpersonal conflicts.

Stumpf (undated) completed a path analysis for the questionnaire data from 144 professionals in a government R & D organization. Leadership behavior was not directly related to the subordinates' job satisfaction or performance, but it was related through two moderating or intervening variables that linked the leader's consideration and initiation to subordinates' job satisfaction and performance. The leader's initiation of structure correlated with the subordinates' skill-role compatibility, which, in turn, correlated with the subordinates' job satisfaction. Thus, the R & D professionals' satisfaction with their jobs depended on the extent to which their skills were not in conflict with the demands of their roles, which, in turn, depended on the structuring of the situation by their supervisors.

Curvilinear Effects. Skinner (1969) obtained results indicating that industrial foremen who scored high in consideration experienced lower-than-average grievance and turnover rates among their subordinates. As did Fleishman and Harris (1962), Skinner concluded that the consideration of supervisors bears a curvilinear relationship to the turnover and grievances of employees. As consideration increases, grievances decrease to a point and then level off. But supervisory initiation also had a curvilinear relationship to grievances.

Interaction of Effects. The interacting effects of consideration and initiation of structure were observed to vary, depending on the situation. Thus, considerate foremen could structure without increasing turnover and grievances (Cummins, 1971). Fleishman and Harris (1962) found in using the SBDQ that the consideraton and initiation of structure by foremen interacted to affect the grievances and turnover of employees. Medium and high degrees of consideration, along with low degrees of structure by foremen, were associated with the lowest rates of turnover and grievances of employees. Graen, Dansereau, and Minami (1972a) found, among 660 managers of a large corporation, that for those managers who saw their leader as either extremely high or low in initiating structure, the relationship between their leader's consideration behavior and the managers' performance evaluation was positive. But for those managers who saw their leader as intermediate in initiating structure, the relationship between their leader's consideration and the managers' performance was near zero.

But other studies failed to establish any interaction of initiation and consideration on outcomes. Filley, House, and Kerr (1976) studied three companies to test Fleishman and Harris's (1962) hypothesis that the leader's initiation of structure acts as a mediator of the relationship between the leader's consideration and employees' job satisfaction. Initiating structure was positively and significantly related to satisfaction with the company in all three organizations. Consideration was significantly related to satisfaction with the company and freedom of action in all organizations. The data failed to support the mediating hypothesis. Similarly, as will be examined more fully in Chapter 28, M. G. Evans (1970a) tested the path-goal hypothesis in two organizations. He found that consideration and initiation of structure did not interact in path-goal facilitation but, rather, that consideration and initiation of

structure each acted separately to enhance path-goal instrumentality. The mixed findings suggest that the occurrence of the interaction effect depends on particular circumstances.

Contingent Aspects of the Subordinates. As might have been expected from what has been presented regarding the effects of autocratic leader behavior compounded with authoritarian subordinates, Weed, Mitchell, and Moffitt (1976) found that leaders who initiated more structure with dogmatic subordinates were likely to achieve higher levels of performance, while leaders who exhibited more consideration yielded greater performance among subordinates who were low in dogmatism. In the previously mentioned path analysis by Sheridan and Vredenburgh (1979), greater job experience of the nursing personnel was found to be related to less considerate leadership from the head nurses, which, in turn, increased the subordinates' tension and had mixed effects on their performance.

M. Beer's (1964) industrial study of the effects of leadership behavior on subordinates' fulfillment of needs disclosed that subordinates whose need for self-actualization, esteem, autonomy, production emphasis, and consideration was high were positively motivated by the leader's initiation of structure, contrary to the hypothesis that the leader's consideration would be more effective in motivating subordinates. Abdel-Halim (1981) collected data from 89 lower- and middle-level manufacturing managers and demonstrated that the subordinates' locus of control moderated the effects of the ambiguity and complexity of tasks on the effectiveness of initiation and consideration.

Contingent Aspects of the Leaders. The effects of initiation or consideration appear to depend on whether the leader has a strong need for achievement and is experienced and expert. Assuming that one of the primary functions of a lower-level leader is to maintain the subordinate's job performance at a level that is acceptable to the leader's superior, B. T. Mayes (1979) showed how the leader's need for achievement moderated the relations between the subordinates' job performance and the leader's consideration and initiation of structure. For 180 leader-subordinate dyads, the leader's need for achievement significantly moderated the relationship between the subordinate's job performance and the leader's initiation of structure. Leaders with a high need for achievement who initiated structure obtained a better performance from their subordinates than did leaders with a low need for achievement who also initiated structure.

Another illustration of a contingent effect that is due to the leader was provided by Miklos (1963), who observed that the longer the tenure of school principals who were high in the initiation of structure, the greater the consensus among teachers in their role expectations for teachers and the greater the agreement between teachers and principals. Agreement between teachers and principals was highest when principals were described as being high in both consideration and the initiation of structure.

The expert power of the leader also moderates the effects of initiation and consideration. Path analyses by Martin and Hunt (1980) disclosed that initiation and consideration, when combined directly or indirectly with expert power, linearly enhanced the group's cohesiveness, job satisfaction, and intentions to remain on the job.

Podsakoff, Todor, and Schuler (1983) helped to explain this effect of expert power and leadership. They collected data from 101 employees of a large nonprofit organization who used modified LBDQ scales to describe their supervisors. As the supervisors' initiation of structure increased and if the supervisors were highly expert, the role ambiguity of the subordinates decreased. However, if the leaders who were high in initiation were low in expert power, the reverse occurred—the role ambiguity of the subordinates increased. A similar, although not as extreme, pattern emerged with the increasing consideration of the leaders. Expert considerate leaders generated less role ambiguity in their subordinates, whereas inexpert considerate leaders generated more role ambiguity.

Causal Effects

Cross-lagged Analyses

The limitations of the results of LBDQ surveys in ascertaining whether the described leadership is a cause, a consequence, or a coincidence of group effectiveness, satisfaction, or other valued outcomes has already been noted. Do considerate and structuring leaders promote the satisfaction and productivity of subordinates, or do leaders of satisfied and productive subordinates show them more consideration and tend to initiate less structure? Cross-lagged analyses suggest that the causality is reciprocal. Leaders affect subsequent outcomes and outcomes affect the leaders' subsequent behavior (Greene, 1973, 1974, 1975, 1979a).

Greene (1975) asked first-level managers in insurance, marketing, finance, and research and engineering to describe their own consideration and initiation of structure on the LBDQ. Two subordinates of each of the managers rated their own work satisfaction. Peers of these subordinates rated the subordinates' productivity. The measures were picked up on successive occasions one month apart. Cross-lagged comparisons were made of the leaders' behavior at time 1 correlated with the subordinates' satisfaction or productivity at time 2 and contrasted with the subordinates' satisfaction or performance at time 1 correlated with the leaders' behavior at time 2. The results strongly suggested that considerate leadership resulted subsequently in the increased satisfaction of subordinates. At the same time, the subordinates' productivity resulted subsequently in their managers' increased consideration for them. Finally, the subordinates' productivity resulted subsequently in a reduction in the managers' initiation of structure.

Experimental Effects

Even greater confidence about the cause and effects of initiation and consideration comes from the rare experiment in which the leader's initiation or consideration (or both) is arbitrarily manipulated experimentally and measurements are taken of the subsequent effects on subordinates. Some results were obtained to support the argument that initiation or consideration causes the subsequent improved performance or increased satisfaction of subordinates.

Dawson, Messé, and Phillips (1972) arranged for teachers to increase their initiation of structure deliberately. They found that their students' work-group productivity improved as a consequence. When the teachers subsequently increased their consideration deliberately, the students' work-group productivity again increased as a consequence.

In a laboratory experiment by Gilmore, Beehr, and Richter (1979), 48 participants were subjected to either low or high consideration and low or high structure by specially coached student supervisors who were working with groups of four members each. The LBDQ completed by the members failed to discriminate the behavior of the four types of supervisors, even though the leadership behavior itself had differential effects on the quality of the participants' performance. The quality the participants' performance was highest with leaders who were high in initiation of structure but low in consideration. On the other hand, neither the amount of initiation nor the amount of consideration was related to various measures of satisfaction of the participants.

Finally, as mentioned before, Howell's (1985) experiment demonstrated that if group norms were supportive of high productivity, the leader's initiation and consideration resulted in a rise in productivity and satisfaction.

Summary and Conclusions

It was found possible to cluster hundreds of different bits of leader behavior into two factors—initiation and consideration—although early on, it was recognized that some important elements might still be missing. Twelve factors were found to reasonably exhaust the list: Although factorially and conceptually independent, in their revised measurement with LBDQ-Form XII scales, the leader's tendencies to be considerate and to initiate structure were ordinarily found to correlate moderately with each other.

Personal and situational variables of considerable variety relate to the appearance of consideration and the initiation of structure by the leader. The latter becomes more important when less structure is available to the group. Psychometric reviews of results using the original and revised LBDQ and the SBDQ indicate that the generally negative associations between task-oriented initiation of structure, as measured by the SBDQ, and satisfaction and morale become positive when the coercive elements are removed. But leniency is likely to continue to bias the results along with halo effects when single sources of variance are used to evaluate both leadership and outcomes. Self-ratings seem

unlikely to indicate what leaders do, according to their subordinates. Moreover, many contingencies can be cited as moderators of the relationships. Also, a variety of expanded and alternative factor structures are available for a more detailed study of leadership behavior with the LBDQ-XII.

Causal analyses by cross-lagged surveys and experimentation suggest that consideration both increases the satisfaction of subordinates and is increased by it. The initiation of structure by the leader (if structure is low) improves the subordinates' performance, which, in turn, increases the leader's subsequent consideration and reduces the leader's initiation of structure.

Several components that are variously involved in the different versions of scales that measure the leader's initiation of structure must be taken into account for a full appreciation of their antecedents and their effects on the subordinates' performance. The elements of role- and task clarification are likely to have positive effects on satisfaction and productivity; the autocratic elements in the earlier LBDQs may have negative effects, especially on satisfaction. Consideration, likewise, may contribute differently in different situations to satisfaction and effectiveness as a consequence of its several components, including participatory and consultative decision making and the concern for the welfare of subordinates.

The discrepancy between empirical correlations and conceptual discriminations—the mixture of conceptually distinct items of behavior that the same leaders tend to exhibit—requires looking at more of the LBDQ scales than just initiation and consideration in any single study to understand what is happening. In different settings, different elements moderate the effect of initiation and consideration in their impact on productivity and satisfaction. Beyond this, since the scales of LBDQ-XII are differentially related to different dimensions of the satisfaction of members and the performance of the group, in the interest of uncovering some heretofore hidden complexities of the behavior and influence of leaders, it would seem desirable to explore the possibilities of a multifactor approach, rather than to rest content with a two-factor solution. At the same time, as shall be shown in the next chapter, such a multifactor approach must have room for a general leadership activity factor.

Laissez-faire Leadership versus Motivation to Manage

Few elected or appointed leaders continuously abdicate their responsibilities. Although this laissez-faire style is the least frequently observed by colleagues and subordinates (Bass & Avolio, 1989), many still reveal it in varying amounts. As presidents, Ronald Reagan was one of the highest and Lyndon Johnson one of the lowest in respect to laissez-faire leadership. At the same time, Jimmy Carter displayed such leadership only for some issues. Johnson and Carter immersed themselves in the details of what their administrations had to do. Yet, although Carter ordinarily was involved in great detail, particularly in the creation of his programs, he was much less active in implementing voluntary wage and price guidelines, a macroeconomic strategy that a president can initiate by himself. Carter's absence of much leadership in this regard contrasted with Johnson's, for Johnson was much more willing than was Carter to use his presidential powers of persuasion and bargaining on business and labor. Carter was more restricted in his efforts. Johnson would have earned a low rating for laissez-faire leadership on this issue, whereas Carter would have earned a higher one. At the same time, for most issues, Ronald Reagan, as president, was much more laisssez-faire in style than was Carter or Johnson. His subordinates had free rein to proceed as they thought best. The many scandals that surfaced during and after his administration could be attributed in part to his "hands-off" style with poor choices for subordinates.

Relations among Leadership Styles

The generally positive correlations between factorially and conceptually distinct styles of leadership have already been noted in the preceding chapters. That is,

.leaders who score high in direction, task orientation, and initiation of structure also tend to score high in participation, relations orientation, and consideration. Thus, for 112 managers, Jones, James, and Bruni (1975) found that the leaders' supportiveness correlated .64 with the emphasis on goals and .74 with the facilitation of work. Likewise, the facilitation of interaction correlated .58 with the emphasis on goals and .70 with the facilitation of work. Schriesheim, House, and Kerr (1976) found a median correlation for 10 studies of .52 between the initiation of structure and consideration on the Leader Behavior Description Questionnaire—Form XII. Farrow, Valenzi, and Bass (1980) reported that the frequency of the leaders' *direction*, as seen by their over 1,200 subordinates, correlated .26 with consultation and .13 with *participation*.[1]

Errors of leniency and halo may be involved. Even so, there is a tendency to describe leaders as being more active or less active on several conceptually distinct dimensions concurrently. This tendency may be due to the real behavior of leaders, as well as to subordinates' perceptual biases.

Active managers take the major responsibility for decision making when they are directive and consultative, whereas inactive managers take little or no responsibility as laissez-faire leaders. Laissez-faire leadership correlates about $-.3$ to $-.6$ with various more active leadership styles (Bass & Avolio, 1988).

Active versus Passive Leadership

Active or passive leadership was one of the two dimensions on which Barber (1985) described U.S. presidents.

---

[1]As defined in Chapters 22 and 23, *direction* (italicized) refers only to giving orders with or without explanation. Direction (romanized) includes ordering, persuading, and manipulating. *Participation* (italicized)

Theodore Roosevelt was a continuing bundle of energetic activity; Calvin Coolidge slept 11 hours a day.

Some investigators have studied laissez-faire leadership attitudes and behavior, defining matters in terms of the passivity of leaders; others have examined the motivation and success in becoming active as a leader or manager. Although activity and passivity are two sides of the same coin and the conclusions about them are similar, the theories, models, and methods of the two types of leadership behavior have been considerably different. Bradford and Lippitt (1945) saw laissez-faire leadership as being descriptive of leaders who avoid attempting to influence their subordinates and who shirk their supervisory duties. Such leaders have no confidence in their ability to supervise. They bury themselves in paperwork, stay away from subordinates. They may condone "license." They leave too much responsibility with subordinates, set no clear goals, and do not help their group to make decisions. They tend to let things drift. To some degree, the perceived activity or passivity of the leaders may be affected by the needs of the subordinates. For instance, Niebuhr, Bedeian, and Armenakis (1980) found that among 202 nursing personnel at a Veterans Administration hospital, those who were motivated toward self-goals of achievement, power, and independence perceived their leaders to be less active. Those with strong other-directed goals, such as the need for affiliation, saw their leaders as more active.

Laissez-faire leadership should not be confused with democratic, relations-oriented, participative, or considerate leadership behavior. Nor should it be confused with delegation or management by exception. Delegation implies the leader's active direction of a subordinate to take responsibility for some role or task. The active delegative leader remains concerned and will follow up to see if the role has been enacted or the task has been successfully completed.[2] The leader who practices management by exception allows the subordinate to continue on paths that the subordinate and the leader agreed on until problems arise or standards are not met, at which time the leader intervenes to make corrections. More active leaders monitor their subordinates' performance, searching for discrepancies from accepted standards; more passive leaders wait for the discrepancies to be called to their attention (Hater & Bass, 1988).[3]

The second and opposite approach, which has been studied extensively by McClelland (1975) and Miner (1965), deals with the active end of the spectrum. As was detailed in Chapter 9, McClelland found successful leadership to be undergirded by the need for power and the absence of need for affiliation, coupled with the ability to suppress the need for power. Miner proposed that managers are likely to be more successful to the degree that they are motivated to engage in six prescribed managerial roles: (1) maintaining good relations with superiors, (2) competing for advancement and recognition, (3) being an active and assertive father figure (even if they are women managers), (4) exercising power over subordinates by the appropriate use of positive and negative sanctions, (5) being visibly different from subordinates, and (6) accepting responsibility for administrative details.

Laissez-faire Leadership

Research Beginnings

Democratic and authoritarian leadership[4] was compared with laissez-faire leadership by adults who were instructed how to lead boys' clubs (Lewin, Lippitt, & White, 1939; Lippitt, 1940a). Laissez-faire leaders gave group members complete freedom of action, provided them with materials, refrained from participating except to answer questions when asked, and did not make evaluative remarks. This behavior was in contrast to that of autocratic leaders, who displayed a much greater frequency of order giving, disrupting commands, praise and approval, and nonconstructive criticism. It also contrasted with the behavior of democratic leaders, who gave suggestions and stimulated subordinates to guide themselves. Under laissez-faire conditions, the groups were less well organized, less efficient, and less satisfying to members than under democratic conditions. The work was of poorer quality and less work was done, and, there was more play, frustra-

---

refers only to sharing in the decision process. Participation (romanized) includes consulting, sharing, and delegating.
[2]See Chapter 22.

[3]See Chapter 17.
[4]See Chapter 21.

tion, disorganization, discouragement, and aggression under laissez-faire than under democratic leadership. When groups of boys were required to carry out various projects under a high degree of laissez-faire leadership, they felt a lack of organization to get things done and did not know where they stood. When an autocratic leader was followed by a laissez-faire leader, the group exhibited an initial outburst of aggressive, uncontrolled behavior. This form of behavior subsided during the second and third meetings. Similar outbursts were not observed after the transition from laissez-faire to other forms of leadership. Although it did not stimulate as much aggression as did the autocratic condition, laissez-faire leadership was disliked because it was accompanied by less sense of accomplishment, less clarity about what to do, and less sense of group unity. The investigators (Lippitt & White, 1943; White & Lippitt, 1960) concluded that laissez-faire leadership resulted in less concentration on work and a poorer quality of work than did democratic and autocratic leadership. There was less general satisfaction than from the democratic style, but still somewhat more satisfaction than from the autocratic style that was employed in their study.

Follow-up Studies

Subsequent research suggested that the satisfaction of followers will be lower under laissez-faire leadership than under autocratic leadership if the latter is nonpunitive, appropriate for the followers' levels of competence, or in keeping with the requirements of the situation. Most often, laissez-faire leadership has been consistently found to be the least satisfying and effective management style. The original observations of Lewin, Lippitt, and White have been supported in a variety of survey and experimental investigations of the impact of laissez-faire leadership on subordinates' performance.

Low Productivity. In a study of railroad-section groups, Katz, Maccoby, Gurin, and Floor (1951) found that the groups were unproductive if their supervisors avoided exercising the leadership role and relinquished it to members of the work group. These supervisors also did not differentiate their role from the role of worker. Like their subordinates, they engaged in pro-

duction work rather than spend their time in supervisory functions. Berrien (1961) studied groups that differed in their adaptation to changes in work. Poorly adapted groups felt little pressure from their superiors and appeared to attribute their poor performance to lax discipline. In the same way, Murnighan and Leung's (1976) experiment found that undergraduate participants who were led by uninvolved leaders were less productive in the quality and quantity of the problems they solved and lower in satisfaction in comparison to participants who were led by involved leaders. Argyris (1954) conducted a case study in a bank in which the management recruited supervisors who were interested in security and predictability, disliked hostility and aggression, and wanted to be left alone. The bank's recruitment policy fostered in employees a norm of low work standards and unexpressed dissatisfaction.

Unproductive Attitudes and Behavior. Pelz (1956) reported that the laissez-faire pattern of leadership was negatively related to productivity in a research organization. Similarly, Farris (1972) demonstrated that the less innovative of 21 scientific groups at the National Aeronautics and Space Administration had less peer and managerial leadership. In addition, the leadership of these groups was less task- or relations-oriented and less consultative or participative.

Baumgartel (1957) studied directive, laissez-faire, and participative patterns of leadership behavior. Group members under laissez-faire leadership reported more isolation from the leader and less participation in decision making than did those under directive leadership. The results suggested that laissez-faire leadership contributed to low cohesiveness of the group. Kidd and Christy (1961) studied three patterns of behavior: laissez-faire, active monitoring, and participative leadership. They found that although the speed of processing work was greatest under laissez-faire leadership, there was much less avoidance of errors, particularly in comparison to active-monitoring leadership. Aspegren (1963) compared laissez-faire, directive, and participative patterns of leadership and showed that laissez-faire leadership was associated with lower task motivation and lower satisfaction with superiors. Similarly, W. S. MacDonald's (1967a, 1967b) study of three styles of leadership (laissez-faire, dominant, and democratic) in the Job Corps found that laissez-faire leadership was associated with the highest rates of truancy and delinquency and with the slowest modifications in performance. Wehman, Goldstein, and Williams (1977) reported results from an experiment in which four leadership styles were varied to study their effects on 80 undergraduates' individual risk-taking behavior in group settings and the shift in risk-taking behavior when the responsibility for making decisions moved from the individuals to groups. They found that the shift in such behavior was more likely to occur in laissez-faire-led groups and no-designated-leader groups than in groups led by a democratic or autocratic leader.

Absence of Leaders. In Arensberg and McGregor's (1942) case study of an engineering department without supervisors, a management committee approved the department's plans and checked its progress. The management considered this arrangement to be ideal for creative work. The employees, however, felt insecure and constrained in this overly permissive environment. Boss (1978) studied seven top-level administrative staffs from selected public agencies who engaged in a confrontation team-building program for six days. The only group that showed growth, according to subjective pre–post measures was the group in which the chief executive officer (CEO) was present. The other six groups, in which no CEO was present, either retrogressed or did not change. This finding was consistent with the failures reported in organizational development efforts elsewhere, which were attributable to the lack of support from the CEO (Boss & McConkie, 1976) or the inability of the CEO to understand the objectives and processes of organizational development (Derr, 1972).

When the Therapist Is Not a Leader. Therapeutic and sensitivity training groups are a different matter. Fried (1977) observed that a consultant's "abstinence" from the leadership of a group of mental health workers on a psychiatric hospital ward was therapeutic in its promotion of transference. Such transference also occurs from the role taken by the sensitivity trainer who, by abstaining from providing structure and direction for the group, creates a social vacuum that permits

the group to learn, develop, and structure itself and allows individual members to mature.

Measuring Laissez-faire Leadership and Its Effects

The Multifactor Leadership Questionnaire (MLQ-Form 5) (Bass, 1985c) contains a ten-item scale that directly assesses laissez-faire leadership. The items on the laissez-faire scale were as follows: "only tells me what I have to know to do my job"; "does not seem to care about results"; "avoids making decisions"; "stays out of our way"; "if we don't bother him/her, he/she doesn't bother us"; "does not make a difference to our group's performance"; "is likely to be absent when needed"; "is hard to find when a crisis arises"; "whatever we do is OK with him/her"; and "we don't know where he/she stands on issues."

Respondents indicate how frequently their superior displays each item, with anchors of 0 to 4 in which 0 means "never" and 4 means "frequently, if not always." The scale total correlated .88 with a higher-order factor of passive leadership and $-.11$ with a higher-order factor of active leadership.

Laissez-faire leadership does not seem to be the exact opposite of active leadership. Nonetheless, correlations of laissez-faire leadership were strongly negative for 1,006 respondents' descriptions of their leaders on scales of transformational leadership, as follows: charisma, $-.56$; individualized consideration, $-.55$; intellectual stimulation, $-.47$; and inspirational leadership, $-.49$. Correlations with transactional leadership were .25 with management by exception[5] and $-.28$, with contingent reward.

The expected negative correlations of laissez-faire leadership with the effectiveness of outcomes and subordinates' satisfaction with the leadership generalized across different kinds of leaders, different kinds of situations, and for outcomes with both soft and hard data. Thus, correlations, of $-.49$, $-.39$, $-.34$, $-.29$, $-.45$, $-.41$, $-.60$, and $-.57$, respectively, were reported by

---

[5]Yammarino and Bass (1989) found that the correlations with laissez-faire leadership are negative when the manager actively searches for exceptions and are positive when the manager gets involved only when exceptions are called to his or her attention. Overall management by exception correlated .44 with passive leadership and .16 with active leadership (Bass, 1985a).

their subordinates for 49 division heads, 58 production managers, 75 project leaders, 28 religious ministers, 9 vice presidents, 38 mid-level managers, 186 junior naval officers, and 318 senior naval officers between the laissez-faire leadership of their leaders and the leaders' contribution to the effectiveness of their organizations (Bass & Avolio, 1989).

Comparable negative correlations were found between laissez-faire leadership and superiors' appraisals of the performance and promotability of business managers (Hater & Bass, 1988) and naval officers (Yammarino & Bass, 1989), and with financial outcomes of simulated businesses (Avolio, Waldman, & Einstein, 1988).

Absence of Performance- and Maintenance-oriented Leadership

Misumi (1985) provided a great deal of indirect evidence that the leader's active concern for the subordinates' performance or for the maintainance of relations was consistently better for organizational outcomes than was the *combined* lack of (p)erformance-oriented or (m)aintenance-oriented leadership—pm leadership. For example, he reported that the annual accident rate per hundred for a three-year period of Nishitetsu bus drivers was 79.1 if the bus drivers were supervised by pm dispatchers, who were below the median in performance (P) orientation and maintenance (M) orientation, while it was 44 to 52 per 100 if the dispatchers were above the median on either P, M, or PM (both P and M). Similarly, Misumi found that the job satisfaction of 2,257 employees in 186 Mitsubishi work groups was above average in 28 percent of the pm-led groups but above average in 37–73 percent of the P, M, or PM-led groups. A similar pattern emerged for the employees' satisfaction with the company.

Furthermore, the adequacy of communication was 14.7 under pm leadership and 16.0 to 17.5 under P, M, and PM leadership, respectively. The rated performance was high in only 3 of 92 squads in a bearing manufacturing firm led by pm supervision but it was high in 10, 11, and 16 of the equal total numbers of P, M, and PM-led squads. Similar results with regard to productivity were obtained in surveys in other industrial companies (coal mining, shipbuilding, tire manufacturing, and automobile manufacturing). These surveys

also found that, regardless of the industry, pm leadership ranked last in relation to the productivity of groups, in comparison to P, M, and PM leadership. Only 6 percent of 883 pm engineering project managers were found successful, in contrast to 16, 25, and 52 percent of M, P, and PM project managers, respectively. Among 967 governmental employees, the measures of morale were uniformly lowest under the pm leadership of section chiefs than under the P, M, and PM leadership of such chiefs. The same pattern held for the leadership of Japanese schoolteachers, according to their pupils, and to children's reports about the consequences of their parents' pm, in contrast to P, M, and PM, leadership for the children's understanding, compliance, pride, intimacy, and respect.

Misumi (1985, pp. 251–259) also reported the results of a Japanese experiment in which for groups that were high in the motivation to achieve, the highest productivity occurred with PM supervisors. When the motivation to achieve was low, P-type leadership alone generated the most productivity. But regardless of the group's motivation to achieve, productivity was lowest with pm supervisors.

Ronald Reagan's Effects

Given the negative impact of laissez-faire leadership, how does one explain the effects of President Ronald Reagan's generally laissez-faire leadership style, which was based on his stated belief that he was properly delegating when he sat back and let his subordinates proceed as they thought best. Reagan was able to leave office in 1988 with one of the highest popularity ratings (64–68 percent) of any U.S. president in a public opinion poll. One explanation may be his choice of subordinates. If his subordinates, such as David Stockman, were highly competent, then great achievements were possible. If he had sleazy or incompetent subordinates like Edwin Meese, then the results were disastrous. The disaster was compounded when the subordinate cabinet officer, such as Samuel Pierce of the Housing and Urban Development Department, was an extremely laissez-faire executive himself (Waldman, Cohn, & Thomas, 1989). The astute management of the news helped make it possible to credit Reagan with the successes of his subordinates and to distance him from their failures. He remained the "Teflon president" immune to the many scandals that marred his administration. Furthermore, although Reagan exemplified the laissez-faire leader in much of his behavior, he also was a mass of contradictions in his orientation and style. He was described as the "least informed of the presidents I have known," by former Speaker of the House Tip O'Neill, yet he was highly charismatic. He derided the plight of the disadvantaged as a group, yet often exhibited compassion for an unfortunate individual.

Although it is obviously impossible to evaluate Reagan's overall success and effectiveness as a president at the time of this writing, from this vantage point, his presidency appears to have been a highly mixed bag. Popular tax reform was matched with a mounting gap in the distribution of income between the rich and the poor. Diplomatic victories were matched by the transformation of the United States from the largest creditor nation to the largest debtor nation. The perceptions of Reagan's building of U.S. military strength and power were matched by the country's relative economic decline in competition with Japan and Western Europe. Although his administration exerted leadership in developing improved relations with and solutions to problems in Canada, Angola, and the Middle East, it often followed, rather than led the way to, improved outcomes in the Philippines, Latin America, and the Soviet Union for which it was quick to take credit. An arch-proponent of a balanced budget, Reagan nevertheless instituted policies that resulted in a budget deficit that was larger than the deficits created by all his predecessors combined. The good feelings that the American majority had for him when he left office were coupled with the worsening problems of land despoilation, drugs, child care, and care of the elderly, homelessness, health costs and insurance, education, acid rain, bankruptcies of savings banks, and nuclear waste. Many of these problems were left to be addressed seriously by his successors. To conclude, Ronald Reagan's laissez-faire style did not seem to hurt his overall popularity, but it, no doubt, resulted in considerable ineffectiveness, especially when he had to depend on irresponsible, incompetent, or laissez-faire subordinates and when he made statements or deals without appropriate consultation with more knowledgeable colleagues.

Subordinates' Autonomy and Laissez-faire Leadership

Subordinates' favor autonomy. Laissez-faire leadership provides it but is dissatisfying to subordinates. Is there a contradiction?

Freedom is a mixed blessing. If it means anarchy; the absence of control of oneself or others; the absence of needed organizational sanctions; the concentration of organizational control at the bottom so that individual goals take precedence over organizational goals; and an internally unregulated, leaderless, competitive marketplace for resources in which each member is trying to maximize his or her own self-interests, it is likely to generate organizational ineffectiveness (Miner, 1973; Price, 1968; Tannenbaum, 1968).

If freedom implies the lack of systematic processes in problem solving, it also will result in ineffectiveness of outcomes. Thus, when Maier and Maier (1957) experimented with discussions under free and more systematic styles of leadership, they found that free discussion produced decisions of lower quality than did systematic, controlled, step-by-step discussion. They also noted that freer approaches to problem solving were less effective and less satisfying and yielded less commitment from participants than did systematic problem solving. Thus, when Maier and Solem (1962) compared 50 free-discussion groups with 96 groups of 4 participants each who used problem solving in systematic steps, the quality of the solutions of the free-discussion groups was likely to be lower than that of the systematic groups. Only 12 percent of the free-discussion groups created integrated solutions that met the criteria of success, whereas almost half the systematic groups did so. Maier and Thurber (1969) reported similar results.

Nonetheless, evidence can be mustered to support the contention that employees who feel a great deal of freedom to do their work as they like tend to be more satisfied and productive. March (1955) analyzed patterns of interpersonal control in 15 primitive communities and found that productivity was related to the degree of the groups' autonomy. In A. K. Rice's (1953) study of a weaving shed in India, a type of reorganization that gave workers greater autonomy resulted in increased efficiency and decreased damage.

When Morse and Reimer (1956) arranged for the authority of operative employees in two departments to be increased to strengthen the employees' autonomy, they found that both satisfaction and productivity increased. O'Connell (1968) changed the responsibilities and behavioral patterns of first-level supervisors in an insurance company. Even though the supervisors became bogged down in paperwork to a greater extent than was expected, sales improved and insurance lapse rates declined to some degree.

Meltzer (1956) reported that scientists are most productive when they have freedom to control their research activities. Pelz and Andrews (1966a, 1966b) studied scientists and engineers in several laboratories. They found that the most effective scientists were self-directed and valued freedom, but that these scientists still welcomed coordination and guidance from other members of the organization. Similar results were reported by Weschler, Kahane, and Tannenbaum (1952) and by Tannenbaum, Weschler, and Massarik (1961) for two divisions of a research laboratory.

Indik (1965b) studied 96 organizations of three types and found that the workers' freedom to set their own pace of work was associated with productivity and satisfaction with their jobs. Trow (1957) reported that experimental groups with high degrees of autonomy provided greater satisfaction to members than did those in which members were dependent on a centralized group structure.

There Is No Contradiction. Laissez-faire leadership does not necessarily imply *effective* autonomy for subordinates. How does one reconcile the two sets of findings that (1) laissez-faire leadership is detrimental to the performance of subordinates and (2) the autonomy of subordinates enhances the subordinates' performance? The answer lies in what the subordinates need to do their job well. If the subordinates are skilled, professional, or self-starting salespeople, they may need consultation, *participation*, or delegation, with the *directive* boundary conditions specified by the leader, the

organization, or even the task itself. Within these boundaries, the leader should permit the already competent and motivated subordinates to complete their work in the manner they think best. This kind of leadership paradoxically requires that the leader exercise authority to permit such freedom of action (Bass, 1960). Active follow-up by the leader is also important because it provides evidence that the subordinates' performance is as expected and shows the subordinates that the leader cares about what they are doing. This type of leadership is not related in any way to laissez-faire leadership, in which the leader does nothing unless asked by colleagues and even then may procrastinate or fail to respond. The laissez-faire leader is inactive, rather than reactive or proactive. He or she does not provide clear boundary conditions; may work alongside subordinates or withdraw into paperwork; and avoids, rather than shares, decision making. Under this type of leadership, the subordinates do not feel free to carry out their jobs as they see fit; instead, they feel uncertain about their own authority, responsibilities, and duties.

Supporting this distinction between working under laissez-faire leadership and being provided with freedom are the results reported by Farris (1972). In a study of 21 research teams, Farris found that the provision of freedom to subordinates was highly related to innovation when the superiors preceded their decision making with consultation with their subordinates. But, when supervisors made little use of consultation beforehand, their provision of freedom was uncorrelated with innovation by their subordinates.

Further indirect support comes from a review of leaderless groups by Desmond and Seligman (1977). In the 28 studies that were reviewed, those groups with more intelligent participants obtained positive results and were likely to be more highly structured by specially prepared audiotapes, preprinted instruction, and instrumented feedback of group opinion, which substituted for the missing leaders. That is, the freedom of the leaderless group could result in productivity if the participants had the competence and information to deal with the situation and obtained the necessary instructions to clarify the boundary conditions within which they could carry on.

What about Delegation, Management by Exception, and Participation? The contrary consequences for the effectiveness of subordinates of the subordinates' freedom and autonomy, on the one hand, and the ineffectiveness of laissez-faire leadership, on the other hand, reside, to some extent, in the confusion of the laissez-faire leadership with the practices of delegation, management by exception, and participative leadership. As has already been shown, although delegation and management by exception are not as satisfying and effective as are more active leadership styles, they nevertheless may contribute to the effectiveness of subordinates and the organization.

The laissez-faire leader does not delineate the problem that needs to be solved or the requirements that must be met, as does the leader who delegates. The laissez-faire leader does not search for deviations from standards or intervene when they are found, as does a leader who practices management by exception. The laissez-faire leader does not engage in extended discussions with subordinates to achieve a consensual decision, as does the participative leader.

The inactivity of the laissez-faire leader—his or her unwillingness to accept responsibility, give directions, provide support, and so on—has been consistently negatively related to productivity, satisfaction, and cohesiveness. Sheer energization, drive, motivation to succeed, and activity are likely to be correlated with successful leadership and influence.[6] A further examination of the qualities that are important to active leaders, in contrast to laissez-faire leaders, is seen in much of McClelland's Leadership Motive Pattern and in Miner's "motivation to manage."

Motivation to Lead and to Manage

Jongbloed and Frost (1985) attributed the differential budgetary growth and success of two Canadian hospital laboratories to the motivation and activity of the directors. The desire of the director of the more successful laboratory "to achieve international recognition for outstanding research was apparent in the energy he devoted to lobbying hospital administrators and Minis-

try of Health officials" (p. 102). The other laboratory director was not similarly motivated and did not engage in lobbying.

Effects on Followers of Active Leadership

Consonant with the conclusions of Chapter 6, more activity by leaders, regardless of the style, is usually associated with the greater satisfaction and effectiveness of their followers. Conversely, more often than not, less activity in any of these active styles is negatively related to the performance and satisfaction of the followers. Thus, for instance, the structuring of expectations contributes positively to the productivity, cohesiveness, and satisfaction of the group. This pattern of behavior is the central factor in leadership when leadership is defined as the initiation and maintenance of structure in expectation and interaction. The leader can accomplish these initiatives through *direction* or *participation*, inspiration or consultation, negotiation or delegation. Whatever the style, it must involve the leader taking action. It is doubtful that leaders in most situations can be of positive value to the group's performance, satisfaction, and cohesiveness without this kind of active structuring unless all such structure has already been provided by other means.

Being active in one style or another or both combined was better than being inactive in both styles. When data collected by Farrow, Valenzi, and Bass (1980) from 1,300 subordinates and their 340 managers describing the pooled frequency of the direction and consultation of the managers were correlated with the effectiveness of the groups, as seen by both the managers and the subordinates, the correlation with effectiveness (.41) was higher than that obtained for direction (.28) or consultation (.37) alone. Even more extreme, the combined direction-consultation index correlated .61 with satisfaction, but consultation alone correlated .52. Bass, Valenzi, Farrow, and Solomon (1975) found overall correlations ranging from .3 to .6 between the behavior of leaders, as seen by their subordinates, and the judged effectiveness of the leaders' work units, regardless of whether the leaders were directive or participative. When *direction*, consultation, *participation*, and delegation were combined, their composite correlated

[6]See Chapter 6.

.36 and .61 with effectiveness and satisfaction, respectively. Similarly, R. Likert's System 4 combined participative management with "high performance, no-nonsense goals, orderly systematic goal setting processes and rigorous assessment of progress in achieving those goals" (R. Likert & J. Likert, 1976). Path analyses reported by R. Likert (1973) demonstrated that managerial leadership, whether task- or relations oriented, contributed both directly and indirectly to the subordinates' satisfaction and productive efficiency. For large samples, the direct correlations between total leadership, subordinates' satisfaction, and total productive efficiency were .49 and .42, respectively. In addition, total managerial leadership correlated .42 with a good organizational climate, .23 with peer leadership, and .27 with a good group process. The latter, in turn, correlated between .25 and .67 with subordinates' satisfaction and total productive efficiency.

Stogdill (1974) reviewed an array of surveys and experiments, mostly containing concurrent analyses of leadership behavior and outcomes, more often than not in temporary, short-term groups and without reference to possible contingent conditions. He concluded that *both* the democratic leadership cluster (participation, relations orientation, and consideration) and the work-related cluster (direction, task orientation, structuring but not autocratic) were more likely to be positively than negatively related to the productivity, satisfaction, and cohesiveness of the group. Participative leadership behavior, as well as leadership behavior that structured followers' expectations, was consistently related to the group's cohesiveness.

As was seen in Chapter 23, Blake and Mouton (1964) argued that 9,9 leadership, which is concerned both with production and with people, is optimal. As was noted earlier, Hall and Donnell (1979) confirmed this contention by showing that the 190 out of 1,878 managers who were the fastest in their career advancement were likely to be high in both task orientation and relations orientation, according to their subordinates. And the slowest advancing 445 managers were clearly 1,1, laissez-faire in style, that is, low in both task orientation and relationship orientation. In an experiment with 80 undergraduates, Medcof and Evans (1986) demonstrated that plodders are the least desirable leaders in business—a finding that agreed with Blake and Mou-

ton's argument. Again, as was noted earlier in this chapter, Misumi (1985) reported PM leadership combining both performance and maintenance orientation was most efficacious in a wide variety of settings compared to P, M, or pm leadership.

Fleishman and Simmons (1970) concluded that leadership that combines high consideration and initiation of structure is most likely to optimize a number of criteria of effectiveness for a variety of supervisory jobs. In agreement, Karmel (1978) concluded that the combination of initiation and consideration—the total activity of leaders in contrast to their inactivity—may be the most important dimensions to investigate. A powerful general factor can be produced if one so decides by the selection of appropriate factor-analytical routines. It may be that pooling a diversity of decision-making styles for a new measure of generalized leadership activity will be useful.

Caveat. There are some obvious examples of instances in which a group may do better with a less active leader. Leadership activity, as such, does not always guarantee the performance, satisfaction, and cohesion of a group. Highly active but coercive, monopolistic, autocratic leadership will contribute more to a group's dissatisfaction and lack of cohesiveness than to a group's productivity. The qualities of the leadership activity must be taken into account. For the leader, doing something is usually, but not always, better than doing nothing. A calm, steady hand at the tiller may be required rather than an impulsive change of course. Moreover, as was noted in Chapter 24, activity in two styles may add little more than activity in one style alone.[7]

Not all activity in interpersonal and organizational settings is conducive to successful leadership, nor is successful leadership associated with the generation of any and all activity in oneself and others. For instance, as was noted in Chapter 9, McClelland's (1985) Leadership Motive Pattern (LMP) includes the tendency of individuals to tell stories on the Thematic Apperception Test (TAT) about inhibiting activity. The more relevant question is whether activity will be influential and whether it will necessarily result in the increased

[7]See Larson, Hunt, and Osborn (1976); Nystrom (1978); and Schriesheim (1982).

performance, satisfaction, and cohesiveness of a group. The answer to this question appears to depend on whether the work-related leadership behavior is autocratic, directive, task oriented, or structuring and whether the person-related leadership behavior is democratic, participative, relations oriented, or considerate. These determinants are in addition to the contingencies that also may have to be taken into account. The activist admonition to "lead, follow, or get out of the way" has to be qualified by adding "with forethought, responsibility, and care." The pressure for action may need to be inhibited.

McClelland's (1975) Leadership Motive Pattern (LMP) is high for individuals who score high on the projective Thematic Apperception Test (TAT) in their need for power but who score low in their need for affiliation and, as was just noted, who exhibit impulse control in their projected inhibition of the expression of power. (They are actually less active than they really are driven to be.) A high LMP index was seen to forecast success in management. Thus, McClelland and Burnham (1976) scored the TAT responses of managers' needs for power, achievement, and affiliation. They found that successful managers—managers whose subordinates were higher in morale and productivity—wrote TAT stories with need for power scores that were above average and with need for achievement scores that were higher than their need for affiliation scores and that their stories contained at least moderate levels of activity inhibition. Again, in a follow-up study of 237 A T & T managers, McClelland and Boyatzis (1982) found that although the high need for achievement predicted the success of lower-level managers, the moderate-to-high need for power, the low need for affiliation, and high scores in activity inhibition—the LMP—predicted the success of most other managers. Progress over 16 years at A T & T correlated an estimated .33 with LMP (McClelland, 1980).

Managerial Role Motivation in Hierarchical Organizations

According to Miner (1965), people differ in their motivation to carry out the roles required of a manager and their success in doing so. Using another projective approach—the Miner Sentence Completion Scale (MSCS), a sentence-completion test—in which examinees, without awareness, project their desires by completing incomplete sentences such as, "Giving orders . . . ," "Athletic contests . . . ," or "My father . . . ," Miner (1965) originated a theory of managerial role motivation, built on role theory, psychoanalytic theory, and the empirical results of Kahn (1956b) and Fleishman, Harris, and Burtt (1955). His theory was directed specifically toward role-taking propensities within the ideal large organization, formalized and rationalized to function bureaucratically. Miner argued that people who "repeatedly associate positive rather than negative emotion" with various managerial role prescriptions are more likely to meet the existing requirements for effectiveness.

Roles and Requisite Motivation. The six managerial role prescriptions presented by Miner, along with the required motivation for success as a manager, were as follows:

1. Managers must behave in ways that do not provoke negative reactions from their superiors. To represent their group upward in the organization and to obtain support for their actions, managers should maintain good relationships with those above them. A generally positive attitude toward those holding positions of authority is required.

2. Since a strong competitive element is built into managerial work, managers must compete for the available rewards, both for themselves and for their groups. If they do not, they may lose ground as functions are relegated to lower their status. Without a willingness to compete, promotion is improbable. To meet this role requirement, managers should be favorably disposed toward engaging in competition.

3. There is a parallel between managerial role requirements and the assertiveness that is traditionally demanded of the masculine role. Both a manager and a father are supposed to take charge, to make decisions, to take such disciplinary action as may be necessary, and to protect others. Even women managers will be expected to follow the essentially masculine pattern of behavior as traditionally defined.[8] A desire to meet the requirements of assertive masculinity will generally

[8]More about this in Chapter 32.

lead to success in meeting certain role prescriptions of the managerial job.

4. Managers must exercise power over subordinates and direct their behavior in a manner that is consistent with organizational and personal objectives. Managers must tell others what to do, when necessary, and enforce their words through the appropriate use of positive and negative sanctions. The person who finds such directive behavior difficult and emotionally disturbing will have difficulty meeting this managerial role prescription.

5. Managers must stand out from their groups and assume positions of high visibility. They cannot use the actions of their subordinates as a guide for their own behavior as managers. Rather, they must deviate from their immediate groups and do things that will inevitably invite attention, discussion, and perhaps criticism from those who report to them. When the idea of standing out from the group, of behaving in a different manner, and of being highly visible elicits feelings of unpleasantness, then behavior appropriate to the role will occur less often than is needed.

6. Managers must "get the work out" and keep on top of routine demands. Administrative requirements of this kind are found in all managerial work, although the specific activities will vary somewhat from one situation to another. To meet these prescriptions, a manager must at least be willing to deal with routines and ideally gain some satisfaction from doing so.

Contradictions. As can be seen, Miner did not mince words. He argued that in a typical bureaucratic hierarchy, what is needed for leadership is an authority-accepting, upward-oriented, competitive, assertive, masculine, power-wielding, tough-minded person who will attend to details. In preparing his role prescriptions, he was selective about which facts about leadership he incorporated and which facts he ignored. A positive attitude toward authority may characterize authoritarian-submissive behavior.[9] An organization of submissive managers would not seem to promise innovation and effectiveness.

Competitive behavior presents many problems for an organization. Managers who are in competition with their peers hide necessary information from each

other and fail to consider the goals of subordinates, attainment of which is important to all concerned. Competition means that managers negotiate with their peers instead of solving problems with them. Decisions are based on power, rather than on merit—again, a consequence that is not calculated to add to organizational effectiveness.

It is true that visibility may help one's own advancement. However, the concern for such visibility may conflict with good team support from subordinates who may feel exploited.

The stern father image and the willingness and need to use sanctions seem to contradict most of the evidence about the costs of coercion and autocratic leadership behavior. If attention to details means the inclusion of sanctions, this prescription can easily be overdone if the manager fails to have a sense of priorities.

Despite these contradictions, considerable support for Miner's theory has been amassed for predicting the success of managers in a hierarchical organization. But, as shall be seen, the contradictions are stronger, in a professional organization of colleagues in which innovation and creativity are priorities, and where cooperation, open communication, expert power, and helping relationships are paramount. For the professional type of organization, Miner laid out a different set of role prescriptions for leadership, accompanied by a different sentence-completion test (MSCS—Form P) than the one created for assessing managers in a hierarchical bureaucracy (MSCS—Form H).

Measuring the Motivation to Manage in Hierarchical Organizations

MSCS—Form H was used to measure managerial role motivation in bureaucratic organizations (Miner, 1965). It contains 40 items, 35 of which are scored. As was just mentioned, the scale is a projective measure in which examinees complete a list of incomplete sentences such as, "Sitting behind a desk, I . . . " A majority of the incomplete sentences refer to situations that are either outside the work environment or are not specifically related to the managerial job. Ordinarily, examinees are unaware of what is being measured, so they are unlikely to distort their responses to present themselves

---

[9]See Chapter 8.

in a good light as managers. Subscales for the motivation to take each of the prescribed managerial roles can be obtained. For instance, completing the incomplete sentence; "When playing cards I . . ." with the response, "I always try to win" would contribute to one's score on the competitive games scale. The response, "I usually become bored" would do the reverse. Table 25.1 shows the subscales of the MSCS and the interpretation of positive responses to the incomplete sentences.

A multiple-choice version was developed by Steger, Kelley, Chouiniere, and Goldenbaum (1977), whose total score correlated .68, .38, .56, and .68 with the original MSCS—Form H in different samples. However, a considerable inflation of scores occurred when the multiple-choice format was used. Respondents did not choose the socially undesirable negative alternatives of the kind they ordinarily produce in response to the open-ended incomplete sentences of the original projective test (Miner, 1977b).

Concurrent Validities. Berman and Miner (1985) obtained results indicating that 75 chief executive and operating officers, executive vice presidents, and group vice presidents who had worked their way upward most successfully through a bureaucratic hierarchy earned significantly higher MSCS scores than did 65 lower-level managers of nearly the same age who had not risen as high in the hierarchy and 26 others, including the founder-entrepreneur and his relatives.

Earlier, Miner (1965) found that the higher the total scores on MSCS—Form H, the higher were the hierarchical level, the performance ratings, and the rated potentials of 81 to 100 managers of research and development (R & D) in a petrochemical firm. Furthermore, the total MSCS scores of 70 department store managers related significantly to the managers' grade levels and potential but not to their rated performance. Likewise, Gantz, Erickson, and Stephenson (1977a) reported that the total MSCS scores of 117 scientists and engineers in a government R & D laboratory related significantly to their peers' ratings of their supervisory potential. For 101 personnel and industrial managers, Miner and Miner (1977) reported a significant relation between total MSCS scores and a composite measure of their success, compensation, and positional level. Miner (1977) reported correlations of .20, .57, and .39, respectively, of MSCS with the performance ratings of 81 R & D managers, 61 oil company managers, and 81 administrators in a large school district. Similar correlations of MSCS scores with levels of position were

Table 25.1 Subscales of the Miner Sentence Completion Scale and Their Interpretation

Subscale of Incomplete Sentences About:	Interpretation of Positive Responses
Authority figures	A desire to meet managerial role requirements in terms of positive relationships with superiors.
Competitive games	A desire to engage in competition with peers in games or sports and thus to meet managerial role requirements in this regard.
Competitive situations	A desire to engage in competition with peers in occupational or work-related activities and thus to meet managerial role requirements in this regard.
Assertive role	A desire to behave in an active and assertive manner involving activities that are often viewed in this society as predominantly masculine and thus to meet managerial role requirements.
Imposing wishes	A desire to tell others what to do and to utilize sanctions in influencing others, thus indicating a capacity to fulfill managerial role requirements in relationships with subordinates.
Standing out from the group	A desire to assume a distinctive position of a unique and highly visible nature in a manner that is congruent with the role requirements of the managerial job.
Routine administrative functions	A desire to meet managerial role requirements regarding activities that are often associated with the day-to-day administrative duties of managerial work.

SOURCE: Miner and Smith (1982, p. 298).

found by Miner (1977a) for 142 personnel and industrial relation managers and for 395 managers from a
variety of firms.

With 82 school administrators in a large city, Miner
(1967) found total MSCS scores to relate significantly
with their compensation, rated performance, and potential but not with their hierarchical level. However,
hierarchical level in the organization was significantly
related to the total MSCS scores of 44 women department store managers (Miner, 1977a) and 50 and 37 textile managers, respectively (Southern, 1976). Two additional analyses reported by Miner (1982a) showed how
MSCS scores were higher for those who were at a
higher organizational level. The mean score for 22 personnel managers who were vice presidents was 5.7, but
it was only 2.4 for 79 personnel managers who were
below the vice presidential level. The mean was 6.8 for
49 CEOs, presidents and group vice presidents, while
it was 0.9 for 49 matched managers at lower levels.
Other concurrent significant differences that were in
line with expectations for the scores on MSCS—Form
H and the organizational level of managers were reported for hospital officers (Black, 1981).

With samples of students, Miner and Crane (1977)
obtained positive findings that related MSCS scores to
the promotion of 47 MBA students to management, to
the selection of a fraternity president among 40 candidates (Steger, Kelley, Chouiniere, & Goldenbaum,
1977), and to the choice among 190 for student offices.
Miner, Rizzo, Harlow, and Hill (1974/1977) also reported
positive findings for undergraduate students in a simulated bureaucratic organization. Finally, Miner and
Crane (1981) found a correlation of .48 between the
MSCS scores of 56 graduate students in management
and the students' tendencies to describe their present
and planned work as more managerial in nature.

Less consistently significant results were obtained
for scores on the subscales. The subscale score dealing
with motivation to enter competitive situations was
most often associated with the criteria for managerial
success. Less often associated with success were the
subscale scores for assertive motivation, the desire to
stand out, and the desire to perform routine administrative functions.

Predictive Validities. Total MSCS scores forecast
the rise in organizational level and subsequent per-

formance ratings of 49 to 81 R & D and marketing
managers in a petrochemical firm (Miner, 1965). Lacey
(1977) found that total MSCS scores were significantly
able to predict the promotion to management of 95 scientists and engineers. Lardent (1977) likewise showed
that the total MSCS scores of 251 candidates sucessfully
forecast graduation from the U.S. Army officer
candidate school at Fort Benning. Butler, Lardent, and
Miner (1983) were able to do the same for 502 West
Point cadets. But Bartol, Anderson, and Schneier
(1980) failed to find concurrent differences in motivation to manage among classes of sophomores, juniors,
and seniors in business schools, and Bartol and Martin
(1980) were unable to find significant changes in the
same MBA students in a longitudinal study in which
the 232 students were assessed with the multiple-
choice form of the MSCS at the beginning of their program and again after graduation. Moreover, unlike the
military findings, no relation was found between the
students' completion of the MBA program and their
MSCS scores, although Bartol and Martin did report
that the MSCS scores of 97 of the graduates were a
significant predictor of these persons' salaries after
graduation. Support for the construct validity of the
MSCS was also obtained in that Bartol and Martin
found correlatons with MSCS scores of .26 and .34 respectively, with the students' desired managerial level
and the level the students thought it was possible for
them to attain.

Validity Contingent on Bureaucratic Hierarchy.
Since the role prescriptions were applicable only to traditional bureaucratic hierarchies, Miner (1965) proposed
and found that the total scores on MSCS—Form H
should be unrelated to the success of professionals outside such highly structured organizations. Although it
is impossible to prove the hypothesis, his argument was
supported by his failure (Miner, 1977a) to find significant relations between the scores on MSCS—Form H
and various criteria of success of 24 to 51 managerial
consultants, 49 faculty members of business schools, 36
to 57 school administrators in small- and medium-size
cities and consolidated districts, and 65 salesmen at an
oil dealership (Miner, 1962a, 1962b).

More convincing support for this argument was obtained by Miner, Rizzo, Harlow, and Hill (1977), who
showed that in simulated low-structure situations, in

which 89 students worked on various case projects in small teams of 4 to 7, scores on MSCS—Form H were unrelated to the students' emergence as leaders. On the other hand, in line with Miner's theory, in a high-structure situation in which students chose to work on current problems in assigned positions in a simulated organization with 6 divisional levels, the total scores on MSCS—Form H of higher-level leaders were highest and the scores of nonleaders and of those who opted to work outside the organization were lowest.

Motivation to Lead in Professional Organizations

Oliver (1982) created an inventory to discriminate reliably between hierarchical and professional organizations, and Miner (1982a) developed MSCS—Form P, another sentence-completion test, to measure professional motivation to deal with success in a professional, in contrast to a hierarchical, organization. The subscales of Form P concern the motivation to acquire knowledge, to act independently, to accept status, to provide help, and to be professionally committed. Motivation on Form P is more likely to correlate with the level and performance of professional leaders than of hierarchical leaders. Miner reported correlations of .51, .55, .42, and .53, respectively, with the professional rank, professional compensation, number of journal articles published, and number of books published of 112 members of the Academy of Management. The correlations of such criterion measures of professional success with the corresponding scores for the motivation to manage on Form H were, respectively, .02, .08, .01, and .09.

Independent support for a different approach to professional organizations was provided by Cornelius and Lane (1984), who collected data for managers in a professionally oriented service organization. The service organization provided instruction in a second language to full-time students for a profit. Here, the investigators failed to obtain positive correlations of McClelland's LMP profile of a high need for power and a low need for affiliation with measures of the performance of an administrative job or the subordinates' morale. In fact, they obtained a negative correlation of −.42 of LMP scores against an administrative efficiency index for the lower level of supervisors. Their analyses were weakened by their failure to include an expression for the activity inhibition of power in their measurement of LMP. Also, the service organization was a hierarchically-arranged group of professionals. However, Cornelius and Lane did find that LMP scores predicted the assignment of managers to more prestigious work centers.

Motivation for Entrepreneurial Leadership

The motivation to manage on the MSCS—Form H failed to relate to the desire of 38 Oregon entrepreneurs to expand. Consequently, Form T was constructed to assess the motivation for entrepreneurial leadership: the motivation to achieve, to take risks, to seek the results of performance, to innovate, to plan, and to set goals. On Form T, the mean for 23 entrepreneurs with faster growing firms was 11.9, while it was 0.5 for 28 entrepreneurs of slow-growth firms and 2.0 for nonentrepreneurs (Smith & Miner, 1984).

Critique

A number of difficulties emerge from Miner's work. Even restricting Miner's motivation to manage to traditional hierarchies fails to account for the contrast between his prescriptions for the managerial role and those, say, of most behavioral scientists who favor democratic, participative, relations-oriented, and considerate leadership. Indeed, conspicuously absent from Miner's results are criteria of the subordinates' satisfaction, productivity, cohesiveness, and growth. As was noted earlier, the satisfaction of subordinates may be strongly associated with considerate and relations-oriented leadership behavior, but the leaders' superiors may evaluate the leaders more favorably for their production emphasis and task orientation. Chapter 22 showed that one leadership style, negotiation or manipulation, was related to the salary levels attained by managers (usually determined by their superiors) adjusted for age, seniority, education, function, and so on. Yet, negotiative or manipulative behavior was the one leadership style that was likely to be negatively related to subordinates' satisfaction and subordinates' ratings of the effectiveness of work groups.

Thus, individual managers may be most successful in hierarchical organizations if they pursue the role prescriptions set forth by Miner, but in the absence of evidence, one can only guess, given R. Likert's (1977b) long-range studies, that their organizations are likely to suffer from the consequences of subordinates' grievances, absences, turnover, and dissatisfaction, as well as from vertical and lateral blockages and filtering of communication. Nevertheless, Miner may be performing an extremely important service in pointing out the fundamental conflict, noted by Argyris (1964a) and Culbert and McDonough (1980), among others, between the integration of the long-term objectives of the individual manager and those of the organization.

In the 1990s and beyond, to survive and prosper, even the largest of hierarchical organizations will require flexibility in meeting the challenges of rapidly changing technologies and markets. Professional-like concerns for commitment, loyalty, and involvement will become increasingly important. Entrepreneurial (or intrapreneurial) attitudes and behavior will also be important for the organization's members. It would seem that some complex combination of what is being measured by Forms H, P, and T would become increasingly relevant in the healthiest of organizations.

Psychometric Criticisms of MSCS. Brief, Aldag, and Chacko (1976, 1977) were critical of the reliability of scoring the sentence-completion test in the original MSCS—Form H. But Miner (1978a) showed that when more experienced raters are used, agreement, as measured by correlations among scorers, runs from .83 to .98. Experienced scorers are also more in agreement in the mean score assigned. The multiple-choice version of MSCS eliminates this issue. Correlations between scores for items on the original and multiple-choice versions were .68, .71, and .38 for three samples of production and office managers, although the subscales tend to be less consistent from one version to the other. Unfortunately, Eberhardt, Yap, and Basuray (1988), according to an analysis of 271 senior business students, failed to find correlations of the subscales, as would have been expected, with corresponding motives assessed by the Steers and Braunstein Manifest Needs Questionnaire. Furthermore, the subscales lacked reliability.

Brief, Aldag, and Chacko (1976, 1977) also called attention to the lack of correlation of the MSCS with results obtained from the Personal Values Questionnaire (PVQ) (England, 1976) and the Self-Description Inventory (SDI) (Ghiselli, 1971), both of which correlate with managerial success. But Miner (1978b) found more problems with the PVQ and SDI as standards than with the MSCS.

Trends in the Motivation to Manage

Although it is not known whether there has been a change since the 1930s in the tendencies toward laissez-faire leadership, several sources of data have suggested that a decline may be occurring in the motivation to manage. Miner (1974a) viewed with alarm what became a sharp reduction over the 20-year period between 1960 and 1980 in the mean MSCS—Form H scores of comparable cross-sectional samples of Oregon business students (Miner & Smith, 1982). The mean data obtained for the four time periods are shown in Table 25.2.[10]

The motivation of male and female students to manage showed similar declines except that motivation continued to decline somewhat among the female students between 1972–73 and 1980, while it leveled off for the male students. In 1960, there was a considerable gap between males and females; by 1980, the gap had practically vanished. According to Miner and Smith (1982), the implications of these findings are that organizations increasingly will be faced with new managers who have less motivation to manage and hence less potential to rise in the organization and less potential to manage effectively.

In the continuing follow-up of the 20-year Management Progress Study of A T & T managers' careers, starting in 1956, the managers' need for advancement, as revealed in interviews, was an important predictor of success; it correlated .44 with the level achieved in 20 years (Bray, Campbell, & Grant, 1974). But in the assessment of a new sample, started in 1977, for the Management Continuity Study, Howard and Bray

[10]Bartol, Anderson, and Schneier (1980) found that during the 1970s, there was an acute reversal of the decline in the motivation to manage of students at Syracuse University and the University of Maryland. They observed that the levels of motivation returned almost to those of 1960. However, the differences in trends in Oregon and Syracuse appear to be due to differences in the training of the scorers of the MSCS (Bartol, Schneier, & Anderson, 1985; Miner, Smith, & Ebrahimi, 1985).

Table 25.2 Patterns of Changes in the Scores on MSCS—Form H among Business Students at the University of Oregon over 20 Years

Years	Number of Students	Male	Female	Both
1960–61	287	3.62	1.59	3.33
1967–68	129	.60	−.07	.52
1972–73	86	−1.99	−1.23	−1.84
1980	124	−1.93	−1.78	−1.86

SOURCE: Adapted from Miner and Smith (1982, p. 300).

(1988) found a considerable decrease in the need for advancement, in contrast to the 1956 sample. The need for self-fulfillment appeared to have taken its place.

Caution is required in interpreting these declines in motivation to manage. Miner and Smith's case rests mainly on students at the University of Oregon, and Howard and Bray's case rests on a single firm, the "old" A T & T before the court-ordered breakup of the company, that is, before its management was forced to shift from a regulated, service-oriented monopolistic utility to a price-sensitive, competitive firm in an unregulated market.

Summary and Conclusions

Uniformly, laissez-faire leaders are downgraded by their subordinates. Productivity, cohesiveness, and satisfaction suffer under such leadership. But laissez-faire leadership should not be confused with the positive effects of legitimate autonomy for subordinates. In contrast to laissez-faire leadership, active, responsible, masculine assertiveness and related behaviors are required for success as a manager in the typical hierarchy, although possibly not to the extremes proposed in Miner's model.

Although consideration, relations orientation, and participation alone promote satisfaction, the combination of high initiation and consideration, high orientation task and relations orientation, and high direction and participation may be most conducive to effective leadership. Depending on which outcome is considered, the next most efficacious combination is active engagement in either one or the other. But the least efficacious is a combination of low initiation and consideration, low task- and relations orientation, and low direction and participation—an equivalent of laissez-faire leadership. However, as illustrated in the leadership of presidents whether leaders are active or passive may depend on the issues and circumstances, not just the personal predelictions of the leaders. For example, a sharp increase in laissez-faire leadership may occur when leaders are notified that their positions are being eliminated or that they are to be transferred in the near future. These situational issues, as they affect leadership and management, are addressed next.

Situational Moderators

Leadership, Environment, and Organization

Leadership and Situations

Chapter 25 just showed how different motivations to manage are involved in bureaucratic, professional, and entrepreneurial settings. Similarly, some optimal, rather than an absolutely high, level of activity is required for leadership to be successful and effective; this level depends on the constraints and challenges faced by the group that is being led. If the performance of American presidents were rated on Osgood's semantic differential scales—active–inactive, strong–weak, and good–bad—no doubt, activity, strength, and goodness would usually go together. However, the 1950s may have been best served by the less active President Dwight D. Eisenhower, whereas the more active Theodore Roosevelt might have created more problems than he would have solved.

Situational demands and the personal attributes of the leader must both be considered in trying to understand the likely effectiveness of the leader. Thus, it is not surprising that Nebeker and Mitchell (1974) found that differences in leadership behavior could be explained by the leader's expectations that a certain style of leadership would be effective in a particular kind of situation. For example, the success of the careers of 310 British and U.S. managers in 28 different companies corresponded to the extent to which the managers' achievement orientation matched their company's support of risk taking. The managers' success was evidenced by the progress of their salaries compared to their age. On the other hand, other matches of orientation and the company situation that were expected to make a difference in the managers' advancement failed to do so (Ansari, Baumgartel, & Sullivan, 1982).

Illustrating the significance of fit in another way,

O'Connor and Farrow (1979) demonstrated the importance for personal satisfaction of matching the amount of structure required by managers in research and production and the managers' preferences for such structure. Similarly, managers reported that they needed to engage in political and manipulative behavior most often in organizations that lacked structure and in which there was much continuing ambiguity about goals and processes and a great many technological uncertainties (Allen, Panian, & Lotz, 1979; Madison, Allen, Porter, et al., 1980).

Trait versus Situation

As was noted in the earlier historical review of leadership theory, the trait approach is not enough for understanding leadership. Above and beyond personal attributes of consequence, the situation can make a difference. Whereas some types of leadership are reported or expected of leaders in all situations, other types of leadership are more specific to particular types of situations (Hemphill, 1950a). For instance, according to a survey by Hemphill, Seigel, and Westie (1951), when the group has a high degree of control over its members, the leader is expected to dominate and actually does so; in groups whose members participate to a high degree, however, these expectations and reports of domination do not occur.

What is required for leadership in a stressful situation is likely to differ from what is needed in calm and steady circumstances. For a given leader in one situation or the other, some subordinates are likely to be more experienced, more motivated, or better adjusted to their situation. The leader may need to deal differently with the various kinds of subordinates. Some leadership behavior is a function of individual differences, but other leadership behavior appears to depend mainly on situational differences or on the interaction of the individual and the situation. Any full account requires the "within-and-between" analysis advocated by Dansereau, Alutto, and Yammarino (1984) in which the percentage of variance in leadership behavior and the percentage of the effects of the leadership on performance and satisfaction can be allocated to the leaders across situations, across the groups led, and to the individual leader-follower relationships within the groups led. Thus, for 116 insurance agents in 31 work groups, Yammarino, Dubinsky, and Hartley (1987) showed that 28 percent of the average correlation of subordinates and supervisors about the subordinates' performance was attributable to the differences among the work groups and their leaders; 14 percent, to differences among the subordinates within the work groups led by the same supervisor; and still less, to peculiar fluctuations of the followers' relations with some leaders, but not others. For a sample of 83 retail sales associates in 26 work groups, only 14 percent could be attributable to differences among the supervisors, while 7 percent was due to supervisor-subordinate relations within the groups.

Stogdill's (1951b) study of transferred naval officers suggested that some behaviors of the transferee in the new situations were characteristic of the transferee himself rather than of the position. These behaviors included his tendency to delegate authority; to spend time in public relations; to evaluate, read, and answer mail; to read technical publications; and to spend time with outsiders. But other behavior, such as the amount of personal contact time; time spent with superiors; and time spent in supervision, coordination, and writing reports, was more a matter of demands of the situation.

Patterning

W. O. Jenkins (1947) reviewed a large number of military studies that indicated that the traits required in a leader are related to the demands of the situation. Stogdill's (1948) review of 124 studies from a broader array of situations suggested that although there may be general traits associated with leadership, the pat-

terns of those traits required for leadership differ with the situation.[1] Subsequently, DuBrin (1963) found that a leadership inventory, consisting of both trait and situational items, correlated significantly with a leadership criterion, whereas neither set of items alone was significantly related to the criterion. Again, O. L. Campbell (1961) reported significant differences among leaders in eight different situations when described on the consideration and initiating structure scales of the Leader Behavior Description Questionnaire (LBDQ).

Leadership Styles

Chapter 23 examined the premium placed on the maturity of subordinates by the Hersey-Blanchard (1977) situational leadership model in determining what leadership model is appropriate. Even Blake and Mouton (1964) would agree that how the 9,9 integrated, highly task- and relations-orientated style properly manifests itself in a leader's behavior will depend on a subordinate's maturity.

Then there is Fiedler's (1967a) contingency model, which is also detailed in Chapter 23. According to Fiedler, relations-oriented leadership is optimal when the situation is neither highly favorable nor highly unfavorable to the leader in terms of his or her esteem, power, and the situation's structure; task-oriented leadership is optimal when the situation is either highly favorable or highly unfavorable to the leader.

As for initiation and consideration,[2] Vecchio (1981), among many others, concluded, from an analysis of LBDQ data from 107 subordinates' descriptions of their supervisors, that a matching of the leader's style to the needs of subordinates and the work setting yields the maximum satisfaction of subordinates with the leadership, although not necessarily with other aspects of the situation, such as with the job or with working conditions. Such matching was seen as the reason why although each of four chief executive officers (CEOs) displayed a different pattern of traits, all four emerged as effective leaders in their four different organizational cultures (Free, 1983).

[1]See Chapter 4.
[2]See Chapter 24.

Leaders Can Alter Situations

In all this, one must keep in mind that leaders are not merely reactive; often they change the situation to suit their own proclivities. Many of the world's most eminent leaders could not be deflected from their pursuits by environmental, organizational, or collegial considerations.[3] Thus, Singh (1982) argued, along the lines of Blake and Mouton, that Indian managers must avoid allowing the situation to dominate them to such an extent that normlessness results. Again, Fiedler advocated training the leader to make the situation better fit the leader's LPC orientation.

Situations Can Alter Leadership

Much has been learned about how the demands of a task and the characteristics of the immediate group members modify the type of leadership that will occur. Less well studied has been the impact of the external environment and the complex organization in which the tasks are to be accomplished and in which the leader's group is embedded. Yet, it is clear that the external environment and the complex organization exert important effects on the leader's behavior in his or her group.

Changes in the complex organization and its external environment ordinarily will bring on changes in its leadership. As organizations mature, the charismatic founders of social movements usually give way to the bureaucratic successors. In the case of the union movement in the United States, unions fight for recognition, then become established institutions, and subsequently may move into an even later stage of fighting for survival. In each stage, the requirements for leadership differ. The low paid, lower skilled immigrants with limited English who made up the members of the United Steel Workers changed to a new generation of highly paid, skilled, English-speaking, better educated members. Leading them required new approaches. Patronage had to give way to persuasion. Newer issues involving the match between the leader and the situation have emerged; these issues reflect societal changes, such as the sharp increase in legislative inter-

vention into the world of work and the relations among employers and employees. Further changes in the leadership of the steel union were necessary to deal with the impact of foreign competition and new technologies.

Theories, Models, and Prescriptions

Increasing attention has been devoted to providing rationales for understanding these personal versus situational effects. Katz and Kahn's (1966) introduction of systems theory to the study of leadership and social interaction is illustrative of such efforts. Most efforts to develop theories, models, and prescriptions for directly fitting the leader's behavior to the situational requirements appear somewhat like Ashby's (1957, 1960) Law of Requisite Variety—the functions evolving within a brain or created within a computer must be differentiated to match the different elements in the outside environment with which they must deal. The variety of the leader's behaviors must coincide with the situational demands that parallel them. Or the explanations take the form of tautologies. The appropriate leadership is that which serves to fix, or to get others to fix, whatever is malfunctioning or is less than optimal in the system.

One also has to remain alert to the possibilities of coincidental correlations between leadership attributes or behavior and situations, since theories may be built on them inadvertently. One needs to see the link of direct or indirect causation of the situation on the leader or the leader on the situation. Thus, organizational size itself may correlate with a more directive leadership style but cannot account for it. Mediating organizational and psychological processes that are connected with both size and leadership are needed to confirm and understand the relationship (Indik, 1965b).

Kerr, Schriesheim, Murphy, and Stogdill (1974) reviewed how situational elements determined whether consideration or initiation of structure was more effective.[4] Among the situational variables found to determine whether the initiation of structure or consideration yielded satisfaction and productivity were the

---

[3]See Chapter 12.

[4]See Chapter 24.

subordinates' need for information, job level, expectations of the leaders' behavior, and perceived organizational independence. Also important were how similar the leaders' attitudes and behavior were to the managerial style of higher management and the leaders' upward influence. In addition, the effects of the task, including whether there were pressures to produce and provisions for intrinsic satisfaction, were significant.

Yukl (1981) specified the situations in which 19 leadership behaviors would be most essential. For the task-oriented behaviors, for instance, Yukl suggested that the leaders' emphasis on performance is needed more when subordinates' errors and deficiencies in the quality of products are costly and difficult to correct or would endanger the health and lives of people. Leaders can structure reward contingencies better when it is possible to measure the subordinates' performance accurately. More role clarification is desirable when the organization has elaborate rules and regulations and subordinates are not familiar with them. Goal setting by leaders is more effective when the outcomes of performance are highly dependent on the subordinates' efforts and are not strongly affected by fluctuating conditions that are beyond the control of subordinates. The dissemination of information by the leaders is most important when the work of subordinates is strongly affected by developments in other parts of the organization and subordinates are dependent on the leaders to keep them informed about the developments. The facilitation of work by leaders is required more when shortages of inputs or inadequate support services would result in the serious and immediate disruption of the work.

Yukl also prescribed a number of relations-oriented leadership behaviors for particular situations. The need for more consideration by the leader occurs, according to Yukl, when the leader works in close proximity to subordinates or must interact frequently with them owing to the nature of the task. Praise and recognition by the leader become more important when subordinates are not able to get much direct feedback about their performance from the work itself or from clients, customers, or co-workers. The facilitation of interaction by the leader is essential when the organizational unit is large and contains competing groups or factions.

This chapter focuses on environmental and organizational factors, external to the organization, that influence leader-subordinate relations inside the organization. Subsequent chapters examine group, task, and other situational factors of consequence.

Leadership and the External Environment

Stable versus Turbulent Environment

Systems theory suggests that what takes place outside a system is likely to affect what takes place inside it. This emphasis on organizations as open systems contrasts with the earlier approaches of economists, engineers, and behaviorists. Now more attention is paid to the environmental forces that interact with the organization and continuously modify what is going on inside it. Thus, if a business operates in a stable environment, it is likely to have stable organizational policies and departments similar in structure. If the environment is unstable, policies are less uniform, and greater differences emerge among the various divisions of the firm (Lawrence & Lorsch, 1967b).

The failure of organizational structures to change in response to changing environmental processing requirements led J. A. Miller (1974), who studied leadership behavior in ten organizations, to propose and find support for the argument that the optimal degree of initiation of structure by the leader depends on how much the processes demand such structure when the organization has not already provided it.

Osborn, Hunt, and Bussom (1977), like Miller, proposed to extend Ashby's (1957, 1960) Law of Requisite Variety to understand the relation between environmental demands on the organization and the organization's structure. The organization must possess as much required variety as the variety that can be expected from the environment. Internal variety of organizational structure should correspond to the environmental variety of demand on the organization. Organizations in environments with numerous disturbances should, therefore, contain an equally sophisticated capability to vary important internal characteristics. Similarly, leaders in environments that varied should show more varied behavior than leaders in stable environments. Osborn, Hunt, and Bussom tested whether the consistency of the matching of the leader's behavior with environmental conditions was more valid than an alternative model suggesting that the leader's behavior offsets and compensates (as Miller argued) for the environmental demands. In 60 chapters of a business fraternity, within-chapter variations across selected environmental dimensions gave a measure of environmental variety. Five leadership dimensions from the LBDQ-Form XII[5] for each leader of a fraternity chapter yielded a measure of leadership variety. The overall performance of the chapter was best when environmental variety was low and was mismatched with high leadership variety. However, leadership variety that matched high environmental variety was associated with better performance by the chapter, but the effects were much smaller.

Market Stability. An attribute of the outside environment that is likely to influence the behavior of leaders inside an organization is the stability of the market in which a firm or agency operates. If the firm operates in a stable marketplace, less total leadership is needed and more substitutes for leadership can be employed. Matters can be programmed; policies can be set; and leadership, when needed, can be directive.[6] In a turbulent market, more leadership will be needed, particularly consultation on a continuing basis.

Burns and Stalker (1961) interviewed key people in 20 organizations in a variety of industries. They classified the management methods as either "mechanistic" or "organic." The mechanistic organization was characterized by rule-based, vertical communication patterns, with decision and influence centered at the top levels; organic forms featured lateral communication, adaptability based on learning, and less rigidly defined jobs. The mechanistic style was found to be more appropriate for dealing with stable environments, and the organic style was more suited to changing environments.

The effective firms in a rapidly changing, complex environment involved their lower-level managers in joint departmental decisions. Managers who possessed the competence and knowledge to deal with the environment had more decision-making influence than did those who did not. The effective firms in relatively stable environments concentrated decision making and influence at the top level of management. Lower-level managers in such stable environments found satisfaction from being able to get a quick decision from those at higher levels.

Burns and Stalker found that the executives in a sales-engineering company were required to deal repeatedly with the same customers, suppliers, and regulatory bodies. The demand for direct interaction with the environment was greater for the sales-engineering company, whereas in a clothing company, interaction was accomplished indirectly, mainly in written form.

Executives had less autonomy in the environment when there was less differentiation of customers, greater feedback, and indirect communication with the environment. All these characteristics were associated with the clothing company. As a consequence, the executives in the clothing company spent less time in decision making and more dealing with routine tasks. Their autonomy was more restricted, both horizontally and vertically, compared to that of the sales-engineering executives, whose environmental surroundings were the opposite of those of the clothing firm (Burns & Stalker, 1961).

Firms that had to operate in turbulent fields were more likely to share the power of decision making inside their organization, according to a study by Emery and Trist (1965). In agreement, Lawrence and Lorsch (1967a) compared decision making in the stable container industry with decision making in the more turbulent plastics industry. Again, in the stable environment, the decision-making processes within the container firm were likely to be directive; in the more turbulent environment of the plastics firm, decision-making processes were more likely to be consultative.

Economic, Political, Social, and Legal Influences

Studies of legislative leadership by Peabody (1976) and Rosenthal (1974) suggested that a variety of environmental forces strongly affect the stability of political

---

[5]See Chapter 24.

[6]As defined in Chapters 22 and 23, *direction* (italicized) refers only to giving orders with or without explanation. Direction (romanized) includes ordering, persuading, and manipulating. *Participation* (italicized) refers only to sharing in the decision process. Participation (romanized) includes consulting, sharing, and delegating.

leadership. The same variables can be seen to operate even more intensively in the private sector, where market forces and technological changes often dramatically affect the stability and succession of leadership (Bryson & Kelley, 1978). Performance reviews, in the form of annual elections for the board of directors, periodic audits, and stockholders' meetings by outsiders, can influence the actions of the leadership and the stability of the dominant coalition inside the organization (M. P. Allen, 1974). A change in the law, in resources, or in competing organizations also may force changes in leadership (Pfeffer, 1972b). Groups of clients, unions, professional associations, and regulatory agencies affect how and what will be discussed and decided, both in legislatures and in private organizations, especially with regard to visible and emotional questions. Feature stories, publicity, and exposés can be used to support or destroy the leadership in both locations (Ilchman & Uphoff, 1969).

Using factored questionnaires, Bass, Valenzi, and Farrow (1977) asked 76 managers to rate the extent to which economic, political, social, and legal forces outside their organization influenced and their immediate subordinates. Each of the 277 subordinates described the leadership behavior of the managers. Production, accounting, and finance managers saw economic forces as most important; service, sales, and marketing and personnel managers saw economic forces as least important compared to political, social, or legal forces. But even after partialing out the effects of the managers' personality, background characteristics, and managerial function, Bass, Valenzi, and Farrow found that managers who perceived external economic forces to be important to their supervisor-subordinate relations tended to be more *directive* and manipulative, according to their subordinates. On the other hand, managers who felt that external political, social, and legal forces were more important tended to be more consultative, according to their subordinates.

In a follow-up analysis, Farrow, Valenzi, and Bass (1980) examined 250 managers in profit-making organizations and 95 in nonprofit organizations. In the nonprofit firms, the leaders' styles, as seen by the subordinates, were affected more by the managers' perceptions of outside environmental influences. For example, perceptions of strong economic influences were correlated $-.30$, $-.25$, and $-.21$ with consultation, *participation*, and delegation, respectively, in the nonprofit organizations. The parallel correlations in the profit-making organizations were $-.05$, $-.11$, and $-.02$.

Community leaders differed in their thoughts about which influences affected the developmental needs of their communities, depending on their regional location. Although those in the Southwest believed that local business determined their communities' needs, far fewer leaders from the Northeast did so. At the same time, the leaders from the Northeast thought that nonlocal governments and nonlocal businesses exerted more influence on developmental needs (Olien, Tichenor, & Donohue, 1987).

Economic Conditions. A commonly observed reaction of management to economic recession, loss of markets, and reduced sales and profits is to cut programs that contribute to the improvement of leadership and interpersonal relations within the organization. Training and development are seen as overhead that can be sacrificed to assist the firm's economic balance. During these times, security needs rise among both workers and managers that affect their relationships and problems that must be addressed, such as layoffs, retraining, early retirement, and reductions in compensation and benefits. Franke and Kaul (1978) stirred up controversy over the Hawthorne studies (Roethlisberger, 1947) suggesting that the heightened productivity of the Western Electric personnel at the Hawthorne Works, which had been attributed by the researchers to increased attention by supervisors to human relations and the concerns of the workers, was actually accounted for statistically by an economic downturn in the late 1920s that resulted in an increase in closer supervision and workers' fears that they might lose their jobs.

In the 1980s, there was an escalation of mergers, acquisitions, and leveraged buyouts, aided by favorable investor attitudes and increased tax advantages for company debt over equity[7] which some economists ap-

---

[7]High-risk, high-interest junk bonds were floated to provide the leverage for purchases of an acquisition. Such interest was fully tax-deductible as a business expense. The bonds were to be paid from the earnings and sales of assets of the acquisition whose reduced profits due to the payments and sales of its assets would result in lower tax liabilities.

plauded for shaking up complacent managements but others saw as predatory business practices that benefit the entrepreneurs and managers who are involved at the expense of all the other constituents of the organization. Commitment, loyalty, and involvement suffered. Long-term investment for such as research and development had to be sacrificed in favor of marshaling resources to maintain short-term strength and stock prices. Confusion and anxiety permeated the members of the organization, who were threatened by the loss of their jobs, policy changes, plant closings, and general uncertainty.

The Sociopolitical Ethos. In an interview survey by Bruce (1986), CEOs also mentioned the political environment as being important to what they could accomplish. Mergers in the 1980s could not have been possible in the antitrust environment of the 1960s. Maccoby (1983) pointed out the need to consider the continual change in societal attitudes toward the ethics of work. He identified four ethics in earlier U.S. history, each of which was replaced when its ideals no longer could meet society's social and economic needs. The four dominant ethics were (1) the Protestant or Puritan ethic, (2) the craft ethic, (3) the entrepreneurial ethic, and (4) the career ethic. Each ethic generated different predominant styles of leadership: work orientation, expert orientation, risky competitiveness, and careerism. Likewise, Bass (1960) saw leadership styles affected by the dominance of task orientation in the United States before 1950 giving way to concern in the 1950s for getting along with others, to be followed by an increasing self-orientation (which, indeed, began in the 1960s). Each, in turn, had different effects on the practice of leadership in U.S. organizations. Production and the heroes of production were paramount in a task-oriented society. Marketing, conformity, and interpersonal relationships became the predominant issues of the 1950s, followed by a predicted greater self-oriented focus of the "me-too" era, which occurred from the mid-1960s onward, in which issues, ranging from individual alienation to careerism, became dominant.

A longer psychohistorical focus of societal effects on leadership was proposed by Demause (1982). Demause noted that the common practice of infanticide and abandonment in classical and medieval times pro-

moted the survivors' view that their parents and the leaders who displaced the parents were their saviors. The ambivalence toward children that followed in the next centuries fostered the model of parents and leaders as benevolent autocrats. Between 1800 and 1950, the prevailing practice of treating children as subjects for training and socialization created the model of the leader as the source of contingent reinforcement. Finally, the post-1950 Spock generation created a model of parents and leaders as helpers.

Regulatory Agencies. Ungson, James, and Spicer (1985) surveyed 89 firms in two industries—wood products and high technology—about the effects of regulatory agencies on their planning and goal setting and the need to adjust their organizations to the regulatory agencies' actions. In both industries, managers saw governmental regulatory agencies as more unpredictable and uncontrollable than they did their suppliers of raw material, competitors, customers, and labor. Generally, in the wood-products industry, adjustments in personnel were most likely to occur because of governmental regulatory agencies and least likely to occur because of competitors or investors. But in the high-technology industry, none of the outside factors was as important in affecting the adjustments of personnel.

Ownership. The treatment of executives by a higher authority in 71 large manufacturing firms depended, according to Gomez-Mejia, Tosi, and Hinkin (1987), on whether the firm had dominant outside stockholders. Such stockholders are owners who view the firms primarily as financial investments. They use their power to compensate hired CEOs according to the economic performance of the firms. In firms without such dominant stockholders, which were controlled more by the management itself, the compensation awarded CEOs depended more on the size of their firm's operations than on its performance.

Socioeconomic Status of the Community. Osborn and Hunt (1979) created an index of the socioeconomic level of a community based on its median income per family, mean educational level of its residents, the tendency of residents to vote, and other socioeconomic conditions. For the 60 chapters of a national business fraternity mentioned earlier, the investigators obtained a correlation of .40 between the community status of the chapter leaders and their initiation of structure and .68 with their consideration, as measured by the LBDQ.

Religious Affiliation. L. B. Ward (1965) completed a large-scale survey of top managements in the United States that suggested that the religious affiliation of the top managers in a firm affected the personnel policies promoted within the firm. Personnel practices were more likely to be liberal when the top management was not restricted to members of one religious group. Policies were more likely to be liberal if the top management was exclusively Jewish than if it was exclusively Protestant. The most conservative managements were exclusively Catholic.

Reference Groups

Other environmental influences on leaders and members of any organization are their reference groups—those with whom they compared themselves. Hyman (1942) asked subjects to estimate their status along several dimensions—social, economic, intellectual, physical, and the like. He found that individuals estimated some aspects of their status in relation to family members, other aspects in relation to friends or peers at work, and still other aspects in relation to people in general. Small reference groups were usually more important than were people in general in determining the subjects' satisfaction with their status. Satisfaction with their income was highly dependent on the reference group with which the individuals compared themselves.

Local versus Cosmopolitan. Merton (1949/1957) showed that the identification with different reference groups was associated with variations in patterns of leadership behavior. In a community study, 86 informants identified 379 individuals as persons of some influence. The 30 most influential members of the community were interviewed. Of these 30, 16 were classified as "locals" and 14 as "cosmopolitans" in their reference-group identifications. The two groups differed in attitudes and behavior that were of consequence to their serving as leaders or followers as follows:

Locals	Cosmopolitans
Local patriots	Interested in the world at large
Reluctant to leave the community	Willing to leave the community
Reared locally	Mostly newcomers
Desire to know many people	Selective in their choice of organizations
Members of local fraternal and business groups	Members of national professional societies
Influence rests on complex network of personal relationships	Influence derived from prestige and professional position
Understand the community	Know their job

Multiple Reference Groups. People usually see themselves as members of several reference groups if asked, "What are you?" In Texas, a Texan may say he is an American first. Outside Texas, the Texan may first say Texan, then American, businessman, father, and Episcopalian. Each is a reference group, and the effects are complex. Thus, when Festinger (1949) brought Catholic and Jewish girls together in a small club and asked them to elect officers before the girls' religion was identified, both groups voted as much for nonmembers as for members of their own religion. In a control situation, in which religious identities were disclosed, 64 percent of the Catholics voted for Catholic girls, but the Jewish girls continued to vote equally as often for members of either religion. However, in a large group, in which the voters were only privately identified by religious affiliation, Jewish girls showed the same tendency to vote for members of their own religion as did Catholic girls. The same effects were observed when confederates were alternately identified as Catholics and Jews for the benefit of different groups of voters to rule out any influences of the individual nominee on the outcomes.

To understand and predict a person's interpersonal behavior in a designated social situation, one has to determine his or her various reference groups. For example, if two people collide in a crowded street, they may ignore the collision, they may beg each other's pardon, or one may shove the other. What each person does will depend, to some extent, on whether the interacting persons are male or female; white or black; and upper, middle, or lower class and whether the situation is in North America or Zambia.[8]

Real Outside Networks of Relationships

Leaders usually belong to more groups than do followers. They integrate the various subgroups of a larger group and mediate between the membership groups and the wider community. Thus, J. B. Marks (1959) found that leaders maintained significantly more extra-clique friendship links than did followers and tended to mediate between their groups and the surrounding social environment. Schiffman and Gaccione (1974) found that the opinion leaders in the nursing home industry were administrators who interacted more often with administrators from other nursing homes. However, the leaders who identified with the norms of the in-house group were more strongly supported by members than were the leaders who identified with the norms of the external groups.

The effects of leaders' outside connections are well known. Interlocking company directorates can take considerable advantage of such linkages for the good of their organizations, even though doing so has the potential for corruption. When the boards of social service organizations were composed of high-status (business leaders) rather than middle-status (middle management and professional) members, the organizations were found to be more effective, better financed, and able to provide a higher quality of service (Zald, 1967).

Pettigrew (1973) observed that developing and maintaining a network of contacts outside as well as inside the organization are the means by which many leaders help their subordinates reach their desired objectives. Koulack (1977) involved 44 undergraduates in simulated bargaining situations. Leaders who did all the bargaining were treated by out-group members either with friendliness or with hostility. The leaders who were treated in a friendly manner by the out-group members were rated as more effective by the in-group members.

[8]Chapters 32 to 34 examine the effects of these affiliations of sex, race, ethnicity, and national identity on the emergence and success of leaders and managers.

Organizations and Leadership

Leadership in an organization is determined by the organization's legitimating principles and cultural norms and by the social structure within which it occurs. As the organization matures, so will the strategies of its leadership change (Biggart & Hamilton, 1987). Thus, Pellegrin (1953), Philipsen and Cassee (1965), and Weinberg (1965) observed that institutional requirements determine the characteristics of members who are accepted as leaders. It is apparent that the kind of leader who emerges in an organization and the individual who is successful as a leader and is evaluated as effective as a leader depends on the philosophy of the larger organization in which the leader's group is embedded. The philosophy influences the organization's directors. In turn, its effects move down to successively lower levels of management and contribute to the constraints that are imposed; the structures that are created; and the ways in which people are mobilized, resources are allocated, and performance is evaluated. These, in turn, will affect the patterns of leader-member relations in the organization.

Organizational Philosophy

The organization's philosophy includes its assumptions, values, foci of attention, priorities, and goals and the techniques it promulgates to implement its efforts. Clearly its philosophy and culture overlap and reinforce each other in determining what is the right thing to do and what is important and good.

Some firms concentrate their attention on their financial or physical resources in the search for long-run success. They may adopt Williamson's (1975) view of organizations as internal markets in which members are opportunistic and self-interested, rather than trusting, and conflicts are resolved by fiat, or costly bargaining.

Other firms take their human resources relations into greater account. Using McGregor's (1960) terms, in Theory X firms, top-down decision making predominates. As discussed in Chapter 21, System 1 and System 2 practices (R. Likert, 1961a) are the rule. In Theory Y firms, participative bottom-up decision making and the approaches of System 3 and System 4 are more common. Then there are Theory Z firms.

Ouchi (1981) described Theory Z as the basis for Japanese management and recognized a number of U.S. firms, such as Procter & Gamble, IBM, and Hewlett-Packard, for following Theory Z in their own systems. These firms are characterized by long-term employment, intensive socialization, and clear statements of objectives and values emphasizing cooperation and teamwork. Management policies to implement these approaches include slow promotion from within, the rotation of jobs, the creation of generalists rather than specialists, complex appraisal systems, emphasis on work groups rather than individuals, open communication, consultative decision making, and a relations-oriented concern for employees. In comparison to top-down, Theory X (authoritarian) organizations, Theory Z organizations are more decentralized and have flatter structures—fewer levels of management. When Roberts (1986) compared the reports of 97 managers in a Type Z business firm with those of 147 managers in a Type X organization, she found, not unexpectedly, that subordinates exercised more upward influence in dealing with their bosses in the Type Z than in the Type X organization.

According to Robbins (1983), although Theory Z gives the impression of greater equalization of power and control and "bottom-up" management, in fact, it actually has mixed effects on top management's power and control and, for the most part, increases rather than decreases their top managers' power and control. The decentralization and team decision making of Theory Z increase the equalization of power, but employee-organizational lifelong commitments may increase employees' tolerance for what ordinarily may be the subject of complaints. The emphasis on good human relations may reduce constructive confrontation; generalist career development may reduce the ability to move to another company; and the flatter Theory Z organizations eliminate middle managers who, in taller-structured bureaucracies, for example, filter and control what information gets to top management.

Some of the same firms that Ouchi (1981) saw as Theory Z organizations were to be found among those in Peters and Waterman's (1982) well-known *In Search of Excellence*. Interviews in companies that were iden-

tified as having excellent management systematically differed from those in less well-managed companies in their bias for action, informality, flexibility, intensive communication, temporary task forces, and more acceptance of risk taking.

Different Views of Organization. Organizations may be viewed as rational-structural systems. Metaphorically, in such a view, they are machines composed of interdependent parts, and leadership is a matter of specifying who does what for whom and why. A second view is that organizations are extended families with networks of relations and obligations; in this view, leadership is more concerned with relations, with the socialization and development of subordinates. A third view is that organizations are a political system, a jungle of conflicts of interests and coalitions. According to this view, leadership is based on power and the allocation of scarce resources. A fourth view of the organizations is symbolic. It sees organizations as theaters, with members continually trying to play roles that communicate meaning to others about what is happening. In such a view, the leaders are artists and actors (Bolman, 1986).

Variations in 1,200 managers' and subordinates' perceptions of their organizations had systematic effects on the organizations' leadership styles, according to a factor analysis by Farrow (undated) of managers' and subordinates' descriptions of their organizations using the Bass-Valenzi Management Styles Survey. Organizations were seen to vary in the extent to which they were well managed, required a lot of managerial activity, were mechanistic, and were bottom-up or top-down in their distribution of power and information. Table 26.1 lists the factors and the scales that correlated most highly with them.

The frequency with which different styles of leadership appeared were related to the factored descriptions. For example, more consultative leadership was seen in well-managed firms, more directive leadership was seen in top-down firms, and more *participative* leadership in bottom-up firms.

Effects of Stated Policies. The effects of stated organizational policies on a supervisor's use of rewards and punishment were examined experimentally by Greenberg (1978) and Leventhal and Whiteside (1973),

Table 26.1 Factored Descriptions of the Surrounding Organization and Scales That Most Highly Correlated with Each of the Factors

1. Well-Managed or Poorly-Managed Organization
   .79[a] Harmony: Members do not fight, complain, or disagree.
   .76 Organizational clarity: Assignments are clearly explained and logically structured.
   .76 Organizational order: Activities are planned and organized.
   .71 Clear task objectives: One knows when he or she is doing a good job.
   .71 Warmth and trust: People trust each other in the organization.

2. Much versus Little Managerial Activity
   .78 Amount of managerial activity.
   .76 Importance of external influences.
   .59 Commitment of members.
   .58 Interdependence of members and units.
   .57 Complexity of operations.

3. Mechanistic Rather than Organic Organization
   .80 Much constraint: Organizational arrangements must be followed.
   .62 Strong organizational structure.
   .58 Amount of routine work.

4. Extent to which the Organization Is Bottom Up
   .70 Amount of power by subordinates.
   .60 Amount of discretionary opportunities.
   .52 Independence of members.
   .47 Absence of routine work.

5. Extent to which the Organization Is Top Down
   .79 Amount of the superior's power
   .58 Amount of the superior's information

[a]Factor loading or correlation.
SOURCE: Farrow (undated).

who found that experimental subjects rewarded low performers more when they were instructed to encourage high future performance than when they were instructed to reward on the basis of past performance.[9] Leventhal, Michaels, and Sanford (1972) found that experimental subjects who were given the policy of minimizing conflict allocated more rewards to low performers than did those subjects who were advised to ignore conflict. Landau and Leventhal (1976) reported that subjects who were required to retain only the best performers, compared to those who had to try to retain all workers, gave fewer rewards to low performers. Complicating matters was Graen and Liden's (1980)

[9]As will be seen in Chapter 34, this use of rewards to energize future efforts appears to be more common in developing countries, such as Colombia and India, than in developed countries, such as the United States or Sweden (Ryterband & Thiagarajan, 1968).

finding that the relationship between organizational policies and supervisory behavior may be moderated by the severity of the policy and the supervisor's attributions of the causes of the subordinate's behavior. Here, experimental subjects had to deal with a subordinate who had missed a production deadline. The failure to make the deadline was due to the subordinate in one experimental treatment and was outside the subordinate's control in the other treatment. Company policy was mild in one treatment and severe in the other. The mild policy required the supervisor to issue a verbal warning that the subordinate's pay would be docked if the deadline was missed again. The severe policy was to dock the subordinate for one day's pay. The results demonstrated that the subjects who acted as supervisors were more likely to follow the policy when the cause of missing the deadline was attributed to the subordinate than when it was attributed to a cause out-side the subordinate's control and when the stated company policy was mild rather than severe.

In a field study, Hammer and Turk (1985) showed that when the management philosophy resulted in intentional pressure on 160 first-line supervisors by higher-ups to supervise strictly, there was a significant unique, negative correlation with the supervisors' attention to the maintenance of the work group. The supervisors' perceptions of their authority to fire subordinates were also significantly affected.

Organizational Objectives and Functions

The values, beliefs, and rationales that make up an organization's philosophy affect and are affected by the organization's mission—its purposes and objectives and the functions it performs to accomplish its mission. In turn, the purposes and functions of an organization affect and are affected by its leadership. Systematic differences have been seen among departments of larger organizations, such as those concerned with manufacturing, personnel, finance, marketing, and research and development (R & D). Much has also been written about the different types of leadership that are required for different types of organizations and institutions to meet their systematically different purposes, functions, and membership. Here it is appropriate to sample some of the singularities that have been proposed and observed in such institutional settings as universities, schools, libraries, cooperatives, unions, and the military. Many of these issues were addressed earlier, but less attention was paid to the local organizational scene and its peculiar impact on the requisite leadership.

Goals Differ by Functions. Goals depend on a manager's functions. Thus, Browne (1950a, 1950b, 1950c) and Dearborn and Simon (1958) found that top-ranking executives of a business firm tended to perceive organizational goals in terms of the functions of their own departments. Manufacturing managers believed that the quality of a product and the low costs of production were goals that were important to the firm; sales and marketing managers saw effective advertising, customer service, and the low price of the product as important goals.

In a survey of British managers, Heller (1969a) found that those in personnel and general management functions typically used less directive procedures than did their colleagues in finance and production. Managers who led groups in purchasing, stores, and sales tended to be in between. This finding was consistent with earlier work by Fleishman, Harris, and Burtt (1955), who noted that foremen in manufacturing departments or other departments that worked under time constraints were likely to receive higher merit ratings if they tended to initiate structure more often, while the reverse was true for foremen in service departments. In addition, in the nonmanufacturing service departments with fewer time constraints, considerate supervisors were seen as more proficient. More initiation contributed to greater absenteeism and grievances mainly in manufacturing departments and to turnover in service departments.

Forbes (1985) divided a sample of 246 British and American managers according to their functional areas. He ranked the functional areas according to the presumed degree of uncertainty in the work as follows: personnel and training, R & D, sales and marketing, production, and finance and accounting. The more uncertainty in the function, the more the managers' reported concern for rules, use of authority, search for learning opportunities, and breadth of focus. The managers' interpersonal orientation was recorded in a data bank of results of simulated training exercises (Bass, Burger, et al., 1979). It involved human relations concerns, the ability to listen, greater trust in others, the willingness to discuss feelings, tolerance of conflict, and acceptance of affection and feedback. Interpersonal orientation was higher for those 123 managers in sales, marketing, personnel, and training—functional areas with more people content in the work to be done. Interpersonal orientation was lower for the 123 managers in the functional areas of finance, accounting, production, and R & D, where jobs were lower in "people content."

Manufacturing versus Service. Manufacturing usually demands more routinization and coordination than do service functions. In a study of 787 managers, Child and Ellis (1973) found that managers in manufacturing organizations saw their roles as more formal, better defined, and more routine than did managers in service organizations. Consistent with this, Solomon (1986) found that Israeli firms that engaged in production, public or private, were more oriented toward performance-based rewards and to contingent rewarding than were public or private firms that were engaged in services.

Utilitarian versus Voluntary Organizations. Etzioni (1961) suggested that different dynamics of leadership would be at play in utilitarian organizations that produce goods or services than in normative organizations, such as voluntary professional societies. Activity may be personally costly, and the rewards are different for office holding in voluntary organizations. Relations are likely to be more personal and informal in voluntary organizations (Walker, 1982). But the expected greater power differentials of the leaders and the led in utilitarian compared to voluntary organizations did not surface in an interview and questionnaire survey by Pearce (1983). Pearce (1982) compared four volunteer organizations (newspaper, poverty relief, family planning, and fire department) with four counterpart organizations staffed by regular employees. Interviewers with random samples in each organization concluded that workers in volunteer organizations are much more variable in their performance than are employees of utilitarian organizations. In volunteer organizations, workers were much more likely to ignore their leaders and to work when they wanted to and in the way they wanted to. Paid employees of utilitarian organizations were more likely to work within the constraints of organizational policies and leaders' directives.

Leaders of voluntary organizations differed systematically from those in organizations of employees. In voluntary organizations, authority was invested in the membership as a whole. Their leaders were the representatives of the membership who could assume some of its authority. It was a bottom-up process. Volunteer followers reported significantly more personal influence than did employee followers. In the employing organizations, the employers had the authority, which they could grant top down to the leaders in the organization. Leaders in the voluntary organizations depended much more on their subordinates than did the leaders in the employing organizations.

Leaders in voluntary organizations are likely to be reluctant to be too directive or controlling for fear of losing volunteers (LaCour, 1977). This reluctance results in their tendency to be relations oriented (Rawls, Ulrich, & Nelson, 1973). But Kellogg and White (1987) suggested that matters are more complex. Volunteers exchange their time and service for social and psychic rewards, such as recognition, worthwhile work, and personal growth. The directiveness of leaders, which facilitates the achievement of goals and the satisfaction of the volunteers' needs may be quite appropriate.

In addition, many volunteers are intrinsically motivated by the organization's accomplishment of worthwhile purposes. In a survey study of 127 volunteers in 10 voluntary organizations, Kellogg and White (1987) found that, as expected, the leaders' relations orientation, in the form of support, contributed to the volunteers' satisfaction. But, at the same time, directive role clarification by the leaders enhanced the volunteers' satisfaction with their work, more so if they originally were lower in intrinsic motivation. Presumably, such leaders gave more meaning and purpose to the work for those who were not particularly motivated by it initially. But specifying the work to be done did combine with high intrinsic motivation to promote the volunteers' satisfaction.

Some Illustrative Public Institutions

Governments, universities, schools, and libraries provide evidence of the extent to which organizational policies, purposes, and functions systematically relate to the leadership required.

Governments and Governmental Agencies. As with most long-standing institutions, governments have a history and sphere of operation of their own, apart from the constituencies they represent. Governmental institutions maintain ideals, values, and expert capacities across time. Although their constituencies can influence what the government does, the government may also affect the politics of their constituents and how they are represented (Hargrove, 1988).

Even more than in utilitarian organizations, leaders of governmental institutions, as well as their agencies and departments, are likely to be much more than rational actors pursuing calculated self-interests, knowing their preferences and how to achieve them. Rather, they are strongly influenced by institutional norms, symbols, and rules that have developed historically. Activities are often carried out as a duty or obligation, as well as for self-interest. Helping to maintain the institution may be seen as more important than helping to implement a particular policy. The leaders may have solutions that are looking for problems just as much as problems that are searching for solutions (March & Olsen, 1984). Civil servants, with expert and legitimate power, working within their own professional and institutional norms, may shape policies that depart considerably from a simple balancing of the interests of a diverse constituency (Heclo, 1974).

The leader, manager, or administrator in a governmental agency begins with a different overall mission than his or her counterpart in a private-for-profit firm. The public agency survives as a function of its services in serving the purpose of the public, legislatures, elected officials, and political power blocs. The private firm survives (if it is not subsidized by public money) by producing wanted goals, services, and profits that are consistent with the satisfaction of its owners, managers, employees, and community.

The public-sector firm or agency differs from the private firm in its lack of dependence on its market, immunity from bankruptcy but not from deficit budgets, different legal and formal constraints, greater exposure to political influences, stronger relations with political authorities, greater exposure to public scrutiny, and greater accountability (Lachman, 1985). Also, executives of public organizations operate with more formalization and less autonomy in hiring, firing, or rewarding, than do executives in the private sector (Rainey, 1983). But in an interview of 141 Israeli chief executive officers (40 public; 91 private), all engaged in production, the expected differences about political and market influences did not appear. Likewise, according to Kaminitz (1977) and Palgi (1984), differences in worker participation in public versus private industries in Israel also failed to appear. As expected, however, satisfaction was lower for public-sector leaders. An unexpected finding was that the CEOs of public firms had longer time spans of discretion.

According to still another comparison of Israeli public and private businesses and industries, managers

from private industries were more likely to consult coworkers when they needed help on their own jobs than were managers in government-owned firms (Erez & Rim, 1982). Solomon's (1986) survey of 240 top Israeli executives, half from the public and half from the private sector, found that the differences in perceptions and satisfaction were in line with expectations. There was much greater emphasis on contingent rewards in the private sector, which also was more likely to promote efficient work methods, task clarification, and task autonomy.

Guyot (1962) compared 100 business managers with 147 public administrators. Contrary to expectations, it was the public administrators who were higher in need for achievement and less in need for affiliation than the business managers. They were equal in need for power. U.S. managers, like Israeli managers, generally have been found to be more satisfied in the private sector. For example, managers in business organizations were seen to be better satisfied than were those in military or governmental organizations (Porter & Mitchell, 1967).[10] Compared to business managers, Rainey (1979) found that governmental managers (1) express weaker performance-extrinsic reward "expectancies," (2) are lower on measures of satisfaction, (3) perceive rules about personnel and civil service regulations as constraints on incentives, but (4) show no difference in role perceptions and motivation.

Farrow, Valenzi, and Bass (1980) compared the perceptions of managers in 250 profit-making and 95 not-for-profit U.S. firms and agencies about their environment, organization, task, work group, and leadership styles. As was noted earlier, those in the private sector reported significantly more economic and less political social influence on leader-subordinate relations than did those in the public sector but the same amount of legal influence. The felt constraints and amount of order and structure were significantly higher in the public sector. The managers in the private sector reported more discretionary opportunities, complex tasks, and managerial activities, whereas the managers in the public sector reported significantly more routine work. The power of subordinates was seen to be higher in the public sector. Finally, private-sector managers, in

---

[10]See also Buchanan (1974); Paine, Carroll, and Leete (1966); Rainey (1983); and Rhinehart, Barrell, DeWolfe, et al. (1969).

comparison to public-sector managers, saw themselves as being more active as leaders: more *directive*, negotiative, consultative, and delegative. These results differed from an Israeli survey by Chitayat and Venezia (1984), which reported that senior executives in business organizations displayed less direction and more participativeness than did their counterparts in the public sector. As in all earlier studies, the U.S. managers were more satisfied with their own job and with their supervisors.

The Israeli kibbutz (cooperative) is a mix of service- and production-oriented purposes and of utilitarian and normative character and has strong social and political components. In a simulation study of the work performance of 135 first-level Israeli supervisors from the public and private sectors and from kibbutzim, the leaders of the kibbutzim were most effective when they used direct group participation, in contrast to the private-sector leaders, who were most effective when they assigned goals, and to the public-sector leaders, who did best with participation by representatives (Erez, 1986).

Educational Institutions: Universities. Universities contrast greatly with mainline utilitarian organizations and have been described as organized anarchies. According to Cohen and March (1974), who interviewed 42 university presidents, universities are likely to have problematic goals, unclear technologies, and fluid participation in decision making. Inertia is high in universities. Most issues are of little consequence to the members as a whole, and decisions depend on who happens to be involved at the time they have to be made. There is a weak base of information available. Effective leadership requires managing unobtrusively, providing arenas for discussing a wide variety of problems, facilitating the participation of opposing points of view, and persisting in attempts to accomplish objectives, despite the inertia.

Nevertheless, Drenth (1986) noted that European colleges and universities can be structured to provide more organization and less anarchy. The different structures impose different demands on the leadership. Before 1968, the European university was a collegial organization that tended to be run by a fraternity of scholars organized into autonomous departments. De-

centralization, informality, and a low level of programming and standardization were intended to provide self-fulfillment and the achievement of personal objectives, particularly of the departmental chairmen. The rector fulfilled primarily a ceremonial role, representing the university, chairing traditional sessions, and presiding at other ritual formalities. The rare central decision making was generally based on consensus. Trust, seniority, acceptability, and respect were more effective than were managerial direction and task-oriented leadership.

After the student revolution of 1968, the European university emerged as a political organization in which the power of the individual autonomous chair holder was replaced by that of departmental boards with substantial representation by all layers of participants. The forming of coalitions and alliances and use of bargaining, delaying tactics, resistance, and procedural manipulation became normal parts of organizational decision making. Leadership required participation, negotiating, and conflict management, along with inventiveness and initiative.

Some European universities operate as traditional bureaucracies with standardized and formalized work processes, rules, and prescriptions. The influence of the technostructure is strong, with planning and regulation, forms and records, registration and control. The role of the leader involves timing the bureaucratic machinery and using the control systems available from the standardization of processes, output, and skills. Emphasis is placed on regulations and the routine handling of problems.

Almost opposite in organization are those universities, often newly created, whose structure remains simple. These universities emphasize the centralization of decision making and pay relatively little attention to the formalization and standardization of procedures. There is a sense of a mission, an identification with common objectives, dependence on one person, and instability. The rector is often a dynamic, powerful, task-oriented individual with charismatic features.

It also makes a considerable difference to the leadership of the U.S. university if it is a rich private one or a less-well-endowed public university. Roberts (1986) reported that the charismatic, inspirational style of leadership was more likely to be seen in 45 administrators in a rich, private university than in 61 administrators in a counterpart public university that operated with fewer resources and had to be mainly transactional rather than transformational in leadership.

The leadership styles of administrators in university settings appear to differ from those of managers in business organizations. Roberts (1986) also compared 106 administrators from two universities, with 244 managers from two businesses. She found that the administrators in the universities, in contrast to the business managers, reported using much more competitive impression management by working effectively behind the scenes, by taking action without relevant others' awareness, and by creating favorable impressions on others.

Educational Institutions: Public Schools. Many studies of school principals and superintendents have been cited in the context of other leadership issues. This section summarizes what is known about the particular elements in the school principal's personality and situation that are of consequence to his or her leadership and administration and its effectiveness. Anecdotes and cases suggest that "strong" leadership of a school enhances the effectiveness of the school, but there is no consensus on what is meant by either strong leadership or an effective school (Firestone & Wilson, 1985; Hoy & Ferguson, 1985).

Dwyer (1984) interviewed and observed 42 "successful" principals but found no single factor that could account for the success of those principals. According to Goldberg (1984), however, as with transformational leaders, successful school leaders establish challenging expectations that force students and teachers alike to work harder to support a vision that they collectively adopt and whose implementation they share. For example, Sweeney (1982) found, in a case study of nine New York City elementary schools, a strong association between high expectations of the principal and staff and positive school outcomes.

Manasse (1984) reported that in effective school systems, principals built and shaped their vision while simultaneously involving the staff and students in the development and implementation of that vision and the expectations to support it. Morphet, Johns, and Reller (1982) argued further that by increasing follow-

ers' involvement and responsibility in the administration of the school, the principal can adopt a more positive, proactive change-agent role. Less effective principals react to the demands and constraints in their school systems but do not create them (Firestone & Wilson, 1985). Effective principals indicate to their staffs and students the important and valuable goals for the school. They recognize individual differences not only in *what* individuals can learn but in *how* they learn (Cole, 1984). J. S. Brown (1970) compared 63 business managers and 84 public school administrators. The business managers made choices in a simulation with higher payoff coupled with higher risk and were higher in assessed initiative and achievement-orientation but were no different from the school administrators in decisiveness and self-assurance.

Libraries. Libraries are more circumscribed educational institutions with distinctive patterns of the emergent and successful leadership of their directors and departmental supervisors. Although service should be the main goal of libraries, the goal is in conflict with a sense of elitism and self-serving preservation (Sager, 1982). New technologies to enhance the quality of service conflict with budgetary constraints, acquisitions of books, and political considerations. In addition, libraries are composed of two levels of employees, professional and clerical, whose interests may also conflict.

Dragon (1979) surveyed administrators in three large public libraries with the LBDQ and concluded that the directors and supervisors tended to be higher in initiating structure and lower in consideration than were their counterparts in many other types of organizations. Sparks (1976) found that library administrators, like most other leaders, saw themselves as being more considerate on the LBDQ than their subordinates thought them to be. Consistent with this finding, Hall (1979) noted that students who were graduating from library school preferred consultation to more directive styles of leadership. In the same way, R. J. Solomon (1976) demonstrated that those directors of university departments who earned higher leadership scores (according to their subordinates) led university library departments which were more effective in serving other departments according to the directors of the other departments. On the basis of the results of administering the Jackson Personality Inventory and the Ghiselli Self-Description Inventory to library directors, Moore (1983) described several traits that are essential for success as an academic library director: flexibility and adaptability, willingness to accept change, a stable and equable temperament, emotional balance, and endurance.

Other Institutions. Other kinds of institutions have their own special effects on leader-follower relations, as is discussed in more detail in other chapters. For instance, in hospitals and clinics, outside physicians with expert power exert a strong influence on the in-hospital administration, nurses, and paraprofessionals, in competition with the inside supervisors. The role of guards in prisons increases their authoritarian tendencies, which are tempered by the special exchange relationships that guards develop with prisoners. In the military, technical readiness for combat competes with the maintenance of high-quality relationships for career advancement in a peace-time bureaucracy.

Leadership and Organizational Constraints

The leadership in organizations is affected by the organization's size, structure, complexity, and stability.

Size of an Organization

The size of an organization can be gauged in terms of the number of its members or the amount and monetary value of its output in product or services. Ordinarily, larger organizations will require more structure to constrain the geometrically expanding possibilities of connections and interactions among the growing number of units and members.

The size of an organization was recognized early on as a variable that is of consequence to its leadership. The CEO of a hundred-person organization can get to know each member individually and act accordingly, but such becomes impossible in a thousand-person organization. The compensation of the CEOs is likely to be determined by the size of their operations, not by their profitability, particularly if their boards of directors are mainly members of management and shares in the firm are widely held by the public. Leading an in-

fantry squad has different requirements than leading an infantry division. Emergent and appointed leadership within these respective organizations is likely to be systematically different. Erez and Rim (1982) found that compared to managers in smaller Israeli firms, those in firms with over 600 workers turned more frequently to their co-workers for assistance on their own jobs. The managers were most concerned with getting co-workers to do the jobs to which the co-workers were assigned in firms with 600 to 4,000 workers, in contrast to the larger or smaller firms. In firms with 4,000 to 6,000 workers, the managers most often sought the assistance of their own bosses than did managers in the larger or smaller firms. And managers in firms with up to 600 employees were least likely to use rational tactics with their bosses compared to those in larger organizations.

L. W. Porter (1963a) reported that the overall satisfaction of managers was greater in large than small companies. However, lower levels of management were better satisfied in small companies than in large companies, whereas higher levels of management were better satisfied in large rather than in small companies. But ElSalmi and Cummings (1968) found that small companies fulfilled the needs of top managers more than did large companies. For middle and lower managers, the reverse was true. Size, as such, was not the critical factor. Cummings and ElSalmi (1970) reported that the diversity of roles and the level of the position were more highly related to the satisfaction of needs than was the size of the department or company.

Size itself does not really make the difference. What matters is what size brings along with it. Larger organizational size is ordinarily accompanied by the greater need for structural complexity, more filtered and delayed information, geometric increases in the number of dyadic and group relationships, greater social distance, and additional constraints on change. Although many correlations between organizational size and leadership can be singled out for attention, ordinarily they are discussed in the context of other related mediating variables. For example, Friesen (1983) required a combination of organizational size, organizational structure, and organizational auspices to account for subordinates' descriptions of leaders' behavior in 23 public and private mental health agencies.

Structure and Formalization

Many more obvious differences in leadership patterns occur in organizations that differ substantially in size. One striking difference is how much relationships have to become more structured and formalized in the larger organization. As Robbins (1983, pp. 70–71) noted:

Decision making is different for an organization that has ninety thousand employees than one that has ninety. Job specialization, the creation of a policy manual, or the formation of departments are probably unnecessary when a company has ninety.... As size increases, so does the height of the structure, the number of horizontal units, and the number of rules and regulations.

On the basis of empirical factor studies, Pugh, Hickson, Hinings, and Turner (1968) developed the Aston model, which includes two major organizational factors: the structuring of activities (prescribed work roles) and the centralization of decision making (limits on discretion). These factors represent the two principal strategies of administrative control. Both usually increase as an organization enlarges.

Along with increasing size, the routineness of operations also leads to greater standardization and structuring of relations. Convenience food restaurants represent the ultimate in routine service, accompanied by a high degree of standardization and structure. In addition, as was noted earlier, stable, predictable environments permit organizations to formalize and structure themselves to a higher degree than do unstable or uncertain environments.

Chapin and Tsouderos (1955) studied the case histories of 91 organizations and concluded that as organizations increase in size and differentiation, rank-and-file members become more passive and farther removed from the policy-making centers. Likewise, the executives become farther removed from the activities that they plan and initiate. The long lines of command impose problems in communication.

Structure also reflects the needs of the top leaders of the large organization to maintain maximum control over it. As a consequence, a bureaucratic structure is favored, with specialized jobs, standardization, rules

and regulations, and centralized decision making. But as was mentioned before, even when the top managers favor a more humanistic organizational philosophy, such as Theory Z, they may do so because they can still maintain their desired power and control. Compliance can be maintained through commitment at the lower levels rather than through sanctions. Middle managers do not have to be dominated; they can be eliminated (Robbins, 1983).

Katz and Allen (1985) illustrated the importance of structure in a study of the 86 R & D teams that were embedded in matrix managements in nine firms. The performance of these teams was best when their project manager had more organizational influence and when their functional boss had more influence over the technical details of their work. Their performance was also better when the team members perceived that the project manager and the functional manager had equal influence over their salaries and promotions.

Lanzetta and Roby (1955) contrasted antiaircraft crews of three men each performing all functions with crews arranged in a hierarchical structure. They found that the performance of crews improved with the structure in place, particularly when the work load was heavy. Results also depend on what relations are structured within a group. Naylor and Dickinson (1969) observed that arranging the way the task was to be carried out, but not distributing the work components among the group members, was positively related to the effectiveness of the group.

Structural Clarity. The perceived clarity of structure and roles seems to be particularly important. E. E. Smith (1957) studied experimental groups in which both productivity and satisfaction were found to be related to the degree of role clarity of the members. Similarly, Lenski (1956) noted that group members with low degrees of status crystallization tended to experience difficulty in establishing effective, satisfying patterns of interaction with others. Dyer and Lambert (1953) observed that bomber wings were more efficient when members had a clear recognition of the status structure. In a study conducted by the Life Insurance Agency Management Association (1964a), it was found that agents who reported that the job was accurately described before they were hired were less likely to quit than were those who had been less clearly informed. Similarly, Wanous (1973) showed that newly recruited telephone operators who were told both the good and the bad about the job were less likely to quit than were those who were told only about the good aspects. Trieb and Marion (1969), following a study in two companies, agreed that the extent to which new employees had been fully oriented to their jobs was highly related to the employees' subsequent job satisfaction and loyalty to their companies.

Timing and Need for Structure. Kinder and Kol-mann (1976) found that self-actualization from sensitivity training groups[11] was greatest when leaders' and members' roles were highly structured at first and less structured later on. Similarly, Bridges, Doyle, and Mahan (1968) found that hierarchically undifferentiated groups were more effective than were differentiated groups in the analysis of problems but not in the synthetic phases of problem solving.

Individual Differences. Some leaders work better in unstructured situations, while others work better in structured settings. According to Maas (1950), leaders who projected blame on others exhibited a desirable behavioral change when they led relatively informal, unstructured groups. On the other hand, leaders who absorbed blame showed the desirable change when they led formal, structured groups. When placed in reversed situations, both types of leaders exhibited anxiety and signs of stress. Overall, highly structured organizations, both public and private, were expected to determine the types of individuals who will be chosen to work within them. Those individuals who choose to join such bureaucracies are also particular types of individuals. Most important, highly structured organizations socialize those who work within them. However, the facts about these individuals seem to be quite different from their hypothesized personalities.

In line with Weber's arguments about bureaucracies (1924/1947), Merton (1940) suggested that bureaucrats are likely to be inflexible. They are likely to overemphasize the importance of goals for whose attainment the rules were established. The goals will be displaced by the attention to outmoded rules. Actions will continue to be bound by inapplicable rules.

[11]See Chapter 35.

The career orientation of bureaucrats makes them cautious, conservative, and protective of an entrenched position. They are unwilling to be innovative or to take risks. They are impersonal in their thinking and ignore the concerns of clients and their individual needs. Their formal authority breeds arrogance. Furthermore, the selection and socialization processes induce a bureaucratic personality without a sense of personal identity, little intrinsic interest in work, and uncompromising adherence to rules (Bensman & Rosenberg, 1960).

While the above descriptions of the bureaucrat fit the conventional wisdom about them, Goodsell (1983) marshaled considerable evidence to support contrary arguments: Bureaucrats are human, too. In fact, citing Kohn's (1971) structured interview study of 3,101 men working in public and private bureaucratic organizations, men who worked in bureaucratic firms and public agencies were more, not less, self-directed than those who worked in nonbureaucratic firms and agencies. They were more open-minded, had more personally responsible standards of morality, were more receptive to change, and showed greater flexibility in dealing with problems. In explaining why Weber's, Merton's, and Bensman and Rosenberg's expectations about the bureaucratic mind were unsupported, Kohn suggested that bureaucratic organizations tend to select better educated personnel who are challenged to a great degree by their assignments and whose education makes for greater intellectual flexibility. Also, within the bureaucracy, they are freer from arbitrary actions by their superiors.

Structural Complexity. As an organization increases in age, size, and differentiation in structure, the more complex it becomes. More specialization develops within it. Special staffs arise that often have different interests. More political behavior becomes necessary, which requires more compromise and accommodation. Decision making and implementation processes also become more complicated (Thompson, 1967).

As the complexity of the organization increases, the dynamics within it must change. For example, the number of possible coalitions increases. The greater an organization's complexity, the more leadership positions are required. The positions will be arranged hierarchically, with carefully delineated roles and responsibilities; additional power is attached to each position that is higher in the hierarchy (Bryson & Kelley, 1978).

The complexity of the organization will affect the pattern of succession.[12] The greater the complexity, the more levels any candidate needs to climb to reach the top of the hierarchy. Complexity probably also has an effect on the nature of accession to office. As complexity increases, so does factionalism (Tichy, 1973; Tushman, 1977). A structurally complex organization, such as a major corporation, gives rise to officials who are oriented more toward Theory X in their outlook and who are more concerned than normal about their need for safety and less concerned about ego and self-actualizing needs (Applebaum, 1977).

Hunt, Osborn, and Martin (1979, 1981) completed a line of investigation of that part of a leader's behavior that is required—that is, determined by the structured relationships imposed by the organization—and that part which is discretionary. In a study of 68 army telecommunication units, they found that greater complexity in the structure of the unit coincided with more discretionary leadership to improve role clarity and provide support. However, such discretionary leadership did not deal with work assignments or with rules and procedures. In addition, the amount of discretionary leadership correlated with both performance and satisfaction. At the same time, the role clarity required from the leadership correlated .25 with the subordinates' involvement in their jobs and −.24 with the subordinates' intentions to quit (Osborn & Hunt, 1979)

Tall versus Flat Structures. Flat structured organizations have few hierarchical levels and many members or units at each level; tall-structured organizations have many more levels but fewer members or units at each level. Worthy (1950) maintained that flat-structured organizations such as Sears, Roebuck resulted in the greater satisfaction of employees than did tall-structured organizations such as General Electric. Richardson and Walker (1948) studied a company (IBM) in which the number of vertical levels of organization was reduced and concluded that the reduction of social distance between the management and the workers resulted in improved satisfaction and teamwork.

The reported results are decidedly assorted. Ghiselli and Johnson (1970) obtained some support for Worthy's contention by showing that satisfaction of the needs for esteem, autonomy, and self-actualization was higher in the flat than in the tall organizations they studied. However, satisfaction of the needs for security and social relationships did not differ in the two types of organizations. At the same time, ElSalmi and Cummings (1968) found that at the top levels, tall structures produced less fulfillment than did flat or intermediate structures. For lower levels, tall structures resulted in greater fulfillment.

Porter and Lawler (1964) and Porter and Siegel (1965) surveyed managers in tall or flat organizations that varied in size. In small organizations, the satisfaction of managers was greater in flat than in tall organizations, but the findings were reversed for large companies (with more than 5,000 employees). Generally, tall organizations yielded greater satisfaction of security and social needs, while flat organizations gave greater satisfaction of self-actualization. But structure was not at all related to satisfaction of the needs for esteem and autonomy. Similarly, Esser and Strother (1962) found no relationship between the orientation toward rules by managers and the size or flatness of their organization.

In an analysis of experimental organizations with tall and flat structures, Carzo and Yanouzas (1969) found that tall structures required more time to process decisions, but flat structures required more time to coordinate efforts and resolve conflicts. However, tall organizations were superior in profits and the rate of return.

Span of Control. Another way of looking at the effects of tall and flat structures is by examining the effects of the average number of subordinates supervised by each manager. Each manager must supervise many more subordinates in a flat structure than in a tall structure.[13] For example, Kipnis and Cosentino (1969) found that as the supervisory span of control of 131 supervisors from 5 manufacturing firms increased, the number of official warnings the supervisors used to correct employees' undesirable attitudes and behavior also increased. Goodstadt and Kipnis (1970) experimentally manipulated the leader's span of control so that sub-

---

[12]See Chapter 31.

[13]See Van Fleet (1983) for a further discussion of span-of-control research.

jects were led to believe they were supervising either 3 or 8 subordinates. The subjects who believed they were supervising 8 subordinates spent significantly less time talking to problem workers and threatened to fire them on earlier trials than did subjects who believed they had only 3 subordinates. Likewise Ford (1981) found that when supervisors had larger departments to manage, subordinates felt they were shown less consideration by their supervisors. These results are all consistent with the expectation that when faced with a larger number of subordinates who are reporting directly to them, supervisors will be forced to reduce the amount of time they can spend individually with each subordinate. Although it may be possible to remedy the situation with more group meetings, delegation, and the granting of more autonomy, as was seen in the three just-cited studies, management by exception often emerges. With a large span of control, the supervisor tends to concentrate on deviations from standards and efforts to remedy the situation.

Centralization versus Decentralization

Centralization implies that more decisions are made in the headquarters, nucleus, or central authority of the organization and fewer decisions are possible in the peripheral units. Centralization promotes the greater coordination of efforts and activities among the units and more uniform policies with respect to the common goals of the larger organization. It makes possible a more rapid, concerted reaction of the whole organization.

Decentralization usually brings with it more opportunity to react quickly and flexibly to opportunities and threats to the organization. Less filtering of information can occur that is of consequence to the decisions made by the decentralized units. More "ownership," sense of responsibility, and commitment are posited for the decentralized design. But there are costs to decentralization. Thus, Kanter (1982a) described decentralized units that were so concerned about operating issues that their definition of "long range" was the next quarter. T. A. Mahoney (1967) surveyed 283 organizations, obtaining managers' perceptions on 114 variables. Decentralization was found to be correlated negatively with most criteria of organizational effectiveness. In a survey of 217 executives in 109 firms,

Stagner (1969) found that the decentralization of business enterprises was not related to profitability from sales. However, profitability from capital was significantly higher in centralized than in decentralized firms. Nevertheless, Newman and Summer (1961) outlined a set of guides for determining the degree of decentralization that is desirable for an organization, and W. T. Morris (1967) formulated 40 propositions, along with a set of mathematical models, for evaluating the factors involved in the consequences of decentralization.

Dispersion of Authority and Power. Increases in the authority and autonomy of workers come about as a result of managerial policy and action. But such policy is not necessarily dependent on decentralization, although it is more easily facilitated by higher managers when they work through the few, rather than many, levels of authority of the decentralized organization (Cordiner, 1952; Newman & Logan, 1965; Zald, 1964). Thus, decentralization has been advocated as a method for reducing the concentration of authority in high-level positions and for filtering it down to employees (Kline & Martin, 1958; Kruisinga, 1954). However, the major reasons why managers are motivated to decentralize are that they are usually concerned about problems of coordination. As organizations become larger, with many geographically dispersed subunits involving numerous products, the problems of coordination and responding to local changes induce a tendency toward decentralization (Chandler, 1956, 1962).

Legitimate power is usually disseminated outward when an organization decentralizes. The effects were seen by Baum (1961), who studied the U.S. Civil Service Commission and eight other dependent federal agencies. The commission formulates and enforces policies that must be applied by the agencies in hiring and promoting personnel. Baum found that the decentralization of hiring and promotion were handled effectively only when the agencies accepted and attempted to comply with the policies of the controlling commission. Executives in the more successful agencies regarded decentralization as providing them with the authority they deserved, but the executives in the less successful agencies saw the decentralized function as work.

In Baum's study, decentralization was accompanied

by an increase in the decision-making authority of those in the higher levels of administration. Likewise, M. W. Meyer's (1968) survey of 254 city, county, and state departments of finance found that with the size of the organizations held constant, the number of organizational subunits decreased, but the number of levels of supervision within the subunits increased with the decentralization of decision making. Most important, decentralization was associated with more rules for the evaluation of decisions.

Centralization of Industrial Relations. Baker and France (1954) examined the personnel and industrial relations departments of a sample of firms. They observed that top managers tended to prefer the decentralization of industrial-relations functions so that local problems arising in a specific plant could be solved as they arose. Union officials, on the other hand, preferred the centralization of industrial-relations functions as an aid in industry-wide bargaining. M. Whitehill (1968) surveyed companies in the meat-packing industry and found that union negotiations with centralized structures by means of contacts with the main office resulted in more benefits for employees than did negotiations with decentralized structures involving contacts with local plants.

Centralization and the Competence of Subordinates. Centralization or decentralization may be a consequence rather than a cause. Blau (1968) investigated 250 governmental agencies and found that decentralization was most prevalent in agencies that employed a large number of highly qualified personnel. On the other hand, the presence of automation and poorly qualified personnel in large agencies was accompanied by more vertical levels of organization and tighter managerial control.

Legislative Centralization. Centralization of legislative leadership was seen by Bryson and Kelley (1978) as being likely to give greater enforcement power to the leadership and more stability. But more conflicts are also likely because of reduced consultation and the lack of sharing of information (A. Rosenthal, 1974). Consensual decision making becomes less frequent with centralization (Mechanic, 1962; Pettigrew, 1972). Adversarial relationships will be greater (R. A. Gordon,

1961) unless statesmen appear at the top of the centralized leadership (Selznick, 1951). Centralization promotes coups (S. Kahn, 1970).

Stable versus Changing Organizations

The importance of organizational stability was seen to vary as a function of the size of organizations. England (1967b) reported that managers of middle-sized companies rated organizational stability generally higher in importance than did managers of small companies. Stability was of least importance to managers of large companies.

Using data from 215 governmental departments, M. W. Meyer (1975) found that the stability of organizational structure was lower when the leaders had changed a great deal in the past, when leaders were dependent on a higher authority, and when the leaders maintained close contact with their superiors.

The top managements of stable firms were found by Burns (1957) to differ from those of firms that were growing. Burns (1957) collected diaries for 3 to 5 weeks from 76 British top managers in medium-sized companies. Top managers in expanding firms spent relatively more time in discussions with one another. There was little flow of information up and down the hierarchical structures in the growing than in the stable firms. Again, Kerr (1985) demonstrated, in 89 interviews about the managerial compensation systems of 20 large industrial firms, that compensation was hierarchically based in the stable, steady-state firms that were committed to existing products and markets. On the other hand, compensation was more likely to be performance-based in less stable "evolutionary" firms that were involved in acquisitions, mergers, and joint ventures, sometimes in unfamiliar external markets and technologies.

Other Organizational Constraints

Managers may have to operate under many other organizational constraints that will systematically affect their styles of behavior, performance, and satisfaction. Unionization makes a difference in their behavior. The various task-related, interpersonal, and policy barriers to getting work done are also constraints that affect the style, performance, and satisfaction of supervisors. Also illustrative are the extent to which organizations require secrecy, restrict employees from bypassing the chain of command, and are scarce in resources.

Hare (1957) observed that self-oriented and group-oriented leaders among groups of boys did not differ in aggression at an adult-supervised playground at school, but self-oriented leaders were significantly more aggressive in unsupervised neighborhood play conditions. There were more differences between the situations than between the leadership styles. Disagreement was higher in both styles in the supervised playground, while tension and antagonism were higher in the unsupervised neighborhood play conditions. Similarly, Farrow, Valenzi, and Bass (1980) found that the leadership styles of direction and consultation were greater when more organization, order, and imposed constraints were present. But less manipulativeness by leaders was observed under these constrained conditions if goals were clear and levels of trust among the members were high.

Obstacles. Peters and O'Connor (1980) identified a number of situational variables that are likely to interfere with the supervisors' accomplishment of tasks, such as the lack of ready availability of materials and supplies. Laboratory studies confirmed the importance of the availability of materials and supplies to getting the work done and to job satisfaction (Peters, Fisher, & O'Connor, 1982). Field studies yielded more complex results. From an open-ended questionnaire, completed by 300 national managers of a chain of convenience stores, O'Connor, Peters, Pooyan, et al. (1984) identified 22 organizational constraints on the managers' work. These constraints were the shortage of help; the lack of authority to enforce company standards; bypassed authority; insufficient training; inadequate equipment; inadequate help; frequent, long, and inappropriate meetings; excessive paperwork; unscheduled activities; ignorance of company policies and procedures; an inadequate amount of merchandise; the lack of job-related information; inadequate response time and budgetary support; inappropriate work space; unkept appointments; excessive inventory; insufficient materials and supplies; theft by customers and by employees; work overload; and wrong inventory. For a sample of 1,450 first-, second-, and third-level managers

of the chain of convenience stores, the investigators obtained a correlation of −.40 between the managers' satisfaction with supervision and the extent to which they perceived overall that these constraints were operating in their work settings. These relations held for all three levels of management, although, as expected, satisfaction with supervision was greater at each successive level of management.

Situational constraints may place managers under a double handicap. In addition to making their assignments more difficult, the managers may also be appraised as performing less adequately than is justified by the objective evidence. Steel and Mento (1986) investigated the impact of situational constraints (job-induced obstacles; interpersonal obstacles; and environmental, policy, and procedural constraints) on the objective performance, along with supervisors' appraisals and self-ratings, of 438 branch managers of a finance company. The constraints were highly intercorrelated and formed a single factor scale. The district manager's supervisory appraisals of the branch managers correlated −.36 with the situational constraints faced by the managers. That is, the more constraints faced by the branch managers, the lower were the appraisals they earned. But the constraints had little actual effect on the objective performance of the managers, except possibly on their ability to control past-due accounts.

Requirements of Secrecy. A constraint that limits whether managers can be participative with their subordinates is the extent to which the organization requires secrecy concerning products, techniques, and business strategies. Employees cannot be asked to participate in decisions if much of the information required to discuss such decisions cannot be revealed to them (Tannenbaum & Massarik, 1950).

Chain of Command. The ability or lack of ability to bypass formal organizational lines of communication appeared to affect leaders' evaluations of their subordinates. On the basis of the responses of 395 white-collar employees and managers of the engineering division of a public utility to a questionnaire, Hunt, Osborn, and Schuler (1978) concluded that a manager's approval of subordinates was predicted by the adequacy of the organization's general communication and planning and how much the manager received orders out of the chain of command. The manager's disapproval of subordinates was also affected by these out-of-the-chain-of-command orders, over which the manager had no control.

Unionization. Although leader-subordinate relations within an organization would seem to be mediated by whether the subordinates belonged to a strong or weak union or to none at all, few empirical comparisons have been made. One would expect, for example, that arbitrary, capricious, coercive management would be highly constrained if workers had a second route to upward influence via a strong and effective union. It is more likely that such management would result in unionization that, in turn, would reinforce management's rule-bound leadership in place of arbitrariness. A rare empirical study of the effect of unionization on supervisory-subordinate relations within a firm was completed by Hammer and Turk (1985), who collected data from 160 first-line supervisors in 12 sections of a factory with an employee union. The percentage of workers who belonged to the union varied from zero to 82 percent, depending on the section. Regression analyses showed that the "density" of union members in a section contributed uniquely to the section supervisor's emphasis on performance, "going by the book," and sense of a clear authority to discipline. This last result could be explained by the union contract. The supervisors' use of discipline and penalties against subordinates was regulated. It was power granted to the supervisor through negotiations between management and labor, specified in the union contract. Supervisors, abiding by the contract, knew the rights they had both to reward and to punish; so did their unionized subordinates. On the other hand, union stewards, according to E. L. Miller (1966), need to remain mindful of the employees' rights and interests.

Leadership and Organizational Culture

Intertwined with the philosophy, purposes, functions, and structure of the organization is its culture. Pericles identified the four aspects of the culture of Athens as an organized polity that made it so valuable to its citizenry. First, it was open, democratic, and optimistic about its citizens' individual capabilities. Job assignments and promotions were based on merit, and the individual's dignity was upheld. Everyone was equal before the law. Second, its culture promoted beauty, good taste, and personal satisfaction in home, work, and play. Third, it was a culture of innovation; it provided the models for others to follow. Fourth, it encouraged an alignment of the interests of the individual citizen with those of the state (Clemens & Mayer, 1987).

Contents of an Organizational Culture

Weick (1979) suggested that the primary function of organizations is "sense making." Organizational members develop a set of mutually acceptable ideas and beliefs about what is real, what is important, and how to respond. The culture of an organization is this shared learned pattern of behavior, transmitted from one generation to the next (Deal & Kennedy, 1982). It includes the values that are shared by the members, the heroes who exemplify the organization's values, the rituals that provide for the expressive bonding of members and cultural learning, and the stories that transmit the culture's values and ideas. The contents of a culture that may be studied are listed in Table 26.2.

Two investigations are illustrative. Martin, Feldman, Hatch, and Sitkin (1983) collected three types of stories that members told to assert the distinctiveness of their own organizational impact on how the organizational culture communicates what is to be expected from its leadership. The stories told about (1) whether the big boss was human and, when presented with an opportunity to perform a status-equalizing act, did or did not do so, (2) rule breaking (for instance, a senior manager broke a rule and was confronted by a junior person), and (3) how the boss reacted to mistakes. Rosen (1985) completed an ethnographic study of an advertising agency that demonstrated how the senior management manipulated the language, gestures, and context of a breakfast ritual to ensure acceptance of the goals and practices of the company. This ritual reinforced and reaffirmed the bureaucratic structure of the organization and its capitalistic values.

Table 26.2 Frequently Studied Cultural Forms

Cultural Form	Definition
Rite	Relatively elaborate, dramatic, planned sets of activities that consolidate various forms of cultural expressions into one event, which is carried out through social interactions, usually for the benefit of an audience.
Ceremonial	A system of several rites connected with a single occasion or event.
Ritual	A standardized, detailed set of techniques and behaviors that manage anxieties but seldom produce intended technical consequences that are of practical importance.
Myth	A dramatic narrative of imagined events, usually used to explain the origins or transformations of something. Also, an unquestioned belief about the practical benefits of certain techniques and behaviors that is not supported by demonstrated facts.
Saga	An historical narrative describing the unique accomplishments of a group and its leaders, usually in heroic terms.
Legend	A handed-down narrative of some wonderful event that is based in history but has been embellished with fictional details.
Story	A narrative based on true events—often a combination of truth and fiction.
Folktale	A fictional narrative.
Symbol	Any object, act, event, quality, or relation that serves as a vehicle for conveying meaning, usually by representing another thing.
Language	A particular form or manner in which members of a group use vocal sounds and written signs to convey meanings to each other.
Gesture	A movement of a part of the body used to express meaning.
Physical setting	Those things that surround people physically and provide them with immediate sensory stimuli as they carry out culturally expressive activities.
Artifact	Material objects manufactured by people to facilitate culturally expressive activities.

SOURCE: Adapted from Trice (1984, p. 655).

Jung's (1971) psychology provides a useful fourfold view of widely divergent organizational cultures. These cultures are bureaucracies with sense-thinking managers, matrix organizations with intuitive-thinking leaders, organic organizations with intuitive-feeling leaders, and familiar cultures with sensing-feeling members (Mitroff, 1983).

Assumptions. Basic assumptions about the nature of reality, time, space, human nature, and the environment are taken for granted at a preconscious level by those who are embedded in the organization's culture. There is a greater level of awareness about the interrelated values, and the art, technology, and behavior that emerges is visible but not necessarily "decipherable." It often takes an outsider to understand the cultural connections of the observable products and behavior to the underlying values and preconscious assumptions. Early in its development, an organizational culture is the "glue" that holds the organization together

as a source of identity and distinctive competence. But in an organization's decline, its culture can become a constraint on innovation, since it is focused on the organization's past glories (Schein, 1985).

Normative Values. To describe a particular organization's culture, Kilmann and Saxton (1983) list eight questions that the organizational culture answers: (1) What makes sense; what can be talked about? (2) Who am I; where do I belong? (3) Who rules; how, why, and by what means? (4) What are the unwritten rules of the game for what really counts; how do I stay out of trouble? (5) Why are we here and for what purposes? (6) What is our history, geography, and the structure we build? (7) What are the stories about ourselves and others? and (8) What are our morality and ethics? Are people basically good or evil? The Kilmann-Saxton (1983) cultural-gap survey asks organizational members to describe the strength of their organization's norms. The norms deal with task support, task innovation, social relationships, and autonomy of individual members all of which are expected to contribute to an organization's performance and satisfaction. Low scores are seen to reflect gaps in the organization's culture that are required for better performance and satisfaction.

To focus more specifically on those aspects of a corporate culture that contribute to organizational excellence, Sashkin (1986, 1988) extracted seven explicit and three implicit core values or beliefs from Peters and Waterman (1982). Included were task-relevant values, such as being the best at what the company does, attending to details in doing a job, superior quality and service, importance of economic growth and profits, and managers as "hands-on doers," not just planners and administrators. Other values were more concerned with relationships: people, as individuals, are important; people in the organization should be innovators and should take risks without feeling that they will be punished if they fail; informality is important to improve the flow of communication throughout the organization; and people should have fun doing their work.

All these values should be made explicit in a recognized organizational philosophy that is developed and supported by those at the top. Sashkin constructed the Organizational Beliefs Questionnaire to measure respondents' estimations of whether others in their organization subscribed to such beliefs as "People in this organization believe in being the very best at what we do." Construct validation was obtained by showing greater variance among rather than within 46 organizations. A total score reflecting the endorsement of values that promote excellence was found to be higher in more effective organizations.

Cultural Transmitters. Kouzes and Posner (1987) emphasized the importance of the leader in transmitting the organization's culture and values. The organization contains a network of "priests," who maintain and bless the values; "storytellers," who watch over the values; and "gossips," who are key transmitters of the culture (Deal & Kennedy, 1982).

The Leader as Culture Builder

The organization's culture derives from its antecedent leadership. It also affects its subsequent leader-subordinate relationships in a variety of ways. Anecdotal evidence and argumentation abound in considering how an organization's leadership influences its culture. For Schein (1985), leadership is critical to the creation and maintenance of culture. Bass (1985a) suggested that while transactional leaders work within their organizational culture, transformational leaders change them. Tichy and Ulrich (1984) thought that the transformational leader needs to understand and realign the organization's culture as a way of providing meaning by making sense of symbols and events.

Hickman and Silva (1984) argued that the two bases of effective organizational performance are strategic thinking and culture building by the leaders. Strategic thinking creates the vision of a firm's future. The vision becomes a reality when the leaders build a culture that is dedicated to the vision. In contrast to transactional leadership, the leaders here are visionary executives who integrate creative insight and sensitivity to "forge the strategy-culture alloy." These leaders combine versatility, focus, and patience to maintain the organization's highly effective performance over the long term.

According to Kiefer and Senge (1984), such leadership pushes for a "metanoic" organization, building on such assumptions as people are inherently good, honest, trustworthy, and purposeful; everyone has a unique contribution to make; and complex problems require local solutions. Leaders who build such cultures need to have personalities with a deep sense of vision and purposefulness. They are aligned around that vision and can balance reason and intuition, as well as empower others (Kiefer, 1986; Senge, 1980). Such leaders display much individualized consideration (Bass, 1985a). They facilitate and teach. They "create" rather than "maintain" and are personally involved with the development of key managers (Senge, 1984, 1986).

For Schein (1985), one is likely to see a constant interplay between culture and leadership. Leaders create the mechanisms for cultural embedding and reinforcement. Cultural norms arise and change because of what leaders tend to focus their attention on, their reactions to crises, their role modeling, and their recruitment strategies. For Schein, the organizational culture is taught by its leadership.

Leadership and Organizational Climate. An important feature of an organization's culture is its climate—the subjective feelings about the organization among those who work within it. The climate directly affects how these persons relate to each other. As might be expected, Kozlowski and Doherty (1989) showed that the quality of leader-subordinate relations was directly related to the satisfaction felt about the organization's climate. Halpin and Croft (1962) found systematic connections among scales measuring different aspects of a school's organizational climate and leadership and the response of teachers. Sheridan and Vredenburgh (1978a) showed that the head nurses' consideration and initiation of structure in a hospital could be explained partly by the turnover among staff members and the administrative climate, as measured by an instrument developed by Pritchard and Karasick (1973). J. L. Franklin (1975) examined similar relations in a broader organizational context. Particularly important to an organization's climate are how clear its leaders make the organization's goals to the members and convey a sense that the climate is one in which there is a high degree of trust among its members.

For 78 executives described by 407 subordinates, Bass, Valenzi, Farrow, and Solomon (1975) used stepwise regression to determine that in organizations described as more trusting, more participative leadership behavior was observed. In organizations that the subordinates perceived as having clear goals, the managers were described as more directive, more likely to consult with their subordinates, and more likely to share decision making with the subordinates. In a follow-up with descriptions by over 1,200 subordinates of their superiors' leadership behavior and aspects of the organization, Farrow, Valenzi, and Bass (1980) found that consultation was most frequent when organizational goals were clear and levels of trust were high. Similarly according to Hunt, Osborn, and Schuler (1978), an organization with overall practices that promoted the clarity of jobs and clear standards increased the leaders' supportive behavior toward their subordinates. Again Child and Ellis (1973) concluded that more delegation by the superior was seen if work roles were clear and much discretion was perceived in the organization's climate.

In a survey study of 440 Indian managers from 7 organizations, Ansari (1988) found that whether the climate was "favorable" or "unfavorable" affected the managers' efforts to influence. If the climate was favorable, participative managers said they were more individually considerate to their subordinates and less likely to try to block or defy their bosses, task-oriented managers said they increased the use of their expertise and reasoning with both their bosses and their subordinates, and bureaucrats said they were more likely to challenge their subordinates and be ingratiating toward their boss. If the climate was unfavorable, participative managers were more likely to use coalition tactics and to manipulate their subordinates and were ingratiating and negotiating with their bosses. The task-oriented managers said they were less defiant toward their bosses, and the bureaucrats said they were more assertive with their subordinates and more transactional and diplomatic with their bosses.

Founders of Organizational Cultures

The creation of much of the organizations' cultures is attributed to their entrepreneurial founders (Pettigrew, 1973; 1979). For example, Schein (1983) noted that a founder creates a culture from a preconceived "cultural paradigm" in his or her head. Then, the founder's and successor's leadership shapes the culture and the mechanisms to restrain it. But Schein and others assumed that a monolithic culture of shared values emerges that is guided and controlled by the founder. Martin, Sitkin, and Boehm's (1985) detailed interview study of a young and growing electronics manufacturing firm in Silicon Valley, California, with 700 employees suggested that the founders' values may conflict to some extent with those of various constituencies in the firm. In this case, although 72 percent of the employees' explanations of the company's origins, quality control, and turnover were in agreement with the founders' interpretations, 19 percent were not.

Some founders, such as Steven Jobs of Apple Computer, who do not have previous leadership and management experience or much formal education, form companies and originate corporate cultures that they must leave to others to manage. However, in general, the facts are otherwise. Among the CEOs of the fastest growing companies in the United States, three-fourths were founders of their companies, and 83 percent, like Walt Disney of Disney Productions or Ray Kroc of McDonald's, never made plans to retire. They were not just inspired originators; they also had the credentials for long-term tenure. All but 19 percent were college graduates; 46 percent held graduate degrees, mostly in engineering; and half had managerial experience in a Fortune 500 company before founding their own company (Nicholson, 1983).

Founders of Countercultures

John DeLorean and Hyman Rickover are examples of founders of countercultures. Martin and Siehl (1983) described John DeLorean's counterculture, which was built within General Motors in reaction to GM's dominant cultural values of deference to authority, invisibility, and loyalty. The heads of divisions of General Motors (GM), despite some degree of autonomy, were expected to conform closely to GM's dominant values. Deference to authority was expressed, for instance, in the way

> subordinates were expected to meet their superiors from out of town at the airport, carry their bags, pay their hotel and meal bills, and chauffeur them around day and night. The higher the status of the superior, the more people would accompany him on the flight and the larger the retinue that would wait at the airport. (p. 57)

DeLorean enraged his boss by failing to meet him at the airport and thereby signaling disrespect for his boss's authority. He also created and recounted stories about the foolish extravagances of subordinates who catered to the whims of visiting VIPs. In the GM culture, invisibility was expressed in such ways as maintaining standardized offices; eating together in the executive dining room; and adopting a uniform dress code of dark suit, white shirt, and blue or black tie. Again, DeLorean violated these rules, for example, in requesting a brighter, more modern and attractive office decor and dressing in a more fashionable but still conservative continental mode. Loyalty in the GM culture was expressed by not voicing criticisms in front of the corporate management. DeLorean invented stories to interpret the costs to GM of "group think" and conformity.

DeLorean's counterculture was an attempt to support the value of productivity instead of deference, of objective measures of performance instead of subjective indicators of conformity, and of independence instead of blind loyalty. But his deviance remained within tolerable limits until he left to found his own company, which had notorious consequences. It remained for Roger Smith, a new CEO, to reshape GM's dominant culture.

Hyman Rickover almost singlehandedly constructed a powerful naval counterestablishment in the Nuclear Reactors Branch of the U.S. Navy (Polmar & Allen, 1981). This branch became a separate elite nuclear establishment in control de facto by 1980 of one-third of the U.S. naval fleet! Rickover formed this counterestablishment for his self-satisfaction and to coincide with his personal views of what was wrong with the U.S. Navy's values and practices, in general, and the Naval Academy at Annapolis, in particular. His manufactured culture included horrendous stress interviews that were of questionable validity for applicants, generally favoring graduates of NROTC rather than of the academy. Discipline was extreme, focused on overlearning and dedication. There was an intense emphasis on both detailed direction and the practice of management by exception, which involved the bypassing of channels and weekly reports written personally to Rickover. There was an unrelenting pressure to work and study. Rickover, himself, set the workaholic pace in a Spartan office with Spartan lunches. He was almost always in civilian dress. Expertise took precedence over rank, and specialization, over general management.

As civilian chief of the Naval Reactors Branch of the Atomic Energy Commission and later, of the Department of Energy and the U.S. Navy's chief for nuclear propulsion, Rickover was the nuclear organization's network center. For two decades after he would have been retired by the U.S. Navy, he maintained his power, authority, and budget, bypassing the navy and going directly to Congress. Although experiments with nuclear reactors for propulsion preceded him, he made himself the mythological originator. He rejected cost considerations in the decisions over whether to build nuclear or conventional fleets. Only nuclear submarines and surface vessels were valued. The result of all this was a large first-rate, nuclear navy, built at the expense of a larger, possibly more nationally useful, conventional fleet. A higher price was paid in financial and human costs than was necessary. The human costs were evidenced ultimately in the failure to maintain a sufficient number of volunteers for the nuclear submarine fleet (Polmar & Allen, 1982).

Promoting Changes in the Dominant Culture

But one does not have to construct a counterculture to improve the existing culture. The issue to which top management is particularly sensitive is the leadership required for managing organizational change in its culture. Such change is necessitated by new marketing requirements, new technologies, and new kinds of personnel (Bass, 1985a; Bennis & Nanus, 1985).

Leavitt (1986) and Tichy and Devanna (1986), among others, provided book-length advice, consistent with research results about transformational leaders, on how to accomplish the needed changes in the organizational culture. It is essential for top management to articulate the change that is required. The message may be of a vision that entails *directive* and persuasive leadership; it may permit modifications and contributions from others. Changes, consistent with the message, are introduced in the structure, processes, and practices, and sufficient participation is encouraged to generate commitment, loyalty, and involvement, accompanied by full two-way communication with adequate feedback loops. Desired role and behavioral models of leadership begin at the top and are encouraged at each successive level below. Furthermore, leaders who are concerned about organizational renewal will seek to foster organizational cultures and climates that are hospitable and conducive to creativity, problem solving, risk taking, and experimentation. Kane (1984) described how the General Electric culture was changed in this way by the transformational leadership of Jack Welch. First, there was articulation of the changes that were desired. Next, the necessary changes in structure, processes, and practices were made and were widely communicated. Finally, new role and behavioral models were established.

According to Wilkins and Bristow (1987), when trying to promote cultural changes in an organization, say to shift it from a service to a market orientation, such as occurred in A T & T, leaders should first honor the past, returning to it for inspiration and instruction and

identifying past objectives, principles, and still-successful approaches that will be maintained. As Gardner (1988b, p. 6) pointed out, "Leaders must understand the interweaving of continuity and change . . . in long-term purposes and values." Promotions should be made to ensure that these older values can survive despite the oncoming changes. Ceremonial events are needed to mourn the loss of the cherished past. Finally, changes should be organic, developing out of new ways that are already desired and providing reinforcement for new incremental efforts that are attempted and successful.

Organizational Culture and Manipulation by Management. Mitchell (1985) contrasted the values explicit in two empirical studies of successful enterprises. One was Peters and Waterman's (1982) *In Search of Excellence,* which identified 62 firms that had a history of growth, economic success, and innovativeness over a 25-year period.[14] The other was Levering, Moskowitz, and Katz's (1984) *The 100 Best Companies to Work for in America.* These were the 100 companies that employees said they liked to work for. Only 21 of the 100 best-liked firms showed up among the 62 excellently managed companies mentioned by Peters and Waterman. Peters and Waterman considered the management of the task-effective culture to be manipulative. That is, in such a culture people are valued not for themselves but as being instrumental to productivity. Employees' values are shaped to increase their commitment to productivity, the institution, and the maintenance of the work ethic. The manipulation is not done through conviction but through myths, fables, and fairy tales about values that the management itself does not necessarily believe in. As Mitchell (1985, p. 353) stated:

> Peters and Waterman say: "all the companies we interviewed [from Boeing and McDonald's] were quite simply rich tapestries of anecdote, myth and fairy tale" (p. 75). . . . the great leader "is concerned with the tricks of the pedagogue, the mentor, the linguist, the more successfully to become the value shaper, the exemplar, the making of meanings" (p. 82).

[14]The excellently managed firms actually do not appear to provide greater returns on investment to shareholders than do their less well-managed counterparts. However, they do seem to be less risky investments in that the price of their stocks is less variable (Simpson & Ireland, 1987).

In contrast, many of the 100 best companies to work for, according to their employees, stressed more truly relations-oriented values, such as making employees feel they were part of a team or family, encouraging open communication, encouraging suggestions, promoting from within, enabling people to feel pride in their products or services, sharing profits, reducing social distance, making the workplace as pleasant as possible, encouraging the employees' participation in community service, matching employee savings funds, avoiding layoffs whenever possible, showing concern for the employees' health, and providing training and the reimbursement of tuition.

Specific policy statements about these values were found among many of the 100 best-liked firms. For instance, Apple Computer stated that employees should be able to trust the motives and integrity of their supervisors. Armstrong declared that management should respect the dignity and inherent rights of the individual, maintain high moral and ethical standards, and reflect honesty, integrity, reliability, and forthrightness. According to the policy statements of Doyle, Dane, & Bernbach, employees and the firm may refuse to work on advertising accounts for ethical reasons or on accounts that may have negative effects on the public. Other firms focused on statements about the need for mutual trust and respect (Moog); honesty (Rolm); and dignity, fairness, kindness, and the professional treatment of all individuals and organizations with whom they work (Celestial Seasonings).

Mitchell (1985) concluded that what seems to be the best-managed firms may be different from those for whom employees most like to work. The management of the former creates a culture, with its symbols and myths, to get employees to work harder and better; the management of the latter seems genuinely to care about the quality of the experience of everyone in the firm. In the former, management may practice consideration but really believe in exploitation; in the latter, a truer concern for others is seen in their employees' evaluations.

The Effects of the Organization's Culture on the Leader

Schein (1985) suggested that culture manages management more than management manages culture. For instance, a strong organizational culture, with values and internal guidelines for more autonomy at lower levels, can prevent top management from increasing its personal power at the expense of middle management (Rubin & Berlew, 1984).

Trice and Beyer (1984, p. 666) noted that

> managers need to learn to . . . assess not only the technical consequences of any activities and programs, but also their possible ceremonial, expressive consequences. . . . Also, they need to learn and practice effective ceremonial skills. Some flair for the dramatic and the ability to be expressive in speech, writing, and gestures could be an asset in meeting the ceremonial requirements of managerial roles.

Managers particularly need to attend to the conservativeness, reflected in rites and ceremonials, that can hinder efforts to change the organization. They need to modify the rites and ceremonials, when it is possible to do so, to fit with the desired new directions for the organization. They can invent new rites to replace the old, some of which symbolize the value of change itself (Hedberg, Nystrom, & Starbuck, 1976). One example is the ceremonial introduction of a new product or process to replace an older one.

Lombardo (1983) described three corporations, A, B, and C, each of whose different cultures (highly task oriented, highly pragmatic, and highly considerate of others) resulted in the development of parallel differences among their respective managers. In the same way, Roberts's (1986) survey of the styles used by 350 business managers and university administrators with their subordinates, peers, and bosses described earlier found that managers in Type Z organizations (Japanese-style organizations) were less likely to be directive than were their counterparts in Type A (authoritarian, top-down organizations).

Effects of Clan and Market Cultures. Kerr and Slocum (1987) identified two types of corporate reward systems that give rise to two different cultures—clan and market—and characteristically different leadership experiences. Table 26.3 details the characteristics of the clan and market cultures. In the clan culture, one's superior defines and evaluates, usually subjectively, one's managerial performance. There is promotion from within, often connected with one's need for fur-

Table 26.3 Contrasting Organizational Cultures

Aspect of the Culture	Type of Culture	
	Clan	Market
Relationship of the Individual and the Organization	Fraternal Long-term commitment Mutual interests; shared fate Hierarchical	Contractual Short-term commitment Self-interests, utilitarian Depends on the contract
Relationship among Organizational Members	Price in membership Interdependence Identification with peers Pressure to conform Stress on teamwork	Independence from peers Limited interaction Little pressure to conform Stress on individual initiative
Process of Acculturation	Long socialization. Superiors are mentors, role models, and agents of socialization. The "rich" normative structure governs a wide range of behaviors.	Little socialization. Superiors are distant; are negotiators and allocators of resources. The "lean" normative structure governs few behaviors.

SOURCE: Adpated from Kerr and Slocum (1987, pp. 102 and 104).

ther development. People are expected to do more than just what is agreed in contracts. Loyalty to the organization is exchanged for commitment to it (Ouchi, 1981).

A contrasting market culture develops from a performance-based contingent-reward system. One's role is specifically defined and evaluated by objective, financial outcomes. There is much less need for superior-subordinate interaction or concern for the subordinates' socialization and development. Presumably, the clan culture provides more potential for transformational leadership and the market culture, for transactional leadership.

Effects of Kibbutz Ownership. The effects of the culture of kibbutzim on their top officials' leadership of firms that the kibbutzim owned as cooperatives was contrasted with the leadership of counterpart publicly and privately owned business firms by Chitayat and Venezia (1984). It was found that among a sample of 224 Israeli senior executives, the business executives were more *directive*, negotiative, and delegative and less *participative* than were the general managers of firms owned by the kibbutzim. They also had relatively greater power and were more assertive, but they did not differ from the executives of the kibbutzim-owned

firms in the amount of consultation they did or how well informed they were.

Instrumentality and Expressiveness in the Culture. Santner (1986) used the High School Characteristics Index to describe two schools, one with a low instrumental, low expressive school climate and the other with a high instrumental, high expressive school climate,[15] to show the different effects of the two climates on the character of those who emerged as student leaders in the two situations. In the low instrumental, low expressive school, personality-tested dominance and friendliness discriminated the formal leaders of official school groups as well as the informal leaders whom their peers distinguished from the nonleaders. In addition, in this low instrumental, low expressive school, highly achievement-oriented girls were most likely to be the formal leaders and lower achievement-oriented boys were more likely to be the informal leaders. But, in the high instrumental, high expressive school, tested dominance was the only significant

[15]A highly instrumental climate is one in which rewards are contingent on the appropriate performance of subordinates and means are more important than ends. In an expressive climate, there is more spontaneity, more actions based on sentiments and feelings rather than on carefully thought-out means to ends.

factor that differentiated the leaders from the non-leaders.

Summary and Conclusions

How the leader and subordinates relate to each other within the group depends on societal influences, real outside relationships, and reference groups in the minds of both. For example, leaders who see economic externalities as most important tend to be more directive, but leaders who believe social or political influences from the outside to be more important tend to be more participative.

The surrounding organization and its policies, size, structure, and culture are of particular consequence to leader-subordinate interactions. Although the organization and its culture influence what is expected of the leaders and what they will do, the leaders in turn, shape their organizations and culture to fit their needs. The leader's discretionary and nondiscretionary behavior depends on organizational and environmental considerations. But equally important is the immediate group in which the leadership occurs—the subject that is discussed next.

Leaders and Their Immediate Groups

Earlier chapters explored the interacting nature of leader-follower relations. This chapter concentrates on the effects of the group qua group on its leadership and the effects of the leadership on its group of members as a collective entity. What a leader does will depend on the attributes of the group as a whole (Barnlund, 1962; Carter, Haythorn, Shriver, & Lanzetta, 1951), just as what the group does depends on the leader.

Importance of the Group

The attitudes and activities of the group transcend those of its individual members. Group norms can survive even if all the members are changed. Members behave differently when they are isolated from each other than when they are all together. The leader's dyadic relations with each of his or her subordinates may not reflect the leader's relations with the same subordinates as a group.

The group's drive, cohesion, selection of goals, and attainment of goals are likely to be influenced by the leader. Individual members will be affected by the leader's relationship to the group. Thus, individual subordinates may react differently to a leader when they are alone with the leader than when they are in a group with the leader.

A number of other aspects of leader-group relations go beyond the relations of the leader and each of the individual members. The group narrows the range of possible leader–individual subordinate interactions in the interests of equity and time and because of the group's expectations about the leader. The leader's reactions to the group may have a stronger impact on the members than may the leader's reactions to them as individuals. Again, supervisors are evaluated on the basis of the performance of their groups rather than on the performance of individual members of the groups (Schriesheim, Mowday, & Stogdill, 1979).

The focus on the performance of the work group, rather than on the performance of the individual employee, is likely to be greater when labor is stronger and unionized. The group's relation to the leader will be more important than will the individual employee's relation to the leader (Bramel & Friend, 1987).

Deindividuation

The group effect becomes especially strong if "deindividuation" occurs in its members, that is, if the group members lose their identity as individuals and merge themselves into the group. In such a case, the members lose much of their inhibitions and behave uncharacteristically (LeBon, 1897). The disinhibition of deindividuation makes it easier for group members to discuss intimate problems with a stranger whom they expect never to see again than with friends or relatives. Festinger, Pepitone, and Newcomb (1952) studied groups of students who were required to discuss personal family matters. They confirmed that the students experienced less restraint in doing so under a condition of deindividuation, which minimized the attention they paid to one another as individuals. Deindividuation constituted a satisfying state of group affairs associated with increased group attractiveness when it was present. In the same way, Rosenbaum (1959) and Leipold (1963) found that participants preferred to maintain a greater psychosocial distance between themselves and their partners when potentially unfavorable evaluations might be fed back to them than when no such information was anticipated.

Individual identity is ordinarily stressed if rewards are anticipated; deindividuation is more likely to occur if punishment is expected. Furthermore, deindividuation will increase with anonymity, the level of emotional arousal, and the novelty of the situation. The loss of inhibition will be reflected in less compliance with outside authority and more conforming to the demands of the in-group. Responses are more immediate, and there is less self-awareness and premeditation. The collective mission is stressed over the individual's needs. Disinhibition and the loss of self-identity unleash the energy to accomplish great feats if they have constructive direction. They also facilitate the rabble rouser. We become inhibited from ordinary social constraints when we lose ourselves in a crowd. The riot-inciting leader can generate mindless mob violence.

Overt and Covert Effects

Particularly in Japan, the group is likely to have a strong influence on its leader. Thus, Furukawa (1981) showed, in a survey of 1,576 Japanese managers, that managers establish their primary management objective from among a set of possibilities after judging how it fits with their work group's interests and favorability to them.

Leader-member relations are also affected less overtly by the group. Some of the assumptions that determine an organizational culture are fantasies that are shared by members in a group that is embedded in the larger organization (Kets de Vries & Miller, 1984a). Idealization or devaluation of the leader and dependence on him or her is one such shared fantasy. One group, as a group, in the same larger organization will be dependent on whoever is assigned the job of group leader. Another group, without the same assumptions, will display more independence or counterdependence, regardless of who is appointed leader. A leader of a group with a clique who behaves the same way as the leader of another group without a clique will be evaluated differently by the two groups. E. R. Carlson (1960) showed that groups that contain cliques will be less satisfied with their leaders than will groups that are free from such cliques.

Team-Member Exchange Effects. Group effects appear to augment the leader's impact on the satisfaction of the individual members. Thus, Seers (undated) extended Graen's (1976) concept of the quality of the dyadic leader-member exchange to the quality of the team-member exchange. Items that correlated most highly with the factor of the quality of the team-member exchange among 178 hourly employees who worked in one of 19 teams, included "how often I vol-

unteer extra help to the team" and "how often others on the team help me to learn better work methods." Eighteen percent of a team member's work satisfaction was accounted for by the favorable quality of the member's exchange relation with the team leader. At the same time, an additional 4 percent was due to the quality of the exchange relation with the team. The comparable figures for a member's satisfaction with co-workers were 11 percent owing to the quality of the leader-member exchange and 27 percent owing to the quality of the team-member exchange.

Properties of the Group

The means and variances in the attributes of individual members make a difference to the leadership of the group and its patterns of influence. Thus, Dyson, Godwin, and Hazelwood (1976) were able to link members' consensus to the influence of decisions in homogeneous but not in heterogeneous groups.

D. G. Bowers (1969) found that the leaders' importance will be greater for work groups composed of particular kinds of employees. Among 1,700 work groups from 22 organizations, Bowers observed that groups made up of longer-service, older, and less educated members attached greater importance to the supervisor and his or her direct influence on their behavior. The effects were especially relevant in administrative, staff, production, and marketing groups. In better educated, shorter-service, younger groups, especially those whose members were primarily female, such as clerical and service groups, less importance was given to the role of the supervisor and greater importance was given to the behavior of peer members in the group.

The leader's contribution to the group's productivity is likely to be reduced by faulty group-interaction processes (Steiner, 1972) or enhanced by "assembly bonus effects" (Collins & Guetzkow, 1964) that occur mainly with difficult tasks (Shaw & Ashton, 1976). That is, above and beyond individual members' capabilities to deal with the task they face, faulty leader-group interactions may result in performance that is worse than if the members had been free to work alone and to remain uninfluenced by the leader. When members work in a well-led group, their performance is likely to be better than what might have been expected from a simple pooling of their individual capabilities as members (Bass, 1980).

The Group's Development

As shown in Figure 27.1, the developmental stage of the group as a group is important to the emergence of leaders and the effects of leadership. For example, different leaders emerged in successive stages of therapy in a psychiatric ward (S. Parker, 1958). Likewise, Sterling and Rosenthal (1950) reported that leaders and followers change with different phases of the group process; the same leaders reoccur when the same phases return. Kinder and Kolmann (1976) found that in 23-hour marathon groups, gains in self-actualization were greatest when initially highly structured leadership roles were maintained early in the groups' development and then switched to low-structured leadership roles later in the groups' development. Similarly, Okanes and Stinson (1974) concluded that more Mach-

iavellian persons were chosen as informal leaders early in the development when groups could still improvise; when the groups had become more highly structured, however, Machiavellian persons were less likely to be chosen as leaders. Vecchio (1987) concluded that the one aspect of the Hersey-Blanchard model (1977) that had validity was the utility of using directive leadership early in the group's development and then employing more participative leadership for the group as it matured.

On the basis of a review of the literature, Stogdill (1959, 1972) identified three possible main effects of the leader on organized groups: productivity, drive, and cohesiveness. The rational model (see Figure 27.1) created by Schriesheim, Mowday, and Stogdill (1979) suggested that a group's drive and cohesiveness interact with each other to generate a group's productivity. In the model, supportive or relations-oriented leadership behavior interacts with instrumental or task-oriented leadership behavior to promote a group's drive and cohesiveness. All this occurs in the context of the

Figure 27.1. Model Linking Leadership to Group Outcomes

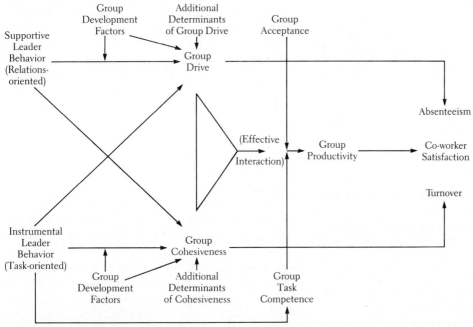

SOURCE: *Adapted from Schriesheim, Mowday, and Stogdill (1979). Modifications are shown in parentheses. Effects of feedback of group outcomes on leadership are not shown.*

group's development, which also contributes to the group's drive (directed energization) and cohesiveness (mutual attraction of members) and results in more effective interaction among its members. Then, if the group has competence to complete the task and accepts the responsibility for doing so, its productivity increases, the satisfaction of members with each other is greater, and the members' tendency to be frequently absent or to quit is reduced.

Phases in the Development of Groups

The consistency and importance of the phases in a group's development were noted and observed by many investigators. Leaders have to learn to respect these phases. Thus, Terborg, Castore, and DeNinno (1975) demonstrated that groups must work together for some time before they can begin to behave as a team and that the performance of a team is positively or negatively related to cohesiveness at different stages of the team's development.

In one of the early studies of group development, Bales (1950) observed that small groups exhibit phases in their problem-solving behavior. Bales and Strodtbeck (1951)[1] demonstrated that, after an introductory polite stage, the second phase in the development of small groups tends to involve a great deal of tension because of the members' competition for leadership and the stabilization of the status structure. Thus, Heinicke and Bales (1953) observed that emergent leaders tended to be rated high in initiating suggestions and opinions in the first session and at the beginning of the second session, but during the second session, they began to engage in an active struggle for status. After consolidating their position in the second session, they became less active in the third and fourth sessions, permitting other members to play more active roles. But the leaders' opinions and suggestions were still accepted, and they did not have to make as much effort to win their points.

Geier (1967) completed a detailed study of the first two stages of unstructured small experimental groups. Geier instructed some participants in a group task. Members entered their groups without an assigned

role. The leader was the member whom the members perceived by consensus as having made the most successful attempt to influence the group. Stage 1 involved the rapid and painless elimination of contenders with negative characteristics. The second stage involved an intense struggle for leadership and the further elimination of competitors. Only 2 of 80 members in the various small groups studied made no effort to gain leadership. Those who were uninformed, unparticipative, rigid, and hindered the attainment of goals were eliminated first. Attempts to recruit lieutenants and to gain the members' support were most obvious in Stage 2. The roles of lieutenant developed in 11 of 16 groups. Of the 11 lieutenants, 7 had been contenders for leadership in Stage 1.

Tuckman (1965) reviewed some 60 studies involving experimental, training, and therapeutic groups. An analysis of these studies suggested two additional stages of development through which the groups had to go to reach full group maturity. The first two stages of forming and storming were the same as the already mentioned stages of politeness followed by conflict. *Forming* was characterized by testing and orientation; *storming* was characterized by intragroup conflict, status differentiation, and emotional response. The third stage was *norming*, characterized by the development of group cohesion, norms, and intermember exchange, and the fourth stage was *performing*, marked by functional role interrelations and the effective performance of tasks. These stages of forming, storming, norming, and performing could overlap in some groups and alternate in others (Heinen & Jacobsen, 1976). The emergence and success of the different kinds of leadership that were needed clearly could be connected to each of these phases.

The development of small groups continues into further stages (Gersick, 1985). About halfway through the life cycle of problem-solving groups (which presumably have reached the fourth, performing, stage), the groups re-form themselves. During this re-formation, groups reevaluate their progress to date, reach agreement on final goals, revise their plans for completing their assigned task, and refocus their effort toward completing the task. Following this re-formation, they concentrate more of their efforts on the critical aspects of performing the task and focus on accomplishing their task to

[1]See also Borgatta and Bales (1953b), Heinicke and Bales (1953), and Philip and Dunphy (1959).

meet stated requirements. Near the completion of the task, efforts are made to shape the team product so it will fit environmental demands. Work is finalized, consistent with the requirements of the situation.

Effective leadership allows groups to move systematically through these necessary stages. Groups that are unable to develop a differentiated leader-follower role structure will be unable to engage in the effective performance of tasks (Borgatta & Bales, 1953b). Conversely, groups with a high degree of consensus about their leadership will be more effective and better satisfied than will those that do not reach such a consensus.

Phases and Outcomes. Stogdill (1972) suggested that the cohesiveness, drive, and productivity of a group is closely related to the developmental stages of groups and what is required of the group's leader. The group's drive appears in every stage, but the arousal and tensions of the second stage of storming most closely reflect the amount of that drive. The specific tasks that the group is motivated to perform, however, may differ across the stages. Thus, for instance, in the second stage, the group's drive is directed toward evolving a structure for the group; in the third stage, it operates to develop greater cohesiveness; and in the last stage, it is directed toward the successful completion of the group's task. In the third stage, norming, in which roles have finally been accepted and communication has improved, group cohesiveness emerges. In the fourth and final stage, effective performance of the task, group productivity is seen.

The functions of the leader depend on the stage of a group's development. For instance, relations-oriented leadership behavior would contribute to the group's need to develop cohesiveness in the third stage (norming) and task-oriented leadership behavior would facilitate the group's accomplishment of the task in the fourth stage (performing).

Phases and Role Boundaries. The group's development can be seen in the stabilization of the role boundaries of the individual members, including those of the leader. The role-boundary set for an individual—his or her limits—encompasses the acts that the other group members will accept from him or her. Boundaries are established by fairly stable role expectations that are often conveyed by the leader. In group experiments by Gibb (1961), one leader with a permissive leadership style was followed by another with a restrictive style, and vice versa. In other groups, one leader was followed by another with the same style. Group members accepted and responded more readily to leaders who followed other leaders with the same style of either latitude or restriction in the members' prescribed range of behaviors. The members were also less defensive and more productive in problem solving. Expectations were built quickly, with minimum cues, and survived over long periods. Esteemed and influential members, those frequently nominated as such in sociometric tests, tended to stay within the realistic boundaries prescribed by the group. Individuals who were less frequently chosen were more likely to violate the boundary specifications. (Perhaps those who were chosen more often had a wider range of behaviors and more role space in which to move.) The members responded to an individual member's role actions outside the role boundaries by pretending not to see or hear the behavior, ignoring it, subtle fighting, open rebellion, isolating the member, or forcing his or her withdrawal.

Given powerful norms, groups tended to select goals and perform activities that were commensurate with the norms. To exert influence, the behavior and goals of the leader had to be consonant with the group's goals. But high levels of defensiveness in the group prevented the effective exercise of such influence.

Groups undergo an orderly reduction in defensiveness as they mature, according to J. R. Gibb (1964). While a group is forming, its members remain superficial and polite to each other, and trust is low. After members have learned to trust each other (presumably after some storming), they learn how to make effective decisions and gain greater control over the choice of goals in the norming phase. With these better goals, they can make better use of the group's resources in their performance.

Leadership and a Stable Structure

A stable structure of relations must be developed for a group to become cohesive (Heinen & Jacobsen, 1976; Sherwood & Walker, 1960; Tuckman, 1965). Leaders have important effects on a group's development of a stable structure (Heslin & Dunphy, 1964). Recognizing this fact, Bion (1961) found that if the discussion leader of a therapy group failed to provide structure, the members, striving to arrive at a structure, sought a leader among themselves. As was discussed in previous chapters, during the early stages of a group's development, members may want and accept more direction. At this time, leaders may exert a greater influence on the stabilization of a group's role structures and thus have a greater impact on the group's cohesiveness.

Leaders differ in how much they affect the extent to which the intended structure of relations within the group and its input and outputs is the enacted structure. In a study of 39 work groups in three organizations, Inderrieden (1984) found that along with the uncertainty of the task, the leaders' need for power and self-actualization were the strongest predictors of the actual structure of the work groups.

In a study of Japanese nursery school children, Toki (1935) observed that early separation of an emergent leader from the group resulted in a disintegration of the structure of the group. The structure was more likely to hold up when the emergent leader left late in the group's development. When an adult leader was introduced, the structure built around the child leader collapsed.

Effects of Groups on Their Leaders

Differences among groups that are likely to affect what the leader can and will do include the group's drive, cohesiveness, size, compatibility, norms, and status. Earlier chapters looked at some of these effects from a variety of different perspectives.

Drive and Cohesiveness

The motivation of a group includes its drive and cohesiveness. The drive of a group refers to its level of directed energization; the cohesiveness of the group refers to the level of attachment of the members to the group and its purposes. Clearly, the two are related in that both will increase with the extent to which the group and its activities are valued by the members. Nevertheless, many investigations have focused on one or the other; others have merged the concepts of group drive and group cohesiveness by focusing on the

members' loyalty, involvement, and commitment to the group (Furukawa, 1981). Stogdill (1972) conceived group drive to be the arousal, freedom, enthusiasm, or esprit of the group and the intensity with which members invest their expectations and energy on behalf of the group. Steiner (1972) defined group motivation similarly as the willingness of members to contribute their resources to the collective effort. Zander (1971) found such motivation to depend on the members' desires to achieve success and to avoid failure—on the value to them of successful outcomes, as well as their previous history of success (Zander, 1968) and pressures for high performance (Zander, Medow, & Dustin, 1964).

Although group drive and cohesiveness ordinarily are correlated, Stogdill (1972) concluded, from a review of 60 studies, that under certain circumstances, the level of group drive conditions the relationship between productivity and cohesiveness. Under routine operating conditions and low drive, productivity and cohesiveness tend to be negatively related, while under high drive, they tend to be positively related. The seemingly paradoxical findings are readily explained when group drive is studied along with productivity and cohesiveness. When the group's drive is high, members' energies are directed toward the group's goals. If the group is also cohesive, the members will work collectively and productively toward that goal. On the other hand, if the group's drive is low, the member's energies will be directed elsewhere. If the group also remains cohesive, the members will reinforce each other's tendencies to ignore the group's productive goals and seek satisfaction from unproductive activities.

Effects of Drive

Bass, Flint, and Pryer (1957b) demonstrated that the motivation of all the members of a group affected the success of the leader. When all members are initially equal in status, an individual is more likely to become influential as a group leader if he or she attempts more leadership than do others. However, among highly motivated members, such attempted leadership was found to exert little effect on who emerged as a leader to influence the group's decision. In the same way,

Hemphill, Pepinsky, Shevitz, et al. (1954) showed that group members attempted to lead more frequently when the rewards for solving a problem were relatively high and they had a reasonable expectation that efforts to lead would contribute to the accomplishment of the task. Durand and Nord (1976) observed that those subordinates in a textile and plastics firm who felt that their success or failure was in the hands of forces outside their control (and, therefore, were presumably lower in group motivation) tended to see their supervisors as initiating more structure and showing less consideration.

A group's drive is likely to be high when members are highly committed. Members are more likely to want to expend energy for such groups. Gustafson (1968) manipulated commitment of the members to their discussion groups by varying the extent to which grades for a course depended on the groups' performance. Less role differentiation into leaders, task specialists, and social-emotional specialists was perceived by members with either a strong commitment or a weak commitment; that is, the three functions were not differentiated, but the groups showed less social-emotional behavior when their members were highly committed. In an analysis of 1,200 to 1,400 subordinates' descriptions of their groups, Farrow, Valenzi, and Bass (1980) found that directive leadership and delegative leadership were seen more frequently when the subordinates' commitment to the groups was high.

Effects of Cohesiveness

Group cohesiveness has been defined in a variety of other ways in addition to the average member's attraction to the group (Bass, 1960). It has also been defined as all the forces acting on members to remain in the group (Festinger, 1950), the level of the group's morale and associated attitudes among the members of a group (C. E. Shaw, 1976), the individual needs satisfied and expectancies from group membership, in contrast to alternatives offered elsewhere (Cartwright, 1965), and the extent to which members reinforce each others' expectations about the value of maintaining the identity of the group (Stogdill, 1972). Other investigators have identified cohesiveness in terms of variables that are highly correlated with a group's cohesiveness, such as the members' commitment to the group, the presence of peer pressure, the felt support from the group, and the absence of role conflict and ambiguity in the group. The meaning of cohesiveness could also be extended to include attaching a high value to group activities, to group solidarity, to willingness to be identified as a member of the group, and to being in agreement about norms, structure, and roles.

Implications of Expectations, Solidarity, and Identification. Borgatta, Cottrell, and Wilker (1959) studied groups that differed in the members' expectations about the value of group activities. The higher the initial expectation, the higher the final level of satisfaction for groups as a whole. Leaders of low-expectation groups changed their assessments more than did leaders of high-expectation groups.

The ease of the flow of influence between the leader and followers was expected to be associated with cohesive social relations (Turk, Hartley, & Shaw, 1962). Theodorson (1957) found that the roles of task leader and social leader were combined in cohesive groups but were separated in poorly integrated groups. Weak group cohesiveness provided a condition under which those who scored high in sociability would attempt to develop cooperation through increased interaction, while those who scored low in sociability would tend to remain passive (Armilla, 1967).

Gergen and Taylor (1969) demonstrated that high-status participants, when presented to a group in a "solidarity setting," tended to meet the group's expectations but failed to meet expectations when they were presented in a "productivity setting." Low-status participants in the productivity context presented themselves more positively; in the solidarity condition, they became more self-demeaning.

Acceptance of a group's leaders is linked to identification with the in-group. Thus, Bulgarian or Yemenite immigrants to Israel identified themselves first as Jewish, then second as Bulgarians or Yemenites. As a consequence, they could more easily support and follow Israeli leaders. On the other hand, Israeli immigrants who identified themselves first as Germans, Americans, or Moroccans were more likely to accept the Israeli leaders only if their self-evaluation was not rooted in the old country (Eisenstadt, 1952).

Podsakoff, Todor, Grover, and Huber (1984) collected data from 1,116 mainly male employees working in a variety of city and state governmental agencies, as well as some hospital pharmacists. Cohesiveness significantly increased the employees' satisfaction with supervisors who practiced a good deal of contingent rewarding. It significantly decreased satisfaction with supervisors who engaged in a lot of noncontingent punishment. Cohesion had no significant effect on satisfaction with supervisors who were contingent punishers or noncontingent rewarders. According to Dobbins and Zaccaro (1986), cohesiveness moderated the effects of leaders' consideration and initiation of structure on subordinates' satisfaction among 203 military cadets. Leaders' consideration and initiation of structure was correlated more highly with subordinates' satisfaction in cohesive compared to uncohesiveness groups. For 131 hourly employees in a manufacturing firm in the Midwest who completed anonymous mailed questionnaires, commitment to the Protestant ethic affected the relation of the leaders' behavior to the employees' job satisfaction (Brief & Aldag, 1977). Conversely, O'Reilly and Roberts (1978) showed that subordinates' low aspirations for mobility reduced the impact of the leaders' behavior on the subordinates' satisfaction and performance.

Implications for Structuring. Arguing that norms, structure, and roles are clearer in cohesive groups, J. F. Schriesheim (1980) proposed that initiation of structure by the leader is redundant in cohesive groups. But more initiation by the leader is likely in groups in which cohesiveness is low, groups that have less of a normative influence on members, and groups in which the members are more likely to be dependent on the leader than on the group. An analysis of data from 43 work groups in a public utility supported Schriesheim's proposition by showing that satisfaction with supervision, role clarity, and self-rated performance correlated much more highly with initiation of structure by the leader if the groups were low rather than high in cohesiveness. Schriesheim also expected that the leaders' consideration would contribute to the subordinates' role clarity only in groups whose cohesiveness was high. Again, her supposition was borne out. She found a correlation of .31 between the leaders' consideration

and the subordinates' role clarity in highly cohesive groups but corresponding correlations of .05 and −.04 in groups in which cohesiveness was medium or low. Schriesheim inferred from these results that highly cohesive groups provide members with clear roles and that clarity is reinforced by supportive, considerate leaders. Such groups have little need for additional initiation of structure from their leaders. Conversely, according to Farrow, Valenzi, and Bass (1980), consultative leadership will yield more satisfaction by subordinates if the leader feels that members are highly committed to the group and its goals. House and Dessler (1974) suggested that the leader may need to structure such groups less tightly.

Effects of the Group's Agreement about a Leader. The leadership process is affected by whether the immediate group is in agreement on who shall lead it. Agreement among the members about who should lead was found to be correlated with a greater cohesiveness of the group (Shelley, 1960a) and with more frequent attempts to lead (Banta & Nelson, 1964). Bales and Slater (1955) obtained results showing that three different roles of members tended to emerge in groups that did not reach a consensus on who should lead: an active role, a task-specialist role, and a best-liked-person role. In groups that had attained such a consensus, less role differentiation occurred; the active and task specialist roles were performed by the same member. Harrell and Gustafson (1966) reported that in groups lacking consensus, an active task-specialist role emerged along with a best-liked-member role. Role differentiation occurred less in both their high- and low-consensus groups than occurred in Bales and Slater's study. In addition, attractive groups and those with the most interesting tasks tended to exhibit the least role differentiation.

Harmony and Cooperativeness. Consultation by the group leader was more frequent in work groups that were described by their members as harmonious and free of conflict (Bass, Valenzi, Farrow, & Solomon, 1975). Groups with cooperative members, compared to groups with competitive members, were more likely to develop leaders, evaluate fellow members more favorably, show less hostility, and solve their problems as a group more rapidly (Raven & Eachus, 1963). This finding is consistent with the conventional wisdom that suggests that it usually benefits the organization to encourage competition among groups with independent tasks but that competition should be discouraged within the groups.

Compatible Members. Groups that are composed of compatible rather than incompatible members are better able to elect competent leaders. They also are better able to use the resources and abilities of members, since they are more likely to elect leaders who allow the highly competent members enough freedom to express themselves and to influence the groups' performance (W. C. Schutz, 1955). Lester (1965) found that the emergent leader among the highly task-oriented members of an American Mount Everest climbing expedition was able to be more relations oriented.

Thelen et al. (1954) factor-analyzed the self- and group descriptions made by members of a discussion group. Five clusters of members were identified. Cluster A, composed of members who rejected fighting and pairing, made significantly more leadership attempts than did any other group. It preferred structure and cohesiveness, which prevent undue domination and intimacy. Cluster B, with ego needs for intimate relationships, showed little interest in differences in status. Cluster C, which preferred to avoid power struggles or responsibility, rejected competition for leadership. Cluster AC, which rejected fighting, supported and looked to the leader to support their status needs. Cluster BC, which accepted fighting, supported the leader and attempted to mediate conflicts to maintain the group's cohesion.

Other group variables affecting a group's leadership included its size, stability, status, norms, and goals.

Effects of the Group's Size

Increased size affects a group's leadership because it brings with it reduced opportunities to lead, more responsibilities and demands on the leader, and a possible widening of the span of control.[2] As the size of the group increases, the number of interactional relationships among members increases at an extremely rapid rate. Graicunas (1937) deduced that a leader with two

subordinates can interact with them singly and in combination, the contacts can be initiated by the leader or by the subordinates, and 6 relationships are possible. With 4 subordinates, the number of relationships is 44 and with 6 subordinates, the number of relationships is 222. Graicunas concluded that executives should not have more than 4 or 5 subordinates reporting to them directly because of the time required for personal contacts. Nevertheless, surveys of industrial executives[3] indicated that corporation presidents may have from 1 to 25 assistants reporting to them. The average in the several surveys ranged from 5 to 9 immediate assistants.

Opportunities to Lead. The size of the group affects the emergence of a leader. Bass and Norton (1951) reported that the opportunity of any single member to take on the functions of leadership in a group decreased as the number of members increased.[4] In agreement, Hare (1962) reviewed several studies which suggested that as the size of the group increases, individual members have less opportunity to talk and to attempt to lead; that is, fewer members can initiate leadership acts. In parallel, Warner and Hilander's (1964) study of 191 voluntary organizations in a community found that the involvement and participation of members decreased as the size of the organization increased. However, to the contrary, J. H. Healy (1956) found that for chief executives of corporations the subordinates' involvement in policy making was greater as the number of immediate subordinates increased.

As the size of the group increases, more differences appear in the members' tendencies to be talkative and attempts to be influential (Bales & Slater, 1955). In groups that ranged from 2 to 12 members, Bass and Norton (1951) reported that such differences increased directly with the increase in the size of the groups and reached the maximum in groups of 6 members. But contrary to most researchers, Kidd (1958) found no relation between the size of a group and increases in the differences among members' influence in groups of 2, 4, or 6 members. Also, Blankenship and Miles (1968)

[2]For a detailed review of the effects of span of control in relation to the size of the group, see House and Miner (1969).
[3]The studies were by Dale (1952), Entwisle and Walton (1961), J. H. Healy (1956), and F. W. Mahler (1961).
[4]Evidence that the opportunity for leadership tends to decrease as the size of the group increases was also provided by Bales, Strodtbeck, Mills, and Roseborough (1951); Dawe (1934); and Stephan (1952).

noted that the size of the units they led was less important to the decision-making behavior of executives than was their organizational level.

Changes in Leadership Style and Effects. Hemphill (1950b) studied groups with leaders whom the group members considered to be superior. He found that as the size of the groups increased, the members made greater demands on the leaders. Larger groups made significantly stronger demands on the leaders' strength, reliability, predictability, competence to do the job, coordination, impartial enforcement of rules, and structure. At the same time, larger groups required less consideration from the leaders for individual members.

Pelz (1951) observed that small groups were better satisfied with leaders who took their part than with those who sided with the organization; large groups (10 or more members) were better satisfied with leaders who supported the organization. Medalia's (1954) results indicated that as the size of the work unit increased, the worker's perception of their leaders as "human relations minded" decreased. Goodstadt and Kipnis (1970) found that as the size of the groups increased, supervisors tended to spend less time with poor workers and to give fewer pay raises to good workers. Again, in 100 randomly selected chapters of the League of Women Voters, J. Likert (1958) found that officers engaged in more activities as the chapters increased in size, but the chapter presidents exhibited less interest in individual members' ideas. Consistent with all these findings, Schriesheim and Murphy (1976) found, through a subgroup moderator analysis, that the leaders' initiation of structure was related to satisfaction of members in larger work groups and that the leaders' consideration was related to the satisfaction of members in smaller groups. However, Greene and Schriesheim (1980) showed that instrumented leadership was actually most influential in affecting drive and cohesiveness in larger work groups, while supportive leadership was most influential in smaller work groups.

A meta-analysis by Wagner and Gooding (1987) of 7 to 19 studies of the effects of participative leadership on various outcomes found that the positive correlation of perceived participation with perceived satisfaction of subordinates remained at .44 and .42, respectively, in small and large groups, but the correlation

between participative leadership as perceived by members and their acceptance of decisions fell from .44 to .31 in small and large groups, respectively. When independent sources of leadership and outcome data were correlated that were free of single-source bias, the results again fell for the acceptance of decisions (from .27 to .20) and for satisfaction (from .25 to .03). Thus, overall, participatory leadership practices generally had more salutory effects in small than in large groups.

Kipnis, Schmidt, and Wilkinson (1980) reported that when trying to be influential, supervisors of large groups were likely to choose impersonal tactics, such as assertiveness, and sanctions and appeals to a higher authority, rather than more personal influence tactics, such as ingratiation and bargaining. In small groups, relatively more personal and relatively fewer impersonal tactics were employed by the same supervisors. This finding may explain why a small span of control does not produce close supervision (Bell, 1967; Udell, 1967).

Changes in Requirements. Thomas and Fink (1963) reviewed several studies which concluded that as groups enlarged, the leaders had to deal with more role differentiation, more role specialization, and more cliques. Slater (1958) noted that the stabilization of a group's role structure became increasingly difficult with the increased size of the group.

Hare (1952) studied boys in groups ranging from 5 to 12 members. Leaders were found to yield more influence on decisions in the smaller groups, but the leaders' level of skill was not related to influence. The larger groups demanded more skill from their leaders, and in large groups, the skill of leaders was positively correlated with the increased movement of members toward group consensus. In a comprehensive summary of personal factors found to be associated with leadership in natural and experimental groups, R. D. Mann (1959) noted that in groups of 7 or under, intelligence seemed a little more important to leadership than did adjustment, but in larger groups, adjustment increased slightly and intelligence decreased slightly in correlation with leadership.

Antecedents. Guion (1953) and G. D. Bell (1967) found that first-line supervisors tended to supervise fewer subordinates as the complexity of the job increased. The number of the subordinates of chief executives tended to increase with the growth of the size of firms, according to J. H. Healy (1956). His results suggested that individuals differ in their ability to interact and that many who become leaders of very large organizations are able to interact with 12 to 15 or more assistants without feeling overburdened or pressured for time. Indik (1964) surveyed 116 organizations that ranged in size from 15 to 3,000 members and found that as organizations increase in size, they take on more operative members before they add new supervisors.

Confounds. Indik (1963, 1965a) cautioned that most generalizations about the effects of size are confounded by other factors. Two of these confounds are the greater cohesiveness to be found in the smaller group and the optimum size of the group's task. In a survey of 5,871 workers from 228 factory groups that ranged from 5 to 50 members, Seashore (1954) found that the smaller groups were also more cohesive. The same was true for the conference groups studied by N. E. Miller (1950).

As was just noted, demands on a leader's initiatives increase with an increase in the group's size and the potential of the leader or members to interact individually with each other decreases as the group enlarges. If additional members are superfluous and unnecessary as far as the completion of the group's task is concerned, effectiveness and satisfaction are likely to suffer with an increase in the number of members. For any given task, there is an optimum-size group. Two people or even one person may be adequate and optimal for many tasks; five or six appear to be optimal for discussion groups (Bass, 1960). A larger number of different kinds of experts is likely to be needed for complex tasks whose completion requires skills and knowledge from many disciplines. The leader may need to cope with groups that are suboptimal or too large for the group's task. When the group is too large for the task, the leader may need to initiate more structure so members do not get in each other's way. When the group is too small for the task, the leader may need to provide for more time and resources or reduce the goals.

Effects of the Status and Esteem of the Group

Some groups in a large organization are seen as more valuable and critical to the organization's success than are other groups. For example, line groups are likely to be considered more important than are staff groups. The prestige may also vary. Thus, the biology department may be perceived as more prestigious than may the agriculture department at a university. Groups of skilled craftsmen may be thought of as more prestigious than may groups of line operatives. The reputations of groups of the same type may vary as well. For instance, one biology department may be viewed as ossified, while another is seen as being at the forefront of the field. Similarly, one group of skilled craftsmen may be seen as quarrelsome, recalcitrant, and hard to please, whereas another may be considered highly efficient, competent, and dependable. Fried (1988) showed that within organizations such as hospitals, the relative power of the nurses, administrative personnel, and physicians were seen, particularly by the nurses, to depend on the centrality, nonsubstitutability, and coping with uncertainty of their respective roles.

Leadership within these different groups is likely to be affected in several ways. It will be easier to attract and hold members in the groups that have higher status and esteem. These more highly valued groups will have relatively more influence with their leaders. In turn, their leaders will have more influence when they represent their groups in dealings with a higher authority and with representatives of other groups at the same organizational level.

Effects of the Group's Norms

The group's norms (its definition of tasks, goals, the paths to the goals, and the appropriate relationships among members) strongly affect what a leader can accomplish in the group as well as who will emerge as the leader. In turn, the leader often has an impact on group outcomes by influencing the group's norms.

Frame of Reference. Sherif's conception of the social norm exerted a marked influence on research on leadership. In an autokinetic experience, Sherif (1936) seated a subject in a darkened room and asked the person to observe a spot of light projected on a screen.

The subject reported the distance that the light appeared to move. The average distance for several trials was recorded as the subject's individual norm. When the subject was later placed with a confederate of the experimenter who uniformly reported a distance that varied markedly from that reported by the participant, the subject tended to change estimates to conform with the group norm. Asch (1952) obtained similar results when a subject was asked to judge the length of lines after six confederates of the experimenter had rendered judgments that defied the senses. The confederates uniformly declared that the really shorter of two lines was longer. It was the norm of these confederates, not any single emergent leader, that influenced many of the subjects.

Other demonstrations of the effect of group norms showed how these norms moderate whether actual leadership behavior will be perceived as such. Thus, in an experimental comparison, Lord and Alliger (1985) found that the correlation of group members' perceptions of emergent leadership with actually observed leadership behaviors is greater when norms are established for members to be systematic rather than to remain spontaneous. Likewise, Phillips and Lord (1981) demonstrated that if a group was described as effective, but members were led to believe that the group's success could be explained by other factors than the leader, the group's performance had less of an effect on the members' ratings of the leader.

The Group's History of Successes or Failures. Some groups and organizations have histories of success and high performance that contribute to their esteem, while others have histories of failure and low performance. For instance, different United Fund agencies were found by Zander, Forward, and Albert (1969) to be consistently successful or consistently unsuccessful in meeting the goals of their fund drives. In the same way, Denison (1984) reported consistencies in the rate of return on investments by companies over a five-year period. Some companies tend to do well continually; others always do poorly. Histories of success give rise to norms of success and high performance, while histories of failure give rise to norms of failure and low performance. Thus, Farris and Lim (1969) found that high-performance groups had higher expectations of their future success as groups than did low-perform-

ance groups. Leaders whose accession to office coincides with a failure when the groups have been accustomed to success will no doubt earn more blame than ordinary. Conversely, leaders whose accession coincides with the success of previously failing groups will gain an unusual amount of credit, which may not be justified. According to experimental results obtained by Howell (1985), a role-conflict condition will arise for members when performance norms are low but the leader is high in the initiation of structure, particularly in the pressure to produce.

Conformity and Deviation. Ordinarily, when a discrepancy exists between the opinion of one member and the rest of the group, the deviating member tends to move closer to the group norm. But if an extreme deviate refuses to yield, he or she will be personally rejected by the other members (Festinger, 1950, 1954; Schachter, 1951). Gerard (1953) and Berkowitz and Howard (1959) obtained results to indicate that leaders directed most of their communications to such deviates. If a deviate was unreceptive to accepting the majority point of view, the group tended to expel the deviate from the group psychologically. Raven's (1959a) report of the results of an experiment noted that deviates would shift toward the norm if they could express their opinions, both privately and in public. Presumably, the leader could make a difference by encouraging such expression by the deviates.

Conformity to Norms and the Leader. Scioli, Dyson, and Fleitas (1974) found that when conformity was demanded by college groups, the most dominant members became the groups' instrumental (task-oriented) leaders. Thibaut and Strickland (1956) obtained results indicating that as the group's pressure to conform increased (often pushed by the leader), more members increased in conformity under a "group set" and decreased in conformity under a "task set."[5] At the same time, McKeachie (1954) reported that the members' conformity to the norms of their groups and liking for the groups were greater in leader-oriented than in group-oriented classes.

Newcomb (1943) conducted a study of social values on a college campus. He found that the most influen-

[5]Under a task set, subjects were instructed to focus their attention on the task; under a group set, they were to concentrate on the group.

tial members represented the dominant values of the campus. Those who conformed in conduct but not in attitude possessed social skills but maintained close ties to their families. Those who conformed in attitude but not in conduct tended to lack social skills but regarded the conformity of attitudes to be a mark of community acceptance and superior intelligence. Similarly, Sharma (1974) found that Indian students who were activists and prominent as leaders of demonstrations were concerned primarily with student issues, not with social change. The attitudes of these student activists tended to reflect the traditional values of their communities toward religion, caste, marriage, and family. Likewise, in a study of modernization in India that sampled 606 heads of households engaged in agriculture, Trivedi (1974) found that although opinion leaders may have accepted innovations in agriculture, they, like Sharma's (1974) student activists, adhered to traditional religious beliefs and convictions. They differentiated agricultural from religious activities more fully in the process. (But in the United States in the late 1960s and early 1970s, in France in 1968, as in China in 1919 and 1989, the norms of student activists placed them in the vanguard of reform and revolutionary change.)

In a Hungarian study, Merei (1949) formed groups that were composed of submissive nursery school children. When placed in separate rooms, each group developed its own role structure, rules for play, and routine of activities. After these had become stabilized, a child with strong propensities to lead in play activities was introduced into each group. Although the new members were widely successful in gaining leadership positions, they were not able to change the norms and procedural rules of the groups. The groups had more of an impact on the leaders than the leaders had on the groups. Consistent with this finding, Bates (1952) showed that the closer that the behavior of individuals comes to realizing the norms of the group, the higher are these individuals' likely position as leaders in the group. However, many other investigators found that group leaders ranked higher in the assimilation of group norms because they were highly influential in the formation of the norms.[6] Although leaders may be influential in establishing group norms, once the norms

are adopted, they are expected to observe the norms (Hare, 1962).

O. J. Harvey (1960) found that formal leaders conformed more to group norms than did informal (sociometrically identified) leaders or other group members, especially under conditions of uncertainty. Mulder (1960) also found that the judgment of leaders was most influenced by other members when they, the leaders, were appointed in an ambiguous situation. But the emergent, informal leaders were the least influenced in the ambiguous situation without established norms.

When the Leader Can Deviate. The fact that leaders tend to be prime exemplars of their groups' value systems is not to suggest that they are slaves to the groups' norms (Rittenhouse, 1966). In fact, they may deviate considerably from the norms in various aspects of their conduct. In a study of sociometric cliques among teachers, Rasmussen and Zander (1954) found that leaders were less threatened than were followers by deviation from their subgroup's norms. Leaders appeared secure enough to feel they could depart from the norms without jeopardizing their status. Similarly, Harvey and Consalvi (1960) found that the member who was second highest in status as a leader of a group was significantly more conforming than was the member who was at the top or bottom of the status hierarchy. The leader conformed the least, but not significantly less than the lowest-status member. Likewise, Hughes (1946) observed that members of industrial work groups let "rate busters" know in forceful terms that their violation of group norms would not be tolerated. However, the leaders of the work groups were allowed more freedom to deviate from certain group norms than were other members whose positions were less secure.

The Leader's Need for Early Conformity. As was detailed in previous chapters, Hollander (1958, 1960, 1964) suggested that the early conformity of leaders to the norms of their groups gains for them "idiosyncracy credits" that enable them to deviate from the norms at later dates without their groups' disapproval. A large body of research (Hollander, 1964) supported this hypothesis. The lesson for would-be leaders who wish to bring about changes in groups is that they usually must first accept the groups' current norms to be accepted

[6]See Borgatta (1955b); Jones, Gergen, and Jones (1963); Kates and Mahony (1958); Katz, Libby, and Strodtbeck (1964); E. M. Mumford (1959); Tannenbaum and Bachman (1966); and Turk (1961).

by the groups. Practical politicians often can bring about more change by first identifying with a country's current norms and then moving the country ahead with statesmanship that takes the country where it would not have gone without the politician's direction. Franklin Delano Roosevelt's leadership of the isolationist United States into World War II is an illustration.

Acceptance and the Leader's Freedom to Deviate. In a study of personnel in the U.S. Air Force, Biddle, French, and Moore (1953) found that the closer the attitudes of crew chiefs were to the policies of the U.S. Air Force, the stronger were their attempts to lead. Chiefs who accepted their role as supervisors used their influence to further the institutional goals and purposes. But the amount of such attempted leadership was not related to the extent to which the chiefs were accepted by the crew members. However, crew chiefs who were accepted by their groups deviated further from the norms and policies than those who were not accepted.

Leadership and the Group's Goals. Without doubt, the group's purpose or goal is the predominant norm of a group. Studies of experimental groups indicate that members readily accept or commit themselves to the defined task and seem to develop other norms in support of the norms of the task. Once the members understand and agree on the group's goal, the goal operates as a norm against which the members evaluate each other's potential for leadership. Goode and Fowler (1949) observed, in a small industrial plant, that the informal groups supported the company's production goals despite the workers' low satisfaction with their jobs. The authors attributed this outcome to leadership that provided clear statements of the groups' goals; clear definitions of the members' roles; and strong, congruent group pressures toward conformity from within and outside the informal group.

Members differ in their commitment to the goals of a group. The greater a member's responsibility for attaining a goal, the stronger his or her commitment to the goal. Ordinarily, leaders exhibit more concern than do followers for the group's attainment of its goals. The attainment of goals is used by members as a criterion for evaluating the group's performances. Once members agree on their expectations for a group, these

expectations operate as a norm that induces pressure for compliance, making routine leadership easier. The expectations also make leadership that attempts to move the group away from its chosen paths more difficult.

Stability of the Group

The group's stability affects its leadership. B. D. Fine (1970) studied 151 members of an unstable pool of workers and 582 workers who were assigned to stable groups in a refinery. The groups did not differ significantly in coordination, communication, participation, decision making, satisfaction, or mental health. The unstable groups were higher than were the stable groups in motivation and the resolution of conflict. Leaders of stable groups were significantly higher in their facilitation of interaction but not in support, the emphasis on goals, or the facilitation of work. Leaders of unstable groups exercised less control, and the workers in these groups expressed less need for freedom.

Other Group Effects

The group variables affecting leadership that have been discussed so far should be considered suggestive rather than exhaustive. For example, the source of information makes a difference. On the one hand, Woods (1984) observed more participative leadership in quality circles than in other group activities in manufacturing firms. Likewise, significantly more quality circles than other types of groups perceived their leaders to be highly participative. Nevertheless, the leaders themselves perceived no differences in their own behavior in the two situations.

Experience in a another group affects the attitudes toward leadership of those who subsequently become leaders and presumably their performance as leaders. Akhtar and Haleem (1980) showed that newly promoted superiors in an Indian hydroelectric power station exhibited the same attitudes toward initiation and consideration as those attitudes that had been the norm in the groups of employees from which they had come.

Bushe (1987) studied 415 managers' attitudes toward quality-of-work-life (QWL) projects. Those who were involved in permanent problem-solving groups were most favorable and those in temporary groups were least favorable toward such projects in comparison to those with no experience in problem solving in QWL groups.

To conclude, many other attributes of groups, as groups, are likely to influence the results with their leaders and managers: the sources of information; the age of the groups; the leaders' and members' earlier experiences elsewhere; whether the groups are part of a larger organization, are temporary or permanent, and are easy or difficult to enter; and whether the membership is homogeneous or heterogeneous. Each of these attributes is likely to influence what is required of the persons who emerge as the leaders and what leadership behavior is most likely to be effective.

Impact of the Leader on the Group's Drive and Cohesiveness

The preceding chapters were replete with illustrations of the impact of the leader's competence, personality, and style on the outcomes of the group. Here, I wish to call attention only to the leader's effects on the group's drive and cohesiveness and the variables that are closely allied with them.

Impact on the Group's Drive

As detailed in Chapter 12, charismatic and inspirational leadership have strong effects on the drive of a group since they correlate highly with individual members' reports of extra efforts. But because of the lack of interest in empirical research before 1980 on the effects of inspirational and charismatic leadership, the evidence that leadership affects a group's drive is sparse, according to a review by Schriesheim, Mowday, and Stogdill (1979). Nevertheless, Greene and Schriesheim (1977, 1980) examined leadership behavior and group drive using a longitudinal design with 123 work groups. Using cross-lagged correlational, cross-lagged path, and corrected dynamic correlational analyses, they found that both instrumental (task-oriented) and supportive (relations-oriented) leadership behavior were causally antecedent to the groups' drive.

Medow and Zander (1956) found that group members who were in positions of centrality—and, therefore, more likely to exert leadership—exhibit more con-

cern for the group's goals than do members in peripheral positions.[7] Central members select goals in terms of the group's probability of success, are more insistent that the group be correct, exhibit a stronger desire for the group's success, and perceive themselves to have more influence than other members perceive themselves to have.

The presence of a leader can help the group members remain interested in the goal of a task. Zander and Curtis (1965) reported that group members whose task performance was poorer than they expected tended to lower their aspirations. But they did not downgrade or reject the task as much when a leader was present.

Those who exert leadership tend to feel more responsible for the outcomes of their groups. E. Pepitone (1952) found that the more responsible a member's role, the greater his or her concern for the success of the group. E. J. Thomas (1957) reported that when members were highly dependent on each other for the performance of a task, those who were able to facilitate the performance of other members worked harder for the group.

Zander (1971) showed that the leader's feedback about the group's performance and the leader's reward practices had a positive impact on the group's desire to achieve success. The absence of a leader to clarify the requirements of the task and the goals of the group resulted in the group's spending much time in clarification and in the quest for orderliness. Members of unorganized groups (J. R. P. French, 1941) and members of groups under a laissez-faire type of leadership (Lippitt, 1940a) frequently expressed a desire to get things organized, to buckle down to work, and to stick to the job that was supposed to be done.

In a large-scale Swedish study, Norrgren (1981a) observed that the positive behavioral intentions of managers exerted considerable influence on the quality of the relations among the members of their work groups. The positive intentions also motivated their subordinates to perform and increased how much challenge and stimulation the subordinates felt that they received from their jobs. J. Likert's (1958) previously cited study that showed how the size of the chapters of the League of Women Voters influenced the chapter presi-

[7] See Chapter 30 for more about the effects of central and peripheral positions on leadership.

dents, found that, in turn, members were more active when the presidents were interested in their ideas (as in smaller chapters) and when the officers of the chapter believed that the members should have relatively high degrees of influence on policies and activities. The members participated less actively in chapter activities when they felt pressure from the president, but participated more actively under pressure from the leaders of their project discussion groups, as well as from their peers.

Impact on the Group's Cohesiveness

Democratic, participative, and relations-oriented leadership behavior was found to contribute to the cohesiveness of groups in a number of studies.[8] Smith (1948) obtained a positive correlation between group cohesion and supportive leadership in area-management teams in English social agencies but not among local social work groups in these agencies. Similarly, task-oriented, directive leadership behavior was seen to increase cohesiveness according to many other investigations.[9] Both types of leadership behavior were found to contribute to the cohesiveness of groups in still other studies.[10] A leader of a work group who combines high concerns for the task with high concerns for relations, such as Misumi's high Performance (P) and high Maintenance (M) leader, was expected to establish group-shared attitudes favoring a high level of performance. Indeed, such performance norms were the highest under Japanese leaders of the PM type (mean = 17.3), followed by M-type leaders (mean = 16.5), P-type leaders (mean = 16.3), and pm-type leaders (mean = 15.8). Using Jackson's (1960) return-potential model of norms, Sasaki and Yamaguchi (1971) obtained results that were parallel to Misumi's for 160 second-year Japanese junior high school students in 32 groups—16 groups of boys and 16 groups of girls. The point of maximum return (the point maximally approved by the group members) varied as follows: PM, 25.0; P, 20.0 M, 16.3; and pm, 18.8. The degree of agreement among members about a behavioral norm differed with the styles of their leaders as follows: PM, 3.02; P, 1.71; M, 1.63; and pm, 1.99.

Group Moderators of the Leader's Impact

How leadership behavior affects the group's drive and cohesiveness depends, to some extent, on the characteristics of the group. The same leadership that may contribute to motivated and cohesive subordinates in one kind of group may fail to do so in another. Greene and Schriesheim's (1980) analysis of 123 work groups revealed that instrumental leadership had strong effects on drive and cohesiveness, particularly in large and new groups. The reverse was true for supportive leadership, which exerted the most influence on drive and cohesiveness in small and in recently established groups.

Leana (1983) manipulated the same variables in an experiment on how the style of leadership and cohesiveness affected "groupthink." Groupthink is extreme concurrence-seeking in decision-making groups (Janis, 1972). Concurrence-seeking overrides the realistic appraisal of alternative courses of action and vigilant information processing (Janis & Mann, 1977). It results in faulty decision making. Janis (1982) hypothesized that concurrence-seeking or groupthink would occur more readily in cohesive groups with directive leaders. Other conditions that would generate groupthink included stress and pressure for a solution, insulation of the group from outside sources of information, and the lack of adequate procedures for finding and evaluating information. Leanna (1982) created experimental conditions for groupthink but varied whether the leader was directive or participative and whether the 4-member groups that were drawn from a total of 208 college students were high or low in cohesiveness. In contrast to participative leadership, directive leadership produced more groupthink, which was reflected in incomplete canvassing of alternatives, the failure to discuss alternatives, and decisions that were strongly based on the leader's preferences. But unexpectedly, high cohesiveness did not result in more such groupthink than did low cohesiveness. In fact, high cohesiveness actu-

[8]The studies were by Lewin (1939), R. Likert (1961a, 1967), Lippitt (1940a, 1940b) and Mann and Baumgartel (1952), among others. See also Chapters 21, 22, and 23.
[9]The studies were by Berkowitz (1953a); P. J. Burke (1966a, 1966b); Katzell, Miller, Rotter, and Venet (1970); Keeler and Andrews (1963); and Stogdill (1965a).
[10]See Christner and Hemphill (1955); Greene and Schriesheim (1977, 1980); Hemphill, Seigel, and Westie (1951); and Trieb and Marion (1969).

ally widened the search for information. The effects of style of leadership and cohesiveness were independent of each other.

Impact of the Leader on the Assembly Bonus Effect

Many of the chapters of this book have looked at what leaders do to increase the effectiveness of the performance of their subordinates, individually or collectively. But what can the leader do to reduce the faulty processes among the subordinates and increase the assembly bonus effect? For instance, when alternatives are to be considered, the leader can promote a brainstorming session to avoid criticism. According to Fox (1988) faulty processes can best be reduced by the leader's increasing the fairness of the "playing field." Although openness is generally desired among all members, at the outset, the leader can make it possible for members to make contributions without being identified so that the parochialism of their efforts and their fears of retaliation for criticisms are reduced and the efforts are evaluated on their merits, without regard to the status, esteem, and power of the source. In this way, newcomers will not be constrained and the group members will not have to spend as much time being tactful about why each other's naive ideas will not work. Such anonymous inputs can be attained when the leader asks the members to submit prediscussion inputs anonymously, when the members are hooked into an electronic network, or when the leader presents to the group a summary of the inputs without identifying the sources.

The leader can make more effective use of the group by assigning subparts of the task to those individuals whose competencies best match the requirements of the subparts (Bass, 1960). He or she can also prevent premature closure in the group's evaluation of alternatives (E. R. Alexander, 1979).

A questioning set helps members to evaluate alternatives systematically. What current resource could be substituted, modified, combined, omitted, or reversed? (Osborn, 1953). The "rush to judgment" that often occurs can be avoided. Frequently, only one solution gets most of the group's attention.

The leader can encourage a more even distribution of participation by encouraging inactive members and discouraging the monopolizers. On the other hand, the leader can make for a more effective group outcome by recognizing the differences in the competencies of the members. To some degree, the leader may have to encourage the participation of the more competent members and discourage the participation of the less competent members.

The leader can clarify the group's goals and ensure agreement about them and an understanding of them. The leader can help get the group to view its problem in such a way that the problem can be reorganized to be handled efficiently. Even when the group feels satisfied with its solution, its return to the same problem a second time is likely to generate an even better solution (Maier & Hoffman, 1960b).

More of the assembly bonus effect can be obtained by arranging for the cross-training of members. One can fill another's shoes in case of absence. Regularly scheduled meetings ordinarily will help (Dyer & Lambert, 1953), as will other ways of improving communications among the members.[11]

Summary and Conclusions

Team–leader effects go beyond those of each of the individual members interacting with the leader. There may be an assembly bonus effect for the team so that the team does better than the sum of its members. Or, faulty processes may result in the team doing worse. The leader makes a difference in which outcome occurs. In turn, the leader is affected in many ways by the group. Thus, leadership systematically depends on the phase of the group's development in which the leadership is occurring as well as on the group's history. As newly formed groups progress, they find it necessary to resolve contests for influence and to develop role structure and cohesiveness before they can engage in the effective performance of tasks. Leaders are expected to provide role structure, maintain goal direction, and resolve interpersonal problems. If leaders fail to fulfill their expected roles, new leaders tend to emerge.

Group drive and group cohesiveness make consider-

[11]See Chapter 30.

able differences in what is required of the leader and what the leader is able to do. Likewise, the size of the group affects the leadership. The larger the group, the more difficult it becomes for any member to acquire leadership. Large groups make greater demands on their leaders than do small ones.

Groups develop norms that define the appropriate conduct of the members. Once a norm has become stabilized in the mutual expectations of members, members bring strong pressures to bear on the individual who deviates from the norm. The greater the extent to which members assimilate the norms and values of a group, the greater the probability of their emergence as leaders. As leaders, they tend to act as strong exponents of these group norms and tend to conform to them. However, once leaders have consolidated their position, they are likely to be granted considerable latitude in departing from the same norms. The goals of a group operate as group norms in terms of which the members evaluate the group's performance. Leaders exhibit a stronger concern for and commitment to their groups' goals and work harder for their groups' success than do followers. Other aspects of the group, as a group, that affect the requirements for success as a leader include the group's stability, the group's status and esteem, the group's frame of reference, and the group's past history.

Leaders have systematic effects on the drive of their groups, although little attention has been paid to this aspect of charismatic and inspirational leadership. Both directive and participative leadership can contribute to group cohesiveness, as can the interest and concern that the leader shows for the group. Inspirational leadership would be expected to increase the group's cohesiveness.

We now turn from variables about the group and its members, to the tasks faced by the group and how these interact with the leader's behavior.

Leadership, Task, and Technology

The tasks faced by the group, by the organization, and by its individual members affect and are affected by the leadership. The roles required by the tasks have consequences for the outcomes of the members' satisfaction, the group's productivity, and the organization's performance. In the same way, the leadership involved in the tasks to be accomplished is intimately linked to the technology used.

Singled out for special attention has been the extent to which the task is structured and the members' roles to accomplish it are clear. These factors, in turn, are expected to moderate the leader's directive or participative style and its effects on outcomes. At least 48 reasonably rigorous laboratory and survey efforts to verify this path-goal theory were reported in a review by Indvik (1986b). However, before I review path-goal theory and its validity, I will first examine the more general issue of the extent to which various requirements of tasks have been linked with leadership and leadership-outcome relationships.

The Leader's Competence and the Requirements of Tasks

The requirements of tasks affect whether a leader is needed, who emerges as a leader, how the leader behaves, and what kinds of leadership behavior result in the greater productivity and satisfaction of the followers. Thus, some of the earliest research on leadership in small groups was carried out in the Soviet Union by Chevaleva-Ianovskaia and Sylla (1929), who observed that no leadership arose in 888 spontaneous preschool groups unless special problems occurred.

Early on, the requirements of the task situation were seen to determine the traits that distinguish those who are chosen to lead in a particular situation. Thus, Caldwell and Wellman (1926) showed that the basis of choice varied according to the activities for which lead-

ers were picked by their junior high school classmates. For example, physical abilities determined the selection of athletic leaders. Nevertheless, among the students who were studied, scholarship was high among chosen leaders in all designated situations. Again, Dunkerley (1940) found that college women who were selected as intellectual leaders were superior in judgment, initiative, and intellectual ability and those who were picked as social leaders were superior in dress and appearance. Those who were chosen as religious leaders were least neurotic, while those who were chosen as social leaders were most neurotic.

Effects of the Transfer of Leaders

Although there is some consistency in a leader's performance in different situations, there is also systematic change in what happens when a leader is transferred to new assignments and tasks. For instance, Stogdill, Shartle, Scott, et al. (1956) studied 20 naval officers who were to be transferred to new positions and the 20 officers whom they were to replace. After several months in their new positions, the transferred officers were found to have shifted their patterns of work performance, but not of interpersonal behavior, to resemble those of the officers they had replaced. In other words, the officers tended to transfer their patterns of interpersonal behavior from one assignment to another but changed their patterns of work performance in response to the task requirements of the new assignments. In a similar way, Carter, Haythorn, Shriver, and Lanzetta (1951) found, in a small group experimental study, that the behavior of leaders differed from one situation to another, depending on the requirements of the group task.

The individual who emerges as the leader in one group tends to acquire leadership status when placed in other groups, particularly if the different groups are performing similar tasks. A change in task may permit new leaders to emerge. Barnlund (1962) rotated group members through a set of different tasks and through groups with changing memberships. The highest degree of leadership transferability occurred between literary and construction tasks and the lowest degree, between coordination and mathematical tasks. Changes in both task and group membership were found to condition the emergence of specific individuals as leaders. However, Borg and Tupes (1958) and Blake, Mouton, and Fruchter (1954) reported consistency of behavior in the same leader performing in different groups with varying tasks. Nevertheless, the general trend of the research that was reviewed supports the hypothesis that groups tend to accept as leaders those members who exhibit characteristics and abilities that will facilitate the accomplishment of the group's specific task. Furthermore, leaders tend to change certain aspects of their behavior in response to changes in the demands of the group's task.[1]

Leader's Ability and Requirements of Tasks

As was seen in Chapter 7, the emergence of leadership is correlated with how much the emergent leader's abilities are relevant to the tasks that the group faces. Different tasks call for different abilities, and the leaders who emerge have difference competencies that are relevant to the requirements of the different tasks. Thus, Carter and Nixon (1949a) performed a complicated experiment in which the leadership performance of 100 high school boys was measured by teachers' ratings, nominations by students, school-activity records, and observer's ratings in three group tasks. A 7-hour battery of tests was also administered. It was found that the boys' scores on the mechanical ability test coincided with leadership in mechanical tasks on all criteria. Scores on the numerical test and for persuasiveness were correlated with leadership in intellectual tasks, while the scores on the work-fluency and clerical tests predicted leadership in clerical tasks on all criteria. Scores on the reasoning test were positively related to leadership in all tasks on all criteria, and the scores on the musical-interest test were negatively related.

Clifford and Cohn (1964) described how different attributes of group members related to their nomination by colleagues for nine different leadership positions. Nominations for the role of planner were significantly related to having ideas and being smart, friendly, liked, empathic, and a good influence. Nominations for swimming captain were significantly correlated with being good at swimming and being a good influence. A different pattern of characteristics was associated with each role, but none of the attributes was significantly related to being chosen for the role of banquet chairman.

Again, as was noted in Chapter 7, experimenters observed the effects of task ability on leadership processes by providing different amounts of advance information to different members of a group. Outcomes were different with different types of tasks. Hemphill, Pepinsky, Shevitz, et al. (1956) reported that individuals who were given task-relevant information before an experiment scored higher in attempted leadership in assembly and construction tasks but not in strategic and discussion tasks.

Competence Relative to Subordinates' Abilities.

The competence of the leader for the task and how the leader behaves as a consequence are moderated by the subordinates' ability to handle the task. If supervisors believe their subordinates have the requisite skills, the supervisors are more likely to be consultative, *participative*,[2] or delegative (Heller, 1969a) and so they should be (Hersey & Blanchard, 1977). It seems equally true that if the the subordinates do have the skills and interest for the particular tasks of consequence, their productivity and satisfaction will be greater if supervisors permit them to participate partially or fully in the decision-making process. Full participation will be less than optimum when the subordinates do not have the requisite skills and interest.

The Leader's Personality and the Requirements of Tasks

Not only do group tasks determine which abilities are important for leadership, they are also linked to personality factors that seem to promote the choice of leaders.

---

[1]A further examination of how the change in the requirements of a task from one situation to another affects the transfer of leadership appears in Chapter 31.

[2]As defined in Chapters 22 and 23, *participation* (italicized) refers only to sharing in the decision process. Participation (romanized) includes consulting, sharing, and delegating. *Direction* (italicized) refers only to giving orders with or without explanation. Direction (romanized) includes ordering, persuading, and manipulating.

Wardlow and Greene (1952) reported that adolescent girls with high scores on tests measuring their adjustment to school and home and health problems were preferred by peers who were working with them on an intellectual task. Megargee, Bogart, and Anderson (1966) asked pairs of participants, one with a high score and one with a low score on a dominance test, to perform two different tasks. When the instructions emphasized the task, the dominant participants did not emerge as leaders significantly more often than did their partners. However, when leadership was emphasized in the instructions, the dominant members emerged as leaders in 90 percent of the pairs.

B. B. Roberts (1969) administered a battery of personality tests to leaders and followers who were studied under different conditions. Concrete and practical-thinking persons were chosen as leaders in structured tasks by all group members, but they were chosen only by the practical and concrete choosers for unstructured tasks. The theoretically oriented members were chosen as leaders in unstructured tasks by abstract, theoretical followers. W. W. Burke (1965) found that followers who worked under a socially distant leader rated their groups as more satisfying and productive in a decision-making task than on a code-solving task. Dubno (1963) obtained results which indicated that the effectiveness of groups was higher when quality rather than the speed of performing a task was emphasized by their leaders and when the leaders reached decisions more quickly than did the other members. But Hoyt and Stoner (1968) failed to confirm that the risky decisions made by groups were due to the leadership of risk-prone members. With leadership effects held constant, group discussions still produced group decisions that were riskier than the mean of the individual decisions of members. Nevertheless, as will be detailed later, the risk behavior of the leader is likely to depend on his or her speed in reaching decisions, on the organization's stage of development, and on whether the group is at an early or late phase in problem solving. The task requirements of newly formed groups and organizations are different from those of mature groups and organizations, and what is required of their leaders at these different stages is also likely to be different. Furthermore, just as the patterns of interpersonal behavior do not change substantially but the patterns of work performance do change when leaders are trans-

ferred, the leader's initiation of structure and directive leadership are more likely to shift with the changing demands of tasks than are the leader's consideration and relations orientation (Ford, 1981). Finally, although more frequent initiation and direction actually may be seen in highly structured task situations (Stech, 1981; Wolcott, 1984), they also may be superfluous and less conducive to productivity and satisfaction than is leadership that is less directive and structuring.

The Subordinates' Personality and the Requirements of Tasks

Indvik (1986b) surveyed 467 nonacademic staff at a university and found that subordinates' perceptions of their ability and preference for structure systematically affected what kinds of leadership behavior, under various task circumstances, generated elevated expectations, satisfaction, and meritorious performance. For subordinates who preferred structure, participative leadership messages were most effective when formalization of the organization was low and when the importance of the work group was high. For subordinates who did not prefer structure, participative leadership messages enhanced their satisfaction when the task was highly structured, the importance of the work group was low, and the formalization of the organization was high.

Important Dimensions of Tasks

Valenzi, Miller, Eldridge, et al. (1972) reviewed previous research on the impact of leadership behavior on the requirements of tasks and concluded that the degree of structure, routineness, complexity, and interdependence of tasks and the intellectual, rather than the manipulative, requirements systematically alter the amount and kind of leadership that will be most effective. On the basis of this review, a survey was conducted. Using stepwise regression analyses, Bass, Valenzi, Farrow, and Solomon (1975) found, for 78 managers described by their 407 subordinates, that tasks with clear objectives were seen to result in more *direction* and consultation by the managers. Routine tasks were associated with less *participative* leadership and more complex tasks, with negotiative leadership, and with more frequent delegation. Other dimensions that were isolated were autonomy or discretionary opportunities. If subordinates had to engage in planning, coordination, and other managerial activities, again delegation was reported to be more frequent among their leaders. The correlation of superior-subordinate relations to structure was particularly strong. With much structure, more *direction* was seen. This finding was confirmed in an unpublished follow-up by the author with 340 managers and over 1,300 subordinates.

Structure

Leadership of groups and individuals with structured compared with unstructured tasks have been considered in a great many studies.[3] For instance, Hill and Hughes (1974) reported that leaders displayed more socioemotional behaviors, both positive and negative, when subordinates performed unstructured as opposed to structured tasks. Widely used to examine the effects of structure is House and Dessler's (1974) measure of task structure, a ten-item questionnaire on which respondents describe the extent to which their tasks are simple, repetitive, and unambiguous.

"Structure" refers to the extent to which role relations are loosely or tightly arranged. "Task structure" also refers to the extent to which what needs to be done is specified and certain. For example, Lawrence and Lorsch (1967b) assumed that task structure went from the lowest to the highest as one moved from fundamental research to applied research, to sales, and finally to production. In six organizations, they found that production personnel (whose work was most specified and certain) and fundamental-research personnel (whose tasks were least specified and certain) both preferred task-oriented leaders, whereas members in the sales subsystem (which had moderately specified and certain work) preferred more interpersonal, socially oriented leaders.

Fiedler's Contingency Model. A tenet of Fiedler's (1967a) contingency model was based on the effect of task structure. For Fiedler, task structure creates a more favorable situation for the leader. A task-oriented leader will be more effective when there is either a great deal of task structure or very little task structure.

[3]See, for example, Fiedler (1964), Hunt (1967), Shaw and Blum (1966), and Wofford (1971).

A relations-oriented leader will be more effective if task structure is moderate. Although the conclusions remain controversial (see, for instance, Graen, Alvares, Orris, & Martella, 1970; Graen, Orris, & Alvares, 1971), considerable empirical support for this proposition was presented in Chapter 23. However, the effects of task structure may be much weaker than are other situational elements that favor the leader (W. Hill, 1969a).

Some Effects on Leadership Behavior and Outcomes. Wofford (1971) observed that unstructured tasks elicited more achievement-oriented and organizing managerial behavior than did structured tasks. Lord (1975) found that the degree of task structure in a situation was negatively related to the occurrence of facilitative leadership behavior. An unexpected curvilinear effect emerged; instrumental (task-directed) leadership was most effective with tasks that were moderate in structure.

Shaw and Blum (1966) found that structured problems were better served by directive supervision. Thus, when the problem on which five-person groups were working was highly structured so that clear procedures could be followed, directive supervision led to quick results. Yet, when leaders did initiate structure a great deal, as was seen in a study by Badin (1974) of 42 work groups in a manufacturing firm, their effectiveness was reduced if the groups were already highly structured. The correlation of effectiveness and initiating structure was −.56. But in the less structured of the 42 groups, the effectiveness of the groups correlated .20 with the extent to which the first-line supervisors initiated structure.

Filley, House, and Kerr (1979) found that task structure moderated the relationship between participation and performance and between participation and the attitudes of subordinates. Participative leadership had no effect or was contraindicated when tasks were machine paced, mechanized, and highly structured in other ways. But when tasks were unstructured, the effects of participative leadership on both the attitudes and productivity of subordinates were consistently positive.

Hanaway (1985) examined the effects of the uncertainty of tasks on the initiating and search behavior of 18 upper-level and 32 lower-level administrators of school districts. The lower-level administrators were observed to be more reticent to take actions when conditions were uncertain, but the results for the upper-level administrators were less clear.

Role Clarity. Generally, people, particularly those with a great need for structure, prefer to work in clear settings. Valenzi and Dessler (1978) showed that among 284 employees in two electronics firms, satisfaction was uniformly high when role clarity was high. The leaders' consideration promoted even more satisfaction. In addition, Benson, Kemery, Sauser, and Tankesley (1985) found that a high need for clarity was related to low job satisfaction among 370 university employees above and beyond the effects of their role ambiguity on the employees' dissatisfaction.

The determination of perceived role ambiguity or perceived role clarity is a way to discern how much structure exists in a group. Kinicki and Schriesheim, (1978) studied the role clarity of 173 freshmen in 16 classes, as measured by Rizzo, House, and Lirtzman's (1970) scale dealing with clear, planned objectives; clear responsibilities; clear expectations; and clear explanations of what has to be done. They found that students were more satisfied with relations-oriented teachers, particularly when role clarity in the situation was low. But the students were more productive with directive teachers when role clarity was low, not when it was high. As Siegall and Cummings (1986) demonstrated, satisfaction with supervision is enhanced if a subordinate's role is initially ambiguous and if the supervisor contributes to clarifying the role by issuing instructions and directions.

Fulk and Wendler (1982) found, among 308 clerical and managerial employees, that role clarity was associated with nonpunitive, task-oriented leadership and contingent reward. Such leadership was satisfying, but role clarity could also emerge as a consequence of arbitrary and punitive leadership behavior that was dissatisfying. Congruently, Schriesheim and Murphy (1976) failed to find that role clarity moderated the relationship between any kind of leadership behavior and the satisfaction and performance of subordinates.

To try to make more sense out of this evidence, I will say more about the extent to which structure and role clarity affect the impact of leadership on performance and satisfaction when, later in this chapter, I review path-goal theory and the specific tests used to try to validate it.

Clarity of Objectives. Nagata (1965) observed that groups with goal-relevant tasks enabled leaders to exercise more influence on the members than did groups in which the tasks were not relevant to the goal. To some extent, clear objectives may substitute for structured relationships or clear role relationships in getting the job done, particularly if little coordination is required. Multiple regression analyses by Bass, Farrow, and Valenzi (1977) for 250 managers and their 924 subordinates suggested that the effectiveness of work groups was significantly greater if the mangers had clear objectives. Furthermore, where these organizational members were competent and motivated to attain their objectives and could operate independently or in cooperation with each other, the effectiveness of their performance was strongly associated with the clarity of their objectives and the adequacy of their resources.

Autonomy and Discretionary Opportunities

One's felt autonomy and discretion to do one's job appear to be complex perceptions that are affected by various factors, such as the organization's technology and the frames of reference shared with co-workers, as well as the style of leadership employed. Presumably, leaders who initiate a great deal of structure by definition, reduce their subordinates' autonomy. But leaders' consideration should enhance subordinates' feelings of autonomy. Thus, Ferris and Rowland (1981) suggested that the leaders' initiation of structure and consideration systematically affect the subordinates' perceptions of autonomy in this way, which, in turn, may or may not contribute to the subordinates' performance.

The same leadership will have different effects, depending on whether subordinates' autonomy is high or low. Thus, Johns (1978) found a correlation of .29 between the leaders' initiation of structure and the subordinates' job satisfaction when 232 union employees reported that their autonomy was high and a correlation of .01 when they indicated that their autonomy was low. The leaders' consideration and the subordinates' job satisfaction correlated only .20 when the subordinates' autonomy was high but correlated .52 when it was low.

As might be expected, data analysis begun by Bass and Valenzi (1974) for over 1,300 subordinates' descriptions of 340 managers indicated that, if leaders' were viewed as delegative and negotiative, their subordinates felt in possession of more discretionary opportunities. Leaders were also less likely to be seen as *directive* under such conditions (Bass, Valenzi, Farrow, & Solomon, 1975).

Amabile and Gryskiewicz (1987) interviewed 120 research and development (R & D) scientists to elicit two critical incidents from each of them, one incident to illustrate the occurrence of high creativity and the other, to provide an instance of low creativity. Consistent with what has been said about participative leadership and creativity, in describing the incidents of high creativity, over 74 percent of the interviewees mentioned freedom to decide what to do and how to do one's work, a sense of control over one's work and ideas, freedom from contraints, and an open atmosphere. This finding agrees with conclusions reached by Andrews and Farris (1967) and others, although Amabile and Gryskiewicz hastened to add that there is a limit to the amount of such freedom, for it must be bounded by the team supervisor's coordination of the team's overall efforts (Pelz & Andrews, 1966b).

In presenting these incidents of high creativity, one-third to one-half the 120 scientists revealed that their leaders' enthusiasm, interest, and commitment to new ideas and challenges encouraged their creativity.[4] The supportive leadership was seen in the willingness to take risks, to provide recognition for success, and to clarify what was needed. The leaders accepted failure without destructive criticism and avoided excessive evaluations. Such leaders did not dwell on the status quo. Keller (1989) reported that the productivity of 30 project *research* teams correlated .57 with the intellectual stimulation of their leaders but close to zero with the same leadership in 36 *project* development teams.

Routineness versus Variations in Tasks

Jobs can require that employees carry out the same few tasks in a repetitive cycle or may involve a greater variety of tasks that are more variable in sequence. The optimal performance by leaders depends on whether the work involves uniform, recurring, repetitive tasks

[4]Here, there is consistency with the effects of the transformational leadership factors of inspirational leadership, intellectual stimulation, and individualized consideration.

or considerable variability in the requirements of tasks (Valenzi, Miller, Eldridge, et al., 1972).

In their classic study of workers on the assembly line, Walker and Guest (1952) emphasized the extent to which supervision was likely to be more directive when the tasks to be performed were extremely routine. Likewise, Bass, Valenzi, Farrow, and Solomon (1975) reported more directive leadership as well as less supervisory delegation in work groups that were carrying out routine tasks. Similarly, Ford (1981) showed that in 35 departments in a book publishing firm, a bank, and a university, the routineness of work uniquely correlated .36 with the extent to which the departmental manager initiated structure but only .05 with his or her consideration as a leader.

In a study involving 16 departments in 10 organizations, R. H. Hall (1962) distinguished between uniform, easily routinized, and standardized activities and nonuniform, difficult-to-routinize, and creative activities. He found that departments and hierarchical levels whose activities were more nonroutine were also less bureaucratic than were those departments and levels that were oriented toward routine activities. In nonroutine situations, the atmosphere was more personal, had less hierarchical emphasis, and required fewer procedures and regulations. Consistent with all these findings, Heller and Yukl (1969) found that production and finance managers (who supervised more routinized work) tended to use centralized decision making, while general and personnel managers (who supervised less routinized work) were more participative.

The linkage of routineness to the greater initiation of structure by leaders is consistent with the hypothesis, verified by Kipnis (1984) for several levels of managers in Australia and the United States, that employees who work on routine tasks are likely to be devalued by their supervisors. But despite this finding, Jiambalvo and Pratt (1982) reported that in four Big-8 accounting firms, considerate leadership behavior by senior accountants increased the involvement in tasks among staff assistants who performed relatively simple tasks more than it did among those who performed relatively complex tasks.

Variety. Hackman and Oldham's (1975) Job Diagnostic Survey included job variety as an important variable that was likely to relate to the motivation to work. Using ratings based on the survey, Johns (1978) showed that with job variety, the leaders' initiation of structure generated greater job satisfaction and fewer intentions to quit among subordinates. Without such variety, the leaders' initiation of structure was unrelated to the subordinates' satisfaction and increased their intentions to quit. However, the leaders' consideration was strongly associated with satisfaction, regardless of whether the job was varied or routine. Yet, only when variety was absent was the leaders' lack of consideration associated with the subordinates' intentions to quit. In contrast, Brief, Aldag, Russell, and Rude (1981) found, in an investigation of police officers, relatively little of the expected effects of the variety of job skills on the favorability of the police officers' attitudes toward the citizenry.

In a study that distinguished working on uniform and nonuniform tasks, Pelz (cited in Litwak, 1961), found a higher correlation between the motivation to work and productivity when those engaged in nonuniform tasks were permitted by their supervisors to make their own job decisions. But for those involved with uniform tasks, there was a higher correlation between motivation and productivity when freedom to make decisions was restricted. Nonetheless, Katz, Maccoby, and Morse (1950) found that supervisors of high-producing sections were significantly more likely to give general rather than close supervision, even though they were supervising routine clerical work in a life insurance company. However, in a subsequent study of less routine railroad work (Katz, Maccoby, Gurin, & Floor, 1951), little difference was found between the closeness of supervision by foremen of high- and low-producing sections.

In these and the many other related studies that followed,[5] R. Likert could find no diminution in the utility of participative (System 4) leadership in routine jobs as compared to those with more variety. But Griffin (1980) suggested otherwise. He contrasted the leadership-outcome relations among employees who had "high-scope" tasks (varied, involving, and autonomous) and those who had "low-scope" (simple, routine) tasks. In his first survey of 129 employees, the scope of the employees' tasks did not correlate with the leadership

style of their supervisors. However, for a subset of employees with high-scope jobs but a low need for personal growth, directive supervision subsequently resulted in greater satisfaction. On the other hand, employees with low-scope jobs were more satisfied with their subsequent supervision if their supervisors were more supportive and practiced more management by exception. Such supervisors were described by such statements as, "My supervisor doesn't bother me as long as I do a good job" and "My supervisor leaves me alone and lets me work."

Although passive management by exception generally has been downgraded by subordinates as a satisfying style of supervision,[6] the results here suggest that employees in low-scope jobs prefer and feel better when their supervisors practice management by exception. This suggestion was confirmed in a survey of 195 full-time employees by Algattan (1985). When the scope of the tasks that subordinates performed was low and the subordinates had little need for growth, the leaders' maintenance of the status quo was more positively related to outcomes than was more active direction, participation, or task-oriented leadership.

To conclude, while studies have shown that leadership tends to be directive with routine operations, such directiveness may not necessarily be useful. Whether or not subordinates are satisfied with routine or varied tasks depends on their need for growth. In addition, job variety may substitute for considerate leadership as a satisfier.

Complexity of Tasks

Bell (1967) viewed the complexity of tasks in terms of the degree of predictability of the demands of the work, the amount of discretion exercised, the extent of responsibility, and the number of different tasks performed. Among supervisors in a hospital, he found that the more complex the subordinates' tasks or the supervisor's job, the narrower was the supervisor's span of control. But the complexity of tasks did not influence how closely the subordinates were supervised. Barrow's (1976) study indicated that leaders exhibited more task orientation when faced with more complex tasks, but the complexity of the tasks did not affect

[5]See Chapter 21.

[6]See Chapter 17.

their tendency to be punitive. However, Cuthbertson (1982), in a survey of 175 subordinates and their 25 supervisors in a central office of a school district, found more directive leadership than she expected in relation to the complexity of the tasks involved. Among 61 to 68 telecommunications units, Osborn and Hunt (1979) obtained contrasting patterns of correlations with leadership, the structural complexity of the units led, and the difficulty of the units' tasks. They found that the leadership that was required was unrelated to the complexity of the units led or the difficulty of the tasks. However, the actual amount of support and role clarification by the leaders, as expected, correlated between .24 and .31 with structural complexity of the units but unexpectedly between $-.30$ and $-.42$ with the difficulty of the task.

Barrow (1976) observed, in a simulation using 120 male college students as leaders, that more initiation of structure was caused by increasing the complexity of the task, but autocratic behavior was generated more by the poor performance of workers than by increasing the complexity of the task, while considerate leadership was evoked by improvements in the workers' performance. Relevant to these results, Wofford (1971) found that a personal-interaction (relations-oriented) manager was more effective for complex operations, whereas a self-oriented, autocratic manager was more suited to situations with simple work schedules.

Hammer and Turk (1985) showed that supervisors were less likely to perform group-maintenance activities if they supervised employees who worked with intensive technology, such as in a repair shop or an R & D laboratory, whose tasks were complex and nonroutinized. On the other hand, supervisors of workers who were engaged in long-linked technologies, such as mass-production assembly lines and whose tasks were interdependent were more likely to engage in network activities. In addition, supervisors in the intensive-technology situation felt, to a greater extent, that they had the authority to reward subordinates, whereas supervisors in the long-linked technology settings felt they had more authority to discharge employees and, in turn, were less likely to be seen as experts.

Increasing Complexity of Tasks. The effects of the increasing complexity of tasks on requirements for

leadership are illustrated by the changing military scene. Those who are now being selected to serve as military leaders in the next several decades will have to operate under conditions for which there is less public consensus than existed in World War II. They will be expected to know how to use minimal force in unconventional little conflicts in which they will be trying to keep the peace. Fighting, when it occurs, will be more intense, lethal, and destructive. For this type of fighting, an understanding of the local values of what is right, good, and important, along with intellectual sensitivity, will be particularly important. Officers will be required to respond thoughtfully to increasingly ambiguous circumstances. They will need to inspire subordinates with a vision of the future that strengthens the subordinates' loyalty and commitment rather than merely fosters the subordinates' grudging obedience (Gal, 1986).

Difficulty of Tasks. A factor analysis of 104 different experimental tasks by M. E. Shaw (1963b) disclosed three factors that contribute to the effects of the complexity of tasks: (1) the difficulty of tasks (the number of operations, skills, and knowledge required to complete the task), (2) the multiplicity of correct solutions, and (3) the requirements for cooperation (integrated efforts). C. G. Morris (1966a, 1966b) found that as the difficulty of the tasks increased for groups, there was a concomitant increase in the leaders' and members' attempts to structure answers, propose solutions, and seek evaluations. However, tasks of intermediate difficulty generated the highest frequency of attempts to structure the problem, followed by tasks that were the most difficult; easy tasks produced the most irrelevant interactions. At the same time, Nagata (1966) found that groups with easy tasks exhibited more role differentiation and permitted leaders to exercise more influence than did groups with difficult tasks. Nevertheless, Bass, Pryer, Gaier, and Flint (1958) observed fewer attempts to lead in groups with easy problems.

When it was arranged for students to instruct others on easy and hard tasks in a laboratory setting, the "instructors" used less punishment when trainees performed difficult tasks than when they performed easy ones. A meta-analysis by Tubbs (1986) of 87 studies that tested Locke's (1968) hypotheses on how the difficulty and specificity of goals enhance the speed and quantity of work that subordinates perform provided further indirect evidence that motivating leaders (in this case the experimenter) are more structuring with specific, difficult goals than are leaders who tell subordinates just to do their best or do not tell them anything about the goals. Difficult goals resulted in the higher motivation and performance of participants in short-term laboratory studies, but according to the meta-analysis, such results were somewhat less likely to materialize in survey studies of workers who were engaged in longer-term assignments, perhaps because sometimes assignments may be too difficult, as noted next.

The pressure of time and the need to meet deadlines contribute to the difficulty of tasks. For research scientists and engineers, Hall and Lawler (1971) found that the pressure to do high-quality work and to help the company attain its financial goals contributed to the successful performance of their research laboratories. Andrews and Farris (1972) also reported that time pressures experienced by scientists and engineers correlated positively with their subsequent performance. However, pressure that was perceived as unreasonable or excessive resulted in poor performance or decreased performance. Such excessive pressure can result in the setting of unrealistically high goals (Forward & Zander, 1971).

Multiplicity of Solutions. Shaw and Blum (1966) noted that directive supervision was more effective if the problem called for agreement on a single solution, whereas participation paid off when multiple, divergent solutions were needed. They had groups of five members each perform three tasks that required different types of solutions. Directive supervision was more effective when the problem called for a single final decision or involved the convergence of judgments into some final product. On the other hand, when the problem required multiple, divergent final solutions, participative approaches were more effective.

Participative leadership is suggested by the voluminous evidence that groups achieve better solutions to problems with multiple alternative possibilities than does their average member working alone (Bass, 1960). (Nonetheless, the group decision may not be as good as the decision achieved by the best member working

alone.) This assembly bonus effect (Steiner, 1972) occurs unless individual members already have the requisite information to solve the problem alone, for instance, when every member is a professional expert who is highly trained to deal with the same standard types of problems in the same way. There will be less of an assembly bonus if the addition of members produces interference rather than nonredundant information. Thus, according to Heller (1969a), the primary reason that managers in 15 firms reported using participative leadership was to improve the technical quality of complex decisions. In fact, some form of consultation is mandatory in highly technically oriented organizations, for the available technical expertise does not fully reside with their supervisors but is distributed, to some degree, among the subordinates.

The difficulty of a task is in the eye of the beholder. Manz, Adsit, Campbell, and Mathison-Hance (1988) surveyed 3,580 managers in a large firm about the hindrances to their performance. Better performing managers paid more attention to external hindrances, such as inadequate appraisal systems and the absence of opportunities for promotion. Poorer performers focused more on deficiencies in skills, such as the lack of interpersonal or technical abilities.

Required Cooperation and Interdependence of Tasks. Conflicting evidence has emerged here. Requisite cooperation and the interdependence of tasks among subordinates has been found to be promoted by participative leadership in some research studies. Other investigations have failed to find any effects, and evidence from still other laboratory and survey studies suggests that when subordinates engage in interdependent tasks, directive leadership and initiation of structure by the leader are more efficacious.

O'Brien (1969b) theorized that the equalization of power and participative leadership would be appropriate for tasks that require a great deal of cooperation, whereas a power differential between the superior and the subordinates would be more effective in situations in which subordinates carry out tasks independently of each other. Vroom and Mann's (1960) results were illustrative. Vroom and Mann studied drivers and positioners in a package-delivery company. The positioner's job required a high degree of interdependence and considerable interaction with co-workers and with the supervisor. The driver's job involved little interpersonal interaction and considerable independence in work activity. In line with expectations, the positioners favored democratic leaders and the drivers preferred authoritarian leaders.

Although, Bass, Valenzi, Farrow, and Solomon (1975) failed to find statistically significant correlations between leadership styles and the interdependence of tasks of work-group members, larger-scale follow-up analysis as initiated by Bass and Valenzi (1974) indicated that more *directive* leadership and consultative leadership were associated with the interdependence of tasks, but negotiative leadership was greater when members worked independently of each other. However, Ford (1981), in a survey of 25 departmental managers and their 445 departmental associates, found that the amount of interdependence in the work flow within the departments did not help to account for the variance in the initiation of structure or consideration by the managers beyond that already explained by the routineness or uncertainty of departmental tasks. On the other hand, Lord and Rowzee's (1979) laboratory experiment with 4-person groups showed that when tasks required a high degree of interdependence among the subjects, more frequent directive leadership behaviors emerged: developing the orientation, developing plans, and promoting coordination. Consistent with these results, Fry, Kerr, and Lee (1986) found that among 22 high school and college teams in 8 sports, winning coaches of highly interdependent sports teams (such as basketball) were described by their players as displaying more initiation of structure and less consideration than were winning coaches of sports teams, such as golf, that required little or no interdependence. Coaches of winning teams that were highly interdependent also displayed more initiation and less consideration than did coaches of losing teams that were highly interdependent.

To adequately explain these results requires the consideration of another variable—the competence of the team members. Directive leadership to clarify roles may have been needed more when team members must work in collaboration but the team members are novices. Participative leadership that is focused on commitment becomes more important for high-quality collaborative efforts when the members are already trained and experienced.

Required Interdependencies among Members. Thompson (1967) distinguished among three kinds of interdependencies: pooled, sequential, and reciprocal. In the pooled circumstance, each individual such as the baseball player at bat performs alone, but the results have collective effects. In the sequential effect, one person, such as a running quarterback in a football play for whom others will block the opposition, depends on others earlier in a sequence. Reciprocal interdependence occurs when each person must interact with others, such as in basketball. Leadership and management in conditions of pooled interdependence require continuing attention to tactical judgments and the development of individual performers, but cohesiveness may not be as important. In sequential performance, leadership and management must attend more to planning and the preparation of the team. The requirements for performance are tighter and more highly specified and scheduled and cohesiveness is more important. In reciprocal interdependence, satisfactory mutual adjustments are of the greatest importance and necessitate that the most attention be paid to relationships and continuing cooperation (Keidel, 1984).

Kabanoff and O'Brien (1979) studied leadership when members of a group either had to *coordinate* their efforts (work on subtasks arranged in an order of precedence) or *collaborate* (work simultaneously with each other on every subtask). Groups that had to coordinate their efforts were more productive, especially when the leaders were more task competent. But the leaders' task competence was irrelevant to productivity in the collaborative task situation. This finding may be explained by a suggestion of Hill and Hughes (1974) that there is a greater emphasis on the leaders' socioemotional function than on their task function in the collaborative situation. As a consequence, their task competence is relatively less important when collaboration is required.

Socioemotional versus Task Requirements

As was just observed, a distinction that is important for understanding what type of competence will be demanded of a leader is whether socioemotional or task requirements will be emphasized for leadership. This is the most frequent role differentiation that occurs in discussion groups. When the demands of the task are high in groups, being liked does not contribute much to leadership, and socioemotional skills are not highly valued (Slater, 1955). On the other hand, in social and personal-development groups, such as therapy groups, sensitivity training groups, social clubs, and gangs, the socioemotional function will be emphasized. As was concluded in Chapter 23, in most kinds of groups, both types of leadership usually need to be present. Thus, A. S. Miles (1970) reported that student leaders who rated high on both task ability and socioemotional ability were considered most influential. Empirically, the differentiation between the two types of abilities often is not found. For instance, Gustafson and Harrell (1970) observed relatively little differentiation between task and socioemotional roles in experimental groups. Similarly, V. Williams (1965) noted that some types of group structures were able to operate effectively without differentiating task specialists from socioemotional specialists.

To sort out the effects, Olmsted (1954) gave one set of groups instructions that were designed to induce socioemotional concerns for group processes and the satisfaction of members. The directions given to the second set of groups emphasized the accomplishment of tasks and maintenance of impersonal relationships among members. The most talkative members in the task-directed groups talked longer than did their counterparts in the socioemotional groups, perhaps as the result of a group norm related to the intensity of participation. Task-directed groups tended to develop stable leadership-status structures, while members of socioemotional groups continued to jockey for position for a longer time.

Slater (1955) found that the amount of agreement among members in discussion groups moderated the effects. In groups that achieved a high degree of consensus on solutions to problems, the highest participator (who was more likely to be a leader than a follower) usually received the highest rating for helping the group meet the requirements of its task. In low-consensus groups, the highest participator was not rated high in this regard.

Sociotechnical Design. There has been increasing interest in designing tasks and work to take account of both the task and the socioemotional requirements. Considerable consultation with the workers is seen as fundamental to establishing the bases for meeting both the requirements of the task and the workers' socioemotional needs. Participative leadership becomes mandatory in the actual operations and is built into the design. For instance, *minimal critical specification* is a principle of sociotechnical design. According to this principle, the design process should identify what is essential to be accomplished in a task, and no more should be specified than what is essential. For example, although the design process may be precise about what needs to be done, it should leave maximum latitude about the method the employee may use to accomplish the task. Again, the *multifunctional* principle of sociotechnical design proposes that for an organization to be sufficiently adaptive to meet environmental demands, it is necessary for its members to be willing and able to perform more than one function or to perform the same function in a variety of ways to meet changing circumstances. Clearly, both task-oriented and relations-oriented leadership are needed to obtain the requisite employee performance and the commitment of employees to such fluid arrangements (Bass & Barrett, 1981).

Phases in Group Problem Solving

The requirements of the task change as a group progresses in its solution of a problem. Given these changing requirements during the course of group problem solving, Valenzi, Miller, Eldridge, et al. (1972) concluded that effective leadership for one phase of problem solving may be different than it is for another phase. Early on, the group usually engages in the divergent generation of alternatives. In this phase, broad participation is needed; as a consequence, Doyle (1971) considered democratic leaders to be most effective. But in the convergent, final, synthesizing phase, when coordination becomes more important, groups with leaders of high status were particularly effective. Becker and Baloff (1969) also suggested that optimal leader-subordinate relations may depend on whether the group's immediate task involves information processing, the generation of alternatives, or decision making.

Ghiselli (1966a) observed experimental groups at various stages of problem solving. The presence of a strongly self-confident decision maker, along with highly intelligent, confident, and cohesive followers, was associated with the better performance of the group in the later stages of the group's development. Nonetheless, initial performance was poor in its early storming phase. Presumably, such confidence, competence, and motivation generated many conflicting alternatives that later formed the basis of high-quality decisions.

Sample and Wilson (1965) also studied groups in different phases of problem solving. They found that task-oriented leaders quickly structured the group procedures during the planning phase and were then able to play a more relaxed role in the operational phase. Relations-oriented leaders, on the other hand, tended to hold group discussions during the planning stage, and the work did not get organized. As a result, these leaders had to try to organize procedures during the operational stage, with only partial success. In such circumstances, groups under task-oriented leaders performed more effectively.

Type of Task

Carter and Nixon (1949b) found that different participants emerged as leaders, depending on whether intellectual, clerical, or mechanical-assembly tasks were involved. Carter, Haythorn, and Howell (1950) studied the effects of six types of tasks (reasoning, intellectual construction, clerical, discussion, motor cooperation, and mechanical assembly) on leadership in initially leaderless groups. Although there was some generality of leadership performance across all tasks, two clusters of tasks made a difference in who emerged as a leader. The leaders of the intellectual tasks were different from the leaders of the tasks involving doing things with one's hands.

As was mentioned earlier, C. G. Morris (1966a, 1966b) varied the type of task and the difficulty of the task for 108 groups. The variance in the leaders' behavior was related more to the type of task than to the difficulty of the task. Discussion tasks elicited significantly more structuring of problems and more explana-tory and defensive comments by leaders. Production tasks resulted in more structuring of proposed solutions, disagreement, and procedural comments. Problem-solving tasks were similar to discussion tasks but led to more irrelevant activity and less structuring of problems.

Korten (1968) suggested that if the final product of a task was practical, more directive supervision was in order. If the outcome was theoretical, then participation was likely to be more useful.

Tasks at Different Organizational Levels. Systematic changes in the type of tasks that are performed occur as leaders move up the organizational ladder.[7] The different types of tasks call for different kinds of leadership. At the production and operations levels, the processes are direct and concrete. Work and service are with tangible materials and methods that are accomplished by people, tools, and machines. At these levels, leaders deal with issues of routines, pacing, meeting deadlines, balancing the need for immediate production or service with the need for the development of individual subordinates and the need to prepare subordinates for future operations. Trust is based on personal contact and knowledge. Leadership involves face-to-face interaction and interpersonal skills. At higher organizational levels, leadership deals much more with buffering the rational production at lower levels from the turbulence of the external environment. At these levels, the subordinates' operations are monitored indirectly, and the coordination and integration of efforts with the market and the external environment become the tasks of consequence (Jaques, 1978).

Not unexpectedly, Bass, Valenzi, Farrow, and Solomon (1975) found that the more subordinates' work involved planning, coordination, evaluation, and other managerial activities, the more frequently their superior was likely to delegate decision making to them. However, follow-up analyses on a larger scale added that such subordinates were also given more direction.

Leadership and Changes in the Organization's Tasks. As the organization ages, the tasks change at higher levels and, consequently, the type of leadership that is needed also changes. Brenner (1972) and Lavoie and Culbert (1978), among others, describe the com-

[7]See Chapter 20.

monly observed progression of organizations through development, maturity, and decline. Different tasks arise as the organization matures. Different stages of an organization's development call for the emergence of different styles of executive leadership in the different phases. Early on, the tasks of a business enterprise are to develop products, processes, and procedures; create a demand for them; build loyalty to a brand; find a significant niche in the market; develop personnel and new technology; attract financing; and so on. Later, the tasks may require more attention to cost containment, divestment, maintaining the share of the market, and integrating new product lines with older ones. The founders who conceive and originate organizations that grow and thrive, for example, are more prone to take calculated risks than are their counterparts who must deal with old, declining organizations.[8] Leadership that is predictable and that works within the established rules and procedures and under greater formal constraints is more characteristic of mature organizations than of those in the early stages of their development.

In the established organization in a stable environment, the executive must be able to serve as a transactional leader who works within the institutionalized values and systems. The executive leader serves as a steward, balancing out the strongly developed interests of the different constituencies that may be in conflict with each other. Much political compromise and accommodation are needed. During periods of gestation, birth, development, resolution, re-formation, and renewal, the executive's tasks require more transformational leadership, greater persistence and effort, and greater inspirational and charismalike behavior.[9] New strategies and commitments to new values and new systems are required. The cycle of development, maturity, and decline is not inevitable. Rather, intervention by transformational managers can provide for the renewal of an organization through reform or revolution (Normann, 1977).

Impact of Automation and Computers on Leadership. By 1990, over 80 percent of the office workers were using computers. Thus, office supervisors had to be reasonably familiar with computers and the

complexities of computer systems. The same was true for blue-collar supervision as automation increased in factories, mills, and warehouses.

In addition to the rapid expansion of technological capabilities are the concomitant changes in organizational arrangements and leadership. In the U.S. military, on-line instant communication makes it possible to link the U.S. president with the local combat commander on the battle site, bypassing many organizational echelons. Likewise, FAX and electronic mail make for instant communication and potential control across continents, oceans, and organizational levels. Increasingly, the centralization of decision making or overcontrol of the local commander is the result. Similarly, tighter reins by higher-level executives are made possible by computer systems. Although the greatest emphasis has been placed on the impact of automation on stable, repetitive, processing systems, computer-assisted creative designing and engineering are now commonplace for production and service processes. Computerized planning and control models are also available for real-time planning and control by higher-level executives.

Word processing and office automation increase the productivity of individual typists. Nevertheless, supposedly to take advantage of the automation, the individualized dyadic relationship of the manager and the typist may be severed and replaced with an anonymous pool of typists. The consequential loss for both the manager and the secretary of the quality of their relationship may be the price paid for greater typing productivity.

First-line supervisors become more like area supervisors when advanced manufacturing computer technology or computer integrated manufacturing is put in place. It is somewhat uncertain whether such area supervisors will be shop-floor experts or engineering-trained personnel with some shop experience. Minimally, the new technology brings about more changes in the role of the first-line supervisor than in the roles of personnel at almost any other level in the hierarchy, but the new role is relatively routine and readily analyzed (Ettle, 1986).

According to Kraemer and Danziger (1984), computerization at the workplace increases the closeness of the supervisor with those at the bottom of the hierarchy. The supervisors lose some of their potential for

---

[8]See Chapter 26.
[9]See Chapter 12.

upward influence, while those who are higher up feel a greater sense of control. The pressure of time and the importance of deadlines increase. These changes enhance the possibilities of bureaucratic management. But the effects may be counterproductive. Applebaum (1982) noted that computer programming applied to the construction industry resulted in the reliance on authoritarian and mechanistic procedures. The outcome was inefficient and irrational; control of the work process was decreased instead of increased.

However, Kerr, Hill, and Broedling (1986) offered a more balanced perspective. They suggested that automation should have its biggest effects on workers whose work had been labor intensive, closely supervised, and required little discretion and judgment. Obviously, the supervisors of such workers would be responsible for more sophisticated equipment. Nevertheless, computerized systems directly give the upper management detailed information on the individual worker, such as his or her error rate and deadlines that are missed. Upper managers can bypass the first-level supervisor to obtain such information. The supervisor will then be expected to explain the reasons for the worker's deviation from the production plans. Further conflicts of interest arise for the first-level supervisor, who now faces demands from a specialized staff of systems analysts and programmers, along with those from the traditional line superiors, subordinates, and staff personnel: "first-line supervisors will have to be more technically proficient, as well as more highly skilled in human relations than their predecessors" (p. 114).

Computerization can also eliminate the need for management controls for it can provide direct feedback from work performed on the task without any supervisory intervention. The self-managed employee can be provided by computer with continued feedback about his or her performance along with the information needed to improve it.

In contrast to the findings of Kraemer and Danzinger (1984), Kerr, Hill, and Broedling (1986) inferred that first-line supervisors will move farther from their subordinates and closer to middle managers. They reasoned that computerization reduces the time that supervisors need to spend in planning and scheduling work; documenting records and reports; engaging in coordination and control; organizing the subordinates' work; and maintaining quality and efficiency, safety

and cleanliness, and machinery and equipment. Presumably, spans of control can be increased. Nonetheless, the first-line supervisor's role does not seem to be diminished, for computerization facilitates his or her service as a boundary spanner; a maintainer of relations with other units; or a selector, trainer, and motivator of subordinates. Computerization makes it possible for first-line supervisors to operate more like middle managers, relative to the total organization, rather than remain oriented toward dealing mainly with subordinates (Hill & Kerr, 1984).

The increasing technology and computerization of the task suggests that in more technologically advanced organizations, the power motive may become less important than the need for achievement as a predictor of success in advancement to higher levels of management. As was noted in Chapter 10, McClelland (1975) demonstrated that individuals who scored high on the Thematic Apperception Test in the need for power and the inhibition of power tended to emerge as more successful leaders in a variety of situations. However, when McClelland and Boyatzis (1982) examined whether the leadership-motive pattern was predictive of the long-term managerial success of technical and nontechnical managers at A T & T, the power-motive pattern was related to significantly higher levels of advancement after 8 to 16 years with the company only for nontechnical managers. For the technically trained and experienced managers, the need for achievement, rather than the power motive, predicted advancement into the next several echelons of the firm.

Path-Goal Theory: The Explanation of Task Effects on Leadership

Beginning with Georgopolous, Mahoney, and Jones (1957) and delineated by M. G. Evans (1970a) and House (1971), path-goal theory stimulated the search for an explanation of how the nature of the group's task systematically affects whether consideration, initiation of structure, or their interplay makes more of a contribution to the group's satisfaction and effectiveness. Rightfully, the theory has been modified on a continuing basis by experimental failures. According to T. R. Mitchell (1979), path-goal theory calls for the leader to provide subordinates with coaching, guidance, and the rewards necessary for satisfaction and effective performance necessitated by the subordinates' abilities to meet the particular task requirements and attain the designated goals. Focus is on ways for the leader to influence subordinates' perceptions of the clarity of the paths to goals and the desirability of the goals themselves. Leadership behavior that is best suited for increasing motivation depends on the subordinate's personal characteristics and the demands of the task. Valued rewards should be awarded contingent on effective performance.[10]

An Exchange Theory of Leadership

Path-goal theory is an exchange theory of leadership. It attempts to explain why contingent reward works and how contingent reward influences the motivation and satisfaction of subordinates. In its earliest version by Georgopolous, Mahoney, and Jones (1957), it focused on the need for leaders to "point out the paths to successful effort" (Bass, 1965, p. 150). Leaders do so by "increasing personal payoffs to subordinates for work-goal attainment, and making the path to these pay-offs easier to travel by clarifying it, reducing roadblocks and pitfalls, and increasing the opportunities for personal satisfaction en route" (House, 1971, p. 324).

Path instrumentalities are the subordinate's subjective estimates that his or her performance will lead to the accomplishment of the goal and that achievement of the goal will result in ends desired by the subordinate. The leader enhances the subordinate's motivation, performance, and satisfaction by clarifying and enhancing path instrumentalities (Yukl & Van Fleet, 1986). This cognitive-perceptual explanation of path-goal theory can be matched in terms of operant behavior and reinforcement theory, according to Mawhinney and Ford (1977), to account for the path-goal phenomenon.

The Leader's Role

Leaders can affect a subordinate's efforts in several ways in the path-goal process. They can clarify the subordinate's role, that is, what they expect the subordinate to do. They can make the rewards to the subordinate more dependent on his or her satisfactory performance. They can increase the size and value of the

rewards (M. G. Evans, 1970a). Specific leadership behaviors that contribute to the follower's attainment of the goal are providing support to the follower; alleviating boredom and frustration with work, especially in times of stress; coaching; providing direction; and fostering the follower's expectations that his or her efforts will lead to the successful completion of the task (Fiedler & House, 1988).

But, early on, House and Mitchell (1974) recognized that path-goal leadership, as such, was only needed and useful in certain circumstances. The leader needs to complement only what is missing in a situation to enhance the subordinate's motivation, satisfaction, and performance. What is missing is determined by the environment, the task, and the competence and the motivation of the subordinate (Fiedler & House, 1987). Thus, the subordinate's productivity is enhanced if the leader provides needed structure to clarify means and ends if they are missing or unclear to the subordinate. This contribution of the leader is particularly apparent in jazz ensembles, in which a deviation-counteracting loop is observed that involves the leader's interpretation, criticism, and adjustments of the ensemble. The need for such correction is increased by the variety of selections the ensemble plays, the availability to them of new musical numbers, the difficulty of the numbers played, the lack of rehearsal time, and so on (Voyer & Faulkner, 1986).

Given clear tasks and roles, the supervisor contributes to continued productivity by consideration, support, and attention to the subordinates' personal and interpersonal needs for satisfying relationships (Fiedler & House, 1988). If what is missing can be supplied in other ways by the organization, such as through policies, regulations, improved communications, channels of information, contingent reward schemes, counseling services, and so on, substitutes for the leadership[11] may result in the same outcomes that would have been expected from the appropriate leadership.

The Path-Goal Linkage

The exchange involved in path-goal theory is seen when subordinates perceive high productivity to be an easy "path" to attain personal goals and, as a consequence, they are productive. Directive leadership in-

[10]See Chapter 17.

[11]See Chapter 30.

creases the promise of reward to the subordinates for their performance and makes the paths to their goals clearer and easier. Accordingly, such directive leadership is needed only if the task is complex, difficult, or ambiguous and its goals are unclear. Whether the subordinates are self-reinforcing and have a great need for autonomy, growth, achievement, or affection will also make a difference. On the other hand, if subordinates are faced with simple but boring or dangerous tasks, a leader may do better by being supportive and considerate rather than directive. Too much motivation among subordinates, evidenced by a state of high anxiety, may call for calming support from the leader rather than any talk about contingent (uncertain) rewards that will increase such anxiety. Supportive confidence building may be required rather than more drive (Yukl, 1981).

Efforts to Test the Theory

Translated into experiments, considerate leadership behavior (or supportive relations-oriented leadership) was expected to correlate more highly with satisfaction and productivity in structured than in unstructured situations. The initiation of structure was expected to correlate more highly with satisfaction and productivity in unstructured than in structured situations. These expectations fit with the conventional wisdom that "chaos is the midwife of dictatorship" (Durant, 1957). Unfortunately, more initiation of structure is likely to be seen when the group task is already structured (Bass, Valenzi, Farrow, & Solomon, 1975).

Despite a considerable amount of general empirical support for it, path-goal theory is complex, which makes it difficult to test the theory's deduced relationships. Furthermore, too much rigor may be required of such tests, and sampling and measurements may be inadequate to meet the requirements (Yukl & Van Fleet, 1986). Thus, it is not surprising that a wide array of empirical results, sometimes contradictory, have emerged from the hundred or more published surveys and experiments that tested various propositions derived from path-goal theory.

Supportive Results

Reviews of the empirical literature are available in reports by House and Mitchell (1974) and Schriesheim and Kerr (1974). Both these reviews tended to confirm the theory, as did a meta-analysis by Indvik (1986a) involving 87 empirical tests. In addition, House and Dessler (1974) demonstrated that, as predicted, the available task structure generally determined whether the initiation of structure and consideration by the leader would contribute to the subordinates' satisfaction, positive expectations, and role clarity. Earlier, House (1971) found support *a posteriori* in several studies cited in earlier chapters.[12] In specific *a priori* tests of the theory, House found, as expected, that the satisfaction of subordinates was associated with the extent to which the leader's initiation of structure reduced role ambiguity. Likewise, Meheut and Siegel (1973) observed that the leader's initiation that was role clarifying was positively related to the subordinates' satisfaction with management by objectives. A more complicated finding was that the more autonomous the subordinates, the more the leader's initiation of structure correlated with the subordinates' satisfaction, but the less the leader's initiation correlated with the subordinates' performance. At the same time, as the scope of the subordinates' task decreased, the leader's consideration correlated more with the subordinate's satisfaction and performance. Also supportive were direct tests of the theory by Dessler (1973), who found that with the leader's consideration held constant, the leader's initiation of structure correlated less with the subordinates' satisfaction and role clarity as the ambiguity of the task decreased.

Schriesheim and DeNisi (1981) studied how the variety of tasks in a job, feedback, and dealing with others moderated the impact of the initiation of structure on satisfaction with supervision among 110 employees who were working in a medium-size plant and among 205 employees of a medium-size manufacturer. The variety of tasks was expected to require more initiation of structure for the employees' satisfaction with supervision. Such initiation would be redundant with routine jobs (House & Dessler, 1974) and when feedback was already structured and subordinates dealt a lot with others. The results confirmed the moderating effect of all three task variables.

---

[12]The studies were by Fleishman, Harris, and Burtt (1955); Halpin (1954); Mulder, van Eck, and de Jong (1971); Mulder and Stemerding (1963); Rush (1957); and Sales (1972).

Mixed and Nonsupportive Results

Szilagyi and Sims (1974) obtained data from 53 administrative, 240 professional, 117 technical, and 231 service personnel at multiple levels of occupational skills in a hospital. Although the results supported path-goal propositions concerning the demands of the task and the relationship between the leader's initiation of structure and the subordinates' satisfaction, they failed to do so for the relationship between the leader's initiation of structure and the subordinates' performance. Similarly, Stinson and Johnson (1975) tested hypotheses derived from the path-goal theory of leadership that the correlations between the leader's initiation of structure and satisfaction variables and role-clarity variables are more positive under conditions of low task structure, low task repetitiveness, and high task autonomy than under high task structure, high task repetitiveness, and low task autonomy. The leader's consideration and the subordinates' satisfaction and role clarity were expected to be more positively related under structured, repetitive, dependent conditions than under unstructured, unrepetitive, autonomous conditions. The subjects were military officers, civil service personnel, and project engineers. The results were consistent with path-goal theory with respect to consideration but tended to be contrary to the theory regarding the initiation of structure.

Contrary to path-goal theory, the leader's consideration is still generally found to result in the higher satisfaction of subordinates, regardless of the characteristics of the task (Johns, 1978; Miles & Petty, 1977). Thus, J. F. Schriesheim and C. A. Schriesheim (1980) surveyed 290 managerial and clinical employees in 9 different jobs at 5 levels in the operations divisions of a large public utility. Contrary to path-goal theory, they found that regardless of the task structure, organizational level, or type of job, supportive (considerate) leadership explained 63 percent of the variance in the subordinates' satisfaction with their supervisors after instrumental leadership (initiation) was partialled out. But, as predicted, instrumental leadership (after supportive leadership was partialled out) contributed 17 percent to accounting for the variance in role clarity. However, again this covariance was unmoderated by the task structure, organizational level, or type of job.

Likewise, Seers and Graen (1984) found that without reference to leadership, performance and satisfaction outcomes directly depended on the characteristics of the task, as well as on the subordinates' need for growth. In the same way, the satisfactory quality of the leader-subordinate relationship independently added to the prediction of the outcomes of performance and satisfaction without reference to the task and the subordinates' needs that also were related to the outcomes.

Wolcott (1984) tested path-goal predictions for library supervisors and the performance of their reference librarians and catalogers. Contrary to path-goal predictions, the initiation of more structure contributed to better performance when the task structure was already high than when it was low. The librarians' high educational level and low need for independence were seen to be possible explanations for the results.

Generally, the initiation of structure still frequently increases tensions, especially when consideration is low (Miles & Petty, 1977; Schriesheim & Murphy, 1976) and when the initiation of structure measure continues to contain coercive, threatening items, along with direction and order giving. In turn, this linkage of direction and coercion is a consequence of dependence on empirical rather than conceptual analyses for developing measurements. Although autocrats tend to want to structure situations, conceptually, one can direct without being a threatening autocrat. For over 1,300 subordinates of their 340 managers, the correlation between being coercive and being directive was only .38, according to Farrow, Valenzi, and Bass (1980).

In a first study, Greene (1979a) showed that, as expected, instrumental (structuring) leadership behavior was correlated positively with the satisfaction and performance of 119 engineers, scientists, or technicians if they faced tasks with little structure. But such instrumental leadership was negatively correlated with satisfaction and minimally with performance when the tasks were more structured. Considerate or supportive leadership, as expected from the theory, increased the correlation with intrinsic satisfaction (but not with performance or extrinsic satisfaction) as the task structure increased.

In a second study, Greene (1979b) tested several assumptions about causation that underlie the theory.

The findings supported the theory, except, again, for the hypotheses concerning the subordinates' performance. Downey, Sheridan, and Slocum (1975) found only partial support for the path-goal predictions, and J. P. Siegel (1973) and Szilagyi and Sims (1974b) found none. Dessler and Valenzi (1977) failed to find moderator effects across supervisory levels. T. R. Mitchell (1979) concluded that the findings were stronger for the consideration hypothesis than for the structuring hypothesis and stronger for satisfaction as a criterion than for performance.

Indvik (1985, 1986a) completed a meta-analysis of 48 path-goal studies involving 11,862 respondents. Task structure, as such, was measured in some of the studies; in the remainder, low job level was accepted as an indicator of high task structure, as was large organizational size. As expected, when structure was absent from the work environment, directive, structuring leadership behavior contributed to the intrinsic motivation of subordinates, their satisfaction with the leader, and their overall satisfaction, but, surprisingly, it failed to add to role clarity, as such. However, contrary to expectations, directive, structuring leadership contributed to the subordinates' performance when the structure was high but not when the structure was low.

Considerate, supportive leadership behavior in a highly structured work setting, did enhance motivation, satisfaction, performance, and role clarity, as expected. In a related meta-analytic report, Indvik (1986b) concluded that participative leadership provided the most overall satisfaction to subordinates who preferred and experienced a low task structure. Furthermore, when the task structure was high, achievement-oriented leadership behavior was related to increased intrinsic satisfaction among subordinates but decreased extrinsic satisfaction and performance for those subordinates with a high need for achievement.

Efforts to Reconcile the Theory with the Mixed Results

Johns (1978) suggested that much more is "missing" that the leader may supply efficaciously than just task structure, as measured by House and Dessler's (1974) scale about the extent to which tasks are simple, repetitive, and unambiguous. Johns (1978) argued for using a broader measurement of the scope of a job for determining what could be missing from it; such a measurement would be Hackman and Oldham's (1975) index based on variety, autonomy, the significance of the job, feedback from the job, and the identity that the job provides to its occupant. Johns (1978) found that Sims, Szilagyi, and Keller's (1976) Job Characteristics Inventory, which measures the scope of a job, provided a measure to moderate more consistently the relationships between leadership behavior and the satisfaction of subordinates than task structure alone could do.

Coercive versus Noncoercive Initiation of Structure. The measures of leadership behavior are obtained most often from the Leader Behavior Description Questionnaire—Form XII (LBDQ-XII) and less so from the Supervisory Behavior Description Questionnaire (SBDQ).[13] Schriesheim and Von Glinow (1977) first noted that path-goal predictions of job satisfaction were less likely to be supported when a more coercive measure, such as the SBDQ scale of the initiation of structure, had been used.[14] Schriesheim and VonGlinow then demonstrated, with 230 maintenance workers, that if a coercion-loaded scale was used, reverse results were obtained for the path-goal predictions for job satisfaction. But when coercion-free scales (the LBDQ and the LBDQ-XII) or items from them were employed, path-goal predictions were confirmed if task structure and role clarity were used to moderate the relationship between the leader's consideration and initiation of structure and the employees' job satisfaction.

Conditions Affect What Leaders Can Do. A second source of contradictory findings results from the fact that leaders tend to be more directive when it is easier for them to do so, such as when roles are clear, conditions are structured, and jobs are routine (Bass, Valenzi, Farrow, & Solomon, 1975). But such structuring would seem to be redundant for productivity when conditions are already structured. Rather, it would seem that such direction is needed more when conditions are unstructured, for in such unstructured situations, it might be argued that the group wants some

---

[13]See Chapter 24, which discusses the coercive elements in the SBDQ that are absent from the LBDQ.
[14]See, for example, Downey, Sheridan, and Slocum (1975, 1976) and J. P. Siegel (1973).

direction from the leader, not just the leader's sympathy. Nevertheless, Indvik's (1985, 1986a) previously mentioned meta-analysis proved otherwise—directive, structuring leadership contributed to subordinate performance when structure was high, not when it was low.

Attributes of Leaders and Subordinates. The leader's personality also needs to be taken into account in the structured situation, given Farrow and Bass's (1977) finding that highly *directive* leaders tend primarily to be satisfied authoritarians. In addition, the subordinates' personality needs to be considered. Griffin (1979) proposed a set of prescriptions combining path-goal theory and the subordinates' need for achievement and self-actualization. Griffin called for achievement-oriented, consultative leadership for self-actualizing subordinates with "big" jobs. But for self-actualizers in routine jobs of little scope, supportive leadership (consideration without consultation) was required. For "big" jobs performed by occupants who are uninterested in self-actualization, directive leadership (structuring without threat) was seen as most needed. For occupants of routine jobs who have no need for self-actualization, maintenance leadership behavior (management by exception) was suggested.

Schriesheim and Schriesheim (1980) added other subordinate variables that are likely to act as path-goal moderators of the leader-outcome relationships. These variables included the subordinates' need for affiliation, authoritarianism, ability, training, and experience relative to the demands of the task and their internalization of professional norms and standards. Similarly, Abdel-Halim (1981) found that the subordinates' locus of control (internal or external) had important effects on the path-goal leader-outcome relationships associated with the ambiguity of the role and the complexity of the job.

Algattan (1985) examined the extent to which the scope of the subordinates' task, strength of the need for growth, and locus of control moderated leader-outcome relationships for two periods, two months apart. At each time period, if the subordinates' locus of control was external, the scope of their tasks and the strength of their need for growth increased the extent to which both participative and directive leadership

contributed to their satisfaction and performance. But if the subordinates' locus of control was internal, task-oriented leadership, as such, was of more importance to their satisfaction and performance. However, a cross-lagged analysis of the correlations for the two time periods failed to support the existence of causality in the relationships.

Craig (1983) attempted to show the importance of subordinates' self-esteem to path-goal leader-outcome relationships but failed to find the expected interactions. Wolcott (1984) found no effect on the relationships from differences in the subordinates' need for independence. Keller (1987) argued that the discomfort of role ambiguity may differ from one subordinate to another. Some people who may want to clarify and structure their roles themselves are unlikely to be enthusiastic about a leader who initiates structure even if the task is unstructured or ambiguous. Subordinates with high levels of education, such as R & D professionals, who may have internalized professional norms that provide them with role clarity may not need or want the leader to initiate structure. Some subordinates may actually enjoy the unstructured nature of a task; they may have a low need for clarity and prefer to create their own structure. Thus, compared to task structure, the subordinates' need or lack of need for clarity was seen to be a more important moderator of the correlations between the leader's initiation of structure and the subordinates' satisfaction and performance.

In a survey of 477 professionals employed in four R & D organizations, Keller (1988) employed Rizzo, House, and Lirtzman's (1970) role-ambiguity scale to measure the subordinate's perceived task clarity, as well as Ivancevich and Donnelly's (1974) scale to measure the subordinate's felt need for clarity on the job. He found that the need for clarity had a moderating effect on the initiation of structure–satisfaction relationship for both concurrent data and data gathered one year later. The higher a subordinate's felt need for clarity, the stronger was the relationship between the leader's initiation of structure and the subordinate's job satisfaction. The subordinate's need for clarity was similarly found to moderate the initiation of structure-performance relationship in the largest of the R & D organizations. But, as proposed, the actual clarity of the task for the subordinates, as such, failed to serve as a moderator for these leader-outcome relationships. In the same way, Kroll and Pringle (1985) failed to find the expected effects of the leader's directiveness on the satisfaction of 43 middle managers in marketing. Kroll and Pringle explained the results by noting that managers rated the ambiguous situation as a positive experience, particularly if they judged the amount of direction they received to be the amount they actually desired.

A Comprehensive Study. Using data from a survey of 467 nonacademic staff at a university, Indvik (1988) completed tests of 17 hypotheses that involved directive, supportive, participative, and achievement-oriented leadership behavior and the expectancies that increased effort would improve performance and that such improved performance would yield valued outcomes. Also measured were intrinsic satisfaction with work, extrinsic satisfaction with pay and promotion, and satisfaction with one's superior. The subordinate's performance was appraised by the superior. Indvik examined the task structure, norms of the work group, and organizational formalization as situational moderators of the relations between leadership behavior and subordinate outcomes. Personal subordinate moderators included the need for achievement and preference for environmental structure. Hierarchical stepwise re-

gression analyses[15] provided support for only 7 of the 17 hypotheses tested.

Moderators that had significant effects included the subordinates' preference for structure and need for achievement. However, Indvik concluded that generally, because of its low reliability, the subordinates' preference for structure had a weak moderating effect on the relations of leadership behavior to subordinate outcomes. Directive and achievement-oriented leadership behaviors were too highly correlated with each other to be distinguishable.

Indvik recommended that future studies should measure transformational leadership behavior instead of the transactional leadership behaviors on which path-goal research has concentrated, for it is likely that transformational leadership behavior is more sensitive to task structure and the characteristics of subordinates.

Integration of Findings. Neider and Schriesheim (1988) constructed a comprehensive path-goal model, shown in Figure 28.1, that attempts to incorporate much of the consistent findings about the process and the variables of consequence.

[15]In a stepwise regression analysis, predictors are added according to their contribution to the overall prediction of outcomes. In a hierarchical regression, they are added in a predetermined order. The order used was based on path-goal propositions.

Figure 28.1. An Integrated Path Goal Perspective of Motivation and Leadership

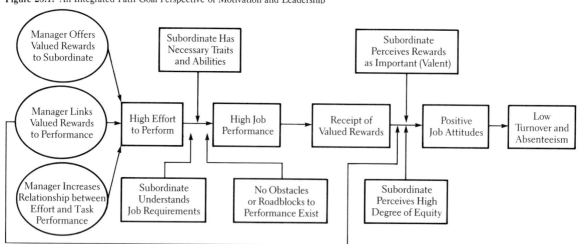

SOURCE: *Neider and Schriesheim (1988).*

In the model, the manager stimulates the subordinate's effort by offering valued rewards and linking them to the subordinate's effort and performance. How much the effort yields high performance depends on the subordinate's knowledge, skills, and abilities, as well as on the absence of hurdles to performing the job. The rewards received by the subordinate, if valued and equitable, create satisfaction and encourage the subordinate to remain on the job.

Summary and Conclusions

The requirements of the task systematically moderate how different leadership behaviors affect what happens in the group. The characteristics of the task that make a difference include its structure, clarity, provisions for the subordinate's use of discretion, routineness, variety, complexity, difficulty and interdependencies, and automation. As the task is different at different phases in a group's development and at different organizational levels, so is the requisite leadership.

Path-goal theory has been widely tested and modified to account for the impact of the task on optimum leader-subordinate relations. Currently, it suggests that to obtain the subordinate's effective performance and satisfaction, the leader must provide structure if it is missing and must supply rewards that are contingent on the adequate performance of the subordinate. To do so, leaders must clarify the desirability of the goals for the subordinates, a role seemingly suited for transformational leaders. But the efficacy in doing so will depend on such personal characteristics as the subordinates' need for clarity. However, the ambiguity of the situation may also be a source of stress. It is the issue that will be examined next.

Stress and Leadership

Individuals, groups, and organizations that are confronted with threats to their steady states of well-being will experience stress. Rowney and Cahoon (1988) noted that the burnout scores among individuals who work in the same unit are more similar than those of individuals who work in different units doing similar kinds of work. In many instances, the available leadership makes the difference in the prevention or occurrence of stress and burnout. Leadership can be the source of increased stress; it can provide for avoiding or coping with it. Thus, Graham (1982) found that with professional employees of a county extension service, job stress was lower when the leaders of their district program were described as higher on the Leader Behavior Description Questionnaire (LBDQ)[1] in both the initiation of structure and in consideration.

The Nature of Stress

Dynamics

Stress occurs to individuals, groups, and organizations when their situation is overly complex, ambiguous, and unclear, as well as highly motivating and demanding in relation to the competence or structural adequacy to deal with the demands. Stress results in emotional arousal; frustration; defensiveness in fight or flight; and physiological symptoms, such as sweating, heavier breathing, or increased heart beat. One's state of anxiety is a perceptual manifestation of such objective conditions of stress (Spielberger, 1972) and was measured on the job by Schriesheim and Murphy (1976) with the 20-item State Anxiety subscale of the State-Trait Anxiety Inventory (Spielberger, Gorsuch, & Lushene, 1970).

[1]See Chapter 24.

The ordinary healthy reaction of an individual, group, or organization to dissatisfaction with the current state of affairs is to examine fully what prevents the attainment of the more desired state, then to consider various alternative courses of action, and finally to take appropriate steps to achieve the goal. But if motivation is high, if obstacles are severe, or if remaining in the current state is threatening to one's welfare or survival, malfunctions occur in the coping process. There may be no time to deliberate about choices among actions. There may be communication outages or severe information overloads. The mobilization of autonomic energy occurs with the felt emotional arousal and related symptoms of stress. Such arousal narrows perceptions and limits the ability to think creatively (Lazarus, 1966). Memory and cognitive functions become impaired (Weschler, 1955).

Faulty Decision Making

Decision making under stress becomes faulty. Instead of careful analysis and calculation or the effective use of the intuition of the expert based on learning and experience, the stressed individual will fall back on nonproductive intuitive reactions that satisfy his or her immediate personal emotional needs rather than the objective requirements of the situation. As Simon (1987, p. 62) noted "Lying, for example, is much more often the result of panic than of Machiavellian scheming." When Sorokin (1943) examined reports of the reactions of groups and communities to the calamities of famine, war, and revolution, he found that a calamity tended to intensify emotional arousal, distort cognitive processes, focus attention on the calamity and away from other features of the environment, hasten disintegration of the self, and decrease rationality of behavior.

Stress among Managers

Stress among managers is commonplace. In response to 17 questions, such as how much in the last month they felt nervous and stressed (0 = never to 4 = very often a problem), several hundred each of Japanese managers furnished an overall mean of 1.59; Indian managers, a mean of 1.37; and American managers, a mean of 1.33. The average manager in the three countries experienced a stressful experience at least once a month (Ivancevich, Schweiger, & Ragan, 1986). The figures for U.S. managers were much lower in response to questions about their experiencing stress daily, somatic symptoms, anxiety, and social disfunctioning and much higher for their reports of job-induced stress ("I am not sure of exactly what is expected of me") and the discharge of job tension off the job (Matteson & Ivancevich, 1982). The use of tobacco, alcohol, tranquilizers, sedatives, and other drugs are commonly efforts by managers and professionals to cope with job stress, as are physical exercise, socializing with friends, and recreational activities (Latack, 1986).

Stress Is Multifaceted

A variety of different antecedent conditions may give rise to stress in groups. To some degree, the observed and appropriate leadership behavior will depend on the particular antecedents that were involved. Bass, Hurder, and Ellis (1954) identified four emotionally arousing stress experiences with different antecedents: (1) frustration is likely to be felt when highly prized positive goals are unattainable because of inability or difficulties in the path to the goals, (2) fear occurs when escape from noxious conditions is threatened by obstacles in the path, (3) anxiety is aroused when these paths, obstacles, and goals become unclear (fear and frustration turn to anxiety with increasing uncertainty), and (4) conflicts arise when one faces incompatible choices of goals. Potentially high risks and costs compete with the anticipated benefits of a course of action.

After examining the physiological reactions and the cognitive and psychomotor performance of 200 college men under experimentally induced frustration, fear, anxiety, and conflict, Bass, Hurder, and Ellis (1954) concluded that performance under these various stress

conditions would decrease or increase in contrast to a stress-free condition depending on which tasks and skills were involved, which type of stress was imposed, and the initial level of arousal of the participants. Differences among the men were also large.

Individual Differences

Leader-subordinate dyadic analysis would seem particularly important in understanding leadership in threatening situations. What one subordinate may see as an invigorating challenge, another may perceive as a stress-laden threat. It is all in the eye of the beholder. As McCauley (1987, p. 1) put it: "A challenging, rewarding task for one person may be flooded with stress and anxiety for others. How one appraises self and situation makes all the difference."

According to Bunker (1986), less stress in the same threatening conditions are felt by those who are generally optimistic, who believe that such conditions are matters of their own fate and not controlled by external forces, who can tolerate ambiguity and uncertainty, and who feel they can improve their own abilities. Such confidence is enhanced with experience. The effects of stress and anxiety are reduced as experience is gained with the same threats (Benner, 1984). The effect of experience is similar to the effects of preparation, overlearning, and overtraining.

Stress can also vary from one individual to another as a consequence of deep-seated feelings of inadequacy that surface in aggression or overdependence when real or imagined threats occur. People differ from each other in this intrapsychic tension.[2] Levinson (1980) conceived of stress as a consequence of such intrapsychic tension—the increased gap between one's ego ideal (the partly conscious image of oneself at one's future best) and one's current self-image.

Situational Differences

The study of leadership under stressful conditions has often treated stress as a homogeneous situation. Yet, the same stressful experience can stem from a variety of precipitating conditions, and the variety of possible reactions to it may depend on the different precipitat-

[2]See Chapter 12.

ing conditions. Thus, research on disasters has found systematic differences in community reactions to warnings of tornadoes and warnings of floods. Communities react much more quickly to threats of tornadoes than to the threats of floods.

Combat Conditions

Military combat is illustrative of both the situational and personal elements that are of consequence to the generation of stress and the reactions to it. The actions and coping of soldiers in conditions of combat stress are a response to a situational and personal complex of antecedent and mediating variables. Whether soldiers and their leaders will actively carry out their duties, become passive, or collapse will depend on the amount of surprise and uncertainty in the battle; the weather and terrain; and, particularly, whether the operations are mobile and offensive or static and defensive. Stress is likely to be higher in the enforced passivity of the static or defensive condition that generates a feeling of helplessness (Gal & Lazarus, 1975). Again, individual differences in personality, family problems, and prior exposure to combat will be of importance. Active "fighters" are more intelligent and masculine and have more leadership potential (Egbert, Meeland, Cline, et al., 1957). Winners of medals are more persevering, decisive, and devoted to duty (Gal, 1983).

One's role in combat makes a difference. The higher physiological responses of Israeli officers compared with enlisted men is coupled with fewer somatic complaints and breakdowns among the officers. Leaders are more emotionally aroused but appear to suffer much less decrement in their performance during combat than do enlisted men, although generally, as in the Israeli-Arab confrontations, the officers were much more at risk than were the enlisted personnel. Gal and Jones (1985) suggest that one's perceived role as a leader provides a sense of mastery and control and causes one to concentrate on tasks that distract attention from the realistic dangers.

Role Stress

Kahn, Wolfe, Quinn, et al. (1964) showed that two distinct sources of stress could be identified in organizations: role conflict and role ambiguity. Each has differ-

ent antecedents and consequences. Role conflict involves contradictory requirements, competing demands for one's time, and inadequate resources. Role ambiguity involves the lack of clarity about tasks and goals and uncertainty about the requirements of one's job.[3] Latack (1986, p. 380) noted how managers and professionals tried either to control role ambiguity, role conflict, and role overload or to escape from them. To control role ambiguity, they "try to see the situation as an opportunity to learn and develop new skills" (p. 380). To escape from role ambiguity, they "try to do their best to get out of the situation gracefully." To control role conflict, they "work on changing policies which caused this situation." To escape from role conflict, they "separate themselves as much as possible from the people who created this situation."

Role Overload. To role conflict and ambiguity, Latack (1986) added role overload as a source of stress. To control role overload, managers and professionals "try to be very organized so they can keep on top of things." To escape from role overload, they "set their own priorities based on what they like to do." When the Job-Related Tension Index of Kahn, Wolfe, Quinn, et al. (1964) was completed by 113 Canadian managers for R. E. Rogers (1977), four factors were extracted from the results. These factors were a too-heavy work load, self-doubts, a sense of insufficient authority and influence upstairs, and the need to make unpopular decisions against their better judgment.

Shaw and Weekley (1985) also found actual qualitative overload to be stressful. Nonetheless, other investigators did not conclude that work overload was necessarily stressful to managers. S. Carlson (1951) found that it was normal for most Swedish executives to report being overloaded and having little time for family or friends.[4] A business management survey of 179 company presidents and board chairmen obtained results indicating that the average executive worked approximately 63 hours per week but did not feel overworked, although over 70 percent thought they did not have enough time for thinking and planning (Anonymous, 1968). But W. E. Moore (1970) observed that de-

---

[3]House and Rizzo (1972a, 1972b) and Rizzo, House, and Lirtzman (1970) also conceived of role conflict and role ambiguity as critically distinct phenomena.
[4]See Chapter 16.

tailed chores involving problems in communication and operations interfered with the effective use of the managers' time. Yet Jaques (1966) noted that hard work and long hours were not sufficient conditions for producing stress symptoms in executives. Rather, stress conditions are generated from within the manager as responses to impossible standards of achievement or tasks that are perceived as overly difficult.

The conclusions about work overload are seen in the extent to which some harried executives are aggressively involved in achieving more in less time. As discussed before in Chapter 10, such executives have an habitual sense of the urgency of time (Friedman & Rosenman, 1974). They are labeled Type A personalities; many are highly stressed, as is evidenced by their proneness to heart disease. Nevertheless, many other harried Type As are not under such stress. The difference is that those Type As who are subject to heart disease are also depressed, tense, and generally prone to illness. They are not generally healthy, talkative, self-confident, and in control of their situations (Friedman, Hall, & Harris, 1985).

Stress and Motivation

As was already noted, stress occurs when the group's drive is too high for the demands of the task. When members are blocked from obtaining a goal or from escaping from a noxious condition, their stress increases with their increasing motivation to obtain the goal or escape the situation. Thus, Tjosvold (1985b) found that although executives made effective decisions under moderate levels of motivation, when faced with a crisis, their performance deteriorated and quick solutions requiring the least effort were chosen instead of high-quality ones.

Since cohesiveness and commitment imply heightened motivation to attain goals, more stress should be seen in cohesive than in noncohesive groups. When J. R. P. French (1941) frustrated groups of cohesive teammates and groups of strangers who were lower in cohesiveness, the more cohesive teams experienced greater fear and frustration. Similarly, Festinger (1949) reported that more complaints that were suggestive of stress appeared among more cohesive groups. Also, M. E. Wright (1943) found that more cohesive pairs of friends exhibited more aggression when frustrated than did pairs whose cohesiveness was lower.

Given a high degree of group drive, the group members' perceived inability to obtain the group's goals or to escape from danger increases the likelihood of stress. Groups that are unable to interact easily or that do not have the formal or informal structure that enables quick reactions are likely to experience stress (Bass, 1960). Panic ensues when members of a group lack superordinate goals—goals that transcend the self-interests of each participant. Mintz (1951) found that, when members of an experimental group in a crisis sought uncoordinated individual reward (or the avoidance of individual punishment), panic was likely to ensue. If the group was organized and perceived a single goal for all, such panic did not materialize. Similarly, in an analysis of anxiety in aerial combat, D. G. Wright (1946) concluded that an aircrew could cope with stress when a common threat was perceived and when a common goal and action toward it were maintained under an apparent plan of action. Clearly, the leader who can transform a group of members with different self-interests into a group with goals that transcend their own self-interests will make it possible for the group to cope more effectively with potentially stressing circumstances.

Stress and Structure

The individual is stressed when highly motivated to escape threat or to obtain highly valued goals, but is unable to respond adequately, unready to react, untrained, and inexperienced. Increased preparedness and overlearning are ways of helping the individual to cope with anticipated stressful situations. At the group or organizational level, the reliability and predictability of the group's response become necessary. Everyone needs to know what everyone else is likely to do. Roles must be clear and free of conflict and ambiguity. Structure, through an informal or formal organization, becomes important. Thus, Isenberg (1981) demonstrated, in an experiment with four-person groups who were making decisions under the stress of the pressure of time, that the structure of relations increased and leadership became more salient; differences in how much time the members were able to speak increased. Again,

Gladstein and Reilly (1985) found that when stress was induced in a business simulation by introducing threats and the pressure of time, decision making became centralized. A small number of members had a lot more influence than did others in the group than when time pressure and threatening events were absent.

When a group does not have the necessary structure to meet emergencies and threats, the initiation of such a structure by a strong leader is seen as needed and useful to the group. Path-goal formulations[5] examine such requisite leadership behavior when the roles of workers are unclear. When subordinates have clear perceptions of their work roles, the leader's initiation of structure is redundant. However, the leader's initiation of structure should help highly motivated subordinates with less clear role perceptions to perform their jobs and thus increase their satisfaction and performance. Schriesheim and Murphy (1976) found that job stress, like the lack of structure, moderated the initiation of structure–job satisfaction relationship, as expected. In J. R. P. French's (1941) previously cited investigation, eight organized groups (with elected leaders) and eight unorganized groups were studied. Frustration was produced by requiring the groups to work on unsolvable problems. Unorganized groups showed a greater tendency to split into opposing factions, whereas the previously organized group exhibited greater social freedom, cohesiveness, and motivation. The greater the differentiation of function the occurred with organization, the greater was the interdependence of members and unity of the group as a whole.

The need for structure at the macro-level, as well as at the individual level, was seen by Sorokin (1943). In times of disaster, ideal human conduct is associated with a well-integrated system of values, in conformity with the ethical values of the larger society, and little discrepancy between values and conduct. But individuals who engage in anti-social and delinquent behavior (murder, assault, robbery, looting, and the like) tend to be guided by self-centered, materialistic, disillusioned ideologies and are not integrated into a larger organized effort. The wanton massacre of inmates of a penitentiary in New Mexico in early 1980 by berserk fellow prisoners was partly attributable to the lack of organization in the prisoners' rebellion, as well as to the sudden complete availability of drugs (Hollie, 1980).

[5]See Chapter 28.

Gal and Jones (1985) noted that a strong informal structure within a military unit helped reduce the perceived stress of combat. Elite units, with strong bonds between comrades and leaders, were found to suffer less stress, as evidenced by much lower psychiatric casualty rates, despite greater exposure than ordinary units to the risks of high-intensity battle.

A Model of Group Responses to Stress

Janis and Mann (1977) looked at responses under stress that were induced by conflict in the face of an impending threat and the risks and costs of taking action to avoid stress. They argued that the completely rational approach to an authentic warning of impending danger would be a thorough examination of objectives, values, and alternative courses of action. Costs and risks would be weighed. A final choice would be based on a cost-benefit analysis. Included in the effective process would be development, careful implementation, and contingency planning. But such vigilance, thorough search, appraisal, and contingency planning are likely to be short-circuited as a consequence of emotional arousal and the socioemotional phenomena generated by the impending threat. Various defective reactions to the warnings of danger are likely to occur. These reactions include adherence to the status quo, too hasty change, defensive avoidance, and panic.

Unconflicted Adherence to the Steady State. One inadequate reaction is the hasty decision that dealing with the threat involves more serious costs and risks than doing nothing. The threat is not perceived, as such, or it is disbelieved. People remain in their homes despite slowly rising flood waters and warnings to evacuate. An inadequate analysis, in which appropriate information is ignored, sees the costs of evacuation as greater than the risks of remaining. This response is less likely in the case of sudden threats such as tornado warnings. Analogously, the energy crises of 1973 and 1979 had built up for 20 years in the face of inertia to cope with them adequately. The threats to the environment of the depletion of the ozone layer, acid rain, and the Greenhouse Effect likewise failed in the 1980s to mobilize the necessary public support for a political effort to deal with the threats. But in 1941, full national commitment and mobilization to deal with the Japanese threat, signaled by the attack on Pearl Harbor, was instantaneous.

Staw, Sandelands, and Dutton (1981) pointed to the increased rigidity in organizations when threatened. Consistent with this, Gladstein and Reilly (1985) engaged 128 MBA students in a full six-day business simulation to show that threatening events and the pressure of time each systematically constrain decision-making processes by reducing the amount of information used by the groups before they reach their decisions.

Hasty Change

If the costs and risks of taking action to deal with a perceived threat are thought to be low, a new course of action is adopted, often too hastily, without an adequate examination of the threat, risks, and long-term implications. Thus, individuals who experience a high degree of tension from an intense structural strain in the social or political fabric become susceptible to the influence of those rebel leaders who promise to restructure the situation quickly, particularly if the established leadership fails to do so (Downton, 1973). A field investigation by Torrance and staff (1955) reported that aircrews who were "forced down" and faced simulated difficulties of surviving in "enemy" territory tended to turn to immediate but ineffective solutions to their problems and to concede more to comfort as their stress increased. For example, as the hardships increased, they chose to travel on roads in "enemy" territory instead of traveling over routes where they were less likely to be seen.

Rapid decisive leadership is valued highly under conditions of perceived threat to the group. Executives and politicians incrementally "put out one fire after another," drifting into a new policy to cope with each successive threat, rather than formulating a new policy based on a thorough search, appraisal, and plan (Lindbloom, 1959).

Defensive Avoidance

When the risks of change are seen to be high and the current course of action is maintained because of fatalism and a sense that no better course can be found, the various Freudian mechanisms, such as rationalization, displacement, fantasy, and denial, provide psychologi-cal defenses to avoid the threat, rather than to cope rationally with the danger. Particularly common to managers in large organizations, according to Janis (1972), are procrastination, shifting responsibility (buck-passing), and bolstering—providing social support for quickly seizing on the least objectionable choice. These are defective ways of dealing with a threat.

Hypervigilance (Panic). If the threat contains time pressures and deadlines and if individual motivation to escape the threat is high, hypervigilance (panic) may set in. Defective search is illustrated by the failure to take the time to choose a satisfactory escape route from a fire. Instead, a person in panic, in a highly suggestible state, simply starts imitating what everybody else is doing, failing to anticipate the consequences of blocking common exits. According to a review by A. L. Strauss (1944), the major factors in panic are (1) conditions that weaken individuals physically, (2) the reduced mental ability and lessened capacity to act rationally, (3) heightened emotionality, tension, and imagination, which facilitate impulsive action, (4) heightened suggestibility and contagion, which may precipitate flight, and (5) the loss of contact with leaders and a predisposition to follow those at hand.

When disaster strikes, panic is not the first reaction of most people. The acute fear and attempts to flee the disaster occur only when immediate danger is perceived and individuals see their escape routes blocked (Quarantelli, 1954). Exacerbating the panic reaction is a strong sense of isolation. For some, the unadaptive reaction is to freeze in place or to become blinded to the events occurring around them. When the atomic bomb was dropped on Hiroshima, many people ceased to feel (Lifton, 1967). Nevertheless, there are others who begin trying to cope with the disaster if they receive no formal directions from authorities.

Leadership Under Stress

Informal leadership and temporary groups may emerge if the formal authorities and emergency services cannot deal with the crisis (Mileti, Drabek, & Haas, 1975). The direct removal of the threats and obstacles that are the source of stress may be facilitated. Drive and anxiety may be reduced by providing informal and formal leadership support and an increasing sense of security. Individuals, groups and organizations that are frozen into inertia and disbelief when they are seriously threatened may be aroused and alerted. Faced with hasty, poorly thought-out decisions, leaders may delay the premature disclosure of options and call for a reconsideration of proposals. When their followers are engaged in defensive avoidance, leaders may bring them back to reality. Panic can be reduced or avoided by strong leadership that points the way to safety.

Thus, leaders can help their groups to cope with stress in many ways. Nonetheless, they also can cause more of it. Yet, as shall be seen, in general, groups with leaders are likely to cope better with stress than are those without leaders. Groups and organizations that are under stress expect and desire more directiveness from leaders. Moreover, whoever takes the role of leader during times of social stress will be expected to revise goals, define common objectives, restructure situations, and suggest solutions to deal with the sources of stress and conflict (Downton, 1973). But as shall also be seen, although directive leadership is most expected, desired, and successful when stress is high, it may not always be the most effective style.

The personality-leader linkage will be affected by stress. Under conditions with short, unpredictable time pressures in which unusual physical and emotional exertion is required, such as in military combat, more charismatic leadership will be seen, in contrast to military leadership in noncombat operations (Bass, 1985a). Personal assertiveness may be a stronger determinant of emergence as a leader under stress in contrast. It may be less important in determining emergence as a leader in unstressed circumstances.

Leadership May Contribute to Stress

Unfortunately, leadership may be the cause, rather than the amelioration, of stressful conditions that result in emotionally driven actions by the followers and poorer long-term outcomes. And the leaders who emerge are likely to be different from those in unstressed situations. They may actually contribute to the stress. Political leaders manufacture crises to enhance their own power, to divert public attention from the real problems, and to gain public support for their arbitrary actions.

Those who are elected to office may be more prone to stress themselves. Sanders and Malkis (1982) manipulated the importance and difficulty of a problem and external incentives involving recognition of esteem and success. They found that Type A (stress-prone) personalities were nominated more often as leaders than were Type B personalities. However, the fewer Type Bs who were chosen as leaders tended to be more effective as individuals in the assigned task than were the Type As.

Many studies have reported that for subordinates their immediate supervisor is the most stressful aspect of their work (e.g., Herzberg, 1966). The tyrannical boss is the most frequently mentioned source of stress (McCormick & Powell, 1988).

Numerof, Seltzer, and Bass (1989) unexpectedly found that when other transformational factors[6] were held constant, intellectually stimulating leaders increased the felt stress and job "burnout" of their subordinates. Misumi (1985) reported the results of a series of experiments that showed that production-prodding leadership with instructions such as, "Work more quickly," "Work accurately," "You could do more," and "Hurry up, we haven't much time left" generated detectable physiological symptoms of stress. The systolic and diastolic blood pressure of experimental subjects increased, as did their galvanic skin responses. In similar laboratory experiments, such production-prodding leadership caused feelings of hostility and anxiety about the experiment.

Among a sample of police officers, half their "harmful stressors" were the administrative styles of their superiors (Griggs, 1985). Stressful conditions affect what is expected of a leader, who attempts to lead, and who emerges as a leader. In stressful conditions, leaders differ in the extent to which they promote the attainment of goals, the satisfaction of members, and the survival of their groups.

Nystrom and Starbuck (1984) suggested that top managers can guide organizations into crises and intensify the crises by blindness, rigidity, and the inability to unlearn their inadequate old ways of doing things. In the same way, Sutton, Eisenhardt, and Jucker (1986) thought that the Atari Corporation's decline and immi-

[6]See Chapter 12.

nent collapse was due to its management's rigidity in continuing to market products that no longer were selling and their failure to develop new products.

Sometimes the decrement in leadership performance may be a consequence of the external imposition of handicaps on the leaders. Thus, the loss of support from a higher authority may weaken the leaders' influence, control of needed resources, and continued attention to the organization's purposes. During the early years of the Reagan administration, with a director, James Watt, emphasizing deregulation and showing a lack of sympathy for environmental concerns, the Environmental Protection Agency (EPA) came under clear and unclear threats to its mission from its own leadership, coupled with serious staff and budget cuts. A survey of 181 EPA managers and staff showed a consequential deterioration in their optimism, satisfaction, and identification with the organization and in the quality of supervisor-subordinate relations (Morganthau & Hager, 1981).

Effects of Prolonged Stress. Prolonged stress from internal or external challenges that are too great for the group to deal with can result in the group's demise. What leads to the death of some groups and the survival of others over a long period of time? Survival of a group, organization, or community under prolonged stress is closely dependent on leadership that is able to maintain the group or organization's integrity, drive, and goal direction. Such leadership needs to work with the increased cohesion and deal with the reduced performance of tasks by groups that are under continued threat.[7] But instead of helping to stave off decline and death, the leadership may contribute to the prolonged stress of the group, organization, or community and to its eventual demise.

F. E. Parker (1923, 1927) sent questionnaires to some 3,000 consumer cooperative societies. Among those that had failed, the most frequent reasons were (1) inefficient leadership and management, (2) declining interest and cooperative spirit among the members, (3) factional disputes among the members, and (4) members' interference with the management. Blumenthal (1932) attributed the decline of social and fraternal groups in small towns to the departure of young people (the towns' best leadership potential) to the cities.

Munro's (1930) study of community service organizations found that ineffective organizations that were less likely to survive were characterized by ineffective leadership, the lack of political sagacity, unwise policies and tactics, spasmodic work, and overorganized and duplicated services. Kolb (1933) and Sorokin (1943) observed that without religious purposes and a commitment to an integrative ideology of religion, such as were fostered by leadership, rural communities were less likely to survive disasters. In reviewing the decline and fall of special-interest groups in rural communities, Kolb and Wileden (1927) pointed to factional competition for leadership and irreconcilable differences between leaders and followers.

Most communes cannot survive for any considerable period without strong leadership to maintain discipline and control (Gide, 1930; May & Doob, 1937). Conversely, a whole commune can commit suicide when led to it by a highly charismatic, paranoid leader, as was the case in Jonestown, Guyana, in 1978. The same situation almost occurred in Germany, when Hitler pleaded for a Götterdämmerung in 1945 for all Germany, turning in frustration from his fantasy of being Odin, the Savior, to becoming Odin, the Destroyer.

Successful but Not Necessarily Effective Leadership

The leadership that succeeds in influencing followers may not be most effective in stressful situations, particularly in the long run. It may result in faulty decisions made too hastily or defensive reactions, although it is likely to contribute positively to the escape from panic situations.

Stress, Hasty Decision Making, and Directive Leadership

Crisis provokes a centralization of authority (Hermann, 1963). Berkowitz (1953b) found that both governmental and industrial groups were more likely to accept leadership when the problem was urgent. When followers are under stress, they are likely to accept readily the speedy decisions of directive, task-oriented, structuring

---

[7]See Lanzetta (1955); Lanzetta, Haefner, Langham, and Axelrod (1954); and Torrance (1961).

leaders. But speedy decisions do not necessarily provide the best solutions to the problems facing the followers.

It is not the speed of the decision or the leader's directiveness that may result in inadequate solutions to the stressful circumstances. It is rapid decision making without the opportunity in advance for careful structuring and support. For as shall be seen, rapid decision making generally is sought in crises and disasters and will be effective if the decisions are not hastily made at the last minute but are based on advanced warning, preparation, and organization, along with commitment and support.

As Janis and Mann (1977) noted, when a threat is finally perceived, it generates the desire for prompt decisive action. Leadership becomes centered in one or a few persons who gain increased power to decide for the group. The price for the rapid, arbitrary dictation is abuse, corruption, and the loss of freedom when power is placed in the hands of the dictator. Hertzler (1940) examined 35 historical dictatorships and concluded that they arose during crises and when sudden change was desired. In addition, Downton (1973) suggested that followers who are stressed by ambiguity become easily influenced by aggressive, powerful leaders who promise to reduce the ambiguity and restructure the situation.

Alwon (1980) argued that administrators of social agencies must adopt a strong, directive style (even if it means changing their leadership style) during times of crisis to avoid dangers and to seize opportunities. In emergencies, when danger threatens, subordinates want to be told what to do and to be told in a hurry. They perceive that they have no time to consider alternatives. Rapid, decisive leadership is demanded (Hemphill, 1950b). Five hundred groups were described on questionnaires by members on a variety of dimensions formulated by Hemphill. The adequacy of various leadership behaviors was correlated with the groups' characteristics. Hemphill concluded that in frequently changing and emerging groups, leaders who failed to make decisions quickly would be judged inadequate.

Considerable evidence is available to support the contention that leaders speed up their decision making as a consequence of stress. Their failure to do so leads

to their rejection as leaders (Korten, 1962; Sherif & Sherif, 1953). Acceptance of their rapid, arbitrary decisions without consultation, negotiation, or *participation*[8] is also increased. A leader who can react quickly in emergencies will be judged better by followers than one who cannot.

Flanagan, Levy, et al. (1952) found that, according to respondents, "taking prompt action in emergency situations" was a critical behavior that differentiated those who were judged to be better military officers from those whose performance was judged to be worse. Large-scale surveys of American soldiers during World War II by Stouffer, Suchman, DeVinney, et al. (1949) confirmed that particularly at lower levels in the organization, the military stressed the rapidity of response to orders from a higher authority despite the fact that a unit actually operated under battlefield conditions relatively infrequently.

When rapid decisions are called for, executives are likely to become more directive than participative (Lowin, 1968). Consistent with this finding, the more organizations wish to be prepared for emergency action, the more they are likely to stress a high degree of structure, attention to orders, and authoritarian direction. Fodor (1976, 1978) demonstrated that industrial supervisors who were exposed to the stress of simulated, disturbing subordinates became more autocratic in dealing with the situation. College students did likewise (Fodor, 1973b). From half to two-thirds of 181 airmen, when asked for their opinions about missile teams, rescue teams, scientific teams, or other small crews facing emergencies, strongly agreed that they should respond to the orders of the commander with less question than under normal conditions. In an emergency, the commander was expected to "check more closely to see that everyone is carrying out his responsibility." A majority felt that "the commander should not be 'just one of the boys'" (Torrance, 1956–57).

In a survey of Dutch naval officers' performance by Mulder, de Jong, Koppelaar, and Verhage (1986), the officers were more favorably evaluated by their superiors

[8]As defined in Chapters 22 and 23, *direction* (italicized) refers only to giving orders with or without explanation. Direction (romanized) includes ordering, persuading, and manipulating. *Participation* (italicized) refers only to sharing in the decision process. Participation (romanized) includes consulting, sharing, and delegating.

if they were seen to make more use of their formal power in crisis situations than in noncrisis situations. In crisis conditions, both the superiors and the subordinates of the officers looked for more authoritative direction from the officers. At the same time, the officers were evaluated more favorably by their subordinates if they were seen to be more openly consultative in noncrisis situations than in crisis situations. Moreover, the referent power of the officers in the eyes of the subordinates correlated .55 with their consultativeness under noncrisis conditions but the corresponding correlation was .10 in crisis conditions. The officers relied more on formal and expert power in crisis conditions than in noncrisis conditions, according to their subordinates.

Similarly, militant, decisive, aggressive leadership is demanded during the unstable period of a union's organization as it goes from one emergency to the next. Under stress, strength and activity take on more importance for leadership. After the struggle for survival is over and the union is recognized, the leadership is required to change. Now it must exhibit more willingness to compromise and to cooperate (Selekman, 1947). Confrontation must change to consultation.

Individuals who are more predisposed toward direction and the initiation of structure are more likely to try to take charge when their groups are stressed. They will preempt the leadership role from members who would consult with others before taking action. Given the authoritarian-submissive syndrome, authoritarians who are assigned to the roles of subordinates will be more ready to submit unquestioningly to the dictates of whoever has been assigned the role of leader. Lanzetta (1953) found that aggressive members were more likely to emerge as successful leaders when laboratory groups were stressed by harassment, space, and time restrictions than when no stress was induced. Along similar lines, Ziller (1954) concluded that leaders who accepted responsibility for their groups' action under conditions of uncertainty and risk were also relatively unconcerned about what the groups thought about the issues.

The same results appeared in still a different context. Firestone, Lichtman, and Colamosca (1975) showed that initially leaderless groups with assertive leaders responded more frequently and more rapidly to a confederate member's "diabetic reaction" than did groups whose leaders were less assertive. In such emergencies, unassertive leaders tended to be replaced. The holding of the American diplomatic staff in Tehran in 1979–80 is a classic example of how an external threat dramatically increased the followers' (in this case, the American public's) support for strong leadership to deal with the threats. Ranks were closed, dissension was muted, and rapid decision making was sought from President Jimmy Carter with little examination of the causes, intensity, and risks of the threats or of the costs of taking actions to deal with them. If anything, President Carter failed to come on as strongly and decisively as demanded, although he was more effective in ultimately obtaining the release of the hostages. In the face of crises, nations condemn the vacillating, indecisive leader and applaud the would-be hero-savior (Hook, 1943). President Ronald Reagan was much more popular for being seen as bold and decisive in dealing with the Lebanese crisis in 1983, yet the actions were disasterous.

When calamity threatens, followers want immediate action to escape. The leader's attempts to influence them will be accepted and complied with more readily than when such stress is absent. Although a participative discussion may make for better solutions, holding one to generate a high-quality decision to which the group is committed may be unacceptable. The commitment will come from the followers' restriction of the options they think they have. The leader who shows initiative, inventiveness, and decisiveness is valued most (Barnard, 1948). Helmreich and Collins (1967) observed that participants who faced a fearful experimental situation showed less of a preference for the company of peers and favored being in a leader-dominated group. Polis (1964) also found that under stress, individuals tended to manifest a need for strong leadership and to continue their association with the group. Again, Wispé and Lloyd (1955) concluded that among 43 sales agents, those who generally were less secure and more anxious were also more in favor of their superiors making decisions for them.

One reversal of the call for rapid-decision leadership in crisis conditions was found by Streib, Folts, and LaGreca (1985) in 36 retirement communities. Most residents were ordinarily satisfied to let others make the decisions for them, but they wanted the chance to be involved in decision making if crises arose or the stability of the community was threatened.

Directive Leadership and Prolonged Stress. When the stress is chronic or prolonged, the same tendencies toward directive leadership and acceptance of it are observed. During World War II, Japanese-American residents of California were subjected to isolation, loss of subsistence, threat to loved ones, enforced idleness, and physiological stress because of internment. As a consequence, the internees were apathetic and blindly obedient to influence (Leighton, 1945). Similarly, Fisher and Rubinstein (1956) reported that experimental participants who were deprived of sleep for 48 to 54 hours showed significantly greater shifts in autokinetic judgments, which indicated that they were more susceptible than normal to the social influence of their partners.

Hall and Mansfield (1971) studied the longer-term effects of stress and the response to it in three research and development organizations. The stress was caused by a sudden drop in available research funds, which resulted in strong internal pressures for reduced spending and the increased search of new funds. As would be expected, the response to the threat was to increase the control and direction by the top management and to reduce consultation with the researchers. Subsequently, the effect on the researchers over two years was to decrease their satisfaction and identification with the organization. However, their research performance was unaffected.

To conclude, directive leadership will be preferred and be successful in influencing followers under stress. But such leadership may be counterproductive in the long run.

Leadership and Defensive Avoidance

As was already noted, often it is the political leadership that contrives the threats, crises, and ambiguities. For centuries, political leaders have used real or imagined threat to increase the cohesiveness among their followers and to gain unquestioning support for their own dictates. The common scenario begins with economic weakness and dislocation, followed by international complications, revolution and sometimes civil war, and finally a breakdown of political institutions. The dictator organizes ready-made immediate solutions that soothe, flatter, and exalt the public but do not promote its well-being. Blame is directed elsewhere.

When business and governmental leaders are seen to consult and share decisions with subordinates in times of crises (Berkowitz, 1953b), it is often because they seek bolstering from their subordinates about the wisdom of their already-chosen solutions. Also, they would like to spread the responsibility for the decision from themselves to their group.

We-They Relations. "We-they" discrimination is encouraged by leaders of groups that are in competition and conflict with each other. In-group–out-group differences are magnified. The power of the leaders of the groups is strengthened. Deviants are not tolerated. Thus, Mulder and Stemerding (1963) found, as expected, that when individuals feel threatened from outside, they tend to depend on strong leaders. The leaders, in turn, promote a variety of defense mechanisms as pseudo-solutions to the stressful problems facing their constituents. Scapegoats are found to account for the social malaise and economic failures. Fanciful promises of a bountiful future are put forth and accepted. Real social, economic, and political issues are avoided and imagined dragons are slain.

Avoidance can be accomplished by physical self-segregation. This was observed by Hayashida (1976) in the in-group and out-group relations of leaders in organizations under the stress of conflicting ideas with outsiders. The leaders of 146 students in an evangelical Christian organization, whose stated beliefs diverged from the cosmopolitan culture of the campus, isolated themselves formally and informally from the rest of the campus. They coped with intergroup conflict by avoiding it.

Leadership and Panic

The ready acceptance of leadership, which may encourage maladaptive hasty decision making and defensiveness, is also seen in panic conditions. But here, leadership generally seems to offset maladaptive reactions to the panic. Kugihara, Misumi, Sato, and Shigeoka (1982) simulated a panic situation of 672 undergraduates in groups of six. In each group, one student was elected leader. Successful escape from the panic was more likely when the leader was in the same room as the other members than when the leader was placed in another room and was unable to determine the disposition of the members. Conceding to others was higher, and less jamming and aggression occurred when the leader was present. Other Japanese experiments with simulated panic demonstrated that the greater the ratio of trained leaders to followers, the faster was the escape and the less the jamming and aggression (Misumi & Peterson, 1987).

Hamblin (1958b) found that followers were more willing to accept the influence of leaders during crises than during noncrisis periods. They gave leaders more responsibility and were seen as more competent in coping with the panic that had been induced experimentally. In the same way, A. L. Klein (1976) observed, in an experimental study of panic conditions of too many people trying to escape through the same door, that the stress group preferred a strong leader rather than a leader who was elected under low stress and was more highly acceptable. Acceptance and election, which gave the accepted legitimate leader control of the group's fate under conditions of low stress, was replaced, under conditions of high stress, by the group's choice of a less legitimate but stronger leader, whom the members thought was endowed with more competence.

Stress and Effectiveness as a Leader

Leadership that is effective in coping with stress implies leadership that results in rationally defensible, high-quality decisions; the appropriate use of available information, skills, and resources; and the enhanced performance of followers in reaching their goals, despite the threats and obstacles to doing so. House and Rizzo (1972b) and Gillespie and Cohen (1984), among others, showed the importance of leaders in helping their groups effectively cope with conflict and stress. In this respect, individual differences among managers are apparent. Lyness and Moses (1989) were able to separate 258 high-potential A T & T managers by the managers' comfort in ambiguous environments. According to Moses and Lyness (1988), adaptive managers

have a broad perspective, are sensitive to feedback, and use both intuition and logic to deal effectively with ambiguity. They are comfortable in doing so. Managers who are inflexible in their approach also react to ambiguity but are uncomfortable and ineffective in dealing with it. Still other managers ignore or are overwhelmed by ambiguity. The adaptive managers were seen by Lyness and Moses to cope far better with stress in assessment centers than were those who are overwhelmed by ambiguity.

Coping by Changing Leaders

Groups, organizations, and communities under stressful conditions may remedy the inadequacies of their leadership by changing it. Thus, Lanzetta (1953) found that different leaders emerged in the same groups as more stressful conditions were imposed. Similarly, Hamblin (1958b) observed that members of experimental groups, when facing genuine crisis situations, tended to replace their old leaders with new ones if the old leaders were unable to cope with the crises.

Coping by Task- and Relations-Oriented Leadership

There is a mix of evidence about the importance of task structuring and supportive, relations orientation to effective leadership under stressful conditions. Although many studies have found that task-oriented leadership is most likely to be effective under stressful conditions, more often, both task-oriented and relations-oriented performance make for effective leadership under stress. Thus, Numerof and Seltzer (1986) showed that having a superior who scored high on the LBDQ both in the initiation of structure and in consideration was associated with lower burnout among subordinates. And as shall be seen, leaders who were high in both task- and relations orientation were most effective in coping with stress conditions in a series of Japanese experiments. At the same time, task-oriented leaders, who scored low on Fiedler's Least Preferred Co-worker (LPC) Questionnaire, were found by Kim and Organ (1982) to be more sensitive to choosing competent subordinates when stressed by the pressure for effective task outcomes. Sample and Wilson (1965) also found that groups with task-oriented leaders performed better than those with person-oriented leaders under conditions of stress but not under routine conditions. However, reversed results were obtained by Fiedler, O'Brien, and Ilgen (1969), in a study of American volunteers in Honduras, who found that low-LPC, task-oriented leaders were more effective in relatively stress-free villages, whereas high-LPC, relations-oriented leaders exerted a more therapeutic effect in villages that were under more stress. The reversal may be a function of how task orientation was measured. It may be that in both stressed and nonstressed situations, although relations-oriented, supportive, considerate leadership generally contributes to adaptive performance and satisfaction in the groups and organizations that are led, task-oriented, instrumental, structuring leadership becomes essential, especially when stress and conflict are high. Such task structuring may still contribute to performance in the nonstressed condition, but it may be less essential. Overall, the requirements for effective leadership will vary somewhat under different conditions of stress.

Dealing with Combat Conditions

High morale and less stress are found in soldiers during combat who had confidence in their commanders (Gal & Jones, 1985). This confidence is seen in the judged professional competence of the commander, belief in his credibility, and the perception that he cares about his troops. But under continuing combat stress, professional competence becomes particularly important, accroding to Kalay's (1983) study of Israeli soldiers in Lebanon in 1982.

Dealing with Conflict

Among 84 randomly selected faculty members from 20 departments of two universities, R. Katz (1977) found that the amount of affective and substantive conflict in departments contributed to the felt tension (.49 and .47) and the department's perceived lack of effectiveness (−.28 and −.29). At the same time, for departments that were in conflict, the leader's initiation of structure correlated more highly with the department's effectiveness than when such conflict was absent. The correlation between the leader's initiation of structure in a department and its effectiveness was .63 when af-

fective conflict was high and only .29 when affective conflict was low. The correlation between initiation and effectiveness was .51 when substantive conflict was high and .38 when substantive conflict was low. In an experiment to confirm these findings, participants were hired to perform routine tasks. For a routine coding task, the initiation of structure correlated .46 with productivity when conflict was high and −.62 when conflict was absent. Less clear results materialized with a cross-checking task. Consistent with these findings, Katz, Phillips, and Cheston (1976) demonstrated that more directive, structured, preemptory "forcing" can often be more effective in resolving interpersonal conflicts than "problem solving."

Dealing with Role Stress

LaRocco and Jones (1978) concluded that for 3,725 U.S. Navy enlisted personnel, supportive leadership and the facilitation of interaction contributed to job satisfaction and satisfaction with the U.S. Navy. Nonetheless, more initiation of structure was needed to alleviate the effects of stress, such as by structuring work and emphasizing goals, increasing role clarity, and reducing role ambiguity. Consistent with these results, 54 subordinates of 19 units heads in a national black social services organization, who revealed little on-the-job anxiety, generated a correlation of −.45 between their unit head's initiation of structure and a 17-item measure of their unit's performance (Schriesheim & Murphy, 1976). But the corresponding correlation was .15 for subordinates with strong job anxiety. For the leader's consideration, the figures were reversed: .41 between consideration and performance when anxiety was low and −.24 when anxiety was high.

Dealing with Panic

Strauss (1944) observed six factors that reduce panic. These factors are (1) calm, intelligent leadership, (2) group discipline and morale, (3) rational action according to a plan, (4) prior training, (5) sound physical health, and (6) attention directed toward a realistic appraisal of conditions and alternatives.

The effect of clear, unambiguous direction can be seen in Japanese experiments by Sugiman, Misumi, and Sako (1983) and by Sugiman and Misumi (1984).

These experiments demonstrated that in an emergency, the speedier evacuation from a simulated underground shopping arcade of a railroad station by city employees was obtained when the leader told one of the subjects "Follow me" and led the way to the exit than when the leader gave instructions to the subject indicating the exit in a loud voice and with large gestures. The investigators suggested that the "follow me" method using one subject worked because small groups tend to congregate amid leaders. However, the "follow me" method worked better when one leader was involved with four other persons rather than eight others (Sugiman & Misumi, 1988).

The most effective leaders in helping groups to escape from panic conditions display performance(P)-maintenance(M) leadership. In the previously mentioned study by Kugihara, Misumi, Sato, and Shigeoka (1982) in which a panic situation was simulated in 6-person groups, the percentage of successful escaping, the degree of jamming, and aggressiveness was measured. Four styles of leadership were compared. The percentage of successful escaping was highest and aggression was lowest in the PM condition, in which leaders focused on both performance planning and the maintenance of relationships, rather than focusing on only one or the other or neither. PM leadership behavior was seen as most appropriate by the subjects. In addition, Misumi and Sako (1982) found it was important first to provide the support and encouragement and then to concentrate on the requirements of performance, rather than vice versa.

Kugihara and Misumi (1984) compared subjects who dealt with a maze under fearful and unfearful conditions. Consistent with the previously cited Japanese experiments of reaction to simulated panic, they found that PM leadership generated the least fear, the largest amount of planning, and the least unreasonable felt pressure from the leader compared with P leadership or M leadership alone or the absence of both.

Dealing with Disasters

A body of observation, commentary, and research on coping with disasters points to the critical contributions of leaders and public managers who are well organized, well prepared, and well trained to provide both the needed instrumental and supportive leadership (Harman, 1984). At the mass populace and community levels, this translates into leadership that provides credible warning systems and the advanced preparation for when disasters actually strike. The absence of such effective leadership and management is marked by maladaptive coping, defensiveness by the public, and exascerbation of panic reactions. At the organizational level, Mitroff, Shrivastava, and Udwadia (1987) advocated both technical and behavioral preparation by organizations for crisis. Management needs early warning systems, high-quality control, and crisis command centers. Among other things, employees need training in security and detection, as well as emotional preparation for emergencies.

Weinberg (1978) reviewed 30 cases of the behavior of groups during disasters: earthquakes, blizzards, accidents, and hurricanes. Trained judges examined each case history. Weinberg found that breakdown occurs in situations of high stress when there is an absence of appropriate leadership. Effective coping occurs with leadership that provides the needed support, structure, and preparations. For example, acccording to Hammerschlag and Astrachan (1971), in the Kennedy Airport "snow-in" of February 1969, the assembled people became passive, compliant, helpless, and without initiative and indigenous leadership. Salvation was predicated on the arrival of some technical authority who could ensure their deliverance—a "leader," the "omnipotent one," who would clear runways, facilitate their departure, feed the hungry, and make everyone happy. The persons in the snow-in never became collaborating groups; there was no task that could have unified them. They developed a sense of abandonment, which was internalized as a retribution for some fantasied wrongdoing. Food swindling and hoarding began to occur. The people did not see the need to initiate planning and coordinating with other groups.

The Need for Structure. Tests of the Lawrence–Douglas County, Kansas, emergency preparedness system demonstrated that the structure needs to be ready for future disasters and that there must be a strong chain of command. Resources must be well organized and the staff highly trained (Watson, 1984). City-wide drills for ambulance drivers were seen to have paid off in the handling of the Hyatt Regency disaster in Kansas City (Ross, 1982). Similar conclusions about the preparation for emergencies were reached in Alexandria, Virginia's, dealing with a disasterous flood (Harman, 1984).

The need for structure and prepared response is the reason why local public service agencies, such as the police, fire, ambulance services and public works departments are the critical human resources whose effective utilization is paramount in times of crisis (Dynes, 1970; Kartez, 1984). Furthermore, the available leadership of these resources makes a difference in the effectiveness of the organized response to disasters. The most effective organizations maintain their own identity and do not depend on outside help from volunteers. The least effective organizations have an amorphous structure, and their leadership is elected or composed of quasi-professional persons who operate with volunteers who are not subject to discipline (Form & Nosow, 1958). In metropolitan Dade County, Florida, emergencies are dealt with by stripped-down administrative processes, rapid decision making, and emergency powers to mobilize resources when needed. Such occurred in handling the Mariel boatlift and the influx of Haitians (Stierheim, 1984). Failure to plan ahead for contingencies such as the loss of access to the disaster site, as occurred in the Flixborough, England, disaster in 1974, resulted in chaotic evacuation and impeded the arrival of emergency services (Bodycombe, 1982). Yet, a preset structure and roles can be vulnerable to destruction and may prove too rigid for appropriate responses to disasters, such as earthquakes (Lanzara, 1983). Contingent planning, which sets priorities of response on the basis of past experiences and future expectations of natural and man-made calamities, is necessary (Spencer, 1981). Minor crises, such as the shortage of supplies, that disrupt work can be the subject of similar contingent planning (Bensahel, 1981).

The Need for Communication Plans. Planning for emergencies calls for the planning of communication strategies. The news media overreact at first. The available information is likely to be sketchy or incorrect, and the location and timing of an emergency are likely to be inconvenient. Communication plans are essential for the effective management of a crisis (Clark, 1986). Potentially destructive rumors need to be squelched (McSweeney, 1976). A center can be set up to provide frequent news about the disaster to the public (Kemp, 1984), along with an emergency resource catalog of suppliers of services and equipment (Ross, 1982). A survey of 1,500 companies to find who was responsible for getting crisis information to employees indicated that 55 percent of the corporations had such a plan to alert personnel and deal with emergencies (Anonymous, 1984).

Communication plans should be prepared for the worst possibilities. They should be formulated especially in developing countries, where information is distributed mainly by word of mouth (Hall, 1985).

The Need to Use Past Experience. Recurrent disasters can be the source of learning and of the improvement of responses to them. Personnel managers learned how to handle pay for employees who are trapped by a snowstorm and the kinds of nonperishable supplies that should be stored (Garlitz, 1983). In reviewing the Mount St. Helens volcanic disaster, Kartez (1984) suggested that the response to emergencies can be more effective when recurring individual and organizational patterns have been recognized and institutional plans are developed with these patterns in mind.

The importance of learning is also demonstrated by the fact that the most highly organized preparation exists in communities that have had repeated and recent experiences with similar types of disasters (Mileti, Drabek, & Haas, 1975). Furthermore, organizations that deal with predictable kinds of disaster, such as recurrent floods, are likely to be more effective than are those that attempt to cope with unfamiliar or erratic calamities, such as volcanic eruptions or once-in-a-lifetime earthquakes (Cuny, 1983). But learning may also have negative consequences. Community leaders will increase their delay in communicating warnings with the amount of prior experience they have had with such warnings. Previous experiences with a disaster may condition a false sense of security (We had our "once-in-a-hundred-years flood" last year) (Mileti, Drabek, & Haas, 1975).

Dealing with Prolonged Stress

The survival of a group under conditions of extreme hardship is dependent of the competent exercise of the leadership role and the maintenance of the group's unity and goal direction and of communication. Under conditions of extreme hardship and stress, a group's chances of survival are enhanced when it has a leader who maintains its integrity, keeps it realistically informed of the situation confronting it, fulfills the expectations of members, is willing to act outside the bounds of stated authority, maintains its commitment and goal direction, and is able to transform members' personal concerns into concerns for achieving the group's goals. Evidence of the importance of this type of leadership is contained in Stockdale's (1987) autobiographical account of how, as the senior ranking American officer in an extremely stressful Vietnamese prisoner-of-war camp, he provided a purposeful and meaningful structure for the prisoners, establishing priorities and rules, stressing the need to resist early, and determining the conditions under which to take torture. He emphasized cohesion with the rule that all were to go home together.

To illustrate both the task-oriented and supportive actions that leaders can take to help subordinates who are reacting maladaptively to continued stress, Figure 29.1 shows an actual packet guide, *Stress in Battle*, prepared by the British Army's Personnel Research Establishment for noncommissioned officers and junior commanders to carry into combat. Note that some stress reaction is considered normal and requires no remediation. Note also the importance of leaders being both supportive and attentive to keep the stressed soldier assigned to specific tasks or to help with small jobs.

The detrimental effect of the inadequate performance of leaders of groups that are under stress, that is, the failure to provide the needed support and structure, was observed by Torrance (1961). Torrance conducted an extensive, outstanding program of research on military groups that were undergoing training for survival. The following leadership behaviors and group conditions were found to produce an adverse effect on the survival of a group: (1) conflict between various echelons of leadership, (2) the failure of the formal leader to accept the informal leadership structure, (3) the formation of cliques, some with resources and others without, (4) the leader's isolation from the remainder of the group, (5) the reduction of the power of the group, with the resulting hostility toward the leader, (6) the leader's abdication of customarily performed leadership roles or functions, (7) the unwillingness of the designated leader to act outside of authority, (8) the group's attempt to function without a designated leader, (9) the leader's failure to fulfill the group's expectations, and (10) the leader's failure to resolve the members' feelings of isolation and loneliness. Stress resulting from differences in values among members or between the leader and the members, the failure of members to give realistic information to others about what they were doing, and the members' failure to give mutual support and to sacrifice their personal goals for the group's goals also tended to jeopardize survival. Transformational leadership was missing.

Requirements with Different Stress Conditions

Leadership that deals effectively with stress cannot be summed up in one simple proposition. For instance, anxious groups and groups that are in conflict call for different types of responses from the leader. For anxious personnel, the leader needs to direct attention to the specifics of their problems. For groups that are facing severe conflicts, the leaders must make possible a full analysis of the costs and benefits of pursuing one goal rather than another. Although active, directive, structuring, and transformational leadership are needed, the nature of conflict—socioemotional, interpersonal, or task related—may make some difference in the extent to which initiation of structure by the leader will contribute to effectiveness (Guetzkow & Gyr, 1954; R. Likert & J. Likert, 1976). But if the leader has the ability and authority and if the situation generates stress, pressure, and tension to achieve success, directive leadership is still the most likely to be effective (Rosenbaum & Rosenbaum, 1971).

In dealing with inertia or defensive avoidance among followers, the leader must challenge outworn decisions and stimulate the followers to rise beyond their own self-serving rationalizations. Followers need to be made

Figure 29.1. Combat Stress and Treatment

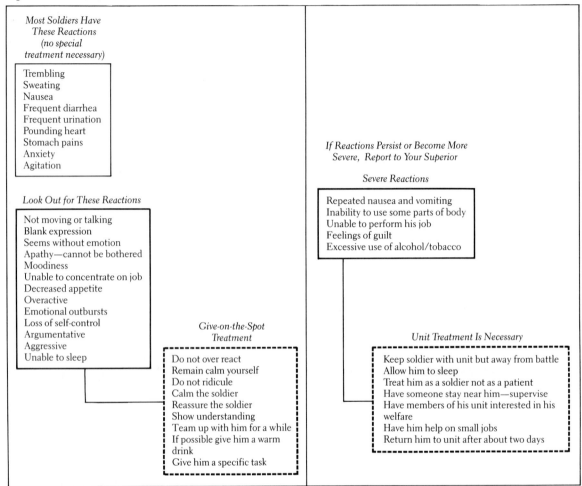

*Most Soldiers Have
These Reactions
(no special
treatment necessary)*

Trembling
Sweating
Nausea
Frequent diarrhea
Frequent urination
Pounding heart
Stomach pains
Anxiety
Agitation

Look Out for These Reactions

Not moving or talking
Blank expression
Seems without emotion
Apathy—cannot be bothered
Moodiness
Unable to concentrate on job
Decreased appetite
Overactive
Emotional outbursts
Loss of self-control
Argumentative
Aggressive
Unable to sleep

*Give-on-the-Spot
Treatment*

Do not over react
Remain calm yourself
Do not ridicule
Calm the soldier
Reassure the soldier
Show understanding
Team up with him for a while
If possible give him a warm
drink
Give him a specific task

*If Reactions Persist or Become More
Severe, Report to Your Superior*

Severe Reactions

Repeated nausea and vomiting
Inability to use some parts of body
Unable to perform his job
Feelings of guilt
Excessive use of alcohol/tobacco

Unit Treatment Is Necessary

Keep soldier with unit but away from battle
Allow him to sleep
Treat him as a soldier not as a patient
Have someone stay near him—supervise
Have members of his unit interested in his
welfare
Have him help on small jobs
Return him to unit after about two days

SOURCE: *Adapted from "Part 1: Combat Stress and Treatment," in* Stress and Battle: A Guide for NCO's
and Junior Commanders *(courtesy of the Army Personnel Research Establishment, United Kingdom).*

aware of their rationalizations and defense mechanisms that conflict with their true values and interests (Reed & Janis, 1974; Rokeach, 1971). Radical speakers attempt to do so by confronting audiences with the contradictions and inconsistencies of popular, accepted points of view.

The Nature of the Task. The task makes a difference in the effects of leadership in groups under the pressure to reach decisions quickly. Dubno (1968) assembled experimental groups, some with fast decision-making leaders and others with slow decision-making leaders. Congruent groups were those with fast decision-making leaders and tasks that required speed and fast decision making. Incongruent groups were those with slow decision-making leaders but with tasks that still required speedy performance and quick decisions. With appointed leaders, the most effective groups were those with slow decision-making leaders who urged the members to arrive at high-quality solutions under the pressure of speed. For groups with emergent leaders, the most effective were those with fast decision-making leaders who stressed the high quality of the members' performance.

Butler and Jones (1979) also saw that the task made a difference for 776 U.S. Navy ship personnel. They found that when the risks of accidents were high and hazards from equipment were evident (as among engineering personnel), leadership was unrelated to the occurrence of accidents (presumably, structure was already very high). But, in the work setting of deck personnel, in which environmental hazards were less evident and personnel were less experienced and hence less clear and competent about tasks, hazards, and goals, the occurrence of accidents was lower when leaders emphasized goals and facilitated interaction. More of any kind of leadership (support, emphasis on goals, and the facilitation of work and interaction) seemed to reduce multiple accidents for deck personnel but was irrelevant for the accidents rates of engineering personnel.

The Intelligence and Experience of the Leader. In coping with conflict with their own superior officer, subordinate leaders' experience and intelligence appear to have opposite effects (Fiedler, Potter, Zais, & Knowlton, 1979).[9] Among those 158 infantry squad leaders who perceived a very high degree of stress in their relations with their immediate superiors, the squad leaders' experience, but not their tested intelligence, correlated with their rated performance as leaders (Fiedler & Leister, 1977b). When perceived stress was low, experience correlated between −.20 and .00 with rated performance. When perceived stress was high, experience correlated between .39 and .66 with rated performance. For the 45 first sergeants in the U.S. Army who were studied by Knowlton (1979), correlations between their rated performance and their intelligence correlated between .51 and .78 when they perceived little conflict between themselves and their superiors. The correlations ranged from −.04 to .24 when such perceived conflict was high. Similar findings were obtained by Zais (1979) for line and staff officers in nine army battalions; by Frost (1983), for 123 first-level and second-level superiors in an urban fire department; by Potter (1978), for 103 Coast Guard officers; and by Borden (1980), who collected data from 45 company commanders, 37 company executive officers, 106 platoon leaders, 42 first sergeants, and 163 platoon

sergeants in a combat infantry division. Here, the leaders' intelligence correlated .44 with their performance when their conflict with their own superior was low; .31, when the conflict was moderate; and −.02, when the conflict was high.

Given the importance of preparedness in coping with stress, the positive impact of experience in dealing with conflict is not unexpected, but the reverse effects for intelligence are yet to be explained. In a bureaucracy, the highly intelligent subordinate leader may be a threat to his or her superiors, who, in turn, downgrade the subordinate's performance. Conflict with superiors appears to be more disturbing to the potentially creative, intelligent, subordinate leader. The leader who is in conflict with higher authority is likely to have less "influence upstairs," which reduces the leader's likely effectiveness and ability to use his or her intelligence.

Fiedler's (1982) cognitive-resource theory is an effort to explain the findings. Fiedler assumed that the intelligent leader's contributions to the group's effectiveness depend on his or her direction of plans, decisions, and ideas. But under stressful conditions, the quality of such plans, decisions, and ideas is associated more highly with the leader's experience than with his or her intelligence. The highly intelligent leader will focus on problems that are not directly relevant to the task and will rely on intellectual solutions to tasks, when the tasks may not be amenable to intellectual solutions. A nondirective intelligent leader will make even less of a contribution to groups under stress, primarily because he or she will prolong the decision-making process, be inactive, or perform poorly.

The cognitive-resource interpretation was supported by data about the effectiveness of staff leaders of U.S. Army mess halls, U.S. Army squad leaders, and leaders of public health teams (Fiedler, 1986). Cognitive-resource theory explained why leaders with fluid intelligence (with the ability to solve new and unusual problems) contributed to high-quality decisions and effective analyses of problems when stress was low but leaders with crystallized intelligence (with the ability to solve problems on the basis of previous learning and experience) did better when stress was high (Fiedler & McGuire, 1987). An in-basket simulation, completed by 34 ROTC cadets in either a threatening military atmo-

[9]This idea was introduced in Chapter 7.

sphere or under relaxed conditions, found that while the contributions of the cadets' crystallized intelligence to the effectiveness of their leadership remained the same under high or low stress, the contribution of their fluid intelligence (analysis of problems, decisiveness, and planning and organizing) to their effectiveness was significantly lower under the high stress (McGuire, 1987).

In a study of 130 Coast Guard officers, Potter and Fiedler (1981) found that the contribution of intelligence to performance was not related to conflict with one's boss in carrying out routine staff work, but it was negatively correlated with the effectiveness of decision making for those officers who engaged in policy-making when conflict with their own boss was high. Fiedler, Potter, and McGuire (1988) concluded that the stress of conflict with one's superiors may interfere with the leader's ability to develop plans and make sound judgments, to communicate these plans to the group, and to supervise and monitor their implementation. However, they noted that the available evidence suggests that such conflict primarily interferes with the leader's ability to analyze the problem and make sound judgments and decisions rather than with the communication of these plans or the implementation of these decisions, plans, and strategies.

Transformational Leadership and Dealing with Stress

Transformational leadership contributes to effective leadership under stress. To illustrate, charismatic transformational leaders tend to keep their "cool" when faced with threats to their lives. Mahatma Gandhi, Franklin Delano Roosevelt, Kemal Atatürk, Benito Mussolini, Kwame Nkrumah, and Ronald Reagan displayed composure and a presence of mind when faced with attempts to assassinate them. They were not easily frightened, disconcerted, or thrown off balance but remained calm and maintained their sense of humor in the face of danger or a crisis (Willner, 1968). They were like medal-winning heroes of military combat. According to Gal's (1985a) analysis of 77 Israeli medal winners in the Yom Kippur War contrasted with ordinary soldiers, the medal winners exhibited more leadership,

perseverance under stress, decisiveness, devotion to duty, and emotional stability.

What Transformational Leadership Adds

It should be kept in mind that transformational leadership does not replace transactional leadership; it adds to it (Waldman, Bass, & Yammarino, 1989). Transformational leadership augments transactional leadership, as seen in initiation and consideration (Seltzer & Bass, 1987). It adds substantially to helping individuals, groups, and organizations that are under conflict and stress. While transactional leadership can provide for structure and consideration, transformational leadership adds to it by helping the followers transcend their own immediate self-interests, increase their awareness of the larger issues, and shift the goals away from personal safety and security toward achievement and self-actualization. The transformational leader may have the charisma[10] to satisfy the followers' frustrated need for identity and feeling of the lack of social support. Thus, in a study of 57 communes over a 4-year period, Bradley (1987) showed that the presence or absence of charisma in the commune's leader contributed to the commune's likelihood of survival. Communes were least likely to survive if their members were strongly seeking charismatic leadership that was not provided. Those with charismatic leaders were most likely to survive, as were those that did not seek such leadership.

The transformational leader may reveal the individualized consideration to convert crises into developmental challenges. He or she may provide the intellectual stimulation to promote subordinates' thoughtful, creative, adaptive solutions to stressful conditions, rather than hasty, defensive, maladaptive ones.

As was shown in the preceding section, a transactional leader can be influential in groups that are under stress. Such a leader can supply solutions for the immediate needs that members perceive they have. Such leadership will provide immediate satisfaction but may not be effective in the long term. What is required is a transformational leader who can evoke higher-level needs, such as for the common good and who can

---

[10]Transformational leadership includes the factors of charisma, inspirational leadership, intellectual stimulation, and individualized consideration (Bass, 1985a). See Chapter 12.

move the group into a fully vigilant search for long-term solutions. Mulder, Ritsema van Eck, and de Jong (1971) studied leadership patterns in a Dutch navy flotilla on active duty. The usual interpersonal and task-oriented factor emerged, but what distinguished crisis from noncrisis leadership was that in crises, the leadership was intense, powerful, and self-confident (leadership that characterizes the charismatic transformational leader[11]), whereas in noncrisis situations, it took the form of the "mild" person-leader relationship.

Effects on Stress and Burnout

More direct evidence of the effects of transactional and transformational leadership were accumulated by Seltzer, Numerof, and Bass (1987). In that study, a total of 277 MBA students who held full-time jobs completed the Personal Stress Symptom Assessment (Numerof, Cramer, & Shachar-Hendin, 1984), in which they indicated how often they experienced headaches, fatigue, irritability, loss of appetite, insomnia, inability to relax, and so on. They also completed the Gillespie-Numerof Burnout Inventory (Numerof & Gillespie, 1984), responding to such items as, "I'm fed up with my job" and "My job has me at the end of my rope." Felt stress and burnout correlated .58. The 277 respondents described their immediate superiors on the Multifactor Leadership Questionnaire (Bass, 1985c). Table

[11]See Chapter 12.

29.1 shows the first-order correlations of the scores for the transformational and transactional leadership of the superiors and the felt stress and burnout of their subordinates. Seltzer, Numerof, and Bass (1987) concluded that 14 percent of the variance in the reported symptoms of stress and 34 percent of the variance in feelings of burnout could be attributed to the lack of transformational leadership and contingent rewarding as well as to more frequent practice of management by exception by the leader.

Multiple regression analyses suggested that if the other factors were held constant, reported stress was lessened if the respondents were working under charismatic and individually considerate leaders but was raised somewhat when the respondents were workng under intellectually stimulating leaders. As for transactional leadership, contingent rewarding was modestly associated with less stress and management by exception with more stress. The pattern was the same for feelings of burnout, but the relations with leadership were much stronger.

Transcending the Immediate

Rather than the autocratic, rapid decision making that the ready-to-be-influenced group demands of the leader, effective leadership in stressful situations organizes group efforts of followers in ways that help to promote vigilance, thorough search, thorough ap-

Table 29.1 First-order Correlations of Transactional and Transformational Leadership of Superiors and the Stress and Burnout Felt by Their Subordinates

Leadership	Symptoms of Stress (N = 285)	Felt Burnout (N = 296)
Transformational		
Charisma	−.17**	−.53**
Individualized consideration	−.18**	−.47**
Intellectual stimulation	−.11*	−.36**
Transactional		
Contingent rewards	−.09*	−.43**
Management by exception	.11*	.22**

**p < .01, r = .14.
*p < .05, r = .10.

Source: Adapted from Numerof, Seltzer, and Bass (1987).

praisal, and contingency planning to avoid defective coping with a threat. Bolstering can be minimized by encouraging devil's advocates. Heterogeneity, rather than homogeneity, can be pursued by selecting members for the group who will promote harder-to-attain creativity rather than quick and easy decision making. Considering the distinctions between frustration, fear, anxiety, and conflict (Bass, Hurder, & Ellis, 1954), to be effective under stress, the leader must be transformational—able to rise above what the group sees as its immediate needs and appropriate reactions. The leader must arouse an inert group about the significance of threats and the group's lack of preparedness. The leader must alter the inert group's willingness to live with frustration rather than make efforts to deal more adequately with obstacles in its path to positive goals. Again, to be effective, instead of catering to the group's immediate needs and fears, the leader may need to calm the demands for hasty change. An effective leader may need to be transformational in identifying and publicizing the inadequacy of defensive pseudo-solutions. The effective leader is transformational in providing superordinate goals that transcend self-interests for the hypervigilant group in a state of panic. Clear, confident direction is important for effective leadership when panic is imminent. But transactional leadership may also be important in planning ahead.

Planning Ahead

Crises can be prevented or their stressful effects mitigated by effective political leaders who plan ahead (Yarmolinsky, 1987). Effective transactional leaders set up early warning mechanisms to avoid surprises that arise from hasty ill-conceived responses. Active practice of management by exception can result in the rational recognition of potential crises. Appropriate searches for information can be instituted without hasty defensiveness. Nevertheless, it is the transformational leader who sounds and articulates the need for early warnings and mobilizes the organization to avoid the emergency or to prepare for it (Tichy & Devanna, 1986). Such leaders devise strategies to avoid or defuse the crisis and persuade immediate subordinates and peers to accept the proposed strategies and mobilize in support of

them. In this regard, political leaders take on an important teaching function (Yarmolinsky, 1987).

By planning ahead, by anticipating potential crises, and by preparing the group for crises, industrial supervisors will be more effective than if they deal only with immediate problems. Studies of leadership behavior in a public utility company, an insurance office, an automobile plant, and in heavy industry found that supervisors of groups with better production records more often engaged in long-range planning and anticipated future problems rather than limited themselves to day-to-day operations (D. Katz, 1951).

Dealing with the Loss of Markets

If a sales crisis hits, business crumbles, and a large number of employees have to be laid off, management can do much to alleviate the resulting distress by setting realistic expectations, keeping employees informed, implementing even-handed layoff policies, allowing employees to leave with dignity, helping displaced employees find new jobs, and providing ceremonies to reduce frustration and anger. In handling the reduced demand for products and plant closings, the management of IBM usually promotes the employees' felt and actual job security by redeploying displaced employees elsewhere, encouraging early retirements, discontinuing overtime and the temporary employment by others, and contracting out work to subcontractors in times of temporary surplus loads (Greenhalgh, McKersie, & Gilkey, 1986). This is the model that the larger and better-known Japanese firms have also pursued.

Dealing with Mergers

Schweiger, Ivancevich, and Power (1987) noted that when a firm is acquired by another, the employees in the firm that was taken over are stressed by the loss of identity, purpose, and ego ideal. Shock, anger, disbelief, depression, and helplessness are frequent responses, as is anxiety because of the lack of information. The employees see the resignations and forced departure of others as a loss of talent as well as a threat to their security. Survival in the reorganization becomes an obsession. Transformational leadership is needed to deal with the merger of the acquired firm's culture and that of the firm that is taking over. It may contribute to creating a new culture in the acquired firm or to a new one that transcends both firms. The contingent-reward system for the future needs to be clearly communicated as well as feedback on how it is working. Again, support, consideration, and commitment at each level of supervision in the acquired firm is essential to cope with the subordinates' stress. It is particularly important, if it is possible to do so, for those with leadership responsibilities in the acquired firm to

> get information about the acquiring firm for their subordinates; identify counterparts in the other firm and make contact and help subordinates to understand that their counterparts in the acquiring firm are not the bad guys and, in many cases, are in a situation similar to their own. (Schweiger, Ivancevich, & Power, 1987, p. 135)

At all levels in the firm, transformational leadership can help subordinates and colleagues to end their previous attachments to the scene before the takeover. It can help reduce the tensions of disengagement, accompanied by the disidentification with the old situation and disenchantment with the new that may produce disorientation without anchors to the past or the future. Leaders can help colleagues and subordinates work through their denials and anger and move toward acceptance of the new situation (Tichy & Devanna, 1986). Assistance with outplacement may buffer the losses experienced by those squeezed out of the organization by the merger.

Transforming Crises into Challenges

Effective transformational leaders can halt crises by disclosing opportunities, arousing courage, and stimulating enthusiasm. The key here, according to Nystrom and Starbuck (1984), is the need for the leaders to be intellectually stimulating, to foster unlearning, and to eliminate the fixation on old ways of doing things. When the cyanide-lacing of Tylenol struck Johnson and Johnson in 1982, the public relations department had no plans for dealing with such a crisis. The chief executive officer rejected any half-way steps to gloss over the disaster and actually converted the marketing disaster into an opportunity to gain credit for good citizenship and regain the firm's market share by introducing a more tamper-proof Tylenol at a time of great public consciousness and publicity about the problem (Snyder, 1983).

Pines (1980) summarized the ways that leaders can provide support to make subordinates "hardier" and to maintain their high-quality performance and decision making despite the presence of stressful conditions. Dramatic changes can be presented as challenges, not as disturbances. Stress can become challenging if the leaders select subordinates for the stressful conditions who prefer a vigorous, fast-paced lifestyle and have the knowledge, intelligence, and preparation to cope adequately with the stress. The subordinates' sense that the control of their fate can be enhanced and their sense of powerlessness, can be lessened. The subordinates' involvement and commitment can offset their focus on the deleterious effects of the stress. For example, rather than paying attention to the dangerous exposure that he or she sees when looking down a vertical cliff face, the exposed climber should focus on the holds and grips that are available immediately in front of him or her.

McCauley (1987) pointed to a number of transformational and transactional ways that leaders can enhance the subordinates' performance by converting a potentially stressful situation into a challenging one. The leader needs to ensure that there will be positive outcomes and that the subordinates know what they are. Although they may be difficult, goals can be set that are clear and attainable. Interim rewards for progress can be given. More generally, taxing conditions can be converted into problems to be solved. Self-confidence can be increased, as can the tolerance for ambiguity, uncertainty, and working in new and unfamiliar conditions. Situations that are beyond one's control can be faced with the recognition that one may be unable to change an undesired state of affairs. The situation may need to be redefined, goals may need to be changed, and patience may be needed (seemingly insurmountable problems sometimes disappear when they are ignored).

Aside from their better effects on subordinates, leaders who view situations as challenges, rather than crises, tend to be more open to ideas and suggestions from their subordinates, which enables them to reach more effective decisions. This tendency was shown by

Tjosvold (1984a), who conducted an experiment in which the focal "managers" led confederates of the experimenter in dealing with an issue of the rotation of jobs, which was either a crisis condition, a challenging condition, or of minor consequence. The "managers" who thought they were in a crisis situation were most closed-minded. Not only did they feel that they disagreed most with their subordinates, but they were the least interested in hearing more from their subordinates, demonstrated less knowledge of their subordinates' arguments, and were least likely to change from their original position. In contrast, the managers who thought they were in a challenging situation were most likely to explore and incorporate the subordinates' views (even opposing views) into their own. They most indicated the desire to hear more arguments. They most incorporated specific information from subordinates to make a complex integrated decision that would likely promote both the simulated company's profits and the employees' satisfaction.

Consistent with Tjosvold's results, Blake and Mouton (1985a) observed that flight captains were able to respond to a crisis situation more effectively if they readily received information and feedback from their flight crews and were open to it. Similar results were obtained for supervisors of fighters of forest fires. To deal with crises effectively, the subordinates need to be ready and willing to provide their leaders with information and feedback and the leaders need to be ready and willing to accept it.

Enhancing Identification and Social Support

Felt stress is likely to be reduced if the individual can be made to feel part of a larger entity. The insecurity of feeling isolated is replaced by the security of a sense of belonging. Transformational leaders can create a sense of identity with a social network of support. Pines (1980) cited research which demonstrated that people with the social support of close friends, relatives, and group associations have lower mortality rates than do those without such social support.

During prolonged bombardments, the social support of children in kibbutzim made them less anxious than Israeli urban children. The loss of such social ties, ostracism, and isolation can be deadly among primitive peoples. Ganster, Fusilier, and Mayes (1986) reported that for 326 employees of a large contracting firm, social support from their supervisors, co-workers, family members, and friends moderately buffered the experience of strain. The strains included somatic complaints, depression, role ambiguity, role conflict, and frustration about the underutilization of skills. Nelson's (1978) survey of the experiences of 30 child care workers in dealing with child care crises found that crises were dealt with most effectively when the leader was supportive, respectful, and calm; had confidence; clarified the situation; and prepared for future crises. On the other hand, crises were dealt with ineffectively by the leader who displayed authoritarian attitudes and behavior, lack of support, loss of control, and poor communication.

As was seen in Chapter 12, followers may be under their own intrapsychic tensions, feeling personally inadequate because of the gap between their self-perceived images of what they are and what they ideally should and would like to be. Their stress will be increased if they feel they cannot reduce the gap. The frustration may result in aggression and feelings of dependence. To help followers cope with their frustration, self-aggrandizing leaders make themselves the object of identification for the followers (Downton, 1973), but socially directed leaders show their individualized consideration in providing opportunities for their followers to develop themselves (Levinson, 1980).

Summary and Conclusions

Stress situations can be categorized in a variety of ways, and emergent and effective leadership will vary accordingly. Groups may be frustrated by unattainable goals. They may fear impending dangers. They may be anxious because of unclear and ambiguous demands. They may be in conflict over competing demands or with other groups. Groups may be in a state of inertia that they perceive is less risky and costly than an active response to warnings of danger. They may be aroused to respond impulsively, defensively, or in panic. Threats to survival may be internal or external, substantive or interpersonal.

It is not necessarily the speed of decision making nor

the directiveness of leadership that is sought or commonly found during crises that makes a decision maladaptive. Rather, the inadequacy of the decision is due to the hastiness with which it is formulated and evaluated and to the lack of preparation and commitment to it. Such hasty directive leadership will also be sought when followers must endure prolonged stress. In the same way, real or imagined threat will result in the acceptance of leaders who encourage defensive avoidance. Likewise, panic will heighten the followers' susceptibility to be influenced by decisions that will be maladaptive.

The emergent leader will do what is immediately required to provide the group with ways of coping with the stress. Rapid direction, initiation of structure, and task-oriented leadership will make the leader more likely to successfully influence the group to succeed. At the same time, the group will be more susceptible to such influence.

Both demagogues and statesmen can be influential but not necessarily effective in times of crisis, as can transactional and transformational leaders. The transactional demagogue can assure inactive followers that the warnings are unimportant and persuade impulsive followers that simple solutions are acceptable. He or she can convince defensive followers by bolstering them and shifting responsibility for the crisis, and he or she can sway panicking followers with other-worldly solutions. The demagogue can successfully lead the popular, easier search for internal subversion when complex external problems are paramount.

The effective leader (who, of course, must also suc-cessfully influence followers) is a transforming statesman who addresses the inert followers by shaking them out of their torpor in the face of impending dangers or by rousing them to work toward what, at first, may seem to be unobtainable goals. The transforming statesman shows followers the inadequacies of simple solutions and defensive avoidance. Superordinate goals are provided for the hypervigilant, and motivation and initiation of structure are provided for the adequate search, appraisal of alternatives, and contingency plans.

The survival of a group is dependent on a type of leadership that is able to keep members and subgroups working together toward a common purpose, to maintain productivity at a level that is sufficient to sustain the group or to justify its existence, and to satisfy the members' expectations of the leader and the group. Competent leadership is especially needed in times of crisis to unite the efforts of members and to strengthen the group's cohesiveness around a common purpose. A group that desires to survive will prevent leaders of contending factions from destroying its legitimacy.

Different types of stress call for different types of leadership behavior. More task-oriented structuring may be required in many stressful circumstances; the creation of supportive groups will be important for the leader's effectiveness in other situations. Ordinarily, both are important.

Crowding, a potential source of stress, is also illustrative of the relevance of physical and interpersonal space to leadership. These subjects are addressed next.

Space, Networks, Leadership, and Its Substitutes

Importance of Spatial and Social Arrangements

Leadership depends on interaction. Interaction depends on physical proximity, social and organizational propinquity, and networks of open channels of communications. And so, not surprisingly, the emergence and success of leadership depend on such physical and social arrangements. Such arrangements may also be possible substitutes for leadership.

Interaction Potential

Interaction potential is the likelihood that any two individuals will interact with each other. The more the individuals interact, the more one is likely to influence or lead the other. Although the purpose of interaction with another person may often be to give or receive information, to play, or to do other things that are unrelated to attempts to lead, many interactions are attempts to influence and to lead. Whatever increases the potential for interaction is also likely to increase attempts to lead. Successful leadership requires such attempts and, as such, is likely also to be correlated with interaction potential.

Physical proximity and the availability of channels of communication increase interaction potential. Thus, in reviewing studies of the effect of the spatial arrangement of participants in a small group, C. D. Ward (1968) concluded that the distance between participants was the most important single factor that influenced interaction. It was even more important than friendship. But friendship, familiarity, similarity, and other social factors also increase the potential to interact (Bass, 1960). Furthermore, the interaction of individuals may be a consequence of their freedom and autonomy from a higher authority. Some jobs permit

more autonomy from a superior. This greater autonomy, in turn, increases the time that individuals spend communicating with others (Yammarino & Naughton, 1988).

Organizational proximity of members also increases their potential to interact and to communicate. With ecco analysis, members of an organization report whether they received a particular message and if they received it, the time of receipt and the immediate source of the message. Using ecco analysis, Davis (1968b) showed that organizational proximity makes a difference in the extent to which informal communications for a particular oral message will be received. Thus, the percentage of higher level supervisors and managers who reported receiving information about parking or layoffs originated by those at the top of the organization was more than reported by assistant foremen and foremen at lower levels. As messages moved downward through the system, the time of receipt increased along with delays and blockages.

Physical barriers would be expected to decrease the interaction between those with such barriers between them. But the opposite seems to be true, according to 99 employees in two high-tech firms surveyed by Hatch (1987). Interaction in offices appears to be positively related to the height of the partitions between offices, the number of partitions, and the use of a door or a secretary. The only negative effect on interaction (which would be expected according to Stech, 1981) is when a desk is positioned away from the office entrance.

Leadership and Physical Space

It follows that the spatial proximity of the leader to the led systematically enhances the influence process and the quality of the exchange between the leader and the led. Conversely, the distance between them reduces the possibilities of influence and the quality of their exchange. It is not surprising that the traditional Inuit culture was highly individualistic rather than cooperative or competitive (Mead, Mirsky, Landes, et al., 1937). The low population density of the Arctic meant that the opportunity for contact among people was low. And without such an opportunity, the amount of influence and leadership was severely limited. Worthy (undated) noted that the rise of organized civilizations required the development of management that could occur only with denser settlements. Stable agriculture, animal husbandry, and fishing were needed to support the requisite density of population in which such organizing leadership was possible as well as necessary for civilizations to emerge. Particularly important was agriculture that needed irrigation works to support it.

Leadership and Physical Proximity

Schrag (1954) found physical proximity to be an important determinant of leadership among prison inmates. Toki (1935) studied the effects on groups of children of the introduction of physical distance to separate them from their adult leaders. The early separation and distancing of the leaders had much more deleterious effects on the groups that were early in their development than did such separation later on. Podsakoff, Todor, Grover, and Huber's (1984) analysis[1] for 1,946 employees' descriptions of the reinforcement behavior of their superiors indicated that the greater the spatial distance between the superior and the subordinates, the significantly more likely was the superior to practice noncontingent punishment and the less likely was the superior to practice either contingent or noncontingent reward. Other direct and indirect linkages to the leadership–physical proximity relationship are seen in territorial behavior, choice of friends, communication patterns, and physical arrangements.

Leadership and Territoriality. Territoriality implies ownership of physically closer space and has similar effects on efforts to influence and the processes of influencing. Our interaction will be higher with those

[1] Detailed in Chapter 17.

who are within the boundaries of what we consider to be our territory. Our interaction and potential for leadership expand if we can stretch those boundaries and contract if the boundaries are contracted. Territoriality is one of the major phenomena of interest to students of animal behavior. One of the primary functions of leadership in animal societies appears to be the location and protection of territory (Allee, 1945, 1951; Allee, Emerson, Park, et al., 1949). It has its counterpart in the attitudes of delinquent gangs about their own "turf" and domestic firms about foreign imports.

Friendship. The potential to influence others is seen indirectly in the effects of proximity and distance on choice and acceptance. Willerman and Swanson (1952) found that sorority girls who lived in the same house chose each other as friends significantly more often than did girls who lived in more scattered locations in town. Proximity contributed to mutual choice. Maisonneuve (1952) and Priest and Sawyer (1967) also found proximity to be a factor in interpersonal choice, as did Gullahorn (1952), who studied the interactions of female clerks seated in rows separated by filing cabinets. Interaction within rows was greater than that across rows. Within rows, the clerks related more with those near them than with those seated at a distance. When distance did not operate as a factor, friendship was the next most important influence on the clerks' choice of others with whom to interact.

Streufert (1965) indicated that attitudes toward a member who deviates from group norms become more unfavorable as the distance between the member and the respondent increases. In the same way, attitudes toward a conforming member become more favorable as the member's proximity to the respondent increases.

Proximity of distance between persons may also be a consequence, rather than a cause, of the relations between those who are engaged in interactions. Willis (1966) observed that individuals stand closer to one another when talking to friends and assume a greater distance when talking to strangers or persons of high status. Again, Little (1965) observed pairs of individuals in various situations. The distance between pairs of individuals in interaction was found to increase as their relationship changed from that of friend to acquaintance to stranger. Distance between pairs increased as the impersonality of the situation increased from living room to office to street corner.

Effect of Distance on Communication.

Indirect evidence of the effects of distance on influence processes are also seen in studies of communication. Gullahorn (1952) observed that greater distance between the work locations of clerical personnel led to less communication among them. Allen and Gerstberger (1973) discovered that communication among product engineers was significantly higher with an open, nonterritorial, office layout than with the traditional arrangements of office walls and assigned permanent workplaces. To the contrary, Hage (1974) found that the more the departments of an organization were physically dispersed, the more intensive were committee and departmental meetings and unscheduled communications. Also, there were fewer interactions *within* physically dispersed departments and more frequent interactions *between* physically dispersed departments. In explanation, Klauss and Bass (1982) concluded that physical distance among organizational entities increases the physical need for coordination, as shown by the increased volume of communication between distant organizational units. Although physical distance may initially hamper interpersonal communication over time, social structure compensates for physical distance and barriers (Barnlund & Harland, 1963). Similarly, modern technology provides alternative modes of communication to help overcome the factors of distance. Conrath (1973a) noted that when authority was involved in an interaction, communications were in writing; when task issues were involved, the telephone was used instead.

Bass, Klauss, and DeMarco (1977) found that as physical distance increases among members of an organization at the same organizational level, there is a direct increase in the use of the telephone instead of face-to-face meetings for interacting with colleagues. But as the hierarchical distance in the number of organizational levels between a manager and a colleague increased along with physical distance, Bass, Klauss, and DeMarco, agreeing with Conrath's (1973) findings, found an increase in the use of memos instead of face-to-face contact or the telephone. The introduction of electronic mail is likely to moderate these effects of physical distance, as such, on collegial efforts to influence each other.

Leadership and Physical Location.

The respective physical locations of individuals make a difference. The group discussant who grabs the chalk and controls the blackboard at a meeting can influence what ideas are singled out for attention. A. M. Rose (1968) identified job occupants who, because of their physical locations, take on "ecologically influential" roles of leadership. Their leadership is not based on personal, social, or psychological traits. These persons are influential because they occupy a position that permits them to mediate ideas among several societal groups. Beauticians, barbers, bartenders, and traveling salespeople are examples of such leaders. In the same way, those who settled at the crossroads of several communities before the advent of the telephone were more likely to emerge as leaders.

As was noted in the last chapter, the physical presence of formal leaders helped their groups to cope better with a panic situation. Likewise, Ronan, Latham, and Kinne (1973) demonstrated that when supervisors of timber workers stayed on the job with the workers after assigning goals, they generated more output from their crews that did those supervisors who assigned goals but did not stay on the job. Supervisors who remained on the job could effectively stress the importance of reaching or exceeding the goal and serve as reminders and monitors.

Seating Arrangements.

Seating arrangements are not as trivial a matter as they might seem. A major difficulty in beginning serious peace negotiations among the United States, the Viet Cong, the South Vietnamese, and the North Vietnamese was disagreement over the shape of the table, round or square. A considerable amount of research has been completed on the extent to which one's influence in a small discussion group is dependent on the location of one's seat in relation to the rest of the group. Traditionally, the appointed leader took his or her place at the head of the table and those who were near in status to the appointed leader were grouped around him or her. Low-status people, as in feudal times, gathered "below the salt." This pattern is still maintained in informal groups, according to several studies. Leaders in small discussion groups tend to gravitate toward the head of the table (Sommer, 1959).[2] In simulated juries, Strodtbeck and Hook (1961) found that those who sat at the end of the table were more likely to be elected jury foreman. For V-shaped arrangements, those with higher status outside the group gravitate toward the apex (Bass & Klubeck, 1952). When the leader does not occupy the head position, other members tend to sit opposite, rather than alongside, him or her. When more than one leader or person of high status is present, these persons tend to seat themselves symmetrically around one end of the table (Sommer, 1961). Members as a whole tend to seat themselves closer to status peers than to members who are higher or lower than themselves in status (Lott & Sommer, 1967). In a study of 88 supervisors and their managers, Bass and Wurster (1953b) found that the first-level supervisors sat on one side of a long table while their second-level superiors sat down on the other side of the table. Again, more dominant members of a group were observed by Hare and Bales (1963) to choose central seats and to do most of the talking.

Group members sitting at end positions of a rectangular arrangement participate more and are rated as wielding more influence than are those at the sides (Strodtbeck & Hook, 1961). Lécuyer (1976) found, with French undergraduates, that the leader's position at the end of a rectangular table enhanced the leader's ability to direct the group.

H. Harris (1949) suggested that a semicircular or V-arrangement, such as for a panel discussion, isolates those at the ends and spotlights those at the center. But Bass and Klubeck (1952) failed to find any such differences when the status of participants outside the group was taken into account. Howells and Becker (1962) seated two group members on one side of a table and three members on the opposite side. A greater number of leaders than would be expected by chance emerged on the side with two seats. C. D. Ward (1968) studied groups of strangers seated in a circle with several empty seats. Those individuals facing the largest number of other members were most likely to be judged as leaders by other group members.

Are you more likely to interact and influence someone sitting next to you or across the table from you? The evidence is mixed. Steinzor (1950) noted that when members of a discussion group were seated in a circle, an individual seated opposite a member who had just stopped talking, rather than one alongside the member, tended to speak next. Similarly, Festinger, Schachter, and Back (1950) showed that individuals who were positioned opposite each other interacted more than did those standing side by side. However, Sommer (1959) found that persons in neighboring seats interacted more than did persons in distant locations. Those in corner positions interacted more than did those who sat side by side or opposite one another. Felipe (1966) also found that such spatial arrangements similarly affected the rates of interaction. It may be that one is more likely to speak to the group after someone else across the table has just finished, but to respond privately to those adjacent.

Seating arrangements are also a consequence of the purposes of meetings. Sommer (1965) reported that casual groups prefer corner seating, cooperating groups sit side by side, coacting groups sit at a distance, and competing groups sit opposite one another.[3] Stech (1983) suggested that managers who preferred relations-oriented leadership or task-oriented leadership could affect their success by choosing various layouts for their offices, which determine the seating arrangements of them and those who visit their offices. Some of his differentiations are shown in Table 30.1.

Leadership and Psychosocial Space

The impact of psychosocial space on leadership is mapped by sociometry. The choice of friends, work partners, and leaders can be displayed in two or three dimensions of space and the correlated networks and linkages can be seen. Moreno (1934/1953) invented this approach to examine patterns of interaction. He asked each member of a group to choose among the others according to some criterion, such as whom he

[2] See also, Lécuyer (1976), Lott and Sommer (1967), and Sommer (1961).

[3] For more on the effects of propinquity and location, see the reviews by Barker (1968), Dogan and Rokkan (1969), Klopfer (1969), Mehrabian (1968a), M. Patterson (1968), and Sommer (1967, 1969).

Table 30.1 Office Layout to Enhance a Manager's Relations Orientation or Task Orientation

Relations-Oriented Layout	Task-Oriented Layout
1. The desk is placed against the wall. The manager turns away from the desk to talk with visitors.	1. The desk is placed so the visitors are seated across from the manager.
2. An informal conversation area is used. For example, the manager and visitor can sit side by side at a coffee table.	2. Most of the space for visitors consists of large, formal furniture.
3. All participants in a conversation are seated on the same level.	3. The manager's chair elevates him or her to a physically higher level than that of others.
4. The office door is open.	4. The office door is closed, and a secretary acts as a buffer.
5. The office space is relatively small and the seats are fairly close together.	5. The office space is large, and furniture is placed so that there are large distances between persons.

SOURCE: Stech (1983, pp. 73-74).

or she liked best. Usually, the large share of choices were garnered by just a few individual members. Figure 30.1 presents a sociometric diagram for a group of eight members. Only the first and second choices are shown. Member A, who received five choices, is the most highly preferred member of the group. Members B and E, who did not receive any choices, are isolates.

Here are some of the kinds of questions asked members of groups and organizations from which interaction and the influence process can be discerned and mapped. With whom do you spend your work time? Whom do you contact in your organization if you have a particular problem? Whom do you avoid? We are more likely to contact and to spend more time with those we esteem, those we regard as important, those with whom we are more familiar, those whom we regard as friends, and those whom we think are more like us than different from us. Those who are esteemed, competent, knowledgeable, familiar, friends, or similar

to us have more potential to interact with us than do those who are unesteemed, incompetent, strangers, and different from us. The latter have less potential to interact with us and, therefore, are less likely to be able to influence us. This conclusion is supported by considerable evidence.

Sociometrics of Leadership

Different uses have been made of sociometry in the study of leadership. H. H. Jennings (1943) used sociometry to distinguish the choice of leaders from the choice of others. She found that group members are much more selective in choosing leaders than they are in choosing friends or roommates. R. L. French (1951) studied the choice structure of companies of naval recruits and found that the frequency of sick-bay attendance was negatively related to sociometric choice by peers but leadership ratings were positively related to sociometric scores. Yet in a study of bomber crews, Roby (1953) found that the sociometric scores of members were unrelated to ratings of the effectiveness of the crews. Nevertheless, as with a preponderance of military studies, Levi, Torrance, and Pletts (1954) observed that the effectiveness of aircrews was enhanced when the officially designated leader was also the sociometrically chosen leader of the crew. The formal and informal structures were congruent.[4]

Massarik, Tannenbaum, Kahane, and Weschler

Figure 30.1. Sociometric Diagram

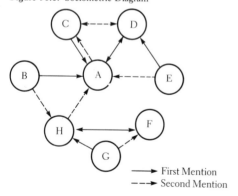

→ First Mention
- - → Second Mention

[4]This congruence, as was noted in Chapter 15, was likely to minimize conflicts between status and esteem. Chapter 36 provides a detailed review of the utility of peer nominations, or "buddy ratings," for forecasting success as a military officer.

(1953) used five sociometric indexes in studying an organization. The indexes were (1) relations prescribed by the organizational chart, (2) perceived relations, (3) reported interactions, (4) preferred interactions, and (5) rejected interactions. Preferred interactions were more highly related to the members' satisfaction than were prescribed or reported interactions. The members re-

lated more freely and were better satisfied under participative than under more directive leadership.

College Presidents' Relationships. The leadership role of college presidents can be more fully appreciated by examining with whom they spend their time, as is shown in Figure 30.2. The sociogram is that of an aver-

Figure 30.2. Administrative Sociogram

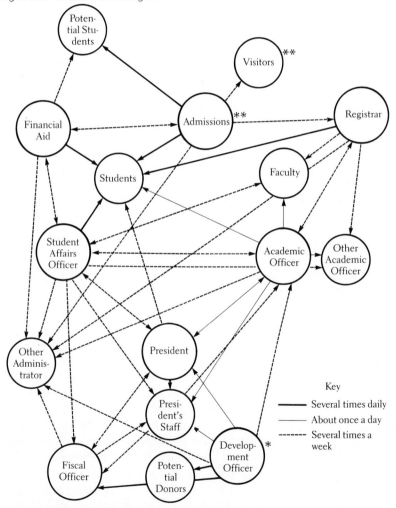

*The development officer responded to the questionnaire but the position was not listed. Other large circles represent officers who responded and whose positions were listed.

**Small circles represent positions listed, but persons occupying the positions did not respond to a questionnaire.

SOURCE: Astin and Scherrei (1980, p. 46).

age president and is based on interviews with 44 presidents and those with whom they spend their time.

It can be seen that the average university president is fairly isolated. Most of his contacts center on his inner circle of staff and vice presidents. The isolation is broken mainly by contacts with students. Only 11 percent of the 44 presidents reported daily contacts with faculty members, while 18 to 21 percent reported daily contact with visitors and students.

A factor analysis of these data uncovered four types of college presidents: bureaucrats, intellectuals, egalitarians, and counselors. The bureaucrats spent more of their time with their academic and fiscal vice presidents and their staffs. They tended to communicate to others indirectly through their staffs. These presidents were perceived by faculty members and other administrators as remote, ineffective, inefficient, and closed. The intellectuals spent relatively more of their time with faculty members and other administrators whom they perceived as intellectuals. Egalitarians and counselors spent more time with students and faculty respectively and those individuals involved in student and faculty affairs. They tended to be more highly rated by faculty and students (Astin & Scherrei, 1980).

Communal Relationships. Bradley (1987) found that different sociometric patterns emerged in communes with different types of leaders. Sociograms were constructed of the responses to the questions of whether the relations with each other member in a communal network were loving, optimistic, and exciting. Figure 30.3 shows the systematic differences in sociograms for when the commune's charismatic leader lives in the commune or is an absentee and distant leader. It also gives examples of communes that have and do not have the potential for charismatic leadership to emerge.

The sociometry clarifies a variety of findings. Charismatic leadership, particularly when the leader is in residence, coincides with many more members in affectionate connection with each other. Others are more loving and exciting when the charismatic leader is present. The least communal linkage is to be seen in a commune without the potential for the emergence of a charismatic leader.

Sociometrics of Interaction Potential

Sociograms are sensitive to interaction potential because of their interpersonal attractiveness and familiarity and how they affect leadership.

Effects of Interpersonal Attractiveness. Sociometric analyses and other interpersonal assessment procedures make possible the study of interpersonal attractiveness and its effects. Variables of consequence here include esteem, popularity, likeability, and perceived friendliness. Each of these variables has been found to increase interaction potential and, therefore, attempts to lead and successful leadership. Frequency of contact may increase esteem and less often may decrease such admiration. Some interaction between individuals is usually necessary before they can increase or decrease their evaluation of each other. If the interaction or its effects is unrewarding, mutual esteem between the individuals is likely to lessen.

Individuals are more likely to interact, the more they value each other and the more they value the interaction among them (Bass, 1960). Thus, Blau (1954a) found that the more esteemed members of a law enforcement agency were contacted by the rest of the group more frequently. Conversely, Festinger and Hutte (1954) reported that people tended to talk least to those toward whom they felt indifferent.

Mutual esteem, familiarity, contact, and influence are interdependent. When sorority women chose the seven most and seven least valued members of their sorority, correlations of .48 to .58 emerged between the tendency to be mentioned at all and being selected as a competent leader (Bass, Wurster, Doll, & Clair, 1953). Similar results were obtained with salesmen.[5] The tendency to be mentioned (visibility) correlated positively with sociometrically rated value, ability, and influence as a salesman (Bass, 1960). Bovard (1951b) reported that more pleasant interactions yielded greater attraction among members. But Festinger and Kelley (1951) found that unpleasant interactions resulted in no change in mutual attraction. However, according to Seashore (1954), the longer duration of shared group friendship yielded greater cohesiveness among 228 fac-

[5]See Chapter 11.

Figure 30.3. An Example of the Communion Structure in a Commune from Each Charismatic Type

Loving AND Improving   Loving   Loving AND Exciting

RESIDENT CHARISMATIC COMMUNE

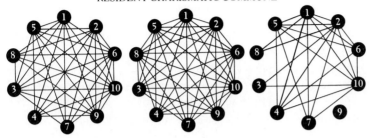

ABSENTEE CHARISMATIC COMMUNE

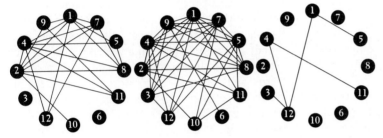

HIGH CHARISMATIC POTENTIAL COMMUNE

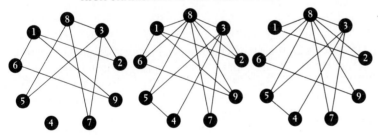

LOW CHARISMATIC POTENTIAL COMMUNE

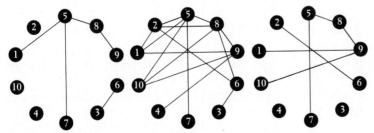

SOURCE: *Excerpt from* Charisma and Social Structure *by Raymond Trevor Bradley. Copyright © 1987 by Raymond Trevor Bradley. Published by Paragon House Publishers.*

tory groups. Similarly, a mean increase in "likeability" among dramatics participants over an 11-week rehearsal period was found by Timmons (1944). If mutual esteem increases interaction, it should also increase effectiveness, and such was found by Van Zelst (1952a). Carpenters and bricklayers were paired either with work partners they chose sociometrically or arbitrarily. Sociometrically assembled pairs were considerably more productive than were pairs who were assembled arbitrarily.

Kelley (1950) presented information to some college students that a visiting instructor would be warm but told other students that the visiting instructor would be cold. The students asked more questions of the "warm" instructor than of the "cold" one. They formed more positive impressions of the "warm" instructor and more negative impressions of the "cold" instructor even though the instructor behaved in the same way in both conditions.

Generally, physically attractive persons tend to make more favorable impressions on others and to be contacted more frequently and for longer periods (Berscheid & Walster, 1969). But the converse has also been seen. Subjects tend to terminate interactions with physically handicapped persons more quickly (Kleck, Ono, & Hastorf, 1966). Similarly, subjects working with supposed mentally ill persons talk less, initiate less conversation, and express opinions that are less representative of their beliefs (Farina, Allen, & Saul, 1966).

Effects of Familiarity. The potential to interact with another particular member increases as the group becomes smaller. Open network connections among members will also increase the likelihood of interaction. In addition, familiarity, as such, breeds interaction, and interaction breeds familiarity. The more intimate or familiar we are with one another, the more likely we are to interact. The more we interact, the more intimate we become (Bass, 1960). Thelen (1954) noted that subgroups that are composed of friends are likely to have more energy to spend in participation than are subgroups composed of strangers.

Intimacy and familiarity are not identical. Caplow and Forman (1950) found that the length of residence in a college community merely increased the number of one's acquaintances rather than the intensity of rela-

tionships with one's neighbors. We can be familiar without being intimate. According to Klauss and Bass (1982), data from a large governmental agency indicated that the familiarity of a colleague with a focal person was associated directly with the frequency of their contact during any given week, as well as with the length of their acquaintanceship. Likewise, intimacy among 75 college students was a function of the frequency and amount of hours of contact among the students (Fischer, 1953).

In studying a rumor's origin and spread, Festinger, Cartwright, Barber, et al. (1947) observed that people are less restrained in talking about such rumors to close friends than to mere acquaintances. Similarly, Hare and Hare (1948) noted a positive correlation between the amount of social activity and the number of family friends among 70 families in a veteran's housing project. Increased congeniality of members was noted by Curtis and Gibbard (1955) with the members' increased experience with each other in both voluntary and compulsory college groups. Likewise, Seashore (1954) found that the members' attraction for each other was greater in factory groups in wich the members were friends for longer periods of time. Finally, Faunce and Beegle (1948) found that cliques at a teenage farmers' camp gradually developed on the basis of newly emerged familiarities, although they were initially formed around homogeneity of age, sex, and country of origin. Bass (1960) advanced two reasons for the increase in interaction as a function of the familiarity and intimacy of members of groups and organizations: (1) members feel more secure in interacting with each other than with strangers and (2) since they can predict each other's actions, they can interact with less difficulty.

Morgan and Sawyer (1967) found that schoolboys prefer strict equality in the distribution of rewards, both with friends and with others. (One sees this preference repeatedly when one is involved in experimental gaming with college students.) Nevertheless, although they prefer equality, friends are willing to accept inequality if one friend thinks that the other friend may want it. But ordinarily friends are less willing to accept inequality. Familiarity with what the other will expect facilitates the ability to reach agreement about how rewards should be distributed.

Effectiveness in the form of goal attainment tends to be associated with increased interaction. If so, effectiveness should also be associated with increased familiarity and/or intimacy. Husband (1940) found that pairs of close friends took less time than pairs of strangers to solve problems in code, puzzles, and arithmetic. Similarly, Goodacre (1953) reported that the members of the more effective of 26 infantry squads in handling field problems had a greater tendency to socialize together after hours. However, Horsfall and Arensberg (1949), in a study of a shoe factory, failed to find any relationship between productivity and the tendencies of its supervisors to interact frequently.

Klauss and Bass (1982) reported that for 577 governmental professionals, their colleagues thought that the more familiar focal persons were more trustworthy, informative, and dynamic than were the less familiar focal persons. Colleagues also felt more satisfied in their relations with these more familiar focal persons. A correlation of .27 emerged between familiarity and perceived effectiveness of relations. But the length of acquaintanceship between the colleagues and the focal persons was unrelated to these measures of effective communication. A higher frequency of interaction between colleagues and focal persons, however, correlated with satisfaction and effectiveness but not with the colleagues' judgments of the trustworthiness and informativeness of the focal persons.

Effects of Similarity. Individuals interact more with those who are like them than those who are unlike them (Bass, 1960). Thus, Pfiffner (1951) observed that employees of the same age, physical attractiveness, marital status, education, and race tend to group together. Strangers first associate on the basis of their homogeneity of sex, age, and place of origin, according to Faunce and Beegle's (1948) study of campers. Likewise, Caplow and Forman (1950) found that interaction among neighbors in a university community was greater if families were homogeneous in occupation, number of children in the family, length of residence, and type of housing. Similarly, in the more turbulent neighborhoods of Chicago, leaders of 181 public and private human service organizations who had similar racial or educational backgrounds were more likely to establish cooperative relations with one another than

were those from different backgrounds (Galaskiewicz & Shatin, 1981).

Effects of Status. T. Burns (1954) reported that middle managers spent more time with superiors than with subordinates, while the reverse was true for first-level supervisors. Likewise, Guest (1956) and Piersol (1958) reported that first-level supervisors spent more time with their subordinates than with their superiors. Zajonc and Wolfe (1966) found that managers in high-level positions and those performing staff functions maintained the widest range of formal contacts within the organization, but these informal contacts did not seem to follow a distinct pattern associated with hierarchical level or function.

Formal versus Informal Organization. Stogdill (1949) asked members of organizations to estimate the amount of time they actually spent with other members. Sociometric charts of these working relationships were superimposed on the formal organizational chart to determine the correspondence between the formally specified and the actual working relationships. Such a determination would make it possible to diagnose communication and interactional problems within the organization. Such a chart is shown in Figure 30.4. It should be noted that in this figure, the vice president, rather than the president, is the focus of working interactions. Department heads A and B also tend to be foci of interactions. Department head C is bypassed by his subordinates, who do not interact much with each other, which suggests that the department head is not an effective leader of his group. With such a pattern of interactions, it is apparent that coordination is effected either by the vice president or by the cross-departmental contacts among section heads. The dominant trend of contact here is upward rather than downward. This trend is consistent with the commonly observed latent pressure to communicate upward more than downward. Such efforts to initiate interactions with superiors may serve more to reduce anxiety and to increase feelings of security and less to communicate about issues of work (A. Kadushin, 1968; Schwartzbaum & Gruenfeld, 1969).

Stogdill (1951a) plotted the number of times each of 22 officers in a small U.S. navy organization was mentioned as a work partner by his peers. Those officers

Figure 30.4. Sociometric Diagram Superimposed on Organization Chart

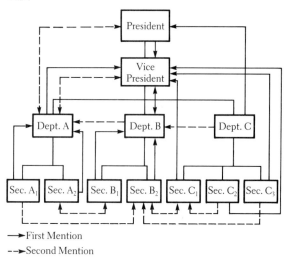

→ First Mention
-→ Second Mention

who occupied high-level positions tended to mention subordinates and outsiders more frequently and superiors less frequently than did officers in lower-level positions. The same trend was observed in the scores for the number of mentions received. High levels of responsibility were related to more total mentions given and received and to more mentions received from members inside one's own unit and from superiors. Scope of authority was not significantly related to any sociometric scores. Those who delegated most freely tended to be mentioned most frequently as work partners by members inside their own units.

To conclude, sociometric preferences for contact, communication, and work map the actual patterns of influence in an organization. They may be quite independent of the authority structure and are more likely to correspond with friendship, familiarity, and mutual esteem. Sociometric descriptions of actual contacts, communicants, and work partners do the same.

Leadership and Psychosocial Distance

Differences in status can be either emphasized or minimized in the search for organizational effectiveness. Status differences can be accented by the physical characteristics of one's office, dress, and privileges, as

well as more subtle social calibrations, such as the use of "Sir" or "Madam" by a younger person addressing an older one. Status differences can be minimized by uniform offices, dress, and privileges, as well as by casual speech, familiar address, self-disclosure, and humor. Claims of common views, common leadership, cooperativeness, sympathy, and understanding also reduce the perceived differences in status (Drake & Moberg, 1986).

Seeman (1960) studied teachers' and principals' perceptions of the differences in their status in 27 public school systems and found that teachers who perceived wide differences between their status and that of the principal tended to describe the principal as being high in changeable behavior and leadership but low in domination. Principals who rated themselves high in status and saw sharp differences between their status and that of their teachers were described by their teachers as communicative, changeable in behavior, and effective as leaders. In an earlier study, Seeman (1950) found that teachers who favored wide differences in status in society and in organizations tended to prefer a directive rather than a group-oriented style of leadership. The number of teachers with these preferences was considerably greater than expected.[6] Rettig, Despres, and Pasamanick (1960) obtained results which indicated that persons in professional positions who perceived wide differences in status among various occupations tended to attach greater importance to personal freedom than did those who perceived narrow differences.

Differences in status can give rise to physical, psychological, and social distancing. McKenzie and Strongman (1981) compared the way British police superintendents, inspectors, and constables placed figurines to indicate how each of them would be positioned for an ordinary conversation between them. The figurines were placed at a greater distance for conversations with those of higher status (the superintendents). The superintendents then set up placements with larger distances between them and those of lower status.

Psychosocial distance in sentiment appears to be increased for the high-status person who has coercive

---

[6]This number has fallen substantially since 1950, as evidenced by the increasing demand of teachers to participate in the design of curricula and the governance of schools.

power over the low-status person and decreased for the low-status person. The prison guard distances himself from the prisoner (Zimbardo, 1973) but the hostage appears to come closer in sentiment to the terrorist captor (Eckholm, 1985).

Controversy continues about whether such social distance is necessary or desirable for leadership and organizational effectiveness. Social and behavioral theorists, such as J. R. Gibb (1964) and Argyris (1962), saw greater costs to leaders and organizations in which psychosocial distance is maintained. More virtue was seen in reducing the psychosocial distance among organizational members and in maintaining close, personal relations among those of different status and at various levels in the organization. On the other hand, Martin and Sims (1956), Jameson (1945), and Pfiffner (1951) argued strongly for maintaining such psychosocial distance to promote organizational effectiveness.

In a questionnaire on what respondents thought was required to succeed in business, administered to 107 MBA students, Bass (1968c) found a factor endorsing the maintenance of social distance and prerogatives. This factor was correlated with the students' perceptions of the importance of personal gain as a motivator to students with strong economic values and to students with less human or social concerns, as revealed in simulated budgeting decisions. Working managers saw somewhat less utility in maintaining such social distance than did the MBA students. Also less supportive of maintaining social distance were those managers with human relations training (Bass, 1970b).

Advantages of Maintaining Distance

Proponents of the maintenance of psychosocial distance from followers suggest that leaders thereby enhance their power and effectiveness. Leaders do so by limiting access to themselves and accenting the difference between their status, esteem, ability, and power and those of their followers. They avoid personal self-disclosures and intimacy with their followers and employ various symbolic separations. (Emperors, sultans, and kings vied with each other as to the height of their thrones above their audience chambers, so they could literally talk down to their subjects from "on high.") Such social distance may either promote the legitimacy

of the leader and follower roles or be a consequence of it.[7]

By maintaining psychosocial distance, a leader can remain impartial, task directed, and free of emotional concern for individual followers. A general can order individual groups of soldiers to a high risk of death for the sake of expected victory. A manager who would have difficulty discharging an incompetent personal secretary might find it easier to lay off a hundred employees several levels below in the hierarchy.

Barnard (1946a) suggested that the maintenance of psychosocial distance in an organization serves several other functions. It may help coordination, protects members from the need to compete for leadership, and acknowledges the importance of the individual's special contribution. It also protects the integrity of the individual in that it acknowledges certain rights, privileges, and obligations that pertain to his or her position. Furthermore, it obviates the necessity of unfavorable comparisons between individuals who differ in training and ability.

Social distance can reduce the amount of extraneous talking between employees that interferes with their productivity. Such extraneous talking may, on occasion, replace work and thus have distracting and deleterious effects on the productive efforts of individual members. Thus, Ingham, Levinger, Graves, and Peckham (1974) observed that individuals did not work quite as hard when they were paired with one or two others than when they worked alone.

Costs of Maintaining Distance

The costs of psychosocial distancing can be high. They can include more defensive behavior by followers, loss of contact, poorer quality of communications, the poorer selection of goals, less commitment to the group's goals, incipient revolt, and organizational rigidity. Barnard (1946a) observed that psychosocial distance can limit the adaptability of the organization, distort the system of distributive justice, and exalt the symbolic function at the expense of efficient performance. In the same vein, Reykowski (1982) inferred that

[7] See Chapter 15. Conversely, when presidents such as Jimmy Carter walk down the street in their inaugural parades or such as Mikhail Gorbachev, move into a crowd to chat they are ceremoniously reducing social as well as physical distance.

the more socially distant from us are other persons, the less is our tendency to maintain equal exchange relationships with them. One may dehumanize psychosocially distant persons and show less concern for justice in dealing with them.

There seems to be some optimal psychosocial distance between the leader and his or her subordinates. Carp, Vitola, and McLanathan (1963) found that effective leaders had a perceptual set that enabled them to maintain optimal psychological distance from subordinates—neither so close that they were hampered by emotional ties nor so distant that they lost emotional contact. Consistent with this finding, in writing about what it takes to be a successful captain of a ship in the U.S. Navy, Mack and Konetzni (1982, p. 3) described this optimum:

> The successful commanding officer ... must learn to become as one with his wardroom and his crew; yet, at the same time, he must remain above and apart. This unique relationship has been the subject of study and story for centuries. It changes; yet it is timeless. It is a skill that must be mastered in turn by each commander if he is to carry out his task with success.

To reduce the social distance between a senior executive and operating employees, to move it closer to the optimum, the executive practices "walk-around" management. Going further, General Joseph Stilwell greatly reduced the psychosocial distance between himself and his enlisted personnel. Stilwell was known for his tendency to wear an unmarked private's uniform, lead infantry marches on foot, and eat in the enlisted men's mess (Tuchman, 1971).

Variations in Preferences and Effects

The optimal social distance between the leader and the follower appears to vary from one leader-follower relationship to another. Differences in preferences will occur for both leaders and followers. The effects of psychosocial distance depend on such personal factors as the leader's and followers' motivation to achieve and their degree of friendship. The effects of distance also depend on situational factors like the favorableness of the situation to the leader.

Effects of the Motivation to Achieve. W. W. Burke (1965) studied different combinations of leaders and followers, each differentiated by their scores for social distance and the need to achieve. In a group situation that varied in tenseness, followers with a strong need to achieve rated the situation as more tense under a socially close leader than did followers with a strong need to achieve who were under a socially distant leader. Followers with a weak need to achieve rated the situation as less tense under socially close than under socially distant leaders. Followers with a strong need to achieve rated socially close leaders as more autocratic than they did socially distant leaders. Followers with a weak need to achieve rated the socially distant leaders as more autocratic. At the same time, regardless of the followers' needs for achievement, socially distant leaders were rated more effective in a coding task and socially close leaders were rated more effective in a human relations task. Overall, followers with a socially distant leader considered their groups to be less productive and less satisfying than did those with a socially close leader.

Networks

Social distance and status differences can be increased or decreased by the network available or imposed. A network is a set of people connected by friendship, influence, work, or communications.[8] Within organizations, it is a reciprocating set of relationships that stabilizes the manager's world and gives it predictability (Sayles, 1964). A manager's network is likely to include vertical, horizontal, and diagonal segments with mutual contacts with his or her boss and superior of the boss, with his or her subordinates and their subordinates, and many other colleagues at the same level or at higher and lower levels. It is also likely to include individuals outside the organization, such as consultants, clients, and suppliers. Network analysis is the study of the links that bind such people and their positions.

Networks can be formed in a variety of ways and for a variety of purposes. Clearinghouses of information can serve as the centers of networks of influence. The

---

[8]Networks obviously can be mapped in sociograms as produced by sociometry.

insurance industry encourages social responsibility and community leadership by its individual member companies in this manner (Karson, 1979). Brown and Detterman's (1987) longitudinal study of the community networks of leaders in a large metropolitan center found that a formal leadership program increased contacts among the white but not among the black participants. New networks emerged and old ones were strengthened for addressing community problems. Underlying the networks were the social establishment, political leaders, business leaders, and community activists.

The vertical, diagonal, and lateral dyads, each of which may be formal or informal, make up the organizational network such as shown in Figure 30.5. The dyadic relations particularly important to the focal manager are displayed. It can be seen here that relations between other members of the organization may be important to a third member. For instance, the dyadic relations between a director and his associate director may have consequences for a staff scientist, who has no direct connection with either person.

A more powerful analysis of networks may be provided by triadic analysis (Holland & Leinhardt, 1976). An analysis for three members could show, for instance, two members linked to a third, but the third member not reciprocating. Bradley (1987) reported systematic differences in which the type of triads appearing in communes were a function of whether the charismatic leader of the commune was in residence or was an absentee leader.

The typical supervisor's network of communications is composed of links to his or her subordinates, to one or more peers and superiors, and to outsiders, as well as to libraries; data bases; computers; and oral, written, and electronic communication. At least one-third of the supervisor's time is spent mainly in face-to-face contact with subordinates (Jablin, 1985), but these links may not be seen as important and challenging as those with outsiders (Whitely, 1984).

Importance of Networks

Ordinarily, a manager's network operates on a transactional exchange relationship. Managers get information, services, and resources in exchange for promises, returned favors, support, and recognition (Kaplan & Mazique, 1983). Nonetheless, networks are important to both transformational and transactional leaders. For instance, old networks are broken up and new ones are established in a changing organization. The transformational leader manages "to foster a new set of social networks with new flows and ties" (Tichy & Devanna, 1986, p. 193). Managers also develop networks of lateral reciprocal exchanges with their peers. Such trading connections enable them to get their own department's work done (Kaplan & Mazique, 1983).

Networking supports one's image in the organization. Managers earn esteem by linking themselves to winning causes (Kotter, 1979), and such alliances promote their advancement. Few managers can function without the linkage of their networks (McCall, Morrison, & Hanman, 1978). With the exponential increase in knowledge and the knowledge worker, communication networks have taken on an ever-increasing role of importance in the success or failure of organizations (Cleveland, 1985).

Effects of Network Centrality on Leadership

The performance and the effects of leaders depend on the leaders' centrality in the networks, their domain of influence, and their contacts and connections in the networks (McElroy & Schrader, 1987). In an analysis of

Figure 30.5. Organizational Network

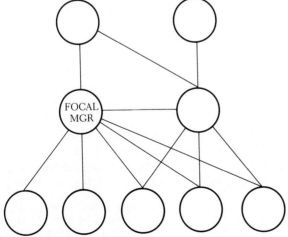

SOURCE: *Adapted from Graen and Scandura (1987, p. 203), by permission of JAI Press Inc., Greenwich, Conn.*

140 full-time nonsupervisory employees of a newspaper publishing company, Brass (1984) showed that perceived influence and promotion to a supervisory position depended on one's location in the networks of work flow, communication, and friendship. Contacts beyond the normal work requirements were important in the acquisition of influence, particularly by technical core employees. Also important to perceived influence were the critical importance of one's position to operations and one's centrality in the networks.

Insko, Thibaut, Moehle, et al. (1980) showed that when 432 students were organized into trading groups, the group through which all trade had to be channeled made the most money and emerged as the leading group. Such functional centrality was also seen to be important to leadership by Tropp and Landers (1979), who examined the relationship of emergent leadership to the frequency of passes to field-hockey teammates. Spatial centrality was not as important as functional centrality to effective plays. And although the leader of a jazz ensemble is its central figure, his role is tempered by the number of criticisms received and disagreements on interpretations, which affect the quality of the performance (Voyer & Faulkner, 1986).

Open and Closed Channels. The mutual influence of leaders and followers depends on how open or closed the channels of communication are between them. Thus, those who have access to the political leaders and decision makers in a community are more likely to be influential in the community (Bockman & Gayk, 1977). Again, group members can influence each other more readily if they are in open communication with each other.

The openness of a channel between superior and subordinate must be two way. That is, both must be perceived as being ready to communicate and to listen (Redding, 1972). Both verbal and nonverbal behavior (such as eye gaze, posture, tone of voice, and facial expressions) can signal such readiness or lack of it (Tjosvold, 1984b). The subordinates' satisfaction with their work and with their superiors is strongly related to their perception of the possibilities of open communication with their superior (Pincus, 1986).

The direction of the flow of information in a channel between the superior and the subordinate and the superior's style of relating to the subordinate will depend on who initially has more information that is relevant to their joint task. As reported in Chapter 22, Shapira (1976) confirmed that if the superior initially possesses more information than the subordinate about what needs to be done, the superior will be more *directive* with the subordinate; if the superior initially possesses less information about what needs to be done, the superior will be more consultative or *participative.*[9]

The use of a channel appears to depend more on its openness and accessibility than on the perceived quality of the information that can be obtained from it (Allen, 1966) or the ease of its use (Gerstberger & Allen, 1968). Thus, neighborhood leaders who have common membership in different organizations tend to have more open cooperative relations with one another (Galaskiewicz & Shatin, 1981). More upward communication channels will be used in hierarchical organizations if trust is present and aspirations for mobility are high (Level & Johnson, 1978; O'Reilly & Roberts, 1974). Horizontal flows of unsolicited information will be increased by reductions in organizational constraint (Albaum, 1964) and increases in the organization's technological certainty (Randolph & Finch, 1977).

Network Preferences. To accommodate their own influence and work preferences, U.S. presidents differed in the networks of staff assistants they constructed. Dwight D. Eisenhower's immediate staff reported indirectly to him through his chief of staff, Sherman Adams. John F. Kennedy was the center of a network of his immediate staff. Lyndon B. Johnson used the telephone extensively to extend his network of direct contacts. Jimmy Carter created groups of staff assistants, each of whom dealt comprehensively and independently with a single different source, and he related directly to each group. Ronald Reagan, like Eisenhower, depended heavily on a chief of staff to screen and funnel the staff's recommendations.

The self-interests of the senders and receivers of information will contribute to distorting or shutting

---

[9]As defined in Chapters 22 and 23, *direction* (italicized) refers only to giving orders with or without explanation. Direction (romanized) includes ordering, persuading, and manipulating. *Participation* (italicized) refers only to sharing in the decision process. Participation (romanized) includes consulting, sharing, and delegating.

down channels by tactics of overloading, circumventing, or reinterpreting the organization's policies and regulations (P. J. Frost, 1986). Leaders can informally expand their networks to increase their own influence. For instance, Admiral Hyman Rickover greatly increased his control and influence by building a large network of his nuclear-trained officers, all of whom reported directly to him each week and bypassed the official channels (Polmar & Allen, 1981).

Effective Communications

Systematic effects on the success of the leader and the effectiveness of those led emerge as a consequence of the communication pattern fostered by the leader, policy, motivation and training.

Leadership and Styles of Communication. An important aspect of a manager's leadership style is the way he or she communicates with colleagues and subordinates. Thus, under authoritarian managers, networks with restricted communications take less time to plan than do groups led with less direction and structure. However, the results of the planning are likely to be less efficient in accomplishing the required tasks (Snadowsky, 1972).

Table 30.2 shows the correlations between leadership and communication styles that Klauss and Bass

(1982) obtained when 71 subordinates described the leadership and communication styles of their 28 focal managers. It can be seen that participative leadership[10] correlated highly with being seen as an informal, frank, open, and two-way communicator—a careful transmitter and a careful listener. Trustworthiness and informativeness, but not dynamism, were also highly correlated with participative styles of leadership. *Directive* leadership was less highly correlated with careful transmission, being open and frank and a careful listener, but not at all with being informal and a careful listener. Dynamism was highly correlated with *directiveness* but at the expense of trustworthiness. Being negotiative and manipulative was unrelated to the style of communication.

Posner and Kouzes (1988b) obtained even stronger linkages between transformational leadership and the communication styles of 146 senior managers according to their 998 subordinates. Transformational leadership was measured by the Leadership Practices Inventory (Kouzes & Posner, 1987). The five factors (challenging the process, inspiring a shared vision, enabling others to act, modeling the way, and encouraging the heart) correlated between .40 and .68 with the trustworthiness, informativeness, and dynamism of the

[10]Consulting, *participating*, and delegating.

Table 30.2 Correlations between Communication Styles, Credibility, and Leadership Styles as Seen by 71 Subordinates of 28 Focal Managers[a]

Communication Style and Credibility	Style of Leadership				
	Directive	Negotiative	Consultative	Participative	Delegative
Communication style					
Careful transmitter	.37	.08	.63	.59	.64
Open and two way	.36	.06	.70	.65	.61
Frank	.42	.04	.50	.45	.36
Careful listener	.15	−.08	.51	.55	.59
Informal	.18	−.01	.53	.55	.55
Credibility					
Trustworthy	.19	−.03	.57	.54	.57
Informative	.31	−.05	.59	.58	.63
Dynamic	.49	−.08	.38	.25	.14

[a]Underlined values are significant at $p < .01$.
Source: Adapted from Klauss and Bass (1982).

communication styles, as measured by Klauss and Bass (1982). For instance, inspirational envisioning correlated .56 with trustworthiness, .58 with informativeness, and .68 with dynamism.

Effective Leadership. Ordinarily, open, easy, ready communications contribute not only to the extent to which the leader and the group can influence each other but to the extent to which they will be effective. On the basis of research with B-29 aircrews, Roby and Forgays (1953) argued that crews who could send information faster to "decision stations" could solve problems faster. In a report on maintenance in four medium bomber wings, Bates (1953) inferred that in the two better-performing maintenance systems, there was more contact between subgroups. The system's leaders were usually involved in such contacts. Torrance (1954b) noted that plane crews in simulated survival exercises were most likely to "survive" if communications were resumed among scattered crew members, leading to a clarification of the situation. Again, such resumption of communication was usually connected to the initiatives of the formal or emerging leadership.

The leadership is often responsible for the ease with which members of a group can communicate with each other. Thus, O'Reilly (1977) found that decision making by subordinates was improved if they could readily make use of their supervisors as sources of information. Such easy communication correlated highly with the described effectiveness of 500 work groups (Bass, 1954b) and for teams engaged in naval ordinance testing (Weschler & Shepard, 1954). Leaders who schedule regular meetings with their groups make for more effective group operations. Thus, Dyer and Lambert (1953) found that in two medium bomber wings, regular meetings of personnel were scheduled in the wing with a better record of performance and effectiveness but not in the less effective wing. In addition, the executive officer of the superior wing was a more active communicator of information to others in the wing. Likewise, Habbe (1952) noted that in an individual plant with regularly scheduled meetings of work groups, workers felt freer to talk about their problems with the foremen and favored more such meetings than did workers of a plant without such regular meetings.

Generally, the imposition of a complex hierarchical structure tends to impede the flow of information, particularly the flow upward. The formal channels may need to be bypassed to reduce the difficulties of communication (Wilensky, 1967). The formal authority structure supposedly enables the necessary flow of technical information, but an informal structure may be needed to increase the ease of the flow, according to a study of an R & D organization by Allen and Cohen (1969). Upward communication that must be relayed through intermediate levels often suffers greatly from filtering by officials at these intermediate levels. The problem is particularly severe for U.S. presidents; the advice and judgment of foreign-area experts at the working level is filtered by intermediaries to give the presidents more of what the intermediaries believe is consistent with the presidents' beliefs and stated policies than with the realistic facts about pending crises (L. R. Anderson, 1983).

Communication and Successful Performance. The successful performance of social service professionals, industrial managers, and military officers[11] was found by Klauss and Bass (1982) to relate to aspects of the way they were seen to communicate. However, the results depended on whether the questionnaire descriptions were obtained from their subordinates, peers, or supervisors. The more successful social service professionals were seen as more open and two-way communicators by their subordinates and peers but less trustworthy by their supervisors. The more successful industrial managers were described by their supervisors as more careful transmitters, more frank, and more informative. The more successful military officers were described by their subordinates as more careful listeners and as more open and two way in their communications but were seen as less careful transmitters by their peers.

Successful leadership hinges on access to information.[12] Those leaders who successfully influenced community opinion about public affairs, education, and family planning among 450 households in a South African black township were found by Heath and Bekker (1986) to have greater exposure to newspapers and tele-

---

[11]Success was measured by the extent to which their salaries were greater than predicted by their age, sex, education, and years of service and by the size of the operations for which they were responsible.
[12]See Chapter 7.

vision than were those who were not influential. In comparison to the nonleaders, the leaders were more active in interpersonal communication than were those who were not leaders.[13] The network opinion leaders also had more contact with white change agents.

Media of Communication

Networks may be built on consistent patterns of oral, written, or electronic contacts or combinations thereof. The medium will make a difference in what happens and how things happen.

Oral versus Written Communication. Channels of oral communication are favored over channels based on written messages. Face-to-face meetings are favored over telephone conversations (Lee & Lee, 1956). Oral communication is promoted by the cultural norms of information sharing in the organization. Written communications are substituted in the absence of such norms (Dewhirst, 1971b). Crucial information can be communicated orally through successive channels more readily than can routine information, which is better tranmitted in writing. Thus, Davis (1968b) found that routine information on parking was poorly communicated orally down the managerial hierarchy, while information on a production-oriented layoff was very well communicated orally. Nevertheless, in a survey of 72 business supervisors, Level (1972) found that in dealing with each of 10 problems at the workplace, the supervisors thought that oral communication followed by written communication was likely to be most effective.

Electronic Communication Networks. When the oral and written channels are joined by electronic communication and information systems, the network of the individual organizational member is greatly expanded. The time spans between interchanges are greatly decreased, and the overload of information becomes a much greater problem than does the underload. Although the concern for privacy and security are heightened, some of the problems that are due to organizational distance decrease. With the filtering and transmission of information by electronic mail, delays are eliminated. What originates at a high managerial level in the organization can quickly reach those at the lowest managerial level. Likewise, electronic mail provides instant contact between physically distant employees at the same organization level.

Fulk, Schmitz, and Ryn (1989) found that more electronic mail was received by R & D supervisors than nonsupervisors. It also had more impact on the supervisors. But electronic mail was more likely to be originated by those with keyboard skills. It was more likely to be sent to known users and if use was encouraged by company policy. Electronic communications and teleconferencing eliminate a good deal of the nonverbal cues that help clarify the information transmitted and the support for continued interaction among senders and receivers. Nonverbal cues, such as eye contact, dress, facial expression, and gestures, that are available in face-to-face interactions are missing. What are likely to be affected when face-to-face interactions and their nonverbal cues are absent are the clarification of the transmitted information and contextual embellishments (Birdwhistell, 1970). With telecommunication, senders may be less inhibited because their feelings can be disguised more readily.

Siegel, Dubrovsky, Kiesler, and McGuire (1986) compared the efficiency of communication, participation, and interpersonal behavior of 144 undergraduates in 3-member groups who discussed their career choices in one of 3 ways: face to face, by computer mail, or mediated by computer. When the groups were linked by computer, the members made fewer remarks than they did face to face and took longer to make their group decisions. The amount of participation in the discussion was more evenly distributed, and the members' behavior was more uninhibited (the members felt freer to use strong and inflammatory expressions). More overall influence appeared to have occurred in the computer-mediated condition in that the groups' decisions shifted farther away from the members' initial individual choices than did the decisions that followed face-to-face discussions. Rawlins (1983) found that with audio-only teleconferencing by 20 4-person groups the assigned leaders did not retain as much of their leadership roles as they did in face-to-face meetings. Rather, the leadership roles were more widely shared if the groups had a teleconference without a face-to-face meeting.

Closed-circuit television comes much closer to face-

[13]See Chapter 6.

to-face communication in its ability to supply the non-verbal cues that Mehrabian (1968a), for instance, found so important. Mehrabian concluded that facial expression ordinarily accounts for half of what is communicated. When eye contact is low or absent, individuals come across as less positive, warm, and friendly (Kleck & Nuessle, 1968). Short (1973), Craig and Jull, (1974) and Rawlins (1983) all reported that face-to-face problem solving took longer than did problem solving by means of audio telecommunications.

Although closed-circuit television makes more of the visual nonverbal cues possible, there are still differences between it and face-to-face meetings as media for linking members in problem-solving tasks. Televised conferencing is less likely to provide the same amount of opportunities for social feedback, sociopsychological distance is likely to be greater among members, and the ability of individual members to control the flow of communication is limited. But the evidence of the differential effects of face-to-face meetings and televised conferencing is mixed. Strickland, Guild, Barefoot, and Paterson (1978) found that when members of a problem-solving group are linked by closed-circuit television networks, rather than by face-to-face meetings, they are less likely to agree on a leader. However, Nicol (1983) reported that a clearer task-leadership hierachy emerged for 20 groups who held closed-circuit television conferences than for 13 groups who met face to face to solve a problem. No differences were seen in the extent to which socioemotional leaders clearly emerged in the two media. Television conferencing comes still closer to a face-to-face meeting with the use of FAX for the instantaneous exchange of documents.

Closed-circuit television can be organized into different kinds of more restricted or less restricted channels of communication. For example, Pagery and Chapanis (1983) compared problem solving by closed-circuit television when central switching made it possible for only one participant to talk at a time and an arrangement in which participants at each station were freer to intervene. Although members in the groups under the central-switching arrangement took longer to solve problems and used fewer and longer messages than did those in the less controlled condition, there was little difference in the effects of the two arrangements on the leadership processes.

Effects of Group or Organizational Task

Networks of communication in an organization can result from the demands of authority, the demands for information, the demands of particular tasks, the bonds of friendship, or the more formal status characteristics of organizations. The purpose served by a network will affect how information is transmitted within it. For example, communication in an authority network will typically be more formalized than will communication in a friendship network (Bass & Ryterband, 1979). Heise and Miller (1951) concluded that the task faced by the network is a determinant of the leadership and the group behavior that are likely to occur. The uniqueness of the solution, the number of decisions to be made, and the amount of previous structure are all involved. For example, G. B. Cohen (1969) studied groups who performed an information-processing task and found that centrality facilitated their performance most when the tasks were highly interdependent.

Leadership in Experimental Communication Networks

Communication networks circumscribe who can communicate with whom, thereby affecting interactions, the group's performance, and the potential leadership process. The control of the channels of communication among members of a group has been used widely to examine systematically the effects on performance and leadership of the network of arrangements provided. Bavelas (1950) originated a laboratory experiment to study the effects of systematic changes in who among five participants could communicate directly with each of the other participants. Bavelas dealt poker hands to the five members of a group. The members could communicate with each other only by written messages. The object was to select the one best poker hand from the combined cards of all the members. The groups differed in communication channels, as shown in Figure 30.6.

In the circle arrangement, the members had an equal opportunity to send messages to and receive messages from the member in the position to their left and the member in the position to their right. In the chain, members in peripheral positions could send messages

Figure 30.6. Communications Networks

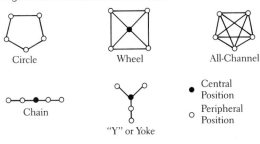

Circle   Wheel   All-Channel

Chain   "Y" or Yoke

● Central Position

○ Peripheral Position

Bavelas networks

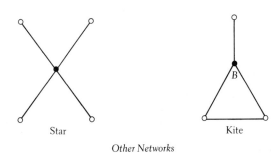

Star   Kite

Other Networks

through intermediaries toward the position in the center. In the wheel, four of the members had equal opportunities to send messages to the person in the center and could also communicate with adjacent members. In the Y, three members could send messages to a fourth person in the central position, but the fifth member was required to communicate with the member in the center through another member. In the star, all communications had to flow through the central position. The kite added an open channel between two of the peripheral positions. These networks contrasted with the all-channel network in which any member could send messages to any other member.

The Standard Design

Subsequently, Leavitt (1951) developed a standardized task that was free of the potential bias that could occur from differences among members who knew how to play poker. At the beginning of each trial, each of five participants was given a card on which five of six symbols were printed; one symbol was missing from each card, and each card lacked a different symbol. The problem each time was to have the group discover and record the one symbol that everyone had in common. The participants were seated around a circular table and were separated from each other by five vertical partitions. They passed messages to each other through open interconnecting slots—the only way of communicating among participants. Leavitt analyzed the pattern of messages that developed and the speed with which the problem was solved when a particular network of channels was open for use.[14] Results are reported below.

Centrality of Individuals of Networks. Bavelas (1950) developed an index of network centrality for the different communication networks shown in Figure 30.6. Centrality was seen to be greatest in the wheel and decreased in the following order: Y, chain, and circle. The star network was regarded as more centralized than was the kite network.

Individual centrality can exist in three ways. A person in a network can be more spatially central, more central in terms of the exchange of information by the network, or more central in terms of the decisions of the network. The greater the inequalities in the opportunities for different members of the network to communicate, the more the members will differ in centrality.

Ordinarily, central positions and those who occupy them have greater power because of their greater access to information and to the control of its distribution. This power makes those in central positions more influential with those who occupy peripheral positions in the Bavelas-Leavitt networks—a finding that was confirmed in numerous studies.[15] The network member who occupied a position of centrality was most likely to emerge as the leader. However, Abrahamson (1969) removed the partitions that prevented group members from seeing each other. In the face-to-face situation, central members emerged as leaders only when no dominance owing to personality was present. Abrahamson concluded that an individual's centrality contributes to his or her emergence as a leader only

[14]Reviews of the method and outcomes of research can be found in Cartwright and Zander (1960), Glanzer and Glaser (1961), and Mulder (1963).
[15]See, for example, Cohen, Bennis, and Wolkon (1961); M. L. Goldberg (1955); and Shaw, Rothschild, and Strickland (1957).

when physical isolation prevents personality factors from having an impact.

The star and Y networks are most centralized because one member has a central position and all the others occupy peripheral positions. The circle and all-channel networks are least centralized, since all members have equal opportunities to communicate.

Effects of Network Centralization. Centralization of a network has important effects on the network's performance. Bales (1953) observed that since the group member who was able to control the communication network was most likely to emerge as the leader, the emergence of leadership was more frequent in the star network (Figure 30.6), with its one central position, than in other networks (see also, Shaw & Rothschild, 1956).

Leavitt (1951) found that speed in solving problems, agreement on who is the leader, satisfaction with the group, and development of an organization were highly correlated with the centrality index of the communication network. That is, it took the least time to solve problems, agree on leadership, and so on when there was one clear central position, such as in the Y. It took more time in the chain and the most time in the circle, in which there was no central position. The circle network experienced difficulty in developing a stable structure for problem solving. However, Burgess (1969) showed that differences in the performance of the various structures of networks tended to disappear once groups had worked under a given arrangement for a time and had attained a steady state—particularly if contingent reinforcement was used to influence their performance.

Development of Centralization. Consistent informal roles emerged within the restrictions of the formal networks, more so in some networks, less so in others. Little informality was possible in the wheel network. The highly restricted wheel network rapidly developed a stable hierarchy that conformed to the formal demands of the system. In that network, the central person sent out information to all participants once he or she had received information from all. In contrast, all-channel groups could display much more variety in the informal organizations they built, particularly in distributing answers. Some evolved a system in which

each person sent answers to every other member, while others developed patterns identical to the wheel or to the chain. Those groups that were formally restricted to the circle network had the greatest difficulty in developing and maintaining a single formal pattern of communications. Over many trials, they tended to fluctuate in the particular patterns of communication they used, especially in exchanging answers (Guetzkow & Simon, 1955).

Usually, a network that began with a central position or informally developed a centralizing procedure was able to complete the task faster with fewer errors (Mulder, 1960). Thus, Cohen, Robinson, and Edwards (1969), who studied groups who were required to solve experimental problems of organization found that centralized problem-solving systems were developed by all subgroups in both the wheel and the all-channel networks. However, such centralization was likely to give rise to less-satisfying peripheral jobs, as well as less opportunity for members as a whole to modify their own organization, to learn about how the organization operated, to be flexible, and to be creative when new challenges were imposed on the group (Bass & Ryterband, 1979). More will be said about this later.

Roles and Role Structures. Persons who occupy central positions carry out different tasks from those who occupy peripheral positions. For example, only the person in the central position spends a great deal of time compiling data, forming solutions, and transmitting answers. Those in peripheral positions spend more of their time receiving information (Guetzkow & Simon, 1955).

Using 76 5-person groups with Leavitt designs, Guetzkow (1960, 1961) found that 3 types of roles and role structure tended to emerge. The central person tended to receive information, formulate answers, and send answers. The peripheral person sent his or her own missing information and received answers. The re-layer passed on his or her and other information and relayed answers. The wheel and all-channel networks tended to develop 2-level structures consisting of a central person and 4 peripheral persons. One-third of the circle groups developed 3-level structures consisting of a central person and 4 peripheral persons. One-third of the circle groups developed 3-level structures consisting of a central person, 2 relayers, and 2 peripheral persons. Two-thirds of the circle groups did not develop organized structures of mutually supporting roles. Groups with differentiated role structures solved the problem faster than did those that remained undifferentiated. The central persons and the relayers perceived the structure more accurately than did the peripheral persons in all except the all-channel groups. They also sent more messages containing proposals for the organization and nominated themselves more often as leaders.

Stability of Leadership. A. M. Cohen (1962) observed greater continuity of leadership in communication networks when members could elect their leaders. Cohen and Bennis (1961) studied groups with changing structures. They found that groups that had changed from a wheel to a circle network tended to organize themselves into a more efficient chain system, but with different leaders than were present in the wheel network. Also, networks with elected leaders retained the same leaders longer than did those that were not permitted to elect leaders.

Central versus Peripheral Involvement. Zander and Forward (1968) found that participants who were in central positions developed a stronger desire for their groups' success than did participants in peripheral positions. Participants whose need to avoid personal failure exceeded their need for personal success tended to become more concerned about their group's performance than were participants whose needs were reversed in strength.

Centrality and Satisfaction. Centralized groups typically have one member at their hub. In routine tasks, the more centralized the structure, the more efficiently members solve problems, but the less those in the more numerous peripheral positions are satisfied (Cohen, 1964). Shaw and Rothschild (1956) found that the occupant of the central position in a star design was more greatly satisfied; otherwise, the members' dissatisfaction did not differ in the various network structures. Using the same designs, Shaw, Rothschild, and Strickland (1957) determined that the satisfaction of members was a joint function of centrality and the amount of support the members received. Central members, more than peripheral members, tried to change the opinion of those who disagreed, but if the central members failed, their satisfaction changed more than did that of the peripheral members. The satisfaction of members was also found to differ with their position in the system (Cohen, Robinson, & Edwards, 1969); it was somewhat higher in decentralized organizations. More specifically, Vannoy and Morrissette (1969) obtained results which suggested that satisfaction with a role in the network was related to its centrality, whereas satisfaction with one's group was related to the effectiveness of the network's operations.

In an experimental effort to detect the underlying elements that were of consequence, Trow (1957) studied groups of participants who were matched according to their scores on the need for autonomy. Some members were led to believe that they occupied positions of centrality and others were led to believe that they occupied positions of dependence. The autonomous situation provided greater satisfaction than the dependent situation. The effect of centrality on satisfaction was positive but not significant.

Access to Information and Its Distribution. Trow (1957) analyzed the interacting effects of providing the occupant of a position in a communications network with access to information and with access to communication channels with others. Perceived status was more a matter of access to the communication channels than to knowledge. On the other hand, Guetzkow (1954) found that persons in central positions had better knowledge and understanding of the network than did persons in peripheral positions. Changing the information available to members had an effect similar to that of changing the centrality of their position or the channels available to their position (M. E. Shaw, 1954a). In a follow-up of this earlier finding, M. E. Shaw (1963a) studied the influence of the availability of information in various networks. Group members with an informational advantage were found to enter the discussion earlier, to initiate more task-oriented communications, to find their suggestions accepted more frequently, and to be rated by others as contributing more to the group's task than were members who had no previous information about the problem. Likewise, Gilchrist, Shaw, and Walker (1954) varied the information available to the four members of a wheel network. They found that the centrality of a position was directly related to the emergence of the leader and to the satisfaction but variations in availability of information were not.

Other Contingent Factors. Planning opportunities make a difference. Thus, members are more likely to learn how to use their own position for the best advantae of the group when the group is given the opportunity to plan between trials, particularly if members are connected with each other by open channels (Guetzkow & Dill, 1957). The members are also likely to develop different patterns of communication, depending on the amount and type of previous experience they have had with alternative networks (A. R. Cohen, 1964).

The placement of persons of lower or higher status or esteem in key positions can alter the outcomes of communication networks. For G. B. Cohen (1969), the presence of high-status members in positions of centrality facilitated the networks' performance. Nevertheless, low-status members became more effective in positions of centrality. Cohen concluded that in a pluricentral social system, the various centers of influence should have easy access to communication with all parts of the organization. Consistent with this conclusion, Mohanna and Argyle (1960) assigned sociometrically popular and unpopular participants to wheel and circle networks. They found that wheel groups with esteemed central members learned faster than did the other groups and required less time and fewer messages to solve the problem.[16]

Networks and Effective Leadership Style

The type of communication network imposed on the group determines which kind of leadership will be most effective. When the central member of the wheel or yoke network and a designated member in the all-channel network are instructed to be coercive (to use the power of their position to require compliance rather than to be persuasive) and to use logic and information to convince, all three types of networks make fewer er-

[16]As was noted in Chapter 15, efficiency is increased and conflict is reduced in organizations when one's esteem is congruent with the importance of the position to which one is assigned.

rors in information. However, the relative superiority of coercion over persuasion is greatest in the wheel network, is less great in the yoke network, and least apparent in the all-channel network. But under all three conditions, as may be expected, members are less satisfied with coercion than with persuasion. In the all-channel and yoke networks, the same or similar amounts of errors in decision making occur with persuasive and coercive leadership. Only in the wheel network are there fewer errors of decision under coercive than under persuasive leadership (Shaw & Blum, 1966; Shepard, 1956).

M. E. Shaw (1955) compared democratic and authoritarian (order-giving) leaders of the different communication networks and found that networks made less of a difference than did leadership style. Speed and accuracy of performance were greater under authoritarian than under democratic leadership, but the members' satisfaction with and nominations for leadership were greater under a democratic style of leadership.

Personal Factors

The placement of individuals with particular personal attributes in central positions or the use of participants who have some strong personal characteristics may systematically affect the outcomes of a communication network. However, M. E. Shaw (1960) failed to find that the homogeneity of members of a network in such attributes as intelligence, acceptance of authority, and individual prominence changed, depending on whether centralized or decentralized structures resulted in more satisfaction and efficiency. But Trow (1957) observed that the stronger the desire of participants for autonomy, the higher was the correlation between the participants' satisfaction and the extent to which they believed they occupied positions of centrality.

Cohen and Foerst (1968) studied groups composed of repressors (members who repress or deny anxiety) and sensitizers (members who react to anxiety and worry). They found that leadership was significantly more continuous in the groups of repressors than in the groups of sensitizers. The groups of repressors developed centralized systems earlier than did the groups of sensitizers. Nevertheless, when given the opportunity, both types of groups rejected the all-channel network in favor of the centralized structure.

The centralized networks produce the fastest solutions with the fewest errors in the simplest kind of problem-solving situation, such as finding the common symbol. But the superiority of the centralized star, wheel, or yoke disappears when the problem is made more complex by adding "noise" to the communications. For instance, when participants have to solve anagram problems for which they may or may not need information from each other, noise—complicated and possibly irrelevant information in the communication system—causes differences in the efficiency of the various nets to differ. Thus, the effectiveness of a communication network depends on the characteristics of the task. No one network is always best (Glanzer & Glaser, 1961).

Implications for Organizational Leadership

The results of the research just presented indicate that groups with a member in a position of centrality are more efficient than are those groups without differentiated role structures. Members who occupy positions of centrality that enable them to exercise control over the flow of information are most likely to emerge as leaders. They are also better satisfied with their groups than are the peripheral members. Several studies suggest that personality factors may mitigate the relation between centrality and leadership. But a highly submissive member may become a more active participant in the group's activities when placed for a time in a position of centrality.

Organizations are composed of networks and contain one or more of the types described earlier. Moreover, the networks in a particular organization will be interrelated and may vary from well-structured networks carrying regular task-related messages to loose informal networks (Guetzkow & Simon, 1955).

In real-world organizations, communications are involved in the exercise of authority, the exchange of information, the completion of specific tasks, friendship, or status. In communication networks based on authority and those based on information, the information typically flows in opposite directions. That is, information in networks that are based on authority flows from the persons who are in positions of authority down to the subordinates. In contrast, in many networks that are based on information, the information primarily flows upward from those who provide information to those who collect that information for use in decision making; as a consequence, the potential for conflict is great.[17]

Uses. Network experiments can be used to simulate some particular organizational problem. In one such simulation by Hesseling and Konnen (1969), five participants represented each of five separate departments of a manufacturing company: sales, R & D, planning and production, organizational methods, and purchasing and subcontracting. All participants received complete information about the procedures of the company and a functional description of their respective departments. They were also given the necessary information to contribute to the decision-making process in their respective departmental roles. The purpose of the simulation was to discover, within a time limit of five 15-minute periods, the best working combination of the product's design, delivery time, and price so they would be able to accept or reject a customer's order. The participants were given sufficient time to discuss as a team how to organize the different department roles. Only written communication could be passed among the five departmental heads. The participants were left to form their own network. The analysis focused on what kinds of networks emerged in such circumstances to yield the best combination of outputs. Centralization might promote speed of decision but quality of decision would depend on other factors.

It may be impossible to translate these laboratory and simulation findings directly to large organizations. Yet these laboratory networks are analogous to real organizational ones. The chain is seen in the vertical and horizontal serial-communication linkages in an organization shown in Figure 30.7 The meeting of the board of directors is an all-channel network. The typical line organization is a yoke. For many specific operations in an organization, persons will find themselves at the hub of the wheel (Dubin, 1958).

[17]Detailed in Chapter 15.

Figure 30.7. Examples of Operational Networks

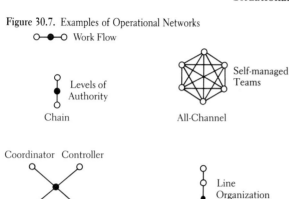

SOURCE: *R. Dubin, Stability of human organizations. In M. Haire (Ed.),* Modern Organizational Theory. *New York: Wiley, 1959, 1962.*

Substitutes for Leadership

Kerr (1977) and Kerr and Jermier (1978) reasoned that since social, organizational, and physical arrangements can be organized to improve the performance of individuals, teams, and organizations, when the demands of a task are known, ways can be found to provide mechanisms and alternatives for the various functions of the formal leader.

Forms of Circumstantial Moderators

Howell, Dorfman, and Kerr (1986) classified moderators of leadership performance and its effects as neutralizers, enhancers, supplements, and substitutes for leadership.[18] Of most interest to subsequent research have been the substitutes for leadership.

Neutralizers. Neutralizers make it impossible for leaders to influence the outcomes of the subordinates'

[18]In terms of multiple regression analysis, employed to test for these moderators of the effects of leadership on outcomes, if $\hat{y} = ax + bz$, when x is leadership behavior, z is the moderator, and $\hat{y}$ is predicted subordinate performance, then:

z is a *neutralizer* if b is negative and z, although correlated with x, does not correlate with $\hat{y}$

z is an *enhancer* if b is positive and z does not correlate with $\hat{y}$

z is a *supplement* if it correlates with $\hat{y}$ adding to the correlation of x with $\hat{y}$

z is a *substitute* if it correlates with $\hat{y}$ while x adjusted for z does not.

performance (Howard & Joyce, 1982). For instance, a leader who is supportive and considerate will have little or no impact on highly authoritarian subordinates. The subordinates' authoritarianism neutralizes the leader's support, which ordinarily would promote better performance outcomes (Weed, Mitchell, & Moffitt, 1976). Neutralizers do not directly correlate with the outcomes but cancel the leader-outcome relationship. Thus, in examining data from 558 staff members of 25 nursing homes, Sheridan, Hogstel, and Fairchild (1985) expected and found that the effects of the supervisors' leadership activities would be significantly weaker in nursing homes with policies and practices that resulted in uncertain work goals and the lack of sufficient rewards for the subordinates' good performance. Another potential neutralizer was the location of the nursing home. The responses of staff members (such as quitting) to poor leadership behavior were expected to be neutralized in small-town locations because there were few alternative jobs available to staff members. Other likely leadership neutralizers include cohesive work groups with antimanagement norms; subordinates who fail to respect the leader's competence; antiauthoritarian subordinates, with an internal locus of control and a high need for independence; union, civil service, or other institutional constraints that prevent the leader from influencing the distribution of organizational rewards; the leader's lack of upward influence; subordinates who do not share the leader's or the organization's goals and objectives; subordinates who do not depend on the leader for resources; and subordinates who work at a physical distance from the leader (Howell, Bowen, Kerr, et al., undated).

Enhancers. Enhancers augment the leader-outcome relationship. A supportive leader who also has influence with a higher authority will have more of an impact on the outcomes of the subordinates' performance than one who does not have such influence. Influence with higher-ups enhances the effect of the leadership on the subordinates' performance.

The same variables, such as the norms of a cohesive work group, may neutralize or enhance the effect of the leader. If the cohesive group's norms are counter to the leader's and the organization's objectives, the cohesion will offset the effect of the leader on the members' performance. If the cohesive group's norms are in alignment with the leader's and the organization's objectives, the cohesive norms will enhance the leader's effects on the members. Summarizing research through 1988, Howell, Bowen, Kerr, et al. (undated) concluded that the following enhancers should increase the impact of supportive relationship-oriented behavior by leaders: cohesive work groups with pro-management norms; the leader with important, highly visible organizational responsibility; the leader with a great deal of upward and lateral influence; the leader with a strong resource base and subordinates who are highly dependent on the leader for resources; and an organizational culture that is supportive of management. The effects on outcomes of the leaders' task-oriented guidance will be enhanced by these situational conditions, as well as by such others as the subordinates' respect for the leader's competence; the leader's reward power; the existence of a visible, influential champion of the leader within or outside the organization[19] a crisis atmosphere exists; or a set of superordinate goals is present.

Supplements. Supplements for leadership contribute to effects on the subordinates' performance but do not cancel out or augment the leader's direct effects. Computerized decision-support systems exemplify designed supplements to leadership. These are pre-planned approaches to solving designated kinds of problems that attempt to parallel systematically the behavior and thought processes of decision makers and can be used to supplement leaders' judgments. They do not substitute completely for the leaders. Rather, they are used by leaders to make a final integrated decision (Wedley & Field, 1984).

Howell and Dorfman (1981) demonstrated that for 220 hospital workers, such supplements could be seen in the extent to which their intrinsic task satisfaction, routinization, and task feedback contributed directly to the employees' commitment or satisfaction or both without inhibiting or augmenting the leaders' more direct influence on the same outcomes. Again, in a study

of university counselors, Howard and Joyce (1982) demonstrated that good peer relationships supplemented the leaders' consideration and initiation.

Substitutes. Substitutes for leadership are variables that make the leadership impossible or unnecessary. When substitutes for leadership are present, leadership itself would be expected to be of little or no consequence to the satisfaction and performance of subordinates. Logically and empirically, substitutes directly affect the performance of subordinates, while the leadership does not. The substitutes act like neutralizers to cancel the leader's effect on the outcomes of the subordinates' performance (Howell, Dorfman, & Kerr, 1986).

Interviews with those who were responsible for supervisory professionals, such as research directors and nursing supervisors, talked repeatedly about substitutes for leadership in professional settings. The work itself emerged and directed the professional worker without the need for the leaders to intervene (Wall, 1986). Thus, a highly predictable work flow, as a consequence of bureaucratization and centralization, can substitute for control by supervisors (Comstock & Scott, 1977).

In predicting the subordinates' commitment to an organization Kerr and Jermier (1978) and Howell and Dorfman (1982) found that the formalization of an organization is a strong substitute for the leader's assigning of work. Formalization is less of a substitute for the leader's specification of the rules and is somewhat less of a substitute for role clarification by the leader in the prediction of employees' satisfaction. Howell and Dorfman (1986) found that organizational formalization was a weak substitute for the leader's specifying procedures in the prediction of the satisfaction of professionals. Further indirect support showing that organizational formalization could moderate and substitute for leadership in affecting outcomes for subordinates was obtained by Freeston (1987) and Podsakoff, Todor, Grover, and Huber (1984). Kerr and Jermier (1978) and Kerr and Slocum (1981) found that the subordinates' ability, professional orientation, and desire for autonomy made the addition of task direction from the leader counterproductive.

In the same way, Sheridan, Vredenburgh, and Abel-

[19]Both J. Edgar Hoover's and Hyman Rickover's postponed retirement and continued success as leaders over many decades within the FBI and the U.S. Navy, respectively, depended, in great part, on the extent to which they had many congressmen who championed their causes.

son (1984) reported that for 98 supervisors and head nurses and their 670 nurses in four hospitals, the nurses' education, group cohesion, and available work technology substituted for the head nurses' leadership in directly and indirectly affecting the nurses' job performance. The administrative climate of the hospitals acted as neutralizers.

Much of what are considered conscious acts of leadership today were attributable in static traditional societies to highly internalized norms, rules, and values. Compliance was a matter of habit and the avoidance of guilt or shame. Except for outlaws, one did what one was expected to do, without explicit direction, monitoring, and reinforcement by a leader (Gardner, 1986a).

The features of sociotechnological jobs and organizational designs, such as those advanced by Cherns (1976), are a particularly important source of substitutes for leadership. For example, the computer display itself can give immediate, direct feedback to the employee who is working at a computer terminal about the employee's absolute speed and errors as well as the employee's performance. The display can be contrasted with previous work, standards, and norms. Organizational feedback about performance, which is ordinarily transmitted through supervision, can be sent directly to the employee to promote self-monitoring and self-evaluation. Team operations in which members share responsibility for achieving team objectives can be rewarded on the basis of the team's productivity without supervisory intervention. The team as a whole and its individual members, rather than a supervisor, become the substitute sources for planning, directing, and controlling.

Jones (1983) showed that the work flow could be controlled as much by the task structure of the role formalization as by the leader's use of reinforcement. In a study of 220 hospital personnel, Howell and Dorfman (1981) obtained partial validation of the hypothesis that to deal with role ambiguity and conflict, the subordinate's ability and experience and the formal organization, in some instances, could substitute for specific supportive leadership behaviors that ordinarily boost the subordinate's job satisfaction and organizational commitment.

Substitutes for leadership were analyzed as moderators of leader-outcome relationships. Podsakoff, To-dor, Grover, and Huber (1982) used moderated regression analysis to test for the effects of substitutes for leadership on the relationship between leaders' contingent-reward behavior and subordinates' satisfaction. Change in the variance explained by the addition of the interaction term (leadership behavior × substitute) to the regression equation was used as the potential indicator of the effect of substitution.

In line with suggestions of Howard and Joyce (1982) Sheridan, Vredenburgh, and Abelson (1984) used path analysis to detect substitutes for leadership. To obtain path coefficients, they treated leadership as a function of expected substitutes and outcomes, as a function of leadership, of substitutes, and of substitutes combined with leadership. Thus, they used substitutes as a predictor of both the leadership behavior itself and of the outcomes.

Applications

These neutralizers, enhancers, supplements, and substitutes can be designed into systems, as needed. Jacobs and Jaques (1987) pointed to the extent to which supervision can be more effective if, independent of it, the structure in the situation is designed to exert demands on the individual employee that are relevant to accomplishing the work to be done.

Howell, Dorfman, and Kerr (1986) suggested that coercive, autocratic leadership can be neutralized by removing the control of rewards and penalties from the leader. Inadequate leadership can be enhanced by team building to increase supportive norms. Selecting mature subordinates may provide a substitute for stable leadership. Assigning an assistant to a manager may act to supplement the manager's leadership.

A study by Tyagi (1985) of 168 life insurance salespersons showed that variations in jobs, such as in the opportunities they provided for using a variety of skills, enhancing the significance of the task, and allowing for autonomy, combined to account for 47 percent of the variance in the intrinsic motivation of the salespersons. But these variations in jobs had far less effect on the salespersons' extrinsic motivation, accounting for only 18 percent of it. In contrast, the leaders' trust and support, interaction and facilitation, and psychological and hierarchical influence combined to account for 38 percent of the salespersons' extrinsic motivation but only 16 percent of their intrinsic motivation. The variety of skills, significance of the task, and autonomy that were built into the job could substitute more for the leadership in intrinsically motivating the salespersons' and less inextrinsically motivating them. Both types of motivation contributed to improvements in the salespersons' work performance.

Group processes also can substitute for leadership. P. B. Smith (1984) found that the manager's role in area management teams of British social workers was relatively unimportant in predicting the effectiveness of the team compared to group process variables, such as the personal involvement of members and the low denial of conflict.

Substitutes for leadership are also seen as possible when reward systems can operate independently of the leader (commissions, piecework, incentives, and profit sharing) and when expert staff personnel are available directly to subordinates without the leader's intervention (Howell, Bowen, Kerr, et al., undated).

Pitner (1988) validated 11 of 13 hypotheses concerning possible substitutes for leadership in the educational context. Staff contributions, differences in teaching, and the structure of the organization could serve as substitutes for leadership in affecting the subordinates' performance and attitudes, according to 450 surveyed teachers from 47 schools.

Autonomous Work Groups. Substitution for formal supervision and leadership is seen most particularly when autonomous work groups are created and self-management[20] is introduced. Autonomous work groups and self-management by individual members of an organization are two ways in which group processes and individual dynamics are structured to eliminate formal supervision and yet achieve or better the results obtained with formally assigned leaders.

Autonomous work groups can operate without direct supervision. For the omitted supervisor's contribution, they substitute collective control by the work-group members of the pace of work, distribution of tasks, and training of new members (Gulowsen, 1972). The supervisor is made redundant if the members of the work group have functionally interrelated tasks and are col-

lectively responsible for the end products. Roles may still be differentiated. One member may still be central; others peripheral. The members must have a variety of skills so they can handle many or most of the groups' tasks. Feedback along with evaluation of the work group as a whole are also necessary. Wall, Kemp, Jackson, and Clegg (1986) completed a study of the long-term effects of using such autonomous work groups in manufacturing in Britain. They found that supervisory routines could be eliminated with no noticeable effects on the subordinates' motivation or performance. They also found enhanced intrinsic job satisfaction among the members but only temporary increases in extrinsic job satisfaction.

Self-management. As was discussed in Chapter 7, building on Bandura's (1977) social learning theory, Manz (1986) argued for fostering self-planning, self-direction, self-monitoring, and self-control, which could replace otherwise needed supervision. For the individual and the group, self-management calls for self-observations, specifications of goals, cuing strategies, rehearsal, self-evaluation, and self-reinforcement (Manz & Sims, 1980). After difficult or unappealing but necessary tasks are identified, each of these processes can be incorporated into an individual's everyday job performance. Thus, self-observation can be promoted by keeping a daily log of what one has discussed with others on the telephone. Goal specification occurs when one sets schedules and priorities for oneself. Cuing is illustrated by the example of a checkout board that was placed at the exit of a manager's office to remind her to leave word for her secretary where she was going and when she would be back. Rehearsal occurs when one makes a sales presentation into a tape recorder and then listens to one's performance, correcting it as deemed necessary. Self-evaluation is aided by keeping charts of one's progress in improving the quality or quantity of one's performance. Self-reinforcement is accomplished by building natural rewards for the performance of tasks. It may be done by searching for features of the task activities that give one a feeling of purpose, competence, and self-control (Manz, 1983). Contrary to what might have been expected, Manz and Angle (1985) noted from what was seen in an insurance firm that such self-management resulted in increased

[20]Discussed earlier in Chapter 7.

compliance by sales personnel with the company's procedures and goals.

The Paradox: Leadership Is Required for Substitutions

To a considerable degree, self-management by groups and individuals requires considerable delegation by a higher authority. Furthermore, higher-ups provide examples, guidance, encouragement, and support. Manz and Sims (1986b) note that self-managed autonomous groups require a "superleader" who is external to the groups. Such an external leader helps the groups become self-monitoring, set their own goals, criticize and reinforce themselves, and plan and assign tasks by themselves instead of depending on the superleader.

Helping others to shift to self-control from external control requires dealing with a variety of problems. There is a self-serving bias in attributing one's poor performance to situational rather than personal factors. Coordination may suffer. Individuals differ in the need for autonomy. Whether the concern is about the employee's developing proficiencies or the employee's current results will make a difference. Self-control with guidance from an external leader is likely to be more directly relevant to the individual's development and internalization of the desired and required job behavior. External control may be sufficient for monitoring results (Manz, Mossholder, & Luthans, 1983). With no formally appointed leader in each group, members have to be willing and able to take on the leadership task and maintenance functions, as needed by the group.

Summary and Conclusions

Physical, organizational, and spatial factors have direct and indirect influence on leader-member relationships. Studies of interpersonal space indicate that individuals interact more frequently with those who are located close to them than with those who are farther away. The member who occupies the head position at the table tends to assume leadership. Leaders tend to gravitate toward head positions and are expected to do so. Members who occupy head positions tend to be more influential than do those who occupy side or peripheral positions. Members tend to maintain greater physical

distance between themselves and members who are of a higher or lower status than between themselves and their peers in status. Differences in status and social distance tend to be valued when the consequences of social interaction may be unpleasant and when effective group performance is desired by group members.

Individuals who live or work in close proximity to each other also exhibit a higher rate of mutual sociometric choice than do those who are situated at a greater distance from each other. At the same time, the quality of personal interaction and achievement by the group may be facilitated by some degree of psychosocial distance between the leader and the followers. Individuals prefer greater social distance between themselves and their competitors than between themselves and those with whom they cooperate.

Research on networks in organizations and in experimental communication networks has indicated that the member who occupies a position of centrality tends to emerge as leader. That member has greater access to communication than do other members and is thus better able to coordinate and direct the group's activities. Groups with positions of centrality within them are more efficient than those with undifferentiated role structures.

The openness of channels is directly related to the information available to a leader and, therefore, to the leader's ability to exert influence. Regular meetings usually (but not always) provide more continuing communications and promote the group's performance. The member who occupies a position of centrality is better satisfied with the group than are members in peripheral positions. Personal factors, such as the need for autonomy and ascendancy, moderate these effects. The experimental results tend to confirm parallel real-world organizational networks.

Social, organizational, and physical rearrangements of how work is accomplished can be used to neutralize, enhance, supplement, or substitute for leadership. Such rearrangements may include setting up autonomous work groups and encouraging self-management. These rearrangements can benefit organizations by reducing the costs of supervision and increasing the employees' commitment, reducing the need for the persistence and the transfer of leadership, the subject that is discussed next.

Persistence, Transfer, and Succession of Leadership

Persistence

Margaret Thatcher and Lyndon Johnson are two of the many world-class leaders whose efforts to reach the top began with initiatives displayed in childhood and continued unabated through adolescence into adulthood. As adults, such leaders obtain their reputation as successful leaders in one situation and then transfer that reputation for successful leadership to other similar situations. Some gain sufficient esteem and experience in these early efforts to succeed as leaders in almost any situation they enter (Bogardus, 1928; Cowley, 1931). Success in one political office serves as a steppingstone to other offices. Failure in one office may immobilize or destroy one's political career (Burns, 1978).

Reasons for the Persistence of Success

Although tasks and goals can be different from situation to situation, some amount of interpersonal competence is required from any leader. So there is likely to be some amount of generalizability about who emerges as leader in different situations. In the same way, personal characteristics, such as energy, intelligence, assertiveness, task orientation, need for power, and other personal traits will promote the persistence of the same persons to emerge as leaders in a variety of times and places. Thus, since considerable consistency is found in intelligence and various personality traits from childhood to adulthood, consistency will also be found in the trait-associated tendencies of children to become leaders and the potential of these children to become leaders as adults. For example, C. M. Cox's (1926) analyses of the biographies of 300 outstanding military, religious, and political leaders frequently found traits of behavior above normal in the childhoods of these leaders, such as the desire to excel, intelligence, insight, self-esteem, and forcefulness—traits usually related to leadership.

The persistence of an individual's attempts, success, and effectiveness as a leader across situations and time periods may be augmented by a consistent "ability to perceive the needs and goals of a constituency and to adjust one's personal approach to group action accordingly" (Kenny & Zaccaro, 1983, p. 678). It is also strengthened by the continuous power that a leader may hold during the various stages in a group's development (Quiggins & Lashbrook, 1972). Persistence in leadership will be bolstered further by the implicit beliefs of followers that regardless of the environmental complexities to be faced, more persistence is a virtue in leaders and shows their sense of responsibility (Graves, 1985).

Such persistence in leadership behavior is seen as characteristic of successful chief executives, manifested in their consistent support of a theme, shifting attention to that theme, granting authority down the line to support the theme, encouraging experimentations about the theme, and developing and maintaining contacts about it throughout the system (Peters, 1980). Such persistence pays off. Staw and Ross (1980) found that marketing managers whose scenarios revealed a persistence in the same strategy as situations changed were evaluated more favorably by practicing administrators than managers whose scenarios showed that they tended to shift strategies to try to accommodate transient changes in conditions.

Effects of the Age of Leaders and Followers

Although there is persistence in leadership, systematic changes occur as a function of age. That is, the requirements for success as a leader are likely to mirror the developmental stages of the leaders and the led. Early on, immaturity, raucousness, and playfulness are required. Later, these characteristics are replaced by demonstrated task and interpersonal competence.

These changes have been demonstrated in studies of children at various ages. For example, observations of the spontaneous play of nursery school children by a 1-minute sampling procedure indicated the existence of two approaches to leading others: persuasion and coercion. Such authoritative leadership behavior continued to be seen among 3–5 year olds by Barner-Berry (1982) in the ongoing informal leadership of a child even after the succession of a new formal leader. The emerging leader was also readily observed in primary school at an early age (Mey, 1936). At this age, children attempt to become leaders to satisfy their desire to influence others, and such emergent leaders tend to be tyrants or stimulators. But later, attempts to organize become more common. With continuing maturation, consistency in attempts and successful leadership increase, while rivalry among would-be leaders decreases (Toki, 1935). Increasing age brings further changes in the behavior that contributes to the success of a leader. For instance, Tryon (1939) found that among 12-year-old girls, leaders were daring and humorous, but among 15-year-old girls, the friendly, enthusiastic, and happy ones were more successful leaders. Among European adolescents, the emphasis on coercion was observed to change with maturation to a persuasive appeal to ideals (Winkler-Hermaden, 1927). Horrocks and Thompson (1946) studied the friendship choices of boys and girls aged 10–17, by administering sociometric tests two weeks apart. They discovered that the fluctuation in the choices of boys and girls of the same age did not differ. However, older boys and girls tended to name the same individual both times as friends, while younger children showed less overlap on the two lists. These results suggested that sociometric choices tended to stabilize in later adolescence.[1]

Persistence in School and Onward

I. J. Levi (1930) obtained a correlation of .19 in the leadership activity of the same group of students in elementary school and later in high school. But the correlation was .52 when these children's leadership performance in junior high school was compared with their performance in high school. And D. P. Page (1935) found that the first-year leadership rank at West Point correlated .67 with fourth-year leadership rank.

Several early studies also determined that leadership in elementary school, high school, and college was predictive of later leadership in adult business and social activities. Courtenay (1938), for example, found that leadership in extracurricular activities as an adolescent was more highly related to various criteria of success as an adult than were scholarship or academic achievement. In other words, leadership, rather than scholarship, was the best predictor of later leadership.[2] Williams and Harrell (1964) reported a significant correlation of .24 between leadership in undergraduate activities and later success in business five years later, as measured by the salary level achieved. Roskens (1958) found significant correlations, ranging from .37 to .63, between college leadership and postcollege leadership. At the same time, postcollege leadership was not highly related to grades in college or to parents' occupational status.

Russell, Mattson, Devlin, and Atwater (1986) obtained a correlation of .18 between high school leadership, as measured by a self-report biodata questionnaire, and subsequent peer ratings as a leader at the U.S. Naval Academy. Similarly, Yammarino and Bass (1989) found that grades for military proficiency at the U.S. Naval Academy correlated with the successful patterns of leadership behavior of the same men as shipboard lieutenants as much as eight years later, but their academic grades at the academy were not correlated with their subsequent leadership performance.

Persistence of Leadership in Experimental Groups

As early as 1904, Terman (1904) reported an experimental verification of the consistency of leadership behavior in schoolchildren from one problem to the next. Borgatta, Couch, and Bales (1954) observed that new

---

[1]The specific traits that are important to leadership are likely to change with changes in society. The pattern has to be rechecked for each generation. Therefore, the results reported here are valid only for the generation in which the data were collected; they may not apply to other generations.

[2]See also, Clem and Dodge (1933), I. J. Levi (1930), D. P. Page (1935), and J. R. Shannon (1929).

groups were more effective if they contained "great men" who had been identified in old groups for their ability, assertiveness, and social success. The "great men" continued to be influential in the new groups. Highly esteemed, active, able persons continued to succeed as leaders in groups with different members that were faced with similar tasks. Blake, Mouton, and Fruchter (1954) reported that the leaders' contribution to the groups' decisions and dominance, as rated by different observers in different situations, yielded consistent individual differences among raters, despite the variation in the situation and the groups' composition. They also noted that as the task and groups were altered, self-ratings and ratings of others were most consistent when they were concerned with leadership and interest. They were less consistent when they were concerned with the effectiveness and satisfaction of others.

Borgatta, Couch, and Bales (1954) found that initially effective leaders tended to emerge as leaders in group after group to which they were assigned. Bass and Norton (1951) analyzed test-retest performance in initially leaderless discussions held a week apart; the test-retest measure of successful leadership was .90. Carter, Haythorn, and Howell (1950) studied the emergence of leaders in groups of college students who were performing the same task again after about four months. The test-retest correlations, which depended on the nature of the task, ranged from .39 for discussion tasks to .88 for motor-coordination tasks.

Rosenberg, Erlick, and Berkowitz (1955) studied small groups that were required to cooperate in tilting an apparatus in such a manner as to move a small bar up a ramp. The persistence of leadership was highly significant among the various regroupings of members. Gordon and Medland (1965a) obtained peer nominations and ratings in small military units before and eight weeks after the reconstitution of the units. Peer nominations for leadership correlated .80 to .90 between the two situations.

Attempted leadership also shows consistencies across different task conditions. Hemphill, Pepinsky, Shevitz, et al. (1954) found an average correlation of .45 between assessments of attempted leadership by the same members of groups engaged in four different tasks: reasoning, instruction, assembly, and strategy.

But as will be discussed in more detail later, this consistency across tasks will depend on the similarity of the tasks. Thus, for example, as groups develop, the same successful leaders will reemerge as the same developmental tasks need to be completed. Sterling and Rosenthal (1950) reported that when leaders and followers changed roles in different phases of their groups' development, the same leaders tended to emerge as similar phases of development recurred.

Persistence of Leadership in Industry and Elsewhere

The consistencies in leadership behavior found among developing individuals and groups and in small laboratory groups were also observed among supervisors, managers, and other institutional leaders across times and places. Furthermore, those who were more effective in one situation and time were likely to be more effective at other times and in similar kinds of locations.

Consistency of Leadership Behavior. Holloway and Wolleat (1981) examined the interaction styles and supervisory behavior of trainees and concluded that individual preferences for different kinds of supervisory interactions were stable. Over a 3-month period, Greene (1976a) reported rate-rerate coefficients of .60 and above for contingent reward behavior and for contingent punitive behavior by supervisors. Similar results were found for contingent reward by Szilagyi (1980b) and Sims (1977) over 3-, 6-, and 12-month intervals. Sakamaki (1974) studied the descriptions of 339 Japanese first-level bank supervisors and second-level bank managers who remained in their same positions for two years by their more than 1,800 subordinates and colleagues in the two successive years. Rate-rerate correlations of .35 and .74, respectively, were found for their leaders' orientation toward performance; the corresponding correlations for orientation toward maintenance leadership were .53 and .59.

Similar evidence about the consistency of transformational and transactional leadership was obtained for a small sample of executives with a six-month test-retest analysis of their subordinates' descriptions of their behavior (Bass & Avolio, 1989). The mass of case and anecdotal evidence available on world-class leaders also supports the contention that leadership behavior is consistent across times and similar situations.

Persistence of Effective Leadership. Considerable evidence is available concerning the tendency of the same leaders to be effective, given the same task requirements with new groups. The impressive set of field studies of first-line supervisors is illustrative.

H. Feldman (1937) studied 22 work groups that shared in savings on operating costs. One year after the project began, supervisors of groups with high savings were assigned to groups with low savings, and vice versa. The order of merit of the supervisors remained practically the same despite the change in assignments. Many of the differences among groups were associated with the leaders—not with the groups they were leading. The supervisors' assignments were then shifted by chance, and the same results occurred. The relative order of performance of the groups depended on who led the groups. The groups with previously low savings records that were subsequently led by high-savings leaders later had high savings, while those with high previous savings that were subsequently led by low-savings leaders later had low savings.

In the same way, J. M. Jackson (1953b) arranged for the supervisors of telephone line crews with high morale to change places with the supervisors of crews with low-morale. A retest of the crews four months later showed a significant shift in the scores for morale, with the previously low groups scoring high and the previously high groups scoring low. Each supervisor tended to receive a score in his second group that was similar to that obtained in his first group. No such significant changes occurred in a set of control groups. Wyndham and Cooke (1964) also studied work groups in which the supervisors exchanged places. They found that the performance of previously ineffective groups improved under previously effective supervisors, but the performance of previously effective groups declined under supervisors of previously ineffective groups.

F. L. W. Richardson (1961) studied work groups in which the only way found to improve productivity and morale was by transferring troublesome leaders out of their groups. N. A. Rosen (1969) obtained ratings of workers' preferences for eight foremen in an upholstering shop. Foremen who were high and low in prefer-

ence then changed places. The greater the workers' consensus in the first and tenth weeks that the new foreman "is our leader," the greater was the increase in productivity and cohesiveness in the eleventh and sixteenth weeks. The findings suggested that the new foremen were evaluated in terms of their ability to help the group. In another experiment by N. A. Rosen (1970b), large changes in the preference for foremen were associated with large gains in productivity following reassignment, while small changes in preference were associated with small gains or losses in productivity.

The effects of charismatic founders can dominate an organization's culture long after the founders are gone.[3] Salaman (1977) illustrated this fact in the case of a small, successful manufacturing firm that continued to be influenced by a charismatic leader even after he had retired and was no longer present on the scene.

To conclude, both logic and empirical results attest to the persistence of leadership behavior and its effects from childhood onward. However, such persistence will depend, to some extent, on the occurrence of leadership in past, present, and future situations that are similar in leadership requirements. Thus, Bass (1960) analyzed the results of eight studies that reported 18 correlations between successful performance in initially leaderless group discussions and successful performance as a leader in "real life." Although the median correlation was .38, the 18 correlations ranged from −.25 to .68. The correlations were higher, the more similar the real life situation to a leaderless group discussion.

Transfer of Leadership

Borrowing from the general psychology of transfer, Bass (1960) developed a model to account for the conditions in which the positive and negative transfer of leadership behavior occurs. Among the major propositions were these:

- Positive transfer (transfer that facilitates performance) from an old to a new situation will be greater, the more the new situation is similar to the old one and the more the new situation calls

[3]See Chapter 12.

for the same leadership behavior as the old one to attain goals.

- Negative transfer (transfer that is detrimental to performance) will be greater the more the new situation, different from the old one and requiring new modes of leadership, is responded to with the old ways of behaving to achieve goals. The new situation is responded to as if it were similar to the old when it actually is not. It is perceived as requiring the old ways of leadership behavior when actually new ways are necessary.

Military-to-Civilian Transfer

There is considerable experimental evidence to confirm the positive transfer of leadership, some of which has already been cited. Thus, as many as 70 U.S. Army generals retire annually to enter civilian life at an age and with the skills and experience commensurate with civilian executive levels into which they move. Ordinarily, the transfers are successful, despite the failure to prepare adequately for the transfer by careful self-analysis and an analysis of the situation to which they transfer (Whelan, 1981).

What transfers positively, say, if one examines the move from high-level military leadership to civilian leadership? Hill (1984) mentioned these characteristics:

1. Contacts with top government and foreign officials and specialists.
2. Relevant experience in dealing with boards and staffs.
3. Effective skills in presentation, persuasion, and communication.
4. Experience in strategic planning and decision making.
5. Emphasis on clear definitions of authority and responsibility.
6. Experience with integrating operations, such as planning with research and development.

Dwight D. Eisenhower illustrated the positive transfer that is possible from a successful military career to performance as university president and president of the United States.

But military-civilian differences also may be a source of negative transfer effects for military officers taking civilian positions for the following reasons:

1. A less authoritarian and more collegial style is required.
2. Civilian employees have a great deal more latitude (say to strike) than do military personnel.
3. Delegation and coordination in civilian business and industry requires much more than giving orders and expecting unqualified compliance.
4. The lack of cost control in the military and profit orientation in civilian firms may be problems for ex-military leaders.
5. The ex-military leaders may lack experience in assessing and making calculated marketing risks.

The career of Ulysses S. Grant illustrated this negative transfer. Grant was successful as the commander of the victorious wartime Union Army, although he had previously been a repeated failure as an officer in peacetime, as a clerk in a store, and as a small businessman. Later, he was also a failure as U.S. president (McFeely, 1981).

Transfer of Specialists

Administrators in one area of specialty readily transfer to another position in the same specialty area. For example, deans of medical schools who change jobs move into other deanships or vice presidencies at their own or other medical schools. A few return to faculty positions, retire, or take up administrative posts outside medical schools (Wilson & McLaughlin, 1984).

However, such specialization may result in negative transfer effects. Kotter (1982b) noted that when general managers adapt themselves to one specific context, they will find it difficult to transfer to a different context. For a general manager in one organization and industry to become general manager in another organization and industry requires the ability to learn new things rapidly and to establish new relationships.

Experience as a manager, per se, is not what is important. Rather, whether the transfer of experience will be positive or negative depends on the relevance of the experience of the old position to the new position. Kennedy (1985) found that while time in service and the number of previous positions held added less than

1 percent to the accuracy of predicting successful leadership performance as a military officer, the assessed relevance of the previous positions added 20 percent to the accuracy in predicting successful leadership performance.

Evidence of the Effects of Positive Transfer

Positive transfer of attempted and successful leadership has been seen when groups move from one similar situation to another and if the issues they face are similar. Even if the membership changes, the same leadership may persist.

Effects of Similar Tasks. Katz, Blau, Brown, and Strodtbeck (1957) reported that groups exhibited a tendency to return to the same leader when the task performed in time 2 was similar to that performed in time 1. Again, as was noted earlier, Bass and Norton (1951) reported a correlation of .90 between successful leadership displayed by members of leaderless group discussions held a week apart. The composition of the groups and the problems discussed were the same. When one discussion was an examination and the other was not, the correlation remained as high as .86 (Bass, 1954a), but the correlation dropped to .75 when 2 members of each group of 7 were coached on how to lead between the test and retest situations (Klubeck & Bass, 1954).

An examination of situational data collected in the screening of candidates for the Office of Strategic Services (OSS, 1948)[4] further illustrated the effects of similar tasks. Positive transfer was evidenced by the increasing correlation of leadership ratings of the candidates' performance on other situational tests with their rated performance in leaderless discussions as the other situational tests became more similar to open discussions. The correlation with leadership in discussions was .30 with leadership in cooperatively constructing a giant toy; .47, with leadership in solving a problem of crossing a brook; .48, with leadership in a personal interview; and .56, with leadership displayed in a debate.

As posited by the transfer model, the transfer of leadership behavior decreases when tasks differ from an old

[4]U.S. Agency which was the forerunner of the Central Intelligence Agency (C.I.A.).

to a new situation, especially when a change from a purely intellectual activity to purely manual-mechanical activities is involved. Thus, Carter, Haythorn, and Howell (1950) found that although leaders in reasoning tasks also tended to emerge as leaders in intellectual and clerical tasks, they did not do so in mechanical tasks. Leaders in mechanical tasks tended to emerge as leaders in motor coordination tasks, but not in intellectual tasks. In an earlier study, Carter and Nixon (1949a) found a tendency for the same person to emerge as leader in clerical and intellectual tasks, but not in mechanical tasks. Thus, no transfer or even a negative transfer seems most likely when the transfer of leadership to be effected is from group tasks of the "head" to tasks of the "hand."

Effects of Similarity of Issues. The positive transfer of successful opinion leadership was reported by Jacoby (1974), who found that opinion leaders' influence overlapped in different areas. The degree of overlap of influence increased with the increase in the similarity of issues about which opinions were sought.

Effects of Changes in Membership. As long as the task stays the same in a new situation, recomposing the group membership does not seem to reduce the positive transfer effects greatly. Various experimental attempts have been made to determine whether the same individuals will emerge as leaders when members are reassigned to new groups with different combinations of leaders and followers. Bass (1949) found a correlation of .72 between the initial leadership status attained by group members in leaderless discussion groups and leadership status attained in reassembled discussion groups. Bass and Wurster (1953a) obtained correlations ranging from .51 to .66 between measures of leadership status in groups that differed in the composition of members and the problems to be discussed. Even when, in addition to changing the groups' composition, a year instead of a week intervened between the test and retest, the tendency to emerge as a discussion leader on the test and the retest correlated .53 (Bass & Coates, 1952). Arbous and Maree (1951) obtained a median correlation of .67 between the extent to which administrative candidates displayed successful leadership when they were appointed discussion leaders and the extent to which they displayed successful leadership in initially leaderless discussions. Similar research by Carter, Haythorn, Meirowitz, and Lanzetta (1951) yielded a correlation of .55. When, in addition to changing the composition of the membership, the type of discussion problem was varied systematically, the correlation in consistency of success was still .58 (Bass & Coates, 1953).

Nevertheless, subtle effects can be seen when the composition of the members of a group is changed. Cloyd (1964) found that the same members tended to perform the same function in successive groups but that different functions, if needed, were performed by members. An analysis of leaders' comments in discussions that had different purposes indicated to J. T. Wood (1977) that the same leaders can be successful in a variety of discussion situations with divergent goals, members, and constraints if they adapt their oral behaviors to meet varying goals and compensate for failures at previous meetings. Other members also readjust.

Members adjust for each other's behavior when they find themselves in new groups. For example, Haythorn (1952) combined and recombined the members of experimental groups. Members were rated on aggressiveness, initiative, confidence, submissiveness, sociability, leadership, and the like. Haythorn found that when one member in a group was rated high on one of these variables, other members were all rated low. It appeared that when one member exhibited a high degree of a given behavior, the other members attempted to adapt to the situation by reducing their behaviors in the same area of role performance. Similarly I. S. Bernstein (1964) removed the dominant male from a group of rhesus monkeys. During the month of his removal, the remaining males increased their dominance and social activities. Upon his return, the dominant male assumed his former position and the social activities of the other males was reduced.

Effects of Changing Task and Organizational Location. In the study mentioned earlier, Sakamaki (1974) found that the performance (P) orientation scores (according to subordinates) of 121 first-line Japanese supervisors who were not transferred correlated .35 from one year to the next. For maintenance (M) orientation, the rate-rerate correlation was .53. For nontransferred

second-line supervisors, the respective correlations were .74 and .59. But for 133 transferred first-line supervisors, the corresponding correlations dropped to .03, and −.07, and for 19 transferred second-line managers, the corresponding correlations dropped to .29 and −.08. The lack of consistency in leadership orientation for the transferred supervisors compared to those who did not transfer could be attributed to a change in the composition of their subordinates who rated them, as well as to a change in their positions and social context.

Misumi and Mannari (1982) clarified the importance of the similarity or difference between the old and new situations of transferred supervisors. When 67 Japanese bank managers were transferred to jobs with similar work content and social context, they tended to exhibit the same P and M orientations, as revealed in rate-rerate correlations by subordinates of .56 and .42, respectively. But when 23 other bank managers were transferred to different kinds of departments in different branches, the rate-rerate correlations dropped to .10 and −.06, respectively.

Evidence of the Effects of Negative Transfer

In this area, one has to rely more on anecdotal evidence and interpretive hindsight. Although negative transfer is a theoretical possibility as well as observable in real life, it is difficult to create experimentally. The manual-mechanical tasks have to be completely free of any discussion, any verbal or intellectual components, or any interaction requirements. All individual traits that are likely to promote positive transfer need to be controlled, such as general ability, interpersonal competence, external status, and external esteem of the participants in the groups that are shifted from "head" to "hand" tasks.

Nonetheless, many observers have described how earlier success in an old situation fixates the behavior of the leader, making him or her less effective in a new, different situation that requires a new approach to problems. For example, a technical supervisor who has been a successful leader in a situation that demands precision exactness may fail to deal with the challenge of decision making in the absence of complete information when promoted to the position of general manager

(Pearse, Worthington, & Flaherty, 1954). Similarly the business executive may transfer his successful profit-making practices to running a government agency with disastrous results (Fishman, 1952). Merton (1940) singled out the stereotyped bureaucrat who adopts measures as a leader in keeping with past training. Under new conditions, not recognized as significantly different, the very soundness of the training leads to the bureaucrat's adoption of the wrong procedures. Furthermore, continued success in day-to-day routines makes the bureaucrat unable to change or see the need to change when the conditions under which the bureaucracy was organized are changed.

Negative transfer may explain the ill-fated attempt at administrative reforms in Zaire in 1973, in which the local chieftaincies were changed by rotating the chiefs outside their areas of origin. Although the failure of the policy was attributed by Schatzberg (1982) to the lack of timely consultation, it would seem that there must have been considerable negative transfer because of the loss of legitimacy, understanding, and applicability of a chief's approach when he was moved from his home area to another.

Shifting leaders from situations that are favorable to them and in which they have experienced effectiveness to situations that are unfavorable to them should produce negative transfer. The leaders' earlier success should result in their continuing to attempt the same leadership in the new situation with a consequential decrement in effective outcomes, as would be inferred from Fiedler's (1967) Contingency Theory.[5] The garrison commander may not do as well when in a front-line command. The effective leader in emergencies may be unsuccessful and ineffective elsewhere. Thus, Elkin, Halpern, and Cooper (1962) observed that the individuals who tended to emerge as leaders in experimentally created mobs were not popular under other circumstances. Likewise, what is likely to make a leader effective in the early stage of development of a sensitivity training group seems to reverse in later stages of development. Data from 158 members and leaders of 20 such groups showed that trainers who were considered to have little need for control and affection tended to elicit the most favorable reactions during an early pe-

riod of a group and the most negative reactions at a later time (Schutz & Allen, 1966).

Negative transfer occurs when a new situation requires values different or opposite to those fitting the old situation. Thus, the political appointments of conservative, private-sector executives to administer public housing programs to which they were ideologically opposed, resulted in their corrupt and wasteful violations of the barest minimum standards of public service (Montgomery, 1989).

A well-documented case of negative transfer of leadership was described by Roberts (1984) and Roberts and Bradley (1987). A school district superintendent in a midwestern suburban community unexpectedly gained a state-wide reputation in educational and business circles for success as an energetic, innovative, and visionary leader who had converted the threat of a budgetary crisis into an opportunity for improvements in the district. Her transformational leadership had a dramatic impact on the district. Her charisma resulted in some of her followers becoming cultlike. However, when she subsequently served for two years as commissioner of education for the state, none of the successful transformational leadership was seen. No cultlike following developed. No attributions of extraordinary talents and abilities were heard; no strong bonds of affection were forged with constituents. Instead, there was strong criticism of her leadership style and actions. What had worked well in a school district in crisis was counterproductive in the larger state system.

Succession

The process of succession is an examination of the transfer process from another vantage point. Antecedents that promote the more effective replacement of one leader by another and the consequences of replacing one leader with another provide a further opportunity to see how the positive and negative transfer of leadership may occur (Gordon & Rosen, 1981).

House and Singh (1987) pointed to the importance of the executive succession process—a phenomenon in all groups and organizations that survive. In the succession process, much power is transferred along with control of the organization's relations to its outside envi-

[5]See Chapter 23.

ronment. A change of executives is often associated with major changes in the organization. The succession is a focal point of political processes within the organization (Zald, 1965). Decisions about the succession express the particular political preferences of the organization's constituencies (Pfeffer & Salancik 1974, Salancik & Pfeffer, 1974). The change of leaders is often accompanied by a change of the political environment that casts the replaced leader in an unfavorable light (Rockman, 1984). It is no wonder that most incumbent chief executives give top priority to the question of succession (Bruce, 1986). Except for a major reorganization, the retirement of the chief executive probably causes more job changes down the line than does any other event.

The average tenure in office of chief operating executives in industry appears similar to those in higher education and hospital administration. The median tends to be little more than five years, although implicitly the expected term of office may often be closer to ten years (Wilson & McLaughlin, 1984). Thus, succession, at the highest levels, at least, is a frequent occurrence for organizations. If the successor comes from within the organization, there may be a wave of other promotions at lower levels. If the succession comes from outside, then the organization that supplied the successor must find a replacement so it, too, will be engaged in a succession process. The rate of succession will increase in periods of prosperity and growth as organizations multiply and expand.

Purposes Served by the Succession Process

Although Flament (1956) and Pryer, Flint, and Bass (1962) reported that experimental groups tended to remain effective as long as they did not change leaders, in the political arena, in particular, the choosing of new leaders is an occasion for renewal. In both capitalist and socialist countries, innovations, new policies, new priorities, and revised budgets usually accompany the succession of new leadership. Yet some leaders may be chosen as caretakers. When a change of leaders is mandated, such as at the end of four or eight years for a U.S. president, the successor may be chosen to provide continuity. Thus, Blake and Mouton (1985b) showed that four twentieth century U.S. presidents who chose

their successors tended to choose a leader similar to their own management style. But, the styles of the nine successors who were not chosen by the previous president tended to be different from those of their predecessors.

A change in management because of poor organizational performance is a way that the organization attempts to be adaptive (Helmich & Brown, 1972). The failure to change leadership will reduce such adaptivity, for failing firms have lower rates of succession than do nonfailing firms (Schwartz & Menon, 1985).

In choosing the top managing successors of an organization, one is likely to be contributing to changes in the organization's strategies and to what is to be valued by the organization. In searching for successors for the chief executive, one seeks organizational renewal. There may be need to dip down into the next generation of managers with less seniority to find the leadership required for such changes. The organization's structure is likely to be affected. For example, Hambrick and Mason (1984) hypothesized that if the successors are highly educated professional managers, the organization is likely to see them introduce more thorough planning systems, complex coordination devices, budgeting details, and complex incentive-compensation schemes.

Succession is an opportunity for organizational members to participate in a process that may significantly shift the organization's direction. The expenditure of time and effort in the process reaffirms the importance of the position to the organization and adds to the power of the position (Pfeffer, 1981b). Succession offers opportunities for coalitions of interests within organizations to communicate, exercise preferences, and negotiate the organization's future (Gephart, 1978).

The Search Committee. The particular representation of organizational members on the search committee for the successor enhances the status of their various constituencies in the organization. The quality of the committee's search process adds legitimacy to the chosen successor's leadership (Hollander, 1985). The search committee is an important source of information to the successor about the organization's current normative expectations, values, and distribution of power (Birnbaum, 1987a). That meeting with outside prospects can provide sources of new objectives, values, information, and methods has received less recognition.

Antecedents of Succession

As Trow (1960) noted, it is difficult to sort out the antecedents from the consequences of the succession in leadership. New leadership may enhance a group's performance, but the group's performance may determine the rate of succession. Nevertheless, one can attempt to tease out the conditions that affect the rate of succession.

The turnover of executives may be due to ill-health, deaths, or unexpected voluntary retirements and resignations for other personal reasons. When Campion and Mitchell (1986) compared 140 former executives and managers with 143 current ones in the same organization, the leavers reported less satisfying job characteristics, more problems of adjustment and socialization, unmet job expectations, and more job stress than did those currently in the organization. House and Singh (1987) listed the following personal traits that help to reduce such turnover: psychological hardiness (optimism, vigorous involvement, commitment to rather than alienation from self), the need for achievement, and the ability to cope with stressful conditions. Particularly important contributors to voluntary resignations are the executives' perceptions of their own power to influence their organization and their felt need for such power.

Firms that lack internal consensus exhibit more internal conflict, which leads to higher rates of executive turnover compared to organizations with internal consensus. Again, turbulent environments are antecedents of executive turnover. Such turbulence doubled annual voluntary resignations of chief executives between 1974 to 1984 (Weschler, 1984).

Involuntary Change. The antecedent condition that most often precipitates an involuntary change of leadership is failure by the group or organization that is attributed to the leadership. Sometimes the attribution is accurate but other times, the leader is the scapegoat for the group or organization's shortcomings. Considerable evidence supports the contention that an organization's failure stimulates a change of its leaders.

Firms with solvency problems (increased debt/equity ratios) change leadership more frequently than do firms without such problems (Pfeffer & Leblebici, 1973). The high turnover of 576 top managers in 31 Fortune 500 firms was associated with the firms' poor financial performance (Wagner, Pfeffer, & O'Reilly, 1984). While 45 percent of bankrupt firms changed chief executives, only 19 percent of a comparable sample of healthy firms did so (Schwartz & Menon, 1985).

The extent to which managers of baseball teams with the poorest season's records are most likely to be changed is well known (Grusky, 1963a). Path analyses by Allen, Panian, and Lotz (1979) confirmed that poor records, rather than other related elements, resulted in the replacement of managers of baseball teams. In the same way, Hamblin (1958b) demonstrated that groups change leaders informally if the leaders do not have a way of helping the groups out of crises. Such changes in leaders will be accelerated if the members have complex rather than simple personalities (Schroder, Streufert, & Welden, 1964). Conversely, Goldman and Fraas (1965) found that subordinates were more likely to choose leaders who had been more successful earlier with the group's task. But Daum (1975) failed to find such results.

Other factors contribute to the turnover in leaders. Virany, Tushman, and Romanelli (1985) concluded, from an analysis of the succession events of corporate-level executives in 37 firms, that although performance was most important in generating the change of executives, such changes were actually driven by strategic reorientations in high-performance firms. Consistent with this finding, Smith and White's (1987) analysis of the succession of 370 chief executive officers in the 25-year history of 173 Fortune 1000 firms showed that the current strategy of the firm tended to dictate the career specialty from which the new chief executive was drawn. Graham and Richards (1979) reached similar conclusions for the railroad industry.

It is not surprising that the increased movement of marketing executives into top management coincides with the increased focus of firms on their marketing. When there is increased emphasis on cost containment accountants come to the fore. Increased strategic concern for production and the quality of products brings engineers into top management.

When persistent organizational problems remain unmanaged and when there is a failure to cope with critical contingencies, the chief executive loses support and is likely to be replaced (Thompson, 1967). Along with the declining performance of their organizations, increasing difficulties in management increase the rate of succession (James & Soref, 1981). Thus, Helmich (1978), in a study of 54 petrochemical firms, found that the rate of presidential turnover was increased with mergers, acquisitions, and the increased dispersal of operations.

Osborn, Jauch, Martin, and Glueck (1981) demonstrated that the rate of executive succession increased with the firms' volatility in profitability and unstable financial strategies. As with turbulent economic environments, the rate of succession was also greater for organizations in more turbulent ownership, supplier relationships, and socioeconomic environments.

Downton (1973) argued that successful transactional leaders must continue to meet their obligations to their followers or be replaced. This statement suggests that transformational leaders should be able to maintain themselves in office longer since they have focused more on long-term considerations. Thus, the Soviet leadership, for example, survived for 70 years, to some extent, on Lenin's admonitions early in the century and promises for a better life for all the workers, peasants, and intelligensia.

Effects of Organizational Size. Among the possible antecedents of the rate of executive succession is the size of the organization. Grusky (1961) reported that the rate of succession of chief executive officers was directly related to the firm's size. But when Salancik and Pfeffer (1980) examined the tenure of the chief executives of 84 U.S. corporations, the executives' tenure was unrelated to the corporations' size. Gordon and Becker (1964) suggested that the relationship of organizational size to the rate of executive succession was complicated by other factors that accompany organizational size. Thus, for instance, larger firms have more ready inside replacements and would be expected to exhibit higher rates of succession as a consequence. However, insiders who reach the top serve longer terms in their positions (Helmich, 1976). Kriesberg (1962, 1964) further suggested that the differences among industries and in technology has to be taken into account.

Salancik, Staw, and Pondy (1980) examined the turnover of the heads of 20 university departments. They found that turnover increased with a department's size but was lower if the department had been more successful in receiving outside grants. Turnover was also lower in departments in which there was agreement about how knowledge in one area was relevant in another area, as reflected in the departments' ability to organize a long string of courses in their curricula. In another study, Pfeffer and Moore (1980) also found that the size of a department was of consequence. They also obtained positive associations between the length of tenure of its heads, departmental consensus, and the seniority of its faculty.

Effects of Age. Differences in the age of top managers and others in a firm contributed to more rapid turnover of top management, according to Wagner, Pfeffer, and O'Reilly (1984). Evidently, the increasing age gap, presumably due to the older-than-ordinary senior managers, brings on pressure to accelerate the succession process.

Concentration of Ownership. Although tenure was related to changes in profit margins, Salancik and Pfeffer (1980) found that it depended on the concentration of stock ownership. Tenure was unrelated to the corporation's performance for owner-managed firms but was related positively to profit margins for externally controlled firms and to stock market rates of return for management-controlled firms. According to McEachern (1975) and Allen and Panian (1982), in general, the rate of succession was likely to be greater if the management was under external control than if it was free wheeling and only in control of itself.

Selection of Insider or Outsider as Successor. Some investigators have concluded that poor organizational performance moves the organization to choose an outsider as successor; other investigators have concluded the opposite. And still others have found middle-range organizational performance to be most conducive to choosing an outsider. The differences may be explained partly by the nature of the organizations involved. For example, Allen, Panian, and Lotz (1979) found that outside succession was more disruptive to the performance of a baseball team than was bringing up a new manager from the inside; nonetheless, there was a greater tendency to go outside for a new manager when the previous year's performance had been poor. In the same way, Virany and Tushman (1986) showed that of the 59 minicomputer firms that were performing poorly tended to make more senior management appointments from the outside than did those firms whose performance was better. Likewise, Otten and Teulings (1970) found, in an analysis of the succession histories of 34 Dutch department heads in different organizations, that low initial levels of performance in departments were a positive incentive to select outsiders as successors.

Dalton and Kesner (1985) observed that outside successors were most often chosen by companies that were mid-range in performance. And for a sample of 166 large firms, Lubatkin and Chung (1985) noted that in a crisis of falling profits, fewer outsiders were chosen as successors. Contrary to most other studies, in this study it was the prosperous firms that were more inclined to choose outsiders. Perhaps there is more willingness of outsiders to accept a senior appointment in a prosperous than a failing firm.

In some firms of sufficient age, long-standing policies, management development, and manpower planning, inside successors are identified early and are groomed for the succession. Larger and older firms, such as IBM and Exxon, along with Japanese firms, in general, and those in many other countries, develop their own chief executives and directors of boards who rise from the ranks and are familiar with the firms' people, markets, and products (Pfeffer & Moore, 1980; Tsurumi, 1983b).

In the political arena, outsiders are chosen to exemplify the "new broom sweeping clean." Best (1981) contrasted the original appointments of cabinet members and their replacements for the presidential administrations between 1952 and 1976 in terms of whether they came from inside or outside the government. Only 35 percent were original appointments at the beginning of a presidential term of office; 65 percent were replacements during a term of office. The original appointees were chosen to generate legitimacy and to form a cabinet that the president could trust. They were mainly outsiders to the Washington bureaucracy. However, their replacements later in the same president's administration were primarily insiders with Washington experience and managerial ability.

Consequences of the Succession

Ziller (1965b) obtained results suggesting that the rapid replacement of group leaders provides a means of creating new ideas and that leads to the continued success of the group. But changing leaders can result in a group's decreased performance (Pryer, Flint, & Bass, 1962) because of the disruption of the change and the costs to performance of the personnel turnover (Rogers, Ford, & Tassone, 1961; Trow, 1960). However, as will be seen, the change in leaders need not be disruptive, especially when it is planned and expected. It actually may result in the improved performance of a group or organization in some instances and no change or reduced performance in others. A more complex set of relations must be examined. For instance, Friedman and Saul's (1988) survey of respondents from 235 Fortune 500 firms demonstrated that the morale of the firm following the succession of a new chief executive officer was lower if the predecessor had a long tenure in office.

In 17 experimental groups studied by Pryer, Flint, and Bass (1962), those groups that gained in effectiveness exhibited correlations of .70 and .33 in the stability of the leadership. Among groups whose effectiveness decreased, the same correlations were −.08 and .01. But Gamson and Scotch (1964) concluded that the impact of the change in managers of a baseball team was minimal; the firing of a baseball manager was only a ritual for, as was noted before, Grusky (1963) had found that baseball teams with the poorest records had the highest rates of change in managers. Allen, Panian, and Lotz (1979) then showed that such higher rates of change subsequently resulted in poorer performance by the teams. Their path-analytic examination of managerial succession for 54 seasons showed that baseball teams that replaced a manager during the season subsequently performed worse. However, Eitzen and Yetman (1972) found no relation between the turnover of coaches of basketball teams and the teams' performance records over 40 years. Similarly, Brown (1982) concluded that in the case of 26 National League football teams from 1970 to 1978, there was no difference in the recovery of teams that had steep declines in performance to better winning records when coaches were replaced in midseason because of the teams' poor performance than when the same coaches were retained. Brown (1982) inferred that the changing of coaches in midstream was a scapegoating mechanism that had little subsequent effect on the teams' performance. Smith, Carson, and Alexander (1984) agreed, finding, in an analysis of the succession of 50 Methodist ministers, that the succesion "in and of itself" did not disrupt or improve church leadership and management, as measured by church attendance, membership, property values, and contributions. Likewise, Lieberson and O'Connor (1972) found that changes in the corporate sales, profit, and profit margins of 167 corporations in 13 industries over a 20-year period (1946 to 1965) were not closely related to changes in the corporate presidents or chairmen of the boards.

The results were different when the effects of changes elsewhere in management were analyzed. Although Lieberson and O'Connor concluded that the succession of new presidents or board chairmen accounted for less of the variance in sales, earnings, and profits than differences in either industry or company, Day and Lord (1986) pointed out that the effects of the change of these top executives increased with time, accounting for from 15.2 percent to 31.7 percent of the profit margins when the time lag between the change of management and its subsequent effects was increased to three years. Unlike the changes in the managers of sports teams, changes in top business management did have important, practical effects on the firms' performance. Thomas (1988) reached the same conclusions in a study of large retail firms in Britain.

Again, Salancik and Pfeffer (1977) studied the influence of 172 successive mayors on the revenues, debt, and expenditures of 30 U.S. cities from 1951 to 1968. As Day and Lord (1986) noted, an adjustment had to be made for the size of the cities to uncover the effect of the succeeding mayors on expenditures and indebtedness. Changes in mayors accounted for about 19 percent of the variance in financial outcomes.

Eitzen and Yetman (1972) and Trow (1961) thought that the results best supported a curvilinear model of the relationships—that there is an optimal rate of turnover of leaders. Nevertheless, Schendel, Patton, and

Riggs (1976) found 80 percent of the turnaround strategies associated with the replacement of top managers. Similar results were reported by Graham and Richards (1979) for the railroad industry.

The Analysis Makes the Difference. Day and Lord (1986) also noted that it was necessary to take monetary inflation and the size of the organization into account, in addition to allowing for sufficient lag-time for the effects of the new management on the firm's performance to be seen. But the effects of the changes in management have been most understated by analyses such as those of Lieberson and O'Connor (1972) because the best predictor of future performance is past performance. When the effect of the company's past performance on its future performance is first in the regression analysis, it takes with it much of the effect of the changes in management on future performance. However, as Weiner and Mahoney (1981) demonstrated for a comparable sample of firms, when the management variable is entered first into the equation, it accounts for 75 to 95 percent of the explained variance. The same is true in studies of the performance of baseball teams.

Moderators of the Effects of the Succession

Whether replacing the leader will contribute to the group's or the organization's subsequent performance is also affected by a variety of moderating variables (Gephart, 1978). The reasons for the succession make a difference in its effects on future performance, as does whether the succession is voluntary or forced and whether the departing chief executive is the firm's founder (Johnson, Magee, Nagarajan, & Newman, 1985; Reinganum, 1985). In an analysis of 136 successions, Friedman and Singh (1986) compared the stock market value of shares of firms from 300 days before the announcement of each succession to 100 days after it. The market value declined when the announced reason for the departure of the chief executive was an unexpected disability, was unaffected if the retirement was expected, but increased if the departure was forced or voluntary because of poor performance. The market value of shares of subsidiary firms that performed poorly for 300 days before the succession increased during the next 100 days with announcement of a new chief executive. But the succession had no effect on the parent firms' shares if they had already been doing well.

Other moderators of the effects of succession include whether the successor brings more competence to the position and what changes occur in the style and power of the leadership. The suddenness of the succession, whether the successor is an insider or outsider, and whether there is a consensus in the group or organization will affect whether the change of leadership is beneficial to the group or organization. The industry in which the succession occurs also moderates its effects.

The Successor's Competence. Pfeffer and Davis-Blake (1986) showed, for 22 teams in the National Basketball Association, that when prior performance is controlled, replacing the coach, in general, had no effect on a team's subsequent performance. However, the new coach's greater competence did make a positive contribution to improving the team's performance. A team that replaced its coach with one who had a good prior record and relevant experience or who had brought about improved performance in other teams performed better than did a team whose new coach lacked experience or had performed less adequately in his previous assignments.

Smith, Carson, and Alexander (1984) found comparable results with their sample of Methodist ministers. Those incoming ministers with a previous record of competence had more positive effects on their new church's performance than did those without such a record. Again, Shetty and Perry (1976) found that executives had more of a postsuccession effect on their organizations in a new industry if they possessed the necessary knowledge and relevant influence of consequence.

The Successor's Style and Power. House and Singh (1987) suggested some especially important unknowns that affect the organization's performance following a succession. These unknowns include the effects of the political behavior of the preceding and succeeding executives and how the executives restructure control within the organization, protect their own position, and implement strategic changes. Helmich (1974b) established that the origin and style of a successor to 140

presidents of manufacturing firms influenced the changes and improvements that occurred in the organization. The task-oriented leadership behavior of the successors was greater than that of the predecessors, particularly during the early days of the successors' tenure.

The personal learning opportunities for the successors are also likely to be of consequence (Hall, 1986). The takeover strategies employed by the successors make a difference. Some begin by holding meetings with their new people; others do not. Some are more aware of the social dynamics involved in the succession; others are not. Some may bring allies and assistants with them; others will enter the new post alone (Grusky, 1969). Some may utilize the formal system and depend on their authority, with a resulting increase in tension; others will rely more on informal contacts to learn about what is needed to guide future actions (Gordon & Rosen, 1981). Some fail to consider individual, group, and organizational dynamics, which results in conflict, defensiveness, and organizational regression (Oskarsson & Klein, 1982).

Preselection Political Activity. Welsh and Dehler (1988) examined the amount of organizational politics (lobbying, forming coalitions, and so forth) that was present in 36 colleges that were actively searching for a new dean and the subsequent effects on the activity of the candidate who was eventually chosen during the first three years in office. If a lot of preselection politicking occurred among the faculty, the chosen successor in a college with abundant resources, as would be expected, expended much less effort to acquire resources than did a successor in a college with scarce resources. But unexpectedly, if political activity was low, there were no differences in the activities of the successor. If there was a lot of political activity among the faculty, the successor was expected to engage in more administrative activity if resources were scarce than if they were abundant. However, if resources were abundant, nonadministrative activity was required of the successor if there was little politicking among the faculty.

The Transition. How the transition is handled by organizations and successors is also important. For instance, an organization may resort to an acting appointee before selecting a permanent successor (Gordon & Rosen, 1981). The transition process itself has become an important subject of study to determine whether it foreshadows things to come with the new leader's activities. From the November election through the first day following the inauguration of the new president on January 20, the transition is carefully watched by journalists for signs of what lies ahead during the new administration. Gilmore (1988) pointed out that the successor, whether in government or in industry, needs to consider the past leader's performance, entrenched interests, and the persistence to change in the agency or firm. A new team has to be assembled, agendas changed, a new vision of the organization created, and a reorganization accomplished that is consistent with the new vision. The place of change must be realistic and balanced. Productive working alliances need to be negotiated to provide for the organization's effective management.

Abruptness of the Succession. In this regard, Friedman and Singh's (1986) demonstration of the negative impact of the unexpected succession on stock prices was already mentioned. Jackson (1953b) reported finding a work group emotionally disturbed by the unexpected replacement of its valued foreman. Top management was excoriated and the new foreman was overly devalued. Gordon and Rosen (1981) also noted that changes in leadership that come with little advance notice are especially detrimental to the effectiveness of factory work groups.

The sudden death of an executive, particularly one who is highly visible to the public, which forces an unexpected succession, results in a decline in the market value of the firm (Worrell, Davidson, Chandy, & Garrison, 1986). Trow (1961) concluded that the effects of executive succession on organizational performance will be more positive if the succession is orderly and planned than if the succession is unexpected and the selection of the new chief executive has to be made under the pressure of time. Sorcher (1985) agreed that careful succession planning is needed at each organizational level. Betts and Huntington (1986) noted that long-term instability follows the death of an authoritar-

ian leader if the country is already unstable, if the authoritarian ruler was in office for a long period, and if there is a strong social organization to facilitate antigovernmental actions following the death of the ruler.

Effects of the Succession of Insiders or Outsiders. While bureaucratic maintenance is thought to be favored by the succession of an insider, more organizational change may be obtained by the succession of an outsider. A progression of insiders is seen to slow organizational growth (Helmich, 1974a) and adaptation (Carlson, 1961).

Conflict may be reduced inside the organization by choosing an outsider. For example, upon winning their independence from Turkey in the nineteenth century, the Balkan countries—Greece, Bulgaria, and Rumania—chose petty German princes for their new kings to avoid conflict among the leading noble families, as well as to obtain support from the Great Powers of Britain, Austria-Hungary, France, and Russia. Similarly, Birnbaum (1971) showed that state universities tend to recruit their presidents from the lower administrative levels of other state universities, rather than from their own universities or from nearby colleges in the state, thus both promoting the transfer from elsewhere and restricting conflict inside their own universities. (At the same time, the main source of lower-level administrators were promotions from within the universities.)

Nevertheless, Lubatkin and Chung (1985) found no particular differences in the subsequent performance of successors who were insiders or outsiders. Likewise, Chung, Lubatkin, Rogers, and Owers (1987) concluded, after comparing 80 appointments of insiders to 19 appointments of outsiders as chief executive officers, that although long-term profitability after a succession depended mainly on the firm's profitability before the succession, rather than on the change of leaders, stock prices went up when outsiders but not insiders were hired by high-performing firms. However, only the exceptional new leader from the outside could successfully turn around the poorly performing firm.

Clearly, contextual moderating variables must be examined before one can reach conclusions about the extent to which better organizational performance results from a choice of an insider or an outsider. One needs to know if the outsider has a mandate for change, particularly to change top management and its strategies. One needs to know whether inside successors have been chosen by default because desired outsiders could not be recruited in the face of the organization's poor history of conflict and performance (House & Singh, 1987).

The succession of insiders provides for the continuity of existing programs, management practices, and organizational stability (House & Singh, 1987). The lack of continuity is seen when outsiders are appointed to senior leadership posts in a new presidential administration. Its effects on the U.S. State Department are a loss of coherence in policy-making (Bloomfield, 1984). The change of administration in the Environmental Protection Agency likewise promotes greater distrust between career employees and political appointees, less effective communication, and the inability to handle routine business or to improve the agency's performance over time (Gaertner, Gaertner, & Devine, 1983).

In their survey of senior-ranking human resources officers in 235 Fortune 500 firms, Friedman and Saul (1988) confirmed that the appointment of outside successors to the post of chief executive officer resulted in more postsuccession disruption and turnover of lower-level executives than did the appointment of inside successors. However, overall, outside and inside successors did not appear to have different effects on morale.

In an analysis of the impact of 477 successions, Lubatkin, Chung, Rogers, and Owers (1989) concluded that although stock prices are depressed generally by the occurrence of a succession, the price of the stock is enhanced (indicating that investors are favorably impressed) when the successor is an outsider and the firm is above the average in its performance. Again, for the 15 percent of 136 successors in Friedman and Singh's (1986) analysis who were outsiders, the market value of the parent firm's shares increased. But the value of shares was unaffected if the successor was an insider. Insider-outsider effects of the predecessor were more complex. Forced resignations of a predecessor who was an insider had a more positive effect than a forced resignation of a predecessor who was an outsider, although both events had positive effects. The voluntary

resignation of an executive who originally was an outsider resulted in a much greater increase in the market value of the parent firm's shares than did the voluntary resignation of one who was originally from the inside. Although the expected retirement of an insider had no effect, the expected retirement of an outsider did have a positive effect on the market value of the parent firm's shares.

Welsh and Dehler (1986) questioned a random stratified sample of 960 faculty members from 40 professional colleges of business, education, agriculture, and engineering and followed up the survey with telephone interviews and questionnaires 3 years later. They found that when consensus about issues was low among the faculty of a college, those colleges that selected a dean from the inside experienced greater turnover of deans. Conversely, when consensus was high among the faculty, those colleges that chose a dean from the outside experienced greater turnover. The lowest turnover of deans occurred in colleges with high faculty consensus who selected a dean from the inside.

Differences among Industries. Durbrow (1971) analyzed the biographical sketches of some 5,300 executives in 429 organizations in 10 major industries. The rates of mobility were highest in the aerospace, electronics, and office equipment industries and lowest in the gas utility, electric utility, and chemical industries. Durbrow found that firms with low rates of executive turnover made the highest profits in high-mobility industries and those with high rates of executive turnover made the highest profits in low-mobility industries. Thus, for instance, utility firms were more profitable if they had high rates of succession, but aerospace firms did best if there was a low turnover among their executives.

A Model for Succession

Gordon and Rosen (1981) proposed a model for the dynamics of succession that takes into account variables antedating the arrival and entry of the new leader into the organization, postarrival variables of consequence, and the interaction between the two sets of variables. Included in the prearrival variables are the successor's background, competence, motivation, and orientation, whether the successor came from inside or outside the organization; how well the successor was known in advance by the organization; the organization's previous general experience with the succession process; and how much the organization was specifically involved in selecting the new leader. The new leader's mandate is also important. Postarrival variables include much of what was identified in preceding chapters about the factors that influence leader-follower relationships and how they, in turn, affect productivity and satisfaction.

Summary and Conclusions

Strong evidence has been found to support the view that leadership is transferable from one situation to another. The nature of the demands of the task determines whether the effects of the transfer will be positive or negative. But, in all, there is a tendency for the leader of one group to emerge as the leader when placed in other groups.

Leadership in high school and college tends to be predictive of leadership in adult life. When members of experimental groups are successively reassigned to new groups, the same individuals tend to emerge as leaders. This effect is enhanced when the task is similar from group to group.

When effective and ineffective leaders change places, the performance and morale of formerly ineffective groups tend to improve under effective leaders, but the formerly effective groups suffer from such a change in leaders.

The productivity of groups that change leaders frequently or experience high rates of succession of new leaders tends to decline. But such reductions may be the cause rather than the effect of the rapid turnover of leaders. Moderators of the effect include whether successors are insiders or outsiders and how abruptly changes are made. Another moderator is whether the successor is of the same or opposite sex, a subject of the next chapter.

Diverse Groups

Women and Leadership

The Rise in Women Leaders and Managers

It is not surprising that sex[1] as a difference of consequence in the study of leadership has surged in importance only during the past two decades. It was hardly discussed in Stogdill's (1948) review and in the first edition of this handbook (Stogdill, 1974), although it was seen as a useful subject for future research.

By the late 1980s, there had been women prime ministers in Britain, India, Pakistan, Sri Lanka, the Philippines, and Norway; a governor-general of Canada; and a candidate for the office of U.S. vice president. Women had also come to occupy a quarter of the supervisory positions in U.S. business and industry. A large number of women had taken on important leadership roles in education, defense, health care, and other not-for-profit sectors as well. Earlier in the twentieth century, female world-class leaders had included Eleanor Roosevelt, Jane Addams, Emily Pankhurst, Marie Curie, and Rosa Luxemburg. Prominent as strong leaders in previous centuries had been Eleanor of Aquitaine; Margaret of Denmark, Norway, and Sweden; Elizabeth I of England; and Catherine the Great of Russia. Furthermore, many less well-known women had managed family businesses or

---

[1]Languages, particularly English, evolve because of usage, not because of logic or consistency. Hence, words that are used incorrectly often come into vogue. Such has been the case with the use of *gender* to mean one of the two sexes.

Men and women are two clearly different biological types, distinguished by a variety of physical and physiological differences. They are the two—the only two—different sexes. Their social and behavioral similarities and differences are looked at in terms of their membership in one sex rather than the other.

Until it was incorrectly applied by social scientists, *gender* was only a grammatical term. In English, there are *three* grammatical genders: male, female, and neutral. Nonetheless, by the 1980s, *gender differences*, a term that probably originated as a Victorian euphuism, had primarily supplanted *sex differences* in the social sciences. Although differences between the two sexes are now most often relabeled differences between two genders, and the social and behavioral blends are *androgynous*, not *neutral*, I have chosen to remain in the minority and to continue to call male-female differences differences between the sexes.

were chosen to replace their deceased husbands in political office or worked as supervisors mainly of other women in offices, in hospitals, or in the telephone industry. Nevertheless, these women were but a small percentage of all the women in the population and a small percentage in contrast to men in leadership positions everywhere.

And still, in the mid-1980s, little more than 5 percent of the members of the U.S. House of Representatives and 2 percent of the members of the U.S. Senate were women. Similarly, only 10 percent of the West German parliament were women. Few women served in the cabinets and ministries of the world's democracies (Kruse & Wintermantel, 1986). However, the sex distribution in office holding seemed to be a bit more equitable in U.S. state and local governments. The continuing failure of women to move en masse into positions of political leadership compared to their somewhat better success in the private sector may be due to the fact that women were granted the right to work before they were granted the right to vote (Apfelbaum & Hadley, 1988). Similarly, women leaders of social movements, such as Margaret Sanger, Emma Goldman, Simone de Beauvoir, or Betty Friedan have been but a small percentage in comparison to the men who have sparked and organized social revolutions and reforms (Apfelbaum & Hadley, 1986).

Increase in MBAs. In 1974, Michigan State University reported twice the proportion of women students in business as it had in 1969. Stanford University noted a similar doubling in a 3-year period from 1971 to 1974 (Chambers, 1974). From 1971 to 1976, the number of women who were enrolled in MBA programs in American universities tripled (L. Werner, 1979). Figure 32.1 shows the sharp rise in the absolute and proportional amounts of women who received MBA degrees or the equivalent between 1956 and 1986. By the late 1980s, parity of the sexes had been reached in many business schools.

Figure 32.1. Closing the Gap

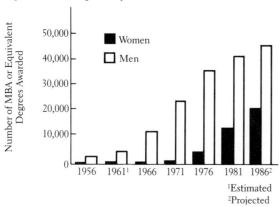

¹Estimated
²Projected

SOURCE: *U.S. Department of Education (1986). Adapted from the* Wall Street Journal *(March 24, 1986, Section 4, p. 11D). Reprinted by permission of the* Wall Street Journal, *© Dow Jones & Company, Inc. (1986). All Rights Reserved Worldwide.*

Increase in Management. There has been a marked increase in the proportion of women in managerial and leadership positions in the past two decades. Although women made up less than 5 percent of middle managers and less than 2 percent of executives in business in the early 1970s (M. W. Meyer, 1975), between 1970 and 1980, gains for women in top leadership roles were registered, especially in the mass media, universities, private foundations, and cultural institutions (Dye & Strickland, 1982). Between 1970 and 1980, the total number of women managers and administrators in the U.S. work force increased over 100 percent. Just between 1972 and 1986, the percentage of women in managerial positions rose from 19 to over 30 percent (Hymowitz & Schellhardt, 1986). In the military, 10 percent of the U.S. naval officers were women by 1987, and by 1980, a woman was serving as the commanding general of a large U.S. army post (Beck, 1980). But by and large, more women in proportion to men were concentrated in the lower levels of management. By 1985, for example, while only 2.7 percent of the top executives and directors of A T & T were women and 8.3 percent and 15 percent were division and district managers, respectively, 22 percent were second-level supervisors and 38.7 percent were first-level supervisors (Hymowitz & Schellhardt, 1986). Proportionately more women than men had attained management jobs in service firms, such as A T & T, rather than in industrial

firms like Dupont, Exxon, or General Motors, where the percentage hovered around 8 percent. The percentages were generally much higher for retailing and trade. For instance, in 1985, the proportion of women managers reached 61 percent in Federated Stores and 64 percent in Bank America.

Many more women, such as Mary Kay, had become company founders and effective leaders of large enterprises. As of 1981, among 112 publicly traded firms headquartered in one metropolitan center, one-fifth reported having at least one woman member of the board of directors. Firms in consumer-related industries were most likely (5 of 10) to have a woman director, while holding companies and firms in the extraction industries had none. Also women had more opportunities to become insider directors (managers elevated to the Board of Directors in the same firm) in small than in large firms (Harrigan, 1981).

Society in Transition

Except when such male-favored characteristics as upper-body strength are required, the roles of women in society are primarily culturally determined. Childbearing has its obvious universal effects, but most of what women can and do is culture based. Thus, in a survey of 224 mainly subsistence-level societies, Murdock (1937) showed that although men generally hunted and trapped and women usually gathered and prepared food, few occupations were entirely relegated anywhere to only one sex. (An exception was hunting sea mammals, which would be hard on pregnant women.)

We are in a period of transition. Much of the cultural support is diminishing for maintaining sex differences in leadership and, more important, for maintaining different attitudes, beliefs, and values about women leaders. Equal employment legislation and U.S. Supreme Court decisions had dramatic effects, as had the movement of a majority of adult women into the full-time work force. Some jobs are still seen as more male relevant and others as more female relevant, and the sexes are still segregated in many firms according to their positions. Nonetheless, by 1977, over 75 percent of women disagreed that some work is meant for men and other work is meant for women—an increase of 21 percentage points from 1962. Younger women in 1977 were even more likely to disagree, which suggests that even more extreme rejection by women of the duality of work roles is becoming the norm (Thornton & Freedman, 1979).

Early research by Hall and Locke (1938) and E. Livingstone (1953) found that women, particularly in industry, were often reluctant to assume supervisory responsibilities. The times, indeed, are "a-changing." After two decades of social turbulence, the women's liberation movement, and cultural changes and after federal legislation prohibiting sex discrimination in employment practices (Title VII of the Civil Rights Act of 1964 and the affirmative action program of the Equal Employment Opportunity Commission), along with the increase in the proportion of women in the world of work, the issue of women as leaders now looms large in research and policy considerations. One indication of the change in attitudes toward women was the steadily increasing percentage of people in nationally representative samples surveyed between 1937 and 1978 in Gallup polls who were willing to vote for a woman for president: 1937, 31 percent; 1949, 48 percent; 1958, 52 percent; 1967, 57 percent; and 1978, 76 percent (Anonymous, 1983).

The attitudes and sex-related stereotypes about women as managers that both women (Kravetz, 1976) and men (Tavris, 1977) hold are changing. M. M. Wood's (1976) survey of approximately 100 male and female managers found that most managers thought that women are winning increased acceptance in the business environment. A comparison of 1965 and 1985 studies of executives' attitudes about women in business showed that executives' perceptions had changed greatly. In the 1985 survey, executives were more likely to think women want positions of authority and felt more comfortable about working for a female boss (Sutton & Moore, 1985).

Data from Powell, Posner, and Schmidt (1984) illustrate the changes that have occurred. In contrast to stereotypic expectations, they found that the 130 women managers in their sample placed a greater emphasis on their careers than on their family life and had a greater concern for production than for social relationships; furthermore, the women managers rated ambition, ability, and skill as being more important than did the 130 male managers in the sample. Neverthe-

less, for a long time to come, women, in general, will face disadvantages in opportunities for managerial and leadership positions.

Constraints on Opportunities for Leadership

Leadership opportunities for women in the past tended to be limited to women's issues and jobs in institutions: women's suffrage, sororities, nunneries, all-girls' schools, and telephone operator supervisors. But even presidents of colleges for women often were men. Although the vast majority of public school teachers were women, they remained a minority of higher-level school administrators (Estler, 1975). According to Sutton and Moore's (1985) survey of executives' attitudes about women as leaders in business, most respondents in 1985, male or female, still believed that women have to be exceptional to succeed in business. Moreover, the women in the poll were less optimistic about their opportunities than were the men who were queried. The women thought they still had to struggle more to rise in the business world and were likely to earn less than their male counterparts.[2] Nevertheless, despite Litter's (1976) finding that in almost all samples, women executives reported they had suffered from discrimination, women who are managers (as well as men who are managers) have a higher degree of job satisfaction than do their nonsupervisory counterparts (Keaveny, Jackson, & Fossum, 1976). These women appear to enjoy their positions and to hold the same expectations of them as do male supervisors (Brief & Oliver, 1976). Many other studies have found little or no difference in the job satisfaction of female and male leaders.

Obstacles and Conflicts

Even when women are promoted to managerial positions, they continue to face a variety of barriers to their upward mobility. In some jobs, the obstacle may be the reluctance to send women traveling with men (Donnelly, 1976). The rotation of jobs for managerial devel-

[2]In reading this section, as with much of this chapter, given the rapidity of societal change, the reader will have to be careful in distinguishing the conclusions reached by the year in which they were made.
[3]See, for instance, Bartol (1974, 1975), Bartol and Wortman (1976), Herrick (1973), and Jacobson and Effertz (1974).

opment may require a woman to relocate, which means that either her husband must also relocate or the couple must live apart in a "commuter marriage." Carroll (1987) argued that the biggest obstacle that women leaders (at least the married ones) face is coping with the conflict between career and family. It is not surprising that among the few sex differences found by Morrison, White, and Van Velsor (1987), women executives felt less equal than did their male counterparts to the demands placed on their time and energy in their daily lives. Supportive husbands may be especially important. The homemaking chores of married women who are working may call for husbands who are willing to share homemaking duties. Among 657 Israeli managers and human service professionals, 57 percent of whom were women, the burnout and exhaustion from stress at work were ameliorated for the women by the amount of support they received in their lives in general, but for the men, it was the support they received at work that helped prevent burnout from stress at work (Etzioni, 1984).

Fewer Opportunities for Necessary Experience and Contacts

Women's lesser experience with team sports than men's has limited their ability to participate effectively in management teams (Hennig & Jardim, 1977). Women do not know the rules (Harragan, 1977). "Old boy" networks make it more difficult for women executives to obtain the information that is necessary to fulfill the monitoring role of the manager effectively.

Women do not frequent men's athletic clubs, they may be excluded from some social clubs, and they may be unable to entertain visitors. These are all situations in which important information may be gathered and in which important decisions may be made. In Finland, male executives may gather in a sauna to negotiate with male union leaders. Above and beyond this social exclusion, women may remain outsiders in a male-dominated organization. In a survey of 76 men and 64 women in a newspaper publishing firm, Brass (1985) found that on the average, the women were rated as being less influential than the men, although they did not differ in the number of others whom they had to contact at work or in their centrality to the formal networks. However, they were not well integrated into the men's networks, including the organization's dominant coalition. According to Symons (1986), who interviewed 67 women professionals and managers in France and Canada, gaining entry, establishing credibility, and managing their sexual identification in the "corporate tribe" is a process of being continuously retested. (The situation is different for men, who need to pass their test of admission and acceptance only once.) Such testing is particularly salient for the token woman middle manager when feminist issues surface in the organization (Rose, 1980).

Fraker (1984) noted a number of other more subtle obstacles for women who are trying to move up the corporate ladder. Women may be seen as unable to "fit in" with the small informal, all-male group that constitutes upper management. In addition, they may be delegated less authority than are their male counterparts for assigned responsibilities, according to a survey by Sherman, Ezell, and Odewahn (1987). They may not receive the same constructive feedback from their male superiors as do their male counterparts. And they may feel uncomfortable and reluctant to discuss personal matters. Furthermore, Bayes and Newton (1978) observed that a woman leader and her subordinates ordinarily have little social experience regarding a woman's possession of the legitimate power to control and protect the boundaries of an adult group, to stand alone as a figure of authority, and to evaluate the output of other adults.

Naïveté. A survey by Radin (1980) of 100 women in upper-, middle-, and entry-level positions in state and local governmental agencies found that the women overrated education and hard work as prerequisites for advancement and underestimated political awareness. The women tended to be ignorant of the political games played within an organization. Yet, a woman's success as a manager, argued Hennig and Jardim (1977) and Trahey (1977), requires competing with men in a system that the men understand better and with which the men are more familiar and comfortable.

Concepts of Women and of Leadership Remain Antithetical

Carpeno (1976) found that for 100 professional staff members of a regional high school system, statements about female leaders indicated doubt and uneasiness about their future. Frank and Katcher (1977) concluded, from a survey of 104 male and 44 female medical students, that the men tended to stereotype the women's behavior and to exclude them from positions of leadership in dissection groups in anatomy courses. Among 1,000 male executives who were surveyed by Bowman, Worthy, and Greyser (1965), 44 percent expressed mildly unfavorable to strongly unfavorable attitudes toward women in management; in general, these men believed that women are temperamentally ill suited for leadership positions. In the same way, a survey of 2,000 executive readers of the *Harvard Business Review* (Bowman, Worthy, & Greyser, 1965) reported that 41 percent of the men were opposed to women in executive roles; many readers thought that women were not suitable. Both men and women in the sample believed that women's opportunities for advancement were limited. Similarly, a 1971 Louis Harris poll of representative working women showed a strong preference for a male boss over a female boss (White, 1981). Likewise, Brenner (1970) found, in a nationwide survey of managers, that the four traits that were regarded as most important for an upper-management position were deemed more likely to be found in men rather than in women. Consistent with both these results, in a study of German students, Kruse and Wintermantel (1986) found that in describing male leaders, the students took it for granted that the leaders would be dominant and competitive, take risks, and be able to make decisions on their own, but for women leaders, these traits had to be stated explicitly. The male leader was the normative leader; the female leader had to fit with the male schematic. In a second study, Kruse and Wintermantel (1986) found that for male students, the concept of man correlated .9 with the concept of manager and .8 with the concept of leadership. The concept of woman correlated −.4 with the concept of manager and −.5 with the concept of leadership. The results for the female students were similar.

When they completed self-reports, both male and female managers showed a preference for stereotypic male (task-oriented) management behaviors (Brenner & Bromer, 1981). Similarly, 1,161 students, using the Bem Sex-Role Inventory (Bem, 1970), chose masculine rather than feminine traits to be sought in the good manager, the good president, and even the female political activist.

Disadvantageous Stereotypes. Four beliefs reinforce unfavorable attitudes toward women as prospects for managerial positions. They were revealed in a factor analysis of 176 male managers' responses to a survey of their attitudes toward women in the world of work. The factors extracted were (1) women lack career orientation, (2) women lack leadership potential, (3) women are undependable, and (4) women are emotionally less stable (Bass, Krusell, & Alexander, 1971). The perceived lack of career orientation is linked to the stereotype that women are less concerned about their jobs. The other stereotypes are built around a mixture of fact and fancy.

Although women may benefit from some positive stereotyping, such as being expected to be more considerate than their male counterparts (Pearson & Serafini, 1984), Heller (1982) found that female leaders are stereotyped negatively at two ends of a continuum. At one extreme, as mother, pet, or sex object, women are considered too submissive or emotional to be effective leaders. At the other extreme, women violate what is expected of them as women and are seen as "iron maidens," as aggressive workaholics, and as domineering and manipulative.

Women are likely to have more difficulty than do men in obtaining the same role legitimacy as leaders. For instance, unlike their male counterparts, new female professors have to establish their legitimacy among students (Richardson & Cook, 1980). Women are faced with the conflict between the stereotypic expectations of them as women and the stereotypic expectations of them as leaders—the latter identified more with maleness. Maleness is associated with the initiation of structure (Pearson & Serafini, 1984).

The female sex-role stereotype labels women as less competent but warmer emotionally than men. The stereotype of the effective manager matches the masculine stereotype of the effective manager: competent, tough, and emotionally cold. Miner (1965) reflected the accepted stereotype that there are parallel role requirements for being a manager and being a man.[4] Both a manager and a man need to be able to take charge, to make decisions, to be assertive, and to take disciplinary action, but women managers in hierarchical organizations must follow masculine behavior patterns, accord-

---

[4]See Chapter 25.

ing to Miner. During the early years of their managerial experience, women tend to identify with the masculine stereotype of a successful manager to overcome their perceived female inadequacies (Hennig, 1971).

The stereotypic concepts of being a woman and of being a leader were viewed as incompatible (V. E. Schein, 1973, 1975). Surveys tended to report large differences in the traits attributed to women and to successful middle managers. Survey data also indicated the popular belief that women make inferior leaders (Bowman, Worthy, & Greyser, 1965). Women themselves tended to subscribe early on to the different stereotypes of managers and of women. O'Leary (1974) and McClelland (1965b) both found that women as a group described themselves as different from or even opposite to men as a group on traits that are supposedly required for management. In confirmation, Frantzve (1979) found a positive relation between masculinity scores on the Bem Sex-Role Inventory and the tendency to emerge as a leader in 49 initially leaderless discussions in groups of men and women. Again, Brenner and Bromer (1981) found, in self-reports by 66 male and 66 female managers in metropolitan New York, that both sexes had a significant preference for behaviors that reflect the male stereotype. By 1989, however, female managers', but not male managers', views may have changed. Thus, 420 male middle managers surveyed by Brenner, Tomkiewicz, and Schein (1989) still clung to the male managerial stereotype reported 15 years earlier by Schein (1973, 1975) although 173 female counterparts no longer equated management with masculine traits.

Broverman, Vogel, Broverman, et al. (1972) asked 100 college students to indicate the characteristics, attitudes, and behaviors in which men and women differed. A second group then rated the extent to which the traits mentioned most frequently by the first group were typical of adult men or women. The female role stereotype that emerged did not fit with what is usually deemed important for effective leadership and management. A woman was regarded as less aggressive, more dependent, and more emotional. She did not hide her emotions, was subjective, easily influenced, and submissive. She enjoyed art and literature, but not mathematics and science. She was excitable in minor crises, passive, uncompetitive, illogical, home oriented,

unskilled in business, sneaky, and unfamiliar with the ways of the world. Her feelings were easily hurt. She was unadventurous, indecisive, cried easily, rarely acted as a leader, and lacked self-confidence. She was uncomfortable about being aggressive, unambitious, unable to separate feelings from ideas, conceited about her appearance, talkative, tactful, gentle, aware of other's feelings, religious, interested in her own appearance, neat, quiet, had a strong need for security, and easily expressed tender feelings.

Such stereotypes may result in self-imposed attitudinal barriers to women's entrance into positions of leadership. They may also cause women to be reluctant to assert themselves for the fear of being seen as aggressive or to display their ambition to achieve for the fear of failure (Heller, 1982).

Female leaders are supposedly more attentive to upward communications from their subordinates; males are expected to be more effective in downward directiveness. Stereotyped female leaders are expected to be more indirect and nonconfrontational and to use influence tactics, such as helplessness, personal reward, and hints, whereas leaders are expected more often to use direct, forthright influence tactics based on expertise, authority, and logic. Generally, these stereotypes do not necessarily reflect realities (Hall & Donnell, 1979; Rice, Instone, & Adams, 1984; Szilagyi, 1980a).

If a woman leader adopts more accommodative, participative leadership behavior, she faces criticism for being too passive. But if she adopts an autocratic or task-oriented leadership behavior or a more directive style, she may be seen as too aggressive and masculine. Powell (1982), among others, showed that sex differences, as such, are related not to being a good manager but to differences in sex-role identities—to how women and men are supposed to differ in the way they behave. For example, in mixed company, a woman may be inhibited by the attitudes she holds about the appropriateness of women attempting to take initiatives in such situations (O'Leary, 1974). Her inhibitions may be reinforced by the mixed reaction of others if she succeeds (Jacobson & Effertz, 1974). Nevertheless, Hyman (1980) suggested that people still perceive woman managers to be either tough, aggressive, unyielding, and autocratic or unassertive, good workers. As a consequence, women leaders may not be able to use their power as directly as can men (Johnson, 1976). Nevertheless, although women may be expected to display less dominance and competitiveness in mixed-sex groups, Bunker and Bender (1980) suggested that female managers are as competitive as are their male counterparts, but they compete in different ways. At the same time, Hollander and Yoder (1980) concluded, from a research review, that observed differences in the leadership behavior of women and men can be attributed mainly to the interrelationship of the role expectations, style, and task demands of particular circumstances.

According to Bayes and Newton (1978), subordinates respond to a woman leader partly as an individual and partly according to the cultural stereotype of woman. The responses of subordinates to a woman leader may be due to their socialized expectations about women in general, which are likely to conflict with the more appropriate response to the woman as a manager and hence who is involved in a role that they consider to be primarily masculine.

Stereotypes have their effects on behavior. We expect women to be more submissive, so we have trouble taking orders from women, no matter what they are like individually. Women leaders themselves are in conflict when they face a divergence in what is expected from them in their role as managers and in their role as females. But do the stereotypes reflect reality? Do women actually differ from men in traits that are of consequence to leadership as they differ in the stereotype? A variety of answers emerges. For example, women are supposed to be less task oriented than are men. Such was actually found true when the Orientation Inventory (Bass, 1967c), a direct measure, was used for male and female counterparts from adolescence to middle age and for many student and occupational groups, except for one group of senior women at the University of California, Berkeley. But no sex differences appeared when the Least Preferred Co-worker (LPC) score,[5] a more disguised measurement, was used by Chapman (1975) and by J. M. Ward (1977) to determine the task- and relations orientation of male and female students and by Schneier (1978), in a study of emerging leaders. And Okanes and Murray (1980)

[5]See Chapter 23.

found that the scores of 51 female managers on the Mehrabian achievement scale were significantly higher than those of 51 male managers. Furthermore, evidence has accumulated that the need to achieve is a complex of styles and orientations and that men score higher in mainly the competitive aspects of achievement. The differences in men's and women's scores for the desire for mastery (a component of achievement), that is, the higher scores of men than of women, tend to diminish with experience. The same happens to the higher scores of women on orientation to work, another component of achievement (Deaux, 1985). Also, male executives are more comfortable than are female executives about achievement when the criteria for excellence are clearly specified and when conformity to authority is desirable (Morrison, White, & Van Velsor, 1987).

Advantageousness of Stereotypes. All these stereotypes may work to a woman manager's advantage. If women managers are not expected to perform well and are seen to operate under handicaps (Terborg & Ilgen, 1975), then if they do perform well, their performance may be attributed to extra effort and competence and may be considered more worthy of reward than that of comparable male managers. Kanter (1977c) and Alban and Seashore (1978) argued that the stereotypic female role requirement that women deal effectively with people offsets the disadvantages to a woman of the stereotypic submissive, nurturing role requirements. Similarly, Larwood and Wood (1977) pointed out, in agreement with what was detailed in preceding chapters, that the effective manager can make use of both the supposedly masculine competence, task orientation, and initiative and the supposedly more feminine concern for people, feelings, and relationships. However, the strength of popular beliefs cannot be ignored. Thus, Powell and Butterfield (1979) found that 694 business students still described the good manager in masculine terms, as did Miner (1974) in his conception of the motivation to manage.

Harassment

Despite its illegality, sexual harassment is experienced by a sizable proportion of women in the workplace (Graham, 1986). Sexual favors may be demanded for women's advancement, and sexual threats may force women into resigning their positions. Sexual harassment may be a hostile response, unrelated to the quality of a woman's job performance, whose goal is to eliminate her as a competitor for advancement. Sexual harassment may be a form of displaced aggression in which the woman colleague is seen as the weaker and safer target of hostility arising from frustration than the powerful male boss who is the cause of the frustration. Both men and women in the workplace have to learn how to relate to each other comfortably without the usually more powerful man misinterpreting the woman's friendliness and sociability as a readiness for sexual intimacy. Nevertheless, men and women who work together may fall in love with each other.

Sexual Relationships

Real and imagined love affairs between men and women in the same corporation are seen as sexual opportunism and are likely to affect the performance of and the favoritism shown to the junior partner—usually the women in the case. Collins (1983) noted that love between managers is dangerous because it may challenge formal superior-subordinate and customary peer relationships. The dominant male–submissive female personal relationship may take precedence over formal organizational requirements and affect political alliances. According to a survey of offices by Quinn (1977), two-thirds of 130 employees found office romances to cause much gossip; one-third, to provoke complaints and hostilities; and one-fifth, to result in distorted communication, threats to the unit's reputation, and lower morale and output. While one-third of the female supervisors of the men who were involved in these affairs openly discussed the situation, only 6 percent of the male supervisors of the women who were involved said they did so. According to Quinn's 130 respondents, once executives learned that co-workers were romantically entangled, they were twice as likely to fire the woman involved. Female executives were less forgiving in this regard than were male executives.

Segregation of Work Roles by Sex

Coser (1980) noted that one-half of all women at work can be found in just 21 occupations. Many studies have shown that it is common to find jobs held either by women only or by men only within firms (Bielby & Baron, 1984; Gutek, 1985). This phenomenon occurs in Portugal, Britain, the Soviet Union, Ireland, and elsewhere, as well as in North America. The jobs held exclusively by women are likely to be both lower paid and less likely to lead to advancement into administrative or executive positions; they are more likely to be transient opportunities and to call for less training and commitment. When women seek to enter or to be promoted into a position, such as management, into which they previously were excluded, they are likely to be judged to be less suitable for such a position if it has been male dominated (Gutek, 1988). This likelihood may not necessarily be due to a personal bias of the decision maker; rather, it may be a result of actual or assumed pressure from a higher authority (Larwood, Gutek, & Gattiker, 1984).

The more one sex dominates an occupation, the more that performance in it is expected to conform to stereotypes about the sex of the occupants. As long as most nurses are women, expectations continue about the low pay for them and the warm and loving care expected from them. As long as management in most industries and institutions remains male dominated, high pay, task orientation, aggressiveness, and competitiveness are expected. Women are seen as better suited for traditional woman's work as a nurse and less well suited for traditional man's work as a manager (Konrad & Gutek, 1987).

Women in Assistant and Service Roles. The sex segregation of work accustoms us to see women in auxiliary and service roles. Numerous surveys and observers' analyses substantiate that being a woman legitimates the performance of a service role as a nurse, secretary, or administrative assistant (O'Leary, 1974; Schein, 1973). R. S. Weiss (1956) noted this linkage of women to service roles in a study of the allocation and acceptance of responsibility in a governmental agency. Reinforcing this linkage is the masculine value for men to prefer to receive nurturance and emotional support from women rather than other men, according to a survey by Burda and Vaux (1987).

Women tend to be counseled accordingly. Weisman, Morlock, Sack, and Levine (1976) observed that the counseling of women who were denied entry into medical school was different from the counseling of men who were denied entry. Men were encouraged to re-apply to other medical schools or to try to obtain a doc-torate in a related field. Women were reminded of the obstacles they would continue to face if they tried to continue in medicine. They were encouraged to change to more sex-role-accepted professions such as nursing. Such inadequate career counseling and the lack of successful female role models were seen as key factors in reducing women's choice of higher-status ca-reers (Heinen, McGlauchin, Legeros, & Freeman, 1975; Lannon, 1977).

Women in Solo Roles

Women often find themselves to be the only member of their sex in a group or organization of men. This solo status further handicaps their integration into net-works of consequence.

Tokenism. Often, the woman in the solo role is a token of simulated enlightenment who is at a consider-able disadvantage in trying to succeed (Izraeli, 1983; Spangler, Gordon, & Pipkin, 1978). Especially if a woman is the token member of a group, her perform-ance faces closer scrutiny. She is under more pressure to conform to stereotypic expectations about women. Differences between men and women are exaggerated, and the token woman is fitted into preexisting stereo-types of what is expected from her (Kanter, 1977a, 1977b). The effects of being a token woman or man were observed by Berle, Biscone, Katz, et al. (1981) in 26 leaderless group discussions in which one member was of one sex and the rest of the members were of the other sex.

As a token, a woman may be thought to have been hired because of affirmative action guidelines rather than for her qualifications (Northcraft & Martin, 1982). On blue-collar jobs, the token woman may experience considerable hostility (O'Farrell & Harlan, 1982). Fur-thermore, token women are more likely to be sexually harassed (Gutek & Morasch, 1982).

In all, tokenism generates many questions about the solo woman leader in a male-dominated organization. How much does the visibility and pressure to perform result in more insecurity and resentment in the token woman? How much are the token woman's attempts to lead met with resistance from the dominant males because of her token status (Adams & Yoder, 1985)?

Stereotyped Expectations of the Solo Woman. Men are likely to attribute a solo woman's success to her sexuality (Lockheed, 1975). When many men and few women are available, the women are expected to fall into their service and assisting roles (Guttentag & Secord, 1983). Frantzve's (1982) analysis of leaderless groups discussions found that when men and women were systematically placed in solo roles among mem-bers of the opposite sex, such isolation from others of the same sex particularly inhibited the woman in an otherwise male group, but not vice versa. Solo females, but not solo males, were least likely to initiate propos-als, were interrupted most, and were most often ig-nored. However, according to a survey by Frantzve (1985), women in solo status learn to cope with their isolation by using humor, "playing the game," working hard and competently, and relying on outside support systems. And being distinctive may have its advantages at times. If the group's task appears to be more relevant to the experience of the woman, as a woman, she may become the resident expert on the subject for the men who form the remainder of the group. The choice of the task can result in a bias in favor of the woman in the situation (Maccoby & Jacklin, 1974).[6] But in the aggregate, women are handicapped by a variety of addi-tional disadvantageous stereotypes and expectations.

Handicaps in Promotion and Mentoring

Although more women are moving into higher-level management positions, especially in selected industries such as banking, publications, cosmetics, and retailing, overall, with more than two-thirds of the working-age women now holding jobs, the promotion of women into positions of leadership, especially at higher levels, has not kept pace (Apfelbaum & Hadley, 1986). Wom-en's entry into management is also handicapped by male administrators' tendencies to discriminate against female employees in personnel decisions involving se-lection, promotion, and supervision (Gutek & Stevens, 1979; Rosen & Jerdee, 1974). Such discriminatory prac-

---

[6]Witness the rapid movement of women into management in consum-er-oriented and service-oriented industries, such as banking, publica-tions, cosmetics, and retailing, in contrast to their much lower participa-tion in management in manufacturing, chemicals, and mining.

tices have been justified on the basis of the higher absenteeism and turnover of women and women's lack of
geographic mobility, particularly if they are married or
have children (Robie, 1973). Absenteeism and turnover
rates among women are higher than those among men
at all age levels (U.S. Department of Labor, 1977), often
as a consequence of child care problems and their husbands' relocation. In the movement to upgrade women
at work, it is especially important to provide adequate
day care for their children, more challenging jobs for
women, and the opportunity for the individual woman
to decide about relocation instead of being treated as
a class who follow in the wake of their husbands' career
moves.

Fewer high-level women are available to serve as
mentors. Their number is reduced further by the
"queen bees," who are uninterested or unsuited for
such mentoring (Riger & Galligan, 1980). Queen bees
tend to be antifeminine. They are primarily interested
in preserving their unusual status in a world of men
(Staines, Tavris, & Jayaratne, 1974). Fortunately, however, they do not represent the majority of high-level
woman executives, more of whom are supportive of
their younger junior women managers (Terborg, Peters,
Ilgen, & Smith, 1977). Bowen (1985) compared 18 male
with 14 female mentors of female protégés. Although
the cross-sex pairing created problems, such as jealousy
among spouses, the most salient problem, regardless of
the sex of the mentor, was the resentment of co-
workers.[7]

Women indicated they need more help than do men
in rising in the organization (Van Velsor, 1987). Men
who occupy most of the higher-level positions are
thought to be less willing to serve as mentors for young
women managers. Nevertheless, women reported having received more help from mentors than did their
male manager counterparts, according to Shapiro's
(1985) survey of 75 middle and top male managers and
67 comparable female managers.

Hoffmann and Reed (1981) concluded, from interviews of both clerks and supervisors in a Fortune 500
firm, that the lower rate of promotion of women was
self-imposed rather than due to discrimination. They
found that promotion was directly dependent on both
men's and women's motivation for advancement. How-

[7]See Chapter 35 for a detailed discussion about mentoring.

ever, although marriage increased the motivated men's
efforts to be promoted into management, marriage decreased such efforts to be promoted among similarly
motivated women. Women who sought and accepted
promotion were disproportionately those who had
avoided marriage and parenthood.

Status, Sex, and Leadership

The lower status of women in American society is illustrated by what happens when a large number of
women enter an occupation: The occupation's prestige
and desirability are lowered (Touhey, 1974). The high
prestige of an occupation is linked to the presence of
a large majority of men in it (Bartol & Bartol, 1975).
Thus, the prestige of clerical work declined when
women replaced men in it during the American Civil
War.

Lockheed (1975) noted that women's lack of influence, found in small-group research, has been attributed to sex-role socialization. Yet, much of it really is a
consequence of the lower status of women. The conflict can be observed in stereotyped expectations of
dominant male and subservient female that occurs
when women are assigned to lead men. Chapter 11
noted the extent to which one's success as a leader is
associated with the status one is accorded. Women in
our society remain handicapped in their efforts to become leaders by their lower status than men's. Illustrative of the impact of sex status was Megargee's (1969)
finding that when participants were paired with their
own sex, those who scored high in dominant personality tended to assume leadership, but when paired
with the opposite sex, males assumed leadership even
when they were submissive personalities. Presumably,
as women's status has increased relative to men since
1969, much less difference in influence, if any, is likely
to be found between the sexes in 1990.

In most cultures, the male's position has higher status than the female's. But considerable variation exists,
ranging from those societies in which men and women
are almost equal in status, as is the case among the Arapesh, to those in which women are higher in status
as, for example, among the Tchambuli. When women
are higher in status than men, they are more likely to
lead. The higher-status woman is dominant; the man

is less responsible and more dependent. The woman makes the choice; the man is chosen (Mead, 1935).

Strodtbeck (1951) contrasted three cultural groups within the United States—Navaho, Mormon, and mainstream American—by arranging discussions between husband and wives from the three groups. Mormon husbands were most likely to lead discussions because in the patriarchal Mormon culture, the status of men is higher than that of women. Navaho husbands were least likely to lead discussions because women traditionally have more status and are more active and demanding in the Navaho culture. Results for the mainstream American spouses were in between the Mormons and the Navahos.

Even among two different geographic regions that presumably have the same general culture, differences in status and leadership appeared. Thus, for example, women undergraduates in New York reported "playing dumb" much more frequently when on a date than did women undergraduates from the West Coast (Wallin, 1950). Again, such regional differences are likely to have decreased, if not disappeared, since 1950.

Male candidates for managerial positions are rated as more promising than are equally qualified female candidates on such dimensions as acceptability and potential for service (Gutek & Stevens, 1979; Rosen, Jerdee, & Prestwich, 1975). When Ezell, Odewahn, and Sherman (1982) surveyed 360 male and female managers in state public welfare organizations, they found that on their entry into management and their promotion to higher levels, the women's leadership potential was more likely to be judged on their past performance and the men's was judged according to future expectations about them, even though the men's and women's competencies and motivation were seen to be the same. As a consequence, judgments about the men could be more subjective.

More Stress

Given the handicaps, conflicts, and disadvantageous stereotypes with which women managers have to cope, it is not surprising to learn, from a longitudinal study by Cooper and Davidson (1982) of 135 top female executives in Britain, that compared with their 500 male counterparts, the women executives manifested more

symptoms of stress, such as migraine headaches, increased cigarette smoking, use of drugs, excessive drinking, and marital problems. Consistent with these findings, Ottaway and Bhatnagar (1988) reported that both U.S. and Indian female managers described themselves as more conflicted and hard driving than did their male counterparts. Similarly, Greenglass (1988) found, among 114 Canadian first-level supervisors in governmental social services, that the women were much more likely to describe themselves as Type A personalities (stress prone) and the men more often called themselves Type B personalities. In coping with stress, especially if they were Type As, the women engaged in more wishful thinking as well as more effort to change the situation or their own behavior than did the men. These results may explain why although women in management may experience more stress than do their male counterparts, they may cope better with it. Reports of disasters have noted that although women generally are more open in revealing their emotions, they appear to survive the stress of prolonged isolation, cold (or heat), and hunger. Women fared better when the Donner Pass wagon train was trapped in the High Sierras and with the stress of prolonged siege during the bombings of London in World War II. On occasion, only the women walked out alive from disastrous crossings of the Mojave Desert in the covered wagon days.

Socialization, Sex, and Leadership

In our society, we are socialized primarily within the nuclear family in a culture that defines sex roles as total roles that define our sense of self and our behavior. The sex role pertains to all aspects of life and takes precedence over situation-specific work roles if they are incompatible. Dominance and independence are associated with masculine roles, and submissiveness, passivity, and nurturance, with feminine roles. Desirable femininity, culturally defined, emphasizes giving and the avoidance of aggressiveness and domination (Broverman, Broverman, Clarkson, et al., 1970). On the basis of a meta-analytic review of 172 social psychology studies, Eagly and Crowley (1986) concluded that the male helping role is to be chivalrous and heroic, whereas the female helping role is to be caring and nurturant.

Even the exceptions among women seem to be a consequence of the differences in the nuclear family in which the women were raised. Vogel, Broverman, Broverman, et al. (1970) and Almquist (1974) found that women who chose nontraditional careers—those that were historically occupied by men—were raised in families in which the mother worked full time. Generally, the nuclear family is likely to discourage women from choosing nontraditional careers. In addition, even if high school students of both sexes have similar aspirations for college and the choice of careers, the male students receive significantly more parental attention and pressure to pursue their aspirations (Goodale & Hall, 1976).

Riger and Galligan (1980) pointed out that socialization may account for the development in females of traits and behaviors, such as the unwillingness to take risks, that are counter to the demands of the management role. Men learn to see risk taking as an opportunity for success as well as failure, whereas women focus more on the failure aspect of risk taking (Henning & Jardim, 1977).

The different socialization of men and women may explain why being firstborn is more helpful to women's than to men's subsequent attainment of positions of leadership. For women, but not for men, Sandler and Scalia (1975) found a significantly greater likelihood for firstborns to serve as presidents or other officers of organizations. Particularly in large families (Bossard & Boll, 1955) and families with working mothers, the eldest daughters are delegated authority and expected to take on many family responsibilities, such as caring for younger siblings (Clausen & Clausen, 1973). Klonsky (1978) found that the eldest daughters in large lower-class families received significantly higher-than-average leadership ratings in high school sports from their coaches. In the same way, Hennig and Jardim (1977) observed that being firstborn was a common characteristic in a sample of 25 successful top-level women leaders.

Other parental practices in rearing daughters also have been seen to make a difference in the subsequent leadership of the girls as adolescents and adults. Parental warmth and discipline contribute to the development of a girl's subsequent performance as a leader, especially if leadership is fostered by the mother as the family's authority figure (Bronfenbrenner, 1961). However, Hennig and Jardim (1977) found that their fathers' encouragement was important to women who achieved success in management.

Psychosocial Development. For Freud (1922), the sex difference in psychosocial development was the reason for the maleness-centering of leadership in the family, culture, art, and civilization. Differential psychosocial development was also the cause of the more passive life goals of females. According to Bernardez (1983), differences in socialization between males and females result in some males' unconscious fear of female power. This fear bars such males from submission, passivity, and dependence on women. But other males also create fantasies that woman leaders are perfect mothers who are selfless, totally accepting, abnegating, nurturing, and without aggression and criticism. When women do not fulfill these expectations, such men direct irrational anger and criticism toward them. To avoid this reaction, some female leaders unconsciously try to minimize their ability and visibility.

Male-Female Differences in Leadership Potential

Males tend to emerge as leaders more than do females in numerous studies of mixed-sex groups (Aries, 1976) and they, the females, tend to differ from men in their activity and influence in small-group experiments (Lockheed & Hall, 1976). Status and sex-role stereotyping handicap the elevation of women to leadership positions. Moreover, socialization as a female itself contributes to the reduced motivation to lead (Estler, 1975). But which actually observed differences in traits affect men's and women's respective tendencies to attempt to lead and to succeed as leaders? Are the differences observed in adolescent girls retained by adult women, particularly women who have chosen to enter management and who have become experienced managers? Do systematic changes in male-female differences in such traits occur that are associated with societal change? These are some of the questions I will now try to answer.

Verbal and Nonverbal Communication Skills

There are systematic differences between men's and women's styles of conversation and communication as a consequence of their differential socialization. There are also sex differences in cultural stereotypes about communication skills.

Women tend to be seen as better communicators (Hyman, 1980). Case (1985) intensively analyzed tapes of mixed-sex meetings of management students and identified speech that was assertive and authoritative as a male style. Such speech featured informal pronunciation, imperative construction, interjections, competitive/aggressive talk, slang, depersonalization, and use of the third person. The female style was personal and facilitative and was characterized by intensifiers, conjunctions, passive agreement, tag questions, and proof from personal experience. Speech that combined elements of each style, which was supportive and assertive in language, was most influential.

Seifert (1984) illustrated the perverse and pervasive stereotyping of the inadequacy of females for leadership. Seifert led male and female participants to believe they were working with male and female leaders, when they were all receiving the same standardized communications from the experimenter. Those male and female participants who received the notes from the supposed male leaders rated the notes as clearer than did those participants who received notes from the supposed female leaders.

In an assessment of 422 A T & T managers reported by Howard and Bray (1988), women were superior in one of their oral presentations and scored slightly but significantly higher than did the men on a test of verbal ability. The women assessees also had better written communication skills, but no differences were observed for other oral presentations dealing with solutions to simulated managerial problems.[8] Maccoby and Jacklin (1974) also reported that women were superior to men in communication skills, but subsequent analyses have suggested that this difference is weak (Hyde, 1981). According to a laboratory experiment by Steckler and Rosenthal (1985), the voices of females were perceived to sound more competent verbally

[8]See Chapter 36.

when women were speaking to their peers. Also, women have been found to be superior in encoding and decoding nonverbal cues (Hall & Halberstadt, 1981). Howard and Bray (1988) found that their woman assessees were judged to be more sensitive and socially objective. Deaux (1976b) concluded, from a review of studies, that in being more sensitive to nonverbal cues, women try to minimize social distance while men use nonverbal behavior to maintain social distance and to assert their status.

To maintain their social distance and assert their status (Denmark, 1977), men more frequently initiate nonreciprocated touching of women, which declares their dominance or higher status. Women look more at the speaker than do men. But in a mutual gaze, women will lower their eyes first. Men more frequently use the direct stare as a threat, while women use it as sexual provocation. Smiling, often a submissive gesture, is more frequent among women. The use of nonverbal power plays is unacceptable if used by women (Henley, 1973a, 1973b).

Cognitive Skills

Howard and Bray (1988) concluded, from their intensive assessment of A T & T managers, that in addition to the just-mentioned slight but significant superiority of women in verbal ability, men scored higher on a test of general information but both men and women contributed equally to the functioning of two discussion groups and did equally well in the planning, organizing, and decision-making aspects of an in-basket test. The women were somewhat more creative on the in-basket test.

Reviews by Shields (1975) and Wittig (1976) and a meta-analysis by Hyde (1981) found some support for sex differences favoring men in spatial visualization. Block and Kolakowski (1973) attributed this difference to a sex-linked chromosome.

Maccoby and Jacklin (1974) concluded that particularly from adolescence onward, males are superior to females in mathematical ability, but a meta-analysis of studies suggested that the effects were small (Hyde, 1981), although males dominated in the achievement of extremely high scores in mathematics (Benbow &

Stanley, 1983). However, if the trends continue, any differences in cognitive skills that are unfavorable to the leadership potential of women will diminish. Rosenthal and Rubin (1982) pointed out that in the preceding 20 years, females showed significant gains relative to their male counterparts in verbal, numerical, and spatial skills. However, women may still consider their thought processes to be different. Myers and McCaulley (1985) reported systematic differences on the Myers-Briggs Type Inventory of the self-descriptions of 1,051 men and 181 women who were attending management-development programs at the Center for Creative Leadership between 1979 and 1983. Some of the difference may have been due to the greater proportion of men in upper management and the greater proportion of women in middle management and staff positions. As Table 32.1 shows, the women more frequently typed themselves as predominantly intuitive and feeling, while the men more frequently typed themselves as predominantly sensing and thinking.

Personality, Values, and Interests

When it comes to actual rather than stereotypic differences between men and women, those women who become leaders tend to be similar in personality to their male counterparts. The personality differences between boys and girls and adult men and women, in general, fade when male and female managers are compared.

Nevertheless, some sex differences remain in identification, self-confidence, moral values, interpersonal concerns, and use of power. What may be involved are differences in attitudes toward authority, tendencies to conform, sex-role orientation, and attitudes toward oneself. These may be continuing differences in traits between the sexes that are ordinarily of consequence to leadership. But they still may fail to result in differences between men's and women's attempts to lead and successes and effectiveness as leaders. For instance, although the women in a mixed-sex group may not be as assertive as the men, they may attempt as much leadership as the men because they are equal in experience or in expertise in the task at hand. They may be as successful leaders as the men because followers happen to be more attentive to the knowledge of the members. Although female executives may prefer to take fewer risks than do male executives, Muldrow and Bayton (1979) demonstrated that their effectiveness was as good as their male counterparts because the quality of their decisions matched that of the male executives.

Needs, Motives, and Interests. A meta-analysis of 63 social psychology studies by Eagly and Steffen (1986) found that men were, on the average, more aggressive than were women. But the results for many other differences in traits between the sexes may appear more frequently for students and inexperienced adults and disappear among more mature managers. Thus, Morrison, White, and Van Velsor (1987) could find few sex differences in a large data bank of interviews and assessments of male and female executives. On the other hand, female MBA students in four periods between 1960 and 1980 (as shown in Table 25.5) obtained mean scores that were lower than their male counterparts in their motivation to manage (orientation toward authority, competitiveness, assertiveness, comfort in exercising power, obtaining visibility, and taking care of detail) (Miner & Smith, 1982). And among 232 MBA students, the mean score for the motivation to manage was 7.04 for males and 3.24 for females (Bartol & Martin, 1986). But for samples of male and female store managers and school administrators, Miner (1974a) could find no differences between the men's and the women's motivation to manage.

Further illustrating the impermanence of sex differences in personality, Miner (1965) found that the motivation of women changed with training and experience in a similar way to that of men. Comparable results

Table 32.1 Differences between Male and Female Managers on the Myers-Briggs Type Indicator

Dominant Type	1,051 Men (percentage)	181 Women (percentage)
Sensing	29.4	13.8
Intuitive	22.3	38.1
Thinking	41.1	32.6
Feeling	7.2	15.4

SOURCE: Adapted from Myers and McCaulley (1985).

were reported by Morrison and Sebald (1974). Female executives were similar to male executives on self-esteem, motivation, and mental ability. In a number of additional studies,[9] female executives differed from female employees in general in the same way that male executives differed from male employees in general. Again, after reviewing the evidence, Terborg (1977) concluded that, on the whole, women who become managers have motives that are similar to those of male managers. Concomitantly, women who are experienced managers show no differences in leadership abilities from their experienced male counterparts (Caudrea, 1975). Pfeffer and Shapiro (1978) observed that managerial women are different from women in general; they are less likely to have traditional female characteristics and are more likely, either by temperament or by accommodation to the stereotyped male role (Hennig, 1971), to be analytical, rationally oriented, and personally competitive (Lannon, 1977). In a study of 27 women in middle management in a variety of organizations, Banfield (1976) found that all but two incorporated masculine characteristics; 17 were identified as masculine in self-concept and role behavior, only 1 was identified as feminine, and the other 9 were identified as androgynous. Consistent with the stereotype of the good manager as masculine (Powell & Butterfield, 1979), Schein (1975) found that women thought a good manager was more unlike themselves than did men.

In developing a leadership-orientation scale for the Women's Strong Vocational Interest Blank, Casey (1975) found that the interests of women leaders varied significantly from those of women nonleaders. The leaders indicated a preference for positions of eminence, freedom of thought, challenge, and interpersonal contact; the nonleaders favored artistic activities.

Larwood and Wood (1977) agreed that women in general have been found to differ from men in traits of consequence to leadership, such as the need for achievement, the fear of success, assertiveness, self-esteem, the need for power, the need for dominance, self-reliance, dependence, the preference for taking risks, and competitiveness. These differences may result in women's failure, when first placed in leadership roles, to seek their maximum advantage and their tendency

to seek compromises too quickly when cooperation is required. But Larwood and Wood interpret the results of experimental findings of such sex differences as transitory evidence of the women's relative lack of familiarity with the leadership tasks involved. With experience, the sex differences disappear. At the same time, with societal change, the differences in traits of men and women, in general (even among adolescents), that are of consequence to leadership may be disappearing. By 1986, Santner (1986) found no differences in the cognitive skills, dominance, friendliness, task orientation, and motivation to achieve of male and female high school leaders, although female students were more likely to head formal groups and male students were more likely to lead informal groups. The decade in which data have been collected to analyze male-female differences is likely to be an important modifier of the results. An exception is male-female differences in interests. There has been surprisingly little change in the patterns of males' and females' interests, according to an analysis by Hansen (1988) of the Women's Strong Vocational Interest patterns of 500 women in general in the 1930s; 1,000, in the 1960s; 300, in the 1970s; and 500, in the 1980s.

In all these decades, women, in general, tended to be more interested than men, in general, in art, music, drama, writing, social science, and nature and to be less interested in realistic and mechanical activities. The only areas in which formerly sizable male-female differences disappeared in the 1980s were in teaching, mathematics, and scientific activities. This finding may have some implications for the movement of women into positions of leadership in hi-tech industries.

Reactions to Conflict. Women may differ from men in how they react to obstacles and to conflicts not faced by men, which may affect their potential as leaders. Larwood and Wood (1977) saw that women were more likely to withdraw psychologically from organizations when they faced obstacles to their promotion to higher management levels. Role conflict with home-making may be a second source of psychological withdrawal from the organization. When faced with opportunities to share a reward, men may be more likely than are women to initiate competition for the whole reward. In comparison, women may first try to cooper-

[9]Bartol (1976a); Brief and Aldag (1975); Brief and Oliver (1976); and Matteson, McMahon, and McMahon (1974).

ate; they will enter competition only in retaliation when others reject their initial efforts to cooperate (Terhune, 1970; J. A. Wall, 1976).

In the 1960s, the implication was drawn that women had to adapt to a managerial model that conformed to the male stereotype of our culture. Women's traits had to be altered so they could become more consistent with those of male managers. But more recently, it has been noted that if and when there are personality differences between men and women, the two sexes can complement each other in management. Mixed-sex teams should be more creative (Loden, 1985). The leadership behavior of women, in contrast to that of their male counterparts in the same situation, may be positively enhanced by their greater recognition of and response to the needs of others and greater sensitivity to interpersonal cues. To the degree that women, in general, are less assertive, they may make better leaders in situations in which such assertiveness would be threatening and likely to arouse competitiveness and defensiveness in followers (Larwood & Wood, 1977).

Sex-Role Identification. An obvious sex difference that remains at all levels of maturity and experience is sex-role identification, or the tendency to engage in what has been generally regarded as masculine or feminine activities. Howard and Bray (1988) found sex-role identification to be the biggest difference in their personality assessments of male and female managers at A T & T. Such sex-role identification, if masculine, predicts stronger aspirations for management (Powell & Butterfield, 1981). It seems to have taken over two decades of research to recognize that the various available masculinity and femininity scales appear to measure, respectively, the tendencies to be directive and assertive and the tendencies to be nurturing and interpersonally concerned. Men score higher on the former scales, and women score higher on the latter scales. But as is consistent with the conclusions of Chapter 23, the best supervisors score higher on both scales (Motowidlo, 1981, 1982). However, even this positive association of androgyny with successful leadership in small groups seems to dissipate as groups continue to develop over time, according to a study of the development of ten groups by Spillman, Spillman, and Reinking (1981).

Sex Differences in Self-confidence. A less obvious exception to the general disappearance of differences in the traits of the two sexes as one moves from adolescent students to experienced managers is the continued lower self-confidence of females compared to males (White, 1981). This lower self-confidence was correlated with relatively lower self-esteem and less willingness to take risks because of a greater fear of failure. Females also may feel uncomfortable with too much success, although this issue has remained controversial.[10] These propensities may contribute to a lesser career orientation and a lower desire to compete for advancement (Hennig & Jardim, 1977), as well as to greater tendencies to conform (Eagly & Carli, 1981) and to avoid attempting to be influential (Eagly, 1983).

According to Maccoby and Jacklin (1974), females had less confidence in their abilities across a wide variety of activities, such as achieving good grades in tasks requiring manual dexterity, solving puzzles, and the ability to deal with emergencies. As in the desire to project stereotyped femininity (Ireson, 1976), in the past, females, more so than males, tended to predict lower performance for themselves than was warranted by their intelligence (Crandall, Katkovsky, & Preston, 1962) and presented themselves as dependent and incompetent (Vaught, 1965).

Although the results have not been uniform (Morrison, White, & Van Velsor, 1987; R. S. Schuler, 1975), typical reports, such as those of Schwartz and Waetjen (1976) and Hennig and Jardim (1977), concluded that women managers were observed by their own supervisors to be less confident, more conservative, and less risk taking than were their male counterparts. The lack of confidence in themselves was seen in woman managers' tendencies to attribute personal failure to their lack of ability, rather than to luck or to external forces.

Seifert (1984) completed an experiment in which male and female participants were led to believe they were working with male or female leaders. But all communications (by note) had been prewritten by the experimenter. The female participants rated themselves as less competent than did the male participants. When the outcome of the task was "successful," the

---

[10]See, for instance, Horner (1970), O'Leary (1974), Tresemer (1976), Wood and Greenfeld (1976), and Zuckerman and Wheeler (1975).

female participants attributed more of the reason for success to the "leader" than to themselves than did the male participants. The male participants gave themselves relatively lower ratings and their "leaders" relatively higher ratings when their "leaders" supposedly were male. Despite all these findings, Spence, Helmreich, and Stapp (1975) concluded that women's self-confidence is increasing with the incorporation of more of the stereotyped masculine traits into their own self-concepts.

Sex Differences in Values. Another less obvious difference between the sexes that is of consequence to leadership is men's and women's values, how they develop, and the attitudes associated with them (Gilligan, 1982). For example, public opinion polls always show women in general to be more supportive of peace and less supportive of militarism than are men. Men's competitiveness shows up in the greater importance they attach to equity and fairness in the allocation of rewards. For women, the valuing of such equity is much weaker than, say, the valuing of need, particularly in all-female groups (Brockner & Adsit, 1986). Consistent with this finding, Gilligan (1982) argued that the sexes differ in moral reasoning; women focus on care and responsibility, while men are preoccupied with rights and justice. For a total sample of 187 people with real-life dilemmas, 92 percent of the women and 62 percent of the men were found to show care for others in their reasoning. None of the men ignored justice, while 23 percent of the women did so (Gilligan, 1982).

Women are more concerned with seeing that no one is hurt and that everyone involved in a situation can be accommodated. Men attach more importance to hierarchical relationships; women, to networks and "webs of connection." Chodorow (1985) added that the separation of self from others is valued more by men, while the connection of self to others is valued more by women. Furthermore, when Powell, Posner, and Schmidt (1984) compared the reported values of 130 male and 130 female managers aged 34–45, they obtained results indicating that the women showed more concern for others with respect to ethical issues and religious values.

Sex Differences in Power and in Using Power. The sexes differ systematically in their respective power

and, therefore, their emergence as successful and effective leaders (Eagly, 1983; Henley, 1973a). Women's status relative to men and their legitimacy as leaders reduce their power to lead, as does their supposed lack of expertise. Male leaders can more readily use power to induce members to conform to group norms without losing favor than can female leaders (Denmark & Diggory, 1966). When Ragins (1987, 1988) carefully matched male and female leaders by rank, department, and specialization, she found no difference in the evaluations of the leaders' effectiveness because of their sex but strong differences in their evaluations as a function of their differences in perceived power. In reviewing earlier studies on the subject, she noted that similar results had been reported by many other investigators[11] who had controlled these power-related variables. Sex differences appeared only when there was no control of power-related variables.[12]

To conclude, when it comes to the traits underlying the potential to lead, women are favored by having slightly better verbal skills, but differences in cognitive skills generally are hard to find. With reference to personality traits, women may suffer from a lack of self-confidence, but this trait, along with other personality differences in the needs, values, and interests that are of consequence to leadership, appear to evaporate for those women who move up the corporate ladder.

Male-Female Differences in Leadership Style

Contrary to what may be expected from what has been said so far about male-female socialization and some of the differences uncovered in traits between the sexes, the preponderance of available evidence, particularly from field studies, is that no consistently clear pattern of differences can be discerned in the supervisory styles of female and male leaders. Some studies, especially those conducted in the laboratory, have been able to find differences, but more have not (Osborn & Vicars, 1976). On the one hand, Morrison, White, and

---

[11]These studies included Adams (1978); Day and Stogdill (1972); Dobbins and Platz (1986); Osborn and Vicars (1976); Rice, Instone, and Adams (1984); and Terborg and Shingledecker (1983).
[12]The studies included Bartol and Butterfield (1976); Haccoun, Haccoun, and Sallay (1978); Jacobson and Effertz (1974); Petty and Lee (1975); and Rosen and Jerdee (1973).

Van Velsor (1987) found that female executives did more to personalize their experiences than did male executives. On the other hand, Boulgarides (1984) could find no differences in the personal values or preferred decision-making styles of 108 male and 108 female business managers of the same age.

Evidence of Differences

Bender (1979) concluded, from laboratory studies, that the leadership process was different with female and male leaders. In a survey by Denmark and Diggory (1966), sorority leaders were likely to be described as displaying less authoritarian behavior than were fraternity leaders. Consistent with this finding, schoolteachers described female principals as exhibiting less coercive behavior than did male principals (Kappelman, 1981).

Interpersonal Concerns. With reference to emerging leadership, Deaux (1976b) suggested that women were more likely to seek interpersonal success in groups, in contrast to men's greater concern for being successful in the task. Similarly, Eskilson and Wiley (1976) reported that women attempted to create a more positive group affect than did men. In allocating resources, Vinacke (1969) inferred that women focus more on maintaining harmony, whereas men concentrate on the quality of the individual performance. In the same way, Heinen, McGlauchin, Legeros, and Freeman (1975) suggested that women managers have particular difficulty dealing with interpersonal conflict among subordinates because of their socialization, which encourages them to avoid confrontation.

Differences in Idealized Leadership. In a study by Rosenfeld and Fowler (1976), some differences emerged for the self-described ideal-leader scores of 89 men and 89 women in the idealized behaviors of democratic men and women, although the results for the idealized autocratic styles were the same for both groups. Democratic women emphasized being helpful, affectionate, nurturing, open minded, and accepting blame; democratic men emphasized being mature, forceful, competent, moral, utilitarian, analytical, and valuing people.

Differences in Leadership Behavior. Morsink (1966) found that when female principals were described by both male and female staff members, they were significantly higher on the Leader Behavior Description Questionnaire—Form 12 (LBDQ—XII) than were male principals on representation, persuasiveness, emphasis on production, predictive accuracy, integration of the group, and influence with superiors. Kappelman (1981) obtained similar results in another survey of male and female principals. In some samples but not others, Petty and Bruning (1980) reported some tendency for female supervisors to display more consideration than male supervisors. Millard (1981) obtained results indicating that 38 female managers, compared to a matched sample of male managers, in a large governmental agency were described by their subordinates as being higher in their emphasis on production and orientation toward superiors but lower in their tolerance for freedom and uncertainty.

In an unpublished study in the 1970s, Sleeth and Humphreys (undated) found differences between 122 men and 122 women students at a large urban university in self-descriptions of their leadership behavior, as scored on the LBDQ and Hersey and Blanchard's (1977) Leader Effectiveness and Adaptability Description, as well as assertiveness and endorsement of the work ethic. The women reported themselves to be slightly higher in consideration and the men reported themselves to be higher in task- rather than relations orientation. Similarly, more consideration than initiation of structure was seen in the self-descriptions of 51 first- and second-level women supervisors (DiMarco & Whitsitt, 1975).

Differences in Involvement. Eskilson (1975) reported that the women who emerged as leaders of three-person laboratory groups showed more intensive involvement with the task than did the men who emerged as leaders. Similar results appeared for coalition forming in a competitive high-risk game (Lirtzman & Wahba, 1972). The female executives were thought to be more concerned than their male counterparts about achieving organizational goals and following rules and policies (Hyman, 1980), but the male executives were more comfortable with intellectual authority

(Morrison, White, & Van Velsor, 1987). Bass (1985a) reported that women managers display less management by exception than their male counterparts, which again points to women's greater tendency to be involved in their subordinates' activities. Associated with this tendency may be the different ways in which female and male supervisors appear to view poor performance by their subordinates. In a laboratory simulation of a workplace, Dobbins (1985) found that women supervisors were more supportive in their leadership generally if the subordinates were women. Male supervisors were supportive only if they had inferred that the cause of the poor performance was stable and was due to causes outside the subordinate's personal control, in which case they thought that close monitoring of the poorly performing subordinate was more appropriate.

Evidence of Little or No Difference

The preceding studies found some tendencies for women leaders to be more relations oriented and involved than their male counterparts. However, a larger array of evidence has failed to establish any consistent differences.

Girls and women do differ from boys and men on many attributes. These attributes may be associated with emergence as a leader. But the differences between the sexes blur if one contrasts women and men who already have achieved status as leaders. Once they are legitimated as leaders, the preponderance of research suggests that women actually do not behave differently from men in the same kind of positions. Most often, reviews and analyses of both field and laboratory studies concluded that little or no effects of sex on leadership style were obtained, whether the leaders are describing themselves or are being described by their subordinates.[13] Thus, among 100 male and 100 female executives at the same middle-management level in federal agencies, Muldrow and Bayton (1979) found no differences in their handling of six personnel decisions, although the women described themselves as less likely to take risks. And, Carpeno (1976) found no differences

[13]See, for instance, Bartol (1973, 1974); Bartol and Butterfield (1976); Bartol and Wortman (1975, 1976); Chapman (1975); Day and Stogdill (1972); Martin (1972); Remland, Jacobson, and Jones (1983); Roussel (1974); and Wexley and Hunt (1974).

because of sex on the Leadership Opinion Questionnaire.

Michener and Schwertfeger (1972) reported no differences between men's and women's preference for the use of coercive power or for withdrawing from the situation, although men, if liked, were more likely to be persuasive. In a study of a simulated work setting, Baker, DiMarco, and Scott (1975) obtained no significant differences between the way men and women allocated rewards or penalties. Again, in a longitudinal field study, Szilagyi (1980a) failed to discern any differences in men or women leaders' administration of rewards or punishments, according to their subordinates of both sexes. Likewise, Butterfield and Powell (1981) obtained no differences in the ratings of the styles of male and female managers. Osborn and Vicars (1976) also found no sex differences in the initiation of structure or the amount of consideration of supervisors, according to their subordinates in residences for the men. Similarly, Thomas (1982) reported no differences in the supervisory orientations of 252 male and 285 female business students or in the students' responses on in-basket tests. No sex differences in preferred solutions to the LEAD situational leadership questionnaire appeared among the male and female management students. Also, Birdsall (1980) reported that both men and women managers use the same masculine communication style.

Success and Effectiveness of Women Leaders

When women rather than men are placed in supervisory and leadership roles, how well are they accepted and followed by their subordinates? How meritorious is their performance as appraised by their superiors? How good is the performance of the groups they lead? How satisfied are their subordinates? Does the sex of the leader make a difference in whether the group attains its objectives and satisfies its needs? Are the productivity and satisfaction of the group affected by the sex of the leader? As Rice, Bender, and Vitters (1980) commented, answering these questions is complicated by the extent to which most available studies depend on subjective ratings that tend to reflect sex bias. Such a distortion was observed by Elrick (1977) in a case study of a "self-analytic" learning group of six women and nine men that found the tendency to deny that a woman was leading the group early in the group's development.

Same Behavior but Evaluated Differently

As was just concluded, the preponderance of results suggests that there is little evidence that women actually behave differently from male leaders in similar roles (Adams & Yoder, 1985). But although women managers may behave the same way as their male counterparts and have the same effects on their groups, they are likely to be evaluated differently (Feild & Caldwell, 1979; Seifert, 1984). Thus, a meta-analysis by Dobbins and Platz (1986) of eight studies comparing male and female leaders on the LBDQ measures of initiation and consideration revealed mean effects owing to sex differences that were close to zero. Nevertheless, Dobbins and Platz obtained a significant mean difference in these studies in the ratings of effectiveness that favored the men. And Wheelan (1975) reported that for 72 female and 72 male undergraduates, women were ranked lower than were men in leadership in mixed-sex 6-person groups, despite the greater participation by the women.

Likewise, male and female supervisors can behave the same way, yet be evaluated differently according to their sex. The same style displayed by a female and a male supervisor may have different effects on subordinates' satisfaction with their supervision (Petty & Lee, 1975; Rosen & Jerdee, 1973). In one case, Hansen (1974) could find no significant differences in support or goal facilitation by supervisors that were associated with their sex; nevertheless, subordinates of both sexes were more dissatisfied if their supervisor was a woman. This finding may have been due to the reports by women supervisors themselves that they had less autonomy or, as was found in other studies, that they, as women supervisors, had less influence with higher authority (South, Bonjean, Corder, & Markham, 1982). Subordinates may also favor male managers because male managers are generally more experienced (Liden, 1985).

In all, one is forced to conclude, along with Denmark (1977), that in a majority of cases, differences between male and female leaders are more a matter of stereotyped expectations than actual fact.

A reason for the perceptions of the differences between the leadership of men and of women in the absence of actual differences in behavior between the sexes was demonstrated by Geis, Boston, and Hoffman (1985). These researchers contrasted how first viewing all-male and all-female authority role models in television commercials affected the immediately subsequent leadership performance and leadership evaluations of 276 undergraduates in 4-person mixed-sex discussions. Although the men and women performed equally as leaders in the discussions, their equal performance was recognized only by those who were subjected to the all-female authority figures. Those who viewed the all-male authority figures recognized only the males as leaders in their own discussions.

Jago and Vroom (1982) found that females who were perceived to be autocratic were negatively evaluated, while males who were perceived to be autocratic received positive evaluations. Again, illustrating the difference in evaluations, Denmark (1980) contrasted the reaction of 384 students to a hypothetical male or female professor who had written an "outspoken" or a conciliatory letter in response to a suggestion made at a faculty meeting. Although the conciliatory style was favored by the students, the conciliatory female professor was rated as less of a leader, less interesting, less sophisticated, less strong, and less fair than her male counterpart. The outspoken woman professor was particularly downgraded by the female students. In the same way, Moore (1984) found that in evaluations of performance, masculine behaviors (ambition, self-reliance, independence, and assertiveness) were valued more highly than were feminine behaviors (affection, gentleness, and understanding), particularly for female high performers.

Different Reasons Applied. There are also differential attributions for why men and why women succeed or fail. A man's success is more likely to be attributed to ability, but a woman's success will be attributed to hard work, good luck, or an easy task (Deaux & Emswiller, 1974). Conversely, a woman's failure will be attributed to her lack of ability, but a man's failure will be attributed to bad luck, task difficulty, or lack of effort (Cash, Gillen, & Burns, 1977; Feather & Simon, 1975). Forsyth and Forsyth (1984) used female confederates as leaders who behaved either in a task-oriented or in an interpersonally concerned way in mixed-sex groups. When the group was successful with a female leader, both the leader and the male subordinates attributed the success to luck. With a male leader, the group attributed the success to the leader's ability.

The attributions for the successful and unsuccessful leadership of women by men are related to men's attitude toward women as managers. For 143 male participants who evaluated a scenario of the performance of a woman manager, those with more favorable attitudes toward women as managers were more likely to attribute success to the women's ability and effort rather than to luck or the value of the job. With such favorable attitudes, they were less likely to attribute failure to the woman's lack of ability or effort (Garland & Price, 1977; Stevens & DeNisi, 1980).

Other Distorting Factors. As noted earlier, men are more likely to explain a woman's success as a leader as being due to her sexuality rather than to her job-relevant competencies if she is in a solo position (Lockheed, 1975). Devaluations of a woman's successful performance are also more likely to occur if the job appears to be inappropriate for women or when the outcome of the work effort is ambiguous.

When 96 experienced managers were asked by Wiley and Eskilson (1982) to evaluate the performance of a hypothetical male or female supervisor who used his or her expert or reward power to influence a subordinate successfully, the managers evaluated the male supervisor more favorably when he employed expert rather than reward power. But the female supervisor was evaluated more favorably when she used her reward-based power. The investigators thought these results were possibly due to the greater credibility of men as experts.

Evaluations come closer to reality when work objectives are clear and the job fits sex-appropriate stereotypes. Evaluations are closer to reality for female nursing administrators than for female engineering supervisors. Discrimination disappears if objective rea-

sons for success are available (Riger & Galligan, 1980). In fact, with equally high levels of objective performance by men and women, participants explicitly evaluated women more favorably than they did men in overreaction to the women's success, which is unexpected in the stereotype (Bigoness, 1976). Other distorting tendencies favoring women also occur.

Distortions favoring the woman leader were seen in subordinates and peer evaluations of leadership performance by Jacobson and Effertz (1974). They found that women leaders in experimental small groups were judged less harshly than were male leaders when performance levels did not meet the groups' expectations. And unexpected success by a woman was considered to deserve more praise than the same unexpected success by a man (Taynor & Deaux, 1973).

The Group's Performance and the Sex of the Leader

Again, the evidence is mixed. A few studies show that groups do better with female leaders, some studies show that groups do better with male leaders, and the majority have found no differences that are due to the sex of the leader.

Women Leaders Are More Effective. Contrary to what they had hypothesized, Eskilson and Wiley (1976) found, in a study with 144 undergraduates, that female-led groups were more productive than were those led by males. And from a review of the literature between 1979 and 1984, Smith (1986) concluded that on creative tasks, groups led by women outperform groups led by men.

Women Leaders Are Less Effective. Several studies pointed to the negative effects of women in leadership posts. In an employee attitude survey, Hansen (1974) found that women supervisors had less impact than men supervisors on the climate of their departments, as evidenced by the correlations between supervisors' attitudes and ratings of the groups' climate. Roussel (1974) examined the effects of the sex of 40 department heads on teachers' ratings of the departmental climate in 10 high schools. Departments headed by men were rated higher in esprit and intimacy; departments headed by women were rated higher in hindrances.

Yerby (1975) assigned 192 male and female undergraduates to small problem-solving groups according to their positive or negative attitudes toward female leaders. All groups were led by women. The groups' performance was associated with the attitudes of their members toward females as leaders. Such attitudes also resulted in the lower group morale of male subordinates under female leaders. Rice, Bender, and Vitters (1980) completed a laboratory study of 288 West Point cadets assigned to 72 4-person groups led by females and males with all roles of subordinates taken by males. They found that groups with male leaders did better on two assigned tasks than did groups led by females.

Male and Female Leaders Do Not Differ in Effectiveness. Bartol (1978) concluded, in a review of the results of laboratory studies, that the sex of the leader generally were not a consistent factor in determining the group's productivity. Nor, according to Larwood, Wood, and Inderlied (1978), did the effectiveness of the performance of managers in field studies appear to be associated consistently with their sex. B. A. Hall (1975) reported no difference in the effectiveness of the assertiveness training of women as a function of the sex of the group leader.

Emergence as a Leader

What little evidence is available is decidedly mixed. Some studies, particularly those before 1970, pointed to the difference between women and men in mixed-sex groups. No doubt this difference is likely to disappear with the liberation of women and the efforts to increase their assertiveness. For some tasks and for the continuing expectations of participants about the appropriateness of the leadership role for women (Hollander, 1983), men are seen as more likely to attempt leadership or emerge as leaders in mixed-sex circumstances (Eskilson & Wiley, 1976). As noted earlier, even when women are generally more dominant, they have tended to defer to men for leadership (Megargee, 1969). Attempts to lead, as seen in the initiation of structure and the amount of talking, was found by Strodtbeck and Mann (1956) to be greater for men in jury deliberations. Again, at a Mormon institution,

Brigham Young University, Oddou (1983) found that men emerged more frequently than women as leaders of mixed-sex work groups.

However, Schneier and Bartol (1980) examined sex differences in the emergence of leaders in 52 task groups in a personnel administration course over a 15-week period. They found no significant differences when leadership was assessed by sociometric choice or when it was based on observational data from Bales's interaction process analyses. And, Ross, Davidson, and Graham (1985) reported that 165 women who worked for a major domestic airline scored higher in performance at centers to assess their management and leadership potential than did 215 men. These results were attributed to the relative bias-free situation.

Subordinates' Satisfaction and the Sex of the Leader

The expected conflict between fulfilling the stereotyped role of a woman and fulfilling the role of a manager have already been noted. Yet, the satisfaction of subordinates appears to be unrelated to whether supervisors fulfill appropriate sex-role stereotypes (Bartol & Wortman, 1975; Millard, 1981; Osborn & Vicars, 1976). It is difficult to divorce the subordinates' attitudes and expectations about women leaders from the subordinates' job satisfaction under female or male leaders. Nevertheless, many studies have reported little difference in the job satisfaction of subordinates as a function of the sex of their supervisor.[14] For instance, Terborg and Shingledecker (1983) could find no differences about staying in or quitting a job between 331 male and female employees under female supervisors and 132 employees working for male supervisors except that of all the employees, the male subordinates under male supervisors were most unclear about how their own performance was evaluated. Again, Adams's (1976) survey of the 276 subordinates of 18 chain store managers failed to find differences in the subordinates' satisfaction with supervision that were due to the sex of the managers. But numerous other studies[15] have reported a preference for male supervisors, again with

[14]See, for example, Bartol (1974, 1975), Bartol and Wortman (1975), N. R. F. Maier (1970a), Millard (1981), and Osborn and Vicars (1976).
[15]Brief and Oliver (1976), Osborn and Vicars (1976), and Renwick and Tosi (1978).

other relevant factors affecting the preference. For example, among blue-collar employees surveyed by Haccoun, Haccoun, and Sallay (1978), satisfaction was higher with male supervisors.

Confounds. Even when, as in a study by Goetz and Herman (1976) of the subordinates of department managers in a large retail store chain, it was found that employees working for women managers were more satisfied with their supervision than were employees working for men, the effects of sex could be accounted for mainly by other differences, such as commission versus noncommission payments plans and the composition of the work units. In the same way, Osborn and Vicars (1976) reported that the effects of the sex of the supervisor could be explained by other factors. One such factor may be the duration of the leader-subordinate relationship. In a short-term laboratory study, Rice, Bender, and Vitters (1980) showed that male West Point cadets with traditional attitudes toward women as army officers were less satisfied in their interactions in a short exercise with appointed female leaders than were egalitarian male or female subordinates. But in summer training, an experience of longer duration, the correlation disappeared (Adams, Prince, Instone, & Rice, 1984). In cadet training programs that lasted six weeks, no consistency in the correlation of these attitudes with satisfaction was obtained, regardless of the sex of the leader or the subordinate (Rice, Instone, & Adams, 1984).

The leader's influence "upstairs" is another confounding factor. Trempe, Rigny, and Haccoun (1985) demonstrated, from their findings with 197 semiskilled employees, 52 percent of whom were women, that although the sex of a supervisor was irrelevant to an employee's satisfaction, the supervisor's influence with a higher authority was important and male supervisors were seen to have such greater influence (Terborg, 1977). Similarly, Taylor and Ilgen (1979) completed a survey of employees with female and male supervisors and could find no difference in the employees' satisfaction with their supervision that were associated with the sex of their supervisors. But in comparison to employees working under male supervisors, the employees working for female managers thought that their supervisors had less reward power.

The revealed wisdom and early research hinted that even women workers generally prefer male superiors. As White (1981) noted, a 1971 poll of working women showed that they strongly preferred a male rather than a female boss. But by the 1980s, studies of college women were suggesting that women preferred women as bosses. The same changes were occurring for preferred opinion leaders. By 1975, on most topics, men revealed no preferences in selecting opinion leaders on the basis of the leaders' sex, but women were exhibiting a distinct preference for women leaders except on political issues (Richmond & McCroskey, 1975). As shall be seen later, more educated subordinates had become more favorably inclined toward women as leaders than had less educated subordinates. But male subordinates' attitudes toward women superiors have remained less sanguine.

Performance Appraisals of Women Managers and Officers

Again, the evidence is mixed. On the one hand, as has already been noted, there is a bias toward men in positions of leadership. Nevertheless, such distortion tends to dissipate with performance appraisals that are based on intensive observation or extensive experience. Many field studies have found no difference in the performance appraisals assigned to men and women, although such findings have not been uniform.

Schwartz and Waetjen (1976) reported that 95 percent of employers of female managers rated their job performance as excellent, very good, or good (probably no different than their leniency-prone ratings of male managers). According to a review by J. E. Smith (1986), when managers are rated by their peers or superiors, no consistent sex differences appear. This finding was confirmed in a meta-analysis by Dobbins and Platz (1986).

Deaux (1976a) obtained no difference in the rated performance of men and women retail store managers. M. M. Wood (1975, 1976) and Wood and Greenfeld (1976) also found little difference in the rated performance of men and women managers in several field analyses. Likewise, the A T & T assessment center's predictions of the managerial potential of 1,097 women were similar to those for men; the distribution of the assessors' ratings for men and women were similar (Ritchie & Moses, 1983).

Some Differences on Specific Aspects of Performance. In a few studies, women leaders received higher or lower ratings than did male leaders on some particular kinds of performance. Thus, a survey by M. M. Wood (1976) suggested that male managers tended to rate their female peers highly in decision making, competence, and ability to handle emotions. Women were seen to bring fresh outlooks to business problems and to offer useful insights into marketing problems involving female customers. They were regarded as tending to reduce intense feelings of competition between male managers.

Rosen and Jerdee (1973) completed three experiments with in-basket evaluations to examine cross-sex role behavior by women supervisors. Although friendly, helpful leadership was rated as more effective whether the supervisor was male or female, a reward style was evaluated as more effective for male than for female supervisors. At the same time, Petty and Lee (1975) obtained results suggesting that consideration by female supervisors is more highly related to the satisfaction of subordinates than is the same consideration by male supervisors. Petty and Lee inferred that because more consideration is expected from women, when it fails to materialize, it is more likely to result in the subordinates' dissatisfaction.

In an analysis using 192 male middle managers, R. A. Patterson (1975) found females to receive lower ratings than males on evaluations of performance and promotability. Although, as was mentioned earlier, male cadets were satisfied to serve under female cadet leaders in summer training, female cadet leaders at West Point earned lower staff appraisals than did male cadet leaders for their performance in summer camp. The performance appraisals of 86 female cadets during summer training, compared to those for a random sample of male cadets, were found by Adams and Hicks (undated) to show that in assigned formal leadership roles, female leaders were rated poorer in overall performance. Rice, Instone, and Adams (1984) reported these same results for larger samples. The female leaders were rated as having less capacity for increased respon-

sibility, less ability to organize and coordinate the efforts of others, less initiative, forcefulness, and aggressiveness, and less ability to adjust to new or changing situations and stresses than were the male leaders.

Moderating Effects of Subordinates, Task, and Situation

Effects of the Sex of Subordinates

After a review of the available evidence, Chapman and Luthans (1975) concluded that sex differences in leadership depended on the group and the situation involved. For instance, Haccoun, Haccoun, and Sallay (1978) found that although nondirective styles were favored for women, the sex of both the supervisor and the subordinate determined the group's performance. However, when differences between the success and effectiveness of the leadership of men and women do occur, they may be due partly or fully to differences in other moderating factors, such as the men's and women's age, education, experience, level in the organization, and extent of professional training.

Success of the Leader of the Same or Opposite Sex. Whether the subordinate and the leader are of the same or opposite sex affects the likelihood of the success of the leader. Thus, in 3-person groups, female leaders were least likely to succeed when the other two members were men; they were most likely to succeed when the other two members were women (Eskilson, 1975). Consistent with these results, Aries (1976) observed that males displayed more leadership than did females in mixed groups of males and females than in same-sex situations. Likewise, Megargee, Bogart, and Anderson (1966) found, in a study of various combinations of dominant and submissive men and women in two experimental tasks, that dominant men paired with submissive men and women and dominant women paired with submissive women tended to appoint themselves as leaders. But dominant women paired with submissive men tended to appoint the men as leaders. The dominant women avoided attempting to lead male partners. Among 144 undergraduates in 48 3-person groups, Eskilson and Wiley (1976) observed that although typical sex-role expectations resulted in male leaders receiving more requests for direction, both sexes addressed more directive behavior toward groups of their own sex.

Petty and Lee (1975) found that male subordinates of female supervisors rated their supervisors as lower in consideration and higher in initiating structure than did female subordinates of female supervisors or subordinates of either sex of male supervisors. But it is not known whether the ratings reflected the actual differences in the behavior of the female supervisors toward female and male subordinates or differences in the way subordinates perceived the same behavior by female and male supervisors. The male subordinates with female supervisors felt less satisfaction with their work and with their supervisors. Since women are expected to exhibit more consideration, and generally do, Petty and Lee suggested that when female supervisors display lack of consideration, their inconsiderate behavior has more of an effect on their subordinates' dissatisfaction than similar inconsiderate behavior by male supervisors.

As was noted early in the chapter, the placement of women in leadership positions over men generates status-reversal conflict, particularly for men with traditional attitudes toward the role of women, with the consequential negative impact on the men's performance found by Yerby (1975). Early on, Whyte (1949) described such a status reversal in restaurants in which waitresses gave orders to countermen. Although the countermen accepted such orders, they did so with resentment and hostility.

Men who work for women may feel a greater reluctance to disclose difficulties because they want to protect their own feelings of superior status and do not want to be seen as lacking strength. Zammuto, London, and Rowland (1979) studied how resident advisory assistants in dormitories dealt with their supervisors as a consequence of whether the assistants and the supervisors were men or women. Both female and male assistants were less likely to withdraw when they were in conflict with female rather than male supervisors. Also, highly committed male assistants were more likely to try to smooth over differences, to compromise, and to confront, if the supervisor was female.

But contrary to expectations, Frantzve (1979) failed to find much effect on whether males or females emerged as leaders in initially leaderless groups when she systematically varied the number of females from 0 to 6 in 6-person groups. Opposite results were found in the field studies of West Point cadets by Rice, Instone, and Adams (1984). Similarly, Lonetto and Williams (1974) found that regardless of the sex of the group, the same personal factors, such as a member's intelligence and self-orientation, were related to the men's and women's emergence as leaders for 31 male and 31 females in 3-person undergraduate groups. In the same way, Kanter (1977b) noted that when all-male and all-female groups were given a specific assignment, the interactional patterns and leadership styles within each group were similar. Likewise, among a group of experienced managers, Gaudreau (1975) could find no differences in leadership competencies associated with their sex. Compared to male cadet subordinates under male or female cadet leaders, female cadet subordinates under female cadet leaders generally described their leaders less favorably. They attributed greater influence to hard work by subordinates and attributed less influence to the leaders' skill.

Effectiveness of the Leader of the Same or Opposite Sex. Eisman (1975) found that in marathon encounter groups of one sex or the other, in which a goal is to promote self-disclosure for therapeutic purposes, more such disclosure occurred when groups were led by a person of the opposite instead of the same sex. But most studies that dealt with short-term, less emotionally involved performances found the contrary to be true: Same-sex supervision was better. When supervised by a woman rather than a man, females performed better on mechanical tasks (Larwood, O'Carroll, & Logan, 1977), standard mathematics tests (Pheterson, Goldberg, & Keisler, 1971), and mathematical word problems (Hoffman & Maier, 1967). Again groups with same-sex leaders were reported by Bullard and Cook (1975) to develop a better group atmosphere than were groups led by opposite-sex leaders. However, no differences in productivity were found.

Satisfaction with the Leader of the Same or Opposite Sex. The subordinates' sex and other personal characteristics have to be considered to find much difference in the actual attitudes of subordinates toward female or male supervisors. Yerby (1975) reported that subordinates' attitudes were a complex interaction of the sex composition of the subordinate groups and the leader's sex. In the laboratory study of 72 teams of male cadets led by males or females described earlier, Rice, Bender, and Vitters (1980) found that the male subordinates with traditional attitudes toward women were lower in overall team morale when led by women. Traditionalists attributed their groups' success more to luck and less to the leaders' shared work when led by women. For those subordinates with liberal attitudes, the leaders' sex did not matter as much. Nevertheless, male subordinates, as a whole, thought that women leaders contributed more to the group's performance but that the expert ability of male leaders was more important to their own individual performance. This finding was consistent with Garland and Price's (1977) results. Garland and Price found that men with favorable views toward women managers attributed the managers' success to factors, such as ability and effort, and avoided attributions of success to luck and the difficulty of the task. These attributions differed from those of more traditional men that women succeed because of good luck, easy tasks, or extra effort (Deaux & Emswiller, 1974).

Petty and Lee (1975) reported the tendency for male subordinates to be more dissatisfied with female supervisors who were high in the initiation of structure and to be more satisfied when both male and particularly female supervisors were more considerate. Petty and Miles (1976) noted that considerate leadership behavior by female supervisors of social service agencies (as well as the initiation of structure by male supervisors) was most conducive to the subordinates' satisfaction with supervision. But when larger samples were employed, Bowman, Worthy, and Greyser (1965) found that among 2,000 active executives, 86 percent of the men and 77 percent of the women reported that men were uncomfortable working for women executives. Consistent with what was reported earlier about stereotypes of women's lack of leadership potential (Bass, Krusell, & Alexander, 1971), 41 percent of the men were unfavorable toward women as managers; women respondents were less unfavorable.

A national sample of male managers and executives revealed negative expectations about married women executives. They felt that married women could not handle the responsibilities of home and career (Rosen, Jerdee, & Prestwich, 1975). On the basis of field research using participant observations, S. S. Mayes (1979) concluded that women in authority elicited hostility and dependence in men, who resist the changes in sex-role behavior involved in promoting women into positions of authority over men. The men fear that such change will destroy the traditional norms of family and relations between the spouses.

Few men talk openly about such hostility, but they continue to harbor much resentment. "Behind every woman manager is a man who thinks she got the job only because she's a woman" (Wessel, 1986, p. 20D). When in competition for a job, it is difficult for a man to accept defeat on the basis of qualifications; it is easier for him to blame the woman's success on affirmative action.

Although many women have been found to prefer working for a man (Ferber, Huber, & Spitze, 1979; Robie, 1973), women with higher levels of education were more favorable toward women managers. Younger college women indicated they were looking forward to working for a woman (Koff, 1973; Terborg, Peters, Ilgen, & Smith, 1977). Undergraduate women appear to be more favorable toward working for women leaders than are male students, who are slower to change their outlook (Welsh, 1979).

Wheeless and Berryman-Fink (1985) suggested that compared to male respondents, female respondents perceive female managers to be more competent communicators, regardless of their previous experience in working for a woman manager. Yet Hollander and Neider (1978) found that women, but not men, generated more negative critical incidents about female rather than male leaders. But when Petty, Odewahn, Bruning, and Thomason (1976) employed larger samples, they found that regardless of the sex of the supervisor or the subordinates, the subordinates' satisfaction with supervision was positively correlated with all leadership behaviors except the emphasis on production. Similarly, Bartol (1974), in a study of 100 undergraduates in 24 same-sex and mixed-sex teams of four members playing a business game, failed to find that dominant (counterstereotype) women had a detrimental effect on the subordinates' satisfaction. Again, Fallon and Hollander (1976) reported no difference in the satisfaction of undergraduate males and females with their elected male and female leaders of mixed-sex groups. But the male leaders were seen by both male and female members as more influential and better able to deal with the tasks.

Effects of the Task

Hollander and Yoder (1980) pointed out that some tasks, such as mechanical construction, are seen as masculine, while others, such as child care, are seen as feminine. Men are more likely to take the lead in dealing with stereotypically masculine tasks, and women are likely to do so with feminine tasks. In the latter case, women who ordinarily might not accept leadership roles will think it is legitimate to do so when dealing with a task that is relevant to them. Since leadership in a mixed-sex group is less customary for women, women may be more sensitive to the need to be competent in dealing with the task (Eskilson & Wiley, 1976). Beckman (1984) found that with married couples, in general, it was the wife who tended to dominate the decision processes about fertility and contraception. However, interviews with 376 Egyptian villagers indicated that it was the husband who dominated the basically economic decision for the family to migrate to find better employment opportunities (McDevitt & Gadalla, 1985–86).

Similarly, Bass (1965a) reported that *directive*[16] and persuasive wives were more acceptable as leaders in working with their husbands on an experimental task that dealt with household issues, but they were unacceptable as leaders if the task involved issues within the real organization in which the husband worked. Carbonell (1984) also demonstrated that females with leadership ability were less likely to display leadership in interactions with males when they were dealing with masculine tasks. Again, Musham (1980) found that women, in general, and men whose role preferences were androgynous were more likely to emerge as lead-

ers if the tasks were socioemotional. Men, in general, and androgynous women emerged as leaders when task-oriented leadership was required.

Career Advancement of Women Leaders and Managers

Personal and Family Factors

Women leaders are less likely to have explicitly oriented themselves toward careers as leaders, according to interviews by Apfelbaum and Hadley (1986). Nonetheless, Fagenson's (1986) survey of 260 women entrepreneurs and managers who had reached low, middle, or high levels in their organizations found that the women advanced in their careers because of personal orientations as well as organizational opportunities. Those who were higher in the organization gave more weight to their careers than to their personal lives, were more committed to their organizations, and were more satisfied with their jobs than were those at a lower level. At the same time, those in higher-level positions also thought their organization was more concerned about the growth of their careers, and that they were more likely to be included in the informal power structure in after-hours activities.

Women are thought to overemphasize the task at hand rather than its implications for future achievement. They concentrate on their current activities either because they personally have not learned to set goals or because they believe they are unlikely to be promoted. Also, they remain more concerned than men about their interpersonal relations either because of socialization or because they must remain in the same "dead-end" position (Kanter, 1977a).

Family Considerations. Carroll (1987) examined the personal and family factors that were of consequence to a sample of 609 women and to a comparable representative sample of 365 men who were in state legislatures or the federal administration. Although 24 and 31 percent, respectively, of the female political appointees in the Carter and Reagan administrations had never been married, the corresponding figures for the male appointees were 4 and 12 percent, respectively. Over 80 percent of the men but only half the women ap-

[16]As defined in Chapters 22 and 23, *direction* (italicized) refers only to giving orders with or without explanation. Direction (romanized) includes ordering, persuading, and manipulating.

pointed were currently married. The pattern was the same for state senators and state representatives, although the differences that were due to sex were not as extreme. On the other hand, while 80 to 100 percent of the married women officials reported having very supportive husbands, only 58 to 72 percent of their male counterparts indicated that they had very supportive wives. The men were more likely than were the women to have at least one child under age 12. The women who were elected to the state legislature, compared to the men, more often felt it was important "to my running for office that my children were old enough for me to feel comfortable about not being home as much."

Affiliations. Personal affiliations were also important for the women officials. From 64 to 81 percent were members of at least one major women's organization, such as the American Association of University Women. Except for the federal appointees in the Reagan administration, many were also members of at least one feminist organization such as the National Organization for Women. They also tended to belong to organizations of women public officials and women's business and professional organizations.

Attractiveness. Riger and Galligan (1980) noted that personal attractiveness may be disadvantageous for female applicants who are seeking managerial positions that are believed to require predominantly male attributes, such as ambition, decisiveness, and rationality (Heilman & Saruwatari, 1979). But countering this "dumb blonde" syndrome is the fact that physically attractive women are likely to find more office doors readily open to them and to be granted longer interviews. Then (1988) found that, in the judgments of 35 male and 37 female students in a simulation experiment, very attractive women were rated higher than were average-looking or unattractive women in their potential for promotion to top management. The unattractive women received the lowest ratings, despite their being seen as more masculine in their potential for promotion as well as more suitable as a co-worker or a friend.

Competence and Motivation. Larwood and Kaplan (1980) surveyed 80 women bank officers concerning the reasons for their success. These women thought that the ability to make decisions and their demonstration of competence were most important. Successful officers were distinguished from unsuccessful ones by their greater interest in learning from male models and in their decision-making ability. They reported themselves to be successful, despite their lower evaluation of their self-confidence. At the same time, the women middle managers studied by Banfield (1976) emphasized their human relations skills, participative decision making, sacrifice of femininity, and reluctance to assert themselves. As a group, they revealed well-integrated personalities with high levels of self-esteem.

According to Litterer (1976), the successful woman executive was characterized by the ability to move socially between informal male and female groups. She could be part of the important informal communication networks of both groups. Similarly, Bartol (1978) distinguished between women managers and women in general, finding that compared to non-career-oriented women managers, the career-oriented women managers saw themselves as more broad-minded, dominating, efficient, and independent.

According to Koff and Handlon (1975), women who are more likely to advance are motivated to do so. Their motivation is evidenced by their desire to achieve, their previous successes, and their personal commitment to developing their careers. Those who are career oriented are either pioneers, sensitive to the climate, or support seekers. The *pioneers* are innovators, initiators, risk takers, and high achievers. They enjoy challenges, are not easily discouraged. They have a positive sense of self-worth, and expect to be successful. They also expect to operate independently and autonomously and to be rewarded for their achievements. They feel a sense of accomplishment from handling increased responsibilities. The *climate sensitives* are more responsive to the psychological climate around them and to approval and recognition from the top management. The *support seekers* need stroking and hand holding. Their upward path needs to be cleared of external obstacles and resistances. These women are easily discouraged, readily loose confidence, and do not like to take risks. But support from a higher authority is important for most women with successful careers in management.

Support from a Higher Authority. Hennig and Jardim (1977) found that 25 women who had reached the higher executive level in major corporations were similar to each other in many respects. All were firstborn children.[17] Their fathers, with whom they tended to be close, had encouraged them to be independent, self-reliant, and risk taking. As children, they had been active in team games. The encouragement, support, and help of a male superior with whom they had developed a close relationship tended to be critical to their success. Van Velsor (1987) confirmed the importance to the success of the careers of 22 women executives of help from above. This support from a higher authority is, no doubt, of considerable consequence to the managerial advancement of men as well, except that the powerful person of consequence to a woman's promotion has to be an enlightened member of the opposite sex.

Organizational Factors

Wood (1975) argued that women have to be more competent and work harder to rise in a corporation than do their male counterparts. Although women have been concentrated at the lower levels of management, their failure to advance may be partly due to the fact that most of them have less seniority and experience than their male counterparts. But contrary to expectations, when Tsui and Gutek (1984) examined a representative sample of 217 male and 78 female middle managers in a large corporation with business in computers, education, and finance, they found that the women had a faster rate of promotion, higher performance appraisals, and more merit increases.

A further illustration of the organizational aspect of success is that historically, women were more likely to advance in smaller firms (Bowman, Worthy, & Geyser, 1965). Today, however, it is the larger firms that have the best developed affirmative action programs and more standardized promotion programs that are likely to inhibit sex biases (Donnelly, 1976). Probably as another consequence of better affirmative action programs in the larger organizations, Dreher, Dougherty, and Whitely (1988) found that for 486 business school

alumni, the usual lower management salaries for women than for men were less common in larger than in smaller organizations.

Despite affirmative action programs, Gutek (1988) noted that women appear to have only one real route to high-level positions. They must have the opportunity to enter the organization (made increasingly possible as a consequence of affirmative action) with a professional job of reasonably high status—one that traditionally was more often likely to be given to men. And such an opportunity in the late 1980s is a realistic expectation. Graves and Powell (1988) found no sex discrimination in 483 campus interviews by outside organizational recruiters; the results were the same for both male and female recruiters. But affirmative action is unlikely to help women move up the corporate ladder from female-dominated, low-status jobs. Furthermore, affirmative action programs are a mixed blessing, according to a survey by Chacko (1982). Women managers who thought they had been hired because of affirmative action by the organization rather than because of their abilities were less committed to the organization and were less satisfied with their work, supervision, and co-workers. They also experienced more role conflict and role ambiguity than did the women managers who believed that their sex status was not important to their selection.

In larger firms, most women enter managerial ranks in staff rather than in line positions. In these positions, they can become specialists and earn credit and acceptance from male colleagues for their skills, expertise, and competence in performing tasks (Hennig & Jardim, 1977; Jacobson & Kock, 1977). But for advancement, they need to move into more general management.

Reasons for the Failure of Careers

In contrast to the upward mobile women, those with the necessary seniority and experience who fail to rise, avoid increased responsibility, challenges, and risks. They are passive and lack ambition and energy. They are low in self-esteem and motivated by the need for security. They view their peers as family. Promotion conflicts with their loyalty to their peers, since it may mean the need to sever relations with friends.

[17]This finding is consistent with the earlier discussions about the greater responsibilities that parents place on their eldest daughters and the effects on the daughters' subsequent performance as leaders.

The failure to perform effectively as a manager will result in reduced self-confidence and motivation. The failure reinforces the negative stereotypes about women's potential for management (Schwartz & Waetjen, 1976). The two main reasons for women's failure as managers, according to a survey of 100 male managers, were the women's unwillingness to help other women and their tendency to be overdemanding at times, particularly of other women (M. M. Wood, 1976). Women are first expected to behave in a feminine manner by showing their subordinates more consideration and less direction than would be expected from male leaders (Bartol & Butterfield, 1976). But, as was mentioned earlier, many women who achieve high status tend to reveal a "queen-bee syndrome" and downgrade women at lower levels in the organization (Staines, Tavris, & Jayaratne, 1973). Again, as was noted earlier, women managers who attributed their hiring to their sex status rather than to their potential contribution to the firm suffered more role conflict and role ambiguity, which were likely to interfere with their effectiveness as leaders (Chacko, 1982).

Special Tactics for Women

Although no differences appeared in the upward-influence tactics of women and men, according to a mailed survey of 486 business school alumni by Dreher, Dougherty, and Whitely (1988), Larwood and Wood (1977) suggested special tactics for the women managers to use to promote their success in an organization. Even more than male managers, women managers need to ensure their superiors of their competence by earning the right credentials and receiving competitive job offers and outside acclaim (M. M. Wood, 1975). Learning how to befriend, give, and receive help from men without letting it become a sexual encounter is important. Pearson (1980) concluded, from a study of the choices of 60 employers in the human services field who had viewed videotapes of 6 employment interviews, that female applicants who combined a warm cooperative style with goal-oriented leadership skills were most likely to be preferred by their employers.

It is not just important to be in a network. One must have the right network of contacts that are relevant to one's profession, one's business, and one's interests.

Pragmatic business contacts are likely to be more useful than are general meetings with other women managers (Cox, 1986).

The woman manager needs to act and dress more like a manager and less like a secretary. She can take a visible seating position at meetings (Donnelly, 1976). She can make sure to inform superiors about her activities. Like the male manager, the woman manager can profit from an apprentice role with several superiors. Sometimes, she may find it useful to exploit her stereotypic differences by requesting assignments to ensure that "the woman's point of view is represented." Depending on the situation, the woman manager needs to be able to play the female role or the managerial role, whichever is appropriate (Trahey, 1977). As was already mentioned, she needs to know how to deal with sexual advances and sexual harassment. Almost all the women executives surveyed by Litterer (1976) had experienced sexual advances from male executives, but practically none reported having an affair with someone in their own organization. The traditional "casting couch" demand on an entertainer for a successful career evidently is present but not required for success as a woman manager. Women need to learn how to use and react to power effectively (Instone, Major, & Bunker, 1983). They must convert aggressiveness into assertiveness and initiative and need to appreciate their own competencies better (Wood, 1975).

After a review of interview and assessment data on more successful and less successful women executives, Morrison, White, and Van Velsor (1987) concluded that executive women may actually differ little from their male counterparts on most matters that count, but unlike the men, they must confront two sets of demands. To be successful,

> [they have] to show their toughness and independence and at the same time count on others. They [must] contradict the stereotypes that their male executives and coworkers have about women—they [must] be seen as different, "better than women" as a group [yet they must not] . . . forfeit all traces of femininity, because that would make them too alien to their superiors and colleagues. . . . [They must] do what *wasn't* expected of them, while doing enough of what *was* expected of them as women to gain ac-

ceptance. The capacity to combine the two consistently, to stay within a narrow band of acceptable behavior, is the real key to success. (p. 4)

Women in leadership positions need to make special adjustments that are not required of their male counterparts. Satisfaction with one's job and with one's life in general tend to be correlated. However, Kavanagh and Halpern (1977) found them uncorrelated for women at higher levels of university leadership. This lack of correlation may be partly due to the fact that, as was mentioned earlier, women executives are less likely to have husbands to assist with the social and home-care demands on their time (Harlan, 1976). Women executives are less likely to be married than are their male counterparts and are less likely to have children (Jusenius, 1976). But those who are married and are mothers face role conflicts that are best handled by what Hall (1972) described as structural role redefinition—changing the demands within the conflicting roles of homemaker and manager—rather than trying to meet the conflicting demands of both.

Summary and Conclusions

Because situational changes are rapidly occurring for women in leadership roles, earlier research may need to be discounted. Despite the many continuing handicaps to movement into positions of leadership owing to socialization, status conflicts, and stereotyping, progress is being made. Some consistent differences remain between boys and girls and less so, among adult men and women managers and leaders. Characteristics that are usually linked to masculinity are still demanded for effective management. Nevertheless, most differences in male and female leaders tend to be accounted for by other controllable or modifiable factors, although women will continue to face conflicts in their decisions to play the roles of wives and mothers as well as of managers and leaders.

The rise of feminism and affirmative action has been accompanied by a flood of analyses of sex differences in leadership to the point where by 1985, Dobbins was calling for a moratorium on such studies. Society is changing from a time when smart women played dumb to a time when assertiveness training is now commonplace for women. Yet, it would seem necessary to continue to give careful consideration to the underlying dynamics and dimensions of importance to success and effectiveness of women leaders. The same careful consideration is necessary for the development of a new appreciation of racial and ethnic differences in leadership, the issue that is dealt with next.

Leadership, Blacks, Hispanics, and Other Minorities

By the late 1980s, thousands of blacks had sought and been elected or appointed to public office. Blacks were mayors of Los Angeles; Detroit; Washington, D.C.; Chicago; Philadelphia; Atlanta; and New York City. Other minorities, such as Hispanics, have achieved similar success in San Antonio and Miami. We are now seeing black general officers and Hispanic admirals. Blacks are taking leading roles in sports, entertainment, and the Democratic Party. Asian Americans have reached teh U.S. Senate. Blacks, Hispanics, Asian Americans, and members of ethnic minorities have achieved prominence as business and professional leaders. But in comparison to mainstream Americans, members of these minority groups face systematic differences in the likelihood of their emerging as leaders and the probabilities of their success.

Most of the available research on leadership of minorities deals with blacks as leaders or subordinates. Considerably less is known about Hispanics and ethnic minorities. Although Jewish Americans have reached positions of leadership in government and in selected industries, such as retailing and the communications media that far exceed their 2.5 percent of the population, they still remain outsiders in their access to careers in line management. Often they reach the top via professional accomplishments as lawyers, accountants, or scientists (Korman, 1988). There is also a dearth of information on the movement of Italian Americans, Polish Americans, Greek Americans, and other ethnic groups into top-level positions of leadership, although highly visible members of these groups appeared in industry and government in the 1980s.

At this time, one can only comment briefly on Asian Americans and Native Americans as leaders or subordinates. Similarly, there is little available data on the sub-

ject of leadership among the handicapped or older employees.

Blacks and Leadership

Blacks Are a Subculture

The next chapter will look at leadership in other cultures. But blacks in the United States are not members of another culture. Rather, they form an American subculture that is tied to the majority culture's institutions without clear boundaries to mark off their society from the larger white society and is sensitive to the norms and values of the majority culture (Liebow, 1967). Blacks have adopted the cultural patterns of the dominant white society (Baldwin, Glazer, Hook, et al., 1966). Unlike Hispanics in general, black Americans' perceptions about family, friends, society, love, work, and money are fairly similar to those of white Americans. Blacks and whites are psychoculturally close (Cunningham, 1984). In fact, Pinkney (1969) found that middle-class blacks tend to overconform to white middle-class standards of behavior. Nevertheless the status ascribed to blacks by whites remains low. As Bass, Cascio, McPherson, and Tragash (1976) noted, in a study of 315 managers' responses to a racial-awareness questionnaire, many agreed that the "system" is biased against blacks and that blacks are excluded from the mainstream. Even potential black leaders may restrict themselves. Thus, Gump (1975) found that black female college students were more likely to see their future roles as wives and mothers, whereas white female college students were oriented more toward their own career development than toward fulfilling the traditional woman's role.

Among 359 black executives surveyed by E. E. Jennings (1980), 45 percent still believed that racial prejudice was the most important impediment to the further progress of their careers. Nevertheless, the 350-year legacy of the master-slave relationship is giving way by fits and jumps, prompted by war, civil strife, legislation, and education, to the rise of a sizable number of black Americans into positions of leadership. The 359 black executives in Jennings's survey were located primarily in large organizations, mainly in manufacturing, real estate, insurance, or finance industries. They performed the same functions that provide for the faster success of whites—marketing, manufacturing, and finance. Higher education and personal contacts were important to their being recruited.

Race Relations in Transition

Experimental research lags behind the changes in attitudes and behavior since the 1940s resulting from desegregation, the civil rights movement, and affirmative action. Moreover, the scant research that was available prior to the mid-1960s was of little relevance to an understanding of the attitudes and behavior of blacks and whites in the 1980s. For example, consider Goode and Fowler's (1949) finding that the tough, autocratic, punitive foreman was most effective for maximizing productivity among marginal,[1] predominantly black workers in a Detroit bumper grinding and polishing shop.

This section first examines the situational constraints and personal factors associated with the emergence of blacks as leaders. It then considers the performance and satisfaction of black leaders and the extent to which such performance is contingent on the racial composition of their subordinates. It also looks at the supervision of black subordinates by whites.

Emergence of Blacks as Leaders

There is a rich store of biographical literature on black political, community, educational, and religious leaders, ranging from the leaders of slave insurrections like Nat Turner to the reform leaders, Frederick Douglass and Martin Luther King, Jr. To work within the "system" (Booker T. Washington), to modify it (W. E. B. du

[1]Marginal workers in this context were the last hired and first fired from the automobile assembly plants, the source of better-paying jobs.

Bois), to destroy it (Malcolm X), or to lead it (Jesse Jackson) have been the different goals of the emergent, charismatic, political leaders.

There is continuity in leadership among blacks. According to a longitudinal study by Tripp (1986), the black student activists of the 1960s continued to be involved in community activities in 1969 and 1978. But entry into leadership positions in business and industry, except for a few black service-oriented industries, such as insurance and undertaking, is mainly a consequence of the equal opportunities legislation of the 1960s. The entry of blacks into military leadership was stimulated by President Harry S. Truman's orders to integrate the armed forces in the late 1940s, which was followed by continuing increases in the proportion of blacks, particularly in the all-volunteer army.

Thus, when legislation, higher authority, or political climate demand it, such as occurred earlier in the military and more recently in industrial and educational organizations, blacks have been advanced into higher-level positions. There are now black generals, company presidents, and university chancellors. School desegregation and affirmative action have opened opportunities for education and advancement of blacks and made visible the movement of blacks into higher-status positions. Formalized recruitment procedures and personnel policies with responsible documentation have resulted in large increases in the advancement of minorities, particularly in larger organizations (Braddock, 1984). The legal impediments to political leadership have changed drastically since the restrictions on black voting rights were lifted in 1964. Especially where blacks form a majority of large minority voting blocs, such as in the Deep South or in the inner cities, blacks have succeeded in being elected to office in large numbers.

Some black politicians have gained large white constituencies. Whites may support blacks for leadership to demonstrate their liberalism. In a laboratory experiment using pairs of high- and low-dominant white and black coeds performing a clerical task in which one participant had to assume the role of leader and the other of follower, Fenelon (1966) found, contrary to expectations, that black women assumed the role of leader twice as often as did white women, no matter what their relative scores on dominance. The white women with high scores on dominance thought it more important to show their egalitarian attitudes than to become leaders.

Individual Factors. Black girls, in particular, in comparison to white girls, seem to become much more self-assertive and independent; their parents expect them to mature earlier. Even as preschoolers, black girls may already be required to carry considerable responsibility for younger siblings. Early on, they are exposed to strong dominant mothers as role models (Baumrind, 1972). Although white Americans tend to be addicted joiners of groups and associations, black Americans are even more extreme in this regard. Memberships in associations are a springboard to leadership experiences and political influence. Concrete, visible issues, such as the right to vote, the integration of schools, and the lack of access to public accommodations, have mobilized black followers. But when these concrete issues are resolved and when only more amorphous or less visible issues remain, such as whites-only school board membership, leadership and organization become blunted and the willingness of individuals to serve as followers declines (Davis, 1982). Without salient black issues, blacks are less likely to assume leadership roles even when they form a sizable proportion of the membership of an organization.

Underrepresentation. Despite their high proportions in some types of organizations, such as labor unions, blacks continue to be underrepresented in positions of leadership. For example, Lamm (1975) found that among 30 union locals with black members in the San Francisco Bay Area, only 10 had blacks in leadership positions in proportion to their number in the membership; in 10 locals, blacks were proportionally underrepresented among the leadership, and in the remaining 10 locals, there were no black leaders. Similarly, despite their overrepresentation for excellence in athletics, blacks remain underrepresented in leadership positions, such as football quarterbacks or team managers.

More generally, blacks remain greatly underrepresented in management in both the public and private sectors, except in special circumstances. Thus, in a study of black MBAs, Brown and Ford (1977) found that relative to their white counterparts, black MBAs had lower opportunities for promotion and advancement. Again, Fernandez (1981) found the biggest gap between aspirations and expectations of upward mobility among black male managers. And according to Jones (1986), 84 percent of the black MBAs from the top 5 graduate schools reported that considerations of race had a negative impact on their performance appraisals, pay, assignments, recognition, and promotions. Nonetheless, black managers could advance when conditions were favorable. For 194 black managers with MBAs who were working in larger organizations, advancement occurred more often when they had more seniority, were in line rather than staff positions, and had help from mentors. They were also helped by their social activities (Nkomo & Cox, 1987).

The entry of blacks and whites into positions of leadership was likely to follow different paths. The importance of a religious ministerial practice as a route to leadership for black men is well known. What is less well known is how the route to leadership often differs for black women and white women. Mottl's (1977) interview study of the different career paths of white and black women reform leaders found that the school bureaucracy was immediately accessible to white women who became involved as teachers and middle-class mothers. Their ease of entry from home into school politics was related to the closeness of the schools, particularly the elementary schools, to family life. Black women leaders began and ended up in community organizations.

Constraints on Blacks as Leaders in America

Lower rates of achievement and leadership can be attributed to possible personal in-born deficits or to educational or cultural deprivation. Or, they may be due to blocked opportunities because of cultural conflict and discrimination (Bowman, 1964).

Cognitive and Interpersonal Abilities. In Chapters 4 and 7, it was concluded that leaders need to be more intelligent (but not too much more so) than those they lead. Whatever the reason, blacks score lower on tests of general cognitive ability. Although over 30 percent of whites score in the 108 to 134 IQ range, only 3.3 percent of blacks do so. Blacks with the same amount of education as whites (but not necessarily the same quality of education), who apply for the same jobs or admission to the same colleges score considerably lower in general cognitive abilities, and these black-white differences are resistant to change (Gottfredson, 1986). More intellectually demanding jobs tend to employ proportionately fewer blacks. Reviewing the research evidence, Schmidt and Hunter (1974) concluded that the lower average job performance of blacks from cognitive-ability tests is accurately predicted from their lower average test scores. The lower scores of blacks than whites are not due to test biases. In fact, if anything, the job performance of blacks has been overestimated from their test results.

Howard and Bray (1988) reported a similar amount of black-white differences in their large-scale assessment project. Minorities, mainly black employees of A T & T, were in the twenty-second percentile in tested cognitive abilities, while whites were at the fifty-seventh percentile. Whites also scored better in general information and on in-basket decision making. But the minorities did just as well as the whites on interpersonal skills, oral presentations, and group-participation exercises. In all, only 29 percent of the minorities were seen as having middle-management potential, compared to 50 percent of the whites.

Despite these continuing black-white differences, it must also be clear that a sizable percentage (29 percent in this instance) of blacks have the potential to be leaders. More generally, 25 percent of the blacks are still higher in tested intelligence than 50 percent of whites. Although they may be proportionately fewer than the number of whites who are available, a substantial number of blacks with the necessary cognitive skills are available for positions of leadership (Elliot & Penner, 1974). And such leadership, for instance in the black community, is related to ability, as reflected in the educational level that is attained.

Education. J. J. Cobb (1974) showed that those blacks who were nominated as the most influential members in their black communities were well educated in diverse fields. The educational levels of black executives who were surveyed by E. E. Jennings (1980) were similar to those of their white counterparts.

In 1970, 1 in 10 whites had completed at least 4 years of college, but fewer than 1 in 20 blacks had done so. Only 15 percent of the blacks aged 55–64 had completed high school, compared to 45 percent of the whites. Among those aged 20 and 21, 82 percent of the whites and 50 percent of the blacks had completed high school. But the educational gap between blacks and whites has narrowed considerably since 1970. By the 1980s, blacks were actually entering college in greater number and obtaining more years of education than were whites of the same level of intelligence (Manning & Jackson, 1984). Nevertheless, it is the lack of educational attainment, reflected in large dropout rates, coupled with the often inferior quality of education that is available, that continues to be a factor in keeping lesser proportions of blacks than whites in comparable positions of political, educational, military, and industrial leadership.

Socioeconomic Status. Socioeconomic status, one key to leadership, remains much lower for blacks than for whites in almost every respect. The incomes of blacks are lower and unemployment rates are higher than those of whites. Nevertheless, it is a mistake to equate impoverishment with race. Half the blacks do not live in slums. And there is a small black upper class; this "high society" of black professionals and businessmen is characterized by conspicuous consumption and the excessive formation of clubs because of their exclusion from their counterpart white society (Frazier, 1966). There is a larger black middle class, although the plurality of blacks falls into a lower class. The black class structure is unlike the white structure. Whites mainly see themselves as middle class with small proportions in the upper and lower classes (Drake & Cayton, 1966).

Family Life. For the population as a whole, black family life is less stable than white family life. Black children are much less likely to live with both parents, and black women are more likely to encounter marital discord than are white women. Moynihan's (1965) well-publicized analysis concluded, from these types of differences, that black fathers, often transients, failed to provide their children with support, discipline, or direction. Hill (1971) countered by pointing with pride to five strengths of intact black families: the adaptability of family roles, strong kinship bonds, a strong work orientation, a strong religious orientation, and a strong achievement orientation.

An interesting question is whether the absence of fathers as role models for children who are raised only by their mothers reduces the leadership potential in either childhood or later life. Actually, strong, dominant mothers have been most significant for many world leaders. Fatherless children may have to take on initiatives and responsibilities earlier, although evidence suggests that fatherless boys who lack a masculine role model with which to identify, develop personalities that are marked by impulsivity, academic failure and indifference, immature dependence, and effeminacy (I. Katz, 1974). Role models for black boys often are provided by older street gang leaders and older brothers.

The educational impact of fatherlessness seems minimal. Whiteman and Deutsch (1968) found no relationship between black children's reading skills and the intactness of their families. Similarly, the national survey by Coleman et al. (1966) found that the presence or absence of a father was not a factor in the scholastic attitudes or achievement of lower-class black or white students. Also, Feld and Lewis (1967) found practically no relationship between family intactness and school anxiety.

Relevant to their adolescent and adult tendencies to influence rather than to be influenced, young black girls, especially those in lower middle-class black families, are likely to become highly self-assertive and independent, despite authoritarian treatment from their parents. In particular, their mothers provide strong, dominant role models. Parental warmth is moderate but the parents discourage infantile behavior. Early maturity of behavior is expected of the daughters, who are required to assume considerable responsibility for the care of the younger siblings at an early age (Baumrind, 1971; Billingsley, 1968; Ladner, 1971).

The Slum Subculture. But any study of blacks as leaders would be incomplete if it ignored that large subset of blacks who are the disadvantaged poor. The slum subculture contains its own ethos, which is a more important determinant of behavior than is being black. The characteristics of this subculture include the absence of a sheltered childhood, early initiation into sex, female-centered families, authoritarianism, marginality, helplessness, resignation, fatalism, dependence, inferiority, the lack of impulse control, the inability to defer gratification, a belief in the superiority of males, and tolerance for psychological pathology (H. Lewis, 1965).

There are strategies for survival in the slums, according to Rainwater (1966), and presumably black leaders in the ghetto become masters of such strategies. First, to obtain immediate gratification, one needs to make oneself interesting and attractive to others to manipulate and to seduce them, even though one really has little to exchange. The second strategy is to resort to force and violence. Concerns center on trouble with the law, toughness and masculinity, cleverness in manipulating others, excitement and thrills, and luck and autonomy (W. B. Miller, 1965). At the same time, lower-class black youths miss the socialization experiences to prepare them for the world of work that are obtained by white working-class youths (Himes, 1965).

The culturally disadvantaged have a generalized distrust of organizations. The contingencies between effective work and its positive outcomes are weak. Supervisors who see themselves as considerate and supportive may be seen by their culturally disadvantaged subordinates as hostile and untrustworthy—evaluations that are unlikely to foster success in an organization (Triandis, 1984).

Marginality and Stress. Marginality can be an asset. The marginal person who lives at the boundary of two world views has two ways of looking at problems and of finding answers to them. The acculturation of black or Hispanic subordinates to the mainstream varies. High "biculturals" have their feet planted firmly in both the mainstream and the minority. According to an experiment by Garza, Romero, Cox, and Ramirez (1982), high biculturals, whether they are Chicano (Mexican American) or black, attempt more leadership in simulated, nonsupportive groups, mixed with Chicanos, blacks, and whites if they are externally oriented. They ask for more opinions and evaluations and make more clarifying remarks.

Nevertheless, to capture the constraining effects on individual blacks who are attempting to succeed as leaders, particularly in a white world, one must attend to the stress created by marginality. At the extreme, black managers may be alone in a white-dominated organization, solo pioneers seen by many as tokens of integration. They face anxieties from internal conflicts (such as between their higher visibility and their lower social status) and confusion from external inconsistencies (such as policies of racial equality but incidents of apparent prejudice). They lack exposure to the informal networks of consequence (Jones, 1973). They may lack accessibility to superiors and respect, appreciation, and encouragement from them (Human & Hofmeyr, 1984). Many black managers feel isolated and alienated. They may suffer from culture shock and a loss of identity. They report difficulties in adjusting to the cues and norms of the corporate environment. They experience value conflicts and may remain uncomfortable among whites. Even though mentoring or counseling could be helpful, they avoid getting involved for fear that the information they reveal will be used against them. As with other disadvantaged groups, their families are unlikely to understand what they do. They often feel a lot of rage against whites' subtle devaluation of them. Therefore, it is not surprising that blacks suffer from high blood pressure at twice the rate of whites (B. M. Campbell, 1982).

Succession Problems. Black leaders, whether of social movements or in politics, have often been highly charismatic. One has only to think of Martin Luther King, Jesse Jackson, or Malcolm X. But as often occurs with charismatic leaders,[2] they do not leave strong organizations behind them. Because of this, their successors can command little of their influence (Davis, 1982).

Financial Support. In contrast to comparable white leaders, black leaders usually must run underfunded organizations that limit their growth. They must concentrate their efforts on money raising, face bankruptcy, and curtail their programs. By the 1980s, a number of traditional black organizations experienced reductions of up to 90 percent in their operating capital. Many newer black organizations (and subsidized black businesses as well) have collapsed in proportionately greater numbers than was expected from the experience of white organizations (Davis, 1982).

Funds to support black organizations have shifted since 1970 from predominantly black to primarily white corporate sources. The influence of whites on black organizational development is also seen in the extent to which whites and the white media select and identify black leaders to be and foster leaders of assimilation rather than leaders of protest or black nationalism (Davis, 1982).

[2]See Chapter 12.

Personal Attributes Associated with Black Leadership

As with whites, the leadership potential shows up early in the lives of black individuals. According to personal interviews and surveys of 221 black men and women who were serving in elected positions in North Carolina in 1977, evidence of leadership within the black community began as early as elementary school. Each experience as a leader or a follower in the family, school, church, or community was seen as an opportunity for learning and developing leadership potential (Buie, 1983). But there are also systematic aspects that are particular to black leaders.

Black Values and Black Leadership. As was indicated in Chapter 11, individuals who "typify the group norm" will be more esteemed than are those who reject or depart from it. Grossack (1954a) found that blacks who were attracted to black activities and who valued the Negro race as such, were more esteemed by fellow blacks than were those who were indifferent to black activities, who rejected blacks, or who disliked black heroes. And so it follows, as Kirkhart (1963) showed, that college students who were accepted for group leadership and external leadership positions were those who identified themselves with their own racial group. Dellums (1977) thought that black political leaders must fully identify with "black politics," a commitment to the eradication of the oppression of minorities. Lamm (1975) noted that black union leaders, despite their own high incomes, identified themselves with the black working class and had more favorable attitudes toward blacks. They were also antiwhite and anti-Semitic in attitude. Fifty percent were identified as "Race Men." Compared with 27 percent of the members of the black middle class who were identified as "Uncle Toms" (subscribing to the white value structure), only 6 percent of these black union leaders could be so identified. On this question of values, blacks who aspire to positions of leadership may be faced with a conflict between the black movement's concerns for social, political, and economic equality and the achievement and individualism that are likely to be of more importance in white organizational life.

Differences in the leadership potential of blacks and whites are likely to accrue from the differences in the personal values expressed by black and white college students. According to Fichter (1966) and Bayer and Boruch (1969), in comparison to white college students, black students placed a greater emphasis on being helpful to others and to society. They were less concerned than were whites about experiencing leadership, making money, and being autonomous. Traditionally, blacks sought high-status, open occupations with little interaction and competition with whites, such as teaching in all-black schools (Porat & Ryterband, 1974). But the occupations they sought broadened by the late 1960s (Bayer & Boruch, 1969) as affirmative action opened new opportunities in the professions and industry. Nevertheless, educated blacks continue to concentrate much more than their white counterparts in education and social service occupations and remain greatly underrepresented in business, engineering, science, and medicine. Black students continue to express more interest in the former than the latter occupations.

The differences in aspirations and access are reinforced by the different networks of contacts and information that are available to blacks and whites and by continued segregated living (Spilerman, 1977). Black managers remain convinced of the importance of "the system" to their own job satisfaction. Wright, King, Berg, and Creecy (1987) found that organizational rather than personal factors accounted for most of the explained variance in the job satisfaction of black managers.

Job Satisfaction of Black Leaders. Overall, satisfaction that their needs were being met was lower among black leaders and professionals than among their white counterparts. Slocum and Strawser (1972) found that black certified public accountants (CPAs) reported higher deficiencies in the fulfillment of their needs than did other CPAs. Black CPAs felt significantly more deprived in compensation, opportunities to help people, to make friends, for independent thought and action and feelings of self-fulfillment and of self-esteem. E. E. Jennings (1980) reported that black executives felt their progress as a group had been slower than that of women and was likely to be slower over the next 15 years. Moreover, O'Reilly and Roberts (1973) reported that overall job satisfaction was significantly higher for white than for nonwhite female registered nurse supervisors. On the other hand, contrary to King

and Bass's (1974) prediction, Scott and Moore (1981) discovered, in a survey of the assessed value of management by objectives (MBO) to 77 black managers and 61 white managers, supervisors, and professionals, that although both racial groups were favorable toward the use of MBO, blacks found more value in MBO than did whites for doing their jobs and for the organization. Black leaders of navy squads scored lower than did white squad leaders on Rotter's Internal-External Control Scale (W. R. Allen, 1975b). Again, Alper (1975) observed that, compared with white newly hired college graduates, black graduates gave the contextual rather than the intrinsic elements of work significantly higher ratings in importance.

Motivational Differences. Watson and Barone (1976) noted that black managers were lower in power motivation. Yet, in a study of 23 black and 75 white supervisors, Miner (1977c) found the black supervisors to be higher than their white counterparts in the motivation to manage (namely, good relations with superiors, competitiveness, masculinity, assertiveness, visibility, and willingness to deal with routines). Consistent with Miner, Thomas (1982) obtained results indicating that black male and female business students were more task oriented in their supervisory orientation than were comparable white students. Vinson and Mitchell (1975) showed that black managers assigned higher ratings than did white managers to the importance of obtaining autonomy, self-fulfillment, friendship, and promotion.

These results may reflect the extent to which middle-class blacks conform more than do their white counterparts to what the blacks believe to be the white norms. Black-white values and orientation probably depend more on the segments of the respective occupational groups from which they are drawn. Black managers may be more task oriented than their white counterparts, whereas black ministers may be more concerned about social issues than are their white counterparts.

Differences in Self-esteem. Studies in the 1960s found that, on the average, blacks had lower self-esteem than did whites (Ruhe, 1972) even when they were given evidence that their abilities were equal to those of whites (Lefcourt & Ladwig, 1965). Such lack of self-esteem affected their assertiveness, desire to be integrated, and expectations of success in their careers (Crain & Weisman, 1972).

However, in a large scale-study of over 5,000 blacks and whites in 25 Northern metropolitan areas, Crain and Weisman (1972) found that the lower self-esteem of blacks was more common among blacks who were born in the South. The self-esteem of blacks who were born in the North tended to be as high as or higher than that of whites. Furthermore, the lack of self-esteem among blacks and its implication for black leadership (Proshansky & Newton, 1968) had to be discounted, to some extent, as a factor in the 1980s, considering the rapid increase in the 1970s of successful black models in sports, television, and politics and the opening up of opportunities for qualified black professionals and managers in the white world of work that was stimulated by programs to foster diversity. With the rise of the black movement, the "new" black person has come to value assertiveness and a feeling of greater control over fate (Ruhe, 1972). The findings of L. Campbell's (1983) survey of 20 black women leaders in rural southern communities illustrate the changes that have occurred in the South. On various self-report instruments, these leaders described themselves as high in self-esteem and in feelings of expertise, competence, and internal control. They were high in the need for achievement and felt they had the concrete personal resources to influence others and to fulfill their groups' expectations.

Another sign of higher self-esteem was seen in a study of U.S. Navy squad leaders. Black leaders chose themselves as the best squad leader in their company more often than did white leaders (W. R. Allen, 1975a).

Disappearance of Differences. A number of studies reported little or no personal differences owing to race. For instance, Dexter and Stein (1955) found little difference among women leaders on campuses as a function of race in masculinity, personality, and speed of association. And Barati (1981) could find no significant differences in the preferred leadership styles or attitudes toward subordinates of 160 black and white undergraduates of both sexes. Again, in better controlled and more recent studies, especially studies of individuals who have already achieved positions of leadership,

black-white differences in values, motivation and other personal attributes have tended to disappear. For example, among those blacks who have attained leadership and management positions much less difference has been found between their values and the values of their white counterparts. Watson and Barone (1976) failed to detect such differences in self-concept on England's (1967a) Personal Values Questionnaire or in the need for achievement and for affiliation. And W. R. Allen (1975b) could find no significant differences between black and white naval squad leaders' levels of aspiration and expectancy of success.

Performance of Blacks and Whites as Leaders

Shull and Anthony (1978) found that among 21 black and 56 white participants in a supervisory training program, the blacks were less willing to support harsh punishment for violation of organizational rules than were the whites, especially when the subordinates had a history of good performance. Otherwise, there was little difference in the way blacks and whites thought they would handle disciplinary problems and role conflicts. Somewhat different findings emerged when Stogdill and Coady (1970) used the Ideal Form of the Leadership Behavior Description Questionnaire (LBDQ) in a study of two vocational high schools. The white students thought that consideration was the most highly regarded pattern for ideal leaders, whereas the black students thought that initiating structure was most important.

The importance of the race of the supervisor was shown by Richards and Jaffee (1972), who completed a laboratory study in which groups consisting of two white undergraduate males and a black or white supervisor played a business game. Trained observers rated the white supervisors significantly higher than the black supervisors on human relations skills and administrative-technical skills. Their ratings were based on checklists of effective and ineffective behaviors, as well as overall graphic ratings. The observers also used Bales's Interaction Process Analysis to assess the leaders' and subordinates' behavior. The white supervisors of the all-white groups of subordinates engaged in significantly more signs of solidarity, giving suggestions, and giving orientation, which lent support to King and Bass's (1974) hypothesis that white supervisors will be more directive and less passive about relationships than will black supervisors when dealing with predominantly white subordinates. However, Bartol, Evans, and Stith (1978) suggested that the evaluative data may have been biased, since all the observers were white.

Experiments before the early 1960s with biracial teams working on intellectual-type problem-solving tasks showed that blacks spoke less and, therefore, exerted less effort to be influential than did whites (Katz & Benjamin, 1960; Katz, Goldston, & Benjamin, 1958). But, possibly reflecting societal shifts in the 1960s, as was mentioned earlier, Fenelon and Megargee (1971) obtained contrary results with the female college students who had described themselves as either high or low in dominance. Despite the white women's personal dominant tendencies, the white women yielded to the black women with whom they interacted, apparently to avoid the implication of prejudice.

World-Class Black Leaders Are More Likely to Be Charismatic. Bass, Avolio, and Goodheim (1987) asked sets of students to describe the transformational and transactional leadership behavior of world-class leaders. Among the 69 leaders, 3 were black and almost all the rest were white. The blacks, Andrew Young and Martin Luther King, were at the top of the scale in charisma, and Malcolm X was not far behind. All three were also near the top of the sample in intellectual stimulation. For Davis (1982) this finding was to be expected, for he felt that "the needs and experiences of the black population may dictate a greater emphasis on transformational leadership" (p. 194). Jesse Jackson illustrated these charismatic and transformational tendencies in the 1984 and 1988 presidential election campaigns.

Leaders of black movements are characterized by their satisfaction of mutual problems and the resulting injustices. They focus much on group identity and the need for a sense of community. While leaders in the white mainstream more often direct their attention to conserving resources and the status quo, leaders of minorities, such as the blacks, must more often be transformational in their concern for social change (Burns,

1978), as well as for unmet social needs and for inequities in the distribution of opportunities (Thompson, 1963).

Importance of the Subordinate's Race

An examination of black and white supervisors is likely to require knowledge of whether the subordinates are black or white. Thus, a study by Rosen and Jerdee (1977) illustrated the expectation that a leader's effective supervisory style depends on the racial composition of the group he or she is supervising. Rosen and Jerdee administered a decision exercise to 148 business students. The students evaluated the extent to which participative decision-making styles were appropriate when supervising work groups of various organizational statuses and minority composition. Significantly less participation was seen likely to be efficacious with minority subordinates. Such subordinates were judged to be less competent and less concerned with the organization's goals.

A line of evidence that indirectly indicates that race will affect interactions between leaders and subordinates comes from studies reviewed by Sattler (1970) on the influence of race on behavior in interviews. Respondents tended to give socially desirable responses to interviewers of races other than their own, responses which were socially "correct" or acceptable, whether or not they reflected the respondents' true feelings. Lower-class respondents were even more likely to be sensitive to the interviewer's race than were middle- and upper-class respondents.

The Hard-Core Unemployed as Subordinates. Although many whites are numbered among the hard-core unemployed, blacks are heavily overrepresented. Therefore, the literature about their supervision has relevance, particularly the possibly extra need for supervisors to be both generally supportive and controlling. This need was demonstrated by Friedlander and Greenberg (1971) and by the National Industrial Conference Board (1970). Both studies found that the hard-core unemployed wanted supervisory support in terms of friendliness, courtesy, and encouragement. The need for supervisors to intervene with the interpersonal difficulties of the hard-core unemployed (Goodman, 1969; Hodgson & Brenner, 1968; Morgan, Blonsky, & Rosen, 1970) and possibly to provide close supervision (Triandis & Malpass, 1971) was suggested, even though such close supervision might prove dissatisfying (Goodale, 1973).

Beatty (1974) found generally positive correlations between the extent to which 21 hard-core unemployed black women described their supervisor's consideration on the Supervisory Behavior Description Questionnaire (SBDQ) and their earnings and performance over a 2-year period. Supervisory initiation on the SBDQ[3] was negatively associated with the black women's work performance. W. S. MacDonald (1967b) found somewhat different results in Job Corps centers with large percentages of black trainees. Positive incentives had little value in shaping behavior. Nor was verbal reproof of much use, in contrast to setting and policing goals and applying sanctions for infractions by the group, which caused the infractions to drop 60 percent in two weeks.

Black Supervisor with Black Subordinates. Traditionally, blacks were limited to leading other blacks. Black supervisors with mainly black subordinates were expected by King and Bass (1974) to be highly concerned about how their subordinates felt about them. Therefore, they were expected to be less directive than were white supervisors of blacks. Adams (1978) reported that although both black and white subordinates perceived their black supervisors to be more considerate, the 11 percent of the subordinates in a retail organization who were black gave their black superiors particularly high ratings for consideration over their white counterparts. However, as was noted in Chapter 29, for 19 black social service agency heads supervising 54 counselors of black inner-city clients, Schriesheim and Murphy (1976) found that more such consideration was helpful mainly in low-stress job settings, whereas more initiation of structure was helpful when stress was high in this situation of blacks supervising blacks.

Black leaders often face the problem of having to earn the trust of their black subordinates, since the latter see them as having been co-opted into the white power structure (M. L. King, 1968). Delbecq and Kaplan (1968) studied the managerial effectiveness of local leaders in neighborhood opportunity centers in an urban ghetto. Clients served by the centers thought that the directors were conservative, unwilling to permit the community to be involved in decision making, and ineffective in negotiations with leaders in the larger community. Subordinates in the centers sought immediate change and action through social protest, marches, and rallies. The directors tended to see such activism by subordinates as a threat to their own self-esteem and to their leadership position. They knew that the higher authority was opposed to demonstrations and, therefore, felt like "men in the middle" between conflicting demands from subordinates and from the higher authority. At the same time, King and Bass (1974) suggested that in comparison to white supervisors, black supervisors of black subordinates may have more difficulty identifying with a white higher authority than with their black work group. Yet, the black supervisor may need additional symbols of authority as well as higher-level support to make his or her position credible.

Black supervisors of black subordinates in particular may have to be able to converse fluently in the "street language" (or Black English) of their subordinates and the general American English of their superiors and to be flexible about both (Kochman, 1969).

Black Supervisor with White Subordinates. King and Bass (1974) suggested that, in comparison with whites supervising whites, black supervisors with mainly white subordinates would be expected to engage more often in general rather than close supervision and to allow or encourage subordinates to initiate boss-subordinate interactions. Doing so would reduce the possible feelings of status incongruity[4] among the white subordinates. The minority-majority status inversion that occurs when blacks supervise whites may generate, for status-conscious whites, a conflict between wanting to avoid the black supervisor and the need to interact with him or her (Blalock, 1959). Such whites may also suffer from a sense of lost status as a consequence of the required interaction with a black superior (Blalock, 1967). Even if the black leader has status as an expert, hostility and the loss of status may be experienced, particularly by lower-status white sub-

---

[3]SBDQ initiation includes autocratic items (see Chapter 24).

[4]See Chapter 15.

ordinates (Winder, 1952). In a retail organization, in which 88 percent of 406 subordinate managers were white, the black male superiors, as predicted by King and Bass, were perceived by the white subordinate managers to exhibit more consideration than did their white male counterparts. But as was noted earlier, their black subordinates were more extreme in perceiving the black superiors as more considerate (Adams, 1978).

The job of black supervisors of white subordinates may be made more difficult, according to Richards and Jaffee (1972), by white subordinates who go out of their way to hinder the effectiveness of their black supervisors. For this and other reasons, King and Bass (1974) suggested that it is particularly important for black supervisors of whites to have the full support of higher authority.

King and Bass (1974) also noted that the small number of black leaders in organizations, particularly blacks who supervise whites, makes them more visible than their white counterparts. This visibility, King and Bass suggested, should cause the black supervisors to have more anxiety about succeeding, a greater sensitivity to negative data regarding the activities they supervise, a possible overreaction to such data, and a greater need for external confirmation of the value of the group's and the leader's performance.

White Supervisor with Black Subordinates. King and Bass (1974) suggested that white supervisors were likely to be more *directive*[5] and less consultative when supervising groups with predominantly black subordinates than when supervising groups of white subordinates. They would be more likely to undervalue the capabilities of black subordinates; the rejection of black workers, in turn, would cause the workers to perform poorly (I. Katz, 1968, 1970). White supervisors would want black subordinates to respect them rather than to like them and to be concerned primarily with pleasing (probably white) higher authority. Furthermore, King and Bass (1974, p. 256) noted

Whites supervising blacks often reflect . . . in private conversations, a feeling of walking on eggshells. This feeling may well be reflected in (a) greater censoring

[5]As defined in Chapters 22 and 23, *direction* (italicized) refers only to giving orders with or without explanation. Direction (romanized) includes ordering, persuading, and manipulating. *Participation* (italicized) refers only to sharing in the decision process. Participation (romanized) includes consulting, sharing, and delegating.

of responses and reactions by white supervisors when most of their subordinates are black, (b) less spontaneity in supervisory-subordinate relations, and (c) less certainty on the part of white supervisors as to how rigidly to enforce company rules on procedures.

Reciprocally, black subordinates may be less willing to discuss personal problems with a white as opposed to a black supervisor. This statement is consistent with Sattler's (1970) research review, which indicates that black clients prefer black counselors.

Consistent with King and Bass's (1974) suggestion that white supervisors would be more *directive* with their black subordinates, Kipnis, Silverman, and Copeland (1973) found that although they mentioned similar kinds of problems with their black and white subordinates, white supervisors in mixed situations reported using more coercion, such as suspensions, more frequently when dealing with black than with white subordinates.

Kraut (1975a) also noted that white managers often are apprehensive about supervising new black subordinates, but they frequently react by giving special help to the new black employees. White supervisors' concerns about black subordinates range from fear of the reactions of white customers to the subordinates to how to handle mixed-race social events.

There are also more subtle differences in the way whites in positions of leadership interact with blacks in comparison to whites. When white undergraduates interviewed job applicants who were confederates, trained by Word, Zanna, and Cooper (1974) to give the same responses to the interviewers' questions, they maintained less eye contact with the black applicants than with the white applicants. They were less likely to lean forward and more likely to sit farther away. The interviews were shorter, and the interviewers made more errors in their speaking. These were all indications of a negative interaction.

Confirmation of the negative effects of such an interaction came when the white interviewers deliberately treated the white job applicants to the same subtle features of the negative interaction by not leaning forward, sitting farther away, and making the interviews shorter. The white job applicants reported that they were more nervous and performed less effectively in the interview than did the white applicants who were treated to a positive interaction with the interviewers. This study corroborated the surveys and commentary mentioned earlier that suggested that new black professional employees experience many stresses above and beyond what would be expected for white employees and their new, usually white, superiors.[6] Moreover, when blacks are involved in intellectual-type tasks, their performance tends to be affected adversely if they are led to believe that it is being compared with that of equivalent whites (Katz, Epps, & Axelson, 1964; Katz & Greenbaum, 1963) especially if anxiety levels are high.

Black or White Leaders with Mixed Racial Groups. No simple generalizations are possible here. Some studies reported that whether the supervisor was black or white did not matter. For instance, in groups of mixed racial composition, Adams (1978) could find no differences in satisfaction or job problems among 406 subordinates in a retail organization (88 percent of whom were white) that were associated with whether their supervisor was a black male, a white male, or a white female. Nor did the subordinates' satisfaction depend on whether the subordinates were black or white. The specific behavior of leaders, rather than their race or the race of their subordinates, may be a much more important influence on the subordinates' performance and satisfaction. Schott (1970) found that among nonwhite principals with integrated staffs, the job satisfaction of faculty members was highly related to the principals' reconciliation of demands, tolerance of uncertainty, persuasiveness, tolerance of freedom, assumption of roles, consideration, predictive accuracy, and integration of the group, as measured by the LBDQ-XII.

When subordinates comprise a mixed group of black and white employees, King and Bass (1974) suggested that the group will lack cohesion, which should result in the need for more directive behavior by supervisors, black or white.[7] Conversely, when groups of subordinates are racially homogeneous, cohesion probably will be higher and will result in the possibility of more participative supervisory styles by both black and white supervisors. But experiments failed to support these conjectures. Hill and Hughes (1974) and Hill and Ruhe

[6]See, for instance, E. W. Jones (1973), T. R. Mitchell (1969), Nason (1972), and C. H. Williams (1975).
[7]See Chapter 22.

(1974), who conducted a laboratory experiment in which undergraduate student participants had to compare black and white leaders under conditions in which the subordinate dyads were black, white, or both, employed both black and white observers. The one significant difference in Bales Interaction Process Analyses observations which emerged showed that both the black and the white leaders of the black dyads were less *directive* than were the leaders of the white or mixed dyads on a fairly structured knot-tying task. (Of the three tasks, the knot-tying task was expected to require the most *directive* behavior from the leaders who possessed the knot-tying knowledge.) Hill and Ruhe (1974) reported no difference in the total time each supervisor talked during the three tasks, regardless of the racial composition of the subordinate pairs, and Allen and Ruhe (1976) found no difference in the supervision of mixed dyads involved in ship-routing and knot-tying tasks.

But some investigations did show that it made a difference whether a black or white was in charge of a mixed-race group and that subordinates acted differently, depending on their race. According to Mayhand and Grusky (1972), when black supervisors adopt a close and punitive style of leadership with a mixed group of black and white subordinates, the black subordinates are likely to be more vocal than are the white subordinates in opposing the leaders. But the white subordinates may show their dissatisfaction by reducing their output. Thus, whites in this situation may be more accommodating in attitude but not in behavior to coercive black supervisors. Hill and Fox (1973) noted, on the basis of a study of 17 racially mixed rifle squads in a training battalion of the U.S. Marines that white squad leaders reported giving proportionately more reprimands, but also more praise, to white subordinates than to black subordinates. And the praise white leaders reported giving to white subordinates was more than given by black leaders to white subordinates.

In a previously mentioned study of 288 male naval recruits, W. R. Allen (1975a) formed 64 experimental groups of 4 members each, 25 percent black, 50 percent black, and 75 percent black. The supervisors were black or white. The leaders, regardless of whether they were black or white, experienced increasing supervisory difficulties as the relative proportion of blacks increased in the groups they were supervising. But the subordinates' SBDQ descriptions of the consideration or initiation of their leaders failed to account for any of the results. Furthermore, black leaders were less expressive in their behavior and were generally more inhibited. White-supervised groups performed tasks faster than did black supervised groups. Allen explained that these results were because of status incongruence and social stress.

In another previously cited study, W. S. Parker (1976) administered the Survey of Organizations[8] to a sample of 17 white supervisors and all the 16 black supervisors in 3 plants with a total of 427 supervisors and 7,286 hourly employees. A total of 72 black and 36 white subordinates described the 33 supervisors. Smaller percentages of Chicano supervisors and subordinates were also involved in the racially mixed work groups. When the four leadership-effectiveness measures derived from the Survey of Organizations were examined, significant differences were found between the black and the white supervisors. Compared to the white supervisors, the black supervisors were rated significantly more favorably by their subordinates for managerial support, emphasis on goals, and facilitation of work. The difference for the facilitation of interaction was in the same direction but was not statistically significant. Furthermore, according to Parker, blacks achieved higher ratings from their black and white subordinates because black supervisors were seen as giving more support, as stimulating a contagious enthusiasm for doing a good job, as emphasizing the task to be completed, and as removing roadblocks to doing a good job. Also when white subordinates were the minority in their work group, they tended to rate their white supervisor more favorably on managerial support than did white subordinates who were in the majority in their own work group. This finding was an exception to the general finding, to be discussed next, that subordinates did not give more favorable ratings to supervisors of their own race.

Are Performance Evaluations of Black Leaders Biased?

A world-wide leadership survey was completed by the U.S. Army in each of its major commands (Penner, Ma-

[8]See Chapter 21.

lone, Coughlin, & Herz, 1973). Data were obtained by asking about one-third of the 30,735 respondents to complete a written questionnaire describing the leadership of their immediate superior; another third, to complete the questionnaire describing the leadership of one of their immediate subordinates; and the final third, to complete the questionnaire describing their own leadership. In addition to various demographic items and a single measure of satisfaction with the overall performance of the individual described, the questionnaire used in the study included a list of 43 specific items of behavior that are commonly observed in U.S. Army leaders. About half these 43 behaviors were derived fairly directly from the SBDQ and LBDQ. For each behavior, three questions were asked: "How often does he?" "How often should he?" and "How important was this to you?" The first question is a measure of perceived actual performance; the second, a statement of expectations; and the third, an indicator of the criticality of the behavior according to the respondent.

Table 33.1 presents a summary analysis of the data reported by Penner, Malone, Coughlin, and Herz (1973) on the differences of the supervisors', self, and subordinates' overall satisfaction with white and non-white commissioned and noncommissioned officers. It can be seen that at the three higher levels, the superiors gave higher evaluations to white than to nonwhite leaders, and the subordinates did the reverse, favoring nonwhites. Self-ratings of satisfaction generally were the same for whites and nonwhites. Since the percentage of nonwhites decreased with the increasing level of the raters, so that in each instance more subordinates than superiors were nonwhite, the results could be a consequence of the overvaluing of leaders of one's own race.

White and nonwhite field-grade officers differed in the list of behaviors that correlated most highly with how satisfied they were with their own overall performance. The list for nonwhite field-grade officers contained seven negative items to be avoided. The list for white field-grade officers contained only one such negative item of behavior. Thus, in evaluating themselves, the nonwhite field grade officers were satisfied with their own overall performance if they avoided doing negative things such as "hesitating to take action,"

Table 33.1 Mean Satisfaction with Overall Performance of U.S. Army Leaders

Rank of Ratees	Raters		
	Superiors	Self	Subordinates
Field-Grade Officers			
White	5.65 (715)[a]	5.58 (1,867)	5.45 (3,843)
Nonwhite	5.24 (63)	5.61 (122)	5.66 (375)
Company-Grade Officers			
White	5.36 (1,227)	5.16 (2,240)	5.07 (2,129)
Nonwhite	5.26 (155)	5.13 (128)	5.24 (441)
Senior Noncommissioned Officers			
White	5.32 (2,116)	5.45 (1,988)	5.00 (1,943)
Nonwhite	5.22 (314)	5.45 (505)	5.22 (548)
Junior Noncommissioned Officers			
White	5.02 (3,265)	4.95 (2,385)	4.78 (1,117)
Nonwhite	5.08 (697)	5.05 (695)	4.81 (251)

[a]Numbers in parentheses refer to the number of leaders rated.

SOURCE: Adapted from Penner, Malone, Coughlin, and Herz (1973).

"failing to show appreciation for priorities of work," or "making it difficult for subordinates to use initiative." On the other hand, the white field-grade officers were satisfied with their own overall performance if they did positive things such as "being technically competent to perform their duties," "seeking additional and more important responsibilities," and "being aware of the state of their unit's morale and doing all they can to make it high." Penner, Malone, Coughlin, and Herz attributed this difference to the discrimination experienced by the nonwhite officers in the 1950s and early 1960s when they first entered service, when it was more important for nonwhite officers to avoid making mistakes than it was for them to stand out in a positive manner.

Further Evidence of Bias. A variety of different kinds of bias have been demonstrated, but the effects have been decidedly mixed. Hammer, Kim, Baird, and Bigoness (1974) asked participants to rate workers who were shown performing on videotape according to an objective criterion of effectiveness. Raters and workers included whites and blacks of both sexes. Although high performers were generally rated as more effective than were low performers, the researchers also found that blacks rated blacks higher than whites, whites rated whites higher than blacks, and greater differences were seen between high- and low-performing whites than between high- and low-performing blacks.

Explanations for the good or poor performance of blacks and whites are systematically different. Similar to what was found for the performance of women compared to that of men in the last chapter, the attributions given blacks for high performance were that they were lucky or highly motivated. Equally high-performing whites were seen as able and well educated. Poorly performing blacks were perceived as showing their lack of ability and education; poorly performing whites, their anxiety and lack of luck or motivation (Pettigrew, Jemmott, & Johnson, 1984).

Bigoness (1976) found that raters tended to give higher ratings to poorly performing blacks than to poorly performing whites, yet rated high-performing whites and blacks similarly. Bartol, Evans, and Stith (1978) concluded, after a review of studies,[9] that there was a tendency to evaluate black leaders more heavily on relations-oriented rather than task-oriented factors.

[9]The studies were by Beatty (1973), Drucker and Schwartz (1973), Huck and Bray (1976), and Richards and Jaffee (1972).

Thus, for example, Beatty (1973) found that sponsoring employers' perceptions of social behaviors, such as friendliness and acceptance by others, had a greater influence on the employers' performance ratings of new black supervisors than did perceptions of the new blacks' task-related behaviors. At the same time, Richards and Jaffee (1972) obtained results suggesting that subordinates with more liberal attitudes were more likely to give their black supervisors higher ratings, especially on human relations skills, than were subordinates with less liberal attitudes. This finding may account for the different results obtained in field and laboratory studies by Kraiger and Ford (1985), who completed a meta-analysis of 59 studies involving almost 15,000 black and white ratees. The negative effect of race was substantial for the field studies but close to zero in the laboratory studies, for most laboratory studies are done in college settings where norms for racial equality and against racial bias are likely to be greater than in the field. Nonetheless, reports of bias have not been uniform in either setting. There has been a remarkable diversity of findings.

Burroughs (1970) studied black girls and white girls in discussion groups. White followers rated black leaders higher when they exhibited a high quality of performance. But Hall and Hall (1976) found no differences because of race or sex in undergraduates' ratings of a case of an effective personnel administrator. And Durojaiye (1969) studied the effects of sex and race on sociometric choice among schoolchildren aged 8–11. Although these children preferred friends of their own sex and race, neither sex nor race influenced their choice of leaders. However, Richards and Jaffee (1972) found that, as a whole, white trained observers judged black leaders more harshly than they did white leaders. Vinson and Mitchell (1975) reported the opposite; they noted that black managers received higher performance ratings mostly from white superiors than did white managers. Schmidt and Johnson (1973) found no differences in peer evaluations among supervisory trainees, whereas among naval squad leaders, W. R. Allen (1975b) found that white leaders received significantly higher ratings from white subordinates than from black subordinates. Similarly, black subordinates chose their black leader as best squad leader in the company more often than they chose their white

leader. Finally, Cox and Krumboltz (1958) and Dejung and Kaplan (1962) found, in early nonsupervisory situations, that ratees received significantly higher evaluations from persons of their own race. In the same way, Flaugher, Campbell, and Pike (1969) found that black medical technicians were rated significantly higher by black than by white supervisors.

Some Implications. No simple answers emerge to the question about whether racial considerations bias evaluations of performance. As long as one must depend on subjective evaluations of black and white leaders, it will be necessary to be sensitive to the potential for bias in their evaluations, although often such biases may fail to show up in particular instances. One can imagine some circumstances in which superiors will lean over backwards to give unearned higher evaluations to black supervisors but other situations in which prejudice may cause lower-than-deserved ratings. Black subordinates and superiors may feel the need to overvalue members of their own race or may set extra-high standards for them. Student participants' ratings in transitory experimental settings may be freer or more biased by the students' generalized feelings about race in comparison to the ratings by long-time organizational colleagues of the performance of familiar associates. But such colleagues also may be more biased or less biased, depending on their general racial attitudes.

Individual differences may override any possible generalizations. Thus, Bass, Cascio, McPherson, and Tragash (1976) collected the responses of 315 managers and professional employees in a large light-manufacturing establishment on 109 racial awareness items. A factor analysis revealed that the respondents differed reliably among themselves to the extent to which they agreed that the effectiveness of blacks in leadership and management is generally influenced by (1) bias in the system, (2) the limited implementation of affirmative action policies, (3) incompetence of black employees in general, (4) the failure to include black employees in the system in a real way, and (5) the need of black employees to build self-esteem.

Personal Strategies for Blacks

Again, as with women, blacks need to adopt personal strategies. Blacks can make themselves more valued by enhancing their competence through higher education, particularly in fields, such as engineering or business, in which they have been scarce. They can avoid resegregating themselves in white schools to develop as much experience and comfort in working in a white world. They can seek entry into firms with good track records for developing and promoting blacks. They can seek sponsors and mentors in those firms. They can prepare themselves to be at the margin of two influences, accepting and maintaining both the desirability of their black identity and the organization's values.

Henderson (1986) suggested that individual blacks need such specific strategies to anchor themselves in corporate America. They must strengthen their own leadership skills and develop a healthy and secure home life. Bowman (1964) used the path-goal hypothesis to sum up what blacks need to consider in their efforts to succeed. In addition to pursuing education, they must believe that their efforts will pay off for them and they must learn to cope with the various social and organizational barriers that stand in their way.

Black leaders as a group can assist in the process of upgrading those who come along behind them. Black leaders in the emerging black middle class need to channel their political energy, talent, and imagination for constructive ends, particularly to help cope with the problems of lower-class blacks (Loury, 1985).

Walters (1985) called for a shift in political strategy from the protest movements of the 1960s and 1970s. Consultation needs to replace confrontation. The black community must be reconstructed internally by strengthening its common resource base and its common frame of reference. The newer strategy will be harder to pursue because the issues have become so complex that black leaders may have difficulty with their constituencies because of the additional information and comprehension that are required (Davis, 1987). Black leaders face a strong challenge in unifying the diverse sectors of their community (Jacob, 1985).

Other Minorities and Leadership

Hispanics

Hispanics are a rapidly increasing minority in the United States. Between 1970 and 1980, they accounted for 23 percent of the growth in the population. During that time, they climbed from 4.5 to 6.4 percent of the U.S. population, in contrast to blacks, who remained almost stable at 11.7 percent. But these figures do not indicate their concentrations in the Southwest, where, for example, they constitute 21 percent of the population of Texas and 19 percent of the population of California.

As immigrants and their descendants from Mexico, Puerto Rico, and Cuba, as well as from the many other countries of Central and South America, Hispanics are far from homogeneous. Coming from middle-class backgrounds, the Cuban Americans have moved much more rapidly into positions of political and business leadership than those who came from the Mexican peasant class. The long-established Hispanics, who form 32 percent of the population of New Mexico and from whom some of the governors of the state have come, are far different from the Puerto Ricans in the ghettos of New York City. The immigrant Chilean engineer of European descent has little in common with the former Indian peasant from Nicaragua or El Salvador (Estrada, undated).

Nevertheless, Hispanics do share cultural commonalities that are likely to affect their emergence and success as leaders, as well as their attitudes and performance as subordinates. But handicapping their prospects for leadership is the fact that like the blacks, a large proportion of Hispanics suffer from lower educational achievement and higher dropout rates. They are more likely to be found in service and blue-collar occupations and to face poverty and language barriers. In large proportions, they are newcomers and younger than the general population. For the most part, we can only infer how Hispanics differ from Anglo mainstreamers in their attitudes and behavior as leaders and as subordinates from what is known primarily about how they differ from mainstreamers in selected attitudes and values that are likely to affect leader-subordinate interactions.

Differences in Attitudes and Values. Hispanics tend to be more collectivistic[10] than are mainstream Americans, who tend to be more individualistic. Unlike

---

[10]Collectivism versus individualism will be discussed in more detail in the next chapter.

a mainstream American, an individual Hispanic who is faced with such decisions as whether to join the U.S. Navy will worry about how other Hispanics view the action. The other Hispanics are not likely to favor such a decision, and the individual will worry about how this disfavor will affect his family. Ridicule and the loss of cultural identity may be seen as a cost of entry into the mainstream (Triandis, 1981).

In contrast to mainstream Americans, Hispanics are more intensely attached to their nuclear and extended families and are more concerned about meeting family obligations and sacrificing their own interests for the sake of their families. Compared to the strong pull of the family, they are ambivalent about work environments (Triandis, Marin, Hui, et al., 1982). As with members of collectivist cultures in general, Hispanics have difficulty separating the person from the role taken by the person (Rojas, 1982). They tend to emphasize cooperation and assistance as opposed to competition and rivalry, which is also likely to affect their performance as leaders (Ross, Triandis, Chang, & Marin, 1982; Triandis, Ottati, & Marin, 1982). They are more optimistic about interpersonal interactions and are less likely to feel that criticism by another person will be constructive (Triandis, Marin, Lisansky, & Betancourt, 1984).

The collectivist values to which Hispanics subscribe, more than do those in the mainstream, that are likely to affect their performance as leaders include being sensitive, loyal, respected, dutiful, gracious, and conforming. Mainstreamers are more likely to emphasize being honest and being moderate (Triandis, Kashima, Lisansky, & Marin, 1982). Consistent with this finding, Hispanics are more likely than are mainstreamers to favor supervisors who provide social support and consideration even if the supervisors are not well organized (Triandis, Hui, Lisansky, et al., 1982). Supervisors are likely to find it useful to keep in mind that unacculturated Hispanic subordinates may be hostile and distrustful of the out-group and the establishment. Links between behavior and reward will be less clear. These subordinates will be ambivalent about their self-esteem and see themselves as a bundle of roles, rather than as a bundle of traits. They will accept and favor social, sex, and power differentiation and will tolerate inefficiency. Furthermore, they will view competence in a

task to be less important than agreeableness, conscientiousness, and getting along with others, and will favor equality over equity. In addition, they will tend to favor group over individual assignments but may not necessarily value participative decision making (Triandis, 1984).

These analyses, mainly about male Hispanics, do not account for the greater acceptance of responsibilities and leadership in school sports by lower-class Puerto Rican girls in comparison to their matched black or white lower-class counterparts. Klonsky (1987) attributed such results to the closer attention that Puerto Rican girls receive from their overprotective mothers (as observed by Cahill, 1967) and less neglect of them by their fathers than is true for other lower-class children. In general, socialization is greater among Puerto Rican girls than among their black or white classmates.

Supervisor-Subordinate Relations. A little evidence has accrued about the impact of black or white supervisors on mixed Hispanic–mainstream groups. For example, Hill and Fox's (1974) examination of the extent to which black and white squad leaders reprimanded or praised their black, white, and Puerto Rican subordinates found that the squad leaders treated all their subordinates similarly. As was noted earlier, although it was expected that one minority group would favor another, Parker (1976) found that Chicano subordinates of black and of white industrial supervisors gave the white supervisors significantly higher ratings on support, emphasis on goals, and facilitation of work and of interaction than they did their black supervisors.

Asian Americans

Already tagged as our "hi-tech coolies," Asian Americans have burst into the U.S. scientific and professional community in record numbers, although they were only 1.5 percent of the population in 1980. Asian Americans are likely to be as collectivistic as the Hispanics (Hsu, 1981), with a strong sense of family obligations and concerns about their own acculturation.

In 1985, they constituted 8 percent of the professionals and technicians in the United States, but made up only 1.3 percent of the managers and executives. Much of this difference may be due to racial prejudice, but some of it may also be due to the ambivalence of

Asian Americans toward integration and socialization into the American mainstream's values, attitudes, and behaviors. In conflict is a cultural background that stresses modesty and the stereotype of Asian Americans as being passive and retiring rather than assertive, which is needed for leadership (Yu, 1985).

With their family support for education, their large overrepresentation at leading American universities, and their acceptance as professionals and technicians, they are likely to experience an upward trend in such employment unless a backlash occurs. But their movement into management in proportions representative of their numbers in technical and professional work is likely to lag, despite Agor's (1986a) finding that, along with women, Asian Americans in general have more intuitive ability than mainstreamers, critical for decision making at higher levels of management.

Native Americans

Little can be said about this country's most impoverished minority, whose members are undereducated and live mainly under tribal councils that discourage participatory democracy and collaborate with state bureaucracies to maintain the status quo. The leadership of their many famous chiefs of the past is only a memory. Most reservation Indians remain repressed and apathetic (Adams, 1984). Many others have faded into the general population.

The observed leadership tends to differ from one tribal culture to another; for example, although in most tribes men are the leaders, women play a more important role among the Navahos. Intensive analyses of anthropological reports are needed to sift out the patterns of consequence. Illustrative of the possibilities was a study by Dekin (1985) of the Inupiat[11] of northern Alaska who live in the Point Barrow area.

Dekin observed that in community meetings, Inupiat leaders need to conform to Inupiat social norms, which would confuse unsophisticated mainstream Americans. Indulgence, indifference, acquiescence, noncompetitiveness, and tolerance are highly valued among the Inupiat and are socialized in childhood. The deeply held values are reflected in the unwillingness to impose one's will on others to divert or correct

[11]The Inupiat are an Inuit (Eskimo) people.

them, particularly if others have already expressed their points of view.

Community development and planning among the Inupiat are particularly difficult because of traditional leadership patterns. Whoever speaks first determines what will be accepted. Avoidance of conflict, and an unwillingness to impose on others or to correct them are the rule. Those with recognized leadership roles, such as the city mayor, must speak first. In public meetings, others are reluctant to disagree with the leaders, so all acquiesce even though they do not privately agree with them. The followers are tolerant but uncommitted. Elections and the secret balloting can produce results that diverge markedly from what was expressed openly at public meetings. Some politicians and North Slope administrators take advantage of these norms by attaining a false consensus in public hearings, despite the fact that if private voting had been allowed, quite different opinions would have been revealed.

The Inupiats' tolerance and indulgence of deviation by followers may be misinterpreted by outsiders as apathy. Rather, these traits represent their reluctance to impose decisions on others if decisions are made at all. Decisions, which must be made by a single leader, are consciously avoided, if possible, even if doing so means delays or inaction. The Inupiat norms also mean that public safety officers, clerks, and accountants, who must abide by impersonal rules of enforcement in the face of differences of opinion, cannot be selected from among the Inupiat.

Other Ethnic Groups

To the original migrants from the British Isles and northern Europe to North America have been added the immigrants to the New World from southern and eastern Europe. Among these immigrants and the descendants who continue to identify with them are the Italian Americans.

Italian Americans. Italian Americans moved rapidly into positions of leadership in government and industry. The next chapter will discuss some of the attitudes of leaders in Italy. This section points to some elements that may continue to contribute to the performance of Italian Americans from the paucity of controlled research on what may distinguish their leadership from the mainstream.

Prud'homme and Baron (1988) found that Italian Canadians have a pattern of irrational beliefs that is likely to influence their interactions with others and that is different from the beliefs of mainstream Canadians. Social approval ("It is essential that one be loved or approved of by virtually everyone in his community") was more fully endorsed by the Italian Canadians than the English Canadians in their study. This need for social approval is consistent with Rutonno and McGoldrick's (1982) finding that Italian Americans tend to build a network with distant relatives of the same age. In contrast to the beliefs of English Canadians, those of Italian Canadians contained more irrational fatalism ("Unhappiness is caused by outside circumstances, and the individual has no control over it"). This finding by Prud'homme and Baron fit with the sense of resignation to events that Spiegel (1982) observed among Italian ethnics. Prud'homme and Baron also found irrationally high self-expectations in their Italian-Canadian sample ("One must be perfectly competent, adequate, and achieving to consider oneself worthwhile") and the necessity for perfect solutions ("There is always a right or perfect solution to every problem, and it must be found or the results will be catastrophic").

There are other elements that may be of consequence to leadership among those who identify with their Italian American heritage. For example, the Italian-American community tends to be as cohesive as is the Italian-American family, with its emphasis on strong family ties (Ziegler & Richmond, 1972).

Italian Americans have moved into top leadership positions in every walk of American life, as witnessed by Lee Iacocca in industry, Amadeo Giannini in banking, Vince Lombardi in sports, Antonin Scalia on the Supreme Court, and Mario Cuomo in politics. However, the extent to which Italian Americans may face the extra hurdles in achieving line-management roles that Jewish Americans seem to face is not known.

Jewish Americans. Korman (1988) reviewed the research evidence on the Jewish experience in America and concluded that despite the liberalization that has occurred in the mainstream in the past half century; despite the fact that they have built and managed many successful organizations; despite their prominence and visibility in medicine, law, academia, art, music, and literature, and in the local, state, and federal governments; despite strong family support in their development, Jewish Americans remain absent from managerial and executive roles in the overwhelming majority of the largest and most important American corporations, ranging from oil and chemicals to foods and commercial banking. Paradoxically, they serve in these same industries as professionals, staff personnel, and consultants. In some sense, here, there is a parallel to the experience of women in general, to Asian Americans, and to other nonmainstreamers in the past several decades.

Although Jews form only 2.5 percent of the U.S. population, 10 percent of college graduates identify themselves as Jewish, so it would be expected that they would be overrepresented rather than underrepresented, as they are in management positions. Consistent with this, Powell (1969) found, in a survey of 239 executives from a variety of industries, that over 23 percent said that being Jewish hindered an executive's career but less than 2 percent said that being Gentile had the same impact. Over 63 percent thought being Jewish kept one from being promoted, compared to the 24 and 20 percent, respectively, who said the same about being Mormon or Roman Catholic. But the comparable figures were under 4 percent for Episcopalians, Methodists, Congregationalists, Lutherans, and Presbyterians.

The executives did not base their opinions on lack of competence, morality, and motivation or on outright discrimination. However, they believed that Jews, Mormons, and Catholics cannot develop the network of necessary friendships inside and outside the firm as easily as can Protestant mainstreamers and cannot meet the criteria of social acceptability, compatability, and "fitting in" in the company. The beliefs, in turn, may be supported by stereotypes, such as that Jews are overly aggressive. The continued exclusion of qualified Jews as well as Asian Americans and other ethnic minorities from line management appears to be based primarily on the belief that they are not socially acceptable, which, in turn, reinforces the self-perceptions of the ethnics that they are indeed outside the mainstream.

Quinn, Kahn, Tabor, and Gordon (1968) found that although 139 executives in the Cleveland-Akron area were generally unprejudiced in the abstract, in that they agreed that Jewish persons should be hired or promoted to important management positions on the same basis as everyone else, when it came to a concrete decision, a fifth indicated they would choose a Gentile over a Jew with equal qualifications.

Korman's thesis is that Jews remain outsiders in a "catch 22" bind. For instance, they are excluded from higher levels of management because they are not members of the right social clubs, and they are excluded as members of the clubs partly because they have not attained the higher levels of management (Zweigenhaft, 1980).

But there also has been systematic exclusion from entering the corporation at the bottom. When it was still legal to do so, 50 percent of the requests for management applicants to the California Public Employment Service explicitly discriminated against Jews, as did 27 percent in Chicago (Waldman, 1956). Most public and private employment agencies in many other cities continued to accept such open discriminatory requests well into the 1960s.

Jewish executives are likely to be found in representative numbers only in sales functions and in states such as New York, New Jersey, Pennsylvania, and Illinois that have large Jewish populations. But they were less likely to be promoted to higher positions in corporate headquarters in the 1960s and 1970s. And they are still highly underrepresented on corporate boards of directors (Korman, 1988). However in the mid-1980s, much depends on differences in industries and specific firms. For example, 27 percent of senior managers in the apparel industry are Jewish, as are 21 percent in retail and supermarket chains and 10 percent in textiles and publishing, but 8 percent are in the aerospace industry and in the soap and cosmetics industries, and less than 1 percent can be found in the petroleum industry. Within industries, they are more prevalent in the smaller firms. And when they do attain top management positions, it is because of their staff or outside status as lawyers, accountants, scientists, or engineers, not from their promotion through line management (Korman, 1988).

Despite all the progress of the past half century in moving minorities into positions of business and industrial leadership, company policies can still account for much of the continuing discrimination. The exclusion of Jews from entry into line management in those industries with few Jewish executives also occurs as a consequence of the corporate policy not to recruit graduates from even highly prestigious schools with more than 30 percent Jewish enrollments (Slavin & Pradt, 1982) in contrast to recruiting graduates from comparable schools with low percentages of Jewish students. Corporate policy also modifies the potential of prejudicial managers to make biased decisions. Although only 29 percent of the managers who would prefer to discriminate against Jews in recruiting, hiring, and promotion to management positions said they would act on their biases if they believed their company was concerned about equal opportunity; 68 percent would do so if they thought their company did not care (Quinn, Kahn, Tabor, & Gordon, 1968).

There is only indirect evidence about differences in the leadership and leadership preferences of Jews and Gentiles. For instance, Jewish Americans are more likely to support liberal political leaders and are much less affected in this regard than are Gentiles by their income levels, which ordinarily reduce such liberal preferences. Ward (1965) found that when the top management of a firm was composed of Jews, rather than of Gentiles, the firm's personnel policies and practices were likely to be more liberal. However, firms that had both Jewish and Gentile senior managers were even more liberal.

The Physically Impaired

What is likely to affect the performance of physically impaired people, both as leaders and as followers, is the tendency for normal people to cut short and to distort interactions with them. Presumably, such behavior may reduce the success of handicapped people in leadership positions.[12] Nonetheless, a physical impairment need not be an impediment. Franklin D. Roosevelt still provides an inspiring model of a person who lost the use of his legs midway in his political career but was able to overcome the adversity. Deaf-blind Helen Keller is another such inspiration.

[12]See Chapter 6.

Few controlled studies were unearthed that compared impaired and unimpaired supervisors in their leadership of impaired and unimpaired subordinates. When 133 deaf subordinates of 21 deaf and 21 hearing supervisors described the supervisors on the LBDQ-Form XII in a survey analyzed by Sutcliffe (1980), no differences were revealed except that the deaf subordinates rated their deaf supervisors higher in orientation to higher authority. But Sutcliffe found in interviews that the deaf supervisors achieved the same quality of leadership as the hearing supervisors by keeping their communications short and to the point. They avoided communicating over the heads of their subordinates. Furthermore, the deaf supervisors tended to be more charismatic than did the hearing supervisors.

Baker, DiMarco, and Scott (1975) noted a compensatory reaction in the supervisory reinforcement of blind workers. In an experiment with subjects who acted as supervisors, the subjects were more likely to administer rewards to blind workers than to sighted workers for identical performance. The opening of more job opportunities for the physically impaired through concerted affirmative action efforts and through the advent of physical and sensory computer aids should lead to more research on their supervision.

Older Workers

The aging of the American population will make the leadership and supervision of older workers of increasing importance. Legislative sanctions against mandatory retirement are likely to increase the average age of managers and supervisors. Again, discrimination and stereotyping need to be overcome. A meta-analysis by Waldman and Avolio (1986) found that although objective studies comparing the job performance of younger and older employees could find little difference between the employees, the subjective performance appraisals by their supervisors were biased in favor of the younger workers. A decrease in sensory and memory functions does accompany aging, but greater experience appears to compensate for these declines. As Simon (1987) concluded, intuition depends directly on the richness of experiences.[13]

According to a survey of 189 nonfaculty staff members at a university who were aged 18 to 70, LBDQ ratings of their supervisors' initiation of structure was more predictive of the younger employees' satisfaction. For the older workers, their supervisors' consideration was more important (Gallagher, 1983).

Leadership by older managers appears to fit what older subordinates require from their supervision. Older managers (aged 40–55) in comparison to younger ones (aged 20–29) were found, in a survey of 200 business school graduates, to be less autocratic and more skilled in human relations; they were also regarded as more efficient and gathered more information before making a decision (Pinder & Pinto, 1974). Campbell (1987) suggested that although older leaders have the advantage of experience and are likely to remain calmer under stress, they may display less decisiveness, have less energy to implement decisions, and not be able to handle new and creative ideas as well as can younger leaders. However, with a mailed survey administration of the LBDQ, returned by 127 program supervisors of community mental health centers as well as by their superiors and their subordinates, Campbell (1981) obtained only slight differences in the LDBQ descriptions of the younger and older supervisors by their superiors. The differences in the subordinates' descriptions of the leadership behavior of younger and older program supervisors were inconsequential.

Older subordinates are likely to react differently from younger ones to different styles displayed by their leaders. Selvin (1960) examined older and young military trainees under three types of leadership—persuasive, weak, and arbitrary. For the trainees as a whole, arbitrary leadership generated the most tension and escape activities, and persuasive leadership generated the least. In addition, older and younger trainees reacted differently to the leadership styles. Under persuasive leadership, the younger trainees tended to exhibit aggressive behavior, such as fighting with each other. Under arbitrary leadership, the younger trainees exhibited relatively personal forms of withdrawal behavior, such as attending mass entertainments and sports events and concentrating on their hobbies. Older trainees under the arbitrary leader tended to respond with anger.

---

[13]Although I presented examples in Chapter 10 of the potential decline in effectiveness of leadership that may accompany advanced age, I can

also cite Armand Hammer, Claude Pepper, Conrad Adenauer, and Colonel Sanders as a few of the examples of effective, aged leaders.

Summary and Conclusions

The many changes that have occurred in this area in recent years suggest the need to discount the findings of many of the earlier studies. But discriminatory constraints still ride heavily on black leaders and emerging leaders from other minorities. Leadership styles are affected by whether leaders and subordinates each are black or white. However, relatively little is known as yet about black leaders' supervision of whites or mixed groups, although some evidence is beginning to appear. Even less is known about Hispanics, Asian Americans, and those from other racial and ethnic groups as leaders and as subordinates. In each group, different factors may be important. Hispanics share an emphasis on collectivism over the mainstream emphasis on individualism. While educational achievement is lower for blacks and Hispanics, it is higher than the mainstream for Asian Americans and for Jewish Americans, and although both groups are prominent in corporate America as staff members and consultants, they remain outsiders and are underrepresented in the seats of power in much of American industry. Equally little known but likely to increase in importance for study is the impact of age and physical handicaps on supervisory-subordinate relationships when differences in prejudice may outweigh differences in performance. From examining leadership in the subcultures of the United States, I now turn to a discussion of leadership patterns in other cultures and countries.

Leadership in Different Countries and Cultures

The Importance and Pace of Internationalization

The internationalization of business took several new twists in the 1980s. European, Japanese, and even Third World multinational corporations increased in number and importance relative to the previously dominant U.S. multinational corporations. They increased their presence greatly in the United States, itself, which resulted in a new much more frequent intercultural mix of foreign ownership and management and North American employees.[1] Globalization of efforts also intensified, so that a manager of research and development (R & D) in the United States could be in immediate contact by electronic mail with a sizable number of immediate subordinates in France and Germany who were engaged in a common project. In addition, Japanese cars began to be assembled in the United States by North American employees under Japanese supervisors for export to Japan. The socialist Second World increasingly is seeking investment and technology from the First World.

Along with its economic integration, a one-world "pop" culture has emerged from the world market for television, concerts by rock stars, and fashions. Multinational military teams and peace-keeping forces have become commonplace. The First and Second Worlds remain responsible for the advanced education of numerous current and future leaders of Third World nations.

The internationalization of institutions affecting leadership continues to grow. The industrialized societies of Europe, Japan, and the Anglo-American world are converging. For example, the traditional Japanese values of lifetime commitment are becoming less important. In diverse countries like Argentina, India, Israel, Nigeria, and Pakistan, employment in business and industry has resulted in many converging values (Miner, 1984). Such converging values were seen by Podsakoff, Dorfman, Howell, and Todor (1986) who compared Mexican and U.S. employees who were working for the same Maquiladora firms (firms along the border in Mexico that assemble U.S.-made components for distribution of the final products in the United States). They found little difference in the way the Mexican and U.S. employees in the same firms conceptualized leaders' rewarding and disciplinary behaviors and their effects. Similarly, Smith, Tayeb, Peterson, et al. (1986) found that questionnaire items dealing with relationships, such as those on the consideration scale of the Leader Behavior Description Questionnaire (LBDQ) or on Misumi's (1985) maintenance (M) orientation scale maintained the same factor structure in the United States, Britain, Japan, and Hong Kong. Yet, there were variations across national boundaries for items on the scales of initiation of structure and performance (P) orientation. And, as shall be seen from the considerable research on leadership that has been completed in individual countries, ranging from Australia to Zaire, there are even differences in the concept and meaning of leadership as one crosses national and cultural boundaries. The differences in socialization in the various nations of the world give rise to different conceptions of leadership. What is good leadership will vary. Even the English word *leader* may not be directly translatable! For instance, it does not easily translate into French, Spanish, or German, so *le leader, el lider,* and *der leiter* may be used instead of the available French, Spanish, or German words, *le meneur, el jefe,* or *der Führer* that tend to connote only leadership that is directive (Graumann, 1986).

---

[1]Publicly owned manufacturing companies in the United States whose headquarters were in Britain, Japan, Germany, the Netherlands, France, and elsewhere were concentrated in such states as California, Connecticut, Illinois, Massachusetts, Michigan, New Jersey, New York, Ohio, Pennsylvania, and Texas.

Issues of Consequence

Given the continuing internationalization and the observed cross-cultural differences, this chapter will try to answer such questions as, How much is it possible to generalize the results of leadership research from one country to another? How transferable are managers with experience and education from one country to another? How do managerial decision-making practices and leadership styles vary in different cultures? Are some dimensions of leadership universally relevant while others are culturally relative?[2]

Similarities and Differences

Some behaviors, attributes, causes, and effects are found everywhere in similar fashion. But other elements tend to be concentrated in some cultures and countries rather than others.

Universal Tendencies. The chapter will consider unique or unusual leadership practices that appear to be associated with a particular cultural background. To understand leadership under such circumstances requires the examination of the unusual institutions of that culture. But such an exploration does not preclude the discovery of universal tendencies, that is, tendencies that are common to a wide variety of cultures and countries. For example, using standard survey procedures in 12 countries and clusters of countries, ranging from the United States and Britain to India and Japan, Bass, Burger, Doktor, and Barrett (1979) found that managers everywhere wanted to be more proactive and to get work done by using less authority. In the same way, managers with higher rates of career advance-

ment everywhere saw themselves as having a higher effective intelligence.

Helping to wash out cross-cultural effects may be the more powerful transcending organizational effects of the multinational corporation. For example, to see if the original Early Identification of Management Potential assessment program in the United States could be validated cross-nationally, the analyses were replicated with 800 Exxon managers from Norway, Denmark, and the Netherlands (Laurent, 1970). Success as a manager was measured by salary adjusted for age and organization's salary structure. Table 34.1 shows the extent to which the results generalized across four countries.

The same traits and measurements of ability in Norway, Denmark, and the Netherlands were predictive of the success of North American managers, as well as of managers in other countries who were working in the same multinational corporation. Cassens (1966a, 1966b) obtained similar results using the same biographical information blank for selecting Exxon executives with samples of nearly 400 Latin Americans working in their native country (Venezuela and elsewhere) and 200 North American managers. There may be several reasons for this similarity. First, universal traits could be involved for relatively uniform tasks. Second, Exxon may tend to recruit "Americanized" Europeans and Latin Americans. Third, socialization processes that occur after one enters an organization may result in uniform requirements that transcend cultures.

Cross-cultural Differences. Bass, Burger, et al. (1979) concluded that, more often than not, national boundaries did make a considerable difference in managers' goals, preferences for taking risks, pragmatism, interpersonal competence, effective intelligence, emotional stability, and leadership style. National boundaries also affected the degree to which these attributes were associated with the speed of promotion. Consistent with these findings, on the basis of a survey of 1,768 managers in a single multinational firm, Griffeth, Hom, DeNisi, and Kirchner (1980) found that 52 percent of the variance in managers' attitudes could be accounted for by their nationality. Again, Bass (1977) demonstrated, by using Exercise Organization (Bass, 1975d), that, in general, for North American managers, productivity and satisfaction are greater when they complete plans developed in their own group than

[2]For additional coverage, particularly on leadership among children, in education, and in small groups, the reader should consult Triandis's (1980) *Handbook of Cross-Cultural Psychology*, volumes 4 and 5. For earlier research reviews, the reader may consult Harbison and Myers (1959), who published a collection of field studies on comparative management and leadership in various countries. This work was followed by Haire, Ghiselli, and Porter's (1966) survey comparison of managers in 14 countries. Available two-country or multiple-country comparisons made possible reviews by Barrett and Bass (1976), Boddewyn and Nath (1970), Nath (1969), and K. H. Roberts (1970). Other works of consequence included those by Farmer and Richman (1964), Fayerweather (1959), and McClelland (1961). Studies generally tended to be based on interviews, but Nath (1969) uncovered 20 survey reports, mostly of comparisons of students in two countries.

Table 34.1 The Forecasting Accuracy of a Common Battery of Tests and Measurements
for the Early Identification of Exxon Managers in Four Countries

Test	United States	Norway	Denmark	The Netherlands
Part A	.44	.59	.61	.55
Part B	.64	.65	.57	.62
Part C	.33	.29	.34	.27
Part D	.52	.43	.34	.45

SOURCE: Adapted from Laurent (1970).

when they carry out plans assigned by another group. But actually, North Americans are extreme in this regard, compared to nationals from selected countries of Europe, Latin America, and Japan. Objective efficiency was 14 percent higher for North Americans carrying out their own rather than others' plans. Similar results were obtained for Irish (13 percent) and French (12 percent) managers but not for Danish or German managers for whom it did not make any difference whose plans were followed. In between in these effects were British, Colombian, Italian, Swiss, Belgian, Dutch, and Japanese managers. Although the managers from all the countries studied rated their own plans as better than those assigned by others to their group, the French managers were most exaggerated in this competitive effect.

The same method may place a greater burden on the leader in one country than in another. For example, Miskin and Gmelch (1985) contrasted the requirements for leadership of quality-control teams in Japan and the United States and argued that Japan's organizational culture (mainly in its larger and better firms and agencies) of entire careers spent in the same organization, security of employment, gradual upward mobility, strong familial relationships, and collective decision making provides more ready-made support for the quality-control effort than does the U.S. organizational culture, with its short-term company loyalty, tough-minded management, rugged individualism, and ambitious upward mobility. In the United States, therefore, the leader of the quality-control team needs to provide more emphasis on the socioemotional components of the group's cooperation, involvement, commitment, and long-term loyalty, which is already present in the Japanese team.

The Unit of Study

The cultural and nation states which tend to be compared are somewhat arbitrary. In the aggregate, countries and cultures differ from each other in the environments that systematically affect leader-follower relations. They may differ from each other in language, religion, values, attitudes, beliefs, education, social organization, technology, wealth, politics, and law (Terpstra, 1978). National boundaries make a convenient difference. But they may or may not be coterminous with cultural boundaries. The Dutch-speaking Flemings are culturally closer in many respects to their Dutch neighbors in the Netherlands than to their Wallonian French-speaking Belgian countrymen. Nevertheless, it is the national boundaries between the Netherlands and Belgium, not the cultural boundaries between the Dutch and French speakers, that determine the educational institutions, legal forces, political effects, and economic considerations that are of consequence to understanding leadership and management. On the other hand, cultural boundaries are likely to have a greater impact on values, sentiments, ideals, language, and role models. Thus, it is not surprising that Weissenberg (1979) was able to show that German-speaking managers varied significantly in their judgments of the importance of 6 of 11 life goals, depending on whether they came from Austria, West Germany, or German Switzerland. Among the nationals from these three countries, the Austrians placed relatively more emphasis on service; the West Germans, on leadership, independence, and prestige; and the Swiss Germans, on wealth and duty.

The combined culture-country effect can be seen when persons from one culture move into a country dominated by another culture. Kelley and Worthley (1981) found that Japanese Americans in financial institutions in Hawaii have managerial attitudes that lie between those of Japanese and American managers. The same kind of result was reported by Zurcher, Meadow, and Zurcher (1965) for Mexican bank officers and employees who were working in Mexico and comparable Chicanos and Anglos who were working in the United States.

Countries Clustered by Cultures. Countries tend to cluster by culture. Thus, North American managers (excluding those in French Canada) tend to cluster with their British cousins on numerous dimensions of leadership behavior and attitudes. Together, they form part of an even larger Anglo-American cluster that includes Australia, Canada, New Zealand, and South Africa. With over 160 countries containing several hundred cultures, it becomes important to try to merge comparisons into a framework of a set of fewer but larger clusters of nations and cultures. Clusters of countries provide a way of displaying cross-cultural results in summary form. The labels provide a preliminary identification of leadership patterns that are likely to be found and the basis for predictions and explanations of what will be found. They may have practical value. For example, they make it possible to determine relevant policies for the transfer of executives from all Germanic countries rather than from Germany, Austria, and Switzerland on a one-by-one basis. Comparisons can concentrate on a dozen clusters, rather than on 160 individual countries.

Ronen and Shenkar (1985) synthesized eight previous efforts[3] to cluster countries according to their similarities and differences in the importance of work, satisfaction with work, autocratic versus democratic attitudes toward work, personal values (such as pragmatism, achievement, decisiveness, and orderliness), and interpersonal values (such as conformity, recognition, and benevolence). The results are shown in Figure 34.1. Geography, history, language, religions, and technological development strongly influenced the clustering.

[3]See, for example, Haire, Ghiselli, and Porter (1966); Hofstede (1976, 1980); and Ronen and Kraut (1977).

Thus, there are more commonalities than differences among the Anglo countries, for example, in the importance they attach to the individual. In addition to language, these countries also have in common a high wealth per capita, democratic forms of government, and a British heritage. Anglo countries differ in particular from the Far Eastern, Near Eastern, and Arab clusters of countries, which for instance, place much more of a premium on authority than do the Anglos. The Anglo cluster was seen by Kipnis, Schmidt, Swaffin-Smith, and Wilkinson (1984), who found no differences in the various strategies used by 360 American, Australian, and English managers to achieve their personal objectives. Likewise, Posner and Low (1988) reported more similarities than differences in the value placed on organizational stakeholders and personal traits by 426 Australian and 1,498 U.S. managers.

In addition to geographic, historical, religious, and (except for Finland) language affinities, the Scandinavian countries even more than the Anglo-American countries, strongly support parliamentary democracy in government and industrial democracy at the workplace.

Language, industrial development, and attitudes toward work, among other things, tie together the Germanic nations of Central Europe. In turn, Latin Europe—France, Italy, Portugal, and Spain—is separated from its Germanic neighbors by generally later technical development, history, language, and more uniformity in Catholicism. The distinctiveness of the difference is evidenced in the much slower introduction of organizational development and related participative leadership practices.

The Latin European and Latin American clusters separate the colonizers from the colonized. The Latin European countries are more advanced in their development and more stable politically for the most part. France, Italy, and Spain have accelerated in technical development. They also tend to be more homogeneous ethnically and racially in their populations than are the Latin American countries.

Common to the Latin cultures, both the Latin European and the Latin American, are Roman law and the lack of a consensual basis, which are seen to strengthen the centralization of authority of the state (Faucheux

Figure 34.1. A Synthesis of Country Clusters

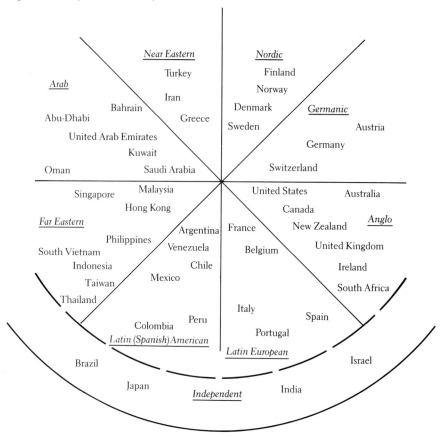

SOURCE: *Adapted from Ronen and Shenkar (1985, p. 449).*

& Rojot, 1979). The Latin cultures also share a lower capacity for openness, trust, and the rational expression of feelings, in contrast to the Anglo cluster. Competence is more likely to be overruled in the Latin than the Anglo cluster by considerations of formal status. The tolerance for uncertainty and ambiguity is likely to be lower. The transfer of programs and practices, such as management by objectives or organizational development, from the Anglo to the Latin world is fraught with impediments, including the greater Latin than Anglo institutionalized centralization of decision making, bureaucratic protection, and state intervention and the lesser importance of internal organizational processes in comparison to the class struggle and to social movements that are external to the individual organization (Faucheux, Amado, & Laurent, 1982).

There is also more hidden game playing in the Latin than in the Anglo organization.

In addition to sharing a common Spanish language and colonial heritage, Spanish America has common patterns of leadership and decision making. For instance, Heller (1969b) stated that South American boards of directors do not seem to abide by standards of Anglo-American efficiency. He also saw common values and habits in Argentina and Chile, each with its own different Latin American subculture, that were deleterious to the effectiveness of organizations. In 59 out of 68 business organizations he observed, board meetings were held without precirculated minutes and agendas. Consequently, the boards spent some 38 percent of their time reexamining the same subject matter that they had previously discussed. Furthermore, the organizations did not carry out decisions that had been reached by the boards. Heller also noted that the managers in these countries tended to equate authority with rapid decision making and to stress its importance. Whereas Anglo-American managers commonly will try to gather more information before they make a decision, Heller sensed that senior managers were expected to make quick decisions in Argentina, Chile, and Uruguay.

Adding to the inefficiency of decision making is the Latin American propensity to rely on intuition, emotional arguments, and justifications, according to McCann (1964). Thought proceeds in a series of direct perceptions of truths. The truths concern the object being contemplated, independent of any demonstrated reasoning process. The truths are neither verifiable nor repeatable. The tendency is toward action that is improvised—that is undertaken without conscious planning. When planning is done, projects may be considered completed after they have been planned (*projectismo*).

The countries in the Far Eastern cluster build on their shared Confucian and Buddhist heritage and a "shame" culture. Unlike the West's "guilt" culture, in which individuals are largely accountable to themselves, in the "shame" culture, interpersonal behavior is more restrained. The verdicts of others are more acceptable, as is parental authority (Ronen, 1986). The boundaries between self and others are unclear. Challenge is less of a personal and more of a collective goal (Metzger, 1977). Little importance is attached to having sufficient time for personal and family life. One's obligation to the family is strong, but being the family breadwinner is what is important, not spending time with the family (Eberhard, 1971). Work and duty are more important than are leisure and enjoyment (Dawson, Haw, Leung, et al., 1971). It is more important to comply with legitimate authority. Personal aggrandizement and advancement are valued less than is recognition by one's peers. Achievement is tied to team efforts (Shenkar & Ronen, 1987). More so than for Americans or Europeans, it is important to do things right and to comply with legitimate authority (Latham, 1988).

Missing from the Shenkar-Ronen clusters are the Second World countries of Eastern Europe, which are mainly Slavic and all socialist, as well as the Third World countries of black Africa. These omissions reflect the lack of available comparative studies. Nevertheless, there are important differences in the values of Second World citizens, such as the Russians, and First World citizens. The Soviets are more likely to regard compromise as a personal loss and perhaps unethical as well. They are much more supportive of the use of punishment as a deterence (Cunningham, 1984). Difference between Russian speakers and those from the West are revealed in the Russians' preference for consecutive rather than simultaneous translation. Ordinarily, the meaning of Russian sentences is more dependent on how they end than are, for example, English sentences. Russians are more comfortable about the accuracy of consecutive translation, while Anglos are likely to prefer simultaneous translation that takes less time.

As will be noted later, the Soviet economic system and the Russian historical heritage result in different supervisor-subordinate relationships than those in the First World. The People's Republic of China, a mix of socialism with a Far Eastern heritage, is still another story. References will also be made to the unusual leadership that emerges in selected black African countries, such as Nigeria, and Islamic countries, such as Saudi Arabia.

Brazil, Japan, India, and Israel do not fall into any of the clusters in Figure 34.1. Unlike Spanish America, in Brazil, Portuguese, Indian, and African influences have had the strongest impact. In contrast to the overly rapid decision making observed by Heller in Spanish-American Argentina, Chile, and Uruguay, Harbron (1965) noted the opposite tendency in Portuguese-American Brazil. Traditional Brazilian managers running inherited family factories practice *jeitinhos*, finding little solutions and avoiding dealing with big problems for which they have had no experience. They are characterized by languid, compromising, "wait and see" attitudes. Despite this type of leadership, Brazil has undergone a remarkable economic expansion since 1965 that has involved robust (and sometimes ruthless) enterpreneurial activity that is not often seen in Spanish America.

Although Japan, China, and Korea have common roots in the Confucian ideology of harmony through proper obedient behavior according to one's prescribed role in one's family, village, and society, Confucianism took a different path in Japan than in Korea or China. The result is that in China and Korea, people feel a more personalized loyalty to individuals, family, and kinship and in Japan, people have a greater loyalty to an organization. (The role of the Samurai, *joeishikimoku*, formulated in the twelfth century, placed more emphasis on ability and common causes than on blood relations.) There is a greater acceptance of top-down leadership in China and Korea and a greater acceptance of bottom-up leadership in Japan. In Japan, by being competent in playing one's proper role in the organization and being committed to the organization, one can aspire to rise to the top. Among South Koreans and Chinese in Singapore, Taiwan, and Hong Kong, only members of the family clan who own a firm can aspire to top positions. In Japan, harmony is achieved with leadership that fosters consensus through much participation; harmony is achieved among Koreans and Chinese by leadership that seeks consensus through much more planning and control by the leader (Castaldi & Soerjanto, 1988).

Japan's history and technological development diverged widely from those of other Far Eastern countries. Professional management appeared earlier in Japan, even earlier than in the West. The history of entrepreneurial activity in Japan was likewise quite different from that found elsewhere in Asia.

Japanese, Korean, and Chinese leadership and management practices are different in numerous ways, despite their common emphasis on collective responsibility and in-group concerns (Fukuda, 1983). Likewise, the preferred management styles of Japanese business students were found to differ significantly from those of Thai business students (Neranartkomol, 1983). In Japan, the Far Eastern collectivistic loyalty to the family is converted into loyalty to the organization. India's different technological development, colonial history, and heterogeneity of ethnic and language groups and Israel's unique history and development keep them separate from the Anglo cluster.

Within-cluster Differences. Despite these cultural clusters, considerable differences are possible among the countries that are clustered on the basis of similar cultures. For example, Hines and Wellington (1974) found that both entrepreneurs and middle managers in New Zealand who were native to Britain had a much higher need for achievement than did those who were native to Australia and New Zealand. Shouksmith (1987) further pointed to the sharp cultural differences in work values and social orientation of the Europeans (*pakahas*) and Maoris in New Zealand. The same can be said for the small but growing number of black leaders and managers in South Africa in contrast to their white counterparts (Hofmeyer, 1987).

Although the United States and Britain are both in the Anglo cluster, considerable differences are often noted between managers from the two countries. In the United States, it is polite to be friendly whether or not you really mean it; in Britain, it is impolite to be friendly if you do not mean it (Terry, 1979). With respect to information about the firm and the job, in the United States, the shop supervisor who represents management is more important to workers' performance than is the shop steward who represents the union; the reverse is true in Britain (Earley, 1986).

In an in-basket simulation, U.S. management trainees responded more favorably than did their English counterparts to both praise and criticism and attached more value to social interaction (Earley, 1985). The results suggest that a contingent reinforcement style of leadership is likely to be more effective with U.S. than with English subordinates.

In particular, Britons are more class conscious. Speech, dress, and style limit mobility and acceptance. It is still much more unusual in Britain than the United States to move out of the working class into the higher ranks of political and business leadership (Newman, 1985). Nor are the leaders likely to be as oriented to the postindustrial world as are their counterparts in the United States, Europe, or Japan. Public school education stresses the need for middle- and upper-class Britons to develop a commanding social presence with grace, wit, eloquence, self-possession, and subtlety; technical and business education are considered to be of less value (Hampden-Turner, 1983).

Although the U.S. and British cultures are similar in many respects, British managers are regarded as less aggressive and less ambitious than are their North

American cousins. British employees are more likely to regard their jobs as a right and privilege, not something to be earned. Work is less of a focal point in their lives than it is for Americans. British employees see themselves as members of their community; Americans, as members of their company. British managers are more likely than are their American counterparts to dislike and distrust foreigners, to be more averse to risk taking, to be fonder of tradition and formality and less accepting of change, to be more class conscious, to want to see more structure, and to follow precedents rather than written codes (Terry, 1979).

Countries in the Latin American cluster vary widely in many ways that are of consequence to leadership. Mexico is characterized by its *mestizo* majority; Argentina, by its diverse European ethnic groups. Venezuela is thoroughly Latin; Chile is more north and Latin European.

Aside from the obvious effects on them of the differences in their economic, political, and social systems, the Chinese in the People's Republic of China diverge from the Chinese in Hong Kong, Taiwan, and Singapore. Unlike those in off-shore locations, Selden (1971) found that subordinate officials in Mainland China were expected to interpret, modify, and adapt policies that were initiated higher up in the system. Another difference is the greater stress in the People's Republic of China on cooperation among workers and relatively less emphasis on the promotion of managers. These differences were revealed in surveys of Chinese managers' judgments of the importance of various work goals in the People's Republic of China, Hong Kong, Taiwan, and Singapore (Shenkar & Ronen, 1987). They were also seen between 49 managers in the People's Republic of China and 49 managers in Hong Kong by Birnbaum and Wong (undated). Managers in the People's Republic of China valued power differences, risk taking, individualism, and assertive masculinity considerably less than did their Hong Kong counterparts. Consistent with this finding, according to Lindsay and Dempsey (1985), collectivism is shown in the attention that managers of firms in the People's Republic of China pay to the lower-level needs of workers and by the managers' holistic concern for workers and for their lifetime employment.

Within-country Differences. As was seen in the preceding chapter, the blacks in the United States do not form a separate culture from the whites. However, the various ethnic groups, such as the Hispanics, do form separate cultures, particularly if they are first-generation immigrants.

Cross-cultural differences among managers in task- and relations orientations and styles may sometimes be overweighed by within-country political effects. For example, within-country differences in the orientation of leaders were seen as being especially significant in Italy by Gallino (1975). Three types of Italian managers were observed: the liberal, the lay humanist, and the Christian socialist. These types varied in how they conceived the manager's role and functions, how subordinates should be trained, their use of formal organizational techniques, their models of economic development, their investment preferences, and their attitudes toward the work force and the representation of workers. "Liberal" managers were more often found in older, established private companies operating in relatively traditional productive and technological sectors; lay humanists, in newer, recently established private companies operating in the advanced production and technological sectors; and the Christian socialist, in companies run fully or partly by the state. The liberal managers were task oriented and profit maximizing, the lay humanists were more concerned about relations and people, and the Christian socialists were oriented toward the public good and the collectivity.

Chowdhry and Pal (1960) also warned against focusing on an overall pattern of values among people within one country, such as India, which could obscure the differences between subgroups in that country. Furthermore, emphasizing the overall patterns of values among countries could miss the commonalities among similar subgroups within these countries. Thus, Singh, Arya, and Reddy (1965) reported that patterns of leadership behavior in Indian villages systematically differed with the leaders' socioeconomic status, caste, and occupation. Similarly, Gopala and Hafeez (1964) reported, for a sample of Indian supervisors, that high educational attainment was associated with favorable attitudes toward employees, while the lack of education was associated with a production orientation. But what is even as much or more of consequence to leadership in countries such as India are the divisions among communities caused by religion, language, and region.

To conclude, the unit of study one uses to examine how nationality and culture affect leadership may be clusters of countries with cultural affinities, individual countries within the same or different clusters, and subgroups within countries. Different conclusions may be reached, depending on which unit is used.

Origins of Leaders

Differences among countries are the rule rather than the exception when one investigates the origins of their leaders in the public and private sectors.[4] Thus, countries may vary in the extent to which their managements are drawn from all social classes or from the upper or lower portions of society. Japan is an almost classless society in that one can climb to positions of leadership through demonstrated capabilities certified by admission and passage through elite universities. At the other extreme, McClelland (1961) noted that 54 percent of Turkey's business leaders came from the upper middle and upper classes. On the other hand, in a socialist country such as Poland, 96 percent of the managers reported that they came from the working or

[4]An exception was seen in nonindustrial societies, where Greenbaum (1977) found that whether or not the village head inherited or was elected or appointed to the post was unrelated to family, economic, or other societal factors in an analysis of 616 societies described in Murdock's Ethnographic Atlas (1967).

lower middle classes. In between was a country like the United States, whose managers were drawn somewhat more uniformly from all classes. And as Table 34.2 shows, neither the working classes nor the aristocracy and upper classes are the prime sources of managers in the private sector in Mexico or Italy. In Turkey, managers in the public sector come from much different class backgrounds than do managers in the private sector; in contrast, managers in both sectors in Italy have much more similar backgrounds.

Curiously, despite their public service leadership, it was not the established landed gentry in Britain who sparked industrialization and the moves toward modernity. Generally, the founders of new industry came from dissenting minorities. In England, leaders of the industrial revolution were drawn out of proportion from the Methodist and other dissenting religious groups. In Roman Catholic France, until the Revocation of the Edict of Nantes in 1685, the source was the Protestant Huguenots. In Colombia, much of business development was due more to the minority of Antioquian miners than to the landowning latifundists. In India, it was due to the Parsee minority, and in Southeast Asia, to the Chinese minority. In the Western World, the Jewish minority played an important entrepreneurial role (Hagen, 1962).

Differences in History and Institutions

Cross-country comparisons of the differences in the origins of leaders need to consider what are often almost unique circumstances within a given country. For instance, religion and history (the Roman Catholic

Table 34.2 Social-Class Background of Managers in the United States, Italy, Turkey, Mexico, and Poland (percentage)

	Private Firms				Public Organizations		
Social Class[a]	United States	Italy	Turkey	Mexico	Italy	Turkey	Poland
Working class	22	8	0	12	2	4	40
Lower middle class	26	49	18	30	53	54	56
Middle class	32	26	28	39	22	25	4
Upper middle class and above	20	16	54	19	22	17	0

[a]Based on the father's occupation.

SOURCE: Adapted from McClelland (1961).

ethos and the return of French entrepreneurs to France after the British takeover of Canada in 1763) were seen to have retarded the emergence of French Canadians as leaders in Canadian industry and business (Pelletier, 1966).

To a large degree, the preceding chapters were a review of what is known about the antecedents and effects of leadership in the United States, buttressed, to some extent, by relevant work elsewhere. In many ways, studies of leadership in the United States, with its cultural emphasis on individualism, action rather than contemplation, pragmatism, and egalitarianism, cannot capture the diversity of relationships found in other countries, which are influenced by their own histories and institutional peculiarities. In many ways, the U.S. experience has been unique for the development of leadership. Alexis de Tocqueville drew attention to this uniqueness in *Democracy in America* (1832/1966), which was based on his travels in the United States:

These Americans are the most peculiar people in the world. You'll not believe it when I tell you how they behave. In a local community in their country a citizen may conceive of some need which is not being met. What does he do? He goes across the street and discusses it with his neighbor. Then what happens? A committee comes into existence and then the committee begins functioning on behalf of that need. And you won't believe this but it is true. All of this is done without reference to any bureaucrat. All of this is done by the private citizens on their own initiative. (Quoted in Miller & Hustedde, 1987, p. 91)

The military historian S. L. A. Marshall (1964) noted the surprise in 1917 of the European trainers of the American Expeditionary Force to be sent to France that the U.S. draftees responded naturally to discipline and that a high percentage of them were potential leaders. Getting this army ready was not the formidable task they originally envisaged on the basis of their European experience.

An institutional peculiarity of the United States is its litigiousness. That is, the country has about 18 lawyers for every 10,000 inhabitants. Legal education is an important source of American leaders in government and business, but it is much less important in most other First World countries. Japan has one lawyer per 10,000 people. In Japan, one's behavior following an ambiguous agreement is much more important than is the written contract, whose words are critical for the North American. Close attention must be paid to the Japanese intimations of their needs without explicit statements of them. To the Japanese, qualifiers are more important than are definite positives and negatives (Morita, 1981). Nor do France (2 lawyers per 10,000) or West Germany (4 lawyers per 10,000), whose languages are more explicit, depend as much on lawyers as a source of their leaders as does the United States (Lee & Schwendiman, 1982).

In decided contrast to the United States, historically, in Britain, managing in business or industry (other than finance) was not the occupation of a gentleman. The eldest son inherited the estate; the younger sons went into the armed services or the church. Middle-class sons went into the professions, the civil service, or the family business. Until recently, a businessman who wanted a title had to work hard for public causes, devoting less time to business and more to public service. But business is now finally becoming respectable; finance always was (R. Stewart, 1966).

In Britain, public school education (actually private, elitist boarding schools), followed by matriculation at Oxford University or Cambridge University was the basis for careers in finance, the civil service, foreign service, the military, and the Church of England (Copeman, 1955). According to an analysis of the educational backgrounds of 3,682 of the British elite by D. P. Boyd (1974), the importance of the public schools and Oxford and Cambridge universities to careers changed little between 1939 and 1971. Social-class traditions and entrance into management as a consequence of social class and academic (nonmanagement) education continue to remain strong.

In Britain, the importance of class and the "right" schools has been coupled with a lack of mobility within the firm. In the traditional British firm, each department was a self-contained unit in which members frequently spent much of their whole careers. In consequence, the members of a department were exposed to a limited range of management attitudes and ideas. They became so immersed in their department's way of thinking that they were unlikely to be able to think outside this pattern of beliefs (R. Stewart, 1966).

Leadership in the Public and Private Sectors

Some common patterns have been observed across what at first would appear to be extremely different cultural settings. Wilkinson (1964) noted that Confucian China and Victorian England emphasized the same developmental requirements for leaders in the public sector. Good manners, good form, and classical cultural training better fitted amateurs for governmental service in comparison to experts with technical or professional education. Civil servants were drawn from the landed gentry and those of middle-class origin who went to the same schools and adopted the accent, dress, and mannerisms of the upper class. Of course, particularly in the People's Republic of China, leadership in the public sector now originates quite differently. A detailed study by M. Sheridan (1976) of five prominent women Party leaders in the People's Republic of China indicated that they came from families of manual and service workers. They earned merit in their political, familial, and work roles and became models for others. But by the 1990s, as in the Soviet Union, the new leaders are likely to come increasingly from the favored classes of Party officials, military officers, managers, and intellectuals.

In France, the major route to political leadership and ministerial office is not, as in Britain or present-day Germany, through election to parliament; rather it is often through experience in the civil service and the French president's or premier's confidence in the official with such experience. This same source of governmental leaders was seen in Bismarck's Germany (Dogan, 1979). But as was noted in Chapter 31, only later in their administration do U.S. presidents draw their cabinet officers from within the government. Early on, presidents seek politically acceptable leaders, for the most part, from business, education, agriculture, and other nonpolitical institutions.[5]

Meritocracies. In France and Belgium, educational achievement, a source of income from property, and

bourgeois origins underlie the leadership of industry and government. Elite cadres dominate the management of business and government on the basis of a level of education that is not ordinarily attained by children from the working classes. Particularly important is a degree from those highly selective *grandes écoles* of technology, administration, and the military. Leadership in nonremunerative high-prestige fields is pursued by those with income from property. In Japan as well, educational achievement, based on graduation from the highly selective and prestigious Tokyo University, is a key to success in business or government.

Strong class divisions characterize the Soviet Union. Party officials, the military, intellectuals, and industrial and scientific technocrats are the upper classes. The workers and peasants are the lower classes. In a production-oriented economy, engineering or technical training is almost mandatory for advancement in industry. Still a different and changing pattern is seen in West Germany. Since World War II, there have been increasing opportunities for people of working-class origins to advance into positions of top leadership in business and governmental service. Before 1945, such leadership was dominated by the landed, business, and military aristocracy (Granick, 1962b).

Family. In India, the managing-agency system was the basis for the development of large-scale indigenous private and public enterprise, as well as of foreign subsidiaries. The agency promoted, financed, and managed the reorganization of India with capital from London. It was rigidly structured, highly characterized, personal, and likely to be a family unit dominated by one person, the *karta* or head of the extended Indian family, responsible for its other members and with authority over them.

A high degree of authority is exercised and obedience demanded in the Indian family system. Children are taught obedience to their elders. This obedience continues into adulthood, as is seen in the lack of delegation in management. Yet subtle constraints prevent the head from giving directions without consulting with senior members of the family (Chowdhry & Tarneja, 1961). At the same time, it is difficult for nonfamily members to advance into upper management positions. There is a sharp gap between middle and upper

[5]In 1989, President Bush may have changed this tendency, to a considerable extent, by beginning with the appointment of many more cabinet officers with governmental and political experience.

management, unlike, say, the situation in firms in the United States.

The leadership of a country by the few large landowning families, *latifundismo*, is still strong in many Latin American countries and is a prime cause of revolutionary action. The leaders of business and government in Chile spring from such a landed aristocracy (Harbron, 1965). In other Latin American countries, the technocrats of public and private enterprise, who are of middle-class backgrounds, are leading the social-change efforts. Thus, Mexico is a "guided democracy" run by self-made millionaires, an industrial elite, top governmental bureaucrats, and political figures with middle-class origins. In countries such as Argentina and Peru, the rise of industrial managers from the middle classes occurred with the post-1945 industrial expansion. Lauterbach (1963) observed, in interviews in 13 Latin American countries, that family relationships are important to the emergence as a leader, particularly outside the major industrial centers. There is a lack of specialization. The same person, family, or executive office can administer a wide variety of enterprises. Immediate objectives predominate. Competition is accepted in the abstract, but it is in actuality a bothersome condition to be restrained by public or private action.

Cultural and Institutional Change

Hofstede (1984) pointed to the observed increase in individualism among the 50 countries whose IBM employees were surveyed between 1968 and 1972. Just as the route to political leadership changed in Mainland China, so a change in social and political developments occurred in Quebec. In the early 1960s, over half the French Canadian families wanted at least one of their sons to become a priest; only 6 percent wanted to see any of them in business rather than in professions such as medicine or law. Ecclesiastical leadership was sought. The society's elite were given a classical education. By the 1980s, Quebec's political, social, and economic modernization had been accompanied by a sharp shift in orientation toward business leadership as a substitute for religious leadership (Lapierre & Toulouse, 1984).

In Spain, one saw a rapid shift from a highly controlled authoritarian government under Franco between 1939 and 1975 to a liberal parliamentary democracy. The protection and regulation of the Franco regime was replaced by the need for leaders of business who could survive in a highly competitive environment with aggressive unions, changing political ideologies, and autonomous regional governments. Spain's joining the European Common Market has added a new challenge of foreign competition and the opportunity of an enlarged market. In Spain, leaders who are adaptable are seen to be of particular importance (Anzizu & Nuenos, 1984).

Shouksmith (1987) pointed to the changes in the 1980s in the meaning of work for New Zealanders. After a history of full employment, New Zealand faced a situation in which disadvantaged, older, and unskilled workers were finding it increasingly difficult to obtain and keep jobs. And jobs, themselves, were being deskilled by automation. The social values of the Maoris were becoming increasingly important in the work force as were women.

A common set of antiauthoritarian values emerged in the First World following World War II. These values emphasized democratic participation in the decisions of organizations and government. According to repeated national surveys, this postwar generation remained more oriented toward freedom of opportunity. It represented a systematic change from the preceding generation, who, particularly in Germany and Italy, grew up under fascism and elsewhere, under systems of privileged classes (Inglehart, 1981). However, although sharp social, economic, and political changes may occur in a country, strong underlying historical continuities remain. For instance, centralization is still characteristic in France. Its most recent appearance occurred with the accession of socialist President François Mitterand and the nationalization of 90 percent of France's banking, its entire steel industry, and half of its major electrical, data processing, and pharmaceutical industries and its public works construction. Since the Middle Ages and the counterreformation, there has been a centralized government and industry, submission to hierarchy, lack of autonomy, antieconomic attitudes, and a strong civil service in France. Today, centralization continues, with its top management originating in three *grandes écoles* and the meritocracy of the *grande corps*. These favored few remain the symbolic expression of society, whether they work in the public or private sector (Aubert, Ramanantsoa, & Reitter, 1984).

Origins of Women Leaders. The origins of women leaders and their opportunities can be quite different in different countries. For example, in Egypt, women leaders seem to come from wealthy families, in which females had the requisite educational opportunities and could obtain social prominence and visibility by being active in social work (Khuri, 1981). In Italy, the 1 percent of business executives who are women are likely to come from families who own their own businesses; nevertheless, a woman has headed Italtel, the top telecommunications company in the country. In Britain, the universities are becoming a source of women managers. Between 1965 and 1983, Singapore's national policy of support for training programs for women, flextime, and child care and its publicized positive attitudes toward women rapidly increased the opportunities for women and their supply in administration and management from hardly any to 18 percent. By 1982, in Israel, proportionately more female than male supervisors were being elected to offices of blue-collar unions (Izraeli, 1982).

Culture, Country, and Attributes of Leadership

The values, beliefs, norms, and ideals that are embedded in a culture affect the leadership behavior, goals, and strategies of organizations (Dill, 1958; Negandhi & Reimann, 1972). Four dimensions of values that are of particular consequence are traditionalism versus modernity, particularism versus universalism, idealism versus pragmatism, and collectivism versus individualism. Linked with these dimensions, and also likely to differ across cultures and countries, are attributes such as competitiveness, the preference for taking risks, a sense of duty, interpersonal competencies, communication skills, effective intelligence, and needs such as for achievement, affiliation, and power. Interests, goals, and objectives also differ and likewise contribute to differences in leadership style (Dawson, Haw, Leung, & Whitney, 1971; Negandhi & Estafen, 1967).

Traditionalism versus Modernity

The strength of traditionalism in Pakistan, the strength of modernism in Sweden, and the mix of both strengths in Japan are well known. Traditionalism emphasizes the family, class, revealed truths, reverence for the past, and ascribed status. Modernism stresses merit, rationality, and progress (Inkeles, 1966). The traditional leader is likely to be the oldest, usually male, head of the family. The status of women is relatively low. Corruption may be a way of life and an accepted means of supplementing a bureaucrat's income (Davis, Ming, & Brosnan, 1986). As a society receives more modern education, it shifts toward modern attitudes. At a certain point, the most educated may revert to a semitraditional point of view and lead a revival of traditionalism, such as has been seen in Iran and elsewhere in the Islamic world.

In traditional societies, such as in rural Indonesia, time is preindustrial and agricultural in orientation. There is no sense of urgency nor the pressure of time. Life is naturally paced; punctuality and long-range planning are unimportant (Davis, Ming, & Brosnan, 1986). There is a multiple instead of a single time frame (E. T. Hall, 1976). With a multiple time frame, the explicit and implicit times to meet may be different, making coordination and decentralization more difficult (Ronen, 1986).

Traditional societies are more responsive to authoritative leadership. A modernist leader like Kemal Atatürk in a traditional society like the former Osmanli Turkey often had to resort to autocratic and coercive methods to promote change. Such a response to authority could be the cause of delay in modernization. Moreux (1971) observed that progress in a traditional semirural French Canadian community was held back by its one wealthy charismatic leader.

The valuing of modernity rather than of tradition is likely to be accompanied by a reduction in the sense of obligations to family and friends. The more traditional French Canadian managers are likely to choose family over business obligations when they are in conflict, whereas the less traditional English Canadians will do the reverse (Auclair, 1968). Differential effects on successful leadership are likely to follow. Strong traditionalists are unlikely to be willing or able to lead their followers toward modernity but will be more influential when attempting to turn the clock back.

Within societies that were changing from traditionalism to modernity, systematic differences among students and managers could be observed. Along with the traditionalism of 138 Botswana students, Ulin (1976) measured their elitism, prejudice, anomie, and authoritarianism. Ulin found that the students were ambivalent about traditionalism and authoritarianism but showed strong anomic and elitist convictions; they held strong anti-Asiatic prejudices and weaker antiwhite attitudes, but they were not biased against other tribes of Africans. In Iraq, a survey of 232 managers by Ali (1982) found that traditional tribalisms were more common in smaller organizations, among older managers, and among those with a lower income.

Particularism versus Universalism

A particularistic value orientation implies institutionalized obligations to friends, whereas the universalistic value orientation stresses institutionalized obligations to society and places a lesser emphasis on interpersonal considerations (Parsons & Shils, 1959). In the particularistic value orientation, family relations and friendships take precedence over considerations of merit and equity. Particularism with reference to work is likely to be more common in a Latin developing country; universalism, in the Anglo-American world. As was cited before, Zurcher (1968) contrasted Mexican, Mexican-American, and American bank officers and employees. As expected, the Mexicans were more particularistic than were the Mexican Americans, and the Mexican Americans were more particularistic than were the Anglo-Americans. Beyond this, the bank officers, as a whole, were more universalistic than the line employees of the same ethnicity. Such universalism correlated with job satisfaction and plans to continue working in the bank (Zurcher, Meadow, & Zurcher, 1965).

Decisions about Compensation. Evidence of cross-cultural differences in particularism versus universalism among managers comes from an analysis by Bass, Burger, et al. (1979) of the responses to Exercise Compensation (Bass, 1975b) of 4,255 managers from the same 12 national groups. The respondents had to decide the percentage salary increase to recommend for each of 10 engineers who differed in merit, job context, and personal problems. A universalistic response was seen in those managers who awarded salary increases only for merit. Particularism was indicated by the focus on various personal problems rather than on merit as the basis for awarding an increase.

Although the 4,255 managers as a whole recommended only 82 percent as much of an increase for the engineer in the tenth percentile in merit as for the engineer at the fiftieth percentile, the Indian managers gave him 103 percent of the average performing engineer's increase. Only in India was the poor performer given more of an increase than the average performer. Ryterband and Thiagarajan (1968) suggested that in India, a salary increase is seen as a stimulator, rather than a reward for meritorious performance, as is true in developed countries. They reported a similar tendency for Colombian in contrast to U.S. and Scandinavian managers. For each individual manager in the sample of 4,255, the standard deviation in his recommendations for 8 engineers in the fiftieth percentile in merit was calculated by Bass, Burger, et al. (1979). The results confirmed the earlier findings by Ryterband and Thiagarajan that in the less developed countries, family, job insecurity, alternative offers, lack of job prestige, and so on justify such differentials. However, managers from more developed countries (except from Japan) tend to justify salary differentials for people doing the same job only by merit differences among the job occupants. Japan differs from the West in that salary increases do not accompany meritorious promotions. Westerners have difficulties in appreciating these "empty promotions" (Yokochi, 1989a). Consistent with these conclusions, Beatty, McCune, and Beatty (1988) captured the policies that differentiated 41 Japanese from 63 U.S. managers. Again, U.S. managers emphasized job performance while the Japanese focused on other elements in deciding on pay increases. Similar to Bass, Burger, et al.'s (1979) findings, the Japanese managers were much less likely to vary the increases for the different employees than were the American managers.

Attitudes toward merit and competence were also reflected in the differential decisions of more particularistic Greek and the more universalistic U.S. personnel directors and students when rating hypothetical applicants for positions in accounting and finance. Triandis (1963) asked 100 American students, 100 Greek students, 32 American personnel directors, and 20 Greek personnel directors to rate 32 candidates who differed systematically in competence, age, sex, race, religion, sociability, and wealth. For the American personnel directors, 54 percent of the variance in the ratings of the candidates was accounted for by whether the candidates were described as highly competent or barely competent. But such competence accounted for only 24.8 percent of the ratings of the Greek personnel directors. Competence was even more important to the American students, whereas sociability was particularly important to the Greek students.

Idealism versus Pragmatism

Pragmatists look for what will work; idealists search for the truth. Pragmatists are opportunistic (England, 1967a). Idealism is greatest and the pragmatic orientation is rare among theology students, regardless of their cultural background (England, 1970). Curiously, *Webster's Third International Dictionary* of 1933 included "active and skilled in business" in the definition of pragmatic. Managers from different countries are more like each other in pragmatism than like compatriots who are not managers (England, 1970). Nonetheless, national differences in judging what is right, good, and important to managers showed up strongly in England, Dhingra, and Agarwal's (1974) survey of over 2,600 managers in five countries, as can be seen in Table 34.3. While the primary orientation of 66 percent of the Japanese, 61 percent of the Koreans, and 58 per-

cent of Americans was pragmatic, it was so only for 40 percent of the Australians and 34 percent of the Indians. Moralism (idealism) was the primary value orientation only for 11 percent of the Koreans and 12 percent of the Japanese; however, it was much higher among the Australians (40 percent) and the Indians (44 percent). The relatively greater extent of pragmatism among Japanese managers underlies their task- and relations orientation toward employees based on pursuing leadership that works (Yokochi, 1989b).

England and Lee (1974) found pragmatism, as measured by their Personal Values Questionnaire, to be related to the success of managers in the United States, Australia, India, and Japan. The success of the careers of these approximately 2,000 managers was indexed by their income adjusted for their age. In all four countries, successful managers were more likely to hold pragmatic values emphasizing productivity, profitability, and achievement. Similarly, for the 5,122 managers in 12 countries who were administered Exercise Objectives (Bass, 1975a) by Bass, Burger, et al. (1979), there were wide variations among the managers of different nationalities on all five budgeting decisions, in their willingness to spend money to deal with each of the problems involving safety, settlement of a strike, improvement of managers' morale, improvement of the quality of a product, and cleaning up a stream that the company was polluting. Whereas 71 percent of Latin American managers chose to clean up the stream, only 46 percent of Japanese managers did so. In a replication by Palmer, Veiga, and Vora (undated), 82 percent of the Indian managers chose to clean up the stream, but only 61 percent of U.S. managers did so. And the

Table 34.3 Primary Value Orientations of Managers from Five Countries

Country	Number	Percentage with a Primary Orientation of		
		Pragmatism	Moralism (Idealism)	Other
Japan	394	66	11	23
Korea	223	61	12	27
United States	1,071	58	31	11
Australia	351	40	40	20
India	623	34	44	22

SOURCE: Adapted from England, Dhingra, and Agarwal (1974, p. 20).

decision of Indian and U.S. managers to reject such expenditures in Exercise Objectives was higher among those with stronger pragmatic values (economic, political, and theoretical) and lower among those with altruistic or idealistic values (social, aesthetic, and religious).

Among the managers studied by Bass, Burger, et al. (1979), significant interactions were found between nationality and the managers' rate of advancement and the tendency to be idealistic or pragmatic about two of the budgeting decisions. For instance, in general, the slower-climbing managers favored the idealistic decision to accept a costly wage agreement to settle a strike immediately, whereas in India, the faster-climbing managers did so more frequently than did the slower-rising managers. It may be that in India, idealism is more favored for leadership than is pragmatism. In a study of student leaders and nonleaders in India, Kumar (1965) found that unlike the usual results for American or European students, Indian student leaders scored high on theoretical and religious interests, while nonleaders scored high on economic and social values. But Govindarajan (1964) observed that Indian high school leaders were more interested than were nonleaders in professional and technical jobs. They more frequently mentioned salary, prestige, and status as reasons for choosing a job.

Variations across countries in pragmatism as opposed to idealism were seen in a multinational survey of IBM personnel completed by Hofstede (1978). Factor scores varied greatly in national norms for personal acquisitiveness in contrast to social concerns. Japanese personnel were most acquisitive and Scandinavians were most socially concerned. The factor scores were as follows: Japan, 95; Germany, 73; Italy, 70; Britain, 66; United States, 62; Latin America, 61; Belgium, 54; India, 50; France, 43; Iberia, 37; the Netherlands, 14; Scandinavia, 10. (These factor scores for 50 nations can be found in Hofstede [1980].)

Collectivism versus Individualism

In her seminal study of 13 primitive societies, Mead (1939) contrasted those societies that were cooperative or collective with those that were individualistic or competitive. In cooperative societies, one is more concerned with one's relations with others, and achievement of the team and one's group is more important than is one's personal achievement. In individualistic societies, self-interest dominates.

In the People's Republic of China, collectivism makes it possible to maintain the system of regular meetings of workers to critique a company's performance. In a quantitative survey of 46 U.S., 203 Mexican, and 503 Taiwan Chinese employees working in the same electronics manufacturing plants in Taiwan and on the U.S.-Mexican border, Dorfman and Howell (1988) found, as expected, that the Mexican and Taiwanese employees were more collectivistic in their beliefs than were the U.S. employees.

Collectivism in Japan. The collectivistic, cooperative Japanese downplay their own individual intelligence. To make much of it would be a threat to the group's harmony, equality, and achievement and would meet with criticism. In Japan, one's concern is for members of one's in-group, not for those in temporary groups or out-groups. But despite the importance of group and collective action in collective societies such as Japan, group-over-individual effects will fail to materialize in the ordinary laboratory study in which unacquainted students are temporarily brought together. In such studies, loyalty to the team and acceptance of its influence will not necessarily be seen because the team is not a real in-group for the participants. Thus, Klauss and Bass (1974) found the greatest anticonformity in such temporary groups of Japanese managers compared to 12 other nationalities. Frager (1970) did likewise in studying conformity and anticonformity in Japan with students as subjects. Concerns for the shared values and goals of the organization will override concerns for one's immediate work unit.

Collectivism in Japan is reflected in the structure of corporations. Individual stock ownership is small and of little consequence, and the corporation's board of directors often is identical with its management. What is stressed are cooperation, consensus, and working for the goals of the majority of company members and optimizing benefits for all. Promotion is from inside. The organization is expected to defend the employees' interests. Loyalty to the firm and a sense of duty are paramount. Although, as was noted earlier, collectivism is expressed more in China and Korea as loyalty to one's family, family-oriented collectivism is also seen in those companies in Japan that are family owned, when, in addition in being born or marrying into the family, the future company leaders may be legally adopted as sons and heirs (Abegglen, 1984).

Collectivism in Japan goes a long way to explain the greater success in Japan of an American idea, the quality control circle. According to a 1983 survey by the Japan Union of Scientists and Engineers, such small-group activities were in effect in more than 80 percent of the Japanese companies with over 1,000 employees and in 50 percent of the companies with 100 to 1,000 employees. Attendance was 90 percent (Ishikawa, undated). In turn, the Japanese attention to quality was dramatized by Gavin (1983), who compared 9 U.S. and 7 Japanese manufacturers of room air-conditioners. The technology, equipment, and product were identical. During the period studied, the U.S. firms averaged 63.5 defects per 100 units on the assembly line and the Japanese firms averaged .95. The U.S. firms averaged 10.5 service calls the first year per 100 units, whereas Japanese firms averaged .60. The cost of failures for the U.S. firms was 4.0 percent of sales but 1.3 percent for the Japanese firms. At the same time, the output of the Japanese firms was also higher. Productivity in the U.S. firms averaged 1.3 units per labor hour, compared to the Japanese average of 1.8 units per labor hour.

Comparisons for the printed circuit-board industry in the two countries unearthed similar results. The error rate in American firms averaged 5 percent, but in the Japanese firms, it averaged .05 percent. The error rates were lower in the Japanese firms even though the Japanese produced more complex boards that are ordinarily more prone to errors. The Japanese also dealt with much more variety in the product. The yield was 70 percent in the United States but 92 percent in Japan. The U.S. firms produced approximately 1,200 styles, whereas the Japanese firms produced approximately 17,000 styles. At that time, the refinement of the printed circuits in the United States was 15-millimeter spacing compared to Japan, where it was 4-millimeter spacing.

Collectivism explains the antipathy of Japanese managers toward individualistic behavior. "Scapegoating"

is avoided by collective responsibility although ultimate responsibility rests with the highest ranking overseer of a project or enterprise. Criticism of performance is for the betterment of the organization and is seen to be directed toward the task or project for which the group has accepted responsibility, although the leader remains ultimately responsible (Yokochi, 1989b). Even the introduction of a new idea that does not emanate from one's group may be seen as selfish or inconsiderate. Innovators may resign because their successful, accepted ideas were embarrassing and disruptive (Hornstein, 1986). In contrast to the results for Britain and the Netherlands, cooperativeness is more likely to be rewarded with advancement in Japan, according to Rosenstein's (1985) analysis of the results of the performance of several thousand managers on selected exercises that were correlated with their rates of advancement.

In Bass, Burger, et al.'s (1979) analysis of the results for Exercise Compensation, discussed earlier, Japanese managers stood apart from the managers in the other developed countries in that they awarded a hypothetical engineer in the nintieth percentile in merit only 138 percent of the average salary increase, in contrast to the 162 percent favored by managers from elsewhere, and paid more attention to the engineer's personal problems. However, when Howard, Shudo, and Umeshima (1983) compared the surveyed attitudes and values of Japanese and American managers, they inferred that although the Japanese attached greater importance to socially beneficial values in contrast to the American's emphasis on individuality and being straightforward, the Japanese had a higher motivation for money and advancement, but these were to be achieved through collective action. Japanese managers may score puzzlingly low in their *preference* for good relations with their colleagues (Hofstede, 1980) because such collective feeling is a matter of obligation to them, not a personal preference (Atsumi, 1979).

In the West, the managerial or administrative decision, itself, is much more discrete and separable from its implementation, which is to follow. In Japan, the making of the decision is seen as the beginning of a search for the best way to implement it. In the West, the decision is ordinarily identified with an individual;

in Japan, it is more often a collective action (P. B. Smith, 1984a). More will be said about this difference later in the chapter.

Individualism in the United States. The "take charge, individual initiative" of U.S. managers contrasts with the more collegial approaches preferred elsewhere (Bennett, 1986). The participation of individual students is prized in the North American classroom but not as much in classrooms elsewhere. Among the IBM employees and supervisors in 50 nations surveyed by Hofstede (1980), those in the United States were most extreme in their individualism, which was seen as a contributor to greatness. Elsewhere, as among the Chinese, it was not. Individualism was high in the Anglo cluster of countries and lowest in some of the Latin American and Far Eastern countries and Pakistan.

Foreign managers who work in the United States see this difference from their own cultural backgrounds. Repeated apologies for a late report by a Japanese may produce anger in a North American. An Arab's polite, social circumlocutions may produce frustration in the North American. The Latin American's small talk and socializing to enhance relations before getting down to work is seen as time wasting by a North American. North American managers are likely to want more autonomy than Swiss superiors want to give them.

Organizational role concepts are different in Japan than in the West. The Japanese operate their large organizations with lack of specificity about the nature of each member's job and area of authority and responsibility. According to a 1960 survey, one-quarter of the larger firms had no organizational chart, and only one-third had rules delineating the authority for the chief of the general affairs division or for the chief of the accounting division (Keizai Doyukai, 1960). When Japanese are asked what their job is, they are likely to reply that they are members of a particular company instead of saying what they do (Tsutomu, 1964). Associated with this lack of specificity is a lack of career specialization (Mannari & Abegglen, 1963). The ambiguous organization works effectively because of the group orientation of its members, the members' willingness to work organically with each other, their taking into ac-

count not only a particular role requirement but who happens to be filling it. The group orientation is accompanied by strong peer pressure (Abegglen, 1958). Hesseling and Konnen (1969) reported that during a decision-making simulation, the Japanese managers were extremely critical of their peers compared to the Dutch managers. In this situation, the Japanese managers appeared to combine behaviors that Westerners would consider to be incompatible.

Commitment, Involvement, Loyalty, and Collectivism. Collectivistic values strengthen commitment, involvement, and loyalty. The life-time employment assignments in Japan are well known. However, what may be less well known is that, as Abegglen (1958) noted, the employer is generally more obligated than is the employee. Complicating the issue of lifetime employment are the two levels of discourse in Japan. *Tatemae* is the polite open communication; *honne* is when the communication expresses true feelings about the matter. Lifetime employment is expected at the time of employment. Employees will continually express, as required, the sense of lifetime commitment to their organization, which is *tatemae,* and only reveal their true feelings, *honne,* on the day before they leave to take a job with another firm (Yokochi, 1989b). According to Marsh and Mannari (1971), rates of quitting and the piracy of managers indicated that there is actually considerable movement from one firm to another among Japanese employees. For example, during one decade, one-fourth of the Japanese manufacturing employees left their place of employment annually, and two-thirds of them did so voluntarily. Despite these facts, both Japanese managers and workers tend to believe that and act as if they have permanent employment. Organizational loyalty is high. Anyone who was not loyal would be regarded as a person of lesser moral principles and deserving of punishment (Yokochi, 1989b). Promotions take place at regular intervals, but an "up-or-out" policy actually results in either continued promotion upward or early retirement (Kezai Doyukai, 1960). Many exceptions to lifetime arrangements can be found even in well-known larger Japanese firms (Pucik, 1981). In an analysis of the personnel records of the Kikkoman Shoyu Company over 60 years beginning in 1918, Lawrence (1984) found considerable variation in the provision for lifetime employment, compensation based on seniority, and ideological identification with the firm as one's family. The practices and beliefs were transitory, rather than deeply fixed, and depended much on the economic effects, especially the effects of World War II. While much of the practices and beliefs in lifetime commitments is true for the largest and wealthiest Japanese firms and agencies, they disappear in the smaller firms that are less secure economically, such as those job shops that depend on maintaining contract work for the larger organizations.

Nonetheless, in comparison to the responses of successful U.S., Australian, and Indian managers, England and Lee (1974) found that successful Japanese managers were most likely to emphasize loyalty. Among the 12 nationalities studied by Bass, Burger, et al. (1979), the life goal of duty—dedication to ultimate values, ideals, and principles—was among the top 3 in importance for 46 percent of the Japanese and 34 percent of Indian managers, at one extreme, and 7 to 9 percent of the German, Austrian, Scandinavian, and British managers, at the other. Japanese workers tend to merge their company and family life. Thus, whereas 56 percent of the Japanese workers in the early 1960s perceived the company to be at least equal in importance to their personal lives, only 24 percent of the North Americans felt the same way (Whitehill, 1964). According to a questionnaire administered by Whitehill and Takezawa (1968) to approximately 2,000 Japanese workers, 57 percent thought of their company as "a part of my life at least equal in importance to my personal life," whereas only 22 percent of the U.S. workers responded similarly.

Loyalty to the In-group. As was already noted for the Japanese, in collective societies, people see themselves as members of in-groups and extended families who protect their interests in exchange for their loyalty. Satisfaction for doing a job that is well recognized by one's peers is sought, in contrast to doing a job well by one's own standards. Job and family life are more closely linked (Hofstede, 1984).

According to Leung's (1983) study of how rewards are allocated, although more individualistic American students, consistent with the universalism of reward for merit, used the principal of equity (each according to his or her contribution) to reward both in-group and out-group members, more collectivistic Hong Kong Chinese students used equity for rewarding out-group members and equality for rewarding in-group members.

The values of a culture affect individual expectations of organizational rewards (England & Koike, 1970). In the individualistic United States, workers believe they receive wages in exchange for services. However, in the collectivistic Orient, compensation is considered to be an obligation of the employer, who is responsible for the employees' welfare; thus compensation is less likely to be related to the services performed than to the individual's needs. Under such circumstances it is difficult to introduce performance appraisal (Gellerman, 1967).

Loyalty to close friends takes on special relationships in a number of countries and can markedly affect patterns of influence. Particularism flourishes. For example, in the Philippines, *pakkisama*, which expresses all-encompassing friendship, results in intense loyalty to one's boss and the formation of cliques. In Greece, one speaks of *philotimo*—the strong bond of affection and loyalty between friends—which again fosters the formation of cliques. In Nigeria, loyalty to other members of one's tribe transcends objective considerations, and patterns of loyalty are strong. In this situation, as in those in which employers feel more obligated to satisfy the needs of their employees than to provide rewards for merit, objective merit ratings, promotions, and salary recommendations based on performance become impossible. The ratings will reflect tribal relationships rather than performance.

Personal Values, Motives, and Goals

Nowotny (1964) focused attention on the differences between the European and U.S. management philosophies. Nowotny attributed the emphasis on stability, convention, quality, and diversity to the European respect for the past. The U.S. management's differential focus on the future resulted in a focus on vitality, mobility, informality, abundance, quantity, and organization. But by the late 1980s, many of these differences were likely to have disappeared as U.S. management was made less secure by the faster growth in industrial and economic power of Europe and Japan and the loss of many whole industries to them, as well as by the dislocations and vast restructurings of U.S. firms. Certainly, U.S. management had become much more concerned about the quality of its products. Many more now worked in mature or declining firms that had been growing in the 1960s. In turn, European and Japanese firms had adopted many of the practices of U.S. management in their own efforts to internationalize.

Barrett and Ryterband (1968) found that managers from developing countries, such as Colombia and India, assigned less importance to meeting competition than did managers from the United States, Britain, and the Netherlands. Managers from developed countries placed greater stress on the objectives of growth and competition. Conversely, the maintenance of satisfactory organizational operations appeared to be more important to those from the developing countries. England, Dhingra, and Agarwal (1974) noted that for North American managers, organizational stability was a means to attain the objective of profitability; for Indian managers, organizational stability was an end in itself.

The Need for Achievement, Affiliation, and Power. Illustrative of the many available studies, McClelland (1961) reported systematic differences among approximately 200 managers from the United States, Italy, Turkey, and Poland in their *n* achievement, *n* affiliation, and *n* power scores. The rankings for the four countries, from highest to lowest, were as follows: *n* achievement—the United States, Poland, Italy, and Turkey; *n* affiliation—Italy, Turkey, the United States, and Poland; and *n* power—the United States, north Italy, Turkey, south Italy, and Poland. Kanungo and Wright (1983) found that British managers had a greater need for achievement than did French managers. However, regardless of national differences, a high need for achievement contributed to entrepreneurial drive, as evidenced in analyses in Turkey (Bradburn, 1963), Nigeria (LeVine, 1966), Brazil (Angelini, 1966), Iran (Tedeschi & Kian, 1962), South Africa (Morsbach, 1969), India (Singh, 1969, 1970), and Trinidad (Mischel,

1961). McClelland and Winter (1969) were also able to demonstrate that a program that increased *n* achievement also resulted in the increased entrepreneurial activities of Indian and Mexican businessmen.

Personal Goals. In Exercise Life Goals (Bass, 1975e), 3,082 managers from the 12 nationalities surveyed by Bass, Burger, et al. (1979) rated the importance of 11 life goals to themselves. Although high percentages of managers everywhere ranked self-realization as first, second, or third, the Japanese were highest (74 percent) and the Indians were lowest (42 percent) in this tendency. Leadership was ranked first, second, or third by 51 percent of the Germans and Austrians and least frequently by the Dutch (20 percent) for whom expertise (50 percent) was most important. Expertise was lowest for the Italians (22 percent) than for any of the other 11 groups. Stereotypes to the contrary, the British managers were relatively highest in emphasizing pleasure (29 percent), followed by the Scandinavians (26 percent), and the Dutch (20 percent), while the Spaniards (9 percent) and Latin Americans (10 percent) were relatively low in stressing pleasure, and the Indians (6 percent), Germans (4 percent), and Japanese (2 percent) were the lowest in this regard. (The Japanese managers may have been most sensitive to the social desirability of the goals.)

When nationalities were compared, wealth—to amass a personal fortune—was most important to the Indian and North American managers and least important to the Japanese. Independence was most important to the Germans and Austrians and least important to the Indians. Prestige was most important to the Latin Americans and least important to the Japanese for whom duty (already mentioned) was most important. Service was most important to the Scandinavians (31 percent), the French (30 percent), and the Spaniards (29 percent), and security was most important to the Scandinavians (36 percent), the British (34 percent), and the Italians (32 percent).

Kanungo and Wright (1983) surveyed managers' attitudes in Canada, France, Japan, and Britain to determine the job outcomes the managers sought. The British and the French managers were most different. The British sought self-actualization and the French sought security and good working conditions. The British-

French distinctness was seen within Canada in a survey by McCarrey, Gasse, and Moore (1984) in the difference in work values between Anglophone managers on the west coast of Canada and their Francophone counterparts in Quebec. The Francophone managers attached greater importance to being loving and helpful and placed more emphasis on work that allowed them to be creative and imaginative. The Anglophones attached more importance to work that provided independence and prestige and allowed them to be clean, neat, and tidy.

According to England, Dhingra, and Agarwal's (1974) survey, dignity, prestige, security, and power were far more important to Indian than to American or Australian managers. Al-Hajjeh (1984) found that Middle Eastern managers placed more emphasis on security than did a comparable sample of Americans.

Smallest-space mapping of the personal goals of managers of various nationalities by Shenkar and Ronen (1987) showed that the meaning of a particular goal may be different in various countries. For instance, to attain higher earnings is seen as both an intrinsic and extrinsic goal in Western countries like Canada, Britain, West Germany, and France, but it is a purely extrinsic goal for managers in the People's Republic of China. Shenkar and Ronen attributed this attitude of Chinese managers both to Confucian philosophy and to Maoist admonitions that material incentives are likely to lead to anticollective self-interest, power, and privileges.

Personal Values. Bigoness and Blakely (1989) extracted four factors from the rankings by managers from 12 countries of the importance of 18 instrumental values (Rokeach, 1973). The four factors were: (1) Supportiveness (cheerful, forgiving, helpful, and loving); (2) Dependability (clean, obedient, polite, responsible, and self controled); (3) Strength (broadminded, capable, and courageous); and (4) Intelligence (imaginative, independent, and intellectual).

Overall, there was considerable agreement among the managers from the 12 countries about the relative order of value of the factors (1-strength, 2-intelligence, 3-dependability, 4-supportiveness). Nevertheless, there remained sizeable mean divergences of opinion according to nationality. Thus, consistent with Bass, Burger,

et al.'s (1979) 12-nation study about the Japanese strong concern for peers and the French lack of such concern, the Japanese managers were the highest in their relative ranking of the importance of supportiveness; the lowest were the French. Again, the Japanese tied the Brazilians in relatively valuing dependability most highly. The Swedes were relatively least concerned with the value of such dependability. Strength was of prime importance to the Brazilians and relatively of least consequence to the U.S. managers. The Brazilians and Italians valued intelligence most highly; the Danes and Australians attached relatively least value to intelligence. The other nationals from Britain, Germany, the Netherlands, and Norway were at neither extreme on any of the four factors.

Aversion to Risk Taking. Bass, Burger, et al. (1979) noted which of 12 nationalities were above or below the median on 18 indicators of the tendency to take risks or the preferences for doing so, according to the managers' responses to various training exercises. U.S. managers had the least aversion to taking risks in that they were below the median on only 11 percent of the 18 indicators. The results for the remaining 11 nationalities were as follows: the Japanese, 33 percent; the Dutch, French, and Scandinavians, 39 percent; the Latin Americans, 40 percent; the British and Indians, 50 percent; the Italians, Spanish, and Portuguese, 56 percent; and the Belgians, Germans, and Austrians, 61 percent. Cummings, Harnett, and Stevens (1971) also ordered nationalities according to their preferences for avoiding financial or physical risks. Again, managers in the United States had the least aversion to risks. Managers in Greece, Scandinavia, and Central Europe were the most risk aversive, while Spanish managers were in between. In Howell and Dorfman's (1988) comparative analysis, the aversion to take risks or the avoidance of uncertainty was higher among the Taiwan Chinese and Mexican employees than among those from the United States.

Hornstein (1986) illustrated the propensity of North American managers to take risks in contrast to the Japanese managers' aversion to doing so. Only 15 percent of the American managers but 40 percent of the Japanese managers said they had never acted courageously during their careers. Ronen (1986) also concluded that

North American managers are much more aggressive risk takers than are their counterparts elsewhere, such as in Indonesia, Burma, Turkey, and Egypt.

A somewhat different picture emerged in Hofstede's (1980) 50-nation survey. The avoidance of uncertainty, one of the dimensions examined referred to the propensity to be less accepting of personal risk and to be uncomfortable in unpredictable and unclear situations. Greece and the Latin American countries of Panama, Peru, El Salvador, Uruguay, and Guatemala were particularly high in this preference. At the other end of the spectrum were the Southeastern Asian countries of Singapore, Hong Kong, and Malaysia; the Scandinavian countries of Sweden and Denmark; and the Commonwealth-linked Jamaica, Great Britain, and Ireland.

Other Personal Traits

Numerous other cross-cluster and cross-country differences in personality have been reported. Consistent with the generally obtained differences between the Far Eastern and Anglo clusters, Gill (1983) found, using Cattell's Sixteen Personal Factors Questionnaire, that Singapore-Chinese managers described themselves as significantly more reserved, serious, conservative, assertive, expedient, trusting, group dependent, and relaxed than did comparable North American or British managers. They also saw themselves as significantly less imaginative and tough-minded.

Scores on the Myers-Briggs Type Indicator for 206 Latin-American and 875 U.S. managers were in line with expected Anglo-Latin American differences, according to Osborn and Osborn (1986), who reported that 78 percent of the Latin Americans described themselves as sensory-intuitives, while only 52 percent of the North Americans did so. The Latin Americans also saw themselves as more judgmental (87 percent) than did the North Americans (70 percent) and less perceptive. In addition, the Latin Americans tended to express significantly more their desire for inclusion with and control of others and affection for them than did North Americans on Schutz's FIRO-B.

In their comparison of the attitudes of executives from five countries or clusters, Cummings, Harnett, and Stevens (1971) found Spanish managers to be fatalistic, somewhat suspicious, and conciliatory. North Americans were at the other extreme: self-determined, trusting, and belligerent. Scandinavians and central European executives were in between in their attitudes. Greek managers were highly suspicious and conciliatory but more like North Americans in believing they were the masters of their own fate.

In a study of 329 managers and technicians from 22 countries in South and Central America, Africa, Asia, and the Middle East, Gruenfeld and MacEachron (1975) found that managers from the less developed countries were more field dependent than were managers from the developed countries. Gruenfeld and MacEachron concluded that since they were more field dependent, those from the developing countries were likely to be more conforming to authority and more personal and attentive rather than impersonal. According to Yokochi (1989b), Japanese managers are unusual in the extent to which they repeatedly express appreciation for long-past services to indicate they remain indebted for favors rendered. They also repeat apologies for their inadequacies. These are *tatemae*, not deep-seated feelings (*honne*).

Satisfaction of Needs

Haire, Ghiselli, and Porter (1966) surveyed approximately 3,600 managers from 14 countries on how important were each of the needs in Maslow's hierarchy and how much each of the needs were fulfilled. Mozina (1969) used the same questionnaire to survey 500 managers from Yugoslavia, as did Clark and McCabe (1970) for over 1,300 Australian managers and Badawy (undated) for middle managers in Saudi Arabia. In agreement with Bass, Burger, et al.'s findings (1979), all these studies found that Maslow's (1954) higher-level needs, such as for self-actualization and esteem, were judged important by managers everywhere. But generally, the fulfillment of these higher-level needs was deemed inadequate. The lowest-level physiological needs, of relatively little importance, were seen to be fairly well satisfied. The need for security, considered to be important, was relatively highly fulfilled. (No doubt this would be less true in the late 1980s.) Again, broad national variations emerged. Managers from the developing countries perceived all the needs to be more important to them than did managers from developed countries and reported a greater sense of unfulfill-ment. At the other extreme, managers from the north European countries tended to place the least impor-tance on all the needs. Consistent with what was con-cluded in Chapter 10 about the greater job satisfaction of those at higher levels in their organization, the man-agers' perceptions of the fulfillment of their needs de-pended everywhere on their hierarchical rank in their organizations. Higher managers, especially in Japan, consistently indicated more fulfillment of all the needs than did lower managers.

Perceived Stress and Conflict

Particular conflicts and sources of stress are salient for leaders and managers in different countries and cul-tures. Rogers (1977) found in a U.S.-Canadian compari-son that whereas decision making was the more impor-tant source of stress for U.S. managers, both work load and decision making were equally frequent sources of stress for Canadian managers. But even sharper differ-ences appeared when English and French Canadian managers were analyzed by Auclair (1968). Male French Canadian managers placed a higher value on their role as the head of the family than did English Canadian managers. Consequently, the French Cana-dian managers perceived a great deal of stress from the conflicting role demands of family and business. In comparison, the English Canadian managers placed less value on their role in the family and experienced less conflict with the role demands of their business organization.

An in-depth interview survey of 30 managers in the Paris area was conducted by COFREMCA (1978). What seemed particularly salient in the French manag-ers' attitudes and values was the conflict between the valuing of their own work and their self-actualization as professionals, the lack of warmth and understanding in work relations, insecurity among the older managers, and competitiveness—particularly in large firms.

Indian supervisors may face various kinds of role conflict special to the Indian scene. Although indus-trial supervisors were observed to be more production oriented than human relations oriented (Bhatt & Pa-thak, 1962), Indian workers expected their foremen to

do more in the way of settling personnel problems and grievances, clarifying work difficulties, and improving work methods and conditions. In other respects, as well, foremen perceived that they were required to per-form duties that were not legitimately part of their jobs, such as training new men on the job, arranging wage agreements, and checking supplies (Sequeira, 1964). Yoga (1964) obtained such results in 11 Indian plants in 3 types of industries (textiles, processing, and engineering). Nonetheless, Ivancevich, Schweiger, and Ragan (1986) found that a sample of approximately 300 Indian managers reported little difference from their approximately 175 North American counterparts in their felt global stress, job stress, or somatic symptoms of stress. If anything, the Indian managers felt less daily stress and were less anxious. In fact, it was a compara-ble sample of over 200 Japanese managers who felt sig-nificantly more global stress, more daily stress, more job stress, more somatic symptoms of stress, and more anxiety than did their Indian or North American counterparts.

The Soviet manager faces fundamental conflicts in contradictory demands from an inflexible system of production quotas and from determining rewards and punishments for performance. These demands are in-tertwined with conflicts and defenses that are rooted in Russia's Mongol- and Byzantine-influenced past. There is an entrenched bureaucracy and an emphasis on secrecy—characteristics that have long been part of the Russian culture (Pipes, 1974). These characteristics are reflected in Lenin's model of close-knit, mutually supportive working relationships with immediate sub-ordinates whose advice may be sought but who are ex-pected to conform to their superiors' dictates (Bass & Farrow, 1977a). Loyalty and support for one's superiors is exchanged for their protection from the larger out-side system (Ryapolov, 1966). Leaders and their imme-diate subordinates become excessively dependent on each other to buffer the demands of the larger system (Granick, 1960).

Central planning pits the leaders of small groups and their immediate subordinates against the arbitrary, dis-tant, demanding central authority. To survive within the system, the small groups must back each other up, for they must engage in unauthorized activities, such as falsifying plans to meet quotas. For example, central planning overestimates of available supplies result in shortages of vital parts. The factory that needs the supplies will need to hire *tolkhachi*, who live permanently near the bases of supply to obtain necessary materials, even shipping them by briefcase, if necessary (Ryapolov, 1966). Assembled items may be declared ready for shipment and distribution even though parts are missing. If a higher-up in the larger system wants to "get" the plant director, the success of the director's coverup will depend on his immediate subordinates' loyalty to him. It remains to be seen whether Mikhail Gorbachev's reforms will have made much change in the system in the 1990s and how much *glasnost* (openness) and *perestroika* (restructuring) will have ameliorated any of the patterns just mentioned.

Unlike his Soviet counterpart, who must conceal productive capacity, hoard resources, sacrifice quality of the products, or even falsify reports to meet inflexible production quotas from central planning, the plant director in the People's Republic of China does not face the same demands from central authority. Rather, more such pressure is likely to arise from the plant's work force, coupled with much greater flexibility to adjust plans, even weekly, on the basis of experience. "Democratic" centralism in China involves massive participation by workers in the management of enterprises (Richman, 1967). The post-Maoist reforms that are moving China into a market economy have added to the pressure on managers, who now must run a profitable enterprise. Like the Japanese, Chinese managers also appear to be displaying relatively high levels of stress. The political repression of the democratic movement in 1989 may exacerbate such stress.

Variations in Competencies in Different Countries

Various abilities associated with leadership have been found to differ across countries. Thus, Britons were found to be more realistic about their own performance than were Southeast Asians; they were more accurate in estimating how correct they had been in answering questions (Wright et al., 1977). Cross-cultural differences have been observed in social perceptual skills, interpersonal competence, effective intelligence, and efficient work habits.

Social Perceptual Skills. Bass, Alexander, Barrett, and Ryterband (1971) calculated empathy and projection scores for managers from 12 national groupings based on the managers' rankings of their own life goals, as well as those of the other members of their training group. The similarity of their self-rankings was also obtained. With an index of 1.00 implying perfect empathic matching of estimates with actualities and zero implying no matching, the British (.35) and Japanese (.30) were highest in empathic matching and the Latin Americans (.03) were the lowest. The British (.62) and Dutch (.62) were highest in the projection of their own rankings on others, and the Indians (.31) and Iberians (.34) were lowest. To some extent, the results were attributable to the usual similarity among the participants' self-rankings (Bass, Burger, et al., 1979).

The average similarity of participants in their self-rankings was only .15 in India, with its 16 major language groups and many religions and castes. It was even lower for the United States (.11), with its multiplicity of ethnic, racial, and religious groups, and lowest for Latin America (.05), where data included managers drawn from recent European immigrant groups from many countries, those of old Spanish or Portuguese stock, as well as mestizos and multiethnics. In general, in Europe, with greater uniformity of religion, language, and centralized education, the average similarities ranged from .23 for France to .39 for Britain. Japan (.27) was also more homogeneous.

Managers everywhere assumed themselves to be more similar to their colleagues than they actually were. The distortion was greatest for U.S. managers and Latin Americans. At the other extreme, the Iberian managers' projections of similarity were closest to their actual similarity.

Interpersonal Competence. A factor analysis of 60 self-ratings on Exercise Self-Appraisal (Bass, 1975f) of actual and preferred behavior by Bass, Burger, et al. (1979) revealed, for over 1,000 managers, seven factors that are involved in interpersonal competence: (1) preferred awareness, (2) actual awareness, (3) submissiveness, (4) reliance on others, (5) favoring group decision making, (6) concern for good human relations, and (7) cooperative relationships with peers. With reference to the first factor, which deals with preferences for awareness of the feelings of others, self-understanding, accepting feedback from others, listening to others, and concern for the welfare of subordinates, the Spanish and Portuguese managers were the highest and the Germans and Austrians were the lowest among the 12 national groupings. The Germans and Austrians were also lowest on the second factor of actual awareness.

Indian managers were the most concerned about rules and Japanese managers were the least concerned. The Japanese felt the least conflict about the more ambiguous organizational arrangements to which they are accustomed. (Unspoken rules must be understood. Otherwise one is regarded as an "untrained person" [Yokochi, 1989b].) The Indian managers saw themselves as most dependent on a higher authority; the German/Austrian managers saw themselves as the least dependent. The Italian managers saw themselves as being lowest in depending on others in problem solving, and, as expected, the Japanese were highest in this regard, as well as in the actual preference to imitate others when solving problems. U.S. managers stood out in their preference for group decision making, whereas the Spanish, Portuguese, and Italian managers were lowest in this regard. In keeping with stereotypes, French managers were the lowest in their reported actual cooperative peer relations and the Dutch were the highest. On other specific ratings, such as the willingness to discuss feelings with others, the French managers again were lowest among the 12 national groupings and the Italian and Japanese managers were the highest.

Self-ratings that discriminated faster- from slower-climbing managers varied from one country to another. For example, in France, Spain, and Portugal, especially, the faster-climbing managers were more concerned than were the slower climbers about their dependence on a higher authority.

Task Competence. In Bass, Burger, et al.'s (1979) analysis, the Japanese were highest in the desire to be objective rather than intuitive, and their preference for persistence was even more extreme relative to other nationalities. Furthermore, they strongly favored being proactive rather than reactive and preferred long-term to short-term views. Moreover, the Japanese managers also saw themselves as actually very high (in comparison to the results for the 11 other nationalities) in actual objectivity, persistence, proactivity, and long-term thinking. On the other hand, the French tended to be most critical of themselves in their self-appraisals of their actual objectivity, persistence, proactivity, and long-term thinking.

In Exercise Communications (Bass, 1975g), Leavitt's one-way/two-way problem is completed. Senders transmit verbally a pattern of six dominoes when two-way communications are permitted. If communications are one way only, receivers must reconstruct the pattern without seeing the original and cannot ask questions. Consistent with their actual and preferred self-appraisals, the objective results of Exercise Communication for 12 nationalities showed the Japanese managers to be highest in the number of correct placements, both in one-way and two-way communications (Bass, Burger, et al., 1979). This finding is consistent with the higher mean scores on intelligence tests reported for the Japanese compared to other nationals (Hathaway, 1984). The faster-climbing Japanese managers, in particular, were able to achieve this degree of accuracy in the fastest time for one-way communications. Close behind them in accuracy with one-way communications were the Germans and the Austrians.

Indian managers did the poorest; they were relatively slow and inaccurate. These results may be attributable to the Japanese familiarity with ideographic communication and to the fact that for Indian managers, English, the language of business, is usually their second or third language.

Differences in Leadership Across Cultures

Requisites of Leadership

There are both universalities and variations in the requirements for leadership across cultures and countries. No doubt, instant communication, world-wide media, trade, travel, multinational enterprises, and the transfer of technology have all contributed to the convergence of requirements for leadership on a worldwide basis. Even in widely disparate cultures, such as

Zambia and Bangladesh, Ali, Humbalo, Khaleque, and Rahman (1982) found that managers shared common concerns about their salaries, political pressures, regionalism, communication breakdowns, and ways of coping with conflict. I have already alluded to the more general pragmatism of business and industrial managers and idealism among leaders of social movements. A survey of 115 white (*pakeha*) male and female managers and 19 Maori male managers in New Zealand, reported by Anderson (1983), found that the degree of *pakeha*-Maori mix of their work groups influenced not how their leadership behavior contributed to the effectiveness of the work groups, but only the difficulty of its implementation.

Nevertheless, particularly in the less developed areas of the world as well as those with the strongest local traditions, there are still other important differences in what is required for leadership. Mead's (1930, 1935, 1939) anthropological comparisons clearly showed that what it takes to be a leader varies across primitive cultures.

The aggressive, efficient, ambitious Manus leader in Oceania would have been rejected by the Dakota Indians, who valued mutual welfare, conforming to the group, generosity, and hospitality. Individualism, the lack of political integration, and lack of need to comply with leadership characterized the Bachiga of Central Africa; obedience, respect for the chief, and cooperative effort with little room for rivalry were the norm among the Bathonga. With their consciousness of position and conformity to rank in a clear hierarchy, the Samoans followed a completely different style of leadership from that pursued by the individualistic Inuits, who considered no person's importance relative to another. Leadership among the Iroquois was achieved through behavior that was socially rewarding to others, such as generosity, cooperation, and hospitality. But among the Kwakiutl, the ideal chieftain was one who could successfully compete financially against other chiefs. What appeared to be demanded of the leader was quite different among the Arapesh of New Guinea, who have no strict ownership of land or scale of success, and the Ifugao of the Philippines, where land ownership has been concentrated and where the landowner is the ideal of success.

Thus, it is not surprising that the patterns of leader-subordinate behavior in industrialized societies vary considerably across countries and across cultures. Although such extreme effects of cultural differences may not be seen in the modern industrialized world, nevertheless considerable differences emerge in what managers think is required for success in the top, middle, and lower levels of management.

Explicit and Implicit Theories of Leadership. As we move from one culture or country to another, we see systematic differences in what is regarded as important for effective leadership and explanations for why this is so. An important source of differences in leadership among countries is a consequence of these different explicit and implicit theories about leader-subordinate relationships. It was to be expected that the belief in participative management would originate in Scandinavia and North America—countries in which political democracy and the importance of the individual were deeply embedded.

According to Lau (1977), Far Eastern cultures have a less-differentiated view of reality. X does not cause Y; rather X and Y affect each other. There is also less abstract thinking. The consequences are a less clear allocation of responsibilities and less organized planning in Chinese firms. At the same time, Confucian principles resulted, in both prerevolutionary and postrevolutionary China, in perceptions of managers as linchpins, mediating the effects of the work environment on their subordinates (Shenkar & Ronen, 1987).

Beliefs about leadership in Japan are imbedded in a cultural matrix of beliefs about the important relations between members of a group. The concept of *amae*, of dependence on another person's kindness and goodwill, is central to leadership in Japan. It places a debt on the person who is loved that must be repaid and binds the leader to the group. Subordinates would be angered by a leader who failed to provide *amae*. *Wa*, group harmony, which balances individual needs and desires with the good of the group and fosters mutual cooperation, would be lost. It is appropriate for superiors to look to subordinates for advice (Lee & Schwendiman, 1982).

Consistent with what has just been said, according to Sullivan, Suzuki, and Kondo's (1984) survey of responses to designed scenarios by 100 U.S. and 266 Japanese managers, the Japanese, more than the Americans, subscribed to an implicit social model to control performance, rather than to an implicit model of the rational-economic individual. In the social model, the individual is thought to be submerged in the work group, so the social entity, the group, rather than the individual, must be monitored, assigned responsibility, and rewarded. At the same time, Japanese tradition called for leaders to be men of exemplary moral courage, self-sacrifice, and benevolence. To this list was added the now widely accepted espousal of Charles Protzman's[6] requirement in post–World War II Japan that the leader be transformational in securing the faith and respect of those under him (Tsurumi, 1982).

Post–World War II Germany saw the rejection of the *Führerprincip* of omniscient command and unquestioning obedience to orders. As a counter, the Allied military occupation imposed industrial democracy, which coupled with the growth of participatory education, resulted in the current norm in West Germany for subordinates to expect to be consulted about decisions. Yet, consistent with the earlier German tradition, once the leader has made the decision, subordinates expect to carry it out to the best of their ability. At the same time, the explicit *Harzburger* model (Hohn, 1962) appeared in post–World War II Germany—a model that was more consistent with the *Führerprincip*. According to the model, the leader must be directive. However, the leader is required to delegate permanent areas of task responsibilities to "co-workers," rather than to give short-term orders. Job descriptions must be carefully written. Subordinates must assume responsibilities within their prescribed area of consequence, along with accepting 315 organizational rules. The approach replaces patriarchical-authoritarian direction with bureaucratic-authoritarian direction. It allows for little subordinate participation or upward influence. Only economic goals are seen as legitimate.

The *Harzburger* model remains highly controversial, particularly among those German scholars and managers who espouse participative management and the emphasis on human relations (Grunwald & Bernthal, 1983). Nevertheless, along with its use in Austria and

Switzerland, the popularity of the Harzburg Model was evidenced in a survey by Topfer (1978), who found that 16 percent of 355 West German firms were using it.

More implicit in India is the preference of many subordinates for a dependent personal relationship, rather than a contractual one, with their leader. Such subordinates seek a nurturant leader and accept authority and status differences (Sinha, 1984). Endemic underemployment results in overstaffing and leadership that must take cognizance of legitimate inefficiencies.

Modern Egypt is a rapidly industrializing, urbanizing amalgam of cultures: Pharaonic, Arab, Turkish, Levantine, and European. The favorite expression is the fatalistic *inshallah*, if God wills. On the one hand, an easygoing attitude about work, relationships, and accomplishments dominates leader-subordinate relations. On the other hand, Egyptian leadership in organizations has been strongly affected by Egypt's widespread use of large public organizations to pursue its development. These organizations follow the higher structured and centralized bureaucratic patterns in socialistic and other developing countries (Badran & Hinings, 1981).

Traits Judged Important for Top, Middle, and Lower Management. Bass, Burger, et al. (1979) analyzed the choices of managers in their selection, from a list of 25 traits, of the 5 most important traits and the 5 least important traits required for top, middle, and lower managers using Exercise Supervise (Bass, 1975c), developed from original lists by L. W. Porter (1959). Indexes reflecting the choices of 3,401 managers yielded significant variations across 12 countries in many of the attributes for the three management levels. For example, Dutch managers saw no difference in the imagination needed for lower and middle managers, but managers everywhere else called for more imagination in successively higher levels of management. Being systematic was judged most important for lower-level managers in Italy, Spain, Portugal, and Latin America, but more necessary for middle managers everywhere else. Managers everywhere were expected to be more careful, the lower their organizational level. But the Dutch thought it was most important for middle managers. The French judged it most important for lower

[6]One of the U.S. consultants who introduced statistical quality control in Japan in the 1950s.

and middle managers to be sharpwitted. The U.S. and British managers put a premium on being resourceful; the Japanese saw intuition as far more important than logic. Sociability was seen as important for top managers by faster accelerating managers more than by slower ones in the Netherlands, Belgium, Italy, Spain, Portugal, Latin America, and India. Slower-rising managers saw such sociability as more important for top management in Britain, Scandinavia, and France.

Required Superior-Subordinate Relations. Germany, Japan, the United States, and the Soviet Union illustrate the systematic differences that are likely to appear in different countries. Luther's concept of the "calling," serving God by doing one's best in one's occupation, continues to be a strong influence on the extent to which the German subordinate expects to carry out decisions once they have been reached. The required informal mutual defense pacts that provide for the survival of both superiors and subordinates in the Soviet system have already been mentioned, as has the extent to which in some cultures, such as the Japanese, the organization assumes a particular importance in one's life. In turn, the importance of the organization affects what is required of Japanese superior-subordinate relations.

The supervisor has different relevance to the worker in Japan. Not only is the supervisor likely to be more involved in the subordinate's off-the-job life, but the supervisor will be accorded more status off the job. Whereas 44 percent of Japanese workers would offer their supervisor their seat on a crowded bus, only 2 percent of Americans said they would do so (Whitehill & Takezawa, 1968).

In the Soviet Union, the need to "beat the system" may produce mutual suspicion between the superior and the subordinate. Both may face cuts in pay of 25 percent below base salary if their performance is not up to expectations (Anonymous, 1970).

Required Masculinity. National boundaries produce different conclusions about the importance of masculinity to management. Chapter 32 reported Bartol and Butterfield's (1976) finding that sex-role stereotypes bias the performance evaluation of U.S. managers' behavior and that masculinity is favored. But

Izraeli and Izraeli (1985) found no such bias when the study was replicated with Israeli instead of American managers.

Consistent differences appear in the strength of masculine and feminine traits across national boundaries, according to a study of 30 nations by Williams and Best (1982). Associated with these differences, Williams and Best found instrumental traits to be linked with masculinity and expressive traits to be linked with femininity. Chapters 25 and 32 noted that the U.S. data strongly indicated that both male and female respondents thought that masculinity (assertiveness, ambition, and task orientation) is required for success in management. Yet among 1,600 Australian high school students, Bottomley and Sampson (1977) reported comparable results only for male respondents. But unlike the boys, a majority of the Australian girls believed that the attributes of both men and women contribute to one's competence in dealing with leadership tasks.

Hofstede's (1980) 50-country survey unearthed a dimension of masculinity. Masculinity was high among IBM personnel in countries in which roles were clearly differentiated for men and women. In these countries such as Japan, assertive and dominant men, along with nurturing women, were favored. Work, money, material goods, and performance were emphasized, rather than play. There was admiration for *machismo*, for the successful achiever, for speed, and for size. In countries that were low in masculinity such as Sweden, there was endorsement of the following attitudes: men can be nurturant, sex roles are fluid, there should be equality between the sexes, unisex and androgeny are ideal, the quality of life is important, work is a means to the good life, people and the environment are important, interdependence is valued, being of service is more important than being ambitious, and small and slow are beautiful. Highest in such masculinity were IBM respondents from Japan, followed closely by the Germanic cluster; Jamaica; the Latin American countries of Venezuela, Equador, Mexico, and Colombia; and Catholic Italy and Ireland. Lowest in masculinity were IBM personnel from the Scandinavian countries of Sweden, Norway, Denmark, and Finland and from the Netherlands. More job stress is likely for leaders in countries with a high masculinity index. In addition, leadership is likely to be more caring and relations oriented in countries with personnel who are low in masculinity and less so in countries with personnel who are high in masculinity.

After noting that Australia and New Zealand scored only a little above the mean in Hofstede's masculinity index, Shouksmith (1987) suggested that the dimension has been mislabeled, since the pattern of life in Australia and New Zealand traditionally is so masculine in orientation. Shouksmith suggested that the dimension really describes the extent to which good living rather than work is valued, along with compatibility with coworkers. If one looks at the country-by-country results, one sees that the complex mixture of attitudes results in the differences among countries being due to different elements. Japan's high masculinity index fits with its emphases on the importance of work over leisure and the strong belief in sex-role differentiation. Sweden accepts the equality of the sexes to earn its low masculinity index and may have as strong interests in recreation as does New Zealand.

Hofstede's masculinity index generally indicates countries in which smaller percentages of women will reach positions of leadership. The low masculinity index obtained for Sweden is reflected in the highest labor-participation rate of females in the world. Yet, as Barrett (1973) noted, opportunities for higher-level positions remain much more limited for women in Sweden than in many other countries, such as Britain, France, Portugal, and the United States, all of which have a much higher masculinity index than does Sweden.

Styles of Leadership

Considerable national and cultural differences have been found in required, preferred, and observed leadership that is autocratic or democratic, participative or directive, relations oriented or task oriented, considerate or structuring, and active or laissez-faire—the styles discussed earlier in Chapters 21 through 25. The cultural differences become even more apparent if the data are gathered from those who are most freely socialized within a given culture, that is, from those who

endorse the core beliefs of the culture. Thus, Dorfman and Howell (1988) demonstrated that in Taiwan, directive leadership displayed by one's superiors correlated .44 with subordinates' satisfaction with work for those subordinates who had strong beliefs in the key cultural values of the Chinese culture. The correlation was only .19 for those who did not have such strong beliefs in their culture.

Autocratic versus Democratic Leadership

R. Likert (1963) argued that democratic leadership and System 4, as described in Chapter 21, is most likely to be effective in any productive organization, regardless of the culture or the country. Despite the wide variations in leadership preferences and behavior, Likert's argument is that, regardless of culture, there is one best way to lead. The System 4 *participatory*[7] approach was successfully introduced into Japan whose management has ordinarily been seen as a benevolent autocracy (System 2) practicing System 3 consultation (Sakano, 1983). In support of Likert's contention, Misumi (1974) applied a System 4 strategy in 1970 in a large shipyard in Japan, using group meetings for group problem solving, goal setting, and decision making in an effort to reduce accidents among 4,000 workers. Accidents per man hours worked ($\times 10^5$) declined from 30 in 1969 to 12 in 1973.

Close rather than general supervision was found to be favored by workers in countries that are high in power distance and authoritarianism, such as Peru (Whyte, 1963) and Thailand (Deyo, 1978). Among North American workers and others in the Anglo cluster, however, the opposite is usually the case. Thus, at the other end of the spectrum, as expected, 500 Australian managers from the Anglo cluster indicated their strong endorsement of democratic managerial beliefs, such as the capacity of subordinates to display initiative, the utility of sharing information, and the importance of self-control (Stening & Wong, 1983).

[7]The convention used in Chapter 22 is continued here. Participation (in roman type) includes consultation (the superior decides), *participation* (shared decisions), and delegation (the subordinate decides). *Participation* (in italics) is limited to joint decision making by superiors and subordinates. Direction (in roman type) refers to initiatives by the leader that involve *direction* (telling), persuasion (selling), and bargaining. *Direction* (in italics) is limited to telling and giving orders.

In the role playing in Exercise Supervise (Bass, 1975c), an equal number of "passive," "moderately involved," and "vitally interested" subordinates meet in a counterbalanced order with a democratic, autocratic, and persuasive "supervisor." Although on a chance basis, 33 percent of the participants should prefer to work again with a democratic supervisor, Bass, Burger, et al. (1979, p. 167) found that French managers were most in favor of doing so (63 percent) and Japanese managers relatively least in favor of doing so (40 percent) among 12 nationalities; the other of 10 European, American, and Asian nationalities were in between in their preferences. In this same analysis, the preference of those participants who played the supervisory roles to work again with passive, uninvolved subordinates was highest among Indian managers (47 percent) and lowest among the Japanese (12 percent). Again, the preference by chance was 33 percent. Latin Americans (19 percent) differed in their preference from Latin Europeans (33 percent). Likewise, North Americans (32 percent), Germans (33 percent), and Scandinavians (31 percent) differed from Britons (22 percent) in this regard.

Power Distance. The subscription to democratic leadership was found to be surprisingly high by Haire, Ghiselli, and Porter (1966) across the 14 countries they studied. But, compared to U.S. managers, managers elsewhere indicated little acceptance of what would be required for such democratic leadership, such as agreement that employees as well as supervisors have the potential to exhibit initiative, share leadership, and contribute to the problem-solving process in organizations. The researchers concluded, on the basis of data from the early 1960s, that introducing democratic leadership into most other countries at that time would be "a little like building the techniques and practices of a Jeffersonian democracy on a basic belief in the divine right of kings" (p. 130).

Chapter 14 discussed the extent to which greater power differences between the leader and the led accent the greater potential for the leader to be authoritarian, directive, persuasive, or coercive. Less power difference would be expected to produce more participative leadership. In line with this hypothesis, Mulder (1976) saw large power differences, or power distance, between the leader and the led associated with the fear of disagreeing with one's superior. In Hofstede's (1980) survey, the same connections were revealed. Coercive, autocratic leadership was more common in countries in which the power distance between superiors and subordinates was high; more democratic styles were practiced in countries in which the power distance was low.

Among the 50 countries studied, those with IBM personnel who were highest in reported power distance included Malaysia, Indonesia, Singapore, and the Philippines from Southeast Asia; the Spanish-American countries of Mexico, Guatemala, Panama, Equador, Colombia, Venezuela, and Peru; India; the Middle Eastern countries; and the West African countries. At the lower end of the spectrum in power distance were the Anglo, Nordic, and Germanic clusters of countries and Israel and Costa Rica. Greater acceptance of an autocratic style of leadership was to be expected and found in the countries that were high in power distance and a democratic style, in the countries that were low in power distance. Somewhat consistent with Hofstede's results was the conclusion reached by Redding and Casey (1975) that managers in Malaysia, Indonesia, Thailand, and the Philippines favored an autocratic style, those in Singapore and Hong Kong were somewhat less favorable toward it, and those in western countries favored it the least. Al-Hajjeh (1984) concluded, from a survey of 25 North American and 25 Middle Eastern managers, that the Middle Easterners supported more autocratic leadership and the Americans did the reverse. Compared to the Americans, the Middle Easterners felt less positive about the capacity of subordinates and a greater need to provide them with detailed instructions. Again, Gebert and Steinkamp (undated) found, from 218 interviews with representative indigenous manufacturers in Nigeria in West Africa, that economic success was thought to depend on discipline and rules whenever possible. In the same way, Kenis (1977) compared the attitudes toward leadership of 150 Turkish and 147 American first-line supervisors in bank branches in Ankara and Istanbul. The Turks favored more autocratic and directive leadership, in contrast to the Americans who favored more democratic, participative, considerate leadership. Kenis attributed his results to the authoritarianism inherent in the Turkish culture.

Authoritarianism. Authoritarianism, as measured by the *F* Scale, influences the acceptance of autocratic rather than democratic behavior.[8] The *F* Scale has been administered to student groups in many different countries. Thus, as was just noted, Turkish students are likely to score higher and American students are likely to score lower on the scale. Indian students usually score high as well (Meade & Whittaker, 1967). Meade's (1967) experimental replication in India of the classic Lewin, Lippitt, and White (1939) study of leadership found that both productivity and satisfaction in boys' groups were higher under autocratic than under nonautocratic leadership in India.

Sinha (1976) agreed that authoritarian leadership is optimum in India. Such leadership features task orientation and strong personal involvement and effort by the leader. More democratic processes are possible only after the structure has become firm for the employees and moderate productivity has been achieved. In support, Singh and Arya (1965) studied 40 sociometrically identified leaders in a village in India. Given the strong authoritarian norm, it was not surprising that leaders were found to be significantly more authoritarian than were nonleaders. Leaders preferred task-oriented leaders to other types, but both leaders and nonleaders rejected the self-interested leader. However, neither Kakar (1971) nor Jaggi (1977) could find similar support for favoring the autocratic mode in India.

Variations have also been observed within Asia in the perceived power distance and in autocratic leadership behavior. The specific issues involved in a given country are likely to make a difference as well. Ishikawa (1986) compared the favored and perceived distribution of power of managers and employees in nine Asian countries. Employers viewed participation by workers relatively more favorably in India, Korea, and Japan than in Pakistan and Taiwan. Power distance regarding decisions about management policy, personnel, working conditions, and workplace issues generally was greatest in Thailand and least in Sri Lanka. In Japan, power distance was seen as being lower on workplace

issues and higher on questions of management policy. In India and elsewhere, perceived power distance also depended on which issues were involved. But, in general, workers in Taiwan perceived the strongest relation between one's position in the hierarchy and one's power.

Paternalism. Paternalism in the culture affects the acceptance of authoritarian leadership. The sense of paternalism was higher among the Taiwan Chinese and Mexican employees than among the U.S. employees working for the same company. Using data on employees in Taiwan, Mexico, and the United States, Dorfman and Howell (1988) emerged with a fifth factor, paternalism, to add to Hofstede's factors. When paternalism was strong, employees subscribed to expecting job security and to be looked after as a person by their company and not only as a worker.

Farmer and Richman (1965) rated a number of countries on paternalism, using a review of the literature and reports from experts. They concluded that Japan was most strongly paternalistic, as evidenced by policies of lifetime employment, age-grade lockstep promotions and salary increases, and the companies' provision of housing, recreational facilities, and shrines for worship for their employees. Other countries that were high in paternalism included Egypt, Chile, Germany, India, France, Mexico, and Saudi Arabia. At the other end of the spectrum were the United States, Britain, the Soviet Union, and Yugoslavia.

Paternalism, featuring the autocratic patron and compliant followers, takes a variety of forms in Latin America. It dominates indigenous Brazilian industry. The traditional worker identifies with the *patrāo*, the patriarchial owner to whom he is a ward, not a member of an organization headed by the patron. In rural Guatemalan factories, immediate supervisors are of local origin. As members of the *padrones* work force, they have limited authority; they can only suggest, not order. On the other hand, if the workers are not unionized, the foreign engineer and the owner or his white-collar surrogates treat workers like children, physically abusing them, as well as dealing directly with their complaints (M. Nash, 1958).

Trust. Nationalities vary in their willingness to trust others and the way they deal with a lack of trust. In

[8]See Chapters 9 and 22.

Italy, trust may be publicly expressed but privately denied, for Italy's history has been characterized by oppressive surface regimentation first by foreign occupiers, then by domestic autocratic governments. But a strong defense of the liberty of the individual and his or her family have been maintained. Outer and inner acceptance have been separated by making the world truly a stage in which the relations between the leader and the led play a dramatic part (Barzini, 1964). Levels of trust influence the willingness of subordinates to work with democratic leaders, according to Williams, Whyte, and Green (1966), who found that the level of trust among Peruvians was generally low. Within countries, organization and status affect the willingness to trust others. For example, Senner (1971) obtained results showing that Brazilian bankers were similar to American college students in that both groups were more trusting than were Peruvian white-collar workers. The bankers' levels of trust reflected their above-average socioeconomic status in Brazil. Likewise Negandhi and Prasad (1971) found that Indian managers in U.S. subsidiaries in India showed more trust in their subordinates than did Indian managers in indigenous Indian firms.

Participative and Directive Leadership

A survey by Sirota (1968) of the attitudes of IBM employees in 46 countries toward supervision indicated their preference for consultation (the superior still makes the decision) and participative, joint decision making, although directive leadership was seen as being more common. In other studies, Israeli managers revealed more actual participatory leadership than they said they supported ideologically (Vardi, Shirom, & Jacobson, 1980). Australian managers were the reverse; ideologically, they endorsed participatory practices, but they were actually less supportive of them in practice (Clark & McCabe, 1970). As would be expected from Chapters 22 and 25, the managers who consulted were viewed most favorably by subordinates and the managers who practiced a lot of persuasion, especially the ones with "no style," were viewed least favorably, particularly in Britain. Participative managers in Britain were not seen as good counselors; many subordinates objected to the number of meetings they called (Sadler, 1970). Consistent with these results, Chaney (1966) found that whereas more productive U.S. scientists had more frequent communications with their superiors and their colleagues, the reverse was true for British scientists—the more productive ones had less frequent communications with their superiors.

As seen in an analysis by Sadler and Hofstede (1972) of IBM employees from Australia, Brazil, Britain, and Japan (shown in Table 34.4), the preferred management style for the majority of IBM employees was consultative, but there were distinct differences among countries. For example, in Brazil, an additional 29 per-

Table 34.4 Preferred and Perceived Leadership Styles of IBM Employees (percentage)

Leadership Style	Australia	Britain	Brazil	Japan
Preferred				
Directive	1	5	8	1
Persuasive	25	25	21	42
Consultative	65	61	42	44
Participative	9	9	29	13
Perceived				
Directive	22	14	23	19
Persuasive	32	30	24	26
Consultative	30	34	17	26
Participative	5	8	12	10
None of these	11	14	24	19

SOURCE: Adapted from Sadler and Hofstede (1972).

cent of the employees preferred *participative* leadership. At the same time, the preference for consultation was considerably higher in Australia and Britain than in Brazil or Japan. Little *participative* leadership was perceived anywhere. These results were consistent with data gathered through the Management Styles Survey in the United States, Spain, Sweden, Finland, and India (Bass, Valenzi, Farrow, & Solomon, 1975). Consultation is preferred over participation everywhere and is more frequently seen everywhere. In all the countries in the IBM survey and in those just mentioned, *directive* supervision was favored less by the vast majority of subordinates. Although, as noted in Chapter 22, the leader's directiveness tended to correlate positively with the subordinates' satisfaction with the leader, it did not do so as strongly as did participation. According to Bass, Burger, et al. (1979), the relative preference for participative leadership in decision making was highest among the Italians and the Japanese. Participative leadership was self-appraised (in Exercise Self-Appraisal) as highest among the Italian managers and lowest among the Dutch and Japanese managers.

Howell and Dorfman (1988) found that participative leadership had stronger effects on the satisfaction and commitment of U.S. employees than on their Mexican counterparts. The correlations for the North Americans were .49 with satisfaction with work, .69 with satisfaction with supervision, and .65 with satisfaction with job performance. The comparable correlations for the Mexican employees were .26, .49, and .09, respectively. At the same time, as Dorfman and Howell (1988) hypothesized, *directive* leadership correlated between .38 and .50 with the Taiwan Chinese and Mexican employees' satisfaction with the leader and commitment to the organization. For the North Americans, working in similar settings, the correlations of *directiveness* and the subordinates' satisfaction were only .22 and .25 (Howell & Dorfman, 1988). Differences in the cohesiveness of the work groups could not substitute for the effects of differences in the leaders' *directiveness.*

Consultation and Two-way Communication. A multinational sample of IBM managers thought they did more consulting than their subordinates thought

they did. Among the 178 managers, 71 percent saw themselves as using a "consulting" leadership style, but only 29 percent of their employees agreed with them (Sadler & Hofstede, 1972). A contradiction probably contributed to the discrepancy. In Haire, Ghiselli, and Porter's (1966) 14-country study noted earlier, it was found that whereas 3,600 managers professed favorable beliefs toward participative leadership and sharing information, they also believed that the average individual preferred to be directed and wanted to avoid responsibility. Similar results were reported by Clark and McCabe (1970) for an additional 1,300 managers in Australia and by Cummings and Schmidt (1972) for a small sample of Greek managers.

These national differences in preferences for certain styles of leadership were seen with considerable consistency across studies. The percentages of managers of a country who preferred two-way over one-way communication in doing Exercise Communication (Bass, 1975g) correlated across nationalities .82 with Haire, Ghiselli, and Porter's (1966) survey measure of the propensity to share information and objectives (Barrett & Franke, 1969). Consultation is the most popular style of decision making among U.S. and Japanese managers. U.S. and Japanese managers were also the highest among those of 12 nationalities in seeing two-way communications as less frustrating than one-way communications. The relatively least frustrated by one-way communications were the Belgians, the Germans/Austrians, and the French. All the Japanese managers who were sampled preferred two-way communications, both as senders and receivers. Almost identical results occurred for the U.S. managers. The Dutch, Belgians, German, Austrians, French, and Indians seemed somewhat more tolerant of one-way communications as senders, but not as receivers (Bass, Burger, et al., 1979).

A. S. Tannenbaum (1974) contrasted the extent to which employees participated both informally and formally in decision making in Italy, Austria, the United States, Yugoslavia, and an Israeli kibbutz. As expected, subordinates and superiors were closest in agreement about their job satisfaction and mental adjustment in Yugoslavia and in the Israeli kibbutz, where workers formally participated in organizational decision-making processes. They were farthest apart in Italy, where employees did not participate in decisions, either formally or informally, despite Italian legislation supporting such participation.

Legally Required versus Actual Participation. According to the International Research Group on Democracy in Europe (IDE), the percentage of decisions for which formal rules of *participation* apply was seen to vary in what had been legalized as of 1981 within 12 European countries and Israel. The countries that were the highest in these percentages were Yugoslavia (76 percent), Italy (66 percent), Norway (64 percent), and Sweden (61 percent). Those that were lowest were Great Britain (21 percent) and Israel (23 percent) (IDE, 1981). Elden (1986) argued that in countries with highly legislated programs for industrial democracy, such as Norway, participative decision making in the workplace may be preached more often than practiced. In Yugoslavia, with its strong legislative support for the participation of workers through workers' councils, Kolaja (1965) observed that actually only about 40 percent of the decisions were instituted by workers and supervisors and 60 percent of the decisions were initiated by higher-level managers. This situation may be contrasted to that of the United States where, without such legislation, it was possible to find establishments that held participatory meetings in which blue-collar supervisors and workers initiated 52 percent of decisions and management was responsible for introducing only 48 percent of the ideas (Rosenberg, 1977). When Jacob and Ahn (1978) examined the participation of workers in six socialist and nine nonsocialist countries, they found that whether or not a country was socialist had little effect. Nor was the technological level of the workers in the different countries of any consequence. Rather, participation in influencing decisions depended on whether the management style, work culture, and formal industrial relations system of the country gave individual workers the feeling that they had the power to determine their conditions of work.

Participation and Perceived Influence. Comparisons were made in the perceived influence of workers and supervisors among 12 European countries and Israel with surveys by the IDE (1979). Although perceived influence by workers was lowest for Israelis and

highest for the Yugoslavs, legalized participation was not strongly associated with actual perceived influence on the decision process in most of the other European countries (IDE, 1981a, 1981b). In Israel and Belgium, workers felt relatively less influential in comparison to workers elsewhere in Europe in about 16 decisions. In Yugoslavia, workers felt relatively more influential in comparison to workers elsewhere. Danish supervisors perceived themselves as being highest in influence compared to supervisors elsewhere; Belgian supervisors felt the least influential. German and French top managers thought they were the most influential, and Scandinavian and Yugoslavian top managers felt the least influential.

Top-down decision making accompanies the power distance that is prevalent in West Africa and in the Arab countries of the Middle East even for minor matters (Pezeshkpur, 1978), as well as in Turkey. Thus, Ottih (1981) observed a low level of delegation and participation by subordinates in decision making in Nigerian banks, where decision making was highly centralized and highly favored by management. Ergun and Onaran (1981) suggested that *direction* and negotiation were "natural" in Turkey. As was mentioned before, Kenis (1977) concluded that Turks favored directive leadership. Nonetheless, in the survey of Turkish electric utility employees by Ergun and Onaran (1981), the employees reported similar satisfaction with whether their supervisors were directive or participative. Correlations ranged between .32 and .42 in the satisfaction of subordinates and the tendencies of their supervisors to be described as more active in any one of five styles ranging from *directive* to delegative.

Manipulative versus Participative Tactics. Bass and Franke (1972) administered the Organizational Success Questionnaire to 1,064 university students from 6 countries in their native languages. The students were applying for summer jobs in other countries. The students' nationality strongly influenced how they varied in their endorsement of political, manipulative approaches to success in getting ahead in management, such as bluffing, rather than social, participative approaches, such as openly committing oneself.[9] All 6 na-

[9]See Chapter 9.

tionalities tended to favor the participative approaches and to reject the political manipulative ones. In addition, the Germans were highest among the 6 nationalities in their endorsement of openly committing themselves, but they were lowest in finding it important to share in decision making. The Swedes were highest in endorsing the fostering of mutual trust and leveling with others and lowest in the political withholding of information, maintaining social distance, compromising for delay, and initiating but retarding actions. Students from the United States were highest in endorsing the establishment of mutual objectives and lowest in endorsing bluffing and making political alliances. The French were highest in supporting the participative arranging of group discussions and sharing in decision making, as in the making of political alliances.

Although they were relatively high in their willingness to share in decision making, the British were lowest in their endorsement of openly committing themselves and fostering mutual trust. They were also highest in their endorsement of withholding information for release when it would do the most good. Whereas the Dutch were next to the highest among the six nationalities in favoring the fostering of mutual trust, they were the lowest in endorsing the establishment of mutual objectives, leveling with others, and arranging for group decisions. They also were the highest in their support for maintaining social distance and initiating actions but then retarding their progress.

The participative endorsements for the 6 countries as a whole correlated .89 with Haire, Ghiselli, and Porter's (1966) managers' preferences in the same countries for sharing information and objectives. Furthermore, endorsement of the participative approaches for the six countries correlated .77 with the countries' national wealth, as measured by the per capita gross national product.

Meaning and Practice in Japan. Franke (1984) compared 149 Japanese managers' and 1,373 U.S. managers' tendency to endorse these same participative and political approaches. The Japanese significantly endorsed all the political approaches to a much greater degree than did the North American managers. Although they agreed that their success could be enhanced by participative decision making with subordi-

nates, it was the Americans who were more in favor of leveling with others, openly committing themselves, establishing mutual objectives, fostering mutual trust, and arranging for group discussions.

Some of these differences between the Japanese and Americans' endorsements of participative decisions may have been due to the extent to which such practices are discretionary for American leaders but institutionalized in Japan. Participation may take on a different character in a country like Japan from what is ordinarily practiced elsewhere. In traditional Japan, negative votes in a group were rare. The members of a group faced the loss of esteem, ridicule, and offense to others if they deviated from the "will of the group," as announced by the group leader. The leader, in turn, had to divine intellectually and emotionally, "with his belly," *haragei*, what the group needed and wanted as a group (Kerlinger, 1951). The description is still valid for modern Japan.

To a Western observer, leader-subordinate relations in which complete subordinate obedience is given to decisions announced by the leader may seem authoritarian-submissive. Actually, leadership in Japan, as seen in the *ringi* method, is a blend of full consultation all around and a seeming intolerance for deviation when consensus has been reached. In the West, consultation is initiated by the leader, who asks for the subordinates' opinions and suggestions before deciding. In Japan, consultation, as seen in the *ringi* system, begins with *nemawashi*, the sounding out of opinions of colleagues about ideas, then formally submitting to one's superior what has emerged in consultation with them (P. B. Smith, 1984a). *Nemawashi* also may involve middle managers talking to subordinates individually about how upper management really feels about an issue before it is to be discussed in public by their group of subordinates (Yokochi, 1989b).

Misumi (1984) noted several important features of *ringi*. First, many people, who are directly or indirectly involved, learn about the proposal. Consensus has developed among many in the organization before the decision reaches the top management. The experience and knowledge of all who are involved is applied to the decision, which enhances its quality. (Thus, Maguire and Pascale, 1978, found that the quality of decisions in Japanese firms was correlated with the extent to which the decisions came from below. This was not true for American firms in which the quality of the decision was better if more time was spent studying the issues.) Second, the wide involvement in the process of people at all levels in the organization means that the decision can be quickly implemented if it is authorized. (This was of great assistance in Japan's rapid change over the last century.) Third, the originator of the idea gets training in management development. Fourth, the *ringi* method fits the large firm, as well as the smaller, family-owned, paternalistic company. However, when Japanese supervise North American workers, they are less consultative than are American supervisors; communication and cultural barriers inhibit the *ringi* practice with American workers (Beatty, Owens, & Jenner, undated).

Meaning and Practice in China. China represents still another variant. Lindsay and Dempsey (1985) suggest that decision making in the People's Republic of China can only be described as "semiparticipative." It blends group criticism and group discussion without group decision making with the avoidance of strong public disagreements. There are strictly patterned discussion flows and a strong dependence on authority.

Meaning and Practice in Britain and France. Decision-making processes take a different form in Britain than in France. According to Graves (1973), British managers do not consider all alternatives, and greater conflict occurs in regard to the value of various alternatives; nevertheless, once a decision is reached, there is more commitment to it. French managers place more weight on alternatives but may be less committed to the alternative selected for implementation. The felt pressure of subordinates to participate in decisions may depend more on individual differences, for, while the superior-subordinate relationship is defined impersonally in many countries, in France, it is defined in personal terms (Inzerilli & Laurent, 1983).

Multinational Subsidiaries versus Indigenous Firms. Heller and Wilpert (1981) surveyed the extent to which decision making was directive (with or without explanation), consultative, joint, or delegated among 625 boss-subordinate dyads in 29 firms in 8 countries. The results varied by country from most di-

rective to most participative. Israel was most directive, and Sweden was most participative. But the authors noted that the type of firm had to be taken into account. For example, more *direction* was found in indigenous German firms than in German multinational corporations. German subsidiaries of multinational firms headed by other nationals were the most participative. Similarly, Negandhi and Prasad (1971) obtained results indicating that managers in North American subsidiaries in Argentina, Brazil, India, the Philippines, and Uruguay found it more comfortable to delegate than did indigenous managers in locally owned firms in the same countries. Whether employees in North American subsidiaries of Japanese multinationals are satisfied or tend to quit appeared to depend on whether the management is more under Japanese or American influence. Japanese employees are more satisfied with Japanese managers and practices than are U.S. employees (Yokochi, 1989b).

Effects of Legitimacy and Cultural Expectations. While a participatory style may work well for leaders and with subordinates in the United States, where it is culturally legitimated, considerably less effective outcomes may be found in other countries in which participation is less expected and appreciated. For example, in Saudi Arabia, Algattan (1985) compared the effectiveness of participatory leadership on U.S. and mainly Asian and African workers. Participative leadership was more effective with the U.S. workers and was related to their greater need for the scope of the task, growth, and an inner locus of control in comparison to Asian and African employees.

In a seminal field experiment, Coch and French (1948) found a marked increase in productivity by North American work groups who were permitted to participate in goal-setting decisions that affected them, in contrast to findings with control groups that were not permitted to participate. But the same experiment failed with Norwegian factory workers because Norwegian workers, who have a lower need for autonomy, did not see participation as legitimate to the extent that American workers did (French, Israel, & Ås, 1960). Again, Locke, Latham, and Erez (1987) showed, in laboratory comparisons, that such group participation in goal setting was unnecessary in the United States where, serendipitously, the experimenter had been friendly and supportive when instructing the subjects. In Israel, the experimenter had been more curt. In Puerto Rico, when the manager of a new Harwood Manufacturing plant began to encourage employees to participate in problem-solving meetings, turnover increased sharply! It was found that the workers in Puerto Rico had decided that if the management was so ignorant of the answers to its problems that it had to consult employees, the company was poorly managed and was unlikely to survive (Marrow, 1964b). In the same way, Israeli sailors were more satisfied with expected legitimate directive leadership than with participative leadership (Foa, 1957).

Relations-oriented and Task-oriented Leadership

Considerable agreement across countries was reported by Blake and Mouton (1970) in what managers regard as ideal. Among almost 2,500 managers from the United States, South Africa, Canada, Australia, the Middle East, and South America in GRID seminars, most agreed that the "9,9" management style[10] (integrated concern with both production and people) was the ideal for their company. But much of the uniformity across countries could be attributed to indoctrination in the course. There was more concern generally for productivity when managers described their own actual behavior. In the same way, Howell and Dorfman (1988), comparing Chinese, Mexican, and American employees in electronics manufacturing plants, concluded that supportive leadership generally had similar positive effects on satisfaction and commitment in all these samples. Moreover, the cohesiveness of the work groups could often substitute for the supportive leadership by generating the satisfaction and commitment. Ayman and Chemers (1983) and Kakar (1971) reached similar conclusions.

The self-, interaction, and task orientations (Bass, 1967b) of leaders and nonleaders have been studied in many different countries, including Poland (Dobruszek, 1967), Britain (Cooper, 1966; R. Cooper & Payne, 1967), and India (Muttayya, 1977) with results generally similar to what was found in U.S. samples.[11] For example, Muttayya found that among 275 diverse formal and informal Indian leaders and nonleaders that the leaders were more task oriented, as expected. As elsewhere, self-orientation among leaders was associated with less commitment to principled public conduct. Likewise, the importance of the vertical dyad linkage on the quality of superior-subordinate relationships was as applicable in Japan and elsewhere as in the United States (Wakabayashi & Graen, 1984).

But cross-national differences in the relevance of task and relations orientation have been found using the Least Preferred Coworker (LPC) questionnaire. Bennett (1977), for example, found that high-performing managers in the Philippines had a low score (task oriented) while their counterparts in Hong Kong had high LPC scores (relations oriented).

The Japanese Example. As noted earlier, the Japanese place a particular premium on the quality of relationships with others. A variety of empirical studies and case analyses have corroborated this finding. Among the 12 national groups studied by Bass, Burger, et al. (1979), the Japanese managers were relatively high or highest in preferred awareness of self-understanding, listening to others with understanding, and accepting warmth and affection from others. They were also highest in their willingness to discuss feelings with others and to cooperate, rather than to compete, with their peers and in seeing the need for top management to be tolerant. At the same time, they remained relatively high among the nationalities in their actual and preferred task orientation relative to their human relations orientation, which admittedly was also strong in an absolute sense. The task centeredness of the Japanese managers appeared more acceptable than it would for British managers, according to White and Trevor (1983), for the Japanese were considered more committed, expert, and socially close (P. B. Smith, 1984a). Task orientation is expected to be high in Japan for it is connected directly with acceptance of the organization's mission and goals. Relations orientation is beyond discussion. It is a given in the Japanese scene upon which depend survival and success (Yokochi, 1989b).

Bolon and Crain (1985) compared the responses of 40 Japanese and 39 U.S. managers and executives in

---

[10]See Chapter 23.
[11]See Chapter 10.

how they would handle a problem subordinate. The Japanese were found to take significantly more steps in dealing with the subordinate. They invested more effort in trying to understand the situation. On the other hand, U.S. male managers (but not female managers) more often attempted to resolve the situation by firing the subordinate or forcing him or her to quit.

When American, Indian, and Japanese managers were compared by Ivancevich, Schweiger, and Ragan (1986), it was found that the Japanese felt they obtained more social support from their bosses than did the Indian or American managers. For Indians and Americans, spouses and relatives were more important providers of such social support.

The greater emphasis on the human side of enterprise by Japanese managers compared to U.S. managers is seen in their differential response to intensified price competition. Americans will cut their human resources expenditures while maintaining their capital equipment, plant, and material resources. They will seek financial and legal solutions to deal with the competition rather than technical ones. The Japanese will try to save their human resources; they will avoid layoffs, discharges, and wage reductions to reduce labor costs, although they will withhold bonuses. If personnel costs must be cut, they will reduce their own salaries and make use of quality circle and other "bottom-up" suggestions to reduce costs. They will reduce the costs of production by increasing the flexibility of their operations and replacing workers with automation, but they transfer and retrain the displaced workers. The Japanese approach requires a high degree of coordination and good working relations between R & D, manufacturing, and marketing, as well as commitment, loyalty, and involvement by employees (Tsurumi, 1983).

The Japanese attention to relationships was made more specific by Hall and Hall (1987), who pointed to the unusual degree to which the Japanese place a premium on listening and the value of agreement. Questions should not be posed unless they have answers or the answers can be found beforehand by asking the questions in advance of a meeting. Proposals should not be refused outright but should be taken under consideration. If finally rejected, the reasons need to be fully stated with politeness and apologies. The transformational factor of individualized consideration as mea-

sured by the Multifactor Leadership Questionnaire emerges from a different set of items in Japan because such consideration is expected from one's supervisor although it remains unspoken. Guidance from the supervisor and acceptance by the subordinate is an unsaid rule governing their relationship (Yokochi, 1989a).

Westerners who interact with Japanese will be more successful if they pay attention to the need for patience. Impatient behavior will be interpreted as bad manners and a lack of sincerity. Uncontrolled emotion will be considered as weakness and in bad taste. But patience may not help the Western negotiator. The Japanese remain ethnocentric in their business activities in Japan itself. They will make special efforts to buy Japanese products, whenever possible, rather than buy them abroad. They will infringe on Western patents (no infringement according to Japanese law) and continue to rely on more expensive Japanese suppliers. The "old-boy" networks are particularly strong in Japan and difficult for foreigners to penetrate.

Initiation versus Consideration

Substantial differences in the initiation of structure and consideration have been found among managers from different countries. For instance, Anderson (1983) did not find that consideration by leaders contributed to the effectiveness of managers in a mixed cultural setting in New Zealand. In the Bass, Burger, et al. (1979) 12-nation data for Exercise Supervise, although there was an overall trend to see the need for more consideration by leaders at lower levels of management, the French regarded being considerate as relatively unimportant at all levels of management, as did the Latin Americans. On the other hand, the Germans and Austrians thought it highly important for lower, middle, and top managers. Consideration was emphasized by fast-rising but not by slow-climbing managers in Italy, Spain, Portugal, and the United States; it was deemphasized by those with accelerated careers in Belgium, Scandinavia, France, Latin America, and India.

L. R. Anderson (1966a, 1966b) studied discussion groups composed of American and Indian graduate students. The leader's effectiveness, as rated by the American students, was positively correlated to both the leader's consideration and initiation. But ratings of the leader's effectiveness by Indian students were correlated only with the leader's consideration scores.

Differences in Psychometric Properties. Culture may affect the psychometric properties involved in measuring initiation and consideration. As was noted earlier, the factor structures of leadership behavior descriptions in the United States, Britain, Japan, and Hong Kong systematically differed especially in which questionnaire items correlated with the initiation of structure (Smith, Tayeb, Peterson, et al., 1986). In the same way, Ayman and Chemers (1982) emerged with a single factor instead of the two factors of initiation and consideration for European in contrast to U.S. managers as described by their respective subordinates. When K. F. Mauer (1974) administered the Leadership Opinion Questionnaire to a sample of 190 mine overseers and shift bosses in the South African gold mining industry, neither a varimax rotation nor an orthogonal target rotation of the two extracted factors approximated the findings of U.S. and Canadian researchers. An oblique target rotation produced a South African solution that was closest to the North American solution.

The correlation between the factors was much higher than that found in other studies. Nevertheless, Matsui, Ohtsuka, and Kikuchi (1978) were able to replicate and extend Fleishman and Peters's (1962) U.S. results with 79 Japanese supervisors. As with the U.S. results, they found that considerate Japanese supervisors (as seen by their subordinates on the Supervisory Behavior Description Questionnaire) were higher in self-inventoried benevolence on L. V. Gordon's Survey of Interpersonal Values. The supervisors' initiation of structure, as described by their subordinates, was lower if the supervisors reported themselves to be higher in valuing independence.

Laissez-faire Leadership
versus the Motivation to Manage

In data collected between 1968 and 1972, the preference to be more influential was high among managers from all 12 nations studied by Bass, Burger, et al. (1979). But it was highest among Japanese, Spanish, and German managers and relatively low among French and Dutch managers. During this same period, the en-

dorsement of active intervention by the leader, in contrast to laissez-faire behavior, was seen by Bass and Franke (1972) to relate to a country's rate of economic growth. Bass and Franke obtained a correlation of .93 in the ranking of 6 industrialized countries between the rate of economic growth of the country for 9 preceding years and the extent to which students from those countries endorsed a manager's being both more participative and more political to achieve success in a career.

Some consistency with these results was obtained by Keys, Edge, Heinza, et al. (1986), who compared the self-descriptions of 214 Korean, 101 Philippine, and 97 U.S. middle managers about how active they were in their relations with others in dealing with various issues. The issues were expected to make a difference, since the Asians were more likely to be more collectivistic and the Americans, more individualistic. The North Americans reported themselves more likely than did the Filipinos or Koreans to threaten their subordinates to obtain compliance with requests. Americans also more frequently ordered subordinates to "do what I want done." Furthermore, the U.S. middle managers were most likely to say that they would disagree openly with their boss and remind the boss about matters if he or she procrastinated. However, the Korean managers were most likely to indicate that they would confront their boss if treated unfairly, while the Filipinos were most likely to indicate a reluctance to go over their boss's head to a higher authority. Less collectivistic than the Filipinos or Koreans, the Americans were more likely to actively complain to their boss if their peers got out of line; they were almost most likely to remind their peers of rules and policies.

Motivation to Manage. Collectivisim and individualism had different effects on the motive to manage others in hierarchical settings. Projective results on the strength of the motivation to manage within bureaucracies, as revealed by scores on the Miner Sentence Completion Scale (MSCS)[12] by foreign and U.S. students in American schools, were quite different. Consistent with the decline in American MSCS scores between 1960 and 1980, noted by Miner and Smith (1982) and Miner, Smith, and Ebrahimi (1985), American stu-

[12]See Chapter 25.

dents were found to score much lower than Asian or African students. Ebrahimi (1985c) found that the motivation to manage, as measured by the MSCS, was significantly higher in a combined sample of Japanese, Korean, Taiwanese, Philippine, Malaysian, and Chinese students and a separate sample of Thai students than in a sample of American students. All were attending schools in the United States, and the samples were 26 to 29 percent female. U.S. students were lowest in MCSC scores compared to samples of students from elsewhere. The MSCS scores were successively higher for students from India, Iran, Thailand, and Nigeria. Some of these differences could be attributed to personal differences among the students. For example, the Nigerian sample contained more students with undergraduate degrees in business. The foreign students studying in the United States may be an unusual sample of more ambitious, adventuresome, assertive individuals, who are more highly socialized to Western mores and higher in class and education than those who remain at home. At the same time, the results suggest that these Asian and African students could fit more readily into management in the highly bureaucratized organizations in which they are likely to find employment when they return home. Consistent with these results, Wachtel (1988) found that prospective managers from Mexico were higher in managerial motivation than were their American counterparts.

Transformational and Transactional Leadership

Howell and Dorfman (1988) expected charismatic leadership to have a considerable impact on Mexican and American employees' satisfaction with work and with supervision. Although the expected effects were positive on both samples, the impact of charismatic leadership was greater on the North American employees, for whom correlations of .50 and .70 were found, compared to the Mexican employees for whom the correlations were .29 and .57. (Some of the darker history of charismatic Mexican political leaders may have been a drag on the Mexican results.)

The U.S. samples also generated higher correlations between transactional contingent rewarding (.48 and .73) and the measures of satisfaction with work and

with supervision, in contrast to the Mexican results (.19 and .58). Likewise, the effects of contingent punishment were greater for the U.S. than for the Mexican samples. Also, contingent reinforcement was found to have positive effects on satisfaction and organizational commitment in Taiwan (Dorfman & Howell, 1988).

According to Yokochi (1989a), Japanese managers at the level of the CEO and several rungs below are much more transformational than transactional. Their subordinates are likely to indicate with the Multifactor Leadership Questionnaire that their leaders take full responsibility for their actions (as a matter of tradition) and are generous in giving concrete guidance. The leaders are highly respected and trusted. The leaders encourage sacrifice by subordinates and at the same time make extra efforts to assure subordinates of their feelings and concern for the welfare of the subordinates and their families. Subordinates are challenged with new ideas and tasks. As noted elsewhere, it is the firm or agency, not the leaders, that provides unspoken rewards and promotions.

Early (1988) pointed to important cross-cultural differences in the effectiveness of contingent rewarding. He noted that since English workers did not value praise, criticism, or general conversation with their superiors, as did American or Ghanaian workers (Early, 1984), English workers would be less likely to be influenced by contingent rewarding. The English workers, particularly those in heavy industry, would distrust feedback from their supervisors (Blumberg, 1968; Goodman & Whittingham, 1969). The transactional factor of contingent reward is complicated in Japan by unspoken expectations of reward as well as obligations. For example, the failure to be promoted would be a consequence of failure to meet unspoken expectations. Strict rules of *tatamae* prohibit one explicitly seeking rewards or professing open expectations of them. Unspoken needs are those which will be fulfilled with successful leader-follower performance. This *honne* is well understood although not by those unaccustomed to the system (Yokochi, 1989a). Even more complicating is the fact that Japanese employees do not differentiate themselves from their supervisors and managers but see all collectively as members of the company. Promotion is from within the organization so that shared common mottos, values, and goals are maintained by workers and management. Pay differentials are small and are decided (along with promotions) not by one's immediate superior but by the amorphous company consistent with its standards, values, history, and traditions. Even more of a problem for the Japanese is management by exception since it is difficult for them to appreciate such a supervisory–subordinate relationship. For them, it would be a matter of custom and tradition for a supervisor to be more concerned about the subordinate.

Leadership in the Multinational Firm

International organizations, both collegial and hierarchical, have been around for a long time. Currently, managers and employees from the world's different nations work together at the United Nations, the World Bank, the World Court, and a host of other international agencies. Among these international organizations, most of the available research on leader-subordinate relations appears in studies of multinational businesses that begin with management and industrial activities in one country and spread to others as they go beyond importing and exporting to manufacturing, marketing, and research in the other countries through subsidiaries organized for these purposes.

The United States dominated the multinational scene in the 1960s. But a dramatic change occurred by the late 1980s, with the rise in the importance of European and Japanese multinational corporations, (MNC's) along with those from the Third World. Regardless of origins, MNC's are becoming truly globalized with shares owned, with components assembled, and with markets, personnel, and research deriving increasingly from many countries.

Is Convergence Occurring?

On the one hand, we have seen, for instance, in the Exxon studies that forecast success as a manager (Laurent, 1970) or the Arab-American homogenization of perceived leadership styles within their multinational firms (Algattan, 1985) that multinational firms are a force for global convergence. At the same time, Hofstede's (1980) research showed that considerable

differences still remained among the different nationals working for IBM.

Nationals of a country may differ in what they do when they are at home and when they go abroad. Thus, Takamiya (1979) observed that Japanese firms in the United States and in Europe were not providing lifetime job security or Japanese-style company welfare programs for their employees. Nonetheless, the Japanese firms abroad were found to be highly productive and to maintain the same high-quality standards that they did at home. The success of the firms appeared to be more a consequence of their attention to production management and high-quality standards than to Japanese-style human relations practices (Hayes, 1981). Pascale and Maguire (1980), following a study of 13 Japanese firms operating in both Japan and the United States, came to similar conclusions. They found that the location of Japanese plants in Japan or the United States was more important to supervisory-subordinate relations than the fact that the management was Japanese. Absenteeism was lower in Japan; more was spent on employee benefits in the United States.

The Multinational Corporations Differ

Likewise, multinational corporations, such as General Motors (United States), L. M. Ericsson (Sweden), Unilever (Britain), Mitsubishi (Japan), and Ciba-Geigy (Switzerland), originating as they did in different countries, vary considerably in their approaches to coordination, the balancing of requirements, decision making, and power relationships (Doz & Prahalad, 1984).

Parent, Host, and Third-Country Nationals

Little has been reported about the specific leader–subordinate relationships of supervisors of one nationality and subordinates of another. They may be operating together at the headquarters in the parent country, in a host country, or in a third country. Either the leader or the subordinate may be a parent-country national (PCN), a host-country national (HCN), or a third-country national (TCN).

Of considerable importance to the leader-subordinate relationship is the multinational firm's organization and methods of decision making. Perlmutter

(1969) saw three possibilities that were likely to have an impact on PCN, HCN, and TCN leadership relations.

- Ethnocentric: The home country is superior to the foreign organization in all respects and all decisions and methods will be controlled by the home country. PCNs monopolize the power and status.
- Polycentric: The organization is host oriented, since foreign cultures are different and local people are able to make the best decisions about the firm's progress. HCNs are more equal in power to PCNs.
- Geocentric: The organization is world oriented, and a balanced view is taken of the local national interests and the objectives of the multinational firm. Managerial positions are filled by people having the most talent, regardless of their national background. TCNs have as much status and power as PCNs and HCNs.

According to Perlmutter, as a multinational organization matures, it moves from ethnocentric to geocentric organizational patterns. Presumably, cultural origins become less significant in the decision-making process with increasing maturity. Ethnocentricity may be maintained longer by Japanese firms. Polycentrism may be the only stage for some service firms such as convenience foods franchises; geocentrism may be reached early in other industries which find comparative advantages in integrating activities in different countries to obtain their financing and supplies, their research, development, and manufacturing, and marketing their products.

Differences in Satisfaction and Valuation. A job satisfaction survey completed by Peter (1969) for Shell, a British-Dutch multinational corporation, illustrates the significance of employees' identification as PCNs, HCNs, or TCNs. Non-Europeans were much more dissatisfied with the company's image than were Europeans. Moreover, among all the nationals, the PCNs, the British and the Dutch, were relatively most satisfied with the company as a place to work and with opportunities to obtain responsibility and authority.

The work location of the managers, their willingness to work abroad, and their experience in working abroad affect their values. Ex-patriates are different from managers who stay home. Yeh (1988) generally could not find Hofstede's patterns in power distance, avoidance of uncertainty, individualism, and masculinity when PCN and TCN managers (63 American and 356 Japanese) were compared with HCN managers (2,237 Taiwanese) working for firms in Taiwan.

Linkage to Uniformity. PCNs and TCNs tend to impose parent-country headquarters' managerial patterns on their host-country peers and subordinates, according to interviews with 248 HCNs and PCNs by Zeira (1975). This finding was corroborated by Al-Jafary and Hollingsworth (1983). Although an Arab organization, as such, would have been expected to operate more autocratically than a U.S. or European multinational firm, among 337 managers of 10 multinational organizations in the Persian Gulf region, both U.S. and Arab managers saw their organizations operating in a Survey of Organizations Systems 3 (consultative) mode and leaning toward Systems 4, an even more participative style.

According to headquarters' PCN personnel directors, multinational uniformity facilitated comparisons of managers in subsidiaries in different countries (Zeira, 1975). Uniformity was also thought to keep up the firm's reputation in different countries and to make it easier to introduce policy changes. HCNs disagreed. A majority thought that PCNs maintain uniformity of policies and practices for their own self-interests. The HCNs believed that the PCNs (and the TCNs) at higher management levels in the local subsidiaries were not motivated to make local improvements and to meet local needs. They thought that the PCNs' insensitivity to the expectations of local HCNs resulted in many conflicts. The HCNs were particularly critical of the tendency of multinational firms to centralize decisions, which makes it impossible to adapt to the needs of the local marketplace. They mistrusted their PCN superiors and believed that their promotion to a higher level was prevented by their not being nationals of the parent country (Zeira, 1975).

PCN Benefits. Because the PCNs are representative of their multinational corporations, they can achieve entry into the upper-class social life of the local communities beyond what they could reach in their previous positions at international headquarters at home. PCNs obtain special benefits as part of their compensation abroad, which makes it possible for them to enjoy a standard of living that is considerably higher than that of their local peers and higher than what they can expect when they return home.

Why PCNs Fail. Despite the extra benefits for working abroad, the failure rates of PCNs are high. Over one-third return from overseas assignments prematurely. Incidents of divorce, alcoholism, and drug abuse are high (Chesanow, 1984). PCNs may experience anxiety over their transfer, a disorientation from culture shock, social dislocation, anxiety about being separated from family and friends, and feelings of having been abandoned by headquarters. They may sense that they lack the necessary influence and local technical assistance. They may have physical problems. Re-entry problems on returning home also need to be faced (Ronen, 1986).

A survey of 105 U.S. multinational firms by Tung (1979) suggested that the most important reasons for a PCN's failure to function effectively in a foreign environment were: (1) the inability of the manager's spouse and family to adjust to a different physical or cultural environment, (2) the manager's inability to adapt to a different physical or cultural environment, (3) the manager's emotional immaturity, (4) the manager's inability to cope with the larger responsibilities posed by the overseas work, (5) the manager's lack of technical competence for the job assignments, and (6) the manager's lack of motivation to work overseas.

Company inattention to proper selection and training of PCNs were particularly important sources of failure. Ratings of the reported rigor of selection, training, and preparation of personnel for overseas assignments correlated $-.63$ with failure rates reported by the 105 firms (Tung, 1979).

PCNs can fail because they erroneously adopt the wrong leadership style for the host country. For instance, probably because of their low estimation of the capabilities and discipline of their Melanesian host employees in Papua New Guinea, an Australian firm adopted a rational-economic, authoritarian, hierarchical leadership approach that was incompatible with tra-

ditional styles of Melanesian leadership. Performance and job satisfaction suffered, and the project had to be abandoned following large sunk costs (Ronen, 1986).

In England, Holland, Belgium, and West Germany, most HCNs felt that to avoid failure, PCNs would need to adapt their leadership style to fit the prevailing pattern in the host country, rather than to emphasize uniformity with the multinational parent country. PCNs need to understand the local nonverbal language and clients' and employees' expectations. A sore point is the larger benefit package often provided the PCN compared to the HCN (Zeira & Banai, 1981).

Suggested Remedial Actions. A survey of 402 corporate employees with overseas experience concluded that selection based on interviews and psychological analyses of the candidates and their families is likely to be more useful in placing employees in foreign assignments than is depending on training alone to provide employees with the means to cope with cultural problems and communication barriers (Dotlich, 1982).

At the same time, a phenomenon that may help PCNs in a foreign assignment is the socialization process, seen in the general tendency to shift attitudes from the norms of the parent country toward the norms of the host country. For example, Lee and Larwood (1983) found that a sample of 33 U.S. ex-patriate managers in Korea shifted significantly closer to the mean of 105 native Korean managers and away from the mean of 74 U.S. managers in the United States in favoring more nonmaterialism, less materialism, more security, less achievement, less competition, more reflectiveness, less activity, and more subjectivity in relationships.

Expatriate managers agreed that the adaptability of families, interpersonal and leadership skills, and technical and language competence are required for the success of PCN managers. They also pointed to the importance of respect for the laws and people of the host country (Gonzalez & Negandhi, 1967; Rubin, Askling, & Kealey, 1977). In a policy-capturing analysis, Russell and Dickinson (1978) identified the factors from 75 attributes found in what it takes to be successful in work in other countries: the acceptability of the assignment to the candidate and the family, skill in interpersonal relations, skill in planning and organizing, and language and technical ability. Thirty-nine upper-middle managers in international divisions of their companies used these factors to judge 60 profiles, half of which were for candidates for jobs in hardship posts, the other half in relatively comfortable foreign assignments. The acceptability of the assignment to the candidate and the family weighed more heavily in the decisions of the 39 managers than all the other factors. Skill in interpersonal relationships weighed more heavily than skill in planning and organizing, proficiency in the language of the host country, and technical ability. Adaptability weighed more heavily than did technical ability and proficiency in the language of the host country.

Staffing with HCNs. A survey of PCN West German male middle managers in a German multinational corporation found them likely to doubt the competence of their HCN subordinates (particularly in Latin America and Europe rather than in the United States) but not of their own peers or supervisors (Miller & Cattaneo, 1982). Consistent with this finding, more HCNs are used in developed countries than in developing countries where qualified HCNs are less readily available. Nevertheless, when efforts are made to locate, select, and train HCNs, dramatic increases can be achieved in the percentage of HCN managers in a developing country, as was illustrated by Nestlé, the Swiss multinational firm, in its Ivory Coast subsidiary (Salmons, 1977).

Multinational firms can attract potentially more productive and accommodating types of HCNs into their ranks than can comparable domestic firms. For example, Vansina and Taillieu (1970) showed that highly task-oriented Flemish business school graduates preferred to work for U.S. or German companies than for their own Belgian organizations.

North American and European multinationals employ HCNs at all levels of management, particularly in developed countries. The reasons for staffing with HCNs include familiarity with the culture, knowledge of the local language, reduced costs, and good public relations (Tung, 1979). TCNs are most likely to be used as a consequence of their competence and technical expertise. PCNs, likewise, are selected for technical competence and are more likely to be used when starting up a foreign enterprise.

Japanese multinationals are most likely to continue to employ PCNs for top- and middle-management positions in their foreign operations (Tung, 1982), in the belief that HCNs or TCNs will not be able to understand, transmit, and maintain the desired organizational culture and policies and communicate easily with the Japanese home office. However, the interest of U.S. multinational corporations in the local employment of HCNs, rather than PCNs, has increased, and their interest in training PCNs for work abroad has decreased. It is uncertain how this change in interest will influence the movement of local HCNs into the headquarters offices and into top management positions (Latham, 1988), but it does suggest that fewer U.S. PCNs will be able to have experience in foreign assignments as they move up the corporate ladder.

Summary and Conclusions

Although internationalization proceeds apace as we become a unified global economy, cultural and national differences continue to have a strong effect on leader-follower relationships. Countries and cultures can be clustered to provide the bases for useful classifications.

The cultural dimensions of consequence to leadership in a given society include traditionalism, particularism, collectivism, and idealism compared to the valuing of modernity, universalism, individualism, and pragmatism. In the same way, the needs for achievement, affiliation, and the power of subordinates and supervisors have different effects on leader-follower relations in different cultures.

Although some argue that there is one best way to manage, considerable evidence points to the greater effectiveness of autocratic leadership behavior in authoritarian cultures and of democratic leadership behavior in democratic cultures. The same is seen for direction versus participation, task orientation versus relations orientation, and initiation versus consideration.

Within the multinational firm, leader-subordinate relations will be affected by whether the firm is ethnocentric, polycentric, or geocentric and whether the individuals involved are from the parent country of the organization, the host country, or a third country. The success rate of PCNs in foreign assignments can be improved considerably by attention to their assessment and training.

Improving Leadership and Leadership Research

Development, Education, and Training for Leadership and Management

"**A**re leaders born or made?" has been the age-old question. Indeed, one's genes contribute to one's intelligence and activity levels, which, we have seen, are associated with leadership. Childhood experiences make their mark as well on one's facility with language, which is also of consequence to leadership. To some extent, leaders are "born" and developed at an early age. But, at the same time, much can be done with their development, education, and training to "make" them leaders. To understand the performance of a leader requires an examination of his or her family background, early childhood development, and educational and role models, along with the social and political learning experiences, informal and formal, that the person encounters as an adult that shapes his or her performance as a leader.

Differences in individual development formed the basis of a theory of transformational leadership by Kuhnert and Lewis (1987), who suggested that such leadership reflects the mature adult development of personal standards and transcendental values in the leader. In contrast, those who pursue only transactional approaches have been arrested at lower levels of development that are built around their own immediate needs, feelings, and interpersonal connections.

Developmental Issues

Chapter 31 pointed to the persistence of leadership tendencies from childhood to adolescence and from adolescence to adulthood. This chapter looks at the factors that contribute to such persistence.

Family Influences

Cox's (1926) study of 300 eminent historical personages noted the appearance among them in childhood of intelligence, self-confidence, assertiveness, and orientation toward achievement. Likewise, Barton (1984) noted that as children, those who subsequently became community leaders displayed greater-than-ordinary role diversity, flexibility in dealing with others, and other signs of leadership potential.

Each girl in H. H. Jennings's (1943) sociometric analysis[1] was asked to describe the different members of her family and to name the member whom she most closely resembled. The leaders (in terms of sociometric choice and offices held) were found to identify themselves with the member of the family whom they described as sociable, reliable, and encouraging. Nonleaders identified themselves with the family members who they said tended to express discouragement, anxiety, and worry.

Childhood and adolescent relationships at home result in tendencies to emerge as a leader during these formative years. Of possible significance are birth order, family size, and parental treatment.

Birth Order. Some studies, such as Day's (1980) analysis of promotion among 116 health care professionals, found that being either firstborn or last born was conducive to advancement compared to being born in between. To explain such results, theorists attributed different personality developments to the eldest and youngest children and those born in between.

[1]See Chapter 11 for more details.

Compared with his or her siblings, the oldest child in a family was thought to be less dominant, less aggressive, less self-confident, and less inclined toward leadership because of the inexperience and insecurity of the parents with their firstborn child and the need for the oldest child to adjust from an only-child family to a family in which attention toward children is divided (Goodenough & Leahy, 1927). Nonetheless, the firstborn has the advantage of more early interaction with adults and adult language. As was noted in Chapter 33, the firstborn are also likely to be given family responsibilities earlier and are expected to mature faster. In comparison with their siblings, youngest children were reported to be more disobedient, more persistent, and more likely to be pampered and helped when help was no longer necessary, as well as disregarded when family or personal decisions were to be made (Hurlock, 1950). In all, taken by itself, it would seem that birth order may or may not make a difference, depending on other aspects of family life, such as the family's income, parental expectations, a full-time working mother, and so on. In low-income families or families with working mothers, the firstborn, particularly, girls, tend to be given considerable responsibilities early on for caring for their siblings.

Size of the Family. Maller (1931) found that the tendency of a child to work in a group for a group goal, rather than alone for an individual prize, is greatest among children with three or four siblings and is less among children of smaller or larger families. Cooperativeness was rated highest among these children from families with the optimal number of children, but persistence was greatest among children from the larger families.

Treatment by Parents. Jane Addams, Champ Clark (an American politician), Clara Barton, the Mayo Brothers, William E. Gladstone, Robert E. Lee, Woodrow Wilson, Benjamin Franklin, and George Washington are among the many historical leaders whose lives illustrate the significance of either a mother or father in determining the career of the future leader (Bogardus, 1934). Among more recent political leaders, parents had a strong positive influence on the development as leaders of Charles de Gaulle, Franklin D.

Roosevelt, Douglas MacArthur, Harry Truman, Winston Churchill, Dwight D. Eisenhower, and Jimmy Carter.

A comparison of children reared in orphanages with children reared by parents suggested the importance of parental interaction or the lack of it. H. H. Anderson (1937) found that nursery school children who were living with their parents interacted more with others and initiated and attempted more leadership than did children from a nursery in an orphanage.

B. M. Bishop (1951) noted that when interacting with a neutral adult, children tend to transfer to the new situation the pattern of interaction they have developed with their mothers. If their mothers are directive, interfering, and critical, the children tend to be inhibited, reluctant, or noncooperative in their interactions with others. If negativism and rebellion against authority are fostered in interactions with parents, they will be reflected in aggressive behavior against others, such as fighting, threatening, and boasting. Or they may result in a withdrawal into fantasy. The normal, maturing child can accept parental and school authority and is cooperative with his or her family and teachers (L. B. Murphy, 1947).

Children from homes in which the children participate in decisions were found by A. L. Baldwin (1949) to be more active, socially outgoing, intelligent, curious, original, constructive, and domineering. C. T. Meyer (1947) concluded that sociability and cooperativeness were greater when parents were clear and consistent, explained decisions to their children, offered opportunities for decision making, had rapport with their children, and better understood their children's problems.

Overprotective parents who deny their children opportunities to experience risks and mistakes commensurate with their maturity seem to restrict their children's development. Such children may exhibit, as adults, irresponsibility, carelessness, overconfidence, and other characteristics that are likely to interfere with their success as leaders. Experiences of success and failure that promote the learning of social skills, of what can and cannot be done in most groups, are missed by such children.

Parents who neglect or ignore their children create a pattern of behavior in children that is also likely to interfere with their leadership potential (except possibly in an antisocial group such as a group of delinquents). Such children often exhibit symptoms like stealing, lying, cruelty, and other attention-getting behavior. Rejected children are often distrustful, are strongly motivated to seek praise, and feel persecuted and indulge in self-pity (Bass, 1960).

Conflicting demands by the mother and father promote behavior in the children that is detrimental to the children's effective and successful interaction with others. The most nervous behavior in children occurs when parents issue conflicting negative demands. Disobedience is greatest when parents issue conflicting positive demands (Meyers, 1944). Consistency from parents and the high standards set by them may be important clues to the early development of future leaders.

Parents as Models. W. A. Anderson (1943) showed that parents' leadership behavior was a model for their children. In a rural New York area, Anderson found that the social participation of an individual is a family tendency. If the father participated, so did the mother. If both participated, the children usually did also. But, Bass (1954a) was unable to find significance between college students' success as leaders in initially leaderless discussions and the extent to which each of their parents had been considerate of them or had initiated interactions with them when they were children.

To add to what was said in the preceding chapter about the importance of socioeconomic background to the emergence of leaders in different countries, the father's occupation and background make a distinct difference in whether their sons emerge as loyalist political leaders, such as Ngo Dinh Diem, Fulgencio Batista, Lazaro Cárdenas, and Jacques Necker, or revolutionary political leaders, such as Ho Chi Minh, Fidel Castro, Pancho Villa, or Maximilien Robespierre.[2] A comparison of 50 loyalist leaders with 50 revolutionary leaders by Rejai and Phillips (1988) found that the loyalists's fathers were much more likely than the revolutionaries' fathers to have been governmental of-

[2]Loyalists, in the sense used here, were those leaders who were best known for their efforts to maintain old unreconstructed regimes. Revolutionaries were those leaders who were best known for their efforts to overthrow the old regimes.

ficials, military officers, bankers, industrialists, professionals, or members of the landed gentry.

Single Parenting: The Importance of a Strong Mother. In the late 1980s, about 25 percent of American children are being raised by one parent, in 90 percent of the cases, the mother who is divorced or never been married. The divorced or unwed father may still play an important amicable role, but one may speculate that if single parenthood results in a strong mother and an absent father, the pattern replicates the family conditions that gave rise to many prominent world-class leaders whose fathers were weak, absent, or died early. The importance of maternal authority was noted in Chapter 32 (Bronfenbrenner, 1961). Dominating mothers whose sons remain attracted and close to them figured in the lives of Franklin Delano Roosevelt, Douglas MacArthur, Winston Churchill, and many others. Consistent with this, interviews with 30 chief executive officers (CEOs) who were selected because of their success as business leaders found that they tended to have strong role models. Most of the time, these role models were their mothers (Piotrowski & Armstrong, 1987). Freud was quoted as saying: "A man who has been the indisputable favorite of his mother keeps for life the feeling of a conqueror, that confidence of success that often induces real success" (Jones, 1953, p. 5).

Parental Standards. Day's (1980) compared 58 health care professionals who were promoted and 58 who were not. Those who were promoted were much more likely to express a recurring theme in interviews about having had a family background that emphasized a strong work ethic. Gibbons's (1986) in-depth interview with transformational and transactional managers found that the transformational executives were much more likely to describe parents who set high educational standards and who provided a family life that was neither extremely lavish nor extremely disadvantaged. And in the just-mentioned study of 30 CEOs, Piotrowski and Armstrong (1987) found that of those who discussed their childhood, most said that they had favorable family conditions during childhood and adolescence. In line with these findings, Hall (1983) observed that charismatic leaders were given more responsibilities as children and felt a lot of respect from their elders. As may be seen most clearly with Charles de Gaulle's childhood, conviction, ideology, and the need to restore *la gloire de la France* were instilled in him by his early family life just after the ignominious defeat of France by the Prussians in 1870. The values and goals of the future French leader were strongly affected for life (Hoffman & Hoffman, 1970).

Leadership was more likely to be displayed by elementary school boys whose parents instilled high standards as well as granted responsibilities and scope for independent action to their sons (Hoffman, Rosen, & Lippitt, 1960). Consistent with this finding, Klonsky (1983) noted that occupants of leadership positions on boys' teams had parents who made more demands for achievement and provided more discipline accompanied by more maternal warmth. Girls who became team leaders were given more responsibilities by their families but less parental warmth.

Parental ambitions may also direct the child toward social success and influence. A family atmosphere of high-quality relationships with parents and siblings also makes a difference (Bass, 1960). Leaders are more likely to make the transition into adolescence without the pains of separation from family, without a sense of becoming isolated, and without the need to compensate for feelings of helplessness (Levinson & Rosenthal, 1984).

Opportunities in Childhood and Adolescence

Murphy (1947) suggested that an adult's performance in groups was likely to be affected by his or her security or anxiety that was developed in relations experienced with other children during the school years. Of consequence to the emergence of democratic or authoritarian tendencies is the respect for individuals fostered by school and residential areas, frustration or happiness in peer groups, and feelings of being respected or excluded from school and social groups.

Practice in leadership is afforded by school and outside activities. Such experiences enhance a person's esteem in solving problems with other members of the group. They provide opportunities to interact with the opposite sex in a socially approved manner and enable the individual to learn more about following, coopera-

tion, competition, and leading others. Adolescence affords the developing leader the opportunity to learn to change his or her behavior as situational demands change to maintain success and effectiveness in interactions with others. Social proficiencies, learned during adolescence, can foster an individual's success in interacting with others as an adult. Social and athletic proficiencies may make a difference in an adolescent's success as an adult leader, depending on the adult environment. Again, the social graces, etiquette, and grooming learned in childhood and adolescence may prove significant. Finally, experiences in extracurricular activities and dating afford opportunities to practice and transfer leadership and to see the success or failure of different attempts to lead (Bass, 1960). Gibbons's transformational managers had a lot of experience as leaders in high school and college. Likewise Hall (1983) noted that charismatic leaders reported more childhood experiences as leaders. Such extracurricular experiences in high school tend to predict subsequent leadership activities in college and in military academies (Yammarino & Bass, 1989a). Again, participation in varsity spots in the naval academy is predictive of subsequent success as a naval officer (Atwater & Yammarino, 1989).

Parents' and teachers' guidance and enlarging of responsibilities can be important to the developing leader. The encouragement of intellectual self-exploration and increasing equalization of power relations with parents and teachers will also contribute (Bass, 1960).

Marginality. After examining the childhood environment of 15 twentieth-century world-class charismatic leaders, Willner (1968) concluded that almost all were socially and psychologically at the margins of several classes, religions, or ethnic affiliations. For example, Kemal Atatürk, the founding father of modern Turkey, grew up at the borders of the Christian Greek and Moslem Turkish cultures. The 15 leaders were also likely to have plural identifications that gave them multiple perspectives, a more flexible view of society, and ways of communicating and responding more convincingly and empathically to a broader spectrum of people. This heterogeneity in background was likely to be augmented by a wider range of experience, by the mobility of the family, and by the exposure to various environments during childhood and adolescence.

Advantaged Childhood. Children from higher-class family backgrounds also were likely to have a wider range of experiences. Prior to the advent of universal education and class mobility, upper- and middle-class family backgrounds were ordinarily requisite for the emergence of leaders even of the proletariat. As was concluded in Chapter 4, socioeconomic status contributes to one's emergence as a leader, and, as was noted in the last chapter, the middle and upper classes generally provide a majority of the world's future managers. Until recently, America's labor leaders seldom came from working-class backgrounds. Leaders of the "workers'" revolutions, from Lenin to Castro, came from middle-class, not working-class or peasant backgrounds. Orlans (1953) observed that many of our great presidents (Washington, Jefferson, and both Roosevelts) tended to come from an aristocratic class, from a background that provided them with a great deal of opportunity to examine and evaluate new ideas, as well as the freedom to pursue a political career.

Educational Issues

Illustrating the shaping of future leaders was Britain's educational system. The leaders and administrative officials of the British Empire at its zenith received from their public schools, such as Eton and Harrow, a general education in self-discipline, team work, and group loyalty that created an aura of command and habits of superiority with "a facade of crisp decisiveness." Their classical education included nothing about modern science, technology, modern languages, or the social sciences. Little attention was paid to innovation and creativity, but a skill and capacity for social role taking, coupled with a sense of self-esteem and a need for achievement, were sufficient to make for reasonably effective leaders and officials for the world arena (Burns, 1978).

The 1,200 members of the Indian Civil Service, most of them British, were of this elite. Their public school and university education had imbued them with a con-

tempt for money making and corruption, pride in the ideals of fair play, open justice, and the duty to make improvements and to maintain an efficient and properly recorded administration. "They were Plato's guardians—a caste apart, bred and trained to be superior" (Lapping, 1985). But they also were handicapped by the class consciousness instilled in them by family and schooling. A good percentage of British leaders still originate from the same public schools (D. P. Boyd, 1974).

Secondary Education

Large-scale efforts to provide leadership training for high school students have been conducted by the American Management Association, the Center for Creative Leadership, the 4H program, and other organizations that are interested in the development of young people.

It was among educators in primary and secondary school settings that evaluative research on leadership education first appeared. For example, Fretwell (1919) gave elected leaders in junior high school responsibility for managing athletic and playground activities. A leadership club was formed to plan and discuss the activities. Fretwell concluded that such experience provided opportunities for leadership and initiative. In the same way, Mayberry (1925) observed that participation in the student government provided training in social purpose, initiative, and cooperation.[3]

A number of controlled experiments were completed. For example, Eichler and Merrill (1933) asked each member of high school classes to rate each other on leadership. Experimental and control groups were paired on the basis of the ratings. Experimental groups were given lectures on leadership methods or participated in discussions about leadership. New ratings were collected. The experimental groups gained more than the control groups in such ratings of leadership, but not to a significant degree. Similarly, G. G. Thompson (1944) studied nursery school children under two programs. In one, the teacher acted in an impersonal manner and gave help only when needed. In the sec-

---

[3]For other early examples, see E. W. Hastings (1926), Lavoy (1928), G. C. Meyers (1923), A. M. Nash (1927), and E. L. Thorndike (1916).

ond, the teacher took an active part in play and helped the children to adjust to each other. The children in the second group showed significant gains in ascendance, social participation, and leadership.

McCandless (1942) studied two cottages of boys in a training school. Both began with adult supervisors, but the experimental cottage became self-governing. Sociometric ratings of intermember popularity were highly correlated with dominance at the beginning. Four months later, the most dominant boys lost in popularity in the experimental cottage, but not in the control cottage.

Zeleny (1940b) compared recitation and group discussion as methods of teaching sociology. Students in the discussion classes gained more in dominance and sociability than did those in the recitation classes and recorded slightly higher gains in knowledge of the subject. Again, Zeleny (1941, 1950) gave student leaders instruction in techniques of leadership and guided practice in the use of these techniques. Students found the training interesting and thought that it helped them adapt better to the social demands made on them.

More recently, an unusual educational effort has focused on gifted children to help them to perform better as leaders. Familiarity with the characteristics of leaders, creativity, and divergent thinking are followed by role playing, observing, and analyzing the leadership of others. Then comes practice in exercises and real-life leadership experiences (Black, 1984).

Higher Education

Education for leadership is seen as being of major importance in higher education. Cleveland (1980) argued that "equipping minds for leadership ought to be what's 'higher' about higher education." According to the results of a survey,

> between 500 and 600 campuses are paying attention to developing their students as leaders, either in the classroom or in extracurricular activities and programs. The extracurricular activities often originate either in a student development office or in direct student initiative. The academic courses may be loosely divided into two categories: those that draw mainly on social psychological and management

studies literature, the traditional homes of leadership studies; and liberal arts academic courses that place the study of leadership in the context of both the humanities and social sciences. . . . (Spitzberg, 1987, p. 4)

Many methods are applied.[4] At the College of Wooster, in addition to formal course work, students spend 3 to 5 days observing national leaders on the job. A consortium of universities in North Carolina conducts a fellows program that included summer internships and attendance at an annual leadership training program at the Center for Creative Leadership. Mentoring programs are provided at the University of California at Irvine. The ethical responsibilities of leadership are stressed in a sequence of courses at the University of San Diego (Spitzberg, 1987). The doors will open in 1992 on an integrated four-year undergraduate leadership studies program in the newly formed Jepson School of Leadership at the University of Richmond. Gardner (1987a) has laid out a leadership development program for community colleges.

The U.S. military academies invest a considerable amount of their cadets' and midshipmen's years in education for leadership. Students begin by learning to work effectively in highly disciplined subordinate roles before being given positions of increasing leadership responsibility. These opportunities for leadership are experienced in their campus lives and in summer field and sea settings. These experiences add to the formal study of the subject, observational study, self-study, and reflections. The students' development as leaders is appraised periodically and feedback is provided for remedial efforts (Katz, 1987; Prince, 1987).

Increasingly, U.S. business schools are providing education in leadership and related behavior and skills to increase the students' capacity to exert personal influence, to make proper use of power, to motivate others, to negotiate and mediate effectively, and to take initiatives. The American Assembly of Collegiate Schools of Business completed a ten-year project to assist schools of management in programmatic efforts in this regard (Zoffer, 1985). Orpen (1982) showed that MBAs had achieved a higher level of position and salary after five

---

[4]For more details about curricula and programs, see Clark, Freeman, and Britt (1987).

years than had a matched sample of non-MBAs, but whether the credentials of the education that is associated with the degree are of consequence remain unknown.

A college degree, a college education, and socioeconomic status are likely to be confounded in their effects on the subsequent emergence of persons in managerial and leadership positions. Nevertheless, there is value in the actual education beyond just being identified as a college graduate. In the Management Progress Study (Bray, Campbell, & Grant, 1974), 274 college graduates who had been hired for first-level management jobs at A T & T and 148 who had been hired without college degrees participated in a 3-day assessment center. The college graduates were judged by the assessors to have a higher potential for middle management. After 20 years, the modal college graduate had reached the third level of management, but the modal noncollege graduate had reached only the second level of management. Furthermore, those who had come from better-rated colleges were at a higher level of management at A T & T (Howard, 1986). This finding was consistent with a correlation of .32 between the ranking of the universities from which 80 Japanese graduates came and the appraisals for their potential for promotion that they received after 3 years (Wakabayashi & Graen, 1984).

Continuing Adult Education and Development

Education for leadership occurs in the context of the current stage of development in which the leader is found. On the basis of analogies from developmental learning over the adult life cycle, Bryson and Kelley (1978) suggested that leaders go through stages. Ideally, a developmental learning process occurs in which capacities and skills that are gained in one stage should prepare the adult leader for new and bigger tasks and responsibilities in later stages. One should learn to be a leader by receiving appropriate feedback while serving as a leader; one should be promoted to higher levels of leadership responsibilities because of one's past performance as a leader and one's promise of future performance.

The development of executives is a logical progression over time. The nature of this progression and how

to manage it needs to be understood. The progression of abilities needs to be specified. There should be a conceptual linkage between leadership at lower levels of an organization and at more senior levels. The executive's development can be conceived of as a process of acquiring successively more complex cognitive maps and other necessary competencies over time. As the skills required for successful operation at a higher level are accumulated, the executive becomes ready to move to that level (Jacobs & Jaques, 1987). However, there may be innate limits on the conceptual and cognitive skills that can be developed through education and experience.

Paradoxically, the additional power that accrues with rising status in the organization may increasingly inhibit continued learning. Rising power may bring about reduced negative feedback from colleagues. It may also bring about the greater monopolization of discussions and decisions by the leader, the induction of fear in others from the leader's aura of power, the distancing of relationships with others, isolation from below, and exemption from appraisal by others. All these problems can be avoided by the rising executive conscious of them and their effects (Kaplan, Drath, & Kofodimos, 1985).

Technical and professional competence often tend to be valued over competence as a supervisor and a leader. The successful engineer who moves into a management position or the successful teacher who becomes a school principal continues to focus on the technical aspects of the work to be done and does poorly in getting his or her colleagues to function at their full potential (Kotter, 1985b). Nevertheless, subsequent progress in management appears to be much more a matter of general higher education than specialization in business, engineering, social science, or the humanities. For example, little difference in the level achieved after 20 years at A T & T was found among those who entered the firm with different educational majors (Howard, 1986). Although engineering majors earn higher grades than do nonengineering majors while they are midshipmen at Annapolis, they do not appear to perform any better as leaders when they subsequently serve as naval officers (Yammarino & Bass, 1989).

The importance of travel to the career development

and personal change in political leaders has been overlooked. When Rejai and Phillips (1988) contrasted 50 loyalist political leaders with 50 revolutionaries, they found that travel reinforced the politicization of the loyalists that was begun at home and at school. However, for the revolutionaries, travel was radicalizing and transforming and helped them to develop standards against which to measure their own countries. This was especially evident in 1989 in the People's Republic of China. However, travel may become of less consequence in a world linked by television.

Career Issues

Individual and Organizational Alignment

The education and development of adult leaders requires the combined efforts of the individual and the organization. The development of adult leaders is largely a matter of self-development abetted by opportunities provided by the organization. Both individual motivation and organizational stimulation are involved in the avoidance of managerial and professional obsolescence. The individual's need for achievement and opportunities for organizational participation were the 2 most important among 12 possible determinants for avoiding obsolescence, according to a survey of 451 U.S. Air Force officers and civilian personnel (Shearer & Steger, 1975). To avoid obsolescence Shearer and Steger deemed experience to be more important for managers and continuing education more important for professionals. Managers also need to maintain clear perspectives about their organization. For instance, those who work in senior civil service positions in the government must understand the historical, social, and political context of their jobs. The Federal Executive Institute places a heavy emphasis on this objective (Wood, 1985).

Careers need to fit purposes that are aligned with the organization's strategic direction. At the same time, managers should be flexible in the face of shifts in opportunities and conditions. Such flexibility includes tentative choices and evaluations that are subject of revision, multiple small careers at low levels, few plateaus, continued new challenging assignments, tak-

ing risks, and experiencing small failures (Gaertner, 1988).

Career Planning. Effective career planning is interactive. Career development is enhanced by the joint efforts of the developing leader to remain resilient in the face of adversity and by the organization to encourage such resilience by feedback and positive reinforcement. The developing leader needs career resilience, career insight, and career identity, which are furthered by creating and implementing a vision of his or her future in the context of expectations about the organization's future. Contingency plans are needed to maintain flexibility (London, 1985). Thus, those 77 middle managers who were judged by a higher-level committee to be more adaptive to changing role demands demonstrated more openness to different ideas and used simpler decision-making processes than did those who were judged to be less adaptive. They were higher in self-esteem and presumably more likely to attempt leadership (Morrison, 1977).

Expectations reflect promotion to higher levels or the failures to do so. For example, the expectations of all 270 managers whose careers at A T & T were studied over 20 years, measured annually, declined sharply during the first 5 years of employment. However, after the fifth year, the expectations of those who subsequently attained fourth- to sixth-level executive positions at the end of the 20-year period turned around and began a steady movement upward. The expectations of those who attained only third-level positions after 20 years remained about the same after the fifth year, while the expectations of those who ended their 20 years at the first or second levels of management continued to decline steadily after the fifth year (Howard & Bray, 1988).

Leader-Subordinate Relations

The prospective leader's behavior develops in concert with those who are directly above or below him or her in the hierarchy. The leader may develop different interlocking behavior with each of his or her subordinates. Along with a general normative relationship, roles played by both will be worked out for designated situations (Graen, 1976). The quality of this leader-member exchange early in one's career contributes to one's successful movement up the corporate ladder later on. Early promotion is an important predictor of future success (E. H. Schein, 1985).

Of particular consequence will be the latitude granted subordinates, the leader's support of the subordinates' activities, and the leader's attention to the subordinates' development (Graen & Cashman, 1975). Challenging assignments provided early contribute to one's success at subsequent stages of one's career as a manager (Vicino & Bass, 1978). For instance, Bray and Howard (1983) found that only 30 percent of the college recruits at A T & T who were predicted to reach middle management actually attained it 8 years later if they had not experienced a challenging job early on. Of those who had been predicted to fail to reach middle management, 61 percent attained it if they had experienced a more challenging job earlier.

The exchange develops into a role relationship that may rigidify or be flexible, depending on a variety of individual and organizational factors. Some people engage in role-making experiences; others do not. The quality of the relationships becomes even more important to one's success in a career than one's initially tested ability. According to a 13-year panel study by Wakabayashi and Graen (1984) of 85 Japanese college graduates, those who had higher-quality vertical exchange relationships in their first 3 years of employment, as reflected in their speed of promotion and bonuses, were most likely to demonstrate greater progress at 7 and 13 years of employment. Those with a lower tested ability on entrance to their firms could make up for it in their advancement by early higher-quality dyadic relationships.

Career Paths

In some kinds of organizations, only one route is open. One must enter at the bottom to climb to the top. For example, entry into the military officer corps requires admission and graduation from a military academy, ROTC, or an officers' candidate school. Promotion is from within; the direct transfer from civilian life to a high-level position in the military is not possible (except during wartime). Career paths in business and industry are much less circumscribed. As was noted in Chapters 32 and 33, women and ethnic minorities who become senior managers are less likely to come up through the ranks of line management and are more likely to emerge into top management from staff, technical, or professional careers inside or outside the organization.

Union leaders can come from the rank and file, from staff professional service, or directly from the outside (Schwartz & Hoyman, 1984). Educational leaders ordinarily begin as teachers. Loyalists leaders were much more likely than were revolutionary leaders to have been employed early on in governmental service, according to Rejai and Phillips's (1988) analysis of 100 political figures.

Currently, voters pay little attention to the job experience of candidates for the most important job in the world, president of the United States. Although candidates talk much about it, voters are more attentive to the emotional uplift provided by the candidates. Nonetheless, presidents who have experience as state governors tend to earn higher ratings for their performance as leaders and crisis managers than do those who have served as vice presidents. (This conclusion, however, did not help Michael Dukakis, governor of Massachusetts, defeat George Bush, vice president, in the 1988 presidential election.)

Mobility of Managers. Better opportunities elsewhere may cause people to change careers. Thus, whether U.S. Air Force officers intended to remain in service or become civilians depended on how attractive they viewed civilian life and how oriented they were toward their occupation (O'Connell, 1986). Or, personnel may become alienated from their current organizational and professional responsibilities as a consequence of violated and unmet expectations; the loss of satisfaction with colleagues; and changes in their own beliefs, interests, values, and maturation (Korman, Wittig-Berman, & Lang, 1981).

Mobility is valued. Managers measure their success in terms of their rate of mobility and fear stagnation if they remain too long in one position (Veiga, 1981). But mobility may be deterred as well for many individual and organizational reasons. Older people may feel less mobile and more concerned about their job security (J. Hall, 1976). They are likely to perceive themselves as less marketable. Company benefits that cannot be transferred will hamper the consideration of job changes (Albrook, 1967). Community ties also inhibit one from moving away, which may be required when one changes jobs. In the same way, other deterrents to geographic mobility are a spouse's career requirements and children's educational needs. Thus, Veiga (1983) studied the mobility of 1,216 managers from 3 manufacturing firms. The average time the managers spent in a particular position, as expected, was affected by their own perceived marketability, the value of company benefits, the importance of job security, and somewhat less by their and their families' ties to their communities. Dissatisfaction with their current position, as expected, increased the managers' willingness to consider changing employers. Likewise, in a study of 283 managers by Campion and Mitchell (1986), such dissatisfaction predicted the managers' resignation from managerial positions and from the organization. But quitting was also predicted by the lack of socialization into the firm, the lack of adjustment, unmet job expectations, and being under more stress. With a survey of almost 4,000 U.S. Air Force personnel, a good percentage of whom were noncommissioned officers, Watson (1986) showed that both opportunities elsewhere and commitment to the U.S. Air Force were important. The lack of commitment and the availability of civilian opportunities together correlated .74 with thoughts of leaving the air force and searching elsewhere. The lack of commitment and thoughts of leaving combined to correlate .79 with intentions to leave the air force, and these intentions correlated .71 with actual quitting.

Mount (1984) surveyed 483 managers of a multinational corporation who were working in the same metropolitan area about their job satisfaction and whether they were establishing their career, were advancing in it, or were maintaining a well-established career. Managers who were getting established were more satisfied than were those who were further along in their careers. This lesser satisfaction may be one reason for changing careers. For example, engineers who are seeking more important and better paying positions shift into line management or become responsible for train-ing, quality control, or research; the change ordinarily is a promotion within the same organization (Bain, 1985). They are more likely to switch into management if they have entrepreneurial, affiliative, and assertive interests; they are less likely to switch if they have strong investigative and artistic interests (Sedge, 1985).

Careerism

Managers who were on a career plateau (a long period without promotion) were found to have timed their career moves less adequately than did those who did not experience such plateaus (Veiga, 1981). For the highly ambitious, it is argued, career development is enhanced by the ability to move within three to four years into different areas of management and leadership in different organizations. Such mobility is seen to pay off in more rapid advancement to higher organizational levels. For the ambitious, concern for career advancement takes precedence over their loyalty and commitment to their currént organization (Feldman, 1985). Such careerism is a serious threat to organizational effectiveness. Feldman sees in it anticipatory dissatisfaction with jobs that do not contribute to the advancement of one's career, the lack of involvement in one's job and loyalty to one's organization, increased job turnover, inauthentic interpersonal relationships, and absorption in self-interests.

Career Failures. Careerism may result in fast-track rapid promotions and short-term job assignments but derailment later at higher levels because of failure to develop one's competencies and power to perform at higher levels of management and to align one's self-interests with the needs of the organization (Kovach, 1986). According to a comparison by their superiors of 86 successful senior managers and 83 who had been derailed, Lombardo, Ruderman, and McCauley (1987) found that the termination of career advancement was seen to be due to personal flaws that did not show up quickly as the fast tracker moved from one assignment to another but became visible only when higher-level complexities were faced. These managers may not have been politically astute, able to think strategically, or able to make high-quality decisions in the face of ambiguous conditions, or they may have lacked leadership competencies. Also, the derailed managers were more likely to be abrasive, to be untrustworthy, and to be unstable. Early remedial action, feedback, coaching, and mentoring might have helped some of those who were sidetracked. Along with personal development, haphazard, short job-hopping needs to be discouraged. Instead systematic moves are needed to increase one's experience in different aspects of the organization with successive broadening increases in responsibility lasting up to two years (Reibstein, 1986).

Costs to the Organization. Careerism among its personnel can lay a heavy burden on organizations, in both the private and public sectors. For example, careerism was seen by Hauser (1984) to degrade the effectiveness of the U.S. military services. In peacetime, there is an absence of lateral entry from higher-level civilian positions into the military, which results in a shortage of credible challenges to whatever is the conventional wisdom in the military. Careers tend to be short. The ideal officer is a generalist, not a specialist. Transfers are frequent; advancement is rapid for many. Coupled with early retirement, the transitory aspects of military careers contribute to conformity and the avoidance of risks. These tendencies are further reinforced by the military's centralization of evaluation and "whole man" concepts of promotion.

Value of Training

The widespread belief in training was noted by Alpander (1986) who found that over 80 percent of the first-level supervisors in 155 Fortune 500 companies are asked to attend in-house training programs of 1 to 4 hours at least once a year; 75 percent, programs that last 5 to 12 hours; and 37 percent, programs that last 13 to 40 hours. Almost all the supervisors participate in such a longer program at least once in 5 years.

Without taking the trouble to examine the available research, critics continue to argue that leadership training lacks theoretical or empirical grounding; is seldom evaluated; and is faddish, depending more on faith than on facts (Rice, 1988). Following a comprehensive review, Latham (1988, p. 574) strongly disagreed:

The scientific leadership training literature is not dominated by fads.... [S]elf-regulation techniques,

Leader Match, role motivation theory, LMX, and double-loop learning have been systematically evaluated for more than a decade, and their evaluation is on-going.... these leadership training programs are grounded in theory; ... the training programs have been subject to repeated investigations; and ... the training has been evaluated empirically. Many of the evaluations included follow-up data collected from three months to five years subsequent to the training. Moreover, the dependent variables for evaluating the training programs included observable behaviors.

Numerous scientific comparisons of trained and untrained managers have been completed to ascertain the extent to which the trained but not the untrained managers changed their attitudes and behaviors, used what they learned, and contributed to more effective operations of their organization. Nevertheless, it may be that the perception of little available evaluation of leadership training is due to the large amount of training that occurs and the extent to which most such training is evaluated cursorily by asking the trainees how satisfied they were with the experience. So, although the number of actual published research comparisons is large, it seems small in contrast to the actual amount of training that is provided. The large body of published research provides confidence in the theoretical underpinnings and factual substantiation of the conclusions reached. We have come a long way from the earliest reports of leadership training in industry and the armed services that were primarily statements about the value of leadership training, descriptions of programs, and discussions of problems.[5] A review of important evaluative studies will be presented later.

Assessing Needs

For convenience, I will first concentrate on the processes and techniques that are applied to training and education for leadership and then will consider the contents and purposes of such training. Whatever the education or training effort, its effectiveness in improv-

[5]See, for instance, Dietz (1943), W. T. Foster (1929), Greenly and Mapel (1943), MacKechnie (1944), McFeely and Mussmann (1945), and R. S. Miller (1943).

ing leadership performance depends first on identifying what needs improvement and then on demonstrating or helping the trainee or student discover how to change his or her perceptions, cognitions, attitudes, and behavior. Experiences must be provided in which the trainee can exhibit the appropriate leadership and instructors, observers, and other trainees can give the trainee feedback about the adequacy and effects of the trainee's efforts (Bass & Vaughan, 1966). But much hinges on the correct identification of the trainee's need for training or education. Moreover, there are two other necessary prelearning conditions, namely the trainee's desire to know and the trainee's sense of role (Akin, 1987).

Top-down and Bottom-up Approaches. The assessment of needs can be initiated in the organization from the top down or from the bottom up. An illustrative top-down approach began with informal meetings with the senior management to identify the training and developmental needs of British social work managers. Priorities were then established among the 15 identified skills by the 66 managers below them. Sharp differences had to be taken into account between the openness of the subordinate managers and their superiors (Leigh, 1983). An illustrative bottom-up approach began in a large Texas Human Resources agency with a survey of 636 subordinates' evaluations of the supervisory styles of their immediate superiors. From these evaluations, a plan for improved supervision was extracted (Russell, Lankford, & Grinnell, 1984).

The importance of using both superiors' and subordinates' assessments of needs was seen in a survey of approximately 7,000 first- and second-level white- and blue-collar supervisors that found the supervisors to be overly confident about their own human relations skills (Bittel & Ramsey, 1983). (Supervisors have biased perceptions of their leadership consideration; subordinates' descriptions tend not to be as favorable as the supervisors' self-descriptions [Weissenberg & Kavanagh, 1972; Bass & Yammarino, 1989].) At the same time, the supervisors were much less confident about how well they could stimulate the improvement of productivity.

Training officers differ considerably about the ap-

propriate source of the assessment of their needs—their higher-ups or their subordinates. The previously mentioned 155 training officers in different Fortune 500 companies were surveyed by Alpander (1986) concerning the training needs of first-line supervisors. A third of the respondents thought that the need of a given supervisor for training should be decided by his or her immediate boss; 18 percent, felt the decision should be made by higher-ups; and 14 percent, by the staff. Others mentioned volunteering and various forms of joint-decision making. Clearly, some combination of sources makes the most sense.

Content. Although one might argue that some of the contents from most or all the preceding chapters should be included in leadership training, the programs are much more limited. For instance, Alpander asked the training officers to indicate what should be and has been included in first-line supervisory training programs. The content emphasized and the percentage of the 155 respondents indicating that the content was actually included in their own first-line supervisory training programs was as follows: how to feed back the results of performance evaluations to employees (92 percent), how to delegate (90 percent), how to improve listening skills (83 percent), how to improve personal leadership effectiveness (80 percent), and how to encourage and obtain the subordinates' participation in decision making (74 percent).

At least 70 percent also identified the following as most representative of the content of their training program: how to make the work environment conducive for self-motivation, how to improve the quality of the product, how to ensure that established goals are perceived as realistic and relevant by the employees, how to assign specific duties to employees, and how to assist employees to understand their role in relation to the company's overall objectives.

Programs to teach particular concepts and models of leadership such as those described in earlier chapters clearly include content about the concepts and models being taught. Many of these will be discussed later. Joynt (1981–82) expressed an additional educational requirement for managers: Managers need to learn how to do research and become "intelligent consumers." They need to be able to examine which theories are relevant and applicable to their own circumstances and which are not.

Extraneous Factors

Training may not be needed as much as a change of facilities, resources, or organizational policies. Organizational policies and practices may be at fault, not the performance of individual leaders. The burden for improvement should not be shifted to the individual manager who will only be frustrated because his or her attempts to improve himself or herself do not matter as long as the organization as a whole remains unchanged (Dreilinger, McElheny, Rice, & Robinson, 1982).

Methods of Leadership Training

According to Hultman (1984), since leaders are action oriented, the educational methods used should stress action, not theory. The methods employed should reflect the participants' working conditions. Particularly if the leaders and managers have considerable power, opportunity must be afforded them for reflection on their style of leadership. The leaders and managers may confuse power with leadership and fail to lead others because of their power and interest in maintaining their power (Maccoby, 1982). In the same vein, J. G. Anderson (1984) argued that leaders can learn to identify their own workplace behaviors that help or hinder them in reaching their goals. They can be systematically aided in this endeavor with appropriate methods.

Training for leadership in any organizational context can be provided in many different ways. Individuals may receive training on or near their jobs. They may be coached by their immediate superiors. They may be given guided job experience on a planned basis. They may train as understudies—assistants to those in a higher position. They may serve a formal management apprenticeship or internship. They may rotate through a variety of jobs by planned transfers. They may be placed in a special trainee position or be given special project assignments. They may be provided feedback from surveys and process consultation.

Off-the-job leadership training can be obtained by participation in trade and professional associations and civic projects and from formal classrooms or work-

shops. Within these forms of training, didactic and experiential training may be given by lecture, case or problem discussion groups, and role playing. Or, games and simulation with mock managerial in-baskets can be used. Computer-assisted instruction, interactive programs, and programmed instruction can also be employed, along with less structured sensitivity training. Stimulated by social learning theory, behavioral role modeling, the integration of didactic with experiential techniques is also available for effective leadership training.

Lectures and Discussion

Among the methods to be examined here, lectures are the least popular with training directors (Carroll, Paine, & Ivancevich, 1972), although a meta-analysis of the effectiveness of management training programs by Burke and Day (1986) found that lectures have a positive value. Discussion groups are relied on heavily in most leadership programs even when many lecture, film, and other didactic presentations are used. Lectures (or their surrogates—films, prepared videotapes, and television) can arouse audiences, provide information, and stimulate thinking. Films and videotapes have the advantage of making use of master lecturers and performers, carefully worked-out scripts, and standardization and development based on evaluative tests. Close detail can be shown; animation and special effects can be put to good use. Music and artwork can provide desired emphases. Interviews with real model leaders can be presented. But without an interactive program, the easy interaction of discussion is absent. Most comparisons of lecture versus discussion approaches to instructing leaders to change their ways of behaving (for example, Levine & Butler, 1952), however, suggest that the discussion of issues in small groups is likely to be more effective, particularly if attitudes must be changed before the new ways will be accepted and adopted by the trainees.

According to L. A. Allen (1957), discussion provides experience in working with others to reach decisions. The experience can promote the potential leadership of the members by preparing them to use the group discussion as a means for reaching effective decisions. Again, Riegel (1952) suggested that case discussions, in particular, can provide experience in objective ways of thinking about common leadership problems. The need to study issues in terms of possible causes and effects is emphasized. Trainees exchange and evaluate each other's solutions to such problems. They develop an awareness of the need for more than single, simple answers to complex problems.

Some Positive Findings. Maier (1953), among others, demonstrated the effectiveness of training using problem-solving discussions. He compared the performance of 176 trained supervisors with 144 untrained ones. The supervisors with eight hours of training in groups were found more likely to bring about acceptance of change in their groups. Argyris (1965) used lectures and case discussions in the laboratory training of senior executives. No significant change followed the lectures, but some measures of skill in interpersonal relations improved after the case discussions.

Discussions may be ineffective poolings of ignorance or they can be adequately stimulated, directed, and provided with resources to promote learning. Mann and Mann (1959c) compared the effects of free-discussion groups and task-directed groups on behavior as described by members. Members of task-directed discussion groups changed significantly more than did those in free-discussion groups in friendliness, desirability as a friend, leadership, attainment of goals, cooperativeness, and general adjustment.

No Differences Found. Numerous reports have failed to confirm the expectation that discussions are more effective than are lectures. For instance, DiVesta (1954) compared lectures and group discussions as vehicles for training in human relations and found them to be equally effective. However, the discussion groups did show slight gains in favorable attitudes toward the initiation of structure. Mahoney, Jerdee, and Korman (1960) compared case analyses, group discussions, and lectures as methods for training in management development and likewise found no significant difference among the methods. All the groups gained in a test of knowledge, probably as a result of practice.

Both Discussion and Lecture Can Be Useful. Experiments have focused on the wrong issue. Discussions and lectures are suitable for different objectives,

different situations, and different personnel. As a result of a research survey on leadership training, Filley and Jesse (1965) developed a set of hypotheses suggesting the conditions under which more didactic, trainer-oriented training and more discussionlike, trainee-oriented training will be effective. Again, Burke and Day's (1986) meta-analysis found that both lectures and a combination of lectures and discussions could be useful in management education.

House (1965) studied the attitudes of 43 managers toward trainee-oriented (more discussion) and trainer-oriented (more lecture) training and found that 24 preferred a combination of the 2 methods, while 12 preferred trainee-oriented and 7 preferred trainer-oriented training.

Discussions can reinforce lectures. Discussions are useful when a lecture needs clarification and amplification. Learning from a lecture or film is facilitated if it is followed by small "buzz groups" to share opinions, raise questions, and consider alternatives. The conclusions of each buzz group can be shared with the other groups and the trainer. This promotion of 2-way communication increases the motivation of trainees and enables them to test their understanding.

Live television makes it possible for one instructor to lecture or to conduct training discussions with groups of leadership trainees at different sites. However, what are needed for such teleconference training are ways to maintain the trainees' attention in the absence of personal contact with the trainer. The trainees need to be willing and able to talk back to the distant trainer and to learn what is happening in other groups. High-quality graphics are also required, and a face-to-face meeting with the trainer is desirable (Smeltzer & Davey, 1988).

Role Playing

Various behavioral adjustments methods, developed by psychiatrists and social and clinical psychologists, have been adapted to the training of leaders. Psychodrama and sociodrama, originated by Moreno (1955) in the 1930s, require participants (alone or with other actors) to act out various leadership problems under different conditions of audience participation in discussion groups (Lippitt, Bradford, & Benne, 1947). Role playing is a variant. It requires one member to play the role of leader and other members to play the roles of followers. The purpose of playing a role, rather than reading or talking about a solution to an interpersonal problem without a script, is to improve learning and retention and to promote transference from the learning situation to the leadership performance on the job. Bradford and Lippitt (1952) suggested that interpersonal skills may be hard to teach by only providing verbal or intellectual reasons for behaving in a certain way without actually helping to produce the ability to behave in the desired way. Didactic approaches, by themselves, may reduce successful leadership behavior by adding to anxiety rather than to understanding.

Role playing quickly became one of the most popular leadership training methods. Many possible uses were seen for it. Trainees might practice what they eventually had to do. Role playing might serve as a diagnostic technique. Group discussion following the role playing might focus on examining specific interchanges experienced in the role plays. Different ways of solving problems could be tested by role players. Other trainees could gain vicariously from observing the success or failure of various attempts during role plays. Standards could be set for handling specific situations (J. R. P. French, 1944b).[6]

As was expected, Lonergan (1958) and Lawshe, Brune, and Bolda (1958) observed that participants in role playing tended to regard it as beneficial in increasing their understanding of human relations problems. Furthermore, the latter found that about twice as many participants preferred the leader role to the follower role. Similarly, Mann and Mann (1959a, 1959b) demonstrated that experience in role playing improved role-playing ability as judged by the individual, other role players, and observers. When they compared ratings of participants' behavior under role playing and group discussions, they found that the participants improved more in interpersonal adjustment after role playing than after group discussion.

Role playing appears to add to leaders' skills in dealing with human relations problems. For example, So-

lem (1960) arranged for small teams drawn from 440 supervisors to meet either in 22 case discussion groups or in 23 multiple role-playing exercises. They role played or discussed 1 of 2 problems, concerning either the assignment of a new truck to a crew of utility repairmen or how to change a work procedure. When role playing the new-truck problem, a participant took the part of the crew's foreman and another acted as a repairman. In the new-truck case discussion, the teams talked about solutions to the problem. The change-of-work-procedure problem was handled similarly as a role play or case discussion. Among the role-playing teams, 46 percent developed integrated, new solutions to the problems. That is, instead of assigning a new truck to the man with the oldest truck, they replaced the oldest truck but enabled each repairman to switch to a newer truck. But only 15 percent of the case discussants did likewise. More integrated solutions were also developed for the role played change-of-work procedures than for the case discussion.

The positive effects of role playing tend to depend on a variety of circumstances. Thus, for instance, Lawshe, Bolda, and Brune (1959) studied five groups under different conditions of feedback. They found that role playing and subsequent discussion increased the participants' sensitivity and orientation toward employees when the participants were required to criticize their own performance and when the human relations point of view was presented to them in a strong, emotional manner. Similarly, Harvey and Beverly (1961) found that role playing has a significant positive effect on changes of opinion, but authoritarian participants gained more from role playing than did those who were not authoritarian. However, Elms and Janis (1965) found that counternorms were accepted to a high degree only under conditions of overt role playing (as opposed to nonovert role playing) and only if large monetary rewards were paid. Trittipoe and Hahn (1961) studied participants in role-playing groups and problem-solving groups. Both observers and followers rated participants higher in role playing if they also rated them higher in problem solving. In turn, those who were rated higher in both were rated higher in leadership and class standing.

Some experiments that were less favorable to role playing also were completed. Mann and Mann (1960)

---

[6]See also, Corsini, Shaw, and Blake (1961); A. F. Klein (1956); Speroff (1957); Stahl (1953, 1954); Symonds (1947); Wolozin (1948); and Zander (1947). Corsini, Shaw, and Blake's (1961) survey of the various role-playing methods included an annotated bibliography of 102 references.

compared the experience of participants in role-playing and task-oriented groups. Contrary to their hypothesis, they observed that participants in the task-oriented problem-solving groups changed more in leadership and general adjustment than those in the role-playing groups. In addition, Hanson, Morton, and Rothaus (1963) found that role-playing situations involving the evaluation of followers' personality traits induce a critical posture in the leader and a submissive role for followers, whereas working on a problem in goal setting and planning permitted followers to be more active. In a study of 200 officer trainees, Tupes, Carp, and Borg (1958) noted that the ability to play roles was not related to ratings of leadership effectiveness but to personality scores. In the aforementioned experiments, both role reversal and multiple role playing were used extensively.

Role Reversal. When supervisors appear to be unable to appreciate the views of subordinates, they may be asked to play the role of a subordinate while someone else plays the role of supervisor. Supervisors in such role reversals may gain insight into what is affecting their subordinates. Furthermore, having to verbalize a position promotes the shift toward that new viewpoint (Bradford & Lippitt, 1952; Speroff, 1954).

Multiple Role Playing. An audience is divided into small teams, and each member of the teams receives instructions to play a particular role. Following the role plays within each team, the audience reassembles and shares experiences (Maier & Zerfoss, 1952). The different teams can be given different instructions, so the effects of these differences on what occurs during the interactions among the players is revealed during the critique by the audience after the groups reassemble as a whole.

Role Playing Combined with Videotaping. Videotape feedback of role plays has become commonplace in leadership training. Illustrative of the use of videotape replay was a training program of American overseas advisers, who viewed a videotape of their interactions with an actor who was trained to play the role of a foreigner. The trainees' performance was critiqued as they watched the tape. Learning was more effective and was retained longer in the videotaped role-playing group than in a control group that only read the training manual about the same issue (P. H. King, 1966).

Ivancevich and Smith (1981) compared role playing and videotaped feedback with a lecture and role playing without videotaping and with a control group without training. They evaluated the performance of 60 sales mangers in dealing with their sales representitives in clarifying goals, openness, giving information, and supportiveness in simulated goal-setting interviews before and after training. In addition, surveys of the 160 sales representatives subordinate to the managers 3 months after training, found that improvement had indeed been greatest for the managers who were trained with videotaping in clarifying goals and supportiveness. But role playing without videotaping was as successful as role playing with videotaping in improving openness and the giving of information. And according to the subordinates, both training groups of managers did equally better than the control group in giving feedback and challenging their subordinates. The subordinate sales representatives in the trained groups also did better than the sales reps of the control group of untrained managers in increasing orders they received per sales presentation, but no differences were obtained in the new accounts generated by the subordinate sales reps of the trained and untrained groups of managers. In all, videotaped feedback following training appeared to do as well or better than did traditional role playing in improving the managers' performance in its effects on the sales reps. Both trained groups of managers generally showed such improvements in contrast to the untrained control groups of managers.

Availability. Role plays can be packaged for self-administration by the role players.[7] For example, Shackleton, Bass, and Allison (1982) provided participants with a booklet of self-administering instructions that made it possible for them to experience and obtain results comparing the five leadership styles—*directive, negotiative, consultative, participative,* and *delegative*—presented in Chapter 22. Packaged videotapes and interactive computerization can create highly realistic settings and role requirements for training.

---

[7]Such "off-the-shelf" leadership training materials are widely distributed by commercial publishers.

Simulation

Other facsimiles of real leadership situations are created by means of the in-basket technique and by games.

The In-basket Technique. Participants are given a booklet that essentially reproduces the contents of a manager's in-basket, along with some general information about the organization in which the manager is located. They must decide what actions to take to dispose of the items before leaving on a trip (Frederiksen, 1962a, 1962b). Good performance is associated with a good sense of priorities, planning ahead, and the appropriate use of available information (Zoll, 1969). Butler and Keys (1973) reported comparisons between 33 first-line supervisors who took a traditional course on the fundamentals of supervision and 30 supervisors who carried out a series of group discussions based on their handling of the in-basket items. The "fundamentals" groups showed no significant improvement in tested knowledge on "How Supervise" (File & Remmers, 1971) or the Supervisory Inventory on Human Relations (Kirkpatrick, 1954). But the in-basket discussion group improved significantly on both instruments. Commensurate with the significant gains in knowledge registered by the "in-basket" participants, in the next several months, back on the job, their subordinates reported more changes for the in-basket discussion participants in their behavior as supervisors, particularly in their "people orientation" and in innovation on Marvin's (1968) Management Matrix. Little or no such change was found for those who took the traditional course on the principles of leadership.

Games. Organizational, institutional, and business games are living cases. Trainees must make sequential decisions and then live with them (Leavitt & Bass, 1964). Outcomes from leadership performance have fairly rapid consequences. Success and failure are more fully objective and observable than is true for role playing in general. Over 30,000 executives participated in one or more of the hundred-or-so business games that appeared in the first five years following the introduction by the American Management Association of its Top Management Decision Simulation in 1956 (L. Stewart, 1962). This prototype business game and most

of its successors confront teams of players with sets of decisions that require them to decide at each successive play how much to budget for raw materials, plant, equipment, advertising, research, and labor. Players usually need to make decisions on what prices to set for their products, whether to borrow money, and whether to build plants. They may negotiate with "suppliers" and "union officals." When the game is used for leadership training, teams may compete against each other or against a computer model.

Organizational games, such as UPPOE (Bass, 1964), create leadership problems. Player-managers must literally obtain the cooperation of player-workers to produce for a "market" paper products made by cutting, assembling, and stapling. Players can be hired and fired; they can speed up, slow down, or strike. Tangible products and raw materials are processed, bought, and sold.

Cases can be recast into in-basket tests and games. For example, ED/AD/EX, used in training programs in the United States, Spain, and India, incorporates interpersonal, strategic, and value aspects of the environment in which a school principal has to operate (Immegart, 1987).

The "Looking Glass," developed by the Center for Creative Leadership (McCall & Lombardo, 1982), is a carefully constructed simulation of the organization of a real glass manufacturer. It attempts to reproduce faithfully in simulation the required arrangements among the managers of the real company. Relevant financial data and information about products are included and must be factored into the communications and decisions making. Up to 20 executive positions are filled in the top four levels of the simulated glass manufacturer. The training involves a period, such as a day, to complete the simulation exercise and a subsequent period for individual and group feedback. Learning is enhanced by systematic feedback of the performance of participants in the simulation. But here, there is a need to "teach for transfer" with structure to support the transfer to the back-home job of what had been learned in the simulation, according to Kaplan, Lombardo, and Mazique's (1985) 6 month follow-up evaluation back on the job.

Despite their widespread use, evaluations of simulations are hard to come by. However, Raia (1966) showed that a business game, simple or complex, can add more to the performance on a final examination about case problems than can discussions and readings about the cases.

Computer-assisted and Programmed Instruction

Hausser, Blaiwes, Weller, and Spencer (1974) described computer-assisted instruction (CAI) in teaching interpersonal skills to U.S. Navy commanders. With the PLATO system and an instructional programming language, TUTOR, Hausser and Spencer (1975) applied CAI to interpersonal skill training in feedback, communication, goal setting, problem solving, decision making, effective rewards and punishments, and the use of power and authority. Compared to controls who received the same pre- and posttest assessments and were involved in the same duties as recruiting officers, those who were trained with CAI learned considerably more.

Videotapes and films can be included as part of computer-regulated programs and can be incorporated in training as stimuli, response alternatives, and feedback.[8] Preston and Chappel (1988) contrasted randomly assigned groups of undergraduates to computer-based training, computer-based training with videotaped vignettes, and group discussions with the videotaped vignettes. They found that any one of three training methods could improve performance on tests of knowledge about principles of leadership equally well.

"Decision Point: A Living Case Study" is an interactive computer program that provides the trainee with a high-fidelity audiovisual simulation of the different phases of managerial experiences. It begins with the trainee being offered and accepting a position with a firm to help manage its marketing problems. Political issues arise, along with personnel grievances, conflicts among departments, and questions of credit policy. Ten decisions need to be made. In each instance, four alternatives are provided. A written debriefing is provided by the computer about the adequacy of each of the chosen decisions, along with explanations.

By 1985, one survey of Fortune 500 firms indicated that over half of them were already beginning to make use of CAI (Hassett & Dukes, 1986). CAI is the technically most advanced version of programmed instruction.

Programmed Instruction. With programmed instruction, instruction is programmed into concrete steps. Trainees must generate or choose the correct answer to a question before proceeding to the next question. Efforts have been made to use programmed instruction (PI) to teach effective human relations. For example, the American Management Association has sponsored PRIME, a programmed textbook for training supervisors. "Cultural assimilators" are programmed texts that have been developed and evaluated to teach leadership training and good human relations relevant to a designated culture (Fiedler, 1968).

It is difficult to write an effective program if what is to be taught involves shadings of opinion, sensitivity to fuzzy socioemotional issues, and unclear ideas about the order of steps in which learning can take place (Bass & Barrett, 1981). Nevertheless, Hynes, Feldhusen, and Richardson (1978) obtained positive results in a controlled experimental study of a three-stage program to train high school students to be better leaders. PI, coupled with lectures, yielded improvements in understanding and attitudes in the first stage, whereas experiential approaches failed to do so in the second and third stages. Positive effects have also been obtained with cultural assimilators (Fiedler, 1968).

Behavioral Modeling

Behavioral modeling is a composite method based on social learning theory. In contrast to the more "mindless" Skinnerian operant learning or the emphasis on insightful discovery in learning, Bandura (1977) argued with experimental support that learning is facilitated if models are provided with information in advance of the consequences of engaging in a specific behavior. Action is foresightful. People are more attentive and active in organizing what is to be learned if they are provided with models to follow. In observational learning, anticipation of a reinforcer influences not only what is observed but what goes unnoticed. Learning from the model is increased when the consequences of the model's behavior are highly valued.

---

[8] The NeXt personal computer is an elegant effort to exploit this multimedia process.

Goldstein and Sorcher (1974) showed how this theoretical approach could be applied to training first-line supervisors. Pilot experiments followed, which were generally supportive (Kraut, 1976).[9] For instance, in an experiment by Latham and Saari (1979), for 2 hours each week for 9 weeks, 20 supervisors engaged in training that dealt with (1) orienting a new employee, (2) giving recognition, (3) motivating a poor performer, (4) correcting poor work habits, (5) discussing a potential disciplinary action, (6) reducing absenteeism, (7) handling a complaining employee, (8) decreasing turnover, and (9) overcoming resistance to change.

Each session followed the same plan after an introduction: (1) a film showing a model supervisor effectively handling a situation, followed by a set of three to six learning points that were shown in the film immediately before and after the model was presented, (2) group discussion of the effectiveness of the model in exhibiting the desired behaviors (to promote retention), (3) practice in role playing the desired behaviors in front of the entire class, and (4) feedback from the class about the effectiveness of each trainee in demonstrating the desired behaviors.

The learning points shown in the film were posted in front of the trainee who played the role of supervisor. For example, points to handle a complaint included (1) avoiding responding with hostility or defensiveness, (2) asking for and listening openly to the employee's complaint, (3) restating the complaint for a thorough understanding, (4) recognizing and acknowledging the employeee's viewpoint, (5) stating one's position nondefensively, when necessary, and (6) setting a specific date for a follow-up meeting.

Positive reactions to the program were sustained over an 8-month period. In contrast to 20 supervisors in a control group, the experimental trainees scored significantly higher on a test of the knowledge necessary to transfer the principles learned in class to different types of job-related problems. The experimental trainees were also more effective in role plays resolving supervisor-employee problems and in earning higher evaluations of their job performance from their superiors one year after training then were the supervisors in the control group, although they had been equiva-

lent in rated performance with the control group one month before training.

Computer-assisted Behavioral Modeling. Because behavioral modeling has discrete components and pursues a systematic series of steps, it lends itself readily to CAI. CAI behavioral modeling programs have been developed to help train supervisors. In these programs, supervisors operate interactively with a computer to learn how to orient new employees, deal with resentment, resolve conflicts, inform the union of a change, and terminate employees (Development Dimensions International, 1983).

Differential Effects. Fox (1989) unearthed 13 reports of the positive effects of using behavioral modeling to improve supervisory skills. Yet despite its effectiveness in promoting the learning of leadership behavior, behavioral modeling may produce varied and unwanted results.

Manz and Sims (1986a) contrasted three separate modeling interventions for leadership behavior. Videotapes provided models of contingent-reward leadership, contingent-reprimand leadership, and goal-setting leadership for randomly selected students assigned to 10 leader-subordinate dyads. A fourth control group did not view any tape. Pre-post measures of the three styles of leadership behavior and the controls' performance were obtained. Overall, modeling generated significantly more change than was observed in the control condition. As expected, the subordinates' satisfaction with the leader increased with increased contingent reward (.61) and increased goal setting (.35) but not with the increased contingent reprimand. Moreover, the coefficients from path analyses showed that the contingent-reward model directly promoted contingent-rewarding leadership behavior (.21). However, the contingent-reprimand model not only resulted in increased reprimanding (.16), but *reduced* contingent rewarding ($-.55$) and goal setting ($-.43$). Finally, the goal-setting model failed to enhance goal-setting leadership significantly and increased reprimanding leadership (.22). Thus, the theoretical basis for the modeling has to be considered in determining whether behavioral role modeling will be productive or counterproductive. Hakel (1976), Locke (1977), and McGehee and Tullar (1978) cautioned against its uncritical adoption.

[9]See also, King and Arlinghaus (1976) and Moses and Ritchie (1976).

Training in Specific Leadership Skills. In addition to behavioral role modeling to cope with specific leadership problems, one also sees much training in skills that are necessary to fulfill a leader's responsibilities adequately. Goldstein (1980) noted the continuing work on the training of raters and the improving of performance evaluations by supervisors. He also found that much of what is available for evaluating training in leadership skills, such as how to handle disciplinary problems, is anecdotal. But illustrative of controlled experimental evaluations of such training was a small sample investigation by Douglas (1977), who examined the efficacy of the systematic training of group leaders using operationally defined leadership skills in a group interaction. Compared to the leaders in an alternate placebo group, those who were trained to use both the reflective-supportive (considerate) and the command-response (directive) styles employed these styles consistently and appropriately. The trained leaders also used the associated verbal responses more consistently and appropriately than did the leaders in the placebo condition. As with Manz and Sims's (1986a) results, another finding was that the effects on the leaders' behaviors overlapped regardless of the theoretical orientation, which suggests that when leadership skills are being taught, there are likely to be spillover effects across skills and orientations. Training leaders in one skill, such as how to use a particular verbal response style, may reduce or increase their ability to use another leadership style. Conceivably, leaders simultaneously can increase their integration of their task and relations orientation (as advocated in Chapter 23).

Sensitivity Training

It was at a social workers' conference on leadership in 1946 that Kurt Lewin and his graduate students at the Massachusetts Institute of Technology stumbled serendipitously into sensitivity training. The conferees judged students' observations about the interpersonal processes that occurred during the conference to be more valuable to their learning than the formal leadership topics that the conferees discussed. The idea took root that all participants in discussion groups could become observers and that the sharing of their observations would provide insight into the leadership processes in general. In addition, individuals could learn about their adequacy in interaction with others and what they might do to improve. The learning process was facilitated by eliminating the formal agenda before a group convened (Bradford, Gibb, & Benne, 1964). The group trainer, on the surface at least, abdicated the leadership role. The social vacuum that was created as a consequence of beginning without an agenda or a leader revealed the individual participants' differences in abilities and willingness to attempt and succeed in initiating structure. The ambiguous situation gave participants the opportunity to try out new ways of carrying out various task and maintenance leadership activities that were of use to the group. The feedback from the other participant-observers reinforced the new attempts that worked well and indicated the inadequacy of other less successful attempts to lead. For this reason, the situation was seen as a "laboratory," a place for experimenting.

Trainers establish themselves as ambiguous authority figures, provide group members with information needed for analyzing group processes, and encourage participation and openness. They do not structure the group discussion: instead, they throw the entire burden of initiative back on the group members. Feedback sessions are used to suggest that the participants' demands for direction and structure from the trainer inhibit the examination of group processes and the development of insight into role relationships.

Theory. Theoretical supports for sensitivity training and its variants are diverse. In addition to Lewin's (1939) topological existentialism, they include analytic theory, Bion's (1948, 1961) fight-or-flight analyses, Moreno's (1955) sociopsychological focus, Berne's (1964) transactional analysis, Perls's (1969) gestalt therapy, Maslow's (1965) humanistic psychology, and Argyris's (1987) double-loop learning.

Variants. Numerous variants have been developed. Sensitivity (or laboratory) training, using the T- (for training) group, focused on interpersonal learning during the 1950s and onward. The *encounter group,* which arose in the 1960s, provides a more intensive experience in openness; the self-examination of hostilities, defenses, and feelings; self-awareness; and personal growth. *Team building* engages people who work as a group, along with their supervisor, in sensitivity training but often with issues relevant to work and organization.

Training may begin with a task and structure, then gradually become less structured. A *marathon* nonstop training weekend may be used. Two or more trainers who meet with a much larger-than-ordinary *cluster group* may be employed. Many organizations have developed unique programs, incorporating some aspects of the sensitivity training laboratory (Morton & Bass, 1964). Actually, many of the elements of sensitivity training, such as participation and feedback, have found their way into training and human resources management, in general. They also can be seen in numerous self-development programs, ranging from group therapy to the physically demanding Outward Bound programs. Sensitivity training has also been "instrumented" so no trainer is needed. In such a case, all instructions come from written materials or directions or directors outside the training group (Blake & Mouton, 1964). More will be said later about this form of training.

The numerous variants of sensitivity training all attempt to accomplish one or more of the following changes in attitude or behavior by the trainee-leaders: (1) greater sensitivity to the needs and desires of followers, (2) greater openness and sharing of information, (3) greater sharing of decision-making responsibilities with followers, (4) more intimate, friendly, and egalitarian interaction with followers, and (5) less structuring, personal dominance, and pushing exclusively for productive output.

Most of the research concerned with the effects of sensitivity training has attempted to determine whether such change has occurred. Although testimonials do not constitute evidence of consequence, Wedel (1957) surveyed 333 former participants in laboratory training and found that they tended to regard the training as valuable in improving their human relations skills. Nonetheless, critics continually questioned whether these objectives were being met in sensitivity training programs. Studies of the impact of sensitivity training on trainees' attitudes, perceptions, and behavior yielded a mix of results. Likewise, the detailed examination of the impact of sensitivity training on the groups and organizations to which the trainees returned resulted in a complex of conclusions concerning the costs and benefits of the training. Cohesiveness may be increased but performance may be impaired. It may be difficult to transfer what is appropriate in training to what is appropriate back on the job. Generalizations about the effects of sensitivity training are made difficult because of its many variations, described earlier.

Changes in Trainees' Attitudes. The majority of studies indicated that sensitivity training results in significant changes in interpersonal attitudes: more favorable attitudes toward subordinates, a stronger human relations orientation, and greater awareness of interpersonal dynamics. For example, Bunker and Knowles (1967) and P. B. Smith (1964, 1975) reported significant changes in attitudes in participants as a consequence of laboratory training. Schutz and Allen (1966) found that the effects of laboratory training resulted in more changes in the attitudes and personality of those in the experimental group than of those in the control group. Tests administered before and six months after training indicated more changes in feelings and behavior toward other people and toward themselves and more changes in the perceptions of others' behavior and feelings toward themselves than occurred for control groups. The participants indicated greater friendliness, sensitivity, and tolerance toward others after training.

When Golembiewski and Carrigan (1970) conducted a mild reinforcement session one year after the initial sensitivity training of managers, they found that changes in attitudes persisted over a period of 18 months for the group that received reinforcement. But Belasco and Trice (1969b) reported that the changes associated with training alone were small, whereas training combined with testing was more effective in producing changes. The most significant changes were in morale, self-concept, and role expectations.

Asquith and Hedlund (1967) administered a before-and-after questionnaire to 20 management trainees in a chemical firm. They noted that although improvements in attitudes toward human relations practices were obtained, the participants exhibited no significant changes in attitudes toward consideration, the initiation of structure, supervision, or management. Blake and Mouton (1966) studied managers and union officers from the same plant and found that instrumental sensitivity training resulted in significant improvements in the attitudes of both groups. But H. B. Stephenson (1966); Biggs, Huneryager, and Delaney (1966); and Asquith and Hedlund (1967) all obtained results indicating that laboratory training produced no significant changes in attitudes toward leadership behaviors, as measured by such instruments as the Leadership Opinion Questionnaire (LOQ).[10] Similarly, Kernan (1963) obtained before-and-after responses to attitude and personality items from two experimental groups and a control group but found no significant changes in the attitudes or personalities of those in the T-groups or the control group.

Changes in Trainees' Perceptions. In line with the primary objective of training to increase perceptual sensitivity, a content analysis by R. H. Solomon (1976) found leaders' statements of the effects of the laboratory training of undergraduates to include increased personal awareness, improved interpersonal relations, and improvements, as well as frustrations, in their leadership skills. Bass (1962b) asked members of a training group to record their self-perceived moods at five different intervals during sensitivity training. He found that skepticism decreased and that concentration and depression increased for awhile and then leveled off, but anxiety did not increase as expected.

Several studies were concerned with changes in self-concept and in perceptions of others. T. Gordon (1955) found that leader-trainees tended to describe their behavior in terms that were similar to their conception of an ideal leader and that laboratory training produced changes toward greater conformity with such ideal behavior. Burke and Bennis (1961) reported that perceptions of actual self and ideal self were closer at the end than at the beginning of training. Bass (1962a) noted significant increases in perceptual sensitivity to interpersonal relations after training. Sensitivity was positively related to peer ratings of influence in the group. But Greiner, Leitch, and Barnes (1968) were unable to demonstrate that instrumented sensitivity training (to be described later) produced significant changes in trainees' perceptions. Likewise, Kassarjian (1965) reported no significant changes in orientation toward self or others as a result of sensitivity training.

A central problem here is that as trainees become more sensitive to the issues and dimensions of consequence, they also become much more modest about the adequacy of their attitudes and behavior. Thus, after a week of feedback from colleagues in instrumented sensitivity training workshops about their own concerns for people and productivity, there is a sharp decline from preworkshop self-ratings about the extent to which the trainees are "9,9", highly concerned in an integrated way about the productivity of people. Among 647 participants, 59.8 percent saw themselves as "9,9" before the workshop but only 13.4 percent saw themselves as "9,9" at the end of the week (Blake, 1986).

Changes in Trainees' Behavior. Typical of improvements reported were those found by Boyd and Ellis (1962) when each participant's supervisor, two of his peers, and two of his subordinates were interviewed in the sixth week and again in the sixth month following training at the Hydroelectric Power Commission of Ontario. Controls were also interviewed in the same manner. Improvements were noted in 64 percent of the sensitivity trainees but only in 23 percent of the controls. The trainees changed more than the controls in increased listening; better interpersonal understanding; better contributions at meetings; increased tolerance and flexibility; and, to a lesser extent, self-confidence and effective expression. Similarly, Bunker (1965b) questioned trainees and their co-workers one year after participation in a laboratory training program. The co-workers reported that the participants gained significantly more than did a control group in interpersonal skills, openness, and understanding of social relationships. Likewise, Morton and Bass (1964) studied 97 managers who listed more than 350 incidents of behavioral change during the six months following an instrumented laboratory experiment in management development. The most frequently mentioned changes dealt with improved working relationships and self-understanding.

M. B. Miles (1965) obtained results showing that sensitivity training resulted in the unfreezing of participation and greater receptivity to feedback, although change was found in consideration and initiating structure (M. B. Miles, 1960). Buchanan and Brunstetter (1959) used T-group methods to train 60 engineers in

[10]See Chapter 24.

supervisory positions. Afterwards, subordinates evaluated the supervisors from the trained group as being more desirable supervisors than they did those from the control group.

R. Harrison (1962) asked participants in laboratory training to describe themselves and 10 associates before and after training. The trained group increased the number of interpersonal and emotional words they used to describe themselves but not others. In another study, R. Harrison (1966) found that 115 laboratory trainees, three months after training, used more terms indicating their awareness of interpersonal relations and fewer terms expressing the manipulation of behavior. In a similar fashion, Oshry and Harrison (1966) administered before-and-after tests to middle managers. The items in which changes occurred suggested that after training, the managers viewed themselves as more human and less impersonal, saw a closer connection between meeting personal needs and getting work done, understood that they were a significant part of the problem, yet saw no connection between their new perceptions and how to translate them into action. These effects were strongest for those who participated most intensely in the laboratory training.

Harrison and Lubin (1955b) studied person-oriented and work-oriented subjects in homogeneous and heterogeneous training groups. Person-oriented members were rated as behaving more expressively and warmly and as forming stronger ties to their homogeneous group. Contrary to the hypothesis, work-oriented members were perceived as learning more than person-oriented members. Members who preferred low structure exceeded those who preferred high structure in "understanding self" and "understanding others." The members of the high-structure group believed themselves to be capable and active in discussion but avoided the examination of interpersonal relations. Although a majority of studies showed that sensitivity training can induce changes in behavior, the effects appear to be moderated by the personality of the trainees.

Effects on Group and Organizational Performance. The preceding studies were designed to determine whether sensitivity training results in changes in the attitudes or behavior of the trainees themselves. The most pragmatic criterion of the effect of training, however, is whether it results in changes in the per-

formance or responses of the groups supervised by the leaders who have received sensitivity training. Unfortunately, the outcomes are complex and multiple. Thus, when Blake, Mouton, and Fruchter (1962) factor analyzed various measures of instrumented T-group outcomes, they found that group cohesion and group accomplishment loaded on separate factors. T-groups could increase cohesion at the expense of productivity, or vice versa, as will be detailed later.

Blake, Mouton, Barnes, and Greiner (1964) studied the management of a large petroleum company engaged in instrumented training. They concluded that the employees' productivity increased as a result of changes in the managers towards a "9,9" leadership style after they were trained. Miles, Milavsky, Lake, and Beckhard (1965) found that sensitivity training resulted in both changes in managers' attitudes and the improved productivity of departments. Beckhard (1966) and Kuriloff and Atkins (1966) also attributed improved operating efficiency to the effects of T-group programs. Unfortunately, the controls in these studies were inadequate. The research was conducted during a long economic upswing when, in general, the profits of businesses were increasing.

Friedlander (1967) compared four work groups that participated in team training with eight similar groups that did not. The trained groups improved in problem solving, mutual influence, and personal involvement more than did the control groups. But there were no significant differences in changes in interpersonal trust, the approachability of leaders, or the evaluation of training sessions.

Weschler and Reisel (1959) studied a sensitivity training group over a period of one year. An emotionality index increased steadily through 30 sessions, but group productivity varied from week to week.

Less saluatory effects on effectiveness and productivity of sensitivity training were seen by Mosvick (1971), who analyzed eight studies of scientists and engineers that used control groups. In four of the studies[11] the subjects were trained by lectures and discussion. In the other four studies,[12] the groups were given T-group training. Mosvick found that the standard

[11]Carron (1964), Miner (1960b), Moon and Hariton (1958), and Mosvick (1966).

[12]Asquith and Hedlund (1967), Buchanan and Brunstetter (1958), Kernan (1963), and Underwood (1965).

methods of training in human relations were more effective than were the T-group methods with technically oriented supervisors. Similarly, in a massive analysis of field data, D. G. Bowers (1973) found strong indications in 23 organizations of less positive effects of T-group training on the subsequent improvements of the organization's performance, in contrast to survey feedback without the T-group experience. Despite the plethora of empirical research on the effects of sensitivity training, Goldstein (1980) complained about the absence of an adequate theory to account for the various results, such as those reported by P. B. Smith (1975, 1976) who had concluded that it is not known if the effects occur in all types of groups, why effects are detected with some measures but not with others, and why certain effects occur at all.

Cohesion versus Productivity. Additional evidence suggested that sensitivity training may improve the relations within a group at the expense of impairing the group's subsequent performance of a task. For example, Deep, Bass, and Vaughan (1967) studied 93 business students who were assigned to simulated companies to play a business game. Some had undergone sensitivity training as intact groups 15 weeks earlier, while others came from diverse sensitivity training groups. The intact groups performed significantly more poorly than did those composed of separately trained members, but they described themselves as higher in cooperation and openness. In the same way, Stinson (1970) studied five control groups, five groups trained as intact teams, and five composed of members assigned to different training groups that were equated on the basis of gross profits earned in a prior business game. The fragmented and control groups outperformed the intact groups in gross profit but declined in cohesiveness, whereas the intact groups were highest in cohesiveness but lowest in productivity. Likewise, Underwood (1965), in a study of 15 training and 15 control groups, found that the T-groups changed more than did the controls, but training had an adverse effect on productivity. Hellebrandt and Stinson (1971) reported similar findings.

To a considerable degree, the belief that organizational productivity increases as a result of sensitivity training tends to rely on inadequately controlled stud-

ies. When controls are more adequate, sensitivity trained groups and their trainees may prove no different nor less productive than control groups (Weschler & Reisel, 1959). Subsequent group learning and problem solving may be lower under some previously sensitivity trained leaders but not among others (Maloney, 1956). Reviews by House (1967, 1968) and findings presented by Goodall (1971) agreed that sensitivity training induces changes, particularly in attitudes, but it also can induce anxiety, confusion, and uncertainty.

Buchanan (1969) found that only 2 of 66 studies analyzed made adequate use of control groups. However, from a review of the literature, Campbell and Dunnette (1968) concluded that laboratory training did change behavior in the laboratory, but, as will be discussed next, there was less conclusive evidence for the transfer of such training to the job situation. P. B. Smith (1975) was able to collect a sufficient number of studies that has satisfactory controls, repeated measure designs, and a minimal duration of 20 hours of training. Unfortunately, the pretest sensitization of participants and the raters' awareness of who participated in training still could not be controlled in most of these studies. Although Smith found 78 reports of significant effects of training on one or more scores after training, only 31 studies employed designs that assessed the persistence of the effects. But 21 studies did report long-term effects, which supports the conclusion that a high degree of cohesiveness usually appears at the end of sensitivity training groups (Stinson, 1970). However, the impact on productivity is more problematic, depending on individual differences (Cooper & Levine, 1978) and the "back home" circumstances to which the training is to be transferred (Argyris, 1969; Bass, 1967c).

Problems in the Transfer of Sensitivity Training. Pugh (1965), among others, called attention to the problem of transferring what is learned in the artificially contrived T-group setting to the real world. Thus, Oshry and Harrison (1966) found that the new diagnostic orientations that middle managers learned during sensitivity training could not be converted into action back on the job because the managers saw no clear connection between their new perceptions and their jobs. To promote the positive transfer of training, Bass (1967c) suggested that in parallel with sensitivity training groups, simulations of the back-home organization involving supervisory, managerial, and organizational issues should be brought into the training laboratory. Bamforth (1965) went farther. As a consequence of the failure of the within-plant T-group members to transfer their learning to on-the-job problems, Bamforth changed the role of the T-group trainer to that of a consultant to regularly functioning, formal work-group meetings. In these meetings, he helped the groups to recognize their boss-subordinate difficulties, anxieties about using or not using authority, relationships with colleagues, role classifications, difficulties in communication, resistance to the disclosure of initially unrecognized dynamics, and other sociopsychological problems. To prevent fadeout of the effects of an off-site team-building program, A. R. Bass (1983) organized regular private follow-up meetings between the supervisor and each subordinate. The 135 participants who had such individual follow-ups with their supervisors exhibited less loss of learning than did 71 controls who did not have such individual follow-up meetings.

Ethical Concerns. K. F. Taylor (1967) charged that sensitivity training is based on questionable objectives—the development of group cohesiveness, confidence in compliance with the norms of the training culture, and disruption of the trainees' personal integrity. Similarly, Lakin (1969) questioned the ethical basis of laboratory training on the gounds that untrained and improperly trained trainers are often employed and that the method takes advantage of group pressure to impose the trainers' values on the trainees, uses scapegoating and demands for consensus and for conformity to accomplish its objectives, and invades the individual's privacy. The sensitivity training experience can be a highly stressful one for some participants and can result in psychological casualties. However, these are infrequent and controllable with an ethical training staff. But the slight risk of such occurrences needs to be offset from an ethical point of view by large benefits for most other participants (Cooper, 1975).[13]

Instrumented and 'Packaged' Sensitivity Training. The standardization of techniques can increase the re-

liability and reduce the variability of results with sensitivity training. Groups can undergo standardized processes that involve instrumented, self-administered, repeated questionnaires for data gathering; analysis; discussion; role plays; in-basket simulations; cases; audiotaped or videotaped instructions; and other types of experiential exercises for sensitivity training. The instruments either create a process similar to a T-group or focus on more specific socioemotional learning experiences. Seven standards are proposed for developing such "ready-to-use" learning programs: (1) a scientific review of what is known about the processes, (2) identification of the behavioral dimensions of consequence that are to be the subjects of learning, (3) effective reinforcement, (4) reliable and valid measures of change, (5) adequate follow-up, (6) the control of necessary antecedent conditions and associated consequences, and (7) adequate norms (Bass, 1977).

Blake and Mouton (1962a) pioneered the instrumentation of sensitivity training, the "most radical innovation in T-group training" (Weschler & Schein, 1962). They removed the trainer. The managerial grid training (Blake & Mouton, 1964) that emerged was widely adopted as a substitute for sensitivity training with trainers. Self-administered, "instrumental" training was seen to give trainees greater responsibility for learning, as well as to be more likely to be transferred. It gave participants more respect for systematic data analysis and was cheaper to conduct (Shepard, 1964). Its content fit with theory and research on the need and ways for supervisors to integrate task- and relations orientation, as advocated in Chapter 23.

Berzon, Reisel, and Davis (1969) evaluated a 10-session instrumented audiotape program for self-directed personal growth groups entitled Planned Experiences for Effective Relating (PEER). They reported a positive change in self-concept. Worden (1976) found that although no immediate personality differences could be detected between the experimental and control subjects, 25 of 67 youths who were subjected to PEER reported, in a 6-month follow-up, that they had made use of leadership skills learned in PEER. Similarly, Vicino, Krusell, Bass, et al. (1973) evaluated the effects of PROCESS (Krusell, Vicino, Manning, et al., 1971, 1982), a program of eight exercises (12 in the 1982 revision), self-administered by booklet, for personal and in-

---

[13]For further critiques along these lines, the reader may wish to consult Back (1972), Coghill (1967), Golembiewski and Blumberg (1970), Marrow (1964b), Odiorne (1963), and Stock (1964).

terpersonal development. A field experiment using a holdout control procedure yielded results indicating that the undergraduate participants improved their concept of themselves, were more able to see themselves as their peers did, and reacted favorably to the total experience. Similar results were obtained with 219 members of a women's religious order.

It would seem that less expensive instrumented approaches can be substituted for the more expensive T-group without much loss of effect. Whether either approach should be included in a leadership training program must take into account the question of whether the learning, even it if has saluatory effects on the individual trainee, can be applied in the real-life setting to which the trainee returns. If not, it may be that Bamforth's (1965) solution of incorporating sensitivity training and process learning into on-the-job activities will be more efficacious.

On-the-Job Leadership Training and Development

Learning and development occur during the performance of regularly assigned duties and may be as effective as formalized training programs. On-the-job efforts can include learning from experience, self-study, special assignments, the rotation of jobs, on-the-job coaching, mentoring, and attendance at meetings of professional associations (Phillips, 1986).

Learning from Experience

It is evident that much learning can accrue from experience. According to Lombardo (1986), 86 senior executives who were interviewed were able to list 286 key events in their careers that generated 529 "lessons." The findings from these lessons, as well as from interviews with over 300 executives, suggested that although everyone appears to value learning from mistakes, successful executives admit making them, while unsuccessful ones try to hide or deny their failures or blame them on others. It is necessary for successful executives to understand what went wrong, to accept the consequences, and to avoid similar circumstances in the future. High performers drew many more lessons from these experiences than did low performers. They

learned skills and attitudes that they needed to overcome obstacles to complete their work. Involvement with others forced an examination of their personal values. Failures led successful managers to confront their own limitations. Five types of assignments were seen to have special importance for the development of managers: project assignments, line-to-staff shifts, start-ups, fix-its, and assignments involving a major change in scope.

Rudman, Ohlott, and McCauley (1988) surveyed 346 mid-level managers and executives from nine Fortune 500 companies to identify and classify the on-the-job developmental opportunities they had experienced. The 103 descriptive items were correlated with global ratings of the jobs' developmental potential and then factor analyzed. Particularly important to development were a supportive boss and opportunities to establish personal credibility. Having to deal with intense pressure and with responsibilities for downsizing were also seen as important opportunities. These sources of development were linked to from 5 to 31 specific lessons unearthed by Lindsey, Holmes, and McCall (1987) that were learned from the opportunity. For example, learning how to be comfortable with ambiguous situations appears to accrue from the lesson learned in holding a job for which there is an absence of strategic direction.

Interviews and questionnaires with 41 New York Telephone managers revealed numerous on-the-job events and developmental opportunities that provided important lessons. A quarter to a half of the respondents mentioned increased responsibilities, special projects, exposure to role models, self-initiated activities, and learning from negative experiences as being most salient for their learning of skills and broader perspectives (Valerio, 1988).

Copeman (1971) collected detailed experiences from 109 CEOs about those they felt had contributed most to the development of various competencies, such as their ability to negotiate or formulate policies. On-the-job opportunities, such as taking charge of a division or serving as assistant to the president were often mentioned. Similar results were reported by Davies and Easterby-Smith (1984) for 60 British managers. A study at Honeywell (1981) indicated that on-the-job experiences were the primary source of development of much managerial knowledge, skill, and ability, including effective decision making and problem solving, communication, delegation, empathy, resolution of conflicts, knowledge about business, knowledge of the products, business trends, and knowledge of costs. Baxter (1953) found such on-the-job opportunities for learning to be as effective as formal supervisory training.

McCall and McCauley (1986) summarized other characteristics of jobs that help develop managers. Important characteristics are assignments with broad responsibilities, trouble-shooting assignments, early experience in leadership positions, and staff positions[14] at corporate headquarters. Also valuable are assignments with project task forces and newly created departments. In addition, career development is enhanced by working in those mainline functional areas that are central to the organization's business (Kotter, 1982a). Moreover, although moving among important job assignments is essential, sufficient time has to be spent in an assignment for it to contribute to the development of one's career (Gabarro, 1985).

Lindsey, Holmes, and McCall (1987) examined the extent to which job assignments differ in their developmental potential by identifying the kinds of experiences that over 400 executives said provided them with lessons and changed them. For instance, one experience that the executives thought made a big difference in their development was their move into staff jobs, such as business or product planning, which forced them to develop new ways of thinking about some strategic element of the business. These jobs often involved exposure to top executives and the executives' assignment to corporate headquarters.

Learning and Development from Challenging Assignments. Jobs enhance development if they are challenging. Exxon managers whose entry-level jobs provided such challenges were more likely to be seen as meritorious six years later (Vicino & Bass, 1978) than were those whose jobs did not provide such challenges. In the A T & T assessment program (Bray & Howard, 1983), candidates with assessed potential were more likely to reach middle management if they were as-

signed challenging jobs. In a questionnaire survey of 118 managers, McCall and McCauley (1986) found that assignments involving overcoming the past and dealing with inadequate, resistant staffs contributed to perceived growth as a manager. The less experienced the manager, the more the assignment is seen to have the potential for development. However, challenges can be too great. For instance, the assignment to a difficult boss appeared to detract from a job's developmental value for a manager.

Learning from One's Superior. Superiors can have a positive influence on their subordinates' managerial styles (Marshall & Stewart, 1981), as was noted earlier in describing the "falling-dominoes" effect (Bass, Waldman, Avolio, & Bebb, 1987). Subordinates are more likely to model their own leadership style on that of their superiors of they perceive their immediate supervisors to be successful and competent. Aspiring military cadets are likely to select for role models those superiors who they believe are charismatic (Clover, 1989). Also, they parallel their superior's occupational values if they think their superiors are considerate (Weiss, 1978).

Coaching

Coaching refers to training, that is, guidance and feedback about specific efforts involved in a task, the performance of a job, and the handling of assignments; mentoring refers to advising and guiding education and career development. A coach is more likely to be one's immediate superior, although peers can coach each other. A mentor may be an immediate superior, but is often found at considerably higher levels in the organization than the protégé and among those with much more experience than the protégé.

In addition to receiving coaching and mentoring from superiors and peers, subordinates may obtain counseling from staff professionals in individual and group sessions. Subordinates also may contribute to their superiors' education. Smith, Organ, and Near (1983) considered this behavior to be an aspect of good "organizational citizenship." Furthermore, leaders and managers can learn from colleagues and their own subordinates, as well as from others whom they may encounter in their work (McCall and McCauley, 1986).

[14]Staff assignments after line experience are advantageous, but being limited only to staff positions, as chapters 32 and 33 noted, limits advancement for women and ethnic "outsiders."

The careers of leaders within the organization may be shaped by consultants, advisers, and sponsors who are not necessarily coaches or mentors. Advisers can provide specific information and facilitate the solution of specific problems; sponsors can use their power to provide opportunities for experiences that are necessary for advancement (Wood & Hertz, 1982).

Coaching Activities. Mills (1986) asked 207 subordinate managers to describe, in a 25-item questionnaire, the coaching practices of their immediate superiors. The factors that emerged included (1) emphasizing self-development and self-discovery, (2) offering constructive ways to improve, (3) conducting regular coaching interviews, (4) being a good listener, (5) delegating and challenging subordinates to perform, (6) and setting realistic standards. All these coaching behaviors contributed to the subordinates' satisfaction with the coaching.

Coaching can occur when superiors use consultation to solicit subordinates' reactions and then offer advice on how the subordinates should deal with the issue. It can also be done after the subordinate represents the superior at a meeting and discusses the experience with the superior or in superior-subordinate discussions of the extent to which preset objectives have been met.

Ineffective and Effective Coaching. Coaching is likely to be ineffective if relations between the coached subordinate and the coaching superior are ambiguous because the subordinate does not trust the coach. It is also likely to be ineffective if the superior sees the subordinate as a rival, if the subordinate's need for dependence is ignored, of the superior is intolerant or does not allow sufficient time for coaching, and if the superior withholds information to maintain power out of hostility toward the subordinate or to feel more secure (Tannenbaum, Kallejian, & Weschler, 1954).

Coaching is likely to work well if the subordinate can identify with the coach and if the coach provides a good model, if the coach and the subordinate are open and trusting with each other, if both accept responsibilities fully, and if the subordinate is provided with suitable rewards and recognition for his or her improvement (H. Levinson, 1962). In addition, coaches will be more effective if they set clear standards, if they appreciate their subordinates' interests and abilities, if they practice delegation coupled with appropriate follow-up, and if they encourage subordinates to complete assignments (Goodacre, 1963). Coaching thrives in a climate of confidence, a climate in which subordinates respect the integrity and capability of their superiors.

Coaching is expected to take greatest advantage of the possibilities of individualized instruction. It can concentrate on those specific problems that subordinates find hardest to deal with. It can attend to those specific performances that subordinates find hardest to improve. It may provide the kind and quality of feedback that can have a great impact on subordinates (Mace, 1950).

Several experiments provided evidence that, as expected, coaching could improve leadership performance. Wexley and Jaffee (1969) compared 10 control groups, 10 groups with approval of the leader "as is" after the first session, and 10 groups with early coaching of the leader. Both observers and followers reported significant changes in the leaders in the direction of greater human relations orientation toward those who were coached. Similarly, Maloney (1956) reported that group cohesiveness and participation but not group learning were improved when a leader followed a precisely coached method for implementing discussion. Likewise, Klubeck and Bass (1954) found that 20 coached, compared to 120 uncoached, sorority women with some leadership potential were more likely to emerge as leaders of initially leaderless group discussions.

Mentoring

Of 122 recently promoted persons in business, two-thirds indicated that they had mentors (M. C. Johnson, 1980). Mentored personnel earned higher overall compensation than did those without mentors (Roche, 1979). Again, personnel with mentors in a large health-business firm believed they had more career opportunities, promotions, security, and recognition than did those without mentors (Fagenson, undated). Zey's (1984) more than 100 interviews with middle and senior managers found about a third reporting that their careers benefited from the opportunity. The popularity of mentoring reflects the interest, both of individual employees and of their organizations, in the career development of individual employees (Clutterbuck, 1982b; Collins & Scott, 1978).

Mentoring tends to be paternalistic in that it provides a role model for the protégé to follow (Levinson, Darrow, Klein, et al., 1978). Mentors use their greater knowledge, experience, and status to help their protégés and do more than merely act supportive or give advice. They may assist in the organizational visibility and advancement of the protégés by informing higher-ups about how good a job the protégés are doing (M. C. Johnson, 1980; Shapiro, 1985). Kram (1983) described the process involved in 18 mentor-protégé relationships as beginning with phased-in initiation, followed by cultivation, separation, and redefinition. During the process, the mentors provided protégés with sponsorship, exposure and visibility, coaching, counseling, protection, friendship, and challenging assignments. The mentors acted as role models and as a source of acceptance and confirmation.

Benefits of Mentoring. Mentoring can help to retain subordinates. It is likely to increase the subordinates' self-esteem and satisfaction with their work and with the progress of their careers. Mentoring can also help protégés to cooperate in joint efforts (Hunt & Michael, 1983) and to use their intelligence more fully to make a contribution to the organization's success (Fiedler & Leister, 1977a).

The mentors' own advancement is facilitated if their replacements are considered to be adequately prepared to step into their shoes. Advancement is also facilitated if the performance of developing subordinates is used as a criterion for evaluation and reward by the mentors' superiors (Jennings, 1967a). In addition, mentors accumulate respect, power, and future access to information from those individuals they have helped to develop. They spread their influence elsewhere, both inside and outside their organization, through their former protégés. Successful mentors are also likely to gain esteem among their peers (Kram, 1980). Mentoring can be a creative, satisfying, and rejuvenating experience for the mentors (Levinson, Darrow, Klein, et al., 1978).

Mentors can inform protégés about how the organization works (Johnson, 1980) and about the uses of power, of integrity, and of the artistic and craftsmanlike

elements in effective management (Zaleznik, 1967). They can help women protégés, in particular, to integrate their career and family responsibilities and are particularly important for the success of the careers of women managers without family connections in the firm (Kram, 1980). At the same time, mentoring appears to be more helpful in the early careers of young managers and professionals from higher socioeconomic backgrounds (Whitely, Dougherty, & Dreher, 1988).

Conditions for Effective Mentoring. Numerous publications (see, for example, Tyson & Birnbrauer, 1983) have laid out the prescriptions for good coaching or mentoring. As Clawson (1980) observed in 38 superior-subordinate relationships, some mentor-protégé arrangements work well, while others do not. Effective mentoring requires executives who can tolerate emotional interchanges and who are able to accept conflict as a dispute over substance, not as a personal attack (Zaleznik, 1967).

In addition to being sufficiently empathic to the needs of protégés, according to Levinson, Darrow, Klein, et al. (1978), mentors should be older and have about 8 to 15 years more experience than their protégés. The authors argued that a greater disparity in age results in a generation gap that interferes with mentoring, while less disparity gives rise to a peer relation, rather than a mentoring relation. Bowen and Zollinger (1980) suggested that mentors should be of the same sex, if possible, although female mentors are likely to be scarce. Nevertheless, male mentors react more favorably to female protégés, particularly if the female protégés are unmarried, but they are more willing to act as mentors toward married than unmarried men. Mentors are also more favorable toward protégés whom they regard as better in job performance.

Hunt and Michael (1983) argue that mentors should be highly placed, powerful, and knowledgeable—that they need to be executives who will not be threatened by their protégés' potential to equal or surpass them. Such mentors will be more effective, since individuals value the positive feedback they receive from those they esteem much more than from those they do not value (Bass, Wurster, & Alcock, 1961). Therefore, the protégés will place a premium on feedback from mentors who are higher in authority in the system and who they believe are experienced, knowledgeable, and es-teemed (Bass, 1985a).

Successful competent and considerate mentors are likely to serve as role models for their protégés. Results from studies of leader-subordinate modeling (Adler, 1982; Korman, 1976), suggest that protégés will model themselves after mentors if they regard the mentors as competent and if they believe their mentors are in control of their paths to valued rewards and to organizational advancement. Furthermore, protégés are more likely to model the leadership styles of their mentors if the mentors are easy to identify with and are personally attractive to the protégés (Bass, 1985a).

Clawson (1979) listed the characteristics of superiors that are likely to contribute to the subordinates' ability to learn a lot from their superiors. The psychological predispositions of effective coaches and mentors included relations orientation, even temperament, tolerance for ambiguity, valuing the organization, liking of the subordinate, and respect for the subordinate's intelligence. Self-perceptions of effective superiors included that of being a teacher, setting an example, being directive and instinctive, providing clear feedback, and avoiding being too critical. The behavior of effective coaches and mentors involved taking time to understand subordinates, informality, listening with understanding, providing new perspectives, and sponsoring subordinates with higher management.

Clawson's (1979) subordinates were likely to say they learned a lot from superiors if they, the subordinates, were also more relations oriented, if they respected and liked their superior and perceived themselves in the role of a learner dealing with relevant assignments. Subordinates showed their interest by responding enthusiastically and adaptively to the superior's guidance. Although similar requirements and benefits are suggested for effective cross-sex mentoring (Clawson & Kram, 1984), women mangers are thought to need and benefit more from mentoring, despite the shortage of women mentors (Warihay, 1980). Women managers find mentors useful because they are less likely than are men to have access to information networks (Rosen, Templeton, & Kirchline, 1981), to be more isolated tokens (Kanter, 1977b), to have to overcome stereotypes about women lacking leadership potential (Mas-sengill & DiMarco, 1979), and to learn their way around a male-dominated organization with male-oriented norms and standards of behavior (Noe, 1988).

Job Rotation

Management development may be built around job rotation—the transfer of trainees from one job to another to provide a succession of educational and developmental experiences. In a survey of 1,958 lower and middle managers Lawler (1964) reported that the managers tended to be more satisfied with their jobs if they remained in the same position for relatively shorter periods. They were more satisfied, in particular, with their opportunities for self-actualization if they were moved more frequently.

Increased family and housing difficulties in the 1980s, caused by frequent relocation, may have changed this attitude. Resistance to accepting a rotation that requires relocating in an undesireable location has increased. Moreover, the two-career family now requires opportunities for both spouses in the new location. Firms may have need to develop substitute training approaches to meet the objectives of job rotation.

The effect on those who must work in departments whose leaders are frequently changed to provide rotational opportunities for the leaders are both negative and positive. The negative effects include the loss of interest, holding actions, and laissez-faire leadership by the leader who knows that he or she will be transferred soon. Important stable programs may be difficult to maintain. The "lame duck" leader may lose legitimate power in the eyes of the subordinates. New relations will have to be established by outsiders with the incoming new leader.

The positive effects are also apparent. Necessary changes and new ideas are likely to coincide with the incoming new leader, and better connections between the new leader's old and new departments are likely. Rotation provides both the leader and the departments with new challenges. It is expected to increase identification with the whole organization, rather than with a single area. A comparison of the British tendency to maintain narrow specialization in a single functional area with the Japanese tendency to expect managers to work anywhere in the firm might shed further light on the utility of rotation. Unfortunately, little experimental evidence is available about any of the expected positive effects of rotation. Maier, Hoffman, and Read (1963) studied superior-subordinate communications in situations in which the superior had formerly occupied the job of his subordinate. In comparison with a control group in which the superior had not occupied the job of his subordinate, they found, with surprise, that previous occupancy of the job did not facilitate superior-subordinate communication.

Survey Feedback

Feedback about performance on the job is critical if learning is to occur from work experiences. This is why survey feedback from peers, subordinates, and clients, as well as superiors, based on standardized questionnaires, can play an important part in leadership development. Such feedback is now common in leadership training and education programs. R. D. Mann (1961) found more change in supervisors of experimental than of control departments as a consequence of survey feedback. D. G. Bowers (1973) reported that survey feedback promoted more improvement than did other developmental interventions, such as sensitivity training or individual consultation.

Bass (1976) described the use in leadership development of the computerized feedback of subordinates' anonymous descriptions of their leaders' *directive*, negotiative, consultative, *participative*, and delegating behavior;[15] the leader's power to decide relative to the subordinates; and various perceptions about the organization and the group in which they worked. The subordinates' satisfaction with and perceptions of the effectiveness of the leaders' performance were also appraised. The leaders' self-perceptions were obtained on the same variables. Feedback by individual counselors or in workshops provided the leaders with a profile of the data and discrepancies from norms among their own, subordinates', and normative descriptions of their

performance. Attention was then focused on which data and discrepancies were important to try to change and how change might be attempted and evaluated. R. J. Solomon (1976) showed that such feedback could result in the improved performance of library departments supervised by department heads who received the feedback.

Yukl (1982) fed back more specifically observable leadership behavior in 23 categories using subordinates', peers', and superiors' descriptions of what they regarded as optimal behavior for effectiveness in the position occupied by the leader. Again, the focus of training was on the discrepancies between actual and desired behaviors. A similar strategy was adopted by Bass and Avolio (1989) for feeding back to managers, on an item-by-item and factor-by factor basis, their transformational and transactional leadership as seen by their subordinates. The saluatory effects obtained will be discussed later.

For three successive years, a sample of 148 Xerox managers received feedback on 44 behaviors from their subordinates on their management of tasks, management of change, communication, leadership, and delegation, as well as how much they involved their employees and helped to develop them. Eighty-three percent of the managers used the feedback to create action plans for improvement. Subsequently, their management style was judged by their employees to be improving (Deets & Morano, 1986).

The considerable hortatory literature about giving and receiving feedback can be summarized as suggesting that feedback should be about the recipient's observed behavior, not the recipient's personality, motivation, or intentions. The receipt of adequate feedback from others and from one's environment requires that the recipient solicit or be open to accepting it. Often the reverse is true. Managers are prone to close out the opportunities for learning when faced with difficult and threatening problems (Argyris, 1982). But instead of shutting out, ignoring, or denying such inputs, it is important to examine in what ways changes could be made to improve the situation. Feedback, coupled with personal reflection, can be used to expand self-awareness and to strengthen relationships with colleagues (May & Kruger, 1988).

---

[15]As defined in Chapters 22 and 23, *direction* (italicized) refers only to giving orders with or without explanation. Direction (romanized) included ordering, persuading, and manipulating. *Participation* (italicized) refers only to sharing in the decision process. Participation (romanized) includes consulting, sharing, and delegating.

Purposes and Content of Leadership Training

Improving Leaders' Attitudes, Skills, and Knowledge

Early leadership training programs[16] stressed increasing the supervisor's human relations knowledge, skills, and ability, especially with reference to problems of interaction among his or her subordinates, as one of the basic goals of training.

Improved Attitudes and Knowledge. Katzell (1948) found that 73 supervisors scored significantly higher on a test of human relations attitudes (How Supervise) after an 8-week training course. Canter (1951), using the same test, studied supervisors in insurance companies. He found significant gains in scores on how to supervise, general facts and principles, and estimates of the group's opinion. He also found that large gains in understanding the psychological principles of supervising others and better insight into subordinates' attitudes were obtained through supervisory training. Similarly, Goodacre (1955) and Neel and Dunn (1960) administered tests of knowledge of human relations practices to members of training groups; significant gains in knowledge were obtained in both studies. But Hand and Slocum (1970) reported no change in knowledge of human relations, self-actualization, motivation, interpersonal relations, or participation as a consequence of a training program for middle managers.

Results obtained by R. D. Miller (1969) indicated that leadership training also improves attitudes toward the importance of the leadership role. Papaloizos (1962) reported that about one-third of the participants in a human relations training program exhibited favorable changes in attitude toward subordinates. Following similar training, Mayo and Dubois (1963) found that the gain in leadership ratings was correlated positively with final course grades but not with other criteria. Likewise, Cassel and Shafer (1961) gave students direct training in human relations and leadership. Test scores revealed significant gains in leadership and social insight but not in sociometric preference or personality tensions and needs. But House and Tosi (1963) found

[16]For example, Canter (1949), Katzell (1948), Maier (1948), Mold (1947), and Vonachen et al. (1946).

that a 40-week training course produced no important advantages for management trainees in job satisfaction and other measures of performance over a control group. Because of the substantive and processual differences in the contents of different leadership and human relations training programs, no single generalization is possible about their efficacy.

Improved Self-perceptions. As noted before, programs which provide feedback purport to increase the accuracy of a leader's self-image. Trice (1959) reported significant changes in self-perception in a trained group but not in a control group. Members of the experimental group who changed the most described themselves as more flexible after training. In a study of human relations training for middle managers, Hand and Slocum (1970) obtained results indicating that acceptance of oneself and others was significantly improved in a immediate posttest, but the significance had disappeared 90 days later. To improve self-perception was the objective of several democratic leadership training studies. Although Gassner, Gold, and Snadowsky (1964) found no significant increase between the actual and ideal self for members of either the experimental or control groups, they found that the experimental group increased significantly in knowledge of democratic leadership, but the control group did not.

Improved Decision Making. Decision making was also often targeted for improvement. For instance, employing 83 undergraduates trained in human relations techniques and 75 who were not, Madden (1977) reported that leaders who received human relations training made significantly more accurate postdiscussion decisions than did untrained leaders, but they were no different in their satisfaction with the decision-making process.

Theory-based Training. Following Ellis's rational theory of therapy, an example of theory-based training was conducted by R. E. Johnson (1980), who showed, with a controlled training experiment, that beliefs in "rational leadership" could be inculcated. However, as Tetrault, Schriesheim, and Neider (1988) pointed out, it is necessary to separate the question of the utility of the training effort based on a theory and the validity of the theory. It is possible to observe a training program that improves the performance of the leaders although it is based on an invalid theory or a theory about which positive evidence is lacking.

Training in Success and Effectiveness as a Leader

In research reports, training procedures can seldom be described in complete detail. For this reason, it is difficult to determine the particular methods which participants have learned in the training that they may use to gain and hold a position of leadership. Nonetheless, a number of studies have shown overall that direct training in the techniques of leadership can improve trainees' leadership and effectiveness in groups.

Opportunity to Emerge as a Leader. Jennings (1952b) studied two groups of 20 production supervisors over 16 training sessions. The experimental group was subdivided into discussion groups to solve case problems. At the end of the first session, the emergent leaders were removed and placed in a separate group. Thus, new leaders were forced to emerge in the second session. These leaders were also removed and placed in the leadership pool. Successive sessions permitted the rise of new leaders. In the control group, the appointed discussion leader presented a problem and helped the group arrive at a solution. Six months later, more members of the experimental group than of the control group were rated above average in effectiveness.

Training for Leading Discussions. Training can also improve the likelihood that discussions will be effective. Thus, Maier (1953) demonstrated that discussion groups with skilled leaders produced better decisions than did those with unskilled leaders. Maier (1950) studied groups of foremen with a leader and three followers with and without training. Leaders of the 44 experimental groups were given 8 hours of lectures, discussions, and role playing, whereas the leaders of the 36 control groups were untrained. Maier found that the trained leaders had more success than the untrained leaders in inducing their groups to accept change and compromise. Subsequently, Maier and Hoffman (1960a) demonstrated that groups with

trained leaders produced discussions of higher quality than those with untrained leaders. Again, Maier and Hoffman (1964) and Maier and Solem (1962) found that leaders who used a problem-solving approach helped their groups to achieve higher-quality solutions than did leaders who applied financial incentives or concentrated on a solution. Barnlund (1955) also demonstrated that trainees who were given discussion leadership training regulated participation more and exhibited a greater ability to resolve conflict in group discussions.

Training and Education in Leadership Styles

Training programs have been developed and evaluated to train individuals to be more successful leaders and how to use each of the major styles of leadership enumerated in Chapters 21 through 25. Thus, the University of Michigan's pioneering survey research feedback programs reduced autocratic and increased democratic leadership behavior.[17] R. Likert (1977b) summarized the many completed evaluations of the approach. Vroom and Yetton (1973) created and subsequently evaluated a program that teaches when various forms of participation or direction are rationally more appropriate.[18] Blake and Mouton's (1964) Managerial Grid Training and Hersey and Blanchard's (1982a) situational leadership programs centered on the development of improved task and interpersonal relationships[19] with some concerns about their evaluation. Fiedler and Mahar (1979b) developed a program to train managers to deal with the situations they face as a function of their scores on the Least Preferred Coworker (LPC) questionnaire,[20] and summarized 12 validity studies of the efficacy of the program. Numerous programs, beginning with Fleishman's (1953b), focused on increasing the consideration behavior of supervisors[21] and evaluations of the efforts. And Miner (1965) trained managers in how to increase their motivation to manage[22] with some effort to evaluate the attempts.

Democratic Leadership. Eichler and Merrill (1933) and Zeleny (1941) found that students gained from di-

[17]See Chapter 21.
[18]See Chapter 22.
[19]See Chapter 23.
[20]See Chapter 23.
[21]See Chapter 24.
[22]See Chapter 25.

rect training in democratic leadership and ways to improve human relations. In the same way, A. K. Healy (1962) noted that training in democratic leadership enabled school children to gain in carrying out the leadership role and in their sociometric scores. The status of sociometric isolates was improved in the democratic setting, as was academic achievement. Similarly, Spector (1958) obtained significant improvement in human relations attitudes among U.S. Air Force cadets as a result of such training. Bavelas (1942) trained three adult leaders in the democratic leadership of community center activities and three controls received no training. The trained leaders greatly reduced the number of leader-initiated activities and the giving of orders and increased the number of activities in which children exercised responsibility, but the control group made no such changes. Under trained leaders, the children showed more interest, enthusiasm, and initiative in planning projects.

Lippitt (1949) gave community leaders in intergroup relations a two-week workshop in democratic leadership group discussion, role playing, and sociodrama. Both the participants and the observers reported that the trainees became more proficient in handling problems of intergroup relations as a result of the workshop. Likewise, Maier and Hoffman (1961) demonstrated that supervisors who were trained to pursue democratic solutions led groups to a more effective and creative solution of a problem in changing work methods than did those without such training. Similarly, Baum, Sorensen, and Place (1970) found that workers' answers to a questionnaire indicated an increase in actual and desired organizational control after their supervisors had completed a course; the change was in the direction of more democratic control.

PM Leadership. For PM leadership training, the ideal leader is "an adaptive perceiver of employees' needs and a diagnostician of how these needs can be met. Feedback processes from employees to their supervisors are central" (Peterson, 1989, p. 34). Supervisors must focus on whether their behavior is experienced by employees as having sufficient planning, performance, and maintenance content. Misumi (1985) reported that a program to teach Japanese shipyard supervisors his theory of performance-maintenance (PM) leadership stressing the need for both task- and relations orientation resulted in a reduction of accidents at work. Cognitive discrepancies on P and M scores between self- and others' ratings decreased. Although the morale and PM scores[23] of nontrained supervisors dropped because of deleterious changes in the company, the PM scores of the trainees did not. Their superiors judged that the performance of 56 of the 71 trained supervisors showed considerable to substantial improvement.

Leader Match. According to Fiedler's contingency model, the leaders' effectiveness depends on the leaders' LPC scores and on whether the situation is favorable. Since LPC is seen as a kind of invariant personality attribute, it follows that leadership effectiveness can best be increased by teaching leaders how to make situations more favorable to themselves. Fiedler, Chemers, and Mahar (1976) developed a self-paced programmed instruction workbook, *Leader Match* that teaches leaders how to (1) assess their own leadership style based on their LPC scores, (2) assess the amount of situational favorability, and (3) change the situation so it matches their style.

Fiedler and Mahar (1979b) reviewed 12 studies that demonstrated the validity of the training effort. Five studies were conducted in civilian organizations and 7 were conducted in military settings. The performance evaluations were collected from 2 to 6 months after training, and some included measures before and after training. The performance evaluations of 423 trained leaders were compared with those of 484 leaders without Leader Match training who were randomly assigned to control groups. Generally, although not uniformly, supportive results were obtained. For example, in Fiedler and Mahar's (1979b) field experiment with 190 ROTC cadets, Leader Match training was administered to the cadets before they attended 4 weeks of advanced summer camp, where they were selected at random to serve in several different leadership positions for 24-hour periods. An analysis of commissioned and noncommissioned officers' evaluations of the cadets' performance, as well as peer ratings, showed that

[23]See Chapter 23.

the 155 male and 35 female cadets with training tended to perform better than did the 176 male and 39 female cadets in the control group.[24]

A meta-analysis by Burke and Day (1986) lent confidence that Leader Match generalized in its effectiveness across situations, as measured by superiors' ratings. In a study of the effects of leadership training on productivity and safety, Fiedler, Bell, Chemers, and Patrick (1984) combined Leader Match training, which emphasizes the need to change situations, and behavioral-modeling training, which teaches necessary leadership behavior that is independent of the situation. No attempt was made to separate the effects of the two types of training. The two training methods together increased productivity and decreased accidents. A five-year follow-up evaluation showed a continuation of the positive effects of the combined training on productivity and safety (Fiedler, Wheeler, Chemers, & Patrick, 1988).

Schriesheim and Hosking (1978) were troubled with Leader Match because they found too many problems in the contingency model itself to warrant using it for remedial actions by specific individuals in specific situations. And Jago and Ragan (1986b) used a computer simulation to show that Leader Match was inconsistent with the contingency model. But Chemers and Fiedler (1986) argued that the wrong assumptions had been made. Jago and Ragan (1986b) disagreed. Kabanoff (1981) also noted that Leader Match was inconsistent with the contingency model and suggested alternative explanations for the results of using Leader Match. Rice and Kastenbaum (1983) inferred that the positive effects of Leader Match are due to its sensitizing leaders to the possibility that they can change their situations. Leader Match, as may many other kinds of training, may exert its positive effects because it bolsters the confidence of leaders who receive the training. Frost (1986) evaluated Leader Match against an alternative training method and a control group. As with other studies, experienced managers who received Leader Match training changed their situational control in accordance with the Leader Match prescrip-

tions. In the alternative method, trainees were also taught successfully how to change their situation control, but no mention was made of their LPC score or its implications. The performance of the trainees in this alternative condition improved in the same way as did the performance of those who received regular Leader Match training. Frost suggested that the results were due to increases in the leaders' confidence, not to feedback on their leadership style (LPC) around which Leader Match training is organized. Frost concluded, from the results of his aforementioned experiment, that for experienced managers, at least, behavioral modeling or other methods of teaching that require leadership behavior that is independent of the situation are likely to be more effective than is Leader Match.

Leader-Member Exchange (LMX). LMX training[25] is aimed at improving the dyadic exchange relations of leaders with members of the group. A controlled experiment completed by Graen, Novak, and Sommerkamp (1982) showed that supervisors who were specifically trained in maintaining high-quality leader-member exchange relationships, in contrast to supervisors who received a placebo experience, improved the productivity of their subordinates over 16 percent; their subordinates' motivation and loyalty were increased and their role conflict and role ambiguity were reduced. Similarly, Scandura and Graen (1984) found that LMX training compared to a control group improved the level of reciprocal understanding and helpfulness between supervisors and subordinates. As a consequence of LMX training, initially "outgroup" subordinates perceived increased support from their supervisors. The weekly productive output and job satisfaction of the subordinates were also increased.

Participative Leadership. Sensitivity training has been seen by Argyris (1969) as key to the development in leaders of receptivity to participative leadership. Sensitivity training, according to Argyris, moves people to become trusting, open, and experimenting with their own ideas and feelings and to own up to them. Moreover, such people can help others to become more so. Without sensitivity training, supervisors will

---

[24]Similar findings were obtained by Chemers and Mahar (1978); Csoka and Bons (1978); Fiedler, Mahar, and Schmidt (1976); and Leister, Borden, and Fiedler (1977).

[25]See Chapter 18.

be more inclined to remain directive in their leadership. The argument is that those who have been through sensitivity training will be more comfortable with participative approaches with their subordinates. But others believe that sensitivity training can produce more manipulative leadership as well (Bass, 1967c).

Training efforts to promote participative or directive leadership were described by A. J. Franklin (1969), Herod (1969), and House (1962). Franklin administered a test of knowledge of group theory to groups of disadvantaged youths. Test scores after training were related to the groups' cohesiveness, but not to a significant degree. Herod (1969) demonstrated that a group-centered training program for college women resulted in the enhancement of participative leadership practices after training. At the end of four months, however, the leaders had regressed to their original positions. House (1962) trained one group in a participative style of leadership and another in a directive style. The more directive method, along with elevated course requirements, was associated with a significant decrease in absences and a significant increase in the number of trainees who completed the course. In one of the few evaluations of the Hersey-Blanchard situational leadership model, 60 executive managers completed a training course on when it was appropriate to tell, sell, participate, or delegate. After completing training, they scored significantly higher on a situational leadership examination than did a control group (Hersey, Angelini, & Carakushansky, 1982). By means of a controlled experiment with workshop supervisors, Crookall (1987) obtained positive results in a more comprehensive evaluation of a group trained in situational leadership in contrast with a control group.

Vroom-Yetton Deductive Model. Chapter 22 described Vroom and Yetton's deductive model for choosing which leadership style to use. Seven decision rules provided guidance to the leader on how directive or participative to be. The Vroom and Yetton training program encourages trainees to see the discrepancies between their way of dealing with a set of standardized cases and the rational model's solution. Detailed analyses are also provided to trainees in answer to such questions as, What circumstances cause the trainee to be-

have in a directive fashion, and what circumstances cause the trainee to behave participatively? What rules of the model did the trainees violate most frequently and least frequently? Does the leadership style displayed by the trainees reflect more concern with getting decisions that are high in quality or with getting decisions that are accepted? Does the leadership style reflect more concern about time pressure or about the development of subordinates? Jago and Vroom (1975) also pursued survey feedback for training by asking subordinates of the trainees to indicate how they think their superior would respond to each Vroom-Yetton case problem.

The Vroom-Yetton model has been found useful in teaching leaders to use different decision processes in different situations and as a way of increasing effectiveness of decisions. Training involves teaching trainees how to analyze various situations to choose the amount of direction or participation that is likely to produce that best decision. Managers who are trained to use the model are more likely to select an appropriate decision-making style (Field, 1982; Vroom & Jago, 1978). The model requires learning to make it useful in everyday situations (Wexley & Latham, 1981), but performance aids can be provided. Personal computer programs provide instant profiles of rules violated by a decision, feasible alternatives, and qualitative effects of the decision for sets of problems of the expanded Vroom-Jago (1988) model. Nonetheless, questions about the Vroom-Yetton training model remain because of its extensive dependence on leaders' self-reports (Schriesheim & Kerr, 1977b). Field (1979) added a number of other problems that weaken confidence in Vroom and Yetton's conclusions, including the effects of social desirability, the lack of external validity, and the biases of experimenters (see also Tetrault, Schriesheim, & Neider, 1988).

Consideration or Initiation of Structure. Efforts here have been twofold, to show, first, that supervisors' attitudes toward initiation and consideration as measured by the LOQ can be changed with training and, second, that this change can also be measured by the Leader Behavior Description Questionnaire (LBDQ). As was noted in Chaper 24, coercive elements were involved in earlier versions of the LBDQ. As a consequence, reductions in initiation and increases in consideration were sought in training.

The results of numerous controlled experiments using the LOQ and the LBDQ to measure improvements have been mixed. Comparisons were difficult because of the extent to which the training itself varied in emphasis, quality, and extent, for there is no single standardized program about how to teach leaders to change their initiation and consideration.

Fleishman (1953b) and Harris and Fleishman (1955) examined the initiation and consideration scores of 39 International Harvester supervisors following a training program. The supervisors' consideration scores increased in means and variances, but the supervisors maintained their heightened consideration scores only if they returned to superiors who were similarly higher in consideration. At the same time, the questionnaire was administered to a control group of foremen who had not taken the course. Compared to the controls, the trainee group exhibited more of a reduction in initiating structure and more of an increase in consideration. Likewise, Stroud (1959) reported that after training, supervisors were described by their superiors as more considerate.

Fifty supervisors of an Australian government railways department were randomly selected and assigned by Tharenou and Lyndon (undated) to receive training and 50 were similarly selected and assigned to a control group. A 2-week residential course trained participants in the skills of planning and relating. Measures of consideration and initiation were obtained before and after training from the supervisors, as well as from 100 male subordinates of the supervisors. Compared to those of the untrained controls, both the trainees' self-rated and subordinate-rated consideration and initiation were increased. Similarly, Deitzer (1967) studied an experimental and control group of district sales managers in an insurance company before, 4 weeks after, and 12 weeks after a training program to increase consideration and the initiation of structure. The experimental group outperformed the control group after training on all criterion variables: the number of new agents recruited, the volume of new policies sold by the agent working under the manager, and the like. The manag-

ers' consideration was positively related to the volume of sales, both 4 and 12 weeks after training; the managers' initiation of structure was related to sales 12 weeks later. However, Bendo (1984) failed to find any significant changes in the LBDQ scores of 126 supervisors who were subjected to Leader Effectiveness Training, a standardized training program.

Savan (1983) contrasted a trained and control group of supervisors and found that a simulation exercise dealing with initiation and consideration conducted between immediate pre- and postmeasurements failed to shift LOQ scores. Nevertheless, 6 months after training, there was a notable improvement in the job performance of the trained supervisors compared to the control group. On the other hand, Painter (1984) measured the LOQ scores of public welfare supervisors and their subordinates' descriptions of the supervisors on the LBDQ 2 months before and after training in interpersonal skills but failed to find any significant effects of the training. Likewise, in a similar pre-post LOQ measurement of 40 restaurant managers and LBDQ assessments of them by their 380 subordinate employees, Anghelone (1981) was unable to find much change in the attitudes or performance of the managers as a consequence of a management training program.

Hand and Slocum (1972) conducted a training program to raise supervisors' consideration scores; 18 months later, they found the supervisors' job performance more highly rated as a consequence. Biggs, Huneryager, and Delaney (1966) found that a 2-week training course resulted in more favorable attitudes toward consideration and less favorable attitudes toward initiating structure. Carron (1964) also obtained data to indicate that supervisors became less strongly oriented toward structuring and authoritarianism as a result of a training effort. Again, Schwartz, Stillwell, and Scanlon (1968) studied two groups of insurance supervisors, one of which moved toward more consideration and less emphasis on production after training and the other of which moved toward more initiation of structure. And although Herod (1969) and M. B. Miles (1965) obtained results from a training program that produced a more considerate attitude toward group processes, they found no significant change in attitudes toward consideration and structure. Carron (1964) noted that although attitudes towards initiating structure and authoritarianism decreased immediately after training, no significant changes were apparent 17 months later. Ayers (1964) found that feedback did little to enhance the effects of training, as measured by changes in attitudes toward consideration and initiation of structure. Similarly, H. B. Stephenson (1966) observed that the training of 449 management trainees in management development produced no significant change in their attitude scores on the LOQ initiation and consideration.

Stogdill (1970) developed a set of films, each depicting a different pattern of LBDQ-XII leadershp behavior: consideration, initiation of structure, tolerance of freedom, and production emphasis. The films were shown to 35 sorority presidents. Each film was followed by a discussion period that was designed to induce insight into the whys and wherefores of the patterns of behavior. Leaders were described by 5 sorority members before training and 3 months after on the LBDQ-XII. The results suggested that leadership behavior was more logically related to the performance of groups after training than before. Stogdill and Bailey (1969) showed the 4 films to small groups of boys in 3 vocational high schools, along with a fifth film on representation. After seeing each movie, the groups discussed the supervisor's behavior. The investigators found that the discussion of the movies exerted a favorable effect on the groups' responses to supervision. In another experiment, Stogdill, Coady, and Zimmer (1970) attempted to influence students' attitudes toward the different supervisory roles by using the films. The results suggested that discussion of the films affected the students' adjustment to supervision. Insight and understanding facilitated favorable response to supervision.

In sum, although results cannot be guaranteed, it appears possible for training programs to increase consideration behavior in leaders, as measured by the LBDQ, sometimes even when the changes are not revealed by comparable shifts in attitudes, as measured by the LOQ. And when the measurement of initiation includes coercive behavior, reductions in such initiation can be induced with training.

Motivation to Manage. By means of a lecture, Miner (1961b) successfully increased the favorableness of the attitudes of 72 research and development supervisors as measured by the Miner Sentence Completion Scale[26] toward accepting responsibility for their leadership role above and beyond their professional roles. He further reported that training resulted in more favorable attitudes toward supervisory work and obtained a small positive correlation between favorable changes in attitudes and changes toward more effective supervisory performance (Miner, 1960b, 1965). Finally, both college students and business managers who took a course with Miner (1965) improved their attitudes toward the acceptance of responsibility, authority, and the willingness to initiate remedial action. Five years later, the business managers who had taken the course had significantly better promotion records than did a control group.

Miner (1988) reviewed previous research on training to increase the motivation of managers and noted its uniqueness in emphasizing how to deal with ineffective subordinates. He further argued that the effectiveness of other training programs, such as Leader Match or behavioral modeling, as seen in Frost's (1986) experiment depend on their sensitizing trainees to the management role.

Transformational Leadership. Although specific behavioral skills can be taught, in training transformational leaders, the emphasis needs to be on education and development, not on skill training alone (Avolio & Gibbons, 1988). Gibbons (1986) reported that in contrast to managers who were transactional, managers who were nominated by their colleagues and described by their subordinates as transformational on the Multifactor Leadership Questionnaire[27] said that their performance primarily reflects their whole integrated person, not specific skills taught in brief workshops that may or may not fit their deeply held values and self-concepts.

Transformational programs of education make use of feedback, as do many other management-development approaches. In this instance, the feedback from colleagues is about one's transformational performance as a charismatic, inspirational, individually considerate and intellectually stimulating leader and how

[26]See Chapter 25.
[27]See Chapter 12.

much one practices the transactional processes of contingent reward and management by exception (Bass & Avolio, 1989). Discrepancies between self and colleagues and self and norms are used to generate ideas and plans for improvement. In an illustrative program, feedback of MLQ results was used to increase the transformational leadership behavior of 250 executives and their direct reports (including the Chief Executive Officer and top four levels of management) of a large Canadian financial institution (Howell & Avolio, 1989). In this program emphasis was also placed on examining the organization's culture as it is and envisioning what it and its goals and objectives should be.

How meaning can be provided to organizational considerations and how long-term strategies can be articulated and implemented are also addressed in developmental efforts. New organizations can by designed and social roles and networks can be arranged (Tichy & Devanna, 1986).

Developing and sharing personal and organizational visions along with their planned implementation can be provided in organizational planning simulations, such as Exercise Venture (Link, Thiagarajan, Trbovich, & Vaughan, 1970) or by a review and discussion of testimonials of what leaders have said about how they do it (Kouzes & Posner, 1985).

Crookall (1987) compared the transactional and transformational leadership training of shop instructors of the Canadian correctional service. The instructors are employed for their trade skills and must manage inmates who are ordinarily low in motivation and education. Twenty of the instructors completed a 3-day program on the Hersey-Blanchard situational leadership model (Hersey & Blanchard, 1977). Another 20 instructors received 3 days of education about transformational leadership (Avolio & Bass, 1989). Still another 20 instructors served as an untrained control group. The situational leadership training was seen by participants and their bosses as a review of good basic supervisory practices; the transformational leadership training was considered to be more of a personal development experience.

Three months before training and 3 months after training, the inmates' supervisors rated the work habits and productivity of both trained groups as significantly improved, but not those of the control group. The

length of the inmates' voluntary stay in the shop programs increased by 50 percent for both sets of trained instuctors and remained unchanged for the control group. Pre- and postchanges in inmates' case descriptions prepared by case managers who did not know about the training experiment registered significant improvement in the inmates' personal growth and development, but no changes occurred for the control group. However, only the transformational program significantly improved the inmates' citizenship behavior and respect for the supervisors. No significant reduction in disciplinary offenses was reported in any of the 3 groups, although the inmates' supervisors reported the need to intervene less often as a consequence of training; they also reported less contraband, sabotage, and complaints from inmates about the staff.

In addition, transformational leadership education resulted in dramatic changes in some of the instructors. One instructor changed from a chronic complainer to a problem solver. Another had inmates asking to be assigned to him for the first time in ten years. Complaints about another instructor for being boring and repetitive were no longer made. And a fourth instructor broke with the tradition of his discipline to take the lead in introducing computerized equipment.

The results of this experiment suggest that transformational leadership education is not a substitute for situational or transactional leadership training. Rather, as is argued elsewhere (Bass, 1985a), transformational leadership can augment transactional leadership. Training in situational leadership can profitably followed by education in transformational leadership.

It must be kept in mind, as Burns (1978) suggested, that transformational leadership requires a broad educational process. Such leadership cannot be manipulated; it must be a joint search for truth by the teacher and the students in which the students are moved "to higher stages of moral reasoning and hence to higher levels of principled judgment..." (p. 449).

Programmatic Applications

Management Development Programs

Management development usually refers to the total long-term off-the-job and on-the-job educational process, whereas supervisory training refers to shorter courses. A full-blown program may accomplish much more than what may be possible with shorter independent training courses. Thus, Guetzkow, Forehand, and James (1962) reported that a one-year management development course changed behavior significantly more than did training courses of short duration.

Management development programs serve other organizational functions. Recruiting is facilitated if prospective applicants know that such a program is available. An organizational-growth strategy can be maintained efficiently when candidates for newly opening positions are already in training. In turn, the growth strategy provides for more possibilities for promotion as a source of reward for managers at lower levels and may reduce defensive competition of promotion (Luttwak, 1976).

Evaluative Impressions. The National Industrial Conference Board (1964) surveyed 167 firms' experience with management development. In evaluating the effectiveness of such programs, 57 percent of the firms expressed the belief that the programs were valuable, but only 14 percent reported evidence in support of this belief.[28]

The National Industrial Conference Board (1963) surveyed 1,074 recently recruited college graduates who had attended management development programs sponsored by their employers. About 40 percent of those who had hoped that the programs would prepare them for promotion felt disappointed and regarded the programs as of little value to themselves or to the company. They preferred instruction that would prepare them for the tasks of specific jobs rather than for human relations and general management. But executives with experience have a different point of view. K. R. Andrews (1966) received 6,000 replies from executives who had attended one of 39 different university programs in management development. Although about 85 percent saw no relationship between attending the courses and their subsequent advances in salary, the benefits they most frequently mentioned were

increased understanding of self and others, greater tolerance for differences in opinion, and heightened awareness of alternative solutions to problems. Structured lectures and didactic teacher-led classwork were regarded as more valuable than unstructured group discussions and informal contacts with faculty and students.

Attitudes and Self-reported Changes. Leadership training of some sort figures strongly in most management development programs, although training is likely to be provided in many other nonsupervisory management functions. In fact, M. W. McCall (1976) suggested that too much emphasis has been placed on leadership training and not enough on the many other varied aspects of a manager's work, although the opposite can also be argued.

Despite the previously-noted evidence to the contrary that training fails to shift LOQ scores (Anghelone, 1981; Savan, 1983; Painter, 1984), numerous other examples of successful changes in attitudes as a consequence of longer-term development programs have appeared. For instance, C. W. Nelson (1967) conducted a training course for top-level managers in a plant, who in turn, conducted a similar course for their lower-level managers. Nelson found that not only did significant changes in attitude occur, but that a retest one year later showed that the effects persisted. Similarly, E. H. Schein (1967) demonstrated that a two-year course in management education produced a significant change in attitudes toward human relations. Again Valiquet (1968) reported a significant change in attitudes and behavior among managers who participated in a one-year training program. R. S. Barrett (1965) found significant change in attitudes, but not in performance, following the completion of an executive development program.

Blake's (1960) study of a management development program in Norway found that the 67 participants reported a greater understanding of other people, themselves, and social trends and more self-confidence in dealing with superiors, peers, and subordinates. Waaler (1962) studied another 194 executives in an management development program in Norway. Participants from the firms with the "best" programs, when compared with those in firms with the "poorest" programs,

---

[28]Other similar kinds of evaluative studies were reported by K. R. Andrews (1966), Basil (1964), Habbe (1950), Jerkedal (1967), Merrell (1965), Oberg (1962), Roethlisberger (1954), and Wikstrom (1961). A handbook (Taylor & Lippitt, 1975) and texts (see, for example, Herbert & Yost, 1978) on management education and development are also available.

reported greater nearness, warmth, and understanding of their employees; more informality with employees; greater predictability of behavior; letting employees know what to expect; and reduced pressure on subordinates.

Specialized Leadership Training and Education

Training programs about how to lead scientists, engineers, technicians, entrepreneurs, military personnel, nurses, schoolteachers, sales personnal, and so on are programs to which much specialized effort has been devoted. The MBA curriculum at universities is another specialized program aimed at preparing students for general business leadership. Entrepreneurial motivation has also been promoted through achievement training. Other specialized programs prepare leaders to work with minorities and in other cultures. Some of these specialized efforts are noted next.

Science and Engineering Supervisors. Although supervision and leadership become major responsibilities for engineers and scientists as they progress in their organizations, their preparation for these responsibilities is left until they have graduated from their professional schools and are at work. But considerable evidence has been attained that such post-graduate efforts generally are efficacious. Moon and Hariton (1958) gave 50 engineering supervisors 30 hours of instruction on methods of self-improvement and greater job efficiency. Lectures were followed by role-playing sessions in which each participant acted out problems in human relations. A questionnaire administered to 67 subordinates of the trained group and to 67 subordinates of untrained supervisors indicated greater improvement for the trained group in understanding the subordinate as an individual, expressing recognition for good work, giving subordinates an opportunity to express their side of a story, and showing more interest in the employees' progress. Carron (1964) administered training over a 6-months period to 23 scientists in supervisory positions, using lectures, discussions, and role playing. A battery of tests was administered to the experimental and a control group immediately before and after training and again 17 months later. The experimental group decreased significantly in authoritarianism and initiating structure, whereas the control group

did not. Mosvick (1966) examined 4 different training methods in a study of 55 engineers in supervisory positions. Three attitude scales and 2 behavioral measures were administered before and after training to experimental and control groups. Members of the trained group showed significant improvement in behavior but not in attitudes; their ability to analyze a simulated communication-conflict situation also improved.

Military Leaders. U.S. military officers (numbering almost 300,000 in the mid-1980s) form an elite profession with its own code and customs and its own politics and culture. They study, train, and prepare for conflicts, ranging from terrorist attacks to conventional invasions of Western Europe that one hopes will never come and maintain a world-wide surveillance of military threats against North America and elsewhere (Morganthau & Horrock, 1984). The amount of required training in the military is also greatly increased by the demand that the military continue to be at the cutting edge of new technology. It is also increased by the steady stream of military personnel to civilian life who need to be replaced.

There is a heavy continuing investment in leadership training for military leaders at all levels. Space prohibits any detailed examination of the special classroom and field exercises that are featured in such training. However, a typical evaluative study was reported by Hood, Showel, and Stewart (1967), who compared U.S. Army squad leaders who received leadership preparation training with a control group of leaders who did not. The trained leaders received higher effectiveness ratings, their squads showed higher spirit, and their followers scored higher on proficiency tests. Descriptions by followers indicated that trained leaders initiated more structure, exercised better control of field exercises, and demonstrated more adequacy in briefing and giving information. Their subordinates were less willing to reenlist, however, and showed less favorable attitudes toward the army. Again, in a study of infantry leaders, Rittenhouse (1968) found that graduates of schools for noncommissioned officers-leaders in the infantry exceeded a control group in their rate of promotion and number of awards, but not in leadership evaluations. Another typical analysis was by Lange, Rittenhouse, and Atkinson

(1968), who presented films of leadership situations followed by group discussion as a method of training military leaders. The groups that discussed the films were more effective than were the control groups in solving leadership problems.

Showel, Taylor, and Hood (1966) found that automated instruction was as effective as conventional methods in training noncommissioned officers in the U.S. Army. Hood, Showel, and Stewart (1967) evaluated three methods for training noncommissioned officers. Recycling consisted of lectures and discussions of leadership principles, followed by a repetition of the course. The integrated system involved lectures, group discussions, films, and role playing of human relations problems. The short course presented formal training in a four-week leader-preparation course. The trainees' scores on written and performance tests of proficiency at the end of recycling were significantly higher than those of the control group. The integrated system and the short course also produced higher scores on written tests, but the differences were not statistically significant. Other examples of effective leadership training for military officers have been discussed in earlier chapters as demonstrations of various principles of consequence (see, for example, Eden & Shani, 1982; Fiedler & Garcia, 1987).

MBA Education.   Education for up to two years that leads to the MBA is broadly based in those institutions that follow the guidelines of the American Assembly of Collegiate Schools of Business. In these schools students receive instruction in applied behavioral science, management information systems, business policy and planning, applied mathematics, and applied economics, as well as in the functional areas of production, human resources management, marketing, finance, and accounting. A major problem for graduates appears to be the lack of opportunity to ply the skills they learned. For example, Hilgert (1965) surveyed MBA graduates who were out of school an average of 8 years, 61 percent of whom were in middle or top management. Seventy-three percent thought that their MBA skills were used only marginally or not at all. Gutteridge (1973) reported that employers regarded the MBA's advantage over the non-MBA as only temporary. Herbert (1972)

found no clear effect of MBA education on job performance. But according to Herbert (1977), 82 supervisors of MBAs and non-MBAs gave MBAs better reputational ratings on technical skills, initiative, responsibility, motivation, judgment, and problem solving but not on better human relations or supervisory skills. The results were not affected by whether the ratees were in staff or line positions.

Jenkins, Reizenstein, and Rodgers (1984) surveyed 110 presidents of Fortune 500 companies and 124 personnel directors from the same firms, along with 450 business school alumni, 93 deans, and 302 faculty members. They found that 57 to 60 percent of the respondents believed the program should focus strongly on quantitative analysis and that an even greater percentage supported an emphasis on decision making. But 32 to 45 percent of these samples thought that MBA programs should deemphasize short-term decision making in favor of long-term strategic planning. The percentage who were satisfied with the extent to which leadership skills were developed among MBAs ranged from 36 to 50 percent. The deans, personnel directors, and alumni were more satisfied and the presidents and faculty members were less satisfied. Satisfaction with the interpersonal skills of MBAs ranged from 28 percent to 46 percent; those in the business community were less satisfied and the academics more so in this regard. Only pluralities ranging from 21 to 43 percent were satisfied with the managerial skills of MBAs.

Interviews with 600 senior executives tended to be consistent with the foregoing findings. Seventy percent thought that business school education was pretty good, and 49 percent regarded the MBA degree as somewhat or very important to getting ahead in their own company, although 86 percent thought that too little application and too much theory were taught.

Executive Development Programs.   These programs are to be found in at least 60 schools of management in the United States. The content parallels that to be covered in the MBA program with variations, depending on the management level of the trainees, the length of the program, and whether a certificate or degree will be awarded. The programs can be made more effective with commitment from outside sponsors to continued executive development and its importance to executive career planning, the use of assessment centers[29] to provide individualized developmental guidance, effective needs analysis, computer networks to link executives in their offices with university faculties, more attention to executive leadership and self-development, and an international perspective, along with custom-made programs for individual organizations (Watson, 1988).

Entrepreneurial and Achievement Motivation. Building on earlier theory and research about the need for achievement, McClelland and Winter (1969) designed workshops to instill a greater need for achievement in entrepreneurs. These workshops were conducted in developed as well as in developing countries, such as Mexico and India. Black entrepreneurs in South Africa were also singled out for attention. Increasing the entrepreneurs' need for achievement was expected to increase their willingness to expand their spheres of activity and their willingness to take on more challenges and responsibility.

The workshops involved showing how the need for achievement is revealed in its projections in the Thematic Apperception Test and how one could increase the achievement thematic content in responding to the test. Generalization about achievement and entrepreneurial activities followed. Positive effects of the training were reported (McClelland & Winter, 1969). Since the need for achievement is of consequence to management, in general, achievement training has been applied to managers, in general. Illustrative were results reported by Boer (1985) in a study of the effects of achievement training on the performance of South African factory management teams (in contrast to control teams who were not trained). The productivity of labor was increased and turnover and absenteeism were reduced in the trained but not in the control groups.

Leadership of and by Minorities. "Awareness" training, mainly for white male managers about special issues of working with women, blacks, and the disadvantaged became commonplace following the passage of affirmative action legislation (Anonymous, 1968b).

[29]Discussed in Chapter 36.

In some instances, heightened awareness has produced overreactions and backlash (L. A. Johnson, 1969). One of the few such programs to be extensively evaluated was reported by Bass, Cascio, McPherson, and Tragash (1976). Following the identification of 5 factors differentiating issues of awareness of managers about affirmative action for black employees,[30] PROSPER (Bass, Cascio, & McPherson, 1972), a self-administered program, was developed. The booklet for PROSPER that each participant receives begins with a pretraining assessment on the 5 factors. Next, a case of an insubordinate black engineer is presented, and the participants have to make in-basket decisions. Each participant then is assigned a role as one of 5 different managers in a firm gathered to discuss the case; each of the roles is built around 1 of the 5 factors. The participants verbalize favorable positions on one of the factors while they hear favorable information about the other 4. Significant increases in the scores for more favorable attitudes towards working with black employees were achieved by 2,293 managers. After 3 to 5 months, 298 managers still showed some of the increase on all 5 factors. Cascio and Bass (1976) further analyzed the specific role-playing effects of PROSPER and found that the results were in the direction of expectations. PROFAIR, a comparable attitude-change program for working with women (Bass, 1971), was developed out of a survey of attitudes towards working with women.

Special programs to train black leaders were illustrated by Katz and Cohen's (1962) "assertion" training to increase self-confidence among blacks. Beatty (1973) completed a study about the training of black supervisors and the importance of their superiors' expectations.

Assertiveness training for women became popular in the 1970s. For example, Heinen, McGlauchlin, Legeros, and Freeman (1975) increased self-awareness and self-confidence in 19 of 20 women managers with such training. Numerous other programs to train women as leaders have been conducted, programs predicated on the supposition that women have unique problems[31] which cannot be effectively resolved only through changing the organizational culture. Woman leaders

[30]See Chapter 33.
[31]See Chapter 32.

need to adjust to the organization as well. Nevertheless, a survey of 101 female and 121 male managers by Alpander and Gutman (1976) indicated that both sexes perceived similar training needs. Be that as it may, Brenner (1972) developed recommendations for designing special enrichment programs for women by using male role training for women so that women learn to adopt more acceptable managerial characteristics.

Hart (1975) designed and evaluated a training program in leadership for adult women based on Hersey and Blanchard's life-cycle theory (1972). Training that focused on interpersonal skills, leadership theory, lifestyles, and the importance of motivation to be a leader resulted in increasing the self-esteem and self-confidence of the trainees in contrast to the controls. Compared to the controls, the trainees also perceived themselves as better able to make decisions, as more active, as more in control of their lives, and as having a greater knowledge of listening skills.

Training Leaders for Foreign Assignments. Space prohibits much discussion about preparing managers for overseas assignments.[32] The lack of such preparation is extremely costly (Tung, 1979). On the basis of surveys and interviews, Zeira (1975) suggested that multinational firms need to equip parent-country nationals and third-country nationals who are expected to serve as managers abroad with adequate knowledge of the complex human problems of international enterprises and with self-confidence to adapt their leadership behavior to the needs of the subsidiary. Tung (1979) found that 26 of 105 U.S. multinationals ran training programs to prepare personnel for overseas assignments. About half these programs used environmental briefings, cultural orientations, and language training. A few used culture assimilators, sensitivity training, and field experience.

Mitchell and Foa (1969) studied American leaders with non-American followers. They found that leaders were rated more effective when they were trained in the norms of the followers. Again, Chemers, Fiedler, Lekhyananda, and Stolurow (1966) demonstrated that training leaders in the culture of a foreign nation, as

opposed to training them in the geography of the nation, resulted in higher levels of group performance and rapport in tasks involving subjects from two different cultures. L. R. Anderson (1965) trained leaders in their own culture's style of leadership or in the style characteristic of another culture and then assigned them to intercultural task groups. Those who were trained in other cultural styles led groups that were more effective in creativity tasks but not in negotiation tasks.

In line with Fiedler's contingency model, Chemers (1969) found that intercultural training tended to modify the situation in the direction of making it more favorable for the low LPC (task-oriented) leader, who then showed more consideration than did the high LPC (relations-oriented) leader.

Training Community Leaders. Training for community leaders is a well-established strategy. Long (1986) presented an evaluation of Ohio's cooperative extension leadership workshops for community development and their positive contributions to the community. Rossing and Heasley (1987) described a design for rural and agricultural leadership training programs. Similarly, Miller (1986) detailed West Virginia University's plan in which its faculty contributes directly to community leadership training. Of particular consequence to the success of any of these programs is accurate identification of the community leaders for participation in the training efforts (Desruisseaux, 1986).

Community leadership training programs have been sparked by a national effort of the U.S. Chamber of Commerce to provide cross-fertilizing education and training that are grounded in workshops for prospective leaders from a single community who are drawn from local industry, government, unions, law enforcement agencies, agriculture, hospitals, and volunteer and welfare agencies. In addition to the informational learning that is possible, important lasting networks can be established across organizational boundaries that benefit the community and its development. For instance, such a leadership educational program was provided to 227 rural citizens of Montana. Classroom and on-site experiences were both useful in enhancing the leaders' self-image, skills, and understanding (Wil-

---

[32]See Chapter 34 for relevant contextual issues.

liams, 1981). Brown and Detterman (1987) agreed and added that participation in community leadership classes promoted increased contacts among the community leaders. In turn, Rossing and Heasley (1987) noted that involvement in public affairs was promoted by such community leadership training.

Factors That Affect Training Outcomes

Numerous researchers have investigated factors that influence the outcomes of leadership training. Personal attributes of trainees, composition of the training group, follow-up strategies, behavior of the trainer, congeniality of the environment to which the person returns, and numerous other factors have been found to influence behavior after instruction.

Criteria of Effective Training

The strength of the effects of training which are found depends on the criteria employed to assess the effects. Thus, Burke and Day (1986) completed meta-analyses of the results of 70 managerial training studies. They contrasted four types of criteria employed in the studies: subjective learning, objective learning, subjective behavior, and objective results. Subjective learning was obtained from the trainees' self-reports about what they thought they had learned from the training. Objective learning was based on tests or measurements of learning during and after training. Subjective behavior was again taken from self-reports about the trainee's performance after training, and objective results were based on independent measures of the trainee's performance as a consequence of training. For all four criteria as a whole, the authors concluded that managerial training is moderately effective and that the effectiveness of the training methods can be generalized to new situations. Thus, when the measured learning outcomes were subjective, the effects were all positive for general management, self-awareness, and human relations training. Nonetheless, self-awareness and human relations training generated stronger effects of subjective learning outcomes that did general management training. When learning outcomes were measured objectively, positive effects were also obtained for all four

types of training. But training in motivation emerged as relatively most effective and training in problem solving as relatively least effective. With subjective behavioral outcomes, the effects of general management, human relations, and self-awareness training were again all positive, and self-awareness was the greatest in this regard. When objective results were used as criteria, the effects of training were again all positive, and human relations training showed the strongest of these positive effects.

When subjective learning outcomes were the criterion, positive outcomes were seen to have been achieved with sensitivity training, behavioral modeling, and lecture-discussuion-role play or practice. Similarly, positive effects on objective learning criteria were obtained for lecture, lecture-discussion, and lecture-discussion-role play or practice. Against subjective behavior outcomes, positive effects were obtained for lecture and lecture-discussion, Leader Match, sensitivity training, behavioral modeling, and combinations of these methods. Sensitivity training and behavioral modeling demonstrated the strongest positive effects. Thus, in all, it would seem that regardless of how training outcomes are measured, the average study reveals a positive effect. However, different types of training will emerge as stronger or weaker in effect, depending on the outcome measures employed.

Composition of the Training Group

The composition of sensitivity training groups has figured strongly in evaluative studies. Illustrating this type of experiment, Harrison and Lubin (1965b) studied participants in groups that were homogeneous or heterogeneous in the personal attributes of the members. The finding that most learning occurred in heterogeneous groups was interpreted as suggesting that members' feelings of cohesiveness and emotional satisfaction may not be appropriate criteria for evaluating the effects of training groups, since ordinarily, much more conflict tends to be experienced in heterogeneous groups once the polite facades have been removed. On the other hand, a number of commentators and a survey of participants and their superiors by Williams (1982) strongly advocated the need for a women-only management course in which many of the more subtle issues of socialization, discrimination, harassment, and influence can be discussed more openly than when both men and women are participants and instructors.

Difference among Trainees

The effectiveness of training, in general, is known to be influenced by the trainee. Some individuals profit more from leadership training than do others. As was mentioned earlier, Klubeck and Bass (1954) studied 140 girls from 7 sororities who were divided into 20 groups composed of 1 member from each of the 7 sororities. The groups engaged in leaderless discussion problems. Observers rated each girl on leadership, influence on the discussion, and other behaviors. The average scores were used to rank the girls from 1 to 7 in each group. Between the first and second leaderless group discussion sessions, some of the girls were given private instruction on how leaders behave. Trained girls who initially ranked 3 in their groups gained significantly more than did those who received no training. Trained girls who initially ranked 6 in their groups did not gain significantly more than those without training. Girls who were initially ranked higher in leadership profited more from training than did those who ranked low.

Lennung and Ahlberg (1975) compared the gains of 17 managers who received sensitivity training with an untrained control sample 5 to 7 months after training. Most striking were the greater variances of the trained compared to the untrained samples in attitudes, awareness, and observed and objectively measured behaviors, which suggests that the effects of training depended on individual differences and differences in the situations to which trainees returned.

Schein and Bennis (1965) studied a complex of organizational and personal variables related to perceived and observed change following laboratory training. Verified change was defined as change reported by the trainee and two associates in the organization. The security and power of the trainee's position in the organization and unfreezing by the trainee during training were significantly related to verified behavioral change. Prior anticipation of change by the trainee was negatively related to verified change.

Noe's (1986) model of requirements for effective training suggests the need for leadership trainees to believe in the assessments of their strengths and weaknesses. They must value the outcomes of training and think that they can achieve the outcomes. They must believe that the training fits with the resources they have available on the job and that the organization will support them if they make use of their learning.

Zenger (1974) made a strong case for integrating the assessment of managers with their training. Differences in trainees' motivation figured in Gruenfeld's (1966) report that participants who paid part of their tuition devoted themsleves more intensely to the program, found it more difficult, and benefited more, as measured by a rating scale and test of values.

Attributes of the Trainer

Rosen, Georgiades, and McDonald (1980) found that the gain in a multiple-choice examination of leadership knowledge and principles among 39 groups of U.S., British, and Canadian trainees from the profit and not-for-profit sectors was correlated with the instructors' experience (.31) and professional academic training (.20), specific training to teach the course (.65), and status of the instructor as an outside professor or consultant (.59). Also contributing to the gain was the support provided by the organization (.38), the price paid for the course (.37), and the number of hours allocated to the course (.45).

Bednar and Heisler (1985) contrasted 38 more effective and less effective industrial training instructors who described their own communication styles. The instructor's effectiveness was judged by their management and professional trainees. Instructors who were judged more effective saw themselves as more open, dramatic, animated, and relaxed than those who judged themsleves less effective. They also thought they left more of a lasting impression about what they had said and how they had said it.

Casualties. The trainer is likely to be particularly important to the outcomes of sensitivity training. Much of the rationale for instrumented self-guided training is based on the known variance in outcomes that are due to differences in trainers' motivation and skills. Casualties in training have been linked to hostile trainers, for instance. The amount of learning has been similarly affected by such trainers. Lieberman, Yalom, and Miles (1973) studied 206 trainees led by different types of encounter-group trainers. They found that casualties among trainees were greatest (12 percent) when the trainers were autocratic, aggressive, charismatic, and convinced of their own beliefs. Other types of trainers with high casualty rates were impersonal, uncaring trainers (11 percent); highly controlling trainers (10 percent); and laissez-faire trainers (8 percent). On the other hand, there were few or no casualties when the laboratory was trainerless and conducted by instrumented audiotape or when trainers were benevolent, caring, group oriented, or participative. Learning was also likely to be greater with such trainers. Learning correlated −.33 with casualty rates, contrary to the expectations of those who see value in making the learning a highly stressful experience.

According to C. L. Cooper (1969), participants in sensitivity training tended to identify with the trainers when they thought the trainers were attractive. As a result, they became more like the trainers in attitude and behavior as training progressed. Psathas and Hardert (1966) obtained results indicating that trainers in sensitivity training groups formulate implicit norms that indicate to members what the norms of the groups should be. Thus, the trainers play a significant role in determining the groups' values and norms. Zigon and Cannon (1974) found similarly that students in group discussions whose appointed leaders were seen as genuine and respected were more likely to transfer what was learned in the groups.

Follow-up Reinforcing Practice and Feedback

To transfer to the job what has been learned during training, trainees need to receive continuing opportunities to practice what has been learned. This practice, in turn, needs to be coupled with feedback or self-reinforcement about the trainees' practice efforts. Wexley and Nemeroff (1975) described a self-feedback mechanism for promoting the transfer of leadership training to the job. For six weeks following training, supervisory trainees completed a daily behavioral checklist to record their supervisory behaviors. On each day, they noted whether they had done such things as praised

subordinates, thanked subordinates for suggestions and told them how they would be followed up, called subordinates together to discuss mutual assistance, gave help as requested, and assigned jobs without interfering until the jobs were completed. Further transfer was promoted by the trainer, who met twice for individual consultation with trainees on the job to review progress and to arrange for the trainees to try out and evaluate the effects of the newly learned behaviors.

Congruence of Training and the Organizational Environment

Organizational factors that have an impact on the effectiveness of supervisory training include the organizational climate, the trainee's immediate superior, upper management, and various other components.

Organizational Climate. Zaleznik (1951) explained the failure of a human relations training program to help trainees solve their work problems on the basis of an inadequate initial diagnosis of supervisory difficulties and on the irrelevance of the training to the problems. Sykes (1962) conducted a case study of a firm in which participants in a managment development program regarded the training as unsuccessful because top management was unwilling to correct grievances and unsatisfactory conditions toward which they had become sensitized during the discussion sessions. Again, a deterioration in human relations resulted from an attempt at supervisory training when a program conflicted with unionism, when recruitment for a program was inadequate, and when a program itself was seen as an effort to indoctrinate a captive audience (Form & Form, 1953).

Both House (1968) and Glube and Margerison (1967) concluded that the organizational climate is extremely important in the development of managers. Baumgartel and Jeanpierre (1972) studied 240 managers who had participated in a management development program. The respondents came from 200 different industrial and commercial firms. Whether managers could apply what they had learned in training was seen to depend on the freedom they had to set personal goals, consideration by higher management of the feelings of lower management, the organization's stimulation and approval of innovation and experimentation, the organization's desire for executives to make use of information given in management courses, and free and open communication among management groups.

Immediate Superior. Most important to whether training will modify behavior back on the job is the trainee's immediate superior. F. C. Mann (1951) found that foremen who changed more as a consequence of training in leadership received more encouragement from their superiors, expected greater personal benefit from training, felt more secure in their relations with their superiors, and perceived they had a greater opportunity to try out new ideas on the job. Consistent with this finding, Hariton (1951) observed that supervisory training increased employees' satisfaction when the supervisors were encouraged by their superiors to use the principles they had learned in training.

Conversely, Fleishman (1953b) and Harris and Fleishman (1955) reported that supervisors who were trained in a human relations orientation appeared to experience role conflict when they returned to their jobs to work under superiors who exhibited a markedly different pattern of behavior. Supervisory training to increase consideration behavior resulted in a much greater shift in some trainees' behavior than the shift that occurred for other trainees when organizational conditions were taken into account. Supervisors who returned to their work after human relations training tended to endorse a more considerate attitude toward employees and to be described by employees as high in consideration if the superiors of the supervisors endorsed considerate attitudes and behaved in a considerate manner. There was a nonsignificant tendency for supervisors to be described as high in initiating structure when their superiors exhibited a similar pattern of behavior. Those supervisors who returned from training to work under a superior who was low in consideration and high in initiating structure (including being coercive) experienced the greatest role conflict, as measured by the discrepancy between their observed behavior and their ideas about how they ought to behave. No such relationship was found for control supervisors who had not taken the training course in human relations. Thus, the supervisors' leadership behavior tended to be highly conditioned by the attitudes and behavior of their superiors (Fleishman, Harris, & Burtt, 1955).

Haire (1948), W. Mahler (1952), and many others since have argued that for leadership training to be effective, the entire management of the organization should be subjected to the same or similar program. It is self-defeating to train lower-level managers in a style of supervision that is incompatible with that of their superiors.

Other Organizational Constraints. Despite the generally observed positive effects of leadership training programs, the effects can be constrained or nullified, according to an interview study by Campisano (1984). The content of the program may be irrelevant to the daily activities of the supervisor or can suffer from redundancy. Furthermore, the interviewees stated that technical competence and management structure were more critical to performance in their organization than was training in leadership skills. Steele, Zane, and Zalkind (1970) reported that perceived pressures from associates, particularly peers, reduced the trainees' involvement (according to consultants) in changed activities 20 months after instruction. On the other hand, Carroll and Nash (1970) reported that 45 foremen in a management development program thought the training was more applicable to the job if they were more highly motivated toward promotion, were more satisfied with the organization, and had sufficient freedom to perform their functions.

Training often must be supported by other specific organizational actions to result in the desired effects. Specific organizational practices, congruent with the training effort, need to be developed and institutionalized on the basis of a comprehensive analysis of organizational, managerial, and technical/professional needs (Dreilinger, McElheny, Robinson, & Rice, 1982). Thus, a supervisory training program to reduce employees' absenteeism actually lowered absenteeism only when quantitative data about the absences of their own subordinate personnel were fed back to supervisors following training (Mann & Sparling, 1956). Similarly, training programs for women managers were seen to require buttressing by encouraging upper-level managers to be supportive of female middle managers and by helping husbands to understand the importance of their support in assuring the success of their wives on the job (Brenner, 1972).

The Need for Programmatic Integration. Van Velsor (1984) summarized what is needed for leadership training and education to have an impact. The organization must show that it supports what is to be learned. The trainee must be willing to participate in the training. The need for training must be perceived. The program should deal with relevant problems and should provide sufficient interaction with peers and valid feedback. Follow-up activities should include postsession debriefing, maintenance of alumni groups, consultation, follow-up training as needed, and reward for improvement and the application of what has been learned.

The promotion of the trainees should be integrated with their development and focused on individualized needs that are aligned with those of the organization (Cunningham & Leon, 1986). Day's (1980) interview survey of 116 health care professionals showed that the professionals tended to connect promotion with training. Of those interviewed, 67 percent noted that following promotion, their organizations made an effort to prepare them for their new responsibilities with training (mostly on-the-job training).

At the same time, Alpander's (1986) survey of 155 corporate training officers found that less than 1 percent reported a direct relationship of promotion to undergoing supervisory training. However, 52 percent reported some indirect contribution of training to the trainees' subsequent advancement. But 31 percent reported that training was of little or no consequence to promotion. At the upper level of an organization, Hall (1986) noted the difficulties involved in connecting executive succession with the learning of individual executives. Most planned executive development focuses on task rather than personal learning. Classroom activities, rather than the exploitation of learning from experience, are emphasized. But such learning from educational and personal experiences needs to be integrated into planning for succession.

Bunker (1986) attributed the success of management training in Japan to the firms' subscription to the proposition that their employees need to be developed before the firms can make a profit. Thus, employees and their development are highly valued. Japanese firms see themselves as educational institutions that are engaged in life-time learning with their employees. "The company is the business school!" Training is "just in time," that is, it is systematically provided just as managers need new skills to take on new roles. Much attention is paid to socialization to the organization.

New members of Japanese firms receive 2 to 8 weeks of initial residential training in a cohort of other new recruits. This training is followed by extensive job rotation during the next 2 years to develop familiarity with various functions and departments. Later on, training is provided to deal with obsolescence and burnout, along with new challenges. Training provides the basis for employees at all levels to fit into and make contributions in a consultative organizational culture.

Summary and Conclusions

Early developments contribute to the making of a successful leader. Of importance are one's parents and the standards they set and the challenges they provide commensurate with one's maturation. Equally important are the leadership opportunities and the experiences one has in childhood, adolescence, and adulthood. Education also plays an important role. Leadership training and education need to be designed around what will be required when trainees and students take on leadership responsibilities.

Experiential training approaches have been favored over highly structured didactic lectures alone for leadership education and training, but new kinds of highly structured experiences, such as those provided by behavioral modeling, have demonstrated the desired training effects. Nevertheless, sensitivity training or its variants, such as team building, continues to be widely practiced. Considerable research is available about its effects. Positive results depend, to some extent, on opportunities for the transfer of learning into appropriate organizational settings. On-the-job leadership training, such as with coaching and mentoring, seems to be widely practiced but is underresearched.

Studies are available about some of the training effects of the leadership styles advocated in earlier chapters. Special attention is also given to examining ways to train leaders to work effectively with minorities and the disadvantaged, along with specific programs to prepare people for foreign assignments.

Research indicates, not unexpectedly, that the effectiveness of training depends on the trainee, the trainer, the composition of the training group, follow-up rein-forcement and feedback, and particularly whether there is congruence between the training and the organizational environment for which the trainee is being prepared. In all, meta-analyses of available evaluative studies have provided evidence that leadership and management training, education, and development are usually effective. Effective training adds to valid assessment, the subject that follows next.

Assessment and Forecasting of Leaders' and Managers' Performance

Many of the earlier chapters looked at designated personal factors that are antecedents of success as a leader. Later chapters considered situational conditions that moderate the effects. This chapter examines how these factors can be usefully combined into predictors to optimize forecasting of the success of leaders. It also looks at how such predictive data can be extracted from assessments of performance in contrived and real-life settings.

The uses of assessment are twofold. By whatever means it is done, assessment provides the basis for choosing from among candidates for leadership and management posts. It also provides useful information for the counseling and further development of incumbent leaders. The group or organization clearly benefits from the valid selection of its leaders instead of relying on haphazard processes, ranging from casual and ill-informed choices to those involving hidden agendas, politics, nepotism, and bribery (Immegart, 1987). Organizational effectiveness is enhanced by the increased assignment of those who are best able to fill leadership positions. A valid assessment increases the tendency of the status of members of the organization to be correlated more highly with their ability and esteem and reduces the potential conflicts caused by incongruities among status, esteem, and ability.[1] In the same way, counseling and development that are based on valid measurements rest on much firmer ground than do management counseling and development that are based exclusively on impressions and feelings. Thus, Knight and Weiss (1980) demonstrated in an experiment that leaders who were perceived to have been

chosen by a competent agent were judged by other group members to have greater expertise than were those who were selected by a less competent agent. They were also more influential.

To assess the traits, personal factors, and individual dispositions related to leadership, the combinations of predictive assessments have included tests and judgments of capacity, achievement, and verbal and nonverbal communication styles; interests, attitudes, and values; sociability, initiative, confidence, and popularity; task and relations orientation; and status, family, educational background, and work history. For example, Miner (1960a) and Nash (1966) reported patterns for forecasting managerial success that were consistent with the personal factors connected with leadership discussed in earlier chapters. These patterns involved energy, risk taking, verbal fluency, confidence, independence, and the desire to be persuasive. Mahoney, Jerdee, and Nash (1960, 1961) showed that the success of 468 managers in Minnesota-based companies was predicted by work-related, business-related, and higher-level occupational interests. These concerned interest in leadership, independence, moderate risk, and work that was not closely detailed. Also predictive were intelligence, better education, more activities in more organizations, and self-reported dominance. In the same way, Ghiselli (1971) predicted managerial progress from a battery of tests of intelligence, supervisory ability, self-assurance, decisiveness, self-actualization, and motivation to achieve.

In addition to information generated from tests and simulations, the predictive data have been supplied by observers, interviewers, outsiders, superiors, peers, subordinates, and the assessees themselves. The assess-

[1]See Chapter 15.

857

...ar way of systemati-
...ultiple and diverse

...either subjective
...ection, develop-
...k samples, tests,
...ources will be combined
...ive observers may do just as good
...uned process observers in identifying which
...individuals in a group are emerging as its leaders (Stein, 1977).

The methods of combining the predictors of success as a leader are either statistical, judgmental, or both. Clinical judgment or a mechanical pooling of the information in some objective systematic way may be used. To aid the judgment, the objective or subjective information or both may be displayed in profiles or printed in narrative reports. The mechanical combining may be based on unit or differential weighting of the information. Again, the weighting can be a matter of judgment or multiple regression analysis to minimize error in the predictions (Sawyer, 1966).

Judgmental Approaches

Pure judgments of the readiness of job incumbents for promotions into positions that require more leadership are commonly used. These judgments may be obtained from observers. More often, they are obtained from the supervisors of the incumbents or from higher management. Such judgments can be a part of standard performance appraisals, and as was noted in Chapter 31, such early appraisals of performance as a leader are likely to predict subsequent success as a leader. They can also be based on observations of leadership performance in work samples and situational tests, as well as on the actual performance of a job. Simulations of management situations, paper-and-pencil simulations in the form of standardized managerial-in-basket tests, initially leaderless group discussions (LGDs), and other small-group exercises can be used to generate the observations from which judgments are derived. Other ways of judging the potential for leadership are to be found in supervisors' opinions and performance appraisals, interviews, references, and recommendations.

In addition to judgments of the assessee's overall leadership performance, discrete elements can be singled out for examination and decision. These elements can then be formed into scores for standardized processing.

Judgments from Simulations

In-basket Tests. These tests simulate the typical contents of a manager's in-basket. The items may include telephone messages, brief memos, detailed reports, letters, directives, complaints, and junk mail about a recently vacated management position. The individual examinee is instructed to imagine that he or she has just taken over the position and has a limited time, such as one hour, to decide how to handle each item (Frederiksen, 1962b, 1966; Frederiksen, Saunders, & Ward, 1957). Realism can be added with telephone calls and visual presentations (Lopez, 1966). An element that is deemed important in the test is ambiguity (Gill, 1979). Although the common problems faced by all managers need to be sampled (Stewart & Stewart, 1976), Brass and Oldham (1976) argued that the more representative and appropriate the in-basket sample to the examinee's particular future management situation, the better the test results predict that performance.

As many as nine independent factors were uncovered in a Sears in-basket test (Bentz, 1967), but Gill (1979) concluded that most factor analyses of in-basket results, including Meyer's (1970a), emerge with just two factors: a relations dimension of supervision and an intellectual dimension of planning and administration. Highly reliable results can be obtained with standardized scoring procedures employed by adequately trained judges of the examinee's responses (Richards & Jaffee, 1972). Interviews with the examinees after they complete the in-basket test can augment the accuracy of the predictions obtained from it (Clutterbuck, 1974).

The results of the in-basket tests of IBM supervisors were found by Wollowick and McNamara (1969) to correlate .32 with increases in management responsibility during the 3 years following testing. Judgments of the examinees' organizing and planning ability and work standards, garnered from an in-basket test, correlated .27 and .44, respectively, with the managerial level they achieved at A T & T 8 years later (Bray & Grant, 1966) and .19 and .24, with the level they achieved 20 years later (Howard & Bray, 1988). Similar findings were reported by Meyer (1963) for manufacturing supervisors at General Electric and by Lopez (1966) for managers at the Port Authority of New York. These investigators agreed that judgments and scores from in-basket tests add considerably to the accuracy of forecasting success as a manager that is not possible with ordinary paper-and-pencil tests of capacity and interests.

Small-group Exercises. In the simplest form of small group exercise, the initially leaderless discussion group (LGD) is assigned a problem to discuss to reach a group decision. Observers judge who emerges as a leader, initiatives displayed by each participant, and other aspects of interpersonal performance, such as the motivation of others, persuasiveness in expression, and skills in dealing with others to handle the problems to be solved. Bass (1954a) reported correlations of these observers' judgments of LGDs of .44, .53, and .38 with rated merit among the 348 ROTC cadets as cadet officers obtained 6 months to a year later. A similar correlation of .47 was found in predicting subsequent nominations for positions of fraternity leadership from earlier performance in an LGD. Similarly, Arbous and Maree (1951) obtained a correlation among 168 South African administrative trainees of .50 between the LGD and the trainees' rated capacity a year later as administrators. Vernon (1950) found, among 123 personnel, a correlation of .33 between the LGD and their rated suitability for foreign service. Mandell (1950b) validated the LGD in the same way for shipyard foremen as did Weislogel (1953) for candidates for military officers; Gleason (1957), for U.S. Army trainees; and Handyside and Duncan (1954), for British supervisors who were followed up for 4 years.

The LGD became a routine part of most assessment centers. Vernon (1950) found a correlation of .75 between judgments based on a 1-hour LGD and judgments by assessors after 3 days of activities at an assessment center.

Although the quantity of talk in an LGD reflects attempts to lead, the quality actually affects a person's success in leading (Bottger, 1984). Those who are rated highly by observers see themselves as more assertive, competitive, self-confident, and willing to function au-

tonomously, whereas those who are rated less effective view themselves as cooperative, disciplined, and tactful (Hills, 1985).

More complex small-group simulations are specifically constructed exercises for small groups of candidates that can be observed by assessors whose judgments are shaped by what they see. Roskin and Margerison (1983) presented examples of simulations that involved the organizing of a team effort whose problem content required little special information or experience but that could bring out the differences in the leadership and managerial skills and attitudes of the participants. These simulations were (1) the production of a set of prototype greeting cards, (2) the building of a monument from material provided, (3) the solution of a case problem, both individually and corporately, (4) the construction and flying of paper airplanes, and (5) the selection of an employee from a number of candidates. Judgments based on observations of 39 elements in the managers' behavior during these simulations that were related to the compatibility of their behavior with the situation and how they dealt with cognitive and perceptual complexity detected those managers who were most likely to be high achievers. But scores of leadership attitudes and opinions on paper-and-pencil tests alone failed to relate to the managers' performance.

Two simulated business situations from which judgments of performance could be gleaned for predictions of leadership were described by Dunnette (1970). Six participants were told they were managing an investment fund and had to buy and sell stocks to make profits for their investors. Stock quotations were changed every five minutes, and other information was presented at predetermined intervals. Organizing skills, working cooperatively with other people, handling a large amount of information, and other group-process and cognitive variables were judged from each participant's behavior. In the second simulated business situation, the six participants were asked to play roles as managerial trainees. Each participant had to plan a project and to make a 10-minute presentation justifying the project and its budget. After the six presentations, the participants engaged in an hour's discussion about the merits of the various projects. Skills in judgment, planning and organizing, proficiency in oral communication, and effectiveness in working in competitive situations could be judged with some accuracy from the emergent behaviors.

Judgments from Speeches and Essays

The essays written by candidates, managers, and leaders and their speeches can form the basis of judgments about their future performance. Thus, Winter (1987) demonstrated that the contents of the inaugural addresses of U.S. presidents could be judged and coded to obtain valid inferences of their leadership-motivation patterns and that such patterns, in turn, were predictive of the success of their administrations. Speech writers provided the specific words, but the leaders reviewed and modified the text. House, Woycke, and Fodor (1988) extended the work to Canadian prime ministers.[2]

Judgments from On-the-Job Performance

Superiors' judgments, evaluations by peers, and self-reports of leaders about their performance on the job may all be employed. Generally, consistencies are likely to be found between superiors' and peers' ratings, although superiors are prone to emphasize getting the work done and peers are more likely to emphasize cooperativeness. Self-reports tend to be inflated (although some managers may have better insight than do others) and may be unrelated to judgments obtained by peers or superiors. For example, Lawler (1967a) found a correlation of .52 between the superiors' and peers' ratings of the job ability of 113 middle and top managers; the agreement on the rated quality of the managers' job performance was .38. On the other hand, correlations were close to zero between the managers' self-reports and the peers' or superiors' ratings of the managers' ability and performance. A meta-analysis by Harris and Schaubroeck (1988) of 11 to 36 reported correlations found a high correlation, on average, between peers' and superiors' ratings but much lower adjusted correlations between self-reports and superiors' ratings or between self-reports and peers' ratings. Agreement between self-reports and others' ratings was lower for managers and professionals than for

blue-collar and service employees. Whether the rating format was dimensional or global had little effect on the agreement.

Judgments by Superiors. Organizations commonly use superiors' judgments to decide who to hire, transfer, and promote and to forecast future success as a leader and a manager in the positions for which the candidates are to be chosen. Equally common are supervisors' and trainers' judgments of prospective future position holders while they are enrolled in training and education programs. For example, the cumulative *military* performance grades awarded by superiors at Annapolis correlated .25 with subsequent fitness reports of 186 U.S. Navy officers serving in the fleet as much as a decade later; they also predicted the tendency of subordinates to describe the officers as charismatic. However, cumulative *academic* performance grades at Annapolis were not predictive (Yammarino & Bass, 1989). This finding was consistent with the failure, more often than not, to find significant correlations between undergraduate college grades and success in business and industry (see, for example, Schick & Kunnecke, 1982) or with better ratings of on-the-job performance (Pallett & Hoyt, 1968). The record for postgraduate grades has been somewhat better (Weinstein & Srinivasan, 1974), although generally, the predictive postgraduate grades of consequence emerged mainly in specific elective courses (Marshall, 1964).

From the research on the persistence of leadership in Chapter 31, we can infer that supervisors' performance appraisals of managers' behavior as leaders and as managers become more consistent with the greater opportunity to observe the managers in action and when the managers are observed in several positions by several supervisors. At the same time, the predictive validity of superiors' judgments will suffer to the extent that they overweight the technical proficiency and manipulative styles of the candidates (Farrow, Valenzi, & Bass, 1981) and the requirements of the new positions are different from those of the old ones. Successful performance in a lower-level position will not necessarily be predictive of performance in a higher-level position that requires cognitive complexity (Jacobs & Jaques, 1987).

Brush and Schoenfeldt (1980) proposed a procedure

[2]Results of work with this approach were discussed in Chapters 9 and 12.

that would direct supervisors' ratings toward a systematic evaluation of current subordinates on dimensions of consequence to the future positions that the subordinates might hold. They argued that it is even possible to evaluate blue-collar workers from their observed behavior on the job on dimensions relevant to supervisory positions to which they might aspire. Schippmann and Prien (1986) obtained such judgments of 47 candidates for first-level supervisory jobs in a steel company from 29 supervisors. The dimensions arranged for the supervisors' judgments included (1) representational skills, (2) supervisory ability, (3) ability to analyze and evaluate information to define problems, (4) knowledge and ability to work with mechanical devices, (5) ability to manage/orchestrate current activities effectively, (6) ability to decide and act, (7) ability to follow through to achieve closure on a task, and (8) administrative ability. Satisfactory reliabilities were achieved, but self-assessments were much more lenient than were the supervisors' ratings.

Judgments by Peers. Peer "buddy" ratings by cadets at West Point or at officers candidate schools (OCS) were found to be the best single predictor of subsequent success as a regular U.S. Army officer (Haggerty, Johnson, & King, 1954). Thus, a correlation of .51 was obtained between peers ratings at West Point and the rated success of infantry officers 18 months later and a correlation of .42 was obtained between peer ratings in OCS and the combat performance of officers (Baier, 1947). Similar results were reported for the U.S. Marine Corps (Wilkins, 1953; Williams & Leavitt, 1947b) and the U.S. Air Force (USAF 1952a, 1952b). Ricciuti (1955) found fellow midshipmen's ratings of aptitude for service more predictive of the subsequent performance of naval officers than ratings made at the U.S. Naval Academy by their Navy officers. Further validations of peer ratings in military settings were reported by Hollander (1965) and by Amir, Kovarsky, and Sharan (1970).

All these reported studies focused on predicting the success of junior officers, but Downey, Medland, and Yates (1976) extended the findings to senior officers. They found that ratings by 1,656 colonels of each other forecast who would be promoted to general. The correlation was .47.

In industry, Kraut (1975b) obtained peer ratings from 156 IBM middle-level managers and 83 higher-level executives attending a month-long training program. Two factors emerged from 13 ratings: impact and tactfulness. These factors correlated .35 and .37, respectively, with the performance appraisals of the higher-level executives but close to zero with the performance appraisals of the middle managers once they were back on the job. However, the peer ratings of impact correlated with the subsequent number of promotions received by both the middle managers and the executives. These predictions from peer judgments were much more likely to be correlated with subsequent success than were predictions obtained from the training staff of the month-long program.

Judgments by peers are often in the form of nominations of the one or several associates with whom the rater is acquainted. Nominations for the most and the least valued have been employed. But to be predictive of subsequent success, the nominations must be positive. Kaufman and Johnson (1974) showed, in two studies of ROTC cadets, that being nominated for being a most effective cadet officer during the school year correlated between .36 and .43 with independent criteria of performance as a platoon leader at summer camp. But being nominated as being *least* effective as an officer did not correlate as negatively as expected with such leadership at summer camp. For this, correlations were −.03 and .16 in the two studies.

Mumford (1983) was impressed with the validity of peer ratings but found the need for a better theoretical understanding of the reasons for it. It would seem that peer ratings are valid because they are likely to be influenced by so many of the personal elements that contribute to success as a leader discussed in Chapters 6, 7, 8, and 11—competence, popularity, and especially esteem, which are likely to persist and be transferred to subsequent leadership positions as the individual ratee moves upward.

Judgments by Subordinates. As was noted in Chapter 35, more and more feedback programs for developing managers are surveying the managers' subordinates. Such information from subordinates is also likely to be predictive of future success as a manager. However, the accuracy of the predictions derived from such information would suffer to the degree that the subordinates overweight sentimentality, the likability of the candidate, and the extent to which the future position's requirements differ greatly from the current one. Nevertheless, Hater and Bass (1988) showed that among 56 Federal Express managers, those who were rated higher in transformational leadership and lower in laissez-faire leadership by their subordinates were significantly more likely to be judged by senior managers as having a greater potential for leadership. Similar results were found by Yammarino and Bass (1989) for junior naval officers.

Of course, it is one thing to use superiors', peers', and subordinates' ratings in research; it is another thing to use them in operations. The colleagues' and candidates' resistance and distortions may increase when the ratings are to be employed by a higher authority to decide on a promotion and the colleagues see themselves competing with the candidate for the promotion.

Self-disclosure. Most survey feedback asks managers to describe their own behavior. These results are then fed back to the managers, along with the judgments of peers, subordinates, and superiors. The self-ratings are not likely to be as useful to the prediction of future success as are the discrepancies between them and others' judgments. The discrepancies will be especially useful for developmental counseling and training.

Although most answers to questionnaires that ask managers to describe or evaluate their own behavior suffer from a variety of errors, autobiographical material dealing with a person's early history of the challenge of and self-determination over important life decisions can be the basis of valid judgments by trained reviewers of the material (Ezekiel, 1968). Candidates may be asked to write about their high school and college experiences, their peak experiences, their jobs and organizations five years into the future, and their obituaries (what they expect and hope will be said about them and their performance).

Judgments from Personnel Procedures

The procedures upon which judgments are based include interviewing, projective testing, meeting with a board, and obtaining references and recommendations.

Judgments from Interviews. The standardized interview from which the interviewer forms judgments about the candidate ordinarily covers the candidate's family, education, and work history. Also often discussed are the candidate's expressed objectives, strong and weak points, hopes and fears, social values, interests, and attitudes toward the organization and toward interpersonal relationships. The accuracy of these self-descriptions is higher for the information that the candidate believes can be independently corroborated (Cascio, 1975).

The interviews vary widely in how they are organized, the time devoted to them, the probing skills of the interviewer, the extent to which the interviewer is trained to provide a similar stimulating situation for each candidate, and so on. A deliberate effort may be made to place stress on the candidate to observe his or her ability to cope with it. Admiral Hyman Rickover conducted over 20,000 such stressful interviews in the process of choosing personnel for the nuclear surface ship and submarine program. However, there appeared to be little standardization in what he did. Furthermore, anecdotal evidence suggests that what he did made little contribution to his accuracy in predicting the subsequent performance of officers in the nuclear fleet (Polmar & Allen, 1981).

Early reviews of the validity of interviews for predicting performance were not supportive (Wagner, 1949). Upward of 80 studies led Mayfield (1964) to conclude that it was mainly intelligence that could be predicted satisfactorily from an interview. However, subsequent improvements in the interview process, especially when covered with other personnel procedures, have revealed considerable utility of judgments based on interviews. Wiesner and Cronshaw (1988) completed a meta-analysis of 150 reported efforts to validate the interview. Structured interviews produced validity coefficients twice as high, on average, than unstructured interviews.

Huse (1962) compared the ratings made by interviewers of 107 managers in 37 firms and the ratings of the same managers by the managers' superiors. Consistent with Mayfield's findings, the interviewers' and superiors' ratings of the intellectual capacity of the managers correlated .26. But they also correlated on various other aspects as well: leadership, .38; creativeness, .27; and overall effectiveness, .16. When the interviewers' leadership judgments were combined with the results of projective and objective tests, the multiple prediction of the superiors' ratings of the managers' leadership reached .44. Likewise, 20 experienced supervisors who were rated as highly effective by their superiors were matched by Glaser, Schwartz, and Flanagan (1958) with 20 less effective supervisors of similar experience, age, and scores on a paper-and-pencil test. The judgments combined with the test scores correlated .34 with discriminating more effective and less effective supervisors; the results of the interview added to the accuracy of the discrimination. Similarly, Howard and Bray (1988) reported that interviews with candidates who were assessed 20 years earlier could detect a number of attributes of consequence to the managers' success at A T & T. They found a correlation of .30 in the interviewers' judgments of the interviewees' range of interests and the managerial level attained by the assessees 20 years later. The interviewers' judgments of the assessees' need for advancement correlated .44 with the level attained by the assessees 20 years later.[3]

Careful attention to the job requirements of the position for which candidates are being considered and the use of multiple trained interviewers appear to make a difference in the validity of the interview. Russell (1978) arranged for 5 trained interviewers to assess 66 senior managers in a Fortune 500 firm who were candidates for positions as general managers. The candidates were assessed on 9 dimensions that a focus group had generated to describe the task and process responsibilities of the position. Accomplishments, disappointments, and developmental activities were discussed in the interviews. The interviewers prepared a report on the candidates for discussion at a meeting to reach consensual decisions about the candidates' readiness for promotion to the position and the candidates' developmental needs. The consensual judgments of understanding, analyzing, and setting direction for a business correlated .32 with the bonuses that were awarded; .26,

with the quality of the candidates' relations with customers and other outsiders; and .23, with staffing performance. The pooled interview judgments of organizational acumen (understanding of the corporate environment to achieve both individual and unit objectives) also correlated .36 with superiors' appraisals of the candidates' nonfiscal performance. In another vein, Herriot and Rothwell (1983) found that the judgments of recruiters, based on their interviews with graduating students, added to the accuracy of predictions of the applicants' suitability above what was obtained from the applicants' résumés alone.

Other studies pointed to what was important in the interviews. For instance, Rasmussen (1984) observed that credentials listed on résumés and verbal behavior had more influence than did nonverbal behavior on judgments of qualifications. Still other studies pointed to ways of improving the contribution to assessment of judgments from interviews. For example, Dipboye, Fontenelle, and Garner (1984) found that reading the application before the interview increased the amount of correct information collected during the interview.

Projective Tests. Responses to projective tests can also form the basis of valid judgments by trained clinicians. The relation of Miner's sentence-completion test to managerial performance was noted in Chapter 25. Huse (1962), for example, found the results of projective tests to correlate with the ratings of 107 managers by their superiors, as follows: persuasiveness, .33; leadership, .26; overall effectiveness, .21; social skills, .18; planning, .18; creativeness, .17; intellectual capacity, .13; and motivation and energy, .03.

Judgments by Boards. It is centuries-old military and naval practice to have candidates appear before boards of officers to present their credentials and to be interviewed, following which, the combined judgments of the board members are used to decide whether to accept or reject the candidates for selection or promotion. Such boards are also used to screen teachers and managers in civil service systems. However, some of the processes that affect the decisions of such boards are just beginning to be known.[4]

---

[3]This research on the value of the interview for predicting managerial performance appeared in the context of its use in assessment centers. More will be said later about the validity of the interview for forecasting the subsequent performance of leaders when the validity and utility of assessment centers are examined.

[4]To be discussed later in the context of assessment centers.

Judgments from References and Recommendations. The judgments of former superiors, colleagues, and acquaintances are routinely and almost universally used. Yet, little has been published on their validity as predictors of success as leaders and managers. Illustrative of what is possible, however, was G. W. McLaughlin's (1971) predictions of the first year of success of cadets at West Point from ratings about them by their high school teachers and coaches. Ratings of the charisma (personal magnetism, bearing, and appearance) and situational behavior (moral and ethical values, cooperation and teamwork, commonsense, and judgment) were the best predictors of the leadership and followership performance of the cadets during their first year at the academy. Athletic coaches and mathematics teachers provided the most valid ratings.

Mechanical Methods

Objective tests provide samples or signs of individual differences in cognition and behavior related to leadership that aim to predict the subsequent performance of leaders. Responses to the test items are unit weighted rather than differentially weighted when they are totaled to form a score, since identical results will be obtained when results with more than four or five items are to be summed (Gulliksen, 1950). Keys are developed to score those items that correlate with emergent, successful, or effective leadership.

Special Keys

It has often been possible to develop a specially cross-validated key for the Strong-Campbell Vocational Interest Blank to discriminate among those who subsequently achieve more success as leaders in their organizations. The inventory is examined item by item (Laurent, 1968), which takes advantage of the extent to which values and interests are important to success as a leader. For example, Harrell and Harrell (1975) developed such a key with the Strong-Campbell for predicting high from low earning managers among MBAs from Stanford University 5 years after graduation. They also keyed responses to the Guilford-Zimmerman Personality Inventory and a survey of personal history in the same way. The total high-earners key predicted earnings of the graduates at 5, 10, 15, and 20 years after graduation; the correlations were .52, .39, .33 and .44, respectively (Harrell & Harrell, 1984). For 443 Exxon managers, a key was developed from answers to the Guilford-Zimmerman Temperament Survey that correlated .31 with their success, as measured by their salaries adjusted for their age, education, seniority, and function. The key correlated .23 with their effectiveness as ranked by their superiors (Laurent, 1968).

Goodstein and Schrader (1963) developed a managerial potential key using the items of the California Psychological Inventory (CPI)—a collection of personality items. The content of items included in the key that were found valid in differentiating managers from non-managers were consistent with much of what was said in earlier chapters about the personality requirements for successful leadership. The items were about masculinity, the need for achievement, dominance, status, self-acceptance, and tolerance. In support, Rawls and Rawls (1968) compared 30 high-rated with 30 low-rated utilities executives using the CPI. High-rated executives scored higher than did low-rated executives in dominance, status, sociability, self-acceptance, and so on. The 206 items of the key were subsequently reduced to 34 by Gough (1984) in a study evaluating the items against measures of the success of military officers and bank managers. The reduced management-potential key correlated .88 and .89 with Goodstein and Schrader's much longer version.

The most positive items in the revised management-potential scale were also consistent with the discussions in earlier chapters. They dealt with being optimistic about the future, able to create good impressions, interpersonally effective, self-confident, relatively free of instability and conflict, and realistic in thinking and social behavior. Gough (1984) also reported considerable consistency between the keyed management-potential scores and descriptions of the respondents by their fellow college students, by their spouses, and by assessment staffs.

Scored Application and Biodata Blanks. Responses to standardized, operational questions on application blanks and biographical information blanks can be similarly keyed to forecast leadership and management performance. Kirkpatrick (1960, 1966) constructed such a key from an 11-page biographical questionnaire. The key was constructed to sort out above-average, average, and below-average Chamber of Commerce executives. A 5-year follow-up study demonstrated the ability of the key to discriminate 80 "high-salary" from 81 "low-salary" managers who were otherwise matched in age and size of their employing organization. Along with higher salaries, as such, as evidence of greater success as an executive, it was also observed that the higher salaried executives were more likely to place a heavy emphasis on their careers, participate actively in community affairs, and enjoy excellent health. Again, the items that formed the key and discriminated more successful from less successful executives of the Chamber of Commerce were consistent with general findings about the antecedents and concomitants of successful leadership discussed earlier. According to the key, the more successful Chamber of Commerce executives came from a middle-class background, spent a happy childhood in a stable family, received a good education, engaged in many extracurricular activities in high school and college, held leadership positions in many of the organizations to which they belonged, and displayed communication skills in debating, dramatics, and editorial work.

A similar type of key, developed for scoring the biographical information blanks of 443 Exxon managers, correlated above .50 with their success and above .30 with their ranked effectiveness (Laurent, 1968). Similarly, Drakeley and Herriot (1988) used data from 41 scorable items of a biographical inventory completed by 420 officers of the British Royal Navy and then cross-validated on a further sample of 282 officers. Three separate keys could be constructed to predict ratings for professional performance, leadership, and commitment. When cross-validated, the professional-performance key correlated .50 with appraised professional performance, the leadership key correlated .20 with appraised leadership, and the commitment key correlated .24 with remaining in the program.

A promising variant is one that emphasizes past accomplishments. The accomplishment record developed and validated by Hough (1984) correlated with subsequent job success (Hough, Keyes, & Dunnette, 1983). Again, biographical information, generated from retrospective life-history essays primarily about past accomplishments that were completed by first-year Annapolis midshipmen, was used to develop a biodata questionnaire. Then, 917 midshipmen who were entering Annapolis completed the scored and keyed questionnaire. The scales that were developed predicted, in cross-validation, subsequent military performance, academic performance, and peer ratings of leadership at the U.S. Naval Academy (Russell, Mattson, Devlin, & Atwater, 1986).

Data from Small-Group Exercises. Small-group exercises also generate objective results that can be mechanically correlated with the future performance of leaders or managers. For example, in Bass, Burger, et al.'s (1979)[5] large-scale study of managers from 12 national clusters, Exercise Life Goals was administered to 3,082 managers who were above or below the median in their own rate of advancement. In this exercise, the managers had to rank the importance to themselves of 11 life goals. Those managers who had advanced more rapidly in their careers, attached more importance to leadership, expertise, prestige, and duty, whereas the slower climbing managers favored self-realization, affection, security, and pleasure.

In a small-group budgeting exercise in the large-scale study just described, the fast-track managers in all the nations studied were more cautious about allocating funds for safety, labor relations, management development, research and development, and controlling water pollution. Nevertheless, in another small-group exercise that asked for recommendations about salary increases, the fast-track managers granted larger increases than did the slow-track managers. In Exercise Supervise, the accelerated managers gave more weight to the importance of generosity, honesty, and fairmindedness.

In other small-group exercises, fast-track, compared to slow-track, managers rated themselves higher in self-understanding and their preference for being more task oriented, although they also saw themselves as interpersonally competent. In addition, the fast-track managers revealed more objective signs of effective intelligence, objectivity, proactivity, and long-term views;

---

[5]Detailed in Chapter 34.

they were slower but more accurate in a two-way communication exercise. Many other objective signs differentiating fast-track from slow-track managers tended to vary country to country.

Combinatory Procedures

Multiple cutoffs, unit weighting, and optimal weighting are possible. When multiple cutoffs are employed, only applicants or candidates whose scores on selected tests are above a certain level are accepted; all others are rejected. When scores are unit weighted, they are merely added together in a combined prediction; the scores need to be standardized with means of 0 and standard deviations of 1 to give equal weighting to them if they are added together to form a single prediction. Such standardized scores can be differentially weighted on the basis of a multiple regression equation or can be accepted or rejected for inclusion, as well as differentially weighted, by a stepwise regression process to optimize the prediction of effectiveness.

Multiple Cutoffs. Mahoney, Sorenson, Jerdee, and Nash (1963) administered the Wonderlic Intelligence test, an empathy test, the Strong Vocational Interest Blank, the CPI, and a personal-history questionnaire to 468 managers from 13 Minnesota-based firms. Panels of executives ranked the examinees on global or overall effectiveness in carrying out their functions as managers. For half the sample, the ability of each of the 98 measures from the test battery to discriminate between the top and the bottom third of the managers in ranked effectiveness was analyzed. These managers were grouped into 6 discriminating clusters. One cluster that separated effective from ineffective managers included having the interests of a sales manager, purchasing agent, and president of a manufacturing firm. The second cluster dealt with the lack of interest in dentistry, printing, and farming. A high score on the intelligence test and self-rated dominance on the CPI formed the bases of the third and fourth clusters. One's educational level and one's wife's educational level and work was the fifth cluster, and engagement in many sports and hobbies, offices held, and high school memberships was the sixth cluster.

An optimum cutoff was determined for deciding whether a manager "passed" or "failed" each cluster. To be predicted as "acceptable," a manager had to be above the cutoff point for 5 of the 6 clusters. For example, an acceptable manager was one who was above the cutoffs in the interests of a sales manager, intelligence, dominance, education, and extracurricular activities.

The other half of the sample was held out for cross-validation. The same multiple cutoffs were used; 45.5 percent of the managers in the cross-validation sample were accepted and 54.5 percent were rejected. Of those who were accepted, 62 percent had been ranked high in effectiveness on the job and 29 percent had been ranked low. But of those who were rejected, only 38 percent had been ranked high in effectiveness and 71 percent had been ranked low.

Unit Weighting. Campbell, Dunnette, Lawler, and Weick (1970) reviewed studies of the value of various measures that are usually included in test batteries, such as intelligence, interests, personality, and biographical information, for predicting leadership and management potential in designated locations. For instance, salaries of supervisors and executives, adjusted for length of service and age, were predicted with correlations above .20 at Minneapolis Gas by 15 to 18 scale scores (Jurgensen, 1966). The promotability of managers at Jewel Tea (Meyer, 1963) and of sales managers at the American Oil Company (Albright, 1966) could similarly be predicted. But mixed results were reported by Tenopyr and Ruch (1965) for various technical managers at North American Aviation.

Selover (1982) combined into an advancement-potential score 5 measures that had been obtained from newly hired personnel at Prudential Insurance and were found to predict the rate of advancement 4 to 5 years later. Correlations ranging from .35 and .40 were seen between the advancement-potential scores, similarly derived, and the rate of advancement in 3 additional samples of newly hired employees.

Ghiselli (1971) identified 13 traits of managerial talent and developed a questionnaire, the Self-Description Inventory, to measure them. He then related the scores on the 13 traits to supervisors' ratings of effectiveness. Ten of the 13 scores related significantly to the criteria. These predictive scores dealt with supervisory ability, the need for occupational status, intelligence, self-actualization, self-assurance, decisiveness, and the lack of the need for security.

Basically negative conclusions about the value of tests and biographical information for predicting general success as a manager were reached by Brenner (1963) at Lockheed Aircraft. But with managers in the same company, Flanagan and Krug (1964) showed that it was necessary to differentiate whether one was trying to predict success and effectiveness in supervision, creativity, organization, research, engineering, or sales. For each, a differently weighted optimization was required.

Multiple Regression: Optimal Weighting of Predictors. The Sears program for predicting managerial performance extended over a period of 35 years. The test battery that evolved tapped intellectual abilities, personality, values, and interests. Its results predicted the promotability of executives and the satisfaction of subordinates with operating efficiency, relationships, and

their own personal satisfactions. Multiple regression was used to weight the test scores optimally to minimize the errors of the predictions. Illustrative are the results for 48 store managers and 42 higher-level managers shown in Table 36.1.

The Sears battery of psychological tests for predicting the performance of executives included measures to tap flexible intellectual functioning by using the Sears adaptation of the California F-Scale of authoritarianism. The battery included a number of tests that were constructed to measure creative ingenuity and ability to initiate change, tests for preference for complexity, a scored biographical-history form, an adjective checklist, a verbal-fluency test, and a self-rating of role definition.

To assess administrative skill and decision making, Sears devised a special in-basket test, along with two leaderless group problem-solving situations. In addition, three problem-solving simulations were designed. The Guilford-Martin Personality Inventory was modified especially to measure emotional stability and com-

Table 36.1 Multiple Correlations between Scores for the Morale of Sears Employees and Scores on the Test Battery for Executives Who Were Responsible for Supervising the Employees

Areas of Employee Morale	Multiple Correlations with Executive Test Battery Scores[a]	
	48 Store Managers	42 Executives
I. Operating Efficiency		
a. Effectiveness of administration	.77	.51
b. Technical competence of supervision	.74	.43
c. Adequacy of communication	.59	.61
II. Personal Relations		
a. Supervisor-employee relations	.68	.54
b. Confidence in management	.59	.52
III. Individual Satisfactions		
a. Status and recognition	.69	.62
b. Identification with the company	.51	.52
IV. Job and Conditions of Work		
a. Working conditions	.36	.40
b. Overall morale score	.47	.54

[a]All correlations significant are at the 1 or 5 percent level of confidence.

SOURCE: Adapted from Bentz (1968, p. 71).

petitive drive. The multiple correlation of the combination of predictor measures with various criteria, such as superiors' ratings, ranged from .49 to above .80.

The Thurstone Test of Mental Ability, the Guilford-Martin Personality Inventory, the Allport-Vernon Study of Values, and the Kuder Interest Inventory were used to predict success as a Sears' purchasing manager. Multiple correlations ranging from .32 to .57 were attained against various criteria of job performance and management potential. A similar battery for predicting the long-term performance of managers of Sears stores yielded measures that correlated from .37 to .61 when optimally combined (Bentz, 1983, 1987).

Exxon's Early Identification of Management Poten-

tial (EIMP) was another prominent effort to use multiple regression to optimize the prediction of managers' success from a battery of predictors. The combination of tests included the Miller Analogies Test, the Strong-Vocational Interest Inventory, the Guilford-Zimmerman Temperament Inventory, and a specially keyed and scored biographical information blank (Laurent, 1968). The accuracy of the multiple regression predictions is shown in Table 34.1. In the United States, the multiple prediction correlated between .33 and .64 with managers' success (salary adjusted for age, seniority, and function). In Norway, Denmark, and the Netherlands, the comparable multiple correlations ranged from .27 to .65 (Laurent, 1970). Figure 36.1 shows how

Figure 36.1. Optimally Weighted Performance of Exxon Managers High, Middle, and Low in Success

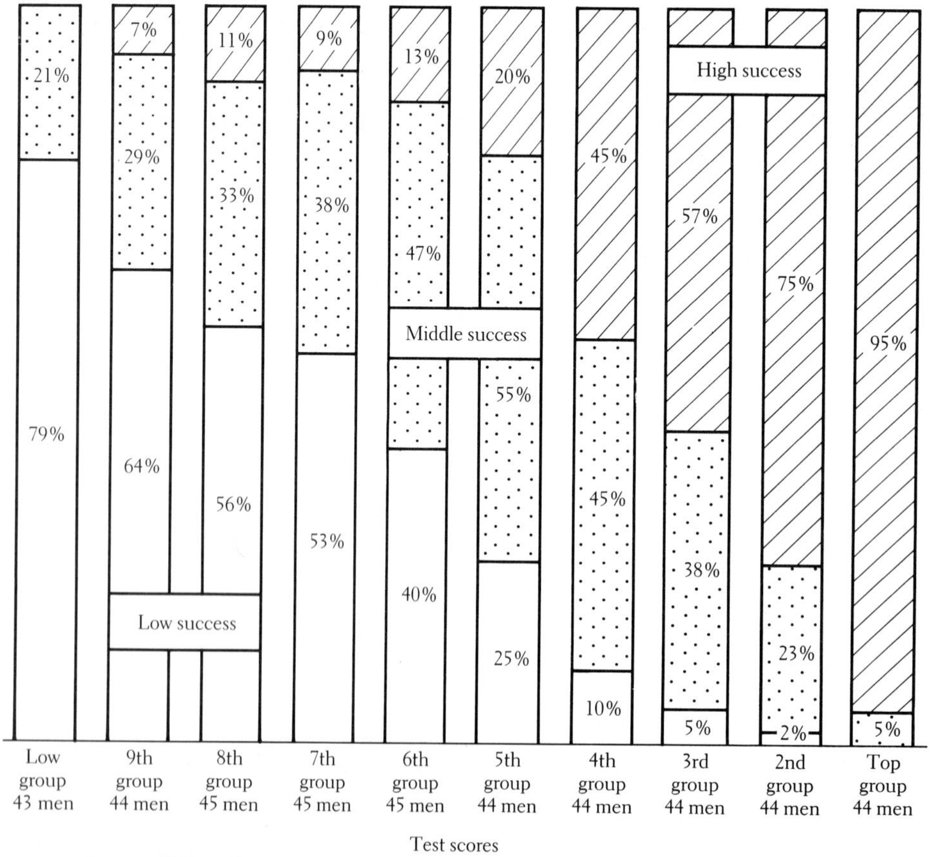

SOURCE: *Laurent (1968, p. 15).*

the higher success of managers was related to their higher optimally weighted scores on the EIMP test battery (Laurent, 1968).

Similar correlations were obtained in predicting the subsequent overall managerial effectiveness of the examinees, according to rankings by higher-level executives. For predicting managerial effectiveness, the multiple correlations ranged from .37 for managers in oil exploration and production to .66 for managers in traffic and purchasing. Again, the multiple correlations predicted success as a manager (suitably adjusted for education, seniority, function, etc.) from .67 for marketing managers to .82 for employee relations managers.

The predictive validity of the EIMP battery appeared to increase steadily with the years between testing and the measurement of the criteria during 3- to 12-year follow-ups. Sparks (1989) attributed the increase to improvements in the criteria. Also, he inferred that the EIMP measures of reasoning, judgment, and temperament make more of a contribution when higher levels of management are attained.

A derivative of the EIMP battery is the Manager Profile Record (MPR) based on the biographical data, the keyed Guilford-Zimmerman Temperament Inventory, and other tested judgmental elements. New item analysis and new validations were completed for the MPR against criteria for the level of responsibility attained by over 15,000 managers in a variety of industries, including banking, chemical, glass, paper, hotel, steel and so on. Validity coefficients ranged from .36 to .85. The work was repeated for first-line supervisors across a variety of situations, from utilities plants to data-processing offices. Validations for 8,765 first-line supervisors yielded correlations ranging from .25 to .37 between the Supervisory Profile Record and the appraisal of the supervisors' on-the-job performance as meeting or exceeding the requirements of the job.[6]

In a somewhat different approach, a set of multiple regression predictions was developed by Saville (1984) for the Occupational Personality Questionnaire (OPQ)

to measure the potential for a variety of different team roles and leader/subordinate types of roles. The output was standardized against a norm group of 527 British managers and professionals. Meaningful correlations were found between supervisors' appraisals of the performance of 440 British managers and OPQ predictive scores. For instance, a score on persuasiveness, extracted from optimally weighted scoring of the OPQ results, as predicted, correlated .27 with being appraised as having a commercial flair and .28 with being appraised as a good negotiator.

Situational and Procedural Moderators

Although the preceding Exxon findings showed considerable variation in multiple regression outcomes for different criteria, different countries, and different functions, the results everywhere were positive and both practically and statistically significant. Above and beyond these findings, within an Exxon U.S. subsidiary, Vicino and Bass (1978) showed that the accuracy of the predictions could be substantially enhanced by paying attention to what happened subsequently to 140 newly hired managers. Six years after employment, the managers were more successful and effective than predicted by the EIMP battery if they had initially been assigned to a supervisor they perceived to have influence with a higher authority, had personalities different from their first supervisor, were more satisfied with the challenges of their first task, and were under less stress in the two years before their measured success and effectiveness. Elsewhere, Berlew and Hall (1966) also showed that the degree of first-year challenge sensed by managers added to the prediction of their subsequent success.

Similarly, Ghiselli (1968a) reported results demonstrating that motivational factors interacted with personality traits that were predictive of the job success of managers. The need for job security was the strongest and the need for power was the weakest moderator in producing interactions between traits and success. Thus, whether managers had a low or a high need for security affected the extent to which their assertiveness correlated with their success as managers. In the same way, whether a score showing a high need for power forecast success as a leader depended on

[6]Drawn from the manuals and Technical Reports 1, 2, and 3 for the Manager Profile Record and the Supervisory Profile Record of Richardson, Bellows & Henry Company. Although by no means identical, similar results were obtained in different functional areas.

whether it was coupled with a strong sense of responsibility (Winter, 1989).

Time. Although Moore (1981) found that it did not matter whether librarians came to their assignments as a first or second career choice, the librarians' patterns of personality and leadership were closer to norms for the general population than they had been 20 years earlier. Similarly, when Harrell and Harrell (1984) applied stepwise regression equations to ability and personality predictions of the success of MBAs from Stanford University in achieving high salaries 5, 10, 15, and 20 years after graduation, different predictors emerged. For example, high earnings at the end of 5 years were predicted by orientation to high earnings, but after 20 years, the best combination of predictors of high earnings from the measures obtained 20 years earlier were youth, interest in sales management, a projective measure of the need for power, and a scored background survey.

Organization. Still another modifier of regression predictions is organizational purpose. Szilagyi and Schweiger (1984) pointed to the need to keep an organization's strategies in mind when trying to forecast the patterns of ability, personality, and experience that will best match candidates with the requirements of a job. Hambrick and Mason (1984) argued that the organization's character and performance will correlate with the particular personal attributes and experience of its senior managers. The differential weightings in multiple regression predictions of success in a rapidly growing organization are likely to be different from those in a mature or declining organization. The weightings of predictors of success as a combat officer are likely to be different from the weightings for optimizing the prediction of success as a garrison officer.

Criteria of Success. Obviously, how success is measured will affect the differential weightings that optimize a multiple regression prediction of success. A majority of studies have depended on subjective evaluations of success as a leader provided by superiors and a higher authority. These evaluations may suffer from various sources of bias by raters, such as halo and leniency. They may be subject to the quirks of memory and different raters' values.

Objective approaches to measuring success have also varied and, as a consequence, have led to different prediction results. At one extreme, as was noted in Chapter 4, many investigations before 1948 defined success as occupying a position of leadership, that is, holding an office or some position of responsibility. The level reached by a manager in an organization was often seen as an appropriate measure of success. This definition was improved by adjustments. Blake and Mouton (1964) used a managerial achievement quotient to evaluate the progress of managers' careers in a single organization; the level of the positions was divided by the managers' chronological age. Younger managers at higher organizational levels were seen to be more successful than were older managers at lower levels. Hall and Donnell (1979) slightly modified the formula. They continued to assume that regardless of the actual organization, managers worked in organizations of eight levels. To generate a realistic index number, they further assumed that all managers' careers are in eight-level organizations. Bass, Burger, et al. (1979) adjusted the quotient by dividing the current level of the manager by the actual number of levels in the organization, then multiplying by the size of the organization. They argued that managers of larger organizations who are at the same place on their respective organizational ladders as managers of smaller organizations were more successful.

Another criterion of managerial success was the amount of salary or compensation earned (Harrell & Harrell, 1975). But the compensation should be adjusted for age, function, experience, seniority, inflation and so forth (Farrow, Bass & Valenzi, 1977; Sparks, 1966).

Sex and Race. The sex and race of examinees may be of some limited consequence in moderating predictive accuracy. Women do about as well as men when undergoing assessment, according to an analysis by Ritchie and Moses (1983) of the overall scores obtained by 1,097 female managers at A T & T. The assessment center's predictions for the progress of their careers at the end of 7 years were as valid as those for male managers. Similar results for women and for men were reported by Moses and Boehm (1975) and for black women compared to white women (Huck & Bray,

1975). But subsequently, a meta-analysis to be discussed later found that the predictive validity of assessment programs was higher when the percentage of women assessees was higher. A validity of .38 based on multiple correlations of the Exxon EIMP battery and managerial success was found for 67 black males; of .31, for 80 white females; and .53, for 685 white males (Sparks, 1989).

Judgments Integrated with Mechanical Methods

Profiling, Typing, and Narrative Integrated Descriptions

Here the information obtained mechanically from tests and measures is combined into a display, summarized into a categorical type by its pattern, or reported in a narrative. From these displays, categorizations, or narratives, judgments about the potential or performance of leaders can be made. For instance, the results of the Myers-Briggs test are arranged to sort examinees into different combinations of sensors, feelers, thinkers, and judges and then the different types are related to the managers' and leaders' performance (McCaulley, 1989).

The individual examinee's capacity, interest, and personality scores are typically categorized, profiled, or converted into narratives. The scores are shown in contrast to norms for the individual's class, organization, occupation, and so on. Then judgments are made from the profiles. For example, Dicken and Black (1965) administered a test battery to candidates for promotion. The battery included the Otis Quick Scoring Mental Ability Test, the Strong Vocational Interest Blank, the Minnesota Multiphasic Personality Inventory, and other measures of aptitude and knowledge. Narrative reports of about 500 words were written for each candidate from the results. After reading the reports, four psychologists rated each candidate on effective intelligence, personal soundness, drive and ambition, leadership and dominance, likableness, responsibility and conscientiousness, ability to cooperate, and overall potential. Three to seven years later, officials from the two firms in which the examinees worked rated them on the same variables. The median correlations between the psychologists' and the officials' follow-up ratings were .38 and .33 in the two firms.

In similar fashion, Albrecht, Glaser, and Marks (1964) had 3 psychologists rank the potential of 31 prospective district marketing managers in budgeting effectiveness, sales performance, interpersonal relationships, and overall. Their rankings were clinical judgments based on combining objective and projective test results, as well as results from an interview and a personal-history form. Although the test scores alone correlated .20, on the average, with subsequent success as a manager, the predictions of the psychologists based on the combined results of tests, interviews, and personal history correlated between .43 and .58 with the managers' subsequent job performance. When tests, interviews, and personal history are combined further in this way with individual and small group exercises, the total effort becomes an assessment center.

Assessment Centers

In the European tradition, the identification of potential leaders tended to make use of inferences based on observations, personality tests, and interviews. The assessment-center fit readily with the European approach. As early as 1923, following on experience in World War I, boards of psychologists and officers were forming judgments of candidates for leadership positions in the German army from observing the candidates in a roundtable discussion and from other tests and methods (Simoneit, 1944). Comparable developments took place in Great Britain (Garforth, 1945). By the 1940s, the British had organized country-house retreats for civil service and industrial candidates to meet with assessors. The candidates were then observed in formal exercises, as well as in informal interactions, by the psychologists and management assessors; the result was valid assessments of the chosen candidates' future performance (Vernon, 1948, 1950).

During World War II, the Office of Strategic Services (1948) created a similar assessment program for candidates for special agents and spies that was based on the psychological theories of Henry Murray (1938). In addition to the usual testing, the candidates were systematically subjected to cognitive and physical group exercises, along with stress interviews. Decisions were made on the basis of the assessors' ratings, which were formed from their observations of the candidates' performance in the various exercises (Murray & Mac-Kinnon, 1946). The interest in assessment programs generated the establishment of a civilian assessment center in 1949 at the University of California, Berkeley (MacKinnon, 1960), and programs at Standard Oil of Ohio (SOHIO) in 1953 (Finkle & Jones, 1970) and at IBM (Kraut, 1972), General Electric (Meyer, 1972), and Sears (Bentz, 1971) by the late 1950s. The modern assessment-center approach spread rapidly around the world (Thornton & Byham, 1982). But most prominent was the assessment center program launched in 1956 at A T & T as a long-term research study of the development of the careers of A T & T managers (Bray, Campbell, & Grant, 1974).

As MacKinnon (1975) noted, "assessment center" may refer to a physical facility, such as the Berkeley's Institute of Personality Assessment Research; a standardized assessment program, such as SOHIO's Formal Assessment of Corporate Talent; or the bringing together of a group of candidates for assessment. By the end of the 1970s, several thousand centers and programs were in operation.

Methods

All the individual and group testing activities discussed so far in this chapter have been used in assessment centers and take from a half day to five days. These activities may include paper-and-pencil and projective tests of values, interests, and personality; tests of cognitive abilities and reading and writing skills; and observers' judgments of the performance on in-basket tests, interviews, role-playing exercises, organizational simulations, and leaderless group discussions requiring cooperation or competition. What is special about the assessment center is its use of the pooled judgments of staff psychologists and managers who have been assigned as observers. The judgments are based on their observations of the candidates in action and the inferences they draw from the test results to reach consensual decisions about the leadership potential of each candidate. The observers also use consensus to predict each candidate's likely performance as a manager and other aspects of the candidate's future performance. From 10 to 52 variables that are assumed to be related to managerial performance may be judged by the team of observers in this way (Howard, 1974).

According to a survey of assessment centers by Bender (1973), the typical center uses 6 assessors, including psychologists and managers at several levels above the candidates. Usually, candidates are processed in multiples of 6, which is seen as an optimal number for interactions and observations. For example, 12 candidates at a time were processed by Macy's in interviews, group discussions, and in-basket tests. Six executives from top and middle management formed the assessment team (Anonymous, 1975). Unless the information is withheld to avoid contaminating follow-up research, feedback of the consensual judgments is given to candidates in most centers to contribute to the candidates' developmental efforts.

Variables

Because of the prominence of the A T & T Management Progress Study and the availability of materials from Development Dimensions International derived from it, the 25 variables deemed important for success at A T & T have been incorporated, in whole or in part, in a good many assessment programs elsewhere. These variables are general mental ability, oral and written communication skills, human relations skills, personal impact, perception of threshold social cues, creativity, self-objectivity, social objectivity, behavioral flexibility, need for the approval of superiors, need for the approval of peers, inner work standards, need for advancement, need for security, goal flexibility, primacy of work, Bell Telephone value orientation, realism of expectations, tolerance of uncertainty, ability to delay gratification, resistance to stress, range of interests, energy, organization and planning, and decision making (Bray, Campbell, & Grant, 1974, pp. 19–20).

The 25 assessment variables were logically grouped into 7 categories, as follows:

1. Administrative skills—a good manager has the ability to organize work effectively and to make high-quality decisions.
2. Interpersonal skills—the forceful personality

makes a favorable impression on others with good oral skills.

3. Intellectual ability—a good manager learns quickly and has a wide range of interests.

4. Stability of performance—a good manager is consistent in his or her performance, even under stressful conditions or in an uncertain environment.

5. Motivation to work—a good manager will find positive areas of satisfaction of life; he or she is concerned with doing a good job for its own sake.

6. Career orientation—a good manager wants to advance quickly in the organization but is not as concerned about a secure job; the manager does not want to delay rewards for too long a time.

7. Lack of dependence on others—a good manager is not as concerned about getting approval from superiors or peers and is unwilling to change his or her life goals.

Administrative skills were found to be assessed best by the manager's performance on the in-basket test. An evaluation of the interpersonal skills was procured from the observer teams' judgment of the manager's performance in group exercises. A measure of intellectual ability was reliably obtained from standardized general ability tests. A measure of stability of performance was acquired from the individual's performance in the simulations. A motivation-to-work measure was obtained from projective tests and the interview, with some contribution from the simulations. Career orientation was seen both in interviews and projective tests and, to some extent, in the personality questionnaires. A measure of dependence was gained mostly from the projective tests (Bray, Campbell, & Grant, 1974).

Dunnette (1971) concluded, from a review of factor analyses of these variables, not only for the A T & T assessment programs but for those at IBM, SOHIO, and elsewhere, that the underlying factors included overall activity and general effectiveness, organizing and planning, interpersonal competence, cognitive competence, motivation to work, personal control of feelings, and resistance to stress.[7] Empirical studies by

Sackett and Hakel (1979) and Tziner (1984) also led to questioning of whether more than just a few dimensions could account for all 25 variables or their factor clusters. Despite this questioning, the surplus of variables may be useful for diagnosis and counseling (Thornton & Byham, 1982). Moreover, the correlations between the ratings of the dimensions on the same exercise are often a lot higher than the correlations for ratings of any one of the dimensions between exercises (Sackett & Dreher, 1982), which suggests that just a few global measures are involved.

Exercise Order Effects? Bycio (1988) found a slight effect of no practical significance on ratings earned by participants at an assessment center, depending on the order in which the participants took various exercises and completed questionnaires. About 1 percent of the variance in ratings could be accounted for by which of 11 orders of center activities the participants were assigned.

Prescreening

Much prescreening of candidates for assessment occurs. For instance, in one year, 1974, Macy's interviewed 2,000 prospective candidates for participation in an assessment center in New York City. Of these prospective candidates, only 500 candidates were processed through the assessment center (Anonymous, 1975). Self-selection also serves as prescreening. Ordinarily, participation from within an organization is voluntary after candidates (such as those at Michigan Bell) have learned that they have been nominated for participation in the assessment center by their supervisors, sometimes with higher-level approval. Self-nominations may also be possible.

Psychometric testing can be used advantageously to prescreen candidates before engaging them in the expense of the total assessment process. For example, for a sample of 80 A T & T prospects, the Gordon Personality Profile and Gordon Personality Inventory tests were administered before the prospective candidates could participate in an assessment center. Four of the scores on the tests correlated with the subsequent assessment based on the full 3-day program, as follows: ascendancy, .46; sociability, .32; original thinking, .37; and vigor, .21. A specially scored biographical question-

[7]Note the similarity of these factors with much of what was presented in earlier chapters on personal factors associated with leadership.

naire alone correlated .48 with the results of the 3 days of assessments. If a composite score based on the biographical questionnaire and the measures of ascendancy and original thinking had been in effect, 84 percent of those scoring in the lowest or "D" category would have been detected as not acceptable to the assessors after 3 days, while only 16 percent would have been deemed acceptable. It was reckoned that over $2,000 per successful candidate could be saved by installation of such a screening program (Moses & Margolis, 1979). In the same way, Dulewicz and Fletcher (1982) found that scores on an intelligence test but not previous specialized experience contributed to the candidates' performance and assessment based on the situational exercises of an assessment center. Thus, preassessment intelligence tests could be used to screen prospects for assessment. Also ignored for 40 years have been the possibilities of prescreening with a single LGD since, as mentioned earlier, a correlation of .75 was reported by Vernon (1950) between the results about candidates obtained in a one-hour LGD and the results of a full assessment at an assessment center.

Reliability of Assessments

Agreement among assessors has been subjected to numerous analyses to provide estimates of the reliability of the assessments. Fewer test-retest estimates are available.

Agreement among Assessors. Observers' independent ratings of assessees correlated .74 in their ratings on the average and .76 in corresponding rankings of 12 participants in the various segments of a 2-day IBM assessment program (Greenwood & McNamara, 1967). Comparable median correlations of .68 and .72 were reported for A T & T's program (Grant, 1964). For the SOHIO program, correlations of assessments between psychologists and managers who served as assessors ranged from .74 for the assessment of the drive of assessees to .93 for the judgment of the amount of assessees' participation.

Schmitt (1977) reported that when a team of 4 assessors evaluated 101 middle management prospects over a 4-month period, mean interrater correlations before the raters' discussion of the ratings ranged from .46 for the rating of assessees' inner work standards to .88 for

the ratings of assessees' oral communication skills. After the assessors discussed their first ratings, the intercorrelations rose to .74 and .91, respectively, but the opinion of no one assessor shifted more than that of any other (Schmitt, 1977), which suggests that mutual influence had occurred. However, in an analysis of the participation of 2,640 candidates in an assessment program to determine their suitability for training as U.S. Navy officers, Herriot, Chalmers, and Wingrove (1985) found that a discussion among the assessors changed the opinions of those assessors who had deviated from the majority opinion, depending on their rank as officers and whether they were above or below the majority in the rating they had initially given a candidate.

In an overall review, Howard (1984) concluded that correlations among assessors tended to be at least .60 in most cases, rising to as high as .99. This agreement was not affected by whether rankings or ratings were used or by whether the assessors were psychologists or managers, but, as will be noted later, meta-analytic results from 47 studies (Gaugler, Rosenthal, Thornton, & Bentson, 1987) showed that psychologists were more valid assessors than were managers.

Correlations among raters are increased most by the consensual discussions they hold. Before such discussions, median correlations range from .50 (Tziner & Dolan, 1982) to .76 (Borman, 1982). After the discussions, the median correlations are likely to rise to .80 or above (Sackett & Dreher, 1982) and as high as .99 (Howard, 1974). This increase may reflect more shared information or it may be a matter of the raters' influence on each other.

Agreement among assessors depends on how much training they receive in making ratings in general and in making ratings about performance in specific exercises. For example, Richards and Jaffee (1972) obtained an increase in interrater agreement as a result of the assessors' training in rating the performance on in-basket tests. They found increases in interrater agreement from .46 to .78 on ratings of human relations skills and of .58 to .90 on ratings of administrative/technical skills.

Test-Retest Reliability. A test-retest reliability of .77 was reported for the A T & T assessment center's testing of men 1-month apart. The test-retest reliability obtained for women candidates was .70, .68 for black candidates of both sexes, and .73 for white candidates of both sexes (Moses & Boehm, 1979; Moses & Margolis, 1979).

Predictive Validity

Reviews by Huck (1973) and Klimoski and Strickland (1977) concluded that assessment centers generated valid predictive information. This conclusion was corroborated in a meta-analysis by Hunter and Hunter (1984), which obtained median corrected correlations of .63 for predicting managerial potential from assessments and .43 for predicting on-the-job performance. But these findings appeared to be inflated according to a more extended meta-analysis by Gaugler, Rosenthal, Thornton and Bentson (1987) that was based on 47 studies of assessment centers involving 12,235 participants. The 107 validity coefficients between the assessment centers' forecasts for candidates and criterion appraisals of the managerial performance and advancement of the candidates (corrected for sampling error, restrictions in range, and unreliability of the criteria) averaged .37.

In the Management Program Study at A T & T, assessments were followed up for 8 years to see if they could predict the promotion of assessees into middle management. Of those assessees who were predicted to succeed, 42 percent did succeed, while only 7 percent of those predicted to fail actually attained middle-management positions (Bray, Campbell, & Grant, 1974). A correlation of .44 was found between 5,943 men who were designated as more than acceptable, acceptable, less than acceptable, or not acceptable by the consensus of the assessors' judgments and whether the men had subsequently earned 2 promotions in the 8 years following the assessment. The overall managerial level that the candidates achieved at the end of 20 years continued to be accurately forecast by the assessments obtained 20 years earlier. Intelligence scores, motivation and personality measures obtained from psychometric instruments, and the results of interviews and in-basket tests all contributed positively to the accuracy of the predictions (Howard & Bray, 1988). The assessment collected 20 years previously also predicted satisfaction, self-confidence, and emotional adjustment.

Similarly, at IBM, Wollowick and McNamara (1969) found a correlation of .37 between the assessment by the assessment center and increased responsibility assigned to candidates. In a follow-up, Hinrichs (1978a) obtained a correlation of .46 between the overall judgments of the assessment center and the level of management reached by the candidates after 8 years. Again, at SOHIO, a correlation of .64 was achieved between assessments and superiors' appraisals of the candidates' potential 6 to 27 months afterwards. The correlation remained stable in forecasting appraisals up to 5 years later (Carleton, 1970). In the A T & T and IBM studies, the assessment center's results for each candidate were *not* seen subsequently by their superiors who were responsible for the on-the-job appraisals and promotions of the candidates, so the validity correlations could not be inflated by such contamination as they might have been in other studies.[8]

Howard (1974) noted that the components at various assessment centers differed in the contributions they made to the accuracy of forecasts. For example, at A T & T, the overall assessment and situational tests had the highest predictive validities; at SOHIO, projective and psychometric tests were particularly important overall; at IBM, some elements in each of the procedures tended to contribute to the prediction of promotion.

From a study of 19 managers in 3 days of assessment and 4 months of follow-up training, Cunningham and Olshfski (1985) concluded that assessment centers, as ordinarily constituted, were better detectors of the variables of socioemotional leadership skills than of the variables of task-leadership skills, but the two tended to be correlated.

Moderating Effects on the Validities. According to the extended meta-analysis by Gaugler, Rosenthal, Thornton, and Bentson (1987), the validity of an assessment center's forecast depended on the criterion of success which was predicted by the assessment. On the average, according to the validities obtained (weighted by sample size and corrected for attenuation and the unreliability of the criterion), the candidates' potential for promotion, rated by supervisors and a higher authority, was better predicted (.53) than was the candi-

---

[8]As will be noted later, even when it is possible, such contamination does not appear to occur.

dates' rated current on-the-job-performance (.36), rated performance in training (.35), or actual advancement in their careers (.36). The least valid predictions were for appraisals by supervisors of the same on-the-job dimensions rated at the assessment center (.33). The assessment center's focus on the current job requirements of candidates appears to be less useful than its concentration on the candidates' possible future job assignments. An extreme case was illustrated by Turnage and Muchinsky (1984), who found no validity in a 1-day program for predicting candidates' currently appraised job performance but valid predictions of the candidates' potential after 5 years and their appraised career potential.

The purpose of the validation effort also made a difference. When the effort was for research purposes, the correlation between assessment predictions and subsequent appraisals of success was .48. However, the correlation was lower if the purpose of the effort was for selection (.41), early identification of promise (.46), or promotion (.30). Overall judgments of the candidates' participation in an assessment center's activities appear to be better predictors of the candidates' advancement and salary increases than are the performance appraisals they receive from their supervisors. In turn, the assessments appear to be better predictors of the appraised on-the-job performance than are objective measures of such performance (Turnage & Muchinsky, 1984).

It also seems that the consensual decisions and the pooled ratings of assessors may yield a less accurate prediction than one made by optimally weighing the independent assessors' ratings and using mechanical pooling of the assessors' ratings by means of multiple regression analysis (Tziner, 1987).

Contrary to expectations, although Borman, Eaton, Bryan, and Rosse (1983) could find no evidence of significant individual differences in the validity of the raters' judgments, the aforementioned meta-analyses suggested that validities were higher if the assessors were psychologists rather than managers, if the percentage of female assessees was greater, and if the percentage of minority assessees was smaller.

Some exercises generated ratings with higher predictive validities than did others (Sackett & Dreher, 1982). Validities were also higher when a broader array of exercises were employed and if peer ratings were provided by the assessees of each other. On the other hand, the validity of assessment-center predictions was little affected by other expected influences such as the ratio of assessees to assessors, the number of days of observation, the number of days that the assessors were trained, and the hours the assessors spent in integrating information. Criterion contamination accruing from providing feedback to assessees and their supervisors also had little of the expected effect on the validities.

Validity of Other Applications. Specialized assessment centers have been created and found valid for predicting successful performance in institutional settings, such as educational and military organizations. For instance, Schmitt, Noe, Merrit, and Fitzgerald (1984) extended the use of assessment centers to forecast success as a school administrator. The specially developed assessment center featured activities and exercises that are relevant to schools, rather than to business and industry. The assessments correlated between .20 to .35 with appraisals of the job performance of the administrators by teachers and administrative staff; however, the assessments failed to correlate with promotions or salary increases. Again, centers were found to be valid and useful for assessing military recruits (Borman, 1982), naval officers (Gardner & Williams, 1973), Canadian female military officers (Tziner & Dolan, 1982), managers of law enforcement agencies (McEvoy, 1988) and civil service and foreign service administrators (Anstey, 1966; Vernon, 1950; Wilson, 1948).

Utility. Because thousands of dollars may have to be spent per candidate, many essays on the cost-effectiveness of assessment centers have been produced (see, for example, Byham & Thornton, 1970). Cascio's and Sibley's (1979) quantitative analysis of the hypothetical utility of assessment centers was based on assumptions about the costs, validities, and gains to the organization as a consequence of improvements in the accuracy of prediction provided by the assessment center. Cascio showed the numerous parameters that had to be considered and the optimal arrangements that were possible if the designated costs, validities, and benefits were involved.

Dunnette (1970) initially raised the question of whether the additional cost of assessment-center procedures, in contrast to less expensive mechanical methods, added sufficiently to the validity of prediction. For instance, Glaser, Schwartz, and Flanagan (1958) had determined that assessments of 227 supervisors from individual interviews, an LGD session, a role-playing situation, and a simulated management-work situation when combined with 2 paper-and-pencil tests yielded multiple correlations of only .30 to .33. Yet the two paper-and-pencil tests alone correlated .23 and .25 with the appraised effectiveness of the supervisors on the job. On the other hand, the A T & T; SOHIO; and, particularly, the IBM studies showed considerable augmentation of the validity of predictions (up to multiple correlations of .62) when the results of an in-basket test, LGD, and biographical information blank were added to information gained from a personality test (Wollowick & McNamara, 1969). But such augmentation was not the case in an assessment of 37 prospects for supervisory positions at Caterpiller Tractor (Bullard, 1969).

Cost estimates have ranged up to $5,000 per assessment-center examinee,[9] including space and materials as well as the assessors' and assessees' time and travel costs without even considering staff salaries. Much less expensive alternatives are the use of standardized machine-scored cognitive and personality psychometric tests. However, the validities of these tests are less likely to reach as high as what is possible when they are combined with the situational tests and other procedures of the assessment center. Another alternative is to rely on recommendations, individual interviews, committee reviews of credentials, and previous performance appraisals. Again, such approaches are unlikely to yield the same accuracies of prediction. Nor does actuarial prediction that is based on multiple regression yield more accurate predictions than do assessors' ratings, according to an analysis based on 24 predictors of the growth of the salaries of 254 managers 1, 3, and 5 years after the managers had been assessed (Howard, 1984). To the extent that one mistake in the selection or promotion of a manager might cost the organization grievously, raising the validity of decisions about selection and promotion, say, from .25 to .50, by

using assessment centers instead of other less thorough efforts can be readily justified and can explain the widespread popularity of assessment centers. Thus, Hogan and Zenke (1986) showed that with a sample of 115 persons applying for seven school principalships, selected exercises at an assessment center yielded a large gain in performance (valued in dollars) over the traditional interview procedures. Nevertheless, Tziner (1987) suggested that it is still an open question as to whether much less expensive alternatives can achieve sufficiently accurate predictions to justify using them instead of the procedures of full-blown assessment centers.

MacKinnon (1975) enumerated a number of other benefits that can be obtained from an assessment center. The assessment center is an educational experience for the assessees and even more so for the managers who serve as observers. Assessees may perform better after returning to their jobs (Campbell & Bray, 1967). Lorenzo (1984) demonstrated that experience as an assessor resulted in proficiency in interviewing others, as well as obtaining and presenting relevant information about the candidates and their managerial qualifications. Assessors also increased their proficiency in preparing concise written reports about this information.

But intangible costs may also need to be considered. The centers may promote organizational stagnation in that assessees will be favored who are most similar in attitudes and values to current managers and, hence, organizational change may be stifled. Another possible negative effect is that the assessment center may establish crown princes whose future success becomes a self-fulfilling prophecy of the organization. Conversely, a candidate who receives a poor assessment may be denied opportunities to show what he or she can really do in the organization. In addition, the stressfulness of the assessment experience may invalidate it. Finally, those who are not nominated for participation at an assessment center may feel left out (Howard, 1974; MacKinnon, 1975).

Ideally, the procedures and variables to be assessed in a particular assessment center should stem from an analysis of the requirements of the jobs for which the candidates are being considered. Then assessment procedures to tap the identified dimensions that match

[9]In 1980 dollars.

these requirements should follow (Thornton & By-ham, 1982). Worbois's (1975) selected 12 assessment variables in this way and predicted supervisory ratings of the subsequent performance of candidates with a correlation of .39. As was noted in the preceding meta-analyses, specific dimensions of the candidate's current on-the-job-performance are harder to predict than is the candidate's overall future performance or potential as a manager.

Summary and Conclusions

The predispositions of the individual that are linked to the person's performance as a leader, which were discussed in previous chapters, can be assessed and combined in various ways to forecast success and effectiveness. Pure judgment and expectations of supervisors and higher authority on the basis of current on-the-job performance are commonly used, often as part of performance appraisals; the judgments of peers and subordinates can also be considered, as can references from sources outside the organization. Clinical judgments from psychological instruments and interviews with employees are another alternative. Simulations make it possible to observe and judge the performance of employees in standardized problem settings. These simulations include managerial in-basket tests, small-group exercises, and LGDs. The reliability and validity of forecasting success with such pure judgments can be increased through the standardization of judgmental requirements, the pooling of judgments, and the training of the judges.

Valid scores from psychometric tests, application blanks, and biographical-information blanks can be obtained, often through the use of specially constructed discriminating keys. The scores can be combined mechanically with or without the use of multiple regression. They also can be combined mechanically with judgments. Conversely, judgments can be formed out of observations and information attained from such tests and measurements. The procedures of assessment centers have become a popular means of combining scores on psychometric tests with observations of candidates in a variety of simulations that are relevant to current and future positions. The final pooling may or may not justify the expense entailed in terms of providing more accurate predictions of future potential of leaders and managers than may predictions obtained by less expensive alternatives. This is one of the remaining questions for future research to settle.

Leadership Issues
for the Twenty-first Century

Research on leadership and its widespread applications are coming of age. Their effects can be seen in the awakening in much of industry to the people side of its enterprise, in corporate mission statements, in the principles that U.S. presidents set forth for their staffs, in professional education and in the established research centers, educational curricula, and nationwide community programs dedicated to leadership. We can only wonder about how much the results of studies of leadership, popularized in college courses, best-selling books, and the mass media, contributed to the implicit theories of leadership espoused by college students in the 1980s. For, the students believe that the productivity and morale of workers depend on leaders who are concerned about the work to be done, are participatory, and offer praise and rewards for good performance (Graves, 1983). Would these same three clusters of leadership behavior have emerged among college students in 1950? The predictions about leadership and management in the year 2000 that were made in the mid-1960s and a few years later erred mainly in that the predicted developments came sooner than expected (Bass, 1967e; Bass & Ryterband, 1974). The predictions made today are likely to be equally conservative.

Paradigm shifts that took place in the 1970s and 1980s are likely to settle into new concentrations of research efforts. For instance, there is likely to be far more research on transformational factors, such as charismatic and inspirational leadership, and on the cognitive processes that are involved in leader-subordinate relationships. In addition, there is likely to be much more sorting out of the personal and situational factors that drive a given group of leader and subordinates, rather than the continuing advocacy of the importance of one or the other.

The love of controlled survey and laboratory studies will extend increasingly to a wider array of methods. In the same way, issues will be broadened by the cross-fertilization of interests of the behavioral, social, and political sciences. Contributions to the field of both substance and methods will increase from non-American sources, particularly from Europe and Asia. Concerns about the equitable distribution of power will be increasingly shared with concerns about the equitable distribution of information.

There is also likely to be increasing consolidation, as well as reanalysis, of earlier findings about leadership and the outcomes of leadership that questioned whether various contingencies were merely transient phenomena. The cultural, social, and economic changes that took place in the last half of the century, may require, as Tucker (1983) suggested, a reexamination of the instruments, structures, and relationships established earlier.

Much will be learned as new nations become complex industrialized societies, for the leadership and management that emerge will need to fit with the cultural realities of the different nations. For instance, new leadership styles in the People's Republic of China that emerge as it moves toward somewhat of a market economy will be affected by two cultural imperatives: the collective principles of Marxism and the rich 3,000-year-old Chinese philosophical heritage (Liancang, 1987). How long the democratic momentum that crashed into the entrenched bureaucracy in 1989 will be curbed remains to be seen.

Considerations in Looking Ahead

Six considerations guide our peering at the future of research on leadership and its application: extrapolation from the past, societal changes, new technologies, organizational trends, changes in personnel practices, and new paradigms.

Extrapolation

First, we look ahead by extrapolation. For example, much of the methodological course for the 1990s and beyond has been set by trends that began in the 1970s and 1980s for more longitudinal research relative to one-time, cross-sectional studies. More integrated field and laboratory studies will appear, along with the use of more sophisticated evaluations of the interactional processes of leaders, not only with subordinates but with superiors, peers, and clients.

Societal Changes

The substance of research on leadership is influenced considerably by what is happening in society as a whole. The majority of the American work force has shifted from manufacturing to service and information work. Organizational life in the public sector and health care have become of increasing interest. Opportunities to increase productivity, particularly its quality, have become more and more dependent on effective human relationships and the development of personnel. In the same way, when humans are replaced with robots and computers, more higher-level personnel specialists, supervisors, and team development are likely to be required. Mandated in much of Western Europe, industrial democracy remains voluntary in the United States, where it is increasingly becoming a fact of life through enlightened managements and employee-ownership plans. At the same time, the percentage of the work force in labor unions continues to decline, particularly in the private sector.

Demographics will inexorably work their will. The average U.S. employee in the 1990s and beyond will be older. Declines in the birthrates in the 1970s were reflected in the late 1980s by shortages of workers in many industries, by unfilled enlistment quotas in the military, and by fewer applicants for college. The greying of America will make labor more of a scarce resource and will increase the trend toward automation, the movement of labor-intensive industry out of the country, and the acceptance of more immigrants

(Jones, 1988). The percentage of more relations-oriented personnel in the U.S. labor force has increased with the sharp increase in the employment of women. A plural society of varied ethnicity and race is replacing the ideal of a single amalgamated society. The multinational firm, with its worldwide outlook, continues to expand. Multinational firms are just as likely to be headquartered in Japan, Britain, Germany, or elsewhere as in the United States. Dual careers and two wage earners in the family are now the rule. Five of every six men over age 65 are moving into a new leisure class of retirees. Foreign investment in the United States has risen sharply, particularly since 1985. A considerable percentage of U.S. personnel are now working for foreign-owned firms. There is an increasing need to remain competitive in the world marketplace with the Pacific Rim nations and with the rapidly unifying European Economic Community.

Forms of government and economic systems began changing in the 1980s from Argentina to Poland, from the Philippines to the Soviet Union. Japan's industry is maturing; Britain's class structure is shifting. The U.S. hegemony in 1945 in economic power has been replaced by the distribution of such power across many nations. These economic and political changes bring new, continuing challenges for leaders at many levels in those countries in government, industry, and education.

The public is numbed by the threats of ecological crises, a nuclear winter, and exploding populations. Concern about corruption, business ethics, and social responsibilities continues, but deregulation has made the concern more a matter of private conscience than of public sanction—a situation that is likely to continue until regulation is reestablished. Leadership research and development will reflect these societal developments. Mentoring will play an increasingly important role (Zey, 1988). Furthermore, a premium will be placed not only on the junior managers' abilities to deal with the human factor but on the attention to quality and costs. More statesmanship and a world outlook will increasingly be required of senior managers, who also will need to remain vigilant in the face of merger mania and corporate takeovers.

The increasing importance of the highly equipped and highly trained individual soldier and the small team in the all-volunteer armed services will focus attention on approaches to promoting stability and cohesiveness through better leadership. Educational leadership in the 1990s is also likely to take a sharp turn in the face of declining enrollments. Compliance with laws regarding energy, pollution, and waste will be more difficult as limits and restrictions are severely tightened. These restrictions, along with increasingly competitive market forces, accelerating technological advances, and rapid societal changes, will further reduce the tolerance for laissez-faire leadership. But care will have to be taken to avoid a drift back to the promotion of autocratic behavior in the guise of active leadership, particularly in periods of high unemployment and job insecurity.

New Technologies

New technologies open up the possibilities of new research methods. They also create new substantive leadership issues. Networks of personal computers and interactive programming will increase greatly the opportunities for survey studies and the experimental manipulation of leader-follower variables. Advances in miniaturization and telemetry will no doubt be put to good use in the direct observation of leader-subordinate behavior and physiological reactions. As electronic mail crosses oceans and cultural boundaries instantly, leaders will face new opportunities and challenges. To date, behavioral research on management information systems has not reached its full potential, but a breakthrough in empirical research, spearheaded by new models, may be in the offing.

Leadership and the Information Revolution. According to Cleveland (1985), the character of the leadership role is systematically changing under the shock of the information revolution. This revolution is evidenced by the rapidly changing distribution of the work force in the United States. In 1920, 9 percent of the work force was engaged in knowledge and educational services; in 1955, 29 percent; and in 1975, 50 percent. In 2000, it is estimated that 66 percent of the work force will be involved in such services. The generation, communication, storage, and retrieval of information have been increasing exponentially in speed and amount. Older approaches to getting work done

may provide little guidance for the future. Six interlinked characteristics of information may radically alter the leader-follower relationship. The agenda for research on leadership in the future will entail dealing with these properties of information.

1. Information is expandable. The more we have, the more we use and the more useful it can become. Information is not a scarce resource; only time and the capacity of people limit its growth. (Of course, it is possible to be overloaded with information so that decisions become delayed or less than optimum.)
2. Information is compressible. It can be concentrated, integrated, summarized, and miniaturized in its manipulation and storage. It requires little energy and the depletion of few physical resources.
3. Information can replace land, labor, and capital. Whole libraries can be packed into a computerized data bank. Automation replaces people. Organized data reduce localized inventory requirements.
4. Information is transportable. Telecommunications makes physical meeting sites unnecessary. People can work together globally.
5. Information is diffusive. It leaks. Despite efforts to maintain secrecy, the leakage is wholesale and pervasive.
6. Information is shareable. An information-rich environment is "a sharing environment . . . the standards, rules, conventions, and codes are going to be different from those created to manage the zero-sum bargains of market economics" (Cleveland, 1985, p. 32).

Technological advances in the social sciences will serve in a similar way. When involved in operations research models, researchers now can deal with "fuzzy sets" of objectives as they affect decision-making processes instead of being limited to the unrealistic single-objective function. When involved with different sources of information, researchers can now make use of the multiscaling of categorizations.

Organizational Change

The world of computerized management information systems and the change in organizations, predicted over 30 years ago by Leavitt and Whisler (1958) for the 1980s, has arrived. Yet, there is little research on how managers' interactions with each other and with superiors, peers, subordinates, and clients have been altered. Middle management is being squeezed out, as Leavitt and Whisler predicted, because senior management can be linked by computer directly to lower levels of supervision and to the operations themselves. It was estimated that more than a million U.S. managers and staff professionals lost their jobs during the 1980s and that over a third of the middle management positions were eliminated (Byrne & Zellner, 1988). The tenure of the average manager in a single firm that was 12 years in 1970 has been reduced to 7 years in 1990. Much of the information processing that was formerly done by management and staff has been taken over by computers.

Cost cutting, mergers, and acquisitions also contributed to the decrease in the number of managers in a particular firm (Tomasko, 1987). The decrease was accompanied by a reduction in the number of layers in management hierarchies with larger spans of control for those who remained.

With an expanding economy, newly formed firms appear to absorb most of the managers who were made redundant in their former companies. But the trend in the decline of the percentage of managers in the U.S. work force from its high of above 10 percent in 1980 is expected to continue well into the twenty-first century. In the 1990s, managers are more likely to be concerned about their personal goals and capabilities than about those of their firm. The psychological contract of managers' loyalty to the firm is being broken (P. Hirsch, 1987; Marks, 1988).

Senior managers, in particular, see themselves as needing to watch out warily for their near-term performance. Everything that can be quantified will be quantified, and tighter controls will be imposed. Thus, senior managers will avoid risk taking, along with long-term investment in research and development (Levinson, 1988). All these tendencies could be reversed by a political reaction to the bankruptcies of leveraged by-outs which were unable to meet the excessive debt payments they incurred. The political reaction might result in highly protected senior managements unable to be moved out of office. Government intervention is already beginning to happen. A 1989 New York State law requires that the Board of Directors consider the costs to the community of accepting a takeover bid as well as the benefits to the shareholders.

Changes in Personnel Practices

Another consideration that may help to predict likely future developments in substantive research on leadership and its applications is the discernment of dissatisfaction with the adequacy of current personnel practices. According to a survey in early 1988 (Anonymous, 1988b), the needs of human resource management that were not being handled well at that time but were seen as requiring a great deal of emphasis at least until 1993 were succession planning, human resource productivity, and organizational design. Less important practices that also needed improvement were team building, the measurement of morale, performance aids, job design, the stress of career development, and outplacement.

New Paradigms

A last consideration is the possibility of new revolutionary paradigms that can affect both future methods and the content of leadership research. We have already seen the rapid impact on leadership theory and research of the cognitive revolution in psychology. Recent developments in the mathematics of dealing with irregularities, reversals in trends, and seemingly chaotic conditions may be applied to modeling the natural discontinuities in leader-follower relationships. The physical sciences may suggest new ways of looking at short-lived phenomena, for example, the emergence of instant leadership in a crisis followed by its equally instant disappearance. The willingness to accept two distinct ways of dealing with the same phenomenon, as is common in wave and particle physics, may lead leadership theorists to treat simultaneously the leader's and subordinates' different rationales for what is happening. Cause-and-effect analyses may be seen as the exception to mutual interactions between the leader and group outcomes. Given the issues that have dominated leadership theory and research in the past several decades, the societal, technological, and organizational changes; and possible new shifts in thinking, a broadening of methodological and substantive issues is to be sought and expected in the field in the near future.

Methodological Issues

Causal Relations

In examining how leadership relates to outcomes, we continue to be faced with which is cause and which is effect. Thus, Kernberg (1984) stated that breakdowns in work effectiveness that are erroneously attributed to failures of leadership are often due to regressions (in the psychoanalytical sense) in environmental, organizational, and group factors. The regressive leadership is an effect rather than a cause. Supervisors may be supportive because they have productive subordinates, or subordinates may be productive because they have supportive supervisors (Bass, 1965c). Some investigations (see, for example, Greene, 1974) have shown that subordinates cause their leader's behavior. Other studies (see, for instance, Dawson, Messé, & Phillips, 1972) have found that the leader's behavior is a cause of the subordinates' performance. Still others (such as Jacobs, 1970) have pointed to mutual causality in an exchange in which the subordinate complies because of the leader's promise and the leader rewards the subordinate for the compliance.

Although they still form a distinct minority, a sizable number of causal studies of leadership have appeared since 1970. Of 89 studies of leadership between 1970 and 1975 reviewed by Hunt, Osborn, and Schriesheim (1977), almost all the 17 laboratory studies but only 24 percent of the 72 field studies concentrated on causal relations. Despite the shortcomings of laboratory studies, they still make the collection of causal data convenient—something that is much more difficult to accomplish in the field. However, it is edifying to see the increasing effort to combine laboratory experiments with field studies and to search the field for corroboration of laboratory findings. But care is required, especially about the need for highly reliable measures. Regression strategies to determine cause and effect, such as path analysis, require highly reliable measures and

strong-enough relationships to permit the testing of alternative models.

The 1980s saw an upsurge in interest in upward influence (see, for example, Kipnis & Schmidt, 1983). It is likely that a greater number of studies will be conducted of the reciprocity involved in the effects of upward and downward influence, such as was done by Deluga (1987), who showed that subordinates' upward influence is depressed more by transactional than by transformational leaders. More generally, we are likely to see more work on how leaders are influenced by the individuals and teams they have been elected or appointed to lead.

Laboratory versus Field Studies

The 5-year review by Hunt, Osborn, and Schriesheim (1977) of 6 major journals found that 72 field studies and 17 laboratory investigations focused mainly on supervisors' behavior and reactions to it. In the field, actual managers and their associates in a wide variety of organizations were the subjects of inquiry. In the laboratory, superior-subordinate relations were simulated by students. A fundamental question has been posed about whether the temporariness of laboratory situations can faithfully represent the real-world relationship. Osborn and Vicars (1976) noted a particular source of error in trying to generalize from laboratory studies of leader-follower relations. Short-term laboratory situations tend to evoke the behavior of participants on the basis of available stereotypes. Extensive interpersonal contact in real life provides a more realistic basis for behavior.

Field studies, by their very nature, are fraught with internal and external threats to the validity of their data and measurements. Nonetheless, although laboratory experiments provide rigor and control, the exclusive reliance on laboratory studies is and should be avoided. As Meehl's (1967) paradox indicates, the more aseptic and controlled the laboratory study, the greater the precision of its outcome. For physics, such greater precision increases confidence in the generality of the finding; in the social sciences, it does just the opposite. Ideally, laboratory studies should be planned in conjunction with fieldwork.

In controlled laboratory experiments, students are

usually the subjects. When there is disagreement between the findings from such experiments and field studies of operating supervisors and employees, the greater rigor and control in the experiments often leads to greater confidence in the conclusions reached in them rather than in the field, although at times, field studies may have obtained results that are closer to the truth. Thus, Fodor (1976) showed that the results of laboratory experiments, even when practicing supervisors instead of students were the subjects, may be quite different for leadership research from the results obtained in the field. In a rare laboratory study that utilized industrial supervisors as subjects, Fodor found that, in comparison to control subjects, those supervisors who were exposed to a group stress situation responded by giving significantly fewer pay raises and lower performance evaluations to compliant workers. However, field studies (such as Goodstadt & Kipnis, 1970) had found just the opposite; in those studies, compliant workers received significantly more pay increases under group stress as opposed to control conditions. Nor were the laboratory results with supervisors consistent with the results that Fodor (1974) obtained with students. In all, we are likely to see an increase in efforts to examine and report laboratory experiences jointly with tests of the same hypotheses in the field.

The Erroneous Law of Small Numbers

The law of large numbers states that large random samples will be highly representative of the population from which they are drawn. The law of small numbers assumes erroneously that small samples will be similarly representative. Tversky and Kahneman (1971) demonstrated that the belief in the law of small numbers leads to highly inflated estimates of the amount of information contained in studies that use small samples. Schmidt and Hunter (1980) thought that much of the variation from situation to situation in the observed relationships in small samples can be considered random departures from a relatively simple overall generalization. The overall generalization does not need to be qualified by the particular situation involved. For example, in examining the relationship between individual competence and job performance, Schmidt, Hunter, and Urry (1976) showed that the samples were

usually too small to produce acceptable levels of statistical power. Thus, if the true relation between, say, scores on intelligence tests and the success of leaders is really about .35, any sample of 30 to 50 would yield a result that was statistically significant from zero only 25 to 50 percent of the time. For a statistical power of .90, to reject statistically the zero relationship 90 percent of the time when the true one is .35, sample sizes of 200 or more are needed.

Erroneous Interpretations of Small Differences. We may look at ten small-sample studies of scores on intelligence tests as they relate to leadership performance and find that half are statistically significant and half are not. Then, we try to infer a reason for the different findings, when, in fact, the differences in the various samples are random and can be accounted for by the law of large numbers. The obvious implication is our need to be cautious in interpreting the meaning of situational variance when the data from the different situations are each based on small samples. With contingent analyses using small samples, we will err considerably in rejecting the null hypothesis at the 5 percent level of confidence that no differences exist between different contingencies. Thus, Hunter and Schmidt (1978) noted that 28 percent of the time (at the 5 percent level of confidence) we could erroneously infer differential relationships between, say, intelligence and performance for 30 black leaders compared to 30 white leaders when no true difference exists.

The problem is far from academic. Hunt, Osborn, and Schriesheim's (1977) review of 89 reports found that 20 percent used samples as small as 30 or even fewer in analyses of data. The problem is compounded when we deal with leadership because ordinarily only small samples of leaders are available unless the organization is very large. Thus, we may need to reexamine carefully how much contingent results occur because of the low power of the sampling on which many are based.

Meta-analysis offers the opportunity to test how random are the various results obtained from the pool of small-sample studies of the same relationship and to arrive at a mean effect size for a given relationship. Here, however, we have to be cognizant of the inflation in the estimated effect size resulting from the adjustments for criterion unreliability and restriction in range. These adjustments may be highly unrealistic because they are based on assumptions about infinitely repeated measurements and samples with the full range of possibilities. Nevertheless, as has been noted, meta-analysis helps to tease out reliable contingent effects from those that are ephemeral, transient, or a consequence of random variation from a true mean relationship. In the 1990s and beyond, any leader-follower phenomenon that can be meta-analyzed will be meta-analyzed.

Erroneous Conclusions from Small Effects. Exacerbating the problem of small samples is the small size of many of the mean effects that emerge. It requires little in the way of systematic errors to distort or confound these relatively small-sized mean effects. These systematic errors creep into the scene for a number of reasons, according to Webster and Starbuck (1987). There are broad characteristics of people, such as intelligence, that correlate with leadership and with outcomes when it is possible that there may be no direct relation between the leadership and the outcomes. It may be that leaders tend to be more intelligent and that better outcomes require more intelligence, but there may be no direct link between the leadership and the outcomes. The failure to consider a contaminating third variable may result in the unwarranted blowing up of the importance of many small mean effects. Thus, Woodward (1965) found that decision-making processes within an organization depended on the organization's technology and structure. Many subsequent studies elaborated on this finding. However, Gerwin (1981) showed that the modest results obtained tended to disappear when the size of the organization was held constant. Multiple-regression control variables are likely to become the rule, rather than the exception, in the research to come.

Erroneous Conclusions from Convenience Sampling

Convenience and feasibility have often dictated that the "sample" studied was actually a selected complete subpopulation, rather than a random representation of a complete population. All the supervisors of a Canadian department store are surveyed or interviewed, rather than a representative sample of all Canadian retail sales supervisors. Researchers still have to rely too much on convenience samples—samples that are most often obtained from larger rather than smaller organizations. The organizations must be cooperative and supportive or the data can be collected only on the outside or by an unobtrusive participant-observer. The combination of large organizations with accessible personnel systems, data banks, mailed surveys, and telephone interviewing will increase the possibilities of large-scale representative sampling.

Single-source Variance. Convenience also leads to the reliance on the same respondent for descriptions or evaluations of the leader's behavior and the outcomes of the leadership. Methods for correcting for the built-in correlation that is due to such single-source variance have been developed. They include removing from the data the first general factor that is assumed to be due to the rater's propensities (Podsakoff & Organ, 1986), using one respondent to describe the leader and another to describe the outcome, and the varient approach of breaking the analysis of covariance into that between the leaders and that between multiple respondents rating the same leader (Avolio, Bass, & Yammarino, 1988). However, so far, no one corrective action seems to be free of problems.

Measurement Problems

Need for Balanced Use of Standardized Measures. A wide diversity of environmental, task, group, interpersonal, and personal variables have been employed, each to a lesser extent, usually in multivariate fashion, as antecedent conditions, correlates, or moderators. Standardized scales for some variables, such as for role clarity and for role conflict, have been adopted, despite the many different but closely parallel conceptualizations of leadership style. Instruments, such as Fiedler's Least Preferred Co-worker (LPC) scale and some form of the Leader Behavior Description Questionnaire (LBDQ) have dominated research on leadership in the past 40 years. This use of common standardized instruments has made possible a great deal of comparisons across studies. It has already been noted how even small changes in instruments may lead to large differences in outcomes. But this concentration of leadership measures has kept the research establishment from looking at many other, possibly more important, aspects of leadership behavior. A balance is needed. On the one hand, researchers need to avoid inventing new measures of the same attributes when old ones with satisfactory reliability and validity are available. On the other hand, concentrated efforts with measures other than the most popular ones are needed, particularly if they can be joined in a nomothetic network with the well-used instruments.

Limitations. Elaborate theories may spin out tales of curvilinear complexity and multiplicative effects. Yet, 50 years of analyses based on such efforts have usually added little beyond error to the prediction equation. Theory building should not go too far beyond what is empirically possible. Although contingency models intuitively are appealing (Yntema & Torgerson, 1961), contingency hypotheses (how X relates to Y depends on Z), Korman (1973) noted, should be entertained in a theory only if they are empirically supported and necessary. Consistent with what has already been said about the erroneous interpretation of small differences, we may see a return to the positing of simpler relations based on larger samples.

Most observational studies use the single, mutually exclusive, coding of the various categorizations of observed data. But such coding is no longer necessary. Statistical and computer programs are now available to analyze the multiple coding of multipurpose activities, multiple contacts, and simultaneous roles played (Martinko & Gardner, 1985).

Cross-lagged correlational analyses to demonstrate leader-subordinate relationships also have their limitations. For instance, Greene (1976a) noted that initial changes in leadership behavior between Time 1 and Time 2 may fail to be associated with parallel changes in subordinates during that same period, but they may show up between Time 2 and Time 3. Thus, three, not two, data collection points are needed. In addition, it is difficult, if not impossible, to rule out the possibilities of confounding uncontrolled changes in third variables on both the leader and the subordinate. Hence, the increased use of repeated measurements over many time

periods is likely, such as that reported by Howard and Bray (1988).

Yukl (1982) noted that factor-scaled questionnaires fail to include important items of leadership behavior that are correlated with two or more factors. Infrequent behaviors are also likely to be missed. Frequency is overemphasized while the leader's sequencing, timing, and style of execution are neglected. Often, the context in which the behavior appears is also missed. Richer materials are also likely to be obtained from questionnaires if in addition to the items that purport to be objective behavioral descriptions, researchers allow for more items that tap the gut feelings of the observers and their estimates about the potential for future assignments of the leader being observed. We need to avoid, because of special interest in the leader-subordinate dyad, eliminating descriptions and evaluations of overall leader-group relations, for it is clear that both are important. Conversely, items about the interaction of the leader with the whole group will fail to provide information about the leader's relations with each individual member of the group (Yammarino & Bass, 1988).

Simple versus Complex Hypothesis Testing. We face a dilemma. On the one hand, "the chain of relationships between leader behavior and outcome is long and complex" (Lieberman, 1976a). Thus, much of what needs to be understood is missed if we simply try to relate leadership behavior, particularly generalized leadership behavior, to final group outcomes. The relation must be considered in terms of the group's norms, cohesiveness, and so on, as well as of the leader's characteristics. Members' expectations may be more important in determining group outcomes than anything the leader can do. Multivariate analyses, complex models, and contingent and moderator analyses need to be used. On the other hand the limitations have been noted in measurements and the extent to which situational variations from one small sample to another are likely to be random, not true, effects. At the same time, second- or higher-order interactions are likely to render inconsistent simple moderator effects from large sample to large sample. Thus, when faced with complex models, we need to be more open to experience greater clinical understanding of data that demand less mathematical rigor (Bass, 1974; L. G. Cronbach, 1975).

Models may be built *a priori* on the basis of logic and prior information and then tested to see if they fit the data obtained in the test. Or models can be built *a posteriori* to fit the obtained data. There are problems with each approach. Korman and Tanofsky (1975) pointed out that *a priori* models are hard to use because of the difficulties of accurately estimating the necessary parameters. Yet, *a posteriori* empirical models may be fraught with psychometric error. They may be likely to exploit random effects. Both kinds of models may be more helpful in identifying the important elements for study, rather than discerning the final true relationships.

Field studies can reflect the complexities of the real world, but laboratory studies and their controls do not provide the solution to dealing with complexity. For instance, in the study of the effects of sex differences on leadership, the short-term, artificial nature of leadership created in the laboratory results in participants relying on stereotypes that influence their responses to the leader. This reliance on stereotypes is less likely to occur in field studies in which leader-subordinate relations are long term. The laboratory engenders exaggerated sex-role demands so that the effects of sex differences in the laboratory are not replicated in the field setting (Osborn & Vicars, 1976).

Need for Qualitative Methods. These methods may be more suitable to providing confidence in the results when complex hypotheses are involved. Bryman, Bresnen, Beardsworth, and Keil (1988) examined the situational factors that construction project leaders take into account when deciding what style of leadership to adopt. Interviews revealed that site managers continually adjusted their leadership styles to suit varying circumstances, such as the pressure of time, the personality of their subordinates, and the degree of control they had. The authors suggested that qualitative research can uncover a wider array of contextual variables. Such variables are grounded in people's experiences and, therefore, are more accessible to leaders and researchers alike.

The search for meaning and significance in the be-

haviors of leaders and their followers, as well as in related events, is aided by qualitative research (Van Maanen, 1979). The actions of people can be explained in terms of the total context in which they occur instead of the isolated or manipulated elements within the situation (H. Smith, 1975).

Qualitative research is likely to begin with deductions from a theory or a set of general propositions (Orpen, 1987) and then to proceed as a detective might to track down patterns, searching for consistencies in the qualitative information. Qualitative research need not begin with precoded systems but can depend on analytic inductions (Strong, 1984). Creativity and controlled imagination are required to move from the specific findings to general conclusions (Mintzberg, 1979). Thus, movement is a circular process involving the search for and collection of specific data, development of crude hypotheses, then the examination of the data (or new data) to see how well the inferred hypotheses fit the data (Brogdan & Taylor, 1975). More of such qualitative research is needed and is likely to find its way into the study of leadership as the limitations of quantitative methods in dealing with organizational complexities become increasingly apparent (Orpen, 1987).

McCall and Lombardo (1978) advocated more leadership research using the ethnographic methods of the unstatistical naturalists to detect the subtleties and nuances involved in the leadership process. Greater attention needs to be paid to unconscious motives that affect the leaders' and the followers' perspectives. Often, qualitative research can deal better with the art and craft in leadership than can the more objective qualitative analysis. That is, there is much art in leadership that is difficult or impossible to put into a test tube. Nevertheless, there is much regularity in this art that can be made understandable by detecting and describing the patterns that appear.

Orpen (1987) regretted that, for the most part, qualitative and quantitative research are likely to parallel or remain independent of each other, rather than being integrated even though they could do much to complement each other. This complementarity was demonstrated by Gibbons (1986), for example, who made use of both quantitative surveys and in-depth interviews of the same executives.

A risk in qualitative research is that we may learn more about the investigator than about the complex scene being investigated. Chafee (1987) noted the divergent conclusions reached by four investigators who looked at the same qualitative data about college presidents. The investigators' conclusions diverged, she argued, because the investigators came from different theoretical traditions: organizational theory, leadership theory, strategic theory, and anthropology. The same key words had different meanings for them. That is, the researchers used the same terminology but drew different inferences from the same qualitative data base.

Theoretical Biases. The disciplinary backgrounds, theoretical preferences, and preconceptions also limit the range of research. Reviews of research and opinions on leadership, of which hundreds are available, tend to consider the same collections of studies over and over again. Thus, the same misconceptions have been perpetuated year after year during the past five decades. Researchers adhere to incorrect theories despite much evidence to the contrary (Staw, 1976). Additional research has not alleviated the problem because much of it is formulated in terms of a few widely publicized hypotheses. When research fails to support popular hypotheses, it tends to be ignored on the grounds that the research instruments were inadequate or the sample was poorly selected. These questions are not raised, of course, when positive results are obtained. Negative research results are much less likely to be published. Thus, it appears that the accretion of new publications does little to change opinion regarding the nature of the relationship between leader behavior and group performance.

Webster and Starbuck (1987) pointed to another handicapping bias in research on leadership. Within each research discipline—industrial/organizational psychology, social psychology, sociology, political science, educational administration, and so on—there are shared sets of beliefs, values, and techniques. The empiricists in each discipline favor certain sets of variables of consequence to measure. Thus, the dimensions of leaders' and subordinates' behavior that are examined and the methods employed to do so continue to be narrow (Greene, 1976c). The narrowness depends on the

disciplinary background (behaviorial, social, or political science) of the investigator. There appears to be relatively little consensus on substantive issues of consequence (Campbell, 1982), particularly across interdisciplinary boundaries. Despite this lack of consensus, we are likely to see, in the 1990s and beyond, an increase in the use of common methods in the study of leadership, depending on whether the investigator is a behavioral, social, or political scientist, but with a continuing wide range of substantive foci.[1] Nevertheless, some developments in the 1980s, such as the focus on transformational leadership (Bass, 1985a), have made it possible to use the same theoretical framework to study small-group and world-class leaders. More of this integration is likely to occur in the 1990s and beyond.

Leniency Effects. The leniency bias showed up in the findings by Perlmutter (1954) that the greater the leaders' abilities to influence other group members, the greater were the number of favorable traits applied to the leaders and the more socially desirable the traits attributed to them. Schriesheim, Kinicki, and Schriesheim (1979) demonstrated the strong leniency effect in the LBDQ-XII consideration scale. (A specific leader earns higher LBDQ scores from respondents who give favorable ratings to leaders in general.) Similar leniency is likely to be found in related measures of leaders' relations orientation, participation, and support. Such leniency may account for much of the association between subordinates' descriptions of their leaders' consideration and the subordinates' satisfaction. Measures of the initiation of structure that are free of coercive items and measures of consideration that are free of leniency (if such is possible) will provide more precise measurements against which to pit situational and personal variables for study. The Multifactor Leadership Questionnaire's scales to measure transformational and transactional leadership appear relatively freer of leniency effects (Bass & Avolio, 1989).

Errors in Leaders' Self-ratings. In earlier chapters, it was repeatedly pointed out that there is little or no relation between leaders' self-descriptions and descrip-

---

[1]A new journal, the *Leadership Quarterly,* has as one of its purposes to provide a single forum for research on leadership from the different disciplines.

tions of leaders by their subordinates or their superiors. Leaders' self-ratings and self-reports are suspect. Thus, in an intensive interview study and work flow analysis of 34 pairs of supervisors and subordinates, Webber (1980) found that the supervisors reported they initiated almost twice as much verbal interaction with their subordinates as the subordinates perceived had occurred. At a considerably lower level, subordinates also overestimated the extent to which they initiated interactions with their superior.

Leaders' self-ratings have consistently been found to relate poorly or not at all to various dependent variables (Schriesheim & Kerr, 1977b). Most are probably contaminated by social desirability (Schriesheim & Kerr, 1974). They contain self-serving, self-vindicating biases and are likely to generate descriptions of what leaders think is expected of them in their organization and society, rather than an accurate portrayal of their behavior relative to other leaders. The manager who assures everyone that there is always full consultation on subordinates' problems since the manager's door is always open is not uncommon. Then there is the self-described "democratic" manager who announces that the organization is going to be democratic or else sanctions will be imposed.

No wonder so little correlation is found between subordinates' perceptions of what the leader does, what they think he will do, and what he should do, on the one hand, and the leader's self-reports on the same issues, on the other hand. Thus, Rees and O'Karma (1980) observed that city department managers and their subordinates differed significantly in how the managers would behave in different situations described by the LEAD questionnaire. Holton (1984) reported similar discrepancies between leaders of a Cooperative Extension Service program and their staff subordinates. Again, Nanko (1981) noted that although 1,800 elementary school teachers, using the LBDQ, judged that their supervisor was doing a poor job, each of the supervisors saw themselves as doing a good job. The correlations of responses from the two sources were close to zero. Burt (1984) found that 32 heads of hospital departments gave themselves better ratings on the LBDQ than their 379 employees gave them. In the same way, according to Dalessio (1983), working business students and their bosses disagreed about their

bosses' leadership. As was noted earlier, supervisors see themselves as having larger and more important jobs than their bosses say the supervisors have (Haas, Porat, & Vaughan, 1969).

Leaders generally see themselves as more transformational than subordinates see them (Bass & Avolio, 1988). According to a survey with the Multifactor Leadership Questionnaire of a representative sample of 186 surface fleet officers in the U.S. Navy, the correlations of the self- versus the subordinate's ratings of leadership were only .21 for charismatic leadership and .21 for individualized consideration (Bass & Yammarino, 1989). The self-subordinate correlations for the remaining five scales were close to zero.

In Birnbaum's (1986) survey of 252 college presidents about the effectiveness of the institutional leadership of the average president, their predecessors, and themselves, the presidents gave themselves a mean rating of 77.3; the average president, 65.6; and their predecessors, 52.0, on a scale of 0 to 100. A serious issue raised by these discrepant results is the reliance that so many studies of chief executive officers (CEOs) place on interviews with CEOs about themselves. Given the low or even zero correlations between what leaders do and their colleagues' descriptions of their behavior, we need to proceed with great care in drawing any inferences from leader-only data. The author's experiences in meeting with small groups of CEOs suggest CEOs are likely to be highly selectively biased in their self-descriptions. This is not to say that the leaders' self-descriptions are necessarily incorrect and the colleagues' descriptions of the leaders are necessarily correct. Rather, it is important for researchers to avoid depending solely on leaders' self-descriptions. Moreover, leaders obviously differ. Some are much more congruent than others in the extent to which their self-reports match those provided by their colleagues. Such congruence with their subordinates can promote the subordinates' morale (Browne & Neitzel, 1952), the quality of the leader-subordinate relationships (Graen & Schiemann, 1978), satisfaction with communications (White, Crino, & Hatfield, 1985), and superiors' evaluations of the leaders (Bass & Yammarino, 1989).

Probably the most effective aspect of management and leadership development is the provision of feedback to promote greater accuracy between self-reports and those received from others. More studies that demonstrate the increasing congruence and subsequent outcomes generated from the provision of such feedback should be conducted. Training and research efforts will, over time, make greater use of superiors', peers', and subordinates' ratings and less of leaders' self-ratings of their purported behavior. But, as will be discussed later, leaders' perceptions, attributions, cognitions, and opinions will continue to be of considerable research importance as a link to what leaders actually do.

Other Systematic Errors. Among all the biases in perceptions and ratings, a few are most salient in the study of leadership. One such tendency is for subordinates to see more good in their own relations with their leader than in the quality of leader-subordinate relations observed elsewhere. Adams, Prince, Instone, and Rice (1984) found that when 400 freshman cadets at West Point described good leadership incidents, the incidents usually involved their interactions with their leaders, whereas the cadets perceived bad leadership to occur mainly in other units. This perception may be part of the larger phenomenon of "we-they" bias, that is, seeing "our group" as better than "their group." In the future, the use of multiple sources of information with demonstrable convergent validity and suitable corrections of such self-other bias will be more routine.

Consistent with earlier work, [2] Larson (1982) and Larson, Lingle, and Scerbo (1984) demonstrated that raters' responses to LBDQ descriptions of leaders who were viewed in action on a videotape were affected by whether the respondents were cued before viewing the tape about whether they were looking at a leader who was known to be effective or ineffective. Such cuing before they observed the videotape of the leader in action moved them to selectively encode into memory different kinds of information. Given their implicit theories about the effects of initiation and consideration, the raters saw the supposedly effective leader as higher in both.

Binning and Fernandez (1986) showed that another bias in the LBDQ descriptions was due to the differential availability to the rater's memory of the different

items. The availability of items to the rater's memory is greater the more familiar, dramatic, specific, positively salient, retrievable, and imaginable the items of leadership behavior are in the LBDQ. An average correlation of .48 was found between the extent to which an item of leadership behavior was seen as descriptive of a leader and the availability to memory of the item. The correlation was higher if information about the leader was more limited. In the future standardized corrections in the LBDQ and similar questionnaires are likely to be introduced to adjust for these availability biases.

An aspect of the bias in self-fulfilling prophecy was detected by Schoorman (1988), who verified that the supervisors of 354 subordinates who had originally participated in the decision to hire the subordinates tended to bias their subsequent performance appraisals of a subordinate in a favorable direction if they had supported the decision to hire and tended to do the reverse if they had opposed the original decision to hire the subordinate.

These consistencies among persons because of their individual predilections and the tendency to be influenced by personal memories reinforce the need to have multiple sources of data about leaders and about outcomes attributed to the leaders. Or else, as was mentioned earlier, corrections need to be made to allow for single-source bias when only a single source of information is possible, such as when a dyadic analysis of the leader with each subordinate calls for each subordinate to describe both the felt quality of relations with the leader and how much the subordinate is committed to the organization's goals.

Phillips and Lord (1986) noted that leadership questionnaires need to be designed according to the type of accuracy being sought, that is, whether it is behavioral or classificatory. Also, the theory (or lack of it) underlying the questionnaire needs to be taken into account when the questionnaire is employed to assess interventions that attempt to change leadership behavior.

Dyadic versus Group Relations

At times, the felt need to describe leaders' performance in terms of their one-on-one relationships with each of their subordinates is more conceptually pleasing than

[2]See, for example, Binning and Lord (1980).

empirically fruitful. However, the dyadic approach can be applied with considerable utility to a variety of research questions. For example, sanctioning, punitive leadership behavior seems to be the result, rather than the cause, of the inadequate performance of specific subordinates. It follows that dyadic analysis should reveal strong differential dealings of supervisors with their subordinates on the basis of the leaders' differential judgments about each of their subordinates. Indeed, we are likely to find a variety of important consequences stemming from Hollander's (1978) observation that leaders have "A" lists and "B" lists of subordinates. The As are closer; and the Bs are more distant. Work-oriented leaders are likely to relegate the more incompetent of their subordinates to the B list and to treat them more punitively. But the As will be expected to be more loyal and obedient and will be required to maintain higher standards of performance. However, person-oriented leaders may exert extra effort with their black sheep and may perhaps even think that their most competent subordinates are sources of conflict because their performance exceeds the group's norms. The linkages to LPC are apparent.

Several different approaches have originated to tease out individual, dyadic, and group effects. One approach is to hold leader-group effects constant to see what happens within each leader's group. Vecchio (1982) obtained data on attitudes and performance from in-group and out-group members of 48 4-man military groups. Within-group leader-member differences predicted attitudes but only after between-group leader differences were held constant; performance outcomes appeared to be unaffected by dyadic or group leadership. Katerberg and Hom (1981) used a stepwise hierarchical regression analysis. They first determined the contribution of each of 31 U.S. Army National Guard units, as a unit, to LBDQ descriptions of the units' leaders, then the contribution of the individuals within the units. Although the effects of within-unit variations in LBDQ scores were stronger than between-unit variations, both significantly predicted the subordinates' reactions.

Still another approach uses an adaptive process regression that involves first determining the artificially assembled groups of an original pool of subordinates that will result in the best possible predictions. The na-

ture of these groups then gives the investigator an idea of which possible groupings may moderate the dyadic leader-subordinate relationship. Berkes and Rauch (1981) found such artificial clusters among 800 police officers. One moderating cluster involved those officers who were operating under less specified procedures and another involved officers who were younger, better educated, and more interdependent in their work. Less role clarifying and more participative leadership was required for satisfying the young, educated, interdependent officers.

The use of dyadic analyses of leaders' relations with individual peers, individual superiors, and relevant others will continue to increase owing to the continuing interest in leader-member exchange theory (Graen, 1976) and its quantitative possibilities. However, allowance clearly has to be made for leaders not only to relate, on some dimensions at least, in the same way to every group member but to the generation of effects that transcend the average member. For instance, an assembly bonus effect in productivity may be due to a leader's structuring the group as a whole, which goes beyond the contributions of the group's members.

The most ambitious, comprehensive, and possibly defensible effort, the *varient*[3] approach, was developed by Dansereau, Alutto, and Yammarino (1984), who used this method to reexamine the reports that originally supported the importance of the individual leader-member exchange dyad over the leader-group relationship on how much negotiating latitude the leader provides each member and the group as a whole. The analyses concluded that both individual-member effects and group effects may be equally salient (Nachman, Dansereau, & Naughton, 1983).

The Varient Approach. According to Yammarino (1988), the varient approach is a paradigm for formulating and testing theories that explicitly considers both the involved variables and entities (the individual, the group, and/or higher levels of analysis). Developed by Dansereau, Alutto, and Yammarino (1984), the approach has been used in a series of studies of leadership to clarify (1) the differences among leaders in their average leadership style (ALS) and their vertical dyad

[3]*Varient* is not a misspelling of *variant*; it stands for *vari(able) ent(ities)*.

linkages (VDL) or leader-member exchanges (LMX) (see, for example, Markham, Dansereau, Alutto, & Dumas, 1983). Superior-subordinate communications have also been profitably analyzed by the varient method (Dansereau & Markham, 1987).

Mathematical theory lies behind the analytical procedure of the paradigm, within and between analysis (WABA), which provides computerized tests. These tests examine the practical and statistical significance of the observed average differences among groups as well as the practical and statistical significance of the differences observed within the groups. For example, 20 leaders, each with their own 10 followers, may be found to differ practically and statistically. But the followers under a given leader may also differ on the variable or correlation being analyzed. For example, in the ALS plan of inquiry, leaders have a similar relationship with each member of their group, but the leaders' relations with members differ from one group to another. In the VDL/LMX approach, leaders have a different relationship with each member in their group; these different relationships are "managed" by the designated leader, and leaders of other groups act similarly. Both ALS and VDL/LMX inferences are important.

A higher level of effects may need to be examined. Whole departments or organizations and their different policies may affect the leaders' relations with their group members as a whole, as well as with various individual members.

Nomological networks of variables can be clarified by WABA procedures. For example, a leadership behavior may be related or unrelated to two outcomes. Or, the two outcome variables may be related, but the leadership behavior may be related to one outcome, not to the other. Another possibility is that the two outcome variables may be unrelated, and leadership behavior may be related to one outcome, but not to the other. The leader's dyadic and group relations may affect the members' satisfaction but not the members' productivity, for instance.

Moderator variables and contingency effects can be identified with WABA. One possibility is that variables are directly related; leadership behavior, for instance, directly affects outcomes. Another possibility is that a relationship between two variables (leadership behav-

ior and an outcome, for example) is dependent or contingent on the values of a third variable, such as company regulations. This indirect contingency is a moderated effect. Here, the leadership behaviors could relate strongly to dyadic and group outcomes in departments with few regulations but not in departments with many regulations (Dansereau, Alutto, Markham, & Dumas, 1982).

The Variety of Approaches

New methods will continue to proliferate. The method of choice for study and application depends on the way the leader-follower phenomenon is conceptualized. Among the most prominent approaches are cognitive and information processing, phenomenology, motivation, and psychodynamics and behavioral observations and reports. At the one extreme are cognitive investigators who focus on perceptions, causal attributions, and expectations. At the other extreme are behavioral investigators who concern themselves with stimulating conditions, behavioral repertoires, and reinforcements that are contingent on the subordinates' performance. The vast array of possible variables to study must continually be pruned. For surveys and experiments to be manageable, researchers single out for study different aspects of the total process of leader-follower interactions. But the models they construct that focus on one aspect or another are not necessarily inconsistent with each other; the potential exists for considerable integration among the models.

As was noted in Chapter 4, by the 1940s, a variety of methods were available to study leadership, including observation and time sampling, sociometry, position and office holding, the analysis of biographies and case histories, and judged requirements for leadership. Measurements were being obtained from psychological tests, questionnaires, rating scales, and interviews. Dimensionalizing by factor analysis was possible (but time consuming). Along with refinements in these procedures since the 1940s, promising new methods emerged.

Cognitive and Information-processing Methods. Applications of new methods (or new applications of old methods) have accompanied the emergence of interest in cognitive and information processes in lieu of descriptions of the behavior of leaders and followers. The focus is on the leaders' and followers' schema for actively organizing information and the scripts they employ to give specific meanings to situations. Prototypes help interpret the world of leadership. Information about specific situations is encoded, stored, and retrieved in terms of category structures and inferential strategies (Pervin, 1985).

Cognitive-perceptual methods, first developed in the 1940s and 1950s to study learning and decision-making processes, the dynamics of personality, and counseling were subsequently introduced into the study of leadership. These methods include protocol analysis, stimulated recall, and the repertory grid. In protocol analysis, individuals' thoughts, feelings, and emotions are recorded as they engage in the activity under investigation. With stimulated recall, the audio or video record of the activity or the protocol is played back, and the individuals describe more fully the thoughts, ideas, and feelings they had when the activity was in progress (Burgoyne & Hodgson, 1984). To construct a repertory grid, a respondent sorts out colleagues noting the categories used to differentiate them (Kelly, 1955). Coghill (1981) showed the profitability of studying the perceptual categories that managers naturally use to assess each other. He applied Kelly's repertory-grid method with 90 managers to provide data to illustrate the importance of perceptual mediation, personal constructs, and implicit theories.

Phenomenological and Perceptual Methods. The methodology of another line of cognitive inquiry has been phenomenological. The inability to resolve the controversy surrounding Fiedler's (1967a) Contingency Theory after more than three decades of theorization and empirical research led Bar-Tal (1989) to argue that what may be most important in understanding leadership is to determine the leader's and followers' phenomenological fields rather than to continue to pursue a positivistic, mechanistic, or statistical explanation of their interaction. To expedite this methodology, the researcher may disclose as much about himself or herself to the focal leader as does the leader to the researcher. Basic emotional processes can then be explored, along with remote and accessible aspects of their respective lives. Barriers to knowing and sharing between the researcher and the leader are expected to be minimized in this way (Massarik, 1983).

If the focus is on perception or cognition, rather than behavior, methods that exploit attribution phenomena can be applied with profit to the leader-follower relationship. The behavior of leaders toward their subordinates appears to be strongly determined by the reasons (ability or motivation) the leaders give for their subordinates' performance—how much it is a matter of luck or the situation or under the subordinates' control. In the same way, the subordinates' attributions of the reasons for the leaders' behavior will strongly relate to the subordinates' satisfaction. Leaders whom subordinates perceive to be willing but incompetent seem to be more forgivable than are leaders whom subordinates perceive to be competent but unwilling.

As was already noted, conscious perceptions can determine a leader's subsequent efforts. Thus, Nebeker and Mitchell (1974) found that differences in leadership behavior could be explained by the leaders' expectations that a certain style of leadership would be effective in a given situation. At the same time, subordinates' descriptions of their leader's behavior may be distorted by their implicit theories about leadership, particularly when they lack real information about the situation and are inclined, therefore, to fall back on stereotypes (Schriesheim & deNisi, 1978). The use of cognitive, as opposed to exclusively behavioral, methods is likely to parallel the same continuing developments in psychology, in general.

Still underutilized are sociometric designs, such as the "Work With" sociometry[4] of Stogdill and Haase (1957) that provides a measure of interaction structures that could be applied to a variety of research designs. Three-dimensional holographic sociometry (Bradley, 1987) is in its infancy. It is likely to have a promising future as it opens up the contributions of the sociometric structure of triadic relationships within an organization to the performance of leaders.

---

[4]Sociograms plot the choices by organizational members of those with whom they would most prefer to work.

Motivational and Psychodynamic Methods. Documents, recordings, and protocols can be analyzed from particular theoretical perspectives and coding models based on motivational and psychoanalytical theories. The projective inferential methodology, pioneered by Winter (1973) to analyze the needs and values of leaders from their speeches, documents, and biographical materials, was detailed in Chapter 9. The approach is likely to provide important empirical support and understanding in studies of charismatic and inspirational leadership. Less prominent is the inductive methodology that Demause (1982) derived from psychoanalysis. Demause argued that a group's fantasies, shared by the leader and his or her followers, which play a crucial role in charismatic leadership, can be detected from a psychoanalytic examination of the leader's and followers' speeches, documents, and body language. The group's fantasies can be teased out from the metaphors and similes that the leader and followers use, and body language, feeling tones, and emotional states can be significant. Thus the "killing" of bills and "dead" halts in negotiations are relevant to the psychohistorian, as are unusual or gratuitous word usages (in the 1988 presidential campaign, the "L word," for example, implied that "liberal" is a dirty word). Unusual repetition and phrasing in discussions, speeches, documents, and minutes of meetings imply potent messages for the psychoanalyst. Symbolism has obvious implications; even its absence during long periods without imagery may be symptomatic of the severe repression of the group's fantasy (Scheidlinger, 1980).

Increasingly, metaphors from science will be used for taxonomies as, for example, such as Field (1989b) did likening leaders to stars, pulsars, quasars, and black holes. (*Stars* communicate positive expectations to followers and induce positive performance. *Pulsars* communicate positive, but unsustainable and unrealistic, expectations. *Quasars* are pessimistic but followers succeed despite them. *Black holes'* pessimism is a drag on followers.)

Zaleznik (1984) reviewed a number of promising schemes for looking at the "text" of leadership—the meanings, intentions, and motives that are subconscious as well as conscious in the spoken or written words employed. The deeper structure underlying the surface interactions of the leader and the followers can be discerned from thematic interpretation. Such interpretation requires grasping a multiplicity of complex conceptual structures in the text. These structures may be cultural or social forces or individual values, meanings, and intentions. They may be seen in the linguistic study of speech patterns or of the formation of symbols. Hidden meanings and unconscious ideas and fantasies are brought to light. The percentage of positive, neutral, and negative words and phrases, emotional or nonemotional; the percentage references to the past, present, conditional, or future; the percentage of action verbs; the percentage of interruptions, hidden reversals or recycling, and delayed responses and silences, all may be clues to what is hidden in the text.

The formation of groups and movements can be organized around such shared fantasies and provide the basis for displacing personal inadequacies. For instance, Demause applied a psychoanalytical coding scheme to the Nixon Tapes to complete a fantasy analysis of them. The analysis found that the leader's personal embarrassments can become substitutes for policy; goals can disappear while actions become irresistible.

Psychohistory has been the psychoanalysts' exclusive turf. However, documentary analyses (House, 1988b) and survey methodology (Bass, Avolio, & Goodheim, 1987) are beginning to be applied to psychohistory. Indeed, if motivational analysis is to move off the controversial psychoanalyst's couch, it will need to take individual, political, and social psychology, as well as relevant aspects of sociology and anthropology, into account to understand the performance of historical figures (Strozier & Offer, 1985). In the hands of psychoanalysts, psychohistory has been limited to an understanding of collective actions from an individualistic orientation. It has focused too much on neurotic mechanisms and the inner person, whose ideas and thoughts are interpreted by an analyst who is far distant in place and time from the leader (Gay, 1985).

Recourse to more objective methods that are also projective techniques is likely to move researchers toward establishing more confidence in the findings about the hidden and unconscious motives and the implicit theories of leadership that affect interactions. For example, Boal, Hunt, and Sorenson (1988) constructed a "Leadership Quotes" questionnaire. Respondents indicated whether each of 133 famous quotations, such as "People are more easily led than driven," "The world needs able men who can create and lead others," or "Happy the kings whose thrones are founded on their peoples' hearts," were related to leadership and whether the leadership was effective or ineffective. Multiple factors emerged that dealt with the direction of activities, influential interactions, legitimate power to lead, and the initiation of structure.

In the future, we are likely to see more joining of motivational analyses of the biographies of world-class leaders, analyses of their speeches and writings, news accounts of their performance, and evaluations of them by historians and political scientists. Much of this joining is already to be seen, for example, in the work of House, Woycke, and Fodor (1988).

Behavioral Methods. Behavioral accounts are still the most popular. Purely behavioral explanations cannot be dismissed. One can look at leadership as a perceptual phenomenon under certain conditions or as a behavioral phenomenon under other conditions and accurately explain what is happening in both instances. Research on leadership has been heavily dependent on subordinates' reported perceptions of their leaders' behavior. Yet, Gilmore, Beehr, and Richter (1979) demonstrated, in a laboratory setting, that participants failed to perceive that their leaders (who had been instructed to be high or low in initiation and consideration) actually differed in their behavior. Nevertheless, higher-quality work by the subordinates resulted if the leaders' behavior was actually high rather than low in initiation and consideration. The lowest-quality work occurred when the leader's actual initiation of structure was high but the leader's consideration was low. It is clear that studies that do not depend solely on perceptions are still needed.

Among the promising behaviorally oriented methods is one that shifts attention away from the leader's *frequency* of behavior to the leader's intensity of behavior. Influenced by opponent process theory, Sheridan, Kerr, and Abelson (1982) examined the *intensity*, rather than the frequency, of a leader's actions. Seven dimensions of leadership behavior were scaled: task direction, participation, consideration, performance feedback, integrity, performance reward, and representation. Inten-

sive task direction was illustrated by "taking time to instruct subordinates in proper work techniques in their jobs." The lack of intensive task direction was illustrated by "bringing new employees into the group without providing any direction or indication of their job responsibilities."

The use of multidimensional scaling in the study of leadership has also not been exploited as much as it could be. One example was provided by Misumi (1985), who described the use of the Quantification of Pattern Classification as a multidimensional scaling method for assigning quantitative values to categorizations of leadership and their effects.

At the same time, not to be ignored are old methods that are applied to new taxonomies of leadership behavior. For example, Van Fleet and Yukl (1986b) trained students to code over 2,500 entries for each of 23 behavior categories as the students encountered them in biographies and autobiographies of military leaders. Clarifying work roles, setting goals, monitoring the environment, planning, and inspiration were the most frequent entries. Bass, Avolio, and Goodheim (1987) asked students to complete the Multifactor Leadership Survey questionnaire about the world-class leaders whose biographies they read. Again, inspirational leadership emerged as an important factor, along with other transformational factors.

Davis and Luthans (1984) demonstrated the usefulness of idiosyncratic observational efforts. They observed over time what happens when a single leader, in this case, a production manager, takes a specific action: the introduction of a new scheduling form with complete instructions and deadlines. The investigators found that the new form resulted in improvements in the quality and quantity of production that could be explained from the cause-effect linkages in what they were able to observe in detail.

The Leadership Observation System (LOS) was developed by Luthans and Lockwood (1984) to be used by trained participants and observers to record independently the behavior of managers using time sampling. Twelve leadership behavior categories with numerous subcategories emerged from a Delphi process that began with 100 categories of possible managerial behaviors. A typical category was planning/coordinating. Within this category were subcategories, such as setting goals and objectives. In a study of 120 managers in a number of organizations, Lockwood (1981) found that LOS had greater convergent and discriminant validity than did parallel descriptions of the same managers with the LBDQ—Form XII or the Managerial Behavior Scales. Different conclusions about the managers' consideration and initiation of structure were reached when the different methods were applied.

At odds with Strong's (1984) atheoretical approach to ethnographic analysis has been the construction of new observational procedures based on explicit theories and models. Although observational studies of leadership are not new, among the most promising current approaches are those that use observations of leadership based on a formal model of interrelated measurements. Particularly notable has been the emergence of increasingly sophisticated methodologies to observe behaviors and their linkage to theory in their construction. SYMLOG (Bales, Cohen, & Williamson, 1979) uses teams of 4 or 5 observers each of whom are on their own time schedule. The observers pick out salient acts of the members of academic self-study groups. Twenty-six general behaviors of a member, such as "active, dominant, talks a lot," and 26 value descriptions, such as "making other feel happy" can be recorded and profiled in terms of 3 dimensions: friendly versus unfriendly, dominant versus submissive, and instrumentally controlled versus emotionally expressive. Members rate each other on these dimensions. Their images of each other reflect the polarization or unification of the group. The observed leadership behaviors and inferred values are examined for their decisive influence on the polarization or unification.

Even more closely tied to theory, Komaki, Zlotnick, and Jensen (1986) began with a theory-based taxonomy of supervisory behavior and then proceeded to develop appropriate observational measures. The taxonomy included three categories based on the theory of operant conditioning: antecedents, monitoring, and the consequences of performance. Further classification broke down the observed supervisory behavior into own and solitary performance and work and non-work-related behavior. Archival records could be consulted in addition to observed work samples and others' reports and self-reports about designated actions. Satisfactory in-

terrelater reliabilities were obtained, along with differential patterns of effective and ineffective supervisory behavior (Komaki, 1986). The results are particularly promising because they can be linked to the voluminous psychological research that deals with operant conditioning.

Martinko and Gardner (1984a) designed and utilized a model involving field observation of the external and work environment, competencies, needs, and causal attributions of the leaders. Also included were categories of behavior (such as planning, organizing, directing, and rewarding) and outcomes. With the procedures and model, the time and event patterns of more effective and less effective school principals could be readily distinguished. For instance, in comparison to those principals who were low performers, those who were high performers used more diverse media for communication and initiated more contacts with teachers and students. Again, Metcalfe (1984) analysed the behavior of leaders in taped appraisal interviews. A behavior that distinguished effective from ineffective interviewers was the greater frequency with which the leaders invited participation from the followers.

Along with the theory-based observations of behavior for research on leadership, behavioral modeling is likely to continue to be a method of choice for training supervisors. Increasingly, simulations that feature interactive computer programs portraying problem situations will become common. Research on maximizing the utility of such programs and evaluating their impact on the performance of leaders will be a likely effort in the decades ahead.

Simulation. Simulation offers the opportunity to examine perceptions, cognitions, motivations, and behaviors simultaneously. In the live field study, observers have no control over what they are observing. This fact places a premium on high-fidelity simulation as a method of inquiry. With high-fidelity simulation, the antecedent conditions and contingencies can be controlled, to a considerable degree, and time can be compressed to facilitate the observational processes and linkages to outcomes. The future is likely to see increasing reliance on simulations to provide opportunities for research on cognitive processes as well as on observed behavior.

Developed from earlier attempts with small-group

exercises, in-baskets tests, computerized business games, and larger organizational games, high-fidelity simulations have become a fine art that provides opportunities to manipulate variables experimentally in laboratory conditions that approach field studies. Subjects may be hired for a week to do, as far as they are concerned, real clerical work in a seemingly real office.

Computer simulations provide complete visual and auditory displays in which leader-subordinate relations can be examined. Complex business games that last for as many as four months are conducted in which many of the elements of real-world decisions must be dealt with satisfactorily and in which leaders may find themselves involved in labor negotiations and real boards of directors.

As was illustrated in Chapter 35, the Looking Glass represents a finely developed simulation to parallel in miniature a real glass manufacturing company. The Looking Glass re-creates for the players the hierarchy of positions, the necessary requirements, and interactions to run a sample organization. Salient variables can be manipulated in a collapsed time frame. Follow-up critiques of players in these simulations make it possible to gain insight into the processes and relationships that are perceived to be of consequence to the players (McCall & Lombardo, 1982). Videotaping can store the experience for later intensive analysis.

Computer and mathematical modeling are another approach to simulation that has a great deal of unexploited potential. Zahn and Wolf (1981) used the Markov model to chain events that related the current hypothetical task-oriented or relations-oriented performance of supervisors to future states of supervisory-sory-subordinate relationships. The model could be manipulated to see designed hypothetical effects on outcomes. Long-term behavior was determined to be highly variable and versatile. Both the leader and the subordinates could influence the system.

The Need to Use Multiple Methods. I have already alluded to the fact that no one approach is fully adequate, by itself, to understand the leadership process. Yukl (1982) noted that cognitive processes, for instance, are unlikely to be reliably detected from observation alone. Yukl and Van Fleet (1982) found, when analyzing four studies to identify effective patterns of leadership behavior among military cadets and U.S. Air Force

officers, that different results will materialize when nonquestionnaire methods, such as the critical incidents technique, are employed than when questionnaires are used in the same situation. They noted that leadership consideration was important for effective leadership in the critical incidents analyses but not in the questionnaire surveys, whereas coordination was important for effective leadership in the questionnaire surveys but not in the critical incidents studies.

There will continue to be proponents of one method over another. Likewise, there will continue to be proponents of a cognitive-perceptual approach and advocates of a behavioral approach to understanding. Nevertheless, a full account of leader-outcome results will require the use of multiple methods in the same situation. Nonetheless, both approaches will be needed for comprehensive explanations.

Substantive Issues

In a discipline, consensus about a new paradigm or a new method usually develops slowly. Nevertheless, a number of new substantive issues quickly aroused attention in the 1970s and 1980s and are likely to generate continuing interest in the 1990s and beyond. And the centuries-old, person-versus-situation controversy is likely to remain with us. Thus, Jago (1982) believed that much more still needs to be done to compare the validity of universal and contingent theories of leadership juxtaposed against whether leadership traits or leadership behaviors are being examined. To some degree, the evidence supporting one position or the other remains incomplete, inconclusive, contradictory, or controversial. Therefore, as one looks back on the earlier chapters of this book, one finds that although a good deal has been accomplished substantively, much more still needs to be done.

Personal Factors Associated with Leadership

There has been a renewal of interest in the personal factors of leadership. Although research designed solely to isolate the characteristics of leaders was thought to have reached the point of diminishing returns, it has been revived in a new form with the emergence of interest in the life-span development of the leader, particularly the transformational leader. The need to learn more about what contributes to the self-confidence, self-determination, and freedom from inner conflict of the charismatic leader is apparent. These quests for a greater understanding of personality and the personality dynamics that affect the leader's performance transcend situational considerations. Programmatic efforts to look at personality, as such, are also suggested by the developments of assessment centers, as well as long-term predictions of success as a manager.

Paige (1977) proposed a hypothesis that still awaits empirical confirmation: Leaders choose tasks and engage in them on the basis of personal considerations, such as their age. Thus, what could be a tempting challenge to a 40-year-old executive would be sidestepped by his or her 60-year-old counterpart.

More often than not, even when there is a lack of supporting evidence, personality is seen as interacting with situational variables to account for leadership and group performance. It may be more important in some situations than in others and with some people more than with others. It may be dominant in cultural settings where, to be a leader, one must epitomize the authoritarianism rooted in the culture. Autocrats may behave the way they do because of their personalities; democrats may behave the way they do as a consequence of both their personalities and other immediate situational and personal considerations (Farrow & Bass, 1977).

Research that is designed to test the effects on the group of the interaction of the characteristics of the leader and the followers generally has been effective in producing valuable insights into leader-follower relations. The research in the 1950s and 1960s on different combinations of authoritarian leaders and followers continues to suggest designs that could be used to test the effects of other leader-follower characteristics. Although such has been done with reference to the need for achievement, the need for affiliation, internal and external loss of control, and so on, many other personality dimensions can be examined in the same way to test the interaction of the leader's personality, values, and behaviors with the followers' personalities, values, and behaviors and the effect of such interaction on the group. Interest is strong in examining how the leader's style of thinking, as measured by the Myers-Briggs

Type Inventory, interacts with the followers' styles. To be kept in mind is the likelihood that extreme homogeneity in leader-follower characteristics may be dysfunctional to satisfactory problem solving by the group that requires flexibility and creativity.

A Less-ordered Role

Suggestions continue to be made that research on leadership—in addition to its narrowness—has been concentrating on the wrong thing. The aim of science is to understand. Understanding is checked by prediction. Adequate prediction can produce control. Practitioners are anxious to provide such control when their understanding is far from perfect. Research on leadership is faulted when it fails to improve such control immediately. Basic research should be judged on whether it contributes to understanding.

The failure of adequate prediction to make the suitable control of behavior possible may also be partly a consequence of the unpredictable and uncontrollable elements in the real-world performance of leaders. Mintzberg (1973) and many others since have concluded that instead of a systematic, steady, orderly attack on one problem at a time, the practicing manager is more likely to be observed devoting short bursts of time to different problems. Frequently interrupted, the manager unsystematically responds to a diversity of demands from superiors, peers, clients, and subordinates. (This behavior helps explain the popularity of management training in time management.) Given the large array of diverse situations that are the daily regimen of the general manager, M. W. McCall (1977) suggested that much of the research to determine which type of leadership style is most effective in particular conditions may remain an impractical academic exercise because the demand characteristics of the manager's role result in the manager optimizing his or her performance by "proficient superficiality" (Mintzberg, 1973) and never giving sufficient time to different problems to deal with each of them fully and adequately.

Leader-Member Exchange. In addition to seeing the leader's role as less orderly, Graen (1976) shifted attention away from the unilateral and consistent group-oriented behavior of the leader toward a focus on the mutual role relationships of the leader with each different member of the group. The quality of this reciprocal relationship contains considerable explanatory value, and researchers should continue to explore its antecedents and consequences with methods described earlier to ascertain its importance relative to average leader-group effects. Nonetheless, Dienesch and Liden (1986) argued that for it to be more fully utilized, LMX needs to be conceived as a multidimensional variable involving perceived contributions, loyalty, and affect. Research is needed on the different ways the leader-member relation varies and the different outcomes that will occur as a consequence.

Succession and Retention of the Leadership Position

Various personal characteristics (rate of talking and interaction, capacity to interact, ability to perform the task, dominance, the exclusive possession of information, the initiation of spontaneity, the provision of freedom to the group, and acceptance of group members) have been found to be associated with emergence as a leader. It has not been demonstrated, however, that these are the same variables that enable the leader to retain his or her role. Thus, there is a need for research that isolates the factors that facilitate the retention of a position of leadership once it has been attained. There is an abundance of evidence on factors that contribute to the emergence of a leader. There is a dearth of research on factors that enable a leader to consolidate his or her position once it has been obtained. In the same way, the characteristics required to win election to political office may be quite different from those required for success and effectiveness as an officeholder.

Issues of Succession. Increasing empirical attention to the replacement and succession problem would seem to have great utility. There are many issues to be explored in this regard. Nathan (1989) concluded that whether the succession had a positive, negative, or no effect on the organization depended on the study's method, criterion of effectiveness, and level of analysis. Thus, individual differences among successors will account positively for succession effects; continuing poor organizational performance will account for negative succession effects. Important questions needing future research include: What are optimum rates of succession for different types of groups, organizations, or institutions? How is the succession used as a tool of strategic change? How do successors cope best with initial resistance? Do the dynamics of the succession process change over time?

Many other questions about the succession process can be posed: Does the successor ignore the former occupant's performance, see it competitively, or attempt to build on it? Should the former occupant be involved in the choice of the successor? Does the former occupant help or hinder the succession process? When occupants are "lame ducks" and must give up office in a designated amount of time, how does this requirement shape their objectives, planning, and power?

An important problem that has been ignored concerns the effects of training on the retention of the leadership role. What kind of training strengthen or weaken an individual's chances of retaining the leadership position?

Leadership and Power

Those who tend to conceive leadership as nothing but a form of social power obscure important relationships between leadership and power and restrict the range of research on the problem. Therefore, more research is needed on the interaction of leadership behavior and personality with power. Questions such as the following remain:

1. Will followers respond positively to a leader with power who exhibits task-oriented rather than relations-oriented behavior?

2. How will the personality of the followers and the urgency to complete the task affect their response?

3. Are there patterns of a leader's personality that may mitigate, to some degree, the adverse effects of coercive and reward power?

4. Can a sense of humor exert a strong moderating effect here?

5. Will coercive power and strong control be more readily accepted when the leader's and followers' values are highly similar than when they are not?

6. What factors tend to legitimate different forms of power among members of a group?

7. What factors tend to legitimate different forms of power in the eyes of observers who are not members of the group?

8. What contributes to a leader continuing to be held in high regard despite one mistake after another?

9. How do presidents and television evangelists maintain their power and charisma, regardless of the quality of their performance? What are the limits to the possibilities of "damage control"?

Research on the equalization of power has been attended by serious difficulties. Appropriate control organizations are seldom available for comparative purposes when some form of power equalization is introduced into a firm. External forces are almost impossible to control. The effects of social, political, and economic factors may be stronger than any variations that can be introduced into a firm. Simulated organizations may provide a better setting for the study of the equalization of power in the large organization.

Research on role conflict, conducted primarily in formal organizations, is also deficient with respect to experimental controls. Here, again, it would be advantageous to study role conflict in simulated organizations in which conflict-inducing demands could be varied and controlled. Research is needed to determine the extent to which various styles of the personality and behavior of leaders are subject to role conflict.

We need to know more about how controversy—conflicts of ideas—can result in creative outcomes. Tjosvold (1985d) pointed to the importance of goal interdependence, confirmation, and collaborative influence in this regard. Knowledge of these factors would be relevant for strategic decision making, policy setting, and participative leadership.

A small number of competently executed studies is available on the legitimation of the leadership role. More studies are needed. Little is still known about what makes a leader legitimate and why and what the effects of such legitimacy are. The importance of the subject merits a much higher rate of activity in this area. In future research, it would be desirable to deter-

mine the effect of variations in the followers' characteristics, as well as variations in leader's characteristics. One would like to known, for example, for what types of follower a given characteristic or pattern of behavior tends to legitimate the leadership role. In addition, it would be useful to know under what conditions a given pattern of leadership behavior would be regarded as legitimate or illegitimate and by what type of follower. From a practical point of view, the problem of the legitimation of leaders is one that should be given high priority in future research.

The suppressive effects of power on followers suggest the need for more subtle approaches to data collection than direct questioning. We should also be seeing more multiple methods examining the same power-leadership issues. Authority and responsibility, linked to power but conceptually different, could be examined more fully in their distribution as sources of organizational pathology.

Use of Contingent Reward and Punishment. Podsakoff and Schriesheim (1985) enumerated a number of unanswered questions about the leader's use of contingent reinforcement for which research is needed. What is the best sequencing of contingent and noncontingent rewards and punishments (when necessary)? How do they interact? Can contingent punishment for poor performance work if it is offset by promises of rewards for appropriate performance? What rewards make promises more or less effective? How important are specificity and focus on the subordinate's performance or products to the efficacy of contingent praise for good performance, as Kanouse, Gumpert, and Canavan-Gumpert (1984) suggested? How does contingent reinforcement of the individual affect the group? How does contingent reinforcement of the group affect the individual?

Leadership Styles

To some degree, all research on leadership styles prior to Burns's (1978) introduction of the concepts of transformational versus transactional leadership could be conceived of as being about democratic, autocratic, or laissez-faire leadership, which takes us back to where it all began in 1938 with Lewin and Lippitt's seminal experiment. Each of these three styles is described by either the amount of overall activity of the leaders or the extent to which the leaders are oriented toward being completely work oriented or completely person oriented.

Ordinarily, the leaders' performance will be better if they are more active than inactive. But activity does not guarantee effective satisfied and cohesive groups. A number of hypotheses need to be tested further. For instance, it has been suggested that leaders tend to be more autocratic and directive when it is easier and more comfortable for them to be so because of their own personalities and because goals are clear and structure is given. But it has also been proposed that leaders really need to be directive and structuring when goals are not clear and structure is not given. Another suggestion is that leaders tend to be more democratic, participative, relations oriented, and considerate when they are concerned about the need for input and reactions from subordinates. Again, how much different personality and situational demands play their parts can be tested in designated organizational settings to determine the importance of selection in contrast to the training of leaders.

Many dimensions of autocratic and democratic leadership have been proposed on which the different styles of leaders can be described. The relationships among some of the dimensions have been clarified and altered. Borrowing from work-motivation theory, some researchers have purged the initiation-of-structure scales of their coercive components and have relabeled them instrumental (to the success of the task). Similarly, consideration now is seen as supportive leadership, and its focus is now on the leader's attention to the different needs of the subordinates, rather than to the automatic use of group methods.

The situational-leadership approach, such as is found in the Hersey-Blanchard model, and an approach arguing for one best way of integrating task and relations orientation, as advocated by Blake and Mouton, need to be compared with a variety of methods and measurement instruments. There ought to be studies that make the comparisons in simulated organizations and in controlled laboratory settings, as well as in content analyses of documents and time-sampling observations in the field.

It should be clear that factor analyses can establish

only how leaders are distributed empirically in the eyes of observers of their performance on given dimensions such as *directive*, negotiative, consultative, *participative*, or delegative.[5] However, leaders in real-life positions tend to reveal performance on all the dimensions but in different amounts, although the dimensions are conceptually distinct but not empirically uncorrelated.

One can stress the utility of consultation (the manager's most frequent style) as a useful style in general. But as Vroom (1976b) noted, concrete situations may demand otherwise. And leaders do change their styles in response to situational conditions (Hill & Hughes, 1974).

The differential effects of task-related and person-related clusters of leadership styles suggest that two central needs are a response-allocation analysis, to sort out conceptually the different styles from each other, and more factorial analyses to see the empirical communalities among the styles. Researchers need to take into account the well-established negative impact on the group of the inactivity of the laissez-faire leader with the possibly but not necessarily positive impact of various types of active intervention by the leader.

Theory and research are needed about the different kinds of considerate behavior. Consideration, as measured by the LBDQ, tends to be noncontingent unlike the contingent rewarding of the MLQ. For instance, LBDQ items about how much the leader helps and does favors for the group are without reference to the group's performance. Nor does LBDQ consideration correlate highly with the individualized consideration factor score of the MLQ (Seltzer & Bass, 1990) which tends to concentrate on how much the leader is concerned about the differential development needs of the followers.

Transformational and Transactional Leadership

Prior to the 1980s, behavioral research on leadership concentrated on the transactional exchange between the leader and the led. The leader clarified what

---

[5]As defined in Chapters 22 and 23, *direction* (italicized) refers only to giving orders with or without explanation. Direction (romanized) includes ordering, persuading, and manipulating. *Participation* (italicized) refers only to sharing in the decision process. Participation (romanized) includes consulting, sharing, and delegating.

needed to be done and the benefits to the self-interests of the followers for compliance. In the new paradigm, the transformational leader moved the followers to transcend their own interests for the good of the group, organization, or society (Bass, 1985a; Burns, 1978). Paraphrasing Zaleznik (1977), transformational leaders, like charismatics, attract strong feelings of identification from their subordinates.

The 1980s were a decade in which empirical research was initiated with this new paradigm in mind.[6] Much more still needs to be done, especially in teasing out the dynamics involved. Some empirical support was obtained about the followers' strong beliefs in the leader as a person. Do these beliefs go beyond the leader's actual competence? Followers have faith that the leader will make it possible for the group to succeed. Are they justified in their faith? Do the followers willingly give the leader too much power to act in crises? Do such leaders transform followers into leaders?

Generally, transformational leadership augments transactional leadership (Waldman, Bass, & Yammarino, 1988). But under what conditions do they conflict? How can one add to the fostering of the pursuit of group and organizational goals (in transformational leadership) to the promotion of self-interests (in transactional leadership)?

Needed Research on Intellectual Stimulation.
Mueller (1980) described the "leading-edge" leader who deals with "fuzzy futures." This type of leader is able to simplify problems and to get to the crux of complex matters while the rest of the crowd is still trying to identify the problem.[7] Research is needed on this "rapid reification" and how to integrate and relate a charismatic component with the logical and intuitive attributes of such transformational leadership.

Needed Research on Charisma and Inspirational Leadership.
Researchers who are interested in studying the transformational leader will have to be prepared to make use of psychodynamic variables associated with charisma. Managers, ministers, battalion commanders, teachers, coaches, and directors can be found

who fit the description of persons to whom followers form deep emotional attachments and who, in turn, inspire their followers to transcend their own interests for superordinate goals—for higher goals than the followers previously recognized. Even in hardened bureaucracies, there are leaders with knowledge of the system, good connections, and the ability to mobilize and husband resources who keep their eyes on the bigger issues and take the risks required for "creative administration," which gives them the large amount of idiosyncrasy credit necessary to arouse in subordinates complete faith and trust in them and a willingness to strive for the higher goals they set forth as challenges for the group.

We are likely to see much more theory and research about the inspirational process. Thus, a line of investigation such as proposed by Field and Van Seters (1989) is likely to spring from the combining of the self-altering prophecies of the Pygmalion and Galatean effects to generate an energized group, organization, or society of high expectations in which members act with positive expectations about each other—labeled the Metharme effect by Field (1989) after the daughter of Pygmalion and Galatea.

Dealing with Stress and Conflict.
Well into the next century, investigators should be continuing to search for answers to such questions as, In what ways can a leader move followers toward acceptance of superordinate goals? How can followers be aroused to self-transcendence? How does a leader move a group from complacency, hasty responses, inertia, or defensiveness in the face of threat to complete and adequate vigilance? If a group is focused primarily on its lower-level needs for safety and security, how does a leader move it toward concern for recognition and achievement? If a group is under stress that is too high for coping with the complexity of the situation, how does the leader steady and calm the group? Crouch and Yetton (1987) add: What should be done for managers who want to be participative but who have poor skills in conflict management? Are there high costs for such managers who bring their subordinates together to resolve conflicts among them?

Opportunities should be expanded for learning more about crisis management from the increased willing-

---

[6]See Chapter 12.
[7]This type of leadership is discussed in Chapter 12 as intellectual stimulation, one of the factors in transformational leadership.

ness of the decision makers to air their mistakes. The disclosure by U.S. and Soviet decision makers in 1989, 27 years after the Cuban missile crisis in 1962, of how each side misread the other's intentions and almost jointly precipitated World War III is illustrative (Keller, 1989).

Likewise, Whyte's (1989) addition to the factors that underlie group think may further elucidate the events when leadership fails during a crisis. Wyte noted the tendency for the group to polarize around the point of view that was initially dominant in the group. This tendency usually frames the leader's and group's decision as a choice between two or more unattractive options. Threats are not seen as possible opportunities. Risk seeking occurs as a way of gambling for a reasonable chance to avoid the certain losses.

The Hierarchy of Effectiveness. A hierarchy of leader-outcome relationships based on survey questionnaire methods and routines has been established in a number of industrial, educational, and military settings. Transformational leadership, particularly charismatic leadership, correlates above .70 with the subordinates' satisfaction with the leader and the leader's perceived effectiveness. The transactional contingent reward correlates closer to .40 with these same outcomes. Transactional passive management by exception correlates closer to zero with these outcomes (Yammarino & Bass, 1989). Will this pattern of correlations hold up when it is suitably corrected for single-source bias? It has been found to hold when subjectively rated outcomes from superiors are independently obtained from subordinates' descriptions of the leader (Hater & Bass, 1988; Yammarino & Bass, 1989). But will it hold up when outcomes are objective measures? One bit of support has been found by Onnen (1987) who obtained correlations of the growth in church membership and church attendance of close to .30 with the transformational leadership of Methodist ministers but near zero for the ministers' transactional leadership. Another bit of support was found by Avolio, Waldman, and Einstein (1988) for leadership and objective outcomes in business games. Systematic studies of the more conceptually differentiated personal communication style of the transformational leader, along with his or her mastery of impression management and authenticity, will be important.

Then researchers need to examine the conditions that promote the emergence of the transformational leader and how to facilitate this emergence. They need to determine the consequences of moving from an emphasis on social exchange, which characterizes the transactional leader, to leadership that mobilizes and directs members toward higher objectives. They need to study the costs and obvious dangers, as well as the benefits, of transformational leadership. A step in this direction is to examine the differences between self-oriented and prosocial leaders (Bass, 1989).

Collective Motivation. An interesting research issue is raised by the question of how collective motivation is promoted in organizations. Collective motivation by employees was seen by Lawler (1982) to be a matter of outcomes that they valued occurring from the performance of the organization and their own contributions to that performance. But Staw (1984) argued that such collective motivation depends on the employees' identification with the organization and their contributions to the organization's performance. Transformational leadership theory would go further and imply that collective motivation would be generated by the employees' identification with their leader, and the employees' and their leader's identification with the organization and its goals and values.

Micro-Macro Opportunities. Hollander (1985) remained dissatisfied with the overconcentration of research on the microleadership of small groups. More macroleadership studies are needed of how leaders affect the strategic functions of institutions and organizations. The transformational-transactional distinction offers an avenue for tying together research on microleadership and macroleadership. As was seen in Chapter 12, transformational leadership—charismatic, intellectually stimulating, inspirational leadership—can be manipulated in the laboratory, reliably observed in small groups that are playing business games, rated reliably in large organizations at all levels, and used to differentiate among world-class leaders. At the same time, the paradigm lends itself to investigations across the disciplines of political science, organizational science, anthropology, sociology, and psychology. It can be readily discussed by psychoanalysts.

Needed Research in Selection and Training. Researchers need to learn how to train the average supervisor in the sensitivities and interpersonal competencies that are required of a transformational leader. They need to determine how to select potential transformational leaders who may not show up as well on many currently available predictors of transactional leadership. Above all, they need to overcome the parochialism that has characterized empirical research on leadership, which has focused on the easier-to-study transactional leadership.

Contraindications. Theory and research are needed on the costs and dangers of transformational leaders. Thus, Bennis (1989) pointed to the destructive consequences of only considering such successful transformational leaders as Steven Jobs or Lee Iacocca as heroes. Again, Bass (1985a) speculated on organizational and societal circumstances that might militate against the success and effectiveness of transformational leaders and Spangler and Braiotta (in press) located such an example: chairmen of audit committees of boards of directors. Trasactional leadership appears just as effective as transformational leadership. Contingent reward and active management by exception correlated .43 and .39, respectively, with effectiveness judged by colleagues in accounting and auditing inside and outside the firm. Parallel correlations with effectiveness of individualized consideration and intellectual stimulation were .40, .30, and .25, respectively.

Leaders as Organizational Politicians

Although the evidence (possibly as a consequence of social desirability) points to a general rejection of Machiavellian approaches (withholding information, bluffing, agreeing but delaying, and maintaining social distance), organizational decisions often can be understood as a consequence of coalition formation, negotiations, and other political processes. Decisions are based on the relative power of those involved, rather than on the merits of the issue.[8] But Culbert and McDonough (1980) considered effective brokering inside and outside their own groups as a challenge for leaders. Inside the group, the leader should try to negotiate arrangements with the subordinates that make for the best possible mix of subordinates serving their own interests and meeting the needs of the group. Externally, the leader as a representative can often do much to increase the group's resources and opportunities through effective negotiations with higher authority and with outsiders. Whereas such negotiating behavior with individual subordinates seems to be a counterproductive leadership style in the eyes of the subordinates,[9] the leader's successful playing of the role of broker still seems worthy of further exploration. The effective political use of authority and power is still a highly underresearched area. Particularly important and underresearched is how the would-be organizational politician can be converted into an organizational statesman. It is possible to be an "honest broker" for whom the marshaling of the evidence becomes as significant as the relative interests of the parties in the negotiation. In this regard, the similarities and differences between legislative leadership and executive leadership need to be more fully examined. We are likely to see a continuing interest in the specifics of the influence tactics employed by leaders and managers to obtain desired outcomes from their superiors, with subordinates, with their organization, and with outsiders (Kipnis, Schmidt, Swaffin-Smith, & Wilkinson, 1984) and the use of increasingly refined instruments in doing so (Schriesheim & Hinken, 1986).

Hermann, Snyder, and Cunningham (1980) posed a number of questions about the way the organizational politician uses staffs, advisers, and confidants. How are they chosen? To what extent do they insulate the leader from the rest of the organization? To what extent do they amplify distant or reduce incoming and outgoing communications by the leader?

Drake and Moberg (1986) called for research on how leaders modify their language to create consistent forms of calibration and impression. Contingencies in the phrasing of requests need to be examined. Tactics need to be related to desired outcomes. The effective use of disclaimers needs to be better understood, along with other ways in which the forms of language can foster interaction.

---

[8]Chapter 9, in particular, looked at individual differences in this regard; Chapters 11–13 discussed the more general issues involved.

[9]See Chapter 22.

Ethics

Both the legislative and the organizational politician may adopt influence tactics that border on the unethical. Flagrant lying, cheating, and stealing are clearly unethical managerial practices. But the extent to which white lies, cutting corners on standards, and making unauthorized use of company or governmental property are clearly unethical is seen to vary with the circumstances and individual differences in the concepts of right and wrong. Despite the importance that it should have, this is a severely underresearched area of empirical research on managerial and leadership behavior. A 1988 Louis Harris poll of 1,031 office workers and 150 senior executives reported that while 89 percent of the employees thought that it was very important for managers to be honest, upright, and ethical in their dealings with employees and the community, only 41 percent said this was actually true of their current employers (Anonymous, 1988a).

Weber (1989) found in interviews with 37 managers that they reasoned morally to conform to majority opinion and organization rules rather than for any universal principles of morality. For Burns (1978), the fostering of moral virtue was fundamental to being a transformational leader. The self-seeking charismatic, by definition, could not be truly a transformational leader. Howell (1988) and Bass (1989) suggested that many charismatic leaders have two faces. They can show their prosocial one, which is transforming, and keep their self-aggrandizing face from interfering with the process.

For Kuhnert and Lewis (1987), the transformational leader develops from a concern for personal goals and agendas to mature higher levels of values and obligations. At the highest level of development are to be found the endorsement of universal ethical principles of justice, the equality of human rights, and respect for human dignity. There is a belief in and a commitment to these principles as valid and as an end in themselves. Thus, the values of life and liberty led Paige (in press) to argue that the pursuit of nonviolent means for dealing with problem solving has to be a central focus in the education of political leaders. Somewhat less idealistic are the extent to which values are relative to the group and circumstance; sometimes, they may be in conflict with each other. But the organization and society are maintained by doing what is right. At the other extreme, the ethical sense is absent; one obeys the rules to avoid being punished (Kohlberg, 1969).[10]

Chapter 10 reviewed the few studies that could be found that dealt with managers' attitudes toward corrupt practices. Revealing to a competitor one's own company's bid for a payoff was almost universally condemned, but petty payoffs from outside contractors for awarding them contracts was much less frowned upon. Insider trading is seen as more a matter of illegality[11] than of immorality (Pitt, 1985).

An experimental program was launched in 1986 to apply Misumi's (1985) PM leadership in seven mainland Chinese factories, hospitals, and agencies. A "character function of leadership" was added to the survey feedback process with emphasis on the moral character of the leader. Along with elements of effective human relations familiar to the West was included in moral character "the commitment to remain within the law and resist temptations for personal gain" (Peterson, 1989, p. 33). Also included was willingness to follow the Communist Party line even when personal views were in conflict with it.

In the West, organizations of professionals, such as those in the health professions or in public accounting, generally tend to monitor the violations of their rules on a case-by-case basis. But beyond this monitoring, critical incidents survey methods used by the American Psychological Association (1953) are available for gathering both clear-cut and borderline incidents of immoral behavior by managers and the various alternative ways that managers and leaders could have used that were morally acceptable in terms of informed consensual opinion or universal standards. We are likely to see such an effort made within the next several decades in the fields of organizational management, probably led by the accounting profession. In addition, we are likely to see questions of commitment to ethical behavior added to survey feedback.

A Model for Ethical Analysis. For Socrates, ethics was the search for the good life in which one's actions are in accord with the truth. According to Steidlmeier

---

[10]Illustrative of people at this level are those who faulted President Richard M. Nixon not for trying to subvert the law but for getting caught.

[11]In some countries, such as Japan, it is not even illegal.

(1987), ethics is creative, searching for human fulfillment and choosing it as good and beautiful. Ethics is practical in purpose. It seeks the full flowering of the human person and excellence in the actualization of the human capacity. Moral virtues are the life-giving patterns of behavior; moral vices are destructive patterns.

Most discussions of professional ethics focus on the destructive vices. They are negative and guilt ridden. The focus is on what should not be, rather than on what should be. Discussions are defensive and dogmatic. Steidlmeier accented the positive. He suggested that we need to clarify our world view and our principles, which should be integrated into our educational and developmental processes. Unfortunately, principles of self-regulation and codes of conduct are often in conflict with the avoidance of the costs and the maintenance of one's competitive edge. There is a need to recognize the costs and a need to share them among stockholders, management, employees, and the public to gain society-wide benefits. Weber (1989) pointed to the need to examine how the organization impinges on the manager's maturity of moral reasoning. Beyond this, there is a need to determine the connection between moral reasoning and moral behavior and how each depends on the issue involved.

Needed is a model that can fit both the hortatory literature on business ethics and social responsibility and the survey evidence of current managerial beliefs and practices. Forrest, Cochran, Ray, and Robin (1989) made such an attempt but were unable to account for the ethical opinions of 315 surveyed managers and 577 surveyed teachers. The investigators extracted four bipolarities from the prescriptive literature: (1) economic versus social purpose; (2) company policy versus individual manager discretion; (3) recurring versus one-time problems; and (4) utilitarian versus ideological decision rules.

Organizational Citizenship. Conceptualizing organizations as a collection of constituencies (March & Simon, 1958) remains a powerful source for understanding the individual leader's performance. Much of leaders' success with their subordinates may depend on how well they negotiate arrangements with other units. By now, the need to focus more attention on the manager's horizontal interactions with peers in other units

and with clients (Dubin, 1962b) has become a platitude. However these leader-leader interactions could be studied with considerable profitability (Hermann, Snyder, & Cunningham, 1980).

In opposition to the political balancing of self-interests, a new concept that is taking shape, which transcends the formal horizontal or vertical relationship. It is that of the good organizational citizen who goes beyond his or her immediate self-interests to promote the well-being of the organization, its members, and society as a whole. "Whistle-blowers" are illustrative. There is need both in the public and private sectors to provide more support for the valid "whistleblowers" and less for their corrupt superiors. More often than not, the "whistleblower" is likely to suffer more punishment than the corrupt superior.

What may follow the "me-too" generation of the past 30 years is more good organizational citizenship. Or there may be a reversion to the "my-group" generation of the 1950s (and like the Japanese of today) that was concerned primarily with peer pressures. What happens will have considerable implications for leadership.

Ethical resolve continues to remain more important than philanthropical concerns to senior management according to surveys of several hundred CEOs in 1989 and 1988 but less important than legal or economic considerations. Not does it appear to relate one way or another to the corporation's financial performance (Aupperle & Simmons, 1989). Nevertheless, research on ethics of business leaders is likely to increase substantially in the next several decades.

Criteria of Effective Leadership

In a review of 89 studies published between 1970 and 1975, Hunt, Osborn, and Schriesheim (1977) reported that 61 percent used only a single criterion of effective leadership, 43 percent of which emphasized performance. However, a greater use of multiple criteria was noted in field studies. Most field studies (81 percent) used criteria obtained from a different informational source than the predictors.

Studies have been conducted on the response of followers' beliefs, satisfaction, and behavior, as well as group productivity, drive, and cohesiveness, to leadership behavior. However, certain variables, such as group productivity and the satisfaction of followers, have been overemphasized at the expense of other variables. For instance, followers' efforts, which presumably should be affected by transformational leadership, in particular, have tended to be neglected as an outcome that is due to leadership.

Evaluations Are Relative and Subject to Change.

Evaluations of leaders are subject to revision. Shartle (1956) observed that ten years too late, a firm might discover it had fired its most effective manager. Often vilified while he was in office, President Harry S. Truman's performance was upgraded considerably in the years that followed. Seen as being more interested in playing golf then in taking decisive actions, President D. Eisenhower was later found to have played an active role in substituting clandestine forces in Iran, Central America, and elsewhere for open displays of U.S. military power—actions that had delayed devastating effects on those countries and on subsequent U.S. relations with them and indirectly led to the Bay of Pigs fiasco and two constitutional crises in the United States. Donald Burr, at first evaluated as a hero who devised a radical new approach to managing airlines, became the villain who failed to consult with others and overexpanded Peoples Airlines to the point where it was thrust into bankruptcy.

Evaluations are relative. Well known are the stories about executives who introduce belt-tightening measures into a department, ride roughshod over subordinates to reduce costs, maximize immediate productivity, and are promoted to repeat the process higher up, leaving behind a shambles of dissatisfaction and conflict to be blamed on their successors.

Peters and Waterman's (1982) popular assessment of exemplary firms that represent excellence in management was based on a highly subjective evaluation of excellent management. When a fuller analysis of the firms' financial performance was compared with those of 1,000 firms evaluated by Forbes, the performance of these firms was seen to be not particularly different (Aupperle, Acar, & Booth, 1986).

What scholars view as effective leadership and how the followers view the same performance may be quite different. In contrast to presidents from Woodrow Wilson through Richard M. Nixon who fulfilled nearly 75 percent of their campaign pledges, Jimmy Carter did almost as well. Nevertheless, Carter was seen as a failure by the public because he did not fulfill the major campaign promises that were important to voters—reducing unemployment and reducing inflation (Krukones, 1985). The discrepancies between scholarly appraisals and the public's evaluation of a leader's performance are particularly apparent in the case of demagogues.

There is a need to distinguish between the successful influence of the leader and his or her long-term effectiveness, as determined by the contribution of the influence to attaining the long-term goals and well-being of the organization or the nation. For instance, researchers need to broaden the criteria of consequence and to attach the appropriate longer-term value of leadership to the development of followers, the organization, and the nation (McCall, 1977). Human resources accounting is an effort in this direction. As managerial accountants increasingly become interested in the behavioral side of a firm's assets and liabilities, there should be increasing opportunities to measure such effects (Caplan & Landekich, 1974). Utility analysis is a promising tool (Cascio & Ramos, 1986). But considerable care will be required to weed out the cause-effect relationships.

Additional questions about the evaluations of the effectiveness of leaders were posed by Hermann, Snyder, and Cunningham (1980). Who determines the criteria for effective leadership and what difference does it make? (Shareholders will emphasize stock prices; employees, job satisfaction). Are output measures, such as the size of profits, votes obtained, or church membership, sufficient measures of the effectiveness of leaders, or are leadership process variables more important? How do researchers avoid having the leader directly influence the judges to render favorable judgments about his or her effectiveness, a phenomenon examined by Dubin (1979).

Linkages, Moderators, and Substitutes

Why does the behavior of the leader affect the group's outcomes? Why do the group's outcomes affect a leader's behavior? The leadership roles serve the necessary functions of maintaining role structure, role freedom, goal direction, and cohesive group action in the performance of a task. The leadership roles do not necessarily specify the patterns of behavior required but, rather, the purposes to be served by them. These purposes include dealing with goal direction and individual members' goals, relations within the group, maintaining the group's role structure, constraints and freedom, individual and group motivation, individual satisfaction and group cohesion, and the group's norms and requirements.

In the emergent situation, leadership is created by the group in response to its own necessities even though an impatient member may impose himself or herself upon the group before the group expresses a demand for such services. In formal organizations, the necessity is acknowledged by the appointment or election of leaders. The effective performance of a task is usually dependent on the appointed or emergent leader's enactment of the leadership roles to carry out the necessary functions. How are the role enactments affected by changes in membership, task, and organization? Are there satisfactory substitutes for leadership, such as the overtraining of followers, computerization and automation, or policies and regulations? How far can self-management be taken with such substitutes?

Computers can be substituted for the supervisor in the monitoring and feedback (to both employees and a higher authority) of the individual employee's productivity, wasting of time, frequency of errors, and presence at or absence from the work station. Computers can troubleshoot and inform employees about corrections they should make and how to make them. Are such monitoring and feedback likely to be favorably accepted by the employee, in contrast to less close human monitoring? Are some aspects more coercive than others? What about this type of monitoring and feedback represents a diminution of the job for the employee, with its associated effects of increasing boredom, dissatisfaction, and loss of self-esteem?

A Systems Approach

Katz and Kahn (1966) pointed the way. A systems approach looks at the leader as someone embedded in a system with multiple inputs from the environment, the organization, the immediate work group supervised, the task, the leader's behavior, and his or her relation-

ships with subordinates and outputs in terms of effective performance and satisfactions (Bass, 1976). Hunt, Osborn, and Schriesheim (1977) thought this kind of systems view of contingent variables was particularly important for future research. For instance, studies of military leadership confirmed that combat and noncombat conditions require different patterns of effective leadership behavior. Such differences are likely to vary by the level of officers. Upward and lateral influence in the system can be as important as downward influence to the accomplishment of missions (Van Fleet & Yukl, 1986). Gal (1989) argued that military leadership in the 1990s will be derived from the commitment of subordinates to rise to the challenge of complex, risky, uncertain, and dangerous situations.

According to Demming (1986), managers need to know whether the system in which they are involved is stable and predictable. Are the system's goals and norms stable? Inefficiencies that show up repeatedly call for managers' efforts to improve the situation. Any one positive outcome, such as the satisfaction of customers or meeting the competition by itself, may mean little to the overall health of the system. Again, zero-defects programs or new equipment alone may be of little consequence to the system. The management needs to focus proactively on the constant improvement of the design and processes of the system that lie within its capabilities.

Much needs to be learned about how leaders manage the boundary between what is inside and outside their mission in the larger organization and how to protect it. How do they create the necessary environment for productivity within their boundaries? To what must they attend and what can they ignore? How do they help others to make sense of arrangements and situations (Gilmore, 1982)?

Adams and Yoder (1985) advocated that particular attention should be paid to the need to consider leader-subordinate relations in the broader setting in which actions take place—the wider organization and external environment—as was done in Chapter 26. Hermann, Snyder, and Cunningham (1980) noted the absence of research on how a leader's behavior is affected by a variety of specific contextual issues. Will a number of groups need to be coordinated or can one group handle the problems? Is the organizational problem a crisis or is it routine? Is the problem familiar or unfamiliar to the organization? Is the leadership to be with immediate subordinates or at a distance? Similarly, Behling and Schriesheim (1976) and Schriesheim and Neider (1988a) saw the need for more future research about the externally oriented activities of managers with higher authority, other department heads, clients, and the community. In all, a more complex set of roles will be seen as part of managerial leadership.

The application of a systems approach to leadership was reflected in the principles set forth for senior executives by the Center for Creative Leadership. Executive leaders need to get in touch at different levels in the organization with "what is really going on." They need to articulate a vision with clear goals, standards, and priorities, along with a plan for developing a climate that will support the effort. Key leaders at various levels of the organization will need to set examples of such support. Periodic measurements of the effort and its success are required. Risk taking and trust building need to be encouraged. Competitiveness that reduces information sharing needs to be discouraged. Suitable appraisal and reward systems for outstanding individual and team accomplishments should follow, with continuing attention to effective personnel staffing, development, and succession to fit the programmatic effort.

In contrast to microlevel research on the leader in relation to his or her subordinates and immediate superiors and to macrolevel research on the aggregated data that relate to the total organization and its environment, mesolevel research involves the individual leader, on the one hand, and the total organization and environment surrounding the leader on the other. More such mesolevel research is needed (House, 1988a).

Discretionary Possibilities and Nondiscretionary Requirements

A few efforts have been made to identify the discretionary opportunities that shape the leader's behavior. Much more is needed to know what is and is not under a leader's control. Such knowledge should reduce subordinates' unrealistic expectations about the leader, as well as the leader's own experiences of violated expectations. In selection and placement testing, researchers should be able to generate higher validity coefficients between personality attributes and that portion of a leader's behavior that is discretionary.

Delegation

Delegation remains a relatively unexplored management option despite the evidence of the important contribution to organization effectiveness. Thus, Miller and Toulouse (1986) showed that the extent to which delegation of authority was practiced in 97 small businesses in Quebec correlated .31 with profitability and .34 with sales growth of the business relative to the others in the same industry. The effects of delegation were stronger than any others examined which included the effects of the business strategies employed, how they were devised, and the CEOs personal characteristics.

Studies of the delegative process are likely to be important in future research on leadership with more fine tuning of delegation as a style of leadership. Delegation is clearly not participation. Although Vroom and Yelton (1973); Bass, Valenzi, Farrow, and Solomon (1975); and Leana (1986, 1987), among others, contributed to some understanding of delegation, it still remains the least researched style.

As a step forward in the research effort, Schriesheim and Neider (1988) conceived of three forms of delegation instead of one. Research is needed to learn whether each of the forms are likely to interact differently with the motivation, commitment, satisfaction, and performance of subordinates:

Advisory delegation, in which	the subordinate makes the decision after first getting a recommendation from the leader.
Informational delegation, in which	the subordinate makes the decision after first getting needed information from the leader.
Extreme delegation, in which	the subordinate makes the decision without any input from the leader.

Of the three forms, advisory delegation is likely to coincide with a strong commitment by the subordinates.

Delegation has been regarded as the style at the

other end of the continuum of styles from autocratic directive leadership. Yet, an autocrat may delegate because of lack of time to handle the problem directly. A transactional leader may delegate in exchange for subordinate support. A transformational leader will use delegation to develop his or her subordinates. A consultive leader may delegate as a result of being convinced of the subordinate's competence and motivations to handle the problem. Delegation may be the choice of a participant consensus. A laissez-faire leader may delegate to avoid blame for possible failure.

There is a need to conceptualize delegation as a process and to research what makes it effective or ineffective.

Contingent Models

Personal traits that are associated with the emergence of a leader appear to transcend situational demands. It is still axiomatic that some of the variance in the emergence and effectiveness of leadership is due to personal traits, and some is due to situational and interactive factors. Nevertheless a meta-analysis by Lord, DeVader, and Alliger (1986) of data from Mann (1959) and additional data suggested that both Stogdill (1948) and Mann seriously underestimated the importance of personal traits relative to situational effects. The meta-analysis showed that the theoretical mean correlations between such traits as intelligence, extroversion, and assertiveness and emergence as a leader were much higher than was realized when suitable adjustments were made for the restrictions in range of the subjects of the studies and for the unreliability of the measures employed. Also taken into account in the meta-analysis was the likelihood of random variation from one study to the next, which explained much of the situational variance and argued against the need for a great concern with contingent explanations. That is, assertiveness for example, is necessary for leaders, regardless of the situation.

But contingent models are still required to explain how the styles required for effective leadership vary with the demands of a situation. For example, Barbieri (1983) used path analyses to show that much of the 39 percent of the variance in the revenues from the sales of *mature* products that were generated by marketing managers and their sales representatives could be accounted for by the managers' extroversion, relations orientation, and intuitive thinking. But the revenues from the sales of *innovative* products were accounted for by the managers' task orientation and the sales representatives' experience, practical orientation, and intelligence. At the same time, the branch managers' unwillingness to delegate was not a contingent effect; it contributed positively to the sales of both kinds of products.

In sum, despite meta-analytic support for the generalizing across situations of personal traits associated with the emergence of leadership such as intelligence, assertiveness, and extroversion, applications of contingent models of leadership are likely to remain prolific sources of further examination and validation, particularly with reference to the styles of leadership that are most effective in designated circumstances. More causal, longer-term, larger-scale contingent studies of styles of leadership and their effectiveness are likely to appear during the coming decades.

Assessment

Research on the various assessment methods employed and their integration into decisions about assessees need to be studied further. The phrasing of over 100 such research questions emerged from a brainstorming session on the subject (Jeswald, 1971), most of which still remain unanswered or partly unanswered two decades later. For example, much more remains to be discovered about the kinds of biodata that can be profitably used for assessment.

The development and evaluation of more sophisticated theory-based, in contrast to empirically originated, biodata forms of greater validity are needed. These forms can be developed and evaluated by asking questions that generate responses that are more likely to be related to the personal styles that are of consequence to subsequent performance as a leader. Thus, researchers can ask questions about how the applicant coped with "the most important challenge you faced" or "your most disappointing experience." Appropriate scoring, consistent with theoretical expectations, can be developed (Kuhnert & Russell, 1989). A list of such dynamic items for application blanks was suggested by

Bass and Barrett (1972)—for example: "May we consult your present employer?"

In this endeavor, as well as in the development of new psychological tests and measurements, experimental findings about personality and social psychology can be put to better use. More complex simulations that duplicate critical aspects of on-the-job performance should be employed. The subtleties of the deep structures involved can be introduced into such simulations. More should be done to assess creative, flexible intelligence, as well as less socially desirable aspects of personality that may influence leadership behavior, such as dogmatism and authoritarianism. More research is needed on newer personality dimensions that are of consequence, such as the tolerance for ambiguity. A lot more needs to be known about the abilities needed to cope with higher-level managerial responsibilities, including the ability to translate ideas into actions. More sophisticated assessments of leaders' performance in decision-making processes are desirable. Justification of the greater expense of assessment centers over ordinary selection methods calls for more utility analyses like the analysis presented by Cascio and Ramos (1986). The contextual conditions surrounding the assessment process also need to be taken more fully into account (Bentz, 1987).

Leadership Development, Training, Persistence, and Succession

On the one hand, researchers can point with pride to the large array of positive evidence about the efforts to train leaders and the success that has been experienced.[12] On the other hand, it is still possible to decry the many continuing inadequacies of training.

Leadership development is a continuing process. Thus, researchers need to learn a lot more about how experience with subordinates, peers, and superiors, as well as with family and friends, shapes one's subsequent performance as a leader. Research on the persistence and transfer of leadership has produced a convincing body of evidence which indicates that one's past success as a leader contributes to one's future success as a leader.

[12]See Chapter 35.

What experiences are necessary to make an effective leader? Does one need to be trained in business to be an effective industrial leader? Does one need to be trained in theology to make an effective pope? Does one need to be a lawyer to be an effective legislative leader? Does one need legislative experience to be an effective president?

Kuhnert and Lewis (1987) raised a number of unanswered substantive questions about the development of transformational leadership. Are there observable changes in the transformational leaders' behavior as a function of the leaders' personalities? Is transactional leadership a less mature developmental phase than is transformational leadership? Are the leaders' developmental phases invariant? Does one have to be a transactional leader before he or she can become transformational? What happens when leaders and followers operate at different developmental levels?

The Genetic Factor. The nature-nurture controversy is by no means settled. Advances in genetics and biology need to be incorporated into leadership models. Large-scale studies of heredity suggest that genes contribute to energy levels, intelligence, interests, assertiveness, a sense of well-being, and the ability to take risks, even job satisfaction, and need to be taken into account in any complete examination of leadership. There are remarkable correlations in these kinds of traits and outcomes among identical twins reared apart, in contrast to genetically unrelated people.

The Purposes of Training. On the one hand, Stogdill (1974) faulted research on training for focusing too much on the extent to which training produces attitudinal and behavioral changes in the trainees. He demanded more evidence on the impact of the training of leaders on followers. Yet, researchers still need to link particular training efforts with particular behavioral changes. For instance, training may understandably increase a trainee's sensitivities; nevertheless, such increased sensitivities may be counterproductive on the job. Sensitivity training may incapacitate the leader for coping with strong opposition, threats, and challenges to the legitimacy of his or her status. What would be at fault here is not the training as such, but an inadequate analysis of the situational demands on the leader. We are beginning to see much greater precision in such analyses. Over time, it is expected that the application of sophisticated analyses of the manager's, administrator's, and leader's roles to training will be much more intensive.

Improvements in Evaluation. Evidence of the utility of the focus on specific behavioral training and its specific effects is to be found in the attention now being paid to behavioral objectives, behavioral modeling, and applications of social learning theory. But in many evaluative studies of leadership training, it is impossible to determine the method or combination of methods that were employed. Evaluative reports need to describe in detail both the method of training and the content that was taught. In addition, more attention needs to be paid to the various threats to the validity of training designs and their evaluations (Kane, 1976). For example, for the purposes of unbiased evaluations, if possible, superiors should not know who has received training and who has not after trainees return to their jobs. Likewise, trainees should not be told whether they are serving as experimental subjects or controls (as in holdout designs).

Multinationalism and Diversity

The globalization of industry will mean increasing attention to international managers, as such, with the probable submergence of surface differences in national styles and performance but with needed increases in attention to underlying differences in institutions, cultures, and governments. At the same time, with the rise in power and influence and the further economic development of countries whose cultures are alien to the West, attitudes, values, interests, and beliefs that are different from those in the West and that affect leader-follower relations will emerge. They are likely to emphasize tradition and collectivism more heavily.

In the United States, studies of black, Hispanic, Asian-American, and women leaders will continue to increase, reflecting their movement into higher levels of leadership and management in industry, government, and education. A greater openness to the line management of Jewish Americans and Asian Americans is likely to increase with the increasing technological requirements for remaining competitive. As more

women move into the higher reaches of management, we may see more of an emphasis on androgyny than on masculinity as being favorable for effective management (Adams & Yoder, 1985). Extensive commentaries will be replaced by more empirical studies. More empirical studies will also be needed if we consider how quickly outdated conclusions from them can become.

Because of the emotional content involved, care needs to be taken not to accept at face value leaders' and subordinates' cross-race and cross-sex opinions and descriptions. At the same time, more attention has to be paid to the underlying feelings of rejection, contempt, guilt, and threat in mainstreamers and outsiders that do not surface because of superficial socialization, socially desirable responses, or mistrust of the investigators. This is another reason why empirical monitoring of such dimensions as the self-confidence of blacks, women, Hispanics, and particularly Asian Americans is essential. It should be recognized that an effective, polite, mutual acceptance can be maintained at one level while underneath, a wall of misunderstanding still exists.

Little is known about Anglo-Hispanic leader-subordinate relations. Yet the Spanish-surnamed group is fast becoming a large U.S. minority. Research here will be made particularly difficult by the wide differences among the Chicanos, the Puerto Ricans, the Cuban Americans, and the large immigrant groups from elsewhere in Latin America.

So far, the preponderance of evidence endorses the need for minority members who serve as leaders in majority environments to emulate the original white, male manager. However, more and timely research will be needed on the accommodations made by minority members to the duality of their roles as both managers and members of a minority group. Leadership is also a completely different matter for minority community leaders, who ordinarily need to identify more with their own subculture than do their followers.

Summary and Conclusions

A review of the preceding chapters suggests that some topics and research designs have been overworked while other important questions remain relatively unexplored. An enormous amount of original, creative research was coupled with a wasteful repetition of tests of shopworn hypotheses and a general disregard for negative results. The atheoretical research published before 1965 was too unfocused, but much of the research based on naive, uncritical theorizing that followed retarded the process of new discoveries. Nevertheless, much has been accomplished.

Accomplishments

Critics complain that leadership is fundamentally antidemocratic and antithetical to the nonleader's rights of expression and power sharing. Other critics complain that despite all the research, nothing is known about leadership. They declare that leadership is a figment of the imagination. For them, leadership as a research subject is moribund and has reached a "dead-end." Nonetheless, this and the preceding 36 chapters attest to the health and well-being of the subject. Indeed, the past several decades produced a wide range of new and challenging substantive issues, including implicit leadership, substitutes for leadership, prototypicality effects, transformational leadership, impression management, self-management, and upward influence. Other issues, such as charismatic leadership, which had been narrowly focused, spread in interest across many fields and disciplines.

Considerable advances occurred in the development and usage of theories. Linkages were forged to general theories, for example, between contingent reinforcement leadership and the general theory of reinforcement. Testable theories were constructed and tested. No longer does one have to wait for the demise of the theorist before a theory of leadership will be abandoned or modified because of its failure to be supported empirically.

The ability to accurately predict future leadership performance increased substantially during the past half century. A few studies took advantage of the miniaturization of physiological recording by radio or the advent of the personal computer. More will be doing so in the future. The same is true for electronic mail and other forms of telecommunication, which will also increase in importance in linking leaders and subordinates who are distant from each other.

New complex and effective research designs are now available. These designs would be equally useful for testing other relationships that have not been explored. The production of critically needed information could be greatly accelerated by feeding new combinations of variables into research designs that have been demonstrated to be effective. Efforts are increasing to bring together the active leaders, organizational consultants, and research investigators to discern common problems and interests and to increase the focus of this research on realities and the application of research results (see, for example, Clark & Clark, 1989).

In the social sciences, old theories used to wither away with the retirement of the originators and their disciples. However, although some theories of leadership have gone or are going this route, other theories of leadership, such as path-goal theory and the contingency theories, have by no means withered. Rather, they have been systematically tested and reshaped as a consequence of the results of tests. And new models have been fashioned on top of them.

The preceding suggestions for future research indicate that the possibilities are far from exhausted. Leadership presents a lively, challenging field for research and innovative applications.

Optimism or Pessimism? The optimist sees the wine bottle as half full; the pessimist sees it as half-empty (and sour to boot). It is easier to be destructive than constructive, particularly when one lacks information. In every field of research, there are always "know-nothings" who argue that the past years have essentially been a waste and it is now necessary to start afresh. Miner (1975) proposed that the concept of leadership be abandoned altogether. Since then, he changed his mind. M. W. McCall (1977) thought that leadership would remain an enigmatic subject because of its many definitions, but in Chapter 1, I noted that the definitions were evolving in a systematic fashion and that, at any rate, the diverse definitions do not seem to detract from model and theory building. The many models and theories that sprang forth in the past three decades are not as divergent and conflicting as one might expect from the diverse definitions of leadership on which they may be built. Ways are needed to juxtapose one model with another to test which one yields more plausible explanations. Fiedler and associates tested Fiedler's contingency theory; Vroom and associates tested their deductive model; Likert and his associates produced massive amounts of support for System 4. Points of theoretical disagreement can be found and critical experiments developed, as was done by Locke, Latham, and Erez (1987) and Blake and Mouton (1985) to determine which model better fits the data.

To some extent, the problem may be that each theoretical point of view is supported by a different array of measurements and situational circumstances. Part of the problem may also be that situational factors determine some kinds of leadership behavior but not others. Autocratic leaders—rigid, inflexible, and self-assured—may try to lead in any situation in which they are placed. Democratic leaders may attempt to lead only if they feel competent and supported in the particular situation. The nondiscretionary behavior of leaders will be determined by organizational and environmental matters that are not within their control. But the leaders' discretionary performance will be much more a matter of their personal predelictions than of situational differences alone.

It is one thing to say that researchers know nothing because they do not obtain consistent results. The lack of consistency may be attributable to a lack of knowledge. Yet, it may be that to achieve consistent results requires accounting for a complexity of variables and as researchers do so, they increase their understanding of what is happening. What are needed are better measurements; a broader appreciation of which situational variables are more important and which are less so (Korman, 1974); and, as was noted earlier, larger samples. Calas (1986) and Calas and Smircich (1987) joined the "cry and dismay" about the narrow substantive themes and methodological means of the past in what has been published about leadership by its establishment of scientific investigators. Nevertheless, they believe that the field has the potential to become much more open to broader approaches in the search for understanding; the acceptance of expanded horizons; more adequate connections with salient substantive issues of the real world outside the community of researchers; and learning from experience, observation, and narrative interpretations of meaning about what they write, as well as from continued dependence on field surveys and controlled experiments.

The choice of topics needs to be broadened to reflect more of the long-lasting issues that leaders, as well as the leadership-research establishment, confront. However, whereas one side of the establishment has continued to complain about the substantive and methodological narrowness of research in the field, its opponents have been equally vociferous about the need for more rigor and discipline. Both types of investigators make contributions, particularly when they can join forces or they can pursue the expansion of horizons from a disciplinary or interdisciplinary basis.

Some collectively disparage the thousands of research studies of leadership.[13] But T. R. Mitchell (1979) concluded that theory and research were continuing to develop and that much of what had been done was being used in practice. "There was reason for controlled optimism. Yet the challenges are still there for the years ahead." His words remain true a decade later.

This book should provide an antidote for the arguments of those contining to bemoan the supposed unknowable, elusive, mysterious nature of leadership. For, I expect and hope that I have been able to show that a considerable body of theory, method, evidence, and understanding is available about how, why, and under what conditions leadership, in all its rich variations—implied, observed, described, and/or evaluated—energizes and exerts its influence sometimes for the worse, more often for the better.

---

[13]About 7,500 have been cited here.

Glossary

This glossary has been prepared because some readers may be unfamiliar with particular specialized terms in statistics; management; and the behavioral, social, and political sciences that were mentioned in the text but not defined or fully discussed. The glossary may also be helpful to readers from abroad who are less familiar with some American colloquialisms that appear in the text. The terms that are discussed more fully in the text are likely to be found in the subject index rather than in this glossary.

A

Accountability Members of an organization who are given responsibility and authority are held answerable for the results.

Achievement motive (nAch) Motivation to seek high performance and success.

Acquiescent response set Agreement with statements, regardless of their content.

Action research Research whose objective includes the implemented solution of the research problem using the diagnosis of the problem, the collection of data, and the analysis and feedback of data.

Adaptation level An individual's expectations and experience set a standard against which events or objects are perceived.

Ad hoc group A temporary group established to deal with a problem or problems. (See *Task force*)

Affect (noun) Feeling, emotional reaction.

Affiliation motive (nAff) The motivation to belong and to be with other people.

Affirmative action Positive programs to increase opportunities for the employment and promotion of members of disadvantaged groups.

Algorithm A procedure used to solve a set of problems by an explicit formula.

Alienation A generalized sense of meaninglessness, helplessness, and social isolation that contributes to the disinhibition of personal controls against engaging in deviant behavior.

Altruism Helping others with no obvious benefit to oneself and with few expectations for personal gain.

Analog A physical, mechanical, or electrical model of an object or concept about which measurements and calculations can be made.

Androgenous Combining attitudes and behavior of both males and females.

Anglos Mainstreamers in U.S. Southwest.

Anomie The reduced social control against deviant behavior that is due to a disregard of norms and standards.

Anxiety Generalized, diffuse apprehension.

A posteriori Explanations are offered after the facts are known.

Application blank A personnel form to elicit information about an individual's personal characteristics, background, and experience.

A priori Hypotheses are formulated before the facts are known.

Arbitration A situation in which a third party renders the decision for two parties who are in conflict.

Artifact The results of an arbitrary method, rather than the true state of affairs.

Artificial intelligence The emulation of the problem-solving, linguistic, and other capabilities of human beings by means of a computer.

Assumed similarity We assume that we are like other people in values, interests, beliefs, and personality. (See *Projection*)

Attenuation Reduction from a theoretically true correlation because of the unreliability of one or both measures correlated.

Attitude An affective, evaluative, relatively enduring reaction, positive or negative, toward an object or proposition.

Attribution theory A theory of the way people impute intentions to other persons or situations.

Auditing Verification of the validity of data, statements, and records.

Autokinetic effect A stationary light that, when viewed in a dark room, appears to move.

Autonomy The degree of freedom in carrying out an assignment.

Aversive reinforcement Reinforcing conditions that inhibit the reinforced behavior; negative reinforcement.

B

Batch production The production of quantities of similiar items, rather than mixes of items.

Behavior modification Changing behavior by changing the consequences of that behavior. Desired new behavior is rewarded (positively reinforced); undesired old behavior is punished (negatively reinforced).

Behavior shaping Behavior modification in which small increments of behavior are reinforced in the direction of the desired behavior until a final desired result is achieved.

Biased sample A sample that is unrepresentative because of one or more sources of systematic error.

Binary Involving two digits or states.

Biographical information blank (See *Application blank*)

Boundary-spanning roles Liaison roles that connect departments or organizations with each other and with the environment.

Bounded rationality Managers make the best decisions they can within the constraints of limited information about possible alternatives and the consequences of the alternatives.

Brainstorming The generation of ideas without evaluating them; a maximum number of ideas can be generated in a limited time.

Buffering Actions or events to seal off processes from external variations.

Bureaucracy An organization that is operated on the basis of rules, regulations, and orderliness and that focuses on legitimacy, the duties of jobs, and the rights of office. It is characterized by standardization, hierarchical control, specified authority, and responsibilities.

Bureaucratic personality The preference for rules, regulations, and order in running organizations.

Burnout Emotional, mental and physical exhaustion resulting from continuing exposure to stress.

Business game A simulation of a business operated by two or more players competing with other businesses in a common market.

C

Career plateau A prolonged halt in promotion up the corporate ladder.

Centralization The degree of concentration of authority in a central location at the top of the organization.

Chain of command The hierarchy of authority in an organization from top to bottom. Members are supposed to know to whom they should report and who reports to them.

Change agent An individual who guides the process of group or organizational change.

Channel The communication path along which information flows.

Chicano Mexican American.

Classical organization theory Early efforts to identify the principles of effective management.

Code A system for representing information and rules.

Coefficient alpha The internal consistency or reliability of a test or measure based on the average intercorrelation among its items.

Cognition A mental event in which perceptions, memories, beliefs, and thoughts are processed.

Cognitive complexity The sensing of many narrow segmented categories in behavior or events, rather than a few broad classifications.

Cognitive dissonance The holding of incompatible beliefs and cognitions.

Cognitive dissonance theory The theory that it is unpleasant to maintain strongly held beliefs that clash with facts and that people are motivated to resolve the incompatibility by maintaining the beliefs and denying the facts.

Cognitive framework The categories and their connections into which individuals place events, behaviors, objects, attributes, and concepts.

Cohesiveness The forces that hold a group together; the attractiveness of a group for its members and the members for one another.

Collective bargaining The negotiation and administration of agreements between labor and management about wages, working conditions, benefits, and other labor-management issues.

Commitment Strong, positive involvement; continuing concern.

Common factor The statistical representation of a factor underlying two or more variables.

Communality The sum of squares of factor loadings for a designated variable; the total variance that is due to the factors that this variable shares with all other variables in an intercorrelated set.

Communication overload The receipt of excessive amounts of information so that the information cannot be processed satisfactorily.

Compliance Acting that is consistent with rules, norms, or influence by others.

Compression of salaries Because of changes in labor market conditions, newly hired employees may begin employment at salaries that are near to or the same as those with seniority, more experience, but similar other credentials.

Compulsory arbitration A negotiation in which the arbiter's decision is binding on the parties in conflict.

Computer-assisted instruction (CAI) Instruction by computers that substitutes for human instruction.

Computer program A set of instructions, arranged in proper sequence, to cause a computer to perform a desired set of operations.

Concept A mental image formed from a set of observations; a definition that labels and provides meaning to the observed reality.

Conflict management Intervening, as needed, to avoid, reduce or resolve conflicts.

Confrontation A situation in which parties in conflict directly face, oppose, and resist each other on the issues.

Consensus An emotionally and intellectually acceptable group decision.

Construct (See *Concept*)

Content analysis An objective, systematic, and usually quantitative description of communications as observed, recorded, or documented.

Contingency table A display of the frequency of individuals or cases, classified according to two or more attributes.

Continuous processing Inputs of energy and materials are transformed into products in a flow for a period of time such as occurs in a petrochemical refinery.

Controlling The process of monitoring and correcting organizational activities to see that they conform to plans.

Co-optation A situation in which authorities choose their successors, colleagues, and assistants.

Coordination Integration of the activities of the separate parts of a group or organization.

Correlation coefficient The relationship between two variables obtained from the same set of cases. It can range from $+1.00$ through 0.00 to -1.00. It is the ratio of how much one (standardized) variable's changes coincide with the changes in the other (standardized) variable.

Counterculture A culture that is radically divergent from the mainstream culture of the society of which it is a part.

Coup Illegitimate, sudden seizure of power. Also, a sudden, surprising victory.

Covariance The mean of the products of the deviations of each of two variables from its own mean.

Criterion A standard of performance; the measure against which other measures are calibrated.

Critical incidents method A performance appraisal in which the supervisor keeps a record over a period of time of the behaviors of each subordinate that are critical to the performance of the job. Also, a survey method for collecting desired and undesired critical behaviors from a sample of employees.

Cross-lag The correlation of earlier data on

one variable with later data from another variable and vice versa.

Cross-validation Scoring keys developed using a first sample are validated using a second sample.

D

Damage control Explanations to offset the effects of a leader's failures and mistakes.

Decentralization The delegation of power and authority from a central, higher authority to lower levels of the organization, which often results in smaller, self-contained organizational units.

Decision making Identifying and selecting a course of action to solve a problem.

Decode To convert coded data into readable and meaningful information.

Deindividuation A state of being in which an individual in a collection of people does not feel personally identifiable by others.

Delphi method A method by which expert opinion is surveyed and compiled and then each expert evaluates the compilation.

Demand characteristics Explicit and implicit perceptual cues of what behavior is expected in a situation.

Departmentalization The grouping into departments of similar, logically connected work activities.

Dependent variable A variable whose changes are the consequences of changes in other variables.

Dialectical inquiry method A method in which decision makers first examine their assumptions, then negate their assumptions, and then create countersolutions that are based on the negated assumptions.

Differentiation Separating and focusing on the differences between individuals, groups, and the activities in an organization.

Discriminant function An optimal weighting of a set of variables to show the maximum statistical discrimination between two groups.

Discrimination (social) The acceptance or rejection of people solely on the basis of their age, sex, race, ethnicity, or membership in a particular group or organization.

Division of labor The breakdown of a complex task into components so that different individuals are responsible for a limited set of more closely connected or similar activities, instead of the task as a whole.

Dogmatism A close-minded rigid style with beliefs that are authoritarian in content.

Downsizing Making smaller.

Dramaturgy Managing impressions by controlling information or cues to be imparted to others.

Dual-careers family A family in which both the husband and wife hold jobs or otherwise pursue careers.

Dyad A two-person group.

Dynamic correlation A correlation of a predictor with successive criteria that change as the criteria change in time.

E

Efficiency The use of minimum costs and resources in achieving organizational objectives.

Ego The part of one's personality that is oriented toward acting reasonably and realistically. (See *Id* and *Superego*)

Ego ideal A partly conscious image of oneself at one's future best.

Empathy The internalization of the feelings of another person.

Encoding The translation of information into a series of symbols for communication.

Equity The fairness of rewards and punishments; a situation in which the ratio of outcomes to inputs for a person is equal to the same ratio for comparison persons.

Ethnocentrism The rejection of foreigners, aliens, and out-groups; the extreme favoring of one's own group. Also belief that the home country is superior to other countries and that methods that work at home can be exported elsewhere. (See *Geocentrism* and *Polycentrism*)

Expectancy An estimate or judgment of the likelihood that some outcome or event will occur.

Expectancy theory The theory that an effort to achieve high performance is a function of the perceived likelihood that high performance can be achieved and will be rewarded if achieved and that the reward will be worth the effort that is expended.

Experiment The manipulation of one or more independent variables and the control of other related variables to observe one or more dependent variables.

Experimental control The elimination or holding of some variables constant to exam-

ine the effects of other variables that are allowed to vary.

External environment The environment outside the organization or the independent group.

External validity The conclusiveness with which findings can be generalized to other populations and settings.

Extrinsic rewards Pay, promotion, and fringe benefits, apart from the satisfaction that is derived from the work itself.

F

F test A test that determines whether the greater variance in the means among groups compared to the variance within the groups cannot be accounted for by chance.

Factor analysis A statistical technique to extract the smallest number of underlying factors accounting for a larger set of variables.

Factor loading The correlation of any particular variable with an extracted factor.

Factor matrix A matrix whose entries are the factor loadings obtained from a factor analysis.

Factor validation The validity of scores derived from a factor analysis.

Fear of success The fear that envy and dislike by others will accompany one's success.

Feedback The receivers' expression of their reaction to the sender's message or actions. Also, information about the results of one's behavior, efforts, or performance that can result in correction and control.

Field experiment The use of the controlled laboratory method in a real-life setting.

Field study The examination of the relations and interactions among variables in real-life settings but without the manipulation of variables as in a field experiment.

Field theory The theory that social behavior is a function of one's environment, as well as of one's attitudes and personality.

First impression One's impression of others that is formed early in a relationship and that often has a lasting impact.

First-line managers Managers who are at the lowest level in the management hierarchy and who are responsible only for the work of operating employees, not for the work of other managers.

First-order factors Factors that are extracted from an original set of variables.

Flexible organization An organization in

which the policies, structure, relationships, and jobs are loosely defined and open to alteration.

Forecasting The prediction of outcomes and future trends.

Formal authority Legitimate or position power; the right to exert influence because of one's hierarchical position in the organization.

Formal group A group that is created by a formal authority and is directed toward achieving specific objectives.

Formalization A situation in which rules, policies, and procedures in organizations are written and institutionalized. (See *Bureaucracy*)

Functional organization An organization that is departmentalized so that those engaged in the same functional activity, such as marketing, are grouped into one department.

G

Game theory The explanation of the behavior of rational people in competitive and conflict situations.

Gender Grammatical categories, male, female, and neuter, such as he, she, and it. Commonly misapplied to the two biologically distinct sexes, male and female.

General factor The factor present in every variable of the set.

General manager An individual who is responsible for all departments within a larger division, such as a manufacturing plant.

Geocentrism A world view of management, operations, and opportunities rather than one limited to a single nation or nationality (ethnocentrism) or an independent collection of countries (polycentrism).

Grapevine The paths through which informal communications are passed in an organization.

Group decision support system A computerized information system in a group meeting to make better use of information for group decisions.

Group think Faulty processes resulting in group decisions that are poorer than those of the individual members working alone.

H

Halo effect The influence of overall impressions on the rating of a specific characteristic.

Hawthorne effect The performance of employees who receive special attention will be better simply because the employees received that attention.

Hedonism Motivation that is attained by gaining pleasure and avoiding pain.

Heuristics "Rule of thumb" solutions to problems that are based on past experience, rather than explicit formulas.

Hierarchical factor analysis The systematic organization of a factor solution from the simplest two-factor solution to a complex of many factors.

Hierarchical organization In a hierarchical organization, except for the member at the top, each member has a superior and except for those at the bottom, each member has one or more subordinates.

Higher-order factors Factors that are extracted from a set of first-order factors (also called second-order factors).

Higher-order interactions The analysis of the interacting effects of three or more independent variables.

Human resource information system A computerized collection, storage, maintenance, and retrieval system for an organization's information about its personnel.

Hygiene factors Benefits that cause dissatisfaction with the job if they are not present but that do not add to satisfaction if they are present.

Hypothesis A conditional prediction about the relationship among concepts or among variables, often generated from a theory, that is subjected to empirical verification.

I

Id The part of the personality that is the repository of basic drives and unsocialized impulses, including sex and aggression.

Ideology A strongly held set of values, attitudes, and beliefs that explain the world.

Implicit theories The tendencies of individuals to weave characteristics of others or characteristics of events into explanatory patterns.

In-basket test A test in which an examinee is given a booklet that contains a sample of memos, bulletins, notes, letters, and reports representing a manager's in-basket and is scored on the way the individual prepares to deal with various issues contained in the material.

Incremental adjustments Problem solving in which each successive action represents a small change.

Independent variable A variable that is manipulated in an experiment whose changes are considered to be the cause of changes in other variables (the dependent variables); variables selected in a survey for the same purpose.

Informal communication Communication that is not officially sanctioned. (See *Grapevine*)

Informal group A group that voluntarily arises from the needs of individuals and the attraction of people to one another because of common values and interests; an unofficial group that is created without the sanction of a higher organizational authority.

Informal organization The relationships between members of an organization that are based on friendship, propinquity, and personal and social needs.

Ingratiation An attempt to influence other persons by flattering them.

Insider trading Trading of stocks and bonds on knowledge from inside the firm that is not available to the public.

Integration The joining of elements to work together in a unified way.

Internal environment Workers, managers, technology, working conditions, and the culture in the organization.

Internalized Behavior, compliance, and conformity are consistent with one's beliefs and values.

Internal locus of control The belief that rewards that one receives result from one's own efforts, rather than because of chance or the effects of others.

Internal validity The conclusiveness with which the effects of the experimental treatments are established in an experiment.

Intrapsychic tension Conflicts within an individual.

Intrinsic rewards Satisfaction from doing the work itself apart from the pay, promotion, and benefits; feelings of growth, esteem, and achievement from doing a job well.

Introjection The unconscious or subconscious attribution of others' motives to oneself.

Ipsative scores A set of scores generated for the same person, rather than a single score per person generated for a set of persons.

J

Job A collection of tasks grouped together similarly in a number of similar positions in a given organization.

Job enlargement The combining of various operations at a similar level into one job to provide more variety for workers.

Job enrichment Providing a job with more challenge, meaning, autonomy, and responsibility.

Job satisfaction Attitudes and feelings about one's job.

Job scope The number of separate operations a particular job requires before a cycle is repeated.

Job specialization The division of work into standardized, simplified tasks.

L

Laboratory study Research in which the effects of extraneous factors that are irrelevant to the problem are minimized by isolating the research in an artificial setting; elements thought to be important in real life are reproduced and manipulated under controlled conditions.

Lame duck A leader whose power has declined because his or her tenure in the leadership position is near its end.

Lateral (or horizontal) communication Communication between departments of an organization that generally follows the work flow, thus providing a direct channel for coordination and problem solving.

Lateral (or horizontal) relationship Direct contact between members of different departments at the same hierarchical level that bypasses the chain of command in their own department.

Learned helplessness A condition in which persons become passive, depressed, and unable to learn to cope with the situation.

Leniency bias The tendency to be more favorable and positive than is justified by evidence.

Libido Psychic energy that is expended in satisfying different needs.

Likert scale A scale in which respondents are asked to indicate how much they agree or disagree with an attitudinal statement.

Line personnel Those managers and workers who are directly responsible for achieving organizational goals (in contrast to staff personnel who provide support services for the line personnel).

Linear programming The optimal allocation of limited resources to attain a goal.

Linguistics The scientific study of language.

Locus of control The degree to which individuals are controlled by their internal motives, habits, and values, rather than by external forces.

Logic Principles and criteria of validity in thought and demonstration; the application of truth tables, the relations of propositions, and the consistency of deductions and assumptions.

Long-linked technology Serial interdependence between work activities; one task can be performed only after another task has been completed.

M

Management by objectives (MBO) A formal set of procedures to review the progress toward common goals of organizational superiors and their immediate subordinates.

Management information system (MIS) A formal, usually computerized, system to provide management with information.

Management science (See *Operations research*)

Manipulation An attempt to influence others in which the manipulator tries to conceal the effort from the target of the influence.

Marginality The position of people at the boundary between two societies who are often uncertain about their identity and status.

Markov model The mathematical transformation of one set of states and events into another.

Mathematical model A facsimile of reality in mathematical terms; a description of a process and parameters and their relationships to one another and to environments.

Matriarchal A female-dominated family or society in which the woman (wife or mother) is most influential.

Matrix organization An organization in which each subordinate reports to both a functional (or divisional) manager and to a project (or group) manager.

MBA Master of Business Administration.

Mechanistic organization An organization in which the operations are rule based.

Mediation A situation in which a third party assists two parties in conflict to reach agreement.

Mentors Individuals who pass on the benefits of their knowledge and experience to younger and less experienced individuals.

Message Encoded information sent by a sender to a receiver.

Mestizo Mixed Indian and European.

Meta-analysis Estimation of the true correlation between two variables from the distribution of sample correlations corrected for the different size of samples, restrictions in range, and unreliabilities of measurement.

Middle managers Managers at the middle levels of the organizational hierarchy who are responsible for the direction of the lower-level supervisors reporting to them.

Mission The stated purposes of the organization.

Model A facsimile that captures the important essentials of reality; may be conceptual, mathematical, or physical.

Modeling Learning by imitation; behaving in the same way as observed in another person to make a certain response.

Moderated regression analysis An optimal prediction equation that includes the effects of moderator variables.

Moderator variable A variable that affects the influence of a second variable on other variables.

Monotonic Numbers arranged so that each is larger (or smaller) than the one preceding it in the sequence.

Multinational corporation (MNC) A corporation with operations and divisions in numerous countries but that is controlled by headquarters in one country.

Multinational firm An organization that locates, trades, or produces products or offers services in several countries.

Multiple regression The optimal weighting of a set of predictor variables to minimize the error of prediction of a criterion.

Myth A dramatic narrative of imagined events and fantasies, usually to explain origins and developments.

N

Negative reinforcement (See *Aversive reinforcement*)

Network A pattern of interconnections among individuals, groups, or organizations.

Nominal group technique The pooling of the ideas of individuals without their meeting to generate or accumulate the pool of ideas.

Nomological network The web of logical connections among constructs.

Nomothetical network (See *Nomological network*)

Nonprogrammed decisions Specific solutions that emerge from unstructured processes to deal with nonroutine problems.

Normative model A model that prescribes a solution to a problem.

Normative scores Raw scores scaled in relation to those of the rest of the population, for example percentiles and standard scores.

Norms Shared group expectations about behavior; socially defined and enforced standards about how the world should be interpreted and how one should behave in it.

NROTC Naval Reseach Officers' Training Corps for the U.S. Navy.

O

Objectives The targeted goals of individuals, groups, or organizations toward which resources and efforts are channeled.

Oblique dimensions Dimensions inclined toward each other at some angle other than 90°, representing their correlation; not orthogonal.

Occupation A collection of similar jobs existing in different firms.

One-way communication Any communication from the sender without a reply from the receiver.

Open system A system that transforms inputs from its environment to outputs to its environment; its general principles may explain organizational behavior.

Operant conditioning A behavioral modification technique in which cued responses are strengthened (more likely to be repeated) as a result of reinforcements (consequences of the behavior).

Operational definition A specification of the procedures or operations by which a concept is sensed and measured.

Operations research Mathematical techniques for modeling, analysis, and solution of management problems.

Organic organization An organization in which operations are subject to modification through learning from feedback.

Organizational climate Employees' atti-

tudes toward the organization and their satisfaction with it.

Organizational conflict Disagreement between organizational members and groups over the allocation of scarce resources, how to engage in interdependent work activities; disagreements arising from different assumptions, goals, identifications, or statuses.

Organizational culture The norms, values, attitudes, and beliefs, evidenced in myths, stories, jargon, and rituals, that are shared by organizational members.

Organizational design The creation of the organizational structure that is most appropriate for the strategy, people, technology, and tasks of the organization.

Organizational development A long-range effort to improve an organization's problem-solving and renewal process.

Organizational goals An organization's purpose, mission, and objectives that form the bases of its strategy.

Organizational structure The arrangement and interrelationship of the various components and positions in an organization.

Organization chart A diagram displaying the functions, departments, and positions in an organization.

Orthogonal dimensions Dimensions that are at right angles to each other; uncorrelated, independent dimensions.

Overload The lack of capacity to meet performance expectations.

P

p value The probability of a given outcome or event, on a scale from 0.00 (not possible) to 1.00 (certain).

Parsimonious The simple but accurate explanation of a phenomenon that avoids more complicated explanations because the simplified one is adequate.

Partial reinforcement A schedule of reinforcement in which rewards are given intermittently.

Patriarchical A male-dominated family or society in which the men are much more in power and control than are the women.

Perception An immediately sensed experience of other persons or objects, modified and organized by the perceiver's personal characteristics and by social influences.

Perceptual defense A selective perception

in which a person substitutes innocuous perceptions for unpleasant stimuli.

Performance appraisal An evaluation of an individual's performance by comparing it to standards or objectives.

Personal construct A concept that is used by a particular individual to categorize events and other persons' behaviors.

Personality The dynamic organization of the abilities, attitudes, beliefs, and motives of a particular individual that contribute to the individual's reaction to his or her environment.

Phenomenological Of or related to comprehending the environment above and beyond the objective environment.

Placebo A substance or a condition, used as an experimental control, that should have no effects relevant to the experiment.

Policy General guidelines for decision making.

Policy capturing A multiple regression procedure in which the regression weights underlying the policies that influenced the decision-makers are determined.

Polycentrism The view that because countries are different, local control is best for organizing operations.

Population The total collection of people or cases from which a sample is drawn.

Position power Power that is inherent in the formal position occupied by the incumbent.

Positive reinforcer The consequence of behavior that is desirable, pleasant, or needed. When linked to the behavior, the positive reinforcer increases the probability that the behavior will be repeated in the same or similar situations.

Post hoc analysis A statistical analysis that is chosen after the experimental data have been collected, not as a part of the original design of the experiment.

Power structure A set of relationships among different members or units of an organization that is based on the differences in power among them.

Prejudice A negative evaluation of a person because of the person's sex, age, race, ethnicity, or membership in another group or organization.

Primary effect The predominant effect of the first information received about persons, objects, or issues upon learning, retention, judgment, or opinion about them.

Prisoner's dilemma The choice when a better outcome for one player is incompatible with the choice resulting in a better outcome for a competing player. This dilemma leads to both players making choices that have unfavorable results for both of them.

Probability sample A sample chosen in such a way that every member of the population has a known, usually equal, probability of being included.

Process consultation Consultation in which members of an organization are helped to understand and change the ways in which they work together.

Productivity Performance relative to resources; output divided by input; quantity and quality of output in a given period.

Programmed decisions Solutions to routine problems determined by rules, procedures, or habits.

Projection The attribution of one's own motives to others, usually unconciously or subconciously. (See *Assumed similarity*)

Propinquity Physical proximity.

Prototype An idealized image or the first of its kind on which copies are based.

Psychological contract Mutual expectations between an individual and an organization or between subordinates and superiors of how work is to be performed and how they will relate to each other; the rights, privileges, and obligations of each to each other.

Psychosocial Psychological elements combine with social aspects to affect relationships.

Purpose The primary role of an organization in society in producing goods or services.

Q

Q-technique A technique in which a set of paired scores is correlated across different variables for two persons or cases.

Quality circle Periodic meetings of employees and management personnel to solve quality, production, and related problems.

Quality control The process that ensures that goods and services meet predetermined standards.

Quality of work life The value of work that takes into account the well-being of the employee as well as that of the organization.

R

R & D Research and development.

R-technique A technique in which the paired scores on two variables are correlated for a number of persons or cases.

Random sample A probability sample in which members are drawn in a random manner from a list of prospects that enumerates the population.

Rational approach An approach in which conclusions are arrived at by reasoning.

Rational-economic man A theory that fully informed people are motivated primarily by money and self-interest.

Real-time operation An operation in which an event is controled by information generated by the event.

Recency effect The predominant effect of the most recent information received on learning, retention, judgment, or opinion about persons, objects, or issues.

Reference group A group with whom we identify and compare ourselves.

Reflect The sign of a variable is changed so the variable is now opposite in meaning.

Refreezing A process in which new behavior becomes the norm through support and reinforcement.

Reinforcement The consequence of behavior that influences whether the behavior will be evoked again under the same or similar stimulus conditions.

Reinforcement schedule The pattern of reinforcement that can affect how quickly behavior is modified, shaped, and learned and how resistant it is to change or to extinction.

Relative deprivation The tendency to be dissatisfied with one's own status and compensation relative to that of those with whom we compare ourselves, to expectations, and to comparable conditions.

Reliability The consistency of measurement, as seen in the stability of scores over time or in the equivalence of scores on two forms of a test af the same attributes. (See *Coefficient alpha*)

Representative sample A sample that is composed of different members proportionate to their types in the population.

Response sets A systematic way of answering a question that is not directly related to the content of the question but to the form of the question and the alternative answers.

Risky shift The tendency for groups to make a decision that is less conservative than one that would be made alone by each of its individual members.

Rite An elaborate, dramatic, ceremonial activity that consolidates cultural expressions into a social event.

Rites of passage Rites in which a person passes from an organizational outsider to an organizational insider. They convey the organization's norms and values symbolically. In society, they include, for example, confirmation, graduation, and marriage.

Ritual A fixed way of enacting a set of rites within an organizational culture.

Role A socially defined pattern of behavior that is expected of an individual in a designated function in a particular position within a group, organization, or society.

Role ambiguity A condition of uncertainty about what is expected and what role behavior will be accepted and rewarded.

Role boundaries Limits of the role behavior that are expected.

Role conflict A situation in which persons are faced with meeting conflicting demands. Conflict can arise between values within a role, between competing roles, or from the demands of others.

Role overload A situation in which role requirements exceed the limits of time, resources, and capabilities.

Role perception What an individual sees are the behaviors needed to enact a role.

Rotation Moving factor axes and their hyperplanes around the 0,0 coordinate to allow more points representing factor loadings to fall in these hyperplanes.

ROTC Reserve Officers' Training Corps for the U.S. Army or U.S. Air Force.

S

Sample A portion of a population that is selected for study in lieu of the complete population.

Sampling error Deviation of any sample statistic from the population value.

Satisfice The choice of a suboptimal alternative when making a decision that meets some minimal criteria of acceptance.

Scapegoating The displacement of hostility toward a weaker available target when the source of frustration is too powerful or not available for attack.

Scientific method The systematic use of deduction, induction, and verification of predictions by the collection of relevant data.

Selective perception Sensing some aspects

of the environment while ignoring other aspects.

Self-actualization   Using one's capacities fully in meaningful, personally satisfying endeavors.

Self-concept   The way people perceive and evaluate themselves.

Self-fulfilling prophecy   The expectation of a reality influences the fulfillment of that reality.

Self-serving bias   Bias to judge oneself favorably, crediting oneself for successes but blaming others and external factors for failures.

Semantic differential rating   Graphic scale with defined extremes, such as a term at one end and its antonym at the other, but undefined anchors in between.

Sense making   Attributing meaning to experience.

Significance   (See *Statistical significance*)

Simple stucture   A structure in which a rotation solution is achieved so that each variable is maximally correlated with as few factors as possible; the variance of the factor loadings is maximized in the VARIMAX solution.

Simulation   The representation of the necessary elements of some object, phenomenon, system, or environment to facilitate control and study. The representation mirrors or maps the effects of various changes in the original, enabling the researcher or trainee to study, analyze, and understand the original by means of the behavior of the model.

Single-source bias   An inflated value that occurs when the same rater supplies the information for the pairs of variables to be correlated.

Smallest-space analysis and mapping   The mathematical procedure to locate and display optimally in two dimensions, a sample of individuals or cases according to their respective distances in measurements from each other.

Social desirability   A response set to answer questions about oneself in the socially approved manner.

Social determinism   The view that the course of history emerges only as an expression, instrument, or consequence of historical laws.

Social distance   The acceptable degree of closeness (physical, social, or psychological) between leaders and subordinates and between members of particular ethnic groups.

Socialization   Learning the norms of one's group, organization, or society and acquiring its distinctive values, beliefs, and characteristics.

Social loafing   A condition in which workers reduce or withhold effort on a group task.

Socioemotional   Interpersonal; dealing with the social and emotional aspects of the relations between people.

Sociometric measure   A measure based on the nominations of peers; who chooses whom can provide a display of the informal structure of relations in a group.

Specialization   The performance of only some specific part of a whole collection of tasks by an individual worker.

Specification equation   An equation that indicates a designated individual's performance on a test in terms of factor subscores weighted by factor loadings.

Specific factor   The statistical representation of some variable based on only one variable in contrast to common factors which are based on two or more variables.

Staff   Individuals or groups who provide line personnel with advice and services.

Stakeholders   Individuals and groups who gain from the organization's successes and lose from its failures.

Standard deviation   A measure of how much variability is present in a set of scores. It is the square root of the variance.

Statistical prediction   Objective judgments about people based on data combined by means of formulas or mechanical methods.

Statistical significance   The probability that a given mean statistic could not have occurred by chance alone.

Statistical test   A mathematical procedure for determining the probability that obtained results are due to chance.

Stepwise multiple regression analyses   Analyses in which one predictor variable at a time is added to the regression equation. The process is halted when the next step adds more error than predictive value to the optimal combination of predictors.

Stereotype   A standard image applied to all members of the same group that ignores the variations among them.

Strategic planning   The formulation of an organization's objectives and how to achieve them.

Stratified random sample   A probability sample whose members are selected by dividing the population into several categories, then selecting respondents randomly from each category. (See *Representative sample*)

Structure   A pattern of prescribed or observed consistencies in relations among members of a group or organization.

Sunk costs   Money spent or resources already used.

Superego   The part of the personality that is oriented toward doing what is regarded as morally right and proper: one's conscience, ego ideal, and ideal self-image.

Superordinate goals   Goals around which divergent parties can rally to collaborate to achieve the goals.

Switch hitter   Ambidextrous; one who can respond in alternative ways.

Symbols   Emblems, tokens, and signs representing ideas, terms, and objects.

Synergy   Cooperative efforts among people or units that generate more motivation than would the isolated operation of the units or people.

System boundary   The boundary between the system and its environment. It is rigid in a closed system (not interactive with its environment) and flexible in an open system (interactive with its environment).

T

t-test   A test that determines whether the average statistics for two samples of subjects cannot be accounted for by chance.

Task force   A temporary group established to address a specific problem. (See *Ad hoc group*)

Tautology   Circular reasoning; for example, arguing that A caused B because B caused A.

Team building   Improving relationships among members and the accomplishment of the task by diagnosing problems in team processes affecting the team's performance.

Territoriality   An innate drive in many species of animals to defend their own habitat.

Theory   A system of concepts, rules about the interconnections of the concepts, and ways of linking the concepts to observed facts.

Theory X   A theory that assumes that the average worker dislikes work, is lazy, has little ambition, and must be directed or threatened with punishment to perform adequately.

Theory Y   A theory that assumes the average worker can enjoy work and be committed, involved, and responsible.

Triad A three-person group.

U

Unfreezing Making old ways unacceptable so that changes are readily accepted and can occur.

Unobtrusive measures Measures obtained without the knowledge of the persons studied.

V

Valence The values or motivating strength of a reward to an individual.

Validity The accuracy or correctness of a method or measurement according to expert opinion, its predictive ability, or its correlation with a construct representing its true meaning.

Values What people consider right, good, and important.

Variable Any quantity that may take on several points on a dimension.

Variance The mean of the sum of squares of the deviations of each of a set of scores from its mean; the square of the standard deviation.

Varimax A solution in factor analysis in which the rotation achieves a maximum variation among the factor loadings so that variables correlate as highly as possible with as few factors as possible and as low as possible with as many other factors as possible.

Verification The collection of facts to support or refute hypotheses.

Vertical communication Communication up or down the chain of command.

W

Walk-around management Top managers visit with employees at their workplace.

Whistle-blowers Employees who voluntarily report infractions of the rules, violations of ethics, or illegal actions by other members of the organization.

Z

Zero loading A loading in a factor analysis, a correlation between a variable and a factor so small that it can be attributed to a chance difference from zero.

References

Aaronovich, G. D., & Khotin, B. I. (1929). The problem of imitation in monkeys. *Novoye v Refleksologii i Fiziologii Nervnoy Systemi, 3,* 378–390.

Abdel-Halim, A. A. (1980a). Effects of higher order need strength on the job performance–job satisfaction relationship. *Personnel Psychology, 33,* 335–347.

Abdel-Halim, A. A. (1980b). Effects of person-job compatibility on managerial reactions to role ambiguity. *Organizational Behavior and Human Performance, 26,* 193–211.

Abdel-Halim, A. A. (1981). Personality and task moderators of subordinate responses to perceived leader behavior. *Human Relations, 34,* 73–88.

Abdel-Halim, A. A. (1982). Social support and managerial affective responses to job stress. *Occupational Behaviour, 3,* 281–295.

Abdel-Halim, A. A. (1983a). Effects of task and personality characteristics on subordinate responses to participative decision making. *Academy of Management Journal, 26,* 477–484.

Abdel-Halim, A. A. (1983b). Power equalization, participative decision-making, and individual differences. *Human Relations, 36,* 683–704.

Abdel-Halim, A. A., & Rowland, K. M. (1976). Some personality determinants of the effects of participation: A further investigation. *Personnel Psychology, 29,* 41–55.

Abegglen, J. C. (1958). *The Japanese factory: Aspects of its social organization.* New York: Free Press.

Abegglen, J. C. (1984). *Management succession and organizational continuity in present-day Japan.* Paper, 75th Anniversary Colloquium, Harvard Business School, Boston.

Aboud, J. (1968). The interactive effect of group cohesion and supervisory style on the productivity of college students on a motor skill test. *Dissertation Abstracts, 29,* 1853.

Abrahamson, M. (1966). *Interpersonal accommodation.* Princeton, NJ: Van Nostrand.

Abrahamson, M. (1967). *The professional in the organization.* Chicago: Rand McNally.

Abrahamson, M. (1969). Position, personality, and leadership. *Psychological Record, 19,* 113–122.

Abramson, L. Y., Seligman, M. E. P., & Teasdale, J. D. (1978). Learned helplessness in humans: Critique and reformulation. *Journal of Abnormal Psychology, 87,* 49–74.

ABS (American Behavioral Scientist). (1965). *The guide to recent publications in the social and behavioral sciences.* New York: American Behavioral Scientist.

Ackerson, L. (1942). *Children's behavior problems: Relative importance and intercorrelations among traits.* Chicago: University of Chicago Press.

Ackoff, R. L., & Emery, F. E. (1972). *On purposeful systems.* Chicago: Aldine-Atherton.

Adair, J. (1973). *Action-centered leadership.* New York: McGraw-Hill.

Adams, E. F. (1976). *Influences of minority supervisors on subordinate attitudes.* Unpublished manuscript.

Adams, E. F. (1978). A multivariate study of subordinate perceptions of and attitudes toward minority and majority managers. *Journal of Applied Psychology, 63*(3), 277–288.

Adams, H. (1984). Red powerlessness: Bureaucratic authoritarianism on Indian reservations. *Cornell Journal of Social Relations, 18*(1), 28–40.

Adams, J., & Hicks, J. M. (undated). *Leadership performance appraisal ratings during cadet field training.* Unpublished manuscript.

Adams, J., Instone, D., Rice, R. W., & Prince, H. T., II. (1981). *Critical incidents of good and bad leadership.* Paper, American Psychological Association, Los Angeles.

Adams, J., Priest, R. F., & Prince, H. T., II. (1986). Achievement motive: Analyzing the validity of the wofo. *Psychology of Women Quarterly, 9,* 357–369.

Adams, J., Prince, H., II, Instone, D., & Rice, R. W. (1984). West Point: Critical incidents of leadership. *Armed Forces and Society, 10,* 597–611.

Adams, J., & Yoder, J. D. (1985). *Effective leadership for women and men.* Norwood, NJ: Ablex.

Adams, J. S. (1963). Wage inequities, productivity and work quality. *Industrial Relations, 3,* 9–16.

Adams, J. S., & Romney, A. K. (1959). A functional analysis of authority. *Psychological Review, 66,* 234–251.

Adams, S. (1952). Effect of equalitarian atmospheres upon the performance of bomber crews. *American Psychologist, 7,* 398.

Adams, S. (1953). Status congruency as a variable in small group performance. *Social Forces, 32,* 16–22.

Adams, S., & Fyffe, D. (1969). *The corporate promotables.* Houston, TX: Gulf.

Adjutant General's Department (1919). *The personnel system of the United States Army.* Washington, DC: U.S. Army.

Adkinson, D. M. (1983). The vice presidency as apprenticeship. *Presidential Studies Quarterly, 13,* 212–218.

Adler, S. (1982). *Subordinate imitation of supervisor behavior: The role of supervisor power and subordinate self-esteem.* Paper, International Congress of Applied Psychology, Edinburgh.

Adorno, T. W., Frenkel-Brunswik, E., Levinson, D. J., & Sanford, R. N. (1950). *The authoritarian personality.* New York: Harper.

Agor, W. H. (1986a). *The logic of intuitive decision-making: A research-based approach for top management.* New York: Quorum Books.

Agor, W. H. (1986b). The logic of intuition: How top executives make important decisions. *Organizational Dynamics, 14*(3), 5–18.

Aiken, E. G. (1965a). Changes in interpersonal descriptions accompanying the operant conditioning of verbal frequency in groups. *Journal of Verbal Learning and Verbal Behavior, 4,* 243–247.

Aiken, E. G. (1965b). Interaction process analysis changes accompanying operant conditioning of verbal frequency in small groups. *Perceptual and Motor Skills, 21,* 52–54.

Aiken, M., & Bacharach, S. B. (1985). Environmental influences on authority and consensus in organizations. *Research in the Sociology of Organizations, 4,* 351–377.

Aiken, W. J., Smits, S. J., & Lollar, D. J. (1972). Leadership behavior and job satisfaction in state rehabilitation agencies. *Personnel Psychology, 25,* 65–73.

AIR (American Institute for Research). (1961). *Situational problems for leadership training. Part IV—categorized bibliography of leadership research literature.* Washington, DC: American Institute for Research.

Ajzen, I., & Fishbein, M. (1980). *Understanding attitudes and predicting social behavior.* Englewood Cliffs, NJ: Prentice-Hall.

Akhtar, S. S., & Haleem, A. (1980). Differences between newly-promoted supervisors and workers with regard to "consideration" and "initiating structure." *Journal of Psychological Researches, 24,* 90–95.

Akin, G. (1978). Grounded theory doesn't come easily: A response to Dunn and Swierczek. *Journal of Applied Behavioral Science, 15,* 557–559.

Akin, G. (1987). Varieties of managerial learning. *Organizational Dynamics, 16*(2), 36–48.

Akin, G., & Hopelain, D. (1986). Finding the culture of productivity. *Organizational Dynamics, 14*(3), 19–32.

Al-Hajjeh, A. A. (1984). Managerial leadership and work-related values of American and Middle Eastern nationals: A cross-cultural study. *Dissertation Abstracts International, 45*(6A), 1850.

Al-Jafary, A., & Hollingsworth, A. T. (1983). An exploratory study of managerial practices in the Arabian Gulf region. *Journal of International Business Studies, 14,* 143–152.

Alban, B. T., & Seashore, E. W. (1978). Women in authority: An experienced view. *Journal of Applied Behavioral Science, 14,* 21.

Albaum, G. (1964). Horizontal information flow: An explanatory study. *Academy of Management Journal, 7,* 21–33.

Albrecht, P. A., Glaser, E. M., & Marks, J. (1964). Validation of a multiple-assessment procedure for managerial personnel. *Journal of Applied Psychology, 48,* 351–360.

Albright, L. (1966). *A research study of the Vernon Psychological Laboratory Test Battery and other measures for field sales managers.* Chicago: American Oil Co. (Reported in Campbell, Dunnette, et al., 1970, 191.)

Albrook, R. C. (1967, May). Participative management: Time for a second look. *Fortune, 75,* 166–170; 197–200.

Alcorn, R. S. (1974). Leadership and stability in mid-nineteenth century America: A case study of an Illinois town. *Journal of American History, 61,* 685–702.

Aldag, R. J., & Brief, A. P. (1977). Relationships between leader behavior variability indicies and subordinate responses. *Personnel Psychology, 30,* 419–426.

Aldag, R. J., & Brief, A. P. (1981). *Managing organizational behavior.* St. Paul, MN: West Publishing.

Alderfer, C. P. (1967). An organizational syndrome. *Administrative Science Quarterly, 12,* 440–460.

Alderfer, C. P. (1969). Job enlargement and the organizational context. *Personnel Psychology, 22,* 418–426.

Alderfer, C. P. (1970). Management development and intergroup relations. *Experimental Publications System, American Psychological Association,* No. 206A.

Alderfer, C. P. (1972). *Existence, relatedness, and growth: Human needs in organizational settings.* New York: Free Press.

Alexander, E. R. (1979). The design of alternatives in organizational contexts: Pilot study. *Administrative Science Quarterly, 24,* 382–404.

Alexander, F. (1942). *Our age of unreason.* Philadelphia: Lippincott.

Alexander, K. D. (1984a). The promise and perils of worker participation in management. *American Journal of Economics and Sociology, 43,* 197–204.

Alexander, L. D. (1979a). The effect level in the hierarchy and functional area have on the extent Mintzberg's roles are required by managerial jobs. *Proceedings, Academy of Management,* Atlanta, GA, 186–189.

Alexander, L. D. (1979b). The effect of level in the hierarchy and functional area on the extent to which Mintzberg's managerial roles are required by managerial jobs. *Dissertation Abstracts, 40,* 2156A.

Alford, R. R., & Scoble, H. M. (1968). Community leadership, education, and political behavior. *American Sociological Review, 33,* 259–272.

Algattan, A. A. (1985). *The path-goal theory of leadership: An empirical and longitudinal analysis.* Unpublished manuscript.

Algattan, A. R. A. (1985). *Test of the path-goal theory of leadership in the multinational domain.* Paper, Academy of Management, San Diego, CA.

Ali, A. J. (1982). An empirical investigation of managerial value systems for working in Iraq. *Dissertation Abstracts International, 43*(7A), 2429.

Ali, M. R., Humbalo, R., Khaleque, A., & Rahman, A. (1982). *Intergroup conflict in industry: A cross-cultural study.* Paper, International Congress of Applied Psychology, Edinburgh.

Alkire, A. A., Collum, M. E., Kaswan, J., & Love, L. R. (1968). Information exchange and accuracy of verbal communication under social power conditions. *Journal of Personality and Social Psychology, 9,* 301–308.

Allee, W. C. (1945). Social biology of subhuman groups. *Sociometry, 8,* 21–29.

Allee, W. C. (1951). *Cooperation among animals, with human implications.* New York: Schuman.

Allee, W. C., Emerson, A. E., Park, O., Park, T., & Schmidt, K. P. (1949). *Principles of animal ecology.* Philadelphia: Saunders.

Allegro, J. T., Bagchus, P. M., & Hofstee, W. K. (1970). Konstruktie van een gedwongen keuzeleiderschapsschaal (LOS). *Nederlands Tijdschrift Psychologie Grensgebieden, 25,* 451–463.

Allen, L. A. (1957). Does managerial development develop managers? *Personnel, 34,* 18–25.

Allen, L. A. (1958). *Management and organization.* New York: McGraw-Hill.

Allen, L., & Sutherland, R. (1963). *Role conflict and congruences.* Austin, TX: Hogg Foundation.

Allen, M. P. (1974). The structure of interorganizational elite cooptation. *American Sociological Review, 39,* 393–406.

Allen, M. P., & Panian, S. K. (1982). Power, performance and succession in the large corporation. *Administrative Science Quarterly, 27,* 538–547.

Allen, M. P., Panian, S. K., & Lotz, R. E. (1979). Managerial succession and organizational performance: A recalcitrant problem revisited. *Administrative Science Quarterly, 24,* 167–180.

Allen, P. (1981). Managers at work: A large scale study of the managerial job in New York City government. *Academy of Management Journal, 24,* 613–619.

Allen, R. W., Madison, D. L., Renwick, P. A., & Mayes, B. T. (1979). Organizational politics: Tactics and characteristics of its actors. *California Management Review, 22*(1), 77–83.

Allen, T. H. (1981). Situational management roles: A conceptual model. *Dissertation Abstracts International, 42* (2A) 465.

Allen, T. J. (1966). Studies of the problem-solving process in engineering design. *IEEE Transactions on Engineering Management, EM-13*(2), 72–83.

Allen, T. J., & Cohen, S. I. (1969). Information flow in research and development laboratories. *Administrative Science Quarterly, 14,* 12–19.

Allen, T. J., & Gerstberger, P. G. (1973). A field experiment to improve communications in a product engineering department: The non-territorial office. *Human Factors, 15*(5), 487–498.

Allen, T. J., Lee, D. M. S., & Tushman, M. L. (1980). R & D performance as a function of internal communication, project management, and the nature of the work. *IEEE Transactions on Engineering Management, 27*(1), 2–12.

Allen, W. R. (1975a). Black and white leaders and subordinates: Leader choice and ratings, aspirations and expectancy of success. In D. Frederick & J. Guiltinan (Eds.), *New challenges for the decision sciences.* Amherst, MA: Northeast Region of the American Institute for Decision Sciences.

Allen, W. R. (1975b). A comparative analysis of black and white leadership in a naturalistic setting. *Dissertation Abstracts International, 36,* 2516.

Allen, W. R., & Ruhe, J. A. (1976). Verbal behavior by black and white leaders of biracial groups in two different environments. *Journal of Applied Psychology, 61,* 441–445.

Alloy, L. B., & Abramson, L. Y. (1982). Learned helplessness, depression, and the illusion of control. *Journal of Personality and Social Psychology, 42,* 1114–1126.

Allport, F. H. (1924). *Social psychology.* Boston: Houghton Mifflin.

Allport, F. H. (1962). A structuronomic conception of behavior: Individual and collective. *Journal of Abnormal Social Psychology, 64,* 3–30.

Allport, G. W., & Vernon, P. E. (1933). *Studies in expressive movement.* New York: Hafner Publishing.

Allport, G. W., Vernon, P. E., & Lindzey, G. (1960). *A study of values.* Boston: Houghton Mifflin.

Allswang, J. M., & Bova, P. (1964). *NORC social research 1941–64: An inventory of studies and publications in social research.* Chicago: University of Chicago, National Opinion Research Center.

Almquist, E. M. (1974). Sex stereotypes in occupational choice: The case for college women. *Journal of Vocational Behavior, 5,* 13–21.

Alpander, G. G. (1974). Planning management training programs for organizational development. *Personnel Journal, 53,* 15–21.

Alpander, G. G. (1986). Conceptual analysis of supervisory training programs in major U. S. corporations. *Proceedings, Academy of Management,* Chicago, 103–107.

Alpander, G. G., & Guttman, J. E. (1976). Contents and techniques of management development programs for women. *Personnel Journal, 55,* 76–79.

Alper, S. W. (1975). Racial differences in job and work environment priorities among newly hired college graduates. *Journal of Applied Psychology, 60,* 132–134.

Alsikafi, M., Jokinen, W. J., Spray, S. L., & Tracy, G. S. (1968). Managerial attitudes toward labor unions in a southern city. *Journal of Applied Psychology, 52,* 447–453.

Altman, I. (1966). Aspects of the criterion problem in small group research, II. Analysis of group tasks. *Acta Psychologica, 25,* 199–221.

Altman, I., Pendleton, C., & Terauds, A. (1960). *Annotations of small group research studies.* Arlington, VA: Human Sciences Research.

Alutto, J. A., & Acito, F. (1974). Decisional participation and sources of job satisfaction: A study of manufacturing personnel. *Academy of Management Journal, 17,* 160–167.

Alutto, J. A., & Belasco, J. A. (1972). A typology for participation in organizational decision making. *Administrative Science Quarterly, 17,* 117–125.

Alutto, J. A., & Hrebiniak, L. G. (1975). *Research on commitment to employing organizations: Preliminary findings on a study of managers graduating from engineering and MBA programs.* Paper, Academy of Management, New Orleans.

Alvarez, R. (1968). Informal reactions to deviance in simulated work organizations. *American Sociological Review, 33,* 895–912.

Alwon, G. J. (1980). Response to agencywide crisis: A model for administrative action. *Child Welfare, 59,* 335–346.

Amabile, T. M., & Gryskiewicz, S. S. (1987). *Creativity in the R & D laboratory* (Tech. Rep. No. 30). Greensboro, NC: Center for Creative Leadership.

American Psychological Association (1953). *Ethical standards of psychologists.* Washington, DC: American Psychological Association.

Amir, Y., Kovarsky, Y., & Sharan, S. (1970). Peer nominations as a predictor of multistage promotions in a ramified organization. *Journal of Applied Psychology, 5,* 462–469.

Anderhalter, D. F., Wilkins, W., & Rigby, M. K. (1952). *Peer rating relationships between officer and peer—candidate predictions of effectiveness as a company grade officer in the U.S. Marine Corps and the ability to predict estimated officer effectiveness of peers* (Tech. Rep. No. 2). St. Louis, MO: Washington University, Department of Psychology.

Anderson, B., & Nilsson, S. (1964). Studies in the reliability and validity of the critical incident technique. *Journal of Applied Psychology, 48*, 398–413.

Anderson, C. L. (1969). *Community health.* St. Louis, MO: C. V. Mosby.

Anderson, C. R. (1977). Locus of control, coping behaviors, and performance in a stress setting: A longitudinal study. *Journal of Applied Psychology, 62*, 446–451.

Anderson, C. R., Hellriegel, D., & Slocum, J. W., Jr. (1977). Managerial response to environmentally induced stress. *Academy of Management Journal, 20*, 260–272.

Anderson, C. R., & Schneier, C. E. (1978). Locus of control, leader behavior and leader performance among management students. *Academy of Management Journal, 21*, 690–698.

Anderson, D. R. (1974). Leadership effectiveness in education as related to congruence between human behavior types and leadership styles. *Dissertation Abstracts International, 34*, 6887.

Anderson, H. H. (1937a). An experimental study of dominative and integrative behavior in children of pre-school age. *Journal of Social Psychology, 8*, 335–345.

Anderson, H. H. (1937b). Domination and integration in the social behavior of young children in an experimental play situation. *Genetic Psychology Monographs, 19*, 341–408.

Anderson, H. H. (1939). Domination and social integration in the behavior of kindergarten children and teachers. *Genetic Psychology Monographs, 21*, 287–385.

Anderson, H. H. (1940). An examination of the concepts of domination and integration in relation to dominance and ascendance. *Psychological Review, 47*, 21–37.

Anderson, H. H., & Brewer, J. E. (1946). Studies of teachers' classroom personalities, II: Effects of teachers' dominative and integrative contacts on children's classroom behavior. *Applied Psychological Monographs,* No. 8.

Anderson, J. E. (1984). The management of wage-price policies in the Johnson and Carter administrations. *Policy Studies Journal, 12*, 733–745.

Anderson, J. G. (1984). When leaders develop themselves. *Training & Development Journal, 38*(6), 18–22.

Anderson, L. E., & Balzer, W. K. (1988). *The effects of timing of leaders' opinions on problem solving groups: A field experiment.* Paper, Society for Industrial and Organizational Psychology, Dallas.

Anderson, L. R. (1964). *Some effects of leadership training on intercultural discussion groups* (Tech. Rep.). Urbana: University of Illinois, Group Effectiveness Research Laboratory.

Anderson, L. R. (1965). Some effects of leadership training on intercultural discussion groups. *Dissertation Abstracts, 25*, 6796.

Anderson, L. R. (1966a). *Initiation of structure, consideration, and task performance in intercultural discussion groups.* Urbana: University of Illinois, Group Effectiveness Research Laboratory. Unpublished report.

Anderson, L. R. (1966b). Leader behavior, member attitudes, and task performance of intercultural discussion groups. *Journal of Social Psychology, 69*, 305–319.

Anderson, L. R. (1983). Management of the mixed-cultural work group. *Organizational Behavior and Human Performance, 31*, 303–330.

Anderson, L. R., & Fiedler, F. E. (1964). The effect of participatory and supervisory leadership on group creativity. *Journal of Applied Psychology, 48*, 227–236.

Anderson, L. R., Karuza, J., & Blanchard, P. N. (1977). Enhancement of leader power after election or appointment to undesirable leader roles. *Journal of Psychology, 97*, 59–70.

Anderson, N. (1923). *The hobo: The sociology of the homeless man.* Chicago: University of Chicago Press.

Anderson, R. C. (1959). Learning in discussions—a resume of the authoritarian–democratic studies. *Harvard Educational Review, 29*, 201–215.

Anderson, R. M. (1964). Activity preferences and leadership behavior of head nurses. *Nursing Research, 13*, 239–242, 333–337.

Anderson, W. A. (1943). The family and individual social participation. *American Sociological Review, 8*, 420–424.

Andreoli, V. A. (1975). *Effect of a leader's threat to behavioral freedom.* Doctoral dissertation, University of North Carolina, Chapel Hill, NC.

Andrews, F. M., & Farris, G. F. (1967). Supervisory practices and innovations in scientific teams. *Personnel Psychology, 20*, 497–515.

Andrews, F. M., & Farris, G. F. (1972). Time pressure and performance of scientists and engineers: A five-year panel study. *Organizational Behavior and Human Performance, 8*, 185–200.

Andrews, I. R., & Henry, M. M (1963). Management attitudes toward pay. *Industrial Relations, 3*, 29–40.

Andrews, J. D. W. (1967). The achievement motive and advancement in two types of organizations. *Journal of Personality and Social Psychology, 6*, 163–168.

Andrews, K. R. (1966). *The effectiveness of university management development programs.* Boston: Harvard University, Graduate School of Business Administration.

Andrews, L. C. (1918). *Leadership and military training.* Philadelphia: Lippincott.

Andrews, P. (1984). Performance, self-esteem and perceptions of leadership emergence: A comparative study of men and women. *Western Journal of Speech Communication, 48*, 1–13.

Andrews, R. E. (1955). *Leadership and supervision, a survey of research findings: A management report.* Washington, DC: U.S. Civil Service Commission.

Andrisani, P. J., & Nestel, G. (1976). Internal-external control as contributor to and outcome of work experience. *Journal of Applied Psychology, 61*, 156–165.

Angelini, A. L. (1966). Measuring the achievement motive in Brazil. *Journal of Social Psychology, 68*, 35–44.

Anghelone, J. D. (1981). The effect of a management training seminar upon the transfer of leadership skills to actual on the job performance. *Dissertation Abstracts International, 43* (4A), 1124.

Anikeeff, A. M. (1957). The effect of job satisfaction upon attitudes of business administrators and employees. *Journal of Social Psychology, 45*, 277–281.

Anonymous (undated, a). *Participants' perceptions of inter-organizational relations.* Unpublished manuscript.

Anonymous (undated, b). *Stability of managerial values.* Unpublished manuscript.

Anonymous (1945/1946). Informal social organizations in the Army. *American Journal of Sociology, 51,* 365-370.

Anonymous (1955, April). How to succeed. *Business Week,* p. 128.

Anonymous (1968a, March). How 179 chief executives waste their time. *Business Management, 33,* 12-14.

Anonymous. (1968b). Awareness training. *Industrial relations news.* New York: Industrial Relations Counselors.

Anonymous (1970, June 11). Russia sets program of wage incentives in scientific work. *Wall Street Journal,* 12.

Anonymous (1972). Women and business: Agenda for the seventies. *Business Environment Studies.* New York: General Electric Co.

Anonymous (1975). Macy's assessment center helps predict executive success. *Personnel News and Views, 5,*(4), 16-18.

Anonymous (1977). Library administrators: Time to show them the door? *Wilson Library Bulletin, 51,* 636-638.

Anonymous (1978a). What do 50 presidents and chief executive officers think about communications? *Journal of Organizational Communication, 8,* 3-11.

Anonymous (1978, May/June). The only way. *Execu-Time: The Newsletter on Effective Use of Executive Time,* 25.

Anonymous (1979, October 8). How to spot the hotshots. *Business Week, 62,* 67-68.

Anonymous (1983, April 18). 29% say they wouldn't elect a woman president, poll says. *New York Times,* B1.

Anonymous (1984). How to develop a crisis communications plan. *Office Administration and Automation, 45*(11), 55-57.

Anonymous (1985). *OPQ Manual.* Esher, Surrey, England: Saville & Holdsworth.

Anonymous (1987, May 11). Notre Dame's "Father Ted" bids farewell. *Newsweek,* p. 75.

Anonymous (1988a). Managers need to be tougher on workplace slackers. *Success, 35*(5), 30.

Anonymous (1988b, September 1). Survey says staffing issues big concern for next 5 years. *Decisions.* Newsletter, Management Decision Systems, Boston, MA.

Ansari, M. A. (1988). *Leadership styles and influence strategies: Moderating effect of organizational climate.* Paper, International Congress of Psychology, Sydney, Australia.

Ansari, M. A., Baumgartel, H., & Sullivan, G. (1982). The personal orientation–organizational climate fit and managerial success. *Human Relations, 35,* 1159-1177.

Ansbacher, H. L. (1942). German military psychology. *Psychological Bulletin, 39,* 370-392.

Ansbacher, H. L. (1948). Attitudes of German prisoners of war: A study of the dynamics of national-socialistic followership. *Psychological Monographs, 62,* 1-42.

Anstey, E. (1966). The civil service administrative class and the diplomatic service: A follow-up. *Occupational Psychology, 40,* 139-151.

Anthony, W. P. (1978). *Participative management.* Reading, MA: Addison-Wesley.

Antia, K. (1969a). Job satisfaction: Facts versus fiction. *Experimental Publications System, American Psychological Association,* No. 113A.

Antia, K. (1969b). Cognitive factors in an organization—a new era in emergence. *Experimental Publications System, American Psychological Association,* No. 096A.

Anzizu, J. M., & Nuenos, P. (1984). *Leadership under sociopolitical change: Business enterprise in Spain.* Paper, 75th Anniversary Colloquium, Harvard Business School, Boston.

Apfelbaum, E., & Hadley, M. (1986). Leadership MS-Qualified: II. Reflections on and critical case study investigation of contemporary women leaders. In C. F. Graumann & S. Moscovici (Eds.), *Changing conceptions of leadership.* New York: Springer-Verlag.

Applebaum, H. A. (1982). Construction management: Traditional versus bureaucratic methods. *Anthropological Quarterly, 55,* 224-234.

Applebaum, S. H. (1977). The motivation of government administrators within a closed climate. *Akron Business and Economic Review, 8,* 26-32.

Aral, S. O., & Whelan, R. K. (1974). *Leadership styles in urban societies.* Tucson: University of Arizona, Institute of Government Research.

Arbous, A. G., & Maree, J. (1951). Contributions of two group discussion techniques to a validated test battery. *Occupational Psychology, 25,* 73-89.

Arensberg, C. M., & McGregor, D. (1942). Determination of morale in an industrial company. *Applied Anthropology, 1,* 12-34.

Arensberg, C. M., & Tootell, G. (1957). Plant sociology: Real discoveries and new problems. In M. Komarovsky (Ed.), *Common frontiers of the social sciences.* New York: Free Press.

Argyle, M., & Dean, J. (1965). Eye-contact, distance, and affiliation. *Sociometry, 28,* 289-304.

Argyle, M., Gardner, G., & Ciofi, F. (1958). Supervisory methods related to productivity, absenteeism, and labour turnover. *Human Relations, 11,* 23-40.

Argyris, C. (1953). Some characteristics of successful executives. *Personnel Journal, 32,* 50-63.

Argyris, C. (1954). Human relations in a bank. *Harvard Business Review, 32,* 63-72.

Argyris, C. (1957). *Personality and organization.* New York: Harper.

Argyris, C. (1960). *Understanding organizational behavior.* Homewood, IL: Dorsey.

Argyris, C. (1961). Organizational leadership. In L. Petrullo & B. M. Bass (Eds.), *Leadership and interpersonal behavior.* New York: Holt, Rinehart & Winston.

Argyris, C. (1962). *Interpersonal competence and organizational effectiveness.* Homewood, IL: Irwin-Dorsey.

Argyris, C. (1963). In defense of laboratory education. *Training Directors Journal, 17,* 21-30.

Argyris, C. (1964a). *Integrating the individual and the organization.* New York: Wiley.

Argyris, C. (1964b). T-groups for organizational effectiveness. *Harvard Business Review, 42,* 60–74.

Argyris, C. (1965). Explorations in interpersonal competence—II. *Journal of Applied Behavioral Science, 1,* 255–269.

Argyris, C. (1969). The incompleteness of social-psychological theory: Examples from small group, cognitive consistency, and attribution research. *American Psychologist, 24,* 893–908.

Argyris, C. (1970). *Intervention theory and method.* Reading, MA: Addison-Wesley.

Argyris, C. (1973). Personality and organization theory revisited. *Administrative Science Quarterly, 18,* 141–167.

Argyris, C. (1976). *Increasing leadership effectiveness.* New York: Wiley.

Argyris, C. (1980). Some limitations of the case method: Experiences in a management development program. *Academy of Management Review, 5,* 291–298.

Argyris, C. (1982). The executive mind and double-loop learning. *Organizational Dynamics, 11*(2), 5–22.

Argyris, C. (1983). Action science and intervention. *Journal of Applied Behavioral Science, 19,* 115–140.

Argyris, C. (1987). Crafting a theory of practice: The case of organizational paradoxes. In R. Quinn & K. Cameron (Eds.), *Paradox and transformation: Towards a theory of change in organization and management.* Boston: Pitman.

Aries, C. (1976). Interaction patterns and themes of male, female, and mixed groups. *Small Group Behavior, 7,* 7–18.

Arlen, E. (1957). *Leadership and human relations: A bibliographic review.* Chicago: University of Chicago, Industrial Relations Center.

Armilla, J. (1967). Predicting self-assessed social leadership in a new culture with the MMPI. *Journal of Social Psychology, 73,* 219–225.

Armstrong, P. (1983). Class relationships at the point of production: A case study. *Sociology, 17,* 339–358.

Aronoff, J., & Mess, L. A. (1971). Motivational determinants of small-group structure. *Journal of Personality and Social Psychology, 3,* 319–324.

Aronson, E., & Cope, V. (1968). My enemy's enemy is my friend. *Journal of Personality and Social Psychology, 8,* 8–12.

Aronson, E., & Worchel, P. (1966). Similarity versus liking as determinants of interpersonal attractiveness. *Psychonomic Science, 5,* 157–158.

Arrington, R. E. (1943). Time sampling in studies of social behavior: A critical review of techniques and results with research suggestions. *Psychological Bulletin, 40,* 81–124.

Arvey, R. D., Davis, G. A., & Nelson, S. M. (1984). Use of discipline in an organization: A field study. *Journal of Applied Psychology, 69,* 448–460.

Arvey, R. D., & Ivancevich, J. M. (1980). Punishment in organizations: A review, propositions, and research suggestions. *Academy of Management Review, 5,* 123–132.

Arvey, R. D., & Neel, C. W. (1974). Moderating effects of employee expectancies on the relationship between leadership consideration and job performance of engineers. *Journal of Vocational Behavior, 4,* 213–222.

Asch, S. E. (1946). Forming impressions of personalities. *Journal of Abnormal and Social Psychology, 41,* 258–290.

Asch, S. E. (1952). *Social psychology.* New York: Prentice-Hall.

Ashbrook, J. B. (1967). Ministerial leadership in church organization. *Ministry Studies, 1,* 3–32.

Ashby, W. R. (1957). *An introduction to cybernetics.* New York: Wiley.

Ashby, W. R. (1960). *Design for a brain.* New York: Wiley.

Ashby, W. R. (1968). Variety, constraint, and the law of requisite variety (1956). In W. Buckley (Ed.), *Modern systems research for the behavioral scientist.* Chicago: Aldine.

Ashford, S. J., & Cummings, L. L. (1981). Strategies for knowing: When and from whom do individuals seek feedback. *Proceedings, Academy of Management, 41,* 161–165.

Ashford, S. J., & Cummings, L. L. (1983). Feedback as an individual resource: Personal strategies of creating information. *Organizational Behavior and Human Performance, 32,* 370–398.

Ashour, A. S. (1973a). The contingency model of leadership effectiveness: An evaluation. *Organizational Behavior and Human Performance, 9,* 339–355.

Ashour, A. S. (1973b). Further discussion of Fiedler's contingency model of leadership effectiveness. *Organizational Behavior and Human Performance, 9,* 369–376.

Ashour, A. S., & England, G. (1971). Subordinate's assigned level of discretion as a function of leader's personality and situational variables. *Experimental Publications System, American Psychological Association, 12,* No. 466-1.

Ashour, A. S., & Johns, G. (1983). Leader influence through operant principles: A theoretical and methodological framework. *Human Relations, 36,* 603–626.

ASME (American Society of Mechanical Engineers). (1960). *50 years progress in management, 1910–1960.* New York: American Society of Mechanical Engineers.

Aspegren, R. E. (1963). A study of leadership behavior and its effects on morale and attitudes in selected elementary schools. *Dissertation Abstracts, 23,* 3708.

Asquith, R. H., & Hedlund, D. E. (1967). Laboratory training and supervisory attitudes. *Psychological Reports, 20,* 618.

Assael, H. (1969). Constructive role of interorganizational conflict. *Administrative Science Quarterly, 14,* 573–582.

Astin, A. W., & Scherrei, R. A. (1980). *Managing leadership effectiveness.* San Francisco: Jossey-Bass.

Atkinson, J. W. (Ed.) (1958). *Motives in fantasy, action and society.* Princeton, NJ: Van Nostrand.

Atkinson, J. W. (1964). *An introduction to motivation.* Princeton, NJ: Van Nostrand.

Atkinson, J. W., & Walker, E. L. (1956). The affiliation motive and perceptual sensitivity to faces. *Journal of Abnormal and Social Psychology, 53,* 38–41.

Atsumi, R. (1979). Tsukiai—Obligatory personal relationships of Japanese white-collar company employees. *Human Organization, 38,* 63–70.

Atwater, L. (1988). The relative importance of situational and individual variables in predicting leader behavior: The surprising impact of subordinate trust. *Group & Organization Studies, 13*(3), 290–310.

Atwater, L., & White, M. (1985). *Behavior and effectiveness of first-line supervisors* (NPRDC Tech. Rep. 86–5). San Diego, CA: Navy Personnel Research and Development Center.

Atwater, L., & Yammarino, F. J. (1989). *Predictors of military leadership. A study of midshipmen leaders at USNA* (ONR Tech. Rep. 7). Binghamton: State University of New York, Center for Leadership Studies.

Aubert, N., Ramanantsoa, B., & Reitter, R. (1984). *Nationalization, managerial power and societal change: A field study in France 1982–1983.* Paper, 75th Anniversary Colloquium on Leadership, Harvard Business School, Boston.

Auclair, G. (1968). *Managerial role conflict: A cross-cultural comparison.* Paper, American Psychological Association, San Francisco.

Aupperle, K. E., Acar, W., & Booth D. E. (1986). An empirical critique of *In Search of Excellence*: How excellent are the excellent companies? *Journal of Management, 12,* 499–512.

Aupperle, K. E., & Simmons, E. B., III. (1989). *Have CEO's of large firms changed their CSR orientations during the Reagan presidency?* Paper, Academy of Management, Washington, DC.

Austin, T. W. (1981). What can managers learn from leadership theories? *Supervisory Management, 26*(7), 22–31.

Ausubel, D. P. (1955). Socioempathy as a function of sociometric status in an adolescent group. *Human Relations, 8,* 75–84.

Ausubel, D. P., & Schiff, H. M. (1955). Some intrapersonal and interpersonal determinants of individual differences in socioemphatic ability among adolescents. *Journal of Social Psychology, 41,* 39–56.

Avolio, B. J., & Bass, B. M. (1988). Transformational leadership, charisma, and beyond. In J. G. Hunt, B. R. Baliga, H. P. Dachler, & C. A. Schriesheim, *Emerging Leadership Vistas.* Lexington, MA: D. C. Heath.

Avolio, B. J., Bass, B. M., & Yammarino, F. J. (1988). *An alternative strategy for reducing biases in leadership ratings.* Paper, Academy of Management, Anaheim, CA.

Avolio, B. J., & Gibbons, T. C. (1988). Developing transformational leaders: A life span approach. In J. Conger & R. Kanungo (Eds.), *Charismatic leadership: The elusive factor in organizational effectiveness.* New York: Wiley.

Avolio, B. J., & Howell, J. M. (undated). *Developing transformational leaders.* Unpublished manuscript.

Avolio, B. J., Waldman, D. A., & Einstein, W. O. (1988). Transformational leadership in a management game simulation. *Group & Organization Studies, 13,* 59–80.

Ayer, J. G. (1968). *Effects of success and failure of interpersonal and task performance upon leader perception and behavior* (Tech. Rep. No. 26). Urbana: University of Illinois, Group Effectiveness Research Laboratory.

Ayers, A. W. (1964). Effect of knowledge of results on supervisor's post-training test scores. *Personnel Psychology, 17,* 189–192.

Ayman, R., & Chemers, M. M. (1982). *The relationship of managerial behavior to effectiveness and satisfaction in Mexico.* Paper, International Congress of Applied Psychology, Edinburgh.

Ayman, R., & Chemers, M. M. (1983). Relationship of supervisory behavior ratings to work group effectiveness and subordinate satisfaction among Iranian managers. *Journal of Applied Psychology, 68*(2), 338–341.

Ayman, R., & Chemers, M. M. (1986). The emic/etic approach to leadership orientation job satisfaction of Mexican managers. Paper, International Congress of Applied Psychology, Jerusalem.

Ayman, R., & Chemers, M. M. (1989). *The effect of leadership match on subordinate satisfaction in Mexican organizations: Some moderating influences of self-monitoring.* Unpublished manuscript.

Babikan, K. (1981). The leader-entrepreneur in the public sector. In F. I. Khuri (Ed.), *Leadership and Development in Arab Society.* Beirut: American University of Beirut, Center for Arab and Middle East Studies.

Bachand, C. (1981). Boards of directors in Canadian government enterprises: An exploratory research. *Dissertation Abstracts International, 42*(3A), 1289.

Bachman, J. G. (1968). Faculty satisfaction and the dean's influence: An organizational study of twelve liberal arts colleges. *Journal of Applied Psychology, 52,* 55–61.

Bachman, J. G., Bowers, D. G., & Marcus, P. M. (1968). Bases of supervisory power: A comparative study in five organizational settings. In A. S. Tannenbaum (Ed.), *Control in organizations.* New York: McGraw-Hill.

Bachman, J. G., Smith, C., & Slesinger, J. A. (1966). Control, performance, and satisfaction: An analysis of structural and individual effects. *Journal of Personality and Social Psychology, 4,* 127–136.

Bachrach, A. J., Candland, D. K., & Gibson, J. T. (1961). Group reinforcement of individual response experiments in verbal behavior. In I. A. Berg & B. M. Bass (Eds.), *Conformity and deviation.* New York: Harper.

Back, K. W. (1948). Interpersonal relations in a discussion group. *Journal of Social Issues, 4,* 61–65.

Back, K. W. (1951). Influence through social communication. *Journal of Abnormal and Social Psychology, 46,* 9–23.

Back, K. W. (1972). *Beyond words: The story of sensitivity training and the encounter movement.* New York: Basic Books.

Backman, C. W., & Secord, P. F. (1959). The effect of perceived liking on interpersonal attraction. *Human Relations, 12,* 379–384.

Backner, B. L. (1961). "Attraction-to-group," as a function of style of leadership, follower personality, and group composition. *Dissertation Abstracts, 22,* 628.

Badawy, M. K. (undated). *Managerial attitudes and need orientations of mideastern executives: An empirical cross-cultural analysis.* Cleveland, OH: Cleveland State University. Unpublished manuscript.

Badin, I. J. (1974). Some moderator influences on relationships between consideration, initiating structure, and organizational criteria. *Journal of Applied Psychology, 59,* 380–382.

Badran, M., & Hinings, B. (1981). Strategies of administrative control and contextual constraints in a less-developed country: The case of Egyptian public enterprise. *Group & Organization Studies, 2*(1), 3–21.

Bagozzi, R. P., & Phillips, L. W. (1982). Representing and testing organizational theories: A holistic construal. *Administrative Science Quarterly, 77,* 459–489.

Baier, D. E. (1947). Note on "A review of leadership studies with particular reference to military problems." *Psychological Bulletin, 44,* 466–467.

Bailey, F. G. (1983). *The tactical uses of passion.* Ithaca, NY: Cornell University Press.

Bailey, H. D. (1966). *An exploratory study of selected components and processes in educational organizations.* Doctoral dissertation, University of California, Berkeley.

Bain, T. (1985). *Why a manager? The mid-career behavior of engineers.* Paper, Academy of Management, San Diego, CA.

Baird, J. E., Jr. (1977). Some nonverbal elements of leadership emergence. *The Southern Speech Communication Journal, 42,* 352–361.

Baird, J. E. (1980). Enhancing managerial credibility. *Personnel Journal, 59,* 1001–1002.

Baker, A. J. (1982). The problem of authority in radical movement groups: A case study of lesbian-feminist organization. *Journal of Applied Behavioral Science, 18,* 323–341.

Baker, B. O., & Block, J. (1957). Accuracy of interpersonal prediction as a function of judge and object characteristics. *Journal of Abnormal and Social Psychology, 54,* 37–43.

Baker, H., & France, R. R. (1954). *Centralization and decentralization in industrial relations.* Princeton, NJ: Princeton University, Industrial Relations Section.

Baker, L. D., DiMarco, N., & Scott, W. E., Jr. (1975). Effects of supervisor's sex and level of authoritarianism on evaluation and reinforcement of blind and sighted workers. *Journal of Applied Psychology, 60,* 28–32.

Baker, R. A., Ware, J. R., Spires, G. H., & Osborn, W. C. (1966). The effects of supervisory threat on decision making and risk taking in a simulated combat game. *Behavioral Science, 11,* 167–176.

Bakke, E. W. (1959). *A Norwegian contribution to management development.* Bergen: Norwegian School of Economics & Business Administration.

Balcazar, F. E., Hopkins, B. L., & Suarez, Y. (1985–86). A critical objective review of performance feedback. *Journal of Organizational Behavior Management, 7*(3–4), 65–89.

Baldwin, A. L. (1949). The effects of home environment on nursery school behavior. *Child Development, 20,* 49–62.

Baldwin, J., Glazer, N., Hook, S., Myrdal, G., & Podhoretz, N. (1966). Liberalism and the Negro: A round-table discussion. In B. E. Segal (Ed.), *Racial and ethnic relations.* New York: Thomas Y. Crowell.

Baldwin, L. E. (1932). *A study of factors usually associated with high school male leadership.* Master's thesis, Ohio State University, Columbus.

Bales, R. F. (1950). *Interaction process analysis.* Reading, MA: Addison-Wesley.

Bales, R. F. (1953). The equilibrium problem in small groups. In T. Parsons, R. F. Bales, & E. A. Shils (Eds.), *Working papers in the theory of action.* New York: Free Press.

Bales, R. F. (1958a). Task roles and social roles in problem-solving groups. In E. E. Maccoby, T. M. Newcomb, & E. L. Hartley (Eds.), *Readings in social psychology.* New York: Holt.

Bales, R. F. (1958b). Role and role conflict. In E. E.. Maccoby, T. M. Newcomb, & E. L. Hartley (Eds.), *Readings in social psychology.* New York: Holt.

Bales, R. F., & Cohen, S. P. (1980). *SYMLOG.* New York: Free Press.

Bales, R. F., Cohen, S. P., & Williamson, S. A. (1979). *SYMLOG: A system for the multiple level observation of groups.* New York: Free Press.

Bales, R. F., & Slater, P. E. (1955). Role differentiation in small decision-making groups. In T. Parsons & R. F. Bales (Eds.), *Family, socialization, and interaction processes.* New York: Free Press.

Bales, R. F., & Strodtbeck, F. L. (1951). Phases in group problem-solving. *Journal of Abnormal and Social Psychology, 46,* 485–495.

Bales, R. F., Strodtbeck, F., Mills, T., & Roseborough, M. E. (1951). Channels of communication in small groups. *American Social Review, 16,* 461–468.

Baliga, B. R., & Hunt, J. G. (1988). An organizational life cycle approach to leadership. In J. G. Hunt, B. R. Baliga, H. P. Dacher, & C. A. Schriesheim, *Emerging leadership vistas.* Lexington, MA: D. C. Heath.

Balk, W. L. (1969). Status perceptions of management "peers." *Academy of Management Journal, 4,* 431–437.

Ball, R. S. (1938). The predictability of occupational level from intelligence. *Journal of Consulting Psychology, 2,* 184–186.

Ballou, A. (1897). *The Hopedale community.* Lowell, MA: Thompson & Hill.

Balma, M. J., Maloney, J. C., & Lawshe, C. H. (1958a). The role of the foreman in modern industry. II. Foreman identification with management, work group productivity, and employee attitude toward the foreman. *Personnel Psychology, 11,* 367–378.

Balma, M. J., Maloney, J. C., & Lawshe, C. H. (1958b). The role of the foreman in modern industry. III. Some correlates of foreman identification with management. *Personnel Psychology, 11,* 535–544.

Baltzell, E. D. (1958). *Philadelphia gentlemen: The making of a national upper class.* New York: Free Press.

Baltzell, E. D. (1980). *Puritan Boston and Quaker Philadelphia.* New York: Free Press.

Balyeat, R. R. (1972). Leader and administrative behavior exhibited by participants of the Administrator Change Agent Program, the University of Tennessee, 1968–1970. *Dissertation Abstracts International, 32,* 6024.

Bamforth, K. (1965). T-group methods within a company. In G. Whitaker (Ed.), *ATM occasional papers 2.* Oxford: Basil E. Blackwell.

Bandura, A. (1977). *Social learning theory.* Englewood Cliffs, NJ: Prentice-Hall.

Bandura, A. (1982). Self-efficacy mechanism in human agency. *American Psychologist, 37,* 122–147.

Bandura, A., & Huston, A. C. (1961). Identification as a process of incidental learning. *Journal of Abnormal and Social Psychology, 63,* 311–318.

Bandura, A., Ross, D., & Ross, S. A. (1962a). "Vicarious" reinforcement and imitation. Stanford, CA: Stanford University. Unpublished manuscript.

Bandura, A., Ross, D., & Ross, S. A. (1962b). *An experimental test of the status envy, social power, and the secondary reinforcement theories of identificatory learning.* Stanford, CA: Stanford University. Unpublished manuscript.

Bandura, A., Ross, D., & Ross, S. A. (1963). A comparative test of the status envy, social power, and secondary reinforcement theories of identificatory learning. *Journal of Abnormal and Social Psychology, 67,* 527–534.

Banfield, E. E. (1976). Women in middle management positions: Characteristics, training, leadership style, limitations, rewards, and problems. *Dissertation Abstracts International, 37,* 1952–1953.

Banfield, E., & Wilson, J. Q. (1963). *City politics.* Cambridge, MA: Harvard University Press.

Bankart, C. P., & Lanzetta, J. (1970). Performance and motivation as variables affecting the administration of rewards and punishments. *Representative Research in Social Psychology, 1,* 1–10.

Banks, O. (1960). *The attitudes of steelworkers to technical change.* Liverpool: Liverpool University Press.

Banta, T. J., & Nelson, C. (1964). Experimental analysis of resource location in problem-solving groups. *Sociometry, 27,* 488–501.

Bar-Tal, Y. (1989). What can we learn from Fiedler's contingency model? *Journal for the Theory of Social Behaviour, 19,* 79–96.

Bar-Yosef, R., & Schild, E. O. (1966). Pressures and defenses in bureaucratic roles. *American Journal of Sociology, 71,* 665–673.

Barati, M. E. (1981). Comparison of preferred leadership styles, potential leadership effectiveness, and managerial attitudes among black and white, female and male management students. *Dissertation Abstracts International, 43*(4A), 1271.

Barber, J. D. (1965). *The law makers.* New Haven, CT: Yale University Press.

Barber, J. D., (1966). *Power in committees: An experiment in the government process.* Chicago: Rand McNally.

Barber, J. D. (1985). *Presidential character: Predicting performance in the White House* (3rd ed.). Englewood Cliffs, NJ: Prentice-Hall.

Barbieri, E. A. (1983). Trait patterns for effective marketing performance. *Dissertation Abstracts International, 44*(12A), 3790.

Bare, R. (1956). A factor analytic description of the performance of enlisted personnel. *USN Bureau of Naval Personnel and Technology Bulletin, 56-1,* 1–37.

Barker, R. G. (1942). The social interrelations of strangers and acquaintances. *Sociometry, 5,* 169–179.

Barker, R. G. (1968). *Ecological psychology.* Stanford, CA: Stanford University Press.

Barlow, J. A. (1981). Mass line leadership and thought reform in China. *American Psychologist, 36,* 300–309.

Barnard, C. I. (1938). *The functions of the executive.* Cambridge, MA: Harvard University Press.

Barnard, C. I. (1939). *Dilemmas of leadership in the democratic process.* Princeton, NJ: Princeton University Press.

Barnard, C. I. (1946a). Functions and pathology of status systems in formal organizations. In W. F. White (Ed.), *Industry and society.* New York: McGraw-Hill.

Barnard, C. I. (1946b). The nature of leadership. In S. D. Hoslett (Ed.), *Human factors in management.* New York: McGraw-Hill.

Barnard, C. I. (1948). *Organization and management.* Cambridge, MA: Harvard University Press.

Barnard, C. I. (1951). Functions of status systems in formal organizations. In R. Dubin (Ed.), *Human relations in administration.* Englewood Cliffs, NJ: Prentice-Hall.

Barnard, C. I. (1952). A definition of authority. In R. K. Merton, A. P. Gray, B. Hockey, & H. C. Selvin (Eds.), *Reader in bureaucracy.* New York: Free Press.

Barner-Berry, C. (1982). An ethological study of a leadership succession. *Ethology & Sociobiology, 3,* 199–207.

Barnes, L. B. (1960). *Organizational systems and engineering groups: A comparative study of two technical groups in industry.* Boston: Division of Research, Harvard Business School.

Barnes, R. M., & Englert, N. A. (1946). *Bibliography of industrial engineering and management literature to January 1, 1946* (5th ed.). Dubuque, IA: W. C. Brown.

Barnlund, D. C. (1955). Experiments in leadership training for decision-making groups. *Speech Monographs, 22,* 1–14.

Barnlund, D. C. (1962). Consistency of emergent leadership in groups with changing tasks and members. *Speech Monographs, 29,* 45–52.

Barnlund, D. C., & Harland, C. (1963). Propinquity and prestige as determinants of communication networks. *Sociometry, 26,* 467–479.

Baron, A. S. (1977). Selection, development and socialization of women. *Business Quarterly, 42,* 61.

Baron, R. A. (1984). Reducing organizational conflict: An incompatible response approach. *Journal of Applied Psychology, 69,* 272–279.

Barrett, G. V., & Bass, B. M. (1976). Cross-cultural issues in industrial and organizational psychology. In M. D. Dunnette (Ed.), *Handbook of industrial and organizational psychology.* Chicago: Rand McNally.

Barrett, G. V., & Franke, R. H. (1969). *Communication preference and performance: A cross-cultural comparison.* Paper, American Psychological Association, Washington, DC.

Barrett, G. V., & Ryterband, E. C. (1968). *Cross-cultural comparisons of corporate objectives on exercise objectives.* Paper, American Psychological Association, San Francisco.

Barrett, N. S. (1973). Have Swedish women achieved equality? *Challenge, 16*(6), 14–20.

Barrett, R. S. (1963). Performance suitability and role agreement: Two Factors related to attitudes. *Personnel Psychology, 16,* 345–357.

Barrett, R. S. (1965). Impact of the executive program on the participants. *Journal of Industrial Psychology, 3,* 1–13.

Barrett, R. S. (1966). The influence of the supervisor's requirements on ratings. *Personnel Psychology, 19,* 375–388.

Barrow, J. C. (1975). An empirical framework of leadership effectiveness and investigation of leader-subordinate-task causality relationships. *Dissertation Abstracts International, 35,* 3631.

Barrow, J. C. (1976). Worker performance and task complexity as causal determinants of leader behavior, style, and flexibility. *Journal of Applied Psychology, 61,* 433–440.

Barrow, J. C. (1977). The variables of leadership: A review and conceptual framework. *Academy of Management Review, 2,* 231–251.

Bartlett, C. J. (1959). Dimensions of leadership behavior in classroom discussion groups. *Journal of Educational Psychology, 50*, 280–284.

Bartlett, F. C. (1926). The social psychology of leadership. *Journal of National Institutional and Industrial Psychology, 3*, 188–193.

Bartol, K. M. (1973). *Male and female leaders in small work groups.* East Lansing: Michigan State University Press.

Bartol, K. M. (1974). Male vs. female leaders: The effect of leader need for dominance on follower satisfaction. *Academy of Management Journal, 17*, 225–233.

Bartol, K. M. (1975). The effect of male versus female leaders on follower satisfaction and performance. *Journal of Business Research, 3*, 33–42.

Bartol, K. M. (1976a). Relationship of sex and professional training area to job orientation. *Journal of Applied Psychology, 61*, 368–370.

Bartol, K. M. (1976b). Expectancy theory as a predictor of female occupational choice and attitude toward business. *Academy of Management Journal, 19*, 669–675.

Bartol, K. M. (1978). The sex structuring of organizations: A search for possible causes. *Academy of Management Review, 3*, 805–815.

Bartol, K. M., Anderson, C. R., & Schneier, C. E. (1980). Motivation to manage among college business students: A reassessment. *Journal of Vocational Behavior, 17*, 22–32.

Bartol, K. M., & Bartol, R. A. (1975). Women in managerial and technical positions: The United States and the Soviet Union. *Industrial Labor Relations Review, 28*, 524–534.

Bartol, K. M., & Butterfield, D. A. (1976). Sex effects in evaluating leaders. *Journal of Applied Psychology, 61*(4), 446–454.

Bartol, K. M., Evans, C. L., & Stith, M. T. (1978). Black vs. white leaders: A comparative review of the literature. *Academy of Management Review, 3*, 293–304.

Bartol, K. M., & Martin, D. C. (1986). *Effects of business school training on motivation to manage: A longitudinal study.* Paper, Academy of Management, Chicago.

Bartol, K. M., Schneier, C. E., & Anderson, C. R. (1985). Internal and external validity issues with motivation to manage research: A reply to Miner, Smith, and Ebrahimi. *Journal of Vocational Behavior, 26*, 299–305.

Bartol, K. M., & Wortman, M. S. (1975). Male versus female leaders: Effects on perceived leader behavior and satisfaction in a hospital. *Personnel Psychology, 28*, 533–547.

Bartol, K. M., & Wortman, M. S. (1976). Sex effects in leader behavior self-descriptions and job satisfaction. *Journal of Psychology, 94*, 177–183.

Bartol, K. M., & Wortman, M. S., Jr. (1979). Sex of leader and subordinate role stress: A field study. *Sex Roles, 5*, 513–518.

Barton, R. S. (1984). *Cognitive and developmental aspects of empowerment: An empirical comparison between citizen leaders and non-leaders (attributions, self-efficacy).* Doctoral dissertation, University of Oregon, Eugene.

Barzini, L. (1964). *The Italians.* London: Atheneum.

Basil, D. C. (1964). *Executive development: A comparison of small and large enterprise.* Minneapolis: University of Minnesota Press.

Bass, A. R. (1964). Some determinants of supervisory and peer ratings. *Dissertation Abstracts, 24*, 5526.

Bass, A. R., Fiedler, F. E., & Krueger, S. (1964). *Personality correlates of assumed similarity (ASo) and related scores* (Tech. Rep. No. 19). Urbana: University of Illinois, Group Effectiveness Research Laboratory.

Bass, B. M. (undated). *Supervisory judgement of employee ability and employee job satisfaction.* Unpublished report.

Bass, B. M. (1949). An analysis of the leaderless group discussion. *Journal of Applied Psychology, 33*, 527–533.

Bass, B. M. (1953). Effects of the nature of the problem on LGD performance. *Journal of Applied Psychology, 37*, 96–99.

Bass, B. M. (1954a). The leaderless group discussion. *Psychological Bulletin, 51*, 465–492.

Bass, B. M. (1954b). Feelings of pleasantness and work group efficiency. *Personnel Psychology, 7*, 81–91.

Bass, B. M. (1955a). Authoritarianism or acquiescence? *Journal of Abnormal and Social Psychology, 51*, 616–623.

Bass, B. M. (1955b). *Interrelations among measurements of leadership and associated behavior.* Baton Rouge: Louisiana State University. Unpublished report.

Bass, B. M. (1955c). *Behavior in groups. III. Consistent differences in the objectivity measured performance of members and groups.* Baton Rouge: Louisiana State University. Unpublished report.

Bass, B. M. (1956). Leadership opinions as forecasts of supervisory success. *Journal of Applied Psychology, 40*, 345–346.

Bass, B. M. (1957a). Leadership opinions and related characteristics of salesmen and sales managers. In R. M. Stogdill & A. E. Coons (Eds.), *Leader behavior: Its description and measurement.* Columbus: Ohio State University, Bureau of Business Research.

Bass, B. M. (1957b). Behavior in groups. *Third Annual ONR Report.* Baton Rouge: Louisiana State University.

Bass, B. M. (1958). Leadership opinions as forecasts of supervisory success: A replication. *Personnel Psychology, 11*, 515–518.

Bass, B. M. (1959). Great men or great times? *Adult Leadership, 8*, 7–10.

Bass, B. M. (1960). *Leadership, psychology, and organizational behavior.* New York: Harper.

Bass, B. M. (1961a). Conformity, deviation, and a general theory of interpersonal behavior. In I. A. Berg & B. M. Bass (Eds.), *Conformity and deviation.* New York: Harper.

Bass, B. M. (1961b). Some aspects of attempted, successful, and effective leadership. *Journal of Applied Psychology, 45*, 120–122.

Bass, B. M. (1961c). Some observations about a general theory of leadership and interpersonal behavior. In L. Petrullo & B. M. Bass (Eds.), *Leadership and interpersonal behavior.* New York: Holt, Rinehart & Winston.

Bass, B. M. (1962a). Mood changes during training laboratory. *Journal of Applied Psychology, 46*, 361–364.

Bass, B. M. (1962b). *Orientation Inventory.* Palo Alto, CA: Consulting Psychologists Press.

Bass, B. M. (1962c). Reactions to "Twelve Angry Men" as a measure of sensitivity training. *Journal of Applied Psychology, 46*, 120–124.

Bass, B. M. (1963). Amount of participation, coalescence, and probability of decision making discussions. *Journal of Abnormal and Social Psychology*, 67, 92–94.

Bass, B. M. (1964). Business gaming for organizational research. *Management Science*, 10, 545–556.

Bass, B. M. (1965a). *Orientation and reactions to coercive, persuasive, and permissive leadership* (Tech. Rep. No. 4). Pittsburgh: University of Pittsburgh, Office of Naval Research.

Bass, B. M. (1965b). *Social behavior and the orientation inventory* (Tech. Rep. No. 9). Pittsburgh: University of Pittsburgh, Office of Naval Research.

Bass, B. M (1965c). *Organizational psychology.* Boston: Allyn & Bacon.

Bass, B. M. (1966a). A plan to use programmed group exercises to study cross-cultural differences in management behavior. *International Journal of Psychology*, 1, 315–322.

Bass, B. M. (1966b). Effects on the subsequent performance of negotiators of studying issues or planning strategies alone or in groups. *Psychological Monographs*, 80, No. 6.

Bass, B. M. (1967a). Combining management training and research. *Training & Development Journal*, 21(4), 2–7.

Bass, B. M. (1967b). Some effects on a group of whether and when the head reveals his opinion. *Organizational Behavior and Human Performance*, 2, 375–382.

Bass, B. M. (1967c). Social behavior and the orientation inventory: A review. *Psychological Bulletin*, 68, 260–292.

Bass, B. M. (1967d). The anarchist movement and the T group: Some possible lessons for organizational development. *Journal of Applied Behavioral Science*, 3, 211–227.

Bass, B. M. (1967e). Implications of behavioral science in the year 2000. In *Management 2000.* New York: American Management Association.

Bass, B. M. (1968a). Ability, values, and concepts of equitable salary increases in exercise compensation. *Journal of Applied Psychology*, 52, 299–303.

Bass, B. M. (1968b). *A preliminary report on manifest preferences in six cultures for participative management* (Tech. Rep. No. 21). Rochester, NY: University of Rochester, Management Research Center.

Bass, B. M. (1968c). How to succeed in business according to business students and managers. *Journal of Applied Psychology*, 52, 254–262.

Bass, B. M. (1970a). When planning for others. *Journal of Applied Behavioral Science*, 6, 151–171.

Bass, B. M. (1970b). Errata: How to succeed in business according to business students and managers. *Journal of Applied Psychology*, 54, 103.

Bass, B. M. (1971). *PROFAIR—an affirmative action program for women employees.* Scottsville, NY: Transnational Programs.

Bass, B. M. (1974). The substance and the shadow. *American Psychologist*, 29, 870–886.

Bass, B. M. (1975a). *Exercise objectives.* Scottsville, NY: Transnational Programs.

Bass, B. M. (1975b). *Exercise compensation.* Scottsville, NY: Transnational Programs.

Bass, B. M. (1975c). *Exercise supervise.* Scottsville, NY: Transnational Programs.

Bass, B. M. (1975d). *Exercise organization.* Scottsville, NY: Transnational Programs.

Bass, B. M. (1975e). *Exercise life goals.* Scottsville, NY: Transnational Programs.

Bass, B. M. (1975f). *Exercise self appraisal.* Scottsville, NY: Transnational Programs.

Bass, B. M. (1975g). *Exercise communication.* Scottsville, NY: Transnational Programs.

Bass, B. M. (1975h). *Exercise organization.* Scottsville, NY: Transnational Programs.

Bass, B. M. (1975i). *PEX—a program of exercises in management and organizational development.* Scottsville, NY: Transnational Programs.

Bass, B. M. (1975j). *Program of exercises for management and organizational psychology.* Scottsville, NY: Transnational Programs.

Bass, B. M. (1976). A systems survey research feedback for management and organizational development. *Journal of Applied Behavioral Science*, 12, 215–229.

Bass, B. M. (1977). Utility of managerial self-planning on a simulated production task with replications in twelve countries. *Journal of Applied Psychology*, 62, 506–509.

Bass, B. M. (1980). Team productivity and individual member competence. *Small Group Behavior*, 11, 431–504.

Bass, B. M. (1981). Individual capability, team response, and productivity. In E. A. Fleishman & M. D. Dunnette (Eds.), *Human performance and productivity.* New York: Erlbaum.

Bass, B. M. (1982). Intensity of relation, dyadic-group considerations, cognitive categorization, and transformational leadership. In J. G. Hunt, U. Sekaran, & C. A. Schriesheim (Eds.), *Leadership beyond establishment views.* Carbondale: Southern Illinois University Press.

Bass, B. M. (1983a). Leadership and management in the 1980's. In A. Glickman (Ed.), *The changing composition of the work force.* New York: Lawrence Erlbaum.

Bass, B. M. (1983b). *Organizational decision-making.* Homstead, IL: Richard D. Irwin.

Bass, B. M. (1983c). Issues involved in relations between methodological rigor and reported outcomes in evaluation of organizational development. *Journal of Applied Psychology*, 68, 197–199.

Bass, B. M. (1983d). Leadership, participation and non-trivial decision-making. In J. G. Hunt & C. A. Schriesheim (Eds.), *New frontiers in leadership research.* New York: Oxford University Press.

Bass, B. M. (1985a). *Leadership and performance beyond expectations.* New York: Free Press.

Bass, B. M. (1985b). Leadership: Good, better, best. *Organizational Dynamics*, 13(3), 26–40.

Bass, B. M. (1985c). *The multifactor leadership questionnaire—form 5.* Binghamton: State University of New York.

Bass, B. M. (1987). *Producing more new model leadership* (Working Paper No. 86-113). Binghamton: State University of New York, School of Management.

Bass, B. M. (1988a). The inspirational processes of leadership. *Journal of Management Development, 7*(5), 21-31.

Bass, B. M. (1988b). Evolving perspectives on charismatic leadership. In J. Conger & J. B. Kanungo (Eds.), *Charismatic leadership: The illusive factor in organizational effectiveness.* San Francisco: Jossey-Bass.

Bass, B. M. (1988c). Policy implications of transformational leadership. In R. W. Woodman & W. A. Pasmore (Eds.), *Research in organizational change and development.* Greenwich, CT: JAI Press.

Bass, B. M. (1989). The two faces of charismatic leadership. *Leaders Magazine, 12*(4), 44-45.

Bass, B. M., Alexander, R. A., Barrett, G. V., & Ryterband, E. C. (1971). Empathy, projection and negation in seven countries. In L. E. Abt & B. F. Reiss (Eds.), *Progress in clinical psychology: Industrial applications.* New York: Grune & Stratton.

Bass, B. M., & Avolio, B. J. (1987). *Biases in leadership ratings* (Working Paper No. 87-124). Binghamton: State University of New York.

Bass, B. M., & Avolio, B. J., (1988). *Prototypicality, leniency and generalized response set in rated and ranked transformational and transactional leadership descriptions.* (Report Series 88-2), Binghamton: State University of New York, Center for Leadership Studies. Also: (1989). Potential biases in leadership measures: How prototypes, leniency, and general satisfaction relate to ratings and rankings of transformational and transactional leadership constructs. *Educational and Psychological Measurement, 49,* 509-527.

Bass, B. M., & Avolio, B. J. (1989). *Manual: The Multifactor Leadership Questionnaire.* Palo Alto, CA: Consulting Psychologists Press.

Bass, B. M., Avolio, B. J., & Goodheim, L. (1987). Biography and the assessment of transformational leadership at the world-class level. *Journal of Management, 13,* 7-19.

Bass, B. M., & Barrett, G. V. (1972). *Man, work and organizations: An introduction to industrial and organizational psychology.* Boston: Allyn & Bacon.

Bass, B. M., & Barrett, G. V. (1981). *People, work and organizations: An introduction to industrial and organizational psychology.* Boston: Allyn & Bacon.

Bass, B. M., Binder, M. J., & Breed, W. (1967). *Profitability and good relations: Which is cause and which is effect?* (Brief No. 4). Pittsburgh: University of Pittsburgh, Management Research Center.

Bass, B. M., Burger, P. C., Doktor, R., & Barrett, G. V. (1979). *Assessment of managers: An international comparison.* New York: Free Press.

Bass, B. M., Cascio, W. F., & McPherson, J. W. (1972). *PROSPER—an affirmative action for black employees.* Scottsville, NY: Transnational Programs.

Bass, B. M., Cascio, W. F., McPherson, J. W., & Tragash, H. J. (1976). PROSPER—training and research for increasing management awareness about affirmative action in race relations. *Academy of Management Journal, 19,* 353-369.

Bass, B. M., & Coates, C. H. (1952). Forecasting officer potential using the leaderless group discussion. *Journal of Abnormal and Social Psychology, 47,* 321-325.

Bass, B. M., & Coates, C. H. (1953). *Situational and personality factors in leadership in ROTC.* Baton Rouge: Louisiana State University.

Bass, B. M., & Dunteman, G. (1963). Behavior in groups as a function of self, interaction, and task orientation. *Journal of Abnormal and Social Psychology, 66,* 419-428.

Bass, B. M., Dunteman, G., Frye, F., Vidulich, R., & Wambach, H. (1963). Self, interaction, and task orientation inventory scores associated with overt behavior and personal factors. *Educational and Psychological Measurement, 23,* 101-116.

Bass, B. M., & Farrow, D. L. (1977a). Quantitative analyses of biographies of political figures. *Journal of Psychology, 97,* 281-296.

Bass, B. M., & Farrow, D. L. (1977b). *A phoenix arises: The importance of manager and subordinate personality in contingency leadership analysis.* Paper, Western Academy of Management, Sun Valley, ID.

Bass, B. M., Farrow, D. L., & Valenzi, E. R. (1977). *A regression approach to identifying ways to increase leadership effectiveness* (Tech. Rep. No. 77-3). Rochester, NY: University of Rochester, U.S. Army Research Institute for the Behavioral and Social Sciences.

Bass, B. M., & Flint, A. W. (1958a). *Some effects of power, practice and problem difficulty on success as a leader* (Tech. Rep. No. 18). Baton Rouge: Louisiana State University.

Bass, B. M., & Flint, A. W. (1958b). *Comparison of the construct validation of three objective measures of successful leadership.* Baton Rouge: Louisiana State University.

Bass, B. M., Flint, A. W., & Pryer, M. W. (1957a). *Group effectiveness as a function of attempted and successful leadership.* Baton Rouge: Louisiana State University.

Bass, B. M., Flint, A. W., & Pryer, M. W. (1957b). *Effects of status-esteem conflict on subsequent behavior in groups.* Baton Rouge: Louisiana State University.

Bass, B. M., & Franke, R. H. (1972). Societal influences on student perceptions of how to succeed in organizations: A cross-national analysis. *Journal of Applied Psychology, 56,* 312-318.

Bass, B. M., Gaier, E. E., Farese, F. J., & Flint, A. W. (1957). An objective method for studying behavior in groups. *Psychological Reports, 3,* 265-280. Also: Bass, B. M. (1960). Measures of average influence and change in agreement of rankings by a group of judges. *Sociometry, 23,* 195-202.

Bass, B. M., Gaier, E. L., & Flint, A. W. (1956). *Attempted leadership as a function of motivation interacting with amount of control.* Baton Rouge: Louisiana State University.

Bass, B. M., Hurder, W. P., & Ellis, N. (1954). *Human stress tolerance* (Final Tech. Rep.). Baton Rouge: Louisiana State University, USAF Aero-Medical Lab.

Bass, B. M., Klauss, R., & DeMarco, J. J. (1977). *Factors influencing communication style* (Tech. Rep. No. 4). Syracuse, NY: Syracuse University.

Bass, B. M., & Klubeck, S. (1952). Effects of seating arrangement of leaderless group discussions. *Journal of Abnormal and Social Psychology, 47,* 724-727.

Bass, B. M., Krusell, J., & Alexander, R. A. (1971). Male managers' attitudes toward working women. *American Behavioral Scientist, 15,* 221-236.

Bass, B. M., & Leavitt, H. J. (1963). Some experiments in planning and operating. *Management Science, 9,* 574-585.

Bass, B. M., McGehee, C. R., Hawkins, W. C., Young, P. C., & Gebel, A. S.

(1953). Personality variables related to leaderless group discussion behavior. *Journal of Abnormal and Social Psychology, 48,* 120–128.

Bass, B. M., & Mitchell, C. W. (1976). Influences on the felt need for collective bargaining by business and science professionals. *Journal of Applied Psychology, 61,* 770–773.

Bass, B. M., & Norton, F. M. (1951). Group size and leaderless discussions. *Journal of Applied Psychology, 35,* 397–400.

Bass, B. M., Pryer, M. W., Gaier, E. L., & Flint, A. W. (1958). Interacting effects of control, motivation, group practice, and problem difficulty on attempted leadership. *Journal of Abnormal and Social Psychology, 56,* 352–358.

Bass, B. M., & Rosenstein, E. (1977). Integration of industrial democracy and participative management: U.S. and European perspectives. In B. T. King, S. S. Streufert, & F. E. Fiedler (Eds.), *Managerial control and organizational democracy.* Washington, DC: Victor Winston & Sons.

Bass, B. M., & Ryterband, E. C. (1974). Work and organizational life in 2001. In M. D. Dunnette (Ed.), *Work and nonwork in the year 2001.* Monterey, CA: Brooks/Cole.

Bass, B. M., & Ryterband, E. C. (1979). *Organizational psychology* (2nd ed.). Boston: Allyn & Bacon.

Bass, B. M., & Shackleton, V. J. (1979). Industrial democracy and participative management: A case for synthesis. *Academy of Management Review, 4,* 393–404.

Bass, B. M., & Thiagarajan, K. M. (1969). Differential preferences for long- vs. short-term payoffs in India and the United States. *Proceedings, International Congress of Applied Psychology.* Amsterdam: Swets & Zeitlinger.

Bass, B. M., & Valenzi, E. R. (1973). *PROFILE.* Scottsville, NY: Transnational Programs.

Bass, B. M., & Valenzi, E. R. (1974). Contingent aspects of effective management styles. In J. G. Hunt & L. L. Larson (Eds.), *Contingency approaches to leadership.* Carbondale: Southern Illinois University Press.

Bass, B. M., Valenzi, E. R., & Farrow, D. L. (1977). *External environment related to managerial style* (Tech. Rep. No. 77-2). Rochester, NY: University of Rochester, U.S. Army Research Institute for the Behavioral and Social Sciences. Also: (1977). *Proceedings, International Conference on Social Change and Organizational Development,* Dubrovnik, Yugoslavia.

Bass, B. M., Valenzi, E. R., & Farrow, D. L. (1978). *Discriminant functions to identify ways to increase leadership effectiveness.* Paper, Eastern Academy of Management, New York.

Bass, B. M., Valenzi, E. R., Farrow, D. L., & Solomon, R. J. (1975). Management styles associated with organizational, task, personal, and interpersonal contingencies. *Journal of Applied Psychology, 60,* 720–729.

Bass, B. M., & Vaughan, J. A. (1965). *The psychology of learning for managers.* New York: American Foundation for Management Research.

Bass, B. M., & Vaughan, J. A. (1966). *Training in industry: The management of learning.* Belmont, CA: Brooks/Cole.

Bass, B. M., Waldman, D. A., Avolio, B. J., & Bebb, M. (1987). Transformational leadership and the falling dominoes effect. *Group & Organization Studies, 12,* 73–87.

Bass, B. M., & White, O. L. (1951). Situation tests. III. Observers' ratings of leaderless group discussion participants as indicators of external leadership status. *Educational and Psychological Measurement, 11,* 355–361.

Bass, B. M., & Wurster, C. R. (1953a). Effects of the nature of the problem on LGD performance. *Journal of Applied Psychology, 37,* 96–99.

Bass, B. M., & Wurster, C. R. (1953b). Effects of company rank on LGD of oil refinery supervisors' performance. *Journal of Applied Psychology, 37,* 100–104.

Bass, B. M., Wurster, C. R., & Alcock, W. (1961). A test of the proposition: We want to be esteemed most by those we esteem most highly. *Journal of Abnormal and Social Psychology, 63,* 650–653.

Bass, B. M., Wurster, C. R., Doll, P. A., & Clair, D. J. (1953). Situational and personality factors in leadership among sorority women. *Psychological Monographs, 67,* 1–23.

Bass, B. M., & Yammarino, F. J. (1988). *Leadership: Dispositional and situational.* (ONR Tech. Rep. No. 1). Binghamton: State University of New York, Center for Leadership Studies.

Bass, B. M., & Yammarino, F. J., (1989). *Transformational leaders know themselves better* (ONR Tech. Rep. No. 5). Binghamton: State University of New York, Center for Leadership Studies.

Bassett, G. A., & Meyer, H. H. (1968). Performance appraisal based on self-review. *Personnel Psychology, 21,* 421–430.

Batchelder, R. L., & Hardy, J. M. (1968). *Using sensitivity training and laboratory method: An organizational case study in the development of human resources.* New York: Association Press.

Bateman, T. S., Strasser, S., & Dailey, R. C. (1983). Toward proper specification of the effects of leader punitive behavior: A research note. *Journal of Management, 8,* 83–93.

Bates, A. P. (1952). Some sociometric aspects of social ranking in a small, face-to-face group. *Sociometry, 15,* 330–342.

Bates, F. L. (1953). *The coordination of maintenance activities in bomb wings: Synchronization and performance.* Chapel Hill: University of North Carolina, Institute for Research and Social Science.

Batkins, J. F. (1982). A descriptive study of power: Exploring directors' styles, staff climates and organizational efficiency in human services. *Dissertation Abstracts International, 43*(2B), 505.

Baum, B. H. (1961). *Decentralization of authority in a bureaucracy.* Englewood Cliffs, NJ: Prentice-Hall.

Baum, B. H., Sorensen, P. F., & Place, W. S. (1970). The effect of managerial training on organizational control: An experimental study. *Organizational Behavior and Human Performance, 5,* 170–182.

Baumgartel, H. (1956). Leadership, motivations, and attitudes in research laboratories. *Journal of Social Issues, 12,* 23–31.

Baumgartel, H. (1957). Leadership style as a variable in research administration. *Administrative Science Quarterly, 2,* 344–360.

Baumgartel, H., Bennis, W. G., & DeNitish, R. (1967). *Readings in group development for managers and trainers.* New York: Asia Publishing House.

Baumgartel, H., & Goldstein, J. W. (1967). Need and value shifts in college training groups. *Journal of Applied Behavioral Science, 3,* 87–101.

Baumgartel, H., & Jeanpierre, F. (1972). Applying knowledge in the back home setting. *Journal of Applied Behavioral Science, 8,* 674–694.

Baumrind, D. (1971). Current patterns of parental authority. *Developmental Psychology Monographs, 4* (4, Part 2).

Baumrind, D. (1972). An exploratory study of socialization effects on black children: Some black-white comparisons. *Child Development, 43,* 261–267.

Bavelas, A. (1942). Morale and the training of leaders. In G. Watson (Ed.), *Civilian morale.* Boston: Houghton Mifflin.

Bavelas, A. (1948). Some problems of organizational change. *Journal of Social Issues, 4,* 48–52.

Bavelas, A. (1950). Communication patterns in task-oriented groups. *Journal of Acoustical Society of America, 22,* 725–730.

Bavelas, A. (1960). Leadership: Man and function. *Administrative Science Quarterly, 4,* 491–498.

Bavelas, A., Hastorf, A. H., Gross, A. E., & Kite, W. R. (1965). Experiments on the alteration of group structure. *Journal of Experimental Social Psychology, 1,* 55–70.

Baxter, B. (1953). A training evaluation study. *Personnel Psychology, 6,* 403–417.

Baxter, B., & Cassidy, R. (1943). *Group experience, the democratic way.* New York: Harper.

Bayer, A. E., & Boruch, R. F. (1969). *The black student in American colleges,* Research Report No. 4(2). Washington, DC: American Council on Education.

Bayes, M., & Newton, P. M. (1978). Women in authority: A sociopsychological analysis. *Journal of Applied Behavioral Science, 14,* 7–20.

Beach, B. H., & Beach, L. R. (1978). A note on judgments of situational favorableness and probability of success. *Organizational Behavior and Human Performance, 22,* 69–74.

Beam, H. H. (1975). *Effectiveness and satisfaction as a function of managerial style and technological complexity in a Navy work environment.* Doctoral dissertation, University of Michigan, Ann Arbor.

Beatty, J. R., McCune, J. T., and Beatty, R. W. (1988). A policy-capturing approach to the study of United States and Japanese managers' compensation decisions. *Journal of Management, 14,* 465–474.

Beatty, J. R., Owens, A. E., & Jenner, S. R. (undated). Perceptual differences of leadership styles between Japanese supervisors and U. S. subordinates. Unpublished manuscript.

Beatty, R. W. (1973). Blacks as supervisors: A study of training job performance and employer expectations. *Academy of Management Journal, 10,* 191–206.

Beatty, R. W. (1974). Supervisory behavior related to job success of hard-core unemployed over a two-year period. *Journal of Applied Psychology, 59,* 38–42.

Beatty, R. W., & Schneier, C. E. (1972). Training the hard-core unemployed through positive reinforcement. *Human Resource Management, 11,* 11–17.

Bechard, J. E. (1971). *The college of education at Michigan State University as an organization: A survey of the perceptions of its students, faculty and administrators.* Doctoral dissertation, Michigan State University, East Lansing.

Bechtel, R. B., & Rosenfeld, H. M. (1966). Expectations of social acceptance and compatibility as related to status discrepancy and social motives. *Journal of Personality and Social Psychology, 3,* 300–349.

Bechterew, W., & Lange, A. (1924/1931). Die Ergebnisse des Experiments auf dem Gebiete der kollektiven Reflexologie. *Zeitschrift für angewandte Psychologie, 24,* 224–254. (Reported in G. Murphy & L. Murphy, *Experimental social psychology,* New York: Harper, 1931.)

Beck, M. (1980, February 18). Women in the armed forces. *Newsweek,* 34–36, 39–42.

Becker, M. H. (1970). Sociometric location and innovativeness: Reformulation and extension of the diffusion model. *American Sociological Review, 35,* 267–304.

Becker, S. W., & Baloff, N. (1969). Organization structure and complex problem solving. *Administrative Science Quarterly, 14,* 260–271.

Beckhard, R. (1966). An organization improvement program in a decentralized organization. *Journal of Applied Behavioral Science, 2,* 3–25.

Beckhard, R. (1969). *Organizational development: Strategies and models.* Reading, MA: Addison-Wesley.

Beckman, L. J. (1984). Husbands' and wives' relative influence on fertility decisions and outcomes. *Population & Environment: Behavioral & Social Issues, 7,* 182–197.

Bednar, D. A., & Heisler, W. J. (1985). Relationships between communicator style and instructional effectiveness in an industrial training setting. *Proceedings, Academy of Management,* San Diego, CA, 114–118.

Bedrosian, H. (1964). An analysis of vocational interests at two levels of management. *Journal of Applied Psychology, 48,* 325–328.

Beebe, R. J. (1975). The least preferred co-worker score of the leader and the productivity of small interacting task groups in octants II and IV of the Fiedler contingency model. *Dissertation Abstracts International, 35,* 3642.

Beehr, A., & Gupta, N. (1987). Organizational management styles, employee supervisory status, and employee responses. *Human Relations, 40,* 45–57.

Beer, M. (1964). *Leadership, employee needs, and motivation.* Doctoral dissertation, Ohio State University, Columbus.

Beer, M. (1968). Needs and need satisfaction among clerical workers in complex and routine jobs. *Personnel Psychology, 21,* 209–222.

Beer, M., Buckhout, R., Horowitz, M. W., & Levy, S. (1959). Some perceived properties of the differences between leaders and nonleaders. *Journal of Psychology, 47,* 49–56.

Beer, S. (1966). *Decision and control.* New York: Wiley.

Behling, O., Gifford, W. E., & Tolliver, J. M. (1980). Effects of grouping information on decision making under risk. *Decision Sciences, 11,* 272–283.

Behling, O., & Schriesheim, C. (1976). *Organizational behavior: Theory, research, and application.* Boston: Allyn & Bacon.

Belasco, J. A. (1973). Educational innovation: The impact of organizational and community variables on performance contract. *Management Science, 20*, 498–506.

Belasco, J. A., & Trice, H. M. (1969a). *The assessment of change in training and therapy.* New York: McGraw-Hill.

Belasco, J. A., & Trice, H. M. (1969b). Unanticipated returns of training. *Training & Development Journal, 23*, 12–17.

Bell, D. (1956). *Work and its discontents.* Boston: Beacon Press.

Bell, G. B. (1951). *The relationship between leadership and empathy.* Doctoral dissertation, Northwestern University, Evanston, IL.

Bell, G. B. (1967). Determinants of span of control. *American Journal of Sociology, 73*, 100–109.

Bell, G. B., & French, R. L. (1950). Consistency of individual leadership position in small groups of varying membership. *Journal of Abnormal and Social Psychology, 45*, 764–767.

Bell, G. B., & Hall, H. E. (1954). The relationship between leadership and empathy. *Journal of Abnormal and Social Psychology, 49*, 156–157.

Bell, T. O. (1969). A study of personality characteristics of school superintendents in relation to administrative behavior. *Dissertation Abstracts, 29A*, 2049–2050.

Bell, W., Hill, R. J., & Wright, C. R. (1961). *Public leadership: A critical review with special reference to adult education.* San Francisco: Chandler.

Bellingrath, G. C. (1930). *Qualities associated with leadership in extracurricular activities of the high school.* New York: Teachers College Contributions to Education.

Bellows, R. M. (1959). *Creative leadership.* Englewood Cliffs, NJ: Prentice-Hall.

Bellows, R. M., Gilson, T. Q., & Odiorne, G. S. (1962). *Executive skills: Their dynamics and development.* Englewood Cliffs, NJ: Prentice-Hall.

Bem, D. J. (1970). *Beliefs, attitudes, and human affairs.* Belmont, CA: Brooks/Cole.

Benbow, C. P., & Stanley, J. C. (1983). Sex differences in mathematical reasoning: More Facts. *Science, 222*, 1029–31.

Bender, I. E., & Hastorf, A. H. (1950). The perception of persons: Forecasting another person's responses on three personality scales. *Journal of Abnormal and Social Psychology, 45*, 556–561.

Bender, J. M. (1973). What is "typical" of assessment centers? *Personnel, 50*(4), 50–57.

Bender, L. R. (1979). *Women as leaders: The impact of leader attributes of masculinity and femininity and of follower attributes toward women.* Doctoral dissertation, State University of New York at Buffalo.

Bendix, R. (1974). *Work and authority in industry.* Berkeley: University of California Press.

Bendo, J. J. (1984). Application of counseling and communication techniques to supervisory training in industry. *Dissertation Abstracts International, 45*(3B), 1050.

Benezet, L. T., Katz, J., & Magnusson, F. W. (1981). *Style and substance: Leadership and the college presidency.* Washington, DC: American Council on Education.

Benne, K. D. (1943). *A conception of authority.* New York: Teachers College, Columbia University.

Benne, K. D., Bradford, L. P., & Lippitt, R. (1964). The laboratory method. In L. P. Bradford, J. R. Gibb, & K. D. Benne (Eds.), *T-group theory and laboratory method.* New York: Wiley.

Benne, K. D., & Sheats, P. (1948). Functional roles of group members. *Journal of Social Issues, 4*, 41–49.

Benner, P. E. (1984). *Stress and satisfaction on the job.* New York: Praeger.

Bennett, A. (1986, February 12). American culture is often a puzzle for foreign managers in the U.S. *Wall Street Journal*, 33.

Bennett, E. B. (1955). Discussion, decisions, commitment and consensus in "group decision." *Human Relations, 8*, 251–273.

Bennett, E. (1963). *Human factors in technology.* New York: McGraw-Hill.

Bennett, E. B. (1971). Discussion, decisions, commitment, and consensus in "group decision." *Human Relations, 8*, 251–273.

Bennett, M. (1977). Testing management theories culturally. *Journal of Applied Psychology, 62*, 578–581.

Bennis, W. G. (1959). Leadership theory and administrative behavior: The problems of authority. *Administrative Science Quarterly, 4*, 259–301.

Bennis, W. G. (1961). Revisionist theory of leadership. *Harvard Business Review, 39*(1), 26–36, 146–150.

Bennis, W. G. (1963). Effecting organizational change: A new role for the behavioral scientist. *Administrative Science Quarterly, 8*, 125–165.

Bennis, W. G. (1964). Goals and meta-goals of laboratory training. In W. G. Bennis (Ed.), *Interpersonal dynamics, essays and readings on human interaction.* Homewood, IL: Dorsey.

Bennis, W. G. (1965). Theory and method in applying behavioral science to planned organizational change. *Journal of Applied Behavioral Science, 1*, 337–360.

Bennis, W. G. (1966a). *Changing organizations.* New York: McGraw-Hill.

Bennis, W. G. (1966b). Changing organizations. *Journal of Applied Behavioral Science, 2*, 247–263.

Bennis, W. G. (1966c). Organizational developments and the fate of bureaucracy. *Industrial Relations Review, 7*, 41–55.

Bennis, W. G. (1969). *Organizational development: Its nature, origins, and prospects.* Reading, MA: Addison-Wesley.

Bennis, W. G. (1970). *American bureaucracy.* Chicago: Aldine.

Bennis, W. G. (1976). *The unconscious conspiracy: Why leaders can't lead.* New York: AMACOM.

Bennis, W. G. (1982, May). Leadership transforms vision into action. *Industry Week*, 54–56.

Bennis, W. G. (1983, April). Transformative leadership. *Harvard University Newsletter.*

Bennis, W. G. (1984). The 4 competencies of leadership. *Training & Development Journal, 38*(8), 14–19.

Bennis, W. G. (1989). *Why leaders can't lead: The unconscious conspiracy continues.* San Francisco: Jossey-Bass.

Bennis, W. G., Benne, K. D., & Chin, R. (1962). *The planning of change: Readings in the applied behavioral sciences.* New York: Holt, Rinehart & Winston.

Bennis, W. G., Berkowitz, N., Affinito, M., & Malone, M. (1958). Authority, power, and the ability to influence. *Human Relations, 11,* 143–155.

Bennis, W. G., & Nanus, B. (1985). *Leaders: The strategies for taking charge.* New York: Harper & Row.

Benoit-Smullyan, E. (1944). Status, status types, and status interrelations. *American Sociological Review, 9,* 151–161.

Bensahel, J. G. (1981). Are you ready to cope with those minor crises? *International Management, 36*(2), 24–25.

Bensimon, E. M. (1987). *The meaning of good presidential leadership: A frame analysis.* Paper, National Meeting of the Association for the Study of Higher Education, Baltimore.

Bensman, J., & Givant, M. (1975). Charisma and modernity: The use and abuse of a concept. *Social Research, 42,* 570–614.

Bensman, J., & Rosenberg, B. (1960). The meaning of work in bureaucratic society. In M. R. Stein, A. J. Vidich, & D. M. White (Eds.), *Identity and anxiety: Survival of the person in mass society.* Glencoe, IL: Free Press.

Benson, P. G., Kemery, E. R., Sauser, W. I., & Tankesley, K. E. (1985). Need for clarity as a moderator of the role ambiguity–job satisfaction relationship. *Journal of Management, 11,* 125–130.

Bentz, V. J. (undated). *Leadership, a study of social interaction.* Unpublished manuscript.

Bentz, V. J. (1964). *The Sears experience in the investigation, description, and prediction of executive behavior.* Chicago: Sears, Roebuck. Unpublished report.

Bentz, V. J. (1967). The Sears experience in the investigation, description and prediction of executive behavior. In F. R. Wickert & D. F. McFarland (Eds.), *Measuring executive effectiveness,* Chap. 7, 147–205. New York: Appleton-Century-Crofts.

Bentz, V. J. (1968). The Sears experience in the investigation, description and prediction of executive behavior. In J. A. Myers, Jr. (Ed.), *Predicting managerial success.* Ann Arbor, MI: Foundation for Research on Human Behavior.

Bentz, V. J. (1971). *Validity of Sears assessment center procedures.* Paper, American Psychological Association, Washington, DC.

Bentz, V. J. (1983). *Research findings from personality assessment of executives.* Paper, Sixth Annual Symposium on Applied Behavioral Science, Virginia Polytechnical Institute, Blacksburg.

Bentz, V. J. (1987). *Explorations of scope and scale: The critical determinant of high-level effectiveness* (Tech. Rep. No. 31). Greensboro, NC: Center for Creative Leadership.

Ben-Yoav, O., Hollander, E. P., & Carnevale, P. J. D. (1983). Leader legitimacy, leader-follower interaction, and followers' ratings of the leader. *Journal of Social Psychology, 121,* 111–115.

Benze, J. G., Jr. (1985). Presidential reorganization as a tactical weapon: Putting politics back into administration. *Presidential Studies Quarterly, 15,* 145–157.

Berelson, B., & Steiner, G. A. (1964). *Human behavior: An inventory of scientific findings.* New York: Harcourt, Brace & World.

Berg, I. A., & Bass, B. M. (1961). *Conformity and deviation.* New York: Harper.

Bergen, H. B. (1939, April). Finding out what employees are thinking. *Conference Board Management Record,* 53–58.

Bergen, S. A. (1986). *Project Management,* New York: Basil Blackwell.

Berger, C., and Braduc, J. (1982). *Language and social knowledge: Uncertainty in interpersonal relations.* London: Arnold.

Berger, C. R. (1969). The effects of influence feedback and need influence on the relationship between incentive magnitude and attitude change. *Dissertation Abstracts International, 30,* 385–386.

Berger, P. L. (1963). Charisma and religious innovation: The social location of Israelite prophecy. *American Sociological Review, 28,* 940–949.

Bergum, B. O., & Lehr, D. J. (1963). Effects of authoritarianism on vigilance performance. *Journal of Applied Psychology, 47,* 75–77.

Berkes, L. J., & Rauch, C. F., Jr. (1981). The use of the adaptive process regression program to analyze leadership effectiveness in a police organization. *Proceedings, Academy of Management,* San Diego, CA.

Berkowitz, L. (1953a). An exploratory study of the roles of aircraft commanders. *USAF Human Resources Research Center and Research Bulletin, No. 53–65,* 1–27.

Berkowitz, L. (1953b). Sharing leadership in small, decision-making groups. *Journal of Abnormal and Social Psychology, 48,* 231–238.

Berkowitz, L. (1954). Group standards, cohesiveness, and productivity. *Human Relations, 7,* 509–519.

Berkowitz, L. (1956a). Personality and group position. *Sociometry, 19,* 210–222.

Berkowitz, L. (1956b). Social desirability and frequency of influence attempts as factors in leadership choice. *Journal of Personality, 24,* 424–435.

Berkowitz, L. (1956c). Group norms among bomber crews: Patterns of perceived crew attitudes, "actual" crew attitudes, and crew liking related to aircrew effectiveness in Far Eastern combat. *Sociometry, 19,* 141–153.

Berkowitz, L. (1957a). Effects of perceived dependency relationships upon conformity to group expectations. *Journal of Abnormal and Social Psychology, 55,* 350–354.

Berkowitz, L. (1957b). Liking for the group and the perceived merit of the group's behavior. *Journal of Abnormal and Social Psychology, 54,* 353–357.

Berkowitz, L. (1960). Some factors affecting the reduction of overt hostility. *Journal of Abnormal and Social Psychology, 60,* 14–21.

Berkowitz, L. (1969). *Advances in experimental social psychology,* Vol. 4. New York: Academic Press.

Berkowitz, L. (1970). *Advances in experimental social psychology,* Vol. 5. New York: Academic Press.

Berkowitz, L., & Connor, W. H. (1966). Success, failure, and social responsibility. *Journal of Personality and Social Psychology, 4,* 664–669.

Berkowitz, L., & Daniels, L. R. (1963). Responsibility and dependency. *Journal of Abnormal and Social Psychology, 66,* 429–436.

Berkowitz, L., & Daniels, L. R. (1964). Affecting the salience of the social responsibility norm; Effects of past help on the response to dependency relationships. *Journal of Abnormal and Social Psychology, 68,* 275–281.

Berkowitz, L., & Haythorn, W. (1955). *The relationship of dominance to leadership choice.* San Antonio, TX: Crew Research Laboratory, AF Personnel & Training Reserve Center, Randolph AF Base, LN-55-8.

Berkowitz, L., & Howard, R. C. (1959). Reactions to opinion deviates as affected by affiliation need (n) and group member interdependence. *Sociometry, 22,* 81–91.

Berkowitz, L., & Levy, B. I. (1956). Pride in group performance and group-task motivation. *Journal of Abnormal and Social Psychology, 53,* 300–306.

Berkowitz, L., & Lundy, R. M. (1957). Personality characteristics related to susceptibility to influence by peers or authority figures. *Journal of Personality, 25,* 306–316.

Berkowitz, L., & Macaulay, J. R. (1961). Some effects of differences in status level and status stability. *Human Relations, 14,* 135–148.

Berkowitz, N. H., & Bennis, W. G. (1961). Interaction patterns in formal service-oriented organization. *Administrative Science Quarterly, 6,* 25–50.

Berle, N. S., Biscone, C. G., Katz, B., Lane, M. E., et al. (1981). *Gender isolation: All alone in a crowd.* Paper, Academy of Management, San Diego, CA.

Berlew, D. E. (1974). Leadership and organizational excitement. In D. A. Kolb, I. M. Rubin, and J. M. McIntyre (Eds.), *Organizational psychology.* Englewood Cliffs, NJ: Prentice-Hall.

Berlew, D. E., & Hall, D. T. (1966). The socialization of managers: Effects of expectations on performance. *Administrative Science Quarterly, 11,* 207–223.

Berlew, D. E., & Heller, D. (1983). Style flexibility—tools for successful leaders. *Legal Economics, 9*(6), 34–37.

Berlyne, D. E. (1950). Novelty and curiosity as determinants of exploratory behavior. *British Journal of Psychology, 41,* 68–80.

Berlyne, D. E. (1955). The arousal and satiation of perceptual curiosity in the rat. *Journal of Comparative and Physiological Psychology, 48,* 238–246.

Berlyne, D. E. (1960) *Conflict, arousal, and curiosity.* New York: McGraw-Hill.

Berman, F. E., & Miner, J. B. (1985). Motivation to manage at the top executive level: A test of the hierarchic role motivation theory. *Personnel Psychology, 38,* 377–391.

Bernard, J. (1928). Political leadership among North American Indians. *American Journal of Sociology, 34,* 296–315.

Bernard, L. L. (1926). *An introduction to social psychology.* New York: Holt.

Bernard, L. L. (1927). Leadership and propaganda. In J. Davis & H. E. Barnes, *An introduction to sociology.* New York: Heath.

Bernardez, T. (1983). Women in authority: Psychodynamic and interactional aspects. *Social Work with Groups, 6*(3–4), 43–49.

Bernardin, H. J. (1976). The influence of reinforcement orientation on the relationship between supervisory style and effectiveness criteria. *Dissertation Abstracts International, 37,* 1018.

Bernardin, H. J., & Alvares, K. M (1975). The effects of organizational level on perceptions of role conflict resolution strategies. *Organizational Behavior and Human Performance, 14,* 1–9.

Berne, E. (1964). *Games people play.* New York: Grove Press.

Bernhard, L. A., & Walsh, M. (1981). *Leadership: The key to the professionalization of nursing.* New York: McGraw-Hill.

Bernhardt, R. G. (1972). *A study of the relationships between teachers' attitudes toward militancy and their perceptions of selected organizational characteristics of their schools.* Doctoral dissertation, Syracuse University, Syracuse, NY.

Bernstein, B. L., & Lecomte, C. (1979). Supervisory-type feedback effects: Feedback discrepancy level, trainee psychological differentiation, and immediate responses. *Journal of Counseling Psychology, 26,* 295–303.

Bernstein, I. S. (1964). Group social patterns as influenced by removal and later reintroduction of the dominant male Rhesus. *Psychological Reports, 14,* 3–10.

Bernstein, M. D. (1971). Autocratic and democratic leadership in an experimental group setting: A modified replication of the experiments of Lewin, Lippitt, and White, with systematic observer variation. *Dissertation Abstracts International, 31,* 6712.

Bernstein, M. H. (1958). *The job of the federal executive.* Washington, DC: Brookings Institution.

Berrien, F. K. (1961). Homeostasis theory of groups—implications for leadership. In L. Petrullo & B. Bass (Eds.), *Leadership and interpersonal behavior.* New York: Holt, Rinehart & Winston.

Berry, D. S., & McArthur, L. Z. (1986). Perceiving character in faces: The impact of age-related craniofacial changes on social perception. *Psychological Bulletin, 100,* 3–18.

Berscheid, E., & Walster, E. (1969). *Interpersonal attraction.* Reading, MA: Addison-Wesley.

Berzon, B., Reisel, J., & Davis, D. (1969). PEER: An audio-tape program for self-directed small groups. *Journal of Human Psychology, 9,* 71–87.

Besco, R. O., & Lawshe, C. H. (1959). Foreman leadership as perceived by superiors and subordinates. *Personnel Psychology, 12,* 573–582.

Besco, R. O., Tiffin, J., & King, D. C. (1959). Evaluation techniques for management programs. *Journal of American Sociology and Training of Directors, 13,* 13–27.

Beshers, J. (1962). *Urban social structure.* New York: Free Press of Glencoe.

Best, J. J. (1981). Presidential cabinet appointments: 1953-1976. *Presidential Studies Quarterly, 11,* 62–66.

Bettin, P. J., & Kennedy, J. K., Jr. (1985). *Measuring leadership experience based on the leader's relevant work history.* Paper, Academy of Management, San Diego, CA.

Betts, R. K., & Huntington, S. P. (1986, August 13). When a dictator dies, how much turmoil will follow? *Wall Street Journal*, 22.

Beutler, L. E., Jobe, A. M., & Elkins, D. (1974). Outcomes in group psychotherapy: Using persuasion theory to increase treatment efficiency. *Journal of Consulting and Clinical Psychology, 42*, 547–553.

Beyer, J. M. (1981). Managerial ideologies and the use of discipline. *Proceedings, Academy of Management*, San Diego, CA, 259–263.

Beyer, J. M., & Trice, H. M. (1984). A field study of the use and perceived effects of discipline in controlling work performance. *Academy of Management Journal, 27*, 743–764.

Bhanos, A. P. (1973). *The entroper: An information theory analysis of democratic leadership and group behavior.* INSEAD Monograph. Unpublished.

Bhaskar, R. (1978). *Problem solving in semantically rich domains.* Doctoral dissertation, Carnegie-Mellon University, Pittsburgh.

Bhatt, L. J., & Pathak, N. S. (1962). A study of functions of supervisory staff and the characteristics essential for success as viewed by a group of supervisors. *Manas, 9*, 25–31.

Bhushan, L. I. (1969). A scale of leadership preference. *Psychological Studies, 14*, 28–34.

Bibby, D. L. (1955). An enlargement of the job for the worker. Paper, Texas Personnel and Management Association. Austin: University of Texas.

Biddle, B. J., French, J. R. P., & Moore, J. V. (1953). *Some aspects of leadership in the small work group.* Ann Arbor: University of Michigan, Institute of Social Research.

Biddle, B. J., & Thomas, E. J. (1966). *Role theory: Concepts and research.* New York: Wiley.

Biddle, T., & Fisher, C. D. (1987). *Performance appraisal interview: A review of research* (ONR Tech. Rep. No. 8). College Station: Texas A & M University, Department of Management.

Bielby, T. W., & Baron, J. N. (1984). A woman's place is with other women: Sex segregation within organizations. In B. F. Reskin (Ed.) *Sex segregation in the workplace: Trends, explanations, remedies.* Washington, DC: National Academy Press.

Bierstedt, R. (1950). An analysis of social power. *American Sociology Review, 15*, 730–736.

Bies, R. J., & Shapiro, D. L. (1986). *It's not my fault, but it's for the greater good: The influence of social accounts on perceptions of managerial legitimacy.* Paper, Academy of Management, Chicago.

Biggane, J. F., & Stewart, P. A. (1965). Job enlargement: A case study. *Personnel Administration, 10*, 22–32, 39–40.

Biggart, B. W., & Hamilton, G. G. (1987). An institutional theory of leadership. *Journal of Applied Behavioral Science, 23*, 429–441.

Biggart, N. (1981). Management Style as strategic interaction: The case of Governor Ronald Reagan. *Journal of Applied Behavioral Science, 17*, 291–308.

Biggs, D. A., Huneryager, S. G., & Delaney, J. J. (1966). Leadership behavior: Interpersonal needs and effective supervisory training. *Personnel Psychology, 19*, 311–320.

Bigoness, W. J. (1976). Effect of applicant's sex, race, and performance

on employer's performance ratings: Some additional findings. *Journal of Applied Psychology, 61*, 80–84.

Bigoness, W. J., & Blakely, G. L. (1989). *A cross-national study of managerial values.* Paper, Academy of Management, Washington, DC.

Bigoness, W. J., Ryan, R., & Hamner, W. C. (1983). Moderators of leader reward behavior. In G. R. Reeves and J. R. Sweigert (Eds.), *Proceedings, American Institute for Decision Sciences*, Boston, 412–414.

Billingsley, A. (1968). *Black families in white America.* Englewood Cliffs, NJ: Prentice-Hall.

Binder, A., Wolin, B. R., & Terebinski, S. J. (1965). Leadership selection when uncertainty is minimal. *Psychonomic Science, 3*, 367–368.

Binder, A., Wolin, B. R., & Terebinski, S. J. (1966). Learning and extinction of leadership preferences in small groups. *Journal of Mathematical Psychology, 3*, 129–139.

Binet, A. (1900). *La suggestibilité.* Paris: Schleicher.

Bingham, W. V. (1927). Leadership. In H. C. Metcalf, *The psychological foundations of management.* New York: Shaw.

Bingham, W. V., & Davis, W. T. (1924). Intelligence test score and business success. *Journal of Applied Psychology, 8*, 1–22.

Binning, J. F., & Fernandez, G. (1986). *Heuristic processes in rating of leader behavior: Assessing item-induced availability biases.* Paper, American Psychological Association, Washington, DC.

Binning, J. F., & Lord, R. G. (1980). Boundary conditions for performance cue effects on group process ratings: Familiarity versus type of feedback. *Organizational Behavior & Human Performance, 26*, 115–130.

Bion, W. R. (1948). Experiences in groups. *Human Relations, 1*, 314–320, 487–496.

Bion, W. R. (1961). *Experiences in groups.* New York: Basic Books.

Bird, C. (1940). *Social psychology.* New York: Appleton-Century.

Birdsall, P. (1980). A comparative analysis of male and female managerial communication style in two organizations. *Journal of Vocational Behavior, 16*, 183–196.

Birdwhistell, R. L. (1970). *Kinesics and context.* Philadelphia: University of Philadelphia Press.

Birnbaum, P. H., & Wong, G. Y. Y. (undated). *Cultural values of managers in the People's Republic of China and Hong Kong.* Unpublished manuscript.

Birnbaum, R. (1971, Spring). Presidential succession: An inter-institutional analysis. *Educational Record*, 133–145.

Birnbaum, R. (1986). Leadership and learning: The college president as intuitive scientist. *The Review of Higher Education, 9*(4), 381–395.

Birnbaum, R. (1987a). *Presidential searches and the discovery of organizational goals.* Paper, Leadership Research Conference, Council for Liberal Learning of the Association of American Colleges, Wingspread, Racine, WI.

Birnbaum, R. (1987b). *Individual preferences and organizational goals: Consistency and diversity in the futures desired by campus leaders.* Paper, Association for the Study of Higher Education, Baltimore.

Birnbaum, R. (1987c). *The implicit leadership theories of college and university presidents.* Paper, Association for the Study of Higher Education, Baltimore.

Birnbaum, R. (1988a). *Responsibility without authority: The impossible job of the college president.* National Center for Postsecondary Governance and Finance, Teachers College, Columbia University, New York.

Birnbaum, R. (1988b). *How colleges work: The cybernetics of academic organization & leadership.* San Francisco: Jossey-Bass.

Birnbrauer, H., & Tyson, L. A. (1984). Flexing the muscles of technical leadership. *Training & Development Journal, 38*(8), 48–52.

Bish, J., & Schriesheim, C. (1974). *An exploratory dimensional analysis of form XII of the Ohio State leadership scales.* Paper, Academy of Management, Seattle.

Bishop, B. M. (1951). Mother-child interaction and the social behavior of children. *Psychological Monographs, 65,* No. 328.

Bishop, D. W. (1964). *Relations between tasks and interpersonal success and group member adjustment.* Master's thesis, University of Illinois, Urbana.

Bishop, D. W. (1967). *Group member adjustment as related to interpersonal and task success and affiliation and achievement motives* (Tech. Rep. No. 23). Urbana: University of Illinois, Group Effectiveness Research Laboratory.

Bishop, R. C., & Hill, J. W. (1969). Job enlargement vs. job change and their effects on contiguous but non-manipulated work groups. *Experimental Publications System, American Psychological Association,* No. 107A.

Bishop, R. C., & Hill, J. W. (1971). Effects of job enlargement and job change in contiguous but non-manipulated jobs as a function of workers' status. *Journal of Applied Psychology, 55,* 175–181.

Bither, S. W. (1971). *Personality as a factor in management team decision making.* University Park: Pennsylvania State University, College of Business Administration.

Bittel, L. R., & Ramsey, J. E. (1983). New dimensions for supervisory training and development. *Training & Development Journal, 37*(3), 12–20.

Bizman, A., & Fox, S. (1984). Managers' perception of the stability of workers' positive and negative behaviors. *Journal of Applied Psychology, 69,* 40–43.

Bjerstedt, A. (1956). The interpretation of sociometric status scores in the classroom. *Nordisk Psykologi, 1–2,* 8–14.

Black, C. H. (1981). *Managerial motivation of hospital chief administrators in investor-owned and not-for-profit hospitals.* Doctoral dissertation, Georgia State University, Atlanta.

Black, J. D. (1984). *Leadership: A new role model particularly applicable to gifted youth.* Unpublished manuscript.

Blackmar, F. W. (1911). Leadership in reform. *American Journal of Sociology, 16,* 626–644.

Blades, J. W. (1976). The influence of intelligence, task ability and motivation on group performance. *Dissertation Abstracts International, 37,* 1463.

Blades, J. W., & Fiedler, F. E. (1973). *Participative management, member intelligence, and group performance* (Tech. Rep. No. 73–40). Seattle: University of Washington, Organizational Research.

Blaihed, S. A. (1982). The relationship between leadership behavior of the chief executive officer in the hospital and overall hospital performance. *Dissertation Abstracts International, 43*(7A), 2169.

Blain, I. (1964). *Structure in management.* London: National Institute of Industrial Psychology.

Blake, R. R. (1960). Applied group dynamics training laboratories. *Journal of the American Society of Training Directors, 14,* 21–27.

Blake, R. R. (1986). Personal communication.

Blake, R. R., & Mouton, J. S. (1961a). *Group dynamics—Key to decision making.* Houston, TX: Gulf.

Blake, R. R., & Mouton, J. S. (1961b). Perceived characteristics of elected representatives. *Journal of Abnormal and Social Psychology, 62,* 693–695.

Blake, R. R., & Mouton, J. S. (1961c). Power, people and performance reviews. *Advanced Management, 26,* 13–17.

Blake, R. R., & Mouton, J. S. (1961d). Union-management relations: From conflict to collaboration. *Personnel, 38,* 38–51.

Blake, R. R., & Mouton, J. S. (1962a). The instrumented training laboratory. In I. R. Weschler & E. H. Schein (Eds.), *Issues in training.* Washington, DC: NTL-NEA.

Blake, R. R., & Mouton, J. S. (1962b). The intergroup dynamics of win-lose conflict and problem-solving collaboration in union-management relations. In M. Sherif (Ed.), *Intergroup relations and leadership.* New York: Wiley.

Blake, R. R., & Mouton, J. S. (1964). *The managerial grid.* Houston, TX: Gulf.

Blake, R. R., & Mouton, J. S. (1965). A 9,9 approach for increasing organizational productivity. In E. H. Schein & W. G. Bennis (Eds.), *Personal and organizational change through group methods.* New York: Wiley.

Blake, R. R., & Mouton, J. S. (1966). Some effects of managerial grid seminar training on union and management attitudes toward supervision. *Journal of Applied Behavioral Science, 2,* 387–400.

Blake, R. R., & Mouton, J. S. (1978). *The new managerial grid.* Houston, TX: Gulf.

Blake, R. R., & Mouton, J. S. (1981a). Management by grid® principles or situationalism: Which? *Group & Organization Studies, 6,* 439–455.

Blake, R. R., & Mouton, J. S. (1981b). Theory and research for developing a science of leadership. *Journal of Applied Behavioral Science, 18,* 275–291.

Blake, R. R., & Mouton, J. S. (1982a). Grid® principles versus situationalism: A final note. *Group & Organization Studies, 7,* 211–215.

Blake, R. R., & Mouton, J. S. (1982b). A comparative analysis of situationalism and 9,9 management by principle. *Organizational Dynamics, 10,* 20–43.

Blake, R. R., & Mouton, J. S. (1985a). Effective crisis management. *New Management, 3*(1), 14–17.

Blake, R. R., & Mouton, J. S. (1985b). Presidential (grid) styles. *Training & Development Journal, 39*(3), 30–34.

Blake, R. R., & Mouton, J. S. (1985c). *The managerial grid III.* Houston, TX: Gulf.

Blake, R. R., Mouton, J. S., Barnes, L. B., & Greiner, L. E. (1964). Breakthrough in organization development. *Harvard Business Review, 42,* 133–155.

Blake, R. R., Mouton, J. S., & Bidwell, A. C. (1962). Managerial grid. *Advanced Management, 1,* 12–15.

Blake, R. R., Mouton, J. S., & Fruchter, B. (1954). The consistency of interpersonal behavior judgments made on the basis of short-term interactions in three-man groups. *Journal of Abnormal and Social Psychology, 49,* 573–578.

Blake, R. R., Mouton, J. S., & Fruchter, B. (1962). A factor analysis of training group behavior. *Journal of Social Psychology, 58,* 121–130.

Blalock, H. M. (1959). Status consciousness: A dimensional analysis. *Social Forces, 37,* 243–248.

Blalock, H. M., Jr. (1967). *Toward a theory of minority-group relations.* New York: Wiley.

Blanchard, K., & Johnson, S. (1982). *The one minute manager.* New York: William Morrow.

Blank, W., Weitzel, J. R., & Green, S. G. (1987). Situational leadership theory: A test of underlying assumptions. *Journal of Management.*

Blankenship, L. V., & Miles, R. E. (1968). Organizational structure and managerial decision behavior. *Administrative Science Quarterly, 13,* 106–120.

Blau, P. M. (1954a). Patterns of interaction among a group of officials in a government agency. *Human Relations, 7,* 337–348.

Blau, P. M. (1954b). Cooperation and competition in a bureaucracy. *American Journal of Sociology, 59,* 530–535.

Blau, P. M. (1955). *The dynamics of bureaucracy.* Chicago: University of Chicago Press.

Blau, P. M. (1960). Patterns of deviation in work groups. *Sociometry, 23,* 245–261.

Blau, P. M. (1964). *Exchange and power in social life.* New York: Wiley.

Blau, P. M. (1968). The hierarchy of authority in organizations. *American Journal of Sociology, 73,* 453–467.

Blau, P. M., & Scott, W. R. (1962). *Formal organizations.* San Francisco: Chandler.

Blauner, R. (1964). *Alienation and freedom: The factory worker and his industry.* Chicago: University of Chicago Press.

Bleda, P. R., Gitter, G. A., & D'Agostino, R. B. (1977). Enlisted men's perceptions of leader attributes and satisfaction with military life. *Journal of Applied Psychology, 62,* 43–49.

Bledsoe, J. C., Brown, S. E., & Dalton, S. L. (1980). Perception of leadership behavior of the school business manager. *Perceptual and Motor Skills, 50,* 1147–1150.

Block, C. J., & Kennedy, J. K., Jr. (1986). *The effects of variations in leader behavior.* Paper, American Psychology Association, New York.

Block, D. R., & Kolakowski, D. (1973). Further evidence of sex-linked major-gene influence on human spatial visualizing ability. *American Journal of Human Genetics, 25,* 1–14.

Block, P. (1986). *The empowered manager.* San Francisco: Jossey-Bass.

Blood, M. R., & Hulin, C. L. (1967). Alienation, environmental characteristics, and worker responses. *Journal of Applied Psychology, 51,* 284–290.

Bloomfield, L. P. (1984, Summer). What's wrong with transitions. *Foreign Policy, 55,* 23–39.

Blum, R. (1953). *The study of groups.* Washington, DC: George Washington University, Human Resources Research Office.

Blumberg, L. U. (1955). Community leaders: The social bases and social-psychological concomitants of community power. *Dissertation Abstracts, 15,* 638.

Blumberg, P. (1968). *Industrial democracy: The sociology of participation.* London: Constable.

Blumenthal, A. (1932). *Small town stuff.* Chicago: University of Chicago Press.

Blumenthal, K. (1986, March 24). Room at the top: U.S. industry, despite some advances, remains mostly devoid of women in senior posts. *Wall Street Journal,* Sec. 4, pp. 7, 9.

Blumenthal, W. M. (1956). *Codetermination in the German steel industry.* Princeton, NJ: Princeton University, Industrial Relations Section.

Blyth, D. E. (1987). *Leader and subordinate expertise as moderators of the relationship between directive leader behavior and performance.* Doctoral dissertation, University of Washington. (Reported in F. E. Fiedler & R. J. House [1987] *Leadership theory and research: A report of progress.* International Reviews of I/O Psychology. New York: Wiley.)

Boal, K. B., & Bryson, J. M. (1987). Charismatic leadership: A phenomonological and structural approach. In J. G. Hunt, B. R. Baliga, H. P. Dachler, & C. A. Schriesheim, *Emerging leadership vistas.* Lexington, MA: D. C. Heath.

Boal, K. B., Hunt, J. G., & Sorenson, R. L. (1988). *Leadership folk theories and second phase development work on the Leadership Quotes Questionnaire.* Paper, Western Academy of Management, Big Sky, MT.

Bobbitt, H. R. (1978). *Organizational behavior understanding and prediction* (2nd ed.). Englewood Cliffs, NJ: Prentice-Hall.

Bockman, S., & Gayk, W. F. (1977). Political orientations and political ideologies. *Pacific Sociological Review, 20,* 536–552.

Boddewyn, J., & Nath, R. (1970). Comparative management studies: An assessment. *Management International Review, 10,* 3–11.

Bodycombe, B. (1982, November). How to manage disasters—in advance. *Management Today, 41,* 44, 46.

Boer, J. H. (1985). Organization climate, NACH training and organization performance in clothing manufacturing factories. *Dissertation Abstracts International, 46,*(10A), 3087.

Bogard, H. M. (1960). Union and management trainees: A comparative study of personality and occupational choice. *Journal of Applied Psychology, 44,* 56–63.

Bogardus, E. S. (1918). *Essentials of social psychology.* Los Angeles: University of Southern California Press.

Bogardus, E. S. (1928). World leadership types. *Sociology and Social Research, 12,* 573–599.

Bogardus, E. S. (1929). Leadership and attitudes. *Sociology and Social Research, 13,* 377–387.

Bogardus, E. S. (1931). Leadership and social situations. *Sociology and Social Research, 16,* 164–170.

Bogardus, E. S. (1934). *Leaders and leadership.* New York: Appleton-Century.

Bohleber, M. E. (1967). Conditions influencing the relationships between leadership style and group structural and population characteristics. *Dissertation Abstracts, 28,* 776–777.

Boise, W. B. (1965). Supervisors' attitudes toward disciplinary actions. *Personnel Administration, 28,* 24–27.

Bolda, R. A. (1959). Employee attitudes related to supervisory and departmental effectiveness. *Engineering and Industrial Psychology, 1,* 31–39.

Bollett, R. M. (1972). The effect of leader presence on change in a personal growth group. *Dissertation Abstracts International, 32,* 4340.

Bolman L. (1973). Some effects of trainers on their groups: A partial replication. *Journal of Applied Behavioral Science, 9,* 534–539.

Bolman, L. (1986). *Concepts of leadership and power in innovating organizations: Machines, families, jungles and theatres.* Paper, Conference on Innovations & Management in the 1990's. Carlsbad, Czechoslovakia.

Bolman, L. G. & Deal, T. E. (1984). *Modern approaches to understanding and managing organizations.* San Francisco: Jossey-Bass.

Bolon, D. S., & Crain, C. R. (1985). Decision sequence: A recurring theme in comparing American and Japanese management. *Proceedings, Academy of Management,* San Diego, CA, 88–92.

Bond, J. R., & Vinacke, W. E. (1961). Coalitions in mixed-sex triads. *Sociometry, 24,* 61–75.

Bonjean, C. M. (1963). Community leadership: A case study and conceptual refinement. *American Journal of Sociology, 67,* 672–681.

Bonjean, C. M. (1964). Class, status, and power reputation. *Sociology and Social Research, 49,* 69–75.

Bonjean, C. M. (1966). Mass, class, and the industrial community: A comparative analysis of managers, businessmen, and workers. *American Journal of Sociology, 72,* 149–162.

Bonner, H. (1959). *Group dynamics.* New York: Ronald Press.

Bonney, M. E. (1943). The consistency of sociometric scores and their relationship to teacher judgments of social success and to personality self-ratings. *Sociometry, 6,* 409–424.

Bonney, M. E. (1946a). A study of mutual friendships on the elementary, high school and college levels. *Sociometry, 9,* 21–47.

Bonney, M. E. (1946b). A study of the sociometric process among sixth-grade children. *Journal of Educational Psychology, 37,* 359–372.

Bonney, M. E. (1947a). Popular and unpopular children: A sociometric study. *Sociometry Monographs,* No. 9.

Bonney, M. E. (1947b). Sociometric study of agreement between teacher judgments and student choices. *Sociometry, 10,* 133–146.

Bonney, M. E. (1949). A study of friendship choices in college in relation to church affiliation, in-church preferences, family size, and length of enrollment in college. *Journal of Social Psychology, 29,* 153–166.

Bonney, M. E., & Powell, J. (1953). Differences in social behavior between sociometrically high and sociometrically low children. *Journal of Educational Research, 46,* 481–495.

Bons, P. M. (1974). *The effect of changes in leadership environment on the behavior of relationship and task-motivated leaders.* Doctoral dissertation, University of Washington, Seattle.

Bons, P. M., Bass, A. R., & Komorita, S. S. (1970). Changes in leadership style as a function of military experience and type of command. *Personnel Psychology, 23,* 551–568.

Bons, P. M. & Fiedler, F. E. (1976). Changes in organizational leadership and the behavior of relationship- and task-motivated leaders. *Administrative Science Quarterly, 21,* 433–472.

Boone, T. A. (1981). Ipsative to normative scaling: A modification of the "leader effectiveness adaptability description—self " scales. *Dissertation Abstracts International, 42*(3B), 1228.

Bord, R. J. (1975). Toward a social-psychological theory of charismatic social influence processes. *Social Forces, 53,* 486–497.

Borden, D. F. (1980). *Leader-boss, stress, personality, job satisfaction and performance: Another look at the interrelationship of some old constructs in the modern large bureaucracy.* Doctoral dissertation, University of Washington, Seattle.

Borg, W. R. (1956). Leadership reactions in situational tests. *American Psychologist, 11,* 379.

Borg, W. R. (1957). The behavior of emergent and designated leaders in situational tests. *Sociometry, 20,* 95–104.

Borg, W. R. (1960). Prediction of small group role behavior from personality variables. *Journal of Abnormal and Social Psychology, 60,* 112–116.

Borg, W. R., & Tupes, E. C. (1958). Personality characteristics related to leadership behavior in two types of small group situational problems. *Journal of Applied Psychology, 42,* 252–256.

Borg, W. R., Tupes, E. C., & Carp, A. (1959). Relationships between physical proficiency and measures of leadership and personality. *Personnel Psychology, 12,* 113–126.

Borgatta, E. F. (1954). Analysis of social interaction and sociometric perception. *Sociometry, 17,* 7–32.

Borgatta, E. F. (1955a). Analysis of social interaction: Actual, role playing, and projective. *Journal of Abnormal and Social Psychology, 51,* 394–405.

Borgatta, E. F. (1955b). Attitudinal concomitants to military statuses. *Social Forces, 33,* 342–347.

Borgatta, E. F. (1960). Small group research—a trend report and bibliography. *Current Sociology, 9,* 173–272.

Borgatta, E. F. (1961). Role-playing specifications, personality, and performance. *Sociometry, 24,* 218–233.

Borgatta, E. F. (1962). A systematic study of interaction process scores, peer and self-assessments, personality and other variables. *Genetic Psychology Monographs, 65,* 219–291.

Borgatta, E. F., & Bales, R. F. (1953a). Interaction of individuals in reconstituted groups. *Sociometry, 16,* 302–320.

Borgatta, E. F., & Bales, R. F. (1953b). Task and accumulation of experience as factors in the interaction of small groups. *Sociometry, 16,* 239–252.

Borgatta, E. F., & Bales, R. F. (1953c). The consistency of subject behavior and the reliability of scoring in interaction process analysis. *American Sociological Review, 18,* 566–569.

Borgatta, E. F., & Cottrell, L. S. (1956). On the classification of groups. In

J. L. Moreno (Ed.), *Sociometry and the science of man*. New York: Beacon House.

Borgatta, E. F., Cottrell, L. S., & Mann, J. H. (1958). The spectrum of individual interaction characteristics: An interdimensional analysis. *Psychological Reports, 4*, 279–319.

Borgatta, E. F., Cottrell, L. S., & Wilker, L. (1959). Initial expectation, group climate, and the assessments of leaders and members. *Journal of Social Psychology, 49*, 285–296.

Borgatta, E. F., Couch, A. S., & Bales, R. F. (1954). Some findings relevant to the great man theory of leadership. *American Sociological Review, 19*, 755–759.

Borgatta, E. F., & Eschenbach, A. E. (1955). Factor analysis of Rorschach variables and behavior observations. *Psychological Reports, 1*, 129–136.

Borgatta, E. F., & Evans, R. R. (1967). Behavioral and personality expectations associated with status positions. *Multivariate Behavior Research, 2*, 153–173.

Borgatta, E. F., Ford, R. N., & Bohrnstedt, G. W. (1968). The Work Components Study (WCS): A revised set of measures for work motivation. *Multivariate Behavior Research, 3*, 403–413.

Borgatta, M. L. (1961). Power structure and coalitions in three person groups. *Journal of Social Psychology, 55*, 287–300.

Borland, C. (1974). *Locus of control, need for achievement and entrepreneurship*. Doctoral dissertation, The University of Texas, Austin.

Borman, W. C. (1982). Validity of behavioral assessment for predicting military recruiter performance. *Journal of Applied Psychology, 67*, 3–9.

Borman, W. C., Eaton, N. K., Bryan, J. D., & Rosse, R. L. (1983). Validity of Army recruiters behavioral assessment: Does the assessor make a difference? *Journal of Applied Psychology, 68*, 415–419.

Borowiec, W. A. (1975). Persistence and change in the gatekeeper role of ethnic leaders: The case of the Polish-American. *Polish Anthropology, 1*, 21–40.

Bose, S. K. (1955). Employee morale and supervision. *Indian Journal of Psychology, 30*, 117–125.

Boshoff, A. B. (1969). A comparison of three methods for the evaluation of managerial positions. *Psychologia Africana, 12*, 212–221.

Boss, G. P. (1976). Essential attributes of the concept of charisma. *The Southern Speech Communication Journal, 41*, 300–313.

Boss, R. W. (1978). The effects of leader absence on a confrontation team-building design. *Journal of Applied Behavioral Science, 14*, 469–478.

Boss, R. W. (1983). Team building and the problem of regression: The personal management interview as an intervention. *Journal of Applied Behavioral Science, 19*, 67–83.

Boss, R. W., & McConkie, M. L. (1976). *An autopsy and an OD failure*. Boulder, CO: University of Colorado. (Reported in Boss, 1978.)

Bossard, J. H. S., & Boll, E. S. (1955). Personality roles in the large family. *Child Development, 26*, 71–78.

Bottger, P. C. (1984). Expertise and air time as bases of actual and perceived influence in problem-solving groups. *Journal of Applied Psychology, 69*, 214–221.

Bottomley, M., & Sampson, S. (1977). The case of the female principal: Sex role attitudes and perceptions of sex differences in ability. *Australian and New Zealand Journal of Sociology, 13*, 137–140.

Boulanger, F., & Fischer, D. G. (1971). Leadership and the group-shift phenomenon. *Perceptual and Motor Skills, 33*, 1251–1258.

Boulgarides, J. D. (1984). A comparison of male and female business managers. *Leadership & Organization Development Journal, 5*(5), 27–31.

Bovard, E. W., Jr. (1948). Social norms and the individual. *Journal of Abnormal and Social Psychology, 43*, 62–69.

Bovard, E. W. (1951a). Group structure and perception. *Journal of Abnormal and Social Psychology, 46*, 398–405.

Bovard, E. W. (1951b). The experimental production of interpersonal affect. *Journal of Abnormal and Social Psychology, 46*, 521–528.

Bovard, E. W. (1952). Clinical insight as a function of group process. *Journal of Abnormal and Social Psychology, 47*, 534–539.

Bowden, A. O. (1926). A study of the personality of student leaders in the United States. *Journal of Abnormal and Social Psychology, 21*, 149–160.

Bowden, G. T. (1947). The adaptive capacity of workers. *Harvard Business Review, 25*, 527–542.

Bowen, D. D. (1985). Were men meant to mentor women? *Training and Development Journal, 39*(2), 31–34.

Bowen, D. D., & Zollinger, P. I. (1980). *Mentoring and the careers of women managers*. Paper, Academy of Management Meetings, Detroit.

Bowers, D. G. (1963). Self-esteem and the diffusion of leadership style. *Journal of Applied Psychology, 47*, 135–140.

Bowers, D. G. (1964a). Self-esteem and supervision. *Personnel Administration, 27*, 23–26.

Bowers, D. G. (1964b). Organizational control in an insurance company. *Sociometry, 27*, 230–244.

Bowers, D. G. (1969). *Work organizations as dynamic systems* (ONR Tech. Rep.). University of Michigan, Ann Arbor.

Bowers, D. G. (1971). *Development techniques and organizational climate: An evaluation of the comparative importance of two potential forces for organizational change* (ONR Tech. Rep.). University of Michigan, Ann Arbor.

Bowers, D. G. (1973). OD techniques and their results in 23 organizations: The Michigan ICL study. *Journal of Applied Behavioral Science, 9*, 21–43.

Bowers, D. G. (1975). *Navy manpower: Values, practices, and human resources requirements*. Ann Arbor: University of Michigan, Institute for Social Research.

Bowers, D. G. (1976). *Systems of organization*. Ann Arbor: University of Michigan Press.

Bowers, D. G. (1983). What would make 11,500 people quit their jobs? *Organizational Dynamics, 11*, 5–19.

Bowers, D. G., & Franklin, J. (1975). *Survey guided development: Data based organizational change.* Ann Arbor, MI: University of Michigan, Institute for Social Research.

Bowers, D. G., & Seashore, S. E. (1966). Predicting organizational effectiveness with a four-factor theory of leadership. *Administrative Science Quarterly, 11,* 238–263.

Bowers, D. G., & Seashore, S. E. (1967). Peer leadership within work groups. *Personnel Administration, 30,* 45–50.

Bowers, J. J. (1976). *Relationship between organizational variables and contemporary practices in small private liberal arts colleges in the State of Ohio.* Doctoral dissertation, Ohio State University, Columbus.

Bowers, R. V. (1966). *Studies on behavior in organizations: A research symposium.* Athens: University of Georgia Press.

Bowin, R. B. (1977). Attitude change toward a theory of managerial motivation. In J. B. Miner (Ed.), *Motivation to manage.* Atlanta, GA: Organizational Measurement Systems Press.

Bowman, G. W., Worthy, N. B., & Greyser, S. A. (1965). Are women executives people? *Harvard Business Review, 43*(4) 14–28, 164–178.

Bowman, H. J. (1964). Perceived leader behavior patterns and their relationships to self-perceived variables—responsibility, authority, and delegation. *Dissertation Abstracts, 25,* 3340.

Bowman, L. E. (1927). An approach to the study of leadership. *Journal of Applied Sociology, 11,* 315–321.

Boyatzis, R. R. (1982). *The competent manager: A model for effective performance.* New York: Wiley.

Boyce, M. W. (1964). Management by committee. *Personnel Practice Bulletin, 20,* 47–51.

Boyd, B. B., & Jensen, J. M. (1972). Perceptions of the first-line supervisor's authority: A study in superior-subordinate communication. *Academy of Management Journal, 15,* 331–342.

Boyd, D. P. (1974). Research note: The educational background of a selected group of England's leaders. *Sociology, 8,* 305–312.

Boyd, J. B., & Ellis, J. (1962). *Findings of research into senior management seminars.* Toronto: Personnel Research Department, The Hydro-Electric Power Commission of Ontario.

Boyd, J. T., Jr. (1989a). *Are military leaders more or less transformational than their superiors?* Unpublished manuscript.

Boyd, J. T., Jr. (1989b). *Are military leaders becoming more or less transformational?* Unpublished manuscript.

Boyd, N. K. (1972). *Negotiation behavior by elected and appointed representatives serving as group leaders or as spokesmen under different cooperative group expectations.* Doctoral dissertation, University of Maryland.

Boyles, B. R. (1968). The interaction between certain personality variables and perceived supervisory styles and their relation to performance and satisfaction. *Dissertation Abstracts, 28*(11B), 4788–4789.

Bradburn, N. M. (1963). N achievement and father dominance in Turkey. *Journal of Abnormal and Social Psychology, 67,* 464–468.

Braddock, J. H., II. (1984). *Recruitment and selection of minorities in high-tech organizations: A sociological perspective.* Paper, ONR Conference on Minorities Entering High Tech Careers, Pensacola, FL.

Bradford, D. L., & Cohen, A. R. (1973). *Managing for excellence: The guide to developing high performance in contemporary organizations.* New York: Wiley.

Bradford, D. L., & Cohen, A. R. (1984). The postheroic leader. *Training & Development Journal, 38*(1), 40–49.

Bradford, L. P., & French, J. R. P. (1948). Introduction: The dynamics of the discussion group. *Journal of Social Issues, 4,* 2–8.

Bradford, L. P., Gibb, J. R., & Benne, K. D. (1964). *T-group theory and laboratory method.* New York: Wiley.

Bradford, L. P., & Lippitt, R. (1945). Building a democratic work group. *Personnel, 22*(3), 142–148.

Bradford, L. P., & Lippitt, R. (1952). Role-playing in management training. In M. J. Dooher & V. Marquis (Eds.), *The development of executive talent.* New York: American Management Association.

Bradley, G. W. (1978). Self-serving biases in the attribution process: A reexamination of the fact or fiction question. *Journal of Personality and Social Psychology, 36,* 56–71.

Bradley, R. T. (1984). *Charisma and social structure: A relational analysis of power and communion in communes.* Unpublished working manuscript, University of Minnesota. (Cited in Trice & Beyer, 1984.)

Bradley, R. T. (1987). Charisma and social structure: A study of love and power. *Wholeness and transformation.* New York: Paragon House.

Bradshaw, H. H. (1970). Need satisfaction, management style, and job level in a professional hierarchy. *Experimental Publications System, American Psychological Association, 8,* No. 289-1.

Brady, G. F., & Helmich, D. L. (1982). Leadership style in the boardroom. *Directors & Boards, 6*(3), 46.

Brainard, S. R., & Dollar, R. J. (1971). Personality characteristics of leaders identifying with different student subcultures. *College Student Personnel, 12,* 200–203.

Bramel, D., & Friend, R. (1987). The work group and its vicissitudes in social and industrial psychology. *Journal of Applied Behavioral Science, 23,* 233–253.

Bramwell, B. S. (1944). The order of merit: The holders and their kindred. *Eugenics Review, 36,* 84–91.

Brandon, A. C. (1965). Status congruence and expectations. *Sociometry, 28,* 272–288.

Brass, D. J. (1984). Being in the right place: A structural analysis of individual influence in an organization. *Administrative Science Quarterly, 29,* 518–539.

Brass, D. J. (1985). Men's and women's networks: A study of interaction patterns and influence in an organization. *Academy of Management Journal, 28,* 327–343.

Brass, D. J., & Oldham, G. R. (1976). Validating an in-basket test using an alternative set of leadership scoring dimensions. *Journal of Applied Psychology, 61,* 652–657.

Braun, D. D. (1976). Alienation and participation: A replication comparing leaders and the "mass." *Journal of Political and Military Sociology, 4,* 245–259.

Bray, D. W., Campbell, R. J., & Grant, D. L. (1974). *Formative years in business: A long-term AT&T study of mangerial lives.* New York: Wiley-Interscience.

Bray, D. W., & Grant, D. L. (1966). The assessment center in the measurement of potential for business management. *Psychological Monographs*, 80(17), No. 625.

Bray, D. W., & Howard A. (1983). The AT&T longitudinal studies of managers. In K. W. Shaiel (Ed.), *Longitudinal studies of adult psychological development*. New York: Guilford Press.

Brayfield, A. H., & Crockett, W. H. (1955). Employee attitudes and employee performance. *Psychological Bulletin*, 52, 396-424.

Brenner, M. H. (1963). *Management selection test validation*. Lockheed California Company, Industrial Relations Research Department. (Reported in Campbell, Dunnette, et al., 1970, 193.)

Brenner, M. H. (1972). Management development for women. *Personnel Journal*, 51, 165-169.

Brenner, M. M. (1970). *Management development activities for women*. Paper, American Psychological Association, Miami.

Brenner, O. C., & Bromer, J. A. (1981). Sex stereotypes and leaders' behavior as measured by the agreement scale for leadership behavior. *Psychological Reports*, 48, 960-962.

Brenner, O. C., Tomkiewisz, J., & Schein, V. E. (1989). The relationship between sex role stereotypes and requisite management characteristics revisited. *Academy of Management Journal*, 32, 662-669.

Brewer, E., & Tomlinson, J. W. C. (1964). The manager's working day. *Journal of Industrial Economics*, 12, 191-197.

Bridges, E. M., Doyle, W. F., & Mahan, D. F. (1968). Effects of hierarchical differentiation on group productivity, efficiency, and risk taking. *Administrative Science Quarterly*, 13, 305-319.

Brief, A. P., & Aldag, R. J. (1975). Male-female differences in occupational values within majority groups. *Journal of Vocational Behavior*, 6, 305-314.

Brief, A. P., & Aldag, R. J. (1977). Work values as moderators of perceived leader behavior-satisfaction relationships. *Sociology and Working Occupations*, 4, 99-112.

Brief, A. P., Aldag, R. J., & Chacko, T. I. (1976). The Miner sentence completion scale: A psychometric appraisal. *Proceedings, American Institute for Decision Sciences*, San Francisco, 171-172.

Brief, A. P., Aldag, R. J., & Chacko, T. I. (1977). The Miner sentence completion scale: An appraisal. *Academy of Management Journal*, 20, 635-643.

Brief, A. P., Aldag, R. J., Russell, C. J., & Rude, D. E. (1981). Leader behavior in a police organization revisited. *Human Relations*, 34, 1037-1051.

Brief, A. P., & Hollenbeck, J. R. (1985). An exploratory study of self-regulating activities and their effects on job performance. *Journal of Occupational Guidance*, 6, 197-208.

Brief, A. P., & Motowidlo, S. J. (1986). Prosocial organizational behaviors. *Academy of Management Review*, 11, 710-725.

Brief, A. P., & Oliver, R. L. (1976). Male-female differences in work attitudes among retail sales managers. *Journal of Applied Psychology*, 61, 526-528.

Briggs, S. R., Cheek, J. M., & Buss, A. H. (1980). An analysis of the self-monitoring scale. *Journal of Personality and Social Psychology*, 38, 679-686.

Brillhart, J. K., & Jochem, L. M. (1964). Effects of different patterns on outcomes of problem solving discussions. *Journal of Applied Psychology*, 48, 175-179.

Brim, O. G. (1954). The acceptance of the new behavior in child-rearing. *Human Relations*, 7, 473-491.

Brindisi, J. G. (1976). *Role satisfaction of community school council members*. Doctoral dissertation, Florida Atlantic University, Boca Raton.

Brinker, P. A. (1955). Supervisor's and foremen's reasons for frustration. *Personnel Journal*, 34, 101-103.

Brinton, C. (1930). Clubs. In *Encyclopaedia of the social sciences*. New York: Macmillan.

Brockhaus, R. H. (1975). I-E locus of control scores as predictors of entrepreneurial intentions. *Proceedings, Academy of Management*, New Orleans, LA, 433-435.

Brockhaus, R. H. (1980). Risk taking propensity of entrepreneurs. *Academy of Management Journal*, 23, 509-520.

Brockner, J., & Adsit, L. (1986). The moderating impact of sex on the equity-satisfaction relationship: A field study. *Journal of Applied Psychology*, 71, 585-590.

Brogdan, R., & Taylor, S. J. (1975). *Introduction to qualitative research methods*. New York: Wiley.

Brogden, H. E., & Thomas, W. F. (1943). The primary traits in personality items purporting to measure sociability. *Journal of Psychology*, 16, 85-97.

Broich, K. (1929). Führeranforderungen in der Kindergruppe. *Zeitschrift für angervandte Psychologie*, 32, 164-212.

Brollier, C. L. (1984). Managerial leadership in hospital-based occupational therapy. *Dissertation Abstracts International*, 45,(5B), 1433.

Broman, W. K. (1974). *The relationship of administrative processes to the innovativeness of public secondary schools*. Doctoral dissertation, State University of New York, Buffalo.

Bronfenbrenner, U. (1961). Some familial antecedents of responsibility and leadership in adolescents. In L. Petrullo & B. M. Bass (Eds.), *Leadership and interpersonal behavior*. New York: Holt, Rinehart & Winston.

Bronfenbrenner, U., Harding, J., & Gallwey, M. (1958). A review and theoretical framework for the study of interpersonal perception. In D. C. McClelland (Ed.), *Talent and society*. Princeton, NJ: Van Nostrand.

Brooks, E. (1955). What successful executives do. *Personnel*, 32, 210-225.

Broverman, I. K., Broverman, D. M., Clarkson, F. E., Rosenkrantz, P. S., & Vogel, S. R. (1970). Sex-role stereotypes and clinical judgments of mental health. *Journal of Consulting and Clinical Psychology*, 34, 1-7.

Broverman, I. K., Vogel, S. R., Broverman, D. M., Clarkson, F. E., & Rosenkrantz, P. S. (1972). Sex-role stereotypes: A current appraisal. *Journal of Social Issues*, 28, 59-78.

Brown, A. (1979). *Personal value systems of Western Australian managers*. Master of Commerce Thesis, University of Western Australia, Perth.

Brown, A. F. (1967). Reactions to leadership. *Educational Administrative Quarterly, 3*, 62–73.

Brown, D. (1987). *Leadership and organization transformation: A competency model.* Doctoral dissertation, Fielding Institute, Santa Barbara, CA.

Brown, D. S. (1964). Subordinates' views of ineffective executive behavior. *Academy of Management Journal, 7*, 288–299.

Brown, G. B. (1982). Leader behavior and faculty cohesiveness in Christian schools. *Dissertation Abstracts International, 43*(7A), 2170.

Brown, H. A., & Ford, D. L., Jr. (1977). An exploratory analysis of discrimination in the employment of black MBA graduates. *Journal of Applied Psychology, 62*, 50–56.

Brown, J. F. (1936). *Psychology and the social order.* New York: McGraw-Hill.

Brown, J. S. (1970). Risk propensity in decision making: A comparison of business and public school administrators. *Administrative Science Quarterly, 15*, 473–481.

Brown, K. A., & Mitchell, T. R. (1986). Influence of task interdependence and number of poor performers on diagnoses of causes of poor performance. *Academy of Management Journal, 29*, 412–424.

Brown, L. D., & Detterman, L. B. (1987). Small interventions for large problems: Reshaping urban leadership networks. *Journal of Applied Behavioral Science, 23*, 151–168.

Brown, M. (1933). *Leadership among high school principals.* New York: Teachers College Contribution to Education.

Brown, M. (1934). Leadership among high school pupils. *Teachers College Record, 35*, 324–326.

Brown, M. C. (1982). Administrative succession and organizational performance: The succession effect. *Administrative Science Quarterly, 27*, 1–16.

Brown, S. C. (1931). Some case studies of delinquent girls described as leaders. *British Journal of Educational Psychology, 1*, 162–179.

Brown, S. M. (1979). Male versus female leaders: A comparison of empirical studies. *Sex Roles, 5*, 595–611.

Browne, C. G. (1949). A study of executive leadership in business. I. The R, A, and D scales. *Journal of Applied Psychology, 33*, 520–526.

Browne, C. G. (1950a). An exploration into the use of certain methods for the study of executive function in business. *Dissertation Abstracts, 58*, 51–57.

Browne, C. G. (1950b). Study of executive leadership in business. II. Social group patterns. *Journal of Applied Psychology, 34*, 12–15.

Browne, C. G. (1950c). Study of executive leadership in business. III. Goal and achievement index. *Journal of Applied Psychology, 34*, 82–87.

Browne, C. G. (1951). Study of executive leadership in business. IV. Sociometric pattern. *Journal of Applied Psychology, 35*, 34–37.

Browne, C. G., & Cohn, T. S. (1958). *The study of leadership.* Danville, IL: Interstate.

Browne, C. G., & Neitzel, B. J. (1952). Communication, supervision, and morale. *Journal of Applied Psychology, 36*, 86–91.

Browne, C. G., & Shore, R. P. (1956). Leadership and predictive abstracting. *Journal of Applied Psychology, 40*, 112–116.

Browne, M. A., & Mahoney, M. J. (1984). Sport psychology. *Annual Review of Psychology, 35*, 605–625.

Browne, P. J., & Golembiewski, R. T. (1974). The line-staff concept revisited: An empirical study of organizational images. *Academy of Management Journal, 17*, 406–417.

Browning, R. P., & Jacob, H. E. (1964). Power motivation and political personality. *Public Opinion Quarterly, 28*, 75–90.

Bruce, J. S. (1986). *The intuitive pragmatists: Conversations with chief executive officers* (Special Report). Greensboro, NC: Center of Creative Leadership.

Bruce M. M. (1953). The prediction of effectiveness as a factory foreman. *Psychological Monographs, 67*, 1–17.

Brumbach, R. B. (1971). Authenticity and theories of administrative behavior. *Administrative Science Quarterly, 16*, 108–112.

Brumback, G. B., & Vincent, J. W. (1970). Factor analysis of work performed data for a sample of administrative, professional, and scientific positions. *Personnel Psychology, 23*, 101–107.

Brunner, E. DeS. (1928). *Village communities.* New York: Doubleday Doran.

Brush, D. H., & Schoenfeldt, L. F. (1980). Identifying managerial potential: An alternative to assessment centers. *Personnel, 57*, 68–76.

Bryant, D. W. (1972). A simulation depicting concepts of leadership. *Dissertation Abstracts International, 32*, 6548.

Bryant, G. W. (1968). Ideal leader behavior descriptions of appointed and sociometrically chosen student leaders. *Dissertation Abstracts, 28*, 3497.

Bryman, A., Bresnen, M., Beardsworth, A., & Keil, T. (1988). Qualitative research and the study of leadership. *Human Relations, 4*(1), 13–30.

Bryson, J., & Kelley, G. (1978). A political perspective on leadership emergence, stability, and change in organizational networks. *Academy of Management Review, 3*, 712–723.

Buchanan, B. (1974). Government managers, business executives, and organizational commitment. *Public Administration Review, 34*, 339–347.

Buchanan, P. C. (1965). Evaluating the effectiveness of laboratory training in industry. In *Explorations in human relations training and research,* No. 1. Washington, DC: National Training Laboratories.

Buchanan, P. C. (1969). Laboratory training and organization development. *Administrative Science Quarterly, 14*, 466–480.

Buchanan, P. C., & Brunstetter, P. H. (1959). A research approach to management improvement. *Journal of American Social Training Directors, 13*, 18–27.

Buck, V. E. (1963). Job pressures on managers: Sources, subjects, and correlates. *Dissertation Abstracts, 24*, 2164–2165.

Buckley, H. A. (1970). Organizational congruence in perceptions of leader effectiveness. *Dissertation Abstracts International, 31*, 2337.

Buckley, W. (Ed.) (1968a). *Modern systems research for the behavioral scientist.* Chicago: Aldine.

Buckley, W. (1968b). Society as a complex adaptive system. In W.

Buckley (Ed.), *Modern systems research for the behavioral scientist*. Chicago: Aldine.

Buckley, W. F. (1979, September 22). Let's define that "leadership" that Kennedy says we need. *Press-Bulletin*, Binghamton, NY, 4A.

Bucklow, M. (1966). A new role for the work group. *Administrative Science Quarterly, 11*, 59–78.

Bugental, D. E. (1964). A study of attempted and successful social influence in small groups as a function of goal-relevant skills. *Dissertation Abstracts, 25*, 660.

Bugental, J. F., & Lehner, G. F. J. (1958). Accuracy of self-perception and group-perception as related to two leadership roles. *Journal of Abnormal and Social Psychology, 56*, 396–398.

Buie, S., Jr. (1983). The emergence process of black elected leadership in North Carolina. *Dissertation Abstracts International, 44*(3A), 620.

Bullard, J. F. (1969). *An evaluation of the assessment center approach to selecting supervisors*. Caterpillar Tractor, Corporate Personnel, Peoria, IL.

Bullard, P. D., & Cook, P. E. (1975). Sex and workstyle of leaders and followers: Determinants of productivity. *Psychological Reports, 36*, 545–546.

Bunce, V. (1981). *Do new leaders make a difference?: Executive succession and public policy under capitalism and socialism*. Princeton, NJ: Princeton University Press.

Bundel, C. M. (1930). Is leadership losing its importance? *Infantry Journal, 36*, 339–349.

Bunker, B. B. (1986). Management training in Japan: Lessons for America. *Proceedings, OD Network Conference*, New York, 182–184.

Bunker, B. B., & Bender, L. R. (1980). How women compete: A guide for managers. *Management Review, 69*, 55–62.

Bunker, D. R. (1965a). Individual applications of laboratory training. *Journal of Applied Behavioral Science, 1*, 131–148.

Bunker, D. R. (1965b). The effect of laboratory education upon individual behavior. In E. H. Schein & W. G. Bennis (Eds.), *Personal and organizational change through group methods*. New York: Wiley.

Bunker, D. R., & Knowles, E. S. (1967). Comparison of behavioral changes resulting from human relations laboratories of different lengths. *Journal of Applied Behavioral Science, 3*, 505–523.

Bunker, K. A. (1986). Coping with the "mess" of stress: An assessment-based research project. *Journal of Management Development, 4*, 68–82.

Bunyi, J. M., (1982). An experimental study of leadership emergence in heterogeneous groups. *Dissertation Abstracts International, 43*(8A), 2492.

Buono, A. F., & Bowditch, J. L. (1989). *The human side of mergers and acquisitions: Managing collisions between people, cultures, and organizations*. San Francisco: Jossey-Bass.

Burda, P. C., & Vaux, A. C. (1987). The social support process in men: Overcoming sex-role obstacles. *Human Relations, 40*, 31–43.

Bureau of Business Research (1962). *Leader behavior description questionnaire—form XII*. Columbus: Ohio State University, College of Commerce and Administration.

Burgess, R. L. (1968). Communication networks: An experimental re-evaluation. *Journal of Experimental Social Psychology, 4*, 324–337.

Burgess, R. (1969). Communication networks and behavioral consequences. *Human Relations, 22*, 137–159.

Burgoyne, J. G., & Hodgson, V. E. (1984). An experiential approach to understanding managerial action. In J. G. Hunt, D. Hosking, C. A. Schriesheim, & R. Stewart (Eds.), *Leaders and managers: International perspectives on managerial behavior and leadership*. New York: Pergamon.

Burke, E. (1790/1967). *Reflections on the revolution in France*. New York: Dutton.

Burke, K. (1950). *Rhetoric of motives*. New York: Prentice-Hall.

Burke, M. J., & Day, R. R. (1986). A cumulative study of the effectiveness of mangerial training. *Journal of Applied Psychology, 71*, 242–245.

Burke, P. J. (1966a). Authority relations and disruptive behavior in the small group. *Dissertation Abstracts, 26*, 4850.

Burke, P. J. (1966b). Authority relations and disruptive behavior in small discussion groups. *Sociometry, 29*, 237–250.

Burke, P. J. (1967). The development of task and social-emotional role differentiation. *Sociometry, 30*, 379–392.

Burke, P. J. (1971). Task and social-emotional leadership role performance. *Sociometry, 34*, 22–40.

Burke, P. J. (1974). Participation and leadership in small groups. *American Sociological Review, 39*, 832–843.

Burke, R. J. (1969). A plea for systematic evaluation of training. *Training & Development Journal, 23*, 24–29.

Burke, R. J., Weitzel, W., & Weir, T. (1978). Characteristics of effective employee performance review and development interviews: Replication and extension. *Personnel Psychology, 31*, 903–919.

Burke, R. J., & Wilcox, D. S. (1971). Bases of supervisory power and subordinate job satisfaction. *Canadian Journal of Behavioral Sciences, 3*, 183–193.

Burke, R. L., & Bennis, W. G. (1961). Changes in perception of self and others during human relations training. *Human Relations, 14*, 165–182.

Burke, R. L., & Wilcox, D. S. (1969). Effects of different patterns and degrees of openness in superior-subordinate communication on subordinate job satisfaction. *Academy of Management Journal, 1*, 319–326.

Burke, W. W. (1964). Leadership behavior as a function of the leader, the follower, and the situation. *Dissertation Abstracts, 24*, 2992.

Burke, W. W. (1965). Leadership behavior as a function of the leader, the follower, and the situation. *Journal of Personality, 33*, 60–81.

Burke, W., Richley, E. A., & DeAngelis, L. (1985). Changing leadership and planning processes at the Lewis Research Center, National Aeronautics and Space Administration. *Human Resource Management, 24*(1), 81–90.

Burks, F. W. (1938). Some factors related to social success in college. *Journal of Social Psychology, 9*, 125–140.

Burnett, C. W. (1951a). Leadership on the college campus. *Educational Research Bulletin, 30,* 34-41.

Burnett, C. W. (1951b). Validating campus leadership. *Educational Research Bulletin, 30,* 67-73.

Burnham, L. E., & Lee, H. E. (1963). *Correlations between seven leadership criteria and selected variables.* Stanford, CA: Stanford University.

Burns, J. H. (1934). *Psychology and leadership.* Fort Leavenworth, KS: Command and General Staff School Press.

Burns, J. M. (1978). *Leadership.* New York: Harper & Row.

Burns, T. (1954). The directions of activity and communication in a departmental executive group: A quantitative study in a British engineering factory with a self-recording technique. *Human Relations, 7,* 73-97.

Burns, T. (1957). Management in action. *Operational Research Quarterly, 8,* 45-60.

Burns, T., & Stalker, G. M. (1961). *The management of innovation.* Chicago: Quadrangle Books.

Burnstein, E. (1969). An analysis of group decision involving risk ("the risky shift"). *Human Relations, 22,* 381-395.

Burnstein, E., & Zajonc, R. B. (1965a). Individual task performance in a changing social structure. *Sociometry, 28,* 16-29.

Burnstein, E., & Zajonc, R. B. (1965b). The effect of group success on the reduction of status incongruence in task-oriented groups. *Sociometry, 28,* 349-362.

Burroughs, W. A. (1970). The study of white females' voting behavior toward two black female collaborators in a modified leaderless group discussion. *Dissertation Abstracts International, 30,* 5063.

Burroughs, W. A., & Jaffee, C. L. (1969). Verbal participation and leadership voting behavior in a leaderless group discussion. *Psychological Record, 19,* 605-610.

Bursk, E. C. (1956). *Human relations for management: The newer perspective.* New York: Harper.

Burt, J. M. (1984). Relationships between leadership behavior and employee absenteeism and turnover in community hospitals' departments. *Dissertation Abstracts International, 45*(6B), 1723.

Burwen, L. S., & Campbell, D. T. (1957a). A comparison of test scores and role-playing behavior in assessing superior vs. subordinate orientation. *Journal of Social Psychology, 46,* 49-56.

Burwen, L. S., & Campbell, D. T. (1957b). The generality of attitudes toward authority and nonauthority figures. *Journal of Abnormal and Social Psychology, 54,* 24-31.

Busch, P. (1980). The sales manager's bases of social power and influence upon the salesforce. *Journal of Marketing, 44,* 91-101.

Busche, G. R. (1987). Temporary or permanent middle management groups? Correlates with attitudes in QWL change projects. *Group & Organization Studies, 12,* 23-37.

Butler, D. C., & Miller, N. (1965). Power to reward and punish in social interaction. *Journal of Experimental Social Psychology, 1,* 311-322.

Butler, J. L., & Keys, J. B. (1973). *A comparative study of simulation and traditional methods of supervisory training in human resource development.* Paper, Academy of Management, Boston.

Butler, M. C., & Jones, A. P. (1979). Perceived leader behavior, individual characteristics, and injury occurrence in hazardous work environments. *Journal of Applied Psychology, 64,* 299-304.

Butler, R. P. (1971). A study of the effects of incentive feedback and manner of presenting the feedback on leader behavior. *Dissertation Abstracts International, 31,* 4377-4378.

Butler, R. P., Lardent, C. L., & Miner, J. B. (1983). A motivational basis for turnover in military officer education and training. *Journal of Applied Psychology, 68,* 496-506.

Butler, W. P. (1961). Job satisfaction among foremen—case study no. 2. *Personnel Practice Bulletin, 17,* 5-14.

Butterfield, D. A. (1969). An integrative approach to the study of leadership effectiveness in organizations. *Dissertation Abstracts, 29,* 3122.

Butterfield, D. A., & Bartol, K. M. (1977). Evaluators of leader behavior: A missing element in leadership theory. In J. G. Hunt & L. L. Larson (Eds.), *Leadership: The cutting edge.* Carbondale: Southern Illinois University Press.

Butterfield, D. A., Posner, B. Z., & Powell, G. N. (1982). *Applicability of the good manager profile to presidents and presidential candidates.* Paper, International Association of Applied Psychology, Edinburgh.

Butterfield, D. A., & Powell, G. N. (1981). Effect of group performance, leader sex, and rater sex on ratings of leader behavior. *Organizational Behavior and Human Performance, 28,* 129-141.

Butterfield, D. A., & Powell, G. N. (1985). *Leadership in the public sector: Presidential candidates as chief executive officers.* Paper, Academy of Management, San Diego, CA.

Buttgereit, H. (1932). Führergestalten in der Schulklass. *Zeitschrift für angewardte Psychologie, 43,* 369-413.

Byars, L. L., & Crane, D. P. (1969). Training by objectives. *Training & Development Journal, 23,* 38-48.

Bychowski, G. (1948). *Dictators and disciples from Caeser to Stalin.* NY: International Universities Press.

Bycio, P. (1988). Exercise order and assessment center performance. *Proceedings, Academy of Management,* Anaheim, CA, 264-267.

Byham, W. C., Adams, D., & Kiggins, A. (1976). Transfer of modeling training to the job. *Personnel Psychology, 29,* 345-349.

Byham, W. C., & Thornton, G. C., III, (1970). "Assessment centers: A new aid in management selection." *Studies in Personnel Psychology, 2*(2), 21-35.

Byrne, D. (1961). Interpersonal attraction and attitude similarity. *Journal of Abnormal and Social Psychology, 62,* 713-715.

Byrne, D. (1965). Authoritarianism and response to attitude similarity-dissimilarity. *Journal of Social Psychology, 66,* 251-256.

Byrne, D. (1971). *The attraction paradigm.* New York: Academic Press.

Byrne, D., & Clore, G .L. (1966). Predicting interpersonal attraction toward strangers presented in three different stimulus modes. *Psychonomic Science, 4,* 239-240.

Byrne, D., Clore, G. L., & Worchel, P. (1966). Effect of economic similarity-dissimilarity on interpersonal attraction. *Journal of Personality and Social Psychology, 4,* 220-224.

Byrne, D., & Griffitt, W. (1966a). A developmental investigation of the law of attraction. *Journal of Personality and Social Psychology, 4,* 699–703.

Byrne, D., & Griffitt, W. (1966b). Similarity versus liking: A clarification. *Psychonomic Science, 6,* 295–296.

Byrne, D., Griffitt, W., & Golightly, C. (1966). Prestige as a factor in determining the effect of attitude similarity-dissimilarity on attraction. *Journal of Personality, 34,* 434–444.

Byrne, D., & Nelson, D. (1965a). The effect of topic importance and attitude similarity-dissimilarity on attraction in a multistranger design. *Psychonomic Science, 3,* 449–450.

Byrne, D., & Nelson, D. (1965b). Attraction as a linear function of proportion of positive reinforcements. *Journal of Personality and Social Psychology, 1,* 659–663.

Byrne, J. A., & Zellner, W. (1988, September 12). Caught in the middle: Six managers speak out on corporate life. *Business Week,* pp. 80–88.

Byrnes, J. L. (1973). *A study of certain relationships among perceived supervisory style, participativeness and teacher job satisfaction.* Doctoral dissertation, Syracuse University, Syracuse, NY.

Cahill, I. D. (1967). Child-rearing practices in lower socioeconomic ethnic groups. *Dissertation Abstracts, 27*(9A), 3139.

Calas, M. B. (1986). *The unavoidable contextual and cultural bases of attribution of leadership research: A literature/literary critique.* Academy of Management, Chicago.

Calas, M. B., & Smircich, L. (1987). Reading leadership as a form of cultural analysis. In J. G. Hunt, B. R. Baliga, H. P. Dachler, & C. A. Schriesheim (Eds.), *Emerging leadership vistas.* Lexington, MA: D.C. Heath.

Calder, B. J. (1977). An attribution theory of leadership. In B. M. Staw and G. R. Salancik (Eds.), *New directions in organizational behavior.* Chicago: St. Clair.

Caldwell, D. F., & O'Reilly, C. A., III. (1982). Boundary spanning and individual performance: The impact of self-monitoring. *Journal of Applied Psychology, 67,* 124–127.

Caldwell, O. W. (1920). Some factors in training for leadership. In *Fourth Yearbook, National Association of Secondary School Principals,* Washington, DC.

Caldwell, O. W., & Wellman, B. (1926). Characteristics of school leaders. *Journal of Educational Research, 14,* 1–15.

Calloway, D. W. (1985). The promise and paradoxes of leadership. *Directors and Boards, 9*(2), 12–16.

Calvin, A. D., Hoffmann, F. K., & Harden, E. D. (1957). The effect of intelligence and social atmosphere on group problem-solving behavior. *Journal of Social Psychology, 45,* 61–74.

Camealy, J. B. (1969). Management development training: Multiple measurement of its effect when used to increase the impact of a long term motivational program. *Dissertation Abstracts, 29A,* 4136–4137.

Cameron, K. S., & Ulrich, D. O. (1986). Transformational leadership in colleges and universities. In J. C. Smart (Ed.), *Higher education: Handbook of theory and research,* Vol. 2. New York: Agathon Press.

Cammalleri, J. A., Hendrick, H. W., Pittman, W. C., Jr., Blout, H. D., &

Prather, D. C. (1973). Effects of different leadership styles on group accuracy. *Journal of Applied Psychology, 57,* 32–37.

Cammann, C., & Nadler, D. A. (1976). Fit control systems to your managerial style. *Harvard Business Review, 54,* 65–72.

Campbell, B. M. (1982, December 12). Black executives and corporate stress. *New York Times Magazine, 35,* 37–39, 100, 102, 104–107.

Campbell, D. P. (1969). SVIB managerial orientation scores of outstanding men. *Personnel Psychology, 22,* 41–44.

Campbell, D. P. (1987). Inklings. *Issues and Observations, 7*(2), 7–8.

Campbell, D. T. (1953). *A study of leadership among submarine officers.* Columbus: Ohio State Univesity, Personnel Research Board.

Campbell, D. T. (1955). An error in some demonstrations of the superior social perceptiveness of leaders. *Journal of Abnormal and Social Psychology, 51,* 694–695.

Campbell, D. T. (1956). *Leadership and its effect upon the group.* Columbus: Ohio State University, Bureau of Business Research.

Campbell, D. T. (1969). Reforms as experiments. *American Psychologist, 24,* 409–429.

Campbell, D. T., Burwen, L. S., & Chapman, J. P. (1955). *Assessing attitudes toward superiors and subordinates through direct attitude statements.* Evanston, IL: Northwestern University, Department of Psychology.

Campbell, D. T., & Damarin, F. L. (1961). Measuring leadership attitudes through an information test. *Journal of Social Psychology, 55,* 159–176.

Campbell, D. T., & Fiske, D. W. (1959). Convergent and discriminant validation by the multi-trait multi-method matrix. *Psychological Bulletin, 55,* 81–105.

Campbell, D. T., & McCormack, T. H. (1957). Military experience and attitudes toward authority. *American Journal of Sociology, 62,* 482–490.

Campbell, D. T., & Mehra, K. (1958). Individual differences in evaluations of group discussions as a projective measure of attitudes toward leadership. *Journal of Social Psychology, 47,* 101–106.

Campbell, D. T., & Stanley, J. C. (1963). *Experimental and quasi-experimental designs for research.* Chicago: Rand McNally.

Campbell, E. (undated). *A sociometric study of day care children.* Unpublished manuscript.

Campbell, H. (1953). Some effects of joint consultation on the status and role of the supervisor. *Occupational Psychology, 27,* 200–206.

Campbell, J. D. (1952). Subjective aspects of occupational status. *American Psychologist, 7,* 308.

Campbell, J. D., & Radke-Yarrow, M. (1956). Interpersonal perception and behavior in children's groups. *American Psychologist, 11,* 416.

Campbell, J. P. (1966). *Identification and enhancement of managerial effectiveness. IV. Management training.* Greensboro, NC: Richardson Foundation.

Campbell, J. P. (1977). The cutting edge of leadership. An overview. In J. G. Hunt and L. L. Larson (Eds.), *Leadership: The cutting edge.* Carbondale: Southern Illinois University Press.

Campbell, J. P. (1982). Editorial: Some remarks from the outgoing editor. *Journal of Applied Psychology, 67*, 691–700.

Campbell, J. P., & Dunnette, M. D. (1968). Effectiveness of T-group experiences in managerial training and development. *Psychological Bulletin, 70*, 73–104.

Campbell, J. P., Dunnette, M. D., Lawler, E. E., & Weick, K. E. (1970). *Managerial behavior, performance, and effectiveness.* New York: McGraw-Hill.

Campbell, J. W. (1948). An attitude survey in a typical manufacturing firm. *Personnel Psychology, 1*, 31–39.

Campbell, L. (1983). Black women community leaders in the rural south: A study in power and influence. *Dissertation Abstracts International, 45*(2B), 719.

Campbell, M. P. (1981). Leadership behavior of community mental health centers' program supervisors in Michigan as perceived by program supervisors, immediate superordinates, and immediate subordinates. *Dissertation Abstracts International, 42*(12B), 4743.

Campbell, M. V. (1958). *Self-role conflict among teachers and its relationship to satisfaction, effectiveness, and confidence in leadership.* Doctoral dissertation, University of Chicago, Chicago.

Campbell, O. L. (1961). The relations between eight situational factors and high and low scores on the leadership behavior dimensions of instructional supervisors. *Dissertation Abstracts, 22*, 786.

Campbell, R. J., & Bray, D. W. (1967). Assessment centers: An aid in management selection. *Personnel Administration, 30*(2), 6–13.

Campbell, V., Lange, C. J., & Shanley, F. J. (1968, June). Relationships among leader effectiveness ratings, intelligence and job knowledge. *Bibliography of Publications.* Washington, DC: Human Resources Research Office.

Campion, J. E. (1969). Effects of managerial style on subordinates' attitudes and performance in a simulated organization setting. *Dissertation Abstracts International, 30*, 881.

Campion, M. A., & Mitchell, M. M. (1986). Management turnover: Experiential differences between former and current managers. *Personnel Psychology, 39*, 57–69.

Campisano, J. F. (1984). Case study: Factors perceived to affect on-the-job use of leadership program content. *Dissertation Abstracts International, 45*(11A), 3294.

Canter, R. R., Jr. (1949). *An experimental study of a human relations training program.* Doctoral dissertation, Ohio State University, Columbus.

Canter, R. R. (1951). A human relations training program. *Journal of Applied Psychology, 35*, 38–45.

Capelle, M. H. (1967). Concurrent validation of the Leadership Opinion Questionnaire for college student leadership. *Dissertation Abstracts, 27*, 3607.

Caplan, E. H., & Landekich, S. (1974). *Human resource accounting: Past, present and future.* New York: National Association for Accountants.

Caplan, R. D., Cobb, S., French, J. R. P., Jr., Harrison, V., & Pinneau, S. R., Jr. (1975). *Job demands and workers' health.* Washington, DC: U.S. Government Printing Office.

Caplow, T. (1956). A theory of coalitions in the triad. *American Sociological Review, 21*, 489–493.

Caplow, T. (1968). *Two against one: Coalitions in triads.* Englewood Cliffs, NJ: Prentice-Hall.

Caplow, T., & Forman, R. (1950). Neighborhood interaction in a homogeneous community. *American Sociological Review, 15*, 357–366.

Carbone, T. C. (1981). Theory X and theory Y revisited. *Managerial Planning, 29*(6), 24–27.

Carbonell, J. L. (1984). Sex roles and leadership revisited. *Journal of Applied Psychology, 69*, 44–49.

Carew, D. K., Parisi-Carew, E., & Blanchard, K. H. (1986). Group development and situational leadership: A model for managing groups. *Training & Development Journal, 40*(6), 46–50.

Carey, H. H. (1942). Consultative supervision and management. *Personnel, 18*, 286, 295.

Carleton, F. O. (1970). *Relationships between follow-up evaluations and information developed in a management assessment.* Paper, American Psychological Association, Miami Beach.

Carlson, E. R. (1960). Clique structure and member satisfaction in groups. *Sociometry, 23*, 327–337.

Carlson, H. B., & Harrell, W. (1942). An analysis of Life's "ablest congressman" poll. *Journal of Social Psychology, 15*, 153–158.

Carlson, R. E., & James, L. R. (1971). *Sampling managerial behavior: A functional time analysis.* Life Insurance Agency Management Association. Unpublished report.

Carlson, R. O. (1961). Succession and performance among school superintendents. *Administrative Science Quarterly, 6*, 210–227.

Carlson, R. O. (1962). *Executive succession and organizational change.* Chicago: University of Chicago, Midwest Administrative Center.

Carlson, S. (1951). *Executive behavior.* Stockholm: Strombergs.

Carlyle, T. (1841/1907). *Heroes and hero worship.* Boston: Adams.

Carney, R. W. (1982). A call for authority. *Management World, 11*(10), 41–44.

Caro, R. (1974). *The power broker: Robert Moses and the fall of New York.* New York: Knopf.

Caro, R. (1982). *The Years of Lyndon Johnson.* New York: Knopf.

Carp, F. M., Vitola, B. M., & McLanathan, F. L. (1963). Human relations knowledge and social distance set in supervisors. *Journal of Applied Psychology, 47*, 78–80.

Carpeno, L. (1976). Expectations of male/female leadership styles in an educational setting. *Dissertation Abstracts International, 37*, 1482.

Carpenter, C. R. (1963). Societies of monkeys and apes. In C. H. Southwick (Ed.), *Primate social behavior.* Princeton, NJ: Van Nostrand.

Carpenter, H. H. (1970). *The relationship between certain organizational structure factors and perceived needs satisfaction of classroom teachers.* Doctoral dissertation, University of Houston, Houston, TX.

Carpenter, H. H. (1971). Formal organizational structural factors and perceived job satisfaction of classroom teachers. *Administrative Science Quarterly, 16*, 460–465.

Carr, R. W. (1971). *A study of the job satisfaction of high school principals.* Doctoral dissertation, University of Michigan, Ann Arbor.

Carrell, J. B. (1974). Sensitivity training: Effects on perceived self-ideal of self congruence. *Dissertation Abstracts International, 34,* 3863-3864.

Carrier, H. D. (1984). An empirical investigation of the competing values of leadership. *Dissertation Abstracts International, 45*(3B), 1051.

Carroll, S. J. (1987). *Gender difference and the contemporary leadership crisis.* Paper, Wingspread Seminar on Leadership Research, Racine, WI.

Carroll, S. J., & Gillen, D. J. (1987). Are the classical management functions useful in describing managerial work? *Academy of Management Review, 12,* 38-51.

Carroll, S. J., & Nash, A. N. (1970). Some personal and situational correlates of reactions to management development training. *Academy of Management Journal, 13,* 187-196.

Carroll, S. J., Jr., Olian, J. D., & Giannantonio, C. M. (1988). Mentor reactions to proteges: An experiment with managers. *Proceedings, Academy of Management,* Anaheim, CA, 273-276.

Carroll, S. J., Paine, F. T., & Ivancevich, J. J. (1972). The relative effectiveness of training methods—expert opinion and research. *Personnel Psychology, 25,* 495-509.

Carroll, S. J., & Taylor, W. H. (1968). The study of the validity of a self-observational central-signaling method of work sampling. *Personnel Psychology, 21,* 359-364.

Carroll, S. J., & Taylor, W. H. (1969). Validity of estimates by clerical personnel of job time estimates. *Journal of Applied Psychology, 53,* 164-166.

Carroll, S. J., & Tosi, H. L. (1970). Goal characteristics and personality factors in a management-by-objectives program. *Administrative Science Quarterly, 15,* 295-305.

Carron, T. J. (1964). Human relations training and attitude change: A vector analysis. *Personnel Psychology, 17,* 403-422.

Carson, A. (1985). Participatory management beefs up the bottom line. *Personnel, 4*(7), 45-48.

Carson, J. O., & Schultz, R. E. (1964). A comparative analysis of the junior college dean's leadership behavior. *Journal of Experimental Education, 32,* 355-362.

Carter, G. C. (1949). Student traits and progression through college. *Journal of Educational Psychology, 40,* 306-308.

Carter, L. F. (1953). Leadership and small group behavior. In M. Sherif & M. O. Wilson (Eds.), *Group relations at the crossroads.* New York: Harper.

Carter, L. F. (1954). Evaluating the performance of individuals as members of small groups. *Personnel Psychology, 7,* 477-484.

Carter, L. F., Haythorn, W., & Howell, M. (1950). A further investigation of the criteria of leadership. *Journal of Abnormal and Social Psychology, 45,* 350-358.

Carter, L. F., Haythorn, W., Meirowitz, B., & Lanzetta, J. T. (1951). The relation of categorizations and ratings in the observation of group behavior. *Human Relations, 4,* 239-254.

Carter, L. F., Haythorn, W., Shriver, B., & Lanzetta, J. T. (1951). The behavior of leaders and other group members. *Journal of Abnormal and Social Psychology, 46,* 589-595.

Carter, L. F., & Nixon, M. (1949a). An investigation of the relationship between four criteria of leadership ability for three different tasks. *Journal of Psychology, 27,* 245-261.

Carter, L., & Nixon, M. (1949b). Ability, perceptual, personality, and interest factors associated with different criteria for leadership. *Journal of Psychology, 27,* 377-388.

Cartwright, D. (1951). Achieving change in people: Some applications of group dynamics theory. *Human Relations, 4,* 381-393.

Cartwright, D. (1959a). A field theoretical conception of power. In D. Cartwright (Ed.), *Studies in social power.* Ann Arbor: University of Michigan, Institute for Social Research.

Cartwright, D. (1959b). *Studies in social power.* Ann Arbor, MI: University of Michigan, Institute for Social Research.

Cartwright, D. (1965). Influence, leadership, control. In J. G. March (Ed.), *Handbook of organizations.* Chicago: Rand McNally.

Cartwright, D., & Zander, A. (1960). *Group dynamics—research and theory.* Evanston, IL: Row, Peterson.

Cartwright, D. S., & Robertson, R. J. (1961). Membership in cliques and achievement. *American Journal of Sociology, 66,* 441-445.

Carzo, R., & Yanouzas, J. N. (1969). Effects of flat and tall organization structure. *Administrative Science Quarterly, 14,* 178-191.

Cascio, W. F. (1974). Functional specialization, culture, and preference for participative management. *Personnel Psychology, 27,* 593-603.

Cascio, W. (1975). Accuracy of verifiable biographical information blank responses. *Journal of Applied Psychology, 60,* 767-769.

Cascio, W. F. (1982). *Costing human resources: The financial impact of behavior in organizations.* Boston: Kent.

Cascio, W. F., & Bass, B. M. (1976). The effects of role play in a program to modify attitudes towards black employees. *Journal of Social Psychology, 92,* 261-266.

Cascio, W. F., & Ramos, R. A. (1986). Development and application of a new method for assessing job performance in behavioral/economic terms. *Journal of Applied Psychology, 71,* 20-28.

Cascio, W. F., & Sibley, V. (1979). The utility of the assessment center as a selection device. *Journal of Applied Psychology, 64,* 107-118.

Case, C. M. (1933). Leadership and conjuncture. *Sociology and Social Research, 17,* 510-513.

Case, S. S. (1985). A sociolinguistic analysis of the language of gender relations, deviance, and influence in managerial groups (intergroup language differences). *Dissertation Abstracts International, 46*(7A), 2006.

Casey, T. J. (1975). The development of a leadership orientation scale on the SVIB for women. *Measurement and Evaluation Guide, 8,* 96-100.

Cash, T. F., Gillen, B., & Burns, D. S. (1977). Sexism and "beautyism" in personnel consultant decision making. *Journal of Applied Psychology, 29,* 80–85.

Cashman, J., (1975). *The nature of leadership in the vertical dyad: The team building process.* Doctoral dissertation. University of Illinois, Urbana.

Cashman, J., Dansereau, F., Jr., Graen, G., & Haga, W. J. (1976). Organizational understructure and leadership: A longitudinal investigation of the managerial role-making process. *Organizational Behavior and Human Performance, 15,* 278–296.

Cashman, J. F., & Snyder, R. A. (1980). Perceptions of leaders' behavior: Situational and personal determinants. *Psychological Reports, 46,* 615–624.

Cassel, R. N. (1961). A construct validity study of leadership and social insight tests for 200 college freshmen students. *Journal of Genetic Psychology, 99,* 165–170.

Cassel, R. N., & Haddox, G. (1959). Comparative study of leadership test scores for gifted and typical high school students. *Psychological Reports, 5,* 713–717.

Cassel, R. N., & Sanders, R. A. (1961). A comparative analysis of scores from two leadership tests for Apache Indian and Anglo-American youth. *Journal of Educational Research, 55,* 19–23.

Cassel, R. N., & Shafer, A. E. (1961). An experiment in leadership training. *Journal of Psychology, 51,* 299–305.

Cassens, F. P. (1966a). Cross cultural dimensions of executive life history antecedents (biographical information). *Dissertation Abstracts, 27,* 291.

Cassens, F. P. (1966b). *Cross cultural dimensions of executive life history antecedents (biographical information).* Greensboro, NC: Creativity Research Institute, Richardson Foundation.

Castaldi, R. M. (1982). An analysis of the work roles of chief executive officers in small furniture manufacturing firms. *Dissertation Abstracts International, 44*(4A), 1184.

Castaldi, R. M., & Soerjanto, T. (1988). *Post-confucianism management practices and behaviors: A comparison of Japan versus China and South Korea.* Paper, Western Academy of Management, Big Sky, MT.

Cates, J. N. (1965). Disclosure of role conflict through critical incidents. *Sociology and Social Research, 49,* 319–329.

Cattell, J. McK. (1906). *American men of science.* New York: Science Press.

Cattell, R. B. (1934). Friends and enemies: A psychological study of character and temperament. *Character and Personality, 3,* 54–63.

Cattell, R. B. (1942). The concept of social status. *Journal of Social Psychology, 15,* 293–308.

Cattell, R. B. (1946). *Description and measurement of personality.* New York: World Book.

Cattell, R. B. (1951). New concepts for measuring leadership in terms of group syntality. *Human Relations, 4,* 161–184.

Cattell, R. B. (1952). *Factor analysis.* New York: Harper.

Cattell, R. B. (1953). On the theory of group learning. *Journal of Social Psychology, 37,* 27–52.

Cattell, R. B. (1957). A mathematical model for the leadership role and other personality-role relations. In M. Sherif & M. O. Wilson (Eds.), *Emerging problems in social psychology.* Norman: University of Oklahoma.

Cattell, R. B. (1966). Psychological theory and scientific method. In R. B. Cattell (Ed.), *Handbook of multivariate experimental psychology.* Chicago: Rand McNally.

Cattell, R. B., Saunders, D. R., & Stice, G. F. (1953). The dimensions of syntality in small groups. *Human Relations, 6,* 331–356.

Cattell, R. B., & Stice, G. F. (1953). *The psychodynamics of small groups.* Urbana: University of Illinois, Laboratory Personality Assessment and Group Behavior.

Cattell, R. B., & Stice, G. F. (1954). Four formulae for selecting leaders on the basis of personality. *Human Relations, 7,* 493–507.

Caudrea, P. A. (1975). Investigation of sex differences across job levels. *Dissertation Abstracts International, 36,* 1957B.

Caul, J. L. (1976). *A comparative study of student, teacher, and principal perceptions of organizational structure between middle schools with high levels and those with low levels of middle school concept implementation.* Doctoral dissertation, Michigan State University, East Lansing, MI.

Cederblom, D. (1982). The performance appraisal interview: A review, implications and suggestions. *Academy of Management Review, 7,* 219–227.

Cell, C. P. (1974). Charismatic heads of state: The social context. *Behavioral Science Research, 4,* 255–304.

Centers, R. (1948). Motivational aspects of occuptional stratification. *Journal of Social Psychology, 28,* 187–217.

Centers, R., & Bugental, D. E. (1966). Intrinsic and extrinsic job motivations among different segments of the working population. *Journal of Applied Psychology, 50,* 193–197.

Chacko, T. I. (1982). Women and equal employment opportunity: Some unintended effects. *Journal of Applied Psychology, 67,* 119–123.

Chafee, E. E. (1987). *Variations on a theme: Leadership.* Paper, Association for the Study of Higher Education, Baltimore.

Chafetz, J. S., & Dworkin, A. G. (1984). Work pressure similarity for homemakers, managers and professionals. *Free Inquiry in Creative Sociology, 12*(1), 47–50.

Chaffee, E. E. (1985). Three models of strategy. *Academy of Management Review, 10,* 89–98.

Chambers, P. (1974). No easy path for women managers. *International Management, 2,* 46–48.

Chandler, A. D. (1956). Management decentralization: A historical analysis. *Business History Review, 30,* 111–174.

Chandler, A. D., Jr. (1962). *Strategy and structure: Chapters in the history of the industrial enterprises.* Cambridge, MA: M.I.T. Press.

Chaney, F. B. (1966). A cross-cultural study of industrial research performance. *Journal of Applied Psychology, 50,* 206–210.

Chaney, M. V., & Vinacke, W. E. (1960). Achievement and nurturance in triads varying in power distribution. *Journal of Abnormal and Social Psychology, 60,* 175–181.

Chang, M. (1982). *A re-examination of Weber's theory of charismatic authority: The case of Mao Tse-tung and the Chinese communist party.* Paper, North Central Sociological Association Conference.

Chanin, M. N., & Schneer, J. A. (1984). A study of the relationship between Jungian personality dimensions and conflict-handling behavior. *Human Relations, 37,* 863–879.

Chapin, F. S. (1924a). Socialized leadership. *Social Forces, 3,* 57–60.

Chapin, F. S. (1924b). Leadership and group activity. *Journal of Applied Sociology, 8,* 141–145.

Chapin, F. S. (1926). Activities of college students: A study in college leadership. *School & Society, 23,* 212–216.

Chapin, F. S. (1931). Research studies of extra-curricular activities and their significance in reflecting social changes. *Journal of Educational Sociology, 11,* 491–498.

Chapin F. S. (1945). *Community leadership and opinion in Red Wing.* Minneapolis: University of Minnesota Press.

Chapin, F. S. (1950). Sociometric stars as isolates. *American Journal of Sociology, 56,* 263–267.

Chapin, F. S., & Tsouderos, J. E. (1955). Formalization observed in ten voluntary associations: Concepts, morphology, process. *Social Forces, 33,* 306–309.

Chapman, J. B. (1975). Comparisons of male and female leadership styles. *Academy of Management Journal, 18,* 645–650.

Chapman, J. B., & Luthans, F. (1975). The female leadership dilemma. *Public Personnel Management, 4,* 173–179.

Chapman, L. J., & Campbell, D. T. (1957a). An attempt to predict the performance of three-man teams from attitude measures. *Journal of Social Psychology, 46,* 277–286.

Chapman, L. J., & Campbell, D. T. (1957b). Response set in the F scale. *Journal of Abnormal and Social Psychology, 54,* 129–132.

Chapple, E. D., & Donald, G., Jr. (1946). A method of evaluating supervisory personnel. *Harvard Business Review, 24,* 197–214.

Charters, W. W. (1964). *Teacher perceptions of administrator behavior.* St. Louis: Washington University.

Charters, W. W., & Gage, N. L. (1963). *Readings in the social psychology of education.* Boston: Allyn & Bacon.

Chassie, M. B. (1984). Vertical dyadic linkage information: Predictors and processes determining quality superior-subordinate relationships. *Dissertation Abstracts International, 46*(1A), 199.

Cheek, S. K. (1987). *Recent state initiatives: The governor as policy leader: The governor as chief administrator.* Paper, Academy of Management, New Orleans.

Chemers, M. M. (1969). Cross-cultural training as a means for improving situational favorableness. *Human Relations, 22,* 531–546.

Chemers, M. M., & Ayman, R. (1985). Leadership orientation as a moderator of the relationship between job performance and job satisfaction of Mexican managers. *Personality and Social Psychology Bulletin, 11,* 359–367.

Chemers, M. M., & Fiedler, F. E. (1986). The trouble with assumptions: A reply to Jago and Ragan. *Journal of Applied Psychology, 71,* 560–563.

Chemers, M. M., Fiedler, F. E., Lekhyananda, D., & Stolurow, L. M. (1966). Some effects of cultural training on leadership in heterocultural task groups. *International Journal of Psychology, 1,* 301–314.

Chemers, M. M., & Mahar, L. (1978). *Amigos two: A comparison of LEADER MATCH with alternative managerial training.* Seattle: University of Washington. Unpublished manuscript.

Chemers, M. M., Rice, R. W., Sundstrom, E., & Butler, W. (1975). Leader esteem for the least preferred co-worker score, training, and effectiveness: An experimental examination. *Journal of Personality and Social Psychology, 31,* 401–409.

Chemers, M. M., & Skrzypek, G. J. (1972). Experimental test of the contingency model of leadership effectiveness. *Journal of Personality and Social Psychology, 24,* 172–177.

Cherns, A. (1976). The principles of sociotechnical design. *Human Relations, 29,* 783–792.

Cherry, C. (1957). *On human communication.* Cambridge, MA: M.I.T. Press.

Chesanow, N. (1984, April). Getting cultured: Class acts for foreign-bound. *Savvy,* 72–77.

Chesterfield, R., & Ruddle, K. (1976). A case of mistaken identity: Ill-chosen intermediaries in a Venezuelan agricultural extension programme. *Community Development Journal, 11,* 53–59.

Chevaleva-Ianovskaia, E., & Sylla, D. (1929). Essai d'une étude sur les enfants meneurs. *Journal of Psychology, 26,* 604–612.

Chhokar, J. S., & Wallin, J. A. (1984). A field study of the effect of feedback frequency on performance. *Journal of Applied Psychology, 69,* 524–530.

Child, J. (1973). Strategies of control and organizational behavior. *Administrative Science Quarterly, 18,* 1–17.

Child, J. (1974). Managerial and organizational factors associated with company performance. *Journal of Management Studies, 11,* 13–27.

Child, J., & Ellis, T. (1973). Predictors of variation in managerial roles. *Human Relations, 26,* 227–250.

Child, J., Pearce, S., & King, L. (1980). Class perceptions and social identification of industrial supervisors. *Sociology, 14,* 363–399.

Chitayat, G., & Venezia, I. (1984). Determinants of management styles in business and nonbusiness organizations. *Journal of Applied Psychology, 69,* 437–447.

Chodorow, N. (1985). Gender, relation, and difference in psychoanalytic perspective. In H. B. Eisenstein & A. Jardine (Eds.), *The future of difference.* New Brunswick, NJ: Rutgers University Press.

Chow, E. N., & Grusky, O. (1980). Productivity, aggressiveness, and supervisory style. *Sociology and Social Research, 65,* 23–36.

Chowdhry, K., & Newcomb, T. W. (1952). The relative abilities of leaders and nonleaders to estimate opinions of their own groups. *Journal of Abnormal and Social Psychology, 47,* 51–57.

Chowdhry, K., & Pal, A. D. (1960). Production planning and organizational morale. In J. A. Rubenstein & C. J. Haberstroh (Eds.), *Some theories of organization.* Homewood, IL: Dorsey.

Chowdhry, K., & Tarneja, R. (1961). India. In *Developing better managers: An eight-nation study.* New York: National Industrial Conference Board.

Christensen, L. (1970). Validity of person-perception accuracy scores. *Perceptual and Motor Skills, 30,* 871–877.

Christie, L., Luce, D., & Macy, J. (1952). *Communication and learning in task oriented groups* (Tech. Rep. No. 231). Cambridge, MA: M.I.T., Research Lab of Electronics.

Christie, R. (1952). Changes in authoritarianism as related to situational factors. *American Psychologist, 7,* 307–308.

Christie, R. (1954). Authoritarianism re-examined. In R. Christie & M. Jahoda (Eds.), *Studies in the scope and method of "The Authoritarian Personality."* New York: Free Press.

Christie, R., & Cook, P. (1958). A guide to published literature relating to the authoritarian personality through 1956. *Journal of Psychology, 45,* 171–179.

Christie, R., & Geis, F. L. (1970). *Studies in Machiavellianism.* New York: Academic Press.

Christner, C. A., & Hemphill, J. K. (1955). Leader behavior of B-29 commanders and changes in crew members' attitudes toward the crew. *Sociometry, 18,* 82–87.

Chung, K. H., Lubatkin, M., Rogers, R. C., & Owers, J. E. (1987). Do insiders make better CEOs than outsiders? *The Academy of Management EXECUTIVE, 1,* 323–329.

Chung, K. S. (1970). Teacher-centered management style of public school principals and job satisfaction of teachers. ERIC *Document Reproduction Service* (Ms. No. EDO42-259).

Chyatte, C. (1949). Personality traits of professional actors. *Occupations, 27,* 245–250.

Cialdini, R. B., Petty, R. E., & Cacioppo, J. T. (1981). Attitude and attitude change. *Annual Review of Psychology, 32,* 357–404.

Clark, A. W., & McCabe, S. (1970). Leadership beliefs of Australian managers. *Journal of Applied Psychology, 54,* 1–6.

Clark, A. W., & McCabe, S. (1972). The motivation and satisfaction of Australian managers. *Personnel Psychology, 25,* 625–638.

Clark, B. R. (1956). Organizational adaptation and precarious values: A case study. *American Sociological Review, 21,* 327–336.

Clark, J. K. (1986). Anticipating chain reactions. *Public Relations Journal, 42*(8), 6–7.

Clark, K. E., & Clark, M. B. (Eds.) (1989). *Measures of leadership.* Greensboro, NC: Center for Creative Leadership.

Clark, M. B., Freeman, F. H., & Britt, S. K. (1987). *Leadership education '87: A source book.* Greensboro, NC: Center for Creative Leadership.

Clark, R. A. (1953). Analyzing the group structure of combat rifle squads. *American Psychologist, 8,* 333.

Clarke, H. I. (1951). Definition of a leader: Roosevelt? Toscanini? Hitler? Adams? Dillinger? *Group, 13,* 7–11.

Clausen, G. (1965). *Risk taking in small groups.* Doctoral dissertation, University of Michigan, Ann Arbor.

Clausen, J. A., & Clausen, S. R. (1973). The effects of family size on parents and children. In J. T. Fawcett (Ed.), *Psychological perspectives on population.* New York: Basic Books.

Clawson, J. G. (1979). *Superior-subordinate relationships in managerial development.* Doctoral dissertation, Harvard University, Cambridge, MA.

Clawson, J. G. (1980). Mentoring in managerial careers. In C. B. Derr (Ed.), *Work, family, and career.* New York: Praeger.

Clawson, J. G., & Kram, K. E. (1984, May-June). Managing cross-gender mentoring. *Business Horizons, 27*(3), 22–32.

Cleeton, G. U., & Mason, C. W. (1934). *Executive ability—its discovery and development.* Yellow Springs, OH: Antioch Press.

Clelland, D. A., & Form, W. H. (1964). Economic dominants and community power: A comparative analysis. *American Journal of Sociology, 69,* 511–521.

Clem, O. M., & Dodge, S. B. (1933). The relation of high school leadership and scholarship to post-school success. *Peabody Journal of Education, 10,* 321–329.

Clemens, J. K., & Mayer, D. F. (1987). *The classic touch: Lessons in leadership from Homer to Hemingway.* Homewood, IL: Dow Jones–Irwin.

Clement, P. A. (1983). An investigation on the validity of the Vroom-Yetton model of leadership. *Dissertation Abstracts International, 45*(3B), 994.

Clements, R. V. (1958). *Managers: A study of their careers in industry.* London: Allen & Unwin.

Cleveland, H. (1980). Learning the art of leadership: The worldwide crisis in governance demands new approaches. Unpublished manuscript.

Cleveland, H. (1985). *The knowledge executive: Leadership in an information society.* New York: Dutton.

Cleven, W. A., & Fiedler, F. E. (1956). Interpersonal perceptions of open-hearth foremen and steel production. *Journal of Applied Psychology, 40,* 312–314.

Clifford, C., & Cohn, T. S. (1964). The relationship between leadership and personality attributes perceived by followers. *Journal of Social Psychology, 64,* 57–64.

Cline, T. A. (1974). *A study of the relationships between Colorado Community College faculty members' attitudes toward collective negotiations and their perceptions of the management styles used in their colleges.* Doctoral dissertation, University of Colorado, Boulder, CO.

Cline, V. B., & Richards, J. M. (1960). Accuracy of interpersonal perception—a general trait? *Journal of Abnormal and Social Psychology, 60,* 1–7.

Cline, V. B., & Richards, J. M. (1961). The generality and accuracy of interpersonal perception. *Journal of Abnormal and Social Psychology, 62,* 446–449.

Cline, V. B., & Richards, J. M. (1963). Cline & Richards' reply to O'Connor's methodological note. *Journal of Abnormal and Social Psychology, 66,* 195–196.

Clingenpeel, R. E. (1971). Leadership in a technical organization. *Dissertation Abstracts International, 32,* 3680–3681.

Clover, W. H. (1989). Transformational leaders: Team performance, leadership ratings and first hand impressions. In K. E. Clark & M. B. Clark (Eds.), *Measures of Leadership.* West Orange, NJ: Leadership Library of America.

Cloyd, J. S. (1964). Functional differentiation and structure of informal groups. *Sociology Quarterly, 5,* 243–250.

Clutterbuck, D. (1974, May). Acid test for management potential. *International Management,* 54–57.

Clutterbuck, D. (1982a). How much does success depend upon a helping hand from above? *International Management, 37,* 17–19.

Clutterbuck, D. (1982b). The whittling away of middle management. *International Management, 37,* 10–16.

Coates, C. H., & Pellegrin, R. J. (1957). Executives and supervisors: Contrasting self-perceptions and conceptions of each other. *American Sociological Review, 22,* 217–220.

Coates, J. (1984). *Personality and situational variables as determinants of the distribution of power in a company organization.* Doctoral dissertation, University of Toronto.

Cobb, J. J. (1974). Leadership and decision-making in a black community: An inter-disciplinary analysis and study. *Dissertation Abstracts International, 34,* 4451.

Cobb, K. (1952). Measuring leadership in college women by free association. *Journal of Abnormal and Social Psychology, 47,* 126–128.

Coch, L., & French, J. R. P. (1948). Overcoming resistance to change. *Human Relations, 1,* 512–532.

Cochran, W. G. (1963). *Sampling techniques* (2nd ed.). New York: Wiley.

Coffin, T. E. (1944). A three-component theory of leadership. *Journal of Abnormal and Social Psychology, 39,* 63–83.

COFREMCA (1978). A psychological study of the attitudes of French managers. *International Study of Management and Organization, 8,* 22–38.

Coghill, C. J. (1981). *Managerial role perception in organization.* Doctoral dissertation, University of the Witwatersrand, Johannesburg, South Africa.

Coghill, M. A. (1967). *Sensitivity training.* Ithaca, NY: Cornell University, Industrial and Labor Relations Library.

Cohen, A. M. (1962). Changing small group communication networks. *Administrative Science Quarterly, 6,* 443–462.

Cohen, A. M., & Bennis, W. G. (1961). Continuity of leadership in communication networks. *Human Relations, 14,* 351–367.

Cohen, A. M., Bennis, W. G., & Wolkon, G. H. (1961). The effects of continued practice on the behaviors of problem-solving groups. *Sociometry, 24,* 416–431.

Cohen, A. M., & Foerst, J. R. (1968). Organizational behaviors and adaptations to organizational change of sensitizer and represser problem-solving groups. *Journal of Personality and Social Psychology, 8,* 209–216.

Cohen, A. M., Robinson, E. L., & Edwards, J. L. (1969). Experiments in organization embeddedness. *Administrative Science Quarterly, 4,* 208–221.

Cohen, A. R. (1954). The effects of individual self-esteem and situational structure on threat-oriented reactions to power. *Dissertation Abstracts, 14,* 727–728.

Cohen, A. R. (1955). Social norms, arbitrariness of frustration, and status of the agent of frustration in the Frustration-Aggression Hypothesis. *Journal of Abnormal and Social Psychology, 51,* 222–226.

Cohen, A. R. (1958). Upward communication in experimentally created hierarchies. *Human Relations, 11,* 41–53.

Cohen, A. R. (1959). Situational structure, self-esteem, and threat-oriented reactions to power. In D. Cartwright (Ed.), *Studies in social power.* Ann Arbor: University of Michigan, Institute for Social Research.

Cohen, A. R. (1964). Communication networks. *Personnel Administration, 27,* 18–24.

Cohen, D., Whitmyre, J. W., & Funk, W. H. (1960). Effect of group cohesiveness and training upon creative thinking. *Journal of Applied Psychology, 44,* 319–322.

Cohen, D. J., & Lindsley, O. R. (1964). Catalysis of controlled leadership in cooperation by human stimulation. *Journal of Child Psychology, 5,* 119–137.

Cohen, D., & March, J. G. (1974). *Leadership and ambiguity.* New York: McGraw-Hill.

Cohen, E. (1956). Stimulus conditions as factors in social change. *American Psychologist, 11,* 407.

Cohen, E. (1957). The effect of members' use of a formal group as a reference group upon group effectiveness. *Journal of Social Psychology, 46,* 307–310.

Cohen, G. B. (1969). *The task-tuned organization of groups.* Amsterdam: Swets & Zeitlinger.

Cohen, J. (1968). Job satisfaction as a function of philosophy of work style among professionals and executives. *Dissertation Abstracts, 29,* 1196.

Cohen, J. (1970). *Secondary motivation.* Chicago: Rand McNally.

Cohn, T. S., Fisher, A., & Brown, V. (1961). Leadership and predicting attitudes of others. *Journal of Social Psychology, 55,* 199–206.

Colby, A. H., & Zak, R. E. (1988). *Transformational leadership: A comparison of Army and Air Force perceptions* (Report 88-0565). Air Command and Staff College, Air University, Maxwell AFB, AL.

Cole, C. T. (1947). Rural leadership—its origin and development. *Journal of Educational Sociology, 21,* 184–188.

Cole, J. F. (1984). High school reform. *Educational Leadership, 41* 38–40.

Coleman, J. S., et al. (1966). *Equality of educational opportunity.* Washington, DC: U.S. Department of Health, Education, and Welfare, U.S. Government Printing Office.

Coles, L. W. (1972). A study of the differential effects of two leadership training styles on United Methodist adult groups. *Dissertation Abstracts International, 32,* 4913.

Collaros, P. A., & Anderson, L. R. (1969). Effect of perceived expertness upon creativity of members of brainstorming groups. *Journal of Applied Psychology, 2,* 159-163.

Collins, A. K. (1957). *Developing leadership in a small plant: A critical account of an experimental training program.* Doctoral dissertation, Cornell University, Ithaca, NY.

Collins, B. E., & Guetzkow, H. (1964). *A social psychology of group processes for decision-making.* New York: Wiley.

Collins, E. G. C. (1983). Managers and lovers. *Harvard Business Review 61*(5), 142-153.

Collins, E. G. C., & Scott, P. (1978). Everyone who makes it has a mentor. *Harvard Business Review, 56*(4), 89-101.

Collins, O., Dalton, M., & Roy, D. (1946). Restriction of output and social cleavage in industry. *Applied Anthropology, 5,* 1-14.

Collins, O. F., Moore, D. G., & Unwalla, D. B. (1964). *The enterprising man.* East Lansing: Michigan State University, Bureau of Business and Economic Research.

Colmen, J. G., Fiedler, G. O., & Boulger, J. R. (1954). Methodological considerations in determining supervisory training needs. *American Psychologist, 9,* 350.

Colyer, D. M. (1951). The good Foreman—as his men see him. *Personnel, 28,* 140-147.

Comrey, A. L., High, W. S., & Wilson, R. C. (1955a). Factors influencing organizational effectiveness. VI. A survey of aircraft workers. *Personnel Psychology, 8,* 79-99.

Comrey, A. L., High, W. S., & Wilson, R. C. (1955b). Factors influencing organizational effectiveness. VII. A survey of aircraft supervisors. *Personnel Psychology, 8,* 245-257.

Comrey, A. L., Pfiffner, J. M., & Beem, H. P. (1952). Factors influencing organizational effectiveness. I. The U.S. Forest Survey. *Personnel Psychology, 5,* 307-328.

Comstock, D. E., & Scott, W. R. (1977). Technology and structure of subunits: Distinguishing individual and work efforts. *Administrative Science Quarterly, 22,* 177-202.

Conant, E. H., & Kilbridge, M. D. (1965). An interdisciplinary analysis of job enlargement: Technology, costs, and behavioral implications. *Industrial Labor Relations Review, 18,* 377-395.

Conant, R. C., & Ashby, R. W. (1970). Every good regulator of a system must be a model of the system. *International Journal of Systems and Science, 1,* 89-97.

Conference Research (1950, March). *Process of administrative conference.* University of Michigan, Ann Arbor.

Conger, J. A., & Kanungo, R. N. (1987). Toward a behavioral theory of charismatic leadership in organizational settings. *Academy of Management, 12,* 637-647.

Conger, J. A., & Kanungo, R. N. (1988). Behavioral dimensions of charismatic leadership. In J. A. Conger & R. N. Kanungo (Eds.), *Charismatic leadership, The elusive factor in organizational effectiveness.* San Francisco: Jossey-Bass, 78-97.

Connors, M., Lindsey, G., & Miller, R. (1976). *The NASA teleconferencing system: An evaluation.* Moffett Field, CA: Ames Research Center, National Aeronautical and Space Administration.

Conover, P. J., Mingst, K. A., & Sigelman, L. (1980). Mirror images in Americans' perceptions of nations and leaders during the Iranian hostage crisis. *Journal of Peace Research, 17,* 325-337.

Conradi, E. (1905). Song and call-notes of English sparrows when reared by canaries. *American Journal of Psychology, 16,* 190-198.

Conway, M. (1915). *The crowd in peace and war.* New York: Longmans, Green.

Cook, D. M. (1968). The impact on managers of frequency feedback. *Academy of Management Journal, 11,* 263-277.

Cooley, C. H. (1902). *Human nature and the social order.* New York: Scribners.

Cooley, C. W. (1956). *Social organization.* Glencoe, IL: Free Press.

Cooley, W. W., & Lohnes, P. R. (1971). *Multivariate data analysis.* New York: Wiley.

Cooper, C. L. (1969). The influence of the trainer on participant change in T-groups. *Human Relations, 22,* 515-530.

Cooper, C. L. (1975). How psychologically dangerous are T-groups and encounter groups? *Human Relations, 28,* 249-260.

Cooper, C. L., & Levine, N. (1978). Implicit values in experimental learning groups: Their functional and dysfunctional consequences. In C. L. Cooper & C. Alderfer (Eds.), *Advances in experimental social processes.* New York: Wiley.

Cooper, C. L., & Mangham, I. L. (Eds.). (1971). *T-groups: A survey of research.* New York: Wiley.

Cooper, G. L., & Davidson, M. J. (1982). The high cost of stress on women managers. *Organizational Dynamics, 10*(4), 44-53.

Cooper, R. (1966). Leader's task relevance and subordinate behavior in industrial work groups. *Human Relations, 19,* 57-84.

Cooper, R., & Payne, R. (1967). *Personality orientations and performance in football teams: Leader's and subordinates' orientations related to team success* (Report No. 1). Birmingham, England: University of Aston, Organizational Group Psychology.

Copeland, N. (1942). *Psychology and the soldier.* Harrisburg, PA: Military Service Publishing.

Copeland, N. (1944). *The art of leadership.* London: Allen.

Copeman, G. H. (1955). *Leaders of British industry: A study of the careers of more than a thousand public company directors.* London: Gee.

Copeman, G. (1971). *The chief executive and business growth.* London: Leviathan House.

Cordiner, R. J. (1952). *Problems of management in a large decentralized organization.* New York: American Management Association.

Corey, L. G. (1971). People who claim to be opinion leaders: Identifying their characteristics by self-report. *Journal of Marketing, 34,* 48-53.

Cornelius, E. T., III, & Lane, F. B. (1984). The power motive and managerial success in a professionally oriented service industry organization. *Journal of Applied Psychology, 69,* 32-39.

Cornwell, J. M. (1983). *A meta-analysis of selected trait research in the leadership literature.* Paper, Southeastern Psychological Association, Atlanta, GA.

Corsini, R. J., Shaw, M. E., & Blake, R. R. (1961). *Roleplaying in business and industry.* New York: Free Press.

Corsino, L. (1982) Malcolm X and the Black Muslim movement: A social psychology of charisma. *Psychohistory Review, 10,* 165–184.

Coser, R. L. (1980). Women and work. *Dissent, 27,* 51–55.

Cosier, R. A., & Aplin, J. C. (1980). Effects of delegated choice on performance. *Personnel Psychology, 33,* 581–593.

Coste, M. M. (1962). Caracterisation de la perception empathique du choix sociometrique. *Revue Francaise de Sociologie, 3*(4), 407–414.

Cotton, G. C., & Cotton, E. G. (1982). *Marginality orientation and LPC: Evidence that task-oriented persons are more "marginal."* Paper, International Congress of Applied Psychology, Edinburgh.

Couch, A., & Carter, L. F. (1953). A factorial study of the related behavior of group members. *American Psychologist, 8,* 333.

Courtenay, M. E. (1938). Persistence of leadership. *School Review, 46,* 97–107.

Courtney, D., Greer, F. L., & Masling, J. M. (1952). *Leadership identification and acceptance.* Philadelphia: Institute for Research in Human Relations.

Courtney, D., Greer, F. L., Masling, J. M., & Orlans, H. (1953). *Naval, neighborhood, and national leadership.* Philadelphia: Institute for Research in Human Relations.

Cowley, W. H. (1928). Three distinctions in the study of leaders. *Journal of Abnormal and Social Psychology, 23,* 144–157.

Cowley, W. H. (1931). Traits of face-to-face leaders. *Journal of Abnormal and Social Psychology, 26,* 304–313.

Cox, C. M. (1926). *The early mental traits of three hundred geniuses.* Stanford: Stanford University Press.

Cox, D. (1953). *Women's attitudes to repetitive work.* London: National Institute of Industrial Psychology.

Cox, J. A., & Krumboltz, J. D. (1958). Racial bias in peer ratings of basic airmen. *Sociometry, 21,* 292–299.

Cox, M. (1986, March 24). Clearer connections: The nebulous networks of the 70's give way to pragmatic business contacts. *Wall Street Journal,* 19D.

Coye, R. W. (1982). Subordinate responses to ineffective leadership. *Dissertation Abstracts International, 43*(6A), 2070.

Coyle, G. L. (1948). *Group work with American youth.* New York: Harper.

Cozan, L. W. (1959). Job enlargement and employee satisfaction. *Personnel Journal, 38,* 95–96.

Craft, J. R. (1943). Measure of a man: Officer candidate rating scale. *Occupations, 22,* 214.

Craig, J. G., & Jull, G. W. (1974). *Teleconferencing studies: Behavioral research and technological implications.* Ottawa: Communications Research Centre, Department of Communication.

Craig, R. D. (1983). Policy capturing in the evaluation of self-esteem as a moderator of the relationship between supervisory style and subordinate satisfaction in the path-goal theory of leadership. *Dissertation Abstracts International, 44*(9B), 2928.

Crain, R. L., & Weisman, C. S. (1972). *Discrimination, personality, and achievement.* New York: Seminar Press.

Crandall, V. C. (1969). Sex differences in expectancy of intellectual and academic reinforcement. In C. P. Smith (Ed.), *Achievement-related motives in children.* New York: Russell Sage Foundation.

Crandall, V. J., Katkovsky, W., & Preston, A. (1962). Motivational and ability determinants of young children's intellectual achievement behaviors. *Child Development, 33,* 643–661.

Crannell, C. W., & Mollenkopf, W. G. (1946). Combat leadership. In F. Wickert (Ed.), *Psychological research in problems of redistribution* (Research Rep. No. 14). Army Air Forces Aviation Psychology Program.

Cratty, B. (1981). *Social psychology in athletics.* Englewood Cliffs, NJ: Prentice-Hall.

Crawford, A. B. (1928). Extra-curriculum activities and academic work. *Personnel Journal, 7,* 121–129.

Crawford, K. S., Thomas, E. D., & Fink, J. J. (1980). Pygmalion at sea: Improving the work effectiveness of low performers. *Journal of Applied Behavioral Science, 16,* 482–505.

Creager, J. A., & Harding, F. D. (1958). A hierarchical factor analysis of foreman behavior. *Journal of Applied Psychology, 42,* 197–203.

Cribbin, J. J. (1981). *Leadership: Strategies for organizational effectiveness.* New York: AMACOM.

Criswell, J. H. (1961). The sociometric study of leadership. In L. Petrullo & B. Bass (Eds.), *Leadership and interpersonal behavior.* New York: Holt, Rinehart & Winston.

Crockett, W. H. (1955). Emergent leadership in small, decision-making groups. *Journal of Abnormal and Social Psychology, 51,* 378–383.

Crockett, W. H., & Meidinger, T. (1956). Authoritarianism and interpersonal perception. *Journal of Abnormal and Social Psychology, 53,* 378–382.

Crockett, W. J. (1981, May). Dynamic subordinancy. *Training & Development Journal, 35,* 155–164.

Cronbach, L. G. (1975). Beyond the two disciplines of scientific psychology. *American Psychologist, 30,* 116–127.

Cronbach, L. J. (1955). Processes affecting scores on "understanding of others" and assumed "similarity." *Psychological Bulletin, 52,* 117–193.

Cronbach, L. J., & Glaser, G. C. (1953). *Psychological tests and personnel decisions.* Urbana: University of Illinois Press.

Cronbach, L. J., Hartmann, W., & Ehart, M. E. (1953). *Investigation of the character and properties of assumed similarity measures* (Tech. Rep. No. 7). Urbana: University of Illinois, Group Effectiveness Research Laboratory.

Cronin, T. (1980). *The state of the presidency* (2d ed.). Boston: Little, Brown.

Cronin, T. E. (1984). Thinking and learning about leadership. *Presidential Studies Quarterly, 14*(1), 22–34.

Cronshaw, S. F., & Lord, R. G. (1987). Effects of categorization, attribution, and encoding processes on leadership perceptions. *Journal of Applied Psychology, 72*(1), 97–106.

Crookall, P. (1989). *Management of inmate workers: A field test of transformational leadership and situational leadership.* Doctoral dissertation, University of Western Ontario, London, Ontario.

Crouch, A. (1986, August). *Effects of manager and subordinate needs for dominance on manager willingness to legitimize conflict and subordinate performance.* Paper, Academy of Management, Chicago.

Crouch, A. (1987). An equilibrium model of management group performance. *Academy of Management Review, 12,* 499–510.

Crouch, A. G., & Yetton, P. (1987). Manager behavior, leadership style, and subordinate performance: An empirical extension of the Vroom-Yetton conflict rule. *Organizational Behavior & Human Decision Processes, 39,* 384–396.

Crouch, A., & Yetton, P. (1988). Manager-subordinate dyads: Relationships among task and social contact, manager friendliness and subordinate performance in management groups. *Organizational Behavior & Human Decision Processes, 41,* 65–82.

Crouch, E. H. (1926). Public school training for leadership. *Peabody Journal of Education, 3,* 230–231.

Crow, W. J. (1957a). The need for representative design in studies of interpersonal perception. *Journal of Consulting Psychology, 21,* 323–325.

Crow, W. J. (1957b). The effect of training upon accuracy and variability of interpersonal perception. *Journal of Abnormal and Social Psychology, 55,* 355–359.

Crow, W. J., & Hammond, K. R. (1957). The generality of accuracy and response sets in interpersonal perception. *Journal of Abnormal and Social Psychology, 54,* 384–390.

Crowe, B. J., Bochner, S., & Clark, A. W. (1972). The effects of subordinates' behavior on managerial style. *Human Relations, 25,* 215–237.

Crozier, M. (1984). *The bureaucratic phenomenon.* Chicago: University of Chicago Press.

Csoka, L. S. (1974). A relationship between leader intelligence and leader rated effectiveness. *Journal of Applied Psychology, 59,* 43–47.

Csoka, L. S. (1975). Relationship between organizational climate and the situational favorableness dimension of Fiedler's contingency model. *Journal of Applied Psychology, 60,* 273–277.

Csoka, L. S., & Bons, P. M. (1978). Manipulating the situation to fit the leader's style—Two validation studies of LEADER MATCH. *Journal of Applied Psychology, 63,* 295–300.

Csoka, L. S., & Fiedler, F. E. (1972a). *Leadership and intelligence: A contingency model analysis.* Paper, American Psychological Association, Honolulu.

Csoka, L. S., & Fiedler, F. E. (1972b). The effect of military leadership training: A test of the contingency model. *Organizational Behavior and Human Performance, 8,* 395–407.

Culbert, S. A., & McDonough, J. (1980). *The invisible war: Pursuing self-interests at work.* New York: Wiley.

Culbert, S. A., & McDonough, J. (1985). *Radical management: Power politics and the pursuit of trust.* New York: Free Press.

Cullers, B., Hughes, C., & McGreal, T. (1973). Administrative behavior and student dissatisfaction: A possible relationship. *Peabody Journal of Education, 50,* 155–163.

Cummin, P. C. (1967). TAT correlates of executive performance. *Journal of Applied Psychology, 51,* 78–81.

Cummings, L. L., & ElSalmi, A. M. (1968). Empirical research on the bases and correlates of managerial motivation: A review of the literature. *Psychological Bulletin, 70,* 127–144.

Cummings, L. L., & ElSalmi, A. M. (1970). The impact of role diversity, job level, and organizational size on managerial satisfaction. *Administrative Science Quarterly, 15,* 1–10.

Cummings, L. L., Harnett, D. L., & Stevens, O. J. (1971). Risk, fate conciliation and trust: An international study of attitudinal differences among executives. *Academy of Management Journal, 14,* 285–304.

Cummings, L. L., & Schmidt, S. M. (1972). Managerial attitudes of Greeks: The roles of culture and industrialization. *Administrative Science Quarterly, 17,* 265–272.

Cummings, L. L., & Schwab, D. P. (1973). *Performance in organizations: Determinants and appraisal.* Glenview, IL: Scott, Foresman.

Cummings, L. L., & Schwab, D. P. (1978). Designing appraisal systems for information yield. *California Management Review, 20,* 18–25.

Cummings, L. L., & Scott, W. E. (1965). Academic and leadership performance of graduate business students. *Business Perspectives, 1,* 11–20.

Cummins, R. C. (1970). An investigation of a model of leadership effectiveness. *Proceedings, American Psychological Association,* 599–600.

Cummins, R. C. (1971). Relationship of initiating structure and job performance as moderated by consideration. *Journal of Applied Psychology, 55,* 489–490.

Cummins, R. C. (1972). Leader-member relations as a moderator of the effects of leader behavior and attitude. *Personnel Psychology, 25,* 655–660.

Cunningham, C. J. (1964). *Measures of leader behavior and their relation to performance levels of county extension agents.* Doctoral dissertation, Ohio State University, Columbus.

Cunningham, I., & Leon, P. (1986). Focusing managerial development. *Journal of European Industrial Training, 10(8),* 23–26.

Cunningham, R. B., & Olshfski, D. F. (1985). Evaluating task leadership: A problem for assessment centers. *Public Personnel Management, 14,* 293–299.

Cunningham, S. (1984, September). Culture plays important role in our beliefs. *APA Monitor,* 8–9.

Cuny, F. (1983). *Disasters and development.* Oxford: Oxford University Press.

Curfman, M. (1939). *An experimental investigation of some of the influences of authoritarian and democratic atmospheres on the behavior of small groups.* Master's thesis, Stanford University, Palo Alto, CA.

Curtis, B., Smith, R. E., & Smoll, F. L. (1979). Scrutinizing the skipper: A study of behaviors in the dugout. *Journal of Applied Psychology, 64,* 391–400.

Curtis, Q. F., & Gibbard, H. A. (1955). *The acquiring of membership in established groups* (Final Tech. Rep.). Morgantown: West Virginia University.

Cushman, J. H. (1989, January 14). Air traffic controllers and U.S. reach accord. *New York Times,* p. 6.

Cussler, M. (1958). *The woman executive*. New York: Harcourt, Brace & World.

Cuthbertson, P. J. (1982). The effects of contingency variables on leadership style. *Dissertation Abstracts International, 43*(5A), 1361.

Cyert, R. M., & March, J. G. (1963). *A behavioral theory of the firm*. Englewood Cliffs, NJ: Prentice-Hall.

Daft, R. L. (1983). *Organizational theory and design*. St. Paul, MN: West Publishing.

Dagirmanjian, S. (1981). The work experience of service staff in mental health service organizations and its relationship to leadership style and organizational structure. *Dissertation Abstracts International, 43*(5B), 1609.

Dahl, R. A. (1957). The concept of power. *Behavioral Science, 2*, 201–215.

Dahl, R. A. (1961). *Who governs?* New Haven, CT: Yale University Press.

Dahl, R. A. (1968). Power. In *International Encyclopedia of the Social Sciences*, Vol. 12. New York: Macmillan and Free Press.

Dahl, R. A., March J., & Nastair, D. (1957). Influence ranking in the United States Senate. Cited in R. A. Dahl, The concept of power, *Behavioral Science, 2*, 201–215.

Dale, E. (1952). *Planning and developing the company organization structure*. New York: American Management Association.

Dale, E. (1955). Centralization versus decentralization. *Advanced Management, 20*, 11–16.

Dalessio, A. (1983). Subordinates' leadership preferences and leader-subordinate understanding. *Dissertation Abstracts International, 45*(5B), 1611.

Dalessio, A., & Davis, D. D. (1986). *Predicting innovation among R & D scientists and engineers*. Paper, American Psychological Association, Washington, DC.

Daley, D. M. (1986). Humanistic management and organizational success: The effect of job and work environment characteristics on organizational effectiveness, public responsiveness, and job satisfaction. *Public Personnel Management, 15*(2), 131–142.

Dalton, D. R., & Kesner, I. F. (1985). Organizational performance as an antecedent of inside/outside chief executive succession: An empirical assessment. *Academy of Management Journal, 28*, 749–762.

Dalton, G. W., Barnes, L. B., & Zaleznik, A. (1968). *The distribution of authority in formal organizations*. Boston: Harvard University, Graduate School of Business Administration.

Dalton, G. W., Lawrence, P. R., & Greiner, L. E. (Eds.). (1970). *Organizational change and development*. Homewood, IL: Irwin-Dorsey.

Dalton, M. (1950). Conflicts between staff and line managerial officers. *American Sociological Review, 15*, 342–351.

D'Angelo, R. V. (1973). *The influence of three styles of leadership on the process and outcome of an organization development effort*. Doctoral dissertation, University of California, Berkeley.

Daniel, T. (1985). Managerial behaviors: Their relationship to perceived organizational climate in a high-technology company. *Group & Organization Studies, 10*, 413–428.

Daniels, L. R., & Berkowitz, L. (1963). Liking and response to dependency relationships. *Human Relations, 16*, 141–148.

Dansereau, F., Alutto, J. A., Markham, S. E., & Dumas, M. (1982). Multiplexed leadership and supervision: An application of within and between analysis. In J. G. Hunt, U. Sekaran, and C. A. Schriesheim (Eds.), *Leadership: Beyond establishment views*. Carbondale: Southern Illinois University Press.

Dansereau, F., Alutto, J. A., & Yammarino, F. J. (1984). *Theory testing in organizational behavior: The varient approach*. Englewood Cliffs, NJ: Prentice-Hall.

Dansereau, F., Cashman, J., & Graen, G. (1973). Instrumentality theory and equity theory as complementary approaches in predicting the relationship of leadership and turnover among managers. *Organizational Behavior and Human Performance, 10*, 184–200.

Dansereau, F., & Dumas, M. (1977). Pratfalls and pitfalls in drawing inferences about leadership behavior in organizations. In J. G. Hunt and L. L. Larson (Eds.), *Leadership: The cutting edge*. Carbondale: Southern Illinois University Press.

Dansereau, F., Graen, G., & Haga, W. J. (1975). A vertical dyad linkage approach to leadership in formal organizations. *Organizational Behavior and Human Performance, 13*, 46–78.

Dansereau, F., & Markham, S. E. (1987). Superior-subordinate communication: Multiple levels of analysis. In F. Jablin, L. Putnam, K. Roberts, & L. Porter (Eds.), *Handbook of organizational communication*. Newbury Park, CA: Sage.

Danzig, E. R., & Galanter, E. H. (1955). *The dynamics and structure of small industrial work groups*. Philadelphia: Institute for Research in Human Relations.

Danzig, E. R., & Siegel, A. I. (1955). *Emergent leadership in a civil defense evacuation exercise*. Philadelphia: Institute for Research in Human Relations.

Darley, J. G., Gross, N., & Martin, W. E. (1952). Studies of group behavior factors associated with the productivity of groups. *Journal of Applied Psychology, 36*, 396–403.

Darley, J. M., & Berscheid, R. (1967). Increased liking as a result of the anticipation of personal contact. *Human Relations, 20*, 29–40.

Dashiell, J. F. (1930). Personality traits and the different professions. *Journal of Applied Psychology, 14*, 197–201.

Daugherty, R. A., & Walters, T. J. (1969). Closure flexibility, field dependence, and student leadership. *Perceptual and Motor Skills, 29*, 256–258.

Daum, J. W. (1975). Internal promotion: A psychological asset or debit? A study of the effects of leader origin. *Organizational Behavior and Human Performance, 13*, 404–413.

Davenport, W. G., Brooker, G., & Munro, N. (1971). Factors in social perception: Seating position. *Perceptual and Motor Skills, 33*, 747–752.

Davies, D. R., & Tune, G. S. (1970). *Human vigilance performance*. New York: American Elsevier.

Davies, J., & Easterby-Smith, M. (1984). Learning and developing from managerial work experiences. *Journal of Management Studies, 2*, 169–183.

Davies, J. C. (1954). Charisma in the 1952 campaign. *American Political Science Review, 48,* 1083–1102.

Davies, J. C. (1963). *Human nature in politics.* New York: Wiley.

Davis, F. J. (1954). Conceptions of official leader roles in the air force. *Social Forces, 32,* 253–258.

Davis, G. (1975). The maturation of Theodore Roosevelt: The rise of an "affective leader." *The History of Childhood Quarterly, 3,* 43–74.

Davis, H. J., Ming, L. W., & Brosnan, T. F. (1986). *The Farmer-Richman model: A bibliographic essay emphasizing applicability to Singapore and Indonesia.* Paper, Academy of Management, Chicago.

Davis, J. A. (1929). A study of 163 communist leaders. *American Sociological Society, 24,* 42–45.

Davis, J. A., & Warnath, C. F. (1957). Reliability, validity, and stability of a sociometric rating scale. *Journal of Social Psychology, 45,* 111–122.

Davis, K. (1951). Learning to live in informal groups. *Advanced Management, 16,* 17–19.

Davis, K. (1957). Management by participation. *Management Review, 46,* 69–79.

Davis, K. (1963). The case for participative management. *Business Horizons, 6,* 55–60.

Davis, K. (1962). *Human relations at work.* New York: McGraw-Hill.

Davis, K. (1968a). Attitudes toward the legitimacy of management efforts to influence employees. *Academy of Management Journal, 11,* 153–161.

Davis, K. (1968b). Success of chain of command oral communications in a manufacturing management group. *Academy of Management Journal, 11,* 379–387.

Davis, K. E. (1982). The status of black leadership: Implications for black followers in the 1980s. *Journal of Applied Behavioral Science, 18,* 309–322.

Davis, L. E., & Valfer, E. S. (1966). Studies in supervisory job design. *Human Relations, 19,* 339–352.

Davis, L. E., & Werling, R. (1960). Job design factors. *Occupational Psychology, 34,* 109–132.

Davis, R. A. (1987). *Concensus and neoconservatism in the black community: A theoretical analysis of black leadership.* Paper, American Sociological Association, Chicago.

Davis, R. C. (1942). *The fundamentals of top management.* New York: Harper.

Davis, T. R. V., & Luthans, F. (1979). Leadership reexamined: A behavioral approach. *Academy of Management Review, 4,* 237–248.

Davis, T. R., & Luthans, F. (1984). Defining and researching leadership as a behavioral construct: An idiographic approach. *Journal of Applied Behavioral Science, 20,* 237–251.

Davitz, J. R. (1955). Social perception and sociometric choice of children. *Journal of Abnormal and Social Psychology, 50,* 173–176.

Dawe, H. C. (1934). The influence of size of kindergarten group upon performance. *Child Development, 5,* 295–303.

Dawson, C. A. (1969). Leadership and achievement: The effects of teaching styles on first-grade children. *Dissertation Abstracts, 29,* 2648–2649.

Dawson, J. E. (1970). *Consideration and ICS: Instructor leadership influencing student performance.* East Lansing: Michigan State University, Human Learning Research Institute.

Dawson, J. E., Messé, L. A., & Phillips, J. L. (1972). Effect of instructor-leader behavior on student performance. *Journal of Applied Psychology, 56,* 369–376.

Dawson, J. L. M., Haw, H., Leung, A., & Whitney, R. E. (1971). Scaling Chinese traditional-modern attitudes and the GSR measurement of "important" versus "unimportant" Chinese concepts. *Journal of Cross-Cultural Psychology, 2,* 1–27.

Day, C. (1909). Industrial leadership. *Yale Review, 18,* 21–33.

Day, C. M. (1980). Promotions of health care personnel in hospitals: Heuristic decision-making. *Dissertation Abstracts International, 42(3A),* 1290.

Day, D. R. (1961). Basic dimensions of leadership in a selected industrial organization. *Dissertation Abstracts, 22,* 3760.

Day, D. R. (1968). *Descriptions of male and female leader behavior by male and female subordinates.* Urbana: University of Illinois, Department of Industrial Administration.

Day, D. R., & Stogdill, R. M. (1972). Leader behavior of male and female supervisors: A comparative study. *Personnel Psychology, 25,* 353–360.

Day, D. V., & Lord, R. G. (1986). *Executive leadership and organizational performance: Suggestions for a new theory and methodology.* Paper, Academy of Management, Chicago. Also: (1988). *Journal of Management, 14,* 453–464.

Day, R. C., & Hamblin, R. L. (1964). Some effects of close and punitive styles of supervision. *American Journal of Sociology, 69,* 499–510.

Deal, T. E., & Kennedy, A. A. (1982). *Corporate cultures: The rite and rituals of corporate life.* Reading, MA: Addison-Wesley.

Dean, L. R. (1954). Union activity and dual loyalty. *Industrial Labor Relations Review, 7,* 449–460.

Dearborn, D. C., & Simon, H. A. (1958). Selective perception: A note on the departmental identifications of executives. *Sociometry, 21,* 140–144.

Deaux, K. (1976a). *Self-evaluations of male and female managers.* Unpublished manuscript.

Deaux, K. (1976b). *The behavior of women and men.* Monterey, CA: Brooks/Cole.

Deaux, K. (1985). Sex and gender. *Annual Review of Psychology, 36,* 49–81.

Deaux, K., & Emswiller, T. (1974). Explanations of successful performance on sex-linked tasks: What is skill for the male is luck for the female. *Journal of Personality and Social Psychology, 29,* 80–85.

DeBolt, J. W., Liska, A. E., & Weng, B. R. (1976). Replications of associations between internal locus of control and leadership in small groups. *Psychological Reports, 38,* 470.

DeCarlo, C. R., & Robinson, O. W. (1966). *Education in business and industry.* New York: Center for Applied Research in Education.

deCharms, R. (1957). Affiliation motivation and productivity in small groups. *Journal of Abnormal and Social Psychology, 55*, 222–226.

deCharms, R. (1968). *Personal causation.* New York: Academic Press.

deCharms, R., & Hamblin, R. I. (1960). *Structural factors and individual needs in group behavior.* St. Louis, MO: Washington University.

deCharms, R., & Rosenbaum, M. E. (1960). Status variables and matching behavior. *Journal of Personality, 29*, 492–502.

Deci, E. L. (1972). The effects of contingent and noncontingent rewards and controls on intrinsic motivation. *Organizational Behavior and Human Performance, 8*, 217–229.

Deckop, J. (1987). Top executive compensation and the pay-for-performance issue. In D. B. Balkin & L. R. Gomez-Mejia (Eds.), *New perspectives in compensation.* Englewood Cliffs, NJ: Prentice-Hall.

Deep, S. D., Bass, B. M., & Vaughan, J. A. (1967). Some effects on business gaming of previous quasi-T-group affiliations. *Journal of Applied Psychology, 51*, 426–431.

Deets, L. E. (1931). The origins of conflict in the Hutererische communities. *Publications of American Social Societies, 25*, 125–135.

Deets, N., & Morano, R. (1986). Xerox's strategy for changing management styles. *Management Review, 75*(3), 31–35.

Deets, N. R., & Tyler, D. (1986). How Xerox improved its performance appraisals. *Personnel Journal, 65*(4), 50–52.

DeGrazia, A. (1949). *Human relations in public administration: An annotated bibliography from the fields of anthropology, industrial management, political science, psychology, public administration, and sociology.* Chicago: Public Administration Clearing House.

DeGrove, J. M., & Kammerer, G. M. (1964). Urban leadership during change. *American Academy of Political Social Science, 353*, 95–106.

Deitzer, B. A. (1967). *Measuring the effectiveness of a selected management development program.* Doctoral dissertation, Ohio State University, Columbus.

Dejung, J. W., & Kaplan, H. (1962). Some differential effects of race of rater and ratee on early peer ratings of combat attitude. *Journal of Applied Psychology, 26*, 370–374.

Dekin, A. (1985). *Planning input from communities—politics and participation.* Paper, Alaska Anthropological Association, Anchorage.

Dekmejian, R. H., & Wyszomirski, M. J. (1972). Charismatic leadership in Islam: The Mahdi of the Sudan. *Comparative Studies in Society and History. 14*, 193–214.

Delbecq, A. L., & Kaplan, S. J. (1968). The myth of the indigenous community leader: A case study of managerial effectiveness within the "War on Poverty." *Academy of Management Journal, 11*, 11–25.

Dellums, R. V. (1977). Black leadership: For change or for status quo? *Black Scholar, 8*, 2–5.

Dellva, W. L., McElroy, J. C., & Schrader, C. B. (1987). *A longitudinal network analysis of formal versus emergent leadership.* Paper, Academy of Management, New Orleans.

DeLong, A. (1971). Dominance-territorial criteria and small group structure. *Comparative Group Studies, 2*, 235–266.

DeLong, A. J. (1970). Seating position and perceived characteristics of members of a small group. *Cornell Journal on Social Relations, 5*, 135–151.

DeLora, J. R., & Barber, W. F. (1963). *Dimensions of occupational status-images as they relate to recruitment and retention of personnel.* San Diego, CA: San Diego State College, Bureau of Business Research.

Delson, S. (1986). *Leadership in a public institution of higher education during a period of declining enrollment and declining resources.* Doctoral dissertation, Columbia University Teachers College, New York.

Deluga, R. (1986). *Employee influence strategies as possible coping mechanisms for role conflict and role ambiguity.* Paper, Eastern Psychological Association, New York.

Deluga, R. J. (1988a). Relationship of transformational and transactional leadership with employee influencing strategies. *Group & Organization Studies, 13*, 456–467.

Deluga, R. (1988b). The politics of leadership: The relationship between task-people leadership and subordinate influence strategies. *Journal of Organizational Behavior, 9*, 359–366.

Delunas, E. E. (1983). Temperament, personality, and managerial effectiveness: Keirsey-Myers leadership styles. *Dissertation Abstracts International, 44*(4A), 1027.

Demause, L. (1982). *Foundations of psychohistory.* New York: Creative Roots.

Dember, W. N., & Earl, R. W. (1957). Analysis of exploratory, manipulatory, and curiosity behaviors. *Psychological Review, 64*, 91–96.

DeMeuse, K. P. (1986). A compendium of frequently used measures in industrial/organizational psychology. *The Industrial-Organizational Psychologist, 23*(2), 53–59.

Demming, W. E. (1986). *Drastic changes for Western management.* Madison, WI: Center for Quality and Productivity Improvement.

Denhardt, R. B. (1987). Images of death and slavery in organizational life. *Journal of Management, 13*, 543–556.

DeNisi, A. S., & Pritchard, R. D. (1978). Implicit theories of performance as artifacts in survey research: A replication and extension. *Organizational Behavior and Human Performance, 21*, 358–366.

DeNisi, A. S., Randolph, W. A., & Blencoe, A. G. (1983). Potential problems with peer feedback. *Academy of Management Journal, 26*, 457–464.

Denison, D. R. (1984). Bringing corporate culture to the bottom line. *Organizational Dynamics, 13*(2), 5–22.

Denmark, F. L. (1977). Styles of leadership. *Psychology of Women Quarterly, 2*, 99–113.

Denmark, F. L. (1980). Psyche: From rocking the cradle to rocking the boat. *American Psychologist, 35*, 1057–1065.

Denmark, F. L., & Diggory, J. C. (1966). Sex differences in attitudes toward leaders' display of authoritarian behavior. *Psychological Reports, 18*, 863–872.

Dennardt, R. B. (1970). Leadership style, worker involvement, and deference to authority. *Sociological and Social Research, 54*, 172–180.

Dent, J. K. (1959). Organizational correlates of the goals of business managements. *Personnel Psychology, 12*, 365–396.

Dent, J. K., & de la Paz, R. (1961). Union security and management attitudes. *Personnel Psychology, 14,* 167–182.

Denton, R. T. (1976). The effects of differing leadership behaviors on the job satisfaction and job performance of professional mental health workers. *Dissertation Abstracts International, 37,* 3183.

Derber, M. (1970). Crosscurrents in workers' participation. *Industrial Relations, 9,* 123–136.

Derber, M., Chalmers, W. E., Edelman, M. T., & Triandis, H. C. (1965). *Plant union-management relations.* Urbana: University of Illinois Press.

Derr, B. C. (1972). Successful entry as a key to successful organization development in big city school systems. In W. Burke & H. A. Hornstein (Eds.), *The social technology of organization development.* Fairfax, VA: NTL Learning Resources.

Desmond, R. E., & Seligman, M. (1977). A review of research on leaderless groups. *Small Group Behavior, 8,* 3–24.

Desruisseaux, P. (1986). Foundations are asked to help train and encourage new leaders. *Chronicle of Higher Education, 32*(9), 19.

Dessler, G. (1972). *A test of the path-goal theory of leadership.* Paper, Academy of Management, Minneapolis, MN.

Dessler, G. (1973). *An investigation of the path-goal theory of leadership.* Doctoral dissertation, Baruch College, City University of New York.

Dessler, G., & Valenzi, E. R. (1977). Initiation of structure and subordinate satisfaction: A path analysis test of path-goal theory. *Academy of Management Journal, 20,* 251–259.

de Tocqueville, A. (1832/1966). *Democracy in America.* New York: Harper & Row.

Deutsch, M. (1949). An experimental study of the effects of cooperation and competition upon group process. *Human Relations, 2,* 199–232.

Deutsch, M. (1973). *The resolution of conflict: Constructive and destructive processes.* New Haven, CT: Yale University Press.

Deutsch, M., & Gerard, H. B. (1954). *A study of normative and informational social influences upon individual judgment* (Tech. Rep.), Contract NONR-285(10). New York: New York University.

Deutsch, M., & Krauss, R. M. (1960). The effect of threat upon interpersonal bargaining. *Journal of Abnormal and Social Psychology, 61,* 181–189.

Deutschberger, P. (1947). The structure of dominance. *American Journal of Orthopsychiatry, 17,* 343–351.

Development Dimensions International. (1983). *Behavior modeling through computer-assisted instruction, 2*(3), 1–3.

Devereux, E. C. (1960). Community participation and leadership. *Journal of Social Issues, 16,* 29–45.

Devereaux, G. (1955). Charismatic leadership and crisis. In W. Muensterberger and S. Axelrod (Eds.), *Psychoanalysis and the Social Sciences.* New York: International University Press.

Devine, I. B. (1983). Organizational crisis and individual response: The case of the Environmental Protection Agency. *Dissertation Abstracts International, 44*(11A), 3474.

Devine, R. P. (1977). Opinion influence roles: Opinion leaders, opinion followers, and isolates. *Dissertation Abstracts International, 37*(12A), 7977.

DeVries, D. L. (in press). Teams-games-tournament. *Simulation and Games, 7,* 21–33.

DeVries, M. F. (1977). Crisis leadership and the paranoid potential: An organizational perspective. *Bulletin of the Menninger Clinic, 41,* 349–365.

Dewhirst, H. D. (1971a). Impact of organizational climate on the desire to manage among engineers and scientists. *Personnel Journal, 50,* 196–203.

Dewhirst, H. D. (1971b). Influence of perceived information-sharing norms on communication channel utilization. *Academy of Management Journal, 14,* 305–315.

Dewhirst, H. D., Metts, V., & Ladd, R. T. (1987). *Exploring the delegation decision: Managerial responses to multiple contingencies.* Paper, Academy of Management, New Orleans.

Dexter, E. S., & Stein, B. (1955). The measurement of leadership in white and negro women students. *Journal of Abnormal and Social Psychology, 51,* 219–221.

Deyo, F. C. (1978). The cultural patterning of organizational development: A comparative case study of Thailand and Chinese industrial enterprises. *Human Organization, 37,* 68–72.

Dhanagare, D. N. (1968). Perception of leader's competence and the rates of positive-negative reactions in work-groups. *Indian Psychological Review, 4,* 126–133.

Dicken, C. F., & Black, J. D. (1965). Predictive validity of psychometric evaluations of supervisors. *Journal of Applied Psychology, 49,* 34–37.

Dickinson, Z. C. (1937). *Compensatory industrial effort.* New York: Ronald Press.

Dickson, J. W. (1980). Perceptions of direct and indirect participation in British companies. *Journal of Applied Psychology, 65,* 226–232.

Dienesch, R. M. (1985). *A three dimensional model of leader-member exchange: An empirical test.* Paper, Academy of Management, Chicago.

Dienesch, R. M., & Liden, R. C. (1986). Leader-member exchange model of leadership: A critique and further development. *Academy of Management Review, 11,* 618–634.

Diesing, P. (1971). *Patterns of discovery in the social sciences.* Chicago: Aldine-Atherton.

Dieterly, D. L., & Schneider, B. (1974). The effect of organizational environment on perceived power and climate: A laboratory study. *Organizational Behavior and Human Performance, 11,* 316–337.

Dietz, W. (1943). Training new supervisors in the skill of leadership. *Personnel, 19,* 604–608.

Dill, D., & Pearson, A. W. (1984). The effectiveness of project managers: Implications of a political model of influence. *IEEE Transactions on Engineering Management, 31*(3), 138–146.

Dill, W. R. (1958). Environment as an influence on managerial autonomy. *Administrative Science Quarterly, 2,* 409–443.

DiMarco, M., & Gustafson, D. (1975). Attitudes of coworkers and managers toward hard-core employees. *Personnel Psychology, 28,* 65–76.

DiMarco, N., & Whitsitt, S. E. (1975). A comparison of female supervisors in business and government organizations. *Journal of Vocational Behavior, 6*, 185-196.

Dion, K. L. (1985). Sex, gender, and groups: Selected issues. In V. O'Leary, R. K. Unger, & B. Strudler-Wallston (Eds.), *Women, gender, and social psychology*. Hillsdale, NJ: Lawrence Erlbaum Associates.

Dipboye, R. L., Fontenelle, G. A., & Garner, K. (1984). Effects of previewing the application on interview process and outcomes. *Journal of Applied Psychology, 69*, 118-128.

Dittes, F. E., & Kelley, H. H. (1956). Effects of different conditions of acceptance upon conformity to group norms. *Journal of Abnormal and Social Psychology, 53*, 100-107.

Dittes, J. E. (1959). Attractiveness of group as function of self-esteem and acceptance by group. *Journal of Abnormal and Social Psychology, 59*, 77-82.

DiVesta, F. J. (1954). Instructor-centered and student-centered approaches in teaching a human relations course. *Journal of Applied Psychology, 38*, 329-335.

DiVesta, F. J., Meyer, D. L., & Mills, J. (1964). Confidence in an expert as a function of his judgments. *Human Relations, 17*, 235-242.

Dixon, N. (1984). Participative management: It's not as simple as it seems. *Supervisory Management, 29*(12), 2-8.

Dobbins, G. H. (1985). Effects of gender on leaders' responses to poor performers: An attributional interpretation. *Academy of Management Journal, 28*, 587-598.

Dobbins, G. H., & Platz, S. J. (1986). Sex differences in leadership: How real are they? *Academy of Management Review, 11*(1), 118-127.

Dobbins, G. H., & Russell, J. M. (1986). The biasing effects of subordinate likeableness of leaders' responses to poor performers: A laboratory and a field study. *Personnel Psychology, 39*, 759-777.

Dobbins, G. H., & Zaccaro, S. J. (1986). The effects of group cohesion and leader behavior on subordinate satisfaction. *Group & Organization Studies, 11*, 203-219.

Dobruszek, Z. (1967). Badanie postaw kierowniczych za pomoca "Inwentarza postaw i pogladow" B. M. Bassa. [A study on the leadership attitudes with "Orientation inventory" of B. M. Bass.] *Przeglad Psychologiczny, 15*.

Dobruszek, Z. (1971). Leadership attitudes measured by the Bass Orientation Inventory. *Polish Psychological Bulletin, 2*, 31-35.

Dodd, S. C. (1955). Diffusion is predictable: Testing probability models for laws of interaction. *American Sociological Review, 20*, 392-401.

Dogan, M. (1979). How to become a minister in France: Career pathways 1870-1978. *Comparative Politics, 12*(1), 1-26.

Dogan, M., & Rokkan, S. (1969). *Quantitative ecological analysis in the social sciences*. Cambridge, MA: M.I.T. Press.

Doll, R. E., & Gunderson, E. K. (1969). The relative importance of selected behavioral characteristics of group members in an extreme environment. *Experimental Publications System, American Psychological Association*, No. 097A.

Doll, R. E., & Longo, A. A. (1962). Improving the predictive effectiveness of peer ratings. *Personnel Psychology, 15*, 215-220.

Dommermuth, W. P. (1965). *The road to the top: A study of the careers of corporation presidents*. Austin: University of Texas, Bureau of Business Research.

Donley, R. E., & Winter, D. G. (1970). Measuring the motives of public officials at a distance: An exploratory study of American presidents. *Behavioral Science, 15*, 227-236.

Donnelly, C. (1976, August). Keys to the executive powder room. *Money, 5*, 28-32.

Dorfman, P. W., & Howell, J. P. (1988). Dimensions of national culture and effective leadership patterns. *Advances in International Comparative Management, 3*, 127-150.

Doroschenko, O. (1928). Der Einfluss des Milieus auf den Inhalt und den Aufbau frei entstehender Kollektive in vorschulpflichtigen Alter. *Zeitschrift für angewandte Psychologie, 30*, 150-167.

Dossett, D. L., Cella, A., Greenberg, C. I., & Adrian, N. (1983). *Goal setting, participation and leader supportiveness effects on performance*. Paper, American Psychological Association, Anaheim, CA.

Dotlich, D. L. (1982). International and intercultural management development. *Development Journal, 36*(10), 26-31.

Douglas, W. S. (1977). An evaluation of experimental procedures for the systematic training of group leaders. *Dissertation Abstracts International, 36*, 4255.

Douglis, M. B. (1948). Social factors influencing the hierarchies of small flocks of the domestic hen; Interactions between resident and part-time members of organized flocks. *Physiological Zoology, 21*, 147-182.

Douvan, E. (1956). Social status and success strivings. *Journal of Abnormal and Social Psychology, 52*, 219-223.

Dow, T. (1969a). The theory of charisma. *Sociological Quarterly, 10*, 306-318.

Dow, T., Jr. (1969b). The role of charisma in modern African development. *Social Forces, 46*, 328-336.

Dowd, J. (1936). *Control in human societies*. New York: Appleton-Century.

Dowell, B. E., & Wexley, K. N. (1978). Development of a work behavior taxonomy for first-line supervisors. *Journal of Applied Psychology, 63*, 563-572.

Dowling, W. F. (1975). At General Motors: Systems 4 builds performance and profits. *Organizational Dynamics, 3*(3), 23-38.

Downey, H. K., Sheridan, J. E., & Slocum, J. W., Jr. (1975). Analysis of relationships among leader behavior, subordinate job performance and satisfaction: A path goal approach. *Academy of Management Journal, 18*, 253-262.

Downey, H. K., Sheridan, J. E., & Slocum, J. W., Jr. (1976). The path-goal theory of leadership: A longitudinal analysis. *Organizational Behavior and Human Performance, 16*, 156-176.

Downey, R. C., Medland, F. F., & Yates, L. G. (1976). Evaluation of a peer rating system for predicting subsequent promotion of senior military officers. *Journal of Applied Psychology, 61*, 206-209.

Downing, J. (1958). Cohesiveness, perception, and values. *Human Relations, 11*, 157-166.

Downs, A. (1967). *Inside bureaucracy.* Boston: Little, Brown.

Downton, J. V. (1973). *Rebel leadership: Commitment and charisma in the revolutionary process.* New York: Free Press.

Doyle, W. J. (1970). The effects of leader achieved status on hierarchically differentiated group performance. *Dissertation Abstracts International, 30,* 2747.

Doyle, W. J. (1971). Effects of achieved status of leader on productivity of groups. *Administrative Science Quarterly, 16,* 40-50.

Doz, Y., & Prahalad, C. K. (1984). Patterns of strategic control within multinational corporations. *Journal of International Business Studies, 15*(2), 55-72.

Drachkovitch, M. M. (1964). Succession and the charismatic leader in Yugoslavia. *Journal of International Affairs, 18*(1), 54-66.

Dragon, A. C. (1979). Leader behavior in changing libraries. *Library Research, 1*(1), 53-66.

Drake, B. H., & Moberg, D. (1986). Communicating influence attempts in dyads: Linguistic sedatives and palliatives. *Academy of Management Review, 11,* 567-584.

Drake, R. M. (1944). A study of leadership. *Character & Personality, 12,* 285-289.

Drake, St. C., & Cayton, H. (1966). The world of the urban lower-class Negro. In R. J. Murphy & H. Elinson (Eds.), *Problems and prospects of the Negro movement.* Belmont, CA: Wadsworth.

Drakeley, R. J., & Herriot, P. (1988). Biographical data, training successes and turnover. *Journal of Occupational Psychology, 61,* 145-152.

Draper, N. R., & Smith, H. (1966). *Applied regression analysis.* New York: Wiley.

Dreher, G. F., Dougherty, T. W., & Whitely, W. (1988). Influence tactics and salary attainment: A study of sex-based salary differentials. *Proceedings, Academy of Management,* Anaheim, CA, 346-350.

Dreher, G. F., & Sackett, P. R. (1983). *Perspectives on employee staffing and selection: Readings and commentary.* Homewood, IL: Richard D. Irwin.

Dreilinger, C., McElheny, R., Rice, D., & Robinson, B. (1982). The promise of leadership-style training: An outdated myth? *Training & Development Journal, 36*(8), 69-71.

Dreilinger, C., McElheny, R., Robinson, B., & Rice, D. (1982, Oct.). Beyond the myth of leadership-style training: Planned organizational change. *Training & Development Journal, 36*(10), 70-74.

Drenth, P. J. D. (1986). *The university and its leadership: A look from the rector's office.* Presidential Address, Division of Organizational Psychology, International Association of Applied Psychology, Jerusalem, Israel.

Drenth, P. J. D., & Koopman, P. L. (1984). A contingency approach to participative leadership: How good? In J. G. Hunt, D. Hosking, C. A. Schriesheim, & R. Stewart (Eds.), *Leaders and managers: International perspectives on managerial behavior and leadership.* New York: Pergamon.

Drory, A., & Ben-Porat, A. (1980). Leadership style and leniency bias in evaluation of employees' performance. *Psychological Reports, 46,* 735-739.

Drory, A., & Gluskinos, V. M. (1980). Machiavellianism and leadership. *Journal of Applied Psychology, 65,* 81-86.

Drought, N. E. (1967). The operations committee: An experience in group dynamics. *Personnel Psychology, 20,* 153-163.

Drucker, E. H., & Schwartz, S. (1973). *The prediction of AWOL, military skills, and leadership potential.* Alexandria, VA: Human Resources Research Organization.

Drucker, P. F. (1946). *Concept of the corporation.* New York: John Day.

Drucker, P. F. (1954). *The practice of management.* New York: Harper.

Du Vall, E. W. (1943). *Personality and social group work.* New York: Association Press.

Dubin, R. (1958). *The world of work.* Englewood Cliffs, NJ: Prentice-Hall.

Dubin, R. (1962a). Business behavior behaviorally viewed. In G. B. Strother (Ed.), *Social science approaches to business behavior.* Homewood, IL: Dorsey.

Dubin, R. (1962b). Stability of human organizations. In M. Haire (Ed.), *Modern organizational theory.* New York: Wiley.

Dubin, R. (1965). Supervision and productivity: Empirical findings and theoretical considerations. In R. Dubin, G. C. Homans, F. C. Mann, & D. C. Miller (Eds.), *Leadership and productivity.* San Francisco: Chandler.

Dubin, R. (1979). Metaphors of leadership: An overview. In J. G. Hunt & L. L. Larson (Eds.), *Crosscurrents in leadership.* Carbondale: Southern Illinois University Press.

Dubin, R., & Spray, S. L. (1964). Executive behavior and interaction. *Industrial Relations, 3,* 99-108.

Dubno, P. (1963). Decision time characteristics of leaders and group problem solving behavior. *Journal of Social Psychology, 59,* 259-282.

Dubno, P. (1965). Leadership, group effectiveness, and speed of decision. *Journal of Social Psychology, 65,* 351-360.

Dubno, P. (1968). Group congruency patterns and leadership characteristics. *Personnel Psychology, 21,* 335-344.

DuBrin, A. J. (1963). Trait and situational approaches in the development of a leadership inventory. *Journal of Industrial Psychology, 1,* 28-37.

DuBrin, A. J. (1964). Trait and interpersonal self descriptions of leaders and nonleaders in an industrial setting. *Journal of Industrial Psychology, 2,* 51-55.

Duchon, D., Green, S. G., & Tabor, T. D. (1986). Vertical dyad linkage: A longitudinal assessment of antecedents, measures, and consequences. *Journal of Applied Psychology, 71,* 56-60.

Duffy, P. J. (1973). *Lateral interaction orientation: An expanded view of leadership.* Doctoral dissertation, Southern Illinois University, Carbondale.

Dulany, D. (1975). *Converging operations.* Unpublished note.

Dulewicz, V., & Fletcher, C. (1982). The relationship between previous experience, intelligence and background characteristics of participants and their performance in an assessment centre. *Journal of Occupational Psychology, 55,* 197-207.

Duncan, P. K., & Bruwelheide, L. R. (1985-86). Feedback: Use and possible behavioral functions. *Journal of Organizational Behavior Management, 7*(3–4), 91–114.

Duncan, W. J. (1984). Perceived humor and social network patterns in a sample of task-oriented groups: A re-examination of prior research. *Human Relations, 37,* 895–907.

Dunkerley, M. D. (1940). A statistical study of leadership among college women. *Student Psychology and Psychiatry, 4,* 1–64.

Dunn, W. N., & Swierczek, F. W. (1976). Planned organizational change: Toward grounded theory. *Journal of Applied Behavioral Science, 13,* 135–157.

Dunnette, M. D. (1966). *Identification and enhancement of managerial effectiveness. II. Research problems and research results in the identification of managerial effectiveness.* Greensboro, NC: Richardson Foundation.

Dunnette, M. D. (1967). The motives of industrial managers. *Organizational Behavior and Human Performance, 2,* 176–182.

Dunnette, M. D. (1970). *Multiple assessment procedures in identifying and developing managerial talent* (ONR Tech. Rep. 4000). Minneapolis: University of Minnesota.

Dunnette, M. D. (1971). Multiple assessment procedures in identifying and developing managerial talent. In P. McReynolds (Ed.), *Advances in psychological assessment,* Vol. I. Palo Alto, CA: Science and Behavior Books.

Dunnette, M. D. (1986). Describing the role of the middle manager. *Is the Role of the Middle Manager Really Different?* Symposium, American Psychological Association, New York.

Dunnette, M. D., & Campbell, J. P. (1968). Laboratory education: Impact on people and organizations. *Industrial Relations, 8,* 1–27.

Dunnette, M. D., Campbell, J. P., & Argyris, C. (1968). *A symposium: Laboratory training.* Minneapolis: University of Minnesota, Industrial Relations Center.

Dunnette, M. D., Lawler, E. E., Weick, K. E., & Opsahl, R. L. (1967). The role of financial compensation in managerial motivation. *Organizational Behavior and Human Performance, 2,* 175–216.

Dunnington, R. A., Sirota, D., & Klein, S. M. (1963). *Research for organization theory and management action.* Paper, Industrial Relations Research Association, Boston.

Dunphy, D. C. (1963). The social structure of urban adolescent peer groups. *Sociometry, 26,* 230–246.

Dunteman, G. H. (1966). Self, interaction, and task-orientation scores and their relationship to promotability ratings. *Journal of Industrial Psychology, 4,* 20–26.

Dunteman, G., & Bass, B. M. (1963). Supervisory and engineering success associated with self, interaction, and task orientation scores. *Personnel Psychology, 16,* 13–22.

Dupuy, R. E., & Dupuy, T. N. (1959). *Brave men and great captains.* New York: Harper & Row.

Dupuy, R. E., & Dupuy, T. N. (1984). *Brave men and great captains.* Fairfax, VA: Hero.

Durand, D. E., & Nord, W. R. (1976). Perceived leader behavior as a function of personality characteristics of supervisors and subordinates. *Academy of Management Journal, 19,* 427–438.

Durand, D. E., & Shea, D. (1974). Entrepreneurial activity as a function of achievement motivation and reinforcement control. *Journal of Psychology, 88,* 57–63.

Durant, W. (1957). *The reformation.* New York: Simon & Schuster.

Durbrow. B. R. (1971). *Inter-firm executive mobility.* Doctoral dissertation, Ohio State University, Columbus.

Durham, L. E., & Gibb, J. R. (1960). *An annotated bibliography of research, 1947–1960.* Washington, DC: National Training Laboratories.

Durkheim, E. (1947). *The division of labor in society.* New York: Free Press.

Durojaiye, M. O. (1969). Patterns of friendship and leadership choices in a mixed ethnic junior school: A sociometric analysis. *British Journal of Educational Psychology, 39,* 88–89.

Dustin, D. S., & Davis, H. P. (1967). Authoritarianism and sanctioning behavior. *Journal of Personality and Social Psychology, 6,* 222–224.

Duxbury, M. L., Armstrong, G. D., Drew, D. J., & Henly, S. J. (1984). Head nurse leadership style with staff nurse burnout and job satisfaction in neonatal intensive care units. *Nursing Research, 33*(2), 97–104.

Dwivedi, R. S. (1983). Management by trust: A conceptual model. *Group & Organization Studies, 8,* 375–405.

Dwyer, D. C. (1984). The search for instructional leadership: Routines and subtleties in principal's role. *Educational Leadership, 41,* 32–37.

Dye, T. R., & Strickland, J. (1982). Women at the top: A note on institutional leadership. *Social Science Quarterly, 63,* 333–341.

Dyer, J. L., & Lambert, W. E. (1953). *Coordination of flying activities in bomb wings: Integration and performance.* Chapel Hill: University of North Carolina, Institute for Research in Social Science.

Dyer, J. L., Lambert, W. E., & Tracy, G. (1953). *Attitudes toward selected elements of organization and the performance of bomb squadrons.* Chapel Hill: University of North Carolina, Institute for Research in Social Science.

Dyer, W. G. (1972). *Modern theory and method in group training.* New York: Van Nostrand Reinhold.

Dyer, W. G., & Dyer, J. H. (1984). The M*A*S*H generation: Implications for future organizational values. *Organizational Dynamics, 13*(1), 66–79.

Dymond, R. F. (1949). A scale for the measurement of empathic ability. *Journal of Consulting Psychology, 13,* 127–133.

Dynes, R. R. (1969). *Organized behavior in disaster.* Columbus: Ohio State University, Disaster Research Center.

Dynes, R. R. (1970). *Organized behavior in disasters.* Lexington, MA: D. C. Heath.

Dyson, J. W., Fleitas, D. W., & Scioli, F. P. (1972). The interaction of leadership personality, and decisional environments. *Journal of Social Psychology, 86,* 29–33.

Dyson, J. W., Godwin, P. H., & Hazelwood, L. A. (1976). Group composition, leadership orientation, and decisional outcomes. *Small Group Behavior, 7,* 114–128.

Eaglin, R. G. (1970). An experimental study of the effect of positive, negative, and no verbal reinforcers on assigned leaders in eight-member decision making groups. *Dissertation Abstracts International, 31,* 3688–3689.

Eaglin, R. G. (1973). The effect of verbal reinforcement on leader behavior. *Journal of College Student Personnel, 14,* 71–76.

Eagly, A. H. (1970). Leadership style and role differentiation as determinants of group effectiveness. *Journal of Personality, 38,* 509–524.

Eagly, A. H. (1983). Gender and social influence: A social psychological analysis. *American Psychologist, 38,* 971–981.

Eagly, A. H., & Carli, L. L. (1981). Sex of researchers and sex-typed communications as determinants of sex differences in influenceability: A meta-analysis of social influence studies. *Psychological Bulletin, 90,* 1–20.

Eagly, A. H., & Crowley, M. (1986). Gender and helping behavior: A meta-analytic review of the social psychological literature. *Psychological Bulletin, 100,* 283–308.

Eagly, A. H., & Steffen, V. J. (1986). Gender and aggressive behavior: A meta-analytic review of the social psychological literature. *Psychological Bulletin, 100,* 309–330.

Earley, C. P. (1985). The role of praise and criticism across cultures: A study of the U.S. and England. *Proceedings, Academy of Management,* 206–209.

Earley, P. C. (1984). Social interaction: The frequency of use and valuation in the U.S., England, and Ghana. *Journal of Cross-Cultural Psychology, 15,* 477–485.

Earley, P. C. (1985). Influence of information, choice and task complexity upon goal acceptance, performance, and personal goals. *Journal of Applied Psychology, 70,* 481–491.

Earley, P. C. (1986a). An examination of the mechanisms underlying the relation of feedback to performance. *Proceedings, Academy of Management,* Chicago, 214–218.

Earley, P. C. (1986b). Supervisors and shop stewards as sources of contextual information in goal setting: A comparison of the United States with England. *Journal of Applied Psychology, 71,* 111–117.

Earley, P. C. (1987). Intercultural training for managers: A comparison of documentary and interpersonal methods. *Academy of Management Journal, 30,* 685–698.

Earley, P. C. (1988). *Contributions of intercultural research to the understanding of performance feedback.* Paper, Society for Industrial and Organizational Psychology, Dallas.

Eaton, J. W. (1952). Controlled acculturation: A survival technique of the Hutterites. *American Sociological Review, 17,* 331–340.

Eberhard, W. (1971). *Moral and social values of the Chinese: Collected essays.* Washington, DC: Chinese Materials and Research Aids Service Center.

Eberhardt, B. J., Yap, C. K., & Basuray, M. T. (1988). A psychometric evaluation of the multiple choice version of the Miner Sentence Completion Scale. *Educational and Psychological Measurement, 48,* 119–126.

Ebrahimi, B. (1985a). *The use of international managerial talent to overcome the potential talent shortage facing multinational corporations.* Paper, Southern Management Association, Orlando, FL.

Ebrahimi, B. (1985b). *The cultural dynamics of managerial motivation among potential managers from the Far East and the United States.* Paper, Academy of Management, San Diego, CA.

Ebrahimi, B. (1985c). Measuring the effects of cultural and other explanatory variables on motivation to manage of potential managers from five countries: A case of theory building and theory testing in cross-cultural research. *Dissertation Abstracts International, 46(2A),* 469–470.

Eckerman, W. C. (1964). The relationship of need achievement to production, job satisfaction, and psychological stress. *Dissertation Abstracts, 24,* 3446.

Eckholm, E. (1985, July 1). Hostage bond to captors is common. *New York Times,* A11.

Edel, E. C. (1966). A study in managerial motivation. *Personnel Administration, 29,* 31–38.

Edel, E. C. (1968). "Need for success" as a predictor of managerial performance. *Personnel Psychology, 21,* 231–240.

Eden, D. (1984). Self-fulfilling prophecy as a management tool: Harnessing pygmalion. *Academy of Management Review, 9,* 64–73.

Eden, D. (1988). Pygmalion, goal setting, and expectancy: Compatible ways to boost productivity. *Academy of Management Review, 13,* 639–652.

Eden, D., & Leviatan, U. (1975). Implicit leadership theory as a determinant of the factor structure underlying supervisory behavior scales. *Journal of Applied Psychology, 60,* 736–741.

Eden, D., & Ravid, G. (1982). Pygmalion vs. self-expectancy: Effects of instructor- and self-expectancy on trainee performance. *Organizational Behavior and Human Performance, 30,* 351–364.

Eden, D., & Shani, A. B. (1982). Pygmalion goes to boot camp: Expectancy, leadership, and trainee performance. *Journal of Applied Psychology, 67,* 194–199.

Edinger, L. J. (1964). Political science and political biography (II): Reflections in the study of leadership. *Journal of Politics, 26,* 648–676.

Edinger, L. J. (1967). *Political leadership in industrialized societies.* New York: Wiley.

Edwards, C., & Heery, E. (1985). The incorporation of workplace trade unionism? Some evidence from the mining industry. *Sociology, 19,* 345–363.

Edwards, J. E., & Rode, L. G. (1986). *A path analytic approach to the construct validation of selected leadership scales.* Paper, Academy of Management, Chicago.

Edwards, M. T. (1973). *Leader influence and task set.* Master's thesis, State University of New York, Buffalo.

Edwards, W. (1955). The theory of decision making. *Psychological Bulletin, 51,* 380–417.

Egbert, R. L., Meeland, R., Cline, V. B., Forgy, E. W., Spickter, M. W., & Brown, C. (1957, December). *Fighter 1: An analysis of combat fighters and non-fighters.* (HumRRO Tech. Rep. No. 44). Presidio of Monterey, CA: U.S. Army Leadership Human Research Unit.

Eichler, G. A. (1934). *Studies in student leadership.* Doctoral dissertation, Pennsylvania State College, State College, PA.

Eichler, G. A., & Merrill, R. R. (1933). Can social leadership be improved by instruction in its technique? *Journal of Educational Sociology, 7*, 233–236.

Eisenberger, R. (1972). Explanation of rewards that do not reduce tissue needs. *Psychological Bulletin, 77*, 319–339.

Eisenstadt, S. N. (1952). The process of absorption of new immigrants in Israel. *Human Relations, 5*, 223–246.

Eisenstadt, S. N. (1954). Studies in reference group behavior. 1. Reference norms and the social structure. *Human Relations, 7*, 191–216.

Eisenstadt, S. N. (1968). *Max Weber: On charisma and institution building—selected papers.* Chicago: University of Chicago Press.

Eisman, E. J. (1975). The effects of leader sex and self-disclosure on member self-disclosure in marathon encounter groups. *Dissertation Abstracts International, 36*, 1429.

Eitzen, R., & Yetman, N. (1972). Managerial change, longevity, and organizational effectiveness. *Administrative Science Quarterly, 17*, 110–116.

Ekvall, G., & Arvonen, J. (1984). *Leadership styles and organizational climate for creativity: Some findings in one company* (Report 1). Stockholm: Faradet.

Elden, Max. (1986). Sociotechnical systems ideas as public policy in Norway: Empowering participation through worker-managed change. *Special Issue: Sociotechnical Systems: Innovations in Designing High-Performance Systems, Journal of Applied Behavioral Science, 22*, 239–255.

Elgie, D. M., Hollander, E. P., & Brice, R. W. (1988). Appointed and elected leaders' responses to favorableness of feedback and level of task activity from followers. *Journal of Applied Social Psychology, 18*, 1361–1370.

Elgood, C. (1976). *Handbook of management games.* London: Gower Press.

Elkin, F., Halpern, G., & Cooper, A. (1962). Leadership in a student mob. *Canadian Journal of Psychology, 16*, 199–201.

Elkins, D. (1958). Some factors related to the choice-status of ninety eighth-grade children in a school society. *Genetic Psychology Monographs, 58*, 207–272.

Elliot, J. D. (1953). Increasing office productivity through job enlargement. *The human side of the office manager's job* (Office Management Series, No. 134). New York: American Management Association.

Elliott, O., & Penner, D. D. (1974). The impact of social structure and organizational change. In H. L. Fromkin & J. J. Sherwood (Eds.), *Intergrating the organization.* New York: Free Press.

Ellis, H. (1904). *A study of British genius.* London: Hurst & Blackett.

Ellis, R. A. (1956). Social status and social distance. *Sociology and Social Research, 40*, 240–246.

Ellis, R. J., & Adamson, R. S. (undated). *Antecedents of leadership emergence.* Unpublished manuscript.

Ellis, R. J., Adamson, R. S., Deszca, G., & Cawsey, T. F. (undated). *Self-monitoring and leadership emergence.* Unpublished manuscript.

Elms, A. C., & Janis, I. L. (1965). Counter-norm attitudes induced by consonant vs. dissonant conditions of role-playing. *Journal of Experimental Research in Personality, 1*, 50–60.

Elrick, M. (1977). The leader, she: Dynamics of a female-led self-analytic group. *Human Relations, 30*, 869–878.

ElSalmi, A. M., & Cummings, L. L. (1968). Managers' perceptions of needs and need satisfactions as a function of interactions among organizational variables. *Personnel Psychology, 21*, 465–477.

Elson, J. A. (1965). *Abstracts of personnel research reports* (USAF PRL Tech. Rep. No. 65-23). Brooks Field, TX: U.S. Air Force Personnel Research Center.

Emerson, R. M. (1964). Power-dependence relations: Two experiments. *Sociometry, 27*, 282–298.

Emerson, R. W. (1841/1891). *Essays: First series on history.* New York: T. Y. Crowell.

Emery, D. A. (1959). Managerial leadership through motivation by objectives. *Personnel Psychology, 12*, 65–79.

Emery, F. E., & Thorsrud, E. (1969). *The form and content in industrial democracy.* London: Tavistock.

Emery, F. E., & Trist, E. L. (1965). The causal texture of organizational environments. *Human Relations, 18*, 21–32.

Emmet, D. (1966). *Rules, roles, and relations.* New York: St. Martin's Press.

Engel, G. V. (1970). Professional autonomy and bureaucratic organization. *Administrative Science Quarterly, 15*, 12–21.

England, G. W. (1967a). Personal value systems of American managers. *Academy of Management Journal, 10*, 53–68.

England, G. W. (1967b). Organizational goals and expected behavior of American managers. *Academy of Management Journal, 10*, 107–117.

England, G. W. (1970). *Personal value systems analysis as an aid to understanding organizational behavior: A comparative study in Japan, Korea, and the United States.* Paper, Exchange Seminar on Comparative Organizations, Amsterdam.

England, G. W. (1972). *Personal value systems of Australian managers.* Minneapolis: University of Minnesota, Industrial Relations Center.

England, G. W. (1976). *The manager and his values: An international perspective.* Cambridge, MA: Ballinger.

England, G. W., Agarwal, N. C., & Dhingra, O. P. (1973). *Personal value systems of Indian managers.* Minneapolis: University of Minnesota Press.

England, G. W., Dhingra, O. P., & Agarwal, N. C. (1974). *The manager and the man: A cross-cultural study of personal values.* Kent, OH: Kent State University Press.

England, G. W., & Koike, R. (1970). Personal value systems of Japanese managers. *Journal of Cross-Cultural Psychology, 1*, 21–40.

England, G. W., & Lee, R. (1971). Organizational goals and expected behavior among American, Japanese, and Korean managers—a comparative study. *Academy of Management Journal, 14*, 425–438.

England, G. W., & Lee, R. (1974). The relationship between managerial values and managerial success in the United States, Japan, India, and Australia. *Journal of Applied Psychology, 59*, 411–419.

England, G. W., & Weber, M. L. (1972). *Managerial success: A study of value and demographic correlates* (ONR Tech. Rep.). Minneapolis: University of Minnesota, Center for the Study of Organizational Performance and Human Effectiveness.

Entwisle, D. R., & Walton, J. (1961). Observations on the span of control. *Administrative Science Quarterly, 5*, 522–533.

Eoyang, C. K. (1983). Symbolic transformation of belief systems. In L. Pondy, P. Frost, E. Morgan, & T. Dandridge (Eds.), *Organizational symbolism*. New York: JAI Press.

Epstein, C. F. (1970). Encountering the male establishment: Sex status limits on women's careers in the professions. *American Journal of Sociology, 75*, 965–982.

Epstein, G. F. (1969). Machiavelli and the devil's advocate. *Journal of Personality and Social Psychology, 11*, 38–41.

Epstein, S. (1956). An experimental study of some of the effects of variations in the clarity and extent of a supervisor's area of freedom upon his supervisory behavior. *Dissertation Abstracts, 16*, 2513.

Eran, M. (1966). Relationship between self-perceived personality traits and job attitudes in middle management. *Journal of Applied Psychology, 50*, 424–430.

Erez, M. (1979). *Correlates of leadership style: Field-dependence and social intelligence versus social orientation.* Unpublished manuscript.

Erez, M. (1980). Correlates of leadership style: Field-dependence and social intelligence versus social orientation. *Perceptual and Motor Skills, 50*, 231–238.

Erez, M. (1986). The congruence of goal-setting strategies with sociocultural values, and its effects on performance. *Journal of Management, 12*, 83–90.

Erez, M., & Arad, R. (1986). Participative goal-setting: Social, motivational, and cognitive factors. *Journal of Applied Psychology, 71*, 591–597.

Erez, M., Earley, P. C., & Hulin, C. L. (1985). The impact of participation on goal acceptance and performance: A two-step model. *Academy of Management Journal, 28*, 50–66.

Erez, M., & Kanfer, F. H. (1983). The role of goal acceptance in goal setting with task performance. *Academy of Management Review, 8*, 454–463.

Erez, M., & Rim, Y. (1982). The relationships between goals, influence, tactics, and personal and organizational variables. *Human Relations, 35*, 871–878.

Ergun, T., & Onaran, O. (1981). Managerial styles as a means of improving an organization: The Turkish Electricity Authority case. *Turkish Public Administration Annual, 8*, 45–67.

Erikson, E. (1964). *Insight and responsibility.* New York: W. W. Norton.

Erikson, E. (1968). *Identity, youth, and crisis.* New York: W. W. Norton.

Erikson, E. (1969). *Gandhi's truth.* New York: W. W. Norton.

Eskilson, A. (1975). Sex composition and leadership in small groups. *Dissertation Abstracts International, 35*, 5694.

Eskilson, A., & Wiley, M. G. (1976). Sex composition and leadership in small groups. *Sociometry, 39*, 183–194.

Essa, L. M. (1983). Expectations of the head nurse's qualifications, leadership behavior and role in Egyptian hospitals. *Dissertation Abstracts International, 44*(6B), 1780.

Esser, N. J., & Strother, G. B. (1962). Rule interpretation as an indicator of style of management. *Personnel Psychology, 15*, 375–386.

Estler, S. E. (1975). Women as leaders in public education. *Signs, 1*, 363–386.

Estrada, L. F. (undated). *Hispanic youth: Demographic realities and constraints.* Unpublished manuscript.

Etkin, W. (Ed.). (1964). *Social behavior and organization among vertebrates.* Chicago: University of Chicago Press.

Ettle, J. (1986). *The first-line supervisor and advanced manufacturing technology.* Ann Arbor, MI: Industrial Technology Institute.

Etzioni, A. (1959). Lower levels of leadership in industry. *Sociology and Social Research, 43*, 209–212.

Etzioni, A. (1961). *A comparative analysis of complex organizations.* New York: Free Press.

Etzioni, A. (1965). Dual leadership in complex organizations. *American Sociological Review, 30*, 688–698.

Etzioni, A. (1984). Moderating effect of social support on the stress-burnout relationship. *Journal of Applied Psychology, 69*, 615–622.

Evan, W. M., & Simmons, R. G. (1969). Organizational effects of inequitable rewards: Two experiments in status inconsistency. *Administrative Science Quarterly, 4*, 224–237.

Evan, W. M., & Zelditch, M. (1961). A laboratory experiment on bureaucratic authority. *American Sociological Review, 26*, 883–893.

Evans, G. C. (1960). Validity of ascendance measurements in group interaction. *Psychological Reports, 7*, 114.

Evans, M. G. (1968). *The effects of supervisory behavior upon worker perception of their path-goal relationships.* Doctoral dissertation, Yale University, New Haven, CT.

Evans, M. G. (1969). Conceptual and operational problems in the measurement of various aspects of job satisfaction. *Journal of Applied Psychology, 53*, 93–101.

Evans, M. G. (1970a). The effects of supervisory behavior on the path-goal relationship. *Organizational Behavior and Human Performance, 5*, 277–298.

Evans, M. G. (1970b). Leadership and motivation: A case concept. *Academy of Management Journal, 13*, 91–102.

Evans, M. G. (1972). Leadership behavior: Demographic factors and agreement between subordinate and self-descriptions. *Personnel Psychology, 25*, 649–653.

Evans, M. G. (1973). A leader's ability to differentiate: The subordinate's perception of the leader and subordinate's performance. *Personnel Psychology, 26*, 385–395.

Evans, M. G. (1974). Extensions of a path-goal theory of motivation. *Journal of Applied Psychology, 59*, 172–178.

Evans M. G., & Dermer, J. (1974). What does the least preferred coworker scale really measure? A cognitive interpretation. *Journal of Applied Psychology, 59*, 202–206.

Evenson, W. L. (1959). Leadership behavior of high school principals. *National Association of Secondary School Principals Bulletin, 43*, 96–101.

Exline, R. V. (1960). Interrelations among two dimensions of sociometric status, group congeniality and accuracy of social perception. *Sociometry, 23,* 85–101.

Exline, R. V., & Ziller, R. C. (1959). Status congruency and interpersonal conflict in decision-making groups. *Human Relations, 12,* 147–162.

Eysenck, H. J. (1985). *Personality and individual differences: A natural science approach.* New York: Plenum.

Ezekiel, R. S. (1968). The personal future and Peace Corps competence. *Journal of Personality and Social Psychology Monograph Supplement,* Part 2, 8, 1–26.

Ezell, H. F., Odewahn, C. A., & Sherman J. D. (1982). Women entering management: Differences in perceptions of factors influencing integration. *Group & Organization Studies,* 243–253.

Fagenson, E. (undated). *The mentor advantage: Career and job attributes considered.* Unpublished manuscript.

Fagenson, E. A. (1986). Women's work orientations: Something old, something new. *Group & Organization Studies, 11,* 75–100.

Fahey, W., & Harris, R. (1987). *Excellence in Command.* Conference on Military Leadership: Tradition and Future Trends. U.S. Naval Academy, Annapolis, MD.

Fairhurst, G. T., Green, S. G., & Snavely, B. K. (1984). Face support in controlling poor performance. *Human Communication Research, 11,* 272–295.

Falbo, T. (1977). Multidimensional scaling of power strategies. *Journal of Personality and Social Psychology, 35,* 535–547.

Fallon, B. J., & Hollander, E. P. (1976). *Sex-role stereotyping in leadership: A study of undergraduate discussion groups.* Paper, American Psychological Association, Washington, DC.

Fanelli, A. A. (1956). A typology of community leadership based on influence and interaction within the leader subsystem. *Social Forces, 34,* 332–338.

Farina, A., Allen, J., & Saul, G. (1966). The role of the stigmatized person in affecting social relationships. *Journal of Personality, 71,* 421–428.

Farley, R., & Hermalin, A. (1971). Family stability: A comparison of trends between blacks and whites. *American Sociological Review, 36,* 1–17.

Farmer, R. N., & Richman, B. M. (1964). A model for research in comparative management. *California Management Review, 1,* 55–68.

Farmer, R. N., & Richman, B. M. (1965). *Comparative management and economic progress.* Homewood, IL: Irwin.

Farris, G. F. (1971a). *Colleagues' roles and innovation in scientific teams* (Working Paper No. 552-71). Cambridge, MA: Alfred P. Sloan School of Management, M.I.T.

Farris, G. F. (1971b). *Executive decision making in organizations: Identifying the key men and managing the process* (Working Paper No. 551-71). Cambridge, MA: Alfred P. Sloan School of Management, M.I.T.

Farris, G. F. (1971c). Organizing your informal organization. *Innovation,* No. 25, 2–11.

Farris, G. F. (1972). The effect of individual roles on performance in innovative groups. *R&D Management,* No. 3.

Farris, G. F., & Lim, F. G. (1969). Effects of performance on leadership, cohesiveness, influence, satisfaction, and subsequent performance. *Journal of Applied Psychology, 53,* 490–497.

Farrow, D. L. (1976). *A path-analytic approach to the study of contingent leader behavior.* Doctoral dissertation, University of Rochester, Rochester, NY.

Farrow, D. L. (1984). *Impact of authoritarianism on organizational functioning.* Paper, International Conference on Authoritarianism and Dogmatism, Potsdam, NY.

Farrow, D. L., & Bass, B. M. (1977). *A phoenix emerges: The importance of manager and subordinate personality in contingency leadership analyses* (Tech. Rep. 77-1). Rochester, NY: Univeristy of Rochester.

Farrow, D. L., Bass, B. M., & Valenzi, E. R. (1977). *A manager's tendencies to be participative associated with his perceptions of the environment outside his organization.* Paper, Academy of Management, Orlando, FL.

Farrow, D. L., Valenzi, E. R., & Bass, B. M. (1979). *A regression approach to identifying ways to increase leadership effectiveness.* Paper, American Psychological Association, New York.

Farrow, D. L., Valenzi, E. R., & Bass, B. M. (1980). *A comparison of leadership and situational characteristics within profit and non-profit organizations.* Paper, Academy of Management, Detroit.

Farrow, D. L., Valenzi, E. R., & Bass, B. M. (1981). *Managerial political behavior, executive success and effectiveness.* Paper, Academy of Management, San Diego, CA.

Fast, R. G. (1964). *Leader behavior of principals as it relates to teacher satisfaction.* Master's thesis, University of Alberta, Edmonton.

Fathi, A. (1965). Leadership and resistance to change: A case from an under-developed area. *Rural Sociology, 30,* 204–212.

Faucheaux, C. (1984). Leadership, power and influence within social systems. *Symposium on the Functioning of Executive Power.* Case Western University, Cleveland, OH.

Faucheux, C., Amado, G., & Laurent, A. (1982). Organizational development and change. *Annual Review of Psychology, 33,* 343–370.

Faucheux, C., & Rojot, J. (1979). Social psychology and industrial relations: A cross-cultural perspective. In G. M. Stephenson & C. J. Brotherton (Eds.), *Industrial relations: A social psychological approach.* New York: Wiley.

Faulkner, R. O. (1962). *Concise dictionary of Middle Egyptian.* London: Oxford.

Faunce, D., & Beegle, J. A. (1948). Cleavages in a relatively homogeneous group of rural youth: An experiment in the use of sociometry in attaining and measuring integration. *Sociometry, 11,* 207–216.

Fauquier, W., & Gilchrist, J. (1942). Some aspects of leadership in an institution. *Child Development, 13,* 55–64.

Fay, P. J., & Middleton, W. C. (1943). Judgment of leadership from the transmitted voice. *Journal of Social Psychology, 17,* 99–102.

Fayerweather, J. (1959). *The executive overseas.* Syracuse, NY: Syracuse University Press.

Fayol, H. (1916). *Administration industrielle et generale.* Paris: Dunod.

Fearing, F. (1927). Psychological studies of historical personalities. *Psychological Bulletin, 24,* 521–539.

Feather, N. T., & Simon, J. G. (1975). Reactions to male and female success and failure in sex-linked occupations: Impressions of personality, causal attributions, and perceived likelihood of different consequences. *Journal of Personality and Social Psychology, 31,* 20–31.

Fedor, D. B., Buckley, M. R., & Eder, R. W. (undated). *Subordinate perceptions of supervisor feedback intentions.* Unpublished manuscript.

Feffer, M., & Phillips, L. (1953). Social attainment and performance under stress. *Journal of Personality, 22,* 284–297.

Feierabend, R. L., & Janis, I. L. (1954). An experimental comparison of two ways of organizing positive and negative arguments in persuasive communications. *American Psychologist, 9,* 362–363.

Feil, M. H. (1950). *A study of leadership and scholastic achievement in their relation to prediction factors.* Doctoral dissertation, Ohio State University, Columbus.

Feild, H. S., & Caldwell, B. E. (1979). Sex of supervisor, sex of subordinate, and subordinate job satisfaction. *Psychology of Women Quarterly, 3,* 391–399.

Feinberg, M. R. (1953). Relation of background experience to social acceptance. *Journal of Abnormal and Social Psychology, 48,* 206–214.

Feitler, F. C. (1971). *A study of relationships between principal leadership styles and organizational characteristics of elementary schools.* Doctoral dissertation, Syracuse University, Syracuse, NY.

Feitler, F. C., & Blumberg, A. (1971). Changing the organizational character of a school. *Elementary School Journal, 71,* 206–215.

Feld, S., & Lewis, J. (1967). *The assessment of achievement anxieties in children.* Mental Health Study Center, National Institute of Mental Health, Washington, DC.

Feldman, D. C. (1985). The new careerism: Origins, tenets and consequences. *The Industrial-Organizational Psychologist, 23,* 39–44.

Feldman, D. C. (1986). Why no good deed goes unpublished. *The Industrial-Organizational Psychologist, 24,* 39–41.

Feldman, H. (1937). *Problems in labor relations.* New York: Macmillan.

Feldman, J. (1974). Race, economic class and the intention to work. *Journal of Applied Psychology, 59,* 179–186.

Feldman, R. A. (1967). Three types of group integration: Their relationship to power, leadership, and conformity behavior. *Dissertation Abstracts, 27,* 2202–2203.

Feldman, S. P. (1986). Culture, charisma, and the CEO: An essay on the meaning of high office. *Human Relations, 39,* 211–228.

Felipe, N. (1966). Interpersonal distance and small group interaction. *Cornell Journal of Social Relations, 1,* 59–64.

Fellner, D. J., & Sulzer-Azaroff, B. (1985). Occupational safety: Assessing the impact of adding assigned or participative goal-setting. *Journal of Organizational Behavior Management,* 3–24.

Fenchel, G. H., Monderer, J. H., & Hartley, E. L. (1951). Subjective status and the equilibrium hypothesis. *Journal of Abnormal and Social Psychology, 46,* 476–479.

Fenelon, J. R. (1966). *The influence of race on leadership prediction.* Master's thesis, University of Texas, Austin.

Fenelon, J. R., & Megargee, E. I. (1971). The influence of race on the manifestation of leadership. *Experimental Publications System, American Psychological Association, 10,* No. 380–12.

Fenichel, O. (1945). *The psychoanalytic theory of neurosis.* New York: W. W. Norton.

Fensterheim, H., & Tresselt, M. E. (1953). The influence of value systems on the perception of people. *Journal of Abnormal and Social Psychology, 48,* 93–98.

Ferber, M., Huber, J., & Spitze, G. (1979). Preference for men as bosses and professionals. *Social Forces, 58,* 466–476.

Ferguson, L. W. (1950). The L.O.M.A. merit rating scales. *Personnel Psychology, 3,* 193–216.

Fermi, L. (1966). *Mussolini.* Chicago: University of Chicago Press.

Fernandez, P. (1981). *Racism and sexism in corporate life: Changing values in American business.* Lexington, MA: D. C. Heath.

Fernberg, O. F. (1979). Regression in organizational leadership. *Psychiatry, 42*(1), 24–39.

Ferris, A. E. (1965). *Organizational relationships in two selected secondary schools: A comparative study.* Doctoral dissertation, Columbia University, New York.

Ferris, G. R. (1985). Role of leadership in the employee withdrawal process: A constructive replication. *Journal of Applied Psychology, 70,* 777–781.

Ferris, G. R., & Rowland, K. M. (1981). Leadership, job perceptions, and influence: A conceptual integration. *Human Relations, 34,* 1069–1077.

Festinger, L. (1949). The analysis of sociograms using matrix algebra. *Human Relations, 2,* 153–158.

Festinger, L. (1950). Informal social communication. *Psychological Review, 57,* 271–282.

Festinger, L. (1954). A theory of social comparison processes. *Human Relations, 7,* 117–140.

Festinger, L., Cartwright, D., Barber, K., Fleisch, J., Gottsdinker, J., Keyson, A., & Leavitt, G. (1947). A study of a rumor: Its origin and spread. *Human Relations, 1,* 464–486.

Festinger, L., Gerard, H. B., Hymovitch, B., Kelley, H. H., & Raven, B. (1952). The influence process in the presence of extreme deviates. *Human Relations, 5,* 327–346.

Festinger, L., & Hutte, H. A. (1954). An experimental investigation of the effect of unstable interpersonal relations in a group. *Journal of Abnormal and Social Psychology, 49,* 513–522.

Festinger, L., & Kelley, H. H. (1951). *Changing attitudes through social contact.* Ann Arbor, MI: Research Center for Group Dynamics.

Festinger, L., Pepitone, A., & Newcomb, T. (1952). Some consequences of de-individuation in a group. *Journal of Abnormal and Social Psychology, 47,* 382–389.

Festinger, L., Schachter, S., & Back, K. (1950). *Social processes in informal groups: A study of a housing project.* New York: Harper.

Festinger, L., & Thibaut, J. (1951). Interpersonal communication in small groups. *Journal of Abnormal and Social Psychology, 46,* 92–99.

Festinger, L., Torrey, J., & Willerman, B. (1954). Self-evaluation as a function of attraction to the group. *Human Relations, 7,* 161–174.

Fichter, J. H. (1966). Career preparation and expectations of Negro college seniors. *Journal of Negro Education*, 35, 322–335.

Fiechtner, B., & Krayer, K. J. (1986). Variations in dogmatism and leader-supplied information: Determinants of perceived behavior in task-oriented groups. *Group & Organization Studies*, 11, 403–418.

Fiedler, F. E. (1953a). Quantitative studies in the role of therapists' feelings toward their patients. In O. H. Mowrer (Ed.), *Psychotherapy: Theory and research*. New York: Ronald Press.

Fiedler, F. E. (1953b). The psychological distance dimension in interpersonal relations. *Journal of Personality*, 22, 142–150.

Fiedler, F. E. (1953c). *Assumed similarity measures as predictors of team effectiveness in surveying* (Tech. Rep. No. 6). Urbana: University of Illinois, Bureau of Research Service.

Fiedler, F. E. (1954a). Interpersonal perception and sociometric structure in prediction of small team effectiveness. *American Psychologist*, 8, 365.

Fiedler, F. E. (1954b). Assumed similarity measures and predictors of team effectiveness. *Journal of Abnormal and Social Psychology*, 49, 381–388.

Fiedler, F. E. (1955). The influence of leader-keyman relations on combat crew effectiveness. *Journal of Abnormal and Social Psychology*, 51, 227–235.

Fiedler, F. E. (1956). *Social perception and group effectiveness* (Annual Technical Report). Urbana: University of Illinois.

Fiedler, F. E. (1957). A note on leadership theory: The effect of social barriers between leaders and followers. *Sociometry*, 20, 87–94.

Fiedler, F. E. (1958). *Leader attitudes and group effectiveness*. Urbana: University of Illinois Press.

Fiedler, F. E. (1961). Leadership and leadership effectiveness traits: A reconceptualization of the leadership trait problem. In L. Petrullo & B. M. Bass (Eds.), *Leadership and interpersonal behavior*. New York: Holt, Rinehart & Winston.

Fiedler, F. E. (1962). Leader attitudes, group climate, and group creativity. *Journal of Abnormal and Social Psychology*, 65, 308–318.

Fiedler, F. E. (1963). *A contingency model for the prediction of leadership effectiveness* (Tech. Rep. No. 10). Urbana: University of Illinois, Group Effectiveness Research Lab.

Fiedler, F. E. (1964). A contingency model of leadership effectiveness. In L. Berkowitz (Ed.), *Advances in experimental social psychology*, Vol. 1. New York: Academic Press.

Fiedler, F. E. (1965). Engineering the job to fit the manager. *Harvard Business Review*, 43(5), 115–122.

Fiedler, F. E. (1966). The effect of leadership and cultural heterogeneity on group performance: A test of the contingency model. *Journal of Experimental Social Psychology*, 2, 237–264.

Fiedler, F. E. (1967a). *A theory of leadership effectiveness*. New York: McGraw-Hill.

Fiedler, F. E. (1967b). The effect of inter-group competition on group member adjustment. *Personnel Psychology*, 20, 33–44.

Fiedler, F. E. (1968). The effect of culture training on leadership, organizational performance, and adjustment. *Naval Research Review*, 7–13.

Fiedler, F. E. (1970a). Leadership experience and leader performance: Another hypothesis shot to hell. *Organizational Behavior and Human Performance*, 5, 1–14.

Fiedler, F. E. (1970b). *Personality, motivational systems, and behavior of high and low LPC persons* (Tech. Rep. No. 70–12). Seattle: University of Washington, Department of Psychology.

Fiedler, F. E. (1971a). *Leadership*. New York: General Learning Press.

Fiedler, F. E. (1971b). Note on the methodology of the Graen, Orris, and Alveres studies testing the contingency model. *Journal of Applied Psychology*, 55, 202–204.

Fiedler, F. E. (1971c). Validation and extension of the contingency model of leadership effectiveness: A review of empirical findings. *Psychological Bulletin*, 76, 128–148.

Fiedler, F. E. (1971d). *Personality and situational determinants of leader behavior* (Tech. Rep.). Seattle: University of Washington, Department of Psychology.

Fiedler, F. E. (1972a). Personality, motivational systems, and behavior of high- and low-LPC persons. *Human Relations*, 25, 391–412.

Fiedler, F. E. (1972b). Predicting the effects of leadership training and experience from the contingency model. *Journal of Applied Psychology*, 56, 114–119.

Fiedler, F. E. (1972c). The effects of leadership training and experience: A contingency model interpretation. *Administrative Science Quarterly*, 17, 453–470.

Fiedler, F. E. (1973). The contingency model—a reply to Ashour. *Organizational Behavior and Human Performance*, 9, 356–368.

Fiedler, F. E. (1974). The contingency model—new directions for leadership utilization. *Journal of Contemporary Business*, 3, 65–79.

Fiedler, F. E. (1977a). What triggers the person-situation interaction in leadership. In D. Magnusson & N. S. Endler (Eds.), *Personality at the crossroads: Current issues in interactional psychology*. Hillsdale, NJ: Erlbaum.

Fiedler, F. E. (1977b). A rejoinder to Schriesheim and Kerr's premature obituary of the contingency model. In J. G. Hunt & L. L. Larson (Eds.), *Leadership: The cutting edge*. Carbondale: Southern Illinois University Press.

Fiedler, F. E. (1977c). Situational control and dynamic theory of leadership. In B. King, F. E. Fiedler, & S. Streufert (Eds.), *Managerial control and organizational democracy*. Washington, DC: W. H. Winston & Sons.

Fiedler, F. E. (1978). The contingency model and the dynamics of the leadership process. In L. Berkowitz (Ed.), *Advances in experimental social psychology*, Vol. 11. New York: Academic Press.

Fiedler, F. E. (1982). *Are leaders an intelligent form of life? The role of cognitive processes in leadership performance* (Organizational Research Tech. Rep. 82–1). Seattle: University of Washington.

Fiedler, F. E. (1984). *The contribution of cognitive resources and leader behavior to organizational performance* (Organizational Research Tech. Rep. 84–4). Seattle: University of Washington.

Fiedler, F. E. (1986). The contribution of cognitive resources and leader behavior to organizational performance. *Journal of Applied Social Psychology*, 16(6), 532–548.

Fiedler, F. E. (1987, July). Structured management training in underground mining—five years later. *Technology Transfer Seminar*, Bureau of Mines Information Circular No. 9145, 149–153.

Fiedler, F. E., Bell, C. H., Chemers, M. M., & Patrick, D. (1984). Increasing mine productivity and safety through management training and organization development: A comparative study. *Basic & Applied Social Psychology, 5*, 1–18.

Fiedler, F. E., Bons, P. M., & Hastings, L. (1975). The utilization of leadership resources. In W. T. Singleton & P. Spurgeon (Eds.), *Measurement of human resources.* London: Taylor & Francis.

Fiedler, F. E., & Chemers, M. M. (1974). *Leadership and effective management.* Glenview, IL: Scott, Foresman.

Fiedler, F. E., Chemers, M. M., & Mahar, L. (1976). *Improving leadership effectiveness: The LEADER MATCH concept.* New York: Wiley.

Fiedler, F. E., Fiedler, J., & Camp, S. (1971). Who speaks for the community? *Journal of Applied Social Psychology, 1*, 324–333.

Fiedler, F. E. & Garcia, J. E. (1987). *New approaches to effective leadership: Cognitive resources and organizational performance.* New York: Wiley.

Fiedler, F. E., Hartmann, W., & Rudin, S. A. (1953). *The relationship of interpersonal perception to effectiveness in basketball teams* (Tech. Rep. No. 3). Urbana: University of Illinois, Bureau of Research Services.

Fiedler, F. E., & Hoffman, E. L. (1962). Age, sex, and religious background as determinants of interpersonal perception among Dutch children: A cross-cultural validation. *Acta Psychologica, 20*, 185–195.

Fiedler, F. E., & House, R. J. (1988). Leadership: A report of progress. In C. Cooper (Ed.), *International review of industrial and organizational psychology.* Greenwich, CT: JAI Press.

Fiedler, F. E., & Leister, A. F. (1977). Leader intelligence and task performance: A test of a multiple screen model. *Organizational Behavior and Human Performance, 20*, 1–14.

Fiedler, F. E., & Mahar, L. (1979a). A field experiment validating contingency model leadership training. *Journal of Applied Psychology, 64*, 247–254.

Fiedler, F. E., & Mahar, L. (1979b). The effectiveness of contingency model training: Validation of LEADER MATCH. *Personnel Psychology, 32*, 45–62.

Fiedler, F. E., Mahar, L., & Schmidt, D. (1976). *Four validation studies of contingency model training* (Organizational Research Tech. Rep. No. 75–70). Seattle: University of Washington.

Fiedler, F. E., & McGuire, M. A. (1987). Paper, Third Army Leadership Conference, Kansas City, MO.

Fiedler, F. E., & Meuwese, W. A. T. (1963). Leaders' contribution to task performance in cohesive and uncohesive groups. *Journal of Abnormal and Social Psychology, 67*, 83–87.

Fiedler, F. E., Meuwese, W. A. T., & Oonk, S. (1961). An exploratory study of group creativity in laboratory tasks. *Acta Psychologica, 18*, 100–119.

Fiedler, F. E., & Nealey, S. M. (1966). *Second-level management.* Washington, DC: U.S. Civil Service Commission.

Fiedler, F. E., O'Brien, G. E., & Ilgen, D. R. (1969). The effect of leadership style upon the performance and adjustment of volunteer teams operating in successful foreign environment. *Human Relations, 22*, 503–514.

Fiedler, F. E., Potter, E. H., & McGuire, M. A. (1988). *Stress and effective leadership decisions.* Paper, International Congress of Psychology, Sydney, Australia.

Fiedler, F. E., Potter, E. H., III, Zais, M. M., & Knowlton, W. A., Jr. (1979). Organizational stress and the use and misuse of managerial intelligence and experience. *Journal of Applied Psychology, 64*, 635–647.

Fiedler, F. E., Warrington, W. G., & Blaisdell, F. J. (1952). Unconscious attitudes as correlates of sociometric choice in social groups. *Journal of Abnormal and Social Psychology, 47*, 790–796.

Fiedler, F. E., Wheeler, W. A., Chemers, M. M., & Patrick, D. (1987). Structured management training in underground mining: A five year follow-up. *Training & Development Journal, 41*(9), 40–43.

Field, R. H. G. (1979). A critique of the Vroom-Yetton contingency model of leadership behavior. *Academy of Management Review, 4*, 249–257.

Field, R. H. G. (1982). A test of the Vroom-Yetton normative model of leadership. *Journal of Applied Psychology, 67*, 523–532.

Field, R. H. G. (1989a). The self-fulfilling prophecy leader: Achieving the metharme effect. *Journal of Management Studies, 26*, 151–175.

Field, R. H. G. (1989b, May-June). Leaders as stars, pulsars, quasars, and black holes. *Business Horizons*, 1–5.

Field, R. H. G., & Van Seters, D. A. (1988). Management by expectations: The power of positive prophecy. *Journal of General Management, 14*(2), 19–33.

Field, S. (1984). Leadership style and job satisfaction among human service workers. *Dissertation Abstracts International, 45*(7A), 2255.

File, Q. W. (1945). The measurement of supervisory quality in industry. *Journal of Applied Psychology, 29*, 323–337.

File, Q. W., & Remmers, H. H. (1971). *How supervise?* New York: Psychological Corporation.

Filella, J. F. (undated). *Upward influence tactics of Spanish bank managers.* Unpublished manuscript.

Filella, J. F. (1971). *Exercise life goals: Guess work or interpersonal perception?* (Tech. Rep. No. 40). Rochester, NY: University of Rochester, Management Research Center.

Filley, A. C. (1975). *Interpersonal conflict resolution.* Glenview, IL: Scott, Foresman.

Filley, A. C., & Grimes, A. J. (1967). *The bases of power in decision processes.* Paper, Academy of Management, New York.

Filley, A. C., & House, R. J. (1969). *Managerial process and organizational behavior.* Glenview, IL: Scott, Foresman.

Filley, A. C., House, R. J., & Kerr, S. (1976). *Managerial process and organizational behavior* (2nd ed.). Glenview, IL: Scott, Foresman.

Filley, A. C., & Jesse, F. C. (1965). Training leadership style: A survey of research. *Personnel Administration, 28*, 14–21.

Fiman, B. G. (1973). An investigation of the relationships among supervisory attitudes, behaviors, and outputs: An examination of McGregor's theory Y. *Personnel Psychology, 26*, 95–105.

Finch, F. H., & Carroll, H. A. (1932). Gifted children as high school leaders. *Pediatrics Seminar, 41*, 476–481.

Fine, B. D. (1970). Comparison of work groups with stable and unstable membership. *Experimental Publications System, American Psychological Association, 9*, No. 333-1.

Fine, S. A. (1963). *A functional approach to a broad scale map of work behavior.* Paper, American Psychological Association, San Francisco.

Fine, S. E. (1977). *Job analysis for heavy equipment operators.* Washington, DC: International Union of Operating Engineers.

Finkle, R. B., & Jones, W. S. (1970). *Assessing corporate talent: A key to managerial manpower planning.* New York: Wiley-Interscience.

Finley, R. M., Jr. (1970). *Evaluation of behavior predictions from projective tests given in a management assessment center.* Paper, American Psychological Association, Miami Beach, FL.

Finn, D. (1969). *The corporate oligarch.* New York: Simon & Schuster.

Fiorelli, J. S. (1988). Power in work groups: Team members' perspectives. *Human Relations, 41*, 1–12.

Firestone, I. J, Lichtman, C. M., & Colamosca, J. V. (1975). Leader effectiveness and leadership conferral as determinants of helping in a medical emergency. *Journal of Personality and Social Psychology, 31*, 243–248.

Firestone, W. A., & Wilson, B. L. (1985). Using bureaucratic and cultural linkages to improve instruction: The principal's contribution. *Educational Administrative Quarterly, 21*(2), 7–30.

Fischer, P. H. (1953). An analysis of the primary group. *Sociometry, 16*, 272–276.

Fischman, J. (1987). Type A on trial. *Psychology Today, 21*(2), 42–50.

Fishbein, M., Landy, E., & Hatch, G. (1969a). Some determinants of an individual's esteem for the least preferred co-worker: An attitudinal analysis. *Human Relations, 22*, 173–188.

Fishbein, M., Landy, E., & Hatch, G. (1969b). A consideration of two assumptions underlying Fiedler's contingency model for prediction of leadership effectiveness. *American Journal of Psychology, 82*, 457–473.

Fisher, B. M., & Edwards, J. E. (1988). Consideration and initiating structure and their relationships with leader effectiveness: A meta-analysis. *Best Papers Proceedings, Academy of Management*, Anaheim, CA, 201–205.

Fisher, C. D. (1979). Transmission of positive and negative feedback to subordinates: A laboratory investigation. *Journal of Applied Psychology, 64*, 533–540.

Fisher, S., & Rubinstein, I. (1956). The effects of moderate sleep deprivation on social influence in the autocratic situation. *American Psychologist, 11*, 411.

Fisher, S. C. (1982). *Institutions, authority and the structure of doctor/patient communication.* Paper, Society for the Study of Social Problems.

Fishman, L. (1952). Limitations of the business executive as government administrator. *Journal of Business, 25*, 89–94.

Fisk, G. (1964). *The frontiers of management psychology.* New York: Harper.

Fiske, D. W. (1979). Two worlds of psychological phenomena. *American Psychologist, 34*, 733–739.

Fiske, D. W., & Cox, J. A., Jr. (1960). The consistency of ratings by peers. *Journal of Applied Psychology, 44*, 11–17.

Fiske, D. W., & Maddi, S. R. (1961). *Functions of varied experience.* Homewood, IL: Dorsey.

Fitzsimmons, S. J., & Marcuse, F. L. (1961). Adjustment in leaders and non-leaders as measured by the sentence completion projective technique. *Journal of Clinical Psychology, 17*, 380–381.

Flament, C. (1956). Changements de roles et adaptation la tache dans des groupes de travail utilisant divers riseaux de communications. *Années Psychologia, 56*, 411–431.

Flanagan, J. C. (1949). Critical requirements: A new approach to employee evaluation. *Personnel Psychology, 2*, 419–425.

Flanagan, J. C. (1951). Defining the requirements of the executive's job. *Personnel, 28*(1), 28–35.

Flanagan, J. C. (1954). The critical incident technique. *Psychology Bulletin, 51*, 327–358.

Flanagan, J. C. (1961). Leadership skills: Their identification, development, and evaluation. In L. Petrullo & B. M. Bass (Eds.), *Leadership and interpersonal behavior.* New York: Holt, Rinehart & Winston.

Flanagan, J. C., & Krug, R. E. (1964). Testing in management selection: State of the art. *Personnel Administration, 27*(2), 3–5.

Flanagan, J. C., Levy, S., et al. (1952). *Development of an objective form of the leaders reaction test.* Pittsburgh, PA: American Institute for Research.

Flaugher, R. L., Campbell, J. T., & Pike, L. W. (1969). Ethnic group membership as a moderator of supervisor's ratings. *ETS Bulletin PR-69-5.* Princeton, NJ: Educational Testing Service.

Fleishman, E. A. (1951). *Leadership climate and supervisory behavior*, Personnel Research Board, Columbus: Ohio State University.

Fleishman, E. A. (1953a). The measurement of leadership attitudes in industry. *Journal of Applied Psychology. 37*, 153–158.

Fleishman, E. A. (1953b). Leadership climate, human relations training, and supervisory behavior. *Personnel Psychology, 6*, 205–222.

Fleishman, E. A. (1953c). The description of supervisory behavior. *Journal of Applied Psychology, 37*, 1–6.

Fleishman, E. A. (1956). Differences between military and industrial organizations. In R. M. Stogdill & C. L. Shartle (Eds.), *Patterns of administrative performance.* Columbus: Ohio State University, Bureau of Business Research.

Fleishman, E. A. (1957a). A leader behavior description for industry. In R. M. Stogdill & A. E. Coons (Eds.), *Leader behavior: Its description and measurement.* Columbus: Ohio State University, Bureau of Business Research.

Fleishman, E. A. (1957b). The leadership opinion questionnaire. In R. M. Stogdill & A. E. Coons (Eds.), *Leader behavior: Its description and measurement.* Columbus: Ohio State University, Bureau of Research.

Fleishman, E. A. (1960). *Leadership opinion questionnaire.* Chicago: Science Research Associates.

Fleishman, E. A. (1972). *Examiner's manual for the supervisory behavior description questionnaire.* Washington, DC: Management Research Institute.

Fleishman, E. A. (1973). Twenty years of consideration and structure. In E. A. Fleishman & J. G. Hunt (Eds.), *Current developments in the study of leadership.* Carbondale: Southern Illinois University Press.

Fleishman, E. A. (1989a). *Examiner's manual for the Leadership Opinion Questionnaire (LOQ) (Revised).* Chicago: Science Research Associates.

Fleishman, E. A. (1989b). *Examiner's manual for the Supervisory Behavior Description (SBD) Questionnaire (Revised).* Chicago: Science Research Associates.

Fleishman, E. A., & Harris, E. F. (1962). Patterns of leadership behavior related to employee grievances and turnover. *Personnel Psychology, 15,* 43–56.

Fleishman, E. A., Harris, E. F., & Burtt, H. E. (1955). *Leadership and supervision in industry.* Columbus: Ohio State University, Bureau of Educational Research.

Fleishman, E. A., & Peters, D. R. (1962). Interpersonal values, leadership attitudes, and managerial "success." *Personnel Psychology, 15,* 127–143.

Fleishman, E. A., & Salter, J. A. (1961). Humanizing relationships in a small business. *Advanced Management, 26,* 18–20.

Fleishman, E. A., & Salter, J. A. (1963). Relation between the leader's behavior and his empathy toward subordinates. *Journal of Industrial Psychology, 1,* 79–84.

Fleishman, E. A., & Simmons, J. (1970). Relationship between leadership patterns and effectiveness ratings among Israeli foremen. *Personnel Psychology, 23,* 169–172.

Flemming, E. G. (1935). A factor analysis of the personality of high school teachers. *Journal of Applied Psychology, 19,* 596–605.

Fletcher, C., & Williams, R. (1976). The influence of performance feedback in appraisal interviews. *Journal of Occupational Psychology, 49,* 75–83.

Flint, A. W., Bass, B. M., & Pryer, M. W. (1957a). *Esteem and successful leadership* (Tech. Rep. No. 11). Baton Rouge: Louisiana State University.

Flint, A. W., Bass, B. M., & Pryer, M. W. (1957b). *Esteem, status, motivation, and attraction to the group* (Tech. Rep. No. 9). Baton Rouge: Louisiana State University.

Flocco, E. C. (1969). An examination of the leader behavior of school business administrators. *Dissertation Abstracts International, 30,* 84–85.

Flowers, M. L. (1976). Laboratory study of some implications of Janis' groupthink hypothesis. *Dissertation Abstracts International, 36,* 4197.

Flyer, E. S., Barron, E., & Bigbee, L. (1953). Discrepancies between self-descriptions and group ratings as measures of lack of insight. *USAF Human Resources Research Center Research Bulletin,* No. 53–55.

Foa, U. G. (1956). A test of the foreman-worker relationship. *Personnel Psychology, 9,* 469–486.

Foa, U. G. (1957). Relation of worker's expectation to satisfaction with supervisor. *Personnel Psychology, 10,* 161–168.

Foa, U. G. (1960). Some correlates of the empathy of the workers with the foreman. *Journal of Applied Psychology, 44,* 6–10.

Foa, U. G., Mitchell, T. R., & Fiedler, F. E. (1971). Differential matching. *Behavioral Science, 16,* 130–142.

Fodor, E. M. (1973a). Group stress, ingratiation, and the use of power. *Journal of Social Psychology, 91,* 345–346.

Fodor, E. M. (1973b). Disparagement by a subordinate, ingratiation, and the use of power. *Journal of Psychology, 84,* 181–186.

Fodor, E. M. (1974). Disparagement by a subordinate as an influence on the use of power. *Journal of Applied Psychology, 59,* 652–655.

Fodor, E. M. (1976). Group stress, authoritarian style of control, and use of power. *Journal of Applied Psychology, 61,* 313–318.

Fodor, E. M. (1978). Simulated work climate as an influence on choice of leadership style. *Personality and Social Psychology Bulletin, 4,* 111–114.

Fodor, E. M. (1984). The power motive and reactivity to power stresses. *Journal of Personality and Social Psychology, 47,* 853–859.

Fodor, E. (1987). *Motive pattern as an influence on leadership in small groups.* Paper, American Psychological Association. New York.

Fodor, E. M., & Farrow, D. L. (1979). The power motive as an influence on the use of power in an industrial simulation. *Journal of Personality and Social Psychology, 37,* 2091–2097.

Fodor, E. M., & Smith, T. (1982). The power motive as an influence on group decision making. *Journal of Personality and Social Psychology, 42,* 178–185.

Fogarty, M. P. (1956). *Personality and group relations in industry.* New York: Longmans, Green.

Follert, V. (1983). Supervisors' power: An exchange model of leadership. *Psychological Reports, 52,* 740.

Follett, M. P. (1918). *The new state.* Gloucester, MA: Peter Smith.

Foote, A. E. (1970). *Managerial style, hierarchical control, and decision making in public television stations.* Doctoral dissertation, Ohio State University, Columbus.

Forbes, J. B. (1985). The relationship between management styles and functional specialization. *Group & Organization Studies, 10,* 95–111.

Ford, B. L., & McCaffrey, A. (1966). An exploratory investigation of "power" among nursery-school children by the method of resource process analysis. *Cornell Journal of Social Relations, 1,* 33–43.

Ford, J. B. (1980). The effects of covert power on the inhibition of structural change. *Dissertation Abstracts International, 41*(5A), 2316.

Ford, J. D. (1981). Departmental context and formal structure as constraints on leader behavior. *Academy of Management Journal, 24,* 274–288.

Ford, R. C. (1983). Delegation without fear. *Supervisory Management, 28*(7), 2–8.

Forehand, G. A., & Gilmer, B. (1964). Environmental variation in studies of organizational behavior. *Psychological Bulletin, 62,* 361–382.

Forehand, G. A., & Guetzkow, H. (1961). The administrative judgment test as related to descriptions of executive judgment behaviors. *Journal of Applied Psychology, 45,* 257–261.

Forlano, G., & Watson, G. (1937). Relation between success in military training and intelligence, extroversion, and adequacy. *Journal of Social Psychology, 8,* 243–249.

Form, W. H. (1945). Status stratification in a planned community. *American Sociological Review, 10,* 605–613.

Form, W. H., & Form, A. L. (1953). Unanticipated results of a foreman training program. *Personnel Journal, 32,* 207–212.

Form, W. H., & Nosow, S. (1958). *Community in disaster.* New York: Harper.

Form, W. H., & Sauer, W. L. (1963). Labor and community influentials: A comparative study of participation and imagery. *Industrial Labor Relations Review, 17,* 3–19.

Forrest, P. J., Cochran, D. S., Ray, D. F., & Robin, D. P. (1989). *Factors which influence ethical business judgments: A managerial and societal comparison.* Paper, Academy of Management, Washington, DC.

Forsyth, D. R., & Forsyth, N. M. (1984). *Subordinates' reactions to female leaders.* Paper, Eastern Psychological Association, Baltimore.

Fortune (1946). The management poll. *34*(4), 5–6.

Fortune (1969). Special issue on American youth. *57*(1), 66–148.

Forward, J., & Zander, A. (1971). Choice of unattainable group goals and effects on performance. *Organizational Behavior and Human Performance, 6,* 184–199.

Foster, J. P. (1976). *Perceptions of principals' behavior as rated by teachers, students, and principals in junior high schools in Chattanooga, Tennessee.* Doctoral dissertation, Virginia Polytechnic Institute and State University, Blacksburg.

Foster, W. T. (1929). Education for leadership in business. *School Society, 29,* 734–736.

Foti, R. J., & Cohen, B. A. (undated). *Self-monitoring and leadership emergence.* Unpublished manuscript.

Foti, R. J., Fraser, S. L., & Lord, R. G. (1982). Effects of leadership labels and prototypes on perceptions of political leaders. *Journal of Applied Psychology, 67,* 326–333.

Foundation for Research on Human Behavior (1954). *Leadership patterns and organizational effectiveness.* Ann Arbor, MI: Foundation for Research on Human Behavior.

Fouriezos, N., Hutt, M., & Guetzkow, H. (1950). Measurement of self oriented needs in discussion groups. *Journal of Abnormal and Social Psychology, 45,* 682–690.

Fowler, E. M. (1982, December 15). Careers: Discontent of middle managers. *New York Times,* p. D17.

Fox, A. M. (1967). Temperament and attitude correlates of leadership behavior. *Educational Psychology Measurement, 27,* 1167–1168.

Fox, D., Lorge, I., Weltz, P., & Herrold, K. (1953). Comparison of decisions written by large and small groups. *American Psychologist, 8,* 351.

Fox, H., Walton, S. D., Kirchner, W. K., & Mahoney, T. A. (1954). *Leadership and executive development: A bibliography.* Minneapolis: University of Minnesota Press.

Fox, T. G. (1973). *The influence of manifest and latent social identities on medical school faculty attitudes.* Doctoral dissertation, University of Michigan, Ann Arbor.

Fox, V. (1947). A study of the promotion of enlisted men in the army. *Journal of Applied Psychology, 31,* 298–305.

Fox, W. M. (1954). *An experimental study of group reaction to two types of conference leadership.* Doctoral dissertation, Ohio State University, Columbus.

Fox, W. M. (1957). Group reaction to two types of conference leadership. *Human Relations, 10,* 279–289.

Fox, W. M. (1974). *Least preferred coworker scales: Research and development* (Tech. Rep. No. 70-5). Gainesville, FL: University of Florida, College of Business Administration.

Fox, W. M. (1976). Reliabilities, means, and standard deviations for LPC scales: Instrument refinement. *Academy of Management Journal, 19,* 450–461.

Fox, W. M. (1982). A test of Octant I of Fiedler's contingency model with training dependent coaching task groups. *Replications in Social Psychology, 2*(1), 47–49.

Fox, W. M. (1987–88, Winter). Improving performance appraisal systems. *National Productivity Review, 7*(1), 20–27.

Fox, W. M. (1988). *Effective group problem solving.* San Francisco: Jossey-Bass.

Fox, W. M. (1989). *Behavior modeling: An overview.* Unpublished manuscript.

Fox, W. M., Hill, W. A., & Guertin, W. N. (1973). Dimensional analyses of least preferred co-worker scales. *Journal of Applied Psychology, 57,* 192–194.

Foyal, H. (1949). *General and industrial management* (C. Storrs, Trans.). London: Pitman.

Frager, R. (1970). Conformity and anticonformity in Japan. *Journal of Personality and Social Psychology, 15,* 203–210.

Fraker, S. (1984). Why women are not getting to the top. *Fortune, 109*(8), 40–45.

Fram, E. H., & DuBrin, A. J. (1981). Time-span orientation: A key factor of contingency management. *Personnel Journal, 60*(1), 46–48, 61.

Frank, E. J. (1973). *Cognitive complexity and leadership: The effect of perceptual sensitivity on leadership success.* Doctoral dissertation, Purdue University, Lafayette, IN.

Frank, H. H., & Katcher, A. H. (1977). The qualities of leadership; How male medical students evaluate their female peers. *Human Relations, 30,* 403–416.

Frank, L. K. (1939). Dilemma of leadership. *Psychiatry, 2,* 343–361.

Frank, L. L., & Hackman, J. R. (1975). A failure of job enrichment: The case of the change that wasn't. *Journal of Applied Behavioral Science, 11,* 413–436.

Frank, R. S. (1971). The relationship between dogmatism, preference for self-actualizing values, and indirect discussion leadership styles—as influenced by two group procedures. *Dissertation Abstracts International, 32,* 3025.

Franke, R. H. (1984). *Contrasts and changes in Japanese and American managerial attitudes between 1960 and 1980.* Paper, Academy of Management, Boston.

Franke, R., & Kaul, J. (1978). The Hawthorne experiments revisited: First statistical interpretation. *American Sociological Review, 43,* 623-643.

Frankfort, H., Frankfort, H. A., Wilson, J. A., & Jacobsen, T. (1949) *Before philosophy.* Baltimore: Penguin Books.

Franklin, A. J. (1969). The relationship between leadership training in group dynamics and the development of groups among disadvantaged youth. *Dissertation Abstracts, 29,* 2090-2091.

Franklin, J. L. (1975). Relations among four social-psychological aspects of organizations. *Administrative Science Quarterly, 20,* 422-433.

Frantzve, J. (1979). *The influence of gender composition of leaderless group discussions on ratings of effectiveness.* Doctoral dissertation, University of Georgia, Athens, GA.

Frantzve, J. L. (1982). *Gender isolation as an influence on behavior.* Paper, International Congress of Applied Psychology, Edinburgh.

Frantzve, J. L. (1985). *Organizational women: Fiction and fact.* Paper, American Psychological Association, Los Angeles.

Frazier, E. F. (1966). "Society": Status without substance. In R. J. Murphy & H. Elinson (Eds.), *Problems and prospects of the Negro movement.* Belmont, CA: Wadsworth.

Frederiksen, N. (1962a). In-basket tests and factors in administrative performance. In H. Guetzkow (Ed.), *Simulation in social science: Readings.* Englewood Cliffs, NJ: Prentice-Hall.

Frederiksen, N. (1962b). Factors in in-basket performance. *Psychological Monographs, 76*(22), No. 541.

Frederiksen, N. (1966). Validation of a simulation technique. *Organizational Behavior and Human Performance, 1,* 87-109.

Frederiksen, N., Saunders, D. R., & Ward, B. (1957). The in-basket test. *Psychological Monographs: General and Applied, 71*(9), Whole No. 438.

Free, V. (1983). CEOs and their corporate cultures—new game plans. *Marketing Communications, 8*(6), 21-27.

Freeman, G. L., & Taylor, E. K. (1950). *How to pick leaders.* New York: Funk & Wagnalls.

Freeman, L. C., Fararo, T. J., Bloomberg, W., & Sunshine, M. H. (1963). Locating leaders in local communities: A comparison of some alternative approaches. *American Sociological Review, 28,* 791-798.

Freemesser, G. F., & Kaplan, H. B. (1976). Self-attitudes and deviant behavior: The case of the charismatic religious movement. *Journal of Youth and Adolescence, 5*(1), 1-9.

Freeston, K. (1987). Leader substitutes in educational organizations. *Educational Administration Quarterly, 23*(2), 45-59.

French, E. B., & Magee, J. J. (1972). The incidence of the emotionally disturbed within the administrative units of a large organization. *Personnel Psychology, 3,* 535-543.

French, E. G. (1956). Motivation as a variable in work-partner selection. *Journal of Abnormal and Social Psychology, 53,* 96-99.

French, J. L., & Rosenstein, J. (1984). Employee ownership, work attitudes, and power relationships. *Academy of Management Journal, 27,* 861.

French, J. R. P. (1941). The disruption and cohesion of groups. *Journal of Abnormal and Social Psychology, 36,* 361-377.

French, J. R. P. (1944a). Organized and unorganized groups under fear and frustration. *University of Iowa, Student and Child Welfare, 20,* 231-308.

French, J. R. P. (1944b). Retraining an autocratic leader. *Journal of Abnormal and Social Psychology, 39,* 224-237.

French, J. R. P. (1950). Field experiments: Changing group productivity. In J. G. Miller (Ed.), *Experiments in social process.* New York: McGraw-Hill.

French, J. R. P. (1956). A formal theory of social power. *Psychological Review, 63,* 181-194.

French, J. R. P., Jr. (1957). An experimental study of resistance to influence. In *Annual Report.* Ann Arbor: University of Michigan, Research Center Group.

French, J. R. P., Israel, J., & Ås, D. (1960). An experiment on participation in a Norwegian factory. *Human Relations, 13,* 3-19.

French, J. R. P., Kay, E., & Meyer, H. H. (1966). Participation and the appraisal system. *Human Relations, 19,* 3-20.

French, J. R. P., Morrison, W., & Levinger, G. (1960). Coercive power and forces affecting conformity. *Journal of Abnormal and Social Psychology, 61,* 93-101.

French, J. R. P., & Raven, B. (1959). The bases of social power. In D. Cartwright (Ed.), *Studies in social power.* Ann Arbor: University of Michigan, Institute for Social Research.

French, J. R. P., Sherwood, J. J., & Bradford, D. L. (1966). Change in self-identity in a management training conference. *Journal of Applied Behavioral Science, 2,* 210-218.

French, J. R. P., & Snyder, R. (1959). Leadership and interpersonal power. In D. Cartwright (Ed.), *Studies in social power.* Ann Arbor: University of Michigan, Institute for Social Research.

French, J. R. P., & Zander, A. (1949). The group dynamics approach. In A. Kornhauser (Ed.), *Psychology of labor-management relations.* Champaign, IL: Industrial Relations Research Association.

French, R. L. (1949). Morale and leadership. In *Human factors in undersea warfare.* Washington, DC: National Research Council.

French, R. L. (1950). Verbal output and leadership status in initially leaderless discussion groups. *American Psychologist, 5,* 310-311.

French, R. L. (1951). Sociometric status and individual adjustment among naval recruits. *Journal of Abnormal and Social Psychology, 46,* 64-72.

French, W. L., Bell, C. H., & Zawacki, R. A. (Eds.). (1978). *Organizational development: Theory, practice and research.* Dallas: Business Publications.

Frenkel, E. (1936). Studies in biographical psychology. *Character and Personality, 5,* 1-34.

Fretwell, E. K. (1919). Education for leadership. *Teachers College Record, 20,* 324-352.

Freud, S. (1913/1946). *Totem and taboo.* New York: Vintage Books.

Freud, S. (1922). *Group psychology and the analysis of ego*. London: International Psychoanalytical Press.

Freud, S. (1922/1939). *Moses and monotheism*. New York: A. A. Knopf.

Freud, S., & Bullitt, C. (1932). *Thomas Woodrow Wilson: A psychological study*. New York: Houghton Mifflin.

Frey, M. W. (1963). An experimental study of the influence of disruptive interaction induced by authoritarian-equalitarian, leader-follower combinations upon the decision-making effectiveness of small groups. *Dissertation Abstracts, 25*, 897.

Freyer, F. W. (1964). *An evaluation of level of aspiration as a training procedure*. Englewood Cliffs, NJ: Prentice-Hall.

Fried, B. J. (1988). Power acquisition in a health care setting: An application of strategic contingencies theory. *Human Relations, 41*, 915–927.

Fried, K. W. (1977). Some effects of the leader's abstinent role on group experience. *Group, 1*, 118–131.

Friedland, W. H. (1964). For a sociological concept of charisma. *Social Forces, 43*(1), 18–26.

Friedlander, F. (1963). Underlying sources of job satisfaction. *Journal of Applied Psychology, 47*, 246–250.

Friedlander, F. (1966a). Importance of work versus nonwork among socially and occupationally stratified groups. *Journal of Applied Psychology, 50*, 437–441.

Friedlander, F. (1966b). Performance and interactional dimensions of organizational work groups. *Journal of Applied Psychology, 50*, 257–265.

Friedlander, F. (1967). The impact of organizational training laboratories upon the effectiveness and interaction of ongoing work groups. *Personnel Psychology, 20*, 289–307.

Friedlander, F., & Greenberg, S. (1971). Effect of job attitudes, training, and organizational climate on performance of the hard-core unemployed. *Journal of Applied Psychology, 55*, 287–295.

Friedlander, F., & Margulies, N. (1969). Multiple impacts of organizational climate and individual value systems upon job satisfaction. *Personnel Psychology, 22*, 171–183.

Friedlander, F., & Pickle, H. (1968). Components of effectiveness in small organizations. *Administrative Science Quarterly, 13*, 289–304.

Friedman, G. (1961). *The anatomy of work*. New York: Free Press.

Friedman, H. S., DiMatteo, M. R., & Taranta, A. (1980). A study of the relationship between individual differences in nonverbal expressiveness and factors of personality and social interaction. *Journal of Research in Personality, 14*, 351–364.

Friedman, H. S., Hall, J. A., & Harris, J. M. (1985). Type A behavior, nonverbal expressive style, and health. *Journal of Personality and Social Psychology, 48*, 1299–1315.

Friedman, H. S., Prince, L. M., Riggio, R. E., & DiMatteo, M. R. (1980). Understanding and assessing nonverbal expressiveness: The affective communication test. *Journal of Personality and Social Psychology, 39*, 331–351.

Friedman, H. S., & Riggio, R. E. (1981). Effect of individual differences in nonverbal expressiveness on transmission of emotion. *Journal of Nonverbal Behavior, 6*, 96–104.

Friedman, M., & Rosenman, R. H., (1974). *Type A behavior and your heart*. New York: Knopf.

Friedman, S. D., & Saul, K. (1988). *Internal consequences of CEO succession events in large corporations*. Paper, Academy of Management, Anaheim, CA.

Friedman, S. D., & Singh, H. (1986). *CEO succession events and market reactions: The effects of reason, successor origin, and contact*. Unpublished manuscript.

Friedman, S. T. (1969). Relation of parental attitudes toward child rearing and patterns of social behavior in middle childhood. *Psychological Reports, 24*, 575–579.

Friedrich, C. (1961). Political leadership and the problem of charismatic power. *Journal of Politics, 23*, 19.

Friesen, B. J. (1983). Organizational and leader behavior correlates of the line worker job satisfaction and role clarity. *Dissertation Abstracts International, 44*(8A), 2581.

Fritz, R. (1986). The leader as creator. In J. D. Adams (Ed.), *Transforming leadership*. Alexandria, VA: Miles River Press.

Fromm, E. (1941). *Escape from freedom*. New York: Farrar & Rinehart.

Frost, D. E. (1983). Role perceptions and behavior of the immediate supervisor: Moderating effects on the prediction of leadership effectiveness. *Organizational Behavior and Human Performance, 31*, 123–142.

Frost, D. E. (1986). A test of situational engineering for training leaders. *Psychological Reports, 59*, 771–782.

Frost, D. E., Fiedler, F. E., & Anderson, J. W. (1983). The role of personal risk-taking in effective leadership. *Human Relations, 36*, 185–202.

Frost, P. J. (1986). Power, politics and influence. In L. W. Porter, L. L. Putnam, K. H. Roberts, & E. M. Jablin (Eds.), *The handbook of organizational communication*. Beverly Hills, CA: Sage.

Frost, P. J., & Hayes, D. C. (1979). An exploration in two cultures of a model of political behavior in organizations. In G. W. England, A. R. Negandhi, & B. Wilpert (Eds.), *Organizational functions in a cross-cultural perspective*. Kent, OH: Kent State University Press.

Fruchter, B., & Skinner, J. A. (1966). Dimensions of leadership in a student cooperative. *Multivariate Behavioral Research, 1*, 437–445.

Fry, L. W., Kerr, S., & Lee, C. (1986). Effects of different leader behaviors under different levels of task interdependence. *Human Relations, 39*, 1067–1082.

Frye, R. L., & Spruill, J. (1965). Type of orientation and task completion of elementary-grade students. *Journal of Genetic Psychology, 106*, 45–49.

Fujii, D. S. (1977). A dyadic, interactive approach to the study of leader behaviors. *Dissertation Abstracts International, 37*, 5415–5416.

Fukuda, K. (1983). Japanese and Chinese management practices: Uncovering the differences. *Mid-Atlantic Journal of Business, 21*(2), 35–44.

Fulk, J., Schmitz, J., & Ryn, D. (1989). *Communications in R&D via electronic mail.* Center for Innovation Management Studies, Lehigh University, Lehigh, PA.

Fulk, J., & Wendler, E. R. (1982). Dimensionality of leader-subordinate interactions: A path-goal investigation. *Organizational Behavior and Human Performance, 30,* 241–264.

Fultiner, J. D. (1972). School principals look at leader behavior: The problem of interpersonal needs. *Dissertation Abstracts International, 32,* 6036.

Furukawa, H. (1981). Management objectives, conditions in workunit, and leadership behavior. *Psychologia: An International Journal of Psychology in the Orient, 24,* 176–184.

Gabarro, J. J. (1979). Socialization at the top: How CEO's and subordinates evolve interpersonal contracts. *Organizational Dynamics, 7,* 3–23.

Gabarro, J. J. (1985). Taking charge: Stages in management succession. *Harvard Business Review, 64*(3), 110–123.

Gabarro, J. J., & Kotter, J. P. (1980). Managing your boss. *Harvard Business Review, 58,* 92–100.

Gaertner, G. H., Gaertner, K. N., & Devine, I. (1983). Federal agencies in the context of transition: A contrast between democratic and organizational theories. *Public Administration Review, 43,* 421–432.

Gaertner, K. N. (1988). Managers' careers and organizational change. *Academy of Management Executive, 2,* 311–318.

Gaertner, K. N., & Gaertner, G. H. (1985). Performance-contingent pay for federal managers. *Administration and Society, 17*(1), 7–20.

Gage, N. L., & Exline, R. V. (1953). Social perception and effectiveness in discussion groups. *Human Relations, 6,* 381–396.

Gal, R. (1983). Courage under stress. In S. Breznitz (Ed.), *Stress in Israel.* New York: Van Nostrand Reinhold.

Gal, R. (1985a). *Combat stress as an opportunity: The case of heroism.* Paper, Northeast Regional Conference of the Inter-University Seminar on Armed Forces and Society, Albany, NY.

Gal, R. (1985b). Commitment and obedience in the military: An Israeli case study. *Armed Forces and Society, 11,* 553–564.

Gal, R. (1986). Unit morale: From a theoretical puzzle to an empirical illustration: An Israeli example. *Journal of Applied Social Psychology, 16,* 549–564.

Gal, R. (1987). *Yesterday's conventional warfare—Tomorrow's nuclear warfare? Lessons from the Israeli experience.* Paper, Conference on Military Leadership, Annapolis, MD.

Gal, R., (1989). *Military leadership for the 1990's: Commitment-derived leadership.* Unpublished manuscript.

Gal, R., & Jones, F. D. (1985). *Psychological aspects of combat stress: A model derived from Israeli and other combat experiences.* Unpublished manuscript.

Gal, R., & Lazarus, R. S. (1975). The role of activity in anticipating and confronting stressful situations. *Journal of Human Stress, 1*(4), 4–20.

Gal, R., & Manning, F. J. (1987). Morale and its components: A cross-national comparison. *Journal of Applied Social Psychology, 17,* 369–391.

Galanter, M. (1982). Charismatic religious sects and psychiatry: An overview. *American Journal of Psychiatry, 139,* 1539–1548.

Galaskiewicz, J., & Shatin, D. (1981). Leadership and networking among neighborhood human service organizations. *Administrative Science Quarterly, 26,* 434–448.

Galinsky, M. J., & Schopler, J. H. (1980). Structuring co-leadership in social work training. *Social Work with Groups, 3*(4), 51–63.

Gallagher, A. (1983). The older worker: The relationship between job satisfaction and supervisor style. *Dissertation Abstracts International, 45*(2A), 460.

Gallino, L. (1975). Three types of Italian top managers. *International Student Management Organization, 5,* 43–70.

Gallo, P. S., & McClintock, C. G. (1962). Behavioral, attitudinal, and perceptual differences between leaders and non-leaders in situations of group support and non-support. *Journal of Social Psychology, 56,* 121–133.

Galsworthy, J. (1931). *Maid in waiting.* London: W. Heineman.

Galton, F. (1869). *Hereditary genius.* New York: Appleton.

Galton, F. (1890). *English men of science: Their nature and nurture.* New York: Appleton, Century.

Gamson, W. A. (1965). Experimental studies of coalition formation. In L. Berkowitz (Ed.), *Advances in experimental social psychology.* New York: Academic Press.

Gamson, W. A. (1968). *Power and discontent.* Homewood, IL: Dorsey.

Gamson, W. A., & Scotch, N. (1964). Scapegoating in baseball. *American Journal of Sociology, 70,* 69–70.

Ganster, D. C., Fusilier, M. R., & Mayes, B. T. (1986). Role of social support in the experience of stress at work. *Journal of Applied Psychology, 71,* 102–110.

Gantt, H. L. (1916). *Industrial leadership.* New Haven, CT: Yale University Press.

Gantz, B. S., Erickson, C. O., & Stephenson, R. W. (1977a). Measuring the motivation to manage in a research and development population. In J. B. Miner (Ed.), *Motivation to manage.* Atlanta, GA: Organizational Measurement Systems Press.

Gantz, B. S., Erickson, C. O., & Stephenson, R. W. (1977b). Some determinants of promotion in a research and development population. In J. B. Miner (Ed.), *Motivation to manage.* Atlanta, GA: Organizational Measurement Systems Press.

GAP (Group for the Advancement of Psychiatry). (1974). Problems of psychiatric leadership. *GAP Report, 8,* 925–946.

Garbin, A. P., & Bates, F. L. (1966). Occupational prestige and its correlates: A re-examination. *Social Forces, 44,* 295–302.

Gardner, B. B., & Whyte, W. F. (1945). The man in the middle. *Applied Anthropology, 4,* 1–28.

Gardner, C. A., Jr. (1971). *Faculty participation in departmental administrative activities.* Doctoral dissertation, University of Michigan, Ann Arbor.

Gardner, E. F., & Thompson, G. G. (1956). *Social relations and morale in small groups.* New York: Appleton-Century-Crofts.

Gardner, G. (1956). Functional leadership and popularity in small groups. *Human Relations, 9,* 491–509.

Gardner, J. W. (1961). *Excellence: Can we be equal and excellent too?* New York: Harper.

Gardner, J. W. (1965a). *The anti-leadership vaccine.* New York: The Carnegie Corporation, Annual Report.

Gardner, J. W. (1965b). *Self-renewal.* New York: Harper & Row.

Gardner, J. W. (1981). *Leadership: A sampler of the wisdom of John Gardner.* Minneapolis: University of Minnesota, Hubert H. Humphrey Institute.

Gardner, J. W. (1986a). *The nature of leadership: Introductory considerations* (Leadership Paper 1). Washington, DC: Independent Sector.

Gardner, J. W. (1986b). The tasks of leadership (Leadership Paper No. 2). Washington, DC: Independent Sector.

Gardner, J. W. (1987a). Leadership: The role of community colleges in developing the nation's young potential leaders. *Community, Junior and Technical College Journal, 57*(5), 16–21.

Gardner, J. W. (1987b). Leaders and followers. *Liberal Education, 73*(2), 4–8.

Gardner, J. W. (1988a). *The task of motivating* (Leadership Paper No. 9). Washington, DC: Independent Sector.

Gardner, J. W. (1988b). *Renewing: The leader's creative task* (Leadership Paper No. 10). Washington, DC: Independent Sector.

Gardner, J. W. (1989). *On leadership.* New York: Free Press.

Gardner, K. E., & Williams, A. P. O. (1973). A twenty-five year follow-up of an extended interview selection procedure in the Royal Navy. *Occupational Psychology, 47,* 1–13.

Gardner, N. D. (1974). *Group leadership.* Washington, DC: National Training and Development Service Press.

Gardner, W. L., & Martinko, M. J. (1985). *Impression management: An observational study.* Paper, Academy of Management, San Diego.

Gardner, W. L., & Martinko, M. J. (1988). Impression management: An observational study linking audience characteristics with verbal self-presentations. *Academy of Management Journal, 31,* 42–65.

Garforth, F. I. de la P. (1945). War office selection boards. *Occupational Psychology, 19,* 97–108.

Garland, H. (1984). Relation of effort-performance expectancy to performance in goal-setting experiments. *Journal of Applied Psychology, 69,* 79–84.

Garland, H., & Beard, J. F. (1979). Relationship between self-monitoring and leader emergence across two task situations. *Journal of Applied Psychology, 64,* 72–76.

Garland, H., & Price, K. H. (1977). Attitudes toward women in management and attributions for their success and failure in managerial position. *Journal of Applied Psychology, 62,* 29–33.

Garlitz, G. F. (1983). Learning from worksite traumas. *Personnel Administrator, 28*(4), 28–34.

Garrison, K. C. (1933). A study of some factors related to leadership in high school. *Peabody Journal of Education, 11,* 11–17.

Gartner, D., & Iverson, M. A. (1967). Some effects of upward mobile status in established and *ad hoc* groups. *Journal of Personality and Social Psychology, 5,* 390–397.

Garza, R. T., Romero, G. J., Cox, G., & Ramirez, M. (1982). Biculturalism, locus of control, and leader behavior in ethnically mixed small groups. *Journal of Applied Social Psychology, 12,* 237–253.

Gassner, S. M., Gold, J., & Snadowsky, A. M. (1964). Changes in the phenomenal field as a result of human relations training. *Journal of Psychology, 58,* 33–41.

Gast, I. F. (1984). Leader discretion as a key component of a manager's role. In J. G. Hunt, D. Hosking, C. A. Schriesheim, & R. Stewart (Eds.), *Leaders and managers: International perspectives on managerial behavior and leadership.* New York: Pergamon.

Gaston, T. L. (1983). *Factors enabling psychologically healthy individuals (managers) to function in the less-than-optimal organizational system.* Doctoral dissertation, George Washington University, Washington, DC.

Gates, T. J. (1972). Change in selected personality variables of high ranking federal executives during a residential executive training program. *Dissertation Abstracts International, 32,* 6196.

Gatzke, H. W. (1973). Hitler and psychohistory. *American History Review, 78,* 394–401.

Gaudreau, P. A. (1975). Investigation of sex differences across job levels. *Dissertation Abstracts International, 36,* 1957B.

Gaugler, B. B., Rosenthal, D. B., Thornton, G. C., III, & Bentson, C. (1987). Meta-analysis of assessment center validity. *Journal of Applied Psychology, 72,* 493–511.

Gauthier, W. J., Jr. (1975). *The relationship of organizational structure, leader behavior of the principal and personality orientation of the principal to school management climate.* Doctoral dissertation, University of Connecticut, Storrs.

Gavin, D. A. (1983). Quality on the line. *Harvard Business Review, 61*(5), 65–75.

Gay, P. (1985). Forward. In C. B. Strozier & D. Offer, (Eds.), The leader. *Psychohistorical Essays.* New York: Plenum.

Gebel, A. S. (1954). Self-perception and leaderless group discussion status. *Journal of Social Psychology, 40,* 309–318.

Gebert, D., & Steinkamp, T. H. (undated). *Selfconcept, leadership style and economic success of entrepreneurs in Nigeria.* Bayreuth University, FRG. Unpublished manuscript.

Geertz, C. (1977). Centers, kings and charisma: Reflections on the symbolics of power. In J. Ben-David and T. N. Clark (Eds.), *Culture and its creators: Essays in honor of Edward Shils.* Chicago: University of Chicago Press.

Geertz, C. (1983). Reflections on the symbolics of power. In C. Geertz (Ed.), *Local knowledge.* New York: Basic Books.

Gehrman, G. H. (1970). *An investigation of the relationship between participation and organizational climate: An empirical study of the perceptions of high school senior students, teachers, principals and district superintendents in innovative vs. noninnovative schools.* Doctoral dissertation, University of Massachusetts, Amherst.

Geier, J. G. (1963). A descriptive analysis of an interaction pattern resulting in leadership emergence in leaderless group discussion. *Dissertation Abstracts, 26,* 2919–2920.

Geier, J. G. (1967). A trait approach to the study of leadership in small groups. *Journal of Communication, 17,* 316-323.

Geis, F. L., Boston, M., & Hoffman, N. (1985). Sex of authority role models and achievement by men and women: Leadership performance and recognition. *Journal of Personality and Social Psychology, 49,* 636-653.

Geissler, E. M. (1984). Personality characteristics and feelings of power-powerlessness in nurse and non-nurse leaders. *Dissertation Abstracts International, 45*(7B), 2101.

Gekoski, N. (1952). Predicting group productivity. *Personnel Psychology, 5,* 281-291.

Gellerman, S. W. (1967). Passivity, paranoia, and "pakikisama." *Columbia Journal of World Business, 2,* 59-66.

Gellert, E. (1961). Stability and fluctuation in the power relationships of young children. *Journal of Abnormal and Social Psychology, 62,* 8-15.

Gemmill, G. R., & Heisler, W. J. (1972). Fatalism as a factor in managerial job satisfaction, job strain, and mobility. *Personnel Psychology, 25,* 241-250.

Gemmill, G. R., & Thamhain, H. J. (1974). Influence styles of project managers: Some project performance correlates. *Academy of Management Journal, 17,* 216-224.

Geneen, H., & Moscow, A. (1984). *Managing.* New York: Doubleday.

General Electric Company (1957). *The effective manufacturing foreman.* Schenectady, NY: General Electric Co.

George, C. S., Jr. (1972). *The history of management thought.* Englewood Cliffs, NJ: Prentice-Hall.

George, E. I., & Abraham, P. A. (1966). A comparative study of leaders and non-leaders among pupils in secondary schools. *Journal of Psychological Researches, 10,* 116-120.

George, J. R., & Bishop, L. K. (1971). Relationship of organizational structure and teacher personality characteristics to organizational climate. *Administrative Science Quarterly, 16,* 467-475.

George, N. (1958). *Supervisors' thinking on current issues.* Dayton, OH: National Management Association.

George, W. L. (1922). Mastery of men. *Harpers, 144,* 657-665.

Georgi, C. (1963). *The literature of executive management.* New York: Special Libraries Association.

Georgopoulos, B. S. (1965). Normative structure variables and organizational behavior. *Human Relations, 18,* 155-169.

Georgopoulos, B. S., Mahoney, G. M., & Jones, N. W. (1957). A path-goal approach to productivity. *Journal of Applied Psychology, 41,* 345-353.

Georgopoulos, B. S., & Tannenbaum, A. S. (1957). A study of organization effectiveness. *American Sociological Review, 22,* 534-540.

Gephart, R. P., Jr. (1978). Status degradation and organizational succession: An ethnomethodological approach. *Administrative Science Quarterly, 23,* 553-581.

Gerard, H. B. (1953). The effect of different dimensions of disagreement on the communication process in small groups. *Human Relations, 6,* 249-271.

Gerard, H. B. (1954). The anchorage of opinions in face-to-face groups. *Human Relations, 7,* 313-325.

Gerard, H. B. (1957). Some effects of status, role clarity, and group goal clarity upon the individual's relations to group progress. *Journal of Personality, 25,* 475-488.

Gergen, K. J. (1969). *The psychology of behavior exchange.* Reading, MA: Addison-Wesley.

Gergen, K. J., & Taylor, M. G. (1969). Social expectancy and self-presentation in a status hierarchy. *Journal of Experimental Social Psychology, 5,* 79-92.

Gersick, C. J. G. (1985). *Time and transition in work teams: Towards a new model of group development.* [Reported in B. B. Morgan, A. S. Glickman, et al. (1986). *Measurement of team behaviors in a Navy environment.* Orlando, FL: Center of Excellence for Simulation and Training Technology, Naval Training Systems Center.]

Gerstberger, P. G., & Allen, T. J. (1968). Criteria used by research and development engineers in the selection of an information source. *Journal of Applied Psychology, 52,* 272-279.

Gerth, H., & Mills, C. W. (1952). A sociological note on leadership. In J. E. Hulett & R. Stagner (Eds.), *Problems in social psychology.* Urbana: University of Illinois Press.

Gerth, H., & Mills, C. W. (1953). *Character and social structure.* New York: Harcourt, Brace.

Gerwin, D. (1981). Relationships between structure and technology. In P. C. Nystrom & W. H. Starbuck (Eds.), *Handbook of organizational design.* New York: Oxford University Press.

Gesell, A. L., & Thompson, H. (1934). *Infant behavior: Its genesis and growth.* New York: McGraw-Hill.

Getzels, J. W. (1963). Conflict and role behavior in an educational setting. In W. W. Charters & N. L. Gage (Eds.), *Readings in the social psychology of education.* Boston: Allyn & Bacon.

Getzels, J. W., & Guba, E. G. (1954). Role, role conflict, and effectiveness: An empirical study. *American Sociological Review, 19,* 164-175.

Getzels, J. W., & Guba, E. G. (1957). Social behavior and the administrative process. *School Review, 55,* 423-441.

Ghiselin, B. (1987). Images. *Issues and Observations, 7*(4), 8-9.

Ghiselli, E. E. (1959). Traits differentiating management personnel. *Personnel Psychology, 12,* 535-544.

Ghiselli, E. E. (1960). Individuality as a factor in the success of management personnel. *Personnel Psychology, 13,* 1-10.

Ghiselli, E. E. (1963a). The validity of management traits in relation to occupational level. *Personnel Psychology, 16,* 109-113.

Ghiselli, E. E. (1963b). Intelligence and managerial success. *Psychological Reports, 12,* 898.

Ghiselli, E. E. (1964). Maturity of self-perception in relation to managerial success. *Personnel Psychology, 17,* 41-48.

Ghiselli, E. E. (1966a). Psychological properties of groups and group learning. *Psychological Reports, 19,* 17-18.

Ghiselli, E. E. (1966b). *The validity of occupational aptitude tests.* New York: Wiley.

Ghiselli, E. E. (1968a). Interaction of traits and motivational factors in the determination of the success of managers. *Journal of Applied Psychology, 52*, 480–483.

Ghiselli, E. E. (1968b). Some motivational factors in the success of managers. *Personnel Psychology, 21*, 431–440.

Ghiselli, E. E. (1971). *Explorations in managerial talent.* Pacific Palisades, CA: Goodyear.

Ghiselli, E. E., & Barthol, R. P. (1953). The validity of personality inventories in the selection of employees. *Journal of Applied Psychology, 37*, 18–20.

Ghiselli, E. E., & Barthol, R. P. (1956). Role perceptions of successful and unsuccessful superiors. *Journal of Applied Psychology, 40*, 241–244.

Ghiselli, E. E., & Johnson, D. A. (1970). Need satisfaction, managerial success, and organizational structure. *Personnel Psychology, 23*, 569–576.

Ghiselli, E. E., & Lodahl, T. M. (1958a). The evaluation of foremen's performance in relation to the internal characteristics of their groups. *Personnel Psychology, 11*, 179–187.

Ghiselli, E. E., & Lodahl, T. M. (1958b). Patterns of managerial traits and group effectiveness. *Journal of Abnormal and Social Psychology, 57*, 61–66.

Ghiselli, E. E., & Siegel, J. P. (1972). Leadership and managerial success in tall and flat organization structures. *Personnel Psychology, 25*, 617–624.

Ghiselli, E. E., & Wyatt, T. A. (1972). Need satisfaction, managerial success, and attitudes toward leadership. *Personnel Psychology, 3*, 413–420.

Gibb, C. A. (undated). *Leadership.* Unpublished manuscript.

Gibb, C. A. (1947). The principles and traits of leadership. *Journal of Abnormal and Social Psychology, 42*, 267–284.

Gibb, C. A. (1949). Some tentative comments concerning group Rorschach pointers to the personality traits of leaders. *Journal of Social Psychology, 30*, 251–263.

Gibb, C. A. (1950). The sociometry of leadership in temporary groups. *Sociometry, 13*, 226–243.

Gibb, C. A. (1951). An experimental approach to the study of leadership. *Occupational Psychology, 25*, 233–248.

Gibb, C. A. (1954). Leadership. In G. Lindzey (Ed.), *Handbook of social psychology.* Cambridge, MA: Addison-Wesley.

Gibb, C. A. (1958). An interactional view of the emergence of leadership. *Australian Journal of Psychology, 10*, 101–110.

Gibb, C. A. (1969a). Leadership. In G. Lindzey & E. Aronson (Eds.), *The handbook of social psychology,* 2nd ed., Vol. 4. Reading, MA: Addison-Wesley.

Gibb, C. A. (1969b). *Leadership: Selected readings.* Baltimore: Penguin Books.

Gibb, J. R. (1954). *Factors producing defensive behavior within groups* (Annual Tech. Rep.). Boulder: University of Colorado, Human Relations Lab.

Gibb, J. R. (1961). Defense level and influence potential in small groups.

In L. Petrullo & B. M. Bass (Eds.), *Leadership and interpersonal behavior.* New York: Holt, Rinehart & Winston.

Gibb, J. R. (1964). The T-group as a climate for trust formation. In L. P. Bradford, J. R. Gibb, & K. D. Benne (Eds.), *T-group theory and laboratory methods: Innovation in re-education.* New York: Wiley.

Gibb, J. R., Platts, G. N., & Miller, L. F. (1951). *Dynamics of participative groups.* St. Louis, MO: John S. Swift.

Gibbard, G. S., Hartman, J. J., & Mann, R. D. (1974). *Analysis of groups: Contribution to the theory, research, and practice.* San Francisco: Jossey-Bass.

Gibbons, T. C. (1986). *Revisiting the question of born vs. made: Toward a theory of development of transformational leaders.* Doctoral dissertation, Fielding Institute, Santa Barbara, CA. Also: Paper, OD Network Conference, New York.

Gibson, A. K. (1974). *The achievement of sixth grade students in a midwestern city.* Doctoral dissertation, University of Michigan, Ann Arbor.

Gibson, J. L., Ivancevich, J. M., & Donnelly, J. H., Jr. (1973). *Organizations: Structure, processes, behavior.* Dallas: Business Publications.

Gide, C. (1930). *Communist and cooperative colonies.* New York: Crowell.

Giffin, K., & Ehrlich, L. (1963). The attitudinal effects of a group discussion on a proposed change in company policy. *Speech Monographs, 30*, 377–379.

Giffort, D., & Ayman, R. (1988). *Leadership style, situational control and subordinate job satisfaction.* Paper, Academy of Management, Anaheim, CA.

Gilbert, E. M. (1972). *Teaching styles prevalent in satisfying and dissatisfying college credit courses as perceived by adult students.* Doctoral dissertation, Ohio State University, Columbus.

Gilbert, G. R. (1985). Building highly productive work teams through positive leadership. *Public Personnel Management, 14*, 449–454.

Gilchrist, J. C. (1952). The formation of social groups under conditions of success and failure. *Journal of Abnormal and Social Psychology, 47*, 174–187.

Gilchrist, J. C., Shaw, M. E., & Walker, L. C. (1954). Some effects of unequal distribution of information in a wheel group structure. *Journal of Abnormal and Social Psychology, 49*, 554–556.

Gill, R. W. T. (1979). The in-tray (in-basket) exercise as a measure of management potential. *Journal of Occupational Psychology, 52*, 185–197.

Gill, R. W. T. (1983). *Personality profiles of Singapore-Chinese, British and American managers: A cross-cultural comparison.* Paper, Third Asian Regional Conference on Cross-Cultural Psychology, Bangi, Malaysia.

Gillen, D. J., & Carroll, S. J. (1985). Relationship of managerial ability to unit effectiveness in more organic versus more mechanistic departments. *Journal of Management Studies, 22*, 668–676.

Gillespie, D. F., & Cohen, S. E. (1984, Fall). Causes of worker burnout. *Children and Youth Services Review, 6*, 115–124.

Gillespie, H. R. (1980). An investigation of current management/leadership style of manufacturing executives in American industry. *Dissertation Abstracts International*, 41(7A), 3177.

Gillespie, J. B. (1980). The phenomenon of the public wife: An exercise in Goffman's impression management. *Symbolic Interaction*, 3(2), 109–126.

Gilligan, C. (1982). *In a different voice*. Cambridge, MA: Harvard University Press.

Gilligan, C. (1986a). Remapping development: The power of divergent data. In L. Cirillo & S. Wapner (Eds.), *Value presuppositions in theories of human development*. Hillside, NJ: Erlbaum Associates.

Gilligan, C. (1986b). Remapping the moral domain: New images of self in relationship. In T. Heller, M. Sosna, & D. Wellbery (Eds.), *Reconstructing individualism: Autonomy, individuality, and the self in western thought*. Palo Alto, CA: Stanford University Press.

Gilman, G. (1962). An inquiry into the nature and use of authority. In M. Haire (Ed.), *Organization theory in industrial practice*. New York: Wiley.

Gilmore, D. C., Beehr, T. A., Richter, D. J. (1979). Effects of leader behaviors on subordinate performance and satisfaction: A laboratory experiment with student employees. *Journal of Applied Psychology*, 64, 166–172.

Gilmore, T. N. (1982). Leadership and boundary management. *Journal of Applied Behavioral Science*, 18, 343–356.

Gilmore, T. N. (1988). *Making a leadership change: How organizations and leaders can handle leadership transitions successfully*. San Francisco: Jossey-Bass.

Ginsburg, L. R. (1971). Small group performance: The effects of the interaction of leader and member orientation on the effectiveness and attractiveness of small groups. *Dissertation Abstracts International*, 32, 3682.

Gintner, G., & Linkskold, S. (1975). Rate of participation and expertise as factors influencing leader choice. *Journal of Personality and Social Psychology*, 32, 1085–1089.

Ginzberg, E., & Reilley, E. W. (1957). *Effecting change in large organizations*. New York: Columbia University Press.

Gioia, D. A., & Sims, H. P. (1985). On avoiding the influence of implicit leadership theories in leader behavior descriptions. *Educational and Psychological Measurement*, 45, 217–232.

Gioia, D. A., & Sims, H. P. (1986). Cognition-behavior connections: Attribution and verbal behavior in leader-subordinate interactions. *Organizational Behavior and Human Decision Processes*, 37, 197–229.

Gitter, A. G., Black, H., & Fishman, J. E. (1975). Effect of race, sex, nonverbal communication and verbal communication on perception of leadership. *Sociological and Social Research*, 60, 46–57.

Gitter, A. G., Black, H., & Goldman, A. (1975). Role of nonverbal communication in the perception of leadership. *Perceptual and Motor Skills*, 40, 463–466.

Gitter, A. G., Satow, Y., & Goldman, A. (1968). Leadership: Non-verbal communication and mode of presentation of stimuli. *CRC Report*, No. 25, Boston University.

Gitter, A. G., & Walkley, J. (1968). Nonverbal communication: Leader-follower perception and mode of presentation. *CRC Report*, No. 21, Boston University.

Given, W. B. (1949). *Bottom-up management: People working together*. New York: Harper.

Gjestland, D. S. (1982). *Leadership and the bases of power*. Doctoral dissertation, University of California, Santa Barbara.

Gladstein, D. L., & Reilly, N. P. (1985). Group decision making under threat: The tycoon game. *Academy of Management Journal*, 28, 613–627.

Gladstone, R. (1989, July 31). Auto unions and companies lose to Japan. Binghamton, NY: *Binghamton Press & Sun-Bulletin*, Business Section, 5.

Glanzer, M. (1958). Curiosity, exploratory drive, and stimulus satiation. *Psychological Bulletin*, 55, 302–315.

Glanzer, M., & Glaser, R. (1961). Techniques for the study of group structure. II. Empirical studies of the effects of structure in small groups. *Psychological Bulletin*, 58, 1–27.

Glaser, B. G., & Strauss, A. L. (1967). *The discovery of grounded theory*. Chicago: Aldine.

Glaser, R., Schwartz, P. A., & Flanagan, J. C. (1958). The contribution of interview and situational performance procedures to the selection of supervisory personnel. *Journal of Applied Psychology*, 42, 69–73.

Gleason, W. J. (1957). Predicting Army leadership ability by modified leaderless group discussion. *Journal of Applied Psychology*, 41, 231–235.

Glickman, A. S., Hahn, C. P., Fleishman, E. A., & Baxter, B. (1969). *Top management development and succession: An exploratory study*. New York: Macmillan.

Glube, R. H., & Margerison, C. J. (1976). Managerial leadership. *Journal of European Training*, 5, 76–101.

Gluskinos, U. M., & Kestleman, B. (1970). *Management and union leaders' perception of work needs as compared with self-reported needs*. Paper, American Psychological Association, Miami Beach, FL.

Goble, F. (1972). *Excellence in leadership*. New York: American Management Association.

Godfrey, E. P., Fiedler, F. E., & Hall, D. M. (1959). *Boards, management, and company success*. Danville, IL: Interstate.

Goetz, T. E., & Herman, J. B. (1976). *Effects of supervisor's sex and subordinate sex on job satisfaction and productivity*. Washington, DC: American Psychological Association.

Goffman, E. (1959). *The presentation of self in everyday life*. Garden City, NY: Doubleday.

Goffman, I. W. (1957). Status consistency and preference for change in power-distribution. *American Sociological Review*, 22, 275–281.

Golb, E. F., & Fiedler, F. E. (1955). *A note on psychological attributes related to the score assumed similarity between opposites (ASo)* (Tech. Rep. No. 12). Urbana: University of Illinois, Group Effectiveness Research Laboratory.

Gold, H. A. (1962). The importance of ideology in sociometric evaluation of leadership. *Group Psychotherapy*, 15, 224–230.

Gold, R. (1951–52). Janitors versus tenants: A status-income dilemma. *American Journal of Sociology, 57*, 486–493.

Goldberg, H., & Iverson, M. A. (1965). Inconsistency in attitude of high status persons and loss of influence: An experimental study. *Psychological Reports, 16*, 673–683.

Goldberg, M. (1984). The essential points of a nation at risk. *Educational Leadership, 41*, 15–16.

Goldberg, M. L. (1955). Leadership and self-attitudes. *Dissertation Abstracts, 15*, 1457–1458.

Goldberg, P. (1983). *The intuitive edge: Understanding and developing intuition*. Boston: Houghton Mifflin.

Goldberg, S. C. (1954). Three situational determinants of conformity to social norms. *Journal of Abnormal and Social Psychology, 49*, 325–329.

Goldberg, S. C. (1955). Influence and leadership as a function of group structure. *Journal of Abnormal and Social Psychology, 51*, 119–122.

Golden, O. (1955). *Executive development: A bibliographic review*. Chicago: University of Chicago, Industrial Relations Center.

Goldfarb, W. (1949). Characteristics of 200 active merchant marine officers. In G. G. Killinger (Ed.), *Psychobiological Program of War Shipping Administration*. Stanford, CA: Stanford University Press.

Goldman, M., & Fraas, L. A. (1965). The effects of leader selection on group performance. *Sociometry, 28*, 82–88.

Goldring, P. (1967). *Role of distance and posture in the evaluation of interactions*. Paper, American Psychological Association, Washington, DC.

Goldstein, A. P., & Sorcher, M. (1974). *Changing supervisory behavior*. New York: Pergamon.

Goldstein, I. L. (1980). Training in work organizations. *Annual Review of Psychology, 31*, 229–272.

Golembiewski, R. T. (1961). Three styles of leadership and their uses. *Personnel, 38*(4), 34–45.

Golembiewski, R. T. (1967). *Organizing men and power*. Chicago: Rand McNally.

Golembiewski, R. T., & Blumberg, A. (1970). *Sensitivity training and the laboratory approach: Reading about concepts and applications*. Itasca, IL: Peacock.

Golembiewski, R. T., & Carrigan, S. B. (1970). The persistence of laboratory-induced changes in organization styles. *Administrative Science Quarterly, 15*, 330–340.

Gomberg, W. (1966). The trouble with democratic management. *Transaction, 3*, 30–55.

Gomez-Mejia, L. R., Page, R. C., & Tornow, W. W. (1982). A comparison of the practical utility of traditional statistical, and hybrid job evaluation approaches. *Academy of Management Journal, 25*, 790–809.

Gomez-Mejia, L. R., Tosi, H., & Hinkin, T. (1987). Managerial control, performance, and executive compensation. *Academy of Management Journal, 30*, 51–70.

Gonzalez, R., & Negandhi, A. (1967). *The United States overseas executive: His orientation and career patterns*. East Lansing: Michigan State University Press.

Good, L. R., & Good, K. C. (1974). Similarity to a group and desire for leadership status. *Psychological Reports, 34*, 759–762.

Goodacre, D. M. (1951). The use of a sociometric test as a predictor of combat unit effectiveness. *Sociometry, 14*, 148–152.

Goodacre, D. M. (1953). Group characteristics of good and poor performing combat units. *Sociometry, 16*, 168–179.

Goodacre, D. M. (1955). Experimental evaluation of training. *Journal of Personnel Administration and Industrial Relations, 2*, 143–149.

Goodacre, D. M. (1963). Stimulating improved management. *Personnel Psychology, 16*, 133–134.

Goodale, J. G. (1973). Effects of personal background and training on work values on the hard-core unemployed. *Journal of Applied Psychology, 57*, 1–9.

Goodale, J. G., & Hall, D. T. (1976). Inheriting a career: The influence of sex, values, and parents. *Journal of Vocational Behavior, 8*, 19–30.

Goodall, K. (1971). Casualty lists from group encounters. *Psychology Today, 5*, 28.

Goodchilds, J. D., & Smith, E. D. (1964). The wit and his group. *Human Relations, 17*, 23–31.

Goode, C. E. (1951). Significant research on leadership. *Personnel, 27*, 342–350.

Goode, W. J. (1960). Norm commitment and conformity to role-status obligations. *American Journal of Sociology, 66*, 246–258.

Goode, W. J., & Fowler, I. (1949). Incentive factors in a low morale plant. *American Sociological Review, 14*, 618–624.

Goodenough, F. L. (1930). Inter-relationships in the behavior of young children. *Child Development, 1*, 29–48.

Goodenough, F. L., & Leahy, A. M. (1927). The effects of certain family relationships upon the development of personality. *Pedagogical Seminary, 34*, 45–71.

Goodman, J. F. B., & Whittingham, T. G. (1969). *Shop stewards in British industry*. London: McGraw-Hill.

Goodman, P. S. (1967). An empirical examination of Elliott Jaques' concept of time span. *Human Relations, 20*, 155–170.

Goodman, P. S. (1969). Hiring, training, and retaining the hard-core. *Industrial Relations, 9*, 54–66.

Goodsell, C. T. (1983). *The case for bureaucracy: A public administration polemic*. Chatham, NJ: Chatham House.

Goodstadt, B. E., & Hjelle, L. A. (1973). Power to the powerless: Locus of control and the use of power. *Journal of Personality and Social Psychology, 27*, 190–196.

Goodstadt, B. E., & Kipnis, D. (1970). Situational influences on the use of power. *Journal of Applied Psychology, 54*, 201–207.

Goodstein, L. D., & Schrader, W. (1963). An empirically-derived managerial key for the California Psychological Inventory. *Journal of Applied Psychology, 47*, 42–45.

Gopala, K. K. M., & Hafeez, A. (1964). A study of supervisors' attitude towards employees and production in relation to some personal factors. *Indian Journal of Applied Psychology, 1*, 78–83.

Gorbachev, M. (1988, December 8). Excerpt from speech to U.N. on major Soviet military cuts. *New York Times*, A16.

Gorden, R. L. (1952). Interaction between attitude and the definitions of the situation in the expression of opinion. *American Sociological Review, 17*, 50–58.

Gordon, C. W., & Adler, L. McK. (1963). *Dimensions of teacher leadership in classroom social systems: Pupil effects on productivity, morale, and compliance*. Los Angeles, CA: University of California, Department of Education.

Gordon, F. E., & Strober, M. H. (1975). *Bringing women into management*. New York: McGraw-Hill.

Gordon, G., & Becker, G. (1964). Organization size and managerial succession: A re-examination. *American Journal of Sociology, 70*, 215–222.

Gordon, G. E., & Rosen, N. (undated). *Critical factors in leadership succession*. Unpublished manuscript.

Gordon, G. E., & Rosen, N. (1981). Critical factors in leadership succession. *Organizational Behavior and Human Performance, 27*, 227–254.

Gordon, L. V. (1952). Personal factors in leadership. *Journal of Social Psychology, 36*, 245–248.

Gordon, L. V. (1963). *Gordon personal inventory: Manual*. New York: Harcourt, Brace & World.

Gordon, L. V. (1966). *Work environment preference schedule—WEPS*. Preliminary manual.

Gordon, L. V. (1970). Measurement of bureaucratic orientation. *Personnel Psychology, 23*, 1–11.

Gordon, L. V. (1975). *Measurement of interpersonal values*. Chicago: Science Research Associates.

Gordon, L. V., & Medland, F. F. (1965a). The cross-group stability of peer ratings of leadership potential. *Personnel Psychology, 18*, 173–177.

Gordon, L. V., & Medland, F. F. (1965b). Leadership aspiration and leadership ability. *Psychological Reports, 17*, 388–390.

Gordon, R. A. (1961). *Business leadership in the large corporation*. Berkeley: University of California Press.

Gordon, T. (1954). Leadership: Shall it reside in the leader or the group? *American Journal of Nursing, 54*, 1087–1088.

Gordon, T. (1955). *Group-centered leadership—a way of releasing the creative power of groups*. Boston: Houghton Mifflin.

Gordon, T. (1977). *Leadership effectiveness training, L.E.T.: The no-lose way to release the productive potential of people*. New York: Wyden Books.

Gorman, A. H. (1963). *The leader in the group: A conceptual framework*. New York: Teachers College, Columbia University, Bureau of Publications.

Gorn, G. J., & Kanungo, R. N. (1980). Job involvement and motivation: Are intrinsically motivated managers more job involved? *Organizational Behavior and Human Performance, 26*, 265–277.

Gorton, R. A. (1976). *School administration: Challenge and opportunity for leadership*. Dubuque, IA: W. C. Brown.

Gottfredson, L. S. (1986). Societal consequences of the g factor in employment. *Journal of Vocational Behavior, 29*, 379–410.

Gottheil, E., & Lauterbach, C. G. (1969). Leader and squad attributes contributing to mutual esteem among squad members. *Journal of Social Psychology, 77*, 69–78.

Gottheil, E., & Vielhaber, D. P. (1966). Interaction of leader and squad attributes related to performance of military squads. *Journal of Social Psychology, 68*, 113–127.

Gough, H. G. (1969). A leadership index on the California psychological inventory. *Journal of Counseling Psychology, 16*, 283–289.

Gough, H. G. (1984). A managerial potential scale for the California Psychology Inventory. *Journal of Applied Psychology, 69*, 233–240.

Gough, H. G. (1987). *Administrator's guide for the California psychological inventory*. Palo Alto, CA: Consulting Psychologists Press.

Gough, H. G. (1989). Testing for leadership with the California psychological inventory. In K. E. Clark & M. B. Clark (Eds.), *Measures of leadership*. West Orange, NJ: Leadership Library of America.

Gough, H. G., McClosky, H., & Meehl, P. (1952). A personality scale for social responsibility. *Journal of Abnormal and Social Psychology, 47*, 73–80.

Gouldner, A. W. (1947). Attitudes of "progressive" trade-union leaders. *American Journal of Sociology, 52*, 389–392.

Gouldner, A. W. (1950). *Studies in leadership*. New York: Harper.

Gouldner, A. W. (1954). *Patterns of industrial bureaucracy*. New York: Free Press. Also: (1965). Yellow Springs, OH: Antioch Press.

Gouldner, A. W. (1957). Cosmopolitans and locals: Toward an analysis of latent social roles. *Administrative Science Quarterly, 2*, 281–306.

Gouldner, A. W. (1960). The norm of reciprocity: A preliminary statement. *American Sociological Review, 25*, 161–178.

Gouldner, A. W. (1965). *Studies in leadership*. London: Russell & Russell.

Gourley, H. V. (1963). Patterns of leadership in decision-making in a selected county. *Dissertation Abstracts, 23*, 3717.

Govindarajan, T. N. (1964). Vocational interests of leaders and nonleaders among adolescent school boys. *Journal of Psychological Research, 8*(3), 124–130.

Gowin, E. B. (1915). *The executive and his control*. New York: Macmillan.

Gowin, E. B. (1918). *The selection and training of the business executive*. New York: Macmillan.

Gowin, E. B. (1919). *Developing executive ability*. New York: Ronald Press.

Grace, H. A. (1954). Conformance and performance. *Journal of Social Psychology, 40*, 333–335.

Graeff, C. L. (1983). The situational leadership theory: A critical view. *Academy of Management Review, 8*, 285–291.

Graen, G. (1976). Role making processes within complex organizations. In M. D. Dunnette (Ed.), *Handbook of industrial and organizational psychology*. Chicago: Rand McNally.

Graen, G. (1978). *Role-making processes of leadership development*. Paper, American Association for the Advancement of Science, Washington, DC.

Graen, G., Alvares, K., Orris, J. B., & Martella, J. A. (1970). Contingency model of leadership effectiveness: Antecedent and evidential results. *Psychological Bulletin, 74*, 285–296.

Graen, G., & Cashman, J. F. (1975). A role-making model of leadership in formal organizations: A developmental approach. In J. G. Hunt & L. L. Larson (Eds.), *Leadership frontiers*. Kent, OH: Kent State University Press.

Graen, G., Cashman, J. F., Ginsburgh, S., & Schiemann, W. (1977). Effects of linking-pin quality upon the quality of working life of lower participants: A longitudinal investigation of the managerial understructure. *Administrative Science Quarterly, 22*, 491–504.

Graen, G., Dansereau, F., & Minami, T. (1972a). Dysfunctional leadership styles. *Organizational Behavior and Human Performance, 7*, 216–236.

Graen, G., Dansereau, F., & Minami, T. (1972b). An empirical test of the man-in-the-middle hypothesis among executives in a hierarchical organization employing a unit-set analysis. *Organizational Behavior and Human Performance, 8*, 262–285.

Graen, G., Dansereau, F., & Minami, T., & Cashman, J. (1973). Leadership behaviors as cues to performance evaluation. *Academy of Management Journal, 16*, 611–623.

Graen, G., & Ginsburgh, S. (1977). Job resignation as a function of role orientation and leader acceptance: A longitudinal investigation of organizational assimilation. *Organizational Behavior and Human Performance, 19*, 1–17.

Graen, G. B., Liden, R. C., & Hoel, W. (1982). Role of leadership in the employee withdrawal process. *Journal of Applied Psychology, 67*, 868–872.

Graen, G., Novak, M. A., & Sommerkamp, P. (1982). The effects of leadership-member exchange and job design on productivity and satisfaction: Testing a dual attachment model. *Organizational Behavior and Human Performance, 30*, 109–131.

Graen, G., Orris, J. B., & Alvares, K. M. (1971). Contingency model of leadership effectiveness: Some experimental results. *Journal of Applied Psychology, 55*, 196–201.

Graen, G., Orris, J., & Johnson, T. (1973). Role assimilation in a complex organization. *Journal of Vocational Behavior, 3*, 395–420.

Graen, G. B., & Scandura, T. A. (1986). Toward a psychology of dyadic organizing. In B. M. Staw & L. L. Cummings (Eds.), *Research in organizational behavior*, Vol. 9. Greenwich, CT: JAI Press.

Graen, G. B., Scandura, T. A., & Graen, M. R. (1986). A field experimental test of the moderating effects of growth need strength on productivity. *Journal of Applied Psychology, 71*, 484–91.

Graen, G., & Schiemann, W. (1978). Leader-member agreement: A vertical dyad linkage approach. *Journal of Applied Psychology, 63*, 206–212.

Graham, E. (1986, March 24). My lover, my colleague: As on the job romance flourishes firms finding adapting touchy but essential. *Wall Street Journal*, Section 4, 25–26.

Graham, F. C. (1982). Job stress in Mississippi cooperative extension service county personnel as related to age, gender, district, tenure, position and perceived leadership behavior of immediate supervisors. *Dissertation Abstracts International, 43*(7A), 2180.

Graham, G. H. (1969). Theories X and Y in the teaching of management. *Collegiate News Views, 22*, 15–18.

Graham, J. W. (1987). The essence of leadership: Fostering follower autonomy, *not* automatic followership. In J. G. Hunt (Ed.), *Emerging leadership vistas*. Elmsford, NY: Pergamon.

Graham, K. R., & Richards, M. D. (1979). Relative performance deterioration, management and strategic change in rail-based holding companies. *Proceedings, Academy of Management*, Atlanta, GA, 108–112.

Graham, W. K. (1968). Description of leader behavior and evaluation of leaders as a function of LPC. *Personnel Psychology, 21*, 457–464.

Graham, W. K. (1969). Comparison of job attitude components across three organizational levels. *Personnel Psychology, 22*, 33–40.

Graham, W. K. (1970). Leader behavior, esteem for least preferred coworker, and group performance. *Experimental Publications System, American Psychological Association*, No. 192A. Also: (1973). *Journal of Social Psychology, 90*, 59–66.

Graham, W. K., & Calendo, J. R. (1969). Personality correlates of supervisory ratings. *Personnel Psychology, 22*, 483–487.

Graham, W. K., & Gleno, T. (1970). Perception of leader behavior and evaluation of leaders across organizational levels. *Experimental Publications System, American Psychological Association*, No. 144A.

Graicunas, V. A. (1937). Relationship in organization. In L. Gulick & L. Urwick (Eds.), *Papers on the science of administration*. New York: Institute of Public Administration.

Granick, D. (1960). *The Red executive*. Garden City, NY: Doubleday.

Granick, D. (1962). Business and class in Europe. In D. Granick (Ed.), *The European executive*. New York: Doubleday.

Grant, D. L. (1932). Leadership in the fraternity. *Journal of Higher Education, 3*, 257–261.

Grant, D. L. (1955). A factor analysis of managers' ratings. *Journal of Applied Psychology, 39*, 283–286.

Grant, D. L. (1964). Situational tests in the assessment of managers. Part II: Contributions to the assessment process. In *The Executive Study Conference; Management games in selection and development*. Princeton, NJ: Educational Testing Service.

Grant, D. L., & Bray, D. W. (1969). Contributions of the interview to assessment of management potential. *Journal of Applied Psychology, 53*, 24–34.

Grant, D. L., Katkovsky, W., & Bray, D. M. (1967). Contributions of projective techniques to assessment of management potential. *Journal of Applied Psychology, 51*, 226–232.

Graumann, C. F. (1986). Changing conceptions of leadership: An introduction. In C. F. Graumann & S. Moscovici (Eds.), *Changing conceptions of leadership*. New York: Springer-Verlag.

Graves, D. (1972). Reported communication ratios and informal status in managerial work groups. *Human Relations, 25*, 159–170.

Graves, D. (1973). The impact of culture upon marginal attitudes, beliefs and behavior in England and France. In D. Graves (Ed.), *Man-*

agement research: A cross cultural perspective. San Francisco: Jossey-Bass.

Graves, L. M. (undated). *Implicit beliefs about supervision: An exploration of their dimensionality and relationship to subordinate satisfaction.* Unpublished manuscript.

Graves, L. M. (1983). Implicit leadership theory: A comparison to two-dimensional leadership theory. *Proceedings, Eastern Academy of Management,* Pittsburgh, PA, 93-95.

Graves, L. M. (1985). Effects of leader persistence and environmental complexity on leadership perceptions: Do implicit beliefs discourage adaption to complex environments? *Group & Organization Studies, 10,* 19-36.

Graves, L. M., & Powell, G. N. (1988). An investigation of sex discrimination in recruiters' evaluations of actual applicants. *Journal of Applied Psychology, 73,* 20-29.

Gray, L. N., Richardson, J. T., & Mayhew, B. H. (1968). Influence attempts and effective power: A re-examination of the unsubstantiated hypothesis. *Sociometry, 31,* 245-258.

Green, C. N. (1972). Relationships among role accuracy, compliance, performance evaluation and satisfaction within managerial dyads. *Academy of Management Journal, 15,* 205-215.

Green, C. N. (1975). The reciprocal nature of influence between leader and subordinate. *Journal of Applied Psychology, 60,* 187-193.

Green, G. H. (1948). Insight and group adjustment. *Journal of Abnormal and Social Psychology, 43,* 49-61.

Green, N. E. (1950). Verbal intelligence and effectiveness of participation in group discussion. *Journal of Educational Psychology, 41,* 440-445.

Green, S. G., & Liden, R. C. (1980). Contextual and attributional influences on control decisions. *Journal of Applied Psychology, 65,* 453-458.

Green, S. G., & Mitchell, T. R. (1979). Attributional processes of leaders in leader-member interactions. *Organizational Behavior and Human Performance, 23,* 429-458.

Green, S. G., & Nebeker, D. M. (1974). *Leader behavior: Autonomous or interactive?* (Tech. Rep. No. 74-62). Seattle: University of Washington, Organizational Research.

Green, S. G., & Nebeker, D. M. (1977). The effects of situational factors and leadership style on leader behavior. *Organizational Behavior and Human Performance, 19,* 368-377.

Green, S. G., Nebeker, D. M., & Boni, M. A. (1974). *Personality and situational effects in leader behavior* (Tech. Rep. No. 74-55). Seattle: University of Washington, Organizational Research.

Greenbaum, L. (1977). Cross-cultural study of the use of elections for selection of the village headman. *Behavioral Science and Research, 12,* 45-49.

Greenberg, J. (1978). Equity, motivation, and the effects of past rewards on allocation decisions. *Personality and Social Psychology Bulletin, 4,* 131-134.

Greenberg, J. (1988). Cultivating an image of justice: Looking fair on the job. *Academy of Management EXECUTIVE, 2*(2), 155-157.

Greenberg, J., & Leventhal, G. S. (1976). Equity and the use of over-reward to motivate performance. *Journal of Personality and Social Psychology, 34,* 179-190.

Greene, C. N. (1972). Relationships among role accuracy, compliance, performance, evaluation, and satisfaction within managerial dyads. *Academy of Management Journal, 15,* 205-215.

Greene, C. N. (1973). A longitudinal analysis of relationships among leader behavior and subordinate performance and satisfaction. *Proceedings, Academy of Management,* Boston, 438-439.

Greene, C. N. (1974). The path-goal theory of leadership: A replication and an analysis of causality. *Proceedings, Academy of Management,* Seattle, 47.

Greene, C. N. (1975). The reciprocal nature of influence between leader and subordinate. *Journal of Applied Psychology, 60,* 187-193.

Greene, C. N. (1976a). A longitudinal investigation of performance-reinforcing behaviors and subordinate satisfaction and performance. *Proceedings, Midwest Academy of Management,* St. Louis, MO, 157-185.

Greene, C. N. (1976b). *Causal connections among cohesion, drive, goal acceptance, and productivity in work groups.* Paper, Academy of Management, Kansas City, MO.

Greene, C. N. (1976c). Disenchantment with leadership research: Some causes, recommendations, and alternative directions. In J. G. Hunt & L. L. Larson (Eds.), *Leadership: The cutting edge.* Carbondale: Southern Illinois University Press.

Greene, C. N. (1979a). Questions of causation in the path-goal theory of leadership. *Academy of Management Journal, 22,* 22-41.

Greene, C. N. (1979b). A longitudinal investigation of modifications to a situational model of leadership effectiveness. *Proceedings, Academy of Management,* Atlanta, GA, 52-58.

Greene, C. N., & Organ, D. W. (1973). An evaluation of casual models linking the received role with job satisfaction. *Administrative Science Quarterly, 18,* 95-103.

Greene, C. N., & Podsakoff, P. M. (1979). *Effects of withdrawal of a performance-contingent reward on supervisory influence and power.* Indiana University, Bloomington, IN, working paper. Also: (1981). *Academy of Management Journal, 24,* 527-542.

Greene, C. N., & Schriesheim, C. (1977). *Causal paths among dimensions of leadership, group drive, and cohesiveness: A longitudinal field investigation.* Paper, Academy of Management, Orlando, FL.

Greene, C. N., & Schriesheim, C. A. (1980). Leader-group interactions: A longitudinal field investigation. *Journal of Applied Psychology, 65,* 50-59.

Greenfield, T. B. (1968). Research on the behavior of educational leaders: Critique of a tradition. *Alberta Journal of Educational Research, 14,* 55-76.

Greenfield, T. B., & Andrews, J. H. M. (1961). Teacher leader behavior. *Alberta Journal of Educational Research, 7,* 92-102.

Greenglass, E. R. (1988). Type A behavior and coping strategies in female and male supervisors. *Applied Psychology: An International Review, 37,* 271-288.

Greenhalgh, L., McKersie, R. B., & Gilkey, R. W. (1986). Rebalancing the workforce at IBM: A case study of redeployment and revitalization. *Organizational Dynamics, 14*(4), 30–47.

Greenly, R. S., & Mapel, E. B. (1943). The development of executive talent. *Personnel, 19,* 628–634.

Greenwald, A. G. (1980). The totalitarian ego: Fabrication and revision of personal history. *American Psychologist, 35,* 603–618.

Greenwood, J. M., & McNamara, W. J. (1967). Interrater reliability in situational tests. *Journal of Applied Psychology, 51,* 101–106.

Greenwood, J. M., & McNamara, W. J. (1969). Leadership styles of structure and consideration and managerial effectiveness. *Personnel Psychology, 22,* 141–152.

Greer, C. R., & Labig, C. E. (1987). Employee reactions to disciplinary action. *Human Relations, 40,* 507–524.

Greer, F. L. (1953). Neighborhood leaders. In D. Courtney et al. (Eds.), *Naval, neighborhood, and national leadership.* Philadelphia: Institute for Research in Human Relations.

Greer, F. L. (1954, May). *Leadership identification and acceptance.* Status Report. Washington, DC: Institute for Research in Human Relations.

Greer, F. L. (1960). *Leader indulgence and group performance.* Washington, DC: General Electric Company. Also: (1961). *Psychological Monographs, 75,* No. 516.

Greer, F. L., Galanter, E. H., & Nordlie, P. G. (1954). Interpersonal knowledge and individual and group effectiveness. *Journal of Abnormal and Social Psychology, 49,* 411–414.

Gregory, R. A. (1986). *Leadership education in institutions of higher education: An assessment.* Greensboro, NC: Center for Creative Leadership.

Greiner, L. E. (1972). Evolution and revolution as organizations grow. *Harvard Business Review, 50*(4), 37–46.

Greiner, L. E., Leitch, D. F., & Barnes, L. B. (1968). The simple complexity of organizational climate in a government agency. In R. Tagiuri & G. H. Litwin (Eds.), *Organizational climate.* Boston: Harvard University, Graduate School of Business Administration.

Greller, M. M. (1978). The nature of subordinate participation in the appraisal interview. *Academy of Management Journal, 21,* 646–658.

Greller, M. M. (1980). Evaluation of feedback sources as a function of role and organizational development. *Journal of Applied Psychology, 65,* 24–27.

Greller, M. M., & Herold, D. M. (1975). Sources of feedback: A preliminary investigation. *Organizational Behavior and Human Performances, 13,* 244–256.

Grey, R. J., & Kipnis, D. (1976). Untangling the performance appraisal dilemma: The influence of perceived organizational context on evaluative processes. *Journal of Applied Psychology, 61,* 329–335.

Griffeth, R. W., Hom, P. W., DeNisi, A., & Kirchner, W. (1980). A multivariate multinational comparison of managerial attitudes. *Proceedings, Academy of Management,* Detroit, 63–67.

Griffin, R. W. (1979). Task design determinants of effective leader behavior. *Academy of Management Review, 4,* 215–224.

Griffin, R. W. (1980). Relationships among individual, task design, and leader behavior variables. *Academy of Management Journal, 23,* 665–683.

Griffitt, W. B. (1968). Anticipated reinforcement and attraction. *Psychonomic Science, 11,* 355.

Griffitt, W. B. (1969). Attitude evoked anticipatory responses and attraction. *Psychonomic Science, 14,* 153–155.

Griggs, D. F. (1985). Police stress and management style. *Dissertation Abstracts International, 46*(4A), 1094.

Groh, D. (1986). The dilemma of unwanted leadership in social movements: The German example before 1914. The G. F. Graumann & S. Moscovici (Eds.), *Changing conception of leadership.* New York: Springer-Verlag.

Gronlund, N. E. (1955a). Acquaintance span and sociometric status. *Sociometry, 18,* 62–68.

Gronlund, N. E. (1955b). Sociometric status and sociometric perception. *Sociometry, 18,* 122–128.

Gronn, P. C. (1983). Talk as work: The accomplishment of school administration. *Administrative Science Quarterly, 28,* 1–21.

Gross, B. M. (1965). What are your organization's objectives? A general systems approach to planning. *Human Relations, 18,* 195–215.

Gross, E. (1961). Dimensions of leadership. *Personnel Journal, 40,* 213–218.

Gross, N., & Harrott, R. E. (1965). *Staff leadership in public schools.* New York: Wiley.

Gross, N., Martin, W. E., & Darley, J. G. (1953). Studies of group behavior: Leadership structures in small organized groups. *Journal of Abnormal and Social Psychology, 48,* 429–432.

Gross, N., Mason, W. S., & McEachern, A. W. (1958). *Explorations in role analysis.* New York: Wiley.

Gross, N., McEachern, A. W., & Mason, W. S. (1966). Role conflict and its resolution. In B. J. Biddle & E. J. Thomas (Eds.), *Role theory: Concepts and research.* New York: Wiley.

Grossack, M. M. (1953). Cues, expectations, and first impressions. *Journal of Psychology, 35,* 245–252.

Grossack, M. M. (1954a). Perceived Negro group belongings and social rejection. *Journal of Psychology, 38,* 127–130.

Grossack, M. M. (1954b). Some effects of cooperation and competition upon small group behavior. *Journal of Abnormal and Social Psychology, 49,* 341–348.

Grosser, D., Polansky, N., & Lippitt, R. (1951). A laboratory study of behavioral contagion. *Human Relations, 4,* 115–142.

Grove, A. S. (1986, April 7). Tapping into the leader who lies within us. *Wall Street Journal, 22,* col. 3.

Gruenfeld, L. W. (1962). A study of the motivation of industrial supervisors. *Personnel Psychology, 15,* 303–314.

Gruenfeld, L. W. (1966). Effects of tuition payment and involvement on benefit from a management development program. *Journal of Applied Psychology, 50,* 396–399.

Gruenfeld, L. W., & Arbuthnot, J. (1968). Field independence, achievement values and the evaluation of a competency related dimension on the least preferred coworker (LPC) measure. *Perceptual and Motor Skills, 27,* 991–1002.

Gruenfeld, L. W., & Foltman, F. F. (1967). Relationship among supervisors' integration, satisfaction, and acceptance of a technological change. *Journal of Applied Psychology, 51,* 74–77.

Gruenfeld, L., & Kassum, S. (1973). Supervisory style and organization effectiveness in a pediatric hospital. *Personnel Psychology, 26,* 531–544.

Gruenfeld, L. W., & MacEachron, A. E. (1975). A cross national study of cognitive style among managers and technicians. *International Journal of Psychology, 10*(1), 27–55.

Gruenfeld, L. W., Rance, D. E., & Weissenberg, P. (1969). The behavior of task oriented (low LPC) and socially oriented (high LPC) leaders under several conditions of social support. *Journal of Social Psychology, 79,* 99–107.

Gruenfeld, L. W., & Weissenberg, P. (1966). Supervisory characteristics and attitudes toward performance appraisals. *Personnel Psychology, 19,* 143–151.

Grunstad, N. L. (1972). *The determination of leader behavior from the interaction of Fiedler's LPC and situation favorableness.* Doctoral dissertation, Ohio State University, Columbus.

Grunwald, W., & Bernthal, W. F. (1983). Controversy in German management: The Harzburg model experience. *Academy of Management Review, 8,* 233–241.

Grusky, O. (1959). Organizational goals and the behavior of informal leaders. *American Journal of Sociology, 65,* 59–67.

Grusky, O. (1961). Corporate size, bureaucratization, and managerial succession. *American Journal of Sociology, 67,* 261–269.

Grusky, O. (1963). Managerial succession and organizational effectiveness. *American Journal of Sociology, 69,* 21–31.

Grusky, O. (1969). Succession with an ally. *Administrative Science Quarterly, 14,* 155–170.

Guest, R. H. (1956). Of time and the foreman. *Personnel, 32,* 478–486.

Guest, R. H. (1957). Job enlargement, a revolution in job design. *Personnel Administration, 20,* 9–16.

Guest, R. H. (1962a). *Organizational change: The effect of successful leadership.* Homewood, IL: Irwin-Dorsey.

Guest, R. H. (1962b). Managerial succession in complex organizations. *American Journal of Sociology, 68,* 47–56.

Guest, R. H., Hersey, P., & Blanchard, K. H. (1977). *Organizational change through effective leadership.* Englewood Cliffs, NJ: Prentice-Hall.

Guetzkow, H. (1951). *Groups, leadership, and men: Research in human relations.* Pittsburgh: Carnegie Press.

Guetzkow, H. (1954). *Organizational development and restrictions in communication.* Pittsburgh: Carnegie Institute of Technology.

Guetzkow, H. (1960). Differentiation of roles in task-oriented groups. In D. Cartwright & A. Zander (Eds.), *Group dynamics.* Evanston, IL: Row, Peterson.

Guetzkow, H. (1961). Organizational leadership in task-oriented groups.

In L. Petrullo & B. M. Bass (Eds.), *Leadership and interpersonal behavior.* New York: Holt, Rinehart & Winston.

Guetzkow, H., & Dill, W. R. (1957). Factors in the organizational development of task-oriented groups. *Sociometry, 20,* 175–204.

Guetzkow, H., Forehand, G. A., & James, B. J. (1962). An evaluation of educational influence on administrative judgment. *Administrative Science Quarterly, 6,* 483–500.

Guetzkow, H., & Gyr, J. (1954). An analysis of conflict in decision-making groups. *Human Relations, 7,* 367–382.

Guetzkow, H., & Kriesberg, M. (1950). *Executive use of the administrative conference.* New York: American Management Association.

Guetzkow, H., & Simon, H. A. (1955). The impact of certain communication nets upon organization and performance in task oriented groups. *Management Science, 31,* 43–49.

Guilford, J. P. (1954). *Psychometric methods.* New York: McGraw-Hill.

Guilford, J. P. (1967). *The nature of human intelligence.* New York: McGraw-Hill.

Guilford, J. P., & Guilford, R. B. (1939). Personality factors D,R,T, and A. *Journal of Abnormal and Social Psychology, 34,* 21–36.

Guilford, J. S. (1952). Temperament traits of executives and supervisors measured by the Guilford Personality Inventories. *Journal of Applied Psychology, 36,* 228–233.

Guion, R. M. (1953). The employee load of first line supervisors. *Personnel Psychology, 6,* 223–244.

Guion, R. M., & Gottier, R. F. (1965). Validity of personality measures in personnel selection. *Personnel Psychology, 18,* 135–164.

Gullahorn, J. T. (1952). Distance and friendship as factors in the gross interaction matrix. *Sociometry, 15,* 123–134.

Gulliksen, H. (1950). *Theory of mental tests.* New York: Wiley.

Gulowsen, J. (1972). A measure of work group harmony. In L. E. Davis & J. C. Taylor (Eds.), *Design of jobs.* Hammondsworth, U.K.: Penguin.

Gump, J. P. (1975). Comparative analysis of black women's and white women's sex-role attitudes. *Journal of Consulting and Clinical Psychology, 43,* 858–863.

Gurin, G., Veroff, J., & Feld, S. (1960). *Americans view their mental health: A nationwide interview study.* New York: Basic Books.

Gurnee, H. (1936). *Elements of social psychology.* New York: Farrar & Rinehart.

Gusfield, J. R. (1966). Functional areas of leadership in social movements. *Sociology Quarterly, 7,* 137–156.

Gustafson, D. P. (1968). The effect of commitment to the task on role differentiation in small unstructured groups. *Academy of Management Journal, 11,* 457–458.

Gustafson, D. P. (1969). The effect of commitment to the task on role differentiation in small unstructured groups. *Dissertation Abstracts, 29,* 2357.

Gustafson, D. P., & Harrell, T. W. (1970). A comparison of role differentiation in several situations. *Organizational Behavior and Human Performance, 5,* 299–312.

Gutek, B. A. (1985). *Sex and the workplace: Impact of sexual behavior and harassment on women, men and organizations.* San Francisco: Jossey-Bass.

Gutek, B. A. (1988). Sex segregation and women at work: A selective review. *Applied Psychology: An International Review, 37*(2), 103–120.

Gutek, B. A., & Morasch, B. (1982). Sex ratios, sex role spillover and sexual harassment of women at work. *Journal of Social Issues, 38*, 55–74.

Gutek, B. A., & Stevens, D. A. (1979). Differential responses of males and females to work situations which evoke sex role stereotypes. *Journal of Vocational Behavior, 14*, 23–32.

Guttentag, M., & Secord, P. F. (1983). *Too many women? The sex ratio question.* Beverly Hills, CA: Sage.

Gutteridge, T. G. (1973). MBA recruitment and utilization: A comparison of two perspectives. *Personnel Journal, 52*(4), 293–303.

Guyot, J. F. (1962). Government bureaucrats are different. *Public Administration Review, 22*, 195–202.

Guzzardi, W. (1965). *The young executives.* New York: New American Library.

Gwertzman, B. (1983, March 17). Reagan reaffirms goal for Lebanon. *New York Times,* A9.

Gyr, J. W. (1972). Is a theory of direct visual perception adequate? *Psychological Bulletin, 77*, 246–261.

Haas, J. A., Porat, A. M., & Vaughan, J. A. (1969). Actual versus ideal time allocations reported by managers: A study of managerial behavior. *Personnel Psychology, 22*, 61–75.

Habbe, S. (1947). Job attitudes of life insurance agents. *Journal of Applied Psychology, 31*, 111–128.

Habbe, S. (1950). *Company programs of executive development.* New York: National Industrial Conference Board.

Habbe, S. (1952). Does communication make a difference? *Management Record, 14*, 414–416, 442–444.

Haccoun, D. M., Haccoun, R. R., & Sallay, G. (1978). Sex differences in the appropriateness of supervisory styles: A nonmanagement view. *Journal of Applied Psychology, 63*, 124–127.

Hackman, J. R. (1969). Toward understanding the role of tasks in behavioral research. *Acta Psychologica, 31*, 97–128.

Hackman, J. R., & Lawler, E. E. (1971). Employee reactions to job characteristics. *Journal of Applied Psychology Monograph, 55*, 259–286.

Hackman, J. R., & Moon, R. G. (1950). Are leaders and followers identified by similar criteria? *American Psychologist, 5*, 312 (Abstract).

Hackman, J. R., & Oldham, G. R. (1975). Development of the job diagnostic survey. *Journal of Applied Psychology, 60*, 159–170.

Hafeez, A. (1971). A study of ascendance-submission among engineering, humanities, and science students, employed engineers and supervisors. *Indian Journal of Social Work, 32*, 95–98.

Hage, J. (1974). *Communication and organizational control: Cybernetics in health and welfare settings.* New York: Wiley.

Hage, J., & Aiken, M. (1967). Relationship of centralization to other structural properties. *Administrative Science Quarterly, 12*, 72–92.

Hage, J., & Aiken, M. (1969). Routine technology, social structure, and organization goals. *Administrative Science Quarterly, 14*, 366–376.

Hagen, E. E. (1962). *On theory of social change.* Homewood, IL: Dorsey.

Haggerty, H. R., Johnson, C. C., & King, S. H. (1954). Evaluation of ratings on combat performance of officers, obtained by mail. *American Psychologist, 9*, 388 (Abstract).

Hahn, C. P. (1959). *Collection of data for utilization of situational problems for training in those leadership behaviors essential for effective performance as a junior officer.* Washington, DC: American Institute for Research.

Hahn, C. P., & Trittipoe, T. G. (1961). *Situational problems for leadership training: III. Review for petty officers of leadership research.* Washington, DC: Naval Contract Report, Institute for Research.

Haiman, F. S. (1951). *Group leadership and democratic action.* Boston: Houghton Mifflin.

Hain, T. (1972). *Determinants of changes in supervisory styles: An empirical test.* Paper, Midwest Academy of Management, Notre Dame, IN.

Hain, T. (1974). *The development of a behavioral forecasting index* (Tech. Rep.). Detroit: General Motors. Unpublished manuscript.

Hain, T., & Tubbs, S. (1974). *Organizational development: The role of communication in diagnosis, change and evaluation.* Paper, International Communication Association.

Hain, T., & Widgery, R. (1973). *Organizational diagnosis: The significant role of communication.* Paper, International Communication Association.

Haire, M. (1948). Some problems of industrial training. *Journal of Social Issues, 4*, 41–47.

Haire, M., Ghiselli, E. E., & Porter, L. W. (1963). Cultural patterns in the role of the manager. *Industrial Relations, 2*, 95–117.

Haire, M., Ghiselli, E. E., & Porter, L. W. (1966). *Managerial thinking: An international study.* New York: Wiley.

Haislip, O. L., Jr. (1986). C4 = effective leadership. *Supervision, 48*(4), 14–16.

Hakel, M. D. (1976). Some questions and comments about applied learning. *Personnel Psychology, 29*, 361–369.

Hakel, M. D., Hollman, D., & Dunnette, M. D. (1968). Stability and change in the social status of occupations over 21 and 42 year periods. *Personnel and Guidance Journal, 46*, 762–764.

Halal, W. E. (1974). Toward a general theory of leadership. *Human Relations, 27*, 401–416.

Halberstam, D. (1983). *The best and the brightest.* New York: Penguin.

Haley, M. J. (1983). Relationship between internal-external locus of control beliefs, self-monitoring and leadership style adaptability. *Dissertation Abstracts International, 44*(11B), 3563.

Hall, A. (1986, March 31). Developments to watch. *Business Week,* 73.

Hall, B. A. (1975). *The effect of sex of the leader on the development of assertiveness in women undergoing group assertive training.* Doctoral dissertation, University of Missouri, Kansas City.

Hall, D. T. (1972). A model of coping with role conflict: The role behavior of college educated women. *Administrative Science Quarterly, 17*, 471–486.

Hall, D. T. (1986). Dilemmas in linking succession planning to individual executive learning. *Human Resource Management, 25*, 235–265.

Hall, D. T., Bowen, D. D., Lewicki, R. J., & Hall, F. F. (1975). *Experiences in management and organizational behavior.* Chicago: St. Clair Press.

Hall, D. T., & Lawler, E. E. (1970). Job characteristics and pressures and the organizational integration of professionals. *Administrative Science Quarterly, 15,* 271–281.

Hall, D. T., & Lawler, E. E. (1971). Job pressures and research performance. *American Scientist, 59*(1), 64–73.

Hall, D. T., & Mansfield, R. (1971). Organizational and individual response to external stress. *Administrative Science Quarterly, 16,* 533–547.

Hall, D. T., & Schneider, B. (1972). Correlates of organizational identification as a function of career pattern and organizational type. *Administrative Science Quarterly, 17,* 340–350.

Hall, D. T., Schneider, B., & Nygren, H. T. (1970). Personal factors in organizational identification. *Administrative Science Quarterly, 15,* 176–190.

Hall, E. T. (1976). *Beyond culture.* New York: Doubleday.

Hall, E. T., & Hall, M. R. (1987). *Hidden differences: Doing business with the Japanese.* New York: Doubleday.

Hall, F. S., & Hall, D. T. (1976). Effects of job incumbents' race and sex on evaluations of managerial performance. *Academy of Management Journal, 19,* 476–481.

Hall, H. E. (1953). *Empathy, leadership and art.* Master's thesis, Louisiana State University, Baton Rouge.

Hall, J. (1976). To achieve or not: The manager's choice. *California Management Review, 18,* 5–18.

Hall, J. (1979). Student preference for leadership styles. *Assistant Librarian, 72*(6), 86–88.

Hall, J., & Donnell, S. M. (1979). Managerial achievement: The personal side of behavioral theory. *Human Relations, 32,* 77–101.

Hall, J., & Williams, M. S. (1966). A comparison of decision-making performances in established and ad hoc groups. *Journal of Personality and Social Psychology, 3,* 214–222.

Hall, J. A., & Halberstadt, A. G. (1981). Sex roles and nonverbal communication skills. *Sex Roles, 7,* 273–287.

Hall, L. K. (1983). *Charisma: A study of personality characteristics of charismatic leaders.* Doctoral dissertation, University of Georgia, Athens.

Hall, P., & Locke, H. W. (1938). *Incentives and contentment: A study made in a British factory.* London: Pitman.

Hall, R. H. (1962). Intraorganizational structural variation: Application of bureaucratic model. *Administrative Science Quarterly, 7,* 295–308.

Hall, R. H. (1977). *Organizations, structure and process* (2nd ed.). Englewood Cliffs, NJ: Prentice-Hall.

Hall, R. L. (1955). Social influence on the aircraft commander's role. *American Sociological Review, 20,* 292–299.

Hall, R. L. (1956). *Predicting bomber crew performance from the aircraft commander's role.* San Antonio, TX: Lackland Air Force Base, Crew Research Laboratory.

Hall, R. L. (1957). Group performance under feedback that confounds responses of group members. *Sociometry, 20,* 297–305.

Hall, R. L. (1985). The Indian context. *Public Relations Journal, 41*(2), 13–15.

Halperin, K., Synder, C. R., Shenkel, R. J., & Houston, B. K. (1976). Effect of source status and message favorability on acceptance of personality feedback. *Journal of Applied Psychology, 61,* 85–88.

Halpin, A. W. (1953). *Studied in air crew composition. X. The combat leader behavior of B-29 aircraft commanders.* Columbus: Ohio State University, Personnel Research Board.

Halpin, A. W. (1954). The leadership behavior and combat performance of airplane commanders. *Journal of Abnormal and Social Psychology, 49,* 19–22.

Halpin, A. W. (1955a). The leadership ideology of aircraft commanders. *Journal of Applied Psychology, 39,* 82–84.

Halpin, A. W. (1955b). The leader behavior and leadership ideology of educational administrators and aircraft commanders. *Harvard Educational Review, 25,* 18–32.

Halpin, A. W. (1956a). *The leader behavior of school superintendents.* Columbus: Ohio State University, College of Education.

Halpin, A. W. (1956b). The behavior of leaders. *Educational Leadership, 14,* 172–176.

Halpin, A. W. (1957a). The leader behavior and effectiveness of aircraft commanders. In R. M. Stogdill & A. E. Coons (Eds.), *Leader behavior: Its description and measurement.* Columbus: Ohio State University, Bureau of Business Research.

Halpin, A. W. (1957b). *Manual for the leader behavior description questionnaire.* Columbus: Ohio State University, Bureau of Business Research.

Halpin, A. W. (1957c). The observed leader behavior and ideal leader behavior of aircraft commanders and school superintendents. In R. M. Stogdill & A. E. Coons (Eds.), *Leader behavior: Its description and measurement.* Columbus: Ohio State University, Bureau of Business Research.

Halpin, A. W. (1966). *Theory and research in administration.* New York: Macmillan.

Halpin, A. W., & Croft, D. B. (1962). *The organizational climate of schools.* St. Louis, MO: Washington University.

Halpin, A. W., & Winer, B. J. (1957). A factorial study of the leader behavior descriptions. In R. M. Stogdill & A. E. Coons (Eds.), *Leader behavior: Its description and measurement.* Columbus: Ohio State University, Bureau of Business Research.

Halsey, G. D. (1938). *How to be a leader.* New York: Harper.

Hambleton, R. K., Blanchard, K. H., & Hersey, P. (1977). *Maturity scale—self rating form.* San Diego, CA: Learning Resources.

Hambleton, R. K., & Gumpert, R. (1982). The validity of Hersey and Blanchard's theory of leader effectiveness. *Group & Organization Studies, 7,* 225–242.

Hamblin, R. L. (1958a). Group integration during a crisis. *Human Relations, 11,* 67–76.

Hamblin, R. L. (1958b). Leadership and crises. *Sociometry, 21,* 322–335.

Hamblin, R. L., Miller, K., & Wiggins, J. A. (1961). Group morale and competence of the leader. *Sociometry, 24,* 295–311.

Hambrick, D. C. (1981). Environment, strategy, and power within top management teams. *Administrative Science Quarterly, 26,* 255–276.

Hambrick, D. C., & Mason, P. A. (1984). Upper echelons: The organization as a reflection of its top managers. *Academy of Management Review, 9,* 193–206.

Hammer, S. (1978, September). When women have power over women. *Ms. Magazine, 7*(3), 49.

Hammer, T. H., & Dachler, P. (1973). *The process of supervision in the context of motivation theory* (Tech. Rep. No. 3). College Park, MD: University of Maryland, Department of Psychology.

Hammer, T. H., & Turk, J. (1985). *Organizational determinants of leader behavior and authority.* Paper, Academy of Management, San Diego. Also: (1987). *Journal of Applied Psychology, 71,* 674–682.

Hammer, W. C., Kim, J. S., Baird, L., & Bigoness, W. J. (1974). Race and sex as determinants of ratings by potential employers in a simulated work-sampling task. *Journal of Applied Psychology, 59,* 705–711.

Hammerschlag, C. A., & Astrachan, B. M. (1971). The Kennedy airport snow-in: An inquiry into intergroup phenomena. *Psychosomatics, 34,* 301–308.

Hampden-Turner, C. (1983). *Gentlemen and tradesmen.* Boston: Routledge & Kegan Paul.

Hanawalt, N. G., Hamilton, C. E., & Morris, M. L. (1943). Level of aspiration in college leaders and nonleaders. *Journal of Abnormal and Social Psychology, 38,* 545–548.

Hanawalt, N. G., & Richardson, H. M. (1944). Leadership as related to the Bernreuter personality measures: IV. An item analysis of responses of adult leaders and non-leaders. *Journal of Applied Psychology, 28,* 397–411.

Hanawalt, N. G., Richardson, H. M., & Hamilton, R. J. (1943). Leadership as related to Bernreuter personality measures: II. An item analysis of responses of college leaders and non-leaders. *Journal of Social Psychology, 17,* 251–267.

Hanaway, J. (1985). Managerial behavior, uncertainty and hierarchy. *Human Relations, 38,* 1085–1100.

Hand, H. H., & Slocum, J. W. (1970). Human relations training for middle management: A field experiment. *Academy of Management Journal, 13,* 403–410.

Hand, H. H., & Slocum, J. W. (1972). A longitudinal study of the effects of a human relations training program on managerial effectiveness. *Journal of Applied Psychology, 56,* 412–417.

Handy, C. B. (1976). *Understanding organizations.* Baltimore: Penguin Books.

Handyside, J. D., & Duncan, D. C. (1954). Four years later: A follow-up of an experiment in selecting supervisors. *Occupational Psychology, 28,* 9–23.

Hanfmann, E. (1935). Social structure of a group of kindergarten children. *American Journal of Orthopsychiatry, 5,* 407–410.

Hankins, F. H. (1931). Fraternal orders. In E.R.A. Seligman (Ed.), *Encyclopedia of the social sciences.* New York: Macmillan.

Hanna, N. E. (1973). *Organizational variables and innovativeness in collegiate nursing institutions: A comparative study.* Doctoral dissertation, University of Michigan, Ann Arbor.

Hannah, M. E. (1974). Situational aspects of leadership in a high school. *Dissertation Abstracts International, 35,* 2990.

Hansen, J. C. (1988). Changing interests of women: Myth or reality? *Applied Psychology: An International Review, 37,* 133–150.

Hansen, P. (1974). *Sex differences in supervision.* Paper, American Psychological Association, New Orleans.

Hanson, P. G., Morton, R. B., & Rothaus, P. (1963). The fate of role stereotypes in two performance appraisal situations. *Personnel Psychology, 16,* 269–280.

Hansson, R. O., & Fiedler, F. E. (1973). Perceived similarity, personality, and attraction to large organizations. *Journal of Applied Social Psychology, 3,* 258–266.

Harbison, F., & Myers, C. (1959). *Management in the industrial world.* New York: McGraw-Hill.

Harbron, J. D. (1965). The dilemma of an elite group: The industrialist in Latin America. *Inter-American Economic Affairs, 19,* 43–62.

Hardesty, D. L., & Jones, W. S. (1968). Characteristics of judged high potential management personnel—the operations of an industrial assessment center. *Personnel Psychology, 21,* 85–98.

Harding, L. W. (1949). Twenty-one varieties of educational leadership. *Educational Leadership, 6,* 299–302.

Hardy, R. C. (1971). Effect of leadership style on the performance of small classroom groups: A test of the contingency model. *Journal of Personality and Social Psychology, 19,* 367–374.

Hardy, R. C. (1972). A development study of relationships between birth order and leadership style for two distinctly different American groups. *Journal of Social Psychology, 87,* 147–148.

Hardy, R. C. (1975). A test of poor leader-member relations cells of the contingency model on elementary school children. *Child Development, 45,* 958–964.

Hardy, R. C., & Bohren, J. F. (1975). The effect of experience on teacher effectiveness: A test of the contingency model. *Journal of Psychology, 89,* 159–163.

Hardy, R. C., Sack, S., & Harpine, F. (1973). An experimental test of the contingency model on small classroom groups. *Journal of Psychology, 85,* 3–16.

Hare, A. P. (1952). A study of interaction and consensus in different sized groups. *American Sociological Review, 17,* 261–267.

Hare, A. P. (1953). Small group discussions with participatory and supervisory leadership. *Journal of Abnormal and Social Psychology, 48,* 273–275.

Hare, A. P. (1957). Situational differences in leader behavior. *Journal of Abnormal and Social Psychology, 55,* 132–135.

Hare, A. P. (1962). *Handbook of small group research.* New York: Free Press.

Hare, A. P. (1972). Bibliography of small group research 1959–1969. *Sociometry, 35,* 1–150.

Hare, A. P., & Bales, R. F. (1963). Seating position and small group interaction. *Sociometry, 26,* 480–486.

Hare, A. P., Borgatta, E. F., & Bales, R. F. (1955). *Small groups: Studies in social interaction.* New York: Knopf.

Hare, A. P., & Hare, R. T. (1948). Family friendship within the community. *Sociometry, 11*, 329–334.

Hargrove, E. C. (1987). *Jimmy Carter as President*. Paper, Conference on the Presidency, Princeton University, Princeton, NJ.

Hargrove, E. (1988). Two conceptions of institutional leadership. In B. Jones (Ed.), *Political leadership from political science perspectives*. Lawrence: University of Kansas Press.

Hargrove, E. C., & Nelson, M. (1984). *Presidents, politics, and policy*. Baltimore: Johns Hopkins University Press.

Hariton, T. (1951). *Conditions influencing the effects of training foremen in human relations principles*. Doctoral dissertation, University of Michigan, Ann Arbor.

Harlan, A. (1976). *Psychological coping patterns of male and female managers*. Paper, Academy of Management, Kansas City, MO.

Harlow, R. F. (1957). *Social science in public relations: A survey and analysis of social science literature bearing upon the practice of public relations*. New York: Harper.

Harman, D. (1984). Lessons learned about emergency preparedness. *Public Management, 66*(3), 5–8.

Harmon, H. H. (1967). *Modern factor analysis*. Chicago: University of Chicago Press.

Harmon, H. H., & Jones, W. H. (1966). Factor analysis by minimizing residuals (Minres). *Psychometrika, 31*, 351–368.

Harnquist, K. (1956). *Adjustment: Leadership and group relations in a military training situation*. Stockholm: Almquist & Wiksell.

Harper, S. F., & Gordon, O. H. (1958). *Executive development: A bibliographic review*. Chicago: University of Chicago, Industrial Relations Center.

Harragan, M. L. (1977). *Games mother never taught you*. New York: Rawson.

Harrell, A. M., & Stahl, M. J. (1981). A behavioral decision theory approach for measuring McClelland's trichotomy of needs. *Journal of Applied Psychology, 66*, 242–244.

Harrell, T. W. (1961). *Managers' performance and personality*. Cincinnati, OH: South-Western.

Harrell, T. W. (1966). *Personality differences between extreme performers during a fourth discussion session* (Tech. Rep. No. 12). Stanford, CA: Stanford University, Graduate School of Business.

Harrell, T. W. (1969). The personality of high earning MBA's in big business. *Personnel Psychology, 22*, 457–463.

Harrell, T. W. (1983). *The high earners scale at 20 years out* (Research Paper No. 689). Stanford, CA: Stanford University, Graduate School of Business.

Harrell, T. W., & Alpert, B. (1979). The need for autonomy among managers. *Academy of Management Review, 4*, 259–267.

Harrell, T. W., Burnham, L. E., Hunt, R. S., & Lee, H. E. (1964). *Reliability and intercorrelations for thirteen leadership criteria* (Tech. Rep. No. 8). Stanford, CA: Stanford University, Graduate School of Business.

Harrell, T. W., Burnham, L. E., & Lee, H. E. (1963). *Correlations between seven leadership criteria* (Tech. Rep. No. 4). Stanford, CA: Stanford University, Graduate School of Business.

Harrell, T. W., & Gustafson, D. P. (1966). *Division groups with a trend away from role differentiation* (Tech. Rep. No. 13). Stanford, CA: Stanford University, Graduate School of Business.

Harrell, T. W., & Harrell, M. S. (1975). *A scale for high earners* (ONR Tech. Rep. No. 7). Stanford, CA: Stanford University, Graduate School of Business.

Harrell, T. W., & Harrell, M. S. (1984). *Stanford MBA careers: A 20 year longitudinal study*. Stanford, CA: Stanford University, Graduate School of Business.

Harrell, T. W., & Lee, H. E. (1964). *An investigation of the product moment intercorrelations among small group leadership criteria* (Tech. Rep. No. 6). Stanford, CA: Stanford University, Graduate School of Business.

Harrigan, K. R. (1981). Numbers and positions of women elected to corporate boards. *Academy of Management Journal, 24*, 619–625.

Harris, B. M. (1964). Leadership prediction as related to measures of personal characteristics. *Personnel Administration, 27*, 31–34.

Harris, C. R., & Heise, R. C. (1964). Tasks, not traits—the key to better performance review. *Personnel, 41*, 60–64.

Harris, E. F., & Fleishman, E. A. (1955). Human relations training and the stability of leadership patterns. *Journal of Applied Psychology, 39*, 20–25.

Harris, H. (1949). *The group approach to leadership testing*. London: Routledge & Kegan Paul.

Harris, K. W. (1968). *Change in role requirements of superintendents over the last quarter-century*. Doctoral dissertation, Ohio State University, Columbus.

Harris, L. (1987). *Inside America*. New York: Vintage Press.

Harris, M. M., & Schaubroeck, J. (1988). A meta-analysis of self-superior, self-peer, and peer-supervisor ratings. *Personnel Journal, 41*, 43–62.

Harris, R. (1987). *Excellence in command*. Conference on military leadership: Traditions and future trends. U.S. Naval Academy, Annapolis, MD.

Harrison, A. M. (1978). *The operational definition of managerial roles*. Doctoral dissertation, University of Cape Town, South Africa.

Harrison, C. W., Rawls, J. R., & Rawls, D. J. (1971). Differences between leaders and nonleaders in six-to-eleven-year-old children. *Journal of Social Psychology, 84*, 269–272.

Harrison, E. L. (1982). Training supervisors to discipline effectively. *Training and Development Journal, 36*(11), 111–113.

Harrison, R. (1962). The impact of the laboratory on perceptions of others by the experimental group. In C. Argyris (Ed.), *Interpersonal competence and organizational effectiveness*. Homewood, IL: Dorsey.

Harrison, R. (1966). Cognitive change and participation in a sensitivity-training laboratory. *Journal of Consulting Psychology, 30*, 517–520.

Harrison, R. (1970). Choosing the depth of organizational intervention. *Journal of Applied Behavioral Science, 6*, 181–202.

Harrison, R. (1984). Leadership and strategy for a new age. In J. D. Adams (Ed.), *Transforming work*. Alexandria, VA: Miles River Press.

Harrison, R., & Lubin, B. (1965a). Personal style, group composition, and learning. Part I. *Journal of Applied Behavioral Science, 1,* 286–294.

Harrison, R., & Lubin, B. (1965b). Personal style, group composition, and learning. Part II. *Journal of Applied Behavioral Science, 1,* 294–301.

Harrison, T. M. (1985). Communication and participative decision making: An exploratory study. *Personnel Psychology, 38,* 93–116.

Harrow, M., Astrachan, B. M., Tucker, G. J., Klein, E. B., & Miller, J. C. (1971). The T-group and study group laboratory experience. *Journal of Social Psychology, 85,* 225–237.

Harsanyi, J. C. (1962a). Measurement of social power, opportunity costs, and the theory of two-person bargaining games. *Behavioral Science, 7,* 67–80.

Harsanyi, J. C. (1962b). Measurement of social power in n-person reciprocal power situations. *Behavioral Science, 7,* 81–91.

Hart, L. B. (1975). Training women to become effective leaders: A case study. *Dissertation Abstracts International, 35,* 6977.

Hart, P., & Mellons, J. (1970). Management youth and company growth: A correlation? *Management Decision, 4,* 50–53.

Hartley, R. E. (1960a). Relationships between perceived values and acceptance of a new reference group. *Journal of Social Psychology, 51,* 181–190.

Hartley, R. E. (1960b). Norm compatibility, norm preference, and the acceptance of new reference groups. *Journal of Social Psychology, 52,* 87–95.

Hartmann, H. (1970). Codetermination in West Germany. *Industrial Relations, 9,* 137–147.

Hartson, L. D. (1911). The psychology of the club: A study in social psychology. *Pedagogical Seminary, 18,* 353–414.

Harvey, E. (1968). Technology and the structure of organizations. *American Sociological Review, 33,* 247–259.

Harvey, O. J. (1953). An experimental approach to the study of status relations in informal groups. *American Sociological Review, 18,* 357–367.

Harvey, O. J. (1960). Reciprocal influence of the group and three types of leaders in an unstructured situation. *Sociometry, 23,* 57–68.

Harvey, O. J. (1963). *Motivation and social interaction.* New York: Ronald Press.

Harvey, O. J., & Beverly, G. D. (1961). Some personality correlates of concept change through role playing. *Journal of Abnormal and Social Psychology, 63,* 125–130.

Harvey, O. J., & Consalvi, C. (1960). Status and conformity to pressure in informal groups. *Journal of Abnormal and Social Psychology, 60,* 182–187.

Harvey, O. J., Hunt, D. E., & Schroder, H. M. (1961). *Conceptual systems and personality organization.* New York: Wiley.

Harville, D. L. (1969). Early identification of potential leaders. *Journal of College Student Personnel, 10,* 333–335.

Hassett J., & Dukes, S. (1986). The new employee trainer: A floppy disk. *Psychology Today, 20*(9), 30–32.

Hastings, E. W. (1926). Is pupil training for leadership a worthwhile feature? *American Physical Education Review, 31,* 1080–1085.

Hastings, R. E. (1964). Leadership in university research teams. *Dissertation Abstracts, 24,* 2723.

Hastorf, A. H. (1965). The reinforcement of individual actions in a group situation. In L. Krasner & L. P. Ullmann (Eds.), *Research in behavior modification.* New York: Holt, Rinehart & Winston.

Hastorf, A. H., Schneider, D., & Polefka, J. (1969). *Person perception.* Reading, MA: Addison-Wesley.

Hatch, M. J. (1987). Physical barriers, task characteristics, and interaction activity in research and development firms. *Administrative Science Quarterly, 32,* 387–399.

Hatch, R. S. (1962). *An evaluation of a forced-choice differential accuracy approach to the measurement of supervisory empathy.* Englewood Cliffs, NJ: Prentice-Hall.

Hater, J. J., & Bass, B. M. (1988). Supervisors' evaluations and subordinates' perceptions of transformational and transactional leadership. *Journal of Applied Psychology, 73,* 695–702.

Hathaway, B. (1984, September). Question value of IQ tests. *APA Monitor,* 10.

Hauser, W. L. (1984). Careerism vs. professionalism in the military. *Armed Forces and Society, 10,* 449–463.

Hausman, H. J., & Strupp, H. H. (1955). Non-technical factors in supervisors' ratings of job performance. *Personnel Psychology, 8,* 201–217.

Hausser, D., Blaiwes, A. S., Weller, D., & Spencer, G. (undated). *Applications of computer-assisted instruction to interpersonal skill training* (Tech. Rep. 74-C-0100-1). Orlando, FL: NAVTRAEQUIPCEN.

Hausser, D., & Spencer, G. (1975). *Application of computer-assisted instruction to interpersonal skill training.* Ann Arbor, MI: Institute for Social Research.

Havighurst, R. J., & Russell, M. (1945). Promotion in the armed services in relation to school attainment and social status. *School Review, 53,* 202–211.

Havighurst, R. J., & Taba, H. (1949). *Adolescent character and personality.* New York: Wiley.

Havron, M. D., & McGrath, J. E. (1961). The contribution of the leader to the effectiveness of small military groups. In L. Petrullo & B. M. Bass (Eds.), *Leadership and interpersonal behavior.* New York: Holt, Rinehart & Winston.

Hawkins, C. H. (1962). A study of factors mediating a relationship between leader rating behavior and group productivity. *Dissertation Abstracts, 23,* 733.

Hay, R., & Gray, E. (1974). Social responsibilities of business managers. *Academy of Management Journal, 17,* 135–143.

Hayashida, C. T. (1976). The isolation of leadership: A case study of precarious religious organization. *Review of Religious Research, 17,* 141–152.

Hayden, S. J. (1955). Getting better results from post-appraisal interviews. *Personnel, 31,* 541–550.

Hayes, R. H. (1981). Why Japanese factories work. *Harvard Business Review, 59*(4), 56–66.

Haynes, P. D. (1972). *A comparison of perceived organizational characteristics between selected work stoppage and non-work stoppage school districts in the state of Michigan.* Doctoral dissertation, Western Michigan University, Kalamazoo.

Hays, S., & Thomas, W. N. (1967). *Taking command.* Harrisburg, PA: Stackpole.

Haythorn, W. W. (1952). *The influence of individual group members on the behavior of coworkers and on the characteristics of groups.* Doctoral dissertation, University of Rochester, Rochester, NY.

Haythorn, W. W. (1953). The influence of individual members on the characteristics of small groups. *Journal of Abnormal and Social Psychology, 48,* 276–284.

Haythorn, W. W. (1954a). *Relationships between sociometric measures and performance in medium bomber crews in combat* (AFPTRC-TR-54-101). San Antonio, TX: Lackland Air Force Base Crew Research Laboratory, AF Personnel & Training Reserve Center.

Haythorn, W. W. (1954b). *An analysis of role distribution in B-29 crews* (AFPTRC-TR-54-104). San Antonio, TX: Lackland Air Force Base Crew Research Laboratory, AF Personnel & Training Reserve Center.

Haythorn, W. W. (1956). The effects of varying combinations of authoritarian and equalitarian leaders and followers. *Journal of Abnormal and Social Psychology, 53,* 210–219.

Haythorn, W. W. (1985). *Requirements for a sequential, progressive development system.* Paper, American Psychological Association, Los Angeles.

Haythorn, W. W., Couch, A., Haefner, D., Langham, P., & Carter, L. F. (1956a). The behavior of authoritarian and equalitarian personalities in groups. *Human Relations, 9,* 57–74.

Haythorn, W. W., Couch, A., Haefner, D., Langham, P., & Carter, L. F. (1956b). The effects of varying combinations of authoritarian and equalitarian leaders and followers. *Journal of Abnormal and Social Psychology, 53,* 210–219.

Hazel, J. T., Madden, J. M., & Christal, R. E. (1964). Agreement between worker-supervisor descriptions of the worker's job. *Journal of Industrial Psychology, 2,* 71–79.

Healy, A. K. (1962). Effects of changing social structure through child leaders. *Dissertation Abstracts, 23,* 2233.

Healy, J. H. (1956). *Executive coordination and control.* Columbus: Ohio State University, Bureau of Business Research Monograph.

Hearn, G. (1957). Leadership and the spatial factor in small groups. *Journal of Abnormal and Social Psychology, 54,* 269–273.

Heath, C. W. (1945). *What people are: A study of normal young men.* Cambridge, MA: Harvard University Press.

Heath, C. W., & Gregory, L. W. (1946). What it takes to make an officer. *Infantry Journal, 58,* 44–45.

Heath, M. R., & Bekker, S. J. (1986). *Identification of opinion leaders in public affairs educational matters and family planning in the township of Atteridgeville* (Research Finding Comm N-142). Pretoria, South Africa: Human Sciences Research Council.

Heclo, H. (1974). *Modern social politics in Britain and Sweden.* New Haven: Yale University Press.

Hedberg, B. (1981). How organizations learn and unlearn. In P. C. Nystrom and W. H. Starbuck (Eds.), *Handbook of organizational design,* Vol. 1. London: Oxford University Press.

Hedberg, B. L. T., Nystrom, P. C., & Starbuck, W. H. (1976). Camping on seesaws: Prescriptions for a self-designing organization. *Administrative Science Quarterly, 21,* 41–65.

Hefty, J. C. (1972). The relationships between the value orientations, leader behavior, and effectiveness of secondary school principals in selected middle sized school systems. *Dissertation Abstracts International, 32,* 4286–4287.

Hegarty, W. H. (undated). *Using subordinate ratings to elicit behavioral changes in supervisors.* Morgantown: West Virginia University.

Hegel, G. F. (1830/1971). Philosophy of mind. (Trans. W. Wallace.) *Encyclopedia of the philosophical sciences.* Oxford: Clarendon Press.

Heider, F. (1958). *The psychology of interpersonal relations.* New York: Wiley.

Heifetz, R. L., & Sinder, R. M. (1987). Political leadership: Managing the public's problem solving. In R. B. Reich (Ed.), *The power of public ideas.* New York: Ballinger.

Heilman, M. E., Cage, J. H., Hornstein, H. A., & Herschlag, J. K. (1984). Reactions to prescribed leader behavior as a function of role perspective: The case of the Vroom-Yetton model. *Journal of Applied Psychology, 69,* 50–60.

Heilman, M. E., & Guzzo, R. A. (1978). The perceived cause of work success as a mediator of sex discrimination in organizations. *Organizational Behavior and Human Performance, 21,* 346–357.

Heilman, M. E., Hornstein, H. A., Cage, J. H., & Herschlag, J. K. (1984). Reactions to prescribed leader behavior as a function of role perspective: The case of the Vroom-Yetton model. *Journal of Applied Psychology, 69,* 50–60.

Heilman, M. E., & Saruwatari, L. R. (1979). When beauty is beastly: The effects of appearances and sex on evaluations of job applicants for managerial and nonmanagerial jobs. *Organizational Behavior and Human Performance, 23,* 360–372.

Heinen, J. S., & Jacobsen, E. (1976). A model of task group development in complex organizations and a strategy of implementation. *Academy of Management Review, 1,* 98–111.

Heinen, J. S., McGlauchin, D., Legeros, C., & Freeman, J. (1975). Developing the woman manager. *Personnel Journal, 54,* 282–286.

Heinicke, C., & Bales, R. F. (1953). Developmental trends in the structure of small groups. *Sociometry, 16,* 7–38.

Heintz, R. K., & Preston, M. G. (1948). The dependence of the effect of the group on the individual upon the character of the leadership. *American Psychologist, 3,* 269–270 (Abstract).

Heise, G. A., & Miller, G. A. (1951). Problem-solving by small groups using various communication nets. *Journal of Abnormal and Social Psychology, 46,* 327–335.

Heisler, W. J. (1974). A performance correlate of personal control beliefs in an organizational context. *Journal of Applied Psychology, 59,* 504–506.

Heiss, J. S. (1963). The dyad views the newcomer: A study of perception. *Human Relations, 16,* 241–248.

Heizer, J. H. (1969). A study of significant aspects of manager behavior. *Academy of Management Journal, 3*, 386–387.

Heizer, J. H. (1972). Manager action. *Personnel Psychology, 3*, 511–521.

Helfrich, M. L., & Schwirian, K. P. (1968). The American business-man—entrepreneur or bureaucrat? *Bulletin of Business Research, 1*, 6–9.

Hellebrandt, E. T., & Stinson, J. E. (1971). The effects of T-group training on business game results. *Journal of Applied Psychology, 77*, 271–272.

Heller, F. A. (1969a). *Managerial decision making*. London: Human Resources Center, Tavistock Institute of Human Relations.

Heller, F. A. (1969b). The role of business management in relation to economic development. *International Journal of Comparative Sociology, 10*, 292–298.

Heller, F. A. (1972a). *Managerial decision making: A study of leadership styles and power sharing among senior managers*. New York: Harper & Row.

Heller, F. A. (1972b). Research on five styles of managerial decision making. *International Student Management Organization, 11*, 85–104.

Heller, F. A. (1976). The decision process: An analysis of power-sharing at senior organizational levels. In R. Dubin (Ed.), *Handbook of work, organization, and society*. Chicago: Rand McNally.

Heller, F. A., & Clark, A. W. (1976). Personnel and human resources development. *Annual Review of Psychology, 27*, 405–435.

Heller, F. A., & Wilpert, B. (1981). *Competence and power in managerial decision-making: A study of senior levels of organization in eight countries*. London: Wiley.

Heller, F. A., & Yukl, G. (1969). Participation, managerial decision-making, and situational variables. *Organizational Behavior and Human Performance, 4*, 227–241.

Heller, T. (1982). *Women and men as leaders*. New York: Praeger.

Heller, T. (1985). Changing authority patterns: A cultural perspective. *Academy of Management Review, 10*, 488–495.

Heller, T., & Stein, P. T. (1978). Explaining the relationship of leadership status to high verbal participation. *Personality and Social Psychology Bulletin, 4*, 356.

Heller, T., & Van Til, J. (1982). Leadership and followership: Some summary propositions. *Journal of Applied Behavioral Science, 18*, 405–414.

Helmich, D. L. (1974a). Predecessor turnover and successor characteristics. *Cornell Journal of Social Relations, 9*, 249–260.

Helmich, D. L. (1974b). Organizational growth and succession patterns. *Academy of Management Journal, 17*, 771–775.

Helmich, D. L. (1975). Corporate succession: An examination. *Academy of Management Journal, 18*, 429–441.

Helmich, D. L. (1976). Succession: A longitudinal look. *Journal of Business Research, 4*, 335–364.

Helmich, D. L. (1978). Leader flows and organizational process. *Academy of Management Journal, 21*, 463–478.

Helmich, D., & Brown, W. (1972). Successor type and organizational change in the corporate enterprise. *Administrative Science Quarterly, 17*, 371–381.

Helmich, D. L., & Erzen, P. E. (1975). Leadership style and leader needs. *Academy of Management Journal, 18*, 397–402.

Helmreich, R. L., & Collins, B. E. (1967). Situational determinants of affiliative preference under stress. *Journal of Personality and Social Psychology, 6*, 79–85.

Helson, H. (1964). *Adaptation-level theory*. New York: Harper & Row.

Hemphill, J. K. (1949a). The leader and his group. *Journal of Educational Research, 28*, 225–229, 245–246.

Hemphill, J. K. (1949b). *Situational factors in leadership*. Columbus: Ohio State University, Bureau of Educational Research.

Hemphill, J. K. (1950a). *Leader behavior description*. Columbus: Ohio State University, Personnel Research Board.

Hemphill, J. K. (1950b). Relations between the size of the group and the behavior of "superior" leaders. *Journal of Social Psychology, 32*, 11–22.

Hemphill, J. K. (1952). *Leadership in small groups* (Tech. Rep.). Columbus: Ohio State Leadership Studies.

Hemphill, J. K. (1954). *A proposed theory of leadership in small groups* (Tech. Rep.). Columbus: Ohio State University, Personnel Research Board.

Hemphill, J. K. (1955). Leadership behavior associated with the administrative reputations of college departments. *Journal of Educational Psychology, 46*, 385–401.

Hemphill, J. K. (1959). Job descriptions for executives. *Harvard Business Review, 37*(5), 55–67.

Hemphill, J. K. (1960). *Dimensions of executive positions*. Columbus: Ohio State University, Bureau of Business Research.

Hemphill, J. K. (1961). Why people attempt to lead. In L. Petrullo & B. M. Bass (Eds.), *Leadership and interpersonal behavior*. New York: Holt, Rinehart & Winston.

Hemphill, J. K., & Coons, A. E. (1957). Development of the leader behavior description questionnaire. In R. M. Stogdill & A. E. Coons (Eds.), *Leader behavior: Its description and measurement*. Columbus: Ohio State University, Bureau of Business Research.

Hemphill, J. K., Griffiths, D. E., & Frederiksen, N. (1962). *Administrative performance and personality: A study of the principal in a simulated elementary school*. New York: Teachers College, Columbia University.

Hemphill, J. K., & McConville, C. B. (1962). *The effect of "human" vs. "machine" set on group problem solving procedures*. Princeton, NJ: Educational Testing Service.

Hemphill, J. K., & Pepinsky, P. N. (1955). *Leadership acts*. Columbus: Ohio State University, Personnel Research Board.

Hemphill, J. K., & Pepinsky, P. N., Kaufman, A. E., & Lipetz, M. E. (1956). The effects of reward and expectancy on motivation to lead. *American Psychologist, 11*, 379 (Abstract).

Hemphill, J. K., & Pepinsky, P. N., Kaufman, A. E., & Lipetz, M. E. (1957). Effects of task motivation and expectancy of accomplishment upon attempts to lead. *Psychological Monographs*, No. 451.

Hemphill, J. K., & Pepinsky, P. N., Shevitz, R. N., Jaynes, W. E., & Christner, C. A. (1954). *Leadership acts. I. An investigation of the relation between possession of task relevant information and attempts to lead.* Columbus: Ohio State University, Personnel Research Board.

Hemphill, J. K., & Sechrest, L. B. (1952). A comparison of three criteria of aircrew effectiveness in combat over Korea. *Journal of Applied Psychology, 36,* 323–327.

Hemphill, J. K., Seigel, A., & Westie, C. W. (1951). *An exploratory study of relations between perceptions of leader behavior, group characteristics, and expectations concerning the behavior of ideal leaders.* Columbus: Ohio State University, Personnel Research Board.

Hemphill, J. K., & Westie, C. M. (1950). The measurement of group dimensions. *Journal of Psychology, 29,* 325–342.

Hencley, S. P. (1960). *A typology of conflict between school superintendents and their reference groups.* Doctoral dissertation, University of Chicago, Chicago.

Hencley, S. P. (1961). The school superintendent and his role: A conflict typology. *Educational Research Bulletin, 40,* 57–67.

Henderson, D. B. (1977). Identification and analysis of the relationship between self-actualization and leadership style in selected graduate students in educational administration. *Dissertation Abstracts International, 37,* 4894.

Henderson, E. (1986). Blacks in corporate America: Is there a future? *Personnel Journal, 65*(1), 12–14.

Henderson, J. C., & Nutt, P. C. (1980). The influence of decision style on decision-making behavior. *Management Science, 26,* 371–386.

Hendrick, C., & Brown, S. R. (1971). Introversion, extraversion, and interpersonal attraction. *Journal of Personality and Social Psychology, 20,* 31–35.

Hendrick, H. (1989). Perceptual accuracy of self and others and leadership status as functions of cognitive complexity. In K. E. Clark & M. E. Clark (Eds.), *Measures of leadership.* West Orange, NJ: Leadership Library of America.

Hendrix, W. H., & McNichols, C. W. (1982). Organizational effectiveness as a function of managerial style, situational environment, and effectiveness criterion. *Journal of Experimental Education, 52,* 145–151.

Heneman, H. G. (1971). *An empirical investigation of expectancy theory predictions of job performance.* Paper, Academy of Management, Atlanta, GA.

Heneman, H. G., III. (1973). Impact of performance on managerial pay levels and pay changes. *Journal of Applied Psychology, 58,* 128–130.

Henley, N. M. (1973a). The politics of touch. In P. Brown (Ed.), *Radical psychology.* New York: Harper & Row.

Henley, N. M. (1973b). Status & sex: Some touching observations. *Bulletin of the Psychonomic Society, 2,* 91–93.

Hennig, M. (1971, March). What happens on the way up. *MBA,* 8–10.

Hennig, M., & Jardim, A. (1977). *The managerial woman.* Garden City, NY: Doubleday.

Hennigar, J., & Taylor, R. G. (1980). A study of the correlation between general administrative style and openness to change. *Journal of Instructional Psychology, 7*(1), 6–12.

Henning, D. A., & Moseley, R. L. (1970). Authority role of a functional manager: The controller. *Administrative Science Quarterly, 15,* 482–489.

Henning, H. (1929). Ziel und Möglichkeiten der experimentellen Charakterprüfung. *Jahrbuch der Charakterologie, 6,* 213–273.

Henry, W. E. (1949). The business executive: The psycho-dynamics of a social role. *American Journal of Sociology, 54,* 286–291.

Henson, H. H. (1934). *Analysis of leadership.* New York: Oxford University Press.

Herbert, T. T. (1972). *Philosophy and design of graduate business programs: Evaluative feedback and implications.* Paper, Midwest Academy of Management, Notre Dame, IN.

Herbert, T. T. (1977). The MBA and job performance: Evidence from appraisals. *Akron Business and Economic Review, 8,* 35–40.

Herbert, T. T., & Deresky, H. (1987). General managers should match their missions. *Organizational Dynamics, 15*(3), 40–51.

Herbert, T. T., & Yost, E. B. (1978). *Management education and development.* Westport, CT: Greenwood.

Herman, J. E. (1973). *The objective environment and organizational attitudes.* Paper, Midwest Academy of Management, Chicago.

Hermann, C. P. (1963). Some consequences of crisis which limit the viability of organizations. *Administrative Science Quarterly, 8,* 61–82.

Hermann, M. G., & Kogan, N. (1968). Negotiation in leader and delegate groups. *Journal of Conflict Resolution, 12,* 332–344.

Hermann, M. G., & Milburn, T. W. (Eds.). (1977). *A psychological examination of political leaders.* New York: Free Press.

Hermann, M. G., Snyder, R. C., & Cunningham, L. L. (1980). Leadership: Some trends, challenges and opportunities. *Mershon Center Quarterly Report* (Ohio State University), *5*(3), 1–8.

Hernandez, S. R., & Kaluzny, A. D. (1982). Selected determinants of performance within a set of health service organizations. *Proceedings, Academy of Management,* New York, 52–56.

Herod, J. (1969). Characteristics of leadership in an international fraternity for women and influence on the leaders' attitudes of a group centered leader training experience. *Dissertation Abstracts, 29,* 3461–3462.

Herold, D. M. (1974). *Mutual influence processes in leader-follower relationships.* Doctoral dissertation, Yale University, New Haven, CT.

Herold, D. M. (1977). Two-way influence processes in leader-follower dyads. *Academy of Management Journal, 20,* 224–237.

Herold, D. M., & Greller, M. M. (1977). Feedback. The definition of a construct. *Academy of Management Journal, 20,* 142–147.

Heron, A. R. (1942). *Sharing information with employees.* Stanford, CA: Stanford University Press.

Herrick, J. S. (1973). Work motives of female executives. *Public Personnel Management, 2,* 380–388.

Herring, W. H. (1972). A study of the effect of high and low congruence of role expectations by superiors, managers, and subordinates upon the performance of managers. *Dissertation Abstracts International*, 37, 3493.

Herriot, P., Chalmers, C., & Wingrove, J. (1985). Group decision-making in an assessment centre. *Journal of Occupational Psychology*, 58, 309–312.

Herriot, P., & Rothwell, C. (1983). Expectations and impressions in the graduate selection interview. *Journal of Occupational Psychology*, 56, 303 314.

Hersey, P., Angelini, A. L., & Carakushansky, S. (1982). The impact of situational leadership and classroom structure on learning effectiveness. *Group & Organization Studies*, 7, 216–224.

Hersey, P., & Blanchard, K. H. (1969a). Life cycle theory of leadership. *Training & Development Journal*, 23, 26–34.

Hersey, P., & Blanchard, K. H. (1969b). *Management of organizational behavior.* Englewood Cliffs, NJ: Prentice-Hall.

Hersey, P., & Blanchard, K. H. (1972). The management of change. Change and the use of power. *Training & Development Journal*, 26(1), 6; (2), 20–24; (3), 6–10.

Hersey, P., & Blanchard, K. H. (1973). *Leader effectiveness and adaptability description-self.* Escondido, CA: Center for Leadership Studies.

Hersey, P., & Blanchard, K. H. (1974). So you want to know your leadership style? *Training & Development Journal*, 28(2), 22–37. Also: (1981). 35(6), 34–54.

Hersey, P., & Blanchard, K. H. (1977). *Management of organizational behavior: Utilizing human resources.* Englewood Cliffs, NJ: Prentice-Hall.

Hersey, P., & Blanchard, K. H. (1982a). *Management of organization behavior: Utilizing human resources* (4th ed.). Englewood Cliffs, NJ: Prentice-Hall.

Hersey, P., & Blanchard, K. H. (1982b). Leadership style: Attitudes and behaviors. *Training & Development Journal*, 36(5), 50–52.

Hertzler, J. O. (1940). Crises and dictatorships. *American Sociological Review*, 5, 157–169.

Herzberg, F. I. (1966). *Working and the nature of man.* New York: Crowell.

Herzberg, F., Mausner, B., Peterson, R. O., & Capwell, D. F. (1957). *Job attitudes: Review of research and opinion.* Pittsburgh: Psychological Service of Pittsburgh.

Herzberg, F., Mausner, B., & Snyderman, B. B. (1959). *The motivation to work.* New York: Wiley.

Heslin, J. A., Jr. (1966). *A field test of the Likert theory of management in an ADP environment.* Master's thesis, American University, Washington, DC.

Heslin, R., & Dunphy, D. (1964). Three dimensions of member satisfaction in small groups. *Human Relations*, 17, 99–112.

Hespe, G., & Wall, T. (1976). The demand for participation among employees. *Human Relations*, 29, 411–428.

Hesseling, P., & Konnen, E. E. (1969). Culture and subculture in a decision-making exercise. *Human Relations*, 22, 31–51.

Hetzler, S. A. (1955). Variation in role-playing patterns among different echelons of bureaucratic leaders. *American Sociological Review*, 20, 700–706.

Hewitt, J. P., & Stokes, R. (1975). Disclaimers. *American Sociological Review*, 40, 1–11.

Heyns, R. W. (1948). *Effects of variation in leadership on participant behavior in discussion groups.* Doctoral dissertation, University of Michigan, Ann Arbor.

Heyns, R. W. (1950). Factors determining influence and decision satisfaction in conferences requiring pooled judgments. *Proceedings, Administrative Conference*, University of Michigan, Ann Arbor.

Hickman, C. R., & Silva, M. A. (1984). *Creating excellence: Managing corporate culture, strategy, and change in the New Age.* New York: New American Library.

Hicks, C. F. (1972). An experimental approach to determine the effect of a group leader's programmed nonverbal facial behavior upon group member's perception of the leader. *Dissertation Abstracts International*, 32, 4778–4779.

Hicks, J. A., & Stone, J. B. (1962). The identification of traits related to managerial success. *Journal of Applied Psychology*, 46, 428–432.

Hickson, D. J., Hinings, C. R., Less, C. A., Schneck, R. E., & Pennings, J. M. (1971). A strategic contingencies theory of intraorganizational power. *Administrative Science Quarterly*, 16, 216–229.

Hickson, D. J., Pugh, D. S., & Pheysey, D. C. (1969). Operations technology and organization structure: An empirical reappraisal. *Administrative Science Quarterly*, 14, 378–397.

High, W. S., Goldberg, L. L., & Comrey, A. L. (1955). Factored dimensions of organizational behavior. II. Aircraft workers. *Educational and Psychological Measurement*, 15, 371–382.

High, W. S., Goldberg, L. L., & Comrey, A. L. (1956). Factored dimensions of organizational behavior. III. Aircraft supervisors. *Educational and Psychological Measurement*, 16, 38–53.

High, W. S., Wieson, R. C., & Comrey, A. L. (1955). Factors influencing organizational effectiveness. VIII. A survey of aircraft foremen. *Personnel Psychology*, 8, 355–368.

Higham, J. (1978). *Ethnic leadership in America.* Baltimore: Johns Hopkins Press.

Hilgard, E. R., Sait, E. M., & Magaret, G. A. (1940). Level of aspiration as affected by relative standing in an experimental social group. *Journal of Experimental Psychology*, 27, 411–421.

Hilgert, R. L. (1965). The expectations of part-time MBA students. Paper *Proceedings, Image and impact of education for business*. American Association of Collegiate Schools of Business, St Louis, MO.

Hill, J. W., & Hunt, J. G. (1970). *An investigation of the relationship between employee need satisfaction and perceived leadership of two levels of management.* Carbondale: Southern Illinois University, Department of Management.

Hill, K. D., & Kerr, S. (1984). The impact of computer integrated manufacturing systems on the first-line supervisor. *Journal of Organizational Behavior Management*, 6, 81–97.

Hill, N. (1976). Self-esteem: The key to effective leadership. *Administrative Management*, 31(8), 24.

Hill, R. (1984). From war room to boardroom. Professional soldiers excelling as managers. *International Management, 39*(4), 22–28.

Hill, R. (1985). The business leader with the Shakespearean touch. *International Management, 40*(9), 71–76.

Hill, R. B. (1971). *The strength of black families.* New York: National Urban League.

Hill, R. E. (1971, April). The leadership role as a factor in commitment and satisfaction among registered nurses. *Dissertation Abstracts International, 31,* 6314.

Hill, T. A. (1973). *An experimental study of the relationship between the opinionatedness of a leader and consensus in group discussions of policy.* Doctoral dissertation, Indiana University, Bloomington.

Hill, T. E., & Schmitt, N. (1977). Individual differences in leadership decision making. *Organizational Behavior and Human Performance, 19,* 353–367.

Hill, W. (1969a). The validation and extension of Fiedler's theory of leadership effectiveness. *Academy of Management Journal, 12,* 33–47.

Hill, W. (1969b). A situational approach to leadership effectiveness. *Journal of Applied Psychology, 53,* 513–517.

Hill, W. A. (1973). Leadership style: Rigid or flexible? *Organizational Behavior and Human Performance, 9,* 35–47.

Hill, W. H., & Fox, W. A. (1973). Black and white marine squad leaders' perceptions of racially mixed squads. *Academy of Management Journal, 16,* 680–686.

Hill, W. H., & Hughes, D. (1974). Variations in leader behavior as a function of task type. *Organizational Behavior and Human Performance, 11,* 83–96.

Hill, W. H., & Ruhe, J. A. (1974). Attitudes and behaviors of black and white supervisors in problem solving groups. *Academy of Management Journal, 17,* 563–569.

Hillery, J. M., & Wexley, K. N. (1974). Participation effects in appraisal interviews conducted in a training situation. *Journal of Applied Psychology, 59,* 168–171.

Hills, D. A. (1985). Prediction of effectiveness in leaderless group discussions with the adjective check list. *Journal of Applied Social Psychology, 15,* 443–447.

Hills, F. S. (1979). The pay-for-performance dilemma. *Personnel, 56*(5), 23–31.

Hills, R. J. (1963). The representative function: Neglected dimension of leadership behavior. *Administrative Science Quarterly, 8,* 83–101.

Himes, J. S. (1965). Some work-related deprivations of lower-class Negro youths. In L. A. Ferman, J. A. Kornbluh, & A. Haber (Eds.), *Poverty in America.* Ann Arbor: University of Michigan Press.

Hines, G. H., & Wellington, V. U. (1974). Achievement motivation levels of immigrants in New Zealand. *Journal of Cross-Cultural Psychology, 5,* 37–47.

Hinings, C. R., Hickson, D. J., Pennings, J. M., & Schneck, R. E. (1974). Structural conditions of intraorganizational power. *Administrative Science Quarterly, 19,* 22–44.

Hinken, T. R., & Schriesheim, C. A. (1986). *Influence tactics used by subordinates: A theoretical and empirical analysis and refinement of the Kipnis, Schmidt, and Wilkinson scales.* Paper, Academy of Management, Chicago.

Hinken, T. R., & Schriesheim, C. A. (1989). Development and application of new scales to measure the French and Raven (1959) bases of social power. *Journal of Applied Psychology, 74,* 561–567.

Hinrichs, J. R. (1969). Comparison of "real life" assessments of management potential with situational exercises, paper-and-pencil ability tests, and personality inventories. *Journal of Applied Psychology, 53,* 425–433.

Hinrichs, J. R. (1978a). An eight-year follow-up of a management assessment center. *Journal of Applied Psychology, 63,* 596–601.

Hinrichs, J. R. (1978b). *Practical management for productivity.* New York: Van Nostrand Reinhold, Chapter 6.

Hinton, B. L., & Barrow, J. C. (1975). The superior's reinforcing behavior as a function of reinforcements received. *Organizational Behavior and Human Performance, 14,* 123–149.

Hinton, B. L., & Barrow, J. C. (1976). Personality correlates of the reinforcement propensities of leaders. *Personnel Psychology, 29,* 61–66.

Hirsch, J. (1987, August 2). College leaders read "How to." *New York Times,* Education section, 9.

Hirsch, P. (1987). *Pack your own parachute: How to survive mergers, takeovers, and other corporate disasters.* Reading, MA: Addison-Wesley.

Hise, R. T. (1968, Fall). The effect of close supervision on productivity of simulated managerial decision-making groups. *Business Studies,* North Texas State University, pp. 96–104.

Hites, R. W. (1953). A questionnaire for measuring leader-identification. *American Psychologist, 8,* 368.

Hites, R. W., & Campbell, D. T. (1950). A test of the ability of fraternity leaders to estimate group opinion. *Journal of Social Psychology, 32,* 95–100.

Hobert, R., & Dunnette, M. D. (1967). Development of moderator variables to enhance the prediction of managerial effectiveness. *Journal of Applied Psychology, 51,* 50–64.

Hobhouse, L. T., Wheeler, G. C., & Ginsberg, M. (1930). *The material culture and social institutions of the simpler peoples.* London: Chapman & Hall.

Hocking, W. E. (1924). Leaders and led. *Yale Review, 13,* 625–641.

Hodge, J. W. (1976). The relationship between styles of supervision and need satisfaction of two levels of management employees. *Dissertation Abstracts International, 37,* 1987.

Hodgetts, R. M. (1968). Leadership techniques in the project organization. *Academy of Management Journal, 11,* 211–219.

Hodgson, J. D., & Brenner, M. H. (1968). Successful experience: Training hard-core unemployed. *Harvard Business Review, 46*(5), 148–156.

Hodgson, R. C., Levinson, D. J., & Zaleznik, A. (1965). *The executive role constellation.* Boston: Harvard University Press.

Hoffman, E. L., & Rohrer, J. H. (1954). An objective peer evaluation scale: Construction and validity. *Educational and Psychological Measurement, 14,* 332–341.

Hoffman, L., Rosen, S., & Lippitt, R. (1960). Parental coerciveness, child autonomy, and the child's role at school. *Sociometry, 23,* 15–22.

Hoffman, L. R. (1958). Similarity of personality: A basis for interpersonal attraction? *Sociometry, 21,* 300–308.

Hoffman, L. R. (1974). Review of leadership and decision-making. *Journal of Business, 47,* 593–598.

Hoffman, L. R., Burke, R. J., & Maier, N. R. F. (1965). Participation, influence, and satisfaction among members of problem-solving groups. *Psychological Reports, 16,* 661–667.

Hoffman, L. R., Harburg, E., & Maier, N. R. F. (1962). Differences and disagreement as factors in creative group problem solving. *Journal of Abnormal and Social Psychology, 64,* 206–214.

Hoffman, L. R., & Maier, N. R. F. (1967). Valence in the adoption of solutions by problem-solving groups: II. Quality and acceptance as goals of leaders and members. *Journal of Personality and Social Psychology, 6,* 175–182.

Hoffman, L. R., & Smith, C. G. (1960). Some factors affecting the behaviors of members of problem-solving groups. *Sociometry, 23,* 273–291.

Hoffman, M. L. (1956). Conformity to the group as a defense mechanism. *American Psychologist, 11,* 375.

Hoffman, P. J., Festinger, L., & Lawrence, D. H. (1954). Tendencies toward group comparability in competitive bargaining. *Human Relations, 7,* 141–159.

Hoffman, R. H. (1968). *An analysis of factors affecting leadership in an industrial firm.* MBA thesis, Ohio State University, Columbus.

Hoffman, S., & Hoffman, I. (1970). The will to grandeur: deGaulle as political artist. In D. A. Rustow (Ed.), *Philosophers and kings: Studies in leadership.* New York: George Braziller.

Hoffmann, C., & Reed, J. S. (1981, Winter). Sex discrimination?—The XYZ affair. *Public Interest, 62,* 21–39.

Hofmeyer, K. (1987). Training and development of black management. In B. M. Bass, & P. J. D. D. Drenth (Eds.), *Advances in organizational psychology: An international review.* Beverly Hills, CA: Sage.

Hofstede, G. (1976). Nationality and espoused values of managers. *Journal of Applied Psychology, 61,* 148–155.

Hofstede, G. (1978, January 20). Private correspondence.

Hofstede, G. (1979). Value systems in forty countries. In L. H. Eckensberger, W. J. Lonner, & Y. H. Poortinga (Eds.), *Cross-cultural contributions to psychology.* Lisse, The Netherlands: Swets & Zeitlinger.

Hofstede, G. (1980). *Culture's consequence: International differences in work related values.* Beverly Hills, CA: Sage.

Hofstede, G. (1984). The cultural relativity of the quality of life concept. *Academy of Management Review, 9,* 389–398.

Hogan, J., & Zenke, L. (1986). Dollar-value utility of alternative procedures for selecting school principals. *Educational and Psychological Measurement, 46,* 935–945.

Hogan, R. (1969). Development of an empathy scale. *Journal of Consulting and Clinical Psychology, 33,* 307–316.

Hogan, R., Raskin, R., & Fazzini, D. (undated). *The dark side of charisma.* Unpublished manuscript.

Hogue, J. P., Otis, J. L., & Prien, E. P. (1962). Assessments of higher-level personnel: VI. Validity of predictions based on projective techniques. *Personnel Psychology, 15,* 335–344.

Hohn, R. (1962). *Menschenführung im Handel.* Bad Harzburg: Verlag für Wissenschaft, Wirtschaft, und Technik.

Holden, R. (1954). Relationships between perceived leadership perceptions of the ideal, and group productivity in small classroom groups. *Dissertation Abstracts, 14,* 1994.

Holding, D. H. (1969). *Experimental psychology in industry.* Baltimore: Penguin.

Holland, P. W., & Leinhardt, S. (1976). Local structure in social networks. In D. R. Heise (Ed.), *Sociological Methodology.* San Francisco: Jossey-Bass.

Hollander, E. P. (1954). Authoritarianism and leadership choice in a military setting. *Journal of Abnormal and Social Psychology, 49,* 365–370.

Hollander, E. P. (1956). The friendship factor in peer nominations. *Personnel Psychology, 9,* 435–448.

Hollander, E. P. (1957). The reliability of peer nominations under various conditions of administration. *Journal of Applied Psychology, 41,* 85–90.

Hollander, E. P. (1958). Conformity, status, and idiosyncrasy credit. *Psychological Review, 65,* 117–127.

Hollander, E. P. (1960). Competence and conformity in the acceptance of influence. *Journal of Abnormal and Social Psychology, 61,* 365–369.

Hollander, E. P. (1961a). Some effects of perceived status on responses to innovative behavior. *Journal of Abnormal and Social Psychology, 63,* 247–250.

Hollander, E. P. (1961b). Emergent leadership and social influence. In L. Petrullo & B. M. Bass (Eds.), *Leadership and interpersonal behavior.* New York: Holt, Rinehart & Winston.

Hollander, E. P. (1964). *Leaders, groups, and influence.* New York: Oxford University Press.

Hollander, E. P. (1965). Validity of peer nominations in predicting a distance performance criterion. *Journal of Applied Psychology, 49,* 434–438.

Hollander, E. P. (1966). *Leadership style, competence, and source of authority as determinants of active and perceived influence* (Tech. Rep.). Buffalo: State University of New York.

Hollander, E. P. (1971). Style, structure, and setting in organizational leadership. *Administrative Science Quarterly, 16,* 1–10.

Hollander, E. P. (1978). *Leadership dynamics: A practical guide to effective relationships.* New York: Free Press.

Hollander, E. P. (1983). Women and leadership. In H. H. Blumberg, A. P. Hare, V. Kent, & M. Davies (Eds.), *Small Groups and Social Interaction,* Vol. 1. New York: Wiley.

Hollander, E. P. (1985). Leadership and power. In G. Lindzey and E. Aronson (Eds.), *The handbook of social psychology.* New York: Random House.

Hollander, E. P. (1986). On the central role of leadership processes. *International Review of Applied Psychology, 35,* 39–52.

Hollander, E. P. (1987). *College and university leadership from a social psychological perspective: A transactional view.* Paper, Invitational Interdisciplinary Colloquium on Leadership in Higher Education, National Center for Postsecondary Governance and Finance, Columbia University, New York.

Hollander, E. P., & Bair, J. T. (1954). Attitudes toward authority-figures as correlates of motivation among aviation cadets. *Journal of Applied Psychology,* 38, 21-25.

Hollander, E. P., Fallon, B. J., & Edwards, M. T. (1977). Some aspects of influence and acceptability for appointed and elected leaders. *Journal of Psychology,* 95, 289-296.

Hollander, E. P., & Julian, J. W. (1968). Leadership. In E. F. Borgatta & W. W. Lambert (Eds.), *Handbook of personality theory and research.* Chicago: Rand McNally.

Hollander, E. P., & Julian, J. W. (1969). Contemporary trends in the analysis of leadership processes. *Psychological Bulletin,* 71, 387-397.

Hollander, E. P., & Julian, J. W. (1970). Studies in leader legitimacy, influence, and innovation. In L. Berkowitz (Ed.), *Advances in experimental social psychology,* Vol. 5. New York: Academic Press.

Hollander, E. P., Julian, J. W., & Perry, F. A. (1966). *Leader style, competence, and source of authority as determinants of actual and perceived influence* (Tech. Rep. No. 5). Buffalo: State University of New York.

Hollander, E. P., & Neider, L. L. (1978). *Critical incidents and rating scales in comparing "good"-"bad" leadership.* Paper, American Psychological Association, Toronto.

Hollander, E. P., & Sauaser, E. R. (1953). *A further consideration of peer nominations on leadership in the Naval Air Training Program* (Medical Research Report). Pensacola, FL: U.S. Naval School of Aviation.

Hollander, E. P., & Webb, W. B. (1955). Leadership, followership, and friendship: An analysis of peer nominations. *Journal of Abnormal and Social Psychology,* 50, 163-167.

Hollander, E. P., and Yoder, J. (1980). Some issues in comparing women and men as leaders. *Basic Applied Social Psychology,* 1, 267-280.

Hollie, P. (1980, February 4). Officers recapture New Mexico prison without resistance. *New York Times,* A1, D9.

Hollingshead, A. B. (1949). *Elmtown's youth: The impact of social classes on adolescents.* New York: Wiley.

Hollingsworth, A. T., & Al-Jafary, A. R. A. (1983). Why supervisors don't delegate and employees won't accept responsibility. *Supervisory Management,* 28(4), 12-17.

Hollingworth, L. S. (1926). *Gifted children.* New York: Macmillan.

Hollingworth, L. S. (1939). What we know about the early selection and training of leaders. *Teachers College Record,* 40, 575-592.

Hollman, R. W. (1973). *A study of the relationships between organizational climate and managerial assessment of management by objectives.* Doctoral dissertation, University of Washington, Seattle.

Holloman, C. R. (1965). The leadership role of military and civilian supervisors in a military setting as perceived by supervisors and subordinates. *Dissertation Abstracts,* 26, 2903-2904.

Holloman, C. R. (1967). The perceived leadership role of military and civilian supervisors in a military setting. *Personnel Psychology,* 20, 199-210.

Holloman, C. R. (1968). Leadership and headship: There is a difference. *Personnel Administration,* 31(4), 38-44.

Holloman, C. R. (1986). "Headship" vs. leadership. *Business and Economic Review,* 32(2), 35-37.

Holloman, C. R., & Hendrick, H. W. (1972). Adequacy of group decisions as a function of decision-making process. *Academy of Management Journal,* 15, 175-184.

Holloway, E. L., & Wolleat, P. L. (1981). Style differences of beginning supervisors: An interactional analysis. *Journal of Counseling Psychology,* 28, 373-376.

Holmes, J. S. (1969). Comparison of group leader and nonparticipant observer judgments of certain objective interaction variables. *Psychological Reports,* 24, 655-659.

Holt, R. T. (1952a). *An exploratory study of the French cabinets of the first legislature of the Fourth Republic* (Tech. Rep. No. 2). Minneapolis: University of Minnesota.

Holt, R. T. (1952b). *An analysis of the problem of stability and cohesive membership in coalitions* (Tech. Rep. No. 3). Minneapolis: University of Minnesota.

Holton, P. B. (1984). Leadership styles of program leaders in the cooperative extension service in New England. *Dissertation Abstracts International,* 46(2A), 329.

Holtzman, W. H. (1952). Adjustment and leadership: A study of the Rorschach test. *Journal of Social Psychology,* 36, 179-189.

Homans, G. C. (1950). *The human group.* New York: Harcourt, Brace.

Homans, G. C. (1958). Social behavior as exchange. *American Journal of Sociology,* 63, 597-606.

Homans, G. C. (1961). *Social behavior: Its elementary forms.* New York: Harcourt, Brace.

Honeywell Corporate Human Resources and Corporate Employee Relations. (1981). *Honeywell management development survey: Corporate findings.* Minneapolis, MN: Honeywell.

Hood, P. D. (1963). *Leadership climate for trainee leaders: The army AIT platoon.* Washington, DC: George Washington University, Human Resources Research Office.

Hood, P. D., Showel, M., & Stewart, E. C. (1967). *Evaluation of three experimental systems for noncommissioned officer training.* Washington, DC: George Washington University, Human Resources Office.

Hook, S. (1943). *The hero in history.* New York: John Day.

Hooker, E. R. (1928). Leaders in village communities. *Social Forces,* 6, 605-614.

Hooper, D. B. (1969). Differential utility of leadership opinions in classical and moderator models for the prediction of leadership effectiveness. *Dissertation Abstracts International,* 30, 13.

Hoover, N. R. (1987). *Transformational and transactional leadership: A test of the model.* Doctoral dissertation, University of Louisville, Louisville, KY.

Hopfe, M. W. (1970). Leadership style and effectiveness of department chairmen in business administration. *Academy of Management Journal, 13,* 301–310.

Hopkins, T. K. (1964). *The exercise of influence in small groups.* Totowa, NJ: Bedminster Press.

Hoppock, R. (1935). *Job satisfaction.* New York: Harper.

Hoppock, R., Robinson, H. A., & Zlatchin, P. J. (1948). Job satisfaction researches of 1946–1947. *Occupations, 27,* 167–175.

Hord, S. M., Hall, G. E., & Stiegelbauer, S. M. (1984). How principals work with other change facilitators. *Education and Urban Society, 17,* 89–109.

Hornaday, J. A., & Aboud, J. (1971). Characteristics of successful entrepreneurs. *Personnel Psychology, 24,* 141–153.

Hornaday, J. A., & Bunker, C. S. (1970). The nature of the entrepreneur. *Personnel Psychology, 23,* 47–54.

Horne, H. H. (1931). *The essentials of leadership.* Nashville, TN: Cokesbury Press.

Horne, J. H., & Lupton, T. (1965). The work activities of "middle" management—an exploratory study. *Journal of Management Studies, 2,* 14–33.

Horner, M. S. (1972). Toward an understanding of achievement-related conflicts in women. *Journal of Social Issues, 28,* 157–176.

Horner, M. S. (1970). Femininity and successful achievement: A basic inconsistency. In J. Bardwick, E. Douvan, M. S. Horner, & D. Gutmann (Eds.), *Feminine psychology and conflict.* Monterey, CA: Brooks/Cole.

Hornstein, H. (1986). *Managerial courage: Revitalizing your company without sacrificing your job.* New York: Wiley.

Horrocks, J. E., & Thompson, G. G. (1946). A study of the friendship fluctuations of rural boys and girls. *Journal of Genetic Psychology, 69,* 189–198.

Horrocks, J. E., & Wear, B. A. (1953). An analysis of interpersonal choice relationships of college students. *Journal of Social Psychology, 38,* 87–98.

Horsfall, A. B., & Arensberg, C. M. (1949). Teamwork and productivity in a shoe factory. *Human Organization, 8,* 13–26.

Horwitz, M. (1954). The recall of interrupted group tasks: An experimental study of individual motivation in relation to group goals. *Human Relations, 7,* 3–38.

Horwitz, M., Goldman, M., & Lee, F. J. (1955). *Effects of two methods of changing a frustrating agent on reduction of hostility* (Preliminary Report). Urbana: University of Illinois, Bureau of Educational Research.

Hosking, D. M. (1978). *A critical evaluation of Fiedler's predictor measures of leadership effectiveness.* Doctoral dissertation, University of Warwick, Warwick, England.

Hosmer, L. T. (1982). The importance of strategic leadership. *Journal of Business, 3*(2), 47–57.

Hostiuck, K. T. (1970). *The perceived pressure and perceived norm compatibility of reference groups as influences on executives' political behavior.* Doctoral dissertation, Ohio State University, Columbus.

Hough, L. M. (1984). Development and evaluation of the "accomplishment record" method of selecting and promoting professionals. *Journal of Applied Psychology, 69,* 135–146.

Hough, L. M., Keyes, M. A., & Dunnette, M. D. (1983). An evaluation of three "alternative" selection procedures. *Personnel Psychology, 36,* 261–276.

House, P. W., & Covello, V. (1984). The phenomenon of the mandarins. *Bureaucrat, 13*(3), 30–34.

House, R. J. (1962). An experiment in the use of management training standards. *Academy of Management Journal, 5,* 76–81.

House, R. J. (1965). Managerial reactions to two methods of management training. *Personnel Psychology, 18,* 311–320.

House, R. J. (1967). T-group education and leadership effectiveness: A review of the empiric literature and a critical evaluation. *Personnel Psychology, 20,* 1–32.

House, R. J. (1968). Leadership training: Some dysfunctional consequences. *Administrative Science Quarterly, 12,* 556–571.

House, R. J. (1971). A path goal theory of leader effectiveness. *Administrative Science Quarterly, 16,* 321–338.

House, R. J. (1972). Some new applications and tests of the path-goal theory of leadership. Unpublished manuscript.

House, R. J. (1974). Path-goal theory of leadership. *Journal of Contemporary Business, 3,* 81–97.

House, R. J. (1977). A 1976 theory of charismatic leadership. In J. G. Hunt & L. L. Larson (Eds.), *Leadership: The cutting edge.* Carbondale: Southern Illinois University Press.

House, R. J. (1984). *Power in organizations: A social psychological perspective.* Toronto: University of Toronto. Unpublished manuscript.

House, R. J. (1985). *Research contrasting the behavior and effect of reputed charismatic versus reputed non-charismatics.* Paper, Administrative Science Association of Canada, Montreal.

House, R. J. (1988a). Leadership research: Some forgotten, ignored, or overlooked findings. In J. G. Hunt, B. R. Baliga, H. P. Dachler, & C. A. Schriesheim, *Emerging leadership vistas.* Lexington, MA: D. C. Heath.

House, R. J. (1988b). Power and personality in complex organizations. In L. L. Cummings & B. M. Staw (Eds.), *Research in Organizational Behavior, 10,* 305–357.

House, R. J., & Baetz, M. L. (1979). Leadership: Some empirical generalizations and new research directions. *Research in Organizational Behavior, 1,* 341–423.

House, R. J., & Dessler, G. (1974). The path goal theory of leadership: Some post hoc and a priori tests. In J. G. Hunt & L. L. Larson (Eds.), *Contingency approaches to leadership.* Carbondale: Southern Illinois University Press.

House, R. J., Filley, A. C., & Gujarati, D. N. (1971). Leadership style, hierarchical influence, and the satisfaction of subordinate role expectations: A test of Likert's influence proposition. *Journal of Applied Psychology, 55,* 422–432.

House, R. J., Filley, A. C., & Kerr, S. (1971). Relation of leader consideration and initiation structure to R and D subordinates' satisfaction. *Administrative Science Quarterly, 16,* 19–30.

House, R. J., & Kerr, S. (1973). Organizational independence, leader behavior, and managerial practices: A replicated study. *Journal of Applied Psychology, 58,* 173–180.

House, R. J., & Miner, J. B. (1969). Merging management and behavioral theory: The interaction between span of control and group size. *Administrative Science Quarterly, 14,* 451–464.

House, R. J., & Mitchell, T. R. (1974). Path-goal theory of leadership. *Journal of Contemporary Business, 3,* 81–97.

House, R. J., & Rizzo, J. R. (1972a). Toward the measurement of organizational practices: Scale development and validation. *Journal of Applied Psychology, 56,* 388–396.

House, R. J., & Rizzo, J. R. (1972b). Role conflict and ambiguity as critical variables in a model of organizational behavior. *Organizational Behavior and Human Performance, 7,* 467–505.

House, R. J., & Singh, J. V. (1987). Organizational behavior. Some new directions for I/O psychology. *Annual Review of Psychology, 38,* 669–718.

House, R. J., Spangler, W. D., & Woycke, J. (1989). *Personality and charisma in the U.S. presidency.* Unpublished manuscript.

House, R. J., & Tosi, H. L. (1963). An experimental evaluation of a management training program. *Academy of Management Journal, 6,* 303–315.

House, R. J., Tosi, H. L., Rizzo, J. R., & Dunnock, R. C. (1967). *Management development: Design, evaluation, and implementation.* Ann Arbor: University of Michigan, Bureau of Industrial Relations.

House, R. J., Wigor, L. A., & Schulz, K. (1970). *Psychological participation, leader behavior, performance and satisfaction: An extension of prior research and a motivation theory interpretation.* Paper, Eastern Academy of Management, East Lansing, MI.

House, R. J., Woycke, J., & Fodor, E. (1986). *Research contrasting the motives and effects of reputed charismatic versus reputed non-charismatic U.S. presidents.* Paper, Academy of Management, Chicago.

House, R. J., Woycke, J., & Fodor, E. M. (1988). Charismatic and non-charismatic leaders: Differences in behavior and effectiveness. In J. A. Conger & R. N. Kanungo, *Charismatic leadership: The elusive factor in organizational effectiveness.* San Francisco: Jossey-Bass.

Houser, J. D. (1927). *What the employer thinks.* Cambridge, MA: Harvard University Press.

Houston, G. C. (1961). *Manager development: Principles and perspectives.* Homewood, IL: Irwin.

Hovey, D. E. (1974). The low-powered leader confronts a messy problem: A test of Fiedler's theory. *Academy of Management Journal, 17,* 358–362.

Howard, A. (1974). An assessment of assessment centers. *Academy of Management Journal, 17,* 115–134.

Howard, A. (1986). College experiences and managerial performance. *Journal of Applied Psychology, 71,* 530–552.

Howard, A., & Bray, D. W. (1988). *Managerial lives in transition: Advancing age and changing times.* New York: Guilford Press.

Howard, A., & Bray, D. W. (1989). Predictors of managerial success over long periods of time. In M. B. Clark & K. E. Clark (Eds.), *Measures of leadership.* West Orange, NJ: Leadership Library of America.

Howard, A., Shudo, K., & Umeshima, M. (1983). Motivation and values among Japanese and American managers. *Personnel Psychology, 36,* 883–898.

Howard, D. S. (1968). Personality similarity and complementarity and perceptual accuracy in supervisor-subordinate relationships. *Dissertation Abstracts, 28,* 4789–4790.

Howard, P. W., & Joyce, W. F. (1982). *Substitutes for leadership: A statistical refinement.* Paper, Academy of Management, New York.

Howat, G., & London, M. (1980). Attributions of conflict management strategies in supervisor-subordinate dyads. *Journal of Applied Psychology, 65,* 172–175.

Howell, C. E. (1942). Measurement of leadership. *Sociometry, 5,* 163–168.

Howell, J. M. (1985). *A laboratory study of charismatic leadership* (Working Paper No. 85-35). London, Ontario: School of Business Administration, University of Western Ontario.

Howell, J. M. (1988). Two faces of charisma: Socialized and personalized leadership in organizations. In J. Conger & R. Kanungo (1988), *Charismatic leadership: The illusive factor in organizational effectiveness.* San Francisco: Jossey-Bass.

Howell, J. M., & Avolio, B. J. (1989). *Transformational versus transactional leaders: How they impart innovation, risk-taking, organizational structure and performance.* Paper, Academy of Management, Washington, DC.

Howell, J. M., & Frost, P. J. (1988). A laboratory study of charismatic leadership. *Organizational Behavior and Human Decision Processes, 43,* 243–269.

Howell, J. P., Bowen, D., Kerr, S., Dorfman, P. W., & Podsakoff, P. M. (undated) *Substitutes for leadership.* Unpublished manuscript.

Howell, J. P., & Dorfman, P. W. (1981). Substitutes for leadership: Test of a construct. *Academy of Management Journal, 24,* 714–728.

Howell, J. P., & Dorfman, P. W. (1986). Leadership and substitutes for leadership among professional and nonprofessional workers. *Journal of Applied Behavioral Science, 22,* 29–46.

Howell, J. P., & Dorfman, P. W. (1988). *A comparative study of leadership and its substitutes in a mixed cultural work setting.* Unpublished manuscript.

Howell, J. P., Dorfman, P. W., & Kerr, S. (1986). Moderator variables in leadership research. *Academy of Management Review, 11,* 88–102.

Howells, L. T., & Becker, S. W. (1962). Seating arrangement and leadership emergence. *Journal of Abnormal and Social Psychology, 64,* 148–150.

Howton, F. W. (1969). *Functionaries.* Chicago: Quadrangle Books.

Hoy, W. L., & Ferguson, J. (1985). A theoretical framework and exploration of organizational effectiveness of schools. *Educational Administrative Quarterly, 21*(2), 117–134.

Hoy, W. K., Tarter, C. J., & Forsyth, P. (1978). Administrative behavior and subordinate loyalty: An empirical assessment. *Journal of Educational Administration, 16,* 29–38.

Hoyt, G. C., & Stoner, J. A. (1968). Leadership and group decisions involving risk. *Journal of Experimental and Social Psychology, 4,* 275–284.

Hsu, C. C., & Newton, R. R. (1974). Relation between foremen's leadership attitudes and the skill level of their work groups. *Journal of Applied Psychology, 59,* 771–772.

Hsu, F. L. K., (1981). *American and Chinese: Passage to differences* (3rd ed.). Honolulu: University of Hawaii Press.

Huck, J. R. (1973). Assessment centers: A review of external and internal validities. *Personnel Psychology, 26,* 191–212.

Huck, J. R., & Bray, D. W. (1976). Management assessment center evaluations and subsequent job performance of white and black females. *Personnel Psychology, 29,* 13–30.

Huertas, S. C., & Powell, L. (1986). Effect of appointed leadership on conformity. *Psychological Reports, 59,* 679–682.

Hughes, E. C. (1945). Dilemmas and contradictions of status. *American Journal of Sociology, 50,* 353–359.

Hughes, E. C. (1946). The knitting of racial groups in industry. *American Sociological Review, 11,* 512–519.

Hulet, R. E. (1958). Leadership behavior in independent and fraternity houses. *Dissertation Abstracts, 19,* 1015.

Hulin, C. L. (1962). The measurement of executive success. *Journal of Applied Psychology, 46,* 303–306.

Hulin, C. L. (1966). Job satisfaction and turnover in a female clerical population. *Journal of Applied Psychology, 50,* 280–285.

Hulin, C. L., & Blood, M. R. (1968). Job enlargement, individual differences, and worker responses. *Psychological Bulletin, 69,* 41–55.

Hultman, G. (1984). Managerial work, organizational perspectives, and the training of managers. *Scandinavian Journal of Educational Research, 28,* 199–210.

Human, L., & Hofmeyr, K. (1984). Black managers in a white world: Strategy formulation. *South African Journal of Business Management, 15,* 96–104.

Humes, J. F. (1947). The use and results of instructional demonstrations for supervisory training groups. *American Psychologist, 2,* 338–339.

Hummel, R. P. (1973). *Charisma in politics: Psycho-social causes of revolution as preconditions of charismatic outbreaks within the framework of Weber's epistemology.* Master's thesis, New York University.

Hummel, R. P. (1975). Psychology of charismatic followers. *Psychological Reports, 37,* 759–770.

Hunsaker, P. L., & Cook, C. W. (1986). *Managing organizational behavior.* Reading, MA: Addison-Wesley.

Hunt, D. M., & Michael, C. (1983). Mentorship: A career training and development tool. *Academy of Management Review, 8,* 475–485.

Hunt, J. E. (1968). Expectations and perceptions of the leadership behavior of elementary school principals. *Dissertation Abstracts, 28,* 4852–4853.

Hunt, J. G. (1967). Fiedler's leadership contingency model: An empirical test in three organizations. *Organizational Behavior and Human Performance, 2,* 290–308.

Hunt, J. G. (1971). Leadership-style effects at two managerial levels in a simulated organization. *Administrative Science Quarterly, 16,* 476–485.

Hunt, J. G., & Hill, J. W. (1971). *Improving mental hospital effectiveness: A look at managerial leadership* (Tech. Rep. No. 71-4). Carbondale: Southern Illinois University.

Hunt, J. G., Hill, J. W., & Reaser, J. M. (1971). *Consideration and structure effects in mental hospitals: An examination of two managerial levels* (Tech. Rep. No. 71-1). Carbondale: Southern Illinois University.

Hunt, J. G., Hill, J. W., & Reaser, J. M. (1973). Correlates of leadership behavior at two managerial levels in a mental institution. *Journal of Applied Psychology, 3,* 174–185.

Hunt, J. G., & Larson, L. L. (1974). *Contingency approaches to leadership.* Carbondale: Southern Illinois University Press.

Hunt, J. G., & Larson, L. L. (1975). *Leadership frontiers.* Kent, OH: Kent State University Press.

Hunt, J. G., & Larson, L. L. (1977). *Leadership: The cutting edge.* Carbondale: Southern Illinois University Press.

Hunt, J. G., & Liebscher, V. K. C. (1973). Leadership preference, leadership behavior, and employee satisfaction. *Organizational Behavior and Human Performance, 9,* 59–77.

Hunt, J. G., & Osborn, R. N. (1978). A multiple approach to leadership for managers. In J. Stinson & P. Hersey (Eds.), *Leadership for practitioners.* Athens: Ohio University, Center for Leadership Studies.

Hunt, J. G., Osborn, R. N., & Larson, L. L. (1973). *Leadership effectiveness in mental institutions* (NIMH Final Tech. Rep.). Carbondale: Southern Illinois University, Department of Administrative Sciences.

Hunt, J. G., Osborn, R. N., & Larson, L. L. (1975). Upper level technical orientation and first level leadership within a noncontingency and contingency framework. *Academy of Management Journal, 18,* 476–488.

Hunt, J. G., Osborn, R. N., & Martin, H. J. (1979). *A multiple influence model of leadership.* Unpublished manuscript. Also: (1981). Tech. Rep. No. 520. Carbondale: Southern Illinois University Press.

Hunt, J. G., Osborn, R. N., & Schriesheim, C. A. (1977). *Omissions and commissions in leadership research.* Unpublished manuscript.

Hunt, J. G., Osborn, R. N., & Schriesheim, C. A. (1978). Some neglected aspects of leadership research. *Proceedings, Midwest Academy of Management Meetings,* Bloomington, IN, 364–375.

Hunt, J. G., Osborn, R. N., & Schuler, R. S. (1978). Relations of discretionary and nondiscretionary leadership to performance and satisfaction in a complex organization. *Human Relations, 31,* 507–523.

Hunt, J. G., & Schuler, R. S. (1976), *Leader reward and sanctions: behavior relations criteria in a large public utility.* Carbondale: Southern Illinois University. Department of Administrative Sciences.

Hunt, J. G., Sekaran, U., & Schriesheim, C. A. (Eds.). (1981). *Leadership: Beyond establishment views.* Carbondale: Southern Illinois University.

Hunter, A., & Fritz, R. (1985). Class, status, and power structures of community elites: A comparative case study. *Social Science Quarterly, 66,* 602–616.

Hunter, E. C., & Jordan, A. M. (1939). An analysis of qualities associated with leadership among college students. *Journal of Educational Psychology, 30,* 497–509.

Hunter, F. (1953). *Community power structure.* Chapel Hill: University of North Carolina Press.

Hunter, F. (1959). *Top leadership, U.S.A.* Chapel Hill: University of North Carolina Press.

Hunter, J. E., & Hunter, R. F. (1984). Validity and utility of alternative predictors of job performance. *Psychological Bulletin, 96,* 72–98.

Hunter, J. E., & Schmidt, F. L. (1978). Differential and single group validity of employment tests by race: A critical analysis of three recent studies. *Journal of Applied Psychology, 63,* 1–11.

Hunter, O. N. (1959). *Relationship between school size and discrepancy in perceptions of ten superintendents' behavior.* Doctoral dissertation, Washington University, St. Louis, MO.

Huntford, R. (1984). *Scott and Amundsen: The race to the South Pole.* London: Pan.

Hurlock, E. B. (1950). *Child development.* New York: McGraw-Hill.

Hurwitz, J. I., Zander, A. F., & Hymovitch, B. (1953). Some effects of power on the relations among group members. In D. Cartwright & A. Zander (Eds.), *Group dynamics.* Evanston, IL: Row, Peterson.

Husband, R. W. (1940). Cooperative versus solitary problem solution. *Journal of Social Psychology, 11,* 405–409.

Huse, E. F. (1962). Assessments of higher level personnel: IV. The validity of assessment techniques based on systematically varied information. *Personnel Psychology, 15,* 195–205.

Huss, C. (1973). A *study of planned organizational change in the structure and functioning of Indian hospitals.* Doctoral dissertation, School of Economics, Delhi University, Delhi, India.

Hussein, A. L. (1969). *Factors emerging from favorableness judgments of basic interview data in six occupational fields.* Doctoral dissertation, Ohio State University, Columbus.

Hutchins, E. B., & Fiedler, F. E. (1960). Task-oriented and quasi-therapeutic role functions of the leader in a small military group. *Sociometry, 23,* 393–406.

Hutchins, G. B. (1923). Leadership, an opportunity and a challenge to industrial employees. *Industrial Management, 66,* 76–77.

Hyde, J. S. (1981). How large are cognitive gender differences? A meta-analysis using w2 and d. *American Psychologist, 36,* 892–901.

Hyman, B. (1980). Responsive leadership: The woman manager's asset or liability? *Supervisory Management, 25*(8), 40–43,

Hyman, H. H. (1942). The psychology of status. *Archives of Psychology,* No. 269.

Hyman, H. H., & Singer, E. (1968). *Readings in reference group theory and research.* New York: Free Press.

Hyman, S. (1954). *The American presidency.* New York: Harper & Row.

Hymowitz, C., & Schellhardt, T. D. (1986, March 24). The glass ceiling: Why women can't seem to break the invisible barrier that blocks them from the top jobs. *Wall Street Journal,* Section 4, 1, 4–5.

Hynes, K., Feldhusen, J. F., & Richardson, W. B. (1978). Application of a three-stage model of instruction to youth leadership training. *Journal of Applied Psychology, 63,* 623–628.

Ickes, W. J., & Barnes, R. D. (1977). The role of sex and self-monitoring in unstructured dyadic interactions. *Journal of Personality and Social Psychology, 35,* 315–330.

IDE (Industrial Democracy in Europe), International Research Group. (1979). Participation: Formal rules, influence, and involvement. *Industrial Relations, 18,* 273–294.

IDE (Industrial Democracy in Europe), International Research Group. (1981a). Industrial democracy in Europe: Differences and similarities across countries and hierarchies. *Organization Studies, 2,* 113–129.

IDE (Industrial Democracy in Europe), International Research Group. (1981b). *Industrial democracy in Europe.* Oxford: Clarendon Press.

Ilchman, W. F., & Uphoff, N. T. (1969). *The political economy of change.* Berkeley: University of California Press.

Ilgen, D. R., Fisher, C. D., & Taylor, M. S. (1979). Consequences of individual feedback on behavior in organizations. *Journal of Applied Psychology, 64,* 349–371.

Ilgen, D. R., & Fujii, D. S. (1976). An investigation of the validity of leader behavior descriptions obtained from subordinates. *Journal of Applied Psychology, 61,* 642–651.

Ilgen, D. R., & Knowlton, W. A., Jr. (1980). Performance attributional effects on feedback from superiors. *Organizational Behavior and Human Performance, 25,* 441–456.

Ilgen, D. R., Mitchell, T. R., & Frederickson, J. W. (1981). Poor performers: Supervisors' and subordinates' responses. *Organizational Behavior and Human Performance, 27,* 386–410.

Ilgen, D. R., & O'Brien, G. (1974). Leader-member relations in small groups. *Organizational Behavior and Human Performance, 12,* 335–350.

Ilgen, D. R., Peterson, R. B., Martin, B. A., & Boeschen, D. A. (1981). Supervisor and subordinate reactions to performance appraisal sessions. *Organizational Behavior and Human Performance, 28,* 311–330.

Ilgen, D. R., & Terborg, J. R. (1975). Sex discrimination and sex-role stereotypes: Are they synonymous? No! *Organizational Behavior and Human Performance, 14,* 154–157.

Iliad of Homer (1720/1943). A. Pope (Trans.). New York: Heritage Press.

Immegart, G. (1987). *Selection and training of headmasters.* Paper, II World Basque Congress, Bilbao, Spain.

Inderrieden, E. J. (1984). Empirical investigation of the expanded work group structure model: The effects of leader needs and behavioral characteristics (technology, size, environment). *Dissertation Abstracts International, 46*(2A), 470.

Indik, B. P. (1963). Some effects of organization size on member attitudes and behavior. *Human Relations, 16,* 369–384.

Indik, B. P. (1964). The relationship between organization size and supervisory ratio. *Administrative Science Quarterly, 9,* 301–312.

Indik, B. P. (1965a). Organization size and member participation: Some empirical tests of alternative explanations. *Human Relations, 18,* 339–350.

Indik, B. P. (1965b). *Three studies of organizational and individual dimensions of organizations* (Tech. Rep. No. 15). New Brunswick, NJ: Rutgers, The State University.

Indik, B. P., & Berrian, F. K. (1968). *People, groups, and organizations.* New York: Teachers College Press.

Indik, B. P., Georgopoulos, B. S., & Seashore, S. E. (1961). Superior-subordinate relationships and performance. *Personnel Psychology, 14,* 357–374.

Indvik, J. (1985). *A path-goal theory investigation of superior-subordinate relationships.* Doctoral dissertation, University of Wisconsin, Madison.

Indvik, J. (1986a). Path-goal theory of leadership: A meta-analysis. *Proceedings, Academy of Management,* Chicago, 189–192.

Indvik, J. (1986b). *A path-goal theory investigation of achievement-oriented and participative leader message behaviors.* Paper, Academy of Management, Chicago.

Indvik, J. (1988). *A more complete testing of path-goal theory.* Paper, Academy of Management, Anaheim, CA.

Infante, D. A., & Gordon, W. E. (1985). Superiors' argumentativeness and verbal aggressiveness as predictors of subordinates' satisfaction. *Human Communication Research, 12,* 117–125.

Ingham, A. G., Levinger, G., Graves, J., & Peckham, V. (1974). The Ringlemann effect: Studies of group size and group performance. *Journal of Experimental Social Psychology, 10,* 371–384.

Inglehart, R. (1981). Value change in the uncertain 1970's. In G. Dlugos, & K. Weiermair (Eds.), *Management under differing value systems: Political, social, and economical perspectives in a changing world.* Berlin: deGruyter.

Ingmire, B. D. (1968). Relationships between creativity scores and leadership behavior in a group of high school seniors. *Dissertation Abstracts, 29,* 1365.

Ingraham, L. C. (1981). Leadership, democracy, and religion: Role ambiguity among pastors in Southern Baptist churches. *Journal for the Scientific Study of Religion, 20,* 119–129.

Inkeles, A. (1966). The modernization of man. In M. Weiner (Ed.), *Modernization.* New York: Basic Books.

Inkson, J. H. K., Hickson, D. J., & Pugh, D. S. (1968). *Administrative reduction of variance in organizations and behavior.* Paper, British Psychological Society.

Inkson, J. H. K., Payne, R. L., & Pugh, D. S. (1967). Extending the occupational environment. *Occupational Psychology, 41,* 33–49.

Inskon, A., Thibaut, J. W., Moehle, D., Wilson, M., Diamond, W. D., Gilmore, R., Solomon, M. R., & Lipsitz, A. (1980). Social evolution and the emergence of leadership. *Journal of Personality and Social Psychology, 39,* 431–448.

Institute for Social Research. (1954). *Task order 2* (Annual Report). Ann Arbor: University of Michigan.

Instone, D., Major, B., & Bunker, B. B. (1983). Gender, self confidence, and social influence strategies: An organizational simulation. *Journal of Personality and Social Psychology, 44,* 322–333.

Inzerilli, G., & Laurent, A. (1983). Managerial views of organization structure in France and USA. *International Studies of Management and Organization, 13,* 97–118.

Ippoliti, P. (1989). *The transformational transactional differences between new business and established business leaders.* Doctoral dissertation, Temple University, Philadelphia.

Ireson, C. J. (1976). *Effects of sex role socialization on adolescent female achievement.* Paper, Pacific Sociological Association, San Diego, CA.

Irwin, F. A., & Poole, G. E. (1940). *Student leadership in community clubs.* New Jersey S.T.C. Student Education.

Isenberg, D. G. (1981). Some effects of time-pressure on vertical structure and decision-making accuracy in small groups. *Organizational Behavior and Human Performance, 27,* 119–134.

Ishikawa, A. (undated) *Developing the creative potential of the organization in the changing environment: A Japanese experience.* Unpublished manuscript.

Ishikawa, A. (1986). *The meaning of power for Asian workers.* Paper, Fourth International Workshop on Capitalist and Socialist Organizations, Budapest, Hungary.

Ivancevich, J. M. (1970). An analysis of control, bases of control, and satisfaction in an organizational setting. *Academy of Management Journal, 13,* 427–436.

Ivancevich, J. M. (1974). A study of a cognitive training program: Trainer styles and group development. *Academy of Management Journal, 17,* 428–439.

Ivancevich, J. M. (1976). Effects of goal setting on performance and job satisfaction. *Journal of Applied Psychology, 61,* 605–612.

Ivancevich, J. M. (1979). An analysis of participation in decision making among project engineers. *Academy of Management Journal, 22,* 253–269.

Ivancevich, J. M. (1982). Subordinate's reactions to performance appraisal interviews: A test of feedback and goal-setting techniques. *Journal of Applied Psychology, 67,* 581–587.

Ivancevich, J. M. (1983). Contrast effects in performance evaluation and reward practices. *Academy of Management Journal, 26,* 465–476.

Ivancevich, J. M., & Baker, J. C. (1970). A comparative study of the satisfaction of domestic U.S. managers and overseas U.S. managers. *Academy of Management Journal, 13,* 69–77.

Ivancevich, J. M., & Donnelly, J. H. (1970a). Leader influence and performance. *Personnel Psychology, 23,* 539–549.

Ivancevich, J. M., & Donnelly, J. H. (1970b). An analysis of control, bases of control, and satisfaction in an organizational setting. *Academy of Management Journal, 13,* 427–436.

Ivancevich, J. M., & Donnelly, J. H. (1974). A study of role clarity and need for clarity for three occupational groups. *Academy of Management Journal, 17,* 28–36.

Ivancevich, J. M., & Matteson, M. T. (1980). *Stress and work: A managerial perspective.* Glenview, IL: Scott, Foresman.

Ivancevich, J. M., Matteson, M. T., & Preston, C. (1982). Occupational stress, Type A behavior, and physical well being. *Academy of Management Journal, 25,* 373–391.

Ivancevich, J. M., & McMahon, J. T. (1982). The effects of goal setting, external feedback, and self generated feedback on outcome variables: A field experiment. *Academy of Management Journal, 25,* 359–372.

Ivancevich, J. M., Schweiger, D. M., & Ragan, J. W. (1986). *Employee stress, health, and attitudes: A comparison of American, Indian, and Japanese managers.* Paper, Academy of Management, Chicago.

Ivancevich, J. M., & Smith, S. V. (1981). Goal setting interview skills training: Simulated and on-the-job analyses. *Journal of Applied Psychology, 66,* 697–705.

Iverson, M. A. (1964). Personality impression of punitive stimulus persons of differential status. *Journal of Abnormal and Social Psychology, 68,* 617–626.

Izard, C. E. (1959). Personality correlates of sociometric status. *Journal of Applied Psychology, 43,* 89–93.

Izard, C. E. (1960). Personality similarity and friendship. *Journal of Abnormal and Social Psychology, 61,* 47–51.

Izraeli, D. N. (1982). Avenues into leadership for women: The case of union officers in Israel. *Economic and Industrial Democracy, 3,* 515–529.

Izraeli, D. N. (1983). Sex effects or structural effects? An empirical test of Kanter's theory of proportions. *Social Forces, 62,* 153–165.

Izraeli, D. N., & Izraeli, D. (1985). Sex effects in evaluating leaders: A replication study. *Journal of Applied Psychology, 70,* 540–546.

Jaap, T. (1982). Trends in management development: Introducing theory "P"—A British organizational model. *Training & Development Journal, 36*(10), 57–62.

Jablin, F. M. (1980). Superior's upward influence, satisfaction, and openness in superior-subordinate communication: A reexamination of the "Pelz effect." *Human Communication Research, 6,* 210–220.

Jablin, F. M. (1981). An exploratory study of subordinates' perceptions of supervisory politics. *Communication Quarterly,* 269–275.

Jablin, F. M. (1985). Task/work relationships: A life-span perspective. In M. L. Knapp & G. R. Miller (Eds.), *Handbook of interpersonal communication.* Beverly Hills, CA: Sage.

Jack, L. M. (1934). An experimental study of ascendent behavior in preschool children. *University of Iowa Study of Child Welfare, 9,* 5–65.

Jackson, J. M. (1953a). *The relation between attraction, being valued, and communication in a formal organization.* Ann Arbor: University of Michigan, Institute for Social Research.

Jackson, J. M. (1953b). The effect of changing the leadership of small work groups. *Human Relations, 6,* 25–44.

Jackson, J. M. (1960). Structural characteristics of norms. In G. E. Jensen (Ed.), *Dynamics of instructional groups.* Chicago: University of Chicago Press.

Jackson, M. L., & Fuller, F. F. (1966). Influence of social class on students' evaluations of their teachers. *Proceedings, American Psychological Association,* New York, 269–270.

Jackson, S. (1986, March 24). BW/Harris Poll: How executives rate a B-school education. *Business Week.*

Jacob, J. E. (1985). Black leadership in a reactionary era. *Urban League Review, 9*(1), 42–45.

Jacob, P. E., & Ahn, C. (1978). *Impetus for worker participation.* Paper, International Sociological Association, Uppsala, Sweden.

Jacobs, H. L. (1976). A critical evaluation of Fiedler's contingency model of leadership effectiveness in its application to interdisciplinary task-groups in public school settings. *Dissertation Abstracts International, 36,* 4912.

Jacobs, M., Jacobs, A., Feldman, G., & Cavior, N. (1973). Feedback II—the "credibility gap": Delivery of positive and negative and emotional and behavioral feedback in groups. *Journal of Consulting and Clinical Psychology, 41,* 215–223.

Jacobs, T. O. (1970). *Leadership and exchange in formal organizations.* Alexandria, VA: Human Resources Research Organization.

Jacobs, T. O., & Jaques, E. (1987). Leadership in complex systems. In J. Zeidner (Ed.), *Human productivity enhancement.* New York: Praeger.

Jacobsen, E. N. (1984). The subordinate: A moderating variable between leader behavior and effectiveness. *Dissertation Abstracts International, 45*(7B), 2296.

Jacobson, E. (1951). Foremen and stewards, representatives of management and the union. In H. Guetzkow (Ed.), *Groups, leadership, and men.* Pittsburgh: Carnegie Press.

Jacobson, E. (1971). *Depression.* New York: International Universities Press.

Jacobson, E., Charters, W. W., & Lieberman, S. (1951). The use of role concept in the study of complex organizations. *Journal of Social Issues, 7,* 18–27.

Jacobson, E., & Seashore, S. E. (1951). Communication practices in complex organizations. *Journal of Social Issues, 7,* 28–29.

Jacobson, M. B., & Effertz, J. (1974). Sex roles and leadership: Perceptions of the leaders and the led. *Organizational Behavior and Human Performance, 12,* 383–396.

Jacobson, M. B., & Kock, W. (1977). Women as leaders: Performance evaluation as a function of method of leader selection. *Organizational Behavior and Human Performance, 20,* 149–157.

Jacoby, J. (1968). Creative ability of task-oriented versus person-oriented leaders. *Journal of Creative Behavior, 2,* 249–253.

Jacoby, J. (1974). The construct validity of opinion leadership. *Public Opinion Quarterly, 38,* 81–89.

Jacoby, J., Mazursky, D., Troutman, T., & Kuss, A. (1984). When feedback is ignored: Disutility of outcome feedback. *Journal of Applied Psychology, 69,* 531–545.

Jaffee, C. L. (1968). Leadership attempting: Why and when? *Psychological Reports, 23,* 939–946.

Jaffee, C. L., Cohen, S. L., & Cherry, R. (1972). Supervisory selection program for disadvantaged or minority employees. *Training & Development Journal, 26,* 22–27.

Jaffee, C. L., & Lucas, R. L. (1969). Effects of rates of talking and correctness of decision on leader choice in small groups. *Journal of Social Psychology, 79,* 247–254.

Jaffee, C. L., Richards, S. A., & McLaughlin, G. W. (1970). Leadership selection under differing feedback conditions. *Psychonomic Science, 20,* 349–350.

Jaffee, C. L., & Skaja, N. W. (1968). Conditional leadership in a two-person interaction. *Psychological Reports, 23,* 135–140.

Jaggi, B. (1977). Job satisfaction and leadership style in developing countries: The case of India. *International Journal of Communication Sociology, 3*, 230–236.

Jago, A. G. (1978a). A test of spuriousness in descriptive models of participative leader behavior. *Journal of Applied Psychology, 63*, 383–387.

Jago, A. G. (1978b). Configural cue utilization in implicit models of leader behavior. *Organizational Behavior and Human Performance, 22*, 474–496.

Jago, A. G. (1982). Leadership: Perspectives in theory and research. *Management Science, 28*, 315–336.

Jago, A. G., & Ragan, J. W. (1986a). The trouble with LEADER MATCH is that it doesn't match Fiedler's contingency model. *Journal of Applied Psychology, 71*, 555–559.

Jago, A. G., & Ragan, J. W. (1986b). Some assumptions are more troubling than others: Rejoinder to Chemers and Fiedler. *Journal of Applied Psychology, 71*, 564–565.

Jago, A. G., & Vroom, V. H. (1974). Predicting leader behavior from a measure of behavioral intent. *Proceedings, American Institute for Decision Sciences*, Chicago, 503–505.

Jago, A. G., & Vroom, V. H. (1975). Perceptions of leadership style: Superior and subordinate descriptions of decision-making behavior. In J. G. Hunt & L. L. Larson (Eds.), *Leadership frontiers*. Carbondale: Southern Illinois University Press.

Jago, A. G., & Vroom, V. H. (1980). An evaluation of two alternatives to the Vroom/Yetton normative model. *Academy of Management Journal, 23*, 347–355.

Jago, A. G., & Vroom, V. H. (1982). Sex differences in the incidence and evaluation of participative leader behavior. *Journal of Applied Psychology, 67*, 776–783.

Jain, S. C. (1971). *Indian manager: His social origin and career*. Bombay, India: Somaiya Publications.

Jambor, H. (1954). *Discrepancies in role expectations for the supervisory position*. Doctoral dissertation, University of Minnesota, Minneapolis.

James, D. R., & Soref, M. (1981). Profit constraints on managerial autonomy: Managerial theory and the unmaking of the corporation president. *American Sociological Review, 46*, 1–18.

James, G., & Lott, A. J. (1964). Reward frequency and the formation of positive attitudes toward group members. *Journal of Social Psychology, 62*, 111–115.

James, J. (1951). A preliminary study of the size determinant in small group interaction. *American Sociological Review, 16*, 474–477.

James, L. R., & White, J. F. (1983). Cross-situational specificity in managers' perceptions of subordinate performance, attributions, and leader behavior. *Personnel Psychology, 36*, 809–856.

James, W. (1880). Great men, great thoughts, and their environment. *Atlantic Monthly, 46*, 441–459.

James, W. (1917). *Selected papers on philosophy*. New York: E. P. Dutton.

Jameson, S. H. (1945). Principles of social interaction. *American Sociological Review, 10*, 6–12.

Janda, K. F. (1960). Towards the explication of the concept of leadership in terms of the concept of power. *Human Relations, 13*, 345–363.

Janis, I. L. (1962). Psychological effects of warnings. In G. W. Baker &

D. W. Chapman (Eds.), *Man and society in disaster*. New York: Basic Books.

Janis, I. L. (1972). *Victims of groupthink: A psychological study of policy decisions and fiascos*. Boston: Houghton Mifflin.

Janis, I. L. (1982). *Groupthink* (2nd ed.). Boston: Houghton Mifflin.

Janis, I. L., & Feshbach, S. (1953). Effects of fear-arousing communications. *Journal of Abnormal and Social Psychology, 48*, 78–92.

Janis, I. L., & Mann, L. (1977). *Decision making: A psychological analysis of conflict, choice, and commitment*. New York: Free Press.

Jansen, D. G., Winborn, B. B., & Martinson, W. D. (1968). Characteristics associated with campus social-political action leadership. *Journal of Counseling Psychology, 15*, 552–562.

Jaques, E. (1952). *The changing culture of a factory*. New York: Dryden Press.

Jaques, E. (1956). *Measurement of responsibility*. Cambridge, MA: Harvard University Press.

Jaques, E. (1966). Executive organization and individual adjustment. *Journal of Psychosomatic Research, 10*, 77–82.

Jaques, E. (1976). *A general theory of bureaucracy*. London: Heinemann.

Jaques, E. (1978). *General theory of bureaucracy*. Exeter, NH: Heinemann Books.

Jaques, E. (1982). *The form of time*. London: Heinemann.

Jaques, E. (1985). A look at the future of human resources work via stratified systems theory. *Human Resource Planning, 8*, 233–237.

Jarrard, L. E. (1956). Empathy: The concept and industrial applications. *Personnel Psychology, 9*, 157–167.

Javier, E. O. (1972). *Academic organizational structure and faculty/administrator satisfaction*. Doctoral dissertation, University of Michigan, Ann Arbor.

Jaynes, W. E. (1956). Differences between jobs and between organizations. In R. M. Stogdill & C. L. Shartle (Eds.), *Patterns of administrative performance*. Columbus: Ohio State University, Bureau of Business Research.

Jencks, C., Bartlett, S., Corcoran, M., Crouse, J., Eaglesfield, D., Jackson, G., McClelland, K., Mueser, P., Olneck, M., Schwartz, J., Ward, S., & Williams, J. *Who gets ahead? The determinants of economic success in America*. New York: Basic Books.

Jenkins, C. D. (1976). Recent evidence supporting psychologic and social risk factors for coronary disease. *New England Journal of Medicine, 294*, 987–994, 1033–1038.

Jenkins, C. D. (1978). Behavioral risk-factors in coronary artery disease. *Annual Review of Medicine, 29*, 543–562.

Jenkins, C. D., Rosenman, R. H., & Zyzanski, S. (1974). Prediction of clinical coronary heart disease by a test for the coronary prone behavior pattern. *New England Journal of Medicine, 290*, 1271–1275.

Jenkins, C. D., Zyzanski, S., & Rosenman, R. H. (1976). Risk of new myocardial infarction in middle-aged men with manifest coronary heart disease. *Circulation, 53*, 342–347.

Jenkins, D. H., & Blackman, C. A. (1956). *Antecedents and effects of administration behavior*. Columbus: Ohio State University, College of Education.

Jenkins, G. D., & Lawler, E. E. (1981). Impact of employee participation in pay plan development. *Organizational Behavior and Human Performance, 28,* 111–128.

Jenkins, J. G. (1948). The nominating technique, its uses and limitations. In D. Krech & R. S. Crutchfield (Eds.), *Theory and problems of social psychology.* New York: McGraw-Hill.

Jenkins, J. G., et al. (1950). *The combat criteria in naval aviation.* Washington, DC: U.S. Navy, Division of Aviation Medicine, Bureau of Medicine and Surgery.

Jenkins, R. L., Reizenstein, R. C., & Rodgers, E. C. (1984). Probing opinions: Report cards on the MBA. *Harvard Business Review, 62*(5), 20–30.

Jenkins, W. O. (1947). A review of leadership studies with particular reference to military problems. *Psychological Bulletin, 44,* 54–79.

Jennings, E. E. (1952a). The frustrated foreman. *Personnel Journal, 31,* 86–88.

Jennings, E. E. (1952b). Forced leadership training. *Personnel Journal, 31,* 176–179.

Jennings, E. E. (1954). The dynamics of forced leadership training. *Journal of Personnel Adminstration and Industrial Relations, 1,* 110–118.

Jennings, E. E. (1955). Democratic supervision works only in the right climate. *Personnel Journal, 33,* 296–299.

Jennings, E. E. (1960). *An anatomy of leadership: Princes, heroes, and supermen.* New York: Harper.

Jennings, E. E. (1962). *The executive: Aristocrat, bureaucrat, democrat.* New York: Harper & Row.

Jennings, E. E. (1966). *The executive in crisis.* East Lansing: Michigan State University.

Jennings, E. E. (1967a). *Executive success: Stresses, problems, and adjustments.* New York: Appleton-Century-Crofts.

Jennings, E. E. (1967b). *The mobile manager: A study of the new generation of top executives.* Doctoral dissertation, University of Michigan, Ann Arbor.

Jennings, E. E. (1980, April). *Profile of a black executive.* Cited in World of Work Report, p. 28.

Jennings, H. H. (1943). *Leadership and isolation.* New York: Longmans, Green.

Jennings, H. H. (1944). Leadership—a dynamic re-definition. *Journal of Educational Sociology, 17,* 431–433.

Jennings, H. H. (1947). Leadership and sociometric choice. *Sociometry, 10,* 32–49.

Jensen, M. B., & Morris, W. E. (1960). Supervisory ratings and attitudes. *Journal of Applied Psychology, 44,* 339–340.

Jensen, R. J. (1977). Leadership in contemporary American labor unions: Adaptation and renewal. *Communication Quarterly, 25*(2), 29–33.

Jerdee, T. H. (1964). Supervisor perception of work group morale. *Journal of Applied Psychology, 48,* 259–262.

Jerkedal, A. (1967). *Top management education: An evaluation study.* Stockholm: Swedish Council for Personnel Administration.

Jeswald, T. A. (1971). Research needs in assessment—A brief report of a conference. *The Industrial Psychologist, 9*(1), 12–14.

Jiambalvo, J., & Pratt, J. (1982). Task complexity and leadership effectiveness in CPA firms. *Accounting Review, 57,* 734–750.

Joe, V. C. (1971). Review of the internal-external control construct as a personality variable. *Psychological Reports, 28,* 619–640.

Johns, G. (1978). Task moderators of the relationship between leadership style and subordinate responses. *Academy of Management Journal, 21,* 319–325.

Johnson, A. C., Peterson, R. B., & Kahler, G. E. (1968). Historical changes in characteristics of foremen. *Personnel Journal, 47,* 475–481, 499.

Johnson, A. L., Luthans, F., & Hennessey, H. W. (1984). The role of locus of control in leader influence behavior. *Personnel Psychology, 37,* 61–75.

Johnson, D. E. (1969). *A comparison between the Likert management systems and performance in Air Force ROTC detachments.* Doctoral dissertation, University of Minnesota, Minneapolis.

Johnson, D. E. (1970). *Concepts of air force leadership.* Maxwell AF Base, AL: Air University.

Johnson, D. M., & Smith, H. C. (1953). Democratic leadership in the college classroom. *Psychological Monographs, 67,* No. 11.

Johnson, D. W., & Johnson, F. P. (1975). *Joining together: Group theory and group skills.* Englewood Cliffs, NJ: Prentice-Hall.

Johnson, E. W. (1988). *Management and labor: Breaking away.* Chicago: DePaul University.

Johnson, L. A. (1969). *Employing the hard-core unemployed.* New York: American Management Association.

Johnson, M. C. (1980). Speaking from experience: Mentors—the key to development and growth. *Training & Development Journal, 34*(7), 55–57.

Johnson, P. (1976). Women and power: Toward a theory of effectiveness. *Journal of Social Issues, 32,* 99–110.

Johnson, P. O., & Bledsoe, J. C. (1973). Morale as related to perceptions of leader behavior. *Personnel Psychology, 26,* 581–592.

Johnson, P. V., & Marcrum, R. H. (1968). Perceived deficiencies in individual need fulfillment of career army officers. *Journal of Applied Psychology, 52,* 457–461.

Johnson, R. D. (1970). *An investigation of the interaction effects of ability and motivational variables in task performance.* Doctoral dissertation, Indiana University, Bloomington.

Johnson, R. E. (1980). A significance of rational behavior training in the leadership development of first-line supervisors. *Dissertation Abstracts International, 41*(2A), 597.

Johnson, R. H. (1973). *Initiating structure, consideration, and participative decision making: Dimensions of leader behavior.* Doctoral dissertation, Michigan State University, East Lansing.

Johnson, R. J. (1954). Relationship of employee morale to ability to predict responses. *Journal of Applied Psychology, 38,* 320–323.

Johnson, R. J. (1963). Two approaches to the prediction of group responses. *Journal of Applied Psychology, 47,* 158–160.

Johnson, R. W., & Ryan, B. J. (1976). A test of the contingency model of leadership effectiveness. *Journal of Applied Social Psychology, 6,* 177–185.

Johnson, W. G. (1969). On-the-job affirmation of self and stated level of job satisfaction and their relation to perceived supervisory climate. *Dissertation Abstracts International, 30,* 424.

Johnson, W., Magee, R. P., Nagarajan, N. J., & Newman, H. A. (1985). An analysis of the stock price reaction to sudden executive deaths: Implications for the managerial labor market. *Journal of Accounting and Economics, 7,* 151–174.

Johnston, G. (undated, a). *A study of teacher loyalty to the principal: Rule administration and hierarchical influence of the principal.* Unpublished manuscript.

Johnston, G. (undated, b). *Relationships among teachers' perceptions of the principal's style, teachers' loyalty to the principal.* Unpublished manuscript.

Johnston, R. W. (1981). Leader-follower behavior in 3-D. Part 1. *Personnel, 58*(4), 32–42.

Joiner, C. W., Jr. (1985). Making the "Z" concept work. *Sloan Management Review, 26*(3), 57–63.

Jones, A. J. (1938). *The education of youth for leadership.* New York: McGraw-Hill.

Jones, A. P., James, L. R., & Bruni, J. R. (1975). Perceived leadership behavior and employee confidence in the leader as moderated by job involvement. *Journal of Applied Psychology, 60,* 146–149.

Jones, E. (1953). *The life and work of Sigmund Freud,* Vol. 1. New York: Basic Books.

Jones, E. E. (1954). Authoritarianism as a determinant of first-impression formation. *Journal of Personality, 23,* 107–127.

Jones, E. E. (1964). *Ingratiation.* New York: Appleton-Century-Crofts.

Jones, E. E., & deCharms, R. (1957). Changes in social perception as a function of the personal relevance of behavior. *Sociometry, 20,* 75–85.

Jones, E. E., Gergen, K. J., Gumpert, P., & Thibaut, J. W. (1965). Some conditions affecting the use of ingratiation to influence performance evaluation. *Journal of Personality and Social Psychology, 1,* 613–625.

Jones, E. E., Gergen, K. J., & Jones, R. E. (1963). Tactics of ingratiation among leaders and subordinates in a status hierarchy. *Psychological Monographs, 77,* No. 566.

Jones, E. E., & Pittman, T. S. (1982). Toward a general theory of strategic self-preservation. In J. Suls (Ed.), *Psychological perspectives on the self.* Hillsdale, NJ: Erlbaum.

Jones, E. E., & Wortman, C. (1973). *Ingratiation: An attributional approach.* Morristown, NJ: General Learning Press.

Jones, E. W. (1973). What it's like to be a black manager. *Harvard Business Review, 51*(3), 108–116.

Jones, E. W. (1986). Black managers: The dream deferred. *Harvard Business Review, 64*(3), 84–93.

Jones, G. R. (1983). Forms of control and leader behavior. *Journal of Management, 9,* 159–172.

Jones, H. R., & Johnson, M. (1972). LPC as a modifier of leader-follower relationships. *Academy of Management Journal, 15,* 185–196.

Jones, M. E. (1988, October 1). Business must prepare for changes in the 1990s. *Press & Sun Bulletin,* Binghamton, NY, p. 3A.

Jones, R. E., & Jones, E. E. (1964). Optimum conformity as an ingratiation tactic. *Journal of Personality, 32,* 436–458.

Jones, R. E., & Melcher, B. H. (1982). Personality and the preference for modes of conflict resolution. *Human Relations, 35*(8), 649–658.

Jongbloed, L., & Frost, P. J. (1985). Pfeffer's model of management: An expansion and modification. *Journal of Management, 11,* 97–110.

Jordan, A. M., & Hunter, E. C. (1939). An analysis of quality associated with leadership among college students. *Journal of Educational Psychology, 30,* 497–509.

Jordan, P. C. (1986). Effects of an extrinsic reward on intrinsic motivation: A field experiment. *Academy of Management Journal, 29,* 405–412.

Jöreskog, K. G., & Sorbos, D. (1978). *LISREL VI: Analysis of linear structure.* See J. S. Long, (1983). *Covariance structure models: An introduction to LISREL.* Beverly Hills, CA: Sage.

Joynt, P. (1981/1982). Contingency research as a management strategy. *Journal of General Management, 7*(2), 24–35.

Julian, J. W. (1964). Leader and group behavior as correlates of adjustment and performance in negotiation groups. *Dissertation Abstracts, 24,* 646.

Julian, J. W., & Hollander, E. P. (1966). *A study of some role dimensions of leader-follower relations* (Tech. Rep. No. 1). Buffalo, NY: State University of New York.

Julian, J. W., Hollander, E. P., & Regula, C. R. (1969). Endorsement of the group spokesman as a function of his source of authority, competence, and success. *Journal of Personality and Social Psychology, 11,* 42–49.

Jung, C. G. (1971). *Psychological types* (R. F. C. Hall, Trans.). Princeton, NJ: Princeton University Press.

Jung, C. K. (1968). *Analytical psychology: Its theory and practice.* New York: Pantheon Books.

Jurgensen, C. E. (1966). *Report to participants on adjective word sort.* Minneapolis: Minneapolis Gas Company. Unpublished manuscript. Reported in Campbell, Dunnette et al. (1970), pp. 188–190.

Jurma, W. E. (1978). Leadership structuring style, task ambiguity, and group member satisfaction. *Small Group Behavior, 9,* 124–134.

Jusenius, C. L. (1976). Economics. *Signs: Journal of Women in Culture and Society, 2,* 177–189.

Justis, R. T. (1975). Leadership effectiveness: A contingency approach. *Academy of Management Journal, 18,* 160–167.

Kabanoff, B. (1981). A critique of LEADER MATCH and its implications for leadership research. *Personnel Psychology, 34,* 749–764.

Kabanoff, B. (1985a). *Do feelings of cooperativeness and assertiveness affect the choice of conflict management mode?* Paper, Academy of Management, San Diego, CA.

Kabanoff, B. (1985b). Potential influence structures as sources of interpersonal conflict in groups and organizations. *Organizational Behavior and Human Decision Processes, 36,* 113–141.

Kabanoff, B., & O'Brien, G. E. (1979). Cooperation structure and the relationship of leader and member ability to group performance. *Journal of Applied Psychology, 64,* 526–532.

Kaczka, E. E., & Kirk, R. V. (1967). Managerial climate, work groups, and organizational performance. *Administrative Science Quarterly, 12,* 253–272.

Kadushin, A. (1968). Games people play in supervision. *Social Work, 13,* 23–32.

Kadushin, C. (1968). Power, influence, and social circles: A new methodology for studying opinion makers. *American Sociological Review, 33,* 685–699.

Kaess, W. A., Witryol, S. L., & Nolan, R. E. (1961). Reliability, sex differences, and validity in the leadership discussion group. *Journal of Applied Psychology, 45,* 345–350.

Kagay, M. (1988, June 14). Workers want their employers to listen to them, survey shows. *New York Times,* A25.

Kahn, R. L. (1951). An analysis of supervisory practices and components of morale. In H. Guetzkow (Ed.), *Groups, leadership, and men.* Pittsburgh: Carnegie Press.

Kahn, R. L. (1956a). *Employee motivation.* Ann Arbor: University of Michigan, Bureau of Industrial Relations.

Kahn, R. L. (1956b). The prediction of productivity. *Journal of Social Issues, 12,* 41–49.

Kahn, R. L. (1958). Human relations on the shop floor. In E. M. Hugh-Jones (Ed.), *Human relations and modern management.* Amsterdam: North-Holland Publishing.

Kahn, R. L. (1960). Productivity and job satisfaction. *Personnel Psychology, 13,* 275–287.

Kahn, R. L., & Boulding, E. (1964). *Power and conflict in organizations.* New York: Basic Books.

Kahn, R. L., & Katz, D. (1953/1960). Leadership practices in relation to productivity and morale. In D. Cartwright & A. Zander (Eds.), *Group dynamics.* New York: Harper & Row.

Kahn, R. L., & Morse, N. C. (1951). The relationship of productivity to morale. *Journal of Social Issues, 7,* 8–17.

Kahn, R. L., & Quinn, R. P. (1970). Role stress: A framework for analysis. In A. McLean (Ed.), *Mental health and work organizations.* Chicago: Rand McNally.

Kahn, R. L., & Tannenbaum, A. S. (1957). Leadership practices and member participation in local unions. *Personnel Psychology, 10,* 277–292.

Kahn, R. L., Wolfe, D. M., Quinn, R. P., Shoek, J. D., & Rosenthal, R. A. (1964). *Organizational stress: Studies in role conflict and ambiguity.* New York: Wiley.

Kahn, S. (1970). *How people get power.* New York: McGraw-Hill.

Kaiser, H. F. (1958). The varimax criterion for analytic rotation in a factor analysis. *Psychometrika, 23,* 187–200.

Kakar, S. (1971). Authority patterns and subordinate behavior in Indian organizations. *Administrative Science Quarterly, 16,* 295–307.

Kalay, E. (1983). *The commander in stress situations in IDF combat units during the "Peace for Galilee" campaign.* Paper, Third International Conference on Psychological Stress and Adjustment in Time of War and Peace, Tel Aviv, Israel.

Kamano, D. K., Powell, B. J., & Martin, L. K. (1966). Relationship between ratings assigned to supervisors and their ratings of subordinates. *Psychological Reports, 18,* 158.

Kamerman, J. B. (1981). A *"scrutinization" of charisma: Charismatic authority and control in the work of the symphony orchestra conductor.* Paper, Eastern Sociological Society, New York.

Kaminitz, H. (1977). The employers' approach to participation. In O. Karmi & A. Saar (Eds.), *Proceedings, International Seminar on Workers Participation.* Israel: Bar Ilan University, The Israel Institute of Productivity and the Institute for the Advancement of Labor Relations.

Kanareff, V. T., & Lanzetta, J. T. (1960). Effects of task definition and probability or re-enforcement upon the acquisition and extinction of imitative responses. *Journal of Experimental Psychology, 60,* 340–348.

Kane, D. E. (1984). A *General Electric case study: Four critical steps to cultural change.* Unpublished manuscript.

Kane, J. D. (1976). The evaluation of organizational training programs. *Journal of European Training, 5,* 289–338.

Kanouse, D. E., Gumpert, P., & Canavan-Gumpert, D. (1984). The semantics of praise. In J. H. Harvey, W. Ickes, & R. F. Kidd (Eds.), *New directions in attributional research,* Vol. 3. Hillsdale, NJ: Erlbaum.

Kanter, R. M. (1972). *Commitment and community.* Cambridge, MA: Harvard University Press.

Kanter, R. M. (1976). Why bosses turn bitchy. *Psychology Today, 11*(5), 56–59, 88–91.

Kanter, R. M. (1977a). *Men and women of the corporation.* New York: Basic Books.

Kanter, R. M. (1977b). Some effects of proportions on group life: Skewed sex ratios and responses to token women. *Journal of Sociology, 82,* 965–990.

Kanter, R. M. (1977c). Women in organizations: Sex roles, group dynamics, and change strategies. In A. G. Sargent, *Beyond sex roles.* St. Paul, MN: West Publishing.

Kanter, R. M. (1982a). Dilemmas of participation: Issues in implementing participatory quality-of-work-life programs. *National Forum, 62*(2), 16–19.

Kanter, R. M. (1982b). Dilemmas of managing participation. *Organizational Dynamics, 11*(1), 5–27.

Kanter, R. M. (1983). *The change masters.* New York: Simon & Schuster.

Kanungo, R. (1966). Sociometric rating and perceived interpersonal behavior. *Journal of Social Psychology, 68,* 253–268.

Kanungo, R. N., & Wright, R. (1983). A cross-cultural comparative study of managerial job attitudes. *Journal of International Business Studies, 14,* 115–129.

Kanungo, S. C., Mathur, J. S., & Chatterjee, B. B. (1965). Perceptions of leadership roles in rural settings. *Manas, 12,* 127–143.

Kaplan, A. (1964). *The conduct of inquiry: Methodology for behavioral science.* San Francisco: Chandler.

Kaplan, E. M., & Cowen, E. L. (1981). Interpersonal helping behavior of industrial foremen. *Journal of Applied Psychology, 66,* 633–638.

Kaplan, H. R., Tausky, C., & Bolaria, B. S. (1969). Job enrichment. *Personnel Journal, 48,* 791–798.

Kaplan, R. E. (1986). The warp and woof of the general manager's job. In B. Schneider & D. Schoorman (Eds.), *Facilitating work effectiveness.* Lexington, MA: Lexington Books.

Kaplan, R. E., Drath, W. H., & Kofodimos, J. R. (1985). *High hurdles: The challenge of executive self-development* (Tech. Rep. No. 25). Greensboro, NC: Center for Creative Leadership.

Kaplan, R. E., Lombardo, M. M., & Mazique, M. S. (1985). A mirror for managers: Using simulation to develop management teams. *Journal of Applied Behavioral Science, 21,* 241–253.

Kaplan, R. E., & Mazique, M. (1983). *Trade routes: The manager's network of relationships* (Tech. Rep. No. 22). Greensboro, NC: Center for Creative Leadership.

Kappelman, S. K. (1981). *Teachers' perceptions of principals' bases of power in relation to principals' styles of leadership.* Doctoral dissertation, University of New Orleans, New Orleans.

Karasick, B., Leidy, T. R., & Smart, B. (1968). Characteristics differentiating high school leaders from nonleaders. *Purdue Opinion Panel Poll Report, 27,* 18.

Karmel, B. (1978). Leadership: A challenge to traditional research methods and assumptions. *Academy of Management Review, 3,* 475–482.

Karson, S. G. (1979). Insurance industry and social responsibility. *Journal of Contemporary Business, 8,* 103–114.

Kartez, J. D. (1984). Crisis response planning. *Journal of the American Planning Association, 50*(1), 9–21.

Kassarjian, H. H. (1965). Social character and sensitivity training. *Journal of Applied Behavioral Science, 1,* 433–440.

Kast, F. E., & Rosenzweig, J. E. (1972). General systems theory: Applications for organization and management. *Academy of Management Journal, 15,* 447–465.

Katerberg, R., & Hom, P. W. (1981). Effects of within-group and between-groups variation in leadership. *Journal of Applied Psychology, 66,* 218–223.

Kates, S. L., & Mahone, C. H. (1958). Effective group participation and group norms. *Journal of Social Psychology, 48,* 211–216.

Katz, D. (1949). Employee groups: What motivates them and how they perform. *Advanced Management, 14,* 119–124.

Katz, D. (1951). Survey research center: An overview of the human relations program. In H. Guetzkow (Ed.). *Groups, leadership and men.* Pittsburgh: Carnegie Press.

Katz, D., & Kahn, R. L. (1951). Human organization and worker motivation. In L. R. Tripp (Ed.), *Industrial productivity.* Madison, WI: Industrial Relations Research Association.

Katz, D., & Kahn, R. L. (1966, 1978). *The social psychology of organizations.* New York: Wiley.

Katz, D., Maccoby, N., Gurin, G., & Floor, L. (1951). *Productivity, supervision, and morale among railroad workers.* Ann Arbor: University of Michigan, Institute for Social Research.

Katz, D., Maccoby, N., & Morse, N. C. (1950). *Productivity, supervision, and morale in an office situation.* Ann Arbor: University of Michigan, Institute for Social Research.

Katz, D. J. (1987). *Introduction.* Conference on Military Leadership: Traditions and Future Trends, U.S. Naval Academy, Annapolis, MD.

Katz, E., Blau, P. M., Brown, M. L., & Strodtbeck, F. L. (1957). Leadership stability and social change: An experiment with small groups. *Sociometry, 20,* 36–50.

Katz, E., & Lazarsfeld, P. F. (1955). *Personal influence: The part played by people in the flow of mass communications.* New York: Free Press.

Katz, E., Libby, W. L., & Strodtbeck, F. L. (1964). Status mobility and reactions to deviance and subsequent conformity. *Sociometry, 27,* 245–260.

Katz, F. E. (1965). Explaining informal groups in complex organizations: The case for autonomy in structure. *Administrative Science Quarterly, 10,* 204–221.

Katz, I. (1967). Some motivational determinants of racial differences in intellectual achievement. *International Journal of Psychology, 2,* 1–12.

Katz, I. (1968). Factors influencing Negro performance in the desegregated school. In M. Deutsch, I. Katz, & A. R. Jensen (Eds.), *Social class, race, and psychological development.* New York: Holt, Rinehart & Winston.

Katz, I. (1970). Experimental studies of Negro-white relationships. In L. Berkowitz (Ed.), *Advances in experimental social psychology,* Vol. 5. New York: Academic Press.

Katz, I. (1974). Cultural and personality factors in minority group behavior: A critical review. In M. L. Fromkin & J. J. Sherwood (Eds.), *Integrating the organization.* New York: Free Press.

Katz, I., & Benjamin, L. (1960). Effects of white authoritarianism in biracial work groups. *Journal of Abnormal and Social Psychology, 61,* 448–456.

Katz, I., & Cohen, M. (1962). The effects of training Negroes upon cooperative problem solving in biracial teams. *Journal of Abnormal and Social Psychology, 64,* 319–325.

Katz, I., Epps, E. G., & Axelson, L. J. (1964). Effect upon Negro digit-symbol performance of anticipated comparison with whites and with other Negroes. *Journal of Abnormal and Social Psychology, 69,* 77–83.

Katz, I., & Greenbaum, G. (1963). Effects of anxiety, threat, and racial environment on task performance of Negro college students. *Journal of Abnormal and Social Psychology, 66,* 562–567.

Katz, I., Goldston, J., & Benjamin, L. (1958). Behavior and productivity in biracial work groups. *Human Relations, 11,* 123–141.

Katz, R. L. (1974). Skills of an effective administrator. *Harvard Business Review, 52*(5), 90–102.

Katz, R. (1977). The influence of group conflict on leadership effectiveness. *Organizational Behavior and Human Performance, 20,* 265–286.

Katz, R., & Allen, J. J. (1985). Project performance and the locus of influence in the R & D matrix. *Academy of Management Journal, 28,* 67–87.

Katz, R., & Farris, G. (1976). *Does performance affect LPC?* Boston: Massachusetts Institute of Technology. Unpublished manuscript.

Katz, R., Phillips, E., & Cheston, R. (1976). *Methods of conflict resolution—a re-examination.* Boston: Massachusetts Institute of Technology. Unpublished manuscript.

Katzell, R. (1987). *How leadership works.* Paper, Conference on Military Leadership: Traditions and Future Trends, United States Naval Academy, Annapolis, MD.

Katzell, R. A. (1948). Testing a training program in human relations. *Personnel Psychology, 1,* 319–329.

Katzell, R. A. (1962). Contrasting systems of work organization. *American Psychologist, 17,* 102–111.

Katzell, R. A., Barrett, R. S., Vann, D. H., & Hogan, J. M. (1968). Organizational correlates of executive roles. *Journal of Applied Psychology, 52,* 22–28.

Katzell, R. A., & Guzzo, R. A. (1983). Psychological approaches to productivity improvement. *American Psychologist, 38,* 468–472.

Katzell, R. A., Miller, C. E., Rotter, N. G., & Venet, T. G. (1970). Effects of leadership and other inputs on group processes and outputs. *Journal of Social Psychology, 80,* 157–169.

Kaufman, G. G., & Johnson, J. C. (1974). Scaling peer ratings: An examination of the differential validities of positive and negative nominations. *Journal of Applied Psychology, 59,* 302–306.

Kaufman, R. A., Hakmiller, K. L., & Porter, L. W. (1959). The effects of top and middle management sets on the Ghiselli self-description inventory. *Journal of Applied Psychology, 43,* 149–153.

Kavanagh, M. J. (1969). Subordinates' satisfaction as a function of their supervisor's behavior. *Dissertation Abstracts International, 30,* 1391–1392.

Kavanagh, M. J. (1972). Leadership behavior as a function of subordinate competence and task complexity. *Administrative Science Quarterly, 17,* 591–600.

Kavanagh, M. J. (1975). Expected supervisory behavior, interpersonal trust and environmental preferences. Some relationships based on a dyadic model of leadership. *Organizational Behavior and Human Performance, 13,* 17–30.

Kavanagh, M. J., & Halpern, M. (1977). The impact of job level and sex differences on the relationship between life and job satisfaction. *Academy of Management Journal, 20,* 66–73.

Kavanagh, M. J., MacKinney, A. C., & Wolins, L. (1970). Satisfaction and morale of foremen as a function of middle manager's performance. *Journal of Applied Psychology, 54,* 145–156.

Kavanagh, M. J., & York, D. R. (1972). Biographical correlates of middle managers' performance. *Personnel Psychology, 25,* 319–332.

Kavcic, B., Rus, V., & Tannenbaum, A. S. (1971). Control, participation, and effectiveness in four Yugoslav industrial organizations. *Administrative Science Quarterly, 16,* 74–86.

Kay, B. R. (1959). Key factors in effective foreman behavior. *Personnel, 36,* 25–31.

Kay, B. R. (1963). Prescription and perception of the supervisory role: A rolecentric interpretation. *Occupational Psychology, 37,* 219–227.

Kay, E., French, J. R. P., & Meyer, H. H. (1962). A study of the performance appraisal interview. *Behavioral Research Science.* New York: General Electric.

Kay, E., & Meyer, H. H. (1962). The development of a job activity questionnaire for production foremen. *Personnel Psychology, 15,* 411–418.

Kay, E., Myer, H. H., & French, J. R. P. (1965). Effects of threat in a performance appraisal interview. *Journal of Applied Psychology, 49,* 311–317.

Kearny, W. J. (1979). Pay for performance? Not always. *MSU Business Topics, 27,* 5–16.

Keaveny, T. J. (1972). The impact of managerial values on managerial behavior. *Dissertation Abstracts International, 32,* 6708.

Keaveny, T. J., Jackson, J. H., & Fossum, J. A. (1976). *Sex differences in job satisfaction.* Paper, Academy of Management, Kansas City, MO.

Keeler, B. T., & Andrews, J. H. M. (1963). Leader behavior of principals, staff morale, and productivity. *Alberta Journal of Educational Research, 9,* 179–191.

Kegan, R. (1982). *The evolving self: Problem and process in human development.* Cambridge, MA: Harvard University Press.

Kegan, R., & Lahey, L. L. (1984). Adult leadership and adult development: A constructivist view. In B. Kellerman (Ed.), *Leadership: Multidisciplinary perspectives.* Englewood Cliffs, NJ: Prentice-Hall.

Kehoe, D. A. (1976). The interpersonal basis of consensus on emergent leadership in small discussion groups. *Dissertation Abstracts International, 36,* 5231–5232.

Keichel, W., III. (1983, May 30). Wanted: Corporate leaders. *Fortune,* 135–140.

Keidel, R. W. (1984). Baseball, football, and basketball: Models for business. *Organizational Dynamics, 12*(3), 5–18.

Keizai Doyukai 1958 Survey Report. (1960). The structure and function of top management of large enterprises in Japan. In N. Kazuo (Ed.), *Big business executives in Japan.* Tokyo: Diamond Press.

Keller, N. R. (1983). The emergence of expertise in small groups. *Dissertation Abstracts International, 45*(2B), 724.

Keller, R. T. (1987). *A test of the path-goal theory of leadership with need for clarity as a moderator in research and development organizations.* Paper, Academy of Management, New Orleans.

Keller, R. T. (1989a). A test of the path-goal theory of leadership with need for clarity as a moderator in research and development organizations. *Journal of Applied Psychology, 74,* 208–212.

Keller, R. T. (1989b). *Toward a contingency theory of leader behavior and creative versus incremental innovative outcomes in research and development project groups: Report on the first wave of data.* Bethlehem, PA: Lehigh University, Center for Innovation Management Studies.

Keller, R. T., & Szilagyi, A. D. (1976). Employee reactions to leader reward behavior. *Academy of Management Journal, 19,* 619–627.

Keller, W. (1989, January 30). '62 missile crisis yields new puzzle. *New York Times,* A2.

Kellerman, B. (1987). *The politics of leadership in America: Implications for higher education in the late 20th century.* Paper, Invitational Interdisciplinary Colloquium on Leadership in Higher Education, National Center for Postsecondary Governance and Finance, Teachers College, Columbia University, New York.

Kelley, H. H. (1950). The warm-cold variable in the first impressions of persons. *Journal of Personality, 18,* 431-439.

Kelley, H. H. (1951). Communication in experimentally created hierarchies. *Human Relations, 4,* 39-56.

Kelley, H. H. (1973). The processes of causal attribution. *American Psychologist, 28,* 107-128.

Kelley, H. H., & Arrowood, A. J. (1960). Coalitions in the triad: Critique and experiment. *Sociometry, 23,* 231-244.

Kelley, H. H., & Michela, J. L. (1980). Attribution theory and research. *Annual Review of Psychology, 31,* 457-501.

Kelley, H. H., & Shapiro, M. M. (1954). An experiment on conformity to group norms where conformity is detrimental to group achievement. *American Sociological Review, 19,* 667-677.

Kelley, H. H., & Thibaut, J. W. (1954). Experimental studies of group problem solving and process. In G. Lindzey (Ed.), *Handbook of social psychology.* Cambridge, MA: Addison-Wesley.

Kelley, L., & Worthley, R. (1981). The role of culture in comparative management: A cross-culture perspective. *Academy of Management Journal, 24,* 164-173.

Kelley, R. E. (1988). In praise of followers. *Harvard Business Review, 66*(6), 141-148.

Kelley, W. R. (1968). The relationship between cognitive complexity and leadership style in school superintendents. *Dissertation Abstracts, 28,* 4910-4911.

Kellogg, C. E., & White, D. D. (1987). *Leader behaviors and volunteer satisfaction with work: The effect of volunteer motivation level.* Paper, Academy of Management, New Orleans.

Kelly, G. (1955). The psychology of personal constructs. New York: W. W. Norton.

Kelly, J. (1963). A study of leadership in two contrasting groups. *Sociological Review, 11,* 323-336.

Kelly, J. (1964). The study of executive behavior by activity sampling. *Human Relations, 17,* 277-287.

Kelman, H. C. (1953). Attitude change as a function of response restriction. *Human Relations, 6,* 185-214.

Kelman, H. C. (1958). Compliance, identification, and internalization: Three processes of attitude change. *Journal of Conflict Resolution, 2,* 51-60.

Kelman, H. C. (1970). A social-psychological model of political legitimacy and its relevance to black and white student protest movements. *Psychiatry, 33,* 224-246.

Kemp, R. L. (1984). The city manager's role in emergency management. *Public Management, 66*(3), 9-12.

Kemp, R. M. (1983). Effective management of high technology projects. *Dissertation Abstracts International, 43*(12A), 4017.

Kenan, T. A. (1948). *A method of investigating executive leadership.* Doctoral dissertation, Ohio State University, Columbus.

Kenis, I. (1977). A cross-cultural study of personality and leadership. *Group & Organization Studies, 2,* 49-60.

Kennan, N., & Hadley, M. (1986). The creation of political leaders in the context of American politics in the 1970s and 1980s. In C. F. Graumann & S. Moscovici (Eds.), *Changing conceptions of leadership.* New York: Springer-Verlag.

Kennedy, J. E., & O'Neill, H. E. (1958). Job content and workers' opinions. *Journal of Applied Psychology, 42,* 372-375.

Kennedy, J. K. (1982). Middle LPC leaders and the contingency model of leadership effectiveness. *Organizational Behavior and Human Performance, 30,* 1-14.

Kennedy, J. (1985). *Measuring leadership experience based on relevant work history.* Paper, American Psychological Association, Los Angeles.

Kennedy, P. A. (1983). Leadership: An influential increment. *Dissertation Abstracts International, 44*(4B), 1268.

Kenny, D. A., & Zaccaro, S. J. (1983). An estimate of variance due to traits in leadership. *Journal of Applied Psychology, 68,* 678-685.

Kerlinger, F. N. (1951). Decision-making in Japan. *Social Forces, 30,* 36-41.

Kern, A. G., & Bahr, H. M. (1974). Some factors affecting leadership climate in a state parole agency. *Pacific Sociological Review, 17,* 108-118.

Kernan, J. P. (1963). *Laboratory human relations training—its effects on the personality of supervisory engineers.* Doctoral dissertation, New York University, New York.

Kernberg, O. F. (1979). Regression in organizational leadership. *Psychiatry, 42*(1), 24-38.

Kernberg, O. F. (1984). Regression in organizational leadership. In M. F. R. Kets de Vries (Ed.), *The irrational executive: Psychoanalytic explorations in management.* New York: International Universities Press.

Kerr, C., Dunlop, J. T., Harbison, F., & Myers, C. A. (1961). Industrialism and world society. *Harvard Business Review, 39*(1), 113-122.

Kerr, J. L. (1985). Diversification strategies and managerial rewards: An empirical study. *Academy of Management Journal, 28,* 155-179.

Kerr, S. (1973). Ability- and willingness-to-leave as moderators of relationships between task and leader variables and satisfaction. *Journal of Business Research, 1,* 115-128.

Kerr, S. (1975). On the folly of rewarding A, while hoping for B. *Academy of Management Journal, 18,* 769-783.

Kerr, S. (1977). Substitutes for leadership: Some implications for organizational design. *Organization and Administrative Sciences, 8,* 135-146.

Kerr, S., Hill, K. D., & Broedling, L. (1986). The first-line supervisor: Phasing out or here to stay. *Academy of Management Review, 11,* 103-117.

Kerr, S., & Jermier, J. (1978). Substitutes for leadership: Their meaning and measurement. *Organizational Behavior and Human Performance, 22,* 374-403.

Kerr, S., & Schriesheim, C. (1974). Consideration, initiating structure, and organizational criteria—an update of Korman's 1966 review. *Personnel Psychology, 27,* 555-568.

Kerr, S., Schriesheim, C. A., Murphy, C. J., & Stogdill, R. M. (1974). Toward a contingency theory of leadership based upon the consideration and initiating structure literature. *Organizational Behavior and Human Performance, 12,* 62-82.

Kerr, S., & Slocum, J. W., Jr. (1981). Controlling the performances of people in organizations. In P. C. Nystrom & W. H. Starbuck (Eds.), *Handbook of organizational design,* Vol. 2. New York: Oxford University Press.

Kerr, J., & Slocum, J. W., Jr. (1987). Managing corporate culture through reward systems. *Academy of Management Executive, 1*(2), 99-108.

Kerr, W. A. (1947). Labor turnover and its correlates. *Journal of Applied Psychology, 31,* 366-371.

Kerr, W. A., & Speroff, B. J. (1951). *Measurement of empathy.* Chicago: Psychometric Affiliates.

Kessing, F. M., & Kessing, M. M. (1956). *Elite communication in Samoa: A study of leadership.* Stanford, CA: Stanford University Press.

Kessler, C. C. (1968). Differences between subordinates who are successful and less successful in meeting superiors' demands. *Dissertation Abstracts, 28,* 3866-3867.

Ketchel, J. M. (1972). *The development of methodology for evaluating the effectiveness of a volunteer health planning organization.* Doctoral dissertation, Ohio State University, Columbus.

Kets de Vries, M. F. R. (1980). *Organizational paradoxes. Clinical approaches to management.* London: Tavistock.

Kets de Vries, M. F. R. (1984). Managers can drive their subordinates mad. In M. F. R. Kets de Vries (Ed.), *The irrational executive. Psychoanalytic explorations in management.* New York: International Universities Press.

Kets de Vries, M. F. R., & Miller, D. (1984a). Group fantasies and organizational functioning. *Human Relations, 37,* 111-134.

Kets de Vries, M. F. R., & Miller, D. (1984b). *Leadership in organizations: Review, synthesis and application.* Paper, 75th Anniversary Colloquium Series, Harvard Business School, Boston.

Kets de Vries, M. F. R., & Miller, D. (1985). Narcissism and leadership: An object relations perspective. *Human Relations, 38,* 583-601.

Kets de Vries, M. F. R., & Miller, D. (1986). Personality, culture, and organization. *Academy of Management Review, 11,* 266-279.

Key, R. C. (1974). *A study of perceived organizational characteristics in persistent disagreement school districts and nonpersistent disagreement districts in the San Francisco Bay area.* Doctoral dissertation, University of Southern California, Los Angeles.

Key, V. O., Jr. (1961). *Public opinion and American democracy.* New York: Knopf.

Keys, B., Edge, A. G., Heinza, D. D., Randall, C., & Case, T. (1986). *A cross-national study to evaluate differences between leadership relationships of managers in the U.S.,Philippines, and Korea.* Paper, Academy of Management, Chicago.

Khandwalla, P. (1973). Effect of competition on the structure of top management control. *Academy of Management Journal, 16,* 285-295.

Khemka, K. C. (1968). Perception of leadership status in a free operant group discussion situation as a function of the knowledge of reinforcement contingency. *Dissertation Abstracts, 29,* 1189.

Khuri, F. I. (Ed.). (1981). *Leadership and development in Arab society.* Beirut, Lebanon: American University of Beirut, Center for Arab and Middle East Studies.

Kidd, J. A., & Christy, R. T. (1961). Supervisory procedures and work-team productivity. *Journal of Applied Psychology, 45,* 388-392.

Kidd, J. S. (1958). Social influence phenomena in a task-oriented group. *Journal of Abnormal and Social Psychology, 56,* 13-17.

Kiechel, W., III. (1983, May). Wanted: Corporate leaders. *Fortune,* 135-140.

Kiefer, C. (1986). Leadership in metanoic organizations. In J. D. Adams (Ed.), *Transforming leadership.* Alexandria, VA: Miles River Press.

Kiefer, C., & Senge, P. (1984). Metanoic organizations. In J. D. Adams (Ed.), *Transforming work.* Alexandria, VA: Miles River Press.

Kiernan, J. P. (1975). A critical appreciation of Sundkler's leadership types in the light of further research. *African Studies, 34,* 193-201.

Kiesler, C. A., & Corbin, L. H. (1965). Commitment, attraction, and conformity. *Journal of Personality and Social Psychology, 2,* 890-895.

Kiesler, C. A., & Kiesler, S. B. (1969). *Conformity.* Reading, MA: Addison-Wesley.

Kiesler, C. A., Kiesler, S. B., & Pallak, M. (1967). The reactions to norm violations. *Journal of Personality, 35,* 585-599.

Kiessling, R. J., & Kalish, R. A. (1961). Correlates of success in leaderless group discussion. *Journal of Social Psychology, 54,* 359-365.

Kiggundu, M. N. (1983). Task interdependence and job design: Test of a theory. *Organizational Behavior and Human Performance, 31,* 145-172.

Kight, S. S., & Smith, E. E. (1959). Effects of feedback on insight and problem-solving efficiency in training groups. *Journal of Applied Psychology, 43,* 209-211.

Kilborn, P. T. (1989, July 16). Nations call for action on environment. *New York Times,* A7.

Kilbourne, C. E. (1935). The elements of leadership. *Journal of Coast Artillery, 78,* 437-439.

Kilbridge, M. D. (1960). Do workers prefer larger jobs? *Personnel Journal, 37,* 45-48.

Kilbridge, M. D. (1961). Do they want larger jobs? *Supervisory Management, 6*(4), 25-28.

Kilcourse, T. (1985). A framework for training influential managers. *Journal of the European Industrial Training, 9*(4), 23-26.

Kilmann, R. H., & Saxton, M. J. (1983). *Organizational cultures: Their assessment and change.* San Francisco: Jossey-Bass.

Kilmann, R. H., & Thomas, K. W. (1975). Interpersonal conflict-handling behavior as a reflection of Jungian personality dimensions. *Psychological Reports, 37,* 971-980.

Kim, J. S., & Schuler, R. S. (1976). Contingencies of the effectiveness of participation in decision making and goal setting. Paper, Eastern Academy of Management, Washington, DC.

Kim, K. I., & Organ, D. W. (1982). Determinants of leader-subordinate exchange relationships. *Group & Organization Studies, 7*, 77–89.

Kimberly, J. R., & Evanisko, M. J. (1981). Organizational innovation: The influence of individual organizational and contextual factors on hospital adoption of technological and administrative innovations. *Academy of Management Journal, 24*, 689–713.

Kincheloe, S. C. (1928). The prophet as a leader. *Sociology and Social Research, 12*, 461–468.

Kinder, B. N., & Kolmann, P. R. (1976). The impact of differential shifts in leader structure on the outcome of internal and external group participants. *Journal of Clinical Psychology, 32*, 857–863.

Kinder, D. R. (1981). President, prosperity, and public opinion. *Public Opinion Quarterly, 45*(1), 1–21.

King, B., Streufert, S., & Fiedler, F. E. (Eds.) (1978). *Managerial control and organizational democracy*. New York: Halsted Press.

King, C. D., & Van de Vall, M. (1969). *Dimensions of workers' participation in managerial decision-making*. Paper, Industrial Relations Research Association, New York.

King, C. E. (1962). *Sociology of small groups*. New York: Pageant Press.

King, D. C., & Bass, B. M. (1974). Leadership, power, and influence. In H. L. Fromkin & J. J. Sherwood (Eds.), *Integrating the organization*. New York: Free Press.

King, H. D., & Arlinghaus, C. G. (1976). *Interaction management validated in the steel industry*. Unpublished manuscript.

King, M. L., Jr. (1968). The role of the behavioral scientist in the civil rights movement. *Journal of Social Issues, 24*, 1–12.

King, P. H. (1966). *A summary of research in training for advisory roles in other cultures by the behavioral sciences laboratory*. Wright-Patterson Air Force Base, OH: Aerospace Medical Research Laboratories.

Kingsley, L. (1967). Process analysis of a leaderless counter-transference group. *Psychological Reports, 20*, 555–562.

Kinicki, A. J., & Schriesheim, C. A. (1978). Teachers as leaders: A moderator variable approach. *Journal of Educational Research, 70*, 928–935.

Kipnis, D. (1958). The effects of leadership style and leaderless power upon the inducement of an attitude change. *Journal of Abnormal and Social Psychology, 57*, 173–180.

Kipnis, D. (1960). Some determinants of supervisory esteem. *Personnel Psychology, 13*, 377–392.

Kipnis, D. (1964). Mobility expectations and attitudes toward industrial structure. *Human Relations, 17*, 57–72.

Kipnis, D. (1972). Does power corrupt? *Journal of Personality and Social Psychology, 24*, 33–41.

Kipnis, D. (1976). *The powerholders*. Chicago: University of Chicago Press.

Kipnis, D. (1984). Technology, power and control. *Research in the Sociology of Organizations, 3*, 125–156.

Kipnis, D., Castell, P. J., Gergen, M., & Mauch, D. (1976). Metamorphic effects of power. *Journal of Applied Psychology, 61*, 127–135.

Kipnis, D., & Cosentino, J. (1969). Use of leadership powers in industry. *Journal of Applied Psychology, 53*, 460–466.

Kipnis, D., & Lane, W. P. (1962). Self-confidence and leadership. *Journal of Applied Psychology, 46*, 291–295.

Kipnis, D., & Schmidt, S. M. (1982). *Profiles of organizational influence strategies (Form M)*. San Diego, CA: University Associates.

Kipnis, D., & Schmidt, S. M. (1983). An influence perspective on bargaining within organizations. In M. H. Bazerman and R. J. Lewicki (Eds.), *Negotiating in organizations*. Beverly Hills, CA: Sage.

Kipnis, D., Schmidt, S., Price, K., & Stitt, C. (1981). Why do I like thee: Is it your performance or my orders? *Journal of Applied Psychology, 66*, 324–328.

Kipnis, D., Schmidt, S. M., Swaffin-Smith, C., & Wilkinson, I. (1984). Patterns of managerial influence: Shotgun managers, tacticians, and bystanders. *Organizational Dynamics, 12*(3), 58–67.

Kipnis, D., Schmidt, S. M., & Wilkinson, I. (1980). Intraorganizational influence tactics: Explorations in getting one's way. *Journal of Applied Psychology, 65*, 440–452.

Kipnis, D., Silverman, A., & Copeland, C. (1973). Effects of emotional arousal on the use of supervised coercion with black and union members. *Journal of Applied Psychology, 57*, 38–43.

Kipnis, D., & Vanderveer, R. (1971). Ingratiation and the use of power. *Journal of Personality and Social Psychology, 17*, 280–286.

Kipnis, D., & Wagner, C. (1967). Character structure and response to leadership. *Journal of Experimental Research in Personality, 1*, 16–24.

Kirchner, W. K. (1961). Differences between better and less effective supervisors in appraisal of their subordinates. *American Psychologist, 16*, 432–433 (Abstract).

Kirchner, W. K., & Belenker, J. (1955). What employees want to know. *Personnel Journal, 33*, 378–379.

Kirchner, W. K., & Reisberg, D. J. (1962). Differences between better and less effective supervisors in appraisal of subordinates. *Personnel Psychology, 15*, 295–302.

Kirkhart, R. O. (1963). Minority group identification and group leadership. *Journal of Social Psychology, 59*, 111–117.

Kirkpatrick, D. L. (1954). *Evaluating human relations programs for industrial foremen and supervisors*. Doctoral dissertation, University of Wisconsin, Madison.

Kirkpatrick, J. J. (1960). *Background history factors that lead to executive success*. Paper, American Psychological Association, Chicago.

Kirkpatrick, J. J. (1966). *Five-year follow-up study of the American Chamber of Commerce standard application for employment form*. Washington, DC: U.S. Chamber of Commerce.

Kirmeyer, S. L., & Lin, T. (1987). Social support: Its relationship to observed communication with peers and superiors. *Academy of Management Journal, 30*, 138–151.

Kirscht, J. P., & Dillehay, R. C. (1967). *Dimensions of authoritarianism: A review of research and theory*. Lexington: University of Kentucky.

Kirscht, J. P., Lodahl, T. M., & Haire, M. (1959). Some factors in the selection of leaders by members of small groups. *Journal of Abnormal and Social Psychology, 58,* 406-408.

Kiser, S. L. (1955). *The American concept of leadership.* New York: Pageant Press.

Klapp, O. E. (1948). The creation of popular heroes. *American Journal of Sociology, 54,* 135-141.

Klaus, D. J., & Glasser, R. (1970). Reinforcement determinants of team proficiency. *Organizational Behavior and Human Performance, 5,* 33-67.

Klauss, R. (1981). *Senior executive service competencies: A superior manager's model.* Unpublished manuscript.

Klauss, R., & Bass, B. M. (1974). Group influence of individual behavior across cultures. *Journal of Cross-cultural Psychology, 5,* 236-246.

Klauss, R., & Bass, B. M. (1981). *Impact of communication.* New York: Academic Press.

Klauss, R., & Bass, B. M. (1982). *Interpersonal communications in organizations.* New York: Academic Press.

Klauss, R., Flanders, L., Fisher, D., & Carlson, D. (1981a). *Senior executive service competencies: A superior manager's model.* Washington, DC: U.S. Office of Personnel Management.

Klauss, R., Flanders, L., Fisher, D., & Carlson, D. (1981b). *Analyzing managerial roles in the Federal government.* Paper, Academy of Management, San Diego, CA.

Klebanoff, H. E. (1976). Leadership: An investigation of its distribution in task-oriented small groups. *Dissertation Abstracts International, 36,* 3614.

Kleck, B., Ono, H., & Hastorf, A. H. (1966). The effects of physical space upon face-to-face interaction. *Human Relations, 19,* 425-436.

Kleck, R. E., & Nuessle, W. (1968). Congruence between the indicative and communicative functions of eye contact in interpersonal relations. *British Journal of Social and Clinical Psychology, 7,* 241-246.

Klein, A. F. (1956). *Role playing in leadership training and group problem solving.* New York: Association Press.

Klein, A. L. (1975). Changes in leadership appraisal as a function of the stress of a simulated panic situation and task outcome. *Dissertation Abstracts International, 36,* 1970.

Klein, A. L. (1976). Changes in leadership appraisal as a function of the stress of a simulated panic situation. *Journal of Personality and Social Psychology, 34,* 1143-1154.

Klein, S. M. (1964). Work pressure and group cohesion. *Dissertation Abstracts, 24,* 3448.

Klein, S. M., & Maher, J. R. (1966). Education and satisfaction with pay. *Personnel Psychology, 18,* 195-208.

Klein, S. M., & Maher, J. R. (1968). Educational level, attitudes, and future expectations among first-level management. *Personnel Psychology, 21,* 43-53.

Klein, S. M., & Maher, J. R. (1970). Decision-making autonomy and perceived conflict among first-level management. *Personnel Psychology, 23,* 481-492.

Klein, S. M., & Ritti, R. R. (1970). Work pressure, supervisory behavior,

and employee attitudes: A factor analysis. *Personnel Psychology, 23,* 153-167.

Klepinger, B. W. (1980). The leadership behavior of executives of social service organizations as related to managerial effectiveness and employee satisfaction. *Dissertation Abstracts International, 41*(5A), 2295.

Klimoski, R. J., Friedman, B. A., & Weldon, E. (1980). Leader influence in the assessment of performance. *Personnel Psychology, 33,* 389-401.

Klimoski, R. J., & Hayes, N. J. (1980). Leader behavior and subordinate motivation. *Personnel Psychology, 33,* 543-555.

Klimoski, R. J. & Strickland, W. J. (1977). Assessment centers—valid or merely prescient. *Personnel Psychology, 30,* 353-361.

Kline, B. E., & Martin, N. H. (1958). Freedom, authority, and decentralization. *Harvard Business Review, 36*(3), 69-75.

Klonsky, B. G. (1978). *Family structure, socialization, and aspects of female social and personality development: Some neglected leads and unfinished business.* Paper, American Psychological Association, Toronto.

Klonsky, B. G. (1983). The socialization and development of leadership ability. *Genetic Psychology Monographs, 108,* 95-135.

Klonsky, B. G. (1987). *The socialization and development of leadership ability and responsibility in female adolescents: A multi-ethnic analysis.* Unpublished manuscript.

Klopfer, P. H. (1962). *Behavioral aspects of ecology.* Englewood Cliffs, NJ: Prentice-Hall.

Klofper, P. H. (1969). *Habitats and territories: A study of the use of space by animals.* New York: Basic Books.

Klubeck, S., & Bass, B. M. (1954). Differential effects of training on persons of different leadership status. *Human Relations, 7,* 59-72.

Kmetz, J. T., & Willower, D. J. (1982). Elementary school principals' work behavior. *Educational Administration Quarterly, 18,* 62-78.

Knapp, D. E., & Knapp, D. (1966). Effect of position on group verbal conditioning. *Journal of Social Psychology, 69,* 95-99.

Knapp, M. L., Stohl, C., & Reardon, K. (1981). Memorable messages. *Journal of Communication, 31,* 27-42.

Knickerbocker, I. (1948). Leadership: A conception and some implications. *Journal of Social Issues, 4,* 23-40.

Knight, M. E. (1952). *The German executive: 1890-1933.* Stanford, CA: Stanford University Press.

Knight, P. A. (1984). Heroism versus competence: Competing explanations for the effects of experimenting and consistent management. *Organizational Behavior and Human Performance, 33,* 307-322.

Knight, P. A., & Weiss, H. M. (1980). Effect of selection agent and leader origin on leader influence and group member perceptions. *Organizational Behavior and Human Performance, 26,* 7-21.

Knowles, E. S. (1967). *A bibliography of research: 1960-1967.* Washington, DC: NTL Institute for Applied Behavioral Science.

Knowles, H. P., & Saxberg, B. O. (1971). *Personality and leadership.* Reading, MA: Addison-Wesley.

Knowles, M. C. (1963). Group assessment in staff selection. *Personnel Practice Bulletin, 19,* 6-16.

Knowlton, W. (1979). *The effects of stress, experience, and intelligence on dyadic leadership performance.* Doctoral dissertation, University of Washington, Seattle.

Knowlton, W. A., & Mitchell, T. R. (1980). Effects of causal attributions on a supervisor's evaluation of subordinate performance. *Journal of Applied Psychology, 65,* 459–466.

Koch, H. L. (1933). Popularity in preschool children: Some related factors and a technique for its measurement. *Child Development, 4,* 164–175.

Koch, S. (1959). Formulation of the person in the social context. In S. Koch (Ed.), *Psychology: A study of a science,* Vol. 3. New York: McGraw-Hill.

Koch, S. (1963). Investigations of man as socius. In S. Koch (Ed.), *Psychology: A study of a science,* Vol. 6. New York: McGraw-Hill.

Kochan, T. A., Cummings, L. L., & Huber, G. P. (1976). Operationalizing the concepts of goals and goal incompatibilities in organizational behavior research. *Human Relations, 29,* 527–544.

Kochan, T. A., Schmidt, S. M., & de Cotiis, T. A. (1975). Superior-subordinate relations: Leadership and headship. *Human Relations, 28,* 279–294.

Kochman, T. (1969). "Rapping" in the black ghetto. *Transaction, 6,* 26–34.

Koff, L. A. (1973). Age, experience and success among women managers. *Management Review, 62,* 65–66.

Koff, L. A., & Handlon, J. H. (1975). Women in management—Key to success or failure. *Personnel Administration, 20*(2), 24–28.

Koford, C. B. (1963). Group relations in an island colony of Rhesus monkeys. In C. H. Southwick (Ed.), *Primate social behavior.* Princeton, NJ: Van Nostrand.

Kohlberg, L. (1969). Stage and sequence: The cognitive-developmental approach to socialization. In D. A. Goslin (Ed.), *Handbook of socialization theory and research.* Skokie, IL: Rand-McNally.

Kohn, A. (1986). How to succeed without even vying. *Psychology Today, 20*(9), 22–28.

Kohn, M. L. (1971). Bureaucratic man: A portrait and an interpretation. *American Sociological Review, 36,* 461–474.

Kohs, S. C., & Irle, K. W. (1920). Prophesying army promotion. *Journal of Applied Psychology, 4,* 73–87.

Kohut, G. F. (1983). Women in management: Communicative correlates of sex role identity and leadership style toward the development of a managerial self-concept. *Dissertation Abstracts International, 44*(6A), 1625.

Kohut, H. (1976). Creativeness, charisma, group psychology. In J. E. Gedo & G. H. Pollock (Eds.), *Psychological issues 34/35.* New York: International Universities Press.

Kohut, H. (1977). *The restoration of the self.* New York: International Universities Press.

Koile, E. A., & Draeger, C. (1969). T-group member ratings of leader and self in human relations laboratory. *Journal of Psychology, 72,* 11–20.

Kolaja, J. (1965). *Workers' councils: The Yugoslav experience.* London: Tavistock.

Kolaja, J., Able, R. L., Ferguson, J. P., Mathews, W. R., Jr., Porter, H. M., & Ramsey, L. (1963). An organization seen as a structure of decision-making. *Human Relations, 16,* 351–357.

Kolb, J. H. (1933). *Trends of country neighborhoods.* Madison: University of Wisconsin, Agriculture Experimental Station.

Kolb, J. H., & Wileden, A. F. (1927). *Special interest groups in rural society.* Madison: University of Wisconsin, Agriculture Experimental Station.

Kolstad, A. (1944). Attitudes of employees and their supervisors. *Personnel Journal, 20,* 241–250.

Komaki, J. L. (1981, February). Applied behavior analysis. *The Industrial Psychologist, 19,* 7–9.

Komaki, J. L. (1982). Why we don't reinforce: The issues. *Journal of Organizational Behavior Management, 4*(3–4), 97–100.

Komaki, J. L. (1986). Toward effective supervision: An operant analysis and comparison of managers at work. *Journal of Applied Psychology, 71,* 270–279.

Komaki, J. L., Collins, R. L., & Penn, P. (1982). The role of performance antecedents and consequences in work motivation. *Journal of Applied Psychology, 67,* 334–340.

Komaki, J. L., Desselles, M. L., & Bowman, E. D. (1989). Definitely not a breeze: Extending an operant model of effective supervision to teams. *Journal of Applied Psychology, 74,* 522–529.

Komaki, J. L., Zlotnick, S., & Jensen, M. (1986). Development of an operant-based taxonomy and observational index of supervisory behavior. *Journal of Applied Psychology, 71,* 260–269.

Konar-Goldband, E., Rice, R. W., & Monkarsh, W. (1979). Time-phased interrelationships of group atmosphere, group performance, and leader style. *Journal of Applied Psychology, 64,* 401–409.

Konovsky, M. A. (1986). *Antecedents and consequence of informal leader helping behavior: A structural equation modeling approach.* Doctoral dissertation, Indiana University, Bloomington.

Konrad, A., & Gutek, B. A. (1987). Theory and research on group composition: Applications to the status of women and ethnic minorities. In S. Oskamp & S. Spacapan (Eds.), *Interpersonal processes: The Claremont symposium on applied social psychology.* Newbury Park, CA: Sage.

Koontz, H., & O'Donnell, C. (1955). *Principles of management.* New York: McGraw-Hill.

Koontz, H., O'Donnell, C., & Weihrich, H. (1958). *Management.* New York: McGraw-Hill.

Kopelman, R. E., & Reinharth, L. (1982). Research results: The effect of merit-pay practices on white collar performance. *Compensation Review, 14*(4), 30–40.

Korman, A. K. (1964). Job satisfactions of the first-line supervisors. *Personnel Administration, 27,* 35–37.

Korman, A. K. (1966). "Consideration," "initiating structure," and organizational criteria. *Personnel Psychology, 18,* 349–360.

Korman, A. K. (1968). The prediction of managerial performance: A review. *Personnel Psychology, 21,* 295–322.

Korman, A. K. (1971). Expectancies as determinants of performance. *Journal of Applied Psychology, 55,* 218–222.

Korman, A. K. (1973). On the development of contingency theories of leadership: Some methodological considerations and a possible alternative. *Journal of Applied Psychology, 58,* 384–387.

Korman, A. K. (1974). Contingency approaches to leadership: An overview. In J. G. Hunt & L. L. Larson (Eds.), *Contingency approaches to leadership.* Carbondale: Southern Illinois University Press.

Korman, A. K. (1976). A hypothesis of work behavior revisited and an extension. *Academy of Management Review, 1,* 50–63.

Korman, A. K. (1988). *The outsiders. Jews and corporate America.* Lexington, MA: Lexington Books.

Korman, A. K., & Tanofsky, R. (1975). Statistical problems of contingency models in organizational behavior. *Academy of Management Journal, 18,* 393–397.

Korman, A. K., Wittig-Berman, U., & Lang, D. (1981). Career success and personal failure: Alienation in professionals and managers. *Academy of Management Journal, 24,* 342–360.

Kornhauser, A. W., & Sharp, A. A. (1932). Employee attitudes. *Personnel Journal, 10,* 393–404.

Korotkin, A. L., & Yarkin-Levin, K. (1985). *A study of leadership competency requirements and job performance dimensions.* Unpublished manuscript.

Korten, D. C. (1962). Situational determinants of leadership structure. *Journal of Conflict Resolution, 6,* 222–235.

Korten, D. C. (1968). Situational determinants of leadership structure. In D. Cartwright & A. Zander (Eds.), *Group dynamics: Research and theory.* New York: Harper & Row.

Kotter, J. P. (1978). Power, success and organizational effectiveness. *Organizational Dynamics, 6,* 26–40.

Kotter, J. P. (1979). *Power in management.* New York: AMACOM.

Kotter, J. P. (1982a). *The general managers.* New York: Free Press.

Kotter, J. P. (1982b). What effective general managers really do. *Harvard Business Review, 60*(6), 156–167.

Kotter, J. P. (1985a). Never underestimate the power of your subordinates. *Working Woman, 10*(12), 19–22.

Kotter, J. P. (1985b, October 20). Looking for more Iacoccas. Why business has so few leaders. *New York Times,* p. 2F.

Kotter, J. P. (1987). *The leadership factor.* New York: Free Press.

Kotter, J. P., & Lawrence, P. R. (1974). *Mayors in action.* New York: Wiley.

Koulack, D. (1977). Effect of outgroup responses on perceptions of leader effectiveness. *Social Forces, 55,* 959–965.

Kouzes, J. M., & Posner, B. Z. (1985, January). When are leaders at their best? *Santa Clara Magazine, 27*(3), 2–6.

Kouzes, J. M., & Posner, B. Z. (1987). *The leadership challenge: How to get extraordinary things done in organizations.* San Francisco: Jossey-Bass.

Kovach, B. E. (1986). The derailment of fast-track managers. *Organizational Dynamics, 15*(2), 41–48.

Kozlowski, S. W. J., & Doherty, M. L. (1989). Integration of climate and leadership: Examination of a neglected issue. *Journal of Applied Psychology, 74,* 546–553.

Kraemer, K. L., & Danziger, J. N. (1984). Computers and control in the work environment. *Public Administration Review, 44*(1), 32–42.

Kraiger, K., & Ford, J. K. (1985). A meta-analysis of ratee race effects in performance ratings. *Journal of Applied Psychology, 70,* 56–65.

Kraitem, M. H. (1981). An investigation of current management/leadership style of top financial executives in the United States. *Dissertation Abstracts International, 42*(2A), 774.

Kram, K. E. (1980). *Mentoring process at work: Developmental relationships in managerial careers.* Doctoral dissertation, Yale University, New Haven, CT.

Kram, K. E. (1983). Phases of the mentor relationship. *Academy of Management Journal, 26,* 608–625.

Krauft, C., & Bozarth, J. (1971). Democratic, authoritarian, and laissez-faire leadership with institutionalized mentally retarded boys. *Mental Retardation, 9,* 7–10.

Kraut, A. I. (1969). Intellectual ability and promotional success among high level managers. *Personnel Psychology, 22,* 281–290.

Kraut, A. I. (1972). A hard look at management assessment centers and their future. *Personnel Journal, 51,* 317–326.

Kraut, A. I. (1975a). The entrance of black employees into traditionally white jobs. *Academy of Management Journal, 18,* 610–615.

Kraut, A. I. (1975b). Prediction of managerial success by peer and training-staff ratings. *Journal of Applied Psychology, 60,* 14–19.

Kraut, A. I. (1976). Developing managerial skills via modeling techniques: Some positive research findings—a symposium. *Personnel Psychology, 29,* 325–369.

Kraut, A. I., & Scott, G. J. (1972). Validity of an operational management assessment program. *Journal of Applied Psychology, 56,* 124–129.

Kravetz, D. (1976). Sex role concepts of women. *Journal of Consulting Clinical Psychology, 44,* 437–443.

Krech, D., & Crutchfield, R. S. (1948). *Theory and problems of social psychology.* New York: McGraw-Hill.

Kreitner, R. (1981). Managerial reaction to the term behavior modification. *Journal of Organizational Behavior Management, 3*(2), 53–58.

Krejci, J. (1976). Leadership and change in two Mexican villages. *Anthropological Quarterly, 49,* 185–196.

Kremer, J., & Mack, D. (1983). Pre-emptive game behavior and the emergence of leadership. *British Journal of Social Psychology, 22,* 19–26.

Kriesberg, L. (1962). Careers, organization size, and succession. *American Journal of Sociology, 68,* 355–359.

Kriesberg, L. (1964). Reply. *American Journal of Sociology, 70,* 223.

Krishnan, B. (1965). The leadership qualities among the college students as assessed by the "L" scale of the Mysore Personality Inventory. *Psychological Studies, 10,* 23–36.

Kroen, C. W. (1968). Validation of Herzberg's theory of job motivation and its relationship to leadership style. *Dissertation Abstracts, 28,* 5225–5226.

Kroll, M. J., & Pringle, C. D. (1985). Individual differences and path-goal theory: The role of leader directiveness. *Southwest Journal of Business and Economics, 2*(3), 11-20.

Krout, M. H. (1942). *Introduction to social psychology.* New York: Harper.

Kruglanski, A. W. (1969). Some variables affecting interpersonal trust in supervisor-worker relations. *Dissertation Abstracts, 29,* 3219.

Kruisinga, H. J. (1954). *The balance between centralization and decentralization in managerial control.* Oxford: Blackwell.

Krukones, M. G. (1985, Winter). The campaign promises of Jimmy Carter: Accomplishments and failures. *Presidential Studies Quarterly, 15*(1), 136-144.

Krumboltz, J. D., Christal, R. E., & Ward, J. H. (1959). Predicting leadership ratings from high school activities. *Journal of Educational Psychology, 50,* 105-110.

Kruse, L., & Wintermantel, M. (1986). Leadership Ms-Qualified: I. The gender bias in everyday and scientific thinking. In C. F. Graumann & S. Moscovici (Eds.), *Changing conceptions of leadership.* New York: Springer-Verlag.

Krusell, J., Vicino, F. L., Manning, M. R., Ryterband, E. C., Bass, B. M., & Landy, D. A. (1972). *PROCESS—A program of self-administered exercises for personal and interpersonal development.* Scottsville, NY: Transnational Programs.

Krusell, J., Vicino, F., Manning, M. R., Ryterband, E. C., Bass, B. M., & Landy, D. A. (1982). Personal and interpersonal development: A self-administered workbook. San Diego, CA: University Associates.

Kuenzli, A. E. (1959). Preferences for high and low structure among prospective teachers. *Journal of Social Psychology, 49,* 243-248.

Kugihara, N., & Misumi, J. (1984). An experimental study of the effect of leadership types on followers' escaping behavior in a fearful emergency maze-situation. *Japanese Journal of Psychology, 55,* 214-220.

Kugihara, N., Misumi, J., Sato, S., & Shigeoka, K. (1982). Experimental study of escape behavior in a simulated panic situation: II. Leadership in emergency situation. *Japanese Journal of Experimental Social Psychology, 21,* 159-166.

Kuhnert, K. W., & Lewis, P. (1987). Transactional and transformational leadership: A constructive/developmental analysis. *Academy of Management Review, 12,* 648-657.

Kuhnert, K. W., & Russell, C. J. (1989). Theory and practice in the selection and development of organizational leaders. *Journal of Management,* in press.

Kumar, P. (1965). A study of value-dimensions in student leadership. *Psychological Studies, 10,* 73-79.

Kumar, P. (1966). Certain personal factors in student leadership. *Journal of Psychological Researches, 10,* 37-42.

Kunczik, M. (1974). The ASo-(LPC) value in the contingency model of effective leadership: Critical overview and suggestion of an alternative interpretation. *Kölner Zeitschrift für Soziologie und Sozialpsychologie, 26,* 115-137.

Kunczik, M. (1976a). Empirische Überprüfung des Kontingenzmodells effektiver Führung. Teil 1. [Empirical test of the contingency model of leadership effectiveness.] *Kölner Zeitschrift für Soziologie und Sozialpsychologie, 28,* 517-536.

Kunczik, M. (1976b). Empirische Überprüfung des Kontingenzmodells effektiver Führung. Teil 2: Beprüfung anhand von Ausbildungsgruppen der Bundeswehr [Empirical test of the contingency model of leadership effectiveness. Part 2: Examination with the aid of the training groups of the federal armed services.] *Kölner Zeitschrift für Soziologie und Sozialpsychologie, 28,* 738-754.

Kunz, D. K., & Hoy, W. K. (1976). Leadership style of principals and the professional zone of acceptance of teachers. *Educational Administration Quarterly, 12,* 49-64.

Kureshi, A., & Fatima, B. (1984). Power motive among student leaders and non-leaders: Testing the affective-arousal model. *Journal of Psychological Researches, 28*(1), 21-24.

Kuriloff, A. H. (1963). An experiment in management—putting theory Y to the test. *Personnel Journal, 40,* 8-17.

Kuriloff, A. H. (1966). *Reality in management.* New York: McGraw-Hill.

Kuriloff, A. H., & Atkins, S. (1966). T group for a work team. *Journal of Applied Behavioral Science, 2,* 63-93.

Kurke, L. B., & Aldrich, H. E. (1979). *Mintzberg was right!: A replication and extension of "the nature of managerial work."* Paper, Academy of Management, Atlanta, GA. Also: (1983). *Management Science, 29,* 975-984.

Kurukawa, H. (1981). Management objectives, conditions in workunit, and leadership behavior. *Psychologia—An International Journal of Psychology in the Orient, 24,* 176-184.

Kuykendall, J., & Unsinger, P. C. (1982). The leadership styles of police managers. *Journal of Criminal Justice, 10,* 311-321.

L'Etang, H. (1970). *The pathology of leadership.* New York: Hawthorn Books.

Labak, A. S. (1973). The study of charismatic college teachers. *Dissertation Abstracts International, 34,* 1258B.

Labovitz, G. H. (1972). More on subjective executive appraisal: An empirical study. *Academy of Management Journal, 18,* 289-302.

Lacey, L. (1977). Discriminability of the Miner sentence completion scale among supervisory and nonsupervisory scientists and engineers. In J. B. Miner (Ed.), *Motivation to manage.* Atlanta, GA: Organizational Measurement Systems Press.

Lachman, R. (1985). Public and private sector differences: CEOs' perceptions of their role environments. *Academy of Management Journal, 28,* 671-680.

LaCour, John A. (1977). Organizational structure: Implications for volunteer program outcomes. *Journal of Voluntary Action Research, 6,* 41-47.

Ladner, J. A. (1971). *Tomorrow's tomorrow: The black woman.* New York: Doubleday.

Ladouceur, J. (1973). *School management profile and capacity for change.* Doctoral dissertation, University of Toronto, Toronto, Ontario.

LaGaipa, J. J. (1969). Biographical inventories and style of leadership. *Journal of Psychology, 72,* 109-114.

Lahat-Mandelbaum, B. S., & Kipnis, D. (1973). Leader behavior dimensions related to students' evaluation of teaching effectiveness. *Journal of Applied Psychology, 58,* 250-253.

Laing, R. D., Phillipson, H., & Lee, A. R. (1966). *Interpersonal perception: A theory and a method of research.* New York: Springer-Verlag.

Laird, D. A., & Laird, E. C. (1956). *The new psychology for leadership.* New York: McGraw-Hill.

Lake, D. G., & Martinko, M. J. (1982). *The identification of high performing principals* (Working Paper). Tallahassee: Florida State University. (Cited in Martinko & Gardner, 1984.)

Lakin, M. (1969). Some ethical issues in sensitivity training. *American Psychologist, 24,* 923-928.

Lambert, R. (1971). Classement de portraits selon la valeur présumée au commandement et attribution de traits de personnalité. *Bulletin du Centre d'Etudes et Recherches Psychotechniques, 20,* 41-51.

Lamm, H. (1973). Intragroup effects on intergroup negotiation. *European Journal of Social Psychology, 3,* 179-192.

Lamm, R. (1975). Black union leaders at the local level. *Industrial Relations, 14,* 220-232.

Lammers, C. J. (1967). Power and participation in decision-making in formal organizations. *American Journal of Sociology, 73,* 201-216.

Lana, R. E., Vaughan, W., & McGinnies, E. (1960). Leadership and friendship status as factors in discussion group interaction. *Journal of Social Psychology, 52,* 127-134.

Lanaghan, R. C. (1972). *Leadership effectiveness in selected elementary schools.* Doctoral dissertation, University of Illinois, Urbana-Champaign.

Land, K. C. (1969). Principles of path analysis. In E. F. Borgatta (Ed.), *Sociological methodology.* San Francisco: Jossey-Bass.

Landau, S. B., & Leventhal, G. S. (1976). A simulation study of administrators' behavior toward employees who receive job offers. *Journal of Applied Social Psychology, 6,* 291-306.

Landsberger, H. A. (1961). The horizontal dimension in bureaucracy. *Administrative Science Quarterly, 6,* 299-332.

Landy, D., McCue, K., & Aronson, E. (1969). Beyond Parkinson's Law: III. The effect of protractive and contractive distractions on the wasting of time on subsequent tasks. *Journal of Applied Psychology, 3,* 236-239.

Landy, F. J., Barnes, J. L., & Murphy, K. R. (1978). Correlates of perceived fairness of performance evaluation. *Journal of Applied Psychology, 63,* 751-754.

Landy, F. J., & Farr, J. L. (1980). Performance rating. *Psychological Bulletin, 87,* 72-107.

Lane, R. E. (1961). *Political life.* Glencoe, IL: Free Press.

Lane, T. F. E. (1985, October). Take a lead from your followers. *Chief Executive,* p. 11.

Lange, C. J., Campbell, V., Katter, R. V., & Shanley, F. J. (1958). *A study of leadership in army infantry platoons.* Washington, DC: Human Resources Research Office.

Lange, C. J., & Jacobs, T. O. (1960). *Leadership in army infantry platoons: Study II.* Washington, DC: Human Resources Research Office.

Lange, C. J., Rittenhouse, C. H., & Atkinson, R. C. (1968, June). *Films and group discussions as a means of training leaders.* Washington, DC: Human Resources Research Office.

Langer, E. J., Blank, A., & Chanowitz, B. (1978). The mindlessness of ostensibly thoughtful action. *Journal of Personality and Social Psychology, 36,* 635-642.

Langer, W. C. (1972). *The mind of Adolf Hitler.* New York: Basic Books.

Lannon, J. M. (1977). Male vs. female values in management. *Management International Review, 17,* 9-12.

Lansing, F. W. (1957). Selected factors of group interaction and their relation with leadership performance. *International Journal of Sociometry, 1,* 170-174.

Lanzara, G. F. (1983). Ephemeral organizations in extreme environments: Emergence, strategy, and extinction. *Journal of Management Studies, 20(1),* 71-95.

Lanzetta, J. T. (1953). *An investigation of group behavior under stress* (Task Order V). Rochester, NY: University of Rochester.

Lanzetta, J. T. (1955). Group behavior under stress. *Human Relations, 8,* 29-52.

Lanzetta, J. T., Haefner, D., Langham, P., & Axelrod, H. (1954). Some effects of situational threat on group behavior. *Journal of Abnormal and Social Psychology, 49,* 445-453.

Lanzetta, J. T., & Hannah, T. E. (1969). Reinforcing behavior of naive trainers. *Journal of Personality and Social Psychology, 11,* 245-252.

Lanzetta, J. T., & Haythorn, W. W. (1954). *Instructor-crew influence on attitude formation in student crews* (TR-54-79). San Antonio, TX: Crew Research Laboratory, Air Force Personnel and Training Reserve Center.

Lanzetta, J. T., & Roby, T. B. (1955). *Group performance as a function of work-distribution patterns and task load* (CRL-LN-55-4). San Antonio, TX: Crew Research Laboratory, Air Force Personnel and Training Reserve Center.

Lanzetta, J. T., & Roby, T. B. (1956). Effects of work-group structure and certain task variables on group performance. *Journal of Abnormal and Social Psychology, 53,* 307-314.

Lanzetta, J. T., & Roby, T. B. (1957). Group learning and communication as a function of task and structure "demands." *Journal of Abnormal and Social Psychology, 55,* 121-131.

Lanzetta, J. T., & Roby, T. B. (1960). The relationship between certain group process variables and group problem-solving efficiency. *Journal of Social Psychology, 52,* 135-148.

Lanzetta, J. T., Wendt, G. R., Langham, P., & Haefner, D. (1956). The effects of an "anxiety reducing" medication on group behavior under threat. *Journal of Abnormal and Social Psychology, 52,* 103-108.

Lapiere, R. T. (1938). *Collective behavior.* New York: McGraw-Hill.

Lapiere, R. T., & Farnsworth, P. R. (1936). *Social psychology.* New York: McGraw-Hill.

Lapierre, L., & Toulouse, J. M. (1984). *La graine a monseigneret.* 75th Anniversary Colloquium on Leadership, Harvard Business School, Boston.

Lapping, B. (1985). *End of empire.* London: Granada.

Lardent, C. L. (1977). *An assessment of the motivation to command among U.S. army officer candidates* (Tech. Rep.). Washington, DC: U.S. Army Research Institute for the Behavioral and Social Sciences.

Larkin, R. W. (1975). Social exchange in the elementary school classroom: The problem of teacher legitimation of the social power. *Sociological Education, 48,* 400–410.

LaRocco, J. M., & Jones, A. P. (1978). Co-worker and leader support as moderators of stress-strain relationships in work situations. *Journal of Applied Psychology, 63,* 629–634.

Larsen, K. S., & Larsen, K. J. (1969). Leadership, group activity and sociometric choice in service sororities and fraternities. *Perceptual and Motor Skills, 28,* 539–542.

Larson, A. (1968). *Eisenhower: The president nobody knew.* New York: Popular Library.

Larson, C. J. (1975). Leadership in three black neighborhoods. *Phylon, 36,* 260–268.

Larson, J. R. (1980). *Some hypotheses about the causes of supervisory performance feedback behavior.* Paper, Academy of Management, Detroit, MI.

Larson, J. R. (1982). Cognitive mechanisms mediating the impact of implicit theories of leader behavior on leader behavior ratings. *Organizational Behavior and Human Performance, 29,* 129–140.

Larson, J. R., Jr. (1984). The performance feedback process: A preliminary model. *Organizational Behavior and Human Performance, 33,* 42–76.

Larson, J. R., Jr. (1986). Supervisors' performance feedback to subordinates: The impact of subordinate performance valence and outcome dependence. *Organizational Behavior and Human Decision Processes, 37,* 391–408.

Larson, J. R. (1989). The dynamic interplay between employees' feedback-seeking strategies and supervisors' delivery of performance feedback. *Academy of Management Review, 14,* 408–422.

Larson, J. R., Jr., Glynn, M. A., Fleenor, C. D., & Scontrino, M. P. (1985). Exploring the dimensionality of managers' performance feedback to subordinates. *Proceedings, Academy of Management,* San Diego. Also: (1986). *Human Relations, 39,* 1083–1102.

Larson, J. R., Jr., Lingle, J. H., & Scerbo, M. M. (1984). The impact of performance cues on leader-behavior ratings: The role of selective information availability and probabilistic response bias. *Organizational Behavior and Human Performance, 33,* 323–349.

Larson, L. L., Hunt, J. G., & Osborn, R. N. (1974). Correlates of leadership and demographic variables in three organizational settings. *Journal of Business Research, 2,* 335–347.

Larson, L. L., Hunt, J. G., & Osborn, R. N. (1976). The great hi-hi leader behavior myth: A lesson from Occam's razor. *Academy of Management Journal, 19,* 628–641.

Larson, L. L., & Rowland, K. M. (1973). Leadership style, stress, and behavior in task performance. *Organizational Behavior and Human Performance, 9,* 407–420.

Larson, L. L., & Rowland, K. M. (1974). Leadership style and cognitive complexity. *Academy of Management Journal, 17,* 37–45.

Larwood, L., Gutek, B. A., & Gattiker, U. (1984). Perspectives on institutional discrimination and resistance to change. *Group & Organization Studies, 9*(3), 333–352.

Larwood, L., & Kaplan, M. (1980). Job tactics of women in banking. *Group & Organization Studies, 5,* 70–79.

Larwood, L., O'Carroll, M., & Logan, J. (1977). Sex role as a mediator of achievement in task performance. *Sex Roles, 3,* 109–114.

Larwood, L., & Wood, M. M. (1977). *Women in management.* Lexington, MA: D. C. Heath.

Larwood, L., Wood, M. M., & Inderlied, S. D. (1978). Training women for management: New problems, new solutions. *Academy of Management Review, 3,* 584–593.

Lasher, W. F. (1975). *Academic governance in university professional schools.* Doctoral dissertation, University of Michigan, Ann Arbor.

Lassey, W. R., & Fernandez, R. R. (1976). *Leadership and social change.* La Jolla, CA: University Associates.

Lasswell, H. (1948). *Power and personality.* New York: W. W. Norton.

Lasswell, H. D., & Kaplan, A. (1950). *Power and society.* New Haven, CT: Yale University Press.

Lasswell, H. D., Lerner, D., & Rothwell, C. E. (1952). *The comparative study of elites.* Stanford, CA: Stanford University Press.

Latack, J. C. (1986). Coping with job stress: Measures and future directions for scale development. *Journal of Applied Psychology, 71,* 377–385.

Latham, G. (1988). Human resource training and development. *Annual Review of Psychology, 39,* 545–582.

Latham, G. P., & Baldes, J. J. (1975). The "practical significance" of Locke's theory of goal setting. *Journal of Applied Psychology, 60,* 122–124.

Latham, G. P., Erez, M., & Locke, E. A. (1988). Resolving scientific disputes by the joint design of crucial experiments by the antagonists: Application to the Erez-Latham dispute regarding participation in goal setting. *Journal of Applied Psychology Monographs, 73,* 753–772.

Latham, G. P., & Lee, T. W. (1986). Goal setting. In E. A. Locke (Ed.), *Generalizing from laboratory to field settings.* Lexington, MA: Lexington Books.

Latham, G. P., & Saari, L. M. (1979). Importance of supportive relationships in goal setting. *Journal of Applied Psychology, 64,* 151–156.

Latham, G. P., & Steel, T. P. (1983). The motivational effects of participation versus goal setting on performance. *Academy of Management Journal, 26,* 406–417.

Latta, J. A., & Emener, W. G. (1983). State vocational rehabilitation agency leadership behavior styles. *Journal of Rehabilitation Administration, 7,* 141–148.

Lau, A. W., Newman, A. R., & Broedling, L. A. (1980). The nature of managerial work in the public sector. *Public Administration Review, 40*(5), 513–520.

Lau, A. W., & Pavett, C. M. (1980). The nature of managerial work: A comparison of public and private sector managers. *Group & Organization Studies, 5,* 453–466.

Lau, S. (1977). *Managerial styles of traditional Chinese firms.* Doctoral dissertation, University of Hong Kong, Hong Kong.

Laughlin, R. A. (1973). *A study of organizational climate perceived by faculty in Colorado community junior colleges.* Doctoral dissertation, University of Colorado, Boulder.

Laurent, H. (1968). Research on the identification of management potential. In J. A. Myers (Ed.), *Predicting managerial success*. Ann Arbor, MI: Foundation for Research on Human Behavior.

Laurent, H. (1970). Cross-cultural cross-validation of empirically validated tests. *Journal of Applied Psychology, 54*, 417–423.

Lauterbach, A. (1954). *Men, motives, and money: Psychological frontiers of economics*. Ithaca, NY: Cornell University Press.

Lauterbach, A. (1963). Management aims and development needs in Latin America. *Business History Review, 39*, 557–572, 577–588.

Lavoie, D., & Culbert, S. A. (1978). Stages in organization and development. *Human Relations, 31*, 417–438.

Lavoy, K. R. (1928). Leaders, born or made. *School Social, 28*, 683–684.

Lawler, E. E., III. (1964). How long should a manager stay in the same job? *Personnel Administration, 27*, 6–8, 27.

Lawler, E. E., III. (1965). Managers' perceptions of their subordinates' pay and of their superiors' pay. *Personnel Psychology, 18*, 413–422.

Lawler, E. E., III. (1966a). *Identification and enhancement of managerial effectiveness: I. Current practices in industry and government for identifying and developing managers*. Greensboro, NC: Richardson Foundation.

Lawler, E. E., III. (1966b). *Identification and enhancement of managerial effectiveness: III. The role of motivation in managerial effectiveness*. Greensboro, NC: Richardson Foundation.

Lawler, E. E., III. (1966c). Managers' attitudes toward how their pay is and should be determined. *Journal of Applied Psychology, 50*, 273–279.

Lawler, E. E., III. (1966d). The mythology of management compensation. *California Management Review, 9*, 11–22.

Lawler, E. E., III. (1967a). Management performance as seen from above, below, and within. *Journal of Applied Psychology, 51*, 247–253.

Lawler, E. E., III. (1967b). How much money do executives want? *Personnel Management Abstracts, 12*, 1–8.

Lawler, E. E., III. (1969). Job design and employee motivation. *Personnel Psychology, 22*, 426–435.

Lawler, E. E., III. (1982). Increasing worker involvement to enhance organizational effectiveness. In P. S. Goodman (Ed.), *Changes in organizations*. San Francisco: Jossey-Bass.

Lawler, E. E., III. (1984). Leadership in participative organizations. In J. G. Hunt, D. Hosking, C. A. Schriesheim, & R. Stewart (Eds.), *Leaders and managers: International perspectives on managerial behavior and leadership*. New York: Pergamon.

Lawler, E. E., III. (1985). Education, management style, and organizational effectiveness. *Personnel Psychology, 38*, 1–26.

Lawler, E. E., III. (1986). *High-involvement management: Participative strategies for improving organizational performance*. San Francisco: Jossey-Bass.

Lawler, E., III. (1987). The design of effective reward systems. In J. W. Lorsch (Ed.). *Handbook of organizational behavior*. Englewood Cliffs, NJ: Prentice-Hall.

Lawler, E. E., III, & Hackman, J. R. (1969). Impact of employee participation in the development of pay incentive plans: A field experiment. *Journal of Applied Psychology, 53*, 467–471.

Lawler, E. E., III, & Hall, D. H. (1970). Relationship of job characteristics to job involvement, satisfaction, and intrinsic motivation. *Journal of Applied Psychology, 54*, 305–312.

Lawler, E. E., III, & Mohrman, S. A. (1987). Unions and the new management. *Academy of Management Executive, 1*, 293–300.

Lawler, E. E., III, Mohrman, A. M., Jr., & Resnick, S. M. (1984). Performance appraisal revisited. *Organizational Dynamics, 13*(1), 20–35.

Lawler, E. E., III, & Porter, L. W. (1963). Perceptions regarding management compensation. *Industrial Relations, 3*, 41–49.

Lawler, E. E., III, & Porter, L. W. (1966). Predicting managers' pay and their satisfaction with their pay. *Personnel Psychology, 19*, 363–374.

Lawler, E. E., III, & Porter, L. W. (1967a). The effect of performance on job satisfaction. *Industrial Relations, 7*, 20–28.

Lawler, E. E., III, & Porter, L. W. (1967b). Antecedent attitudes of effective managerial performance. *Organizational Behavior and Human Performance, 2*, 122–142.

Lawler, E. E., III, Porter, L. W., & Tannenbaum, A. (1968). Managers' attitudes toward interaction episodes. *Journal of Applied Psychology, 52*, 432–439.

Lawler, E. J., (1975). An experimental study of factors affecting the mobilization of revolutionary coalitions. *Sociometry, 38*, 163–179.

Lawler, E. J., (1983). Cooptation and threats as "Divide and Rule" tactics. *Social Psychology Quarterly, 46*, 89–98.

Lawrence, B. S. (1984). Historical perspective: Using the past to study the present. *Academy of Management Review, 9*, 307–312.

Lawrence, H. (1968). The effectiveness of a group-directed vs. a worker-directed style of leadership in social group work. *Dissertation Abstracts, 28*, 4712.

Lawrence, L. C., & Smith, P. C. (1955). Group decision and employee participation. *Journal of Applied Psychology, 39*, 334–337.

Lawrence, P. R. (1958). *The changing of organizational behavior patterns: A case study of decentralization*. Boston: Harvard Business School.

Lawrence, P. R., & Lorsch, J. W. (1967a). *Organization and environment*. Cambridge, MA: Harvard University Press.

Lawrence, P. R., & Lorsch, J. W. (1967b). Differentiation and integration in complex organizations. *Administrative Science Quarterly, 12*, 1–47.

Lawrie, J. W. (1966). Convergent job expectations and ratings of industrial foremen. *Journal of Applied Psychology, 50*, 97–107.

Lawshe, C. H., Bolda, R. A., & Brune, R. L. (1959). Studies in management training evaluation: II. The effect of exposures to role playing. *Journal of Applied Psychology, 43*, 287–292.

Lawshe, C. H., Brune, R. L., & Bolda, R. A. (1958). What supervisors say about role playing. *Journal of American Social Training of Directors, 12*, 3–7.

Lawshe, C. H., & Nagle, B. F. (1953). Productivity and attitude toward supervisor. *Journal of Applied Psychology, 37*, 159–162.

Lazar, I. (1953). *Interpersonal perception—a selected review of the literature*. Urbana: University of Illinois.

Lazarsfeld, P., Berelson, B., & Gaudet, H. (1948). *The people's choice* (2nd ed). New York: Columbia University Press.

Lazarus, R. S. (1966). *Psychological stress and the coping process*. New York: McGraw-Hill.

Leana, C. (1983). *The effects of group cohesiveness and leader behavior on defective decision processes: A test of Janis' groupthink model*. Paper, Academy of Management, Dallas.

Leana, C. R. (1984). *Antecedents and consequences of delegation*. Doctoral dissertation, University of Houston, Houston, TX.

Leana, C. R. (1985). A partial test of Janis' groupthink model: Effects of group cohesiveness and leader behavior on defective decision making. *Journal of Management, 11*, 5–17.

Leana, C. R. (1986). Predictors and consequences of delegation. *Academy of Management Journal, 29*, 754–774.

Leana, C. R. (1987). Power relinquishment vs. power sharing: Theoretical clarification and empirical comparison of delegation and participation. *Journal of Applied Psychology, 72*, 228–233.

Learned, E. P., Ulrich, D. N., & Booz, D. R. (1951). *Executive action*. Boston: Harvard University Press.

Leavitt, H. J. (1951). Some effects of certain communication patterns on group performance. *Journal of Abnormal and Social Psychology, 46*, 38–50.

Leavitt, H. J. (1962). Unhuman organization. *Harvard Business Review, 40*, 90–98.

Leavitt, H. J. (1986). *Corporate pathfinders*. New York: Dow-Jones-Irwin and Penguin Books.

Leavitt, H. J., & Bass, B. M. (1964). Organizational psychology. *Annual Review of Psychology, 15*, 371–398.

Leavitt, H. J., & Mueller, R. A. H. (1951). Some effects of feedback on communication. *Human Relations, 4*, 401–410.

Leavitt, H. J., & Whisler, T. L. (1958). Management in the 1980's. *Harvard Business Review, 36*, 41–48.

LeBon, G. (1897). *The crowd*. New York: Macmillan.

Lécuyer, R. (1976). Social organizations and spatial organization. *Human Relations, 29*, 1045–1060.

Lee, D. M. (1976). Subordinate perceptions of leadership behavior: A judgmental approach. *Dissertation Abstracts International, 37*, 2555–2556.

Lee, F. J., Horwitz, M., & Goldman, M. (1954). Power over decision making and the response to frustration in group members. *American Psychologist, 9*, 413–414 (Abstract).

Lee, H. C. (1965). Do workers really want flexibility on the job? *Personnel, 42*, 74–77.

Lee, H. E., & Harrell, T. W. (1965). *Relation between talking and sociometric choices* (Tech. Rep.). Stanford, CA: Stanford University, Graduate School of Business.

Lee, I. J., & Lee, L. L. (1956). *Handling barriers in communication*. New York: Harper.

Lee, S. M. (1969). Organizational identification of scientists. *Academy of Management Journal, 3*, 327–337.

Lee, S. M., & Schwendiman, G. (Eds.). (1982). *Japanese management: Cultural and environmental considerations*. New York: Praeger.

Lee, Y., & Larwood, L. (1983). The socialization of expatriate managers in multinational firms. *Academy of Management Journal, 26*, 657–665.

Lefcourt, H. M., & Ladwig, G. W. (1965). The effect of reference groups upon Negroes' task persistence in a biracial competitive game. *Journal of Personality and Social Psychology, 1*, 668–671.

Lefkowitz, M., Blake, R. R., & Mouton, J. S. (1955). Status factors in pedestrian violation of traffic signals. *Journal of Abnormal and Social Psychology, 51*, 704–706.

Lehman, H. C. (1937). The creative years in science and literature. *Science Monitor, 45*, 65–75.

Lehman, H. C. (1942). Optimum ages for eminent leadership. *Science Monitor, 54*, 162–175.

Lehman, H. C. (1947). The age of eminent leaders, then and now. *American Journal of Sociology, 52*, 342–356.

Lehman, H. C. (1953). *Age and achievement*. Princeton, NJ: Princeton University Press.

Lehman, H. C., & Witty, P. A. (1927). Play activity and school progress. *Journal of Educational Psychology, 18*, 318–326.

Leib, A. (1928). Vorstellungen und Urteile von Schülern über Führer in der Schulklass. *Zeitschrift für Angewandte Psychologie, 30*, 241–346.

Leigh, A. (1983). Analyzing management training needs in British social work. *Social Policy and Administration, 17*, 249–259.

Leighton, A. H. (1945). *The governing of men: General principles and recommendations based on experiences at a Japanese relocation camp*. Princeton, NJ: Princeton University Press.

Leik, R. K. (1965). "Irrelevant" aspects of stooge behavior: Implications for leadership studies and experimental methodology. *Sociometry, 28*, 259–271.

Leipold, W. E. (1963). *Psychological distance in diadic interview*. Doctoral dissertation, University of North Dakota, Grand Forks.

Leister, A., Borden, D., & Fiedler, F. E. (1977). Validation of contingency model leadership training: LEADER MATCH. *Academy of Management Journal, 20*, 464–470.

Lemann, T. B., & Solomon, R. L. (1952). Group characteristics as revealed in sociometric patterns and personality ratings. *Sociometry, 15*, 7–90.

Lennerlöf, L. (1965a). The formal authority of the supervisor. *Psychology Research Bulletin, 5*, 22–31.

Lennerlöf, L. (1965b). Attitudes to supervisory motivation. *Psychology Research Bulletin, 5*, 1–22.

Lennerlöf, L. (1968). *Supervision: Situation, individual, behavior effect*. Stockholm: Swedish Council for Personnel Administration.

Lennox, R. D., & Wolfe, R. N. (1984). Revision of the self-monitoring scale. *Journal of Personality and Social Psychology, 46*, 1349–1364.

Lennung, S. A., & Ahlberg, A. (1975). The effects of laboratory training: A field experiment. *Journal of Applied Behavioral Science, 11*, 177–188.

Lenski, G. E. (1956). Social participation and status crystallization. *American Sociological Review, 21*, 458–464.

Leopold, L. (1913). *Prestige*. London: Fisher & Unwin.

Lepkowski, M. L., Sr. (1970). *Cooperative decision making as related to* supportive relations and communication in the senior high school. Doctoral dissertation, University of Buffalo, Buffalo, NY.

Lerea, L., & Goldberg, A. (1961). The effects of socialization upon group behavior. *Speech Monographs, 28,* 60–64.

Lerner, H. H. (1952). Bibliography on leadership and authority in local communities. *Bulletin of World Federation on Mental Health, 4* (Suppl.).

Lerner, H. (1974). Early origins of envy and devaluation of women: Implications for sex role stereotypes. *Bulletin of the Menninger Clinic, 38,* 538–553.

Lerner, M. J., & Becker, S. (1962). Interpersonal choice as a function of ascribed similarity and definition of the situation. *Human Relations, 15,* 27–34.

Lerner, M. J., Dillehay, R. C., & Sherer, W. C. (1967). Similarity and attraction in social contexts. *Journal of Personality and Social Psychology, 5,* 481–486.

Lesieur, F. G. (1958). *The Scanlon plan.* Cambridge, MA: M.I.T. Press.

Lester, D., & Genz, J. L. (1978). Internal-external locus of control, experience as a police officer, and job satisfaction in municipal police officers. *Journal of Police Science and Administration, 6,* 479–481.

Lester, J. T. (1965). *Correlates of field behavior. Behavioral research during the 1963 Mount Everest expedition* (Tech. Rep. No. 1). San Francisco: Berkeley Institute of Psychological Research.

Lester, R. I. (1981). Leadership: Some principles and concepts. *Personnel Journal, 60,* 868–870.

Leung, K. (1983). *The impact of cultural collectivism on reward allocation.* Master's thesis, University of Illinois, Urbana.

Level, D. A. (1972). Communication effectiveness: Method and situation. *Journal of Business Communication, 10,* 19–25.

Level, D. A., & Johnson, L. (1978). Accuracy of information flows within the superior/subordinate relationship. *Journal of Business Communication, 15*(2), 12–22.

Leventhal, G. S., Michaels, J. W., & Sanford, D. (1972). Inequity and inter-personal conflict: Reward allocation and secrecy about rewards as methods of preventing conflict. *Journal of Personality and Social Psychology, 23,* 88–102.

Leventhal, G. S., & Whiteside, H. D. (1973). Equity and the use of reward to elicit high performance. *Journal of Personality and Social Psychology, 25,* 75–88.

Levering, R., Moskowitz, M., & Katz, M. (1984). *The 100 best companies to work for in America.* Reading, MA: Addison-Wesley.

Levi, A. M., & Benjamin, A. (1977). Focus and flexibility in a model of conflict resolution. *Journal of Conflict Resolution, 21,* 405–423.

Levi, I. J. (1930). Student leadership in elementary and junior high school and its transfer into senior high school. *Journal of Educational Research, 22,* 135–139.

Levi, M. A. (1954). *A comparison of two methods of conducting critiques* (AFPTRC-TR54-108). San Antonio, TX: Lackland AFB, Crew Research Laboratory, AF Personnel & Training Reserve Center.

Levi, M. A., Torrance, E. P., & Pletts, G. O. (1954). Sociometric studies of combat air crews in survival training. *Sociometry, 17,* 304–328.

Levine, J., & Butler, J. (1952). Lecture vs. group discussion in changing behavior. *Journal of Applied Psychology, 36,* 29–33.

Levine, J., Laffal, J., Berkowitz, M., Lindemann, J., & Drevdahl, J. (1954). Conforming behavior of psychiatric and medical patients. *Journal of Abnormal and Social Psychology, 49,* 251–255.

LeVine, R. (1966). *Dreams and deeds: Achievement motivation in Nigeria.* Chicago: University of Chicago Press.

Levine, S. (1949). An approach of constructive leadership. *Journal of Social Issues, 5,* 46–53.

Levinger, G. (1959). The development of perceptions and behavior in newly formed social power relationships. In D. Cartwright (Ed.), *Studies in social power.* Ann Arbor: University of Michigan, Institute for Social Research.

Levinger, G., Morrison, H. W., & French, J. R. P. (1957). Coercive power and forces affecting conformity. *American Psychologist, 12,* 393 (Abstract).

Levinson, D. J. (1959). Role, personality, and social structure in the organizational setting. *Journal of Abnormal and Social Psychology, 58,* 170–180.

Levinson, D. J., Darrow, C. M., Klein, E. G., Levinson, M. H., & McKee B. (1978). *The seasons of a man's life.* New York: Knopf.

Levinson, H. (1962). A psychologist looks at executive development. *Harvard Business Review, 40,* 69–75.

Levinson, H. (1968). *The exceptional executive: A psychological conception.* Cambridge, MA: Harvard University Press.

Levinson, H. (1970). *Executive stress.* New York: Harper & Row.

Levinson, H. (1980a). Criteria for choosing chief executives. *Harvard Business Review, 58*(4), 113–120.

Levinson, H. (1980b). Power, leadership, and the management of stress. *Professional Psychology, 11,* 497–508.

Levinson, H. (1984). Management by guilt. In M. F. R. Kets de Vries (Ed.), *The irrational executive. Psychoanalytic explorations in management.* New York: International Universities Press.

Levinson, H. (1988). You won't recognize me: Predictions about changes in top-management characteristics. *Academy of Management Executive, 2*(2), 119–125.

Levinson, H., & Rosenthal, S. (1984). *CEO: Corporate leadership in action.* New York: Basic Books.

Levy, B. I. (1954). *A preliminary study of informal crew conferences as a crew training adjunct* (AFPTRC-TR-54-87). San Antonio, TX: Lackland AFB, Crew Research Laboratory, AF Personnel & Training Reserve Center.

Levy-Leboyer, C., & Pineau, C. (1981). Caracteristiques organisationnelles, style de leadership et réussite dans la recherche bio-medicale. *Revue de Psychologie Appliquée, 31,* 201–235.

Lewin, A., & Craig, J. R. (1968). The influences of level of performance on managerial style: An experimental object-lesson in the ambiguity of correlation data. *Organizational Behavior and Human Performance, 3,* 440–458.

Lewin, K. (1939). Field theory and experiment in social psychology: Concepts and methods. *American Journal of Sociology, 44*, 868–896.

Lewin, K. (1943). Forces behind food habits and methods of change. *Bulletin of the Natural Resources Council, 108*, 35–65.

Lewin, K. (1947a). Frontiers in group dynamics: Concept, method and reality in social science, social equilibria and social change. *Human Relations, 1*, 5–41.

Lewin, K. (1947b). Group decision and social change (1944). In T. Newcomb & E. Hartley (Eds.), *Readings in social psychology*. New York: Holt.

Lewin, K. (1951). *Field theory in social science: Selected theoretical papers*, D. Cartwright (Ed.). New York: Harper & Row.

Lewin, K., & Lippitt, R. (1938). An experimental approach to the study of autocracy and democracy: A preliminary note. *Sociometry, 1*, 292–300.

Lewin, K., Lippitt, R., & White, R. K. (1939). Patterns of aggressive behavior in experimentally created social climates. *Journal of Social Psychology, 10*, 271–301.

Lewis, D. R., & Dahl, T. (1976). Time management in higher education administration: A case study. *Higher Education, 5*, 49–66.

Lewis, G. F. (1960). A comparison of some aspects of the backgrounds and careers of small businessmen and American business leaders. *American Journal of Sociology, 65*, 348–355.

Lewis, H. (1965). Child rearing among low-income families. In L. A. Ferman, J. L. Kornbluh, & A. Haber (Eds.), *Poverty in America*. Ann Arbor: University of Michigan Press.

Lewis, H. S. (1974). Leaders and followers: Some anthropological perspectives. *Addison-Wesley Module in Anthropology No. 50*. Reading, MA: Addison-Wesley.

Lewis, P., Kuhnert, K., & Maginnis, R. (1987). Defining military character. *Parameters: U.S. Army War College Quarterly, 17*(2), 33–41.

Lewis, R., & Stewart, R. (1961). *The managers: A new examination of the English, German, and American executive*. New York: New American Library.

Ley, R. (1966). Labor turnover as a function of worker differences, work environment, and authoritarianism of foremen. *Journal of Applied Psychology, 50*, 497–500.

LIAMA. (1964a). "Realistic" job expectations and survival. *Life Insurance Agency Management Association, 2*, File No. 432.

LIAMA. (1964b). Agent attitude: A study of attitudes and performance among ordinary agents. *Life Insurance Agency Management Association, 11*, File No. 440.

Liancang, X. (1987). Recent developments in organizational psychology in China. In B. M. Bass, P. J. D. Drenth, & P. W. Weissenberg (Eds.), *Advances in organizational psychology: An international review*. Beverly Hills, CA: Sage.

Lichtenberg, P., & Deutsch, M. (1954). *A descriptive review of research on the staff process of decision-making* (AFPTRC-TR-54-129). San Antonio, TX: Air Force Personnel & Training Reserve Center.

Lichtheim, M. (1973). *Ancient Egyptian literature. Vol. 1: The old and middle kingdoms*. Los Angeles: University of California Press.

Lichtman, C. M. (1968). An interactional analysis of structural and individual variables in a work organization. *Dissertation Abstracts, 29*, 675–676.

Lichtman, C. M. (1970). Some intrapersonal response correlates of organizational rank. *Journal of Applied Psychology, 54*, 77–80.

Liden, R. C. (1981). *Contextual and behavioral factors influencing perceptions of ineffective performance and managerial responses*. Doctoral dissertation, University of Cincinnati, Cincinnati, OH.

Liden, R. C. (1985, February). Female perceptions of female and male managerial behavior. *Sex Roles, 12*, 3–4.

Liden, R. C., Ferris, G. R., & Dienesch, R. M. (1988). The influence of causal feedback on subordinate reactions and behavior. *Group & Organization Studies, 13*, 348–373.

Liden, R. C., & Graen, G. (1979). The impact of leader-member exchange on job resignation. *Proceedings, American Institute for Decision Sciences*, New Orleans, 348–350.

Liden, R., & Graen, G. (1980). Generalizability of the vertical dyad linkage model of leadership. *Academy of Management Journal, 23*, 451–465.

Liden, R. C., & Mitchell, T. R. (1985). Reactions to feedback: The role of attributions. *Academy of Management Journal, 28*, 291–308.

Lieberman, A. (1969). *The effects of principal leadership on teacher morale, professionalism, and style in the classroom*. Doctoral dissertation, University of California, Los Angeles.

Lieberman, M. A. (1976a). Change induction in small groups. *Annual Review of Psychology, 27*, 217–250.

Lieberman, M. A. (1976b). People-changing groups: The new and not so new. In S. Areli (Ed.), *The American handbook of psychiatry*. New York: Basic Books.

Lieberman, M. A., Yalom, I. D., & Miles, M. B. (1973). *Encounter groups: First facts*. New York: Basic Books.

Lieberman, S. (1954). The relationship between attitudes and roles: A natural field experiment. *American Psychologist, 9*, 418–419 (Abstract).

Lieberman, S. (1956). The effects of changes in roles on the attitudes of role occupants. *Human Relations, 9*, 385–402.

Lieberson, S., & O'Connor, J. F. (1972). Leadership and organizational performance: A study of large corporations. *American Scoiological Review, 37*(2), 117–130.

Liebow, E. (1967). *Tally's corner*. Boston, MA: Little, Brown.

Liem, M. A., & Slivinski, L. W. (1975). A comparative study of middle and senior management dimensions and job types in the Canadian public service. *Studies in Personnel Psychology, 6*, 21–34.

Lifton, P. D. (1985). Individual differences in moral development: The relation of sex, gender, and personality to morality. *Journal of Personality, 53*, 306–334.

Lifton, R. J. (1967). *Death in life: Survivors of Hiroshima*. New York: Random House.

Likert, J. (1958). *Leadership for effective leagues*. Washington, DC: League of Women Voters.

Likert, R. (1932). A technique for the measurement of attitudes. *Archives of Psychiatry, 52,* 140.

Likert, R. (1940). *Morale and agency management.* Hartford, CT: Life Insurance Sales Research Bureau.

Likert, R. (1947). *A program of research on the fundamental problems of organizational human behavior.* Ann Arbor, MI: Survey Research Center, Institute for Social Research.

Likert, R. (1955). Developing patterns of management. I. *American Management Association, General Management Series,* No. 178. New York.

Likert, R. (1956). Developing patterns of management. II. *American Management Association, General Management Series,* No. 182. New York.

Likert, R. (1958). Effective supervision: An adaptive and relative process. *Personnel Psychology, 11,* 317–332.

Likert, R. (1959). Motivational approach to management development. *Harvard Business Review, 37,* 75–82.

Likert, R. (1961a). *New patterns of management.* New York: McGraw-Hill.

Likert, R. (1961b). An emerging theory of organizations, leadership and management. In L. Petrullo & B. M. Bass (Eds.), *Leadership and interpersonal behavior.* New York: Holt, Rinehart & Winston.

Likert, R. (1963). Trends toward a world-wide theory of management. *Proceedings, International Management Congress, 2,* 110–114.

Likert, R. (1967). *The human organization.* New York: McGraw-Hill.

Likert, R. (1973). Human resource accounting: Building and assessing productive organizations. *Personnel, 50,* 8–24.

Likert, R. (1975). Improving cost performance with cross-functional teams. *Conference of Board of Records, 92,* 51–59.

Likert, R. (1977a). Management styles and the human component. *Management Review, 66,* 23–28, 43–45.

Likert, R. (1977b). *Past and future perspectives on system 4.* Paper, Academy of Management, Orlando, FL.

Likert, R., & Bowers, D. G. (1973, March). Improving the accuracy of P/L reports by estimating the change in dollar value of the human organization. *Michigan Business Review,* 15–24.

Likert, R., & Fisher, S. (1977). MBGO: Putting some team spirit into MBO. *Personnel, 54*(1), 41–47.

Likert, R., & Katz, D. (1948). Supervisory practices and organizational structures as they affect employee productivity and morale. *American Management Association, Personnel Series,* No. 120.

Likert, R., & Likert, J. G. (1976). *New ways of managing conflict.* New York: McGraw-Hill.

Likert, R., & Likert, J. G., (1978). A method for coping with conflict in problem-solving groups. *Group & Organization Studies, 3,* 427–434.

Limerick, D. C. (1976). Authority: An axis of leadership role differentiation. *Psychologia Africana, 16,* 153–172.

Lindbloom, C. (1959). The science of "muddling through." *Public Administration Review, 19,* 79–99.

Lindeman, E. C. (1933). *Social education.* New York: New Republic.

Lindemuth, M. H. (1969). *An analysis of the leader behavior of academic deans as related to the campus climate in selected colleges.* Doctoral dissertation, University of Michigan, Ann Arbor.

Lindgren, H. C. (1954). *Effective leadership in human relations.* New York: Hermitage House.

Lindsay, C. P., & Dempsey, B. L. (1985). Experiences in training Chinese business people to use U.S. management techniques. *Journal of Applied Behavioral Science, 21,* 65–78.

Lindsey, E., Holmes, V., & McCall, M. W., Jr. (1987). *Key events in executive lives* (Tech. Rep. No. 32). Greensboro, NC: Center for Creative Leadership.

Lindzey, G. (1954). *Handbook of social psychology.* Reading, MA: Addison-Wesley.

Lindzey, G., & Aronson, E. (1969). *Handbook of social psychology.* Reading, MA: Addison-Wesley.

Lindzey, G., & Kalnins, D. (1958). Theoretic apperception test: Some evidence bearing on the "hero assumption." *Journal of Abnormal and Social Psychology, 57,* 76–83.

Lindzey, G., & Urdan, J. A. (1954). Personality and social choice. *Sociometry, 17,* 47–63.

Link, H. C. (1944). The definition of social effectiveness and leadership through measurement. *Education and Psychological Measurement, 4,* 57–67.

Link, J. R., Thiagarajan, K. M., Trbovich, N. D., & Vaughan, J. A. (1970). *Exercise venture.* Scottsville, NY: Transnational Programs.

Link, R. (1971, June). Alienation. *Sweden Now,* 36–40.

Linton, R. (1945). *The cultural background of personality.* New York: Appleton-Century-Crofts.

Lipetz, M. E., & Ossorio, P. G. (1967). Authoritarianism, aggression, and status. *Journal of Personality and Social Psychology, 5,* 468–472.

Lipham, J. M. (1960). *Personal variables related to administrative effectiveness.* Doctoral dissertation, University of Chicago, Chicago.

Lippa, R. (1978). The effect of expressive control on expressive consistency and on the relation between expressive behavior and personality. *Journal of Personality, 46,* 438–461.

Lippitt, R. (1940a). *An analysis of group reaction to three types of experimentally created social climates.* Doctoral dissertation, State University of Iowa, Iowa City.

Lippitt, R. (1940b). An experimental study of the effect of democratic and authoritarian group atmospheres. *University of Iowa Studies in Child Welfare, 16,* 43–95.

Lippitt, R. (1942). The morale of youth groups. In G. B. Watson (Ed.), *Civilian morale.* Boston: Houghton Mifflin.

Lippitt, R. (1943a). The psychodrama in leadership training. *Sociometry, 6,* 286–292.

Lippitt, R. (1943b). From domination to leadership. *Journal of the National Association of Women Deans and Counselors, 6,* 147–152.

Lippitt, R. (1949). *Training in community relations.* New York: Harper.

Lippitt, R., Bradford, L. P., & Benne, K. D. (1947). Sociodramatic clarification of leader and group roles as a starting point for effective group functioning. *Sociatry, 1,* 82–91.

Lippitt, R., Polansky, N., Redl, F., & Rosen, S. (1952). The dynamics of power. *Human Relations, 5,* 37–64.

Lippitt, R., Thelen, H., & Leff, E. (undated). Unpublished memorandum.

Lippitt, R., Watson, J., & Westley, B. (1958). *The dynamics of planned change.* New York: Harcourt, Brace.

Lippitt, R., & White, R. K. (1943). The social climate of children's groups. In R. G. Baker, J. S. Kounin, & H. F. Wright (Eds.), *Child behavior and development.* New York: McGraw-Hill.

Lippitt, R., & White, R. (1960). Leader behavior and member reactions in three social climates. In I. D. Cartwright & A. Zander (Eds.), *Group dynamics.* New York: Harper & Row.

Lippitt, R., & Zander, A. (1943). A study of boys' attitudes toward participation in the war effort. *Journal of Social Psychology, 17,* 309–325.

Lippmann, W. (1922). *Public opinion.* New York: Harcourt, Brace.

Lipset, S. M. (1985). Feeling better: Measuring the nation's confidence. *Public Opinion, 8*(37), 6–9, 56–58.

Lirtzman, S., & Wahba, M. (1972). Determinants of coalitional behavior of men and women: Sex roles or situational requirement? *Journal of Applied Psychology, 56,* 406–411.

Lischeron, J. A., & Wall, T. D. (1975). Employee participation: An experimental field study. *Human Relations, 28,* 863–884.

Litman-Adizes, T., Raven, B. H., & Fontaine, G. (1978). Consequences of social power and causal attributions for compliance as seen by powerholder and target. *Personality and Social Psychological Bulletin, 4*(2), 260–264. (Cited in House, 1974.)

Litterer, J. A. (1976). *Life cycle changes of career women: Assessment and adaptation.* Paper, Academy of Management, Kansas City, MO.

Little, K. B. (1965). Personal space. *Journal of Experimental Social Psychology, 1,* 237–247.

Litwak, E. (1961). Models of organization which permit conflict. *American Journal of Sociology, 67,* 177–184.

Litwin, G. H. (1968). Climate and motivation: An experimental study. In R. Tagiuri & G. H. Litwin (Eds.), *Organizational climate.* Boston: Harvard University, Graduate School of Business Administration.

Litwin, G. H., & Stringer, R. A. (1966). *The influence of organizational climate on human motivation.* Paper, Conference of the Foundation for Research on Human Behavior, Ann Arbor, MI.

Litwin, G. H., & Stringer, R. A. (1968). *Motivation and organizational climate.* Boston: Harvard University, Graduate School of Business Administration, Division of Research.

Litzinger, W. D. (1965a). Interpersonal values and leadership attitudes of branch bank managers. *Personnel Psychology, 18,* 193–198.

Litzinger, W. D. (1965b). The motel entrepreneur and the motel manager. *Academy of Management Journal, 8,* 268–281.

Litzinger, W., & Schaefer, T. (1982). Leadership through followership. *Business Horizons, 25*(5), 78–81.

Litzinger, W. D., & Schaefer, T. E. (1986). Something more—The nature of transcendent management. *Business Horizons, 29*(2), 68–72.

Livingstone, E. (1953). Attitudes of women operatives to promotion. *Occupational Psychology, 27,* 191–199.

Livingstone, S. (1969). Pygmalion in management. *Harvard Business Review, 47,* 81–89.

Lloyd, H. (1964). *Biography in management studies.* New York: Humanities Press.

Locke, E. A. (1968). Toward a theory of task motivation and incentives. *Organizational Behavior and Human Performance, 3,* 157–190.

Locke, E. A. (1970). The supervisor as motivator: His influence on employee performance and satisfaction. In B. M. Bass, R. Cooper, & J. A. Haas (Ed.), *Managing for accomplishment.* Lexington, MA: D. C. Heath.

Locke, E. A. (1977). The myths of behavior mod in organizations. *Academic Management Review, 4,* 131–136.

Locke, E. A., Latham, G. P., & Erez, M. (1987). *3-way interactive presentation & discussion: A unique approach to resolving scientific disputes: Designing crucial experiments.* Paper, Conference of the Society for Industrial and Organizational Psychology, Atlanta, GA.

Locke, E. A., Latham, G., Saari, L. M., & Shaw, K. N. (1981). Goal setting and task performance: 1969–1980. *Psychological Bulletin, 90,* 125–152.

Locke, E. A., Motowidlo, S. J., & Bobko, P. (1986). Using self-efficacy theory to resolve the conflict between goal-setting theory and expectancy theory in organizational behavior and industrial/organizational psychology. *Journal of Social and Clinical Psychology, 4,* 328–338.

Locke, E. A., & Schweiger, D. M. (1979). Participation in decision making: One more look. In B. Staw & L. L. Cummings (Eds.), *Research in organizational behavior,* Vol. 1. Greenwich, CT: JAI Press.

Locke, E. A., Schweiger, D. M., & Latham, G. P. (1986). Participation in decision making: When should it be used? *Organizational Dynamics, 14*(3), 65–79.

Lockheed, M. E. (1975). Female motive to avoid success: A psychological barrier or a response to deviancy? *Sex Roles, 1,* 41–50.

Lockheed, M. E., & Hall, K. P. (1976). Conceptualizing sex as a status characteristic: Applications to leadership training strategies. *Journal of Social Issues, 32,* 111–124.

Lockwood, D. L. L. (1981). The assessment of an observational system to measure leadership behaviors. *Dissertation Abstracts International, 42*(11A), 4870.

Lodahl, A. (1982). *Crisis in values and the success of the Unification Church.* Bachelor of arts thesis in sociology, Cornell University, Ithaca, NY. (Cited in Trice & Beyer, 1986.)

Loden, M. (1985). *Feminine leadership, or, how to succeed in business without being one of the boys.* New York: Times Books.

Lohmann, M. R. (1961). *Top management committees: Their functions and authority.* New York: American Management Association.

Loken, R. D. (1951). *Why they quit, a survey of Illinois employees who quit their jobs in 1949; retail, clerical, manufacturing.* Urbana: University of Illinois Press.

Lombardo, M. M. (1983). I felt it as soon as I walked in. *Issues & Observations, 3*(4), 7–8.

Lombardo, M. M. (1986). Questions about learning from experience. *Issues & Observations, 6*(1), 7–10.

Lombardo, M. M., Ruderman, M. N., & McCauley, C. D. (1987). *Explanations of success and derailment in upper-level management positions*. Paper, Academy of Management, New York.

London, M. (1985). *Developing managers*. San Francisco: Jossey-Bass.

London, M., & Mone, E. M. (1987). *Career management and survival in the workplace*. San Francisco: Jossey-Bass.

Lonergan, W. G. (1958). Management trainees evaluate role playing. *Journal of American Society of Training Directors, 12*, 20–25.

Lonetto, R., & Williams, D. (1974). Personality, behavioral and output variables in a small group task situation: An examination of consensual leader and non-leader differences. *Canadian Journal of Behavioral Sciences, 6*, 59–74.

Long, R. J. (1979). Desires for and patterns of worker participation in decision making after conversion to employee ownership. *Academy of Management Journal, 22*, 611–617.

Long, R. J. (1982). *Determinants of managerial desires for various types of employee participation in decision making*. Paper, International Congress of Applied Psychology, Edinburgh.

Long, R. J. (1988). Factors affecting managerial desires for various types of employee participation in decision making. *Applied Psychology: An International Review, 37*, 15–34.

Long, R. L. (1986). An evaluation of Ohio Cooperative Extension Service leadership workshops in a community development context. *Dissertation Abstracts International, 46*, 1899–1900.

Longnecker, C. O., Sims, H. P., & Gioia, D. A. (1987). Behind the mask: The politics of employee appraisal. *Academy of Management Executive, 1*(3), 183–193.

Longshore, J. M. (1987). *The associative relationship between transformational leadership styles and group activity*. Doctoral dissertation, Nova University, Boca Raton, FL.

Lopez, F. M. (1966). *Evaluating executive decision making: The in-basket technique* (AMA Research Study 75). New York: American Management Association.

Lopez, F. M. (1970). *The making of a manager*. New York: American Management Association.

Lord, R. G. (1975). Group performance as a function of leadership behavior and task structure. *Dissertation Abstracts International, 35*, 6155.

Lord, R. G. (1976). Group performance as a function of leadership behavior and task structure: Toward an explanatory theory. *Organizational Behavior and Human Performance, 17*, 76–96.

Lord, R. G. (1977). Functional leadership behavior: Measurement and relation to social power and leadership perceptions. *Administrative Science Quarterly, 22*, 114–133.

Lord, R. G. (1985). An information processing approach to social perceptions, leadership perceptions and behavioral measurement in organizational settings. In B. M. Staw & L. L. Cummings (Eds.), *Research in organizational behavior*, Vol. 7. Greenwich, CT: JAI Press.

Lord, R. G., & Alliger, G. M. (1985). A comparison of four information processing models of leadership and social perceptions. *Human Relations, 38*, 47–65.

Lord, R. G., Binning, J., Rush, M. C., & Thomas, J. C. (1978). Effect of performance and leader behavior on questionnaire ratings of leader behavior. *Organizational Behavior and Human Performance, 21*, 27–39.

Lord, R. G., DeVader, C. L., & Alliger, G. M. (1986). A meta-analysis of the relation between personality traits and leadership perceptions: An application of validity generalization procedures. *Journal of Applied Psychology, 71*, 402–410.

Lord, R. G., Foti, R. J., & DeVader, C. L. (1984). A test of leadership categorization theory: Internal structure, information processing, and leadership perceptions. *Organizational Behavior and Human Performance, 34*, 343–378.

Lord, R. G., Foti, R. J., & Phillips, J. S. (1982). A theory of leadership categorization. In J. G. Hunt, U. Sekaran, & C. Schriesheim (Eds.), *Leadership: Beyond establishment views*. Carbondale: Southern Illinois University.

Lord, R. G., & Rowzee, M. (1979). Task interdependence, temporal phase, and cognitive heterogeneity as determinants of leadership behavior and behavior-performance relations. *Organizational Behavior and Human Performance, 23*, 182–200.

Lord, R. G., & Smith, J. E. (1983). Theoretical, information processing and situational factors affecting attribution theory models of organizational behavior. *Academy of Management Review, 8*, 50–60.

Lorenzo, R. V. (1984). Effects of assessorship on managers' proficiency in acquiring, evaluating, and communicating information about people. *Personnel Psychology, 37*, 617–634.

Lorge, I., Fox, D., Davitz, J., & Brenner, M. (1958). A survey of studies contrasting the quality of group performance and individual performance, 1920–1957. *Psychological Bulletin, 55*, 337–370.

Lorsch, J. W. (1970). Introduction to the structural design of organizations. In G. W. Dalton, P. R. Lawrence, & J. W. Lorsch (Eds.), *Organizational structure and design*. Homewood, IL: Dorsey.

Lott, B. E. (1961). Group cohesiveness: A learning phenomenon. *Journal of Social Psychology, 55*, 275–286.

Lott, B. E., & Lott, A. J. (1960). The formation of positive attitudes toward group members. *Journal of Abnormal and Social Psychology, 61*, 297–300.

Lott, D. F., & Sommer, R. (1967). Seating arrangements and status. *Journal of Personality and Social Psychology, 7*, 90–95.

Loury, G. C. (1985, Spring). The moral quandary of the black community. *Public Interest, 79*, 9–22.

Low, L. (1948). Resolving employee resistance to new personnel policies: A case study. *Personnel Psychology, 1*, 185–196.

Lowin, A. (1968). Participative decision making: A model, literature, critique, and prescription for research. *Organizational Behavior and Human Performance, 3*, 68–106.

Lowin, A., & Craig, J. R. (1968). The influence of level of performance on managerial style: An experimental object-lesson in the ambiguity of correlation data. *Organizational Behavior and Human Performance, 3*, 440–458.

Lowin, A., Hrapchak, W. J., & Kavanagh, M. J. (1969). Consideration and initiating structure: An experimental investigation of leadership traits. *Administrative Science Quarterly, 14,* 238–253.

Lowry, R. P. (1968). *Who's running this town? Community leadership and social change.* New York: Harper & Row.

Loye, D. (1977). *The leadership passion.* San Francisco: Jossey-Bass.

Loyer, M. des A., & O'Reilly, R. R. (1985). *Assessing the impact of education on leadership effectiveness of graduates.* Paper, American Educational Research Association, Chicago.

Lubatkin, M. H., & Chung, K. H. (1985). *Leadership origin and organizational performance in prosperous and declining firms.* Paper, Academy of Management, San Diego, CA.

Lubatkin, M. H., Chung, K. H., Rogers, R. C., & Owers, J. E. (1989). Stockholder reactions to CEO changes in large corporations. *Academy of Management Journal, 32,* 47–68.

Lucas, C. (1965). Task performance and group structure as a function of personality and feedback. *Journal of Social Psychology, 66,* 257–270.

Luchins, A. S., & Luchins, E. H. (1961). On conformity with judgments of a majority or an authority. *Journal of Social Psychology, 53,* 303–316.

Luckie, W. R. (1963). Leader behavior of directors of instruction. *Dissertation Abstracts, 25,* 1960.

Luecke, D. S. (1973). The professional as organizational leader. *Administrative Science Quarterly, 18,* 86–94.

Lueder, D. C. (1985). Don't be mislead by LEAD. *Journal of Applied Behavioral Science, 21,* 143–151.

Luft, J. (1969). *Of human interaction.* Palo Alto, CA: National Press.

Luithlen, W. F. (1931). Zur psychologie der initiative und der Führereigenschaften. *Zeitschrift für angewandte Psychologie, 39,* 56–122.

Lull, P., Fund, F., & Piersol, D. (1955). What communication means to the corporate president. *Advancement in Management, 20,* 17–20.

Lundberg, G. A., & Beazley, V. (1948). Consciousness of kind in a college population. *Sociometry, 11,* 59–74.

Lundgren, D. C., & Knight, D. J. (1974). Leadership styles and member attitudes in T groups. *Personality and Social Psychology Bulletin, 74,* 263–266.

Lundquist, A. (1957). *Arbetsledare och arbetsgrupp.* Stockholm: Personal Administrativa Rådet.

Lundy, R. M. (1956). Assimilative projection and accuracy of prediction in interpersonal perceptions. *Journal of Abnormal and Social Psychology, 52,* 33–38.

Lundy, R. M., Katkovsky, W., Cromwell, R. L., & Shoemaker, D. J. (1955). Self acceptability and descriptions of sociometric choices. *Journal of Abnormal and Social Psychology, 51,* 260–262.

Lupfer, M. B. (1965). Role enactment as a function of orientation, expectations, and duration of interaction. *Dissertation Abstracts, 25,* 5376–5377.

Luthans, F. (1977). *Organizational behavior* (2nd ed.). New York: McGraw-Hill.

Luthans, F. (1986). *Fifty years later: What do we know about managers and managing.* Presidential address, Academy of Management, Chicago.

Luthans, F. (1988). Successful vs. effective real managers. *Academy of Management Executive, 2*(2), 127–132.

Luthans, F., & Kreitner, R. (1975). *Organizational behavior modification.* Glenview, IL: Scott, Foresman.

Luthans, F., & Larsen, J. K. (1986). How managers really communicate. *Human Relations, 39,* 161–178.

Luthans, F., & Lockwood, D. L. (1984). Toward an observation system for measuring leader behavior in natural settings. In J. G. Hunt, D. Hosking, C. A. Schriesheim, & R. Stewart (Eds.), *Leaders and managers: International perspectives on managerial behavior and leadership.* New York: Pergamon Press.

Luthans, F., Rosenkrantz, S. A., & Hennessey, H. W. (1985). What do successful managers really do? An observation study of managerial activities. *Journal of Applied Behavioral Science, 21,* 255–270.

Luthans, F., Walker, J. W., & Hodgetts, R. M. (1969). Evidence on the validity of management education. *Academy of Management Journal, 4,* 451–457.

Luttbeg, N. R. (1968). The structure of beliefs among leaders and the public. *Public Opinion Quarterly, 32,* 398–409.

Luttwak, E. N. (1976). *The grand strategy of the Roman empire.* Baltimore, MD: Johns Hopkins University Press.

Lyda, M. L. (1964). *Research studies in education: 1953–1963.* Bloomington, IN: Phi Delta Kappa.

Lyle, J. (1961). Communication, group atmosphere, productivity, and morale in small task groups. *Human Relations, 14,* 369–379.

Lynd, R. S., & Lynd, H. M. (1929). *Middletown.* New York: Harcourt, Brace.

Lyness, K. S., & Moses, J. L. (1989). *Ambiguity, uncertainty and chance in organizations: Assessing behavior and improving coping styles.* Boston, MA: Allen & Unwin (in preparation).

Lynn, L. E., Jr. (1985). Managers in the Reagan administration. *Bureaucrat, 14*(1), 41–45.

Lynton, R. P., & Pareek, U. (1967). *Training for development.* Homewood, IL: Dorsey-Irwin.

Maas, H. S. (1950). Personal and group factors in leaders' social perception. *Journal of Abnormal and Social Psychology, 45,* 54–63.

Macaulay, S. (1963). Noncontractual relations in business. *American Sociological Review, 28,* 55–67.

Maccoby, E. E., & Jacklin, C. N. (1974). *The psychology of sex differences.* Stanford, CA: Stanford University Press.

Maccoby, E. E., Newcomb, T. M., & Hartley, E. L. (1958). *Readings in social psychology.* New York: Holt, Rinehart & Winston.

Maccoby, M. (1976/1978). *The gamesman.* New York: Simon & Schuster. Also: (1974). New York: Bantam Books.

Maccoby, M. (1979). Leadership needs of the 1980's. *Current Issues in Higher Education, 2,* 17–23.

Maccoby, M. (1981). *The leader: A new face for American management.* New York: Ballantine Books.

Maccoby, M. (1982). The leader. *NABW (National Association of Bank Women) Journal, 58*(3), 25–28.

Maccoby, M. (1983). Management: Leadership and the work ethic. *Modern Office Procedures, 28*(5), 14, 16, 18.

Maccoby, M. (1988). *Why work: Leading the new generation.* New York: Simon & Schuster.

Maccoby, N. (1949). The relationship of supervisory behavior and attitudes to group productivity in two widely different industrial settings. *American Psychologist, 4*, 283 (Abstract).

Macdonald, D. A. (1969). The relationship between leadership orientation and group productivity and satisfaction: The residence hall adviser and his section. *Dissertation Abstracts International, 30*, 391.

MacDonald, W. S. (1967a). Responsibility and goal establishment: Critical elements in Job Corps programs. *Perceptual and Motor Skills, 24*, 104.

MacDonald, W. S. (1967b). Social structure and behavior modification in Job Corps training. *Perceptual and Motor Skills, 24*, 142.

Mace, M. L. (1950). *The growth and development of executives.* Boston, MA: Harvard Business School, Division of Research.

Machiavelli, N. (1513/1962). *The prince.* New York: Mentor Press.

Machiavelli, N. (1532/1950) *The discourses.* London: Routledge & Kegan Paul.

MacIver, R. M. (1947). *The web of government.* New York: Macmillan.

Mack, W. P., & Konetzni, A. H., Jr. (1982). *Command at sea* (4th ed.). Annapolis, MD: Naval Institute Press.

MacKechnie, A. R. (1944). Importance and development of leadership in our small unit commanders. *Military Review, 24*, 9–12.

MacKenzie, R. A. (1969). The management process in 3-D. *Harvard Business Review, 47*(6), 80–87.

MacKinney, A. C. (1967). *Conceptualizations of a longitudinal study of manager performance.* Ames: Iowa State University, Industrial Relations Center.

MacKinney, A. C. (1968). *The longitudinal study of manager performance: Phase I variables.* Ames: Iowa State University. Unpublished report.

MacKinney, A. C., Kavanagh, M. J., Wolins, L., & Rapparlie, J. H. (1970). *Manager development project: Summary of progress through June 1969.* Ames: Iowa State University.

MacKinney, A. C., Wernimont, P. F., & Galitz, W. O. (1962). Has specialization reduced job satisfaction? *Personnel, 39*, 8–17.

MacKinney, A. C., Wolins, L., Kavanagh, M. J., & Rapparlie, J. H. (1971). *Manager development project. Progress through June 1971—a summary report.* Dayton, OH: Wright State University.

MacKinnon, D. W. (1960). The highly effective individual. *Teachers College Record, 61*, 367–378.

MacKinnon, D. W. (1975). *An overview of assessment centers* (Tech. Rep. No. 1). Greensboro, NC: Center for Creative Leadership.

MacLennan, B. W. (1975). The personalities of group leaders: Implications for selection and training. *International Journal of Group Psychotherapy, 25*, 177–183.

MacMillan, I. C., & George, R. (1975). Corporate venturing: Challenges for senior managers. *Journal of Business Strategy, 5*, 34–43.

MacNaughton, J. D. (1963). A study of foremen's communication. *Personnel Practice Bulletin, 19*, 10–19.

Madden, F. M. (1977). The effect of human relations training on group leaders' decisions and members' satisfaction. *Dissertation Abstracts International, 38*, 52.

Madique, M. A. (1980). Entrepreneurs, champions, and technological innovation. *Sloan Management Review, 21*(2), 59–76.

Madison, D. L., Allen, R. W., Porter, L. W., Renwick, P. A., & Mayes, B. T. (1980). Organizational politics: An exploration of managers' perceptions. *Human Relations, 33*, 79–100.

Madsen, D., & Snow, P. G. (1983). The dispersion of charisma. *Comparative Political Studies, 16*, 337–362.

Mael, F. (1986). *Trading latitude for lieutenancy: The exchange component of the leader member exchange model of leadership.* Masters thesis, Wayne State University, Detroit, MI.

Maguire, M. A., & Pascale, R. T. (1978). Communication, decision-making and implementation among managers in Japanese and American managed companies in the United States. *Sociology and Social Research, 63*, 1–22.

Maher, J. P. (1976). Situational determinants of leadership behavior in task-oriented small groups. *Dissertation Abstracts International, 37*, 693–694.

Mahler, F. W. (1961). The span of control in sixty Australian undertakings. *Personnel Practice Bulletin, 17*, 35–40.

Mahler, W. (1952). Trends in management training: A composite training and development program. In M. J. Dooher & V. Marquis (Eds.), *The development of executive talent.* New York: American Management Association.

Mahoney, G. M. (1953). *Supervisory and administrative practices associated with worker attitudes toward an incentive system.* Ann Arbor: University of Michigan, Institute for Social Research.

Mahoney, T. A. (1955). *What do managers do?* Minneapolis: University of Minnesota, Industrial Relations Center.

Mahoney, T. A. (1961). *Building the executive team.* Englewood Cliffs, NJ: Prentice-Hall.

Mahoney, T. A. (1967). Managerial perceptions of organizational effectiveness. *Management Science, 14*, 76–91.

Mahoney, T. A., Frost, P., Crandall, N. F., & Weitzel, W. (1972). The conditioning influence of organization size upon managerial practice. *Organizational Behavior and Human Performance, 8*, 230–241.

Mahoney, T. A., Jerdee, T. H., & Carroll, S. I. (1965). The job(s) of management. *Industrial Relations, 4*, 97–110.

Mahoney, T. A., Jerdee, T. H., & Korman, A. (1960). An experimental evaluation of management development. *Personnel Psychology, 13*, 81–98.

Mahoney, T. A., Jerdee, T. H., & Nash, A. N. (1960). Predicting managerial effectiveness. *Personnel Psychology, 13*, 147–163.

Mahoney, T. A., Jerdee, T. H., & Nash, A. N. (1961). *The identification of management potential.* Dubuque, IA: W. C. Brown.

Mahoney, T. A., Sorenson, W. W., Jerdee, T. H., & Nash, A. N. (1963). Identification and prediction of managerial effectiveness. *Personnel Administration, 26,* 12–22.

Mahoney, T. A., & Weitzel, W. (1969). Managerial models of organizational effectiveness. *Administrative Science Quarterly, 14,* 357–365.

Mai-Dalton, R. (1975). *The influence of training and position power on leader behavior* (Tech. Rep. No. 75-72). Seattle: University of Washington, Organizational Research.

Maier, N. R. F. (1948). A human relations program for supervisors. *Industrial Labor Relations Review, 1,* 443–464.

Maier, N. R. F. (1950). The quality of group decisions as influenced by the discussion leader. *Human Relations, 3,* 155–174.

Maier, N. R. F. (1953). An experimental test of the effect of training on discussion leadership. *Human Relations, 6,* 161–173.

Maier, N. R. F. (1960). Screening solutions to upgrade quality: A new approach to problem-solving under conditions of uncertainty. *Journal of Psychology, 49,* 217–231.

Maier, N. R. F. (1963). *Problem-solving discussions and conferences: Leadership methods and skills.* New York: McGraw-Hill.

Maier, N. R. F. (1965). *Psychology in industry.* Boston: Houghton Mifflin.

Maier, N. R. F. (1967). Assets and liabilities in group problem solving: The need for integrative function. *Psychological Review, 74,* 239–249.

Maier, N. R. F. (1968). The subordinate's role in the delegation process. *Personnel Psychology, 21,* 179–191.

Maier, N. R. F. (1970a). Male versus female discussion leaders. *Personnel Psychology, 23,* 455–461.

Maier, N. R. F. (1970b). *Problem solving and creativity in individuals and groups.* Belmont, CA: Brooks/Cole.

Maier, N. R. F. (1973). *Psychology in industrial organizations.* Boston: Houghton Mifflin.

Maier, N. R. F., & Danielson, L. E. (1956). An evaluation of two approaches to discipline in industry. *Journal of Applied Psychology, 40,* 319–323.

Maier, N. R. F., & Hoffman, L. R. (1960a). Using trained "developmental" discussion leaders to improve further the quality of group decisions. *Journal of Applied Psychology, 44,* 247–251.

Maier, N. R. F., & Hoffman, L. R. (1960b). Quality of first and second solutions to group problem-solving. *Journal of Applied Psychology, 44,* 278–283.

Maier, N. R. F., & Hoffman, L. R. (1961). Organization and creative problem solving. *Journal of Applied Psychology, 45,* 277–280.

Maier, N. R. F., & Hoffman, L. R. (1963). Seniority in work groups: A right or an honor? *Journal of Applied Psychology, 47,* 173–176.

Maier, N. R. F., & Hoffman, L. R. (1964). Financial incentives and group decision in motivating change. *Journal of Social Psychology, 64,* 355–368.

Maier, N. R. F., & Hoffman, L. R. (1965). Acceptance and quality of solutions as related to leaders' attitudes toward disagreement in group problem solving. *Journal of Applied Behavioral Science, 1,* 373–386.

Maier, N. R. F., Hoffman, L. R., & Read, W. H. (1963). Superior-subordinate communications: The relative effectiveness of managers who held their subordinates' positions. *Personnel Psychology, 16,* 1–12.

Maier, N. R. F., & Maier, R. A. (1957). An experimental test of the effects of "developmental" vs. "free" discussions on the quality of group decisions. *Journal of Applied Psychology, 41,* 320–323.

Maier, N. R. F., & McRay, P. (1972). Increasing innovation in change situations through leadership skills. *Psychological Reports, 31,* 343–354.

Maier, N. R. F., & Sashkin, M. (1971). Specific leadership behaviors that promote problem solving. *Personnel Psychology, 24,* 35–44.

Maier, N. R. F., & Solem, A. R. (1952). The contribution of a discussion leader to the quality of group thinking: The effective use of minority opinions. *Human Relations, 5,* 277–288.

Maier, N. R. F., & Solem, A. R. (1962). Improving solutions by turning choice situations into problems. *Personnel Psychology, 15,* 151–158.

Maier, N. R. F., Solem, A. R., & Maier, A. A. (1957). *Supervisory and executive development: A manual for role playing.* New York: Wiley.

Maier, N. R. F., & Thurber, J. A. (1969). Problems in delegation. *Personnel Psychology, 22,* 131–139.

Maier, N. R. F., & Zerfoss, L. F. (1952). MRP: A technique for training large groups of supervisors and its potential use in social research. *Human Relations, 5,* 177–186.

Maissonneuve, J. (1952). Selective choices and propinquity. *Sociometry, 15,* 135–140.

Majchrzak, A. (1987). Effects of management policies on unauthorized absence behavior. *Journal of Applied Behavioral Science, 23,* 501–523.

Major, K. D. (1988). *Dogmatism, visionary leadership, and effectiveness of secondary schools.* Doctoral dissertation, University of LaVerne, LaVerne, CA.

Major, M. (1984). Delegating authority without losing control. *Today's Office, 19*(5), 45–46.

Majumder, R. K., MacDonald, A. P., & Greever, K. B. (1977). A study of rehabilitation counselors: Locus of control and attitudes toward the poor. *Journal of Counseling Psychology, 24,* 137–141.

Maller, J. B. (1925). Cooperation and competition: An experimental study in motivation. *Teachers College Contributions to Education,* No. 384.

Maller, J. B. (1931). Size of family and personality of offspring. *Journal of Social Psychology, 2,* 3–25.

Malloy, H. (1936). Study of some of the factors underlying the establishment of successful social contacts at the college level. *Journal of Social Psychology, 7,* 205–228.

Malone, F. (1984). Cognitive style and leader adaptability of managers. *Dissertation Abstracts International, 45*(5A), 1268.

Maloney, F. C. (1979). A study of the relationship between leadership behavior and particular personality characteristics of women elementary principals in public and Roman Catholic schools. *Dissertation Abstracts International, 39*(8A), 4633.

Maloney, R. M. (1956). Group learning through group discussion: A group discussion implementation analysis. *Journal of Social Psychology, 43,* 3–9.

Manasse, A. L. (1984). Principals as leaders of high performing systems. *Educational Leadership, 41,* 42–46.

Manchester, W. (1978). *American Caesar: Douglas MacArthur, 1880–1964.* Boston: Little, Brown.

Manchester, W. (1988). Manchester on leadership. *Modern Maturity, 31*(5), 40–46, 108–111.

Mandell, M. M. (1949). Supervisors' attitudes and job performance. *Personnel, 26,* 182–183.

Mandell, M. M. (1950a). The administrative judgment test. *Journal of Applied Psychology, 34,* 145–147.

Mandell, M. M. (1950b). Validation of group oral performance test. *Personnel Psychology, 3,* 179–185.

Mandell, M. M. (1956). Supervisory characteristics and ratings: A summary of recent research. *Personnel, 32,* 435–440.

Mandell, M. M., & Duckworth, P. (1955). The supervisor's job: A survey. *Personnel, 31,* 456–462.

Mangee, C. (1976). *A study of the perceived behaviors of elementary school principals and the organizational climate of elementary schools.* Doctoral dissertation, University of Michigan, Ann Arbor.

Manheim, H. L. (1960). Intergroup interaction as related to status and leadership differences between groups. *Sociometry, 23,* 415–427.

Manis, J. G., & Meltzer, B. N. (1967). *Symbolic interaction: A reader in social psychology.* Boston: Allyn & Bacon.

Mann, F. C. (1951). Changing superior-subordinate relationships. *Journal of Social Issues, 7/8,* 56–63.

Mann, F. C. (1961). Studying and creating change. In W. Bennis, K. Benne, & R. Chin (Eds.), *The planning of change.* New York: Holt, Rinehart & Winston.

Mann, F. C. (1965). Toward an understanding of the leadership role in formal organization. In R. Dubin (Ed.), *Leadership and productivity.* San Francisco: Chandler.

Mann, F. C., & Baumgartel, H. (1952). *Absences and employee attitudes in an electric power company.* Ann Arbor: University of Michigan, Survey Research Center.

Mann, F. C., & Baumgartel, H. (1953). *The supervisor's concern with cost in an electric power company.* Ann Arbor: University of Michigan, Survey Research Center.

Mann, F. C., & Dent, J. K. (1954a). The supervisor—member of two organizational families. *Harvard Business Review, 32*(6), 103–112.

Mann, F. C., & Dent, J. K. (1954b). *Appraisals of supervisors and attitudes of their employees in an electric power company.* Ann Arbor: University of Michigan, Survey Research Center.

Mann, F. C., & Hoffman, L. R. (1960). *Automation and the worker: A study of social change in power plants.* New York: Holt, Rinehart & Winston.

Mann, F. C., Indik, B. P., & Vroom, V. H. (1963). *The productivity of work groups.* Ann Arbor: University of Michigan, Survey Research Center.

Mann, F. C., & Sparling, J. E. (1956). Changing absence rates: An application of research findings. *Personnel, 32,* 392–408.

Mann, F. C., & Williams, L. K. (1962). Some effects of the changing work environment in the office. *Journal of Social Issues, 18,* 90–101.

Mann, J. H. (1960). The relationship between role playing ability and interpersonal adjustment. *Journal of General Psychology, 62,* 177–183.

Mann, J. H., & Mann, C. H. (1959a). The effect of role-playing experience on role-playing ability. *Sociometry, 22,* 64–74.

Mann, J. H., & Mann, C. H. (1959b). Role playing and interpersonal adjustment. *Journal of Counseling Psychology, 6,* 148–152.

Mann, J. H., & Mann, C. H. (1959c). The importance of group task in producing group-member personality and behavior changes. *Human Relations, 12,* 75–80.

Mann, J. H., & Mann, C. H. (1960). The relative effectiveness of role playing and task oriented group experience in producing personality and behavior change. *Journal of Social Psychology, 51,* 313–317.

Mann, J. W. (1961). Group relations in hierarchies. *Journal of Social Psychology, 54,* 283–314.

Mann, R. D. (1959). A review of the relationships between personality and performance in small groups. *Psychological Bulletin, 56,* 241–270.

Mann, R. D. (1961). Dimensions of individual performance in small groups under task and social-emotional conditions. *Journal of Abnormal and Social Psychology, 62,* 674–682.

Mann, R. D., Gibbard, G. S., & Hartman, J. J. (1967). *Interpersonal styles and group development: An analysis of the member-leader relationship.* New York: Wiley.

Mannari, H., & Abegglen, J. (1963, Winter). The educational background of Japan's industrial leaders. *Bessatsu chuo koron: Keiei mondai,* 190–197.

Mannheim, B. F., Rim, Y., Grinberg, B. (1967). Instrumental status of supervisors as related to workers' perceptions and expectations. *Human Relations, 20,* 387–396.

Manning, W. H., & Jackson, R. (1984). College entrance examinations: Objective selection or gatekeeping for the economically privileged. In C. R. Reynolds & R. T. Brown (Eds.), *Perspectives on bias in mental testing.* New York: Plenum.

Mansour, J. M. (1969). Leadership behavior and principal-teacher interpersonal relations. *Dissertation Abstracts International, 30,* 526.

Manton, E. J. (1972). An analysis of the psychological consequences of organizational boundary relevance. *Dissertation Abstracts International, 32,* 6708–6709.

Manz, C. C. (1983). Improving performance through self-leadership. *National Productivity Review, 2*(3), 288–297.

Manz, C. C. (1986). Self-leadership: Toward an expanded theory of self-influence processes in organizations. *Academy of Management Review, 11,* 585–600.

Manz, C. C., Adsit, D. J., Dennis, J., Campbell, S., & Mathison-Hance, M. (1988). Managerial thought patterns and performance: A study of perceptual patterns of performance hindrances for higher and lower performing managers. *Human Relations, 41,* 447–465.

Manz, C. C., & Angle, H. L. (1985). *Does group self-management mean a loss of personal control?: Triangulating a paradox.* Paper, Academy of Management, San Diego, CA.

Manz, C. C., Mossholder, K. W., & Luthans, F. (1983). *A contemporary perspective of control in organizations: A social learning view.* Paper, Academy of Management, Dallas.

Manz, C. C., & Sims, H. P., Jr. (1980). Self-management as a substitute for leadership: A social learning theory perspective. *Academy of Management Review, 5,* 361–367.

Manz, C. C., & Sims, H. P. (1984). Searching for the "unleader": Organizational member views on leading self-managed groups. *Human Relations, 37,* 409–424.

Manz, C. C., & Sims, H. P., Jr. (1986a). Beyond imitation: Complex behavioral and affective linkages resulting from exposure to leadership training models. *Journal of Applied Psychology, 71,* 571–578.

Manz, C. C., & Sims, H. P. (1986b). Leading self-managed groups: A conceptual analysis of a paradox. *Economic and Industrial Democracy, 7,* 141–165.

Manz, C. C., & Sims, H. P. (1987). Leading workers to lead themselves. The external leadership of self-managing work teams. *Administrative Science Quarterly, 32,* 106–129.

Mao, T. (1967). *Selected works of Mao Tse-tung.* Peking: Foreign Language Press.

Marak, G. E. (1964). The evolution of leadership structure. *Sociometry, 27,* 174–182.

Maranell, G. M. (1970). The evaluation of presidents: An extension of the Schlesinger polls. *Journal of American History, 57,* 104–113.

March, J. C., & March, J. G. (1978). Performance sampling in social matches. *Administrative Science Quarterly, 23,* 454–465.

March, J. G. (1955). Group autonomy and internal group control. *Social Forces, 33,* 322–326.

March, J. G. (1956). Influence measurement in experimental and semi-experimental groups. *Sociometry, 19,* 260–271.

March, J. G. (1965). *Handbook of organizations.* Chicago: Rand McNally.

March, J. G., & Olsen, J. P. (1984). The new institutionalism: Organizational factors in political life. *American Political Science Review, 78,* 734–749.

March, J. G., & Simon, H. A. (1958). *Organizations.* New York: Wiley.

Marchant, M. P. (1976). *Participative management in academic libraries.* Westport, CT: Greenwood.

Marchetti, P. V. (1953). Some aspects of the manager-employee relationship in the retail grocery. *American Psychologist, 8,* 402.

Marcus, J. T. (1961). Transcendentalism and charisma. *Western Political Quarterly, 14,* 237.

Marcus, P. M. (1960). Expressive and instrumental groups: Toward a theory of group action. *American Journal of Sociology, 66,* 54–59.

Marcus, P. M. (1962). Group cohesion and worker productivity: A dissenting view. *Personnel Administration, 25*(3), 44–48, 57.

Marder, E. (1960). *Leader behavior as perceived by subordinates as a function of organizational level.* Master's thesis, Ohio State University, Columbus.

Margerison, C., & Glube, R. (1979). Leadership decision making: An empirical test of the Vroom and Yetton model. *Journal of Management Studies, 16,* 45–55.

Margerison, C., & Kakabadse, A. (1984). *How American chief executives succeed.* New York: American Management Association.

Margiotta, F. D. (1976). A military elite in transition: Air Force leaders in the 1980's. *Armed Forces and Society, 2,* 155–184.

Margolin, J. B. (undated). *The application of Heider's theory to the effect of perceived cooperation or competition on the transfer of hostility.* Unpublished manuscript.

Markham, S. E. (1988). The pay-for-performance dilemma revisited: An empirical example of the importance of group effects. *Journal of Applied Psychology, 73,* 172–180.

Markham, S. E., Dansereau, F., Alutto, J. A., & Dumas, M. (1983). Leadership convergence: An application of within and between analysis to validity. *Applied Psychological Measurement, 7,* 63–72.

Marks, A. R. (1954). *An investigation of modifications of job design in an industrial situation and their effects on some measures of economic productivity.* Doctoral dissertation, University of California, Berkeley.

Marks, J. B. (1954). Interests, leadership, and sociometric status among adolescents. *Sociometry, 17,* 340–349.

Marks, J. B. (1959). Interests and group formation. *Human Relations, 12,* 385–390.

Marks, M. L. (1988). The disappearing company man. *Psychology Today, 22*(9), 34–39.

Marks, M. R., & Jenkins, L. W. (1965). *"Initiate structure" and "Consideration"—their surprising and general relation to global ratings or rankings* (Tech. Rep.). Rochester, NY: University of Rochester.

Marple, C. H. (1933). The comparative susceptibility of three age levels to the suggestion of group versus expert opinion. *Journal of Social Psychology, 4,* 176–186.

Marquis, D. G. (1962). Individual responsibility and group decisions involving risk. *Industrial Management Review, 3,* 8–23.

Marquis, D. G., Guetzkow, H., & Heyns, R. W. (1951). A social psychological study of the decision-making conference. In H. Guetzkow (Ed.), *Groups, leadership, and men.* Pittsburgh, PA: Carnegie Press.

Marrow, A. J. (1964a). *Behind the executive mask.* New York: American Management Association.

Marrow, A. J. (1964b). Risks and uncertainties in action research. *Journal of Social Issues, 20,* 5–20.

Marrow, A. J., Bowers, D. G., & Seashore, S. E. (1968). *Management by participation.* New York: Harper & Row.

Marrow, A. J., & French, J. R. P. (1946a). Changing a stereotype in industry. *Personnel, 22,* 305–308.

Marrow, A. J., & French, J. R. P. (1946b). A case of employee participation in a non-union shop. *Journal of Social Issues, 2,* 29–34.

Marsh, M. K., & Atherton, R. M., Jr. (1981–2). Leadership, organizational type, and subordinate satisfaction in the U.S. army: The hi-hi paradigm sustained. *Journal of Social Relations, 9,* 121–143.

Marsh, R. M., & Mannari, H. (1971). Lifetime commitment in Japan: Roles, norms, and values. *American Journal of Sociology, 76,* 795–812.

Marshall, G. L. (1964). *Predicting executive achievement.* Doctoral dissertation, Harvard University, Cambridge, MA.

Marshall, H. R. (1958). Factors relating to the accuracy of adult leaders' judgments of social acceptance in community youth groups. *Child Development, 29,* 417–424.

Marshall, J., & Stewart, R. (1981). Managers' job perceptions: Their overall frameworks and working strategies. *Journal of Management Studies, 18,* 177–190.

Marshall, S. L. A. (1964). *World War I.* New York: American Heritage.

Marston, A. (1964). Personality variables related to self-reinforcement. *Journal of Psychology, 58,* 169–175.

Martin, A. R. (1969). Morale and productivity: A review of the literature. *Public Personnel Review, 30,* 42–45.

Martin, D. C. (1987). Factors influencing pay decisions: Balancing managerial vulnerabilities. *Human Relations, 40,* 417–430.

Martin, H. J., & Hunt, J. G. (1981). *Discretionary leadership: Theory and measurement.* Paper, Midwest Academy of Management, Carbondale, IL.

Martin, J., Feldman, M. S., Hatch, M. J., & Sitkin, S. B. (1983). The uniqueness paradox in organizational stories. *Administrative Science Quarterly, 28,* 438–453.

Martin, J., & Harder, J. (1988). *Bread and roses: Justice and the distribution of financial and socio-emotional rewards in organizations* (Research Paper No. 1010). Stanford, CA: Stanford University, Graduate School of Business.

Martin, J., Scully, M., & Levitt, B. (1988). *In justice and the legitimation of revolution: Damning the past, excusing the present, and neglecting the future.* Unpublished manuscript.

Martin, J., & Siehl, C. (1983). Organizational culture and counterculture: An uneasy symbiosis. *Organizational Dynamics, 12*(2), 52–64.

Martin, J., Sitkin, S. B., & Boehm, M. (1985). Founders and the elusiveness of a cultural legacy. In P. J. Frost, L. F. Moore, M. R. Louis, C. C. Lundberg, & J. Martin (Eds.), *Organizational culture.* Beverly Hills, CA: Sage.

Martin, N. H. (1959). The levels of management and their mental demands. In W. L. Warner & N. H. Martin (Eds.), *Industrial man.* New York: Harper & Row.

Martin, N. H., & Sims, J. H. (1956). Thinking ahead: Power tactics. *Harvard Business Review, 34*(6), 25–36, 140.

Martin, R. (1972). *Decentralized school management: Professional staff and client perception.* Doctoral dissertation, University of California, Los Angeles.

Martin, T. N., & Hunt, J. G. (1980). Social influence and intent to leave: A path-analytic process model. *Personnel Psychology, 33,* 505–528.

Martin, W. E., Gross, N., & Darley, J. G. (1952). Studies of group behavior: Leaders, followers, and isolates in small organized groups. *Journal of Abnormal and Social Psychology, 47,* 838–842.

Martin, W. J. (1980). *The managerial behavior of high school principals.* Doctoral dissertation, The Pennsylvania State University, University Park.

Martin, W. J., & Willower, D. J. (1981). The managerial behavior of high school principals. *Educational Administration Quarterly, 17,* 69–90.

Martinko, M. J., & Gardner, W. L. (1984a). The observation of high performing educational managers: Methodological issues and managerial implications. In J. G. Hunt, D. Hosking, C. A. Schriesheim, & R. Stewart (Eds.), *Leaders and managers: International perspectives on managerial behavior and leadership.* New York: Pergamon.

Martinko, M. J., & Gardner, W. L. (1984b). *The behavior of high performing educational managers: An observational study.* Department of Management, Florida State University, Tallahassee, FL.

Martinko, M. J., & Gardner, W. L. (1985). Beyond structured observation: Methodological issues and new directions. *Academy of Management Review, 10,* 676–695.

Martinko, M. J., & Gardner, W. L. (1987). The leader/member attribution process. *Academy of Management Review, 12,* 235–249.

Marvin, P. (1968). *Management goals: Guidelines and accountability.* Homewood, IL: Dow Jones-Irwin.

Marwell, G. (1966). Types of past experience with potential work partners: Their effects on partner choice. *Human Relations, 19,* 437–447.

Marwell, G., & Schmitt, D. (1967). Dimensions of compliance-gaining behavior: An empirical analysis. *Sociometry, 30,* 350–364.

Masling, J. M. (1953). The Bainbridge study. In D. Courtney (Ed.), *Naval, neighborhood, and national leadership.* Philadelphia: Institute for Research in Human Relations.

Masling, J. M., Greer, F. L., & Gilmore, R. (1955). Status, authoritarianism, and sociometric choice. *Journal of Social Psychology, 41,* 297–310.

Maslow, A. H. (1954). *Motivation and personality.* New York: Harper.

Maslow, A. H. (1965). *Eupsychian management: A journal.* Homewood, IL: Dorsey.

Mason, D. J. (1957). Judgments of leadership based upon physiognomic cues. *Journal of Abnormal and Social Psychology, 54,* 273–274.

Mason, W. A. (1964). Sociability and social organization in monkeys and apes. In L. Berkowitz (Ed.), *Advances in experimental social psychology.* New York: Academic Press.

Massarik, F. (1983). Searching for essence in executive experience. In S. Srivastva (Ed.), *The executive mind.* San Francisco: Jossey-Bass.

Massarik, F., Tannenbaum, R., Kahane, M., & Weschler, I. R. (1953). Sociometric choice and organizational effectiveness: A multi-relational approach. *Sociometry, 16,* 211–238.

Massengill, D., & DiMarco, N. (1979). Sex-role stereotypes and requisite management characteristics: A current replication. *Sex Roles, 5,* 561–570.

Masuda, Y. (1980). *The information society.* Bethesda, MD: World Future Society.

Mathews, D. R. (1954). *The social background of political decision-makers.* New York: Random House.

Mathews, J. E. (1963). Leader behavior of elementary principals and the group dimensions of their staffs. *Dissertation Abstracts, 25,* 2318.

Matsui, T., Ohtsuka, Y., & Kikuchi, A. (1978). Consideration and structure behavior as reflections of supervisory interpersonal values. *Journal of Applied Psychology, 63,* 259–262.

Matteson, M. T. (1976). Attitudes toward women as managers: Sex or role differences? *Psychological Reports, 39,* 166.

Matteson, M. T., & Ivancevich, J. M. (1982). Stress and the medical technologist: I. A general overview. *American Journal of Medical Technology, 48,* 163-168.

Matteson, M. T., McMahon, J. F., & McMahon, M. (1974). Sex differences and job attitudes: Some unexpected findings. *Psychological Reports, 35,* 1333-1334.

Matthews, J. (1951). *Research on the development of valid situational tests of leadership. 1. Survey of the literature.* Pittsburgh: American Institute for Research.

Matthews, S. (1980). The gentle art of delegation. *Accountancy* (UK), *91,* 104-106, 122, 124.

Mauer, J. G. (1969). *Work role involvement of industrial supervisors.* East Lansing: Michigan State University, Bureau of Business and Economic Research.

Mauer, K. F. (1974). The utility of the leadership opinion questionnaire in the South African mining industry. *Journal of Behavioral Science, 74,* 67-72.

Maurice, M., & Sellier, F. (1979). Societal analysis of industrial relations: A comparison between France and West Germany. *British Journal of Industrial Relations, 7,* 322-336.

Mausner, B. (1953). Studies in social interaction. III. Effect of variation in one partner's prestige on the interaction of observer pairs. *Journal of Applied Psychology, 37,* 391-393.

Mausner, B. (1954a). The effect of prior reinforcement on the interaction of observer pairs. *Journal of Abnormal and Social Psychology, 49,* 65-68.

Mausner, B. (1954b). The effects of one partner's success in a relevant task on the interaction of observer pairs. *Journal of Abnormal and Social Psychology, 49,* 557-560.

Mausner, B. (1966). *Situational and personal factors in social interaction* (Tech. Rep.). Glenside, PA: Beaver College.

Mausner, B., & Bloch, B. L. (1957). A study of the additivity of variables affecting social interaction. *Journal of Abnormal and Social Psychology, 54,* 250-256.

Mawhinney, T. C. (1982). Maximizing versus matching in people versus pigeons. *Psychological Reports, 50,* 267-281.

Mawhinney, T. C., & Ford, J. D. (1977). The path goal theory of leader effectiveness: An operant interpretation. *Academy of Management Review, 2,* 398-411.

May, G. D., & Kruger, M. J. (1988). The manager within. *Personnel Journal, 67*(2), 56-65.

May, M. A., & Doob, L. W. (1937). *Competition and cooperation* (Bulletin No. 25). New York: Social Science Research Council.

May, O. P., & Thompson, C. L. (1973). Perceived levels of self-disclosure, mental health, and helpfulness of group leaders. *Journal of Counseling Psychology, 20,* 349-352.

Mayberry, B. A. (1925). Training for leadership by means of student government. *Journal of the National Educational Association, 14,* 186.

Mayberry, H. T. (1943). Measuring leadership qualities of officer candidates. *Texas Personnel Review, 2,* 79-83.

Mayes, B. T. (1979). *Leader needs as moderators of the subordinate job performance-leader behavior relationship.* Paper, Academy of Management, Atlanta, GA.

Mayes, S. S. (1979). Women in positions of authority: A case study of changing sex roles. *Signs: Journal of Women in Culture and Society, 4,* 556-568.

Mayfield, E. C. (1964). The selection interview: A re-evaluation of published research. *Personnel Psychology, 17,* 239-260.

Mayfield, E. C. (1970). Management selection: Buddy nominations revisited. *Personnel Psychology, 23,* 377-389.

Mayhand, E., & Grusky, O. (1972). A preliminary experiment on the effects of black supervisors on white and black subordinates. *Journal of Black Studies, 2,* 461-470.

Mayo, E., & Lombard, G. F. F. (1944). *Teamwork and labor turnover in the aircraft industry of Southern California* (Report No. 32). Cambridge, MA: Harvard Business School.

Mayo, G. C., & DuBois, P. H. (1963). Measurement of gain in leadership training. *Educational Psychology Measurement, 23,* 23-31.

Mazlish, B. (1976). *The revolutionary ascetic: Evolution of a political type.* New York: Basic Books.

McCaffree, K. M. (1961). Union membership policies and labor productivity among asbestos workers. *Industrial Labor Relations Review, 14,* 227-234.

McCall, G. J., & Simmons, J. L. (1966). *Identities and interactions.* New York: Free Press.

McCall, M. W., Jr. (1974). The perceived cognitive role requirements of formal leaders. Paper, American Psychological Association, New Orleans, LA.

McCall, M. W., Jr. (1976). Leadership research: Choosing gods and devils on the run. *Journal of Occupational Psychology, 49,* 139-153.

McCall, M. W., Jr. (1977). *Leaders and leadership: Of substance and shadow* (Tech. Rep. No. 2). Greensboro, NC: Center for Creative Leadership.

McCall, M. W. (1978). Conjecturing about creative leaders. *Journal of Creative Behavior, 14,* 225-234.

McCall, M. W., Jr., & Lombardo, M. M. (Eds.). (1978). *Leadership: Where else can we go?* Durham, NC: Duke University Press.

McCall, M. W., Jr., & Lombardo, M. M. (1982). Using stimulation for leadership and management research: Through the looking glass. *Management Science, 28,* 533-549.

McCall, M. W., Jr., & Lombardo, M. M. (1983). *Off the track: Why and how successful executives get derailed* (Tech. Rep. No. 21). Greensboro, NC: Center for Creative Leadership.

McCall, M. W., Jr., & McCauley, C. D. (1986). *Developmental experiences in managerial work: A literature review* (Tech. Rep. No. 26). Greensboro, NC: Center for Creative Leadership.

McCall, M. W., Jr., Morrison, A. M., & Hanman, R. L. (1978). *Studies of managerial work: Results and methods* (Tech. Rep.). Greensboro, NC: Center for Creative Leadership.

McCall, M. W., & Segrist, C. A. (1980). *In pursuit of the manager's job:*

Building on Mintzberg (Tech. Rep. No. 14) Greensboro, NC: Center for Creative Leadership.

McCandless, B. R. (1942). Changing relationships between dominance and social acceptability during group democratization. *American Journal of Orthopsychiatry, 12,* 529-535.

McCann, E. C. (1964). An aspect of management philosophy in the United States and Latin America. *Academy of Management Journal, 7,* 149-152.

McCarrey, M. W. & Edwards, S. A. (1972). Hierarchies of scientist goal objects: Individual characteristics and performance correlates. *Journal of Applied Psychology, 3,* 271-272.

McCarrey, M. W., Ganse, Y., & Moore, L. (1984). Work value goals and instrumentalities: A comparison of Canadian west-coast Anglophone and Quebec City Francophone managers. *International Review of Applied Psychology, 33,* 291-303.

McCauley, C. D. (1987). Stress and the eye of the beholder. *Issues & Observations, 7*(3), 1-16.

McCaulley, M. H. (1989). *The Myers-Briggs type indicator and leadership.* Gainesville, FL: Center for Applications of Psychological Type.

McClelland, D. C. (1961). *The achieving society.* Princeton, NJ: Van Nostrand.

McClelland, D. C. (1965a). Toward a theory of motive acquisition. *American Psychologist, 20,* 321-333.

McClelland, D. C. (1965b). Achievement motivation can be developed. *Harvard Business Review, 43*(6), 6-24, 178.

McClelland, D. C. (1965c). N achievement and entrepreneurship: A longitudinal study. *Journal of Personality and Social Psychology, 1,* 389-392.

McClelland, D. C. (1966a). Does education accelerate economic growth? *Economic Development and Cultural Change, 14,* 257-278.

McClelland, D. C. (1966b). Longitudinal trends in the relation of thought to action. *Journal of Consulting Psychology, 30,* 479-483.

McClelland, D. C. (1970). The two faces of power. *Journal of International Affairs,* 29-47.

McClelland, D. C. (1975). *Power: The inner experience.* New York: Irvington Publishers (distributed by Halstead Press).

McClelland, D. C. (1980). Motive dispositions: The merits of operant and respondent measures. In L. Wheeler (Ed.), *Review of personality and social psychology.* Beverly Hills, CA: Sage.

McClelland, D. C. (1985). *Human motivation.* Glenview, IL: Scott, Foresman.

McClelland, D. C., & Boyatzis, R. E. (1982). Leadership motive pattern and long-term success in management. *Journal of Applied Psychology, 67,* 737-743.

McClelland, D. C., & Burnham, D. H. (1976). Power is the great motivator. *Harvard Business Review, 54*(2), 100-110.

McClelland, D. C., & Clark, R. A. (1953). Antecedent conditions for affective arousal. In D. C. McClelland, J. W. Atkinson, R. A. Clark, & E. L. Lowell (Eds.), *The achievement motive.* New York: Appleton-Century-Crofts.

McClelland, D. C., Davis, W. N., Kalin, R., & Warner, R. (1972). *The drinking man.* New York: Free Press.

McClelland, D. C., & Winter, D. G. (1969). *Motivating economic achievement.* New York: Free Press.

McClintock, C. G. (1963). Group support and the behavior of leaders and nonleaders. *Journal of Abnormal and Social Psychology, 67,* 105-113.

McClintock, C. G. (1966). The behavior of leaders, non-leaders, non-joiners, and non-leader joiners under conditions of group support and non-support. In R. V. Bowers (Ed.), *Studies on behavior in organizations.* Athens: University of Georgia Press.

McConkie, M. L. (1979). A clarification of the goal setting and appraisal process in MBO. *Academy of Management Review, 4,* 29-40.

McConkie, M. L. (1984). *The symbolic meanings of leadership.* Paper, International Congress of Psychology, Acapulco.

McCormick, C. P. (1938). *Multiple management.* New York: Harper.

McCormick, C. P. (1949). *The power of people: Multiple management up to date.* New York: Harper.

McCormick, J., & Powell, B. (1988, April). Management for the 1990's. *Newsweek,* 47-48.

McCroskey, J. C. (1977). *Oral communication apprehension: A summary.* Unpublished manuscript.

McCroskey, J. C., et al. (1981). *Individual differences among employees, management communication style and employee satisfaction: Replication and extension.* Paper, Eastern Communication Association, Pittsburgh.

McCuen, T. L. (1929). Leadership and intelligence. *Education, 50,* 89-95.

McCullough, G. E. (1975). The effects of changes in organizational structure: Demonstration projects in an oil refinery. In L. E. Davis & A. B. Cherns (Eds.), *The quality of working life. Vol. 2: Cases and commentary.* New York: Free Press.

McCurdy, H. G., & Eber, H. W. (1953). Democratic versus authoritarian: A further investigation of group problem-solving. *Journal of Personality, 22,* 258-269.

McCurdy, H. G., & Lambert, W. E. (1952). The efficiency of small human groups in the solution of problems requiring genuine cooperation. *Journal of Personality, 20,* 478-494.

McDevitt, T. M. & Gadalla, S. M. (1985-86). Special issue: Migration intentions and behavior: Third World perspectives. *Population & Environment: Behavioral & Social Issues, 8,* 98-119.

McDonnell, J. F. (1974). An analysis of participative management as a choice of leadership style. *Dissertation Abstracts International, 35,* 1339.

McDonough, Edward F., III, & Kinnunen, R. M. (1984). Management control of new product development projects. *IEEE Transactions on Engineering Management, 31*(1), 18-21.

McEachern, W. A. (1975). *Managerial control and performance.* Lexington, MA: D. C. Heath.

McElroy, J. C. (1982). A typology of attribution leadership research. *Academy of Management Review, 7,* 413-417.

McElroy, J. C. (1985). Inside the teaching machine: Integrating attribution and reinforcement theories. *Academy of Management, 11,* 123–141.

McElroy, J. C., & Schrader, C. B. (1986). Attribution theories of leadership and network analysis. *Journal of Management, 12,* 351–362.

McEvoy, G. M. (1988). Predicting managerial performance: A seven year assessment center validation study. *Proceedings, Academy of Management,* Anaheim, CA, 277–281.

McFarland, C., & Ross, M. (1982). Impact of causal attributions on affective reactions to success and failure. *Journal of Personality and Social Psychology, 43,* 937–946.

McFeely, W. M., & Mussmann, W. W. (1945). Training supervisors in leadership. *Personnel, 21,* 217–223.

McFeely, W. S. (1981). *Grant: A biography.* New York: Norton.

McFillen, J. M. (1977). The organizing and managing of organizational behavior: A review of first edition organizational behavior texts. *Academy of Management Review, 2,* 355–359.

McFillen, J. M. (1978). *The role of power, supervision, and performance in leadership productivity* (Working Paper). Columbus: Ohio State University, College of Administrative Sciences.

McFillen, J. M., & New, J. R. (1978). *Situational determinants of supervisor attributes and behavior* (Working Paper). Columbus: Ohio State University, College of Adminstrative Sciences.

McFillen, J. M., & New, J. R. (1979). Situational determinants of supervisor attributions and behavior. *Academy of Management Journal, 22,* 793–809.

McGahan, F. E. (1941). Factors associated with leadership ability. *Texas Outlook, 25,* 37–38.

McGehee, W., & Thayer, P. W. (1961). *Training in business and industry.* New York: Wiley.

McGehee, W., & Tullar, W. L. (1978). A note on evaluating behavior modification and behavior modeling as industrial training techniques. *Personnel Psychology, 31,* 477–484.

McGinnies, E., & Ferster, C. B. (1971). *The reinforcement of social behavior.* Boston: Houghton Mifflin.

McGrath, J. E. (1964). *Leadership behavior: Some requirements for leadership training.* Washington, DC: Office of Career Development, U.S. Civil Service Commission.

McGrath, J. E., & Altman, J. (1966). *Small group research: A synthesis and critique.* New York: Holt, Rinehart & Winston.

McGregor, D. (1944). Conditions of effective leadership in the industrial organization. *Journal of Consulting Psychology, 8,* 55–63.

McGregor, D. (1960). *The human side of enterprise.* New York: McGraw-Hill.

McGregor, D. (1966). *Leadership and motivation.* Cambridge, MA: M.I.T. Press.

McGregor, D. (1967). *The professional manager.* New York: McGraw-Hill.

McGregor, D., & Arensberg, C. (1940). The genesis of attitudes toward management. *Psychological Bulletin, 37,* 433–434.

McGruder, J. (1976). *The community reintegration centers of Ohio: A case analysis in community based corrections.* Doctoral dissertation, Ohio State University, Columbus.

McGuire, C., Lammon, M., & White, G. D. (1953). Adolescent peer acceptance and valuations of role behaviors. *American Psychologist, 8,* 397 (Abstract).

McGuire, J. W. (1962). *Interdisciplinary studies in business behavior.* Cincinnati, OH: Southwestern.

McGuire, M. A. (1987). *The contribution of intelligence to leadership performance on an in-basket test.* Master's thesis, University of Washington, Seattle.

McHenry, J. J. (1986). *Activity and responsibility differences between first-level and middle managers: The effects of job function.* Paper, American Psychological Association, Washington, DC.

McIntosh, N. J. (1988). *Substitutes for leadership: Review, critique and suggestion.* Paper, Academy of Management, Anaheim, CA.

McKeachie, W. J. (1954). Individual conformity to attitudes of classroom groups. *Journal of Abnormal and Social Psychology, 49,* 282–289.

McKelvey, W. W. (1969). Exceptional noncomplementarity and style of interaction between professional and organization. *Administrative Science Quarterly, 14,* 21–32.

McKenna, E. (undated). *A situational perspective of the leadership role of the chief accountant in industry.* Unpublished manuscript.

McKenna, E. F. (1972). *Leadership styles in industry.* Master's thesis, University of Lancaster, Lancaster, England.

McKenzie, I. K., & Strongman, K. T. (1981). Rank (status) and interaction distance. *European Journal of Social Psychology, 11,* 227–230.

McLachlan, J. F. (1974). Therapy strategies, personality orientation and recovery from alcoholism. *Canadian Psychiatric Association Journal, 19,* 25–30.

McLarney, W. J. (1962). *Management training.* Homewood, IL: Irwin.

McLaughlin, F. E. (1971). Personality changes through alternate group leadership. *Nursing Research, 20,* 123–130.

McLaughlin, G. W. (1971). *The use of high school faculty ratings to predict USMA fourth class performance.* West Point, NY: United States Military Academy, Office of Institutional Research.

McMahon, J. T. (1972). The contingency theory: Logic and method revisited. *Personnel Psychology, 25,* 697–710.

McMartin, J. A. (1970). Two tests of an averaging model of social influence. *Journal of Personality and Social Psychology, 15,* 317–325.

McMurry, R. N. (1947). The problem of resistance to change in industry. *Journal of Applied Psychology, 31,* 580–593.

McMurry, R. N. (1974). *The maverick executive.* New York: AMACOM.

McNamara, V. D. (1968). *Leadership, staff, and school effectiveness.* Doctoral dissertation, University of Alberta, Alberta, Canada.

McNaul, J. P. (1969). *Behavioral patterns among professionals in a research and development environment.* Doctoral dissertation, Stanford University, Stanford, CA.

McNerney, W. J. (1962). *Hospital and medical economics.* Chicago: Hospital Research and Educational Trust.

McSweeney, J. P. (1976). Rumors—enemy of company morale and community relations. *Personnel Journal, 55*, 435–436.

Mead, M. (1930). *Growing up in New Guinea—A comparative study of primitive education.* New York: Morrow.

Mead, M. (1935). *Sex and temperament in three primitive societies.* New York: Morrow.

Mead, M. (1939). *From the South Seas—Coming of age in Samoa.* New York: Morrow.

Mead, M., Mirsky, M., Landes, R., Edel, M. M., Goldman, I., Quain, B., Mishkin, B., & Zessner, W. (1937). *Cooperation and competition among primitive peoples.* New York: McGraw-Hill.

Meade, R. D. (1967). An experimental study of leadership in India. *Journal of Social Psychology, 72*, 35–43.

Meade, R. D., & Whittaker, J. D. (1967). A cross-cultural study of authoritarianism. *Journal of Social Psychology, 72*, 3–7.

Mechanic, D. (1962). Sources of power of lower participants in complex organizations. *Administrative Science Quarterly, 7*, 349–364.

Medalia, N. Z. (1954). Unit size and leadership perception. *Sociometry, 17*, 64–67.

Medalia, N. Z. (1955). Authoritarianism, leader acceptance, and group cohesion. *Journal of Abnormal and Social Psychology, 51*, 207–213.

Medalia, N. Z., & Miller, D. C. (1955). Human relations leadership and the association of morale and efficiency in work groups: A controlled study with small military units. *Social Forces, 33*, 348–352.

Medcof, J. W., & Evans, M. G. (1986). Heroic or competent? A second look. *Organizational Behavior and Human Decision Processes, 38*, 295–304.

Medland, F. F., & Olans, J. J. (1964). *Peer rating stability in changing groups* (Tech. Research Note, No. 142). Washington, DC: U.S. Army, Personnel Research Office.

Medley, F. (1986). Head nurse leadership style and staff nurse job satisfaction. *Florida Nursing Review, 2*(2), 17–18.

Medow, H., & Zander, A. (1965). Aspirations for the group chosen by central and peripheral members. *Journal of Personality and Social Psychology, 1*, 224–228.

Meehl, P. (1967). Theory testing in psychological physics. *Philosophy of Science, 34*, 103–115.

Meek, C. B. (1987). Review of C. M. Rosen, C. J. Klein, & K. Young (1986), Employee ownership in America: The equity solution. *Academy of Management Review, 2*, 389–392.

Megargee, E. I. (1969). Influence of sex roles on the manifestation of leadership. *Journal of Applied Psychology, 53*, 377–382.

Megargee, E. I., Bogart, P., & Anderson, B. J. (1966). Prediction of leadership in a simulated industrial task. *Journal of Applied Psychology, 50*, 292–295.

Mehaffey, T. D. (1973). The effects of a T-group experience on clients with measured high and low dependency needs. *Dissertation Abstracts International, 33*, 3299–3300.

Meheut, Y., & Siegel, J. P. (1973). *A study of leader behavior and MBO success.* Toronto: University of Toronto, Faculty of Management Studies. Unpublished manuscript.

Mehrabian, A. (1968a). Inference of attitude from the posture, orientation, and distance of a communicator. *Journal of Consulting Clinical Psychology, 32*, 296–308.

Mehrabian, A. (1968b). Communication with words. *Psychology Today, 2*(4), 53–56.

Mehrabian, A. (1969). Significance of posture and position in the communication of attitude and status relationships. *Psychological Bulletin, 71*, 359–372.

Mehrabian, A. (1970). *Tactics of social influence.* Englewood Cliffs, NJ: Prentice-Hall.

Meier, K. (1988). Bureaucratic leadership in public organizations. In B. Jones (Ed.), *Political leadership from political science perspectives.* Lawrence: University of Kansas Press.

Meindl, J. R., & Ehrlich, S. B. (1987). The romance of leadership and the evaluation of organizational performance. *Academy of Management Journal, 30*, 90–109.

Meindl, J. R., Ehrlich, S. B., & Dukerich, J. M. (1985). The romance of leadership. *Administrative Science Quarterly, 30*, 78–102.

Melcher, A. J. (1976). Participation: A critical review of research findings. *Human Resources Management, 15*(2), 12–21.

Mellon, S. J. (1975). Instrumentality—expectancy theory of work motivation. *Dissertation Abstracts International, 36*, 1490.

Meltzer, L. (1956). Scientific productivity in organizational settings. *Journal of Social Issues, 12*, 32–40.

Meltzer, L., & Salter, J. (1962). Organization structure and the performance and job satisfaction of physiologists. *American Sociological Review, 27*, 351–362.

Mendell, J. S., & Gerjuoy, H. G. (1984). Anticipatory management or visionary leadership: A debate. *Managerial Planning, 33*(3), 28–31, 63.

Mendenhall, M. E. (1983). Self-monitoring as a determinant of leader emergence. *Dissertation Abstracts International, 44*(7B), 2284.

Merei, F. (1949). Group leadership and institutionalization. *Human Relations, 2*, 23–39.

Merrell, V. D. (1965). *An analysis of university sponsored executive development programs.* Los Angeles: University of California, School of Public Administration.

Merriam, C. E. (1926). *Four American party leaders.* New York: Macmillan.

Merriam, C. E., & Gosnell, H. E. (1929). *The American party system.* New York: Macmillan.

Merron, K., Fisher, D., & Torbert, W. R. (1987). Meaning making and management action. *Group & Organization Studies, 12*, 274–286.

Merton, R. K. (1940). Bureaucratic structure and personality. *Social Forces, 18*, 560–568.

Merton, R. K. (1949, 1957). *Social theory and social structure.* New York: Free Press.

Merton, R. K. (1969). The social nature of leadership. *American Journal of Nursing, 69*, 2614–2618.

Merton, R. K., Gray, A. P., Hockey, B., & Selvin, H. C. (1952). *Reader in bureaucracy*. New York: Free Press.

Merton, R. K., & Kitt, A. S. (1950). Contributions to the theory of reference group behavior. In R. K. Merton & P. F. Lazarsfeld (Eds.), *Studies in the scope and method of "The American Soldier."* New York: Free Press.

Mesics, E. A. (1960). *Training in organizations: Business, industrial, and government*. Bibliography Series No. 4. Ithaca, NY: Cornell University, New York State School of Industrial and Labor Relations.

Mesics, E. A. (1964). *An annotated bibliography on education and training in organizations*. Ithaca, NY: Cornell University, New York State School of Industrial and Labor Relations.

Metcalf, H. C. (1931). *Business leadership*. New York: Pitman.

Metcalfe, B. A. (1984). Microskills of leadership: A detailed analysis of the behaviors of managers in the appraisal interview. In J. Hunt, D. M. Hosking, C. A. Schriesheim, and R. Stewart (Eds.), *Leaders and managers: International perspectives on managerial behavior and leadership*. New York: Pergamon.

Mettal, W. G. (1973). Human relations training and creative problem-solving competence in adolescents. *Dissertation Abstracts International, 33,* 3288.

Metzger, T. A. (1977). *Escape from predicament*. New York: Columbia University Press.

Meuwese, W. A. T., & Fiedler, F. E. (1965). *Leadership and group creativity under varying conditions of stress* (Tech. Rep.). Urbana: University of Illinois, Group Effectiveness Research Laboratory.

Mey, W. (1936). Spontaneous and elective leadership in school classes. *Pädagogische Studien und Kritiken, 12,* 1–82.

Meyer, C. T. (1947). The assertive behavior of children as related to parent behavior. *Journal of Home Economics, 39,* 77–80.

Meyer, E. C. (1980). Leadership: A return to the basics. *Military Review, 60*(7), 4–9.

Meyer, E. C. (1983). Leadership—A soldier's view. *Washington Quarterly, 6*(3), 169–174.

Meyer, H. D. (1961). *An exploratory study of the executive position description questionnaire in the Jewel Tea Co., Inc.* Paper, Conference on the Executive Study, Princeton, NJ.

Meyer, H. D. (1963). *A four year study of management promotions in the Jewel Tea Co. as related to three measures of achievement motivation*. Chicago: Jewel Tea Co. (Reported in Campbell, Dunnette, et al., 1970, 190–191.)

Meyer, H. H. (1951). Factors related to success in human relations aspect of work-group leadership. *Psychological Monographs, 65,* No. 320.

Meyer, H. H. (1959). A comparison of foreman and general foreman conceptions of the foreman's job responsibility. *Personnel Psychology, 12,* 445–452.

Meyer, H. H. (1963). *The in-basket test as measure of foreman performance*. Management Development and Employee Relations Services, General Electric.

Meyer, H. H. (1968). Achievement motivation and industrial climates.

In R. Tagiuri & G. H. Litwin (Eds.), *Organizational climate*. Boston: Harvard University, Graduate School of Business Administration.

Meyer, H. H. (1970a). The validity of the in-basket test as a measure of managerial performance. *Personnel Psychology, 23,* 297–307.

Meyer, H. H. (1970b). *Improving supervisor-employee relations in the shop*. Unpublished manuscript.

Meyer, H. H. (1972). *Assessment centers at General Electric*. Paper, Development Dimensions Orientation Conference, San Francisco.

Meyer, H. H. (1975). The pay for performance dilemma. *Organizational Dynamics, 3*(3), 39–50.

Meyer, H. H., Kay E., & French, J. R. P. (1965). Split roles in performance appraisal. *Harvard Business Review, 43*(1), 123–129.

Meyer, H. H., & Walker, W. B. (1961). Need for achievement and risk preferences as they relate to attitudes toward reward systems and performance appraisal in an industrial setting. *Journal of Applied Psychology, 45,* 251–256.

Meyer, H. H., Walker, N. B., & Litwin, G. H. (1961). Motive patterns and risk preferences associated with entrepreneurship. *Journal of Abnormal and Social Psychology, 63,* 570–574.

Meyer, M. W. (1968). The two authority structures of bureaucratic organization. *Administrative Science Quarterly, 13,* 211–228.

Meyer, M. W. (1975). Leadership and organizational structure. *American Journal of Sociology, 81,* 514–542.

Meyers, A. K., & Miller, N. E. (1954). Failure to find a learned drive based on hunger: Evidence for learning motivated by "exploration." *Journal of Comparative and Physiological Psychology, 47,* 428–436.

Meyers, C. E. (1944). The effect of conflicting authority on the child. *University of Iowa Study on Child Welfare, 20,* 31–98.

Meyers, G. C. (1923). Training for leadership. *School and Society, 17,* 437–439.

Meyers, L. C. (1970). Some effects of facilitator training on the attitudes and performances of people in leadership positions. *Dissertation Abstracts International, 31,* 2962–2963.

Michaelson, F. J. (1951). *Some motivational aspects of leadership*. Doctoral dissertation, Ohio State University, Columbus.

Michaelson, L. K. (1973). Leader orientation, leader behavior, group effectiveness, and situational favorability: An empirical extension of the contingency model. *Organizational Behavior and Human Performance, 9,* 226–245.

Michels, R. (1915). *Political parties*. New York: Macmillan.

Michener, A., & Burt, M. R. (1974). Legitimacy as a base of social influence. In J. T. Tedeschi (Ed.), *Perspectives on social power*. Chicago: Aldine.

Michener, A., Fleishman, J., Elliot, G., & Skolnick, J. (1976). Influence use and target attributes. *Journal of Personality and Social Psychology*.

Michener, A., & Schwertfeger, M. (1972). Liking as a determinant of power tactic preference. *Sociometry, 35,* 190–202.

Michener, H. A., & Burt, M. R. (1975a). Components of "authority" as determinants of compliance. *Journal of Personnel Psychology, 31,* 606–614.

Michener, H. A., & Burt, M. R. (1975b). Use of social influence under varying conditions of legitimacy. *Journal of Personality and Social Psychology, 32,* 398–407.

Michener, H. A., & Lawler, E. J. (1975). Endorsement of formal leaders: An integrative model. *Journal of Personality and Social Psychology, 31,* 216–223.

Middleton, W. C. (1941). Personality qualities predominant in campus leaders. *Journal of Social Psychology, 13,* 199–210.

Miklos, E. (1963). *Dimensions of conflicting expectations and the leader behavior of principals.* Doctoral dissertation, University of Alberta, Edmonton.

Miles, A. S. (1970). Dimensions of student leadership at Cornell University. *Dissertation Abstracts International, 30,* 2856.

Miles, C. S. (1985). *Leadership effectiveness of professional home economists in Cornell cooperative extension.* Doctoral dissertation, Cornell University, Ithaca, NY.

Miles, M. B. (1960). Human relations training: Processes and outcomes. *Journal of Consulting Psychology, 7,* 301–306.

Miles, M. B. (1965). Changes during and following laboratory training: A clinical experimental study. *Journal of Applied Behavioral Science, 1,* 215–242.

Miles, M. B., Milavsky, J. R., Lake, D. G., & Beckhard, R. (1965). *Organizational improvement: Effects of management team training in Bankers Trust.* New York: Bankers Trust Company, Personnel Division.

Miles, P. L. (1934). Leadership. *Infantry Journal, 41,* 183–188, 276–283.

Miles, R. E. (1964a). Attitudes toward management theory as a factor in managers' relationship with their superiors. *Academy of Management Journal, 7,* 308–314.

Miles, R. E. (1964b). Conflicting elements in managerial ideologies. *Industrial Relations, 4,* 77–91.

Miles, R. E., & Ritchie, J. B. (1968). Leadership attitudes among union officials. *Industrial Relations, 8,* 108–117.

Miles, R. H., & Petty, M. M. (1977). Leader effectiveness in small bureaucracies. *Academy of Management Journal, 20,* 238–250.

Mileti, D. S., Drabek, T. E., & Haas, J. E. (1975). *Human systems in extreme environments: A sociological perspective.* Boulder: University of Colorado, Institute of Behavioral Science.

Milewicz, J. C. (1983). *An exploratory study in the behavioral dimensions of a channel of distribution: An assessment of the power, leadership, control, and performance linkages.* Doctoral dissertation, University of Alabama, Tuscaloosa.

Milgram, S. (1965a). Liberating effects of group pressure. *Journal of Personality and Social Psychology, 1,* 127–134.

Milgram, S. (1965b). Some conditions of obedience and disobedience to authority. *Human Relations, 18,* 57–76.

Milkovich, G. T., & Anderson, P. H. (1972). Management compensation and secrecy policies. *Personnel Psychology, 25,* 293–302.

Mill, C. R. (1953). Personality patterns of sociometrically selected and sociometrically rejected male college students. *Sociometry, 16,* 151–167.

Millard, R. J. (1981). A comparative analysis of male and female management style and perceived behavior patterns. *Dissertation Abstracts International, 42*(3B), 1219.

Miller, A. (1988, April 25). Stress on the job; it's hurting morale and the bottom line! How can workers and bosses cope? *Newsweek,* 40ff.

Miller, A. H. (1920). *Military leadership.* New York: Putnam.

Miller, D. (1983). The correlates of entrepreneurship in three types of firms. *Management Science, 29,* 770–791.

Miller, D., & Friesen, H. (1980). Momentum and revolution in organizational adaptation. *Academy of Management Journal, 22,* 591–614.

Miller, D., & Toulouse, J-M. (1986, Winter). Strategy, structure, CEO personality and performance in small firms. *American Journal of Small Business,* 47–62.

Miller, D. B. (1986). *Managing professionals in research and development.* San Francisco: Jossey-Bass.

Miller, D. C. (1968). Using behavioral science to solve organizational problems. *Personnel Administration, 31,* 21–29.

Miller, D. C., & Dirksen, J. L. (1965). The identification of visible, concealed, and symbolic leaders in a small Indiana city: A replication of the Bonjean-Noland study of Burlington, North Carolina. *Social Forces, 43,* 548–555.

Miller, D. C., & Schull, F. A. (1962). The prediction of administrative role conflict resolutions. *Administrative Science Quarterly, 7,* 143–160.

Miller, D. T., & Ross, M. (1975). Self-serving biases in the attribution of causality: Fact or fiction? *Psychological Bulletin, 82,* 213–225.

Miller, E. L. (1966). Job attitudes of national union officials: Perceptions of the importance of certain personality traits as a function of job level and union organizational structure. *Personnel Psychology, 19,* 395–410.

Miller, E. L. (1969). Job satisfaction of national union officials. *Personnel Psychology, 22,* 261–274.

Miller, E. L., & Cattaneo, R. (1982). Some leadership attitudes of West German expatriate managerial personnel. *Journal of International Business Studies, 13*(1), 39–50.

Miller, F. B. (1960). *Personnel research contributions by U.S. universities.* (Bulletin No. 42). Ithaca, NY: Cornell University, New York State School of Industrial and Labor Relations.

Miller, F. B., & Coghill, M. A. (1961). *The historical sources of personnel work.* Ithaca, NY: Cornell University, New York State School of Industrial and Labor Relations.

Miller, F. G., & Remmers, H. H. (1950). Studies in industrial empathy. II. Management's attitudes toward industrial supervision and their estimates of labor attitudes. *Personnel Psychology, 3,* 33–40.

Miller, G. A. (1967). Professionals in a bureaucracy: Alienation among individual scientists and engineers. *American Sociological Review, 32,* 755–768.

Miller, G. J. (1987). *Administrative dilemmas: The role of political leadership.* Working paper. St. Louis, MO: Washington University.

Miller, J. A. (1973a). *Structuring/destructuring: Leadership in open systems.* (Tech. Rep. No. 64). Rochester, NY: University of Rochester, Management Research Center.

Miller, J. A. (1973b). *A hierarchical structure of leadership behaviors* (Tech. Rep. No. 66). Rochester, NY: University of Rochester, Management Research Center.

Miller, J. A. (1974). *Leadership in open systems.* Doctoral dissertation, University of Rochester, Rochester, NY.

Miller, J. G. (1955). Toward a general theory for the behavioral sciences. *American Psychologist, 10,* 513–531.

Miller, J. G. (1971a). The nature of living systems. *Behavioral Science, 16,* 277–301.

Miller, J. G. (1971b). Living systems: The group. *Behavioral Science, 16,* 302–398.

Miller, K. I., & Monge, P. R. (1986). Participation, satisfaction, and productivity: A meta-analytic review. *Academy of Management Journal, 29,* 727–753.

Miller, L., & Hamblin, R. L. (1963). Interdependence, differential rewarding, and productivity. *American Sociological Review, 28,* 768–778.

Miller, L. C., & Hustedde, R. J. (1987). Group approaches. In D. E. Johnson, L. R. Meiller, & G. F. Summers (Eds.), *Needs assessment: Theory and methods.* Ames: Iowa State University Press.

Miller, N. E. (1950). *Effects of group size on group process and member satisfaction.* Ann Arbor: University of Michigan, Proceedings of the Administrative Conference.

Miller, N. E., & Dollard, J. (1941). *Social learning and imitation.* New Haven, CT: Yale University Press.

Miller, P. (1951). *Democratic leadership in secondary education.* Doctoral dissertation, Ohio State University, Columbus.

Miller, P. (1953). *Leadership in secondary education.* Columbus: Ohio State University, Personnel Research Board.

Miller, R. B. (1962). Task description and analysis. In R. M. Gagne (Ed.), *Psychological principles in system development.* New York: Holt, Rinehart & Winston.

Miller, R. D. (1969). A systems concept of training. *Training & Development Journal, 23,* 4–14.

Miller, R. E., & Murphy, J. V. (1956). Social interactions of Rhesus monkeys: I. Food-getting dominance as a dependent variable. *Journal of Social Psychology, 44,* 249–255.

Miller, R. S. (1943). Developing leadership in young officers. *Military Review, 23,* 11–12.

Miller, R. W. (1986). Extending university resources in support of volunteer development: Evaluation of a pilot effort. *Journal of Voluntary Action Research, 15*(1), 100–115.

Miller, S. J. (1970). *Prescription for leadership: Training for the medical elite.* Chicago: Aldine-Atherton.

Miller, W. B. (1965). Focal concerns of lower-class culture. In L. A. Ferman, J. L. Kornbluh, & A. Haber (Eds.), *Poverty in America.* Ann Arbor: University of Michigan Press.

Mills, J. (1986). Subordinate perceptions of managerial coaching practices. *Proceedings, Academy of Management,* Chicago, 113–116.

Mills, T. M. (1953). Power relations in three-person groups. *American Sociological Review, 18,* 351–357.

Mills, T. M. (1954). The coalition pattern in three-person groups. *American Sociological Review, 19,* 657–667.

Mills, T. M. (1957). *Group structure and the newcomer: An experimental study of group expansion.* Oslo, Norway: Oslo University Press.

Mills, T. M. (1964). *Group transformation: An analysis of a learning group.* Englewood Cliffs, NJ: Prentice-Hall.

Mills, T. M., & Rosenberg, S. (1970). *Readings in the sociology of small groups.* Englewood Cliffs, NJ: Prentice-Hall.

Milner, E. (1948). Student preferences concerning teaching method and class structuring. *American Psychologist, 3,* 233–234 (Abstract).

Milton, O. (1952). Presidential choice and performance on a scale of authoritarianism. *American Psychologist, 7,* 597–598 (Abstract).

Miner, J. B. (1960a). The Kuder preference record in management appraisal. *Personnel Psychology, 13,* 187–196.

Miner, J. B. (1960b). The effect of a course in psychology on the attitudes of research and development supervisors. *Journal of Applied Psychology, 44,* 224–231.

Miner, J. B. (1961). The validity of the PAT in the selection of tabulating machine operators: An analysis of productive power. *Journal of Projective Techniques, 25,* 330–333.

Miner, J. B. (1962a). Conformity among university professors and business executives. *Administrative Science Quarterly, 7,* 96–109.

Miner, J. B. (1962b). Personality and ability factors in sales performance. *Journal of Applied Psychology, 46,* 6–13.

Miner, J. B. (1963). Occupational differences in the desire to exercise power. *Psychological Reports, 13,* 18.

Miner, J. B. (1965). *Studies in management education.* New York: Springer-Verlag.

Miner, J. B. (1967). *The school administrator and organizational character.* Eugene: University of Oregon, Center for the Advanced Study of Educational Administration.

Miner, J. B. (1968). The early identification of managerial talent. *Personnel and Guidance Journal, 46,* 586–591.

Miner, J. B. (1973). *The management process: Theory, research and practice.* New York: Macmillan.

Miner, J. B. (1974a). Motivation to manage among women: Studies of business managers and educational administrators. *Journal of Vocational Behavior, 5,* 197–208.

Miner, J. B. (1974b). Student attitudes toward bureaucratic role prescriptions and the prospects for managerial talent shortages. *Personnel Psychology, 27,* 605–613.

Miner, J. B. (1975). The uncertain future of the leadership concept: An overview. In J. G. Hunt & L. L. Larson (Eds.), *Leadership frontiers.* Kent, OH: Kent State University Press.

Miner, J. B. (Ed.). (1977a). *Motivation to manage: A ten year update on the "studies in management education" research.* Atlanta, GA: Organizational Measurement Systems Press.

Miner, J. B. (1977b). Implications of managerial talent projections for management education. *Academy of Management Review, 2*, 412–420.

Miner, J. B. (1977c). Motivational potential for upgrading among minority and female managers. *Journal of Applied Psychology, 62*, 691–697.

Miner, J. B. (1978a). Twenty years of research on role motivation theory of managerial effectiveness. *Personnel Psychology, 31*, 739–760.

Miner, J. B. (1978b). The Miner sentence completion scale: A re-appraisal. *Academy of Management Journal, 21*, 283–294.

Miner, J. B. (1982a). The uncertain future of the leadership concept: Revisions and clarifications. *Journal of Applied Behavioral Science, 18*, 293–307.

Miner, J. B. (1982b). A note on theory and research for developing a science of leadership. *Journal of Applied Behavioral Science, 18*, 536–538.

Miner, J. B. (1984). Participation and management. In B. Wilpert & A. Sorge (Eds.), *International perspectives on organizational democracy.* New York: Wiley.

Miner, J. B. (1986). Managerial role motivation training. *Journal of Managerial Psychology, 1*(1), 25–30.

Miner, J. B., & Brewer, J. F. (1976). The management of ineffective performance. In M. D. Dunnette (Ed.), *Handbook of industrial and organizational psychology.* New York: Rand-McNally.

Miner, J. B., & Crane, D. P. (1977). The continuing effects of motivational shifts among college students. In J. B. Miner (Ed.), *Motivation to manage.* Atlanta, GA: Organizational Measurement Systems Press.

Miner, J. B., & Crane, D. P. (1981). Motivation to manage and the manifestation of a managerial orientation in career planning. *Academy of Management Journal, 24*, 626–633.

Miner, J. B., & Miner, M. G. (1977). Managerial characteristics of personnel managers. In J. B. Miner (Ed.), *Motivation to manage.* Atlanta, GA: Organizational Measurement Systems Press.

Miner, J. B., Rizzo, J. R., Harlow, D. N., & Hill, J. W. (1974). Role motivation theory of managerial effectiveness in simulated organizations of varying degrees of structure. *Journal of Applied Psychology, 59*, 31–37. Also: (1977). In J. B. Miner (Ed.), *Motivation to manage.* Atlanta, GA: Organizational Measurement Systems Press.

Miner, J. B., & Smith, N. R. (1982). Decline and stabilization of managerial motivation over a 20-year period. *Journal of Applied Psychology, 67*, 297–305.

Miner, J. B., Smith, N. R., & Ebrahimi, B. (1985). Further considerations in the decline and stabilization of managerial motivation: A rejoinder to Bartol, Anderson, and Schneier (1980). *Journal of Vocational Behavior, 26*, 290–298.

Mintz, A. (1951). Non-adaptive behavior. *Journal of Abnormal and Social Psychology, 46*, 150–159.

Mintzberg, H. (1968). *The manager at work—determining his activities, and programs by structured observation.* Doctoral dissertation, M.I.T. Sloan School of Management, Cambridge, MA.

Mintzberg, H. (1970). Structured observation as a method to study managerial work. *Journal of Management Studies, 7*, 87–104.

Mintzberg, H. (1971). Managerial work: Analysis from observation. *Management Science, 18B*, 97–110.

Mintzberg, H. (1973). *The nature of managerial work.* New York: Harper & Row.

Mintzberg, H. (1975). The manager's job: Folklore and fact. *Harvard Business Review, 53*(4), 49–61.

Mintzberg, H. (1979). An emerging strategy of 'direct' research. *Administrative Science Quarterly, 26*, 583–589.

Mintzberg, H. (1983). *Power in and around organizations.* Englewood Cliffs, NJ: Prentice-Hall.

Mintzberg, H., & Waters, J. A. (1982). Tracking strategy in an entrepreneurial firm. *Academy of Management Journal, 25*, 465–499.

Mischel, W. (1961). Preference for delayed reinforcement and social responsibility. *Journal of Abnormal and Social Psychology, 62*, 1–7.

Mischel, W. (1965). Predicting the success of Peace Corps volunteers in Nigeria. *Journal of Personality and Social Psychology, 1*, 510–517.

Miskin, V. D., & Gmelch, W. H. (1985). Quality leadership for quality teams. *Training & Development Journal, 39*(5), 122–129.

Misshauk, M. J. (1968). *The relation of supervisor skill mix to employee satisfaction and productivity.* Doctoral dissertation. Ohio State University, Columbus.

Misumi, J. (1974). *Action research on the development of leadership, decision-making processes and organizational performance in a Japanese shipyard.* Paper, International Congress of Applied Psychology, Liege, Belgium.

Misumi, J. (1984). Decision making in Japanese groups and organizations. In B. Wilpert & A. Sorge (Eds.), *International yearbook of organizational democracy*, Vol. 2. Chichester: Wiley.

Misumi, J. (1985). *The behavioral science of leadership. An interdisciplinary Japanese research program.* Ann Arbor: University of Michigan Press.

Misumi, J., & Mannari, N. (1982). The empirical study concerning the validity of the measurement of the leadership behavior in industrial organizations. *Proceedings, Japanese Organizational Science Association.* (Cited in J. Misumi, 1985, 284–290.)

Misumi, J., & Peterson, M. F. (1985). The performance-maintenance (PM) theory of leadership: Review of a Japanese research program. *Administrative Science Quarterly, 30*, 198–223.

Misumi, J., & Peterson, M. F. (1987). Supervision and leadership. In B. M. Bass, P. J. D. Drenth, & P. Weissenberg, (Eds.), *Advances in organizational psychology: An international review.* Beverly Hills, CA: Sage.

Misumi, J., & Sako, H. (1982). An experimental study of the effect of leadership behavior on followers' behavior of following after the leader in a simulated emergency situation. *Japanese Journal of Experimental Social Psychology, 21*(1), 49–59. (Cited in J. Misumi, 1985.)

Misumi, J., & Seki, F. (1971). Effects of achievement motivation on the effectiveness of leadership patterns. *Administrative Science Quarterly, 16*, 51–59.

Misumi, J., & Shirakashi, S. (1966). An experimental study of the effects of supervisory behavior on productivity and morale in a hierarchical organization. *Human Relations, 19*, 297–307.

Misumi, J., Takeda, T., & Seki, F. (1967). An empirical study of the effects of managerial and supervisory behavior of PM pattern on productivity and morale, particularly need for achievement in an hierarchical organization. *Japanese Journal of Educational and Social Psychology, 7,* 27–42. (Cited in J. Misumi, 1985.)

Misumi, J., & Tasaki, T. (1965). A study of the effectiveness of supervisory patterns in a Japanese hierarchical organization. *Japanese Psychological Research, 7,* 151–162. (Cited in J. Misumi, 1985.)

Mitchell, B. N. (1969). The black minority in the CPA profession. *Journal of Accounting, 128*(3), 41–48.

Mitchell, J. O. (1975). Assessment center validity: A longitudinal study. *Journal of Applied Psychology, 60,* 573–579.

Mitchell, T. R. (1969). *Leader complexity, leadership style, and group performance.* Doctoral dissertation, University of Illinois, Urbana.

Mitchell, T. R. (1970a). The construct validity of three dimensions of leadership research. *Journal of Social Psychology, 80,* 89–94.

Mitchell, T. R. (1970b). Leader complexity and leadership style. *Journal of Personality and Social Psychology, 16,* 166–174.

Mitchell, T. R. (1972). Cognitive complexity and group performance. *Journal of Social Psychology, 86,* 35–43.

Mitchell, T. R. (1979). Organizational behavior. *Annual Review of Psychology, 30,* 243–281.

Mitchell, T. R. (1981). *Leader attributions and leader behavior: First stage testing of theoretical model* (Tech. Rep. No. 522). Seattle: University of Washington, School of Business.

Mitchell, T. R. (1985). Review of in search of excellence versus the 100 best companies to work for in America: A question of perspective and values. *Academy of Management Review, 10,* 350–355.

Mitchell, T. R., & Albright, D. W. (1972). Expectancy theory predictions of the satisfaction, effort, performance, and retention of naval aviation officers. *Organizational Behavior and Human Performance, 8,* 1–20.

Mitchell, T. R., Biglan, A., Oncken, G. R., & Fiedler, F. E. (1970). The Contingency Model: Criticism and suggestions. *Academy of Management Journal, 13,* 253–267.

Mitchell, T. R., & Foa, U. G. (1969). Diffusion of the effect of cultural training of the leader in the structure of heterocultural task groups. *Australian Journal of Psychology, 21,* 31–43.

Mitchell, T. R., Green, S. G., & Wood, R. E. (1981). An attributional model of leadership and the poor performing subordinate: Development and validation. In B. M. Staw and L. L. Cummings (Eds.), *Research in organizational behavior.* Greenwich, CT: JAI Press.

Mitchell, T. R., & Kalb, L. S. (1981). Effects of outcome knowledge and outcome valence on supervisor's evaluations. *Journal of Applied Psychology, 66,* 604–612.

Mitchell, T. R., & Kalb, L. S. (1982). Effects of job experience on supervisor attributions for a subordinate's poor performance. *Journal of Applied Psychology, 67,* 181–188.

Mitchell, T. R., Larson, J. R., & Green, S. G. (1977). Leader behavior, situational moderators and group performance: An attributional analysis. *Organizational Behavior and Human Performance, 18,* 254–268.

Mitchell, T. R., & Liden, R. C. (1982). The effects of the social context on performance evaluations. *Organizational Behavior and Human Performance, 29,* 241–256.

Mitchell, T. R., & Scott, W. G. (1987). Leadership failures, the distrusting public, and prospects of the administrative state. *Public Administration Review, 47,* 445–452.

Mitchell, T. R., Smyser, C. M., & Weed, S. E. (1975). Locus of control: Supervision and work satisfaction. *Academy of Management Journal, 18,* 623–630.

Mitchell, T. R., & Wood, R. E. (1979). *An empirical test of an attributional model of leaders' responses to poor performance.* Paper, Symposium on Leadership, Duke University, Durham, NC.

Mitchell, T. R., & Wood, R. E. (1980). Supervisor's responses to subordinate poor performance: A test of an attributional model. *Organizational Behavior and Human Performance, 25,* 123–138.

Mitchell, V. F. (1968). The relationship of effort, abilities, and role perceptions to managerial performance. *Dissertation Abstracts, 29,* 360.

Mitchell, V. F. (1970). Needs satisfactions of military commanders and staff. *Journal of Applied Psychology, 54,* 282–287.

Mitchell, V. F., & Porter, L. W. (1967). Comparative managerial role perceptions in military and business hierarchies. *Journal of Applied Psychology, 51,* 449–452.

Mitroff, I. (1983). *Stakeholders of the organization mind.* San Francisco: Jossey-Bass.

Mitroff, I. I. (1978). Systematic problem solving. In M. W. McCall & M. M. Lombardo (Eds.), *Leadership: Where else can we go?* Durham, NC: Duke University Press.

Mitroff, I. I., & Kilmann, R. H. (1976). On organization stories: An approach to the design and analysis of organization through myths and stories. In R. H. Kilmann, L. R. Pondy, & D. P. Slevin (Eds.), *The management of organization design,* Vol. 1. New York: Elsevier North-Holland.

Mitroff, I. I., Shrivastava, P., & Udwadia, F. E. (1987). Effective crisis management. *Academy of Management Executive, 1,* 283–292.

Mitscherlich, A. (1967). Changing patterns of authority: A psychiatric interpretation. In L. J. Edinger (Ed.), *Political leadership in industrialized societies.* New York: Wiley.

Moede, W. (1920). *Experimentelle Massenpsychologie.* Leipzig: Hirzel.

Moffie, D. J., Calhoon, R., & O'Brien, J. K. (1964). Evaluation of a management development program. *Personnel Psychology, 17,* 431–440.

Mohanna, A. I., & Argyle, M. (1960). A cross-cultural study of structured groups with unpopular central members. *Journal of Abnormal and Social Psychology, 60,* 139–140.

Mohr, L. B. (1971). Organizational technology and organizational structure. *Administrative Science Quarterly, 16,* 444–459.

Mohr, L. B. (1977). Authority and democracy in organizations. *Human Relations, 30,* 919–947.

Mohrman, A., & Lawler, E. (1983). Motivation and performance appraisal behavior. In F. Landy, S. Zedeck & J. Cleveland, (Eds.), *Performance measurement and theory.* Hillsdale, NJ: Erlbaum.

Mold, H. P. (1947). Outline of a complete training program. *Personnel Journal, 26*(2), 75–79.

Mold, H. P. (1952). Management builds itself—a case study in conference training. In M. J. Dooher & V. Marquis (Eds.), *The development of executive talent.* New York: American Management Association.

Moloney, M. M. (1979). *Leadership in nursing: Theory, strategies, action.* St. Louis: C. V. Mosby.

Moment, D., & Zaleznik, A. (1963). Role development and interpersonal competence. Boston: Harvard University, Graduate School of Business Administration.

Monge, P. R., & Kirste, K. K. (1975). *Proximity, location, time, and opportunity to communicate.* San Jose: California State University.

Montgomery, P. (1989). Inside job: How a HUD program grew into a slush fund for Republican insiders. *Common Cause, 15*(4), 17–20.

Moon, C. G., & Hariton, T. (1958). Evaluating an appraisal and feedback training program. *Personnel, 35,* 37–41.

Mooney, J. D., & Reiley, A. C. (1931). *Onward industry: The principles of organization and their significance to modern industry.* New York: Harper.

Moore, B. V. (1927). The May conference on leadership. *Personnel Journal, 6,* 124–128.

Moore, B. V., Kennedy, J. E., & Castore, G. F. (1946). *The work, training, and status of supervisors as reported by supervisors in industry.* State College: Pennsylvania State College.

Moore, D. P. (1984). Evaluating in-role and out-of-role performers. *Academy of Management Journal, 27,* 603–618.

Moore, H. T. (1921). The comparative influence of majority and expert opinion. *American Journal of Psychology, 32,* 16–20.

Moore, H. T., & Gilliland, A. R. (1921). The measurement of aggressiveness. *Journal of Applied Psychology, 5,* 97–118.

Moore, J. C. (1968). Status and influence in small group interactions. *Sociometry, 31,* 47–63.

Moore, J. C. (1969). Social status and social influence: Process considerations. *Sociometry, 32,* 145–158.

Moore, J. V. (1953a). *A factor analysis of subordinate of noncommissioned officer supervisors* (Research Bulletin No. 53-6). San Antonio, TX: USAF Human Resources Research Center.

Moore, J. V. (1953b). *Factor analytic comparisons of superior and subordinate ratings of the same NCO supervisors.* (Tech. Rep. No. 53-24). San Antonio, TX: USAF Human Resources Research Center.

Moore, J. V., & Smith, R. G. (1953). Some aspects of noncommissioned officer leadership. *Personnel Psychology, 6,* 427–443.

Moore, L. B. (1968). Managerial time. *Management Review, 9,* 77–85.

Moore, L. H. (1932). Leadership traits of college women. *Sociology and Social Research, 17,* 44–54.

Moore, L. H. (1935). Leadership traits of college women. (II.) *Sociology and Social Research, 20,* 136–139.

Moore, L. I. (1976). The FMI: Dimensions of follower maturity. *Group & Organization Studies, 1,* 203–222.

Moore, M. M. (1981). First career, second career, and alternative career academic librarians: A study in personality and leadership differentials as related to managerial talent. *Dissertation Abstracts International, 42*(1A), 7.

Moore, M. M. (1983). "New blood" and managerial potential in academic libraries. *Journal of Academic Librarianship, 9*(3), 142–147.

Moore, W. E. (1970). *The professions: Roles and rules.* New York: Russell Sage Foundation.

Moos, M., & Koslin, B. (1951). Political leadership reexamined: An empirical approach. *Public Opinion Quarterly, 15,* 563–574.

Morall, H. H. (1974). *The relationship between perceived participation in school management and morale of selected black and nonblack teachers and students in Volusia County, Florida senior high schools.* Doctoral dissertation, University of Miami, Miami, FL.

Moranian, T., Gruenwald, D., & Reidenbach, R. (Eds.). (1965). *Business policy and its environment.* New York: Holt, Rinehart & Winston.

Mordechai, E. (1966). Relationships between self-perceived personality and job attitudes in middle management. *Journal of Applied Psychology, 50,* 428–430.

Moreno, J. L. (1934/1953). *Who shall survive?* Beacon, NY: Beacon House.

Moreno, J. L. (1940). Time as a quantitative index of interpersonal relations. *Sociometry, 3,* 62–80.

Moreno, J. L. (1955). *Sociodrama: A method for the analysis of social conflicts.* Beacon, NY: Beacon House.

Moreno, J. L. (1960). *The sociometry reader.* New York: Free Press.

Moreux, C. (1971). Specificite culturelle du leadership en milieu rural Canadien-Francais. *Sociologie et Societes, 3,* 229–258.

Morgan, B. S., Blonsky, M. R., & Rosen, H. (1970). Employee attitudes towards a hard-core hiring program. *Journal of Applied Psychology, 54,* 473–478.

Morgan, W. R., & Sawyer, J. (1967). Bargaining, expectations, and the preference for equality over equity. *Journal of Personality and Social Psychology, 6,* 139–149.

Morganthau, T., & Hager, M. (1981, October 19). The 'Ice Queen' at E.P.A. *Newsweek,* pp. 67–68.

Morganthau, T., & Horrock, N. (1984, July 9). The new warriors. *Newsweek,* 32–33.

Morita, A. (1981). Yes, no, or the importance of however. *Industrial Management, 23*(4), 12–15.

Morphet, E. L., Johns, R. L., & Reller, T. L. (1982). *Educational organization and administration: Concepts, practices and issues.* Englewood Cliffs, NJ: Prentice-Hall.

Morris, C. G. (1966a). Task effects on group interaction. *Journal of Personality and Social Psychology, 4,* 545–554.

Morris, C. G. (1966b). Effects of task characteristics on group process. *Dissertation Abstracts, 26,* 7477.

Morris, C. G., & Fiedler, F. E. (1964). *Application of a new system of interaction analysis to the relationship between leader attitudes and behavior in problem solving groups.* Urbana: University of Illinois, Department of Psychology.

Morris, C. G., & Hackman, J. R. (1969). Behavioral correlates of perceived leadership. *Journal of Personality and Social Psychology, 13,* 350–361.

Morris, D. R. (1966). *Washing of the spears.* London: Jonathan Cape.

Morris, R. T., & Seeman, M. (1950). The problem of leadership: An interdisciplinary approach. *American Journal of Sociology, 56,* 149–155.

Morris, W. T. (1967). *Decentralization in management systems: An introduction to design.* Columbus: Ohio State University Press.

Morrison, A. M., White, R. P., & Van Velsor, E. (1987). The narrow band. *Issues & Observations, 7*(2), 1–7.

Morrison, R. F. (1977). Career adaptivity: The effective adaptation of managers to changing role demands. *Journal of Applied Psychology, 62,* 549–558.

Morrison, R. F., & Sebald, M. (1974). Personal characteristics differentiating female executives from female nonexecutive personnel. *Journal of Applied Psychology, 59,* 656–659.

Morrow, H. G. (1971). Consensus of observed leader behavior and role expectations of the elementary school principal. *Dissertation Abstracts International, 31,* 5856.

Morrow, I. J., & Stern, M. (1989). Stars, adversaries, producers, and phantoms at work: A new leadership typology. In K. E. Clark & M. B. Clarke (Eds.), *Measures of leadership.* West Orange, NJ: Leadership Library of America.

Morsbach, H. (1969). A cross-cultural study of achievement motivation and achievement values in two South African groups. *Journal of Social Psychology, 79,* 267–268.

Morse, J. J., & Wagner, F. R. (1978). Measuring the process of managerial effectiveness. *Academy of Management Journal, 21,* 23–35.

Morse, N. C. (1953). *Satisfactions in the white collar job.* Ann Arbor: University of Michigan, Institute for Social Research.

Morse, N. C., & Reimer, E. (1956). The experimental change of a major organizational variable. *Journal of Abnormal and Social Psychology, 52,* 120–129.

Morse, N. C., Reimer, E., & Tannenbaum, A. S. (1951). Regulation and control in hierarchical organizations. *Journal of Social Issues, 7,* 41–48.

Morsink, H. M. (1966). *A comparison of the leader behavior of fifteen men and fifteen women secondary school principals in Michigan.* Unpublished manuscript.

Morton, R. B., & Bass, B. M. (1964). The organizational training laboratory. *Training Directors Journal, 18,* 2–18.

Moser, R. P. (1957). The leadership patterns of school superintendents and school principals. *Administrator's Notebook, 6,* 1–4.

Moses, J. L., & Boehm, V. R. (1975). Relationship of assessment-center performance to management progress of women. *Journal of Applied Psychology, 60,* 527–529.

Moses, J. L., & Margolis, J. P. (1979). *Assessing the assessor.* Paper, International Congress of Assessment Center Method, New Orleans, LA.

Moses, J. L., & Ritchie, R. J. (1976). Supervisory relationships training: A behavioral evaluation of a behavioral modeling program. *Personnel Psychology, 29,* 337–343.

Moses, L. L., & Lyness, K. S. (1988). Individual and organizational responses to ambiguity. In F. D. Schoorman & B. Schneider (Eds.), *Facilitating work effectiveness.* Lexington, MA: Lexington Books.

Moss, G. (1974). How community leaders view extension. *Journal of Extension, 13*(3), 8–15.

Most, R. (1989). Hypotheses about the relationship between leadership and intelligence. In K. E. Clark & M. B. Clark (Eds.), *Measures of leadership.* Greensboro, NC: Center for Creative Leadership.

Mostofsky, D. I. (Ed.). (1970). *Attention: Contemporary theory and analysis.* New York: Appleton-Century-Crofts.

Mosvick, R. K. (1966). *An experimental evaluation of two modes of motive analysis instruction in an industrial setting.* Doctoral dissertation, University of Minnesota, Minneapolis.

Mosvick, R. K. (1969). *Twenty years of experimental evaluation of human relations training in the United States and Great Britain, 1949–1969.* St. Paul, MN: Macalester College. Unpublished manuscript.

Mosvick, R. K. (1971). Human relations training for scientists, technicians, and engineers: A review of the relevant experimental evaluations of human relations training. *Personnel Psychology, 24,* 275–292.

Motowidlo, S. J. (1981). A scoring procedure for sex-role orientation based on profile similarity indices. *Educational and Psychological Measurement, 41,* 735–744.

Motowidlo, S. J. (1982). Sex role orientation and behavior in a work setting. *Journal of Personality and Social Psychology, 42,* 935–945.

Mott, P. E. (1972). *The characteristics of effective organizations.* New York: Harper & Row.

Mottl, T. L. (1977). School movements as recruiters of women leaders: Boston's school movements of the 1960's and 1970's. *Urban Education, 12,* 3–14.

Mount, M. K. (1983). Comparisons of managerial and employee satisfaction with a performance appraisal system. *Personnel Psychology, 36,* 99–110.

Mount, M. K. (1984). Managerial career stage and facets of job satisfaction. *Journal of Vocational Behavior, 24,* 340–354.

Mouton, J. S., & Blake, R. S. (1970). Issues in transnational organization development. In B. M. Bass, R. Cooper, & J. A. Haas (Eds.), *Managing for accomplishment.* Lexington, MA: D. C. Heath.

Mowday, R. T. (1978). The exercise of upward influence in organizations. *Administrative Science Quarterly, 23,* 137–156.

Mowday, R. T. (1979). Leader characteristics, self-confidence, and methods of upwards influence in organizational decision situations. *Academy of Management Journal, 22,* 709–725.

Mowrer, O. H. (1939). Authoritarianism vs. self government in the management of children's aggressive (anti-social) reactions as a preparation for citizenship in a democracy. *Journal of Social Psychology, 10,* 121–127.

Moyer, D. C. (1954). *Teachers' attitudes toward leadership as they relate to teacher satisfaction.* Doctoral dissertation, University of Chicago, Chicago.

Moynihan, D. P. (1965). Employment income, and ordeal of the Negro family. In T. Parsons & K. B. Clark (Eds.), *The Negro American.* Boston: Houghton Mifflin.

Mozina, S. (1969). Management opinion on satisfaction and importance of psychosocial needs in their jobs. *Proceedings, International Congress of Applied Psychology,* Amsterdam.

Mudd, S. A. (1968). Group sanction severity as a function of degree of behavior deviation and relevance of norm. *Journal of Personality and Social Psychology, 8,* 258–260.

Mueller, R. K. (1980). Leader-edge leadership. *Human Systems Management, 1,* 17–27.

Mulder, M. (1959). Power and satisfaction in task oriented groups. *Acta Psychologica, 16,* 178–225.

Mulder, M. (1960). Communication structure, decision structure, and group performance. *Sociometry, 23,* 1–14.

Mulder, M. (1963). *Group structure, motivation and group performance.* The Hague: Mouton.

Mulder, M. (1971). Power equalization through participation? *Administrative Science Quarterly, 16,* 31–38.

Mulder, M. (1976). Reduction of power differences in practice: The power instance reduction theory and its applications. In G. Hofstede & M. S. Kassem (Eds.), *European contributions to organization theory.* Assen, Netherlands: Van Gorcum.

Mulder, M., de Jong, R. D., Koppelaar, L., & Verhage, J. (1986). Power, situation, and leaders' effectiveness: An organizational field study. *Journal of Applied Psychology, 71,* 566–570.

Mulder, M., & Stemerding, A. (1963). Threat, attraction to group, and need for strong leadership. *Human Relations, 16,* 317–334.

Mulder, M., van Dijk, R., Stirwagen, T., Verhagen, J., Soutendijk, S., & Zwerzerijnen, J. (1966). Illegitimacy of power and positiveness of attitude towards the power person. *Human Relations, 19,* 21–37.

Mulder, M., van Eck, R., & de Jong, R. D. (1971). An organization in crisis and non-crisis situations. *Human Relations, 24,* 19–41.

Mulder, M., & Wilke, H. (1970). Participation and power equalization. *Organizational Behavior and Human Performance, 5,* 430–448.

Muldrow, T. W., & Bayton, J. A. (1979). Men and women executives and processes related to decision accuracy. *Journal of Applied Psychology, 64,* 99–106.

Mullen, J. H. (1954). The supervisor assesses his job in management. *Personnel, 31,* 94–108.

Mullen, J. H. (1965). Differential leadership modes and productivity in a large organization. *Academy of Management Journal, 8,* 107–126.

Mullen, J. H., (1966a). Personality polarization as an equilibrating force in a large organization. *Human Organization, 25,* 330–338.

Mullen, J. H. (1966b). *Personality and productivity in management.* New York: Columbia University Press.

Muller, H. P. (1970). Relationship between time-span of discretion, leadership behavior, and Fiedler's LPC scores. *Journal of Applied Psychology, 54,* 140–144.

Mulligan, L., & Mulligan, G. (1981). Reconstructing restoration science: Styles of leadership and social composition of the early royal society. *Social Studies of Science, 11,* 327–364.

Mumford, E. (1906/1907). Origins of leadership. *American Journal of Sociology, 12,* 216–240, 367–397, 500–531.

Mumford, E. (1909). *The origins of leadership.* Chicago: University of Chicago Press.

Mumford, E. M. (1959). Social behavior in small work groups. *Sociological Review, 7,* 137–157.

Mumford, M. D. (1983). Social comparison theory and the evaluation of peer evaluations: A review and some applied implications. *Personnel Psychology, 36,* 867–81.

Mumford, M. D., Fleishman, E. A., Levin, K. Y., Korotkin, A. L., & Hein, M. B. (1988). *Taxonomic efforts in the description of leadership behavior: A synthesis and cognitive interpretation.* Fairfax, VA: George Mason University Center for Behavioral and Cognitive Studies.

Munch, P. A. (1945). *Sociology of Tristan da Cunha: Results of the Norwegian scientific expedition to Tristan da Cunha, 1937–1938.* Oslo: I Kommisjon Hos Jacob Dybwad, No. 13.

Munro, W. B. (1930). Civic organization. In *Encyclopaedia of the social sciences.* New York: Macmillan.

Munson, C. E. (1981). Style and structure in supervision. *Journal of Education for Social Work, 17,* 65–72.

Munson, E. L. (1921). *The management of men.* New York: Holt.

Murchison, C. (1935). The experimental measurement of a social hierarchy in Gallus Domesticus. *Journal of General Psychology, 12,* 3–39.

Murdoch, P. (1967). Development of contractual norms in a dyad. *Journal of Personality and Social Psychology, 6,* 206–211.

Murdock, G. P. (1937). Comparative data on the decision of labor by sex. *Social Forces, 15,* 551–553.

Murdock, G. P. (1967). *Ethnographic atlas.* Pittsburgh: University of Pittsburgh Press.

Murnighan, J. K., & Leung, T. K. (1976). The effects of leadership involvement and the importance of the task on subordinates' performance. *Organizational Behavior and Human Performance, 17,* 299–310.

Murphy, A. J. (1941). A study of the leadership process. *American Sociological Review, 6,* 674–687.

Murphy, L. B. (1947). Social factors in child development. In T. M. Newcomb & E. L. Hartley (Eds.), *Readings in social psychology.* New York: Holt.

Murphy, V. V., & Corenblum, A. F. (1966). Loyalty to immediate superior at alternate hierarchical levels in a bureaucracy. *American Journal of Sociology, 72,* 77–85.

Murray, F. (1988). *A study of transformational leadership and organizational effectiveness in selected small college settings.* Doctoral dissertation, Kent State University, Kent, OH.

Murray, H. A. (1938). *Explorations in personality.* New York: Oxford University Press.

Murray, H. A., & MacKinnon, D. W. (1946). Assessment of OSS personnel. *Journal of Consulting Psychology, 10,* 76–80.

Musham, Catherine (1980). The relationship between leadership emergence, sex-role adaptability and interpersonal behavior. *Dissertation Abstracts International, 41*(11B), 4310.

Mussen, P. H., & Porter, L. W. (1959). Personal motivations and self-conceptions associated with effectiveness and ineffectiveness in emergent groups. *Journal of Abnormal and Social Psychology, 59,* 23–27.

Musser, S. J. (1987). *Charismatic empowerment: Stimulating self-actualization or creating dependency.* Paper, Academy of Management, New Orleans, LA.

Musser, S. J., & Martin, Y. (1988). *An initial study of the influence and conflict management strategies employed by socialized charismatic leaders.* Unpublished manuscript.

Muttayya, B. C. (1977). Personality and value orientations of Panchayat leaders, informal leaders and non-leaders: A comparative study. *Behavior Science Community Development, 11,* 1–11.

Myer, H. E., & Fredian, A. J. (1959). Personality test scores in the management hierarchy: Revisited. *Journal of Applied Psychology, 43,* 212–220.

Myers, I. B. (1962). *The Myers-Briggs type indicator.* Palo Alto, CA: Consulting Psychologists Press.

Myers, I. B., & McCaulley, M. H. (1985). *Manual: A guide to the development and use of the Myers-Briggs type indicator.* Palo Alto, CA: Consulting Psychologists Press.

Myers, M. S. (1966). Conditions for manager motivation. *Harvard Business Review, 44*(1), 58–71.

Myers, M. S. (1968). Every employee a manager. *California Management Review, 10,* 9–20.

Nachman, S., Dansereau, F., & Naughton, T. J. (1983). Negotiating latitude: A within- and between-groups analysis of a key construct in the vertical dyad linkage theory of leadership. *Psychological Reports, 53,* 171–177.

Nachman, S., Dansereau, F., & Naughton, T. J. (1985). Levels of analysis and the vertical dyad linkage approach to leadership. *Psychological Reports, 57,* 661–662.

Nafe, R. W. (1930). A psychological description of leadership. *Journal of Social Psychology, 1,* 248–266.

Nagata, Y. (1965). The effects of task structure upon group organization process in terms of the relevance of the individual's goal oriented activities. *Japanese Journal of Psychology, 36,* 56–66.

Nagata, Y. (1966). Effects of task structure on the process of group organization in terms of the difficulty of the task. I. *Psychological Reports, 18,* 566.

Nagel, J. N. (1968). Some questions about the concept of power. *Behavioral Science, 13,* 129–137.

Nagle, B. F. (1954). Productivity, employee attitude, and supervisor sensitivity. *Personnel Psychology, 7,* 219–232.

Nahabetian, H. J. (1969). *The effects of a leader's upward influence on group member satisfaction and task facilitation.* Doctoral dissertation, University of Rochester, Rochester, NY.

Nanko, R. A. (1981). The relationship between the perceptions of leadership behavior of supervisors and anxiety levels of teachers. *Dissertation Abstracts International, 42*(5A), 1949.

Narain, R. (1955). Two decades of studies of leadership traits. *Shiksha, 8,* 80–94.

Narayanan, S., Venkatachalam, R., & Bharathiar, U. (1982). Leadership effectiveness and adaptability among small hosiery units. *Managerial Psychology, 3*(2), 40–47.

Nash, A. M. (1927). Training for leadership here and now. *Training School Bulletin, 24,* 10–14.

Nash, A. N. (1965). Vocational interests of effective managers: A review of the literature. *Personnel Psychology, 18,* 21–37.

Nash, A. N. (1966). Development of an SVIB key for selecting managers. *Journal of Applied Psychology, 50,* 250–254.

Nash, J. B. (1929). Leadership. *Phi Delta Kappan, 12,* 24–25.

Nash, M. (1958). *Machine age Maya: The industrialization of a Guatemalan community* (Memoirs No. 87). Menasha, WI: American Anthropological Association.

Nason, R. W. (1972). Dilemma of black mobility in management. *Business Horizons, 15,* 57–68.

Nath, R. (1969). A methodological review of cross-cultural management research. In J. Boddewyn (Ed.), *Comparative management and marketing.* Glenview, IL: Scott, Foresman.

Nathan, B. R. (1989). CEO succession and organizational performance: Towards an integrative resolution of a recalcitrant problem. Unpublished manuscript.

Nathan, B. R., & Alexander, R. A. (1985). The role of inferential accuracy in performance rating. *Academy of Management Review, 10,* 109–115.

Nathan, B. R., Hass, M. A., & Nathan, M. L. (1986). *Meta-analysis of Fiedler's leadership theory: A figure is worth a thousand words.* Paper, American Psychological Association, Washington, DC.

National Industrial Conference Board. (1948). *Decentralization in industry.* New York: National Industrial Conference Board.

National Industrial Conference Board. (1963). *College graduates assess their company training.* New York: National Industrial Conference Board.

National Industrial Conference Board. (1964). *Developing managerial competence: Changing concepts and emerging practices.* New York: National Industrial Conference Board.

National Industrial Conference Board. (1970). *Managing programs to employ the disadvantaged* (Studies in Personnel Policy No. 219). New York: National Industrial Conference Board.

National Institute of Industrial Psychology. (1952). *Joint consultation in British industry.* London: Staples Press.

National Research Council. (1943). *Psychology for the fighting man.* New York: Penguin Books.

Naumann-Etienne, M. (1975). *Bringing about open education: Strategies for innovation and implementation.* Doctoral dissertation, University of Michigan, Ann Arbor.

Nayar, P. K. B. (1969). *Leadership bureaucracy and planning in India.* New Delhi: Associate Publishing House.

Naylor, J. C., & Dickinson, T. L. (1969). Task structure, work structure, and team performance. *Journal of Applied Psychology, 3,* 167–177.

Nealey, S. M., & Blood, M. R. (1968). Leadership performance of nursing supervisors at two organizational levels. *Journal of Applied Psychology, 52,* 414–422.

Nealey, S. M., & Fiedler, F. E. (1968). Leadership functions of middle managers. *Psychological Bulletin, 5,* 313–329.

Near, J. P., & Miceli, M. P. (1986). Retaliation against whistle blowers: Predictors and effects. *Journal of Applied Psychology, 71,* 137–145.

Nebeker, D. M. (1975). Situational favorability and environmental uncertainty: An integrative study. *Administrative Science Quarterly, 20,* 281–294.

Nebeker, D. M., & Hansson, R. O. (1972). *Confidence in human nature and leader style* (Tech. Rep. No. 72-37). Seattle: University of Washington, Organizational Research.

Nebeker, D. M., & Mitchell, T. R. (1974). Leader behavior: An expectancy theory approach. *Organizational Behavior and Human Performance, 11,* 355–367.

Neel, R. G., & Dunn, R. E. (1960). Predicting success in supervisory training programs by the use of psychological tests. *Journal of Applied Psychology, 44,* 358–360.

Negandhi, A. R., & Estafen, B. D. (1967). A research model to determine the applicability of American management know-how in differing cultures and/or environments. In S. B. Prasad (Ed.), *Management in international perspective.* New York: Appleton-Century-Crofts.

Negandhi, A. R., & Prasad, S. B. (1971). *Comparative management.* New York: Appleton-Century-Croft.

Negandhi, A. R., & Reimann, B. C. (1972). A contingency theory of organization re-examined in the context of a developing country. *Academy of Management Journal, 15,* 137–146.

Neider, L. L. (1980). An experimental field investigation utilizing an expectancy theory view of participation. *Organizational Behavior and Human Performance, 26,* 425–442.

Neider, L. L., & Schriesheim, C. A. (1988). Making leadership effective: A three stage model. *Journal of Management Development, 7*(5), 10–20.

Neilsen, E. H., & Rao, M. V. H. (1987). The strategy-legitimacy nexus: A thick description. *Academy of Management Review, 12,* 523–533.

Nelson, C. W. (1949). *The development and evaluation of a leadership attitude scale for foremen.* Doctoral dissertation, University of Chicago, Chicago.

Nelson, C. W. (1950). *Differential concepts of leadership and their function in an industrial organization.* Paper, American Psychological Association, State College, PA.

Nelson, C. W. (1967). A new approach to the development of institutional leadership and communication: A challenge to deans. *Journal of National Association of National Deans' Counselors, 30,* 132–137.

Nelson, J. E. (1978). Child care crises and the role of the supervisor. *Child Care Quarterly, 7,* 318–326.

Nelson, P. D. (1963). *An evaluation of a popular leader* (Report No. 63-9). U.S. Navy Medical Neuropsychiatric Research Unit, San Diego, CA.

Nelson, P. D. (1964a). Similarities and differences among leaders and followers. *Journal of Social Psychology, 63,* 161–167.

Nelson, P. D. (1964b). Supervisor esteem and personnel evaluations. *Journal of Applied Psychology, 48,* 106–109.

Nelson, P. D. & Berry, N. H. (1966). *Dimensions of peer and supervisor ratings in a military setting* (Report No. 66-1). U.S. Navy Medical Neuropsychiatric Research Unit, San Diego, CA.

Neranartkomol, P. (1983). Attitudes toward managerial styles and need satisfaction: A comparison of Thai and Japanese business students. *Dissertation Abstracts International, 45*(6A), 1813.

Neubauer, W. (1982). Dimensionale Struktur der impliziten Fuhrungstheorie bei Vorgesetzten. [Dimensional structure of the implicit leadership theory among supervisors.] *Psychologie und Praxis, 26*(1), 1–11 (Abstract).

Neuberger, O. (1983). Fuhren als widerspruchliches Handeln. [Leadership and its dilemmas.] *Psychologie und Praxis, 27*(1), 22–32.

Neuman, G. A., & Edwards, J. E. (1988). *The effect of organizational development interventions on satisfaction and attitudes.* Paper, Academy of Management, Anaheim, CA.

Neumann, A. (1987). *Strategic leadership: The changing orientations of college presidents.* Paper, Association of the Study of Higher Education, Baltimore.

Neustadt, R. (1960). *Presidential power.* New York: Wiley.

Neustadt, R. E. (1980). *Presidential power: The politics of leadership from FDR to Carter.* New York: Wiley.

Newcomb, T. M. (1943). *Personality and social change.* New York: Holt, Rinehart & Winston.

Newcomb, T. M. (1956). The prediction of interpersonal attraction. *American Psychologist, 11,* 575–586.

Newcomb, T. M. (1961). *The acquaintance process.* New York: Holt, Rinehart & Winston.

Newcomb, T. M., Turner, R. H., & Converse, P. E. (1965). *Social psychology.* New York: Holt, Rinehart & Winston.

Newcomer, M. (1955). *The big business executive: The factors that made him, 1900–1950.* New York: Columbia University Press.

Newell, A., & Simon, H. A. (1972). *Human problem solving.* Englewood Cliffs, NJ: Prentice-Hall.

Newman, B. (1985, May 6). A Briton needn't pay much heed to class; he knows his place. *Wall Street Journal,* 1, 26.

Newman, R. G. (1983). Thoughts on superstars of charisma: Pipers in our midst. *American Journal of Orthopsychiatry, 53,* 201–208.

Newman, W. H., & Logan, J. (1965). *Business policies and central management.* Cincinnati, OH: Southwestern.

Newman, W. H., & Summer, C. E. (1961). *The process of management: Concepts, behavior, practice.* Englewood Cliffs, NJ: Prentice-Hall.

Newport, G. (1962). A study of attitudes and leadership behavior. *Personnel Administration, 25,* 42–46.

Newsome, R. R. (1972). Risky decisions of leaders and their groups. *Dissertation Abstracts International, 32,* 4849.

Newstetter, W. I., Feldstein, M. J., & Newcomb, T. M. (1938). *Group adjustment.* Cleveland, OH: Western Reserve University Press.

Newsweek (1980, February 18). Women in the armed forces. 34–36, 39–42.

Nichol, E. A. (1948). Management through consultative supervision. *Personnel Journal, 27,* 207–217.

Nicholls, J. R. (1985). A new approach to situational leadership. *Leadership and Organization Development Journal, 6*(4), 2–7.

Nicholson, R. (1983). Managing emerging businesses. *Managing, 3*(3), 21–25.

Nicol, J. H. (1983). Video-mediated communication and leadership emergence in small groups. *Dissertation Abstracts International, 44*(11A), 3196.

Nie, N. H., Bent, D. H., & Hull, C. H. (1970). *SPSS: Statistical package for the social sciences.* New York: McGraw-Hill.

Nie, N. H., Powell, G. B., Jr., & Prewitt, K. (1969). Social structure and political participation: Developmental relationships. *American Political Science Review, 63,* 361–378, 808–832.

Niebuhr, R. E., Bedeian, A. G., & Armenakis, A. A. (1980). Individual need states and their influence on perceptions of leader behavior. *Social Behavior and Personality, 8,* 17–25.

Niebuhr, R. E., & Davis, K. R., Jr. (1984). Self-esteem: Relationship with leader behavior perceptions as moderated by the duration of the superior-subordinate dyad association. *Personality and Social Psychology Bulletin, 10,* 51–59.

Niehoff, B. P., Enz, C., & Grover, R. A. (1989). *The impact of top management actions on employee attitudes.* Paper, Academy of Management, Washington, DC.

Nietzche, F. (1883/1974). Thus spoke Zarathustra. In O. Levy (Ed.), *The complete works of Friederich Nietzche.* New York: Gordon Press.

Nietzsche, F. W. (1888/1936). *The Antichrist.* Magdeburg: Nordland-Verlag.

Nightingale, D. V. (1981). Participation in decision-making: An examination of style and structure and their effects on member outcomes. *Human Relations, 34,* 1119–1133.

Nimmo, D. (1970). *The political persuaders.* Englewood Cliffs, NJ: Prentice-Hall.

Ninane, P. (1970). Réactions des leaders de groupe aux décisions de leur supérieur hiérarchique. *Bulletin d'Etudes, Recherches de Psychologie, 19,* 113–130.

Ninane, P., & Fiedler, F. E. (1970). Member reactions to success and failure of task groups. *Human Relations, 23,* 3–13.

Nisbett, M. A. (1986). The leader—boss or coach? *Canadian Banker, 93*(1), 54–57.

Nix, H. L., Dressel, P. L., & Bates, F. L. (1977). Changing leaders and leadership structure: A longitudinal study. *Rural Sociology, 42,* 22–41.

Nix, H. L., Singh, R. N., & Cheatham, P. L. (1974). Views of leader respondents compared with random respondents' views. *Journal of Community Development and Society, 5,* 81–91.

Nkomo, S. M., & Cox, T., Jr. (1987). *Individual and organizational factors affecting the upward mobility of black managers.* Paper, Academy of Management, New Orleans.

Noe, R. A. (1986). Trainees' attributes and attitudes: Neglected influences on training effectiveness. *Academy of Management Review, 11,* 736–749.

Noe, R. A. (1988). Women and mentoring: A review and research agenda. *Academy of Management Review, 13,* 65–78.

Nolting, O. F. (1941). *Management methods in city government.* Chicago: International City Managers Association.

Nord, W. R. (1969). Social exchange theory: An integrative approach to social conformity. *Psychological Bulletin, 71,* 174–208.

Norfleet, B. (1948). Interpersonal relations and group productivity. *Journal of Social Issues, 4,* 66–69.

Norman, A. K. (1964). "Consideration" and "initiating structure" and organizational criteria. *Personnel Administration, 27,* 35–37.

Norman, R. D. (1953). The interrelationships among acceptance-rejection, self-other identity, insight into self, and realistic perception of others. *Journal of Social Psychology, 37,* 205–235.

Norman, W. T. (1963). Toward an adequate taxonomy of personality attributes: Replicated factor structure in peer nomination personality ratings. *Journal of Abnormal and Social Psychology, 66,* 574–583.

Normann, R. (1977). *Management for growth.* New York: Wiley.

Norrgren, F. (1981a). *Managers' beliefs, behavioral intentions and evaluations with respect to participation* (Report No. 6, 3). Göteborg, Sweden: University of Göteborg, Department of Applied Psychology.

Norrgren, F. (1981b). *Subordinate reactions to different managerial beliefs about participation* (Report No. 6, 2). Göteborg, Sweden: University of Göteborg, Department of Applied Psychology.

Northcraft, G., & Martin, J. (1982). Double jeopardy: Resistance to affirmative action from potential beneficiaries. In B. A. Gutek (Ed.), *Sex-role stereotyping and affirmative action policy.* Los Angeles: University of California, Institute for Industrial Relations.

Northway, M. L. (1946). Some challenging problems of social relationships. *Sociometry, 9,* 187–198.

Northway, M. L., Frankel, E. B., & Potashin, R. (1947). Personality and sociometric status. *Sociometry Monographs, 11.*

Northwood, L. K. (1953). The relative ability of leaders and non-leaders as expert judges of fact and opinions held by members of the community of which they are a part. *Dissertation Abstracts, 13,* 898.

Notcutt, B., & Silva, A. L. M. (1951). Knowledge of other people. *Journal of Abnormal and Social Psychology, 46,* 30–37.

Novak, M. A., & Graen, G. B. (1985). *Perceived leader control as a moderator of personal leader resources contributing to leader-member exchange.* Paper, Academy of Management, San Diego, CA.

Nowotny, O. H. (1964). American vs. European management philosophy. *Harvard Business Review, 42*(2), 101–108.

Null, E. J., & Smead, W. H. (1971). Relationships between the political orientation of superintendents and their leader behavior as perceived by subordinates. *Journal of Educational Research, 65,* 103–106.

Numerof, R. E., Cramer, K. D., & Shachar-Hendin, S. A. (1984). Stress in health administrators: Sources, symptoms, and coping strategies. *Nursing Economics, 2,* 270–279.

Numerof, R. E., & Gillespie, D. F. (1984). *Predicting burnout among health service providers.* Paper, Academy of Management, Boston.

Numerof, R. E., & Seltzer, J. (1986). *The relationship between leadership* factors, burnout, and stress symptoms among middle managers. Paper, Academy of Management, Chicago.

Nunnally, J. C. (1967). *Psychometric theory.* New York: McGraw-Hill.

Nutt, P. C. (1986). Tactics of implementation. *Academy of Management Journal, 29*, 230–261.

Nuttin, J. R. (1984). *Motivation, planning, and action: A relational theory of behavioral dynamics.* Hillsdale, NJ: Erlbaum.

Nutting, R. L. (1923). Some characteristics of leadership. *School & Society, 18*, 387–390.

Nwaobasi, J. O. (1981). Relationship between administrative management system, selected demographic variables and level of job satisfaction: An analysis of principal-teacher perceptions. *Dissertation Abstracts International, 43*(1A), 38.

Nydegger, R. V. (1971). *Leadership status and verbal behavior in small groups as a function of schedule of reinforcement and level of information processing complexity.* Paper, American Psychological Association, Washington, DC.

Nye, J. R. (1968). Role performance in situations of conflicting role definitions. *Dissertation Abstracts, 29*, 1301.

Nystrom, P. C. (1978). Managers and the hi-hi leader myth. *Academy of Management Journal, 21*, 325–331.

Nystrom, P. C. (1986). Comparing beliefs of line and technostructure managers. *Academy of Management Journal, 29*, 812–819.

Nystrom, P. C., & Starbuck, W. H. (1984). To avoid organizational crises, unlearn. *Organizational Dynamics, 12*(4), 53–65.

Oaklander, H., & Fleishman, E. A. (1964). Patterns of leadership related to organizational stress in hospital settings. *Administrative Science Quarterly, 8*, 520–531.

O'Barr, W. M. (1982). *Linguistic evidence: Language, power, and strategy in the courtroom.* New York: Academic Press.

Oberg, W. (1962). *The university's role in executive education: A report to the participating companies.* East Lansing: Michigan State University, Graduate School of Business Administration.

Oberg, W. (1972, Spring). Charisma, commitment, and contemporary organization theory. *Business Topics, 20*, 18–32.

Obradovic, J. (1970). Participation and work attitudes in Yugoslavia. *Industrial Relations, 9*, 161–169.

Obradovic, J. (1975). Workers' participation: Who participates? *Industrial Relations, 14*, 32–44.

O'Brien, G. E. (1969a). Group structure and measurement of potential leader influence. *Australian Journal of Psychology, 21*, 277–289.

O'Brien, G. E. (1969b). Leadership in organizational settings. *Journal of Applied Behavioral Science, 5*, 45–63.

O'Brien, G. E. (1970). Group structure and productivity. *Australian Military Forces Resource Report, No. 7-70.*

O'Brien, G. E., & Harary, F. (1977). Measurement of the interactive effects of leadership style and group structure upon group performance. *Australian Journal of Psychology, 29*, 59–71.

Obrochta, R. J. (1960). Foremen-worker attitude patterns. *Journal of Applied Psychology, 44*, 88–91.

O'Connell, J. J. (1968). *Managing organizational innovation.* Homewood, IL: Irwin.

O'Connell, M. J. (1986). *The impact of institutional and occupational values on Air Force officer career intent.* Paper, Academy of Management, Chicago.

O'Connor, E., & Farrow, D. L. (1977). *Environmental constraints, organizational structures and preferred patterns of managerial behavior.* Paper, Southeastern Psychological Association, Hollywood, FL.

O'Connor, E. J., & Farrow, D. L. (1979). A cross-functional comparison of prescribed versus preferred patterns of managerial structure. *Journal of Management Studies, 16*, 222–234.

O'Connor, E. J., Peters, L. H., Pooyan, A., Weekley, J., Blake, F., & Erenkrantz, B. (1984). Situational constraint effects on performance, affective reactions, and turnover: A field replication and extension. *Journal of Applied Psychology, 69*, 663–672.

O'Connor, J. (1932). *Characteristics of successful executives.* Hoboken, NJ: Stevens Institute of Technology.

O'Connor, J. R. (1972). The relationship of kinesic and verbal communication to leadership perception in small group discussion. *Dissertation Abstracts International, 32*, 6589.

O'Connor, W. F. (1963). A note on the Cline and Richards' studies on accuracy of interpersonal perception. *Journal of Abnormal and Social Psychology, 66*, 194–195.

Oddou, G. R. (1983). The emergence of leaders in natural work groups: A test of self-monitoring theory. *Dissertation Abstracts International, 44*(7B), 2284.

O'Dempsey, K. (1976). Time analysis of activities, work patterns and roles of high school principals. *Administrator's Bulletin, 7*, 1.

Odier, C. (1948). Valeur et valence du chef. *Schweizerisches Archiv für Neurologisches Psychiatrie, 61*, 408–410.

Odiorne, G. S. (1963). The trouble with sensitivity training. *Training Directors Journal, 17*(2), 9–20.

O'Donovan, T. R. (1962). Differential extent of opportunity among executives and lower managers. *Academy of Management Journal, 5*, 139–149.

O'Farrell, B., & Harlan, S. L. (1982). Craftworkers and clerks: The effect of male co-worker hostility on women's satisfaction with non-traditional jobs. *Social Problems, 29*(3), 252–264.

Offerman, L. R. (1984). Short-term supervisory experience and LPC score: Effects of leader's sex and group sex composition. *Journal of Social Psychology, 23*, 115–121.

Offerman, L. R., Schroyer, C. J., & Green, S. K. (1986). *Behavioral consequences of leader attributions for subordinate performance.* Paper, American Psychological Association, Washington, DC.

Office of Strategic Services (O.S.S.) Assessment Staff. (1948). *Assessment of men: Selection of personnel for Office of Strategic Services.* New York: Rinehart.

Ogbuehi, D. A. (1981). The correlates of leadership effectiveness of managers in selected private and semi-public organizations in Nigeria. *Dissertation Abstracts International, 42*(4A), 1383.

Okanes, M. M., & Murray, W. (1980). Achievement and Machiavellianism among men and women managers. *Psychological Reports, 46,* 783–788.

Okanes, M., & Stinson, J. E. (1974). Machiavellianism and emergent leadership in a management simulation. *Psychological Reports, 35,* 255–259.

Oldham, G. R. (1975). The impact of supervisory characteristics on goal acceptance. *Academy of Management Journal, 18,* 461–475.

Oldham, G. R. (1976). The motivational strategies used by supervisors: Relationships to effectiveness indicators. *Organizational Behavior and Human Performance, 15,* 66–86.

O'Leary, V. E. (1974). Some attitudinal barriers to occupational aspirations in women. *Psychological Bulletin, 81,* 809–826.

Olien, C. N., Tichenor, P. J., & Donohue, G. A. (1987). Role of Mass Communication. In D. E. Johnson, L. R. Miller, L. C. Miller, & G. F. Summers (Eds.), *Needs assessment: Theory and methods.* Ames: Iowa University Press.

Olive, B. A. (1965). *Management: A subject listing of recommended books, pamphlets, and journals.* Ithaca, NY: Cornell University, Graduate School of Business and Public Administration.

Oliver, J. E. (1982). An instrument for classifying organizations. *Academy of Management Journal, 25,* 855–866.

Oliverson, L. R. (1976). Identification of dimensions of leadership and leader behavior and cohesion in encounter groups. *Dissertation Abstracts International, 37,* 136–137.

Olmstead, J. A. (1974). *Development of leadership assessment simulations.* Arlington, VA: U.S. Army Research Institute for the Behavioral and Social Sciences.

Olmstead, J. S., Lackey, L. L., & Christenson, H. E. (1975). *Leadership actions as evaluated by experienced company grade officers.* Alexandria, VA: Human Resources Research Organization.

Olmstead, M. S. (1954). Orientation and role in the small group. *American Sociological Review, 6,* 741–751.

Olmsted, D. W. (1954). Organizational leadership and social structure in a small city. *American Sociological Review, 19,* 273–281.

Olmsted, D. W. (1957). Inter-group similarities of role correlates. *Sociometry, 20,* 8–20.

Olsen, M. E. (1968). *The process of social organization.* New York: Holt, Rinehart & Winston.

O'Neill, H. E., & Kubany, A. J. (1959). Observation methodology and supervisory behavior. *Personnel Psychology, 12,* 85–95.

Onnen, M. K. (1987). *The relationship of clergy leadership characteristics to growing or declining churches.* Doctoral dissertation, University of Louisville, Louisville, KY.

Opsahl, R. L., & Dunnette, M. D. (1966). Role of financial compensation in industrial motivation. *Psychological Bulletin, 66,* 94–118.

O'Reilly, C. A. (1977). Supervisors and peers as information sources, group supportiveness, and individual decision-making performance. *Journal of Applied Psychology, 62,* 632–635.

O'Reilly, C. (1984). *Charisma as communication: The impact of top management credibility and philosophy on employee involvement.* Paper, Academy of Management, Boston.

O'Reilly, C. A., III, & Puffer, S. M. (1983). *Positive effects from negative sanctions: The impact of rewards and punishments in a social context.* Paper, Academy of Management, San Diego, CA.

O'Reilly, C. A., III, & Roberts, K. H. (1973). Job satisfaction among whites and nonwhites: A cross-cultural approach. *Journal of Applied Psychology, 57,* 295–299.

O'Reilly, C. A., & Roberts, K. H. (1974). Information filtration in organizations: Three experiments. *Organizational Behavior and Human Performance, 11,* 253–265.

O'Reilly, C. A., III, & Roberts, K. H. (1978). Supervisor influence and subordinate mobility aspirations as moderators of consideration ratings and structure. *Journal of Applied Psychology, 63,* 96–102.

O'Reilly, C. A., III, & Weitz, B. A. (1980). Managing marginal employees: The use of warnings and dismissals. *Administrative Science Quarterly, 25,* 467–484.

Orlans, H. (1953). *Opinion polls on national leaders* (Rep. No. 6). Washington, DC: Institute for Research on Human Relations.

O'Roark, A. M. (1986). *Bass-Valenzi decision modes and Myers-Briggs dominant functions: Management perspectives and preferences.* Paper, International Congress of Applied Psychology, Jerusalem.

Orpen, C. (1978). The relationship between job satisfaction and job performance among Western and tribal black employees. *Journal of Applied Psychology, 63,* 263–265.

Orpen, C. (1982). Effects of MBA training in managerial success. *Journal of Business Education, 57*(1), 152–154.

Orpen, C. (1987). The role of qualitative research in management. *South African Journal of Business, 18,* 250–254.

Orr, D. B. (1960). A new method for clustering jobs. *Journal of Applied Psychology, 44,* 44–49.

Osborn, A. R. (1953). *Applied imagination: Principles and procedures of creative thinking.* New York: Scribner.

Osborn, R. N., & Hunt, J. G. (1974). An empirical investigation of lateral and vertical leadership at two organizational levels. *Journal of Business Resources, 2,* 209–221.

Osborn, R. N., & Hunt, J. G. (1975a). An adaptive-reaction theory of leadership: The role of macro variables in leadership research. In J. G. Hunt & L. L. Larson (Eds.), *Leadership frontiers.* Carbondale: Southern Illinois University Press.

Osborn, R. N., & Hunt, J. G. (1975b). Relations between leadership, size, and subordinate satisfaction in a voluntary organization. *Journal of Applied Psychology, 60,* 730–735b.

Osborn, R. N., & Hunt, J. G. (1979). *Environment and leadership: Discretionary and nondiscretionary leader behavior and organizational outcomes.* Unpublished manuscript.

Osborn, R. N., Hunt, J. G., & Bussom, R. S. (1977). On getting your own way in organizational design: An empirical illustration of requisite variety. *Organization and Administrative Sciences, 8,* 295–310.

Osborn, R. N., Hunt, J. G., & Jauch, L. R. (1980). *Organization theory: An integrated approach.* New York: Wiley.

Osborn, R. N., Hunt, J. G., & Pope, R. (1973). *Lateral leadership, satisfaction, and performance.* Paper, Academy of Management, Boston.

Osborn, R. N., Hunt, J. G., & Skaret, D. J. (1977). Managerial influence in a complex configuration with two unit heads. *Human Relations, 30,* 1025–1038.

Osborn, R. N., & Jackson, D. H. (1988). Leaders, riverboat gamblers, or purposeful unintended consequences in the management of complex, dangerous technologies. *Academy of Management Journal, 31,* 924–947.

Osborn, R. N., Jauch, L. R., Martin, T. N., & Glueck, W. F. (1981). The event of CEO succession, performance, and environmental conditions. *Academy of Management Journal, 24,* 183–191.

Osborn, R. N., & Vicars, W. M. (1976). Sex stereotypes: An artifact in leader behavior and subordinate statisfaction analysis? *Academy of Management Journal, 19,* 439–449.

Osborn, T. N., & Osborn, D. B. (1986). Leadership profiles in Latin America: How different are Latin American managers from their counterparts? *Issues & Observations, 6*(2), 7–10.

Oshry, B. I., & Harrison, R. (1966). Transfer from here-and-now to there-and-then: Changes in organizational problem diagnosis stemming from T-group training. *Journal of Applied Behavioral Science, 2,* 185–198.

Oskarsson, H., & Klein, R. H. (1982). Leadership change and organizational regression. *International Journal of Group Psychotherapy, 32,* 145–162.

O'Toole, J. (1985). *Vanguard management.* New York: Doubleday.

Ottaway, R. N., & Bhatnagar, D. (1988). Personality and biographical differences between male and female managers in the United States and India. *Applied Psychology: An International Review, 37,* 201–212.

Otten, A. J. W., & Teulings, A. W. M. (1970). Buitenstaanders en Krachtfiguren. [Outsiders and powerfigures.] *Mens en Onderneming, 24,* 296–313.

Ottih, L. O. (1981). Managerial decentralization in Nigerian banks: Case studies of selected banks. *Dissertation Abstracts International, 42*(7A), 3280.

Ouchi, W. (1981). *Theory Z: How American business can meet the Japanese challenge.* Reading, MA: Addison-Wesley.

Ouchi, W. G., & Maguire, M. A. (1975). Operational control: Two functions. *Administrative Science Quarterly, 20,* 559–569.

Oxford English Dictionary. (1933). London: Oxford University Press.

Pacinelli, R. N. (1968). Rehabilitation counselor job satisfaction as it relates to perceived leadership behavior and selected background factors. *Dissertation Abstracts, 29,* 1863.

Page, B. I. (1984). Presidents as opinion leaders: Some new evidence. *Policy Studies Journal, 12,* 649–661.

Page, D. P. (1935). Measurement and prediction of leadership. *American Journal of Sociology, 41,* 31–43.

Page, E. C. (1985). Political authority and bureaucratic power. A comparative analysis. Brighton, Sussex: Wheatsheaf Books.

Page, M. L. (1936). The modification of ascendant behavior in preschool children. *University of Iowa Study on Child Welfare, 12,* 69.

Page, R. C. (1987). The position description questionnaire. In S. Gael (Ed.), *Handbook of job analysis.* New York: Wiley.

Page, R. C., & Tornow, W. W. (1987). *Managerial job analysis: Are we further along?* Paper, Society for Industrial Organizational Psychology, Atlanta, GA.

Page, R. H., & McGinnies, E. (1959). Comparison of two styles of leadership in small group discussion. *Journal of Applied Psychology, 43,* 240–245.

Pagery, P. D., & Chapanis, A. (1983). Communication control and leadership in telecommunications by small groups. *Behavior and Information Technology, 2*(2), 179–196.

Paige, G. D. (in press). Nonviolent global problem solving and tacks of political leadership studies. *International Political Science Review.*

Paige, G. D. (1972). *Political leadership.* New York: Free Press.

Paige, G. D. (1977). *The scientific study of political leadership.* New York: Free Press.

Paine, F. T., Carroll, S. J., & Leete, B. A. (1966). Need satisfactions of managerial level personnel in a government agency. *Journal of Applied Psychology, 50,* 247–249.

Painter, L. C. (1984). Leadership orientation and behavior following interpersonal skill training: Perceptions of supervisors and subordinates (Consideration, structure, management). *Dissertation Abstracts International, 45*(6A), 1631.

Palgi, M. (1984). *Theoretical and empirical aspects of workers' participation in decision-making—A comparison between Kibbutz and non-Kibbutz industrial plants in Israel.* Doctoral dissertation, Hebrew University, Jerusalem.

Pallett, J. E., & Hoyt, D. P. (1968). College curriculum and success in general business. *Journal of College Personnel, 9*(4), 238–245.

Palm, L. B. (1976). A study of videotaped behavior and its relationship to perceived leadership behavior. *Dissertation Abstracts International, 36,* 4930–4931.

Palmer, D. D., Veiga, J. F., & Vora, J. A. (undated). *Managerial value profiles as predictors of policy decisions in a cross-cultural setting.* Unpublished manuscript.

Palmer, F. H., & Myers, T. I. (1955). Sociometric choices and group productivity among radar crews. *American Psychologist, 10,* 441–442.

Palmer, G. J. (1962a). Task ability and effective leadership. *Psychological Reports, 10,* 863–866.

Palmer, G. J. (1962b). Task ability and successful and effective leadership. *Psychological Reports, 11,* 813–816.

Palmer, G. J., & McCormick, E. J. (1961). A factor analysis of job activities. *Journal of Applied Psychology, 45,* 289–294.

Palmer, J., & Byrne, D. (1970). Attraction toward dominant and submissive strangers: Similarity versus complementarity. *Journal of Experimental Research in Personality, 4,* 108–115.

Palmer, M. (1971). The application of psychological testing to entrepreneurial potential. *California Management Review, 13*(3), 32–38.

Palmer, W. J. (1974). Management effectiveness as a function of personality traits of the manager. *Personnel Psychology, 27,* 283–295.

Pandey, J. (1976). Effects of leadership style, personality characteristics and methods of leader selection on members' leaders' behavior. *European Journal of Social Psychology, 6,* 475–489.

Pandey, J., & Bohra, K. A. (1984). Ingratiation as a function of organizational characteristics and supervisory styles. *International Review of Applied Psychology, 33*, 381–394.

Paolillo, J. G. (1981a). Manager's self-assessments of managerial roles: The influence of hierarchical level. *Journal of Management, 7*, 43–52.

Paolillo, J. G. (1981b). Role profiles for managers at different hierarchical levels. *Proceedings, Academy of Management*, San Diego, CA, 91–94.

Papaloizos, A. (1962). Personality and success of training in human relations. *Personnel Psychology, 15*, 423–428.

Park, B. E. (1988). When world leaders get sick—Disease, disability and danger. *Leaders, 11*(2), 36–38.

Parker, F. E. (1923). *Consumers' cooperative societies in the United States in 1920*. Washington, DC: U.S. Department of Labor Bulletin No. 313.

Parker, F. E. (1927). *Cooperative movements in the United States in 1925 (other than experimental)*. Washington, DC: U.S. Department of Labor Bulletin No. 437.

Parker, S. (1958). Leadership patterns in a psychiatric ward. *Human Relations, 11*, 287–301.

Parker, T. C. (1963). Relationships among measures of supervisory behavior, group behavior, and situational characteristics. *Personnel Psychology, 16*, 319–334.

Parker, T. C. (1965). The psychological environment and work group behavior. *Personnel Administration, 28*, 26–31.

Parker, W. S., Jr. (1976). Black-white differences in leader behavior related to subordinates' reactions. *Journal of Applied Psychology, 61*, 140–147.

Parks, M. R. (1985). Interpersonal communication and the quest for personal competence. In M. L. Knapp & G. R. Miller (Eds.), *Handbook of interpersonal communication*. Beverly Hills, CA: Sage.

Parsons, C. K., Herold, D. M., & Leatherwood, M. L. (1985). Turnover during initial employment: A longitudinal study of the role of causal attributions. *Journal of Applied Psychology, 70*, 337–341.

Parsons, C. K., Herold, D. M., & Turlington, B. (1981). *Individual differences in performance feedback preferences*. Paper, Academy of Management, San Diego, CA.

Parsons, T. (1951). *The social system*. New York: Free Press.

Parsons, T., & Shils, E. A. (Eds.). (1959). *Toward a general theory of action*. Cambridge, MA: Harvard University Press.

Parten, M. B. (1932). Social participation among preschool children. *Journal of Abnormal and Social Psychology, 27*, 243–269.

Parten, M. B. (1933). Leadership among preschool children. *Journal of Abnormal and Social Psychology, 27*, 430–440.

Partridge, E. DeA. (1934). Leadership among adolescent boys. *Teachers College Contributions to Education*, No. 608.

Pascal, B. (1660/1950). *Pensées*. New York: Pantheon.

Pascale, R. T., & Maguire, M. A. (1980). Comparison of selected work factors in Japan and the United States. *Human Relations, 33*, 433–455.

Pascarella, P., & Cook, D. D. (1978). Can you win? *Industrial Week, 196*(2), 75–84.

Pasmore, W. A., & Sherwood, J. J. (Eds.). (1978). *Socio-technical systems: A source book*. LaJolla, CA: University Associates.

Patch, A. M. (1943). Some thoughts on leadership. *Military Review, 23*, 5–7.

Patchen, M. (1962). Supervisory methods and group performance norms. *Administrative Science Quarterly, 7*, 275–294.

Patchen, M. (1964). Participation in decision-making and motivation. What is the relation? *Personnel Administration, 27*(6), 24–31.

Patchen, M. (1970). *Participation, achievement, and involvement on the job*. Englewood Cliffs, NJ: Prentice-Hall.

Patchen, M. (1974). The locus and basis of influence on organizational decisions. *Organizational Behavior and Human Performance, 11*, 195–221.

Pate, L. E., & Heiman, D. C. (1981). *A test of the Vroom-Yetton decision model in seven field settings*. Paper, Academy of Management, San Diego, CA.

Patten, T. H. (1968a). *The foreman: Forgotten man of management*. New York: American Management Association.

Patten, T. H. (1968b). Merit increases and the facts of organization life. *Management of Personnel Quarterly, 7*, 30–38.

Patterson, M. (1968). Spatial factors in social interactions. *Human Relations, 21*, 351–361.

Patterson, M. L., & Holmes, D. S. (1966). Social interaction correlates of the MPI extroversion-introversion scale. *American Psychologist, 21*, 724–725.

Patterson, M. L., & Sechrest, L. B. (1967). *Impression formation and interpersonal distance*. Evanston, IL: Northwestern University. Unpublished manuscript.

Patterson, R. A. (1975). Women in management: An experimental study of the effects of sex and marital status on job performance ratings, promotability ratings and promotion decisions. *Dissertation Abstracts International, 36*, 3108–3109B.

Patton, W. M. (1954). Studies in industrial empathy: III. A Study of supervisory empathy in the textile industry. *Journal of Applied Psychology, 38*, 285–288.

Pavett, C. M. (1983). Evaluation of the impact of feedback on performance and motivation. *Human Relations, 36*, 641–654.

Pavett, C. M., & Lau, A. W. (1982). Managerial roles, skills and effective performance. *Proceedings, Academy of Management*, New York, 95–99.

Pavett, C. M., & Lau, A. W. (1983). Managerial work: The influence of hierarchical level and functional specialty. *Academy of Management Journal, 26*, 170–177.

Payne, R. (1963). Leadership and perceptions of change in a village confronted with urbanism. *Social Forces, 41*, 264–269.

Payne, R. G., & Hauty, G. T. (1955). The effect of psychological feedback upon work decrement. *Journal of Experimental Psychology, 50*, 343–351.

Payne, R. L., & Pheysey, D. C. (1971). Organization structure and sociometric nominations amongst line managers in three contrasted organizations. *European Journal of Social Psychology, 1,* 261–284.

Peabody, R. L. (1962). Perceptions of organizational authority: A comparative analysis. *Administrative Science Quarterly, 6,* 463–482.

Peabody, R. L. (1964). *Organizational authority: Superior-subordinate relationships in three public organizations.* New York: Atherton Press.

Peabody, R. L. (1976). *Leadership in Congress.* Boston: Little, Brown.

Peabody, R. L., & Rourke, F. E. (1964). Public bureaucracies. In J. G. March (Ed.), *Handbook of service organizations.* New York: Atherton Press.

Pearce, J. L. (1980). Apathy or self interest? The volunteer's avoidance of leadership roles. *Journal of Voluntary Action Research, 9*(1–4), 85–94.

Pearce, J. L. (1982). Leading and following volunteers: Implications for a changing society. *Journal of Applied Behavioral Science, 18,* 385–394.

Pearce, J. L. (1983). Comparing volunteers and employees in a test of Etzioni's compliance typology. *Journal of Voluntary Action Research, 12*(2), 22–30.

Pearce, J. L., & Porter, L. W. (1986). Employee responses to formal performance appraisal feedback. *Journal of Applied Psychology, 71,* 211–218.

Pearce, J. L., Stevenson, W. B., & Perry, J. L. (1985). Managerial compensation based on organizational performance: A time series analysis of the effects of merit pay. *Academy of Management Journal, 28,* 261–278.

Pearse, R. F., Worthington, E. I., & Flaherty, J. J. (1954). A program for developing tools engineers into manufacturing executives. *ASTE Tool Engineering Conference Papers,* 22T5, Detroit.

Pearson, B. E. (1980). Women's entry into managerial positions at human service agencies: Effect of applicant's locus of control and leadership style on employer preference for applicants. *Dissertation Abstracts International, 41*(5A). 1958.

Pearson, J. C., & Serafini, D. M. (1984). Leadership behavior and sex role socialization: Two sides of the same coin. *Southern Speech Communication Journal, 49,* 396–405.

Pearson, W. M., & Sanders, L. T. (1981). State executives' attitudes toward some authoritarian values. *State and Local Government Review, 13,* I(2), 73–79.

Peck, E. M. (1931). A study of the personalities of five eminent men. *Journal of Abnormal and Social Psychology, 26,* 37–57.

Peck, S. M. (1966). *The rank-and-file leader.* New Haven, CT: College & University Press.

Pedersen, D. M., Shinedling, M. M., & Johnson, D. L. (1971). Effects of sex examiner and subject on children's quantitative test performance. *Journal of Personality and Social Psychology, 19,* 114–118.

Pedigo, P. R. (1986). *Impact of information technology on middle management.* Paper, American Psychological Association, Washington, DC.

Peirce, J. R. (1970). Effects of selected organizational variables on the behavioral style of the industrial supervisor. *Dissertation Abstracts International, 31,* 3047–3048.

Pellegrin, R. J. (1952). *Status achievement in youth groups: Elements of group adjustment in relation to social mobility.* Doctoral dissertation, University of North Carolina, Chapel Hill.

Pellegrin, R. J. (1953). The achievement of high status and leadership in the small group. *Social Forces, 32,* 10–16.

Pellegrin, R. J. (1969). The interaction of physical and psychological distance in dyadic transactions. *Dissertation Abstracts International, 30,* 373.

Pellegrin, R. J., & Coates, C. H. (1957). Executives and supervisors: Contrasting definitions of career success. *Administrative Science Quarterly, 2,* 506–517.

Pelletier, G. (1966, Fall). Business management in French Canada. *Business Quarterly—Canada Management Journal,* 56–62.

Pelz, D. C. (1949). The effect of supervisory attitudes and practices on employee satisfaction. *American Psychologist, 4,* 283–284.

Pelz, D. C. (1951). Leadership within a hierarchical organization. *Journal of Social Issues, 7,* 49–55.

Pelz, D. C. (1952). Influence: A key to effective leadership in the first-line supervisor. *Personnel, 29,* 209–217.

Pelz, D. C. (1953). *The influence of the supervisor with his department as a condition of the way supervisory practices affect employee attitudes.* Doctoral dissertation, University of Michigan, Ann Arbor.

Pelz, D. C. (1956). Some social factors related to performance in a research organization. *Administrative Science Quarterly, 1,* 310–325.

Pelz, D. C., & Andrews, F. M. (1964). Detecting causal priorities in panel study data. *American Sociological Review, 29,* 836–848.

Pelz, D. C., & Andrews, F. M. (1966a). *Scientists in organizations: Productive climates for research and development.* New York: Wiley.

Pelz, D. C., & Andrews, F. M. (1966b). Autonomy, coordination, and stimulation in relation to scientific achievement. *Behavioral Science, 11,* 89–97.

Penfield, R. V. (1971). Identifying effective supervisors. *Personnel Journal, 50,* 209–212.

Penfield, R. V. (1974). Time allocation patterns and effectiveness of managers. *Personnel Psychology, 27,* 245–255.

Penner, D. D., Malone, D. M., Coughlin, T. M., & Herz, J. A. (1973). Satisfaction with U.S. Army leadership. *U.S. Army War College, Leadership Monograph Series,* No. 2.

Pennings, J. M. (1975). The relevance of the structured-contingency model for organization effectiveness. *Administrative Science Quarterly, 20,* 393–407.

Pennington, D. F., Haravey, F., & Bass, B. M. (1958). Some effects of decision and discussion on coalescence, change, and effectiveness. *Journal of Applied Psychology, 42,* 404–408.

Penzer, W. N. (1969). Educational level and satisfaction with pay: An attempted replication. *Personnel Psychology, 22,* 185–199.

Pepinsky, H. B., & Pepinsky, P. N. (1961). Organization, management strategy, and team productivity. In L. Petrullo & B. M. Bass (Eds.), *Leadership and interpersonal behavior.* New York: Holt, Rinehart & Winston.

Pepinsky, H. B., Pepinsky, P. N., Minor, F. J., & Robin, S. S. (1957).

Team productivity as related to the confirmation or contradiction by management of its commitments to an appointed leader. Columbus: Ohio State University, Personnel Research Board.

Pepinsky, H. B., Pepinsky, P. N., Minor, F. J., & Robin, S. S. (1959). Team productivity and contradiction of management policy commitments. *Journal of Applied Psychology, 43*, 264-268.

Pepinsky, H. B., Pepinsky, P. N., & Pavlik, W. B. (1956). *Motivational factors in individual and group productivity: I. Successful task accomplishment as related to task relevant personal beliefs.* Columbus: Ohio State University, Personnel Research Board.

Pepinsky, P. N., Hemphill, J. K., & Shevitz, R. N. (1955). *Leadership acts. II. The relation between needs for achievement and affiliation to lead under conditions of acceptance and rejection.* Columbus: Ohio State University Research Foundation.

Pepinsky, P. N., Hemphill, J. K., & Shevitz, R. N. (1958). Attempts to lead, group productivity, and morale under conditions of acceptance and rejection. *Journal of Abnormal and Social Psychology, 57*, 47-54.

Pepinsky, P. N., Pepinsky, H. B., & Pavlik, W. B. (1956). *Motivational factors in individual and group productivity. III. The effects of task complexity and time pressure upon team productivity.* Columbus: Ohio State University, Personnel Research Board.

Pepinsky, P. N., Pepinsky, H. B., & Pavlik, W. B. (1960). The effects of task complexity and time pressure upon team productivity. *Journal of Applied Psychology, 44*, 34-38.

Pepinsky, P. N., Pepinsky, H. B., Robin, S. S., & Minor, F. J. (1957). *The effects of induced orientation and type of task upon group performance and group member morale.* Columbus: Ohio State University, Personnel Research Board.

Pepitone, A. (1958). Attributions of causality, social attitudes, and cognitive matching processes. In R. Tagiuri and L. Petrullo (Eds.), *Person perception and interpersonal behavior.* Stanford, CA: Stanford University Press.

Pepitone, A. (1964). *Attraction and hostility.* New York: Atherton Press.

Pepitone, A., & Kleiner, R. (1957). The effects of threat and frustration on group cohesiveness. *Journal of Abnormal and Social Psychology, 54*, 192-199.

Pepitone, A., & Reichling, G. (1955). Group cohesiveness and the expression of hostility. *Human Relations, 8*, 327-337.

Pepitone, E. (1952). *Responsibility to the group and its effect on the performance of the members.* Doctoral dissertation, University of Michigan, Ann Arbor.

Peppers, L., & Ryan, J. (1986). Discrepancies between actual and aspired self: A comparison of leaders and nonleaders. *Group & Organization Studies, 11*, 220-228.

Peres, S. H. (1962). Performance dimensions of supervisory positions. *Personnel Psychology, 15*, 405-410.

Perlmutter, H. V. (1954). Impressions of influential members of discussion groups. *Journal of Psychology, 38*, 223-234.

Perlmutter, H. V. (1969). The tortuous evolution of the multinational corporation. *Columbia Journal of World Business, 4*(1), 9-18.

Perls, F. (1969). In John O. Stevens (Ed.), *Gestalt theory verbatim.* Layfayette, CA: Real People Press.

Perrow, C. (1967). A framework for the comparative analysis of organizations. *American Sociological Review, 32*, 194-208.

Perrucci, R., & Pilisak, M. (1970). Leaders and ruling elites: The interorganizational bases of community power. *American Sociological Review, 35*, 1040-1057.

Perry, D., & Mahoney, T. A. (1955). In-plant communications and employee morale. *Personnel Psychology, 8*, 339-353.

Person, H. S. (1928). Leadership as a response to environment. *Educational Record Supplement No. 6, 9*, 10-21.

Pervin, L. A. (1985). Personality: Current controversies, issues and directions. *Annual Review of Psychology*, 83-114.

Peter, H. (1969). *Cross-cultural survey of managers in ten countries.* Paper, American Psychological Association, Washington, DC.

Peters, L. H., Fisher, C. D., & O'Connor, E. J. (1982). The moderating effect of situational control of performance variance on the relationship between individual differences and performance. *Personnel Psychology, 35*, 609-621.

Peters, L. H., Hartke, D. D., & Pohlmann, J. T. (1985). Fiedler's contingency theory of leadership: An application of the meta-analysis procedure of Schmidt and Hunter. *Psychological Bulletin, 97*, 274-285.

Peters, L. H., & O'Connor, E. J. (1980). Situational constraints and work outcomes: The influences of a frequently overlooked construct. *Academy of Management Review, 5*, 391-397.

Peters, T. J. (1979). Leadership: Sad facts and silver linings. *Harvard Business Review, 57*(6), 164-172.

Peters, T. J. (1980). A style for all seasons. *Executive, 6*(3), 12-16.

Peters, T. J., & Austin, N. K. (1985). Managing by walking around. *California Management Review, 28*, 9-34.

Peters, T. J., & Waterman, R. H. (1982). *In search of excellence.* New York: Harper & Row.

Petersen, E., Plowman, E. G., & Trickett, J. M. (1962). *Business organization and management.* Homewood, IL: Irwin.

Petersen, P. B., & Lippitt, G. L. (1968). Comparison of behavioral styles between entering and graduating students in officer candidate school. *Journal of Applied Psychology, 52*, 66-70.

Petersen, R. B. (1969). Worker participation in the enterprise: The Swedish experience. *Proceedings, Industrial Relations Research Association*, New York.

Peterson, M. F. (1985a). Experienced acceptability: Measuring perceptions of dysfunctional leadership. *Group & Organization Studies, 40*, 447-477.

Peterson, M. F. (1985b). *Paradigm struggles in leadership research: Progress in the 1980's.* Paper, Academy of Management, San Diego, CA.

Peterson, M. F. (1988). PM theory in Japan and China: What's in it for the United States? *Organizational Dynamics, 16*, 22-38.

Peterson, M. F., Phillips, R. L., & Duran, C. A. (1989). A comparison of Japanese performance-maintenance measures with U.S. leadership scales. *Psychologia—An International Journal of Psychology in the Orient, 32*, 58-70.

Petrullo, L., & Bass, B. M. (1961). *Leadership and interpersonal behavior.* New York: Holt, Rinehart & Winston.

Pettigrew, A. (1972). Information control as a power resource. *Sociology, 6,* 187–204.

Pettigrew, A. M. (1973). *The politics of organizational decision-making.* London: Tavistock.

Pettigrew, A. M. (1979). On studying organizational cultures. *Administrative Science Quarterly, 24,* 570–581.

Pettigrew, T. F., Jemmott, J. B., & Johnson, J. T. (1984). *Race and the questioner effect: Testing the ultimate attribution error.* University of California, Santa Cruz. Unpublished manuscript.

Petty, M. M., & Bruning, N. S. (1980). A comparison of the relationships between subordinates' perceptions of supervisory behavior and measures of subordinates' job satisfaction for male and female leaders. *Academy of Management Journal, 23,* 717–725.

Petty, M. M., & Lee, G. K. (1975). Moderating effects of sex of supervisor and subordinate on relationships between supervisory behavior and subordinate satisfaction. *Journal of Applied Psychology, 60,* 624–628.

Petty, M. M., & Miles, R. H. (1976). Leader sex-role stereotyping in a female-dominated work culture. *Personnel Psychology, 29,* 393–404.

Petty, M. M., Odewahn, C. A., Bruning, N. S., & Thomason, T. L. (1976). *An examination of the moderating effects of supervisor sex and subordinate sex upon the relationships between supervisory behavior and subordinate outcomes in mental health organizations.* Unpublished manuscript.

Petty, R. E., & Cacioppo, J. T. (1980). *Attitudes and persuasion. Classic and contemporary approaches.* Dubuque, IA: W. C. Brown.

Petty, R. E., Harkins, S. G., & Williams, K. D. (1980). The effects of group diffusion of cognitive effort on attitudes: An information processing view. *Journal of Personality and Social Psychology, 38,* 81–92.

Pezeshkpur, C. (1978). Challenges to management in the Arab world. *Business Horizons, 21,* 47–55.

Pfeffer, J. (1972a). Merger as a response to organizational interdependence. *Administrative Science Quarterly, 17,* 383–395.

Pfeffer, J. (1972b). Interorganizational influence and managerial attitudes. *Academy of Management Journal, 15,* 317–330.

Pfeffer, J. (1977). The ambiguity of leadership. *Academy of Management Review, 2,* 104–112.

Pfeffer, J. (1981a). Management as symbolic action: The creation and maintenance of organizational paradigms. In L. L. Cummings & B. Staw (Eds.), *Research in organizational behavior,* Vol. 3. Greenwich, CT: JAI Press.

Pfeffer, J. (1981b). *Power in organizations.* Boston: Pitman.

Pfeffer, J., & Davis-Blake, A. (1986). Administrative succession and organizational performance: How administrator experience mediates the succession effect. *Academy of Management Journal, 29,* 72–83.

Pfeffer, J., & Leblebici, H. (1973). Executive recruitment and the development of interfirm organizations. *Administrative Science Quarterly, 18,* 449–461.

Pfeffer, J., & Leblebici, M. (1973). The effect of competition on some dimensions of organizational structure. *Social Forces, 52,* 268–279.

Pfeffer, J., & Moore, W. L. (1980). Average tenure of academic department heads: The effects of paradigm, size, and departmental demography. *Administrative Science Quarterly, 25,* 387–406.

Pfeffer, J., & Salancik, G. R. (1974). Organizational decision making as a political process: The case of a university budget. *Administrative Science Quarterly, 19,* 135–151.

Pfeffer, J., & Salancik, G. R. (1975). Determinants of supervisory behavior: A role set analysis. *Human Relations, 28,* 139–153.

Pfeffer, J., & Salancik, G. R. (1978). *The external control of organizations: A resource dependence perspective.* New York: Harper & Row.

Pfeffer, P., & Shapiro, S. J. (1978). Personnel differences in male and female MBA candidates. *Business Quarterly, 43,* 77–80.

Pfiffner, J. M. (1948). A pattern for improved supervisory leadership. *Personnel, 24,* 271–280.

Pfiffner, J. M. (1951). *The supervision of personnel: Human relations in the management of men.* Englewood Cliffs, NJ: Prentice-Hall.

Pfiffner, J. M., & Sherwood, F. P. (1960). *Administrative organization.* Englewood Cliffs, NJ: Prentice-Hall.

Pfiffner, J. M., & Wilson, R. C. (1953). "Management-mindedness" in the supervisory ranks: A study of attitudes in relation to status. *Personnel, 30,* 122–125.

Phares, E. J. (1973). *Locus of control: A personality determinant of behavior.* Morristown, NJ: General Learning Press.

Pheterson, G. I., Goldbert, P. A., & Kiesler, S. B. (1971). Evaluation of the performance of women as a function of their sex, achievement, and personal history. *Journal of Personality and Social Psychology, 19,* 114–118.

Pheysey, D. C. & Payne, R. L. (1970). *The Hemphill group dimensions description questionnaire: A British industrial application.* Birmingham: University of Aston, Industrial Administration Research Unit.

Pheysey, D. C., Payne, R. L., & Pugh, D. S. (1971). Influence of structure at organizational and group levels. *Administrative Science Quarterly, 16,* 61–73.

Philip, H., & Dunphy, D. (1959). Developmental trends in small groups. *Sociometry, 22,* 162–174.

Philips, B. N. (1954). Relationship of process behavior to the task efficiency of small face-to-face groups. *American Psychologist, 9,* 449.

Philipsen, H. (1965a). Het meten van leiderschap. *Mens en Onderneming, 19,* 153–171.

Philipsen, H. (1965b). Medezeggenschap in de vorm van werkoverleg. In C. J. Lammers (Ed.), *Medezeggenschap en overleg in het bedrijf.* Utrecht: Het Spectrum.

Philipsen, H., & Cassee, E. T. (1965). Verschillen in de wijze van leidinggeven tussen drie typen organisaties. *Mens en Onderneming, 19,* 172–174.

Phillips, J. J. (1986). Training supervisors outside the classroom. *Training & Development Journal, 40*(2), 46–49.

Phillips, J. S. (1984). The accuracy of leadership ratings. A cognitive categorizational perspective. *Organizational Behavior and Human Performance, 33,* 125–38.

Phillips, J. S., & Lord, R. G. (1981). Causal attributions and perceptions of leadership. *Organizational Behavior and Human Performance, 28,* 143–163.

Phillips, J. S., & Lord, R. G. (1982). Schematic information processing and perceptions of leadership in problem-solving groups. *Journal of Applied Psychology, 67,* 486–492.

Phillips, J. S., & Lord, R. G. (1986). Notes on the practical and theoretical consequences of implicit leadership theories for the future of leadership measurement. *Journal of Management, 12,* 31–41.

Phillips, R. L. (1972). *A study of twenty-one variables relating to leader legitimation.* Doctoral dissertation, Ohio State University, Columbus.

Phillips, T. R. (1939). Leader and led. *Journal of the Coast Artillery, 82,* 45–58.

Pickle, H., & Friedlander, F. (1967). Seven societal criteria of organizational success. *Personnel Psychology, 20,* 165–178.

Pieper, F. (1958). *Modular management and human leadership.* Minneapolis, MN: Methods Press.

Piersol, D. T. (1958). Communication practices of supervisors in a midwestern corporation. *Advanced Management, 23,* 20–21.

Pierson, J. F. (1984). Leadership styles of university and college counsel center directors: Perspectives from the field (personality type, job satisfaction, consideration, initiation of structure). *Dissertation Abstracts International, 45*(2A), 418.

Pigors, P. (1933). Leadership and domination among children. *Sociologus, 9,* 140–157.

Pigors, P. (1935). *Leadership or domination.* Boston: Houghton Mifflin.

Pigors, P. (1936). Types of leaders in group work. *Sociology and Social Research, 21,* 3–17.

Pinard, J. W. (1932). Tests of perseveration. *British Journal of Psychology, 23,* 5–19.

Pinchot, J., III. (1985). *Intrapreneuring.* New York: Harper & Row.

Pincus, J. D. (1986). Communication satisfaction, job satisfaction, and job performance. *Human Communication Research, 12,* 395–419.

Pinder, C. C., & Pinto, P. R. (1974). Demographic correlates of managerial style. *Personnel Psychology, 27,* 257–270.

Pinder, C., Pinto, P. R., & England, G. W. (1973). *Behavioral style and personal characteristics of managers* (Tech. Rep.). Minneapolis: University of Minnesota, Center for the Study of Organizational Performance and Human Effectiveness.

Pines, M. (1980). Psychological hardiness. *Psychology Today, 14*(2), 38–39.

Pinkney, A. P. (1969). *Black Americans.* Englewood Cliffs, NJ: Prentice-Hall.

Pinnell, R. I. (1984). *The relationships between locus of control, communication apprehension, power orientations and leadership styles.* Doctoral dissertation, University of Denver, Denver, CO.

Piotrowski, C., & Armstrong, T. R. (1987). Executive leadership characteristics portrayed on CNN's pinnacle. Reported in *Behavioral Science Newsletter,* Book XVI, Vol. 23.

Pipes, R. (1974). *Russia under the old regime.* New York: Weidenfeld & Nicolson.

Pitkin, W. B. (1931). *The psychology of achievement.* New York: Simon & Schuster.

Pitner, N. J. (1988). Leadership substitutes: Their factorial validity in educational organizations. *Educational and Psychological Measurement, 48,* 307–315.

Pitt, L. F. (1985). Managerial attitudes towards corruption—A pilot study. *South African Journal of Business Management, 16,* 27–30.

Plato. (1945). *The republic,* F. M. Cornford (Trans.). New York: Oxford University Press.

Plutarch. (1909). *Plutarch's complete works.* New York: T. Y. Crowell.

Plutarch. (1932). *Lives of the noble Grecians and Romans.* New York: Modern Library.

Podsakoff, P. M. (1982). Determinants of a supervisor's use of rewards and punishments: A literature review and suggestions for further research. *Organizational Behavior and Human Performance, 29,* 58–83.

Podsakoff, P. (1987). *Leader reward and punishment behavior: A methodological and substantive review* (Working Paper). Bloomington: Indiana University.

Podsakoff, P. M., Dorfman, P. W., Howell, J. P., & Todor, W. D. (1986). Leader reward and punishment behaviors: A preliminary test of a culture-free style of leadership effectiveness. *Advances in International Comparative Management, 2,* 95–138.

Podsakoff, P. M., & Organ, D. W. (1986). Self-reports in organizational research. Problems and prospects. *Journal of Management, 12,* 31–41.

Podsakoff, P. M., & Schriesheim, C. A. (1985a). Field studies of French and Raven's bases of power: Critique, reanalysis, and suggestions for future research. *Psychological Bulletin, 97,* 387–411.

Podsakoff, P. M., & Schriesheim, C. A. (1985b). Leader reward and punishment behavior: A methodological and substantive review. In B. Staw & L. L. Cummings (Eds.), *Research in organizational behavior.* San Francisco: Jossey-Bass.

Podsakoff, P. M., & Todor, W. D. (1983a). *Individual differences as moderators of leader reward and punishment behaviors* (Working Paper). Bloomington: Indiana University.

Podsakoff, P. M., & Todor, W. D. (1983b). *An analysis of the nature of the moderators of leader reward and punishment behaviors.* Bloomington: Indiana University. Unpublished manuscript.

Podsakoff, P. M., & Todor, W. D. (1985). Relationships between leader reward and punishment behavior and group processes and productivity. *Journal of Management, 11,* 55–73.

Podsakoff, P. M., Todor, W. D., Grover, R. A., & Huber, V. L. (1984). Situational moderators of leader reward and punishment behaviors: Fact or fiction? *Organizational Behavior and Human Performance, 34,* 21–63.

Podsakoff, P. M., Todor, W. D., & Schuler, R. S. (1983). Leader expertise as a moderator of the effects of instrumental and supportive leader behaviors. *Journal of Management, 9,* 173–185.

Podsakoff, P. M., Todor, W. D., & Skov, R. (1982). Effect of leader contingent and non-contingent reward and punishment behaviors on subordinate performance and satisfaction. *Academy of Management Journal, 25,* 810-821.

Poitou, J. P. (1969). Pouvoir coercitif et interdépendence. *Année Psychologique, 69,* 435-453.

Polansky, N., Lippitt, R., & Redl, F. (1950a). An investigation of behavioral contagion in groups. *Human Relations, 3,* 319-348.

Polansky, N., Lippitt, R., & Redl, F. (1950b). The use of near-sociometric data in research on group treatment process. *Sociometry, 13,* 39-62.

Polis, T. (1964). A note on crisis and leadership. *Australian Journal of Psychology, 16,* 57-61.

Polmar, N., & Allen, T. B. (1981). *Rickover: Controversy and genius. A biography.* New York: Simon & Schuster.

Ponder, Q. D. (1958). *Supervisory practices of effective and ineffective foremen.* Doctoral dissertation, Columbia University, New York.

Pondy, L. R. (1967). Organizational conflict: Concepts and models. *Administrative Science Quarterly, 12,* 296-320.

Pondy, L. R. (1976). Leadership is a language game. In M. McCall & M. Lombardo (Eds.), *Leadership: Where else can we go?* Durham, NC: Duke University Press.

Pondy, L. R. (1977). The other hand clapping: An information processing approach to organizational power. In T. H. Hammer & S. B. Bacharach (Eds.), *Reward systems and power distributions.* Ithaca, NY: Cornell University Press.

Pondy, L. (1983). Union of rationality and intuition in management action. In S. Srivastva & Associates (Eds.), *The executive mind.* San Francisco: Jossey-Bass.

Porat, A. M., & Ryterband, E. C. (1974). Career performance, choice and attainment for members of minority groups. In H. L. Fromkin & J. J. Sherwood (Eds.), *Integrating the organization.* New York: Free Press.

Porras, J. I., & Anderson, B. (1981). Improving managerial effectiveness through modeling-based training. *Organizational Dynamics, 9*(4), 60-77.

Porras, J. I., & Berg, P. O. (1976). The impact of organizational development. *Academy of Management Review, 1,* 249-266.

Porter, A. (1965). Validity of socioeconomic origin as a predictor of executive success. *Journal of Applied Psychology, 49,* 11-13.

Porter, L. W. (1958). Differential self-perceptions of management personnel and line workers. *Journal of Applied Psychology, 42,* 105-108.

Porter, L. W. (1959). Self-perceptions of first-level supervisors compared with upper-management personnel and operative line workers. *Journal of Applied Psychology, 43,* 183-186.

Porter, L. W. (1961a). A study of perceived need satisfaction in bottom and middle management jobs. *Journal of Applied Psychology, 45,* 1-10.

Porter, L. W. (1961b). Perceived trait requirements in bottom and middle management jobs. *Journal of Applied Psychology, 45,* 232-236.

Porter, L. W. (1962). Job attitudes in management: I. Perceived deficiencies in need fulfillment as a function of job level. *Journal of Applied Psychology, 46,* 375-384.

Porter, L. W. (1963a). Job attitudes in management: II. Perceived importance of needs as a function of job level. *Journal of Applied Psychology, 47,* 141-148.

Porter, L. W. (1963b). Job attitudes in management: III. Perceived deficiencies in need fulfillment as a function of line versus staff type of job. *Journal of Applied Psychology, 47,* 267-275.

Porter, L. W. (1963c). Job attitudes in management: IV. Perceived deficiencies in need fulfillment as a function of size of company. *Journal of Applied Psychology, 47,* 386-397.

Porter, L. W. (1964). *Organizational patterns of managerial job attitudes.* New York: American Foundation for Management Research.

Porter, L. W., Allen, R. W., & Angle, H. L. (1981). The politics of upward influence in organizations. In B. Staw & L. Cummings (Eds.), *Research in organizational behavior.* Greenwich, CT: JAI Press.

Porter, L. W., & Ghiselli, E. E. (1957). The self perceptions of top and middle management personnel. *Personnel Psychology, 10,* 397-406.

Porter, L. W., & Henry, M. M. (1964a). Job attitudes in management: V. Perceptions of the importance of certain personality traits as a function of job level. *Journal of Applied Psychology, 48,* 31-36.

Porter, L. W., & Henry, M. M. (1964b). Job attitudes in management: VI. Perceptions of the importance of certain personality traits as a function of line versus staff type of job. *Journal of Applied Psychology, 48,* 305-309.

Porter, L. W., & Kaufman, R. A. (1959). Relationships between a top-middle management self-description scale and behavior in a group situation. *Journal of Applied Psychology, 43,* 345-348.

Porter, L. W., & Lawler, E. E. (1964). The effects of "tall" versus "flat" organizational structures on managerial job satisfaction. *Personnel Psychology, 17,* 135-148.

Porter, L. W., & Lawler, E. E. (1965). Properties of organization structure in relation to job attitudes and behavior. *Psychological Bulletin, 64,* 23-51.

Porter, L. W., & Lawler, E. E. (1968). *Managerial attitudes and performance.* Homewood, IL: Irwin-Dorsey.

Porter, L. W., Lawler, E. E., & Hackman, J. R. (1975). *Behavior in organizations.* New York: McGraw-Hill.

Porter, L. W., & Mitchell, V. F. (1967). Comparative study of need satisfactions in military and business hierarchies. *Journal of Applied Psychology, 51,* 139-144.

Porter, L. W., & Siegel, J. (1965). Relationships of tall and flat organization structures to the satisfaction of foreign managers. *Personnel Psychology, 18,* 379-392.

Posner, B. Z., & Kouzes, J. M. (1988a). Development and validation of the Leadership Practices Inventory. *Educational and Psychological Measurement, 48,* 483-496.

Posner, B. Z., & Kouzes, J. M. (1988b). Relating leadership and credibility. *Psychological Reports, 63,* 527-530.

Posner, B. Z., & Low, P. S. (1988). *Australian and American management values: A preliminary investigation.* Paper, Western Academy of Management, Big Sky, MT.

Posner, B. Z., & Schmidt, W. H. (1984). Values and the American manager: An update. *California Management Review, 3,* 202–216.

Posthuma, A. B. (1970). *Normative data on the least preferred coworkers scale (LPC) and the group atmosphere questionnaire (GA)* (Tech. Rep. No. 70-8). Seattle: University of Washington, Organizational Research.

Potter, E. H. (1978). *The contribution of intelligence and experience to the performance of staff personnel.* Doctoral dissertation, University of Washington, Seattle.

Potter, E. H., III, & Fiedler, F. E. (1981). Stress and the utilization of staff member intelligence and experience. *Academy of Management Journal, 24,* 361–376.

Powell, G. N. (1982). Sex-role identity and sex: An important distinction for research on women in management. *Basic and Applied Social Psychology, 3,* 67–79.

Powell, G. N., & Butterfield, D. A. (1979). The "good manager": masculine or androgynous? *Academy of Management Journal, 22,* 395–403.

Powell, G. N., & Butterfield, D. (1980). The female leader: Attributional effects of group performance. *Psychological Reports, 47,* 891–897.

Powell, G. N., & Butterfield, D. (1981). A note on sex-role identity effects on managerial aspirations. *Journal of Occupational Psychology, 54,* 299–301.

Powell, G. N., & Butterfield, D. (1984). The "high-high" leader rides again. *Group & Organization Studies, 9,* 437–450.

Powell, G. N., Posner, B. Z., & Schmidt, W. H. (1984). Sex effects on managerial value systems. *Human Relations, 37,* 909–921.

Powell, R. M. (1952). Sociometric analysis of informal groups—Their structure and function in two contrasting communities. *Sociometry, 15,* 367–399.

Powell, R. M. (1956). An experimental study of role taking, group status, and group formation. *Sociology and Social Research, 40,* 159–165.

Powell, R. M. (1969). *Race, religion, and the promotion of the American executive.* Columbus: Ohio State University Press.

Powell, R. M., & Nelson, D. H. (1969). The business executive's self-image versus his image of the politician. *Personnel Journal, 48,* 677–682.

Powell, R. M., & Stinson, J. E. (1971). *Individual and organization impact of laboratory training.* Paper, Academy of Management, Atlanta, GA.

Powell, R. M., Thrasher, J. D., Darrough, D., et al. (1951). The nature and extent of group organization in a girls' dormitory: A sociometric investigation. *Sociometry, 14,* 317–339.

Pratt, J., & Jiambalvo, J. (1982). Determinants of leader behavior in an audit environment. *Accounting, Organizations and Society, 7,* 369–379.

Precker, J. A. (1952). Similarity of valuings as a factor in selection of peers and near-authority figures. *Journal of Abnormal and Social Psychology, 47,* 406–414.

Prentice, D. B., & Kunkel, B. W. (1930). College contributions to intellectual leadership. *School & Society, 32,* 594–600.

Prentice, W. C. H. (1961). Understanding leadership. *Harvard Business Review, 39*(5), 143–151.

Presthus, R. V. (1960). Authority in organizations. *Public Administration Review, 20*(2), 86–91.

Presthus, R. (1964). *Men at the top: A study in community power.* New York: Oxford University Press.

Presthus, R. (1965). *Behavioral approaches to public administration.* University, AL: University of Alabama Press.

Preston, J. C. & Chappel, K. E. (1988). *Assessment of three training methods used to teach managers leadership.* Paper, International Congress of Psychology, Sydney, Australia.

Preston, M. G., & Heintz, R. K. (1949). Effects of participatory vs. supervisory leadership on group judgement. *Journal of Abnormal and Social Psychology, 44,* 345–355.

Prestridge, V., & Wray, D. (1953). *Industrial sociology: An annotated bibliography.* Champaign: University of Illinois, Institute of Labor and Industrial Relations.

Price, B. (1974). A study of leadership strength of female police executives. *Journal of Police Science and Administration, 2,* 219–226.

Price, J. L. (1968). *Organizational effectiveness: An inventory of propositions.* Homewood, IL: Irwin.

Price, J. L. (1976). *Cadres, commanders and commissars: The training of the Chinese communist leadership.* Boulder, CO: Westview Press.

Price, K. H., & Garland, H. (1981). Compliance with a leader's suggestions as a function of perceived leader/member competence and potential reciprocity. *Journal of Applied Psychology, 66,* 329–336.

Price, M. A. (1948). *A study of motivational factors associated with leadership behavior of young women in a private school.* Doctoral dissertation, Ohio State University, Columbus.

Prien, E. P. (1963). Development of a supervisor position description questionnaire. *Journal of Applied Psychology, 47,* 10–14.

Prien, E. P., & Culler, A. R. (1964). Leaderless group discussion participation and inter-observer agreements. *Journal of Social Psychology, 62,* 321–328.

Prien, E. P., & Lee, R. J. (1965). Peer ratings and leaderless group discussions for evaluation of classroom performance. *Psychological Reports, 16,* 59–64.

Prien, E. P., & Liske, R. E. (1962). Assessments of higher level personnel. III. Rating criteria: A comparative analysis of supervisor ratings and incumbent self rating of job performance. *Personnel Psychology, 15,* 187–194.

Priest, R. F., & Sawyer, J. (1967). Proximity and peership: Bases of balance in interpersonal attraction. *American Journal of Sociology, 72,* 633–649.

Prieto, A. C. (1975). *An investigation of the relationship between participative group management in elementary schools and the needs satisfaction of elementary classroom teachers.* Doctoral dissertation, University of New Orleans, New Orleans, LA.

Prince, H. T. (1987). *Leader development at the U.S. Military Academy.* Paper, Conference on military leadership: Traditions and trends. United States Naval Academy, Annapolis, MD.

Pritchard, R., & Karasick, B. (1973). The effects of organizational climate on managerial job performance and job satisfaction. *Organizational Behavior and Human Performance, 9,* 110–119.

Prosh, F. (1928). The basis on which students choose their leaders. *American Physical Education Review, 33,* 265–267.

Proshansky, H., & Newton, P. (1968). The nature and meaning of Negro self-identity. In M. Deutsch, I. Katz, & A. Jensen (Eds.), *Social class, race, and psychological development.* New York: Holt, Rinehart & Winston.

Proshansky, H. M., & Seidenberg, B. (1965). *Basic studies in social psychology.* New York: Holt, Rinehart & Winston.

Prothero, J., & Fiedler, F. E. (1974). *The effects of situational change on individual behavior and performance: An extension of the contingency model* (Tech. Rep. No. 74-59). Seattle: University of Washington, Organizational Research.

Prud'homme, L., & Baron, P. (1988). Irrational beliefs and ethnic background: Ellis' theory revisited. *Applied Psychology: An International Review, 37,* 301–310.

Pryer, M. W., & DiStefano, M. K. (1971). Perceptions of leadership behavior, job satisfaction, and internal-external control across three nursing levels. *Nursing Review, 20,* 534–537.

Pryer, M. W., Flint, A. W., & Bass, B. M. (1962). Group effectiveness and consistency of leadership. *Sociometry, 25,* 391–397.

Psathas, G., & Hardert, R. (1966). Transfer interventions and normative patterns in the T Group. *Journal of Applied Behavioral Science, 2,* 149–169.

Psychological Services. (1953). *Bibliography on military leadership: Annotations of selected studies from scientific, technical, and related publications.* Maxwell Air Force Base, AL: Air Research and Development Command, Human Resources Research Institute.

Pucik, V. (1981). Promotions and intraorganizational status differentiation among Japanese managers. *Proceedings, Academy of Management,* San Diego, CA, 59–62.

Puckett, E. S. (1958). Productivity achievements: A measure of success. In F. G. Lesieur (Ed.), *The Scanlon plan.* Cambridge, MA: M.I.T. Press.

Puffer, J. A. (1905). Boys' gangs. *Pedagogical Seminary, 12,* 175–213.

Pugh, D. (1965). T-group training from the point of view of organizational theory. In G. Whitaker (Ed.), *ATM Occasional Papers 2.* Oxford: Basil E. Blackwell.

Pugh, D. S., Hickson, D. J., Hinings, C. R., & Turner, C. (1968). Dimensions of organization structure. *Administrative Science Quarterly, 13,* 65–105.

Pugh, D. S., Hickson, D. J., Hinings, C. R., & Turner, C. (1969). The context of organizational structures. *Administrative Science Quarterly, 14,* 91–112.

Pulakos, E. D., & Wexley, K. N. (1983). The relationship among perceptual similarity, sex, and performance ratings in manager-subordinate dyads. *Academy of Management Journal, 26,* 129–139.

Punch, K. F. (1967). *Bureaucratic structure of schools and its relationship to leader behavior.* Toronto: Ontario Institute for Studies in Education. Unpublished manuscript.

Punch, K. F. (1968). Bureaucratic structure in schools and its relationships to leader behavior: An empirical study. *Dissertation Abstracts, 29,* 448–449.

Purcell, K., Modrick, J. A., & Yamahiro, R. (1960). Item vs. trait accuracy in interpersonal perception. *Journal of General Psychology, 62,* 285–292.

Purcell, T. V. (1953). *The worker speaks his mind on company and union.* Cambridge, MA: Harvard University Press.

Purcell, T. V. (1954). Dual allegiance to union and management (a symposium). 2. Dual allegiance to company and union packinghouse workers. A Swift-UPWA Study in a crisis situation (1949–1952). *Personnel Psychology, 7,* 45–58.

Purcell, T. V. (1960). *Blue collar man: Patterns of dual allegiance in industry.* Cambridge, MA: Harvard University Press.

Puryear, E. F. (1971). *Nineteen stars.* Washington, DC: Coiner.

Quaglieri, P. L., & Carnazza, J. P. (1985). Critical inferences and the multidimensionality of feedback. *Canadian Journal of Behavioral Science, 17,* 284–293.

Quarantelli, E. L. (1954). The nature and conditions of panic. *American Journal of Sociology, 60,* 267–275.

Queener, E. L. (1951). *Introduction to social psychology.* New York: Sloan.

Quiggins, J. G., & Lashbrook, W. B. (1972). *Task and socio-emotional leadership in ongoing groups: A theoretical perspective.* Paper, Western Speech Communication Association, Honolulu.

Quinn, R. E. (1977). Coping with cupid: The formation, impact, and management of romantic relationships in organizations. *Administrative Science Quarterly, 22,* 30–45.

Quinn, R. E. (1984). Applying the competing values approach to leadership: Towards an integrative framework. In J. G. Hunt, D. Hosking, C. A. Schriesheim, & R. Stewart (Eds.), *Leaders and managers: International perspectives on managerial behavior and leadership.* New York: Pergamon.

Quinn, R. E. (1988). *Beyond rational management: Mastering the paradoxes and competing demands of high performance.* San Francisco: Jossey-Bass.

Quinn, R. E., & Cameron, K. (1983). Organizational life cycles and shifting criteria of effectiveness: Some preliminary evidence. *Management Science, 29,* 33–51.

Quinn, R. E., Dixit, N., & Faerman, S. R. (1987). *Perceived performance: Some archetypes of managerial effectiveness and ineffectiveness.* Institute for Government and Policy Studies, Nelson A. Rockefeller College of Public Affairs and Policy, State University of New York at Albany.

Quinn, R. E., & Hall, R. H. (1983). Environments, organizations, and policy makers: Towards an integrative framework. In R. H. Hall and R. E. Quinn (Eds.), *Organization theory and public policy: Contributions and limitations.* Beverly Hills, CA: Sage.

Quinn, R. P., Kahn, R. K., Tabor, J. M., & Gordon, L. K. (1968). *The chosen few: A study of discrimination in executive selection.* Ann Arbor: University of Michigan, Institute for Social Research.

Quinn, R. P., & Kent, J. T. (1967). *Big fish, little fish: A "competitive" approach to organizational primary groups.* Paper, American Psychological Association, Washington, DC.

Rabi, M. M. (1967). *The political theory of Ibn Khaldun.* Leiden: Brill.

Rabow, J., Fowler, F., Bradford, D., Hofeller, M., & Shibuya, Y. (1966). The role of social norms and leadership in risk-taking. *Sociometry, 29,* 16-27.

Rackham, N. (1971). *Developing interactive skills.* Northampton, England: Wellens Publishing.

Racz, L. L. (1971). A study of teacher alienation and its relationship to individual needs and leadership behavior. *Dissertation Abstracts International, 31,* 6319.

Radin, B. A. (1980). Leadership training for women in state and local government. *Public Personnel Management, 9*(2), 52-60.

Radke, M., & Klisurich, D. (1947). Experiments in changing food habits. *Journal of American Diet Association, 23,* 403-409.

Radloff, R., & Helmreich, R. (1968). *Groups under stress.* New York: Appleton-Century-Crofts.

Ragins, B. R. (1987). *Power and leadership effectiveness: A study of subordinate evaluations of male and female leaders.* Doctoral dissertation, University of Tennessee, Knoxville.

Ragins, B. R. (1988). Does gender matter? An investigation of potential artifacts in research on subordinate evaluations of male and female managers. *Proceedings, Academy of Management,* Anaheim, CA, 356-360.

Rahim, M. A. (1983). A measure of styles of handling interpersonal conflict. *Academy of Management Journal, 26,* 368-376.

Rahim, M. A. (1986). *A new measure of bases of leader power.* Paper, Academy of Management, Chicago.

Rahim, M. A. (1988). The development of a leader power inventory. *Multivariate Behavioral Research, 23,* 491-503.

Raia, A. P. (1966). A study of the educational value of management games. *Journal of Business, 39,* 339-352.

Raiffa, H., & Schlaifer, R. (1961). *Applied statistical decision theory.* Boston: Harvard University, Graduate School of Business Administration.

Rainey, H. G. (1979). Reward expectancies, role perceptions, and job satisfaction among government and business managers: Indications of commonalities and differences. *Proceedings, Academy of Management,* Atlanta, GA, 357-361.

Rainey, H. G. (1983). Public agencies and private firms. *Administration and Society, 15,* 207-242.

Rainio, K. (1955). *Leadership qualities: A theoretical and an experimental study on foremen.* Helsinki: Academiae Scientiarum Fennicae.

Rainwater, L. (1966). Crucible of identity: The Negro lower-class family. *Daedalus, 95,* 172-216.

Ralston, D. A. (1985). Employee ingratiation: The role of management. *Academy of Management Review, 10,* 477-487.

Rambo, W. W. (1958). The construction and analysis of a leadership behavior rating form. *Journal of Applied Psychology, 42,* 409-415.

Randle, C. W. (1956). How to identify promotable executives. *Harvard Business Review, 34,* 122-134.

Randolph, W. A., & Finch, F. E. (1977). The relationship between organization technology and the direction and frequency dimensions of task communications. *Human Relations, 30,* 1131-1145.

Rao, N. R. K. (1982). An investigation of the impact of the supervisor's reinforcement contingency on his behavior in a dyadic interaction with a subordinate. *Dissertation Abstracts International, 43*(2A), 497.

Raskin, A. H. (1976, June 11). The workers' voice in German companies. *New York Times,* D7.

Rasmussen, G., & Zander, A. (1954). Group membership and self-evaluation. *Human Relations, 7,* 239-251.

Rasmussen, K. G., Jr. (1984). Nonverbal behavior, verbal behavior, resume credentials, and selection interview outcomes. *Journal of Applied Psychology, 69,* 551-556.

Rasmussen, R. L. (1976). The principal's leadership behavior in unusually successful and unsuccessful elementary schools. *Education Research Quarterly, 1,* 18-29.

Rath, K. C., & Sahoo, M. S. (1974). Socio-economic status of Panchayat leaders and their role in agricultural production. *Social Cultural, 5,* 25-28.

Raube, S. A. (1947). *Factors affecting employee morale.* New York: National Industrial Conference Board.

Raudsepp, E. (1962). Career satisfactions: Money means less than sense of accomplishment. *Machine Design, 34,* 99-102.

Raudsepp, E. (1981). Delegate your way to success. *Computer Decisions, 13*(3), 157-158, 163-164.

Raven, B. H. (1959a). The dynamics of groups. *Review of Education Research, 29,* 332-343.

Raven, B. H. (1959b). Social influence on opinion and the communication of related content. *Journal of Abnormal and Social Psychology, 58,* 119-128.

Raven, B. H. (1965a). *A bibliography of publications relating to the small group.* Los Angeles: University of California, Department of Psychology.

Raven, B. H. (1965b). Social influence and power. In I. D. Steiner & M. Fishbein (Eds.), *Current studies in social psychology.* New York: Holt, Rinehart & Winston.

Raven, B. H., & Eachus, H. T. (1963). Cooperation and competition in means-interdependent triads. *Journal of Abnormal and Social Psychology, 67,* 307-316.

Raven, B. H., & French, J. R. P. (1957). An experimental investigation of legitimate and coercive power. *American Psychologist, 12,* 393.

Raven, B. H., & French, J. R. P. (1958a). Group support, legitimate power, and social influence. *Journal of Personality, 26,* 400-409.

Raven, B. H., & French, J. R. P. (1958b). Legitimate power, coercive power, and observability in social influence. *Sociometry, 21,* 83-97.

Raven, B. H., Kelley, H. H., & Shapiro, M. M. (1954). An experiment on conformity to group norms where conformity is detrimental to group achievement. *American Sociological Review, 19,* 667-677.

Raven, B. H., & Kruglanski, A. W. (1970). Conflict and power. In P. Swingle (Ed.), *The structure of conflict.* New York: Academic Press.

Raven, B. H., & Shaw, J. I. (1970). Interdependence and group problem-solving in the triad. *Journal of Personality and Social Psychology, 14,* 157–165.

Rawlins, C. L. (1983). Teleconferencing and the leadership of small groups. *Dissertation Abstracts International, 44*(8A), 2562.

Rawls, D. J., & Rawls, J. R. (1968). Personality characteristics and personal history data of successful and less successful executives. *Psychological Reports, 23,* 1032–1034.

Rawls, J., Ulrich, R., & Nelson, O. (1973). A comparison of managers entering or re-entering the profit and non-profit sectors. *Academy of Management Journal, 3,* 616–623.

Ray, B. (1989). *The relationship of job satisfaction, individual characteristics, and leadership behaviors to corporate culture beliefs and climate for change.* Doctoral dissertation, East Texas State University, Commerce, TX.

Read, P. B. (1974). Source of authority and the legitimation of leadership in small groups, *Sociometry, 37,* 180–204.

Read, W. H. (1962). Upward communication in industrial hierarchies. *Human Relations, 15,* 3–15.

Ready, R. K. (1964). Leadership in the 1960's. *California Management Review, 6,* 37–46.

Reals, W. H. (1938). Leadership in the high school. *School Review, 46,* 523–531.

Reaser, J. M., Vaughan, M. R., & Kriner, R. E. (1974). *Military leadership in the seventies: A closer look at the dimension of leadership behavior.* Alexandria, VA: Human Resources Research Organization.

Reavis, C. A., & Derlega, V. J. (1976). Test of a contingency model of teacher effectiveness. *Journal of Educational Research, 69,* 221–225.

Reddin, W. J. (undated). Management style diagnosis test. Fredericton, N.B.: Organizational Tests.

Reddin, W. J. (1970). *Managerial effectiveness.* New York: McGraw-Hill.

Reddin, W. J. (1977). An integration of leader-behavior typologies. *Group & Organization Studies, 2,* 282–295.

Redding, S. G., & Casey, T. W. (1975). Managerial beliefs among Asian managers. *Proceedings, Academy of Management,* New Orleans, LA, 351–355.

Redding, W. C. (1972). *Communication within the organization: An interpretive review of theory and research.* New York: Industrial Communications Council.

Redl, F. (1942). Group emotion and leadership. *Psychiatric, 5,* 573–596.

Redl, F. (1948). Resistance in therapy groups. *Human Relations, 1,* 307–313.

Reed, H. D., & Janis, I. L. (1974). Effects of a new type of psychological treatment on smokers' resistance to warnings about health hazards. *Journal of Consulting and Clinical Psychology, 42,* 748.

Reeder, R. R. (1981). The importance of the superior's technical competence in the subordinates' work. *Dissertation Abstracts International, 42*(6A), 2830.

Rees, R. T., & O'Karma, J. G. (1980). Perception of supervisor leadership style in a formal organization. *Group & Organization Studies, 5,* 65–68.

Regula, C. R. (1967). *Quality and quantity of contributions as determi-*

nants of perceived ability (Tech. Rep.). Buffalo: State University of New York, Department of Psychology.

Regula, R. C., & Julian, J. W. (1973). The impact of quality and frequency of task contributions on perceived ability. *Journal of Social Psychology, 89,* 115–122.

Reibstein, L. (1986, March 24). The not-so-fast track: Firms try promoting hotshots more slowly. *Wall Street Journal,* 23.

Reid, F. T. (1970). Impact of leader style on the functioning of a decision-making group. *Archives of General Psychiatry, 23,* 268–276.

Reider, N. (1944). Psychodynamics of authority with relation to some psychiatric problems in officers. *Bulletin of the Menninger Clinic, 8,* 55–58.

Reidy, R. J., Jr. (1976). *A comparative analysis of selected public elementary community school administrative systems and public elementary non-community school administrative systems using the Likert administrative systems model.* Doctoral dissertation, University of Connecticut, Storrs.

Reif, W. E., Newstrom, J. W., & St. Louis, R. D. (1976). Sex as a discriminatory variable in organizational reward decisions. *Academy of Management Journal, 19,* 469–476.

Reif, W. E., & Schoderbek, P. P. (1966). Job enlargement: Antidote to apathy. *Management Personnel Quarterly, 5,* 16–23.

Reilly, J. W., & Robinson, F. P. (1947). Studies of popularity in colleges: II. Do dormitory arrangements affect popularity? *Educational and Psychological Measurement, 7,* 327–330.

Reilly, R. R. (1970). A study of the effect of task-irrelevant factors on leader selection. *Dissertation Abstracts International, 30,* 3551.

Reilly, R. R., & Jaffee, C. L. (1970). Influences of some task-irrelevant factors on leader selection. *Psychological Record, 20,* 535–539.

Reinganum, M. R. (1985). The effect of executive succession on stockholder wealth. *Administrative Science Quarterly, 30,* 46–60.

Reininger, K. (1929). Das soziale Vehalten von Schulneulingen. *Wien Arbeiten für pädagogische Psychologie, 7,* 14.

Reitz, H. J. (1971). Managerial attitudes and perceived contingencies between performance and organizational response. *Proceedings, Academy of Management,* Atlanta, GA, 227–238.

Rejai, M. (1980). Theory and research in the study of revolutionary personnel. In T. B. Burr (Ed.), *Handbook of political conflict.* New York: Free Press.

Rejai, M., & Phillips, K. (1979). *Leaders of revolution.* Beverly Hills, CA: Sage.

Rejai, M., & Phillips, K. (1988). Loyalists and revolutionaries: Political elites in comparative perspective. *International Political Science Review, 9,* 107–118.

Remland, M. (1981). Developing leadership skills in nonverbal communication: A situational perspective. *Journal of Business Communication, 18*(3), 17–29.

Remland, M. S. (1984). Leadership impressions and nonverbal communication in a superior-subordinate interaction. *Communication Quarterly, 32*(1).

Remland, M., Jacobson, C., & Jones, T. (1983). Effects of psychological gender and sex-incongruent behavior on evaluations of leadership. *Perceptual and Motor Skills, 57,* 783–789.

Remmelin, M. K. (1938). Analysis of leaders among high school seniors. *Journal of Experimental Education, 6,* 413–422.

Remmers, L. J., & Remmers, H. H. (1949). Studies in industrial empathy: I. Labor leaders' attitudes toward industrial supervision and their estimate of managements' attitudes. *Personnel Psychology, 2,* 427–436.

Renck, R. (1955). Morale in four key groups in industry. *Conference on employee attitude surveys.* Chicago: University of Chicago, Industrial Relations Center.

Renck, R. (1957). *Morale in industrial organizations.* Chicago: University of Chicago, Industrial Relations Center.

Renwick, P. A., & Tosi, H. (1978). The effects of sex, marital status, and educational background on selection decisions. *Academy of Management Journal, 21,* 93–103.

Rettig, S., Despres, L., & Pasamanick, B. (1960). Status stratification and status equalization. *Journal of Social Psychology, 52,* 109–117.

Reykowski, J. (1982). Social motivation. *Annual Review of Psychology, 33,* 123–154.

Reynolds, F. J. (1944). Factors of leadership among seniors of Central High School, Tulsa, Oklahoma. *Journal of Education Research, 37,* 356–361.

Reynolds, H. H. (1966). Efficacy of sociometric ratings in predicting leadership success. *Psychology Reports, 19,* 35–40.

Rhinehart, J. B., Barrell, R. P., DeWolfe, A. S., Griffin, J. E., & Spaner, F. E. (1969). Comparative study of need satisfaction in government and business hierarchies. *Journal of Applied Psychology, 53,* 230–235.

Ricciuti, H. N. (1955). Ratings of leadership potential at the U.S. Naval Academy and subsequent officer performance. *Journal of Applied Psychology, 39,* 194–199.

Rice, A. K. (1953). Productivity and social organization in an Indian weaving shed. *Human Relations, 6,* 297–329.

Rice, A. K. (1958). *Productivity and social organization: The Ahmedabad experiment.* London: Tavistock.

Rice, A. K. (1963). *The enterprise and its environment.* New York: Humanities Press.

Rice, A. K. (1965). *Leadership for leadership—interpersonal and intergroup relations.* New York: Humanities Press.

Rice, B. (1986, December). Dealing with difficult bosses. *U.S. Air,* 32–39.

Rice, B. (1988). Work or perk? *Psychology Today, 22*(11), 26, 28–29.

Rice, R. W. (1976). The esteem for least preferred co-worker (LPC) score: What does it measure? *Dissertation Abstracts International, 36B,* 5360–5361.

Rice, R. W. (1978a). Psychometric properties of the esteem for least preferred co-worker (LPC scale). *Academy of Management Review, 3,* 106–118.

Rice, R. W. (1978b). Construct validity of the least preferred co-worker score. *Psychology Bulletin, 85,* 1199–1237.

Rice, R. W. (1979). Reliability and validity of the LPC scale: A reply. *Academy of Management Review, 4,* 291–294.

Rice, R. W. (1981). Leader LPC and follower satisfaction: A review. *Organizational Behavior and Human Performance, 28,* 1–25.

Rice, R. W., Bender, L. R., & Vitters, A. G. (1980). Leader sex, follower attitudes toward women, and leadership effectiveness: A laboratory experiment. *Organizational Behavior and Human Performance, 25,* 46–78.

Rice, R. W., & Chemers, M. M. (1973). Predicting the emergence of leaders using Fiedler's contingency model of leadership effectiveness. *Journal of Applied Psychology, 57,* 281–287.

Rice, R. W., & Chemers, M. M. (1975). Personality and situational determinants of leaders' behavior. *Journal of Applied Psychology, 60,* 20–27.

Rice, R. W., Instone, D., & Adams, J. (1984). Leader sex, leader success, and leadership process: Two field studies. *Journal of Applied Psychology, 69,* 12–32.

Rice, R. W., & Kastenbaum, D. R. (1983). The contingency model of leadership: Some current issues. *Basic and Applied Social Psychology, 4,* 373–392.

Richard, J. E. (1959). *A president's experience with democratic management.* Occasional Paper No. 18. Chicago: University of Chicago, Industrial Relations Center.

Richards, G. L., & Inskeep, G. C. (1974, Spring). The middle manager—his continuing education and the business school. *Collegiate News and Views,* 5–7.

Richards, S. A., & Cuffee, J. U. (1972). Behavioral correlates of leadership effectiveness in interacting and counteracting groups. *Journal of Applied Psychology, 56,* 377–381.

Richards, S. A., & Jaffee, C. L. (1972). Blacks supervising whites: A study of interracial difficulties in working together in a simulation organization. *Journal of Applied Psychology, 56,* 234–240.

Richardson, F. L. W. (1961). *Talk, work, and action.* Ithaca, NY: Cornell University, New York State School of Industrial and Labor Relations.

Richardson, F. L. W., & Walker, C. R. (1948). *Human relations in an expanding company.* New Haven, CT: Yale University, Labor and Management Center.

Richardson, H. M. (1940). Communality of values as a factor in friendships of college and adult women. *Journal of Social Psychology, 11,* 303–312.

Richardson, H. M., & Hanawalt, N. G. (1943). Leadership as related to Bernreuter personality measures: I. College leadership in extracurricular activities. *Journal of Social Psychology, 17,* 237–249.

Richardson, H. M., & Hanawalt, N. G. (1944). Leadership as related to Bernreuter personality measures: III. Leadership among men in vocational and social activities. *Journal of Applied Psychology, 28,* 308–317.

Richardson, H. M., & Hanawalt, N. G. (1952). Leadership as related to the Bernreuter personality measures: V. Leadership among adult females in social activities. *Journal of Social Psychology, 36,* 141–153.

Richardson, J. T. (1969). Expertise, power, leadership and personal influence. An integration of theory and experimental evidence. *Dissertation Abstracts. 29,* 3221.

Richardson, J. T., Mayhew, B. H., & Gray, L. N. (1969). Differentiation, restraint, and the asymmetry of power. *Human Relations, 22,* 263–274.

Richardson, L. W., & Cook, J. A. (1980). *Classroom authority management of male and female university professors.* Paper, American Sociological Association, New York.

Richardson, R. (1971). *Fair pay and work.* London: Heinemann.

Richman, B. (1967). Capitalists and managers in Communist China. *Harvard Business Review, 45,* 57–71, 78.

Richman, B. M., & Farmer, R. N. (1974). *Leadership, goals, and power in higher education.* San Francisco: Jossey-Bass.

Richmond, A. H. (1954). Conflict and authority in industry. *Occupational Psychology, 28,* 24–33.

Richmond, V. P., & McCroskey, J. C. (1975). Whose opinion do you trust? *Journal of Communication, 25*(3), 42–50.

Riecken, H. W. (1952). Some problems of consensus development. *Rural Sociology, 17,* 245–252.

Riecken, H. W. (1953). Popularity and conformity to group norms. *American Psychologist, 8,* 420–421.

Riecken, H. W. (1958). The effect of talkativeness on ability to influence group solutions of problems. *Sociometry, 21,* 309–321.

Riedel, J. E. (1974). *A comparison of principal, teacher and student perceptions of selected elementary school principals' effectiveness.* Doctoral dissertation, University of Southern California, Los Angeles.

Riedesel, P. L. (1974). Bales reconsidered: A critical analysis of popularity and leadership differentiation. *Sociometry, 37,* 557–564.

Riegel, J. W. (1952). *Executive development: A survey of experience in fifty American corporations.* Ann Arbor: University of Michigan Press.

Riegel, J. W. (1955). *Employee interest in company success—how can it be stimulated and maintained?* Ann Arbor: University of Michigan, Bureau of Industrial Relations.

Riger, S., & Galligan, P. (1980). Women in management: An explanation of competing paradigms. *American Psychologist, 35,* 902–910.

Riggio, R. E. (1986). Assessment of basic social skills. *Journal of Personality and Social Psychology, 51,* 649–660.

Riggio, R. E., & Friedman, H. S. (1986). Impression formation: The role of expressive behavior. *Journal of Personality and Social Psychology, 50,* 421–427.

Riker, W. H. (1986). *Art of political manipulation.* New Haven, CT: Yale University Press.

Riley, M. W., & Cohn, R. (1958). Control networks in informal groups. *Sociometry, 21,* 30–49.

Riley, M. W., & Flowerman, S. H. (1951). Group relations as a variable in communications research. *American Sociological Review, 16,* 174–176.

Rim, Y. (1965). Leadership attitudes and decisions involving risk. *Personnel Psychology, 18,* 423–430.

Rim, Y. (1981). Childhood, values and means of influence in marriage. *International Review of Applied Psychology, 30,* 507–520.

Rim, Y., & Mannheim, B. F. (1964). Factors related to attitudes of management and union representatives. *Personnel Psychology, 17,* 149–165.

Ring, K. (1964). Some determinants of interpersonal attraction in hierarchical relationships: A motivational analysis. *Journal of Personnel, 32,* 651–665.

Ring, K., & Kelley, H. H. (1963). A comparison of augmentation and reduction as modes of influence. *Journal of Abnormal and Social Psychology, 66,* 95–102.

Rios, R. M. (1972). The comparative effects of tape-led and leaderless groups. *Dissertation Abstracts International, 32,* 6769.

Ritchie, J. B., & Miles, R. E. (1970). An analysis of quality and quality of participation as mediating variables in the participative decision making process. *Personnel Psychology, 23,* 347–359.

Ritchie, R. J., & Moses, J. L. (1983). Assessment center correlates of women's advancement into middle management: A 7-year longitudinal analysis. *Journal of Applied Psychology, 68,* 227–231.

Rittenhouse, C. H. (1968). *A follow-up study of NCO leaders school graduates.* Washington, DC: Human Resources Research Office.

Rittenhouse, J. D. (1966). Conformity behavior in sixth grade leaders. *Dissertation Abstracts, 26,* 6212.

Rizzo, J. R., House, R. J., & Lirtzman, S. I. (1970). Role conflict and ambiguity in complex organizations. *Administrative Science Quarterly, 15,* 150–163.

Roach, D. E. (1956). Factor analysis of rated supervisory behavior. *Personnel Psychology, 9,* 487–498.

Roach, J. M. (1976). *Recent initiatives in labor-management cooperation.* Houston, TX: National Center for Productivity and Quality of Working Life.

Roadman, H. E. (1964). An industrial use of peer ratings. *Journal of Applied Psychology, 48,* 211–214.

Robbins, S. P. (1983). The theory Z organization from a power-control perspective. *California Management Review, 25,* 67–75.

Roberts, A. H., & Jessor, R. (1958). Authoritarianism, punitiveness, and perceived social status. *Journal of Abnormal and Social Psychology, 56,* 311–314.

Roberts, B. B. (1969). The leader, group, and task variables of leader selection in college. *Dissertation Abstracts, 29,* 2360–2361.

Roberts, D. M. (1950). *Leadership in teen-age groups.* New York: Association Press.

Roberts, K. A. (1970). On looking at an elephant: An evaluation of cross-cultural research related to organizations. *Psychological Bulletin, 74,* 327–350.

Roberts, K. A., Blankenship, L. V., & Miles, R. E. (1968). Organizational leadership, satisfaction, and productivity. *Academy of Management Journal, 11,* 401–422.

Roberts, N., & King, P. (1988). Policy entrepreneurs: Catalysts for innovative public policy. *Proceedings, Academy of Management,* Anaheim, CA, 313–317.

Roberts, N. C. (1984). *Transforming leadership: Sources, processes, consequences.* Paper, Academy of Management, Boston.

Roberts, N. C. (1986). Organizational power styles: Collective and competitive power under varying organizational conditions. *Journal of Applied Behavioral Science, 22,* 443–458.

Roberts, N. C., & Bradley, R. T. (1987). *Limits to charisma.* Paper, Conference on Charisma, McGill University, Montreal.

Robie, E. A. (1973). Challenge to management. In E. Ginzberg & A. M. Yohalem (Eds.), *Corporate library: Women's challenge to management.* Baltimore: Johns Hopkins University Press.

Robins, A. R., Willemin, L. P., & Brueckel, J. E. (1954). Exploratory study of echelon differences in efficiency ratings. *American Psychologist, 9,* 457.

Robinson, D. D. (1970). Predicting police effectiveness from self reports of relative time spent in task performance. *Personnel Psychology, 23,* 327–345.

Robinson, H. A. (1954). Job satisfaction researches of 1953. *Personnel Guide Journal, 33,* 26–29.

Robinson, H. A., Conners, R. P., & Whitacre, G. H. (1966). Job satisfaction researches of 1964–65. *Personnel Guide Journal, 45,* 371–379.

Roby, T. B. (1952). The influence of subgroup relationships on the performance of group and subgroup tasks. *American Psychologist, 7,* 313–314.

Roby, T. B. (1953). *Relationships between sociometric measures and performance in medium-bomber crews* (Res. Bull. No. 53-18). San Antonio, TX: Lackland Air Force Base, Human Resources Research Center.

Roby, T. B. (1961). The executive function in small groups. In L. Petrullo & B. Bass (Eds.), *Leadership and interpersonal behavior.* New York: Holt, Reinhart & Winston.

Roby, T. B. (1968). *Small group performance.* Chicago: Rand McNally.

Roby, T. B., & Forgays, D. G. (1953). *A problem solving model of communication in B-29 crews* (Tech. Rep. No. 53-32). San Antonio, TX: Lackland Air Force Base, Human Resources Research Center.

Roby, T. B., & Lanzetta, J. T. (1958). Considerations in the analysis of group tasks. *Psychological Bulletin, 55,* 88–101.

Roby, T. B., Nicol, E. H., & Farrell, F. M. (1963). Group problem solving under two types of executive structure. *Journal of Abnormal and Social Psychology, 67,* 550–556.

Roche, G. R. (1979). Much ado about mentors. *Harvard Business Review, 57*(1), 17–28.

Rock, M. L., & Hay, E. N. (1953). Investigation of the use of tests as a predictor of leadership and group effectiveness in a job evaluation situation. *Journal of Social Psychology, 38,* 109–119.

Rockman, B. A. (1984). *The leadership question: The presidency and the American system.* New York: Praeger.

Roe, A. (1956). *The psychology of occupations.* New York: Wiley.

Roethlisberger, F. J. (1941). *Management and morale.* Cambridge, MA: Harvard University Press.

Roethlisberger, F. J. (1945). The foreman: Master and victim of double talk. *Harvard Business Review, 23,* 283–298.

Roethlisberger, F. J. (1954). The territory and skill of the administrator. In L. Sayles (Ed.), *Addresses on industrial relations, 1954 series.* Bulletin No. 22. Ann Arbor: University of Michigan, Bureau of Industrial Relations.

Roethlisberger, F. J., & Dickson, W. J. (1947). *Management and the worker.* Cambridge, MA: Harvard University Press.

Roethlisberger, F. J., Lombard, G. F. F., & Renken, H. O. (1954). *Training for human relations: An interim report.* Boston: Harvard University, Graduate School of Business Administration.

Roff, M. (1950). A study of combat leadership in the air force by means of a rating scale: Group differences. *Journal of Psychology, 30,* 229–239.

Rogers, C. R. (1951). *Client-centered therapy.* Boston: Houghton Mifflin.

Rogers, M. S., Ford, J. D., & Tassone, J. A. (1961). The effects of personnel replacement on an information-processing crew. *Journal of Applied Psychology, 45,* 91–96.

Rogers, R. E. (1977). Components of organizational stress among Canadian managers. *Journal of Psychology, 95,* 265–273.

Rohde, K. J. (1951). *Dominance composition as a factor in the behavior of small leaderless groups.* Doctoral dissertation, Northwest University, Evanston, IL.

Rohde, K. J. (1952). The relation of authoritarianism of the aircrew member to his acceptance by the airplane commander. *American Psychologist, 7,* 310–311.

Rohde, K. J. (1954a). *Individual executive ability as a factor in the performance of small groups* (Tech. Rep. No. 17). Columbus: Ohio State University, Personnel Research Board.

Rohde, K. J. (1954b). *Variations in group composition with respect to individual task ability as a factor in group behavior* (Tech. Rep. No. 18). Columbus: Ohio State University, Personnel Research Board.

Rohde, K. J. (1954c). An evaluation of the extent to which task ability of the man in charge of a group is determinative of that group's success in performing the task. *American Psychologist, 9,* 569 (Abstract).

Rohde, K. J. (1958). Theoretical and experimental analysis of leadership ability. *Psychological Reports, 4,* 243–278.

Rojas, L. (1982). *Salient mainstream and Hispanic values in a Navy training environment: An anthropological description* (ONR Tech. Rep. No. 22). Champaign: University of Illinois, Department of Psychology.

Rokeach, M. (1971). Long-range experimental modification of values, attitudes and behavior. *American Psychologist, 26,* 453–459.

Rokeach, M. (1972). A theory of organization and change within value-attitude systems. In G. D. Paige (Ed.), *Political leadership: Readings for an emerging field.* New York: Free Press.

Roman, D. D. (1986). *Managing projects: A systems approach.* New York: Elsevier.

Romanelli, E., & Tushman, M. L. (1983). *Executive leadership and orga-*

nizational outcomes: An evolutionary perspective (Rep. No. 130). New York: Columbia University, Center for Career Research and Human Resources Management.

Ronan, W. W. (1970). Individual and situational variables relating to job satisfaction. *Journal of Applied Psychology, 54,* 1–31.

Ronan, W. W., Latham, G. P., & Kinne, S. B. (1973). Effects of goal setting and supervision of worker behavior in an industrial situation. *Journal of Applied Psychology, 58,* 302–307.

Ronen, S. (1986). *Comparative and multinational management.* New York: Wiley.

Ronen, S., & Kraut, A. I. (1977). Similarities among countries based on employee work values and attitudes. *Columbia Journal of World Business, 12,* 89–96.

Ronen, S., & Shenkar, O. (1985). Clustering countries on attitudinal dimensions: A review and synthesis. *Academy of Management Review, 10,* 435–454.

Ronken, H. O., & Lawrence, P. R. (1952). *Administering changes.* Boston: Harvard University, Graduate School of Business Administration.

Rooker, J. L. (1967). The relationship of need achievement and need affiliation to leader behavior. *Dissertation Abstracts, 28,* 4426.

Rosch, E. (1975). Cognitive representations of semantic categories. *Journal of Experimental Psychology, 104,* 192–233.

Rose, A. M. (1962). Alienation and participation: A comparison of group leaders and the "Mass." *American Sociological Review, 27,* 834–838.

Rose, A. M. (1968). The ecological influential: A leadership type. *Sociology and Social Research, 52,* 185–192.

Rose, E. (1982). The anatomy of mutiny. *Armed Forces and Society, 11,* 561–574.

Rose, R. (1963). The emergence of leaders. *New Society, 2(5),* 12–13.

Rose, S. O. (1980). *Betwixt and between: Women and the exercise of power in middle management positions.* Paper, Eastern Sociological Society, Philadelphia.

Roseborough, M. E. (1953). Experimental studies of small groups. *Psychological Bulletin, 50,* 275–303.

Rosen, B., & Jerdee, T. H. (1973). The influence of sex-role stereotypes on evaluations of male and female supervisory behavior. *Journal of Applied Psychology, 57,* 44–48.

Rosen, B., & Jerdee, T. H. (1974). Influence of sex role stereotypes on personnel decisions. *Journal of Applied Psychology, 59,* 9–14.

Rosen, B., & Jerdee, T. H. (1977). Influence of subordinate characteristics on trust and use of participative decision strategies in a management simulation. *Journal of Applied Psychology, 62,* 628–631.

Rosen, B., & Jerdee, T. H. (1978). Effects of decision permanence on managerial willingness to use participation. *Academic Management Journal, 21,* 722–725.

Rosen, B., Jerdee, T. H., & Prestwich, T. L. (1975). Dual career mutual adjustment: Potential effects of discriminatory managerial attitudes. *Journal of Marriage and the Family, 37,* 565–572.

Rosen, B., Templeton, M. E., & Kirchline, K. (1981). First few years on the job: Women in management. *Business Horizons, 24,* 26–29.

Rosen, C. M., Klein, C. J., & Young, K. (1986). *Employee ownership in America: The equity solution.* Lexington, MA: D. C. Heath.

Rosen, H. (1961a). Managerial role interaction: A study of three managerial levels. *Journal of Applied Psychology, 45,* 30–34.

Rosen, H. (1961b). Desirable attributes of work: Four levels of management describe their job environments. *Journal of Applied Psychology, 45,* 156–160.

Rosen, H., & Rosen, R. A. H. (1955). *The union member speaks.* New York: Prentice-Hall.

Rosen, H., & Weaver, C. G. (1960). Motivation in management: A study of four managerial levels. *Journal of Applied Psychology, 44,* 386–392.

Rosen, M. (1985). Breakfast at Spiro's: Dramaturgy and dominance. *Journal of Management, 11(2),* 31–48.

Rosen, N., Greenhalgh, L., & Anderson, J. C. (undated). *The cognitive structure of industrial/labor relationships.* Unpublished manuscript.

Rosen, N. A. (1961). How supervise?—1943–1960. *Personnel Psychology, 14,* 87–100.

Rosen, N. A. (1969). *Leadership change and work-group dynamics.* Ithaca, NY: Cornell University Press.

Rosen, N. A. (1970a). Open systems theory in an organizational subsystem: A field experiment. *Organizational Behavior and Human Performance, 5,* 245–265.

Rosen, N. A. (1970b). Demand characteristics in a field experiment. *Journal of Applied Psychology, 54,* 163–168.

Rosen, N. A., Georgiades, N. J., & McDonald, G. (1980). An empirical test of a leadership contingency model for teaching behavioral science concepts to managers. *Journal of Occupational Psychology, 53,* 1–10.

Rosen, S. (1954). Some effects of previous patterns of aggression on interpersonal relations in new groups. *American Psychologist, 9,* 459 (Abstract).

Rosen, S., Levinger, G., & Lippitt, R. (1961). Perceived sources of social power. *Journal of Abnormal and Social Psychology, 62,* 439–441.

Rosenbach, W. E., & Mueller, R. (1988). *Transformational and transactional leadership effectiveness.* Paper, International Congress of Psychology, Sydney, Australia.

Rosenbaum, D. E. (1988, November 9). Democrats keep solid hold on Congress. *New York Times,* A24.

Rosenbaum, L. L., & Rosenbaum, W. B. (1971). Morale and productivity consequences of group leadership style, stress, and type of task. *Journal of Applied Psychology, 55,* 343–348.

Rosenbaum, M. E. (1959). Social perception and the motivational structure of interpersonal relations. *Journal of Abnormal and Social Psychology, 59,* 130–133.

Rosenberg, M. (1956). Misanthropy and political ideology. *American Sociological Review, 21,* 690–695.

Rosenberg, M., & Pearlin, L. I. (1962). Power-orientations in the mental hospital. *Human Relations, 15,* 335–350.

Rosenberg, R. D. (1977). *A dual process model of worker participation at* the blue-collar level. Doctoral dissertation, Technion-Israel Institute of Technology, Haifa.

Rosenberg, S., Erlick, D. E., & Berkowitz, L. (1955). Some effects of varying combinations of group members on group performance measures and leadership behaviors. *Journal of Abnormal and Social Psychology, 51,* 195–203.

Rosener, L., and Schwartz, P. (1980). Women, leadership and the 1980's: What kind of leaders do we have? In *New leadership in the public interest.* New York: NOW Legal Defense and Education Fund.

Rosenfeld, E. (1951). Social stratification in a "classless" society. *American Sociological Review, 16,* 766–774.

Rosenfeld, J. M., & Smith, M. J. (1967). Participative management: An overview. *Personnel Journal, 46,* 101–104.

Rosenfeld, L. B., & Fowler, G. D. (1976). Personality, sex, and leadership style. *Communications Monographs, 43,* 320–324.

Rosenman, R. H., & Friedman, M. (1971). The central nervous system and coronary heart disease. *Hospital Practice, 6,* 87–97.

Rosenman, R. H., & Freidman, M. (1974). Neurogenic factors in pathogenesis of coronary heart disease. *Medical Clinics of North America, 58,* 269–279.

Rosenstein, E. (1970). Histadrut's search for a participation program. *Industrial Relations, 9,* 170–186.

Rosenstein, E. (1976). *Workers' participation in management: Problematic issues in the Israeli system.* Binghamton: State University of New York, Systems Research Working Paper.

Rosenstein, E. (1977). Workers' participation in management: Problematic issues in the Israeli system. *Industrial Relations Journal, 8,* 55–69.

Rosenstein, E. (1985). Cooperativeness and advancement of managers: An international perspective. *Human Relations, 38,* 1–22.

Rosenthal, A. (1974). *Legislative performance in the states: Explorations in committee behavior.* New York: Free Press.

Rosenthal, D., & Frank, J. D. (1956). Psychotherapy and the placebo effect. *Psychological Bulletin, 53,* 294–302.

Rosenthal, R. (1978). Combining results of independent studies. *Psychological Bulletin, 85,* 185–193.

Rosenthal R. (1979a). The "file-drawer" problem and tolerance for null results. *Psychological Bulletin, 86,* 638–641.

Rosenthal, R. (Ed.). (1979b). *Skill in nonverbal communication.* Cambridge, MA: Oelgeschlager, Gunn, & Hain.

Rosenthal, R., Hall, J. A., DiMatteo, M. R., Rogers, P. L., & Archer, D. (1979). *Sensitivity to nonverbal communication: The PONS test.* Baltimore: Johns Hopkins University Press.

Rosenthal, R., & Jacobson, L. (1968). *Pygmalion in the classroom: Teacher expectation and pupils' intellectual development.* New York: Holt, Rinehart & Winston.

Rosenthal, R., & Rubin, D. B. (1982). Further meta-analytic procedures for assessing cognitive gender differences. *Journal of Educational Psychology, 74,* 708–712.

Roskens, R. W. (1958). The relationship between leadership participation in college and after college. *Dissertation Abstracts, 19,* 473.

Roskin, R., & Margerison, C. (1983). The effectiveness of some measures of managerial effectiveness. *Human Relations, 36,* 865–882.

Roslow, S. (1940). Nation-wide and local validation of the P.Q. or Personality Quotient Test. *Journal of Applied Psychology, 24,* 529–539.

Ross, I. C., & Zander, A. (1957). Need satisfaction and employee turnover. *Personnel Psychology, 10,* 327–338.

Ross, J. D., Davidson, S., & Graham, W. K. (1986). *Sex differences in pre and mid-management assessment center performance.* Paper, Academy of Management, San Diego, CA.

Ross, M. G., & Hendry, C. E. (1957). *New understandings of leadership.* New York: Association Press.

Ross, R. B. (1982). Emergency planning paid off. *Security Management, 26*(9), 62–65.

Ross, R. R., & Gendreau, P. (1980). *Effective correctional treatment.* New York: Butterworth.

Ross, W., Triandis, H. C., Chang, B., & Marin, G. (1982). *Work values of Hispanics and mainstream Navy recruits* (ONR Tech. Rep. No. 8). Champaign: University of Illinois.

Rosse, J. G., & Kraut, A. I (1983). Reconsidering the vertical dyad linkage model of leadership. *Journal of Occupational Psychology, 56,* 63–71.

Rossel, R. D. (1970). Instrumental and expressive leadership in complex organizations. *Administrative Science Quarterly, 15,* 306–316.

Rossing, B. E., & Heasley, D. K. (1987). Enhancing public affairs participation through leadership development education: Key questions for community development research and practice. *Journal of the Community Development Society, 18* (2), 98–116.

Rothbart, M. (1968). Effects of motivation, equity, and compliance on the use of reward and punishment. *Journal of Personality and Social Psychology, 8,* 143–147.

Rothe, H. F. (1946). Output rates among butter wrappers: II. *Journal of Applied Psychology, 30,* 320–327.

Rothe, H. F. (1947). Output rates among machine operators: I. Distributions and their reliability. *Journal of Applied Psychology, 31,* 484–489.

Rothe, H. F. (1949). The relation of merit ratings to length of service. *Personnel Psychology, 2,* 237–242.

Rothe, H. F. (1960). Does higher pay bring higher productivity? *Personnel, 37,* 20–38.

Rothe, H. F. (1961). Output rates among machine operators: III. A non-incentive situation in two levels of business activity. *Journal of Applied Psychology, 45,* 50–54.

Rothe, H. F., & Nye, C. T. (1958). Output rates among coil winders. *Journal of Applied Psychology, 42,* 182–186.

Rothe, H. F., & Nye, C. T. (1959). Output rates among machine operators: II. Consistency related to methods of pay. *Journal of Applied Psychology, 43,* 417–420.

Rothman, R. A., & Perrucci, R. (1970). Organizational careers and professional expertise. *Administrative Science Quarterly, 15,* 282–293.

Rothwell, R., Freeman, C., Horsley, A., Jervis, V. T. P., Robertson, A. B., & Townsend, J. (1974). SAPPHO updated—Project SAPPHO phase II. *Research Policy, 3,* 258–291.

Rotter, J. B. (1966). Generalized expectancies for internal versus external control of reinforcement. *Psychological Monographs, 80,* No. 609.

Roucek, J. S. (1934). The social value of women's club work. *Sociology and Social Research, 18,* 453–461.

Roussel, C. (1974). Relationship of sex of department head to department climate. *Administrative Science Quarterly, 19,* 211–220.

Rowland, K. M., & Scott, W. E. (1968). Psychological attributes of effective leadership in a formal organization, *Personnel Psychology, 21,* 365–377.

Rowney, J. I. A., & Cahoon, A. R. (1988). *A preliminary investigation of burnout dimensions in intact work groups.* Paper, International Congress of Psychology, Sydney, Australia.

Roy, N. K., Jaiswal, N. K., & Shankar, J. (1974). Socio-economic characteristics of leaders and followers in a rural society. *Social Culture, 5,* 43–48.

Rubenowitz, S. (1962). Job-oriented and person-oriented leadership. *Personnel Psychology, 15,* 387–396.

Rubenowitz, S., & Norrgren, F. (1980). The effectiveness of participation in ten Swedish plants. *Department of Applied Psychology,* University of Göteborg, 4(1).

Rubin, B. D., Askling, L. R. & Kealy, D. J. (1977). Cross-cultural effectiveness: An overview. In D. S. Hoopes (Ed.), *Intercultural communications: State of the art overview.* Pittsburgh: Sietar.

Rubin, G. J. (1972). A modified contingency model for leadership effectiveness. *Dissertation Abstracts International, 32,* 6710–6711.

Rubin, I. M., & Berlew, D. E. (1984). The power failure in organizations. *Training & Development Journal, 38(1),* 35–38.

Rubin, I. M., & Goldman, M. (1968). An open system model of leadership performance. *Organizational Behavior and Human Performance, 3,* 143–156.

Rubin, J. Z., Lewicki, R. J., & Dunn, L. (1973). *The perception of promisors and threateners.* Paper, American Psychological Association, Montreal.

Ruch, F. L. (1953). *Bibliography on military leadership.* Los Angeles: Psychological Services.

Ruderman, M. N., Ohlott, P. J., & McCauley, C. D. (1989). *Assessing opportunities for leadership development.* In K. E. Clark & M. B. Clark (Eds.), *Measures of leadership.* West Orange, NJ: Leadership Library of America.

Rudin, S. A. (1964). Leadership as a psychophysiological activation of group members: A case experimental study. *Psychological Reports, 15,* 577–578.

Rudin, S. A., et al. (1952). *Some empirical studies of the reliability of social perception scores.* Urbana: University of Illinois.

Rudraswamy, V. (1964). An investigation of the relationships between perceptions of status and leadership attempts. *Journal of Indian Academy of Applied Psychology, 1,* 12–19.

Ruhe, J. A. (1972). *The effects of varying racial compositions upon attitudes and behaviors of supervisors and subordinates in simulated work groups.* Doctoral dissertation, University of Florida, Gainsville.

Ruiz de Gauna, R. (1988). *El liderazgo en Bernard M. Bass: Su analisis, componentes y aplicacion.* Doctoral dissertation, Universidad de Deusto, Bilbao, Spain.

Runyon, K. E. (1973). Some interactions between personality variables and management styles. *Journal of Applied Psychology, 57,* 228–294.

Rupe, J. C. (1951). When workers rate the boss. *Personnel Psychology, 4,* 271–290.

Rus, V. (1970). Influence structure in Yugoslav enterprise. *Industrial Relations, 9,* 149–160.

Rush, C. H., Jr. (undated). Group dimensions of air crews. Columbus: Ohio State University, Personnel Research Board.

Rush, C. H. (1957). Leader behavior and group characteristics. In R. M. Stogdill & A. E. Coons (Eds.), *Leader behavior: Its description and measurement.* Columbus: Ohio State University, Bureau of Business Research.

Rush, M. C., Thomas, J. C., & Lord, R. G. (1977). Implicit leadership theory: A potential threat to the internal validity of leader behavior questionnaires. *Organizational Behavior and Human Performance, 20,* 93–110.

Rushlau, P. J., & Jorgensen, G. Q. (1966). *Interpersonal relationships: A review.* Salt Lake City: University of Utah, Regional Rehabilitation Research Institute.

Rusmore, J., & Baker, H. (1987). *Executive performance in four organizational levels and two kinds of intellectual ability.* Paper, Society for Industrial and Organizational Psychology, Atlanta, GA.

Rusmore, J. T. (1961). Use of the executive position description questionnaire in a study of managers in the Pacific Telephone and Telegraph Company. *Proceedings, Conference on the Executive Study,* Princeton, NJ.

Rusmore, J. T. (1984). *Executive performance and intellectual ability in organizational levels.* San Jose, CA: San Jose State University, Advanced Human Systems Institution.

Russell, B. (1938). *Power.* London: Allen & Unwin.

Russell, C. J., Mattson, J., Devlin, S. E., & Atwater, D. (1986). *Predictive validity of biodata items generated from retrospective life experience essays.* Paper, Society for Industrial and Organizational Psychology, Chicago.

Russell, P. A., Lankford, M. W., & Grinnell, R. M., Jr. (1984). Administrative styles of social work supervisors in a human service agency. *Administration in Social Work, 8(1),* 1–16.

Russell, P. W., Jr. (1978). *The selection of managers for overseas corporate assignments.* Doctoral dissertation, Colorado State University, Fort Collins.

Russell, P. W., Jr., & Dickinson, T. L. (1978). *Factors affecting overseas success in industry.* Paper, Society for Intercultural Education, Training and Research, Phoenix, AZ.

Rutonno, M., & McGoldrick, M. (1982). Italian families. In M. McGoldrick, J. K. Pearce, & J. Giordano (Eds.), *Ethnicity and family therapy.* New York: Guilford Press.

Ryapolov, G. (1966). I was a Soviet manager. *Harvard Business Review, 44(1),* 117–125.

Rychlak, J. F. (1963). Personality correlates of leadership among first level managers. *Psychological Reports, 12,* 43–52.

Ryterband, E. C., & Barrett, G. V. (1970). Managers' values and their relationship to the management of tasks: A cross-cultural comparison. In B. M. Bass, R. C. Cooper, & J. A. Haas (Eds.), *Managing for accomplishment.* Lexington, MA: D. C. Heath.

Ryterband, E. C., & Thiagarajan, K. M. (1968). *Managerial attitudes toward salaries as a function of social and economic development* (Tech. Rep. No. 24). Rochester, NY: University of Rochester, Management Research Center.

Sabath, G. (1964). The effect of disruption and individual status on person perception and group attraction. *Journal of Social Psychology, 64,* 119-130.

Sackett, P. R., & Dreher, G. F. (1982). Constructs and assessment center dimensions: Some troubling empirical findings. *Journal of Applied Psychology, 67,* 401-410.

Sackett, P. R., & Hakel, M. D. (1979). Temporal stability and individual differences in using assessment information to form over-all ratings. *Organizational Behavior and Human Performance, 23,* 120-137.

Sadler, P. J. (1970). Leadership style, confidence in management, and job satisfaction. *Journal of Applied Behavioral Science, 6,* 3-19.

Sadler, P. J., & Hofstede, G. H. (1972). Leadership styles: Preferences and perceptions of employees of an international company in different countries. *Mens en Onderneming, 26,* 43-63.

Safire, W. (1975). *Before the fall: An inside view of the pre-Watergate White House.* New York: Doubleday.

Sager, D. J. (1982). *Participatory management in libraries.* Metuchen, NJ: Scarecrow Press.

Sakamaki, Y. (1974). The effects of the factors of group structure and the degree of group members' perceptions of leadership functions. *Japanese Journal of Experimental Social Psychology, 14,* 139-146.

Sakano, N. (1983). Leadership styles: Japanese school administrators and Japanese corporate managers. *Dissertation Abstracts International, 45*(1A), 77.

Sakoda, J. M. (1952). Factor analysis of OSS situational tests. *Journal of Abnormal and Social Psychology, 47,* 843-852.

Salaman, G. (1977). A historical discontinuity: From charisma to routinization. *Human Relations, 30,* 373-388.

Salancik, G. R., Calder, B. J., Rowland, K. M., Leblebici, H., & Conway, M. (1975). Leadership as an outcome of social structure and process: A multidimensional analysis. In J. G. Hunt & L. L. Larson (Eds.), *Leadership frontiers.* Carbondale: Southern Illinois University Press.

Salancik, G. R., & Meindl, J. R. (1984). Corporate attributions as strategic illusions of management control. *Administrative Science Quarterly, 29,* 238-254.

Salancik, G. R., & Pfeffer, J. (1974). The bases and use of power in organizational decision making: The case of a university. *Administrative Science Quarterly, 19,* 453-473.

Salancik, G. R., & Pfeffer, J. (1977). Constraints on administrator discretion: The limited influence of mayors on city budgets. *Urban Affairs Quarterly, 12,* 475-498.

Salancik, G. R., & Pfeffer, J. (1980). Effects of ownership and performance on executive tenure in U.S. corporations. *Academy of Management Journal, 23,* 653-664.

Salancik, G. R., Pfeffer, J., & Kelly, J. P. (1978). A contingency model of influence in organizational decision making. *Pacific Sociological Review, 21,* 239-256.

Salancik, G. R., Staw, B. M., & Pondy, L. R. (1980). Administrative turnover as a response to unmanaged organizational independence. *Academy of Management Journal, 10,* 422-437.

Saleh, S. D., & Otis, J. L (1964). Age level and job satisfaction. *Personnel Psychology, 17,* 425-430.

Saleh, S. D., Prien, E. P., Otis, J. L., & Campbell, J. T. (1964). The relation of job attitudes, organization performance, and job level. *Journal of Industrial Psychology, 2,* 59-65.

Sales, C. A., Levanoni, E., & Saleh, S. D. (1984). Satisfaction and stress as a function of job orientation, style of supervision and the nature of the task. *Engineering Mangement International, 2,* 145-153.

Sales, S. M. (1964). *A laboratory investigation of the effectiveness of two industrial supervisory dimensions.* Master's thesis, Cornell University, Ithaca, NY.

Sales, S. M. (1966). Supervisory style and productivity: Review and theory. *Personnel Psychology, 19,* 275-286.

Sales, S. M. (1972). Authoritarianism: But as for me, give me liberty, or give me a big, strong leader I can honor, admire, respect and obey. *Psychology Today, 8,* 94, 143.

Salipante, P., & Goodman, P. (1976). Training, counselling and retention of the hard-core unemployed. *Journal of Applied Psychology, 61,* 1-11.

Salmons, S. (1977). Africans get a taste for the top. *International Management, 32,* 39-41.

Salter, J. T. (1935). *Boss rule: Portraits in city politics.* New York: McGraw-Hill.

Samelson, F. (1986). Authoritarianism from Berlin to Berkeley: On social psychology and history. *Journal of Social Issues, 42,* 191-208.

Sample, J. A., & Wilson, T. R. (1965). Leader behavior, group productivity, and rating of least preferred co-worker. *Journal of Personality and Social Psychology, 1,* 266-270.

Sampson, E. E. (1964). *Approaches, contexts, and problems: A book of readings of social psychology.* Englewood Cliffs, NJ: Prentice-Hall.

Sampson, E. E., & Brandon, A. C. (1964). The effects of role opinion deviation on small group behavior. *Sociometry, 27,* 261-281.

Sampson, R. V. (1968). *The psychology of power.* New York: Random House.

Sanders, E. P. (1968). Evolutionary performance, managerial abilities, and change: An explanatory investigation of organizations. *Journal of Applied Psychology, 52,* 362-365.

Sanders, G. S., & Malkis, F. S. (1982). Type A behavior, need for control, and reactions to group participation. *Organizational Behavior and Human Performance, 30,* 71-86.

Sanderson, D., & Nafe, R. W. (1929). Studies in rural leadership. *American Sociological Review, 23,* 163-175.

Sandler, B. E., & Scalia, F. A. (1975). The relationship between birth order, sex, and leadership in a religious organization. *Journal of Social Psychology, 95*, 279–280.

Sanford, F. H. (1950). *Authoritarianism and leadership: A study of the follower's orientation to authority*. Philadelphia, PA: Institute for Research in Human Relations.

Sanford, F. H. (1951). Leadership identification and acceptance. In H. Guetzkow (Ed.), *Groups, leadership, and men*. Pittsburgh: Carnegie Press.

Sanford, N. (1986). A personal account of the study of authoritarianism: Comment on Samelson. *Journal of Social Issues, 42*, 209–214.

Santee, R. T., & Vanderpol, T. L. (1976). Actors status and conformity to norms—Study of student evaluations of instructors. *Sociological Quarterly, 17*, 378–388.

Santner, B. (1986). *The relationship of dominance, friendliness, task orientation, achievement motivation, intelligence, gender, and race to high school student leadership*. Doctoral dissertation, Fordham University, New York.

Sarachek, B. (1968). Greek concepts of leadership. *Academy of Management Journal, 11*, 39–48.

Sarbin, T. R., & Jones, D. S. (1955). The assessment of role-expectations in the selection of supervisory personnel. *Educational and Psychological Measurement, 15*, 236–239.

Sargent, J. F., & Miller, G. R. (1971). Some differences in certain communication behaviors of autocratic and democratic leaders. *Journal of Communication, 21*, 233–252.

Saris, R. J. (1969). *The development of a 13th subscale to the Leader Behavior Description Questionnaire—Form XII entitled "Responsibility Deference."* Doctoral dissertation, University of Idaho, Moscow.

Sarkesian, S. C. (1985). Leadership and management revisited. *Bureaucrat, 14*(1), 20–24.

Sasaki, K., & Yamaguchi, M. (1971). An experimental study of the effect of leadership on the formation of group norms. *Bulletin of the Faculty of Sociology, Kansai Gakuin University, 22*, 209–226. (Cited in Misumi, 1985.)

Sashkin, M. A. (undated). *A new approach to understanding and creating organizational excellence*. Unpublished manuscript.

Sashkin, M. (1972). Leadership style and group decision effectiveness: Correlational and behavioral tests of Fiedler's contingency model. *Organizational Behavioral and Human Performance, 8*, 347–362.

Sashkin, M. (1986). The visionary leader. *Training & Development Journal, 40*(5), 58–61.

Sashkin, M. (1988). The visionary leader. In J. A. Conger and R. N. Kanungo (Eds.), *Charismatic leadership: The elusive factor in organizational effectiveness*. San Francisco: Jossey-Bass.

Sashkin, M., & Burke, W. W. (1989). *Understanding and assessing organizational leadership*. In K. E. Clark & M. B. Clark (Eds.), *Measures of leadership*. West Orange, NJ: Leadership Library of America.

Sashkin, M., & Fulmer, R. M. (1985). *Toward an organizational leadership theory*. Paper, Biennial Leadership Symposium, Texas Tech University, Lubbock, TX.

Sashkin, M., & Fulmer, R. M. (1988). Toward an organizational leader-

ship theory. In J. G. Hunt, B. R. Baliga, H. P. Dachler, & C. A. Schriesheim (Eds.), *Emerging leadership vistas*. Lexington, MA: Lexington Books, D. C. Heath.

Sashkin, M., & Huddle, G. (1988). The principal's leadership role in creating effective schools. In J. G. Hunt (Ed.), *Emerging leadership vistas*. Lexington, MA: Lexington Books, D. C. Heath.

Sashkin, M., Taylor, F. C., & Tripathi, R. C. (1974). An analysis of situational moderating effects on the relationships between least preferred co-worker and other psychological measures. *Journal of Applied Psychology, 59*, 731–740.

Sato, S., Kugihara, N., Misumi, J., & Shigeoka, K. (1984). Experimental study of escape behavior in a simulated panic situation: III. Effect of the PM leadership conditions. *Japanese Journal of Experimental Social Psychology, 24*, 83–91.

Sattler, J. M. (1970). Racial "experimenter effects" in experimentation, testing, interviewing, and psychotherapy. *Psychological Bulletin, 73*, 137–160.

Saunders, C. S., & Scamell, R. (1982). Intraorganizational distributions of power: Replication research. *Academcy of Management Journal, 25*, 192–200.

Saunders, J., Davis, J., & Monsees, D. M. (1974). Opinion leadership in family planning. *Journal of Health and Social Behavior, 15*, 217–227.

Savan, M. (1983). The effects of a leadership training program on supervisory learning and performance. *Dissertation Abstracts International, 45*(4A), 1193.

Savery, L. K., & Swain, P. S. (1985). Leadership style: Differences between expatriates and locals. *Leaderhip and Organizational Development Journal, 6*(4), 8–11.

Saville, P. (1984). Occupational personality questionnaires. *Personnel Management, 16*(2), 47.

Sawyer, J. (1966). Management *and* prediction, clinical *and* statistical. *Psychological Bulletin*, 178–200.

Sayles, L. R. (1958). *Behavior of industrial work groups*. New York: Wiley.

Sayles, L. R. (1963). *Individualism and big business*. New York: McGraw-Hill.

Sayles, L. R. (1964). *Managerial behavior: Administration in complex organizations*. New York: McGraw-Hill.

Sayles, L. (1979). *Leadership: What effective managers really do . . . and how they do it*. New York: McGraw-Hill.

Scandura, T. A., & Graen, G. (1984). Moderating effects of initial leader-member exchange status on the effects of a leadership intervention. *Journal of Applied Psychology, 69*, 428–436.

Scandura, T. A., Graen, G. B., & Novak, M. A. (1986). When managers decide not to decide autocratically: An investigation of leader-member exchange and decision influence. *Journal of Applied Psychology, 71*, 579–584.

Schachter, S. (1951). Deviation, rejection, and communication. *Journal of Abnormal and Social Psychology, 46*, 190–207.

Schachter, S., Ellerston, N., McBride, D., & Gregory, D. (1951). An experimental study of cohesiveness and productivity. *Human Relations, 4*, 229–238.

Schachter, S., Willerman, B., Festinger, L., & Hyman, R. (1961). Emotional disruption and industrial productivity. *Journal of Applied Psychology, 45*, 201–213.

Schanck, R. L. (1932). A study of a community and its group and institutions conceived of behavior of individuals. *Psychological Monographs, 43*, No. 2.

Schatzberg, M. G. (1982). Le mal Zairois: Why policy fails in Zaire. *African Affairs, 81*, 337–348.

Scheffler, I., & Winslow, C. N. (1950). Group position and attitude toward authority. *Journal of Social Psychology, 32*, 177–190.

Scheidlinger, S. (1980). The psychology of leadership revisited: An overview. *Group, the Journal of the Eastern Group Psychotherapy Society, 4*, 1–17.

Schein, E. H. (1967) Attitude change during management education. *Administrative Science Quarterly, 11*, 601–628.

Schein, E. H. (1983). The role of the founder in creating organizational culture. *Organizational Dynamics, 12*, 13–28.

Schein, E. H. (1985). *Organizational culture and leadership: A dynamic view.* San Francisco: Jossey-Bass.

Schein, E. H., & Bennis, W. G. (1965). *Personal and organizational change through group methods.* New York: Wiley.

Schein, E. H., & Lippitt, G. L. (1966). Supervisory attitudes toward the legitimacy of influencing subordinates. *Journal of Applied Behavioral Science, 2*, 199–209.

Schein, E. H., & Ott, J. S. (1962). The legitimacy of organizational influence. *American Journal of Sociology, 67*, 682–689.

Schein, V. E. (1973). The relationship between sex role stereotypes and requisite management characteristics. *Journal of Applied Psychology, 57*, 95–100.

Schein, V. E. (1975). Relationship between sex role stereotypes and requisite management characteristics among female managers. *Journal of Applied Psychology, 60*, 340–344.

Schell, H. (1951). *Technique of administration: Administrative proficiency in business.* New York: McGraw-Hill.

Schendel, D. G., Patton, G. R., & Riggs, J. (1976). Corporate turnaround strategies: A study of profit decline and recovery. *Journal of General Management, 3*, 3–11.

Schenk, C. (1928). Leadership. *Infantry Journal, 33*, 111–122.

Schere, J. L. (1981). Tolerance of ambiguity as a discriminating variable between entrepreneurs and managers. *Proceedings, Academy of Management,* San Diego, CA, 404–408.

Schick, G. J., & Kunnecke, B. F. (1982). Do high grades, top schools, or an advanced degree lead to job security and extraordinary salary progression? *Interfaces, 12*(1), 9–18.

Schiff, H. (1954). Judgmental response sets in the perception of sociometric status. *Sociometry, 17*, 207–227.

Schiffer, I. (1973). *A psychoanalytic look at mass society.* Toronto: University of Toronto Press.

Schiffer, I. (1983). *Charisma: A psychoanalytic look at mass society.* Toronto: University of Toronto Press.

Schiffman, L. G., & Gaccione, V. (1974). Opinion leaders in institutional markets. *Journal of Marketing, 38*, 49–53.

Schilit, W. K. (1987). Upward influence activity in strategic decision making: An examination of organizational differences. *Group & Organization Studies, 12*, 343–368.

Schilit, W. K., & Locke, E. A. (1982). A study of upward influence in organizations. *Administrative Science Quarterly, 27*, 304–316.

Schiller, M. (1961). A new approach to leadership assessment. *Personnel Psychology, 14*, 75–86.

Schippmann, J. S., & Prien, E. P. (1986). Psychometric evaluation of an integrated assessment procedure. *Psychological Reports, 59*, 111–122.

Schlacter, J. L. (1969). *Increased participation in the decision-making process among field crews in the Ohio Department of Highways: A field study.* Doctoral dissertation, Ohio State University, Columbus.

Schlenker, B. R. (1980). *Impression management: The self-concept, social identity, and interpersonal relations.* Monterey, CA: Brooks/Cole.

Schlesinger, L., Jackson, J. M., & Butman, J. (1960). Leader-member interaction in management committees. *Journal of Abnormal and Social Psychology, 61*, 360–364.

Schmid, J., & Leiman, J. M. (1957). The development of hierarchical factor solutions. *Psychometrika, 22*, 53–61.

Schmidt, F. L., & Hunter, J. E. (1974). Racial and ethnic bias in psychological tests: Divergent implications of two definitions of test bias. *American Psychologist, 28*, 1–8.

Schmidt, F. L., & Hunter, J. E. (1977). Development of a general solution to the problem of validity generalization. *Journal of Applied Psychology, 62*, 529–540.

Schmidt, F. L., & Hunter, J. E. (1980). The future of criterion-related validity. *Personnel Psychology, 33*, 41–58.

Schmidt, F. L., & Hunter, J. E. (1981). Employment testing: Old theories and new research findings. *American Psychologist, 36*, 1128–1137.

Schmidt, F. L., Hunter, J. E., & Urry, V. W. (1976). Statistical power in criterion-related validity studies. *Journal of Applied Psychology, 61*, 473–485.

Schmidt, F. L., & Johnson, R. H. (1973). Effect of race on peer ratings in an industrial setting. *Journal of Applied Psychology, 57*, 237–241.

Schmidt, R. E. (1985). Management in a leaderless environment. *Bureaucrat, 14*(3), 30–32.

Schmidt, S. M., & Kipnis, D. (1984). Managers' pursuit of individual and organizational goals. *Human Relations, 37*, 781–794.

Schmidt, W. H., & Posner, B. Z. (1986). Values and expectations of federal service executives. *Public Administration Review, 46*, 447–454.

Schmitt, D. R. (1969). Punitive supervision and productivity: An experimental analog. *Journal of Applied Psychology, 2*, 118–123.

Schmitt, N. (1977). Interrater agreement in dimensionality and combination of assessment center judgments. *Journal of Applied Psychology, 62*, 171–176.

Schmitt, N., Noe, R. A., Merrit, R., & Fitzgerald, M. P. (1984). Validity of assessment center ratings for the prediction of performance ratings and school climate of school administrators. *Journal of Applied Psychology, 69,* 207-213.

Schnake, M. E. (1986). Vicarious punishment in a work setting. *Journal of Applied Psychology, 71,* 343-345.

Schneider, A. L. (1969). *A study of characteristics of outstanding first line supervisors.* Master's thesis, Ohio State University, Columbus.

Schneider, B. (1970). Relationships between various criteria of leadership in small groups. *Journal of Social Psychology, 82,* 253-261.

Schneider, B. (1972). Organizational climate: Individual preferences and organizational realities. *Journal of Applied Psychology, 56,* 211-217.

Schneider, B. (1973). The perception of organizational climate: The customer's view. *Journal of Applied Psychology, 57,* 248-256.

Schneider, D. J. (1973). Implicit personality theory: A review. *Psychological Bulletin, 79,* 294-309.

Schneider, D. J. (1981). Tactical self-presentations: Toward a broader conception. In J. T. Tedeschi (Ed.), *Impression management and social psychological research.* New York: Academic Press.

Schenider, D. J., Hastorf, A. H., & Ellsworth, P. C. (1979). *Person perception.* Reading, MA: Addison-Wesley.

Schneider, J. (1937). The cultural situation as a condition for the achievement of fame. *American Sociology Review, 2,* 480-491.

Schneider, J., & Mitchel, J. O. (1980). Functions of life insurance agency managers and relationships with agency characteristics and managerial tenure. *Personnel Psychology, 33,* 795-808.

Schneier, C. E. (1978). The contingency model of leadership: An extension to emergent leadership and leader's sex. *Organizational Behavior and Human Performance, 21,* 220-239.

Schneier, C. E., & Bartol, K. M. (1980). Sex effects in emergent leadership. *Journal of Applied Psychology, 65,* 341-345.

Schock, B. F., & Matthews, L. B. (1974). Identifying extension opinion leaders. *Journal of Extensions, 12,* 16-24.

Schoderbek, P. P. (1968). The use of job enlargement in industry. *Personnel Journal, 47,* 796-801.

Schoderbek, P. P., & Reif, W. E. (1969). *Job enlargement: Key to improved performance.* Ann Arbor: University of Michigan, Bureau of Industrial Relations.

Schoen, D. R. (1957). Human relations: Born or bogle? *Harvard Business Review, 35*(6), 41-47.

Schoennauer, A. W. (1967). Behavior patterns of executives in business acquisitions. *Personnel Administration, 30*(2) 27-32.

Schon, D. A. (1963). Champions for radical new inventions. *Harvard Business Review, 41*(2), 77-86.

Schoorman, F. D. (1988). Escalation bias in performance appraisals: An unintended consequence of supervisor participation in hiring decisions. *Journal of Applied Psychology, 73,* 58-62.

Schopler, J., & Matthews, M. W. (1965). The influence of the perceived causal locus of partner's dependence on the use of the interpersonal power. *Journal of Personality and Social Psychology, 2,* 609-612.

Schott, J. L. (1970). *The leader behavior of non-white principals in inner-city elementary schools with integrated teaching staffs under conditions of high and low morale.* Doctoral dissertation, Purdue University, Lafayette, IN.

Schrag, C. (1954). Leadership among prison inmates. *American Sociological Review, 19,* 37-42.

Schrage, H. (1965). The R & D entrepreneur: Profile of success. *Harvard Business Review, 43*(6), 56-61.

Schrank, W. R. (1968). The labeling effect of ability grouping. *Journal of Educational Research, 62,* 51-52.

Schregle, J. (1970). Forms of participation in management. *Industrial Relations, 9,* 117-122.

Schreiber, E. M. (1978). Education and change in American opinions on a woman for president. *Public Opinion Quarterly, 42,* 171-182.

Schriesheim, C. A. (1979a). The similarity of individual directed and group directed leader behavior descriptions. *Academy of Management Journal, 22,* 345-355.

Schriesheim, C. A. (1979b). Social desirability and leader effectiveness. *Journal of Social Psychology, 108,* 89-94.

Schriesheim, C. A. (1982). The great high consideration–high initiating structure leadership myth: Evidence on its generalizability. *Journal of Social Psychology, 116,* 221-228.

Schriesheim, C. A., Bannister, B. D., & Money, W. H. (1979). Psychometric properties of the LPC scale: An extension of Rice's review. *Academy of Management Review, 4,* 287-290.

Schriesheim, C. A., & DeNisi, A. S. (1978). *The impact of implicit theories on the validity of questionnaires.* Unpublished manuscript.

Schriesheim, C. A., & DeNisi, A. S. (1979). Task dimensions as moderators of the effect of instrumental leader behavior: A path-goal approach. *Proceedings, Academy of Management,* Atlanta, GA, 103-106.

Schriesheim, C. A., & DiNisi, A. S. (1981). Task dimensions as moderators of the effects of instrumental leadership: A two-sample replicated test of path-goal leadership theory. *Journal of Applied Psychology, 66,* 589-597.

Schriesheim, C. A., & Hinken, T. R. (1986). *Influence tactics used by subordinates: A theoretical and empirical analysis and refinement of the Kipnis, Schmidt, and Wilkinson subscales.* Paper, Academy of Management, San Diego, CA.

Schriesheim, C. A., Hinken, T. R., & Tetrault, L. A. (1988). *The validity of measuring "leader" reinforcement behavior by questionnaire: An examination of the leader reward and punishment questionnaire (LRPQ).* Unpublished manuscript.

Schriesheim, C. A., & Hosking, D. (1978). Review essay of Fiedler, F. E., Chemers, M. M., & Mahar, L. Improving leadership effectiveness: the leader match concept. *Administrative Science Quarterly, 23,* 496-505.

Schriesheim, C. A., House, R. J., & Kerr, S. (1976). Leader initiating structure: A reconciliation of discrepant research results and some empirical tests. *Organizational Behavioral and Human Performance, 15,* 297-321.

Schriesheim, C. A., & Kerr, S. (1974). Psychometric properties of the Ohio State leadership scales. *Psychological Bulletin, 81,* 756-765.

Schriesheim, C. A., & Kerr, S. (1977a). R. I. P. LPC: A response to

Fiedler. In J. G. Hunt & L. L. Larson (Eds.), *Leadership: The cutting edge*. Carbondale: Southern Illinois University Press.

Schriesheim, C. A., & Kerr, S. (1977b). Theories and measures of leadership: A critical appraisal of present and future directions. In J. G. Hunt & L. L. Larson (Eds.), *Leadership: The cutting edge*. Carbondale: Southern Illinois University Press.

Schriesheim, C. A., Kinicki, A. J., & Schriesheim, J. F. (1979). The effect of leniency of leader behavior descriptions. *Organizational Behavioral and Human Performance, 23*, 1–29.

Schriesheim, C. A., Mowday, R. T., & Stogdill, R. M. (1979). Crucial dimensions of leader-group interactions. In J. G. Hunt & L. L. Larson (Eds.), *Cross-currents in leadership*. Carbondale: Southern Illinois University Press.

Schriesheim, C. A., & Murphy, C. J. (1976). Relationship between leader behavior and subordinate satisfaction and performance: A test of some situational moderators. *Journal of Applied Psychology, 61*, 634–641.

Schriesheim, C. A., & Neider, L. L. (1988a). *The coming new phase of leadership theory and development*. Unpublished manuscript.

Schriesheim, C. A., & Neider, L. L. (1988b). *Distinctions among subtypes of perceived delegation and leadership decision-making: A theoretical and empirical analysis*. Paper, Society for Industrial and Organizational Psychology, Atlanta, GA.

Schriesheim, C. A., & Neider, L. L. (1988c). *Subtypes of management delegation: An extension of the Vroom and Yetton conceptualization*. Unpublished manuscript.

Schriesheim, C. A., & Stogdill, R. M. (1975). Differences in factor structure across three versions of the Ohio State leadership scales. *Personnel Psychology, 28*, 189–206.

Schriesheim, C. A., Tepper, B. J., & Tetrault, L. A. (1988). *The validity of drawing across-octant conclusions from the contingency model of leadership effectiveness: Critique and analysis*. Unpublished manuscript.

Schriesheim, C. A., & Von Glinow, M. A. (1977). The path goal theory of leadership: A theoretical and empirical analysis. *Academy of Management Journal, 20*, 398–405.

Schriesheim, J. F. (1980). The social context of leader-subordinate relations: An investigation of the effects of group cohesiveness. *Journal of Applied Psychology, 65*, 183–193.

Schriesheim, J. F., & Schriesheim, C. A. (1980). A test of the path-goal theory of leadership and some suggested directions for future research. *Personnel Psychology, 33*, 349–370.

Schriver, W. R. (1966). The prediction of worker productivity. *Human Organizations, 25*, 339–343.

Schroder, H. M., Streufert, S., & Welden, D. C. (1964). *The effect of structural abstractness in interpersonal stimuli on the leadership role* (Tech. Rep. No. 3). Princeton, NJ: Princeton University, Office of Naval Research.

Schubert, A., et al. (1974). *A study of nonverbal communication and leadership emergence in task-oriented and informal small group discussions*. Paper, International Communication Association, New Orleans.

Schubert, M. L. (1973). A comparison of the effects of two models of sensitivity training on "level of experiencing." *Dissertation Abstracts International, 34*, 1264.

Schul, B. D. (1975). *How to be an effective group leader*. Chicago: Nelson-Hall.

Schuler, E. A. (1935). A study of the consistency of dominant and submissive behavior in adolescent boys. *Journal of Genetic Psychology, 46*, 403–432.

Schuler, R. S. (1975). Sex, organizational level, and outcome importance: Where the differences are. *Personnel Psychology, 28*, 365–376.

Schuler, R. S. (1976). Participation with supervisor and subordinate authoritarianism: A path goal reconciliation. *Administrative Science Quarterly, 21*, 320–325.

Schuler, R. S., & Kim, J. S. (1978). Employees' expectancy perceptions as explanatory variables for effectiveness of participation in decision making. *Psychological Reports, 43*, 651–656.

Schultz, B. (1974). Characteristics of emergent leaders of continuing problem solving groups. *Journal of Psychology, 88*, 167–173.

Schultz, B. (1980). Communicative correlates of perceived leaders. *Small Group Behavior, 11*, 175–191.

Schultz, G. P. (1951). Worker participation on production problems. *Personnel, 28*, 201–210.

Schulze, R. O. (1958). The role of economic dominants in community power structure. *American Sociological Review, 23*, 3–9.

Schumer, H. (1962). Cohesion and leadership in small groups as related to group productivity. *Dissertation Abstracts, 22*, 3735–3736.

Schuster, J. R., & Clark, B. (1970). Individual differences related to feelings toward pay. *Personnel Psychology, 23*, 591–604.

Schutz, A. (1967). *The phenomenology of the social world*. Evanston, IL: Northwestern University Press.

Schutz, W. C. (1955). What makes groups productive? *Human Relations, 8*, 465–499.

Schutz, W. C. (1961a). On group composition. *Journal of Abnormal and Social Psychology, 62*, 275–281.

Schutz, W. C. (1961b). The ego, FIRO theory, and the leader as completer. In L. Petrullo & B. M. Bass (Eds.), *Leadership and interpersonal behavior*. New York: Holt, Rinehart & Winston.

Schutz, W. C. (1977). *Leaders of schools: FIRO theory applied to administrators*. La Jolla, CA: University Associates.

Schutz, W. C., & Allen, V. L. (1966). The effects of a T-group laboratory on interpersonal behavior. *Journal of Applied Behavioral Science, 2*, 265–286.

Schwartz, A. R., & Hoyman, M. M. (1984). The changing of the guard: The new American labor leader. *Annals of the American Academy of Political and Social Science, 473*, 64–75.

Schwartz, B. (1983). George Washington and the Whig conception of heroic leadership. *American Sociological Review, 48*, 18–33.

Schwartz, E. B., & Waetjen, W. B. (1976). Improving the self-concepts of women managers. *Business Quarterly, 41*, 20–27.

Schwartz, F. C., Stillwell, W. P., & Scanlon, B. K. (1968). Effects of management development on manager behavior and subordinate perception. *Training & Development Journal, 22*(4), 38–50.

Schwartz, K. B., & Menon, K. (1985). Executive succession in failing firms. *Academy of Management Journal, 28*(3), 680–686.

Schwartz, M. M., Jenusaitis, E., & Stark, H. F. (1966). A comparison of the perception of job-related needs in two industry groups. *Personnel Psychology, 19*, 185–194.

Schwartz, M. M., & Levine, H. (1965). Union and management leaders: A comparison. *Personnel Administration, 28*(3), 44–47.

Schwartz, M. M., Stark, H. F., & Schiffman, H. R. (1970). Responses of union and management leaders to emotionally toned industrial relations terms. *Personnel Psychology, 23*, 361–367.

Schwartz, S. (1968). *Tank crew effectiveness in relation to the supervisory behavior of the tank commander.* Washington, DC: George Washington University, Human Resources Research Office.

Schwartz, S. L., & Gekoski, N. (1960). The supervisory inventory: A forced-choice measure of human relations attitude and technique. *Journal of Applied Psychology, 44*, 233–236.

Schwartzbaum, A., & Gruenfeld, L. (1969). Factors influencing subject-observer interaction in an organizational study. *Administrative Science Quarterly, 14*, 443–449.

Schweiger, D. M., Ivancevich, J. M., & Power, F. R. (1987). Executive actions for managing human resources before and after acquisition. *Academy of Management Executive, 1*(2), 127–138.

Schweiger, D. M., & Jago, A. G. (1982). Problem-solving styles and participative decision making. *Psychology Reports, 50*, 1311–1316.

Schweitzer, A. (1984). *The age of charisma.* Chicago: Nelson-Hall.

Schwirian, K. P., & Helfrich, M. L. (1968). Economic role and community involvement of business executives. *Sociology Quarterly, 9*, 64–72.

Schwyhart, W. R., & Smith, P. C. (1972). Factors in the job involvement of middle managers. *Journal of Applied Psychology, 56*, 227–233.

Scioli, F. P., Dyson, J. W., & Fleitas, D. W. (1974). The relationship of personality and decisional structure to leadership. *Small Group Behavior, 5*, 3–22.

Scontrino, M. P. (1972). The effects of fulfilling and violating group members' expectations about leadership style. *Organizational Behavior and Human Performance, 8*, 118–138.

Scontrino, M. P. (1979). *Evaluative performance: A manual for local governments.* Seattle: Washington Local Government Personnel Institute.

Scott, D., & Moore, M. L. (1981). An assessment of a management by objectives program by black and white managers, supervisors, and professionals. *Proceedings, Academy of Management,* San Diego, CA, 219–223.

Scott, E. L. (1956). *Leadership and perceptions of organization.* Columbus: Ohio State University, Bureau of Business Research.

Scott, L. K. (1978). Charismatic authority in the rational organization. *Educational Administration Quarterly, 14*(2), 43–62.

Scott, W. A. (1957). Attitude change through reward of verbal behavior. *Journal of Abnormal and Social Psychology, 55*, 72–75.

Scott, W. A. (1967). *Organizational theory: A behavioral analysis for management.* Homewood, IL: Irwin.

Scott, W. E. (1965). Some motivational determinants of work behavior. *Indiana Business Information Bulletin, 54*, 116–131.

Scott, W. E. (1977). Leadership: A functional analysis. In J. G. Hunt & L. L. Larson (Eds.), *Leadership: The cutting edge.* Carbondale: Southern Illinois University Press.

Scott, W. E., Jr., & Podsakoff, P. M. (1982). Leadership, supervision and behavioral control: Perspectives from an experimental analysis. In L. Frederickson (Ed.), *Handbook of organizational behavior management.* New York: Wiley.

Scott, W. H. (1952). *Industrial leadership and joint consultation.* Liverpool: University Press of Liverpool.

Scott, W. R. (1965). Reactions to supervision in a heteronomous professional organization. *Administrative Science Quarterly, 10*, 65–81.

Scully, M. (1973). The 55 sheepish goats of Dr. Fox. *Chronicle of Higher Education, 8*(4), 1–5.

Seaman, D. F. (1981). *Working effectively with task-oriented groups.* New York: McGraw-Hill.

Seashore, S. E. (1954). *Group cohesiveness in the industrial work group.* Ann Arbor: University of Michigan, Institute for Social Research.

Seashore, S. E., & Bowers, D. G. (1963). *Changing the structure and functioning of an organization.* Ann Arbor: University of Michigan, Institute for Social Research.

Seashore, S. E., & Bowers, D. G. (1970). Durability of organization change. *American Psychologist, 25*, 227–233.

Sechrest, L. B., & Hemphill, J. K. (1954). Motivational variables in the assuming of combat obligation. *Journal of Consulting Psychology, 18*, 113–118.

Secord, P. F., & Backman, C. W. (1964). Interpersonal congruency, perceived similarity, and friendship. *Sociometry, 27*, 115–127.

Sedge, S. K. (1985). A comparison of engineers pursuing alternate career paths. *Journal of Vocational Behavior, 27*, 56–70.

Sedring, D. D. (1969). Models and images of man and society in leadership theory. *Journal of Politics, 31*(1), 1–31.

Seeman, M. (1950). Some status correlates of leadership. In A. G. Grace (Ed.), *Leadership in American education.* Chicago: University of Chicago Press.

Seeman, M. (1953). Role conflict and ambivalence in leadership. *American Sociological Review, 18*, 373–380.

Seeman, M. (1957). A comparison of general and specific leader behavior descriptions. In R. M. Stogdill & E. A. Coons (Eds.), *Leader behavior: Its description and measurement.* Columbus: Ohio State University, Bureau of Business Research.

Seeman, M. (1958). Social mobility and administrative behavior. *American Sociological Review, 23*, 633–642.

Seeman, M. (1960). *Social status and leadership—the case of the school executive.* Columbus: Ohio State University, Educational Research Monograph No. 35.

Seers, A. (undated). *Team-member exchange quality: A preliminary inves-*

tigation of a new construct for role making research. Unpublished manuscript.

Seers, A., & Graen, G. B. (1984) The dual attachment concept: A longitudinal investigation of the combination of task characteristics and leader-member exchange. *Organizational Behavior and Human Performance, 33,* 283–306.

Segard, C. P. (1927). Thirty-three essentials of leadership. *Industrial Psychology, 3,* 270.

Seidman, J., London, J., & Karsh, B. (1951). Why workers join unions. *Annals of the American Academy of Political and Social Science, 274,* 75–84.

Seifert, C. M. (1984). Reactions to leaders: Effects of sex of leader, sex of subordinate, method of leader selection and task outcome. *Dissertation Abstracts International, 45*(12B), 3999.

Seiler, D. A., & Williams, W. E. (1972). Assessing engineers' early job adjustment: A longitudinal approach. *Personnel Psychology, 25,* 687–696.

Seiler, J. A. (1967). *Systems analysis in organizational behavior.* Homewood, IL: Irwin-Dorsey.

Selden, M. (1971). *The Yenan way in revolutionary China.* Cambridge, MA: Harvard University Press.

Seldman, M. L. (1971). An investigation of aspects of marathon-encounter group phenomena: Types of participants and differential perceptions of leaders. *Dissertation Abstracts International, 32,* 3652.

Selekman, B. M. (1924). *Sharing management with the workers.* New York: Russell Sage Foundation.

Selekman, B. M. (1947). *Labor relations and human relations.* New York: McGraw-Hill.

Seligman, L. G. (1964). *Leadership in a new nation.* New York: Atherton Press.

Sells, S. B. (1968). The nature of organizational climate. In R. Tagiuri & G. L. Litwin (Eds.), *Organizational climate: Explorations of a concept.* Cambridge, MA: Harvard University Press.

Selover, R. B. (1970). *Identifying college graduates with high potential for advancement.* Prudential Insurance Company of America. (Reported in Campbell, Dunnette, et al., 1970, 186–187.)

Seltzer, J., & Bass, B. M. (1987). *Leadership is more than initiation and consideration.* Paper, American Psychological Association, New York.

Seltzer, J., & Bass, B. M. (1990). Transformational leadership: Beyond initiation and consideration. *Journal of Management,* in press.

Seltzer, J., & Numerof, R. E. (1988). Supervisory leadership and subordinate burnout. *Academy of Management Journal, 31,* 439–446.

Seltzer, J., Numerof, R. E., & Bass, B. M. (1987). *Transformational leadership: Is it a source of more or less burnout or stress?* Paper, Academy of Management, New Orleans. Also: *Journal of Health and Human Resources Administration* (in press).

Selvin, H. C. (1960). *The effects of leadership.* New York: Free Press.

Selznick, P. (1943). An approach to a theory of bureaucracy. *American Sociological Review, 8,* 47–54.

Selznick, P. (1948). Foundations of the theory of organization. *American Sociological Review, 13,* 25–35.

Selznick, P. (1957). *Leadership in administration: A sociological interpretation.* Evanston, IL: Row, Peterson.

Senge, P. (1980). *System dynamics and leadership* (Working Paper D-3263). Cambridge: Massachusetts Institute of Technology, System Dynamics Group.

Senge, P. (1984). *Systems thinking and the new management style* (Working Paper D-3586-2). Cambridge: Massachusetts Institute of Technology, System Dynamics Group.

Senge, P. (1986). Systems principles for leadership. In J. D. Adams (Ed.), *Transforming leadership.* Alexandria, VA: Miles River Press.

Senger, J. (1971). Managers' perceptions of subordinates' competence as a function of personal value orientation. *Academy of Management Journal, 14,* 415–423.

Senner, E. E. (1971). *Trust as a measure of the impact of cultural differences on individual behavior in organizations.* Paper, American Psychological Association, Washington, DC.

Sequeira, C. E. (1962). Characteristics of effective supervisor. *Manas, 9,* 1–12.

Sequeira, C. E. (1964). Functions of a supervisor. *Indian Journal of Applied Psychology, 1,* 46–54.

Serafini, D. M., & Pearson, J. C. (1984). Leadership behavior and sex role socialization: Two sides of the same coin. *Southern Speech Communication Journal, 49,* 396–405.

Sergiovanni, T. J., Metzcus, R. H., & Burden, L. (1969). Toward a particularistic approach to leadership style: Some findings. *American Education Research Journal, 6,* 62–80.

Seversky, P. M. (1982). Trust, need to control, and the tendency to delegate: A study of the delegation behavior of superintendents. *Dissertation Abstracts International, 43*(9A), 2851.

Sexton, W. P. (1966). *Organizational necessities and individual needs: An empirical study.* Doctoral dissertation, Ohio State University, Columbus.

Sexton, W. P. (1967). Organizational and individual needs: A conflict? *Personnel Journal, 46,* 337–343.

Sgro, J. A., Worchel, P., Pence, E. C., & Orban, J. A. (1980). Perceived leader behavior as a function of the leader's interpersonal trust orientation. *Academy of Management Journal, 23,* 161–165.

Shackleton, V. J., Bass, B. M., & Allison, S. N. (1975). *PAXIT.* Scottsville, NY: Transnational Programs.

Shackleton, V. J., Bass, B. M., & Allison, S. E. (1982). *Survival: The impact of leadership style.* San Diego, CA: University Associates.

Shainwald, R. G. (1974). The effect of self-esteem on opinion leadership. *Dissertation Abstracts International, 34,* 3635.

Shamir, B., House, R. J., & Arthur, M. B. (1988). *The transformational effects of charismatic leadership—A motivational theory.* Unpublished manuscript.

Shannon, C. E., & Weaver, W. (1949). *The mathematical theory of communication.* Urbana: University of Illinois Press.

Shannon, J. R. (1929). The post-school careers of high school leaders and high school scholars. *School Review, 37,* 656–665.

Shapira, Z. (1975). *Expectancy determinants of intrinsically motivated be-*

havior. Doctoral dissertation, University of Rochester, Rochester, NY.

Shapira, Z. (1976). A facet analysis of leadership styles. *Journal of Applied Psychology, 61,* 136–139.

Shapira, Z., & Dunbar, R. L. M. (1980). Testing Mintzberg's managerial roles classification using an in-basket simulation. *Journal of Applied Psychology, 65,* 87–95.

Shapiro, G. L. (1985). *Sex differences in mentoring functions received and valued by managers.* Paper, Academy of Management, San Diego, CA.

Shapiro, M. I. (1971). Initiating structure and consideration: A situationist's view of the efficacy of two styles of leadership. *Dissertation Abstracts International, 31,* 4382–4383.

Shapiro, R. J., & Klein, R. H. (1975). Perceptions of the leaders in an encounter group. *Small Group Behavior, 6,* 238–248.

Sharf, B. F. (1978). A rhetorical analysis of leadership emergence in small groups. *Communication Monographs, 45,* 156–172.

Sharma, C. L. (1955). *Practices in decision-making as related to satisfaction in teaching.* Doctoral dissertation, University of Chicago, Chicago.

Sharma, S. L. (1974). Social value orientations of activist student leaders: A comparative study. *Indian Journal of Social Work, 35,* 67–71.

Sharpe, R. T. (1956). Differences between perceived adminstrative behavior and role-norms as factors in leadership evaluation and group morale. *Dissertation Abstracts, 16,* 57.

Shartle, C. L. (1933). *Some psychological factors in foremanship.* Doctoral dissertation, Ohio State University, Columbus.

Shartle, C. L. (1934). A clinical approach to foremanship. *Personnel Journal, 13,* 135–139.

Shartle, C. L. (1949a). Organization structure. In W. Dennis (Ed.), *Current trends in industrial psychology.* Pittsburgh: University of Pittsburgh Press.

Shartle, C. L. (1949b). Leadership and executive performance. *Personnel, 25,* 370–380.

Shartle, C. L. (1950a). Leadership aspects of administrative behavior. *Advanced Management, 15,* 12–15.

Shartle, C. L. (1950b). Studies of leadership by interdisciplinary methods. In A. G. Grace (Ed.), *Leadership in American education.* Chicago: University of Chicago Press.

Shartle, C. L. (1951a). Leader behavior in jobs. *Occupations, 30,* 164–166.

Shartle, C. L. (1951b). Studies in naval leadership. In H. Guetzkow (Ed.), *Groups, leadership, and men.* Pittsburgh, PA: Carnegie Press.

Shartle, C. L. (1956). *Executive performance and leadership.* Englewood Cliffs, NJ: Prentice-Hall.

Shartle, C. L. (1960). Work patterns and leadership style in administration. *Personnel Psychology, 13,* 295–300.

Shartle, C. L. (1961). Leadership and organizational behavior. In L. Petrullo & B. M. Bass (Eds.), *Leadership and interpersonal behavior.* New York: Holt, Rinehart & Winston.

Shartle, C. L., Brumback, G. B., & Rizzo, J. R. (1964). An approach to dimensions of value. *Journal of Psychology, 57,* 101–111.

Shartle, C. L., & Stogdill, R. M. (1953). *Studies in naval leadership: Methods, results, and applications* (Tech. Rep.). Columbus: Ohio State University, Personnel Research Board.

Shartle, C. L., & Stogdill, R. M. (1966). *Manual for value scale—business firm.* Columbus: Ohio State University, Bureau of Business Research.

Shartle, C. L., Stogdill, R. M., & Campbell, D. T. (1949). *Studies in naval leadership.* Columbus: Ohio State University Research Foundation.

Shaver, E. L. (1931). *Science of leadership.* Boston: Pilgrim Press.

Shaw, C. E. (1976). *A comparative study of organizational climate and job satisfaction at selected public and Catholic secondary schools in Connecticut.* Doctoral dissertation, University of Connecticut, Storrs.

Shaw, D. M. (1960). Size of share in task and motivation in work groups. *Sociometry, 23,* 203–208.

Shaw, E. P. (1965). The social distance factor and management. *Personnel Administration, 28,* 29–31.

Shaw, J. B., & Fisher, C. D. (1986). *Supervisor-subordinate agreement on performance feedback: A field study* (ONR Tech. Rep. No. 7). College Station, TX: Texas A & M University, Department of Management.

Shaw, J. B., & Weekley, J. A. (1985). The effects of objective work-load variations of psychological strain and post-work-load performance. *Journal of Management, 11,* 87–98.

Shaw, M. E. (1954a). Some effects of unequal distribution of information upon group performance in various communication nets. *Journal of Abnormal and Social Psychology, 49,* 547–553.

Shaw, M. E. (1954b). Some effects of problem complexity upon problem solving efficiency in different communication nets. *Journal of Experimental Psychology, 48,* 211–217.

Shaw, M. E. (1955). A comparison of two types of leadership in various communication nets. *Journal of Abnormal and Social Psychology, 50,* 127–134.

Shaw, M. E. (1959a). Some effects of individually prominent behavior upon group effectiveness and member satisfaction. *Journal of Abnormal and Social Psychology, 59,* 382–386.

Shaw, M. E. (1959b). Acceptance of authority, group structure, and the effectiveness of small groups. *Journal of Personality, 27,* 196–210.

Shaw, M. E. (1960). A note concerning homogeneity of membership and group problem solving. *Journal of Abnormal and Social Psychology, 60,* 448–450.

Shaw, M. E. (1961). A serial position effect in social influence on group decisions. *Journal of Social Psychology, 54,* 83–91.

Shaw, M. E. (1963a). Some effects of varying amounts of information exclusively possessed by a group member upon his behavior in the group. *Journal of General Psychology, 68,* 71–79.

Shaw, M. E. (1963b). *Scaling group tasks: A method for dimensional analysis* (Tech. Rep. No. 1). Gainesville: University of Florida.

Shaw, M. E. (1971). *Group dynamics.* New York: McGraw-Hill.

Shaw, M. E., & Ashton, N. (1976). Do assembly bonus effects occur on disjunctive tasks? A test of Steiner's theory. *Bulletin of the Psychonomic Society, 8*, 469-491.

Shaw, M. E., & Blum, J. M. (1964). *Effects of leadership style upon group performance as a function of task structure.* Gainesville: University of Florida. Also: (1966). *Journal of Personality and Social Psychology, 3*, 238-242.

Shaw, M. E., & Gilchrist, J. C. (1956). Intra-group communication and leader choice. *Journal of Social Psychology, 43*, 133-138.

Shaw, M. E., & Harkey, B. (1976). Some effects of congruency of member characteristics and group structure upon group behavior. *Journal of Personality and Social Psychology, 34*, 412-418.

Shaw, M. E., & Penrod, W. T. (1962). Does more information available to a group always improve group performance? *Sociometry, 25*, 377-390.

Shaw, M. E., & Rothschild, G. H. (1956). Some effects of prolonged experience in communication nets. *Journal of Applied Psychology, 40*, 281-286.

Shaw, M. E., Rothschild, G. H., & Strickland, J. F. (1957). Decision processes in communication nets. *Journal of Abnormal and Social Psychology, 54*, 323-330.

Shaw, M. E., & Shaw, L. M. (1962). Some effects of sociometric grouping under learning in a second grade classroom. *Journal of Social Psychology, 57*, 453-458.

Shearer, R. L., & Steger, J. A. (1975). Manpower obsolescence: A new definition and empirical investigation of personal variables. *Academy of Management Journal, 18*, 263-275.

Sheldon, W. H. (1927). Social traits and morphologic type. *Personnel Journal, 6*, 47-55.

Shelley, H. P. (1960a). Focused leadership and cohesiveness in small groups. *Sociometry, 23*, 209-216.

Shelley, H. P. (1960b). Status consensus, leadership, and satisfaction with the group. *Journal of Social Psychology, 51*, 157-164.

Shenkar, O., & Ronen, S. (1987). Structure and importance of work goals among managers in the People's Republic of China. *Academy of Management Journal, 30*, 564-576.

Shepard, H. A. (1956). Superiors and subordinates in research. *Journal of Business, 29*, 261-267.

Shepard, H. A. (1964). Explorations in observant participation. In L. P. Bradford, J. R. Gibb, & K. D. Benne (Eds.), *T-group theory and laboratory method.* New York: Wiley.

Shepherd, C., & Weschler, I. R. (1955). The relation between three interpersonal variables and communication effectiveness: A pilot study. *Sociometry, 18*, 103-110.

Sheppard, D. I. (1967). Relationship of job satisfaction to situational and personality characteristics of terminating employees. *Personnel Journal, 46*, 567-571.

Sheridan, J. E., Hogstel, M., Fairchild, T. J. (1985). *Contextual model of leadership influence on the job performance, absenteeism and turnover of nursing home staff* (Working Paper No. 2). Dallas: Texas Christian University, McNeeley School of Business.

Sheridan, J. E., Kerr, J. L., & Abelson, M. A. (1982). Leadership activa-

tion theory: An opponent process model of subordinate responses to leader behavior. In J. G. Hunt, V. Sekarian, & C. A. Schriesheim (Eds.), *Leadership: Beyond establishment views.* Carbondale: Southern Illinois University Press.

Sheridan, J. E., & Vredenburgh, D. J. (1978a). Usefulness of leadership behavior and social power variables in predicting job tension, performance, and turnover of nursing employees. *Journal of Applied Psychology, 63*, 89-95.

Sheridan, J. E., & Vredenburgh, D. J. (1978b). Predicting leadership behavior in a hospital organization. *Academy of Management Journal, 21*, 679-689.

Sheridan, J. E., & Vredenburgh, D. J. (1979). Structural model of leadership influence in a hospital organization. *Academy of Management Journal, 22*, 6-21.

Sheridan, J., Vredenburgh, D., & Abelson, M. (1984). Contextual model of leadership influence in hospital units. *Academy of Management Journal, 27*, 57-78.

Sheridan, M. (1976). Young women leaders in China. *Signs: Journal of Women in Culture and Society, 2*, 59-88.

Sherif, D. R. (1969). *Administrative behavior: A quantitative case study of six organizations.* Iowa City: University of Iowa, Center of Labor and Management.

Sherif, M. (1936). *The psychology of social norms.* New York: Harper.

Sherif, M. (1962). *Intergroup relations and leadership.* New York: Wiley.

Sherif, M. (1967). *Social interaction: Process and products.* Chicago: Aldine.

Sherif, M., & Sherif, C. W. (1953). *Groups in harmony and tension.* New York: Harper.

Sherif, M., & Sherif, C. W. (1956). *An outline of social psychology.* New York: Harper.

Sherif, M., & Sherif, C. W. (1964). *Reference groups: Explorations into conformity and deviations of adolescents.* New York: Harper & Row.

Sherif, M., White, B. J., & Harvey, O. J. (1955). Status in experimentally produced groups. *American Journal of Sociology, 60*, 370-379.

Sherif, M., & Wilson, M. O. (1953). *Group relations at the crossroads.* New York: Harper.

Sherman, J. D., Ezell, H. F., & Odewahn, C. A. (1987). Centralization of decision making and accountability based on gender. *Group & Organization Studies, 12*, 454-463.

Sherwood, C. E., & Walker, W. S. (1960). Role differentiation in real groups: An extrapolation of a laboratory small-group research finding. *Sociology and Social Research, 45*, 14-17.

Shetty, Y. K., & Perry, N. S. (1976). Are top executives transferable across companies? *Business Horizons, 19*, 23-28.

Shevitz, R. N. (1955). *An investigation of the relation between exclusive possession of information and attempts to lead in small groups.* Doctoral dissertation, Ohio State University, Columbus.

Shields, S. A. (1975). Functionalism, Darwinism, and the psychology of women. *American Psychologist, 30*, 739-754.

Shiflett, S. C. (1973). The contingency model of leadership effectiveness: Some implications of its statistical and methodological properties. *Behavioral Science, 18*, 429-440.

Shiflett, S. C. (1974). Stereotyping and esteem for one's best preferred co-worker. *Journal of Social Psychology, 93*, 55-65.

Shiflett, S. C., & Nealey, S. M. (1972). The effects of changing leader power: A test of situational engineering. *Organizational Behavior and Human Performance, 7*, 371-382.

Shils, E. A. (1950). Primary groups in the American army. In R. A. Merton & P. F. Lazarsfeld (Eds.), *Studies in the scope and method of "The American Soldier."* New York: Free Press.

Shils, E. A. (1954). Authoritarianism: "Right" and "Left." In R. Christie & M. Jahoda (Eds.), *Studies in the scope and method of "The Authoritarian Personality."* New York: Free Press.

Shils, E. A. (1965). Charisma, order, and status. *American Sociological Review, 30*, 199-213.

Shils, E. A., & Janowitz, M. (1948). Cohesion and disintegration in the Wehrmacht in World War II. *Public Opinion Quarterly, 12*, 280-315.

Shima, H. (1968). The relationship between the leader's modes of interpersonal cognition and the performance of the group. *Japanese Psychology Research, 10*, 13-30.

Shlensky, B. (1972). Determinants of turnover in training programs for the disadvantaged. *Personnel Administration, 15*(2), 53-61.

Shorey, P. (1933). *What Plato said.* Chicago: University of Chicago Press.

Short, J. A. (1973). *The effects of medium of communication on persuasion, bargaining, and perceptions of the other.* Cambridge, England: Post Office, Long Range Intelligence Division.

Shostrom, E. L. (1974). *POI manual: An inventory for the measurement of self-actualization.* San Diego, CA: Educational and Industrial Testing Service.

Shouksmith, G. (1987). Emerging personnel values in changing societies. In B. M. Bass, P. J. D. Drenth, & P. Weissenberg (Eds.), *Advances in organizational psychology.* Beverly Hills, CA: Sage.

Showel, M. (1960). Interpersonal knowledge and rated leader potential. *Journal of Abnormal and Social Psychology, 61*, 87-92.

Showel, M., Taylor, E., & Hood, P. D. (1966). *Automation of a portion of NCO leadership preparation training.* Washington, DC: Human Resources Research Organization.

Shrauger, S., & Altrocchi, J. (1964). The personality of the perceiver as a factor in person perception. *Psychological Bulletin, 62*, 289-308.

Shriver, B. (1952). *The behavioral effects of changes in ascribed leadership status in small groups.* Doctoral dissertation, University of Rochester, Rochester, NY.

Shull, F., & Anthony, W. P. (1978). Do black and white supervisory problem solving styles differ? *Personnel Psychology, 31*, 761-782.

Shultz, G. P.. (1975). *Leaders and followers in an age of ambiguity.* New York: New York University Press.

Siegall, M., & Cummings, L. L. (1986). Task role ambiguity, satisfaction, and the moderating effect of task instruction source. *Human Relations, 39*, 1017-1032.

Siegel, A. L., & Ruh, R. A. (1973). Job involvement, participation in decision-making, personal background and job behavior. *Organizational Behavior and Human Performance, 9*, 318-327.

Siegel, J., Dubrovsky, V., Kiesler, S., & McGuire, T. W. (1986). Group processes in computer mediated communication. *Organizational Behavior and Human Decision Processes, 37*, 157-187.

Siegel, J. P. (1969). A study of the relationship among organizational factors, personality traits, job, and leadership attitudes. *Dissertation Abstracts, 29*, 2662-2663.

Siegel, J. P. (1973). *Reconsidering "consideration" in a leadership-path-goal interpretation of satisfaction and performance.* Toronto: University of Toronto. Unpublished manuscript.

Siegel, S. (1956) *Nonparametric statistics for the behavioral sciences.* New York: McGraw-Hill.

Siegenthaler, J. K. (1969). *Decision-making in Swiss labor unions.* Paper, Industrial Relations Research Association, New York.

Sikula, A. F. (1971). *Values, value systems, and their relationships to organizational effectiveness.* Paper, Academy of Management, Atlanta, GA.

Silverman, B. R. (1983). Why the merit pay system failed in the federal government. *Personnel Journal, 62*, 294-302.

Simmons, J. (1986). The CEO: Leading participatory management. *Proceedings, OD Network Conference,* New York.

Simmons, R. G. (1968). The role conflict of the first-line supervisor: An experimental study. *American Journal of Sociology, 73*, 482-495.

Simon, H. A. (1947). *Administrative behavior: A study of decision-making process in administrative organization.* New York: Macmillan.

Simon, H. A. (1957). *Models of man.* New York: Wiley.

Simon, H. A. (1987). Making management decisions: The role of intuition and emotion. *Academy of Management Executive, 1*, 57-64.

Simoneit, M. (1944). *Grundriss der charakterologischen Diagnostik.* Leipzig: Teubner.

Simons, H. W. (1970). Requirements, problems, and strategies: A theory of persuasion for social movements. *Quarterly Journal of Speech, 56*(1), 1-11.

Simonton, D. K. (1986). Presidential personality: Biographical use of the group adjective check list. *Journal of Personality and Social Psychology, 51*, 149-160.

Simpson, D. B., & Peterson, R. B. (1972). Leadership behavior, need satisfactions, and role perceptions of labor leaders: A behavior analysis. *Personnel Psychology, 25*, 673-686.

Simpson, R. H. (1938). A study of those who influence and of those who are influenced in discussion. *Teachers College Contributions to Education.*

Simpson, R. L. (1959). Vertical and horizontal communication in formal organizations. *Administrative Science Quarterly, 4*, 188-196.

Simpson, W. G., & Ireland, T. C. (1987). Managerial excellence and shareholder returns. *American Association of Individual Investors Journal, 9*, 4-8.

Sims, H. P. (1977). The leader as manager of reinforcement contingencies: An empirical example and a model. In J. G. Hunt and L. L.

Larson (Eds.), *Leadership: The cutting edge.* Carbondale: Southern Illinois University Press.

Sims, H. P. (1980). Further thoughts on punishment in organizations. *Academy of Management Review, 5,* 133–138.

Sims, H. P., Jr., & Gioia, D. A. (1984). Performance failure: Executive response to self-serving bias. *Business Horizons,* (1), 64–71.

Sims, H. P., & Manz, C. C. (1981). Social learning theory: The role of modeling in the exercise of leadership. *Journal of Organizational Behavior Management, 3*(4), 55–63.

Sims, H. P., Jr., & Manz, C. C. (1984). Observing leader verbal behavior: Toward reciprocal determinism in leadership theory. *Journal of Applied Psychology, 69,* 222–232.

Sims, H. P., Jr., & Szilagyi, A. D. (1975). Leader reward behavior and subordinate satisfaction and performance. *Organizational Behavior and Human Peformance, 14,* 426–438.

Sims, H. P., & Szilagyi, A. D. (1978). *A causal analysis of leader behavior over three different time lags.* Paper, Eastern Academy of Management, New York.

Sims, H. P., Szilagyi, A. D., & Keller, R. T. (1976). The measurement of job characteristics. *Academy of Management Journal, 19,* 195–211.

Singer, J. E. (1966). The effect of status congruence and incongruence on group functioning. *Dissertation Abstracts, 27,* 1932.

Singer, M. S. (1985). Transformational versus transactional leadership: A study of New Zealand company managers. *Psychological Reports, 57,* 143–146.

Singer, M. S., & Singer, A. E. (1986). Relation between transformational vs. transactional leadership preference and subordinates' personality: An exploratory study. *Perceptual and Motor Skills, 62,* 775–780.

Singer, P. (1969). Toward a re-evaluation of the concept of charisma with reference to India. *Journal of Social Research, 12*(2), 13–25.

Singh, C. B. P., Kumari, R., & Singh, I. K. (1988). *Dynamics of upward influence tactics in Indian organization.* Paper, International Congress of Psychology, Sydney, Australia.

Singh, N. P. (1969). n/Ach among successful-unsuccessful and traditional-progressive agricultural entrepreneurs of Delhi. *Journal of Social Psychology, 79,* 271–272.

Singh, N. P. (1970). n/Ach among agricultural and business entrepreneurs of Delhi. *Journal of Social Psychology, 81,* 145–149.

Singh, P. (1982). Leadership styles: Changing Indian scenario. *Journal of Management (India), 11,* 171–184.

Singh, R. (1983). Leadership style and reward allocation: Does least preferred co-worker scale measure task and relation orientation? *Organizational Behavior and Human Performance, 32*(2), 178–197.

Singh, R., Bohra, K. A., & Dalal, A. K. (1979). Favourableness of leadership situations studied with information integration theory. *European Journal of Social Psychology, 9,* 253–264.

Singh, S. N., & Arya, H. P. (1965). Value-orientations of local village leaders. *Manas, 12,* 145–156.

Singh, S. N., Arya, H. P., & Reddy, S. K. (1965). Different types of local leadership in two north Indian villages. *Manas, 12,* 97–107.

Singleton, T. (1976). A *study of managerial motivation development among college student leaders.* Doctoral dissertation, Georgia State University, Atlanta.

Singleton, T. (1977). Managerial motivation development: College student leaders. In J. B. Miner (Ed.), *Motivation to manage.* Atlanta, GA: Organizational Measurement Systems Press.

Sinha, D., & Kumar, P. (1966). A study of certain personality variables in student leadership. *Psychological Studies, 11,* 1–8.

Sinha, J. B. P. (1976). The authoritarian leadership: A style of effective management. *Indian Journal of Industrial Relations, 2,* 381–389.

Sinha, J. B. P. (1984). A model of effective leadership styles in India. *International Studies of Management and Organization, 14*(3), 86–98.

Sinha, J. B., & Chowdry, G. P. (1981). Perception of subordinates as a moderator of leadership effectiveness in India. *Journal of Social Psychology, 113,* 115–121.

Sirota, D. (1959). Some effects of promotional frustration on employees' understanding of, and attitudes toward, management. *Sociometry, 22,* 273–278.

Sirota, D. (1968). Internatinal survey of job goals and beliefs. Paper, International Congress of Applied Psychology, Amsterdam.

Sisson, E. D. (1948). Forced choice—the new army rating. *Personnel Psychology. 1,* 365–381.

Skinner, E. W. (1969). Relationships between leadership behavior patterns and organizational-situational variables. *Personnel Psychology, 22,* 489–494.

Skrzypek, G. J. (1969). *The relationship of leadership style to task structure, position power, and leader-member relations* (Tech. Rep. No. 34). West Point, NY: U.S. Military Academy, U.S. Army Hospital.

Slater, P. E. (1955). Role differentiation in small groups. *American Sociological Review, 20,* 300–310.

Slater, P. E. (1958). Contrasting correlates of group size. *Sociometry, 21,* 129–139.

Slavin, S. L., & Pradt, M. S. (1982). *The Einstein syndrome: Corporate anti-semitism in America today.* Lanham, MD: University Press of America.

Sleeth, R. G., & Humphreys, L. W. (undated). *Differences in leadership styles among future managers: A comparison of males and females.* Unpublished manuscript.

Sloan, J. W. (1984). The Ford presidency: A conservative approach to economic management. *Presidential Studies Quarterly, 14,* 526–537.

Slocum, J. W., Jr. (1970). Supervisory influence and the professional employee. *Personnel Journal, 49,* 484–488.

Slocum, J. W. (1973). *Organizational climate: Fact or fiction.* Paper, Midwest Academy of Management, Chicago.

Slocum, J. W. (1984). Commentary: Problems with contingency models of leader participation. In J. G. Hunt, D. Hosking, C. A. Schriesheim, and R. Stewart (Eds.), *Leaders and managers: International perspective on managerial behavior and leadership.* New York: Pergamon.

Slocum, J. W., Miller, J. D., & Misshauk, M. J. (1970). Needs, environmental work satisfaction, and job performance. *Training & Development Journal, 24,* 12–15.

Slocum, J. W., & Strawser, R. H. (1972). Racial differences in job attitudes. *Journal of Applied Psychology, 56,* 28–32.

Slusher, A., Van Dyke, J., & Rose, G. (1972). Technical competence of group leaders, managerial role, and productivity in engineering design groups. *Academy of Management Journal, 15,* 197–204.

Smallridge, R. J. (1972). *A study of relationships between perceived management system of elementary schools and the personal needs satisfaction of teachers.* Doctoral dissertation, George Peabody College for Teachers, Nashville, TN.

Smart, J. C. (Ed.). (1986). *Higher education: Handbook of theory and research,* Vol. 2. New York: Agathon Press. (See Cameron, K. S., & Ulrich, D. O., 1986.)

Smelser, W. T. (1961). Dominance as a factor in achievement and perception in cooperative problem solving interactions. *Journal of Abnormal and Social Psychology, 62,* 535–542.

Smeltzer, L. R., & Davey, J. A. (1988). An analysis of management training via telecommunications. *Journal of European Industrial Training, 12*(3), 11–16.

Smircich, L., & Chesser, R. J. (1981). Superiors' and subordinates' perceptions of performance: Beyond disagreement. *Academy of Management Journal, 24,* 198–205.

Smircich, L., & Morgan, G. (1982). Leadership: The management of meaning. *Journal of Applied Behavioral Science, 18,* 257–273.

Smith, A. B. (1971). *Role expectations for and observations of community college department chairmen: An organizational study of consensus and conformity.* Doctoral dissertation, University of Michigan, Ann Arbor.

Smith, A. J. (1957). Similarity of values and its relation to acceptance and the projection of similarity. *Journal of Psychology. 43,* 251–260.

Smith, A. J. (1958). Perceived similarity and the projection of similarity: The influence of valence. *Journal of Abnormal and Social Psychology, 57,* 376–378.

Smith, B. J. (1982). *An initial test of a theory of charismatic leadership based on the responses of subordinates.* Doctoral dissertation, University of Toronto, Toronto.

Smith, B. L., & Smith, C. M. (1956). *International communication and political opinion: A guide to the literature.* Princeton, NJ: Princeton University Press.

Smith, C. A. (1937). Social selection and community leadership. *Social Forces, 15,* 530–545.

Smith, C. A., & Ellsworth, P. C. (1985). Patterns of cognitive appraisal in emotion. *Journal of Personality and Social Psychology, 48,* 813–838.

Smith, C. A., Organ, D. W., & Near, J. P. (1983). Organizational citizenship behavior: Its nature and antecedents. *Journal of Applied Psychology, 68,* 653–663.

Smith, C. B. (1984). Do legitimacy of supervisor and reward contingency interact in the prediction of work behavior? *Human Relations, 37,* 1029–1046.

Smith, C. G., & Ari, O. N. (1964). Organizational control structure and member consensus. *American Journal of Sociology, 69,* 623–638.

Smith, C. G., & Tannenbaum, A. S. (1963). Organizational control structure: A comparative analysis. *Human Relations, 16,* 299–316.

Smith, C. G., & Tannenbaum, A. S. (1965). Some implications of leadership and control for effectiveness in a voluntary association. *Human Relations, 18,* 265–272.

Smith, D. M. (1985). *Cavour.* London: Weidenfeld & Nicolson.

Smith, E. E. (1957). The effects of clear and unclear role expectations on group productivity and defensiveness. *Journal of Abnormal and Social Psychology, 55,* 213–217.

Smith, E. E. (1969). Congruence of self-perception variables for emergent leaders and non-leaders of small task groups. *Dissertation Abstracts International, 30,* 2899.

Smith, E. E., & Kight, S. S. (1959). Effects of feedback on insight and problem solving efficiency in training groups. *Journal of Applied Psychology, 43,* 209–211.

Smith, F. J., & Kerr, W. A. (1953). Turnover factors as assessed by the exit interview. *Journal of Applied Psychology, 37,* 352–355.

Smith, G. A. (1958). *Managing geographically decentralized companies.* Boston: Harvard Business School.

Smith, G. A., & Matthews, J. B. (1967). *Business, society, and the individual: Problems in responsible leadership of private enterprise organizations operating in a free society.* Homewood, IL: Irwin.

Smith, H. (1975). *Qualitative research methods.* New York: McGraw-Hill.

Smith, H. (1976). *The Russians.* New York: Ballantine.

Smith, H. C. (1947). Music in relation to employee attitudes, piece work production, and industrial accidents. *Applied Psychology Monographs,* No. 14.

Smith, H. C. (1964). *Psychology of industrial behavior.* New York: McGraw-Hill.

Smith, H. C. (1966). *Sensitivity to people.* New York: McGraw-Hill.

Smith, H. L., & Krueger, L. M. (1933). *A brief summary of literature on leadership.* Bloomington: Indiana University, School of Education Bulletin.

Smith, J. E. (1986). *Women in management (1979–1984): A review of the literature.* Paper, American Psychological Association, New York.

Smith, J. E., Carson, K. P., & Alexander, R. A. (1984). Leadership: It can make a difference. *Academy of Management Journal, 27,* 765–776.

Smith, L. M. (1967). *Social psychological aspects of school building design.* St. Louis, MO: Washington University.

Smith, M. (1934). Personality dominance and leadership. *Sociology and Social Research, 19,* 18–25.

Smith, M. (1935a). Leadership: The management of social differentials. *Journal of Abnormal and Social Psychology, 30,* 348–358.

Smith, M. (1935b). Comparative study of Indian student leaders and followers. *Social Forces, 13,* 418–426.

Smith, M. (1937). Classifications of eminent men. *Sociology and Social Research, 21,* 203–212.

Smith, M. (1948). Control interaction. *Journal of Social Psychology, 28,* 263–273.

Smith, M., & Nystrom, W. C. (1937). A study of social participation and of leisure time of leaders and non-leaders. *Journal of Applied Psychology, 21,* 251–259.

Smith, M., & White, M. C. (1987). Strategy, CEO specialization, and succession. *Administrative Science Quarterly, 32,* 263–280.

Smith, M. B., Bruner, J. S., & White, R. W. (1956). *Opinions and personality.* New York: Wiley.

Smith, M. C. (1975). *The relationship between the participative management style of elementary school principals as perceived by their teachers and level of teacher morale.* Doctoral dissertation, University of Southern California, Los Angeles.

Smith, M. G. (1942). Mending our weakest links. *Advanced Management, 7,* 77–83.

Smith, N. R. (1967). *The entrepreneur and his firm: The relationship between type of man and type of company.* East Lansing: Michigan State University, Graduate School of Business Administration.

Smith, N. R., & Miner, J. B. (1984). *Motivational considerations in the success of technologically innovative entrepreneurs.* Paper, Entrepreneurship Research Conference, Babson College and Georgia Institute of Technology.

Smith, P. B. (1963). Differentiation between sociometric rankings. *Human Relations. 16,* 335–350.

Smith, P. B. (1964). Attitude changes associated with training in human relations. *British Journal of Social and Clinical Psychology, 3,* 104–112.

Smith, P. B. (1970). *Group processes: Selected readings.* Middlesex, England: Penguin.

Smith, P. B. (1975). Controlled studies of the outcome of sensitivity training. *Psychological Bulletin, 82,* 597–622.

Smith, P. B. (1976). Why successful groups succeed: The implications of T-group research. In C. L. Cooper (Ed.), *Developing social skills in managers.* New York: Wiley.

Smith, P. B. (1984a). The effectiveness of Japanese styles of management: A review and critique. *Journal of Occupational Psychology, 57,* 121–136.

Smith, P. B. (1984b). Social service teams and their managers. *British Journal of Social Work, 14,* 601–613.

Smith, P. B., Moscow, D., Berger, M., & Cooper, C. (1969). Relationships between managers and their work associates. *Administrative Science Quarterly, 14,* 338–345.

Smith, P. B., Tayeb, M., Peterson, M., Bond, M., & Misumi, J. (1986). *On the generality of leadership style measures.* Unpublished manuscript.

Smith, P. C., Kendall, L. M., & Hulin, C. L. (1969). *The measurement of satisfaction in work and retirement.* Chicago: Rand McNally.

Smith, R. B. (1983). Why soldiers fight. Part I. Leadership, cohesion and fighter spirit. *Quality and Quantity, 18*(1), 1–32.

Smith, R. G. (1974). The effects of leadership style, leader position power, and problem solving method on group performance. *Dissertation Abstracts International, 35,* 773–774.

Smith, S., & Haythorn, W. W. (1972). Effects of compatibility, crowding, group size, and leadership seniority on stress, anxiety, hostility, and annoyance in isolated groups. *Journal of Personality and Social Psychology, 22,* 67–79.

Smith, W. P. (1967a). Power structure and authoritarianism in the use of power in the triad. *Journal of Personality, 35,* 65–89.

Smith, W. P. (1967b). Reactions to a dyadic power structure. *Psychonomic Science, 7,* 373–374.

Smith, W. P. (1968). Precision of control and the use of power in the triad. *Human Relations, 21,* 295–310.

Smits, S. J., & Aiken, W. J. (1969). *A descriptive study of supervisory practices as perceived by counselors in state vocational rehabilitation offices.* Bloomington: Indiana University, School of Education.

Smuckler, R. H., & Belknap, G. M. (1956). *Leadership and participation in urban political affairs.* East Lansing: Michigan State University.

Smythe, H. H. (1950). Changing patterns in Negro leadership. *Social Forces, 29,* 191–197.

Snadowsky, A. M. (1969). Group effectiveness as a function of communication network, task complexity, and leadership type. *Dissertation Abstracts International, 30,* 2155.

Snadowsky, A. M. (1972). Communication network research: An examination of controversies. *Human Relations, 25,* 283–306.

Snedden, D. (1930). Aspirational notions of leadership. *School & Society, 31,* 661–664.

Snoek, J. D. (1966). Role strain in diversified role sets. *American Journal of Sociology, 71,* 363–372.

Snyder, L. (1983). An anniversary review and critique: The Tylenol crisis. *Public Relations Review, 9*(3), 24–34.

Snyder, M. (1974). The self-monitoring of expressive behavior. *Journal of Personality and Social Psychology, 30,* 526–537.

Snyder, M. (1979). Self-monitoring processes. In L. Berkowitz (Ed.), *Advances in experimental social psychology, 12,* 86–128. New York: Academic Press.

Snyder, M., & Cantor, N. (1980). Thinking about ourselves and others: Self-monitoring and social knowledge. *Journal of Personality and Social Psychology, 39,* 222–234.

Snyder, M., & Mason, T. C. (1975). Persons, situations, and the control of social behavior. *Journal of Personality and Social Psychology, 32,* 637–644.

Snyder, N., & Glueck, W. F. (1977). *Mintzberg and the planning literature: An analysis and reconciliation.* Paper, Academy of Management, Orlando, FL.

Snyder, N., & Glueck, W. F. (1980). How managers plan—the analysis of managers' activities. *Long Range Planning, 13*(1), 70–76.

Snyder, N. H., & Wheelen, T. L. (1981). Managerial roles: Mintzberg and the management process theorists. *Proceedings, Academy of Management,* San Diego, CA, 249–253.

Snyder, R., French, J. R. P., & Hoehn, A. J. (1955). *Experiments on leadership in small groups* (Research Rep.). Chanute AF Base, IL: Personnel and Training Reserve Center.

Snyder, R. A., & Bruning, N. S. (1985). Quality of vertical dyad linkages: Congruence of supervisor and subordinate competence and role stress as explanatory variables. *Group & Organization Studies, 10,* 81–94.

Snyder, R. A., & Morris, J. H. (1984). Organizational communication and performance. *Journal of Applied Psychology, 69,* 461–465.

Sofer, C. (1955). Reaction to administrative change: A study of staff relations in three British hospitals. *Human Relations, 8,* 291–316.

Sofer, C. (1970). *Men in mid-career: A study of British managers and technical specialists.* New York: Cambridge University Press.

Sofranko, A. J., & Bridgeland, W. M. (1975). Agreement and disagreement on environmental issues among community leaders. *Cornell Journal of Social Relations, 10,* 151–162.

Sola Pool, I. de. (1964). The head of the company: Conceptions of role and identity. *Behavioral Science, 9,* 147–155.

Solem, A. R. (1953). The influence of the discussion leader's attitude on the outcome of group decision conferences. *Dissertation Abstracts, 13,* 439.

Solem, A. R. (1958). An evaluation of two attitudinal approaches to delegation. *Journal of Applied Psychology, 42,* 36–39.

Solem, A. R. (1960). Human relations training: Comparison of case study and role playing. *Personnel Administration, 23,* 29–37.

Solem, A. R., Onachilla, V. J., & Heller, K. Z. (1961). The posting problems technique as a basis for training. *Personnel Administration, 24*(3), 22–31.

Solomon, E. E. (1986). Private and public sector managers: An empirical investigation of job characteristics and organizational climate. *Journal of Applied Psychology, 71,* 247–259.

Solomon, L. (1960). The influence of some types of power relationships and game strategies upon the development of interpersonal trust. *Journal of Abnormal and Social Psychology, 61,* 223–230.

Solomon, L. N., Berzon, B., & Davis, D. P. (1970). A personal growth program for self-directed groups. *Journal of Applied Behavioral Science, 6,* 427–452.

Solomon, L. N., Berzon, B., & Weedman, C. W. (1968). The programmed group: A new rehabilitation resource. *International Journal of Group Psychotherapy, 18,* 199–219.

Solomon, R. H. (1976). Personality changes in leaders and members of personality laboratories. *Dissertation Abstracts International, 36,* 5285–5286.

Solomon, R. J. (1976). An examination of the relationship between a survey feedback O. D. technique and the work environment. *Personnel Psychology, 29,* 583–594.

Sommer, R. (1959). Studies in personal space. *Sociometry, 22,* 247–260.

Sommer, R. (1961). Leadership and group geography. *Sociometry, 24,* 99–110.

Sommer, R. (1965). Further studies of small group ecology. *Sociometry, 28,* 337–348.

Sommer, R. (1967). Small group ecology. *Psychological Bulletin, 67,* 145–152.

Sommer, R. (1969). *Personal space: The behavioral basis of design.* Englewood Cliffs, NJ: Prentice-Hall.

Sonnenfeld, J. (1981). Executive apologies for price fixing: Role biased perceptions of causality. *Academy of Management Journal, 24,* 192–198.

Sorcher, M. (1966). The interaction between participation, urgency and group leader status in small decision-making groups. *Dissertation Abstracts, 26,* 6213.

Sorcher, M. (1985). *Predicting executive success: What it takes to make it into senior management.* New York: Wiley.

Sorcher, M., & Goldstein, A. P. (1972). A behavior modeling approach in training. *Personnel Administration, 35,* 35–41.

Sord, B. H., & Welsch, G. A. (1964). *Managerial planning and control as viewed by lower levels of supervision.* Austin: University of Texas, Bureau of Business Research.

Sorokin, P. A. (1927a). *Social mobility.* New York: Harper.

Sorokin, P. A. (1927b). Leaders of labor and radical social movements in the United States and foreign countries. *American Journal of Sociology, 33,* 382–411.

Sorokin, P. A. (1943). *Man and society in calamity.* New York: Dutton.

Sorokin, P. A., & Berger, C. Q. (1939). *Time budgets of human behavior.* Cambridge, MA: Harvard University Press.

Sorokin, P. A., & Zimmerman, C. C. (1928). Farmer leaders in the United States. *Social Forces, 7,* 33–46.

Sorrentino, R. M., & Boutillier, R. G. (1975). The effect of quantity and quality of verbal interaction on ratings of leadership ability. *Journal of Experimental Social Psychology, 11,* 403–411.

South, E. B. (1927). Some psychological aspects of committee work. *Journal of Applied Psychology, 11,* 348–368.

South, S. J., Bonjean, C. M., Corder, J., & Markham, W. T. (1982). Sex and power in the federal bureaucracy: A comparative analysis of male and female supervisors. *Work and Occupations, 9*(2), 233–254.

Southern, L. J. F. (1976). *An analysis of motivation to manage in the tufted carpet and textile industry of northwest Georgia.* Doctoral dissertation, Georgia State University, Atlanta.

Southwick, C. H. (1963). *Primate social behavior.* Princeton, NJ: Van Nostrand.

Southwick, C. H., & Siddiqi, M. R. (1967). The role of social tradition in the maintenance of dominance in a wild Rhesus group. *Primates, 8,* 341–353.

Spangler, E., Gordon, M. A., & Pipkin, R. M. (1978). Token women: An empirical test of Kanter's hypothesis. *American Journal of Sociology, 84,* 160–170.

Spangler, W. D., & Braiotta L., Jr. (in press). Leadership and corporate audit committee effectiveness. *Group & Organization Studies.*

Sparks, C. P. (1966). *Personnel development series. Humble Oil & Refining Company.* Houston, TX. Unpublished report.

Sparks, C. P. (1989). Testing for management potential. In K. E. Clark & M. B. Clark (Eds.), *Measures of leadership.* West Orange, NJ: Leadership Library of America.

Sparks, R. (1976). Library management: Consideration and structure. *Journal of Academic Librarianship, 2*(2), 66–71.

Spaulding, C. B. (1934). Types of junior college leaders. *Sociology and Social Research, 18,* 164–168.

Spector, A. J. (1953). Factors in morale. *American Psychologist, 8,* 439–440.

Spector, A. J. (1956). Expectations, fulfillment, and morale. *Journal of Abnormal and Social Psychology, 52*, 51–56.

Spector, A. J. (1958). Changes in human relations attitudes. *Journal of Applied Psychology, 42*, 154–157.

Spector, A. J., Clark, R. A., & Glickman, A. S. (1960). Supervisory characteristics and attitudes of subordinates. *Personnel Psychology, 13*, 301–316.

Spector, B. (1987). Transformational leadership: The new challenge for U.S. unions. *Human Resource Management, 26*, 3–16.

Spector, P., & Suttell, B. J. (1957). *Research on the specific leader behavior patterns most effective in influencing group performance*. Washington, DC: American Institute for Research.

Spector, P. E. (1975). Relationships of organizational frustration with reported behavior reactions of employees. *Journal of Applied Psychology, 60*, 635–357.

Spence, J. T., Helmreich, R., & Stapp, J. (1975). Ratings of self and peers on the sex role attributes and their relation to self-esteem and conceptions of masculinity and femininity. *Journal of Personality and Social Psychology, 32*, 29–39.

Spencer, J. F. (1981). Contingency planning. *Handling & Shipping Management, 22*(11), 58–64.

Spencer, L. M. (undated). *The Navy leadership and management education and training program*. Unpublished manuscript.

Speroff, B. J. (1953). The group's role in role playing. *Journal of Industrial Training, 7*, 3–5.

Speroff, B. J. (1954). Rotational role playing used to develop executives. *Personnel Journal, 33*, 49–50.

Speroff, B. J. (1955). Job satisfaction and interpersonal desirability values. *Sociometry, 18*, 69–72.

Speroff, B. J. (1957). The "behind-the-back" way in training leaders. *Personnel Journal, 35*, 411–412, 435.

Sperry, R. (1985). Managers' job definitions and concepts. *Bureaucrat, 14*(3), 14–18.

Spicer, E. H. (1952). *Human problems in technological change*. New York: Russell Sage Foundation.

Spiegel, J. (1982). An ecological model of ethnic families. In M. McGoldrick, J. K. Pearce, & J. Giordano (Eds.), *Ethnicity and family therapy*. New York: Guilford Press.

Spielberger, C. D. (1972). Anxiety as an emotional state. In C. D. Spielberger (Ed.), *Anxiety: Current trends in theory and research*, Vol. 1. New York: Academic Press.

Spielberger, C. D., Gorsuch, R. L., & Lushene, R. E. (1970). *Manual for the state-trait anxiety inventory*. Palo Alto, CA: Consulting Psychologists Press.

Spilerman, S. (1977). Labor market structure, and socioeconomic economic achievement. *American Journal of Sociology, 85*, 551–593.

Spillane, R. (1980). Attitudes of business executives and union leaders to industrial relations: Twenty-three years later. *Journal of Industrial Relations, 22*, 317–325.

Spiller, G. (1929). The dynamics of greatness. *Sociological Review, 21*, 218–232.

Spillman, B., Spillman, R., & Reinking, K. (1981). Leadership emergence-dynamic analysis of the effects of sex and androgyny. *Small Group Behavior, 12*, 139–157.

Spitz, C. J. (1982). The project leader: A study of task requirements, management skills and personal style. *Dissertation Abstracts International, 43* (6A), 2073.

Spitzberg, I. J., Jr. (1986). *Questioning leadership*. Unpublished manuscript.

Spitzberg, I. J. (1987). Paths of inquiry into leadership. *Liberal Education, 73*(2), 24–28.

Spitzer, M. E., & McNamara, W. J. (1964). A managerial selection study. *Personnel Psychology, 17*, 19–40.

Spriegel, W. R., & Mumma, E. W. (1961). *Training supervisors in human relations*. Austin: University of Texas, Bureau of Business Research.

Springer, D. (1953). Ratings of candidates for promotion by co-workers and supervisors. *Journal of Applied Psychology, 37*, 347–351.

Springer, D. (1956). Why employees refuse promotion: A case study. *Personnel, 32*, 457–462.

Sproull, L. S. (1981). Managing education programs: A micro-behavioral analysis. *Human Organization, 40*, 113–122.

Spruill, V. J., Frye, R. L., & Butler, J. R. (1969). Differences in leadership stereotypes between deviants and normals. *Journal of Social Psychology, 79*, 255–256.

Sprunger, J. A. (1949). *The relationship of group morale estimates to other measures of group and leader effectiveness*. Master's thesis, Ohio State University, Columbus.

Srinivasan, V., Shocker, A. D., & Weinstein, A. G. (1973). Measurement of a composite criterion of managerial success. *Organizational Behavior and Human Performance, 9*, 147–167.

Srivastava, S. K., & Kumar, S. (1984). Leadership style and effectiveness of junior and middle level central government officers: A comparative study. *Psychological Studies. 29*, 136–138.

Srivastva, S. (1983). Introduction: Common themes in executive thought and action. In S. Srivastva & Associates, *The executive mind*. San Francisco: Jossey-Bass.

Srole, L. (1956). Social integration and certain corollaries: An exploratory study. *American Sociological Review, 21*, 709–716.

St. John, W. D. (1983). Successful communications between supervisors and employees. *Personnel Journal, 62*(1), 71–77.

Stagner, R. (1950). Stereotypes of workers and executives among college men. *Journal of Abnormal and Social Psychology, 45*, 743–748.

Stagner, R. (1954). Dual allegiance to union and management. 1. Dual allegiance as a problem in modern society. *Personnel Psychology, 7*, 41–46.

Stagner, R. (1962). Personality variables in union-management relations. *Journal of Applied Psychology, 46*, 350–357.

Stagner, R. (1969). Corporate decision making: An empirical study. *Journal of Applied Psychology, 53*, 1–13.

Stagner, R., Chalmers, W. E., & Derber, M. (1958). Guttman-type scales for union and management attitudes toward each other. *Journal of Applied Psychology, 42*, 293–300.

Stagner, R., Derber, M., & Chalmers, W. E. (1959). The dimensionality of union-management relations at the local level. *Journal of Applied Psychology, 43,* 1–7.

Stagner, R., Flebbe, D. R., & Wood, E. V. (1952). Working on the railroads: A study of job satisfaction. *Personnel Psychology, 5,* 293–306.

Stahl, G. R. (1953). Training directors evaluate role playing. *Journal of Industrial Training, 7,* 21–29.

Stahl, G. R. (1954). A statistical report of industry's experience with role playing. *Group Psychotherapy, 6,* 202–215.

Stahl, M. J. (1983). Achievement, power and managerial motivation: Selecting managerial talent with the job choice exercise. *Personnel Psychology, 36,* 775–789.

Staines, G., Tavris, C., & Jayarante, T. E. (1973). The queen bee syndrome. In C.Tavris (Ed.), *The female experience.* Del Mar, CA: CRM. Also: (1974). *Psychology Today 8*(1), 55–58, 60.

Stamp, G. (1981). Levels and types of managerial capability. *Journal of Management Studies, 18*(3), 277–297.

Stampolis, A. (1958). *Employees' atittudes toward unionization, management, and factory conditions.* Atlanta: Georgia State College of Business Administration.

Standard & Poors. (1967). *Register of corporations, directors and executives.* New York: Standard & Poors.

Stander, N. E. (1965). A longitudinal study of some relationships among criteria of managerial performance as perceived by superiors and subordinates. *Journal of Industrial Psychology, 3,* 43–51.

Stanley, D. T., Mann, D. E., & Doig, J. W. (1967). *Men who govern: A biographical profile of federal political executives.* Washington, DC: Brookings Institution.

Stanton, E. S. (1960). Company policies and supervisors' attitudes toward supervision. *Journal of Applied Psychology, 44,* 22–26.

Starch, D. (1943). *How to develop your executive ability.* New York: Harper.

Stark, H. F. (1958). *Trade union administration: Theory and practice.* Doctoral dissertation, Rutgers University, New Brunswick, NJ.

Stark, S. (1953). Toward a psychology of charisma: I. The innovation viewpoint of Robert Tucker. *Psychological Reports, 1,* 1163–1166.

Stark, S. (1969). Toward a psychology of charisma: II. The pathology viewpoint of James C. Davies. *Psychological Reports, 24,* 88–90.

Stark, S. (1970). Toward a psychology of charisma: III. Intuitional empathy, Vorbilder, Fuehrers, transcendence-striving, and inner creation. *Psychological Reports, 26,* 683–696.

Starr, C. G. (1954). *Civilization and the Caesars.* Ithaca, NY: Cornell University Press.

Stauss, G. (1963). The personality vs. organization theory. In D. R. Hampton, C. E. Summer, & R. A. Webber (Eds.), *Organizational behavior and the practice of management.* Glenview, IL: Scott, Foresman.

Staw, B. M. (1976). Organizations and their environments. In M. D. Dunnette (Ed.), *Handbook of industrial and organizational psychology.* Chicago: Rand McNally.

Staw, B. M. (1984). Organizational behavior: A review and reformulation of the Field's outcome variables. *Annual Review of Psychology, 35,* 627–666.

Staw, B. M., & Ross, J. (1980). Commitment in an experimenting society: A study of the attribution of leadership from administrative scenarios. *Journal of Applied Psychology, 65,* 249–260.

Staw, B. M., Sandelands, L. E., & Dutton, J. E. (1981). Threat-rigidity effects in organizational behavior: A multi-level analysis. *Administrative Science Quarterly, 26,* 501–524.

Stech, E. L. (1981). Leadership has a logic all its own. *Hospital Financial Management, 35*(2), 14–18, 24–25.

Stech, E. L. (1983). *Leadership communication.* Chicago: Nelson-Hall.

Steckler, N. A., & Rosenthal, R. (1985). Sex differences in nonverbal and verbal communication with bosses, peers, and subordinates. *Journal of Applied Psychology, 70,* 157–163.

Steel, R. P., & Mento, A. J. (1986). Impact of situational constraints on subjective and objective criteria of managerial job performance. *Organizational Behavior and Human Decision Processes, 37,* 254–265.

Steele, F. I., Zane, D. E., & Zalkind, S. S. (1970). Managerial behavior and participation in a laboratory training process. *Personnel Psychology, 23,* 77–90.

Steele, R. S. (1973). *The physiological concomitants of psychogenic motive arousal in college males.* Doctoral dissertation, Harvard University, Cambridge, MA.

Steele, R. S. (1977). Power motivation, activation, and inspirational speeches. *Journal of Personality, 45,* 53–64.

Steger, J. A., Kelley, W. B., Chouiniere, G., & Goldenbaum, A. (1977). A forced choice version of the Miner sentence completion scale and how it discriminates campus leaders and non-leaders. In J. B. Miner (Ed.), *Motivation to manage.* Atlanta, GA: Organizational Measurement Systems Press.

Steidlmeier, P. (1987). *The paradox of poverty: A reappraisal of economic development policy.* Cambridge, MA: Ballinger.

Stein, R. T. (1971). *Accuracy in perceiving emergent leadership in small groups.* Paper, American Psychological Association, Washington, DC.

Stein, R. T. (1975). Identifying emergent leaders from verbal and nonverbal communications. *Journal of Personality and Social Psychology, 32,* 125–135.

Stein, R. T. (1977). Accuracy of process consultants and untrained observers in perceiving emergent leadership. *Journal of Applied Psychology, 62,* 755–759.

Stein, R. T. (1980). *Assessment centers past and future: A critique of the measures used to assess managerial potential* (Special Report). Greensboro, NC: Center for Creative Leadership.

Stein, R. T. (1982a). Using real-time simulations to evaluate managerial skills. *Journal of Assessment and Central Technologies, 5*(2), 9–15.

Stein, R. T. (1982b). High status group members as exemptors: A summary of field research on the relationship of status to congruence conformity. *Small Group Behavior, 13,* 3–21.

Stein, R. T., Geis, F. L., & Damarin, F. (1973). Perception of emergent leadership hierarchies in task groups. *Journal of Personality and Social Psychology, 28,* 77–87.

Stein, R. T., & Heller, T. (1978). *The relationship of emergent leadership status and high verbal participation in small groups: A review of the literature.* Chicago: University of Illinois at Chicago Circle, Department of Psychology. Unpublished manuscript.

Stein, R. T., & Heller, T. (1979). An empirical analysis of the correlations between leadership status and participation rates reported in the literature. *Journal of Personality and Social Psychology, 37,* 1993–2002.

Stein, R. T., Hoffman, L.R., Cooley, S. J., & Pearse, R. W. (1979). Leadership valence: Modeling and measuring the process of emergent leadership. In J.G. Hunt & L. L. Larson (Eds.), *Crosscurrents in leadership.* Carbondale: Southern Illinois University.

Steiner, D. D., & Dobbins, G. H. (undated). *The role of work values in leader-member exchange.* Unpublished manuscript.

Steiner, I. D. (1965). *Current studies in social psychology.* New York: Holt, Rinehart & Winston.

Steiner, I. D. (1966). Models for inferring relationships between group size and potential group productivity. *Behavioral Science, 11,* 273–283.

Steiner, I. D. (1972). *Group process and productivity.* New York: Academic Press.

Steiner, I. D. (1974). *Task-performing groups.* Morristown, NJ: General Learning Press.

Steiner, I. D., & Dodge, J. S. (1957). A comparison of two techniques employed in the study of interpersonal perception. *Sociometry, 20,* 1–7.

Steiner, I. D., & Field, W. L. (1960). Role assignment and interpersonal influence. *Journal of Abnormal and Social Psychology, 61,* 239–245.

Steiner, I. D., & McDiarmid, C. G. (1957). Two kinds of assumed similarity between opposites. *Journal of Abnormal and Social Psychology, 55,* 140–142.

Steiner, I. D., & Peters, S. C. (1958). Conformity and the A-B-X model. *Journal of Personality, 26,* 229–242.

Steinman, J. I. (1974). *Some antecedents of participative decision making.* Doctoral dissertation, University of California, Berkeley.

Steinmetz, L. L. (1968). Leadership styles and systems management: More direction, less confusion. *Personnel Journal, 47,* 650–654.

Steinzor, B. (1950). The spatial factor in face to face discussion groups. *Journal of Abnormal and Social Psychology, 45,* 552–555.

Stening, B. W., & Wong, P. S. (1983). Australian managers' leadership beliefs, 1970/82. *Psychological Reports, 53,* 274–278.

Stephan, F. E. (1952). The relative rate of communication between members of small groups. *American Sociological Review, 17,* 482–486.

Stephenson, H. B. (1966). The effect of a management training program on leadership attitude and on-the-job behavior. *Dissertation Abstracts, 27,* 1512.

Stephenson, T. E. (1959). The leader-follower relationship. *Sociological Review, 7,* 179–195.

Sterling, T. D., & Rosenthal, B. G. (1950). The relationship of changing leadership and followership in a group to the changing phases of group activity. *American Psychologist, 5,* 311.

Sterngold, J. (1988, November 4). Group bids $20.9 billion for Nabisco. *New York Times,* D1.

Stevens, G. E., & DeNisi, A. S. (1980). Women as managers: Attitudes and attributions for performance by men and women. *Academy of Management Journal, 23,* 355–361.

Stewart, A., & Stewart, V. (1976). *Tomorrow's men today.* London: Institute of Personnel Management/Institute of Manpower Studies.

Stewart, A. J., & Rubin, Z. (1974). The power motive in the dating couple. *Journal of Personal and Social Psychology, 34,* 305–309.

Stewart, A. J., & Winter, D. G. (1976). Arousal of the power motive in women. *Journal of Consulting and Clinical Psychology, 44,* 495–496.

Stewart, B. R. (1978). *Leadership for agricultural industry.* New York: McGraw-Hill.

Stewart, G. T. (1974). Charisma and integration: An eighteenth century North American case. In *Comparative Studies in Society and History, 16*(2), 138–149.

Stewart, L. (1962). Management games today. In J. M. Kibbee, C. J. Craft, & B. Nanus (Eds.), *Management games.* New York: Rinehart.

Stewart, P. A. (1967). *Job enlargement.* Iowa City: University of Iowa, Center for Labor & Management.

Stewart, R. (1965). The use of diaries to study managers' jobs. *Journal of Management Studies, 2,* 228–235.

Stewart, R. (1966). The socio-cultural setting of management in the United Kingdom. *International Labor Review, 94,* 108–131.

Stewart, R. (1967). *Managers and their jobs: A study of the similarities and differences in the way managers spend their time.* London: Macmillan.

Stewart, R. (1976a). *Contrasts in management.* Maidenhead, England: McGraw-Hill.

Stewart, R. (1976b). To understand the manager's job: Consider demands, constraints, choices. *Organizational Dynamics, 4,* 22–32.

Stewart, R. (1982a). *Choices for the manager: A guide to understanding managerial work and behavior.* Englewood Cliffs, NJ: Prentice-Hall.

Stewart, R. (1982b). A model for understanding managerial jobs and behavior. *Academy of Management Review, 7,* 7–13.

Stierheim, M. R. (1984). Crisis management in metropolitan Dade County. *Public Management, 66*(3), 2–4.

Stimpson, D. V., & Bass, B. M. (1964). Dyadic behavior of self-, and interaction-, and task-oriented subjects in a test situation. *Journal of Abnormal and Social Psychology, 68,* 558–562.

Stinson, J. E. (1970). *The differential impact of participation in laboratory training in collaborative task effort in intact and fragmented groups.* Doctoral dissertation, Ohio State University, Columbus.

Stinson, J. E. (1972). "Least preferred coworker" as a measure of leadership style. *Psychological Reports, 30,* 930.

Stinson, J. E., & Hellebrandt, E. T. (1972). Group cohesiveness, productivity, and strength of formal leadership. *Journal of Social Psychology, 87,* 99–105.

Stinson, J. E., & Johnson, T. W. (1975). The path-goal theory of leadership: A partial test and suggested refinement. *Academy of Management Journal, 18,* 242–252.

Stinson, J. E., & Tracy, L. (1974). Some disturbing characteristics of the LPC score. *Personnel Psychology, 24,* 477–485.

Stires, L. K. (1970). Leadership designation and perceived ability as determinants of the tactical use of modesty and self-enhancement. *Dissertation Abstracts International, 30A,* 3551.

Stock, D. (1964). A survey of research on T groups. In L. P. Bradford, J. R. Gibb, & K. D. Benne, *T-group theory and laboratory method.* New York: Wiley.

Stockdale, J. B. (1981). The principles of leadership. *American Educator, 5*(4), 12, 14-15, 33.

Stockdale, J. B. (1987). *Leadership in response to changing societal values.* Paper, Conference on Military Leadership: Traditions and Future Trends, United States Naval Academy, Annapolis, MD.

Stogdill, R. M. (1948). Personal factors associated with leadership: A survey of the literature. *Journal of Psychology, 25,* 35-71.

Stogdill, R. M. (1949). The sociometry of working relations in formal organizations. *Sociometry, 12,* 276-286.

Stogdill, R. M. (1950). Leadership, membership and organization. *Psychological Bulletin, 47,* 1-14.

Stogdill, R. M. (1951a). The organization of working relationships: Twenty sociometric indices. *Sociometry, 14,* 366-374.

Stogdill, R. M. (1951b). Studies in naval leadership, Part II. (Ed.), In H. Guetzkow (Ed.), *Groups, leadership, and men.* Pittsburgh: Carnegie Press.

Stogdill, R. M. (1952). Leadership and morale in organized groups. In J. E. Hulett & R. Stagner (Eds.), *Problems in social psychology.* Urbana: University of Illinois.

Stogdill, R. M. (1955). Interactions among superiors and subordinates. *Sociometry, 18,* 552-557.

Stogdill, R. M. (1957a). *Leadership and structures of personal interaction.* Columbus: Ohio State University, Bureau of Business Research.

Stogdill, R. M. (1957b). *The RAD Scales: Manual.* Columbus: Ohio State University, Bureau of Business Research.

Stogdill, R. M. (1959). *Individual behavior and group achievement.* New York: Oxford University Press.

Stogdill, R. M. (1962). Intragroup-intergroup theory and research. In M. Sherif (Ed.), *Intergroup relations and leadership.* New York: Wiley.

Stogdill, R. M. (1963a). *Manual for the Leader Behavior Description Questionnaire—Form XII.* Columbus: Ohio State University, Bureau of Business Research.

Stogdill, R. M. (1963b). *Team achievement under high motivation.* Columbus: Ohio State University, Bureau of Business Research.

Stogdill, R. M. (1965a). *Managers, employees, organizations.* Columbus: Ohio State University, Bureau of Business Research.

Stogdill, R. M. (1965b). *Manual for job satisfaction and expectation scales.* Columbus: Ohio State University, Bureau of Business Research.

Stogdill, R. M. (1967). The structure of organization behavior. *Multivariate Behavior Research, 2,* 47-61.

Stogdill, R. M. (1968). *Leadership: A survey of the literature. I. Selected topics.* Greensboro, NC: Smith Richardson Foundation.

Stogdill, R. M. (1969). Validity of leader behavior descriptions. *Personnel Psychology, 22,* 153-158.

Stogdill, R. M. (1970). *Effects of leadership training on the performance of sororities.* Columbus: Ohio State University. Unpublished report.

Stogdill, R. M. (1972). Group productivity, drive, and cohesiveness. *Organizational Behavior and Human Performance, 8,* 26-43.

Stogdill, R. M. (1974). *Handbook of leadership* (1st ed.). New York: Free Press.

Stogdill, R. M., (1975). The evolution of leadership theory. *Proceedings, Academy of Management,* New Orleans, LA, 4-6.

Stogdill, R. M., & Bailey, W. R. (1969). *Changing the response of vocational students to supervision: The use of motion pictures and group discussion.* Columbus: Ohio State University, Center for Vocational and Technical Education.

Stogdill, R. M., Bailey, W. R., Coady, N. P., & Zimmer, A. (1971). Improving response to supervision. *Training & Development Journal, 25*(9), 16-22.

Stogdill, R. M., & Coady, N. P. (1970). Preferences of vocational students for different styles of supervisory behavior. *Personnel Psychology, 23,* 309-312.

Stogdill, R. M., Coady, N. P., & Zimmer, A. (1970). *Response of vocational students to supervision: Effects of reinforcing positive and negative attitudes toward different supervisory roles.* Columbus: Ohio State University, Center for Vocational and Technical Education.

Stogdill, R. M., & Coons, A. E. (1957). *Leader behavior: Its description and measurement.* Columbus: Ohio State University, Bureau of Business Research.

Stogdill, R. M., & Goode, O. S. (1957). Effects of the interactions of superiors upon the performances and expectations of subordinates. *International Journal of Sociometry, 1,* 133-145.

Stogdill, R. M., Goode, O. S., & Day, D. R. (1962). New leader behavior description sub-scales. *Journal of Psychology, 54,* 259-269.

Stogdill, R. M., Goode, O. S., & Day, D. R. (1963a). The leader behavior of corporation presidents. *Personnel Psychology, 16,* 127-132.

Stogdill, R. M., Goode, O. S., & Day, D. R. (1963b). The leader behavior of United States senators. *Journal of Psychology, 56,* 3-8.

Stogdill, R. M., Goode, O. S., & Day, D. R. (1964). The leader behavior of presidents of labor unions. *Personnel Psychology, 17,* 49-57.

Stogdill, R. M., Goode, O. S., & Day, D. R. (1965). *The leader behavior of university presidents.* Columbus: Ohio State University, Bureau of Business Research.

Stogdill, R. M., & Haase, K. K. (1957). Structures of working relationships. In R. M. Stogdill (Ed.), *Leadership and structures of personal interaction.* Columbus: Ohio State University, Bureau of Business Research.

Stogdill, R. M., & Koehler, K. (1952). *Measures of leadership structure and organization change.* Columbus: Ohio State University, Personnel Research Board.

Stogdill, R. M., & Scott, E. L. (1957). Responsibility and authority relationships. In R. M. Stogdill (Ed.), *Leadership and structures of personal interaction.* Columbus: Ohio State University, Bureau of Business Research.

Stogdill, R. M., Scott, E. L., & Jaynes, W. E. (1956). *Leadership and role expectations*. Columbus: Ohio State University, Bureau of Business Research.

Stogdill, R. M., & Shartle, C. L. (1948). Methods for determining patterns of leadership behavior in relation to organization structure and objectives. *Journal of Applied Psychology, 32*, 286–291.

Stogdill, R. M., & Shartle, C. L. (1955). *Methods in the study of administrative leadership*. Columbus: Ohio State University, Bureau of Business Research.

Stogdill, R. M., & Shartle, C. L. (1956). *Patterns of administrative performance*. Columbus: Ohio State University, Bureau of Business Research.

Stogdill, R. M., & Shartle, C. L. (1958). *Manual for the Work Analysis Forms*. Columbus: Ohio State University, Bureau of Business Research.

Stogdill, R. M., Shartle, C. L., Scott, E. L., Coons, A. E., & Jaynes, W. E. (1956). *A predictive study of administrative work patterns*. Columbus: Ohio State University, Bureau of Business Research.

Stogdill, R. M., Shartle, C. L., Wherry, R. J., & Jaynes, W. E. (1955). A factorial study of administrative behavior. *Personnel Psychology, 8*, 165–180.

Stogdill, R. M., Wherry, R. J., & Jaynes, W. E. (1953). *Patterns of leader behavior: A factorial study of Navy officer performance*. Columbus: Ohio State University, Bureau of Business Research.

Stohl, C. (1986). The role of memorable messages in the process of organizational socialization. *Communication Quarterly, 34*, 231–249.

Stoltz, R. E. (1959). Factors in supervisors' perceptions of physical science research personnel. *Journal of Applied Psychology, 43*, 256–258.

Stone, D. L., Gueutal, H. G., & MacIntosh, B. (1984). The effects of feedback sequence and expertise of rater on perceived feedback accuracy. *Personnel Psychology, 37*, 487–506.

Stone, G. G., Gage, N. L., & Leavitt, G. S. (1957). Two kinds of accuracy in predicting another's responses. *Journal of Social Psychology, 45*, 245–254.

Stone, P., & Kamiya, J. (1957). Judgments of consensus during group discussion. *Journal of Abnormal and Social Psychology, 55*, 171–175.

Stone, R. C. (1946). Status and leadership in a combat-fighter squadron. *American Journal of Sociology, 51*, 388–394.

Stone, S. (Ed.). (1976). *Management for nurses*. St. Louis, MO: C. V. Mosby.

Stonequist, E. V. (1937). *The marginal man*. New York: Scribner's.

Stoner-Zemel, M. J. (1988). *Visionary leadership, management, and high performing work units*. Doctoral dissertation, University of Massachusetts, Amherst.

Stoodley, B. H. (1962). *Society and self: A reader in social psychology*. New York: Free Press.

Storey, A. W. (1954). A study of member satisfaction and types of contributions in discussion groups with responsibility-sharing leadership. *Dissertation Abstracts, 14*, 737.

Stotland, E. (1954). Peer groups and reactions to power figures. *American Psychologist, 9*, 478.

Stotland, E. (1959). Peer groups and reactions to power figures. In D.

Cartwright (Ed.), *Studies in social power*. Ann Arbor: University of Michigan, Institute for Social Research.

Stotland, E. (1969). *The psychology of hope*. San Francisco: Jossey-Bass.

Stotland, E., Cottrell, N. B., & Laing, G. (1960). Group interaction and perceived similarity of members. *Journal of Abnormal and Social Psychology, 61*, 335–340.

Stotland, E., Thorley, S., Thomas, E., Cohen, A., & Zander, A. (1957). The effects of group expectations and self-esteem upon self-evaluation. *Journal of Abnormal and Social Psychology, 54*, 55–63.

Stotland, E., Zander, A., & Natsoulas, T. (1961). Generalization of interpersonal similarity. *Journal of Abnormal and Social Psychology, 62*, 250–256.

Stouffer, S. A. (1949). An analysis of conflicting social norms. *American Sociological Review, 14*, 707–717.

Stouffer, S. A., Suchman, E. A., DeVinney, L. C., Star, S. A., & Williams, R. M., Jr. (1949). *The American soldier: Adjustment during army life*. Princeton, NJ: Princeton University Press.

Stouffer, S. A., & Toby, J. (1951). Role conflict and personality. *American Journal of Sociology, 56*, 395–406.

Strasser, F. (1983). Techniques: Delicate delegation. *Management World, 12*(4), 32–33.

Strauss, A. L. (1944). The literature on panic. *Journal of Abnormal and Social Psychology, 39*, 317–328.

Strauss, G. (1962). Tactics of lateral relationship: The purchasing agent. *Administrative Science Quarterly, 7*, 161–186.

Strauss, G. (1963). Some notes on power-equalization. In H. J. Leavitt (Ed.), *The social science of organizations: Four perspectives*. Englewood Cliffs, NJ: Prentice-Hall.

Strauss, G. (1966). Participative management: A critique. *ILR Research, Cornell University, 12*, 3–6.

Strauss, G., & Rosenstein, E. (1970). Workers' participation: A critical view. *Industrial Relations, 9*, 197–214.

Stray, H. F. (1934). Leadership traits of girls in girls' camps. *Sociology and Social Research, 18*, 241–250.

Streib, G. F., Folts, W. E., & LaGreca, A. J. (1985). Autonomy, power, and decision-making in thirty-six retirement communities. *Gerontologist, 25*, 403–409.

Streufert, S. (1965). Communicator importance and interpersonal attitudes toward conforming and deviant group members. *Journal of Personality and Social Psychology, 2*, 242–246.

Streufert, S., Streufert, S. C., & Castore, C. H. (1968). Leadership in negotiations and the complexity of conceptual structure. *Journal of Applied Psychology, 52*, 218–223.

Strickland, L. H. (1967). Need for approval and the components of the ASo score. *Perceptual and Motor Skills, 24*, 875–878.

Strickland, L., Guild, P., Barefoot, J., & Paterson, S. (1978). Teleconferencing and leadership emergence. *Human Relations, 31*, 583–596.

Stringer, L. A. (1970). Sensitivity training: An alternative to the T-group method. *Teachers College Record, 71*, 633–640.

Strodtbeck, F. L. (1951). Husband-wife interaction over revealed differences. *American Journal of Sociology, 16*, 468–473.

Strodtbeck, F. L., & Hare, A. P. (1954). Bibliography of small group research: From 1900 through 1953. *Sociometry, 17,* 107–178.

Strodtbeck, F. L., & Hook, L. H. (1961). The social dimensions of a twelve man jury team. *Sociometry, 24,* 397–415.

Strodtbeck, F. L., & Mann, R. D. (1956). Sex role differentiation in jury deliberations. *Sociometry, 19,* 3–11.

Stromberg, R. P. (1967). Value orientation and leadership behavior of school principals. *Dissertation Abstracts, 27,* 2811.

Strong, E. K. (1943). *Vocational interests of men and women.* Stanford, CA: Stanford University Press.

Strong, L. (1956). Of time and top management. *Management Review, 45,* 486–493.

Strong, P. M. (1984). On qualitative methods and leadership research. In J. G. Hunt, D. Hosking, C. A. Schriesheim, & R. Stewart (Eds.), *Leaders and managers: International perspectives on managerial behavior and leadership.* New York: Pergamon.

Stroud, P. V. (1959). Evaluating a human relations training program. *Personnel, 36,* 52–60.

Strozier, C. B., & Offer, D. (1985a). Introduction. In C. B. Strozier & D. Offer (Eds.), *The leader: Psychohistorical essays.* New York: Plenum.

Strozier, C. B., & Offer, D. (1985b). Sigmund Freud and history. In C. B. Strozier & D. Offer (Eds.), *The leader: Psychohistorical essays.* New York: Plenum.

Strube, M. J., & Garcia, J. E. (1981). A meta-analytical investigation of Fiedler's contingency model of leadership effectiveness. *Psychological Bulletin, 90,* 307–321.

Strube, M. J., & Garcia, J. E. (1983). On the proper interpretation of empirical findings: Strube and Garcia (1981) revisited. *Psychological Bulletin, 93,* 600–603.

Strümpfer, D. J. W. (1983). How managers describe themselves in a job context. *South African Journal of Business Management, 14,* 45–52.

Strunk, O. (1957). Empathy: A review of theory and research. *Psychological Newsletter, NYU, 9,* 47–57.

Strupp, H. H., & Hausman, H. J. (1953). Some correlates of group productivity. *American Psychologist, 8,* 443–444.

Stryker, P. (1956). How participative can management get? *Fortune, 54,* 134–136, 217–218, 220.

Stryker, P. (1960). *The character of the executive.* New York: Harper & Row.

Student, K. R. (1968). Supervisory influence and workgroup performance. *Journal of Applied Psychology, 52,* 188–194.

Stumpf, S. (undated). *Leadership behaviors in managing scientists and engineers: A path analytic approach.* Unpublished manuscript.

Sturmthal, A. (1961). The workers' councils in Poland. *Industrial Labor Relations Review, 14,* 379–396.

Sturmthal, A. (1964). *Workers' councils: A study of workplace organization on both sides of the Iron Curtain.* Cambridge, MA: Harvard University Press.

Stymne, B. (1986). Industrial democracy and the worker. *International Review of Applied Psychology, 35,* 101–120.

Styskal, R. A. (1980). Power and commitment in organizations: A test of the participation thesis. *Social Forces, 58,* 925–943.

Suchman, J. (1956). Social sensitivity in the small task-oriented group. *Journal of Abnormal and Social Psychology, 52,* 75–83.

Sugiman, T., & Misumi, J. (1984). Action research on evacuation method in emergent situation: II. Effects of leader: Evacuee ratio on efficiency of follow-direction method and follow-me method. *Japanese Journal of Experimental Social Psychology, 23,* 107–115.

Sugiman, T., & Misumi, J. (1988). Development of a new evacuation method for emergencies: Control of collective behavior by emergent small groups. *Journal of Applied Psychology, 73(1),* 3–10.

Sugiman, T., Misumi, J., & Sako, H. (1983). Action research on evacuation method in emergent situations: I. Comparison between follow-direction method and follow-me method. *Japanese Journal of Experimental Social Psychology, 22,* 95–98.

Sukel, W. M. (1983) Assessing adults' socialization: Attitudes of top, middle, and supervisory managers. *Psychological Reports, 52,* 735–739.

Suliman, N. H. (1981). Leadership in women's associations in Egypt. In F. I. Khuri (Ed.), *Leadership and development in Arab society.* Beirut, Lebanon: American University of Beirut. Center for Arab and Middle East Studies.

Sullivan, J., Suzuki, T., & Kondo, Y. (1984). Managerial theories of the performance control process in Japanese and American work groups. *Proceedings, Academy of Management,* Boston, 98–102.

Summers, G. F. (1987). Democratic governance. In D. E. Johnson, L. R. Meiller, L. C. Miller, & G. F. Summers (Eds.), *Needs assessment: Theory and methods.* Ames: Iowa State University Press.

Survey Research Center. (1948). *Productivity, supervision, and employee morale.* Ann Arbor: University of Michigan.

Susman, G. I. (1970). The concept of status congruence as a basis to predict task allocations in autonomous work groups. *Administrative Science Quarterly, 15,* 164–175.

Sutcliffe, R. E. (1980). A comparative study of leader behavior among deaf and hearing supervisors. *Dissertation Abstracts International, 42(2A),* 496.

Suttell, B. J., & Spector, P. (1955, November). *Research on the specific leader behavior patterns most effective in influencing group performance.* Washington, DC: American Institute for Research.

Sutton, C. D., & Moore, K. K. (1985). Executive women—20 years later. *Harvard Business Review, 63(5),* 42–66.

Sutton, C. D., & Woodman, R. W. (1989). Pygmalion goes to work: The effects of supervisor expectations in the retail setting. *Journal of Applied Psychology, 74*(in press).

Sutton, R. I., Eisenhardt, K. M., & Jucker, J. V. (1986). Managing organizational decline. *Organizational Dynamics, 14(4),* 17–29.

Svalastoga, K. (1950). Note on leaders' estimates of public opinion. *Public Opinion Quarterly, 14,* 767–769.

Swain, R. L. (1971). *Catalytic colleagues in a government R & D organization.* Master's thesis, Massachusetts Institute of Technology, Boston.

Sward, K. (1933). Temperament and direction of achievement. *Journal of Social Psychology, 4,* 406–429.

Swartz, J. L. (1973). *Analysis of leadership styles of college level head football coaches from five midwestern states.* Doctoral dissertation, University of Northern Colorado, Greeley.

Sweeney, A. B., Fiechtner, L. A., & Samores, R. J. (1975). An integrative factor analysis of leadership measures and theories. *Journal of Psychology, 90,* 75–85.

Sweeney, J. (1982). Research synthesis on effective school leadership. *Educational Leadership, 39,* 346–352.

Sweitzer, R. E. (1963). *Role expectations and perceptions of school principals* (Tech Rep.). Stillwater: Oklahoma State University.

Swigart, J. S. (1936). *A study of the qualities of leadership and administrative qualifications of thirty-eight women executives.* Master's thesis, Ohio State University, Columbus.

Swingle, P. G. (1970a). Exploitative behavior in non-zero-sum games. *Journal of Personality and Social Psychology, 16,* 121–132.

Swingle, P. G. (1970b). *The structure of conflict.* New York: Academic Press.

Switzer, K. A. (1975). Peasant leadership: Comparison of peasant leaders in two Colombian states. *International Journal of Comparative Sociology, 16,* 291–300.

Sykes, A. J. M. (1962). The effect of a supervisory training course in changing supervisors' perceptions and expectations of the role of management. *Human Relations, 15,* 227–243.

Sykes, A. J. M. (1964). A study in changing the attitudes and stereotypes of industrial workers. *Human Relations, 17,* 143–154.

Sylvia, D., & Hutchison, T. (1985). What makes Ms. Johnson teach? A study of teacher motivation. *Human Relations, 38,* 841–856.

Symonds, P. M. (1947). Role playing as a diagnostic procedure in the selection of leaders. *Sociatry, 1,* 43–50.

Symons, G. L. (1986). Coping with the corporate tribe: How women in different cultures experience the managerial role. *Journal of Management, 12,* 379–390.

Sypher, B. D., & Zorn, T. E., Jr. (1986). Communication-related abilities and upward mobility. *Human Communication Research, 12,* 420–431.

Szabo, D. M. (1981). *A relationship between job satisfaction of staff nurses with perceptions they hold of their head nurse's leadership behavior.* Master's thesis, Villanova University, Philadelphia.

Szilagyi, A. D. (1980a). Reward behavior of male and female leaders: A causal inference analysis. *Journal of Vocational Behavior, 16,* 59–72.

Szilagyi, A. D. (1980b). Causal inferences between leader reward behavior and subordinate performance, absenteeism, and work satisfaction. *Journal of Occupational Psychology, 53,* 195–204.

Szilagyi, A. D., Jr., & Schweiger, D. M. (1984). Matching managers to strategies: A review and suggested framework. *Academy of Management Review, 9,* 626–637.

Szilagyi, A. D., & Sims, H. P. (1974a). The cross-sample stability of the supervisory behavior description questionnaire. *Journal of Applied Psychology, 59,* 767–770.

Szilagyi, A. D., & Sims, H. P. (1974b). An exploration of the path-goal theory of leadership in a health care environment. *Academy of Management Journal, 17,* 622–634.

Tabb, J. Y., & Goldfarb, A. (1970). *Workers' participation in management expectations and experience.* Elmsford, NY: Pergamon.

Taft, R. (1955). The ability to judge people. *Psychological Bulletin, 52,* 1–23.

Tagiuri, R. (1965). Value orientations and the relationship of managers and scientists. *Administrative Science & Quarterly, 10,* 39–51.

Tagiuri, R. (1969). Person perception. In G. Lindzey & E. Aronson (Eds.), *The handbook of social psychology,* Vol. 3. Reading, MA: Addison-Wesley.

Tagiuri, R., & Kogan, N. (1957). The visibility of interpersonal preferences. *Human Relations, 10,* 385–390.

Tagiuri, R., Kogan, N., & Long, L. M. K. (1958). Differentiation of sociometric choice and status relations in a group. *Psychological Reports, 4,* 523–526.

Tagiuri, R., & Petrullo, L. (1958). *Person perception and interpersonal behavior.* Stanford, CA: Stanford University Press.

Takamiya, M. (1979). *Japanese multinationals in Europe: Internal operations and their public policy implications.* Berlin: International Institute of Management.

Talland, G. A. (1954). The assessment of group opinion by leaders and their influence on its formation. *Journal of Abnormal and Social Psychology, 49,* 431–434.

Talland, G. A. (1957). Rate of speaking as a group norm. *Human Organization, 15,* 8–10.

Tang, T. L., Tollison, P. S., & Whiteside, H. D. (1988). *Top-, middle-, and lower-management attendance and quality circle effectiveness.* Paper, American Psychological Association, Atlanta, GA.

Tanimoto, R. H. (1977). *A field study of MBO in a utility company.* MBA thesis, Pepperdine University, School of Business and Management, Malibu, CA.

Tannenbaum, A. S. (1956a). The concept of organization control. *Journal of Social Issues, 12,* 50–60.

Tannenbaum, A. S. (1956b). Control structure and union functions. *American Journal of Sociology, 61,* 536–545.

Tannenbaum, A. S. (1958). The relationship between personality and group structure. In R. Likert (Ed.), Effective supervision: An adaptive and relative process. *Personnel Psychology, 11,* 317–322.

Tannenbaum, A. S. (1962). An event-structure approach to social power and to the problem of power comparability. *Behavioral Science, 7,* 315–331.

Tannenbaum, A. S. (1963). *Control in organizations: Individual adjustment and organizational performance.* Palo Alto, CA: Stanford University.

Tannenbaum, A. S. (1966). *Social psychology of the work organization.* San Francisco: Wadsworth.

Tannenbaum, A. S. (1968). *Control in organizations.* New York: McGraw-Hill.

Tannenbaum, A. S. (1974). *Hierarchy in organizations: An international comparison.* San Francisco: Jossey-Bass.

Tannenbaum, A. S., & Allport, F. H. (1956). Personality structure and group structure: An interpolative study of their relationships through event-structure analysis. *Journal of Abnormal and Social Psychology, 53,* 272–280.

Tannenbaum, A. S., & Bachman, J. G. (1966). Attitude uniformity and role in a voluntary organization. *Human Relations, 19,* 309–323.

Tannenbam, A. S., & Georgopoulos, B. S. (1957). The distribution of control in formal organizations. *Social Forces, 36,* 44–50.

Tannenbaum, A. S., & Smith, C. G. (1964). Effects of member influence in an organization: Phenomenology versus organization structure. *Journal of Abnormal and Social Psychology, 69,* 401–410.

Tannenbaum, D. E. (1959). Relation of executive leadership to the factor of external authority: A study of board-executive relationships in five family agencies. *Dissertation Abstracts, 22,* 1239.

Tannenbaum, R. (1950). Managerial decision-making. *Journal of Business, 23,* 33–37.

Tannenbaum, R., Kallejian, V., & Weschler, I. R. (1954). Training managers for leadership. *Instructions on Industrial Relations,* UCLA, Los Angeles No. 35.

Tannenbaum, R., & Massarik, F. (1950). Participation by subordinates in the managerial decision-making process. *Canadian Journal of Economic and Political Science, 16,* 408–418.

Tannenbaum, R., & Massarik, F. (1951). Sharing decision making with subordinates. In R. Dubin (Ed.), *Human relations in administration.* Englewood Cliffs, NJ: Prentice-Hall.

Tannenbaum, R., & Schmidt, W. H. (1958). How to choose a leadership pattern. *Harvard Business Review, 36*(2), 95–101.

Tannenbaum, R., Weschler, I. R., & Massarik, F. (1961). *Leadership and organization.* New York: McGraw-Hill.

Tansik, D. A. (1971). *Influences of organizational goal structure upon participant evaluations.* Paper, Academy of Management, Atlanta, GA.

Tarnapol, L. (1958). Personality differences between leaders and non-leaders. *Personnel Journal, 37,* 57–60.

Tarnowieski, D. (1973). *The changing success ethic.* New York: American Management Association, AMACOM survey report series.

Taub, R. P. (1969). *Bureaucrats under stress.* Berkeley: University of California Press.

Taussig, F. W., & Barker, W. S. (1925). American corporations and their executives: A statistical inquiry. *Quarterly Journal of Economics, 40,* 1.

Taussig, F. W., & Joslyn, C. S. (1932). *American business leaders: A study in social origins and social stratification.* New York: Macmillan.

Tavris, C. (1977). Men and women report their views on masculinity. *Psychology Today, 10,* 34–42, 82.

Taylor, B., & Lippitt, G. L. (Eds.). (1975). *Management development and training handbook.* London: McGraw-Hill

Taylor, D. W., Berry, P. C., & Block, C. H. (1958). Does group participation when using brainstorming facilitate or inhibit creative thinking? *Administrative Science Quarterly, 3,* 23–47.

Taylor, F. W. (1911). *Principles of scientific management.* New York: Harper & Brothers.

Taylor, H. (1980). Effective leadership styles. *Canadian Manager* (Canada), *5*(5), 12–13.

Taylor, H. R. (1986). Power at work. *Personnel Journal, 65*(4), 42–49.

Taylor, J. C. (1969). *The conditioning effects of technology on organizational behavior in planned social change.* Ann Arbor: University of Michigan, Institute for Social Research.

Taylor, J. C. (1971). *Technology and planned organizational change.* Ann Arbor: University of Michigan, Institute for Social Research.

Taylor, J. C., & Bowers, D. G. (1972). *Survey of organizations: Toward a machine-scored standardized questionnaire instrument.* Ann Arbor: University of Michigan, Institute for Social Research.

Taylor, K. F. (1967). Some doubts about sensitivity training. *Australian Psychology, 1,* 171–179.

Taylor M., Crook, R., & Dropkin, S. (1961). Assessing emerging leadership behavior in small discussion groups. *Journal of Educational Psychology, 52,* 12–18.

Taylor, M. S. (1981). *The effects of feedback consistency: One test of a model.* Paper, Academy of Management, San Diego, CA.

Taylor, M. S., Fisher, C. D., & Ilgen, D. R. (1984). Individual's reactions to performance feedback in organizations: A control theory perspective. In K. M. Rowland & G. R. Ferris (Eds.), *Research in personnel and human resource management,* Vol 2. Greenwich, CT: JAI Press.

Taylor, M. S., & Ilgen, D. R. (1979). *Employees' reactions to male and female managers: Is there a difference?* Paper, Academy of Management, Atlanta, GA.

Taylor, M. S., & Slania, M. A. (1981). *The moderating effects of chronic self-esteem upon the psychological success cycle.* Paper, Midwestern Psychological Association, Detroit.

Taylor, W. J., Jr. (1983). Leading the Army. *Washington Quarterly, 6*(1), 40–45.

Taynor, J., & Deaux, K. (1973). When women are more deserving than men: Equity, attribution, and perceived sex differences. *Journal of Personality and Social Psychology, 28,* 360–367.

Tead, O. (1929). The technique of creative leadership. *In human nature and management.* New York: McGraw-Hill.

Tead, O. (1935). *The art of leadership.* New York: McGraw-Hill.

Tedeschi, J. T., & Kian, M. (1962). Cross-cultural study of the TAT assessment for achievement motivation: Americans and Persians. *Journal of Social Psychology, 58,* 227–234.

Tedeschi, J. T., Lindskold, S., Horai, J., & Gahagan, J. P. (1969). Social power and the credibility of promises. *Journal of Personality and Social Psychology, 13,* 253–261.

Tedeschi, J. T., Schlenker, B. R., & Lindskold, S. (1972). The exercise of power and influence: The source of influence. In J. T. Tedeschi (Ed.), *Social influence processes.* Chicago: Aldine.

Teller, L. (1961). *Worker participation in business management.* Washington, DC: U.S. Government Printing Office.

Tenopyr, M. L. (1969). The comparative validity of selected leadership scales relative to success in production management. *Personnel Psychology, 22*, 77–85.

Tenopyr, M. L., & Ruch, W. W. (1965). *The comparative validity of selected leadership scales relative to success in production management.* Paper, American Psychological Association, Chicago.

Terauds, A., Altman, I., & McGrath, J. E. (1960). *A bibliography of small group research.* Arlington, VA: Human Sciences Research.

Terborg, J. R. (1977). Women in management: A research review. *Journal of Applied Psychology, 62*, 647–664.

Terborg, J. R., Castore, C. H., & DeNinno, J. A. (1975). *A longitudinal field investigation of the impact of group composition on group performance and cohesion.* Paper, Midwestern Psychological Association, Chicago.

Terborg, J. R., & Ilgen, D. R. (1975). A theoretical approah to sex discrimination in traditionally masculine occupations. *Organizational Behavior and Human Performance, 13*, 352–376.

Terborg, J. R., Peters, L. H., Ilgen, D. R., & Smith, F. (1977). Organizational and personal correlates of attitudes toward women as managers. *Academy of Management Journal, 20*, 89–100.

Terborg, J. R., & Shingledecker, P. (1983). Employee reactions to supervision and work evaluation as a function of subordinate and manager sex. *Sex Roles, 9*(7), 813–824.

Terhune, K. W. (1970). The effects of personality in cooperation and conflict. In P. Swingle (Ed.), *The structure of conflict.* New York: Academic Press.

Terman, L. M. (1904). A preliminary study of the psychology and pedagogy of leadership. *Pedagogical Seminary, 11*, 413–451.

Terman, L. M. (1925). *Mental and physical traits of a thousand gifted children.* Stanford, CA: Stanford University Press.

Terpstra, V. (1978). *The cultural environment of international business.* Cincinnati, OH: Southwestern.

Terreberry, S. (1968). The evolution of organizational environments. *Administrative Science Quarterly, 12*, 590–613.

Terrell, G., & Shreffler, J. (1958). A developmental study of leadership. *Journal of Educational Research, 52*, 69–72.

Terry, P. T. (1979). The English in management. *Management Today 1*(11), 90–97.

Tetrault, L. A., Schriesheim, C. A., & Neider, L. L. (1988). Leadership training interventions: A review. *Organizational Development Journal, 6*(3), 77–83.

Tewel, K. (1986). The urban school principal: The rocky road to instructional leadership. *Carnegie Quarterly, 31*(1), 1–8.

Tharenou, P., & Lyndon, J. T. (undated). *The effect of a supervisory development program on leadership style.* Unpublished manuscript.

Thelen, H. A. (1954). *Dynamics of groups at work.* Chicago: University of Chicago Press.

Thelen, H. A., et al. (1954). *Methods for studying work and emotionality in group operation.* Chicago: University of Chicago, Human Dynamics Laboratory.

Thelen, H. A., Hawkes, T. H., & Strattner, N. S. (1965). Role perception and task performance of experimentally composed small groups. Chicago: University of Chicago, Graduate School of Education.

Thelen, H. A., & Whitehall, J. (1949). Three frames of reference: The description of climate. *Human Relations, 2*, 159–176.

Then, D. A., (1988). *Benefits of beauty: The impact of physical attractiveness, sex and education on social and work evaluations.* Paper, International Congress of Psychology, Sydney, Australia.

Theodorson, G. A. (1957). The relationship between leadership and popularity roles in small groups. *American Sociological Review, 22*, 58–67.

Thiagarajan, K. M. (1968). *A cross-cultural study of the relationships between personal values and managerial behavior* (Tech. Rep. No. 23). Rochester, NY: University of Rochester, Management Research Center.

Thiagarajan, K. M., & Deep, S. D. (1970). A study of supervisor-subordinate influence and satisfacion in four cultures. *Journal of Social Psychology, 82*, 173–180.

Thibaut, J. W. (1950). An experimental study of the cohesiveness of underprivileged groups. *Human Relations, 3*, 251–278.

Thibaut, J. W., & Coules, J. (1952). The role of communication in the reduction of interpersonal hostility. *Journal of Abnormal and Social Psychology, 47*, 770–777.

Thibaut, J. W., & Faucheux, C. (1965). The development of contractual norms in a beginning situation under two types of stress. *Journal of Experimental Social Psychology, 1*, 89–102.

Thibaut, J. W., & Gruder, C. L. (1969). Formation of contractual agreements between parties of unequal power. *Journal of Personality and Social Psychology, 11*, 59–65.

Thibaut, J. W., & Kelley, H. H. (1959). *The social psychology of groups.* New York: Wiley.

Thibaut, J. W., & Riecken, H. W. (1955a). Some determinants and consequences of the perception of social causality. *Journal of Personality, 24*, 113–133.

Thibaut, J. W., & Riecken, H. W. (1955b). Authoritarianism, status, and the communication of aggression. *Human Relations, 8*, 95–120.

Thibaut, J. W. & Strickland, L. H. (1956). Psychological set and social conformity. *Journal of Personality, 25*, 115–129.

Thomas, A. B. (1988). Does leadership make a difference to organizational performance? *Administrative Science Quarterly, 33*, 388–400.

Thomas, E. J. (1957). Effects of facilitative role interdependence on group functioning. *Human Relations, 10*, 347–366.

Thomas, E. J. & Fink, C. F. (1963). Effects of group size. *Psychological Bulletin, 60*, 371–384.

Thomas, J. M. (1969). *The sensitivity hypothesis in laboratory education: Its effect on the organization.* Paper, Industrial Relations Research Association, New York.

Thomas, K. W. (1976). Conflict and conflict management. In M. D. Dunnette (Ed.), *Handbook of industrial and organizational psychology.* Chicago: Rand McNally.

Thomas, K. W., & Schmidt, W. H. (1976). A survey of managerial interests with respect to conflict. *Academy of Management Journal, 19,* 315–318.

Thomas, V. G. (1982). The relationship of race and gender of supervisor, subordinates, and organization to estimated stress and supervisory style in a simulated organization: A study of business administration and management students. *Dissertation Abstracts International, 44*(12B), 3970.

Thomason, G. F. (1967). Managerial work roles and relationships (Part II). *Journal of Management Studies, 4,* 17–30.

Thompson, D. C. (1963). *The Negro leadership class.* Englewood Cliffs, NJ: Prentice-Hall.

Thompson, D. E. (1971). Favorable self-perception, perceived supervisory style, and job satisfaction. *Journal of Applied Psychology, 55,* 349–352.

Thompson, G. G. (1944). The social and emotional development of preschool children under two types of educational programs. *Psychological Monographs, 56,* 1–29.

Thompson, J. D. (1956). Authority and power in "identical" organizations. *American Journal of Sociology, 62,* 290–301.

Thompson, J. D. (1967). *Organizations in action.* New York: McGraw-Hill.

Thompson, J. D. (1969). *Organizations in action: Social science bases of administrative theory.* Paper, American Psychological Association, Washington, DC.

Thomson, H. A. (1970). A comparison of predictor and criterion judgments of managerial performance using the multitrait-multimethod approach. *Journal of Applied Psychology, 54,* 496–502.

Thorndike, E. L. (1916). Education for initiative and originality. *Teachers College Record, 17,* 405–416.

Thorndike, E. L. (1920). Intelligence and its uses. *Harper's Magazine, 140,* 227–235.

Thorndike, E. L. (1936). The relation between intellect and morality in rulers. *American Journal of Sociology, 45,* 321–334.

Thorndike, E. L. (1939). How may we improve the selection, training and life-work of leaders? *Teachers College Record, 40,* 593–605.

Thorndike, E. L. (1940). *Human nature and the social order.* New York: Macmillan.

Thorndike, R. L. (1938). On what type of task will a group do well? *Journal of Abnormal and Social Psychology, 33,* 409–413.

Thorndike, R. L., & Stein, S. (1937). An evaluation of the attempts to measure social intelligence. *Psychological Bulletin, 23,* 275–285.

Thornton, A., & Freedman, D. (1979). Consistency of sex role attitudes of women, 1962–1977: Evidence from a panel study. *American Sociological Review, 44,* 831–842.

Thornton, G. C. (1968). The relationship between supervisory and self-appraisals of executive performance. *Personnel Psychology, 21,* 441–455.

Thornton, G. C. & Byham, W. C. (1982). *Assessment centers and managerial performance.* New York: Academic Press.

Thorsrud, E., & Emery, F. E. (1970). Industrial democracy in Norway. *Industrial Relations, 9,* 187–196.

Thrasher, F. (1927). *The gang.* Chicago: University of Chicago Press.

Throop, R. K. (1972). *An explanatory survey of teacher job satisfaction: A path analysis.* Doctoral dissertation, Syracuse University, Syracuse, NY.

Thucydides. (404 BC/1910). *History of the Peloponnesian War.* New York: Everyman Library.

Thurstone, L. L. (1944). *A factorial study of perception.* Chicago: University of Chicago Press.

Thurstone, L. L., & Chave, E. J. (1929). *The measurement of attitude.* Chicago: University of Chicago Press.

Tichy, N. (1973). An analysis of clique formation and structure in organizations. *Administrative Science Quarterly, 8,* 194–208.

Tichy, N., & Devanna, M. (1986). *Transformational leadership.* New York: Wiley.

Tichy, N., & Ulrich, D. (1983). *Revitalizing organizations: The leadership role.* Graduate School of Business Administration, University of Michigan, Ann Arbor. Unpublished manuscript.

Tichy, N M., & Ulrich, D. O. (1984). The leadership challenge—a call for the transformational leader. *Sloan Management Review, 26*(1), 59–68.

Tierney, W. G. (1987). *Symbolism and presidential perceptions of leadership.* Paper, Association for the Study of Higher Education, Baltimore.

Timaeus, E., & Lück, H. E. (1970). Stereotype Erwartungen bei der Wahrnehmung von Führungskräften in der Wirtschaft. *Psychologische Bundschau, 21,* 39–43.

Timasheff, N. S. (1938). Then power phenomenon. *American Sociological Review, 3,* 499–509.

Timmons, W. M. (1944). Some outcomes of participation in dramatics: II. Likeability and cooperativeness: Relationships between outcomes. *Journal of Social Psychology, 19–20,* 35–51.

Tinbergen, N. (1953). *Social behavior in animals.* London: Methuen Monograph.

Titus, C. H. (1950). *The process of leadership.* Dubuque, IA: W. C. Brown.

Titus, H. E., & Goss, R. G. (1969). Psychometric comparison of old and young supervisors. *Psychological Reports, 24,* 727–733.

Titus, H. E., & Hollander, E. P. (1957). The California F-Scale in psychological research. *Psychological Bulletin, 54,* 47–64.

Tjosvold, D. (1984a). Effects of crisis orientation on managers' approach to controversy in decision making. *Academy of Management Journal, 27,* 130–138.

Tjosvold, D. (1984b). Effects of leader warmth and directiveness on subordinate performance on a subsequent task. *Jounal of Applied Psychology, 69,* 422–427.

Tjosvold, D. (1985a). Implications of controversy research for management. *Journal of Management, 11,* 21–37.

Tjosvold, D. (1985b, August). Stress dosage for problem solvers. *Working Smart, 5.*

Tjosvold, D. (1985c). Power and social context in superior-subordinate interactions. *Organizational Behavior and Human Decision Processes*, 35, 281-293.

Tjosvold, D. (1985d). The effects of attribution and social context on superiors' influence and interaction with low performing subordinates. *Personnel Psychology*, 38, 361-376.

Tjosvold, D., Andrews, I., & Jones, H. (1983). Cooperative and competitive relationships between leaders and subordinates. *Human Relations*, 36, 1111-1124.

Tjosvold, D., Wedley, W. C., & Field, R. H. G. (1986). Constructive controversy, the Vroom-Yetton model, and managerial decision making. *Journal of Occupational Behavior*, 7, 125-138.

Toby, J. (1952). Some variables in role conflict analysis. *Social Forces*, 30, 323-327.

Toch, H., & Smith, H. C. (1968). *Social perception*. Princeton, NJ: Van Nostrand.

Toki, K. (1935). Führer-Gefolgschaftsstruktur in der Schulklasse. [Leader-follower structure in school classes.] *Japanese Journal of Psychology*, 10, 27-56.

Tomasko, R. (1987). *Downsizing*. New York: AMACOM.

Tomassini, L. A., Solomon, I., Romney, M. B., & Krogstad, J. L. (1982). A framework of a cognitive-behavior theory of leader influence and effectiveness. *Organizational Behavior and Human Performance*, 30, 391-406.

Tomekovic, T. (1962). Levels of knowledge of requirements as a motivation factor in the work situation. *Human Relations*, 15, 197-216.

Töpfer, A. (1978). Das Harzburger Modell in der Unternehmungpraxis—Eine Bestandanalyse. *Der Betrieb*, 38, 1802-1803.

Tornow, W. W., & Pinto, P. R. (1976). The development of a managerial job taxonomy: A system for describing, classifying, and evaluating executive positions. *Journal of Applied Psychology*, 61, 410-418.

Toronto, R. S. (1972). *General systems theory applied to the study of organizational change*. Doctoral dissertation, University of Michigan, Ann Arbor.

Torrance, E. P. (1952). *Survival research* (Rep. No. 29). Washington, DC: Human Resources Research Laboratory.

Torrance, E. P. (1953). Methods of conducting critiques of group problem-solving performance. *Journal of Applied Psychology*, 37, 394-398.

Torrance, E. P. (1954a). *Some consequences of power differences on decisions in B-26 crews* (Research Bull. 54-128). San Antonio, TX: USAF Personnel and Training Research Center.

Torrance, E. P. (1954b). The behavior of small groups under the stress conditions of "survival." *American Sociological Review*, 19, 751-755.

Torrance, E. P. (1955a). Some consequences of power differences in permanent and temporary three-man groups. In P. Hare, E. F. Borgatta, & R. F. Bales (Eds.), *Small groups*. New York: Knopf.

Torrance, E. P. (1955b). Perception of group functioning as a predictor of group performance. *Journal of Social Psychology*, 42, 271-281.

Torrance, E. P. (1956-57). Group decision-making and disagreement. *Social Forces*, 35, 314-318.

Torrance, E. P. (1959a). An experimental evaluation of "no-pressure" influence. *Journal of Applied Psychology*, 43, 109-113.

Torrance, E. P. (1959b). The influence of experienced members of small groups on the behavior of the inexperienced. *Journal of Social Psychology*, 49, 249-257.

Torrance, E. P. (1961). A theory of leadership and interpersonal behavior under stress. In L. Petrullo & B. Bass (Eds.), *Leadership and interpersonal behavior*. New York: Holt, Rinehart & Winston.

Torrance E. P., & Aliotti, N. C. (1965). Accuracy, task effectiveness, and emergence of a social-emotional resolver as a function of one- and two-expert groups. *Journal of Psychology*, 61, 161-170.

Torrance, E. P., & Mason, R. (1956). The indigenous leader in changing attitudes and behavior. *International Journal of Sociometry*, 1, 23-28.

Torrance, E. P., & Mason, R. (1958). Instructor effort to influence: An experimental evaluation of six approaches. *Journal of Educational Psychology*, 49, 211-218.

Torrance, E. P., & Staff. (1955). *Survival research. A report of the fourth year of development*. Reno, NV: Stead AFB, CRL Field Unit No. 2.

Tosi, H. (1970). A reexaminatin of personality as a determinant of the effects of participation. *Personnel Psychology*, 23, 91-99.

Tosi, H. (1971). Organization stress as a moderator in the relationship between influence and role response. *Academy of Management Journal*, 14, 7-20.

Tosi, H. (1973). The effect of interaction of leader behavior and subordinate authoritarianism. *Personnel Psychology*, 26, 339-350.

Tosi, H., Aldag, R., & Storey, R. (1973). On the measurement of the environment: An assessment of the Lawrence and Lorsch environment uncertainty questionnaire. *Administrative Science Quarterly*, 18, 27-36.

Touchet, R. E. (1949). *Leadership action: The transmission of information exclusively possessed*. Privately published.

Touhey, J. (1974). Effects of additional women professionals on ratings of occupational prestige and desirability. *Journal of Personality and Social Psychology*, 29, 86-89.

Trahey, J. (1977). *Women and power*. New York: Avon Books.

Trapp, E. P. (1955). Leadership and popularity as a function of behavioral predictions. *Journal of Abnormal and Social Psychology*, 51, 452-457.

Trattnor, J. (1963). Comparison of three methods for assembling aptitude test batteries. *Personnel Psychology*, 16, 230.

Trempe, J., Rigny, A., & Haccoun, R. R. (1985). Subordinate satisfaction with male and female managers: Role of perceived supervisory influence. *Journal of Applied Psychology*, 70, 44-47.

Tresemer, D. (1976). Do women fear success? *Signs: Journal of Women in Culture and Society*, 1, 863-874.

Triandis, H. C. (1959a). Differential perception of certain jobs and people by managers, clerks and workers in industry. *Journal of Applied Psychology*, 43, 221-225.

Triandis, H. C. (1959b). Categories of thought of managers, clerks, and workers in an industry. *Journal of Applied Psychology*, 43, 338-344.

Triandis, H. C. (1959c). A critique and experimental design for the study of the relationship between productivity and satisfaction. *Psychological Bulletin, 56,* 309–312.

Triandis, H. C. (1960). Comparative factorial analysis of job semantic structures of managers and workers. *Journal of Applied Psychology, 44,* 297–302.

Triandis, H. C. (1963). Factors affecting employee selection in two cultures. *Journal of Applied Psychology, 47,* 89–96.

Triandis, H. C. (1967). Interpersonal relations in international organizations. *Organizational Behavior and Human Performance, 2,* 26–55.

Triandis, H. (Ed.). (1980). *Handbook of cross-cultural psychology.* Boston: Allyn & Bacon.

Triandis, H. C. (1981). *Hispanic concerns about the U.S. Navy* (ONR Tech. Rep.). Champaign: University of Illinois.

Triandis, H. (1984). *Selection and retention of minorities in organizations.* ONR Conference on Minorities Entering High Tech Careers, Pensacola, FL.

Triandis, H., Feldman, J., Weldon, D. E., & Harvey, W. M. (1975). Ecosystem distrust and the hard-to-employ. *Journal of Applied Psychology, 60,* 44–56.

Triandis, H. C., Hui, C. H., Lisansky, J., Ottati, V., Marin, G., & Betancourt, H. (1982). *Perceptions of supervisor-subordinate relations among Hispanic and mainstream recruits* (ONR Tech. Rep. No. 11). Champaign: University of Illinois.

Triandis, H. C., Kashima, Y., Lisanky, J., and Marin, G. (1982). *Self-concepts and values among Hispanic and mainstream Navy recruits* (ONR Tech. Rep. No. 7). Champaign: University of Illinois.

Triandis, H. C., & Malpass, R. S. (1971). Studies of black and white interaction in job settings. *Journal of Applied Social Psychology, 1,* 101–117.

Triandis, H. C., Marin, G., Betancourt, H., & Chang, B. (1982). *Acculturation, biculturalism and familism among Hispanic and mainstream Navy recruits* (ONR Tech. Rep. No. 15). Champaign: University of Illinois.

Triandis, H. C., Marin, G., Betancourt, H., Lisansky, J., & Chang, B. (1982). *Dimensions of familism among Hispanic and mainstream Navy recruits* (ONR Tech. Rep. No. 14). Champaign: University of Illinois.

Triandis, H. C., Marin, G., Hui, C. H., Lisansky, J., & Ottati, V. (1982). *Role perceptions of Hispanic and mainstream Navy recruits* (ONR Tech. Rep. No. 24). Champaign: University of Illinois.

Triandis, H. C., Marin, G., Lisansky, J. & Betancourt, H. (1984). Simpatia as a cultural script of Hispanics. *Journal of Personality and Social Psychology, 47,* 1363–1375.

Triandis, H. C., Mikesell, E. H., & Ewen, R. B. (1962). *Some cognitive factors affecting group creativity* (Tech. Rep. No. 5). Urbana: University of Illinois, Group Effectiveness Research Laboratory.

Triandis, H. C., Ottati, V., & Marin, G. (1982). *Social attitudes among Hispanic and mainstream Navy recruits* (ONR Tech. Rep. No. 10). Champaign: University of Illinois.

Triandis, H. C., Vassiliou, V., & Thomanek, E. K. (1966). Social status as a determinant of respect and friendship acceptance. *Sociometry, 29,* 396–405.

Trice, H. M. (1959). A methodology for evaluating conference leadership training. *ILR Research, Cornell University, 5,* 2–5.

Trice, H. M. (1984). Rites and ceremonials in organizational culture. In S. B. Bacharach & S. M. Mitchell (Eds.), *Perspectives on organizational sociology: Theory and research,* Vol. 4. Greenwich, CT: JAI Press.

Trice, H. M., & Beyer, J. M. (1984). Studying organizational cultures through rites and ceremonials. *Academy of Management Review, 9,* 653–669.

Trice, H. M., & Beyer, J. M. (1986). Charisma and its routinization in two social movement organizations. *Research in Organizational Behavior, 8,* 113–164.

Trieb, S. E. (1967). *An analysis of supermarket managerial leadership and its relation to measures of organizational effectiveness.* Doctoral dissertation, Ohio State University, Columbus.

Trieb, S. E., & Marion, B. W. (1969). *Managerial leadership and the human capital of the firm.* Columbus: Ohio State University, College of Agriculture.

Trimble, C. (1968). Teachers' conceptions of leadership behavior of principals as related to principal's perception of this involvement in the decision-making process. *Dissertation Abstracts, 28,* 4432–4433.

Triplett, N. (1898). The dynamogenic factors in pacemaking and competition. *American Journal of Psychology, 9,* 507–533.

Triplett, N. (1900). The psychology of conjuring perceptions. *American Journal of Psychology, 11,* 439–510.

Tripp, L. (1986). Community leadership and black former activists of the 1960s. *Western Journal of Black Studies, 10(2),* 86–89.

Trist, E. L., & Bamforth, V. (1951). Some social and psychological consequences of the longwall method of coal-getting. *Human Relations, 4,* 3–38.

Trist, E. L., Higgin, G. W., Murray, H., & Pollock, A. B. (1963). *Organizational choice.* London: Tavistock.

Trittipoe, T. G., & Hahn, C. P. (1961). *Situational problems for leadership training. Part I—Development and evaluation of situational problems.* Washington, DC: American Institute for Research.

Trivedi, D. N. (1974). Modernization, rationality, opinion leadership or compartmentalization of spheres of activity. *Man in India, 54,* 271–280.

Tronc, K., & Enns, F. (1969). Promotional aspirations and differential role perceptions. *Alberta Journal of Educational Research, 15,* 169–183.

Tropp, K. J., & Landers, D. M. (1979). Team interaction and the emergence of leadership and interpersonal attraction in field hockey. *Journal of Sport Psychology, 1,* 228–240.

Trotter, R. J. (1987). Stop blaming yourself. *Psychology Today, 21(2),* 30–39.

Trow, D. B. (1957). Autonomy and job satisfaction in task-oriented groups. *Journal of Abnormal and Social Psychology, 53,* 204–209.

Trow, D. B. (1960). Membership succession and team performance. *Human Relations, 13,* 259–269.

Trow, D. B. (1961). Executive succession in small companies. *Administrative Science Quarterly, 6,* 228–239.

Trow, D. B., & Herschdorfer, G. (1965). *An experiment on the status incongruence phenomenon* (Tech. Rep.). Binghamton, NY: State University of New York.

Trow, D. B., & Smith, D. H. (1983). Correlates of volunteering in advocacy planning: Testing a theory. In D. H. Smith & J. Van Til (Eds.), *International perspectives on voluntary action research.* Washington, DC: University Press of America.

Troxell, J. P. (1954). Elements in job satisfaction: A study of attitudes among different occupational and status groups. *Personnel, 31,* 199–205.

Troy, D. B. (1961). Executive succession in small companies. *Administrative Science Quarterly, 6,* 228–239.

Truman, H. S. (1958). *Memoirs.* New York: Doubleday.

Trumbo, D. A. (1961). Individual and group correlates of attitudes toward work related change. *Journal of Applied Psychology, 45,* 338–344.

Tryon, C. M. (1939). Evaluations of adolescent personality by adolescents. *Monographs in Social Research and Child Development, 4,* No. 4.

Tscheulin, D. (1973). Leader behavior measurement in German industry. *Journal of Applied Psychology, 57,* 28–31.

Tsui, A. S. (1982). *A role set analysis of mangerial reputation.* Paper, Academy of Management, New York.

Tsui, A. S. (1984). A role set analysis of managerial reputation. *Organizational Behavior and Human Performance, 34,* 64–96.

Tsui, A. S., & Gutek, B. A. (1984). A role set analysis of gender differences in performance, affective relationships, and career success of industrial middle managers. *Academy of Management Journal, 27,* 619–635.

Tsui, A. S., & Ohlott, P. (1986). *Multiple assessment of managerial effectiveness: Consensus in effectiveness models.* Paper, American Psychological Association, Washington, DC. Also: (1988). *Personnel Psychology, 41,* 779–803.

Tsur, E. (1983, November). The kibbutz way of life. Structure and management of the kibbutz. *Kibbutz Studies,* 23–31.

Tsurumi, R. (1982, Spring/Summer). American origins of Japanese productivity: The Hawthorne experiment rejected. *Pacific Basin Quarterly, 7,* 14–15.

Tsurumi, Y. (1983a). *Multinational management: Business strategy and government policy* (2nd ed.). Cambridge, MA: Ballinger.

Tsurumi, Y. (1983b, July 31). U.S. mangers often "technically illiterate" and out of touch. *Washington Post.*

Tsutomu, O. (1964). *Bijinesu man (Business man).* Tokyo: San'ichi Shobo.

Tubbs, M. E. (1986). Goal setting: A meta-analytic examination of the empirical evidence. *Journal of Applied Psychology, 71,* 474–483.

Tubbs, S. L., & Baird, J. W. (1976). *The open person.* Columbus, OH: Charles E. Merrill.

Tubbs, S. L., & Hain, T. (1979). *Managerial communication and its relation to total organizational effectiveness.* Paper, Academy of Management, Atlanta, GA.

Tubbs, S. L., & Moss, S. (1978). Oganizational communication. In S. L. Tubbs, & S. Moss (Eds.), *Human communication.* New York: Random House.

Tubbs, S. L., & Porter, R. G. (1978). *Predictors of grievance activity.* Detroit, MI: General Motors Corporation. Unpublished report.

Tubbs, S. L., & Widgery, R. N. (1978). When productivity lags, check at the top: Are key managers really communicating? *Management Review, 67,* 20–25.

Tuchman, B. W. (1971). *Stilwell and the American experience in China, 1911–45.* New York: Macmillan.

Tucker, J. H. (1983). Leadership orientation as a function of interpersonal need structure: A replication with negative results. *Small Group Behavior, 14,* 107–114.

Tucker, R. C. (1968). The theory of charismatic leadership. *Daedalus, 97,* 731–756.

Tucker, R. C. (1981). *Politics as leadership.* Columbia: University of Missouri Press.

Tucker, R. G. (1970). The theory of charismatic leadership. In D. A. Rustow (Ed.), *Philosophers and kings: Studies in leadership.* New York: Braziller.

Tuckman, B. W. (1965). Developmental sequence in small groups. *Psychological Bulletin, 63,* 384–399.

Tuckman, B. W., & Oliver, W. F. (1968). Effectiveness of feedback to teachers as a function of source. *Journal of Educational Psychology, 59,* 297–301.

Tumes, J. (1972). *The contingency theory of leadership: A behavioral investigation.* Paper, Eastern Academy of Management, College Park, MD.

Tung, R. L. (1979). U.S. multinationals: A study of their selection and training procedures for overseas assignments. *Proceedings, Academy of Management,* Atlanta, Ga, 298–301.

Tung, R. L. (1982). Selection and training of US, European and Japanese multinationals. *California Management Review, 25,* 57–71.

Tupes, E. C., Carp, A., & Borg, W. R. (1958). Performance in role playing situations as related to leadership and personality measures. *Sociometry, 21,* 165–179.

Turk, H. (1961). Instrumental values and the popularity of instrumental leaders. *Social Forces, 39,* 252–260.

Turk, H., Hartley, E. L., & Shaw, D. M. (1962). The expectation of social influence. *Journal of Social Psychology, 58,* 23–29.

Turk, T., & Turk, H. (1962). Group interaction in a formal setting: The case of the triad. *Sociometry, 25,* 48–55.

Turnage, J. J., & Muchinsky, P. M. (1984). A comparison of the predictive validity of assessment center evaluations versus traditional measures in forecasting supervisory job performance: Interpretive implications of criterion distortion for the assessment paradigm. *Journal of Applied Psychology, 69,* 595–602.

Turner, A. N. (1954). Foreman—key to worker morale. *Harvard Business Review, 32*(1), 76–86.

Turner, A. N. (1955). Interaction and sentiment in the foreman-worker relationship. *Human Organization, 14,* 10–16.

Turner, A. N. (1957). Foreman, job, and company. *Human Relations, 10*, 99–112.

Turner, A. N., & Lawrence, P. R. (1965). *Industrial jobs and the worker.* Boston: Harvard University, Graduate School of Business Administration.

Turner, A. N., & Miclette, A. L. (1962). Sources of satisfaction in repetitive work. *Occupational Psychology, 36*, 215–231.

Turner, N. W. (1977). *Effective leadership in small groups.* Valley Forge, PA: Judson Press.

Turner, W. W. (1960). Dimensions of foreman performance: A factor analysis of criterion measures. *Journal of Applied Psychology, 44*, 216–223.

Tushman, M. L. (1977). A political approach to organizations: A review and rationale. *Academy of Management Review, 2*, 206–216.

Tutoo, D. N. (1970). The mask effect of some variables on leadership assessment. *Manas, 17*, 77–83.

Tversky, A., & Kahneman, D. (1971). Belief in the law of small numbers. *Psychological Bulletin, 76*, 105–110.

Tyagi, P. K. (1985, Summer). Relative importance of key job dimensions and leadership behaviors in motivating salesperson work performance. *Journal of Marketing, 49*, 76–86.

Tyler, T. R., Rasinski, K. A., & McGraw, K. M. (1985). The influence of perceived injustice on the endorsement of political leaders. *Journal of Applied Social Psychology, 15*, 700–725.

Tyson, L., & Birnbrauer, H. (1983). Coaching: A tool for success. *Training & Development Journal, 37*(9), 30–34.

Tziner, A. (1984). Predictor of peer rating in a military assessment center: A longitudinal follow-up. *Canadian Journal of Administrative Sciences, 1*, 146–160.

Tziner, A. (1987). The assessment centre revisited: Practical and theoretical considerations. In S. Dolan & R. S. Schuler (Eds.), *Human resource management in Canada.* St. Paul, MN: West Publishing.

Tziner, A., & Dolan, S. (1982). Validity of an assessment center for identifying future female officers in the military. *Journal of Applied Psychology, 67*, 728–736.

Tziner, A., & Elizur, D. (1985). Achievement motive: A reconceptualization and new instrument. *Journal of Occupational Behaviour, 6*, 209–228.

U.S. Air Force. (1951) *A preliminary investigation of the relationship of trainees and pilot officer promotions* (HRRL Rep. No. 3). Washington, DC: Human Resources Research Laboratory.

U.S. Air Force, Air Training Command. (1952a). *Aspects of noncommissioned officer leadership* (Tech. Rep. No. 52-3). Lackland Air Force Base, TX: Human Resources Research Center.

U.S. Air Force, Air Training Command. (1952b). *Research on the evaluation and prediction of officer qualities.* Maxwell Field, AL: Human Resources Research Center.

U.S. Army. (1919). *The personnel system of the United States Army,* Vol. 2. Washington, DC: Adjutant General's Office.

U.S. Army. (1966). *The executive: Philosophy, problems, practices. A bibliographic survey.* Washington, DC: U.S. Government Printing Office.

U.S. Army, Adjutant General's Office, Personnel Research Board. (1952). *A trend study of officer efficiency ratings for the period 1922–1945.* PRS Report 896.

U.S. Department of Commerce. (1971). *The social and economic status of Negroes in the United States, 1970* (BLS Report No. 394). Washington, DC: U.S. Government Printing Office.

U.S. Department of Defense. (1969). *Project one hundred thousand: Characteristics and performance of "new standards" men.* Washington, DC: Assistant Secretary of Defense, Manpower, and Reserve Affairs.

U.S. Department of Labor. (1966). *The Negroes in the United States: Their economic and social situation.* (Bull. No. 1511). Washington, DC: U.S. Government Printing Office.

U.S. Department of Labor. (1970). *Manpower report of the President.* Washington, DC: U.S. Government Printing Office.

U.S. Department of Labor, Bureau of Labor Statistics. (1979). *Women in the labor force: Some new data series.* Washington, DC: U.S. Government Printing Office.

U.S. Department of Labor, Bureau of Labor Statistics. (1977). *U.S. working women: A data book.* Washington, DC: U.S. Government Printing Office.

U.S. Interagency Advisory Group. (1958). *Annotated bibliography on conference leadership and participation.* Washington, DC: U.S. Civil Service Commission.

Udell, J. G. (1967). Am empirical test of hypothesis relating to span of control. *Administrative Science Quarterly, 12,* 420–439.

Uesgi, T. T., & Vinacke, W. E. (1963). Strategy in a feminine game. *Sociometry, 26,* 75–88.

Uhlman, F. W., & Fiedler, F. E. (1958). Choices of fraternity presidents for leadership and maintenance roles. *Psychological Reports, 4,* 498.

Ulin, R. D. (1976). African leadership: National goals and the values of Botswana University students. *Comparative Education, 12,* 145–155

Ulrich, D. N., Booz, D. R., & Lawrence, P. R. (1950). *Management behavior and foreman attitude.* Boston: Harvard University, Graduate School of Business Administration.

Underwood, W. J. (1965). Evaluation of laboratory training. *Training Directors Journal, 19,* 34–40.

Ungson, G. R., James, C., & Spicer, B. H. (1985). The effects of regulatory agencies on organizations in wood products and high technology/electronics industries. *Academy of Management Journal, 28,* 426–445.

Updegraff, H. (1936). *Inventory of youth in Pennsylvania.* Washington, DC: American Youth Commission of the American Council on Education.

Upmanyu, V. V., & Singh, S. (1981). Test of contingency model of leadership effectiveness. *Psychological Studies, 26,* 44–48.

Uris, A. (1953) *Techniques of leadership.* New York: McGraw-Hill.

Uris, A. (1958). Job stress and the executive. *Management Review, 47,* 4–12.

Urry, V. W., & Nicewander, W. A. (1966). Factor analysis of the commander's evaluation report. *U.S. Army Enlisted Evaluation Center, Technical Research Study.*

Urwick, L. F. (1952). *Notes of the theory of organization.* New York: American Management Association.

Urwick, L. F. (1953). *Leadership and morale.* Columbus: Ohio State University, College of Commerce and Administration.

Urwick, L. F. (1957). *Leadership in the twentieth century.* New York: Pitman.

Utecht, R. E., & Heier, W. D. (1976). The contingency model and successful military leadership. *Academy of Management Journal, 19,* 606-618.

Utterback, W. E. (1958). The influence of style of moderation on the outcomes of discussion. *Quarterly Journal of Speech, 44,* 149-152.

Vagts, A. (1942). Age and field command. *Military Review, Ft. Leavenworth, 22,* 36-38.

Vaill, P. B. (1978). Toward a behavior description of high-performing systems. In M. W. McCall, Jr. & M. M. Lombardo (Eds.), *Leadership: Where else can we go?* Durham, NC: Duke University Press.

Vaill, P. B. (1982) The purposing of high-performing systems. *Organizational Dynamics, 10*(2), 23-39.

Valenzi, E. R., & Bass, B. M. (1975). *The Bass-Valenzi Management Styles Profile: A computerized systems survey feedback procedure.* Paper, Academy of Management, New Orleans, LA.

Valenzi, E. R., & Dessler, G. (1978). Relationships of leader behavior, subordinate role ambiguity and subordinate job satisfaction. *Academy of Management Journal, 21,* 671-678.

Valenzi, E. R., Miller, J. A., Eldridge, L. D., Irons, P. W., Solomon, R. J., & Klauss, R. E. (1972). *Individual differences, structure, task, and external environment and leader behavior: A summary* (Tech. Rep. No. 49). Rochester, NY: University of Rochester, Management Research Center.

Valerio, A. M. (1989). Leadership in New York Telephone: A study of the developmental experiences of managers. In K. E. Clark & M. B. Clark (Eds.), *Measures of leadership.* West Orange, NJ: Leadership Library of America.

Valiquet, M. I. (1968). Individual change in management development programs. *Journal of Applied Behavioral Science, 4,* 313-325.

Van de Vall, M., & Bolas, C. (1980). Applied social discipline research or social policy research: The emergence of a professional paradigm in sociological research. *American Sociology, 15,* 128-137.

Van de Ven, A. H. (1976). On the nature, formation, and maintenance of relations among organizations. *Academy of Management Review, 2,* 34-53.

Van de Ven, A. H., & Ferry, D. L. (1980). *Measuring and assessing organizations.* New York: Wiley.

Van Dusen, A. C. (1948). Measuring leadership ability. *Personnel Psychology, 1,* 67-79.

Van Fleet, D. D. (1983). Span of management research and issues. *Academy of Management Review, 26,* 546-552.

Van Fleet, D. D., & Yukl, G. A. (1986a). *A century of leadership research.* Paper, Academy of Management, Chicago.

Van Fleet, D. D., & Yukl, G. A. (1986b). *Military leadership: An organizational behavior perspective.* Greenwich, CT: JAI Press.

Van Laningham, G. (1939). *The study of college leaders.* Master's thesis, Indiana State College, Terra Haute.

Van Maanen, J. (1979). Reclaiming qualitative methods for organizational research. *Administrative Science Quarterly, 26,* 520-527.

Van Meir, E. J. (1972). Leadership behavior of male and female elementary principals. *Dissertation Abstracts International, 32,* 3643.

Van Velsor, E. V. (1984). Can development programs make a difference? *Issues & Observations, 4*(4), 1-5.

Van Velsor, E. (1987). *Breaking the glass ceiling: Can women make it to the top in America's largest corporations?* Reading, MA: Addison-Wesley.

Van Zelst, R. H. (1951). Worker popularity and job satisfaction. *Personnel Psychology, 4,* 405-412.

Van Zelst, R. H. (1952a). Soiometrically selected work teams increase production. *Personnel Psychology, 5,* 175-185

Van Zelst, R. H. (1952b). Empathy test scores of union leaders. *Journal of Applied Psychology, 36,* 293-295.

Vanderslice, V. J. (1988). Separating leadership from leaders: An assessment of the effect of leader and follower roles in organizations. *Human Relations, 41,* 677-696.

Vannoy, J., & Morrissette, J. O. (1969). Group structure, effectiveness, and individual morale. *Organizational Behavior and Human Performance, 4,* 299-307.

Vansina, L. S. (1988). The general manager and organizational leadership. In M. Lambrecht (Ed.), *Corporate revival—Managing in the nineties.* Leuven, Belgium: University Press.

Vansina, L. S., & Taillieu, T. C. (1970). Comparative study of the characteristics of Flemish graduates planning their careers in national or international organizations. In B. M. Bass, R. C. Cooper, & J. A. Haas (Eds.), *Managing for accomplishment.* Lexington, MA: D. C. Heath.

Vardi, Y., Shirom, A., & Jacobson, D. (1980). A study of the leadership beliefs of Israeli managers. *Academy of Management Journal, 23,* 367-374.

Vaughan, M. B. M. (1981). Project phases and role shifts in the work of overseas project managers: A case study of a California-based multinational firm. *Dissertation Abstracts International, 42*(7A), 3282.

Vaughan, W., & McGinnies, E. (1957). Some biographical determiners of participation in group discussion. *Journal of Applied Psychology, 41,* 179-185.

Vaught, G. M. (1965). The relationship of role idenfication and ego strength to sex differences in the rod-and-frame test. *Journal of Personality, 33,* 271-283.

Vecchio, R. P. (1974). *LPC as a measure of socio-emotional and task orientation.* Unpublished manuscript.

Vecchio, R. P. (1975). *Effects of interpersonal attraction, leadership style, and authoritarianism on decision making.* Paper, Midwest Psychological Associaton, Chicago.

Vecchio, R. P. (1977). An empirical examination of the validity of Fiedler's model of leadership effectiveness. *Organizational Behavior and Human Performance, 19,* 180-206.

Vecchio, R. P. (1979). A dyadic interpretation of the contingency model of leadership effectiveness. *Academy of Management Journal, 22,* 590–600.

Vecchio, R. P. (1981). Situational and behavioral moderators of subordinate satisfaction with supervision. *Human Relations, 34,* 947–963.

Vecchio, R. P. (1982). A further test of leadership effects due to between-group variation and within-group variation. *Journal of Applied Psychology, 67,* 200–208.

Vecchio, R. P. (1983). Assessing the validity of Fiedler's contingency model of leadership effectiveness: A closer look at Strube and Garcia. *Psychological Bulletin, 93,* 404–408.

Vecchio, R. P. (1985). Predicting employee turnover from leader-member exchange: A failure to replicate. *Academy of Management Journal, 28,* 478–485.

Vecchio, R. P. (1987). Situational leadership theory: An examination of a prescriptive theory. *Journal of Applied Psychology, 72,* 444–451.

Vecchio, R. P., & Gobdel, B. C. (1984). The vertical dyad linkage model of leadership: Problems and prospects. *Organizational Behavior and Human Performance, 34,* 5–20.

Veen, P. (1972). Effects of participative decision-making in field hockey training: A field experiment. *Organizational Behavior and Human Performance, 7,* 288–307.

Veiga, J. F. (1981). Plateaued versus nonplateaued managers: Career paterns, attitudes, and path potential. *Academy of Management Journal, 24,* 566–578.

Veiga, J. F. (1983). Mobility influences during managerial career stages. *Academy of Management Journal, 26,* 64–85.

Veiga, J. F. (1986). Propensity to give up control in a decision making group: An explanation and a measure. *Proceedings, Academy of Management,* Chicago, 208–212.

Veiga, J. F. (1988). Face your problem subordinates now! *Academy of Management Executive, 2,* 145–152.

Venable, B. (1983). *Principal rule administration behavior, influence, and teacher loyalty.* Dissertation Abstracts International, 44(7A), 2009.

Vengroff, R. (1974). Popular participation and the administration of rural develpment: The case of Botswana. *Human Organization, 33,* 303–309.

Verba, S. (1961). *Small groups and political behavior: A study of leadership.* Princeton, NJ: Princeton University Press.

Vernon, P. E. (1948). The validation of the civil service observation method in the selection of trained executives. *Occupational Psychology, 22,* 587–594.

Vernon, P. E. (1950). The validation of civil service selection board proedures. *Occupational Psychology, 24,* 75–95.

Veroff, J. (1957). Development and validation of a projective measure of power motivation. *Journal of Abnormal and Social Psychology, 54,* 1–8.

Veroff, J., Atkinson, J. W., Feld, S. E., & Gurin, G. (1960). The use of thematic apperception to assess motivation in a nationwide interview study. *Psychological Monographs, 74,* No. 12.

Vertreace, W. C., & Simmins, C. H. (1971). Attempted leadership in the leaderless group discussion as a function of motivation and ego involvement. *Journal of Personality and Social Psychology, 19,* 285–289.

Vicino, F., & Bass, B. M. (1978). Lifespace variables and managerial success. *Journal of Applied Psychology, 63,* 81–88.

Vicino, F. L., Krusell, J., Bass, B. M., Deci, E. L., & Landy, D. A. (1973). The impact of PROCESS: Self-administered exercises for personal and interpersonal development. *Journal of Applied Behavioral Science, 9,* 737–757.

Vielhaber, D. P., & Gottheil, E., (1965). First impressions and subsequent ratings of performance. *Psychological Reports, 17,* 916.

Vienneau, J. (1982). A study of leadership behavior of volunteer administrators in amateur sports organizations in the province of New Brunswick, Canada. *Dissertation Abstracts International, 43*(9B), 2931.

Vinacke, W. E. (1969). Variables in experimental games: Toward a field theory. *Psychological Bulletin, 71,* 293–318.

Vinacke, W. E., & Arkoff, A. (1957). An experimental study of coalitions in the triad. *American Sociological Review, 22,* 406–414.

Vinson, E., & Mitchell, T. R. (1975). *Differences in motivational predictors and criterion measures for black and white employees.* Paper, Academy of Management, New Orleans.

Virany, B., & Tushman, M. L. (1986). *Executive succession: The changing characteristics of top management teams.* Paper, Academy of Management, Chicago.

Virany, B., Tushman, M. L., & Romanelli, E. (1985). A longitudinal study of the determinants and effects of executive succession. *Proceedings, Academy of Management,* San Diego, CA, 186–190.

Virmani, K. G., & Mathur, P. (1984, Spring). Intelligence to use intelligence: Managerial trait theory revisited. *Abhigyan,* 39–48.

Viteles, M. S. (1953). *Motivation and morale in industry.* New York: W. W. Norton.

Viteles, M. S. (1971). The long-range impact of a programme of humanistic studies for business executives on managerial attitudes and behavior. *International Review of Applied Psychology, 20,* 5–24.

Vogel, S. R., Broverman, I. K., Broverman, D. M., Clarkson, F. E., & Rosenkrantz, P. S. (1970). Maternal employment and perception of sex roles among college students. *Developmental Psychology, 3,* 381–384.

Volkerding, J., & Grasha, A. F. (1988). *Status and affect in manager-subordinate relationships.* Paper, American Psychological Association, Atlanta, GA.

Von Baeyer, C. L., Sherk, D. L., & Zanna, M. P. (1981). Impression management in the job interview: When the female applicant meets the male "chauvisnist" interviewer. *Personality and Social Psychology Bulletin, 7,* 45–51.

Von Bertalanffy, L. (1956). General systems theory. *General Systems. Yearbook of the Society for the Advancement of General Systems Theory, 1,* 1–10.

Von Bertalanffy, L. (1962). General system theory—a critical review. *General systems. Yearbook of the Society for the Advancement of General Systems Research, 7,* 1–20.

Vonachen, H. A., et al. (1946). A comprehensive mental hygiene program at Caterpillar Tractor Co. *Industrial Medicine, 15,* 179–184.

Vough, C. (1975). *Tapping the human potential: A strategy for productivity.* New York: AMACOM.

Voyer, J. J., & Faulkner, R. R. (1986). Cognition and leadership in an artistic organization. *Proceedings, Academy of Management,* Chicago, 160–164.

Vroom, V. H. (1959). Some personality determinants of the effects of participation. *Journal of Abnormal and Social Psychology, 59,* 322–327.

Vroom, V. H. (1960a). *Some personality determinants of the effects of participation.* Englewood Cliffs, NJ: Prentice-Hall.

Vroom, V. H. (1960b). The effect of attitudes on perception of organizational goals. *Human Relations, 13,* 229–240.

Vroom, V. H. (1962). Ego-involvement, job satisfaction, and job performance. *Personnel Psychology, 15,* 159–178.

Vroom, V. H. (1964). *Work and motivation.* New York: McGraw-Hill.

Vroom, V. H. (1965). *Motivation in management.* New York: American Foundation for Management Research.

Vroom, V. H. (1966). Organizational choice: A study of pre- and post-decision processes. *Organizational Behavior and Human Performance, 1,* 212–225.

Vroom, V. H. (1974a). Decision making and the leadership process. *Journal of Contemporary Business, 3,* 47–64

Vroom, V. H. (1974b). A new look at managerial decision making. *Organizational Dynamics, 3*(1), 66–80.

Vroom, V. H. (1976a). Can leaders learn to lead? *Organizational Dynamics, 4*(3), 17–28.

Vroom, V. H. (1976b). Leadership. In M. D. Dunnette (Ed.), *Handbook of industrial and organizational psychology.* Chicago: Rand McNally.

Vroom, V. H. (1984). Reflections on leadership and decision-making. *Journal of General Management* (UK), 9(3), 18–36.

Vroom, V. H., & Jago, A. G. (1974). Decision making as a social process: Normative and descriptive models of leader behavior. *Decision Science, 5,* 743–769.

Vroom, V. H., & Jago, A. G. (1978). On the validity of the Vroom-Yetton model. *Journal of Applied Psychology, 63,* 151–162.

Vroom, V. H., & Jago, A. G. (1984). *Leadership and decision-making: A revised normative model.* Paper, Academy of Management, Boston.

Vroom, V. H., & Jago, A. G. (1988). *The new leadership: Managing participation in organizations.* Englewood Cliffs, NJ: Prentice-Hall.

Vroom, V. H., & Mann, F. C. (1960). Leader authoritarianism and employee attitudes. *Personnel Psychology, 13,* 125–140.

Vroom, V. H., & Pahl, B. (1971). Relationship between age and risk taking among managers. *Journal of Applied Psychology, 55,* 399–405.

Vroom, V. H., & Yetton, P. W. (1973). *Leadership and decision-making.*

Pittsburgh: University of Pittsburgh Press. Also: (1974). New York: Wiley.

Vrooman, T. H. (1971). The perceptions and expectations of superintendents and their high school principals with regard to leadership style and delegated formal task-performance. *Dissertation Abstracts International, 31,* 6326–6327.

Vrugt, A. (undated) *Differential social perception and attribution of intent: Testing the effects of nonverbal rule violation.* Amsterdam: Universiteit van Amsterdam, Subfaculteit Psychologie.

Waaler, R. (1962). *Management development: A Norwegian experiment.* Boston: Harvard University, Graduate School of Business Administration.

Wachtel, J. M. (1988). *The effects of cultural variables on managerial motivation: A cross-cultural study of Mexico and the U.S.* Paper, Western Academy of Management, Big Sky, MT.

Waddell, H. L. (1952). How to make your workers want to become foremen. In *Practical approaches to supervisory and executive development.* New York: American Management Association, Personnel Series.

Wager, L. W. (1965). Leadership style, hierarchical influence, and supervisory role obligations. *Administrative Science Quarterly, 9,* 391–420.

Wager, L. W. (1971). The expansion of orgranizational authority and conditions affecting its denial. *Sociometry, 34,* 91–113.

Wagner, J. A., III, & Gooding, R. Z. (1987). Shared influence and organizational behavior: A meta-analysis of situational variables expected to moderate participation-outcome relationships. *Academy of Management Journal, 30,* 524–541.

Wagner, R. (1949). The employment interview: A critical summary. *Personnel Psychology, 2,* 17–46.

Wagner, W. G., Pfeffer, J., & O'Reilly, C. A. (1984). Organizational demography and turnover in top-management groups. *Administrative Science Quarterly, 29*(1), 74–92.

Wagstaff, L. H. (1970). *The relationship between administrative systems and interpersonal needs of teachers.* Doctoral dissertation, University of Oklahoma, Norman.

Wainer, H. A., & Rubin, I. M. (1969). Motivation of research and development entrepreneurs: Determinants of company success. *Journal of Applied Psychology, 53,* 178–184.

Waite, R. G. L. (1977). *The psychopathic god: Adolf Hitler.* New York: Basic Books.

Walberg, H. J. (1971). Varieties of adolescent creativity and the high school environment. *Exceptional Children, 38,* 111–116.

Wakabayashi, M., & Graen, G. B. (1984). The Japanese career progress study: A seven year follow-up. *Journal of Applied Psychology, 69,* 603–614.

Wakabayashi, M., Graen, G., Graen, M., & Graen, M. (1988). Japanese management progress: Mobility into middle management. *Journal of Applied Psychology, 73,* 217–227.

Wald, R. M., & Doty, R. A. (1954). The top executive—a firsthand profile. *Harvard Business Review, 32,* 45–54.

Waldman, D. A., & Avolio, B. J. (1986). A meta-analysis of age differences in job performance. *Journal of Applied Psychology, 71*, 33–38.

Waldman, D. A., & Bass, B. M. (1986). *Adding to leader and follower transactions: The augmenting effect of tranformational leadership* (Working Paper 86–109). Binghamton: State University of New York, School of Management.

Waldman, D. A., Bass, B. M., & Einstein, W. O. (1986). *Effort, performance and transformational leadership in industrial and military settings* (Working Paper 84–78). Binghamton: State University of New York at Binghamton, School of Management.

Waldman, D. A., Bass, B. M., & Einstein, W. O. (1987). Leadership and outcomes of performance appraisal process. *Journal of Occupational Psychology, 60*, 177–186.

Waldman, D. A., Bass, B. M., & Yammarino, F. J. (1988). *Adding to leader-follower transactions: The augmenting effect of charismatic leadership* (ONR Tech. Rep. No. 3). Binghamton: State University of New York, Center for Leadership Studies.

Waldman, L. (1956). Employment discrimination against Jews in the United States . . . 1955. *Jewish Social Studies, 18*, 3. (Cited in Korman, 1988.)

Waldman, S., Cohn, B., & Thomas, R. (1989, August 7). The HUD ripoff. *Newsweek*, 16–22.

Walker, C. R. (1950). The problems of the repetitive job. *Harvard Business Review, 28*, 54–58.

Walker, C. R. (1962). *Modern technology and civilization*. New York: McGraw-Hill.

Walker, C. R., & Guest, R. H. (1952). *The man on the assembly line*. Cambridge, MA: Harvard University Press.

Walker, C. R., Guest, R. H., & Turner, A. N. (1956). *The foreman on the assembly line*. Cambridge, MA: Harvard University Press.

Walker, J. M. (1982). The limits of strategic management in voluntary organizations. *Journal of Voluntary Action Research, 12*, 39–55.

Walker, K. (1974). Workers' participation in management—problems, practice and prospects. *Bulletin of the International Institute of Labor Studies, 12*, 3–35.

Walker, K. F. (1962). Executives' and union leaders' perceptions of each other's attitudes to industrial relations (the influence of stereotypes). *Human Relations, 15*, 183–196.

Walker, K. F. (1975). Mitbestimmung im Management im internationalen Vergleich. [An international comparison of participation in management.] *Soziale Welt, 26*, 150–173.

Walker, T. G. (1976). Leader selection and behavior in small political groups. *Small Group Behavior, 7*, 363–368.

Wall, C. C. (1970). *Perceived leader behavior of the elementary school principal as related to educational goal attainment*. Doctoral dissertation, University of California, Los Angeles.

Wall, J. (1986). *Bosses*. Lexington, MA: D. C. Heath.

Wall, J. A., Jr. (1976). Effects of success and opposing representatives' bargaining orientation on intergroup bargaining. *Journal of Personality and Social Psychology, 33*, 55–61.

Wall, T. D., Kemp, N. J., Jackson, P. R., & Clegg, C. W. (1986). Outcomes of autonomous workgroups: A long-term field experiment. *Academy of Management Journal, 29*, 280–304.

Wallace, R. L. (1972). A comparative study of attitude scores of managers toward employees and toward selected leadership policies in groups of firms which have either discontinued or retained cost reduction sharing plans. *Dissertation Abstracts International, 32*, 7359–7360.

Wallace, S. R. (1971). Some problems associated with management criteria in industry. *Psychonomic Monographs Supplement, 4*, 236–237.

Wallace, W. L., & Gallagher, J. V. (1952). *Activities and behaviors of production supervisors*. New York: Psychological Corporation.

Wallach, M. A., Kogan, N., & Bem, D. J. (1962). Group influence on individual risk takings. *Journal of Abnormal and Social Psychology, 65*, 75–86.

Wallach, M. A., Kogan, N., & Bem, D. J. (1964). Diffusion of responsibility and level of risk taking in groups. *Journal of Abnormal and Social Psychology, 68*, 263–274.

Wallach, M. A., Kogan, N., & Burt, R. (1968). Are risk takers more persuasive than conservatives in group decisions? *Journal of Experimental Social Psychology, 4*, 76–89.

Wallin, P. (1950). Cultural contradictions and sex roles: A repeat study. *American Sociological Review, 15*, 288–293.

Walster, E., Aronson, E., & Abrahams, D. (1966). On increasing the persuasiveness of a low prestige communicator. *Journal of Experimental Social Psychology, 2*, 325–342.

Walter, B. (1966). Internal control relations in administrative hierarchies. *Administrative Science Quarterly, 11*, 179–206.

Walter, N. (undated). *A study of the effects of conflicting suggestions upon judgment in the autokinetic situation*. Unpublished manuscript.

Walters, R. (1985). Imperatives of black leadership: Policy mobilization and community development. *Urban League Review, 9*(1), 20–41.

Walton, R. E. (1972). Interorganizational decision making and identity conflict. In M. Tuite, R. Chisholm, & M. Radnor (Eds.), *Interorganizational decision making*. Chicago: Aldine.

Walton, R. E., & McKersie, R. B. (1965). *A behavioral theory of labor negotiations: An analysis of a social interaction system*. New York: McGraw-Hill.

Walton, R. E., & McKersie, R. B. (1966). Behavioral dilemmas in mixed motive decision-making. *Behavioral Science, 11*, 370–384.

Walton, S. D. (1966). *American business and its environment*. New York: Macmillan.

Wanous, J. P. (1973). Effects of a realistic job preview on job acceptance, job attitudes, and job survival. *Journal of Applied Psychology, 58*, 327–332.

Warbusse, J. P. (1923). *Cooperative democracy*. New York: Macmillan.

Ward, C. D. (1968). Seating arrangement and leadership emergence in small discussion groups. *Journal of Social Psychology, 74*, 83–90.

Ward, J. M. (1977). Normative determinants of leadership. *Dissertation Abstracts International, 37*, 4710.

Ward, L. B. (1965). The ethnics of executive selection. *Harvard Business Review, 43*(2), 6–28.

Ward, L. B., & Athos, A. G. (1972). *Student expectations of corporate life.* Boston: Harvard Business School, Division of Research.

Ward, S. A. (1981). *Rhetorically sensitive supervisory communication: A situational analysis.* Paper, Speech Communication Association, Anaheim, CA.

Wardlow, M. E., & Greene, J. E. (1952). an exploratory sociometric study of peer status among adolescent girls. *Sociometry, 15,* 311–318.

Ware, J. E., Jr., & Williams, R. G. (1974). The Doctor Fox effect. *Chronicle of Higher Education, 9*(9), 3. Reprinted in Boffey, P. M. (1974, November 18).

Warihay, P. B. (1980). The climb to the top: Is the network the route for women. *The Personnel Administrator, 25*(4), 55–60.

Warner, M. LaV. (1923). Influence of mental level in the formation of boys' gangs. *Journal of Applied Psychology, 7,* 224–236.

Warner, W. K., & Hilander, J. S. (1964). The relationship between size of organization and membership participation. *Rural Sociology, 29,* 30–39.

Warner, W. L., & Abegglen, J. C. (1955). *Occupational mobility in American business and industry, 1928–1952.* Minneapolis: University of Minnesota Press.

Warner, W. L., & Martin, N. H. (1959). *Industrial man.* New York: Harper.

Warner, W. L., Meeker, M., & Eells, K. (1949). *Social class in America.* Chicago: Science Research Associates.

Warr, P. B., & Routledge, T. (1969). An opinion scale for the study of managers' job satisfaction. *Occupational Psychology, 43,* 95–109.

Warren, J. M., & Maroney, R. J. (1969). Competitive social interaction between monkeys. In R. B. Zajonc (Ed.), *Animal social psychology.* New York: Wiley.

Warren, N. D. (1958). Job simplification versus job enlargement. *Journal of Industrial Engineering, 9,* 435–439.

Warriner, C. K. (1955). Leadership in the small group. *American Journal of Sociology, 60,* 361–369.

Warwick, D. P. (1975). *The public bureaucracy: Politics, personality, and organization in the U.S. State Department.* Cambridge, MA: Harvard University Press.

Washburne, N. F. (1967). *Rational and interaction decision-making roles in task-oriented groups* (Tech. Rep.). Akron, OH: Akron University.

Wasserman, P. (1959). *Measurement and evaluation of organizational performance: An annotated bibliography.* Ithaca, NY: Cornell University, Graduate School of Business and Public Administration.

Wasserman, P., & Silander, F. S. (1958). Decision-making: An annotated bibliography. Ithaca, NY: Cornell University, Graduate School of Business and Public Administration.

Waters, T. J., & Dougherty, R. A. (1970). Student leadership, mathematics aptitude, and college major. *Psychological Reports, 27,* 406.

Watson, B. M., Jr. (1984). Lawrence, Kansas—Before and after "The Day After." *Public Management, 66*(3), 13–15.

Watson, D. (1971). Reinforcement theory of personality and social system: Dominance and position in a group power structure. *Journal of Personality and Social Psychology, 20,* 180–185.

Watson, D., & Bromberg, B. (1965). Power communication and position satisfaction in task-oriented groups. *Journal of Personality and Social Psychology, 2,* 859–864.

Watson, D., & Friend, R. (1969). Measurement of social-evaluative anxiety. *Journal of Personality and Social Psychology, 33,* 448–457.

Watson, D. L. (1965). Effects of certain social power structures on communication in task-oriented groups. *Sociometry, 28,* 322–336.

Watson, G. B. (1942). *Civilian morale.* New York: Houghton Mifflin.

Watson, J., & Williams, J. (1977). Relationship between managerial values and managerial success of black and white managers. *Journal of Applied Psychology, 62,* 203–207.

Watson, J. G., & Barone, S. (1976). The self-concept, personal values, and motivational orientations of black and white managers. *Academy of Management Journal, 19,* 36–48.

Watson, K. M. (1982). An analysis of communication patterns: A method for discriminating leader and subordinate roles. *Academy of Management Journal, 25,* 107–120.

Watson, O. M., & Graves, T. D. (1966). Quantitative research in proxemic behavior. *American Anthropologist, 68,* 971–985.

Watson, R. (1988). New visions for university sponsored executive education programs. *Academy of Management Executive, 2,* 321–323.

Watson, T. W. (1986). *Full-scale test of an empirical model of turnover.* Paper, Academy of Management, Chicago.

Watson, W., & Michaelsen, L. (1984). Task performance information and leader participation behavior: Effect on leader-subordinate interaction, frustration, and future productivity. *Group & Organization Studies, 9,* 121–144.

Watts, P. (1986). *The wounded leader: Coping with managerial dysfunction.* Paper, OD Network Conference, New York.

Wayne, S. J., & Ferris, G. F. (1988). *Influence tactics, affect, and exchange quality in supervisor-subordinate dyads.* Paper, American Psychological Association, Atlanta, GA.

Wearing, A., & Bishop, D. (1967). *Leader and member attitudes toward co-workers, intergroup competition, and the effectiveness and adjustment of military squads* (Tech. Rep. No. 21). Urbana: University of Illinois, Group Effectiveness Laboratory.

Wearing, A. J., & Bishop, D. W. (1974). The Fiedler contingency model and the functioning of military squads. *Academy of Management Journal, 17,* 450–459.

Weary, G. (1979). Self-serving attributional biases: Perceptual or response distortions. *Journal of Personality and Social Psychology, 37,* 1418–1420.

Weaver, C. H. (1958). The quantification of the frame of reference in labor-management communication. *Journal of Applied Psychology, 42,* 1–9.

Webb, U. (1915). Character and intelligence. *British Journal of Psychology Monograph,* No. 20.

Webber, R. A. (1980). Perceptions of interactions between superiors and subordinates. *Human Relations, 23,* 235–248.

Weber, J. (1989). Managers' moral meaning: An exploratory look at managers' responses to the moral dilemmas. *Proceedings, Academy of Management,* Washington, DC, 333–337.

Weber, M. (1922/1963). *The sociology of religion.* Beacon, NY: Beacon Press.

Weber, M. (1924/1947). *The theory of social and economic organization* (T. Parsons, Trans.). New York: Free Press.

Weber, M. (1946). The sociology of charismatic authority. In H. H. Mills & C. W. Mills (Eds. and Trans.), *From Max Weber: Essays in sociology.* New York: Oxford University Press.

Weber, M. (1957). *The theory of social and economic organization* (T. Parsons, Ed.). New York: Free Press.

Webster, J., & Starbuck, W. H. (1987). Theory building in industrial and organizational psychology. In C. L. Cooper & I. T. Robertson (Eds.), *International review of industrial and organizational psychology,* Vol. 3. New York: Wiley.

Wedel, C. C. (1957). *A study of measurement in group dynamics laboratories.* Doctoral dissertation, George Washington University, Washington, DC.

Wedley, W. C., & Field, R. H. (1982). The Vroom-Yetton model: Are feasible set choices due to chance? *Proceedings, Academy of Management,* New York, 146–150.

Wedley, W. C., & Field, R. H. G. (1984). A predecision support system. *Academy of Management Review, 9,* 696–703.

Weed, S. E., & Mitchell, T. R. (1980). The role of environmental and behavioral uncertainty as a mediator of situation-performance relationships. *Academy of Management Journal, 23,* 38–60.

Weed, S. E., Mitchell, T. R., & Moffitt, W. (1976). Leadership style, subordinate personality, and task type as predictors of performance and satisfaction with supervision. *Journal of Applied Psychology, 61,* 58–66.

Wehman, R., Goldstein, M. A., & Williams, J. R. (1977). Effects of different leadership styles on individual risk-taking in groups. *Human Relations, 30,* 249–259.

Weick, K. (1983). Managerial thought in the context of action. In S. Srivastva & Associates (Eds.), *The executive mind.* San Francisco: Jossey-Bass.

Weick, K. E. (1966). *Identification and enhancement of managerial effectiveness: V. The social psychology of managerial effectiveness.* Greensboro, NC: Richardson Foundation.

Weick, K. E. (1969, 1979). *The social psychology of organizing.* Reading, MA: Addison-Wesley.

Weinberg, C. (1965). Institutional differences in factors associated with student leadership. *Sociology and Social Research, 49,* 425–436.

Weinberg, S. B. (1978). A predictive model of group panic behavior. *Journal of Applied Communication Research, 6*(1), 1–9.

Weiner, B., Frieze, I., Kukla, A., Reed, L., Rest, S., & Rosenbaum, R. (1971). Perceiving the causes of success and failure. In E. E. Jones, D. E. Kanouse, H. H. Kelley, R. E. Nesbett, S. Valins, & B. Weiner (Eds.), *Attribution: Perceiving the causes of behavior.* Morristown, NJ: General Learning Press.

Weiner, N. (1961). *Cybernetics* (2nd ed.). Cambridge, MA: M. I. T. Press.

Weiner, N. (1978). Situational and leadership influence on organizational performance. *Proceedings, Academy of Management,* San Francisco, 230–234.

Weiner, N., & Mahoney, T. A. (1981). A model of corporate performance as a function of environmental, organizational, and leadership influences. *Academy of Management Journal, 24,* 453–470.

Weinstein, A. G., & Srinivasan, V. (1974). Predicting managerial success of master of business administration (MBA) graduates. *Journal of Applied Psychology, 59,* 207–212.

Weinstein, M. S. (1969). Achievement motivation and risk preference. *Journal of Personality and Social Psychology, 13,* 153–172.

Weislogel, R. L. (1953). The development of situational performance tests for various types of military personnel. *American Psychologist, 8,* 464 (Abstract).

Weisman, C. S., Morlock, L. L., Sack, D. G., & Levine, D. M. (1976). Sex differences in response to a blocked career pathway among unaccepted medical school applicants. *Sociology of Work and Occupations, 3,* 187–208.

Weiss, D. J., Davis, R. V., England, G. W., & Lofquist, L. H. (1961). Validity of work histories obtained by interview. *Minnesota Studies of Vocational Rehabilitation, 12,* No. 41.

Weiss, D. S., Davis, R. V., England, G. W., & Lofquist, L. H. (1964). *The measurement of vocational needs.* Minneapolis: University of Minnesota, Studies in Vocational Rehabilitation.

Weiss, H. M. (1977). Subordinate imitation of supervisor behavior: The role of modeling in organizational socialization. *Organizational Behavior and Human Performance, 19,* 89–105.

Weiss, H. M. (1978). Social learning of work values in organization. *Journal of Applied Psychology, 63,* 711–718.

Weiss, R. S. (1956). *Processes of organization.* Ann Arbor: University of Michigan, Survey Research Center.

Weiss, W. (1958). The relationship between judgments of communicator's position and extent of opinion change. *Journal of Abnormal and Social Psychology, 56,* 380–384.

Weiss, W., & Fine, B. J. (undated). *The effect of induced aggressiveness on opinion change* (Tech. Rep. No. 2). Boston: Boston University.

Weissenberg, P. (1979). A comparison of the life goals of Austrian, German-Swiss, and West German (FRG) managers. *Economies et Societies, 13,* 683–693.

Weissenberg, P., & Gruenfeld, L. W. (1966). Relationships among leadership dimensions and cognitive style. *Journal of Applied Psychology, 50,* 392–395.

Weissenberg, P., & Kavanagh, M. J. (1972). The independence of initiating structure and consideration: A review of the literature. *Personnel Psychology, 25,* 119–130.

Weitz, J. (1956). Job expectancy and survival. *Journal of Applied Psychology, 40,* 245–247.

Weitz, J. (1958). Selecting supervisors with peer ratings. *Personnel Psychology, 11,* 25–35.

Weitz, J., & Nuckols, R. C. (1953). A validation of "How Supervise?" *Journal of Applied Psychology, 37,* 7–8.

Wells, L. M. (1963). The limits of authority: Barnard revisited. *Public Administration Review, 23,* 161–166.

Welsh, M. A., & Dehler, G. E. (1986). *The political context and consequences of administrative succession.* Paper, Academy of Management, Chicago.

Welsh, M. A., & Dehler, G. E. (1988). Political legacy of administrative succession. *Academy of Management Journal, 31,* 948–961.

Welsh, M. C. (1979). Attitudinal measures and evaluation of males and females in leadership roles. *Psychological Reports, 45,* 19–22.

Wendt, H. W., & Light P. C. (1976). Measuring "greatness" in American presidents: Model case for international research on political leadership? *European Journal of Social Psychology, 6,* 105–109.

Werdelin, I. (1966). Teacher ratings, peer ratings, and self ratings of behavior in school. *Educational and Psychological Interactions,* No. 11.

Werner, D. S. (1955). *Personality, environment, and decision making.* Ann Arbor, MI: University Microfilm No. 12, 247.

Werner, L. (1979). MBA: The fantasy and the reality. *Working Woman, 4*(12), 37–41.

Wernimont, P. F. (1971). What supervisors and subordinates expect of each other. *Personnel Journal, 50,* 204–208.

Weschler, D. (1955). *Weschler adult intelligence scale: Manual.* New York: Psychological Corporation.

Weschler, I. R., Kahane, M., & Tannenbaum, R. (1952). Job satisfaction, productivity, and morale: A case study. *Occupational Psychology, 26,* 1–4.

Weschler, I. R., & Reisel, J. (1959). *Inside a sensitivity training group.* Los Angeles: University of California, Institute of Industrial Relations.

Weschler, I. R., & Schein, E. H. (Eds.). (1962). *Issues in training.* Washington, DC: NTL-NEA.

Weschler, I. R., & Shepard, C. (1954). Organizational structure, sociometric choice, and communication effectiveness: A pilot study. *American Psychologist, 9,* 492–493.

Weschler, P. (1984). The long haul to the top. *Dun's Business Month, 123*(4), 52–71.

Wessel, D. (1986, March 20). The last angry men. *Wall Street Journal,* 20D.

West, N. (1978). *Leadership with a feminine cast.* San Francisco: R & E Research Associates.

Westburgh, E. M. (1931). A point of view: Studies in leadership. *Journal of Abnormal and Social Psychology, 25,* 418–423.

Westerlund, G. (1952a). *Behavior in a work situation with functional supervision and with group leaders.* Stockholm: Nordisk Rotogravyr.

Westerlund, G. (1952b). *Group leadership: A field experiment.* Stockholm: Nordisk Rotogravyr.

Wetzel, W. A. (1932). Characteristics of pupil leaders. *School Review, 40,* 532–534.

Wexley, K. N., Alexander, R. A., Greenwalt, J. P., & Couch, M. A. (1980). Attitudinal congruence and similarity as related to interpersonal evaluations in manager-subordinate dyads. *Academy of Management Journal, 23,* 320–330.

Wexley, K. N., & Hunt, P. J. (1974). Male and female leaders: Comparison of performance and behavior patterns. *Psychological Reports, 35,* 867–872.

Wexley, K. N., & Jaffee, C. L. (1969). Comparison of two feedback techniques for improving the human relations skills of leaders. *Experimental Publications System, American Psychology Association,* No. 039.

Wexley, K. N., & Latham, G. P. (1981). *Developing and training human resources in organizations.* Glenview, IL: Scott, Foresman.

Wexley, K. N., & Nemeroff, W. F. (1975). Effectiveness of positive reinforcement and goal setting as methods of management development. *Journal of Applied Psychology, 60,* 446–450.

Wheatley, B. C. (1967). The effects of four styles of leadership upon anxiety in small groups. *Dissertation Abstracts, 27,* 3533–3534.

Wheatley, B. C. (1972). Leadership and anxiety: Implications for employer/employee small group meetings. *Personnel Journal, 51,* 17–21.

Wheatley, D. (1972). *A study of the management systems of the junior colleges of the State of Texas.* Doctoral dissertation, University of Houston, Houston, TX.

Wheelan, S. A. (1975). Sex differences in the functioning of small groups. *Dissertation Abstracts International, 35,* 4712–4713.

Wheeler, D., & Jordan, H. (1929). Change of individual opinion to accord with group opinion. *Journal of Abnormal and Social Psychology, 24,* 203–206.

Wheeler, L. (1964). Information seekings as a power strategy. *Journal of Social Psychology, 62,* 125–130.

Wheeler, L. (1970). *Interpersonal influence.* Boston: Allyn & Bacon.

Wheeler, L., Smith, S., & Murphy, D. B. (1964). Behavioral contagion. *Psychological Reports, 15,* 159–173.

Wheeless, V. E., & Berryman-Fink, C. (1985). Perceptions of women managers and their communicator competencies. *Communication Quarterly, 33,* 137–148.

Whelan, W. J. (1981). Senior military leadership and post military careers. *Dissertation Abstracts International, 42*(2A), 839.

Wherry, R. J. (1950). *Factor analysis of Officer Qualifications Form QCL-2B.* Columbus: Ohio State University Research Foundation.

Wherry, R. J. (1959). Hierarchial factor solutions without rotation. *Psychometrika, 24,* 45–51.

Wherry, R. J., & Fryer, D. H. (1949). Buddy ratings—popularity contest or leadership criteria? *Personnel Psychology, 2,* 147–159.

Wherry, R. J., & Olivero, J. (Eds.). (1971). *The Ohio State University computer programs for psychology.* Columbus: Ohio State University, Department of Psychology.

Wherry, R. J., Stander, N. E., & Hopkins, J. J. (1959). *Behavior trait ratings by peers and references* (USAF WADC Tech. Rep. No. 59-360).

Whisler, T. L., & Harper, S. F. (1962). *Performance appraisal: Research and practice.* New York: Holt, Rinehart & Winston.

White, H. C. (1971a). How purchasing managers view leadership. *Journal of Purchasing, 7,* 5–18.

White, H. C. (1971b). Leadership: Some behaviors and attitudes of hospital employees. *Hospital Progress, 52*(10), 46–50; *52*(11), 41–45.

White, H. C. (1971c). Some perceived behavior and attitudes of hospital employees under effective and ineffective supervision. *Journal of Nursing Administration, 1*(1), 49–54.

White, H. C., (1971d). Perceptions of leadership styles by nurses in supervisory positions. *Journal of Nursing Administration, 1*(2), 44–51.

White, H. C. (1972). Identifying the true leader in industrial management. *Industrial Management, 14,* 1–7.

White, J. C. (1964). Attitude differences in identification with management. *Personnel Journal, 43,* 602–603.

White, J. C. (1972). Perceptions of leadership by managers in a federal agency. *Personnel Administration and Public Personnel Review, 1,* 51–56.

White, J. D. (1963). Autocratic and democratic leadership and their respective groups' power, hierarchies, and morale. *Dissertation Abstracts, 24,* 602.

White, J. E. (1950). Theory and method for research in community leadership. *American Sociological Review, 15,* 50–60.

White, J. R. (1983). Cross-situational specificity in managers' perceptions of subordinate performance, attributions, and leader behaviors. *Personnel Psychology, 36,* 809–856.

White, M., & Trevor, M. (1983). *Under Japanese management.* London: Heinemann.

White, M. C. (1981). Achievement, self-confidence, personality traits, and leadership ability: A review of literature on sex differences. *Psychological Reports, 48,* 547–569.

White, M. C., Crino, M. D., & Hatfield, J. D. (1985). An empirical examination of the parsimony of perceptual congruence scores. *Academy of Management Journal, 28,* 732–737.

White, M. C., DeSanctis, G., & Crino, M. D. (1981). Achievement, self confidence, personality traits and leadership ability: A review of the literature on sex differences. *Psychological Reports, 48,* 547–569.

White, R. K., & Lippitt, R. (1960). *Autocracy and democracy: An experimental inquiry.* New York: Harper.

White, R. K., & Lippitt, R. (1968). Leader behavior and member reaction in three social climates. In D. Cartwright & A. Zander (Eds.), *Group dynamics: Research and theory.* New York: Harper & Row.

Whitehill, A. M. (1964). Cultural values and employee attitudes: United States and Japan. *Journal of Applied Psychology, 48,* 69–72.

Whitehill, A. M., & Takezawa, S. (1961). *Cultural values in management-worker relations.* Chapel Hill: University of North Carolina, School of Business Administration.

Whitehill, A. M., & Takezawa, S. (1968). *The other worker.* Honolulu: East-West Center Press.

Whitehill, M. (1968). *Centralized versus decentralized decision-making in collective bargaining: Effects on substantive contract language.* Iowa City: University of Iowa, Center for Labor and Management.

Whitelock, D. (1950). *The beginnings of English society.* London: Penguin.

Whitely, W. (1984). An exploratory study of managers' reactions to properties of verbal communication. *Personnel Psychology, 37,* 41–59.

Whitely, W. (1985). Managerial work behavior: An integration of results from two major approaches. *Academy of Management Journal, 28,* 344–362.

Whitely, W., Dougherty, T. W., & Dreher, G. F. (1988). The relationship of mentoring and socioeconomic origin to managers' and professionals' early career progress. *Proceedings, Academy of Management,* Anaheim, CA, 58–62.

Whiteman, M. (1954). The performance of schizophrenics on social concepts. *Journal of Abnormal and Social Psychology, 49,* 266–271.

Whiteman, M., & Deutsch, M. (1968). Some effects of social class and race on children's language and intellectual abilities. In M. Deutsch, I. Katz, & A. Jensen (Eds.), *Social class, race, and psychological development.* New York: Holt, Rinehart & Winston.

Whitson, S. (1980). *Authority on the crisis of confidence.* Paper, Mid-South Sociological Association, Little Rock, AR.

Whyte, G. (1989). Groupthink reconsidered. *Academy of Management Review, 14,* 40–56.

Whyte, W. F. (1943). *Street corner society: The social structure of an Italian slum.* Chicago: University of Chicago Press.

Whyte, W. F. (1949). The social structure of the restaurant. *American Journal of Sociology, 54,* 302–310.

Whyte, W. F. (1951). Small groups and large organizations. In J. H. Rohrer & M. Sherif (Eds.), *Social psychology at the crossroads.* New York: Harper.

Whyte, W. F. (1953). *Leadership and group participation—an analysis of the discussion group.* Ithaca, NY: Cornell University, New York State School of Industrial and Labor Relations.

Whyte, W. F. (1955). *Money and motivation: An analysis of incentives in industry.* New York: Harper.

Whyte, W. F. (1961). *Men at work.* Homewood, IL: Dorsey.

Whyte, W. F. (1963). Culture, industrial relations and economic development: The case of Peru. *Industrial Labor Relations Review, 16,* 583–593.

Whyte, W. F., & Gardner, B. B. (1945). Human elements in supervision. *Applied Anthropology, 4,* 7.

Whyte, W. H. (1956). *The organization man.* New York: Simon & Schuster.

Wicker, A. W. (1969). Size of church membership and members' support of church behavior settings. *Journal of Personality and Social Psychology, 3,* 278–288.

Wicker, A. W. (1985). Getting out of our conceptual ruts. *American Psychologist, 40,* 1094–1103.

Wickert, F. (1947). *Psychological research on problems of redistribution* (AAF Aviation Psychology Program Research Report No. 14). Washington, DC: U.S. Government Printing Office.

Wickert, F. R. (1951). Turnover and employees' feelings of ego-involvement in the day-to-day operations of a company. *Personnel Psychology, 4,* 185–197.

Widgery, R. N., & Tubbs, S. L. (1975). *Using feedback of diagnostic information as an organizational development strategy.* Paper, International Communication Association.

Wiener, W. (1972). *Selected perceptions and compatibilities of personnel in innovative and non-innovative schools.* Doctoral dissertation, Syracuse University, Syracuse, NY.

Wiesner, W. H., & Cronshaw, S. F. (1988). A meta-analytic investigation of the impact of interview format and degree of structure on the validity of the employment interview. *Journal of Occupational Psychology, 61,* 275–290.

Wiggam, A. E. (1931). The biology of leadership. In H. C. Metcalf (Ed.), *Business leadership.* New York: Pitman.

Wikstrom, W. S. (1961). *Developing better managers: An eight-nation study.* New York: National Industrial Conference Board.

Wikstrom, W. S. (1967). *Managing at the foreman's level.* New York: National Industrial Conference Board.

Wilcox, D. S., & Burke, R. J. (1969). Characteristics of effective employee performance review and development interviews. *Personnel Psychology, 22,* 291–305.

Wilcox, W. H. (1982). *Assistant superintendents' perceptions of the effectiveness of the superintendent, job satisfaction, and satisfaction with the superintendent's supervisory skills.* Doctoral dissertation, University of Missouri, Columbia.

Wildavsky, A. (1964). *Leadership in a small town.* Towanda, NJ: Bedminster Press.

Wile, D. B., Bron, G. D., & Pollack, H. B. (1970). The group therapy questionnaire: An instrument for study of leadership in small groups. *Psychological Reports, 27,* 263–273.

Wilemon, D. L., & Cicero, J. P. (1970). The project manager—anomalies and ambiguities. *Academy of Management Journal, 13,* 269–282.

Wilensky, H. L. (1967). *Organizational intelligence: Knowledge and policy in government and industry.* New York: Basic Books.

Wilensky, H. W. (1957). Human relations in the workplace. In C. Arensberg (Ed.), *Research in industrial human relations.* New York: Harper.

Wiley, M. G., & Eskilson, A. (1982). The interaction of sex and power base on perceptions of managerial effectiveness. *Academy of Management Journal, 25,* 671–677.

Wilkins, A. L., & Bristow, N. J. (1987). For successful organization culture, honor your past. *Academy of Management Executive, 1,* 221–229.

Wilkins, E. H. (1940). On the distribution of extracurricular activities. *School and Society, 51,* 651–656.

Wilkins, E. J., & deCharms, R. (1962). Authoritarianism and response to power cues. *Journal of Personality, 30,* 439–457.

Wilkins, W. L. (1953). From symposium: Selection of personnel for hazardous duties. *American Psychologist, 8,* 294 (Abstract).

Wilkinson, R. (1964). *Gentlemanly power.* London: Oxford University Press.

Willerman, B. (1954). *Organizational involvement as reflected in type of member complaint: An indirect method of measurement* (Tech. Rep. No. 4). Minneapolis: University of Minnesota.

Willerman, B., & Swanson, L. (1952). An ecological determinant of differential amounts of sociometric choices within college sororities. *Sociometry, 15,* 326–329.

Willerman, B., & Swanson, L. (1953). Group practice in voluntary organizations: A study of college sororities. *Human Relations, 6,* 57–77.

Williams, A. S. (1981). Training rural citizens: An evaluation of a leadership training program. *Journal of the Community Development Society, 12*(1) 63–82.

Williams, C. H. (1975). Employing the black administrator. *Public Personnel Management, 4,* 76–83.

Williams, E. (1968). *An analysis of selected work duties and performances of the more effective versus the less effective manager.* Doctoral dissertation, Ohio State University, Columbus.

Williams, F. J., & Harrell, T. W. (1964). Predicting success in business. *Journal of Psychology, 48,* 164–167.

Williams, J. E., & Best, D. L. (1982). *Measuring sex stereotypes: A thirty-nation study.* Beverly Hills, CA: Sage.

Williams, J. L. (1963). *Personal space and its relation to extroversion-introversion.* Master's thesis, University of Alberta, Edmonton.

Williams, J. L. (1969). Group geography and the assumption of leadership. *Dissertation Abstracts International, 30,* 1642.

Williams, L. B., III. (1970). *Superior-subordinate relationships in public elementary schools.* Doctoral dissertation, Rutgers, The State University of New Jersey, New Brunswick.

Williams, L. K., Whyte, W. F., & Green, C. S. (1966). Do cultural differences affect workers' attitudes? *Industrial Relations, 5,* 105–117.

Williams, R. E. (1956). *A description of some executive abilities by means of the critical incident technique.* Doctoral dissertation, Columbia University, New York.

Williams, R. S. (1982). *Developing skills for women in middle management: A case study in course evaluation.* Paper, International Congress of Applied Psychology, Edinburgh.

Williams, S. B., & Leavitt, H. J. (1947a). Group opinion as a predictor of military leadership. *Journal of Consulting Psychology, 11,* 283–291.

Williams, S. B., & Leavitt, H. J. (1947b). Methods of selecting Marine Corps officers. In G. A. Kelly (Ed.), *New methods in applied psychology.* College Park: University of Maryland.

Williams, T. H. (1952). *Lincoln and his generals.* New York: Vantage.

Williams, V. (1965). Leadership types, role differentiation, and system problems. *Social Forces, 43,* 380–389.

Williamson, E. G. (1948). The group origins of student leaders. *Educational and Psychological Measurement, 8,* 603–612.

Williamson, O. E. (1975). *Markets and hierarchies.* New York: Free Press.

Willis, F. N. (1966). Initial speaking distance as a function of the speakers' relationship. *Psychonomic Science, 5,* 221–222.

Willits, R. D. (1967). Company performance and interpersonal relations. *Industrial Management Review, 8,* 91–107.

Willmorth, N. E., Taylor, E. L., Lindelien, W. B., & Ruch, F. L. (1957). *A factor analysis of rating scale variables used as criteria of military leadership* (Research Report No. 57-154). USAF Personnel Training Research Center.

Willner, A. R. (1968). *Charismatic political leadership: A theory.* Princeton, NJ: Princeton University, Center for International Studies.

Willower, D. J. (1960). Leadership styles and leaders' perceptions of subordinates. *Journal of Educational Sociology, 34*, 58–64.

Wilpert, B. (1975). Research on industrial democracy: The German case. *Industrial Relations Journal, 6*, 53–64.

Wilsnack, S. (1974). The effects of social drinking on women's fantasy. *Journal of Personality, 42*, 43–61.

Wilson, A. T. M. (1972). How to appraise. *Management Today*, 99–100, 104–108.

Wilson, B. R. (1975). *The noble savages: The primitive origins of charisma and its temporary survival*. Berkeley: University of California Press.

Wilson, C. L., O'Hare, D., & Shipper, F. (1989). Task cycle theory: The processes of influence. In K. E. Clark & M. B. Clark (Eds.), *Measures of leadership*. West Orange, NJ: Leadership Library of America.

Wilson, M. P., & Curtis, P. (1984). *Leadership in academic medicine*. San Francisco: Jossey-Bass.

Wilson, M. P., & McLaughlin, C. P. (1984). *Leadership and management in academic medicine*. San Francisco: Jossey-Bass.

Wilson, N. A. (1948). The work of the Civil Service Selection Board. *Occupational Psychology, 22*, 204–212.

Wilson, R. C., Beem, H. P., & Comrey, A. L. (1953). Factors influencing organizational effectiveness. III. A survey of skilled tradesmen. *Personnel Psychology, 6*, 313–325.

Wilson, R. C., High, W. S., Beem, H. P., & Comrey, A. L., (1954). A factor analytic study of supervisory and group behavior. *Journal of Applied Psychology, 38*, 89–92.

Wilson, R. C., High, W. S., & Comrey, A. L. (1955). An iterative analysis of supervisory and group dimensions. *Journal of Applied Psychology, 39*, 85–91.

Wilson, S. R. (1971). Leadership, participation, and self-orientation in observed and nonobserved groups. *Journal of Applied Psychology, 55*, 433–438.

Wilson, T. P. (1968). Patterns of management and adaptations to organizational roles—A study of prison inmates. *American Journal of Sociology, 74*, 146–157.

Wilson, W. K. (1938). The challenge of leadership. *Journal of the Coast Artillery, 81*, 363–366.

Winder, A. E. (1952). White attitudes toward Negro-white interaction in an area of changing racial composition. *American Psychologist, 7*, 330–331.

Winder, C. L., & Wiggins, J. S. (1964). Social reputation and social behavior: A further validation of the Peer Nomination Inventory. *Journal of Abnormal and Social Psychology, 68*, 681–684.

Winkler-Hermaden, V. (1927). *Zur Psychologie des Zugführers*. Jena: Fischer.

Winn, A. (1966). Social change in industry: From insight to implementation. *Journal of Applied Behavioral Science, 2*, 170–184.

Winston, S. (1932). Studies of Negro leadership: Age and occupational distribution of 1,608 Negro leaders. *American Journal of Sociology, 37*, 595–602.

Winston, S. B. (1937). Bio-social characteristics of American inventors. *American Sociological Review, 2*, 837–849.

Winter, D. G. (undated). *Predicting long term management success from TAT measures of power motivation and responsibility*. Unpublished manuscript.

Winter, D. G. (1967). *Power motivation in thought and action*. Doctoral dissertation, Harvard University, Cambridge, MA.

Winter, D. G. (1973). *The power motive*. New York: Free Press.

Winter, D. G. (1979a). *Navy leadership and management competencies: Convergence among tests, interviews and performance ratings*. Boston: McBer & Co.

Winter, D. G. (1979b). *An introduction to LMET theory and research*. Boston: McBer & Co.

Winter, D. G. (1987). Leader appeal, leader performance, and the motives profile of leaders and followers: A study of American presidents and elections. *Journal of Personality and Social Psychology, 52*, 96–202.

Winter, D. G., & Barenbaum, N. B. (1989). Responsibility and the power motive in men and women. *Journal of Personality, 53*, 335–355.

Winter, D. G., & Stewart, A. J. (1975). Content analysis as a technique for assessing political leaders. In T. Milburn & H. C. Hermann (Eds.), *A psychological examination of political leaders*. New York: Free Press.

Winter, D. G., & Stewart, A. J. (1978). Power motivation. In H. London & J. Exner (Eds.), *Dimensions of personality*. New York: Wiley.

Wirdenius, H. (1958). *Supervisors at work*. Stockholm: Swedish Council for Personnel Administration.

Wischmeier, R. R. (1955). Group-centered and leader-centered leadership: An experimental study. *Speech Monographs, 22*, 43–48.

Wiseman, R. L., & Schenek-Hamlin, W. (1981). A multidimensional scaling validation of an inductively-derived set of compliance-gaining strategies. *Communication Monographs, 48*, 251–270.

Wispé, L. G. (1955). A sociometric analysis of conflicting role-expectancies. *American Journal of Sociology, 61*, 134–137.

Wispé, L. G. (1957). The success attitude: An analysis of the relationship between individual needs and social role-expectancies. *Journal of Social Psychology, 46*, 119–124.

Wispé, L. G., & Lloyd, K. E. (1955). Some situational and psychological determinants of the desire for structured interpersonal relations. *Journal of Abnormal and Social Psychology, 51*, 57–60.

Wispé, L. G., & Thayer, P. W. (1957). Role ambiguity and anxiety in an occupational group. *Journal of Social Psychology, 46*, 41–48.

Wittenberg, R. M. (1951). Reaching the individual through the group. *Pastoral Psychology, 2*, 41–47.

Wittig, M. A. (1976). Sex differences in intellectual functioning: How much of a difference do genes make? *Sex Roles, 2*, 63–74.

Wittreich, W. (1977). Managerial motivation development: Business managers. In J. B. Miner (Ed.), *Motivation to manage*. Atlanta, GA: Organizational Measurement Systems Press.

Wofford, J. C. (1967). Behavior styles and performance effectiveness. *Personnel Psychology, 20*, 461–495.

Wofford, J. C. (1970). Factor analysis of managerial behavior variables. *Journal of Applied Psychology, 54,* 169-173.

Wofford, J. C. (1971). Managerial behavior, situational factors, and productivity and morale. *Administrative Science Quarterly, 16,* 10-17.

Wofford, J. C. (1981). *An integrative theory of leadership.* Paper, Academy of Management, San Diego, CA.

Wolberg, A. R. (1977). Selecting potential group leaders for training in group techniques. *Transnational Mental Health Newsletter, 19,* 7-8.

Wolcott, C. (1984). The relationship between the leadership behavior of library supervisors and the performance of their professional subordinates (path-goal theory, management). *Dissertation Abstracts International, 45*(5A), 1507.

Wolf, W. B. (1963). Precepts for managers—Interviews with Chester I. Barnard. *California Management Review, 6,* 89-94.

Wolin, B. R., & Terebinski, S. J. (1965). Leadership in small groups: A mathematical approach. *Journal of Experimental Psychology, 69,* 126-134.

Wollowick, H. B., & McNamara, W. J. (1969). Relationship of the components of an assessment centre to management success. *Journal of Applied Psychology, 53,* 348-352.

Wolman, B. (1956). Leadership and group dynamics. *Journal of Social Psychology, 43,* 11-25.

Wolman, B. (Ed.). (1971). *The psychoanalytic interpretation of history.* New York: Basic Books.

Wolozin, H. (1948). Teaching personnel administration by role playing. *Personnel Journal, 27,* 107-109.

Women's Bureau, Employment Standards Administration, U.S. Department of Labor. (1974). *The myth and the reality.* Washington, DC: U.S. Government Printing Office.

Women's Bureau, Employment Standards Administration, U.S. Department of Labor. (1975). *Women workers today.* Washington, DC: U.S. Government Printing Office.

Wonder, B. D., & Cotton, C. C. (1980). Relation of marginality to extroversion-introversion dimension. *Psychological Reports, 47,* 1015-1021.

Wood, F. R., & Hertz, R. (1982). Influential associations in organizations. *Proceedings, Academy of Management,* New York, 399-402.

Wood, J. T. (1977). Leading in purposive discussions: A study of adaptive behavior. *Communication Monographs, 44,* 152-165.

Wood, M. M. (1975). What does it take for a woman to make it in management? *Personnel Journal, 54,* 38-41.

Wood, M. M. (1976). Women in management: How is it working out? *Advanced Mangement Journal, 41,* 22-30.

Wood, M. M., & Greenfeld, S. T. (1976). Women managers and fear of success: A study in the field. *Sex Roles, 2,* 375-387.

Wood, M. T. (1972). Effects of decision processes and task situations on influence perceptions. *Organizational Behavior and Human Performance, 7,* 417-427.

Wood, M. T. (1973). Power relationships and group decision making in organizations. *Psychological Bulletin, 79,* 280-293.

Wood, M. T., & Sobel, R. S. (1970). Effects of similarity of leadership style at two levels of management on the job satisifaction of the first level manager. *Personnel Psychology, 23,* 577-590.

Wood, R. E., & Arasu, S. (undated). *The effects of positive versus negative feedback on role ambiguity.* Unpublished manuscript.

Wood, R. E., & Mitchell, T. R. (1981). Manager behavior in a social context: The impact of impression management on attributions and disciplinary actions. *Organizational Behavior and Human Performance, 28,* 356-378.

Wood, R. S. (1985). Education for leadership. *Bureaucrat, 14*(2), 45-46.

Woods, F. A. (1913). *The influence of monarchs.* New York: Macmillan.

Woods, P. F. (1984). A comparative analysis of supervisory leadership styles in quality circle and non-quality circle groups (manufacturing). *Dissertation Abstracts International, 45*(11A), 3406.

Woodward, C. V. (1974). *Responses of the presidents to charges of misconduct.* New York: Dell.

Woodward, J. (1958). *Management and technology.* London: Her Majesty's Stationery Office.

Woodward, J. (1965). *Industrial organization: Theory and practice.* Oxford: Oxford University Press.

Woodworth, D. G., & MacKinnon, D. W. (1958). *The use of trait ratings in an assessment of 100 Air Force captains.* U.S. Air Force WADA Tech. Note, No. 58-64.

Woodworth, R. S., (1920). The Woodworth personal data sheet. In S.I. Franz (Ed.), *Handbook of mental examination methods.* New York: Macmillan.

Worbois, G. M. (1975). Validation of externally developed assessment procedures for identification of supervisory potential. *Personnel Psychology, 28,* 77-91.

Worchel, P. (1961). Status restoration and the reduction of hostility. *Journal of Abnormal and Social Psychology, 63,* 443-445.

Word, C. O., Zanna, M. P., & Cooper, J. (1974). The nonverbal mediation of self-fulfilling prophecies in interracial interaction. *Journal of Experimental Social Psychology, 10,* 109-120.

Worden, P. E. (1976). The impact of two experimental time-limited leadership training programs on youth. *Dissertation Abstracts International, 36,* 5067.

Worrell, D. L., Davidson, W. N., III, Chandy, P. R., & Garrison, S. L. (1986). Management turnover through deaths of key executives: Effects on investor wealth. *Academy of Management Journal, 29,* 674-694.

Worthy, J. C. (undated). *The first managerial revolution and the origins of civilization.* Unpublished manuscript.

Worthy, J. C. (1950). Organizational structure and employee morale. *American Sociological Review, 15,* 169-179.

Worthy, M. M., Wright, J. M., & Shaw, M. E. (1964). Effects of varying degrees of legitimacy in the attribution of responsibility for negative events. *Psychonomic Science, 1,* 169-170.

Wortman, M. S. (1982). Strategic management and changing leader-follower roles. *Journal of Applied Behaviorial Science, 18,* 371-383.

Wray, D. E. (1949). Marginal men of industry: The foremen. *American Journal of Sociology, 54,* 298-301.

Wright, D. G. (1946). Anxiety in aerial combat. *Research Publication of the Association of Nervous and Mental Disorders, 25,* 116-124.

Wright, D. W. (1972). A comparative study of two leadership styles in goal-bound group discussions. *Dissertation Abstracts International, 32,* 7121.

Wright, G. N., et al. (1977). *Cultural differences in probabilistic thinking: An extension into South East Asia* (Tech. Rep. No. 77-1). London: Brunel University, Decision Analysis Unit.

Wright, J. D., & Hamilton, R. F. (1979). Education and job attitudes among blue-collar workers. *Sociology of Work and Occupations, 67,* 59-83.

Wright, M. E. (1943). The influence of frustration upon social relations of young children. *Character & Personality, 12,* 111-122.

Wright, N. B. (1984-5). Leadership styles: Which are best when? *Business Quarterly* (Canada), *49*(4) 20-23.

Wright, R., King, S., Berg, W. E., & Creecy, R. F. (1987). Job satisfaction among black female managers: A causal approach. *Human Relations, 40,* 489-506.

Wrong, D. H. (1968). Some problems in defining social power. *American Journal of Sociology, 73,* 673-681.

Wrong, D. (1980). *Power: Its forms, bases and uses.* New York: Harper & Row.

Wurster, C. R., & Bass, B. M. (1953). Situational tests: IV. Validity of leaderless group discussions among strangers. *Educational and Psychological Measurement, 13,* 122-132.

Wurster, C. R., Bass, B. M., & Alcock, W. (1961). A test of the proposition: We want to be esteemed most by those we esteem most highly. *Journal of Abnormal and Social Psychology, 63,* 650-653.

Wyatt, S., & Langdon, J. N. (1937). *Fatigue and boredom in repetitive work.* London: Industrial Health Research Board.

Wyndham, A. J., & White, E. (1952). Joint consultation: Case study no. 3. *Personnel Practice Bulletin, 8,* 3-13.

Wyndham, C. H., & Cooke, H. M. (1964). The influence of the quality of supervision on the production of men engaged in moderately hard physical work. *Ergonomics, 7,* 139-149.

Yammarino, F. J. (1988). *The varient approach: Variables, levels of analysis, and WABA* (Working paper 88-142). Binghamton: State University of New York, School of Management.

Yammarino, F. J., & Bass, B. M. (1989a). Long term forecasting of transformational leadership and its effects among naval officers: Some preliminary findings. In K. E. Clark & M. B. Clark (Eds.), *Measures of leadership.* West Orange, NJ: Leadership Library of America. Also: (1988). ONR Tech. Rep. No. 2. Binghamton: State University of New York, Center for Leadership Studies.

Yammarino, F. J., & Bass, B. M. (1989b). *Multiple levels of analysis investigation of transformational leadership* (ONR Tech. Rep. No. 4). Binghamton: State University of New York, Center for Leadership Studies.

Yammarino, F. J., & Dubinsky, A. J. (1989). Superior-subordinate relationships: A multiple level of analysis approach. *Organizational Behavior and Human Decision Processes,* in press.

Yammarino, F. J., Dubinsky, A. J., & Hartley, S. W. (1987). An approach for assessing individual versus group effects in performance evaluations. *Journal of Occupational Psychology, 60,* 157-167.

Yammarino, F. J., & Naughton, T. J. (1987). *Level of analysis and individual versus group directed leader behavior descriptions: An empirical test.* Paper, Academy of Management, New Orelans, LA.

Yammarino, F. J., & Naughton, T. J. (1988). Time spent communicating: A multiple levels of analysis approach. *Human Relations, 41,* 655-676.

Yankelovich, D., & Immerwahr, J. (1983). *Putting the work ethic to work.* New York: Public Agenda Foundation.

Yarmolinsky, A. (1987). *Leadership in crisis situations.* Paper, First Annual Conference on Leadership, Wingfoot, Racine, WI.

Yeager, T. C. (1935). An analysis of certain traits of selected high school seniors interested in teaching. *Teachers College Contribution to Education,* No. 660.

Yeh, R. (1988). Values of American, Japanese and Taiwanese managers in Taiwan: A test of Hofstede's framework. *Proceedings, Academy of Management,* Anaheim, CA, 106-110.

Yerby, J. (1975). Attitude, task, and sex composition as variables affecting female leadership in small problem-solving groups. *Speech Monographs, 42,* 160-168.

Yntema, D. B., & Torgerson, W. S. (1961). Man-machine cooperation in decisions requiring common sense. *IRE Transactions on Human Factors (Electronic), 2,* 20-26.

Yoga, M. (1964). Patterns of supervisory authority. *Journal of the Indian Academy of Applied Psychology, 1,* 44-48.

Yokochi, N. (1989a). *Leadership styles of Japanese business executives and managers: Transformational and transactional.* Doctoral dissertation, United States International University, San Diego, CA.

Yokochi, N. (1989b). Private communication, June 28.

York, M.W. (1969). Reinforcement of leadership in small groups. *Dissertation Abstracts International, 30,* 1643.

York, R. O., & Hastings, T. (1985-6). Worker maturity and supervisory leadership behavior. *Administration in Social Work, 9*(4), 37-47.

Yoshino, M. (1984). *Contrasts and commonalities between early and postwar industrial leaders in Japan.* Paper, 75th Anniversary Colloquium on Leadership, Harvard Business School, Boston.

Yu, W. (1985, September 11). Asian-Americans charge prejudice slows climb to management ranks. *Wall Street Journal,* p. 35.

Yukl, G. A. (1968). Leader personality and situational variables as co-determinants of leader behavior. *Dissertation Abstracts, 29,* 406.

Yukl, G. A. (1969). A situation description questionnaire for leaders. *Educational and Psychological Measurement, 29,* 515-518.

Yukl, G. A. (1970). Leader LPC scores: Attitude dimensions and behavioral correlates. *Journal of Social Psychology, 80,* 207-212.

Yukl, G. A. (1971). Toward a behavioral theory of leadership. *Organizational Behavior and Human Performance. 6,* 414-440.

Yukl, G. A. (1981, 1989). *Leadership in organizations.* Englewood Cliffs, NJ: Prentice-Hall.

Yukl, G. A. (1982). *A behavioral approach to needs assessment for managers.* Paper, Academy of Management, New York.

Yukl, G. A. (1987a). *A new taxonomy for integrating diverse perspectives on managerial behavior.* Paper, American Psychological Association, New York.

Yukl, G. A., (1987b). *Development of a new measure of managerial behavior: Preliminary report on validation of the MPS.* Paper, Eastern Academy of Management, Boston.

Yukl, G. A. (1988). *Development and validation of the managerial practices questionnaire* (Tech. Rep.). State University of New York at Albany.

Yukl, G., & Carrier, H. (1986). An exploratory study on situational determinants of managerial behavior. *Proceedings, Eastern Academy of Management,* New York, 40-43.

Yukl, G., & Hunt, J. B. (1976). An empirical comparison of the Michigan four-factor and Ohio State LBDQ leadership scales. *Organizational Behavior and Human Performance, 17,* 45-65.

Yukl, G. A., & Kanuk, L. (1979). Leadership behavior and the effectiveness of beauty salon managers. *Personnel Psychology, 32,* 663-675.

Yukl, G., & Lepsinger, R. (1989). An integrating taxonomy of managerial behavior: Implications for improving managerial effectiveness. In J. W. Jones, B. D. Steffy, & D. W. Bray (Eds.), *Applying psychology in business: The manager's handbook.* Lexington, MA: Lexington Press.

Yukl, G. A., & Taber, T. (1983). The effective use of managerial power. *Personnel, 60*(2), 37-44.

Yukl, G. A., & Van Fleet, D. D. (1982). Cross-situational, multimethod research on military leader effectiveness. *Organizational Behavior and Human Performance, 30,* 87-108.

Yukl, G., Wall, S., & Lepsinger, R. (1989). *Preliminary report on validation of the managerial practices survey.* In K. E. Clark & M. B. Clark (Eds.), *Measures of leadership.* West Orange, NJ: Leadership Library of America.

Yura, H. (1976). *Nursing leadership: Theory and process.* New York: Appleton-Century-Crofts.

Yuzuk, R. P. (1959). *The assessment of employee morale: A comparison of two measures.* Doctoral dissertation, Ohio State University, Columbus.

Yuzuk, R. P. (1961). *The assessment of employee morale.* Columbus: Ohio State University, Bureau of Business Research.

Zablock, B. (1980). *Charisma and alienation.* New York: Free Press.

Zachary, W. B., & Krone, R. M. (1984). Managing creative individuals in high-technology research projects. *IEEE Transactions on Engineering Management, 31*(1), 37-40.

Zagona, S. V., Willis, J. E., & MacKinnon, W. J. (1966). Group effectiveness in creative problem-solving tasks: An examination of relevant variables. *Journal of Psychology, 62,* 111-137.

Zagona, S. V., & Zurcher, L. A. (1964). Participation, interaction, and role behavior in groups selected from the extremes of the open-closed cognitive continuum. *Journal of Psychology, 58,* 255-264.

Zahn, G. L., & Wolf, G. (1981). Leadership and the art of cycle maintenance: A simulation model of superior-subordinate interaction. *Organizational Behavior and Human Performance, 28,* 26-49.

Zais, M. M. (1979). *The impact of intelligence and experience on the performance of army line and staff officers.* Master's thesis, University of Washington, Seattle.

Zajonc, R. B. (1962). The effects of feedback and probability of group success on individual and group performance. *Human Relations, 15,* 149-163.

Zajonc, R. B. (1969). *Animal social psychology: A reader of experimental studies.* New York: Wiley.

Zajonc, R. B., & Wolfe, D. M. (1966). Cognitive consequences of a person's position in a formal organization. *Human Relations, 19,* 139-150.

Zald, M. N. (1964). Decentralization—myth vs. reality. *Personnel, 41,* 19-26.

Zald, M. N. (1965). Who shall rule? A political analysis of succession in a large welfare organization. *Pacific Sociological Review, 8,* 52-60.

Zald, M. N. (1967). Urban differentiation, characteristics of boards of directors, and organizational effectiveness. *American Journal of Sociology, 73,* 261-272.

Zaleznik, A. (1951). *Foreman training in a growing enterprise.* Boston: Harvard University, Graduate School of Business Administration.

Zaleznik, A. (1956). *Worker satisfaction and development.* Boston: Harvard University, Graduate School of Business Administration.

Zaleznik, A. (1963). The human dilemmas of leadership. *Harvard Business Review, 41*(4), 49-55.

Zaleznik, A. (1965a). The dynamics of subordinacy. *Harvard Business Review, 43*(3), 119-131.

Zaleznik, A. (1965b). Interpersonal relations in organizations. In J. G. March (Ed.), *Handbook of organizations.* Chicago: Rand McNally.

Zaleznik, A. (1966). *Human dilemmas of leadership.* New York: Harper & Row.

Zaleznik, A. (1967). Management disappointment. *Harvard Business Review, 45*(6), 59-70.

Zaleznik, A. (1974). Charismatic and consensus leaders: A psychological comparison. *Bulletin of the Menninger Clinic, 38,* 222-238.

Zaleznik, A. (1975). Psychopathology and politics reconsidered. *Bulletin of the Menninger Clinic, 39*(2), 145-162.

Zaleznik, A. (1977). Managers and leaders: Are they different? *Harvard Business Review, 55*(5), 67-80.

Zaleznik, A. (1980). Why authority fails. *The Executive, 6*(3), 34-40.

Zaleznik, A. (1983). The leadership gap. *Washington Quarterly, 6*(1), 32-39.

Zaleznik, A. (1984). *Leadership as a text: An essay on interpretation.* Paper, 75th Anniversary Colloquium, Harvard Business School, Boston.

Zaleznik, A., Christensen, C. R., & Roethlisberger, F. J. (1958). *The motivation, productivity, and satisfaction of workers.* Boston: Harvard University, Graduate School of Business Administration.

Zaleznik, A., Dalton, G. W., & Barnes, L. B. (1970). *Orientation and conflict in career.* Boston: Harvard University, Graduate School of Business Administration.

Zaleznik, A., & Kets de Vries, M. (1975). *Power and the corporate mind.* Boston: Houghton Mifflin.

Zaleznik, A., & Moment, D. (1964). *The dynamics of interpersonal behavior.* New York: Wiley.

Zammuto, R. F., London, M., & Rowland, K. M. (1979). Effects of sex on commitment and conflict resolution. *Journal of Applied Psychology, 64,* 227-231.

Zand, D. E. (1971). *Collateral organization.* NTL Organizational Development Network. Unpublished manuscript.

Zander, A. (1947). Role playing: A technique for training the necessarily dominating leader. *Sociatry, 1,* 225-235.

Zander, A., (1949). *The problem of resistance in creating social change.* Paper, American Society of Public Administration, New York.

Zander, A. (1950). Resistance to change—its analysis and prevention. *Advanced Management, 15,* 9-11.

Zander, A. (1953) The effects of prestige on the behavior of group members: An audience demonstration. *American Management Association, Personnel Service,* No. 155.

Zander, A. (1968). Group aspirations. In D. Cartwright & A. Zander (Eds.), *Group dynamics: Research and theory* (3rd ed.). New York: Harper & Row.

Zander, A. (1971). *Motives and goals in groups.* New York: Academic Press.

Zander, A., & Cohen, A. R. (1955). Attributed social power and group acceptance: A classroom experimental demonstration. *Journal of Abnormal and Social Psychology, 51,* 490-492.

Zander, A., Cohen, A. R., & Stotland, E. (1957). *Role relations in the mental health professions.* Ann Arbor: University of Michigan, Institute for Social Research.

Zander, A., & Curtis, T. (1962). Effects of social power on aspiration setting and striving. *Journal of Abnormal and Social Psychology, 64,* 63-74.

Zander, A., & Curtis, T. (1965). Social support and rejection of organizational standards. *Journal of Educational Psychology, 56,* 87-95.

Zander, A., & Forward, J. (1968). Position in group, achievement motivation, and group aspirations. *Journal of Personality and Social Psychology, 8,* 282-288.

Zander, A., Forward, J., & Albert, R. (1969). Adaptation of board members to repeated failure or success in their organization. *Organizational Behavior and Human Performance, 4,* 56-76.

Zander, A., & Gyr, J. (1955). Changing attitudes toward a merit rating system. *Personnel Psychology, 8,* 429-448.

Zander, A., & Havelin, A. (1960). Social comparison and interpersonal attraction. *Human Relations, 13,* 21-32.

Zander, A., & Medow, H. (1963). Individual and group levels of aspiration. *Human Relations, 16,* 89-105.

Zander, A., & Medow, H. (1965). Strength of group and desire for attainable group aspirations. *Journal of Personality, 33,* 122-139.

Zander, A., Medow, H., & Dustin, D. (1964). Social influences on group aspirations. In A. Zander & H. Medow (Eds.), *Group aspirations and group coping behavior.* Ann Arbor: University of Michigan, Institute for Social Research.

Zander, A., Medow, H., & Efron, R. (1965). Observers' expectations as determinants of group aspirations. *Human Relations, 18,* 273-287.

Zander, A., & Wolfe, D. (1964). Administrative rewards and coordination among committee members. *Administrative Science Quarterly, 9,* 50-69.

Zavala, A. (1971). Determining the hierarchical structure of a multidimensional body of information. *Perceptual and Motor Skills, 32,* 735-746.

Zdep, S. M. (1968). Reinforcement of leadership behavior in specially constructed groups. *Dissertation Abstracts, 29,* 1599.

Zdep, S. M. (1969). Intra group reinforcement and its effects on leadership behavior. *Organizational Behavior and Human Performance, 4,* 284-298.

Zdep, S. M., & Oakes, W. F. (1967). Reinforcement of leadership behavior in group discussion. *Journal of Experimental Social Psychology, 3,* 310-320.

Zeira, Y. (1975). Overlooked personnel problems of multinational corporations. *Columbia Journal of World Business, 10,* 96-103.

Zeira, Y., & Banai, M. (1981). Attitudes of host-country organizations toward MNC staffing policies: Cross-country and cross-industry analysis. *Management International Review, 2(2),* 38-47.

Zeleny, L. D. (1939). Characteristics of group leaders. *Sociology and Social Research, 24,* 140-149.

Zeleny, L. D. (1940a). Objective selection of group leaders. *Sociology and Social Research, 24,* 326-336.

Zeleny, L. D. (1940b). Experimental appraisal of a group learning plan. *Journal of Education Research, 34,* 37-42.

Zeleny, L. D. (1941). Experiments in leadership training. *Journal of Educational Sociology, 14,* 310-313.

Zeleny, L. D. (1946-47). Selection of compatible flying partners. *American Journal of Sociology, 52,* 424-431.

Zeleny, L. D. (1950). Adaptation of research findings in social leadership to college classroom procedures. *Sociometry, 8,* 314-328.

Zelko, H., & Dance, F. E. X. (1965). *Business and professional speech communication.* New York: Holt, Rinehart & Winston.

Zenger, H. (1974). Third generation manager training. *MSU Business Topics, 21,* 23-28.

Zenter, H. (1951). Morale: Certain theoretical implications of data in the American soldier. *American Sociology Review, 16,* 297-307.

Zerbe, W. J., & Paulhus, D. L. (1985). *Socially desirable responding in organizational behavior.* University of British Columbia, Vancouver. Unpublished manuscript.

Zey, M. G. (1984). *The mentor connection.* Homewood, IL: Dow Jones-Irwin.

Zey, M. G. (1988). A mentor for all reasons. *Personnel Journal, 67(1),* 46-51.

Ziegenhagen, E. A. (1964). *Perceived inconsistencies regarding self and ethnocentric political leadership.* Doctoral dissertation, University of Illnois, Urbana.

Ziegler, S., & Richmond, A. H. (1972). *Characteristics of Italian house-holders in metropolitan Toronto*. Toronto: Ethnic Research Program, Institute for Behavioral Research Centre.

Zierden, W. E. (1980). Leading through the follower's point of view. *Organizational Dynamics, 8*(4), 27–46.

Zigon, F. J., & Cannon, J. R. (1974). Processes and outcomes of group discussions as related to leader behaviors. *Journal of Educational Research, 67,* 199–201.

Zilboorg, G. (1950). Authority and leadership. *Bulletin of the World Federation of Mental Health, 2,* 13–17.

Ziller, R. C. (1954). Four techniques of decision making under uncertainty. *American Psychologist, 9,* 498.

Ziller, R. C. (1955). Scales of judgment: A determinant of the accuracy of group decisions. *Human Relations, 8,* 153–164.

Ziller, R. C. (1957). Four techniques of group decision making under uncertainty. *Journal of Applied Psychology, 41,* 384–388.

Ziller, R. C. (1959). Leader acceptance of responsibility for group action under conditions of uncertainty and risk. *Journal of Psychology, 47,* 57–66.

Ziller, R. C. (1962). The newcomer's acceptance in open and closed groups. *Personnel Administrator, 25,* 24–31.

Ziller, R. C. (1963). Leader assumed dissimilarity as a measure of prejudicial cognitive style. *Journal of Applied Psychology, 47,* 339–342.

Ziller, R. C. (1964). Individuation and socialization: A theory of assimilation in large organizations. *Human Relations, 17,* 341–360.

Ziller, R. C. (1965a). The leader's perception of the marginal member. *Personnel Administrator, 28,* 6–11.

Ziller, R. C. (1965b). Toward a theory of open and closed groups. *Psychological Bulletin, 64,* 164–182.

Ziller, R. C. (1973). *The social self.* New York: Pergamon.

Ziller, R. C., Behringer, R. D., & Jansen, M. J. (1961). The newcomer in open and closed groups. *Journal of Applied Psychology, 45,* 55–58.

Ziller, R. C., Stark, B. J., & Pruden, H. O. (1969). Marginality and integrative management positions. *Academy of Management Journal, 4,* 487–495.

Zillig, M. (1933). Führer in der Schulklasse. [Classroom leaders.] *Industrial Psychotechnologie, 10,* 177–182.

Zimbardo, P. G. (1969). The human choice: Individuation, reason, and order versus deindividuation, impulse, and chaos. In W. J. Arnold & D. Levine (Eds.), *Nebraska symposium on motivation.* Lincoln: University of Nebraska Press.

Zimbardo, P. G. (1973). Social psychology: Tool for improving the human condition. In J. Seigel & M. Reich (Eds.), *Mental Health Reports 6.* Washington, DC: National Institute of Mental Health.

Zimet, C. N., & Fine, H. J. (1955). Personality changes with a group therapeutic experience in a human relations seminar. *Journal of Abnormal and Social Psychology, 51,* 68–73.

Zink, H. (1930). *City bosses in the United States: A study of twenty municipal bosses.* Durham, NC: Duke University Press.

Zoffer, H. J. (1985, October 20). Training managers to take charge. *New York Times,* 2F.

Zola, E. (1902). *The downfall.* New York: Collier.

Zoll, A. A. (1969). *Dynamic management education* (2nd ed.). Reading, MA: Addison-Wesley.

Zollschan, G. K., & Hirsch, W. (1964). *Explorations in social change.* Boston: Houghton Mifflin.

Zorn, T. E. (1988). *Construct system development, transformational leadership and leadership messages among small business owners.* Paper, Speech Communication Association, New Orleans, LA.

Zuberbier, L. W. (1971). Fostering a greater balance of participation in small leaderless discussion groups. *Dissertation Abstracts International, 32,* 3430–3431.

Zuckerman, M., & Wheeler, L. (1975). To dispel fantasies about the fantasy-based measure of fear of success. *Psychological Bulletin, 82,* 932–946.

Zullow, H. M., Oettingen, G., Peterson, C., & Seligman, M. E. P. (1988). Pessimistic explanatory style in the historical record: CAVing LBJ, presidential candidates, and East versus West Berlin. *American Psychologist, 43,* 673–682.

Zurcher, L. A. (1968). Particularism and organizational position: A cross-cultural analysis. *Journal of Applied Psychology, 52,* 139–144.

Zurcher, L. A., Meadow, A., & Zurcher, S. L. (1965). Value orientation, role conflict, and alienation from work: A cross-cultural study. *American Sociological Review, 30,* 539–548.

Zweig, J. P. (1966). The relationships among performance, partisanship in labor-management issues, and leadership style of first line supervisors. *Dissertation Abstracts, 26,* 4801.

Zweigenhaft, R. L. (1980). American Jews: In or out of the upper class? In G. W. Domhoff (Ed.), *Power structure research.* Beverly Hills, CA: Sage.

Author Index

Instone, D., 247, 321, 712, 723, 729, 730, 731, 736, 890
Inzerilli, G., 795
Ippoliti, P., 220
Ireland, T. C., 591
Ireson, C. J., 722
Irle, K. W., 38, 62, 74
Irons, P. W., 615, 618, 623
Isenberg, D. G., 506, 637
Ishikawa, A., 776, 790
Israel, J., 795
Ivancevich, J. J., 819
Ivancevich, J. M., 243, 249, 258, 323, 325, 369, 371, 373, 421, 423, 463, 464, 631, 635, 654, 655, 782, 797, 822
Iverson, M. A., 112, 241, 300
Izard, C. E., 175
Izraeli, D. N., 715, 772, 787

Jaap, T., 474
Jablin, F. M., 291, 344, 345, 349, 671
Jacklin, C. N., 715, 719, 722
Jackson, D. H., 143
Jackson, G., 173
Jackson, J. H., 709
Jackson, J. M., 92, 100, 176, 177, 456, 610, 690, 701
Jackson, M. L., 173
Jackson, P. R., 685
Jackson, R., 741
Jacob, H. E., 130, 149
Jacob, J. E., 753
Jacob, P. E., 793
Jacobs, A., 340
Jacobs, H. L., 506
Jacobs, M., 340
Jacobs, T. O., 14, 16, 48, 51, 84, 114, 214, 274, 405, 406, 457, 684, 813, 860, 883
Jacobsen, E., 598, 599
Jacobsen, E. N., 491
Jacobson, C., 725
Jacobson, D., 791
Jacobson, E., 158, 171, 284, 452
Jacobson, L., 213
Jacobson, M. B., 709, 712, 723, 727, 735
Jacoby, J., 54, 366, 499, 692
Jaffee, C. L., 93, 329, 745, 748, 751, 752, 834, 858, 874
Jaggi, B., 790
Jago, A. G., 18, 443, 445, 464-465, 466, 467, 469-470, 726, 841, 842, 897
Jaiswal, N. K., 172
Jambor, H., 291, 292
James, B. J., 846
James, C., 569
James, D. R., 697
James, G., 330
James, L. R., 349, 352, 388, 389, 390, 476, 494, 544
James, W., 37, 39
Jameson, S. H., 135, 292, 441, 669

Janda, K. F., 15, 225
Janis, I. L., 243, 260, 289, 349, 610, 638, 639, 642, 650, 821
Janowitz, M., 279
Jaques, E., 14, 16, 51, 103, 104, 114, 214, 267, 278, 312, 313, 404, 405, 406, 624, 637, 684, 813, 860
Jardim, A., 710, 718, 722, 735
Jauch, L. R., 14, 386, 697
Javier, E. O., 433
Jayaratne, T. E., 716, 736
Jaynes, W. E., 91, 234, 282, 311, 314, 391, 392, 393, 520, 601, 613, 689
Jeanpierre, F., 853
Jemmott, J. B., 751
Jencks, C., 173
Jenkins, C. D., 157
Jenkins, G. D., 423
Jenkins, J. G., 279
Jenkins, L. W., 522, 528-529
Jenkins, R. L., 848
Jenkins, W. O., 38, 40, 59, 78, 107, 511, 564
Jenner, S. R., 795
Jennings, E. E., 26, 38, 82, 119, 739, 741, 744, 835, 839
Jennings, H. H., 17, 60, 66, 67, 69, 70, 73, 76, 95, 96, 132, 175, 179, 182, 662, 807
Jensen, M., 30, 31, 54, 388-389, 401, 409, 410, 896
Jensen, N. B., 141
Jenusaitis, E., 162
Jerdee, T. H., 32, 119-120, 383, 385, 392, 404, 445, 446, 715, 717, 723, 726, 730, 732, 746, 820, 857, 866
Jerkedal, A., 846
Jermier, J., 45, 682, 683
Jervis, V. T. P., 220
Jesse, F. C., 820
Jessor, R., 126
Jeswald, T. A., 910
Jiambalvo, J., 355, 618
Jobe, A. M., 358
Jochem, L. M., 113
Joe, V. C., 153
Johns, G., 339, 617, 619, 629, 630
Johns, R. L., 578
Johnson, 328
Johnson, A. C., 81, 83
Johnson, A. L., 153
Johnson, C. C., 179, 861
Johnson, D. A., 582
Johnson, D. E., 433
Johnson, D. L., 731
Johnson, D. M., 422, 426
Johnson, E. W., 295
Johnson, J. C., 861
Johnson, J. T., 751
Johnson, L., 672
Johnson, L. A., 849
Johnson, M., 500
Johnson, M. C., 834, 835, 838

Johnson, P., 713
Johnson, P. V., 151, 162
Johnson, R. D., 328
Johnson, R. H., 519, 752
Johnson, S., 319, 324
Johnson, T., 335
Johnson, T. W., 629
Johnson, W., 699
Johnston, G., 307, 308
Johnston, R. W., 52
Jokinen, W. J., 286
Jones, A. J., 60, 91
Jones, A. P., 349, 476, 544, 646, 651
Jones, D. S., 287
Jones, E., 809
Jones, E. E., 125, 126, 137, 211, 235, 342, 607
Jones, E. W., 740, 743, 749
Jones, F. D., 636, 638, 646
Jones, G. R., 24, 45, 230, 684
Jones, H., 303
Jones, H. R., 500
Jones, M. E., 880
Jones, N. W., 46, 626, 627
Jones, R. E., 235, 304, 607
Jones, T., 725
Jones, W. S., 872
Jongbloed, L., 10, 124, 276, 551
Jordan, A. M., 61, 62, 64, 67, 69-70
Jordan, H., 260
Jordan, P. C., 325
Jöreskog, K. G., 418
Joslyn, C. S., 172, 173
Joyce, W. F., 682, 683, 684
Jucker, J. V., 640-641
Julian, J. W., 11, 13, 48, 93, 100, 106, 244, 245, 300, 356, 478, 506
Jull, G. W., 676
Jung, C. G., 52, 587
Jurgensen, C. E., 866
Jurma, W. E., 539-540
Jusenius, C. L., 737
Justis, R. T., 106, 236

Kabanoff, B., 287, 288, 303, 622, 841
Kaczka, E. E., 483
Kadushin, A., 667
Kahane, M., 243, 453, 457, 550, 662-663
Kahler, G. E., 81, 83
Kahn, R. K., 757
Kahn, R. L., 8, 13, 14, 32, 44, 51, 199, 274, 277, 290, 292, 296, 385, 416, 454, 474, 553, 565, 636, 908
Kahn, S., 584
Kahneman, D., 884
Kakar, S., 790, 796
Kalay, E., 646
Kalb, L. S., 353, 365
Kallejian, V., 834
Kalnins, D., 170
Kaluzny, A. D., 540
Kamano, D. K., 290

Subject Index